中国统计年鉴

CHINA STATISTICAL YEARBOOK

2006

（总第25期 No.25）

中华人民共和国国家统计局　编

Compiled by

National Bureau of Statistics of China

中国统计出版社
China Statistics Press

（京）新登字 041 号

图书在版编目(CIP)数据

中国统计年鉴.2006/ 中华人民共和国国家统计局 编
- 北京：中国统计出版社，2006.9
ISBN 7-5037-5001-4

I.中…
II.中…
III.统计资料 - 中国 -2006- 年鉴
IV.C832-54

中国版本图书馆 CIP 数据核字(2006)第 105209 号

中国统计年鉴 -2006

作　　者 / 中华人民共和国国家统计局
责任编辑 / 徐　辉　叶礼奇　郭　栋
E-mail: yearbook@stats.gov.cn
Address: No.57 Yuetan Nanjie, Shanlihe, Beijing 100826
封面设计 / 张　冰
出版发行 / 中国统计出版社
通信地址 / 北京市西城区三里河月坛南街 57 号　邮政编码 / 100826
办公地址 / 北京市丰台区西三环南路甲 6 号
电　　话 / (010)63376898、63376907（发行部）、63376858（编辑部）
印　　刷 / 北京顺义振华印刷厂
经　　销 / 新华书店
开　　本 / 890 × 1240 毫米　1/16
字　　数 / 2150 千字
印　　张 / 67.25
版　　别 / 2006 年 9 月第 1 版
版　　次 / 2006 年 9 月第 1 次印刷
书　　号 / ISBN 7-5037-5001-4/F · 2384
定　　价 / 298.00 元　Price: 298.00 yuan (RMB)

本书附同版本 CD-ROM 一张，光盘内容以书面文字为准。
中国统计版图书，如有印装错误，本社发行部负责调换。

《中国统计年鉴—2006》

编委会和编辑出版人员

China Statistical Yearbook - 2006

EDITORIAL BOARD AND STAFF

编者说明

一、《中国统计年鉴—2006》系统收录了全国和各省、自治区、直辖市2005年经济、社会各方面的统计数据，以及近二十年和其他历史重要年份的全国主要统计数据，是一部全面反映中华人民共和国经济和社会发展情况的资料性年刊。

二、本年鉴正文内容分为25个篇章，即：1.行政区划和自然资源；2.综合；3.国民经济核算；4.人口；5.就业人员和职工工资；6.固定资产投资；7.能源；8.财政；9.价格指数；10.人民生活；11.城市概况；12.环境保护；13.农业；14.工业；15.建筑业；16.运输和邮电；17.国内贸易；18.对外经济贸易；19.旅游；20.金融业；21.教育和科技；22.文化、体育和卫生；23.其他社会活动；24.香港特别行政区主要社会经济指标；25.澳门特别行政区主要社会经济指标。同时附录两个篇章：1.台湾省主要社会经济指标；2.我国经济、社会统计指标同世界主要国家和地区比较。为方便读者使用，各篇章前设有《简要说明》，对本篇章的主要内容、资料来源、统计范围、统计方法以及历史变动情况予以简要概述，篇末附有《主要统计指标解释》。

三、本年鉴所涉及的全国性统计数据，除行政区划、国土面积和森林资源外，均未包括香港、澳门特别行政区和台湾省数据。

四、香港特别行政区和澳门特别行政区的统计是构成国家统计总体的一部分。但根据中华人民共和国“香港特别行政区基本法”和“澳门特别行政区基本法”的有关原则，香港、澳门与内地是相对独立的统计区域，根据各自不同的统计制度和法律规定，独立进行统计工作。本年鉴中香港和澳门特别行政区统计资料分别由香港特别行政区政府统计处、澳门特别行政区政府统计暨普查局提供，国家统计局进行编辑。

五、与2005年版《中国统计年鉴》相比较，本年鉴在统计内容和编辑上主要做了如下修订：

1．在《综合篇》和《人民生活篇》，增加了按东、中、西和东北地区分组的资料。分组方法如下：

东部地区：北京市、天津市、河北省、上海市、江苏省、浙江省、福建省、山东省、广东省、海南省；

中部地区：山西省、安徽省、江西省、河南省、湖北省、湖南省；

西部地区：内蒙古自治区、广西壮族自治区、重庆市、四川省、贵州省、云南省、西藏自治区、陕西省、甘肃省、青海省、宁夏回族自治区、新疆维吾尔自治区；

东北地区：辽宁省、吉林省、黑龙江省。

2．在《人口篇》，将原来千分之一人口变动调查资料替换为2005年全国百分之一人口抽样调查资料，并第一次增加了按地区分组的城乡人口数。

3．根据第一次全国经济普查结果，增加了2004年国内生产总值行业构成资料和全口径工业主要统计指标按注册登记类型、按行业分组的资料，并对能源生产和消费、部分工业产品产量、社会消费品零售总额以及相关的国民经济核算指标的历史数据进行了调整。同时，还将去年因经济普查而简化的工业、建筑业、房地产投资和批发零售贸易业等资料恢复为正常年报内容。

六、本年鉴所使用的度量衡单位，均采用国际统一标准计量单位。

七、本年鉴中部分数据合计数或相对数由于单位取舍不同而产生的计算误差，均未作机械调整。

八、本年鉴凡带有续表的资料，有关注解均列在最后一张续表的下方。

九、符号使用说明:年鉴各表中的“空格”表示该项统计指标数据不足本表最小单位数、数据不详或无该项数据；“#”表示其中的主要项；“*”或“①”表示本表下有注解。

PREFACE

I. *China Statistical Yearbook 2006* is an annual statistics publication, which covers very comprehensive data in 2005 and some selected data series in historically important years and the most recent twenty years at national level and local levels of province, autonomous region, and municipality directly under the central government and therefore, reflects various aspects of China's social and economic development.

II. The yearbook contains the following twenty-five chapters, l. Divisions of Administrative Areas and Natural Resources; 2. General Survey; 3. National Accounts; 4. Population; 5. Employment and Wages; 6. Investment in Fixed Assets; 7. Energy; 8. Government Finance; 9. Price Indices; 10. People's Livelihood; 11. General Survey of Cities; 12. Environment Protection; 13. Agriculture; 14. Industry; 15. Construction; 16. Transport, Post and Telecommunication Services; 17. Domestic Trade; 18. Foreign Trade and Economic Cooperation; 19. Tourism; 20. Financial Intermediation; 21. Education, Science and Technology; 22.Culture, Sports and Public Health; 23. Other Social Activities; 24. Main Social and Economic Indicators of Hong Kong Special Administrative Region (SAR); 25. Main Social and Economic Indicators of Macao Special Administrative Region (SAR). Two chapters listed as the appendices are Main Social and Economic Indicators of Taiwan Province and A Comparison of Economic and Social Indicators among the People's Republic of China and Other Countries/Areas. In brief introduction at the beginning of each chapter, main coverage of this chapter, data sources, statistical coverage, statistical methods and historical changes are concerned. In addition, Explanatory Notes on Main Statistical Indicators are provided at the end of each chapter.

III. The national data in this book do not include that of Hong Kong Special Administrative Region, Macao Special Administrative Region and Taiwan Province except for divisions of administrative areas, territory and forest resources.

IV. Statistics of Hong Kong Special Administrative Region and Macao Special Administrative Region constitute an integral part of the national statistics of China. According to the principles set forth in *the Basic Law of Hong Kong Special Administrative Region*, and *the Basic Law of Macao Special Administrative Region,* statistically Hong Kong, Macao and the mainland of China are three mutually independent regions, and follow their own and different statistical systems in carrying out independent statistical operation. Statistics on Hong Kong Special Administrative Region and Macao Special Administrative Region as included in this yearbook are provided by the Department of Census and Statistics of the Government of Hong Kong Special Administrative Region, the Department of Census and Statistics of the Government of Macao Special Administrative Region, and edited by National Bureau of Statistics.

V. Compared with the *China Statistical Yearbook 2005,* some changes are made in contents and in editing mode, including the following:

1) In chapters on General Survey and People's Livelihood, data are classified into eastern region, central region, western region and northeastern region, which cover following provinces:

Eastern region: Beijing, Tianjin, Hebei, Shanghai, Jiangsu, Zhejiang, Fujian, Shandong, Guangdong and Hainan.

Central region: Shanxi, Anhui, Jiangxi, Henan, Hubei and Hunan.

Western region: Inner Mongolia, Guangxi, Chongqing, Sichuan, Guizhou, Yunnan, Tibet, Shaanxi, Gansu, Qinghai, Ningxia and Xinjiang.

Northeastern region: Liaoning, Jilin and Heilongjiang.

2) In the chapter on Population, data from the annual survey on change of population are substituted by data from the National Sample Survey on 1% of Population conducted in 2005. Information on population by urban and rural residence and by province is added for the first time.

3) Results of the First National Economic Census bring new data into the Yearbook, including gross domestic product by industry, and major industrial statistics of the society by type of ownership and by industry for the year 2004. At the same time, the 2004 statistics compiled on the basis of preliminary reports for manufacturing industry, construction, investment in real estate development, wholesale and retail trades have been recompiled for normal annual statistics.

VI. The units of measurement used in this yearbook are internationally standard measurement units.

VII. Statistical discrepancies due to rounding are not adjusted in the yearbook.

VIII. If a table in the yearbook occupies more than one page, the footnotes pertaining to the table are placed at the end of the last page.

IX. Notations used in the yearbook:

(blank space) indicates that the figure is not large enough to be measured with the smallest unit in the table, or data are unknown or are not available;"#" indicates a major breakdown of the total; and "*"or "①"indicates footnotes at the end of the table.

目 录

CONTENTS

一、行政区划和自然资源

Divisions of Administrative Areas and Natural Resources

简要说明
Brief Introduction
1-1 全国行政区划（2005年底） ……… (3)
Divisions of Administrative Areas in China (End of 2005)
1-2 自然状况 ……… (4)
Natural Conditions
1-3 自然资源 ……… (5)
Natural Resources
1-4 土地状况 ……… (6)
Land Characteristics
1-5 主要山脉基本情况 ……… (6)
Main Mountain Ranges
1-6 主要河流基本情况 ……… (7)
Major Rivers
1-7 河流流域面积 ……… (7)
Drainage Area of Rivers
1-8 内陆水域面积 ……… (8)
Inland Water Area
1-9 湖泊面积 ……… (8)
Area of Lakes
1-10 海区海域及渔场面积 ……… (9)
Sea Area and Areas of Fishing Ground
1-11 浅海滩涂海湾可养殖面积 ……… (9)
Seashore Land Area for Cultivation
1-12 主要矿产基础储量 ……… (10)
Major Mineral Basic Reserves

1-13 各地区主要能源、黑色金属矿产基础储量（2005年）……(11)
Basic Reserves of Major Energy and Ferrous Metals by Region (2005)
1-14 各地区主要有色金属、非金属矿产基础储量（2005年）……(12)
Basic Reserves of Major Non-ferrous Metal and Non-metal Mineral by Region (2005)
1-15 主要城市平均气温（2005年）……(13)
Monthly Average Temperature of Major Cities (2005)
1-16 主要城市平均相对湿度(2005年) ……(14)
Average Relative Humidity of Major Cities (2005)
1-17 主要城市降水量（2005年）……(15)
Monthly Precipitation of Major Cities (2005)
1-18 主要城市日照时数（2005年）……(16)
Monthly Sunshine Hours of Major Cities (2005)
主要统计指标解释 ……(17)
Explanatory Notes on Main Statistical Indicators

二、综合
General Survey

简要说明
Brief Introduction
2-1 各部门机构数……(23)
Grass-roots Units in Various Sectors
2-2 平均每天主要社会经济活动 ……(25)
Selected Indicators on Average Daily Social and Economic Activities
2-3 国民经济和社会发展总量与速度指标 ……(26)
Principal Aggregate Indicators on National Economic and Social Development and Growth Rates
2-4 国民经济和社会发展结构指标 ……(34)
Structural Indicators on National Economic and Social Development
2-5 国民经济和社会发展比例和效益指标 ……(37)
Indicators on National Economic and Social Development
2-6 按区域分的国民经济和社会发展主要指标（2005年）……(40)
Main Indicators of National Economic and Social Development by Eastern, Central, Western and Northeastern Region (2005)
2-7 人均主要工农业产品产量 ……(44)
Per Capita Output of Major Industrial and Agricultural Products
2-8 民族自治地方自然资源 ……(45)
Natural Resources in Minority Nationality Autonomous Areas
2-9 民族自治地方行政区划和人口（2005年）……(45)
Administrative Division and Population of Minority Nationality Autonomous Areas (2005)
2-10 民族自治地方国民经济与社会发展主要指标 ……(46)
Main Indicators on Economic and Social Development in Minority Autonomous Areas
2-11 少数民族分布的主要地区 ……(50)
Geographic Distribution of Minority Nationalities
主要统计指标解释……(51)
Explanatory Notes on Main Statistical Indicators

三、国民经济核算
National Accounts

简要说明
Brief Introduction
3-1 国内生产总值……(57)

Gross Domestic Product
3-2　国内生产总值构成 …………………………………………………………………………（58）
Composition of Gross Domestic Product
3-3　国内生产总值指数（上年=100）……………………………………………………………（59）
Indices of Gross Domestic Product (preceding year=100)
3-4　国内生产总值指数(1978年 =100) …………………………………………………………（60）
Indices of Gross Domestic Product (year of 1978=100)
3-5　分行业增加值及构成（2004年）……………………………………………………………（61）
Value-added and Composition by Sector (2004)
3-6　三次产业贡献率 ……………………………………………………………………………（62）
Share of the Three Industries to the Increase of GDP
3-7　三次产业对国内生产总值增长的拉动 ……………………………………………………（62）
Contribution of the Three Industries to GDP Growth
3-8　地区生产总值和指数 ………………………………………………………………………（63）
Gross Regional Product and Indices
3-9　地区生产总值（2005年）……………………………………………………………………（64）
Gross Regional Product (2005)
3-10　地区生产总值项目结构（2005年）…………………………………………………………（67）
Components of Gross Regional Product (2005)
3-11　支出法国内生产总值 ………………………………………………………………………（68）
Gross Domestic Product by Expenditure Approach
3-12　支出法国内生产总值结构 …………………………………………………………………（69）
Components of Gross Domestic Product by Expenditure Approach
3-13　三大需求对国内生产总值增长的贡献率和拉动 …………………………………………（70）
Share and Contribution of the Three Components of GDP by Expenditure Approach to the Growth of GDP
3-14　支出法地区生产总值（2005年）……………………………………………………………（71）
Gross Regional Product by Expenditure Approach (2005)
3-15　各地区资本形成总额及构成（2005年）……………………………………………………（72）
Gross Capital Formation and Its Composition by Region (2005)
3-16　各地区最终消费支出及构成（2005年）……………………………………………………（73）
Final Consumption Expenditure and Its Composition by Region (2005)
3-17　居民消费水平 ………………………………………………………………………………（74）
Household Consumption Expenditure
3-18　各地区居民消费水平（2005年）……………………………………………………………（75）
Household Consumption Expenditure by Region (2005)
3-19　国际收支平衡表（2005年）…………………………………………………………………（76）
Balance of Payments (2005)
3-20　2002年投入产出基本流量表(中间使用部分) ………………………………………………（77）
Intermediate Use Part of 2002 Input-Output Table
3-21　2002年投入产出基本流量表(最终使用部分) ………………………………………………（80）
Final Use Part of 2002 Input-Output Table
3-22　投入产出直接消耗系数表（2002年）………………………………………………………（82）
Direct Input Coefficient of Input-Output Table (2002)
3-23　投入产出完全消耗系数表（2002年）………………………………………………………（85）
Total Input Coefficients of Input-Output Table (2002)
3-24　资金流量表（实物交易，2003年）…………………………………………………………（88）
Flow of Funds Table (Physical Transaction, 2003)
3-25　资金流量表（金融交易，2003年）…………………………………………………………（88）
Flow of Funds Table (Financial Transaction, 2003)
主要统计指标解释 ……………………………………………………………………………（90）
Explanatory Notes on Main Statistical Indicators

四、人口
Population

简要说明
Brief Introduction
4-1 人口数及构成 …… (99)
Population and Its Composition
4-2 人口出生率、死亡率和自然增长率 …… (99)
Birth Rate, Death Rate and Natural Growth Rate of Population
4-3 各地区人口数和出生率、死亡率、自然增长率（2005年） …… (100)
Total Population and Birth Rate, Death Rate and Natural Growth Rate by Region (2005)
4-4 各地区人口的城乡构成（2005年） …… (101)
Population by Urban and Rural Residence and Region (2005)
4-5 五次全国人口普查人口基本情况 …… (102)
Basic Statistics on National Population Census in 1953, 1964, 1982, 1990 and 2000
4-6 各地区人口平均预期寿命 …… (103)
Population Life Expectancy by Region
4-7 按年龄和性别分人口数（2005年） …… (104)
Population by Age and Sex (2005)
4-8 各地区户数、人口数、性别比和户规模（2005年） …… (105)
Household, Population, Sex Ratio and Household Size by Region (2005)
4-9 各地区分性别、户口登记状况的人口（2005年） …… (107)
Population by Sex, Household Registration Status and Region (2005)
4-10 各地区人口年龄构成和抚养比（2005年） …… (109)
Age Composition and Dependency Ratio of Population by Region (2005)
4-11 各地区按性别和婚姻状况分的人口（2005年） …… (110)
Population by Sex, Marital Status and Region (2005)
4-12 各地区按性别和受教育程度分的人口（2005年） …… (112)
Population by Sex, Educational Attainment and Region (2005)
4-13 各地区按性别分的15岁及15岁以上文盲人口（2005年） …… (114)
Illiterate Population Aged 15 and Over by Sex and Region (2005)
4-14 各地区按家庭户规模分的户数（2005年） …… (115)
Family Households by Size and Region (2005)
4-15 育龄妇女分年龄、孩次的生育状况(2004年11月1日至2005年10月31日) …… (116)
Age-specific Fertility Rate of Childbearing Women by Age of Mother and Birth Order (2004.11.1-2005.10.31)
4-16 各地区0-30岁独生子女数(2005年) …… (117)
Singleton Aged 0-30 by Region (2005)
4-17 各地区家庭户按住房来源分的户数（2005年） …… (118)
Number of Household by Sources of Housing and Region (2005)
4-18 各地区家庭户的住房间数和面积（2005年） …… (119)
Number of Rooms and Floor Space of Family Households by Region (2005)
主要统计指标解释 …… (120)
Explanatory Notes on Main Statistical Indicators

五、就业人员和职工工资
Employment and Wages

简要说明
Brief Introduction
5-1 就业基本情况 …… (125)
Employment

5-2 按三次产业分就业人员数（年底数）…………………………………………………………………………… (126)
Number of Employed Persons at the Year-end by Three Industries
5-3 各地区按三次产业分就业人员数（2005年底）……………………………………………………………… (127)
Number of Employed Persons at the Year-end by Three Industries and Region (2005)
5-4 按城乡分就业人员数（年底数）………………………………………………………………………………… (128)
Number of Employed Persons at the Year-end in Urban and Rural Areas
5-5 按行业分就业人员数（年底数） ……………………………………………………………………………… (130)
Number of Employed Persons at the Year-end by Sector
5-6 各地区按行业分城镇单位就业人员数（年底数）…………………………………………………………… (131)
Number of Employed Persons in Urban Units at the Year-end by Sector and Region
5-7 按登记注册类型和细行业分职工人数（2005年底）………………………………………………………… (134)
Number of Staff and Workers at the Year-end by Status of Registration and Sector in Detail (2005)
5-8 各地区按行业分职工人数（年底数）………………………………………………………………………… (137)
Number of Staff and Workers at the Year-end by Sector and Region
5-9 各地区按行业分国有单位职工人数（年底数）……………………………………………………………… (140)
Number of Staff and Workers in State-owned Units at the Year-end by Sector and Region
5-10 各地区按行业分城镇集体单位职工人数（年底数）………………………………………………………… (143)
Number of Staff and Workers in Urban Collective-owned Units at the Year-end by Sector and Region
5-11 各地区按行业分其他单位职工人数（年底数）……………………………………………………………… (146)
Number of Staff and Workers in Units of Other Types of Ownership at the Year-end by Sector and Region
5-12 各地区按行业分城镇单位专业技术人员数（年底数）……………………………………………………… (149)
Number of Scientific and Technical Personnel in Urban Collective-owned Units at the Year-end by Sector and Region
5-13 各地区按行业分私营企业和个体就业人数（2005年底）…………………………………………………… (152)
Number of Employed Persons in Private Enterprises and Self-employed Individuals at the Year-end by Sector and Region (2005)
5-14 各地区按行业分城镇私营企业和个体就业人数（2005年底） ……………………………………………… (153)
Number of Employed Persons in Urban Private Enterprises and Self-employed Individuals at the Year-end by Sector and Region (2005)
5-15 各地区私营企业就业人数（2005年底）………………………………………………………………………… (154)
Number of Employed Persons in Private Enterprises at the Year-end by Region (2005)
5-16 各地区个体就业人数（2005年底）……………………………………………………………………………… (155)
Number of Self-employed Individuals at the Year-end by Region (2005)
5-17 职工工资总额和指数 ………………………………………………………………………………………… (156)
Total Wages Bill of Staff and Workers and Related Indices
5-18 职工平均工资及指数 ………………………………………………………………………………………… (157)
Average Wage of Staff and Workers and Related Indices
5-19 各地区按行业分职工工资总额 ……………………………………………………………………………… (158)
Total Wages Bill of Staff and Workers by Sector and Region
5-20 按细行业分职工平均工资（2005年）…………………………………………………………………………… (161)
Average Wage of Staff and Workers by Sector in Detail (2005)
5-21 各地区按行业分职工平均工资 ……………………………………………………………………………… (164)
Average Wage of Staff and Workers by Sector and Region
5-22 各地区按行业分国有单位职工平均工资 …………………………………………………………………… (167)
Average Wage of Staff and Workers in State-owned Units by Sector and Region
5-23 各地区按行业分城镇集体单位职工平均工资 ……………………………………………………………… (170)
Average Wage of Staff and Workers in Urban Collective-owned Units by Sector and Region
5-24 各地区按行业分其他单位职工平均工资（年底数）………………………………………………………… (173)
Average Wage of Staff and Workers in Other Ownership Units at the Year-end by Sector and Region
5-25 按登记注册类型分其他单位职工平均工资 ………………………………………………………………… (176)
Average Wage of Staff and Workers in Units of Other Types of Ownership by Registration Status
5-26 各地区国有及国有控股企业就业人数和劳动报酬（2005年） ……………………………………………… (177)
Employed Persons at the Year-end and Earnings in State-owned and State-holding Enterprises by Region (2005)

5-27 各地区职业介绍工作情况（2005年）……（178）
Situations of Careers Service by Region (2005)
5-28 各地区城镇登记失业人员及失业率……（180）
Registered Urban Unemployment Persons and Unemployment Rate by Region
主要统计指标解释……（181）
Explanatory Notes on Main Statistical Indicators

六、固定资产投资
Investment in Fixed Assets

简要说明
Brief Introduction
6-1 全社会固定资产投资……（187）
Total Investment in Fixed Assets in the Whole Country
6-2 按城乡分全社会固定资产投资……（188）
Total Investment in Fixed Assets in the Whole Country by Rural and Urban Area
6-3 各地区按经济类型分全社会固定资产投资……（189）
Total Investment in Fixed Assets in the Whole Country by Ownership and Region
6-4 按资金来源和构成分全社会固定资产投资……（191）
Total Investment in Fixed Assets in the Whole Country by Sources of Funds and Use of Funds
6-5 各地区全社会固定资产投资资金来源……（192）
Sources of Funds of Total Investment in Fixed Assets in the Whole Country by Region
6-6 各地区全社会住宅投资……（193）
Total Investment in Residential Buildings in the Whole Country by Region
6-7 各地区按主要行业分的全社会固定资产投资……（194）
Total Investment in Fixed Assets in the Whole Country by Region and Sector
6-8 各地区全社会建设总规模……（197）
Total Investment in Construction in the Whole Country by Region
6-9 各地区全社会施工、竣工房屋面积和价值……（198）
Value and Floor Space of Buildings under Construction and Completed in the Whole Country by Region
6-10 按资金来源和隶属关系分城镇固定资产投资……（199）
Investment in Fixed Assets in Urban Area by Sources of Funds and Jurisdiction of Management
6-11 按构成和建设性质分城镇固定资产投资……（200）
Investment in Fixed Assets in Urban Area by Use of Funds and Type of Construction
6-12 城镇固定资产投资建设总规模……（201）
Total Investment in Fixed Assets of Construction in Urban Area
6-13 按行业分城镇固定资产投资和建设总规模（2005年）……（202）
Investment in Fixed Assets in Urban Area by Sector and Total Investment in Construction (2005)
6-14 按行业、隶属关系和注册类型分城镇固定资产投资(2005年)……（206）
Investment in Fixed Assets in Urban Area by Sector, Jurisdiction of Management and Registration Status (2005)
6-15 城镇各行业投资资金来源和新增固定资产（2005年）……（210）
Sources of Funds of Investment and Newly Increased Fixed Assets in Urban Area by Sector (2005)
6-16 各地区按行业分城镇固定资产投资……（214）
Investment in Fixed Assets in Urban Area by Region and Sector
6-17 各地区按项目规模分城镇固定资产投资……（217）
Investment in Fixed Assets in Urban Area by Size of Construction and Region
6-18 各地区城镇能源工业投资……（218）
Investment in Energy Industry in Urban Area by Region
6-19 各地区城镇施工、竣工房屋建筑面积和价值……（219）
Value and Floor Space of Buildings under Construction and Completed in Urban Area by Region
6-20 各地区按行业分城镇新增固定资产……（220）
Newly Increased Fixed Assets in Urban Area by Region and Sector

6-21 城镇50万元以上施工、投产项目个数 …… (223)
Number of Construction Projects over 500 Thousand Yuan under Construction and Put into Use in Urban Area
6-22 城镇新增固定资产及交付使用率 …… (224)
Newly Increased Fixed Assets and Rate of Projects of Fixed Assets Completed and Put into Operation in Urban Area
6-23 按行业分城镇50万元以上施工、投产项目个数（2005年） …… (225)
Number of Construction Projects over 500 Thousand Yuan under Construction and Put into Use in Urban Area by Sector (2005)
6-24 新增主要产品生产能力 …… (227)
Newly Increased Production Capacity of Major Production
6-25 全社会主要产品建设规模（2005年） …… (229)
Construction Size of Main Production in the Whole Country (2005)
6-26 农村个人固定资产投资和建房 …… (231)
Individual Investment in Fixed Assets and Buildings Construction in Rural Areas
6-27 房地产开发企业(单位)主要指标 …… (232)
Main Indicators of Enterprises for Real Estate Development
6-28 房地产开发企业(单位)个数 …… (233)
Number of Enterprises for Real Estate Development
6-29 房地产开发企业(单位)从业人员数 …… (234)
Number of Employed Persons in Enterprises for Real Estate Development
6-30 房地产开发企业 (单位)土地开发及购置 …… (235)
Land Development and Purchase of Enterprises for Real Estate Development
6-31 房地产开发企业(单位)建设投资总规模及完成投资(2005年) …… (236)
General Scale of Construction and Actually Completed Investment of Enterprises for Real Estate Development (2005)
6-32 按用途分房地产开发企业(单位)投资完成额 …… (237)
Actually Completed Investment of Enterprises for Real Estate Development by Use
6-33 房地产开发企业(单位)资金来源 …… (238)
Sources of Funds of Enterprises for Real Estate Development
6-34 房地产开发企业(单位)建设房屋建筑面积和造价 …… (239)
Floor Space and Cost of Buildings Developed by Enterprises for Real Estate Development
6-35 按用途分房地产开发企业(单位)新开工房屋面积 …… (240)
Floor Space of Buildings Started This Year by Enterprises for Real Estate Development by Use
6-36 商品房屋销售情况 …… (241)
Selling of Commercial Buildings
6-37 按用途分商品房屋销售面积 …… (242)
Floor Space of Commercial Buildings Sold by Use
6-38 按用途分商品房屋平均销售价格 …… (243)
Average Selling Price of Commercial Buildings by Use
6-39 房地产开发企业(单位)资产负债 …… (244)
Assets and Liabilities of Enterprises for Real Estate Development
6-40 房地产开发企业(单位)经营情况 …… (245)
Operating Statistics of Enterprises for Real Estate Development
6-41 按规模分房地产开发企业(单位)完成投资（2005年） …… (246)
Actually Completed Investment of Enterprises for Real Estate Development by Size of Enterprise (2005)
6-42 房地产开发企业(单位)建设成套住宅竣工与销售情况 …… (247)
Flats of Residential Buildings Completed and Sold by Enterprises for Real Estate Development
6-43 35个大中城市主要指标完成情况（2005年） …… (248)
Main Indicators of Real Estate in 35 Large and Medium-sized Cities (2005)
6-44 在建大型项目基本情况（2005年） …… (250)
Basic Conditions of Large Projects Being Constructed (2005)
主要统计指标解释 …… (252)
Explanatory Notes on Main Statistical Indicators

七、能源
Energy

简要说明
Brief Introduction
7-1 能源生产总量及构成 …… (261)
Total Production of Energy and Its Composition
7-2 能源消费总量及构成 …… (261)
Total Consumption of Energy and Its Composition
7-3 综合能源平衡表 …… (262)
Overall Energy Balance Sheet
7-4 石油平衡表 …… (263)
Petroleum Balance Sheet
7-5 煤炭平衡表 …… (264)
Coal Balance Sheet
7-6 电力平衡表 …… (264)
Electricity Balance Sheet
7-7 能源生产弹性系数 …… (265)
Elasticity Ratio of Energy Production
7-8 能源消费弹性系数 …… (265)
Elasticity Ratio of Energy Consumption
7-9 按行业分能源消费量（2004年） …… (266)
Consumption of Energy by Sector (2004)
7-10 按行业分能源消费量（2005年） …… (268)
Consumption of Energy by Sector (2005)
7-11 能源加工转换效率 …… (270)
Efficiency of Energy Conversion
7-12 平均每天能源消费量 …… (270)
Average Daily Energy Consumption by Type of Energy
7-13 生活能源消费量 …… (271)
Average Annual Energy Consumption for Non-Production Purpose
7-14 人均生活能源消费量 …… (271)
Annual Per Capita Energy Consumption for Non-Production Purpose
7-15 各地区电力消费量 …… (272)
Electricity Consumption by Region
7-16 各地区能源消耗指标（2005年） …… (273)
Indicators of Energy Consumption by Region (2005)
主要统计指标解释 …… (274)
Explanatory Notes on Main Statistical Indicators

八、财政
Government Finance

简要说明
Brief Introduction
8-1 国家财政收支总额及增长速度 …… (281)
Government Revenue and Expenditure and Their Increase Rates
8-2 国家财政分项目收入 …… (281)
Government Revenue by Item
8-3 各项税收 …… (282)
Taxes

8-4 国家财政主要支出项目 …… (282)
Government Expenditure by Main Item
8-5 国家财政按功能性质分类的支出 …… (283)
Government Expenditure by Function
8-6 国家财政用于农业的支出 …… (284)
Government Expenditure For Agriculture
8-7 国家财政用于科学研究的支出 …… (284)
Government Expenditure for Science and Research
8-8 国家财政用于抚恤和社会福利的支出 …… (285)
Government Expenditure for Pension and Social Welfare
8-9 政策性补贴支出 …… (285)
Budgetary Expenditure for Price Subsidies
8-10 中央和地方财政收入及比重 …… (286)
Government Revenue and Ratio of the Central and Local Government
8-11 中央和地方财政支出及比重 …… (286)
Government Expenditure and Ratio of Central and Local Governments
8-12 中央和地方财政主要收入项目（2005年）…… (287)
Main Items of Government Revenue of the Central Government and Local Governments (2005)
8-13 中央和地方财政主要支出项目（2005年）…… (288)
Main Items of Budgetary Expenditure of Central and Local Governments (2005)
8-14 各地区财政收入（2005年）…… (289)
Final Statement of Government Revenue by Region (2005)
8-15 各地区财政支出（2005年）…… (293)
Final Statement of Government Expenditure by Region (2005)
8-16 预算外资金分项目收入 …… (298)
Extra-budgetary Revenue by Item
8-17 预算外资金分项目支出 …… (298)
Extra-budgetary Expenditure by Item
8-18 中央和地方预算外资金收支及比重 …… (299)
Total Extra-budgetary Revenues and Expenditures and Ratio of the Central Government and Local Governments
8-19 国家财政债务发行情况 …… (300)
Government Debts Issuance
8-20 国家财政债务还本付息支出 …… (300)
Government Payment for the Principal and Interest of Debts
8-21 外债余额 …… (301)
Balance of Foreign Debts
8-22 外债风险指标 …… (301)
Risk Indicators on Foreign Debts
主要统计指标解释 …… (302)
Explanatory Notes on Main Statistical Indicators

九、价格指数
Price Indices

简要说明
Brief Introduction
9-1 各种价格指数 …… (311)
Price Indices
9-2 各种价格定基指数 …… (311)
Fixed-base Price Indices
9-3 居民消费价格分类指数（2005年）…… (312)
Consumer Price Indices by Category (2005)

9-4 商品零售价格分类指数（2005年）…… (314)
Retail Price Indices by Category (2005)
9-5 居民消费价格指数和商品零售价格指数 …… (315)
Consumer Price Indices and Retail Price Indices
9-6 各地区居民消费价格分类指数 …… (316)
Consumer Price Indices by Category and Region
9-7 商品零售价格分类指数 …… (324)
Retail Price Indices by Category of Commodities
9-8 各地区农业生产资料价格分类指数 …… (327)
Price Indices of Means of Agricultural Production by Category and Region
9-9 农产品生产价格指数 …… (329)
Indices of Producers' Prices for Farm Products
9-10 各地区农产品生产价格指数 …… (330)
Producers' Prices for Farm Products by Region
9-11 各地区工业品出厂价格指数 …… (331)
Ex-Factory Price Indices of Industrial Products by Region
9-12 按行业分工业品出厂价格指数 …… (332)
Ex-Factory Price Indices of Industrial Products by Sector
9-13 工业品出厂价格分类指数 …… (333)
Ex-Factory Price Indices of Industrial Products
9-14 原材料、燃料、动力购进价格指数 …… (333)
Indices of Purchasing Prices of Raw Materials, Fuels and Power
9-15 各地区固定资产投资价格指数 …… (334)
Price Indices of Investment in Fixed Assets by Region
9-16 按工业行业分工业品出厂价格指数 …… (335)
Ex-Factory Price Indices of Industrial Products by Sector
9-17 房地产价格指数 …… (336)
Price Indices for Real Estate
9-18 全国和35个大中城市房地产价格指数 …… (337)
Price Indices of Real Estate in China and 35 Large and Medium-sized Cities
主要统计指标解释 …… (338)
Explanatory Notes on Main Statistical Indicators

十、人民生活
People's Livelihood

简要说明
Brief Introduction
10-1 人民生活基本情况 …… (345)
People's Life
10-2 城乡居民家庭人均收入及恩格尔系数 …… (347)
Per Capita Annual Income and Engle Coefficient of Urban and Rural Households
10-3 城乡居民人民币储蓄存款 …… (347)
Savings Deposit in Urban and Rural Areas
10-4 各地区城乡居民人民币储蓄存款（年底余额）…… (348)
Savings Deposit of Urban and Rural Household by Region at the Year-end
10-5 城镇居民家庭基本情况 …… (349)
Basic Conditions of Urban Households
10-6 城镇居民家庭基本情况（2005年）…… (350)
Basic Condition of Urban Households (2005)
10-7 城镇居民家庭平均每人全年消费性支出（2005年）…… (350)
Per Capita Annual Living Expenditure of Urban Households (2005)

10-8 东、中、西部及东北地区城镇居民家庭基本情况（2005年）……（352）
Basic Conditions of Urban Households of Eastern, Central, Western and Northeastern Region (2005)
10-9 城镇居民家庭平均每人全年购买主要商品数量 ……（353）
Per Capita Annual Purchases of Major Commodities of Urban Households
10-10 城镇居民家庭平均每百户年底耐用消费品拥有量 ……（353）
Number of Major Durable Consumer Goods Owned Per 100 Urban Households at the Year-end
10-11 东、中、西部及东北地区城镇居民家庭平均每人全年购买的主要商品数量（2005年）……（354）
Per Capita Annual Purchase Major Commodities of Urban Households of Eastern, Central, Western and Northeastern Region (2005)
10-12 东、中、西部及东北地区城镇居民家庭平均每百户年底耐用消费品拥有量（2005年）……（354）
Number of Durable Consumer Goods Owned Per 100 Urban Households of Eastern, Central, Western and Northeastern Region at the Year-end (2005)
10-13 按收入等级分城镇居民家庭平均每人全年购买主要商品数量（2005年）……（355）
Per Capita Annual Purchases of Major Commodities of Urban Households by Level of Income (2005)
10-14 按收入等级分城镇居民家庭平均每百户年底耐用消费品拥有量（2005年）……（356）
Number of Durable Consumer Goods Owned Per 100 Urban Households at Year-end by Level of Income (2005)
10-15 各地区城镇居民平均每人全年家庭收入来源（2005年）……（357）
Per Capita Annual Income of Urban Households by Sources and Region (2005)
10-16 各地区城镇居民家庭平均每人全年消费性支出（2005年）……（358）
Per Capita Annual Consumption Expenditure of Urban Households by Region (2005)
10-17 各地区城镇居民家庭平均每百户耐用消费品拥有量（2005年底）……（364）
Number of Major Durable Consumer Goods Owned Per 100 Urban Households at the Year-end by Region (2005)
10-18 农村居民家庭基本情况 ……（368）
Basic Conditions of Rural Households
10-19 农村居民按纯收入分组的户数占调查户比重 ……（369）
Percentage of Rural Households Grouped by Per Capita Annual Net Income
10-20 农村居民家庭平均每人纯收入 ……（369）
Per Capita Annual Net Income of Rural Households
10-21 各地区农村居民家庭人均纯收入 ……（370）
Per Capita Net Income of Rural Households by Region
10-22 各地区按来源分农村居民家庭人均纯收入（2005年）……（371）
Per Capita Annual Net Income of Rural Households by Sources and Region (2005)
10-23 按收入五等份分农村居民家庭基本情况（2005年）……（372）
Basic Conditions of Rural Households by Five Equal Parts of Income (2005)
10-24 按收入五等份分农村居民家庭平均每人生活消费支出（2005年）……（372）
Per Capita Consumption Expenditure of Rural Households by Five Equal Parts of Income (2005)
10-25 农村居民家庭平均每人生活消费支出构成 ……（373）
Composition of Per Capita Consumption Expenditure of Rural Households
10-26 各地区农村居民家庭平均每人生活消费支出（2005年）……（374）
Per Capita Consumption Expenditure of Rural Households by Region (2005)
10-27 各地区农村居民家庭平均每人生活消费现金支出（2005年）……（375）
Per Capita Cash Consumption Expenditure of Rural Households by Region (2005)
10-28 东、中、西部及东北地区农村居民家庭基本情况（2005年）……（376）
Basic Conditions of Rural Households of Eastern, Central, Western and Northeastern Region (2005)
10-29 农村居民家庭平均每人主要食品消费量 ……（377）
Per Capita Consumption of Major Foods in Rural Households of National at the Year-end
10-30 农村居民家庭平均每百户年底耐用消费品拥有量 ……（377）
Number of Durable Consumer Goods Owned Per 100 Rural Households at the Year-end
10-31 东、中、西部及东北地区农村居民家庭平均每人主要食品消费量（2005年）……（378）
Major Foods Consumption Per Capita in Whole Year of Rural Households of Eastern, Central, Western and Northeastern Region (2005)

10-32 东、中、西部及东北地区农村居民家庭平均每百户年底耐用消费品拥有量（2005年）……………………（378）
Number of Durable Consumer Goods Owned per 100 Rural Households of Eastern, Central, Western and Northeastern Region (2005)
10-33 各地区农村居民家庭平均每人主要食品消费量（2005年）……………………（379）
Per Capita Consumption of Major Food in Rural Households by Region (2005)
10-34 各地区农村居民家庭平均每百户主要耐用消费品拥有量（2005年底）……………………（380）
Number of Durable Consumer Goods Owned Per 100 Rural Households by Region at the Year-end (2005)
10-35 城乡新建住宅面积和居民住房情况 ……………………（382）
Floor Space of Newly Built and Housing Conditions of Urban and Rural Residents
10-36 农村居民家庭住房情况 ……………………（382）
Housing Conditions of Rural Households
10-37 各地区农村居民家庭住房情况（2005年）……………………（383）
Housing Conditions of Rural Households at the Year-end by Region (2005)
主要统计指标解释……………………（384）
Explanatory Notes on Main Statistical Indicators

十一、城市概况
General Survey of Cities

简要说明
Brief Introduction
11-1 全部地级城市数（2005年）……………………（389）
Number of Cities at Prefecture Level (2005)
11-2 沿海开放城市和经济特区城市社会经济指标（2005年）……………………（390）
Main Social and Economic Indicators of Coastal Opening Cities and Cities in Special Economic Zones (2005)
11-3 省会城市和计划单列市主要指标（2005年）……………………（392）
Main Indicators of Provincial Capitals and Separate Planning Cities (2005)
11-4 地级及以上城市国民经济和社会发展主要指标（2005年）……………………（394）
Main Indicators of Economic and Social Development of Cities at Prefecture Level and above (2005)
11-5 城市公用事业基本情况 ……………………（395）
Basic Statistics on City Public Utilities
11-6 各地区城市建设情况（2005年）……………………（396）
Statistics on City Construction by Region (2005)
11-7 各地区城市供水情况（2005年）……………………（397）
Basic Statistics on Tap Water Supply in Cities by Region (2005)
11-8 各地区城市燃气情况（2005年）……………………（398）
Basic Statistics on Supply of Gas in Cities by Region (2005)
11-9 各地区城市集中供热情况（2005年）……………………（399）
Basic Statistics on Heating in Cities by Region (2005)
11-10 各地区城市市政设施（2005年）……………………（400）
Basic Statistics on Municipal Infrastructure in Cities by Region (2005)
11-11 各地区城市公共交通情况（2005年）……………………（401）
Basic Statistics on Public Transportation in Cities by Region (2005)
11-12 各地区城市园林和绿地（2005年）……………………（402）
Basic Statistics on Parks, Gardens and Green Areas in Cities by Region (2005)
11-13 各地区城市环境卫生情况（2005年）……………………（403）
Basic Statistics on Urban Sanitation in Cities by Region (2005)
11-14 各地区城市设施水平（2005年）……………………（404）
Level of Public Facilities in Cities by Region (2005)
主要统计指标解释 ……………………（405）
Explanatory Notes on Main Statistical Indicators

十二、环境保护
Environment Protection

简要说明
Brief Introduction
12-1 环境保护基本情况 …… (409)
Basic Statistics on Environmental Protection
12-2 水资源情况 …… (412)
Water Resources
12-3 供水用水情况 …… (413)
Water Supply and Water Use
12-4 各地区废水排放及处理情况（2005年） …… (414)
Discharge and Treatment of Industrial Waste Water by Region (2005)
12-5 工业按行业分废水排放及处理情况（2005年） …… (416)
Discharge and Treatment of Waste Water by Sector (2005)
12-6 主要城市工业废水排放及处理情况（2005年） …… (417)
Discharge and Treatment of Industrial Waste Water in Major Cities (2005)
12-7 全海域海水水质评价结果（2005年） …… (418)
Ambient Sea Water Quality (2005)
12-8 主要城市空气质量指标（2005年） …… (418)
Ambient Air Quality in Major Cities (2005)
12-9 各地区废气排放及处理情况（2005年） …… (419)
Emission and Treatment of Industrial Waste Gas by Region (2005)
12-10 主要城市工业废气排放及处理情况（2005年） …… (421)
Emission and Treatment of Industrial Waste Gas in Major Cities (2005)
12-11 工业按行业分废气排放及处理情况（2005年） …… (422)
Emission and Treatment of Waste Gas by Sector (2005)
12-12 各地区工业固体废物产生及处理利用情况（2005年） …… (424)
Production, Treatment and Utilization of Industrial Solid Wastes by Region (2005)
12-13 按行业分工业固体废物产生及处理利用情况（2005年） …… (425)
Production, Treatment and Utilization of Industrial Solid Wastes by Sector (2005)
12-14 主要城市工业固体废物产生及处理利用情况（2005年） …… (427)
Emission and Treatment of Industrial Sold Waste in Major Cities (2005)
12-15 各地区城市生活垃圾清运和处理情况（2005年） …… (428)
Collection, Transport and Disposal of Consumption Wastes in Cities by Region (2005)
12-16 主要城市道路交通噪声监测情况（2005年） …… (430)
Monitoring of Urban Road Traffic Noise in Major Cities (2005)
12-17 国控主要城市区域环境噪声监测情况（2005年） …… (431)
Monitoring of Urban Environment Noise in Major Cities under National Control Programme (2005)
12-18 各地区土地利用情况（2005年） …… (432)
Land Use by Region (2005)
12-19 各地区森林资源情况 …… (433)
Forest Resources by Region
12-20 造林面积 …… (434)
Area of Afforestation
12-21 林业重点工程造林面积 …… (435)
Area of Key Afforestation Projects
12-22 各地区湿地面积 …… (436)
Area of Wetlands by Region
12-23 红树林各地类面积 …… (437)
Site Classification and Area of Sharpleaf Mangrove (Rhizophora Apiculata)
12-24 各地区自然保护基本情况（2005年） …… (437)

Basic Situation of Natural Protection by Region (2005)
12-25 地质灾害及防治情况 …… (438)
Geological Disasters and Prevention and Cure
12-26 森林火灾情况 …… (440)
Forest Fires
12-27 森林病虫鼠害防治情况 …… (441)
Prevention of Forest Diseases, Pests and Rats
12-28 环境污染与破坏事故情况 …… (443)
Environment Pollution and Destruction Accidents
12-29 地震灾害情况 …… (444)
Earthquake Disasters
12-30 主要海洋灾害情况（2005年） …… (444)
Major Marine Disasters (2005)
12-31 环境污染治理投资 …… (444)
Investment in the Treatment of Environmental Pollution
12-32 工业污染治理投资来源 …… (445)
Sources of Investment in the Treatment of Industrial Pollution
12-33 工业污染治理投资完成情况 …… (446)
Investment Completed in the Treatment of Industrial Pollution
12-34 林业系统营林固定资产投资资金来源 …… (447)
Sources of Funds of Investment in Fixed Assets for Afforestation in Forest System
12-35 林业系统营林固定资产投资完成情况 …… (448)
Investment in Fixed Assets Completed for Afforestation in Forest System
主要统计指标解释 …… (449)
Explanatory Notes on Main Statistical Indicators

十三、农业
Agriculture

简要说明
Brief Introduction
13-1 农村基层组织和农业基本情况 …… (461)
Basic Conditions of Rural Grass-root Units and Agriculture
13-2 主要农牧渔业生产情况 …… (462)
Output of Farming, Animal Husbandry and Fishery
13-3 农村基层组织情况 …… (463)
Basic Conditions of Rural Grass-root Unit
13-4 乡村从业人员（年底数） …… (464)
Rural Laborers at the Year-end
13-5 各地区耕地面积 …… (465)
Area of Cultivated Land by Region
13-6 农、林、牧、渔业总产值及指数 …… (466)
Gross Output Value of Farming, Forestry, Animal Husbandry and Fishery and Related Indices
13-7 主要农业机械拥有量（年底数） …… (467)
Major Agricultural Machinery at the Year-end
13-8 有效灌溉面积、农用化肥施用量、农村水电站及用电量 …… (469)
Irrigated Area, Consumption of Chemical Fertilizers, Number of Hydropower Stations and Electricity Consumption in Rural Areas
13-9 农村水电建设和发电量 …… (470)
Rural Hydropower Construction and Amount of Electric Power Generation
13-10 灌溉、水库和除涝、治水、治碱情况 …… (471)
Irrigation, Reservoirs, Flood Prevention, Water and Soil Conservation and Improvement of

Saline-Alkaline Land
13-11 各地区水利设施和除涝、治碱面积（2005年）…………（472）
Water Conservancy Facilities and Area with Flood Prevention Measures and Improved Area of Saline-Alkaline Land by Region (2005)
13-12 农村居民家庭生产性固定资产原值（年底数）…………（473）
Original Value of Productive Fixed Assets of Rural Household at the Year-end
13-13 农村居民家庭平均每百户拥有主要生产性固定资产数量（年底数）…………（474）
Number of Major Productive Fixed Assets Per 100 Rural Households at the Year-end
13-14 各地区农村居民家庭土地经营情况（2005年底）…………（475）
Area of Land Managed by Rural Households at the Year-end by Region (2005)
13-15 农作物总播种面积 …………（476）
Total Sown Areas of Farm Crops
13-16 主要农作物种植结构 …………（479）
Planting Structure of Major Farm Crops
13-17 主要农产品产量 …………（480）
Output of Major Farm Products
13-18 主要农产品单位面积产量 …………（483）
Output of Major Farm Products Per Hectare
13-19 主要林产品产量 …………（484）
Output of Major Forest Products
13-20 牲畜饲养情况…………（485）
Number of Livestock
13-21 畜产品产量…………（487）
Output of Livestock Products
13-22 水产品产量…………（489）
Output of Aquatic Products
13-23 主要农产品人均占有量 …………（491）
Per Capita Output of Major Farm Products
13-24 平均每一农林牧渔业从业人员主要农产品生产量 …………（492）
Output of Major Farm Products Per Agricultural Laborer
13-25 农村居民家庭平均每人出售主要农产品 …………（493）
Per Capita Major Farm Products Sold by Rural Households
13-26 农村居民家庭平均每人出售主要畜产品及水产品 …………（494）
Sales of Livestock, Poultry, Small Animals and Fishery Per Capita Rural Household
13-27 主要农产品产量与解放前最高年产量比较 …………（495）
Output of Major Agricultural Products in Comparison with Peak Year Prior to 1949
13-28 受灾面积和成灾面积 …………（496）
Areas Covered and Affected by Natural Disaster
13-29 国营农场基本情况 …………（497）
Basic Statistics on State Farms
主要统计指标解释…………（498）
Explanatory Notes on Main Statistical Indicators

十四、工业
Industry

简要说明
Brief Introduction
14-1 全部工业企业主要经济指标（2004年）…………（505）
Main Economic Indicators of All Industrial Enterprises (2004)
14-2 按行业分全部工业企业主要经济指标（2004年）…………（506）
Main Economic Indicators of All Industrial Enterprises by Sector (2004)

14-3 各地区全部工业企业主要经济指标（2004年）…… (508)
Main Indicators of All Industrial Enterprises by Region (2004)
14-4 按行业分全部国有及规模以上非国有工业企业主要指标（2005年）…… (510)
Main Indicators of State-owned and Non-state-owned Industrial Enterprises above Designated Size by Industrial Sector (2005)
14-5 按行业分全部国有及规模以上非国有工业企业主要经济效益指标（2005年）…… (514)
Main Indicators on Economic Benefit of All State-owned and Non-state-owned Industrial Enterprises above Designated Size by Industrial Sector (2005)
14-6 全部国有及规模以上非国有工业企业主要指标 …… (516)
Main Indicators of All State-owned and Non-state-owned Industrial Enterprises above Designated Size
14-7 全部国有及规模以上非国有工业企业主要经济效益指标(2005年) …… (519)
Main Indicators on Economic Benefit of All State-owned and Non-state-owned Industrial Enterprises above Designated Size (2005)
14-8 按行业分国有及国有控股工业企业主要指标（2005年）…… (520)
Main Indicators of State-owned and State-holding Industrial Enterprises by Industrial Sector (2005)
14-9 按行业分国有及国有控股工业企业主要经济效益指标（2005年）…… (524)
Main Indicators on Economic Benefit of State-owned and State-holding Industrial Enterprises by Industrial Sector (2005)
14-10 国有及国有控股工业企业主要指标 …… (526)
Main Indicators of State-owned and State-holding Industrial Enterprises
14-11 国有及国有控股工业企业主要经济效益指标（2005年）…… (529)
Main Indicators on Economic Benefit of State-owned and State-holding Industrial Enterprises (2005)
14-12 按行业分私营工业企业主要指标（2005年）…… (530)
Main Indicators of Private Enterprises by Industrial Sector (2005)
14-13 按行业分私营工业企业主要经济效益指标（2005年）…… (534)
Main Indicators on Economic Benefit of Private Industrial Enterprises by Industrial Sector (2005)
14-14 私营工业企业主要指标 …… (536)
Main Indicators of Private Industrial Enterprises
14-15 私营工业企业主要经济效益指标（2005年）…… (539)
Main Indicators on Economic Benefit of Private Industrial Enterprises (2005)
14-16 按行业分"三资"工业企业主要指标（2005年）…… (540)
Main Indicators of Industrial Enterprises with Hong Kong, Macao, Taiwan and Foreign Funds by Industrial Sector (2005)
14-17 按行业分"三资"工业企业主要经济效益指标（2005年）…… (544)
Main Indicators on Economic Benefit of Industrial Enterprises with Hong Kong, Macao, Taiwan and Foreign Funds by Industrial Sector (2005)
14-18 "三资"工业企业主要指标 …… (546)
Main Indicators of Industrial Enterprises with Hong Kong, Macao, Taiwan and Foreign Funds
14-19 "三资"工业企业主要经济效益指标（2005年）…… (549)
Main Indicators on Economic Benefit of Industrial Enterprises with Hong Kong, Macao, Taiwan and Foreign Funds (2005)
14-20 按行业分大中型工业企业主要指标（2005年）…… (550)
Main Indicators of Large and Medium-sized Industrial Enterprises by Industrial Sector (2005)
14-21 按行业分大中型工业企业主要经济效益指标（2005年）…… (554)
Main Indicators on Economic Benefit of Large and Medium-sized Industrial Enterprises by Industrial Sector (2005)
14-22 大中型工业企业主要指标 …… (556)
Main Indicators of Large and Medium-sized Industrial Enterprises
14-23 大中型工业企业主要经济效益指标（2005年）…… (559)
Main Indicators on Economic Benefit of Large and Medium-sized Industrial Enterprises (2005)
14-24 主要工业产品产量 …… (560)
Output of Major Industrial Products
14-25 工业产品产量 …… (565)

Output of Industrial Products
14-26 规模以上工业主要产品生产能力（2004年）…………（567）
Production Capacity of Main Products of Industrial Enterprises above Designated Size (2004)
主要统计指标解释 …………（569）
Explanatory Notes on Main Statistical Indicators

十五、建筑业
Construction

简要说明
Brief Introduction
15-1 建筑业企业概况 …………（579）
Main Indicators on Construction Enterprises
15-2 按登记注册类型分建筑业企业主要经济指标（2005年）…………（580）
Main Economic Indicators on Construction Enterprises by Registration Status (2005)
15-3 建筑业企业主要经济指标 …………（582）
Main Economic Indicators on Construction Enterprises
15-4 各地区总承包建筑业企业主要经济指标（2005年）…………（583）
Main Economic Indicators on Construction Enterprises of General Contractors by Region (2005)
15-5 各地区专业承包建筑业企业主要经济指标（2005年）…………（584）
Main Economic Indicators on Construction Enterprises of Professional Contractors by Region (2005)
15-6 各地区建筑业总产值 …………（585）
Total Output Value of Construction by Region
15-7 各地区建筑业增加值 …………（586）
Value-added of Construction by Region
15-8 各地区建筑业企业利税总额 …………（587）
Total Pre-Tax Profits of Construction Enterprises by Region
15-9 各地区建筑业企业利润总额 …………（588）
Total Profits of Construction Enterprises by Region
15-10 各地区建筑业劳动生产率 …………（589）
Labor Productivity of Construction Enterprises by Region
15-11 各地区按登记注册类型分建筑业企业单位数（2005年）…………（590）
Number of Construction Enterprises by Registration Status and Region (2005)
15-12 各地区按登记注册类型分建筑业企业从业人员（2005年）…………（591）
Number of Staff and Workers in Construction Enterprises by Registration Status and Region (2005)
15-13 建筑业企业技术装备情况 …………（592）
Number and Power of Machinery and Equipment Owned by Construction Enterprises
15-14 国有建筑业企业技术装备情况 …………（593）
Number and Power of Machinery and Equipment Owned by State-owned Construction Enterprises
15-15 各地区建筑业总产值（2005年）…………（594）
Total Output Value of Construction by Region (2005)
15-16 各地区按登记注册类型分建筑业总产值（2005年）…………（595）
Total Output Value of Construction by Registration Status and Region (2005)
15-17 各地区按行业分建筑业总产值（2005年）…………（596）
Total Output Value of Construction by Branch and Region (2005)
15-18 各地区按资质等级分总承包建筑业总产值（2005年）…………（597）
Total Output Value of Construction of General Contractors by Qualification Criteria and by Region (2005)
15-19 各地区按资质等级分专业承包建筑业总产值（2005年）…………（598）
Total Output Value of Construction of Professional Contractors by Qualification Criteria and by Region (2005)
15-20 各地区建筑业企业签订合同情况（2005年）…………（599）
Contracts Signed by Construction Enterprises by Region (2005)
15-21 各地区建筑业企业承包工程完成情况（2005年）…………（600）

Completion of Contracted Projects by Construction Enterprises by Region (2005)
15-22 各地区按登记注册类型分建筑业企业实收资本（2005年）……(601)
Paid-up Capitals of Construction Enterprises by Registration Status and Region (2005)
15-23 各地区建筑业企业资产（2005年）……(602)
Assets of Construction Enterprises by Region (2005)
15-24 各地区按登记注册类型分建筑业企业资产（2005年）……(603)
Assets of Construction Enterprises by Registration Status and Region (2005)
15-25 各地区建筑业企业负债及所有者权益（2005年）……(604)
Liabilities and Owners' Equity of Construction Enterprises by Region (2005)
15-26 各地区按登记注册类型分建筑业企业所有者权益（2005年）……(605)
Owners' Equity of Construction Enterprises by Registration Status and Region (2005)
15-27 各地区按登记注册类型分建筑业企业负债（2005年）……(606)
Liabilities of Construction Enterprises by Registration Status and Region (2005)
15-28 各地区建筑业企业总收入（2005年）……(607)
Total Income of Construction Enterprises by Region (2005)
15-29 各地区按登记注册类型分建筑业企业总收入（2005年）……(608)
Total Income of Construction by Registration Status and Region (2005)
15-30 各地区建筑业企业利税总额（2005年）……(609)
Total Pre-Tax Profits of Construction Enterprises by Region (2005)
15-31 各地区按登记注册类型分建筑业企业税金总额（2005年）……(610)
Taxes of Construction Enterprises by Registration Status and by Region (2005)
15-32 各地区按登记注册类型分建筑业企业利润总额（2005年）……(611)
Total Profits of Construction Enterprises by Registration Status and Region (2005)
15-33 各地区按资质等级分总承包建筑业企业利润总额（2005年）……(612)
Total Profits of Construction of General Contractors by Qualification Criteria and by Region (2005)
15-34 各地区按资质等级分专业承包建筑业企业利润总额（2005年）……(613)
Total Profits of Construction of General Contractors by Qualification Criteria and by Region (2005)
15-35 各地区按登记注册类型分建筑业企业工程结算利润（2005年）……(614)
Profits of Project Settlement Accounts of Construction Enterprises by Registration Status and Region (2005)
15-36 各地区建筑业劳动生产率（2005年）……(615)
Labor Productivity of Construction Enterprises by Region (2005)
15-37 建筑业房屋建筑面积……(616)
Floor Space of Buildings of Construction Enterprises
15-38 各地区劳务分包建筑业企业主要指标（2005年）……(617)
Main Indicators of Construction Enterprises of Work Subcontractors by Region (2005)
15-39 勘察设计机构和人员数（2005年）……(618)
Number of Prospecting and Designing Institutions and Their Staff and Workers (2005)
15-40 勘察设计单位营业收入情况（2005年）……(619)
Business Revenue of Prospecting and Designing Institutions (2005)
15-41 建设工程监理企业和人员数(2005年)……(620)
Construction Project Supervision Enterprises and Employees (2005)
15-42 建设工程监理营业收入(2005年)……(621)
Business Revenue of Construction Project Supervision Enterprises (2005)
主要统计指标解释……(622)
Explanatory Notes on Main Statistical Indicators

十六、运输和邮电
Transport, Post and Telecommunication Services

简要说明
Brief Introduction
16-1 各地区交通运输、邮电通信业职工人数（2005年底）……(629)

Number of Staff and Employed Workers in Transport, Post and Telecommunication Services at the Year-end by Region (2005)
16-2 交通运输业基本情况 …… (630)
Basic Conditions of Transport
16-3 各地区运输线路长度（2005年底） …… (631)
Length of Transport Routes at the Year-end by Region (2005)
16-4 运输线路长度 …… (632)
Length of Transportation Routes
16-5 运输线路质量 …… (632)
Quality of Transport Routes
16-6 客运量 …… (633)
Passenger Traffic
16-7 旅客周转量 …… (633)
Passenger-Kilometers
16-8 货运量 …… (634)
Freight Traffic
16-9 货物周转量 …… (634)
Freight Ton-Kilometers
16-10 旅客运输平均运距 …… (635)
Average Transport Distance of Passengers
16-11 货物运输平均运距 …… (635)
Average Transport Distance of Freight
16-12 各地区客运量（2005年） …… (636)
Passenger Traffic by Region (2005)
16-13 各地区旅客周转量（2005年） …… (637)
Passenger-kilometers by Region (2005)
16-14 各地区货运量（2005年） …… (638)
Freight Traffic by Region (2005)
16-15 各地区货物周转量（2005年） …… (639)
Freight Ton-kilometers by Region (2005)
16-16 国家营业铁路基本情况 …… (640)
Basic Statistics on National Railways in Operation
16-17 铁路机车拥有量 …… (640)
Number of Railway Locomotives
16-18 国家铁路客、货车拥有量 …… (641)
Number of National Railway Passenger Coaches and Freight Cars Owned
16-19 国家铁路运输固定资产 …… (642)
Fixed Assets of National Railway Transport
16-20 按货类分国家铁路货物运输量 …… (642)
National Railway Freight Traffic by Category of Cargo
16-21 铁路主要干线客货运输量（2005年） …… (643)
Passenger and Freight Traffic of Principal Trunk Railways (2005)
16-22 铁路主要车站旅客发送量 …… (644)
Number of Passengers Dispatched from Principal Railway Stations
16-23 铁路主要车站货物发送量 …… (645)
Volume of Freight Dispatched from Principal Railway Stations
16-24 国家铁路运输主要财务指标 …… (645)
Financial Indicators of National Railway Transport
16-25 国家铁路运输主要技术经济指标 …… (646)
Principal Economic and Technical Indicators of National Railway Transport
16-26 民用汽车拥有量 …… (647)
Possession of Civil Vehicles
16-27 私人汽车拥有量 …… (649)

Possession of Private Vehicles
16-28 新注册民用汽车数量 …………………………………………………………………………………… (651)
New Registration Statistics on Civil Vehicles
16-29 公路运输汽车拥有量 …………………………………………………………………………………… (653)
Possession of Vehicles for Highway Transportation
16-30 民用运输船舶拥有量 …………………………………………………………………………………… (654)
Possession of Civil Transport Vessels
16-31 私人运输船舶拥有量 …………………………………………………………………………………… (655)
Possession of Private Transport Vessels
16-32 沿海主要港口分货类吞吐量 ……………………………………………………………………………… (656)
Volume of Freight Handled in Major Coastal Ports by Type of Freight
16-33 沿海主要港口货物吞吐量 ………………………………………………………………………………… (656)
Volume of Freight Handled in Major Coastal Ports
16-34 沿海主要港口码头泊位数（2005年底）…………………………………………………………………… (657)
Number of Berths in Major Coastal Ports at the Year-end (2005)
16-35 内河主要港口码头泊位数（2005年底）…………………………………………………………………… (657)
Number of Berths in Major Ports of Inland Rivers at the Year-end (2005)
16-36 民用航空航线及飞机架数 ………………………………………………………………………………… (658)
Number of Civil Aviation Routes and Civil Aircrafts
16-37 民用航空运输量及通用飞行时间 ………………………………………………………………………… (659)
Civil Aviation Traffic and Flying Time of General Aviation
16-38 输油(气)管道长度和运输量（2005年底）……………………………………………………………… (660)
Length and Volume of Petroleum and Gas Pipelines at the Year-end (2005)
16-39 邮电业务基本情况 ……………………………………………………………………………………… (662)
Basic Conditions of Post and Telecommunication Services
16-40 邮电业务量 ……………………………………………………………………………………………… (663)
Business Volume of Post and Telecommunication Services
16-41 邮政局所数及邮递线路(年底数) ………………………………………………………………………… (666)
Post and Telecommunication Services Facilities (Year-end)
16-42 电信主要通信能力（年底数）…………………………………………………………………………… (667)
Main Communication Capacity of Telecommunications (Year-end)
16-43 邮电通信服务水平 ……………………………………………………………………………………… (668)
Level of Post and Telecommunication Services
主要统计指标解释 ………………………………………………………………………………………………… (669)
Explanatory Notes on Main Statistical Indicators

十七、国内贸易
Domestic Trade

简要说明
Brief Introduction
17-1 国内贸易基本情况 ……………………………………………………………………………………… (677)
Basic Conditions of Domestic Trade
17-2 消费品市场交易情况 …………………………………………………………………………………… (677)
Trade of Consumable Markets in Urban and Rural Areas
17-3 社会消费品零售总额 …………………………………………………………………………………… (678)
Retail Sale of Consumer Goods
17-4 按登记注册类型分限额以上批发和零售业、住宿和餐饮业基本情况（2005年）……………………… (679)
Basic Conditions of Enterprises above Designated Size of Wholesale and Retail Trades, Hotels and Catering Services by Status of Registration (2005)
17-5 限额以上批发和零售业、住宿和餐饮业法人企业数 …………………………………………………… (682)
Number of Corporation Units above Designated Size of Wholesale and Retail Trades, Hotels and Catering Services

17-6 限额以上批发和零售业、住宿和餐饮业产业活动单位数 …… (683)
Number of Economic Active Units above Designated Size of Wholesale and Retail Trades, Hotels and Catering Services
17-7 限额以上批发和零售业、住宿和餐饮业从业人数 …… (684)
Number of Persons Employed in Enterprises above Designated Size of Wholesale and Retail Trades, Hotels and Catering Services
17-8 按行业分限额以上批发和零售业商品购、销、存总额（2005年） …… (685)
Total Purchases, Sales and Inventory of Enterprises above Designated Size of Wholesale and Retail Trades by Sector (2005)
17-9 限额以上批发和零售业商品购、销、存总额 …… (686)
Total Purchases, Sales and Inventory of Enterprises above Designated Size of Wholesale and Retail Trades
17-10 限额以上批发和零售业主要商品分类销售额 …… (687)
Sale Values of Enterprises above Designated Size of Wholesale and Retail Trades by Category of Main Commodities
17-11 各地区星级住宿业经营情况 …… (688)
Business of Star-ranking Hotels by Region
17-12 各地区限额以上餐饮业经营情况 …… (689)
Business of Catering Services above Designated Size by Region
17-13 按登记注册类型分限额以上批发、零售企业资产及负债（2005年） …… (690)
Assets and Liabilities of Enterprises above Designated Size of Wholesale and Retail Trades by Status of Registration (2005)
17-14 按行业分限额以上批发、零售企业资产及负债(2005年) …… (692)
Assets and Liabilities of Enterprises above Designated Size of Wholesale and Retail Trades by Sector (2005)
17-15 限额以上批发和零售企业资产及负债 …… (693)
Assets and Liabilities of Enterprises above Designated Size of Wholesale and Retail Trades
17-16 限额以上批发企业资产及负债 …… (694)
Assets and Liabilities of Enterprises above Designated Size of Wholesale Trade
17-17 限额以上零售企业资产及负债 …… (695)
Assets and Liabilities of Enterprises above Designated Size of Retail Trade
17-18 按登记注册类型和行业分限额以上餐饮企业资产及负债(2005年) …… (696)
Assets and Liabilities of Enterprises above Designated Size of Cetering Services by Status of Registration and Sector (2005)
17-19 限额以上餐饮企业资产及负债 …… (697)
Assets and Liabilities of Enterprises above Designated Size of Catering Services
17-20 按登记注册类型分限额以上批发、零售企业主要财务指标(2005年) …… (698)
Main Financial Indicators of Enterprises above Designated Size of Wholesale and Retail Trades by Status of Registration (2005)
17-21 按行业分限额以上批发、零售企业主要财务指标(2005年) …… (700)
Main Financial Indicators of Enterprises above Designated Size of Wholesale and Retail Trades by Sector (2005)
17-22 限额以上批发和零售企业主要财务指标 …… (701)
Main Financial Indicators of Enterprises above Designated Size of Wholesale and Retail Trades
17-23 限额以上批发企业主要财务指标 …… (702)
Main Financial Indicators of Enterprises above Designated Size of Wholesale Trade
17-24 限额以上零售企业主要财务指标 …… (703)
Main Financial Indicators of Enterprises above Designated Size of Retail Trade
17-25 按登记注册类型和行业分限额以上餐饮企业主要财务指标(2005年) …… (704)
Main Financial Indicators of Enterprises above Designated Size of Catering Services by Status of Registration and Sector (2005)
17-26 限额以上餐饮企业主要财务指标 …… (705)
Main Financial Indicators of Enterprises above Designated Size of Catering Services
17-27 按业态分限额以上连锁零售企业基本情况 …… (706)
Basic Conditions of Enterprises above Designated Size of Chain Stores by Business Categories
17-28 按登记注册类型分限额以上连锁零售企业基本情况 …… (709)
Basic Conditions of Enterprises above Designated Size of Chain Stores by Status of Registration

17-29 分地区限额以上连锁零售企业基本情况 …… (711)
Basic Conditions of Enterprises above Designated Size of Chain Stores by Region
17-30 按业态分限额以上连锁餐饮企业基本情况 …… (713)
Basic Conditions of Enterprises above Designated Size of Chain Catering Services by Business Categories
17-31 按登记注册类型分限额以上连锁餐饮企业基本情况 …… (715)
Basic Conditions of Enterprises above Designated Size of Chain Catering Services by Status of Registration
17-32 分地区限额以上连锁餐饮企业基本情况 …… (717)
Basic Conditions of Enterprises above Designated Size of Chain Catering Services by Region
17-33 按登记注册类型分限额以上连锁住宿企业基本情况 …… (719)
Basic Conditions of Enterprises above Designated Size in Chain Hotels by Status of Registration
17-34 分地区限额以上连锁住宿企业基本情况 …… (721)
Basic Conditions of Enterprises above Designated Size of Chain Hotels by Region
17-35 亿元以上商品交易市场基本情况（2005年） …… (722)
Basic Statistics on Commodity Exchange Markets of Turnover above 100 Million Yuan (2005)
17-36 亿元以上商品交易市场摊位分类情况（2005年） …… (723)
Classification of Commodity Transaction Markets of Turnover above 100 Million Yuan (2005)
17-37 各地区亿元以上商品交易市场基本情况 …… (724)
Basic Statistics on Commodity Exchange Markets of Turnover above 100 Million Yuan by Region
主要统计指标解释 …… (725)
Explanatory Notes on Main Statistical Indicators

十八、对外经济贸易
Foreign Trade and Economic Cooperation

简要说明
Brief Introduction
18-1 对外经济贸易基本情况 …… (733)
Foreign Trade and Economic Cooperation
18-2 人民币对主要外币年平均汇价（中间价） …… (734)
Average Exchange Rate of RMB Yuan Against Main Convertible Currencies (Middle Rate)
18-3 货物进出口总额 …… (734)
Total Value of Imports and Exports
18-4 按贸易方式分货物进出口总额 …… (735)
Total Value of Imports and Exports by Way of Trade
18-5 历年出口货物分类金额 …… (736)
Exports Value by Category of Commodities (Customs Statistics)
18-6 历年进口货物分类金额 …… (737)
Imports Value by Category of Commodities (Customs Statistics)
18-7 进出口货物分类金额 …… (738)
Value of Imports and Exports by Category of Commodities (Customs Statistics)
18-8 我国同各国(地区)海关货物进出口总额 …… (740)
Volume of Imports and Exports by Countries and Regions (Customs Statistics)
18-9 出口主要货物数量和金额 …… (744)
Main Export Commodities in Volume and Value (Customs Statistics)
18-10 进口主要货物数量和金额 …… (747)
Main Import Commodities in Volume and Value (Customs Statistics)
18-11 各地区按经营单位所在地分货物进出口总额 …… (749)
Total Value of Imports and Exports by Location of China's Foreign Trade Managing Units
18-12 各地区按境内目的地和货源地分货物进出口总额 …… (750)
Imports Value of Commodities by the Places of Their Destination and Exports Value of Commodities by the Places of Their Origin in China
18-13 各地区外商投资企业货物进出口总额 …… (751)

Value of Imports and Exports of Foreign-funded Enterprises by Region
18-14 利用外资概况 …… (752)
Utilization of Foreign Capital
18-15 按方式分外商投资额 …… (752)
Amount of Foreign Investment by Type
18-16 按国别(地区)分实际外商投资额 …… (753)
Actual Foreign Investment by Countries or Regions
18-17 按行业分外商直接投资（2005年） …… (756)
Foreign Direct Investment by Sector (2005)
18-18 按行业分外商投资企业年底注册登记情况（2005年） …… (757)
Registration Status of Foreign Funded Enterprises by Sector at the Year-end (2005)
18-19 各地区外商投资企业年底注册登记情况 …… (758)
Registration Status of Foreign Funded Enterprises by Region at the Year-end
18-20 按主要国别(地区)分对外直接投资(非金融类) …… (759)
Overseas Direct Investment by Countries or Regions (Non-Finance)
18-21 按行业分对外直接投资（非金融类） …… (760)
Overseas Direct Investment by Sector (non-financial)
18-22 对外经济合作 …… (761)
Economic Cooperation with Foreign Countries or Regions
18-23 按国别(地区)分对外经济合作完成营业额 …… (762)
Turnover of Economic Cooperation with Foreign Countries or Regions
主要统计指标解释 …… (767)
Explanatory Notes on Main Statistical Indicators

十九、旅游
Tourism

简要说明
Brief Introduction
19-1 旅游事业发展情况 …… (773)
Development of Tourism
19-2 国际旅游外汇收入及构成 …… (774)
Foreign Exchange Earnings and Its Composition
19-3 按性别、年龄和事由分外国入境旅游人数 …… (774)
Number of Foreigner Tourists by Sex, Age and Purpose
19-4 按国别分外国入境旅游人数 …… (775)
Number of Foreigner Tourists by Country/Region
19-5 各地区国际旅游外汇收入 …… (776)
Foreign Exchange Earnings by Region
19-6 各地区接待入境旅游人数 …… (777)
Number of International Tourists by Region
19-7 国内旅游情况 …… (777)
Statistics of Domestic Tourism
主要统计指标解释 …… (778)
Explanatory Notes on Main Statistical Indicators

二十、金融业
Financial Intermediation

简要说明
Brief Introduction
20-1 银行系统机构、人员数（2005年底） …… (781)

Number of Institutions and Employed Persons in Finance System at the Year-end (2005)
20-2 金融机构人民币信贷资金平衡表（资金来源） …… (781)
Credit Funds Balance Sheet of Financial Institutions (Sources of Funds)
20-3 金融机构人民币信贷资金平衡表（资金运用） …… (782)
Credit Funds Balance Sheet of Financial Institutions (Uses of Funds)
20-4 金融机构现金收入 …… (782)
Cash Income of Financial Institutions
20-5 金融机构现金支出 …… (782)
Cash Expenditures of Financial Institutions
20-6 金融机构现金投放与回笼 …… (783)
Cash Statistics of Financial Institutions
20-7 国家银行人民币信贷收支（年底余额） …… (784)
Sources and Uses of Credit Funds of National Banks at the Year-end
20-8 货币供应量（年底余额） …… (785)
Money Supply at the Year-end
20-9 货币供应量同比增长率 …… (785)
Percentage Change of Money Supply Over the Last Corresponding Period
20-10 金融机构法定存款利率 …… (786)
Nominal Interest Rates on Deposits of Financial Institutions
20-11 金融机构法定贷款利率 …… (786)
Nominal Interest Rates on Loans of Financial Institutions
20-12 黄金和外汇储备 …… (787)
Gold and Foreign Exchange Reserves
20-13 国有商业银行资产负债表（年底余额） …… (787)
Balance Sheet of State-owned Commercial Banks at the Year-end
20-14 外资银行资产负债表（年底余额） …… (788)
Balance Sheet of Foreign Capital Banks at the Year-end
20-15 国内有价证券分类发行情况（2005年） …… (788)
Issuance of Domestic Securities (2005)
20-16 证券市场基本情况 …… (789)
General Statistics on Securities Markets
20-17 上市公司数量 …… (789)
Summary for Number of Listed Companies
20-18 股票发行量和筹资额 …… (790)
Issued Share and Raised Capital
20-19 股票交易情况 …… (790)
Trading Summary for Stocks
20-20 保险系统机构、人员数（2005年底） …… (791)
Number of Institutions and Employed Persons in Insurance System (Year-end of 2005)
20-21 保险公司业务经济技术指标（2005年） …… (791)
Economic and Technical Indicators of Insurance Companies Funded with Chinese and Foreign Capital (2005)
主要统计指标解释 …… (792)
Explanatory Notes on Main Statistical Indicators

二十一、教育和科技
Education, Science and Technology

简要说明
Brief Introduction
21-1 学校、教职工和专任教师情况（2005年） …… (797)
Basic Statistics on Schools, Teachers and Staff and Full-time Teachers (2005)

21-2　各级各类学历教育学生情况（2005年）…… (798)
Basic Statistics on Students by Level and Type of Education (2005)
21-3　各级各类学校数 …… (799)
Number of Schools by Level and Type of School
21-4　各级各类学校专任教师数 …… (799)
Number of Full-time Teachers by Level and Type of School
21-5　各级各类学校招生数 …… (800)
Number of New Students Enrollment by Level and Type of School
21-6　各级各类学校在校学生数 …… (800)
Number of Students Enrollment by Level and Type of School
21-7　各级各类学校毕业生数 …… (801)
Number of Graduates by Level and Type of School
21-8　研究生和留学生数 …… (801)
Number of Postgraduates and Students Studying Abroad
21-9　分学科研究生情况（2005年）…… (802)
Number of Postgraduate Students by Field of Study (2005)
21-10　高等教育学校（机构）数（2005年）…… (803)
Number of Schools or Institutions of Higher Education (2005)
21-11　高等学校（机构)学生数（2005年）…… (803)
Number of Students in Regular Institutions of Higher Education (2005)
21-12　成人本、专科分学科学生数（2005年）…… (804)
Number of Students in Adult Institutions of Higher Education by Field of Study (2005)
21-13　普通本、专科分学科学生数（2005年）…… (805)
Number of Students in Undergraduate and Junior Colleges by Field of Study (2005)
21-14　网络本、专科分学科学生数（2005年）…… (805)
Number of Students Enrolled in Internet-based Courses by Field of Study (2005)
21-15　中等职业学校（机构)数（2005年）…… (806)
Number of Secondary Vocational Schools (2005)
21-16　中等职业学校（机构)学生分科类情况（2005年）…… (806)
Students in Secondary Vocational Schools by Field of Study (2005)
21-17　职业技术培训机构基本情况（2005年）…… (807)
Basic Statistics on Vocational/Technical Training Institutions (2005)
21-18　普通高中学校和学生情况（2005年）…… (807)
Statistics on Regular Senior Secondary Schools and Students (2005)
21-19　普通初中学校和学生情况（2005年）…… (808)
Statistics on Regular Junior Secondary Schools and Students (2005)
21-20　职业初中学校和学生情况（2005年）…… (808)
Statistics on Vocational Junior Secondary Schools and Students (2005)
21-21　普通小学学校和学生情况（2005年）…… (809)
Statistics on Regular Primary Schools and Students (2005)
21-22　技工学校数、学生数和教职工数 …… (809)
Number of Technical Schools, Students, Teachers and Staff
21-23　各类技工学校情况（2005年）…… (810)
Statistics on Technical Schools (2005)
21-24　学龄儿童入学率和各级普通学校毕业生升学率 …… (810)
Enrollment Rate of School-age Children and Proportion of Students Entering into Schools of Higher Grade
21-25　各地区高等学校普通本、专科学生数（2005年）…… (811)
Number of Students Enrolled in Undergraduate or Specialized Courses in Institutions of Higher Education by Region (2005)
21-26　各地区普通高等学校（机构）教职工情况（2005年）…… (813)
Situations on Teachers and Staff in Regular Schools (Institutions) of Higher Education by Region (2005)

21-27 各地区中等职业学校（机构)学生情况（2005年）…… (814)
Conditions on Students in Secondary Vocational Schools (Institutions) by Region (2005)
21-28 各地区中等职业学校（机构)教职工数(2005年）…… (815)
Number of Teachers and Staff in Secondary Vocational Schools (Institutions) by Region (2005)
21-29 各地区普通高中基本情况（2005年）…… (816)
Basic Statistics on Regular Senior Secondary Schools by Region (2005)
21-30 各地区普通初中基本情况（2005年）…… (817)
Basic Statistics on Regular Junior Secondary Schools by Region (2005)
21-31 各地区职业初中基本情况（2005年）…… (818)
Basic Statistics on Vocational Junior Secondary Schools by Region (2005)
21-32 各地区普通小学基本情况（2005年）…… (819)
Basic Statistics on Regular Primary Schools by Region (2005)
21-33 各地区特殊教育基本情况（2005年）…… (820)
Basic Statistics on Special Education by Region (2005)
21-34 各地区各级普通学校生师比（2005年）…… (821)
Student-Teacher Ratio by Level of Regular Schools by Region (2005)
21-35 每十万人口各级学校平均在校生数（2005年）…… (822)
Number of Students Per 100 000 Inhabitants by Level (2005)
21-36 各地区教育经费情况 …… (823)
Basic Statistics on Educational Funds by Region
21-37 各类学校教育经费情况（2004年）…… (824)
Educational Funds in Various School (2004)
21-38 科技活动基本情况 …… (825)
Basic Statistics on Scientific and Technological Activities
21-39 科学研究与开发机构基本情况 …… (826)
Basic Statistics on Scientific Research and Development Institutions
21-40 大中型工业企业科技活动基本情况 …… (827)
Basic Statistics on Science and Technology Activities of Large-sized and Medium-sized Industrial Enterprises
21-41 高技术行业大中型工业企业科技活动投入情况（2005年）…… (828)
Basic Statistics on Scientific and Technological Activities Funds of Large-sized and Medium-sized Industrial Enterprises in High-tech Industry (2005)
21-42 高技术行业大中型工业企业科技活动产出情况（2005年）…… (828)
Basic Statistics on Scientific and Technological Activities Outputs of Large-sized and Medium-sized Industrial Enterprises in High-tech Industry (2005)
21-43 高等学校科技活动情况 …… (830)
Basic Statistics on Higher Education for Scientific and Technological Activities
21-44 国内、外三种专利申请受理数 …… (831)
Three Kinds of Applications for Patents Received from Domestic and Foreign Country (Region)
21-45 国内、外三种专利申请授权数 …… (832)
Three Kinds of Patents Granted from Domestic and Foreign Country (Region)
21-46 按地区分国内三种专利申请受理数和授权数（2005年）…… (833)
Patent Applications Examined and Granted by Region (2005)
21-47 按国别(地区)分国外专利申请受理数及授权数（2005年）…… (834)
Patent Applications Examined and Granted by Country (Region) (2005)
21-48 按国际标准分类的发明、实用新型专利申请数和授权数 …… (835)
Inventions and Utility Models of Patent Applications Examined and Granted by International Classifications
21-49 国有企事业单位专业技术人员数（年底数）…… (838)
Number of Scientific and Technical Personnel in State-owned Enterprises and Institutions at the Year-end
21-50 开发区高新技术企业主要经济指标（2005年）…… (839)
Main Economic Indicators of High-tech Enterprises in Development Areas (2005)

21-51 各地区技术市场成交额 …… (840)
Transaction Value in Technical Market by Region
21-52 各地区测绘部门生产完成情况（2005年） …… (841)
Statistics on Projects Completed by Surveying and Mapping Departments by Region (2005)
21-53 各地区测绘资料提供情况（2005年） …… (842)
Statistics on Output of Surveying and Mapping Materials by Region (2005)
21-54 各地区气象业务站点及观测项目情况（2005年） …… (843)
Status of Operational Meteorological Stations and Their Observation Items (2005)
21-55 各地区地震监测情况（2005年） …… (845)
Situation of Earthquake Monitoring (2005)
21-56 国家监督抽查产品质量情况 …… (846)
Results of Sampling Check on Product Quality under State Supervision
21-57 各地区产品质量情况（2005年） …… (847)
Quality of Products by Region (2005)
21-58 产品质量监督检查情况（2005年） …… (848)
Results of Sampling Check under Supervision on the Quality of Products (2005)
21-59 各地区出入境货物检验检疫情况（2005年） …… (850)
Quarantine of Freight by Region (2005)
21-60 中国科协系统科技活动情况（2005年） …… (852)
Basic Statistics on Scientific and Technological Activities of China Associations for Science and Technology (2005)
主要统计指标解释 …… (854)
Explanatory Notes on Main Statistical Indicators

二十二、文化、体育和卫生
Culture, Sports and Public Health

简要说明
Brief Introduction
22-1 文化、文物单位机构、人员数（2005年） …… (861)
Number of Institutions and Personnel in Culture and Cultural Relics (2005)
22-2 文化、文物单位数 …… (862)
Number of Institutions for Culture and Cultural Relics
22-3 艺术表演团体演出情况（2005年） …… (863)
Basic Statistics on Performance of Art Troupes (2005)
22-4 艺术表演团体收支情况（2005年） …… (863)
Income and Expenditures of Art Troupes (2005)
22-5 群众艺术馆、文化馆站业务活动及经费情况（2005年） …… (864)
Basic Statistics on Activities and Expenditures of Mass Art Centers and Cultural Centers (2005)
22-6 公共图书馆业务活动及经费情况（2005年） …… (864)
Facilities, Services and Expenditures of Public Libraries (2005)
22-7 博物馆、文物机构业务活动及经费情况（2005年） …… (865)
Facilities, Services and Expenditures of Museums and Cultural Relic Agencies (2005)
22-8 摄制电影片产量 …… (865)
Film Production
22-9 广播、电视事业发展情况 …… (866)
Basic Statistics on Radio and Television Stations
22-10 广播、电视节目制作时间 …… (866)
Production of Radio and Television Programs
22-11 广播、电视宣传基本情况（2005年） …… (866)
Basic Statistics on Radio and Television Programs (2005)
22-12 图书出版分类构成情况（2005年） …… (867)

Composition of Books Published in China (2005)
22-13 各地区少年儿童读物类图书和课本出版情况（2005年） …… (868)
Number of Books Published for Children and Textbooks by Region (2005)
22-14 课本出版情况(2005年) …… (868)
Publication of Textbooks (2005)
22-15 各地区录像制品出版情况（2005年） …… (869)
Publication of Video Products by Region (2005)
22-16 各地区录音制品出版情况（2005年） …… (870)
Publication of Audio Products by Region (2005)
22-17 档案馆机构和人员情况 …… (871)
Statistics on Institution and Personnel of Archives Institution
22-18 国家综合档案馆基本情况 …… (871)
Basic Statistics on National Comprehensive Archives
22-19 我国与外国体育活动交往情况 …… (872)
Visits between Chinese and Foreign Sports Delegations
22-20 群众体育活动情况 …… (872)
Activities of Mass Sports
22-21 体委系统职工人数（2005年） …… (872)
Number of Staff and Workers in Sports Commissions (2005)
22-22 运动员分项创世界纪录情况（2005年） …… (873)
World Records Chalked up by Chinese Athletes by Events (2005)
22-23 运动员获世界冠军情况 …… (873)
World Championships Won by Chinese Athletes
22-24 卫生机构数 …… (874)
Number of Health Institutions
22-25 卫生机构人员数 …… (875)
Number of Employed Persons in Health Institutions
22-26 卫生机构床位数 …… (875)
Number of Beds in Health Institutions
22-27 按市县分卫生机构床位数和卫生技术人员 …… (876)
Beds and Medical Technical Personnel in Health Institutions by City and County Areas
22-28 医院、卫生院平均每院床位和人员数 …… (876)
Average Number of Beds and Persons Engaged Per Hospitals and Health Centers
22-29 各地区卫生机构数、医疗机构床位数（2005年） …… (877)
Number of Health Institutions and Beds by Region (2005)
22-30 各地区卫生机构人员数（2005年） …… (878)
Number of Employed Persons in Health Institutions by Region (2005)
22-31 卫生机构各类人员数 …… (879)
Employed Persons in Health Institutions by Type of Occupation
22-32 各类医疗机构诊疗人次及入院人数（2005年） …… (879)
Number of Visits and Inpatients in Medical Institutions (2005)
22-33 医疗机构病床使用情况（2005年） …… (879)
Utilization of Beds in Medical Institutions (2005)
22-34 城市前十位疾病死亡原因及构成（2005年） …… (880)
Death Rate of 10 Major Diseases in Urban Areas (2005)
22-35 农村前十位疾病死亡原因及构成（2005年） …… (881)
Death Rate of 10 Major Diseases in Rural Areas (2005)
22-36 法定报告传染病发病及死亡情况（2005年） …… (882)
Incidence and Death from Infectious Diseases (2005)
22-37 卫生总费用 …… (882)
Expenditure for Public Health
主要统计指标解释 …… (883)
Explanatory Notes on Main Statistical Indicators

二十三、其他社会活动
Other Social Activities

简要说明
Brief Introduction
23-1 历届全国人民代表大会代表人数 …… (887)
Number of Deputies to All the Previous National People's Congresses
23-2 历届全国政治协商会议委员人数 …… (887)
Number of Deputies to All the Previous Chinese People's Political Consultative Conferences
23-3 妇联干部情况 …… (888)
Cadres of the Women's Federation
23-4 工会组织情况 …… (889)
Basic Statistics on Trade Unions
23-5 劳动争议处理情况 …… (890)
The Disposal of Labor Disputes
23-6 律师、公证和调解工作基本情况 …… (891)
Basic Statistics on Lawyers, Notarization and Mediation
23-7 国内公证文书分类 …… (892)
Domestic Notarial Documents by Type
23-8 涉外公证文书分类 …… (893)
Foreign-Related Notarial Documents by Type
23-9 调解民间纠纷分类 …… (894)
Number of Civil Disputes Mediated by Type
23-10 在押服刑人员基本情况 …… (894)
Basic Statistics of Termers in Custody
23-11 公安机关立案的刑事案件及构成 …… (895)
Criminal Cases Registered in Public Security Organs and Its Composition
23-12 公安机关受理、查处治安案件数 …… (895)
Offense Cases Against Public Order Handled by Public Security Organs
23-13 交通事故情况（2005年） …… (896)
Basic Statistics on Traffic Accidents (2005)
23-14 火灾事故情况（2005年） …… (896)
Basic Statistics on Fires (2005)
23-15 各地区交通事故情况（2005年） …… (897)
Basic Statistics on Traffic Accidents by Region (2005)
23-16 各地区火灾事故情况（2005年） …… (898)
Basic Statistics on Fires by Region (2005)
23-17 检察机关直接立案侦查案件情况（2005年） …… (898)
Cases under Direct Investigation by Procurator's Offices (2005)
23-18 检察机关审查批准、决定逮捕犯罪嫌疑人和提起公诉被告人情况（2005年） …… (899)
Arrests of Criminal Suspects and Defendants Under Public Prosecution Approved by Procurator's Offices (2005)
23-19 检察机关处理申诉案件情况（2005年） …… (899)
Appeals Handled by Procurator's Offices (2005)
23-20 人民法院审理一审案件情况 …… (899)
First Trial Cases by Courts
23-21 人民法院审理刑事一审案件收结案情况（2005年） …… (900)
First Trial Criminal Cases Accepted and Settled by Courts (2005)
23-22 人民法院审理刑事案件罪犯情况 …… (900)
Criminal Cases Heard by Courts
23-23 人民法院审理婚姻家庭、继承一审案件收结案情况（2005年） …… (901)
First Trial Civil Cases of Marriages, Family Affairs and Inheritance Accepted and Settled

by Courts (2005)
23-24 人民法院审理合同纠纷一审案件收结案情况（2005年） …… (901)
First Trial Cases of Contracts Disputes Accepted and Settled by Courts (2005)
23-25 人民法院审理权属、侵权纠纷及其他民事一审收结案情况（2005年） …… (902)
First Trial Cases of Disputes of Right, Infringement of Right and Other Civil Affairs Accepted and Settled by Courts (2005)
23-26 人民法院行政一审案件收结案情况（2005年） …… (902)
First Trial Administrative Cases Accepted and Settled by Courts (2005)
23-27 收养、救助类单位情况 …… (903)
Basis Statistics on Social Welfare and Salvation Institutions
23-28 民政行业单位基本情况 …… (903)
Basic Conditions of Civil Affairs Agencies
23-29 享受补助、救济人员情况 …… (904)
Persons Receiving Subsidies or Relief Funds
23-30 社会福利企业基本情况 …… (904)
Basic Statistics on Social Welfare Enterprises
23-31 各地区城镇社区服务设施基本情况（2005年） …… (905)
Basic Statistics on Community Servicas Facilities in Urban Areas by Region (2005)
23-32 离休和退休费 …… (906)
Pensions for Retired and Resigned Persons
23-33 按企业、事业、机关分的离休和退休费 …… (906)
Pensions for Retired and Resigned Persons by Enterprises, Institutions and State Organizations
23-34 离休和退休人员保险福利费用及构成 …… (907)
Value and Composition of Social Insurance and Welfare for Retired and Resigned Persons
23-35 各地区离休和退休人员数（2005年底） …… (908)
Number of Retired and Resigned Persons at the Year-end by Region (2005)
23-36 参加基本养老保险人数 …… (909)
Number of People Participated in Basic Pension Insurance
23-37 社会保险基本情况 …… (909)
Basic Statistics on Social Insurance
23-38 社会保险基金收支及累计结余 …… (910)
Revenue, Expenses and Reserve of Social Insurance Fund
23-39 分地区基本养老保险情况（2005年） …… (911)
Statistics on Basic Pension Insurance by Region (2005)
23-40 分地区失业保险情况（2005年底） …… (912)
Statistics of Unemployment Insurance at the Year-end by Region (2005)
23-41 分地区基本医疗保险情况（2005年） …… (913)
Statistics of Basic Medical Insurance by Region (2005)
23-42 残疾人事业基本情况 …… (914)
Basic Information of People with Disabilities
23-43 婚姻登记和离婚情况 …… (915)
Number of Marriages and Divorces
主要统计指标解释 …… (916)
Explanatory Notes on Main Statistical Indicators

二十四、香港特别行政区主要社会经济指标
Main Social and Economic Indicators of Hong Kong Special Administrative Region

简要说明
Brief Introduction
24-1 主要统计指标概览 …… (923)
Summary of Key Statistics

24-2 按区议会地区划分的香港陆地面积 …… (927)
Land Area of Hong Kong by District Council District
24-3 土地用途分布情况 …… (928)
Land Usage
24-4 按地区类别及路边情况划分的大气质量(2005年) …… (929)
Air Quality by Area Type and Roadside Condition (2005)
24-5 按种类划分的每日平均产生的固体废物 …… (929)
Daily Average Solid Waste Generation by Type
24-6 人口主要指标 …… (930)
Main Indicators of Population
24-7 劳动人口及失业状况 …… (930)
Labour Force and Unemployment
24-8 按行业划分的就业人数 …… (931)
Employed Persons by Industry
24-9 按每月就业收入划分的就业人数 …… (931)
Employed Persons by Monthly Employment Earnings
24-10 本地生产总值 …… (932)
Gross Domestic Product
24-11 按当年价格计算生产法本地生产总值 …… (932)
Gross Domestic Product by Economic Activity at Current Prices
24-12 按2000年不变价格计算生产法本地生产总值 …… (933)
Gross Domestic Product by Economic Activity at Constant (2000) Prices
24-13 支出法本地生产总值 …… (934)
Gross Domestic Product by Expenditure Component
24-14 本地居民生产总值 …… (934)
Gross National Product
24-15 香港国际收支平衡表 …… (935)
Hong Kong's Balance of Payments Account
24-16 香港国际投资头寸(期末头寸) …… (936)
Hong Kong's International Investment Position (Position as at end of period)
24-17 电力、煤气、水消费量 …… (936)
Electricity, Gas and Water Consumption
24-18 工业生产指数 …… (937)
Index of Industrial Production
24-19 按楼宇种类划分的新落成私人楼宇 …… (937)
Private Buildings Newly Completed by Type of Building
24-20 按楼宇种类划分的获批准可动工兴建私人楼宇 …… (938)
Private Buildings with Consent to Commence Work by Type of Building
24-21 按类型划分的永久性屋宇单位数量(3月底的数字) …… (939)
Number of Permanent Quarters by Type (as at End March of the Year)
24-22 按居所租住权划分的家庭住户数目 …… (939)
Domestic Households by Tenure of Accommodation
24-23 进出香港货物 …… (940)
Inward and Outward Movements of Cargo
24-24 按主要货物装卸地点划分的集装箱吞吐量 …… (940)
Container Throughput by Main Cargo Handling Location
24-25 通讯及互联网服务 …… (941)
Communications and Internet Services
24-26 商品进出口贸易总额 …… (942)
Total Imports and Exports of Goods
24-27 商品进口及出口的主要供应地和去向 …… (942)
Imports and Exports of Goods by Major Supplier and Destination
24-28 商品转口的主要来源和去向 …… (942)

Re-exports of Goods by Major Origin and Destination
24-29 涉及外发中国内地加工的贸易 …… (943)
Trade Involving Outward Processing in the Mainland of China
24-30 按主要服务组别划分的服务出口及进口 …… (943)
Exports and Imports of Services by Major Service Group
24-31 按主要目的地和来源地划分的服务出口及进口 …… (944)
Exports and Imports of Services by Major Destination and Source
24-32 按主要投资者国家/地区划分的外来直接投资头寸及流动 …… (944)
Position and Flow of Inward Direct Investment by Major Investor Country/Territory
24-33 按主要接受投资国家/地区划分的对外直接投资头寸及流动 …… (945)
Position and Flow of Outward Direct Investment by Major Recipient Country/Territory
24-34 按母公司的国家/地区划分的驻港地区总部公司数目 …… (945)
Number of Companies in Hong Kong that are Regional Headquarters by Country/Territory of the Parent Company
24-35 按母公司的国家/地区划分的驻港地区办事处公司数目 …… (946)
Number of Companies in Hong Kong that are Regional Offices by Country/Territory of the Parent Company
24-36 按居住国家/地区划分的访港旅客人数 …… (947)
Visitor Arrivals by Country/Territory of Residence
24-37 政府储备结余(一般收入帐目及各基金) …… (947)
Government's Reserve Balances (General Revenue Account and Funds)
24-38 政府收入(一般收入帐目及各基金) …… (948)
Government Revenue (General Revenue Account and Funds)
24-39 政府支出(一般收入帐目及各基金) …… (949)
Government Spending (General Revenue Account and Funds)
24-40 按用途划分的公共开支 …… (950)
Public Expenditure by Function
24-41 外币兑换率及港汇指数 …… (950)
Exchange Rates and the Effective Exchange Rate Indices
24-42 货币供应量 …… (952)
Money Supply
24-43 股票价格指数、证券交易成交额及市场总值 …… (953)
Index of Share Prices, Value of Stock Exchange Turnover and Market Capitalisation
24-44 居民消费价格指数（2004年10月-2005年9月=100） …… (956)
Consumer Price Indices (Oct. 2004 - Sep. 2005=100)
24-45 按四分位开支组别及商品或服务类别划分的住户每月平均开支 …… (957)
Average Monthly Household Expenditure by Commodity/Service Section by Quartile Expenditure Group
24-46 按年龄/教育程度/经济活动身份划分的2003年至2005年曾使用个人计算机的10岁及以上人士数目 …… (958)
Persons Aged 10 and Over Having Used Personal Computer by Age/ Educational Attainment/Economic Activity Status, 2003 - 2005
24-47 按年龄/教育程度/经济活动身份划分的2003年至2005年曾使用互联网服务的10岁及以上人士数目 …… (959)
Persons Aged 10 and Over Having Used Internet Service by Age/ Educational Attainment/Economic Activity Status, 2003 - 2005
24-48 按行业/就业人数类别划分的2003年至2005年使用个人计算机、连接互联网或有设立网页/网站的机构单位数目 …… (960)
Establishments Using Personal Computers, with Internet Connection or Web Pages/Web Sites by Industry Sector/Employment Size, 2003 - 2005
24-49 按行业/就业人数类别划分的2003年至2005年有通过电子途径预订或购买、获取、售卖或递送货物、服务或资料划分的机构单位数目 …… (961)
Establishments Having Ordered or Purchased, Received, Sold or Delivered Goods, Services or Information through Electronic Means by Industry
24-50 15岁及以上人口教育程度 …… (962)
Educational Attainment of Population Aged 15 and Above

24-51 按教育及培训机构类别划分的学生人数 …… (963)
Student Enrolment by Type of Educational and Training Institution
24-52 医疗卫生条件 …… (965)
Conditions of Public Health
24-53 社会保障 …… (966)
Social Security
《中国统计年鉴》与香港特别行政区统计刊物中使用的指标对照表 …… (967)
A Comparison of Common Statistical Terms Used in China Statistical Yearbook and Publications Compiled by the Census and Statistics Department, the Government of the Hong Kong Special Administrative Region
主要统计指标解释 …… (968)
Explanatory Notes on Main Statistical Indicators

二十五、澳门特别行政区主要社会经济指标
Main Social and Economic Indicators of Macao Special Adminstrative Region

简要说明
Brief Introduction
25-1 主要统计指标概况 …… (979)
Principal Statistical Indicators
25-2 按堂区划分的澳门面积 …… (981)
Land Area of Macao by Parish
25-3 人口主要指标 …… (981)
Main Demographic Indicator
25-4 经济活动人口及失业状况 …… (981)
Labour Force and Unemployment
25-5 按行业划分的就业人口 …… (982)
Employed Population by Industry
25-6 按行业划分的每月工作收入中位数 …… (982)
Median Monthly Employment Earnings
25-7 本地生产总值（按当年价格计算） …… (983)
Gross Domestic Product (At Current Prices)
25-8 支出法本地生产总值 …… (983)
Gross Domestic Product (Expenditure-based Estimates)
25-9 生产法本地生产总值 …… (984)
Gross Domestic Product (Production-based Estimates)
25-10 生产法本地生产总值结构 …… (984)
Structure of Gross Domestic Product (Production-based Estimates)
25-11 电力、燃料及水消耗量 …… (985)
Consumption of Electricity, Fuels and Water
25-12 按用途划分的建成私人房屋单位及建筑面积 …… (985)
Units and Gross Floor Area Completed by End-use
25-13 按用途划分的获批准新动工私人房屋单位及建筑面积 …… (985)
Units and Gross Floor Area Started by End-use
25-14 零售业销售额 …… (986)
Retail Sales
25-15 外地进出澳门货物 …… (986)
External Trade by Mode of Transport
25-16 集装箱流量 …… (986)
Container Flow
25-17 海路集装箱总吞吐量 …… (987)
Seaborne Container Throughput
25-18 通信服务 …… (987)

Communications
25-19 主要商品进出口总额 …… (987)
Values of Major Merchandise Trade
25-20 主要商品进口原产地和出口目的地 …… (988)
Values of Imports and Exports by Major Country/Region
25-21 财政收入 …… (988)
Government Revenue
25-22 财政支出 …… (989)
Government Expenditure
25-23 货币供应 …… (989)
Money Supply
25-24 外币兑换率 …… (990)
Exchange Rates
25-25 居民消费价格指数(1999年10月至2000年9月=100) …… (991)
Consumer Price Index (October/1999 - September/2000=100)
25-26 按双周开支五等分位及商品与服务分类统计之每户双周平均消费开支 …… (992)
Average Biweekly Household Expenditure By Quintile of Biweekly Expenditure Group And Section of Goods and Services
25-27 14岁及14岁以上人口教育程度 …… (993)
Education Levels of Population Aged 14 and Over
25-28 按各类型教育机构统计的学生人数 …… (993)
Students by Type of Educational Institutes
25-29 医疗卫生条件 …… (994)
Health
25-30 按住所租住权划分的家庭住户数目 …… (994)
Number of Households by Tenure of Accommodation
25-31 社会保障基金发放次数及金额 …… (995)
Number of Payments and Amounts of Subsidy Granted by Social Security Fund
主要统计指标解释 …… (996)
Explanatory Notes on Main Statistical Indicators

附录一、台湾省主要社会经济指标
APPENDIX I. Main Social and Economic Indicators of Taiwan Province

附录1-1 主要统计指标概况 …… (1003)
Summary of Key Statistics
附录1-2 面积和人口主要指标 …… (1006)
Main Indicators of Area and Population
附录1-3 劳动力和就业状况 …… (1006)
Labor Force and Employment
附录1-4 本地居民生产总值 …… (1007)
Gross National Product
附录1-5 本地生产总值支出构成 …… (1007)
Expenditures on Gross Domestic Product
附录1-6 本地生产总值部门构成 …… (1008)
Gross Domestic Product by Kind of Economic Activity
附录1-7 农业生产指数 …… (1009)
Index of Agricultural Production
附录1-8 主要农产品产量 …… (1009)
Output of Major Crops
附录1-9 工业生产指数 …… (1009)
Index of Industrial Production

附录1-10 主要工业产品产量 …… (1010)
Output of Major Industrial Products
附录1-11 能源生产和消费 …… (1011)
Production and Consumption of Energy
附录1-12 按用途分的批准动工的建筑面积 …… (1011)
Floor Space of Authorized Construction Projects by the Purpose
附录1-13 铁路和公路客货运量 …… (1012)
Railway and Highway Passenger and Freight Traffic
附录1-14 邮政及电信营运量 …… (1012)
Telecommunication Services
附录1-15 商品进出口贸易总额 …… (1013)
Total Imports and Exports
附录1-16 商品进口来源和出口去向 …… (1014)
Origin of Imports and Destination of Exports
附录1-17 出口与进口商品分类 …… (1015)
Composition of Exports and Imports
附录1-18 旅游人数 …… (1015)
Visitor Arrivals and International Tourists
附录1-19 居民消费价格指数 …… (1015)
Consumer Price Indices
附录1-20 各级政府财政收入净额 …… (1016)
Net Revenue of Treasury
附录1-21 各级政府财政支出净额 …… (1016)
Net Expenditures of Treasury
附录1-22 政府公债 …… (1016)
Government Bonds
附录1-23 主要金融指标 …… (1017)
Principal Financial Indicators
附录1-24 股票交易 …… (1017)
Transactions of Listed Stock
附录1-25 入学率和教育经费 …… (1018)
Net Enrollment Rate and Public Expenditures for Education at Current Market Prices
附录1-26 科技人员数和科研开发经费 …… (1018)
Number of Scientists, Engineers and Technicians and Expenditures for R&D
附录1-27 医院、病床和医务人员情况 …… (1019)
Medical Facilities and Health Personnel
附录1-28 家庭设备普及率 …… (1019)
Percent of Families Owning Household Appliances

附录二、我国经济、社会统计指标同世界主要国家和地区比较

APPENDIX II. A Comparison of Indicators of Economy and Society Among the People's Republic of China and Other Countries/Areas

附录2-1 国土面积和人口 …… (1023)
Territory and Population
附录2-2 按三次产业划分的就业 …… (1024)
Employment by Type of Industry
附录2-3 国内生产总值及其增长率 …… (1025)
Gross Domestic Product and Its Growth Rate
附录2-4 农业生产指数（2005年）…… (1026)
Agricultural Production Indices (2005)
附录2-5 工业生产指数 …… (1027)

Industry Production Indices
附录2-6　中国主要指标居世界位次 …………………… (1028)
Precedence of Main Indicators of China in the World
附录2-7　居民消费价格指数 …………………… (1029)
Consumer Price Indices
附录2-8　进出口贸易额 …………………… (1030)
Total Imports and Exports
附录2-9　国际收支（2005年） …………………… (1031)
Balance of Payments (2005)

1

行政区划和自然资源

Divisions of Administrative Areas and Natural Resources

简要说明

本篇章的主要内容和资料来源

行政区划和自然资源资料主要包括我国行政区划、自然状况、自然资源及开发和利用等资料。

1．“全国行政区划”资料，由民政部根据国务院批准的，截止到上一年末全国行政区划变更情况汇总整理并提供。

2．自然状况包括国土、山脉、河流、海洋、气候等数据资料，由国家统计局综合司根据有关历史资料进行整理和编辑。

3．自然资源包括土地、森林、水利、海洋、矿产、气象等资料。其中，耕地面积来自国家统计局1996年农业普查数据；荒地面积和草原面积来自农业部1991年调查数据；林业用地面积和森林资源数据来自国家林业局1999-2003年第六次全国森林资源清查数据；水利资源数据由水利部提供；海洋资源数据由国家海洋局提供；矿产资源数据由国土资源部提供；气象资料由中国气象局国家气象中心提供。

Brief Introduction

Main Content and Source of Data

Data in this chapter mainly cover China's divisions of administrative areas, natural conditions and the exploitation and utilization of the natural resources.

1) Data on divisions of administrative areas in China are prepared and provided by the Ministry of Civil Affairs on the basis of the changes in the divisions of administrative areas approved by the State Council by the end of the previous year.

2) Data on natural conditions cover land area, mountain ranges, rivers, ocean and meteorological phenomena. Statistics are compiled by the Department of Comprehensive Statistics of the National Bureau of Statistics using relevant historical data.

3) Data on natural resources cover land, forest, water, ocean and mineral resources. Data on cultivated land are from the 1996 agriculture census conducted by the National Bureau of Statistics. Data on undeveloped land and grassland are collected from surveys conducted in 1991 by the Ministry of Agriculture. Data on land occupied by forest industry and on forest resources are prepared according to the 6th National Forest Resource Survey conducted by the National Bureau of Forestry during 1999-2003. Data on water resources are provided by the Ministry of Water Conservancy. Data on oceanic resources are provided by the State Oceanic Administration. Data on mineral resources are provided by the Ministry of Land and Resources. Meteorological data are provided by National Meteorological Center of the China Meteorological Bureau.

1-1 全国行政区划（2005年底）

Divisions of Administrative Areas in China (End of 2005)

单位：个 (unit)

省级区划名称 Provinces, Autonomous Regions and Municipalities	地级区划数 Number of Regions at Prefecture Level	#地级市 Cities at Prefecture Level	县级区划数 Number of Regions at County Level	#县级市 Cities at County Level	#市辖区 Districts under the Jurisdiction of Cities	乡镇级区划数 Number of Regions at Townships Level	#街道办事处 Street Communities	#镇 Towns
全　国 National Total	**333**	**283**	**2862**	**374**	**852**	**41636**	**6152**	**19522**
北京市 Beijing			18		16	314	131	142
天津市 Tianjin			18		15	241	101	120
河北省 Hebei	11	11	172	22	36	2205	242	943
山西省 Shanxi	11	11	119	11	23	1389	193	561
内蒙古自治区 Inner Mongolia	12	9	101	11	21	1112	195	493
辽宁省 Liaoning	14	14	100	17	56	1528	550	602
吉林省 Jilin	9	8	60	20	19	878	254	426
黑龙江省 Heilongjiang	13	12	130	19	65	1273	365	470
上海市 Shanghai			19		18	214	103	108
江苏省 Jiangsu	13	13	106	27	54	1410	281	1019
浙江省 Zhejiang	11	11	90	22	32	1525	298	752
安徽省 Anhui	17	17	105	5	44	1696	241	948
福建省 Fujian	9	9	85	14	26	1101	167	593
江西省 Jiangxi	11	11	99	10	19	1550	123	773
山东省 Shandong	17	17	140	31	49	1931	460	1194
河南省 Henan	17	17	159	21	50	2299	392	841
湖北省 Hubei	13	12	102	24	38	1220	277	733
湖南省 Hunan	14	13	122	16	34	2409	233	1089
广东省 Guangdong	21	21	121	23	54	1585	429	1145
广西壮族自治区 Guangxi	14	14	109	7	34	1232	106	699
海南省 Hainan	2	2	20	6	4	218	18	180
重庆市 Chongqing			40	4	15	1081	112	608
四川省 Sichuan	21	18	181	14	43	4782	238	1865
贵州省 Guizhou	9	4	88	9	10	1543	92	691
云南省 Yunnan	16	8	129	9	12	1455	56	567
西藏自治区 Tibet	7	1	73	1	1	692	9	140
陕西省 Shaanxi	10	10	107	3	24	1745	148	917
甘肃省 Gansu	14	12	86	4	17	1348	121	457
青海省 Qinghai	8	1	43	2	4	422	30	123
宁夏回族自治区 Ningxia	5	5	21	2	8	229	42	94
新疆维吾尔自治区 Xinjiang	14	2	99	20	11	1009	145	229
香港特别行政区 Hong Kong Special Administrative Region								
澳门特别行政区 Macao Special Administrative Region								
台湾省 Taiwan								

1-2 自然状况

Natural Conditions

项目		Item		2005
国土		**Territory**		
国土面积	(万平方公里)	Area of Territory	(10 000 sq.km)	960
海域面积	(万平方公里)	Area of Sea	(10 000 sq.km)	473
海洋平均深度	(米)	Average Depth of Sea	(m)	961
海洋最大深度	(米)	Maximum Depth of Sea	(m)	5377
岸线总长度	(公里)	Length of Coastline	(km)	32000
大陆岸线长度		Mainland Shore		18000
岛屿岸线长度		Island Shore		14000
岛屿个数	(个)	Number of Islands		5400
岛屿面积	(万平方公里)	Area of Islands	(10 000 sq.km)	3.87
气候		**Climate**		
热量分布	(积温≥0℃)	Distribution of Heat	(Accumulated Temperature≥0℃)	
黑龙江北部及青藏高原		Northern Heilongjiang and Tibet Plateau		2000-2500
东北平原		Northeast Plain		3000-4000
华北平原		North China Plain		4000-5000
长江流域及以南地区		Changjiang (Yangtze) River Drainage Area and the Area to the south of it		5800-6000
南岭以南地区		Area to the South of Nanling Mountain		7000-8000
降水量	(毫米)	Precipitation	(mm)	
台湾中部山区		Mid-Taiwan Mountain Area		≥4000
华南沿海		Southern China Coastal Area		1600-2000
长江流域		Changjiang River Valley		1000-1500
华北、东北		Northern and Northeastern Area		400-800
西北内陆		Northwestern Inland		100-200
塔里木盆地、吐鲁番盆地和柴达木盆地		Tarim Basin, Turpan Basin and Qaidam Basin		≤25
气候带面积比例	(国土面积=100)	Percentage of Climatic Zones to Total Area of Territory		
湿润地区	(干燥度<1.0)	Humid Zone	(aridity<1.0)	32
半湿润地区	(干燥度=1.0-1.5)	Semi-Humid Zone	(aridity 1.0-1.5)	15
半干旱地区	(干燥度=1.5-2.0)	Semi-Arid Zone	(aridity 1.5-2.0)	22
干旱地区	(干燥度>2.0)	Arid Zone	(aridity>2.0)	31

注：1.气候资料为多年平均值。

2.岛屿面积未包括香港、澳门特别行政区和台湾省。

a) The climate data refer to the average figures in many years.

b) Island area does not include that of Hong Kong Special Administrative Region, Macao Special Administrative Region and Taiwan Province.

1-3 自 然 资 源

Natural Resources

项 目	Item	2005
土地资源 （万公顷）	**Land Resources (10 000 hectares)**	
耕地面积	Area of Cultivated Land	13004
荒地面积	Area of Undeveloped Land	10800
#宜农荒地	Useable for Agricultural Production	3535
林业用地面积	Area of Afforested Land	28493
#宜林荒山荒地（含宜林沙荒）	Undeveloped Land Usable for Afforestation	5471
草原面积	Area of Grassland	40000
#可利用面积	Utilizable Area	31333
森林资源	**Forest Resources**	
森林面积 （万公顷）	Forest Area (10 000 hectares)	17491
森林覆盖率 (%)	Forest-coverage Rate (%)	18.21
活立木总蓄积量 （万立方米）	Total Standing Stock Volume (10 000 cu.m)	1361810
森林蓄积量 （万立方米）	Stock Volume of the Forest (10 000 cu.m)	1245585
水利资源	**Water Resources**	
大陆	Land	
水资源总量 （亿立方米）	Total Water Resources Volume (100 million cu.m)	28053.1
地表水资源量（河川径流量）	Surface Water Volume	26982.4
地下水资源量	Ground Water Volume	8091.1
地表水与地下水资源重复量	Duplicated Measurement between Surface Water and Groundwater	7020.4
水力资源蕴藏量 （亿千瓦）	Hydropower Resources (100 million kw)	6.76
#可开发量	Developable Resources	3.79
内陆水域总面积 （万公顷）	Inland Water Area (10 000 hectares)	1747
#可养殖面积	Cultivatable Area	675
#已养殖面积	Cultivated Area	467
海洋	Sea	
海洋能源理论蕴藏量 （亿千瓦）	Theoretical Sea-energy Reserves (100 million kw)	6.3
海岸带面积 （万平方公里）	Coastal Area (10 000 sq.km)	28
滩涂面积 （万平方公里）	Sea-beach Area (10 000 sq.km)	2.08
大陆架渔场面积 （万公顷）	Area of Fishing Ground of Continental Shelf (10 000 hectares)	28000
海水可养殖面积 （万公顷）	Cultivatable Area in Marine Areas (10 000 hectares)	260.01
#已养殖面积	Cultivated Area	109.49
浅海滩涂可养殖面积 （万公顷）	Cultivable Area in Shallow Sea and Sea-beaches (10 000 hectares)	242.00
#已养殖面积	Cultivated Area	89.37

注：土地资源为以前清查数，有待进一步勘测；耕地面积为1996年农业普查数据，草原面积为1991年调查数，林业用地面积和森林资源为第六次全国森林资源清查（1999-2003）数；水资源总量及其分组指标为当年数据，其他水利资源数据为1985年评价数。

a) Figures on land resources in the table were obtained from surveys in previous years. The figures are subject to further verification. Figures on area of cultivated land were taken from the 1996's agricultural census. The area of grassland was the figure of 1991's survey. Figures on area of afforested land and forest resources were the figures of the Sixth National Forestry Survey (1999-2003). Total water resources volume and its sub-item indicators are data in 2005, and other indicators in Water Resources were estimated figures in 1985.

1-4 土 地 状 况

Land Characteristics

项 目	Item	面 积 Area	占总面积(%) Percentage to Total Area
总面积 （万平方公里）	**Total Land Area (10 000 sq.km)**	**960**	**100.00**
按地形分: （万平方公里）	**By Topographic Feature (10 000 sq.km)**		
山地	Mountains	320	33.33
高原	Plateaus	250	26.04
盆地	Basins	180	18.75
平原	Plains	115	11.98
丘陵	Hills	95	9.90
按地高分: （万平方公里）	**By Altitude (10 000 sq.km)**		
500米以下	Under 500 m	241.7	25.18
500-1000米	500-1000 m	162.5	16.93
1000-2000米	1000-2000 m	239.9	24.99
2000-3000米	2000-3000 m	67.6	7.04
3000米以上	Above 3000 m	248.3	25.86
按特征分: （万公顷）	**By Land Use (10 000 hectares)**		
耕地	Cultivated Land	13004	13.54
森林	Forests	17491	18.22
内陆水域面积	Water Area in Land	1747	1.82
草地	Area of Grassland	40000	41.67
#可利用草地	Useable Area	31333	32.64
其他	Others	23758	24.75

注：本表数字多为过去清查数。

a) Most figures in this table were obtained from surveys in previous years.

1-5 主要山脉基本情况

Main Mountain Ranges

名 称	Mountain Range	山峰高程(米) Height of Mountain Peak (m)	雪线高程(米) Height of Snow Line (m)	冰川面积(平方公里) Glacier Area (sq.km)
阿尔泰山	Altay Mountains	4374	3000--3200	287
天山	Tianshan Mountains	7435	3600--4400	9548
祁连山	Qilian Mountains	5826	4300--5240	2063
帕米尔	Pamirs	7579		2258
昆仑山	Kunlun Mountains			11639
喀喇昆仑山	Karakorum Mountain	8611	5100--5400	3265
唐古拉山	Tanggula Mountains	6137		2082
羌塘高原	Qiangtang Plateau	6596		3566
念青塘古拉山	Nyainqentanglha Mountains	7111	4500--5700	7536
横断山	Hengduan Mountains	7556	4600--5500	1456
喜玛拉雅山	The Himalayas	8848	4300--6200	11055
冈底斯山	Gangdisi Mountains	7095	5800--6000	2188

1-6 主要河流基本情况
Major Rivers

名 称	River	流域面积 (平方公里) Drainage Area (sq.km)	河 长 (公里) Length (km)	年径流量 (亿立方米) Annual Flow (100 million cu.m)
长 江	Changjiang River (Yangtze River)	1808500	6300	9513
黄 河	Huanghe River (Yellow River)	752443	5464	661
松花江	Songhuajiang River	557180	2308	762
辽 河	Liaohe River	228960	1390	148
珠 江	Zhujiang River (Pearl River)	453690	2214	3338
海 河	Haihe River	263631	1090	228
淮 河	Huaihe River	269283	1000	622

1-7 河流流域面积
Drainage Area of Rivers

流域名称	River	流域面积 (平方公里) Drainage Area (sq.km)	占外流河、内陆河流域面积合计 Percentage to Total (%)
合计	**Total of Out-flowing Rivers and Inland Rivers**	**9559370**	**100.00**
外流河	**Out-flowing Rivers**	**6114728**	**63.97**
黑龙江及绥芬河	Heilongjiang River and Suifenhe River	875342	9.16
辽河、鸭绿江及沿海诸河	Liaohe, Yalujiang and Related Coastal Rivers	345207	3.61
海滦河	Haihe River and Luanhe River	318161	3.33
黄河	Huanghe River (Yellow River)	752443	7.87
淮河及山东沿海诸河	Huaihe and Related Coastal Rivers in Shandong Province	329211	3.44
长江	Changjiang River (Yangtze River)	1808500	18.92
浙闽台诸河	Rivers in Zhejiang, Fujian and Taiwan Provinces	239803	2.51
珠江及沿海诸河	Zhujiang River (Pearl River) and Related Coastal River	580640	6.07
元江及澜仓江	Yuanjiang River and Lancang River	240652	2.52
怒江及滇西诸河	Nujiang River and West Yunnan Rivers	157156	1.64
雅鲁藏布江及藏南诸河	Brahmaputra and Southern Tibet Rivers	396258	4.15
藏西诸河	Western Tibet Rivers	57340	0.60
额尔齐斯河	Ertix River	50000	0.52
内陆河	**Inland Rivers**	**3408659**	**35.66**
内蒙内陆河	Rivers in Inner Mongolia	300067	3.14
河西内陆河	Rivers in Huanghe Upper Reach Area	488301	5.11
准噶尔内陆河	Rivers in Zhunger Basin	316530	3.31
中亚细亚内陆河	Rivers in Central Asia	93130	0.97
塔里木内陆河	Rivers in Tarim Basin	1074810	11.24
青海内陆河	Rivers in Qinghai Province	316285	3.31
羌唐内陆河	Rivers in Qiangtang	721182	7.54
松花江、黄河、藏南闭流区	Blind Drainage Areas of Songhua River, Huanghe River and Southern Tibet	90353	0.95

注：本表所列面积系水利部门量算初步汇总数，有待进一步核实。

a) Figures in the table are obtained from preliminary measurements and tabulated data by water conservancy departments, and are subject to further verification.

1-8 内陆水域面积

Inland Water Area

单位：千公顷 (1 000 hectares)

水域	Water Area	总水面 Total Water Area	#可养殖水面 Cultivatable Water Area	#已养殖水面 Cultivated Water Area	#尚可利用水面 Utilizable Water Area
总计	**Total**	**17471**	**6749**	**4669**	**2080**
池塘	Pool	1922	1922	1858	64
湖泊	Lake	7524	2151	824	1327
水库	Reservoir	2302	1884	1516	368
河沟	Brook	5278	766	347	419
其他	Others	445	26	124	

1-9 湖泊面积

Area of Lakes

湖区	Area of Lakes	湖水面积（平方公里） Area of Lakes (sq.km)	湖水贮量（亿立方米） Reserve of Lakes (100 million cu.m)	#淡水贮量 Reserve of Fresh Water	占湖泊淡水总贮量(%) As Percentage of Total Lake Reserve of Fresh Water (%)
总计	**Total**	**75610**	**7510**	**2150**	**100.0**
青藏高原	Tibet Plateau	36560	5460	880	40.9
东部平原	Eastern Plain	23430	820	820	38.1
蒙新高原	Mongolia and Xinjiang Plateau	8670	760	20	0.9
东北平原	Northeast Plain	4340	200	160	7.4
云南高原	Yunnan Plateau	1100	240	240	11.2
其他	Others	1510	30	30	1.4

1-10 海区海域及渔场面积

Sea Area and Areas of Fishing Ground

名 称	Sea	海域总面积 (千公顷) Sea Area (1 000 hectares)	大陆架渔场面积 (千公顷) Area of Fishing Ground of Continental Shelf (1 000 hectares)	平均深度 (米) Average Depth (m)	最大深度 (米) Maximum Depth (m)
总 计	**Total**	**472700**	**280000**		
渤 海	Bohai Sea	7700	7700	18	70
黄 海	Huanghai Sea	38000	35300	44	140
东 海	Donghai Sea	77000	54900	370	2719
南 海	Nanhai Sea	350000	182100	1212	5559

1-11 浅海滩涂海湾可养殖面积

Seashore Land Area for Cultivation

单位: 千公顷 (1 000 hectares)

地 区	Region	海水可养殖面积 Cultivatable Marine Area	浅 海 Shallow Sea	滩 涂 Sea-beach	港 湾 Harbor
全 国	**National Total**	**2600.11**	**1622.56**	**797.00**	**180.55**
北 京	Beijing	0.44		0.44	
天 津	Tianjin	18.49	10.00	8.49	
河 北	Hebei	111.37	49.66	61.70	
辽 宁	Liaoning	725.84	590.44	92.45	42.95
上 海	Shanghai	3.22		3.22	
江 苏	Jiangsu	139.00	7.87	130.96	0.17
浙 江	Zhejiang	101.46	36.30	57.39	7.77
福 建	Fujian	184.94	77.39	100.76	6.79
山 东	Shandong	358.21	131.68	173.41	53.12
广 东	Guangdong	835.67	664.00	120.00	51.67
广 西	Guangxi	31.95	6.78	22.09	3.08
海 南	Hainan	89.52	48.43	26.09	15.00

1-12 主要矿产基础储量

Major Mineral Basic Reserves

项 目		Item		2005
石油	(万吨)	Petroleum	(10 000 tons)	248972.1
天然气	(亿立方米)	Natural Gas	(100 million cu.m)	28185.4
煤炭	(亿吨)	Coal	(100 million tons)	3326.4
铁矿	(矿石，亿吨)	Iron	(Ore, 100 million tons)	216.0
锰矿	(矿石，万吨)	Manganese	(Ore, 10 000 tons)	21539.8
铬矿	(矿石，万吨)	Chromium Ore	(Ore, 10 000 tons)	521.0
钒矿	(万吨)	Vanadium	(10 000 tons)	1323.5
原生钛铁矿	(万吨)	Titanium Ore	(10 000 tons)	21410.4
铜矿	(铜，万吨)	Copper	(Metal, 10 000 tons)	2856.4
铅矿	(铅，万吨)	Lead	(Metal, 10 000 tons)	1393.4
锌矿	(锌，万吨)	Zinc	(Metal, 10 000 tons)	4269.1
铝土矿	(矿石，万吨)	Bauxite	(Ore, 10 000 tons)	73057.8
镍矿	(镍，万吨)	Nickel	(Metal, 10 000 tons)	270.7
钨矿	(WO_3，万吨)	Tungsten	(WO_3, 10 000 tons)	260.5
锡矿	(锡，万吨)	Tin	(Metal, 10 000 tons)	155.5
钼矿	(钼，万吨)	Molybdenum	(Metal, 10 000 tons)	363.4
锑矿	(锑，万吨)	Antimony	(Metal, 10 000 tons)	95.3
金矿	(金，吨)	Gold	(Metal, tons)	1956.6
银矿	(银，吨)	Silver	(Metal, tons)	59791.0
稀土矿	(氧化物，万吨)	Rare Earths	(REO, 10 000 tons)	1968.5
菱镁矿	(矿石，万吨)	Magnesite Ore	(Ore, 10 000 tons)	173831.3
普通萤石	(矿物，万吨)	Fluorspar Mineral	(Mineral, 10 000 tons)	2536.8
硫铁矿	(矿石，万吨)	Pyrite Ore	(Ore, 10 000 tons)	190328.2
磷矿	(矿石，亿吨)	Phosphorus Ore	(Ore,100 million tons)	37.0
钾盐	(KCl，万吨)	Potassium KCl	(KCl, 10 000 tons)	28891.6
盐矿	(NaCl，亿吨)	Sodium Salt NaCl	(NaCl, 100 million tons)	1816.6
芒硝	(Na_2SO_4，亿吨)	Mirabilite	(Na_2SO_4, 100 million tons)	64.3
重晶石	(矿石，万吨)	Barite Ore	(Ore, 10 000 tons)	9677.1
玻璃硅质原料	(矿石，万吨)	Silicon Materials For Glass Ore	(Ore, 10 000 tons)	138177.6
石墨	(矿物，万吨)	Graphite Mineral (Crystal)	(Mineral, 10 000 tons)	3881.7
滑石	(矿石，万吨)	Talc Ore	(Ore, 10 000 tons)	10995.2
高岭土	(矿石，万吨)	Kaolin Ore	(Ore, 10 000 tons)	60225.9

注：本表资料由国土资源部提供。其中，石油和天然气的数据为剩余可采储量(下表同)。

a) The data in the table are provided by the Ministry of Land and Resources. The data for petroleum and natural gas are the proved remaining reserves. The same as the following table.

1-13 各地区主要能源、黑色金属矿产基础储量（2005年）

Basic Reserves of Major Energy and Ferrous Metals by Region (2005)

地 区	Region	石 油（万吨）Petroleum (10 000 tons)	天然气（亿立方米）Natural Gas (100 million cu.m)	煤 炭（亿吨）Coal (100 million tons)	铁 矿（矿石,亿吨）Iron (Ore, 100 million tons)	锰 矿（矿石,万吨）Manganese (Ore, 10 000 tons)	铬 矿（矿石,万吨）Chromite Ore (Ore, 10 000 tons)	钒 矿（万吨）Vanadium (10 000 tons)	原生钛铁矿（万吨）Titanium Ore (10 000 tons)
全 国	**National Total**	**248972.1**	**28185.4**	**3326.4**	**216.0**	**21539.9**	**521.0**	**1323.5**	**21410.4**
北 京	Beijing	9.0		5.6	3.4			0.2	6.3
天 津	Tianjin	4327.3	367.4	3.0					
河 北	Hebei	12951.8	179.5	71.8	42.1	5.7	4.1	18.7	547.6
山 西	Shanxi			1054.8	6.2	12.9			
内蒙古	Inner Mongolia	5670.9	3970.5	757.9	12.7	17.7	133.7		
辽 宁	Liaoning	17015.3	500.4	54.5	64.7	1167.3			
吉 林	Jilin	15757.8	199.9	16.4	1.6	0.4			
黑龙江	Heilongjiang	53418.3	903.8	77.3	0.5				
上 海	Shanghai								
江 苏	Jiangsu	2402.5	24.5	22.1	2.0			6.1	
浙 江	Zhejiang			0.5	0.1			4.1	
安 徽	Anhui	136.4	0.0	145.5	9.1			22.0	
福 建	Fujian			4.3	3.7	112.4			
江 西	Jiangxi			7.8	1.7			2.2	
山 东	Shandong	29849.2	277.1	108.2	10.1				
河 南	Henan	5876.8	161.3	127.1	0.9			1.0	
湖 北	Hubei	1033.4	39.2	3.3	4.7	878.4		48.3	
湖 南	Hunan			20.4	1.5	5382.8		223.2	
广 东	Guangdong	9.0	0.3	1.9	1.9	203.1			
广 西	Guangxi	122.5	8.5	8.5	1.0	7256.9		153.0	
海 南	Hainan	45.1	11.0	0.9	0.4				
重 庆	Chongqing		1219.5	18.2		1881.5			
四 川	Sichuan	289.0	4295.1	49.2	31.1	30.2		762.2	20807.8
贵 州	Guizhou		9.9	148.9	0.5	2549.8			
云 南	Yunnan	10.5	14.5	74.0	4.5	1204.4	0.1	0.1	
西 藏	Tibet			0.1	0.3		194.5		
陕 西	Shaanxi	16972.9	5450.0	284.1	4.1	346.6	1.1	1.5	
甘 肃	Gansu	9465.2	97.5	49.4	4.0	17.3	131.3	80.9	
青 海	Qinghai	3824.9	1525.3	19.9	0.1		1.6		
宁 夏	Ningxia	95.5	0.5	68.5					
新 疆	Xinjiang	41378.0	6023.6	122.4	3.1	472.5	54.6	0.2	48.7
海 域	Ocean	28310.7	2906.4						

1-14 各地区主要有色金属、非金属矿产基础储量（2005年）

Basic Reserves of Major Non-ferrous Metal and Non-metal Mineral by Region (2005)

地区	Region	铜矿 (铜,万吨) Copper (Metal, 10 000 tons)	铅矿 (铅,万吨) Lead (Metal, 10 000 tons)	锌矿 (锌,万吨) Zinc (Metal, 10 000 tons)	铝土矿 (矿石,万吨) Bauxite (Ore, 10 000 tons)	菱镁矿 (矿石,万吨) Magnesite Ore (Ore, 10 000 tons)	硫铁矿 (矿石,万吨) Pyrite Ore (Ore, 10 000 tons)	磷矿 (矿石,亿吨) Phosphorus Ore (Ore, 100 million tons)	高岭土 (矿石,万吨) Kaolin Ore (Ore, 10 000 tons)
全国	**National Total**	**2856.4**	**1393.4**	**4269.1**	**73057.8**	**173831.3**	**190328.2**	**37.0**	**60225.9**
北京	Beijing			2.6	2.3				
天津	Tianjin								
河北	Hebei	15.1	17.3	176.0	393.8	1240.3	1887.1	2.3	58.3
山西	Shanxi	156.2	1.5	1.3	11729.3		1996.8	1.0	160.2
内蒙古	Inner Mongolia	106.4	224.4	676.3			11394.8	0.1	435.1
辽宁	Liaoning	13.6	14.1	38.0		146077.7	3027.3	0.8	618.3
吉林	Jilin	11.9	4.2	53.6		1.1	1491.3		62.7
黑龙江	Heilongjiang	120.3	5.3	22.3			48.2		
上海	Shanghai								
江苏	Jiangsu	8.6	13.8	36.5			451.7	0.3	1258.2
浙江	Zhejiang	11.8	40.2	68.9			1314.0		535.2
安徽	Anhui	245.6	9.5	15.0			36419.6	0.4	349.8
福建	Fujian	97.3	19.9	44.8	65.3		1169.1		5818.2
江西	Jiangxi	820.1	35.0	48.5			13955.1	0.8	3957.6
山东	Shandong	31.1	6.4	1.2	938.9	26282.0	414.6	0.7	
河南	Henan	10.5	26.7	33.8	18238.3		12619.3	0.1	
湖北	Hubei	181.4	2.8	5.8	141.3		2267.7	8.4	1043.2
湖南	Hunan	39.2	117.7	228.0	176.6		6833.7	2.7	2642.2
广东	Guangdong	66.9	143.4	257.1			33000.1		28024.8
广西	Guangxi	14.9	30.3	193.2	13508.5		5593.8		12818.6
海南	Hainan	2.8	0.3						1896.9
重庆	Chongqing		3.9	14.8	3639.1		1907.1		
四川	Sichuan	85.5	75.6	174.8		180.3	40136.1	3.2	56.1
贵州	Guizhou	0.4	5.9	12.5	21531.4		5451.7	7.0	10.4
云南	Yunnan	259.0	338.6	1495.6	1971.3		8194.2	8.5	399.1
西藏	Tibet	220.5	18.5	1.3				0.2	
陕西	Shaanxi	16.3	12.7	58.1	721.8		646.1		81.1
甘肃	Gansu	191.2	113.0	455.0			4.0		
青海	Qinghai	49.8	93.5	99.7		49.9	96.8	0.6	
宁夏	Ningxia								
新疆	Xinjiang	80.3	19.0	54.4			7.9		
海域	Ocean								

1-15 主要城市平均气温（2005年）

Monthly Average Temperature of Major Cities (2005)

单位：摄氏度 (℃)

城 市	City	1月 Jan.	2月 Feb.	3月 Mar.	4月 Apr.	5月 May	6月 June	7月 July	8月 Aug.	9月 Sept.	10月 Oct.	11月 Nov.	12月 Dec.	年平均 Annual Average
北 京	Beijing	-2.7	-2.8	6.3	16.4	19.8	25.6	27.9	26.0	22.0	14.9	7.5	-2.5	13.2
天 津	Tianjin	-3.9	-3.1	5.4	16.3	19.8	25.7	27.8	25.7	21.7	14.8	7.1	-3.0	12.9
石家庄	Shijiazhuang	-2.1	-1.5	7.9	17.9	20.7	27.8	28.7	25.9	21.8	15.7	9.7	-0.5	14.3
太 原	Taiyuan	-5.7	-2.8	4.6	14.9	19.6	24.5	25.5	22.6	18.3	10.2	4.6	-5.1	10.9
呼和浩特	Hohhot	-11.4	-9.8	0.5	10.7	17.0	23.6	24.8	22.2	16.9	8.5	0.2	-10.9	7.7
沈 阳	Shenyang	-11.3	-10.9	0.4	11.3	16.1	22.0	24.9	24.0	19.1	11.1	2.7	-12.8	8.0
大 连	Dalian	-3.9	-4.7	2.5	10.8	15.4	20.3	24.8	24.2	21.4	14.7	8.9	-3.8	10.9
长 春	Changchun	-15.1	-15.1	-3.1	9.2	15.1	20.9	22.9	22.7	17.2	9.1	-0.5	-15.6	5.6
哈尔滨	Harbin	-16.4	-16.7	-4.0	7.7	14.4	21.7	22.8	22.3	16.3	7.7	-2.3	-16.7	4.7
上 海	Shanghai	3.4	4.3	9.0	17.8	20.7	26.5	29.3	28.3	26.3	19.2	15.2	4.9	17.1
南 京	Nanjing	1.5	3.0	9.0	18.6	21.3	27.6	28.7	26.8	24.8	17.4	13.6	3.8	16.3
杭 州	Hangzhou	3.1	4.4	9.6	19.1	21.2	27.3	29.8	28.4	27.2	19.0	15.1	5.5	17.5
合 肥	Hefei	1.4	2.6	9.2	18.8	21.7	27.5	28.4	26.1	24.3	17.3	13.3	3.6	16.2
福 州	Fuzhou	9.8	10.5	12.8	19.7	22.8	26.3	29.6	29.0	27.6	23.0	19.8	12.2	20.3
南 昌	Nanchang	3.7	4.7	10.6	20.5	22.8	27.5	30.3	28.5	27.1	19.9	15.6	7.0	18.2
济 南	Jinan	-1.5	-1.4	7.2	17.9	21.6	28.6	27.6	25.5	21.3	15.5	10.8	-0.8	14.4
青 岛	Qingdao	-0.7	-0.9	4.7	12.5	16.5	22.3	25.2	24.3	21.5	16.4	11.5	0.4	12.8
郑 州	Zhengzhou	-0.5	0.3	8.7	18.5	21.3	28.2	26.9	25.4	21.3	15.5	11.5	1.9	14.9
武 汉	Wuhan	3.6	3.6	11.1	21.2	23.7	28.5	30.4	27.2	25.3	18.5	14.4	5.8	17.8
长 沙	Changsha	3.3	3.6	11.2	20.8	22.9	27.5	30.4	27.3	24.8	18.4	15.4	6.9	17.7
广 州	Guangzhou	13.7	14.4	17.2	22.6	27.3	27.9	29.9	28.7	28.5	25.8	22.2	15.1	22.8
南 宁	Nanning	11.5	13.4	16.5	22.1	27.7	27.6	28.6	27.7	26.5	23.4	19.5	12.7	21.4
海 口	Haikou	19.0	20.3	20.1	25.4	29.4	29.4	29.4	28.7	28.3	27.0	24.6	19.1	25.1
桂 林	Guilin	6.2	6.3	12.5	20.5	25.3	26.6	29.2	27.9	26.6	21.6	17.8	9.4	19.2
重 庆	Chongqing	7.6	9.4	13.5	20.2	22.8	26.8	29.5	25.9	26.3	17.8	14.4	8.8	18.6
温 江	Wenjiang	4.8	6.3	11.5	18.4	21.4	25.0	25.6	23.3	23.3	16.8	12.5	5.7	16.2
贵 阳	Guiyang	1.8	3.4	8.0	16.1	20.1	22.1	23.3	22.1	21.2	14.9	11.9	4.5	14.1
昆 明	Kunming	10.2	14.0	13.3	18.6	21.7	21.5	21.0	20.4	19.3	16.8	13.0	10.1	16.7
拉 萨	Lhasa	-0.1	3.8	6.7	9.4	11.0	17.5	17.6	16.3	14.6	9.6	4.3	0.5	9.3
西 安	Xi'an	-0.1	1.9	10.0	19.0	22.3	28.0	28.0	24.4	22.0	14.1	9.8	0.7	15.0
兰 州	Lanzhou	-6.7	-3.9	2.8	10.1	14.2	18.3	19.1	18.2	15.0	6.6	0.5	-7.8	7.2
西 宁	Xining	-7.8	-4.4	1.7	8.2	12.5	15.8	17.2	16.7	12.8	5.6	-0.9	-8.2	5.8
银 川	Yinchuan	-7.4	-4.9	4.1	14.1	18.9	24.6	25.3	22.6	18.4	9.7	3.2	-7.8	10.1
乌鲁木齐	Urumqi	-14.7	-14.8	2.4	11.8	17.6	23.1	25.5	21.5	19.0	9.7	-0.1	-10.8	7.5

1-16 主要城市平均相对湿度(2005年)

Average Relative Humidity of Major Cities (2005)

单位：% (%)

城市	City	1月 Jan.	2月 Feb.	3月 Mar.	4月 Apr.	5月 May	6月 June	7月 July	8月 Aug.	9月 Sept.	10月 Oct.	11月 Nov.	12月 Dec.	年平均 Annual Average
北京	Beijing	41	46	31	34	48	60	65	73	59	50	45	36	49
天津	Tianjin	51	53	39	37	50	65	72	78	68	57	60	50	57
石家庄	Shijiazhuang	55	59	34	37	53	50	62	70	65	51	46	38	52
太原	Taiyuan	57	53	34	31	45	49	62	69	69	70	53	44	53
呼和浩特	Hohhot	63	55	33	28	32	34	47	59	55	49	44	50	46
沈阳	Shenyang	66	62	43	50	60	75	79	78	67	61	58	68	64
大连	Dalian	54	54	50	53	61	81	85	86	73	64	60	62	65
长春	Changchun	72	63	46	46	49	72	80	75	63	54	51	65	61
哈尔滨	Harbin	72	65	49	54	48	66	79	74	66	51	55	66	62
上海	Shanghai	72	76	64	64	70	70	76	76	73	70	69	61	70
南京	Nanjing	63	67	54	56	61	59	71	75	79	72	73	57	66
杭州	Hangzhou	71	76	64	62	71	64	67	68	69	75	75	62	69
合肥	Hefei	69	77	62	65	68	66	78	80	79	70	74	58	71
福州	Fuzhou	67	79	67	70	78	75	67	69	67	64	65	59	69
南昌	Nanchang	74	78	70	68	79	74	67	69	70	66	73	57	70
济南	Jinan	44	59	41	41	46	47	72	74	70	55	48	44	53
青岛	Qingdao	57	60	58	57	64	75	81	81	72	58	59	57	65
郑州	Zhengzhou	56	60	45	47	58	53	78	75	76	66	54	40	59
武汉	Wuhan	67	77	62	64	72	70	70	75	77	68	76	55	69
长沙	Changsha	80	79	70	66	79	75	66	72	77	73	75	63	73
广州	Guangzhou	64	81	73	80	80	81	71	77	71	61	64	48	71
南宁	Nanning	79	86	83	84	82	89	82	86	84	79	81	76	83
海口	Haikou	78	84	83	80	75	78	76	79	80	74	77	73	78
桂林	Guilin	75	80	79	76	79	85	72	73	68	61	68	59	73
重庆	Chongqing	80	74	76	73	81	76	72	80	72	86	85	81	78
温江	Wenjiang	80	81	76	70	75	74	81	84	75	80	79	76	78
贵阳	Guiyang	87	85	78	74	80	80	76	78	72	80	83	79	79
昆明	Kunming	58	42	55	48	44	70	73	74	71	73	70	69	62
拉萨	Lhasa	38	27	37	36	52	39	54	65	57	48	30	26	42
西安	Xi'an	63	63	51	47	56	48	63	73	70	74	65	45	60
兰州	Lanzhou	62	63	62	42	60	60	72	71	70	76	67	58	64
西宁	Xining	59	49	54	44	53	59	69	68	71	68	55	48	58
银川	Yinchuan	58	49	34	24	42	38	52	60	57	60	51	51	48
乌鲁木齐	Urumqi	79	76	69	42	40	34	36	52	38	46	76	78	56

1-17 主要城市降水量（2005年）

Monthly Precipitation of Major Cities (2005)

单位：毫米　　　　(millimeters)

城　市	City	1月 Jan.	2月 Feb.	3月 Mar.	4月 Apr.	5月 May	6月 June	7月 July	8月 Aug.	9月 Sept.	10月 Oct.	11月 Nov.	12月 Dec.	全年 Annual Total
北　京	Beijing	1.5	10.0	0.2	17.0	68.4	66.4	96.1	123.4	24.5	1.8	0.4	1.0	410.7
天　津	Tianjin	1.6	6.0		8.5	37.4	170.9	154.2	209.0	29.2	0.9		0.8	618.5
石家庄	Shijiazhuang	1.9	15.5	0.2	11.2	39.6	43.3	89.7	101.7	83.6	2.0		0.8	389.5
太　原	Taiyuan	0.2	5.2	2.5	6.6	37.1	30.8	42.9	77.6	68.4	3.0		0.4	274.7
呼和浩特	Hohhot	0.1	9.3		10.4	15.4	21.3	60.6	92.1	32.3	4.1		2.7	248.3
沈　阳	Shenyang	13.4	5.8		74.4	114.3	132.6	179.9	191.1	48.5	40.8	2.8	18.6	822.2
大　连	Dalian	0.6	13.1	1.8	43.0	134.6	166.0	100.6	173.3	87.1	16.2	12.0	20.2	768.5
长　春	Changchun	2.9	2.1	1.9	38.0	38.7	190.0	166.7	129.7	72.6	25.4	7.3	5.7	681.0
哈尔滨	Harbin	8.2	1.0	3.3	61.3	18.1	117.6	161.8	57.6	44.7	8.8	15.6	9.9	507.9
上　海	Shanghai	73.0	124.9	42.7	33.1	75.6	37.3	118.6	307.4	101.5	39.3	84.7	21.7	1059.8
南　京	Nanjing	25.5	71.1	43.8	80.9	58.6	63.6	235.9	214.9	85.8	37.9	62.9	11.4	992.3
杭　州	Hangzhou	78.2	155.4	70.6	72.7	99.5	26.2	240.7	133.1	60.1	80.3	82.2	39.6	1138.6
合　肥	Hefei	24.5	72.8	51.9	71.7	87.0	44.3	272.0	212.6	134.9	27.1	84.2	8.3	1091.3
福　州	Fuzhou	8.1	138.4	93.4	53.5	352.6	122.4	286.8	96.7	261.4	263.2	17.4	11.5	1705.4
南　昌	Nanchang	91.7	225.8	129.2	166.7	362.7	156.3	97.0	47.1	216.9	90.9	292.1	32.3	1908.7
济　南	Jinan		20.6	0.2	28.9	65.6	118.8	252.9	161.0	286.9	19.2	6.8	4.5	965.4
青　岛	Qingdao		29.0	8.9	10.5	53.1	83.7	63.2	256.7	290.9	21.5	5.8	7.5	830.8
郑　州	Zhengzhou		8.3	9.6	13.3	56.5	132.9	214.4	118.0	133.3	35.3	4.9	2.3	728.8
武　汉	Wuhan	32.9	110.6	46.6	65.9	176.6	179.5	108.6	93.0	150.0	8.3	143.4	1.2	1116.6
长　沙	Changsha	75.1	190.8	106.8	92.2	400.8	272.1	66.7	80.4	47.5	64.4	159.3	44.8	1600.9
广　州	Guangzhou	8.4	35.0	121.2	209.1	395.2	581.5	131.5	371.2	128.9		2.6	1.6	1986.2
南　宁	Nanning	25.9	35.4	62.7	42.2	148.4	393.0	99.3	121.6	145.9	1.9	15.3	27.6	1119.2
海　口	Haikou	8.4	8.6	22.7	56.7	159.4	279.4	148.3	231.0	212.2	22.2	17.3	20.8	1187.0
桂　林	Guilin	49.1	119.4	186.9	82.0	436.3	644.8	68.5	90.4	70.9	13.5	56.0	59.6	1877.4
重　庆	Chongqing	10.3	27.5	69.3	79.4	182.1	137.4	101.7	221.8	62.2	83.4	31.6	13.1	1019.8
温　江	Wenjiang	15.6	13.4	44.9	38.3	75.2	160.9	138.5	212.4	33.3	12.3	16.1	4.7	765.6
贵　阳	Guiyang	25.8	13.1	68.8	54.0	177.7	243.7	184.1	117.9	63.1	54.8	39.7	24.8	1067.5
昆　明	Kunming	12.8	0.2	39.3	8.3	26.1	204.0	169.6	242.1	105.8	90.1	39.2	38.5	976.0
拉　萨	Lhasa	4.1		1.2	7.7	29.5	85.2	104.3	167.2	75.5	21.1			495.8
西　安	Xi'an		9.1	5.6	19.2	43.1	67.1	45.6	127.4	104.2	117.9	2.2		541.4
兰　州	Lanzhou	1.5	4.7	14.8	5.5	106.0	71.5	120.5	32.8	38.8	31.9	3.3	0.1	431.4
西　宁	Xining	1.7	6.2	19.1	8.5	61.7	79.7	106.8	106.3	66.5	26.0	1.6		484.1
银　川	Yinchuan		1.7			13.6	2.0	11.5	19.6	19.7	6.7		0.1	74.9
乌鲁木齐	Urumqi	5.6	4.0	6.5	35.2	25.0	28.6	16.7	86.7	2.0	9.0	33.1	23.9	276.3

1-18 主要城市日照时数（2005年）

Monthly Sunshine Hours of Major Cities (2005)

单位：小时 (hours)

城市	City	1月 Jan.	2月 Feb.	3月 Mar.	4月 Apr.	5月 May	6月 June	7月 July	8月 Aug.	9月 Sept.	10月 Oct.	11月 Nov.	12月 Dec.	全年 Annual Total
北京	Beijing	210.3	160.2	270.8	254.9	261.2	231.7	200.5	185.4	192.3	216.3	192.7	199.8	2576.1
天津	Tianjin	178.4	132.3	244.3	219.5	237.8	229.1	183.4	148.9	199.3	215.9	174.4	184.9	2348.2
石家庄	Shijiazhuang	168.4	98.5	266.0	250.1	247.8	203.5	144.9	170.4	168.0	189.9	195.4	171.2	2274.1
太原	Taiyuan	157.4	147.4	256.7	277.9	271.1	254.2	251.5	243.8	166.1	190.6	220.7	183.5	2620.9
呼和浩特	Hohhot	121.6	151.9	285.2	279.1	313.1	300.3	276.9	236.4	235.0	233.0	209.0	175.3	2816.8
沈阳	Shenyang	148.8	169.5	263.1	211.3	212.2	140.6	166.7	146.5	234.3	220.6	172.8	163.5	2249.9
大连	Dalian	228.2	198.2	269.6	245.7	286.6	246.9	204.4	218.6	235.7	253.4	195.8	166.6	2749.7
长春	Changchun	154.9	196.5	238.3	204.3	228.6	151.0	147.1	188.0	241.9	221.5	190.6	161.9	2324.6
哈尔滨	Harbin	77.5	148.5	245.4	162.0	213.7	234.7	155.1	201.8	212.3	215.4	159.7	107.9	2134.0
上海	Shanghai	113.9	83.0	170.2	195.3	176.5	201.5	154.9	161.4	164.7	159.5	112.6	135.5	1829.0
南京	Nanjing	130.0	98.3	202.1	230.5	184.5	211.1	195.7	138.9	131.5	161.6	106.6	146.7	1937.5
杭州	Hangzhou	92.4	56.4	161.3	200.2	124.0	216.4	180.8	156.4	197.0	132.9	102.6	141.8	1762.2
合肥	Hefei	98.2	75.2	184.6	219.2	194.6	214.0	191.4	141.0	130.3	156.0	95.3	134.3	1834.1
福州	Fuzhou	74.4	34.1	100.3	137.9	66.8	123.8	246.5	154.4	174.8	120.2	111.1	124.9	1469.2
南昌	Nanchang	43.7	51.6	109.2	200.0	106.9	183.4	274.3	222.7	214.7	165.0	86.8	136.2	1794.5
济南	Jinan	197.7	115.5	219.6	249.1	286.5	254.1	159.3	185.7	139.9	194.4	183.9	183.8	2369.5
青岛	Qingdao	201.8	151.9	235.4	256.6	278.8	209.2	160.9	165.3	138.1	210.7	174.5	171.9	2355.1
郑州	Zhengzhou	83.8	79.5	181.5	227.8	186.6	201.5	78.7	139.8	125.4	147.5	146.9	141.9	1740.9
武汉	Wuhan	110.4	51.3	149.5	212.4	170.3	177.5	233.8	173.0	167.4	139.6	110.2	134.3	1829.7
长沙	Changsha	26.8	38.1	80.6	158.4	80.0	149.0	249.4	181.6	144.0	116.9	91.6	106.7	1423.1
广州	Guangzhou	83.9	16.0	52.8	44.3	72.6	61.0	175.3	147.7	146.7	210.6	145.7	131.9	1288.5
南宁	Nanning	33.4	19.7	44.0	92.4	189.6	84.9	231.1	171.0	164.0	170.6	121.7	100.8	1423.2
海口	Haikou	88.4	103.6	104.2	138.6	232.0	165.3	228.4	225.5	180.5	180.4	132.9	60.7	1840.5
桂林	Guilin	37.0	17.1	33.6	109.3	143.0	80.4	246.9	208.2	202.4	174.9	111.4	102.6	1466.8
重庆	Chongqing	12.2	29.7	62.3	125.1	80.6	118.3	179.4	97.2	171.0	17.9	5.9	4.3	903.9
温江	Wenjiang	30.7	26.5	78.2	111.9	94.7	118.0	76.4	77.3	70.7	32.8	30.1	29.7	777.0
贵阳	Guiyang	25.5	51.0	39.2	117.5	106.4	97.2	188.9	97.7	145.9	76.1	49.4	9.3	1004.1
昆明	Kunming	216.4	244.7	188.0	238.0	280.4	105.5	109.6	96.6	114.4	129.7	181.4	149.6	2054.3
拉萨	Lhasa	237.6	208.2	253.6	267.7	273.9	291.7	263.3	206.4	277.8	267.3	284.7	267.8	3100.0
西安	Xi'an	82.3	76.9	198.2	228.3	207.8	253.0	190.6	143.3	153.4	131.9	129.2	154.5	1949.4
兰州	Lanzhou	185.9	180.8	201.5	235.7	251.5	260.0	221.6	215.0	163.8	167.9	184.1	202.1	2469.9
西宁	Xining	186.2	188.2	189.5	253.6	259.1	261.1	198.4	198.6	153.9	161.9	207.0	220.0	2477.5
银川	Yinchuan	165.2	171.6	262.0	273.7	282.2	293.3	262.7	253.9	216.4	225.1	214.2	193.1	2813.4
乌鲁木齐	Urumqi	40.0	88.5	204.7	294.0	311.4	334.8	289.8	270.2	285.3	225.6	109.6	74.8	2528.7

主要统计指标解释

行政区划 指国家对行政区域的划分。根据宪法规定，我国的行政区域划分如下：(1)全国分为省、自治区、直辖市；(2)省、自治区分为自治州、县、自治县、市；(3)自治州分为县、自治县、市；(4)县、自治县分为乡、民族乡、镇；(5)直辖市和较大的市分为区、县；(6)国家在必要时设立的特别行政区。

国土 指中华人民共和国国家管辖下的领土、领海和领空。

气候 指地球与大气之间长期能量交换与质量交换所形成的一种自然环境状态，它是多种因素综合作用的结果。气候既是人类生活和生产的环境要素之一，又是供给人类生活和生产的重要资源。气温、降水、湿度等气象要素的多年平均值是用来描述一个地区气候状况的主要参数，而各种气象要素某年、某月的平均值(或总量)则可以反映出该时期天气气候状况的重要特征。

自然资源 指人类可以直接从自然界获得，并用于生产和生活的物质资源。自然资源一般可以分成可再生资源和非再生资源两大类。可再生资源指在较短时间内可以再生、可以循环利用的资源，包括土地资源、水资源、气候资源、生物资源和海洋资源等。非再生资源指在使用后不能再生的资源，包括矿产资源和地热能源。

土地资源 土地指陆地的表层部分，它主要由岩石、岩石的风化物和土壤构成。土地资源按利用类型可以分为农用地、建筑用地和未利用地。农用地包括耕地、园地、林地、牧草地和水面。建筑用地包括居民点及工矿用地、交通用地和水利设施用地。未利用地指农用地和建筑用地以外的土地，包括滩涂、荒漠、戈壁、冰川和石山等。

耕地面积 指经过开垦用以种植农作物并经常进行耕耘的土地面积。包括种有作物的土地面积、休闲地、新开荒地和抛荒未满三年的土地面积。

林业用地面积 指生长乔木、竹类、灌木、沿海红树林等林木的土地面积，包括有林地、灌木林、疏林地、未成林造林地、迹地、苗圃等。

草地面积 指牧区和农区用于放牧牲畜或割草，植被盖度在5%以上的草原、草坡、草山等面积。包括天然的和人工种植或改良的草地面积。

森林资源 指森林、林木、林地以及依托森林、林木、林地生存的野生动物、植物和微生物。林木指树木和竹子。森林指以乔木为主体的植物群落，是集生的乔木及与共同作用的植物、动物、微生物和土壤、气候等的总体。

活立木总蓄积量 指一定范围内土地上全部树木蓄积的总量，包括森林蓄积、疏林蓄积、散生木蓄积和四旁树蓄积。

森林面积 指由乔木树种构成，郁闭度0.2以上(含0.2)的林地或冠幅宽度10米以上的林带的面积，即有林地面积。森林面积包括天然起源和人工起源的针叶林面积、阔叶林面积、针阔混交林面积和竹林面积，不包括灌木林地面积和疏林地面积。

森林蓄积量 指一定森林面积上存在着的林木树干部分的总材积。它是反映一个国家或地区森林资源总规模和水平的基本指标之一，也是反映森林资源的丰富程度、衡量森林生态环境优劣的重要依据。

森林覆盖率 指一个国家或地区森林面积占土地总面积的百分比。森林覆盖率是反映森林资源的丰富程度和生态平衡状况的重要指标。在计算森林覆盖率时，森林面积包括郁闭度0.2以上的乔木林地面积和竹林地面积，国家特别规定的灌木林地面积、农田林网以及四旁(村旁、路旁、水旁、宅旁)林木的覆盖面积。计算公式为：

$$\text{森林覆盖率（\%）}=\frac{\text{森林面积}}{\text{土地总面积}}\times 100\%$$

水资源 水在自然界中以固体、液体和气态三种聚集状态存在，分布于海洋、陆地(包括土壤)以及大气之中，通过水循环形成水资源。水资源包括经人类控制并直接可供灌溉、发电、给水、航运、养殖等用途的地表水和地下水，以及江河、湖泊、井、泉、潮汐、港湾和养殖水域等。水资源是发展国民经济不可缺少的重要自然资源。

地表水和地下水 陆地上的水因空间分布不同，分为地表水和地下水。地表水指分别存在于河流、湖泊、沼泽、冰川和冰盖等水体中水分的总称，又称陆地水。地下水指储存在地面以下饱和岩土孔隙、裂隙及溶洞中的水。

内陆水域总面积 指江、河、湖泊、池塘、塘堰、水库等各种流水或蓄水的水面占地面积。

海洋 是海和洋的统称。洋为地球表面上相连接的广大咸水水体的主体部分。海为地球表面相连接的广大咸水水体被陆地、岛礁、半岛包围或分隔的边缘部分。

海水可养殖面积 指利用滩涂、浅海、港湾进行鱼、虾、蟹、贝、藻等海水经济动植物的人工养殖的水面面积。

径流 指陆地上接受降水后扣除损耗外，从地表和地下向流域出口断面汇集的水流。径流可分为地表径流、地下径流和壤中流。地表径流指沿地表向河流、湖泊、沼泽、海洋等汇集的水流；地下径流指沿潜水层或隔水层间的含水层，向河流、湖泊、沼泽、海洋等汇集的地下水水流。

径流量 指在一定时段内通过河流某一过水断面的水量，用以反映一个国家或地区水资源的丰歉程度。计算公式为：

径流量=降水量-蒸发量

矿产资源 矿产指由地质作用形成，富集于地壳中或出露于地表达到工农业利用要求的有用矿物。矿产是一种重要的自然资源，是社会发展的重要物质基础。

矿产基础储量 基础储量是查明矿产资源的一部分。它能满足现行采矿和生产所需的指标要求，是控制的、探明的并通过可行性或预可行性研究认为属于经济的、边界经济的部分，用未扣除设计、采矿损失的数量表示。

流域 每条河流都有自己的干流和支流，干支流共同组成这条河流的水系。每条河流都有自己的集水区域，这个集水区域就称为该河流的流域。

外流河 指直接或间接流入海洋的河流。供给外流河河水的区域称为外流区域。

内陆河 指在陆地内部干燥地区，河水沿途消失于沙漠或注入内陆湖泊的河流。供给内陆河河水的区域称为内陆区域。

大陆架 指沿海国家的领海以外，依其陆地领土的全部自然延伸，扩展到大陆边缘的，其宽度依据《联合国海洋法公约》规定的海底区域的海床和底土。大陆架海区水产资源丰富，海底多蕴藏石油、天然气以及其他矿产资源，这些自然资源属沿海国家所有。我国的大陆架为我国领海以外依本国陆地领土的全部自然延伸，扩展到大陆边外缘的海底区域的海床和底土；如果从测算领海宽度的基线量起至大陆边外缘的距离不足200海里，则扩展到200海里。

浅海养殖 指在可养殖的浅海中进行海水经济动植物养殖。

滩涂养殖 指利用位于海边潮间带的软泥或砂泥地带加以平整，筑堤、建坝等进行海水养殖。

港湾养殖 指利用港、湾，或在海边、河口附近的滩涂、洼地拦闸筑堤进行海水养殖。

气温 指空气的温度，我国一般以摄氏度(℃)为单位表示。气象观测的温度表是放在离地面约1.5米处通风良好的百叶箱里测量的，因此，通常说的气温指的是离地面1.5米处百叶箱中的温度。其统计计算方法为：

月平均气温是将全月各日的平均气温相加，除以该月的天数而得。

年平均气温是将12个月的月平均气温累加后除以12而得。

相对湿度 指空气中实际所含水蒸气密度和同温度下饱和水蒸气密度的百分比值。其统计方法与气温相同。

降水量 指从天空降落到地面的液态或固态(经融化后)水，未经蒸发、渗透、流失而在地面上积聚的深度。其统计计算方法为：

月降水量是将全月各日的降水量累加而得。

年降水量是将12个月的月降水量累加而得。

日照时数 指太阳实际照射地面的时间。其统计方法与降水量相同。

Explanatory Notes on Main Statistical Indicators

Divisions of Administrative Areas refers to the division of administrative areas by the state. The Constitution of the People's Republic of China stipulates that the administrative areas in China are divided as: 1) The whole country is divided into provinces, autonomous regions and municipalities directly under the central government; 2) Provinces and autonomous regions are divided into autonomous prefectures, counties, autonomous counties and cities; 3) Autonomous prefectures are divided into counties, autonomous counties and cities; 4) Counties and autonomous counties are divided into townships, nationality townships and towns; 5) Municipalities and large cities are divided into districts and counties, 6) The state shall, when necessary, establish special administrative regions.

Territory refers to territorial land, sea and air space under the administration of the People's Republic of China.

Climate refers to the natural environmental status formed by the long-term exchange of energy and mass between the earth and the air, and is the results of interaction of many factors. Climate is both one of the environment factors and the important resources for the living and production activities of the human being. The average values across several years of meteorological factors such as temperature, rainfall and humidity are used as important parameters to describe the climate of a region, while the average values (or total values) of a given year or month of meteorological factors reflect the key characteristics of climate for that period of time.

Natural Resources refer to material resources that could be obtained from the nature by human being and used for production and living. Natural resources in general can be classified as renewable resources and non-renewable resources. Renewable resources refer to resources that could be renewed and recycled during a relatively short period of time, including land resource, water resource, climate resource, biology resource and marine resource. Non-renewable resources include resources that could not be renewed, such as minerals and geothermal resource.

Land Resource Land refers to the surface of the earth, consisting of mainly rocks and its whethering and earth. Land resource can be classified, by its utilization, as land for agriculture, land for construction and unused land. Land for agriculture includes cultivated land, plantation land, forestland, grassland and waters. Land for construction includes land for residential purpose, for manufacturing and mining, for transportation and for water-conservancy projects. Unused land refers to land other than land for agriculture and construction, including beaches, deserts, Gobi, glaciers and rock mountains.

Area of Cultivated Land refers to area of land reclaimed for the regular cultivation of various farm crops, including crop-cover land, fallow, newly reclaimed land and land laid idle for less than 3 years.

Area of Afforested Land refer to land for trees bamboo, bushes and mangrove, including forest-cover land, bush-covered land, sparse forest land, land planned for afforestation and nurseries of young trees.

Area of Grassland refers to areas of grassland, grass-slopes and grass-covered hills with a vegetation-covering rate of over 5% that are used for animal husbandry or harvesting of grass. It includes natural, cultivated and improved grassland areas.

Forest Resource refers to forests, trees, forestland and wild animals, plants and microorganism that live on forest and trees. Trees include trees and bamboo. Forest refers to the population of clusters of trees and other plants, animals and microorganism as well as the earth and climate that have interactions with the trees.

Total Standing Stock Volume refers to the total stock volume of trees growing in land, including trees in forest, tress in sparse forest, scattered trees and trees planted by the side of villages, farm houses and along roads and rivers.

Forest Area refers to the area of forest where trees and bamboo grow with canopy density above 0.2, including land of natural woods and planted woods, but excluding bush land and thin forest land. It reflects the total areas of afforestation.

Stock Volume of Forest refers to total stock volume of wood growing in forest area, which shows the total size and level of forest resources of a country or a region. It is also an important indicator illustrating the richness of forest resource and the status of forest ecological environment.

Forest Coverage Rate refers to the ratio of area of afforested land to total land area. It is a very important indicator that reflects the status of abundance of forest resource and ecosystem balance. Forest area includes the area of trees and bamboo grow with canopy density above 0.2, the area of shrubby tree according to regulations of the government, the area of forest land inside farm land and the area of trees planted by the side of villages, farm houses and along roads and rivers. The formula for calculating forest coverage rate is as follows:

Forestry coverage rate (%)= (Area of Afforested Land/Area of Total Land) × 100%

Water Resource Water exists in the nature in solid, liquid and gaseous states, is distributed in the ocean, land (including earth) and air, and constitutes the water resource through the circulation of water. Water resource includes the surface water and underground water that is controlled by the human being for irrigation, power-generation, water supply, navigation and cultivation. It also includes rivers, lakes, wells, springs, tides, gulf and water area for cultivation. Water resource as an important natural resource is indispensable for the development of the national economy.

Surface Water and Underground Water Water on earth can be divided into surface water and underground water according to its distribution. Surface water refers to moisture exists in rivers, lakes, swamps, glaciers, icecaps and so on. It is also called land water. The underground water refers to water deposited underground in the cranny and the hole of saturated rock soil and in the water-eroded cave.

Inland Water Area refers to water area of rivers, lakes, ponds, reservoir, etc.

Ocean is the general name for sea and ocean. Ocean refers to the main body of large salt water connected with the earth. Sea refers to the edge areas of the salt water on the earth that are comparted or surrounded by land, island, reef or peninsula.

Marine Cultivatable Areas refer to water areas in beach, shallow sea and lough that are used to breed marine cash propagation, such as fish, shrimp, crab, shellfish, alga and so on.

Runoff refers to the water gathered at the way out of the cross section of drainage area either from the surface or underground after deducting the wastage of the precipitation on the land. Runoff can be divided into surface runoff, underground runoff and within soil runoff. Surface runoff refers to water flow to the rivers, lakes, swamps, and seas on the surface of the earth. Underground runoff refers to water flow to rivers, lakes, swamps, and seas through the water-bearing stratum of confined layer or unconfined layer.

Volume of Runoff refers to the total volume of water running through a certain cross section of a river during a certain period of time, reflecting the water resource condition in a country or a region. The formula for calculating volume or runoff is as follows:

Runoff =Precipitation-Evaporation

Mineral Resources refer to useful minerals that can be used for industrial or agricultural purposes enriched in lithosphere or on earth due to the geological process. Minerals are important natural resources, and important material base for social development.

Ensured Mineral Reserves refer to the actual mineral reserves, which equal to the proven mineral reserves (including industrial reserves and prospective reserves) minus extracted parts and underground losses.

Drainage Area Each river has its own main stream and branches to form the water system of the river. Each river has its own catchment area, which is also called as the drainage area of the river.

Out-flowing Rivers refer to rivers directly or indirectly flowing into the sea. The area providing water to the out-flowing rivers is called as out-flowing area.

Inland Rivers refer to rivers in inland dry areas that die away in desert on the way or infuse into inland lakes. The area providing water to the inland rivers is called as inland area.

Continental Shelf refers to seabed and subsoil of sea floor area that beyond the marginal sea of the coastal countries which stretches naturally of its land territory to continent edge, and its width is defined by the United Nations Marine Convention. The continental shelf area is rich in aquatic products, and its seabed contains petroleum, natural gas and other mineral resources, which belong to the coastal countries. The continental shelf of our country is the natural stretch of its land territory to the continent edge besides the marginal sea of our country. It expands to the seabed and subsoil of the sea floor area to the edge of the continent. If the distance from the baseline of the marginal sea to the continent edge is less than 200 nautical miles, it can be expanded to 200 nautical miles.

Shallow Sea Cultivation refers to the breeding of marine cash propagation in the cultivatable shallow sea.

Sea-beaches Cultivation refers to the level off the ooze and mud in tideland to bank up and build dam to conduct marine cultivation.

Harbor Cultivation refers to marine cultivation conducted in harbors, bays, or the sea-beaches or marshes around seaside and bayou by blocking the gate and banking up the dam.

Temperature refers to the air temperature. China uses centigrade as the unit. The thermometry used for weather observation is put in a breezy shutter, which is 1.5 meters high from the ground. Therefore, the commonly used temperature refers to the temperature in the breezy shutter 1.5 meters away from the ground. The calculation method is as follows:

Monthly average temperature is the summation of average daily temperature of one month divided by the actual days of that particular month.

Annual average temperature is the summation of monthly average of a year divided by 12 months.

Relative Humidity refers to the ratio of actual water vapor pressure to the saturation water vapor density under the current temperature. The statistical method is the same as that of temperature.

Volume of Precipitation refers to the deepness of liquid state or solid state (thawed) water falling from the sky to the ground that has not been evaporated, infiltrated or run off. The calculation method is as follows:

Monthly precipitation is the summation of daily precipitation of a month.

Annual precipitation is the summation of 12 months precipitation of a year.

Sunshine Hours refer to the actual hours of sun irradiating the earth. The calculation method is the same as that of the precipitation.

2

综 合

General Survey

简要说明

本篇章主要内容和资料来源

一、综合资料主要包括国民经济和社会发展综合资料以及民族自治地方社会经济发展情况资料两部分。分别由国家统计局综合司和国家民族事务委员会经济发展司编辑整理。

二、国民经济综合资料是抽取全书的精华，通过对各篇章主要统计指标及其速度、结构、比例和效益等的加工计算，来反映国民经济和社会发展的总体情况。

三、民族自治地方及少数民族统计资料由两部分组成：

一是以地域为主体进行的统计调查。即根据国家民委和国家统计局联合布置的民族自治地方国民经济和社会发展统计报表制度，由有民族自治地方的20个省、自治区、直辖市民委和统计局共同组织实施。统计范围是5个民族自治区、30个自治州、120个自治县（旗）辖区内的全部单位，全国汇总时不重复计算。统计调查方法为全面调查。另外，全国民族自治地方卫生情况由卫生部提供。民族自治地方行政区划资料是根据民政部编辑的《行政区划简册》汇总整理。

二是以民族成分为主体进行的统计调查，主要反映全国少数民族社会发展情况。其中全国少数民族教职员工、学生数据由教育部提供；全国少数民族优秀运动员、教练员数据由国家体育总局提供；全国少数民族文字出版物数据由新闻出版署提供。

四、从1998年年报开始执行国家统计局和国家工行政管理局共同制定的《关于划分企业登记注册类型的规定》。从2003年起开始执行新的《国民经济行业分类》，与以往相比，增加了4个门类，3个大类，28个中类和67个小类。

Brief Introduction

Main Content and Source of Data

I. This chapter consists of two parts: summary data on the national economy and social development and data on the social and economic development of the minority national autonomous areas, which are compiled by the Department of Comprehensive Statistics of the National Bureau of Statistics and by Department of Economic Development of the State Commission on Ethnic Affairs respectively.

II. The summary data on the national economy highlight the overall situation of the economic and social development by presenting key statistics including growth, structure, ratio and efficiency data derived from other chapters.

III. Data on the minority nationality autonomous areas and the minority nationalities are composed of two parts:

(1) Data collected from the surveys conducted by areas. A statistical reporting system on the economic and social development in the minority nationality autonomous areas has been assigned jointly by the State Commission on Ethnic Affairs and the National Bureau of Statistics and implemented by the ethnic affairs commissions and the statistical bureaus of 20 provinces and autonomous regions. The reporting system covers all units under the jurisdiction of the 5 minority nationality autonomous regions, 30 autonomous prefectures and 120 autonomous counties. Duplicated counts are excluded in the national tabulation. Method of data collection is complete investigation In addition, data on the public health of the minority nationality autonomous areas are provided by the Ministry of Public Health, and data on the divisions of administrative areas of the minority nationality autonomous areas are tabulated and prepared in accordance with the *Concise Edition of the Divisions of Administrative Areas* compiled by the Ministry of Civil Affairs.

(2) Data collected from the surveys mainly on the minority nationalities. They chiefly show the social development of the minority nationalities. Among them, data on the students and teaching staff of the minority nationalities are provided by the Ministry of Education; data on the excellent athletes and coaches are provided by the State Sports Administration; and data on the publications of the minority nationality languages are provided by the Press and Publication Administration.

IV. The *Regulation on the Classification of the Registration Status of Enterprises*, jointly developed by the National Bureau of Statistics and the State Industry and Commerce Administration, has been in use in compiling the annual statistics since 1998. The new *Industrial Classification of the National Economy* has been in use since 2003, added 4 new divisions, 3 new divisions, 28 major groups and 67 groups.

2-1 各部门机构数

Grass-roots Units in Various Sectors

部 门	Sector	机构数 Grass-roots Units 2004	2005	2005年比上年增长(%) Increase Rate in 2005 over 2004 (%)
农村基层单位 （万个）	**Rural Grass-roots Units (10 000 units)**			
基层组织	Grass-roots Organizations			
乡政府	Township Governments	1.78	1.66	-6.7
镇政府	Town Governments	1.92	1.89	-1.6
村民委员会	Village Committees	65.27	64.01	-1.9
乡村户数	Numbers of Rural Households	24971	25223	1.0
国营农场 （个）	**State-owned Farms (unit)**	**1928**	**1923**	**-0.3**
国有及规模以上非国有工业企业 （万个）	**Industrial Enterprises of State-owned and Non-state-owned above Designated Size (10 000 units)**	**27.65**	**27.18**	**-1.7**
大型企业	Large Industrial Enterprises	0.21	0.25	17.2
中型企业	Medium-sized Industrial Enterprises	2.56	2.73	6.7
小型企业	Small Industrial Enterprises	24.88	24.21	-2.7
#国有及国有控股企业	State-owned and State-holding Enterprises	3.56	2.75	-22.8
集体企业	Collective-owned Enterprises	1.81	1.59	-11.9
外商及港澳台商投资企业	Enterprises with Funds from Hong Kong, Macao, Taiwan and Foreign Countries	5.72	5.64	-1.4
建筑业企业 （个）	**Construction Enterprises and Units (unit)**	**59018**	**58750**	**-0.5**
邮电业 （个）	**Postal and Telecommunication Services (unit)**			
邮政局所	Postal Offices	66393	65917	-0.7
金融业 （个）	**Financial Intermediation (unit)**	**88218**	**82546**	**-6.4**
银行系统合计	Sub-total of Banking System	88150	82453	-6.5
保险系统机构	Sub-total of Insurance System	68	93	36.8
教育事业	**Education**			
普通高等学校 （所）	Regular Institutions of Higher Education (unit)	1731	1792	3.5
普通中学 （万所）	Regular Secondary Schools (10 000 units)	7.91	7.80	-1.4
#高中	Senior Secondary Schools	1.60	1.61	0.6
初中	Junior Secondary Schools	6.31	6.19	-1.9
普通小学 （万所）	Primary Schools (10 000 units)	39.42	36.62	-7.1
学前教育 （万所）	Pre-school Education (10 000 units)	11.79	12.44	5.5
特殊教育 （所）	Special Schools (unit)	1560	1593	2.1
科技机构 （个）	**Science and Technology Institutions (unit)**	**32723**	**33714**	**3.0**

2-1 续表 continued

部 门	Sector	机构数 Grass-roots Units		2005年比上年增长(%) Increase Rate in 2005 over 2004 (%)
		2004	2005	
艺术事业 (个)	**Art Institutions (unit)**			
#艺术表演团体	Art Performing Troupes	2759	2805	1.7
艺术表演场所	Art Performing Centers	1928	1866	-3.2
#剧场、影剧院	Theaters and Cinemas	1766	1766	0.0
公共图书馆 (个)	**Public Libraries (unit)**	**2720**	**2762**	**1.5**
群众文化事业 (个)	**Mass Cultural Establishments (unit)**	**41402**	**41588**	**0.4**
群众艺术馆	Mass Art Centers	380	447	17.6
文化馆	Cultural Centers	2841	2779	-2.2
文化站	Cultural Stations	38181	38362	0.5
#乡文化站	Township Cultural Centers	34834	34593	-0.7
艺术教育事业 (个)	**Arts Education Establishments (unit)**	**193**	**189**	**-2.1**
其他文化事业 (个)	**Other Cultural Establishments (unit)**	**312876**	**332302**	**6.2**
艺术创作机构	Art Creation Institutions	422	352	-16.6
艺术研究机构	Art Research Institutions	188	188	0.0
艺术展览机构	Art Exhibition Institutions	36	56	55.6
文物事业 (个)	**Cultural Relic Establishments (unit)**	**3965**	**4030**	**1.6**
博物馆	Museums	1548	1581	2.1
文物保护管理机构	Agencies of Historical Relics Preservation	2151	2186	1.6
文物商店	Cultural Relic Shops	106	97	-8.5
广播、电视台 (座)	**Radio and Television Broadcasting Stations (unit)**			
广播电台	Radio Stations	282	273	-3.2
电视台	Television Stations	314	302	-3.8
卫生事业 (个)	**Health Care (unit)**	**297540**	**298997**	**0.5**
#医院、卫生院	Hospitals and Health Centers	60864	60397	-0.8
疗养院	Sanatoriums	292	274	-6.2
门诊部、诊所	Clinics	208794	207404	-0.7
专科防治院（所、站）	Specialized Prevention & Treatment Stations	1583	1502	-5.1
疾病预防控制中心	Center for Disease Control and Prevention	3588	3585	-0.1
妇幼保健院（所、站）	Maternity and Child Care Centers	2998	3021	0.8
民政单位 (个)	**Civil Affairs Departments (unit)**	**103411**	**101442**	**-1.9**
事业单位	Institutions	66884	66533	-0.5
社会福利企业单位	Social Welfare Enterprises	32410	31211	-3.7
行政机关	Administrative Departments	4117	3698	-10.2

注：卫生机构数从2002年起为登记注册数。

a) Number of health institutions since 2002 are registered ones.

2-2 平均每天主要社会经济活动

Selected Indicators on Average Daily Social and Economic Activities

指 标	Item	1978	1989	1997	2005
每天创造的财富	**Daily Production**				
国内生产总值 (亿元)	Gross Domestic Product (100 million yuan)	10.0	46.6	216.4	501.6
第一产业	Primary Industry	2.8	11.6	39.1	63.2
第二产业	Secondary Industry	4.8	19.9	102.9	238.5
#工业	Industry	4.4	17.8	90.2	210.7
建筑业	Construction	0.4	2.2	12.7	27.8
第三产业	Tertiary Industry	2.4	15.0	74.4	199.9
#交通运输仓储和邮政业	Transport, Storage and Post	0.5	2.2	12.6	28.8
批发和零售业	Wholesale and Retail Trade	0.7	4.6	20.0	37.1
财政收入 (亿元)	Government Revenue (100 million yuan)	3.1	7.3	23.7	86.7
财政支出 (亿元)	Government Expenditures (100 million yuan)	3.1	7.7	25.3	93.0
粮食 (万吨)	Grain (10 000 tons)	83.5	111.7	135.4	132.6
棉花 (万吨)	Cotton (10 000 tons)	0.6	1.0	1.3	1.6
油料 (万吨)	Oil-bearing Crops (10 000 tons)	1.4	3.5	5.9	8.4
肉类 (万吨)	Meat (10 000 tons)			14.4	21.2
水产品 (万吨)	Aquatic Products (10 000 tons)	1.3	3.2	9.9	14.0
布 (万米)	Cloth (10 000 m)	3022	5184	6816	13271
原煤 (万吨)	Coal (10 000 tons)	169	289	376	604
发电量 (亿千瓦小时)	Electricity (100 million kwh)	7.0	16.0	31.1	68.5
原油 (万吨)	Crude Oil (10 000 tons)	28.5	37.7	44.0	49.7
粗钢 (万吨)	Crude Steel (10 000 tons)	8.7	16.9	29.8	96.8
钢材 (万吨)	Rolled Steel (10 000 tons)	6.0	13.3	27.3	103.5
水泥 (万吨)	Cement (10 000 tons)	17.9	57.6	140.2	292.8
每天消费量	**Daily National Consumption**				
最终消费支出 (亿元)	Final Consumption Expenditure (100 million yuan)	6.1	30.6	131.9	265.5
居民消费	Resident Consumption	4.8	24.1	101.2	194.3
农村居民	Rural Household	3.0	12.5	39.9	52.1
城镇居民	Urban Household	1.8	11.7	61.2	142.2
政府消费	Government Consumption Expenditure	1.3	6.4	30.7	71.3
能源消费量 (万吨标准煤)	Energy Consumption (10 000 tons of SCE)	157	266	378	612
社会消费品零售总额 (亿元)	Total Retail Sales of Consumer Goods (100 million yuan)	4.3	22.2	85.6	184.0
每天其他经济活动	**Other Daily Economic Activities**				
资本形成总额 (亿元)	Gross Capital Formation (100 million yuan)	3.8	17.3	82.1	218.0
固定资产形成总额	Gross Fixed Capital Formation	2.9	12.1	71.1	212.2
存货增加	Changes in Inventories	0.8	5.2	11.0	5.7
城镇新建住宅面积 (万平方米)	Residential Buildings Completed in Urban Areas (10 000 sq.m)	10.4	54.0	111.2	181.1
农民新建房屋面积 (万平方米)	Private Buildings Completed in Rural Areas (10 000 sq.m)	27.4	185.2	220.8	182.7
客运量 (万人)	Passenger Traffic (10 000 persons)	696	2168	3633	5060
货运量 (万吨)	Freight Traffic (10 000 tons)	682	2708	3502	5102
沿海主要港口货物吞吐量 (万吨)	Cargo Handled at Principal Seaports (10 000 tons)	54	134	249	802
邮电业务总量 (亿元)	Business Volume of Postal and Telecommunication Services (100 million yuan)	0.1	0.3	4.9	33.0
货物进出口总额 (亿美元)	Total Value of Imports and Exports (USD 100 million)	0.6	3.1	8.9	39.0
出口总额	Total Exports	0.3	1.4	5.0	20.9
进口总额	Total Imports	0.3	1.6	3.9	18.1
实际利用外资额 (亿美元)	Foreign Capital Actually Used (USD 100 million)		0.3	1.8	1.7
过夜旅游者人数 (万人次)	Tourists (Overnight Visitors) (10 000 person-times)	0.2	2.6	6.5	12.8
居民新增储蓄额 (亿元)	Outstanding Amount of Savings Deposit (100 million yuan)	0.1	3.8	21.3	58.9
每天人口变动和婚姻	**Daily Population Changes and Marriages**				
出 生 (万人)	Births (10 000 persons)	4.8	6.7	5.6	4.4
死 亡 (万人)	Deaths (10 000 persons)	1.6	2.0	2.2	2.3
结 婚 (万对)	Marriages (10 000 couples)	1.6	2.6	2.5	2.3
离 婚 (对)	Divorces (couples)	781	2063	3282	4890

注：本表价值指标除邮电业务总量按不变价格计算外，其余均按当年价格计算。邮电业务总量2000年及以前按1990年不变价格计算，2001年起按2000年不变价格计算。

a) Figures in value terms in this table are at current prices, except that on the business transaction of post and telecommunications service which is at 1990 constant prices before 2000 and at 2000 constant prices since 2000.

2-3 国民经济和社会发展总量与速度指标

指标		Item		1978
人口与就业		**Population and Employment**		
人口	（万人）	**Population**	(10 000 persons)	
年底总人口		Population at the Year-end		96259
城镇人口		Urban		17245
乡村人口		Rural		79014
男性人口		Male		49567
女性人口		Female		46692
就业	（万人）	**Employment**	(10 000 persons)	
就业人员数		Employment		40152
#职工人数		Staff and Workers		9499
城镇登记失业人数		Urban Registration Unemployment		530
宏观经济		**Macro Economy**		
国民经济核算	（亿元）	**National Accounting**	(100 million yuan)	
国民总收入		Gross National Income		3645.2
国内生产总值		Gross Domestic Product		3645.2
第一产业		Primary Industry		1018.4
第二产业		Secondary Industry		1745.2
第三产业		Tertiary Industry		881.6
支出法国内生产总值		Gross Domestic Product by Expenditure Approach		3605.6
最终消费支出		Government Final Consumption Expenditure		2239.1
居民消费		Household Consumption Expenditures		1759.1
政府消费		Government Consumption Expenditure		480.0
资本形成总额		Gross Capital Formation		1377.9
固定资本形成总额		Gross Fixed Capital Formation		1073.9
存货增加		Changes in Inventories		304.0
货物和服务净出口		Net Export of Good and Service		-11.4
固定资产投资	（亿元）	**Investment in Fixed Assets**	(100 million yuan)	
全社会固定资产投资总额		Total Investment in Fixed Assets		
#国有经济		State-Owned Units		
集体经济		Collective-Owned Units		
私营个体经济		Self-employed Units		
全社会施工房屋面积	（亿平方米）	Floor Space of Buildings under Construction	(100 million sq.m)	
全社会竣工房屋建筑面积	（亿平方米）	Floor Space of Buildings Completed	(100 million sq.m)	
财政	（亿元）	**Government Finance**	(100 million yuan)	
国家财政收入		Government Revenue		1132.3
中　央		Central Government		175.8
地　方		Local Governments		956.5
国家财政支出		Government Expenditures		1122.1
中　央		Central Government		532.1
地　方		Local Governments		590.0
物价总指数（上年=100）		**Price Indices (preceding year=100)**		
居民消费价格指数		Consumer Price Index		100.7
商品零售价格指数		Retail Price Index		100.7
农业生产资料价格指数		Price Indices of Means of Agricultural Production		99.9
工业品出厂价格指数		Ex-Factory Price Indices of Industrial Products		100.1
原材料、燃料、动力购进价格指数		Purchasing Price Indices of Raw Material, Fuel and Power		
固定资产投资价格指数		Investment in Fixed Assets Price Indices		
能源生产与消费	（万吨标准煤）	**Production and Consumption of Energy**	(10 000 tons of SCE)	
能源生产总量		Total Energy Production		62770
能源消费总量		Total Energy Consumption		57144

Principal Aggregate Indicators on National Economic and Social Development and Growth Rates

总量指标		Aggregate Data		速度指标（%）				Indices and Growth Rates (%)		
				指数 Index（2005为以下各年）(2005 as Percentage of the Following Years)				平均增长速度 Average Annual Growth Rate		
1989	1997	2004	2005	1978	1989	1997	2004	1979–2005	1990–2005	1998–2005
112704	123626	129988	130756	135.8	116.0	105.8	100.6	1.1	0.9	0.7
29540	39449	54283	56212	326.0	190.3	142.5	103.6	4.5	4.1	4.5
83164	84177	75705	74544	94.3	89.6	88.6	98.5	-0.2	-0.7	-1.5
58099	63131	66976	67375	135.9	116.0	106.7	100.6	1.1	0.9	0.8
54605	60495	63012	63381	135.7	116.1	104.8	100.6	1.1	0.9	0.6
55329	69820	75200	75825	188.8	137.0	108.6	100.8	2.4	2.0	1.0
13742	14668	10576	10850	114.2	79.0	74.0	102.6	0.5	-1.5	-3.7
378	577	827	839	158.3	222.0	145.5	101.5	1.7	5.1	4.8
17000.9	77653.1	159586.7	183956.1	1204.4	443.8	202.8	111.0	9.7	9.8	9.2
16992.3	78973.0	159878.3	183084.8	1198.7	441.8	198.5	110.2	9.6	9.7	8.9
4228.0	14264.6	20955.8	23070.4	336.0	189.2	132.2	105.2	4.6	4.1	3.5
7278.0	37543.0	73904.3	87046.7	1801.6	611.1	214.6	111.7	11.3	12.0	10.0
5486.3	27165.4	65018.2	72967.7	1540.0	434.0	209.5	110.0	10.7	9.6	9.7
17311.3	81658.5	160280.4	186700.9							
11164.2	48140.6	87032.9	96918.1							
8812.6	36921.5	63833.5	70906.0							
2351.6	11219.1	23199.4	26012.1							
6332.7	29968	69168.4	79559.8							
4419.4	25965.0	65117.7	77464.4							
1913.3	4003.0	4050.7	2095.4							
-185.6	3549.9	4079.1	10223.0							
4410.4	24941.1	70477.4	88773.6		2012.8	355.9	126.0		20.8	14.6
2808.1	13091.7	25027.6	29666.9		1056.5	226.6	118.5		17.3	9.5
570.0	3850.9	9965.7	11969.6		2099.9	310.8	120.1		22.0	12.6
1032.3	3429.4	9880.6	13890.6		1345.6	405.0	140.6		15.9	15.8
	23.0	37.6	43.1			187.4	114.6			8.2
	16.6	20.7	22.8			137.1	110.0			4.0
2664.9	8651.1	26396.5	31649.3	2795.1	1187.6	365.8	119.9	13.1	16.7	17.6
822.5	4226.9	14503.1	16548.5	9413.3	2012.0	391.5	114.1	18.3	20.6	18.6
1842.4	4424.2	11893.4	15100.8	1578.8	819.6	341.3	127.0	10.8	14.1	16.6
2823.8	9233.6	28486.9	33930.3	3023.8	1201.6	367.5	119.1	13.5	16.8	17.7
888.8	2532.5	7894.1	8776.0	1649.3	987.4	346.5	111.2	10.9	15.4	16.8
1935.0	6701.1	20592.8	25154.3	4263.4	1300.0	375.4	122.2	14.9	17.4	18.0
118.0	102.8	103.9	101.8							
117.8	100.8	102.8	100.8							
118.9	99.5	110.6	108.3							
118.6	99.7	106.1	104.9							
126.4	101.3	111.4	108.3							
	101.7	105.6	101.6							
101639	132410	187341	206068	328.3	202.7	155.6	110.0	4.5	4.5	5.7
96934	137798	203227	223319	390.8	230.4	162.1	109.9	5.2	5.4	6.2

2–3 续表 1

指 标	Item	1978
产 业	**Industry**	
农业	**Agriculture**	
农林牧渔业从业人员 (万人)	Employed Persons of Farming, Forestry, Animal Husbandry and Fishery (10 000 persons)	28455.6
农林牧渔业总产值 (亿元)	Gross Output Value of Farming Forestry, Animal Husbandry and Fishery (100 million yuan)	1397.0
主要农产品产量 (万吨)	Output of Major Farm Products (10 000 tons)	
粮 食	Grain	30476.5
棉 花	Cotton	216.7
油 料	Oil-bearing Crops	521.8
甘 蔗	Sugar Cane	2111.6
甜 菜	Beet Roots	270.2
茶 叶	Tea	26.8
水 果	Fruits	657.0
肉 类	Meat	
水产品	Aquatic Products	465.4
工业	**Industry**	
主要工业产品产量	Output of Major Industrial Products	
布 (亿米)	Cloth (100 million m)	110
机制纸及纸板 (万吨)	Machine-Made Paper and Paperboards (10 000 tons)	439
成品糖 (万吨)	Refined Sugar (10 000 tons)	227
家用电冰箱 (万台)	Household Refrigerators (10 000 units)	2.80
房间空气调节器 (万台)	Air Conditioners (10 000 units)	0.02
家用洗衣机 (万台)	Household Washing Machines (10 000 units)	0.04
彩色电视机 (万台)	Color Television Sets (10 000 units)	0.38
原 煤 (亿吨)	Coal (100 million tons)	6.18
原 油 (万吨)	Crude Oil (10 000 tons)	10405
天然气 (亿立方米)	Natural Gas (100 million cu.m)	137.3
发电量 (亿千瓦小时)	Electricity (100 million kwh)	2566
粗 钢 (万吨)	Crude Steel (10 000 tons)	3178
钢 材 (万吨)	Rolled Steel (10 000 tons)	2208
水 泥 (万吨)	Cement (10 000 tons)	6524
国有及限额以上非国有工业企业主要指标	Principal Indicators of Industrial Enterprises of State Ownership and Non-state-owned Above Designated Size	
工业增加值 (亿元)	Gross industrial Output Value (100 million yuan)	
资产总计 (亿元)	Original Value of Fixed Assets (100 million yuan)	
固定资产净值年平均余额(亿元)	Annual Average Balance of Net Value of Fixed Assets (100 million yuan)	
利润总额 (亿元)	Profits (100 million yuan)	
建筑业	**Construction**	
建筑业企业从业人员 (万人)	Number of Employed Persons (10 000 persons)	
建筑业总产值 (亿元)	Gross Output Value (100 million yuan)	
交通运输业	**Transportation**	
客运量 (万人)	Passenger Traffic (10 000 persons)	253993
铁 路	Railways	81491
公 路	Highways	149229
水 运	Waterways	23042
民 航	Civil Aviation	231
货运量 (万吨)	Freight Traffic (10 000 tons)	248946
铁 路	Railways	110119
公 路	Highways	85182
水 运	Waterways	43292
民 航	Civil Aviation	6
管 道	Pipelines	10347
沿海主要港口货物吞吐量 (万吨)	Volume of Freight Handled at Major Coastal Ports(10 000 tons)	19834

Continued

总量指标		Aggregate Data		速度指标 (%)				Indices and Growth Rates(%)		
1989	1997	2004	2005	指数 Index (2005为以下各年) (2005 as Percentage of the Following Years)				平均增长速度 Average Annual Growth Rate		
				1978	1989	1997	2004	1979–2005	1990–2005	1998–2005
32440.5	32677.9	30596.0	29975.5	105.3	92.4	91.7	98.0	0.2	-0.5	-1.1
6534.7	23788.4	36239.0	39450.9	505.5	266.9	148.3	105.7	6.2	6.3	5.1
40754.9	49417.1	46946.9	48402.2	158.8	118.8	97.9	103.1	1.7	1.1	-0.3
378.8	460.3	632.4	571.4	263.7	150.8	124.1	90.4	3.7	2.6	2.7
1295.2	2157.4	3065.9	3077.1	589.7	237.6	142.6	100.4	6.8	5.6	4.5
4879.5	7889.7	8984.9	8663.8	410.3	177.6	109.8	96.4	5.4	3.7	1.2
924.3	1496.8	585.7	788.1	291.7	85.3	52.7	134.6	4.0	-1.0	-7.7
53.5	61.3	83.5	93.5	348.9	174.8	152.4	112.0	4.7	3.6	5.4
1831.9	5089.3	15340.9	16120.1	2453.7	880.0	316.7	105.1	12.6	14.6	15.5
	5268.8	7244.8	7743.1			147.0	106.9			4.9
1151.7	3601.8	4901.8	5107.6	1097.6	443.5	141.8	104.2	9.3	9.8	4.5
189	249	482	484	439.2	256.0	194.7	100.5	5.6	6.1	8.7
1333	2733	5413	6205	1413.5	465.5	227.0	114.6	10.3	10.1	10.8
501	703	1034	912	401.9	182.1	129.9	88.3	5.3	3.8	3.3
671	1044	3008	2987	106680.7	445.3	286.0	99.3	29.5	9.8	14.0
37	974	6390	6765	33822850.0	18053.3	694.5	105.9	60.2	38.4	27.4
825	1254	2533	3036	7588800.0	367.8	242.0	119.8	51.6	8.5	11.7
940	2711	7432	8283	2179794.7	881.2	305.5	111.5	44.8	14.6	15.0
10.54	13.73	19.92	22.05	356.8	209.2	160.6	110.7	4.8	4.7	6.1
13764	16074	17587	18135	174.3	131.8	112.8	103.1	2.1	1.7	1.5
150.5	227.0	414.6	509.4	371.0	338.5	224.4	122.9	5.0	7.9	10.6
5848	11356	22033	25003	974.4	427.5	220.2	113.5	8.8	9.5	10.4
6159	10894	28291	35324	1111.5	573.5	324.2	124.9	9.3	11.5	15.8
4859	9979	31976	37771	1710.6	777.3	378.5	118.1	11.1	13.7	18.1
21029	51174	96682	106885	1638.3	508.3	208.9	110.6	10.9	10.7	9.6
		54805	72187							
		215358	244784				113.7			
		79749	89460				112.2			
		11929	14803				124.1			
1005	2102	2500	2700		268.7	128.5	108.0		6.4	3.2
1283	9126	29021	34552		2693.1	378.6	119.1		22.9	18.1
791376	1326094	1767453	1847018	727.2	233.4	139.3	104.5	7.6	5.4	4.2
113807	93308	111764	115583	141.8	101.6	123.9	103.4	1.3	0.1	2.7
644508	1204583	1624526	1697381	1137.4	263.4	140.9	104.5	9.4	6.2	4.4
31778	22573	19040	20227	87.8	63.7	89.6	106.2	-0.5	-2.8	-1.4
1283	5630	12123	13827	5985.7	1077.7	245.6	114.1	16.4	16.0	11.9
988435	1278218	1706412	1862066	748.0	188.4	145.7	109.1	7.7	4.0	4.8
151489	172149	249017	269296	244.5	177.8	156.4	108.1	3.4	3.7	5.8
733781	976536	1244990	1341778	1575.2	182.9	137.4	107.8	10.8	3.8	4.1
87493	113406	187394	219648	507.4	251.0	193.7	117.2	6.2	5.9	8.6
31	125	277	307	4792.2	989.4	246.0	110.8	15.4	15.4	11.9
15641	16002	24734	31037	300.0	198.4	194.0	125.5	4.2	4.4	8.6
49025	90822	246074	292777	1476.1	597.2	322.4	119.0	10.5	11.8	15.8

2-3 续表 2

指 标		Item		1978
邮电通信业		**Post and Telecommunication Services**		
邮电业务总量	(亿元)	Total Business Revenue	(100 million yuan)	34.1
函 件	(亿件)	Number of Letters Delivered	(10 000 pieces)	28.4
报刊期发数	(万份)	Number of Newspapers and Magazines Distributed	(10 000 copies)	11250
局用电话交换机容量	(万门)	Capacity of Office Telephone Exchanges	(10 000 lines)	406
本地电话年末用户	(万户)	Number of Local Telephone Subscribers at Year-end	(10 000 subscriber)	193
城市		Urban Telephone Subscribers		119
农村		Rural Telephone Subscribers		73
公用电话	(万户)	Public Telephone	(10 000 Subscribers)	1.2
移动电话用户	(万户)	Number of Mobile Telephone Subscribers	(10 000 subscribers)	
国内商业		**Domestic Trade**		
社会消费品零售总额	(亿元)	Total Retail Sales of Consumer Goods	(100 million yuan)	1559
对外贸易		**Foreign Trade**		
货物进出口总额	(亿美元)	Total Value of Exports and Imports	(USD 100 million)	206.4
出口额		Exports		97.5
进口额		Imports		108.9
实际利用外资额		**Utilization of Foreign Capital**		
外商直接投资	(亿美元)	Foreign Direct Investments	(USD 100 million)	
外商其他投资	(亿美元)	Other Foreign Investments	(USD 100 million)	
国际旅游		**International Tourism**		
入境旅游过夜者人数	(万人次)	Number of Tourists (Overnight Visitors)	(10 000 person-times)	72
国际旅游外汇收入	(亿美元)	Foreign Exchange Earnings from Tourism	(USD 100 million)	2.6
金融业		**Financial Intermediation**		
金融机构人民币各项存款余额	(亿元)	Deposits of National Banking System	(100 million yuan)	1135
金融机构人民币各项贷款余额	(亿元)	Loans of National Banking System	(100 million yuan)	1850
股票筹资额	(亿元)	Raised Capital	(100 million yuan)	
保险公司保费金额	(亿元)	Insurance Premium of Insurance Companies	(100 million yuan)	
保险公司赔款及给付金额	(亿元)	Indemnity Expenditure and Payment of Insurance Companies	(100 million yuan)	
教育、科技、文化		**Education, Science and Technology and Culture**		
教育		**Education**		
专任教师数	(万人)	Full-time Teachers	(10 000 persons)	
#普通高等学校		Institutions of Higher Education		20.6
普通中学		Secondary Schools		318.2
普通小学		Primary Schools		522.6
在校学生数	(万人)	Students Enrollment	(10 000 persons)	
#普通高等学校		Institutions of Higher Education		85.6
普通中学		Secondary Schools		6548.3
普通小学		Primary Schools		14624.0
教育经费支出	(亿元)	Government Expenditures on Education	(100 million yuan)	
科技		**Science and Technology**		
科学家、工程师数	(万人)	Number of Scientists and Engineers	(10 000 persons)	
研究与试验发展经费支出	(亿元)	Expenditures on Research and Development	(100 million yuan)	
技术市场成交额	(亿元)	Volume of Transaction in Technical Markets	(100 million yuan)	
文化		**Culture**		
图书出版数量	(亿册)	Number of Books Published	(100 million copies)	37.7
故事影片产量	(部)	Production of Feature Films	(film)	46
电视节目制作时间	(万小时)	Time for TV Programs Production	(10 000 hours)	

Continued

总量指标 Aggregate Data				速度指标(%) Indices and Growth Rates(%)						
				指数 Index（2005为以下各年）(2005 as Percentage of the Following Years)				平均增长速度 Average Annual Growth Rate		
1989	1997	2004	2005	1978	1989	1997	2004	1979–2005	1990–2005	1998–2005
123.5	1773.3	9712.3	12028.5	47362.6	13077.8	910.5	123.8	25.6	35.6	31.8
57.3	68.6	82.8	73.5	258.8	128.3	107.2	88.8	3.6	1.6	0.9
17704	21875	14789	14601	129.8	82.5	66.7	98.7	1.0	-1.2	-4.9
1035	11269	42347	47196	11627.5	4561.4	418.8	111.5	19.3	27.0	19.6
568	7031	31176	35045	18204.9	6169.4	498.4	112.4	21.3	29.4	22.2
440	5244	21025	23975	20113.5	5453.6	457.2	114.0	21.7	28.4	20.9
128	1787	10151	11069	15080.7	8619.5	619.6	109.0	20.4	32.1	25.6
4.0	193.9	2215.0	2681.2	223433.3	67198.0	1382.8	121.0	33.1	50.2	38.9
1.0	1323.3	33482.4	39340.6		4014346.9	2972.9	117.5		94.0	52.8
8101	31253	59501	67177	4310.1	829.2	214.9	112.9	15.0	14.1	10.0
1116.8	3251.6	11545.5	14219.1	6889.1	1273.2	437.3	123.2	17.0	17.2	20.3
525.4	1827.9	5933.2	7619.5	7814.9	1450.2	416.8	128.4	17.5	18.2	19.5
591.4	1423.7	5612.3	6599.5	6060.1	1115.9	463.5	117.6	16.4	16.3	21.1
33.9	452.6	606.3	603.3		1778.4	133.3	99.5		19.7	3.7
3.8	71.3	34.4	34.8		913.4	48.8	101.2		14.8	-8.6
936	2377	4176	4681	6537.6	500.0	196.9	112.1	16.7	10.6	8.8
18.6	120.7	257.4	293.0	11139.2	1575.1	242.6	113.8	19.1	18.8	11.7
10786	82390	241424	287170	25312.4	2662.4	348.5	118.9	22.7	22.8	16.9
14360	74914	178198	194690	10523.8	1355.8	259.9	109.3	18.8	17.7	12.7
	1294	1511	1883			145.5	124.6			4.8
139	773	4318	4932		3554.3	638.3	114.2		25.0	26.1
55	247	1004	1137		2081.7	460.0	113.2		20.9	21.0
39.7	40.5	85.8	96.6	468.9	243.3	238.5	112.6	5.9	5.7	11.5
298.0	358.7	466.8	477.1	149.9	160.1	133.0	102.2	1.5	3.0	3.6
554.4	579.4	562.9	559.2	107.0	100.9	96.5	99.3	0.3	0.1	-0.4
208.2	317.4	1333.5	1561.8	1824.5	750.1	492.1	117.1	11.4	13.4	22.0
4554.0	6017.9	8695.4	8580.9	131.0	188.4	142.6	98.7	1.0	4.0	4.5
12373.1	13995.4	11246.2	10864.1	74.3	87.8	77.6	96.6	-1.1	-0.8	-3.1
	2531.7	7242.6								
	166.8	225.2	256.1			153.5	113.7			5.5
	509.2	1966.3	2450.0			481.1	124.6			21.7
82.0	351.4	1334.4	1551.4		1891.9	441.5	116.3		20.2	20.4
58.6	73.1	64.1	64.0	169.8	109.2	87.6	99.8	2.0	0.6	-1.6
136	88	212	260	565.2	191.2	295.5	122.6	6.6	4.1	14.5
	61.6	211.7	255.4			414.3	120.6			19.4

2-3 续表 3

指 标		Item		1978
家庭、生活、环境		**Family, People's Livelihood and Environment**		
家庭		**Family**		
家庭总户数	(万户)	Total Number of Households	(10 000 households)	20641
城镇居民平均每户家庭人口	(人)	Average Household Size in Urban Areas	(person)	
农村居民平均每户常住人口	(人)	Average Household Size in Rural Areas	(person)	
婚姻		**Marriages and Divorces**		
结婚登记总数	(万对)	Register Number of Marriages	(10 000 couples)	597.8
离婚数	(万对)	Number of Divorces	(10 000 couples)	28.5
居住		**Housing**		
城市人均住宅建筑面积	(平方米)	Per Capita Gross Living Space in Cities	(sq.m)	6.7
农村居民人均住房面积	(平方米)	Per Capita Net Floor Space of Rural Residents	(sq.m)	8.1
生活		**People's Livelihood**		
城镇居民人均可支配收入	(元)	Per Capita Annual Disposable Income of Urban Households	(yuan)	343
农村居民人均纯收入	(元)	Per Capita Net Income of Rural Residents	(yuan)	134
城乡人民币储蓄存款余额	(亿元)	Outstanding Amount of Saving Deposits in Urban and Rural Areas	(100 million yuan)	211
工资		**Wages and Welfare**		
工资总额	(亿元)	Total Wages	(100 million yuan)	569
职工平均工资	(元)	Average Wage of Staff and Workers	(yuan)	615
离休和退休费	(亿元)	Pensions for Retired Staff and Workers	(100 million yuan)	17
卫生		**Health Care**		
医院、卫生院	(个)	Number of Hospitals		64311
医生	(万人)	Number of Doctors	(10 000 persons)	103.3
医院、卫生院床位数	(万张)	Number of Hospital Beds	(10 000 units)	184.7
城市市政建设		**City Construction**		
全年供水总量	(亿吨)	Annual Supply of Tap Water	(100 million tons)	78.8
城市煤气和天然气供气量	(亿立方米)	Volume of Coal Gas and Natural Gas Supply in Cities	(10 000 cu.m)	19.5
排水管道长度	(万公里)	Length of Sewer Pipelines	(10 000 km)	2.0
实有道路长度	(万公里)	Length of Paved Roads	(10 000 km)	2.7
公共交通运营数	(辆)	Number of Public Vehicles under Operation	(unit)	25839
园林绿地面积	(万公顷)	Areas of Green Land	(10 000 hectare)	8
环境、灾害		**Environment and Disaster**		
环境污染治理投资总额	(亿元)	Actual Investment in Implementation of the Project for Pollution Treatment in the Year	(100 million yuan)	
环境污染与破坏事故次数	(起)	Number of Pollution Accidents	(times)	
环境污染直接经济损失	(万元)	Losses Converted into Cash	(10 000 yuan)	
环境污染事故赔罚款金额	(万元)	Amount of Reparations and Fines	(10 000 yuan)	
火灾发生数	(起)	Number of Fire Disasters	(unit)	
火灾损失	(万元)	Fire Loss	(10 000 yuan)	
交通事故发生数	(起)	Number of Traffic Accidents	(unit)	
交通事故损失	(万元)	Loss of Traffic Accidents	(10 000 yuan)	

注：1.本表价值指标除邮电业务总量按不变价格计算外，其余均按当年价格计算。邮电业务总量2000年及以前按1990年不变价格计算，以后按2000年不变价格计算。

2.本表速度指标中，国民总收入、国内生产总值及三次产业增加值、物价指数、农林牧渔业总产值、邮电业务总量、城乡居民收入和平均工资指标均按可比价格计算。固定资产投资平均增长速度按累计法计算。

3.职工人数1997年及以前为全部职工人数，以后为在岗职工人数，两者不可比。

4.2000年及以后保险业务包括外资公司。

5.本表国民核算指标，社会消费品零售总额1997、2004年数据，能源生产总量、能源消费总量和原煤产量2004年数据为经济普查后的调整数。

continued

总量指标		Aggregate Data		速度指标(%)				Indices and Growth Rates(%)		
				指数 Index（2005为以下各年）(2005 as Percentage of the Following Years)				平均增长速度 Average Annual Growth Rate		
1989	1997	2004	2005	1978	1989	1997	2004	1979–2005	1990–2005	1998–2005
27078	32890	36628	39558	191.6	146.1	120.3	108.0	2.4	2.4	2.3
3.55	3.19	2.98	2.96		83.4	92.8	99.3		-1.1	-0.9
4.86	4.35	4.08	4.08		84.0	93.8	100.0		-1.1	-0.8
937.2	914.1	867.1	823.1	137.7	87.8	90.0	94.9	1.2	-0.8	-1.3
75.3	119.8	166.5	178.5	626.3	237.1	149.0	107.2	7.0	5.5	5.1
13.5	17.8	25.0	26.1	389.7	193.4	146.7	104.4	5.2	4.2	4.9
17.2	22.5	27.9	29.7	366.7	172.7	132.0	106.5	4.9	3.5	3.5
1374	5160	9422	10493	607.4	332.8	194.7	109.6	6.9	7.8	8.7
602	2090	2936	3255	624.5	204.3	142.8	106.2	7.0	4.6	4.6
5196	46280	119555	141051	66975.8	2714.4	304.8	118.0	27.3	22.9	14.9
2619	9405	16900	19790	3478.6	755.8	210.4	117.1	14.0	13.5	9.7
1935	6470	16024	18364	546.9	381.1	250.5	112.8	6.5	8.7	12.2
319	1791	4511	5253	30365.3	1644.7	293.3	116.5	23.6	19.1	14.4
61613	67479	60864	60397	93.9	98.0	89.5	99.2	-0.2	-0.1	-1.4
171.8	198.5	190.6	193.8	187.6	112.8	97.6	101.7	2.4	0.8	-0.3
253.8	286.9	304.7	313.5	169.7	123.5	109.3	102.9	2.0	1.3	1.1
393.7	476.8	490.3	502.1	637.2	127.5	105.3	102.4	7.1	1.5	0.6
143.2	193.2	383.0	466.3	2391.3	325.6	241.4	121.7	12.5	7.7	11.6
5.5	12.0	21.9	24.1	1232.4	442.1	201.3	110.0	9.7	9.7	9.1
9.6	13.9	22.3	24.7	916.0	257.1	178.2	110.8	8.5	6.1	7.5
59671	169121	281516	313296	1212.5	525.0	185.2	111.3	9.7	10.9	8.0
38	68	132	147	1796.0	385.2	215.2	111.2	11.3	8.8	10.1
	502.4	1909.8	2388.0			475.3	125.0			21.5
3332	1992	1441	1406		42.2	70.6	97.6		-5.2	-4.3
	8366	36366	10515			125.7	28.9			2.9
	3050	3964	3082			101.0	77.8			0.1
	140280	252704	235941			168.2	93.4			6.7
	154141	167197	136288			88.4	81.5			-1.5
	304217	517889	450254			148.0	86.9			5.0
	184616	239141	188401			102.1	78.8			0.3

a) Figures in value terms in this table are at current prices, except that on the business transaction of post and telecommunications service which is at 1990 constant prices before 2000 and at 2000 constant prices since 2000.

b) The indices and growth rates of the follow indicators are calculated at constant prices: gross national income, gross domestic product, value-added of the tertiary industry, price indices, gross output value of farming, forestry, animal husbandry and fishery, business volume of post and telecommunications, per capita income of urban and rural residents, average wages and welfare. The average annual growth rate of total investment in fixed assets are calculated at the accumulate method.

c) Figures before 1998 on workers and staff refer to all workers and staff, while figures since 1998 refer to fully employed workers and staff. So, the data are not comparable.

d) Insurance business includes foreign insurance company since 2000.

e) Data of indicators of national accounts, data of total retail sales of consumer goods in 1997 and 2004, and data of total energy production, total energy consumption and production of coal in 2004 were modified based on the First National Economic Census results.

2-4 国民经济和社会发展结构指标

Structural Indicators on National Economic and Social Development

单位：% (%)

指标	Item	1978	1989	1997	2005
人口与就业	**Population and Employment**				
人口	**Population**				
城乡结构	Urban and Rural Structure				
城镇	Urban	17.9	26.2	31.9	43.0
乡村	Rural	82.1	73.8	68.1	57.0
性别结构	Sexual Structure				
男	Male	51.5	51.6	51.1	51.5
女	Female	48.5	48.4	48.9	48.5
就业	**Employment**				
产业结构	Industrial Structure				
第一产业	Primary Industry	70.5	60.1	49.9	44.8
第二产业	Secondary Industry	17.3	21.6	23.7	23.8
第三产业	Tertiary Industry	12.2	18.3	26.4	31.4
宏观经济	**Macro Economy**				
国民经济核算	**National Accounting**				
国内生产总值产业结构	Industrial Structure				
第一产业	Primary Industry	27.9	24.9	18.1	12.6
第二产业	Secondary Industry	47.9	42.9	47.5	47.5
第三产业	Tertiary Industry	24.2	32.2	34.4	39.9
固定资产投资	**Investment in Fixed Assets**				
全社会固定资产投资结构	Structure of Total Investment in Fixed Assets				
城镇	Urban			77.0	84.6
农村	Rural			23.0	15.4
资金来源结构	Structure of Funded Sources				
国家预算内资金	State Budget		8.3	2.8	4.4
国内贷款	Domestic Loans		17.3	18.9	17.3
利用外资	Foreign Investment		6.6	10.6	4.2
自筹和其他投资	Self-raising Funds and Others Investment		67.8	67.7	74.1
财政	**Government Finance**				
财政收入结构	Structure of Government Revenue				
中央	Central Government	15.5	30.9	48.9	52.3
地方	Local Governments	84.5	69.1	51.1	47.7
财政支出结构	Structure of Government Expenditures				
中央	Central Government	47.4	31.5	27.4	25.9
地方	Local Governments	52.6	68.5	72.6	74.1
利用外资	**Utilization of Foreign Capital**				
实际利用外资结构	Structure of Foreign Capital Actually Utilized				
对外借款	Loans from Abroad		62.5	18.7	
外商直接投资	Foreign Direct Investment		33.7	70.3	94.5
外商其他投资	Other Foreign Investment		3.8	11.1	5.5
能源	**Energy**				
能源生产总量结构	Structure of Total Energy Production				
原煤	Coal	70.3	74.1	74.1	76.4
原油	Crude Oil	23.7	19.3	17.3	12.6
天然气	Natural Gas	2.9	2.0	2.1	3.3
水电、核电、风电	Hydro-power, Nuclear Power, Wind Power	3.1	4.6	6.5	7.7
能源消费总量结构	Structure of Total Energy Consumption				
煤炭	Coal	70.7	76.1	71.7	68.9
石油	Petroleum	22.7	17.1	20.4	21.0
天然气	Natural Gas	3.2	2.1	1.7	2.9
水电、核电、风电	Hydro-power, Nuclear Power, Wind Power	3.4	4.7	6.2	7.2

2-4 续表 1 continued

单位：% (%)

指 标	Item	1978	1989	1997	2005
产 业	**Industry**				
农业	**Agriculture**				
农林牧渔业产值结构	Structure of Gross Output Value of Agriculture				
#农业	Farming	80.0	62.8	58.2	49.7
林业	Forestry	3.4	4.4	3.4	3.6
牧业	Animal Husbandry	15.0	27.6	28.8	33.7
渔业	Fishery	1.6	5.3	9.6	10.2
工业	**Industry**				
工业企业资产结构	Structure of Capital of Industrial Enterprises				
大型企业	Large Enterprises			54.6	38.8
中型企业	Medium-sized Enterprises			15.3	34.2
小型企业	Small Enterprises			30.1	27.0
建筑业	**Construction**				
建筑业总产值结构	Structure of Gross Output Value of Construction Industry				
国有企业	State-owned Enterprise		68.5	49.6	24.4
集体企业	Collective-owned Enterprises		31.5	43.0	8.1
港澳台商投资企业	Enterprises with Funds from Hong Kong, Macao & Taiwan			0.7	0.5
外商投资企业	Foreign Funded Enterprises			0.8	0.7
其他	Other Enterprises			5.9	66.2
交通运输业	**Transportation**				
货运量结构	Structure of Freight Traffic				
铁 路	Railways	44.2	15.3	13.5	14.5
公 路	Highways	34.2	74.2	76.4	72.1
水 运	Waterways	17.4	8.9	8.9	11.8
民 航	Civil Aviation				
管道输油(气)	Pipelines	4.2	1.6	1.3	1.7
国内商业	**Domestic Trade**				
社会消费品零售总额构成	Composition of Retail Sales of Consumer Goods				
市	Cities	32.4	45.3	59.2	67.1
县	Counties	24.4	16.4	12.8	11.2
县以下	Below Counties	43.2	38.3	28.0	21.7
货物进出口	**Imports and Exports of Goods**				
出口货物结构	Structure of Exports				
初级产品	Primary Goods	53.5	28.7	13.1	6.4
工业制成品	Manufactured Goods	46.5	71.3	86.9	93.6
进口货物结构	Structure of Imports				
初级产品	Primary Goods		19.9	20.1	22.4
工业制成品	Manufactured Goods		80.1	79.9	77.6
国际旅游	**International Tourism**				
来华旅游人数结构	Structure of Tourists Visiting China				
外国人	Foreigners	12.7	6.0	12.9	16.9
港澳同胞	Hong Kong and Macao Compatriots	}86.3	}93.8	83.3	79.7
台湾同胞	Taiwan Compatriots			3.7	3.4
金融业	**Financial Intermediation**				
金融机构资金来源结构	Structure of Sources of Funds in Financial Institutions				
各项存款	Deposits			86.7	95.1
金融债券	Bonds				1.9
对国际金融机构负债	Liability to International Financial Institutions			0.2	0.2
流通中现金	Currency in Circulation			10.7	8.0
其他	Others			2.3	-5.1
金融机构资金运用结构	Structure of Fund Uses in Financial Institutions				
各项贷款	Loans			78.9	64.5
有价证券及投资	Securities and Investment			3.9	11.6
在国际金融机构资产	Capital in International Finance Institutions			0.6	0.3
金银占款	Position for Billion and Silver Purchase			14.2	0.1
外汇占款	Position for Foreign Exchange			1.7	23.6
财政借款	Financial Debts				
教育、科技、文化	**Education, Science and Culture**				
教育	**Education**				
普通学校在校学生结构	Structure of Student Enrollment in Regular Schools				
大学生	College and University Students	0.4	1.2	1.5	7.4
中学生	Secondary School Students	31.1	28.7	32.8	40.9
小学生	Primary School Students	68.5	70.1	65.7	51.7

注：工业企业资产结构1997年为1998年数据。
a) Structure of capital of industry in 1997 are the data in 1998.

2-4 续表 2 continued

单位：% (%)

指 标	Item	1978	1989	1997	2005
普通学校专任教师结构	Structure of Full-time Teachers in Regular Schools				
大学	Colleges and Universities	2.4	4.2	3.9	8.5
中学	Secondary Schools	37.6	36.6	40.3	42.1
小学	Primary Schools	60.0	59.2	55.8	49.4
科技	**Science and Technology**				
科技经费筹集额结构	Structure of Funds for Scientific and Technological Activities				
#政府资金	Government Funds			26.2	23.1
企业资金	Enterprises Funds			44.6	65.5
金融机构贷款	Loans from Banks			13.1	5.3
科技经费内部支出结构	Structure of Internal Expenditures on Scientific and Technological Activities				
#劳务费	Service Fees			19.9	21.4
固定资产购建	Purchases of Fixed Assets			27.5	29.5
#研究与发展经费支出	Research and Development Expenses			45.2	50.7
生活、环境	**People's Livelihood and Environment**				
生活	**People's Livelihood**				
城镇居民消费结构	Consumption Structure of Urban Residents				
食品类	Food	57.5	54.5	46.6	36.7
衣着类	Clothing	13.6	12.3	12.5	10.1
居住	Residence			9.4	10.2
用品及其他	Articles for Daily Use and Others	}28.9	}33.2	31.5	43.0
农村居民消费结构	Consumption Structure of Rural Residents				
食品类	Food	67.7	54.8	55.1	45.5
衣着类	Clothing	12.7	8.3	6.8	5.8
居住	Residence	10.3	19.7	14.4	14.5
用品及其他	Articles for Daily Use and Others	9.3	17.2	23.7	34.2
福利	**Social Welfare**				
离休退休人员结构	Structure of Retired and Resigned Persons				
离休人员	Retired Veterans		7.9	5.5	2.5
退休人员	Retired Persons		92.1	94.5	97.5
离休退休人员保险福利费结构	Structure of Insurance Contribution and Welfare Funds of Retired and Resigned Persons				
离休金	Pensions for Retired Veterans			8.0	5.4
退休金	Pensions for Retired Persons			70.8	84.7
医疗卫生费	Expenses for Medical Care			13.6	5.7
其他	Others			7.6	4.1
卫生	**Health Care**				
卫生技术人员结构	Doctors by Types				
#医生	Doctors	41.9	45.1	45.1	43.5
护师、护士	Nurses	16.5	24.2	27.2	30.3
卫生机构床位结构	Beds in Health Agencies				
市医院	Hospitals at City Level	38.6	52.0	63.5	69.5
县医院	Hospitals at County Level	61.4	48.0	36.5	30.5
环境、灾害	**Environment and Disasters**				
工业污染治理投资结构	Structure of Investment in the Treatment of Industrial Pollution				
治理废水	Waste Water Treatment			62.5	29.2
治理废气	Waste Gas Treatment			24.7	46.5
治理固体废物	Solid Wastes Treatment			5.4	6.0
治理噪声	Noise Abatement			0.7	0.7
其他	Others			6.7	17.6
火灾事故损失额结构	Structure of Fire Losses Converted into Cash				
特大	Extraordinarily Serious Fires			23.7	5.7
重大	Serious Fires			14.5	8.0
一般	Ordinary Fires			61.8	86.3

注：卫生机构床位结构数1997年及以前为医院、卫生院床位结构数。

a) Before 1997, beds in health agencies referred to those in hospitals and clinics.

2-5 国民经济和社会发展比例和效益指标

Indicators on National Economic and Social Development

指 标	Item	1978	1989	1997	2005
人口与就业	**Population and Employment**				
人口	**Population**				
出生率 (‰)	Birth Rate (‰)	18.25	21.58	16.57	12.40
死亡率 (‰)	Death Rate (‰)	6.25	6.54	6.51	6.51
自然增长率 (‰)	Natural Growth Rate (‰)	12.00	15.04	10.06	5.89
就业	**Employment**				
就业者负担人口	Dependency Ratio	1.40	1.04	0.77	0.72
城镇登记失业率 (%)	Registered Unemployment Rate in Urban Areas (%)	5.3	2.6	3.1	4.2
宏观经济	**Macro Economy**				
国民经济核算	**National Accounting**				
全社会劳动生产率 (元/人)	Overall Labor Productivity (yuan/person)	917	3099	11382	24246
第一产业	Primary Industry	353	1292	4095	6664
第二产业	Secondary Industry	2732	6033	22927	49735
第三产业	Tertiary Industry	1938	5469	14943	31195
人均国内生产总值 (元)	Per Capita GDP (yuan)	381	1519	6420	14040
固定资产投资	**Investment in Fixed Assets**				
全社会固定资产投资相当于国内生产总值比例 (%)	Proportion of Investment in Fixed Assets to GDP (%)		26.0	31.6	48.5
全社会房屋建筑面积竣工率 (%)	Rate of Total Floor Space of Buildings Completed in Construction (%)		77.9	72.0	52.8
财政	**Government Finance**				
国家财政收入相当于国内生产总值比例(%)	Proportion of Government Revenue to GDP (%)	31.1	15.7	11.0	17.3
国家财政支出相当于国内生产总值比例(%)	Proportion of Government Expenditures to GDP (%)	30.8	16.6	11.7	18.5
预算外资金收入相当于国家财政收入比例 (%)	Proportion of Extra-budgetary Receipt to Government Revenue (%)	30.7	99.8	32.7	17.8
外债	**Foreign Debts**				
偿债率 (%)	Debt Service Ratio (%)		8.3	7.3	3.1
负债率 (%)	Liability Ratio (%)		9.2	14.5	12.6
债务率 (%)	Foreign Debt Ratio (%)		86.4	63.2	33.6
利用外资	**Utilization of Foreign Capital**				
实际利用外商直接投资额相当于合同利用外商直接投资额比例 (%)	Proportion of Actually Utilized Foreign Direct Investment to Contracted Foreign Direct Investment (%)		60.6	88.7	31.9
能源	**Energy**				
能源生产弹性系数	Elastic Coefficient of Energy Production		1.49		0.98
能源消费弹性系数	Elastic Coefficient of Energy Consumption		1.02		0.97
每万元国内生产总值消耗的能源 (吨标准煤)	Energy Consumption per 10 000 yuan GDP (ton of SCE)	15.7	5.7	1.7	1.2

2-5 续表 1 continued

指　　标	Item	1978	1989	1997	2005
产　业	**Industry**				
农业	**Agriculture**				
每一农林牧渔业从业人员生产量（公斤）	Output of Farm Corps Per Agricultural Laborer (kg)				
粮食	Grain		1276	1528	1598
棉花	Cotton		11.9	14.2	18.9
油料	Oil-bearing Crops		40.5	66.7	101.6
猪牛羊肉	Pork, Beef and Mutton			131.4	203.3
水产品	Aquatic Products		36.0	111.3	168.6
每公顷播种面积农产品产量（公斤）	Output of Farm Crops per Hectare of Sown Area (kg)				
粮食	Grain	2527	3632	4377	4642
棉花	Cotton	445	728	1025	1129
油料	Oil-bearing Crops	839	1233	1743	2149
工业	**Industry**				
总资产贡献率 (%)	Ratio of Total Assets to Industrial Output Value (%)			7.12	11.82
资产负债率 (%)	Assets-Liability Ratio (%)			63.74	57.81
成本费用利润率 (%)	Ratio of Profits to Industrial Cost (%)			2.35	6.42
流动资产周转次数 (次/年)	Number of Times of Annual of Turnover Circulating Funds (times/year)			1.41	2.35
建筑业	**Construction**				
技术装备率 (元／人)	Value of Machinery per Laborer (yuan/person)		2341	4729	9273
产值利税率 (%)	Ratio of Pre-tax Profits to Gross Output Value (%)		5.8	4.2	6.0
全员劳动生产率 (元／人)（按增加值计算）	Overall Labor Productivity (yuan/person) (in terms of value-added per employee)			12089	23427
交通运输业	**Transportation**				
客运量弹性系数	Elastic Coefficient of Passenger Traffic	1.10		0.70	0.44
货运量弹性系数	Elastic Coefficient of Freight Traffic	0.96	0.15		0.89
铁路网密度 (公里／万平方公里)	Railway Density (km/10000 sq.km)	54	59	69	79
公路网密度 (公里／万平方公里)	Highway Density (km/10000 sq.km)	927	1057	1278	2011
铁路货运密度 (万吨公里/公里)	Railway Freight Traffic Density (10 000 tons.km/km)	1034	1827	2011	2747
公路货运密度 (万吨公里/公里)	Highway Freight Traffic Density (10 000 tons.km/km)	3.08	33.27	42.98	45.03
平均每一沿海港口泊位货物吞吐量 (万吨)	Cargo Handled at Seaports per Berth (10 000 tons)		55	68	94
邮电通信业	**Post and Telecommunication Services**				
邮电业务总量弹性系数	Elastic Coefficient of Postal and Telecommunication Services	0.39	4.88	3.46	2.34
电话普及率(含移动电话) (部/百人)	Access to Telephones (include mobile phone) (set/100 persons)			8.1	57.2
移动电话普及率 (部/百人)	Access to Mobile Phones (set/100 persons)			1.1	30.3
国内商业	**Domestic Trade**				
人均社会消费品零售额 (元)	Per Capita Retail Sales of Consumer Goods (yuan)	163	724	2541	5153
对外贸易	**Foreign Trade**				
进出口总额相当于国内生产总值比例(%)	Proportion of Total Value of Imports & Exports to GDP (%)	9.7	24.5	34.1	63.9
国际旅游	**International Tourism**				
每一来华游客花费 (美元)	Expenditure per International Tourist in China (USD)		76	210	244
金融业	**Financial Intermediation**				
金融机构存款相当于国内生产总值比例 (%)	Bank Deposits as Percentage of GDP (%)	31.1	63.5	104.3	156.9
金融机构贷款相当于国内生产总值比例 (%)	Bank Loans as Percentage of GDP (%)	50.8	84.5	94.9	106.3
金融机构现金支出相当于收入比例 (%)	Proportion of Cash Outlay to Cash Receipt in Bank (%)	101.2	101.4	101.0	100.4

2-5 续表 2 continued

指 标	Item	1978	1989	1997	2005
教育、科技、文化	**Education, Science and Technology and Culture**				
教育	**Education**				
学龄儿童净入学率 (%)	Rate of School-age Children Enrollment (%)	95.5	97.4	98.9	99.2
小学升初中 (%)	Rate of Graduates of Primary Schools Entering Junior Secondary Schools (%)	87.7	71.5	93.7	98.4
初中升高中 (%)	Rate of Graduates of Junior Secondary Schools Entering Senior Secondary Schools (%)			51.5	69.7
高中升高等教育 (%)	Rate of Graduates of Senior Secondary Schools Entering Institutions of Higher Education (%)	40.9	38.3	48.6	76.3
普通学校生师比 (%)	Student-Teacher Ratio by Level of Regular Schools (%)				
普通高等学校	Regular Institutions of Higher Education			10.87	16.85
普通高中	Regular Senior Secondary Schools			14.05	18.54
初中	Junior Secondary Schools			17.33	17.80
小学	Primary Schools			24.16	19.43
科技	**Science and Technology**				
研究与试验发展经费支出相当于国内生产总值比例 (%)	R&D Expenditures as Percentage of GDP (%)			0.64	1.34
文化	**Culture**				
每百万人有艺术表演团体 (个)	Number of Troupes per Million Persons (unit)	3.27	2.53	2.15	2.15
每百万人有公共图书馆 (个)	Number of Public Libraries per Million Persons (unit)	1.27	2.23	2.13	2.11
每百万人有博物馆 (个)	Number of Museums per Million Persons (unit)	0.36	0.86	1.04	1.21
家庭、生活、环境	**Family, People's Livelihood and Environment**				
家庭	**Family**				
少儿抚养比 (%)	Dependency Ratio of Children (%)	54.63	41.53	39.58	28.19
老年抚养比 (%)	Dependency Ratio of the Aged (%)	7.97	8.40	9.23	10.69
婚姻	**Marriages and Divorces**				
粗离婚率 (‰)	Divorce Rate (‰)		0.68	0.97	1.37
生活	**People's Livelihood**				
城镇与农村居民收入增长率比例(以农村居民收入指数为1) (1978=100)	Proportion of Growth Rate of Annual Income of Urban Residents to Rural Residents (the Growth Rate of Net Income of Rural Residents =100) (1978=100)		0.40	0.63	0.97
福利	**Welfare**				
离退休费相当于工资总额比例 (%)	Pensions for Retired and Resigned Persons as Percentage of Total Wages (%)		12.2	19.0	26.5
离退休人员相当于在职人员比例 (%)	Proportion of the Number of Workers Who Have Retired or Resigned to the Number of Employed Ones (%)		16.0	22.8	46.9
卫生	**Health Care**				
每万人医生数 (人)	Number of Doctors per 10 000 Persons (person)	10.8	15.6	16.5	15.2
每万人医院、卫生院床位数 (张)	Number of Hospital Beds per 10 000 Persons (unit)	19.3	22.8	23.5	24.5
医疗机构病床使用率 (%)	Utilization Rate of Beds in Health Institutions (%)		81.7	61.7	62.9
城市市政建设	**City Construction**				
用水普及率 (%)	Percentage of Population with Access to Tap Water (%)		47.4	61.2	91.1
用气普及率 (%)	Percentage of Population with Access to Tap Gas (%)		17.8	40.0	82.1
人均公共绿地面积 (平方米)	Per Capita Public Green Areas (sq.m)		1.7	2.9	7.9
环境、灾害	**Environment and Disasters**				
平均每起火灾损失 (元)	Average Loss of per Fire (yuan)			10988	5776
平均每起交通事故损失 (元)	Average Loss of per Traffic Accident (yuan)			6069	4184
平均每起环境污染事故直接经济损失 (元)	Average Direct Loss per Pollution Accident (yuan)			41998	74787

注：1.预算外资金收入相当于国家财政收入比例2005年为2004年数据。
2.工业企业效益1997年为1998年数据。
3.少儿抚养比和老年抚养比1978年、1989年和1997年分别为1982年、1990年和1995年数据。

a) Data on proportion of extra-budgetary receipt to government revenue in 2005 are the data in 2004.
b) Economic efficiency of industry in 1997 were the data in 1998.
c) Figures of dependency ratio of children and the aged in 1978, 1989 and 1997 were the 1982's, 1990's and 1995's data.

2-6 按区域分的国民经济和社会发展主要指标（2005年）

指 标	Item	全国总计 National Total
自然资源	**Natural Resources**	
土地面积 （万平方公里）	Area of Land (10 000 sq.km)	960.0
人口	**Population**	
年底总人口 （万人）	Population at the Year-end (10 000 persons)	130756
劳动就业	**Employment**	
年底就业人员 （万人）	Employment At the Year-end (10 000 persons)	75825
#城镇	Urban Area	27331
年末城镇登记失业率 (%)	Registered Unemployment Rate in Urban Area (%)	4.2
国民经济核算	**National Accounting**	
国内(地区)生产总值（亿元）	Gross Domestic Product (100 million yuan)	183084.8
第一产业	Primary Industry	23070.4
第二产业	Secondary Industry	87046.7
#工业	Industry	76912.9
第三产业	Tertiary Industry	72967.7
人均国内(地区)生产总值 （元）	Per Capita Gross Domestic Product (yuan)	14040
固定资产投资	**Investment in Fixed Assets**	
全社会固定资产投资总额 （亿元）	Total Investment in Fixed Assets (100 million yuan)	88773.6
#房地产开发	Real Estate Development	15909.2
财政	**Government Finance**	
地方财政收入 （亿元）	Local Government Revenue (100 million yuan)	14884.2
地方财政支出 （亿元）	Local Government Expenditure (100 million yuan)	25154.3
对外贸易	**Foreign Trade**	
货物进出口总额 （亿美元）	Total Value of Imports and Exports (100 million USD)	14219.1
出口额	Exports	7619.5
进口额	Imports	6599.5
物价	**Price Indices**	
居民消费价格总指数 （上年=100）	Consumer Price Index (previous year=100)	101.8
农业	**Agriculture**	
主要农产品产量 （万吨）	Output of Major Farm Products (10 000 tons)	
粮食	Grain	48402.2
棉花	Cotton	571.4
油料	Oil-bearing Crops	3077.1

Main Indicators of National Economic and Social Development by Eastern, Central, Western and Northeastern Region (2005)

东部地区 Eastern Region		中部地区 Central Region		西部地区 Western Region		东北地区 Northeastern Region	
绝对数 Absolute Figures	占全国比重 (%) As Percentage of National Total	绝对数 Absolute Figures	占全国比重 (%) As Percentage of National Total	绝对数 Absolute Figures	占全国比重 (%) As Percentage of National Total	绝对数 Absolute Figures	占全国比重 (%) As Percentage of National Total
91.6	9.5	102.8	10.7	686.7	71.5	78.79	8.2
46388	36	35202.0	27.4	35976	28.0	10757	8.4
24810	36	19065	28.0	19448	28.6	4704	6.9
7996	45	3791	21.5	3896	22.1	1956	11.1
3.0		3.8		4.1		4.7	
109924.6	55.6	37230.3	18.8	33493.3	16.9	17140.8	8.7
8681.8	37.7	6204.6	27.0	5924.6	25.8	2192.6	9.5
56673.2	58.5	17412.7	18.0	14331.6	14.8	8505.8	8.8
51120.0	59.8	14914.1	17.5	11839.7	13.9	7549.8	8.8
44569.7	57.2	13613.1	17.5	13237.1	17.0	6442.4	8.3
23768		10608		9338		15982	
45626.3	52.4	16145.6	18.5	17645.0	20.3	7678.8	8.8
9673.4	60.8	2232.0	14.0	2666.2	16.8	1337.6	8.4
8955.0	60.2	2263.7	15.2	2464.8	16.6	1200.6	8.1
11564.4	46.0	4713.9	18.7	6252.7	24.9	2623.3	10.4
12781.6	89.9	415.1	2.9	451.3	3.2	571.1	4.0
6798.0	89.2	244.2	3.2	257.6	3.4	319.7	4.2
5983.5	90.7	170.9	2.6	193.8	2.9	251.3	3.8
101.7		102.1		101.4		101.3	
12766.2	26.4	14778.3	30.5	13438.7	27.8	7419.0	15.3
185.5	32.5	176.4	30.9	209.1	36.6	0.4	0.1
906.4	29.5	1252.5	40.7	766.3	24.9	151.9	4.9

2-6 续表

指　标	Item	全国总计 National Total
工业	**Industry**	
主要工业产品产量	Output of Major Industrial Products	
原煤 (亿吨)	Coal (100 million tons)	22.1
原油 (万吨)	Crude Oil (10 000 tons)	18135.3
发电量 (亿千瓦小时)	Electricity (100 million kwh)	25002.6
粗钢 (万吨)	Crude Steel (10 000 tons)	35324.0
水泥 (万吨)	Cement (10 000 tons)	106884.8
交通运输业	**Transportation**	
铁路营业里程 (公里)	Length of Railways in Operation (km)	75437.6
公路里程 (公里)	Length of Highways (km)	1930543
#高速公路	Expressways	41005
旅客周转量 (亿人公里)	Total Passenger-kilometer (100 million person-km)	17466.7
货物周转量 (亿吨公里)	Total Freight Ton-kilometer (10 million ton-km)	80258.1
邮电通信业	**Post and Telecommunication Services**	
邮电业务总量 (亿元)	Total Business Revenue (100 million yuan)	12028.5
国内商业	**Domestic Trade**	
社会消费品零售总额 (亿元)	Total Retail Sales of Consumer Goods (100 million yuan)	67176.6
教育	**Education**	
普通高等学校	Institutions of Higher Education	
学校数 (个)	Number of Institutions (unit)	1792
招生数 (万人)	New Student Enrollment (10 000 persons)	504.5
在校学生数 (万人)	Student Enrollment (10 000 persons)	1561.8
毕业生数 (万人)	Number of Graduates (10 000 persons)	306.8
卫生	**Health Care**	
卫生机构数 (个)	Number of Hospitals (unit)	298997
#医院、卫生院	Hospitals and Health Centers	60397
卫生技术人员 (万人)	Medical Technical Personnel (10 000 persons)	446.0
#医生	Doctors	193.8
医疗机构床位数(万张)	Number of Hospital Beds (10 000 beds)	335.1
#医院、卫生院	Hospitals and Health Centers	313.5
人民生活	**People's Livelihood**	
城镇居民可支配收入 (元)	Per Capita Disposable Income of Urban Households (yuan)	10493
农村居民人均纯收入 (元)	Per Capita Net Income of Rural Households (yuan)	3255

注：本表中涉及分地区数据相加不等于全国总计的指标，在计算东、中、西和东北地区占全国的比重时，分母为31个省(区、市)相加的合计数。

continued

东部地区 Eastern Region		中部地区 Central Region		西部地区 Western Region		东北地区 Northeastern Region	
绝对数 Absolute Figures	占全国比重 (%) As Percentage of National Total	绝对数 Absolute Figures	占全国比重 (%) As Percentage of National Total	绝对数 Absolute Figures	占全国比重 (%) As Percentage of National Total	绝对数 Absolute Figures	占全国比重 (%) As Percentage of National Total
2.9	12.9	9.2	41.8	8.1	36.9	1.9	8.4
6720.1	37.1	585.3	3.2	4502.4	24.8	6327.5	34.9
11281.9	45.1	5682.8	22.7	6104.3	24.4	1933.7	7.7
19497.2	55.2	7502.5	21.2	4555.4	12.9	3768.8	10.7
55137.0	51.6	24078.9	22.5	22055.1	20.6	5613.8	5.3
16998	23	17457	23.1	27594	36.6	13388	17.7
515791	27	463507	24.0	780339	40.4	170906	8.9
16724	41	10476	25.5	10530.0	25.7	3273.0	8.0
6177.5	40.1	4337.0	28.1	3630.3	23.5	1276.8	8.3
48214.6	67.4	9539.0	13.3	8666.2	12.1	5123.7	7.2
6503.2	54.2	2098.9	17.5	2351.4	19.6	1041.9	8.7
36973.8	54.4	13184.5	19.4	11580.5	17.0	6219.9	9.2
714	39.8	468	26.1	428	23.9	182	10.2
208.3	41.3	138	27.3	109.0	21.6	49.4	9.8
643.1	41.2	426.2	27.3	331.8	21.2	160.7	10.3
129.4	42.2	80.7	26.3	63.7	20.8	33.0	10.7
98780	33.0	68317	22.8	99894	33.4	32006	10.7
16770	27.8	15546	25.7	22890	37.9	5191	8.6
172.2	38.6	113.9	25.5	111.4	25.0	49	10.9
73.7	38.0	47.5	24.5	51.3	26.5	21	11.0
126.7	37.8	82.2	24.5	87.7	26.2	38	11.5
117.8	37.6	77.4	24.7	82.7	26.4	36	11.4
13375		8809		8783		8730	
4720		2957		2379		3379	

a) As the sum of some indicators by region is different from the national total, while calculating the percentage of eastern, central, western and northeastern region to all country, the denominator is the sum of 31 provinces.

2-7 人均主要工农业产品产量

Per Capita Output of Major Industrial and Agricultural Products

年 份 Year	粮 食 (公斤) Grain (kg)	棉 花 (公斤) Cotton (kg)	油 料 (公斤) Oil-bearing Crops (kg)	糖 料 (公斤) Sugar Crops (kg)	茶 叶 (公斤) Tea (kg)	水 果 (公斤) Fruits (kg)	猪牛羊肉 (公斤) Pork, Beef and Mutton (kg)	水产品 (公斤) Aquatic Products (kg)
1978	318.74	2.27	5.46	24.91	0.28	6.87		4.87
1980	326.69	2.76	7.84	29.67	0.31	6.92		4.59
1985	360.70	3.94	15.02	57.53	0.41	11.07		6.71
1986	367.00	3.32	13.82	54.86	0.43	12.63		7.72
1987	371.74	3.92	14.09	51.20	0.47	15.39		8.81
1988	357.72	3.77	11.98	56.17	0.49	15.12		9.63
1989	364.32	3.39	11.58	51.88	0.48	16.38		10.30
1990	393.10	3.97	14.21	63.55	0.48	16.51		10.90
1991	378.26	4.93	14.24	73.16	0.47	18.91		11.74
1992	379.97	3.87	14.09	75.61	0.48	20.95		13.37
1993	387.37	3.17	15.31	64.70	0.51	25.55		15.47
1994	373.46	3.64	16.69	61.63	0.49	29.36		17.98
1995	387.28	3.96	18.67	64.96	0.49	34.98		20.89
1996	414.39	3.45	18.16	68.66	0.49	38.21	30.35	27.01
1997	401.74	3.74	17.54	76.31	0.50	41.37	34.55	29.28
1998	412.42	3.62	18.63	78.82	0.54	43.90	37.02	31.45
1999	405.55	3.05	20.76	66.48	0.54	49.76	37.99	32.91
2000	366.04	3.50	23.40	60.47	0.54	49.30	38.32	33.89
2001	355.89	4.19	22.53	68.05	0.55	52.35	39.52	34.44
2002	356.97	3.84	22.63	80.39	0.58	54.30	40.83	35.64
2003	334.29	3.77	21.82	74.83	0.60	112.68	42.74	36.51
2004	362.22	4.88	23.66	73.84	0.64	118.36	44.57	37.82
2005	371.26	4.38	23.60	72.50	0.72	123.65	47.20	39.20

注：本表计算中所使用的人口数字为年平均人口数（下表同）；2003年起水果产量含果用瓜。

a) Population data calculated in the table refer to the annual average population. The same as the following tables. Since 2003, the output of fruits includes that of fruit melons.

2-7 续表 continued

年 份 Year	布 (米) Cloth (m)	机制纸及纸板 (公斤) Machine-made Paper and Paperboard (kg)	纱 (公斤) Yarn (kg)	原 煤 (吨) Coal (ton)	原 油 (公斤) Crude Oil (kg)	发电量 (千瓦小时) Electricity (kwh)	粗 钢 (公斤) Crude Steel (kg)	水 泥 (公斤) Cement (kg)
1978	11.54	4.59	2.49	0.65	108.82	268.36	33.24	68.23
1980	13.73	5.45	2.98	0.63	107.98	306.35	37.83	81.39
1985	13.96	8.67	3.36	0.83	118.83	390.76	44.52	138.86
1986	15.44	9.36	3.73	0.84	122.51	421.36	48.93	155.66
1987	15.96	10.53	4.03	0.86	123.74	458.75	51.92	171.81
1988	17.06	11.53	4.23	0.89	124.41	494.90	53.95	190.75
1989	16.92	11.92	4.26	0.94	123.04	522.78	55.05	187.99
1990	16.63	12.08	4.07	0.95	121.84	547.22	58.45	184.74
1991	15.79	12.85	4.00	0.94	122.52	588.77	61.70	219.51
1992	16.37	14.81	4.31	0.96	121.97	647.18	69.47	264.57
1993	17.23	16.24	4.26	0.98	123.25	712.34	76.00	312.18
1994	17.73	17.94	4.11	1.04	122.57	778.72	77.70	353.39
1995	21.59	23.34	4.50	1.13	124.54	835.81	79.15	394.74
1996	17.17	21.67	4.21	1.15	129.22	888.10	83.15	403.42
1997	20.23	22.22	4.55	1.12	130.68	923.16	88.57	416.02
1998	19.40	17.11	4.36	1.01	129.61	939.48	93.05	431.50
1999	19.94	17.22	4.52	1.02	127.63	988.60	99.12	457.09
2000	21.94	19.70	5.20	1.03	129.09	1073.62	101.77	472.82
2001	22.80	29.70	5.98	0.91	128.91	1164.29	119.22	519.75
2002	25.18	36.45	6.64	0.95	130.43	1291.78	142.43	566.23
2003	27.44	37.64	7.63	1.34	131.64	1482.91	172.57	669.11
2004	37.20	41.77	9.96	1.54	135.70	1699.98	218.28	745.96
2005	37.15	47.60	11.13	1.69	139.10	1917.79	270.95	819.84

2-8 民族自治地方自然资源

Natural Resources in Minority Nationality Autonomous Areas

项 目	Item	2004	占全国比重(%) Percentage to All Country
总面积 （万平方公里）	**Total Area (10 000 sq.km)**	**611.73**	**63.72**
牧区、半农半牧区草原面积（万公顷）	Area of Grasslands in Pastoral and Semi-pastoral Areas (10 000 hectares)	30000.00	75.0
森林面积 （万公顷）	Area of Forest (10 000 hectares)	5648.00	42.2
森林蓄积量 （亿立方米）	Stock Volume of the Forest(100 million cu.m)	52.49	51.8
水力资源蕴藏量 （亿千瓦）	Hydropower Resources (100 million kw)	4.46	66.0

注：除总面积外，其它资源为以前清查数，有待进一步勘测。

a) The figures of resources, except total area, were obtained from surveys in previous year, and are subject to further verification.

2-9 民族自治地方行政区划和人口（2005年）

Administrative Division and Population of Minority Nationality Autonomous Areas(2005)

省级单位名称	Provinces and Autonomous Regions	地级区划数（个） Number of Regions at Prefecture Level (unit)	#地级市 Cities at Prefecture Level	#自治州 Autonomous Prefectures	县级区划数（个） Number of Regions at County Level (unit)	#县级市 Cities at County Level	#自治县（旗） Autonomous Counties (Qi)	总人口（万人） Total Population in Minority Areas (10 000 persons)	#少数民族人口 Minority Population	少数民族人口占自治地方总人口比重(%) Minority Population as Percentage to Total Population in Minority Areas(%)
全 国	**National Total**	**77**	**31**	**30**	**699**	**66**	**120**	**17507.10**	**8238.95**	**47.06**
河 北	Hebei				6		6	196.17	114.18	58.21
内蒙古	Inner Mongolia	12	9		101	11	3	2386.40	515.76	21.61
辽 宁	Liaoning				8		8	334.64	170.10	50.83
吉 林	Jilin	1		1	11	6	3	330.71	114.06	34.49
黑龙江	Heilongjiang				1		1	25.06	5.26	21.00
浙 江	Zhejiang				1		1	17.73	1.82	10.29
湖 北	Hubei	1		1	10	2	2	446.46	240.80	53.94
湖 南	Hunan	1		1	15	1	7	489.03	360.22	73.66
广 东	Guangdong				3		3	47.68	17.95	37.64
广 西	Guangxi	14	14		109	7	12	4925.00	1898.00	38.54
海 南	Hainan				6		6	157.03	78.42	49.94
重 庆	Chongqing				4		4	252.69	170.05	67.29
四 川	Sichuan	3		3	51	1	4	653.77	369.81	56.57
贵 州	Guizhou	3		3	46	4	11	1588.62	945.79	59.54
云 南	Yunnan	8		8	78	7	29	2124.94	1163.82	54.77
西 藏	Tibet	7	1		73	1		276.00	258.00	93.48
甘 肃	Gansu	2		2	21	2	7	321.61	183.77	57.14
青 海	Qinghai	6		6	35	2	7	327.01	201.92	61.75
宁 夏	Ningxia	5	5		21	2		596.20	214.51	35.98
新 疆	Xinjiang	14	2	5	99	20	6	2010.35	1214.69	60.42

2-10 民族自治地方国民经济与社会发展主要指标

指　　标		Item		1990
人口与就业		**Population and Employment**		
人口	**(万人)**	**Population**	**(10 000 persons)**	
年底总人口		Population at the Year-end		15296
#少数民族人口		Minority Population		6880
就业		**Employment**		
就业人员数	(万人)	Employment	(10 000persons)	7406.44
宏观经济		**Macroeconomic Indicator**		
地区生产总值	**(亿元)**	**Regional GDP**	**(100 million yuan)**	
第一产业		Primary Industry		
第二产业		Secondary Industry		
第三产业		Tertiary Industry		
固定资产	**(亿元)**	**Investment in Fixed Assets**	**(100 million yuan)**	
全社会固定资产投资总额		Total Investment in Fixed Assets		
#国有单位		State-owned Units		259.4
财政	**(亿元)**	**Finance**	**(100 million yuan)**	
地方财政收入		Local Governments Revenue		166.7
地方财政支出		Local Governments Expenditures		304.4
产业		**Industry**		
农业		**Agriculture**		
耕地面积	(万公顷)	Cultivated Areas	(10 000 hectares)	1763.0
灌溉面积	(万公顷)	Irrigated Areas	(10 000 hectares)	764.0
农林牧渔总产值	(亿元)	Gross Output Value of Farming, Forestry, Animal Husbandry and Fishery	(100 million yuan)	
主要农产品产量		Output of Major Farm Products		
粮食产量	(万吨)	Grain	(10 000 tons)	5373.0
棉花产量	(万吨)	Cotton	(10 000 tons)	47.0
油料产量	(万吨)	Oil-bearing Crops	(10 000 tons)	208.0
大牲畜年底头数	(万头)	Large Domestic Animals	(10 000 heads)	5286.0
羊年底头数	(万只)	Goats and Sheep (year-end)	(10 000 heads)	11362.0
猪年底头数	(万头)	Hogs (year-end)	(10 000 heads)	5668.0
工业		**Industry**		
工业总产值	(亿元)	Gross Industrial Output Value	(100 million yuan)	
主要工业产品产量		Output of Major Industrial Products		
布	(亿米)	Cloth	(100 million m)	7.4
机制纸及纸板	(万吨)	Machine-Made Paper and Paperboards	(10 000 tons)	94.1
糖	(万吨)	Sugar	(10 000 tons)	222.6
原煤	(亿吨)	Coal	(100 million tons)	1.21
原油	(万吨)	Crude Oil	(10 000 tons)	1265.0
发电量	(亿千瓦小时)	Electricity	(100 million kwh)	738.8
钢	(万吨)	Steel	(10 000 tons)	368.3
生铁	(万吨)	Pig Iron	(10 000 tons)	417
水泥	(万吨)	Cement	(10 000 tons)	1957.8
木材	(万立方米)	Timber	(10 000 cu.m)	1761.0

注：工业总产值为全部国有和年销售收入500万元以上的非国有工业企业的工业总产值。

Main Indicators on Economic and Social Development in Minority Autonomous Areas

总量指标 Aggregate Data				速度指标（%） Indices and Growth Rates						
				指数 Index (2005年为以下各年) (2005 as Percentage of the Following Years)				平均增长速度 Average Annual Growth Rate		
1995	2000	2004	2005	1990	1995	2000	2004	1991-2005	1996-2005	2001-2005
16044	16818	17311	17507	114.5	109.1	104.1	101.1	0.9	0.9	0.8
7232	7767	8115	8239	119.8	113.9	106.1	101.5	1.2	1.3	1.2
7869.62	8308.89	8808.09	8879.13	119.9	112.8	106.9	100.8	1.2	1.2	1.3
4901.14	**7486.15**	**12518.62**	**15705.93**		**268.4**	**174.0**	**114.9**		**10.4**	**11.7**
1628.55	2022.30	2919.70	3300.20		173.2	131.8	107.3		5.6	5.7
1746.52	2834.43	5347.60	6419.02		350.9	208.4	121.7		13.4	15.8
1526.07	2629.41	4251.32	5986.71		276.0	171.6	112.4		10.7	11.4
1444.0	2477.0	6259.4	8357.7		578.8	337.4	133.5		19.2	27.5
982.6	1552.6	2923.3	3767.5	1452.4	383.4	242.7	128.9	19.5	14.4	19.4
248.1	475.5	825.8	1026.4	615.7	413.7	215.8	124.3	12.9	15.3	16.6
595.1	1172.9	2467.7	3050.4	1002.1	512.6	260.1	123.6	16.6	17.8	21.1
1508.0	2086.4	2048.2	2040.0	115.7	135.3	97.8	99.6	1.0	3.1	-0.4
838.0	935.7	988.7	1033.5	135.3	123.3	110.5	104.5	2.0	2.1	2.0
2536.6	3199.8	4803.4	5349.5	249.4	178.9	136.3	108.1	6.3	6.0	6.4
5801.0	6381.4	6764.4	7186.8	133.8	123.9	112.6	106.2	2.0	2.2	2.4
94.6	146.2	179.9	187.9	399.9	198.7	128.5	104.4	9.7	7.1	5.1
264.0	353.2	397.4	372.0	178.9	140.9	105.3	93.6	4.0	3.5	1.0
5618.0	5565.9	5973.8	5535.0	104.7	98.5	99.4	92.7	0.3	-0.1	-0.1
11906.0	13075.8	16225.8	16390.8	144.3	137.7	125.4	101.0	2.5	3.2	4.6
7240.0	8200.8	7955.7	8526.4	150.4	117.8	104.0	107.2	2.8	1.6	0.8
	3923.5	7822.8	10653.6							
6.9	5.0	2.3	3.5	47.0	50.4	69.4	150.4	-4.9	-6.6	-7.0
191.2	175.5	224.9	272.9	290.0	142.7	155.5	121.3	7.4	3.6	9.2
239.5	498.2	813.0	678.1	304.6	283.1	136.1	83.4	7.7	11.0	6.4
1.66	1.5	2.7	3.8	314.1	229.0	259.9	140.1	7.9	8.6	21.1
1610.0	2291.7	2843.2	2832.5	223.9	175.9	123.6	99.6	5.5	5.8	4.3
1186.5	1712.5	2363.2	3052.2	413.1	257.2	178.2	129.2	9.9	9.9	12.3
699.6	647.1	1321.0	1846.3	501.3	263.9	285.3	139.8	11.3	10.2	23.3
554.7	724.8	1409.7	2086.8	500.4	376.2	287.9	148.0	11.3	14.2	23.6
4295.9	5703.1	8394.5	10155.9	518.7	236.4	178.1	121.0	11.6	9.0	12.2
3257.0	1052.5	276.4	169.4	9.6	5.2	16.1	61.3	-14.5	-25.6	-30.6

a) The statistical coverage of gross industrial output value covers all state-owned industrial enterprises and the non-state-enterprises with annual sales income over 5 million yuan.

2-10 续表

指　　标	Item	1990
建筑业	**Construction**	
建筑业企业人数 (万人)	Number of Employed Persons (10 000 persons)	
建筑业总产值 (亿元)	Gross Output Value (100 million yuan)	
施工房屋面积 (万平方米)	Floor Space of Buildings under Construction (10 000 sq.m)	
竣工房屋面积 (万平方米)	Floor Space of Buildings Completed (10 000 sq.m)	
邮电运输	**Transport, Post and Telecommunication Services**	
铁路营业里程 (万公里)	Railways in Operation (10 000 km)	1.31
公路通车里程 (万公里)	Highways (10 000 km)	29.37
邮电业务总量 (亿元)	Total and Telecommunications Services (100 million yuan)	8.6
邮路及农村投递线路总长度 (万公里)	Length of Postal Routes and Rural Delivery Routes(10 000 km)	88
国内商业	**Domestic Trade**	
社会消费品零售总额 (亿元)	Total Retail Sales of Consumer Goods (100 million yuan)	681.8
对外经济贸易	**Foreign Trade**	
进出口总额 (亿美元)	Total Value of Exports and Imports (USD 100 million)	
出口额	Exports	
进口额	Imports	
国际旅游	**International Tourism**	
国际旅游人数 (万人次)	Number of Foreign Tourists (10 000 persons)	
旅游外汇收入 (亿美元)	Foreign Exchange Earnings from Tourism (USD 100 million yuan)	
金融	**Financial Intermediation**	
金融机构各项存款 (亿元)	Deposits of Financial Institutions (100 million yuan)	
金融机构各项贷款 (亿元)	Loans of Financial Institutions (100 million yuan)	
教育、文化、卫生	**Education, Technology and Culture**	
教育	**Education**	
在校学生数 (万人)	Students Enrollment (10 000 persons)	
普通高等学校	Institutions of Higher Education	13.6
普通中学	Secondary Schools	609.6
普通小学	Primary Schools	1852.9
专任教师数 (万人)	Full-time Teachers (10 000 persons)	
普通高等学校	Institutions of Higher Education	2.8
普通中学	Secondary Schools	41.5
普通小学	Primary Schools	84.8
文化	**Culture**	
出版数量	Publications	
图书 (万册)	Number of Books Published (10 000 copies)	30166.3
杂志 (万册)	Number of Magazines Issued (10 000 copies)	7866.4
报纸 (万份)	Number of Newspapers Issued (10 000 copies)	79119.6
卫生	**Health Care**	
卫生机构 (万个)	Number of Health Institutions (10 000 units)	3.2
卫生机构床位 (万张)	Number of Hospitals and Sanatorium Beds (10 000 units)	35.9
卫生技术人员 (万人)	Medical Personnel (10 000 persons)	48.9

注：2000年及以后铁路营业里程为国家铁路营业里程。

Continued

总量指标 Aggregate Data				速度指标（%） Indices and Growth Rates						
				指数 Index（2005年为以下各年） (2005 as Percentage of the Following Years)				平均增长速度 Average Annual Growth Rate		
1995	2000	2004	2005	1990	1995	2000	2004	1991–2005	1996–2005	2001–2005
	131.6	132.6	141.7			107.7	106.9			1.5
	754.3	1358.4	1794.5			237.9	132.1			18.9
	9231.9	14100.7	15964.4			172.9	113.2			11.6
	5325.9	6893.6	8072.1			151.6	117.1			8.7
1.7	1.43	1.68	1.76			123.4	105.2			4.3
33.21	42.36	55.67	61.95	210.9	186.5	146.2	111.3	5.1	6.4	7.9
78	296.9	729.8	891.8	10370.3	1143.4	300.4	122.2	36.3	27.6	24.6
106.8	109.5	108.1	109.7	124.6	102.7	100.1	101.5	1.5	0.3	0.0
1692.3	2569.8	3677.9	4874.2	714.9	288.0	189.7	132.5	14.0	11.2	13.7
	85.6	173.3	221.5			258.6	127.8			20.9
	49.7	92.4	126.4			254.4	136.8			20.5
	36.0	81.0	95.1			264.5	117.5			21.5
	348.2	388.0	485.4			139.4	125.1			6.9
	7.5	10.2	12.8			169.6	125.9			11.1
	7905.8	13546.0	16323.8			206.5	120.5			15.6
	6548.0	10613.6	11299.7			172.6	106.5			11.5
18.6	34.2	83.5	100.0	735.3	537.6	292.4	119.7	14.2	18.3	23.9
631.88	873.0	1064.9	1277.2	209.5	202.1	146.3	119.9	5.1	7.3	7.9
1889.49	1886.0	1692.9	1667.7	90.0	88.3	88.4	98.5	-0.7	-1.2	-2.4
3.7	3.6	5.8	6.3	223.7	169.3	172.1	108.7	5.5	5.4	11.5
41.47	47.9	57.5	61.1	147.3	147.5	127.7	106.4	2.6	4.0	5.0
85.8	89.9	86.8	88.1	103.8	102.6	97.9	101.4	0.3	0.3	-0.4
42275.0	42309.5	66611.7	45275.5	150.1	107.1	107.0	68.0	2.7	0.7	1.4
7881.0	8332.4	8341.7	15581.5	198.1	197.7	187.0	186.8	4.7	7.1	13.3
94984.8	123276.9	256030.6	166887.4	210.9	175.7	135.4	65.2	5.1	5.8	6.2
2.90	1.60	1.55	1.55	48.4	53.4	96.7	99.8	-4.7	-6.1	-0.7
38.7	38.2	40.0	41.0	114.1	105.9	107.3	102.4	0.9	0.6	1.4
52.7	35.5	47.5	47.8	97.9	90.7	134.6	100.6	-0.1	-1.0	6.1

a) The length of railway in operation since 2000 is national railways.

2-11 少数民族分布的主要地区
Geographic Distribution of Minority Nationalities

人口数为2000年人口普查机器汇总数据。

Figures of population are obtained from the Population Census in 2000.

民 族	Nationality	分布的主要地区	Main Geographic Distribution	人口数(人) Population (person)
蒙古族	Mongolian	内蒙古、辽宁、吉林、河北、黑龙江、新疆	Inner Mongolia, Liaoning, Jilin, Hebei, Heilongjiang and Xinjiang	5813947
回 族	Hui	宁夏、甘肃、河南、新疆、青海、云南、河北、山东、安徽、辽宁、北京、内蒙古、天津、黑龙江、陕西、贵州、吉林、江苏、四川	Ningxia, Gansu, Henan, Xinjiang, Qinghai, Yunnan, Hebei, Shandong, Anhui, Liaoning, Beijing, Inner Mongolia, Tianjin, Heilongjiang, Shaanxi, Guizhou, Jilin, Jiangsu and Sichuan	9816805
藏 族	Tibetan	西藏、四川、青海、甘肃、云南	Tibet, Sichuan, Qinghai, Gansu and Yunnan	5416021
维吾尔族	Uygur	新疆	Xinjiang	8399393
苗 族	Miao	贵州、湖南、云南、广西、重庆、湖北、四川	Guizhou, Hunan, Yunnan, Guangxi, Chongqing, Hubei and Sichuan	8940116
彝 族	Yi	云南、四川、贵州	Yunnan, Sichuan and Guizhou	7762272
壮 族	Zhuang	广西、云南、广东	Guangxi, Yunnan and Guangdong	16178811
布依族	Bouyei	贵州	Guizhou	2971460
朝鲜族	Korean	吉林、黑龙江、辽宁	Jilin, Heilongjiang and Liaoning	1923842
满 族	Manchu	辽宁、河北、黑龙江、吉林、内蒙古、北京	Liaoning, Hebei, Heilongjiang, Jilin, Inner Mongolia and Beijing	10682262
侗 族	Dong	贵州、湖南、广西	Guizhou, Hunan and Guangxi	2960293
瑶 族	Yao	广西、湖南、云南、广东	Guangxi, Hunan, Yunnan and Guangdong	2637421
白 族	Bai	云南、贵州、湖南	Yunnan, Guizhou and Hunan	1858063
土家族	Tujia	湖南、湖北、重庆、贵州	Hunan, Hubei, Chongqing and Guizhou	8028133
哈尼族	Hani	云南	Yunnan	1439673
哈萨克族	Kazak	新疆	Xinjiang	1250458
傣 族	Dai	云南	Yunnan	1158989
黎 族	Li	海南	Hainan	1247814
傈僳族	Lisu	云南、四川	Yunnan and Sichuan	634912
佤 族	Va	云南	Yunnan	396610
畲 族	She	福建、浙江、江西、广东	Fujian, Zhejiang, Jiangxi and Guangdong	709592
高山族	Gaoshan	台湾、福建	Taiwan and Fujian	4461
拉祜族	Lahu	云南	Yunnan	453705
水 族	Shui	贵州、广西	Guizhou and Guangxi	406902
东乡族	Dongxiang	甘肃、新疆	Gansu and Xinjiang	513805
纳西族	Naxi	云南	Yunnan	308839
景颇族	Jingpo	云南	Yunnan	132143
柯尔克孜族	Kirgiz	新疆	Xinjiang	160823
土 族	Tu	青海、甘肃	Qinghai and Gansu	241198
达斡尔族	Daur	内蒙古、黑龙江	Inner Mongolia and Heilongjiang	132394
仫佬族	Mulam	广西	Guangxi	207352
羌 族	Qiang	四川	Sichuan	306072
布朗族	Blang	云南	Yunnan	91882
撒拉族	Salar	青海	Qinghai	104503
毛南族	Maonan	广西	Guangxi	107166
仡佬族	Gelao	贵州	Guizhou	579357
锡伯族	Xibe	辽宁、新疆	Liaoning and Xinjiang	188824
阿昌族	Achang	云南	Yunnan	33936
普米族	Pumi	云南	Yunnan	33600
塔吉克族	Tajik	新疆	Xinjiang	41028
怒 族	Nu	云南	Yunnan	28759
乌孜别克族	Ozbek	新疆	Xinjiang	12370
俄罗斯族	Russian	新疆、黑龙江	Xinjiang and Heilongjiang	15609
鄂温克族	Ewenki	内蒙古	Inner Mongolia	30505
德昂族	De'ang	云南	Yunnan	17935
保安族	Bonan	甘肃	Gansu	16505
裕固族	Yugur	甘肃	Gansu	13719
京 族	Jing	广西	Guangxi	22517
塔塔尔族	Tatar	新疆	Xinjiang	4890
独龙族	Drung	云南	Yunnan	7426
鄂伦春族	Oroqen	黑龙江、内蒙古	Heilongjiang and Inner Mongolia	8196
赫哲族	Hezhen	黑龙江	Heilongjiang	4640
门巴族	Moinba	西藏	Tibet	8923
珞巴族	Lhoba	西藏	Tibet	2965
基诺族	Jino	云南	Yunnan	20899

主要统计指标解释

平均增长速度　计算平均增长速度有两种方法：一种是习惯上经常使用的“水平法”，又称几何平均法，是以间隔期最后一年的水平同基期水平对比来计算平均每年增长(或下降)速度；另一种是“累计法”，又称代数平均法或方程法，是以间隔期内各年水平的总和同基期水平对比来计算平均每年增长(或下降)速度。在一般正常情况下，两种方法计算的平均每年增长速度比较接近；但在经济发展不平衡、出现大起大落时，两种方法计算的结果差别较大。

本《年鉴》内所列的平均增长速度，除固定资产投资用“累计法”计算外，其余均用“水平法”计算。从某年到某年平均增长速度的年份，均不包括基期年在内。如建国四十三年以来的平均增长速度是以1949年为基期计算的，则写为1950-1992年平均增长速度，其余类推。

国民经济行业分类　自2003年定期报表开始使用新的《国民经济行业分类》（GB/T4754-2002）该分类是由国家统计局组织修订，经国家质量监督检验检疫总局批准，于2002年5月10日发布实施。这次修订是在1994年分类标准的基础上，参照联合国《全部经济活动的国际标准产业分类》（ISIC/Rev.3）进行的。修订后的《国民经济行业分类》（GB/T4754-2002）共有门类20个，大类95个，中类396个，小类913个。新增门类4个，大类增加3个，中类增加28个，小类增加67个。

企业(单位)登记注册类型　是以在工商行政管理机关登记注册的各类企业为划分对象，以工商行政管理部门对企业登记注册的类型为依据，将企业登记注册类型分为内资企业、港澳台商投资企业和外商投资企业三大类。内资企业包括国有企业、集体企业、股份合作企业、联营企业、有限责任公司、股份有限公司、私营公司和其他企业；　港澳台商投资企业和外商投资企业分别包括合资经营企业、合作经营企业、独资经营企业和股份有限公司。对不在工商行政管理部门进行登记注册的行政机关、事业单位和社会团体，主要按其经费来源和管理方式进行划分。

国有企业　指企业全部资产归国家所有，并按《中华人民共和国企业法人登记管理条例》规定登记注册的非公司制的经济组织。不包括有限责任公司中的国有独资公司。

集体企业　指企业资产归集体所有，并按《中华人民共和国企业法人登记管理条例》规定登记注册的经济组织。

股份合作企业　指以合作制为基础，由企业职工共同出资入股，吸收一定比例的社会资产投资组建，实行自主经营，自负盈亏，共同劳动，民主管理，按劳分配与按股分红相结合的一种集体经济组织。

联营企业　指两个及两个以上相同或不同所有制性质的企业法人或事业单位法人，按自愿、平等、互利的原则，共同投资组成的经济组织。联营企业包括国有联营企业、集体联营企业、国有与集体联营企业和其他联营企业。

有限责任公司　指根据《中华人民共和国公司登记管理条例》规定登记注册，由两个以上、五十个以下的股东共同出资，每个股东以其所认缴的出资额对公司承担有限责任，公司以其全部资产对其债务承担责任的经济组织。有限责任公司包括国有独资公司以及其他有限责任公司。

股份有限公司　指根据《中华人民共和国公司登记管理条例》规定登记注册，其全部注册资本由等额股份构成并通过发行股票筹集资本，股东以其认购的股份对公司承担有限责任，公司以其全部资产对其债务承担责任的经济组织。

私营企业　指由自然人投资设立或由自然人控股，以雇佣劳动为基础的营利性经济组织。包括按照《公司法》、《合伙企业法》、《私营企业暂行条例》规定登记注册的私营有限责任公司、私营股份有限公司、私营合伙企业和私营独资企业。

其他企业　指上述企业之外的其他内资经济组织。

与港澳台商合资经营企业　指港澳台地区投资者与内地企业依照《中华人民共和国中外合资经营企业法》及有关法律的规定，按合同规定的比例投资设立、分享利润和分担风险的企业。

与港澳台商合作经营企业　指港澳台地区投资者与内地企业依照《中华人民共和国中外合作经营企业法》及有关法律的规定，依照合作合同的约定进行投资或提供条件设立、分配利润和分担风险的企业。

港澳台商独资经营企业　指依照《中华人民共和国外资企业法》及有关法律的规定，在内地由港澳台地区投资者全额投资设立的企业。

港澳台商投资股份有限公司　指根据国家有关规定，经原外经贸部依法批准设立，其中港、澳、台商的股本占公司注册资本的比例达25% 以上的股份有限公司。凡其中港、澳、台商的股本占公司注册资本的比例小于25%的，属于内资企业中的股份有限公司。

中外合资经营企业　指外国企业或外国人与中国内地企业依照《中华人民共和国中外合资经营企业法》及有关法律的规定，按合同规定的比例投资设立、分享利润和分担风险的企业。

中外合作经营企业　指外国企业或外国人与中国内地企业依照《中华人民共和国中外合作经营企业法》及有关法律的规定，依照合作合同的约定进行投资或提供条件设立、分配利润和分担风险的企业。

外资企业　指依照《中华人民共和国外资企业法》及有关法律的规定，在中国内地由外国投资者全额投资设立的企业。

外商投资股份有限公司　指根据国家有关规定，经原外经贸部依法批准设立，其中外资的股本占公司注册资本的比例达25% 以上的股份有限公司。凡其中外资股本占公司注册资本的比例小于25%的，属于内资企业中的股份有限公司。

行政机关、事业单位和社会团体　参照企业登记注册类型，主要按其经费来源和管理方式划分。具体规定如下：

⑴行政机关：包括国家机关和政党机关，原则上均列为“国有”。但有特殊规定的，如供销社等，则列为“集体”。

⑵事业单位：包括经国家机构编制部门和有关业务主管部门批准成立的各类事业单位，不包括实行企业化管理的事业单位。事业单位的划分办法如下：

①由国家财政预算拨款或列入财政预算外资金管理以及经费主要来源于国有主管部门或国有上级单位的事业单位，列为“国有”。

②经费主要来源于集体单位的事业单位，列为“集体”。

③公民个人(或个人合伙)开办的事业单位，列为“私营”。

④上述以外的其他事业单位，如果其经费来源不明确，按管理方式进行归类。

⑶社会团体：包括经民政部门批准成立以及未纳入社会团体管理条例范围的工会、妇联等各类社会团体。社会团体的划分办法如下：

①未纳入民政部社会团体管理条例范围的工会、妇联、共青团、青联、工商联、科协、侨联等社会团体，国家拨款设立的基金会或基金管理组织以及经费主要来源于国有业务主管部门或国有上级单位的社会团体，列为“国有”。

②经费主要来源于集体单位的社会团体，列为“集体”。

③公民个人(或个人合伙)开办的社会团体，划为“私营”。

④上述以外的其他社会团体，如果其经费来源不明确，改按管理方式进行归类。

Explanatory Notes on Main Statistical Indicators

Average Annual Growth Rate Two methods for calculating average annual growth rate are applied, one is often called level approach, or the method of calculating geometric average, which is derived by comparing the level of the last year of the interval with that of the beginning year; the other is called accumulative approach or algebraic average or equation method, which is derived by the summation of the actual figure of each year in the interval divided by the figure in the base year.Usually the results calculated by the two methods are fairly close, but they differed sharply when uneven economic development occurred with striking fluctuations in growth.

The average annual growth rates listed in this statistical yearbook are calculated by level approach except for the growth rate of investment in fixed assets. The base years are not listed when the years are listed for average annual growth rates. For instance, the average annual growth rate of 43 years since 1949 is listed as average annual growth rate of 1950-1992 without listing the base year 1949. And the analogy of this is also the same for the rest of the years.

Industrial Classification of the National Economy The new *Industrial Classification of the National Economy* (GB/T 4754-2002) is introduced starting from the compilation of 2003 annual statistics. The new revision was basedon the 1994 classification and organized by the National Bureau of Statistics taking into consideration of the *International Standards of the Industrial Classification of All Economic Activities* (ISIC/Rev.3) of the United Nations, and the new *Classification* was promulgated by the National Administration of Quality Supervision, Inspection and Quarantine on May 10, 2002. The revised version of the *Industrial Classification of the National Economy* (GB/T 4754-2002) is composed of 20 major divisions, 95 divisions, 396 major groups and 913 groups, including 4 new major divisions, 3 new divisions, 28 major groups and 67 groups.

Registration Status of Enterprises Enterprises are classified into 3 categories, namely domestic-funded enterprises, enterprises with investment from Hong Kong, Macau and Taiwan, and enterprises with foreign investment, in the light of the registration status of an enterprise in industrial and commercial administration agencies. Domestic-funded enterprises include state-owned enterprises, collective-owned enterprises, cooperative enterprises, joint ownership enterprises, limited liability corporations, share-holding corporations Ltd., private enterprises and other enterprises. Included in the enterprises with investment from Hong Kong, Macau and Taiwan and enterprises with foreign investment are joint-venture enterprises, cooperative enterprises, sole investment enterprises and share-holding corporations Ltd. For government agencies, institutions and social organizations which are not requested to be registered in industrial and commercial administration agencies, they are classified mainly by their sources of funds and way of management.

State-owned Enterprises refer to non-corporation economic units where the entire assets are owned by the state and which have registered in accordance with the *Regulation of the People's Republic of China on the Management of Registration of Corporate Enterprises*. Excluded from this category are sole state-funded corporations in the limited liability corporations.

Collective-owned Enterprises refer to economic units where the assets are owned collectively and which have registered in accordance with the *Regulation of the People's Republic of China on the Management of Registration of Corporate Enterprises*.

Cooperative Enterprises refer to a form of collective economic units (enterprises) where capitals come mainly from employees as their shares, with certain proportion of capital from the outside, where production is organized on the basis of independent operation, independent accounting for profits and losses, joint work, democratic management, and a distribution system that integrates remuneration according to work with dividend according to capital share.

Joint Ownership Enterprises refer to economic units established by two or more corporate enterprises or corporate institutions of the same or different ownership, through joint investment on the basis of equality, voluntary participation and mutual benefits. They include state joint ownership enterprises, collective joint ownership enterprises, joint state-collective enterprises, other joint ownership enterprises.

Limited Liability Corporations refer to economic units established with investment from 2-50 investors and registered in accordance with the *Regulation of the People's Republic of China on the Management of Registration of Corporations*, each investor bearing limited liability to the corporation depending on its share of investment, and the corporation bearing liability to its debt to the maximum of its total assets. Limited liability corporations include exclusive state-funded limited liability corporations and other limited liability corporations.

Share-holding Corporations Ltd. refer to economic units registered in accordance with the *Regulation of the People's Republic of China on the Management of Registration of Corporations*, with total registered capitals divided into equal shares and raised through issuing stocks. Each investor bears limited liability to the corporation depending on the holding of shares, and the corporation bears liability to its debt to the maximum of its total assets.

Private Enterprises refer to profit-making economic units invested and established by natural persons, or controlled by natural persons using employed labour. Included in this category are private limited liability corporations, private share-holding corporations Ltd., private partnership enterprises and private-funded enterprises registered in accordance with the *Corporation Law*, *Partnership Enterprises Law* and *Interim Regulations on Private Enterprises* .

Other Domestic-funded Enterprises refer to domestic-funded economic units other than those mentioned above.

Cooperative Enterprises with Funds from Hong Kong Macau and Taiwan established by investors from Hong Kong, Macau and Taiwan with enterprises in the mainland of China in accordance with the *Law of the People's Republic of China on Sino-foreign Cooperative Enterprises* and other relevant laws, where the investment or provision of facilities, and the share of profits and risks is stipulated in the cooperative contract.

Enterprises with Sole (exclusive) Investment from Hong Kong, Macau and Taiwan refer to enterprises established in the mainland of China with exclusive investment from investors from Hong Kong, Macau and Taiwan in accordance with the *Law of the People's Republic of China on Foreign-Funded Enterprises* and other relevant laws.

Share-holding Corporations Ltd. with Investment from Hong Kong, Macau and Taiwan refer to share-holding corporations Ltd. established with the approval from the former Ministry of Foreign Trade and Economic Relations in line with relevant state regulations, where the share of investment from Hong Kong, Macau or Taiwan businessmen exceeds 25% of the total registered capital of the corporation. In case the share of investment from Hong Kong, Macau or Taiwan is less than 25% of the total registered capital, the enterprise is to be classified as domestic-funded share-holding corporation Ltd.

Joint-venture Enterprises with Foreign Investment refer to enterprises jointly established by foreign enterprises or foreigners with enterprises in the mainland of China in accordance with the *Law of the People's Republic of China on Sino-foreign Joint Venture Enterprises* and other relevant laws, where the share of investment, profits and risks is stipulated in the contract.

Cooperation Enterprises with Foreign Investment refer to enterprises jointly established by foreign enterprises or foreigners with enterprises in the mainland of China in accordance with the *Law of the People's Republic of China on Sino-foreign Cooperative Enterprises* and other relevant laws, where the investment or provision of facilities, and the share of profits and risks is stipulated in the cooperative contract.

Enterprises with Sole (exclusive) Foreign Investment refer to enterprises established in the mainland of China with exclusive investment from foreign investors in accordance with the *Law of the People's Republic of China on Foreign-Funded Enterprises* and other relevant laws.

Share-holding Corporations Ltd. with Foreign Investment refer to share-holding corporations Ltd. established with the approval from the Ministry of Foreign Trade and Economic Relations in line with relevant state regulations, where the share of investment from foreign investors exceeds 25% of the total registered capital of the corporation. In case the share of foreign investment is less than 25% of the total registered capital, the enterprise is to be classified as domestic-funded share-holding corporation Ltd.

Government Agencies, Institutions and Social Organizations are classified into following categories by source of funds and way of management taking reference of the registration status of enterprises:

(1) Government agencies: include state and party agencies, classified in principle as state-owned. There are exceptions, such as supply and marketing cooperatives which are classified as collective-owned.

(2) Institutions: include institutions of various types established with the approval by organization and staffing departments of the government, but exclude institutions where enterprise management system is introduced. Institutions are further classified as follows:

(a) Institutions whose main budget is listed in the government budget appropriations or extra-budget funds, or allocated from the budget of their competent government agencies. Such institutions are classified as state-owned.

(b) Institutions whose budget mainly comes from collective units. Such institutions are classified as collective-owned.

(c) Institutions other than those mentioned above whose source of budget is not clear. Such institutions are classified by way of management.

(3) Social organizations: include social organizations established with the approval from the Ministry of Civil Affairs, and organizations that are not covered by social organization management regulations such as trade unions, womens federations etc.. Social organizations are further classified as follows:

(a) Social organizations that are not covered by social organization management regulations of the Ministry of Civil Affairs such as trade unions, womens federations, communist youth leagues, youth associations, industrial and commerce associations, scientists associations, overseas Chinese associations, etc., foundations and fund management organizations established with funds from the state, and social organizations whose funds mainly come from the budget of their competent government agencies. Such institutions are classified as state-owned.

(b) Social organizations whose budget mainly comes from collective units. Such institutions are classified as collective-owned.

(c) Social organizations established by individual or a group of citizens, which are classified as private.

(d) Social organizations other than those mentioned above whose source of budget is not clear. Such organizations are classified by way of management.

3

国民经济核算

National Accounts

简 要 说 明

国民经济核算资料主要包括国内生产总值、投入产出表、资金流量表及国际收支平衡表四个部分。

一、国内生产总值

国内生产总值数据是由国家统计局国民经济核算司根据不同产业部门、不同支出构成的特点和资料来源情况而采用不同方法计算的。国民总收入是在国内生产总值的基础上加上来自国外的净要素收入求得的。

本年鉴公布的国内生产总值以及与之有关的指标数据，最后一年数据不是最终数，还会在获得更多的财务和行政记录等资料后发生变动。如果遇到普查，在能够获得更详细的基础资料的情况下，国内生产总值的历史数据还会发生变动。2005年，根据第一次经济普查资料，按照《经济普查年度GDP核算方案》的要求，重新计算了经济普查年度（即2004年）国内生产总值数据，并利用趋势离差法（即先根据经济普查数据计算出历史数据的趋势值，然后，利用原有历史数据实际值和趋势值的比率修订根据经济普查数据计算的历史数据趋势值，得到新的历史数据修订值），修订了国内生产总值历史数据。本年鉴中的数据是修订以后的数据，2005年数据是在修订后的2004年数据基础上计算出来的。

本年鉴所列分地区的数据来自各省、自治区、直辖市统计局的国民经济核算资料。由于采取分级核算，各地区数据相加不等于全国总计。

二、投入产出表

投入产出表也称部门联系平衡表或产业关联表，它是根据国民经济各部门生产中的投入来源和使用去向纵横交叉组成的一张棋盘式平衡表。它可以用来揭示部门间经济技术的相互依存、相互制约的数量关系。投入产出表由国家统计局国民经济核算司编制。

三、资金流量表

我国资金流量表表式与国际上通用的表式相似，是机构部门与交易项目的矩阵表式。主栏为交易项目，主要反映分配方式和融资工具；宾栏按机构部门分类。机构部门分类是根据机构单位具有的基本特征所进行的部门分类。资金流量表把参与资金活动的主体分为非金融企业、金融机构、政府、住户和国外五个部门。每一部门下设资金来源与资金运用两栏。现行的资金流量表分为两大部分，上半部分为实物交易部分，由国家统计局国民经济核算司编制；下半部分为金融交易部分，由中国人民银行调查统计司编制。

四、国际收支平衡表

国际收支平衡表由国家外汇管理局国际收支司依据国际货币基金组织编写的《国际收支统计手册》第五版编制。

Brief Introduction

Statistics on national accounts include mainly four components, namely, gross domestic product, input-output table, flow of fund table and balance of payments.

I. Gross Domestic Product

Data on GDP are calculated by the Department of National Accounts of the National Bureau of Statistics (NBS) with various approaches in the light of the features of various sectors, various expenditure structures and the data sources. The gross national product can be calculated on the base of GDP and the net factor income from abroad.

Data on gross domestic product and related indicators of the most recent year published in the yearbook are not final and are subject to changes when more information from financial data and administrative records are available. When it happens to be a census year, data of GDP of the past years may also be revised. In 2005, the GDP figures for the year 2004 were recompiled in accordance with the *Programme of Compilation of GDP and National Accounts for the Year of Economic Census* and with the result from the first economic census. GDP data for earlier years were revised by trend deviation approach (trend of historical data were first calculated with data from the census, which was further revised by the ratio between the value of historical data and the trend of historical data, resulting in revised historical data series.). Data for 2005 are compiled on the basis of revised 2004 data.

Regional data in this yearbook are prepared according to the data of national accounts provided by the statistical bureaus of the provinces, autonomous regions and municipalities directly under the central government. The sum of the regional data is not equal to the national total due to the decentralized accounting approach.

II. Input-output Table

Reflecting the sources of the input into, and the utilization of the output from production by various industries of the national economy, the input-output table is used to reveal, in quantitative terms, the interrelated and mutually dependent economic and technological relations between industries.The input-output table of China is compiled by the Department of National Accounts of the National Bureau of Statistics.

III. Flow of Fund Table

Similar to internationally accepted format, the flow of fund table of China constitutes a matrix of institutional sectors by transactions. Items of transactions are expressed as row headings representing forms of distribution and methods of financing. Institutional sectors are shown as column headings, grouped by the characteristics of the transactors. There are 5 groups of institutional sectors in the flow of fund table, namely, non-financial corporations, financial institutions, governments, households, and the rest of the world. Under each sector there are 2 headings: source of fund and utilization of fund. The current flow of fund table is composed of two parts: the first part is the physical (real) transactions compiled by the Department of National Accounts of the National Bureau of Statistics, and the second part is the financial transactions compiled by the Survey and Statistics Department of the People's Bank of China.

IV. Balance of Payments

The balance of payment table is compiled by the Balance of Payment Department of the State Administration of Foreign Exchanges in accordance with the 5th edition of the *Manual on Balance of Payment* prepared by the International Monetary Fund.

3-1 国 内 生 产 总 值

Gross Domestic Product

本表按当年价格计算。

Data in this table are calculated at current prices.

单位：亿元 (100 million yuan)

年 份 Year	国民总收入 Gross National Income	国内生产总值 Gross Domestic Product	第一产业 Primary Industry	第二产业 Secondary Industry	工 业 Industry	建筑业 Construction	第三产业 Tertiary Industry	#交通运输仓储和邮政业 Transport, Storage and Post	#批发与零售业 Wholesale and Retail Trades	人均国内生产总值(元/人) Per Capita GDP (yuan/person)
1978	3645.2	3645.2	1018.4	1745.2	1607.0	138.2	881.6	172.8	265.5	381
1979	4062.6	4062.6	1258.9	1913.5	1769.7	143.8	890.2	184.2	220.2	419
1980	4545.6	4545.6	1359.4	2192.0	1996.5	195.5	994.2	205.0	213.6	463
1981	4889.5	4891.6	1545.6	2255.5	2048.4	207.1	1090.5	211.1	255.7	492
1982	5330.5	5323.4	1761.6	2383.0	2162.3	220.7	1178.8	236.7	198.6	528
1983	5985.6	5962.7	1960.8	2646.2	2375.6	270.6	1355.7	264.9	231.4	583
1984	7243.8	7208.1	2295.5	3105.7	2789.0	316.7	1806.9	327.1	412.4	695
1985	9040.7	9016.0	2541.6	3866.6	3448.7	417.9	2607.8	406.9	878.4	858
1986	10274.4	10275.2	2763.9	4492.7	3967.0	525.7	3018.6	475.6	943.2	963
1987	12050.6	12058.6	3204.3	5251.6	4585.8	665.8	3602.7	544.9	1159.3	1112
1988	15036.8	15042.8	3831.0	6587.2	5777.2	810.0	4624.6	661.0	1618.0	1366
1989	17000.9	16992.3	4228.0	7278.0	6484.0	794.0	5486.3	786.0	1687.0	1519
1990	18718.3	18667.8	5017.0	7717.4	6858.0	859.4	5933.4	1147.5	1419.7	1644
1991	21826.2	21781.5	5288.6	9102.2	8087.1	1015.1	7390.7	1409.7	2087.0	1893
1992	26937.3	26923.5	5800.0	11699.5	10284.5	1415.0	9424.0	1681.8	2735.0	2311
1993	35260.0	35333.9	6887.3	16454.4	14188.0	2266.5	11992.2	2205.6	3198.7	2998
1994	48108.5	48197.9	9471.4	22445.4	19480.7	2964.7	16281.1	2898.3	4338.4	4044
1995	59810.5	60793.7	12020.0	28679.5	24950.6	3728.8	20094.3	3424.1	5467.7	5046
1996	70142.5	71176.6	13885.8	33835.0	29447.6	4387.4	23455.8	4068.5	6379.2	5846
1997	77653.1	78973.0	14264.6	37543.0	32921.4	4621.6	27165.4	4593.0	7314.1	6420
1998	83024.3	84402.3	14618.0	39004.2	34018.4	4985.8	30780.1	5178.4	8084.8	6796
1999	88189.0	89677.1	14548.1	41033.6	35861.5	5172.1	34095.3	5821.8	8788.6	7159
2000	98000.5	99214.6	14716.2	45555.9	40033.6	5522.3	38942.5	7333.4	9629.7	7858
2001	108068.2	109655.2	15516.2	49512.3	43580.6	5931.7	44626.7	8406.1	10787.4	8622
2002	119095.7	120332.7	16238.6	53896.8	47431.3	6465.5	50197.3	9393.4	11950.9	9398
2003	135174.0	135822.8	17068.3	62436.3	54945.5	7490.8	56318.1	10098.4	13480.0	10542
2004	159586.7	159878.3	20955.8	73904.3	65210.0	8694.3	65018.2	12147.6	15249.8	12336
2005	183956.1	183084.8	23070.4	87046.7	76912.9	10133.8	72967.7	10526.1	13534.5	14040

注：1.1980年以后国民总收入(原称国民生产总值)与国内生产总值的差额为国外净要素收入。

2.2004年及以前年份第一产业不包括农林牧渔服务业，交通运输仓储和邮政业包括电信业，但不包括城市公共交通业，批发与零售业包括餐饮业(下表同)。

a) Since 1980, the difference between the Gross Domestic Product and the Gross National Income (formerly, the Gross National Product) has been the net factor income from abroad.

b) In 2004 and preceding years, the primary industry did not include service of farming, forestry, animal husbandry and fishery; transport, storage and post included telecommunication services, but did not include urban public transport; wholesale and retail trades included catering services. The same as in the following table.

3-2 国内生产总值构成

Composition of Gross Domestic Product

本表按当年价格计算。

Data in this table are calculated at current prices.

单位：%　　(%)

年份 Year	国内生产总值 Gross Domestic Product	第一产业 Primary Industry	第二产业 Secondary Industry	工业 Industry	建筑业 Construction	第三产业 Tertiary Industry	#交通运输仓储和邮政业 Transport, Storage and Post	#批发与零售业 Wholesale and Retail Trades
1978	100.0	27.9	47.9	44.1	3.8	24.2	4.7	7.3
1979	100.0	31.0	47.1	43.6	3.5	21.9	4.5	5.4
1980	100.0	29.9	48.2	43.9	4.3	21.9	4.5	4.7
1981	100.0	31.6	46.1	41.9	4.2	22.3	4.3	5.2
1982	100.0	33.1	44.8	40.6	4.2	22.1	4.4	3.7
1983	100.0	32.9	44.4	39.9	4.5	22.7	4.4	3.9
1984	100.0	31.8	43.1	38.7	4.4	25.1	4.6	5.7
1985	100.0	28.2	42.9	38.3	4.6	28.9	4.5	9.7
1986	100.0	26.9	43.7	38.6	5.1	29.4	4.6	9.2
1987	100.0	26.6	43.5	38.0	5.5	29.9	4.5	9.6
1988	100.0	25.5	43.8	38.4	5.4	30.7	4.4	10.8
1989	100.0	24.9	42.9	38.2	4.7	32.2	4.6	9.9
1990	100.0	26.9	41.3	36.7	4.6	31.8	6.2	7.6
1991	100.0	24.3	41.8	37.1	4.7	33.9	6.5	9.6
1992	100.0	21.5	43.5	38.2	5.3	35.0	6.2	10.2
1993	100.0	19.5	46.6	40.2	6.4	33.9	6.2	9.1
1994	100.0	19.6	46.6	40.4	6.2	33.8	6.0	9.0
1995	100.0	19.8	47.2	41.1	6.1	33.0	5.6	9.0
1996	100.0	19.5	47.5	41.4	6.1	33.0	5.7	9.0
1997	100.0	18.1	47.5	41.7	5.8	34.4	5.8	9.3
1998	100.0	17.3	46.2	40.3	5.9	36.5	6.1	9.6
1999	100.0	16.2	45.8	40.0	5.8	38.0	6.5	9.8
2000	100.0	14.8	45.9	40.3	5.6	39.3	7.4	9.7
2001	100.0	14.1	45.2	39.8	5.4	40.7	7.7	9.8
2002	100.0	13.5	44.8	39.4	5.4	41.7	7.8	9.9
2003	100.0	12.6	46.0	40.5	5.5	41.4	7.4	9.9
2004	100.0	13.1	46.2	40.8	5.4	40.7	7.6	9.5
2005	100.0	12.6	47.5	42.0	5.5	39.9	5.7	7.4

3-3 国内生产总值指数

Indices of Gross Domestic Product

本表按可比价格计算。

Data in this table are calculated at constant prices.

(上年=100) (preceding year=100)

年份 Year	国民总收入 Gross National Income	国内生产总值 Gross Domestic Product	第一产业 Primary Industry	第二产业 Secondary Industry	工业 Industry	建筑业 Construction	第三产业 Tertiary Industry	#交通运输仓储和邮政业 Transport, Storage, and Post	#批发与零售业 Wholesale and Retail Trades	人均国内生产总值 Per Capita GDP
1978	111.7	111.7	104.1	115.0	116.4	99.4	113.7	108.9	123.1	110.2
1979	107.6	107.6	106.1	108.2	108.7	102.0	107.8	107.7	108.8	106.1
1980	107.8	107.8	98.5	113.6	112.7	126.7	105.9	105.7	98.7	106.5
1981	105.2	105.2	107.0	101.9	101.7	103.2	110.4	101.9	130.0	103.9
1982	109.2	109.1	111.5	105.6	105.8	103.4	113.0	111.7	103.9	107.5
1983	111.1	110.9	108.3	110.4	109.7	117.1	115.2	110.0	121.9	109.3
1984	115.3	115.2	112.9	114.5	114.9	110.9	119.4	115.0	121.5	113.7
1985	113.2	113.5	101.8	118.6	118.2	122.2	118.3	113.5	128.9	111.9
1986	108.5	108.8	103.3	110.2	109.6	115.9	112.1	112.8	110.6	107.2
1987	111.5	111.6	104.7	113.7	113.2	117.9	114.4	110.0	113.5	109.8
1988	111.3	111.3	102.5	114.5	115.3	108.0	113.2	113.3	114.3	109.5
1989	104.2	104.1	103.1	103.8	105.1	91.6	105.4	104.7	91.7	102.5
1990	104.1	103.8	107.3	103.2	103.4	101.2	102.3	108.6	95.2	102.3
1991	109.1	109.2	102.4	113.9	114.4	109.6	108.8	111.2	104.5	107.7
1992	114.1	114.2	104.7	121.2	121.2	121.0	112.4	110.5	113.1	112.8
1993	113.7	114.0	104.7	119.9	120.1	118.0	112.1	114.5	108.4	112.7
1994	113.1	113.1	104.0	118.4	118.9	113.7	111.0	111.6	109.5	111.8
1995	109.3	110.9	105.0	113.9	114.0	112.4	109.8	114.1	107.7	109.7
1996	110.2	110.0	105.1	112.1	112.5	108.5	109.4	113.6	107.2	108.9
1997	109.1	109.3	103.5	110.5	111.3	102.6	110.7	112.9	110.4	108.2
1998	107.9	107.8	103.5	108.9	108.9	109.0	108.3	110.6	107.8	106.8
1999	107.6	107.6	102.8	108.1	108.5	104.3	109.3	113.4	109.1	106.7
2000	108.9	108.4	102.4	109.4	109.8	105.7	109.7	113.6	110.1	107.6
2001	108.1	108.3	102.8	108.4	108.7	106.8	110.2	111.6	109.3	107.5
2002	109.5	109.1	102.9	109.8	110.0	108.8	110.4	109.9	110.0	108.4
2003	110.6	110.0	102.5	112.7	112.8	112.1	109.5	108.3	111.0	109.3
2004	110.4	110.1	106.3	111.1	111.5	108.1	110.0	117.1	108.1	109.4
2005	111.0	110.2	105.2	111.7	111.6	112.6	110.0	111.7	107.8	109.6

3-4 国内生产总值指数

Indices of Gross Domestic Product

本表按可比价格计算。

Data in this table are calculated at constant prices.

(1978年=100) (year of 1978=100)

年份 Year	国民总收入 Gross National Income	国内生产总值 Gross Domestic Product	第一产业 Primary Industry	第二产业 Secondary Industry	工业 Industry	建筑业 Construction	第三产业 Tertiary Industry	#交通运输仓储和邮政业 Transport, Storage and Post	#批发与零售业 Wholesale and Retail Trades	人均国内生产总值 Per Capita GDP
1978	100.0	100.0	100.0	100.0	100.0	100.0	100.0	100.0	100.0	100.0
1979	107.6	107.6	106.1	108.2	108.7	102.0	107.8	107.7	108.8	106.1
1980	116.0	116.0	104.6	122.9	122.4	129.2	114.2	113.8	107.4	113.0
1981	122.0	122.1	111.9	125.2	124.5	133.3	126.2	116.0	139.6	117.5
1982	133.3	133.1	124.8	132.1	131.7	137.9	142.6	129.5	145.1	126.2
1983	148.2	147.6	135.1	145.8	144.5	161.4	164.3	142.5	176.8	137.9
1984	170.8	170.0	152.6	166.9	166.0	179.0	196.1	163.8	214.8	156.8
1985	193.4	192.9	155.4	197.9	196.2	218.7	231.9	185.9	276.8	175.5
1986	209.9	210.0	160.5	218.2	215.2	253.4	260.0	209.7	306.1	188.2
1987	234.1	234.3	168.1	248.1	243.6	298.7	297.4	230.7	347.3	206.6
1988	260.6	260.7	172.3	284.1	280.8	322.5	336.7	261.5	396.9	226.3
1989	271.4	271.3	177.6	294.8	295.0	295.3	354.8	273.8	363.8	231.9
1990	282.5	281.7	190.7	304.1	304.9	298.8	363.0	297.2	346.5	237.3
1991	308.2	307.6	195.2	346.3	348.8	327.4	395.0	330.5	362.1	255.6
1992	351.5	351.4	204.4	419.5	422.6	396.2	444.0	365.2	409.4	288.4
1993	399.6	400.4	214.0	502.8	507.5	467.5	497.9	418.3	443.9	324.9
1994	452.0	452.8	222.6	595.2	603.5	531.5	552.8	466.8	486.2	363.3
1995	494.2	502.3	233.7	677.7	688.2	597.4	607.1	532.7	523.7	398.6
1996	544.5	552.6	245.6	759.8	774.3	648.2	664.2	605.0	561.2	433.9
1997	593.8	603.9	254.2	839.4	861.9	665.2	735.1	682.8	619.4	469.4
1998	640.6	651.2	263.1	914.2	938.6	725.2	796.4	755.1	667.4	501.4
1999	689.2	700.9	270.5	988.6	1018.6	756.2	870.5	856.2	727.9	534.9
2000	750.6	759.9	277.0	1081.8	1118.3	799.1	955.1	973.0	801.3	575.5
2001	811.1	823.0	284.8	1173.1	1215.2	853.3	1052.6	1085.8	876.0	618.7
2002	888.5	897.8	293.0	1288.4	1336.4	928.3	1162.1	1193.3	963.5	670.4
2003	983.1	987.8	300.3	1451.7	1506.8	1040.4	1272.1	1292.3	1069.2	733.1
2004	1085.4	1087.4	319.3	1613.0	1680.2	1125.0	1399.8	1513.1	1156.1	802.2
2005	1204.4	1198.7	336.0	1801.6	1874.7	1266.9	1540.0	1690.4	1246.4	878.9

3-5 分行业增加值及构成（2004年）

Value-added and Composition by Sector (2004)

本表按当年价格计算。

Data in this table are calculated at current prices.

行业	Sector	增加值（亿元）Value-added (100 million yuan)	增加值构成（%）Composition of Value-added (%)
总　计	**Total**	**159878.3**	**100.0**
第一产业	**Primary Industry**	**21412.7**	**13.4**
农林牧渔业	Farming, Forestry, Animal Husbandry and Fishing	21412.7	13.4
第二产业	**Secondary Industry**	**73904.3**	**46.2**
工业	Industry	65210.0	40.8
采矿业	Mining	7628.3	4.8
制造业	Manufacturing	51748.5	32.4
电力、燃气及水的生产和供应业	Production and Supply of Electricity, Gas and Water	5833.3	3.6
建筑业	Construction	8694.3	5.4
第三产业	**Tertiary Industry**	**64561.3**	**40.4**
交通运输、仓储和邮政业	Transport, Storage and Post	9304.4	5.8
信息传输、计算机服务和软件业	Information Transmission, Computer Services and Software	4236.3	2.6
批发和零售业	Wholesale and Retail Trades	12453.8	7.8
住宿和餐饮业	Hotels and Catering Services	3664.8	2.3
金融业	Financial Intermediation	5393.0	3.4
房地产业	Real Estate	7174.1	4.5
租赁和商务服务业	Leasing and Business Services	2627.5	1.6
科学研究、技术服务和地质勘查业	Scientific Research, Technical Services and Geologic Prospecting	1759.5	1.1
水利、环境和公共设施管理业	Management of Water Conservancy, Environment and Public Facilities	768.6	0.5
居民服务和其他服务业	Services to Households and Other Services	2481.5	1.6
教育	Education	4892.6	3.1
卫生、社会保障和社会福利业	Health, Social Security and Social Welfare	2620.7	1.6
文化、体育和娱乐业	Culture, Sports and Entertainment	1043.2	0.7
公共管理和社会组织	Public Management and Social Organizations	6141.4	3.8

注：本表行业分类为按新国民经济行业分类（GB/T 4754-2002)划分，农林牧渔服务业包括在第一产业中。

a) This table uses the new Industrial Classification of National Economy (GB/T 4754-2002), services of farming, forestry, animal husbandry and fishery are included in the primary industry.

3-6 三次产业贡献率

Share of the Three Industries to the Increase of GDP

本表按可比价格计算。
Data in this table are calculated at constant prices.

单位：% (%)

年份 Year	国内生产总值 Gross Domestic Product	第一产业 Primary Industry	第二产业 Secondary Industry	#工业 Industry	第三产业 Tertiary Industry
1990	100.0	41.9	41.0	39.7	17.1
1991	100.0	7.1	62.8	58.0	30.1
1992	100.0	8.4	64.5	57.6	27.1
1993	100.0	7.8	65.5	59.1	26.7
1994	100.0	6.5	67.9	62.6	25.6
1995	100.0	9.0	64.3	58.5	26.7
1996	100.0	9.5	62.9	58.5	27.6
1997	100.0	6.7	59.7	58.3	33.6
1998	100.0	7.5	60.9	55.4	31.6
1999	100.0	5.9	57.8	55.0	36.3
2000	100.0	4.4	60.8	57.6	34.8
2001	100.0	5.0	46.7	42.1	48.3
2002	100.0	4.5	49.8	44.4	45.7
2003	100.0	3.3	58.5	51.9	38.2
2004	100.0	7.7	52.2	47.7	40.1
2005	100.0	6.3	54.7	47.9	39.0

注：产业贡献率指各产业增加值增量与GDP增量之比。
a) Share of the three industries refers to the proportion of the increment of every industrial value added to the increment of GDP.

3-7 三次产业对国内生产总值增长的拉动

Contribution of the Three Industries to GDP Growth

本表按可比价格计算。
Data in this table are calculated at constant prices.

单位：百分点 (percentage points)

年份 Year	国内生产总值 Gross Domestic Product	第一产业 Primary Industry	第二产业 Secondary Industry	#工业 Industry	第三产业 Tertiary Industry
1990	3.8	1.6	1.6	1.5	0.6
1991	9.2	0.6	5.8	5.3	2.8
1992	14.2	1.2	9.2	8.2	3.8
1993	14.0	1.1	9.2	8.3	3.7
1994	13.1	0.9	8.9	8.2	3.3
1995	10.9	1.0	7.0	6.4	2.9
1996	10.0	0.9	6.3	5.9	2.8
1997	9.3	0.6	5.6	5.4	3.1
1998	7.8	0.6	4.8	4.3	2.4
1999	7.6	0.4	4.4	4.2	2.8
2000	8.4	0.4	5.1	4.9	2.9
2001	8.3	0.4	3.9	3.5	4.0
2002	9.1	0.4	4.5	4.0	4.2
2003	10.0	0.3	5.9	5.2	3.8
2004	10.1	0.8	5.3	4.8	4.0
2005	10.2	0.6	5.6	4.9	4.0

注：产业拉动指GDP增长速度与各产业贡献率之乘积。
a) Contribution of the three industies to GDP growth refers to the growth rate of GDP multiplying the industrial shares.

3-8 地区生产总值和指数

Gross Regional Product and Indices

本表绝对数按当年价格计算，指数按可比价格计算。

Level figures in this table are calculated at current prices while that of indices are at constant prices.

地 区	Region	地区生产总值（亿元） Gross Regional Product (100 million yuan)					指 数（上年=100） Indices (preceding year=100)				
		2001	2002	2003	2004	2005	2001	2002	2003	2004	2005
北 京	Beijing	3710.52	4330.40	5023.77	6060.28	6886.31	111.7	111.5	111.0	114.1	111.8
天 津	Tianjin	1919.09	2150.76	2578.03	3110.97	3697.62	112.0	112.7	114.8	115.8	114.7
河 北	Hebei	5516.76	6018.28	6921.29	8477.63	10096.11	108.7	109.6	111.6	112.9	113.4
山 西	Shanxi	2029.53	2324.80	2855.23	3571.37	4179.52	110.1	112.9	114.9	115.2	112.6
内蒙古	Inner Mongolia	1713.81	1940.94	2388.38	3041.07	3895.55	110.6	113.2	117.6	120.9	123.8
辽 宁	Liaoning	5033.08	5458.22	6002.54	6672.00	8009.01	109.0	110.2	111.5	112.8	112.3
吉 林	Jilin	2120.35	2348.54	2662.08	3122.01	3620.27	109.3	109.5	110.2	112.2	112.1
黑龙江	Heilongjiang	3390.13	3637.20	4057.40	4750.60	5511.50	109.3	110.2	110.2	111.7	111.6
上 海	Shanghai	5210.12	5741.03	6694.23	8072.83	9154.18	110.5	111.3	112.3	114.2	111.1
江 苏	Jiangsu	9456.84	10606.85	12442.87	15003.60	18305.66	110.2	111.7	113.6	114.8	114.5
浙 江	Zhejiang	6898.34	8003.67	9705.02	11648.70	13437.85	110.6	112.6	114.7	114.5	112.8
安 徽	Anhui	3246.71	3519.72	3923.10	4759.32	5375.12	108.9	109.6	109.4	113.3	111.6
福 建	Fujian	4072.85	4467.55	4983.67	5763.35	6568.93	108.7	110.2	111.5	111.8	111.6
江 西	Jiangxi	2175.68	2450.48	2807.41	3456.70	4056.76	108.8	110.5	113.0	113.2	112.8
山 东	Shandong	9195.04	10275.50	12078.15	15021.84	18516.87	110.0	111.7	113.4	115.4	115.2
河 南	Henan	5533.01	6035.48	6867.70	8553.79	10587.42	109.0	109.5	110.7	113.7	114.2
湖 北	Hubei	3880.53	4212.82	4757.45	5633.24	6520.14	108.9	109.2	109.7	111.2	112.1
湖 南	Hunan	3831.90	4151.54	4659.99	5641.94	6511.34	109.0	109.0	109.6	112.1	111.6
广 东	Guangdong	12039.25	13502.42	15844.64	18864.62	22366.54	110.5	112.4	114.8	114.8	113.8
广 西	Guangxi	2279.34	2523.73	2821.11	3433.50	4075.75	108.3	110.6	110.2	111.8	113.2
海 南	Hainan	558.41	621.97	693.20	798.90	894.57	109.1	109.6	110.6	110.7	110.2
重 庆	Chongqing	1765.68	1990.01	2272.82	2692.81	3070.49	109.0	110.2	111.5	112.2	111.5
四 川	Sichuan	4293.49	4725.01	5333.09	6379.63	7385.11	109.0	110.3	111.3	112.7	112.6
贵 州	Guizhou	1133.27	1243.43	1426.34	1677.80	1979.06	108.8	109.1	110.1	111.4	111.6
云 南	Yunnan	2138.31	2312.82	2556.02	3081.91	3472.89	106.8	109.0	108.8	111.3	109.0
西 藏	Tibet	146.04	166.56	189.09	220.34	251.21	112.7	112.9	112.0	112.1	112.1
陕 西	Shaanxi	2010.62	2253.39	2587.72	3175.58	3675.66	109.8	111.1	111.8	112.9	112.6
甘 肃	Gansu	1125.37	1232.03	1399.83	1688.49	1933.98	109.8	109.9	110.7	111.5	111.8
青 海	Qinghai	300.13	340.65	390.20	466.10	543.32	111.7	112.1	111.9	112.3	112.2
宁 夏	Ningxia	337.44	377.16	445.36	537.16	606.10	110.1	110.2	112.7	111.2	110.9
新 疆	Xinjiang	1491.60	1612.65	1886.35	2209.09	2604.19	108.6	108.2	111.2	111.4	110.9

注：本表2001-2003年数据为经济普查后修订的数据。

a) Data from 2001 to 2003 were modified based on China Economic Census results in 2004.

3-9 地区生产总值（2005年）

Gross Regional Product (2005)

本表绝对数按当年价格计算，指数按可比价格计算。

Level figures in this table are calculated at current prices while indices are calculated at constant prices.

单位：亿元 (100 million yuan)

地 区	Region	地区生产总值 Gross Regional Product	第一产业 Primary Industry	第二产业 Secondary Industry	工 业 Industry	建筑业 Construction	第三产业 Tertiary Industry
北 京	Beijing	6886.31	97.99	2026.51	1707.04	319.47	4761.81
天 津	Tianjin	3697.62	112.38	2051.17	1885.04	166.13	1534.07
河 北	Hebei	10096.11	1503.07	5232.50	4665.21	567.29	3360.54
山 西	Shanxi	4179.52	262.42	2353.16	2117.68	235.48	1563.94
内蒙古	Inner Mongolia	3895.55	589.56	1773.21	1477.88	295.33	1532.78
辽 宁	Liaoning	8009.01	882.41	3953.28	3489.58	463.70	3173.32
吉 林	Jilin	3620.27	625.61	1580.83	1363.94	216.89	1413.83
黑龙江	Heilongjiang	5511.50	684.60	2971.68	2696.30	275.38	1855.22
上 海	Shanghai	9154.18	80.34	4452.92	4129.52	323.40	4620.92
江 苏	Jiangsu	18305.66	1461.49	10355.03	9334.69	1020.34	6489.14
浙 江	Zhejiang	13437.85	892.83	7166.15	6349.34	816.81	5378.87
安 徽	Anhui	5375.12	966.49	2221.17	1818.45	402.72	2187.46
福 建	Fujian	6568.93	841.20	3200.26	2842.43	357.83	2527.47
江 西	Jiangxi	4056.76	727.37	1917.47	1455.50	461.97	1411.92
山 东	Shandong	18516.87	1963.51	10628.62	9568.58	1060.04	5924.74
河 南	Henan	10587.42	1892.01	5514.14	4896.01	618.13	3181.27
湖 北	Hubei	6520.14	1082.13	2810.01	2436.55	373.46	2628.00
湖 南	Hunan	6511.34	1274.15	2596.71	2189.91	406.80	2640.48
广 东	Guangdong	22366.54	1428.27	11339.93	10482.03	857.90	9598.34
广 西	Guangxi	4075.75	912.50	1510.68	1264.84	245.84	1652.57
海 南	Hainan	894.57	300.75	220.07	156.16	63.91	373.75
重 庆	Chongqing	3070.49	463.40	1259.12	1023.35	235.77	1347.97
四 川	Sichuan	7385.11	1481.14	3067.23	2527.08	540.15	2836.74
贵 州	Guizhou	1979.06	368.94	826.63	714.24	112.39	783.49
云 南	Yunnan	3472.89	669.81	1432.76	1180.83	251.93	1370.32
西 藏	Tibet	251.21	48.04	63.52	17.48	46.04	139.65
陕 西	Shaanxi	3675.66	435.77	1849.28	1553.60	295.68	1390.61
甘 肃	Gansu	1933.98	308.06	838.56	685.80	152.76	787.36
青 海	Qinghai	543.32	65.34	264.61	203.94	60.67	213.37
宁 夏	Ningxia	606.10	72.08	281.23	229.07	52.16	252.79
新 疆	Xinjiang	2604.19	509.99	1164.79	961.61	203.18	929.41

3-9 续表 1 continued

单位：亿元 (100 million yuan)

地区	Region	交通运输、仓储和邮政业 Transport, Storage and Post	批发和零售业 Wholesale and Retail Trades	住宿和餐饮业 Hotels and Catering Services	金融业 Financial Intermediation	房地产业 Real Estate	其他服务业 Other Services
北　京	Beijing	404.66	654.09	182.81	836.62	455.31	2228.32
天　津	Tianjin	227.16	436.14	70.15	159.24	128.77	512.61
河　北	Hebei	702.00	598.56	115.22	211.17	291.51	1442.08
山　西	Shanxi	351.19	261.24	109.39	122.09	106.48	613.55
内蒙古	Inner Mongolia	360.19	338.12	140.11	67.52	98.32	528.52
辽　宁	Liaoning	509.37	850.33	178.84	212.72	243.99	1178.07
吉　林	Jilin	208.10	345.02	83.39	83.63	112.29	581.40
黑龙江	Heilongjiang	318.39	413.16	103.35	33.48	163.47	823.37
上　海	Shanghai	582.60	840.89	168.31	675.12	676.12	1677.88
江　苏	Jiangsu	741.06	1816.46	287.25	562.42	731.01	2350.94
浙　江	Zhejiang	512.94	1258.21	221.27	674.77	695.82	2015.86
安　徽	Anhui	358.71	397.70	99.25	112.86	219.19	999.75
福　建	Fujian	455.18	584.63	108.77	179.14	321.74	878.01
江　西	Jiangxi	300.60	288.52	67.11	69.55	171.88	514.26
山　东	Shandong	968.64	1387.22	441.26	467.59	653.66	2006.37
河　南	Henan	625.87	616.25	302.23	181.74	298.19	1156.99
湖　北	Hubei	365.71	575.37	155.45	127.32	217.17	1186.98
湖　南	Hunan	366.72	516.51	127.60	123.31	234.93	1271.41
广　东	Guangdong	990.53	2222.72	520.63	673.65	1456.14	3734.67
广　西	Guangxi	225.20	389.43	111.82	90.83	164.26	671.03
海　南	Hainan	64.34	91.67	27.55	12.44	33.61	144.14
重　庆	Chongqing	218.97	277.68	66.56	92.98	143.88	547.90
四　川	Sichuan	380.28	475.16	221.42	262.26	286.23	1211.39
贵　州	Guizhou	115.82	131.50	39.16	71.07	79.53	346.41
云　南	Yunnan	163.08	271.48	74.10	131.66	143.87	586.13
西　藏	Tibet	11.10	19.85	10.96	6.70	9.93	81.11
陕　西	Shaanxi	242.12	293.83	74.67	97.04	105.53	577.42
甘　肃	Gansu	144.70	130.78	53.53	44.73	63.78	349.84
青　海	Qinghai	31.88	35.63	9.38	20.36	14.10	102.02
宁　夏	Ningxia	45.81	38.65	11.33	32.00	22.61	102.39
新　疆	Xinjiang	149.63	145.10	45.70	80.34	55.79	452.85

3-9 续表 2 continued

单位: 亿元 (100 million yuan)

地区	Region	构成 (%) Composition (%)			指数 (上年=100) Indices (preceding year=100)				人均地区生产总值 (元/人) Per Capita Gross Regional Product (yuan/person)
		第一产业 Primary Industry	第二产业 Secondary Industry	第三产业 Tertiary Industry	地区生产总值 Gross Regional Product	第一产业 Primary Industry	第二产业 Secondary Industry	第三产业 Tertiary Industry	
北京	Beijing	1.4	29.5	69.1	111.8	99.2	110.1	113.0	45444
天津	Tianjin	3.0	55.5	41.5	114.7	104.3	117.6	111.7	35783
河北	Hebei	14.9	51.8	33.3	113.4	106.2	115.4	113.2	14782
山西	Shanxi	6.3	56.3	37.4	112.6	94.6	116.2	111.2	12495
内蒙古	Inner Mongolia	15.1	45.5	39.4	123.8	109.1	134.9	118.1	16331
辽宁	Liaoning	11.0	49.4	39.6	112.3	107.9	117.1	108.2	18983
吉林	Jilin	17.3	43.6	39.1	112.1	109.9	111.6	113.6	13348
黑龙江	Heilongjiang	12.4	53.9	33.7	111.6	108.7	112.6	110.8	14434
上海	Shanghai	0.9	48.6	50.5	111.1	91.1	111.5	111.1	51474
江苏	Jiangsu	8.0	56.6	35.4	114.5	102.9	116.0	114.9	24560
浙江	Zhejiang	6.6	53.4	40.0	112.8	101.5	112.7	115.2	27703
安徽	Anhui	18.0	41.3	40.7	111.6	101.7	117.1	110.8	8675
福建	Fujian	12.8	48.7	38.5	111.6	104.2	113.0	112.5	18646
江西	Jiangxi	17.9	47.3	34.8	112.8	106.5	117.1	110.8	9440
山东	Shandong	10.6	57.4	32.0	115.2	104.8	117.9	114.4	20096
河南	Henan	17.9	52.1	30.0	114.2	107.5	117.6	112.8	11346
湖北	Hubei	16.6	43.1	40.3	112.1	104.0	115.2	111.8	11431
湖南	Hunan	19.6	39.9	40.5	111.6	105.7	112.2	113.5	10426
广东	Guangdong	6.4	50.7	42.9	113.8	104.9	115.0	113.7	24435
广西	Guangxi	22.4	37.1	40.5	113.2	107.1	118.4	111.4	8788
海南	Hainan	33.6	24.6	41.8	110.2	106.0	116.9	110.2	10871
重庆	Chongqing	15.1	41.0	43.9	111.5	104.5	112.9	112.3	10982
四川	Sichuan	20.1	41.5	38.4	112.6	105.4	118.0	110.6	9060
贵州	Guizhou	18.6	41.8	39.6	111.6	105.2	112.7	114.0	5052
云南	Yunnan	19.3	41.2	39.5	109.0	106.1	108.1	111.4	7835
西藏	Tibet	19.1	25.3	55.6	112.1	105.5	123.6	109.7	9114
陕西	Shaanxi	11.9	50.3	37.8	112.6	107.7	115.8	110.1	9899
甘肃	Gansu	15.9	43.4	40.7	111.8	105.9	113.2	112.8	7477
青海	Qinghai	12.0	48.7	39.3	112.2	105.0	115.9	110.2	10045
宁夏	Ningxia	11.9	46.4	41.7	110.9	103.2	115.3	108.9	10239
新疆	Xinjiang	19.6	44.7	35.7	110.9	106.5	114.4	109.4	13108

3-10 地区生产总值项目结构（2005年）

Components of Gross Regional Product (2005)

本表按当年价格计算。
Data in this table are calculated at current prices.

单位：亿元 (100 million yuan)

地 区	Region	地区生产总值 Gross Regional Product	劳动者报酬 Compensation of Employees	固定资产折旧 Depreciation of Fixed Assets	生产税净额 Net Taxes on Production	营业盈余 Operating Surplus
北 京	Beijing	6886.31	3114.15	1095.51	1017.05	1659.60
天 津	Tianjin	3697.62	1164.82	515.77	727.37	1289.66
河 北	Hebei	10096.11	4160.01	1254.97	1316.07	3365.06
山 西	Shanxi	4179.52	1496.72	634.89	644.88	1403.03
内蒙古	Inner Mongolia	3895.55	1599.46	544.87	433.21	1318.01
辽 宁	Liaoning	8009.01	3524.91	1288.09	1267.61	1928.40
吉 林	Jilin	3620.27	1618.66	617.51	521.94	862.16
黑龙江	Heilongjiang	5511.50	1950.04	733.35	781.01	2047.10
上 海	Shanghai	9154.18	3269.38	1501.79	1418.96	2964.05
江 苏	Jiangsu	18305.66	7493.67	2960.06	2581.57	5270.36
浙 江	Zhejiang	13437.85	5337.16	1905.37	1909.16	4286.16
安 徽	Anhui	5375.12	2435.13	738.25	747.62	1454.12
福 建	Fujian	6568.93	2890.90	919.33	866.05	1892.65
江 西	Jiangxi	4056.76	1845.67	488.88	502.26	1219.95
山 东	Shandong	18516.87	6529.10	2940.02	2637.77	6409.98
河 南	Henan	10587.42	4691.11	1220.15	1270.84	3405.32
湖 北	Hubei	6520.14	2923.57	1098.99	970.00	1527.58
湖 南	Hunan	6511.34	2939.66	847.17	836.65	1887.86
广 东	Guangdong	22366.54	8832.24	3585.19	3040.37	6908.74
广 西	Guangxi	4075.75	2018.82	496.15	418.47	1142.31
海 南	Hainan	894.57	441.07	142.46	104.56	206.48
重 庆	Chongqing	3070.49	1504.53	376.54	375.70	813.72
四 川	Sichuan	7385.11	3429.66	1246.35	1023.94	1685.16
贵 州	Guizhou	1979.06	914.99	290.33	290.62	483.12
云 南	Yunnan	3472.89	1611.50	512.76	697.73	650.90
西 藏	Tibet	251.21	130.71	57.56	18.19	44.75
陕 西	Shaanxi	3675.66	1510.30	610.93	571.50	982.93
甘 肃	Gansu	1933.98	694.02	300.29	482.87	456.80
青 海	Qinghai	543.32	258.53	102.17	64.53	118.09
宁 夏	Ningxia	606.10	291.91	122.71	78.89	112.59
新 疆	Xinjiang	2604.19	1265.62	373.58	301.82	663.17

3-11 支出法国内生产总值

Gross Domestic Product by Expenditure Approach

本表按当年价格计算。

Data in value terms in this table are calculated at current prices.

年份 Year	支出法国内生产总值(亿元) Gross Domestic Product by Expenditure Approach (100 million yuan)	最终消费支出 Final Consumption Expenditures	资本形成总额 Gross Capital Formation	货物和服务净出口 Net Exports of Goods and Services	资本形成率(投资率)(%) Capital Formation Rate (%)	最终消费率(消费率)(%) Final Consumption Rate (%)
1978	3605.6	2239.1	1377.9	-11.4	38.2	62.1
1979	4092.6	2633.7	1478.9	-20.0	36.1	64.4
1980	4592.9	3007.9	1599.7	-14.7	34.8	65.5
1981	5008.8	3361.5	1630.2	17.1	32.5	67.1
1982	5590.0	3714.8	1784.2	91.0	31.9	66.5
1983	6216.2	4126.4	2039.0	50.8	32.8	66.4
1984	7362.7	4846.3	2515.1	1.3	34.2	65.8
1985	9076.7	5986.3	3457.5	-367.1	38.1	66.0
1986	10508.5	6821.8	3941.9	-255.2	37.5	64.9
1987	12277.4	7804.6	4462.0	10.8	36.3	63.6
1988	15388.6	9839.5	5700.2	-151.1	37.0	63.9
1989	17311.3	11164.2	6332.7	-185.6	36.6	64.5
1990	19347.8	12090.5	6747.0	510.3	34.9	62.5
1991	22577.4	14091.9	7868.0	617.5	34.8	62.4
1992	27565.2	17203.3	10086.3	275.6	36.6	62.4
1993	36938.1	21899.9	15717.7	-679.5	42.6	59.3
1994	50217.4	29242.2	20341.1	634.1	40.5	58.2
1995	63216.9	36748.2	25470.1	998.6	40.3	58.1
1996	74163.6	43919.5	28784.9	1459.2	38.8	59.2
1997	81658.5	48140.6	29968.0	3549.9	36.7	59.0
1998	86531.6	51588.2	31314.2	3629.2	36.2	59.6
1999	90964.1	55636.9	32951.5	2375.7	36.2	61.2
2000	98749.0	61516.0	34842.8	2390.2	35.3	62.3
2001	108972.4	66878.3	39769.4	2324.7	36.5	61.4
2002	120350.3	71691.2	45565.0	3094.1	37.9	59.6
2003	136398.8	77449.5	55963.0	2986.3	41.0	56.8
2004	160280.4	87032.9	69168.4	4079.1	43.2	54.3
2005	186700.9	96918.1	79559.8	10223.0	42.6	51.9

注：支出法国内生产总值不等于国内生产总值是由于计算误差的影响。

a) The gross domestic production by expenditure approach is not equal to gross domestic product due to statistical discrepancies.

3-12 支出法国内生产总值结构

Components of Gross Domestic Product by Expenditure Approach

本表按当年价格计算。

Data in value terms in this table are calculated at current prices.

年份 Year	最终消费支出 Final Consumption Expenditures								资本形成总额 Gross Capital Formation			
	绝对数（亿元） Absolute Figure (100 million yuan)				构成 Composition				绝对数（亿元） Absolute Figure (100 million yuan)		构成（资本形成总额=100） Composition (Gross Capital Formation=100)	
					最终消费支出=100 Final Consumption Expenditures=100		居民消费支出=100 Household Consumption Expenditures=100					
	居民消费支出 Household Consumption Expenditures	农村居民 Rural Household	城镇居民 Urban Household	政府消费支出 Government Consumption Expenditures	居民消费支出 Household Consumption Expenditures	政府消费支出 Government Consumption Expenditures	农村居民 Rural Household	城镇居民 Urban Household	固定资本形成总额 Gross Fixed Capital Formation	存货增加 Change in Inventories	固定资本形成总额 Gross Fixed Capital Formation	存货增加 Change in Inventories
1978	1759.1	1092.4	666.7	480.0	78.6	21.4	62.1	37.9	1073.9	304.0	77.9	22.1
1979	2011.5	1252.9	758.6	622.2	76.4	23.6	62.3	37.7	1153.1	325.8	78.0	22.0
1980	2331.2	1411.0	920.2	676.7	77.5	22.5	60.5	39.5	1322.4	277.3	82.7	17.3
1981	2627.9	1603.8	1024.1	733.6	78.2	21.8	61.0	39.0	1339.3	290.9	82.2	17.8
1982	2902.9	1787.5	1115.4	811.9	78.1	21.9	61.6	38.4	1503.2	281.0	84.3	15.7
1983	3231.1	2010.5	1220.6	895.3	78.3	21.7	62.2	37.8	1723.3	315.7	84.5	15.5
1984	3742.0	2312.1	1429.9	1104.3	77.2	22.8	61.8	38.2	2147.0	368.1	85.4	14.6
1985	4687.4	2809.6	1877.8	1298.9	78.3	21.7	59.9	40.1	2672.0	785.5	77.3	22.7
1986	5302.1	3059.2	2242.9	1519.7	77.7	22.3	57.7	42.3	3139.7	802.2	79.6	20.4
1987	6126.1	3428.9	2697.2	1678.5	78.5	21.5	56.0	44.0	3798.7	663.3	85.1	14.9
1988	7868.1	4174.0	3694.1	1971.4	80.0	20.0	53.0	47.0	4701.9	998.3	82.5	17.5
1989	8812.6	4545.7	4266.9	2351.6	78.9	21.1	51.6	48.4	4419.4	1913.3	69.8	30.2
1990	9450.9	4683.1	4767.8	2639.6	78.2	21.8	49.6	50.4	4827.8	1919.2	71.6	28.4
1991	10730.6	5082.0	5648.6	3361.3	76.1	23.9	47.4	52.6	6070.3	1797.7	77.2	22.8
1992	13000.1	5833.5	7166.6	4203.2	75.6	24.4	44.9	55.1	8513.7	1572.6	84.4	15.6
1993	16412.1	6858.0	9554.1	5487.8	74.9	25.1	41.8	58.2	13309.2	2408.5	84.7	15.3
1994	21844.2	8875.3	12968.9	7398.0	74.7	25.3	40.6	59.4	17312.7	3028.4	85.1	14.9
1995	28369.7	11271.6	17098.1	8378.5	77.2	22.8	39.7	60.3	20885.0	4585.1	82.0	18.0
1996	33955.9	13907.1	20048.8	9963.6	77.3	22.7	41.0	59.0	24048.1	4736.8	83.5	16.5
1997	36921.5	14575.8	22345.7	11219.1	76.7	23.3	39.5	60.5	25965.0	4003.0	86.6	13.4
1998	39229.3	14472.0	24757.3	12358.9	76.0	24.0	36.9	63.1	28569.0	2745.2	91.2	8.8
1999	41920.4	14584.1	27336.3	13716.5	75.3	24.7	34.8	65.2	30527.3	2424.2	92.6	7.4
2000	45854.6	15147.4	30707.2	15661.4	74.5	25.5	33.0	67.0	33844.4	998.4	97.1	2.9
2001	49213.2	15791.0	33422.2	17665.1	73.6	26.4	32.1	67.9	37754.5	2014.9	94.9	5.1
2002	52571.3	16271.7	36299.6	19119.9	73.3	26.7	31.0	69.0	43632.1	1932.9	95.8	4.2
2003	56834.4	16305.7	40528.7	20615.1	73.4	26.6	28.7	71.3	53490.7	2472.3	95.6	4.4
2004	63833.5	17550.6	46282.9	23199.4	73.3	26.7	27.5	72.5	65117.7	4050.7	94.1	5.9
2005	70906.0	19014.1	51891.9	26012.1	73.2	26.8	26.8	73.2	77464.4	2095.4	97.4	2.6

3-13　三大需求对国内生产总值增长的贡献率和拉动

Share and Contribution of the Three Components of GDP by Expenditure Approach to the Growth of GDP

本表按可比价格计算。
Data in value terms in this table are calculated at constant prices.

年　份 Year	最终消费支出 Final Consumption Expenditure		资本形成总额 Gross Capital Formation		货物和服务净出口 Net Exports of Goods and Services	
	贡献率 (%) Share (%)	拉　动 (百分点) Contribution (percentage points)	贡献率 (%) Share (%)	拉　动 (百分点) Contribution (percentage points)	贡献率 (%) Share (%)	拉　动 (百分点) Contribution (percentage points)
1978	39.4	4.6	66.0	7.7	-5.4	-0.6
1979	87.3	6.6	15.4	1.2	-2.7	-0.2
1980	71.8	5.6	26.5	2.1	1.8	0.1
1981	93.4	4.9	-4.3	-0.2	10.9	0.6
1982	64.7	5.9	23.8	2.2	11.5	1.0
1983	74.1	8.1	40.4	4.4	-14.5	-1.6
1984	69.3	10.5	40.5	6.2	-9.8	-1.5
1985	85.5	11.5	80.9	10.9	-66.4	-9.0
1986	45.0	4.0	23.2	2.0	31.8	2.8
1987	50.2	5.8	23.5	2.7	26.2	3.0
1988	49.6	5.6	39.4	4.5	11.0	1.2
1989	39.6	1.6	16.4	0.7	44.0	1.8
1990	47.8	1.8	1.8	0.1	50.3	1.9
1991	65.1	6.0	24.3	2.2	10.5	1.0
1992	72.5	10.3	34.2	4.9	-6.7	-1.0
1993	59.5	8.3	78.6	11.0	-38.1	-5.3
1994	30.2	4.0	43.8	5.7	25.9	3.4
1995	44.7	4.9	55.0	6.0	0.3	
1996	60.1	6.0	34.3	3.4	5.6	0.6
1997	37.0	3.4	-7.4	-0.7	70.4	6.5
1998	57.1	4.4	29.3	2.3	13.6	1.1
1999	76.8	5.8	52.8	4.0	-29.6	-2.2
2000	63.8	5.4	21.7	1.8	14.4	1.2
2001	50.0	4.1	50.1	4.2	-0.1	
2002	43.6	4.0	48.8	4.4	7.6	0.7
2003	35.3	3.5	63.7	6.4	1.0	0.1
2004	38.7	3.9	55.3	5.6	6.1	0.6
2005	36.1	3.7	38.1	3.9	25.8	2.6

注：1.三大需求指支出法国内生产总值的三大构成项目，即最终消费支出、资本形成总额、货物和服务净出口。
2.贡献率指三大需求增量与支出法国内生产总值增量之比。
3.拉动指国内生产总值增长速度与三大需求贡献率的乘积。

a) Three components of GDP by expenditure approach are final consumption expenditure,gross capital formation and net exports of goods and services
b) Share of the three components refers to the proportion of the increment of the three components of GDP to the increment of GDP.
c) Contribution of the three components refers to the growth rate of GDP multiplies the share of the three components.

3-14 支出法地区生产总值（2005年）

Gross Regional Product by Expenditure Approach (2005)

本表按当年价格计算。

Data in value terms in this table are calculated at current prices.

地区	Region	支出法地区生产总值（亿元）Gross Regional Product by Expenditure Approach (100 million yuan)	最终消费支出 Final Consumption Expenditures	资本形成总额 Gross Capital Formation	货物和服务净流出 Net Outflow of Goods and Services	资本形成率（投资率）(%) Capital Formation Rate (%)	最终消费率（消费率）(%) Final Consumption Rate (%)
北京	Beijing	6886.31	3539.49	3580.89	-234.07	52.0	51.4
天津	Tianjin	3697.62	1506.91	1968.45	222.26	53.2	40.8
河北	Hebei	10096.11	4315.20	4628.48	1152.43	45.8	42.7
山西	Shanxi	4103.32	1955.19	2178.45	-30.32	53.1	47.6
内蒙古	Inner Mongolia	3895.55	1713.92	2845.06	-663.43	73.0	44.0
辽宁	Liaoning	8009.01	3822.95	4006.64	179.42	50.0	47.7
吉林	Jilin	3687.40	1906.19	1813.37	-32.16	49.2	51.7
黑龙江	Heilongjiang	5511.50	2660.75	1958.70	892.05	35.5	48.3
上海	Shanghai	9154.18	4418.99	4186.86	548.33	45.7	48.3
江苏	Jiangsu	18305.66	7538.04	9313.16	1454.46	50.9	41.2
浙江	Zhejiang	13437.85	6373.24	6448.72	615.89	48.0	47.4
安徽	Anhui	5375.12	3020.70	2365.01	-10.59	44.0	56.2
福建	Fujian	6568.93	3295.55	2943.65	329.73	44.8	50.2
江西	Jiangxi	4061.76	2117.30	1981.98	-37.52	48.8	52.1
山东	Shandong	18516.87	7954.47	9283.69	1278.71	50.1	43.0
河南	Henan	10587.42	5353.67	5019.81	213.94	47.4	50.6
湖北	Hubei	6520.14	3645.71	2943.58	-69.15	45.1	55.9
湖南	Hunan	6511.34	4036.74	2575.03	-100.43	39.5	62.0
广东	Guangdong	22366.54	11533.44	8383.17	2449.93	37.5	51.6
广西	Guangxi	4075.75	2477.08	1747.42	-148.75	42.9	60.8
海南	Hainan	894.57	468.71	424.33	1.53	47.4	52.4
重庆	Chongqing	3149.10	1803.43	1939.77	-594.10	61.6	57.3
四川	Sichuan	7385.11	4357.69	3326.22	-298.80	45.0	59.0
贵州	Guizhou	1979.06	1627.27	1024.94	-673.15	51.8	82.2
云南	Yunnan	3472.89	2321.75	1989.93	-838.79	57.3	66.9
西藏	Tibet	251.21	184.72	184.14	-117.65	73.3	73.5
陕西	Shaanxi	3675.65	1684.12	2112.14	-120.61	57.5	45.8
甘肃	Gansu	1933.98	1217.63	916.96	-200.61	47.4	63.0
青海	Qinghai	543.32	360.72	369.28	-186.68	68.0	66.4
宁夏	Ningxia	606.10	390.92	475.96	-260.78	78.5	64.5
新疆	Xinjiang	2604.14	1266.52	1606.80	-269.18	61.7	48.6

3-15 各地区资本形成总额及构成（2005年）

Gross Capital Formation and Its Composition by Region (2005)

本表按当年价格计算。

Data in value terms in this table are calculated at current prices.

地区	Region	资本形成总额（亿元） Gross Capital Formation (100 million yuan)	固定资本形成总额 Gross Fixed Capital Formation	存货增加 Change in Inventories	构成（资本形成总额=100） Composition (Total=100) 固定资本形成总额 Gross Fixed Capital Formation	存货增加 Change in Inventories
北京	Beijing	3580.89	3204.65	376.24	89.5	10.5
天津	Tianjin	1968.45	1753.92	214.53	89.1	10.9
河北	Hebei	4628.48	4239.12	389.36	91.6	8.4
山西	Shanxi	2178.45	1897.39	281.06	87.1	12.9
内蒙古	Inner Mongolia	2845.06	2685.22	159.84	94.4	5.6
辽宁	Liaoning	4006.64	3705.99	300.65	92.5	7.5
吉林	Jilin	1813.37	1743.66	69.71	96.2	3.8
黑龙江	Heilongjiang	1958.70	1788.67	170.03	91.3	8.7
上海	Shanghai	4186.86	3743.42	443.44	89.4	10.6
江苏	Jiangsu	9313.16	8739.71	573.45	93.8	6.2
浙江	Zhejiang	6448.72	6269.16	179.56	97.2	2.8
安徽	Anhui	2365.01	2224.31	140.70	94.1	5.9
福建	Fujian	2943.65	2654.95	288.70	90.2	9.8
江西	Jiangxi	1981.98	1922.10	59.88	97.0	3.0
山东	Shandong	9283.69	8798.79	484.90	94.8	5.2
河南	Henan	5019.81	4506.75	513.06	89.8	10.2
湖北	Hubei	2943.58	2804.01	139.57	95.3	4.7
湖南	Hunan	2575.03	2569.24	5.79	99.8	0.2
广东	Guangdong	8383.17	7407.54	975.63	88.4	11.6
广西	Guangxi	1747.42	1699.04	48.38	97.2	2.8
海南	Hainan	424.33	363.37	60.96	85.6	14.4
重庆	Chongqing	1939.77	1862.65	77.12	96.0	4.0
四川	Sichuan	3326.22	3179.92	146.30	95.6	4.4
贵州	Guizhou	1024.94	996.24	28.70	97.2	2.8
云南	Yunnan	1989.93	1755.30	234.63	88.2	11.8
西藏	Tibet	184.14	196.19	-12.05	106.5	-6.5
陕西	Shaanxi	2112.14	2035.20	76.94	96.4	3.6
甘肃	Gansu	916.96	874.52	42.44	95.4	4.6
青海	Qinghai	369.28	364.08	5.20	98.6	1.4
宁夏	Ningxia	475.96	444.82	31.14	93.5	6.5
新疆	Xinjiang	1606.80	1485.17	121.63	92.4	7.6

3-16 各地区最终消费支出及构成（2005年）

Final Consumption Expenditure and Its Composition by Region (2005)

本表按当年价格计算。
Data in value terms in this table are calculated at current prices.

地区	Region	最终消费支出（亿元）Final Consumption Expenditures (100 million yuan)	居民消费支出 Household Consumption	居民消费支出：农村居民 Rural Household	居民消费支出：城镇居民 Urban Household	政府消费支出 Government Consumption	最终消费支出=100 Final Consumption Expenditures=100：居民消费支出 Household Consumption	最终消费支出=100 Final Consumption Expenditures=100：政府消费支出 Government Consumption	居民消费支出=100 Household Consumption Expenditures=100：农村居民 Rural Household	居民消费支出=100 Household Consumption Expenditures=100：城镇居民 Urban Household
北京	Beijing	3539.49	2248.02	184.92	2063.10	1291.47	63.5	36.5	8.2	91.8
天津	Tianjin	1506.91	980.05	122.32	857.73	526.86	65.0	35.0	12.5	87.5
河北	Hebei	4315.20	2944.38	1104.42	1839.96	1370.82	68.2	31.8	37.5	62.5
山西	Shanxi	1955.19	1395.73	424.39	971.34	559.46	71.4	28.6	30.4	69.6
内蒙古	Inner Mongolia	1713.92	1102.15	313.75	788.40	611.77	64.3	35.7	28.5	71.5
辽宁	Liaoning	3822.95	2720.95	569.28	2151.67	1102.00	71.2	28.8	20.9	79.1
吉林	Jilin	1906.19	1392.42	318.40	1074.02	513.77	73.0	27.0	22.9	77.1
黑龙江	Heilongjiang	2660.75	1841.27	434.72	1406.55	819.48	69.2	30.8	23.6	76.4
上海	Shanghai	4418.99	3271.64	184.02	3087.62	1147.35	74.0	26.0	5.6	94.4
江苏	Jiangsu	7538.04	5339.09	1588.27	3750.82	2198.95	70.8	29.2	29.7	70.3
浙江	Zhejiang	6373.24	4705.79	1354.46	3351.33	1667.45	73.8	26.2	28.8	71.2
安徽	Anhui	3020.70	2410.57	884.28	1526.29	610.13	79.8	20.2	36.7	63.3
福建	Fujian	3295.55	2393.17	700.94	1692.23	902.38	72.6	27.4	29.3	70.7
江西	Jiangxi	2117.30	1642.20	816.84	825.36	475.10	77.6	22.4	49.7	50.3
山东	Shandong	7954.47	5435.38	1580.90	3854.48	2519.09	68.3	31.7	29.1	70.9
河南	Henan	5353.67	3817.86	1554.22	2263.64	1535.81	71.3	28.7	40.7	59.3
湖北	Hubei	3645.71	2785.42	815.32	1970.10	860.29	76.4	23.6	29.3	70.7
湖南	Hunan	4036.74	3056.07	1136.41	1919.66	980.67	75.7	24.3	37.2	62.8
广东	Guangdong	11533.44	8989.70	1419.88	7569.82	2543.74	77.9	22.1	15.8	84.2
广西	Guangxi	2477.08	1822.03	738.97	1083.06	655.05	73.6	26.4	40.6	59.4
海南	Hainan	468.71	341.06	126.43	214.63	127.65	72.8	27.2	37.1	62.9
重庆	Chongqing	1803.43	1336.96	350.13	986.83	466.47	74.1	25.9	26.2	73.8
四川	Sichuan	4357.69	3366.47	1328.28	2038.19	991.22	77.3	22.7	39.5	60.5
贵州	Guizhou	1627.27	1230.07	449.45	780.62	397.20	75.6	24.4	36.5	63.5
云南	Yunnan	2321.75	1661.64	603.77	1057.87	660.11	71.6	28.4	36.3	63.7
西藏	Tibet	184.72	83.22	33.87	49.35	101.50	45.1	54.9	40.7	59.3
陕西	Shaanxi	1684.12	1334.48	561.33	773.15	349.64	79.2	20.8	42.1	57.9
甘肃	Gansu	1217.63	893.15	331.22	561.93	324.48	73.4	26.6	37.1	62.9
青海	Qinghai	360.72	210.29	64.15	146.14	150.43	58.3	41.7	30.5	69.5
宁夏	Ningxia	390.92	261.23	77.34	183.89	129.69	66.8	33.2	29.6	70.4
新疆	Xinjiang	1266.52	764.26	238.98	525.28	502.26	60.3	39.7	31.3	68.7

3-17 居民消费水平

Household Consumption Expenditure

本表绝对数按当年价格计算，指数按可比价格计算。

Absolute figures in this table are calculated at current prices, while indices are calculated at constant prices.

年份 Year	绝对数(元) Value (yuan) 全国居民 All Households	农村居民 Rural Household	城镇居民 Urban Household	城乡消费水平对比(农村居民=1) Urban/Rural Consumption Ratio (Urban Household=1)	指数（上年=100） Index (Preceding Year=100) 全国居民 All Households	农村居民 Rural Household	城镇居民 Urban Household	指数(1978=100) Index (1978=100) 全国居民 All Households	农村居民 Rural Household	城镇居民 Urban Household
1978	184	138	405	2.9	104.1	104.3	103.3	100.0	100.0	100.0
1979	208	159	425	2.7	106.9	106.5	102.8	106.9	106.5	102.8
1980	238	178	489	2.7	109.0	108.4	107.2	116.5	115.4	110.2
1981	264	201	521	2.6	108.3	109.8	104.0	126.2	126.8	114.6
1982	288	223	536	2.4	106.8	109.1	100.7	134.8	138.3	115.4
1983	316	250	558	2.2	108.1	110.6	102.1	145.8	153.1	117.9
1984	361	287	618	2.2	112.0	112.9	107.9	163.2	172.8	127.2
1985	446	349	765	2.2	113.5	113.3	111.1	185.2	195.7	141.3
1986	497	378	872	2.3	104.7	102.3	106.7	194.0	200.3	150.8
1987	565	421	998	2.4	106.0	104.9	105.6	205.5	210.0	159.3
1988	714	509	1311	2.6	107.8	105.2	109.7	221.5	221.0	174.7
1989	788	549	1466	2.7	99.8	98.3	100.7	221.0	217.2	176.0
1990	833	560	1596	2.9	103.7	99.2	108.5	229.2	215.4	190.9
1991	932	602	1840	3.1	108.6	105.4	110.7	249.0	227.1	211.4
1992	1116	688	2262	3.3	113.3	108.5	116.1	282.0	246.5	245.3
1993	1393	805	2924	3.6	108.4	104.3	110.4	305.8	257.1	270.8
1994	1833	1038	3852	3.7	104.6	103.1	104.4	320.0	265.0	282.8
1995	2355	1313	4931	3.8	107.8	106.8	107.2	345.1	282.9	303.2
1996	2789	1626	5532	3.4	109.4	114.5	103.4	377.6	323.8	313.6
1997	3002	1722	5823	3.4	104.5	103.1	102.2	394.6	334.0	320.4
1998	3159	1730	6109	3.5	105.9	101.2	105.9	417.8	338.1	339.2
1999	3346	1766	6405	3.6	108.3	105.1	107.0	452.3	355.3	363.0
2000	3632	1860	6850	3.7	108.6	104.5	107.8	491.0	371.3	391.1
2001	3869	1969	7113	3.6	105.7	104.5	103.2	518.8	388.0	403.6
2002	4106	2062	7387	3.6	106.5	105.2	104.2	552.5	408.1	420.5
2003	4411	2103	7901	3.8	106.5	100.3	106.3	588.5	409.5	447.2
2004	4925	2301	8679	3.8	107.4	103.4	106.4	632.3	423.5	475.7
2005	5439	2531	9393	3.7	107.7	106.5	105.8	681.0	451.0	503.3

注：城乡消费水平对比，没有剔除城乡价格不可比的因素（下表同）。

a) The effect of price differentials between urban and rural areas has not been removed in the calculation of the urban/rural consumption ratio. The same as in the following table.

3-18 各地区居民消费水平（2005年）
Household Consumption Expenditure by Region (2005)

本表绝对数按当年价格计算，指数按可比价格计算。
Absolute figures in this table are calculated at current prices, while indices are calculated at constant prices.

地 区	Region	绝对数(元) Value (yuan) 全国居民 All Households	农村居民 Rural Household	城镇居民 Urban Household	城乡消费水平对比（农村居民=1）Urban/Rural Consumption Ratio (Urban Household=1)	指数（上年=100）Index (Preceding Year=100) 全国居民 All Households	农村居民 Rural Household	城镇居民 Urban Household
北 京	Beijing	14835	6635	16683	2.5	106.8	106.1	105.0
天 津	Tianjin	9484	4360	11394	2.6	109.4	105.9	109.6
河 北	Hebei	4311	2449	7927	3.2	110.2	109.8	106.8
山 西	Shanxi	4172	2146	7104	3.3	109.8	109.4	106.9
内蒙古	Inner Mongolia	4620	2460	7103	2.9	111.6	114.6	108.5
辽 宁	Liaoning	6449	3267	8688	2.7	111.3	113.7	107.3
吉 林	Jilin	5135	2467	7556	3.1	110.0	113.3	108.5
黑龙江	Heilongjiang	4822	2419	6958	2.9	112.1	121.2	109.4
上 海	Shanghai	18396	9157	19573	2.1	110.0	116.0	107.8
江 苏	Jiangsu	7163	4207	10199	2.4	113.7	110.2	112.5
浙 江	Zhejiang	9701	5476	14097	2.6	115.9	110.4	116.3
安 徽	Anhui	3888	2177	7136	3.3	110.4	110.4	106.3
福 建	Fujian	6793	3730	10296	2.8	108.5	109.1	106.6
江 西	Jiangxi	3821	2576	7329	2.8	109.6	108.1	109.5
山 东	Shandong	5899	3078	9453	3.1	115.2	113.0	113.2
河 南	Henan	4092	2372	8145	3.4	107.7	105.1	105.2
湖 北	Hubei	4883	2503	8051	3.2	110.6	114.1	108.2
湖 南	Hunan	4894	2855	8477	3.0	111.6	110.3	108.5
广 东	Guangdong	9821	3947	13624	3.5	110.3	114.1	108.7
广 西	Guangxi	3928	2366	7149	3.0	115.7	120.4	107.2
海 南	Hainan	4145	2458	6955	2.8	106.2	107.2	103.9
重 庆	Chongqing	4782	2251	7959	3.5	111.4	112.1	108.6
四 川	Sichuan	4130	2432	7577	3.1	111.0	111.0	106.8
贵 州	Guizhou	3140	1563	7498	4.8	114.7	115.4	110.8
云 南	Yunnan	3749	1913	8285	4.3	110.8	115.3	104.0
西 藏	Tibet	3019	1532	9040	5.9	102.7	106.7	100.1
陕 西	Shaanxi	3594	2024	8234	4.1	109.6	114.0	105.6
甘 肃	Gansu	3453	1812	7410	4.1	109.6	112.7	104.1
青 海	Qinghai	3888	1941	6947	3.6	114.0	125.3	108.6
宁 夏	Ningxia	4413	2231	7495	3.4	113.0	109.5	109.3
新 疆	Xinjiang	3847	1884	7311	3.9	110.7	113.5	106.3

3-19 国际收支平衡表(2005年)
Balance of Payments (2005)

单位：万美元 (USD 10 000)

项目	Type of Transaction	差额 Balance	贷方 Credit	借方 Debit
一.经常项目	**Current Account**	**16081831**	**90358179**	**74276348**
A.货物和服务	Goods and Services	12479770	83688783	71209013
a.货物	Goods	13418910	76248373	62829464
b.服务	Services	-939139	7440410	8379549
1.运输	Transportation	-1302102	1542652	2844755
2.旅游	Travel	753693	2929600	2175907
3.通讯服务	Communication Service	-11817	48523	60340
4.建筑服务	Construction Service	97357	259295	161938
5.保险服务	Insurance Service	-665014	54942	719956
6.金融服务	Financial Service	-1424	14523	15948
7.计算机和信息服务	Computer and Information Service	21768	184018	162251
8.专有权利使用费和特许费	Fees for Patent or Royalty	-516385	15740	532125
9.咨询	Consultation	-86141	532213	618354
10.广告、宣传	Advertisement and Publicity	36052	107573	71521
11.电影、音像	Movies and Audio-video Products	-2010	13386	15395
12.其它商业服务	Other Commercial Service	749703	1688478	938775
13. 别处未提及的政府服务	Government Service not Elsewhere Classified	-12818	49466	62284
B.收益	Income and Profit	1063514	3895910	2832396
1.职工报酬	Compensation of Staff and Workers	151965	333706	181741
2.投资收益	Profit from Investment	911549	3562204	2650655
C.经常转移	Current Transfers	2538547	2773486	234939
1.各级政府	Governments	-17623	4885	22508
2.其它部门	Other Departments	2556170	2768601	212431
二.资本和金融项目	**Capital and Finance Account**	**6296392**	**41895620**	**35599228**
A.资本项目	Capital Account	410179	415515	5336
B.金融项目	Financial Account	5886212	41480105	35593893
1. 直接投资	Direct Investments	6782104	8607126	1825022
1.1 我国在外直接投资	Chinese Direct Investments Abroad	-1130569	56486	1187055
1.2 外国在华直接投资	Foreign Direct Investments in China	7912673	8550641	637967
2. 证券投资	Securities	-493284	2199744	2693027
2.1 资产	Assets	-2615689	7445	2623134
2.1.1 股本证券	Capital Stock			
2.1.2 债务证券	Liability Stock	-2615689	7445	2623134
2.1.2.1 (中)长期债券	(Metaphase) Long-term Bonds	-2548219	7445	2555664
2.1.2.2 货币市场工具	Money Market Tools	-67470		67470
2.2 负债	Liabilities	2122405	2192298	69893
2.2.1 股本证券	Capital Stock	2034600	2034600	
2.2.2 债务证券	Liability Stock	87805	157698	69893
2.2.2.1 (中)长期债券	(Metaphase) Long-term Bonds	56732	126332	69601
2.2.2.2 货币市场工具	Money Market Tools	31073	31366	293
3. 其它投资	Other Investments	-402608	30673235	31075843
3.1 资产	Assets	-4894736	1037124	5931860
3.1.1 贸易信贷	Trade Credits	-2290528		2290528
长期	Long Term	-91621		91621
短期	Short Term	-2198907		2198907
3.1.2 贷款	Loans	-1299313	83356	1382669
长期	Long Term	-150500		150500
短期	Short Term	-1148813	83356	1232169
3.1.3 货币和存款	Currencies and Deposits	-1031734	392166	1423900
3.1.4 其它资产	Other Assets	-273160	561602	834762
长期	Long Term			
短期	Short Term	-273160	561602	834762
3.2 负债	Liabilities	4492127	29636111	25143984
3.2.1 贸易信贷	Trade Credit	2541152	2541152	
长期	Long Term	116893	116893	
短期	Short Term	2424259	2424259	
3.2.2 贷款	Loans	292403	22801334	22508931
长期	Long Term	144438	1634177	1489739
短期	Short Term	147965	21167157	21019192
3.2.3 货币和存款	Currencies and Deposits	1336554	3830371	2493817
3.2.4 其它负债	Other Liabilities	322017	463253	141236
长期	Long Term	46145	59606	13461
短期	Short Term	275872	403647	127775
三. 储备资产	**Reserve Assets**	**-20701600**	**192900**	**20894500**
3.1 货币黄金	Gold Reserves			
3.2 特别提款权	SDR (Special Drawing Rights)	-500		500
3.3 在基金组织的储备头寸	China's Position in IMF (International Monetary Fund)	192900	192900	
3.4 外汇	Foreign Currencies	-20894000		20894000
3.5 其它债权	Other Creditor's rights			
四.净误差与遗漏	**Net Error and Omission**	**-1676623**		**1676623**

注：1.本表贸易数据来自海关统计。
2.本表直接投资贷方数据来自商务部统计和间接申报中的“与土地有关的土地批租和租赁”;借方数据来自间接申报统计。
3.本表其余数据来自间接申报统计。

a) Trade data in the table are from customs statistics.
b) Credit data on direct investment in the table are from statistics and from "Approved Leasing of Land" in indirect reporting, both collected by the Ministry of Commerce, and debit data are from indirect reporting.
c) Other data in the table are from indirect reporting.

3-20 2002年投入产出基本流量表(中间使用部分)

Intermediate Use Part of 2002 Input-Output Table

按当年生产者价格计算。
Data are calculated at producers' prices of 2002.

单位：万元 (10 000 yuan)

产出 Output / 投入 Input	农业 Agriculture	采掘业 Mining and Quarrying	食品制造业 Foodstuff	纺织、缝纫及皮革产品制造业 Textile, Sewing Leather and Furs Products	其他制造业 Other Manufacturing
总投入合计 Total Input	**285787423**	**103171891**	**144807828**	**156354358**	**138916353**
中间投入合计 Intermediate Input	**119482762**	**43505928**	**99835961**	**117744730**	**90229653**
农业 Agriculture	46368196	400482	48665195	14929518	7931416
采掘业 Mining and Quarrying	980425	3522633	578518	509729	893993
食品制造业 Foodstuff	15717460	24150	19517192	2469542	116667
纺织、缝纫及皮革产品制造业 Textile, Sewing, Leather and Furs Products	213490	518175	288534	58077334	4460309
其他制造业 Other Manufacturing	1614621	981772	3445672	2194545	31922391
电力、热力及水的生产和供应业 Production and Supply of Electric Power, Heat Power and Water	3310203	6675985	1601606	2582378	2918722
炼焦、煤气及石油加工业 Coking, Gas and Petroleum Refining	2814692	2673374	351415	465640	995110
化学工业 Chemical Industry	19248702	3577633	4769907	13670509	12591762
建筑材料及其他非金属矿物制品业 Building Materials and Non-metal Mineral Products	900994	717725	829371	327418	722486
金属产品制造业 Metal Products	1162704	4127089	1267906	667973	5347287
机械设备制造业 Machinery and Equipment	3964841	7306034	1268582	2929627	3875755
建筑业 Construction	497113	140575	39328	66420	101527
运输邮电业 Transportation, Post and Telecommunication Services	6152180	3817729	3898697	3335444	4865707
批发零售贸易、住宿和餐饮业 Wholesale and Retail Trades, Hotels and Catering Services	7957970	3175037	7751175	8525567	8187931
房地产业、租赁和商务服务业 Real Estate, Leasing and Business Services	1194941	2002090	3359790	4018055	2640751
金融保险业 Banking and Insurance	4513873	1612782	1146339	1560269	1585900
其他服务业 Other Services	2870359	2232664	1056734	1414760	1071940
增加值合计 Total Value-added	**166304661**	**59665963**	**44971867**	**38609628**	**48686700**
劳动者报酬 Compensation of Employees	133159686	25695041	12041768	18459317	17791707
生产税净额 Net Taxes on Production	5446504	6513463	16584325	6093462	8443995
固定资产折旧 Depreciation of Fixed Assets	7649132	7116017	6419373	5010472	6067509
营业盈余 Operating Surplus	20049338	20341442	9926401	9046378	16383488

3-20 续表

单位：万元

产出 Output / 投入 Input	电力、热力及水的生产和供应业 Production and Supply of Electric Power, Heat Power and Water	炼焦、煤气及石油加工业 Coking, Gas and Petroleum Refining	化学工业 Chemical Industry	建筑材料及其他非金属矿物制品业 Building Materials and Non-metal Mineral Products	金属产品制造业 Metal Products
总投入合计 Total Input	**84781571**	**64483952**	**215726168**	**58045337**	**213653418**
中间投入合计 Intermediate Input	**42321967**	**53278848**	**157633500**	**38958086**	**161963370**
农业 Agriculture	19983	46879	6630650	44797	36820
采掘业 Mining and Quarrying	13643672	37394821	9642000	5614025	19883597
食品制造业 Foodstuff			1661306	1202	
纺织、缝纫及皮革产品制造业 Textile, Sewing, Leather and Furs Products	221071	89675	1460688	460094	561993
其他制造业 Other Manufacturing	331806	196089	3977155	2555284	8221507
电力、热力及水的生产和供应业 Production and Supply of Electric Power, Heat Power and Water	4055205	1604967	10315568	3572869	10665427
炼焦、煤气及石油加工业 Coking, Gas and Petroleum Refining	3392373	3156409	7271507	1757973	6066174
化学工业 Chemical Industry	760984	1113519	80972315	3879191	4294500
建筑材料及其他非金属矿物制品业 Building Materials and Non-metal Mineral Products	180593	151072	1217392	4693308	3355112
金属产品制造业 Metal Products	752453	611561	3407253	3026136	75074277
机械设备制造业 Machinery and Equipment	7732293	1760948	5388156	2940913	8342401
建筑业 Construction	77805	22243	119142	48680	110440
运输邮电业 Transportation, Post and Telecommunication Services	3241727	2963538	7146430	3386468	8713316
批发零售贸易、住宿和餐饮业 Wholesale and Retail Trades, Hotels and Catering Services	3418921	2215739	9280771	3277284	9019176
房地产业、租赁和商务服务业 Real Estate, Leasing and Business Services	709478	679107	4536877	1202562	3505604
金融保险业 Banking and Insurance	2274867	558037	2447272	1783718	1882277
其他服务业 Other Services	1508736	714243	2159017	713582	2230749
增加值合计 Total Value-added	**42459604**	**11205104**	**58092668**	**19087251**	**51690048**
劳动者报酬 Compensation of Employees	9820296	3422128	20406171	9880149	22819739
生产税净额 Net Taxes on Production	8324572	3711262	13351240	4513542	10050860
固定资产折旧 Depreciation of Fixed Assets	12057082	2295399	10376852	3690998	8632348
营业盈余 Operating Surplus	12257655	1776316	13958406	1002562	10187100

continued

(10 000 yuan)

机械设备制造业 Machinery and Equipment	建筑业 Construction	运输邮电业 Transportation, Post and Telecommunication Services	批发零售贸易、住宿和餐饮业 Wholesale and Retail Trades, Hotels and Catering Services	房地产业、租赁和商务服务业 Real Estate, Leasing & Business Services	金融保险业 Banking and Insurance	其他服务业 Other Services	中间使用合计 Total Intermediate Use
444322891	**281326817**	**146064292**	**242910018**	**73139316**	**173306319**	**307507064**	**3134305017**
333721140	**215384929**	**75805409**	**121152599**	**26375147**	**71168199**	**147153749**	**1915715976**
111059	22862990	1316764	12693380		113678	1215546	163387352
2442911	7025824	777986	497301	26722	432647	2049320	105916124
345	246056	361187	18104503	9953	207354	2892178	61329095
1934548	1058879	619770	2058539	272666	378748	8835238	81509752
7263083	10758040	1442646	7801290	1607616	6100944	17194380	107608842
6776944	4167503	2104395	4859462	798105	2361387	5909391	74280115
2221719	7156192	18079701	2911038	262271	508050	2863678	62947316
30438266	10542466	1372514	3987849	333341	654988	18134775	210343221
5821777	30577593	256964	398615	85177	917321	1318824	52471743
62980221	46912747	828340	772648	146754	1930528	2057449	211073326
161357092	25951714	14442299	14273143	2651481	26819656	14587378	305592313
217570	338610	1961900	2304846	1115037	3697728	7555931	18414894
11346933	12759813	16286143	6678045	2066993	2445890	10099726	109204780
20006053	14037234	4253101	12949236	2836347	6479816	17946337	141317694
11947151	14944249	3046150	14608221	7965246	8025661	17503094	101889028
5142131	2350743	7251456	11228354	4985406	7589118	5165042	63077584
3713337	3694276	1404093	5026127	1212033	2504684	11825462	45352797
110601752	**65941888**	**70258883**	**121757419**	**46764169**	**102138121**	**160353315**	**1218589041**
45865651	38985990	30961105	49227169	13759179	23742432	113467464	589504993
22052279	2848851	6110360	40432340	1143905	11241913	7759242	174622113
15039312	7021012	18403662	10020801	5736725	40344121	21524857	187405672
27644510	17086036	14783756	22077109	26124360	26809654	17601752	267056263

3-21 2002年投入产出基本流量表(最终使用部分)

按当年生产者价格计算。

单位：万元

产出 Output / 投入 Input	最终使用 Final Uses 最终消费 Final Consumption Expenditures 居民最终消费 Household Consumption Expenditures 农村居民 Rural Household	城镇居民 Urban Household	小计 Subtotal	政府消费 Government Consumption Expenditures	合计 Total Consumption Expenditures
总投入合计 Total Input					
中间投入合计 Intermediate Input	**162717000**	**362996000**	**525713000**	**191199000**	**716912000**
农业 Agriculture	49328792	55311145	104639937	1641611	106281548
采掘业 Mining and Quarrying	778640	2072984	2851624		2851624
食品制造业 Foodstuff	24895831	46839594	71735425		71735425
纺织、缝纫及皮革产品制造业 Textile, Sewing, Leather and Furs Products	6498773	25810963	32309736		32309736
其他制造业 Other Manufacturing	2463039	10806275	13269314		13269314
电力、热力及水的生产和供应业 Production and Supply of Electric Power, Heat Power and Water	2290655	10451072	12741727		12741727
炼焦、煤气及石油加工业 Coking, Gas and Petroleum Refining	415227	2504000	2919227		2919227
化学工业 Chemical Industry	4982991	9496691	14479682		14479682
建筑材料及其他非金属矿物制品业 Building Materials and Non-metal Mineral Products	995232	4602802	5598034		5598034
金属产品制造业 Metal Products	757054	3173869	3930923		3930923
机械设备制造业 Machinery and Equipment	6166089	23357856	29523945		29523945
建筑业 Construction					
运输邮电业 Transportation, Post and Telecommunication Services	4683771	13024019	17707790	3061651	20769441
批发零售贸易、住宿和餐饮业 Wholesale and Retail Trades, Hotels and Catering Services	14151138	48540636	62691774		62691774
房地产业、租赁和商务服务业 Real Estate, Leasing and Business Services	22260260	32682273	54942533	1018757	55961290
金融保险业 Banking and Insurance	5371883	9431639	14803522		14803522
其他服务业 Other Services	16677625	64890182	81567808	185476981	267044789

Final Use Part of 2002 Input-Output Table

Data are calculated at producers' prices of 2002.

(10 000 yuan)

最终使用 Final Uses					进口	其他	总产出
资本形成总额 Gross Capital Formation			出口	最终使用合计			
固定资本形成总额 Gross Fixed Capital Formation	存货增加 Change in Inventories	资本形成总额 Subtotal	Exports	Total of Final Uses	Imports	Others	Total Output
436321000	**19329000**	**455650000**	**309443175**	**1482005175**	**269424809**	**6008674**	**3134305017**
7727341	3319720	11047060	4741965	122070573	6811579	7141077	285787423
	1923194	1923194	4484215	9259033	16689591	4686326	103171891
	2698465	2698465	8934890	83368780	5270968	5380921	144807828
	125849	125849	54951070	87386655	16304206	3762157	156354358
2595050	1427938	4022988	20802597	53019	8877012	2089623	138916353
			512777	184427	106173	-2646875	84781571
	-349708	-349708	2630030	-219382	5208068	1545155	64483952
	2433750	2433750	21763899	38677331	35881658	2587274	215726168
	-1465234	-1465234	4177256	8310056	1979122	-757340	58045337
3215875	-36342	3179533	15270049	22380505	22669240	2868827	213653418
125817798	7441838	133259636	104448272	267231853	129817405	1316130	444322891
272753592		272753592	1045919	273799511	797672	-10089915	281326817
1975652	424044	2399697	14518826	37687964	2919902	2091450	146064292
9547810	1385486	10933296	28878775	102503845	37981	-873541	242910018
11426735		11426735	10036576	77424601	7718880	1711570	173306319
			218132	15021653	2760460	-2199462	73139316
1261147		1261147	12027927	280333863	5574891	-12604704	307507064

3-22 投入产出直接消耗系数表（2002年）

产出 Output / 投入 Input	农业 Agriculture	采掘业 Mining and Quarrying	食品制造业 Foodstuff	纺织、缝纫及皮革产品制造业 Textile, Sewing Leather and Furs Products	其他制造业 Other Manufacturing
总投入合计 Total Input	**1.0000000**	**1.0000000**	**1.0000000**	**1.0000000**	**1.0000000**
中间投入合计 Intermediate Input	**0.4180826**	**0.4216839**	**0.6894376**	**0.7530633**	**0.6495251**
农业 Agriculture	0.1622472	0.0038817	0.3360674	0.0954851	0.0570949
采掘业 Mining and Quarrying	0.0034306	0.0341433	0.0039951	0.0032601	0.0064355
食品制造业 Foodstuff	0.0549970	0.0002341	0.1347800	0.0157945	0.0008398
纺织、缝纫及皮革产品制造业 Textile, Sewing, Leather and Furs Products	0.0007470	0.0050224	0.0019925	0.3714468	0.0321079
其他制造业 Other Manufacturing	0.0056497	0.0095159	0.0237948	0.0140357	0.2297958
电力、热力及水的生产和供应业 Production and Supply of Electric Power, Heat Power and Water	0.0115827	0.0647074	0.0110602	0.0165162	0.0210106
炼焦、煤气及石油加工业 Coking, Gas and Petroleum Refining	0.0098489	0.0259118	0.0024268	0.0029781	0.0071634
化学工业 Chemical Industry	0.0673532	0.0346764	0.0329396	0.0874329	0.0906428
建筑材料及其他非金属矿物制品业 Building Materials and Non-metal Mineral Products	0.0031527	0.0069566	0.0057274	0.0020941	0.0052009
金属产品制造业 Metal Products	0.0040684	0.0400021	0.0087558	0.0042722	0.0384929
机械设备制造业 Machinery and Equipment	0.0138734	0.0708142	0.0087604	0.0187371	0.0278999
建筑业 Construction	0.0017395	0.0013625	0.0002716	0.0004248	0.0007308
运输邮电业 Transportation, Post and Telecommunication Services	0.0215271	0.0370036	0.0269233	0.0213326	0.0350262
批发零售贸易、住宿和餐饮业 Wholesale and Retail Trades, Hotels and Catering Services	0.0278458	0.0307742	0.0535273	0.0545272	0.0589414
房地产业、租赁和商务服务业 Real Estate, Leasing and Business Services	0.0041812	0.0194054	0.0232017	0.0256984	0.0190096
金融保险业 Banking and Insurance	0.0157945	0.0156320	0.0079163	0.0099791	0.0114162
其他服务业 Other Services	0.0100437	0.0216402	0.0072975	0.0090484	0.0077164
增加值合计 Total Value-added	**0.5819174**	**0.5783161**	**0.3105624**	**0.2469367**	**0.3504749**
劳动者报酬 Compensation of Employees	0.4659396	0.2490508	0.0831569	0.1180608	0.1280750
生产税净额 Net Taxes on Production	0.0190579	0.0631321	0.1145264	0.0389721	0.0607847
固定资产折旧 Depreciation of Fixed Assets	0.0267651	0.0689724	0.0443303	0.0320456	0.0436774
营业盈余 Operating Surplus	0.0701547	0.1971607	0.0685488	0.0578582	0.1179378

Direct Input Coefficient of Input-Output Table (2002)

电力、热力及水的生产和供应业 Production and Supply of Electric Power, Heat Power and Water	炼焦、煤气及石油加工业 Coking, Gas and Petroleum Refining	化学工业 Chemical Industry	建筑材料及其他非金属矿物制品业 Building Materials and Non-metal Mineral Products	金属产品制造业 Metal Products	机械设备制造业 Machinery and Equipment	建筑业 Construction
1.0000000	**1.0000000**	**1.0000000**	**1.0000000**	**1.0000000**	**1.0000000**	**1.0000000**
0.4991883	**0.8262342**	**0.7307111**	**0.6711665**	**0.7580659**	**0.7510780**	**0.7656040**
0.0002357	0.0007270	0.0307364	0.0007718	0.0001723	0.0002500	0.0812684
0.1609273	0.5799090	0.0446956	0.0967179	0.0930647	0.0054981	0.0249739
0.0000000	0.0000000	0.0077010	0.0000207	0.0000000	0.0000008	0.0008746
0.0026075	0.0013907	0.0067710	0.0079265	0.0026304	0.0043539	0.0037639
0.0039137	0.0030409	0.0184361	0.0440222	0.0384806	0.0163464	0.0382404
0.0478312	0.0248894	0.0478179	0.0615531	0.0499193	0.0152523	0.0148137
0.0400131	0.0489487	0.0337071	0.0302862	0.0283926	0.0050002	0.0254373
0.0089758	0.0172682	0.3753477	0.0668304	0.0201003	0.0685048	0.0374741
0.0021301	0.0023428	0.0056432	0.0808559	0.0157035	0.0131026	0.1086906
0.0088752	0.0094839	0.0157943	0.0521340	0.3513835	0.1417443	0.1667553
0.0912025	0.0273083	0.0249768	0.0506658	0.0390464	0.3631528	0.0922476
0.0009177	0.0003449	0.0005523	0.0008386	0.0005169	0.0004897	0.0012036
0.0382362	0.0459578	0.0331273	0.0583418	0.0407825	0.0255376	0.0453558
0.0403262	0.0343611	0.0430211	0.0564608	0.0422140	0.0450259	0.0498965
0.0083683	0.0105314	0.0210307	0.0207176	0.0164079	0.0268884	0.0531206
0.0268321	0.0086539	0.0113443	0.0307297	0.0088100	0.0115730	0.0083559
0.0177956	0.0110763	0.0100081	0.0122935	0.0104410	0.0083573	0.0131316
0.5008117	**0.1737658**	**0.2692889**	**0.3288335**	**0.2419341**	**0.2489220**	**0.2343960**
0.1158305	0.0530694	0.0945929	0.1702143	0.1068073	0.1032259	0.1385790
0.0981885	0.0575533	0.0618898	0.0777589	0.0470428	0.0496312	0.0101265
0.1422135	0.0355964	0.0481020	0.0635882	0.0404035	0.0338477	0.0249568
0.1445792	0.0275466	0.0647043	0.0172720	0.0476805	0.0622172	0.0607338

3-22 续表 continued

投入 Input \ 产出 Output	运输邮电业 Transportation, Post and Telecommunication Services	批发零售贸易、住宿和餐饮业 Wholesale and Retail Trades, Hotels and Catering Services	房地产业、租赁和商务服务业 Real Estate, Leasing & Business Services	金融保险业 Banking and Insurance	其他服务业 Other Services
总投入合计 Total Input	**1.0000000**	**1.0000000**	**1.0000000**	**1.0000000**	**1.0000000**
中间投入合计 Intermediate Input	**0.5189866**	**0.4987551**	**0.4106498**	**0.3606152**	**0.4785378**
农　业 Agriculture	0.0090150	0.0522555	0.0006559	0.0000000	0.0039529
采掘业 Mining and Quarrying	0.0053263	0.0020473	0.0024964	0.0003654	0.0066643
食品制造业 Foodstuff	0.0024728	0.0745317	0.0011965	0.0001361	0.0094052
纺织、缝纫及皮革产品制造业 Textile, Sewing, Leather and Furs Products	0.0042431	0.0084745	0.0021854	0.0037280	0.0287318
其他制造业 Other Manufacturing	0.0098768	0.0321160	0.0352032	0.0219802	0.0559154
电力、热力及水的生产和供应业 Production and Supply of Electric Power, Heat Power and Water	0.0144073	0.0200052	0.0136255	0.0109121	0.0192171
炼焦、煤气及石油加工业 Coking, Gas and Petroleum Refining	0.1237791	0.0119840	0.0029315	0.0035859	0.0093126
化学工业 Chemical Industry	0.0093966	0.0164170	0.0037794	0.0045576	0.0589735
建筑材料及其他非金属矿物制品业 Building Materials and Non-metal Mineral Products	0.0017593	0.0016410	0.0052931	0.0011646	0.0042888
金属产品制造业 Metal Products	0.0056711	0.0031808	0.0111394	0.0020065	0.0066907
机械设备制造业 Machinery and Equipment	0.0988763	0.0587590	0.1547529	0.0362525	0.0474375
建筑业 Construction	0.0134318	0.0094885	0.0213364	0.0152454	0.0245716
运输邮电业 Transportation, Post and Telecommunication Services	0.1114998	0.0274918	0.0141131	0.0282610	0.0328439
批发零售贸易、住宿和餐饮业 Wholesale and Retail Trades, Hotels and Catering Services	0.0291180	0.0533088	0.0373894	0.0387801	0.0583607
房地产业、租赁和商务服务业 Real Estate, Leasing and Business Services	0.0208549	0.0601384	0.0463091	0.1089051	0.0569193
金融保险业 Banking and Insurance	0.0496456	0.0462243	0.0437902	0.0681631	0.0167965
其他服务业 Other Services	0.0096128	0.0206913	0.0144523	0.0165716	0.0384559
增加值合计 Total Value-added	**0.4810134**	**0.5012449**	**0.5893502**	**0.6393848**	**0.5214622**
劳动者报酬 Compensation of Employees	0.2119690	0.2026560	0.1369969	0.1881229	0.3689914
生产税净额 Net Taxes on Production	0.0418334	0.1664499	0.0648673	0.0156401	0.0252327
固定资产折旧 Depreciation of Fixed Assets	0.1259970	0.0412531	0.2327908	0.0784356	0.0699979
营业盈余 Operating Surplus	0.1012140	0.0908860	0.1546952	0.3571863	0.0572402

3-23 投入产出完全消耗系数表（2002年）

Total Input Coefficients of Input-Output Table (2002)

产出 Output / 投入 Input	农业 Agriculture	采掘业 Mining and Quarrying	食品制造业 Foodstuff	纺织、缝纫及皮革产品制造业 Textile, Sewing Leather and Furs Products	其他制造业 Other Manufacturing
农业 Agriculture	0.2432561	0.0248039	0.5021044	0.2337942	0.1304129
采掘业 Mining and Quarrying	0.0440191	0.1069393	0.0499706	0.0658978	0.0776971
食品制造业 Foodstuff	0.0869284	0.0105156	0.1999268	0.0603048	0.0256668
纺织、缝纫及皮革产品制造业 Textile, Sewing, Leather and Furs Products	0.0089923	0.0183939	0.0147448	0.6048778	0.0782547
其他制造业 Other Manufacturing	0.0285444	0.0396383	0.0631511	0.0634510	0.3335000
电力、热力及水的生产和供应业 Production and Supply of Electric Power, Heat Power and Water	0.0364573	0.0992668	0.0446816	0.0667431	0.0690335
炼焦、煤气及石油加工业 Coking, Gas and Petroleum Refining	0.0323018	0.0561393	0.0323092	0.0401625	0.0462484
化学工业 Chemical Industry	0.1640184	0.1104743	0.1545428	0.2968351	0.2580637
建筑材料及其他非金属矿物制品业 Building Materials and Non-metal Mineral Products	0.0094433	0.0162437	0.0150327	0.0129490	0.0170385
金属产品制造业 Metal Products	0.0389931	0.1234360	0.0575337	0.0671289	0.1330431
机械设备制造业 Machinery and Equipment	0.0768008	0.1930703	0.0962218	0.1438696	0.1525202
建筑业 Construction	0.0055329	0.0062839	0.0061208	0.0074069	0.0070399
运输邮电业 Transportation, Post and Telecommunication Services	0.0546660	0.0786838	0.0761790	0.0843390	0.0962454
批发零售贸易、住宿和餐饮业 Wholesale and Retail Trades, Hotels and Catering Services	0.0672450	0.0763635	0.1152681	0.1474065	0.1353065
房地产业、租赁和商务服务业 Real Estate, Leasing and Business Services	0.0277740	0.0496119	0.0575198	0.0804819	0.0631305
金融保险业 Banking and Insurance	0.0359764	0.0396136	0.0391703	0.0485521	0.0455530
其他服务业 Other Services	0.0220226	0.0365464	0.0254476	0.0330896	0.0279319

3-23 续表

投入 Input \ 产出 Output	电力、热力及水的生产和供应业 Production and Supply of Electric Power, Heat Power and Water	炼焦、煤气及石油加工业 Coking, Gas and Petroleum Refining	化学工业 Chemical Industry	建筑材料及其他非金属矿物制品业 Building Materials and Non-metal Mineral Products	金属产品制造业 Metal Products
农业 Agriculture	0.0201210	0.0277919	0.0937298	0.0367707	0.0334391
采掘业 Mining and Quarrying	0.2418676	0.7005087	0.1672406	0.2065048	0.2439564
食品制造业 Foodstuff	0.0107894	0.0132895	0.0330936	0.0167613	0.0158708
纺织、缝纫及皮革产品制造业 Textile, Sewing, Leather and Furs Products	0.0152916	0.0186742	0.0302710	0.0305844	0.0234782
其他制造业 Other Manufacturing	0.0329760	0.0416780	0.0694160	0.1002499	0.1108201
电力、热力及水的生产和供应业 Production and Supply of Electric Power, Heat Power and Water	0.0884986	0.1009992	0.1174452	0.1197669	0.1270100
炼焦、煤气及石油加工业 Coking, Gas and Petroleum Refining	0.0730893	0.1025159	0.0913072	0.0790672	0.0874118
化学工业 Chemical Industry	0.0789468	0.1206713	0.6741066	0.1952896	0.1317334
建筑材料及其他非金属矿物制品业 Building Materials and Non-metal Mineral Products	0.0118680	0.0163255	0.0191844	0.1000137	0.0369436
金属产品制造业 Metal Products	0.0918512	0.1176098	0.1034668	0.1669915	0.6260167
机械设备制造业 Machinery and Equipment	0.2365939	0.2047030	0.1709858	0.2110147	0.2173794
建筑业 Construction	0.0062520	0.0072876	0.0074328	0.0081061	0.0076717
运输邮电业 Transportation, Post and Telecommunication Services	0.0847276	0.1180871	0.1050910	0.1261805	0.1229808
批发零售贸易、住宿和餐饮业 Wholesale and Retail Trades, Hotels and Catering Services	0.0897026	0.1044887	0.1250656	0.1287200	0.1288452
房地产业、租赁和商务服务业 Real Estate, Leasing and Business Services	0.0430894	0.0572728	0.0712012	0.0679630	0.0672774
金融保险业 Banking and Insurance	0.0539255	0.0468244	0.0500436	0.0698353	0.0486218
其他服务业 Other Services	0.0355980	0.0409536	0.0351171	0.0354895	0.0377730

continued

机械设备制造业 Machinery and Equipment	建筑业 Construction	运输邮电业 Transportation, Post and Telecommunication Services	批发零售贸易、住宿和餐饮业 Wholesale and Retail Trades, Hotels and Catering Services	房地产业、租赁和商务服务业 Real Estate, Leasing & Business Services	金融保险业 Banking and Insurance	其他服务业 Other Services
0.0369769	0.1355242	0.0346006	0.1254504	0.0242747	0.0186200	0.0474263
0.1118248	0.1475391	0.1331544	0.0477979	0.0437783	0.0286273	0.0591512
0.0180666	0.0244615	0.0142920	0.1053394	0.0119400	0.0092216	0.0272870
0.0270254	0.0256639	0.0182241	0.0254171	0.0153012	0.0147145	0.0607745
0.0827956	0.1072971	0.0428976	0.0725628	0.0756369	0.0529893	0.1050885
0.0818411	0.0811861	0.0513143	0.0482577	0.0414338	0.0299250	0.0524068
0.0545544	0.0782380	0.1684983	0.0363354	0.0243068	0.0206498	0.0378782
0.2423329	0.1749993	0.0830183	0.0957452	0.0744662	0.0478645	0.1643574
0.0365475	0.1348370	0.0131393	0.0111793	0.0177976	0.0090684	0.0159996
0.3995289	0.3609698	0.0909705	0.0650462	0.1077422	0.0500654	0.0759436
0.6961803	0.2891787	0.2562420	0.1762983	0.3161800	0.1351402	0.1670156
0.0078521	0.0093187	0.0203548	0.0161675	0.0268634	0.0221687	0.0313316
0.1039984	0.1232891	0.1690647	0.0683126	0.0515946	0.0567892	0.0767391
0.1409653	0.1361110	0.0834480	0.1053036	0.0856640	0.0745911	0.1128953
0.0871430	0.1054158	0.0607361	0.0982932	0.0827653	0.1424281	0.0952673
0.0531439	0.0512396	0.0821423	0.0749347	0.0688264	0.0930404	0.0446086
0.0345782	0.0388196	0.0272098	0.0361543	0.0282345	0.0280507	0.0548658

3-24　资金流量表（实物交易，2003年）

单位：亿元

机构部门 Institutional Sectors		非金融企业部门 Non-financial Corporations		金融机构部门 Financial Institutions		政府部门 Governments	
交易项目	Transaction	运用 Utilization	来源 Source	运用 Utilization	来源 Source	运用 Utilization	来源 Source
1.净出口	Net Exports						
2.增加值	Value Added		67652.1		4388.2		12347.7
3.劳动者报酬	Compensation of Laborers	26169.7		1452.8		11301.3	
(1)工资及工资性收入	Wages and Related Income						
(2)单位社会保险付款	Employer's Contribution of Social Securities						
4.生产税净额	Taxes on Production, Net	18594.7		564.5		43.1	20633.5
(1)生产税	Taxes on Production						
(2)生产补贴	Subsidies to Production						
5.财产收入	Income from Properties	7550.0	3805.9	6008.7	6464.0	990.8	345.3
(1)利息	Interest	4957.4	2092.6	5941.3	6464.0	990.8	345.3
(2)红利	Dividend	2592.6	1681.6				
(3)土地租金	Rent on Land Use						
(4)其他	Others		31.7	67.4			
6.初次分配总收入	Total Income from Primary Distribution		19143.6		2826.3		20991.3
7.经常转移	Current Transfer	3756.2	287.1	782.8	572.0	4525.3	9357.3
(1)收入税	Taxes on Income	2836.8		210.8			4465.0
(2)社会保险缴款	Payment to Social Security						4882.9
(3)社会保险福利	Social Security Welfare					4016.4	
(4)社会补助	Allowances	48.3				500.1	
(5)其他	Others	871.0	287.1	572.0	572.0	8.8	9.4
8.可支配总收入	Total Disposable Income		15674.6		2615.4		25823.3
9.最终消费	Final Consumption Expenditure					14808.0	
(1)居民消费	Household Consumption						
(2)政府消费	Government Consumption					14808.0	
10.总储蓄	Savings		15674.6		2615.4		11015.3
11.资本转移	Capital Transfer		5476.7			5476.7	
(1)投资性补助	Investment Allowances						
(2)其他	Other						
12.资本形成总额	Gross Capital Formation	36980.0		71.1		6775.9	
(1)固定资本形成总额	Gross Fixed Capital Formation	36736.8		71.1		6775.9	
(2)存货增加	Changes in Inventories	243.2					
13.其他非金融资产获得减处置	Minus Items from Other Non-financial Capital						
14.净金融投资	Net Financial Investment	-15828.8		2544.4		-1237.2	
15.统计误差	Statistical Discrepancy	1298.1		127.6		696.8	

3-25　资金流量表（金融交易，2003年）

单位：亿元

机构部门 Institutional Sectors		非金融企业部门 Non-financial Corporations		金融机构部门 Financial Institutions		政府部门 Governments	
交易项目	Transaction	运用 Utilization	来源 Source	运用 Utilization	来源 Source	运用 Utilization	来源 Source
净金融投资	Net Financial Investment	-14530.7		2672.0		-540.5	
资金运用合计	Total Utilization	16673.4		55668.3		3872.3	
资金来源合计	Total Sources		31204.0		52996.3		4412.8
通货	Currency in Circulation	222.0		1.0	2468.0	49.4	
存款	Savings Deposits	15776.3		501.9	36159.6	3762.1	
贷款	Loans		23734.8	27958.5	802.0		-1865.2
证券	Securities		1795.6	8257.0	3600.2	114.3	5213.0
保险准备金	Reserves for Insurance Business	157.6			2254.3		939.4
结算资金	Settlement Funds	152.0			169.1		
金融机构往来	Flow Between Financial Institutions			1748.4	1642.7		
准备金	Reserve Funds			3896.8	3910.1		
库存现金	Cash			329.7	289.3		
中央银行贷款	Loans from the Central Bank			1020.0	850.1		
其他（净）	Other (net)	802.5	0.0		857.2	-53.5	5.7
直接投资	Foreign Investment	-12.6	3896.5				
其他对外债权债务	Other Claims or Liabilities on Abroad	-424.8	400.3	2271.7	-6.1		120.0
国际储备资产	Assets in International Serves			9686.0			
国际收支错误与遗漏	Errors and Omission of Balance of Payment		1376.7				

Flow of Funds Table (Physical Transaction, 2003)

(100 million yuan)

住户部门 Households		国内合计 Total of Domestic Sectors		国外部门 Rest of the World		合 计 Total	
运 用 Utilization	来 源 Source	运 用 Utilization	来 源 Source	运 用 Utilization	来 源 Source	运 用 Utilization	来 源 Source
					-2682.1		-2682.1
	33002.2		117390.2				117390.2
30213.9	69151.2	69137.8	69151.2	106.1	92.6	69243.9	69243.9
1431.3		20633.5	20633.5			20633.5	20633.5
537.0	3809.6	15086.5	14424.9	1225.0	1886.6	16311.5	16311.5
537.0	3524.7	12426.6	12426.6			12426.6	12426.6
	249.3	2592.6	1930.9	1225.0	1886.6	3817.5	3817.5
	35.7	67.4	67.4			67.4	67.4
	73780.8		116742.0				116742.0
6646.6	6954.0	15710.8	17170.4	1529.8	70.2	17240.6	17240.6
1417.3		4465.0	4465.0			4465.0	4465.0
4882.9		4882.9	4882.9			4882.9	4882.9
	4016.4	4016.4	4016.4			4016.4	4016.4
	548.4	548.4	548.4			548.4	548.4
346.3	2389.1	1798.1	3257.7	1529.8	70.2	3327.9	3327.9
	74088.2		118201.6				118201.6
52685.5		67493.5				67493.5	
52685.5		52685.5				52685.5	
		14808.0				14808.0	
	21402.7		50708.1		-3493.5		47214.6
		5476.7	5476.7			5476.7	5476.7
7727.7		51554.7				51554.7	
7720.1		51303.9				51303.9	
7.6		250.8				250.8	
13675.0		-846.6		-3493.5		-4340.1	
2447.4		4572.7		-232.2		4340.1	

Flow of Funds Table (Financial Transaction, 2003)

(100 million yuan)

住户部门 Households		国内合计 Total of Domestic Sectors		国外部门 Rest of the World		合 计 Total	
运 用 Utilization	来 源 Source	运 用 Utilization	来 源 Source	运 用 Utilization	来 源 Source	运 用 Utilization	来 源 Source
3726.1		-3725.6					
99326.8		7184.2		106511.1		73868.9	
	95600.7		10909.8		106510.6		73868.9
2320.4	2468.0	148.1		2468.4	2468.0	1589.4	1589.2
36600.1	36159.6	61.5	501.9	36661.5	36661.5	28104.3	28104.3
27959.0	29659.2	547.5	-1152.8	28506.4	28506.4	19916.6	19916.6
9678.0	10608.7	639.7		10317.8	10608.7	7462.1	8020.1
3193.6	3193.6			3193.6	3193.6	2635.1	2635.1
169.1	169.1			169.1	169.1	55.8	55.8
1748.4	1642.7			1748.4	1642.7	1185.9	1345.8
3896.8	3910.1			3896.8	3910.1	1800.8	1640.2
329.7	289.3		40.4	329.7	329.7	141.6	141.6
1020.0	850.1			1020.0	850.1	-635.5	-455.7
891.5	862.9			891.5	862.9	-272.0	-1008.9
-12.6	3896.5	3896.5	-12.6	3883.9	3883.9	4289.7	4289.7
1846.9	514.2	514.2	1846.9	2361.1	2361.1	795.6	795.6
9686.0			9686.0	9686.0	9686.0	6249.7	6249.7
	1376.7	1376.7		1376.7	1376.7	549.8	549.8

主要统计指标解释

国内生产总值(GDP) 指按市场价格计算的一个国家(或地区)所有常住单位在一定时期内生产活动的最终成果。国内生产总值有三种表现形态，即价值形态、收入形态和产品形态。从价值形态看，它是所有常住单位在一定时期内生产的全部货物和服务价值超过同期投入的全部非固定资产货物和服务价值的差额，即所有常住单位的增加值之和；从收入形态看，它是所有常住单位在一定时期内创造并分配给常住单位和非常住单位的初次收入之和；从产品形态看，它是所有常住单位在一定时期内最终使用的货物和服务价值减去货物和服务进口价值。在实际核算中，国内生产总值有三种计算方法，即生产法、收入法和支出法。三种方法分别从不同的方面反映国内生产总值及其构成。

国民总收入(GNI) 即国民生产总值，指一个国家(或地区)所有常住单位在一定时期内收入初次分配的最终结果。一国常住单位从事生产活动所创造的增加值在初次分配中主要分配给该国的常住单位，但也有一部分以生产税及进口税(扣除生产和进口补贴)、劳动者报酬和财产收入等形式分配给非常住单位；同时，国外生产所创造的增加值也有一部分以生产税及进口税(扣除生产和进口补贴)、劳动者报酬和财产收入等形式分配给该国的常住单位，从而产生了国民总收入的概念。它等于国内生产总值加上来自国外的净要素收入。与国内生产总值不同，国民总收入是个收入概念，而国内生产总值是个生产概念。

三次产业 三产业的划分是世界上较为常用的产业结构分类，但各国的划分不尽一致。我国的三次产业划分是：

第一产业是指农、林、牧、渔业。

第二产业是指采矿业，制造业，电力、煤气及水的生产和供应业，建筑业。

第三产业是指除第一、二产业以外的其他行业。

劳动者报酬 指劳动者因从事生产活动所获得的全部报酬。包括劳动者获得的各种形式的工资、奖金和津贴，既包括货币形式的，也包括实物形式的，还包括劳动者所享受的公费医疗和医药卫生费、上下班交通补贴、单位支付的社会保险费、住房公积金等。对于个体经济来说，其所有者所获得的劳动报酬和经营利润不易区分，这两部分统一作为劳动者报酬处理。

生产税净额 指生产税减生产补贴后的余额。生产税指政府对生产单位从事生产、销售和经营活动以及因从事生产活动使用某些生产要素(如固定资产、土地、劳动力)所征收的各种税、附加费和规费。生产补贴与生产税相反，指政府对生产单位的单方面转移支出，因此视为负生产税，包括政策亏损补贴、价格补贴等。

固定资产折旧 指一定时期内为弥补固定资产损耗按照规定的固定资产折旧率提取的固定资产折旧，或按国民经济核算统一规定的折旧率虚拟计算的固定资产折旧。它反映了固定资产在当期生产中的转移价值。各类企业和企业化管理的事业单位的固定资产折旧是指实际计提的折旧费；不计提折旧的政府机关、非企业化管理的事业单位和居民住房的固定资产折旧是按照统一规定的折旧率和固定资产原值计算的虚拟折旧。原则上，固定资产折旧应按固定资产当期的重置价值计算，但是目前我国尚不具备对全社会固定资产进行重估价的基础，所以暂时只能采用上述办法。

营业盈余 指常住单位创造的增加值扣除劳动者报酬、生产税净额和固定资产折旧后的余额。它相当于企业的营业利润加上生产补贴，但要扣除从利润中开支的工资和福利等。

支出法国内生产总值 是从最终使用的角度反映一个国家(或地区)一定时期内生产活动最终成果的一种方法，包括最终消费支出、资本形成总额及货物和服务净出口三部分。计算公式为：

$$\text{支出法国内生产总值} = \text{最终消费支出} + \text{资本形成总额} + \text{货物和服务净出口}$$

最终消费支出 指常住单位为满足物质、文化和精神生活的需要，从本国经济领土和国外购买的货物和服务的支出。它不包括非常住单位在本国经济领土内的消费支出。最终消费支出分为居民消费支出和政府消费支出。

居民消费支出 指常住住户在一定时期内对于货物和服务的全部最终消费支出。居民消费支出除了直接以货币形式购买的货物和服务的消费支出外，还包括以其他方式获得的货物和服务的消费支出，即所谓的虚拟消费支出。居民虚拟消费支出包括如下几种类型：单位以实物报酬及实物转移的形式提供给劳动者的货物和服务；住户生产并由本住户消费了的货物和服务，其中的服务仅指住户的自有住房服务和付酬的家庭雇员提供的家庭和个人服务；金融机构提供的金融媒介服务；保险公司提供的保险服务。

政府消费支出 指政府部门为全社会提供的公共服务的消费支出和免费或以较低的价格向居民住户提供的货物和服务的净支出，前者等于政府服务的产出价值减去政府单位所获得的经营收入的价值，后者等于政府部门免费或以较低价格向居民住户提供的货物和服务的市场价值减去向住户收取的价值。

资本形成总额 指常住单位在一定时期内获得减去处置的固定资产和存货的净额，包括固定资本形成总额和存货增加两部分。

固定资本形成总额 指生产者在一定时期内获得的固定资产减处置的固定资产的价值总额。固定资产是通过生产活动生产出来的，且其使用年限在一年以上、单位价值在规定标准以上的资产，不包括自然资产。可分为有形固定资本形成总额和无形固定资本形成总额。有形固定资本形成总额包括一定时期内完成的建筑工程、安装工程和设备工器具购置(减处置)价值，以及土地改良、新增役、种、奶、毛、娱乐用牲畜和新增经济林木价值。无形固定资本形成总额包括矿藏的勘探、计算机软件等获得减处置。

存货增加 指常住单位在一定时期内存货实物量变动的市场价值，即期末价值减期初价值的差额，再扣除当期由于价格变动而产生的持有收益。存货增加可以是正值，也可以是负值，正值表示存货上升，负值表示存货下降。存货包括生产单位购进的原材料、燃料和储备物资等存货，以及生产单位生产的产成品、在制品和半成品等存货。

货物和服务净出口 指货物和服务出口减货物和服务进口的差额。出口包括常住单位向非常住单位出售或无偿转让的各种货物和服务的价值；进口包括常住单位从非常住单位购买或无偿得到的各种货物和服务的价值。由于服务活动的提供与使用同时发生，一般把常住单位从非常住单位得到的服务作为进口，非常住单位从常住单位得到的服务作为出口。货物的出口和进口都按离岸价格计算。

直接消耗系数 也称为投入系数，记为$a_{ij}(ij=1,2,\cdots,n)$它是指在生产经营过程中第 j 产品(或产业)部门的单位总产出所直接消耗的第 i 产品部门货物或服务的价值量，将各产品(或产业)部门的直接消耗系数用表的形式表现，就是直接消耗系数表或直接消耗系数矩阵，通常用字母A表示。

完全消耗系数 指第 j 产品部门每提供一个单位最终使用时，对第 i 产品部门货物或服务的直接消耗和间接消耗之和。将各产品部门的完全消耗系数用表的形式表现，就是完全消耗系数表或完全消耗系数矩阵，通常用字母B表示。

机构单位 指有权拥有资产和承担负债，能够独立地从事经济活动并与其他实体进行交易的经济实体。

机构部门 将相同性质的机构单位归并在一起，就形成机构部门。资金流量核算将常住机构单位划分为以下四个机构部门：非金融企业部门、金融机构部门、政府部门、住户部门。与常住单位发生经济往来关系的非常住单位组成国外部门，在资金流量核算中也视同机构部门。

非金融企业与非金融企业部门 非金融企业指主要从事市场货物生产和提供非金融市场服务的常住企业，它主要包括从事上述活动的各类法人企业。所有非金融企业归并在一起，就形成非金融企业部门。

金融机构与金融机构部门 金融机构指主要从事金融媒介以及与金融媒介密切相关的辅助金融活动的常住单位，它主要包括中央银行、商业银行和政策性银行、非银行信贷机构和保险公司。所有金融机构归并在一起，就形成金融机构部门。

政府单位与政府部门 政府单位指在我国境内通过政治程序建立的、在一特定区域内对其他机构单位拥有立法、司法和行政权的法律实体及其附属单位。政府单位的主要职能是利用征税和其他方式获得的资金向社会和公众提供公共服务。通过转移支付，对社会收入和财产进行再分配。它主要包括各种行政单位和非营利性事业单位。所有政府单位归并在一起，就形成政府部门。

住户与住户部门 住户指共享同一生活设施、部分或全部收入和财产集中使用、共同消费住房、食品和其他消费品与消费服务的常住个人或个人群体。所有住户归并在一起，就形成住户部门。

非常住单位与国外部门 所有不具有常住性的机构单位都是非常住单位。将所有与我国常住单位发生交易的非常住单位归并在一起，就形成国外部门。

初次分配总收入 初次分配是生产活动形成的净成果在参与生产活动的生产要素的所有者及政府之间的分配。生产活动的净成果是增加值。生产要素包括劳动力、土地、资本。劳动力所有者因提供劳动而获得劳动报酬；土地所有者因出租土地而获得地租；资本的所有者因资本的形态不同而获得不同形式的收入：借贷资本所有者获得利息收入；股权所有者获得红利或未分配利润；政府因直接或间接介入生产过程而获得生产税或支付补贴。初次分配的结果形成各个机构部门的初次分配总收入。各部门的初次分配总收入之和就等于国民总收入，亦即国民生产总值。

经常转移 转移是一个机构单位向另一个机构单位提供货物、服务或资产，而同时并没有从后一机构单位获得任何货物、服务或资产作为回报的一种交易。经常转移包括扣除资本转移外的所有转移。其形式有收入税、社会保险付款、社会补助和其他经常转移。

可支配总收入 在初次分配总收入的基础上，通过经常转移的形式对初次分配总收入进行再次分配。再分配的结果形成各个机构部门的可支配总收入。各部门的可支配总收入之和称为国民可支配总收入。

总储蓄 指可支配总收入用于最终消费后的余额。各部门的总储蓄之和称为国民总储蓄。

资本转移 指一个部门无偿地向另一个部门支付用于非金融投资的资金，是一种不从对方获取任何对应物作为回报的交易。资本转移具有不同于经常转移的两个特征，一是转移的目的是用于投资，而不是用于消费；二是资本转移其实物形式往往涉及除存货和现金以外资产所有权的转移；其现金形式往往涉及除存货以外的资产的处置。资本转移包括投资性补助和其他资本转移。

净金融投资 它反映机构部门或经济总体资金富余或短缺的状况。从实物交易角度看，它是指总储蓄加资本转移收入减资本转移支出减非金融投资后的差额。从金融交易角度看，它是金融资产的增加额减金融负债的增加额之后的差额。

通货 指以现金形式存在于市场流通中的货币，包括本币和外币。

存款 指金融机构接受客户存入的货币款项，存款人可随时或按约定时间支取款项的信用业务。包括活期存款、定期存款、住户储蓄存款、财政存款、外汇存款和其他存款等。

贷款 指金融机构将其所吸收的资金，按一定的利率贷放给客户并约期归还的信用业务。包括短期贷款、中长期贷款、财政贷款、外汇贷款和其他贷款。

证券（不含股票） 由债券购买者承购的或因销售产品而拥有的，可在金融市场上交易并代表一定债权的书面证明。包括政府债券、金融债券、企业债券、商业票据、支付固定收入但不提供法人企业残余价值分享权的优先股等。

股票及其他股权 指股票购买者及直接投资者对其投资企业净资产所拥有的权益。股票是股份公司签发的证明股东投资并按其所持股份享有权益和承担义务的权益性证券。其他股权是机构单位以直接投资的方式用除股票、债权性证券以外的土地、房屋及建筑物、机器设备、存货、资源资产等实物资产，商标、专利权、土地使用权、特许使用权、商誉等无形资产及货币资金直接向其他单位进行的投资。通常以股权证、出资证明书、参与证或类似的单据为凭证。

保险准备金 指对人寿保险准备金和养恤基金的净权益、保险费预付款和未结索赔准备金。

结算资金 指金融机构用于结算目的汇兑在途的资金。

金融机构往来 指各金融机构之间的资金往来，包括同业存放款和同业拆借款。

准备金 指各金融机构在中央银行的存款及缴存中央银行的法定准备金。

中央银行贷款 指中央银行向各金融机构的贷款。

经常项目 包括货物、服务、收益及经常性转移。

货物进出口 指通过我国海关进出口的货物。货物的进出口值都按离岸价格估价。离岸价格可视为进口商在出口商边境领取货物时支付的购买者价格。当进口商领取该货物时，该货物已装载到进口商自己的运载工具或其他运载工具，出口商已为该货物支付了出口税或获得了出口退税。

服务进出口 指常住单位与非常住单位之间相互提供的服务。包括运输服务、旅游服务、通讯服务、建筑服务、保险服务、金融服务、计算机和信息服务、咨询服务、广告、宣传服务、电影音像服务、专有权力使用费和特许费、其他商务服务、政府服务。

收益 指常住单位与非常住单位之间因相互提供生产要素而产生的收入，包括劳动者报酬和投资收益。其中投资收益包括直接投资、证券投资和其他投资的收益和支出，以及直接投资收益的再投资。

资本项目 包括移民转移、债务减免等资本性转移。

金融项目 包括直接投资、证券投资和其他投资。

直接投资 指外国、港澳台地区在我国和我国在外国、港澳台地区以独资、合资、合作及合作勘探开发方式进行的投资。

证券投资 指我国对外国、港澳台地区发行的股票、债券等有价证券和我国购买外国、港澳台地区发行的股票、债券等有价证券。

其他投资 指除直接投资和证券投资以外的所有对外金融资产与负债交易项目。包括外国提供给我国和我国提供给外国的贸易信贷、贷款、货币和存款以及其他资产。

储备资产增减额 指我国在黄金储备、外汇储备、在国际货币基金组织的储备头寸、特别提款权、使用基金信贷等方面本年末与上年末余额之间的差额。负号表示储备资产增加，正号表示储备资产减少。

Explanatory Notes on Main Statistical Indicators

Gross Domestic Product (GDP) refers to the final products at market prices produced by all resident units in a country (or a region) during a certain period of time. Gross domestic product is expressed in three different forms, i.e. value, income, and products respectively. GDP in its value form refers to the total value of all goods and services produced by all resident units during a certain period of time, minus the total value of input of goods and services of the nature of non-fixed assets; in other term, it is the sum of the value-added of all resident units. GDP in the form of income includes the income created by all resident units and distributed to resident and non-resident units. GDP in the form of products refers to the value of all goods and services for final consumption by all resident units minus the net exports of goods and services during a given period of time. In the practice of national accounting, gross domestic product is calculated with three approaches, i.e. production approach, income approach and expenditure approach, which reflect gross domestic product and its composition from different aspects.

Gross National Income (GNI) also known as gross national product, refers to the final result of the primary distribution of the income created by all the resident units of a country (or a region) during a certain period of time. The value-added created by the resident units of a country engaged in production activities is distributed, during the primary distribution, mainly to the resident units of that country, while part of it is distributed to the non-resident units in the form of production tax and import duties (minus subsidies to production and import), remuneration for the labourers and property income. At the meantime, a part of the value-added created abroad is distributed to the resident units of the country in the form of production tax and import duties (minus subsidies to production and import), remuneration for the labourers and property income. The concept of gross national income is thus developed, which equals to the gross domestic product plus the net factor income from abroad. Unlike the gross domestic product which is a concept of production, the gross national income is a concept of income.

Three Industries Classification of economic activities into three branches of industries is a common practice in the world, although the grouping varies to some extent form country to country. In China economic activities are categorized into following industries:

Primary industry: refers to agriculture, forestry, animal husbandry and fishery.

Secondary industry: refers to mining and quarrying, manufacturing, production and supply of electricity, water and gas, and construction.

Tertiary industry: refers to all other economic activities not included in primary or secondary industry.

Labourers Remuneration refers to the whole payment of various forms earned by the labourers from the productive activities they are engaged in. It includes wages, bonuses and allowances the labourers earned in monetary form and in kind. It also includes the free medical services provided to the labourers and the medicine expenses, traffic subsidies and social insurance, housing fund paid by the employers. As the individual economy is concerned, since the labourers remuneration is not easily distinguished from the operating profit, both are treated as labourers remuneration.

Net Taxes on Production refers to the difference of the taxes on production minus the subsidies on production. The taxes on production refers to the various taxes, extra charges and fees levied on the production units on their production, sale and business activities as well as on the use of some factors of production, such as fixed assets, land and labour force in the production activities they are engaged in. In contrast to the taxes on production, the subsidies on production refer to the unilateral government transfer to the production units and are therefore regarded as negative taxes on production. They include subsidies on the loss due to implementation of government policies, price subsidies, etc.

Depreciation of Fixed Assets refers to the depreciation of fixed assets of a given period, drawn in accordance with the stipulated depreciation rate for the purpose of compensating the wear loss of the fixed assets or the depreciation of fixed assets calculated in a fictitious way in accordance with the stipulated unified depreciation rate in the national economic accounting system. It reflects the value of transfer of the fixed assets in the production of the current period. The depreciation of fixed assets in various enterprises and institutions managed as enterprises refers to the depreciation expenses actually drawn. In government agencies and institutions not managed as enterprises which do not draw the depreciation expenses, as well as for the houses of residents, the depreciation of fixed assets is the imputed depreciation, which is calculated in accordance with the stipulated unified depreciation rate. In principle, the depreciation of fixed assets should be calculated on the basis of the repurchased value of the fixed assets. However, there is no actual condition to re-evaluate all the fixed assets in China. Therefore, the above-mentioned methods are temporarily adopted at present.

Operating Surplus refers to the balance of the value added created by the resident units deducting the labourers remuneration, net taxes on production and the depreciation of fixed assets. It is equivalent to the business profit of the enterprises plus subsidies on production, but the wages and welfare expenses paid from the profits should be deducted.

GDP by Expenditure Approach refers to the method of

measuring the final results of production activities of a country (region) during a given period from the perspective of final use. It includes final consumption expenditure, total capital formation and net export of goods and services, i.e.:

GDP by expenditure approach = final consumption expenditure + total capital formation + net export of goods and services

Final Consumption Expenditure refers to the total expenditure of resident units for purchases of goods and services from domestic economic territory and abroad to meet the requirements of material, cultural and spiritual life. It excludes the expenditure of non-resident units on consumption in the economic territory of the country. The final consumption expenditure is broken down into household consumption expenditure and government consumption expenditure.

Households Consumption Expenditure refers to the total expenditure of resident households on the final consumption of goods and services. In addition to the consumption of goods and services bought by the households directly with money, the households consumption expenditure also includes expenditure on goods and services obtained by the households in other ways, i. e. the so-called imputed consumption expenditure, which includes the following: (a) the goods and services provided to the households by the employer in the form of payment in kind and transfer in kind; (b) goods and services produced and consumed by the households themselves, in which the services refer only to the owner-occupied housing and domestic and individual services provided by the paid household workers; (c) financial intermediate services provided by financial institutions; (d) insurance services provided by insurance companies.

Government Consumption Expenditure refers to the expenditure on the consumption of the public services provided by the government to the whole society and the net expenditure on the goods and services provided by the government to the households free of charge or at low prices. The former equals to the output value of the government services minus the value of operating income obtained by the government departments. The latter equals to the market value of the goods and services provided by the government free of charge or at low prices to the households minus the value received by the government from the households.

Total Capital Formation refers to the fixed assets acquired minus those disposed of and the net value of inventory, including the total fixed capital formation and the increase in inventory.

Total Fixed Capital Formation refers to the value of fixed assets acquired minus those disposed of during a given period. Fixed assets are the assets produced through production activities with specified unit value which could be used for over one year, excluding natural assets. Total fixed capital formation can be categorized into total tangible capital formation and total intangible capital formation. The total tangible capital formation include the value of the construction projects, installation projects completed and the equipment, apparatus and instruments purchased as well as the value of land improved, the value of draught animals, breeding stock, animals for milk, wool and for recreational purpose, and the newly increased forest with economic value during a given period. The total intangible capital formation includes the prospecting of minerals, the acquisition of computer software minus the disposal of them.

Increase in Inventory refers to the market value of the change in inventory of resident units during a given period, i.e. the difference of value between the beginning and the end of the period minus the current gains due to the change in prices. The increase in inventory can be positive or negative. A positive value indicates the increase in inventory while a negative value indicates the decrease in stock. The inventory includes the raw materials, fuels and reserve materials purchased by the production units as well as the inventory of finished products, semi-finished products, work-in-progress, etc.

Net Export of Goods and Services refers to the difference of the exports of goods and services minus the imports of goods and services. The imports include the value of various goods and services sold or gratuitously transferred by the resident units to the non-resident units. The imports include the value of various goods and services purchased or gratuitously acquired by the resident units from the non-resident units. Because the provision of services and the use of them happen simultaneously, the acquisition of services by the resident units from abroad is usually treated as import while the acquisition of services by non-resident units in this country is usually treated as export. The export and import of goods are calculated at FOB.

Direct Input Coefficient refers to the volume of products and services of industry *i*, which is consumed directly by industry *j* in the course of its production or business, recorded as a_{ij} (i,j=1,2, … ,n). The direct input coefficient table or direct input coefficient matrix, usually denoted as A, is a table that presents direct input coefficients of all industries.

Total Input Coefficient refers to the volume of products and services of industry *i* which is consumed directly and indirectly by industry *j* in producing each unit of final use. The total input coefficient table or total input coefficient matrix, usually denoted as B, is a table that presents total input coefficients of all industries.

Institutional Units refer to economic entities that are in a position to own assets and incur liabilities, to engage independently in economic activities, and to conduct transactions with other entities.

Institutional Sectors refer groups of institutional units that are homogenous in nature. Following 4 institutional sectors are identified in the flow of fund accounts: non-financial corporations, financial institutions, governments and households, Also treated as an institutional sector is the rest of the world, which is composed of non-resident units that have economic relations with the resident units.

Non-Financial Corporations and the Sector of Non-

Financial Corporations Non-financial corporations refer to resident corporations that are engaged in the production of goods and the provision of non financial services in the market, mainly covering corporate enterprises of various types engaged in the above-mentioned activities. All non-financial corporations make up the sector of non-financial corporations.

Financial Institutions and the Sector of Financial Institutions Financial institutions refer to resident institutions that are engaged in the financial intermediate services or auxiliary financial activities that are closed related with financial intermediate services, mainly covering central banks, commercial banks, policy-related banks, non-banking credit institutions and insurance companies. All financial institutions make up the sector of financial institutions.

Government Units and the Sector of Governments Government units refer to legal entities and their auxiliary units within the territory of China that are established through political process and are empowered with legislative, administrative or judicial rights over other institutional units in a given region. The main function of government units is to acquire funds through taxation or other means, to provide public services to the society and households, and to conduct redistribution of income and properties of the society through transfer payment. Government units cover mainly administrative and non-profit institutional units of various types. All government units make up the sector of governments.

Households and the Sector of Households Households refer to resident individuals or groups of resident individuals who share common living facilities, pool together entire or part of their income and properties at their common disposal, and share their housing, food and other consumer goods and services. All households make up the sector of households.

Non-resident Units and the Rest of the World Non-resident units refer to of units that are of a non-resident nature. All non-resident units that have transactions with resident units make up the sector the rest of the world.

Total Income of Primary Distribution Primary distribution refers to the distribution of net results from production activities among the owners of factors of production and the governments. Factors of production include labour force, land and capitals. Owners of labour force gain remuneration by providing labour. Owners of land receive rents from leasing of land. Owners of capitals get income of various forms depending on the type of capitals: bankers receive income from interest and share holders receive dividends or non-distributed profits. Governments either gain production tax or pay for subsidies by participating directly or indirectly in the production process. Results of primary distribution generate the total income of primary distribution of each sector, and the sum of the total income of primary distribution of all sectors make up the gross national income, or the gross national product.

Current Transfers Transfer refers to the transaction of provision of goods, services or assets by an institutional unit to another institutional unit without receiving any goods, services or assets in return from the recipient. Current transfers refer to all kinds of transfers other than capital transfers, including income tax, payment to social securities, social allowances and other current transfers.

Total Disposable Income Total income of primary distribution is re-distributed through current transfer, resulting in the total disposable income of various institutional sectors. The sum of total disposable income of all institutional sectors makes up the total national disposable income.

Total Savings refer to the total disposable income minus the final consumption. Total savings of all sectors make up the total national savings.

Capital Transfer refers to the free payment from one sector to another sector for non-financial capital formation, and is a transaction that seeks no return from the recipient. The capital transfer differs from the current transfer in 2 aspects: 1) The purpose of the capital transfer is investment rather than consumption. 2) The capital transfer features the transfer of the ownership of the assets other than inventory and cash, and the capital transfer in its monetary form involves the disposal of assets other than inventory. Capital transfer includes investment subsidies and other capital transfers.

Net Financial Investment reflects the surplus or shortage of capitals of institutional sectors or of the economy in general. It refers to total savings plus the income from capital transfer minus payment for capital transfer and the non-financial investment from the point of view of physical transaction. In terms of monetary transaction, it is the difference between the increase in financial assets minus the increase of the financial liabilities.

Currency in Circulation refers to currency that is in circulation in the market, including local and foreign currencies.

Deposits refer to credit transactions by which financial institutions accept deposits from clients who could withdraw their deposit at any time or by agreed time frame. They include current deposit, fixed deposit, household savings deposit, government deposit, foreign exchange deposit and other deposits.

Loans refer to credit transactions by which financial institutions lend their capital to clients at certain level of interest rates, which the latter will repay by agreed time frame. They include short-term loans, medium and long-term loans, government loans, foreign exchange loans and other loans.

Securities (excluding stocks) refer to written certificates representing creditors' rights, purchased by bond holders or owned by selling products, which can be transacted at the financial markets. They include government bonds, financial bonds, corporation bonds, commercial drafts, preferential stocks that provide fixed income without the right to share the residual value of corporations, etc.

Stocks and Other Holding Rights refer to the rights by stockholders and direct investors on the net assets of corporations they invested in. Stocks refer to negotiable securities on creditor's rights, issued by stock companies certifying the investment by stockholders and their rights and duties depending on their stocks. Other holding rights refer to the direct investment by institutional units to other units in forms other than stocks and negotiable securities on creditor's rights, including tangible assets such as land, buildings, machines and equipment, inventory, resources, etc., and intangible assets such as trade marks, patents, rights on land use, licenses, commodity credit, and the capitals. Documents on holding rights usually include certificates on creditor's right, certificates on investment or on participation, etc.

Insurance Reserve Funds refer to reserve fund for life insurance, the net pension fund, advance payment of premium and non-claimed reserves.

Settlement Fund refers to bank fund of financial institutions for settlement that is in the process of remittance.

Transactions Between Financial Institutions refer to flow of capital between financial institutions, including interbank deposits and loans.

Reserve Funds refer to savings of financial institutions in the central bank and designated reserves to the central bank.

Loans from the Central Bank refer to loans from the central bank to financial institutions.

Current Account includes goods, services, earnings and current transfers.

Import and Export of Goods refer to imported or exported goods through Chinese customs. Both import and export of goods are valued at free on board (f.o.b.) prices. Free on board prices can be regarded as the purchaser's prices paid by importers when claiming goods at the boarder of the exporters. When the importer claim the imported goods, the goods have been loaded in importer's carriers or other carriers, and the exporter has paid export duty or received export redeem.

Import and Export of Services refers services provided between resident and non-resident units, including services on transportation, tourism, communications, construction, insurance, banking, computer and information, consultation, advertisements and publicity, as well as film, audio and video services, royalty for patents, trademarks and other special rights, other commercial services, and government services.

Earnings refers income from provision of factors of production between resident and non-resident units, including compensation of labours and earnings from investment. Earnings from investment include earnings from and expenses on direct investment, security investment and other investment, as well as reinvestment of earnings from direct investment.

Capital Account includes capital transfers such as immigration transfer, reduction or exemption of debts, etc..

Financial Account includes direct investment, security investment and other investments.

Direct Investment refers to investment by foreign investors or investors from Hong Kong, Macao and Taiwan in China, or by Chinese investors in foreign countries or in Hong Kong, Macao and Taiwan, in forms of exclusive investment, joint investment, contracted operation and cooperative development,.

Security Investment refers to the issue of stocks and securities by China in foreign countries or in Hong Kong, Macao and Taiwan, and the purchase by Chinese units of stocks and securities issued in foreign countries or in Hong Kong, Macao and Taiwan.

Other Investment refers to all external transactions on financial assets and liabilities other than direct investment and security investment, including trade credits, loans, currency, savings and other assets, provided by foreign countries to China and by China to foreign countries.

Reserve Assets, Net Increase refers to the net balance between the end of the reference year and the end of the previous year, in the gold reserve, foreign exchange reserve, special drawing rights in the International Monetary Fund, and the use of the Funds credits. The increase in the reserve assets is expressed in negative figure and the decrease in the reserve assets is expressed in positive figure.

4

人口
Population

简 要 说 明

一、本篇资料的主要内容

本篇资料反映我国2005年及历年人口方面的基本情况，包括全国及31个省、自治区、直辖市的主要人口统计数据，如：全国历年人口数、城镇人口、乡村人口；2005年各地区人口数、出生率、死亡率、自然增长率、人口负担系数、家庭户规模、人口受教育程度等。

二、本篇的资料来源

本篇资料由国家统计局人口和就业统计司整理。其中表4－1、4－2中1982－1989年的数据根据1982年、1990年两次全国人口普查数据进行了调整；1990－2000年的数据根据2000年全国人口普查数据进行了调整；2001－2004年数据为人口变动情况抽样调查推算数；2005年数据为全国1％人口抽样调查推算数；其余年份为户籍统计数据。表4－3为2005年全国1％人口抽样调查推算数据。表4－4数据来源为全国和各地区1％人口抽样调查主要数据公报。表4－5为五次全国人口普查主要数据。表4－6是根据1990年和2000年全国人口普查数据计算的。表4－7至4－18为2005年全国1％人口抽样调查样本数据。

2005年全国1％人口抽样调查是以全国为总体，各省、自治区、直辖市为次总体，采用分层、多阶段、整群概率比例抽样方法，在全国31个省、自治区、直辖市抽取了2869个县(市、区)、21181个乡(镇、街道)、77417个调查小区的1699万人。经加权后汇总，2005年全国人口出生率为12.40‰，死亡率为6.51‰，自然增长率为5.89‰。按此推算，2005年末全国总人口为130756万人，出生人口为1617万人，死亡人口为849万人，净增人口为768万人。

Brief Introduction

I. Main Content

Data in this chapter show the basic condition of population in 2005 and in previous years of the whole nation and of 31 provinces, autonomous regions and municipalities directly under the central government, such as the national population, urban population and rural population over the years; as well as population, birth rates, death rates, natural growth rates, dependency ratio, household size and education attainment of population by region in 2005.

II. Source of Data

Data in this chapter are prepared by the Department of Population and Employment Statistics of the National Bureau of Statistics. In tables 4-1 and 4-2, figures for 1982-1989 have been adjusted in line with the data from the population censuses of 1982 and 1990, figures for 1990-2000 have been adjusted on the basis of the 2000 population census, figures for 2001-2004 are estimates from the annual national sample survey on population changes, figures for 2005 are estimated from the National Sample Survey of 1% of Population, while figures for other years are statistics derived from household registration. Data in Table 4-3 are estimates from the 2005 National Sample Survey of 1% of Population. Date in Table 4-4 are from the national and provincial communiqués of the key results of the 2005 National Sample Survey of 1% of Population. Data in Table 4-5 present the main results from the five national population censuses. Data in Table 4-6 are compiled from the 1990 and 2000 population censuses. Data in tables 4-7 to 4-18 are the sample results of the 2005 National Sample Survey of 1% of Population.

The National Sample Survey of 1% of Population adopted a multi-stage stratified systematic PPS cluster sampling scheme, taking the whole nation as the population and each province, autonomous region or municipality as the sub-population. A total of 16.99 million people were selected from 77,417 survey districts in 21,181 townships (towns and urban neighborhood committees) in 2,869 counties (cities and districts) of the 31 provinces, autonomous regions and municipalities. The weighted estimation procedure suggested that the birth rate was 12.40 per thousand, the death rate was 6.51 per thousand and the natural growth rate was 5.89 per thousand for China in 2005. Based on these rates, it was further estimated that China had a total population of 1,307.56 million at the end of 2005, with 16.17 million births, 8.49 million deaths and a net increase of 7.68 million people during the year.

4-1 人 口 数 及 构 成

Population and Its Composition

本表各年人口未包括香港、澳门特别行政区和台湾省的人口数据。
Data in this table exclude the population of Hong Kong SAR, Macao SAR and Taiwan Province.

单位：万人 (10 000 persons)

年 份 Year	年底人口数 Total Population (year-end)	按性别分 By Sex				按城乡分 By Residence			
		男 Male		女 Female		城镇 Urban		乡村 Rural	
		人口数 Population	比重(%) Proportion	人口数 Population	比重(%) Proportion	人口数 Population	比重(%) Proportion	人口数 Population	比重(%) Proportion
1978	96259	49567	51.49	46692	48.51	17245	17.92	79014	82.08
1980	98705	50785	51.45	47920	48.55	19140	19.39	79565	80.61
1985	105851	54725	51.70	51126	48.30	25094	23.71	80757	76.29
1989	112704	58099	51.55	54605	48.45	29540	26.21	83164	73.79
1990	114333	58904	51.52	55429	48.48	30195	26.41	84138	73.59
1991	115823	59466	51.34	56357	48.66	31203	26.94	84620	73.06
1992	117171	59811	51.05	57360	48.95	32175	27.46	84996	72.54
1993	118517	60472	51.02	58045	48.98	33173	27.99	85344	72.01
1994	119850	61246	51.10	58604	48.90	34169	28.51	85681	71.49
1995	121121	61808	51.03	59313	48.97	35174	29.04	85947	70.96
1996	122389	62200	50.82	60189	49.18	37304	30.48	85085	69.52
1997	123626	63131	51.07	60495	48.93	39449	31.91	84177	68.09
1998	124761	63940	51.25	60821	48.75	41608	33.35	83153	66.65
1999	125786	64692	51.43	61094	48.57	43748	34.78	82038	65.22
2000	126743	65437	51.63	61306	48.37	45906	36.22	80837	63.78
2001	127627	65672	51.46	61955	48.54	48064	37.66	79563	62.34
2002	128453	66115	51.47	62338	48.53	50212	39.09	78241	60.91
2003	129227	66556	51.50	62671	48.50	52376	40.53	76851	59.47
2004	129988	66976	51.52	63012	48.48	54283	41.76	75705	58.24
2005	130756	67375	51.53	63381	48.47	56212	42.99	74544	57.01

注：1.1982年以前数据为户籍统计数；1982—1989年数据根据1990年人口普查数据有所调整；1990-2000年数据根据2000年人口普查数据进行了调整；2001-2004年数据为人口变动情况抽样调查推算数；2005年数据根据全国1%人口抽样调查数据推算(下表同)。
2.年底人口数和按性别分人口中包括中国人民解放军现役军人，按城乡分人口中现役军人计入城镇人口。

a) Data before 1982 were taken from the annual reports of the Ministry of Public Security. Data in 1982-1989 were adjusted on the basis of the 1990 national population census. Data in 1990-2000 were adjusted on the basis of the estimated on the basis of the 2000 national population census. Data in 2001-2004 have been estimated on the basis of the annual national sample surveys on population changes. Data in 2005 are estimated on the national 1% sample survey on population. (the next table is the same).

b) Total population and population by sex include the military personnel of Chinese People's Liberation Army, the military personnel are classified as urban population in the item of population by residence.

4-2 人口出生率、死亡率和自然增长率

Birth Rate, Death Rate and Natural Growth Rate of Population

单位：‰ (‰)

年 份 Year	出生率 Birth Rate	死亡率 Death Rate	自然增长率 Natural Growth Rate	年 份 Year	出生率 Birth Rate	死亡率 Death Rate	自然增长率 Natural Growth Rate
1978	18.25	6.25	12.00	1993	18.09	6.64	11.45
1980	18.21	6.34	11.87	1994	17.70	6.49	11.21
1981	20.91	6.36	14.55	1995	17.12	6.57	10.55
1982	22.28	6.60	15.68	1996	16.98	6.56	10.42
1983	20.19	6.90	13.29	1997	16.57	6.51	10.06
1984	19.90	6.82	13.08	1998	15.64	6.50	9.14
1985	21.04	6.78	14.26	1999	14.64	6.46	8.18
1986	22.43	6.86	15.57	2000	14.03	6.45	7.58
1987	23.33	6.72	16.61	2001	13.38	6.43	6.95
1988	22.37	6.64	15.73	2002	12.86	6.41	6.45
1989	21.58	6.54	15.04	2003	12.41	6.40	6.01
1990	21.06	6.67	14.39	2004	12.29	6.42	5.87
1991	19.68	6.70	12.98	2005	12.40	6.51	5.89
1992	18.24	6.64	11.60				

4-3 各地区人口数和出生率、死亡率、自然增长率（2005年）

Total Population and Birth Rate, Death Rate and Natural Growth Rate by Region (2005)

地　区	Region	年底人口数（万人）Total Population (year-end) (10 000 persons)	出生率（‰）Birth Rate (‰)	死亡率（‰）Death Rate (‰)	自然增长率（‰）Natural Growth Rate (‰)
全　国	**National Total**	**130756**	**12.40**	**6.51**	**5.89**
北　京	Beijing	1538	6.29	5.20	1.09
天　津	Tianjin	1043	7.44	6.01	1.43
河　北	Hebei	6851	12.84	6.75	6.09
山　西	Shanxi	3355	12.02	6.00	6.02
内蒙古	Inner Mongolia	2386	10.08	5.46	4.62
辽　宁	Liaoning	4221	7.01	6.04	0.97
吉　林	Jilin	2716	7.89	5.32	2.57
黑龙江	Heilongjiang	3820	7.87	5.20	2.67
上　海	Shanghai	1778	7.04	6.08	0.96
江　苏	Jiangsu	7475	9.24	7.03	2.21
浙　江	Zhejiang	4898	11.10	6.08	5.02
安　徽	Anhui	6120	12.43	6.23	6.20
福　建	Fujian	3535	11.60	5.62	5.98
江　西	Jiangxi	4311	13.79	5.96	7.83
山　东	Shandong	9248	12.14	6.31	5.83
河　南	Henan	9380	11.55	6.30	5.25
湖　北	Hubei	5710	8.74	5.69	3.05
湖　南	Hunan	6326	11.90	6.75	5.15
广　东	Guangdong	9194	11.70	4.68	7.02
广　西	Guangxi	4660	14.26	6.09	8.16
海　南	Hainan	828	14.65	5.72	8.93
重　庆	Chongqing	2798	9.40	6.40	3.00
四　川	Sichuan	8212	9.70	6.80	2.90
贵　州	Guizhou	3730	14.59	7.21	7.38
云　南	Yunnan	4450	14.72	6.75	7.97
西　藏	Tibet	277	17.94	7.15	10.79
陕　西	Shaanxi	3720	10.02	6.01	4.01
甘　肃	Gansu	2594	12.59	6.57	6.02
青　海	Qinghai	543	15.70	6.21	9.49
宁　夏	Ningxia	596	15.93	4.95	10.98
新　疆	Xinjiang	2010	16.42	5.04	11.38

注：1.全国年底人口数包括现役军人数，分地区数字中未包括。
2.全国数据未包括香港、澳门特别行政区和台湾省的人口数据。
3.全国数据根据抽样误差和调查误差进行了修正。
4.分地区人口数是根据1%人口抽样调查充分考虑了流动人口的数据，故部分地区人口数与上年不能直接进行对比。

a) The military personnel were included in the national total population, but excluded in the regional total population.
b) The national total population excluded the population of Hong Kong, Macao and Taiwan.
c) The national total population was adjusted according to the sampling error and investigation error.
d) Data of total population by region are data based on 1% Population Sample Survey with careful consideration of floating population. So the data in some regions are not comparable with preceding year.

4-4 各地区人口的城乡构成（2005年）

Population by Urban and Rural Residence and Region (2005)

本表数据来源为全国和各地区1%人口抽样调查主要数据公报。

Data in this table are obtained from Communiqué on major figures of the 1% Population Sample Survey in 2005.

单位：万人 (10 000 persons)

地 区	Region	人口数（11月1日零时） Total Population (zero hour of Nov.1)	城镇人口 Urban Population		乡村人口 Rural Population	
			人口数 Population	比重（%） Proportion	人口数 Population	比重（%） Proportion
全 国	**National Total**	**130628**	**56157**	**42.99**	**74471**	**57.01**
北 京	Beijing	1536	1284	83.62	252	16.38
天 津	Tianjin	1043	783	75.11	259	24.89
河 北	Hebei	6844	2580	37.69	4264	62.31
山 西	Shanxi	3352	1411	42.11	1940	57.89
内蒙古	Inner Mongolia	2386	1126	47.20	1260	52.80
辽 宁	Liaoning	4220	2477	58.70	1743	41.30
吉 林	Jilin	2715	1426	52.52	1289	47.48
黑龙江	Heilongjiang	3818	2027	53.10	1791	46.90
上 海	Shanghai	1778	1584	89.09	194	10.91
江 苏	Jiangsu	7468	3742	50.11	3726	49.89
浙 江	Zhejiang	4894	2742	56.02	2152	43.98
安 徽	Anhui	6114	2170	35.50	3944	64.50
福 建	Fujian	3532	1671	47.30	1861	52.70
江 西	Jiangxi	4307	1593	37.00	2713	63.00
山 东	Shandong	9239	4158	45.00	5081	55.00
河 南	Henan	9371	2872	30.65	6499	69.35
湖 北	Hubei	5707	2465	43.20	3242	56.80
湖 南	Hunan	6320	2338	37.00	3982	63.00
广 东	Guangdong	9185	5573	60.68	3612	39.32
广 西	Guangxi	4655	1565	33.62	3090	66.38
海 南	Hainan	826	373	45.20	453	54.80
重 庆	Chongqing	2797	1264	45.20	1533	54.80
四 川	Sichuan	8208	2709	33.00	5499	67.00
贵 州	Guizhou	3725	1001	26.87	2724	73.13
云 南	Yunnan	4442	1311	29.50	3132	70.50
西 藏	Tibet	276	74	26.65	202	73.35
陕 西	Shaanxi	3718	1384	37.23	2334	62.77
甘 肃	Gansu	2592	778	30.02	1814	69.98
青 海	Qinghai	543	213	39.25	330	60.75
宁 夏	Ningxia	595	252	42.28	343	57.72
新 疆	Xinjiang	2008	746	37.15	1262	62.85

4-5 五次全国人口普查人口基本情况

Basic Statistics on National Population Census in 1953, 1964, 1982, 1990 and 2000

本表未包括香港、澳门特别行政区及台湾省数据。

Data in this table excluded the population of Hong Kong , Macao and Taiwan.

指标	Item	1953	1964	1982	1990	2000
总人口 （万人）	**Total Population (10 000 persons)**	**59435**	**69458**	**100818**	**113368**	**126583**
男	Male	30799	35652	51944	58495	65355
女	Female	28636	33806	48874	54873	61228
性别比（以女性为100）	Sex Ratio (female=100)	107.56	105.46	106.30	106.60	106.74
家庭户规模 （人/户）	**Average Family Size (person/household)**	**4.33**	**4.43**	**4.41**	**3.96**	**3.44**
各年龄组人口 （%）	**Population by Age Group (%)**					
0-14岁	0-14	36.28	40.69	33.59	27.69	22.89
15-64岁	15-64	59.31	55.75	61.50	66.74	70.15
65岁及以上	65 and Over	4.41	3.56	4.91	5.57	6.96
民族人口	**Nationality Population**					
汉族 （万人）	Han Nationality (10 000 persons)	54728	65456	94088	104248	115940
占总人口比重 （%）	Percentage to Total Population (%)	93.94	94.24	93.32	91.96	91.59
少数民族 （万人）	Minority Nationalities (10 000 persons)	3532	4002	6730	9120	10643
占总人口比重 （%）	Percentage to Total Population (%)	6.06	5.76	6.68	8.04	8.41
每十万人拥有的各种受教育程度人口 （人）	**Population with Various Education Attainments Per 100 000 Persons (person)**					
大专及以上	Junior College and Above		416	615	1422	3611
高中和中专	Senior Secondary/Secondary Technical School		1319	6779	8039	11146
初中	Junior Secondary School		4680	17892	23344	33961
小学	Primary School		28330	35237	37057	35701
文盲人口及文盲率	**Illiterate Population and Illiterate Rate**					
文盲人口 （万人）	Illiterate Population (10 000 persons)		23327	22996	18003	8507
文盲率 （%）	Illiterate Rate (%)		33.58	22.81	15.88	6.72
城乡人口 （万人）	**Population by Residence (10 000 persons)**					
城镇人口	Urban Population	7726	12710	21082	29971	45844
乡村人口	Rural Population	50534	56748	79736	83397	80739
平均预期寿命 （岁）	**Life Expectancy (years)**			**67.77***	**68.55**	**71.40**
男	Male			66.28*	66.84	69.63
女	Female			69.27*	70.47	73.33

注：1.历次普查总人口数据中包括了中国人民解放军现役军人。在城乡人口中，中国人民解放军现役军人列为城镇人口统计。

2.1953年总人口数据中包括了间接调查人口，而民族人口、城乡人口中未包括。

3.1964年文盲人口为13岁及13岁以上不识字人口，1982、1990、2000年文盲人口为15岁及15岁以上不识字或识字很少的人。

4.表中“*”号表示为1981年数据。

a) Total population from population censuses includes the military personnel. Military personnel is listed as urban population in population by residence.

b) Total population of 1953 census includes the population from indirect survey, but excludes in the nationality population and urban/rural population.

c) Illiterate population of 1964 census referred to people of 13 years old and over who could not read. Illiterate population of 1982, 1990 and 2000 censuses referred to people of 15 years old and over who could not read or could read very little.

d) Data with "*" in this table are of 1981.

4-6 各地区人口平均预期寿命

Population Life Expectancy by Region

单位：岁 (years old)

地 区	Region	1990年预期寿命 Life Expectancy in 1990	男 Male	女 Female	2000年预期寿命 Life Expectancy in 2000	男 Male	女 Female
全 国	**National Total**	**68.55**	**66.84**	**70.47**	**71.40**	**69.63**	**73.33**
北 京	Beijing	72.86	71.07	74.93	76.10	74.33	78.01
天 津	Tianjin	72.32	71.03	73.73	74.91	73.31	76.63
河 北	Hebei	70.35	68.47	72.53	72.54	70.68	74.57
山 西	Shanxi	68.97	67.33	70.93	71.65	69.96	73.57
内蒙古	Inner Mongolia	65.68	64.47	67.22	69.87	68.29	71.79
辽 宁	Liaoning	70.22	68.72	71.94	73.34	71.51	75.36
吉 林	Jilin	67.95	66.65	69.49	73.10	71.38	75.04
黑龙江	Heilongjiang	66.97	65.50	68.73	72.37	70.39	74.66
上 海	Shanghai	74.90	72.77	77.02	78.14	76.22	80.04
江 苏	Jiangsu	71.37	69.26	73.57	73.91	71.69	76.23
浙 江	Zhejiang	71.78	69.66	74.24	74.70	72.50	77.21
安 徽	Anhui	69.48	67.75	71.36	71.85	70.18	73.59
福 建	Fujian	68.57	66.49	70.93	72.55	70.30	75.07
江 西	Jiangxi	66.11	64.87	67.49	68.95	68.37	69.32
山 东	Shandong	70.57	68.64	72.67	73.92	71.70	76.26
河 南	Henan	70.15	67.96	72.55	71.54	69.67	73.41
湖 北	Hubei	67.25	65.51	69.23	71.08	69.31	73.02
湖 南	Hunan	66.93	65.41	68.70	70.66	69.05	72.47
广 东	Guangdong	72.52	69.71	75.43	73.27	70.79	75.93
广 西	Guangxi	68.72	67.17	70.34	71.29	69.07	73.75
海 南	Hainan	70.01	66.93	73.28	72.92	70.66	75.26
重 庆	Chongqing				71.73	69.84	73.89
四 川	Sichuan	66.33	65.06	67.70	71.20	69.25	73.39
贵 州	Guizhou	64.29	63.04	65.63	65.96	64.54	67.57
云 南	Yunnan	63.49	62.08	64.98	65.49	64.24	66.89
西 藏	Tibet	59.64	57.64	61.57	64.37	62.52	66.15
陕 西	Shaanxi	67.40	66.23	68.79	70.07	68.92	71.30
甘 肃	Gansu	67.24	66.35	68.25	67.47	66.77	68.26
青 海	Qinghai	60.57	59.29	61.96	66.03	64.55	67.70
宁 夏	Ningxia	66.94	65.95	68.05	70.17	68.71	71.84
新 疆	Xinjiang	62.59	61.95	63.26	67.41	65.98	69.14

注：2000年各省人口平均预期寿命是根据各省1990年以来人口变动调查公布的死亡率对2000年人口普查死亡数据修正后计算的。

a) Life expectancy in 2000 by region is calculated by the death data of 2000's Population Census, which modified by the mortality rates from the annual national sample surveys on population changes since 1990.

4-7 按年龄和性别分人口数（2005年）

Population by Age and Sex (2005)

本表是2005年全国1%人口抽样调查样本数据，抽样比为1.325%。

Data in this table are obtained from the 1% Population Sample Survey in 2005. The sampling fraction is 1.325%.

年龄 Age	人口数（人） Population (person)	男 Male	女 Female	占总人口比重（%） Percentage to Total Population (%)	男 Male	女 Female	性别比（女=100） Sex Ratio (female=100)
总计 Total	**16985766**	**8584882**	**8400884**	**100.00**	**50.54**	**49.46**	**102.19**
0-4	907102	499709	407393	5.34	2.94	2.40	122.66
5-9	1060664	577004	483660	6.24	3.40	2.85	119.30
10-14	1353263	721493	631770	7.97	4.25	3.72	114.20
15-19	1443484	749084	694399	8.50	4.41	4.09	107.88
20-24	1036723	499927	536796	6.10	2.94	3.16	93.13
25-29	1110290	539235	571055	6.54	3.17	3.36	94.43
30-34	1445908	711021	734887	8.51	4.19	4.33	96.75
35-39	1651487	813134	838354	9.72	4.79	4.94	96.99
40-44	1475539	732641	742898	8.69	4.31	4.37	98.62
45-49	1147578	575858	571720	6.76	3.39	3.37	100.72
50-54	1236929	622759	614170	7.28	3.67	3.62	101.40
55-59	907435	462421	445014	5.34	2.72	2.62	103.91
60-64	668310	342519	325791	3.93	2.02	1.92	105.13
65-69	564095	286166	277929	3.32	1.68	1.64	102.96
70-74	454955	224027	230928	2.68	1.32	1.36	97.01
75-79	290171	135684	154487	1.71	0.80	0.91	87.83
80-84	156110	66132	89978	0.92	0.39	0.53	73.50
85-89	56582	20475	36107	0.33	0.12	0.21	56.71
90-94	15825	4785	11040	0.09	0.03	0.06	43.35
95+	3319	810	2509	0.02	0.00	0.01	32.28

注：由于各地区数据采用加权汇总的方法，全国1%人口抽样调查样本数据合计与各分项相加略有误差(以下表同)。

a) Because data by region are calculated by the weighted sum method, total data of the 1% Population Sample Survey is not equal to the sum of each item.

4-8 各地区户数、人口数、性别比和户规模（2005年）

Household, Population, Sex Ratio and Household Size by Region (2005)

本表是2005年全国1%人口抽样调查样本数据，抽样比为1.325%。

Data in this table are obtained from the 1% Population Sample Survey in 2005. The sampling fraction is 1.325%.

地区	Region	户数（户） Number of Households (household)	家庭户 Family Household	集体户 Collective Household	人口数（人） Population (person)	男 Male	女 Female	性别比（女=100） Sex Ratio (female=100)
全国	**National Total**	**5391013**	**5286554**	**104459**	**16985766**	**8584882**	**8400884**	**102.19**
北京	Beijing	73787	69594	4192	203582	103122	100461	102.65
天津	Tianjin	46385	44806	1578	138060	69308	68752	100.81
河北	Hebei	272829	270892	1937	906856	455500	451355	100.92
山西	Shanxi	131264	130427	837	444096	225294	218802	102.97
内蒙古	Inner Mongolia	108157	106792	1365	315884	161560	154324	104.69
辽宁	Liaoning	191306	189878	1428	558727	280107	278620	100.53
吉林	Jilin	114033	113403	631	359512	182545	176968	103.15
黑龙江	Heilongjiang	169716	169177	540	505647	255867	249780	102.44
上海	Shanghai	87861	83106	4756	235351	118419	116932	101.27
江苏	Jiangsu	337537	329566	7971	989454	485494	503960	96.34
浙江	Zhejiang	235033	226688	8345	648340	328876	319465	102.95
安徽	Anhui	267231	265023	2208	810095	406651	403444	100.79
福建	Fujian	156154	148892	7262	467922	235254	232669	101.11
江西	Jiangxi	173456	171522	1934	570672	290449	280223	103.65
山东	Shandong	420932	415415	5517	1224142	611975	612167	99.97
河南	Henan	363015	361725	1290	1241616	630613	611003	103.21
湖北	Hubei	244772	242166	2606	755824	384490	371334	103.54
湖南	Hunan	265433	263001	2432	837363	428236	409126	104.67
广东	Guangdong	345573	310146	35427	1217005	616339	600667	102.61
广西	Guangxi	182241	180466	1775	616837	319740	297097	107.62
海南	Hainan	28422	27779	644	109601	57525	52076	110.46
重庆	Chongqing	130399	129342	1057	370367	186623	183744	101.57
四川	Sichuan	368516	366256	2260	1087009	541978	545031	99.44
贵州	Guizhou	142854	142031	823	493715	254202	239513	106.13
云南	Yunnan	163945	161443	2502	589039	303893	285146	106.57
西藏	Tibet	7282	7227	55	36666	18149	18517	98.01
陕西	Shaanxi	151049	149873	1176	492410	248660	243750	102.01
甘肃	Gansu	93512	92736	775	343364	173235	170129	101.83
青海	Qinghai	19566	19245	321	71903	36328	35574	102.12
宁夏	Ningxia	22075	21917	158	78892	39733	39159	101.47
新疆	Xinjiang	76677	76020	657	265815	134718	131097	102.76

4-8 续表 continued

地 区	Region	家庭户人口数(人) Family Household Population (person)	男 Male	女 Female	集体户人口数(人) Collective Household Population (person)	男 Male	女 Female	平均家庭户规模(人/户) Average Family Size (person/household)
全 国	**National Total**	**16570406**	**8354106**	**8216300**	**415360**	**230777**	**184584**	**3.13**
北 京	Beijing	188218	93301	94916	15365	9821	5544	2.70
天 津	Tianjin	130900	65378	65523	7160	3931	3229	2.92
河 北	Hebei	899339	452019	447320	7517	3482	4035	3.32
山 西	Shanxi	440601	223302	217299	3495	1992	1503	3.38
内蒙古	Inner Mongolia	310952	158140	152812	4932	3420	1512	2.91
辽 宁	Liaoning	553971	277593	276378	4756	2514	2241	2.92
吉 林	Jilin	356480	180823	175657	3032	1722	1310	3.14
黑龙江	Heilongjiang	503286	254337	248949	2361	1530	831	2.97
上 海	Shanghai	220576	109480	111096	14775	8939	5836	2.65
江 苏	Jiangsu	958550	469534	489016	30903	15960	14944	2.91
浙 江	Zhejiang	619804	311824	307980	28537	17052	11485	2.73
安 徽	Anhui	801681	401545	400136	8414	5106	3308	3.02
福 建	Fujian	445164	222733	222431	22759	12521	10238	2.99
江 西	Jiangxi	564060	286604	277456	6612	3845	2767	3.29
山 东	Shandong	1203376	600605	602770	20767	11370	9397	2.90
河 南	Henan	1237993	627873	610119	3623	2740	883	3.42
湖 北	Hubei	744987	377712	367275	10836	6778	4058	3.08
湖 南	Hunan	826391	421473	404919	10971	6764	4208	3.14
广 东	Guangdong	1053819	532417	521402	163187	83922	79265	3.40
广 西	Guangxi	610512	316165	294347	6325	3575	2750	3.38
海 南	Hainan	106797	56085	50712	2804	1440	1364	3.84
重 庆	Chongqing	366415	183737	182678	3951	2886	1065	2.83
四 川	Sichuan	1079070	537480	541591	7939	4498	3441	2.95
贵 州	Guizhou	490715	252090	238626	3000	2113	887	3.45
云 南	Yunnan	578788	298092	280695	10251	5801	4450	3.59
西 藏	Tibet	36346	17951	18395	320	198	123	5.03
陕 西	Shaanxi	488076	246030	242046	4334	2629	1705	3.26
甘 肃	Gansu	340445	171212	169233	2919	2024	896	3.67
青 海	Qinghai	70595	35590	35005	1308	738	570	3.67
宁 夏	Ningxia	78435	39417	39018	457	316	141	3.58
新 疆	Xinjiang	264066	133565	130500	1750	1153	597	3.47

4-9 各地区分性别、户口登记状况的人口（2005年）

Population by Sex, Household Registration Status and Region (2005)

本表是2005年全国1%人口抽样调查样本数据，抽样比为1.325%。

Data in this table are obtained from the 1% Population Sample Survey in 2005. The sampling fraction is 1.325%.

单位：人 (person)

地区	Region	人口数 Total			居住在本乡、镇、街道，户口在本乡、镇、街道 Residing in the Township, Towns and Street Communities with Permanent Household Registration There		
		合计 Total	男 Male	女 Female	小计 Sub-total	男 Male	女 Female
全　国	**National Total**	**16985766**	**8584882**	**8400884**	**14956470**	**7559833**	**7396636**
北　京	Beijing	203582	103122	100461	127395	64088	63307
天　津	Tianjin	138060	69308	68752	109521	54925	54597
河　北	Hebei	906856	455500	451355	841012	422905	418107
山　西	Shanxi	444096	225294	218802	404399	205474	198925
内蒙古	Inner Mongolia	315884	161560	154324	255807	130741	125066
辽　宁	Liaoning	558727	280107	278620	471471	237686	233785
吉　林	Jilin	359512	182545	176968	324453	165421	159032
黑龙江	Heilongjiang	505647	255867	249780	456208	231467	224742
上　海	Shanghai	235351	118419	116932	141227	70431	70796
江　苏	Jiangsu	989454	485494	503960	838581	410231	428350
浙　江	Zhejiang	648340	328876	319465	500993	251836	249157
安　徽	Anhui	810095	406651	403444	753916	377898	376018
福　建	Fujian	467922	235254	232669	364564	182054	182510
江　西	Jiangxi	570672	290449	280223	527132	268448	258684
山　东	Shandong	1224142	611975	612167	1117888	558422	559466
河　南	Henan	1241616	630613	611003	1190572	604059	586513
湖　北	Hubei	755824	384490	371334	692569	352732	339838
湖　南	Hunan	837363	428236	409126	776821	397281	379540
广　东	Guangdong	1217005	616339	600667	856030	432917	423113
广　西	Guangxi	616837	319740	297097	574954	299353	275601
海　南	Hainan	109601	57525	52076	95861	50396	45464
重　庆	Chongqing	370367	186623	183744	339248	171213	168034
四　川	Sichuan	1087009	541978	545031	1005145	502538	502607
贵　州	Guizhou	493715	254202	239513	458818	236976	221842
云　南	Yunnan	589039	303893	285146	540976	279122	261853
西　藏	Tibet	36666	18149	18517	35057	17331	17726
陕　西	Shaanxi	492410	248660	243750	459543	231626	227917
甘　肃	Gansu	343364	173235	170129	325728	164233	161496
青　海	Qinghai	71903	36328	35574	64692	32638	32054
宁　夏	Ningxia	78892	39733	39159	70648	35646	35003
新　疆	Xinjiang	265815	134718	131097	235241	119747	115493

4-9 续表 continued

单位：人 (person)

地区	Region	居住在本乡、镇、街道,户口登记地在外乡、镇、街道,离开户口登记地半年以上 Residing in the Township, Towns and Street Communities with Permanent Household Registration Elsewhere, Having been Away from that Places For More Than 6 Months.			居住在本乡、镇、街道,户口待定 Residing in the Township, Towns and Street Communities with Places of Household Registration Unsettled.			原住在本乡、镇、街道,现在国外工作学习 Originally Living in the Townships, Towns and Street Communities, Now Working or Studying Abroad		
		小计 Sub-total	男 Male	女 Female	小计 Sub-total	男 Male	女 Female	小计 Sub-total	男 Male	女 Female
全国	**National Total**	**1945894**	**983525**	**962370**	**82374**	**40905**	**41469**	**1029**	**619**	**410**
北京	Beijing	75285	38568	36718	843	436	407	58	30	28
天津	Tianjin	28075	14134	13941	455	244	210	9	5	4
河北	Hebei	63485	31554	31930	2336	1026	1310	23	15	8
山西	Shanxi	37431	18669	18763	2266	1152	1114	1	0	1
内蒙古	Inner Mongolia	57961	29780	28180	2105	1031	1074	12	7	4
辽宁	Liaoning	85339	41457	43882	1875	941	934	43	24	19
吉林	Jilin	34466	16827	17639	559	278	282	35	20	15
黑龙江	Heilongjiang	48062	23682	24380	1339	694	645	39	25	14
上海	Shanghai	93546	47711	45836	549	264	285	29	13	16
江苏	Jiangsu	144242	71882	72360	6477	3277	3200	154	104	50
浙江	Zhejiang	142667	74669	67998	4626	2339	2287	54	30	23
安徽	Anhui	53222	27249	25973	2944	1496	1448	13	8	5
福建	Fujian	98757	50939	47818	4370	2114	2256	232	147	85
江西	Jiangxi	39027	19761	19266	4503	2233	2270	10	6	4
山东	Shandong	101586	51330	50257	4629	2196	2433	39	27	11
河南	Henan	46278	24181	22097	4736	2351	2385	30	22	8
湖北	Hubei	61315	30814	30501	1923	939	984	16	5	11
湖南	Hunan	58256	29772	28484	2271	1177	1094	15	7	8
广东	Guangdong	351468	178647	172821	9458	4749	4709	50	26	24
广西	Guangxi	39064	18968	20095	2800	1405	1396	19	14	5
海南	Hainan	12944	6725	6219	777	393	385	19	10	9
重庆	Chongqing	29427	14574	14853	1679	830	849	13	6	8
四川	Sichuan	75586	36316	39270	6255	3107	3148	24	17	7
贵州	Guizhou	31883	15760	16124	3007	1464	1542	7	2	4
云南	Yunnan	44911	23225	21686	3115	1527	1588	38	19	19
西藏	Tibet	1464	742	721	145	75	70			
陕西	Shaanxi	31153	16131	15022	1700	894	806	14	8	6
甘肃	Gansu	16278	8311	7968	1356	691	665	1	1	1
青海	Qinghai	6648	3406	3242	558	280	277	4	4	1
宁夏	Ningxia	7444	3691	3754	798	395	402	1	0	0
新疆	Xinjiang	28624	14049	14575	1921	905	1016	30	17	13

4-10 各地区人口年龄构成和抚养比（2005年）

Age Composition and Dependency Ratio of Population by Region (2005)

本表是2005年全国1%人口抽样调查样本数据，抽样比为1.325%。
Data in this table are obtained from the 1% Population Sample Survey in 2005. The sampling fraction is 1.325%.

地区	Region	人口数 (人) Population (person)	0-14岁 Age 0-14	15-64岁 Age 15-64	65岁及以上 Age 65 and Over	总抚养比 (%) Gross Dependency Ratio (%)	少年儿童抚养比 Children Dependency Ratio	老年人口抚养比 Old Dependency Ratio
全 国	**National Total**	**16985766**	**3321029**	**12123681**	**1541056**	**40.10**	**27.39**	**12.71**
北 京	Beijing	203582	20932	160636	22014	26.74	13.03	13.70
天 津	Tianjin	138060	17488	107195	13377	28.79	16.31	12.48
河 北	Hebei	906856	160282	672457	74117	34.86	23.84	11.02
山 西	Shanxi	444096	94573	315280	34244	40.86	30.00	10.86
内蒙古	Inner Mongolia	315884	53884	236945	25056	33.32	22.74	10.57
辽 宁	Liaoning	558727	79560	424584	54583	31.59	18.74	12.86
吉 林	Jilin	359512	52084	279851	27577	28.47	18.61	9.85
黑龙江	Heilongjiang	505647	74876	392334	38437	28.88	19.08	9.80
上 海	Shanghai	235351	21182	186010	28159	26.53	11.39	15.14
江 苏	Jiangsu	989454	153721	728207	107525	35.88	21.11	14.77
浙 江	Zhejiang	648340	103086	476673	68581	36.01	21.63	14.39
安 徽	Anhui	810095	187067	541274	81754	49.66	34.56	15.10
福 建	Fujian	467922	86487	340481	40954	37.43	25.40	12.03
江 西	Jiangxi	570672	143226	379303	48143	50.45	37.76	12.69
山 东	Shandong	1224142	194922	907427	121794	34.90	21.48	13.42
河 南	Henan	1241616	262380	876943	102292	41.58	29.92	11.66
湖 北	Hubei	755824	142736	543773	69314	39.00	26.25	12.75
湖 南	Hunan	837363	156693	595873	84797	40.53	26.30	14.23
广 东	Guangdong	1217005	260401	866533	90071	40.45	30.05	10.39
广 西	Guangxi	616837	146466	411440	58931	49.92	35.60	14.32
海 南	Hainan	109601	25964	74277	9360	47.56	34.96	12.60
重 庆	Chongqing	370367	76551	253202	40614	46.27	30.23	16.04
四 川	Sichuan	1087009	237516	730821	118672	48.74	32.50	16.24
贵 州	Guizhou	493715	139899	313312	40504	57.58	44.65	12.93
云 南	Yunnan	589039	142052	402662	44325	46.29	35.28	11.01
西 藏	Tibet	36666	10010	24397	2259	50.29	41.03	9.26
陕 西	Shaanxi	492410	96302	353629	42480	39.25	27.23	12.01
甘 肃	Gansu	343364	80364	238196	24804	44.15	33.74	10.41
青 海	Qinghai	71903	17307	50254	4341	43.08	34.44	8.64
宁 夏	Ningxia	78892	20438	53701	4753	46.91	38.06	8.85
新 疆	Xinjiang	265815	62580	186012	17223	42.90	33.64	9.26

4-11 各地区按性别和婚姻状况分的人口（2005年）

Population by Sex, Marital Status and Region (2005)

本表是2005年全国1%人口抽样调查样本数据，抽样比为1.325%。

Data in this table are obtained from the 1% Population Sample Survey in 2005. The sampling fraction is 1.325%.

单位：人 (person)

地区	Region	15岁及以上人口 Population Aged 15 and Over	男 Male	女 Female	未婚 Never Married	男 Male	女 Female	初婚有配偶 First Married	男 Male	女 Female
全国	**National Total**	**13664737**	**6786677**	**6878061**	**2619360**	**1524886**	**1094474**	**9824784**	**4801807**	**5022977**
北京	Beijing	182650	92227	90424	42458	24048	18410	125619	62766	62853
天津	Tianjin	120572	59994	60578	25272	13533	11739	86157	43035	43123
河北	Hebei	746574	369699	376876	150192	83326	66866	539078	264338	274740
山西	Shanxi	349524	175754	173769	63950	37514	26437	257429	127362	130068
内蒙古	Inner Mongolia	262000	133393	128607	44045	26679	17367	197268	98619	98649
辽宁	Liaoning	479167	238190	240977	75060	43118	31942	356012	176046	179966
吉林	Jilin	307428	155105	152323	54665	31559	23105	224734	111905	112829
黑龙江	Heilongjiang	430771	216958	213813	67892	39886	28007	321690	159928	161761
上海	Shanghai	214169	107344	106825	45843	25561	20283	150506	75581	74925
江苏	Jiangsu	835732	401541	434191	132857	74717	58140	628557	301591	326966
浙江	Zhejiang	545255	274090	271165	94861	56991	37871	403170	201100	202069
安徽	Anhui	623028	303519	319509	107540	63216	44325	459328	219875	239453
福建	Fujian	381435	188037	193398	81372	46360	35012	267788	130941	136846
江西	Jiangxi	427446	209866	217579	71072	42527	28545	318555	153907	164648
山东	Shandong	1029220	507409	521811	185411	103594	81817	760077	373871	386206
河南	Henan	979235	483364	495872	198308	113209	85099	705908	341961	363947
湖北	Hubei	613088	305444	307644	107940	65272	42668	446127	216780	229347
湖南	Hunan	680670	342170	338500	136313	81936	54377	477887	234618	243268
广东	Guangdong	956604	473198	483406	287066	155264	131802	611909	299796	312113
广西	Guangxi	470371	238765	231606	107908	67455	40453	321121	156264	164857
海南	Hainan	83637	43036	40601	21852	13323	8529	55980	27723	28257
重庆	Chongqing	293816	145638	148178	43319	27417	15903	215741	104593	111148
四川	Sichuan	849493	415877	433616	126300	77715	48585	621161	298556	322606
贵州	Guizhou	353816	178813	175003	63287	39732	23555	254057	123713	130344
云南	Yunnan	446987	228580	218407	85689	54480	31210	320210	157797	162413
西藏	Tibet	26656	13064	13592	9393	5074	4320	14585	7099	7486
陕西	Shaanxi	396108	195982	200127	74375	43747	30628	286807	138574	148233
甘肃	Gansu	263000	130485	132515	50573	29433	21141	189969	92184	97785
青海	Qinghai	54595	27343	27252	10481	6183	4298	38081	18731	19350
宁夏	Ningxia	58454	29123	29330	10563	6003	4560	43550	21412	22138
新疆	Xinjiang	203235	102669	100566	43499	26016	17483	125723	61140	64583

4-11 续表 continued

单位：人 (person)

地 区	Region	再婚有配偶 Re-married	男 Male	女 Female	离 婚 Divorced	男 Male	女 Female	丧 偶 Widowed	男 Male	女 Female
全 国	**National Total**	**301209**	**138947**	**162262**	**135625**	**81486**	**54139**	**783760**	**239551**	**544209**
北 京	Beijing	4056	2069	1987	2869	1341	1528	7647	2003	5644
天 津	Tianjin	2200	1055	1145	1353	672	681	5590	1699	3891
河 北	Hebei	15075	6269	8805	5256	3506	1750	36973	12259	24714
山 西	Shanxi	7808	3326	4482	3057	2187	870	17279	5366	11913
内蒙古	Inner Mongolia	6217	2730	3487	3024	1823	1201	11446	3541	7905
辽 宁	Liaoning	13369	6372	6997	9489	5077	4411	25238	7578	17660
吉 林	Jilin	8274	3908	4366	5021	2980	2040	14735	4753	9982
黑龙江	Heilongjiang	12694	6224	6470	7682	4486	3196	20813	6434	14379
上 海	Shanghai	4155	2027	2128	3749	1883	1866	9916	2293	7624
江 苏	Jiangsu	15531	6746	8785	7100	4229	2871	51686	14258	37428
浙 江	Zhejiang	10913	4427	6486	5436	3439	1997	30874	8133	22741
安 徽	Anhui	10094	4183	5911	4305	2896	1409	41760	13349	28412
福 建	Fujian	6456	2961	3495	3103	2001	1101	22716	5773	16943
江 西	Jiangxi	8445	3974	4471	2974	1906	1069	26399	7553	18846
山 东	Shandong	19451	8284	11168	5773	3819	1954	58507	17841	40666
河 南	Henan	14433	6183	8250	6542	4377	2165	54044	17633	36411
湖 北	Hubei	15139	7081	8058	5363	3367	1996	38519	12944	25575
湖 南	Hunan	15960	7216	8744	6621	4281	2340	43888	14118	29770
广 东	Guangdong	8789	4547	4242	6014	3387	2627	42826	10204	32622
广 西	Guangxi	7024	3471	3553	3785	2442	1343	30533	9133	21400
海 南	Hainan	1110	585	525	556	357	199	4140	1049	3091
重 庆	Chongqing	9418	3992	5426	4458	2562	1896	20880	7075	13805
四 川	Sichuan	26462	11382	15080	10247	6098	4148	65324	22127	43197
贵 州	Guizhou	9847	5116	4730	3845	2450	1395	22780	7802	14978
云 南	Yunnan	11043	5596	5447	4304	2531	1773	25741	8176	17564
西 藏	Tibet	364	191	173	507	127	381	1806	574	1232
陕 西	Shaanxi	9063	4178	4884	3442	2251	1191	22421	7231	15190
甘 肃	Gansu	4831	2311	2520	2345	1478	867	15282	5080	10202
青 海	Qinghai	2003	1042	961	1112	518	595	2918	870	2048
宁 夏	Ningxia	1370	725	645	631	319	312	2340	664	1676
新 疆	Xinjiang	19616	10776	8840	5660	2696	2964	8737	2040	6697

4-12 各地区按性别和受教育程度分的人口（2005年）
Population by Sex, Educational Attainment and Region (2005)

本表是2005年全国1%人口抽样调查样本数据，抽样比为1.325%。
Data in this table are obtained from the 1% Population Sample Survey in 2005. The sampling fraction is 1.325%.

单位：人 (person)

地 区	Region	6岁及6岁以上人口 Population Aged 6 and Over	男 Male	女 Female	未上过学 No Schooling	男 Male	女 Female	小 学 Primary School	男 Male	女 Female
全 国	**National Total**	**15878355**	**7975386**	**7902969**	**1646360**	**450088**	**1196272**	**5285045**	**2581633**	**2703412**
北 京	Beijing	196019	99133	96885	7697	1562	6134	28028	13189	14840
天 津	Tianjin	132069	66091	65978	6603	1599	5004	28890	13865	15025
河 北	Hebei	846198	422303	423895	58381	15437	42944	254380	120194	134185
山 西	Shanxi	416531	210667	205864	21630	6521	15109	124513	58870	65643
内蒙古	Inner Mongolia	298416	152460	145956	31560	9626	21934	83456	40723	42733
辽 宁	Liaoning	532275	266101	266174	25497	6650	18847	145201	68956	76245
吉 林	Jilin	341975	173247	168727	20311	6369	13942	104191	50017	54174
黑龙江	Heilongjiang	481167	243098	238069	30028	8922	21105	138865	65924	72941
上 海	Shanghai	227240	114171	113069	12505	2347	10158	36037	16521	19517
江 苏	Jiangsu	939782	458139	481643	96151	21065	75086	270481	125586	144895
浙 江	Zhejiang	610761	308907	301854	71599	19066	52532	218873	110877	107996
安 徽	Anhui	754241	374549	379692	125436	36404	89033	254019	123724	130295
福 建	Fujian	439048	219551	219498	52608	11290	41318	159882	76763	83118
江 西	Jiangxi	517669	259646	258022	48835	11712	37124	209474	97364	112111
山 东	Shandong	1146600	570312	576288	140084	36119	103965	331391	153174	178217
河 南	Henan	1148451	576801	571650	101730	29115	72615	327316	156399	170917
湖 北	Hubei	715022	361479	353543	78240	19215	59025	227281	109864	117417
湖 南	Hunan	777739	394484	383256	62996	16842	46155	262644	130388	132256
广 东	Guangdong	1144620	575353	569266	67240	14720	52520	372059	175728	196332
广 西	Guangxi	564039	290675	273364	45454	11098	34356	224461	111306	113155
海 南	Hainan	101346	52797	48549	8748	2067	6680	31312	15203	16109
重 庆	Chongqing	348166	174616	173549	37514	10973	26541	147268	74701	72568
四 川	Sichuan	1013364	502405	510959	150815	44863	105952	439004	226276	212728
贵 州	Guizhou	448406	229078	219328	83420	22192	61228	200332	106659	93674
云 南	Yunnan	537098	276207	260891	96592	30641	65950	255810	136154	119656
西 藏	Tibet	32972	16279	16694	15016	6024	8992	14164	8096	6068
陕 西	Shaanxi	465541	233706	231835	44316	13179	31138	145308	69805	75503
甘 肃	Gansu	320059	160557	159501	59141	18388	40753	118587	59212	59375
青 海	Qinghai	65843	33116	32728	14906	4869	10037	22575	11987	10588
宁 夏	Ningxia	71782	35970	35812	11607	3527	8080	24015	12055	11961
新 疆	Xinjiang	243918	123489	120429	19703	7686	12017	85226	42054	43171

4-12 续表 continued

单位：人 (person)

地 区	Region	初 中 Junior Secondary School	男 Male	女 Female	高 中 Senior Secondary School	男 Male	女 Female	大专及以上 College and Higher Level	男 Male	女 Female
全 国	**National Total**	**6088659**	**3316912**	**2771747**	**1975098**	**1120964**	**854134**	**883192**	**505789**	**377404**
北 京	Beijing	63027	34090	28938	49266	24764	24501	48001	25528	22473
天 津	Tianjin	50103	26590	23513	27873	14085	13787	18601	9951	8650
河 北	Hebei	391553	209414	182139	101848	56313	45536	40036	20945	19091
山 西	Shanxi	192850	102839	90011	54343	29927	24415	23197	12510	10687
内蒙古	Inner Mongolia	114065	63948	50117	45675	24899	20775	23660	13264	10397
辽 宁	Liaoning	244140	127992	116147	73033	38466	34568	44404	24036	20367
吉 林	Jilin	143398	76616	66783	51242	27773	23469	22832	12472	10360
黑龙江	Heilongjiang	211122	113125	97997	70264	37978	32286	30888	17149	13741
上 海	Shanghai	81520	42992	38528	56630	29845	26784	40549	22466	18082
江 苏	Jiangsu	370726	195339	175387	138515	78597	59918	63909	37552	26357
浙 江	Zhejiang	212998	117950	95048	74175	41981	32194	33115	19031	14084
安 徽	Anhui	276259	154899	121360	69520	41464	28056	29007	18058	10949
福 建	Fujian	151251	87054	64197	53429	31282	22147	21877	13162	8717
江 西	Jiangxi	183396	103403	79994	56016	34228	21788	19946	12940	7006
山 东	Shandong	479871	265134	214737	144346	84947	59399	50909	30939	19970
河 南	Henan	539866	288691	251175	131090	74911	56179	48450	27685	20765
湖 北	Hubei	276577	153380	123197	96636	57200	39436	36287	21819	14468
湖 南	Hunan	308624	164487	144136	108558	62003	46554	34917	20763	14154
广 东	Guangdong	462511	241625	220886	176299	104690	71609	66510	38590	27920
广 西	Guangxi	215420	121699	93720	56149	33616	22533	22556	12956	9600
海 南	Hainan	41203	22951	18251	14558	9299	5260	5524	3276	2248
重 庆	Chongqing	111705	59813	51892	35557	19413	16143	16122	9716	6406
四 川	Sichuan	309710	167245	142464	78538	43785	34753	35297	20235	15061
贵 州	Guizhou	119830	73200	46630	29927	17874	12053	14897	9153	5743
云 南	Yunnan	132722	80138	52584	33857	19043	14813	18117	10229	7889
西 藏	Tibet	2799	1634	1165	700	362	338	293	163	131
陕 西	Shaanxi	181467	97658	83810	65714	36551	29163	28734	16514	12221
甘 肃	Gansu	92812	53116	39696	35882	21514	14368	13637	8327	5310
青 海	Qinghai	16520	9809	6711	7161	3838	3323	4682	2613	2069
宁 夏	Ningxia	22730	12862	9868	8534	4739	3795	4895	2786	2109
新 疆	Xinjiang	87885	47218	40667	29764	15574	14190	21340	10957	10383

4-13 各地区按性别分的15岁及15岁以上文盲人口（2005年）

Illiterate Population Aged 15 and Over by Sex and Region (2005)

本表是2005年全国1%人口抽样调查样本数据，抽样比为1.325%。

Data in this table are obtained from the 1% Population Sample Survey in 2005. The sampling fraction is 1.325%.

单位：人、%　　(person, %)

地 区	Region	15岁及15岁以上人口 Population Aged 15 and Over	男 Male	女 Female	文盲人口 Illiterate Population	男 Male	女 Female	文盲人口占15岁及以上人口的比重 % to Total Aged 15 and Over	男 Male	女 Female
全 国	**National Total**	**13664737**	**6786677**	**6878061**	**1508706**	**397877**	**1110828**	**11.04**	**5.86**	**16.15**
北 京	Beijing	182650	92227	90424	7152	1393	5759	3.92	1.51	6.37
天 津	Tianjin	120572	59994	60578	5793	1303	4490	4.80	2.17	7.41
河 北	Hebei	746574	369699	376876	53638	13842	39797	7.18	3.74	10.56
山 西	Shanxi	349524	175754	173769	19472	5673	13799	5.57	3.23	7.94
内蒙古	Inner Mongolia	262000	133393	128607	29476	8751	20725	11.25	6.56	16.12
辽 宁	Liaoning	479167	238190	240977	22839	5700	17139	4.77	2.39	7.11
吉 林	Jilin	307428	155105	152323	17994	5436	12558	5.85	3.50	8.24
黑龙江	Heilongjiang	430771	216958	213813	26633	7584	19049	6.18	3.50	8.91
上 海	Shanghai	214169	107344	106825	11213	2019	9194	5.24	1.88	8.61
江 苏	Jiangsu	835732	401541	434191	83702	17528	66174	10.02	4.37	15.24
浙 江	Zhejiang	545255	274090	271165	65172	16687	48485	11.95	6.09	17.88
安 徽	Anhui	623028	303519	319509	119875	34197	85678	19.24	11.27	26.82
福 建	Fujian	381435	188037	193398	49279	10028	39251	12.92	5.33	20.30
江 西	Jiangxi	427446	209866	217579	45038	10308	34730	10.54	4.91	15.96
山 东	Shandong	1029220	507409	521811	127449	31741	95707	12.38	6.26	18.34
河 南	Henan	979235	483364	495872	95891	26929	68962	9.79	5.57	13.91
湖 北	Hubei	613088	305444	307644	74114	17902	56212	12.09	5.86	18.27
湖 南	Hunan	680670	342170	338500	58377	15200	43177	8.58	4.44	12.76
广 东	Guangdong	956604	473198	483406	57370	10634	46735	6.00	2.25	9.67
广 西	Guangxi	470371	238765	231606	40625	9040	31584	8.64	3.79	13.64
海 南	Hainan	83637	43036	40601	8162	1794	6367	9.76	4.17	15.68
重 庆	Chongqing	293816	145638	148178	34244	9658	24586	11.65	6.63	16.59
四 川	Sichuan	849493	415877	433616	141104	40946	100158	16.61	9.85	23.10
贵 州	Guizhou	353816	178813	175003	75750	19190	56560	21.41	10.73	32.32
云 南	Yunnan	446987	228580	218407	89713	27653	62060	20.07	12.10	28.41
西 藏	Tibet	26656	13064	13592	11953	4374	7579	44.84	33.48	55.76
陕 西	Shaanxi	396108	195982	200127	40903	12024	28879	10.33	6.14	14.43
甘 肃	Gansu	263000	130485	132515	54780	16601	38180	20.83	12.72	28.81
青 海	Qinghai	54595	27343	27252	13143	4101	9042	24.07	15.00	33.18
宁 夏	Ningxia	58454	29123	29330	10935	3271	7664	18.71	11.23	26.13
新 疆	Xinjiang	203235	102669	100566	16919	6370	10549	8.32	6.20	10.49

注：本表"文盲人口"指15岁及15岁以上不识字及识字很少人口。

a) Illiterate population in this table refers to the population aged 15 and over, who are unable or very difficult to read.

4-14 各地区按家庭户规模分的户数（2005年）

Family Households by Size and Region (2005)

本表是2005年全国1%人口抽样调查样本数据，抽样比为1.325%。

Data in this table are obtained from the 1% Population Sample Survey in 2005. The sampling fraction is 1.325%.

单位：户 (household)

地 区	Region	家庭户户数 Number of Family Households	一人户 One Person	二人户 Two Persons	三人户 Three Persons	四人户 Four Persons	五人户 Five Persons	六人户 Six Persons	七人户 Seven Persons	八人户 Eight Persons	九人户 Nine Persons	十人及以上户 Ten Persons and Over
全 国	**National Total**	**5286554**	**567455**	**1294464**	**1577147**	**1014177**	**538035**	**199448**	**58212**	**22028**	**8383**	**7205**
北 京	Beijing	69594	10453	20191	25622	8125	3841	948	259	107	33	15
天 津	Tianjin	44806	4036	11363	18937	6345	3108	807	144	51	8	7
河 北	Hebei	270892	20585	59008	77806	64353	31476	13179	3122	934	264	166
山 西	Shanxi	130427	9979	26546	36662	31604	16374	6821	1648	514	163	115
内蒙古	Inner Mongolia	106792	9178	29574	41861	16895	7038	1711	371	110	42	12
辽 宁	Liaoning	189878	16412	54836	72276	26690	14970	3771	663	191	50	19
吉 林	Jilin	113403	6651	27595	44196	19081	11398	3268	779	308	87	40
黑龙江	Heilongjiang	169177	11683	47396	67909	24193	13430	3462	696	303	63	42
上 海	Shanghai	83106	13328	25007	30199	8254	4913	978	285	103	25	14
江 苏	Jiangsu	329566	40678	96182	103101	47492	31067	8044	1942	726	209	126
浙 江	Zhejiang	226688	38743	67072	67211	31749	15671	4729	926	366	142	78
安 徽	Anhui	265023	31079	68162	78502	53199	23483	7499	1988	699	258	155
福 建	Fujian	148892	22655	37027	40613	27541	13724	5018	1444	519	212	139
江 西	Jiangxi	171522	16484	38777	47285	37744	18962	7598	2576	1141	457	498
山 东	Shandong	415415	43930	118917	140097	73550	29139	7908	1304	418	98	56
河 南	Henan	361725	28520	69147	97970	91494	47998	19056	5028	1546	554	411
湖 北	Hubei	242166	23511	63391	75096	46593	23190	7431	1821	720	264	149
湖 南	Hunan	263001	29125	63060	73904	55626	27694	9460	2540	969	361	261
广 东	Guangdong	310146	43421	64847	68221	59159	39055	19500	8378	3981	1696	1888
广 西	Guangxi	180466	20181	36911	44589	39370	23495	9475	3577	1471	670	726
海 南	Hainan	27779	2607	4241	5860	5832	4683	2498	1107	467	234	250
重 庆	Chongqing	129342	18648	37501	39101	20634	9524	2897	660	244	79	55
四 川	Sichuan	366256	51770	100456	103686	61472	32518	11191	3133	1203	455	372
贵 州	Guizhou	142031	12014	28908	36404	32074	19702	8341	2982	987	377	242
云 南	Yunnan	161443	12901	26388	38206	44283	23714	11327	3114	945	340	225
西 藏	Tibet	7227	386	696	1058	1303	1132	829	633	467	305	419
陕 西	Shaanxi	149873	13197	33664	43286	33518	16955	6973	1611	443	145	81
甘 肃	Gansu	92736	6066	15450	23989	21810	14193	7395	2541	825	258	209
青 海	Qinghai	19245	1487	3069	5156	4418	2733	1414	522	223	116	107
宁 夏	Ningxia	21917	1420	4068	6207	4698	3025	1631	553	213	66	37
新 疆	Xinjiang	76020	6324	15016	22135	15077	9831	4291	1867	837	353	290

4-15 育龄妇女分年龄、孩次的生育状况
(2004年11月1日至2005年10月31日)
Age-specific Fertility Rate of Childbearing Women by Age of Mother and Birth Order (2004.11.1-2005.10.31)

本表是2005年全国1%人口抽样调查样本数据，抽样比为1.325%。

Data in this table are obtained from the 1% Population Sample Survey in 2005. The sampling fraction is 1.325%.

年龄 Age	平均育龄妇女人数（人） Average Number of Childbearing Women (person)	出生人数（人） Births (person)	一孩 1st Births	二孩 2nd Births	三孩及以上 3rd Births and over	生育率（‰） Fertility Rate (‰)	一孩 1st Births	二孩 2nd Births	三孩及以上 3rd Births and over
总计 Total	**4676587**	**161042**	**101383**	**50997**	**8662**	**34.44**	**21.68**	**10.9**	**1.85**
15-19	**664051**	**4209**	**3993**	**205**	**11**	**6.34**	**6.01**	**0.31**	**0.02**
15	159681	17	17			0.11	0.11		
16	142241	94	88	5		0.66	0.62	0.04	
17	138374	415	402	12	1	3.00	2.91	0.08	0.01
18	119925	1072	1019	50	3	8.94	8.50	0.42	0.02
19	103829	2611	2466	137	7	25.14	23.75	1.32	0.07
20-24	**540714**	**61889**	**55745**	**5584**	**560**	**114.46**	**103.09**	**10.33**	**1.04**
20	99451	6735	6344	368	23	67.72	63.79	3.70	0.23
21	101725	11016	10302	669	45	108.30	101.27	6.58	0.45
22	113155	13947	12802	1056	89	123.25	113.13	9.33	0.79
23	119600	15891	14169	1564	158	132.87	118.47	13.08	1.32
24	106783	14300	12128	1927	244	133.91	113.58	18.05	2.29
25-29	**581947**	**53367**	**33103**	**17693**	**2571**	**91.70**	**56.88**	**30.40**	**4.42**
25	115252	13794	10829	2614	351	119.69	93.96	22.68	3.05
26	113871	11978	8299	3213	467	105.19	72.88	28.21	4.10
27	110544	10037	6114	3434	488	90.79	55.31	31.07	4.41
28	115952	9082	4511	3966	604	78.32	38.91	34.20	5.21
29	126327	8477	3350	4466	661	67.10	26.51	35.35	5.23
30-34	**758911**	**30521**	**6925**	**20404**	**3192**	**40.22**	**9.12**	**26.89**	**4.21**
30	133869	7660	2390	4618	651	57.22	17.86	34.50	4.86
31	144698	7401	1782	4893	727	51.15	12.31	33.81	5.02
32	153716	6196	1185	4347	665	40.31	7.71	28.28	4.32
33	157343	5055	860	3604	591	32.12	5.46	22.90	3.76
34	169285	4210	709	2943	559	24.87	4.19	17.38	3.30
35-39	**834137**	**9157**	**1275**	**6177**	**1705**	**10.98**	**1.53**	**7.41**	**2.04**
35	169913	3102	452	2195	456	18.26	2.66	12.92	2.68
36	183370	2538	367	1729	441	13.84	2.00	9.43	2.41
37	158828	1605	215	1073	317	10.11	1.35	6.76	1.99
38	153068	1076	125	690	261	7.03	0.82	4.51	1.71
39	168958	836	116	490	230	4.95	0.68	2.90	1.36
40-44	**707521**	**1447**	**240**	**749**	**458**	**2.05**	**0.34**	**1.06**	**0.65**
40	164217	553	84	327	142	3.37	0.51	1.99	0.86
41	177276	378	59	201	117	2.13	0.33	1.13	0.66
42	177644	284	47	120	118	1.60	0.26	0.68	0.66
43	100442	122	20	60	42	1.22	0.20	0.60	0.42
44	87943	110	30	41	40	1.26	0.34	0.46	0.45
45-49	**589306**	**451**	**101**	**185**	**164**	**0.77**	**0.17**	**0.31**	**0.28**
45	96175	84	14	42	28	0.87	0.14	0.44	0.29
46	105700	92	28	38	26	0.87	0.27	0.36	0.25
47	131737	80	14	34	33	0.61	0.11	0.26	0.25
48	128958	100	22	36	41	0.77	0.17	0.28	0.32
49	126735	96	23	36	37	0.76	0.18	0.28	0.29

4-16 各地区0-30岁独生子女数(2005年)

Singleton Aged 0-30 by Region (2005)

本表是2005年全国1%人口抽样调查样本数据，抽样比为1.325%。

Data in this table are obtained from the 1% Population Sample Survey in 2005. The sampling fraction is 1.325%.

单位：人 (person)

地 区	Region	0-30岁人口数 Population Aged 0-30			0-30岁独生子女人数 Singleton Aged 0-30			占同龄人口比重(%) As Percentage of the Same Age (%)		
		合计 Total	男 Male	女 Female	合计 Total	男 Male	女 Female	合计 Total	男 Male	女 Female
全 国	**National Total**	**7163448**	**3710559**	**3452888**	**2098947**	**1188145**	**910801**	**29.30**	**32.02**	**26.38**
北 京	Beijing	76607	39607	37000	40954	21908	19045	53.46	55.31	51.47
天 津	Tianjin	52818	26964	25854	27986	15175	12810	52.98	56.28	49.55
河 北	Hebei	389777	199285	190491	97393	55441	41952	24.99	27.82	22.02
山 西	Shanxi	196122	100555	95566	42059	22547	19512	21.45	22.42	20.42
内蒙古	Inner Mongolia	127362	65632	61730	47941	26539	21403	37.64	40.44	34.67
辽 宁	Liaoning	194696	99170	95526	100759	57758	43001	51.75	58.24	45.02
吉 林	Jilin	135427	69668	65759	64232	36347	27885	47.43	52.17	42.40
黑龙江	Heilongjiang	188030	96357	91673	91460	50552	40908	48.64	52.46	44.62
上 海	Shanghai	85309	42953	42357	49769	25812	23957	58.34	60.09	56.56
江 苏	Jiangsu	366627	186117	180509	172960	95398	77562	47.18	51.26	42.97
浙 江	Zhejiang	248887	127367	121521	92755	56169	36586	37.27	44.10	30.11
安 徽	Anhui	346312	180173	166138	95245	57825	37420	27.50	32.09	22.52
福 建	Fujian	206034	105549	100485	49585	29952	19633	24.07	28.38	19.54
江 西	Jiangxi	259017	136650	122367	58710	35002	23708	22.67	25.61	19.37
山 东	Shandong	465231	239487	225744	157095	99462	57633	33.77	41.53	25.53
河 南	Henan	549829	291683	258147	127266	70578	56687	23.15	24.20	21.96
湖 北	Hubei	292733	154543	138190	94818	54486	40332	32.39	35.26	29.19
湖 南	Hunan	338047	177065	160982	98511	57516	40995	29.14	32.48	25.47
广 东	Guangdong	628728	323224	305504	95962	52684	43278	15.26	16.30	14.17
广 西	Guangxi	285798	153192	132606	50389	28040	22349	17.63	18.30	16.85
海 南	Hainan	54989	29629	25359	8870	4826	4043	16.13	16.29	15.94
重 庆	Chongqing	136017	70287	65730	60781	33731	27050	44.69	47.99	41.15
四 川	Sichuan	421342	214743	206600	158461	85275	73186	37.61	39.71	35.42
贵 州	Guizhou	240761	127171	113590	39572	21573	18000	16.44	16.96	15.85
云 南	Yunnan	288084	151029	137054	45895	23710	22185	15.93	15.70	16.19
西 藏	Tibet	20879	10603	10276	2859	1388	1471	13.69	13.09	14.32
陕 西	Shaanxi	202442	105681	96760	53006	29278	23727	26.18	27.70	24.52
甘 肃	Gansu	154668	79355	75313	30362	16767	13595	19.63	21.13	18.05
青 海	Qinghai	35620	18012	17608	7875	4039	3837	22.11	22.42	21.79
宁 夏	Ningxia	40455	20466	19989	7052	3735	3317	17.43	18.25	16.59
新 疆	Xinjiang	134801	68343	66458	28365	14632	13733	21.04	21.41	20.66

4-17 各地区家庭户按住房来源分的户数（2005年）

Number of Household by Sources of Housing and Region (2005)

本表是2005年全国1%人口抽样调查样本数据，抽样比为1.325%。

Data in this table are obtained from the 1% Population Sample Survey in 2005. The sampling fraction is 1.325%.

单位：户 (household)

地区	Region	合计 Total Number of Household	自建住房 Self-built House	购买商品房 Purchasing Commercial Building	购买经济适用房 Purchasing Economically Affordable Housing	购买原公有住房 Purchasing Former Public-owned Building	租赁公有住房 Renting Public-owned Building	租赁商品房 Renting Commercial Building	其他 Others
全国	**National Total**	**5277716**	**3644340**	**367737**	**152584**	**461939**	**172499**	**301799**	**176818**
北京	Beijing	69565	15532	8415	2212	19148	10187	11494	2577
天津	Tianjin	44728	17430	8466	933	5034	9679	1716	1470
河北	Hebei	270774	211981	14754	7195	21324	4165	7656	3698
山西	Shanxi	130135	87034	5404	8004	13292	4412	5833	6156
内蒙古	Inner Mongolia	106615	54154	14854	3851	17968	2543	9684	3561
辽宁	Liaoning	189770	90992	34033	7541	31246	11185	11563	3209
吉林	Jilin	113312	61590	14511	8818	15497	3914	5424	3558
黑龙江	Heilongjiang	169041	78117	27289	12510	32220	4620	8413	5871
上海	Shanghai	82977	15540	19654	674	15357	11757	18310	1685
江苏	Jiangsu	329179	221916	32301	5675	26940	8265	28348	5734
浙江	Zhejiang	226414	142270	20453	1195	12319	4900	33437	11840
安徽	Anhui	264397	210941	12288	4780	16656	4519	9355	5858
福建	Fujian	148616	92913	9312	3329	7385	4266	17731	13679
江西	Jiangxi	171220	128013	8044	3554	10117	6017	6287	9189
山东	Shandong	415276	325998	19897	9506	29169	7525	13559	9622
河南	Henan	361142	303822	9696	11776	22605	2863	5651	4730
湖北	Hubei	241773	173820	9618	6379	25202	10968	7863	7923
湖南	Hunan	261521	205544	8280	5354	18488	6922	7958	8976
广东	Guangdong	309899	178829	30804	6419	21715	11432	45339	15361
广西	Guangxi	180095	144136	4102	2758	10862	6638	5106	6494
海南	Hainan	27744	18270	761	1186	2649	1754	1349	1776
重庆	Chongqing	129130	89967	11415	4202	7600	4642	5500	5804
四川	Sichuan	365055	287007	17810	6759	21938	8921	11149	11471
贵州	Guizhou	141843	109594	3844	4019	7201	3882	4938	8364
云南	Yunnan	161166	128924	3242	3910	8674	4459	3889	8067
西藏	Tibet	7155	6101	44	84	123	333	169	301
陕西	Shaanxi	149480	108074	5011	7503	13334	4627	6924	4007
甘肃	Gansu	92624	68892	4600	3733	9083	2508	1941	1867
青海	Qinghai	19194	11964	1347	1034	2357	798	726	967
宁夏	Ningxia	21905	13182	2636	1032	2897	763	994	402
新疆	Xinjiang	75972	41795	4851	6661	13539	3033	3492	2600

4-18 各地区家庭户的住房间数和面积（2005年）

Number of Rooms and Floor Space of Family Households by Region (2005)

本表是2005年全国1%人口抽样调查样本数据，抽样比为1.325%。

Data in this table are obtained from the 1% Population Sample Survey in 2005. The sampling fraction is 1.325%.

地 区	Region	家庭户户数（户） Number of Family Households (household)	家庭户人数（人） Population in Family Households (person)	平均每户住房间数（间/户） Number of Rooms per Households (room/household)	人均住房建筑面积（平方米/人） Floor Space of Housing per Capita (sq.m/person)	人均住房间数（间/人） Number of Rooms Per Capita (room/household)
全 国	**National Total**	**5286554**	**16570406**	**3.05**	**28.69**	**0.97**
北 京	Beijing	69594	188218	2.82	24.82	1.04
天 津	Tianjin	44806	130900	2.27	23.49	0.78
河 北	Hebei	270892	899339	3.35	26.05	1.01
山 西	Shanxi	130427	440601	3.45	24.53	1.02
内蒙古	Inner Mongolia	106792	310952	2.39	22.58	0.82
辽 宁	Liaoning	189878	553971	2.24	23.90	0.77
吉 林	Jilin	113403	356480	2.32	21.62	0.74
黑龙江	Heilongjiang	169177	503286	2.11	21.22	0.71
上 海	Shanghai	83106	220576	2.14	26.73	0.81
江 苏	Jiangsu	329566	958550	2.91	36.53	1.00
浙 江	Zhejiang	226688	619804	3.02	40.69	1.10
安 徽	Anhui	265023	801681	3.26	25.13	1.08
福 建	Fujian	148892	445164	3.27	35.39	1.09
江 西	Jiangxi	171522	564060	3.45	33.30	1.05
山 东	Shandong	415415	1203376	2.99	28.14	1.03
河 南	Henan	361725	1237993	3.73	26.56	1.09
湖 北	Hubei	242166	744987	3.02	34.50	0.98
湖 南	Hunan	263001	826391	3.42	34.39	1.09
广 东	Guangdong	310146	1053819	2.95	25.80	0.87
广 西	Guangxi	180466	610512	3.24	27.72	0.96
海 南	Hainan	27779	106797	2.44	20.57	0.63
重 庆	Chongqing	129342	366415	3.02	35.71	1.06
四 川	Sichuan	366256	1079070	3.14	34.74	1.07
贵 州	Guizhou	142031	490715	2.79	24.49	0.81
云 南	Yunnan	161443	578788	2.80	24.23	0.78
西 藏	Tibet	7227	36346	3.77	23.93	0.75
陕 西	Shaanxi	149873	488076	3.23	26.99	0.99
甘 肃	Gansu	92736	340445	4.04	20.73	1.10
青 海	Qinghai	19245	70595	3.10	19.91	0.84
宁 夏	Ningxia	21917	78435	3.06	21.70	0.86
新 疆	Xinjiang	76020	264066	2.79	22.50	0.80

主要统计指标解释

人口数　指一定时点、一定地区范围内有生命的个人总和。

年度统计的年末人口数指每年12月31日24时的人口数。年度统计的全国人口总数内未包括香港、澳门特别行政区和台湾省以及海外华侨人数。

城镇人口和乡村人口　城镇人口是指居住在城镇范围内的全部常住人口；乡村人口是除上述人口以外的全部人口。

出生率（又称粗出生率）　指在一定时期内（通常为一年）一定地区的出生人数与同期内平均人数（或期中人数）之比，用千分率表示。本资料中的出生率指年出生率，其计算公式为：

$$出生率=\frac{年出生人数}{年平均人数}\times 1000‰$$

式中：出生人数指活产婴儿，即胎儿脱离母体时（不管怀孕月数），有过呼吸或其他生命现象。年平均人数指年初、年底人口数的平均数，也可用年中人口数代替。

死亡率（又称粗死亡率）　指在一定时期内（通常为一年）一定地区的死亡人数与同期内平均人数（或期中人数）之比，用千分率表示。本资料中的死亡率指年死亡率，其计算公式为：

$$死亡率=\frac{年死亡人数}{年平均人数}\times 1000‰$$

人口自然增长率　指在一定时期内（通常为一年）人口自然增加数（出生人数减死亡人数）与该时期内平均人数（或期中人数）之比，用千分率表示。计算公式为：

$$人口自然增长率=\frac{本年出生人数-本年死亡人数}{年平均人数}\times 1000‰$$

$$=人口出生率-人口死亡率$$

总抚养比　也称总负担系数。指人口总体中非劳动年龄人口数与劳动年龄人口数之比。通常用百分比表示。说明每100名劳动年龄人口大致要负担多少名非劳动年龄人口。用于从人口角度反映人口与经济发展的基本关系。计算公式为：

$$GDR=\frac{P_{0-14}+P_{65^+}}{P_{15-64}}\times 100\%$$

其中：GDR为总抚养比；

P_{0-14}为0～14岁少年儿童人口数；

P_{65^+}为65岁及65岁以上的老年人口数；

P_{15-64}为15～64岁劳动年龄人口数。

老年人口抚养比　也称老年人口抚养系数。指某一人口中老年人口数与劳动年龄人口数之比。通常用百分比表示。用以表明每100名劳动年龄人口要负担多少名老年人。老年人口抚养比是从经济角度反映人口老化社会后果的指标之一。计算公式为：

$$ODR=\frac{P_{65^+}}{P_{15-64}}\times 100\%$$

其中：ODR为老年人口抚养比；

P_{65^+}为65岁及65岁以上的老年人口数；

P_{15-64}为15～64岁的劳动年龄人口数。

少年儿童抚养比　也称少年儿童抚养系数。指某一人口中少年儿童人口数与劳动年龄人口数之比。通常用百分比表示。以反映每100名劳动年龄人口要负担多少名少年儿童。计算公式为：

$$CDR=\frac{P_{0-14}}{P_{15-64}}\times 100\%$$

其中：CDR为少年儿童抚养比；

P_{0-14}为0～14岁少年儿童人口数；

P_{15-64}为15～64岁劳动年龄人口数。

Explanatory Notes on Main Statistical Indicators

Total Population refers to the total number of people alive at a certain point of time within a given area.

The annual statistics on total population is taken at midnight, the 3lst of December, not including residents in Taiwan province, Hong Kong and Macao and overseas Chinese.

Urban Population and Rural Population Urban population refer to all people residing in cities and towns, while rural population refer to population other than urban population.

Birth Rate (or Crude Birth Rate) refers to the ratio of the number of births to the average population (or mid-period population) during a certain period of time (usually a year), expressed in ‰. Birth rate in the chapter refers to annual birth rate. The following formula is used:

Birth Rate = (Number of Births/Average Number of Population)× 1000‰

Number of births in the formula refers to live births, i.e. when a baby has breathed or showed any vital phenomena regardless of the length of pregnancy.

Annual average number of population is the average of the number of population at the beginning of the year and that at the end of the year. Sometimes it is substituted by the mid-year population.

Death Rate (or Crude Death Rate) refers to the ratio of the number of deaths to the average population (or mid-period population) during a certain period of time (usually a year), expressed in ‰. Death rate in the chapter refers to annual death rate. The following formula is used:

Death Rate= (Number of Deaths/Annual Average Number of Population)× 1000‰

Natural Growth Rate of Population refers to the ratio of natural increase in population (number of births minus number of deaths) in a certain period of time (usually a year) to the average population (or mid-period population) of the same period, expressed in ‰. The following formula is applied:

Natural Growth Rate of Population = [(Number of Births-Number of Deaths)/Average Number of Population]× 1000‰

Natural Growth Rate of Population = Birth Rate-Death Rate

Gross Dependency Ratio also called gross dependency coefficient, refers to the ratio of non-working-age population to the working-age population, express in %. Describing in general the number of non-working-age population that every 100 people at working ages will take care of, this indicator reflects the basic relation between population and economic development from the demographic perspective. The gross dependency ratio is calculated with the following formula:

$$GDR=\frac{P_{0-14}+P_{65+}}{P_{15-64}}\times 100\%$$

Where: GDR is the gross dependency ratio

P_{0-14} is the population of children aged 0-14

P_{65+} is the elderly population aged 65 and over, and

P_{15-64} is the working-age population aged 15-64

Old Dependency Ratio also called old dependency coefficient, refers to the ratio of the elderly population to the working-age population, express in %. It describes the number of the elderly population that every 100 people at working ages will take care of. Old dependency ratio is one of the indicators reflecting the social implication of population aging from the economic perspective. The old dependency ratio is calculated with the following formula:

$$ODR=\frac{P_{65+}}{P_{15-64}}\times 100\%$$

Where: ODR is the old dependency ratio

P_{65+} is the elderly population aged 65 and over, and

P_{15-64} is the working-age population aged 15-64

Children Dependency Ratio also called children dependency coefficient, refers to the ratio of the children population to the working-age population, express in %. It describes the number of children population that every 100 people at working ages will take care of. The children dependency ratio is calculated with the following formula:

$$CDR=\frac{P_{0-14}}{P_{15-64}}\times 100\%$$

Where: CDR is the children dependency ratio

P_{0-14} is the children population aged 0-14, and

P_{15-64} is the working-age population aged 15-64

5

就业人员和职工工资

Employment and Wages

简要说明

一、本篇资料的主要内容

本篇资料反映我国劳动经济方面的基本情况，包括31个省、自治区、直辖市的主要劳动统计数据。如：经济活动人口数，就业人员及职工人数，城镇登记失业人数，职工工资总额，平均工资及指数变化情况等。

二、本篇资料的统计范围

《劳动统计报表制度》的调查范围为法人企业、事业、行政单位（不包括乡镇企业、私营单位和个体工商户）；《人口变动情况抽样调查方案》的调查推算范围为全国人口，本篇资料的统计范围为16岁及以上人口；《乡村社会经济调查方案》的调查范围为全国乡镇以下农村地区；《培训就业统计报表制度》的填报范围为全国就业服务和职业介绍机构；私营企业及个体工商业统计范围为全社会。1990年及以后的经济活动人口、就业人员、城镇和乡村就业人员资料，是根据第五次全国人口普查资料及历年人口变动调查、劳动力调查资料推算的，因此分地区、分类型、分行业的资料相加不等于总计。1998年及以后城镇单位就业人员、职工人数、工资总额、平均工资等指标中不再包括离开本单位仍保留劳动关系人员及其生活费。

三、本篇的资料来源

1.就业基本情况及分组资料、职工工资总额等资料，是国家统计局人口和就业统计司根据《劳动统计报表制度》、《人口变动情况抽样调查方案》、《劳动力调查制度》及《乡村社会经济调查方案》搜集资料，加工整理。

2.职业介绍服务机构及劳动力交流情况、城镇登记失业人数，是劳动和社会保障部根据其《培训就业统计报表制度》整理提供。

3.私营企业及个体工商业就业人员，由国家工商行政管理总局提供。

四、本篇的统计调查方法

劳动统计采用全面调查方法，由各级统计部门逐级上报；人口变动情况抽样调查和劳动力调查采用抽样调查方法；培训、就业统计及私营企业和个体工商业统计利用行政登记资料加工整理。

Brief Introduction

I. Main Content

Data in this chapter show the basic conditions of China's labour economy, including the main data of labour statistics of the whole country and 31 provinces, autonomous regions and municipalities under the direct leadership of the central government, such as the economically active population, number of the employed persons and staff and workers, number of registered unemployed persons in urban areas, total wages and average wages of the staff and workers and the changes in index, etc.

II. Coverage of Statistics

The Comprehensive Labour Statistics Reporting System covers corporate enterprises, institutions and administrative agencies (excluding township enterprises, private units or self-employed business). *The Sample Survey on the Population Changes* covers and estimates the population aged 16 and over of the whole country. *The Rural Social and Economic Survey* covers all rural areas below township level in China. *The Statistical Reporting System on Training and Employment* covers all agencies and units providing employment services. The Statistical Reports on Private Enterprises and Individual Industrial and Commercial Business cover the whole society. Data on economically active population, total employed population and employed population by urban and rural areas since 1990 are estimated on the basis of the 2000 population census, the annual sample surveys on the change of population and the labour force surveys, Breakdown of these data by province, by type of ownership and by industry do not add up to the totals. People leaving their work units with their working records and allowances kept in the work units are not covered in urban employed population, total number of workers and staff, total wage bills, average wage and other related statistics since 1998.

III. Source of Data

(1) Data on basic conditions of employment, total wage bill of workers and staff are collected and compiled through the *Comprehensive Labour Statistics Reporting System, the Sample Survey on the Population Changes*, and the *Rural Social and Economic Survey* by the Department of Population and Employment Statistics of the National Bureau of Statistics.

(2) Data on the employment services and the exchanges of labour force and on the urban registered unemployed persons are collected through the *Statistical Reporting System on Training and Employment* and provided by the Ministry of Labour and Social Security.

(3) Data on the number of persons employed in private enterprises and self-employed persons in industry and commerce are provided by the State Administration for Industry and Commerce.

IV. Survey Methodology

A complete reporting from lower levels to higher levels is used in the labour statistics reporting system. Surveys on population changes and labour force surveys are conducted with sampling scheme. Statistics on training, employment, private enterprises and self-employed individuals are collected and compiled on basis of administrative records.

5-1 就业基本情况

Employment

项　目	Item	2001	2002	2003	2004	2005
经济活动人口　（万人）	**Economically Active Population (10 000 persons)**	**74432**	**75360**	**76075**	**76823**	**77877**
就业人员合计　（万人）	**Total Number of Employed Persons (10 000 persons)**	**73025**	**73740**	**74432**	**75200**	**75825**
第一产业	Primary Industry	36513	36870	36546	35269	33970
第二产业	Secondary Industry	16284	15780	16077	16920	18084
第三产业	Tertiary Industry	20228	21090	21809	23011	23771
就业人员构成(合计=100)	**Composition of Employed Persons (total=100)**					
第一产业	Primary Industry	50.0	50.0	49.1	46.9	44.8
第二产业	Secondary Industry	22.3	21.4	21.6	22.5	23.8
第三产业	Tertiary Industry	27.7	28.6	29.3	30.6	31.4
按城乡分就业人员(万人)	**Number of Employed Persons by Urban and Rural Areas (10 000 persons)**					
城镇就业人员	Urban Employed Persons	23940	24780	25639	26476	27331
#国有单位	State-owned Units	7640	7163	6876	6709.93	6488
城镇集体单位	Urban Collective-owned Units	1291	1122	1000	897.16	810
股份合作单位	Cooperative Units	153	161	173	192.4	188
联营单位	Joint Ownership Units	45	45	44	44.1	45
有限责任公司	Limited Liability Corporations	841	1083	1261	1436	1750
股份有限公司	Share-holding Corporations Ltd.	483	538	592	624.9	699
私营企业	Private Enterprises	1527	1999	2545	2993.73	3458
港澳台商投资单位	Units with Funds from Hong Kong, Macao & Taiwan	326	367	409	469.8	557
外商投资单位	Foreign Funded Units	345	391	454	563	688
个体	Self-employed Individuals	2131	2269	2377	2521.22	2778
乡村就业人员	Rural Employed Persons	49085	48960	48793	48724	48494
#乡镇企业	Township and Village Enterprises	13086	13288	13573	13866	14272
私营企业	Private Enterprises	1187	1411	1754	2023.52	2366
个体	Self-employed Individuals	2629	2474	2260	2065.88	2123
在岗职工人数　（万人）	**Number of Staff and Workers (10 000 persons)**	**10792**	**10558**	**10492**	**10576**	**10850**
国有单位	State-owned Units	7409	6924	6621	6438	6232
城镇集体单位	Urban Collective-owned Units	1241	1071	951	851	769
其他单位	Units of Other Types of Ownership	2142	2563	2920	3287	3849
城镇登记失业人数(万人)	**Number of Registered Unemployed Persons in Urban Areas (10 000 persons)**	**681**	**770**	**800**	**827**	**839**
城镇登记失业率　（%）	**Registered Unemployment Rate in Urban Areas (%)**	**3.6**	**4**	**4.3**	**4.2**	**4.2**

注：本篇章就业人员合计和城镇、乡村就业人员小计1990年至2000年数据根据第五次人口普查资料重新调整，2001年及以后数据根据人口变动抽样调查资料推算，因此，与相应年份的分地区、分注册登记类型、分行业资料的分项数据之和不一致（以下各表同）。

a) From 1990 to 2000, the total number of employed persons, the sub-total of urban and rural employed persons have been adjusted in accordance with the data obtained from the 5th National Population Census. Since 2001, these data are calculated based on the annual population sample survey. As a result, the sum of the data by region, by ownership and by sector is not equal to the total. The same as in the following tables.

5-2 按三次产业分就业人员数（年底数）

Number of Employed Persons at the Year-end by Three Industries

年份 Year	经济活动人口（万人）Economically Active Population (10 000 persons)	就业人员（万人）Total Employed Persons (10 000 persons)	第一产业 Primary Industry	第二产业 Secondary Industry	第三产业 Tertiary Industry	构成（合计=100）Composition in Percentage 第一产业 Primary Industry	第二产业 Secondary Industry	第三产业 Tertiary Industry
1952	21106	20729	17317	1531	1881	83.5	7.4	9.1
1957	23971	23771	19309	2142	2320	81.2	9.0	9.8
1962		25910	21276	2059	2575	82.1	8.0	9.9
1965		28670	23396	2408	2866	81.6	8.4	10.0
1970		34432	27811	3518	3103	80.8	10.2	9.0
1975		38168	29456	5152	3560	77.2	13.5	9.3
1978	40682	40152	28318	6945	4890	70.5	17.3	12.2
1979	41592	41024	28634	7214	5177	69.8	17.6	12.6
1980	42903	42361	29122	7707	5532	68.7	18.2	13.1
1981	44165	43725	29777	8003	5945	68.1	18.3	13.6
1982	45674	45295	30859	8346	6090	68.1	18.4	13.5
1983	46707	46436	31151	8679	6606	67.1	18.7	14.2
1984	48433	48197	30868	9590	7739	64.0	19.9	16.1
1985	50112	49873	31130	10384	8359	62.4	20.8	16.8
1986	51546	51282	31254	11216	8811	60.9	21.9	17.2
1987	53060	52783	31663	11726	9395	60.0	22.2	17.8
1988	54630	54334	32249	12152	9933	59.3	22.4	18.3
1989	55707	55329	33225	11976	10129	60.1	21.6	18.3
1990	65323	64749	38914	13856	11979	60.1	21.4	18.5
1991	66091	65491	39098	14015	12378	59.7	21.4	18.9
1992	66782	66152	38699	14355	13098	58.5	21.7	19.8
1993	67468	66808	37680	14965	14163	56.4	22.4	21.2
1994	68135	67455	36628	15312	15515	54.3	22.7	23.0
1995	68855	68065	35530	15655	16880	52.2	23.0	24.8
1996	69765	68950	34820	16203	17927	50.5	23.5	26.0
1997	70800	69820	34840	16547	18432	49.9	23.7	26.4
1998	72087	70637	35177	16600	18860	49.8	23.5	26.7
1999	72791	71394	35768	16421	19205	50.1	23.0	26.9
2000	73992	72085	36043	16219	19823	50.0	22.5	27.5
2001	74432	73025	36513	16284	20228	50.0	22.3	27.7
2002	75360	73740	36870	15780	21090	50.0	21.4	28.6
2003	76075	74432	36546	16077	21809	49.1	21.6	29.3
2004	76823	75200	35269	16920	23011	46.9	22.5	30.6
2005	77877	75825	33970	18084	23771	44.8	23.8	31.4

5-3 各地区按三次产业分就业人员数（2005年底）

Number of Employed Persons at the Year-end by Three Industries and Region (2005)

地区	Region	就业人员（万人）Total Employed Persons (10 000 persons)	第一产业 Primary Industry	第二产业 Secondary Industry	第三产业 Tertiary Industry	构成（合计=100）Composition in Percentage 第一产业 Primary Industry	第二产业 Secondary Industry	第三产业 Tertiary Industry
全国	**National Total**	**75825.0**	**33970.0**	**18084.0**	**23771.0**	**44.8**	**23.8**	**31.4**
北京	Beijing	920.4	62.2	226.4	631.8	6.8	24.6	68.6
天津	Tianjin	426.9	80.5	173.3	173.1	18.9	40.6	40.5
河北	Hebei	3467.3	1562.3	1048.4	856.6	45.1	30.2	24.7
山西	Shanxi	1476.4	641.8	385.8	448.7	43.5	26.1	30.4
内蒙古	Inner Mongolia	1041.1	560.5	162.8	317.9	53.8	15.6	30.5
辽宁	Liaoning	1978.6	718.9	504.4	755.2	36.3	25.5	38.2
吉林	Jilin	1099.4	523.9	201.8	373.8	47.7	18.4	34.0
黑龙江	Heilongjiang	1625.8	787.7	339.7	498.4	48.4	20.9	30.7
上海	Shanghai	855.9	61.1	331.3	463.5	7.1	38.7	54.2
江苏	Jiangsu	3877.7	1076.7	1493.4	1307.6	27.8	38.5	33.7
浙江	Zhejiang	3202.9	791.1	1339.9	1071.8	24.7	41.8	33.5
安徽	Anhui	3484.7	1778.2	762.7	943.7	51.0	21.9	27.1
福建	Fujian	1868.5	702.5	582.3	583.7	37.6	31.2	31.2
江西	Jiangxi	2107.5	967.4	464.3	675.8	45.9	22.0	32.1
山东	Shandong	5110.8	2056.5	1558.6	1495.6	40.2	30.5	29.3
河南	Henan	5662.4	3138.8	1251.7	1271.9	55.4	22.1	22.5
湖北	Hubei	2676.3	1133.9	521.8	1020.5	42.4	19.5	38.1
湖南	Hunan	3658.3	1962.0	639.4	1056.9	53.6	17.5	28.9
广东	Guangdong	4702.1	1548.7	1443.1	1710.3	32.9	30.7	36.4
广西	Guangxi	2703.1	1518.7	302.1	882.2	56.2	11.2	32.6
海南	Hainan	377.7	215.1	40.1	122.5	57.0	10.6	32.4
重庆	Chongqing	1720.8	779.5	370.6	570.7	45.3	21.5	33.2
四川	Sichuan	4603.5	2329.9	845.8	1427.8	50.6	18.4	31.0
贵州	Guizhou	2215.8	1272.0	228.5	715.3	57.4	10.3	32.3
云南	Yunnan	2461.3	1709.2	245.1	507.0	69.4	10.0	20.6
西藏	Tibet	140.4	86.3	12.9	41.2	61.4	9.2	29.3
陕西	Shaanxi	1882.9	956.4	348.3	578.2	50.8	18.5	30.7
甘肃	Gansu	1347.6	770.5	184.8	392.3	57.2	13.7	29.1
青海	Qinghai	267.6	131.6	46.5	89.6	49.2	17.4	33.5
宁夏	Ningxia	299.6	145.1	66.7	87.8	48.4	22.3	29.3
新疆	Xinjiang	764.3	407.1	101.7	255.4	53.3	13.3	33.4

5-4 按城乡分就业人员数（年底数）

单位：万人

年份 地区	Year Region	合计 Total	城镇 小计 Subtotal	#国有单位 State-owned Units	#集体单位 Collective-owned Units	#股份合作单位 Cooperative Units	#联营单位 Joint Ownership Units	#有限责任公司 Limited Liability Corporations	#股份有限公司 Share Holding Corporations Ltd.
	1978	40152	9514	7451	2048				
	1980	42361	10525	8019	2425				
	1985	49873	12808	8990	3324		38		
	1989	55329	14390	10108	3502		82		
	1990	64749	17041	10346	3549		96		
	1991	65491	17465	10664	3628		49		
	1992	66152	17861	10889	3621		56		
	1993	66808	18262	10920	3393		66		164
	1994	67455	18653	11214	3285		52		292
	1995	68065	19040	11261	3147		53		317
	1996	68950	19922	11244	3016		49		363
	1997	69820	20781	11044	2883		43		468
	1998	70637	21616	9058	1963	136	48	484	410
	1999	71394	22412	8572	1712	144	46	603	420
	2000	72085	23151	8102	1499	155	42	687	457
	2001	73025	23940	7640	1291	153	45	841	483
	2002	73740	24780	7163	1122	161	45	1083	538
	2003	74432	25639	6876	1000	173	44	1261	592
	2004	75200	26476	6710	897	192	44	1436	625
	2005	75825	27331	6488	810	188	45	1750	699
北京	Beijing	920.4	736.3	195.0	23.8	22.5	2.4	149.4	36.4
天津	Tianjin	426.9	248.4	90.1	11.3	1.1	1.3	23.8	10.2
河北	Hebei	3467.3	661.3	347.5	37.7	6.7	0.6	53.4	24.6
山西	Shanxi	1476.4	440.6	252.6	31.1	3.1	0.6	55.8	12.9
内蒙古	Inner Mongolia	1041.1	350.3	162.0	12.4	1.8	0.3	47.0	14.3
辽宁	Liaoning	1978.6	865.1	302.4	41.0	5.5	0.7	67.9	26.8
吉林	Jilin	1099.4	414.2	178.7	21.0	1.9	0.3	27.2	20.4
黑龙江	Heilongjiang	1625.8	676.9	314.1	38.4	24.2	1.0	41.5	41.6
上海	Shanghai	855.9	612.4	141.6	14.7	2.7	1.6	47.9	33.4
江苏	Jiangsu	3877.7	1215.2	283.7	38.7	8.3	1.8	88.1	52.9
浙江	Zhejiang	3202.9	904.3	179.8	30.7	19.5	1.6	150.4	47.9
安徽	Anhui	3484.7	545.5	208.7	30.8	3.9	0.8	52.3	24.8
福建	Fujian	1868.5	555.5	150.9	19.1	5.8	2.7	35.9	16.2
江西	Jiangxi	2107.5	468.7	199.3	18.5	3.5	0.6	27.0	12.2
山东	Shandong	5110.8	1328.6	423.9	65.3	14.9	3.3	189.2	62.0
河南	Henan	5662.4	910.0	404.8	91.2	8.5	1.2	131.5	42.8
湖北	Hubei	2676.3	743.5	313.3	37.2	5.2	2.2	51.0	33.4
湖南	Hunan	3658.3	682.9	259.2	31.0	5.1	0.8	67.9	25.5
广东	Guangdong	4702.1	1612.6	380.2	68.7	10.9	7.7	94.2	36.3
广西	Guangxi	2703.1	427.7	198.9	19.9	1.5	0.8	34.4	11.1
海南	Hainan	377.7	121.7	57.9	4.1	0.4	1.2	4.8	2.9
重庆	Chongqing	1720.8	353.9	122.9	14.0	3.7	5.6	50.3	11.1
四川	Sichuan	4603.5	802.0	316.1	42.2	7.8	1.4	90.6	40.9
贵州	Guizhou	2215.8	281.7	146.7	10.4	1.7	0.7	37.0	10.6
云南	Yunnan	2461.3	410.4	175.3	11.5	2.8	0.2	33.6	12.4
西藏	Tibet	140.4	31.5	16.9	0.5			0.3	0.2
陕西	Shaanxi	1882.9	445.8	249.1	22.4	7.7	0.8	35.6	13.1
甘肃	Gansu	1347.6	263.3	159.0	12.6	4.5	2.4	9.3	3.5
青海	Qinghai	267.6	81.5	32.1	2.2	0.7		4.7	2.6
宁夏	Ningxia	299.6	87.6	38.5	1.4	1.0	0.1	13.0	4.0
新疆	Xinjiang	764.3	360.4	187.0	6.1	0.8	0.3	35.4	12.0

Number of Employed Persons at the Year-end in Urban and Rural Areas

(10 000 persons)

Urban Area				乡　村 Rural Area			
#私营企业 Private Enterprises	#港澳台商投资单位 Units with Funds from Hong Kong, Macao and Taiwan	#外商投资单位 Foreign Funded Units	#个　体 Self-employed individuals	小　计 Subtotal	#乡镇企业 Township and Village Enterprises	#私营企业 Private Enterprises	#个　体 Self-employed Individuals
			15	30638	2827		
			81	31836	3000		
		6	450	37065	6979		
	4	43	648	40939	9367		
57	4	62	614	47708	9265	113	1491
68	69	96	692	48026	9609	116	1616
98	83	138	740	48291	10625	134	1728
186	155	133	930	48546	12345	187	2010
332	211	195	1225	48802	12017	316	2551
485	272	241	1560	49025	12862	471	3054
620	265	275	1709	49028	13508	551	3308
750	281	300	1919	49039	13050	600	3522
973	294	293	2259	49021	12537	737	3855
1053	306	306	2414	48982	12704	969	3827
1268	310	332	2136	48934	12820	1139	2934
1527	326	345	2131	49085	13086	1187	2629
1999	367	391	2269	48960	13288	1411	2474
2545	409	454	2377	48793	13573	1754	2260
2994	470	563	2521	48724	13866	2024	2066
3458	557	688	2778	48494	14272	2366	2123
173.5	21.7	49.6	57.2	184.0	136.2	121.0	27.5
44.5	9.9	41.2	9.8	178.5	79.8	44.2	15.7
72.3	8.5	12.1	93.4	2805.9	1006.5	169.4	176.5
39.0	1.6	2.6	41.1	1035.7	402.3	43.3	41.2
47.1	1.6	2.5	60.2	690.8	232.6	21.1	22.1
189.5	9.8	39.3	178.4	1113.5	601.3	62.7	104.2
77.2	2.6	7.2	75.2	685.2	216.6	10.8	13.8
77.5	3.1	4.3	109.0	948.9	173.0	17.7	46.6
256.7	28.6	61.2	22.4	243.5	201.6	209.1	11.9
397.2	50.4	79.7	189.2	2662.5	1291.7	400.0	132.0
218.5	46.4	53.4	154.8	2298.5	1241.5	316.4	165.3
86.5	3.7	6.7	123.6	2939.2	533.2	79.2	143.2
100.8	99.4	64.0	54.7	1313.0	670.3	33.9	35.2
89.1	7.0	3.1	104.1	1638.8	394.9	45.2	63.6
262.9	25.9	98.2	174.7	3782.2	1653.5	181.3	190.2
72.9	7.3	8.4	136.6	4752.4	1011.9	65.7	137.6
89.7	8.8	13.3	142.0	1932.8	639.3	32.9	86.8
150.8	7.9	6.4	125.8	2975.4	901.8	49.6	70.8
402.0	194.1	108.1	306.3	3089.5	1207.9	124.1	183.3
54.3	5.5	6.2	89.8	2275.4	364.7	29.2	73.8
31.8	1.7	1.7	15.1	256.0	32.0	4.2	6.9
78.5	2.3	4.9	59.9	1366.9	203.9	27.0	31.0
153.2	3.4	6.4	136.2	3801.5	666.8	84.8	114.4
37.4	0.8	1.7	33.7	1934.2	252.1	13.2	26.0
76.1	1.6	1.7	87.3	2050.9	358.2	33.1	58.6
4.1			9.2	108.8	3.1	0.8	2.4
49.2	1.6	1.8	62.4	1437.0	418.2	105.3	87.1
34.3	0.6	0.6	34.7	1084.3	197.9	13.8	21.3
19.2	0.2		19.7	186.0	25.0	8.7	10.5
14.0		1.0	13.9	212.0	62.6	9.4	4.7
58.6	0.7	0.9	57.1	403.9	95.4	8.5	18.8

5-5 按行业分就业人员数（年底数）
Number of Employed Persons at the Year-end by Sector

单位: 万人 (10 000 persons)

年 份 Year	合 计 Total	农、林、牧、渔业 Farming, Forestry, Animal Husbandry and Fishery	采掘业 Mining and Quarrying	制造业 Manufacturing	电力、煤气及水的生产和供应业 Production and Supply of Electricity Gas and Water	建筑业 Construction	地质勘查业水利管理业 Geological Prospecting and Water Conservancy	交通运输仓储和邮电通信业 Transport, Storage, Post & Telecommunication Services
1978	40152	28318	652	5332	107	854	178	750
1980	42361	29122	697	5899	118	993	188	805
1985	49873	31130	795	7412	142	2035	197	1279
1989	55329	33225	842	8547	180	2407	199	1522
1990	64749	34117	882	8624	192	2424	197	1566
1991	65491	34956	905	8839	203	2482	199	1617
1992	66152	34795	898	9106	215	2660	202	1674
1993	66808	33966	932	9295	240	3050	144	1688
1994	67455	33386	915	9613	246	3188	139	1864
1995	68065	33018	932	9803	258	3322	135	1942
1996	68950	32910	902	9763	273	3408	129	2013
1997	69820	33095	868	9612	283	3449	129	2062
1998	70637	33232	721	8319	283	3327	116	2000
1999	71394	33493	667	8109	285	3412	111	2022
2000	72085	33355	597	8043	284	3552	110	2029
2001	73025	32974	561	8083	288	3669	105	2037
2002	73740	32487	558	8307	290	3893	98	2084

5-5 续表 continued

单位: 万人 (10 000 persons)

年 份 Year	批发零售贸易和餐饮业 Wholesale and Retail Trade & Catering Services	金融、保险业 Finance and Insurance	房地产业 Real Estate	社会服务业 Social Services	卫生体育和社会福利业 Health Care, Sports & Social Welfare	教育、文化艺术和广播电影电视业 Education, Culture and Arts, Radio, Film and Television	科学研究和综合技术服务业 Scientific Research and Polytechnic Services	国家机关、政党机关和社会团体 Government Agencies, Party Agencies and Social Organizations	其 他 Others
1978	1140	76	31	179	363	1093	92	467	521
1980	1363	99	37	276	389	1147	113	527	588
1985	2306	138	36	401	467	1273	144	799	1319
1989	2770	205	43	550	518	1426	165	1022	1709
1990	2839	218	44	594	536	1457	173	1079	1798
1991	2998	234	48	604	553	1497	179	1136	1910
1992	3209	248	54	643	565	1520	183	1148	2313
1993	3459	270	66	543	416	1210	173	1030	3740
1994	3921	264	74	626	434	1436	178	1033	4155
1995	4292	276	80	703	444	1476	182	1042	4484
1996	4511	292	84	747	458	1513	183	1093	4563
1997	4795	308	87	810	471	1557	186	1093	4862
1998	4645	314	94	868	478	1573	178	1097	5118
1999	4751	328	96	923	482	1568	173	1102	4969
2000	4686	327	100	921	488	1565	174	1104	5643
2001	4737	336	107	976	493	1568	165	1101	5852
2002	4969	340	118	1094	493	1565	163	1075	6245

5-6 各地区按行业分城镇单位就业人员数（年底数）

Number of Employed Persons in Urban Units at the Year-end by Sector and Region

单位：万人 (10 000 persons)

年 份 Year 地 区 Region		合 计 Total	农、林、牧、渔业 Agriculture, Forestry, Animal Husbandry and Fishing	采矿业 Mining	制造业 Manufacturing	电力、燃气及水的生产和供应业 Production and Supply of Electricity, Gas and Water	建筑业 Construction	交通运输、仓储和邮政业 Transport, Storage and Post
	2003	10969.7	484.5	488.3	2980.5	297.6	833.7	636.5
	2004	11098.9	466.1	500.7	3050.8	300.6	841.0	631.8
	2005	11404.0	446.3	509.2	3210.9	299.9	926.6	613.9
北 京	Beijing	505.6	2.8	2.2	102.4	5.8	41.1	37.1
天 津	Tianjin	194.1	0.8	7.3	77.7	3.4	9.1	11.8
河 北	Hebei	495.6	8.5	27.6	120.3	17.4	33.9	25.6
山 西	Shanxi	360.5	3.6	66.3	72.2	10.1	20.8	20.0
内蒙古	Inner Mongolia	243.0	30.1	17.5	44.0	9.1	13.0	15.9
辽 宁	Liaoning	497.1	28.8	30.5	150.4	16.9	28.3	33.0
吉 林	Jilin	261.9	20.3	13.5	60.4	8.0	13.5	17.9
黑龙江	Heilongjiang	490.4	88.9	45.1	102.5	15.4	36.2	27.9
上 海	Shanghai	333.2	1.5	0.1	118.7	5.4	13.3	32.8
江 苏	Jiangsu	628.8	15.5	14.9	251.6	14.1	27.0	33.0
浙 江	Zhejiang	531.1	1.8	1.8	203.4	10.1	82.5	19.3
安 徽	Anhui	335.3	9.4	28.5	68.3	9.3	27.7	16.1
福 建	Fujian	400.1	7.5	4.2	200.2	8.1	30.6	15.0
江 西	Jiangxi	275.6	14.8	8.8	64.0	9.5	22.4	16.1
山 东	Shandong	891.0	6.5	61.6	336.7	20.2	68.2	29.5
河 南	Henan	700.6	9.5	49.2	155.2	21.7	64.8	32.9
湖 北	Hubei	511.8	30.7	13.0	146.0	13.0	44.1	29.3
湖 南	Hunan	406.3	8.5	10.8	81.1	10.6	53.1	22.4
广 东	Guangdong	904.3	10.6	3.3	360.0	19.6	58.6	47.3
广 西	Guangxi	283.6	13.7	5.2	56.7	8.0	22.6	17.4
海 南	Hainan	74.7	18.4	1.1	7.2	1.9	5.3	4.2
重 庆	Chongqing	215.5	2.1	8.6	54.1	5.8	34.3	13.9
四 川	Sichuan	512.7	9.3	20.5	117.8	15.3	76.7	22.8
贵 州	Guizhou	210.6	3.0	10.9	41.7	6.5	23.9	8.7
云 南	Yunnan	247.0	16.3	6.0	44.5	7.0	18.5	13.1
西 藏	Tibet	18.2	0.5	0.1	0.8	0.8	0.7	0.7
陕 西	Shaanxi	334.2	6.4	18.2	86.2	9.2	19.6	20.4
甘 肃	Gansu	194.3	8.4	9.4	44.2	6.8	13.8	11.7
青 海	Qinghai	42.6	2.3	1.6	6.7	1.7	2.9	3.4
宁 夏	Ningxia	59.7	4.0	5.6	11.3	3.6	4.0	3.1
新 疆	Xinjiang	244.7	61.5	16.0	24.7	5.6	16.1	11.6

注：城镇单位就业人员数不含私营企业和个体。

a) Employed persons in urban units don't include those in private enterprise and self-employed individuals.

5-6 续表 1 continued

单位：万人 (10 000 persons)

年份 Year / 地区 Region		信息传输、计算机服务和软件业 Information Transmission, Computer Service and Software	批发和零售业 Wholesale and Retail Trade	住宿和餐饮业 Hotels and Catering Services	金融业 Financial Intermediation	房地产业 Real Estate	租赁和商务服务业 Leasing and Business Services
2003		116.8	628.1	172.1	353.3	120.2	183.5
2004		123.7	586.7	177.1	356.0	133.4	194.4
2005		130.1	544.0	181.2	359.3	146.5	218.5
北 京	Beijing	19.4	38.8	24.6	15.8	23.3	46.7
天 津	Tianjin	2.4	11.7	3.0	5.1	2.3	6.6
河 北	Hebei	4.7	27.0	5.1	18.1	2.9	4.7
山 西	Shanxi	4.1	21.0	4.0	12.1	1.3	4.8
内蒙古	Inner Mongolia	2.5	7.4	2.6	8.1	1.4	2.7
辽 宁	Liaoning	5.1	16.9	6.1	18.2	6.2	9.5
吉 林	Jilin	3.1	9.6	3.1	9.3	2.8	3.2
黑龙江	Heilongjiang	4.1	21.6	3.8	11.5	4.3	4.6
上 海	Shanghai	4.2	24.4	7.8	15.8	8.2	14.9
江 苏	Jiangsu	6.5	28.9	8.6	22.2	5.8	9.1
浙 江	Zhejiang	4.9	19.2	9.8	19.1	6.2	14.2
安 徽	Anhui	3.2	17.5	2.7	11.2	3.2	4.3
福 建	Fujian	3.5	11.0	4.9	9.9	5.1	4.9
江 西	Jiangxi	2.9	10.2	2.4	8.7	2.4	2.5
山 东	Shandong	5.8	39.8	11.8	24.6	8.5	10.8
河 南	Henan	4.8	48.2	11.0	20.9	5.5	10.3
湖 北	Hubei	4.5	27.6	6.6	13.1	5.9	6.4
湖 南	Hunan	4.2	13.9	7.0	13.7	5.6	4.5
广 东	Guangdong	14.0	40.6	22.2	29.9	20.9	23.5
广 西	Guangxi	3.6	13.7	4.8	7.9	3.1	5.9
海 南	Hainan	0.9	2.9	3.1	1.8	1.4	1.4
重 庆	Chongqing	2.4	9.2	3.1	7.2	3.1	1.8
四 川	Sichuan	5.1	19.1	5.2	17.2	4.3	6.0
贵 州	Guizhou	1.6	12.1	2.7	4.9	3.8	2.4
云 南	Yunnan	2.9	11.4	3.9	7.1	2.0	2.5
西 藏	Tibet	0.3	0.6	0.4	0.6		0.1
陕 西	Shaanxi	3.5	20.0	4.8	9.9	2.4	2.8
甘 肃	Gansu	2.2	8.5	2.5	5.9	1.1	2.1
青 海	Qinghai	0.8	1.7	0.4	1.4	0.2	0.6
宁 夏	Ningxia	0.5	2.1	0.7	2.4	0.7	0.7
新 疆	Xinjiang	2.2	7.6	2.8	5.8	2.3	4.0

5-6 续表 2 continued

单位：万人 (10 000 persons)

年 份 地 区	Year Region	科学研究、技术服务和地质勘查业 Scientific Research, Technical Services, and Geological Prospecting	水利、环境和公共设施管理业 Management of Water Conservancy, Environment and Public Facilities	居民服务和其他服务业 Services to Households and Other Services	教 育 Education	卫生、社会保障和社会福利业 Health, Social Securities and Social Welfare	文化、体育和娱乐业 Culture, Sports and Entertainment	公共管理和社会组织 Public Management and Social Organization
	2003	221.9	172.5	52.8	1442.8	485.8	127.8	1171.0
	2004	222.1	176.1	54.2	1466.8	494.7	123.4	1199.0
	2005	227.7	180.4	53.9	1483.2	508.9	122.5	1240.8
北 京	Beijing	31.6	7.0	10.3	36.8	16.2	14.1	29.7
天 津	Tianjin	5.3	3.6	4.3	17.0	7.7	1.7	13.2
河 北	Hebei	7.6	8.6	2.1	84.0	22.8	4.9	69.8
山 西	Shanxi	5.9	5.0	1.3	46.4	13.9	4.3	43.6
内蒙古	Inner Mongolia	4.1	5.9	0.8	33.0	10.5	3.1	31.2
辽 宁	Liaoning	9.1	10.8	2.1	51.3	21.9	5.2	46.7
吉 林	Jilin	5.8	6.9	1.0	36.8	14.3	3.7	28.7
黑龙江	Heilongjiang	9.4	7.9	5.0	42.5	17.0	3.6	39.2
上 海	Shanghai	13.2	5.1	4.0	25.7	15.5	4.5	18.3
江 苏	Jiangsu	9.2	10.0	1.2	81.8	29.9	5.0	54.7
浙 江	Zhejiang	7.4	5.9	1.0	51.5	23.9	4.6	44.3
安 徽	Anhui	5.3	5.7	0.5	57.5	17.7	4.2	43.2
福 建	Fujian	3.9	3.8	1.2	42.3	12.2	3.2	28.5
江 西	Jiangxi	5.5	4.3	0.6	45.7	14.1	3.3	37.4
山 东	Shandong	8.1	11.4	3.1	104.5	35.4	5.7	98.7
河 南	Henan	11.1	10.6	1.5	107.2	33.1	6.0	97.1
湖 北	Hubei	9.5	9.4	1.4	64.8	25.8	5.5	55.0
湖 南	Hunan	5.9	6.6	0.7	66.2	23.5	4.0	64.0
广 东	Guangdong	12.3	11.9	4.2	98.4	38.2	8.2	80.7
广 西	Guangxi	5.3	5.2	0.7	54.9	17.0	3.3	34.7
海 南	Hainan	1.5	2.1	0.1	8.9	3.0	1.2	8.4
重 庆	Chongqing	5.1	2.7	0.6	31.2	8.8	1.8	19.8
四 川	Sichuan	11.2	7.2	2.0	79.3	26.4	4.9	62.4
贵 州	Guizhou	3.6	2.5	0.8	38.0	8.9	2.0	32.5
云 南	Yunnan	5.6	4.0	0.5	47.0	12.6	3.4	38.8
西 藏	Tibet	0.5	0.2		3.2	1.3	0.6	6.8
陕 西	Shaanxi	12.5	5.3	2.0	51.1	14.0	3.9	41.8
甘 肃	Gansu	4.8	3.9	0.6	30.8	7.6	2.7	27.3
青 海	Qinghai	1.8	0.8	0.2	6.2	2.4	0.6	6.9
宁 夏	Ningxia	1.1	1.8		7.3	2.7	0.9	7.4
新 疆	Xinjiang	4.4	4.3	0.3	32.0	10.8	2.5	30.2

5-7 按登记注册类型和细行业分职工人数（2005年底）

Number of Staff and Workers at the Year-end by Status of Registration and Sector in Detail (2005)

单位：万人 (10 000 persons)

项目	Item	合计 Total	国有单位 State-owned Units	城镇集体单位 Urban Collective-owned Units	其他单位 Units of Other Types of Ownership
全国总计	**National Total**	**10850.3**	**6232.0**	**769.2**	**3849.2**
按企、事业和机关分组	**Grouped by Enterprises, Institutions and Agencies**				
企业	Enterprises	7064.1	2569.6	663.4	3831.1
事业	Institutions	2712.9	2591.4	103.5	18.0
机关	Agencies & Organizations	1073.3	1071.0	2.3	
按国民经济行业分组	**Grouped by Sector**				
农、林、牧、渔业	**Agriculture, Forestry, Animal Husbandry and Fishing**	**414.2**	**392.7**	**8.7**	**12.8**
农业	Agriculture	199.4	194.4	1.0	4.0
林业	Forestry	106.9	104.5	0.5	2.0
畜牧业	Animal Husbandry	27.3	23.6	0.4	3.3
渔业	Fishing	6.8	4.9	0.2	1.7
农、林、牧、渔服务业	Services	73.8	65.3	6.6	1.8
采矿业	**Mining**	**497.6**	**235.7**	**23.5**	**238.4**
煤炭开采和洗选业	Mining and Washing of Coal	342.2	150.8	15.9	175.5
石油和天然气开采业	Extraction of Petroleum and Natural Gas	83.2	52.5	0.7	30.0
黑色金属矿采选业	Mining of Ferrous Metal Ores	16.9	7.4	1.9	7.6
有色金属矿采选业	Mining of Non-ferrous Metal Ores	29.5	14.1	1.9	13.5
非金属矿采选业	Mining and Processing of Nonmetal Ores	24.1	10.0	3.0	11.2
其它采矿业	Mining of Other Ores	1.6	0.8	0.1	0.7
制造业	**Manufacturing**	**3096.5**	**599.0**	**214.4**	**2283.1**
农副食品加工业	Processing of Food from Agricultural Products	104.1	16.0	4.6	83.5
食品制造业	Manufacture of Foods	67.4	9.7	4.2	53.6
饮料制造业	Manufacture of Beverage	69.3	13.4	2.0	54.0
烟草制品业	Manufacture of Tobacco	18.1	15.2	0.5	2.4
纺织业	Manufacture of Textile	271.6	38.3	14.3	219.0
纺织服装、鞋、帽制造业	Manufacture of Textile Wearing Apparel, Footware, and Caps	171.9	6.0	11.2	154.7
皮革、毛皮、羽毛（绒）及其制品业	Manufacture of Leather, Fur, Feather & Its Products	86.1	2.2	3.6	80.3
木材加工及木、竹、藤、棕、草制品业	Processing of Timbers, Manufacture of Wood, Bamboo, Rattan, Palm, and Straw Products	31.5	5.9	4.5	21.0
家具制造业	Manufacture of Furniture	28.6	1.1	2.6	24.9
造纸及纸制品业	Manufacture of Paper and Paper Products	56.6	8.2	5.2	43.2
印刷业和记录媒介的复制	Printing, Reproduction of Recording Media	41.0	13.3	6.8	20.9
文教体育用品制造业	Manufacture of Articles for Culture, Education and Sport Activity	38.4	0.8	2.0	35.7
石油加工、炼焦及核燃料加工业	Processing of Petroleum, Coking, Processing of Nucleus Fuel	54.0	18.4	2.8	32.8
化工原料及化学制品制造业	Manufacture of Chemical Raw Material and Chemical Products	206.3	56.3	12.2	137.7
医药制造业	Manufacture of Medicines	89.3	13.7	3.3	72.3
化学纤维制造业	Manufacture of Chemical Fiber	20.2	2.9	0.7	16.6
橡胶制品业	Manufacture of Rubber	36.8	3.3	3.9	29.6
塑料制品业	Manufacture of Plastic	69.4	2.9	7.0	59.5
非金属矿物制品业	Manufacture of Non-metallic Mineral Products	206.8	45.0	21.9	139.9

5-7 续表 1 continued

单位：万人 (10 000 persons)

项目	Item	合计 Total	国有单位 State-owned Units	城镇集体单位 Urban Collective-owned Units	其他单位 Units of Other Types of Ownership
黑色金属冶炼及压延加工业	Manufacture and Processing of Ferrous Metals	184.2	69.5	10.3	104.4
有色金属冶炼及压延加工业	Manufacture & Processing of Non-ferrous Metals	77.4	24.6	4.4	48.3
金属制品业	Manufacture of Metal Products	91.4	10.4	14.4	66.6
通用设备制造业	Manufacture of General Purpose Machinery	186.6	46.7	22.2	117.7
专用设备制造业	Manufacture of Special Purpose Machinery	156.5	52.5	8.5	95.5
交通运输设备制造业	Manufacture of Transport Equipment	229.5	80.4	15.6	133.5
电气机械及器材制造业	Manufacture of Electrical Machinery & Equipment	161.2	16.3	12.1	132.7
通信设备、计算机及其他电子设备制造业	Manufacture of Communication Equipment, Computer and Other Electronic Equipment	226.9	14.9	3.8	208.2
仪器仪表及文化、办公用机械制造业	Manufacture of Measuring Instrument and Machinery for Cultural Activity & Office Work	55.4	7.1	3.1	45.3
工艺品及其他制造业	Manufacture of Artwork, Other Manufacture	57.7	3.2	6.0	48.5
废弃资源和废旧材料回收加工业	Recycling and Disposal of Waste	2.2	0.8	0.5	0.8
电力、燃气及水的生产和供应业	**Production and Supply of Electric Power and Heat Power**	**293.7**	**205.7**	**5.9**	**82.1**
电力、热力的生产和供应业	Production and Supply of Electric Power and Heat Power	226.8	154.2	3.9	68.6
燃气生产和供应业	Production and Supply of Gas	16.5	9.8	0.2	6.5
水的生产和供应业	Production and Supply of Water	50.5	41.7	1.8	7.0
建筑业	**Construction**	**854.3**	**250.3**	**173.9**	**430.2**
房屋和土木工程建筑业	Construction of Building & Civil Engineering	735.3	215.0	154.2	366.0
建筑安装业	Architectural Installation	82.5	28.4	15.1	39.0
建筑装饰业	Architectural Decoration	22.6	2.4	3.2	17.0
其他建筑业	Other Construction	13.9	4.5	1.3	8.1
交通运输、仓储和邮政业	**Traffic, Transport, Storage and Post**	**579.2**	**421.8**	**29.1**	**128.2**
铁路运输业	Transport Via Railway	166.6	156.3	3.7	6.5
道路运输业	Transport Via Road	154.9	103.5	10.5	41.0
城市公共交通业	Urban Public Traffic	89.6	48.3	2.7	38.5
水上运输业	Water Transport	49.8	28.6	4.2	17.0
航空运输业	Air Transport	21.0	10.9	0.2	9.9
管道运输业	Transport Via Pipeline	1.8	1.2	0.1	0.5
装卸搬运和其他运输服务业	Loading, Unloading, Portage and Other Transport Services	25.2	10.6	6.2	8.4
仓储业	Storage	24.8	18.7	1.3	4.9
邮政业	Post	45.4	43.7	0.2	1.6
信息传输、计算机服务和软件业	**Information Transfer, Computer Services and Software**	**116.8**	**59.3**	**1.3**	**56.2**
电信和其他信息传输服务业	Telecom & Other Information Transfer Services	89.6	56.5	0.9	32.3
计算机服务业	Computer Services	9.7	2.0	0.2	7.5
软件业	Software Industry	17.4	0.8	0.2	16.4
批发和零售业	**Wholesale and Retail Trade**	**508.3**	**204.4**	**85.1**	**218.9**
批发业	Wholesale Trade	270.3	137.9	39.0	93.3
零售业	Retail Trade	238.0	66.4	46.0	125.6
住宿和餐饮业	**Hotels and Catering Services**	**166.5**	**63.3**	**13.1**	**90.1**
住宿业	Hotels	109.8	51.7	8.2	49.9
餐饮业	Catering Services	56.7	11.6	4.8	40.2

5-7 续表 2 continued

单位：万人 (10 000 persons)

项 目	Item	合 计 Total	国有单位 State-owned Units	城镇集体单位 Urban Collective-owned Units	其他单位 Units of Other Types of Ownership
金融业	**Financial Intermediation**	**295.0**	**154.9**	**61.6**	**78.6**
银行业	Bank	240.5	138.2	60.9	41.4
证券业	Security Activities	6.2	1.5		4.7
保险业	Insurance	44.1	13.8		30.3
其他金融活动	Other Financial Activities	4.2	1.4	0.6	2.2
房地产业	**Real Estate**	**132.7**	**43.9**	**7.6**	**81.1**
#房地产开发经营	Development and Management of Real Estate	63.6	16.1	3.7	43.7
物业管理	Property Management	49.9	15.4	2.6	31.9
房地产中介服务	Agency Services for Real Estate	5.1	2.2	0.2	2.7
租赁和商务服务业	**Leasing and Business Services**	**198.8**	**104.8**	**33.2**	**60.8**
租赁业	Leasing	3.5	0.9	0.7	1.9
商务服务业	Business Services	195.3	103.8	32.6	58.9
科学研究、技术服务和地质勘查业	**Scientific Research, Technical Service and Geologic Prospecting**	**212.7**	**179.7**	**3.0**	**29.9**
研究与实验发展	Research and Experimental Development	60.7	56.6	0.2	3.8
专业技术服务业	Professional Technical Services	94.6	72.6	2.1	19.9
科技交流和推广服务业	Services of Science and Technology Exchanges and Promotion	27.1	20.9	0.6	5.6
地质勘查业	Geologic Prospecting	30.4	29.6	0.1	0.7
水利、环境和公共设施管理业	**Management of Water Conservancy, Environment and Public Facilities**	**170.3**	**152.5**	**8.8**	**9.0**
水利管理业	Management of Water Conservancy	46.2	44.8	0.9	0.5
环境管理业	Environmental Management	72.1	63.0	6.5	2.6
公共设施管理业	Management of Public Facilities	52.0	44.7	1.4	5.9
居民服务和其他服务业	**Services to Households and Other Services**	**47.2**	**21.0**	**9.5**	**16.6**
居民服务业	Services to Households	23.3	12.0	3.6	7.7
其他服务业	Other Services	23.9	9.1	5.9	8.9
教育	**Education**	**1444.7**	**1390.8**	**39.0**	**14.9**
#初等教育	Junior Education	596.7	567.2	27.8	1.7
中等教育	Secondary Education	619.6	606.2	8.0	5.4
高等教育	Senior Education	152.7	149.6	0.2	2.9
卫生、社会保障和社会福利业	**Health, Social Security and Social Welfare**	**491.4**	**437.8**	**46.2**	**7.4**
卫生	Health	467.4	416.3	45.0	6.1
社会保障业	Social Security	12.2	10.8	0.4	1.0
社会福利业	Social Welfare	11.8	10.7	0.8	0.3
文化、体育和娱乐业	**Culture, Sports and Entertainment**	**117.0**	**106.2**	**2.4**	**8.5**
新闻出版业	Journalism and Publishing Activities	23.4	22.4	0.2	0.8
广播、电影、电视和音像业	Broadcasting, Movies, Televisions and Audiovisual Activities	40.2	38.2	0.5	1.6
文化艺术业	Cultural and Art Activities	37.9	35.8	1.3	0.7
体育	Sports Activities	8.2	7.6		0.5
娱乐业	Entertainment	7.4	2.2	0.3	4.9
公共管理和社会组织	**Public Management and Social Organization**	**1213.5**	**1208.3**	**2.9**	**2.2**
#中国共产党机关	Organs of Communist Party of China	49.7	49.7		
国家机构	Government Agencies	1123.4	1121.6	1.7	
人民政协和民主党派	People's Political Consultative Conference and Democratic Parties	8.4	8.4		
群众社团、社会团体和宗教组织	Non-Governmental Institutions, Social Organizations and Religion Organizations	20.2	18.6	0.5	1.1

5-8 各地区按行业分职工人数（年底数）

Number of Staff and Workers at the Year-end by Sector and Region

单位：万人 (10 000 persons)

年份 Year 地区 Region		合计 Total	农、林、牧、渔业 Agriculture, Forestry, Animal Husbandry and Fishing	采矿业 Mining	制造业 Manufacturing	电力、燃气及水的生产和供应业 Production and Supply of Electricity, Gas and Water	建筑业 Construction	交通运输、仓储和邮政业 Transport, Storage and Post
	2003	10492.0	459.7	481.0	2898.9	292.3	773.5	609.7
	2004	10575.9	438.1	491.2	2960.0	294.0	777.7	598.4
	2005	10850.3	414.2	497.6	3096.5	293.7	854.3	579.2
北京	Beijing	448.4	2.7	2.0	95.4	5.6	35.1	33.0
天津	Tianjin	169.9	0.8	6.4	71.5	3.1	8.3	10.4
河北	Hebei	483.7	8.5	27.5	118.5	16.9	31.0	25.2
山西	Shanxi	352.1	3.6	65.8	71.1	10.0	20.2	19.6
内蒙古	Inner Mongolia	239.6	30.0	17.3	43.8	9.1	12.7	15.5
辽宁	Liaoning	476.6	28.6	30.3	144.8	16.8	27.6	31.8
吉林	Jilin	257.9	20.2	13.4	59.4	8.0	13.1	17.6
黑龙江	Heilongjiang	455.4	68.3	45.0	98.2	15.1	34.1	27.3
上海	Shanghai	264.8	0.8		95.6	5.3	9.9	26.0
江苏	Jiangsu	602.9	15.0	14.7	245.2	13.9	25.8	31.3
浙江	Zhejiang	511.8	1.8	1.8	200.7	9.9	78.9	18.4
安徽	Anhui	317.4	8.9	27.5	66.2	9.1	23.8	15.3
福建	Fujian	387.0	7.0	4.1	197.8	7.8	28.2	13.7
江西	Jiangxi	264.8	14.6	8.5	62.5	9.2	20.3	15.2
山东	Shandong	871.1	6.4	60.8	333.7	20.0	66.1	29.1
河南	Henan	681.9	9.3	48.7	152.7	21.4	60.0	32.0
湖北	Hubei	452.1	28.0	11.4	119.8	12.0	35.4	27.1
湖南	Hunan	381.2	7.7	10.5	78.4	10.4	43.5	20.3
广东	Guangdong	886.1	10.3	3.2	357.2	19.5	56.4	45.8
广西	Guangxi	268.6	12.6	5.0	54.6	7.7	20.5	16.5
海南	Hainan	72.6	18.1	1.1	6.9	1.9	4.9	4.1
重庆	Chongqing	209.7	2.1	8.5	53.0	5.7	33.8	13.4
四川	Sichuan	492.8	9.1	19.6	115.9	15.0	72.5	22.0
贵州	Guizhou	202.0	2.8	10.6	40.5	6.3	21.6	8.2
云南	Yunnan	235.7	14.8	5.8	43.2	6.7	17.3	12.1
西藏	Tibet	16.3	0.3	0.1	0.8	0.7	0.5	0.6
陕西	Shaanxi	323.2	6.3	17.8	84.4	9.1	18.1	19.1
甘肃	Gansu	188.5	8.2	9.1	43.1	6.8	13.2	11.6
青海	Qinghai	40.9	2.2	1.6	6.5	1.7	2.6	3.3
宁夏	Ningxia	57.4	4.0	5.2	11.1	3.5	3.7	3.0
新疆	Xinjiang	237.8	61.0	14.3	24.3	5.6	15.2	10.7

5-8 续表 1 continued

单位：万人 (10 000 persons)

年份 地区	Year Region	信息传输、计算机服务和软件业 Information Transmission, Computer Service and Software	批发和零售业 Wholesale and Retail Trade	住宿和餐饮业 Hotels and Catering Services	金融业 Financial Intermediation	房地产业 Real Estate	租赁和商务服务业 Leasing and Business Services
	2003	104.0	592.0	159.4	286.2	108.3	167.6
	2004	110.6	550.9	162.6	286.9	120.2	176.3
	2005	116.8	508.3	166.5	295.0	132.7	198.8
北京	Beijing	17.5	34.3	20.4	10.8	19.6	42.3
天津	Tianjin	2.2	8.8	2.2	3.5	1.7	4.5
河北	Hebei	4.2	26.6	5.0	15.0	2.8	4.6
山西	Shanxi	3.6	20.6	3.9	9.6	1.3	4.7
内蒙古	Inner Mongolia	2.5	7.3	2.6	7.1	1.4	2.6
辽宁	Liaoning	4.9	16.1	5.9	13.8	5.8	6.9
吉林	Jilin	3.0	9.3	3.1	8.5	2.8	3.2
黑龙江	Heilongjiang	3.9	20.6	3.5	9.8	4.1	3.9
上海	Shanghai	3.5	15.7	4.6	13.5	4.4	11.1
江苏	Jiangsu	5.5	27.3	7.8	16.8	5.4	8.6
浙江	Zhejiang	4.4	18.3	9.3	15.8	5.7	13.8
安徽	Anhui	2.7	16.5	2.5	8.7	2.9	3.8
福建	Fujian	2.9	10.5	4.7	8.3	4.8	4.7
江西	Jiangxi	2.6	9.9	2.3	7.2	2.3	2.2
山东	Shandong	5.1	38.1	11.2	18.5	8.3	10.6
河南	Henan	4.1	46.9	10.7	17.6	5.4	9.9
湖北	Hubei	4.1	23.6	5.4	11.0	4.9	5.6
湖南	Hunan	3.7	13.3	6.7	10.6	5.3	4.3
广东	Guangdong	13.4	39.4	21.6	27.2	20.5	23.1
广西	Guangxi	2.6	12.9	4.7	7.3	3.0	5.1
海南	Hainan	0.9	2.7	3.1	1.7	1.4	1.3
重庆	Chongqing	2.3	9.1	3.0	5.2	3.0	1.7
四川	Sichuan	4.4	18.6	5.0	13.4	4.0	5.8
贵州	Guizhou	1.5	11.7	2.6	4.5	3.6	2.4
云南	Yunnan	2.6	10.8	3.7	6.7	1.9	2.3
西藏	Tibet	0.3	0.6	0.4	0.6		0.1
陕西	Shaanxi	3.2	19.5	4.5	8.8	2.2	2.8
甘肃	Gansu	2.0	8.2	2.4	5.6	1.0	2.0
青海	Qinghai	0.7	1.5	0.4	1.2	0.2	0.5
宁夏	Ningxia	0.5	2.0	0.7	1.8	0.7	0.5
新疆	Xinjiang	2.0	7.5	2.6	4.8	2.2	3.9

5-8 续表 2 continued

单位：万人 (10 000 persons)

年份 地区	Year Region	科学研究、技术服务和地质勘查业 Scientific Research, Technical Services, and Geological Prospecting	水利、环境和公共设施管理业 Management of Water Conservancy, Environment and Public Facilities	居民服务和其他服务业 Services to Households and Other Services	教育 Education	卫生、社会保障和社会福利业 Health, Social Securities and Social Welfare	文化、体育和娱乐业 Culture, Sports and Entertainment	公共管理和社会组织 Public Management and Social Organization
	2003	206.3	163.9	47.5	1401.7	471.7	122.0	1146.3
	2004	207.6	164.6	47.5	1424.5	476.8	117.7	1170.2
	2005	212.7	170.3	47.2	1444.7	491.4	117.0	1213.5
北京	Beijing	26.0	6.6	8.9	32.8	15.2	12.6	27.2
天津	Tianjin	4.7	3.1	2.2	16.2	6.8	1.5	11.9
河北	Hebei	7.4	8.5	2.1	83.2	22.6	4.8	69.4
山西	Shanxi	5.6	5.0	1.2	45.2	13.7	4.2	43.1
内蒙古	Inner Mongolia	4.0	5.8	0.8	32.7	10.4	3.1	30.8
辽宁	Liaoning	8.8	10.4	2.0	50.2	21.2	5.1	45.8
吉林	Jilin	5.7	6.9	1.0	36.6	14.1	3.7	28.5
黑龙江	Heilongjiang	8.9	7.3	4.8	42.0	16.6	3.5	38.6
上海	Shanghai	11.7	3.8	2.8	22.9	13.5	3.5	16.2
江苏	Jiangsu	8.6	9.3	1.0	80.2	28.5	4.8	53.3
浙江	Zhejiang	6.8	5.5	0.9	49.7	23.1	4.3	42.8
安徽	Anhui	5.1	5.3	0.4	56.3	16.9	4.0	41.4
福建	Fujian	3.7	3.5	1.2	41.4	11.5	3.0	28.0
江西	Jiangxi	5.4	4.0	0.6	44.8	13.6	3.2	36.5
山东	Shandong	7.8	10.9	2.9	103.3	34.6	5.6	97.9
河南	Henan	10.8	10.4	1.4	106.3	32.6	5.8	96.1
湖北	Hubei	8.9	8.5	1.2	62.0	24.9	5.3	53.0
湖南	Hunan	5.6	6.2	0.6	64.7	22.8	3.8	62.8
广东	Guangdong	11.9	11.8	4.1	95.5	37.3	8.0	80.1
广西	Guangxi	5.1	4.8	0.7	51.9	16.5	3.2	33.8
海南	Hainan	1.4	2.0	0.1	8.7	2.9	1.2	8.2
重庆	Chongqing	4.9	2.6	0.6	30.8	8.6	1.7	19.6
四川	Sichuan	10.7	6.7	1.5	77.5	25.3	4.8	61.0
贵州	Guizhou	3.5	2.2	0.8	36.8	8.6	2.0	31.8
云南	Yunnan	5.0	3.7	0.5	45.7	12.1	3.3	37.6
西藏	Tibet	0.5	0.2		2.9	1.0	0.5	6.1
陕西	Shaanxi	12.2	5.1	2.0	49.5	13.6	3.7	41.3
甘肃	Gansu	4.6	3.8	0.3	29.7	7.5	2.6	26.9
青海	Qinghai	1.8	0.6	0.2	6.1	2.4	0.6	6.7
宁夏	Ningxia	1.1	1.8		7.2	2.6	0.8	7.2
新疆	Xinjiang	4.3	4.2	0.3	31.8	10.7	2.4	30.0

5-9 各地区按行业分国有单位职工人数（年底数）

Number of Staff and Workers in State-owned Units at the Year-end by Sector and Region

单位：万人 (10 000 persons)

年份 地区	Year Region	合计 Total	农、林、牧、渔业 Agriculture, Forestry, Animal Husbandry and Fishing	采矿业 Mining	制造业 Manufacturing	电力、燃气及水的生产和供应业 Production and Supply of Electricity, Gas and Water	建筑业 Construction	交通运输、仓储和邮政业 Transport, Storage and Post
	2003	6621.3	433.9	259.7	854.2	220.1	278.7	474.4
	2004	6438.2	412.7	263.3	730.0	214.4	260.6	452.1
	2005	6232.0	392.7	235.7	599.0	205.7	250.3	421.8
北　京	Beijing	178.5	0.9	0.2	12.8	0.9	7.3	12.7
天　津	Tianjin	79.3	0.7	1.1	12.4	2.1	3.1	7.6
河　北	Hebei	342.8	8.0	13.8	46.2	13.8	12.2	21.8
山　西	Shanxi	247.5	3.4	41.9	23.5	7.7	12.7	17.2
内蒙古	Inner Mongolia	159.7	29.0	4.0	3.7	6.0	3.6	13.8
辽　宁	Liaoning	292.4	27.7	17.2	37.0	11.2	9.5	26.9
吉　林	Jilin	176.3	19.7	5.9	17.3	5.7	5.2	13.5
黑龙江	Heilongjiang	286.5	65.8	2.5	31.1	11.7	10.3	24.3
上　海	Shanghai	120.3	0.5		17.6	3.8	4.9	9.5
江　苏	Jiangsu	273.4	13.8	9.7	20.4	7.8	6.0	18.5
浙　江	Zhejiang	172.5	1.6	0.3	7.5	6.6	3.3	10.6
安　徽	Anhui	199.2	8.6	3.8	17.4	6.5	8.4	10.8
福　建	Fujian	144.5	6.5	2.0	6.7	5.3	8.7	10.4
江　西	Jiangxi	191.3	14.3	6.6	18.3	7.3	8.3	13.6
山　东	Shandong	415.8	4.9	40.6	37.4	14.6	15.5	19.1
河　南	Henan	395.3	7.4	16.6	36.3	15.3	19.7	27.2
湖　北	Hubei	300.2	27.1	6.3	37.6	9.3	12.0	21.6
湖　南	Hunan	246.3	7.1	5.8	19.3	8.0	9.6	16.5
广　东	Guangdong	369.9	9.2	1.8	16.1	12.8	14.1	25.2
广　西	Guangxi	188.7	12.0	2.9	18.8	6.6	4.1	11.8
海　南	Hainan	56.6	17.9	1.0	2.3	1.2	3.1	2.7
重　庆	Chongqing	120.1	1.7	5.0	18.9	3.4	5.8	10.5
四　川	Sichuan	303.7	7.8	10.7	34.7	8.6	19.2	16.1
贵　州	Guizhou	140.5	2.7	3.1	15.4	4.8	12.1	7.1
云　南	Yunnan	168.4	14.4	3.1	12.0	3.6	6.5	9.9
西　藏	Tibet	15.4	0.3	0.1	0.4	0.7	0.3	0.6
陕　西	Shaanxi	242.0	5.9	15.0	41.2	7.3	9.8	17.5
甘　肃	Gansu	154.7	7.9	6.6	28.3	6.4	6.7	10.5
青　海	Qinghai	30.9	1.8	0.8	1.4	1.2	1.7	2.7
宁　夏	Ningxia	37.4	3.9	0.2	2.0	2.9	1.7	2.8
新　疆	Xinjiang	181.9	60.4	7.1	5.0	2.4	4.9	8.9

5-9 续表 1 continued

单位：万人 (10 000 persons)

年份 Year 地区 Region	信息传输、计算机服务和软件业 Information Transmission, Computer Service and Software	批发和零售业 Wholesale and Retail Trade	住宿和餐饮业 Hotels and Catering Services	金融业 Financial Intermediation	房地产业 Real Estate	租赁和商务服务业 Leasing and Business Services
2003	63.9	286.3	69.2	176.3	48.8	98.7
2004	66.2	246.3	66.0	166.2	46.8	99.7
2005	59.3	204.4	63.3	154.9	43.9	104.8
北京 Beijing	1.2	6.4	6.0	4.7	3.1	20.8
天津 Tianjin	0.4	2.2	0.7	2.1	0.4	3.1
河北 Hebei	2.8	13.8	3.2	8.5	1.8	2.6
山西 Shanxi	2.9	12.3	2.6	5.5	0.9	2.9
内蒙古 Inner Mongolia	2.2	3.9	1.3	4.4	0.9	1.8
辽宁 Liaoning	2.1	5.6	1.7	7.3	3.0	4.5
吉林 Jilin	2.1	4.1	1.7	4.6	1.4	1.9
黑龙江 Heilongjiang	2.8	9.3	1.9	5.4	2.3	1.9
上海 Shanghai	1.4	4.2	2.3	3.8	1.7	4.8
江苏 Jiangsu	2.4	6.6	2.5	7.5	2.2	4.0
浙江 Zhejiang	1.4	3.1	2.2	7.0	1.6	4.1
安徽 Anhui	2.0	8.1	1.2	5.2	1.1	1.9
福建 Fujian	1.7	4.7	1.4	4.8	1.3	2.9
江西 Jiangxi	1.9	6.7	1.4	4.1	1.4	1.6
山东 Shandong	2.1	12.3	5.3	8.0	2.8	4.2
河南 Henan	2.4	22.3	5.1	8.8	2.4	5.6
湖北 Hubei	3.6	10.9	1.9	7.0	1.9	3.2
湖南 Hunan	1.7	5.2	2.7	4.3	1.6	2.9
广东 Guangdong	6.2	13.6	5.1	13.9	4.6	13.0
广西 Guangxi	1.5	6.5	2.1	4.4	1.4	3.0
海南 Hainan	0.6	1.4	0.8	1.3	0.5	0.7
重庆 Chongqing	1.9	3.5	0.9	2.8	0.9	0.6
四川 Sichuan	3.4	8.0	1.5	7.5	1.3	4.4
贵州 Guizhou	0.6	6.2	1.0	2.2	0.5	1.3
云南 Yunnan	1.7	4.3	1.3	4.2	0.4	1.1
西藏 Tibet	0.3	0.5	0.4	0.6		
陕西 Shaanxi	2.1	9.9	1.7	5.6	1.1	1.9
甘肃 Gansu	1.7	4.5	1.5	3.8	0.6	1.3
青海 Qinghai	0.6	0.9	0.3	0.9	0.1	0.3
宁夏 Ningxia	0.4	1.1	0.3	1.2	0.1	0.3
新疆 Xinjiang	1.1	2.3	1.4	3.2	0.7	1.9

5-9 续表 2 continued

单位：万人 (10 000 persons)

年份 Year / 地区 Region		科学研究、技术服务和地质勘查业 Scientific Research, Technical Services, and Geological Prospecting	水利、环境和公共设施管理业 Management of Water Conservancy, Environment and Public Facilities	居民服务和其他服务业 Services to Households and Other Services	教育 Education	卫生、社会保障和社会福利业 Health, Social Securities and Social Welfare	文化、体育和娱乐业 Culture, Sports and Entertainment	公共管理和社会组织 Public Management and Social Organization
	2003	176.7	147.9	19.9	1340.1	419.1	112.4	1141.1
	2004	179.8	148.0	20.5	1371.6	423.0	107.3	1163.9
	2005	179.7	152.5	21.0	1390.8	437.8	106.2	1208.3
北　京	Beijing	15.4	4.8	2.0	29.4	13.3	9.8	26.8
天　津	Tianjin	3.6	2.9	0.9	16.0	6.5	1.4	11.8
河　北	Hebei	7.1	7.8	1.6	83.2	21.0	4.4	69.3
山　西	Shanxi	5.5	4.8	0.5	44.9	11.4	3.9	43.1
内蒙古	Inner Mongolia	3.8	5.4	0.5	32.3	9.0	3.1	30.8
辽　宁	Liaoning	7.6	9.9	1.1	50.0	19.6	4.8	45.7
吉　林	Jilin	5.2	6.1	0.7	36.3	12.9	3.5	28.4
黑龙江	Heilongjiang	8.3	6.8	3.0	41.7	15.7	3.4	38.5
上　海	Shanghai	10.0	3.0	1.1	22.1	10.8	3.1	16.0
江　苏	Jiangsu	6.8	7.5	0.5	78.9	20.8	4.2	53.2
浙　江	Zhejiang	5.2	3.9	0.5	47.9	19.5	4.0	42.2
安　徽	Anhui	4.9	5.0	0.4	56.2	12.7	3.8	41.3
福　建	Fujian	3.2	3.1	0.7	41.0	9.4	2.7	27.9
江　西	Jiangxi	5.2	3.4	0.4	44.4	12.8	3.2	36.4
山　东	Shandong	6.7	10.1	0.6	99.7	29.5	5.2	97.4
河　南	Henan	9.9	10.1	0.8	74.0	30.3	5.5	95.5
湖　北	Hubei	8.3	7.8	0.5	60.4	23.7	5.1	51.8
湖　南	Hunan	5.2	5.5	0.4	63.6	20.5	3.4	62.7
广　东	Guangdong	8.5	9.2	1.4	93.4	35.6	6.3	79.9
广　西	Guangxi	4.8	4.6	0.2	51.4	16.1	2.9	33.6
海　南	Hainan	1.3	1.8		8.4	2.5	0.9	8.2
重　庆	Chongqing	2.4	2.4	0.4	30.5	7.2	1.7	19.6
四　川	Sichuan	10.4	6.0	1.0	76.9	20.6	4.6	61.0
贵　州	Guizhou	3.0	2.1	0.2	36.2	8.4	1.8	31.7
云　南	Yunnan	4.4	3.3	0.2	45.5	12.0	3.0	37.5
西　藏	Tibet	0.5	0.2		2.9	1.0	0.5	6.1
陕　西	Shaanxi	11.4	5.0	0.9	48.9	12.3	3.5	41.2
甘　肃	Gansu	4.5	3.8	0.3	29.7	7.2	2.6	26.9
青　海	Qinghai	1.8	0.6	0.2	6.1	2.3	0.6	6.7
宁　夏	Ningxia	1.0	1.7		7.1	2.6	0.8	7.2
新　疆	Xinjiang	3.9	4.0	0.2	31.6	10.5	2.4	30.0

5-10 各地区按行业分城镇集体单位职工人数（年底数）

Number of Staff and Workers in Urban Collective-owned Units at the Year-end by Sector and Region

单位：万人 (10 000 persons)

年份 Year 地区 Region	合计 Total	农、林、牧、渔业 Agriculture, Forestry, Animal Husbandry and Fishing	采矿业 Mining	制造业 Manufacturing	电力、燃气及水的生产和供应业 Production and Supply of Electricity, Gas and Water	建筑业 Construction	交通运输、仓储和邮政业 Transport, Storage and Post
2003	950.5	13.9	27.0	287.4	6.8	201.1	36.6
2004	850.7	12.0	25.6	251.0	6.4	183.9	32.6
2005	769.2	8.7	23.5	214.4	5.9	173.9	29.1
北京 Beijing	20.7	0.3	0.2	5.0		4.0	0.7
天津 Tianjin	9.1		0.2	2.9		1.2	0.6
河北 Hebei	36.7	0.4	0.6	12.3	0.1	7.5	1.0
山西 Shanxi	29.8	0.1	3.6	9.2	0.2	2.7	0.6
内蒙古 Inner Mongolia	12.2	0.2	0.5	3.6	0.1	2.2	0.4
辽宁 Liaoning	39.8	0.3	2.0	17.2	0.5	8.6	1.4
吉林 Jilin	20.4	0.1	0.5	8.0	0.1	3.7	1.4
黑龙江 Heilongjiang	37.6	0.7	2.2	14.3	0.3	8.8	1.3
上海 Shanghai	11.0	0.1		2.0	0.1	0.4	0.6
江苏 Jiangsu	36.8	0.6	0.8	10.0	0.3	4.4	1.8
浙江 Zhejiang	29.4	0.1	0.2	5.9	0.4	9.3	0.9
安徽 Anhui	28.2	0.2	3.5	4.3	0.2	5.6	1.9
福建 Fujian	18.2			4.7	0.2	5.4	0.8
江西 Jiangxi	17.6	0.1	0.1	3.2	0.1	8.2	0.8
山东 Shandong	63.3	0.6	1.9	21.6	0.2	13.9	1.3
河南 Henan	88.5	1.2	0.9	15.2	0.1	10.9	2.1
湖北 Hubei	35.6	0.5	1.7	12.5	0.2	8.6	2.2
湖南 Hunan	27.7	0.3	1.4	6.6	0.2	9.3	1.6
广东 Guangdong	67.4	0.2		22.6	1.7	17.8	2.0
广西 Guangxi	18.2	0.1	0.3	4.0	0.1	5.6	1.3
海南 Hainan	3.8	0.1		0.5		1.3	0.1
重庆 Chongqing	13.7	0.5	0.3	4.0	0.1	4.5	0.8
四川 Sichuan	40.9	1.0	0.7	8.4	0.4	15.6	1.6
贵州 Guizhou	9.8		0.2	2.4	0.1	3.3	0.4
云南 Yunnan	10.6	0.1	0.2	2.5	0.1	2.4	0.2
西藏 Tibet	0.3			0.1		0.1	
陕西 Shaanxi	20.7	0.3	0.2	5.8		4.4	0.5
甘肃 Gansu	11.9	0.1	1.0	3.8	0.1	2.3	0.6
青海 Qinghai	2.0	0.1		0.5	0.1	0.5	0.1
宁夏 Ningxia	1.3			0.3		0.3	
新疆 Xinjiang	6.0	0.3	0.1	0.9	0.1	1.1	0.1

5-10 续表 1 continued

单位：万人 (10 000 persons)

年份 Year 地区 Region		信息传输、计算机服务和软件业 Information Transmission, Computer Service and Software	批发和零售业 Wholesale and Retail Trade	住宿和餐饮业 Hotels and Catering Services	金融业 Financial Intermediation	房地产业 Real Estate	租赁和商务服务业 Leasing and Business Services
2003		1.7	122.4	15.2	63.7	6.8	28.4
2004		1.2	103.1	14.2	63.5	7.1	28.7
2005		1.3	85.1	13.1	61.6	7.6	33.2
北京	Beijing	0.1	2.1	1.2		0.8	2.4
天津	Tianjin	0.2	1.6	0.2	0.5		0.3
河北	Hebei		5.8	0.4	4.4	0.1	1.4
山西	Shanxi		4.9	0.4	2.8	0.1	1.5
内蒙古	Inner Mongolia		0.7	0.2	1.9		0.5
辽宁	Liaoning	0.2	2.1	0.4	2.8	0.2	1.5
吉林	Jilin		1.0	0.2	2.6	0.0	0.5
黑龙江	Heilongjiang		3.2	0.4	1.9	0.4	1.1
上海	Shanghai		1.8	0.2		0.2	2.6
江苏	Jiangsu	0.1	4.8	0.4	2.5	0.3	1.4
浙江	Zhejiang		1.4	0.7	2.9	0.2	1.5
安徽	Anhui		3.9	0.1	2.3	0.3	1.4
福建	Fujian	0.1	1.8	0.3	1.5	0.2	0.6
江西	Jiangxi		1.4	0.1	1.7	0.1	0.4
山东	Shandong	0.2	6.4	1.0	4.0	0.8	3.2
河南	Henan		13.6	1.8	5.5	0.2	3.3
湖北	Hubei		3.2	0.3	2.3	0.4	0.5
湖南	Hunan		1.5	0.4	2.9	0.2	0.3
广东	Guangdong	0.1	5.2	1.3	5.4	2.0	4.7
广西	Guangxi		2.6	0.4	1.8	0.1	1.0
海南	Hainan		0.7	0.2	0.3	0.1	0.1
重庆	Chongqing		0.9	0.1	0.7	0.1	0.1
四川	Sichuan		2.5	0.6	3.9	0.2	0.6
贵州	Guizhou		1.4	0.1	1.1	0.2	0.3
云南	Yunnan		2.1	0.3	1.7		0.5
西藏	Tibet		0.1				
陕西	Shaanxi		4.7	0.4	1.8	0.1	0.4
甘肃	Gansu		1.5	0.4	1.2	0.1	0.4
青海	Qinghai		0.2		0.3		0.2
宁夏	Ningxia		0.2	0.1	0.3		
新疆	Xinjiang		1.6	0.1	0.9	0.1	0.4

5-10 续表 2 continued

单位：万人 (10 000 persons)

年 份 地 区	Year Region	科学研究、技术服务和地质勘查业 Scientific Research, Technical Services, and Geological Prospecting	水利、环境和公共设施管理业 Management of Water Conservancy, Environment and Public Facilities	居民服务和其他服务业 Services to Households and Other Services	教育 Education	卫生、社会保障和社会福利业 Health, Social Securities and Social Welfare	文化、体育和娱乐业 Culture, Sports and Entertainment	公共管理和社会组织 Public Management and Social Organization
	2003	3.4	9.8	14.0	55.6	49.3	3.0	4.5
	2004	3.2	9.2	12.6	41.8	47.7	2.6	4.3
	2005	3.0	8.8	9.5	39.0	46.2	2.4	2.9
北 京	Beijing	0.5	0.1	1.3	0.7	1.1	0.1	
天 津	Tianjin	0.1		0.7	0.1	0.2		0.1
河 北	Hebei		0.2	0.4	0.1	1.5	0.2	0.1
山 西	Shanxi		0.2	0.6	0.2	2.2	0.3	0.1
内蒙古	Inner Mongolia		0.2	0.2		1.3		
辽 宁	Liaoning	0.2	0.3	0.5	0.2	1.3		0.1
吉 林	Jilin	0.1	0.6	0.2		1.1	0.1	0.1
黑龙江	Heilongjiang	0.2	0.2	1.6	0.1	0.6		0.1
上 海	Shanghai	0.1	0.3	0.4	0.1	1.8	0.1	0.2
江 苏	Jiangsu	0.2	1.3	0.2	0.6	6.5	0.3	0.1
浙 江	Zhejiang	0.2	1.1	0.2	0.9	3.3	0.1	0.1
安 徽	Anhui	0.1	0.1		0.1	4.0	0.2	0.1
福 建	Fujian	0.1	0.1	0.2		2.0		
江 西	Jiangxi		0.4	0.1		0.6		0.1
山 东	Shandong	0.2	0.3	0.3	2.6	4.4	0.1	0.2
河 南	Henan	0.2	0.1	0.2	30.8	1.7	0.1	0.4
湖 北	Hubei	0.1	0.4	0.2	0.9	0.9		0.6
湖 南	Hunan		0.3	0.1	0.4	2.2	0.1	
广 东	Guangdong	0.4	1.3	0.6	0.8	1.2	0.2	0.1
广 西	Guangxi	0.1	0.1	0.3	0.2	0.2		
海 南	Hainan					0.4		
重 庆	Chongqing		0.1			1.4		0.1
四 川	Sichuan		0.4	0.3	0.1	4.5	0.1	
贵 州	Guizhou		0.1	0.1		0.1		
云 南	Yunnan		0.2	0.1		0.1		0.1
西 藏	Tibet							
陕 西	Shaanxi		0.1	0.4	0.1	1.2	0.1	0.1
甘 肃	Gansu					0.2		
青 海	Qinghai					0.1		
宁 夏	Ningxia							
新 疆	Xinjiang		0.1	0.1		0.1		

5-11 各地区按行业分其他单位职工人数（年底数）

Number of Staff and Workers in Units of Other Types of Ownership at the Year-end by Sector and Region

单位：万人 (10 000 persons)

年份 Year / 地区 Region	合计 Total	农、林、牧、渔业 Agriculture, Forestry, Animal Husbandry and Fishing	采矿业 Mining	制造业 Manufacturing	电力、燃气及水的生产和供应业 Production and Supply of Electricity, Gas and Water	建筑业 Construction	交通运输、仓储和邮政业 Transport, Storage and Post
2003	2920.3	11.9	194.3	1757.4	65.4	293.8	98.7
2004	3287.0	13.4	202.2	1979.0	73.2	333.3	113.7
2005	3849.2	12.8	238.4	2283.1	82.1	430.2	128.2
北 京 Beijing	249.2	1.5	1.7	77.6	4.7	23.8	19.6
天 津 Tianjin	81.5	0.1	5.1	56.2	0.9	4.0	2.2
河 北 Hebei	104.3	0.1	13.1	60.1	2.9	11.2	2.3
山 西 Shanxi	74.8		20.3	38.4	2.1	4.9	1.8
内蒙古 Inner Mongolia	67.7	0.8	12.8	36.4	2.9	6.9	1.3
辽 宁 Liaoning	144.4	0.7	11.0	90.6	5.1	9.5	3.5
吉 林 Jilin	61.2	0.4	7.0	34.0	2.1	4.2	2.7
黑龙江 Heilongjiang	131.3	1.8	40.3	52.8	3.2	15.0	1.6
上 海 Shanghai	133.5	0.3		76.0	1.5	4.6	16.0
江 苏 Jiangsu	292.7	0.6	4.2	214.7	5.8	15.4	10.9
浙 江 Zhejiang	310.0	0.1	1.3	187.3	2.9	66.2	6.9
安 徽 Anhui	90.1	0.1	20.2	44.5	2.5	9.8	2.7
福 建 Fujian	224.3	0.6	2.1	186.4	2.3	14.1	2.6
江 西 Jiangxi	55.9	0.1	1.8	40.9	1.8	3.8	0.9
山 东 Shandong	392.0	0.8	18.3	274.8	5.3	36.8	8.7
河 南 Henan	198.1	0.7	31.2	101.2	6.0	29.4	2.6
湖 北 Hubei	116.3	0.4	3.4	69.6	2.4	14.8	3.2
湖 南 Hunan	107.2	0.3	3.3	52.5	2.2	24.6	2.2
广 东 Guangdong	448.8	0.9	1.4	318.5	5.0	24.5	18.6
广 西 Guangxi	61.7	0.6	1.8	31.7	1.1	10.8	3.4
海 南 Hainan	12.2	0.2		4.2	0.7	0.6	1.3
重 庆 Chongqing	75.9		3.2	30.0	2.2	23.5	2.2
四 川 Sichuan	148.2	0.2	8.1	72.8	6.0	37.7	4.3
贵 州 Guizhou	51.7		7.3	22.8	1.4	6.3	0.7
云 南 Yunnan	56.7	0.4	2.5	28.7	3.0	8.4	2.0
西 藏 Tibet	0.5			0.2		0.2	
陕 西 Shaanxi	60.5	0.1	2.6	37.5	1.8	3.9	1.1
甘 肃 Gansu	21.8	0.2	1.5	10.9	0.2	4.2	0.5
青 海 Qinghai	8.0	0.4	0.8	4.6	0.5	0.4	0.5
宁 夏 Ningxia	18.7	0.1	5.0	8.8	0.6	1.7	0.2
新 疆 Xinjiang	50.0	0.4	7.1	18.4	3.2	9.2	1.7

5-11 续表 1 continued

单位：万人 (10 000 persons)

年 份 Year 地 区 Region		信息传输、计算机服务和软件业 Information Transmission, Computer Service and Software	批发和零售业 Wholesale and Retail Trade	住宿和餐饮业 Hotels and Catering Services	金融业 Financial Intermediation	房地产业 Real Estate	租赁和商务服务业 Leasing and Business Services
	2003	38.4	183.3	75.0	46.2	52.6	40.6
	2004	43.2	201.6	82.4	57.2	66.3	47.9
	2005	56.2	218.9	90.1	78.6	81.1	60.8
北 京	Beijing	16.3	25.8	13.3	6.1	15.7	19.1
天 津	Tianjin	1.6	5.0	1.3	0.9	1.3	1.0
河 北	Hebei	1.3	7.0	1.4	2.1	1.0	0.6
山 西	Shanxi	0.6	3.4	1.0	1.3	0.3	0.2
内蒙古	Inner Mongolia	0.3	2.7	1.0	0.7	0.5	0.3
辽 宁	Liaoning	2.6	8.3	3.7	3.7	2.5	0.9
吉 林	Jilin	0.9	4.1	1.1	1.3	1.3	0.8
黑龙江	Heilongjiang	1.1	8.1	1.2	2.5	1.5	0.9
上 海	Shanghai	2.0	9.8	2.0	9.7	2.6	3.7
江 苏	Jiangsu	2.9	15.9	4.8	6.8	2.9	3.2
浙 江	Zhejiang	3.0	13.8	6.4	6.0	3.8	8.2
安 徽	Anhui	0.7	4.5	1.2	1.3	1.5	0.5
福 建	Fujian	1.1	4.0	3.0	2.0	3.3	1.2
江 西	Jiangxi	0.7	1.7	0.7	1.3	0.8	0.1
山 东	Shandong	2.9	19.4	4.9	6.6	4.8	3.2
河 南	Henan	1.7	11.0	3.8	3.2	2.7	1.0
湖 北	Hubei	0.5	9.5	3.2	1.7	2.6	1.9
湖 南	Hunan	2.0	6.5	3.7	3.3	3.5	1.0
广 东	Guangdong	7.1	20.6	15.2	7.9	14.0	5.5
广 西	Guangxi	1.1	3.8	2.1	1.1	1.5	1.1
海 南	Hainan	0.2	0.7	2.1	0.1	0.8	0.4
重 庆	Chongqing	0.3	4.7	2.0	1.7	2.0	1.0
四 川	Sichuan	1.0	8.1	3.0	1.9	2.6	0.8
贵 州	Guizhou	0.9	4.1	1.5	1.2	2.8	0.8
云 南	Yunnan	0.8	4.4	2.0	0.8	1.5	0.8
西 藏	Tibet		0.1				
陕 西	Shaanxi	1.2	4.8	2.4	1.5	1.0	0.5
甘 肃	Gansu	0.2	2.2	0.5	0.6	0.3	0.3
青 海	Qinghai	0.1	0.4	0.1		0.1	
宁 夏	Ningxia	0.1	0.8	0.4	0.3	0.5	0.1
新 疆	Xinjiang	0.9	3.6	1.0	0.8	1.4	1.6

5-11 续表 2 continued

单位：万人 (10 000 persons)

年份 Year 地区 Region	科学研究、技术服务和地质勘查业 Scientific Research, Technical Services, and Geological Prospecting	水利、环境和公共设施管理业 Management of Water Conservancy, Environment and Public Facilities	居民服务和其他服务业 Services to Households and Other Services	教育 Education	卫生、社会保障和社会福利业 Health, Social Securities and Social Welfare	文化、体育和娱乐业 Culture, Sports and Entertainment	公共管理和社会组织 Public Management and Social Organization
2003	26.2	6.1	13.6	6.1	3.3	6.6	0.7
2004	24.6	7.3	14.4	11.2	6.1	7.8	2.1
2005	29.9	9.0	16.6	14.9	7.4	8.5	2.2
北京 Beijing	10.1	1.7	5.5	2.8	0.8	2.7	0.3
天津 Tianjin	1.0	0.2	0.6			0.1	
河北 Hebei	0.4	0.5	0.1			0.2	
山西 Shanxi	0.1		0.1	0.1	0.1		
内蒙古 Inner Mongolia	0.2	0.2	0.1	0.3	0.1		
辽宁 Liaoning	0.9	0.2	0.5	0.1	0.2	0.3	
吉林 Jilin	0.4	0.1	0.1	0.2	0.1	0.1	
黑龙江 Heilongjiang	0.5	0.3	0.2	0.1	0.3	0.1	
上海 Shanghai	1.6	0.5	1.4	0.6	0.9	0.3	
江苏 Jiangsu	1.6	0.5	0.3	0.7	1.3	0.2	
浙江 Zhejiang	1.4	0.5	0.3	0.9	0.2	0.2	0.5
安徽 Anhui	0.2	0.2			0.1	0.1	
福建 Fujian	0.4	0.3	0.3	0.4	0.1	0.3	
江西 Jiangxi	0.1	0.2		0.4	0.2		
山东 Shandong	0.9	0.5	2.0	1.0	0.7	0.3	0.2
河南 Henan	0.7	0.2	0.3	1.4	0.6	0.2	0.2
湖北 Hubei	0.5	0.3	0.5	0.7	0.2	0.2	0.6
湖南 Hunan	0.4	0.3	0.1	0.7	0.1	0.3	0.1
广东 Guangdong	3.0	1.3	2.0	1.3	0.4	1.5	
广西 Guangxi	0.3	0.1	0.2	0.3	0.2	0.3	0.2
海南 Hainan	0.2	0.2		0.3		0.2	
重庆 Chongqing	2.4	0.1	0.1	0.2		0.1	
四川 Sichuan	0.3	0.3	0.2	0.5	0.2	0.1	
贵州 Guizhou	0.5		0.5	0.5	0.1	0.2	0.1
云南 Yunnan	0.6	0.2	0.2	0.2		0.2	
西藏 Tibet							
陕西 Shaanxi	0.8		0.7	0.6	0.1	0.1	
甘肃 Gansu	0.1		0.1				
青海 Qinghai	0.1						
宁夏 Ningxia	0.1						
新疆 Xinjiang	0.3	0.1	0.1	0.2		0.1	

5-12 各地区按行业分城镇单位专业技术人员数（年底数）

Number of Scientific and Technical Personnel in Urban Collective-owned Units at the Year-end by Sector and Region

单位：万人 (10 000 persons)

年份 Year 地区 Region		合计 Total	农、林、牧、渔业 Agriculture, Forestry, Animal Husbandry and Fishing	采矿业 Mining	制造业 Manufacturing	电力、燃气及水的生产和供应业 Production and Supply of Electricity, Gas and Water	建筑业 Construction	交通运输、仓储和邮政业 Transport, Storage and Post
	2003	3113.0	78.2	66.5	431.6	68.3	160.9	90.0
	2004	3153.1	75.2	70.4	433.6	67.8	163.4	89.8
	2005	3201.0	70.5	65.0	449.5	68.3	178.4	81.9
北京	Beijing	143.5	0.6	0.2	18.2	1.3	12.9	3.8
天津	Tianjin	47.2	0.3	1.1	9.6	0.7	2.9	2.0
河北	Hebei	162.2	1.5	4.2	17.5	3.6	7.2	3.7
山西	Shanxi	96.1	1.2	8.8	11.8	2.3	5.4	2.3
内蒙古	Inner Mongolia	73.2	6.0	1.9	7.4	2.3	2.7	1.8
辽宁	Liaoning	132.6	2.4	3.2	21.4	3.7	5.9	4.6
吉林	Jilin	84.6	4.6	1.7	9.5	2.0	3.1	2.3
黑龙江	Heilongjiang	105.8	10.0	5.0	11.4	2.9	4.6	3.1
上海	Shanghai	69.1	0.2		14.4	1.1	3.5	3.7
江苏	Jiangsu	182.4	1.9	2.3	37.1	3.5	7.0	5.1
浙江	Zhejiang	135.7	0.8	0.3	22.4	2.9	16.8	2.9
安徽	Anhui	100.6	1.3	2.9	9.2	2.2	5.1	2.0
福建	Fujian	96.2	1.3	0.4	21.1	2.0	5.7	2.0
江西	Jiangxi	84.4	1.8	1.0	9.2	1.8	3.4	2.2
山东	Shandong	240.4	2.2	8.3	39.9	5.0	12.1	5.5
河南	Henan	196.8	1.7	5.6	23.6	4.2	11.0	3.0
湖北	Hubei	147.7	3.3	1.3	21.6	3.5	8.0	4.6
湖南	Hunan	127.0	0.9	1.0	14.0	2.3	9.1	2.3
广东	Guangdong	221.4	1.5	0.5	41.7	4.0	11.0	6.9
广西	Guangxi	94.6	2.4	0.9	8.1	2.0	3.8	2.5
海南	Hainan	18.9	2.5	0.2	1.0	0.3	0.6	0.9
重庆	Chongqing	61.8	0.9	1.0	9.3	1.3	6.2	1.7
四川	Sichuan	159.4	3.7	2.3	20.0	4.0	12.6	3.2
贵州	Guizhou	67.8	1.1	1.6	7.2	1.5	3.3	1.0
云南	Yunnan	85.5	4.4	0.7	7.8	1.8	3.2	1.9
西藏	Tibet	3.9			0.1	0.1	0.1	0.1
陕西	Shaanxi	106.3	2.0	3.5	22.7	2.2	3.8	2.7
甘肃	Gansu	53.6	1.7	0.7	6.1	1.2	2.1	1.5
青海	Qinghai	14.2	0.7	0.2	1.0	0.5	0.8	0.5
宁夏	Ningxia	18.3	0.6	0.9	1.7	0.8	1.0	0.4
新疆	Xinjiang	70.0	7.1	3.1	3.5	1.2	3.5	1.7

5-12 续表 1 continued

单位：万人 (10 000 persons)

年份 Year 地区 Region		信息传输、计算机服务和软件业 Information Transmission, Computer Service and Software	批发和零售业 Wholesale and Retail Trade	住宿和餐饮业 Hotels and Catering Services	金融业 Financial Intermediation	房地产业 Real Estate	租赁和商务服务业 Leasing and Business Services
	2003	41.1	101.0	17.5	159.5	29.3	36.4
	2004	44.4	95.0	18.7	157.2	31.8	36.1
	2005	46.8	86.0	19.3	156.2	33.5	38.3
北京	Beijing	10.0	8.2	2.7	7.1	5.1	9.0
天津	Tianjin	1.0	1.6	0.3	2.7	0.4	0.5
河北	Hebei	1.4	4.1	0.8	7.8	0.8	0.9
山西	Shanxi	1.1	2.9	0.5	4.4	0.4	1.0
内蒙古	Inner Mongolia	0.9	1.1	0.3	3.5	0.3	0.6
辽宁	Liaoning	2.2	3.3	0.8	8.9	1.6	1.5
吉林	Jilin	1.1	1.7	0.2	4.7	0.7	1.0
黑龙江	Heilongjiang	1.4	2.6	0.3	5.2	0.8	0.9
上海	Shanghai	1.4	2.4	0.4	5.6	0.9	1.4
江苏	Jiangsu	2.1	4.4	1.1	9.8	1.8	1.9
浙江	Zhejiang	1.8	4.5	1.2	9.0	1.9	2.8
安徽	Anhui	0.9	2.1	0.2	4.1	0.7	0.5
福建	Fujian	1.2	2.0	0.5	4.8	1.1	1.2
江西	Jiangxi	0.9	1.6	0.3	3.8	0.5	0.4
山东	Shandong	1.7	6.8	1.4	9.5	2.5	2.1
河南	Henan	1.3	6.3	1.2	7.7	1.2	1.4
湖北	Hubei	1.8	3.8	0.7	6.5	1.5	1.2
湖南	Hunan	1.4	2.4	1.0	4.9	1.4	0.9
广东	Guangdong	5.1	7.9	1.7	14.1	3.9	3.9
广西	Guangxi	0.9	2.3	0.5	4.2	0.9	1.0
海南	Hainan	0.4	0.4	0.3	0.9	0.3	0.3
重庆	Chongqing	0.4	1.3	0.3	2.3	0.9	0.3
四川	Sichuan	1.6	2.8	0.5	6.8	1.0	1.0
贵州	Guizhou	0.5	1.7	0.2	2.5	1.0	0.5
云南	Yunnan	1.1	2.1	0.4	4.3	0.4	0.6
西藏	Tibet	0.1			0.4		
陕西	Shaanxi	1.2	2.6	0.5	4.3	0.5	0.6
甘肃	Gansu	0.7	0.9	0.2	2.1	0.2	0.3
青海	Qinghai	0.3	0.3	0.1	0.8	0.2	0.1
宁夏	Ningxia	0.3	0.4	0.1	1.2	0.2	0.1
新疆	Xinjiang	0.8	1.7	0.4	2.4	0.5	0.8

5-12 续表 2 continued

单位：万人 (10 000 persons)

年 份 Year 地 区 Region		科学研究、技术服务和地质勘查业 Scientific Research, Technical Services, and Geological Prospecting	水利、环境和公共设施管理业 Management of Water Conservancy, Environment and Public Facilities	居民服务和其他服务业 Services to Households and Other Services	教 育 Education	卫生、社会保障和社会福利业 Health, Social Securities and Social Welfare	文化、体育和娱乐业 Culture, Sports and Entertainment	公共管理和社会组织 Public Management and Social Organization
	2003	112.8	26.3	7.1	1154.2	349.3	60.1	122.8
	2004	112.9	27.6	6.8	1182.6	355.0	56.0	128.8
	2005	113.5	27.7	6.5	1200.9	364.1	54.4	140.3
北 京	Beijing	16.2	1.0	1.7	23.6	11.5	6.4	3.9
天 津	Tianjin	2.8	0.6	0.3	13.5	5.5	0.8	0.7
河 北	Hebei	3.6	1.5	0.6	74.6	17.0	2.2	9.1
山 西	Shanxi	3.1	0.8	0.1	36.9	10.0	2.0	1.3
内蒙古	Inner Mongolia	2.2	1.1	0.1	28.0	7.8	1.7	3.6
辽 宁	Liaoning	5.2	1.6	0.3	42.8	15.9	2.7	4.4
吉 林	Jilin	3.5	1.1	0.1	31.1	10.4	1.8	3.9
黑龙江	Heilongjiang	3.2	1.2	0.2	35.1	11.8	1.9	4.3
上 海	Shanghai	4.4	0.5	0.1	17.1	9.8	1.2	0.9
江 苏	Jiangsu	5.1	1.6	0.2	66.2	21.7	2.3	7.4
浙 江	Zhejiang	4.5	0.9	0.1	41.7	17.3	2.3	1.8
安 徽	Anhui	2.7	0.8	0.1	45.9	12.6	2.6	4.7
福 建	Fujian	2.3	0.5	0.2	37.0	8.3	1.2	3.2
江 西	Jiangxi	2.4	0.6	0.1	38.7	10.1	1.5	4.0
山 东	Shandong	4.4	2.3	0.2	86.7	27.0	2.8	20.0
河 南	Henan	4.8	1.2	0.2	86.1	21.7	2.1	12.6
湖 北	Hubei	4.8	1.6	0.2	52.9	19.7	2.6	8.3
湖 南	Hunan	2.9	0.9	0.2	53.8	17.1	1.4	9.0
广 东	Guangdong	6.8	1.4	0.5	77.9	27.1	2.7	2.9
广 西	Guangxi	2.9	0.8	0.1	43.1	11.8	1.5	4.8
海 南	Hainan	0.5	0.1	0.1	7.3	2.1	0.5	0.4
重 庆	Chongqing	1.9	0.2	0.1	25.0	6.3	0.7	1.6
四 川	Sichuan	6.1	0.8	0.2	65.6	18.5	2.2	6.7
贵 州	Guizhou	2.0	0.3	0.1	31.7	6.4	0.9	4.4
云 南	Yunnan	3.1	0.8	0.1	38.5	9.3	1.6	3.2
西 藏	Tibet	0.2			1.7	0.5	0.2	0.3
陕 西	Shaanxi	5.3	1.2	0.3	37.7	9.5	1.4	4.4
甘 肃	Gansu	2.3	0.7		23.8	5.3	1.0	2.7
青 海	Qinghai	0.9	0.2	0.1	5.2	1.7	0.4	0.5
宁 夏	Ningxia	0.6	0.3		6.2	2.0	0.5	1.0
新 疆	Xinjiang	2.7	1.0	0.1	25.5	8.3	1.4	4.4

5-13 各地区按行业分私营企业和个体就业人数（2005年底）

Number of Employed Persons in Private Enterprises and Self-employed Individuals at the Year-end by Sector and Region (2005)

单位：万人 (10 000 persons)

地区	Region	合计 Total	#制造业 Manufacturing	#建筑业 Construction	#交通运输、仓储和邮政业 Transport, Storage and Post	#批发和零售业 Wholesale and Retail Trade	#住宿和餐饮业 Hotels and Catering Services	#租赁和商务服务业 Leasing and Business Services	#居民服务和其他服务业 Services to Households and Other Services
全国总计	**National Total**	**10724.6**	**2988.1**	**379.6**	**398.9**	**4065.8**	**720.3**	**385.9**	**649.6**
北京	Beijing	379.2	50.8	20.6	8.2	106.2	21.5	42.6	17.0
天津	Tianjin	114.2	37.5	4.3	4.5	37.4	3.7	5.7	4.4
河北	Hebei	511.7	167.7	17.6	27.0	197.2	36.0	4.5	23.0
山西	Shanxi	164.6	36.2	3.7	5.2	72.9	14.0	2.8	10.8
内蒙古	Inner Mongolia	150.5	25.1	5.0	8.5	60.8	16.6	2.9	13.4
辽宁	Liaoning	534.8	122.3	20.5	50.5	192.4	37.9	14.5	29.9
吉林	Jilin	176.9	35.8	4.5	9.6	82.5	13.5	4.5	9.6
黑龙江	Heilongjiang	250.8	42.8	6.7	17.0	102.8	29.6	4.7	18.6
上海	Shanghai	500.1	112.9	31.7	12.5	199.2	14.6	55.5	18.3
江苏	Jiangsu	1118.4	528.2	71.4	21.2	308.0	32.6	24.3	69.8
浙江	Zhejiang	854.9	430.6	18.1	23.5	230.6	35.2	18.9	42.1
安徽	Anhui	432.6	102.7	11.4	23.9	178.9	38.1	7.4	32.9
福建	Fujian	224.6	65.0	5.3	3.2	89.0	11.7	9.3	16.7
江西	Jiangxi	302.0	84.4	5.5	12.7	120.4	23.0	4.6	20.4
山东	Shandong	809.0	284.9	29.8	25.1	294.2	49.0	22.7	48.1
河南	Henan	412.8	90.7	8.5	22.2	179.7	41.8	5.1	33.3
湖北	Hubei	351.4	78.1	10.3	18.2	150.9	29.8	9.4	26.5
湖南	Hunan	397.1	78.3	8.5	13.0	158.2	21.5	66.5	19.1
广东	Guangdong	1015.7	262.3	15.3	14.2	427.1	57.7	25.6	58.2
广西	Guangxi	247.1	43.2	3.5	15.6	114.1	19.9	6.7	15.8
海南	Hainan	58.2	4.6	3.0	3.4	23.1	4.2	2.8	3.8
重庆	Chongqing	196.3	40.0	10.2	6.0	80.5	12.8	8.0	13.2
四川	Sichuan	488.5	95.6	15.1	18.7	197.0	48.0	16.5	36.9
贵州	Guizhou	110.3	18.6	2.3	4.6	44.5	8.5	1.9	7.2
云南	Yunnan	255.1	40.9	26.9	10.0	99.9	27.8	4.6	13.9
西藏	Tibet	16.6	0.9	1.7	0.7	6.1	2.7	0.2	2.1
陕西	Shaanxi	304.1	53.7	4.8	7.3	165.6	25.3	5.9	19.7
甘肃	Gansu	104.1	16.9	4.9	1.9	47.9	13.1	2.3	7.7
青海	Qinghai	58.2	9.4	2.7	1.5	22.1	7.1	0.3	2.9
宁夏	Ningxia	42.0	7.3	2.2	1.0	18.2	3.8	1.3	4.1
新疆	Xinjiang	143.0	20.8	3.5	7.9	58.2	19.5	4.0	10.3

5-14 各地区按行业分城镇私营企业和个体就业人数（2005年底）

Number of Employed Persons in Urban Private Enterprises and Self-employed Individuals at the Year-end by Sector and Region (2005)

单位：万人 (10 000 persons)

地区	Region	合计 Total	#制造业 Manufacturing	#建筑业 Construction	#交通运输、仓储和邮政业 Transport, Storage and Post	#批发和零售业 Wholesale and Retail Trade	#住宿和餐饮业 Hotels and Catering Services	#租赁和商务服务业 Leasing and Business Services	#居民服务和其他服务业 Services to Households and Other Services
全国总计	**National Total**	**6236.1**	**1329.6**	**242.7**	**226.5**	**2534.8**	**465.6**	**302.6**	**427.8**
北京	Beijing	230.7	15.8	8.0	5.0	66.7	15.8	30.2	12.5
天津	Tianjin	54.3	11.3	2.3	2.8	20.1	1.7	3.7	2.4
河北	Hebei	165.8	47.0	6.1	8.0	66.9	13.7	2.3	10.4
山西	Shanxi	80.1	9.1	2.3	1.7	44.1	7.9	1.8	6.1
内蒙古	Inner Mongolia	107.3	15.1	4.1	6.4	45.8	12.6	2.3	10.0
辽宁	Liaoning	367.9	74.8	16.1	30.0	143.9	26.8	13.1	20.8
吉林	Jilin	152.3	30.2	3.8	8.1	73.8	11.0	4.3	8.2
黑龙江	Heilongjiang	186.5	30.0	5.3	13.1	81.7	20.9	4.3	14.8
上海	Shanghai	279.1	46.6	18.8	8.3	111.7	12.3	33.7	12.3
江苏	Jiangsu	586.4	231.7	38.1	12.4	174.8	25.7	17.1	54.5
浙江	Zhejiang	373.2	131.6	9.4	8.7	135.7	19.1	13.6	25.6
安徽	Anhui	210.1	40.5	6.7	12.5	91.0	19.2	5.2	16.4
福建	Fujian	155.4	36.1	4.1	2.5	66.6	8.7	8.7	12.5
江西	Jiangxi	193.2	46.2	4.2	7.4	84.8	16.5	4.0	14.2
山东	Shandong	437.6	132.8	19.0	11.3	177.8	28.5	15.0	24.0
河南	Henan	209.5	33.5	4.7	10.0	98.1	24.1	3.7	20.2
湖北	Hubei	231.7	44.4	8.3	10.8	102.8	20.1	8.7	18.2
湖南	Hunan	276.6	43.2	6.0	7.6	106.2	14.9	64.1	13.6
广东	Guangdong	708.4	142.4	10.7	10.3	309.2	40.0	20.5	43.1
广西	Guangxi	144.1	22.1	2.8	9.0	65.5	13.1	5.4	10.8
海南	Hainan	47.0	3.4	2.8	2.2	19.2	3.0	2.6	2.8
重庆	Chongqing	138.3	24.1	8.1	4.4	59.1	9.2	7.2	9.7
四川	Sichuan	289.4	40.8	11.2	11.7	127.3	28.0	13.0	21.5
贵州	Guizhou	71.1	10.3	1.9	3.0	27.0	5.5	1.6	4.9
云南	Yunnan	163.4	21.0	23.1	6.6	63.1	19.1	4.2	9.8
西藏	Tibet	13.4	0.8	1.3	0.6	4.8	2.2	0.2	1.8
陕西	Shaanxi	111.7	14.4	2.4	2.8	53.2	13.4	5.0	8.8
甘肃	Gansu	69.1	7.7	3.8	1.5	34.2	9.1	1.9	5.1
青海	Qinghai	38.9	5.4	2.3	0.6	16.4	5.1	0.3	2.2
宁夏	Ningxia	28.0	3.3	1.6	0.6	14.0	2.8	1.1	2.5
新疆	Xinjiang	115.7	14.1	3.2	6.7	49.4	15.5	3.8	8.3

5-15 各地区私营企业就业人数（2005年底）
Number of Employed Persons in Private Enterprises at the Year-end by Region (2005)

单位：万个、万人 (10 000 enterprises, 10 000 persons)

地区	Region	户数 Number of Enterprises	就业人数 Number of Employed Persons	#投资者 Employers	城镇就业人数 Number of Employed Persons in Urban Areas	#投资者 Employers	乡村就业人数 Number of Employed Persons in Rural Areas	#投资者 Employers
全国	**National Total**	**430.1**	**5824.1**	**1109.9**	**3458.4**	**721.0**	**2365.6**	**389.0**
北京	Beijing	26.0	294.5	63.9	173.5	42.3	121.0	21.6
天津	Tianjin	7.7	88.7	19.0	44.5	10.4	44.2	8.6
河北	Hebei	12.7	241.7	36.8	72.3	12.8	169.4	24.1
山西	Shanxi	7.1	82.3	16.1	39.0	9.1	43.3	7.0
内蒙古	Inner Mongolia	4.8	68.2	13.6	47.1	10.1	21.1	3.5
辽宁	Liaoning	16.5	252.1	41.6	189.5	34.5	62.7	7.1
吉林	Jilin	6.0	88.0	12.8	77.2	10.3	10.8	2.5
黑龙江	Heilongjiang	6.8	95.2	19.7	77.5	16.6	17.7	3.1
上海	Shanghai	47.4	465.8	100.6	256.7	56.8	209.1	43.8
江苏	Jiangsu	50.7	797.2	114.3	397.2	64.6	400.0	49.7
浙江	Zhejiang	35.9	534.8	82.0	218.5	41.0	316.4	41.0
安徽	Anhui	10.6	165.7	27.0	86.5	16.0	79.2	11.0
福建	Fujian	12.7	134.7	26.8	100.8	21.7	33.9	5.1
江西	Jiangxi	7.1	134.2	18.7	89.1	13.6	45.2	5.1
山东	Shandong	31.5	444.1	92.3	262.9	62.5	181.3	29.8
河南	Henan	13.4	138.6	33.6	72.9	20.3	65.7	13.4
湖北	Hubei	12.9	122.6	34.2	89.7	28.5	32.9	5.6
湖南	Hunan	8.5	200.4	30.1	150.8	17.9	49.6	12.2
广东	Guangdong	44.9	526.1	116.7	402.0	96.6	124.1	20.1
广西	Guangxi	5.2	83.6	14.6	54.3	9.6	29.2	4.9
海南	Hainan	3.2	36.1	7.7	31.8	6.8	4.2	0.9
重庆	Chongqing	7.6	105.4	20.5	78.5	16.2	27.0	4.3
四川	Sichuan	17.9	238.0	45.3	153.2	32.0	84.8	13.2
贵州	Guizhou	4.1	50.7	18.5	37.4	15.6	13.2	2.9
云南	Yunnan	6.6	109.2	17.7	76.1	14.4	33.1	3.2
西藏	Tibet	0.3	5.0	0.6	4.1	0.6	0.8	0.1
陕西	Shaanxi	9.8	154.5	52.0	49.2	12.3	105.3	39.7
甘肃	Gansu	3.8	48.1	10.0	34.3	7.9	13.8	2.0
青海	Qinghai	1.1	27.9	3.0	19.2	2.5	8.7	0.5
宁夏	Ningxia	1.9	23.4	5.1	14.0	3.5	9.4	1.6
新疆	Xinjiang	5.2	67.1	15.2	58.6	14.0	8.5	1.2

5-16 各地区个体就业人数（2005年底）

Number of Self-employed Individuals at the Year-end by Region (2005)

单位：万户、万人 (10 000 households, 10 000 persons)

地区	Region	个体户数 Number of Enterprises	个体就业人数 Number of Employed Persons	城镇 Urban Employed Persons	乡村 Rural Employed Persons
全国	**National Total**	**2463.9**	**4900.5**	**2777.7**	**2122.8**
北京	Beijing	65.2	84.7	57.2	27.5
天津	Tianjin	17.7	25.5	9.8	15.7
河北	Hebei	108.8	270.0	93.4	176.5
山西	Shanxi	42.9	82.3	41.1	41.2
内蒙古	Inner Mongolia	46.8	82.3	60.2	22.1
辽宁	Liaoning	127.4	282.7	178.4	104.2
吉林	Jilin	44.7	88.9	75.2	13.8
黑龙江	Heilongjiang	71.4	155.6	109.0	46.6
上海	Shanghai	28.3	34.3	22.4	11.9
江苏	Jiangsu	175.3	321.2	189.2	132.0
浙江	Zhejiang	172.7	320.1	154.8	165.3
安徽	Anhui	111.0	266.9	123.6	143.2
福建	Fujian	49.5	89.9	54.7	35.2
江西	Jiangxi	67.5	167.7	104.1	63.6
山东	Shandong	168.7	364.9	174.7	190.2
河南	Henan	128.8	274.2	136.6	137.6
湖北	Hubei	101.9	228.8	142.0	86.8
湖南	Hunan	97.5	196.6	125.8	70.8
广东	Guangdong	227.4	489.6	306.3	183.3
广西	Guangxi	101.6	163.6	89.8	73.8
海南	Hainan	11.8	22.1	15.1	6.9
重庆	Chongqing	44.5	90.9	59.9	31.0
四川	Sichuan	153.1	250.6	136.2	114.4
贵州	Guizhou	43.2	59.7	33.7	26.0
云南	Yunnan	72.9	145.8	87.3	58.6
西藏	Tibet	6.2	11.6	9.2	2.4
陕西	Shaanxi	73.1	149.5	62.4	87.1
甘肃	Gansu	31.0	56.0	34.7	21.3
青海	Qinghai	14.5	30.3	19.7	10.5
宁夏	Ningxia	11.0	18.6	13.9	4.7
新疆	Xinjiang	47.7	75.9	57.1	18.8

5-17 职工工资总额和指数

Total Wages Bill of Staff and Workers and Related Indices

年份 Year 地区 Region	工资总额（亿元） Total Wages Bill (100 million yuan)				指数（上年=100） Indices (preceding year=100)			
	合计 Total	国有单位 State-owned Units	城镇集体单位 Urban Collective-owned Units	其他单位 Other Units	合计 Total	国有单位 State-owned Units	城镇集体单位 Urban Collective-owned Units	其他单位 Other Units
1978	568.9	468.7	100.2		110.5	110.1	112.5	
1980	772.4	627.9	144.5		119.4	118.6	123.3	
1985	1383.0	1064.8	312.3	5.9	122.0	121.6	123.0	163.9
1989	2618.5	2050.2	534.4	33.9	113.1	113.5	109.6	157.7
1990	2951.1	2324.1	581.0	46.0	112.7	113.4	108.7	135.7
1991	3323.9	2594.9	658.6	70.4	112.6	111.7	113.4	153.0
1992	3939.2	3090.4	743.2	105.6	118.5	119.1	112.8	150.0
1993	4916.2	3812.7	849.9	253.6	124.8	123.4	114.4	240.2
1994	6656.4	5177.4	1023.3	455.6	135.4	135.8	120.4	179.7
1995	8100.0	6080.2	1182.0	637.8	121.7	117.4	115.5	140.0
1996	9080.0	6792.7	1241.0	761.4	112.1	111.7	105.0	119.4
1997	9405.3	7211.0	1253.4	940.8	103.6	106.2	101.0	123.6
1998	9296.5	6812.5	1021.6	1462.4	100.2	95.8	83.1	156.9
1999	9875.5	7160.8	962.7	1752.0	106.2	105.1	94.2	119.8
2000	10656.2	7612.9	919.0	2124.3	107.9	106.3	95.5	121.3
2001	11830.9	8355.6	864.6	2610.7	111.0	109.8	94.1	122.9
2002	13161.1	8948.6	828.1	3384.4	111.2	107.1	95.8	129.6
2003	14743.5	9693.8	829.4	4220.3	112.0	108.3	100.2	124.7
2004	16900.2	10777.2	838.4	5284.6	114.6	111.2	101.1	125.2
2005	19789.9	12009.2	867.8	6912.8	117.1	111.4	103.5	130.8
北京 Beijing	1520.1	694.9	30.8	794.4	115.6	111.0	90.4	121.2
天津 Tianjin	419.8	212.7	14.4	192.7	111.1	110.8	100.1	112.4
河北 Hebei	716.1	526.1	34.2	155.9	114.5	108.6	109.6	141.6
山西 Shanxi	548.1	394.4	30.2	123.4	120.7	117.4	105.1	138.2
内蒙古 Inner Mongolia	387.7	265.7	13.6	108.4	120.0	113.5	111.5	141.0
辽宁 Liaoning	827.5	540.7	37.5	249.2	113.9	113.3	97.4	118.2
吉林 Jilin	377.4	259.7	18.4	99.3	107.8	105.6	95.5	117.1
黑龙江 Heilongjiang	654.6	412.2	29.1	213.3	110.5	107.1	96.3	120.4
上海 Shanghai	911.9	440.1	25.3	446.5	113.1	107.9	96.0	120.0
江苏 Jiangsu	1252.1	672.7	48.8	530.6	119.2	113.8	101.2	129.2
浙江 Zhejiang	1298.4	667.2	58.6	572.6	129.4	118.2	98.0	151.0
安徽 Anhui	484.1	307.2	27.7	149.3	114.9	109.5	107.0	129.7
福建 Fujian	648.1	299.1	24.8	324.2	115.8	110.9	97.5	122.5
江西 Jiangxi	358.3	272.6	15.7	70.0	117.3	115.2	114.9	127.0
山东 Shandong	1440.3	823.7	73.2	543.4	130.0	106.6	108.6	203.1
河南 Henan	950.0	575.6	90.3	284.0	118.5	115.7	113.4	126.3
湖北 Hubei	652.4	469.8	31.6	151.0	112.6	116.2	113.8	102.3
湖南 Hunan	591.5	408.1	31.5	151.9	115.3	99.9	108.6	201.0
广东 Guangdong	2085.6	1059.0	88.6	938.0	117.8	112.4	104.6	126.1
广西 Guangxi	410.1	301.8	19.1	89.2	116.4	112.9	108.6	132.7
海南 Hainan	104.2	81.5	3.3	19.5	114.1	113.5	109.1	117.4
重庆 Chongqing	345.8	222.5	15.8	107.5	117.6	116.8	96.1	123.4
四川 Sichuan	773.4	543.0	44.4	186.0	114.8	112.2	105.7	125.7
贵州 Guizhou	284.2	202.4	10.2	71.6	120.1	114.0	94.6	148.5
云南 Yunnan	377.2	283.3	10.8	83.1	109.5	107.3	93.7	120.4
西藏 Tibet	46.3	44.8	0.4	1.0	103.9	109.3	139.8	31.7
陕西 Shaanxi	478.0	367.3	16.6	94.1	114.8	113.3	100.6	124.7
甘肃 Gansu	280.0	242.4	11.3	26.3	112.2	113.3	96.1	110.3
青海 Qinghai	78.0	64.8	2.1	11.2	111.9	105.8	91.8	179.7
宁夏 Ningxia	101.6	66.8	2.0	32.7	116.5	117.9	97.2	115.2
新疆 Xinjiang	387.4	287.2	7.6	92.7	108.7	106.7	97.1	116.7

注：1998年及以后工资总额为在岗职工工资总额，指数按可比口径计算（以下各表同）。

a) Data on total wages bill since 1998 refer to wages of fully employed staff and workers, and the indices was calculated on the basis of comparable coverage (The same as in the following tables).

5-18 职工平均工资及指数

Average Wage of Staff and Workers and Related Indices

年份 Year / 地区 Region	平均货币工资（元） Average Money Wage (yuan) 合计 Total	国有单位 State-owned Units	城镇集体单位 Urban Collective-owned Units	其他单位 Units of Other Types of Ownership	指数（上年=100） Indices (preceding year=100) 货币工资 Average Money Wage 合计 Total	国有单位 State-owned Units	城镇集体单位 Urban Collective-owned Units	其他单位 Units of Other Types of Ownership	实际工资 Average Real Wage 合计 Total	国有单位 State-owned Units	城镇集体单位 Urban Collective-owned Units	其他单位 Units of Other Types of Ownership
1978	615	644	506		106.8	107.0	105.9		106.0	106.2	105.1	
1980	762	803	623		114.1	113.9	114.9		106.1	106.0	106.9	
1985	1148	1213	967	1436	117.9	117.3	119.2	137.0	105.3	104.8	106.6	122.5
1989	1935	2055	1557	2707	110.8	110.9	109.2	113.6	95.2	95.4	93.9	97.7
1990	2140	2284	1681	2987	110.6	111.1	108.0	110.3	109.2	109.7	106.6	108.9
1991	2340	2477	1866	3468	109.3	108.5	111.0	116.1	104.0	103.2	105.6	110.5
1992	2711	2878	2109	3966	115.9	116.2	113.0	114.4	106.7	107.0	104.1	105.3
1993	3371	3532	2592	4966	124.3	122.7	122.9	125.2	107.1	105.7	105.9	107.9
1994	4538	4797	3245	6303	134.6	135.8	125.2	126.9	107.7	108.7	100.2	101.5
1995	5500	5625	3931	7463	121.2	117.3	121.1	118.4	103.8	100.4	103.7	101.4
1996	6210	6280	4302	8261	112.9	111.6	109.4	110.7	103.8	102.6	100.6	101.7
1997	6470	6747	4512	8789	104.2	107.4	104.9	106.4	101.1	104.2	101.7	103.2
1998	7479	7668	5331	8972	106.6	106.1	102.5	97.7	107.2	106.7	103.1	98.3
1999	8346	8543	5774	9829	111.6	111.4	108.3	109.6	113.1	112.9	109.7	111.0
2000	9371	9552	6262	10984	112.3	111.8	108.5	111.8	111.4	110.9	107.6	110.9
2001	10870	11178	6867	12140	116.0	117.0	109.7	110.5	115.2	116.2	108.9	109.7
2002	12422	12869	7667	13212	114.3	115.1	111.6	108.8	115.5	116.3	112.7	109.9
2003	14040	14577	8678	14574	113.0	113.3	113.2	110.3	112.0	112.3	112.2	109.3
2004	16024	16729	9814	16259	114.1	114.8	113.1	111.6	110.5	111.1	109.5	108.0
2005	18364	19313	11283	18244	114.6	115.4	115.0	112.2	112.8	113.6	113.2	110.4
北京 Beijing	34191	39067	14695	32324	115.2	114.9	109.5	115.3	113.5	113.2	107.9	113.6
天津 Tianjin	25271	26685	15713	24945	116.2	115.6	119.4	115.8	114.5	113.9	117.6	114.1
河北 Hebei	14707	15291	9041	14835	113.8	112.6	114.2	118.4	112.2	111.0	112.6	116.8
山西 Shanxi	15645	16027	10157	16580	120.9	120.0	125.5	118.1	118.9	118.0	123.4	116.1
内蒙古 Inner Mongolia	15985	16598	10804	15514	120.0	116.8	119.9	129.7	117.6	114.5	117.5	127.2
辽宁 Liaoning	17331	18360	9161	17550	116.1	116.8	108.2	114.7	115.2	115.9	107.3	113.8
吉林 Jilin	14409	14566	8735	15868	115.9	116.2	116.4	111.8	114.3	114.6	114.8	110.3
黑龙江 Heilongjiang	14458	14424	7724	16492	115.1	113.8	119.3	113.0	114.2	112.9	118.4	112.1
上海 Shanghai	34345	36077	22486	33756	114.2	114.5	111.7	113.8	113.1	113.4	110.6	112.7
江苏 Jiangsu	20957	24659	13064	18468	115.1	118.1	115.1	113.0	112.8	115.8	112.8	110.8
浙江 Zhejiang	25896	39048	20567	18958	110.2	116.8	114.2	112.4	108.6	115.1	112.5	110.7
安徽 Anhui	15334	15450	9894	16788	118.6	114.3	126.2	124.8	117.4	113.2	125.0	123.6
福建 Fujian	17146	20897	13811	14947	109.9	112.8	112.2	108.7	107.9	110.7	110.1	106.7
江西 Jiangxi	13688	14276	8952	13140	115.4	116.2	113.7	113.6	113.7	114.5	112.0	111.9
山东 Shandong	16614	19823	11474	14018	115.9	123.7	116.3	116.6	114.6	122.4	115.0	115.3
河南 Henan	14282	14877	10383	14852	117.9	117.1	119.5	118.0	115.5	114.7	117.0	115.6
湖北 Hubei	14419	15585	8923	13062	121.6	119.0	117.3	127.2	118.4	115.9	114.2	123.9
湖南 Hunan	15659	16649	11547	14422	112.4	115.1	116.5	108.3	110.1	112.7	114.1	106.1
广东 Guangdong	23959	28835	13240	21500	108.3	111.0	110.9	106.1	106.2	108.8	108.7	104.0
广西 Guangxi	15461	16113	10684	14852	113.9	113.9	119.8	111.7	110.6	110.6	116.3	108.4
海南 Hainan	14417	14427	8640	16185	113.9	113.9	106.4	115.6	112.4	112.4	105.0	114.1
重庆 Chongqing	16630	18614	11614	14373	115.8	117.5	118.0	112.0	114.9	116.6	117.1	111.1
四川 Sichuan	15826	17898	11067	12812	112.5	113.1	113.4	112.8	110.6	111.2	111.5	110.9
贵州 Guizhou	14344	14681	10506	14161	115.4	114.1	121.7	117.0	114.7	113.4	121.0	116.3
云南 Yunnan	16140	16900	10516	14894	110.7	110.3	110.5	111.9	108.8	108.5	108.7	110.0
西藏 Tibet	28950	29644	12336	19154	93.8	98.3	128.5	31.3	92.4	96.8	126.6	30.8
陕西 Shaanxi	14796	15223	7926	15465	113.6	114.2	107.5	110.7	112.6	113.2	106.5	109.7
甘肃 Gansu	14939	15840	9291	11827	109.7	110.3	109.8	100.5	108.4	109.0	108.5	99.3
青海 Qinghai	19084	21158	10080	13591	110.8	113.2	97.8	120.4	111.1	113.5	98.1	120.8
宁夏 Ningxia	17211	17634	13630	16668	117.7	115.9	128.4	119.7	115.8	114.1	126.4	117.8
新疆 Xinjiang	15558	15364	12738	16503	107.4	106.1	109.9	111.0	106.8	105.5	109.2	110.3

5-19 各地区按行业分职工工资总额

Total Wages Bill of Staff and Workers by Sector and Region

单位：亿元 (100 million yuan)

年份 Year 地区 Region		合计 Total	农、林、牧、渔业 Agriculture, Forestry, Animal Husbandry and Fishing	采矿业 Mining	制造业 Manufacturing	电力、燃气及水的生产和供应业 Production and Supply of Electricity, Gas and Water	建筑业 Construction	交通运输、仓储和邮政业 Transport, Storage and Post
	2003	14743.5	322.6	655.6	3621.4	547.6	905.2	980.7
	2004	16900.2	335.4	821.2	4125.9	640.5	1011.6	1102.4
	2005	19789.9	346.7	1016.3	4821.7	735.7	1237.9	1230.7
北京	Beijing	1520.1	4.5	4.7	237.9	28.8	88.6	89.1
天津	Tianjin	419.8	1.3	18.8	144.9	15.0	22.4	33.0
河北	Hebei	716.1	5.1	60.4	155.7	38.3	39.5	41.0
山西	Shanxi	548.1	3.7	144.3	91.5	18.5	25.8	37.2
内蒙古	Inner Mongolia	387.7	25.6	27.3	63.6	27.4	19.6	29.7
辽宁	Liaoning	827.5	17.5	60.0	233.2	39.8	38.6	62.4
吉林	Jilin	377.4	13.3	26.1	87.5	15.7	15.9	27.6
黑龙江	Heilongjiang	654.6	40.8	78.5	129.8	30.6	47.4	45.4
上海	Shanghai	911.9	2.1	0.3	287.0	22.0	35.1	90.2
江苏	Jiangsu	1252.1	14.0	32.1	408.4	48.1	41.5	69.4
浙江	Zhejiang	1298.4	4.4	3.2	323.1	45.6	142.9	53.6
安徽	Anhui	484.1	7.0	67.3	90.2	16.7	26.4	19.9
福建	Fujian	648.1	6.9	6.8	273.3	20.9	42.0	31.1
江西	Jiangxi	358.3	10.5	11.5	72.4	16.0	22.4	26.9
山东	Shandong	1440.3	8.3	147.6	428.4	44.2	89.9	62.2
河南	Henan	950.0	7.3	104.9	188.4	40.2	70.4	52.0
湖北	Hubei	652.4	17.9	16.8	164.1	23.4	46.8	45.7
湖南	Hunan	591.5	5.2	14.9	113.1	19.1	49.9	35.5
广东	Guangdong	2085.6	10.4	8.1	627.4	67.1	96.7	147.2
广西	Guangxi	410.1	11.1	7.8	78.8	17.5	27.1	29.3
海南	Hainan	104.2	11.6	1.7	8.7	3.5	5.6	8.9
重庆	Chongqing	345.8	2.3	13.0	82.1	12.2	43.0	22.1
四川	Sichuan	773.4	9.3	33.1	164.3	29.2	79.2	38.7
贵州	Guizhou	284.2	3.0	18.2	54.3	16.6	21.2	14.6
云南	Yunnan	377.2	16.8	8.8	74.5	17.9	21.5	23.0
西藏	Tibet	46.3	0.7	0.1	1.0	1.7	1.1	1.8
陕西	Shaanxi	478.0	6.5	35.0	114.0	18.9	20.9	35.5
甘肃	Gansu	280.0	8.1	15.8	63.2	14.5	13.8	19.6
青海	Qinghai	78.0	2.6	3.0	9.5	4.3	4.5	7.0
宁夏	Ningxia	101.6	4.0	12.9	15.3	9.9	5.9	5.6
新疆	Xinjiang	387.4	65.0	33.3	36.0	12.0	32.1	25.4

5-19 续表 1 continued

单位：亿元 (100 million yuan)

年份 Year / 地区 Region		信息传输、计算机服务和软件业 Information Transmission, Computer Service and Software	批发和零售业 Wholesale and Retail Trade	住宿和餐饮业 Hotels and Catering Services	金融业 Financial Intermediation	房地产业 Real Estate	租赁和商务服务业 Leasing and Business Services
	2003	331.3	660.5	175.3	646.8	184.0	271.7
	2004	378.9	719.2	202.2	776.1	222.5	312.2
	2005	461.3	776.5	228.8	947.6	269.5	403.6
北　京	Beijing	121.1	108.7	39.9	98.2	56.9	128.0
天　津	Tianjin	8.2	18.4	3.4	16.6	4.3	7.3
河　北	Hebei	11.3	23.4	4.7	32.6	4.0	5.3
山　西	Shanxi	7.0	17.1	3.7	20.0	1.4	5.0
内蒙古	Inner Mongolia	5.8	8.5	3.7	14.6	1.9	4.3
辽　宁	Liaoning	17.6	23.1	7.2	39.4	9.0	10.2
吉　林	Jilin	7.5	10.1	3.1	17.6	3.7	5.4
黑龙江	Heilongjiang	12.2	24.8	4.1	23.7	6.0	5.0
上　海	Shanghai	23.7	51.5	12.5	71.0	19.4	33.6
江　苏	Jiangsu	22.0	45.9	11.8	59.9	13.2	15.9
浙　江	Zhejiang	23.6	47.1	14.9	79.9	16.3	30.4
安　徽	Anhui	6.3	16.5	2.6	17.5	4.1	4.9
福　建	Fujian	11.7	17.5	5.8	29.2	8.4	7.7
江　西	Jiangxi	5.2	10.5	2.2	15.3	2.9	2.6
山　东	Shandong	17.1	45.0	13.5	51.8	13.6	16.1
河　南	Henan	9.0	44.4	10.6	37.8	7.0	12.9
湖　北	Hubei	9.8	22.1	5.1	22.1	7.9	7.7
湖　南	Hunan	10.7	19.6	8.3	24.0	8.2	6.1
广　东	Guangdong	64.7	93.8	37.1	119.4	50.2	53.3
广　西	Guangxi	7.5	14.8	4.6	17.3	4.2	6.8
海　南	Hainan	4.2	3.1	3.3	4.9	2.1	2.0
重　庆	Chongqing	6.6	12.3	3.3	16.6	4.5	2.6
四　川	Sichuan	14.1	26.3	5.7	36.9	5.9	10.7
贵　州	Guizhou	3.6	11.8	2.5	11.5	3.5	3.2
云　南	Yunnan	6.8	17.4	3.8	15.9	2.5	4.4
西　藏	Tibet	1.3	1.0	0.5	3.0	0.1	0.1
陕　西	Shaanxi	10.4	18.7	4.2	20.4	2.9	3.4
甘　肃	Gansu	3.1	7.2	2.0	10.0	1.1	2.2
青　海	Qinghai	2.0	1.9	0.6	3.0	0.2	0.6
宁　夏	Ningxia	1.7	2.6	0.8	5.3	0.9	0.7
新　疆	Xinjiang	5.6	11.3	3.2	12.1	3.2	5.3

5-19 续表 2 continued

单位：亿元 (100 million yuan)

年份 Year / 地区 Region		科学研究、技术服务和地质勘查业 Scientific Research, Technical Services, and Geological Prospecting	水利、环境和公共设施管理业 Management of Water Conservancy, Environment and Public Facilities	居民服务和其他服务业 Services to Households and Other Services	教育 Education	卫生、社会保障和社会福利业 Health, Social Securities and Social Welfare	文化、体育和娱乐业 Culture, Sports and Entertainment	公共管理和社会组织 Public Management and Social Organization
	2003	427.7	197.6	60.1	2007.3	767.6	210.3	1770.5
	2004	486.4	218.7	66.3	2306.0	881.8	242.6	2050.3
	2005	579.7	249.5	78.5	2650.6	1023.7	265.8	2465.8
北京	Beijing	117.0	17.6	15.9	118.6	64.0	53.8	126.7
天津	Tianjin	18.0	7.0	4.0	40.9	18.4	4.0	33.7
河北	Hebei	16.7	10.3	3.8	120.5	34.4	7.0	101.9
山西	Shanxi	9.6	5.3	1.4	68.2	18.8	6.5	63.1
内蒙古	Inner Mongolia	7.7	7.5	0.8	58.7	18.2	6.0	56.7
辽宁	Liaoning	20.7	13.2	2.6	93.2	38.2	10.1	91.1
吉林	Jilin	10.5	6.9	1.2	57.2	19.6	5.2	43.5
黑龙江	Heilongjiang	18.6	7.7	6.3	72.1	27.4	5.8	68.5
上海	Shanghai	50.6	12.1	5.7	74.4	47.8	14.4	58.4
江苏	Jiangsu	28.0	17.6	2.2	174.0	70.2	13.4	164.5
浙江	Zhejiang	25.0	13.2	2.3	179.6	89.8	16.2	187.4
安徽	Anhui	9.4	6.3	0.6	85.9	26.2	6.0	70.3
福建	Fujian	9.0	5.7	1.8	79.3	24.8	6.4	60.1
江西	Jiangxi	9.0	4.4	0.5	66.1	22.1	4.9	52.7
山东	Shandong	18.0	16.3	7.2	190.5	70.8	12.1	187.7
河南	Henan	20.8	12.1	1.6	147.8	45.7	7.8	129.4
湖北	Hubei	17.6	9.9	1.8	95.7	39.7	8.5	89.8
湖南	Hunan	10.1	8.0	0.9	107.3	43.3	7.1	100.3
广东	Guangdong	47.1	22.1	8.4	232.5	112.0	25.9	262.2
广西	Guangxi	9.8	5.7	0.8	74.7	28.6	5.4	58.3
海南	Hainan	2.2	2.4	0.1	16.0	5.6	2.2	16.2
重庆	Chongqing	10.9	3.8	0.7	51.0	16.3	3.6	38.7
四川	Sichuan	27.1	7.9	2.8	116.7	47.4	8.9	109.5
贵州	Guizhou	6.3	2.7	0.7	50.8	12.4	2.6	44.7
云南	Yunnan	9.2	4.3	0.6	69.1	20.1	4.7	56.0
西藏	Tibet	1.8	0.3		8.5	2.9	1.7	18.8
陕西	Shaanxi	24.8	5.6	2.4	75.6	19.7	5.0	54.2
甘肃	Gansu	8.5	5.0	0.4	47.0	11.5	4.0	43.0
青海	Qinghai	5.7	0.9	0.8	11.9	4.8	1.3	13.4
宁夏	Ningxia	1.9	2.4	0.1	12.9	4.6	1.4	12.6
新疆	Xinjiang	8.1	5.8	0.3	54.0	18.3	4.1	52.3

5-20 按细行业分职工平均工资（2005年）

Average Wage of Staff and Workers by Sector in Detail (2005)

单位：元 (yuan)

项 目	Item	合 计 Total	国有单位 State-owned Units	城镇集体单位 Urban Collective-owned Units	其他单位 Units of Other Types of Ownership
全 国 总 计	**National Total**	**18364**	**19313**	**11283**	**18244**
按企、事业和机关分组	**Grouped by Enterprises, Institutions and Agencies**				
企业	Enterprises	17853	19069	10909	18242
事业	Institutions	18720	18926	13602	18621
机关	Agencies & Organizations	20828	20840	15365	
按国民经济行业分组	**Grouped by Sector**				
农、林、牧、渔业	**Agriculture, Forestry, Animal Husbandry and Fishing**	**8309**	**8230**	**8113**	**10894**
农业	Agriculture	7517	7499	6671	8622
林业	Forestry	7250	7218	7620	8757
畜牧业	Animal Husbandry	7900	7051	8170	14125
渔业	Fishing	10849	10277	9865	12722
农、林、牧、渔服务业	Services	11933	12318	8305	10976
采矿业	**Mining**	**20626**	**20992**	**11268**	**21207**
煤炭开采和洗选业	Mining and Washing of Coal	19423	18821	11917	20654
石油和天然气开采业	Extraction of Petroleum and Natural Gas	30666	30265	8364	31919
黑色金属矿采选业	Mining of Ferrous Metal Ores	17489	19983	9139	17125
有色金属矿采选业	Mining of Non-ferrous Metal Ores	15597	16172	13118	15334
非金属矿采选业	Mining and Processing of Nonmetal Ores	12405	13362	8678	12544
其它采矿业	Mining of Other Ores	14645	13397	6489	16802
制造业	**Manufacturing**	**15757**	**16963**	**9698**	**16012**
农副食品加工业	Processing of Food from Agricultural Products	11215	8919	7839	11864
食品制造业	Manufacture of Foods	13360	10130	8841	14346
饮料制造业	Manufacture of Beverage	13518	11198	7852	14313
烟草制品业	Manufacture of Tobacco	42772	45656	21250	27552
纺织业	Manufacture of Textile	10597	9316	7802	11020
纺织服装、鞋、帽制造业	Manufacture of Textile Wearing Apparel, Footware, and Caps	12437	12092	8756	12726
皮革、毛皮、羽毛（绒）及其制品业	Manufacture of Leather, Fur, Feather & Its Products	12261	9305	10255	12438
木材加工及木、竹、藤、棕、草制品业	Processing of Timbers, Manufacture of Wood, Bamboo, Rattan, Palm, and Straw Products	9927	8808	5534	11211
家具制造业	Manufacture of Furniture	12393	11338	8027	12941
造纸及纸制品业	Manufacture of Paper and Paper Products	12347	12122	8058	12926
印刷业和记录媒介的复制	Printing, Reproduction of Recording Media	14910	16965	9475	15372
文教体育用品制造业	Manufacture of Articles for Culture, Education and Sport Activity	12741	11066	10231	12917
石油加工、炼焦及核燃料加工业	Processing of Petroleum ,Coking, Processing of Nucleus Fuel	25779	26349	13458	26480
化工原料及化学制品制造业	Manufacture of Chemical Raw Material and Chemical Products	15585	13671	10082	16874
医药制造业	Manufacture of Medicines	17121	15669	9553	17745
化学纤维制造业	Manufacture of Chemical Fiber	15352	12663	18276	15726
橡胶制品业	Manufacture of Rubber	13926	11853	9771	14706
塑料制品业	Manufacture of Plastic	13246	11506	9285	13814
非金属矿物制品业	Manufacture of Non-metallic Mineral Products	11568	11910	8534	11935

5-20 续表 1 continued

单位：元 (yuan)

项目	Item	合计 Total	国有单位 State-owned Units	城镇集体单位 Urban Collective-owned Units	其他单位 Units of Other Types of Ownership
黑色金属冶炼及压延加工业	Manufacture and Processing of Ferrous Metals	24220	26331	13947	23838
有色金属冶炼及压延加工业	Manufacture & Processing of Non-ferrous Metals	17534	19100	11258	17312
金属制品业	Manufacture of Metal Products	14806	15391	9157	15966
通用设备制造业	Manufacture of General Purpose Machinery	16474	15775	10223	17945
专用设备制造业	Manufacture of Special Purpose Machinery	16078	14920	9810	17300
交通运输设备制造业	Manufacture of Transport Equipment	19805	18777	10126	21631
电气机械及器材制造业	Manufacture of Electrical Machinery & Equipment	16093	15968	10692	16624
通信设备、计算机及其他电子设备制造业	Manufacture of Communication Equipment, Computer and Other Electronic Equipment	20299	14765	12094	20872
仪器仪表及文化、办公用机械制造业	Manufacture of Measuring Instrument and Machinery for Cultural Activity & Office Work	16941	13727	11319	17862
工艺品及其他制造业	Manufacture of Artwork, Other Manufacture	12461	14832	8970	12747
废弃资源和废旧材料回收加工业	Recycling and Disposal of Waste	15349	18157	11690	14945
电力、燃气及水的生产和供应业	**Production and Supply of Electricity, Gas and Water**	**25073**	**24378**	**18401**	**27302**
电力、热力的生产和供应业	Production and Supply of Electric Power and Heat Power	27037	26730	19360	28170
燃气生产和供应业	Production and Supply of Gas	20606	19659	17125	22166
水的生产和供应业	Production and Supply of Water	17710	16772	16490	23556
建筑业	**Construction**	**14338**	**16361**	**10171**	**14823**
房屋和土木工程建筑业	Construction of Building & Civil Engineering	13825	15793	9690	14383
建筑安装业	Architectural Installation	18780	20653	14688	19003
建筑装饰业	Architectural Decoration	14725	14604	11633	15342
其他建筑业	Other Construction	14875	17255	10302	14307
交通运输、仓储和邮政业	**Traffic, Transport, Storage and Post**	**21352**	**21160**	**10063**	**24578**
铁路运输业	Transport Via Railway	24327	24437	9008	30085
道路运输业	Transport Via Road	14415	14308	9963	15847
城市公共交通业	Urban Public Traffic	16892	16696	11562	17520
水上运输业	Water Transport	31310	32190	9250	35324
航空运输业	Air Transport	49610	42053	23257	58542
管道运输业	Transport Via Pipeline	33162	30112	32398	41288
装卸搬运和其他运输服务业	Loading, Unloading, Portage and Other Transport Services	20626	20523	9477	29132
仓储业	Storage	15128	12772	12371	25299
邮政业	Post	22321	21739	14690	40734
信息传输、计算机服务和软件业	**Information Transfer, Computer Services and Software**	**40558**	**31654**	**25568**	**50509**
电信和其他信息传输服务业	Telecom & Other Information Transfer Services	36941	31590	23165	46863
计算机服务业	Computer Services	52637	32545	28365	58470
软件业	Software Industry	52784	33897	33452	54038
批发和零售业	**Wholesale and Retail Trade**	**15241**	**15729**	**8252**	**17543**
批发业	Wholesale Trade	17953	17550	9248	22270
零售业	Retail Trade	12132	11904	7410	14025
住宿和餐饮业	**Hotels and Catering Services**	**13857**	**13453**	**10213**	**14670**
住宿业	Hotels	14349	13834	10363	15543
餐饮业	Catering Services	12898	11743	9956	13584

5-20 续表 2 continued

单位：元 (yuan)

项 目	Item	合 计 Total	国有单位 State-owned Units	城镇集体单位 Urban Collective-owned Units	其他单位 Units of Other Types of Ownership
金融业	**Financial Intermediation**	**32228**	**32849**	**18890**	**41634**
银行业	Bank	32236	33617	18918	47436
证券业	Security Activities	56418	51604	16703	57987
保险业	Insurance	27104	21335	10116	29756
其他金融活动	Other Financial Activities	48361	46483	16427	58292
房地产业	**Real Estate**	**20581**	**20077**	**13410**	**21558**
#房地产开发经营	Development and Management of Real Estate	22069	20991	12430	23338
物业管理	Property Management	18244	18622	14794	18340
房地产中介服务	Agency Services for Real Estate	23707	18398	11606	29010
租赁和商务服务业	**Leasing and Business Services**	**20992**	**19972**	**13330**	**27023**
租赁业	Leasing	14961	15737	12880	15379
商务服务业	Business Services	21102	20012	13340	27390
科学研究、技术服务和地质勘查业	**Scientific Research, Technical Service and Geologic Prospecting**	**27434**	**26309**	**19899**	**35154**
研究与实验发展	Research and Experimental Development	29054	28597	21935	36366
专业技术服务业	Professional Technical Services	29460	28727	20499	33170
科技交流和推广服务业	Services of Science and Technology Exchanges and Promotion	23574	19860	17911	38608
地质勘查业	Geologic Prospecting	21366	20576	13536	58293
水利、环境和公共设施管理业	**Management of Water Conservancy, Environment and Public Facilities**	**14753**	**14700**	**11409**	**18932**
水利管理业	Management of Water Conservancy	14246	14251	11977	18260
环境管理业	Environmental Management	13117	13034	10701	20933
公共设施管理业	Management of Public Facilities	17407	17416	14305	18077
居民服务和其他服务业	**Services to Households and Other Services**	**16642**	**19108**	**10945**	**16804**
居民服务业	Services to Households	16815	18306	10815	17375
其他服务业	Other Services	16472	20154	11026	16307
教育	**Education**	**18470**	**18622**	**12724**	**19379**
#初等教育	Junior Education	15528	15696	11993	16875
中等教育	Secondary Education	18476	18509	14417	20810
高等教育	Senior Education	29689	29821	24858	23005
卫生、社会保障和社会福利业	**Health, Social Security and Social Welfare**	**21048**	**21760**	**14907**	**17499**
卫生	Health	21133	21851	14904	18381
社会保障业	Social Security	19787	20182	22930	13798
社会福利业	Social Welfare	18992	19815	10685	11093
文化、体育和娱乐业	**Culture, Sports and Entertainment**	**22885**	**23342**	**13734**	**19691**
新闻出版业	Journalism and Publishing Activities	34042	34289	20602	30413
广播、电影、电视和音像业	Broadcasting, Movies, Televisions and Audiovisual Activitie	21654	21521	18605	26104
文化艺术业	Cultural and Art Activities	18450	18668	11325	21207
体育	Sports Activities	23540	23636	14811	22795
娱乐业	Entertainment	16664	19687	11731	15611
公共管理和社会组织	**Public Management and Social Organization**	**20505**	**20531**	**13659**	**16031**
#中国共产党机关	Organs of Communist Party of China	20332	20332	24300	
国家机构	Government Agencies	20521	20530	14595	
人民政协和民主党派	People's Political Consultative Conference and Democratic Parties	22719	22720	5667	
群众社团、社会团体和宗教组织	Non-Governmental Institutions, Social Organizations and Religion Organizations	22245	22519	16128	20449

5-21 各地区按行业分职工平均工资

Average Wage of Staff and Workers by Sector and Region

单位：元 (yuan)

年份 地区	Year Region	合计 Total	农、林、牧、渔业 Agriculture, Forestry, Animal Husbandry and Fishing	采矿业 Mining	制造业 Manufacturing	电力、燃气及水的生产和供应业 Production and Supply of Electricity, Gas and Water	建筑业 Construction	交通运输、仓储和邮政业 Transport, Storage and Post
	2003	14040	6969	13682	12496	18752	11478	15973
	2004	16024	7611	16874	14033	21805	12770	18381
	2005	18364	8309	20626	15757	25073	14338	21352
北京	Beijing	34191	16125	23774	24958	49776	23300	27655
天津	Tianjin	25271	16034	29571	21183	48417	26777	31836
河北	Hebei	14707	5987	21913	13087	22974	11815	16183
山西	Shanxi	15645	10457	22403	12820	18677	12420	18935
内蒙古	Inner Mongolia	15985	8588	16184	14497	30661	11574	19124
辽宁	Liaoning	17331	6165	19655	16241	24025	12743	19521
吉林	Jilin	14409	6419	19139	14503	19581	10608	15498
黑龙江	Heilongjiang	14458	6175	18422	13129	20347	13458	16385
上海	Shanghai	34345	25332	68590	29835	40965	35034	34354
江苏	Jiangsu	20957	9155	21637	16937	34679	16118	22280
浙江	Zhejiang	25896	24410	18756	16446	46311	18837	29218
安徽	Anhui	15334	7827	24473	13651	18269	11425	12999
福建	Fujian	17146	10017	16664	14229	26695	16161	22623
江西	Jiangxi	13688	7193	13618	11921	17274	11152	17885
山东	Shandong	16614	12877	24157	13019	22090	13069	21488
河南	Henan	14282	7922	21958	12666	19089	12450	17290
湖北	Hubei	14419	6319	14900	13669	19523	13275	16718
湖南	Hunan	15659	7152	13698	14474	18302	12078	17452
广东	Guangdong	23959	10163	23841	18019	34042	17375	32589
广西	Guangxi	15461	8725	15936	14626	22510	14032	17961
海南	Hainan	14417	6338	15337	12833	18829	12082	21504
重庆	Chongqing	16630	10676	15458	15533	21190	12860	16399
四川	Sichuan	15826	10152	16826	14275	19460	11234	17672
贵州	Guizhou	14344	10989	17175	13471	26326	11152	17812
云南	Yunnan	16140	11231	15763	17166	26741	13316	19096
西藏	Tibet	28950	20379	15672	13550	26380	19957	28083
陕西	Shaanxi	14796	10323	19912	13422	20906	11418	18595
甘肃	Gansu	14939	9930	17656	14930	21398	9735	17467
青海	Qinghai	19084	11802	18476	14638	25145	15803	21144
宁夏	Ningxia	17211	9758	25827	13555	25876	11754	18817
新疆	Xinjiang	15558	9896	23337	14871	21920	14005	23634

5-21 续表 1 continued

单位：元 (yuan)

年份 Year 地区 Region		信息传输、计算机服务和软件业 Information Transmission, Computer Service and Software	批发和零售业 Wholesale and Retail Trade	住宿和餐饮业 Hotels and Catering Services	金融业 Financial Intermediation	房地产业 Real Estate	租赁和商务服务业 Leasing and Business Services
	2003	32244	10939	11083	22457	17182	16501
	2004	34988	12923	12535	26982	18712	18131
	2005	40558	15241	13857	32228	20581	20992
北京	Beijing	71544	32109	19926	92764	29811	31699
天津	Tianjin	40569	20603	15861	46874	26727	17898
河北	Hebei	27176	8523	9324	21750	14127	11962
山西	Shanxi	20705	8319	9396	20965	10925	10796
内蒙古	Inner Mongolia	24579	11596	14215	20812	13397	16763
辽宁	Liaoning	38283	14213	12360	28542	15343	15167
吉林	Jilin	25690	10123	10109	20381	13212	16679
黑龙江	Heilongjiang	31427	11912	11589	24066	14113	12661
上海	Shanghai	69572	32385	26939	54390	42309	30589
江苏	Jiangsu	41445	16557	15181	35363	24664	19320
浙江	Zhejiang	54870	26150	15973	50972	29200	22939
安徽	Anhui	23751	9889	10159	20099	13964	14877
福建	Fujian	40326	16491	12570	34993	18944	16986
江西	Jiangxi	21025	10560	9713	21333	12733	11834
山东	Shandong	34609	11768	12023	28213	16214	15425
河南	Henan	22227	9742	10274	21743	13464	13448
湖北	Hubei	24150	9367	9582	19817	16296	13145
湖南	Hunan	29834	14627	12477	22881	15376	14344
广东	Guangdong	48972	23954	17423	44171	25113	24463
广西	Guangxi	28600	11383	9931	23545	14566	13364
海南	Hainan	44996	11199	10869	28094	15625	15144
重庆	Chongqing	30895	13769	11382	32578	14854	15645
四川	Sichuan	32828	14138	11072	27519	14613	19399
贵州	Guizhou	23228	10209	9982	25051	9770	13676
云南	Yunnan	26434	15761	10309	23900	13301	19226
西藏	Tibet	47826	16802	14542	49889	21699	18226
陕西	Shaanxi	33726	9452	9366	23128	13956	12080
甘肃	Gansu	16103	8731	8398	17950	11282	11149
青海	Qinghai	29595	13142	14906	23940	11660	12167
宁夏	Ningxia	33315	13172	10404	29232	14388	12010
新疆	Xinjiang	27544	15127	12417	25149	14517	14176

5-21 续表 2 continued

单位：元 (yuan)

年份 Year 地区 Region		科学研究、技术服务和地质勘查业 Scientific Research, Technical Services, and Geological Prospecting	水利、环境和公共设施管理业 Management of Water Conservancy, Environment and Public Facilities	居民服务和其他服务业 Services to Households and Other Services	教育 Education	卫生、社会保障和社会福利业 Health, Social Securities and Social Welfare	文化、体育和娱乐业 Culture, Sports and Entertainment	公共管理和社会组织 Public Management and Social Organization
	2003	20636	12095	12900	14399	16352	17268	15533
	2004	23593	13336	14152	16277	18617	20730	17609
	2005	27434	14753	16642	18470	21048	22885	20505
北京	Beijing	45661	26575	18159	36447	42925	43617	47277
天津	Tianjin	38973	21113	18648	25268	27435	25892	28544
河北	Hebei	22403	12011	18753	14513	15266	14591	14776
山西	Shanxi	17337	10772	11368	15149	13866	15247	14741
内蒙古	Inner Mongolia	19109	13062	10239	18049	17633	19359	18440
辽宁	Liaoning	23775	12697	13274	18583	18097	19771	20053
吉林	Jilin	18252	9900	11396	15684	14109	14300	15456
黑龙江	Heilongjiang	20862	10651	13062	17304	16568	16599	17880
上海	Shanghai	43200	31124	20338	32489	35511	40574	36765
江苏	Jiangsu	32640	18956	22411	21807	24884	28137	31328
浙江	Zhejiang	37031	24368	23834	36644	39757	37564	44413
安徽	Anhui	18432	12310	13981	15317	15608	14978	17020
福建	Fujian	24346	16433	15707	19111	21733	21018	21616
江西	Jiangxi	16738	11053	9460	14881	16451	15517	14561
山东	Shandong	23235	15214	24511	18549	20608	21906	19347
河南	Henan	19690	11812	10644	14093	14259	13736	13653
湖北	Hubei	19890	11718	15239	15477	16026	15943	16950
湖南	Hunan	17990	13052	14307	16625	19125	18438	16092
广东	Guangdong	40625	19296	19755	24571	30689	32926	33027
广西	Guangxi	19123	11989	12026	14513	17785	17006	17385
海南	Hainan	15174	11918	16075	18665	19642	18082	19854
重庆	Chongqing	22583	14659	13530	16753	19193	21265	19940
四川	Sichuan	25303	11961	18309	15149	18868	18865	18006
贵州	Guizhou	18086	12040	9055	13957	14575	12975	14202
云南	Yunnan	18901	11873	11521	15239	16731	14570	15040
西藏	Tibet	33560	14233	26571	29824	28268	31000	31561
陕西	Shaanxi	20053	11099	11263	15310	14495	13429	13351
甘肃	Gansu	18496	13235	10766	15983	15496	15147	16196
青海	Qinghai	31185	14599	31780	19898	20660	20124	20477
宁夏	Ningxia	18051	13633	13712	18256	18081	16287	17520
新疆	Xinjiang	19077	13419	12159	17183	17297	16972	17661

5-22 各地区按行业分国有单位职工平均工资

Average Wage of Staff and Workers in State-owned Units by Sector and Region

单位：元 (yuan)

年份 Year 地区 Region	合计 Total	农、林、牧、渔业 Agriculture, Forestry, Animal Husbandry and Fishing	采矿业 Mining	制造业 Manufacturing	电力、燃气及水的生产和供应业 Production and Supply of Electricity, Gas and Water	建筑业 Construction	交通运输、仓储和邮政业 Transport, Storage and Post
2003	14577	6912	13888	12601	18226	12739	16234
2004	16729	7538	17304	14486	21223	14400	18283
2005	19313	8230	20992	16963	24378	16361	21160
北京 Beijing	39067	23864	23761	27032	57866	30034	27942
天津 Tianjin	26685	16363	31416	18088	49305	29218	30204
河北 Hebei	15291	5941	19123	14578	20877	15680	16489
山西 Shanxi	16027	10678	22281	11181	19172	13652	20002
内蒙古 Inner Mongolia	16598	8652	15167	13598	26626	13248	20084
辽宁 Liaoning	18360	5915	20853	19726	23769	15940	20058
吉林 Jilin	14566	6390	12877	16123	19981	12390	16957
黑龙江 Heilongjiang	14424	6186	11804	13443	20209	15432	16940
上海 Shanghai	36077	25601	69299	30180	37495	35382	35437
江苏 Jiangsu	24659	9007	22742	21936	34440	23329	24294
浙江 Zhejiang	39048	24648	12778	24494	53727	24872	31352
安徽 Anhui	15450	7794	19990	13352	18746	15044	14207
福建 Fujian	20897	9947	13743	20351	27894	18489	23149
江西 Jiangxi	14276	7201	14299	11816	16879	13479	18870
山东 Shandong	19823	14098	27353	14526	21794	16658	23175
河南 Henan	14877	7904	20992	13502	19199	13365	18587
湖北 Hubei	15585	6301	18342	17330	18895	16202	17860
湖南 Hunan	16649	6921	14017	18086	17772	13283	17940
广东 Guangdong	28835	8954	23023	23138	33904	21559	31569
广西 Guangxi	16113	8668	14837	16598	22023	12829	19693
海南 Hainan	14427	6311	15612	11601	16022	14228	19262
重庆 Chongqing	18614	11091	16695	18385	23292	14232	17462
四川 Sichuan	17898	10392	20832	17969	22266	14640	18563
贵州 Guizhou	14681	11014	16106	14149	24237	11818	18959
云南 Yunnan	16900	11272	16793	26150	26665	14711	20477
西藏 Tibet	29644	21182	15833	13918	26380	18039	28611
陕西 Shaanxi	15223	10492	19557	13405	20969	13520	18907
甘肃 Gansu	15840	9837	19465	16458	21251	10870	18425
青海 Qinghai	21158	13855	24503	19339	26449	18921	23448
宁夏 Ningxia	17634	9752	16019	15083	26767	12323	19460
新疆 Xinjiang	15364	9897	21718	14898	22424	14919	25008

5-22 续表 1 continued

单位：元 (yuan)

年 份 地 区	Year Region	信息传输、计算机服务和软件业 Information Transmission, Computer Service and Software	批发和零售业 Wholesale and Retail Trade	住宿和餐饮业 Hotels and Catering Services	金融业 Financial Intermediation	房地产业 Real Estate	租赁和商务服务业 Leasing and Business Services
	2003	26572	11064	10525	23075	16064	15378
	2004	29131	12883	12194	27522	17720	16869
	2005	31654	15729	13453	32849	20077	19972
北 京	Beijing	53418	43886	20344	90674	32669	27475
天 津	Tianjin	38671	26131	15164	49705	28969	13357
河 北	Hebei	27616	9577	9379	23884	15347	12992
山 西	Shanxi	21526	9494	10760	21573	11465	12299
内蒙古	Inner Mongolia	23738	12580	17369	22529	14885	19105
辽 宁	Liaoning	35145	16044	12865	31208	15576	15859
吉 林	Jilin	25303	10923	9921	23723	12693	16971
黑龙江	Heilongjiang	29049	12699	10755	27075	14486	14249
上 海	Shanghai	69232	37470	27408	74296	45940	27501
江 苏	Jiangsu	35441	18152	14436	33301	24388	21465
浙 江	Zhejiang	55653	43823	17890	51240	38646	27649
安 徽	Anhui	22564	10716	10078	22225	15190	14126
福 建	Fujian	38385	20087	12132	35829	21407	17881
江 西	Jiangxi	17254	11207	9757	20280	14383	12557
山 东	Shandong	34525	14320	12017	30134	15876	16395
河 南	Henan	17322	11051	9926	24690	14732	13232
湖 北	Hubei	24319	9572	9246	20077	16173	13323
湖 南	Hunan	25600	18701	12460	23174	17768	14699
广 东	Guangdong	44712	24854	17744	49554	23035	23677
广 西	Guangxi	31494	12224	10644	24795	15341	15355
海 南	Hainan	47798	12940	10306	31609	14636	14973
重 庆	Chongqing	31079	18566	11471	32088	15311	17287
四 川	Sichuan	33782	17695	12867	29269	17607	21772
贵 州	Guizhou	21224	10700	9127	26132	12013	15749
云 南	Yunnan	25942	21802	10708	27314	14789	19886
西 藏	Tibet	47826	17572	14798	50399	23105	18020
陕 西	Shaanxi	27660	10196	8033	21959	14553	13572
甘 肃	Gansu	16098	9542	8960	19246	12436	12142
青 海	Qinghai	30250	15219	16470	25390	14749	16108
宁 夏	Ningxia	33476	13821	10180	30671	17875	12615
新 疆	Xinjiang	27263	19028	13182	27087	18068	14822

5-22 续表 2 continued

单位：元 (yuan)

年份 地区	Year Region	科学研究、技术服务和地质勘查业 Scientific Research, Technical Services, and Geological Prospecting	水利、环境和公共设施管理业 Management of Water Conservancy, Environment and Public Facilities	居民服务和其他服务业 Services to Households and Other Services	教育 Education	卫生、社会保障和社会福利业 Health, Social Securities and Social Welfare	文化、体育和娱乐业 Culture, Sports and Entertainment	公共管理和社会组织 Public Management and Social Organization
	2003	19975	12104	15075	14602	16922	17544	15557
	2004	22976	13314	17447	16435	19310	21206	17638
	2005	26309	14700	19108	18622	21760	23342	20531
北京	Beijing	49145	27815	28627	37924	45684	48809	47461
天津	Tianjin	35707	20545	25014	25352	27892	26519	28664
河北	Hebei	22905	12200	20947	14515	15688	15136	14779
山西	Shanxi	17446	10956	13428	15167	14975	15943	14741
内蒙古	Inner Mongolia	19366	13165	12547	18129	18704	19444	18438
辽宁	Liaoning	22126	12809	15579	18622	18835	20113	20088
吉林	Jilin	18385	9821	13236	15686	14456	14374	15470
黑龙江	Heilongjiang	21278	10788	16877	17313	16840	16620	17882
上海	Shanghai	37924	32248	21658	32913	37535	42259	36842
江苏	Jiangsu	31693	19875	23644	21864	27651	29430	31361
浙江	Zhejiang	39427	27150	32439	37012	41861	38916	44708
安徽	Anhui	18453	12284	14975	15322	17368	15251	17021
福建	Fujian	24489	16920	16932	19093	23193	22053	21629
江西	Jiangxi	16620	11256	10435	14870	16751	15586	14579
山东	Shandong	24262	15207	17031	18749	21857	22375	19376
河南	Henan	19807	11846	12733	14971	14510	13987	13673
湖北	Hubei	20117	11629	17372	15580	16136	16143	17133
湖南	Hunan	17866	12798	14914	16576	19819	17567	16086
广东	Guangdong	40460	19574	23230	24616	31036	36247	33044
广西	Guangxi	19215	12096	20371	14528	17874	17653	17446
海南	Hainan	15113	12169	20654	18750	20587	20025	19852
重庆	Chongqing	26952	15240	13105	16793	20507	21136	19982
四川	Sichuan	25472	12261	22148	15111	20221	19157	18008
贵州	Guizhou	18385	12410	11994	13996	14659	13505	14211
云南	Yunnan	17965	12131	14654	15192	16777	14966	15044
西藏	Tibet	33560	14233	26925	29824	28268	31042	31561
陕西	Shaanxi	20437	11130	11004	15284	15104	13374	13365
甘肃	Gansu	18585	13243	12148	15985	15634	15152	16197
青海	Qinghai	31360	14559	33776	19908	20790	20342	20479
宁夏	Ningxia	17229	13658	16646	18294	18124	16330	17520
新疆	Xinjiang	19065	13614	13682	17214	17278	17048	17668

5-23 各地区按行业分城镇集体单位职工平均工资

Average Wage of Staff and Workers in Urban Collective-owned Units by Sector and Region

单位：元 (yuan)

年份 Year / 地区 Region		合计 Total	农、林、牧、渔业 Agriculture, Forestry, Animal Husbandry and Fishing	采矿业 Mining	制造业 Manufacturing	电力、燃气及水的生产和供应业 Production and Distribution of Electricity, Gas and Water	建筑业 Construction	交通运输、仓储和邮政业 Transport, Storage and Post
	2003	8678	6125	7178	7600	14911	8375	8212
	2004	9814	7052	8772	8598	17024	9234	8846
	2005	11283	8113	11268	9698	18401	10171	10063
北京	Beijing	14695	11087	17169	12343	12949	15369	14529
天津	Tianjin	15713	12618	14765	12376	17841	22482	14885
河北	Hebei	9041	5958	8766	7924	13057	8743	9428
山西	Shanxi	10157	6057	13259	9805	13919	8133	8955
内蒙古	Inner Mongolia	10804	5472	11688	10464	9093	10901	7842
辽宁	Liaoning	9161	9966	6632	8326	11008	9496	7557
吉林	Jilin	8735	6464	7700	7952	8521	8184	7376
黑龙江	Heilongjiang	7724	3944	10654	6554	20161	7944	6552
上海	Shanghai	22486	29389	11500	16630	48728	20138	13996
江苏	Jiangsu	13064	9757	12546	10873	16248	10667	12005
浙江	Zhejiang	20567	31159	19116	14125	20007	16183	20775
安徽	Anhui	9894	3627	13218	8955	12628	8294	6048
福建	Fujian	13811	8651	13500	11602	19938	14572	12129
江西	Jiangxi	8952	4759	7924	7369	16285	8949	6215
山东	Shandong	11474	7525	12532	11260	9204	9889	10653
河南	Henan	10383	6941	11425	8718	11446	10269	7165
湖北	Hubei	8923	6273	8899	8147	10085	8883	9131
湖南	Hunan	11547	8592	12967	9666	15487	10507	9983
广东	Guangdong	13240	11283	13774	11064	25726	9881	15146
广西	Guangxi	10684	7707	15261	9617	21622	10318	10092
海南	Hainan	8640	5552	13726	7912	7468	7503	9506
重庆	Chongqing	11614	9205	12024	10386	20711	11207	11271
四川	Sichuan	11067	8501	7278	10709	16559	9048	9396
贵州	Guizhou	10506	8955	8590	8230	6965	10161	8250
云南	Yunnan	10516	8614	9969	9708	24065	9411	11557
西藏	Tibet	12336	13588	10263	9117		19446	12762
陕西	Shaanxi	7926	7536	16677	7674	8833	7059	7869
甘肃	Gansu	9291	10104	6549	10912	15922	7819	9353
青海	Qinghai	10080	12972	10437	8213	7211	9568	9922
宁夏	Ningxia	13630	9364		8149		11651	4875
新疆	Xinjiang	12738	7158	13652	11574	12463	14354	17877

5-23 续表 1 continued

单位：元 (yuan)

年份 Year 地区 Region	信息传输、计算机服务和软件业 Information Transmission, Computer Service and Software	批发和零售业 Wholesale and Retail Trade	住宿和餐饮业 Hotels and Catering Services	金融业 Financial Intermediation	房地产业 Real Estate	租赁和商务服务业 Leasing and Business Services
2003	12484	6593	8342	14370	12228	11042
2004	18153	7325	9292	16589	13064	11772
2005	25568	8252	10213	18890	13410	13330
北 京 Beijing	19842	14533	13014	62765	16150	12613
天 津 Tianjin	29336	12254	12528	34118	18734	17477
河 北 Hebei	11730	6381	7539	15741	11749	10446
山 西 Shanxi	1656	6734	5813	19503	7229	7979
内蒙古 Inner Mongolia	17925	9047	8481	15078	7669	9585
辽 宁 Liaoning	17266	7838	9003	16011	7068	10680
吉 林 Jilin	6533	6129	6750	13009	13158	10727
黑龙江 Heilongjiang	9024	5330	8098	12721	14937	7832
上 海 Shanghai	33446	20150	15649		22837	22707
江 苏 Jiangsu	20759	8730	13004	20202	17190	14391
浙 江 Zhejiang	23534	15390	13491	39572	21528	22238
安 徽 Anhui	9922	6649	8559	15348	6979	16493
福 建 Fujian	55762	8972	11179	19684	20581	13962
江 西 Jiangxi	6031	6841	7250	15373	8339	7072
山 东 Shandong	35793	7749	10762	21408	12893	11591
河 南 Henan	9699	7147	9809	15215	10721	13393
湖 北 Hubei	9040	6446	8463	13704	10650	8874
湖 南 Hunan	28789	8459	10478	18739	10738	13932
广 东 Guangdong	29264	11992	12746	23003	14417	15076
广 西 Guangxi	7429	7422	7860	20067	13588	8597
海 南 Hainan	4175	5836	10940	11753	11238	7612
重 庆 Chongqing	10534	8298	8891	25062	10462	15712
四 川 Sichuan	11323	8013	8671	21574	13363	9574
贵 州 Guizhou	6538	7629	9239	23965	8335	8173
云 南 Yunnan	11253	8095	8602	15754	10503	9080
西 藏 Tibet		10461	8785			9111
陕 西 Shaanxi	6000	6353	6064	14092	10501	9349
甘 肃 Gansu	11533	7064	7010	12316	8383	9032
青 海 Qinghai		7975	10359	17885	11146	7076
宁 夏 Ningxia	7800	8077	15394	25403	8000	9391
新 疆 Xinjiang	7944	10706	11956	16843	12805	11010

5-23 续表 2 continued

单位：元 (yuan)

年份 地区	Year Region	科学研究、技术服务和地质勘查业 Scientific Research, Technical Services, and Geological Prospecting	水利、环境和公共设施管理业 Management of Water Conservancy, Environment and Public Facilities	居民服务和其他服务业 Services to Households and Other Services	教育 Education	卫生、社会保障和社会福利业 Health, Social Securities and Social Welfare	文化、体育和娱乐业 Culture, Sports and Entertainment	公共管理和社会组织 Public Management and Social Organization
	2003	14541	10380	8713	9308	11685	9429	10748
	2004	15471	10923	8978	10542	12960	10970	11818
	2005	19899	11409	10945	12724	14907	13734	13659
北京	Beijing	22018	12960	13717	18980	24354	15278	25075
天津	Tianjin	19495	13773	13336	16370	14917	16794	9432
河北	Hebei	9138	7149	11550	13520	9574	8462	12855
山西	Shanxi	11900	7150	10174	12568	8321	5457	14661
内蒙古	Inner Mongolia	18874	5411	5763	13590	10538	9429	24444
辽宁	Liaoning	15111	7175	8810	9832	8134	8237	9683
吉林	Jilin	17140	9114	6235	13479	9899	15413	11918
黑龙江	Heilongjiang	14763	7943	6431	18666	10340	10530	16744
上海	Shanghai	26673	16790	18107	23322	33747	26081	31439
江苏	Jiangsu	18788	12443	26583	17967	17750	14136	14921
浙江	Zhejiang	31472	17708	16163	25597	28389	31333	36701
安徽	Anhui	25608	10630	7140	15223	10144	10396	16344
福建	Fujian	14392	10507	10103	16205	15455	9554	14396
江西	Jiangxi	15433	7284	3123	8036	11505	6345	8754
山东	Shandong	16501	8505	13322	13298	12185	15649	10034
河南	Henan	13401	7723	6125	11917	9585	6350	9928
湖北	Hubei	15017	11133	11060	9451	13311	10923	9594
湖南	Hunan	18725	10933	11924	19722	12287	25263	20194
广东	Guangdong	28475	13473	15673	18097	22092	22558	20216
广西	Guangxi	15366	7874	9700	12273	11542	14282	13543
海南	Hainan	20387	8796	10115	9052	13868	14658	22764
重庆	Chongqing	10537	10015	7615	9583	12379	11160	11021
四川	Sichuan	15886	9399	9071	12586	12852	10830	12761
贵州	Guizhou	10466	6296	7154	10151	12085	9750	11153
云南	Yunnan	14635	9668	8077	12363	11145	12762	13188
西藏	Tibet			19500			8600	
陕西	Shaanxi	7721	9894	7284	6502	8473	6116	8644
甘肃	Gansu	11561	9357	6780	21333	11738	9053	14564
青海	Qinghai		15830	13712	7765	15149	9440	14619
宁夏	Ningxia	13742	10165	8800		13005	6842	
新疆	Xinjiang	17475	7634	7766	11372	20320	13154	11163

5-24 各地区按行业分其他单位职工平均工资（年底数）

Average Wage of Staff and Workers in Other Ownership Units at the Year-end by Sector and Region

单位：元 (yuan)

年份 地区	Year Region	合计 Total	农、林、牧、渔业 Agriculture, Forestry, Animal Husbandry and Fishing	采矿业 Mining	制造业 Manufacturing	电力、燃气及水的生产和供应业 Production and Distribution of Electricity, Gas and Water	建筑业 Construction	交通运输、仓储和邮政业 Transport, Storage and Post
	2003	14574	10022	14321	13263	20923	12345	17621
	2004	16259	10298	17345	14569	23933	13405	21537
	2005	18244	10894	21207	16012	27302	14823	24578
北京	Beijing	32324	12696	24496	25445	48593	22423	27943
天津	Tianjin	24945	11386	29829	22437	47213	26004	43143
河北	Hebei	14835	9626	25536	12991	33200	9899	16268
山西	Shanxi	16580	6189	24224	14525	17388	11745	12103
内蒙古	Inner Mongolia	15514	7324	16662	15010	39710	10958	12854
辽宁	Liaoning	17550	15058	20200	16290	25820	12437	20082
吉林	Jilin	15868	7545	25246	15244	19041	10485	11988
黑龙江	Heilongjiang	16492	6297	19305	14755	20891	15158	16005
上海	Shanghai	33756	22952	9333	30120	49084	35927	34474
江苏	Jiangsu	18468	11662	20913	16728	36106	14877	20616
浙江	Zhejiang	18958	14411	19976	16188	32963	18861	27032
安徽	Anhui	16788	18990	27591	14230	17361	10015	13165
福建	Fujian	14947	10913	19603	14072	24420	15398	23887
江西	Jiangxi	13140	9197	11382	12350	18934	10922	12634
山东	Shandong	14018	9661	18326	12947	23403	12734	19373
河南	Henan	14852	9922	22776	12967	18971	12650	12519
湖北	Hubei	13062	7559	11422	12641	22722	13376	14231
湖南	Hunan	14422	11415	13404	13700	20451	12226	19060
广东	Guangdong	21500	23982	25323	18246	37087	20331	35907
广西	Guangxi	14852	9969	17793	14079	25599	16420	14823
海南	Hainan	16185	9450	10270	14045	24335	11504	26742
重庆	Chongqing	14373	9310	13778	14387	17978	12821	13111
四川	Sichuan	12812	9118	12495	12877	15633	10265	17469
贵州	Guizhou	14161	9136	17870	13559	35441	10507	11078
云南	Yunnan	14894	10378	14779	14028	26935	13354	13140
西藏	Tibet	19154	11860	14625	16053		23319	16209
陕西	Shaanxi	15465	7327	22231	14318	20786	11268	18408
甘肃	Gansu	11827	13874	17369	12484	26869	9052	8025
青海	Qinghai	13591	2265	13088	13857	25236	11917	10245
宁夏	Ningxia	16668	10208	26200	13386	21030	11380	11973
新疆	Xinjiang	16503	11656	25037	15028	21705	13630	16532

5-24 续表 1 continued

单位：元 (yuan)

年份 地区	Year Region	信息传输、计算机服务和软件业 Information Transmission, Computer Service and Software	批发和零售业 Wholesale and Retail Trade	住宿和餐饮业 Hotels and Catering Services	金融业 Financial Intermediation	房地产业 Real Estate	租赁和商务服务业 Leasing and Business Services
	2003	42867	13710	12179	31370	18898	23281
	2004	44683	15901	13387	37141	20045	24855
	2005	50509	17543	14670	41634	21558	27023
北　京	Beijing	73213	30565	20342	94408	29913	38939
天　津	Tianjin	42116	20907	16716	46957	26260	32145
河　北	Hebei	26562	8166	9758	25732	12041	11062
山　西	Shanxi	16973	6371	7330	21606	10483	10545
内蒙古	Inner Mongolia	31670	10800	11255	25011	11109	14466
辽　宁	Liaoning	42211	14753	12525	32536	16303	18163
吉　林	Jilin	26686	10325	11074	22830	13782	19115
黑龙江	Heilongjiang	37820	13683	14168	26323	13323	15687
上　海	Shanghai	70758	32450	27469	46332	41419	40918
江　苏	Jiangsu	47661	18427	15756	42894	25679	18775
浙　江	Zhejiang	54958	23183	15609	56103	25576	20651
安　徽	Anhui	27534	11169	10426	20046	14393	14824
福　建	Fujian	42060	15725	12936	44746	17792	16174
江　西	Jiangxi	32818	11154	10016	32670	10444	18136
山　东	Shandong	34590	11483	12294	30005	16939	18070
河　南	Henan	29849	10275	10934	24912	12572	14791
湖　北	Hubei	22934	10137	9893	27209	17159	13890
湖　南	Hunan	33306	12696	12684	26151	14563	13500
广　东	Guangdong	53257	26488	17723	49300	27370	34365
广　西	Guangxi	24726	12691	9643	24085	13933	12030
海　南	Hainan	38728	13093	11089	28066	16701	18138
重　庆	Chongqing	30582	11122	11506	36438	14864	14685
四　川	Sichuan	29717	12506	10614	32996	13250	13562
贵　州	Guizhou	24880	10407	10623	23982	9474	12198
云　南	Yunnan	28070	12602	10320	22782	12972	24064
西　藏	Tibet		16313	19529	36235	15382	21658
陕　西	Shaanxi	43780	10888	11021	38419	13851	8200
甘　肃	Gansu	16316	8284	7986	20360	10480	9573
青　海	Qinghai	26859	10694	12464	28927	9807	15592
宁　夏	Ningxia	32158	13317	9320	27318	13655	11190
新　疆	Xinjiang	27929	14509	11503	26907	12779	14293

5-24 续表 2 continued

单位：元 (yuan)

年份 Year / 地区 Region	科学研究、技术服务和地质勘查业 Scientific Research, Technical Services, and Geological Prospecting	水利、环境和公共设施管理业 Management of Water Conservancy, Environment and Public Facilities	居民服务和其他服务业 Services to Households and Other Services	教育 Education	卫生、社会保障和社会福利业 Health, Social Securities and Social Welfare	文化、体育和娱乐业 Culture, Sports and Entertainment	公共管理和社会组织 Public Management and Social Organization
2003	26061	14560	14046	16163	14102	16121	8765
2004	29346	16717	13975	18439	15145	17481	13070
2005	35154	18932	16804	19379	17499	19691	16031
北京 Beijing	41345	24177	15428	25075	23349	25418	35826
天津 Tianjin	53915	31750	15594	20058	18418	17964	
河北 Hebei	14409	11156	9382	8716	9987	8037	
山西 Shanxi	10400		9712	12019	6299	10758	
内蒙古 Inner Mongolia	13430	19822	9227	10717	12298	13246	5563
辽宁 Liaoning	40589	14680	12797	13923	12468	15248	2929
吉林 Jilin	16843	16991	9138	15897	12894	11058	9000
黑龙江 Heilongjiang	15850	9494	8947	12636	15276	17760	10353
上海 Shanghai	77510	31948	19873	17127	14235	29076	56000
江苏 Jiangsu	38063	22060	16343	18554	16525	23508	
浙江 Zhejiang	28847	16722	13785	27669	25340	17307	17432
安徽 Anhui	16093	13411	8895	8920	13352	9140	
福建 Fujian	24659	13528	16116	21543	14470	14414	
江西 Jiangxi	21725	14516	14308	16235	11835	7140	4355
山东 Shandong	17584	18424	28627	12671	21517	16366	16401
河南 Henan	19874	13218	10363	16023	14654	10063	11799
湖北 Hubei	17192	15243	14178	14558	15740	11156	9129
湖南 Hunan	19656	19404	13436	19486	22284	24704	20314
广东 Guangdong	42573	23761	18406	25363	27022	20513	27455
广西 Guangxi	18624	11200	9518	13172	17322	9978	7796
海南 Hainan	15471	9996	12661	16746	14735	10992	12000
重庆 Chongqing	18222	8985	14987	12857	15689	28907	
四川 Sichuan	20241	9489	13248	21487	16759	13977	
贵州 Guizhou	16392	12497	8368	11190	9756	8046	10522
云南 Yunnan	27913	9867	10989	28444	8724	10007	13497
西藏 Tibet							
陕西 Shaanxi	15016	8899	14577	19009	13500	22094	12806
甘肃 Gansu	16426	9983	4734	11599	12288		
青海 Qinghai	23197	14892	9670	15545	10316		
宁夏 Ningxia	28672	15188	12315	11833	10000		
新疆 Xinjiang	19335	9929	11356	13157	12897	13904	7300

5-25 按登记注册类型分其他单位职工平均工资

Average Wage of Staff and Workers in Units of Other Types of Ownership by Registration Status

单位：元 (yuan)

年份 地区	Year Region	合计 Total	股份合作单位 Cooperative Units	联营单位 Joint Ownership Units	有限责任公司 Limited Liability Corporations	股份有限公司 Share-holding Corporations Ltd.	其他 Others	港、澳、台商投资单位 Units with Funds from Hong Kong, Macao & Taiwan	外商投资单位 Foreign Funded Units
	1993	4966		3741		5171	3279	5147	5315
	1994	6303		4982		6383	4954	6376	6533
	1995	7463		6056		7277	6494	7484	8058
	1996	8261		6856		7623	7131	8334	9383
	1997	8789		7310		7693	7063	9329	10361
	1998	8972	6054	8431	7750	8833	6133	10027	11767
	1999	9829	6709	9501	8632	9720	8425	10991	12951
	2000	10984	7473	10663	9766	11131	10223	11914	14372
	2001	12140	8398	11887	10993	12385	11621	12544	16101
	2002	13212	9484	12451	11997	13850	10242	13756	17892
	2003	14574	10575	13531	13392	15857	10572	14691	19366
	2004	16259	11773	15358	15196	18545	10102	15727	20440
	2005	18244	13913	17669	17153	20800	12009	17273	21902
北京	Beijing	32324	14884	17566	26684	37705	25311	41347	52262
天津	Tianjin	24945	28401	28465	24611	33770	9193	22932	25117
河北	Hebei	14835	10674	22192	16132	13752	8837	15547	14747
山西	Shanxi	16580	8836	12323	17926	14185	8863	9544	13544
内蒙古	Inner Mongolia	15514	9110	12022	15944	15875	10231	9663	16063
辽宁	Liaoning	17550	11364	10646	17148	21874	10163	17164	17448
吉林	Jilin	15868	8778	8347	14349	18836	8591	11615	20010
黑龙江	Heilongjiang	16492	13872	12911	12508	21975	11548	55793	16241
上海	Shanghai	33756	22386	30148	32605	41657	27233	23882	35324
江苏	Jiangsu	18468	13836	14652	18651	21281	13330	16663	19820
浙江	Zhejiang	18958	17938	27516	18439	23645	20068	17484	17697
安徽	Anhui	16788	9615	11214	17508	18585	10404	11376	15896
福建	Fujian	14947	14672	17491	15124	21400	13115	13874	15109
江西	Jiangxi	13140	13004	13195	13208	16391	9487	10212	12340
山东	Shandong	14018	11617	27775	13762	14869	11929	13442	14236
河南	Henan	14852	11776	10539	15048	15307	10813	14914	15402
湖北	Hubei	13062	10100	10218	12442	12504	8444	11949	22064
湖南	Hunan	14422	13104	12907	13692	16780	16276	12898	15804
广东	Guangdong	21500	17673	25032	26407	30694	17476	17007	22604
广西	Guangxi	14852	10331	10641	15224	15526	10913	10762	20243
海南	Hainan	16185	19235	13315	15012	21257	12144	12243	16558
重庆	Chongqing	14373	13242	14288	12977	19440	13673	14794	18510
四川	Sichuan	12812	10783	12168	11743	14635	9329	16834	18656
贵州	Guizhou	14161	11078	9628	13200	18312	9808	11479	17515
云南	Yunnan	14894	11262	14076	14625	18847	10641	14219	16993
西藏	Tibet	19154	17550	18235	21556	16594	11860		
陕西	Shaanxi	15465	18245	12552	14138	16714	12705	15718	24994
甘肃	Gansu	11827	16470	7976	9995	15441	8124	10189	11557
青海	Qinghai	13591	8653	6556	12216	18319	12516	13243	10770
宁夏	Ningxia	16668	11723	13324	17887	14100	11220	15958	19536
新疆	Xinjiang	16503	17477	14997	14837	23209	10061	16430	18268

5-26 各地区国有及国有控股企业就业人数和劳动报酬（2005年）

Employed Persons at the Year-end and Earnings in State-owned and State-holding Enterprises by Region (2005)

地区	Region	就业人员（万人） Number of Employed Persons (10 000 persons)	#女性 Female	职工（万人） Staff and Workers (10 000 persons)	#专业技术人员 Technical Personnel	就业人员劳动报酬（亿元） Earnings of Employed Persons (100 million yuan)	职工工资总额（亿元） Wages of Staff and Workers (100 million yuan)	职工平均工资（元） Average Wage of Staff and Workers (yuan)
全国	**National Total**	**4288.3**	**1435.1**	**4036.4**	**931.1**	**8455.1**	**8119.5**	**20079**
北京	Beijing	190.7	62.6	167.4	48.4	660.9	608.4	36170
天津	Tianjin	80.8	21.6	69.2	16.4	203.6	189.4	27784
河北	Hebei	188.9	62.6	183.8	38.2	320.0	314.6	16888
山西	Shanxi	183.3	53.4	179.2	34.0	322.1	318.0	17848
内蒙古	Inner Mongolia	101.9	34.3	99.7	18.8	163.0	159.9	15830
辽宁	Liaoning	365.1	132.7	352.7	111.2	679.0	666.4	18784
吉林	Jilin	105.7	32.3	103.7	22.5	176.7	173.8	16211
黑龙江	Heilongjiang	250.9	75.4	222.3	34.5	339.6	316.9	14406
上海	Shanghai	155.5	49.6	122.5	29.8	542.9	483.5	38894
江苏	Jiangsu	207.9	75.5	195.6	52.7	454.1	438.0	22229
浙江	Zhejiang	93.6	32.9	87.6	23.6	302.7	290.6	33236
安徽	Anhui	140.9	44.1	133.3	29.4	244.5	236.3	17792
福建	Fujian	73.2	24.9	68.3	15.4	157.0	150.1	22389
江西	Jiangxi	121.2	39.3	114.9	28.2	164.2	158.5	13787
山东	Shandong	249.9	82.1	241.5	47.9	501.8	492.0	20220
河南	Henan	241.3	83.8	233.3	43.8	386.6	379.5	16752
湖北	Hubei	208.1	75.1	197.4	50.0	292.4	283.5	14248
湖南	Hunan	127.0	41.2	114.6	24.7	208.8	196.8	17201
广东	Guangdong	221.2	76.8	213.8	51.1	662.3	642.0	30285
广西	Guangxi	107.3	36.9	100.5	24.5	175.3	168.6	16939
海南	Hainan	36.9	14.1	36.1	6.1	44.1	42.9	11897
重庆	Chongqing	60.6	18.9	58.1	11.7	115.2	112.2	19189
四川	Sichuan	173.0	58.0	163.9	39.0	312.6	300.3	18328
贵州	Guizhou	82.1	24.0	77.9	15.8	141.0	136.7	18082
云南	Yunnan	88.6	30.1	83.5	21.6	162.4	158.5	19013
西藏	Tibet	7.9	2.8	6.9	1.6	19.6	18.8	27743
陕西	Shaanxi	158.3	52.3	152.8	39.9	251.6	246.2	16091
甘肃	Gansu	95.2	32.3	92.4	19.0	156.5	154.2	16606
青海	Qinghai	15.0	5.1	14.2	4.0	33.2	32.4	22650
宁夏	Ningxia	26.5	8.5	24.9	5.4	52.1	50.0	19461
新疆	Xinjiang	129.7	52.0	124.3	22.0	209.3	200.7	15230

5-27 各地区职业介绍工作情况（2005年）

Situations of Careers Service by Region (2005)

单位：万人 (10 000 persons)

地区	Region	本年末职业介绍机构个数（个） Number of Careers Service (unit)	本年末职业介绍机构人数 Staff and Workers in Careers Service	本年登记招聘人数 Total Registered Job Vacancies This Year	本年登记求职人数 Total Registered Job-seekers This Year	#女性 Female	#下岗职工 Laid-off Workers	#失业人员 Unemployment
全国	**National Total**	**35747**	**11.2**	**4039.0**	**4128.9**	**1786.9**	**345.7**	**1330.4**
北京	Beijing	626	0.4	55.0	52.0	20.6		23.5
天津	Tianjin	206	0.1	55.0	76.5	42.1	3.2	73.3
河北	Hebei	2265	0.6	189.3	194.3	92.7	8.1	37.1
山西	Shanxi	653	0.3	33.3	35.2	13.5	5.7	9.3
内蒙古	Inner Mongolia	1443	0.3	64.2	60.8	26.8	10.4	23.3
辽宁	Liaoning	1807	0.5	139.4	171.2	85.3	23.7	97.5
吉林	Jilin	1343	0.3	58.0	63.7	30.0	14.6	27.5
黑龙江	Heilongjiang	1414	0.3	137.7	147.8	61.7	48.0	59.0
上海	Shanghai	507	0.5	160.2	135.7	60.5	15.0	78.3
江苏	Jiangsu	2945	1.0	258.9	264.4	129.5	0.4	118.8
浙江	Zhejiang	2394	0.6	509.7	377.0	145.7	7.3	53.4
安徽	Anhui	1929	0.5	117.3	132.4	57.7	10.2	48.0
福建	Fujian	976	0.3	280.7	215.7	104.5	12.8	30.7
江西	Jiangxi	1239	0.3	160.4	182.3	71.9	21.5	48.5
山东	Shandong	1969	0.7	292.6	280.5	133.0	14.3	124.6
河南	Henan	1443	0.5	113.3	136.8	61.3	37.3	25.2
湖北	Hubei	910	0.3	146.5	133.1	63.0	19.9	56.2
湖南	Hunan	852	0.3	91.3	137.9	70.3	28.7	61.7
广东	Guangdong	1938	0.9	583.6	722.4	260.5	15.7	124.3
广西	Guangxi	407	0.2	94.0	95.5	46.5	6.1	27.7
海南	Hainan	73		18.3	17.5	9.7	1.0	6.4
重庆	Chongqing	336	0.1	32.8	34.3	16.4	2.4	19.8
四川	Sichuan	1717	0.5	125.1	108.5	50.9	10.5	48.5
贵州	Guizhou	410	0.2	25.9	19.5	8.2	3.6	8.8
云南	Yunnan	1865	0.3	70.2	83.0	34.4	6.2	32.4
西藏	Tibet	21		2.2	2.1	0.9		0.1
陕西	Shaanxi	2251	0.6	89.1	105.3	39.1	10.3	14.9
甘肃	Gansu	640	0.2	31.3	28.7	12.6	3.5	9.3
青海	Qinghai	312	0.1	42.8	45.2	9.0	1.1	6.2
宁夏	Ningxia	228	0.1	23.9	32.7	9.9	0.8	6.0
新疆	Xinjiang	628	0.2	37.0	36.9	18.7	3.4	30.1

5-27 续表 continued

单位：万人 (10 000 persons)

地区	Region	#获得职业资格人员 Persons with Certificates	本年职业指导人数 Person-times of Vocational Guidance	本年介绍成功人数 Placed Job-seekers	#女性 Female	#下岗职工 Laid-off Workers	#失业人员 Unemployment	#获得职业资格人员 Persons with Certificates
全国	**National Total**	**699.8**	**2271.6**	**2165.3**	**964.9**	**186.1**	**681.4**	**384.8**
北京	Beijing	8.5	40.0	29.2	11.7		13.9	6.7
天津	Tianjin	15.2	43.0	8.5	4.7	0.4	8.0	4.1
河北	Hebei	42.9	134.8	110.6	48.1	5.2	27.8	32.2
山西	Shanxi	2.1	24.9	20.4	6.7	2.6	3.9	1.8
内蒙古	Inner Mongolia	3.1	35.5	39.7	16.6	5.4	15.5	2.4
辽宁	Liaoning	20.1	91.3	95.4	48.0	10.1	61.1	14.2
吉林	Jilin	8.3	43.3	40.1	18.0	8.5	14.7	5.9
黑龙江	Heilongjiang	8.4	81.6	80.5	34.1	27.8	33.8	6.2
上海	Shanghai	23.5	97.1	51.4	23.3	6.4	30.4	14.6
江苏	Jiangsu	65.9	234.0	161.6	74.9	0.3	70.4	40.6
浙江	Zhejiang	56.8	182.9	203.3	70.7	4.8	27.0	32.4
安徽	Anhui	18.5	54.9	72.2	30.8	7.0	24.3	7.4
福建	Fujian	9.5	88.7	112.7	58.6	8.1	16.8	6.0
江西	Jiangxi	13.6	67.2	99.6	56.1	13.8	26.3	9.9
山东	Shandong	49.4	177.1	162.6	76.0	9.1	57.0	28.0
河南	Henan	19.7	68.5	78.8	31.5	22.4	18.2	13.3
湖北	Hubei	29.7	100.3	87.3	41.6	12.6	35.9	20.1
湖南	Hunan	118.7	98.2	49.2	23.4	9.8	18.9	18.9
广东	Guangdong	113.1	154.3	312.4	151.2	7.2	69.2	67.4
广西	Guangxi	8.0	49.4	46.5	21.4	2.6	10.9	4.6
海南	Hainan	1.6	14.2	9.5	4.4	0.6	2.0	1.0
重庆	Chongqing	6.0	30.1	22.7	10.6	1.4	14.2	3.8
四川	Sichuan	19.5	94.8	58.5	26.0	6.0	26.1	12.8
贵州	Guizhou	1.7	12.3	8.8	3.8	2.1	4.0	1.1
云南	Yunnan	9.8	67.7	53.0	20.8	2.5	19.2	8.9
西藏	Tibet		1.8	1.0	0.5		0.8	
陕西	Shaanxi	12.2	62.4	56.8	21.8	4.9	7.9	10.1
甘肃	Gansu	5.4	25.4	18.6	7.5	1.7	4.8	4.0
青海	Qinghai	1.7	43.3	39.1	8.8	0.3	3.8	1.4
宁夏	Ningxia	1.2	23.0	15.6	5.1	0.7	3.6	0.9
新疆	Xinjiang	5.7	29.6	19.7	8.2	1.8	11.0	4.1

5-28 各地区城镇登记失业人员及失业率

Registered Urban Unemployment Persons and Unemployment Rate by Region

地 区	Region	失业人员（万人） Unemployment (10 000 persons)				失业率（%） Unemployment Rate (%)			
		1990	2003	2004	2005	1990	2003	2004	2005
北 京	Beijing	1.7	7.0	6.5	10.6	0.4	1.4	1.3	2.1
天 津	Tianjin	8.1	12.0	11.8	11.7	2.7	3.8	3.8	3.7
河 北	Hebei	7.7	25.7	28.0	27.8	1.1	3.9	4.0	3.9
山 西	Shanxi	5.5	13.1	13.7	14.3	1.2	3.0	3.1	3.0
内蒙古	Inner Mongolia	15.2	17.6	18.5	17.7	3.8	4.5	4.6	4.3
辽 宁	Liaoning	23.7	72.0	70.1	60.4	2.2	6.5	6.5	5.6
吉 林	Jilin	10.5	28.4	28.2	27.6	1.9	4.3	4.2	4.2
黑龙江	Heilongjiang	20.4	35.0	32.9	31.3	2.2	4.2	4.5	4.4
上 海	Shanghai	7.7	30.1	27.4	27.5	1.5	4.9	4.4	
江 苏	Jiangsu	22.5	41.8	42.9	41.6	2.4	4.1	3.8	3.6
浙 江	Zhejiang	11.2	28.3	30.1	29.0	2.2	4.2	4.1	3.7
安 徽	Anhui	15.2	25.1	26.1	27.8	2.8	4.1	4.2	4.4
福 建	Fujian	9.0	14.6	14.5	14.9	2.6	4.1	4.0	4.0
江 西	Jiangxi	10.3	21.6	22.4	22.8	2.4	3.6	3.6	3.5
山 东	Shandong	26.2	41.3	42.3	42.9	3.2	3.6	3.4	3.3
河 南	Henan	25.1	26.3	31.2	33.0	3.3	3.1	3.4	3.5
湖 北	Hubei	12.7	49.3	49.4	52.6	1.7	4.3	4.2	4.3
湖 南	Hunan	15.9	37.1	43.0	41.9	2.7	4.5	4.4	4.3
广 东	Guangdong	19.2	35.5	35.9	34.5	2.2	2.9	2.7	2.6
广 西	Guangxi	13.9	14.9	17.8	18.5	3.9	3.6	4.1	4.2
海 南	Hainan	3.5	3.6	4.7	5.1	3.0	3.4	3.4	3.6
重 庆	Chongqing		16.2	16.8	16.9		4.1	4.1	4.1
四 川	Sichuan	38.0	33.1	33.3	34.3	3.7	4.4	4.4	4.6
贵 州	Guizhou	10.7	11.2	11.6	12.1	4.1	4.0	4.1	4.2
云 南	Yunnan	7.8	12.1	11.9	13.0	2.5	4.1	4.3	4.2
西 藏	Tibet			1.2				4.0	
陕 西	Shaanxi	11.2	13.9	18.5	21.5	2.8	3.5	3.8	4.2
甘 肃	Gansu	12.5	9.3	9.5	9.3	4.9	3.4	3.4	3.3
青 海	Qinghai	4.2	3.1	3.5	3.6	5.6	3.8	3.9	3.9
宁 夏	Ningxia	4.0	3.8	4.1	4.4	5.4	4.4	4.5	4.5
新 疆	Xinjiang	9.6	9.9	13.3	11.1	3.0	3.5	3.8	3.9

主要统计指标解释

经济活动人口 指在16周岁及以上，有劳动能力，参加或要求参加社会经济活动的人口。包括就业人员和失业人员。

就业人员 指在16周岁及以上，从事一定社会劳动并取得劳动报酬或经营收入的人员。这一指标反映了一定时期内全部劳动力资源的实际利用情况，是研究我国基本国情国力的重要指标。

各单位的就业人员 指在各级国家机关、政党机关、社会团体及企业、事业单位中工作，取得工资或其他形式的劳动报酬的全部人员。包括在岗职工、再就业的离退休人员、民办教师以及在各单位中工作的外方人员和港澳台方人员、兼职人员、借用的外单位人员和第二职业者。不包括离开本单位仍保留劳动关系的职工。各单位的就业人员反映了各单位实际参加生产或工作的全部劳动力。

城镇私营和个体就业人员 城镇私营就业人员指在工商管理部门注册登记，其经营地址设在县城关镇(含县城关镇)以上的私营企业就业人员，包括私营企业投资者和雇工。城镇个体就业人员指在工商管理部门注册登记，并持有城镇户口或在城镇长期居住，经批准从事个体工商经营的就业人员，包括个体经营者和在个体工商户劳动的家庭帮工和雇工。

城镇登记失业人员 指有非农业户口，在一定的劳动年龄内(16周岁至退休年龄)，有劳动能力，无业而要求就业，并在当地就业服务机构进行求职登记的人员。

城镇登记失业率 城镇登记失业人员与城镇单位就业人员(扣除使用的农村劳动力、聘用的离退休人员、港澳台及外方人员)、城镇单位中的不在岗职工、城镇私营业主、个体户主、城镇私营企业和个体就业人员、城镇登记失业人员之和的比。计算公式为:

$$\text{城镇登记失业率}=\frac{\text{城镇登记失业人数}}{(\text{城镇单位就业人员}-\text{使用的农村劳动力}-\text{聘用的离退休人员}-\text{聘用的港澳台及外方人员})+\text{不在岗职工}+\text{城镇私营业主}+\text{城镇个体户主}+\text{城镇私营企业及个体就业人员}+\text{城镇登记失业人数}}\times 100\%$$

职工 指在国有、城镇集体、联营、股份制、外商和港、澳、台投资、其他单位及其附属机构工作，并由其支付工资的各类人员。不包括下列人员：(1)乡镇企业就业人员；(2)私营企业就业人员；(3)城镇个体劳动者；(4)离休、退休、退职人员；(5)再就业的离、退休人员；(6)民办教师；(7)在城镇单位中工作的外方及港、澳、台人员；(8)其他按有关规定不列入职工统计范围的人员。(1998年及以后的数据均为在岗职工数据，其他相关指标如职工工资总额，职工平均工资等指标也从1998年按此口径进行了相应调整)。

国有单位 指资产归国家所有的经济组织。包括按《中华人民共和国企业法人登记管理条例》规定登记注册的非公司制的经济组织，以及中央、地方各级国家机关、事业单位和社会团体。

集体单位 指生产资料归集体所有，并按《中华人民共和国企业法人登记管理条例》规定登记注册的经济组织。

其他单位 包括股份合作单位、联营单位、有限责任公司、股份有限公司、港澳台商投资单位以及外商投资单位等其他登记注册类型单位。

在岗职工 指在本单位工作并由单位支付工资的人员，以及有工作岗位，但由于学习、病伤产假等原因暂未工作，仍由单位支付工资的人员。

工资总额 指各单位在一定时期内直接支付给本单位全部职工的劳动报酬总额。工资总额的计算原则应以直接支付给职工的全部劳动报酬为根据。各单位支付给职工的劳动报酬以及其他根据有关规定支付的工资，不论是计入成本的还是不计入成本的，不论是按国家规定列入计征奖金税项目的，还是未列入计征奖金税项目的，不论是以货币形式支付的还是以实物形式支付的，均包括在工资总额内。

平均工资 指企业、事业、机关单位的职工在一定时期内平均每人所得的货币工资额。它表明一定时期职工工资收入的高低程度，是反映职工工资水平的主要指标。计算公式为:

$$\text{平均工资}=\frac{\text{报告期实际支付的全部职工工资总额}}{\text{报告期全部职工平均人数}}$$

平均工资指数 指报告期职工平均工资与基期职工平均工资的比率，是反映不同时期职工货币工资水平变动情况的相对数。计算公式为:

$$\text{平均工资指数}=\frac{\text{报告期职工平均工资}}{\text{基期职工平均工资}}\times 100\%$$

平均实际工资指数 职工平均实际工资指扣除物价变动因素后的职工平均工资。职工平均实际工资指数是反映实际工资变动情况的相对数，表明职工实际工资水平提高或降低的程度。计算公式为:

$$\text{平均实际工资指数}=\frac{\text{报告期职工平均工资指数}}{\text{报告期城镇居民消费价格指数}}\times 100\%$$

专业技术人员 指从事专业技术工作的人员以及从事专业技术管理工作且已在1983年以前评定了专业技术职称或在1984年以后聘任了专业技术职务的人员。

专业技术人员具体指工程技术人员、农业技术人员、科研人员(自然科学研究、社会科学研究及实验技术人员)、卫生技术人员、教学人员(含高等院校、中等专业学校、技工学校、中学、小学)、民用航空飞行技术人员、船舶技术人员、经济人员、会计人员、统计人员、翻译人员、图书资料、档案、文博人员、新闻、出版人员、律师、公证人员、广播电视播音人员、工艺美术人员、体育人员、艺术人员及政工人员。

专业技术管理人员具体指企业、事业单位的领导；企业、事业单位下设的职能机构、企业的生产车间和辅助车间(或附属辅助生产单位)中从事生产、技术、经济管理和政治工作人员。

按照公务员管理或参照公务员管理的人员不统计为专业技术人员。

Explanatory Notes on Main Statistical Indicators

Economically Active Population refers to the population aged 16 and over who are capable to work, are participating in or willing to participate in economic activities, including employed persons and unemployed persons.

Employed Persons refer to the persons aged 16 and over who are engaged in social working and receive remuneration payment or earn business income. This indicator reflects the actual utilization of total labour force during a certain period of time and is often used for the research on China's economic situation and national power.

Persons Employed in Various Units refer to all the persons working in government agencies of various levels, political and party organizations, social organizations, enterprises and institutions, and receiving wages or other forms of payment. They include fully-employed staff and workers, re-employed retirees, teachers in schools run by the local people, foreigners and Chinese compatriots from Hong Kong, Macao, and Taiwan working in various units, part-time employees, employees of other units working temporarily at current posts, and employees holding the second job, but exclude staff and workers who have left their working units while keeping their labour contract (employment relation) unchanged. This indicator reflects the total number of laborers actually engaged in production or other operations in various units.

Persons Employed in Private Enterprises and Self-Employed Individuals in Urban Areas Persons employed in private enterprises refer to the persons employed in the private enterprises which have been registered at the departments of industrial and commercial administration and are situated at a county town (i.e. a town where the county government is located) for business operation or at urban areas with the level higher than a county town. The self-employed individuals in urban areas refer to persons who hold the certificates of residence in urban areas or have resided in the urban areas for a long time and have been registered at the departments of industrial and commercial administration and approved to be engaged in individual industrial or commercial business, including self-employed persons as well as helpers and hired labourers who work in the individual households engaged in industrial or commercial business.

Registered Urban Unemployed Persons refer to the persons with non-agricultural household registration at certain working ages (16-50 years for male and 16-45 years for females), who are capable of work, unemployed and willing to work, and have been registered at the local employment service agencies to apply for a job.

Registered Urban Unemployment Rate refers to the ratio of the number of the registered unemployed persons to the sum of the number of persons employed in various units (minus the rural labour force, retirees, and Hong Kong, Macao, Taiwan or foreign employees they employ) laid-off workers in urban units, owners and employees in urban private enterprises, urban self-employed individuals and the registered urban unemployed persons. The formula is as follows:

Registered urban unemployment rate = number of registered urban unemployed persons ÷(number of persons employed in urban units - rural labour force employed – retirees employed - Hong Kong, Macao, Taiwan or foreign employees employ + laid-off workers + owners and employees in urban private enterprises + self-employed individuals in urban areas + registered urban unemployed persons) × 100%.

Staff and Workers refer to persons working in, and receive payment from units of state ownership, collective ownership, joint ownership, share holding ownership, foreign ownership, and ownership by entrepreneurs from Hong Kong, Macao, and Taiwan, and other types of ownership and their affiliated units. They do not include 1) persons employed in township enterprises, 2) persons employed in private enterprises, 3) urban self-employed persons, 4) retirees, 5) re-employed retirees, 6) teachers in the schools run by the local people, 7) foreigners and persons from Hong Kong, Macao and Taiwan who work in urban units, and 8) other persons not to be included by relevant regulations. (Data of 1998 and afterward refer to fully employed staff and workers. Other related statistics such as total wage bill and average wage are adjusted since 1998 accordingly).

State-owned Units refer to economic units whose assets are owned by the state. Included are non-corporation units registered according to *Regulation of the People's Republic of China on the Registration of Enterprises and Corporations*, state organs, institutions and social organizations at the central and local levels.

Collective-Owned Units refer to economic units registered according to *Regulation of the People's Republic of China on the Registration of Enterprises and Corporations* where the means of production are collectively owned.

Units of Other Types of Ownership refer to units registered with other types of ownership, including cooperative units, joint ownership units, limited companies, share holding corporations, units invested by entrepreneurs from Hong Kong,

Macao, and Taiwan, and foreign-invested units.

Fully Employed Staff and Workers refer to persons who work in, and receive wages from their working units, as well as persons who have their work posts, but are temporarily absent from work for reasons of study or on sick, injury or maternal leave and still receive wages from their working units.

Total Wages Bill refer to the total remuneration payment to staff and workers in various units during a certain period of time. The calculation of total wages is based on the total remuneration payment to the staff and workers. Therefore, all the wages and salaries and other payments to staff and workers are included in the total wages regardless of their sources, category, and forms (in kind or cash). (Total wages of staff and workers in this yearbook include only total wages of fully employed staff and workers, excluding the living allowances distributed to those who have left their working units while keeping their labour contract/employment relation unchanged).

Average Wage refers to the average wage in money terms per person during a certain period of time for staff and workers in enterprises, institutions, and government agencies, which reflects the general level of wage income during a certain period of time and is calculated as follows:

Average Wage = Total Wages of Staff and Workers at Reference Time /Average Number of Staff and Workers at Reference Time.

Average Wage Indices refers to the ratio of average wage of staff and workers in the report period to that in the base period, which reflects the change of wage of staff and workers at the different period. It is calculated as follows:

Average Wage Indices = Average Wage of Staff and Workers at Reference Time / Average Wage of Staff and Workers at Base Period x 100%

Average Real Wage Indices average real wage of staff and workers refers to the average wage of staff and workers after removing the effects of the price changes and average real wage indices of staff and workers refers to the change of real wage, which reflects the relative increasing or decreasing level of real wage of staff and workers, which is calculated as follows:

Average Real Wage Indices = Average Wage Indices of Staff and Workers at the Reference Time / Urban Consumer Price Indices at Reference Time x 100%

Professional Personnel refers to the persons who are engaged in special professional work or in professional management who got the titles of a professional post before 1983 or who were appointed to professional positions since 1984.

Professional personnel specifically refers to engineering professionals, agricultural professionals, scientific research professionals (natural science researchers, social science researchers and laboratory technicians), health professionals, teaching professionals (including institutions of higher education, specialized secondary schools, technical schools, regular secondary schools, and primary schools), civil aviation professionals, nautical professionals, economic professionals, accounting professionals, statistical professionals, interpretation professionals, library professionals, archives professionals, professionals of culture, arts and cultural relics, newsman and publishing professionals, lawyers, notary professionals, radio and television announcers, industrial arts professionals, sports professionals, artists and political professionals.

Professional management personnel specifically refers to the managers of enterprises and institutions, the personnel engaged in the management of production, techniques, economic and political aspects in the functional departments under the enterprise and institution, production workshops and accessorial workshops (or accessorial production units) under the enterprises.

Professional personnel excluded the personnel managed by or according to the system of civil servants.

6

固定资产投资

Investment in Fixed Assets

简要说明

一、本篇资料的主要内容

本篇资料通过对一定时期全社会建造和购置固定资产活动的数量方面的描述，反映报告期内固定资产投资的规模和速度、固定资产投资的结构和比例关系、固定资产投资的资金来源及固定资产投资的效果等。

二、本篇资料的统计范围

固定资产投资统计的范围包括：城乡建设项目投资，房地产开发投资，城镇和工矿区私人建房投资及国防、人防建设项目投资。

三、本篇的资料来源

跨省、区项目资料来自国务院各部门；农村集体和农村个人固定资产投资资料来自国家统计局农村经济调查总队的乡村社会经济调查；除此以外的固定资产投资统计资料均来自国家统计局固定资产投资统计司统计调查。

四、本篇的统计调查方法

除农村集体和农村个人固定资产投资统计采用抽样调查方法外，其他均为全面统计报表。

五、统计口径的变化

自1997年起，除房地产开发投资、农村集体投资、个人投资及城镇和工矿区私人建房投资外，固定资产投资的统计起点由5万元提高到50万元。为便于比较，对1996年的相应数据作了全面调整，括号内的数为原口径数。

Brief Introduction

I. Main Content

Statistics in this chapter describe activities on the construction and purchase of fixed assets of the whole society during a given period of time, and reflect the size, growth, structure, finance and results of the investment in fixed assets during the reference pe iod.

II. Coverage of Statistics

Statistics on the investment in fixed assets cover the investment in capital construction projects in urban and rural areas, the investment in real estate development, the housing investment by individuals in urban areas and in industrial and mining areas, as well as investment in national defence projects and civil air defence projects.

III. Sources of Data

Data on the trans-regional projects are provided by the various departments under the State Council. Data on the investment in fixed assets in collective units and by individuals in rural areas are provided by the Rural Socio-economic Survey Organization of NBS through its rural social and economic survey. Other data on the investment in fixed assets are from the surveys conducted by the Department of Statistics of Investment in Fixed Assets, NBS.

IV. Method of Data Collection

All data on the investment in fixed assets are collected by the statistical reporting system with complete enumeration, except data on the investment in fixed assets in collective units and by individuals in rural areas, which are collected through sample surveys.

V.Modification of Statistical Standard

Since 1997, the cut-off point of projects to be covered in the investment statistics are modified from an investment of 50, 000 yuan to 500,000 yuan for statistics of investment in fixed assets, except investment in real estate development, rural collective investment, individual investment and housing investment by individuals in urban areas and in industrial and mining areas. For the convenience of comparison, relevant data of 1996 are adjusted accordingly, and figures in brackets are compiled on the basis of the old standard.

6-1 全社会固定资产投资

Total Investment in Fixed Assets in the Whole Country

指　　标	Item	2004	2005	2005年比上年增长(%) Increase Rate in 2005 over 2004 (%)
投资总额　　(亿元)	**Total Investment　　(100 million yuan)**	**70477.4**	**88773.6**	**26.0**
按经济类型分	Grouped by Type of Ownership			
国有经济	State-owned Units	25027.6	29666.9	18.5
集体经济	Collective-owned Units	9965.7	11969.6	20.1
#农　村	Rural	8086.6	9737.9	20.4
私营个体经济	Individuals Economy	9880.6	13890.6	40.6
#农　村	Rural	3362.7	3940.6	17.2
联营经济	Joint Ownership Units	217.5	229.6	5.5
股份制经济	Share Holding Units	17697.9	23536.0	33.0
外商投资经济	Foreign Funded Units	3854.0	4657.1	20.8
港澳台商投资经济	Units with Funds from Hong Kong, Macao and Taiwan	3113.5	3767.3	21.0
其他经济	Others	720.6	1056.5	46.6
按城乡分	Grouped by Urban and Rural Area			
城镇	Urban	59028.2	75095.1	27.2
#房地产开发	Real Estate Development	13158.3	15909.2	20.9
农村	Rural	11449.3	13678.5	19.5
#农村个人	Rural Individuals	3362.7	3940.6	17.2
按资金来源分	Grouped by Sources of Funds			
国家预算内资金	State Budget	3254.9	4154.3	27.6
国内贷款	Domestic Loans	13788.0	16319.0	18.4
利用外资	Foreign Investment	3285.7	3978.8	21.1
自筹资金	Self-raising Funds	41272.6	55105.8	33.5
其他资金	Others	12963.7	15033.0	16.0
按构成分	Grouped by Use of Funds			
建筑安装工程	Construction and Installation	42803.6	53382.6	24.7
设备工具器具购置	Purchase of Equipment and Instruments	16527.0	21422.9	29.6
其他费用	Others	11146.8	13968.1	25.3
房屋建筑面积　(万平方米)	**Floor Space of Buildings　　(10 000 sq.m)**			
施工面积	Floor Space under Construction	376495.1	431123.0	14.5
#住宅	Residential Buildings	217580.5	239769.6	10.2
竣工面积	Floor Space Completed	207019.1	227588.7	9.9
#住宅	Residential Buildings	124881.1	132835.9	6.4

注：1.按资金来源分组为财务拨款数，各项相加不等于投资总额。
　　2.增长速度未扣除价格因素（以下各表同）。

a) Total investment grouped by source of funds refers to financial appropriation, and the subentry figures do not add up to the total.

b) The growth rates are calculated without removing the factor of price. The same as in the following tables.

6-2 按城乡分全社会固定资产投资

Total Investment in Fixed Assets in the Whole Country by Rural and Urban Area

单位：亿元 (100 million yuan)

年份 Year / 地区 Region		全社会投资 Total Investment	城镇 Urban Area	#房地产开发 Real Estate Development	农村 Rural Area	农户 Agricultural Households	非农户 Non-Agricultural Households
	1995	20019.3	15643.7	3149.0	4375.6	2007.9	2367.7
	1996	(22974.0)	(17627.7)	(3216.4)	(5346.3)	(2544.0)	(2802.3)
		22913.5	17567.2	3216.4	5346.3	2544.0	2802.3
	1997	24941.1	19194.2	3178.4	5746.9	2691.2	3055.6
	1998	28406.2	22491.4	3614.2	5914.8	2681.5	3233.3
	1999	29854.7	23732.0	4103.2	6122.7	2779.6	3343.1
	2000	32917.7	26221.8	4984.1	6695.9	2904.3	3791.6
	2001	37213.5	30001.2	6344.1	7212.3	2976.6	4235.7
	2002	43499.9	35488.8	7790.9	8011.1	3123.2	4887.9
	2003	55566.6	45811.7	10153.8	9754.9	3201.0	6554.0
	2004	70477.4	59028.2	13158.3	11449.3	3362.7	8086.6
	2005	88773.6	75095.1	15909.2	13678.5	3940.6	9737.9
北京	Beijing	2827.2	2595.4	1525.0	231.8	17.2	214.6
天津	Tianjin	1495.1	1364.0	327.5	131.1	29.3	101.8
河北	Hebei	4139.7	3307.8	391.5	831.9	237.4	594.5
山西	Shanxi	1826.6	1666.5	178.0	160.1	75.7	84.4
内蒙古	Inner Mongolia	2643.6	2555.3	162.1	88.3	62.1	26.3
辽宁	Liaoning	4200.4	3666.5	874.3	533.9	132.9	401.0
吉林	Jilin	1741.1	1581.3	195.7	159.8	103.1	56.8
黑龙江	Heilongjiang	1737.3	1581.2	267.6	156.1	140.8	15.3
上海	Shanghai	3509.7	3198.6	1246.9	311.1	7.1	304.0
江苏	Jiangsu	8165.4	6218.9	1545.2	1946.5	218.9	1727.6
浙江	Zhejiang	6520.1	4784.7	1456.5	1735.4	254.2	1481.2
安徽	Anhui	2525.1	2126.7	459.4	398.4	210.1	188.3
福建	Fujian	2316.7	1958.3	540.4	358.4	103.0	255.4
江西	Jiangxi	2176.6	1902.7	301.1	273.9	122.1	151.8
山东	Shandong	9307.3	7275.1	977.7	2032.2	347.8	1684.5
河南	Henan	4311.6	3461.2	388.5	850.4	450.2	400.2
湖北	Hubei	2676.6	2387.4	448.0	289.2	121.0	168.2
湖南	Hunan	2629.1	2204.0	457.0	425.1	194.7	230.4
广东	Guangdong	6977.9	5890.1	1591.9	1087.8	196.0	891.9
广西	Guangxi	1661.2	1480.9	286.8	180.3	147.0	33.3
海南	Hainan	367.2	339.2	70.8	27.9	17.7	10.2
重庆	Chongqing	1933.2	1777.1	517.7	156.1	58.3	97.8
四川	Sichuan	3585.2	2991.8	701.4	593.4	216.1	377.3
贵州	Guizhou	998.3	899.3	154.1	98.9	68.2	30.7
云南	Yunnan	1777.6	1592.3	246.9	185.3	138.5	46.8
西藏	Tibet	181.4	181.4	6.0			
陕西	Shaanxi	1882.2	1740.9	299.0	141.3	110.0	31.3
甘肃	Gansu	870.4	786.0	86.6	84.3	51.5	32.8
青海	Qinghai	329.8	310.8	29.1	19.0	10.1	8.9
宁夏	Ningxia	443.3	382.0	74.8	61.3	28.1	33.2
新疆	Xinjiang	1339.1	1210.0	101.7	129.1	71.7	57.4
不分地区	Not Classified by Region	1677.9	1677.9				

6-3 各地区按经济类型分全社会固定资产投资

Total Investment in Fixed Assets in the Whole Country by Ownership and Region

单位：亿元 (100 million yuan)

年份 地区	Year Region	总计 Total	国有经济 State-owned Units	集体经济 Collective-owned Units	#农村 Rural Area	私营个体经济 Individuals Economy	#农村 Rural Area
	1995	20019.3	10898.2	3289.4	2367.7	2560.2	2007.9
	1996	(22974.0)	(12056.2)	(3660.6)	(2802.3)	(3211.2)	(2544.0)
		22913.5	12006.2	3651.5	2802.3	3211.2	2544.0
	1997	24941.1	13091.7	3850.9	3055.6	3429.4	2691.2
	1998	28406.2	15369.4	4192.2	3233.3	3744.4	2681.5
	1999	29854.7	15947.8	4338.6	3343.1	4195.8	2779.6
	2000	32917.7	16504.4	4801.5	3791.6	4709.4	2904.3
	2001	37213.5	17607.0	5278.6	4235.7	5429.6	2976.6
	2002	43499.9	18877.4	5987.4	4887.9	6519.2	3123.2
	2003	55566.6	21661.0	8009.5	6554.0	7720.1	3201.0
	2004	70477.4	25027.6	9965.7	8086.6	9880.6	3362.7
	2005	88773.6	29666.9	11969.6	9737.9	13890.6	3940.6
北京	Beijing	2827.2	821.3	227.3	214.6	193.5	17.2
天津	Tianjin	1495.1	591.4	134.3	101.8	169.5	29.3
河北	Hebei	4139.7	1215.5	786.9	594.5	642.2	237.4
山西	Shanxi	1826.6	797.9	138.6	84.4	223.9	75.7
内蒙古	Inner Mongolia	2643.6	1233.5	73.4	26.3	273.1	62.1
辽宁	Liaoning	4200.4	1245.5	499.0	401.0	813.4	132.9
吉林	Jilin	1741.1	617.6	83.0	56.8	256.1	103.1
黑龙江	Heilongjiang	1737.3	784.1	31.1	15.3	294.0	140.8
上海	Shanghai	3509.7	1202.6	377.3	304.0	433.6	7.1
江苏	Jiangsu	8165.4	2043.6	1901.7	1727.6	1437.4	218.9
浙江	Zhejiang	6520.1	1738.2	1536.8	1481.2	942.1	254.2
安徽	Anhui	2525.1	847.3	224.6	188.3	541.0	210.1
福建	Fujian	2316.7	730.4	293.5	255.4	432.8	103.0
江西	Jiangxi	2176.6	862.3	196.3	151.8	441.3	122.1
山东	Shandong	9307.3	1674.5	2304.7	1684.5	1593.8	347.8
河南	Henan	4311.6	1311.3	554.7	400.2	892.6	450.2
湖北	Hubei	2676.6	997.2	221.1	168.2	421.8	121.0
湖南	Hunan	2629.1	965.0	306.1	230.4	446.3	194.7
广东	Guangdong	6977.9	1957.6	1109.2	891.9	964.5	196.0
广西	Guangxi	1661.2	666.9	63.5	33.3	392.2	147.0
海南	Hainan	367.2	159.7	12.7	10.2	36.9	17.7
重庆	Chongqing	1933.2	766.9	119.7	97.8	357.4	58.3
四川	Sichuan	3585.2	1202.7	418.5	377.3	629.5	216.1
贵州	Guizhou	998.3	537.7	39.8	30.7	161.4	68.2
云南	Yunnan	1777.6	815.3	63.0	46.8	279.4	138.5
西藏	Tibet	181.4	146.9	6.4		11.5	
陕西	Shaanxi	1882.2	990.9	77.6	31.3	224.9	110.0
甘肃	Gansu	870.4	505.5	58.1	32.8	108.6	51.5
青海	Qinghai	329.8	155.5	13.7	8.9	27.7	10.1
宁夏	Ningxia	443.3	189.2	34.6	33.2	89.2	28.1
新疆	Xinjiang	1339.1	557.9	62.4	57.4	159.0	71.7
不分地区	Not Classified by Region	1677.9	1334.9				

6-3 续表 continued

单位：亿元 (100 million yuan)

年份 地区	Year Region	联营经济 Joint Ownership Units	股份制经济 Share Holding Units	外商投资经济 Foreign Funded Units	港澳台商投资经济 Units with Funds From Hong Kong, Macao and Taiwan	其他经济 Others
	1995	118.5	864.0	1555.3	673.6	60.0
	1996	(126.9)	(1035.1)	(1876.7)	(835.5)	(172.0)
		126.8	1034.6	1876.1	835.4	171.8
	1997	123.1	1387.2	1955.9	937.1	165.7
	1998	60.5	1947.0	1639.6	1334.3	119.0
	1999	97.9	2478.9	1433.4	1218.1	144.4
	2000	94.7	4061.9	1313.2	1293.1	139.6
	2001	94.5	5663.5	1415.5	1583.3	141.7
	2002	138.2	8328.8	1685.4	1765.3	198.2
	2003	188.0	12733.6	2533.7	2375.1	345.7
	2004	217.6	17697.9	3854.0	3113.5	720.6
	2005	229.6	23536.0	4657.1	3767.3	1056.5
北京	Beijing	4.2	1141.2	263.3	171.6	4.9
天津	Tianjin	1.8	367.0	161.6	49.7	19.8
河北	Hebei	22.6	1096.9	106.9	161.2	107.5
山西	Shanxi	18.9	601.2	10.3	29.4	6.3
内蒙古	Inner Mongolia	0.9	987.2	22.4	28.3	24.7
辽宁	Liaoning	3.0	1170.1	284.8	149.3	35.2
吉林	Jilin	0.4	639.5	83.8	45.0	15.8
黑龙江	Heilongjiang	1.4	573.3	34.7	9.6	9.0
上海	Shanghai	14.0	875.4	470.6	129.2	6.9
江苏	Jiangsu	5.7	1479.1	806.8	458.3	32.8
浙江	Zhejiang	3.7	1655.2	343.9	246.7	53.4
安徽	Anhui	2.0	711.8	62.6	94.2	41.6
福建	Fujian	7.0	341.7	210.9	265.2	35.2
江西	Jiangxi	2.4	502.1	58.2	81.3	32.8
山东	Shandong	63.2	2747.5	470.3	255.3	197.9
河南	Henan	6.9	1206.0	126.6	116.4	97.1
湖北	Hubei	17.1	739.1	114.5	91.0	74.8
湖南	Hunan	11.8	718.7	45.1	64.6	71.5
广东	Guangdong	20.8	1214.7	678.7	998.2	34.2
广西	Guangxi	5.0	385.2	63.4	68.7	16.1
海南	Hainan	0.9	119.8	23.2	13.1	1.0
重庆	Chongqing	5.0	550.8	59.4	58.3	15.5
四川	Sichuan	0.8	1149.9	59.4	85.3	39.1
贵州	Guizhou	0.9	236.1	12.3	7.6	2.4
云南	Yunnan	0.9	556.6	13.7	27.3	21.5
西藏	Tibet		11.5	0.3		4.7
陕西	Shaanxi	6.0	491.0	24.1	31.2	36.5
甘肃	Gansu	1.0	156.5	16.6	14.0	10.0
青海	Qinghai	0.5	120.2	8.3	1.1	2.7
宁夏	Ningxia	0.1	114.7	9.8	5.0	0.7
新疆	Xinjiang	0.4	532.9	10.3	11.3	5.0
不分地区	Not Classified by Region		343.0			

6-4 按资金来源和构成分全社会固定资产投资
Total Investment in Fixed Assets in the Whole Country by Sources of Funds and Use of Funds

年 份 Year	按资金来源分 Grouped by Sources of Funds				按构成分 Grouped by Use of Funds		
	国家预算内资金 State Budget	国内贷款 Domestic Loans	利用外资 Foreign Investment	自筹和其他资金 Self-raising Fund and Others	建筑安装工程 Construction and Installation	设备工具器具购置 Purchase of Equipment and Instruments	其他费用 Others
投资额(亿元) Investment (100 million yuan)							
1981	269.8	122.0	36.4	532.9	689.8	223.6	47.5
1982	279.3	176.1	60.5	714.5	871.1	291.4	67.9
1983	339.7	175.5	66.6	848.3	993.3	358.3	78.4
1984	421.0	258.5	70.7	1082.7	1217.6	509.2	106.1
1985	407.8	510.3	91.5	1533.6	1655.5	718.1	169.7
1986	455.6	658.5	137.3	1869.2	2059.7	852.0	209.0
1987	496.6	872.0	182.0	2241.1	2475.7	1038.8	277.3
1988	432.0	977.8	275.3	2968.7	3099.7	1305.4	348.8
1989	366.1	763.0	291.1	2990.3	2994.6	1115.8	300.0
1990	393.0	885.5	284.6	2954.4	3008.7	1165.5	342.7
1991	380.4	1314.7	318.9	3580.4	3647.7	1460.2	486.6
1992	347.5	2214.0	468.7	5050.0	5163.4	2125.1	791.6
1993	483.7	3072.0	954.3	8562.4	8201.2	3315.9	1555.2
1994	529.6	3997.6	1769.0	11531.0	10786.5	4328.3	1928.1
1995	621.1	4198.7	2295.9	13409.2	13173.3	4262.5	2583.5
1996	(629.7)	(4576.5)	(2747.4)	(15465.4)	(15153.4)	(4940.8)	(2879.8)
	625.9	4573.7	2746.6	15412.4	15109.3	4926.0	2878.3
1997	696.7	4782.6	2683.9	17096.5	15614.0	6044.8	3282.3
1998	1197.4	5542.9	2617.0	19359.6	17874.5	6528.5	4003.1
1999	1852.1	5725.9	2006.8	20169.7	18795.9	7053.0	4005.7
2000	2109.5	6727.3	1696.3	22577.4	20536.3	7785.6	4595.9
2001	2546.4	7239.8	1730.7	26470.0	22954.9	8833.8	5424.8
2002	3161.0	8859.1	2085.0	30941.9	26578.9	9884.5	7036.6
2003	2687.8	12044.4	2599.4	41284.8	33447.2	12681.9	9437.5
2004	3254.9	13788.0	3285.7	54236.3	42803.6	16527.0	11146.8
2005	4154.3	16319.0	3978.8	70138.7	53382.6	21422.9	13968.1
构成(%) Percentage							
1981	28.1	12.7	3.8	55.4	71.8	23.3	4.9
1982	22.7	14.3	4.9	58.1	70.8	23.7	5.5
1983	23.8	12.3	4.7	59.2	69.5	25.1	5.4
1984	23.0	14.1	3.9	59.0	66.4	27.8	5.8
1985	16.0	20.1	3.6	60.3	65.1	28.2	6.7
1986	14.6	21.1	4.4	59.9	66.0	27.3	6.7
1987	13.1	23.0	4.8	59.1	65.3	27.4	7.3
1988	9.3	21.0	5.9	63.8	65.2	27.5	7.3
1989	8.3	17.3	6.6	67.8	67.9	25.3	6.8
1990	8.7	19.6	6.3	65.4	66.6	25.8	7.6
1991	6.8	23.5	5.7	64.0	65.2	26.1	8.7
1992	4.3	27.4	5.8	62.5	63.9	26.3	9.8
1993	3.7	23.5	7.3	65.5	62.7	25.4	11.9
1994	3.0	22.4	9.9	64.7	63.3	25.4	11.3
1995	3.0	20.5	11.2	65.3	65.8	21.3	12.9
1996	2.7	19.6	11.8	66.0	66.0	21.5	12.5
1997	2.8	18.9	10.6	67.7	62.6	24.2	13.2
1998	4.2	19.3	9.1	67.4	62.9	23.0	14.1
1999	6.2	19.2	6.7	67.8	63.0	23.6	13.4
2000	6.4	20.3	5.1	68.2	62.4	23.7	13.9
2001	6.7	19.1	4.6	69.6	61.7	23.7	14.6
2002	7.0	19.7	4.6	68.7	61.1	22.7	16.2
2003	4.6	20.5	4.4	70.5	60.2	22.8	17.0
2004	4.4	18.5	4.4	72.7	60.7	23.5	15.8
2005	4.4	17.3	4.2	74.1	60.1	24.1	15.7

注：1.1993年及以后的资金来源为财务拨款数。

2.自1997年起，除房地产投资、农村集体投资、个人投资以外，投资统计的起点由5万元提高到50万元。为便于比较，对1996年的相应数据作了全面调整，括号内为原口径数，未加括号的为调整后的新口径数（以下有关各表同）。

a) Since 1993, the sources of funds refer to financial appropriation.

b) Since 1997, the cut-off point of investment statistics is changed from a minimum of 50,000 yuan to the minimum of 500,000 yuan, except statistics on real estate investment, rural collective investment and individual investment. For the convenience of comparison, relevant data of 1996 in this table were adjusted accordingly. Data in parenthesis were based on the old coverage. Data without parethesis are based on the new standard. The relative tables in the chapter are the same.

6-5 各地区全社会固定资产投资资金来源
Sources of Funds of Total Investment in Fixed Assets in the Whole Country by Region

单位：亿元 (100 million yuan)

年份 地区	Year Region	本年资金来源小计 Subtotal of Sources of Funds This Year	国家预算内资金 State Budget	国内贷款 Domestic Loans	利用外资 Foreign Investment	自筹资金 Self-raising Funds	其他资金 Others
	1995	20524.9	621.1	4198.7	2295.9	10647.9	2761.3
	1996	(23419.0)	(629.7)	(4576.5)	(2747.4)	(11197.4)	(4388.4)
		23358.6	625.9	4573.7	2746.6	11151.0	4261.4
	1997	25259.7	696.7	4782.6	2683.9	12556.1	4540.4
	1998	28716.9	1197.4	5542.9	2617.0	14015.6	5344.2
	1999	29754.6	1852.1	5725.9	2006.8	14638.1	5531.6
	2000	33110.3	2109.5	6727.3	1696.3	16317.3	6260.1
	2001	37987.0	2546.4	7239.8	1730.7	18914.0	7556.1
	2002	45046.9	3161.0	8859.1	2085.0	22816.7	8125.2
	2003	58616.3	2687.8	12044.4	2599.4	31449.8	9834.9
	2004	74564.9	3254.9	13788.0	3285.7	41272.6	12963.7
	2005	94590.8	4154.3	16319.0	3978.8	55105.8	15033.0
北京	Beijing	4561.3	142.3	1059.7	70.9	1446.6	1841.8
天津	Tianjin	1828.6	28.5	435.9	122.5	921.1	320.7
河北	Hebei	4160.2	102.7	569.4	84.7	3024.1	379.3
山西	Shanxi	1879.6	63.7	414.2	25.7	1151.9	224.2
内蒙古	Inner Mongolia	2576.5	143.3	514.2	15.4	1696.9	206.8
辽宁	Liaoning	4318.0	173.8	540.2	128.0	2932.7	543.2
吉林	Jilin	1865.2	100.9	229.6	35.9	1182.4	316.3
黑龙江	Heilongjiang	1715.7	99.4	164.5	19.8	1207.5	224.5
上海	Shanghai	4196.1	46.4	952.3	235.6	1928.3	1033.6
江苏	Jiangsu	8578.9	80.1	1258.7	793.3	5271.7	1175.1
浙江	Zhejiang	6997.9	148.1	1450.4	318.9	3717.7	1362.8
安徽	Anhui	2639.8	135.3	488.1	128.5	1552.3	335.7
福建	Fujian	2608.8	163.7	531.4	132.6	1283.4	497.7
江西	Jiangxi	2244.9	155.9	298.6	96.2	1383.8	310.4
山东	Shandong	9490.0	179.3	991.2	423.6	6900.4	995.4
河南	Henan	4446.0	141.4	681.5	64.4	3039.1	519.6
湖北	Hubei	2729.2	221.9	474.9	72.7	1618.4	341.3
湖南	Hunan	2681.7	106.9	358.0	66.0	1787.4	363.4
广东	Guangdong	7741.3	78.0	1365.2	843.0	4095.4	1359.7
广西	Guangxi	1743.3	115.5	307.1	66.4	919.2	335.1
海南	Hainan	388.7	28.3	122.2	25.1	142.9	70.2
重庆	Chongqing	2081.6	116.0	492.5	42.9	943.1	487.0
四川	Sichuan	3671.2	136.1	532.6	59.6	2382.9	560.0
贵州	Guizhou	1037.8	43.9	304.3	8.5	558.8	122.3
云南	Yunnan	1774.7	123.4	483.4	18.0	851.6	298.2
西藏	Tibet	188.9	113.1	5.5	0.3	34.5	35.4
陕西	Shaanxi	1841.2	186.9	329.2	18.0	1029.2	277.8
甘肃	Gansu	871.2	82.4	170.9	14.1	475.5	128.3
青海	Qinghai	323.7	52.4	49.1	2.0	164.5	55.7
宁夏	Ningxia	417.3	42.1	83.9	6.6	223.3	61.5
新疆	Xinjiang	1340.9	209.3	167.5	11.0	754.0	199.1
不分地区	Not Classified by Region	1650.7	593.2	493.1	28.5	484.9	50.9

6-6 各地区全社会住宅投资

Total Investment in Residential Buildings in the Whole Country by Region

单位：亿元 (100 million yuan)

年份 Year / 地区 Region		合计 Total	城镇 Urban Area	#房地产 Real Estate Development	农村 Rural Area	#农户 Agricultural Households
1995		4736.7	3278.2	1753.1	1458.5	1349.9
1996		5198.5	3326.2	1699.2	1872.3	1766.4
1997		5370.7	3319.7	1539.4	2051.0	1890.7
1998		6393.8	4310.8	2081.6	2083.0	1907.2
1999		7058.8	5050.9	2638.5	2007.9	1799.1
2000		7594.1	5435.3	3312.0	2158.9	1946.5
2001		8339.1	6261.5	4216.7	2077.6	1879.5
2002		9407.1	7248.9	5227.8	2158.2	1917.7
2003		10792.3	8624.8	6776.7	2167.5	1875.1
2004		13464.1	11010.1	8837.0	2453.9	2002.2
2005		15427.2	12825.8	10860.9	2601.5	2211.6
北 京	Beijing	877.9	843.5	779.5	34.4	13.6
天 津	Tianjin	273.0	241.3	234.9	31.7	15.4
河 北	Hebei	607.6	458.4	292.1	149.2	128.6
山 西	Shanxi	211.7	164.9	116.9	46.8	46.0
内蒙古	Inner Mongolia	198.2	180.7	114.7	17.5	17.3
辽 宁	Liaoning	753.6	679.5	614.5	74.1	57.4
吉 林	Jilin	211.3	183.5	145.3	27.7	21.2
黑龙江	Heilongjiang	262.4	230.0	174.8	32.5	32.4
上 海	Shanghai	940.8	929.7	920.8	11.1	5.6
江 苏	Jiangsu	1386.5	1210.6	1133.1	175.9	113.1
浙 江	Zhejiang	1377.3	1169.0	1089.5	208.2	158.2
安 徽	Anhui	554.6	379.0	323.4	175.6	146.2
福 建	Fujian	437.9	381.3	363.7	56.7	50.7
江 西	Jiangxi	297.1	228.7	208.2	68.4	65.1
山 东	Shandong	1276.1	1028.9	698.3	247.2	179.4
河 南	Henan	713.6	404.2	271.6	309.4	306.6
湖 北	Hubei	441.6	350.9	317.6	90.7	86.5
湖 南	Hunan	504.8	362.1	306.1	142.7	133.8
广 东	Guangdong	1283.5	1121.0	1065.7	162.6	144.9
广 西	Guangxi	341.6	231.0	190.8	110.6	106.9
海 南	Hainan	78.6	67.9	56.6	10.8	9.9
重 庆	Chongqing	408.5	357.8	300.4	50.7	38.1
四 川	Sichuan	697.6	583.1	473.3	114.5	92.3
贵 州	Guizhou	142.4	101.9	85.9	40.5	39.9
云 南	Yunnan	322.6	235.0	173.4	87.5	83.5
西 藏	Tibet	19.5	19.5	4.3		
陕 西	Shaanxi	369.6	315.6	212.3	54.0	53.6
甘 肃	Gansu	140.0	114.5	61.1	25.5	23.6
青 海	Qinghai	27.8	22.7	16.6	5.1	5.0
宁 夏	Ningxia	63.6	54.2	47.5	9.4	9.4
新 疆	Xinjiang	166.3	135.8	68.0	30.5	27.4
不分地区	Not Classified by Region	39.6	39.6			

6-7 各地区按主要行业分的全社会固定资产投资

Total Investment in Fixed Assets in the Whole Country by Region and Sector

单位：亿元 (100 million yuan)

年份 Year / 地区 Region		合计 Total	农、林、牧、渔业 Agriculture, Forestry, Animal Husbandry and Fishing	采矿业 Mining	制造业 Manufacturing	电力、燃气及水的生产和供应业 Production and Supply of Electricity, Gas and Water	建筑业 Construction	交通运输、仓储和邮政业 Transport, Storage and Post
	2003	55566.6	1652.3	1775.2	14689.5	3962.4	924.4	6289.4
	2004	70477.4	1890.7	2395.9	19585.5	5795.1	964.0	7646.2
	2005	88773.6	2323.7	3587.4	26576.0	7554.4	1119.0	9614.0
北京	Beijing	2827.2	14.2	4.4	261.9	117.1	26.4	240.9
天津	Tianjin	1495.1	13.5	124.3	417.8	57.0	16.3	151.7
河北	Hebei	4139.7	224.3	134.1	1486.4	329.0	22.4	420.5
山西	Shanxi	1826.6	33.0	295.7	547.2	272.3	4.3	217.6
内蒙古	Inner Mongolia	2643.6	113.0	257.6	572.9	631.9	14.4	362.2
辽宁	Liaoning	4200.4	118.6	205.5	1564.0	140.2	67.3	301.6
吉林	Jilin	1741.1	100.0	89.2	650.9	88.7	17.3	175.1
黑龙江	Heilongjiang	1737.3	143.4	216.9	344.6	127.6	20.0	182.7
上海	Shanghai	3509.7	5.6	2.3	873.8	165.4	7.9	416.2
江苏	Jiangsu	8165.4	54.8	31.9	3560.9	632.2	58.5	585.5
浙江	Zhejiang	6520.1	78.8	8.9	2256.7	571.7	39.7	723.7
安徽	Anhui	2525.1	71.6	131.0	593.1	192.7	42.0	246.5
福建	Fujian	2316.7	60.7	21.4	607.2	261.0	39.1	270.9
江西	Jiangxi	2176.6	75.4	42.4	612.6	136.7	12.7	310.3
山东	Shandong	9307.3	246.4	329.8	4435.8	441.0	273.4	405.7
河南	Henan	4311.6	166.6	277.4	1315.8	351.1	26.1	541.4
湖北	Hubei	2676.6	70.9	48.0	744.8	272.7	98.3	292.7
湖南	Hunan	2629.1	82.7	70.7	617.6	232.5	39.3	216.6
广东	Guangdong	6977.9	47.5	19.9	2292.0	670.9	121.6	635.0
广西	Guangxi	1661.2	61.9	26.3	359.2	193.8	8.8	195.7
海南	Hainan	367.2	23.5	0.9	103.9	22.2	2.9	32.5
重庆	Chongqing	1933.2	45.1	36.3	336.4	160.6	35.9	228.3
四川	Sichuan	3585.2	102.4	162.4	860.8	402.2	27.5	278.0
贵州	Guizhou	998.3	24.6	41.6	133.1	239.7	1.9	144.7
云南	Yunnan	1777.6	74.0	69.4	226.8	339.4	7.3	337.5
西藏	Tibet	181.4	12.6	1.6	4.3	16.0	1.8	62.8
陕西	Shaanxi	1882.2	53.8	157.0	280.3	149.7	21.7	241.3
甘肃	Gansu	870.4	41.9	33.8	182.8	93.4	40.1	137.4
青海	Qinghai	329.8	12.6	37.6	69.4	55.7	8.2	58.8
宁夏	Ningxia	443.3	20.4	33.0	98.5	72.7	0.8	44.0
新疆	Xinjiang	1339.1	130.1	293.9	164.4	65.3	15.1	211.6
不分地区	Not Classified by Region	1677.9		382.1		51.9		944.6

6-7 续表 1 continued

单位：亿元 (100 million yuan)

年 份 地 区	Year Region	信息传输、计算机服务和软件业 Information Transmission, Computer Services and Software	批发和零售业 Wholesale and Retail Trades	住宿和餐饮业 Hotels and Catering Services	金融业 Financial Intermediation	房地产业 Real Estate	租赁和商务服务业 Leasing and Business Services	科学研究、技术服务和地质勘查业 Scientific Research, Technical Services, and Geological Prospecting
	2003	1660.7	922.7	423.0	90.2	13143.4	375.5	285.8
	2004	1657.7	1273.0	560.8	136.0	16678.9	420.8	333.1
	2005	1581.8	1716.4	808.8	109.5	19505.3	549.6	435.1
北 京	Beijing	80.6	27.7	24.8	1.6	1549.8	34.8	32.6
天 津	Tianjin	26.5	27.4	5.8	0.6	370.1	6.0	4.6
河 北	Hebei	68.5	159.0	32.3	4.6	618.4	31.9	47.6
山 西	Shanxi	31.2	26.4	9.3	1.7	233.7	1.1	5.3
内蒙古	Inner Mongolia	16.8	60.7	32.8	1.9	191.9	6.2	13.7
辽 宁	Liaoning	41.4	124.1	45.0	17.4	977.6	39.1	26.9
吉 林	Jilin	24.4	46.7	10.6	4.6	230.9	14.5	12.3
黑龙江	Heilongjiang	86.4	36.5	4.1	0.2	315.4	9.5	5.6
上 海	Shanghai	64.9	34.3	35.2	3.1	1384.3	15.6	16.9
江 苏	Jiangsu	80.9	125.2	54.3	2.3	1808.3	56.5	16.0
浙 江	Zhejiang	96.4	59.0	36.9	5.0	1719.9	71.3	10.4
安 徽	Anhui	33.9	41.6	39.6	1.9	628.5	20.9	12.0
福 建	Fujian	68.1	23.7	18.3	6.5	591.4	14.4	4.6
江 西	Jiangxi	66.5	35.8	32.3	3.1	391.2	9.8	4.0
山 东	Shandong	30.0	245.1	65.2	5.4	1467.1	58.6	40.0
河 南	Henan	67.5	114.2	43.6	4.5	817.0	26.8	24.8
湖 北	Hubei	49.6	63.6	33.3	2.7	568.9	12.5	16.2
湖 南	Hunan	53.1	116.0	39.7	4.6	643.9	18.7	14.7
广 东	Guangdong	227.9	77.2	65.4	9.3	1794.6	29.5	26.2
广 西	Guangxi	35.6	25.0	29.1	2.3	387.7	7.3	4.8
海 南	Hainan	14.0	4.2	26.2	2.3	74.8	1.4	1.4
重 庆	Chongqing	40.4	26.2	10.3	3.2	613.5	14.9	1.5
四 川	Sichuan	73.0	43.1	25.1	1.9	839.8	16.2	19.0
贵 州	Guizhou	29.8	13.3	11.6	1.8	200.1	4.0	4.1
云 南	Yunnan	48.1	29.3	26.3	2.8	351.2	3.7	2.8
西 藏	Tibet	12.5	4.8	2.5	1.7	10.2	0.5	0.8
陕 西	Shaanxi	47.7	68.2	23.6	5.3	329.7	11.1	31.9
甘 肃	Gansu	16.3	25.4	9.1	1.7	124.1	7.6	6.5
青 海	Qinghai	1.7	5.0	1.8	0.5	36.0	1.0	1.2
宁 夏	Ningxia	7.6	7.9	3.0	0.4	86.9	0.2	1.6
新 疆	Xinjiang	40.4	19.9	11.6	4.6	148.4	4.1	20.0
不分地区	Not Classified by Region							5.2

6-7 续表 2 continued

单位：亿元 (100 million yuan)

年 份 地 区	Year Region	水利、环境和公共设施管理业 Management of Water Conservancy, Environment and Public Facilities	居民服务和其他服务业 Services to Households and Other Services	教 育 Education	卫生、社会保障和社会福利业 Health, Social Securities and Social Welfare	文化、体育和娱乐业 Culture, Sports and Entertainment	公共管理和社会组织 Public Management and Social Organizations	国际组织 International Organizations
	2003	4365.8	241.6	1671.1	405.8	531.5	2153.7	2.5
	2004	5071.7	313.7	2024.8	516.7	773.4	2437.4	2.0
	2005	6274.3	363.5	2209.2	661.8	857.0	2926.8	0.2
北 京	Beijing	169.0	1.7	63.3	17.3	65.1	93.8	
天 津	Tianjin	179.8	6.0	40.5	9.6	14.7	22.8	
河 北	Hebei	171.2	19.5	115.2	43.6	28.5	182.7	
山 西	Shanxi	63.6	3.3	36.4	9.8	9.0	25.6	
内蒙古	Inner Mongolia	205.3	3.9	33.6	12.3	25.0	87.8	
辽 宁	Liaoning	265.1	14.0	92.8	22.7	33.5	103.4	
吉 林	Jilin	127.3	3.7	43.1	15.3	14.0	72.6	
黑龙江	Heilongjiang	89.8	5.5	48.3	16.8	16.7	67.3	
上 海	Shanghai	298.7	5.2	69.1	18.3	63.4	29.3	
江 苏	Jiangsu	579.7	32.1	152.6	45.2	74.5	214.0	
浙 江	Zhejiang	510.6	37.8	113.5	50.7	37.8	91.4	
安 徽	Anhui	225.9	5.4	58.5	14.9	101.6	63.6	
福 建	Fujian	140.2	6.1	66.6	17.2	18.7	80.5	
江 西	Jiangxi	233.9	2.6	81.8	25.5	20.8	79.2	
山 东	Shandong	354.5	28.3	207.3	49.7	54.0	569.9	
河 南	Henan	237.9	58.2	108.8	32.9	39.4	57.6	
湖 北	Hubei	200.6	4.0	88.0	19.8	25.5	64.4	
湖 南	Hunan	186.9	9.0	75.8	33.1	23.9	150.3	
广 东	Guangdong	487.0	9.1	208.1	53.9	68.9	133.9	
广 西	Guangxi	188.9	7.4	48.5	19.1	10.5	49.1	
海 南	Hainan	22.0	0.8	13.0	4.7	6.0	10.3	
重 庆	Chongqing	219.8	0.6	68.3	19.6	18.2	54.2	
四 川	Sichuan	460.2	45.9	104.9	35.5	24.1	63.3	
贵 州	Guizhou	62.6	1.9	29.7	9.0	8.5	36.3	
云 南	Yunnan	130.3	4.4	41.0	14.2	13.8	55.4	
西 藏	Tibet	8.6	0.4	11.3	2.0	3.0	24.1	
陕 西	Shaanxi	207.3	34.9	98.3	16.0	18.8	85.5	0.2
甘 肃	Gansu	33.7	3.9	40.6	11.9	6.9	53.1	
青 海	Qinghai	12.9	0.5	7.1	1.8	1.7	16.2	
宁 夏	Ningxia	41.1	0.3	12.6	3.0	1.0	8.2	
新 疆	Xinjiang	97.2	7.1	30.5	16.3	9.2	49.4	
不分地区	Not Classified by Region	62.6					231.4	

6-8 各地区全社会建设总规模

Total Investment in Construction in the Whole Country by Region

单位：亿元 (100 million yuan)

年 份 地 区	Year Region	建设总规模 Total Investment in Construction	在建总规模 Total Investment in Projects under Construction	在建净规模 Net Investment in Projects under Construction
	1995	62978.5	52026.7	26239.6
	1996	75188.0	61930.7	31876.7
	1997	81764.4	67126.6	33289.8
	1998	90449.9	74138.2	36186.6
	1999	96183.1	77120.2	36704.3
	2000	102129.2	79951.1	37288.4
	2001	118302.6	95244.0	49400.7
	2002	135312.8	108684.1	57505.9
	2003	163347.6	131733.0	69740.9
	2004	212275.1	175652.6	92728.5
	2005	270926.7	215349.7	116320.9
北 京	Beijing	11841.0	10118.8	4986.7
天 津	Tianjin	6482.7	5677.2	3591.7
河 北	Hebei	8658.5	6259.9	3383.3
山 西	Shanxi	5070.9	4114.5	2116.1
内蒙古	Inner Mongolia	6925.1	5186.1	3183.0
辽 宁	Liaoning	9925.1	7012.0	3970.3
吉 林	Jilin	3801.0	2510.4	1340.0
黑龙江	Heilongjiang	4035.9	2784.7	1585.9
上 海	Shanghai	16437.2	15068.7	6381.3
江 苏	Jiangsu	21863.1	15225.3	8021.7
浙 江	Zhejiang	20916.7	16397.2	8685.2
安 徽	Anhui	8101.1	6414.1	3835.9
福 建	Fujian	8572.6	7822.6	4376.5
江 西	Jiangxi	5429.1	4270.9	2166.5
山 东	Shandong	20738.8	14914.7	8493.6
河 南	Henan	9837.8	6738.6	3774.0
湖 北	Hubei	9453.8	7652.7	4170.8
湖 南	Hunan	7340.4	6319.1	2972.0
广 东	Guangdong	25890.8	21411.6	10179.5
广 西	Guangxi	5656.9	4651.4	2620.5
海 南	Hainan	1199.7	990.3	394.3
重 庆	Chongqing	8355.2	6992.9	4307.8
四 川	Sichuan	11247.7	9068.6	5740.8
贵 州	Guizhou	3781.0	3185.8	1813.0
云 南	Yunnan	6450.6	5816.8	3362.3
西 藏	Tibet	365.1	227.2	89.3
陕 西	Shaanxi	5187.1	4224.6	2137.5
甘 肃	Gansu	2707.5	2119.9	1018.1
青 海	Qinghai	1158.4	952.4	511.5
宁 夏	Ningxia	1343.4	1012.1	618.1
新 疆	Xinjiang	3190.7	2109.6	1021.3
不分地区	Not Classified by Region	8961.9	8099.2	5472.4

6-9 各地区全社会施工、竣工房屋面积和价值

Value and Floor Space of Buildings under Construction and Completed in the Whole Country by Region

年 份 地 区	Year Region	施工房屋建筑面积(万平方米) Floor Space of Buildings under Construction (10 000 sq.m)	#住 宅 Residential Buildings	#商品住宅 Commercial Buildings	竣工房屋建筑面积(万平方米) Floor Space of Buildings Completed (10 000 sq.m)	#住 宅 Residential Buildings	#商品住宅 Commercial Buildings	竣工房屋价 值(亿元) Value of Buildings Completed (100 million yuan)	#住 宅 Residential Buildings	#商品住宅 Commercial Buildings
	1995	215084.6	140451.9	32902.3	145600.1	107433.1	11951.3		3622.7	995.4
	1996	(236308.5)	(155849.3)	(31849.3)	(162849.3)	(122204.5)	(12232.6)		(4505.6)	(1194.3)
		235258.6	155508.9	31849.3	161965.7	121913.4	12232.6		4505.6	1194.3
	1997	230491.0	149658.1	30374.7	166057.1	121101.0	12464.7		4884.6	1269.9
	1998	245755.7	167600.8	36223.0	170904.8	127571.6	14125.7		5441.8	1484.1
	1999	263294.3	181236.4	42590.3	187357.1	139305.9	17640.7	9498.7	6019.9	1831.3
	2000	265293.5	180634.3	50498.3	181974.4	134528.8	20603.3	10078.2	6253.1	2173.6
	2001	276025.4	182767.1	61583.0	182437.1	130419.6	24625.4	10598.5	6501.0	2622.4
	2002	304428.2	193731.0	73208.7	196737.9	134002.1	28524.7	11758.4	7027.4	3191.0
	2003	343741.7	205286.7	91390.5	202643.7	130160.8	33774.6	13421.0	7631.2	4128.9
	2004	376495.1	217580.5	108196.5	207019.1	124881.1	34677.2	15239.6	8320.3	4620.7
	2005	431123.0	239769.6	129078.4	227588.7	132835.9	43682.9	18789.5	10042.3	6060.1
北 京	Beijing	14390.8	8316.2	7283.4	4891.9	3223.0	2841.4	1015.9	612.7	569.8
天 津	Tianjin	6295.2	3451.0	2827.9	2862.9	1687.3	1271.0	372.1	204.3	173.5
河 北	Hebei	18061.6	10187.7	3254.8	11283.6	6424.8	1021.8	734.1	389.4	121.6
山 西	Shanxi	6185.9	4046.8	1766.8	3380.0	2326.2	557.4	270.1	156.4	68.6
内蒙古	Inner Mongolia	6454.1	3248.3	1606.5	3454.0	1881.5	715.6	292.9	137.2	67.5
辽 宁	Liaoning	15665.6	8617.0	5536.4	8260.6	4819.2	2127.8	744.3	367.0	246.0
吉 林	Jilin	5548.2	2773.9	1525.2	3074.4	1438.5	496.1	283.0	104.0	49.3
黑龙江	Heilongjiang	7069.3	3925.7	1922.6	4148.1	2683.4	1039.4	383.1	224.0	108.6
上 海	Shanghai	14477.9	8303.7	8091.8	4873.8	2819.4	2739.9	1213.5	822.1	811.0
江 苏	Jiangsu	36334.4	16805.0	12386.0	20066.8	8128.4	4497.7	1861.8	786.4	591.1
浙 江	Zhejiang	36411.0	17639.6	12009.9	16097.5	7448.3	3208.9	1512.6	766.0	503.1
安 徽	Anhui	12641.9	8375.8	4301.2	7198.2	5080.5	1480.3	546.5	335.2	158.0
福 建	Fujian	17804.8	8832.8	4806.3	7139.8	4004.2	1304.9	464.0	254.4	164.2
江 西	Jiangxi	12418.3	7542.2	3657.2	6479.1	4295.8	1278.8	360.3	204.0	102.2
山 东	Shandong	42020.8	17303.6	8671.3	25926.3	9879.3	3063.5	1999.9	759.1	385.0
河 南	Henan	26647.1	17342.5	3895.4	17956.7	12915.6	1151.4	887.7	527.9	115.9
湖 北	Hubei	12522.4	8125.4	4012.1	7811.9	5268.6	1411.7	568.7	356.8	200.0
湖 南	Hunan	14914.3	9541.6	3799.4	8520.6	6173.3	1386.5	479.4	298.7	134.6
广 东	Guangdong	37046.7	17321.2	11400.0	16242.5	8196.0	3476.7	1742.2	880.5	632.5
广 西	Guangxi	12118.4	9077.5	3165.0	7523.5	6292.6	1090.3	394.1	289.0	91.3
海 南	Hainan	1899.6	1296.4	765.9	790.2	611.2	172.1	80.0	60.4	32.0
重 庆	Chongqing	12975.5	8349.1	5514.7	5842.3	3855.3	1713.6	474.5	280.0	184.1
四 川	Sichuan	19238.1	12080.0	6560.9	9484.2	6102.9	2225.5	545.8	313.5	167.4
贵 州	Guizhou	6433.0	4626.9	2113.2	3415.4	2657.9	567.9	168.5	107.8	45.9
云 南	Yunnan	10517.3	7118.2	2366.5	6811.6	5005.4	729.1	358.8	235.7	91.5
西 藏	Tibet	733.4	275.1	37.1	428.2	172.2	22.1	52.8	17.5	3.4
陕 西	Shaanxi	9174.7	5813.0	2651.7	4505.9	3052.3	677.1	400.7	232.4	102.3
甘 肃	Gansu	5281.3	3265.4	1134.2	2592.2	1783.9	365.5	166.3	95.4	38.5
青 海	Qinghai	1128.5	652.2	335.9	581.7	340.1	74.6	40.9	19.1	7.8
宁 夏	Ningxia	1981.1	1046.7	737.5	1219.4	706.0	420.8	107.8	54.8	39.2
新 疆	Xinjiang	6607.8	4463.2	941.6	4635.8	3559.8	553.5	262.2	150.3	54.1
不分地区	Not Classified by Region	124.1	6.0		89.3	2.7		4.9	0.1	

6-10 按资金来源和隶属关系分城镇固定资产投资

Investment in Fixed Assets in Urban Area by Sources of Funds and Jurisdiction of Management

单位：亿元 (100 million yuan)

年份 Year 地区 Region	按资金来源分 By Sources of Funds					按隶属关系分 By Jurisdiction of Management	
	国家预算内资金 State Budget	国内贷款 Domestic Loans	利用外资 Foreign Investment	自筹资金 Self-raising Funds	其他资金 Others	中央项目 Central Investment	地方项目 Local Investment
1995	569.0	3511.9	2114.1	7940.8	2013.7	4274.5	11369.2
1996	(679.2)	(5247.0)	(3018.4)	(14600.3)	(5340.8)	(4887.7)	(12740.0)
	576.4	3903.2	2475.6	7748.2	3308.9	4887.7	12679.5
1997	631.7	4136.7	2424.5	8722.3	3597.7	5521.6	13672.7
1998	1108.7	4918.0	2377.9	9885.5	4512.1	6121.6	16369.7
1999	1613.8	5249.8	1832.2	10042.9	4893.1	5894.6	17837.3
2000	1795.0	6245.8	1526.2	11227.5	5620.0	6275.6	19946.2
2001	2261.7	6672.5	1570.5	13708.5	6561.4	6586.6	23414.6
2002	2750.8	8167.5	1825.8	16567.7	7723.9	6526.7	28962.0
2003	2360.1	11223.9	2211.7	23617.4	9448.2	6113.6	39698.1
2004	2855.6	12842.9	2706.6	32196.1	12514.5	7524.6	51503.6
2005	3637.9	15363.9	3386.4	44154.5	14369.7	9111.0	65984.1
北京 Beijing	122.0	1048.5	69.0	1259.2	1830.7	362.9	2232.5
天津 Tianjin	28.1	420.3	113.8	824.1	311.1	213.2	1150.8
河北 Hebei	79.4	464.5	78.3	2333.3	372.8	290.1	3017.7
山西 Shanxi	58.5	409.7	25.4	1012.4	213.4	183.2	1483.2
内蒙古 Inner Mongolia	139.1	504.2	15.2	1626.1	203.5	238.5	2316.8
辽宁 Liaoning	164.1	501.9	117.3	2528.2	472.5	476.7	3189.8
吉林 Jilin	84.5	213.3	35.8	1061.2	310.5	235.7	1345.5
黑龙江 Heilongjiang	96.3	160.1	19.6	1067.3	216.4	406.5	1174.7
上海 Shanghai	45.3	925.7	204.7	1715.1	994.3	382.8	2815.8
江苏 Jiangsu	64.5	1118.1	639.3	3701.7	1108.8	308.8	5910.1
浙江 Zhejiang	103.8	1239.8	272.9	2401.1	1245.0	333.4	4451.3
安徽 Anhui	120.5	471.5	46.3	1283.5	319.6	158.8	1967.9
福建 Fujian	140.3	522.3	120.3	980.4	487.1	99.8	1858.5
江西 Jiangxi	112.8	287.7	87.6	1179.8	303.1	62.4	1840.2
山东 Shandong	136.4	803.9	360.0	5204.3	953.1	254.7	7020.4
河南 Henan	108.0	675.1	62.9	2258.9	490.8	203.7	3257.6
湖北 Hubei	195.7	468.3	60.9	1383.7	331.4	330.3	2057.1
湖南 Hunan	81.7	345.2	61.1	1462.2	306.4	175.5	2028.5
广东 Guangdong	60.9	1309.0	702.3	3262.9	1318.3	470.6	5419.5
广西 Guangxi	101.5	302.7	62.7	768.5	327.8	124.8	1356.1
海南 Hainan	25.3	120.9	24.6	121.5	68.4	79.9	259.3
重庆 Chongqing	116.0	484.1	42.9	808.9	473.6	162.6	1614.4
四川 Sichuan	88.8	522.2	58.4	1865.7	542.7	266.8	2725.0
贵州 Guizhou	33.9	296.4	8.5	478.0	122.1	231.1	668.2
云南 Yunnan	105.1	481.7	17.7	729.0	255.8	278.7	1313.6
西藏 Tibet	113.1	5.5	0.3	34.5	35.4	98.6	82.8
陕西 Shaanxi	178.3	323.9	17.8	905.2	274.6	193.4	1547.4
甘肃 Gansu	72.6	163.7	14.0	413.5	123.0	138.7	647.4
青海 Qinghai	46.5	48.5	1.9	153.6	54.2	79.7	231.2
宁夏 Ningxia	37.7	78.5	6.6	172.7	60.6	55.6	326.4
新疆 Xinjiang	183.9	153.7	9.8	673.1	191.4	535.5	674.5
不分地区 Not Classified by Region	593.2	493.1	28.5	484.9	50.9	1677.9	

6-11 按构成和建设性质分城镇固定资产投资

Investment in Fixed Assets in Urban Area by Use of Funds and Type of Construction

单位: 亿元 (100 million yuan)

年份 Year / 地区 Region		投资额 Total Investment	按构成分 By Use of Funds: 建筑安装工程 Construction and Installation	设备、工器具购置 Purchase of Equipment and Instruments	其他费用 Others	按建设性质分 By Type of Construction: #新建 New Construction	#扩建 Expansion	#改建 Reconstruction
	1995	15643.7	9395.1	3758.2	2490.4	4661.7	4488.2	1878.1
	1996	17567.2	10604.2	4375.2	2587.8	5534.3	5173.5	2011.9
	1997	19194.2	11626.2	4633.4	2934.6	6453.3	5528.9	2199.6
	1998	22491.4	13752.4	5127.2	3611.9	7804.7	6083.3	2791.8
	1999	23732.0	15176.4	5190.7	3365.0	7807.5	5992.5	3199.3
	2000	26221.8	16346.0	5846.7	4029.1	8484.5	6390.5	3827.0
	2001	30001.2	18739.0	6509.5	4752.8	9611.3	7410.8	3974.8
	2002	35488.8	21963.3	7268.0	6257.4	12366.1	7936.8	4611.5
	2003	45811.7	28091.3	9300.7	8419.7	18092.4	10249.9	4932.0
	2004	59028.2	36519.2	12455.6	10053.4	24630.1	12274.2	5929.6
	2005	75095.1	46154.1	16439.2	12501.8	34126.6	13154.5	8721.1
北京	Beijing	2595.4	1431.0	320.5	844.0	370.8	485.6	124.3
天津	Tianjin	1364.0	853.2	265.1	245.7	574.6	263.4	116.1
河北	Hebei	3307.8	1979.2	905.1	423.5	1859.2	633.2	280.8
山西	Shanxi	1666.5	1001.2	506.7	158.6	687.8	403.2	342.2
内蒙古	Inner Mongolia	2555.3	1773.5	554.6	227.2	1479.4	554.4	290.2
辽宁	Liaoning	3666.5	2161.3	882.1	623.1	1388.4	636.0	588.3
吉林	Jilin	1581.3	962.5	434.9	183.9	559.2	288.1	436.3
黑龙江	Heilongjiang	1581.2	1021.1	366.6	193.4	629.1	249.6	333.6
上海	Shanghai	3198.6	1859.5	520.1	819.0	1356.0	273.1	207.5
江苏	Jiangsu	6218.9	3689.3	1463.4	1066.2	2870.7	1219.8	464.6
浙江	Zhejiang	4784.7	2912.7	819.5	1052.5	2200.2	659.9	330.1
安徽	Anhui	2126.7	1287.3	453.3	386.1	1003.5	236.9	362.8
福建	Fujian	1958.3	1080.2	434.5	443.6	918.5	296.4	98.1
江西	Jiangxi	1902.7	1243.9	407.3	251.5	882.5	373.0	274.3
山东	Shandong	7275.1	4448.8	1967.2	859.0	3583.5	1706.8	741.0
河南	Henan	3461.2	2318.6	748.3	394.4	1961.6	666.8	343.5
湖北	Hubei	2387.4	1389.4	539.0	459.1	1066.2	390.3	405.0
湖南	Hunan	2204.0	1423.8	417.8	362.3	859.7	296.4	544.3
广东	Guangdong	5890.1	3621.5	1345.2	923.4	2565.2	1004.9	474.4
广西	Guangxi	1480.9	966.3	272.0	242.6	741.4	268.2	137.9
海南	Hainan	339.2	194.4	105.4	39.5	177.2	47.1	20.6
重庆	Chongqing	1777.1	1075.9	267.8	433.4	773.5	214.9	162.6
四川	Sichuan	2991.8	1747.0	582.6	662.3	1291.8	507.2	377.0
贵州	Guizhou	899.3	540.7	198.8	159.8	419.5	117.5	165.1
云南	Yunnan	1592.3	1055.1	252.4	284.8	874.8	242.2	191.6
西藏	Tibet	181.4	158.3	15.3	7.8	98.6	39.8	20.0
陕西	Shaanxi	1740.9	1172.6	289.8	278.5	832.1	302.6	217.2
甘肃	Gansu	786.0	543.0	164.5	78.6	386.4	193.9	99.6
青海	Qinghai	310.8	228.7	55.7	26.5	172.9	61.6	43.1
宁夏	Ningxia	382.0	244.5	92.5	45.0	182.1	41.7	73.8
新疆	Xinjiang	1210.0	865.4	224.4	120.1	339.7	365.7	306.3
不分地区	Not Classified by Region	1677.9	904.6	566.9	206.4	1020.3	114.3	148.8

6-12 城镇固定资产投资建设总规模

Total Investment in Fixed Assets of Construction in Urban Area

单位: 亿元 (100 million yuan)

年 份 Year 地 区 Region	建设总规模 Total Investment in Construction	在建总规模 Total Investment in Projects under Construction	在建净规模 Net Investment in Projects under Construction
1995	56212.4	47651.1	23871.9
1996	67105.8	56584.4	29074.5
1997	72961.9	61379.8	30234.2
1998	81301.8	68223.3	32953.3
1999	86717.2	70997.5	33361.1
2000	91641.7	73255.2	33496.8
2001	106854.6	88031.7	45164.9
2002	122413.7	100673.0	52618.0
2003	147038.7	121978.1	63187.0
2004	192739.3	167566.0	84641.9
2005	247510.3	205611.8	106583.0
北 京 Beijing	11394.5	9904.2	4772.0
天 津 Tianjin	6249.8	5575.3	3489.9
河 北 Hebei	7232.1	5665.4	2788.8
山 西 Shanxi	4826.4	4030.1	2031.7
内蒙古 Inner Mongolia	6810.4	5159.8	3156.7
辽 宁 Liaoning	8990.1	6611.0	3569.3
吉 林 Jilin	3584.4	2453.6	1283.2
黑龙江 Heilongjiang	3864.5	2769.4	1570.6
上 海 Shanghai	15822.1	14764.7	6077.3
江 苏 Jiangsu	18189.0	13497.8	6294.1
浙 江 Zhejiang	17700.1	14916.0	7204.0
安 徽 Anhui	7514.4	6225.8	3647.6
福 建 Fujian	7958.8	7567.2	4121.1
江 西 Jiangxi	5003.3	4119.0	2014.7
山 东 Shandong	17022.1	13230.2	6809.1
河 南 Henan	8587.2	6338.4	3373.8
湖 北 Hubei	8996.4	7484.4	4002.6
湖 南 Hunan	6684.8	6088.6	2741.6
广 东 Guangdong	23911.1	20519.8	9287.6
广 西 Guangxi	5443.4	4618.2	2587.2
海 南 Hainan	1161.6	980.0	384.0
重 庆 Chongqing	8101.3	6895.1	4210.0
四 川 Sichuan	10277.0	8691.4	5363.5
贵 州 Guizhou	3651.4	3155.1	1782.3
云 南 Yunnan	6218.4	5769.9	3315.4
西 藏 Tibet	365.1	227.2	89.3
陕 西 Shaanxi	5014.4	4193.2	2106.1
甘 肃 Gansu	2590.4	2087.1	985.2
青 海 Qinghai	1130.5	943.6	502.7
宁 夏 Ningxia	1249.0	978.9	584.9
新 疆 Xinjiang	3004.3	2052.2	963.9
不分地区 Not Classified by Region	8961.9	8099.2	5472.4

6-13 按行业分城镇固定资产投资和建设总规模（2005年）

单位：亿元

指标	Item	建设总规模 Total Investment in Construction	在建总规模 Total Investment in Projects under Construction	在建净规模 Net Investment in Projects under Construction
全国总计	**National Total**	**247510.3**	**205611.8**	**106583.0**
农、林、牧、渔业	**Agriculture, Forestry, Animal Husbandry and Fishing**	**1849.2**	**1211.4**	**647.4**
农业	Agriculture	438.7	288.0	156.0
林业	Forestry	554.0	400.9	235.6
畜牧业	Animal Husbandry	323.8	194.8	102.2
渔业	Fishing	92.6	59.9	26.7
农、林、牧、渔服务业	Service Activities for Agriculture, Forestry, Animal Husbandry and Fishing	440.0	267.7	130.8
采矿业	**Mining**	**6683.1**	**4978.2**	**2364.9**
煤炭开采和洗选业	Mining and Washing of Coal	3145.9	2665.0	1432.6
石油和天然气开采业	Extraction of Petroleum and Natural Gas	2258.4	1396.3	459.8
黑色金属矿采选业	Mining and Processing of Ferrous Metal Ores	533.3	378.9	172.2
有色金属矿采选业	Mining and Processing of Non-Ferrous Metal Ores	443.3	322.1	175.4
非金属矿采选业	Mining and Processing of Nonmetal Ores	295.9	210.9	129.8
其他采矿业	Mining of Other Ores	6.4	5.0	1.7
制造业	**Manufacturing**	**51872.4**	**39148.1**	**18383.6**
农副食品加工业	Processing of Food from Agricultural Products	1859.8	1249.6	651.4
食品制造业	Manufacture of Foods	1141.9	803.4	411.9
饮料制造业	Manufacture of Beverages	810.4	588.5	327.6
烟草制品业	Manufacture of Tobacco	297.6	234.0	112.8
纺织业	Manufacture of Textile	2346.8	1639.1	-382.8
纺织服装、鞋、帽制造业	Manufacture of Textile Wearing Apparel, Footware, and Caps	823.9	586.2	295.1
皮革毛皮羽毛(绒)及其制品业	Manufacture of Leather, Fur, Feather and Related Products	427.8	319.0	153.1
木材加工及木竹藤棕草制品业	Processing of Timber, Manufacture of Wood, Bamboo, Rattan, Palm, and Straw Products	526.6	347.5	165.8
家具制造业	Manufacture of Furniture	404.4	308.8	139.0
造纸及纸制品业	Manufacture of Paper and Paper Products	1490.2	1106.5	565.8
印刷业和记录媒介的复制	Printing, Reproduction of Recording Media	455.3	291.4	134.9
文教体育用品制造业	Manufacture of Articles For Culture, Education and Sport Activity	206.8	163.7	85.5
石油加工、炼焦及核燃料加工业	Processing of Petroleum, Coking, Processing of Nuclear Fuel	3065.3	2653.6	1798.8
化学原料及化学制品制造业	Manufacture of Raw Chemical Materials and Chemical Products	5825.9	4577.4	2197.9
医药制造业	Manufacture of Medicines	1632.2	1154.8	575.1
化学纤维制造业	Manufacture of Chemical Fibers	591.8	485.4	228.1
橡胶制品业	Manufacture of Rubber	581.3	443.5	250.4
塑料制品业	Manufacture of Plastics	1059.5	742.7	373.5
非金属矿物制品业	Manufacture of Non-metallic Mineral Products	3004.2	2029.1	973.2
黑色金属冶炼及压延加工业	Smelting and Pressing of Ferrous Metals	6575.7	5505.3	2574.2
有色金属冶炼及压延加工业	Smelting and Pressing of Non-ferrous Metals	2355.5	1836.0	972.5
金属制品业	Manufacture of Metal Products	1412.1	920.2	439.6
通用设备制造业	Manufacture of General Purpose Machinery	2056.9	1367.7	688.1
专用设备制造业	Manufacture of Special Purpose Machinery	1593.5	1104.3	520.7
交通运输设备制造业	Manufacture of Transport Equipment	4893.6	3986.1	2049.6
电气机械及器材制造业	Manufacture of Electrical Machinery and Equipment	1768.4	1257.8	669.6
通信设备、计算机及其他电子设备制造业	Manufacture of Communication Equipment, Computers and Other Electronic Equipment	3545.3	2618.0	1074.5
仪器仪表文化办公用机械制造业	Manufacture of Measuring Instruments and Machinery for Cultural Activity and Office Work	380.4	251.8	144.3
工艺品及其他制造业	Manufacture of Artwork and Other Manufacturing	698.3	550.1	238.2
废弃资源和废旧材料回收加工业	Recycling and Disposal of Waste	40.9	26.4	15.5
电力燃气水的生产供应业	**Production and Supply of Electricity, Gas and Water**	**32468.8**	**29528.6**	**16942.3**
电力、热力的生产和供应业	Production and Supply of Electric Power and Heat Power	29522.6	26970.5	15763.0
燃气生产和供应业	Production and Supply of Gas	1079.2	979.7	477.0
水的生产和供应业	Production and Supply of Water	1867.0	1578.4	715.3
建筑业	**Construction**	**1316.7**	**908.5**	**455.9**
房屋和土木工程建筑业	Construction of Buildings and Civil Engineering	1153.7	795.6	398.5
建筑安装业	Building Installation	41.9	23.3	10.5
建筑装饰业	Building Decoration	17.8	7.6	4.2
其他建筑业	Other Construction	103.3	82.0	44.2

Investment in Fixed Assets in Urban Area by Sector and Total Investment in Construction (2005)

(100 million yuan)

投资额 Investment	#新建 New Construction	#扩建 Expansion	#改建 Reconstruction	建筑安装工程投资 Construction and Installation	设备工器具购置 Purchase of Equipment and Instruments	其他费用 Others
75095.1	**34126.6**	**13154.5**	**8721.1**	**46154.1**	**16439.2**	**12501.8**
842.8	**536.7**	**193.4**	**78.2**	**490.5**	**97.3**	**254.9**
218.1	139.6	39.5	22.8	133.1	23.5	61.5
180.1	109.2	54.3	13.8	76.4	5.3	98.4
175.3	119.7	47.1	5.9	97.0	28.2	50.1
45.9	36.7	6.2	1.7	27.9	9.5	8.5
223.4	131.4	46.4	34.0	156.2	30.8	36.5
3234.3	**1534.9**	**816.3**	**830.9**	**2040.9**	**852.2**	**341.2**
1162.9	521.0	225.7	400.8	584.9	434.7	143.4
1463.6	703.3	451.2	293.2	1135.8	198.4	129.4
278.1	140.6	72.5	56.4	143.4	105.6	29.1
182.3	88.4	37.4	52.9	107.6	54.3	20.4
143.3	79.2	28.3	27.3	66.8	58.0	18.4
4.1	2.5	1.2	0.3	2.3	1.3	0.5
20406.6	**10735.0**	**4761.9**	**3845.1**	**9222.9**	**9322.8**	**1860.8**
893.9	519.2	194.3	159.8	440.8	367.3	85.7
543.5	306.1	137.0	79.4	261.3	228.6	53.7
348.7	176.1	89.6	71.2	155.1	161.3	32.3
95.5	7.4	19.8	49.4	32.3	45.8	17.4
1059.2	567.4	291.9	134.3	447.2	529.6	82.4
384.3	261.1	72.1	31.8	219.1	121.4	43.8
202.7	128.8	38.1	23.9	112.7	69.6	20.4
280.9	180.3	59.5	32.1	131.1	124.3	25.5
189.1	128.7	33.5	18.4	105.9	58.7	24.4
549.3	253.5	175.8	103.7	214.7	286.9	47.7
227.5	117.4	40.2	41.1	101.0	106.6	20.0
88.6	60.9	17.3	5.7	53.3	26.5	8.8
801.3	344.0	229.7	209.4	351.1	365.9	84.3
2130.6	1232.9	460.2	370.0	957.0	953.0	220.6
696.1	381.5	153.5	131.2	352.2	257.7	86.2
175.7	82.8	60.6	25.6	64.8	97.9	13.0
200.6	95.5	59.3	35.3	82.0	104.2	14.3
475.4	317.0	76.6	54.4	215.9	216.2	43.3
1393.9	781.5	318.6	239.6	644.7	640.1	109.1
2305.2	659.5	764.6	800.6	932.2	1225.1	147.9
761.2	377.4	199.7	163.2	362.2	338.9	60.1
745.3	486.8	140.7	83.1	358.7	315.4	71.1
1025.2	558.6	222.1	169.9	489.3	429.4	106.4
784.5	442.5	150.2	132.1	393.5	314.3	76.7
1576.5	732.5	358.2	392.6	667.4	754.4	154.7
771.4	441.1	129.5	131.1	360.4	337.0	74.0
1215.6	762.7	193.7	106.9	431.7	703.1	80.8
161.3	87.1	31.3	26.0	70.3	77.5	13.5
305.2	232.5	41.8	20.8	204.5	59.4	41.4
18.5	12.1	2.9	2.3	10.7	6.4	1.4
7286.6	**4688.2**	**1823.0**	**711.4**	**3730.2**	**2562.0**	**994.4**
6503.2	4183.2	1653.9	609.0	3168.8	2429.4	905.0
274.6	191.7	49.5	31.8	191.6	54.3	28.7
508.7	313.3	119.7	70.6	369.7	78.3	60.7
664.3	**388.2**	**129.3**	**62.5**	**476.8**	**96.7**	**90.8**
589.2	344.9	115.5	57.7	434.2	74.4	80.6
26.5	12.4	5.9	2.0	14.6	9.8	2.2
10.9	6.4	1.9	0.8	6.1	3.6	1.2
37.7	24.5	6.0	1.9	22.0	8.9	6.8

6–13 续表

单位：亿元

指　标	Item	建设总规模 Total Investment in Construction	在建总规模 Total Investment in Projects under Construction	在建净规模 Net Investment in Projects under Construction
交通运输、仓储和邮政业	**Transport, Storage and Post**	**36606.8**	**30531.7**	**18116.0**
铁路运输业	Railway Transport	6357.5	5495.0	3777.5
道路运输业	Road Transport	20333.2	16644.9	9068.2
城市公共交通业	Urban Public Transport	4246.2	3789.4	2728.1
水上运输业	Water Transport	3113.1	2758.1	1421.0
航空运输业	Air Transport	1344.5	872.4	561.7
管道运输业	Transport Via Pipelines	155.6	98.6	33.2
装卸搬运和其他运输服务业	Loading, Unloading and Other Transport Services	123.1	92.1	47.0
仓储业	Storage	882.3	748.4	477.9
邮政业	Post	51.3	32.8	17.7
信息传输、计算机服务和软件业	**Information Transmission, Computer Services and Software**	**2824.9**	**1956.7**	**412.0**
电信和其他信息传输服务业	Telecommunications and Other Information Transmission Services	2604.5	1770.9	333.6
计算机服务业	Computer Services	45.5	38.2	15.6
软件业	Software	174.9	147.5	63.2
批发和零售业	**Wholesale and Retail Trade**	**3151.4**	**2155.2**	**1048.7**
批发业	Wholesale Trade	1447.6	1003.8	507.3
零售业	Retail Trade	1703.9	1151.4	546.1
住宿和餐饮业	**Hotel and Catering Services**	**1713.1**	**1318.3**	**580.2**
住宿业	Hotels	1359.9	1121.2	499.7
餐饮业	Catering Services	353.2	197.1	92.3
金融业	**Financial Intermediation**	**212.6**	**140.6**	**59.9**
银行业	Banks	151.3	89.5	32.4
证券业	Security Activities	32.9	31.4	20.6
保险业	Insurance	10.9	4.1	1.8
其他金融活动	Other Financial Activities	17.5	15.6	5.4
房地产业	**Real Estate**	**68209.9**	**59799.2**	**30537.4**
租赁和商务服务业	**Leasing and Business Services**	**1503.2**	**1255.9**	**661.8**
租赁业	Leasing	20.2	4.0	1.2
商务服务业	Business Services	1483.0	1251.9	660.7
科学研究、技术服务和地质勘查业	**Scientific Research, Technical Service and Geologic Prospecting**	**1286.2**	**1096.6**	**567.2**
研究与试验发展	Research and Experimental Development	545.4	480.4	223.8
专业技术服务业	Professional Technical Services	347.8	275.4	134.4
科技交流和推广服务业	Services of Science and Technology Exchanges and Promotion	228.6	196.8	114.1
地质勘查业	Geologic Prospecting	164.4	144.0	95.0
水利、环境和公共设施管理业	**Management of Water Conservancy, Environment and Public Facilities**	**22783.4**	**19775.9**	**10365.8**
水利管理业	Management of Water Conservancy	6026.1	5538.7	3616.0
环境管理业	Environmental Management	1172.8	982.5	471.9
公共设施管理业	Management of Public Facilities	15584.6	13254.7	6298.4
居民服务和其他服务业	**Services to Households and Other Services**	**375.1**	**304.3**	**187.0**
居民服务业	Services to Households	304.9	255.9	164.2
其他服务业	Other Services	70.2	48.4	23.5
教育	**Education**	**5454.9**	**4355.5**	**1866.5**
卫生、社会保障和社会福利业	**Health, Social Security and Social Welfare**	**1370.0**	**1023.3**	**477.3**
卫生	Health	1296.5	982.8	459.5
社会保障业	Social Security	19.5	8.8	3.9
社会福利业	Social Welfare	54.0	31.7	14.3
文化、体育和娱乐业	**Culture, Sports and Entertainment**	**2367.0**	**1965.5**	**966.7**
新闻出版业	Journalism and Publishing Activities	52.1	45.8	23.9
广播、电视、电影和音像业	Broadcasting, Movies, Televisions and Audiovisual Activities	371.9	278.9	77.0
文化艺术业	Cultural and Art Activities	678.9	580.6	271.5
体育	Sports Activities	582.5	521.8	270.7
娱乐业	Entertainment	681.7	538.3	324.1
公共管理和社会组织	**Public Management and Social Organization**	**5461.6**	**4158.4**	**1942.3**
中国共产党机关	Organs of Communist Party of China	58.1	41.0	12.7
国家机构	Government Agencies	4746.9	3639.4	1709.9
人民政协和民主党派	People's Political Consultative Conference and Democratic Parties	16.5	13.1	8.6
群众团体、社会团体和宗教组织	Non-Governmental Institutions, Social Organizations and Religion Organizations	140.0	123.9	54.3
基层群众自治组织	Grass Roots Self-governing Organizations	500.0	341.0	160.5
国际组织	**International Organizations**			

continued

(100 million yuan)

投资额 Investment	#新建 New Construction	#扩建 Expansion	#改建 Reconstruction	建筑安装工程投资 Construction and Installation	设备工器具购置 Purchase of Equipment and Instruments	其他费用 Others
8860.4	**5193.1**	**1488.5**	**1384.8**	**6502.9**	**1163.7**	**1193.9**
1267.7	518.9	206.8	267.6	715.0	359.3	193.4
5581.4	3556.6	810.1	1008.6	4686.4	244.3	650.8
531.1	380.6	21.2	14.3	206.4	173.8	150.9
779.3	384.6	278.3	42.2	475.9	199.8	103.6
302.4	84.4	76.7	25.9	127.1	131.9	43.4
79.6	34.2	44.2	0.7	65.4	9.7	4.5
43.5	18.7	12.5	10.8	31.6	8.4	3.6
258.5	207.5	34.1	12.9	185.2	31.7	41.6
16.9	7.6	4.7	1.8	9.9	4.9	2.1
1561.6	**427.8**	**775.6**	**332.3**	**638.3**	**839.0**	**84.3**
1490.2	377.1	763.6	326.0	599.2	823.9	67.1
18.5	12.4	3.1	2.5	10.8	4.6	3.2
52.9	38.4	8.8	3.9	28.4	10.5	14.0
1532.1	**1095.2**	**239.3**	**137.1**	**1119.8**	**187.2**	**225.1**
672.2	493.4	94.3	48.9	481.2	94.0	97.0
859.9	601.8	145.0	88.2	638.6	93.2	128.1
675.9	**443.4**	**120.3**	**92.2**	**496.2**	**77.1**	**102.6**
456.2	314.4	80.6	53.7	342.1	39.9	74.1
219.8	129.0	39.7	38.5	154.2	37.2	28.4
105.6	**53.4**	**16.0**	**7.6**	**65.2**	**30.1**	**10.4**
77.1	34.7	13.6	4.8	43.7	26.4	7.1
11.3	10.4	0.3	0.3	10.5	0.6	0.2
7.9	2.8	1.5	1.5	4.4	2.4	1.1
9.2	5.5	0.7	0.9	6.6	0.7	2.0
17098.2	**891.9**	**83.1**	**57.5**	**11905.1**	**258.5**	**4934.5**
486.2	**355.5**	**65.1**	**32.0**	**329.5**	**45.2**	**111.5**
14.2	4.5	1.3	0.9	2.4	11.2	0.7
471.9	351.0	63.9	31.1	327.1	34.0	110.8
424.5	**264.2**	**90.1**	**43.8**	**273.1**	**75.7**	**75.7**
177.0	107.6	39.9	15.8	117.5	33.8	25.7
116.0	82.8	13.5	12.6	67.6	17.6	30.9
70.0	53.9	11.7	2.5	50.3	5.1	14.6
61.5	20.0	25.1	12.9	37.7	19.3	4.5
6097.9	**3953.1**	**1341.4**	**717.6**	**4455.8**	**155.1**	**1487.0**
837.6	523.0	189.4	112.8	658.6	31.4	147.6
318.7	208.3	57.9	41.9	219.2	39.9	59.6
4941.7	3221.8	1094.1	562.9	3578.1	83.8	1279.8
135.5	**72.4**	**28.3**	**22.0**	**93.6**	**20.3**	**21.6**
97.6	47.6	25.2	18.0	71.9	9.8	15.9
37.9	24.7	3.1	4.0	21.7	10.5	5.7
1966.9	**1106.4**	**558.9**	**117.8**	**1614.4**	**138.7**	**213.8**
591.8	**278.0**	**173.1**	**49.6**	**405.3**	**135.0**	**51.5**
550.2	247.6	166.4	47.4	370.8	131.8	47.6
11.2	9.0	1.6	0.3	8.7	1.8	0.7
30.4	21.3	5.1	1.9	25.8	1.4	3.2
685.8	**527.1**	**88.0**	**44.3**	**456.4**	**79.2**	**150.2**
16.9	9.7	3.7	0.7	12.5	1.4	3.0
91.1	50.5	20.4	13.8	54.7	21.8	14.6
216.8	176.8	21.5	13.4	128.3	16.3	72.2
159.2	126.7	21.9	3.2	114.9	11.5	32.8
201.9	163.3	20.4	13.2	145.9	28.2	27.7
2438.1	**1582.2**	**362.7**	**154.5**	**1837.1**	**303.4**	**297.6**
25.4	10.7	9.8	1.5	20.9	2.1	2.4
2080.3	1338.9	322.9	134.6	1542.7	282.0	255.6
6.1	3.7	0.6	1.5	3.4	0.2	2.5
41.1	25.7	9.3	2.9	28.1	4.7	8.3
285.3	203.3	20.1	13.8	242.1	14.5	28.7

6-14 按行业、隶属关系和注册类型分城镇固定资产投资(2005年)

单位：亿元

指 标	Item	投资额 Investment	中央 Central Investment	地方 Local Investment
全国总计	**National Total**	**75095.1**	**9111.0**	**65984.1**
农、林、牧、渔业	**Agriculture, Forestry, Animal Husbandry and Fishing**	**842.8**	**47.4**	**795.4**
农业	Agriculture	218.1	21.2	196.8
林业	Forestry	180.1	7.5	172.6
畜牧业	Animal Husbandry	175.3	3.0	172.3
渔业	Fishing	45.9	0.2	45.6
农、林、牧、渔服务业	Service Activities for Agriculture, Forestry, Animal Husbandry and Fishing	223.4	15.5	208.0
采矿业	**Mining**	**3234.3**	**1443.8**	**1790.5**
煤炭开采和洗选业	Mining and Washing of Coal	1162.9	80.8	1082.1
石油和天然气开采业	Extraction of Petroleum and Natural Gas	1463.6	1311.0	152.6
黑色金属矿采选业	Mining and Processing of Ferrous Metal Ores	278.1	36.8	241.4
有色金属矿采选业	Mining and Processing of Non-Ferrous Metal Ores	182.3	5.3	177.0
非金属矿采选业	Mining and Processing of Nonmetal Ores	143.3	9.9	133.4
其他采矿业	Mining of Other Ores	4.1		4.1
制造业	**Manufacturing**	**20406.6**	**1609.5**	**18797.1**
农副食品加工业	Processing of Food from Agricultural Products	893.9	6.1	887.8
食品制造业	Manufacture of Foods	543.5	4.2	539.3
饮料制造业	Manufacture of Beverages	348.7	1.7	347.1
烟草制品业	Manufacture of Tobacco	95.5	66.1	29.4
纺织业	Manufacture of Textile	1059.2	7.0	1052.2
纺织服装、鞋、帽制造业	Manufacture of Textile Wearing Apparel, Footwear, and Caps	384.3	0.7	383.6
皮革毛皮羽毛(绒)及其制品业	Manufacture of Leather, Fur, Feather and Related Products	202.7	0.2	202.5
木材加工及木竹藤棕草制品业	Processing of Timber, Manufacture of Wood, Bamboo, Rattan, Palm, and Straw Products	280.9	0.0	280.9
家具制造业	Manufacture of Furniture	189.1		189.1
造纸及纸制品业	Manufacture of Paper and Paper Products	549.3	0.9	548.4
印刷业和记录媒介的复制	Printing, Reproduction of Recording Media	227.5	7.2	220.3
文教体育用品制造业	Manufacture of Articles For Culture, Education and Sport Activity	88.6		88.6
石油加工、炼焦及核燃料加工业	Processing of Petroleum, Coking, Processing of Nuclear Fuel	801.3	357.6	443.7
化学原料及化学制品制造业	Manufacture of Raw Chemical Materials and Chemical Products	2130.6	311.8	1818.7
医药制造业	Manufacture of Medicines	696.1	4.9	691.2
化学纤维制造业	Manufacture of Chemical Fibers	175.7	19.0	156.7
橡胶制品业	Manufacture of Rubber	200.6	0.3	200.4
塑料制品业	Manufacture of Plastics	475.4	4.3	471.1
非金属矿物制品业	Manufacture of Non-metallic Mineral Products	1393.9	10.4	1383.5
黑色金属冶炼及压延加工业	Smelting and Pressing of Ferrous Metals	2305.2	309.6	1995.7
有色金属冶炼及压延加工业	Smelting and Pressing of Non-ferrous Metals	761.2	80.0	681.1
金属制品业	Manufacture of Metal Products	745.3	13.3	732.0
通用设备制造业	Manufacture of General Purpose Machinery	1025.2	43.4	981.8
专用设备制造业	Manufacture of Special Purpose Machinery	784.5	70.0	714.5
交通运输设备制造业	Manufacture of Transport Equipment	1576.5	258.7	1317.8
电气机械及器材制造业	Manufacture of Electrical Machinery and Equipment	771.4	6.4	765.1
通信设备、计算机及其他电子设备制造业	Manufacture of Communication Equipment, Computers and Other Electronic Equipment	1215.6	20.2	1195.3
仪器仪表文化办公用机械制造业	Manufacture of Measuring Instruments and Machinery for Cultural Activity and Office Work	161.3	3.3	158.0
工艺品及其他制造业	Manufacture of Artwork and Other Manufacturing	305.2	2.5	302.8
废弃资源和废旧材料回收加工业	Recycling and Disposal of Waste	18.5		18.5
电力燃气水的生产供应业	**Production and Supply of Electricity, Gas and Water**	**7286.6**	**2237.1**	**5049.5**
电力、热力的生产和供应业	Production and Supply of Electric Power and Heat Power	6503.2	2194.3	4308.9
燃气生产和供应业	Production and Supply of Gas	274.6	39.2	235.5
水的生产和供应业	Production and Supply of Water	508.7	3.6	505.1
建筑业	**Construction**	**664.3**	**45.3**	**619.0**
房屋和土木工程建筑业	Construction of Buildings and Civil Engineering	589.2	39.8	549.4
建筑安装业	Building Installation	26.5	5.3	21.2
建筑装饰业	Building Decoration	10.9		10.9
其他建筑业	Other Construction	37.7	0.3	37.5

Investment in Fixed Assets in Urban Area by Sector, Jurisdiction of Management and Registration Status (2005)

(100 million yuan)

内　资 Domestic Funds	港澳台商投资 Funds from Hong Kong, Macao and Taiwan	外商投资 Foreign Funded	国有及国有控股 State-owned and State-holding	集　体 Collective- owned	私营个体 Individuals Economy
66670.7	**3767.3**	**4657.1**	**38676.7**	**2231.7**	**9950.0**
823.2	**6.4**	**13.2**	**549.1**	**29.6**	**110.6**
210.5	3.2	4.4	141.7	6.7	24.1
179.0	0.4	0.8	153.7	5.0	7.6
169.0	2.0	4.3	67.2	6.2	42.1
42.7	0.3	2.9	7.8	5.0	19.7
222.0	0.6	0.9	178.7	6.6	17.1
3199.5	**22.6**	**12.2**	**2412.4**	**94.5**	**284.2**
1156.5	6.1	0.4	804.8	64.7	106.6
1453.6	9.9	0.0	1416.5	0.5	3.2
272.3	2.5	3.3	94.9	8.5	87.9
173.7	2.2	6.4	67.0	13.2	37.4
139.3	1.9	2.0	28.1	7.6	47.3
4.0		0.1	1.1	0.0	1.8
15551.5	**1694.9**	**3160.1**	**5791.2**	**643.8**	**3578.5**
766.1	39.7	88.0	119.1	49.7	230.2
430.8	34.9	77.8	66.9	20.2	113.2
287.4	26.5	34.8	76.6	11.3	64.7
95.3	0.0	0.1	91.5	0.1	0.7
864.4	101.9	92.9	120.2	48.5	273.8
256.5	69.0	58.8	16.3	18.9	111.2
132.1	29.4	41.2	21.0	4.6	54.1
237.5	21.1	22.2	25.2	7.7	93.2
137.4	27.3	24.4	11.9	4.2	68.7
366.2	50.2	132.9	117.2	28.3	93.6
187.9	22.5	17.1	41.4	11.9	55.5
49.0	18.2	21.4	3.4	1.5	26.5
771.8	16.8	12.6	497.3	23.6	67.3
1531.0	173.1	426.5	796.9	43.0	261.2
591.0	55.4	49.7	137.7	21.3	100.6
110.8	21.4	43.5	49.2	2.0	21.3
138.3	15.3	47.0	20.0	6.6	42.8
347.6	51.2	76.5	32.7	31.6	129.1
1183.0	113.3	97.7	266.3	41.6	344.9
2032.7	129.9	142.6	1435.7	30.7	148.2
661.7	66.2	33.2	370.8	38.2	80.3
586.4	58.0	100.8	72.1	26.5	236.7
861.6	38.8	124.8	195.1	45.5	269.0
655.1	31.4	98.0	182.3	27.0	178.9
988.0	60.0	528.4	671.3	31.1	184.5
545.1	81.4	144.9	88.7	26.1	156.2
374.4	295.2	545.9	158.2	15.5	68.0
104.0	21.4	35.8	21.3	4.1	25.2
244.1	25.0	36.1	82.8	21.9	74.1
14.0	0.3	4.2	2.1	0.5	4.7
6722.8	**337.6**	**226.2**	**5661.6**	**85.5**	**148.1**
6016.3	313.2	173.7	5076.8	59.9	119.8
215.3	14.0	45.3	156.6	5.4	15.2
491.2	10.4	7.2	428.2	20.2	13.2
656.4	**3.5**	**4.4**	**381.4**	**56.4**	**61.2**
583.8	2.0	3.4	354.5	50.2	48.0
25.1	0.9	0.5	10.8	1.9	4.2
9.9	0.5	0.5	0.7	0.5	3.7
37.6	0.1	0.0	15.3	3.8	5.3

6-14 续表

单位：亿元

指 标	Item	投资额 Investment	中 央 Central Investment	地 方 Local Investment
交通运输、仓储和邮政业	**Transport, Storage and Post**	**8860.4**	**1778.6**	**7081.8**
铁路运输业	Railway Transport	1267.7	1121.8	145.9
道路运输业	Road Transport	5581.4	284.4	5297.0
城市公共交通业	Urban Public Transport	531.1	6.5	524.6
水上运输业	Water Transport	779.3	100.0	679.3
航空运输业	Air Transport	302.4	152.7	149.6
管道运输业	Transport Via Pipelines	79.6	62.6	17.0
装卸搬运和其他运输服务业	Loading, Unloading and Other Transport Services	43.5	2.5	41.1
仓储业	Storage	258.5	38.2	220.3
邮政业	Post	16.9	10.0	6.9
信息传输、计算机服务和软件业	**Information Transmission, Computer Services and Software**	**1561.6**	**753.9**	**807.7**
电信和其他信息传输服务业	Telecommunications and Other Information Transmission Services	1490.2	750.2	740.0
计算机服务业	Computer Services	18.5	3.0	15.6
软件业	Software	52.9	0.8	52.2
批发和零售业	**Wholesale and Retail Trade**	**1532.1**	**45.4**	**1486.6**
批发业	Wholesale Trade	672.2	35.9	636.3
零售业	Retail Trade	859.9	9.5	850.3
住宿和餐饮业	**Hotel and Catering Services**	**675.9**	**11.2**	**664.7**
住宿业	Hotels	456.2	10.9	445.2
餐饮业	Catering Services	219.8	0.2	219.5
金融业	**Financial Intermediation**	**105.6**	**42.9**	**62.7**
银行业	Banks	77.1	34.9	42.3
证券业	Security Activities	11.3	3.3	8.0
保险业	Insurance	7.9	4.5	3.4
其他金融活动	Other Financial Activities	9.2	0.3	9.0
房地产业	**Real Estate**	**17098.2**	**207.9**	**16890.3**
租赁和商务服务业	**Leasing and Business Services**	**486.2**	**10.7**	**475.5**
租赁业	Leasing	14.2		14.2
商务服务业	Business Services	471.9	10.7	461.3
科学研究、技术服务和地质勘查业	**Scientific Research, Technical Service and Geologic Prospecting**	**424.5**	**136.9**	**287.6**
研究与试验发展	Research and Experimental Development	177.0	77.4	99.6
专业技术服务业	Professional Technical Services	116.0	24.1	92.0
科技交流和推广服务业	Services of Science and Technology Exchanges and Promotion	70.0	1.3	68.7
地质勘查业	Geologic Prospecting	61.5	34.2	27.3
水利、环境和公共设施管理业	**Management of Water Conservancy, Environment and Public Facilities**	**6097.9**	**113.9**	**5984.0**
水利管理业	Management of Water Conservancy	837.6	83.3	754.2
环境管理业	Environmental Management	318.7	3.8	314.8
公共设施管理业	Management of Public Facilities	4941.7	26.8	4914.9
居民服务和其他服务业	**Services to Households and Other Services**	**135.5**	**0.6**	**134.9**
居民服务业	Services to Households	97.6	0.2	97.3
其他服务业	Other Services	37.9	0.4	37.6
教育	**Education**	**1966.9**	**224.4**	**1742.5**
卫生、社会保障和社会福利业	**Health, Social Security and Social Welfare**	**591.8**	**38.6**	**553.2**
卫生	Health	550.2	35.8	514.3
社会保障业	Social Security	11.2	2.4	8.8
社会福利业	Social Welfare	30.4	0.3	30.1
文化、体育和娱乐业	**Culture, Sports and Entertainment**	**685.8**	**41.2**	**644.6**
新闻出版业	Journalism and Publishing Activities	16.9	1.8	15.1
广播、电视、电影和音像业	Broadcasting, Movies, Televisions and Audiovisual Activities	91.1	11.6	79.5
文化艺术业	Cultural and Art Activities	216.8	10.1	206.7
体育	Sports Activities	159.2	15.4	143.8
娱乐业	Entertainment	201.9	2.3	199.6
公共管理和社会组织	**Public Management and Social Organization**	**2438.1**	**321.7**	**2116.5**
中国共产党机关	Organs of Communist Party of China	25.4	7.6	17.8
国家机构	Government Agencies	2080.3	309.2	1771.0
人民政协和民主党派	People's Political Consultative Conference and Democratic Parties	6.1	1.0	5.1
群众团体、社会团体和宗教组织	Non-Governmental Institutions, Social Organizations and Religion Organizations	41.1	3.8	37.3
基层群众自治组织	Grass Roots Self-governing Organizations	285.3	0.1	285.2
国际组织	**International Organizations**			

continued

(100 million yuan)

内 资 Domestic Funds	港澳台商投资 Funds from Hong Kong, Macao and Taiwan	外商投资 Foreign Funded	国有及国有控股 State-owned and State-holding	集 体 Collective-owned	私营个体 Individuals Economy
8644.0	**104.7**	**111.7**	**8082.5**	**83.2**	**113.5**
1267.2		0.4	1244.5	9.9	0.5
5505.8	49.8	25.8	5203.1	42.1	42.2
523.0	4.9	3.2	490.0	4.5	4.4
706.2	29.5	43.6	644.2	4.7	27.1
301.8	0.4	0.2	282.8	13.0	
78.3	1.0	0.2	75.5		0.1
41.2	2.0	0.3	26.8	1.2	3.8
204.0	16.6	38.0	99.7	7.8	35.4
16.5	0.4		16.0	0.1	0.0
1152.8	**219.9**	**188.9**	**1192.6**	**4.8**	**10.1**
1093.7	216.4	180.1	1168.6	3.2	2.0
17.0	1.4	0.1	7.6	0.2	3.8
42.2	2.1	8.7	16.4	1.4	4.2
1464.1	**27.6**	**40.4**	**329.0**	**138.3**	**294.3**
660.6	6.6	5.0	166.6	49.5	124.9
803.4	21.0	35.4	162.4	88.8	169.4
586.7	**43.9**	**45.3**	**125.2**	**33.3**	**181.7**
385.9	34.7	35.6	108.2	17.9	92.4
200.8	9.2	9.7	17.0	15.4	89.3
103.3	**1.4**	**0.9**	**73.8**	**9.2**	**0.4**
75.8	1.3	0.1	52.4	8.6	0.0
11.3			10.5	0.0	0.0
7.9	0.1		5.7	0.1	0.0
8.3	0.1	0.8	5.2	0.5	0.3
15126.8	**1213.9**	**757.5**	**3122.0**	**610.3**	**4845.5**
460.6	**15.4**	**10.2**	**217.3**	**39.4**	**39.6**
12.5		1.8	4.7	0.8	5.0
448.1	15.4	8.4	212.5	38.5	34.6
411.5	**4.1**	**8.9**	**356.7**	**3.8**	**10.2**
172.9	0.5	3.6	158.9	0.5	1.6
112.6	0.0	3.4	98.0	1.0	3.9
64.6	3.5	1.9	43.5	2.2	2.5
61.4		0.0	56.4	0.1	2.2
6037.2	**34.2**	**26.5**	**5557.5**	**101.5**	**65.7**
830.0	0.6	7.0	808.0	9.5	2.6
302.7	5.8	10.1	258.3	5.2	8.7
4904.5	27.8	9.4	4491.2	86.8	54.4
132.2	**1.0**	**2.3**	**60.4**	**11.8**	**31.6**
95.6	0.6	1.3	49.5	9.6	18.9
36.6	0.4	1.0	10.9	2.2	12.7
1952.2	**5.6**	**9.1**	**1699.8**	**54.0**	**86.4**
579.7	**2.8**	**9.3**	**502.2**	**13.7**	**30.0**
538.2	2.8	9.2	468.4	11.3	26.7
11.2			10.2	0.0	0.1
30.3		0.1	23.6	2.3	3.2
637.7	**19.8**	**28.3**	**495.4**	**24.4**	**38.4**
16.9			16.0	0.1	0.0
90.4	0.5	0.2	84.4	1.3	1.4
215.2	0.8	0.9	196.1	4.6	3.8
140.0	9.1	10.0	136.9	0.3	0.2
175.2	9.5	17.2	62.0	18.0	32.9
2428.5	**8.1**	**1.5**	**2066.7**	**194.6**	**20.2**
25.4			24.9	0.4	0.1
2071.3	8.0	1.0	1980.2	36.3	11.2
6.1			6.0		
40.6	0.0	0.5	26.3	1.2	0.9
285.2	0.1	0.0	29.3	156.8	7.9

6-15 城镇各行业投资资金来源和新增固定资产（2005年）

单位：亿元

指　　标	Item	本年资金来源合计 Total Funds This Year	国家预算内资金 State Budget	国内贷款 Domestic Loans
全国总计	**National Total**	**80912.3**	**3637.9**	**15363.9**
农、林、牧、渔业	**Agriculture, Forestry, Animal Husbandry and Fishing**	**840.6**	**178.4**	**33.7**
农业	Agriculture	217.6	34.8	7.3
林业	Forestry	177.7	73.3	3.4
畜牧业	Animal Husbandry	170.6	9.0	11.2
渔业	Fishing	50.4	0.3	3.1
农、林、牧、渔服务业	Service Activities for Agriculture, Forestry, Animal Husbandry and Fishing	224.3	61.0	8.8
采矿业	**Mining**	**3404.5**	**22.5**	**471.8**
煤炭开采和洗选业	Mining and Washing of Coal	1234.7	16.6	201.8
石油和天然气开采业	Extraction of Petroleum and Natural Gas	1537.2	3.2	222.9
黑色金属矿采选业	Mining and Processing of Ferrous Metal Ores	287.5	0.6	21.4
有色金属矿采选业	Mining and Processing of Non-Ferrous Metal Ores	196.7	2.0	14.9
非金属矿采选业	Mining and Processing of Nonmetal Ores	144.3	0.0	10.7
其他采矿业	Mining of Other Ores	4.1		0.1
制造业	**Manufacturing**	**20956.7**	**130.3**	**2482.2**
农副食品加工业	Processing of Food from Agricultural Products	911.6	4.2	89.4
食品制造业	Manufacture of Foods	552.0	1.2	46.1
饮料制造业	Manufacture of Beverages	360.0	1.8	30.6
烟草制品业	Manufacture of Tobacco	96.7	1.8	5.9
纺织业	Manufacture of Textile	1073.1	1.7	107.5
纺织服装、鞋、帽制造业	Manufacture of Textile Wearing Apparel, Footware, and Caps	402.4	1.0	19.3
皮革毛皮羽毛(绒)及其制品业	Manufacture of Leather, Fur, Feather and Related Products	209.0	0.2	7.3
木材加工及木竹藤棕草制品业	Processing of Timber, Manufacture of Wood, Bamboo, Rattan, Palm, and Straw Products	287.0	0.4	20.0
家具制造业	Manufacture of Furniture	187.5	0.1	10.3
造纸及纸制品业	Manufacture of Paper and Paper Products	565.9	0.7	91.9
印刷业和记录媒介的复制	Printing, Reproduction of Recording Media	234.4	0.5	13.0
文教体育用品制造业	Manufacture of Articles For Culture, Education and Sport Activity	89.5	0.0	4.4
石油加工、炼焦及核燃料加工业	Processing of Petroleum, Coking, Processing of Nuclear Fuel	834.3	4.1	151.1
化学原料及化学制品制造业	Manufacture of Raw Chemical Materials and Chemical Products	2128.9	10.5	402.8
医药制造业	Manufacture of Medicines	709.0	6.4	80.9
化学纤维制造业	Manufacture of Chemical Fibers	187.0	0.3	27.8
橡胶制品业	Manufacture of Rubber	201.2	0.2	13.0
塑料制品业	Manufacture of Plastics	492.5	0.1	39.0
非金属矿物制品业	Manufacture of Non-metallic Mineral Products	1451.8	1.8	169.2
黑色金属冶炼及压延加工业	Smelting and Pressing of Ferrous Metals	2307.9	0.6	336.3
有色金属冶炼及压延加工业	Smelting and Pressing of Non-ferrous Metals	793.8	16.0	120.6
金属制品业	Manufacture of Metal Products	760.3	0.7	43.5
通用设备制造业	Manufacture of General Purpose Machinery	1065.3	9.5	82.1
专用设备制造业	Manufacture of Special Purpose Machinery	794.8	26.3	71.8
交通运输设备制造业	Manufacture of Transport Equipment	1645.3	22.7	156.3
电气机械及器材制造业	Manufacture of Electrical Machinery and Equipment	807.7	2.7	63.5
通信设备、计算机及其他电子设备制造业	Manufacture of Communication Equipment, Computers and Other Electronic Equipment	1293.3	8.9	231.7
仪器仪表文化办公用机械制造业	Manufacture of Measuring Instruments and Machinery for Cultural Activity and Office Work	172.3	3.9	10.4
工艺品及其他制造业	Manufacture of Artwork and Other Manufacturing	323.1	1.9	34.2
废弃资源和废旧材料回收加工业	Recycling and Disposal of Waste	19.2	0.3	2.2
电力燃气水的生产供应业	**Production and Supply of Electricity, Gas and Water**	**7226.0**	**320.7**	**3130.0**
电力、热力的生产和供应业	Production and Supply of Electric Power and Heat Power	6437.3	255.8	2966.7
燃气生产和供应业	Production and Supply of Gas	275.0	5.7	60.8
水的生产和供应业	Production and Supply of Water	513.8	59.2	102.5
建筑业	**Construction**	**669.5**	**47.4**	**82.1**
房屋和土木工程建筑业	Construction of Buildings and Civil Engineering	594.5	45.1	75.5
建筑安装业	Building Installation	26.9	0.4	2.8
建筑装饰业	Building Decoration	11.1	0.0	0.2
其他建筑业	Other Construction	37.0	1.8	3.6

Sources of Funds of Investment and Newly Increased Fixed Assets in Urban Area by Sector (2005)

(100 million yuan)

利用外资 Foreign Investment	自筹资金 Self-raising Funds	其他资金 Others	投资额 Investment	新增固定资产 Newly Increased Fixed Assets	固定资产交付使用率(%) Rate of Projects of Fixed Assets Completed Put into Operation(%)
3386.4	**44154.5**	**14369.7**	**75095.1**	**45206.6**	**60.2**
18.5	**457.0**	**153.1**	**842.8**	**608.8**	**72.2**
7.2	120.3	48.1	218.1	154.8	71.0
3.7	62.6	34.7	180.1	127.9	71.0
2.8	119.9	27.7	175.3	127.5	72.8
1.2	40.1	5.7	45.9	30.9	67.4
3.6	114.0	36.9	223.4	167.6	75.0
47.1	**2570.5**	**292.6**	**3234.3**	**2015.8**	**62.3**
0.8	954.1	61.4	1162.9	518.2	44.6
34.4	1099.6	177.1	1463.6	1115.1	76.2
1.9	238.7	25.0	278.1	172.0	61.9
7.9	156.9	14.9	182.3	110.6	60.7
2.1	118.0	13.5	143.3	98.6	68.8
	3.2	0.8	4.1	1.3	32.3
2415.6	**14987.6**	**941.0**	**20406.6**	**13276.5**	**65.1**
60.2	701.5	56.4	893.9	594.2	66.5
62.7	415.7	26.4	543.5	355.2	65.3
26.7	282.2	18.7	348.7	216.1	62.0
	87.7	1.2	95.5	52.5	55.0
114.2	804.3	45.4	1059.2	681.8	64.4
80.5	288.1	13.5	384.3	256.0	66.6
43.9	146.2	11.4	202.7	129.6	64.0
23.2	223.2	20.3	280.9	187.4	66.7
20.5	149.3	7.3	189.1	115.3	61.0
115.1	339.5	18.6	549.3	379.5	69.1
20.6	190.4	10.0	227.5	164.3	72.2
27.6	53.8	3.7	88.6	50.6	57.2
10.2	619.7	49.1	801.3	368.0	45.9
280.8	1346.0	88.9	2130.6	1472.7	69.1
26.5	559.3	35.9	696.1	442.2	63.5
29.1	110.9	19.0	175.7	104.5	59.5
35.7	145.7	6.7	200.6	124.8	62.2
68.4	359.8	25.2	475.4	309.1	65.0
115.9	1090.6	74.3	1393.9	952.4	68.3
98.0	1799.7	73.1	2305.2	1571.8	68.2
49.1	565.6	42.3	761.2	499.2	65.6
96.4	585.2	34.5	745.3	493.5	66.2
83.5	848.5	41.8	1025.2	665.2	64.9
67.9	592.0	36.8	784.5	494.7	63.1
175.2	1191.1	100.0	1576.5	924.7	58.7
127.0	588.6	25.8	771.4	508.5	65.9
480.7	545.2	26.8	1215.6	868.6	71.5
37.5	112.5	7.9	161.3	107.6	66.7
36.5	232.3	18.3	305.2	170.3	55.8
2.0	13.2	1.5	18.5	16.3	88.2
172.3	**3159.5**	**443.4**	**7286.6**	**3429.3**	**47.1**
136.1	2697.4	381.3	6503.2	3006.1	46.2
14.3	175.7	18.4	274.6	118.1	43.0
22.0	286.4	43.7	508.7	305.1	60.0
4.6	**449.4**	**86.0**	**664.3**	**374.8**	**56.4**
4.1	389.3	80.4	589.2	327.3	55.6
0.0	21.7	2.1	26.5	21.9	82.4
0.4	10.2	0.3	10.9	8.6	79.1
0.2	28.2	3.2	37.7	17.0	45.1

6-15 续表

单位：亿元

指　　标	Item	本年资金来源合计 Total Funds This Year	国家预算内资金 State Budget	国内贷款 Domestic Loans
交通运输、仓储和邮政业	**Transport, Storage and Post**	**8427.9**	**1069.5**	**2759.5**
铁路运输业	Railway Transport	1288.4	446.2	333.7
道路运输业	Road Transport	5099.7	514.3	1864.4
城市公共交通业	Urban Public Transport	511.3	29.2	178.9
水上运输业	Water Transport	770.3	13.9	226.4
航空运输业	Air Transport	345.5	38.8	98.5
管道运输业	Transport Via Pipelines	81.3	8.1	5.2
装卸搬运和其他运输服务业	Loading, Unloading and Other Transport Services	46.8	5.2	7.1
仓储业	Storage	267.2	13.4	44.9
邮政业	Post	17.3	0.5	0.4
信息传输、计算机服务和软件业	**Information Transmission, Computer Services and Software**	**1559.3**	**17.9**	**103.4**
电信和其他信息传输服务业	Telecommunications and Other Information Transmission Services	1487.1	16.7	97.5
计算机服务业	Computer Services	19.9	0.7	0.3
软件业	Software	52.3	0.5	5.6
批发和零售业	**Wholesale and Retail Trade**	**1568.2**	**4.9**	**96.5**
批发业	Wholesale Trade	696.6	3.3	40.8
零售业	Retail Trade	871.6	1.6	55.7
住宿和餐饮业	**Hotel and Catering Services**	**691.3**	**5.8**	**55.8**
住宿业	Hotels	468.5	5.6	45.9
餐饮业	Catering Services	222.8	0.2	9.9
金融业	**Financial Intermediation**	**106.2**	**3.8**	**0.4**
银行业	Banks	77.9	3.5	0.2
证券业	Security Activities	10.2	0.0	
保险业	Insurance	7.9		0.2
其他金融活动	Other Financial Activities	10.2	0.3	0.0
房地产业	**Real Estate**	**22617.9**	**44.8**	**4010.9**
租赁和商务服务业	**Leasing and Business Services**	**511.7**	**7.7**	**67.1**
租赁业	Leasing	14.7		0.2
商务服务业	Business Services	496.9	7.7	66.8
科学研究、技术服务和地质勘查业	**Scientific Research, Technical Service and Geologic Prospecting**	**424.8**	**87.0**	**27.3**
研究与试验发展	Research and Experimental Development	180.7	42.3	10.4
专业技术服务业	Professional Technical Services	113.4	22.2	7.5
科技交流和推广服务业	Services of Science and Technology Exchanges and Promotion	66.9	4.5	7.8
地质勘查业	Geologic Prospecting	63.8	17.9	1.6
水利、环境和公共设施管理业	**Management of Water Conservancy, Environment and Public Facilities**	**6043.1**	**773.7**	**1411.9**
水利管理业	Management of Water Conservancy	864.3	295.1	150.8
环境管理业	Environmental Management	314.2	68.7	42.1
公共设施管理业	Management of Public Facilities	4864.6	409.9	1219.0
居民服务和其他服务业	**Services to Households and Other Services**	**142.2**	**16.2**	**5.8**
居民服务业	Services to Households	102.7	16.1	3.8
其他服务业	Other Services	39.5	0.1	2.0
教育	**Education**	**2013.1**	**183.5**	**381.2**
卫生、社会保障和社会福利业	**Health, Social Security and Social Welfare**	**594.4**	**70.1**	**71.9**
卫生	Health	553.4	63.1	70.0
社会保障业	Social Security	11.3	2.6	0.3
社会福利业	Social Welfare	29.7	4.4	1.6
文化、体育和娱乐业	**Culture, Sports and Entertainment**	**708.9**	**79.4**	**85.5**
新闻出版业	Journalism and Publishing Activities	23.3	0.9	2.1
广播、电视、电影和音像业	Broadcasting, Movies, Televisions and Audiovisual Activities	91.7	5.6	10.3
文化艺术业	Cultural and Art Activities	212.6	37.5	19.8
体育	Sports Activities	171.7	30.7	25.6
娱乐业	Entertainment	209.6	4.7	27.8
公共管理和社会组织	**Public Management and Social Organization**	**2406.1**	**574.3**	**86.8**
中国共产党机关	Organs of Communist Party of China	25.4	10.1	0.3
国家机构	Government Agencies	2034.3	555.9	73.9
人民政协和民主党派	People's Political Consultative Conference and Democratic Parties	6.1	1.0	
群众团体、社会团体和宗教组织	Non-Governmental Institutions, Social Organizations and Religion Organizations	45.7	2.0	6.3
基层群众自治组织	Grass Roots Self-governing Organizations	294.6	5.3	6.4
国际组织	**International Organizations**			

continued

(100 million yuan)

利用外资 Foreign Investment	自筹资金 Self-raising Funds	其他资金 Others	投资额 Investment	新增固定资产 Newly Increased Fixed Assets	固定资产交付使用率(%) Rate of Projects of Fixed Assets Completed Put into Operation(%)
212.1	**3872.2**	**514.5**	**8860.4**	**5235.8**	**59.1**
30.3	388.4	89.8	1267.7	626.1	49.4
63.8	2359.2	298.0	5581.4	3515.3	63.0
12.6	262.3	28.3	531.1	306.3	57.7
42.4	441.1	46.6	779.3	269.3	34.6
49.6	152.8	5.8	302.4	309.4	102.3
0.2	38.1	29.7	79.6	41.4	52.1
0.3	32.6	1.6	43.5	19.7	45.1
13.0	182.4	13.5	258.5	130.3	50.4
	15.2	1.1	16.9	18.0	106.2
21.2	**1379.0**	**37.8**	**1561.6**	**958.2**	**61.4**
18.4	1319.2	35.3	1490.2	928.2	62.3
0.3	17.6	1.0	18.5	8.3	44.8
2.6	42.3	1.4	52.9	21.6	40.9
30.9	**1275.8**	**160.1**	**1532.1**	**1019.4**	**66.5**
12.3	578.3	61.8	672.2	432.7	64.4
18.6	697.4	98.3	859.9	586.7	68.2
48.0	**531.2**	**50.5**	**675.9**	**431.7**	**63.9**
34.8	346.0	36.2	456.2	271.8	59.6
13.2	185.2	14.4	219.8	160.0	72.8
0.8	**91.1**	**10.1**	**105.6**	**81.5**	**77.2**
	66.3	8.0	77.1	65.5	85.0
	10.1	0.1	11.3	3.8	33.4
	7.2	0.5	7.9	7.1	89.4
0.8	7.5	1.5	9.2	5.1	55.3
274.9	**7821.1**	**10466.2**	**17098.2**	**10419.3**	**60.9**
8.0	**391.3**	**37.6**	**486.2**	**268.5**	**55.2**
	13.8	0.7	14.2	11.2	78.7
8.0	377.5	36.9	471.9	257.3	54.5
10.5	**255.4**	**44.6**	**424.5**	**196.2**	**46.2**
3.8	105.5	18.7	177.0	81.6	46.1
1.8	65.0	16.9	116.0	61.1	52.6
4.2	45.6	4.7	70.0	32.2	46.0
0.7	39.3	4.3	61.5	21.3	34.7
68.0	**3298.6**	**490.8**	**6097.9**	**3068.2**	**50.3**
14.1	347.3	57.0	837.6	480.8	57.4
8.0	168.8	26.6	318.7	182.2	57.2
45.9	2782.4	407.3	4941.7	2405.2	48.7
1.2	**106.0**	**12.9**	**135.5**	**75.4**	**55.6**
1.0	72.1	9.7	97.6	52.5	53.8
0.2	34.0	3.2	37.9	22.9	60.3
15.5	**1253.4**	**179.4**	**1966.9**	**1430.4**	**72.7**
8.0	**406.3**	**38.1**	**591.8**	**391.6**	**66.2**
7.0	381.1	32.1	550.2	359.7	65.4
1.0	6.3	1.0	11.2	10.1	90.5
	18.9	5.0	30.4	21.7	71.5
15.7	**455.5**	**72.8**	**685.8**	**374.7**	**54.6**
0.0	16.6	3.7	16.9	5.5	32.7
0.7	69.1	6.0	91.1	58.0	63.7
0.8	135.5	19.0	216.8	132.0	60.9
3.0	85.3	27.2	159.2	62.9	39.5
11.2	149.1	16.8	201.9	116.3	57.6
13.3	**1393.5**	**338.2**	**2438.1**	**1550.5**	**63.6**
	11.6	3.3	25.4	18.3	72.0
11.1	1136.4	257.1	2080.3	1338.2	64.3
	5.0	0.2	6.1	3.8	62.8
0.8	22.7	13.9	41.1	25.0	60.8
1.4	217.9	63.6	285.3	165.2	57.9

6-16 各地区按行业分城镇固定资产投资

Investment in Fixed Assets in Urban Area by Region and Sector

单位：亿元 (100 million yuan)

年份 地区	Year Region	合计 Total	农、林、牧、渔业 Agriculture, Forestry, Animal Husbandry and Fishing	采矿业 Mining	制造业 Manufacturing	电力、燃气及水的生产和供应业 Production and Supply of Electricity, Gas and Water	建筑业 Construction	交通运输、仓储和邮政业 Transport, Storage and Post
	2003	45811.7	535.0	1551.9	10744.0	3803.9	528.0	5669.0
	2004	59028.2	645.1	2126.3	14657.2	5525.1	526.3	7091.5
	2005	75095.1	842.8	3234.3	20406.6	7286.6	664.3	8860.4
北京	Beijing	2595.4	2.4	3.3	189.0	110.9	5.4	226.2
天津	Tianjin	1364.0	5.0	124.3	350.3	57.0	10.6	147.2
河北	Hebei	3307.8	61.2	119.5	1179.6	320.4	20.0	351.9
山西	Shanxi	1666.5	11.0	271.5	536.6	257.9	4.2	193.2
内蒙古	Inner Mongolia	2555.3	77.4	244.5	568.6	630.3	12.1	359.4
辽宁	Liaoning	3666.5	34.2	182.9	1359.3	138.7	24.6	280.6
吉林	Jilin	1581.3	18.8	87.6	630.9	88.7	13.0	156.5
黑龙江	Heilongjiang	1581.2	41.4	216.8	335.8	127.6	19.6	175.3
上海	Shanghai	3198.6	2.7	2.2	651.6	159.7	6.1	402.3
江苏	Jiangsu	6218.9	12.7	30.9	2172.4	572.3	36.3	535.3
浙江	Zhejiang	4784.7	11.0	2.3	1106.1	510.3	14.2	655.8
安徽	Anhui	2126.7	21.0	130.3	532.3	190.8	38.9	217.7
福建	Fujian	1958.3	12.7	8.9	490.6	240.8	22.7	228.7
江西	Jiangxi	1902.7	19.3	32.4	572.1	120.9	3.7	255.0
山东	Shandong	7275.1	72.0	310.8	3266.4	416.6	216.7	326.8
河南	Henan	3461.2	56.7	203.2	1116.1	348.8	7.5	468.4
湖北	Hubei	2387.4	40.8	38.5	690.4	271.0	9.7	287.0
湖南	Hunan	2204.0	27.7	46.8	516.3	226.6	32.1	181.1
广东	Guangdong	5890.1	15.4	19.1	1559.2	648.4	66.2	628.6
广西	Guangxi	1480.9	36.7	24.7	347.5	192.3	5.3	186.2
海南	Hainan	339.2	13.9	0.9	103.6	22.1	2.3	31.3
重庆	Chongqing	1777.1	31.6	29.7	300.8	156.0	17.4	221.0
四川	Sichuan	2991.8	35.1	72.2	715.2	398.9	5.5	227.6
贵州	Guizhou	899.3	4.9	39.5	127.6	239.4	1.9	127.8
云南	Yunnan	1592.3	29.1	67.2	219.6	337.5	3.2	335.2
西藏	Tibet	181.4	12.6	1.6	4.3	16.0	1.8	62.8
陕西	Shaanxi	1740.9	32.2	145.8	278.0	148.9	10.2	224.8
甘肃	Gansu	786.0	24.0	32.0	178.2	92.6	39.3	131.2
青海	Qinghai	310.8	8.2	37.5	69.0	55.6	8.2	54.8
宁夏	Ningxia	382.0	3.4	33.0	76.1	72.7	0.8	38.5
新疆	Xinjiang	1210.0	67.7	292.1	162.9	64.9	4.8	197.8
不分地区	Not Classified by Region	1677.9		382.1		51.9		944.6

6-16 续表 1 continued

单位：亿元 (100 million yuan)

年 份 地 区	Year Region	信息传输、计算机服务和软件业 Information Transmission, Computer Services and Software	批发和零售业 Wholesale and Retail Trades	住宿和餐饮业 Hotels and Catering Services	金融业 Financial Intermediation	房地产业 Real Estate	租赁和商务服务业 Leasing and Business Services	科学研究、技术服务和地质勘查业 Scientific Research, Technical Services, and Geological Prospecting
	2003	1645.7	791.4	321.3	86.2	11105.3	309.8	281.7
	2004	1638.0	1117.2	438.1	97.6	14547.0	361.7	311.8
	2005	1561.6	1532.1	675.9	105.6	17098.2	486.2	424.5
北 京	Beijing	80.3	14.0	15.8	1.6	1535.0	27.8	31.8
天 津	Tianjin	26.5	23.4	4.8	0.6	339.5	4.9	4.6
河 北	Hebei	66.4	124.9	29.3	4.2	478.1	30.0	47.6
山 西	Shanxi	31.1	25.9	9.0	1.6	187.0	1.1	5.3
内蒙古	Inner Mongolia	15.3	60.4	31.4	1.9	170.3	6.2	13.7
辽 宁	Liaoning	41.1	119.0	38.0	17.4	916.9	37.0	26.8
吉 林	Jilin	24.3	46.6	10.6	4.6	201.2	13.1	12.3
黑龙江	Heilongjiang	86.4	35.8	3.7	0.2	281.6	9.4	5.5
上 海	Shanghai	64.8	25.4	32.0	2.9	1369.9	12.3	15.1
江 苏	Jiangsu	80.7	111.8	49.5	1.4	1627.7	54.2	16.0
浙 江	Zhejiang	96.2	37.9	33.5	4.8	1516.0	49.3	9.5
安 徽	Anhui	33.6	38.4	23.9	1.9	498.2	14.7	12.0
福 建	Fujian	66.8	16.5	14.5	6.4	547.7	11.4	3.9
江 西	Jiangxi	66.4	35.7	32.2	3.1	322.5	9.8	4.0
山 东	Shandong	29.4	214.9	54.6	5.4	1184.9	49.1	40.0
河 南	Henan	65.0	103.5	36.8	4.4	544.2	26.4	19.0
湖 北	Hubei	49.6	62.4	33.2	2.7	478.9	12.5	16.2
湖 南	Hunan	52.8	108.1	38.7	4.3	495.2	18.6	14.7
广 东	Guangdong	227.0	67.6	54.2	9.1	1643.1	28.3	26.2
广 西	Guangxi	35.6	24.5	19.0	2.3	293.2	7.3	4.8
海 南	Hainan	14.0	4.1	18.2	2.2	72.5	1.1	1.4
重 庆	Chongqing	40.1	24.5	9.7	3.0	560.6	14.7	1.4
四 川	Sichuan	70.0	38.6	22.0	1.4	747.2	16.2	18.9
贵 州	Guizhou	29.8	13.0	6.6	1.8	160.1	4.0	4.1
云 南	Yunnan	48.0	28.6	10.9	2.8	266.4	3.1	2.8
西 藏	Tibet	12.5	4.8	2.5	1.7	10.2	0.5	0.8
陕 西	Shaanxi	44.3	67.7	19.2	5.3	305.2	11.0	31.9
甘 肃	Gansu	16.0	24.2	8.1	1.6	96.7	7.0	6.4
青 海	Qinghai	1.7	4.8	1.7	0.5	30.8	1.0	1.2
宁 夏	Ningxia	7.6	6.1	3.0	0.4	77.4	0.2	1.6
新 疆	Xinjiang	38.4	18.9	9.2	4.2	140.0	4.0	19.9
不分地区	Not Classified by Region							

6-16 续表 2 continued

单位：亿元 (100 million yuan)

年份 地区	Year Region	水利、环境和公共设施管理业 Management of Water Conservancy, Environment and Public Facilities	居民服务和其他服务业 Services to Households and Other Services	教育 Education	卫生、社会保障和社会福利业 Health, Social Securities and Social Welfare	文化、体育和娱乐业 Culture, Sports and Entertainment	公共管理和社会组织 Public Management and Social Organizations	国际组织 International Organizations
	2003	4220.2	65.6	1474.1	357.7	479.6	1841.2	0.3
	2004	4890.8	107.6	1803.0	446.9	531.2	2165.6	0.3
	2005	6097.9	135.5	1966.9	591.8	685.8	2438.1	
北京	Beijing	146.1	0.0	53.4	14.9	58.6	78.9	
天津	Tianjin	178.6	1.8	39.5	9.2	14.2	22.1	
河北	Hebei	160.4	6.2	94.3	33.1	22.0	158.6	
山西	Shanxi	63.6	0.9	30.8	8.8	7.9	18.9	
内蒙古	Inner Mongolia	205.2	2.7	32.1	11.8	24.7	87.2	
辽宁	Liaoning	259.1	11.1	85.2	21.4	33.1	40.2	
吉林	Jilin	127.0	3.6	41.7	14.7	13.9	72.1	
黑龙江	Heilongjiang	89.4	5.5	47.4	16.3	16.6	66.8	
上海	Shanghai	296.0	1.4	63.0	17.3	61.1	12.7	
江苏	Jiangsu	575.2	9.7	133.5	40.4	60.0	98.9	
浙江	Zhejiang	475.9	28.8	101.3	35.1	24.5	72.1	
安徽	Anhui	222.9	2.7	54.3	13.8	20.2	59.1	
福建	Fujian	129.7	1.6	54.2	15.7	13.5	72.1	
江西	Jiangxi	232.5	2.2	78.1	24.5	20.2	68.2	
山东	Shandong	327.0	16.4	186.1	44.3	51.8	461.7	
河南	Henan	230.9	7.7	105.5	30.2	29.2	57.6	
湖北	Hubei	194.6	3.5	87.4	19.4	25.4	64.0	
湖南	Hunan	183.9	5.3	64.0	28.2	18.9	140.7	
广东	Guangdong	485.6	6.1	181.1	53.1	62.0	109.7	
广西	Guangxi	188.5	2.2	40.6	18.2	9.7	42.4	
海南	Hainan	19.3	0.3	12.4	4.6	5.5	9.7	
重庆	Chongqing	215.8	0.5	63.4	18.6	17.4	50.6	
四川	Sichuan	444.2	3.7	83.1	29.3	17.5	45.2	
贵州	Guizhou	62.5	1.8	28.0	8.5	8.3	29.7	
云南	Yunnan	127.5	2.6	35.2	13.8	13.6	45.2	
西藏	Tibet	8.6	0.4	11.3	2.0	3.0	24.1	
陕西	Shaanxi	206.1	3.7	92.2	14.9	16.4	83.1	
甘肃	Gansu	31.7	1.1	28.9	10.2	5.9	51.0	
青海	Qinghai	11.3	0.2	5.4	1.7	1.7	15.6	
宁夏	Ningxia	41.0	0.3	9.1	2.9	0.6	7.2	
新疆	Xinjiang	95.1	1.5	24.3	14.7	8.4	41.3	
不分地区	Not Classified by Region	62.6					231.4	

6-17 各地区按项目规模分城镇固定资产投资

Investment in Fixed Assets in Urban Area by Size of Construction and Region

单位：亿元 (100 million yuan)

年 份 / 地 区	Year / Region	500万元以下 Less Than 5 Million Yuan	500万元-1亿元 5-100 Million Yuan	1-5亿元 100-500 Million Yuan	5-10亿元 500 Million-1 Billion Yuan	10亿元以上 1 Billion Yuan and More
	1995	1016.3	3696.7	2493.9	1029.0	3807.5
	1996	1061.6	4198.7	2931.8	1192.5	4371.5
	1997	1115.5	4409.1	3163.0	1282.1	5342.0
	1998	1333.4	5186.6	3585.9	1414.0	6508.7
	1999	1331.0	5821.7	3899.7	1494.3	6164.7
	2000	1246.8	6627.2	4485.1	1706.4	6219.1
	2001	1258.0	7597.6	5301.7	1854.9	6655.6
	2002	1287.4	9335.5	6335.3	2234.8	7505.8
	2003	1384.9	12274.2	8911.0	3286.6	9271.2
	2004	1397.2	14939.7	11576.9	4079.6	13246.6
	2005	1687.8	19892.7	14564.0	5206.1	17835.3
北 京	Beijing	3.2	130.1	288.4	167.3	481.4
天 津	Tianjin	10.0	232.8	233.4	82.1	478.1
河 北	Hebei	90.0	1258.2	762.7	185.7	619.6
山 西	Shanxi	24.1	377.8	374.7	163.6	548.3
内蒙古	Inner Mongolia	66.5	797.9	543.1	207.2	778.4
辽 宁	Liaoning	136.3	982.8	689.8	327.6	655.7
吉 林	Jilin	32.1	518.5	401.7	134.1	299.3
黑龙江	Heilongjiang	38.3	372.3	348.9	144.9	409.2
上 海	Shanghai	24.5	279.9	418.7	235.1	993.5
江 苏	Jiangsu	71.5	1472.2	1412.0	468.3	1249.8
浙 江	Zhejiang	51.8	1006.8	849.9	303.3	1116.3
安 徽	Anhui	66.0	621.6	386.5	149.0	444.2
福 建	Fujian	36.4	516.5	381.8	150.4	332.9
江 西	Jiangxi	33.0	670.6	381.7	151.0	365.3
山 东	Shandong	74.4	2663.9	2036.0	543.2	979.9
河 南	Henan	96.4	1338.8	801.7	211.9	623.8
湖 北	Hubei	82.9	758.2	395.3	117.8	585.2
湖 南	Hunan	70.2	835.9	392.4	92.9	355.6
广 东	Guangdong	95.0	1179.7	1045.0	429.3	1549.3
广 西	Guangxi	98.0	498.5	270.7	79.9	247.0
海 南	Hainan	11.0	74.8	54.3	20.1	108.2
重 庆	Chongqing	44.3	390.6	323.6	139.0	361.9
四 川	Sichuan	93.0	973.6	558.2	212.8	452.8
贵 州	Guizhou	62.9	222.5	118.7	52.8	288.3
云 南	Yunnan	57.1	360.6	255.8	87.5	584.4
西 藏	Tibet	25.5	83.1	43.8	14.3	8.7
陕 西	Shaanxi	44.1	484.9	348.0	166.4	398.4
甘 肃	Gansu	50.7	273.5	136.4	34.7	204.0
青 海	Qinghai	19.7	82.4	54.6	36.6	88.5
宁 夏	Ningxia	12.9	95.7	68.8	22.5	107.2
新 疆	Xinjiang	65.8	337.9	178.0	61.6	465.1
不分地区	Not Classified by Region		0.2	9.5	13.0	1655.2

注：本表不含房地产和城镇工矿区投资。

a) Data in this table exclude real estate investment and investment in industrial and mining areas in urban area.

6-18 各地区城镇能源工业投资

Investment in Energy Industry in Urban Area by Region

单位：亿元 (100 million yuan)

年份 地区	Year Region	合计 Total	煤炭开采及洗选业 Mining and Washing of Coal	石油及天然气开采业 Extraction of Petroleum and Natural Gas	石油及炼焦加工业 Processing of Petroleum, Coking,	电力、热力及燃气的生产和供应业 Production and Supply of Electricity, Gas and Water
	2003	5508.4	436.4	946.0	322.0	3803.9
	2004	7504.8	690.4	1112.3	637.9	5064.2
	2005	10205.6	1162.9	1463.6	801.3	6777.8
北京	Beijing	116.9	0.4	0.0	12.4	104.0
天津	Tianjin	178.4		123.4	8.3	46.7
河北	Hebei	417.3	43.4	24.9	55.3	293.7
山西	Shanxi	602.7	258.8		94.0	249.9
内蒙古	Inner Mongolia	789.7	109.5	22.2	51.1	606.9
辽宁	Liaoning	320.7	25.0	94.9	78.3	122.4
吉林	Jilin	159.9	9.0	66.4	3.2	81.2
黑龙江	Heilongjiang	335.3	40.7	166.4	24.6	103.6
上海	Shanghai	139.0		1.7	5.5	131.8
江苏	Jiangsu	559.9	13.4	12.6	11.1	522.9
浙江	Zhejiang	478.1	0.3		8.9	468.8
安徽	Anhui	294.5	106.8	0.0	13.7	173.9
福建	Fujian	246.8	4.5		11.8	230.4
江西	Jiangxi	133.3	9.4		11.9	112.0
山东	Shandong	764.4	148.6	117.7	104.5	393.6
河南	Henan	497.8	102.9	55.4	18.8	320.8
湖北	Hubei	286.7	3.9	12.9	9.7	260.2
湖南	Hunan	248.7	18.4		15.0	215.3
广东	Guangdong	673.9	0.0	10.2	71.6	592.0
广西	Guangxi	187.1	5.2	0.2	2.6	179.1
海南	Hainan	82.5			62.7	19.9
重庆	Chongqing	163.5	23.7	0.7	3.1	136.1
四川	Sichuan	430.7	28.7	15.9	7.2	378.9
贵州	Guizhou	269.2	32.7	0.5	3.2	232.8
云南	Yunnan	371.3	37.1	0.0	9.6	324.6
西藏	Tibet	15.1		0.0		15.1
陕西	Shaanxi	300.7	36.7	95.7	26.3	142.0
甘肃	Gansu	142.0	13.0	6.1	36.6	86.2
青海	Qinghai	86.0	2.6	30.7		52.7
宁夏	Ningxia	104.5	33.0		2.4	69.1
新疆	Xinjiang	375.1	16.0	262.1	37.7	59.3
不分地区	Not Classified by Region	434.0	39.1	343.0		51.9

6-19 各地区城镇施工、竣工房屋建筑面积和价值

Value and Floor Space of Buildings under Construction and Completed in Urban Area by Region

年份 Year 地区 Region		施工房屋建筑面积(万平方米) Floor Space of Buildings Under Construction (10 000 sq.m)	#住宅 Residential Buildings	竣工房屋建筑面积(万平方米) Floor Space of Buildings Completed (10 000 sq.m)	#住宅 Residential Buildings	竣工房屋价值(亿元) Value of Buildings Completed (100 million yuan)	#住宅 Residential Buildings
	1995	120453.6	68557.9	58631.1	37489.1	4233.4	2171.8
	1996	123011.1	68834.7	61443.4	39450.5	4968.3	2634.2
	1997	120739.3	68568.0	62490.2	40550.2	5280.1	2833.6
	1998	136669.3	83872.8	70166.1	47616.9	6012.6	3358.8
	1999	144319.3	91835.4	79646.1	55868.9	6791.0	4012.2
	2000	151691.3	94441.6	80507.9	54859.9	7014.6	4122.1
	2001	166837.6	103643.6	85278.9	57476.5	7463.5	4463.7
	2002	189973.4	113848.5	93018.3	59793.6	8435.3	4920.0
	2003	221258.1	124386.5	93114.7	54971.5	10126.4	5883.7
	2004	259252.2	142936.6	101033.8	56897.3	11119.0	6144.1
	2005	304904.3	166143.4	118125.8	66141.9	13952.4	7682.8
北京	Beijing	13281.0	7937.5	4344.7	2987.5	957.0	597.1
天津	Tianjin	5210.4	2897.0	2022.9	1305.2	316.9	177.1
河北	Hebei	11164.8	5901.1	5028.8	2562.3	502.1	251.6
山西	Shanxi	4349.6	2540.2	1755.5	1015.4	209.3	110.8
内蒙古	Inner Mongolia	5623.0	2717.4	2669.1	1366.7	268.1	120.0
辽宁	Liaoning	12368.0	6316.0	5018.5	2525.1	601.3	283.6
吉林	Jilin	4580.1	2088.6	2011.3	765.3	246.6	75.8
黑龙江	Heilongjiang	6075.4	3072.6	3266.1	1935.7	349.3	194.5
上海	Shanghai	12801.8	8205.0	3911.3	2759.6	1129.5	816.3
江苏	Jiangsu	24951.8	13547.5	9904.0	5015.8	1221.0	639.0
浙江	Zhejiang	26069.0	13652.6	7869.5	4021.3	1035.3	581.0
安徽	Anhui	8782.3	5240.9	3592.3	2065.3	347.5	197.4
福建	Fujian	10962.8	5522.8	3244.8	1814.2	340.2	197.6
江西	Jiangxi	9273.3	4859.0	4080.1	2251.6	278.3	146.1
山东	Shandong	24379.6	11664.1	9420.6	4455.5	1070.4	525.8
河南	Henan	14063.5	7309.9	6591.8	3574.1	529.2	252.5
湖北	Hubei	8823.7	5318.0	4217.9	2556.1	442.8	268.3
湖南	Hunan	8490.3	4562.6	3175.6	1789.3	324.0	171.2
广东	Guangdong	28943.7	13168.2	9646.5	4825.0	1393.0	736.9
广西	Guangxi	8275.2	5485.6	3867.4	2867.4	277.6	182.0
海南	Hainan	1562.4	1008.7	476.6	336.6	66.7	49.4
重庆	Chongqing	10799.7	6805.3	4020.2	2442.5	413.7	234.8
四川	Sichuan	14225.1	8609.0	4861.2	2787.9	382.4	202.6
贵州	Guizhou	4475.5	2889.4	1683.6	1141.4	118.3	70.4
云南	Yunnan	5777.3	3626.2	2663.6	1633.4	263.2	148.3
西藏	Tibet	733.4	275.1	428.2	172.2	52.8	17.5
陕西	Shaanxi	7505.0	4313.2	2871.6	1594.4	344.7	184.5
甘肃	Gansu	3988.3	2298.4	1309.2	779.9	128.2	71.2
青海	Qinghai	833.1	449.6	286.5	137.5	33.2	14.0
宁夏	Ningxia	1552.1	827.7	815.4	487.0	87.0	45.4
新疆	Xinjiang	4858.9	3028.2	2981.7	2168.0	217.9	119.9
不分地区	Not Classified by Region	124.1	6.0	89.3	2.7	4.9	0.1

6-20 各地区按行业分城镇新增固定资产

Newly Increased Fixed Assets in Urban Area by Region and Sector

单位：亿元 (100 million yuan)

年份 地区	Year Region	合计 Total	农、林、牧、渔业 Agriculture, Forestry, Animal Husbandry and Fishing	采矿业 Mining	制造业 Manufacturing	电力、燃气及水的生产和供应业 Production and Supply of Electricity, Gas and Water	建筑业 Construction	交通运输、仓储和邮政业 Transport, Storage and Post
	2003	28663.9	375.0	1182.9	6646.9	2228.4	344.3	3531.4
	2004	34731.4	458.9	1398.0	9023.3	3110.0	364.6	4237.8
	2005	45206.6	608.8	2015.8	13276.5	3429.3	374.8	5235.8
北京	Beijing	1703.6	2.1	4.9	172.8	73.4	3.1	73.0
天津	Tianjin	719.2	4.1	71.7	186.6	24.5	5.3	66.0
河北	Hebei	1982.4	45.1	89.8	764.7	180.5	17.5	229.5
山西	Shanxi	888.7	7.1	155.0	232.1	120.8	1.3	130.5
内蒙古	Inner Mongolia	1622.6	70.5	156.0	368.9	214.5	9.0	318.6
辽宁	Liaoning	2367.0	26.7	146.4	977.3	95.0	18.9	139.9
吉林	Jilin	985.7	11.8	69.9	384.3	33.4	7.8	97.9
黑龙江	Heilongjiang	1098.1	35.9	198.4	244.2	46.1	12.6	102.7
上海	Shanghai	2195.1	0.9	0.2	591.5	64.7	2.6	132.5
江苏	Jiangsu	4956.7	10.3	29.2	1865.4	486.8	21.4	614.0
浙江	Zhejiang	2715.6	6.5	1.7	743.6	281.5	4.9	289.9
安徽	Anhui	1081.3	11.8	23.2	307.9	101.1	21.4	116.1
福建	Fujian	867.5	7.0	4.0	255.0	83.9	6.0	52.0
江西	Jiangxi	977.8	11.8	17.8	368.2	47.2	3.4	92.5
山东	Shandong	3791.1	44.7	137.2	1851.5	189.5	111.7	100.3
河南	Henan	2362.6	40.6	126.3	784.8	166.2	5.8	377.8
湖北	Hubei	1561.7	34.6	27.2	447.4	214.4	6.4	171.3
湖南	Hunan	1197.3	14.9	27.0	283.9	68.8	20.4	118.5
广东	Guangdong	3668.8	10.5	6.5	958.5	325.4	22.7	426.9
广西	Guangxi	792.0	22.0	10.9	193.5	70.1	3.8	107.7
海南	Hainan	135.9	11.8	0.0	10.9	6.8	1.8	22.5
重庆	Chongqing	1146.6	21.0	21.0	224.8	36.8	16.4	188.8
四川	Sichuan	1325.9	19.3	30.8	379.4	119.1	4.6	130.8
贵州	Guizhou	445.6	3.3	22.5	90.3	48.8	1.8	54.9
云南	Yunnan	767.5	18.5	27.1	101.0	91.8	1.8	123.6
西藏	Tibet	167.6	6.3	1.7	9.7	7.9	1.3	63.8
陕西	Shaanxi	1026.9	24.4	110.0	192.2	73.4	6.3	123.1
甘肃	Gansu	412.3	12.2	21.1	77.8	39.4	22.0	62.2
青海	Qinghai	163.5	5.6	32.6	43.4	9.0	7.0	17.4
宁夏	Ningxia	229.4	3.5	4.2	65.6	34.6	0.9	1.9
新疆	Xinjiang	823.8	63.9	194.9	99.3	37.6	4.9	108.6
不分地区	Not Classified by Region	1026.9		246.5		36.7		580.3

6-20 续表 1 continued

单位：亿元 (100 million yuan)

年份 Year 地区 Region	信息传输、计算机服务和软件业 Information Transmission, Computer Services and Software	批发和零售业 Wholesale and Retail Trades	住宿和餐饮业 Hotels and Catering Services	金融业 Financial Intermediation	房地产业 Real Estate	租赁和商务服务业 Leasing and Business Services	科学研究、技术服务和地质勘查业 Scientific Research, Technical Services, and Geological Prospecting
2003	1053.0	535.5	204.5	71.4	7242.0	171.7	146.7
2004	1153.3	717.4	267.6	111.4	7893.3	160.6	200.4
2005	958.2	1019.4	431.7	81.5	10419.3	268.5	196.2
北京 Beijing	24.8	6.5	1.9	0.0	1174.9	8.8	12.4
天津 Tianjin	12.8	13.3	1.3	0.6	270.5	0.7	1.5
河北 Hebei	39.3	79.2	15.2	2.4	222.2	10.4	23.8
山西 Shanxi	19.6	24.3	8.3	1.2	106.3	0.7	1.3
内蒙古 Inner Mongolia	14.1	47.1	15.2	1.4	113.9	2.0	9.7
辽宁 Liaoning	35.7	91.7	39.7	9.9	462.4	29.8	20.6
吉林 Jilin	17.1	32.7	8.3	4.5	87.0	8.8	6.2
黑龙江 Heilongjiang	44.7	21.3	3.2	0.2	166.1	3.5	2.5
上海 Shanghai	4.0	18.8	24.8	0.6	1092.0	8.5	7.0
江苏 Jiangsu	64.2	79.9	34.0	0.6	1075.5	47.8	5.7
浙江 Zhejiang	41.4	24.0	18.9	4.6	797.7	17.0	8.1
安徽 Anhui	23.0	19.2	8.8	1.3	259.6	5.1	4.2
福建 Fujian	54.8	5.2	10.5	5.9	250.8	3.1	1.2
江西 Jiangxi	19.9	22.9	19.4	2.6	159.7	7.1	1.5
山东 Shandong	21.1	111.8	26.7	3.6	634.7	25.4	8.2
河南 Henan	59.6	81.1	24.4	2.6	308.1	10.7	8.6
湖北 Hubei	31.4	57.3	24.6	3.0	277.5	9.7	7.2
湖南 Hunan	24.3	87.5	24.7	3.9	257.0	9.7	13.0
广东 Guangdong	95.2	26.5	40.1	9.4	1191.7	18.3	9.5
广西 Guangxi	28.1	12.5	14.0	1.6	166.6	5.6	2.8
海南 Hainan	6.0	1.1	8.5	1.4	37.7	0.2	0.5
重庆 Chongqing	49.4	17.0	7.1	2.8	322.4	13.2	1.3
四川 Sichuan	53.1	19.9	11.9	1.0	332.5	5.3	7.1
贵州 Guizhou	22.0	8.8	6.2	1.8	73.0	2.6	1.2
云南 Yunnan	45.5	25.5	8.8	2.2	148.8	3.6	1.2
西藏 Tibet	11.5	4.9	1.8	1.2	8.4	0.1	0.8
陕西 Shaanxi	37.1	37.3	14.5	3.9	148.3	4.7	14.3
甘肃 Gansu	11.2	12.7	3.4	1.7	68.4	3.8	5.9
青海 Qinghai	1.3	3.7	0.7	0.2	13.4	0.3	0.6
宁夏 Ningxia	7.5	8.5	0.4	1.1	68.3	0.1	1.0
新疆 Xinjiang	38.4	17.3	4.5	4.2	124.2	1.9	7.5
不分地区 Not Classified by Region							0.1

6-20 续表 2 continued

单位：亿元 (100 million yuan)

年份 地区	Year Region	水利、环境和公共设施管理业 Management of Water Conservancy, Environment and Public Facilities	居民服务和其他服务业 Services to Households and Other Services	教育 Education	卫生、社会保障和社会福利业 Health, Social Securities and Social Welfare	文化、体育和娱乐业 Culture, Sports and Entertainment	公共管理和社会组织 Public Management and Social Organizations	国际组织 International Organizations
	2003	2222.2	43.2	994.5	263.3	219.9	1186.7	0.3
	2004	2406.5	74.4	1209.5	308.5	243.3	1392.4	0.2
	2005	3068.2	75.4	1430.4	391.6	374.7	1550.5	
北京	Beijing	44.3		31.4	4.8	13.5	51.1	
天津	Tianjin	28.4	0.5	15.3	10.2	0.4	5.6	
河北	Hebei	91.6	3.8	43.9	19.6	12.4	91.5	
山西	Shanxi	38.4	0.6	20.1	6.9	4.0	10.0	
内蒙古	Inner Mongolia	159.8	2.8	32.0	11.6	9.9	65.8	
辽宁	Liaoning	130.7	10.6	60.7	18.1	21.3	31.6	
吉林	Jilin	86.2	3.0	42.0	11.7	30.1	42.9	
黑龙江	Heilongjiang	76.9	5.2	41.4	14.7	18.6	59.7	
上海	Shanghai	143.2	0.8	52.3	7.2	26.7	16.9	
江苏	Jiangsu	350.4	6.4	142.4	19.7	39.2	63.7	
浙江	Zhejiang	294.4	4.2	86.9	20.1	27.5	42.7	
安徽	Anhui	93.4	1.6	31.9	8.9	7.3	35.4	
福建	Fujian	33.9	0.9	31.0	6.6	4.8	51.0	
江西	Jiangxi	77.2	2.2	57.6	18.9	9.0	39.0	
山东	Shandong	145.9	6.7	93.3	23.5	27.0	228.4	
河南	Henan	188.0	5.8	84.8	28.0	17.5	42.2	
湖北	Hubei	112.0	3.1	65.3	14.0	11.6	43.7	
湖南	Hunan	92.1	2.9	39.3	21.2	8.8	79.4	
广东	Guangdong	209.4	4.4	161.8	28.8	22.5	100.7	
广西	Guangxi	78.6	1.2	30.0	14.7	6.6	21.7	
海南	Hainan	10.3	0.1	6.2	2.0	1.0	7.1	
重庆	Chongqing	111.7	0.2	47.6	16.6	7.7	40.5	
四川	Sichuan	107.1	1.3	43.5	15.4	13.1	30.9	
贵州	Guizhou	54.9	1.2	20.1	5.7	4.4	22.2	
云南	Yunnan	79.2	0.7	27.8	9.9	6.0	44.5	
西藏	Tibet	9.8	0.4	13.2	1.5	2.3	21.0	
陕西	Shaanxi	100.0	2.8	61.1	10.3	10.2	52.8	
甘肃	Gansu	11.9	0.6	14.1	6.9	2.8	34.2	
青海	Qinghai	9.0	0.1	4.8	1.1	0.6	12.8	
宁夏	Ningxia	15.6	0.0	7.3	1.8	0.9	6.2	
新疆	Xinjiang	42.6	1.1	21.5	11.1	7.0	33.3	
不分地区	Not Classified by Region	41.2					122.2	

6-21 城镇50万元以上施工、投产项目个数

Number of Construction Projects over 500 Thousand Yuan under Construction and Put into Use in Urban Area

年 份 地 区	Year Region	施工项目 (个) Number of Projects under Construction (unit)	新开工项目 (个) Number of Projects Started This Year (unit)	全部建成投产项目 (个) Number of Projects Completed and Put into Use (unit)	项目建成投产率 (%) Rate of Construction Projects Completed and Put into Use (%)
	1995	169163	103305	102115	60.4
	1996	176487	111211	108256	61.3
	1997	156865	98003	95560	60.9
	1998	172011	116513	102572	59.6
	1999	175253	111690	109355	62.4
	2000	170430	113225	103749	60.9
	2001	173950	118725	106021	60.9
	2002	181363	128224	104087	57.4
	2003	203215	148042	109155	53.7
	2004	215440	152363	113145	52.5
	2005	261535	190755	148753	56.9
北 京	Beijing	1335	583	479	35.9
天 津	Tianjin	1764	1229	823	46.7
河 北	Hebei	13272	11207	7645	57.6
山 西	Shanxi	5080	3755	2975	58.6
内蒙古	Inner Mongolia	8593	7096	6521	75.9
辽 宁	Liaoning	14339	10535	10068	70.2
吉 林	Jilin	5642	4690	3479	61.7
黑龙江	Heilongjiang	6006	4828	4369	72.7
上 海	Shanghai	3630	2252	1883	51.9
江 苏	Jiangsu	13546	10206	8197	60.5
浙 江	Zhejiang	12903	7382	6176	47.9
安 徽	Anhui	10326	7390	5025	48.7
福 建	Fujian	7531	4556	2880	38.2
江 西	Jiangxi	7204	4705	3608	50.1
山 东	Shandong	20671	16368	9893	47.9
河 南	Henan	13493	10468	8864	65.7
湖 北	Hubei	10938	8620	6703	61.3
湖 南	Hunan	11990	9112	6626	55.3
广 东	Guangdong	14420	8679	5888	40.8
广 西	Guangxi	11780	8276	6205	52.7
海 南	Hainan	1241	913	660	53.2
重 庆	Chongqing	5696	3855	3292	57.8
四 川	Sichuan	12651	9348	6625	52.4
贵 州	Guizhou	6483	4686	3869	59.7
云 南	Yunnan	11883	8721	7865	66.2
西 藏	Tibet	2396	1901	1830	76.4
陕 西	Shaanxi	7103	4728	4164	58.6
甘 肃	Gansu	7316	5354	3868	52.9
青 海	Qinghai	2456	1698	1536	62.5
宁 夏	Ningxia	2199	1757	1510	68.7
新 疆	Xinjiang	6379	4930	4439	69.6
不分地区	Not Classified by Region	1269	927	788	62.1

6-22 城镇新增固定资产及交付使用率

Newly Increased Fixed Assets and Rate of Projects of Fixed Assets Completed and Put into Operation in Urban Area

年份 Year / 地区 Region		固定资产投资额 (亿元) Investment in Fixed Assets (100 million yuan)	新增固定资产 (亿元) Newly Increased Fixed Assets (100 million yuan)	固定资产交付使用率 (%) Rate of Projects of Fixed Assets Completed and Put into Operation (%)
	1995	15643.7	10146.2	64.9
	1996	(17627.7)	(13138.7)	(74.5)
		17567.2	13080.6	74.5
	1997	19194.2	14959.9	77.9
	1998	22491.4	17081.3	75.9
	1999	23732.0	18682.7	78.7
	2000	26221.8	20715.2	79.0
	2001	30001.2	21666.3	72.2
	2002	35488.8	24791.9	69.9
	2003	45811.7	28663.9	62.6
	2004	59028.2	34731.4	58.8
	2005	75095.1	45206.6	60.2
北京	Beijing	2595.4	1703.6	65.6
天津	Tianjin	1364.0	719.2	52.7
河北	Hebei	3307.8	1982.4	59.9
山西	Shanxi	1666.5	888.7	53.3
内蒙古	Inner Mongolia	2555.3	1622.6	63.5
辽宁	Liaoning	3666.5	2367.0	64.6
吉林	Jilin	1581.3	985.7	62.3
黑龙江	Heilongjiang	1581.2	1098.1	69.4
上海	Shanghai	3198.6	2195.1	68.6
江苏	Jiangsu	6218.9	4956.7	79.7
浙江	Zhejiang	4784.7	2715.6	56.8
安徽	Anhui	2126.7	1081.3	50.8
福建	Fujian	1958.3	867.5	44.3
江西	Jiangxi	1902.7	977.8	51.4
山东	Shandong	7275.1	3791.1	52.1
河南	Henan	3461.2	2362.6	68.3
湖北	Hubei	2387.4	1561.7	65.4
湖南	Hunan	2204.0	1197.3	54.3
广东	Guangdong	5890.1	3668.8	62.3
广西	Guangxi	1480.9	792.0	53.5
海南	Hainan	339.2	135.9	40.1
重庆	Chongqing	1777.1	1146.6	64.5
四川	Sichuan	2991.8	1325.9	44.3
贵州	Guizhou	899.3	445.6	49.6
云南	Yunnan	1592.3	767.5	48.2
西藏	Tibet	181.4	167.6	92.4
陕西	Shaanxi	1740.9	1026.9	59.0
甘肃	Gansu	786.0	412.3	52.5
青海	Qinghai	310.8	163.5	52.6
宁夏	Ningxia	382.0	229.4	60.1
新疆	Xinjiang	1210.0	823.8	68.1
不分地区	Not Classified by Region	1677.9	1026.9	61.2

6-23 按行业分城镇50万元以上施工、投产项目个数（2005年）

Number of Construction Projects over 500 Thousand Yuan under Construction and Put into Use in Urban Area by Sector (2005)

行业	Sector	施工项目（个） Number of Projects under Construc-tion (unit)	#新开工 Started This Year	全部建成投产项目（个） Number of Projects Completed and Put into Use (unit)	项目建成投产率（%） Rate of Projects Completed & Put into Use (%)
全国总计	**National Total**	**261535**	**190755**	**148753**	**56.9**
农、林、牧、渔业	**Agriculture, Forestry, Animal Husbandry and Fishing**	**12772**	**11105**	**9735**	**76.2**
农业	Agriculture	2572	2160	1837	71.4
林业	Forestry	2054	1664	1431	69.7
畜牧业	Animal Husbandry	2095	1776	1490	71.1
渔业	Fishing	320	258	199	62.2
农、林、牧、渔服务业	Service Activities for Agriculture, Forestry, Animal Husbandry and Fishing	5731	5247	4778	83.4
采矿业	**Mining**	**8958**	**7287**	**5462**	**61.0**
煤炭开采和洗选业	Mining and Washing of Coal	4242	3291	2497	58.9
石油和天然气开采业	Extraction of Petroleum and Natural Gas	330	274	239	72.4
黑色金属矿采选业	Mining and Processing of Ferrous Metal Ores	1497	1257	959	64.1
有色金属矿采选业	Mining and Processing of Non-Ferrous Metal Ores	1259	1042	710	56.4
非金属矿采选业	Mining and Processing of Nonmetal Ores	1578	1375	1038	65.8
其他采矿业	Mining of Other Ores	52	48	19	36.5
制造业	**Manufacturing**	**90627**	**67686**	**49335**	**54.4**
农副食品加工业	Processing of Food from Agricultural Products	5850	4735	3534	60.4
食品制造业	Manufacture of Foods	3244	2498	1662	51.2
饮料制造业	Manufacture of Beverages	2067	1568	1194	57.8
烟草制品业	Manufacture of Tobacco	310	158	165	53.2
纺织业	Manufacture of Textile	5310	4065	2918	55.0
纺织服装、鞋、帽制造业	Manufacture of Textile Wearing Apparel, Footware, and Caps	2946	2238	1594	54.1
皮革毛皮羽毛(绒)及其制品业	Manufacture of Leather, Fur, Feather and Related Products	1345	1008	626	46.5
木材加工及木竹藤棕草制品业	Processing of Timber, Manufacture of Wood, Bamboo, Rattan, Palm, and Straw Products	2480	2062	1582	63.8
家具制造业	Manufacture of Furniture	1356	1073	730	53.8
造纸及纸制品业	Manufacture of Paper and Paper Products	2220	1648	1249	56.3
印刷业和记录媒介的复制	Printing, Reproduction of Recording Media	1531	1157	858	56.0
文教体育用品制造业	Manufacture of Articles For Culture, Education and Sport Activity	712	533	361	50.7
石油加工、炼焦及核燃料加工业	Processing of Petroleum, Coking, Processing of Nuclear Fuel	1282	824	686	53.5
化学原料及化学制品制造业	Manufacture of Raw Chemical Materials and Chemical Products	7438	5645	4089	55.0
医药制造业	Manufacture of Medicines	3201	1983	1457	45.5
化学纤维制造业	Manufacture of Chemical Fibers	394	244	210	53.3
橡胶制品业	Manufacture of Rubber	938	726	514	54.8
塑料制品业	Manufacture of Plastics	3299	2630	1944	58.9
非金属矿物制品业	Manufacture of Non-metallic Mineral Products	7888	6305	4932	62.5
黑色金属冶炼及压延加工业	Smelting and Pressing of Ferrous Metals	3767	2434	2049	54.4
有色金属冶炼及压延加工业	Smelting and Pressing of Non-ferrous Metals	2154	1422	1051	48.8
金属制品业	Manufacture of Metal Products	4860	3813	2691	55.4
通用设备制造业	Manufacture of General Purpose Machinery	6683	5240	3803	56.9
专用设备制造业	Manufacture of Special Purpose Machinery	4311	3214	2268	52.6
交通运输设备制造业	Manufacture of Transport Equipment	4932	3462	2377	48.2
电气机械及器材制造业	Manufacture of Electrical Machinery and Equipment	4302	3060	2156	50.1
通信设备、计算机及其他电子设备制造业	Manufacture of Communication Equipment, Computers and Other Electronic Equipment	2774	1763	1204	43.4
仪器仪表文化办公用机械制造业	Manufacture of Measuring Instruments and Machinery for Cultural Activity and Office Work	888	592	400	45.1
工艺品及其他制造业	Manufacture of Artwork and Other Manufacturing	1982	1459	939	47.4
废弃资源和废旧材料回收加工业	Recycling and Disposal of Waste	163	127	92	56.4
电力燃气水的生产供应业	**Production and Supply of Electricity, Gas and Water**	**15025**	**8992**	**7461**	**49.7**
电力、热力的生产和供应业	Production and Supply of Electric Power and Heat Power	10907	6724	5592	51.3
燃气生产和供应业	Production and Supply of Gas	879	535	373	42.4
水的生产和供应业	Production and Supply of Water	3239	1733	1496	46.2
建筑业	**Construction**	**6393**	**3728**	**2657**	**41.6**
房屋和土木工程建筑业	Construction of Buildings and Civil Engineering	5828	3329	2341	40.2
建筑安装业	Building Installation	195	156	122	62.6
建筑装饰业	Building Decoration	131	98	90	68.7
其他建筑业	Other Construction	239	145	104	43.5

6-23 续表 continued

行业	Sector	施工项目(个) Number of Projects under Construc-tion (unit)	#新开工 Started This Year	全部建成投产项目(个) Number of Projects Completed and Put into Use (unit)	项目建成投产率(%) Rate of Projects Completed & Put into Use (%)
交通运输、仓储和邮政业	**Transport, Storage and Post**	**21795**	**15750**	**13366**	**61.3**
铁路运输业	Railway Transport	1571	1352	1242	79.1
道路运输业	Road Transport	17094	12356	10688	62.5
城市公共交通业	Urban Public Transport	576	363	248	43.1
水上运输业	Water Transport	822	444	282	34.3
航空运输业	Air Transport	213	136	78	36.6
管道运输业	Transport Via Pipelines	53	28	30	56.6
装卸搬运和其他运输服务业	Loading, Unloading and Other Transport Services	173	118	75	43.4
仓储业	Storage	1077	809	600	55.7
邮政业	Post	216	144	123	56.9
信息传输、计算机服务和软件业	**Information Transmission, Computer Services and Software**	**7740**	**5761**	**4959**	**64.1**
电信和其他信息传输服务业	Telecommunications and Other Information Transmission Services	7460	5577	4839	64.9
计算机服务业	Computer Services	106	77	60	56.6
软件业	Software	174	107	60	34.5
批发和零售业	**Wholesale and Retail Trade**	**11021**	**8898**	**7385**	**67.0**
批发业	Wholesale Trade	4980	4045	3468	69.6
零售业	Retail Trade	6041	4853	3917	64.8
住宿和餐饮业	**Hotel and Catering Services**	**4701**	**3721**	**2947**	**62.7**
住宿业	Hotels	2431	1741	1258	51.8
餐饮业	Catering Services	2270	1980	1689	74.4
金融业	**Financial Intermediation**	**857**	**577**	**527**	**61.5**
银行业	Banks	719	468	442	61.5
证券业	Security Activities	13	10	7	53.9
保险业	Insurance	69	53	47	68.1
其他金融活动	Other Financial Activities	56	46	31	55.4
房地产业	**Real Estate**	**5107**	**3675**	**2555**	**50.0**
租赁和商务服务业	**Leasing and Business Services**	**1763**	**1268**	**843**	**47.8**
租赁业	Leasing	110	99	79	71.8
商务服务业	Business Services	1653	1169	764	46.2
科学研究、技术服务和地质勘查业	**Scientific Research, Technical Service and Geologic Prospecting**	**2060**	**1283**	**977**	**47.4**
研究与试验发展	Research and Experimental Development	777	420	298	38.4
专业技术服务业	Professional Technical Services	730	467	376	51.5
科技交流和推广服务业	Services of Science and Technology Exchanges and Promotion	329	227	175	53.2
地质勘查业	Geologic Prospecting	224	169	128	57.1
水利、环境和公共设施管理业	**Management of Water Conservancy, Environment and Public Facilities**	**24477**	**16519**	**12327**	**50.4**
水利管理业	Management of Water Conservancy	5454	3616	2964	54.4
环境管理业	Environmental Management	1963	1324	968	49.3
公共设施管理业	Management of Public Facilities	17060	11579	8395	49.2
居民服务和其他服务业	**Services to Households and Other Services**	**1272**	**1059**	**844**	**66.4**
居民服务业	Services to Households	896	758	611	68.2
其他服务业	Other Services	376	301	233	62.0
教育	**Education**	**16598**	**12005**	**10271**	**61.9**
卫生、社会保障和社会福利业	**Health, Social Security and Social Welfare**	**6118**	**3974**	**3640**	**59.5**
卫生	Health	5458	3490	3218	59.0
社会保障业	Social Security	90	72	67	74.4
社会福利业	Social Welfare	570	412	355	62.3
文化、体育和娱乐业	**Culture, Sports and Entertainment**	**3625**	**2372**	**1881**	**51.9**
新闻出版业	Journalism and Publishing Activities	102	68	44	43.1
广播、电视、电影和音像业	Broadcasting, Movies, Televisions and Audiovisual Activities	712	461	386	54.2
文化艺术业	Cultural and Art Activities	1270	789	623	49.1
体育	Sports Activities	498	279	190	38.2
娱乐业	Entertainment	1043	775	638	61.2
公共管理和社会组织	**Public Management and Social Organization**	**20626**	**15095**	**11581**	**56.2**
中国共产党机关	Organs of Communist Party of China	464	371	149	32.1
国家机构	Government Agencies	17836	12800	10118	56.7
人民政协和民主党派	People's Political Consultative Conference and Democratic Parties	68	50	31	45.6
群众团体、社会团体和宗教组织	Non-Governmental Institutions, Social Organizations and Religion Organizations	465	318	264	56.8
基层群众自治组织	Grass Roots Self-governing Organizations	1793	1556	1019	56.8
国际组织	**International Organizations**				

6-24 新增主要产品生产能力

Newly Increased Production Capacity of Major Production

能力名称	Item	2001	2002	2003	2004	2005
原煤开采 (万吨/年)	Coal Mining (10 000 tons/year)	2720	3419	7443	15441	18377
焦炭 (万吨/年)	Coke (10 000 tons/year)	1014	1169	4092	9284	7337
天然原油开采 (万吨/年)	Petroleum Extraction (10 000 tons/year)	1931	2541	1716	2468	2388
天然气开采 (亿立方米/年)	Extraction of Petroleum and Natural Gas (10 000 cu.m/year)	18	164	54	114	129
铁矿开采 (原矿) (万吨/年)	Iron Ore Mining (10 000 tons/year)	364	303	681	6322	9211
生铁 (万吨/年)	Pig Iron (10 000 tons/year)	580	1143	3030	5643	6873
炼钢 (万吨/年)	Steel-making (10 000 tons/year)	392	616	3240	5283	4565
平炉钢 (万吨/年)	Open Hearth Steel (10 000 tons/year)	5		243	285	140
转炉钢 (万吨/年)	Converter Steel (10 000 tons/year)	64	323	1635	1815	1572
电炉钢 (万吨/年)	Electric Steel (10 000 tons/year)	81	110	282	414	472
铁合金 (万吨/年)	Iron Alloy (10 000 tons/year)	70	61	204	753	877
铜采矿 (原矿) (万吨/年)	Copper Ore Mining (10 000 tons/year)	45	46	106	397	746
铜选矿:	Copper Ore Dressing					
处理原矿 (万吨/年)	Crude Ore Dressing (10 000 tons/year)	84	76	100	414	308
铜含量 (吨/年)	Copper Content (ton/year)	2500	73	14365	13129	20914
铜冶炼 (吨/年)	Copper Smelting (ton/year)	3865	83800	337690	371435	1113448
#电解铜 (吨/年)	Electrolytic Copper (ton/year)		75800	305390	75975	498125
铅锌采矿 (原矿) (万吨/年)	Plumbum/Zinc Ore Mining (10 000 tons/year)	200	241	3206	611	1089
铅锌选矿:	Plumbum and Zinc Ore Dressing					
处理原矿 (万吨/年)	Crude Ore Dressing (10 000 tons/year)	11	2238	151	349	399
铅含量 (吨/年)	Plumbum Content (ton/year)	2200	20998	28915	55045	75000
锌含量 (吨/年)	Zinc Content (ton/year)	25500	25884	31720	107111	115772
铅冶炼 (吨/年)	Plumbum Smelting (ton/year	185100	32900	50320	495241	505852
#电解铅 (吨/年)	Electrolytic Plumbum (ton/year)	132800	5000	16000	169940	261300
锌冶炼 (吨/年)	Zinc Smelting (ton/year)	166351	228760	179819	366105	670732
#电解锌 (吨/年)	Electrolytic Zinc (ton/year)	86700	116500	82000	166310	207040
氧化铝 (吨/年)	Aluminum Oxide (ton/year)	403000	387015	675800	574000	1844360
电解铝 (吨/年)	Electrolytic Aluminum (ton/year)	555446	580664	1827359	1199360	1211171
水力发电 (万千瓦)	Hydraulic Power (10 000 kw)	534	523	1268	1108	1278
火力发电 (万千瓦)	Fire Power (10 000 kw)	1261	3317	2139	3698	5276
核能发电 (万千瓦)	Nuclear Energy Source (10 000 kw)		333		65	2
其他发电 (万千瓦)	Other Power (10 000 kw)	155	161	13	245	167
水泥 (万吨/年)	Cement (10 000 tons/year)	3049	4776	7568	18909	24117
平板玻璃 (万重量箱/年)	Plate Glass (10 000 Weight-box/year)	1802	1530	1173	5660	6875
胶合板 (万立方米/年)	Plywood (10 000 cu.m/year)	107	845	288	1947	2015
硫酸 (吨/年)	Sulfuric Acid (ton/year)	1758752	1345316	1800000	2493088	6267700
烧碱 (吨/年)	Caustic Soda (ton/year)	310381	314600	336310	1152510	1403468
纯碱 (吨/年)	Soda Ash (ton/year)	182110	293502	276600	794367	1152850
电石 (吨/年)	Calcium Carbide (ton/year)	246852	416771	981436	4591529	1097328

注：2003年以前为城镇口径，2004年以后为全社会口径。

a) Figures of 2003 and before cover urban arear only, while figures of 2004 and after cover both urban and rural areas.

6-24 续表 continued

能力名称	Item	2001	2002	2003	2004	2005
合成氨 (吨/年)	Synthetic Ammonia (ton/year)	914821	1324351	1413400	1409454	2284382
氮肥 (吨/年)	Nitrogen Fertilizers (ton/year)	1843418	1133413	2578201	1485925	4424786
磷肥 (吨/年)	Phosphate Fertilizer (ton/year)	1913400	1106226	2066750	2526258	3165465
钾肥 (吨/年)	Potash Fertilizer (ton/year)	198101	126788	137100	1573170	665790
乙烯 (吨/年)	Ethylene (ton/year)	310000	501190	77425	725214	1964562
塑料树脂及共聚物 (吨/年)	Plastic Colophony and Polymer (ton/year)	967707	789786	687846	1124960	4709032
轮胎外胎 (万条/年)	Inner Tube (10 000 units/year)	651	856	1667	4395	3752
轮胎内胎 (万条/年)	Tire (Cover) (10 000 units/year)	104	2060	438	2301	2244
金属切削机床制造 (台/年)	Metal-Cutting Machine Tools (set/year)	2147	1950	41773	15835	41771
拖拉机制造 (台/年)	Tractors (unit/year)	2802	6460	44600		28460
载货汽车制造 (辆/年)	Trucks (unit/year)	75900	80845	37800	180350	134925
客车制造 (辆/年)	Passenger Motor Vehicles (unit/year)	3800	313000	381400	140795	206800
轿车制造 (辆/年)	Cars (unit/year)	95500	419000	361000	1435499	948777
其他汽车制造 (辆/年)	Other Motor Vehicles (unit/year)	19700	19200	14100	72988	130356
民用钢制船舶 (综合吨/年)	Steel Civilian Ships (ton/year)	560000	200050	15105	688082	1373718
电视机 (万部/年)	Television (10 000 units/year)	210	470	234	1762	2715
化学纤维 (吨/年)	Chemical Fiber (ton/year)	323153	297054	875720	3295972	2665296
棉纺锭 (锭)	Cotton Spindles (unit)	467720	1692153	4480113	6741370	13786477
毛纺锭 (锭)	Wool Spindles (unit)	17201	4580	38014	165788	163844
原盐 (万吨/年)	Raw Salt (10 000 tons/year)	2	171	89	368	931
机制糖	Machine-made Sugar					
年生产糖 (吨)	Annual Production Capacity (ton)	120965	592354	999384	986622	696991
日处理原料 (吨)	Raw Materials Processing (ton)	20008	56247	29323	43562	53658
奶粉 (吨/年)	Milk Powder (ton/year)	59341	321330	103572	53570	164923
啤酒 (万吨/年)	Beer (10 000 tons/year)	519	216	229	310	384
白酒 (万吨/年)	Distilled Spirit (10 000 tons/year)	37	62	52	118	316
其他酒 (万吨/年)	Other Spirt (10 000 tons/year)	9	9	16	47	48
卷烟 (箱/年)	Cigarettes (box/year)	680566	274762	435167	1168950	1551074
机制纸 (万吨/年)	Machine-made Paper (10 000 tons/year)	221	407	307	717	1216
机制纸板 (万吨/年)	Machine-made Paperboard (10 000 tons/year)	61	219	152	338	387
自行车 (万辆/年)	Bicycle (10 000 unit/year)	29	281	139	230	508
家用电冰箱 (万台/年)	Household Refrigerator (10 000 unit/year)	81	15	77	264	604
家用洗衣机 (万台/年)	Household Washing Machine (10 000 unit/year)	250	90	213	339	910
新建铁路投产里程 (公里)	Length of Newly-built and Operating Railway (km)	987	2146	931	1305	1281
新建公路 (公里)	Length of New Highways (km)	18210	26086	27440	67730	60374
改建公路 (公里)	Length of Reconstructed Highways (km)	43374	60764	64072	93156	105065
新(扩)建港口码头	Newly-built or Expanded Ports					
年吞吐量 (万吨)	Annual Handling Capacity (10 000 tons/year)	6248	12255	9888	11408	14840
泊位 (个)	Berths (unit)	83	165	116	140	181
商业石油库 (万立方米)	Commercial Petroleum Depot	101	62	205	197	219
商业冷藏库 (万吨)	Commercial Freezers (10 000 tons)	501	41	113	255	492
粮食仓库 (万公斤)	Grain Storehouses (10 000 kg)	864489	976082	249116	141239	139617
粮食仓库 (平方米)	Grain Storehouses (sq.m)	2101035	2383203	732236	316173	480412
高等院校学生席位 (个)	Students Capacity of Universities and Colleges (unit)	585325	717963	809207	993039	1405331
医院病床 (张)	Number of Hospital Beds (unit)	62176	59187	75810	89065	119369
城市自来水供水能力 (万吨/日)	Tap Water Supply Capacity (10 000 tons/day)	1440	849	1020	1405	2067

6-25 全社会主要产品建设规模（2005年）

Construction Size of Main Production in the Whole Country (2005)

能力名称	Item	建设规模 Total Construction Size	本年施工规模 Under Construction This Year	本年新开工 Started This Year	累计新增 Accumulated Newly Increased	本年新增 Newly Increased This Year
原煤开采（万吨/年）	Coal Mining (10 000 tons/year)	85001	75656	41029	22091	18377
焦炭（万吨/年）	Coke (10 000 tons/year)	20629	18481	10099	9483	7337
天然原油开采（万吨/年）	Petroleum Extraction (10 000 tons/year)	3176	2628	2354	2849	2388
天然气开采（亿立方米/年）	Extraction of Petroleum and Natural Gas (10 000 cu.m/year)	154	153	153	143	129
铁矿开采（原矿）（万吨/年）	Iron Ore Mining (10 000 tons/year)	19521	18190	14414	9491	9211
生铁（万吨/年）	Pig Iron (10 000 tons/year)	14668	13501	9794	9184	6873
炼钢（万吨/年）	Steel-making (10 000 tons/year)	11858	10562	4467	5435	4565
#平炉钢（万吨/年）	Open Hearth Steel (10 000 tons/year)	231	231	159	140	140
转炉钢（万吨/年）	Converter Steel (10 000 tons/year)	2892	2727	725	1682	1572
电炉钢（万吨/年）	Electric Steel (10 000 tons/year)	572	568	217	506	472
铁合金（万吨/年）	Iron Alloy (10 000 tons/year)	1669	1544	1077	1016	877
铜采矿（原矿）（万吨/年）	Copper Ore Mining (10 000 tons/year)	1033	1009	737	757	746
铜选矿：	Copper Ore Dressing					
处理原矿（万吨/年）	Crude Ore Dressing (10 000 tons/year)	523	523	325	319	308
铜含量（吨/年）	Copper Content (ton/year)	36615	36615	9015	21814	20914
铜冶炼（吨/年）	Copper Smelting (ton/year)	1986339	1950339	1570207	1196528	1113448
#电解铜（吨/年）	Electrolytic Copper (ton/year)	784375	781675	604375	498125	498125
铅锌采矿（原矿）（万吨/年）	Plumbum/Zinc Ore Mining (10 000 tons/year)	1549	1528	1380	1221	1089
铅锌选矿：	Plumbum and Zinc Ore Dressing					
处理原矿（万吨/年）	Crude Ore Dressing (10 000 tons/year)	749	720	573	464	399
铅含量（吨/年）	Plumbum Content (ton/year)	98750	95700	84300	79050	75000
锌含量（吨/年）	Zinc Content (ton/year)	141772	140172	117172	123872	115772
铅冶炼（吨/年）	Plumbum Smelting (ton/year)	1243256	1242208	931208	557852	505852
#电解铅（吨/年）	Electrolytic Plumbum (ton/year)	821300	821300	436300	261300	261300
锌冶炼（吨/年）	Zinc Smelting (ton/year)	1360238	1278327	817822	674232	670732
#电解锌（吨/年）	Electrolytic Zinc (ton/year)	303045	228045	32040	207040	207040
氧化铝（吨/年）	Aluminum Oxide (ton/year)	11027570	10677570	4177370	2546760	1844360
电解铝（吨/年）	Electrolytic Aluminum (ton/year)	3961788	3219178	1023872	2411281	1211171
水力发电（万千瓦）	Hydraulic Power (10 000 kw)	18090	15190	5973	2693	1278
火力发电（万千瓦）	Fire Power (10 000 kw)	31137	27253	10685	6666	5276
核能发电（万千瓦）	Nuclear Energy Source (10 000 kw)	532	532	201	132	2
其他发电（万千瓦）	Other Power (10 000 kw)	895	849	582	176	167
水泥（万吨/年）	Cement (10 000 tons/year)	63513	58312	34076	30443	24117
平板玻璃（万重量箱/年）	Plate Glass (10 000 Weight-box/year)	17596	17048	9519	7416	6875
胶合板（万立方米/年）	Plywood (10 000 cu.m/year)	2723	2568	2357	2117	2015
硫酸（吨/年）	Sulfuric Acid (ton/year)	11054162	10587492	6491500	7047380	6267700
烧碱（吨/年）	Caustic Soda (ton/year)	4395718	4253501	2229491	1533518	1403468
纯碱（吨/年）	Soda Ash (ton/year)	1490150	1310150	1299950	1153050	1152850
电石（吨/年）	Calcium Carbide (ton/year)	3082977	2577960	2003260	1505225	1097328
合成氨（吨/年）	Synthetic Ammonia (ton/year)	6869482	6333862	2684042	2673782	2284382

6-25 续表 continued

能力名称	Item	建设规模 Total Construction Size	本年施工规模 Under Construction This Year	本年新开工 Started This Year	累计新增 Accumulated Newly Increased	本年新增 Newly Increased This Year
氮肥 (吨/年)	Nitrogen Fertilizers (ton/year)	10699853	9806545	6502050	4817986	4424786
磷肥 (吨/年)	Phosphate Fertilizer (ton/year)	7002655	6214065	3115695	3242395	3165465
钾肥 (吨/年)	Potash Fertilizer (ton/year)	3155066	1542796	652796	746850	665790
乙烯 (吨/年)	Ethylene (ton/year)	7336912	7322612	2641612	1964762	1964562
塑料树脂及共聚物 (吨/年)	Plastic Colophony and Polymer (ton/year)	10715085	10404741	5485937	4987925	4709032
轮胎外胎 (万条/年)	Inner Tube (10 000 units/year)	10801	7677	5206	4240	3752
轮胎内胎 (万条/年)	Tire (Cover) (10 000 units/year)	4499	3444	2619	2249	2244
金属切削机床制造 (台/年)	Metal-Cutting Machine Tools (set/year)	56537	53111	35151	45003	41771
拖拉机制造 (台/年)	Tractors (unit/year)	97460	97460	79960	28460	28460
载货汽车制造 (辆/年)	Trucks (unit/year)	629611	504680	276674	134925	134925
客车制造 (辆/年)	Passenger Motor Vehicles (unit/year)	357241	346337	129045	211750	206800
轿车制造 (辆/年)	Cars (unit/year)	4688524	4198296	1983782	1949005	948777
其他汽车制造 (辆/年)	Other Motor Vehicles (unit/year)	480505	375055	234849	165806	130356
民用钢制船舶 (综合吨/年)	Steel Civilian Ships (ton/year)	8917779	8247779	7294689	1373718	1373718
电视机 (万部/年)	Television (10 000 units/year)	4333	4254	2939	2810	2715
化学纤维 (吨/年)	Chemical Fiber (ton/year)	5150020	4939477	2337251	2880022	2665296
棉纺锭 (锭)	Cotton Spindles (unit)	28098485	22927497	18577161	16293518	13786477
毛纺锭 (锭)	Wool Spindles (unit)	442720	441164	337234	167144	163844
原盐 (万吨/年)	Raw Salt (10 000 tons/year)	1658	1512	1179	961	931
机制糖	Machine-made Sugar					
年生产糖 (吨)	Annual Production Capacity (ton)	1169700	880900	720302	746660	696991
日处理原料 (吨)	Raw Materials Processing (ton)	181959	72101	63399	164168	53658
奶粉 (吨/年)	Milk Powder (ton/year)	380963	292663	211183	239223	164923
啤酒 (万吨/年)	Beer (10 000 tons/year)	846	760	553	386	384
白酒 (万吨/年)	Distilled Spirit (10 000 tons/year)	411	389	368	330	316
其他酒 (万吨/年)	Others (10 000 tons/year)	138	130	59	49	48
卷烟 (箱/年)	Cigarettes (box/year)	5328368	5261368	1491368	1611074	1551074
机制纸 (万吨/年)	Machine-made Paper (10 000 tons/year)	2286	2095	1641	1353	1216
机制纸板 (万吨/年)	Machine-made Paperboard (10 000 tons/year)	732	707	458	401	387
自行车 (万辆/年)	Bicycle (10 000 unit/year)	805	684	533	583	508
家用电冰箱 (万台/年)	Household Refrigerator (10 000 unit/year)	1007	923	516	656	604
家用洗衣机 (万台/年)	Household Washing Machine (10 000 unit/year)	1255	1185	960	910	910
新建铁路投产里程 (公里)	Length of Newly-built and Operating Railway (km)	10628	9490	5747	2719	1281
新建公路 (公里)	Length of New Highways (km)	108172	102011	73487	65705	60374
改建公路 (公里)	Length of Reconstructed Highways (km)	164210	152269	106765	114789	105065
新(扩)建港口码头	Newly-built or Expanded Ports					
年吞吐量 (万吨)	Annual Handling Capacity (10 000 tons/year)	62689	56487	30738	15497	14840
泊位 (个)	Berths (unit)	596	572	272	194	181
商业石油库 (万立方米)	Commercial Petroleum Depot (10 000 cu.m)	319	308	262	231	219
商业冷藏库 (万吨)	Commercial Freezers (10 000 tons)	591	586	556	497	492
粮食仓库 (万公斤)	Grain Storehouses (10 000 kg)	305626	246282	151161	152617	139617
粮食仓库 (平方米)	Grain Storehouses (sq.m)	942889	677443	410127	538535	480412
高等院校：学生席位 (个)	Students Capacity of Universities and Colleges (unit)	3733951	3207957	1498354	1880243	1405331
医院病床 (张)	Number of Hospital Beds (unit)	270829	266654	157612	131163	119369
城市自来水供水能力 (万吨/日)	Tap Water Supply Capacity (10 000 tons/day)	5557	5345	2826	2280	2067

6-26 农村个人固定资产投资和建房

Individual Investment in Fixed Assets and Buildings Construction in Rural Areas

年份 Year 地区 Region	投资总额（亿元）Total Investment (100 million yuan)	#竣工房屋投资 Investment in Buildings Completed	#住宅 Residential Buildings	施工房屋建筑面积（万平方米）Floor Space of Buildings under Construction (10 000 sq.m)	竣工房屋建筑面积（万平方米）Floor Space of Buildings Completed (10 000 sq.m)	#住宅 Residential Buildings	竣工房屋造价（元/平方米）Cost of Buildings Completed (yuan/sq.m)	#住宅 Residential Buildings
1985	478.4	350.1	313.2		78973.0	69542.0	44.0	45.0
1989	892.0	794.2	641.7	74906.0	71026.0	66134.0	112.0	97.0
1990	876.5	777.1	649.8	76819.0	71136.0	67812.0	109.0	96.0
1991	1042.6	912.5	759.3	85405.0	79501.0	74193.0	115.0	102.0
1992	1005.5	937.5	678.5	83392.0	65338.0	60442.0	143.0	112.0
1993	1137.7	1015.4	760.3	57432.0	56012.0	46129.0	181.0	165.0
1994	1519.2	1315.9	1002.7	72283.0	65390.0	57646.0	201.0	174.0
1995	2007.9	1709.4	1349.9	78192.0	73522.0	66230.0	233.0	204.0
1996	2544.0	2250.9	1766.4	96115.0	87277.0	79531.0	258.0	222.0
1997	2691.2	2405.8	1890.7	89309.0	85888.0	77287.0	280.0	245.0
1998	2681.5	2402.2	1907.2	89099.0	83864.0	77031.0	286.0	248.0
1999	2779.6	1908.2	1799.1	89050.0	83244.0	76758.0	229.2	234.4
2000	2904.3	1969.3	1846.8	88231.8	81270.2	75515.3	242.3	244.6
2001	2976.6	1908.2	1775.0	81048.2	74517.5	68799.3	256.1	258.0
2002	3123.2	1956.5	1858.1	80345.0	75125.7	69841.0	260.4	266.0
2003	3201.0	2053.2	1926.9	81123.7	75683.6	69741.1	271.3	276.3
2004	3362.7	2031.0	1933.4	71112.1	65801.5	62303.5	308.7	310.3
2005	3940.6	2190.6	2083.1	73109.2	66604.2	62292.4	328.9	334.4
北京 Beijing	17.2	11.3	10.7	294.8	212.9	198.9	530.4	535.6
天津 Tianjin	29.3	15.0	14.2	317.9	229.8	196.2	653.8	725.4
河北 Hebei	237.4	125.1	119.7	4315.1	3878.8	3587.6	322.5	333.7
山西 Shanxi	75.7	45.7	44.9	1514.2	1319.7	1298.1	346.2	345.8
内蒙古 Inner Mongolia	62.1	20.7	17.0	738.0	710.0	510.0	291.6	333.5
辽宁 Liaoning	132.9	76.2	68.1	2297.5	2276.9	2153.2	334.8	316.2
吉林 Jilin	103.1	21.6	21.0	486.0	472.0	444.3	457.4	473.5
黑龙江 Heilongjiang	140.8	30.1	29.3	898.8	788.7	746.1	381.1	393.3
上海 Shanghai	7.1	5.6	5.6	53.2	53.2	53.2	1050.0	1050.0
江苏 Jiangsu	218.9	121.1	113.1	3128.0	3128.0	2617.0	387.2	432.2
浙江 Zhejiang	254.2	164.2	158.2	3450.0	3112.0	2979.0	527.8	531.0
安徽 Anhui	210.1	110.2	108.9	3028.2	2925.7	2871.0	376.8	379.2
福建 Fujian	103.0	51.7	50.7	3303.0	2159.0	2117.0	239.6	239.6
江西 Jiangxi	122.1	59.4	57.0	2625.0	2101.3	2017.1	282.9	282.3
山东 Shandong	347.8	188.0	177.2	4989.7	4896.9	4561.0	384.0	388.4
河南 Henan	450.2	295.2	274.1	10502.6	9749.3	9312.1	302.8	294.3
湖北 Hubei	121.0	87.2	84.4	2849.7	2758.5	2637.8	316.0	320.1
湖南 Hunan	194.7	134.0	126.7	5100.0	4693.0	4352.0	285.6	291.1
广东 Guangdong	196.0	130.2	128.4	3765.0	3118.0	3034.0	417.6	423.1
广西 Guangxi	147.0	106.4	104.5	3573.3	3412.8	3364.6	311.8	310.5
海南 Hainan	17.7	10.9	10.1	291.5	268.1	258.3	406.9	392.1
重庆 Chongqing	58.3	40.4	37.4	1497.8	1345.0	1229.8	300.3	304.1
四川 Sichuan	216.1	100.2	88.9	3413.0	3189.0	2816.0	314.3	315.8
贵州 Guizhou	68.2	37.8	36.9	1775.8	1554.3	1496.7	242.9	246.4
云南 Yunnan	138.5	83.5	83.5	4413.0	3834.0	3278.0	217.8	254.7
西藏 Tibet								
陕西 Shaanxi	110.0	48.4	47.6	1517.2	1493.3	1451.6	323.8	327.9
甘肃 Gansu	51.5	26.2	23.3	1031.0	1025.0	958.0	255.5	243.0
青海 Qinghai	10.1	5.5	5.0	252.7	252.7	201.0	217.4	250.7
宁夏 Ningxia	28.1	10.7	9.4	264.0	264.0	218.0	404.3	429.3
新疆 Xinjiang	71.7	28.1	27.4	1423.3	1382.4	1334.7	203.3	205.3

6-27 房地产开发企业(单位)主要指标

Main Indicators of Enterprises for Real Estate Development

指标	Item	2002	2003	2004	2005
企业个数 (个)	**Number of Enterprises (unit)**	**32618**	**37123**	**59242**	**56290**
内资	Domestic Funded	28657	33107	53495	50957
#国有	State-owned Enterprises	5015	4558	4775	4145
集体	Collective-owned Enterprises	2488	2205	2390	1796
港、澳、台投资	Enterprises with Funds from Hong Kong, Macao and Taiwan	2884	2840	3639	3443
外商投资	Foreign Funded	1077	1176	2108	1890
平均从业人数 (万人)	**Average Number of Employed Persons (10 000 persons)**	**113.40**	**120.54**	**158.54**	**151.62**
内资	Domestic Funded	101.43	108.69	142.93	136.67
#国有	State-owned Enterprises	20.87	17.96	16.35	14.01
集体	Collective-owned Enterprises	8.97	7.24	5.85	4.10
港、澳、台投资	Enterprises with Funds from Hong Kong, Macao and Taiwan	8.54	7.94	9.56	9.07
外商投资	Foreign Funded	3.43	3.90	6.05	5.87
土地开发及购置 (万平方米)	**Land Development and Purchase (10 000 sq.m)**				
本年土地开发面积	Land Space Developed This Year	19416.0	22166.3	19740.2	22676.2
本年土地购置面积	Land Space Purchased This Year	31356.8	35696.5	39784.7	38253.7
本年完成投资额 (亿元)	**Investment Completed This Year (100 million yuan)**	**7790.9**	**10153.8**	**13158.3**	**15909.2**
#住宅	Residential Buildings	5227.8	6776.7	8837.0	10860.9
#经济适用房屋	Economically Affordable Housing	589.0	622.0	606.4	519.2
资金来源小计 (亿元)	**Sources of Funds (100 million yuan)**	**9750.0**	**13196.9**	**17168.8**	**21397.8**
#国内贷款	Domestic Loans	2220.3	3138.3	3158.4	3918.1
利用外资	Foreign Investment	157.2	170.0	228.2	257.8
自筹资金	Self-raising Fund	2738.5	3770.7	5207.6	7000.4
房屋建筑面积 (万平方米)	**Floor Space of Buildings (10 000 sq.m)**				
施工面积	Floor Space under Construction	94104.0	117526.0	140451.4	166053.3
竣工面积	Floor Space Completed	34975.8	41464.1	42464.9	53417.0
本年新开工面积	Floor Space Started This Year	42800.5	54707.5	60413.9	68064.4
#住宅	Residential Buildings	34719.3	43853.9	47949.0	55185.1
#经济适用房屋	Economically Affordable Housing	5279.7	5330.6	4257.5	3513.4
商品房屋销售面积 (万平方米)	**Floor Space of Selling House (10 000 sq.m)**	**26808.3**	**33717.6**	**38231.6**	**55486.2**
#住宅	Residential Buildings	23702.3	29778.8	33819.9	49587.8
#经济适用房屋	Economically Affordable Housing	4003.6	4018.9	3261.8	3205.0
商品房屋销售价格 (元/平方米)	**Selling Price of House (yuan/sq.m)**	**2250**	**2359**	**2778**	**3168**
#住宅	Residential Buildings	2092	2197	2608	2937
#经济适用房屋	Economically Affordable Housing	1283	1380	1482	1655
实收资本合计 (亿元)	**Total Capital Hold (100 million yuan)**	**6750.9**	**8471.0**	**12545.8**	**13927.0**
#国家资本金	State Capital	325.6	408.3	1974.7	1596.5
资产负债率 (%)	**Ratio of Liabilities to Assets (%)**	**74.9**	**75.8**	**74.1**	**72.7**
经营总收入 (亿元)	**Total Revenue (100 million yuan)**	**7077.9**	**9137.3**	**13314.5**	**14769.3**
#土地转让收入	Land Transferred	225.1	279.7	410.1	341.4

注：1.2004年数据中除企业个数、从业人员平均数、房屋销售价格、住宅竣工套数以及财务指标为经济普查数据外，其他数据均为快报数据(以下表均同)。

2.2004年以前的商品房销售面积和销售额为实际销售统计口径；2005年的销售面积和销售额包括期房和现房(以下表均同)。

a) All figures for 2004 are from annual statistical reports, except figures on number of enterprises, average number of employed persons, selling prices of houses and other financial indicators which are from the economic census. The same as in the following tables.

b) Figures on floor space of houses sold and selling price of houses for 2004 and earlier years refer to houses actually sold out, while figures for 2005 refer to both completed and future houses sold. The same as in the following tables.

6-28 房地产开发企业(单位)个数

Number of Enterprises for Real Estate Development

单位：个 (unit)

年份 Year 地区 Region	企业个数 Number of Enterprises	内资企业 Domestic Funded Enterprises	#国有 State-owned Enterprises	#集体 Collective-owned Enterprises	港、澳、台投资企业 Enterprises with Funds from Hong Kong Macao and Taiwan	外商投资企业 Foreign Funded Enterprises
1997	21286	17202			1989	2095
1998	24378	19960	7958	4538	3214	1204
1999	25762	21422	7370	4127	3167	1173
2000	27303	23277	6641	3492	2899	1127
2001	29552	25509	5862	2991	2959	1084
2002	32618	28657	5015	2488	2884	1077
2003	37123	33107	4558	2205	2840	1176
2004	59242	53495	4775	2390	3639	2108
2005	56290	50957	4145	1796	3443	1890
北京 Beijing	3123	2786	143	26	197	140
天津 Tianjin	974	887	137	32	41	46
河北 Hebei	1169	1111	66	5	37	21
山西 Shanxi	1181	1155	141	31	21	5
内蒙古 Inner Mongolia	1012	1003	35	8	5	4
辽宁 Liaoning	2744	2451	121	29	157	136
吉林 Jilin	758	720	56	4	26	12
黑龙江 Heilongjiang	1050	1012	124	7	21	17
上海 Shanghai	4064	3587	363	188	277	200
江苏 Jiangsu	3810	3384	216	142	277	149
浙江 Zhejiang	3549	3369	150	66	98	82
安徽 Anhui	1909	1803	145	51	56	50
福建 Fujian	2596	1866	225	91	470	260
江西 Jiangxi	1824	1619	170	41	131	74
山东 Shandong	3039	2855	267	166	119	65
河南 Henan	1906	1795	173	58	59	52
湖北 Hubei	1990	1782	213	47	129	79
湖南 Hunan	2006	1853	172	40	101	52
广东 Guangdong	5410	4410	439	511	792	208
广西 Guangxi	1730	1542	196	51	112	76
海南 Hainan	306	263	22	4	26	17
重庆 Chongqing	1862	1752	68	17	84	26
四川 Sichuan	2848	2725	139	67	76	47
贵州 Guizhou	1465	1405	91	32	39	21
云南 Yunnan	875	848	58	9	21	6
西藏 Tibet	21	21	5			
陕西 Shaanxi	933	901	98	24	22	10
甘肃 Gansu	825	770	68	37	31	24
青海 Qinghai	251	237	11	5	11	3
宁夏 Ningxia	304	301	7	2		3
新疆 Xinjiang	756	744	26	5	7	5

6-29 房地产开发企业(单位)从业人员数

Number of Employed Persons in Enterprises for Real Estate Development

单位：人 (person)

年份 地区	Year Region	平均从业人数 Average Number of Employed Persons	内资企业 Domestic Funded Enterprises	#国有 State-owned Enterprises	#集体 Collective-owned Enterprises	港、澳、台投资企业 Enterprises with Funds from Hong Kong Macao and Taiwan	外商投资企业 Foreign Funded Enterprises
	1997	683217	578927			50000	54290
	1998	825888	708738	332834	134939	83784	33366
	1999	880257	767187	312240	127370	80216	32854
	2000	971942	862245	292252	116416	79066	30631
	2001	1062319	949580	257695	109826	81668	31071
	2002	1134009	1014254	208722	89739	85449	34306
	2003	1205355	1086923	179614	72400	79397	39035
	2004	1585428	1429291	163495	58514	95646	60491
	2005	1516150	1366743	140106	40978	90674	58733
北京	Beijing	83859	67818	6278	829	8982	7059
天津	Tianjin	40849	36042	6703	900	1910	2897
河北	Hebei	39573	36950	2723	121	1913	710
山西	Shanxi	31309	30563	5473	1028	627	119
内蒙古	Inner Mongolia	27738	27432	656	118	244	62
辽宁	Liaoning	51692	47078	3027	333	2276	2338
吉林	Jilin	22332	20975	1865	77	643	714
黑龙江	Heilongjiang	35126	34154	4326	139	349	623
上海	Shanghai	91849	71514	9025	2452	9850	10485
江苏	Jiangsu	84653	75361	5668	2412	5896	3396
浙江	Zhejiang	70909	67155	3709	1135	2053	1701
安徽	Anhui	49030	46681	5301	1336	1276	1073
福建	Fujian	48421	34360	5642	1165	9130	4931
江西	Jiangxi	45369	40473	4678	979	3452	1444
山东	Shandong	107894	101797	13620	6911	3921	2176
河南	Henan	53691	50023	6645	1671	1449	2219
湖北	Hubei	67225	61693	9080	1752	3411	2121
湖南	Hunan	66678	62781	5682	1454	2635	1262
广东	Guangdong	149622	124802	15253	11494	18953	5867
广西	Guangxi	35579	32046	4054	675	1998	1535
海南	Hainan	9021	7760	431	63	623	638
重庆	Chongqing	70563	65590	3811	619	3728	1245
四川	Sichuan	86230	82699	4166	1168	1400	2131
贵州	Guizhou	32658	31481	2479	503	860	317
云南	Yunnan	30256	29149	1236	158	876	231
西藏	Tibet	840	840	253			
陕西	Shaanxi	30342	29301	5419	780	668	373
甘肃	Gansu	19958	18510	1599	553	895	553
青海	Qinghai	5467	5185	290	83	219	63
宁夏	Ningxia	8832	8495	165	23		337
新疆	Xinjiang	18585	18035	849	47	437	113

6-30 房地产开发企业(单位)土地开发及购置

Land Development and Purchase of Enterprises for Real Estate Development

单位：万平方米 (10 000 sq.m)

年份 Year 地区 Region	本年完成开发土地面积 Land Space Developed This Year	土地购置费用(亿元) Total Value of Land Purchased (100 million yuan)	待开发土地面积 Land Space Needed to Development	本年购置土地面积 Land Space Purchased This Year
1997	7371.3	247.6	17670.1	6641.7
1998	7730.1	375.4	13530.7	10109.3
1999	9319.6	500.0	13505.2	11958.9
2000	11666.1	733.9	14754.8	16905.2
2001	15315.8	1038.8	14582.1	23409.0
2002	19416.0	1445.8	19178.7	31356.8
2003	22166.3	2055.2	21782.6	35696.5
2004	19740.2	2574.5	39635.3	39784.7
2005	22676.2	2904.4	27522.0	38253.7
北京 Beijing	314.2	239.8	2914.8	773.9
天津 Tianjin	986.3	72.9	760.0	730.0
河北 Hebei	523.0	49.4	216.0	968.6
山西 Shanxi	251.9	23.8	256.2	519.1
内蒙古 Inner Mongolia	350.3	26.3	141.4	1004.5
辽宁 Liaoning	1697.6	168.2	417.5	2432.8
吉林 Jilin	218.4	24.3	13.5	604.9
黑龙江 Heilongjiang	328.5	32.4	104.9	692.5
上海 Shanghai	558.4	170.4	626.6	754.3
江苏 Jiangsu	1827.4	324.2	3981.3	2848.8
浙江 Zhejiang	1311.6	416.4	730.6	1801.9
安徽 Anhui	1067.2	100.5	1504.1	1896.4
福建 Fujian	726.1	134.9	551.3	1822.5
江西 Jiangxi	947.5	59.3	1124.0	1517.9
山东 Shandong	2356.3	172.1	1850.0	3735.9
河南 Henan	973.2	74.8	763.5	2015.8
湖北 Hubei	941.3	80.7	937.9	1530.6
湖南 Hunan	971.5	82.5	1364.4	1763.0
广东 Guangdong	2085.7	213.6	3245.1	2894.1
广西 Guangxi	674.5	44.6	1814.3	1218.1
海南 Hainan	66.7	9.2	101.4	205.2
重庆 Chongqing	916.3	72.8	2046.3	1385.4
四川 Sichuan	669.1	176.7	990.4	2038.3
贵州 Guizhou	247.6	23.7	278.5	519.9
云南 Yunnan	478.5	41.0	188.5	940.5
西藏 Tibet	36.5	0.8	16.1	44.7
陕西 Shaanxi	409.2	38.2	250.9	611.4
甘肃 Gansu	162.3	8.0	109.4	177.6
青海 Qinghai	65.5	4.5	12.1	112.2
宁夏 Ningxia	35.2	9.1	8.7	245.6
新疆 Xinjiang	478.5	9.4	202.1	447.3

6-31 房地产开发企业(单位)建设投资总规模及完成投资(2005年)

General Scale of Construction and Actually Completed Investment of Enterprises for Real Estate Development (2005)

单位: 亿元 (100 million yuan)

地区	Region	计划总投资 Total Investment Planed	自开始建设至本年底累计完成投资 Accumulative Investment Actually Completed Since Starting of Construction up to the End of This Year	#本年完成投资 Investment Completed This Year	#商品房建设投资 Investment in Commercial Buildings
全 国	**National Total**	**65116.74**	**37243.37**	**15909.25**	**11314.91**
北 京	Beijing	7001.14	4535.74	1525.01	730.00
天 津	Tianjin	2728.22	1133.27	327.54	188.08
河 北	Hebei	1213.10	547.34	391.53	289.65
山 西	Shanxi	584.65	322.54	177.99	139.26
内蒙古	Inner Mongolia	396.94	217.90	162.10	130.35
辽 宁	Liaoning	2677.28	1381.71	874.25	642.66
吉 林	Jilin	497.54	264.13	195.73	146.03
黑龙江	Heilongjiang	682.35	409.00	267.63	222.72
上 海	Shanghai	6615.35	4377.12	1246.86	1094.42
江 苏	Jiangsu	6037.50	3481.26	1545.15	1156.16
浙 江	Zhejiang	5458.01	3560.80	1456.49	958.77
安 徽	Anhui	1930.11	845.28	459.44	299.55
福 建	Fujian	2153.63	1075.47	540.39	350.84
江 西	Jiangxi	1173.49	546.12	301.10	214.47
山 东	Shandong	3556.01	1776.44	977.71	687.33
河 南	Henan	1449.85	701.76	388.52	280.18
湖 北	Hubei	1692.03	749.21	447.95	306.73
湖 南	Hunan	1961.26	942.65	456.97	218.31
广 东	Guangdong	7914.98	4923.21	1591.90	1187.52
广 西	Guangxi	1254.19	705.69	286.79	267.50
海 南	Hainan	284.86	167.50	70.85	60.76
重 庆	Chongqing	2599.85	1374.35	517.73	343.12
四 川	Sichuan	1911.05	1271.03	701.45	647.31
贵 州	Guizhou	639.31	346.38	154.12	100.93
云 南	Yunnan	776.94	476.40	246.91	179.56
西 藏	Tibet	14.68	8.66	6.02	3.49
陕 西	Shaanxi	1030.42	536.79	298.95	223.71
甘 肃	Gansu	339.74	217.09	86.60	69.10
青 海	Qinghai	128.86	75.99	29.11	22.10
宁 夏	Ningxia	140.41	107.13	74.78	66.87
新 疆	Xinjiang	272.99	165.44	101.66	87.42

6-32 按用途分房地产开发企业(单位)投资完成额

Actually Completed Investment of Enterprises for Real Estate Development by Use

单位: 万元 (10 000 yuan)

年份 地区	Year Region	本年完成投资额 Investment Completed This Year	住宅 Residential Buildings	#别墅、高档公寓 Villas, High-grade Apartments	#经济适用房屋 Economically Affordable Housing	办公楼 Office Buildings	商业营业用房 Houses for Business Use	其他 Others
	1997	31783702	15393805	1562955	1854959	3889819	4258452	8241626
	1998	36142292	20815647	1818526	2708523	4337956	4758297	6230392
	1999	41032024	26384794	1786233	4370211	3385973	4843349	6417908
	2000	49840529	33119839	2700142	5424365	2978511	5799927	7942252
	2001	63441107	42166760	3699241	5996464	3079470	7553018	10641859
	2002	77909223	52277560	5169632	5890445	3810018	9336107	12485538
	2003	101538009	67766861	6329872	6219833	5083372	13023473	15664303
	2004	131582516	88369532	10736486	6063880	6521963	17237192	19453829
	2005	159092471	108609322	10494059	5191806	7630681	20395282	22457185
北京	Beijing	15250082	7795336	1388641	447648	1961721	1129007	4364018
天津	Tianjin	3275403	2349240	311449	212116	119477	417449	389237
河北	Hebei	3915256	2920522	103885	367261	97133	472660	424941
山西	Shanxi	1779937	1168931	18895	160641	107448	274199	229359
内蒙古	Inner Mongolia	1621002	1147074	16073	93419	38295	385657	49976
辽宁	Liaoning	8742525	6145405	306288	154200	258764	1502775	835581
吉林	Jilin	1957345	1452681	78237	168516	70410	332528	101726
黑龙江	Heilongjiang	2676332	1748422	4206	144341	82290	461664	383955
上海	Shanghai	12468560	9208365	2254954		1021784	1026068	1212343
江苏	Jiangsu	15451539	11330594	1384185	448374	542683	2170202	1408060
浙江	Zhejiang	14564885	10895057	925300	616628	678772	1705982	1285074
安徽	Anhui	4594413	3233619	61564	97301	132116	648456	580222
福建	Fujian	5403902	3637199	177889	116393	107594	478198	1180911
江西	Jiangxi	3010982	2081628	55694	107090	44861	456512	427981
山东	Shandong	9777098	6982621	201843	448910	293873	1287764	1212840
河南	Henan	3885172	2716205	250668	235479	140472	677936	350559
湖北	Hubei	4479501	3176464	79328	134869	134270	447275	721492
湖南	Hunan	4569741	3061462	287819	104720	112671	715375	680233
广东	Guangdong	15918983	10657419	1198674	28557	903167	1722954	2635443
广西	Guangxi	2867915	1907662	111477	74493	60074	453904	446275
海南	Hainan	708494	566217	58395	28350	4335	83257	54685
重庆	Chongqing	5177291	3004026	318975	119534	170832	713916	1288517
四川	Sichuan	7014479	4732924	433830	124637	182078	1264790	834687
贵州	Guizhou	1541209	858733	17268	96273	78362	214316	389798
云南	Yunnan	2469114	1733652	251970	117999	48656	284702	402104
西藏	Tibet	60207	43348	17974	1021	354	13153	3352
陕西	Shaanxi	2989546	2122786	132870	185528	118394	439687	308679
甘肃	Gansu	866044	610986	2339	67500	32537	117840	104681
青海	Qinghai	291130	165786	860	26836	19280	43828	62236
宁夏	Ningxia	747766	475437	15875	18150	27001	206195	39133
新疆	Xinjiang	1016618	679521	26634	245022	40977	247033	49087

6-33 房地产开发企业(单位)资金来源

Sources of Funds of Enterprises for Real Estate Development

单位: 万元 (10 000 yuan)

年份 Year / 地区 Region		本年资金来源小计 Total Funds This Year	国内贷款 Domestic Loans	利用外资 Foreign Investment	#外商直接投资 Foreign Direct Investment	自筹资金 Self-raising Funds	其他资金来源 Others
	1997	38170650	9111902	4608565	3279010	9728831	14547872
	1998	44149422	10531712	3617581	2588698	11669821	18118509
	1999	47959012	11115664	2566022	1804807	13446210	20631956
	2000	59976309	13850756	1687046	1348026	16142122	28192905
	2001	76963877	16921968	1357044	1061150	21839587	36705562
	2002	97499536	22203357	1572284	1241285	27384451	46198961
	2003	131969224	31382699	1700040	1162667	37706891	61060503
	2004	171687669	31584126	2282001	1425587	52075627	85625867
	2005	213978389	39180778	2578111	1714093	70003924	102215576
北京	Beijing	31019234	6807794	385603	292494	6041386	17784451
天津	Tianjin	6216654	1383517	34895	27229	2017535	2780707
河北	Hebei	4131320	682504	34424	32008	1776377	1638015
山西	Shanxi	1917030	249882	476	476	910929	755743
内蒙古	Inner Mongolia	1575542	58734			1181130	335678
辽宁	Liaoning	9372018	1267527	89308	68971	4586225	3428958
吉林	Jilin	2021527	124756	27656	2233	1007776	861339
黑龙江	Heilongjiang	2680717	178057	35300	35300	1362272	1105088
上海	Shanghai	19898767	4830288	405436	152180	5277844	9385199
江苏	Jiangsu	20388268	3927251	331568	208501	6147632	9981817
浙江	Zhejiang	19401586	4338618	65182	55028	4340125	10657661
安徽	Anhui	5430807	757235	67788	49567	2288821	2316963
福建	Fujian	8039279	1568495	148117	118179	2171544	4151123
江西	Jiangxi	3295995	460301	38527	25605	1448201	1348966
山东	Shandong	11054319	1763799	66240	42415	4615810	4608470
河南	Henan	4362980	607493	21029	14471	1809062	1925396
湖北	Hubei	5134411	1004079	18231	1297	1869530	2242571
湖南	Hunan	5069126	765740	49672	27494	2635023	1618691
广东	Guangdong	22335955	3857541	371561	260032	7023311	11083542
广西	Guangxi	3395656	555493	59114	18252	1128707	1652342
海南	Hainan	895072	82386	14892	11257	342075	455719
重庆	Chongqing	6982893	1277531	140419	106909	2189074	3375869
四川	Sichuan	7990172	856565	151273	150655	3413522	3568812
贵州	Guizhou	1951658	493018	6750	1750	639126	812764
云南	Yunnan	3224736	460638	1990	1990	1066295	1695813
西藏	Tibet	69783	9626			24567	35590
陕西	Shaanxi	2998907	411859	12125	9425	1365531	1209392
甘肃	Gansu	946848	160693			413903	372252
青海	Qinghai	309008	20764	375	375	185255	102614
宁夏	Ningxia	730428	104707			245388	380333
新疆	Xinjiang	1137693	113887	160		479948	543698

6-34 房地产开发企业(单位)建设房屋建筑面积和造价

Floor Space and Cost of Buildings Developed by Enterprises for Real Estate Development

年份 地区	Year Region	施工房屋面积(万平方米) Floor Space of Buildings under Construction (10 000 sq.m)	竣工房屋面积(万平方米) Floor Space of Buildings Completed (10 000 sq.m)	房屋建筑面积竣工率(%) Rate of Floor Space of Buildings Completed (%)	竣工房屋价值(万元) Value of Buildings Completed (10 000 yuan)	竣工房屋造价(元/平方米) Cost of Buildings Completed (yuan/sq.m)
	1997	44985.5	15819.7	35.2	18592458	1175
	1998	50770.1	17566.6	34.6	21391927	1218
	1999	56857.6	21410.8	37.7	24675822	1152
	2000	65896.9	25104.9	38.1	28593463	1139
	2001	79411.7	29867.4	37.6	33694469	1128
	2002	94104.0	34975.8	37.2	41416949	1184
	2003	117526.0	41464.1	35.3	52799528	1273
	2004	140451.4	42464.9	30.2	59524820	1402
	2005	166053.3	53417.0	32.2	77522369	1451
北京	Beijing	10748.5	3770.9	35.1	8120198	2153
天津	Tianjin	3470.6	1479.2	42.6	2079119	1406
河北	Hebei	3821.0	1129.9	29.6	1374134	1216
山西	Shanxi	2266.5	667.3	29.4	917262	1375
内蒙古	Inner Mongolia	2111.3	897.1	42.5	978783	1091
辽宁	Liaoning	7058.9	2443.9	34.6	2931979	1200
吉林	Jilin	1890.0	622.8	33.0	676039	1086
黑龙江	Heilongjiang	2630.5	1305.0	49.6	1421490	1089
上海	Shanghai	10462.4	3095.7	29.6	9467702	3058
江苏	Jiangsu	15619.3	5500.1	35.2	7587800	1380
浙江	Zhejiang	15651.7	4130.8	26.4	6714589	1625
安徽	Anhui	5306.9	1816.9	34.2	2027587	1116
福建	Fujian	6107.7	1576.2	25.8	1997996	1268
江西	Jiangxi	4508.2	1561.5	34.6	1309904	839
山东	Shandong	10670.9	3600.4	33.7	4696486	1304
河南	Henan	4903.0	1370.9	28.0	1447233	1056
湖北	Hubei	4804.4	1627.0	33.9	2387899	1468
湖南	Hunan	5050.4	1741.1	34.5	1793351	1030
广东	Guangdong	15110.0	4385.2	29.0	8293512	1891
广西	Guangxi	4082.8	1330.7	32.6	1167764	878
海南	Hainan	921.1	187.1	20.3	345378	1846
重庆	Chongqing	7487.4	2209.8	29.5	2549302	1154
四川	Sichuan	8277.7	2769.9	33.5	2236073	807
贵州	Guizhou	2784.9	711.6	25.6	624806	878
云南	Yunnan	2807.0	857.5	30.5	1090677	1272
西藏	Tibet	43.4	26.5	61.1	43045	1625
陕西	Shaanxi	3175.7	757.2	23.8	1201727	1587
甘肃	Gansu	1438.0	454.9	31.6	511822	1125
青海	Qinghai	422.9	104.1	24.6	126588	1216
宁夏	Ningxia	1049.4	568.1	54.1	590867	1040
新疆	Xinjiang	1371.1	717.4	52.3	811257	1131

6-35 按用途分房地产开发企业(单位)新开工房屋面积

Floor Space of Buildings Started This Year by Enterprises for Real Estate Development by Use

单位：万平方米 (10 000 sq.m)

年份 地区	Year Region	本年新开工房屋面积 Floor Space Started This Year	住宅 Residential Buildings	#别墅、高档公寓 Villas, High-grade Apartments	#经济适用房屋 Economically Affordable Housing	办公楼 Office Buildings	商业营业用房 Houses for Business Use	其他 Others
	1997	14026.98	10996.64	469.72	1720.57	872.44	1462.45	695.44
	1998	20387.90	16637.50	638.60	3466.40	871.50	1938.65	940.25
	1999	22579.41	18797.94	594.06	3970.36	690.29	2198.56	892.62
	2000	29582.64	24401.15	1169.09	5313.32	898.81	3034.77	1247.91
	2001	37394.18	30532.72	1456.69	5795.97	1072.98	4105.40	1683.08
	2002	42800.52	34719.35	2278.17	5279.68	1254.24	4926.48	1900.45
	2003	54707.53	43853.88	2349.29	5330.58	1466.89	6706.80	2679.96
	2004	60413.86	47949.01	2975.69	4257.49	1704.19	7790.81	2969.85
	2005	68064.44	55185.07	2834.97	3513.45	1671.10	7675.47	3532.79
北京	Beijing	2965.93	1983.24	243.87	265.05	294.91	259.68	428.11
天津	Tianjin	1579.45	1287.06	136.58	161.67	77.21	153.85	61.33
河北	Hebei	1970.80	1751.52	31.82	225.80	37.17	138.71	43.40
山西	Shanxi	1156.01	983.90	17.64	163.97	48.41	101.00	22.70
内蒙古	Inner Mongolia	1425.01	1166.32	21.73	93.36	17.67	216.07	24.95
辽宁	Liaoning	3638.39	3040.03	62.99	79.86	47.28	443.54	107.53
吉林	Jilin	1286.14	1079.33	26.28	114.81	22.80	151.84	32.17
黑龙江	Heilongjiang	1485.11	1147.72	9.55	94.82	35.85	232.51	69.04
上海	Shanghai	3055.47	2485.75	284.85		120.09	235.03	214.61
江苏	Jiangsu	6653.24	5253.64	389.59	272.74	146.83	891.27	361.50
浙江	Zhejiang	4859.59	3822.76	287.69	285.44	107.84	446.83	482.16
安徽	Anhui	2623.41	2181.61	27.07	58.90	42.88	309.59	89.33
福建	Fujian	2196.57	1727.38	33.18	61.05	27.16	170.58	271.45
江西	Jiangxi	2490.82	2093.47	27.22	100.61	20.03	321.09	56.23
山东	Shandong	5650.04	4795.05	105.25	254.61	102.36	564.61	188.02
河南	Henan	2150.58	1699.14	86.54	177.27	63.95	342.99	44.50
湖北	Hubei	2292.92	2003.46	44.50	115.47	38.99	170.47	79.99
湖南	Hunan	2106.40	1678.27	112.25	79.67	59.46	291.28	77.38
广东	Guangdong	4989.82	4010.39	342.83	12.50	99.04	494.79	385.61
广西	Guangxi	1633.29	1277.86	49.98	52.45	39.81	238.57	77.05
海南	Hainan	253.39	194.73	25.11	7.57	1.63	50.11	6.92
重庆	Chongqing	2334.75	1824.74	51.03	75.47	46.97	319.53	143.51
四川	Sichuan	3684.37	3074.53	150.00	99.30	37.10	465.02	107.72
贵州	Guizhou	1007.70	783.38	2.39	87.01	32.00	145.84	46.48
云南	Yunnan	1294.43	1073.61	191.28	76.58	25.79	133.81	61.22
西藏	Tibet	38.81	33.43	9.95		0.20	5.18	
陕西	Shaanxi	1234.75	1125.86	43.29	154.91	31.81	60.99	16.09
甘肃	Gansu	389.78	323.94	1.34	50.46	8.87	53.11	3.87
青海	Qinghai	243.06	201.04	0.47	45.50	11.56	26.43	4.03
宁夏	Ningxia	580.85	441.93	9.12	28.57	14.54	110.26	14.13
新疆	Xinjiang	793.55	639.98	9.59	218.04	10.89	130.90	11.78

6-36 商品房屋销售情况

Selling of Commercial Buildings

年 份 地 区	Year Region	房屋销售面积 (万平方米) Floor Space Sold (10 000 sq.m)	#住 宅 Residential Buildings	商品房销售额 (万元) Total Sale of Commercial Buildings (10 000 yuan)	#住 宅 Residential Buildings
	1991	3025.46	2745.17	2378597	2075979
	1992	4288.86	3812.21	4265938	3798493
	1993	6687.91	6035.19	8637141	7291913
	1994	7230.35	6118.03	10184950	7305208
	1995	7905.94	6787.03	12577269	10240705
	1996	7900.41	6898.46	14271292	11069006
	1997	9010.17	7864.30	17994763	14075553
	1998	12185.30	10827.10	25133027	20068676
	1999	14556.53	12997.87	29878734	24137347
	2000	18637.13	16570.28	39354423	32286046
	2001	22411.90	19938.75	48627517	40211543
	2002	26808.29	23702.31	60323413	49578501
	2003	33717.63	29778.85	79556627	65434492
	2004	38231.64	33819.89	103757069	86193667
	2005	55486.22	49587.83	175761325	145637616
北 京	Beijing	3123.42	2823.65	21202099	17399710
天 津	Tianjin	1408.37	1264.38	5710574	5041379
河 北	Hebei	1408.74	1322.32	2623116	2350398
山 西	Shanxi	688.75	619.86	1522069	1163065
内蒙古	Inner Mongolia	1078.80	918.43	1783491	1287226
辽 宁	Liaoning	2564.48	2340.36	7174340	6205959
吉 林	Jilin	830.91	745.92	1568915	1309503
黑龙江	Heilongjiang	1242.81	1048.26	2608815	1963185
上 海	Shanghai	3158.87	2845.70	21613022	19060478
江 苏	Jiangsu	5135.55	4523.14	17249062	14227924
浙 江	Zhejiang	3305.84	2824.65	14148885	11222435
安 徽	Anhui	1907.21	1686.03	4234369	3481041
福 建	Fujian	1913.84	1720.56	6050925	4819032
江 西	Jiangxi	1650.12	1454.51	2522496	1942900
山 东	Shandong	3754.92	3417.75	9106518	7842466
河 南	Henan	1724.82	1539.60	3220147	2553706
湖 北	Hubei	1708.02	1549.19	3865693	3351897
湖 南	Hunan	1842.16	1611.60	2993154	2263639
广 东	Guangdong	5038.91	4546.32	22386643	18863862
广 西	Guangxi	1438.40	1314.37	2896410	2398083
海 南	Hainan	249.43	233.08	729458	665496
重 庆	Chongqing	2017.66	1792.41	4307679	3406768
四 川	Sichuan	3402.49	3028.55	6619495	5111802
贵 州	Guizhou	862.56	774.71	1385781	1012982
云 南	Yunnan	1431.90	1294.95	3100083	2590989
西 藏	Tibet	25.90	24.18	44032	36421
陕 西	Shaanxi	892.01	849.43	1837192	1639682
甘 肃	Gansu	493.21	439.83	954958	764891
青 海	Qinghai	121.04	108.46	221768	182320
宁 夏	Ningxia	377.89	319.16	844726	563186
新 疆	Xinjiang	687.20	606.48	1235410	915191

6-37 按用途分商品房屋销售面积

Floor Space of Commercial Buildings Sold by Use

单位：万平方米 (10 000 sq.m)

年份 地区 Year Region	房屋销售面积 Floor Space Sold	住宅 Residential Buildings	#别墅、高档公寓 Villas, High-grade Apartments	#经济适用房屋 Economically Affordable Housing	办公楼 Office Buildings	商业营业用房 Houses for Business Use	其他 Other
1997	9010.17	7864.30	254.25	1211.85	341.43	634.06	170.38
1998	12185.30	10827.10	345.30	1666.50	400.60	810.80	146.80
1999	14556.53	12997.87	435.74	2701.31	403.43	1003.17	152.06
2000	18637.13	16570.28	640.72	3760.07	436.98	1399.31	230.56
2001	22411.90	19938.75	878.19	4021.47	502.57	1696.15	274.44
2002	26808.29	23702.31	1241.26	4003.61	538.92	2218.58	348.47
2003	33717.63	29778.85	1449.87	4018.87	630.49	2833.10	475.19
2004	38231.64	33819.89	2323.05	3261.80	692.84	3100.29	618.62
2005	55486.22	49587.83	2818.44	3205.01	1096.23	4081.38	720.78
北京 Beijing	3123.42	2823.65	270.77	222.87	184.67	87.40	27.70
天津 Tianjin	1408.37	1264.38	119.60	100.35	43.47	79.12	21.39
河北 Hebei	1408.74	1322.32	26.68	155.81	15.86	60.37	10.19
山西 Shanxi	688.75	619.86	4.51	100.23	15.85	46.53	6.52
内蒙古 Inner Mongolia	1078.80	918.43	22.35	125.33	19.63	131.61	9.14
辽宁 Liaoning	2564.48	2340.36	44.93	71.48	16.14	182.65	25.34
吉林 Jilin	830.91	745.92	31.96	91.03	14.79	63.48	6.72
黑龙江 Heilongjiang	1242.81	1048.26	7.24	151.98	29.01	138.22	27.32
上海 Shanghai	3158.87	2845.70	449.38		97.89	150.20	65.09
江苏 Jiangsu	5135.55	4523.14	297.04	187.04	119.10	440.08	53.23
浙江 Zhejiang	3305.84	2824.65	166.06	160.98	111.39	263.94	105.87
安徽 Anhui	1907.21	1686.03	36.23	63.22	23.63	180.21	17.33
福建 Fujian	1913.84	1720.56	37.18	78.34	21.05	120.76	51.47
江西 Jiangxi	1650.12	1454.51	24.98	90.19	8.75	175.02	11.83
山东 Shandong	3754.92	3417.75	59.94	242.70	37.55	271.69	27.93
河南 Henan	1724.82	1539.60	94.06	181.11	24.85	154.91	5.45
湖北 Hubei	1708.02	1549.19	39.23	111.31	28.98	95.50	34.35
湖南 Hunan	1842.16	1611.60	100.09	67.69	24.00	184.88	21.68
广东 Guangdong	5038.91	4546.32	480.24	33.96	107.76	277.08	107.75
广西 Guangxi	1438.40	1314.37	50.88	42.48	8.78	99.20	16.05
海南 Hainan	249.43	233.08	25.31	18.27	1.92	14.05	0.39
重庆 Chongqing	2017.66	1792.41	108.71	88.74	32.58	177.86	14.80
四川 Sichuan	3402.49	3028.55	92.23	131.99	33.17	317.21	23.57
贵州 Guizhou	862.56	774.71	7.34	78.75	19.70	64.91	3.24
云南 Yunnan	1431.90	1294.95	139.48	139.91	10.33	113.38	13.24
西藏 Tibet	25.90	24.18	11.09			1.72	
陕西 Shaanxi	892.01	849.43	37.87	119.11	10.48	30.29	1.82
甘肃 Gansu	493.21	439.83	1.35	78.30	10.12	39.30	3.96
青海 Qinghai	121.04	108.46	1.57	14.96	8.73	3.57	0.28
宁夏 Ningxia	377.89	319.16	8.47	38.28	8.65	48.09	1.99
新疆 Xinjiang	687.20	606.48	21.72	218.59	7.40	68.16	5.16

6-38 按用途分商品房屋平均销售价格

Average Selling Price of Commercial Buildings by Use

单位: 元/平方米 (yuan/sq.m)

年份 地区	Year Region	房屋平均销售价格 Average Selling Price of Commercial Buildings	住宅 Residential Buildings	#别墅、高档公寓 Villas, High-grade Apartments	#经济适用房屋 Economically Affordable Housing	办公楼 Office Buildings	商业营业用房 Houses for Business Use	其他 Others
	1997	1997	1790	5382	1097	4677	3090	2129
	1998	2063	1854	4596	1035	5552	3170	1837
	1999	2053	1857	4503	1093	5265	3333	1804
	2000	2112	1948	4288	1202	4751	3260	1864
	2001	2170	2017	4348	1240	4588	3274	2033
	2002	2250	2092	4154	1283	4336	3489	1919
	2003	2359	2197	4145	1380	4196	3675	2241
	2004	2778	2608	5576	1482	5744	3884	2235
	2005	3168	2937	5834	1655	6923	5022	2829
北京	Beijing	6788	6162	9827	3541	13517	13828	3525
天津	Tianjin	4055	3987	5435	3110	5022	4725	3602
河北	Hebei	1862	1777	3391	1493	4752	2999	1599
山西	Shanxi	2210	1876	3899	1281	4908	5759	2033
内蒙古	Inner Mongolia	1653	1402	2956	1196	2993	3204	1728
辽宁	Liaoning	2798	2652	5286	2112	3842	4541	3036
吉林	Jilin	1888	1756	3871	1567	3045	3136	2275
黑龙江	Heilongjiang	2099	1873	4238	1511	4119	3276	2682
上海	Shanghai	6842	6698	7720		11867	7101	4983
江苏	Jiangsu	3359	3146	5002	1691	5216	5180	2263
浙江	Zhejiang	4280	3973	6412	2849	5893	7348	3122
安徽	Anhui	2220	2065	3356	1059	3663	3488	2198
福建	Fujian	3162	2801	5558	1631	4293	8512	2207
江西	Jiangxi	1529	1336	2473	718	2893	3080	1289
山东	Shandong	2425	2295	4679	1905	5848	3550	2867
河南	Henan	1867	1659	2572	1159	3059	3765	1326
湖北	Hubei	2263	2164	4297	1191	2665	4049	1453
湖南	Hunan	1625	1405	2283	1048	2794	3416	1427
广东	Guangdong	4443	4149	7331	1383	8316	8105	3535
广西	Guangxi	2014	1825	3007	1440	4132	4343	1950
海南	Hainan	2924	2855	4436	1976	2720	4108	2645
重庆	Chongqing	2135	1901	4295	1485	2408	4462	1950
四川	Sichuan	1945	1688	3502	1129	3406	4283	1533
贵州	Guizhou	1607	1308	2897	1181	3213	4643	2518
云南	Yunnan	2165	2001	2920	1081	2182	3999	2507
西藏	Tibet	1700	1506	1560			4433	
陕西	Shaanxi	2060	1930	3310	1119	3587	5181	1655
甘肃	Gansu	1936	1739	3147	1180	2771	4006	1163
青海	Qinghai	1832	1681	2134	1264	2766	4117	2142
宁夏	Ningxia	2235	1765	3276	1057	3429	5151	2102
新疆	Xinjiang	1798	1509	2504	1396	2708	4237	2215

6-39 房地产开发企业(单位)资产负债

Assets and Liabilities of Enterprises for Real Estate Development

单位: 万元 (10 000 yuan)

年份 地区	Year Region	实收资本 合计 Total Capital Hold	#国家资本金 State Capital	资产总计 Total Assets	累计折旧 Total Depreciation	#本年折旧 Depreciation This Year	负债总计 Total Liabilities	所有者权益 Owners' Equity	资产负债率(%) Assets Liability Ratio
	1997	38120741	2443003	164169597	1756884	410656	125154596	39015001	76.2
	1998	57787310	8418989	195261772	1910386	390176	148572535	46689237	76.1
	1999	45208800	3024487	187448042	2087894	398180	142638782	44809260	76.1
	2000	53029071	2155664	251859857	2992816	577153	190321015	61538842	75.6
	2001	60198577	4717344	285668126	3544631	674683	214357160	71310966	75.0
	2002	67509145	3255888	330431260	3905332	817353	247645673	82785587	74.9
	2003	84710226	4082557	404864877	4508222	968337	306985556	97879321	75.8
	2004	125458025	19747277	617891877	5980181	1391839	457836253	160055624	74.1
	2005	139269809	15964546	721936389	7370146	1573500	525207058	196734103	72.7
北京	Beijing	16993148	1072443	103056653	869775	195749	81559153	21497500	79.1
天津	Tianjin	3735093	838007	20213883	182235	35107	14718393	5495490	72.8
河北	Hebei	1881471	87128	9317561	130276	34355	6477269	2840292	69.5
山西	Shanxi	1293327	86782	5843700	87856	18696	4199940	1643760	71.9
内蒙古	Inner Mongolia	777169	30448	2878239	35264	7502	1950118	928121	67.8
辽宁	Liaoning	7518959	344824	28261273	249518	59905	19413238	8848035	68.7
吉林	Jilin	994137	82482	5386109	67648	13375	4253918	1132191	79.0
黑龙江	Heilongjiang	1762182	252203	7638744	102354	18073	5708433	1930311	74.7
上海	Shanghai	24203716	4892274	119595212	1040222	200743	79610683	39984529	66.6
江苏	Jiangsu	9439982	867470	56214943	344104	84160	42975166	13239777	76.4
浙江	Zhejiang	8156604	440002	59129595	329206	93290	47646137	11483458	80.6
安徽	Anhui	2976285	266769	12152955	115739	28292	8530794	3622161	70.2
福建	Fujian	6181140	820419	26498164	236101	40321	18316962	8181202	69.1
江西	Jiangxi	1982208	201627	7096295	53111	13508	4595949	2500346	64.8
山东	Shandong	5827451	660312	30301374	351349	74694	22384527	7916847	73.9
河南	Henan	2318891	145206	9784926	143625	29277	6816474	2968452	69.7
湖北	Hubei	4236856	679500	16108008	206708	39484	11077697	5030311	68.8
湖南	Hunan	3111604	423175	14079369	145150	35436	9573138	4506231	68.0
广东	Guangdong	15446245	1908726	98426682	1542327	293601	71956925	26469757	73.1
广西	Guangxi	2099130	194373	9670611	100149	33422	6886251	2784360	71.2
海南	Hainan	815064	130849	3511069	67317	9285	3240784	270285	92.3
重庆	Chongqing	3964993	597677	18585424	216441	40866	12883122	5702302	69.3
四川	Sichuan	6865669	460441	27387326	363306	83173	18435223	8952103	67.3
贵州	Guizhou	1008571	83455	5295455	52557	11623	4112023	1183432	77.7
云南	Yunnan	986549	45336	6372805	78863	22056	5087300	1285505	79.8
西藏	Tibet	40034	11223	170306	2404	579	114928	55378	67.5
陕西	Shaanxi	1776992	128759	7493252	86189	19692	5443361	2054663	72.6
甘肃	Gansu	889725	89471	3307253	55260	11530	2104451	1202802	63.6
青海	Qinghai	591882	32279	1206566	6750	1454	598634	607932	49.6
宁夏	Ningxia	424629	30910	2091222	27246	6271	1603373	487849	76.7
新疆	Xinjiang	970103	59976	4861415	81096	17981	2932694	1928721	60.3

6-40 房地产开发企业(单位)经营情况

Operating Statistics of Enterprises for Real Estate Development

单位：万元 (10 000 yuan)

年份 地区	Year Region	经营总收入 Total Revenue	土地转让收入 Land Transferred	商品房屋销售收入 Commercial Houses Sold	房屋出租收入 Houses Leased	其他收入 Others	经营税金及附加 Operating Tax and Extra Charges	营业利润 Operating Profit
1991		2840325	153810	2378597	39221	268697	205551	275239
1992		5285565	427420	4265938	59617	532590	414435	635196
1993		11359074	839281	8637141	106348	1776304	965917	1559223
1994		12881866	959357	10184950	172817	1564742	951029	1674350
1995		17316624	1943981	12582817	257927	2531899	903047	1434087
1996		19687850	1203378	15337647	299899	2846926	927779	179805
1997		22184557	1032847	17552061	387878	3211770	1042143	-103462
1998		29512078	1322454	24084097	493192	3612325	1388134	-106565
1999		30260108	1032492	25550245	627408	3049963	1453611	-350926
2000		45157119	1296054	38968215	953237	3939613	2145704	732836
2001		54716555	1889894	47294194	1173453	4359014	2734549	1254738
2002		70778478	2251311	61457990	1445728	5623449	3701458	2529148
2003		91372734	2797200	81536881	1643335	5395318	4937227	4303655
2004		133144608	4100917	117522041	3055765	8465884	4130409	8579651
2005		147693468	3414314	133167682	2902876	8208596	8452536	11091896
北京	Beijing	16207054	617906	14607572	658061	323515	917069	618439
天津	Tianjin	3886835	143718	2718774	15300	1009043	208642	334622
河北	Hebei	2596193	19458	2515755	4199	56781	147751	83141
山西	Shanxi	1001459	4986	939101	6612	50760	55299	-29811
内蒙古	Inner Mongolia	1706183	4018	1663260	2968	35937	89320	177935
辽宁	Liaoning	6144218	20145	6025782	31680	66611	376911	202318
吉林	Jilin	1407268	4120	1365450	13579	24119	71992	-27743
黑龙江	Heilongjiang	1935485	1331	1912951	1405	19798	98366	30762
上海	Shanghai	20042848	808810	16244503	1308853	1680682	1115655	3054522
江苏	Jiangsu	12297955	151775	11758743	51923	335514	766835	1087992
浙江	Zhejiang	12445303	89791	12058472	45551	251489	756275	1236474
安徽	Anhui	2720528	12785	2643962	17969	45812	165159	89612
福建	Fujian	5483264	151209	5037848	44638	249569	309910	532558
江西	Jiangxi	1687653	32022	1591317	9510	54804	107121	80914
山东	Shandong	7859516	72034	7443000	21415	323067	470494	472925
河南	Henan	2811080	61734	2675030	11543	62773	160582	170010
湖北	Hubei	2814242	41205	2667472	7526	98039	164476	49728
湖南	Hunan	3107663	119943	2492305	39291	456124	171300	49479
广东	Guangdong	22926880	585767	20171851	457328	1711934	1259410	2165778
广西	Guangxi	1924255	79030	1815179	4208	25838	119912	151403
海南	Hainan	432148	23820	391083	773	16472	23784	-49959
重庆	Chongqing	3605726	70550	3164616	67730	302830	201759	212588
四川	Sichuan	5214309	79168	4309151	19679	806311	291772	239676
贵州	Guizhou	1052783	24181	1004045	10211	14346	65298	-2646
云南	Yunnan	2147686	129424	1984361	8162	25739	118469	118744
西藏	Tibet	37435	30	36953	307	145	7145	6064
陕西	Shaanxi	1548383	50051	1352684	8484	137164	73341	-18596
甘肃	Gansu	775484	1648	748235	14152	11449	33986	19858
青海	Qinghai	190067		187966	1009	1092	9409	-3259
宁夏	Ningxia	598769	2360	592296	3037	1076	31532	8421
新疆	Xinjiang	1084796	11295	1047965	15773	9763	63562	29947

6-41 按规模分房地产开发企业(单位)完成投资（2005年）

Actually Completed Investment of Enterprises for Real Estate Development by Size of Enterprise (2005)

单位：万元　　　　(10 000 yuan)

地区	Region	500万元以下 Less Than 5 Million Yuan	500-1000万元 5-10 Million Yuan	1000-3000万元 10-30 Million Yuan	3000-5000万元 30-50 Million Yuan	5000万-1亿元 50-100 Million Yuan	1-5亿元 100-500 Million Yuan	5-10亿元 500-1000 Million Yuan	10亿元以上 1 billion Yuan and More
全国	**National Total**	**683467**	**1119916**	**6869027**	**7654936**	**18010481**	**62909689**	**26409515**	**35435440**
北京	Beijing	2934	5076	68049	88134	316034	3837851	3301226	7630778
天津	Tianjin	253068	7550	36622	87275	251840	1293873	765561	579614
河北	Hebei	8769	35470	211211	244790	625311	1849836	502148	437721
山西	Shanxi	7620	22835	165052	175056	388105	848513	78250	94506
内蒙古	Inner Mongolia	18642	48233	222925	213048	370415	560397	155932	31410
辽宁	Liaoning	13094	43142	306808	344775	810891	3864743	1665474	1693598
吉林	Jilin	5552	38153	150860	175932	365811	742632	263312	215093
黑龙江	Heilongjiang	12545	36969	220821	164917	345871	1205188	328105	361916
上海	Shanghai	2260	6866	57040	69542	371656	4567762	3542406	3851028
江苏	Jiangsu	24797	55216	405023	571785	1777740	6988414	2524120	3104444
浙江	Zhejiang	12383	21589	271860	400885	1101369	5839675	3071216	3845908
安徽	Anhui	23898	59706	349424	275971	722008	1938210	778917	446279
福建	Fujian	16655	28919	236861	302345	792637	2365369	685356	975760
江西	Jiangxi	12051	59825	426326	387152	558964	1094057	159884	312723
山东	Shandong	10623	46642	480229	686255	1701911	4368583	1230300	1252555
河南	Henan	25682	44602	206682	319230	602592	1795263	402585	488536
湖北	Hubei	31482	72591	277315	240134	565382	1560949	741481	990167
湖南	Hunan	37332	52919	281395	329542	735784	2314257	502684	315828
广东	Guangdong	39844	100338	505584	532960	1339255	5235560	2942954	5222488
广西	Guangxi	7396	25501	191675	277344	566989	1347785	297633	153592
海南	Hainan	1166	7448	53752	81169	153758	308923	66844	35434
重庆	Chongqing	7662	26846	181836	232448	617916	1885144	717789	1507650
四川	Sichuan	23294	83539	618272	607996	1122319	2924099	747749	887211
贵州	Guizhou	17221	58459	201681	170952	374009	557693	110239	50955
云南	Yunnan	10321	20066	147117	142187	315753	1033434	305528	494708
西藏	Tibet	234	1736	5220	14572	25252	13193		
陕西	Shaanxi	24998	25584	203230	164671	465816	1496658	234588	374001
甘肃	Gansu	10626	22963	115787	87040	171757	331414	84960	41497
青海	Qinghai	1317	5499	28228	27485	72517	85400	55684	15000
宁夏	Ningxia	4361	18126	64179	117659	194789	270272	78380	
新疆	Xinjiang	15640	37508	177963	121685	186030	384542	68210	25040

6-42 房地产开发企业(单位)建设成套住宅竣工与销售情况

Flats of Residential Buildings Completed and Sold by Enterprises for Real Estate Development

年份 地区	Year Region	住宅竣工套数合计(套) Total Flats of Residential Buildings Completed (sets)	#别墅、高档公寓 Villas, High-grade Apartments	#经济适用房屋 Economically Affordable Housing	住宅销售套数合计(套) Total Flats of Residential Buildings Sold (sets)	#别墅、高档公寓 Villas, High-grade Apartments	#经济适用房屋 Economically Affordable Housing
	1999	1946358	44025	484978			
	2000	2139702	59880	603573			
	2001	2414392	72207	604788			
	2002	2629616	97751	538486			
	2003	3021134	108525	447678			
	2004	4042219	144949	497501			
	2005	3682523	135276	287311	4235372	152339	295302
北 京	Beijing	229293	18295	29409	239019	13921	19609
天 津	Tianjin	92943	5815	9692	108901	6453	9353
河 北	Hebei	80008	667	9424	118891	1505	14032
山 西	Shanxi	41739	363	9143	52186	226	9534
内蒙古	Inner Mongolia	69381	229	9822	88059	1073	13087
辽 宁	Liaoning	221035	2930	7282	240616	3612	8970
吉 林	Jilin	51558	1219	6541	68100	1803	7404
黑龙江	Heilongjiang	111604	146	14926	112511	755	17032
上 海	Shanghai	234388	22733		243675	24820	
江 苏	Jiangsu	358885	17904	23009	373562	17253	18713
浙 江	Zhejiang	249852	9402	18076	222187	8261	16156
安 徽	Anhui	124704	2502	3709	139638	1737	4250
福 建	Fujian	100085	1771	6952	145079	2771	7078
江 西	Jiangxi	93500	1779	12734	106773	768	5507
山 东	Shandong	271853	3505	25411	304469	4574	24809
河 南	Henan	68728	2441	8292	105325	4179	12335
湖 北	Hubei	85622	3321	5752	110412	2885	8257
湖 南	Hunan	111987	5994	9065	100293	3611	3745
广 东	Guangdong	308993	12398	2992	407387	24893	3166
广 西	Guangxi	95029	2298	1426	114537	2516	4118
海 南	Hainan	9151		456	16302	668	724
重 庆	Chongqing	159226	9509	7972	171166	7761	7546
四 川	Sichuan	193114	2660	10228	268065	5102	14436
贵 州	Guizhou	46909	378	6782	68463	372	6753
云 南	Yunnan	54483	3471	8634	97968	6777	12165
西 藏	Tibet	1014	476		760	25	
陕 西	Shaanxi	83459	1031	8918	69038	1890	10363
甘 肃	Gansu	32494	12	5622	39185	86	6528
青 海	Qinghai	6959	52	1680	9956	40	1412
宁 夏	Ningxia	39062	326	4293	29278	507	3779
新 疆	Xinjiang	55465	1649	19069	63571	1495	24441

6-43 35个大中城市主要指标完成情况（2005年）

Main Indicators of Real Estate in 35 Large and Medium-sized Cities (2005)

城市	City	本年完成投资（万元）Investment Completed This Year (1 000 yuan)	#住宅 Residential Buildings	#办公楼 Office Buildings	#商业营业用房 Houses for Business Use	施工房屋面积（万平方米）Floor Space of Buildings under Construction (10 000 sq.m)	竣工房屋面积（万平方米）Floor Space of Buildings Completed (10 000 sq.m)	#住宅 Residential Buildings
总计	**Total**	**96145888**	**64134667**	**6282365**	**10847341**	**87898.55**	**25663.03**	**20904.83**
北京	Beijing	15250082	7795336	1961721	1129007	10748.50	3770.88	2841.42
天津	Tianjin	3275403	2349240	119477	417449	3470.57	1479.22	1270.96
石家庄	Shijiazhuang	1221027	809444	46562	182977	744.45	192.85	173.07
太原	Taiyuan	794350	417845	83621	151390	940.22	225.16	168.80
呼和浩特	Hohhot	358634	231911	30075	88018	559.46	204.37	160.98
沈阳	Shenyang	4135710	3092834	150587	644632	3101.95	1057.74	927.66
大连	Dalian	2653376	1635526	85453	500314	1570.06	390.52	346.45
长春	Changchun	1078762	853860	46257	124365	858.48	303.17	239.56
哈尔滨	Harbin	1401683	767876	66053	256024	1347.75	524.13	386.11
上海	Shanghai	12468560	9208365	1021784	1026068	10462.39	3095.74	2739.91
南京	Nanjing	2961403	2090239	172098	262703	2767.84	640.91	578.35
杭州	Hangzhou	4105706	3192075	263069	338219	4214.23	902.76	705.45
宁波	Ningbo	2594964	1816824	146761	331964	2666.81	706.68	538.05
合肥	Hefei	1913087	1429390	83762	257120	1676.38	514.40	413.77
福州	Fuzhou	2220270	1588398	49015	171875	2023.33	501.43	448.11
厦门	Xiamen	1140742	833250	32964	103585	1523.25	347.56	276.76
南昌	Nanchang	1102169	817308	25741	155641	1193.01	426.50	352.35
济南	Jinan	1210872	966733	40440	102019	903.54	223.89	200.28
青岛	Qingdao	2238370	1623225	138630	180861	2363.76	812.96	680.03
郑州	Zhengzhou	1681013	1254606	87368	262159	1819.03	422.33	362.96
武汉	Wuhan	2979919	2168546	115745	211829	2749.63	816.72	722.25
长沙	Changsha	2556105	1860552	76668	257708	1895.72	550.57	467.65
广州	Guangzhou	5080846	3485030	505040	580572	4846.25	1064.35	802.88
深圳	Shenzhen	4236865	2655340	280407	530721	3058.90	945.78	704.44
南宁	Nanning	1055035	730600	38747	133028	1509.97	414.06	323.70
海口	Haikou	463789	357495	4255	65668	694.10	109.29	96.91
重庆	Chongqing	5177291	3004026	170832	713916	7487.36	2209.82	1713.55
成都	Chengdu	4510228	2944964	148879	765867	3308.75	762.66	597.69
贵阳	Guiyang	911166	454134	64707	105859	1410.27	278.53	232.89
昆明	Kunming	1493527	1137249	22262	112418	1478.38	434.29	380.25
西安	Xi'an	2122861	1459416	110380	340300	2052.85	347.40	302.90
兰州	Lanzhou	531036	338337	27629	66674	819.57	226.59	174.84
西宁	Xining	270717	149093	18830	42681	382.49	97.69	69.00
银川	Yinchuan	566134	346375	22056	161278	762.42	408.13	298.94
乌鲁木齐	Urumqi	384186	269225	24490	72432	486.89	253.96	205.91

6-43 续表 continued

城市	City	房屋销售面积(万平方米) Floor Space Sold (10 000 sq.m)	#住宅 Residential Buildings	房屋销售价格(元/平方米) Selling Price of House (yuan/sq.m)	#住宅 Residential Buildings	本年购置土地面积(万平方米) Land Space Purchased This Year (10 000 sq.m)	本年开发土地面积(万平方米) Land Space Developed This Year (10 000 sq.m)
总计	**Total**	**27265.17**	**24640.14**	**4081**	**3854**	**14324.85**	**8586.86**
北京	Beijing	3123.42	2823.65	6788	6162	773.87	314.24
天津	Tianjin	1408.37	1264.38	4055	3987	729.97	986.33
石家庄	Shijiazhuang	223.20	211.66	1870	1705	103.55	66.46
太原	Taiyuan	218.99	183.38	3575	2903	109.48	29.84
呼和浩特	Hohhot	224.11	194.75	2057	1541	288.00	86.18
沈阳	Shenyang	996.09	931.18	3187	3027	1141.09	515.79
大连	Dalian	594.94	552.47	3747	3580	313.33	399.51
长春	Changchun	340.04	311.75	2393	2272	394.39	30.73
哈尔滨	Harbin	577.42	476.58	2700	2384	342.32	83.80
上海	Shanghai	3158.87	2845.70	6842	6698	754.32	558.42
南京	Nanjing	946.62	895.34	4077	3850	376.88	437.40
杭州	Hangzhou	704.19	620.66	5619	5454	470.53	156.57
宁波	Ningbo	466.98	389.11	5027	4517	207.25	287.90
合肥	Hefei	599.47	537.40	3006	2799	392.16	366.08
福州	Fuzhou	841.32	796.31	3212	2981	275.49	180.53
厦门	Xiamen	326.65	272.32	5503	4744	106.74	16.58
南昌	Nanchang	381.42	359.91	2587	2519	382.19	283.62
济南	Jinan	261.25	241.61	3133	2993	391.76	146.65
青岛	Qingdao	923.92	825.82	3744	3594	406.95	334.46
郑州	Zhengzhou	613.68	556.42	2638	2387	415.16	259.46
武汉	Wuhan	914.06	834.18	3062	2986	772.78	428.83
长沙	Changsha	674.08	610.77	2314	2089	716.38	355.19
广州	Guangzhou	1272.28	1131.24	5366	5041	309.43	139.96
深圳	Shenzhen	1122.8	1019.8	7582	6996	123.7	94.7
南宁	Nanning	455.72	419.99	2605	2388	188.37	167.54
海口	Haikou	192.53	179.09	2650	2529	131.15	30.62
重庆	Chongqing	2017.66	1792.41	2135	1901	1385.40	916.26
成都	Chengdu	1227.33	1109.86	3224	2870	1115.13	209.16
贵阳	Guiyang	368.71	332.33	2169	1801	314.81	109.32
昆明	Kunming	783.12	734.29	2640	2513	227.56	145.47
西安	Xi'an	456.28	435.46	2851	2686	282.55	226.82
兰州	Lanzhou	231.35	203.46	2590	2339	65.40	8.51
西宁	Xining	110.88	99.46	1877	1727	111.41	62.43
银川	Yinchuan	264.37	222.35	2593	2030	131.60	15.64
乌鲁木齐	Urumqi	243.04	225.06	2373	1920	73.80	135.80

6-44 在建大型项目基本情况（2005年）

单位：万元

单位名称	Name of Enterprise	项目名称
中国长江三峡工程开发总公司	China Three Gorges Project Corporation	水利枢纽工程
澜沧江水电开发公司	Lancangjiang Hydropower Corporation	糯扎渡水电站
阳西海滨电力发展有限公司	Yangxi Haibin Power Development Corporation Ltd.	火力发电建设项目
澜沧江水电开发公司	Lancangjiang Hydropower Corporation	小湾水电站
岭东核电有限公司(深圳)	Lingdong Nuclear Power Corporation Ltd. (Shenzhen)	岭澳核电站二期工程
江苏核电有限公司	Jiangsu Nuclear Power Corporation Ltd.	田湾核电站
龙滩水电开发公司	Longtan Hydropower Corporation	龙滩水电站
二滩水电开发公司	Ertan Hydropower Corporation	锦屏水电站一级
华阳电业有限公司后石电厂	Huayang Power Corporation Ltd.	后石电厂
中国三峡总公司	China Three Gorges Project Corporation	溪洛渡水电站
国务院南水北调办公室	Office of the State Council on South-to-North Water Diversion Project	南水北调东、中线一期工程
水利部	Ministry of Water Conservancy	淮河干流整治
水利部	Ministry of Water Conservancy	黄河下游治理
铁道部	Ministry of Railways	武广客运专线
铁道部	Ministry of Railways	郑西客运专线
铁道部	Ministry of Railways	青藏线格尔木至拉萨段
铁道部	Ministry of Railways	机车车辆购置
铁道部	Ministry of Railways	宁西线西安至合肥段
铁道部	Ministry of Railways	渝怀线
铁道部	Ministry of Railways	株六复线
交通部	Ministry of Communications	船舶购置
湖北沪蓉西高速公路建设指挥部	Hubei Construction Headquarters of Shanghai-Chengdu Expressway	宜昌-恩施高速公路
江门市公路局	Highway Bureau of Jiangmen City	九江大桥（G325）市区公路
广东省交通厅	Guangdong Provincial Transportation Bureau	广深沿海高速公路
陕西省高速公路建设集团	Shaanxi Expressway Construction (Group) Corporation	户县--洋县-勉县高速公路
杭州湾大桥工程指挥部	Project Headquarters of Hangzhou Bay Bridge	交通局杭州湾跨海大桥
上海轨道交通十号线发展有限公司	Shanghai Rail Transport Development Corporation Ltd.(Line 10)	上海轨道交通10号线工程
武汉市轨道交通有限公司	Wuhan Rail Transport Corporation Ltd.	轻轨交通二号线
北京市轨道交通建设管理有限公司	Beijing Rail Transport Construction and Management Corporation Ltd.	地铁十号线
广州市地下铁道总公司	Guangzhou Subway Corporation	轨道交通三号线工程
天津港（集团）有限公司	Tianjin Habor (Group) Corporation Ltd.	天津港扩建
上海同盛投资（集团）有限公司	Shanghai Tongsheng Investment (Group) Corporation Ltd.	洋山深水港区一期工程
盐田三期国际集装箱码头有限公司	Yantian International Container Habor (Phase III) Corporation Ltd.	盐田港三期扩建工程
嵊泗县洋山同盛有限公司	Chengci County Yangshzn Tongsheng Corporation Ltd.	洋山深水港集装箱项目一期工程
浦东国际机场二期工程建设指挥部	Construction Headquarters of Second Phase Project of Pudong International Airport	浦东国际机场扩建工程
首都机场集团公司	Capital Airport Holding Company	北京首都国际机场东扩工程
广州白云国际机场有限公司	Guangzhou Baiyun International Airport Corporation Ltd.	白云国际机场迁建工程
中国石油天然气股份公司	PetroChina Company Ltd.	西气东输管道基建项目
中国神华煤制油有限公司	Coal Liquification Corporation Ltd. of China Shenhua Group	煤直接液化项目
惠州中海壳牌石油化工有限公司	CNOOC Huizhou Shell Petrochemical Corporation Ltd.	中海壳牌石化项目
宝钢股份公司宝钢分公司	Bao Steel Branch of Bao Steel Holding Corporation	扩建汽车板及硅钢生产线工程
东方希望包头稀土铝业有限责任公司	East Hope Baotou Rare Earth Metal and Aluminium Corporation Ltd.	东方希望包头铝电项目
奇瑞汽车有限公司	Chery Automobile Corporation Ltd.	汽车及部件
中国第一汽车集团公司	China No.1 Automobile (Group) Corporation	PQ35项目
上海通用汽车有限公司	Shanghai General Motors Corporation Ltd.	上海通用汽车浦东轿车项目
中芯国际集成电路制造公司	Zhongxin International Integrated Circuit Manufacturing Corporation	SMIC厂房1和2
广东省移动通讯有限公司	Guangdong Provincial Mobile Communications Corporation Ltd.	移动电话GSM扩容
广州大学城指挥部	Headquarters for Construction of Guangzhou University City	广州大学城建设
福州地区大学城建设领导小组办公室	Office of Leading Group for Construction of University City	大学城建设
深圳赛博韦尔软件产业园有限公司	Shenzhen Cyberware Software Industry Park Corporation Ltd.	深圳赛博韦尔软件产业园

Basic Conditions of Large Projects Being Constructed (2005)

(10 000 yuan)

Name of Project	开工时间 Starting Time	计划总投资 Total Planned Investment	累计完成投资 Accumulated Investment Completed	累计新增固定资产 Accumulated Newly Increased Fixed Assets
Water Conservancy Project	1994.12	18715440	12246209	1368021
Nozhadu Hydropower Station		3495142	204261	
Thermal Power Construction Project		2800000	15000	
Xiaowan Hydropower Station	2002.01	2773200	901205	
Ling'ao Nuclear Power Station (Second Phase)	2005.01	2674597	249052	692
Tianwan Nuclear Power Station	1999.10	2652668	2574325	12000
Longtan Hydropower Station	2001.07	2429106	1083553	
Jinping Hydropower Station (level 1)	2005.12	2380229	294408	
Houshi Power Plant	1997.01	2290000	1904373	
Xiluodu Hydropower Station	2005.12	2228626	301857	
Eastern and Central Routes of South-to-North Water Diversion Project(First Phase)	2002.01	12400000	379600	
Treatment of Main Stream of Huihe River	1983.02	8489000	431053	77666
Treatment of Lower Stream of Huanghe River	1996.01	1395510	598738	76055
Wuhan-Guangzhou Passenger Railway Lines	2005.09	6900000	299227	
Zhengzhou-Xi'an Passenger Railway Lines	2005.07	3531000	72000	
Qinghai-Tibet Railway (Geermu-Lhasa Section)	2001.06	3309000	2612936	
Purchase of Locomotives		2640600	2687933	2657933
Ningbo-Xi'an Railway (Hefei-Xi'an Section)	2000.05	2189205	2177550	
Chongqing-Huihua Railway	2000.12	1979085	1871000	1871000
Double Tracks Project of Zhuzhou-Liupanshui Railway	1998.03	1967587	1929579	2571
Purchase of Ships		2619590	2361240	864751
Yichang-Enshi Expressway	2004.08	2045163	533250	110158
Jiujiang Bridge (G325) Urban Highway	2003.10	1441000	52090	
Guangzhou-Shenzhen Coastal Expressway	2004.11	1398961	57455	
Huxian-Yangxian-Mianxian Expressway	2002.09	1387831	891151	146500
Hangzhou Bay Bridge	2003.03	1176000	648000	
Project on Shanghai Rail Transport Line 10		2200000	43318	
Light Rail Transport Line 2		1821300	1398	
Subway Line 10	2003.12	1599400	235177	
Project on Rail Transport Line 3	2001.12	1529500	591168	112514
Expansion of Tianjin Habor	2001.01	1524523	615196	158594
Project of Yangshan Deep-water Habor (Phase I)	2002.06	1431000	1911840	
Phase III of Yantian Habor Expansion Project	2005.01	1120000	120488	
Project of Yangshan Deep-water Container Habor (Phase I)	2002.07	1000000	946304	5500
Expansion Project of Pudong International Airport	2005.05	1988300	378986	
Eastern Expansion Project of Beijing Capital International Airport	2004.03	1904000	1015254	
Moving Project of Baiyun International Airport	2000.04	1486200	1486200	1486200
Pipeline Construction Project for West-East Natural Gas Transmission	2005.01	4631400	644513	644513
Coal Liquification Project	2002.10	1690000	326002	
CNOOC-Shell Petrochemical Project	2002.06	3330000	3309000	
Project on Expansion of Steel Plates for Cars and Silicon Steel Production Line	2005.04	2399464	216422	
East Hope Baotou Rare Earth Metal and Aluminium	2002.11	980000	405100	
Motor Vehicles and Parts	1997.03	1613487	900303	68971
PQ35 Project	2003.07	1230000	734439	
Shanghai GM Cars Pudong Project	1997.01	1134370	1194968	159445
SMIC Workshops 1 and 2	2000.08	1230000	2564840	188857
Capacity Expansion of GSM Mobile Phones	2001.06	1390751	1820752	
Construction of Guangzhou University City	2003.03	3000000	1469805	602100
Construction of University City	2003.03	553000	212139	66226
Shenzhen Cyberware Software Industry Park	2000.05	210000	204500	16500

主要统计指标解释

全社会固定资产投资 是以货币形式表现的在一定时期内全社会建造和购置固定资产的工作量以及与此有关的费用的总称。该指标是反映固定资产投资规模、结构和发展速度的综合性指标,又是观察工程进度和考核投资效果的重要依据。全社会固定资产投资按登记注册类型可分为国有、集体、个体、联营、股份制、外商、港澳台商、其他等。

城镇固定资产投资 指城镇各种登记注册类型的企业、事业、行政单位及个体户进行的计划总投资(或实际需要总投资)50万元及50万元以上的建设项目投资、房地产开发投资、城镇和工矿区私人建房投资。县城及以上区域内发生的投资，县及县以上各级政府及主管部门直接领导、管理的建设项目和企业事业单位的投资均为城镇固定资产投资。

房地产开发投资 指各种登记注册类型的房地产开发公司、商品房建设公司及其他房地产开发法人单位和附属于其他法人单位实际从事房地产开发或经营活动的单位统一开发的包括统代建、拆迁还建的住宅、厂房、仓库、饭店、宾馆、度假村、写字楼、办公楼等房屋建筑物和配套的服务设施，土地开发工程（如道路、给水、排水、供电、供热、通讯、平整场地等基础设施工程）的投资；不包括单纯的土地交易活动。

城镇和工矿区私人建房投资 包括市、县城、城关镇、工矿区所辖范围内的全部私人建房，不论其房主是否系本地的常住户口均应包括。

农村投资 包括在农村区域范围内进行固定资产投资活动的企业、事业、行政单位及农村个人投资。

建设总规模 是指在报告期内所有施工项目的计划总投资。这个指标和施工项目相对应。

在建总规模 是指在报告期末所有在建项目的计划总投资。

在建净规模 是指报告期末所有在建项目建成投产尚需的投资总量。

在建净规模＝在建总规模－累计完成投资。

固定资产投资的资金来源 根据固定资产投资的资金来源不同，分为国家预算内资金、国内贷款、利用外资、自筹资金和其他资金。

(1)国家预算内资金：分为财政拨款和财政安排的贷款两部分。包括中央财政的基本建设基金(分经营性基金和非经营性基金两部分)、专项支出(如煤代油专项等)、收回再贷、贴息资金，财政安排的挖潜改造和新产品试制支出、城建支出、商业部门简易建筑支出、不发达地区发展基金等资金中用于固定资产投资的资金；地方财政中由国家统筹安排的资金等。

(2)国内贷款：指报告期固定资产投资单位向银行及非银行金融机构借入的用于固定资产投资的各种国内借款，包括银行利用自有资金及吸收的存款发放的贷款、上级主管部门拨入的国内贷款、国家专项贷款(包括煤代油贷款、劳改煤矿专项贷款等)、地方财政专项资金安排的贷款、国内储备贷款、周转贷款等。

(3)利用外资：指报告期收到的用于固定资产建造和购置的国外资金(包括设备、材料、技术在内)。包括对外借款(外国政府、国际金融组织贷款、出口信贷、外国银行商业贷款、对外发行债券和股票)、外商直接投资及外商其他投资。不包括我国自有外汇资金(国家外汇、地方外汇、留成外汇、调剂外汇和中国银行自有资金发行的外汇贷款等)。计算利用外资时，需要折算成人民币，折算中所使用的外汇汇率按现汇计算，即按使用外汇时的汇率计算。

(4)自筹资金：指固定资产投资单位报告期收到的，由各地区、各部门及企、事业单位筹集用于固定资产投资的预算外资金，包括中央各部门、各级地方和企、事业单位的自筹资金。

(5)其他资金：指在报告期收到的除以上各种资金之外其他用于固定资产投资的资金，包括企业或金融机构通过发行各种债券筹集到的资金、群众集资、个人资金、无偿捐赠的资金及其他单位拨入的资金等。

固定资产投资按国民经济行业分 根据建设项目建成投产后的主要产品或主要用途及社会经济活动性质来确定国民经济行业。一般情况下，一个建设项目或一个企业、事业单位只能属于一种国民经济行业。

固定资产投资按隶属关系分 是按建设单位或企业、事业、行政单位的主管上级机关确定的。

（1）中央：是指中共中央、人大常委会和国务院各部、委、局、总公司以及直属机构直接领导的建设项目和企业、事业、行政单位。这些单位的固定资产投资计划由国务院各部门直接编制和下达，建设中所需物资、主要设备以及建设中的问题都由中央有关部门安排和解决。

（2）地方：是由省（自治区、直辖市）、地区（州、盟、省辖市）、县（旗、县级市）三级政府及业务主管部门直接领导和管理的建设项目、企业、事业、行政单位。地方项目还包括不隶属以上各级政府及主管部门的建设项目和企业、事业单位，如外商投资企业和无主管部门的企业等。

固定资产投资按建设性质分 根据整个建设项目情况来确定。建设项目的性质一般分为新建、扩建、改建和技术改造、迁建、恢复。房地产开发单位、农村投资、城镇工矿区私人建房投资不划分建设性质。

(1)新建：一般指从无到有“平地起家”开始建设的企业、事业和行政单位或建设项目。现有企业、事业、行政单位一般不属于新建。但如有的单位原有基础很小，经过建设后新增的固定资产价值超过该企、事业、行政单位原有固定资产价值(原值)三倍以上的也应作为新建。

(2)扩建：指在厂内或其他地点，为扩大原有产品的生产能力(或效益)或增加新的产品生产能力，而增建主要的生产车间(或主要工程)、分厂、独立的生产线。行政、事业单位在原单位增建业务用房(如学校增建教学用房、医院增建门诊部、病房等)也作为扩建。

现有企、事业单位为扩大原有主要产品生产能力或增加新的产品生产能力，增建一个或几个主要生产车间(或主要工程)、分厂，同时进行一些更新改造工程的，也应作为扩建。

(3)改建和技术改造：指现有企业、事业单位，对原有设施进行技术改造或更新(包括相应配套的辅助性生产、生活福利设施)的建设项目。现有企业、事业单位为适应市场变化的需要，而改变企业的主要产品种类(如军工企业转产民用品等)的建设项目，应作为改建。原有产品生产作业线由于各工序(车间)之间能力不平衡，为填平补齐充分发挥原有生产能力而增建不增加本企业主要产品设计能力的车间，也应作为改建。技术改造是指企业、事业单位在现有基础上，用先进的技术代替落后的技术，用先进的工艺和装备代替落后的工艺和装备，以改变企业落后的技术经济面貌，实现以内涵为主的扩大再生产，达到提高产品质量、促进产品更新换代、节约能源、降低消耗、扩大生产规模、全面提高社会经济效益的目的。技术改造具体包括以下内容：机器设备和工具的更新改造；生产工艺改革、节约能源和原材料的改造；厂房建筑和公共设施的改造；劳动条件和生产环境的改造等。

固定资产投资按构成分　固定资产投资活动按其工作内容和实现方式分为建筑安装工程，设备、工具、器具购置，其他费用三个部分。

(1)建筑安装工程(建筑安装工作量)：指各种房屋、建筑物的建造工程和各种设备、装置的安装工程。包括各种房屋建造工程；各种用途设备基础和各种工业窑炉的砌筑工程及金属结构工程；为施工而进行的各种准备工作和临时工程以及完工后的清理工作等；铁路、道路的铺设，矿井的开凿及石油管道的架设等；水利工程；防空地下建筑等特殊工程；列入房屋工程预算内的暖气、卫生、通风、照明、煤气等设备的价值及装设油饰工程；列入建筑工程预算内的各种管道(蒸汽、压缩空气、石油、给排水等管道)、电力、电讯电缆导线等的敷设工程；以及各种机械设备的安装工程；为测定安装工程质量，对设备进行的试运工作；房地产开发单位进行的商品房屋开发建设工程、土地开发工程。

在安装工程中，不包括被安装设备本身的价值。

(2)设备、工具、器具购置：指建设单位或企、事业单位购置或自制的，达到固定资产标准的设备、工具、器具的价值。新建单位及扩建单位的新建车间，按照设计或计划要求购置或自制的全部设备、工具、器具，不论是否达到固定资产标准均计入“设备、工具、器具购置”中。

(3)其他费用：指在固定资产建造和购置过程中发生的，除上述几项内容以外的各种应分摊计入固定资产的费用。

施工项目　指报告期内进行过建筑或安装施工活动的项目。凡是报告期内施过工的建设项目，不论施工时间长短，均作为施工项目统计。施工项目个数可以反映一定时期固定资产投资的实际规模，与同期全部建成投产项目个数相比，可以从建设速度的角度反映固定资产投资的效果。根据建设项目施工活动的不同性质，施工项目又分为：本年正式施工项目、本年收尾项目和以前年度全部停缓建项目。

全部建成投产项目　工业项目指设计文件规定形成生产能力的主体工程及其相应配套的辅助设施全部建成，经负荷试运转，证明具备生产设计规定合格产品的条件，并经过验收鉴定合格或达到竣工验收标准，与生产性工程配套的生活福利设施可以满足近期正常生产的需要，正式移交生产的建设项目。非工业项目指设计文件规定的主体工程和相应的配套工程全部建成，能够发挥设计规定的全部效益，经验收鉴定合格或达到竣工验收标准，正式移交使用的建设项目。

新增生产能力(或工程效益)　指通过固定资产投资活动而增加的设计能力(或工程效益)，该指标是以实物形态表现的反映固定资产投资成果的指标，也是考核投资经济效果的重要依据之一。

新增生产能力(或工程效益)一般有以下几种表现形式：

(1)用产品数量表示，以工程在单位时间内(一般是一年)所能生产的产品数量(即年产量)表示。如原煤开采用万吨／年表示，化学农药用吨／年表示，拖拉机制造用台／年表示等。某些化工产品由于含量差别较大，按其设计含量计算折合量表示，如硫酸、纯碱、烧碱等。

(2)用单位时间内所能处理的原料数量表示，以工程每天(或小时)所能处理原料的数量表示。如机制糖工程日处理原料吨，食用植物油日处理原料吨，城市污水处理能力用万吨／日表示等。

(3)用新增加的主要设备的数量或容量表示，如新增棉布织机、丝织机等台数，毛纺锭等锭数，发电厂新增发电机组容量用千瓦表示等。

(4)用建筑物容积、容量、面积、长度表示，是非工业项目或工程新增效益的一种表现形式。如铁路投产里程、新建公路、水库容量、粮食仓库、学校学生席位、医院病床、有效灌溉面积等。

根据工程的特点，有时需要用两种或两种以上的复合计量单位表示新增生产能力(或工程效益)，如新增内燃机生产能力同时用年产台数、千瓦数表示等。

为了规范新增生产能力(或工程效益)的名称和计算单位，国家统计局制订了《新增生产能力(或工程效益)目录及代码》。各固定资产投资单位在统计新增生产能力(或工程效益)时，必须按目录中规定的名称、计量单位和代码填报。

房屋建筑面积　指房屋建筑物勒脚以上外墙外围的水平截面面积，包括房屋建筑物的有效面积和结构面积。该指标是从实物形态上反映建设规模和建设成果的重要指标之一，也是检查工程形象进度、计算工程造价、分析投资效果、研究施工任务和建筑材料之间平衡情况的重要依据。

住宅建筑面积　指施工和竣工房屋建筑面积中供居住用的房屋建筑面积。

施工面积　指报告期内施工的全部房屋建筑面积。包括本期新开工的面积和上期开工跨入本期继续施工的房屋面积，以及上期已停建在本期恢复施工的房屋面积。本期竣工和本期施工后又停缓建的房屋，其建筑面积仍计入本期房屋施工面积中。

竣工面积　指在报告期内房屋建筑按照设计要求已经全部完工，达到住人和使用条件，经验收鉴定合格(或达到竣工验收标准)，正式移交使用单位的各栋房屋建筑面积的总和。

房屋建筑面积竣工率　指一定时期内房屋竣工面积占同期房屋施工面积的比率。是从房屋建筑施工速度的角度反映投资效果的指标。

新增固定资产　指报告期内已经完成建造和购置过程，并已交付生产或使用单位的固定资产价值。该指标是表示固定资产投资成果的价值指标，也是反映建设进度，计算固定资产投资效果的重要指标。

项目建设投产率　指一定时期内全部建成投产项目个数与同期施工项目个数的比率。该指标是从建设单位建设速度的角度反映投资效果的指标。

固定资产交付使用率　指一定时期新增固定资产与同期完成投资额的比率。该指标是反映固定资产动用速度，衡量建设过程中宏观投资效果的综合指标。由于新增固定资产是较长时期内形成的结果，而投资额则是当年完成的，因此，该指标一般适宜于反映较长时期内固定资产的动用情况。

商品房销售面积　指报告期内出售商品房屋的合同总面积(即双方签署的正式买卖合同中所确定的建筑面积)。由现房销售建筑面积和期房销售建筑面积两部分组成。

商品房销售额　指报告期内出售商品房屋的合同总价款(即双方签署的正式买卖合同中所确定的合同总价)。该指标与商品房销售面积同口径，由现房销售额和期房销售额两部分组成。

经济适用房　指根据地方经济适用房计划安排建设的政策性住宅。经济是指房屋建筑造价和销售价格低于一般商品住宅；适用是指适合中低收入家庭购买使用。经济适用房主要是由国家统一下达投资计划，房地产公司开发，对外销售；用地一般采用行政划拨或招标投标方式，免收土地出让金；对各种经批准的收费减半征收，开发利润不超过3%；销售价格实行政府指导价。该指标可以分析房地产投资结构，反映中低收入家庭商品住宅的供求平衡情况。

Explanatory Notes on Main Statistical Indicators

Total Investment in Fixed Assets in the Whole Country refers to the volume of activities in construction and purchases of fixed assets and related fees, expressed in monetary terms. It is a comprehensive indicator which shows the size, structure and growth of the investment in fixed assets, providing basis for observing the progress of construction projects and evaluating results of investment. Total investment in fixed assets in the whole country includes, by type of ownership, the investment by the state-owned units, collective units, individuals, joint ownership units, share-holding units, as well as investment by businessmen from foreign countries and from Hong Kong, Macao and Taiwan, and by other units.

Urban Investment in Fixed Assets refers to construction projects involving a total planned (or required) investment of 500, 000 yuan and over by urban enterprises and institutions of various types of ownership, by administrative units and by individuals, investment in real estate development, and housing investment by individuals in urban areas and in industrial and mining areas. In other words, all investments that take place in county towns and urban areas, investment in construction projects under the direct leadership and management of government agencies at and above county levels and investments by enterprises and institutions at and above county levels are covered in urban investment in fixed assets.

Investment in Real Estate Development refers to the investment by the real estate development companies, commercial buildings construction companies and other real estate development units of various types of ownership in the construction of house buildings, such as residential buildings, factory buildings, warehouses, hotels, guesthouses, holiday villages, office buildings, and the complementary service facilities and land development projects, such as roads, water supply, water drainage, power supply, heating, telecommunications, land leveling and other projects of infrastructure. It excludes the activities in pure land transactions.

Investment in Housing Construction in Urban Areas and in Industrial and Mining Areas refers to all private housing construction under the jurisdiction of cities, county towns and industrial and mining areas, no matter whether the owner of the house is registered as the permanent resident in the locality or not.

Investment in Rural Areas refers to investment in fixed assets by enterprises, institutions and individuals in rural areas.

Total Size of Construction refers to the planned total investment for all construction projects during the reference period.

Total Size of Investment in Projects under Construction refers to the planned total investment of all projects under construction at the end of the reference period.

Net Size of Investment in Projects under Construction refers to the required investment of all projects under construction at the end of the reference period.

Net Size of Investment = Total Size of Investment – accumulated completed investment

Sources of Funds for Investment in Fixed Assets include fund from state budget, domestic loans, foreign investment, self-raised funds, and others depending on the source of investment.

(1) Fund from state budget consists of budgetary appropriation and loans from state budget. More specifically, it includes, from the budget of the central government, capital construction fund (operation fund and non-operational fund), special expenses (e.g. expenses on substituting petroleum with coal), loans from repayment, discount fund, expenses on innovation and trial production of new products, expenses on urban construction, expenses on temporary construction by trade departments, development fund for less developed areas, as well as local budgetary fund transferred from the central budget.

(2) Domestic loans refer to loans of various forms borrowed by investing units from banks and non-bank financial institutions during the reference period for the purpose of investment in fixed assets, including loans issued by banks from their self-owned funds and deposit, loans appropriated by higher responsible authorities, special loans by government (including loan for substituting petroleum with coal, special loan for reform-through-labour coal mines), loans arranged by local government from special funds, domestic reserve loan, and working loan, etc..

(3) Foreign Investment refers to foreign funds received during the reference period for the construction and purchase of investment in fixed assets (covering equipment, materials and technology), including foreign borrowings (loans from foreign governments and international financial institutions, export credit, commercial loans from foreign banks, issue of bonds and stocks overseas), foreign direct investment and other foreign investment. Excluded in this category are capitals in foreign exchanges owned by China (foreign exchanges owned by the central and local governments, foreign exchanges retained by enterprises, foreign exchanges by enterprises through regulating mechanism, loans in foreign exchanges issued by the Bank of China with its own fund, etc.). In calculating the utilization of foreign capitals, foreign currencies are converted into Chinese Renminbi applying the current exchange rate when the foreign capitals are actually used.

(4) Self-raised funds refer to extra-budgetary funds for investment in fixed assets received by investing units from central government ministries, local governments, enterprises and institutions, including their self-raised funds.

(5) Others refer to funds for investment in fixed assets received from the sources other than those listed above, including capitals raised through issuing bonds by enterprises or financial

institutions, funds raised from individuals and through donations, and funds transferred from other units.

Investment in Fixed Assets by Sector The classification of construction projects by sector is determined by the major products or the purpose of the projects when they are put into production or use, and by the nature of their social economic activities. In general, one project or one enterprise or institution can only be classified into one sector.

Investment in Fixed Assets by Jurisdiction of Management refers to the classification of investment by the competent authorities under which investment is made by construction units, enterprises, institutions or administrative units.

(1) Central investment refers to the investment in projects or by enterprises, institutions or administrative units which are under the direct leadership and management of the CPC Central Committee, the NPC Standing Committee, the State Council and of the national commissions, ministries, agencies and state-owned large corporations. Various ministries and departments of the State Council prepare and implement plans for investment in fixed assets by those departments, and arrange and ensure the supply of materials and key equipment required for the projects.

(2) Local investment refers to the investment in projects or by enterprises, institutions or administrative units which are under the direct leadership and management of departments under the provincial, prefecture and county governments. Also included are projects by foreign-invested enterprises and enterprises without competent managing authorities.

Investment in Fixed Assets by Type of Construction The construction projects in general can be classified, by the type of construction, into new construction, expansion, reconstruction and technical transformation, moving and restoration. However, investment by type of construction is not applied to investment by real-estate development units, investment in rural areas and investment in housing by urban individuals.

(1) New construction in general refers to newly constructed enterprises, institutions, administrative agencies or independent projects from scratch. Construction in the existing enterprises, institutions or agencies is not considered as new construction. In case the assets of the existing unit is quite small, and the value of newly added fixed assets exceeds the original value of assets by three times, the expansion will be considered as new construction.

(2) Expansion refers to construction of new major production workshop, branch factory or independent production line within a factory or in other locations, for the purpose of increasing the production capacity (or improving efficiency) of the original products. Newly constructed houses for the operation of institutions and administrative organizations (such as the newly constructed buildings for teaching in schools, buildings for clinics or wards in hospitals, etc.) are also classified as expansion.

Also included in the expansion are investments by existing enterprises or institutions in building major production line(s) or branch factory(ies) along with some work on innovation, for the purpose of expending the production capacity of original products or producing new products.

(3) Reconstruction refers to construction projects by existing enterprises or institutions in innovation or technical transformation of the old facilities (including auxiliary production equipment and welfare facilities). Also considered as reconstruction is the construction of new workshops by the existing enterprises or institutions to change the variety of products to meet the market demand (such as the production of civil products by defence industries), or to bring the designed production capacity into full play through a more balanced production process on production lines. Technical transformation refers to replacement of old technology or equipment by new technology or equipment, in order to expand the reproduction through improvement of technology contents in production, to improve product quality, to promote new products, to save energy and reduce consumption and to improve overall social-economic efficiency. Contents of technical transformation include: updating of machinery, equipment and tools; reforming production process by using energy or materials saving technology; construction of factory workshops and transformation of public facilities; improvement of working conditions and environment, etc.

Investment in Fixed Assets by Structure By their contents, investment activities are classified into 3 categories, i.e. construction and installation, purchase of equipment and instrument, and other expenses.

(1) Construction and installation (work volume of construction and installation) refers to the construction of various houses and buildings and installation of various kinds of equipment and instruments. They include construction of various houses; equipment foundations, industrial kilns and stoves, and metal structure work; preparation works for project construction, and clearing up works post project construction; pavement of railways and roads, drilling of mines and putting up of oil pipes; construction of projects of water conservancy; construction of underground air-raid shelters and construction of other special projects; value of equipment for heating, sanitation, ventilation, lighting, gas, painting, etc. that are covered by the budget of housing projects; laying out of various pipelines (for steam, compressed air, petroleum, tap water and sewage) and lines for electric power and for communications; installation of various machinery equipment, testing operation for pre-testing the quality of installation projects, and land and other development work conducted by real estate developers for commercial housing. The value of equipment installed is not included in the value of installation projects.

(2) Purchase of equipment and instruments refers to the total value of equipment, tools, and instruments purchased or self-produced which come up to standards for fixed assets by the construction units or investing enterprises or institutions. Equipment, tools and instruments purchased or self-produced for new workshops by newly established or expanded units are categorized as "purchase of equipment and instruments" no matter whether they come up to the standards for fixed assets.

(3) Other expenses refer to expenses occurring during the

construction or purchase of fixed assets other than those mentioned above.

Projects under Construction refer to projects with construction and installation activities undertaken in the reference period. All projects that have construction activities undertaken during the reference period are reported as projects under construction irrespective of the length of construction work. The number of projects under construction can reflect the actual size of investment in fixed assets during a given period, and when compared with the number of projects completed and put into use during the same period, it demonstrates the results of investment in fixed assets. Depending on the nature of construction activities, projects under construction can also be classified into projects under construction in current year, winding-up projects in current year and stopped or suspended projects in previous years (with preservation work in current year).

Projects Completed and Put into Use Industrial projects refer to the major projects and accessory facilities completed which result in forming production capacity and have been checked and accepted while the living and welfare facilities have been completed and can ensure normal production and formally put into production. Non-industrial projects refer to the major projects and accessory facilities completed which possess the designed capacity and have been checked, accepted and formally put into production.

Newly Increased Production Capacity (or Project Efficiency) refers to the increase of designed capacity (or project efficiency) through investment in fixed assets, which reflects the accomplishment of investment in fixed assets in kind and serves as important basis for evaluating the economic efficiency of investment.

The newly increased production capacity (project efficiency) are usually expressed in one of the following forms:

(1) output of products, i.e. the output that the project can produce during a given period (usually a year). For instance, the capacity in coal mining is expressed in 10,000 tons/year, the capacity in producing chemical pesticides expressed in ton/year, the capacity in producing tractors in tractor/year, etc. For some chemical products where the effective contents differ significantly, the production capacity is expressed as the designed effective content equivalent, such as in the case of sulphuric acid, soda ash, caustic soda, etc;

(2) raw materials processing capacity, i.e. the volume of raw materials that could be processed by the project per day (or per hour), such as tons of materials processed per day by a sugar refining project or edible vegetable oil project, or tons of urban sewage processed per day;

(3) number or capacity of major equipment increased, such as number of cotton or silk looms increased, wool spindles increased, or capacity (in kilowatts) of power generators increased; and

(4) physical measures (volume, capacity, area, and length) of construction, which is typical for non-industrial projects, for instance, the length of railways put into operation, the length of highways, the capacity of reservoirs, the capacity of warehouses, the floor space of housing projects, capacity for new students in schools or beds in hospitals, areas under new irrigation project, etc.

Features of projects sometimes call for combined use of two or more measurement to reflect the increased production capacity (or project efficiency), for instance, the new capacity for the production of internal combustion engines are expressed in sets per year and kilowatts per year simultaneously.

To standardize the nomenclature and unit of measurement for new production capacity (or project efficiency), the National Bureau of Statistics has developed *Nomenclature and Codes for New Production Capacity (Project Efficiency)*. All reporting units with investment activities are required to follow these two nomenclatures in reporting statistics on new production capacity (project efficiency).

Floor Space of Buildings under Construction refers to total floor space of the horizontal section of outer walls above the plinth of the building, including the effective area and the area occupied by the structure. This indicator is one of the important indicators in physical terms to reflect the scale and accomplishment of the construction industry, and important basis for monitoring the progress, calculating the cost, analyzing the efficiency and studying the supply of building materials in relation with the construction projects.

Floor Space of Residential Buildings refers to the floor space of the residential buildings among the total space of buildings under construction or completed.

Floor Space under Construction refers to total floor space of all buildings under construction during the reference period, including floor space of newly started buildings during the reference period, floor space of construction extended from the previous period to the current period, and floor space of construction suspended during the previous period and resumed in the current period. Floor space of construction completed in the current period, and floor space of construction started and then suspended in the current period are also included in the floor space under construction of the current year.

Floor Space of Buildings Completed refers to the floor space of all buildings completed in the reference period, which have been appraised and accepted (or come up to the designed standards) and have been transferred to the owners for use.

Completion Rate of Floor Space of Buildings refers to the ratio of the floor space of buildings completed in certain period of time to the floor space of buildings under construction in the same period. This indicator reflects the investment result from the perspective of the speed of construction.

Newly Increased Fixed Assets refer to the newly increased value of fixed assets, constructed or purchased, that have been transferred to the investors. This is an indicator that demonstrates the results of investment in fixed assets in monetary terms, and an important indicator to reflect the speed of construction and to calculate the efficiency of investment.

Rate of Construction Projects Completed and Put into Use refers to the ratio of the number of construction projects completed and put into use in certain period of time to the number of projects under construction in the same period. This reflects the investment efficiency from the perspective of the speed of projects construction.

Rate of Projects of Fixed Assets Completed and Put into Operation refers to the ratio of the newly increased fixed assets to the total investment made in the same period. This is a comprehensive indicator reflecting the speed of the employment of fixed assets and the investment efficiency at the macro-level. As the newly increase fixed assets is the result of a long period while the investment is completed in the current year, this indicator is expected to be used to reflect the employment of fixed assets over a long period of time.

Area of Commercial Housing Sold refers to total contracted area of commercial housing (i.e. area of floor space as designated in the formal contracts signed by both sides) during the reference time. It constitutes floor space of completed housing and floor space of future housing.

Value of Commercial Housing Sold refer to total value of contracts (i.e. value of sales/purchase for selling/purchase of commercial housing as designated in the contracts signed by both sides) during the reference time. It has the same coverage as the area of commercial housing sold, constituting completed housing and floor space of future housing

Economically Affordable Housing refers to housing constructed according to the state plan for economically affordable housing. Houses of this category featured in low cost in construction and low prices, and therefore are affordable to mid-income or low income households. Economically affordable housing projects are developed by real estate companies under the state investment plan, with the land provided through government allocation or tendering procedures. Developers are exempted from land utilization fees and enjoy another 50% exemption of all other legitimate fees, while their profits are limited to less than 3%, and the completed houses are sold under the government-guided prices. This indicator helps to analyze the investment structure of the real estate industry and the demand and supply of housing for mid or low income households.

7

能 源

Energy

简要说明

一、本篇资料的主要内容

本篇包括的主要内容有能源生产、消费及品种构成，能源生产和消费弹性系数，综合能源平衡表和主要能源品种的单项平衡表，分行业、分主要能源品种的消费量，能源加工转换效率及生活用能源消费量等。从2006年开始，增加单位国内生产总值能耗等指标。

二、本篇资料的统计范围为全社会。

三、本篇的资料来源

7-1表数据来自工业产品产量统计，并以此为依据计算；7-14表数据来自电力企业联合会；其他表的数据均来自历年能源平衡表。

四、关于数据口径与计算的说明

1.一次能源生产量与工业统计数字一致。

2.能源生产与消费弹性系数分别以能源生产、消费增长速度与国内生产总值增长速度相比求得。

3.能源平衡表中，进口量和出口量采用海关统计数据。进口量中包括我国轮船、飞机在国外加油量，出口量中包括外国轮船、飞机在我国加油量。电力折算标准煤系数按平均发电煤耗计算。

4.能源加工转换效率表中，电力折算标准煤系数采用当量值计算，每千瓦小时折0.1229千克标准煤。

5.GDP和工业增加值按2005年价格计算。

6.单位工业增加值能耗的统计范围是全部国有和年主营业务收入500万元及以上的非国有工业法人企业。

Brief Introduction

I. Main Contents

Data in this chapter cover mainly the energy production and consumption and their composition, the elasticity ratio of energy production and consumption, the overall balance of energy and the balance by different types of energy, the consumption of energy by sector and by types of energy, efficiency of energy conversion and the consumption of energy for non-production uses.

II. Data in This Chapter Cover the Whole Country

III. Source of Data

Data in Table 7-1 are calculated on the basis of statistics on output of industrial products, data in Table 7-14 come from the Association of Power Generation Enterprises, and data in other tables in this chapter are from the energy balance sheets over the years.

IV. Notes on Coverage and Calculation of Data:

(1) The data on the production of primary energy are the same as the concerned data of the industrial statistics.

(2) The elasticity ratio of energy production is calculated as the quotient of the growth rate of energy production divided by the growth rate of GDP; and the elasticity ratio of energy consumption is calculated as the quotient of the growth rate of energy consumption divided by the growth rate of GDP.

(3) In the energy balance, the data on the imports and exports are data from the customs statistics. The refueling by Chinese ships and airplanes abroad is included in the imports. The refueling by foreign ships and airplanes in China is included in the exports. The coefficient for conversion of electric power into the standard coal equivalent is calculated according to the average consumption of coal for generating electricity.

(4) In the table on the efficiency of energy conversion, the coefficient for conversion of electric power into the standard coal equivalent is calculated on the basis of heat value equivalent. One kilowatt is equal to 0.1229 kg SCE.

(5) Gross domestic product and gross industrial output value are calculated at 2005's current prices.

(6) The statistical coverage of energy consumption per unit of industrial value-added is all state-owned and non-state-owned industrial enterprises with annual revenue from principal business over 5 million yuan.

7-1 能源生产总量及构成
Total Production of Energy and Its Composition

年 份 Year	能源生产总量 (万吨标准煤) Total Energy Production (10 000 tons of SCE)	占能源生产总量的比重(%) As Percentage of Total Energy Production			
		原 煤 Coal	原 油 Crude Oil	天然气 Natural Gas	水电、核电、风电 Hydro-power, Nuclear Power, Wind Power
1978	62770	70.3	23.7	2.9	3.1
1980	63735	69.4	23.8	3.0	3.8
1985	85546	72.8	20.9	2.0	4.3
1989	101639	74.1	19.3	2.0	4.6
1990	103922	74.2	19.0	2.0	4.8
1991	104844	74.1	19.2	2.0	4.7
1992	107256	74.3	18.9	2.0	4.8
1993	111059	74.0	18.7	2.0	5.3
1994	118729	74.6	17.6	1.9	5.9
1995	129034	75.3	16.6	1.9	6.2
1996	132616	75.2	17.0	2.0	5.8
1997	132410	74.1	17.3	2.1	6.5
1998	124250	71.9	18.5	2.5	7.1
1999	125935	72.6	18.2	2.7	6.6
2000	128978	72.0	18.1	2.8	7.2
2001	137445	71.8	17.0	2.9	8.2
2002	143810	72.3	16.6	3.0	8.1
2003	163842	75.1	14.8	2.8	7.3
2004	187341	76.0	13.4	2.9	7.7
2005	206068	76.4	12.6	3.3	7.7

注：1.电力折算标准煤的系数根据当年平均发电煤耗计算(下表同)。

a) The coefficient for conversion of electric power into SCE (standard coal equivalent) is calculated on the basic of the data on the average coal consumption in generating electric power in the same year. The same as in the following tables.

7-2 能源消费总量及构成
Total Consumption of Energy and Its Composition

年 份 Year	能源消费总量 (万吨标准煤) Total Energy Consumption (10 000 tons of SCE)	占能源消费总量的比重(%) As Percentage of Total Energy Consumption			
		煤 炭 Coal	石 油 Crude Oil	天然气 Natural Gas	水电、核电、风电 Hydro-power, Nuclear Power, Wind Power
1978	57144	70.7	22.7	3.2	3.4
1980	60275	72.2	20.7	3.1	4.0
1985	76682	75.8	17.1	2.2	4.9
1989	96934	76.1	17.1	2.1	4.7
1990	98703	76.2	16.6	2.1	5.1
1991	103783	76.1	17.1	2.0	4.8
1992	109170	75.7	17.5	1.9	4.9
1993	115993	74.7	18.2	1.9	5.2
1994	122737	75.0	17.4	1.9	5.7
1995	131176	74.6	17.5	1.8	6.1
1996	138948	74.7	18.0	1.8	5.5
1997	137798	71.7	20.4	1.7	6.2
1998	132214	69.6	21.5	2.2	6.7
1999	133831	69.1	22.6	2.1	6.2
2000	138553	67.8	23.2	2.4	6.7
2001	143199	66.7	22.9	2.6	7.9
2002	151797	66.3	23.4	2.6	7.7
2003	174990	68.4	22.2	2.6	6.8
2004	203227	68.0	22.3	2.6	7.1
2005	223319	68.9	21.0	2.9	7.2

7-3 综合能源平衡表

Overall Energy Balance Sheet

单位：万吨标准煤 (10 000 tons of SCE)

项 目	Item	1990	1995	2000	2003	2004	2005
可供消费的能源总量	**Total Energy Available for Consumption**	**96138**	**129535**	**136535**	**172129**	**203344**	**222045**
一次能源生产量	Primary Energy Output	103922	129034	128978	163842	187341	206068
回收能	Recovery of Energy		2312	1760	2043	2508	2840
进口量	Imports	1310	5456	14334	20048	26593	26952
出口量(-)	Exports (-)	5875	6776	9633	12989	11646	11447
年初年末库存差额	Stock Changes in the Year	-3219	-491	1097	-814	-1452	-2368
能源消费总量	**Total Energy Consumption**	**98703**	**131176**	**138553**	**174990**	**203227**	**223319**
在总量中:	Consumption by Sector						
1.农、林、牧、渔、水利业	1.Farming,Forestry,Animal Husbandry, Fishery and Water Conservancy	4852	5505	6045	6716	7680	7972
2.工 业	2.Industry	67578	96191	95443	121771	143244	158058
3.建筑业	3.Construction	1213	1335	2143	2860	3259	3409
4.交通运输、仓储和邮政业	4.Transport, Storage and Post	4541	5863	10067	12819	15104	16672
5.批发、零售业和住宿、餐饮业	5.Wholesale, Retail Trade, Hotels and Catering Services	1247	2018	3039	4180	4820	5026
6.其他	6.Others	3473	4519	5852	6819	7839	8789
7.生活消费	7.Non-Production Consumption	15799	15745	15965	19827	21281	23393
在总量中:	Consumption by Usage						
(一) 终端消费	(I) End-use Consumption	94289	124252	132030	166633	194104	212893
#工业	Industry	63239	89473	89266	113725	134442	147982
(二) 加工转换损失量	(II) Losses in Processing and Transformation	2264	3634	2461	3378	3684	3952
#炼焦	Coking	905		525	769	527	658
炼油	Petroleum Refining	326		781	1092	1416	1305
(三) 损失量	(III) Other Losses	2150	3289	4062	4979	5439	6474
平衡差额	**Balance**	**-2565**	**-1641**	**-2017**	**-2862**	**117**	**-1275**

注：1.电力、热力按等价热值折算，因此加工转换损失量中不包括发电、供热损失量。村办工业包括在工业中(下表同)。

2.进口量包括我国飞机、轮船在国外加油量；出口量包括外国飞机、轮船在我国加油量。

a) Electric power and heat are converted on the basic of equal caloric value. Therefore, losses in processing and transformation exclude losses in power generation and heating. Energy consumption of industry include that of village industry. The same as in the following tables.

b) Data on imports include the petroleum consumed by the Chinese airplanes and ships in refueling abroad. Data on exports include the petroleum consumed by the foreign airplanes and ships in refueling in China.

7-4 石油平衡表
Petroleum Balance Sheet

单位：万吨 (10 000 tons)

项 目	Item	1990	1995	2000	2003	2004	2005
可供量	**Total Energy Available for Consumption**	**11435.0**	**16072.7**	**22631.8**	**27540.5**	**32116.2**	**32539.1**
生产量	Output	13830.6	15005.0	16300.0	16960.0	17587.3	18135.3
进口量	Imports	755.6	3673.2	9748.5	13189.6	17291.3	17163.2
出口量(-)	Exports (-)	3110.4	2454.5	2172.1	2540.8	2240.6	2888.1
年初年末库存差额	Stock Changes in the Year	-40.8	-151.0	-1244.6	-68.2	-521.9	128.8
消费量	**Total Energy Consumption**	**11485.6**	**16064.9**	**22439.3**	**27126.1**	**31699.9**	**32535.4**
在消费量中:	Consumption by Sector						
1.农、林、牧、渔、水利业	1.Farming,Forestry,Animal Husbandry, Fishery and Water Conservancy	1033.6	1203.2	1496.9	1681.4	2001.3	2072.9
2.工 业	2.Industry	7321.6	9349.3	10918.5	12886.5	14857.3	14462.6
3.建筑业	3.Construction	327.3	242.8	830.6	1230.6	1422.3	1502.2
4.交通运输、仓储和邮政业	4.Transport, Storage and Post	1683.2	2863.6	5509.4	7093.2	8620.6	9708.5
5.批发、零售业和住宿、餐饮业	5.Wholesale, Retail Trade, Hotels and Catering Services	77.6	333.9	545.0	682.3	818.7	915.6
6.其他	6.Others	757.8	1390.3	1882.7	1916.4	2201.7	2079.2
7.生活消费	7.Non-production Consumption	284.5	682.0	1256.5	1635.8	1778.0	1794.4
在消费量中:	Consumption by Usage						
(一) 终端消费	(Ⅰ) End-use Consumption	9304.7	13676.3	19893.5	24062.8	28062.0	29189.3
#工 业	Industry	5180.4	7095.5	8530.0	9958.7	11344.1	11245.0
(二) 中间消费(用于加工转换)	(Ⅱ) Intermediate Consumption (Consumed in Transformation)	1630.4	2230.0	2352.9	2901.4	3488.2	3190.7
发 电	Power Generation	1234.4	1358.5	1178.2	1491.6	1864.1	1602.0
供 热	Heating	356.3	399.9	427.0	418.0	418.5	407.6
制 气	Gas Production	39.7	51.6	25.9	20.9	10.5	14.4
(三)炼油损失量	(Ⅲ) Losses in Petroleum Refining	295.8	420.1	721.9	970.9	1195.1	1166.7
(四) 损失量	(Ⅳ) Other Losses	254.7	158.6	192.9	161.9	149.7	155.4
平衡差额	**Balance**	**-50.6**	**7.8**	**192.5**	**414.4**	**416.3**	**3.7**

注：1.生产量为原油产量。

2.进口量包括我国飞机、轮船在国外加油量;出口量包括外国飞机、轮船在我国加油量。

a) Data on output refer to the output of crude oil.

b) Data on imports include the petroleum consumed by the Chinese airplanes and ships in refueling abroad. Data on exports include the petroleum consumed by the foreign airplanes and ships in refueling in China.

7-5 煤炭平衡表

Coal Balance Sheet

单位：万吨 (10 000 tons)

项　　目	Item	1990	1995	2000	2003	2004	2005
可供量	**Total Energy Available for Consumption**	**102221.0**	**133461.7**	**128297.1**	**163402.0**	**192265.5**	**214462.1**
生产量	Output	107988.3	136073.1	129921.0	172200.0	199232.4	220472.9
进口量	Imports	200.3	163.5	217.9	1109.8	1861.4	2617.1
出口量(-)	Exports (-)	1729.0	2861.7	5506.5	9402.9	8666.4	7172.4
年初年末库存差额	Stock Changes in the Year	-4238.5	86.8	3664.7	-504.9	-162.0	-1455.4
消费量	**Total Energy Consumption**	**105523.0**	**137676.5**	**132000.0**	**169232.0**	**193596.0**	**216557.5**
在消费量中:	Consumption by Sector						
1.农、林、牧、渔、水利业	1.Farming,Forestry,Animal Husbandry, Fishery and Water Conservancy	2095.2	1856.7	1647.7	1683.3	2251.2	2315.2
2.工　业	2.Industry	81090.9	117570.7	119300.7	156168.5	180135.2	202444.1
3.建筑业	3.Construction	437.6	439.8	536.8	577.2	601.5	603.6
4.交通运输、仓储和邮政业	4.Transport, Storage and Post	2160.9	1315.1	1132.2	1067.3	832.1	815.3
5.批发、零售业和住宿、餐饮业	5.Wholesale, Retail Trade, Hotels and Catering Services	1058.3	977.4	814.6	860.4	871.8	874.4
6.其他	6.Others	1980.4	1986.7	661.0	700.6	731.0	765.9
7.生活消费	7.Non-Production Consumption	16699.7	13530.1	7907.2	8174.7	8173.2	8739.0
在消费量中:	Consumption by Usage						
(一) 终端消费	(I) End-use Consumption	60205.9	66156.1	46821.4	49044.8	59543.7	62154.1
#工　业	Industry	35773.8	46050.3	34122.0	35981.2	46083.0	48040.7
(二) 中间消费 (用于加工转换)	(II) Intermediate Consumption (Consumed in Transformation)	41257.8	69487.6	85178.6	120187.3	134052.3	154403.4
发　电	Power Generation	27204.3	44440.2	55811.2	81976.5	91961.6	103098.5
供　热	Heating	2995.5	5887.3	8794.1	10895.5	11546.6	13542.0
炼　焦	Coking	10697.6	18396.4	16496.4	23639.9	25349.6	31667.1
制　气	Gas Production	360.4	763.7	960.0	1054.8	1316.4	1277.0
(三) 洗选损耗	(III) Losses in Coal Washing and Dressing	4059.3	2032.8	3191.2	2699.3	3633.9	4582.1
平衡差额	**Balance**	**-3302.0**	**-4214.8**	**-3702.9**	**-5830.1**	**-1330.5**	**-2095.4**

注：生产量为原煤产量。

a) Data on output refer to the output of raw coal.

7-6 电力平衡表

Electricity Balance Sheet

单位：亿千瓦小时 (100 million kwh)

项　　目	Item	1990	1995	2000	2003	2004	2005
可供量	**Total Energy Available for Consumption**	**6230.4**	**10023.4**	**13472.7**	**19032.2**	**21972.3**	**24940.8**
生产量	Output	6212.0	10077.3	13556.0	19105.8	22033.1	25002.6
水　电	Hydropower	1267.2	1905.8	2224.1	2836.8	3535.4	3970.2
火　电	Thermal Power	4944.8	8043.2	11141.9	15803.6	17955.9	20473.4
核　电	Nuclear Power		128.3	167.4	433.4	504.7	530.9
进口量	Imports	19.3	6.4	15.5	29.8	34.0	50.1
出口量(-)	Exports (-)	0.9	60.3	98.8	103.4	94.8	111.9
消费量	**Total Energy Consumption**	**6230.4**	**10023.4**	**13471.4**	**19031.6**	**21971.4**	**24940.4**
在消费量中:	Consumption by Sector						
1.农、林、牧、渔、水利业	1.Farming,Forestry,Animal Husbandry, Fishery and Water Conservancy	426.8	582.4	673.0	773.2	808.9	876.4
2.工　业	2.Industry	4873.3	7659.8	9653.6	13899.7	16254.3	18481.7
3.建筑业	3.Construction	65.0	159.6	154.8	189.8	222.1	233.9
4.交通运输、仓储和邮政业	4.Transport, Storage and Post	105.9	182.3	281.2	396.9	449.6	430.3
5.批发、零售业和住宿、餐饮业	5.Wholesale, Retail Trade, Hotels and Catering Services	76.2	199.5	393.6	623.0	735.4	752.3
6.其他	6.Others	202.4	234.2	643.2	911.0	1036.6	1340.9
7.生活消费	7.Non-Production Consumption	480.8	1005.6	1672.0	2238.0	2464.5	2824.8
在消费量中:	Consumption by Usage						
(一) 终端消费	(I) End-use Consumption	5795.8	9278.9	12534.7	17770.9	20550.8	23233.9
#工　业	Industry	4438.7	6915.3	8716.9	12639.0	14833.7	16775.2
(二) 输配电损失量	(II) Losses in Transmission	434.6	744.5	936.7	1260.7	1420.6	1706.5

7-7 能源生产弹性系数
Elasticity Ratio of Energy Production

年 份 Year	能源生产比上年增长 (%) Growth Rate of Energy Production over Preceding Year (%)	电力生产比上年增长 (%) Growth Rate of Electricity Production over Preceding Year (%)	国内生产总值比上年增长 (%) Growth Rate of Gross Domestic Product (GDP) over Preceding Year (%)	能源生产弹性系数 Elasticity Ratio of Energy Production	电力生产弹性系数 Elasticity Ratio of Electricity Production
1985	9.9	8.9	13.5	0.73	0.66
1989	6.1	7.3	4.1	1.49	1.78
1990	2.2	6.2	3.8	0.58	1.63
1991	0.9	9.1	9.2	0.10	0.99
1992	2.3	11.3	14.2	0.16	0.80
1993	3.6	15.3	14.0	0.26	1.09
1994	6.9	10.7	13.1	0.53	0.82
1995	8.7	8.6	10.9	0.80	0.79
1996	2.8	7.2	10.0	0.28	0.72
1997	-0.2	5.0	9.3		0.54
1998	-6.2	2.9	7.8		0.37
1999	1.4	6.2	7.6	0.18	0.82
2000	2.4	9.4	8.4	0.29	1.12
2001	6.6	9.2	8.3	0.80	1.11
2002	4.6	11.7	9.1	0.51	1.29
2003	13.9	15.5	10.0	1.39	1.55
2004	14.3	15.3	10.1	1.42	1.51
2005	10.0	13.5	10.2	0.98	1.32

注：国内生产总值增长速度按可比价格计算(下表同)。
a) The growth rates of GDP are calculated at constant prices. The same as in the following tables.

7-8 能源消费弹性系数
Elasticity Ratio of Energy Consumption

年 份 Year	能源消费比上年增长 (%) Growth Rate of Energy Consumption over Preceding Year (%)	电力消费比上年增长 (%) Growth Rate of Electricity Consumption over Preceding Year (%)	国内生产总值比上年增长 (%) Growth Rate of Gross Domestic Product (GDP) over Preceding Year (%)	能源消费弹性系数 Elasticity Ratio of Energy Consumption	电力消费弹性系数 Elasticity Ratio of Electricity Consumption
1985	8.1	9.0	13.5	0.60	0.67
1989	4.2	7.3	4.1	1.02	1.78
1990	1.8	6.2	3.8	0.47	1.63
1991	5.1	9.2	9.2	0.55	1.00
1992	5.2	11.5	14.2	0.37	0.81
1993	6.3	11.0	14.0	0.45	0.79
1994	5.8	9.9	13.1	0.44	0.76
1995	6.9	8.2	10.9	0.63	0.75
1996	5.9	7.4	10.0	0.59	0.74
1997	-0.8	4.8	9.3		0.52
1998	-4.1	2.8	7.8		0.36
1999	1.2	6.1	7.6	0.16	0.80
2000	3.5	9.5	8.4	0.42	1.13
2001	3.4	9.3	8.3	0.41	1.12
2002	6.0	11.8	9.1	0.66	1.30
2003	15.3	15.6	10.0	1.53	1.56
2004	16.1	15.4	10.1	1.59	1.52
2005	9.9	13.5	10.2	0.97	1.32

7-9 按行业分能源消费量（2004年）

行　业	Sector	能源消费总量（万吨标准煤）Total Energy Consumption (10 000 tons of SCE)	煤炭消费量（万吨）Coal Consumption (10 000 tons)
消费总量	**Total Consumption**	**203227.02**	**193596.00**
农、林、牧、渔、水利业	**Farming,Forestry,Animal Husbandry,Fishery and Water Conservancy**	**7680.00**	**2251.19**
工业	**Industry**	**143244.02**	**180135.20**
采掘业	**Mining and Quarrying**	**12214.98**	**11371.92**
煤炭开采和洗选业	Mining and Washing of Coal	6343.26	10364.73
石油和天然气开采业	Extraction of Petroleum and Natural Gas	3625.65	355.81
黑色金属矿采选业	Mining and Processing of Ferrous Metal Ores	692.08	92.59
有色金属矿采选业	Mining and Processing of Non-Ferrous Metal Ores	623.04	90.11
非金属矿采选业	Mining and Processing of Nonmetal Ores	856.83	467.02
其他采矿业	Mining of Other Ores	74.12	1.66
制造业	**Manufacturing**	**115261.44**	**73097.33**
农副食品加工业	Processing of Food from Agricultural Products	1820.78	1064.15
食品制造业	Manufacture of Foods	1026.11	770.98
饮料制造业	Manufacture of Beverages	848.54	698.13
烟草制品业	Manufacture of Tobacco	238.16	126.01
纺织业	Manufacture of Textile	4550.25	1991.36
纺织服装、鞋、帽制造业	Manufacture of Textile Wearing Apparel,Footware, and Caps	472.82	171.20
皮革、毛皮、羽毛(绒)及其制品业	Manufacture of Leather, Fur, Feather and Related Products	279.28	84.41
木材加工及木、竹、藤、棕、草制品业	Processing of Timber, Manufacture of Wood, Bamboo, Rattan, Palm, and Straw Products	552.48	352.69
家具制造业	Manufacture of Furniture	110.94	26.25
造纸及纸制品业	Manufacture of Paper and Paper Products	3081.35	2713.93
印刷业和记录媒介的复制	Printing, Reproduction of Recording Media	338.32	36.21
文教体育用品制造业	Manufacture of Articles For Culture, Education and Sport Activity	184.09	16.63
石油加工、炼焦及核燃料加工业	Processing of Petroleum, Coking, Processing of Nuclear Fuel	12173.85	15792.68
化学原料及化学制品制造业	Manufacture of Raw Chemical Materials and Chemical Products	20346.88	9960.73
医药制造业	Manufacture of Medicines	1040.60	539.29
化学纤维制造业	Manufacture of Chemical Fibers	1303.03	778.88
橡胶制品业	Manufacture of Rubber	883.72	354.33
塑料制品业	Manufacture of Plastics	1129.29	225.52
非金属矿物制品业	Manufacture of Non-metallic Mineral Products	18088.40	16304.84
黑色金属冶炼及压延加工业	Smelting and Pressing of Ferrous Metals	29702.49	16209.57
有色金属冶炼及压延加工业	Smelting and Pressing of Non-ferrous Metals	6403.53	2093.04
金属制品业	Manufacture of Metal Products	1966.62	269.45
通用设备制造业	Manufacture of General Purpose Machinery	1705.51	340.35
专用设备制造业	Manufacture of Special Purpose Machinery	1146.52	450.60
交通运输设备制造业	Manufacture of Transport Equipment	2079.64	802.90
电气机械及器材制造业	Manufacture of Electrical Machinery and Equipment	1119.35	149.70
通信设备、计算机及其他电子设备制造业	Manufacture of Communication Equipment, Computers and Other Electronic Equipment	1272.02	137.62
仪器仪表及文化、办公用机械制造业	Manufacture of Measuring Instruments and Machinery for Cultural Activity and Office Work	171.55	20.54
工艺品及其他制造业	Manufacture of Artwork and Other Manufacturing	1194.96	608.94
废弃资源和废旧材料回收加工业	Recycling and Disposal of Waste	30.35	6.39
电力、煤气及水生产和供应业	**Electric Power, Gas and Water Production and Supply**	**15767.60**	**95665.95**
电力、热力的生产和供应业	Production and Supply of Electric Power and Heat Power	14578.43	94452.96
燃气生产和供应业	Production and Supply of Gas	535.75	1182.70
水的生产和供应业	Production and Supply of Water	653.41	30.29
建筑业	**Construction**	**3259.00**	**601.53**
交通运输、仓储和邮政业	**Transport, Storage and Post**	**15104.00**	**832.12**
批发、零售业和住宿、餐饮业	**Wholesale, Retail Trade, Hotels and Catering Services**	**4820.00**	**871.79**
其他行业	**Others**	**7839.00**	**730.97**
生活消费	**Non-Production Consumption**	**21281.00**	**8173.20**

Consumption of Energy by Sector (2004)

焦炭消费量（万吨）Coke Consumption (10 000 tons)	原油消费量（万吨）Crude Oil Consumption (10 000 tons)	汽油消费量（万吨）Gasoline Consumption (10 000 tons)	煤油消费量（万吨）Kerosene Consumption (10 000 tons)	柴油消费量（万吨）Diesel Oil Consumption (10 000 tons)	燃料油消费量（万吨）Fuel Oil Consumption (10 000 tons)	天然气消费量（亿立方米）Natural Gas Consumption (100 million cu.m)	电力消费量（亿千瓦小时）Electricity Consumption (100 million kwh)
17267.01	**28749.31**	**4695.76**	**1060.86**	**9895.16**	**4783.48**	**396.72**	**21971.37**
98.69		**220.13**	**1.08**	**1774.30**	**0.66**		**808.87**
16981.13	**28625.49**	**507.40**	**60.89**	**2004.82**	**3570.40**	**293.63**	**16254.29**
129.88	**1313.74**	**70.81**	**6.80**	**347.22**	**44.65**	**77.07**	**1371.36**
46.67		17.79	4.37	65.07	6.15	1.14	576.15
0.21	1313.74	36.56	0.17	176.45	36.16	75.84	358.95
61.62		6.77	0.71	32.67	0.95	0.04	140.04
12.10	0.00	3.07	0.84	16.68	0.33	0.02	144.52
9.29		6.58	0.70	55.16	1.05	0.03	131.60
		0.03	0.01	1.19	0.01		20.11
16795.11	**27302.48**	**403.89**	**53.83**	**1268.32**	**2049.85**	**198.75**	**11303.02**
5.79	0.14	16.07	0.33	42.96	11.82	0.20	202.03
3.88	0.20	7.80	0.33	20.95	14.56	1.49	100.05
1.38	0.43	8.05	0.54	13.40	10.03	0.56	66.71
0.00		0.93	0.03	6.38	1.07	0.28	31.25
2.16	0.20	21.26	2.05	57.55	72.72	0.50	719.32
0.96	0.47	7.95	0.70	28.42	5.49	0.10	72.57
0.29	0.07	4.05	0.37	18.10	10.83	0.02	45.44
1.42	0.10	3.43	1.36	9.22	2.30	0.08	61.56
1.16	0.04	2.28	0.24	5.72	0.21	0.03	20.59
6.81	0.38	8.88	0.91	25.70	26.85	0.37	359.33
0.11		5.89	0.74	7.79	1.45	0.20	78.37
3.20	0.07	3.33	0.35	15.24	2.42		38.32
66.05	25480.02	25.10	2.06	90.92	561.53	19.16	412.85
1131.81	1797.67	45.72	8.70	134.15	406.14	130.63	1849.20
0.82		7.67	0.52	9.75	5.69	0.70	130.92
34.96	8.48	0.74	0.50	8.07	26.19	0.21	225.33
2.77	0.72	9.75	0.27	10.41	17.27	0.38	149.41
1.89	0.10	14.80	0.74	45.10	16.51	0.40	230.16
203.74	11.62	34.41	3.06	231.84	481.04	19.56	1209.25
14596.00	0.11	22.13	1.92	84.10	201.27	7.64	2063.63
260.69	0.44	7.06	2.32	61.15	84.11	2.82	1257.93
73.03	0.10	19.92	2.61	52.72	13.75	0.80	432.79
255.93	0.25	30.37	7.03	61.45	13.27	1.32	279.78
57.57	0.08	23.66	1.69	35.98	7.67	1.97	152.31
59.03	0.10	28.46	10.16	70.68	10.52	3.65	357.67
14.87	0.16	20.69	1.60	51.22	12.57	0.90	222.92
0.78	0.45	10.41	0.82	44.55	26.85	4.68	277.21
2.09	0.06	5.35	1.13	8.96	0.18	0.06	35.35
3.78	0.02	7.33	0.70	14.56	4.01	0.03	215.66
2.15		0.41	0.04	1.30	1.53		5.11
56.13	**9.26**	**32.70**	**0.26**	**389.29**	**1475.90**	**17.81**	**3579.91**
5.75	8.74	27.23	0.21	370.21	1464.95	12.77	3370.46
50.32	0.52	1.63	0.01	17.11	10.94	5.00	34.33
0.06	0.00	3.84	0.04	1.96	0.01	0.04	175.13
16.79		**156.49**		**333.13**	**21.36**	**1.39**	**222.14**
1.79	**123.82**	**2308.46**	**819.71**	**4182.24**	**1150.44**	**11.16**	**449.65**
53.36		**279.80**	**3.63**	**418.99**	**24.98**	**9.18**	**735.35**
10.09		**936.94**	**148.19**	**1068.00**	**15.63**	**14.14**	**1036.58**
105.16		**286.54**	**27.36**	**113.67**		**67.22**	**2464.49**

7-10 按行业分能源消费量（2005年）

行业	Sector	能源消费总量（万吨标准煤）Total Energy Consumption (10 000 tons of SCE)	煤炭消费量（万吨）Coal Consumption (10 000 tons)
消费总量	**Total Consumption**	**223319.30**	**216557.51**
农、林、牧、渔、水利业	**Farming, Forestry, Animal Husbandry, Fishery and Water Conservancy**	**7971.53**	**2315.24**
工业	**Industry**	**158058.37**	**202444.12**
采掘业	**Mining and Quarrying**	**13251.50**	**14214.20**
煤炭开采和洗选业	Mining and Washing of Coal	6916.95	13096.89
石油和天然气开采业	Extraction of Petroleum and Natural Gas	3761.33	338.07
黑色金属矿采选业	Mining and Processing of Ferrous Metal Ores	946.09	112.12
有色金属矿采选业	Mining and Processing of Non-Ferrous Metal Ores	663.56	91.24
非金属矿采选业	Mining and Processing of Nonmetal Ores	862.51	574.22
其他采矿业	Mining of Other Ores	101.06	1.66
制造业	**Manufacturing**	**127683.89**	**81462.09**
农副食品加工业	Processing of Food from Agricultural Products	2034.40	1152.73
食品制造业	Manufacture of Foods	1169.46	814.83
饮料制造业	Manufacture of Beverages	879.57	682.08
烟草制品业	Manufacture of Tobacco	237.68	107.97
纺织业	Manufacture of Textile	4978.35	2141.14
纺织服装、鞋、帽制造业	Manufacture of Textile Wearing Apparel, Footware, and Caps	546.82	191.54
皮革、毛皮、羽毛(绒)及其制品业	Manufacture of Leather, Fur, Feather and Related Products	310.16	84.04
木材加工及木、竹、藤、棕、草制品业	Processing of Timber, Manufacture of Wood, Bamboo, Rattan, Palm, and Straw Products	690.71	348.52
家具制造业	Manufacture of Furniture	128.83	26.01
造纸及纸制品业	Manufacture of Paper and Paper Products	3274.13	3027.87
印刷业和记录媒介的复制	Printing, Reproduction of Recording Media	274.47	36.22
文教体育用品制造业	Manufacture of Articles For Culture, Education and Sport Activity	195.89	16.57
石油加工、炼焦及核燃料加工业	Processing of Petroleum, Coking, Processing of Nuclear Fuel	11881.87	18919.09
化学原料及化学制品制造业	Manufacture of Raw Chemical Materials and Chemical Products	22494.07	11209.03
医药制造业	Manufacture of Medicines	1122.39	573.50
化学纤维制造业	Manufacture of Chemical Fibers	1342.00	760.15
橡胶制品业	Manufacture of Rubber	1079.38	363.18
塑料制品业	Manufacture of Plastics	1446.81	223.61
非金属矿物制品业	Manufacture of Non-metallic Mineral Products	18849.94	16764.28
黑色金属冶炼及压延加工业	Smelting and Pressing of Ferrous Metals	35988.23	19186.70
有色金属冶炼及压延加工业	Smelting and Pressing of Non-ferrous Metals	7188.69	2238.11
金属制品业	Manufacture of Metal Products	2220.38	273.28
通用设备制造业	Manufacture of General Purpose Machinery	1982.12	340.58
专用设备制造业	Manufacture of Special Purpose Machinery	1242.52	456.52
交通运输设备制造业	Manufacture of Transport Equipment	1950.44	730.35
电气机械及器材制造业	Manufacture of Electrical Machinery and Equipment	1191.25	137.82
通信设备、计算机及其他电子设备制造业	Manufacture of Communication Equipment, Computers and Other Electronic Equipment	1474.41	132.29
仪器仪表及文化、办公用机械制造业	Manufacture of Measuring Instruments and Machinery for Cultural Activity and Office Work	194.18	19.76
工艺品及其他制造业	Manufacture of Artwork and Other Manufacturing	1280.68	498.32
废弃资源和废旧材料回收加工业	Recycling and Disposal of Waste	34.06	6.02
电力、煤气及水生产和供应业	**Electric Power, Gas and Water Production and Supply**	**17122.98**	**106767.83**
电力、热力的生产和供应业	Production and Supply of Electric Power and Heat Power	15802.54	105441.07
燃气生产和供应业	Production and Supply of Gas	629.44	1296.18
水的生产和供应业	Production and Supply of Water	691.00	30.58
建筑业	**Construction**	**3409.32**	**603.56**
交通运输、仓储和邮政业	**Transport, Storage and Post**	**16671.81**	**815.34**
批发、零售业和住宿、餐饮业	**Wholesale, Retail Trade, Hotels and Catering Services**	**5026.17**	**874.39**
其他行业	**Others**	**8788.67**	**765.88**
生活消费	**Non-Production Consumption**	**23393.43**	**8738.97**

Consumption of Energy by Sector (2005)

焦炭消费量（万吨） Coke Consumption (10 000 tons)	原油消费量（万吨） Crude Oil Consumption (10 000 tons)	汽油消费量（万吨） Gasoline Consumption (10 000 tons)	煤油消费量（万吨） Kerosene Consumption (10 000 tons)	柴油消费量（万吨） Diesel Oil Consumption (10 000 tons)	燃料油消费量（万吨） Fuel Oil Consumption (10 000 tons)	天然气消费量（亿立方米） Natural Gas Consumption (100 million cu.m)	电力消费量（亿千瓦小时） Electricity Consumption (100 million kwh)
22205.84	**30086.24**	**4853.30**	**1076.84**	**10972.46**	**4242.06**	**479.13**	**24940.39**
63.47		**227.99**	**1.60**	**1837.64**	**0.66**		**876.40**
21960.92	**29959.37**	**461.71**	**57.50**	**2091.27**	**3024.77**	**353.79**	**18481.69**
165.38	**1386.75**	**54.25**	**6.40**	**382.47**	**39.12**	**87.99**	**1476.82**
59.10		15.27	3.26	68.31	5.25	4.46	588.12
0.28	1386.75	26.88	0.17	198.73	32.34	83.46	384.43
78.61		4.81	1.42	35.34	0.65	0.02	205.14
15.32	0.00	3.45	0.74	14.28	0.25	0.02	157.28
12.07		3.82	0.80	64.76	0.63	0.03	113.87
		0.02	0.01	1.05			27.97
21730.99	**28563.58**	**380.77**	**50.74**	**1296.57**	**1828.77**	**239.21**	**13094.79**
8.00	0.07	13.84	0.40	58.30	12.40	0.30	252.75
5.03	0.10	7.69	0.33	22.65	18.11	1.40	114.54
0.97	0.50	7.24	0.54	15.14	13.04	0.55	76.37
0.01		0.78	0.03	5.96	1.46	0.28	35.78
2.81	0.20	17.50	2.05	45.39	44.41	0.61	821.61
1.25	0.24	9.70	0.70	31.09	6.91	0.10	87.40
0.29	0.04	4.50	0.37	15.57	11.90	0.03	54.72
1.70	0.12	4.94	1.09	11.79	2.62	0.12	105.32
0.97	0.03	2.86	0.24	8.81	0.28	0.04	24.22
4.09	0.51	8.42	0.91	26.60	28.60	0.54	406.76
0.14		6.94	0.74	7.35	1.79	0.21	60.57
3.35	0.09	3.87	0.35	13.06	2.56		42.44
72.76	26021.27	21.82	2.06	54.60	391.78	19.52	312.74
1419.94	2513.08	44.05	6.09	145.82	320.79	154.43	2124.70
1.06		7.67	0.52	9.13	5.97	1.06	152.85
48.10	10.62	1.15	0.50	7.89	33.54	0.32	232.65
1.66	0.82	9.54	0.27	10.53	17.69	0.38	208.80
2.46	0.08	12.51	0.74	41.19	18.31	0.60	321.65
195.59	14.17	25.12	3.06	268.70	527.61	26.04	1416.13
19031.77	0.13	22.13	1.92	97.65	187.42	10.68	2544.40
350.13	0.31	6.42	2.32	56.23	89.68	4.23	1469.60
73.56	0.06	17.92	2.64	55.57	17.64	0.75	506.04
327.78	0.15	27.40	5.80	60.19	9.29	1.98	343.95
64.69	0.11	16.56	1.69	28.68	7.10	2.96	182.47
88.19	0.15	36.50	11.08	72.60	11.65	5.37	300.00
15.73	0.26	21.56	1.60	51.86	13.91	1.35	245.21
0.64	0.40	11.03	0.82	51.43	28.37	5.22	327.11
2.58	0.05	3.61	1.13	9.34	0.20	0.09	42.42
3.56	0.01	7.18	0.70	12.23	2.81	0.04	274.96
2.19		0.33	0.04	1.22	0.92		6.64
64.55	**9.04**	**26.69**	**0.36**	**412.23**	**1156.88**	**26.60**	**3910.09**
5.75	8.78	21.14	0.32	399.42	1141.92	18.81	3693.54
58.73	0.26	2.47	0.02	10.27	14.95	7.72	29.79
0.06	0.00	3.08	0.03	2.54	0.01	0.06	186.76
18.38		**172.14**		**386.64**	**14.18**	**1.49**	**233.93**
1.07	**126.87**	**2470.05**	**882.42**	**5019.41**	**1161.02**	**16.43**	**430.34**
64.08		**299.39**	**3.67**	**486.03**	**27.52**	**10.79**	**752.31**
7.59		**918.20**	**106.19**	**1015.06**	**13.91**	**17.20**	**1340.91**
90.33		**303.83**	**25.46**	**136.40**		**79.43**	**2824.81**

7-11 能源加工转换效率

Efficiency of Energy Conversion

单位：% (%)

年 份 Year	总效率 Total Efficiency	发电及电站供热 Electricity Generation and Heating by Power Stations	炼 焦 Coking	炼 油 Petroleum Refining
1983	69.93	36.94	91.18	99.16
1984	69.16	36.95	90.08	99.17
1985	68.29	36.85	90.79	99.10
1986	68.32	36.69	90.63	99.04
1987	67.48	36.75	90.46	98.81
1988	66.54	36.34	90.77	98.76
1989	66.51	36.74	90.30	98.57
1990	67.20	37.34	91.28	97.90
1991	65.90	37.60	89.90	98.10
1992	66.00	37.80	92.70	96.80
1993	67.32	39.90	98.05	98.49
1994	65.20	39.35	89.62	97.48
1995	71.05	37.31	91.99	97.67
1996	71.50	38.30	94.07	97.46
1997	69.23	35.89	92.08	97.37
1998	69.44	37.06	94.97	97.42
1999	69.19	37.04	96.21	97.51
2000	69.04	37.36	96.21	97.32
2001	69.03	37.63	96.50	97.92
2002	69.04	38.73	96.63	96.71
2003	69.40	38.83	96.13	96.80
2004	70.71	39.46	97.61	96.43
2005	71.08	39.92	97.61	96.86

7-12 平均每天能源消费量

Average Daily Energy Consumption by Type of Energy

能源品种	Type of Energy	1990	1995	2000	2001	2002	2003	2004	2005
合计 （万吨标准煤）	**Total (10 000 tons of SCE)**	**270.4**	**359.4**	**379.6**	**392.3**	**415.9**	**479.3**	**556.8**	**611.8**
煤炭 （万吨）	Coal (10 000 tons)	289.1	377.2	361.6	369.9	387.9	463.6	530.4	530.3
焦炭 （万吨）	Coke (10 000 tons)	18.9	29.4	28.6	30.1	33.8	39.7	47.3	60.8
原油 （万吨）	Crude Oil (10 000 tons)	32.2	40.8	58.2	58.5	61.8	68.3	78.8	82.4
燃料油 （万吨）	Fuel Oil (10 000 tons)	9.2	10.2	10.6	10.5	10.6	11.6	13.1	11.6
汽油 （万吨）	Gasoline (10 000 tons)	5.2	8.0	9.6	9.9	10.3	11.2	12.9	13.3
煤油 （万吨）	Kerosene (10 000 tons)	1.0	1.4	2.4	2.4	2.5	2.5	2.9	3.0
柴油 （万吨）	Diesel Oil (10 000 tons)	7.4	11.8	18.6	19.5	21.0	23.0	27.1	30.1
天然气 （亿立方米）	Natural Gas (100 million cu.m)	0.4	0.5	0.7	0.8	0.8	0.9	1.1	1.3
电力 （亿千瓦小时）	Electricity (100 million kwh)	17.1	27.5	36.9	40.3	45.1	52.1	60.2	68.3

7-13 生活能源消费量

Average Annual Energy Consumption for Non-Production Purpose

能源品种	Type of Energy	1990	1995	2000	2001	2002	2003	2004	2005
合计 （万吨标准煤）	**Total (10 000 tons of SCE)**	**15800**	**15745**	**15965**	**16568**	**17527**	**19827**	**21281**	**23393**
煤炭 （万吨）	Coal (10 000 tons)	16700	13530	7907	7830	7603	8175	8173	8739
煤油 （万吨）	Kerosene (10 000 tons)	105	64	72	75	61	56	27	26
液化石油气 （万吨）	Liquefied Petroleum Gas (10 000 tons)	159	534	988	1006	1169	1293	1350	1329
天然气 （亿立方米）	Natural Gas (100 million cu.m)	19	19	32	44	51	57	67	79
煤气 （亿立方米）	Coal Gas (100 million cu.m)	29	57	89	119	125	131	138	145
热力 （万百万千焦）	Heat (10 billion kilo-joule)	8972	12637	23234	23369	26613	33666	41395	51744
电力 （亿千瓦小时）	Electricity (100 million kwh)	481	1006	1672	1839	2001	2238	2465	2825

7-14 人均生活能源消费量

Annual Per Capita Energy Consumption for Non-Production Purpose

年 份 Year	平均每人生活消费能源 (千克标准煤) Annual Per Capita Consumption for Non-production Purpose (Kg of SCE)	煤 炭 (千克) Coal (kg)	电 力 (千瓦小时) Electricity (kwh)	煤 油 (千克) Kerosene (kg)	液化石油气 (千克) Liquefied Petroleum Gas (kg)	天然气 (立方米) Natural Gas (cu.m)	煤 气 (立方米) Coal Gas (cu.m)
1983	106.6	127.7	13.4	1.2	0.6	0.1	1.5
1984	113.5	134.9	15.3	1.4	0.6	0.5	1.5
1985	127.5	149.6	21.3	1.2	0.9	0.4	1.3
1986	127.3	148.3	23.2	1.3	1.1	0.7	1.3
1987	132.1	152.1	26.4	1.2	1.1	0.7	1.6
1988	141.0	159.1	31.2	1.1	1.2	1.4	1.5
1989	139.3	152.4	35.3	1.1	1.4	1.5	2.4
1990	139.2	147.1	42.4	0.9	1.4	1.6	2.5
1991	138.1	142.0	46.9	0.8	1.7	1.6	3.1
1992	133.4	126.1	54.6	0.7	2.0	1.8	4.4
1993	130.6	120.5	61.2	0.6	2.5	1.4	4.5
1994	129.3	109.5	72.7	0.6	3.2	1.7	6.3
1995	130.8	112.3	83.5	0.5	4.4	1.6	4.7
1996	145.5	118.3	93.1	0.5	5.8	1.6	3.9
1997	133.1	99.5	101.8	0.5	6.0	1.7	4.9
1998	115.9	71.5	106.6	0.5	6.2	1.9	6.0
1999	121.4	67.1	118.2	0.6	7.0	2.1	9.3
2000	126.4	62.6	132.4	0.5	7.8	2.6	10.0
2001	130.3	61.6	144.6	0.6	7.9	3.5	9.4
2002	136.9	59.4	156.3	0.4	9.1	4.0	9.8
2003	153.9	63.4	173.7	0.4	10.0	4.4	10.2
2004	164.2	63.1	190.2	0.2	10.4	5.2	10.7
2005	179.4	67.0	216.7	0.2	10.2	6.1	11.1

注：按年平均人口数计算。

a) Data in the table are calculated with the data on the annual average population in each year.

7–15 各地区电力消费量

Electricity Consumption by Region

单位：亿千瓦小时 (100 million kwh)

地 区	Region	1995	2000	2001	2002	2003	2004	2005
北 京	Beijing	261.74	384.43	399.94	439.96	467.61	513.18	570.54
天 津	Tianjin	178.99	234.05	247.94	274.39	305.64	340.04	384.84
河 北	Hebei	602.68	809.34	867.55	965.83	1099.00	1291.40	1501.92
山 西	Shanxi	399.16	501.99	557.58	628.82	725.20	833.01	946.33
内蒙古	Inner Mongolia	186.83	254.21	280.89	320.43	416.44	530.43	667.72
辽 宁	Liaoning	622.81	748.89	764.77	809.45	907.91	1019.78	1110.56
吉 林	Jilin	267.60	291.37	295.08	306.29	338.70	371.79	378.23
黑龙江	Heilongjiang	409.38	442.28	456.86	468.45	493.37	525.47	555.85
上 海	Shanghai	403.27	559.45	592.98	645.71	745.97	821.44	921.97
江 苏	Jiangsu	684.80	971.34	1078.44	1245.14	1505.11	1820.09	2193.45
浙 江	Zhejiang	439.59	738.05	848.40	1010.72	1232.54	1383.69	1642.31
安 徽	Anhui	288.97	338.93	359.59	389.94	445.42	515.69	582.16
福 建	Fujian	261.28	401.51	439.19	496.83	585.74	664.36	756.59
江 西	Jiangxi	181.21	208.15	222.28	246.57	299.53	335.54	391.98
山 东	Shandong	741.07	1000.71	1104.53	1241.74	1395.72	1639.92	1911.61
河 南	Henan	571.48	718.52	808.41	916.25	1041.89	1191.03	1352.74
湖 北	Hubei	414.99	503.02	526.02	561.96	629.20	700.21	788.91
湖 南	Hunan	374.76	406.12	439.78	477.49	545.83	616.80	674.43
广 东	Guangdong	787.66	1334.58	1458.42	1687.83	2031.29	2387.14	2673.56
广 西	Guangxi	220.77	314.44	331.92	356.95	415.83	456.86	510.15
海 南	Hainan	32.00	38.37	42.96	49.00	56.62	67.01	81.61
重 庆	Chongqing		307.61	220.54	248.01	269.26	302.58	347.68
四 川	Sichuan	582.85	521.23	589.57	660.51	759.80	857.02	942.59
贵 州	Guizhou	203.70	287.78	335.19	366.63	399.57	458.69	486.97
云 南	Yunnan	223.71	273.58	320.75	353.20	370.31	454.51	557.25
陕 西	Shaanxi	239.68	292.76	321.54	355.97	404.11	477.03	516.43
甘 肃	Gansu	241.06	295.33	306.09	339.66	398.34	451.74	489.48
青 海	Qinghai	69.02	109.10	111.90	125.51	150.16	189.76	206.56
宁 夏	Ningxia	92.38	136.17	151.81	178.76	212.12	270.01	302.88
新 疆	Xinjiang	119.67	182.98	197.92	214.60	236.10	266.41	310.14

注：2000年及以后为电力公司数。

a) Data from 2000 are obtained from Power Generation Enterprises.

7-16 各地区能源消耗指标（2005年）

Indicators of Energy Consumption by Region (2005)

地 区	Region	单位地区生产总值能耗(等价值) (吨标准煤/万元) Energy Consumption per Unit of GRP (equivalent value) (ton of SCE/10 000 yuan)	单位地区生产总值电耗(等价值) (千瓦小时/万元) Electricity Consumption per Unit of GRP (equivalent value) (kw.h/10 000 yuan)	单位工业增加值能耗 (规模以上，当量值) (吨标准煤/万元) Energy Consumption per Unit of Industrial Value-added (above Designated Size, equivalent value) (ton of SCE/10 000 yuan)
北 京	Beijing	0.80	828.5	1.50
天 津	Tianjin	1.11	1040.8	1.45
河 北	Hebei	1.96	1487.6	4.41
山 西	Shanxi	2.95	2264.2	6.57
内蒙古	Inner Mongolia	2.48	1714.1	5.67
辽 宁	Liaoning	1.83	1386.6	3.11
吉 林	Jilin	1.65	1044.7	3.25
黑龙江	Heilongjiang	1.46	1008.5	2.34
上 海	Shanghai	0.88	1007.2	1.18
江 苏	Jiangsu	0.92	1198.2	1.67
浙 江	Zhejiang	0.90	1222.2	1.49
安 徽	Anhui	1.21	1082.9	3.13
福 建	Fujian	0.94	1151.8	1.45
江 西	Jiangxi	1.06	966.3	3.11
山 东	Shandong	1.28	1032.4	2.15
河 南	Henan	1.38	1277.7	4.02
湖 北	Hubei	1.51	1210.0	3.50
湖 南	Hunan	1.40	1035.8	2.88
广 东	Guangdong	0.79	1195.3	1.08
广 西	Guangxi	1.22	1251.7	3.19
海 南	Hainan	0.92	912.3	3.65
重 庆	Chongqing	1.42	1132.3	2.75
四 川	Sichuan	1.53	1276.3	3.52
贵 州	Guizhou	3.25	2460.6	5.38
云 南	Yunnan	1.73	1604.6	3.55
陕 西	Shaanxi	1.48	1405.0	2.62
甘 肃	Gansu	2.26	2531.0	4.99
青 海	Qinghai	3.07	3801.8	3.44
宁 夏	Ningxia	4.14	4997.7	9.03
新 疆	Xinjiang	2.11	1190.9	3.00

注：地区生产总值和工业增加值按当年价格计算。

a) Gross regional product and industrial value-added are at current prices.

主要统计指标解释

能源生产总量 指一定时期内，全国一次能源生产量的总和。该指标是观察全国能源生产水平、规模、构成和发展速度的总量指标。一次能源生产量包括原煤、原油、天然气、水电、核能及其他动力能(如风能、地热能等)发电量，不包括低热值燃料生产量、生物质能、太阳能等的利用和由一次能源加工转换而成的二次能源产量。

能源消费总量 指一定时期内，全国物质生产部门、非物质生产部门和生活消费的各种能源的总和。该指标是观察能源消费水平、构成和增长速度的总量指标。能源消费总量包括原煤和原油及其制品、天然气、电力，不包括低热值燃料、生物质能和太阳能等的利用。能源消费总量分为终端能源消费量、能源加工转换损失量和能源损失量三部分。

(1)终端能源消费量：指一定时期内，全国生产和生活消费的各种能源在扣除了用于加工转换二次能源消费量和损失量以后的数量。

(2)能源加工转换损失量：指一定时期内，全国投入加工转换的各种能源数量之和与产出各种能源产品之和的差额。该指标是观察能源在加工转换过程中损失量变化的指标。

(3)能源损失量：指一定时期内，能源在输送、分配、储存过程中发生的损失和由客观原因造成的各种损失量，不包括各种气体能源放空、放散量。

能源生产弹性系数 是研究能源生产增长速度与国民经济增长速度之间关系的指标。计算公式为：

$$能源生产弹性系数=\frac{能源生产总量年平均增长速度}{国民经济年平均增长速度}$$

国民经济年平均增长速度，可根据不同的目的或需要，用国民生产总值、国内生产总值等指标来计算，本年鉴是采用国内生产总值指标计算的。

电力生产弹性系数 是研究电力生产增长速度与国民经济增长速度之间关系的指标。一般来说，电力的发展应当快于国民经济的发展，也就是说电力应超前发展。计算公式为：

$$电力生产弹性系数=\frac{电力生产量年平均增长速度}{国民经济年平均增长速度}$$

能源消费弹性系数 反映能源消费增长速度与国民经济增长速度之间比例关系的指标。计算公式为：

$$能源消费弹性系数=\frac{能源消费量年平均增长速度}{国民经济年平均增长速度}$$

电力消费弹性系数 反映电力消费增长速度与国民经济增长速度之间比例关系的指标。计算公式为：

$$电力消费弹性系数=\frac{电力消费量年平均增长速度}{国民经济年平均增长速度}$$

能源加工转换效率 指一定时期内，能源经过加工、转换后，产出的各种能源产品的数量与同期内投入加工转换的各种能源数量的比率。该指标是观察能源加工转换装置和生产工艺先进与落后、管理水平高低等的重要指标。计算公式为：

$$能源加工转换效率=\frac{能源加工转换产出量}{能源加工转换投入量}\times 100\%$$

单位国内生产总值能耗 指一定时期内，一个国家或地区每生产一个单位的国内生产总值所消耗的能源。计算公式为：

$$单位国内生产总值能耗=\frac{能源消费总量}{国内生产总值}$$

单位国内生产总值电耗 指一定时期内，一个国家或地区每生产一个单位的国内生产总值所消耗的电力。计算公式为：

$$单位国内生产总值电耗=\frac{全社会用电量}{国内生产总值}$$

单位工业增加值能耗 指一定时期内，一个国家或地区每生产一个单位的工业增加值所消耗的能源。计算公式为：

$$单位工业增加值能耗=\frac{工业能源消费量}{工业增加值}$$

Explanatory Notes on Main Statistical Indicators

Total Energy Production refers to the total production of primary energy by all energy producing enterprises in the country in a given period of time. It is a comprehensive indicator to show the capacity, scale, composition and development of energy production of the country. The production of primary energy includes that of coal, crude oil, natural gas, hydro-power and electricity generated by nuclear energy and other means such as wind power and geothermal power. However, it excludes the production of fuels of low calorific value, bio-energy, solar energy and the secondary energy converted from the primary energy.

Total Domestic Energy Consumption refers to the total consumption of energy of various kinds by material production sectors, non material production sectors and households in the country in a given period of time. It is a comprehensive indicator to show the scale, composition and development of energy consumption. The total energy consumption includes that of coal, crude oil and their products, natural gas and electricity, However, it excludes the consumption of fuel of low calorific value, bio-energy and solar energy. Total domestic energy consumption can be divided into three parts: final energy consumption, loss during the process of energy conversion, and energy loss.

(1)Final Energy Consumption: It refers to the total energy consumption by material production sectors, non material production sectors and households in the country (region) in a given period of time, but excludes the consumption in conversion of the primary energy into the secondary energy and the loss in the process of energy conversion.

(2)Loss During the Process of Energy Conversion: It refers to the total input of various kinds of energy for conversion, minus the total output of various kinds of energy in the country in a given period of time. It is an indicator to show the loss that occurs during the process of energy conversion.

(3)Energy Loss: It refers to the total of the loss of energy during the course of energy transport, distribution and storage and the loss caused by any objective reason in a given period of time. The loss of various kinds of gas due to gas discharges and stocktaking is excluded.

Elasticity Ratio of Energy Production is an indicator to show the relationship between the growth rate of energy production and the growth rate of the national economy. The formula is:

Elasticity Ratio of Energy Production = Average Annual Growth Rate of Energy Production / Average Annual Growth Rate of National Economy

The average annual growth rate of the national economy can be shown by the gross national product, gross domestic product and other indicators, depending upon the purposes or needs. The gross domestic product is used in calculation of the ratio in this chapter.

Elasticity Ratio of Electricity Production is an indicator to show the relationship between the growth rate of electricity production and the growth rate of the national economy. Generally speaking, the growth rate of electricity production should be higher than that of the national economy.

Its formula is:

Elasticity Ratio of Electricity Production = Average Annual Growth Rate of Electricity Production / Average Annual Growth Rate of National Economy

Elasticity Ratio of Energy Consumption is an indicator to show the relationship between the growth rate of energy consumption and the growth rate of the national economy. The formula is:

Elasticity Ratio of Energy Consumption = Average Annual Growth Rate of Energy Consumption Average Annual Growth Rate of National Economy

Elasticity Ratio of Electricity Consumption is an indicator to show the relationship between the growth rate of electricity consumption and the growth rate of the national economy. The formula is:

Elasticity Ratio of Electricity Consumption = Average Annual Growth Rate of Electricity Average Annual Growth Rate of National Economy

Efficiency of Energy Processing and Conversion refers to the ratio of the total output of energy products of various kinds after processing and conversion and the total input of energy of various kinds for processing and conversion in the same reference period. It is an important indicator to show the current conditions of energy processing and conversion equipment, production technique and management. The formula is:

Efficiency of Energy Processing & Conversion = (Output of Energy After Processing & Conversion / Input of Energy for Processing & Conversion) × 100%

Energy Consumption per Unit of GDP refers to the energy consumption per unit of gross domestic production in a country or the gross region production in a region in the same reference period. The formula is:

Energy Consumption per Unit of GDP = Total Energy Consumption / Gross Domestic Production

Electricity Consumption per Unit of GDP refers to the electricity consumption per unit of gross domestic production in a country or the gross region production in a region in the same reference period. The formula is:

Electricity Consumption per Unit of GDP = Total Electricity Consumption / Gross Domestic Production

Energy Consumption per Unit of Industrial Value-added refers to the energy consumption per unit of industrial value-added in a country or region in the same reference peroid. The formula is:

Energy Consumption per Unit of Industrial Value-added = Total Energy Consumption / Industrial Value-added

8

财 政

Government Finance

简 要 说 明

一、本篇的主要内容和资料来源

本篇反映国家财政收支状况，资料来源于财政部门，资料基础为国家财政决算、预算外资金收支决算和有关财务报表。

国家财政决算由中央级决算和地方总决算组成。省(自治区、直辖市)级决算及其所属州、县(市)总决算汇总组成省(自治区、直辖市)总决算；各省(自治区、直辖市)总决算汇总成地方总决算。

中央级决算、省(自治区、直辖市)级决算和县(市)总决算，由同级主管部门汇总的行政事业单位决算、企业财务决算、基本建设财务决算和金库年报、税收年报等组成。

为了保证决算数据的准确和完整，年度终了以前，各级财政总预算之间，财政总预算和部门单位预算之间，部门单位预算和所属单位预算之间，都对上下级之间的全年预算数据进行核对。年终后各级财政部门、国家金库会同预算缴款单位将决算收入数据进行核对一致，填制对帐单办理签证后，分别按系统上报。

为保持决算口径的一致，财政部每年要制定和颁发各省(自治区、直辖市)总决算表格和中央单位决算表格。各级财政部门和中央主管部门也要结合本部门的具体情况下达有关决算表格。决算表格按国家决算的组成，分为各级财政部门适用的总决算表格和各级主管部门、单位预算机关适用的单位决算表格，决算表数据根据总预算或单位预算会计帐簿填报。

有关财政收支方面的资料，根据决算收支总表、决算收入明细表、决算支出明细表的数据加工整理编制。

预算外资金收支决算和有关财务报表的编报与国家决算的编报基本相同。

二、统计口径的变化和数据调整

针对历年财政收入、财政支出以及各项财政收支之间由于财政体制、预算编列方法的改变，而存在口径不统一的情况，本年鉴对有关数据进行了调整，使各年之间基本可比。主要调整的项目有：

1.财政收入：将1993年及以前各年的国内外债务收入从财政收入中剔除，不再作为财政收入。将1978－1985年财政价格补贴由冲减财政收入改列财政支出。相应地，“国家财政分项目收入”中取消债务收入一项。

2.财政支出：将1993年及以前各年的国内外债务还本付息支出和利用国外借款安排的基本建设支出从财政支出中剔除，不再作为财政支出。将1978－1985年财政价格补贴由冲减财政收入改列财政支出。相应地，“国家财政分项目支出”、“国家财政分费用类别支出”取消债务支出一项，“国家财政分项目支出”中的基本建设支出不再包括利用国外借款安排的基本建设支出，“国家财政分费用类别支出”中的有关项目也进行了调整。从2000年起，财政支出中包括国内外债务付息支出。

3.中央财政和地方财政收支：根据上述财政收入和财政支出的调整，中央财政收支也相应进行了调整，地方支出个别年份有所调整。“中央财政和地方财政收支总额”表，反映的是按当年的财政体制划分的中央、地方财政组织的收入和负责安排的支出状况，由于财政体制的变化和企业隶属关系的变化，对中央、地方财政收支的影响未做调整。此外，中央与地方财政之间还存在着上解、补助和税收返还的关系。因此，“中央财政和地方财政收支总额”表不反映各级财力情况。

预算外资金从1982年开始建立统计制度，预算外收入和预算外支出项目几经变化。1993年由于实施新的财务通则和会计准则，预算外收支范围又一次做了较大调整，国营企业更新改造资金、大修理基金等不再作为预算外资金，因此1992年以前年度与1993年以后年度的预算外资金收支不可比。从1997年起，预算外资金收支不包括纳入预算内管理的政府性基金（收费），与以前各年也不可比。

Brief Introduction

I. Main Content and Source of Data

The data in this chapter show the government revenue and expenditure. The data come from the departments of finance. The data are based on the final state financial accounts, the final accounts of extra-budgetary revenue and expenditure and the concerned financial reports.

The final state financial accounts are composed of the final accounts at the level of central government and the total final accounts at the level of local governments. The total final accounts at the level of local governments are composed of the total final accounts of the governments of provinces, autonomous regions and municipalities directly under the central government. The total final accounts at the provincial (autonomous region, municipality directly under the central government) level are composed of the final accounts at the provincial level and the total final accounts at the level of governments of prefectures and counties (cities).

The final accounts at the central level, at the provincial level and at the county (city) level are respectively composed of the final accounts of the administrative and institutional units, the final financial accounts of enterprises, final financial accounts of capital construction, annual reports on treasury and annual reports on tax revenue, pooled together by the responsible departments at the same level.

In order to ensure the accuracy and completeness of the data of final accounts, the financial departments at different levels should check the budgetary data of the higher and lower levels of the whole year before the end of the year, including the related figures of the total government budgets between different levels, the related figures between the government total budget and the budgets of the departments and the related figures between the budget of the departments and the budgets of the subordinate units. After the end of the year, the financial departments of different levels and the state treasury should check the data of the revenue in the final accounts together with the units which hand over the budget, filled out the accounts checking sheet, made signatures and reported to the higher authorities respectively.

In order to ensure the consistency in the coverage of the final accounts, the Ministry of Finance works out and issues the final accounts forms for the provinces, autonomous regions and municipalities directly under the central government and the final accounts forms for the departments at the central level. The financial departments at various levels and the central government departments should also work out and issue the final accounts forms in the light of the specific conditions of the department to the departments or units at the lower level. The final account forms are designed in accordance with the composition of the state final account and are composed of the total final accounts forms suitable for the financial departments of different levels and the unit final accounts forms suitable for the budgetary agencies of the responsible departments or units. The data for the final accounts are filled out in accordance with the data in the account books of the total budget or unit budget.

Data on the government revenue and expenditure are compiled on the basis of information from the total final accounts table of the revenue and expenditure, the subsidiary table of the final accounts of the revenue, and the subsidiary table of the final accounts of the expenditure.

The procedures for the compilation of the extra-budgetary revenue and expenditure and the related financial tables are basically the same as those for the compilation of the state final accounts.

II. Change of Statistical Coverage and Data Adjustment

Owing to the changes in financial system and in the methods of compiling and listing the items of the budget, the coverage of the government revenue and expenditure and their breakdowns are not consistent over the years. In view of the above situation, the concerned data in this yearbook have been adjusted so as to make them basically comparable over the years. The main adjusted items are as follows:

(1) Government revenue. The revenues from the domestic and foreign debts in 1993 and the previous years are deducted from the government revenue and no longer listed as the component of the government revenue. The financial subsidies for the price adjustment in 1978-1985 were listed formerly as an item to eat up part of the government revenue and are now listed as an item of government expenditure. Correspondingly, the original item revenue from debtsunder the government revenue by itemis cancelled

(2) Government expenditure. The expenditures for repayment of the principal and interest of the domestic and foreign debts in 1993 and the previous years are deducted from the government expenditure and no longer listed as the component of the government expenditure. The financial subsidies on the price adjustment in 1978-1985 were listed formerly as an item to eat up part of the government revenue and are now listed as an item of government expenditure. Correspondingly, the original item expenditure for debts under the government expenditure by account item and the government expenditure by general categories is canceled; the expenditure for capital construction under the government expenditure by account item no longer includes the expenditure for capital construction as a result of the utilization of the foreign loans; the related items under the government expenditure by general categories have also been adjusted. Total government expenditures include the payment for capital and its interest of domestic and foreign debts since 2000.

(3) Revenue and expenditure of the central government and local governments. According to the above-mentioned adjustments in the government revenue and expenditure, adjustments are also made in the revenue and expenditure of the central government correspondingly and in the revenue and expenditure of the local governments in a few years. The table on Total Revenue and Total Expenditure of the Central Government and Local Governments show the revenues and expenditures of the central government and local governments at the current years. The changes in the financial structure and in the subordinate relationship of the enterprises have the impact on the revenues and expenditures of the central government and local governments. However, no adjustments have been made in the data of the past years. In addition, there are also appropriate adaptations made in the specific conditions in the relationship between the central government and local governments: Sometimes some local governments hand certain amount of their funds over to the central government; Sometimes the central government pays subsidies to the difficult provinces and autonomous regions or send back parts of the tax revenue to the local government. Therefore the table on Total Revenue and Total Expenditure of the Central Government and Local Governments does not show the real financial strengths of the governments at different levels.

Data on the extra-budgetary funds have been collected in accordance with the statistical reporting scheme since 1982. Changes have been made in the items in the extra-budgetary revenue and the extra-budgetary expenditure several times. In 1993, new financial general rules and accounting standards were implemented. As a result, significant changes have been made again in the scope of extra-budgetary revenue and extra-budgetary expenditure. The innovation fund and the major repair fund in the state-owned enterprises were no longer listed as the extra-budgetary funds. Therefore the extra-budgetary revenues and the extra-budgetary expenditures in the years before 1993 and since 1993 are not comparable. Starting from 1997, government funds (revenue from fees) were reclassified into budget management and were not included in the extra-budgetary revenues. Therefore, figures since 1997 were not comparable with earlier figures.

8-1 国家财政收支总额及增长速度

Government Revenue and Expenditure and Their Increase Rates

年 份 Year	财 政 收 入 (亿元) Government Revenue (100 million yuan)	财 政 支 出 (亿元) Government Expenditure (100 million yuan)	收 支 差 额 (亿元) Balance (100 million yuan)	增长速度 (%) Increase Rates (%) 财政收入 Government Revenue	增长速度 (%) Increase Rates (%) 财政支出 Government Expenditure	财政收入占国内生产总值的比重(%) Percentage of Government Revenue to GDP (%)
1978	1132.26	1122.09	10.17	29.5	33.0	31.1
1980	1159.93	1228.83	-68.90	1.2	-4.1	25.5
1985	2004.82	2004.25	0.57	22.0	17.8	22.2
1989	2664.90	2823.78	-158.88	13.1	13.3	15.7
1990	2937.10	3083.59	-146.49	10.2	9.2	15.7
1991	3149.48	3386.62	-237.14	7.2	9.8	14.5
1992	3483.37	3742.20	-258.83	10.6	10.5	12.9
1993	4348.95	4642.30	-293.35	24.8	24.1	12.3
1994	5218.10	5792.62	-574.52	20.0	24.8	10.8
1995	6242.20	6823.72	-581.52	19.6	17.8	10.3
1996	7407.99	7937.55	-529.56	18.7	16.3	10.4
1997	8651.14	9233.56	-582.42	16.8	16.3	11.0
1998	9875.95	10798.18	-922.23	14.2	16.9	11.7
1999	11444.08	13187.67	-1743.59	15.9	22.1	12.8
2000	13395.23	15886.50	-2491.27	17.0	20.5	13.5
2001	16386.04	18902.58	-2516.54	22.3	19.0	14.9
2002	18903.64	22053.15	-3149.51	15.4	16.7	15.7
2003	21715.25	24649.95	-2934.70	14.9	11.8	16.0
2004	26396.47	28486.89	-2090.42	21.6	15.6	16.5
2005	31649.29	33930.28	-2280.99	19.9	19.1	17.3

注：1.在国家财政收支中，价格补贴1985年以前冲减财政收入，1986年以后列为财政支出。为了可比，本表将1985年以前冲减财政收入的价格补贴改列在财政支出中。

2.财政收入中不包括国内外债务收入。

3.从2000年起,财政支出中包括国内外债务付息支出。

a) Government price subsidies were listed as negative revenue items prior to 1986, but they have been listed as expenditure items in government accounts since 1986. For comparison purpose, budgetary price subsidies before 1985 were adjusted and listed as expenditure items.

b) Government revenue exclude revenue from domestic and foreign borrowings.

c) Government expenditures include the payment for interest of domestic and foreign debts from 2000.

8-2 国家财政分项目收入

Government Revenue by Item

单位：亿元　　　　(100 million yuan)

年 份 Year	收入合计 Total Government Revenue	各项税收 Taxes	企业收入 Revenue from Enterprises	企业亏损补贴 Subsidies to Loss-making Enterprises	能源交通重点建设基金收入 Revenue Raised from Funds for Key Construction Projects in Energy Industry and Transportation	预算调节基金收入 Revenue Raised from Budget Adjustment Fund	教育费附加收入 Revenue from Extra-charges for Education	其他收入 Other Revenue
1978	1132.26	519.28	571.99					40.99
1980	1159.93	571.70	435.24					152.99
1985	2004.82	2040.79	43.75	-507.02	146.79			280.51
1989	2664.90	2727.40	63.60	-598.88	202.18	91.19		179.41
1990	2937.10	2821.86	78.30	-578.88	185.08	131.21		299.53
1991	3149.48	2990.17	74.69	-510.24	188.22	138.53	28.01	240.10
1992	3483.37	3296.91	59.97	-444.96	157.11	117.47	31.72	265.15
1993	4348.95	4255.30	49.49	-411.29	117.72	102.46	44.23	191.04
1994	5218.10	5126.88		-366.22	53.96	59.10	64.20	280.18
1995	6242.20	6038.04		-327.77	17.42	34.92	83.40	396.19
1996	7407.99	6909.82		-337.40	3.78	11.09	96.04	724.66
1997	8651.14	8234.04		-368.49			103.29	682.30
1998	9875.95	9262.80		-333.49			113.34	833.30
1999	11444.08	10682.58		-290.03			126.10	925.43
2000	13395.23	12581.51		-278.78			147.52	944.98
2001	16386.04	15301.38		-300.04			166.60	1218.10
2002	18903.64	17636.45		-259.60			198.05	1328.74
2003	21715.25	20017.31		-226.38			232.39	1691.93
2004	26396.47	24165.68		-217.93			300.40	2148.32
2005	31649.29	28778.54		-193.26			356.18	2707.83

注：国家财政收入中不包括国内外债务收入。

a) Government revenue from both domestic and foreign borrowings are excluded in this table.

8-3 各 项 税 收
Taxes

单位：亿元 (100 million yuan)

年 份 Year	合 计 Total	#增值税 Value-added Tax	#营业税 Business Tax	#消费税 Consumption Tax	#关 税 Tariffs	#农业各税 Agricultural and Related Tax	#企业所得税 Company Income Tax
1978	519.28				28.76	28.40	
1980	571.70				33.53	27.67	
1985	2040.79	147.70	211.07		205.21	42.05	696.06
1989	2727.40	430.83	487.30		181.54	84.94	700.43
1990	2821.86	400.00	515.75		159.01	87.86	716.00
1991	2990.17	406.36	564.00		187.28	90.65	731.13
1992	3296.91	705.93	658.67		212.75	119.17	720.78
1993	4255.30	1081.48	966.09		256.47	125.74	678.60
1994	5126.88	2308.34	670.02	487.40	272.68	231.49	708.49
1995	6038.04	2602.33	865.56	541.48	291.83	278.09	878.44
1996	6909.82	2962.81	1052.57	620.23	301.84	369.46	968.48
1997	8234.04	3283.92	1324.27	678.70	319.49	397.48	963.18
1998	9262.80	3628.46	1575.08	814.93	313.04	398.80	925.54
1999	10682.58	3881.87	1668.56	820.66	562.23	423.50	811.41
2000	12581.51	4553.17	1868.78	858.29	750.48	465.31	999.63
2001	15301.38	5357.13	2064.09	929.99	840.52	481.70	2630.87
2002	17636.45	6178.39	2450.33	1046.32	704.27	717.85	3082.79
2003	20017.31	7236.54	2844.45	1182.26	923.13	871.77	2919.51
2004	24165.68	9017.94	3581.97	1501.90	1043.77	902.19	3957.33
2005	28778.54	10792.11	4232.46	1633.81	1066.17	936.40	5343.92

注：1.农业各税包括农业税、牧业税、耕地占用税、农业特产税和契税。
2.企业所得税2001年以前只包括国有及集体企业所得税，从2001年起，企业所得税还包括除国有企业和集体企业外的其他所有制企业所得税，与以前各年不可比。
3.增值税不包括进口产品增值税；消费税不包括进口产品消费税。

a) The agricultural and related taxes include the agricultural tax, the animal husbandry tax, the tax on the use of cultivated land, the tax on special agricultural products and the contract tax.

b) Before 2001, the company income tax only included state-owned and collective-owned enterprises income tax. Since 2001, the company income tax also includes the income tax levied on other enterprises except for state-owned and collective-owned enterprises, the figures are not comparable with the previous years.

c) Value-added tax excludes value-added tax on import. Consumption tax excludes consumption tax on imports.

8-4 国家财政主要支出项目
Government Expenditure by Main Item

单位：亿元 (100 million yuan)

年 份 Year	基本建设支出 Expenditure for Capital Construction	增拨企业流动资金 Additional Appropriation for Circulating Capital of Enterprises	挖潜改造资金和科技三项费用 Innovation Funds and Science and Technology Promotion Funds	地质勘探费 Geological Prospecting Expenses	工、交、流通部门事业费 Operating Expenses of the Departments of Industry, Transport and Commerce	支农支出 Expenditure for Supporting Rural Production
1978	451.92		63.24	20.15	17.79	76.95
1980	346.36		80.45	22.57	22.85	82.12
1985	554.56	14.30	103.42	29.58	35.16	101.04
1989	481.70	12.09	146.30	33.16	45.01	197.12
1990	547.39	10.90	153.91	36.19	46.93	221.76
1991	559.62	13.08	180.81	38.34	52.41	243.55
1992	555.90	10.63	223.62	44.07	64.58	269.04
1993	591.93	18.48	421.38	49.06	76.22	323.42
1994	639.72	17.33	415.13	64.13	100.77	399.70
1995	789.22	34.80	494.45	66.32	102.76	430.22
1996	907.44	42.93	523.02	68.56	120.41	510.07
1997	1019.50	52.20	643.20	73.37	136.41	560.77
1998	1387.74	42.36	641.18	83.13	121.56	626.02
1999	2116.57	56.41	766.05	83.69	128.07	677.46
2000	2094.89	71.06	865.24	88.12	150.07	766.89
2001	2510.64	22.71	991.56	99.01	200.12	917.96
2002	3142.98	18.97	968.38	102.89	232.38	1102.70
2003	3429.30	11.95	1092.99	106.94	285.23	1134.86
2004	3437.50	12.44	1243.94	115.45	368.21	1693.79
2005	4041.34	18.17	1494.59	132.70	444.15	1792.40

注：行政管理费中包括公检法司支出和外交外事支出。

a) Administrative expenses includes the expenditure for public security, judicial expenditure, law court expenditure, procuratorial expenditure and expenditure for foreign affairs.

8-4 续表 continued

单位：亿元 (100 million yuan)

年 份 Year	文教、科学、卫生支出 Expenses on Culture, Education, Science and Public Health	抚恤和社会福利救济费 Expenditure for Pension and Social Welfare	国防支出 Expenditure for National Defence	行政管理费 Administrative Expenses	政策性补贴支出 Expenditure on Policy-related Subsidies
1978	112.66	18.91	167.84	49.09	11.14
1980	156.26	20.31	193.84	66.79	117.71
1985	316.70	31.15	191.53	130.58	261.79
1989	553.33	49.60	251.47	261.86	373.35
1990	617.29	55.04	290.31	303.10	380.80
1991	708.00	67.32	330.31	343.60	373.77
1992	792.96	66.45	377.86	424.58	321.64
1993	957.77	75.27	425.80	535.77	299.30
1994	1278.18	95.14	550.71	729.43	314.47
1995	1467.06	115.46	636.72	872.68	364.89
1996	1704.25	128.03	720.06	1040.80	453.91
1997	1903.59	142.14	812.57	1137.16	551.96
1998	2154.38	171.26	934.70	1326.77	712.12
1999	2408.06	179.88	1076.40	1525.68	697.64
2000	2736.88	213.03	1207.54	1787.58	1042.28
2001	3361.02	266.68	1442.04	2197.52	741.51
2002	3979.08	372.97	1707.78	2979.42	645.07
2003	4505.51	498.82	1907.87	3437.68	617.28
2004	5143.65	563.46	2200.01	4059.91	795.80
2005	6104.18	716.39	2474.96	4835.43	998.47

8-5 国家财政按功能性质分类的支出
Government Expenditure by Function

单位：亿元 (100 million yuan)

年 份 Year	支出合计 Total Government Expenditure	经济建设费 Economic Construction	社会文教费 Social, Cultural and Educational Development	国防费 National Defence	行政管理费 Administrative Expenses	其他支出 Other Expenditure
1978	1122.09	718.98	146.96	167.84	52.90	35.41
1980	1228.83	715.46	199.01	193.84	75.53	44.99
1985	2004.25	1127.55	408.43	191.53	171.06	105.68
1989	2823.78	1291.19	668.44	251.47	386.26	226.42
1990	3083.59	1368.01	737.61	290.31	414.56	273.10
1991	3386.62	1428.47	849.65	330.31	414.01	364.18
1992	3742.20	1612.81	970.12	377.86	463.41	318.00
1993	4642.30	1834.79	1178.27	425.80	634.26	569.18
1994	5792.62	2393.69	1501.53	550.71	847.68	499.01
1995	6823.72	2855.78	1756.72	636.72	996.54	577.96
1996	7937.55	3233.78	2080.56	720.06	1185.28	717.87
1997	9233.56	3647.33	2469.38	812.57	1358.85	945.43
1998	10798.18	4179.51	2930.78	934.70	1600.27	1152.92
1999	13187.67	5061.46	3638.74	1076.40	2020.60	1390.47
2000	15886.50	5748.36	4384.51	1207.54	2768.22	1777.87
2001	18902.58	6472.56	5213.23	1442.04	3512.49	2262.26
2002	22053.15	6673.70	5924.58	1707.78	4101.32	3645.77
2003	24649.95	6912.05	6469.37	1907.87	4691.26	4669.40
2004	28486.89	7933.25	7490.51	2200.01	5521.98	5341.14
2005	33930.28	9316.96	8953.36	2474.96	6512.34	6672.66

8-6 国家财政用于农业的支出

Government Expenditure For Agriculture

单位：亿元 (100 million yuan)

年份 Year	合计 Total	支农支出 Expenditure for Supporting Rural Production	农业基本建设支出 Expenditure for Capital Construction	农业科技三项费用 Science & Technology Promotion Funds	农村救济费 Rural Relief Funds	其他 Others	用于农业支出占财政支出的比重(%) Percentage to Total Government Expenditure
1978	150.66	76.95	51.14	1.06	6.88	14.63	13.43
1980	149.95	82.12	48.59	1.31	7.26	10.67	12.20
1985	153.62	101.04	37.73	1.95	12.90		7.66
1989	265.94	197.12	50.64	2.48	15.70		9.42
1990	307.84	221.76	66.71	3.11	16.26		9.98
1991	347.57	243.55	75.49	2.93	25.60		10.26
1992	376.02	269.04	85.00	3.00	18.98		10.05
1993	440.45	323.42	95.00	3.00	19.03		9.49
1994	532.98	399.70	107.00	3.00	23.28		9.20
1995	574.93	430.22	110.00	3.00	31.71		8.43
1996	700.43	510.07	141.51	4.94	43.91		8.82
1997	766.39	560.77	159.78	5.48	40.36		8.30
1998	1154.76	626.02	460.70	9.14	58.90		10.69
1999	1085.76	677.46	357.00	9.13	42.17		8.23
2000	1231.54	766.89	414.46	9.78	40.41		7.75
2001	1456.73	917.96	480.81	10.28	47.68		7.71
2002	1580.76	1102.70	423.80	9.88	44.38		7.17
2003	1754.45	1134.86	527.36	12.43	79.80		7.12
2004	2337.63	1693.79	542.36	15.61	85.87		9.67
2005	2450.31	1792.40	512.63	19.90	125.38		7.22

注：从1998年开始，"农业基本建设支出"包括增发国债安排的支出。

a) Expenditure for agricultural capital construction since 1998 included the expenditure funded from additional issuing national debt.

8-7 国家财政用于科学研究的支出

Government Expenditure for Science and Research

单位：亿元 (100 million yuan)

年份 Year	合计 Total	科技三项费用 Expenditure for S&T Promotion	科学支出 Expenditure for Sciences	科研基建费 Expenditure on Capital Construction of S&T Institutes	其他科研事业费 Other S&T Operating Expenditure
1978	52.89	25.47	15.46	6.66	5.30
1980	64.59	27.57	19.63	11.27	6.12
1985	102.59	44.35	32.00	18.83	7.41
1989	127.87	59.13	38.45	17.91	12.38
1990	139.12	63.48	44.44	17.47	13.73
1991	160.69	73.32	54.15	18.40	14.82
1992	189.26	89.41	57.16	24.55	18.14
1993	225.61	106.56	65.59	33.95	19.51
1994	268.25	114.22	87.90	36.06	30.07
1995	302.36	136.02	96.86	38.00	31.48
1996	348.63	155.01	109.66	48.55	35.41
1997	408.86	189.97	127.12	42.74	49.03
1998	438.60	189.90	151.92	47.28	49.50
1999	543.85	272.80	168.06	52.89	50.10
2000	575.62	277.22	189.03	61.52	47.85
2001	703.26	359.64	223.08	63.37	57.17
2002	816.22	398.60	269.85	69.99	77.78
2003	975.54	416.64	300.79	111.06	147.05
2004	1095.34	483.98	335.93	95.90	179.53
2005	1334.91	609.69	389.14	112.50	223.58

注：表中科研基建费由国家统计局测算，2005年数据为初步数。

a) Expenses on capital construction of S&T institutes are calculated by the National Bureau of Statistics, data of 2005 are preliminary data.

8-8 国家财政用于抚恤和社会福利的支出

Government Expenditure for Pension and Social Welfare

单位：亿元 (100 million yuan)

年 份 Year	合 计 Total	抚恤支出 Pension for Disable and Bereaved Families	离退休费 Expenditure on Retirees	社会救济福利费 Social Welfare and Relief Funds	救灾支出 Expenses on Disaster Relief	其 他 Others
1978	18.91	2.93	2.34	4.62	9.02	
1980	20.31	4.51	3.41	5.36	7.03	
1985	31.15	7.13	4.88	7.71	10.25	1.18
1989	49.60	14.43	8.56	10.80	12.88	2.93
1990	55.04	16.61	9.60	12.07	13.33	3.43
1991	67.32	17.21	10.32	13.18	22.51	4.10
1992	66.45	18.45	12.40	14.36	15.89	5.35
1993	75.27	20.78	14.09	17.01	15.40	7.99
1994	95.14	24.78	20.12	20.55	19.42	10.27
1995	115.46	29.11	22.78	24.19	27.27	12.11
1996	128.03	32.78	10.67	28.98	39.06	16.54
1997	142.14	37.62	13.51	36.57	34.51	19.93
1998	171.26	40.38	16.24	35.29	52.32	27.03
1999	179.88	54.57	19.68	48.52	34.05	23.06
2000	213.03	59.72	23.72	59.71	28.73	41.15
2001	266.68	69.86	30.26	89.99	35.17	41.40
2002	372.97	60.03	41.28	141.63	32.93	97.10
2003	498.82	99.15	42.19	217.69	55.71	84.08
2004	563.46	107.92	49.57	266.58	49.04	89.54
2005	716.39	148.28	55.57	324.22	62.97	125.35

注：1.从1996年起离退休费不包括已划入行政事业单位离退休经费支出类中的由民政部门管理的地方离退休费。
2.从1976年起救灾支出中包括抗震救灾费。

a) Since 1996, the expenditure on retirees excluded the local expenditure for retirees which had been transferred to the pension of administration and run by the department of civil affairs.

b) Since 1976, expenses on disaster relief include the expenses on earthquake relief.

8-9 政策性补贴支出

Budgetary Expenditure for Price Subsidies

单位：亿元 (100 million yuan)

年 份 Year	合 计 Total	粮棉油价格补贴 Subsidies on Price Increases in Grain, Cotton and Edible Oil	平抑物价等补贴 Subsidies on Curbing Price Increase	肉食品价格补贴 Subsidies on Increase in Meat Price	其他价格补贴 Other Price Subsidies
1978	11.14	11.14			
1980	117.71	102.80			14.91
1985	261.79	198.66		33.52	29.61
1989	373.55	262.52		41.29	69.74
1990	380.80	267.61		41.78	71.41
1991	373.77	267.03		42.46	64.28
1992	321.64	224.35		38.54	58.75
1993	299.30	224.75		29.86	44.69
1994	314.47	202.03	41.25	25.41	45.78
1995	364.89	228.91	50.17	24.17	61.64
1996	453.91	311.39	53.38	27.46	61.68
1997	551.96	413.67	43.20	28.25	66.84
1998	712.12	565.04	28.10	26.09	92.89
1999	697.64	492.29	14.25	20.55	170.55
2000	1042.28	758.74	17.71	19.39	246.44
2001	741.51	605.44	16.74	4.55	114.78
2002	645.07	535.24	5.32	1.60	102.91
2003	617.28	550.15	5.15	1.28	60.70
2004	795.80	660.41	5.22	1.28	128.89
2005	998.47	577.91	4.69	0.93	414.94

注：政策性补贴支出，1985年以前冲减财政收入，1986年起作为支出项目列在财政支出中。

a) The government expenditure for price subsidies were listed as a negative revenue item prior to 1986, but they have been listed as a government expenditure item since 1986.

8-10 中央和地方财政收入及比重

Government Revenue and Ratio of the Central and Local Government

年 份 Year	全国（亿元） Total Revenue (100 million yuan)	中央 Central Government	地方 Local Governments	比重（%） Ratio (%) 中央 Central Government	地方 Local Governments
1978	1132.26	175.77	956.49	15.5	84.5
1980	1159.93	284.45	875.48	24.5	75.5
1985	2004.82	769.63	1235.19	38.4	61.6
1989	2664.90	822.52	1842.38	30.9	69.1
1990	2937.10	992.42	1944.68	33.8	66.2
1991	3149.48	938.25	2211.23	29.8	70.2
1992	3483.37	979.51	2503.86	28.1	71.9
1993	4348.95	957.51	3391.44	22.0	78.0
1994	5218.10	2906.50	2311.60	55.7	44.3
1995	6242.20	3256.62	2985.58	52.2	47.8
1996	7407.99	3661.07	3746.92	49.4	50.6
1997	8651.14	4226.92	4424.22	48.9	51.1
1998	9875.95	4892.00	4983.95	49.5	50.5
1999	11444.08	5849.21	5594.87	51.1	48.9
2000	13395.23	6989.17	6406.06	52.2	47.8
2001	16386.04	8582.74	7803.30	52.4	47.6
2002	18903.64	10388.64	8515.00	55.0	45.0
2003	21715.25	11865.27	9849.98	54.6	45.4
2004	26396.47	14503.10	11893.37	54.9	45.1
2005	31649.29	16548.53	15100.76	52.3	47.7

注：1.中央、地方财政收入均为本级收入。
2.本表数字不包括国内外债务收入。

a) The revenue of the central and local governments refers to each own revenue of central government and local governments.
b) Revenue in this table does not include revenue from domestic and foreign borrowings.

8-11 中央和地方财政支出及比重

Government Expenditure and Ratio of Central and Local Governments

年 份 Year	全国（亿元） Total Expenditure (100 million yuan)	中央 Central Government	地方 Local Governments	比重（%） Ratio (%) 中央 Central Government	地方 Local Governments
1978	1122.09	532.12	589.97	47.4	52.6
1980	1228.83	666.81	562.02	54.3	45.7
1985	2004.25	795.25	1209.00	39.7	60.3
1989	2823.78	888.77	1935.01	31.5	68.5
1990	3083.59	1004.47	2079.12	32.6	67.4
1991	3386.62	1090.81	2295.81	32.2	67.8
1992	3742.20	1170.44	2571.76	31.3	68.7
1993	4642.30	1312.06	3330.24	28.3	71.7
1994	5792.62	1754.43	4038.19	30.3	69.7
1995	6823.72	1995.39	4828.33	29.2	70.8
1996	7937.55	2151.27	5786.28	27.1	72.9
1997	9233.56	2532.50	6701.06	27.4	72.6
1998	10798.18	3125.60	7672.58	28.9	71.1
1999	13187.67	4152.33	9035.34	31.5	68.5
2000	15886.50	5519.85	10366.65	34.7	65.3
2001	18902.58	5768.02	13134.56	30.5	69.5
2002	22053.15	6771.70	15281.45	30.7	69.3
2003	24649.95	7420.10	17229.85	30.1	69.9
2004	28486.89	7894.08	20592.81	27.7	72.3
2005	33930.28	8775.97	25154.31	25.9	74.1

注：1.中央、地方财政支出均为本级支出。
2.本表数字2000年以前不包括国内外债务还本付息支出和利用国外借款收入安排的基本建设支出。从2000年起，全国财政支出和中央财政支出中包括国内外债务付息支出。

a) The expenditure of the central and local governments refers to each direct expenditure of the central and local governments.
b) Expenditures before 2000 in this table does not include the payment of the principal and interest of domestic and foreign debts and the expenditure for capital construction using foreign loans. Expenditures of central government and local governments since 2000 include all payment for the principal and interest of domestic and foreign debts.

8-12 中央和地方财政主要收入项目（2005年）
Main Items of Government Revenue of the Central Government and Local Governments (2005)

单位：亿元 (100 million yuan)

项 目	Item	国家财政收入 Total Government Revenue	中央 Central Government	地方 Local Governments
各项税收	**Total Taxes**	**28778.54**	**16051.81**	**12726.73**
消费税	Consumption Tax	1633.81	1633.81	
增值税	Value Added Tax	10792.11	7931.35	2860.76
营业税	Business Tax	4232.46	129.64	4102.82
进口产品消费税、增值税	Consumption Tax and Value Added Tax on Imports	4211.78	4211.78	
资源税	Resource Tax	142.20		142.20
城市维护建设税	Urban Maintenance and Development Tax	795.68	4.66	791.02
企业所得税	Company Income Tax	5343.92	3204.03	2139.89
个人所得税	Personal Income Tax	2094.91	1256.94	837.97
城镇土地使用税	Urban Land Using Tax	137.34		137.34
其他各税	Other Tax	776.33		776.33
关税	Tariffs	1066.17	1066.17	
船舶吨税	Cargo Tax	13.81	13.81	
农业税	Agriculture and Related Taxes	59.41		59.41
契税	Tax on Contracts	735.14		735.14
耕地占用税	Tax on the Use of Arable Land	141.85		141.85
外贸企业出口退税	Tax Rebate to Foreign Trade Company	-4048.94	-4048.94	
证券交易印花税	Stamp Tax on Security Exchange	67.30	65.30	2.00
车辆购置税	Vehicle Purchase Tax	583.26	583.26	
企业亏损补贴	**Subsidies for the Losses of the State-owned Enterprises**	**-193.26**	**-26.69**	**-166.57**
工业企业	Industry Enterprises	-39.08	-17.34	-21.74
商业企业	Commercial Enterprises	-2.69		-2.69
粮食企业	Grain Enterprises	-38.83		-38.83
外贸企业	Foreign Trade Enterprises	-6.99	-6.83	-0.16
农林、水产、气象企业	Agriculture, Forest, Aquaculture and Meteorology Enterprises	-2.51	-2.24	-0.27
其它企业	Other Enterprises	-103.16	-0.28	-102.88
征收排污费和城市水资源费收入	**Fee on Sewage Treatment and Fee on Urban Water Resource**	**163.84**	**11.93**	**151.91**
其他收入	**Other Revenues**	**2543.99**	**508.88**	**2035.11**
教育费附加收入	**Extra-charges for Education**	**356.18**	**2.60**	**353.58**

8-13 中央和地方财政主要支出项目（2005年）

Main Items of Budgetary Expenditure of Central and Local Governments (2005)

单位：亿元 (100 million yuan)

项　目	Item	国家财政支出 Total Expenditure	中央 Central Government	地方 Local Government
基本建设支出	**Expenditure for Capital Construction**	**4041.34**	**1365.56**	**2675.78**
挖潜改造和科技三项费用	**Innovation Funds and Science & Technology Promotion Funds**	**1494.59**	**337.89**	**1156.70**
企业挖潜改造资金	Enterprises Innovation Funds	884.90	15.57	869.33
科技三项费用	Expenditure for Science and Technology Promotion	609.69	322.32	287.37
增拨企业流动资金	**Additional Appropriation for Enterprises' Circulating Capital**	**18.17**	**17.10**	**1.07**
地质勘探费	**Geological Prospecting Expenses**	**132.70**	**39.95**	**92.75**
工业、交通、流通部门事业费	**Operating Expenses of Department of Industry, Transportation and Commerce**	**444.15**	**91.38**	**352.77**
支农支出	**Expenditure for Supporting Rural Production**	**1792.40**	**147.53**	**1644.87**
农、林、水利和气象支出	Expenses of Agriculture, Forest, Irrigation and Meteorology	1607.47	121.82	1485.65
农业综合开发支出	Expenses of Agriculture Comprehensive Development	184.93	25.71	159.22
城市维护建设支出	**Urban Maintenance and Construction Expenditure**	**1393.61**		**1393.61**
城市维护建设费	Urban Maintenance and Construction Expense	1260.64		1260.64
环境保护和城市水资源建设支出	Environmental Protection and Urban Water Resources Construction Expenses	132.97		132.97
文教、科学、卫生事业费	**Operating Expenses for Culture, Education, Science and Health Care**	**6104.18**	**587.67**	**5516.51**
教育事业费	Operating Expenses for Education	3974.83	244.85	3729.98
科学事业费	Operating Expenses for Science	389.14	249.03	140.11
卫生事业费	Operating Expenses for Health	1036.81	21.26	1015.55
文体广播事业费	Operating Expenses for Culture, Sports and Broadcast	703.40	72.53	630.87
抚恤和社会福利救济费	**Pensions and Relief Funds for Social Welfare**	**716.39**	**5.34**	**711.05**
社会保障补助支出	**Social Security Subsidiary Expenses**	**1817.64**	**236.71**	**1580.93**
国防支出	**Expenditure for National Defense**	**2474.96**	**2447.03**	**27.93**
行政管理费	**Expenditure for Government Administration**	**2883.49**	**464.26**	**2419.23**
公检法司支出	**Expenditure for Public Security Agency, Procuratorial Agency and Court of Justice**	**1852.89**	**88.83**	**1764.06**
武装警察部队支出	**Expenditure for Armed Police Troops**	**326.87**	**285.80**	**41.07**
外交外事支出	**Expenditure for Diplomacy**	**99.05**	**86.70**	**12.35**
对外援助支出	**Expenditure for External Assistance**	**74.70**	**74.70**	
支援经济不发达地区支出	**Expenditure for Supporting Undeveloped Areas**	**195.42**	**6.66**	**188.76**
政策性补贴支出	**Expenditure for Price Subsidies**	**998.47**	**591.44**	**407.03**
粮、棉、油价格补贴	Subsidies on Price Increases in Grain, Cotton and Edible Oil	577.91	233.77	344.14
平抑物价和储备糖等补贴	Subsidies on Stabilizing Price Level and Sugar Reserve	4.69	3.08	1.61
肉食价格补贴	Subsidies on Price Increase in Meats	0.93		0.93
其他价格补贴	Other Price Subsidies	414.94	354.59	60.35
其他部门的事业费	**Operating Expenses in Other Department**	**1275.34**	**109.09**	**1166.25**
其他支出	**Other Expenditures**	**2942.55**	**474.55**	**2468.00**
中央预备费	**Central Government Reserve**			
地方预备费	**Local Government Reserve**			
教育费附加支出	**Expenditure on Education Surcharge**	**315.15**		**315.15**
行政事业单位离退休经费	**Expenditure for Retired Persons in Administrative Department**	**1164.83**	**98.85**	**1065.98**
用车购税收入安排的支出	**Expenditure by Using the Vehicle Purchase Tax**	**556.38**	**403.92**	**152.46**
预算外资金改革支出	**Expenditure for the Off-budget administrative reform**			
国内外债务付息支出	**Interest Payment for the Domestic and Foreign Debts**	**815.01**	**815.01**	
国内债务付息支出	Interest Payment for the Domestic Debts	779.65	779.65	
归还向人民银行借款利息	Interest Payment for the Loans from PBC			
国外借款付息支出	Interest Payment for the Foreign Debts	35.36	35.36	

8-14 各地区财政收入（2005年）

Final Statement of Government Revenue by Region (2005)

单位：万元 (10 000 yuan)

地 区	Region	收入合计 Total Revenue	增值税 Value-added Tax	营业税 Operation Tax	企业所得税 Company Income Tax	企业所得税退税 Tax Rebate for Company Income Tax	个人所得税 Individual Income Tax	资源税 Resources Tax
地方合计	**Region Total**	**148842198**	**26442211**	**41028163**	**17459018**	**-7612**	**8379693**	**1421990**
北 京	Beijing	9192098	975976	3837623	1647615		845232	2855
天 津	Tianjin	3318507	642377	964545	414157	-3026	188224	4679
河 北	Hebei	5157017	1210346	1052792	533681		282403	110338
山 西	Shanxi	3683437	1026952	606999	369947	-2	136805	181699
内蒙古	Inner Mongolia	2774553	484469	782709	193550	-4	100684	66395
辽 宁	Liaoning	6752768	1130567	1646848	721990	-114	328052	120494
吉 林	Jilin	2071520	395328	475904	139160	-298	111221	18136
黑龙江	Heilongjiang	3182056	850156	595595	185764	-97	155623	111357
上 海	Shanghai	14173976	2261236	5129265	2491494		1119241	
江 苏	Jiangsu	13226753	2655705	3428176	1776961		661954	28336
浙 江	Zhejiang	10665964	2042343	3243348	1679185	-170	661194	33668
安 徽	Anhui	3340170	577244	781042	300808		124964	45691
福 建	Fujian	4326003	731267	1246076	542646		274137	21436
江 西	Jiangxi	2529236	338739	628395	174115	-149	112649	22884
山 东	Shandong	10731250	1930040	2177928	1108282		388938	182437
河 南	Henan	5376514	879692	1115960	515639	-57	220453	87137
湖 北	Hubei	3755217	659098	913346	390641		174623	32889
湖 南	Hunan	3952651	589327	942450	218340	-488	167566	12247
广 东	Guangdong	18072044	3235854	5557670	2364478		1324252	24270
广 西	Guangxi	2830359	393267	683811	185408	-343	145763	19683
海 南	Hainan	686802	97395	236794	45265		35689	5730
重 庆	Chongqing	2568072	336548	702018	139817		106662	29945
四 川	Sichuan	4796635	710737	1347643	399414	-100	220842	39009
贵 州	Guizhou	1824963	313700	463060	160814	-2078	88973	19754
云 南	Yunnan	3126490	560191	676429	333481	-6	119435	31904
西 藏	Tibet	120312	11824	48721	8879		4475	2399
陕 西	Shaanxi	2753183	553438	692717	205939	-435	102237	68213
甘 肃	Gansu	1235026	253337	315890	84320	-235	51793	21100
青 海	Qinghai	338222	78378	100177	25396		10289	14205
宁 夏	Ningxia	477216	87318	157580	26077		22199	2290
新 疆	Xinjiang	1803184	429362	476652	75755	-10	93121	60810

注：2005年中央本级出口退税增列216.54亿元，增加地方财政本级收入中增值税216.54亿元，这一增加额未在本表中反映。

a) In 2005, 21.654 billion yuan is added to tax rebate for foreign trade company of central level government, corresponding 21.654 billion yuan is added to value-added tax of local government, but the figure is excluded in the table.

8-14 续表 1 continued

单位：万元 (10 000 yuan)

地区	Region	固定资产投资方向调节税 Tax on the Adjustment of the Investment in the Fixed Assets	城市维护建设税 Tax on City Maintenance and Construction	房产税 Tax on Real Estates	印花税 Stamp Tax	城镇土地使用税 Tax on the Use of Urban Land	土地增值税 Land Value Added Tax	车船使用和牌照税 Tax on the Use of Vehicles and Ships
地方合计	**Region Total**	**16816**	**7910187**	**4359577**	**1614651**	**1373444**	**1403140**	**388975**
北京	Beijing	6	388336	352058	108870	32986	23831	31744
天津	Tianjin	51	158763	103040	38301	10124	3555	8791
河北	Hebei	208	292508	110806	51500	44924	8539	9128
山西	Shanxi	40	213095	65997	32805	44980	1530	2922
内蒙古	Inner Mongolia	3031	142453	72100	32516	62537	12422	9362
辽宁	Liaoning	2001	399204	248284	75072	97590	59491	16836
吉林	Jilin	59	131567	76606	16084	23881	6927	5610
黑龙江	Heilongjiang	5	276040	112187	22985	36485	6149	8643
上海	Shanghai	1927	497914	341042	260311	20865	246277	14160
江苏	Jiangsu		706573	401319	164700	67111	227335	23638
浙江	Zhejiang	208	616358	306006	119864	66906	154734	21535
安徽	Anhui		204860	73518	29979	43533	30049	10874
福建	Fujian	103	185544	169576	55267	29400	40785	12662
江西	Jiangxi	44	112715	46618	17435	23083	20895	6847
山东	Shandong	5376	659514	327950	92515	294438	143916	56022
河南	Henan	1	291771	117917	35940	72363	28387	7626
湖北	Hubei		240276	107289	40502	50634	15834	11076
湖南	Hunan		250221	92390	32638	29098	5796	8079
广东	Guangdong	133	643373	619228	205723	86288	188995	71681
广西	Guangxi	778	129157	75414	14113	29218	47896	4704
海南	Hainan		37005	29702	6232	7007	18340	2691
重庆	Chongqing		131586	57507	24646	20740	29273	3913
四川	Sichuan	213	280858	132234	44559	57787	51374	11052
贵州	Guizhou	17	129134	42836	8443	17573	8724	2849
云南	Yunnan	2251	295727	79107	26762	29899	5567	13441
西藏	Tibet		4114		654		296	
陕西	Shaanxi	197	207660	69411	22562	35153	8070	8277
甘肃	Gansu		93582	41993	12475	13880	55	2225
青海	Qinghai	11	23195	9468	2905	984	5	512
宁夏	Ningxia		30388	13553	4304	4939	1783	845
新疆	Xinjiang	156	136696	64421	13989	19038	6310	1230

8-14 续表 2 continued

单位：万元 (10 000 yuan)

地 区	Region	屠宰税 Slaughter Tax	筵席税 Banquet Tax	农业税 Agricultural Tax	农业特产税 Tax on Special Agricultural Products	牧业税 Tax on the Animal Husbandry	耕地占用税 Tax on The Occupancy of Cultivated Land	契 税 Contract Tax
地方合计	**Region Total**	**49**	**16**	**127959**	**466042**	**87**	**1418490**	**7351400**
北 京	Beijing						7405	606775
天 津	Tianjin						8255	163175
河 北	Hebei	7		47204	558		27780	148178
山 西	Shanxi	30		2	308		11477	31881
内蒙古	Inner Mongolia		16	527	1531		60179	45345
辽 宁	Liaoning			5346	6321		36925	389349
吉 林	Jilin	2		996	5024		19660	76259
黑龙江	Heilongjiang			675	9308		14344	86716
上 海	Shanghai						33916	1110419
江 苏	Jiangsu			438			121566	808849
浙 江	Zhejiang			837			122793	691432
安 徽	Anhui			3048			41695	178145
福 建	Fujian				22021		32003	209093
江 西	Jiangxi				4615		48703	149640
山 东	Shandong			54376	11199		310785	520896
河 南	Henan			74	36016		53544	194269
湖 北	Hubei			200	17648		32745	150295
湖 南	Hunan				52831		83729	194456
广 东	Guangdong	10		291	7562		121258	818646
广 西	Guangxi			2669	6167		57559	111791
海 南	Hainan			488	30		3078	19703
重 庆	Chongqing			791	13697		31325	141390
四 川	Sichuan			287	21780		59798	239008
贵 州	Guizhou			103	66828		17211	35059
云 南	Yunnan			5834	172260		25930	83277
西 藏	Tibet						96	
陕 西	Shaanxi				8085		25694	59015
甘 肃	Gansu			395	2236		4286	22283
青 海	Qinghai			21			2707	5788
宁 夏	Ningxia			333			698	15712
新 疆	Xinjiang			3024	17	87	1346	44556

8-14 续表 3 continued

单位：万元 (10 000 yuan)

地 区	Region	国有资产经营收益 State-owned Assets Profit	国有企业计划亏损补贴 Planning Subsidies to Loss-suffering Stated-owned Enterprises	行政性收费收入 Income from Administrative Fees	罚没收入 Penalty and Confiscatory Income	海域场地矿区使用费收入 Income from Use of Sea Area, Field and Diggings	专项收入 Special Project Income	其他收入 Other Income
地方合计	**Region Total**	**3947475**	**-1665673**	**10736983**	**6171631**	**63201**	**6487539**	**1946746**
北 京	Beijing	15442	-502900	245235	188420	11090	329862	43637
天 津	Tianjin	82	-25000	458474	67835	3026	89995	19084
河 北	Hebei	108702	-13901	384858	346513	4050	328512	67383
山 西	Shanxi	31929	-18243	246150	187501	2	480872	27759
内蒙古	Inner Mongolia	147758	-2479	170942	113281		240019	35210
辽 宁	Liaoning	244525	-30478	630022	271868	8532	288998	55045
吉 林	Jilin	159719	-55890	201239	115997	207	109115	39007
黑龙江	Heilongjiang	158829	-21019	202661	115254		225915	28481
上 海	Shanghai	7	-179869	340636	162068		290350	32717
江 苏	Jiangsu	371646	-100212	815291	530529	1651	486895	48292
浙 江	Zhejiang	12918	-424666	265531	584372	743	418430	48395
安 徽	Anhui	46640	-51917	510006	159997		182499	47495
福 建	Fujian	77751	-2477	290876	213993	4897	120693	48254
江 西	Jiangxi	128975	-2025	309246	193782		96294	95736
山 东	Shandong	390287	-42741	1080665	424524	15227	497050	101626
河 南	Henan	364102	-8807	634921	298045	186	303300	128035
湖 北	Hubei	70763	-20073	419491	248581	803	117526	81030
湖 南	Hunan	146547	-37725	469569	276875		229895	188810
广 东	Guangdong	310727	-17660	1034117	603254	7244	524155	340495
广 西	Guangxi	267677	-6926	275233	193485	4056	106123	83656
海 南	Hainan	24816		53947	28458	1297	21133	12002
重 庆	Chongqing	96751	-22477	480942	90923	3	123271	28801
四 川	Sichuan	198651	-21932	505568	212321	1	227695	57836
贵 州	Guizhou	43352	-3761	137595	100969		103746	70062
云 南	Yunnan	86476	-18405	153927	158018		167894	117091
西 藏	Tibet	1683	-9149	16289	5841		3469	20721
陕 西	Shaanxi	291985	-12082	130873	126338	186	119655	29995
甘 肃	Gansu	80741	-12769	98309	44641		84942	19547
青 海	Qinghai	3287	-40	14249	7985		24273	14427
宁 夏	Ningxia	22073		33512	19466		26914	7232
新 疆	Xinjiang	42634	-50	126609	80497		118049	8885

8-15 各地区财政支出（2005年）

Final Statement of Government Expenditure by Region (2005)

单位：万元 (10 000 yuan)

地 区	Region	支出合计 Total Expenditure	基本建设 Expenditure for Capital Construction	企业挖潜改造资金 Expenditure for Innovation Enterprises	地质勘探费 Expenditure for Geological Prospecting	科技三项费用 Expenditure for Science and Technology Promotion	流动资金 Expenditure for Circulating Funds
地方合计	**Region Total**	**251543091**	**26757770**	**8693287**	**927540**	**2873706**	**10653**
北 京	Beijing	10583114	844269	443307	12900	96094	
天 津	Tianjin	4421207	732323	291198	14637	108550	
河 北	Hebei	9791635	735846	211320	26123	74044	
山 西	Shanxi	6687508	505365	16551	22577	43607	896
内蒙古	Inner Mongolia	6818772	1106816	291274	35164	43463	
辽 宁	Liaoning	12043636	1268402	377461	34620	233698	
吉 林	Jilin	6311212	504908	217276	45643	45681	
黑龙江	Heilongjiang	7877854	603916	322273	20735	83400	
上 海	Shanghai	16462550	3692060	2370026	1646	29114	
江 苏	Jiangsu	16733965	1537082	633343	27978	271295	
浙 江	Zhejiang	12655345	924118	572882	30829	340822	
安 徽	Anhui	7130633	641160	232987	47007	37659	
福 建	Fujian	5930663	489241	217375	14443	83179	268
江 西	Jiangxi	5639525	417475	162393	66392	25103	
山 东	Shandong	14662271	704835	573010	27743	194199	3129
河 南	Henan	11160412	1083689	293900	27797	92275	
湖 北	Hubei	7787159	452024	124474	15787	79312	2934
湖 南	Hunan	8734181	749789	168894	58816	81570	
广 东	Guangdong	22890691	2644339	265978	34768	526901	2181
广 西	Guangxi	6114806	699528	143801	31900	36362	
海 南	Hainan	1512421	174881	4969	3724	7497	
重 庆	Chongqing	4873543	733446	97882	7192	48959	
四 川	Sichuan	10821769	1142259	240878	57059	71804	1245
贵 州	Guizhou	5207261	412285	50171	39356	33615	
云 南	Yunnan	7663115	878316	141045	26928	57536	
西 藏	Tibet	1854502	563995	3292	15829	4437	
陕 西	Shaanxi	6389627	580587	96165	49248	43788	
甘 肃	Gansu	4293479	452723	45308	52082	23136	
青 海	Qinghai	1697547	265122	13711	15851	8249	
宁 夏	Ningxia	1602509	384608	33440	13393	12658	
新 疆	Xinjiang	5190179	832363	36703	49373	35699	

8-15 续表 1 continued

单位：万元 (10 000 yuan)

地区	Region	农业支出 Expenditure for Agriculture	林业支出 Expenditure for Forestry	农林水利气象等部门事业费 Expenditure for Operating Expenses of Agriculture, Forestry, Water Conservancy and Meteorology	工业交通部门事业费 Expenditure for Operating Expenses of Departments of Industry & Transportation	流通部门事业费 Expenditure for Operating Expenses of Department of Commerce	文体广播事业费 Expenditure for Operating Expenses of Departments of Culture, Sport& Broadcasting
地方合计	**Region Total**	**8673075**	**4730652**	**3045016**	**3099048**	**428683**	**6308710**
北京	Beijing	276401	86443	63576	73253	2588	250827
天津	Tianjin	87498	12578	28427	19120	254	107471
河北	Hebei	322693	217046	92937	156451	16204	252154
山西	Shanxi	228410	165376	67897	99872	11866	176686
内蒙古	Inner Mongolia	242095	402720	75403	72843	7373	148984
辽宁	Liaoning	434798	140428	129528	235629	18609	217638
吉林	Jilin	213980	169801	42224	80881	16128	148802
黑龙江	Heilongjiang	295465	247210	69143	105351	41300	171198
上海	Shanghai	246078	16569	88560	73701	1928	264465
江苏	Jiangsu	662191	40973	272520	192629	11723	429236
浙江	Zhejiang	578958	88438	194086	242202	14374	374539
安徽	Anhui	289279	112115	75099	85704	10309	166755
福建	Fujian	203307	47881	80618	110708	11545	193357
江西	Jiangxi	268330	118979	69504	97737	16572	144340
山东	Shandong	641754	90511	163582	168799	22258	449415
河南	Henan	353795	151824	135794	97770	17882	368004
湖北	Hubei	322293	159185	93080	105162	30603	191783
湖南	Hunan	402771	226576	89791	125274	29893	219200
广东	Guangdong	451444	143189	523179	205998	54763	508356
广西	Guangxi	231545	150800	92498	51795	7499	177727
海南	Hainan	57985	27698	37268	8399	1223	34663
重庆	Chongqing	130318	149771	30816	30032	3916	104379
四川	Sichuan	416192	426012	108429	181229	22260	281067
贵州	Guizhou	245928	212683	74244	70315	13263	180923
云南	Yunnan	336445	270602	127945	103670	17354	205342
西藏	Tibet	59904	23658	12812	42847	525	37946
陕西	Shaanxi	217540	322987	79430	133808	20243	169811
甘肃	Gansu	136613	233924	54014	40955	3064	128598
青海	Qinghai	62651	71648	14966	18768	388	35564
宁夏	Ningxia	65865	93249	16574	19490	1639	36337
新疆	Xinjiang	190549	109778	41072	48656	1137	133143

8-15 续表 2 continued

单位：万元 (10 000 yuan)

地区 Region	教育事业费 Expenditure for Operating Expenses of Education	科学事业费 Expenditure for Operating Expenses of Department of Science	卫生经费 Expenditure for Public Health	其他部门的事业费 Expenditure for Operating Expenses of Other Departments	抚恤和社会福利救济费 Expenditure for Pensions and Relief Funds for Social Welfare	行政事业单位离退休经费 Expenditure for Retired Persons in Administrative Department
地方合计 Region Total	**37299753**	**1401120**	**10155520**	**11662495**	**7110549**	**10659759**
北京 Beijing	1458723	157439	656229	409578	320515	538247
天津 Tianjin	672034	27989	189803	107850	87061	11609
河北 Hebei	1705374	35192	450870	639754	283309	470734
山西 Shanxi	1020914	20905	281735	317121	196674	363628
内蒙古 Inner Mongolia	786645	19037	208768	371663	147111	401923
辽宁 Liaoning	1421954	46142	343526	580493	449995	533460
吉林 Jilin	741472	27113	207022	298027	231563	361541
黑龙江 Heilongjiang	1065721	33565	280124	434990	238472	227118
上海 Shanghai	1829415	159199	521464	633179	248436	69060
江苏 Jiangsu	2582399	79492	750563	737656	431081	502468
浙江 Zhejiang	2315489	105657	648767	878414	309056	89046
安徽 Anhui	1174312	25687	250223	221585	255928	422244
福建 Fujian	1115121	46787	259305	315885	171429	361597
江西 Jiangxi	879253	22053	218381	325369	251831	200756
山东 Shandong	2487484	76471	544085	706013	406910	646793
河南 Henan	1873208	42928	418057	544269	353006	647891
湖北 Hubei	1188461	25760	311597	289669	341746	281259
湖南 Hunan	1230010	26129	244520	444684	317127	450120
广东 Guangdong	3292088	160063	823633	1221592	417445	1051043
广西 Guangxi	1052608	40725	259931	348461	160274	242239
海南 Hainan	242088	5402	65191	87570	48268	62623
重庆 Chongqing	606598	10855	151757	112232	172664	316635
四川 Sichuan	1405260	48974	495641	354632	377908	593177
贵州 Guizhou	933707	30452	258160	184890	152226	36304
云南 Yunnan	1222810	44405	448073	313012	202968	626054
西藏 Tibet	203794	2800	71090	7123	26916	20474
陕西 Shaanxi	993134	24048	217038	325534	195293	255028
甘肃 Gansu	674831	19916	178431	153022	115760	236013
青海 Qinghai	203132	4810	88611	52633	50659	161040
宁夏 Ningxia	195197	7513	54008	53523	35847	68903
新疆 Xinjiang	726517	23612	258917	192072	113071	410732

8-15 续表 3 continued

单位：万元 (10 000 yuan)

地区	Region	社会保障补助支出 Expenditure on Subsidies to Social Security Programs	国防支出 Expenditure for National Defense	行政管理费 Expenditure for Government Administration	外交外事支出 Expenditure for Foreign Affairs	武装警察部队支出 Expenditure for Armed Police Troops	公检法司支出 Expenditure for Public Security Agency, Procuratorial Agency and Court of Justice
地方合计	**Region Total**	**15809341**	**279337**	**24192313**	**123543**	**410708**	**17640557**
北京	Beijing	250954	3041	691634	1597	2296	843905
天津	Tianjin	372050	2631	259918	6260	2708	318590
河北	Hebei	725068	11700	974398	8429	4937	688198
山西	Shanxi	560873	8877	691631	1456	7227	399587
内蒙古	Inner Mongolia	324628	5679	714427	2358	17528	318539
辽宁	Liaoning	1650379	20848	919584	18811	13588	755499
吉林	Jilin	1048895	7640	451254	3241	15468	358850
黑龙江	Heilongjiang	1098148	5816	695575	2673	19722	477651
上海	Shanghai	720825	4996	689946	10410		880928
江苏	Jiangsu	637112	19687	1821131	6762	25848	1302032
浙江	Zhejiang	289424	13113	1419044	8049	30681	1157530
安徽	Anhui	484508	7222	737823	4957	6407	429256
福建	Fujian	102766	17354	493542	1791	19473	455897
江西	Jiangxi	393028	6111	509527	1065	6973	405794
山东	Shandong	587856	12614	1629489	4639	14300	1021718
河南	Henan	679660	7540	1209591	1396		697993
湖北	Hubei	711377	5465	947952	1767	26600	657104
湖南	Hunan	839972	13346	872580	3070	16312	561809
广东	Guangdong	393745	25971	2225707	6826	70775	2313302
广西	Guangxi	309193	11756	614387	8929	9122	461043
海南	Hainan	117149	4851	149745	1731	6219	102942
重庆	Chongqing	431288	5316	516304	616	14548	332896
四川	Sichuan	804604	18631	1353259	3627	24080	742809
贵州	Guizhou	253478	5173	651549	1483	4420	358349
云南	Yunnan	290334	17433	781218	3680	24068	517079
西藏	Tibet	48352	423	279559	675	2502	81914
陕西	Shaanxi	765679	4679	624333	1345	6096	345306
甘肃	Gansu	475215	1358	425038	2372	3571	204504
青海	Qinghai	136332	1890	156724	1025	3607	81170
宁夏	Ningxia	70364	1679	106901	1226	3437	80944
新疆	Xinjiang	236085	6497	578543	1277	8195	287419

8-15 续表 4 continued

单位：万元 (10 000 yuan)

地 区	Region	城市维护费 Expenditure for City Maintenance	政策性补贴支出 Expenditure for Price Subsidies	支援不发达地区支出 Expenditure for Supporting Underdeveloped Areas	海域开发建设和场地使用费支出 Expenditure for Developing Land and Sea Area	车辆税费支出 Expenditure for Vehicle tax	债务利息支出 Expenditure for Interest of Debts	专项支出 Expenditure for Special Items	其他支出 Other Expenditures
地方合计	**Region Total**	**12606413**	**4070345**	**1887617**	**29776**	**1524608**	**298146**	**5788732**	**23044319**
北 京	Beijing	527159	46158			7161		325194	2193626
天 津	Tianjin	520168	30072	50	3166	4637	2000	90989	309566
河 北	Hebei	460698	210332	61418	2231	45332	234	263773	644836
山 西	Shanxi	288666	93004	57348	225	48679	473	548733	440649
内蒙古	Inner Mongolia	378206	158001	67105	49	79250	12053	190406	189261
辽 宁	Liaoning	793637	259728	43531	5679	29801	108941	264696	692533
吉 林	Jilin	206841	482906	35905	85	21323	45459	80774	200509
黑龙江	Heilongjiang	323133	435750	46490	210	58246		219016	255443
上 海	Shanghai	864610	14229			2657		298953	2730096
江 苏	Jiangsu	1565236	142100	14312	591	46139	11584	436149	1542653
浙 江	Zhejiang	764081	63683	45030	449	18190		374712	763682
安 徽	Anhui	217674	306798	57490	92	32105	1807	156451	639990
福 建	Fujian	166059	63207	42714	2667	19878	12443	104792	706034
江 西	Jiangxi	280059	116081	58894	75	60918		86726	429806
山 东	Shandong	1179667	201713	21612	6210	39116	3830	452000	1580516
河 南	Henan	366284	326166	92653	132	76491	25829	293993	880595
湖 北	Hubei	266545	159085	59211	643	67595	3445	103073	762168
湖 南	Hunan	384270	140534	75300	186	89190	5334	176591	690523
广 东	Guangdong	1061969	137951	141351	4469	7730	834	461588	3711513
广 西	Guangxi	237157	54736	93234	1140	67691	5047	93922	419756
海 南	Hainan	55480	11385	25504	803	9234	579	17558	139792
重 庆	Chongqing	375711	63957	45145		66936	2404	100104	210866
四 川	Sichuan	310157	159060	123912	82	107179	38767	181799	729777
贵 州	Guizhou	129292	34223	131371	58	103984	7513	78803	519043
云 南	Yunnan	269366	52194	166080	110	76350	661	106804	335233
西 藏	Tibet	4329	18997	42145		76788		4041	197335
陕 西	Shaanxi	244267	92081	86645	37	84866	286	67485	342840
甘 肃	Gansu	112309	52429	101781	91	63353	1260	74145	227663
青 海	Qinghai	19197	12486	43667	86	56772	7363	20244	89181
宁 夏	Ningxia	59852	16485	37181	60	13036		24108	94992
新 疆	Xinjiang	174334	114814	70538	150	43981		91110	373842

8-16　预算外资金分项目收入

Extra-budgetary Revenue by Item

单位：亿元 (100 million yuan)

年　份 Year	合　计 Total	行政事业性收　费 Revenue of Administrative and Institutional Units	政府性基金收　入 Revenue of Funds	乡镇自筹、统筹资金 Revenue form Fundraising Programs of Township Governments	地方财政收　入 Revenue of Local Governments	国有企业和主管部门收入 Revenue of State-owned Enterprises and Its Governing Department	其　他收　入 Other Revenues
1978	347.11	63.41			31.09	252.61	
1980	557.40	74.44			40.85	442.11	
1985	1530.03	233.22			44.08	1252.73	
1989	2658.83	500.66			54.36	2103.81	
1990	2708.64	576.95			60.59	2071.10	
1991	3243.30	697.00			68.77	2477.53	
1992	3854.92	885.45			90.88	2878.59	
1993	1432.54	1317.83			114.71		
1994	1862.53	1722.50			140.03		
1995	2406.50	2234.85			171.65		
1996	3893.34	3395.75		272.90	224.69		
1997	2826.00	2414.32		295.78	115.90		
1998	3082.29	1981.92	478.41	337.31		54.67	229.98
1999	3385.17	2354.28	396.51	358.86		50.11	225.41
2000	3826.43	2654.54	383.51	403.34		59.22	325.81
2001	4300.00	3090.00	380.00	410.00		60.00	360.00
2002	4479.00	3238.00	376.00	272.00		72.00	521.00
2003	4566.80	3335.74	287.10	293.14		52.33	598.49
2004	4699.18	3208.42	351.29	213.09		64.12	862.26

注：1993-1995年和1996年的预算外资金收入范围分别有所调整，与以前各年不可比。从1997年起，预算外资金收入不包括纳入预算内管理的政府性基金（收费），与以前各年也不可比。从2004年起，预算外资金收入为财政预算外专户收入。

a) Since adjustment on the coverage of extra-budgetary revenues from 1993 to 1995 and in 1998 has made, the figures are not comparable with the previous years. Since 1997, the extra-budgetary revenues do not include the intra-budgetary government fund (fee), the figures are not comparable with the previous years. Since 2004, the extra-budgetary revenue is the fiscal extra-budgetary revenue in special account.

8-17　预算外资金分项目支出

Extra-budgetary Expenditure by Item

单位：亿元 (100 million yuan)

年　份 Year	合　计 Total	基本建设支　出 Capital Construction	专项支出 Special Expenditure	行政事业费支　出 Operating and Administrative Expenses	城市维护费支　出 Urban Maintenance Expenses	乡镇自筹、统筹支出 Expenditure by Township Governments	其他支出 Other Expenses
1996	3838.32	1490.23	307.27	1254.36		136.39	650.07
1997	2685.54	502.03	311.59	1280.19		288.69	303.04
1998	2918.31	393.98	423.60	1588.28		335.26	177.19
1999	3139.14	539.82		1816.13	127.45	350.34	305.40
2000	3529.01	426.20		2225.09	146.38	387.39	343.96
2001	3850.00	350.00		2500.00	150.00	400.00	450.00
2002	3831.00	260.00		2655.00	160.00	268.00	488.00
2003	4156.36	269.86		2836.55	202.62	283.11	564.22
2005	4351.73	287.28		3133.80	193.82	205.09	531.74

注：1996年预算外资金支出范围有所调整，与以前各年不可比。从1997年起，预算外资金支出不包括纳入预算内管理的政府性基金(收费)，与以前各年也不可比。从2004年起，预算外资金支出为财政预算外专户支出。

a) Because adjustment on the coverage of extra-budgetary expenditures in 1998 has made, the figures are not comparable with the previous years. Since 1997, the extra-budgetary expenditures do not include the intra-budgetary government fund (fee), the figures are not comparable with the previous years. Since 2004, the extra-budgetary expenditure is the fiscal extra-budgetary expenditure in special account.

8-18 中央和地方预算外资金收支及比重

Total Extra-budgetary Revenues and Expenditures and Ratio of the Central Government and Local Governments

项 目 Item	全国（亿元） Total (100 million yuan)	中 央 Central Government	地 方 Local Governments	比重（%） Ratio (%) 中 央 Central Government	地 方 Local Governments
收 入 Revenue					
1986	1737.31	716.63	1020.68	41.2	58.8
1987	2028.80	828.03	1200.77	40.8	59.2
1988	2360.77	907.15	1453.62	38.4	61.6
1989	2658.83	1072.28	1586.55	40.3	59.7
1990	2708.64	1073.28	1635.36	39.6	60.4
1991	3243.30	1381.10	1862.20	42.6	57.4
1992	3854.92	1707.73	2147.19	44.3	55.7
1993	1432.54	245.90	1186.64	17.2	82.8
1994	1862.53	283.32	1579.21	15.2	84.8
1995	2406.50	317.57	2088.93	13.2	86.8
1996	3893.34	947.66	2945.68	24.3	75.7
1997	2826.00	145.08	2680.92	5.1	94.9
1998	3082.29	164.15	2918.14	5.3	94.7
1999	3385.17	230.45	3154.72	6.8	93.2
2000	3826.43	247.63	3578.79	6.5	93.5
2001	4300.00	347.00	3953.00	8.1	91.9
2002	4479.00	440.00	4039.00	9.8	90.2
2003	4566.80	379.37	4187.43	8.3	91.7
2004	4699.18	350.69	4348.49	7.5	92.5
支 出 Expenditure					
1986	1578.37	640.94	937.43	40.6	59.4
1987	1840.75	741.61	1099.14	40.3	59.7
1988	2145.27	842.86	1302.41	39.3	60.7
1989	2503.10	975.87	1527.23	39.0	61.0
1990	2707.06	1037.69	1669.37	38.3	61.7
1991	3092.26	1263.27	1828.99	40.9	59.1
1992	3649.90	1592.81	2057.09	43.6	56.4
1993	1314.30	198.87	1115.43	15.1	84.9
1994	1710.39	225.02	1485.37	13.2	86.8
1995	2331.26	351.38	1979.88	15.1	84.9
1996	3838.32	1034.92	2803.40	27.0	73.0
1997	2685.54	143.91	2541.63	5.4	94.6
1998	2918.31	139.74	2778.57	4.8	95.2
1999	3139.14	164.82	2974.32	5.3	94.7
2000	3529.01	210.74	3318.28	6.0	94.0
2001	3850.00	258.13	3591.87	6.7	93.3
2002	3831.00	259.00	3572.00	6.8	93.2
2003	4156.36	329.32	3827.04	7.9	92.1
2004	4351.73	389.50	3962.23	9.0	91.0

注：1993-1995年和1996年的预算外资金收支范围分别有所调整，与以前各年不可比。从1997年起，预算外资金收支不包括纳入预算内管理的政府性基金（收费），与以前各年也不可比。从2004年起，预算外资金收支为财政预算外专户收支。

a) Because adjustment on the coverage of extra-budgetary revenues and expenditures from 1993 to 1995 and in 1998 has made, the figures are not comparable with the previous years. Since 1997, the extra-budgetary revenues and expenditures do not include the intra-budgetary government fund (fee), the figures are not comparable with the previous years. Since 2004, the extra-budgetary revenue and expenditure is the fiscal extra-budgetary revenue and expenditure in special account.

8-19 国家财政债务发行情况

Government Debts Issuance

单位：亿元 (100 million yuan)

年 份 Year	合 计 Total	国内债务 Domestic Debts	国外借款 Foreign Borrowing	国内其他债务 Other Domestic Debts
1985	89.85	60.61	29.24	
1986	138.25	62.51	75.74	
1987	223.55	63.07	106.48	54.00
1988	270.78	92.17	138.61	40.00
1989	407.97	56.07	144.06	207.84
1990	375.45	93.46	178.21	103.78
1991	461.40	199.30	180.13	81.97
1992	669.68	395.64	208.91	65.13
1993	739.22	314.78	357.90	66.54
1994	1175.25	1028.57	146.68	
1995	1549.76	1510.86	38.90	
1996	1967.28	1847.77	119.51	
1997	2476.82	2412.03	64.79	
1998	3310.93	3228.77	82.16	
1999	3715.03	3702.13		12.90
2000	4180.10	4153.59	23.10	3.41
2001	4604.00	4483.53	120.47	
2002	5679.00	5660.00		19.00
2003	6153.53	6029.24	120.68	3.61
2004	6879.34	6726.28	145.07	7.99
2005	6922.87	6922.87		

注：从1999年开始，国内其他债务项目为债务收入大于支出部分增列的偿债基金。

a) Since 1999, other domestic debts were the sinking fund which come from the excessive part of the revenue from borrowings minus the expenditure for debts.

8-20 国家财政债务还本付息支出

Government Payment for the Principal and Interest of Debts

单位：亿元 (100 million yuan)

年 份 Year	合 计 Total	国内债务还本付息 Payment for the Principal and Interest of Domestic Debts	国外债务还本付息 Payment for the Principal and Interest of Foreign Debts	归还向人民银行借款的利息 Payment of the Interest of Loans from People's Bank	债务收入大于支出部分增列偿债基金 Sinking Fund from the Excessive Part of the Revenue from Borrowings minus the Expenditure for Debts
1980	28.58		24.40	4.18	
1985	39.56		32.59	6.97	
1989	72.37	19.30	45.84	7.23	
1990	190.07	113.42	68.21	8.44	
1991	246.80	156.69	80.22	9.89	
1992	438.57	342.42	80.26	15.89	
1993	336.22	224.30	89.22	22.70	
1994	499.36	364.96	107.17	27.23	
1995	882.96	784.06	71.69	27.21	
1996	1355.03	1266.29	60.76	27.98	
1997	1918.37	1820.40	70.76	27.21	
1998	2352.92	2245.79	76.60	30.53	
1999	1910.53	1792.33	90.99	27.21	12.90
2000	1579.82	1552.21	27.61		3.41
2001	2007.73	1923.42	84.31		
2002	2563.13	2467.71	95.42		19.00
2003	2952.24	2876.58	75.66		3.61
2004	3671.59	3542.42	129.17		7.99
2005	3923.37	3878.51	44.86		

注：从2000年开始，表中数据均为债务还本支出。

a) Since 2000, expenditure in this table refers to payment for the principal of debts.

8-21 外 债 余 额

Balance of Foreign Debts

债务类型	Type of Debts	1999	2000	2001	2002	2003	2004	2005
总计 （亿美元）	**Total (USD 100 million)**	**1518.30**	**1457.30**	**1701.10**	**1713.60**	**1936.34**	**2285.96**	**2810.45**
按债务类型分	**By Type of Debt**							
外国政府贷款	Loans from Foreign Governments	265.60	246.10	237.00	244.23	254.20	322.08	271.95
国际金融组织贷款	Loans from International Financial Institutions	251.39	263.50	275.70	277.02	264.67	251.01	267.88
国际商业贷款	International Commercial Loans	653.80	947.70	972.30	929.10	1051.73	1247.83	1362.62
贸易信贷	Trade Loans			216.10	263.23	365.74	465.04	908.00
按偿还期限分	**By Repayment Terms**							
长期债务余额	Balance of Long-term Debts	1366.50	1326.50	1195.30	1155.60	1165.90	1242.87	1249.02
短期债务余额	Balance of Short-term Debts	151.80	130.80	505.80	558.00	770.44	1043.09	1561.43
构成 (%)	**Percentage (%)**	**100.0**	**100.0**	**100.0**	**100.0**	**100.0**	**100.0**	**100.0**
按债务类型分	**By Type of Debt**							
外国政府贷款	Loans from Foreign Governments	17.5	16.9	13.9	14.5	13.1	14.1	9.7
国际金融组织贷款	Loans from International Financial Institutions	16.5	18.1	16.2	16.4	13.7	11.0	9.5
国际商业贷款	International Commercial Loans	43.1	65.0	57.2	53.5	54.3	54.6	48.5
贸易信贷	Trade Loans			12.7	15.6	18.9	20.3	32.3
按偿还期限分	**By Repayment Terms**							
长期债务余额	Balance of Long Term Debts	90.0	91.0	70.3	67.4	60.2	54.4	44.4
短期债务余额	Balance of Short Term of Debts	10.0	9.0	29.7	32.6	39.8	45.6	55.6

注：2001年及以后外债余额按新口径统计，比2000年及以前的登记债务余额增加了3个月以内贸易项下的对外融资余额。

a) Foreign debts since 2001 are collected by the new standard, the figures increase the foreign loans under the item of international trade loans within 3 months than the debts before 2001.

8-22 外债风险指标

Risk Indicators on Foreign Debts

单位：% (%)

年份 Year	偿债率 Debt Service Ratio	负债率 Liability Ratio	债务率 Foreign Debt Ratio
1985	2.7	5.2	56.0
1986	15.4	7.3	72.1
1987	9.0	9.4	77.1
1988	6.5	10.0	87.1
1989	8.3	9.2	86.4
1990	8.7	13.5	91.6
1991	8.5	14.9	91.9
1992	7.1	14.4	87.9
1993	10.2	13.9	96.5
1994	9.1	17.1	78.0
1995	7.6	15.2	72.4
1996	6.0	14.2	67.7
1997	7.3	14.5	63.2
1998	10.9	15.2	70.4
1999	11.3	15.3	69.5
2000	9.2	13.5	52.1
2001	7.5	14.7	56.8
2002	7.9	13.6	46.1
2003	6.9	13.7	39.9
2004	3.2	13.9	34.9
2005	3.1	12.6	33.6

注：1.本表资料由国家外汇管理局提供。
2.偿债率指偿还外债本息与当年贸易和非贸易外汇收入(国际收支口径)之比。
3.负债率指外债余额与当年国内生产总值之比。
4.债务率指外债余额与当年贸易和非贸易外汇收入(国际收支口径)之比。

a) The table is provided by State Administration of Foreign Exchange.
b) Debt service ratio refers to the ratio of the payment of principal and interest of foreign debts to the foreign exchange receipts from foreign trade and non-trade services of the current year..
c) Liability ratio refers to the ratio of the balance of foreign debts to the gross domestic product of the current year.
d) Foreign debt ratio refers to the ratio of the balance of foreign debts to the foreign exchange receipts from foreign trade and non-trade services of the current year.

主要统计指标解释

财政收入 指国家财政参与社会产品分配所取得的收入，是实现国家职能的财力保证。财政收入所包括的内容几经变化，目前主要包括：

(1)各项税收：包括增值税、营业税、消费税、土地增值税、城市维护建设税、资源税、城市土地使用税、企业所得税、个人所得税、关税、证券交易印花税、车辆购置税、农牧业税和耕地占用税等。

(2)专项收入：包括排污费收入、城市水资源费收入、矿产资源补偿费收入、教育费附加收入等。

(3)其他收入：包括利息收入、基本建设贷款归还收入、基本建设收入、捐赠收入等。

(4)国有企业亏损补贴：此项为负收入，冲减财政收入。主要包括对工业企业、商业企业、粮食企业的补贴。

财政支出 国家财政将筹集起来的资金进行分配使用，以满足经济建设和各项事业的需要，主要包括：

(1)基本建设支出：指按国家有关规定，属于基本建设范围内的基本建设有偿使用、拨款、资本金支出以及经国家批准对专项和政策性基建投资贷款，在部门的基建投资额中统筹支付的贴息支出。

(2)企业挖潜改造资金：指国家预算内拨给的用于企业挖潜、革新和改造方面的资金。包括各部门企业挖潜改造资金和企业挖潜改造贷款资金，为农业服务的县办“五小”企业技术改造补助，挖潜改造贷款贴息资金。

(3)地质勘探费用：指国家预算用于地质勘探单位的勘探工作费用，包括地质勘探管理机构及其事业单位经费、地质勘探经费。

(4)科技三项费用：指国家预算用于科技支出的费用，包括新产品试制费、中间试验费、重要科学研究补助费。

(5)支援农村生产支出：指国家财政支援农村集体(户)各项生产的支出。包括对农村举办的小型农田水利和打井、喷灌等的补助费，对农村水土保持措施的补助费，对农村举办的小水电站的补助费，特大抗旱的补助费，农村开荒补助费，扶持乡镇企业资金，支援农村合作生产组织资金、农村农技推广和植保补助费，农村草场和畜禽保护补助费，农村造林和林木保护补助费，农村水产补助费，发展粮食生产专项资金。

(6)农林水利气象等部门的事业费用：指国家财政用于农垦、农场、农业、畜牧、农机、林业、森工、水利、水产、气象、乡镇企业的技术推广、良种推广(示范)、动植物(畜禽、森林)保护、水质监测、勘探设计、资源调查、干部训练等项费用，园艺特产场补助费，中等专业学校经费，飞播牧草试验补助费，营林机构、气象机构经费，渔政费以及农业管理事业费等。

(7)工业交通商业等部门的事业费：指国家预算支付给工交商各部门用于事业发展的人员和公用经费支出，包括勘探设计费、中等专业学校经费、技术学校经费、干部训练费。

(8)文教科学卫生事业费：指国家预算用于文化、出版、文物、教育、卫生、中医、公费医疗、体育、档案、地震、海洋、通讯、电影电视、计划生育、党政群干部训练、自然科学、社会科学、科协等项事业的人员和公用经费支出以及高技术研究专项经费。主要包括工资、补助工资、福利费、离退休费、助学金、公务费、设备购置费、修缮费、业务费、差额补助费。

(9)抚恤和社会福利救济费：指国家预算用于抚恤和社会福利救济事业的经费。包括由民政部门开支的烈士家属和牺牲病残人员家属的一次性、定期抚恤金，革命伤残人员的抚恤金，各种伤残补助费，烈军属、复员退伍军人生活补助费，退伍军人安置费，优抚事业单位经费，烈士纪念建筑物管理、维修费，自然灾害救济事业费和特大自然灾害灾后重建补助费等。

(10)行政事业单位离退休支出：指实行归口管理的行政事业单位离退休经费。

(11)社会保障补助支出：指国家预算用于社会保障的补助支出，包括对社会保险基金的补助、促进就业补助、国有企业下岗职工补助、补充全国社会保障基金等。

(12)国防支出：指国家预算用于国防建设和保卫国家安全的支出，包括国防费、国防科研事业费、民兵建设以及专项工程支出等。

(13)行政管理费：包括行政管理支出，党派团体补助支出，外交支出，公安安全支出，司法支出，法院支出，检察院支出和公检法办案费用补助。

(14)政策性补贴支出：指经国家批准，由国家财政拨给用于粮棉油等产品的价格补贴支出。主要包括粮、棉、油差价补贴，平抑物价和储备糖补贴，农业生产资料价差补贴，粮食风险基金，副食品风险基金，地方煤炭风险基金等。

(15)债务利息支出：指国家预算中用于偿还国内外债务利息的支出。

中央财政收入和地方财政收入 指按现行分税制财政体制划分的中央本级收入和地方本级收入。1994年实行分税制财政体制以后，属于中央财政的收入包括关税、海关代征消费税和增值税，消费税，中央企业所得税，地方银行和外资银行及非银行金融企业所得税，铁道部门、各银行总行、各保险总公司等集中缴纳的营业税、利润和城市维护建设税，车辆购置税，船舶吨税，增值税的75%部分，证券交易税(印花税)94%部分，个人所得税中的利息所得税，利息所得税之外的个人所得税中央分享的部分，海洋石油资源税。属于地方财政的收入包括营业税，地方企业所得税，利息所得税之外的个人所得税地方分享的部分，城镇土地使用税，固定资产投资方向调节税，城镇维护建设税，房产税，车船使用税，印花税，屠宰税，农牧业税，农业特产税，耕地占用税，契税，土地增值税、国有土地有偿使用收入，增值税25%部分，证券交易税(印花税)6%部分和除海洋石油资源税以外的其他资源税。

中央财政支出和地方财政支出 指根据政府在经济和社会活动中的不同职责，划分中央和地方政府的责权，按照政府的责权划分确定的支出。中央财政支出包括国防支出，武装警察部队支出，中央级行政管理费和各项事业费，重点建设支出以及中央政府调整国民经济结构、协调地区发展、实施宏观调控的支出。地方财政支出主要包括地方行政管理和各项事业费，地方统筹的基本建设、技术改造支出，支援农村生产支出，城市维护和建设经费，价格补贴支出等。

预算外资金收支 预算外资金指国家机关、事业单位和社会团体为履行或代行政府职能，依据国家法律、法规和具有法律效力的规章而收取、提取和安排使用的未纳入国家预算管理的各种财政性资金。其范围主要包括：法律、法规规定的行政事业性收费、政府性基金和附加收入等；国务院或省级人民政府及其财政、计划（物价）部门审批的行政事业性收费；国务院及财政部审批建立的政府性基金、附加收入等；主管部门所属单位集中上缴资金；用于乡镇政府开支的乡自筹和乡统筹资金；其他未纳入预算管理的财政性资金。社会保障基金在国家财政尚未建立社会保障预算制度以前，先按预算外资金管理制度进行管理，专款专用。财政部门在银行开设统一的专户，用于预算外资金收入和支出管理。部门和单位的预算外收入必须上缴同级财政专户，支出由同级财政按预算外资金收支计划和单位财务收支计划统筹安排，从财政专户中拨付，实行收支两条线管理。

债务收入 国家以信用形式筹措的资金，包括财政部对国内商业银行和其他投资者发行的各种政府债券、财政部在国际资金市场发行的外币债券以及国家财政“统借统还”的其他政府外债。

债务还本支出 指国家财政用于偿还国内、国外债务本金支出。

中央财政赤字 指当年中央财政总支出大于中央财政总收入的差额。

Explanatory Notes on Main Statistical Indicators

Government Revenue refers to the revenue of the government finance by means of participating in the distribution of the social products, which is the financial resources for ensuring the government to function. The contents of government revenue have been changed several times. Now it includes the following main items:

(1) Various tax revenues, including value added tax, business tax, consumption tax, land value added tax, tax on city maintenance and construction, resources tax, tax on use of urban land, enterprise income tax, personal income tax, tariff, stamp tax on security transactions, tax on purchase of motor vehicles, tax on agriculture and animal husbandry and tax on occupancy of cultivated land, etc.

(2) Special revenues, including revenues from the fee on sewage treatment, fee on urban water resources, fee for the compensation of mineral resources and extra-charges for education, etc.

(3) Other revenues, including revenue from interest, revenue from the repayment of capital construction loan, revenue from capital construction projects, and donations and grants.

(4) Subsidies for the losses of the state-owned enterprises. This is an item of negative revenue, consisting of subsidies to industrial, commercial and grain purchasing and supply enterprises.

Government Expenditure refers to the distribution and use of the funds the government finance has raised, so as to meet the needs of economic construction and various causes. It includes the following main items:

(1) Expenditure for capital construction: It refers to the non-gratuitous use and appropriation of funds for capital construction in the range of capital construction, outlay of capital as well as the loans on capital construction approved by the government for special purpose or policy purpose and the expenditure with discount paid in an overall way within the amount of the funds appropriated to the departments for capital construction.

(2) Innovation funds of the enterprises: They refer to the funds appropriated from the government budget for the enterprises to tap the latent power, upgrade the technology and carry out innovation, including the innovation fund of the departments, loan of the enterprises for innovation, subsidies on the innovation of the small fertilizer plant, small cement plant, small coal mines, small machinery plant and small steel plant, the expenditure of interest for the loan for innovation.

(3) Geological prospecting expenses: They refer to the expenses appropriated from the government budget to the geological prospecting units for the expenditure of the prospecting work, including the expenditures of the administrative agencies for geological prospecting and their institutional units as well as the geological prospecting expenditure.

(4) expenditures for science and technology promotion: They refer to the expenses appropriated from the government budget for the scientific and technological expenditure, including new products development expenditure, expenditure for intermediate trial and subsidies on important scientific researches.

(5) Expenditure for supporting rural production: It refers to the expenditures appropriated from the government budget for supporting the various expenditures of the rural collective units or households for production, including the subsidies to the small water conservancy projects and well drilling, sprinkling irrigation projects run by the villages; subsidies on the rural water and soil conserving measures; subsidies to the small power stations run by the villages; subsidies to the expenditure for fighting against particularly severe draughts; subsidies on the rural waste land exclamation; fund for supporting the township enterprises; fund for supporting rural cooperative production organizations, subsidies to the expenditure for popularization of the agricultural technologies and plant protection in the rural areas; subsidies to the expenditure for the protection of grasslands and cattle and fowls; subsidies on afforestation and forest protection in rural areas; subsidies on the rural aquatic products industry; special fund for developing grain production.

(6) Operating expenses of the departments of farming, forestry, water conservancy and meteorology etc.: They refer to the expenses appropriated from the government budget for the expenditures of agricultural exclamation, farms, agriculture, animal husbandry, agricultural machinery, forestry, timber industry, water conservancy, aquatic products industry, meteorology, technology popularization in township enterprises, popularization (demonstration) of improved varieties, plant (cattle and fowls, forest) protection, water quality monitoring, prospecting and designing, resources investigation, cadres training, subsidies to horticulture gardens, expenditure of specialized secondary schools, subsidies on the experiments of sowing herbage seeds by flights, expenditures of afforestation agencies and meteorology agencies, expenses for fishery administration and operating expenses for agricultural administration, etc.

(7) Operating expenses of the departments of industry, transport and commerce: They refer to the expenses appropriated from the government budget to cover the expenditure on salaries and operational expenditure of the departments of industry, transport and commerce for the expenditure of business development, including expenses for prospecting and designing, expenditures of specialized secondary schools, expenditures of the technical training schools and expenditures for cadres training, etc.

(8) Operating expenses of the departments of culture, education, science and public health: They refer to the expenses appropriated from the government budget for the expenditures on salaries and operational expenditure of the causes of culture, publication, cultural relics, education, public health, traditional Chinese medical science, free medical services, sports, archives, earthquake, ocean, communications, broadcasting, film and television, family planning; expenditure for training of cadres of government, party and mass organization; expenditures for natural sciences, social sciences, associations for science and technology and the special expenditure for the high-tech researches. They include mainly wages, extra wages, welfare funds, pension for the retirees, stipend, expenses for official business, expenses for equipment purchases, expenses for repairs, business expenses and subsidies to the units which are unable to support their expenditures by their own earnings.

(9) Pension for the disabled or for the families of the bereaved and relief funds for social welfare: They refer to the funds appropriated from the government budget for the expenditures of pension for the disabled or for the families of the bereaved and relief funds for social welfare, including the lump-sum or regular pension paid by the departments of civil affairs to the members of martyrs families and families of those who died for the public interest, pension to the revolutionary disabled, subsidies for permanent disability of various kinds, subsidies to the military martyrs dependents and the demobilized servicemen, expenditure for settling down the demobilized servicemen, operating expenses of the consoling institutions, expenses for management and repair of the commemorative buildings for the martyrs, the expenses managed by the departments of civil affairs for the retirees and those who have quitted their work, expenses for social relief in rural and urban areas, operating expenses for providing relief to the areas of natural calamity and subsidies on the reconstruction after the particularly severe natural calamities, etc.

(10) Expenditure on retirees: It refers to the expenditure on retirees of government agencies and institutions that are covered by the state budget.

(11) Expenses on subsidies to social security system: It refers to expenditure from the state budget for subsidies to social security system, including subsidies to the social insurance fund, subsidies to promoting employment, subsidies to laid-off workers of state-owned enterprises, supplement to national social security funds, etc.

(12) Expenditures for national defence: They refer to the security, including expenses of national defence, expenses of scientific researches on national defence, expenses for building up peoples militia and expenditure for special projects, etc.

(13) Administrative expenses: They include expenditure for administration, subsidies to the parties and mass organizations, diplomatic expenditure, expenditure for public security, judicial expenditure, law court expenditure, procuratorial expenditure and subsidies to the expenses for treating the cases by the public security departments, procuratorial organs and law courts.

(14) Expenditure on policy-related subsidies: It refers to the expenditure appropriated, with the approval of the government, from the state budget for price subsidies on such products as grain, cotton and edible oil. More specifically, it includes subsidies to the difference between the selling prices and purchasing prices of grains, cotton and edible oil, subsidies for curtaining prices and for sugar reserve, subsidies to the difference between the selling prices and purchasing prices of means pf agricultural production, risk fund for grains, risk fund for non-staple food, risk fund for local production of coal, etc.

(15) Expenditure on interest of debts: It refers to expenses from the state budget on paying interest of domestic and foreign debts.

Revenue of the central government and revenue of the local governments: refers to the revenue of the central government and that of the local governments as defined by the decentralized taxation system starting from 1994. In accordance with this system, the revenue of the central government includes tariff, consumption tax and value added tax levied by the customs, consumption tax, income tax of the enterprises subordinate to the central government, income taxes of the local banks, foreign-funded banks and non-bank financial institutions, business tax and profits of railways, head offices of banks, head office of insurance company , which are handed over to the government in a centralized way, tax on city maintenance and construction, tax on purchasing motor vehicles, tonnage tax of ships, 75% of the value added tax, 94% of the tax on stock dealing (stamp tax), interest income tax in the personal income tax, proportion of the personal income tax (other that interest income tax) to be shared by the central government, and tax on ocean petroleum resources,. The revenue of the local governments includes business tax, income tax of the enterprises subordinate to the local government, proportion of the personal income tax (other that interest income tax) to be shared by the central government, tax on the use of urban land, tax on the adjustment of the investment in fixed assets, tax on town maintenance and construction, tax on real estates, tax on the use of vehicles and ships, stamp tax, slaughter tax, tax on agriculture and animal husbandry, tax on special agricultural products, tax on the occupancy of cultivated land, contract tax, value-added tax on land, income from charges on use of state-owned land, 25% of the value added tax, 6% of the tax on stock dealing (stamp tax) and tax on resources other than the ocean petroleum resources.

Expenditure of the central government and expenditure of the local governments: according to the different functions of the central government and local governments in the economic and social activities, the rights of affairs administration are classified between the central government and local governments; and the classification of the expenditure between the central government and local governments are made on the basis of the classification of the rights of affairs administration between them. The expenditure of the central government includes the expenditure for national defence, expenditure for armed police forces, the administrative expenses and various operating expenses at the level of central government, expenditure for key projects and the expenditure of the central government for adjusting the national economic structure, coordinating the development among different regions and exercising the macro-economic regulation and control. The expenditure of the local governments includes mainly the administrative expenses and various operating expenses at the level of local governments, the expenditure for capital construction and technological innovation with the funds raised by the local government, expenditure for supporting rural production, expenditure for city maintenance and construction and expenditure for price subsidies, etc.

Extra-budgetary revenue and expenditure Extra-budgetary fund refers to financial fund of various types not covered by the regular government budgetary management, which is collected, allocated or arranged by government agencies, institutions and social organizations while performing duties delegated to them or on behalf of the government in accordance with laws, rules and regulations. It mainly covers following items: administrative and institutional fees, governmental funds and extra charges that are stipulated by laws and regulations; administrative and institutional fees approved by the State Council and provincial governments and their financial and planning (price management) departments; governmental funds and extra charges established by the State Council and the Ministry of Finance; funds turned over to competent departments by their subordinate institutions; self-raised and collected funds by township governments for their own expenditure; and other financial funds that are not covered in budgetary management. Social security funds are treated as extra-budget fund and managed for its exclusive use, given the circumstance that separate government budgetary system for social security is yet to be designed. Special accounts are opened by the financial departments in banks for the management of revenue and expenditure of extra-budgetary fund. Extra-budgetary revenue and expenditure is managed separately, namely, revenue of institutions and departments must enter into the special accounts of the financial departments at the same administrative level, and their extra-budgetary expenditure is arranged in line with the extra-budget plans and appropriated from these accounts.

Revenue from debts refers to fund raised by the state in credit forms, including various domestic government bonds issued by the Ministry of Finance to commercial banks and other investors, bonds in foreign currencies issued by the Ministry of Finance at the international capital market, and other foreign debts borrowed and to be repaid centrally by the government finance.

Expenditure on repayment of principal of debts refers to the expenditure from government finance on the repayment of principal of domestic and foreign debts.

Deficit of central government finance refers to the difference between the total expenditure and the total revenue of the central government.

9

价格指数
Price Indices

简要说明

一、本篇资料的主要内容

本篇价格指数资料，反映生产、流通、消费与投资等环节的价格变动趋势和变动幅度。主要包括居民消费价格指数、商品零售价格指数、农业生产资料价格指数、工业品出厂价格指数(生产者价格指数)、原材料、燃料和动力购进价格指数、固定资产投资价格指数和房地产价格指数等。

二、本篇的资料来源

价格指数编制由国家统计局城市社会经济调查司组织实施。由各省、自治区、直辖市及抽选出的市、县城市社会经济调查队依据国家统计局统一制定的价格统计调查制度向基层采集原始数据汇总后上报。

三、居民消费、商品零售价格指数

编制居民消费、商品零售价格指数的资料采用抽样调查和重点调查相结合的方法取得，即在全国选择不同经济区域和分布合理的地区，以及有代表性的商品作为样本，对其市场价格进行定期调查，以样本推断总体。目前，国家一级抽选出的调查市、县226个。编制过程按下列几个步骤进行:

1.选择调查地区和调查点。调查地区按照经济区域和地区分布合理等原则，选出具有代表性的大、中、小城市和县作为国家的调查地区，在此基础上选定经营规模大、商品种类多的商场(包括集市和服务网点)作为调查点。

2.选择代表商品和代表规格品。代表商品是选择那些消费量大、价格变动有代表性的商品；代表规格品的确定是根据商品零售资料和近5万户城市居民、6.8万户农村居民的消费支出记帐资料，按照有关规定筛选的。筛选原则：(1)与社会生产和人民生活关系密切；(2)消费(销售)数量(金额)大；(3)市场供应稳定；(4)价格变动趋势有代表性；(5)所选的代表规格品之间差异大。

目前，居民消费价格调查按用途划分为8大类，251个基本分类，各地每月调查600-700种规格产品价格；商品零售价格按用途划分为16个大类，225个基本分类，各地每月调查500种以上的规格产品价格。

3.价格调查方式。采用派员直接到调查点登记调查，同时全国聘请近万名辅助调查员协助登记调查。

4.权数的确定。商品零售价格指数的计算权数主要根据社会商品零售额资料确定;居民消费价格指数的计算权数根据近12万户城乡居民家庭消费支出构成确定。

四、工业品出厂价格指数

工业品出厂价格是工业品第一次出售时的出厂价格。该项调查采用重点调查与典型调查相结合的调查方法。重点调查对象为全部国有企业和年销售收入500万元以上的非国有工业企业;典型调查对象为年销售收入500万元以下的非国有工业企业。

1.选择代表企业的原则：(1)按工业行业选择调查企业，各中类行业原则上都要有调查企业；(2)大型企业应尽量都选上(或占相当大比重)；(3)选择生产正常、稳定的企业作为调查对象；(4)选择企业时要兼顾不同所有制形式。

2.选择代表产品的原则：(1)按工业行业选择代表产品；(2)选择对国计民生影响大的产品；(3)选择生产较为稳定的产品；(4)选择有发展前景的产品；(5)选择具有地方特色的产品。

目前《工业品价格调查目录》包括4000多种产品(9500多个规格)。上述代表产品所代表的行业销售额占当年全国工业品销售总额的90%以上。

3.价格调查方式。采用企业报表形式，每月5万家左右工业企业上报数据资料。

4.权数的确定。编制工业品出厂价格指数所用的权数，用工业品销售额计算。计算资料来源于工业普查数据。若近期没有工业普查数据时，采用工业统计资料和部门统计资料来推算。权数一般五年更换一次。

五、固定资产投资价格指数

固定资产投资价格调查采用重点调查与典型调查相结合的方法。固定资产投资价格调查所涉及的价格是构成固定资产投资额实体的实际购进价格或结算价格。调查的内容包括构成当年建筑工程实体的钢材、木材、水泥、地方材料(如砖、瓦、灰、沙、石等)、化工材料(如油漆等)等主要建筑材料价格；作为活劳动投入的劳动力价格（单位工资）和建筑机械使用费用；设备工器具购置和其他费用投资价格。

1.选择建筑安装工程调查点的原则：(1)样本单位应具有一定覆盖面；(2)投资经济活动代表性强；(3)兼顾不同经济类型；(4)选择重点工程；(5)兼顾国民经济各门类及不同工程类别。

2.选择其他费用调查点的原则：在选择其他费用调查点时，所遵循的原则与建筑安装工程调查点的原则基本相同，特别是要注意选择那些投资额大的工程。但由于其他费用不易取得，所以在实际操作过程中，应同时在建设单位、施工单位开展重点调查，并辅以典型调查(从管理部门取得资料)。

3.价格调查方式。采用企业报表和调查员走访相结合的方式。

4.权数的确定。固定资产投资价格指数的计算权数是建筑安装工程、设备工器具购置和其他费用三者前三年的平均比重。

六、房地产价格指数

从广义上讲，房地产是房产与地产的总称。因此房地产价格调查的内容主要包括以下几个部分:

1.房屋销售价格。从进入房地产市场的渠道看，房屋销售价格包括商品房和二手房两部分。

2.房屋租赁价格。房屋租赁价格包括住宅、办公楼、商业娱乐用房、工业仓储用房和其他用房五部分。

3.土地交易价格。土地交易价格包括居民用地、工业仓储用地、商业旅游娱乐用地和其他用地四部分。

4.物业管理价格。物业管理价格包括住宅、办公楼、商业娱乐用房和工业仓储用房四部分。

房地产价格调查采用重点调查与典型调查相结合的方法。调查方式采用报表与走访相结合的方式。

目前我国房地产价格调查在七十个大中城市开展，调查样本超过1万个。

Brief Introduction

I. Main Content

Data on the price indices in this chapter show the changing trend and the change rates in production, consumption and investment, including mainly consumer price indices of residents, retail price indices, price indices of agricultural means of production, purchasing price indices of farm products, producers' price indices of industrial products, purchasing price indices of raw materials, fuels and power, price indices of investment in fixed assets, and real estate price indices.

II. Source of Data

Statistics on price indices are organized by the Department of Urban Socio-economic Survey, NBS. The urban socio-economic survey organizations of the provinces, autonomous regions and municipalities and of the selected cities and counties collect data from the grassroots units in accordance with the scheme of price survey stipulated by the NBS, tabulate them and report them to the higher agencies.

III. Consumer Price Indices of Residents and Retail Price Indices

Data for calculation of the consumer price indices of residents and the retail price indices in China are collected through a combination of sample surveys and surveys of key units. Areas distributed in different economic regions are selected as the sample areas and the representative commodities are selected as the sample commodities. Regular surveys are conducted to collect data on the market prices. Estimation of population made on the basis of the sample. At present, 226 cities and counties have been selected for this purpose. Following are major steps in the process of calculation of the price indices:

(1) The selection of the areas and places for survey: Based on such principles as regional economic features and reasonable geographic distribution, representative sample areas for the national survey are selected which include large, medium and small cities and counties. When the sample areas are selected, large-scale shops and markets (including fairs and service outlets) with great varieties of commodities are selected as the survey places.

(2) The selection of the representative commodities and their specifications or varieties: The representative commodities are the commodities consumed in large quantity and representative in price changes. The representative specifications or varieties are determined according to the data on the retail sales of commodities and the account data of the residents of close to 50,000 urban households and 68,000 rural households, following the related instructions for selection. In principle, only those specifications or varieties of the commodities can be selected: (a) They are closely related to the social production and people's livelihood; (b) They are sold in large quantities (or large values); (c) The market supply is stable; (d) The changes of their prices are representative in trend; (e) There is great difference among the specifications or varieties selected.

At present, data are collected on about 600-700 specifications each month under 251 basic headings in 8 categories in the consumer price surveys. For the retail price surveys, data are collected on more than 500 specifications each month under 225 basic headings in 16 categories

(3) Data collection: Enumerators are sent to the survey places to take the records of the prices. Nearly 10 thousand assistant enumerators are invited to assist the survey work.

(4) The determination of the weights: The weights for calculation of the retail price indices are determined mainly according to the total retail sales of commodities. The weights for calculation of the consumer price indices are determined according to the composition of the consumption expenditures of close to 120,000 urban and rural households.

IV. Producers' Prices of Industrial Products

Producers' prices of industrial products refer to the price of industrial products when they leave factories. The survey program include the key units survey and typical units survey. The key units refer to all state-owned industrial enterprises and those non-state-owned industrial enterprises with annual sale revenue above 5 million yuan. The typical units refer to the non-state-owned industrial enterprises with annual sale revenue below 5 million yuan.

(1) Principle in selecting the representative enterprises:

(a) Enterprises to be covered in the survey are selected by industrial sectors. In principle, every branch should have enterprises selected; (b) All (or a majority of) large-sized enterprises should be selected; (c) Enterprises with normal and stable production are to be selected; (d) Different types of ownership should be considered in selecting enterprises.

(2) The principle to select the representative products:

(a) The products are selected by industrial sectors; (b) The selected products should have great impact on the national economy and the people's livelihood; (c) The production of the products selected are stable; (d) The foreground of products is representative in trend; (e) The products are typical and with local color.

The present List of Industrial Products for the survey includes over 4,000 products (including 9,500 specifications or varieties). The industrial sales value of the industries represented by these products accounts for more than 90 percent of total industrial sales value.

(3) Data collection: Reports by enterprises are adopted. About 50,000 industrial enterprises report price data every month.

(4) The determination of the weights: The weights for calculation of the producers' price indices of industrial products are determined according to the total sales value of industrial products. Data from the industrial census are used for the calculation. If industrial census data are not available for the reference year, industrial statistical data and statistical data from other agencies will be used to estimate the weights. The weights are replaced every five years.

V. Price Indices for Investment in Fixed Assets

Data on prices of investment in fixed assets are collected by the survey on key units and typical units. The prices of the survey of investment in fixed assets are the actual purchasing prices or balancing prices of entity of investment in fixed assets. The survey content includes the prices of main construction materials that composing the architecture engineering entity in the year, such as steel, timber, cement, local construction materials (such as brick, tile, calcareousness, sand, stone, etc.), chemical materials (such as oil paint, etc.), the price of labor force as input (wages), prices for renting of building machinery and equipment, the purchasing price of equipment, tools and instruments and the prices of others investments.

The following principle to select the sample of price survey of investment in fixed assets should be followed.

(1) The principle to select the prices survey point of construction and installation: (a) Sample units should be a certain coverage; (b) The economic activity of investment is great representative; (c) Different economic types of ownership should be considered; (d) The key projects need to be selected; (e) Give attention to both various branches and types of project.

(2) The principle to select the prices survey point of others investments: The principle to select the prices survey point of others fees is general the same as that of construction and installation, especially to select the projects with great investment value. Since it is not easy to obtain the other fees, it should do the key survey on the construction owner units and building units assisted with typical survey (gotten from the administration department), in the actual operation.

(3) Price survey way: Enterprises reporting system is used together with the enumerators visiting method.

(4) The determination of the weights: The weights for calculation of the price indices of investment in fixed assets are determined according to the average proportion of construction and installation, purchase of equipment, tools and instruments and others investment in the 3 previous years.

VI. Price Indices for Real Estate

The real estate in broad sense refers to the property in terms of buildings and land. Therefore, the price survey on real estate covers the following items:

1) Prices for selling houses and buildings. In terms of the types of houses sold at the market, prices for selling houses include the prices for commercial houses and for second-hand houses.

2) Prices for renting houses and buildings. Included in this category are prices for renting residential housing, office buildings, buildings for business or recreational purposes, buildings for industrial or storage purposes, and housing for other purposes.

3) Prices for land transaction. Included in this category are prices for the transaction of land used for residential housing, for industrial and storage purposes, for business or recreational purposes and for other uses.

4) Prices for property management. Included in this category are prices for residential housing, office buildings, buildings for business or recreational purposes, and buildings for industrial or storage purposes.

Survey on real estate prices employed a combination of survey of key units and survey of typical cases. Data are collected through reporting forms supplemented by interviews.

The survey on real estate prices at present is conducted in 70 large and medium cities, with a sample of over 10,000 units.

9-1 各种价格指数

Price Indices

(上年=100) (preceding year=100)

年 份 Year	居民消费价格指数 Consumer Price Index	城市居民消费价格指数 Urban Areas	农村居民消费价格指数 Rural Areas	商品零售价格指数 Retail Price Index	工业品出厂价格指数 Ex-Factory Price Indices of Industrial Products	原材料、燃料、动力购进价格指数 Purchasing Price Indices of Raw Material, Fuel and Power	固定资产投资价格指数 Investment in Fixed Assets Price Index
1978	100.7	100.7		100.7	100.1		
1980	107.5	107.5		106.0	100.5		
1985	109.3	111.9	107.6	108.8	108.7		
1989	118.0	116.3	119.3	117.8	118.6	126.4	
1990	103.1	101.3	104.5	102.1	104.1	105.6	
1991	103.4	105.1	102.3	102.9	106.2	109.1	109.5
1992	106.4	108.6	104.7	105.4	106.8	111.0	115.3
1993	114.7	116.1	113.7	113.2	124.0	135.1	126.6
1994	124.1	125.0	123.4	121.7	119.5	118.2	110.4
1995	117.1	116.8	117.5	114.8	114.9	115.3	105.9
1996	108.3	108.8	107.9	106.1	102.9	103.9	104.0
1997	102.8	103.1	102.5	100.8	99.7	101.3	101.7
1998	99.2	99.4	99.0	97.4	95.9	95.8	99.8
1999	98.6	98.7	98.5	97.0	97.6	96.7	99.6
2000	100.4	100.8	99.9	98.5	102.8	105.1	101.1
2001	100.7	100.7	100.8	99.2	98.7	99.8	100.4
2002	99.2	99.0	99.6	98.7	97.8	97.7	100.2
2003	101.2	100.9	101.6	99.9	102.3	104.8	102.2
2004	103.9	103.3	104.8	102.8	106.1	111.4	105.6
2005	101.8	101.6	102.2	100.8	104.9	108.3	101.6

9-2 各种价格定基指数

Fixed-base Price Indices

年 份 Year	居民消费价格指数 Consumer Price Index (1978=100)	城市居民消费价格指数 Urban Areas (1978=100)	农村居民消费价格指数 Rural Areas (1985=100)	商品零售价格指数 Retail Price Index (1978=100)	工业品出厂价格指数 Ex-factory Price Indices of Industrial Products (1985=100)	原材料、燃料、动力购进价格指数 Purchasing Price Indices of Raw Material, Fuel and Power (1990=100)	固定资产投资价格指数 Investment in Fixed Assets Price Index (1991=100)
1978	100.0	100.0		100.0			
1980	109.5	109.5		108.1			
1985	131.1	134.2	100.0	128.1	100.0		
1989	209.9	219.2	157.9	203.4	152.8	96.1	
1990	216.4	222.0	165.1	207.7	159.0	100.0	
1991	223.8	233.3	168.9	213.7	168.9	109.1	100.0
1992	238.1	253.4	176.8	225.2	180.4	121.1	115.3
1993	273.1	294.2	201.0	254.9	223.7	163.6	145.9
1994	339.0	367.8	248.0	310.2	267.3	193.4	161.1
1995	396.9	429.6	291.4	356.1	307.1	222.9	170.6
1996	429.9	467.4	314.4	377.8	316.0	231.6	177.4
1997	441.9	481.9	322.3	380.8	315.0	234.6	180.4
1998	438.4	479.0	319.1	370.9	302.1	224.7	180.0
1999	432.2	472.8	314.3	359.8	294.8	217.3	179.3
2000	434.0	476.6	314.0	354.4	303.1	228.4	181.3
2001	437.0	479.9	316.5	351.6	299.2	227.9	182.0
2002	433.5	475.1	315.2	347.0	292.6	222.7	182.4
2003	438.7	479.4	320.2	346.7	299.3	233.4	186.4
2004	455.8	495.2	335.6	356.4	317.6	260.0	196.8
2005	464.0	503.1	343.0	359.3	333.2	281.6	199.9

9-3 居民消费价格分类指数（2005年）

Consumer Price Indices by Category (2005)

(上年=100) (preceding year=100)

项 目	Item	全 国 National Indices	城 市 Urban Indices	农 村 Rural Indices
居民消费价格指数	**Consumer Price Index**	**101.8**	**101.6**	**102.2**
食品	**Food**	**102.9**	**103.1**	**102.5**
粮食	Grain	101.4	101.5	101.3
#大米	Rice	101.2	101.3	101.1
面粉	Flour	100.2	100.2	100.1
淀粉及薯类	Starches and Tubers	105.5	105.9	104.7
干豆类及豆制品	Beans and Bean Products	102.4	102.1	103.0
油脂	Oil or Fat	94.3	94.0	94.4
肉禽及其制品	Meal, Poultry and Their Products	102.5	102.1	103.1
蛋	Eggs	104.6	104.2	105.4
水产品	Aquatic Products	105.9	106.1	105.5
菜	Vegetables	109.1	110.0	106.8
#鲜菜	Fresh Vegetables	110.4	111.0	108.7
调味品	Flavoring	101.4	101.2	101.5
糖	Carbohydrate	104.0	102.9	105.6
茶及饮料	Tea and Beverages	100.1	100.1	100.2
茶	Tea	100.8	100.8	100.7
饮料	Beverages	99.8	99.8	99.8
干鲜瓜果	Dried and Fresh Melons and Fruits	102.2	102.8	100.6
#鲜果	Fresh Fruits	101.6	102.3	99.5
糕点饼干面包	Cake, Biscuit and Bread	100.9	100.8	101.2
奶及奶制品	Milk and Its Products	100.9	100.7	101.9
在外用膳食品	Outward Dinner	102.4	102.6	101.7
其它食品及加工服务费	Other Foods and Manufacturing Services	101.3	101.6	101.0
烟酒及用品	**Tobacco, Liquor and Articles**	**100.4**	**100.3**	**100.5**
烟草	Tobacco	100.4	100.4	100.4
酒	Liquor	100.6	100.4	100.8
吸烟、饮酒用品	Articles for Smoking and Drinking	99.6	99.6	99.8
衣着	**Clothing**	**98.3**	**98.0**	**99.1**
服装	Garments	98.1	97.9	98.7
衣着材料	Clothing Material	100.0	99.7	100.4
鞋袜帽	Footgear and Hats	98.3	97.7	99.4
衣着加工服务费	Clothing Manufacturing Services	101.1	101.1	101.1
家庭设备用品及服务	**Household Facilities, Articles and Services**	**99.9**	**99.7**	**100.3**
耐用消费品	Durable Consumer Goods	98.8	98.6	99.3
家具	Furniture	99.2	98.8	99.9
家庭设备	Household Facilities	98.5	98.4	98.7

9-3 续表 continued

(上年=100) (preceding year=100)

项　目	Item	全　国 National Indices	城　市 Urban Indices	农　村 Rural Indices
室内装饰品	Interior Decorations	99.5	99.0	100.2
床上用品	Bed Articles	99.4	99.1	100.0
家庭日用杂品	Daily Use Household Articles	100.4	100.3	100.5
家庭服务及加工维修服务费	Household Service and Manufacturing Upkeep	104.4	104.1	104.9
医疗保健和个人用品	**Health Care and Personal Articles**	**99.9**	**99.6**	**100.5**
医疗保健	Health Care	99.5	99.2	100.1
医疗器具及用品	Medical Instrument and Articles	97.4	97.7	97.1
中药材及中成药	Traditional Chinese Medicine	96.5	96.8	96.0
西药	Western Medicine	97.7	97.7	97.7
保健器具及用品	Health Care Appliances and Articles	100.0	100.0	99.8
医疗保健服务	Health Care Services	105.2	104.8	105.6
个人用品及服务	Personal Articles and Services	100.8	100.6	101.2
化妆美容用品	Cosmetics	99.4	99.2	100.0
卫生用品	Sanitation Articles	99.4	99.5	99.4
个人饰品	Personal Decorations	101.6	101.9	101.2
个人服务	Personal Services	101.9	101.3	102.6
交通和通信	**Transportation and Communication**	**99.0**	**98.4**	**100.3**
交通	Transportation	101.5	101.1	102.0
交通工具	Transportation Facility	97.3	96.2	98.4
车用燃料及零配件	Fuels and Parts	110.3	110.9	109.5
车辆使用及维修费	Using and Upkeep Fare	102.0	102.2	101.5
市内公共交通费	Incity Traffic Fare	102.2	101.9	103.6
城市间交通费	Intercity Traffic Fare	103.3	102.4	104.3
通信	Communication	96.6	96.2	97.7
通信工具	Communication Facility	84.1	81.1	91.1
通信服务	Communication Service	99.6	99.7	99.6
娱乐教育文化用品及服务	**Recreation, Education and Culture Articles**	**102.2**	**101.3**	**103.8**
文娱用耐用消费品及服务	Durable Consumer Goods for Cultural and Recreational Use and Services	93.8	92.9	95.9
教育	Education	105.1	104.3	106.0
教材及参考书	Teaching Materials and Reference Books	100.9	100.9	100.8
学杂托幼费	Tuition and Child Care	105.4	104.7	106.3
文化娱乐用品	Cultural and Recreational Articles	101.2	101.3	100.6
文化娱乐	Cultural Articles	99.8	99.8	99.9
书报杂志	Newspapers and Magazines	100.8	100.8	100.7
文娱费	Expenditure of Culture and Recreation	102.9	103.0	102.0
旅游及外出	Touring and Outgoing	99.6	99.4	100.5
居住	**Residence**	**105.4**	**105.6**	**105.2**
建房及装修材料	Building and Building Decoration Materials	102.6	102.6	102.7
租房	Renting	101.9	101.6	103.3
自有住房	Private Housing	105.6	106.8	102.0
水电燃料	Water, Electricity and Fuels	108.6	107.7	110.3

9-4 商品零售价格分类指数（2005年）

Retail Price Indices by Category (2005)

(上年=100) (preceding year=100)

项目	Item	全国 National Indices	城市 Urban Indices	农村 Rural Indices
商品零售价格总指数	**Retail Price Index**	**100.8**	**100.5**	**101.4**
食品类	**Food**	**103.1**	**103.3**	**102.8**
粮食	Grain	101.4	101.6	101.2
油脂	Oil or Fat	94.7	94.6	94.8
肉禽及其制品	Meat, Poultry and Their Products	103.0	102.8	103.3
蛋	Eggs	104.7	104.3	105.5
水产品	Aquatic Products	105.8	106.3	104.6
菜	Vegetables	108.1	108.6	107.2
调味品	Flavoring	101.4	101.5	101.3
食糖	Sugar	106.9	106.0	108.0
糖果	Candy	102.6	101.1	104.3
干鲜瓜果	Dried and Fresh Melons and Fruits	101.7	101.9	101.2
糕点饼干面包	Cake, Biscuit and Bread	100.8	100.8	100.9
奶及奶制品	Milk and Its Products	100.9	100.7	101.5
在外用膳食品	Outward Dinner Food	102.8	103.2	101.7
主食	Staple Food	102.2	102.7	101.1
炒菜	Fried Dishes	103.2	103.5	102.3
地方小吃	Local Snack	102.0	102.4	101.2
其它食品	Other Foods	101.2	101.5	100.7
饮料、烟酒	**Beverages, Tobacco and Liquor**	**100.5**	**100.4**	**100.6**
茶及饮料	Tea and Beverages	100.2	100.2	100.3
烟草	Tobacco	100.3	100.3	100.5
酒	Liquor	100.9	100.8	101.0
服装、鞋帽	**Garments, Shoes and Hats**	**97.9**	**97.4**	**99.1**
服装	Garments	97.9	97.4	99.1
鞋袜帽	Footgear and Hats	98.1	97.4	99.5
纺织品	**Textiles**	**99.8**	**99.3**	**100.4**
棉布	Cotton Cloth	101.0	100.3	101.7
棉花化纤混纺布	Blend Cloth	101.2	100.6	101.8
化纤布	Chemical Fiber Cloth	101.2	101.1	101.3
毛织品	Wool	100.3	100.6	99.8
丝织品	Silk	98.6	98.1	99.5
家用电器及音像器材	**Household Appliances, Music and Video Equipment**	**96.3**	**95.9**	**97.3**
文化办公用品	**Cultural and Office Appliances**	**96.7**	**96.0**	**98.2**
日用品	**Articles for Daily Use**	**100.2**	**100.2**	**100.2**
日用百货	General Merchandise for Daily Use	100.0	99.9	100.1
日用杂品	Grocery for Daily Use	100.7	100.6	100.9
体育娱乐用品	**Sports and Recreation Articles**	**98.4**	**98.1**	**99.1**
交通、通信用品	**Transportation and Communication Appliances**	**91.7**	**90.8**	**94.0**
家具	**Furniture**	**99.1**	**98.7**	**100.1**
化妆品	**Cosmetics**	**99.3**	**99.2**	**99.5**
金银珠宝	**Gold, Silver and Jewelry**	**104.4**	**104.6**	**104.1**
中西药品及医疗保健用品	**Traditional Chinese and Western Medicines and Health Care Articles**	**97.6**	**97.7**	**97.4**
医疗器具及用品	Medical Apparatus and Article	98.4	98.6	98.0
中药材及中成药	Traditional Chinese Medicinal Materials and Medicines	96.5	96.6	96.3
西药	Western Medicines	97.8	97.8	97.8
书报杂志及电子出版物	**Books, Newspapers, Magazines and Electronic Publications**	**100.3**	**100.4**	**100.3**
燃料	**Fuels**	**115.4**	**114.3**	**117.4**
建筑材料及五金电料	**Building Materials and Hardware**	**102.1**	**101.9**	**102.5**
建筑装璜材料	Building Decoration Materials	102.3	102.0	102.8
五金电料	Hardware	101.5	101.6	101.3

9-5 居民消费价格指数和商品零售价格指数

Consumer Price Indices and Retail Price Indices

(上年=100) (preceding year=100)

年份 地区	Year Region	居民消费价格指数 Consumer Price Index			商品零售价格指数 Retail Price Index		
		全省（区、市） Province	城市 Urban Areas	农村 Rural Areas	全省（区、市） Province	城市 Urban Areas	农村 Rural Areas
	1994	124.1	125.0	123.4	121.7	120.9	122.9
	1995	117.1	116.8	117.5	114.8	113.5	116.4
	1996	108.3	108.8	107.9	106.1	105.8	106.4
	1997	102.8	103.1	102.5	100.8	100.8	100.7
	1998	99.2	99.4	99.0	97.4	97.4	97.6
	1999	98.6	98.7	98.5	97.0	97.0	97.1
	2000	100.4	100.8	99.9	98.5	98.5	98.5
	2001	100.7	100.7	100.8	99.2	98.9	99.6
	2002	99.2	99.0	99.6	98.7	98.5	99.1
	2003	101.2	100.9	101.6	99.9	99.6	100.5
	2004	103.9	103.3	104.8	102.8	102.1	104.2
	2005	101.8	101.6	102.2	100.8	100.5	101.4
北京	Beijing	101.5	101.5		99.7	99.7	
天津	Tianjin	101.5	101.5		99.9	99.9	
河北	Hebei	101.8	101.4	102.2	101.1	101.0	101.2
山西	Shanxi	102.3	101.7	103.7	100.3	100.0	100.7
内蒙古	Inner Mongolia	102.4	102.0	103.3	101.5	101.5	101.4
辽宁	Liaoning	101.4	100.8	104.0	100.1	100.0	100.9
吉林	Jilin	101.5	101.4	101.9	101.1	101.0	101.5
黑龙江	Heilongjiang	101.2	100.8	102.3	100.4	99.7	102.3
上海	Shanghai	101.0	101.0		99.4	99.4	
江苏	Jiangsu	102.1	102.0	102.4	100.3	100.0	101.1
浙江	Zhejiang	101.3	101.5	101.2	100.9	101.0	100.7
安徽	Anhui	101.4	101.0	101.9	100.6	100.0	101.1
福建	Fujian	102.2	101.9	102.8	100.6	100.3	101.0
江西	Jiangxi	101.7	101.5	102.2	100.9	100.3	101.4
山东	Shandong	101.7	101.1	102.4	100.6	100.4	101.2
河南	Henan	102.1	102.1	102.1	101.7	101.8	101.6
湖北	Hubei	102.9	102.7	103.3	102.1	101.9	102.4
湖南	Hunan	102.3	102.1	102.8	102.3	101.6	103.0
广东	Guangdong	102.3	102.0	102.7	101.8	101.5	102.2
广西	Guangxi	102.4	103.0	101.6	101.1	101.3	101.0
海南	Hainan	101.5	101.3	101.7	100.9	100.4	101.5
重庆	Chongqing	100.8	100.8		98.7	98.7	
四川	Sichuan	101.7	101.7	101.6	100.6	100.1	101.0
贵州	Guizhou	101.0	100.6	102.1	101.3	100.3	102.8
云南	Yunnan	101.4	101.7	101.0	100.1	100.4	99.8
西藏	Tibet	101.5	101.5	100.9	100.8	100.8	100.4
陕西	Shaanxi	101.2	100.9	101.8	100.1	99.8	100.8
甘肃	Gansu	101.7	101.2	103.0	99.9	99.5	100.6
青海	Qinghai	100.8	99.7	103.1	100.7	100.6	101.0
宁夏	Ningxia	101.5	101.6	101.2	100.4	100.5	100.1
新疆	Xinjiang	100.7	100.6	101.2	99.4	99.5	99.3

9-6 各地区居民消费价格分类指数

Consumer Price Indices by Category and Region

(上年=100) (preceding year=100)

年 份 地 区	Year Region	总指数 General Index	食 品 Food	#粮 食 Grain	#油 脂 Oil or Fat	#肉禽及其制品 Meal,Poultry and Products	#蛋 Eggs	#水产品 Aquatic Products	#菜 Vegetables	#鲜 菜 Fresh Vegetables
	2001	100.7	100.0	99.3	91.7	101.6	106.0	97.1	100.9	101.4
	2002	99.2	99.4	98.3	98.7	99.5	102.6	96.7	98.2	98.1
	2003	101.2	103.4	102.3	112.6	103.3	98.6	100.3	117.7	120.5
	2004	103.9	109.9	126.4	118.2	117.6	120.2	112.7	95.1	93.9
	2005	101.8	102.9	101.4	94.3	102.5	104.6	105.9	109.1	110.4
北 京	Beijing	101.5	104.9	104.6	98.0	103.8	104.7	104.7	110.8	111.9
天 津	Tianjin	101.5	103.4	103.8	94.7	104.5	103.5	95.7	112.1	113.2
河 北	Hebei	101.8	102.4	103.1	96.6	102.5	102.8	104.0	100.5	100.4
山 西	Shanxi	102.3	102.7	103.7	94.7	100.9	102.4	105.1	109.1	109.7
内蒙古	Inner Mongolia	102.4	102.9	103.7	96.9	101.7	103.7	100.0	108.0	109.2
辽 宁	Liaoning	101.4	101.8	104.0	86.4	100.4	102.5	102.8	104.9	105.3
吉 林	Jilin	101.5	101.8	104.1	92.1	101.5	103.7	101.5	104.2	105.0
黑龙江	Heilongjiang	101.2	100.1	100.4	91.5	99.5	102.8	99.4	110.8	111.9
上 海	Shanghai	101.0	104.5	103.0	91.2	105.7	105.8	114.2	103.3	103.5
江 苏	Jiangsu	102.1	103.9	100.0	92.4	104.3	104.3	105.4	114.8	116.2
浙 江	Zhejiang	101.3	103.0	98.0	95.2	103.2	107.4	106.0	111.7	112.6
安 徽	Anhui	101.4	102.6	98.2	90.8	103.7	107.4	104.0	116.4	118.1
福 建	Fujian	102.2	103.7	99.8	96.5	103.7	103.6	106.0	111.0	114.0
江 西	Jiangxi	101.7	103.1	100.3	96.2	102.2	107.5	103.2	117.3	120.0
山 东	Shandong	101.7	102.7	100.2	94.6	100.9	104.5	103.4	109.1	109.7
河 南	Henan	102.1	103.4	101.4	92.5	103.3	104.5	102.3	114.2	118.5
湖 北	Hubei	102.9	104.2	100.8	91.7	104.1	105.9	105.4	114.2	116.4
湖 南	Hunan	102.3	102.9	99.4	96.0	99.8	109.0	106.7	121.4	125.0
广 东	Guangdong	102.3	104.7	101.8	99.9	105.8	104.6	109.3	110.2	111.4
广 西	Guangxi	102.4	102.7	101.6	92.2	103.1	103.7	108.0	106.3	108.2
海 南	Hainan	101.5	101.7	100.7	95.3	100.8	106.2	104.0	108.6	110.0
重 庆	Chongqing	100.8	100.1	102.7	83.8	101.4	104.8	104.1	98.7	98.7
四 川	Sichuan	101.7	102.1	102.1	94.2	101.4	105.6	104.5	104.4	105.8
贵 州	Guizhou	101.0	101.3	100.4	88.7	100.8	102.1	106.2	103.7	105.0
云 南	Yunnan	101.4	100.8	103.6	97.9	98.6	104.9	113.7	92.9	92.4
西 藏	Tibet	101.5	101.3	102.1	100.4	104.5	106.9	96.0	101.3	98.7
陕 西	Shaanxi	101.2	101.0	101.3	97.1	100.9	104.5	102.3	102.3	102.6
甘 肃	Gansu	101.7	101.2	102.1	96.9	102.3	104.8	103.0	100.7	101.2
青 海	Qinghai	100.8	101.0	102.0	92.3	101.4	104.0	103.9	103.1	103.3
宁 夏	Ningxia	101.5	101.9	104.1	97.5	103.0	104.4	101.4	99.5	99.5
新 疆	Xinjiang	100.7	98.5	101.9	91.8	96.2	100.8	106.0	93.8	93.4

9-6 续表 1 continued

(上年=100) (preceding year=100)

年份 地区	Year Region	#干鲜瓜果 Dried and Fresh Melons and Fruits	#鲜果 Fresh Fruits	#在外用膳食品 Outward Dinner	烟酒及用品 Tobacco, Liquor and Articles	#烟草 Tobacco	#酒 Liquor	衣着 Clothing	服装 Garments	衣着材料 Clothing Material
	2001	99.9	100.3	100.2	99.7	99.6	99.9	98.1	97.6	98.8
	2002	103.1	103.6	99.9	99.9	99.9	100.1	97.6	97.4	98.9
	2003	103.0	101.8	100.1	99.8	99.8	100.1	97.8	97.6	99.2
	2004	104.0	102.2	104.1	101.2	100.9	102.2	98.5	98.3	100.2
	2005	102.2	101.6	102.4	100.4	100.4	100.6	98.3	98.1	100.0
北京	Beijing	109.5	111.0	105.4	100.0	98.8	100.7	100.1	101.5	99.5
天津	Tianjin	109.6	109.2	104.1	99.7	101.2	103.2	96.3	99.9	100.0
河北	Hebei	109.8	111.6	101.0	99.9	99.4	100.3	98.8	98.7	99.7
山西	Shanxi	99.6	98.6	102.1	100.8	101.1	99.8	97.8	97.0	98.8
内蒙古	Inner Mongolia	104.2	104.8	102.6	100.0	100.2	99.8	100.1	100.3	97.6
辽宁	Liaoning	105.0	104.9	101.4	100.9	100.7	101.1	96.9	97.3	100.8
吉林	Jilin	106.3	106.5	100.5	101.1	101.2	101.1	100.5	99.9	99.5
黑龙江	Heilongjiang	95.3	92.9	100.8	101.3	101.5	100.8	99.3	99.1	101.2
上海	Shanghai	99.4	98.0	104.5	99.7	99.5	99.8	92.1	90.8	105.1
江苏	Jiangsu	98.1	97.5	104.2	100.6	100.4	100.8	98.6	98.5	100.2
浙江	Zhejiang	98.5	98.0	101.6	100.0	99.4	101.1	97.0	96.5	100.7
安徽	Anhui	97.8	97.3	101.2	100.0	100.1	100.0	98.5	98.9	100.0
福建	Fujian	104.8	105.4	102.5	99.8	99.8	100.0	97.1	96.4	100.5
江西	Jiangxi	102.2	101.6	101.4	100.2	99.6	101.2	97.7	97.6	100.8
山东	Shandong	107.0	104.2	101.3	100.3	100.4	100.6	98.2	98.1	99.8
河南	Henan	107.7	111.1	101.3	101.0	101.6	100.3	98.2	97.9	99.4
湖北	Hubei	107.6	109.3	102.3	100.8	100.8	102.1	100.1	100.4	98.6
湖南	Hunan	102.9	102.9	101.7	99.8	100.0	99.3	99.4	99.3	101.0
广东	Guangdong	99.8	99.1	102.8	101.3	101.7	101.6	98.3	98.0	100.7
广西	Guangxi	100.5	99.8	101.5	99.9	100.1	99.7	97.1	96.6	100.9
海南	Hainan	96.1	95.5	100.3	101.2	101.2	101.1	97.0	96.0	99.8
重庆	Chongqing	96.0	92.1	101.4	101.2	101.8	99.8	92.1	94.0	96.3
四川	Sichuan	102.7	100.0	102.8	100.4	100.4	100.6	97.6	97.2	101.5
贵州	Guizhou	100.1	99.5	104.1	100.1	100.2	99.4	99.3	99.9	102.2
云南	Yunnan	101.6	101.1	100.6	103.7	103.5	105.6	98.0	97.5	100.0
西藏	Tibet	92.3	90.4	101.2	102.2	101.2	104.3	100.7	101.3	98.0
陕西	Shaanxi	98.7	96.9	100.8	100.3	100.7	99.4	100.0	99.5	98.9
甘肃	Gansu	102.7	99.2	101.1	97.9	97.7	97.7	97.1	97.0	99.8
青海	Qinghai	97.6	91.6	100.9	100.0	100.0	100.1	97.3	96.5	99.4
宁夏	Ningxia	100.9	100.2	102.1	99.0	98.6	99.3	103.5	104.1	99.9
新疆	Xinjiang	98.1	94.5	100.9	99.3	98.9	99.8	98.4	98.3	100.5

9-6 续表 2 continued

(上年=100) (preceding year=100)

年份 地区	Year Region	鞋袜帽 Footgear and Hats	衣着加工服务费 Clothing Manufacturing Service	家庭设备用品及服务 Household Facilities, Articles and Services	耐用消费品 Durable Consumer Goods	室内装饰品 Interior Decorations	床上用品 Bed Articles	家庭日用杂品 Daily Use Household Articles	家庭服务及加工维修服务费 Household Service and Manufacturing Upkeep
	2001	99.0	100.3	97.7	96.1	98.3	99.3	98.6	101.5
	2002	98.0	99.9	97.5	95.9	98.8	98.7	98.0	101.2
	2003	97.7	100.1	97.4	95.8	98.8	98.4	98.3	101.1
	2004	98.3	100.7	98.6	97.1	99.2	99.3	99.8	101.9
	2005	98.3	101.1	99.9	98.8	99.5	99.4	100.4	104.4
北京	Beijing	96.5	100.8	99.7	99.7	98.2	97.6	99.6	102.5
天津	Tianjin	85.2	99.7	99.1	97.6	95.9	103.2	100.4	107.2
河北	Hebei	98.7	101.2	98.4	97.8	99.0	99.5	99.0	99.4
山西	Shanxi	99.5	102.0	100.4	99.3	97.8	98.8	101.2	109.9
内蒙古	Inner Mongolia	100.2	99.9	100.3	99.4	99.1	99.5	99.9	107.5
辽宁	Liaoning	95.6	100.0	99.7	98.8	96.5	99.4	100.4	106.2
吉林	Jilin	101.9	99.8	99.2	98.0	98.7	99.9	100.4	100.4
黑龙江	Heilongjiang	99.6	99.0	100.2	97.9	99.1	101.9	101.4	102.3
上海	Shanghai	94.5	103.4	100.8	98.6	99.3	96.9	103.4	109.8
江苏	Jiangsu	97.8	104.1	100.2	99.5	100.0	99.7	100.0	104.2
浙江	Zhejiang	97.4	101.6	100.1	98.3	101.0	100.3	101.2	106.4
安徽	Anhui	96.8	99.8	99.3	97.4	103.7	98.9	100.0	102.1
福建	Fujian	98.2	102.1	99.6	98.3	99.2	98.4	100.2	103.8
江西	Jiangxi	97.2	104.2	99.6	97.7	99.1	97.0	100.9	107.1
山东	Shandong	98.0	99.9	100.1	99.9	100.0	98.7	99.7	103.6
河南	Henan	98.3	100.6	99.6	98.8	99.3	100.0	100.1	101.7
湖北	Hubei	99.1	101.7	98.8	97.2	99.1	98.8	100.2	101.4
湖南	Hunan	99.3	102.4	100.7	99.5	100.0	100.0	101.7	107.3
广东	Guangdong	98.7	100.4	100.6	99.3	100.5	99.3	101.3	104.4
广西	Guangxi	97.1	104.2	99.9	99.8	94.8	98.5	99.4	107.1
海南	Hainan	99.6	101.2	100.7	100.3	99.7	97.6	101.2	103.5
重庆	Chongqing	86.1	101.0	100.1	99.1	100.3	99.1	100.3	104.6
四川	Sichuan	98.1	100.8	99.7	98.6	99.1	98.9	99.9	103.8
贵州	Guizhou	97.9	99.4	99.4	99.2	96.4	102.4	98.7	104.9
云南	Yunnan	98.7	99.3	100.4	97.7	102.4	98.8	99.1	118.2
西藏	Tibet	100.9	97.6	99.6	97.8	101.4	99.9	99.1	106.2
陕西	Shaanxi	101.5	100.6	99.8	99.1	96.7	101.7	100.5	101.3
甘肃	Gansu	96.2	101.5	99.4	99.4	99.4	98.7	99.4	100.7
青海	Qinghai	98.5	103.0	99.8	97.7	99.1	102.5	102.6	102.0
宁夏	Ningxia	102.4	103.0	99.1	97.4	102.2	99.7	101.1	100.3
新疆	Xinjiang	97.8	100.9	99.1	98.4	99.0	100.1	98.5	102.3

9-6 续表 3 continued

(上年=100) (preceding year=100)

年 份 地 区	Year Region	医疗保健和个人用品 Health Care and Personal Articles	医疗保健 Health Care	医疗器具及用品 Medical Appliances and Articles	中药材及中成药 Traditional Chinese Medicine	西 药 Western Medicine	保健器具及用品 Health Care Appliances and Articles	医疗保健服务 Health Care Services	个人用品及服务 Personal Articles and Services
	2001	100.0	100.3	98.3	101.4	94.8	97.3	110.5	99.5
	2002	98.8	98.5	97.2	96.6	94.5	97.1	108.2	99.5
	2003	100.9	101.2	101.0	105.0	94.5	98.2	108.9	100.2
	2004	99.7	99.1	102.3	98.9	94.9	98.6	105.2	101.2
	2005	99.9	99.5	97.4	96.5	97.7	100.0	105.2	100.8
北 京	Beijing	98.0	96.8	99.4	91.1	97.2	98.0	100.0	102.4
天 津	Tianjin	97.6	97.6	98.4	95.3	96.2	98.6	100.9	97.4
河 北	Hebei	99.2	98.7	96.6	97.5	98.9	99.3	100.1	100.3
山 西	Shanxi	99.9	99.5	94.5	93.5	97.1	97.7	108.1	100.5
内蒙古	Inner Mongolia	105.7	107.7	93.1	98.4	96.9	99.4	141.0	101.6
辽 宁	Liaoning	99.3	98.9	95.6	97.4	98.0	99.4	100.4	100.3
吉 林	Jilin	98.6	97.8	91.7	95.3	98.5	99.1	100.0	100.6
黑龙江	Heilongjiang	100.0	100.1	99.0	100.8	99.3	100.4	101.1	99.6
上 海	Shanghai	100.3	100.4	99.4	99.2	95.6	100.0	106.5	100.2
江 苏	Jiangsu	100.2	99.4	98.0	97.5	97.8	100.2	102.6	101.9
浙 江	Zhejiang	100.8	100.5	99.1	93.3	96.5	102.0	111.4	101.2
安 徽	Anhui	98.7	96.9	95.3	94.7	95.2	98.3	101.2	102.1
福 建	Fujian	98.8	97.9	94.7	94.7	97.6	100.0	100.9	100.3
江 西	Jiangxi	100.9	99.1	92.4	89.0	95.1	98.9	118.5	103.7
山 东	Shandong	99.7	99.4	97.8	97.0	99.1	101.0	101.7	100.4
河 南	Henan	98.2	97.4	96.9	95.3	96.1	99.2	100.6	100.2
湖 北	Hubei	98.1	97.6	96.6	95.2	97.8	98.2	99.8	99.3
湖 南	Hunan	99.0	97.9	100.2	96.5	98.2	99.2	99.2	101.5
广 东	Guangdong	99.2	99.1	99.7	97.7	98.9	99.9	100.4	99.5
广 西	Guangxi	100.2	99.4	95.8	92.1	97.6	98.2	108.3	101.4
海 南	Hainan	99.7	99.0	99.0	95.0	99.0	97.2	102.1	101.1
重 庆	Chongqing	102.5	104.0	98.7	102.6	101.5	108.8	107.2	98.1
四 川	Sichuan	101.3	101.4	100.0	97.9	98.5	99.5	108.3	100.9
贵 州	Guizhou	100.5	100.5	101.4	99.7	98.0	98.8	104.1	100.6
云 南	Yunnan	102.2	102.7	94.7	100.5	95.5	99.6	126.5	100.4
西 藏	Tibet	100.4	100.5	97.5	100.3	100.7	100.1	101.5	100.1
陕 西	Shaanxi	98.5	97.9	94.8	96.2	97.4	97.9	101.2	100.2
甘 肃	Gansu	103.3	103.1	94.4	95.4	99.5	101.7	118.6	103.5
青 海	Qinghai	102.0	101.0	101.9	98.1	98.6	101.6	104.1	104.9
宁 夏	Ningxia	98.2	96.8	100.5	96.7	94.9	98.8	100.0	101.9
新 疆	Xinjiang	109.3	114.2	100.0	100.8	98.8	99.4	145.7	100.4

9-6 续表 4 continued

(上年=100) (preceding year=100)

年份 地区	Year Region	化妆美容用品 Cosmetics	卫生用品 Sanitation Articles	个人饰品 Personal Decorations	个人服务 Personal Services	交通和通信 Transportation and Communication	交通 Transportation	交通工具 Transportation Facility
	2001	99.8	97.9	97.8	101.7	99.0	101.0	96.4
	2002	99.7	97.3	99.3	101.2	98.1	99.1	95.0
	2003	99.5	97.1	102.9	100.8	97.8	99.5	95.9
	2004	98.8	98.4	104.5	101.8	98.5	100.4	96.5
	2005	99.4	99.4	101.6	101.9	99.0	101.5	97.3
北京	Beijing	105.4	100.8	102.0	102.6	97.5	99.1	95.7
天津	Tianjin	99.0	100.2	98.0	94.8	98.6	104.1	99.3
河北	Hebei	101.2	99.4	100.9	100.0	99.0	100.7	99.1
山西	Shanxi	99.5	97.8	101.8	101.1	98.8	102.1	98.2
内蒙古	Inner Mongolia	100.8	97.4	101.7	104.8	99.8	101.6	98.1
辽宁	Liaoning	98.9	99.5	100.9	100.7	98.7	101.1	98.4
吉林	Jilin	99.4	97.9	102.4	102.6	96.2	101.0	99.7
黑龙江	Heilongjiang	98.8	97.9	102.9	98.3	99.4	101.1	100.8
上海	Shanghai	96.8	98.0	102.8	99.9	97.5	99.9	92.9
江苏	Jiangsu	99.5	100.4	102.3	104.4	98.4	100.8	97.8
浙江	Zhejiang	98.9	99.5	103.2	102.6	98.9	101.0	96.8
安徽	Anhui	99.4	99.5	98.9	104.8	99.3	102.5	98.3
福建	Fujian	100.3	99.0	101.6	100.2	97.7	100.8	96.4
江西	Jiangxi	100.2	98.7	101.7	112.6	99.5	103.2	99.3
山东	Shandong	99.4	99.3	101.1	101.2	99.5	101.8	97.7
河南	Henan	98.9	98.4	101.7	102.0	100.3	102.7	98.5
湖北	Hubei	98.9	98.7	100.2	98.9	101.5	103.6	99.0
湖南	Hunan	100.3	100.8	101.0	104.0	99.3	101.3	97.4
广东	Guangdong	97.5	99.5	101.5	99.9	99.1	100.7	95.0
广西	Guangxi	98.9	101.2	101.2	102.5	101.1	103.2	97.7
海南	Hainan	100.0	100.0	99.6	104.4	100.5	102.0	97.3
重庆	Chongqing	97.5	100.8	101.1	93.4	99.9	102.3	100.0
四川	Sichuan	99.6	100.3	102.4	100.6	100.2	101.9	98.9
贵州	Guizhou	100.0	102.2	100.8	99.2	99.4	102.7	99.3
云南	Yunnan	100.5	98.2	102.8	99.5	98.3	101.0	95.8
西藏	Tibet	100.1	98.6	101.9	99.7	100.2	102.1	99.2
陕西	Shaanxi	100.9	98.7	100.0	101.3	100.6	103.9	99.1
甘肃	Gansu	98.8	98.3	101.0	109.5	97.3	102.0	99.7
青海	Qinghai	98.1	98.2	101.5	115.9	91.8	101.1	100.1
宁夏	Ningxia	100.2	99.3	101.5	105.8	100.5	105.6	97.9
新疆	Xinjiang	99.7	97.2	101.7	103.8	99.5	101.6	98.4

9-6 续表 5 continued

(上年=100) (preceding year=100)

年份 地区	Year Region	车用燃料及零配件 Fuels and Parts	车辆使用及维修费 Using and Upkeep Fare	市内公共交通费 Incity Traffic Fare	城市间交通费 Intercity Traffic Fare	通信 Communication	通信工具 Communication Facility	通信服务 Communication Services
	2001	99.0	100.4	105.8	104.0	96.8	80.5	101.1
	2002	98.5	100.0	101.9	101.8	97.2	83.5	100.3
	2003	108.3	98.9	100.6	101.4	96.1	82.1	99.4
	2004	107.7	101.0	101.0	102.5	96.8	84.3	99.8
	2005	110.3	102.0	102.2	103.3	96.6	84.1	99.6
北京	Beijing	112.6	102.2	100.0	102.3	95.6	75.6	100.0
天津	Tianjin	108.6	101.3	111.8	98.2	94.8	70.5	100.0
河北	Hebei	112.0	101.9	101.2	101.2	97.5	84.8	100.0
山西	Shanxi	112.3	103.2	102.9	105.5	96.1	71.7	100.2
内蒙古	Inner Mongolia	109.5	100.4	101.8	105.3	97.7	91.0	99.5
辽宁	Liaoning	107.5	101.8	101.5	101.3	97.2	74.8	99.9
吉林	Jilin	108.3	106.3	99.8	100.7	92.8	82.4	98.7
黑龙江	Heilongjiang	105.5	101.6	99.6	102.2	98.2	86.3	99.8
上海	Shanghai	113.0	102.5	102.0	100.1	94.9	66.1	100.0
江苏	Jiangsu	110.0	100.0	102.7	99.8	96.2	83.1	99.7
浙江	Zhejiang	111.9	102.9	102.9	101.9	96.4	84.4	100.0
安徽	Anhui	109.1	100.6	103.7	103.8	96.5	85.7	99.2
福建	Fujian	111.1	101.9	99.7	103.3	95.4	79.6	98.8
江西	Jiangxi	109.5	100.4	107.0	103.5	96.5	79.7	100.0
山东	Shandong	110.9	101.8	101.5	106.8	96.9	86.1	100.0
河南	Henan	109.4	103.7	104.6	104.2	97.7	87.4	100.2
湖北	Hubei	109.3	104.4	102.5	106.5	98.7	89.0	100.2
湖南	Hunan	108.8	105.5	101.2	101.1	97.6	89.9	100.0
广东	Guangdong	110.7	100.4	101.2	101.7	97.5	87.5	100.0
广西	Guangxi	109.5	103.7	113.2	104.6	96.6	85.4	100.0
海南	Hainan	108.5	101.0	99.9	105.3	98.3	86.0	100.0
重庆	Chongqing	112.6	100.6	100.0	103.9	98.1	78.9	100.0
四川	Sichuan	109.0	101.1	101.2	103.6	97.6	91.3	99.3
贵州	Guizhou	109.5	103.3	102.5	103.1	97.2	87.9	99.1
云南	Yunnan	112.5	105.7	100.8	102.7	95.9	83.0	98.7
西藏	Tibet	103.5	100.9	99.7	106.4	97.5	95.8	97.7
陕西	Shaanxi	107.0	100.5	102.8	110.9	97.2	85.6	99.4
甘肃	Gansu	104.7	98.7	101.0	106.4	92.7	85.1	95.0
青海	Qinghai	108.0	103.7	100.6	101.5	80.7	72.5	82.7
宁夏	Ningxia	111.1	104.9	108.1	107.7	96.4	84.5	100.0
新疆	Xinjiang	109.5	100.4	102.5	99.3	97.4	88.7	99.7

9-6 续表 6 continued

(上年=100) (preceding year=100)

年份 地区	Year Region	娱乐教育文化用品及服务 Recreation, Education and Culture	文娱用耐用消费品及服务 Durable Consumer Goods and Service for Recreational Use	教育 Education	教材及参考书 Teaching Materials and Reference Books	学杂托幼费 Tuition and Child Care	文化娱乐用品 Cultural and Recreational Articles	文化娱乐 Cultural Articles
	2001	106.6	91.2	113.6	106.1	114.1	101.7	99.4
	2002	100.6	90.5	103.7	99.0	104.0	101.2	98.9
	2003	101.3	92.7	104.3	101.7	104.5	101.3	98.7
	2004	101.3	93.3	103.4	102.8	103.4	101.1	99.4
	2005	102.2	93.8	105.1	100.9	105.4	101.2	99.8
北京	Beijing	99.7	94.9	100.0	100.8	99.9	101.5	99.9
天津	Tianjin	100.0	95.1	100.5	100.9	100.5	103.5	101.6
河北	Hebei	105.0	93.5	108.3	102.1	108.7	100.3	100.0
山西	Shanxi	108.1	95.7	113.3	101.2	114.6	101.7	99.5
内蒙古	Inner Mongolia	100.4	95.3	101.6	100.6	101.6	100.2	99.6
辽宁	Liaoning	106.3	90.8	112.7	101.0	114.0	99.8	99.1
吉林	Jilin	103.0	93.5	106.9	104.1	107.4	101.5	99.3
黑龙江	Heilongjiang	100.2	94.4	101.5	99.0	101.5	100.5	100.4
上海	Shanghai	98.3	85.8	99.5	94.8	100.2	102.6	100.8
江苏	Jiangsu	102.2	93.0	105.1	101.0	105.3	102.3	100.2
浙江	Zhejiang	100.2	95.5	101.3	99.6	101.4	101.2	99.8
安徽	Anhui	100.9	92.2	102.5	106.6	102.4	99.5	98.6
福建	Fujian	104.7	94.7	109.6	101.1	110.3	101.4	100.0
江西	Jiangxi	100.0	93.8	101.0	100.4	101.0	100.8	99.6
山东	Shandong	102.7	95.9	105.0	101.2	105.2	101.0	100.0
河南	Henan	102.6	94.8	105.3	100.2	106.0	100.6	100.0
湖北	Hubei	103.6	93.8	106.5	102.0	106.7	100.5	100.7
湖南	Hunan	103.0	97.7	105.2	101.4	105.5	101.7	99.7
广东	Guangdong	100.3	93.6	102.5	102.4	102.5	100.7	99.0
广西	Guangxi	106.6	92.5	111.5	100.0	112.3	101.8	100.1
海南	Hainan	101.1	93.8	104.2	106.5	104.1	99.7	99.4
重庆	Chongqing	104.1	90.4	112.2	98.4	113.3	100.7	100.6
四川	Sichuan	104.5	95.4	105.2	99.5	105.5	101.0	99.9
贵州	Guizhou	99.0	94.2	101.3	98.8	101.6	100.7	99.3
云南	Yunnan	102.3	88.7	114.0	101.3	115.5	99.5	99.9
西藏	Tibet	99.6	95.6	105.0	100.7	106.1	100.6	100.5
陕西	Shaanxi	100.3	93.5	100.8	98.4	101.1	103.6	98.7
甘肃	Gansu	104.1	93.8	109.6	103.0	109.8	100.4	100.0
青海	Qinghai	103.6	94.6	108.3	100.3	108.7	99.9	101.1
宁夏	Ningxia	99.6	88.6	101.2	102.1	101.1	103.6	99.5
新疆	Xinjiang	98.6	95.0	100.2	98.7	100.4	101.2	98.8

9-6 续表 7 continued

(上年=100) (preceding year=100)

年份 地区	Year Region	书报杂志 Newspapers and Magazines	文娱费 Expenditure of Culture and Recreation	旅游及外出 Touring and Outgoing	居住 Residence	建房及装修材料 Building and Decoration Materials	租房 Renting	自有住房 Private Housing	水电燃料 Water, Electricity and Fuels
	2001	101.9	104.4	100.3	101.2	98.8	108.6	100.0	102.5
	2002	101.0	104.2	95.9	99.9	98.4	104.4	95.4	102.9
	2003	100.4	104.6	95.4	102.1	99.5	103.5	99.1	105.7
	2004	100.6	103.2	100.6	104.9	104.3	103.0	100.9	107.5
	2005	100.8	102.9	99.6	105.4	102.6	101.9	105.6	108.6
北京	Beijing	100.2	101.8	101.8	105.9	103.2	100.0	107.2	108.6
天津	Tianjin	100.0	107.8	100.8	106.7	102.1	102.1	103.6	112.5
河北	Hebei	100.0	101.0	96.4	105.5	101.8	105.3	100.4	109.7
山西	Shanxi	102.8	103.7	99.9	104.5	102.6	101.5	103.7	106.5
内蒙古	Inner Mongolia	100.0	101.0	99.1	106.9	101.4	101.8	105.4	111.5
辽宁	Liaoning	100.5	99.9	96.1	104.5	102.9	101.5	105.8	105.7
吉林	Jilin	101.1	104.4	100.8	107.6	101.9	100.0	105.5	111.5
黑龙江	Heilongjiang	100.8	100.5	97.7	109.4	106.7	101.5	108.4	112.6
上海	Shanghai	101.1	104.1	107.0	102.9	103.9	100.0	106.9	101.0
江苏	Jiangsu	101.8	104.6	100.3	104.4	104.3	101.6	104.2	105.0
浙江	Zhejiang	100.2	102.5	99.8	104.4	103.1	101.6	103.1	106.5
安徽	Anhui	100.0	100.2	96.6	105.3	101.2	101.3	107.0	108.8
福建	Fujian	100.2	103.3	99.6	106.8	101.7	100.1	105.2	112.0
江西	Jiangxi	100.3	102.7	99.3	105.7	101.1	105.4	106.3	109.5
山东	Shandong	100.7	102.6	99.8	105.2	102.0	102.5	104.3	109.2
河南	Henan	100.1	102.3	99.0	106.8	102.5	99.7	108.1	111.4
湖北	Hubei	99.7	100.7	101.8	105.7	102.4	100.0	108.2	109.1
湖南	Hunan	100.9	104.4	98.2	107.3	105.0	101.9	104.9	111.6
广东	Guangdong	101.8	101.4	100.3	104.4	101.3	99.9	105.7	106.9
广西	Guangxi	100.9	105.2	93.1	104.0	102.9	98.8	103.3	106.8
海南	Hainan	99.0	100.4	109.0	105.9	105.2	100.9	105.1	106.7
重庆	Chongqing	100.0	101.3	90.5	103.0	101.2	100.0	106.1	103.6
四川	Sichuan	100.0	103.2	100.2	103.8	101.8	101.2	102.3	106.7
贵州	Guizhou	101.0	102.8	91.4	106.4	101.7	110.1	105.6	111.0
云南	Yunnan	100.3	98.5	96.2	105.9	105.3	103.6	103.4	107.5
西藏	Tibet	100.1	101.3	98.7	106.7	101.6	105.3	100.1	111.1
陕西	Shaanxi	100.0	111.1	99.4	106.7	101.5	109.1	108.7	110.2
甘肃	Gansu	100.3	100.7	94.6	109.1	103.2	101.4	116.4	111.0
青海	Qinghai	100.2	98.7	99.4	106.3	107.0	100.0	105.4	106.9
宁夏	Ningxia	99.9	109.1	107.4	106.3	101.1	110.4	107.7	110.3
新疆	Xinjiang	100.9	103.5	92.3	107.3	105.7	117.2	100.6	109.7

9-7 商品零售价格分类指数

Retail Price Indices by Category of Commodities

(上年=100) (preceding year=100)

年份 Year / 地区 Region	总指数 General Index	食品 Food	#粮食 Grain	#油脂 Oil or Fat	#肉禽及其制品 Meat, Poultry and Their Products	#蛋 Eggs	#水产品 Aquatic Products	#菜 Vegetables	#干鲜瓜果 Dried and Fresh Melons and Fruits
1994	121.7	135.2	148.7	161.4			120.7		
1995	114.8	124.7	134.4	116.3			114.2		
1996	106.1	107.7	107.5	92.1			105.6		
1997	100.8	99.8	92.1	101.6			101.2		
1998	97.4	96.8	96.9	100.7			94.2		
1999	97.0	95.8	96.4	94.4			93.6		
2000	98.5	97.5	90.1	86.2			102.7		
2001	99.2	100.6	101.5	89.3			96.3		
2002	98.7	99.9	98.6	100.1			96.2		
2003	99.9	103.4	102.2	112.5	103.0	98.5	100.3	116.3	102.2
2004	102.8	109.9	126.5	116.8	117.1	119.8	112.5	95.2	104.1
2005	100.8	103.1	101.4	94.7	103.0	104.7	105.8	108.1	101.7
北京 Beijing	99.7	105.9	106.1	96.9	104.0	105.3	107.2	107.4	104.3
天津 Tianjin	99.9	103.5	103.8	94.7	104.5	103.5	95.7	112.1	109.6
河北 Hebei	101.1	102.2	103.1	96.8	102.5	102.8	104.0	98.9	110.4
山西 Shanxi	100.3	102.6	103.6	94.9	101.1	102.4	104.6	107.1	100.9
内蒙古 Inner Mongolia	101.5	102.9	103.8	96.5	102.5	104.1	100.0	107.4	102.1
辽宁 Liaoning	100.1	101.8	104.2	86.1	99.8	102.7	102.2	105.4	104.4
吉林 Jilin	101.1	101.7	103.8	92.5	101.0	103.1	100.7	105.0	106.3
黑龙江 Heilongjiang	100.4	99.8	100.5	89.6	99.7	101.9	100.0	105.8	96.5
上海 Shanghai	99.4	104.7	102.1	91.2	105.5	105.8	114.4	103.4	99.4
江苏 Jiangsu	100.3	103.7	100.1	92.4	104.4	104.8	104.9	111.8	98.8
浙江 Zhejiang	100.9	103.7	98.1	93.6	103.5	107.5	105.7	113.2	99.7
安徽 Anhui	100.6	103.4	98.0	90.3	104.5	108.3	103.9	116.4	98.3
福建 Fujian	100.6	103.8	99.6	97.5	104.0	103.5	105.9	110.4	104.8
江西 Jiangxi	100.9	103.3	98.8	96.1	102.0	107.2	102.6	116.7	101.1
山东 Shandong	100.6	103.2	100.0	95.6	103.0	105.9	104.6	106.3	107.5
河南 Henan	101.7	103.2	100.9	92.5	102.9	105.2	101.3	113.2	107.5
湖北 Hubei	102.1	105.1	100.7	91.8	105.0	103.9	104.4	117.2	106.9
湖南 Hunan	102.3	103.6	100.4	97.5	101.4	108.8	105.9	122.1	99.8
广东 Guangdong	101.8	104.6	102.0	100.1	105.6	105.1	108.9	109.5	99.6
广西 Guangxi	101.1	102.9	101.6	96.4	103.4	103.4	108.2	107.1	97.3
海南 Hainan	100.9	102.4	100.1	98.7	100.9	105.6	104.6	110.3	95.8
重庆 Chongqing	98.7	100.2	102.7	83.8	101.4	104.8	104.9	98.7	96.0
四川 Sichuan	100.6	102.4	102.4	95.1	101.9	105.0	104.7	105.5	102.9
贵州 Guizhou	101.3	101.6	100.0	91.4	101.0	105.2	106.3	104.3	102.4
云南 Yunnan	100.1	100.7	103.3	97.4	99.1	104.5	113.1	91.7	101.4
西藏 Tibet	100.8	102.9	105.9	101.6	104.1	101.8	99.2	97.0	95.1
陕西 Shaanxi	100.1	101.1	101.0	96.1	100.9	105.0	101.3	101.6	101.0
甘肃 Gansu	99.9	101.2	102.8	96.1	103.0	104.5	103.6	99.2	100.3
青海 Qinghai	100.7	100.9	101.1	93.2	102.2	106.2	102.5	102.2	96.7
宁夏 Ningxia	100.4	102.0	104.6	98.2	102.7	104.5	100.9	99.4	100.5
新疆 Xinjiang	99.4	98.2	101.9	90.7	97.8	99.8	103.5	94.5	95.8

9-7 续表 1 continued

(上年=100) (preceding year=100)

年份 Year 地区 Region		饮料烟酒 Beverages, Tobacco and Liquor	服装鞋帽 Garments, Shoes and Hats	纺织品 Textiles	家用电器及音像器材 Household Appliances, Music and Video Equipment	文化办公用品 Cultural and Office Appliances	日用品 Articles for Daily Use	体育娱乐用品 Sports and Recreation Articles	交通、通信用品 Transportation and Communication Appliances
	1994	111.3	119.6	114.7			113.9		
	1995	107.8	116.8	115.4			109.7		
	1996	105.1	108.5	106.4			105.3		
	1997	101.2	103.5	101.9			102.3		
	1998	98.8	99.3	99.1			99.0		
	1999	97.3	97.3	98.0			97.9		
	2000	98.0	99.2	98.6			98.1		
	2001	99.5	98.9	99.1			98.3		
	2002	99.9	97.9	99.4			98.7		
	2003	99.9	97.5	99.3	94.2	95.8	98.5	98.1	91.1
	2004	101.0	98.2	100.0	94.7	96.9	99.6	98.2	91.8
	2005	100.5	97.9	99.8	96.3	96.7	100.2	98.4	91.7
北京	Beijing	100.2	101.3	98.2	97.6	98.2	100.0	97.3	88.5
天津	Tianjin	101.8	96.1	102.2	96.3	98.8	100.4	97.6	88.6
河北	Hebei	100.1	99.1	101.2	95.9	98.0	99.9	99.5	93.3
山西	Shanxi	101.2	98.0	98.7	97.0	97.6	100.3	98.3	88.9
内蒙古	Inner Mongolia	100.1	99.7	99.2	96.4	97.9	99.8	98.7	93.3
辽宁	Liaoning	101.1	96.6	98.9	95.1	96.1	100.2	99.5	89.4
吉林	Jilin	100.7	100.7	99.7	95.8	97.0	100.1	97.9	91.9
黑龙江	Heilongjiang	100.9	97.7	101.1	96.8	97.7	100.5	100.1	91.9
上海	Shanghai	99.6	92.6	99.4	93.1	91.6	100.5	94.7	88.5
江苏	Jiangsu	100.6	98.5	100.0	94.9	96.0	99.8	97.8	90.8
浙江	Zhejiang	100.0	96.7	100.5	96.6	98.0	100.6	99.5	94.2
安徽	Anhui	100.2	97.8	99.5	95.3	96.2	99.3	97.3	93.3
福建	Fujian	99.7	97.2	99.3	96.1	96.4	99.6	98.4	89.9
江西	Jiangxi	100.4	97.7	99.0	96.4	97.0	100.7	98.3	90.8
山东	Shandong	100.4	97.6	99.1	98.2	96.1	99.5	99.1	92.7
河南	Henan	100.6	98.4	99.8	97.2	98.4	99.9	99.6	94.7
湖北	Hubei	100.6	100.7	98.2	96.3	98.4	98.9	102.6	93.1
湖南	Hunan	100.0	99.5	100.3	98.4	99.0	100.7	97.9	92.3
广东	Guangdong	101.3	97.8	99.1	96.6	94.8	101.0	99.9	91.6
广西	Guangxi	101.0	97.5	101.2	96.4	95.8	101.8	100.7	89.5
海南	Hainan	100.9	96.6	98.0	97.0	97.0	100.7	99.8	92.8
重庆	Chongqing	100.4	92.2	98.7	95.6	99.8	100.0	94.1	88.9
四川	Sichuan	100.5	97.4	100.4	96.6	97.1	100.2	98.9	93.0
贵州	Guizhou	100.5	99.7	103.3	96.7	99.8	100.2	101.9	94.8
云南	Yunnan	103.0	97.8	99.3	94.7	90.9	99.8	94.8	93.0
西藏	Tibet	101.8	103.0	99.4	96.1	97.5	99.3	96.4	97.6
陕西	Shaanxi	100.0	100.7	101.6	96.7	97.8	100.5	97.8	92.9
甘肃	Gansu	98.2	96.9	100.1	95.9	97.6	98.4	98.8	93.8
青海	Qinghai	100.3	97.5	100.7	96.5	98.3	101.2	99.6	94.7
宁夏	Ningxia	99.7	103.5	100.0	92.6	94.5	101.1	97.7	88.8
新疆	Xinjiang	99.5	98.1	100.5	96.4	96.7	99.4	97.5	93.5

9-7 续表 2 continued

(上年=100) (preceding year=100)

年份 Year 地区 Region	家具 Furniture	化妆品 Cosmetics	金银珠宝 Gold, Silver and Jewelry	中西药品及医疗保健用品 Traditional Chinese and Western Medicines and Health Care Articles	书报杂志及电子出版物 Books, Newspapers, Magazines and Electronic Publications	燃料 Fuels	建筑材料及五金电料 Building Materials and Hardware
1994		116.4				115.1	
1995		109.9				107.4	
1996		105.0				105.0	
1997		102.3				107.3	
1998		100.5				96.1	
1999		99.6				100.4	
2000		98.9				117.7	
2001		98.8				102.4	
2002		98.4				102.0	
2003	97.8	98.9	108.6	98.4	100.3	109.3	99.7
2004	98.8	98.9	111.6	96.7	101.0	112.4	103.7
2005	99.1	99.3	104.4	97.6	100.3	115.4	102.1
北京 Beijing	97.2	104.1	105.1	95.4	100.2	109.9	99.6
天津 Tianjin	97.2	98.2	102.9	96.5	100.6	112.9	101.6
河北 Hebei	100.3	99.5	104.2	98.5	100.6	114.7	101.3
山西 Shanxi	99.2	99.6	102.9	96.2	102.7	115.0	103.2
内蒙古 Inner Mongolia	100.1	99.1	104.3	98.2	100.2	123.5	101.0
辽宁 Liaoning	99.3	98.7	103.8	97.4	100.5	114.9	102.2
吉林 Jilin	98.4	98.8	104.9	96.9	102.2	118.3	101.4
黑龙江 Heilongjiang	96.7	99.4	105.8	99.9	100.5	118.0	103.5
上海 Shanghai	100.1	96.1	107.3	97.7	98.0	109.1	104.0
江苏 Jiangsu	99.7	99.6	104.7	98.1	100.5	113.7	103.6
浙江 Zhejiang	99.8	98.5	104.7	96.8	99.9	113.1	103.0
安徽 Anhui	100.1	98.9	102.9	95.6	101.2	112.8	102.1
福建 Fujian	99.9	99.5	104.2	97.0	100.3	117.0	101.4
江西 Jiangxi	95.0	99.7	104.6	93.8	100.3	118.4	101.3
山东 Shandong	100.0	99.0	103.4	98.8	100.4	113.3	102.0
河南 Henan	99.1	99.6	103.0	96.0	99.7	118.2	102.1
湖北 Hubei	97.6	99.9	104.2	97.1	101.3	113.8	101.9
湖南 Hunan	98.9	100.1	104.2	97.4	100.9	123.2	105.2
广东 Guangdong	99.2	98.8	105.3	98.9	100.8	115.6	100.8
广西 Guangxi	100.5	98.9	106.1	97.3	100.5	115.0	102.6
海南 Hainan	100.5	100.9	105.0	97.4	99.4	113.4	106.6
重庆 Chongqing	101.3	100.8	104.0	102.6	99.7	107.9	101.3
四川 Sichuan	100.0	101.2	104.6	98.6	99.6	114.0	101.4
贵州 Guizhou	100.5	102.5	103.6	99.0	99.9	118.3	102.8
云南 Yunnan	98.7	98.6	105.2	97.4	99.7	112.5	103.5
西藏 Tibet	99.7	98.3	98.7	100.5	100.0	107.5	99.7
陕西 Shaanxi	99.9	99.7	103.6	96.8	98.9	114.4	101.2
甘肃 Gansu	100.0	100.6	104.0	97.7	98.6	113.0	102.4
青海 Qinghai	98.9	98.1	101.5	98.2	100.4	112.7	102.5
宁夏 Ningxia	96.9	98.1	104.3	96.6	100.3	117.1	101.0
新疆 Xinjiang	99.2	98.4	102.2	99.6	98.9	114.1	103.7

9-8 各地区农业生产资料价格分类指数

Price Indices of Means of Agricultural Production by Category and Region

(上年=100) (preceding year=100)

年份 地区	Year Region	总指数 General Index	小农具 Small Farm Tools	饲料 Forage	产品畜 Production Livestock	役畜 Labour Livestock	半机械化农具 Semi-mechanized Farm Tools
	2003	101.4	99.3	102.0	102.9	106.6	99.4
	2004	110.6	104.3	116.5	127.6	109.2	102.1
	2005	108.3	105.1	103.9	106.5	105.5	102.3
河北	Hebei	106.8	100.5	99.2	106.2	99.7	99.9
山西	Shanxi	113.3	125.8	109.0	114.0	102.4	101.8
内蒙古	Inner Mongolia	108.3	100.7	103.4	109.5	100.9	102.4
辽宁	Liaoning	110.0	106.4	106.4	114.7	104.8	101.6
吉林	Jilin	109.2	98.8	107.2	104.9	99.1	107.8
黑龙江	Heilongjiang	108.6	109.1	108.4	111.2	103.0	100.2
江苏	Jiangsu	106.9	101.2	98.9	101.2	105.1	98.7
浙江	Zhejiang	105.8	104.3	102.7	105.1	102.3	102.2
安徽	Anhui	108.3	111.1	107.6	114.7	110.1	105.0
福建	Fujian	108.1	107.2	102.8	102.5	103.8	100.0
江西	Jiangxi	107.9	106.2	101.3	110.3	106.1	102.2
山东	Shandong	106.2	103.4	102.0	103.2	100.9	100.3
河南	Henan	107.9	103.0	101.3	108.0	104.2	104.2
湖北	Hubei	115.1	111.4	116.7	101.2	121.8	101.8
湖南	Hunan	111.2	109.1	108.3	108.0	109.9	104.4
广东	Guangdong	105.8	102.4	104.2	105.6	105.0	102.3
广西	Guangxi	110.5	106.1	108.9	102.6	123.3	107.4
海南	Hainan	108.9	100.6	103.7	105.5	110.8	99.6
四川	Sichuan	107.2	107.4	103.7	111.5	101.4	104.7
贵州	Guizhou	110.2	109.5	106.9	132.7	117.5	107.8
云南	Yunnan	105.9	101.5	104.5	96.4	106.9	100.9
西藏	Tibet	100.6	103.7	99.1	101.5	101.6	103.2
陕西	Shaanxi	107.2	102.8	106.2	105.1	104.5	102.2
甘肃	Gansu	109.0	105.7	100.3	113.6	113.6	100.8
青海	Qinghai	106.5	101.9	95.8	103.2	99.4	101.2
宁夏	Ningxia	109.3	100.9	107.5	106.6	100.1	104.6
新疆	Xinjiang	105.3	104.9	101.3	89.4	97.3	100.9

9-8 续表 continued

(上年=100) (preceding year=100)

年份 地区	Year Region	机械化农具 Mechanized Farm Machinery	化学肥料 Chemical Fertilizer	农药及农药械 Pesticide and Its Appliances	农用机油 Oil for Farm Machinery	其他农业生产资料 Other Means of Agricultural Production
	2003	98.5	101.6	99.9	107.8	97.0
	2004	102.2	112.8	103.0	108.4	106.3
	2005	102.3	112.8	104.1	111.1	109.4
河北	Hebei	101.3	112.0	101.2	116.6	108.6
山西	Shanxi	101.4	115.9	129.7	109.5	116.4
内蒙古	Inner Mongolia	100.7	118.3	99.0	109.9	105.7
辽宁	Liaoning	98.6	117.0	102.5	115.6	108.6
吉林	Jilin	104.2	115.4	103.5	105.4	104.9
黑龙江	Heilongjiang	102.4	115.3	107.7	117.1	96.2
江苏	Jiangsu	103.7	111.3	102.5	108.0	113.0
浙江	Zhejiang	103.3	110.0	103.7	107.7	105.3
安徽	Anhui	106.2	109.0	103.9	107.9	110.1
福建	Fujian	103.0	114.1	108.5	110.2	105.3
江西	Jiangxi	102.7	113.7	104.4	110.4	110.4
山东	Shandong	100.9	110.0	105.8	109.1	109.9
河南	Henan	101.9	110.7	107.0	110.9	114.2
湖北	Hubei	105.8	120.2	103.9	110.6	109.7
湖南	Hunan	102.6	115.2	105.3	109.9	118.6
广东	Guangdong	102.0	108.0	101.7	107.7	110.7
广西	Guangxi	103.7	112.6	106.0	114.4	122.5
海南	Hainan	107.3	111.1	101.1	113.0	130.3
四川	Sichuan	103.2	107.6	101.1	106.9	112.3
贵州	Guizhou	104.0	111.5	100.0	110.7	103.2
云南	Yunnan	100.6	109.6	106.9	111.1	106.5
西藏	Tibet	98.7	98.7	100.7	99.1	101.3
陕西	Shaanxi	103.0	110.0	103.9	107.6	112.4
甘肃	Gansu	96.9	114.3	103.6	115.1	106.6
青海	Qinghai	102.9	110.1	103.2	113.2	114.7
宁夏	Ningxia	103.7	115.8	113.9	109.4	114.0
新疆	Xinjiang	102.5	110.2	102.8	111.0	105.5

9-9 农产品生产价格指数

Indices of Producers' Prices for Farm Products

(上年＝100) (preceding year=100)

指　标	Item	2003	2004	2005
农产品生产价格指数	**General Price Index of Farm Products**	**104.4**	**113.1**	**101.4**
种植业产品	**Planting Products**	**107.4**	**115.9**	**101.6**
谷物	Cereal	102.3	128.1	99.2
#小麦	Wheat	103.0	131.2	96.4
稻谷	Rice	99.9	136.3	101.6
玉米	Corn	104.6	116.9	98.0
大豆	Beans	120.6	120.2	94.2
油料	Oil-bearing Crops	119.4	116.6	91.3
棉花	Cotton	135.3	79.5	111.8
糖料	Sugar	90.5	104.9	111.6
蔬菜	Vegetable	110.4	105.2	107.2
水果	Fruit	102.0	98.6	107.4
林业产品	**Forestry Products**	**107.0**	**104.6**	**104.8**
牧业产品	**Animal Husbandry Products**	**101.8**	**111.1**	**100.5**
猪（毛重）	Pig (gross weight)	102.9	112.8	97.6
牛（毛重）	Cattle and Buffaloes (gross weight)	101.7	103.9	101.7
羊（毛重）	Sheep and Goats (gross weight)	96.3	103.7	101.7
家禽（毛重）	Poultry (gross weight)	101.0	111.8	105.6
蛋类	Eggs	101.1	112.6	106.4
奶类	Milk	103.7	103.7	99.6
渔业产品	**Fishing Products**	**100.3**	**110.2**	**104.7**
海水鱼类	Seawater Fish	104.0	109.2	104.2
淡水鱼类	Freshwater Fish	98.7	111.5	106.2

9-10 各地区农产品生产价格指数

Producers' Prices for Farm Products by Region

(上年=100) (preceding year=100)

地 区	Region	2004 总指数 General Index	2004 种植业产品 Planting Products	2004 林业产品 Forestry Products	2004 牧业产品 Animal Husbandry Products	2004 渔业产品 Fishing Products	2005 总指数 General Index	2005 种植业产品 Planting Products	2005 林业产品 Forestry Products	2005 牧业产品 Animal Husbandry Products	2005 渔业产品 Fishing Products
全 国	**National Total**	**113.1**	**115.9**	**104.6**	**111.1**	**110.2**	**101.4**	**101.5**	**104.8**	**100.5**	**104.7**
北 京	Beijing	105.8	103.2	111.4	107.4	106.5	103.5	107.2	108.3	101.2	98.4
天 津	Tianjin	108.1	103.1	98.8	113.6	104.4	103.4	103.5	102.0	103.2	103.2
河 北	Hebei	110.1	107.1	112.3	112.1	127.0	102.5	103.9	100.6	100.4	107.1
山 西	Shanxi	110.6	109.1	106.3	113.9	102.8	103.5	104.2	102.2	102.6	102.3
内蒙古	Inner Mongolia	112.0	112.3	99.0	112.5	112.3	103.2	103.1	103.2	103.5	100.2
辽 宁	Liaoning	120.4	117.7	95.0	124.9	117.8	101.5	100.3	101.7	103.3	107.3
吉 林	Jilin	118.1	119.8	250.6	111.8	87.3	100.3	100.8	106.1	98.9	100.2
黑龙江	Heilongjiang	117.3	117.1	83.8	119.6	104.8	101.0	100.5	99.6	102.0	101.0
上 海	Shanghai	110.8	108.1		107.8	114.7	105.7	108.2		102.1	104.9
江 苏	Jiangsu	122.7	125.0	99.4	127.4	111.9	100.3	100.3	104.8	98.5	102.6
浙 江	Zhejiang	116.8	117.0	98.8	131.2	110.3	105.9	109.6	101.3	103.2	104.9
安 徽	Anhui	117.8	117.7	102.8	120.2	110.1	98.7	97.3	107.4	99.7	105.6
福 建	Fujian	106.8	104.7	102.3	113.9	107.0	103.9	105.1	104.0	100.9	103.8
江 西	Jiangxi	119.5	122.6	109.1	125.5	110.6	100.5	98.9	108.1	98.4	105.0
山 东	Shandong	112.3	111.4	110.2	115.1	110.0	102.9	103.4	101.0	102.8	103.3
河 南	Henan	121.9	118.4	103.8	129.3	109.3	100.7	99.8	104.9	102.0	103.0
湖 北	Hubei	121.7	119.6	100.1	128.2	113.7	100.3	97.9	104.8	100.5	109.1
湖 南	Hunan	127.3	118.1	111.1	134.8	111.8	99.5	103.4	99.8	96.5	105.4
广 东	Guangdong	110.7	108.9	108.3	118.1	106.1	103.5	104.5	103.9	100.8	104.6
广 西	Guangxi	118.9	104.1	105.3	132.3	109.9	100.0	107.4	98.4	94.5	97.9
海 南	Hainan	106.4	105.7	106.3	115.2	101.5	102.2	101.0	106.8	98.8	105.0
重 庆	Chongqing	125.5	120.3		128.8	107.8	100.0	102.2	100.6	98.8	105.7
四 川	Sichuan	120.4	121.0	104.4	121.5	109.4	103.2	103.9	102.0	102.3	106.5
贵 州	Guizhou	111.1	110.7	106.0	111.7	106.2	101.8	102.5	102.8	101.0	102.7
云 南	Yunnan	112.9	110.7	115.8	116.8	111.6	104.0	103.9	115.3	100.9	111.3
西 藏	Tibet										
陕 西	Shaanxi	111.7	110.3	95.1	115.9	110.3	104.9	108.5	96.9	96.5	95.4
甘 肃	Gansu	113.1	113.0	100.0	113.7	100.0	103.1	103.3	99.7	102.7	101.4
青 海	Qinghai	108.8	111.5		106.7		103.3	102.2		104.1	
宁 夏	Ningxia	114.2	120.2		109.2	132.9	103.3	103.0		103.5	106.3
新 疆	Xinjiang	100.8	96.8	98.8	103.0	122.9	108.3	118.4	87.3	92.7	96.1

9–11 各地区工业品出厂价格指数

Ex-Factory Price Indices of Industrial Products by Region

(上年=100) (preceding year=100)

地 区	Region	1998	1999	2000	2001	2002	2003	2004	2005
全 国	**National**	**95.9**	**97.6**	**102.8**	**98.7**	**97.8**	**102.3**	**106.1**	**104.9**
北 京	Beijing	95.1	97.8	102.5	99.4	96.6	101.5	103.0	101.3
天 津	Tianjin	94.7	96.4	102.8	95.9	95.9	102.5	104.1	100.1
河 北	Hebei	94.4	95.9	105.3	99.9	99.4	107.1	111.6	104.4
山 西	Shanxi	97.5	95.3	100.9	100.3	103.6	112.2	116.1	110.2
内蒙古	Inner Mongolia	98.0	100.4	102.8	100.1	99.3	103.2	105.1	105.1
辽 宁	Liaoning	95.8	102.0	108.8	98.6	97.8	103.6	107.1	105.1
吉 林	Jilin	96.9	100.1	105.1	100.3	98.6	102.5	105.0	104.3
黑龙江	Heilongjiang	97.7	107.4	122.9	95.9	97.8	111.9	113.1	116.7
上 海	Shanghai	93.9	97.6	102.5	96.7	96.4	101.4	103.6	101.7
江 苏	Jiangsu	94.5	96.1	101.1	99.1	97.6	102.3	106.5	102.6
浙 江	Zhejiang	96.0	96.8	101.1	98.3	96.9	100.6	105.0	102.3
安 徽	Anhui	96.4	92.9	98.9	98.6	99.8	103.5	108.2	103.3
福 建	Fujian	95.7	96.6	100.5	98.1	97.2	100.7	102.6	100.2
江 西	Jiangxi	98.4	96.1	101.0	98.1	98.5	104.0	109.7	108.8
山 东	Shandong	96.0	97.2	105.9	99.1	98.8	103.5	106.4	103.7
河 南	Henan	95.3	95.4	104.0	100.5	98.6	105.0	110.2	106.1
湖 北	Hubei	96.2	97.8	101.7	99.0	98.2	103.5	105.7	104.5
湖 南	Hunan	95.9	98.5	102.9	99.8	99.2	102.6	108.0	105.9
广 东	Guangdong	94.8	97.7	103.4	98.5	96.5	99.3	101.7	101.5
广 西	Guangxi	95.4	95.6	105.5	106.3	95.6	102.8	109.7	104.9
海 南	Hainan					98.7	99.5	100.0	99.5
重 庆	Chongqing	94.6	97.7	98.6	98.1	97.6	100.6	103.3	103.0
四 川	Sichuan	97.3	97.0	98.1	100.4	97.7	100.5	105.4	104.0
贵 州	Guizhou	98.2	99.7	100.4	102.2	98.9	103.4	108.0	107.2
云 南	Yunnan	97.2	98.2	101.2	99.9	98.2	101.4	108.8	104.5
西 藏	Tibet								
陕 西	Shaanxi	96.6	97.9	101.5	100.4	100.7	105.7	107.3	110.4
甘 肃	Gansu	95.2	98.1	107.2	98.5	97.9	110.0	114.3	109.6
青 海	Qinghai	100.7	102.8	108.1	93.7	97.6	105.5	111.2	110.2
宁 夏	Ningxia	97.7	98.4	103.6	100.3	99.7	103.9	110.0	106.2
新 疆	Xinjiang	95.8	100.2	129.4	96.3	97.3	115.1	116.4	116.6

9-12 按行业分工业品出厂价格指数
Ex-Factory Price Indices of Industrial Products by Sector

(上年=100) (preceding year=100)

年份 Year	总指数 General Index	冶金工业 Metallurgical Industry	电力工业 Power Industry	煤炭工业 Coal Industry	石油工业 Petroleum Industry	化学工业 Chemical Industry	机械工业 Machine Building Industry	建筑材料工业 Building Materials Industry
1980	100.5	106.2	98.4	106.4	102.1	98.2	97.5	102.5
1985	108.7	114.3	103.4	117.6	107.2	102.9	111.8	115.4
1989	118.6	121.0	105.9	112.2	108.4	119.4	121.2	123.6
1990	104.1	110.3	107.4	106.2	107.1	101.6	102.8	99.6
1991	106.2	114.2	116.9	113.1	118.8	102.4	102.8	106.1
1992	106.8	114.2	108.8	116.1	115.3	102.7	106.6	111.1
1993	124.0	157.7	135.9	139.7	171.3	108.3	119.7	142.8
1994	119.5	106.8	139.5	122.2	148.7	115.4	109.5	107.6
1995	114.9	105.5	109.5	111.3	121.2	126.2	106.3	106.4
1996	102.9	97.7	113.1	113.7	104.6	103.4	101.6	104.3
1997	99.7	97.3	114.0	108.0	107.4	95.5	98.1	99.6
1998	95.9	93.1	105.5	96.6	93.0	92.9	97.0	96.6
1999	97.6	95.8	100.9	94.8	109.6	96.5	97.0	97.7
2000	102.8	103.3	102.4	98.1	144.3	101.0	97.4	99.6
2001	98.7	98.6	102.3	106.5	99.1	97.1	96.8	99.0
2002	97.8	97.6	100.8	111.6	95.2	97.6	96.2	97.8
2003	102.3	106.8	100.9	107.0	115.6	102.3	97.0	99.6
2004	106.1	116.9	102.4	115.9	114.2	107.7	99.4	103.5
2005	104.9	106.8	104.2	118.2	122.4	106.8	99.3	100.7

9-12 续表 continued

(上年=100) (preceding year=100)

年份 Year	森林工业 Timber Industry	食品工业 Food Industry	纺织工业 Textile Industry	缝纫工业 Tailoring Industry	皮革工业 Leather Industry	造纸工业 Paper Industry	文教艺术用品工业 Cultural, Educational & Handicrafts Articles
1980	104.5	101.2	101.6	100.8	102.4	100.5	101.6
1985	114.9	105.5	104.3	105.1	112.1	113.7	103.2
1989	115.7	114.3	122.4	118.9	118.3	123.0	111.0
1990	94.6	101.0	107.2	109.1	106.3	102.3	107.3
1991	100.4	103.3	104.1	109.0	109.0	102.9	105.8
1992	105.9	106.2	99.3	100.8	112.8	102.7	102.3
1993	131.8	113.5	103.8	117.9	111.8	108.9	110.6
1994	106.9	123.4	136.8	116.1	121.9	106.6	109.1
1995	99.5	123.2	117.3	116.5	121.7	144.5	111.4
1996	98.2	104.2	96.0	108.2	111.3	116.1	101.5
1997	99.3	99.6	98.0	103.9	98.3	94.5	100.0
1998	95.4	98.6	94.1	97.7	98.3	94.1	94.4
1999	100.1	96.7	96.0	98.0	96.8	95.9	93.6
2000	99.2	95.8	104.7	99.4	100.2	99.9	99.2
2001	99.6	100.5	98.7	99.2	100.8	99.7	97.9
2002	98.6	99.6	94.7	98.7	99.3	97.9	97.4
2003	99.3	101.1	102.2	99.9	99.8	98.7	98.6
2004	102.1	106.5	104.7	101.1	101.0	101.3	99.8
2005	101.9	100.9	100.3	100.5	102.5	101.4	100.3

9-13 工业品出厂价格分类指数
Ex-Factory Price Indices of Industrial Products

(上年=100) (preceding year=100)

类 别	Item	1998	1999	2000	2001	2002	2003	2004	2005
全部工业品	**Total Industry Products**	**95.9**	**97.6**	**102.8**	**98.7**	**97.8**	**102.3**	**106.1**	**104.9**
生产资料	**Means of Production**	**95.4**	**98.3**	**105.1**	**98.8**	**97.7**	**103.6**	**107.8**	**106.8**
采掘工业	Mining & Quarrying Industry	98.4	104.5	124.9	100.1	101.9	113.3	118.8	125.8
原材料工业	Raw Materials Industry	93.4	98.2	108.4	99.7	98.0	106.7	110.2	109.8
加工工业	Manufacturing Industry	96.8	97.1	98.6	98.1	96.9	100.2	104.8	102.2
生活资料	**Consumer Goods**	**96.9**	**96.4**	**97.8**	**98.5**	**97.9**	**98.9**	**101.2**	**99.8**
食品类	Food	98.9	97.4	96.0	100.5	99.7	100.9	105.2	100.9
衣着类	Clothing	96.2	96.1	100.6	99.0	98.8	99.8	100.9	100.8
一般日用品	Articles for Daily Use	96.7	96.0	98.0	98.3	97.9	99.5	101.9	101.9
耐用消费品	Durable Consumer Goods	94.0	95.6	96.4	95.3	94.7	95.6	96.2	96.8

9-14 原材料、燃料、动力购进价格指数
Indices of Purchasing Prices of Raw Materials, Fuels and Power

(上年=100) (preceding year=100)

年 份 Year	总指数 General Index	燃料、动力类 Fuel and Power	黑色金属材料类 Ferrous Metals	有色金属材料类 Nonferrous Metals	化工原料类 Raw Chemical Materials	木材及纸浆类 Timber and Paper Pulp	建材类 Building Materials	农副产品类 Agricultural Products	纺织原料类 Textile Materials
1989	126.4	124.7	130.3	127.6	124.4	111.4	122.7	128.9	128.5
1990	105.6	110.7	103.9	97.2	95.6	99.4	115.2	107.8	107.4
1991	109.1	112.9	112.5	101.2	99.8	105.6	101.2	106.8	108.9
1992	111.0	116.4	114.5	112.4	102.6	102.0	118.8	103.4	100.5
1993	135.1	136.7	174.1	115.8	114.3	128.6	140.9	112.2	107.1
1994	118.2	118.0	103.8	110.7	111.7	115.1	114.3	148.3	139.6
1995	115.3	108.7	98.2	128.3	127.2	115.8	102.6	143.1	123.6
1996	103.9	110.2	99.3	92.4	98.0	101.9	102.5	114.7	94.5
1997	101.3	109.3	97.4	96.2	97.1	100.9	99.7	102.0	94.7
1998	95.8	99.1	95.1	88.3	93.6	96.7	98.6	94.5	94.3
1999	96.7	100.9	94.7	98.9	97.6	100.4	98.8	89.8	96.8
2000	105.1	115.4	100.9	110.3	105.6	99.8	101.5	99.9	102.4
2001	99.8	100.2	100.5	95.6	98.4	100.4	98.6	101.2	99.7
2002	97.7	100.1	98.2	96.5	97.5	98.7	98.2	95.7	97.1
2003	104.8	107.4	107.9	105.3	102.9	100.3	99.7	106.7	101.4
2004	111.4	109.7	120.4	120.1	108.9	102.8	105.1	114.2	104.7
2005	108.3	115.0	107.5	114.0	108.3	103.5	103.1	101.7	102.4

9-15 各地区固定资产投资价格指数

Price Indices of Investment in Fixed Assets by Region

(上年=100) (preceding year=100)

地区	Region	2004				2005			
		固定资产投资 Investment in Fixed Assets	建筑安装工程 Construction and Installation	设备工、器具 Purchase of Equipment, Tools and Instruments	其他费用 Others	固定资产投资 Investment in Fixed Assets	建筑安装工程 Construction and Installation	设备工、器具 Purchase of Equipment, Tools and Instruments	其他费用 Others
全国	**National Total**	**105.6**	**108.2**	**99.4**	**103.5**	**101.6**	**101.8**	**99.4**	**103.2**
北京	Beijing	104.3	107.7	95.3	101.3	100.7	100.5	98.4	101.9
天津	Tianjin	107.3	111.3	100.5	101.0	101.2	101.4	99.1	102.6
河北	Hebei	107.0	109.6	103.6	102.1	101.9	101.8	101.9	102.0
山西	Shanxi	105.2	106.5	102.5	102.0	103.0	102.7	104.3	102.5
内蒙古	Inner Mongolia	105.0	105.9	104.1	101.4	103.7	104.5	101.2	103.4
辽宁	Liaoning	104.8	107.5	99.9	102.0	102.8	103.7	101.7	100.9
吉林	Jilin	104.1	105.6	101.1	102.9	102.0	102.5	100.1	103.0
黑龙江	Heilongjiang	105.0	106.3	100.5	102.0	102.2	102.2	101.8	102.9
上海	Shanghai	106.7	110.6	99.4	104.7	100.8	100.9	97.4	103.2
江苏	Jiangsu	109.4	114.1	100.5	107.5	100.9	99.6	100.5	106.5
浙江	Zhejiang	105.9	108.7	102.1	103.4	100.3	99.3	100.3	103.1
安徽	Anhui	106.1	108.1	100.1	105.6	101.0	101.0	100.3	102.3
福建	Fujian	103.4	106.7	96.8	101.3	100.7	101.1	97.6	102.8
江西	Jiangxi	107.4	109.6	100.4	107.4	100.5	99.2	100.3	107.2
山东	Shandong	107.4	110.4	101.1	106.7	102.9	103.7	100.8	103.5
河南	Henan	110.1	113.6	103.9	102.5	101.4	101.3	101.5	101.9
湖北	Hubei	106.0	109.2	99.6	104.7	102.2	102.1	100.7	104.5
湖南	Hunan	105.5	107.9	99.1	103.4	103.6	104.3	100.7	104.1
广东	Guangdong	106.4	109.9	98.4	102.0	101.6	102.3	98.7	102.2
广西	Guangxi	104.6	106.8	99.3	101.6	101.4	101.3	100.8	102.0
海南	Hainan	105.6	109.7	100.0	101.7	101.2	101.4	99.8	103.9
重庆	Chongqing	105.1	107.0	98.8	102.7	102.3	102.2	99.7	104.6
四川	Sichuan	106.8	110.1	99.5	101.7	103.9	105.3	99.8	103.5
贵州	Guizhou	104.9	106.4	103.4	100.5	101.4	101.8	100.5	100.9
云南	Yunnan	108.0	110.4	102.4	105.7	104.6	105.4	102.3	103.9
西藏	Tibet								
陕西	Shaanxi	104.5	106.0	99.7	101.5	103.7	103.7	105.3	100.5
甘肃	Gansu	105.5	106.7	104.8	100.4	102.2	102.4	102.2	100.6
青海	Qinghai	102.8	103.2	100.1	104.4	102.1	102.1	100.7	104.2
宁夏	Ningxia	104.9	107.1	99.1	102.6	102.1	102.2	101.3	101.8
新疆	Xinjiang	104.5	105.8	101.9	100.7	102.8	102.7	104.8	100.0

9-16 按工业行业分工业品出厂价格指数

Ex-Factory Price Indices of Industrial Products by Sector

(上年＝100) (preceding year=100)

行业	Sector	2002	2003	2004	2005
工业品出厂价格指数	**Ex-Factory Price Indices of Industrial Products**	**97.8**	**102.3**	**106.1**	**104.9**
煤炭开采和洗选业	Mining and Washing of Coal	113.0	103.8	116.8	123.2
石油和天然气开采业	Extraction of Petroleum and Natural Gas	94.6	119.1	119.6	129.9
黑色金属矿采选业	Mining and Processing of Ferrous Metal Ores	101.0	110.4	145.3	112.3
有色金属矿采选业	Mining and Processing of Non-Ferrous Metal Ores	100.8	107.2	117.6	119.6
非金属矿采选业	Mining and Processing of Nonmetal Ores	100.2	100.2	105.8	109.4
农副食品加工业	Processing of Food from Agricultural Products	98.5	103.1	114.0	101.1
食品制造业	Foodstuff	99.0	99.7	102.9	101.5
饮料制造业	Manufacture of Beverages	99.2	99.2	100.6	100.6
烟草制品业	Manufacture of Tobacco	103.5	100.6	101.1	100.9
纺织业	Manufacture of Textile	95.2	101.8	104.3	100.5
纺织服装、鞋、帽制造业	Manufacture of Textile Wearing Apparel, Footware, and Caps	99.1	99.8	100.7	99.8
皮革、毛皮、羽毛(绒)及其制品业	Manufacture of Leather, Fur, Feather and Related Products	99.1	99.7	100.9	102.5
木材加工及木、竹、藤、棕、草制品业	Processing of Timber, Manufacture of Wood, Bamboo, Rattan, Palm, and Straw Products	96.8	99.1	102.2	101.8
家具制造业	Manufacture of Furniture	99.0	99.6	101.8	102.7
造纸及纸制品业	Manufacture of Paper and Paper Products	97.6	98.7	101.3	101.4
印刷业和记录媒介的复制	Printing, Reproduction of Recording Media	97.0	97.6	98.1	99.6
文教体育用品制造业	Manufacture of Articles For Culture, Education and Sport Activity	97.9	100.2	102.2	102.0
石油加工、炼焦及核燃料加工业	Processing of Petroleum, Coking, Processing of Nuclear Fuel	96.4	114.7	112.2	118.4
化学原料及化学制品制造业	Manufacture of Raw Chemical Materials and Chemical Products	98.9	103.4	110.2	108.5
医药制造业	Manufacture of Medicines	98.3	98.8	97.8	101.6
化学纤维制造业	Manufacture of Chemical Fibers	93.4	104.5	108.1	104.7
橡胶制品业	Manufacture of Rubber	97.7	100.0	101.0	104.5
塑料制品业	Manufacture of Plastics	96.2	99.8	106.5	105.5
非金属矿物制品业	Manufacture of Non-metallic Mineral Products	97.7	99.6	103.3	100.6
黑色金属冶炼及压延加工业	Smelting and Pressing of Ferrous Metals	98.5	110.1	118.9	104.7
有色金属冶炼及压延加工业	Smelting and Pressing of Non-ferrous Metals	95.4	105.1	118.9	111.7
金属制品业	Manufacture of Metal Products	97.6	100.4	107.4	104.0
通用设备制造业	Manufacture of General Purpose Machinery	98.2	99.8	103.1	101.8
专用设备制造业	Manufacture of Special Purpose Machinery	98.9	99.6	101.8	101.8
交通运输设备制造业	Manufacture of Transport Equipment	96.8	97.9	98.2	98.9
电气机械及器材制造业	Manufacture of Electrical Machinery and Equipment		97.9	103.7	103.2
通信设备、计算机及其他电子设备制造业	Manufacture of Communication Equipment, Computers and Other Electronic Equipment	96.5	93.7	95.1	95.3
仪器仪表及文化、办公用机械制造业	Manufacture of Measuring Instruments and Machinery for Cultural Activity and Office Work	93.1	97.3	98.5	98.7
工艺品及其他制造业	Manufacture of Artwork and Other Manufacturing	95.2	102.1	105.7	103.9
废弃资源和废旧材料回收加工业	Recycling and Disposal of Waste	100.7	111.5	116.9	105.3
电力、热力的生产和供应业	Production and Supply of Electric Power and Heat Power	100.7	100.9	102.4	104.2
燃气生产和供应业	Production and Supply of Gas	101.3	103.3	102.5	105.2
水的生产和供应业	Production and Supply of Water	106.2	105.3	104.1	104.0

9-17 房地产价格指数

Price Indices for Real Estate

(上年=100) (preceding year=100)

项 目	Item	2000	2002	2003	2004	2005
房屋销售价格指数	**Selling Price Indices of Houses**	**101.1**	**103.7**	**104.8**	**109.7**	**107.6**
商品房	Commercial Houses	100.8	103.4	105.0	109.0	107.7
住宅	Residential Buildings	101.4	104.0	105.7	109.4	108.4
经济适用房	Economically Affordable Housing	101.4	101.8	102.6	103.2	103.7
普通住宅	General Residential Buildings	101.5	104.3	106.2	109.8	108.2
多层住宅	Multilayer Buildings	102.3	105.5	106.8	109.9	108.5
高层住宅	High-layer Buildings	102.4	103.0	106.1	109.7	107.6
其他住宅	Other Buildings					115.6
高档住宅	Luxury Residential Buildings	101.3	101.7	104.0	110.0	109.5
别墅	Villas	101.4	102.1	104.3	109.6	109.0
高档公寓	High-grade Apartment	101.1	101.5	103.8	110.3	109.7
非住宅	Non-Residential Buildings	98.7	101.3	102.7	107.1	105.6
办公楼	Office Buildings	98.1	99.8	103.4	108.1	107.2
商业娱乐用房	Business and Entertainment	99.6	102.4	102.3	107.0	104.6
工业仓储用房	Industrial Storage					103.9
其他用房	Others	96.9	102.1	103.7	103.9	103.8
二手房	Second-hand House					107.5
住宅	Residential Buildings					108.4
非住宅	Non-residential Buildings					105.5
土地交易价格指数	**Transactions Price Indices of Land**	**100.2**	**106.9**	**108.3**	**110.1**	**109.1**
居民用地	Land for Residential Building Use	101.0	107.7	112.4	111.6	110.3
高档住宅用地	Luxury Residential Buildings	101.6	101.9	105.9	107.6	120.5
普通住宅用地	General Residential Buildings	100.9	108.4	113.0	111.8	108.9
经济适用房用地	Economically Affordable Housing					105.3
工业仓储用地	Land for Industry Use	98.6	100.4	101.3	104.3	103.6
商业、旅游、娱乐用地	Land for Business Tour and Entertainment	100.4	107.0	104.9	110.4	107.9
其他用地	Land for Other	99.8	106.9	104.4	105.5	106.7
房屋租赁价格指数	**Renting Price Indices of Houses**	**102.4**	**100.8**	**101.9**	**101.4**	**101.9**
住宅	Residential Buildings	114.2	102.0	107.5	102.2	100.5
普通住宅	General Residential Buildings					100.6
高档住宅	Luxury Residential Buildings					100.1
经济适用房	Economically Affordable Housing					101.2
廉租房	Tenement House					100.0
办公楼	Office Buildings	96.2	99.5	99.9	100.2	102.9
写字楼	High-grade Office Buildings	95.2	101.1	100.2	99.9	103.4
普通办公用房	General Office Buildings	96.9	98.6	99.7	100.8	100.8
商业娱乐用房	Business and Entertainment Buildings	99.0	100.2	99.6	102.0	101.7
工业仓库用房	Industrial Storage Buildings	99.6	100.7	100.5	100.9	99.9
其他用房	Other Buildings					104.5
物业管理价格指数	**Property Management Price Indices**					**100.0**
住宅	Residential Buildings					100.1
办公楼	Office Buildings					99.9
商业娱乐用房	Business and Entertainment Buildings					99.8
工业仓储用房	Industrial Storage Buildings					100.4

9-18 全国和35个大中城市房地产价格指数

Price Indices of Real Estate in China and 35 Large and Medium-sized Cities

(上年=100)

(preceding year=100)

地区	Region	房屋销售价格指数 Selling Price Indices of Houses		土地交易价格指数 Transactions Price Indices of Land		房屋租赁价格指数 Renting Price Indices of Houses		物业管理价格指数 Property Management Price Indices
		2004	2005	2004	2005	2004	2005	2005
总计	**Total**	**109.7**	**107.6**	**110.1**	**109.1**	**101.4**	**101.9**	**100.0**
北京	Beijing	103.7	106.7	102.5	103.8	103.4	102.4	100.5
天津	Tianjin	113.5	106.0	116.3	103.9	101.2	101.3	100.2
石家庄	Shijiazhuang	103.6	105.6	100.3	100.2	100.1	100.6	100.2
太原	Taiyuan	106.4	105.6	100.7	102.8	99.6	107.5	100.0
呼和浩特	Hohhot	105.2	111.8	104.1	114.7	101.5	104.7	100.0
沈阳	Shenyang	115.9	107.5	116.2	111.4	99.0	101.5	100.5
大连	Dalian	104.6	109.2	112.9	124.7	98.2	99.0	98.4
长春	Changchun	100.2	101.9	104.6	103.9	100.9	100.5	100.0
哈尔滨	Harbin	104.7	104.6	100.0	107.8	100.6	103.6	100.0
上海	Shanghai	115.9	109.7	120.3	106.9	105.5	103.6	100.5
南京	Nanjing	115.3	108.1	103.0	102.8	105.0	100.0	101.0
杭州	Hangzhou	111.7	109.7	139.4	124.8	107.6	102.4	100.4
宁波	Ningbo	113.9	106.4	108.3	115.9	104.3	104.1	100.5
合肥	Hefei	105.6	106.2	105.4	110.6	100.7	100.3	102.5
福州	Fuzhou	103.6	104.4	108.8	118.6	99.6	101.4	100.3
厦门	Xiamen	107.3	108.0	110.2	108.5	102.3	104.2	100.4
南昌	Nanchang	107.3	108.3	118.8	104.2	101.4	102.5	100.3
济南	Jinan	110.3	107.6	104.4	105.9	103.4	101.0	100.0
青岛	Qingdao	115.3	110.9	101.8	103.4	98.6	103.3	100.2
郑州	Zhengzhou	104.0	107.0	103.9	110.9	99.7	100.1	100.2
武汉	Wuhan	108.4	106.8	102.9	102.6	100.7	100.2	98.9
长沙	Changsha	103.3	102.8	102.1	105.4	103.1	101.7	99.9
广州	Guangzhou	102.7	104.7	100.0	100.0	101.6	103.0	102.1
深圳	Shenzhen	104.6	107.2	103.9	118.1	100.0	101.0	99.2
南宁	Nanning	105.7	104.9	100.0	103.6	100.6	101.6	100.2
海口	Haikou	105.9	102.5	102.7	110.0	96.1	101.9	100.0
重庆	Chongqing	113.9	107.2	105.3	102.9	105.9	103.6	100.1
成都	Chengdu	107.9	109.8	116.3	107.8	102.4	100.4	101.2
贵阳	Guiyang	102.6	102.6	100.6	101.5	99.9	102.5	99.5
昆明	Kunming	102.3	102.9	100.0	103.7	104.2	101.4	100.0
西安	Xi'an	105.0	104.3	102.8	105.9	103.2	100.7	100.4
兰州	Lanzhou	108.7	105.6	100.0	100.0	97.8	100.0	101.4
西宁	Xining	104.0	103.4	106.1	102.9	100.4	99.8	100.0
银川	Yinchuan	104.4	102.7	105.8	103.4	106.1	104.3	100.0
乌鲁木齐	Urumqi	100.7	100.9	102.1	101.4	104.2	100.4	99.8

主要统计指标解释

居民消费价格指数　是反映一定时期内城乡居民所购买的生活消费品价格和服务项目价格变动趋势和程度的相对数，是对城市居民消费价格指数和农村居民消费价格指数进行综合汇总计算的结果。该指数可以观察和分析消费品的零售价格和服务价格变动对城乡居民实际生活费支出的影响程度。

城市居民消费价格指数　是反映一定时期内城市居民家庭所购买的生活消费品价格和服务项目价格变动趋势和程度的相对数。该指数可以观察和分析消费品的零售价格和服务项目价格变动对城镇职工货币工资的影响，作为研究职工生活和确定工资政策的依据。

农村居民消费价格指数　是反映一定时期内农村居民家庭所购买的生活消费品价格和服务项目价格变动趋势和程度的相对数。该指数可以观察农村消费品的零售价格和服务项目价格变动对农村居民生活消费支出的影响，直接反映农民生活水平的实际变化情况，为分析和研究农村居民生活问题提供依据。

商品零售价格指数　是反映一定时期内城乡商品零售价格变动趋势和程度的相对数。商品零售价格的变动直接影响到城乡居民的生活支出和国家的财政收入，影响居民购买力和市场供需的平衡，影响到消费与积累的比例关系。因此，该指数可以从一个侧面对上述经济活动进行观察和分析。

农业生产资料价格指数　指反映一定时期内农业生产资料价格变动趋势和程度的相对数。农业生产资料价格指数分为小农具、饲料、产品畜、役畜、半机械化农具、机械化农具、化学肥料、农药及农药械、农机用油、其他农业生产资料十大类。其编制目的是了解农业生产中物质资料投入价格的变动状况，服务于国民经济核算。1994年以前，农业生产资料价格指数仅仅是商品零售价格指数的一个类别，此后，从商品零售价格指数中分离出来，单独编制。

农产品生产价格指数　是反映一定时期内，农产品生产者出售农产品价格水平变动趋势及幅度的相对数。该指数可以客观反映全国农产品生产价格水平和结构变动情况，满足农业与国民经济核算需要。其中某代表品生产价格指数是通过对全部有出售该产品行为的调查单位的个体指数进行几何平均求得的，类价格指数是通过对其所属的类（或代表品）的价格指数进行加权平均求得的。季度累计价格指数的计算方法与分季指数的计算方法相同。

工业品出厂价格指数　是反映一定时期内全部工业产品出厂价格总水平的变动趋势和程度的相对数，包括工业企业售给本企业以外所有单位的各种产品和直接售给居民用于生活消费的产品。该指数可以观察出厂价格变动对工业总产值及增加值的影响。

原材料、燃料和动力购进价格指数　是反映工业企业作为生产投入，而从物资交易市场和能源、原材料生产企业购买原材料、燃料和动力产品时，所支付的价格水平变动趋势和程度的统计指标，是扣除工业企业物质消耗成本中的价格变动影响的重要依据。

目前，我国编制的原材料、燃料和动力购进价格指数所调查的产品包括燃料动力、黑色金属、有色金属、化工、建材等九大类的近1800种产品。

固定资产投资价格指数　是反映一定时期内固定资产投资品及项目的价格变动趋势和程度的相对数。固定资产投资额是由建筑安装工程投资完成额、设备工器具购置投资完成额和其他费用投资完成额三部分组成的。编制固定资产投资价格指数应首先分别编制上述三部分投资的价格指数，然后采用加权算术平均法求出固定资产投资价格总指数。

该指数可以准确地反映固定资产投资中涉及的各类投资品和取费项目价格变动趋势和变动幅度，消除按现价计算的固定资产投资指标中的价格变动因素，真实地反映固定资产投资的规模、速度、结构和效益，为国家科学地制定、检查固定资产投资计划并提高宏观调控水平，为完善国民经济核算体系提供科学的、可靠的依据。

房地产价格指数　是反映一定时期内房地产价格变动趋势和程度的相对数，包括房屋销售价格指数、房屋租赁价格指数、土地交易价格指数和物业管理价格指数。这四套指数的计算方法相似，均采用由下到上逐级汇总的方法。

Explanatory Notes on Main Statistical Indicators

Urban Consumer Price Indices reflect the trend and degree of changes in prices of consumer goods and services purchased by urban households during a given period. It can be used to observe and analyze the impact of price changes in consumer goods and services on wages (in monetary terms) of urban staff and workers, and provide basis for policy-making concerning the living cost and wages of staff and workers.

Rural Consumer Price Indices reflect the trend and degree of changes in prices of consumer goods and services purchased by rural households during a given period. It can be used to observe the impact of change in retail prices of consumer goods and service prices in rural areas on living expenditure of rural households, and to show the changes in the living standard of peasants. It provides basis for analysis and research on condition of life in rural areas.

Retail Price Indices reflect the trend and degree of change in retail prices of commodities during a given period. The change in retail prices of commodities directly affect the living expenditure of urban and rural residents, government revenue, purchasing power of residents and the equilibrium of market supply and demand, and the ratio of consumption to accumulation. Therefore, the retail price indices are useful to analyze the changes of the above economic activities.

Price Indices of Means of Agricultural Production reflect the trend and degree of changes in prices of means of agricultural production during a given period. Price indices of means of agricultural production are composed of 10 categories including small farm tools, feeds, domestic animals for meat, draught domestic animals, semi-mechanized farm machinery, mechanized farm machinery, chemical fertilizers, pesticides and spraying machinery, fuels for farm machinery and other means of agricultural production. Compilation of these indices helps to understand the changes in prices of input into agricultural production and facilitate the compilation of national account statistics. Before 1994, price indices of means of agricultural production was a sub-category in the in the retail price indices of commodities, and it has been compiled separately since 1994.

Indices of Producers' Prices for Farm Products reflect the trend and degree of changes in producers' prices received by farmers when they sell farm products during a given period. These indices depict the change in the level and structure of producers' prices of farm products of the country and meet the needs of agriculture statistics and national account statistics. The producers' price index of a given product is calculated through geometrical mean of individual indices of all surveyed units who sell such product, and the indices of a product category is obtained through weighted mean of price indices of all products in the category. Method for calculating accumulative quarterly indices is the same as for calculating the distinctive quarterly indices.

Ex-factory Price Indices of Industrial Products reflect the trend and degree of changes in general ex-factory prices of all industrial products during a given period, including sales of industrial products by an industrial enterprise to all units outside the enterprise, as well as sales of consumer goods to residents. It can be used to analyze the impact of ex-factory prices on gross output value and value-added of the industrial sector.

Indices of Purchasing Prices of Raw Materials, Fuels and Power reflect changes in the level and degree of prices paid by industrial enterprises when they purchase production input such as raw materials, fuels and power from the market or from other energy or raw materials producing enterprises. These indices provide important basis for measuring the material consumption of industrial enterprises after removing influence of price changes.

At present, close to 1,800 products in 9 categories, including fuels and power, ferrous metals, non-ferrous metals, chemicals, building materials, are covered in China for the survey to produce indices of purchasing prices of raw materials, fuels and power.

Price Indices of Investment in Fixed Assets reflect the trend and degree of changes in prices of investment goods and projects in fixed assets during a given period. The investment in fixed assets consists of three components, namely the investment in construction and installation, the investment in purchases of equipment and instrument, and the investment in other items. Price indices of investment in fixed assets are calculated as the weighted arithmetic mean of the price indices of the three components of investment in fixed assets.

Removing the factor of price change in the aggregates of investment at current prices, this indicator shows the changes in the prices of commodities and fees involved in the investment of fixed assets, and can be used to observe the actual size, growth, structure, and efficiency of investment in fixed assets and provides reliable and scientific data for government planning, management, decision-making, and further improving the current national accounting system.

Price Indices for Real Estate reflect the trend and degree of changes in prices of real estate during a given period, including price indices for selling houses and buildings, price indices for leasing houses and buildings and price indices for land transaction. The methods for the compilation of the three sets of indices are similar in that they all use bottom-up approach under which data are reported from lower level to higher level.

10

人民生活

People's Livelihood

简 要 说 明

一、本篇资料的主要内容

本篇资料反映我国人民生活现状及变化情况，分为城镇居民生活和农村居民生活两部分。

二、城镇居民生活资料来源

城镇居民生活状况的数据来源于国家统计局城市社会经济调查司的城镇住户调查，是对城镇居民家庭抽样调查汇总的结果。调查内容主要包括家庭人口及其构成、家庭现金收支、主要商品购买数量及支出金额、劳动就业状况、居住状况和耐用消费品的拥有量等。

三、城镇居民生活调查方法

城镇住户调查是由国家统计局城市社会经济调查司组织实施，各省、自治区、直辖市调查队及抽中城市及县的调查队依据国家统计局统一制定的城镇住户调查方案，收集资料并逐级汇总上报。

调查对象在2001年以前为全国非农业住户，2002年以后改为全国城市市区和县城关镇区住户。

城镇住户调查采用固定样本户进行连续记帐的调查方式，每一调查期为3年，每年轮换三分之一。调查户是按“二阶段”、“划类选点”、“等距抽样”随机抽选的。

第一阶段，在全国范围内划类选点直接抽选调查城市。把全国市、县按人口规模划分为特大、大、中、小城市和县城五种类型，然后在此基础上按六大行政区分组。每一行政区内又按城市职工平均工资水平高低排列，再把各城市的职工人数累计起来进行等距抽样，每隔100万职工抽取一个样本城市，作为调查城市。

第二阶段，在抽中的城市内采用多阶段和二相抽样相结合的方法抽取调查户。特大、大城市采用三阶段抽选一相调查样本，即先抽选调查街道，从抽中街道再抽调查居委会、最后从抽中居委会抽选调查户；中小城市及县城采用二阶段抽选一相调查样本，即直接抽选居委会，再从中抽选调查户。第二相样本是在一相样本基础上，采取分层等比例抽选经常性调查户。

按上述办法国家统计局共抽选出调查市、县226个，调查户25000户。加上各地根据同一方案抽选的地方点调查户，共有50000余户。

四、农村居民生活资料来源

农村居民生活状况的数据来源于国家统计局农村社会经济调查司的农村住户抽样调查。主要内容包括农村居民家庭基本情况、生活消费支出、主要消费品消费量、耐用消费品拥有量等。

五、农村居民生活调查方法

农村住户调查是以各省(区、直辖市)为总体，直接抽选调查村，在抽中村中抽选调查户。综合运用多种抽样方法确定住户调查网点。农村住户调查网点分布在全国7100多个村，共抽取了68000多个样本农户。

农村住户调查在95%的概率把握程度下要求抽样误差不得超过±3%。为保证农村住户调查资料的准确性，国家统计局农村经济调查总队为调查户设置了现金和实物两本帐，并聘请了近万名辅助调查员帮助做好记帐工作，及时核实、汇总住户调查资料。

为解决调查户的厌烦情绪及样本老化问题，增强抽样调查网点的代表性，更加准确、及时地反映农村社会经济情况，国家统计局农村社会经济调查司对农村住户调查网点实行样本轮换制度，每五年为一个周期。

Brief Introduction

I. Main Content

Data in this chapter show the conditions of people's livelihood in China, consisting of two parts on the life of urban and rural households respectively.

II. Source of Data on the Livelihood of Urban Residents

Data on the livelihood of the urban residents in this chapter come from the data collected through samples survey on the urban households conducted by the Department of Urban Socio-economic Surveys, NBS. The main content of the survey includes the population in the household and its composition, the cash income and expenditure of the household, the quantity of, and the expenditure on major commodities purchased, the employment of the household members, the housing condition and the possession of the durable consumer goods.

III. Methodology for Urban Household Survey

The survey on the urban households is organized by the Department of Urban Socio-economic Surveys, NBS. The survey organizations of the provinces, autonomous regions and municipalities directly under the central government as well as the survey organizations of the selected cities and counties collect the data in accordance with the survey scheme stipulated by NBS and report them to the higher organization.

Until 2001, the survey covered only non-agricultural households. Starting from 2002, it covers all households in urban areas and county towns.

The survey on the urban households is conducted in such a way that households selected by sampling method keep accounts for successive three years and be interviewed by the enumerators. By a rotation sampling scheme, one third of the old sample households should be replaced by the new sample households every year. The respondent households are selected by the two-stage stratified systematic random sampling scheme.

At the first stage, the cities and counties are firstly classified into 5 categories by their population size, namely the particularly large cities, large cities, medium-sized cities, small cities and counties. Secondly, they are grouped into the 6 administrative regions (northeastern region, north region, eastern region, central region, northwestern region and southwestern region). In each administrative region, the cities and counties are arranged in the order of the average wages of their staff and workers in the urban areas. Thirdly, the number of the staff and workers of the cities are accumulated and the sample cities or counties are selected by a systematic sampling scheme; the sampling interval is one million staff and workers.

At the second stage, the sample households are selected by the multi-stage and two-phase sampling scheme. In the particularly large and large cities, the first phase sample is selected by three-stage sampling method: Firstly, the sample sub-districts are selected; Secondly, the sample residents committees are selected from the sample sub-districts; Thirdly, the sample households are selected from the sample residents committees. In the medium-sized and small cities and counties, the first phase sample is selected by two-stage sampling method: Firstly, the sample residents committees are directly selected; Secondly, the sample households are selected from the sample residents committees. The second phase sample is composed of the sample households which are surveyed in a regular way and these households are selected with stratified sampling method from the households in the first phase sample.

In total, 25,000 households in 226 cities and counties are selected by the National Bureau of Statistics in the above-mentioned approach. Additional local samples are selected by local statistical offices by the same sample design, making the total sample size to reach over 50,000 households.

IV. Source of Data on the Livelihood of Rural Residents

Data on the livelihood of the rural residents come from data collected through the sample survey on the rural households, which is organized by the Department of Rural Socio-economic Surveys, NBS. The main content of the survey includes the basic condition of the rural households, consumption expenditure, consumption of major consumer goods and the quantity of durable consumer goods owned.

V. Methodology for Rural Household Survey

Sample survey on the rural households is conducted by first selecting sample villages and then selecting households in the selected villages in each province, with all rural households in the province as the population. A combination of various sampling approaches are used to identify a total of 68,000 households selected from 7,100 villages throughout the whole country.

It is required that the sampling error should not exceed to ±3%, with confidence of probability as 95%. In order to ensure the accuracy of the data of the survey on the rural households, two accounts are designed for the respondent households by the Rural Socio-economic Survey Organization, NBS, the cash account and the account on goods in kind. Nearly 10 thousand assistant enumerators have been invited to help the households to keep good accounts and check and tabulate the data of the survey.

In order to overcome the boring feeling of the respondent households and solve the problem of aging samples to make the sample more representative of the population and able to reflect the rural social and economic situation more accurately and timely, a rotation sampling scheme is implemented by the Department of Rural Socio-economic Surveys, NBS in selecting the rural sample households, with the cycle of complete rotation being 5 years.

10-1 人民生活基本情况

People's Life

指标名称		Item	1989	1997	2004	2005
就业		**Employment**				
城镇居民家庭每户就业人口	(人)	Average Number of Employed Persons per Urban Household (person)	2.00	1.83	1.56	1.51
农村居民家庭每户整半劳动力	(人)	Average Number of Full/Semi Laborer per Rural Household (person)	2.94	2.79	2.82	2.82
城镇居民家庭每一就业者负担人数	(人)	Number of Dependents per Employee of Urban Household (person)	1.78	1.74	1.91	1.96
农村居民家庭每一劳动力负担人数	(人)	Number of Dependents per Laborer of Rural Household (person)	1.65	1.56	1.45	1.44
城镇登记失业人数	(万人)	Registered Urban Unemployment Persons (10 000 persons)	378	577	827	839
城镇登记失业率	(%)	Registered Urban Unemployment Rate (%)	2.6	3.1	4.2	4.2
本年职业介绍服务机构	(个)	Number of Career Service Organization at the Year-end (unit)		34286	33890	35747
本年登记求职人数	(万人)	Total Registered Job-seekers This Year (10 000 persons)		1162	3583	4129
收入与支出		**Income and Expenditure**				
城镇居民人均可支配收入	(元)	Annual Per Capita Disposable Income of Urban Households (yuan)	1374	5160	9422	10493
农村居民人均纯收入	(元)	Annual Per Capita Disposable Income of Rural Households (yuan)	602	2090	2936	3255
城镇居民人均消费性支出	(元)	Annual Per Capita Consumption Expenditure of Urban Households (yuan)	1211	4186	7182	7943
农村居民人均生活消费支出	(元)	Annual Per Capita Living Expenditure of Rural Households (yuan)	535	1617	2185	2555
人均储蓄存款余额	(元)	Per Capita Balance of Saving Deposit (yuan)	461	3744	9197	10787
生活质量		**Life Quality**				
居民家庭恩格尔系数	(%)	Household's Engle Coefficient (%)				
城镇		Urban	54.5	46.6	37.7	36.7
农村		Rural	54.8	55.1	47.2	45.5
居住条件		Residence Condition				
城市人均住宅建筑面积	(平方米)	Per Capita Building Space in City Areas (sq.m)	13.5	17.8	25.0	26.1
农村人均住房面积	(平方米)	Per Capita Living Space in Rural Areas (sq.m)	17.2	22.5	27.9	29.7
交通条件		Traffic Condition				
城市每万人拥有公交车辆	(标台)	Number of Public Transportation Vehicles per 10 000 Population in City (unit)	2.1	4.5	8.4	8.6
城市人均拥有铺路面积	(平方米)	Per Capita Area of Paved Roads in City (sq.m)	3.2	5.2	10.3	10.9
农村通公路行政村比重	(%)	Percentage of Administrative Village Access to Highway in Rural Area (%)	75.0	85.8	92.9	94.3
城镇每百户拥有家用汽车	(辆)	Number of Family Vehicles Per 100 Urban Households (unit)		0.19	2.18	3.37
农村每百户拥有摩托车	(辆)	Number of Motor Cycles Per 100 Rural Households (unit)	0.95	10.89	36.15	40.70
通信条件		Communication Condition				
电话普及率	(部/百人)	Mobile Telephone Popularization Rate (set/100 persons)	0.98	8.11	50.03	57.22
移动电话普及率	(部/百人)	Mobile Telephone Popularization Rate (set/100 persons)		1.07	25.91	30.26
每千人拥有公用电话数	(部)	Per 1 000 Person Public Telephone (Sets)	0.04	1.57	17.14	20.63
城市公用设施普及占有率		City Public Utility Rate				
用水普及率	(%)	Percentage of Population with Access to Tap Water (%)	47.4	61.2	88.8	91.1
用气普及率	(%)	Percentage of Population with Access to Gas (%)	17.8	40.0	81.5	82.1
人均公共绿地面积	(平方米)	Per Capita Public Green Area (sq.m)	1.7	2.9	7.4	7.9
每万人拥有公共厕所	(座)	Number of Public Toilet per 10 000 Persons (unit)	3.1	3.0	3.2	3.2
人均国内旅游花费	(元)	Per Capita Domestic Expenditure on Tour (yuan)		328.1	427.5	436.1
城镇		Urban		599.8	731.8	737.1
农村		Rural		145.7	210.2	227.6

10-1 续表 continued

指标名称	Item	1989	1997	2004	2005
文化、教育和卫生	**Culture, Education and Sport**				
文化	Culture				
广播人口覆盖率 (%)	Broadcast Covering Rate of Population (%)	73.0	86.0	94.1	94.5
电视人口覆盖率 (%)	TV Covering Rate of Population (%)	77.9	87.6	95.3	95.8
每百户彩色电视机拥有量（部/百户）	Number of Color TV per 100 Households (set)				
城镇	Urban	51.5	100.5	133.4	134.8
农村	Rural	3.6	27.3	75.1	84.0
每百户家用电脑拥有量 （部/百户）	Number of Computer per 100 Households (set)				
城镇	Urban		2.6	33.1	41.5
农村	Rural			1.9	2.1
居民家庭文教娱乐支出比重 (%)	Percentage of Household Expenditure on Education, Culture and Entertainment (%)				
城镇	Urban	11.1	10.7	14.4	13.8
农村	Rural	5.7	9.2	11.3	11.6
教育	Education				
升学率 (%)	Rate of Entering the Higher School (%)				
小学升初中	Entering Middle School from Elementary School	71.5	93.7	98.1	98.4
初中升高级中学	Entering Senior Secondary School from Junior Secondary School	38.3	51.5	62.9	69.7
高中升高等教育	Entering College and University from Senior Secondary School	24.6	48.6	82.5	76.3
平均每一学生占有预算内教育事业费支出 (元)	Budgetary Educational Fund per Student (yuan)				
#普通高校	Regular Institutions of Higher Education		6522.9	5552.5	
普通高中	Regular Senior School		1155.4	1758.6	
普通初中	Regular Junior School		591.4	1246.1	
小学	Primary School		333.8	1129.1	
卫生	Health				
每万人口医院、卫生院床位数 (张)	Number of Hospital Beds per 10 000 Persons (bed)	22.8	23.5	24.0	24.5
每万人口医生数 (人)	Number of Doctor per 10 000 Persons (person)	15.6	16.5	15.0	15.2
人均卫生总费用支出 (元)	Per Capita Expenditure for Public Health (yuan)	76.7	186.4	583.9	
居民家庭医疗保健支出比重 (%)	Percentage of Resident Expenditure on Health Care (%)				
城镇	Urban	1.3	4.3	7.4	7.6
农村	Rural	3.1	3.9	6.0	6.6
社会保障和社区服务	**Social Security and Social Service**				
社会保障	Social Security				
参加基本养老保险职工人数 (万人)	Number of Employee Joining Basic Endowment Insurance (10 000 persons)	4817	8671	12250	13120
参加基本养老保险离退休人数 (万人)	Number of Retiree Joining Basic Endowment Insurance (10 000 persons)	893	2533	4103	4368
参加失业保险职工人数 (万人)	Number of Person Joining Unemployment Insurance (10 000 persons)		7961	10584	10648
参加基本医疗保险人数 (万人)	Number of Person Joining Basic Medical Care System (10 000 persons)		1762	12404	13783
参加农村养老保险人数 (万人)	Number of Person Joining Rural Endowment Insurance (10 000 persons)			5382	5442
人均离休退休费 (元)	Per Capita Retirement Pension (yuan)	1478	5458	9808	10761
社区服务	Social Service				
城镇社区服务设施 (万个)	Number of Urban Community Welfare Facilities (10 000 units)	7.1	13.3	19.8	19.5
城镇便民利民服务网点 (万个)	Number of Urban Community Service Points for Civilian (10 000 units)		30.7	70.4	66.5

注：1.城市人均住宅建筑面积、城市交通状况、城市公用事业资料由建设部提供。
2.城镇居民家庭文教娱乐支出比重1989年为1990年数据。
3.人均卫生总费用支出1989年和1997年分别为1991年和1995年数据。

a) Data of urban per capita residence floor space, traffic, and city public utility are provided by the Ministry of Construction.
b) The percentage of urban household expenditure on education, culture and entertainment in 1989 is the data in 1990.
c) The figures of per capita expenditure for public health in 1989 and 1997 are the data in 1991 and 1995.

10-2 城乡居民家庭人均收入及恩格尔系数

Per Capita Annual Income and Engle Coefficient of Urban and Rural Households

年份 Year	城镇居民家庭人均可支配收入 Per Capita Annual Disposable Income of Urban Households		农村居民家庭人均纯收入 Per Capita Annual Net Income of Rural Households		城镇居民家庭恩格尔系数(%) Engle Coefficient of Urban Households (%)	农村居民家庭恩格尔系数(%) Engle Coefficient of Rural Households (%)
	绝对数(元) Value (yuan)	指数(1978=100) Index	绝对数(元) Value (yuan)	指数(1978=100) Index		
1978	343.4	100.0	133.6	100.0	57.5	67.7
1980	477.6	127.0	191.3	139.0	56.9	61.8
1985	739.1	160.4	397.6	268.9	53.3	57.8
1989	1373.9	182.5	601.5	305.7	54.5	54.8
1990	1510.2	198.1	686.3	311.2	54.2	58.8
1991	1700.6	212.4	708.6	317.4	53.8	57.6
1992	2026.6	232.9	784.0	336.2	53.0	57.6
1993	2577.4	255.1	921.6	346.9	50.3	58.1
1994	3496.2	276.8	1221.0	364.3	50.0	58.9
1995	4283.0	290.3	1577.7	383.6	50.1	58.6
1996	4838.9	301.6	1926.1	418.1	48.8	56.3
1997	5160.3	311.9	2090.1	437.3	46.6	55.1
1998	5425.1	329.9	2162.0	456.1	44.7	53.4
1999	5854.0	360.6	2210.3	473.5	42.1	52.6
2000	6280.0	383.7	2253.4	483.4	39.4	49.1
2001	6859.6	416.3	2366.4	503.7	38.2	47.7
2002	7702.8	472.1	2475.6	527.9	37.7	46.2
2003	8472.2	514.6	2622.2	550.6	37.1	45.6
2004	9421.6	554.2	2936.4	588.0	37.7	47.2
2005	10493.0	607.4	3254.9	624.5	36.7	45.5

10-3 城乡居民人民币储蓄存款

Savings Deposit in Urban and Rural Areas

单位：亿元 (100 million yuan)

年份 Year	年底余额 Outstanding Amount			年增加额 Increased Amount		
	总计 Total	定期 Time Deposits	活期 Demand Deposits	总计 Total	定期 Time Deposits	活期 Demand Deposits
1978	210.6	128.9	81.7	29.0	17.2	11.8
1980	399.5	304.9	94.6	118.5	138.5	-20.0
1985	1622.6	1225.2	397.4	407.9	324.3	83.6
1989	5196.4	4215.4	981.0	1374.2	1366.9	7.3
1990	7119.8	5911.2	1208.6	1923.4	1695.8	227.6
1991	9241.6	7691.7	1549.9	2121.8	1780.5	341.3
1992	11759.4	9425.2	2334.2	2517.8	1733.5	784.3
1993	15203.5	11971.0	3232.5	3444.1	2545.8	898.3
1994	21518.8	16838.7	4680.1	6315.3	4867.7	1447.6
1995	29662.3	23778.2	5884.1	8143.5	6939.5	1204.0
1996	38520.8	30873.4	7647.4	8858.5	7095.2	1763.3
1997	46279.8	36226.7	10053.1	7759.0	5353.3	2405.7
1998	53407.5	41791.6	11615.9	7615.4	5473.7	2141.7
1999	59621.8	44955.1	14666.7	6253.0	3198.5	3054.5
2000	64332.4	46141.7	18190.7	4976.7	1310.3	3666.4
2001	73762.4	51434.9	22327.6	9457.6	4144.5	5313.2
2002	86910.6	58788.9	28121.7	13233.2	7432.0	5801.2
2003	103617.3	68498.6	35118.7	16631.6	9674.5	6957.1
2004	119555.4	78138.9	41416.5	15929.4	9640.6	6288.9
2005	141051.0	92263.5	48787.5	21496.8	14127.2	7369.6

10-4 各地区城乡居民人民币储蓄存款（年底余额）

Savings Deposit of Urban and Rural Household by Region at the Year-end

单位：亿元 (100 million yuan)

地区	Region	城乡储蓄 Total Savings			城镇储蓄 Savings of Urban Household			农户储蓄 Savings of Rural Household		
		2002	2003	2004	2002	2003	2004	2002	2003	2004
全国	**National Total**	**86910.6**	**103617.3**	**119555.4**	**71504.8**	**85439.6**	**98789.2**	**15405.8**	**18177.7**	**20766.2**
总行	Head Office	2.5	6.7	354.4	2.5		354.4			
北京	Beijing	4389.7	5293.5	6122.4	4073.1	4926.5	5692.8	316.6	367.1	429.6
天津	Tianjin	1486.4	1825.3	2116.7	1308.3	1593.8	1815.2	178.1	231.6	301.5
河北	Hebei	4808.3	5457.0	6207.5	3317.5	3804.1	4358.3	1490.8	1652.9	1849.2
山西	Shanxi	2307.3	2781.5	3342.3	1768.7	2103.4	2532.9	538.6	678.2	809.5
内蒙古	Inner Mongolia	1137.9	1355.5	1603.9	959.0	1133.1	1334.5	178.9	222.4	269.4
辽宁	Liaoning	4665.0	5434.7	6048.5	4070.5	4741.8	5339.0	594.5	692.9	709.6
吉林	Jilin	1878.5	2161.4	2405.6	1643.3	1904.9	2114.6	235.1	256.5	291.0
黑龙江	Heilongjiang	2915.7	3342.4	3585.5	2654.5	3033.1	3268.9	261.1	309.3	316.6
上海	Shanghai	3891.5	5103.2	6116.1	3638.9	4789.1	5739.1	252.6	314.0	376.38
江苏	Jiangsu	6276.2	7638.2	8863.1	5333.8	6335.1	7622.0	942.4	1303.1	1241.1
浙江	Zhejiang	5212.7	6452.2	7364.1	3935.4	4878.6	5558.0	1277.3	1573.6	1806.0
安徽	Anhui	2047.5	2475.8	2972.4	1609.1	1961.4	2355.7	438.4	514.4	616.7
福建	Fujian	2430.5	2924.7	3322.3	2157.1	2578.1	2905.7	273.4	346.5	416.5
江西	Jiangxi	1706.6	2015.5	2347.7	1397.2	1647.2	1906.3	309.5	368.3	441.4
山东	Shandong	5803.5	6768.4	7721.5	4355.2	5121.9	5791.4	1448.3	1646.5	1930.1
河南	Henan	4196.0	4919.1	5607.3	3211.7	3796.3	4338.8	984.3	1122.8	1268.5
湖北	Hubei	2754.5	3296.5	3860.7	2364.7	2847.6	3340.7	389.9	448.9	525.0
湖南	Hunan	2576.4	3036.5	3483.2	1947.5	2322.2	2698.0	628.9	714.3	785.3
广东	Guangdong	11813.3	14061.8	16193.4	9633.5	11555.8	13272.8	2179.9	2506.0	2920.6
广西	Guangxi	1733.5	1971.7	2240.1	1453.0	1641.1	1838.4	280.5	330.6	401.7
海南	Hainan	483.5	546.9	615.9	427.4	482.9	546.2	56.2	63.9	69.8
重庆	Chongqing	1582.3	1896.6	2189.7	1260.6	1515.0	1729.1	321.8	381.6	460.6
四川	Sichuan	3665.2	4333.8	5019.4	2886.2	3453.8	3999.8	779.0	880.0	1019.6
贵州	Guizhou	758.7	912.8	1094.6	646.6	773.7	911.0	112.1	139.2	183.5
云南	Yunnan	1499.8	1766.5	2052.1	1243.5	1465.1	1679.2	256.3	301.4	372.9
西藏	Tibet	70.4	91.9	107.5	70.4		107.5			
陕西	Shaanxi	2108.1	2519.9	2948.4	1737.9	2101.0	2459.2	370.2	418.9	489.2
甘肃	Gansu	1042.4	1217.4	1384.9	898.1	1051.8	1193.2	144.3	165.6	191.7
青海	Qinghai	222.4	260.5	299.3	206.3	242.2	278.1	16.1	18.3	21.2
宁夏	Ningxia	306.8	377.7	425.5	269.3	322.0	348.8	37.5	55.7	76.7
新疆	Xinjiang	1137.6	1371.8	1534.7	1024.2	1219.4	1359.1	113.5	152.5	175.6

10-5 城镇居民家庭基本情况

Basic Conditions of Urban Households

项　目	Item	1990	1995	2000	2004	2005
调查户数　（户）	**Number of Households Surveyed (household)**	**35660**	**35520**	**42220**	**50430**	**54496**
平均每户家庭人口　（人）	**Average Household Size (person)**	**3.50**	**3.23**	**3.13**	**2.98**	**2.96**
平均每户就业人口　（人）	**Average Number of Employed Persons Per Household (persons)**	**1.98**	**1.87**	**1.68**	**1.56**	**1.51**
平均每户就业面　（%）	**Proportion of Employment per Household (%)**	**56.57**	**57.89**	**53.67**	**52.35**	**51.01**
平均每一就业者负担人数（包括就业者本人）（人）	**Number of Dependents per Employee (including the employee himself or herself) (person)**	**1.77**	**1.73**	**1.86**	**1.91**	**1.96**
平均每人全部年收入（元）	**Per Capita Annual Income (yuan)**	**1516.21**	**4279.02**	**6295.91**	**10128.51**	**11320.77**
工薪收入	Income of Wages and Salaries	1149.70	3390.21	4480.50	7152.76	7797.54
经营净收入	Net Business Income	22.50	72.62	246.24	493.87	679.62
财产性收入	Income from Properties	15.60	90.43	128.38	161.15	192.91
转移性收入	Income from Transfer	328.41	725.76	1440.78	2320.73	2650.70
#可支配收入	Disposable Income	1510.16	4282.95	6279.98	9421.61	10493.03
平均每人消费性支出（元）	**Per Capita Annual Consumption Expenditures (yuan)**	**1278.89**	**3537.57**	**4998.00**	**7182.10**	**7942.88**
食　品	Food	693.77	1771.99	1971.32	2709.60	2914.39
衣　着	Clothing	170.90	479.20	500.46	686.79	800.51
家庭设备用品及服务	Household Appliances and Service	108.45	263.36	374.49	407.37	446.52
医疗保健	Health Care and Medical Services	25.67	110.11	318.07	528.15	600.85
交通通信	Transport and Communications	40.51	183.22	426.95	843.62	996.72
教育文化娱乐服务	Education, Cultural and Recreation Services	112.26	331.01	669.58	1032.80	1097.46
居住	Residence	60.86	283.76	565.29	733.53	808.66
杂项商品与服务	Miscellaneous Goods and Services	66.57	114.92	171.83	240.24	277.75
平均每人消费性支出构成（人均消费性支出=100）	**Composition of Per Capita Annual Consumption Expenditures (%)**					
食　品	Food	54.25	50.09	39.44	37.73	36.69
衣　着	Clothing	13.36	13.55	10.01	9.56	10.08
家庭设备用品及服务	Household Appliances and Service	10.14	7.44	7.49	5.67	5.62
医疗保健	Health Care and Medical Services	2.01	3.11	6.36	7.35	7.56
交通通信	Transport and Communications	1.20	5.18	8.54	11.75	12.55
教育文化娱乐服务	Education, Cultural and Recreation Services	11.12	9.36	13.40	14.38	13.82
居住	Residence	6.98	8.02	11.31	10.21	10.18
杂项商品与服务	Miscellaneous Goods and Services	0.94	3.25	3.44	3.34	3.50

注：1.本表至10-17表为城镇居民家庭收支抽样调查资料。
2.从2002年起，城镇住户调查对象由原来的非农业人口改为城市市区和县城关镇，本篇章相关资料均按新口径计算，历史数据作了相应调整。

a) Data from the table to 10-17 are obtained from the sample survey on income and expenditures of urban households.

b) Since 2002, the objects of urban households survey are the permanent residents of city districts and county towns. The relative data in the chapter are calculated according to the new standard, and historical data have been adjusted accordingly.

10-6 城镇居民家庭基本情况（2005年）

项目		Item		全国 National
调查户数	（户）	Number of Households Surveyed	(household)	54496
调查户比重	(%)	Proportion	(%)	100.00
平均每户家庭人口	（人）	Average Household Size	(person)	2.96
平均每户就业人口	（人）	Average Number of Employed Persons per Household	(person)	1.51
平均每户就业面	(%)	Proportion of Employment per Household	(%)	51.01
平均每一就业者负担人数（包括就业者本人）	（人）	Number of Dependents per Employee (including the employee himself or herself)	(person)	1.96
平均每人全部年收入	（元）	Per Capita Annual Income	(yuan)	11320.77
平均每人可支配收入	（元）	Per Capita Disposable Income	(yuan)	10493.03
平均每人消费性支出	（元）	Per Capita Annual Consumption Expenditure	(yuan)	7942.88

10-7 城镇居民家庭平均每人全年消费性支出（2005年）

项目	Item	总平均 Average	最低收入户 (10%) Lowest Income Households (first decile)	#困难户 (5%) Poor Households (first five percent)
消费性支出（元）	**Total Consumption Expenditures (yuan)**	**7942.88**	**3111.47**	**2656.41**
食品	Food	2914.39	1475.67	1290.09
#粮食	Grain	242.16	219.24	213.48
肉禽及其制品	Meat, Poultry and Their Products	564.91	343.43	296.26
蛋类	Eggs	71.48	51.69	46.06
水产品	Aquatic Products	188.80	70.33	57.83
奶及奶制品	Milk and Its Products	138.62	50.75	39.44
衣着	Clothing	800.51	243.66	189.78
#服装	Garments	577.00	162.17	125.16
家庭设备用品及服务	Household Facilities, Articles and Services	446.52	109.21	90.39
#耐用消费品	Durable Consumer Goods	213.21	31.15	25.59
医疗保健	Medicine and Medical Services	600.85	232.50	206.52
交通通信	Transport, Post and Communication Services	996.72	228.37	180.86
教育文化娱乐服务	Education, Culture and Recreation Services	1097.46	363.61	293.17
#文娱用品	Consumer Goods for Recreational Use	280.21	43.28	33.48
居住	Residence	808.66	384.08	338.74
#住房	Housing	249.25	58.28	44.02
杂项商品与服务	Miscellaneous Commodities and Services	277.75	74.36	66.86
消费性支出构成（%）	**Total Consumption Expenditures (%)**			
食品	Food	36.69	47.43	48.57
衣着	Clothing	10.08	7.83	7.14
家庭设备用品及服务	Household Appliances and Service	5.62	3.51	3.40
医疗保健	Health Care and Medical Services	7.56	7.47	7.77
交通通信	Transport and Communications	12.55	7.34	6.81
教育文化娱乐服务	Education, Cultural and Recreation Services	13.82	11.69	11.04
居住	Residence	10.18	12.34	12.75
杂项商品与服务	Miscellaneous Goods and Services	3.50	2.39	2.52

Basic Condition of Urban Households (2005)

按收入等级分 (Grouped by Percentile of Households)							
最低收入户 (10%) Lowest Income Households (first decile)	#困难户 (5%) Poor Households (first five percent)	低收入户 (10%) Low Income Households (second decile)	中等偏下户 (20%) Lower Middle Income Households (second quintile)	中等收入户 (20%) Middle Income Households (third quintile)	中等偏上户 (20%) Upper Middle Income Households (fourth quintile)	高收入户 (10%) High Income Households (ninth decile)	最高收入户 (10%) Highest Income Households (tenth decile)
5376	2666	5454	10943	10966	10920	5440	5398
9.87	4.89	10.01	20.08	20.12	20.04	9.98	9.91
3.34	3.38	3.22	3.10	2.95	2.79	2.68	2.64
1.26	1.13	1.45	1.55	1.56	1.54	1.54	1.59
37.72	33.43	45.03	50.00	52.88	55.20	57.46	60.23
2.65	2.99	2.22	2.00	1.89	1.81	1.74	1.66
3377.68	2733.30	5202.12	7177.05	9886.96	13596.66	18687.74	31237.52
3134.88	2495.75	4885.32	6710.58	9190.05	12603.37	17202.93	28773.11
3111.47	2656.41	4295.35	5574.32	7308.06	9410.77	12102.51	19153.73

Per Capita Annual Living Expenditure of Urban Households (2005)

低收入户 (10%) Low Income Households (second decile)	中等偏下户 (20%) Lower Middle Income Households (second quintile)	中等收入户 (20%) Middle Income Households (third quintile)	中等偏上户 (20%) Upper Middle Income Households (fourth quintile)	高收入户 (10%) High Income Households (ninth decile)	最高收入户 (10%) Highest Income Households (tenth decile)
4295.35	**5574.32**	**7308.06**	**9410.77**	**12102.51**	**19153.73**
1926.01	2336.30	2838.83	3425.91	4151.09	5367.27
226.76	232.78	241.91	254.36	264.80	267.05
433.51	514.28	584.52	655.83	716.12	756.41
63.79	68.85	74.15	78.21	84.39	79.86
101.05	133.18	176.00	234.15	314.58	403.67
82.73	110.80	140.44	173.23	206.79	248.28
408.63	565.13	784.56	1010.63	1255.95	1757.59
279.48	397.24	558.99	731.97	929.82	1312.69
171.60	268.81	397.17	546.06	754.85	1287.53
60.73	117.18	188.12	270.35	377.85	663.60
308.13	408.12	561.82	764.91	997.59	1287.67
375.86	536.22	764.70	1074.90	1590.28	3769.58
518.77	720.40	985.68	1336.77	1700.23	2907.99
84.41	152.45	236.60	364.93	493.01	874.88
472.21	580.01	745.49	921.67	1195.48	1897.91
77.75	112.90	200.94	284.80	451.25	903.39
114.14	159.32	229.81	329.92	457.03	878.19
44.84	41.91	38.85	36.40	34.30	28.02
9.51	10.14	10.74	10.74	10.38	9.18
4.00	4.82	5.43	5.80	6.24	6.72
7.17	7.32	7.69	8.13	8.24	6.72
8.75	9.62	10.46	11.42	13.14	19.68
12.08	12.92	13.49	14.20	14.05	15.18
10.99	10.41	10.20	9.79	9.88	9.91
2.66	2.86	3.14	3.51	3.78	4.58

10-8 东、中、西部及东北地区城镇居民家庭基本情况（2005年）

Basic Conditions of Urban Households of Eastern, Central, Western and Northeastern Region (2005)

项　目	Item	东部地区 Eastern Region	中部地区 Central Region	西部地区 Western Region	东北地区 Northeastern Region
调查户数（户）	**Number of Households Surveyed (household)**	**22727**	**10698**	**13821**	**7250**
平均每户家庭人口（人）	**Average Household Size (person)**	**3.00**	**2.95**	**2.96**	**2.86**
平均每户就业人口（人）	**Average Number of Employed Persons per Household (persons)**	**1.58**	**1.51**	**1.47**	**1.40**
平均每户就业面（%）	**Percentage of Employment per Household (%)**	**52.67**	**51.19**	**49.66**	**48.95**
平均每一就业者负担人数（包括就业者本人）（人）	**Number of Dependents per Employee (including the employee himself or herself) (person)**	**1.90**	**1.95**	**2.01**	**2.04**
平均每人全部年收入（元）	**Per Capita Annual Income (yuan)**	**14584.60**	**9393.22**	**9418.36**	**9295.57**
#可支配收入	Disposable Income	13374.88	8808.52	8783.17	8729.96
平均每人消费性支出（元）	**Per Capita Annual Living Expenditures for Consumption (yuan)**	**9922.42**	**6540.92**	**6963.54**	**6835.46**
食　品	Food	3521.29	2491.89	2655.33	2477.65
衣　着	Clothing	860.37	791.43	717.45	806.86
家庭设备用品及服务	Household Facilities, Articles and Services	579.20	372.51	401.26	291.45
医疗保健	Medicine and Medical Services	710.61	474.60	521.51	687.22
交通通信	Transport, Post and Communication Services	1472.14	662.10	778.58	692.53
教育文化娱乐服务	Education, Cultural and Recreation Services	1438.92	865.51	960.93	822.10
居住	Residence	990.41	672.93	692.62	772.83
杂项商品与服务	Miscellaneous Commodities and Services	349.49	209.94	235.87	284.83
平均每人消费性支出构成（人均消费性支出=100）	**Composition of Per Capita Annual Living Expenditures for Consumption (%)**	**100.00**	**100.00**	**100.00**	**100.00**
食　品	Food	35.49	38.10	38.13	36.25
衣　着	Clothing	8.67	12.10	10.30	11.80
家庭设备用品及服务	Household Facilities, Articles and Services	5.84	5.70	5.76	4.26
医疗保健	Medicine and Medical Services	7.16	7.26	7.49	10.05
交通通信	Transport, Post and Communication Services	14.84	10.12	11.18	10.13
教育文化娱乐服务	Education, Cultural and Recreation Services	14.50	13.23	13.80	12.03
居住	Residence	9.98	10.29	9.95	11.31
杂项商品与服务	Miscellaneous Commodities and Services	3.52	3.21	3.39	4.17

10-9 城镇居民家庭平均每人全年购买主要商品数量

Per Capita Annual Purchases of Major Commodities of Urban Households

项 目	Item	1990	1995	1999	2000	2004	2005
粮 食 (千克)	Grain (kg)	130.72	97.00	84.91	82.31	78.18	76.98
鲜 菜 (千克)	Fresh Vegetables (kg)	138.70	116.47	114.94	114.74	122.32	118.58
食用植物油 (千克)	Edible Vegetable Oil (kg)	6.40	7.11	7.78	8.16	9.29	9.25
猪 肉 (千克)	Pork (kg)	18.46	17.24	16.91	16.73	19.19	20.15
牛羊肉 (千克)	Beef and Mutton (kg)	3.28	2.44	3.09	3.33	3.66	3.71
家 禽 (千克)	Poultry (kg)	3.42	3.97	4.92	5.44	6.37	8.97
鲜 蛋 (千克)	Fresh Eggs (kg)	7.25	9.74	10.92	11.21	10.35	10.40
水产品 (千克)	Aquatic Products (kg)	7.69	9.20	10.34	11.74	12.48	12.55
鲜 奶 (千克)	Milk (kg)	4.63	4.62	7.88	9.94	18.83	17.92
水果(瓜果) (千克)	Fresh Melons and Fruits (kg)	41.11	44.96	54.21	57.48	56.45	56.69
坚果及果仁类 (千克)	Nuts and Kernels (kg)	3.21	3.04	3.26	3.30	2.94	2.97
酒 (千克)	Liquor (kg)	9.25	9.93	9.61	10.01	8.94	8.85
煤 炭 (千克)	Coal (kg)	206.04	129.52	115.46	128.07	91.97	84.01

10-10 城镇居民家庭平均每百户年底耐用消费品拥有量

Number of Major Durable Consumer Goods Owned Per 100 Urban Households at the Year-end

项 目	Item	1990	1995	1999	2000	2004	2005
摩托车 (辆)	Motorcycle (unit)	1.94	6.29	15.12	18.80	24.84	25.00
洗衣机 (台)	Washing Machine (set)	78.41	88.97	91.44	90.50	95.90	95.51
电冰箱 (台)	Refrigerator (set)	42.33	66.22	77.74	80.10	90.15	90.72
彩色电视机 (台)	Color Television Set (set)	59.04	89.79	111.57	116.60	133.44	134.80
录放像机 (台)	Video-recorder (set)		18.19	21.73	20.10	17.55	15.49
组合音响 (套)	Hi-Fi Stereo Component System (set)		10.52	19.66	22.20	28.29	28.79
照相机 (架)	Camera (set)	19.22	30.56	38.11	38.40	47.04	46.94
空调器 (台)	Air Conditioner (unit)	0.34	8.09	24.48	30.80	69.81	80.67
淋浴热水器 (台)	Shower (unit)		30.05	45.49	49.10	69.40	72.65
排油烟机 (台)	Smoke Absorber (unit)		34.47	48.62	54.10	65.58	67.93
影碟机 (台)	Video Disc Player (set)			24.71	37.50	63.26	68.07
家用电脑 (台)	Computer (set)			5.91	9.70	33.11	41.52
摄像机 (架)	Pickup Camera (set)			1.06	1.30	3.17	4.32
微波炉 (台)	Oven (unit)			12.15	17.60	41.70	47.61
健身器材 (套)	Healthy Equipment (set)			3.83	3.50	4.22	4.68
移动电话 (部)	Mobile Telephone (unit)			7.14	19.50	111.35	137.00
家用汽车 (辆)	Automobile (unit)			0.34	0.50	2.18	3.37

10-11 东、中、西部及东北地区城镇居民家庭平均每人全年购买的主要商品数量（2005年）

Per Capita Annual Purchase Major Commodities of Urban Households of Eastern, Central, Western and Northeastern Region (2005)

项 目	Item	东部地区 Eastern Region	中部地区 Central Region	西部地区 Western Region	东北地区 Northeastern Region
粮 食 （千克）	Grain (kg)	72.16	80.86	75.57	86.26
鲜 菜 （千克）	Fresh Vegetables (kg)	107.91	120.32	122.56	138.62
食用植物油 （千克）	Edible Vegetable Oil (kg)	8.20	9.80	9.26	11.23
猪 肉 （千克）	Pork (kg)	20.07	19.66	23.14	15.42
牛 羊 肉 （千克）	Beef and Mutton (kg)	3.38	2.63	4.29	5.70
家 禽 （千克）	Poultry (kg)	10.59	7.51	9.99	5.04
鲜 蛋 （千克）	Fresh Eggs (kg)	11.22	10.18	8.03	13.09
水 产 品 （千克）	Aquatic Products (kg)	18.15	9.99	7.17	11.82
鲜 奶 （千克）	Milk (kg)	20.15	13.35	18.71	18.94
水果（瓜果）（千克）	Fresh Melons and Fruits (kg)	57.81	55.14	51.78	66.23
坚果及果仁类 （千克）	Nuts and Kernels (kg)	3.19	2.60	3.15	2.71
酒 （千克）	Liquor (kg)	9.27	7.27	6.17	16.14
煤 炭 （千克）	Coal (kg)	47.64	129.61	78.46	111.09

10-12 东、中、西部及东北地区城镇居民家庭平均每百户年底耐用消费品拥有量（2005年）

Number of Durable Consumer Goods Owned Per 100 Urban Households of Eastern, Central, Western and Northeastern Region at the Year-end (2005)

项 目	Item	东部地区 Eastern Region	中部地区 Central Region	西部地区 Western Region	东北地区 Northeastern Region
摩托车 （辆）	Motorcycle (unit)	37.97	21.76	16.77	9.78
自行车 （辆）	Bicycle (unit)	149.46	113.66	93.57	98.00
家用汽车（辆）	Automobile (unit)	6.11	1.26	2.57	1.26
洗衣机 （台）	Washing Machine (set)	95.85	96.85	95.63	90.98
电风扇 （台）	Electric Fan (set)	205.00	207.67	143.28	63.52
电冰箱 （台）	Refrigerator (set)	94.80	90.73	88.00	83.55
彩色电视机(台)	Color Television Set(set)	146.84	128.98	130.52	119.50
家用电脑（台）	Computer (set)	57.31	33.17	32.28	29.36
组合音响（套）	Hi-Fi Stereo Component System (set)	34.69	24.85	29.94	16.79
录音机 （台）	Tape Recorder (set)	46.89	32.39	34.84	38.66
照相机 （架）	Camera (set)	60.15	37.24	40.63	39.23
空调 （台）	Air conditioner (unit)	122.99	80.28	55.41	9.32
排油烟机（台）	Smoke Absorber (unit)	82.14	53.71	55.85	77.66
移动电话机(部)	Mobile Telephone (unit)	156.08	124.05	130.41	116.85

10-13 按收入等级分城镇居民家庭平均每人全年购买主要商品数量（2005年）

Per Capita Annual Purchases of Major Commodities of Urban Households by Level of Income (2005)

项目	Item	总平均 Average	最低收入户 (10%) Lowest Income Households (first decile)	#困难户 (5%) Poor Households (first five percent)	低收入户 (10%) Low Income Households (second decile)	中等偏下户 (20%) Lower Middle Income Households (second quintile)	中等收入户 (20%) Middle Income Households (third quintile)	中等偏上户 (20%) Upper Middle Income Households (fourth quintile)	高收入户 (10%) High Income Households (ninth decile)	最高收入户 (10%) Highest Income Households (tenth decile)
粮　食（千克）	Grain (kg)	76.98	80.28	79.67	79.29	78.42	77.42	76.85	75.07	67.1
淀粉及薯类（千克）	Starches and Tubers (kg)	12.37	13.05	13.05	12.93	12.67	12.21	12.45	12.06	10.48
食用植物油（千克）	Edible Vegetable Oil (kg)	9.25	8.69	8.26	9.19	9.39	9.62	9.58	8.97	8.39
食用动物油（千克）	Edible Animal Oil (kg)	0.36	0.60	0.67	0.42	0.42	0.34	0.32	0.22	0.15
猪　肉（千克）	Pork (kg)	20.15	15.74	14.36	17.77	19.64	20.88	22.07	22.56	21.95
牛　肉（千克）	Beef (kg)	2.28	1.45	1.26	1.83	2.22	2.48	2.65	2.63	2.45
羊　肉（千克）	Mutton (kg)	1.43	0.98	0.96	1.08	1.39	1.55	1.67	1.67	1.53
家　禽（千克）	Poultry (kg)	8.97	5.51	4.46	7.00	8.31	9.26	10.38	11.31	11.61
鲜　蛋（千克）	Fresh Eggs (kg)	10.40	8.01	7.28	9.75	10.38	10.89	11.07	11.62	10.48
鱼（千克）	Fish (kg)	9.37	5.89	5.20	7.36	8.37	9.45	10.77	12.24	12.97
虾（千克）	Shrimp (kg)	1.21	0.33	0.25	0.60	0.85	1.17	1.55	2.08	2.56
鲜　菜（千克）	Fresh Vegetables (kg)	118.58	105.22	101.44	111.00	116.87	121.07	126.00	127.76	118.79
白　酒（千克）	Liquor (kg)	2.28	2.04	1.80	2.40	2.38	2.39	2.44	2.10	1.80
果　酒（千克）	Fruit Wine (kg)	0.26	0.08	0.06	0.14	0.18	0.25	0.33	0.42	0.56
啤　酒（千克）	Beer (kg)	5.75	2.90	2.31	4.61	5.73	6.32	6.54	6.89	6.76
茶　叶（千克）	Tea (kg)	0.23	0.15	0.14	0.17	0.20	0.23	0.28	0.31	0.32
鲜瓜果（千克）	Fresh Melons & Fruits (kg)	56.69	31.65	27.20	43.78	50.37	60.03	66.19	73.44	76.65
糕　点（千克）	Cake (kg)	4.39	2.24	1.83	3.30	3.83	4.54	5.23	5.86	6.31
鲜　奶（千克）	Milk (kg)	17.92	7.80	6.41	11.70	15.30	18.69	22.56	25.74	26.05
奶　粉（千克）	Milk Powder (kg)	0.52	0.28	0.24	0.42	0.51	0.54	0.59	0.63	0.71
酸　奶（千克）	Yogurt (kg)	3.23	1.00	0.72	2.09	2.55	3.51	3.97	4.71	5.62
男士服装（件）	Men's Clothing (piece)	2.63	1.27	1.06	1.82	2.23	2.66	3.14	3.68	4.21
女士服装（件）	Women's Clothing (piece)	3.60	1.55	1.28	2.32	2.85	3.68	4.35	5.14	6.46
儿童服装（件）	Children's Clothing (piece)	1.11	0.66	0.55	0.87	1.04	1.20	1.23	1.25	1.62
鞋　类（双）	Shoes (pair)	2.58	1.68	1.46	2.16	2.38	2.70	2.86	3.09	3.46

10-14 按收入等级分城镇居民家庭平均每百户年底耐用消费品拥有量（2005年）

Number of Durable Consumer Goods Owned Per 100 Urban Households at Year-end by Level of Income (2005)

项目	Item		总平均 Average	最低收入户 (10%) Lowest Income Households (first decile)	#困难户 (5%) Poor Households (first five percent)	低收入户 (10%) Low Income Households (second decile)	中等偏下户 (20%) Lower Middle Income Households (second quintile)	中等收入户 (20%) Middle Income Households (third quintile)	中等偏上户 (20%) Upper Middle Income Households (fourth quintile)	高收入户 (10%) High Income Households (ninth decile)	最高收入户 (10%) Highest Income Households (tenth decile)
成套家具 （套）	Composite Furniture	(set)	77.55	55.22	50.48	66.56	71.67	78.08	83.00	89.23	100.44
摩托车 （辆）	Motorcycle	(unit)	25.00	14.49	12.80	21.75	24.76	26.80	28.01	26.56	27.98
自行车 （辆）	Bicycle	(unit)	120.04	107.83	101.23	123.24	125.05	121.14	120.66	119.73	114.84
助力车 （辆）	Helping Hand Car	(unit)	9.54	3.20	2.62	5.19	7.92	9.73	11.96	13.18	15.03
家用汽车 （辆）	Automobile	(unit)	3.37	0.29	0.16	0.64	0.91	1.73	3.26	5.57	16.20
洗衣机 （台）	Washing Machine	(unit)	95.51	81.68	76.56	88.95	93.38	96.89	99.50	101.54	103.84
电风扇 （台）	Electric Fan	(unit)	172.18	135.77	126.72	156.09	166.70	172.65	180.73	187.79	203.63
电冰箱 （台）	Refrigerator	(unit)	90.72	65.33	58.72	79.99	87.84	94.08	97.36	99.76	104.10
冰柜 （台）	Freezer	(set)	6.68	4.97	4.37	6.21	5.89	6.50	7.22	8.09	8.44
彩色电视机（台）	Color Television Set	(set)	134.80	107.26	103.73	118.14	123.94	133.73	142.50	152.62	172.30
影碟机 （台）	Video Disc Player	(set)	68.07	45.67	39.27	57.69	63.00	68.48	73.38	78.03	90.86
录音机 （台）	Tape Recorder	(set)	39.26	23.41	22.47	31.34	34.52	39.71	44.18	48.19	53.86
录放像机 （台）	Video-recorder	(set)	15.49	4.80	4.01	7.84	11.26	14.24	19.30	23.42	30.40
家用电脑 （台）	Computer	(set)	41.52	7.34	5.97	15.85	27.58	41.27	54.22	64.19	85.09
组合音响 （套）	Hi-Fi Stereo Component System	(set)	28.79	11.12	9.06	18.03	22.80	28.68	33.20	38.51	52.40
摄像机 （架）	Pickup Camera	(set)	4.32	0.40	0.24	0.89	1.36	3.03	5.06	7.72	16.13
照相机 （架）	Camera	(set)	46.94	13.24	11.36	23.62	33.59	44.90	56.73	70.70	94.92
钢琴 （架）	Piano	(set)	2.25	0.39	0.43	0.65	0.81	1.79	2.82	3.60	7.40
其他中高档乐器 （件）	Other Medium and High Grade Musical Instrument	(unit)	6.63	1.54	0.79	2.54	4.31	6.88	8.73	10.06	12.82
微波炉 （台）	Oven	(unit)	47.61	12.91	9.33	22.96	34.99	49.09	59.83	71.67	83.66
空调器 （台）	Air Conditioner	(unit)	80.67	18.90	14.99	35.24	54.04	76.77	96.38	126.61	178.68
取暖器 （台）	Room Heater	(unit)	35.51	14.85	10.71	23.02	29.61	36.76	43.03	46.74	53.03
电炊具 （台）	Electric Cooking Appliances	(unit)	107.20	80.23	76.07	84.07	96.07	104.43	118.06	130.21	143.47
淋浴热水器（台）	Shower	(unit)	72.65	38.93	34.01	51.98	64.35	75.37	83.32	90.93	100.53
排油烟机 （台）	Smoke Absorber	(unit)	67.93	36.87	32.69	52.56	61.68	71.14	76.32	84.02	88.89
消毒碗柜 （台）	Disinfection Cupboard	(unit)	15.77	3.94	2.49	8.40	10.60	13.70	18.76	25.21	35.49
洗碗机 （台）	Dishwasher	(unit)	0.64	0.10	0.07	0.33	0.41	0.66	0.75	1.02	1.35
饮水机 （台）	Drinking Machine	(unit)	42.40	18.02	14.82	28.73	36.84	43.12	50.41	55.28	62.56
吸尘器 （台）	Dust Catcher	(unit)	13.57	1.68	1.24	3.61	6.68	10.92	17.21	24.89	37.85
健身器材 （套）	Healthy Equipment	(unit)	4.68	0.40	0.20	0.86	1.87	3.70	5.90	8.38	14.97
普通电话 （部）	Telephone	(unit)	94.40	81.18	78.60	88.04	91.35	94.85	98.53	100.89	105.13
移动电话 （部）	Mobile Telephone	(unit)	137.00	61.29	48.28	94.51	119.01	143.65	159.52	174.09	199.76
传真机 （部）	Fax-Machine	(unit)	1.17	0.09	0.02	0.16	0.36	0.74	1.08	1.88	5.54

10-15 各地区城镇居民平均每人全年家庭收入来源（2005年）

Per Capita Annual Income of Urban Households by Sources and Region (2005)

单位：元 (yuan)

地区	Region	可支配收入 Disposable Income	总收入 Total Income	工薪收入 Income of Wages and Salaries	经营净收入 Net Business Income	财产性收入 Income from Properties	转移性收入 Income from Transfers
全　国	**National Average**	**10493.03**	**11320.77**	**7797.54**	**679.62**	**192.91**	**2650.70**
北　京	Beijing	17652.95	19533.33	13666.34	213.70	190.44	5462.85
天　津	Tianjin	12638.55	13563.32	8174.64	665.53	148.15	4574.99
河　北	Hebei	9107.09	9616.80	6346.53	643.84	117.46	2508.96
山　西	Shanxi	8913.91	9538.56	7103.45	350.96	136.38	1947.77
内蒙古	Inner Mongolia	9136.79	9565.14	6669.48	857.63	161.25	1876.78
辽　宁	Liaoning	9107.55	9837.20	6103.41	486.03	95.60	3152.17
吉　林	Jilin	8690.62	9122.99	5905.86	712.86	80.70	2423.57
黑龙江	Heilongjiang	8272.51	8722.47	5478.03	858.68	72.97	2312.80
上　海	Shanghai	18645.03	20602.90	14280.65	798.07	292.17	5232.00
江　苏	Jiangsu	12318.57	13329.95	8397.15	1028.69	240.43	3663.68
浙　江	Zhejiang	16293.77	17877.36	11941.09	1921.75	552.94	3461.58
安　徽	Anhui	8470.68	9184.55	6425.54	620.71	124.59	2013.71
福　建	Fujian	12321.31	13407.60	8791.56	839.36	447.98	3328.70
江　西	Jiangxi	8619.66	9042.45	6222.55	532.56	81.19	2206.16
山　东	Shandong	10744.79	11607.82	9026.55	492.12	151.86	1937.29
河　南	Henan	8667.97	9145.98	6095.49	660.88	95.77	2293.83
湖　北	Hubei	8785.94	9395.10	6576.92	419.74	112.34	2286.09
湖　南	Hunan	9523.97	10106.07	6805.30	872.30	195.60	2232.87
广　东	Guangdong	14769.94	16249.89	12265.04	1043.51	417.25	2524.09
广　西	Guangxi	9286.70	10022.40	6975.39	519.87	176.13	2351.00
海　南	Hainan	8123.94	8670.15	6071.20	661.59	198.15	1739.21
重　庆	Chongqing	10243.46	11079.15	7848.52	492.44	188.22	2549.97
四　川	Sichuan	8385.96	9003.59	5838.27	515.49	211.41	2438.41
贵　州	Guizhou	8151.13	8385.08	5516.18	790.84	90.25	1987.80
云　南	Yunnan	9265.90	9994.65	6170.93	595.45	428.07	2800.20
西　藏	Tibet	9431.18	10659.31	10401.71	43.20	10.41	204.00
陕　西	Shaanxi	8272.02	8902.26	6347.81	179.34	135.15	2239.96
甘　肃	Gansu	8086.82	8738.11	6486.84	373.84	39.58	1837.84
青　海	Qinghai	8057.85	8766.68	5613.79	513.41	62.08	2577.40
宁　夏	Ningxia	8093.64	8744.86	5771.58	956.65	64.44	1952.20
新　疆	Xinjiang	7990.15	8693.67	6553.47	522.14	54.51	1563.54

10-16 各地区城镇居民家庭平均每人全年消费性支出（2005年）

Per Capita Annual Consumption Expenditure of Urban Households by Region (2005)

单位：元 (yuan)

地区	Region	消费性支出 Consumption Expenditure	食品 Food	粮食 Grain	淀粉及薯类 Starches and Tubers	干豆类及豆制品 Beans and Bean Products	油脂类 Oil and Fats	肉禽及制品 Meat, Poultry and Related Products	蛋类 Eggs
全国	**National Average**	**7942.88**	**2914.39**	**242.16**	**23.40**	**38.38**	**85.43**	**564.91**	**71.48**
北京	Beijing	13244.20	4215.56	255.64	30.93	46.38	92.65	649.66	82.42
天津	Tianjin	9653.26	3542.90	257.99	34.41	35.00	87.60	547.20	115.45
河北	Hebei	6699.67	2315.76	219.04	22.22	30.59	109.28	402.39	89.81
山西	Shanxi	6342.63	2056.79	262.10	32.79	28.48	53.58	280.62	75.18
内蒙古	Inner Mongolia	6928.60	2177.63	256.46	25.22	21.06	53.94	384.40	51.16
辽宁	Liaoning	7369.27	2860.98	272.84	35.38	45.33	93.66	480.07	93.81
吉林	Jilin	6794.71	2356.00	242.61	29.39	38.66	69.47	415.01	65.43
黑龙江	Heilongjiang	6178.01	2071.62	255.91	29.62	30.59	71.41	371.49	60.57
上海	Shanghai	13773.41	4940.06	253.51	29.63	68.50	80.00	695.41	76.69
江苏	Jiangsu	8621.82	3205.79	223.34	24.60	53.37	72.26	622.04	74.84
浙江	Zhejiang	12253.74	4140.34	239.47	20.74	52.95	77.62	578.97	56.65
安徽	Anhui	6367.67	2781.50	235.36	19.20	40.65	89.53	572.04	99.61
福建	Fujian	8794.41	3595.20	306.77	22.78	45.30	88.81	794.17	80.78
江西	Jiangxi	6109.39	2495.09	224.96	13.56	47.72	116.44	557.31	56.72
山东	Shandong	7457.31	2512.73	219.23	23.94	32.32	66.11	433.92	95.54
河南	Henan	6038.02	2067.51	228.78	24.75	32.70	66.05	371.16	76.06
湖北	Hubei	6736.56	2625.41	225.11	16.47	42.30	103.30	498.91	58.95
湖南	Hunan	7504.99	2689.39	242.98	13.54	43.51	112.42	582.66	54.52
广东	Guangdong	11809.87	4265.19	284.19	16.42	30.83	97.54	1047.54	55.33
广西	Guangxi	7032.80	2906.73	224.37	15.60	39.43	94.21	876.53	50.93
海南	Hainan	5928.79	2819.96	193.91	10.53	18.34	88.49	810.09	35.10
重庆	Chongqing	8623.29	3135.65	218.13	29.90	39.01	99.77	692.58	73.37
四川	Sichuan	6891.27	2709.69	222.39	24.28	33.02	102.21	657.71	68.98
贵州	Guizhou	6159.29	2458.30	220.00	13.15	30.93	87.74	565.08	54.49
云南	Yunnan	6996.90	2997.06	267.58	18.95	36.84	52.80	522.97	61.32
西藏	Tibet	8617.11	3830.45	356.00	24.99	9.41	138.77	767.82	58.99
陕西	Shaanxi	6656.46	2401.52	240.33	28.15	39.12	75.23	325.32	59.35
甘肃	Gansu	6529.20	2352.82	224.19	27.44	25.43	87.21	358.26	56.95
青海	Qinghai	6245.26	2267.36	243.98	26.11	19.46	64.20	439.53	47.41
宁夏	Ningxia	6404.31	2228.63	237.05	25.87	30.60	77.67	361.94	42.66
新疆	Xinjiang	6207.52	2257.44	252.41	22.04	23.47	79.80	446.99	48.55

10-16 续表 1 continued

单位：元 (yuan)

地区	Region	水产品类 Aquatic Products	菜类 Vegetables	调味品 Condiments	糖类 Sugar	烟草类 Tobacco	酒和饮料 Liquor and Beverages	干鲜瓜果类 Dried and Fresh Melons and Fruits	#坚果及果仁 Nuts and Kernels
全国	**National Average**	**188.80**	**275.52**	**37.04**	**29.01**	**146.02**	**134.72**	**206.31**	**32.35**
北京	Beijing	174.00	294.87	74.99	52.81	139.13	285.99	380.43	72.63
天津	Tianjin	287.03	270.39	61.62	29.98	144.56	204.35	282.58	62.36
河北	Hebei	112.43	254.27	31.40	30.12	118.74	174.65	185.35	23.55
山西	Shanxi	36.77	247.57	24.45	17.09	131.84	84.71	144.14	22.51
内蒙古	Inner Mongolia	50.08	169.50	28.81	20.81	119.99	123.33	172.88	24.86
辽宁	Liaoning	224.24	329.41	49.74	38.89	174.86	163.63	269.80	29.42
吉林	Jilin	113.03	273.87	33.75	28.61	103.26	119.25	235.85	22.15
黑龙江	Heilongjiang	93.17	195.90	32.61	20.64	73.31	94.74	188.22	25.42
上海	Shanghai	573.26	382.63	52.58	65.57	258.80	230.92	333.68	62.69
江苏	Jiangsu	266.16	291.55	39.19	26.05	191.74	133.12	192.83	38.16
浙江	Zhejiang	515.79	335.17	35.83	33.15	325.79	194.19	297.06	54.33
安徽	Anhui	132.38	274.31	35.01	22.86	186.41	207.79	167.60	27.89
福建	Fujian	623.46	335.00	45.09	24.36	129.19	138.37	228.64	31.83
江西	Jiangxi	140.48	271.67	27.90	24.36	105.74	80.83	178.15	27.33
山东	Shandong	146.95	211.92	30.04	19.39	75.49	153.40	206.89	34.28
河南	Henan	43.54	217.28	29.48	17.16	96.56	119.60	146.95	25.05
湖北	Hubei	147.29	305.48	35.70	23.66	153.26	109.13	151.75	27.22
湖南	Hunan	132.31	257.10	26.05	31.28	154.09	94.54	209.38	29.10
广东	Guangdong	405.66	348.64	38.09	39.52	96.20	112.92	237.78	26.67
广西	Guangxi	178.47	266.69	28.24	26.13	65.67	74.56	183.00	26.26
海南	Hainan	398.99	268.93	30.27	18.35	93.95	61.76	145.17	8.36
重庆	Chongqing	122.24	308.14	44.67	34.99	207.50	106.64	182.27	35.00
四川	Sichuan	82.82	274.23	44.38	31.71	153.30	104.59	168.92	30.22
贵州	Guizhou	49.89	240.75	33.28	33.90	194.28	110.25	174.41	27.24
云南	Yunnan	93.37	347.85	29.62	25.27	296.65	103.68	178.86	19.54
西藏	Tibet	124.50	470.82	52.97	114.50	439.73	334.38	240.26	4.19
陕西	Shaanxi	57.49	207.95	36.17	20.23	132.22	104.73	170.54	35.12
甘肃	Gansu	50.45	213.04	34.70	19.42	152.50	132.15	192.89	34.92
青海	Qinghai	59.47	195.48	29.99	26.03	117.44	133.09	163.00	30.79
宁夏	Ningxia	53.22	198.03	28.75	24.17	125.60	98.46	198.80	36.57
新疆	Xinjiang	58.31	205.68	26.05	31.76	82.12	90.12	200.17	39.04

10–16 续表 2 continued

单位：元 (yuan)

地 区	Region	糕点类 Cake	奶及奶制品 Milk and Its Products	其他食品 Other Food	在外用餐 Dining Out	食品加工服务费 Food Processing Service Fees	衣 着 Clothing	服 装 Garments	衣着材料 Clothing Materials
全 国	**National Average**	**61.41**	**138.62**	**62.67**	**607.23**	**1.29**	**800.51**	**577.00**	**9.55**
北 京	Beijing	151.82	270.43	85.13	1147.35	0.93	1184.14	803.19	16.81
天 津	Tianjin	107.90	149.17	80.06	847.23	0.37	698.91	488.89	11.52
河 北	Hebei	50.04	134.25	19.59	330.62	0.97	787.33	551.98	13.19
山 西	Shanxi	45.42	154.26	31.97	405.37	0.45	933.03	689.93	11.75
内蒙古	Inner Mongolia	34.20	120.14	96.01	448.62	1.03	1047.91	733.05	10.21
辽 宁	Liaoning	60.13	140.14	39.16	348.25	1.63	740.83	506.85	7.89
吉 林	Jilin	44.12	105.30	42.30	394.34	1.75	826.21	588.07	7.52
黑龙江	Heilongjiang	35.44	95.60	35.47	386.42	0.51	877.96	605.66	7.04
上 海	Shanghai	132.33	246.88	128.58	1330.94	0.14	940.45	694.12	15.30
江 苏	Jiangsu	57.88	156.29	102.95	675.97	1.60	804.23	588.12	9.73
浙 江	Zhejiang	71.90	155.28	84.66	1063.68	1.44	1264.06	969.77	10.92
安 徽	Anhui	54.43	154.65	52.52	436.24	0.94	763.54	549.04	9.65
福 建	Fujian	56.55	152.34	48.83	474.35	0.43	708.79	549.83	3.30
江 西	Jiangxi	49.56	119.63	79.95	398.70	1.39	647.80	475.90	12.45
山 东	Shandong	68.47	159.61	83.28	484.78	1.47	925.94	665.02	12.43
河 南	Henan	48.58	115.26	41.80	391.46	0.36	806.39	595.33	9.96
湖 北	Hubei	57.33	110.25	46.25	538.65	1.62	806.67	579.78	11.76
湖 南	Hunan	43.36	119.20	85.86	485.94	0.67	790.70	568.38	9.05
广 东	Guangdong	85.25	134.49	65.59	1169.01	0.19	673.90	490.96	1.90
广 西	Guangxi	45.53	99.58	56.66	579.93	1.21	519.96	385.21	7.19
海 南	Hainan	43.47	69.53	24.79	508.14	0.14	309.45	242.37	0.54
重 庆	Chongqing	48.80	168.05	56.11	696.57	6.90	849.53	626.15	4.87
四 川	Sichuan	42.56	138.86	46.17	509.97	3.58	640.91	458.34	9.04
贵 州	Guizhou	46.46	96.40	68.96	437.18	1.15	702.90	500.56	8.25
云 南	Yunnan	78.39	78.23	48.58	755.65	0.45	643.94	488.20	8.26
西 藏	Tibet	38.27	339.90	33.85	280.00	5.28	1051.80	663.21	1.51
陕 西	Shaanxi	64.92	124.31	59.60	655.18	0.70	673.07	474.25	12.91
甘 肃	Gansu	38.37	136.80	96.18	506.48	0.36	806.26	560.26	12.77
青 海	Qinghai	39.17	104.44	99.65	458.59	0.33	690.76	495.13	7.90
宁 夏	Ningxia	36.02	124.17	81.51	483.79	0.31	776.51	567.43	12.94
新 疆	Xinjiang	49.92	113.75	48.13	477.19	1.00	825.98	578.27	13.68

10-16 续表 3 continued

单位：元 (yuan)

地区	Region	鞋类 Shoes	衣着加工服务费 Tailoring and Laundering Service Fees	家庭设备用品及服务 Household Appliances and Services	耐用消费品 Durable Consumer Goods	室内装饰品 Room Decorations	床上用品 Bed Articles	家庭日用杂品 Household Articles for Daily Use	家具材料 Furniture Materials
全国	**National Average**	**176.18**	**6.67**	**446.52**	**213.21**	**16.55**	**39.65**	**138.44**	**2.95**
北京	Beijing	296.16	15.48	852.18	441.98	33.63	53.58	246.90	5.95
天津	Tianjin	160.05	7.95	524.20	294.67	25.89	29.39	135.60	1.18
河北	Hebei	184.62	7.40	414.49	248.44	19.06	39.49	89.45	3.30
山西	Shanxi	192.07	2.40	359.44	195.64	17.49	23.36	98.31	3.07
内蒙古	Inner Mongolia	229.60	11.24	394.37	172.12	29.63	39.78	131.26	3.44
辽宁	Liaoning	182.08	6.62	304.80	93.55	24.78	44.82	115.56	7.63
吉林	Jilin	193.02	8.89	279.58	125.93	7.13	27.54	105.70	1.02
黑龙江	Heilongjiang	218.79	7.93	282.78	121.16	11.37	29.86	98.86	2.95
上海	Shanghai	182.43	12.16	800.30	409.74	31.22	73.92	185.49	1.90
江苏	Jiangsu	163.83	8.27	586.84	286.12	16.32	44.75	184.61	2.37
浙江	Zhejiang	240.57	9.19	609.18	285.25	26.78	74.24	155.03	9.96
安徽	Anhui	177.42	2.91	290.88	153.93	7.83	21.69	90.30	2.13
福建	Fujian	132.38	3.28	455.36	203.70	8.14	37.46	151.20	1.08
江西	Jiangxi	133.30	5.28	426.99	206.77	10.58	38.30	134.12	4.99
山东	Shandong	198.25	8.19	503.36	275.55	20.40	37.78	151.13	2.42
河南	Henan	168.78	5.04	376.27	190.08	13.65	37.74	106.87	4.37
湖北	Hubei	180.43	7.09	371.00	162.59	10.05	26.31	143.88	0.56
湖南	Hunan	178.29	5.08	450.97	204.97	12.84	42.51	152.07	4.77
广东	Guangdong	151.06	4.70	605.12	230.86	16.14	58.36	202.34	0.47
广西	Guangxi	106.05	3.97	420.66	209.65	13.05	38.55	130.11	0.64
海南	Hainan	55.56	1.25	304.05	118.46	9.68	25.78	129.17	1.15
重庆	Chongqing	186.91	5.08	583.50	334.07	30.86	44.19	139.69	0.62
四川	Sichuan	144.35	7.09	422.73	202.60	10.78	32.96	130.60	3.44
贵州	Guizhou	167.04	3.22	335.68	113.47	4.86	26.56	168.03	0.92
云南	Yunnan	128.24	1.32	291.17	131.74	7.64	48.42	84.44	1.66
西藏	Tibet	368.42	5.34	476.27	96.27	41.22	134.85	177.19	8.12
陕西	Shaanxi	152.31	6.75	371.81	177.65	12.68	29.77	126.64	4.28
甘肃	Gansu	175.85	7.51	366.20	186.47	16.28	29.04	115.81	2.72
青海	Qinghai	142.65	5.86	356.53	168.30	17.45	33.56	120.69	6.82
宁夏	Ningxia	160.68	7.98	417.38	225.77	23.35	25.68	120.97	0.55
新疆	Xinjiang	187.79	10.53	309.97	121.97	22.41	22.86	117.92	1.34

10-16 续表 4 continued

单位：元 (yuan)

地 区	Region	家务服务 Household Services	医疗保健 Health Care and Medical Services	交通和通信 Transport and Communications	交 通 Transport	通 信 Communications	教育文化娱乐服务 Education, Culture and Recreation Services	文化娱乐用品 Recreation Articles	教 育 Education
全 国	**National Average**	**35.72**	**600.85**	**996.72**	**499.63**	**497.09**	**1097.46**	**280.21**	**571.33**
北 京	Beijing	70.15	1295.76	1943.48	1100.66	842.82	2186.55	677.36	924.75
天 津	Tianjin	37.47	996.35	998.01	505.26	492.74	1283.70	382.50	716.38
河 北	Hebei	14.75	642.71	772.34	385.26	387.08	795.43	234.71	408.63
山 西	Shanxi	21.56	538.70	604.35	188.51	415.84	932.53	215.48	548.83
内蒙古	Inner Mongolia	18.15	533.36	755.51	320.08	435.44	968.81	263.24	504.77
辽 宁	Liaoning	18.46	751.16	744.02	282.18	461.83	849.53	194.40	529.13
吉 林	Jilin	12.27	675.77	733.50	319.08	414.42	800.22	176.88	502.08
黑龙江	Heilongjiang	18.59	613.15	596.97	232.85	364.12	802.49	180.88	479.85
上 海	Shanghai	98.02	796.82	1983.72	1161.33	822.39	2272.76	647.16	1136.15
江 苏	Jiangsu	52.67	579.32	1050.88	632.27	418.61	1287.90	362.03	656.29
浙 江	Zhejiang	57.92	831.79	2097.41	1298.95	798.46	1849.73	412.50	972.69
安 徽	Anhui	15.00	400.34	676.86	258.97	417.89	666.42	194.04	352.79
福 建	Fujian	53.78	478.41	1048.71	384.29	664.42	1106.95	319.35	531.40
江 西	Jiangxi	32.23	326.46	567.52	191.38	376.14	805.41	184.49	392.81
山 东	Shandong	16.07	579.01	902.32	476.71	425.61	1039.99	328.13	546.64
河 南	Henan	23.58	472.31	636.57	177.07	459.50	805.08	208.65	421.72
湖 北	Hubei	27.61	499.34	649.87	242.81	407.06	904.76	192.73	517.28
湖 南	Hunan	33.81	601.34	801.27	296.19	505.08	1138.67	251.25	582.16
广 东	Guangdong	96.95	704.90	2333.05	1557.60	775.45	1669.09	353.93	755.94
广 西	Guangxi	28.67	466.04	703.39	317.77	385.63	998.87	250.92	528.13
海 南	Hainan	19.81	351.06	728.29	350.96	377.33	652.03	162.66	347.11
重 庆	Chongqing	34.08	629.32	929.92	324.43	605.49	1391.11	359.55	772.52
四 川	Sichuan	42.34	442.83	827.66	402.68	424.99	909.03	230.52	449.68
贵 州	Guizhou	21.85	403.43	625.44	219.51	405.93	811.73	204.82	383.02
云 南	Yunnan	17.26	663.01	930.59	390.74	539.86	775.61	213.22	337.42
西 藏	Tibet	18.62	338.57	1309.95	520.43	789.51	678.26	121.58	428.09
陕 西	Shaanxi	20.80	605.31	630.16	217.62	412.54	1081.92	210.97	701.82
甘 肃	Gansu	15.88	492.23	638.63	243.33	395.30	942.75	257.10	505.90
青 海	Qinghai	9.72	554.11	691.25	347.14	344.11	803.08	218.99	360.52
宁 夏	Ningxia	21.05	535.92	705.69	291.37	414.32	769.97	219.56	388.30
新 疆	Xinjiang	23.47	499.16	757.09	375.77	381.32	741.35	182.77	456.25

10-16 续表 5 continued

单位：元 (yuan)

地区	Region	文化娱乐服务 Recreation Services	居住 Residence	住房 Housing	水电燃料及其他 Water, Electricity, Fuels and Others	杂项商品和服务 Miscellaneous Goods and Services	杂项商品 Miscellaneous Goods	服务 Services
全国	**National Average**	**245.93**	**808.66**	**249.25**	**516.31**	**277.75**	**173.13**	**104.62**
北京	Beijing	584.43	1039.78	456.30	527.67	526.76	334.99	191.76
天津	Tianjin	184.81	1291.60	562.06	658.50	317.58	187.64	129.95
河北	Hebei	152.10	762.08	170.24	569.94	209.51	118.62	90.90
山西	Shanxi	168.22	727.91	269.32	419.61	189.88	106.79	83.09
内蒙古	Inner Mongolia	200.80	722.62	191.90	473.55	328.39	203.77	124.62
辽宁	Liaoning	126.00	792.75	187.89	583.81	325.18	143.95	181.23
吉林	Jilin	121.26	845.45	205.61	603.50	277.98	157.32	120.65
黑龙江	Heilongjiang	141.75	695.23	159.05	505.00	237.81	161.61	76.20
上海	Shanghai	489.44	1412.11	666.78	610.74	627.20	427.84	199.36
江苏	Jiangsu	269.59	794.94	335.01	433.64	311.92	185.10	126.82
浙江	Zhejiang	464.54	1059.36	368.17	641.31	401.88	252.36	149.52
安徽	Anhui	119.59	590.27	157.14	415.22	197.87	95.83	102.04
福建	Fujian	256.20	1071.86	386.22	648.39	329.11	181.24	147.87
江西	Jiangxi	228.11	646.16	197.75	435.29	193.97	118.78	75.19
山东	Shandong	165.22	751.69	209.02	505.87	242.29	169.01	73.28
河南	Henan	174.70	651.98	160.15	457.65	221.91	147.57	74.34
湖北	Hubei	194.74	683.89	156.77	505.71	195.62	136.25	59.37
湖南	Hunan	305.25	771.47	272.70	469.96	261.18	169.06	92.12
广东	Guangdong	559.22	1181.42	278.13	780.28	377.20	244.17	133.03
广西	Guangxi	219.82	769.77	224.73	513.18	247.38	150.21	97.17
海南	Hainan	142.26	585.40	161.76	388.18	178.55	130.41	48.14
重庆	Chongqing	259.03	882.41	365.59	461.71	221.85	162.23	59.62
四川	Sichuan	228.83	705.43	257.25	407.47	232.99	146.72	86.28
贵州	Guizhou	223.89	583.46	102.10	462.81	238.35	160.15	78.20
云南	Yunnan	224.96	543.10	124.48	394.22	152.42	91.97	60.45
西藏	Tibet	128.59	517.53	111.97	386.27	414.27	201.64	212.64
陕西	Shaanxi	169.13	653.40	166.50	458.45	239.26	147.67	91.60
甘肃	Gansu	179.76	680.78	224.96	423.11	249.53	168.66	80.87
青海	Qinghai	223.57	666.38	226.38	393.83	215.79	153.01	62.78
宁夏	Ningxia	162.11	711.21	190.66	483.14	259.00	174.69	84.31
新疆	Xinjiang	102.33	571.72	125.16	406.40	244.80	174.72	70.08

10–17 各地区城镇居民家庭平均每百户耐用消费品拥有量（2005年底）

Number of Major Durable Consumer Goods Owned Per 100 Urban Households at the Year-end by Region (2005)

地 区	Region	成套家具 (套) Composite Furniture (sets)	摩托车 (辆) Motorcycle (unit)	自行车 (辆) Bicycle (unit)	助力车 (辆) Helping Hand Car (unit)	家用汽车 (辆) Automobile (unit)	洗衣机 (台) Washing Machine (set)	电风扇 (台) Electric Fan (set)	电冰箱 (台) Refrigerator (set)
全 国	**National Average**	**77.55**	**25.00**	**120.04**	**9.54**	**3.37**	**95.51**	**172.18**	**90.72**
北 京	Beijing	93.66	6.32	193.71	5.08	14.06	104.96	134.39	104.02
天 津	Tianjin	95.73	8.13	202.40	11.13	3.00	95.80	109.13	97.80
河 北	Hebei	85.83	31.56	194.06	13.19	3.94	95.52	137.87	92.07
山 西	Shanxi	80.79	26.23	157.55	5.76	3.13	99.77	82.95	87.08
内蒙古	Inner Mongolia	74.02	27.43	179.44	6.55	3.64	95.29	61.52	85.51
辽 宁	Liaoning	39.63	7.34	107.42	3.74	1.16	87.88	72.04	88.19
吉 林	Jilin	23.67	15.91	104.23	1.85	1.41	97.02	66.90	84.59
黑龙江	Heilongjiang	40.64	9.19	81.88	0.99	1.51	91.62	51.52	77.88
上 海	Shanghai	104.90	2.70	119.10	23.50	3.80	97.30	230.10	104.40
江 苏	Jiangsu	80.19	27.42	152.85	33.86	4.29	99.38	203.39	91.89
浙 江	Zhejiang	88.47	32.65	123.36	30.12	8.71	91.45	255.90	97.79
安 徽	Anhui	66.88	21.87	124.91	8.42	0.76	97.28	241.93	91.75
福 建	Fujian	83.76	49.39	117.05	6.26	1.70	99.72	238.29	98.43
江 西	Jiangxi	72.08	24.38	107.37	5.24	0.73	95.29	239.11	90.66
山 东	Shandong	91.08	47.55	170.76	17.58	4.47	93.28	166.74	90.96
河 南	Henan	72.52	28.14	166.79	15.60	1.58	98.23	185.61	86.33
湖 北	Hubei	88.05	18.11	93.73	4.55	0.92	95.55	220.87	95.58
湖 南	Hunan	84.55	15.41	43.98	4.08	1.10	96.55	234.79	90.30
广 东	Guangdong	83.39	72.83	112.50	4.35	9.69	97.23	295.99	93.90
广 西	Guangxi	89.74	48.26	123.64	10.38	1.88	91.64	289.23	87.20
海 南	Hainan	59.11	55.43	70.09	3.00	3.52	56.33	182.12	67.00
重 庆	Chongqing	100.33	2.67	3.67	0.67	0.67	100.33	184.67	102.00
四 川	Sichuan	99.67	7.94	69.81	5.71	2.37	97.88	206.24	92.85
贵 州	Guizhou	67.17	7.29	17.08	0.13	1.81	97.10	93.50	86.13
云 南	Yunnan	70.31	21.97	114.03	9.00	7.92	90.07	29.20	78.21
西 藏	Tibet	88.00	7.00	136.00	0.00	3.00	95.00	11.00	88.00
陕 西	Shaanxi	69.30	15.45	126.79	2.16	0.44	98.29	136.04	82.89
甘 肃	Gansu	83.90	10.83	155.88	5.60	0.46	98.35	54.90	89.08
青 海	Qinghai	58.59	6.69	45.09	1.73	1.39	98.41	9.96	80.74
宁 夏	Ningxia	22.07	18.59	130.34	2.83	1.27	89.61	64.19	79.48
新 疆	Xinjiang	62.72	16.04	96.83	2.29	2.81	88.53	53.39	79.72

10-17 续表 1 continued

地 区	Region	冰 柜 (台) Freezer (set)	彩色电视机 (台) Color TV Set (set)	影碟机 (台) Video Disc Player (set)	录音机 (台) Tape Recorder (set)	录放像机 (台) Video Recorder (set)	家用电脑 (台) Computer (set)	组合音响 (套) Hi-Fi Stereo Component System (set)	摄像机 (架) Pickup Camera (set)
全 国	**National Average**	**6.68**	**134.80**	**68.07**	**39.26**	**15.49**	**41.52**	**28.79**	**4.32**
北 京	Beijing	10.09	152.81	71.39	68.89	47.50	89.16	37.30	16.25
天 津	Tianjin	14.53	136.27	56.07	46.20	24.20	51.13	28.80	5.67
河 北	Hebei	15.54	124.34	50.91	41.49	14.00	37.63	22.81	3.98
山 西	Shanxi	8.94	113.69	50.96	37.10	12.07	30.16	17.19	2.58
内蒙古	Inner Mongolia	14.04	113.34	54.85	46.44	8.38	23.17	14.27	2.89
辽 宁	Liaoning	8.19	122.07	50.96	41.68	20.71	32.88	21.60	5.72
吉 林	Jilin	10.33	126.59	59.46	40.79	17.58	30.06	14.06	3.67
黑龙江	Heilongjiang	11.39	112.36	52.63	34.15	11.42	25.94	13.29	4.57
上 海	Shanghai	2.10	176.70	93.00	57.70	26.00	81.10	47.70	9.90
江 苏	Jiangsu	4.58	153.19	63.98	32.70	17.53	46.35	28.33	5.34
浙 江	Zhejiang	4.55	178.62	70.09	39.37	19.11	59.47	36.56	5.24
安 徽	Anhui	4.45	132.42	60.48	39.34	13.74	25.97	22.00	2.39
福 建	Fujian	2.12	164.49	79.83	32.45	13.48	54.89	29.28	3.96
江 西	Jiangxi	2.93	139.31	61.02	26.41	10.38	32.03	24.64	2.35
山 东	Shandong	14.67	118.30	62.67	54.91	18.24	45.64	22.28	5.09
河 南	Henan	7.29	124.62	60.77	35.82	8.39	31.82	17.96	3.11
湖 北	Hubei	5.93	131.71	75.74	28.54	9.84	42.42	31.57	1.99
湖 南	Hunan	4.79	129.23	71.62	27.60	10.60	34.94	32.79	2.83
广 东	Guangdong	0.89	155.26	88.34	47.08	17.23	70.34	56.88	6.41
广 西	Guangxi	3.54	140.39	83.07	28.48	11.17	46.67	36.73	3.36
海 南	Hainan	4.95	117.32	68.49	27.05	10.48	26.21	23.89	2.98
重 庆	Chongqing	4.33	155.33	80.33	24.33	15.00	51.33	42.33	3.67
四 川	Sichuan	3.34	138.87	82.27	29.28	10.55	32.26	30.05	2.74
贵 州	Guizhou	5.96	124.51	79.24	21.36	11.10	23.99	38.71	2.79
云 南	Yunnan	1.59	122.12	80.48	40.13	18.16	29.44	36.61	2.87
西 藏	Tibet	7.00	135.00	77.00	59.00	43.00	19.00	32.00	6.00
陕 西	Shaanxi	2.35	128.90	62.65	42.67	14.79	27.92	23.01	2.11
甘 肃	Gansu	3.71	117.98	61.88	52.52	14.18	22.99	26.53	2.06
青 海	Qinghai	6.44	111.68	67.16	36.03	7.93	21.68	20.80	2.99
宁 夏	Ningxia	1.81	108.64	63.27	24.55	6.53	23.15	21.76	0.67
新 疆	Xinjiang	7.71	105.70	61.73	50.05	13.43	23.86	16.10	3.12

10-17 续表 2 continued

地 区	Region	照相机(架) Camera (set)	钢 琴(架) Piano (set)	其他中高档乐器(件) Other Medium and High Grade Musical Instrument (unit)	微波炉(台) Oven (unit)	空调器(台) Air Conditioner (unit)	取暖器(台) Room Heater (unit)	电炊具(台) Electric Cooking Appliances (unit)	淋浴热水器(台) Shower (unit)
全 国	**National Average**	**46.94**	**2.25**	**6.63**	**47.61**	**80.67**	**35.51**	**107.20**	**72.65**
北 京	Beijing	109.14	4.12	11.32	89.14	146.47	36.06	132.70	97.01
天 津	Tianjin	52.53	1.27	2.67	74.33	102.13	22.40	97.33	86.47
河 北	Hebei	46.47	1.51	5.82	40.27	81.43	18.33	71.29	68.13
山 西	Shanxi	35.20	0.72	5.38	25.59	25.93	11.12	45.13	37.87
内蒙古	Inner Mongolia	35.40	1.11	6.88	26.18	7.64	5.71	156.76	42.59
辽 宁	Liaoning	44.52	2.38	5.70	41.94	14.29	15.43	85.50	60.52
吉 林	Jilin	42.28	1.15	6.87	35.77	4.77	11.63	125.53	42.48
黑龙江	Heilongjiang	32.00	1.57	5.56	29.08	7.18	7.78	162.43	30.47
上 海	Shanghai	85.40	4.30	7.20	95.80	168.30	81.60	180.10	90.30
江 苏	Jiangsu	45.16	2.56	4.04	76.50	123.92	50.35	116.32	82.69
浙 江	Zhejiang	51.35	2.64	7.83	58.24	146.89	45.15	115.30	90.35
安 徽	Anhui	35.84	1.96	7.89	40.54	81.82	44.83	97.06	64.14
福 建	Fujian	47.42	2.85	5.86	70.27	134.86	20.02	138.87	101.02
江 西	Jiangxi	37.35	1.50	7.17	38.93	72.41	80.29	84.02	81.77
山 东	Shandong	57.59	3.02	8.51	42.88	74.40	30.38	90.63	72.42
河 南	Henan	38.92	2.08	6.52	30.36	93.55	37.05	80.31	50.61
湖 北	Hubei	38.33	1.63	5.84	46.86	100.63	65.51	111.99	76.74
湖 南	Hunan	38.28	2.21	8.89	36.92	78.49	75.82	67.64	68.56
广 东	Guangdong	64.52	4.12	9.17	61.05	168.66	12.95	122.64	105.23
广 西	Guangxi	38.34	1.77	5.13	51.11	82.20	33.36	135.94	97.05
海 南	Hainan	21.93	2.01	3.37	20.74	45.80	0.23	127.50	69.48
重 庆	Chongqing	50.67	1.67	5.00	71.00	156.67	42.00	91.00	94.33
四 川	Sichuan	40.20	2.17	4.66	42.72	77.14	45.70	111.48	88.15
贵 州	Guizhou	33.73	1.72	5.06	35.18	10.66	59.68	98.12	55.37
云 南	Yunnan	45.12	2.25	5.18	44.77	0.43	33.99	114.49	64.80
西 藏	Tibet	56.00	0.00	2.00	34.00	5.00	58.00	25.00	25.00
陕 西	Shaanxi	41.67	1.07	8.41	35.04	70.37	21.37	94.00	63.16
甘 肃	Gansu	42.83	1.89	8.67	28.13	3.61	16.26	94.39	59.93
青 海	Qinghai	41.68	1.46	4.70	38.22	0.00	22.06	53.52	43.87
宁 夏	Ningxia	28.08	0.92	4.24	30.91	6.68	9.97	127.31	60.87
新 疆	Xinjiang	37.42	2.23	5.97	19.68	7.02	6.81	77.97	59.58

10-17 续表 3 continued

地区	Region	排油烟机 (台) Smoke Absorber (unit)	消毒碗柜 (台) Disinfection Cupboard (unit)	洗碗机 (台) Dishwasher (unit)	饮水机 (台) Drinking Machine (unit)	吸尘器 (台) Dust Catcher (unit)	健身器材 (套) Healthy Equipment (set)	普通电话 (部) Telephone (unit)	移动电话 (部) Mobile Telephone (unit)	传真机 (部) Fax Machine (unit)
全国	**National Average**	**67.93**	**15.77**	**0.64**	**42.40**	**13.57**	**4.68**	**94.40**	**137.00**	**1.17**
北京	Beijing	93.36	8.73	0.97	57.07	40.09	11.86	106.84	190.00	2.65
天津	Tianjin	85.13	2.60	0.33	40.07	24.67	3.13	93.40	122.13	0.73
河北	Hebei	74.64	4.71	0.76	41.38	12.82	5.06	92.85	124.53	0.89
山西	Shanxi	66.08	2.35	0.33	38.55	6.09	2.06	95.60	109.70	0.70
内蒙古	Inner Mongolia	64.37	1.68	0.23	31.14	11.58	2.07	89.60	128.38	0.62
辽宁	Liaoning	79.01	4.96	0.63	25.49	22.14	3.37	92.74	107.14	0.56
吉林	Jilin	80.46	5.29	0.47	30.22	16.29	5.11	88.73	142.02	0.74
黑龙江	Heilongjiang	75.08	4.65	0.66	32.84	14.97	2.70	85.78	117.02	0.79
上海	Shanghai	82.20	14.10	0.40	59.10	54.40	9.50	102.30	180.90	5.70
江苏	Jiangsu	79.65	6.87	0.81	50.78	17.81	5.59	130.79	120.61	2.18
浙江	Zhejiang	87.96	21.70	0.84	56.87	18.24	6.29	96.84	174.73	3.03
安徽	Anhui	54.86	5.76	0.41	29.92	7.99	3.86	95.94	111.33	0.24
福建	Fujian	65.67	36.62	0.63	35.93	6.26	6.33	106.02	166.34	1.50
江西	Jiangxi	46.22	9.91	0.48	38.35	4.51	1.77	87.80	136.26	0.16
山东	Shandong	87.20	5.72	1.11	65.49	17.39	6.24	92.30	144.34	0.83
河南	Henan	55.60	8.95	0.59	44.83	5.57	3.11	90.93	125.51	0.42
湖北	Hubei	60.42	12.80	0.77	32.29	7.01	2.82	91.91	129.06	0.49
湖南	Hunan	36.96	23.50	0.78	36.03	4.92	4.80	84.96	136.36	1.42
广东	Guangdong	81.61	81.11	1.13	41.95	12.50	8.41	101.40	187.39	2.67
广西	Guangxi	56.90	54.13	0.48	41.92	7.10	3.82	87.79	154.37	1.37
海南	Hainan	53.53	52.19	0.69	30.46	1.92	1.46	97.32	128.37	0.86
重庆	Chongqing	41.67	10.00	0.33	47.33	9.67	5.67	94.33	154.33	1.00
四川	Sichuan	40.76	9.64	0.13	38.55	6.93	3.64	89.96	127.91	0.44
贵州	Guizhou	36.92	26.86	0.20	55.85	5.25	2.75	89.42	119.22	0.58
云南	Yunnan	73.10	11.74	0.83	62.87	8.65	3.95	83.16	130.77	0.72
西藏	Tibet	40.00	8.00	2.00	39.00	7.00	1.00	89.00	112.00	0.00
陕西	Shaanxi	63.83	5.05	0.21	33.99	6.88	3.16	88.88	116.86	0.29
甘肃	Gansu	83.85	3.54	0.74	43.22	7.09	1.78	82.38	120.52	0.23
青海	Qinghai	79.77	5.28	0.72	34.44	8.26	2.11	86.75	126.41	0.81
宁夏	Ningxia	64.59	2.82	0.13	35.60	7.66	2.49	85.10	122.67	0.66
新疆	Xinjiang	76.68	4.56	0.78	32.65	16.24	3.89	87.23	108.61	0.37

10-18 农村居民家庭基本情况

Basic Conditions of Rural Households

项目	Item	2000	2001	2002	2003	2004	2005
调查户数 (户)	**Number of Households Surveyed (household)**	**68116**	**68190**	**68190**	**68190**	**68190**	**68190**
调查户人口 (人)	**Number of Residents Surveyed (person)**						
常住人口	Number of Permanent Residents in the Households Surveyed	286162	283223	281674	279536	278234	277759
平均每户常住人口	Average Number of Permanent Residents Per Household	4.20	4.15	4.13	4.10	4.08	4.08
平均每户整半劳动力	Average Number of Full/Semi Labour Force Per Household	2.76	2.73	2.76	2.80	2.82	2.82
平均每个劳动力负担人口(含本人)	Average Number of Dependents per Employee (including the laborer himself or herself)	1.52	1.52	1.50	1.47	1.45	1.44
平均每人年收入(元)	**Per Capita Annual Income (yuan)**						
总收入	Total Income	3146.21	3306.92	3448.62	3582.42	4039.60	4631.21
工资性收入	Income from Wages and Salaries	702.30	771.90	840.22	918.38	998.46	1174.53
家庭经营收入	Income from Household Operations	2251.28	2325.23	2380.51	2454.96	2804.51	3164.43
财产性收入	Income from Properties	45.04	46.97	50.68	65.75	76.61	88.45
转移性收入	Income from Transfers	147.59	162.82	177.21	143.33	160.03	203.81
现金收入	Cash Income	2381.60	2534.70	2712.95	2929.47	3234.16	3915.50
工资性收入	Income from Wages and Salaries	700.41	769.77	839.17	916.65	997.56	1173.10
家庭经营收入	Income from Household Operations	1498.81	1565.51	1653.65	1822.11	2019.83	2472.34
财产性收入	Income from Properties	38.89	41.05	47.65	53.96	62.59	71.78
转移性收入	Income from Transfers	143.49	158.37	172.48	136.75	154.18	198.31
平均每人年支出(元)	**Per Capita Annual Expenditures (yuan)**						
总支出	Total Expenditure	2652.42	2779.96	2923.60	3024.99	3430.10	4126.91
家庭经营费用支出	Expenditure for Household Operations	654.27	695.97	731.01	755.38	923.92	1189.70
购置生产性固定资产	Purchase of Productive Fixed Assets	63.90	78.13	85.50	101.64	107.74	131.14
税费支出	Taxes and Fees	95.52	91.24	78.70	67.31	37.49	13.10
生活消费支出	Expenses on Household Consumption	1670.13	1741.09	1834.31	1943.30	2184.65	2555.40
转移性和财产性支出	Expenses on Properties and Transfers	168.60	173.53	194.08	157.36	176.30	237.60
现金支出	Cash Expenditure	2140.37	2284.62	2437.72	2537.42	2862.54	3567.31
家庭经营费用支出	Expenditure for Household Operations	544.49	584.80	617.41	638.40	788.55	1052.53
购买生产性固定资产	Purchase of Productive Fixed Assets	63.91	78.13	85.50	101.64	107.74	131.14
税费支出	Taxes and Fees	89.81	86.35	75.58	65.99	36.91	12.91
生活消费支出	Expenses on Household Consumption	1284.74	1364.08	1467.62	1576.64	1754.46	2134.58
转移性和财产性支出	Expenses on Properties and Transfers	157.42	171.26	191.61	154.74	174.88	236.15
平均每人年纯收入(元)	**Per Capita Annual Net Income (yuan)**	**2253.42**	**2366.40**	**2475.63**	**2622.24**	**2936.40**	**3254.93**
工资性收入	Income from Wages and Salaries	702.30	771.90	840.22	918.38	998.46	1174.53
家庭经营纯收入	Income from Household Operations	1427.27	1459.63	1486.54	1541.28	1745.79	1844.53
财产性收入	Income from Properties	45.04	46.97	50.68	65.75	76.61	88.45
转移性收入	Income from Transfers	78.81	87.90	98.19	96.83	115.54	147.42

注：本表至10-34表为农村住户抽样调查资料。

a) Data from this table to 10-34 are obtained from the sample surveys on rural households.

10-19 农村居民按纯收入分组的户数占调查户比重
Percentage of Rural Households Grouped by Per Capita Annual Net Income

项　　目	Item	1990	1995	2000	2004	2005
按纯收入分组户数占调查户比重（%）	**Percentage of Households Grouped by Per Capita Annual Net Income (%)**					
100元以下	Less Than 100 Yuan	0.30	0.21	0.31	0.40	0.65
100-200（元）	100-200 Yuan	1.78	0.36	0.20	0.13	0.11
200-300（元）	200-300 Yuan	6.56	0.78	0.43	0.21	0.20
300-400（元）	300-400 Yuan	12.04	1.47	0.69	0.31	0.31
400-500（元）	400-500 Yuan	14.37	2.30	1.01	0.53	0.41
500-600（元）	500-600 Yuan	13.94	3.37	1.37	0.85	0.57
600-800（元）	600-800 Yuan	20.80	9.54	4.44	2.43	1.88
800-1000（元）	800-1000 Yuan	12.49	11.63	5.72	3.64	2.84
1000-1200（元）	1000-1200 Yuan		11.83	6.75	4.04	3.53
1200-1300（元）	1200-1300 Yuan	12.25	5.38	3.75	2.51	1.97
1300-1500（元）	1300-1500 Yuan		9.74	7.42	5.11	4.40
1500-1700（元）	1500-1700 Yuan	3.48	7.92	7.48	5.69	4.89
1700-2000（元）	1700-2000 Yuan		9.39	10.45	8.57	7.67
2000-2500（元）	2000-2500 Yuan		10.29	14.54	13.69	12.49
2500-3000（元）	2500-3000 Yuan		5.89	10.29	11.76	11.42
3000-3500（元）	3000-3500 Yuan		3.49	7.11	8.85	9.55
3500-4000（元）	3500-4000 Yuan	1.99	1.95	4.76	7.09	7.57
4000-4500（元）	4000-4500 Yuan		1.34	3.44	5.25	5.93
4500-5000（元）	4500-5000 Yuan		0.86	2.40	3.92	4.64
5000元以上	5000 Yuan and over		2.26	7.45	15.02	18.96

10-20 农村居民家庭平均每人纯收入
Per Capita Annual Net Income of Rural Households

单位：元　　(yuan)

项　　目	Item	1990	1995	2000	2004	2005
纯收入	**Net Income**	**686.31**	**1577.74**	**2253.42**	**2936.40**	**3254.93**
按收入来源分	**By Source**					
工资性收入	Wages Income	138.80	353.70	702.30	998.46	1174.53
家庭经营纯收入	Net Income from Household Business	518.55	1125.79	1427.27	1745.79	1844.53
农业收入	Farming	344.59	799.44	833.93	1056.50	1097.71
林业收入	Forestry	7.53	13.52	22.44	34.13	45.77
牧业收入	Animal Husbandry	96.81	127.81	207.35	271.08	283.60
渔业收入	Fishery	7.11	15.69	26.95	36.34	42.52
工业收入	Industry	9.15	13.63	52.67	58.65	61.13
建筑业收入	Construction	12.18	34.53	46.73	49.56	47.12
交通、运输、邮电业收入	Transport, Post and Telecommunication Services	13.45	27.76	63.63	72.90	84.19
批发、零售贸易及餐饮业	Wholesale and Retail Trade and Catering Services	12.69	34.26	78.54	94.07	108.55
社会服务业收入	Social Services	6.55	17.18	28.09	31.26	32.61
文教卫生业收入	Culture, Education and Health Care			6.86	8.35	10.13
其他收入	Others	8.49	41.97	60.08	32.94	31.19
转移性和财产性收入	Transfer Income and Property Income	28.96	98.25	123.85	192.15	235.87

10-21 各地区农村居民家庭人均纯收入
Per Capita Net Income of Rural Households by Region

单位：元 (yuan)

地 区	Region	1990	1995	2000	2002	2003	2004	2005
全 国	**National Average**	**686.31**	**1577.74**	**2253.42**	**2475.63**	**2622.24**	**2936.40**	**3254.93**
北 京	Beijing	1297.05	3223.65	4604.55	5398.48	5601.55	6170.33	7346.26
天 津	Tianjin	1069.04	2406.38	3622.39	4278.71	4566.01	5019.53	5579.87
河 北	Hebei	621.67	1668.73	2478.86	2685.16	2853.38	3171.06	3481.64
山 西	Shanxi	603.51	1208.30	1905.61	2149.82	2299.17	2589.60	2890.66
内蒙古	Inner Mongolia	607.15	1208.38	2038.21	2086.02	2267.65	2606.37	2988.87
辽 宁	Liaoning	836.17	1756.50	2355.58	2751.34	2934.44	3307.14	3690.21
吉 林	Jilin	803.52	1609.60	2022.50	2300.99	2530.41	2999.62	3263.99
黑龙江	Heilongjiang	759.86	1766.27	2148.22	2405.24	2508.94	3005.18	3221.27
上 海	Shanghai	1907.32	4245.61	5596.37	6223.55	6653.92	7066.33	8247.77
江 苏	Jiangsu	959.06	2456.86	3595.09	3979.79	4239.26	4753.85	5276.29
浙 江	Zhejiang	1099.04	2966.19	4253.67	4940.36	5389.04	5944.06	6659.95
安 徽	Anhui	539.16	1302.82	1934.57	2117.56	2127.48	2499.33	2640.96
福 建	Fujian	764.41	2048.59	3230.49	3538.83	3733.89	4089.38	4450.36
江 西	Jiangxi	669.90	1537.36	2135.30	2306.45	2457.53	2786.78	3128.89
山 东	Shandong	680.18	1715.09	2659.20	2947.65	3150.49	3507.43	3930.55
河 南	Henan	526.95	1231.97	1985.82	2215.74	2235.68	2553.15	2870.58
湖 北	Hubei	670.80	1511.22	2268.59	2444.06	2566.76	2890.01	3099.20
湖 南	Hunan	664.24	1425.16	2197.16	2397.92	2532.87	2837.76	3117.74
广 东	Guangdong	1043.03	2699.24	3654.48	3911.90	4054.58	4365.87	4690.49
广 西	Guangxi	639.45	1446.14	1864.51	2012.60	2094.51	2305.22	2494.67
海 南	Hainan	696.22	1519.71	2182.26	2423.20	2588.06	2817.62	3004.03
重 庆	Chongqing			1892.44	2097.58	2214.55	2510.41	2809.32
四 川	Sichuan	557.76	1158.29	1903.60	2107.64	2229.86	2518.93	2802.78
贵 州	Guizhou	435.14	1086.62	1374.16	1489.91	1564.66	1721.55	1876.96
云 南	Yunnan	540.86	1010.97	1478.60	1608.64	1697.12	1864.19	2041.79
西 藏	Tibet	649.71	1200.31	1330.81	1462.27	1690.76	1861.31	2077.90
陕 西	Shaanxi	530.80	962.89	1443.86	1596.25	1675.66	1866.52	2052.63
甘 肃	Gansu	430.98	880.34	1428.68	1590.30	1673.05	1852.22	1979.88
青 海	Qinghai	559.78	1029.77	1490.49	1668.94	1794.13	1957.65	2151.46
宁 夏	Ningxia	578.13	998.75	1724.30	1917.36	2043.30	2320.05	2508.89
新 疆	Xinjiang	683.47	1136.45	1618.08	1863.26	2106.19	2244.93	2482.15

10-22 各地区按来源分农村居民家庭人均纯收入(2005年)

Per Capita Annual Net Income of Rural Households by Sources and Region (2005)

单位：元 (yuan)

地区	Region	纯收入 Net Income	工资性收入 Income from Wages and Salaries	家庭经营纯收入 Income from Household Operations	财产性收入 Income from Properties	转移性收入 Income from Transfers
全国	**National Average**	**3254.93**	**1174.53**	**1844.53**	**88.45**	**147.42**
北京	Beijing	7346.26	4524.25	1778.33	588.04	455.64
天津	Tianjin	5579.87	2720.85	2626.46	152.88	79.68
河北	Hebei	3481.64	1293.50	1988.58	93.74	105.81
山西	Shanxi	2890.66	1177.94	1563.52	62.70	86.49
内蒙古	Inner Mongolia	2988.87	504.46	2223.26	73.05	188.10
辽宁	Liaoning	3690.21	1212.20	2163.49	113.24	201.28
吉林	Jilin	3263.99	510.96	2395.50	148.35	209.19
黑龙江	Heilongjiang	3221.27	464.31	2363.92	230.63	162.41
上海	Shanghai	8247.77	6159.70	774.60	457.52	855.95
江苏	Jiangsu	5276.29	2786.11	2124.97	150.44	214.76
浙江	Zhejiang	6659.95	3238.77	2789.40	278.92	352.86
安徽	Anhui	2640.96	1010.05	1499.25	44.91	86.75
福建	Fujian	4450.36	1650.65	2365.02	98.73	335.96
江西	Jiangxi	3128.89	1227.94	1786.41	25.78	88.76
山东	Shandong	3930.55	1437.57	2258.05	102.80	132.13
河南	Henan	2870.58	853.95	1913.66	35.85	67.13
湖北	Hubei	3099.20	941.64	2049.04	16.81	91.71
湖南	Hunan	3117.74	1228.79	1713.35	42.05	133.55
广东	Guangdong	4690.49	2562.39	1731.97	167.25	228.88
广西	Guangxi	2494.67	907.36	1516.36	18.30	52.66
海南	Hainan	3004.03	473.06	2345.56	55.58	129.83
重庆	Chongqing	2809.32	1088.80	1541.48	30.69	148.35
四川	Sichuan	2802.78	954.89	1681.63	41.59	124.65
贵州	Guizhou	1876.96	583.28	1153.36	35.51	104.81
云南	Yunnan	2041.79	348.31	1530.13	75.52	87.84
西藏	Tibet	2077.90	565.18	1187.13	217.22	108.37
陕西	Shaanxi	2052.63	756.71	1118.91	56.92	120.09
甘肃	Gansu	1979.88	586.71	1263.42	20.57	109.18
青海	Qinghai	2151.46	560.52	1359.56	61.99	169.40
宁夏	Ningxia	2508.89	702.10	1561.94	48.62	196.24
新疆	Xinjiang	2482.15	195.51	2140.76	33.87	112.01

10-23 按收入五等份分农村居民家庭基本情况（2005年）

Basic Conditions of Rural Households by Five Equal Parts of Income (2005)

项　目	Item	低收入户 Low Income Households	中低收入户 Lower Middle Income Households	中等收入户 Middle Income Households	中高收入户 Upper Middle Income Households	高收入户 High Income Households
平均每户常住人口（人）	Average Number of Permanent Residents Per Household	4.58	4.35	4.10	3.86	3.48
平均每户整半劳动力（人）	Average Number of Full/Semi Labour Force Per Household	2.94	2.91	2.85	2.78	2.61
平均每个劳动力负担人口（人）	Average Number of Dependents per Employee (including self)	1.56	1.49	1.44	1.39	1.33
平均每人总收入（元）	Per Capita Annual Income (yuan)	2090.02	3024.44	4022.67	5453.55	10210.56
#现金收入	Cash Income	1538.81	2312.43	3266.32	4659.38	9408.66
平均每人总支出（元）	Per Capita Annual Expenditures (yuan)	2647.00	3036.29	3652.61	4561.23	7515.01
#现金支出	Cash Expenditures	2110.56	2466.16	3057.86	3986.29	6996.58
平均每人纯收入（元）	Per Capita Annual Net Income (yuan)	1067.22	2018.31	2850.95	4003.33	7747.35
工资性收入	Income from Wages and Salaries	321.72	672.22	1043.14	1538.84	3096.99
家庭经营纯收入	Income from Household Operations	662.60	1230.66	1651.88	2230.97	3965.85
财产性收入	Income from Properties	21.93	32.35	46.41	80.90	304.03
转移性收入	Income from Transfers	60.97	83.09	109.52	152.63	380.48

10-24 按收入五等份分农村居民家庭平均每人生活消费支出（2005年）

Per Capita Consumption Expenditure of Rural Households by Five Equal Parts of Income (2005)

单位：元 (yuan)

项　目	Item	低收入户 Low Income Households	中低收入户 Lower Middle Income Households	中等收入户 Middle Income Households	中高收入户 Upper Middle Income Households	高收入户 High Income Households
生活消费总支出	**Consumption Expenditure**	**1548.30**	**1913.07**	**2327.69**	**2879.06**	**4593.05**
食品	Food	796.26	950.12	1120.87	1297.26	1807.58
衣着	Clothing	87.98	108.71	132.39	167.51	276.18
居住	Residence	205.88	249.80	313.19	411.45	758.16
家庭设备用品及服务	Household Appliances and Services	59.60	76.22	95.84	127.60	224.14
交通通讯	Transport and Telecommunications	111.19	153.74	206.96	281.55	539.37
文教娱乐用品及服务	Education, Cultural and Recreation and Services	155.49	209.39	262.18	345.17	571.45
医疗保健	Health Care and Medical Services	106.45	128.52	148.11	183.52	305.10
其他商品及服务	Other Goods and Services	25.45	36.57	48.16	65.00	111.06
生活消费现金支出	**Cash Consumption Expenditure**	**1163.18**	**1486.85**	**1871.00**	**2438.79**	**4195.87**
食品	Food	435.00	553.85	696.97	888.15	1440.14
衣着	Clothing	87.20	108.04	131.88	166.89	275.66
居住	Residence	183.70	221.40	282.23	381.64	729.49
家庭设备用品及服务	Household Appliances and Services	58.98	75.68	94.81	127.42	224.04
交通通讯	Transport and Telecommunications	111.19	153.74	206.96	281.55	539.37
文教娱乐用品及服务	Education, Cultural and Recreation and Services	155.49	209.39	262.18	345.17	571.45
医疗保健	Health Care and Medical Services	106.45	128.52	148.11	183.52	305.10
其他商品及服务	Other Goods and Services	25.17	36.23	47.86	64.46	110.62

10-25 农村居民家庭平均每人生活消费支出构成

Composition of Per Capita Consumption Expenditure of Rural Households

单位：% (%)

指 标	Item	1990	1995	2000	2004	2005
生活消费总支出	**Consumption Expenditure**	**100.00**	**100.00**	**100.00**	**100.00**	**100.00**
食品	Food	58.80	58.62	49.13	47.23	45.48
衣着	Clothing	7.77	6.85	5.75	5.50	5.81
居住	Residence	17.34	13.91	15.47	14.84	14.49
家庭设备用品及服务	Household Appliances and Services	5.29	5.23	4.52	4.08	4.36
交通通讯	Transport and Telecommunications	1.44	2.58	5.58	8.82	9.59
文教娱乐用品及服务	Education, Cultural and Recreation and Services	5.37	7.81	11.18	11.33	11.56
医疗保健	Health Care and Medical Services	3.25	3.24	5.24	5.98	6.58
其他商品及服务	Other Goods and Services	0.74	1.76	3.14	2.21	2.13
生活消费现金支出	**Cash Consumption Expenditure**	**100.00**	**100.00**	**100.00**	**100.00**	**100.00**
食品	Food	41.59	41.10	36.14	35.90	36.11
衣着	Clothing	11.75	10.32	7.41	6.81	6.93
居住	Residence	21.66	17.20	17.98	16.94	16.04
家庭设备用品及服务	Household Appliances and Services	8.20	7.92	5.79	5.07	5.20
交通通讯	Transport and Telecommunications	2.24	3.92	7.25	10.98	11.48
文教娱乐用品及服务	Education, Cultural and Recreation and Services	8.36	11.91	14.53	14.11	13.84
医疗保健	Health Care and Medical Services	5.06	4.94	6.82	7.44	7.87
其他商品及服务	Other Goods and Services	1.13	2.68	4.08	2.74	2.54

10-26 各地区农村居民家庭平均每人生活消费支出（2005年）

Per Capita Consumption Expenditure of Rural Households by Region (2005)

单位：元 (yuan)

地区	Region	生活消费支出合计 Consumption Expenditure	食品 Food	衣着 Clothing	居住 Residence	家庭设备及服务 Household Appliances and Services	交通和通讯 Transport, and Communi-cations	文教、娱乐用品及服务 Education, Cultural and Recreation and Services	医疗保健 Health Care and Medical Services	其他商品及服务 Other Goods and Services
全国	**National Average**	**2555.40**	**1162.16**	**148.57**	**370.16**	**111.44**	**244.98**	**295.48**	**168.09**	**54.52**
北京	Beijing	5315.71	1735.95	378.66	854.35	326.89	615.49	796.99	504.20	103.18
天津	Tianjin	3035.96	1171.39	257.26	614.29	117.11	327.58	328.86	179.18	40.29
河北	Hebei	2165.72	888.37	155.52	398.90	101.49	221.96	225.79	134.77	38.92
山西	Shanxi	1877.70	830.48	202.35	200.56	68.93	160.27	279.54	102.90	32.66
内蒙古	Inner Mongolia	2446.17	1054.26	150.01	334.69	84.41	293.32	309.40	176.44	43.64
辽宁	Liaoning	2805.94	1127.23	221.02	378.21	100.42	300.71	376.93	233.53	67.90
吉林	Jilin	2305.98	1003.22	168.21	256.66	81.92	284.86	261.09	193.57	56.44
黑龙江	Heilongjiang	2544.65	923.59	184.11	526.99	73.77	256.58	277.00	253.52	49.09
上海	Shanghai	7277.94	2683.89	366.44	1319.76	458.11	747.54	936.51	561.72	203.97
江苏	Jiangsu	3567.11	1569.27	191.15	512.47	167.97	363.76	478.94	198.56	84.98
浙江	Zhejiang	5432.95	2061.44	318.86	914.06	260.45	618.26	722.95	415.63	121.31
安徽	Anhui	2196.23	999.79	117.41	344.86	106.36	196.72	256.80	133.68	40.61
福建	Fujian	3292.63	1517.60	186.70	457.26	154.42	365.60	356.54	154.03	100.47
江西	Jiangxi	2483.70	1220.53	124.52	326.20	96.36	229.59	276.26	154.68	55.57
山东	Shandong	2735.77	1087.65	159.73	445.71	136.54	294.37	377.16	188.48	46.13
河南	Henan	1891.57	858.97	132.36	317.97	82.69	159.73	177.66	123.41	38.76
湖北	Hubei	2430.19	1192.26	125.01	310.27	110.04	223.16	271.86	135.37	62.23
湖南	Hunan	2756.43	1433.01	127.89	307.28	114.31	218.96	329.28	168.19	57.50
广东	Guangdong	3707.73	1789.42	143.50	530.30	152.12	411.64	360.73	203.85	116.17
广西	Guangxi	2349.60	1186.71	79.48	379.65	95.47	214.07	226.38	123.39	44.45
海南	Hainan	1969.09	1134.75	66.35	146.00	92.28	178.00	198.70	93.00	60.00
重庆	Chongqing	2142.12	1130.35	95.96	231.15	95.78	163.05	249.71	142.65	33.48
四川	Sichuan	2274.17	1244.36	116.35	234.05	102.13	171.50	225.16	144.45	36.18
贵州	Guizhou	1552.39	819.87	79.59	235.50	61.69	99.22	160.91	71.79	23.82
云南	Yunnan	1789.00	975.72	80.33	225.79	67.03	99.81	182.62	122.33	35.37
西藏	Tibet	1723.76	1185.23	182.45	84.24	81.24	79.26	28.20	44.44	38.70
陕西	Shaanxi	1896.48	812.93	124.36	211.71	83.61	163.17	297.33	165.82	37.55
甘肃	Gansu	1819.58	858.89	92.33	240.74	74.09	155.03	257.88	113.96	26.65
青海	Qinghai	1976.03	893.32	156.11	329.33	83.96	208.43	109.53	152.33	43.03
宁夏	Ningxia	2094.48	922.54	143.09	345.93	77.16	178.47	177.90	198.84	50.55
新疆	Xinjiang	1924.41	803.82	171.40	333.19	68.03	183.00	159.32	169.28	36.38

10-27 各地区农村居民家庭平均每人生活消费现金支出（2005年）

Per Capita Cash Consumption Expenditure of Rural Households by Region (2005)

单位：元 (yuan)

地区	Region	生活消费支出合计 Consumption Expenditure	食品 Food	衣着 Clothing	居住 Residence	家庭设备及服务 Household Appliances and Services	交通和通讯 Transport, and Communi-cations	文教、娱乐用品及服务 Education, Cultural and Recreation and Services	医疗保健 Health Care and Medical Services	其他商品及服务 Other Goods and Services
全国	**National Average**	**2134.58**	**770.69**	**147.94**	**342.33**	**110.92**	**244.98**	**295.48**	**168.09**	**54.14**
北京	Beijing	5273.62	1697.31	378.53	853.21	326.34	615.49	796.99	504.20	101.56
天津	Tianjin	2956.11	1092.20	256.60	614.29	117.10	327.58	328.86	179.18	40.29
河北	Hebei	1916.94	640.06	155.25	398.90	101.47	221.96	225.79	134.77	38.74
山西	Shanxi	1636.83	596.81	202.29	193.57	68.92	160.27	279.54	102.90	32.53
内蒙古	Inner Mongolia	1992.06	645.74	147.19	293.95	84.36	293.32	309.40	176.44	41.66
辽宁	Liaoning	2491.54	837.49	220.15	354.44	100.39	300.71	376.93	233.53	67.90
吉林	Jilin	1990.22	736.86	168.06	207.45	81.89	284.86	261.09	193.57	56.44
黑龙江	Heilongjiang	2295.17	751.02	184.11	450.08	73.77	256.58	277.00	253.52	49.09
上海	Shanghai	7091.46	2497.42	366.44	1319.75	458.11	747.54	936.51	561.72	203.97
江苏	Jiangsu	3137.88	1155.59	191.15	497.99	166.90	363.76	478.94	198.56	84.98
浙江	Zhejiang	5178.56	1835.27	318.46	886.38	260.42	618.26	722.95	415.63	121.19
安徽	Anhui	1797.66	638.93	117.21	310.20	103.63	196.72	256.80	133.68	40.49
福建	Fujian	2928.89	1211.73	186.69	402.89	154.42	365.60	356.54	154.03	96.98
江西	Jiangxi	1946.19	727.55	124.43	281.99	96.34	229.59	276.26	154.68	55.35
山东	Shandong	2470.39	826.92	158.67	442.75	136.54	294.37	377.16	188.48	45.51
河南	Henan	1520.18	533.67	131.94	272.55	82.62	159.73	177.66	123.41	38.59
湖北	Hubei	1813.40	611.09	121.77	278.56	109.36	223.16	271.86	135.37	62.23
湖南	Hunan	2178.48	873.14	127.73	289.36	114.31	218.96	329.28	168.19	57.50
广东	Guangdong	3224.28	1369.96	143.49	466.47	151.96	411.64	360.73	203.85	116.17
广西	Guangxi	1860.36	750.52	79.48	326.66	95.47	214.07	226.38	123.39	44.39
海南	Hainan	1523.85	719.64	66.35	115.88	92.28	178.00	198.70	93.00	60.00
重庆	Chongqing	1494.18	509.51	95.95	204.16	95.68	163.05	249.71	142.65	33.48
四川	Sichuan	1623.02	623.61	116.01	208.05	98.25	171.50	225.16	144.45	35.99
贵州	Guizhou	1095.55	375.37	79.59	224.22	61.66	99.22	160.91	71.79	22.79
云南	Yunnan	1256.84	485.96	80.28	183.70	66.97	99.81	182.62	122.33	35.17
西藏	Tibet	969.45	447.00	177.25	74.97	79.68	79.26	28.20	44.44	38.63
陕西	Shaanxi	1642.78	562.25	124.19	208.85	83.61	163.17	297.33	165.82	37.55
甘肃	Gansu	1295.65	347.30	92.13	228.92	73.80	155.03	257.88	113.96	26.63
青海	Qinghai	1445.35	406.48	154.63	294.85	82.63	208.43	109.53	152.33	36.48
宁夏	Ningxia	1648.53	484.11	143.05	338.45	77.16	178.47	177.90	198.84	50.55
新疆	Xinjiang	1582.17	476.09	166.90	324.04	67.17	183.00	159.32	169.28	36.38

10-28 东、中、西部及东北地区农村居民家庭基本情况（2005年）

Basic Conditions of Rural Households of Eastern, Central, Western and Northeastern Region (2005)

项目	Item	东部地区 Eastern Region	中部地区 Central Region	西部地区 Western Region	东北地区 Northeastern Region
平均每户常住人口（人）	**Average Number of Permanent Residents (per Household) (person)**	**3.93**	**4.10**	**4.32**	**3.58**
平均每户整半劳动力（人）	Average Number of Full Labor Force/ Semi Labor Force (per Household) (person)	2.75	2.89	2.86	2.66
平均每个劳动力负担人口(人)	Average Number of Dependents per Employee (including himself or herself) (person)	1.43	1.42	1.51	1.35
平均每人总收入（元）	**Per Capita Annual Income (yuan)**	**6226.58**	**4051.78**	**3646.02**	**5783.68**
#现金收入	Cash Income	5679.68	3288.39	2806.89	5124.74
平均每人总支出（元）	**Per Capita Annual Expenditures (yuan)**	**5095.32**	**3518.26**	**3447.80**	**5578.19**
#现金支出	Cash Expenditures	4707.16	2963.98	2709.74	5120.81
平均每人纯收入（元）	**Per Capita Annual Net Income (yuan)**	**4720.28**	**2956.60**	**2378.91**	**3378.98**
工资性收入	Wages Income	2198.08	1052.64	674.52	709.68
家庭经营纯收入	Household Business Income	2140.62	1774.92	1537.76	2310.79
财产性收入	Property Income	159.71	36.83	49.30	170.63
转移性收入	Transfer Income	221.87	92.21	117.33	187.88
生活消费总支出（元）	**Living Expenditure (yuan)**	**3408.97**	**2276.90**	**2022.88**	**2557.30**
食品	Food	1435.92	1094.07	1007.17	1009.58
衣着	Clothing	191.46	134.49	112.76	191.00
居住	Residence	537.46	307.16	265.54	403.36
家庭设备用品及服务	Household Facilities, Articles and Services	163.19	97.58	82.55	84.37
交通通讯	Transport, Post and Telecommunications	367.46	197.51	167.54	278.37
文教娱乐用品及服务	Cultural, Educational and Recreational Articles and Services	414.74	260.23	216.46	303.44
医疗保健	Medicines and Medical Services	218.51	137.62	134.64	230.14
其他商品及服务	Other Commodities and Services	80.23	48.26	36.21	57.03
生活消费现金支出（元）	**Consumption Paid in Cash (yuan)**	**3087.44**	**1811.63**	**1521.48**	**2268.69**
食品	Food	1137.01	661.91	532.98	773.78
衣着	Clothing	191.14	133.75	111.88	190.69
居住	Residence	515.88	275.46	240.60	350.88
家庭设备用品及服务	Household Facilities, Articles and Services	162.99	96.99	81.71	84.35
交通通讯	Transport, Post and Telecommunications	367.46	197.51	167.54	278.37
文教娱乐用品及服务	Cultural, Educational and Recreational Articles and Services	414.74	260.23	216.46	303.44
医疗保健	Medicines and Medical Services	218.51	137.62	134.64	230.14
其他商品及服务	Other Commodities and Services	79.71	48.15	35.67	57.03

10–29 农村居民家庭平均每人主要食品消费量
Per Capita Consumption of Major Foods in Rural Households of National at the Year-end

品 名	Item	2000	2001	2002	2003	2004	2005
粮食(原粮)(公斤)	Grain (Unprocessed) (kg)	250.23	238.62	236.50	222.44	218.26	208.85
#小麦	Wheat	80.27	76.81	76.31	73.23	72.39	68.44
稻谷	Rice	126.82	122.89	123.11	119.31	117.40	113.36
大豆	Soybeans	2.53	2.46	2.20	2.05	1.91	1.91
蔬菜 (公斤)	Fresh Vegetables (kg)	106.74	109.30	110.55	107.40	106.61	102.28
食油 (公斤)	Edible Oil (kg)	7.06	7.03	7.53	6.27	5.29	6.01
#植物油	Vegetable Oil	5.45	5.51	5.77	5.31	4.31	4.90
肉禽及制品(公斤)	Meats, Poultry and Related Products (kg)	18.30	18.21	18.60	19.68	19.24	22.42
#猪肉	Pork	13.28	13.35	13.70	13.78	13.46	15.62
牛肉	Beef	0.52	0.55	0.52	0.50	0.48	0.64
羊肉	Mutton	0.61	0.60	0.65	0.76	0.82	0.83
家禽	Poultry	2.81	2.87	2.91	3.20	3.13	3.67
蛋及制品 (公斤)	Eggs and Related Products (kg)	4.77	4.72	4.66	4.81	4.59	4.71
奶及制品 (公斤)	Milk and Related Products (kg)	1.06	1.20	1.19	1.71	1.98	2.86
水产品 (公斤)	Aquatic Products (kg)	3.92	4.12	4.36	4.65	4.49	4.94
食糖 (公斤)	Sugar (kg)	1.28	1.43	1.64	1.24	1.11	1.13
酒 (公斤)	Liquor (kg)	7.02	7.10	7.49	7.67	7.84	9.59
瓜果及制品(公斤)	Fruits and Related Products (kg)	18.31	20.33	18.77	17.54	16.97	17.18
坚果及制品(公斤)	Nuts and Related Products (kg)	0.74	0.82	0.78	0.72	0.73	0.81

10–30 农村居民家庭平均每百户年底耐用消费品拥有量
Number of Durable Consumer Goods Owned Per 100 Rural Households at the Year-end

品 名	Item	2000	2001	2002	2003	2004	2005
洗衣机 (台)	Washing Machine (unit)	28.58	29.94	31.80	34.27	37.32	40.20
电风扇 (台)	Electric Fan (unit)	122.62	129.42	134.26	138.08	141.91	146.35
电冰箱 (台)	Refrigerator (unit)	12.31	13.59	14.83	15.89	17.75	20.10
空调机 (台)	Air Conditioner (unit)	1.32	1.70	2.29	3.45	4.70	6.40
抽油烟机 (台)	Exhaust Fan (unit)	2.75	3.15	3.58	4.11	4.81	5.98
自行车 (辆)	Bicycle (unit)	120.48	120.83	121.32	118.50	118.15	98.37
摩托车 (辆)	Motorcycle (unit)	21.94	24.71	28.07	31.80	36.15	40.70
电话机 (部)	Telephone Set (set)	26.38	34.11	40.77	49.06	54.54	58.30
移动电话 (部)	Mobile Telephone (set)	4.32	8.06	13.67	23.68	34.72	50.20
组合音响 (台)	Hi-Fi Stereo Component System (unit)	7.76	8.67	9.73	10.46	11.48	13.00
寻呼机 (台)	Beep-pager (unit)	7.74	7.07	5.45	3.02	1.92	0.36
黑白电视机(台)	Black and White TV Set (unit)	52.97	50.74	48.14	42.80	37.92	21.77
彩色电视机(台)	Color TV Set (unit)	48.74	54.41	60.45	67.80	75.09	84.00
录放像机 (台)	Video-recorder (unit)	3.30	3.33	3.32	3.51	3.65	3.00
收录机 (台)	Radio Cassette Player (unit)	21.58	20.74	20.41	18.70	17.97	10.98
照相机 (架)	Camera (set)	3.12	3.23	3.34	3.36	3.68	4.05
家用计算机(台)	Computer (set)	0.47	0.69	1.10	1.42	1.90	2.10

10-31 东、中、西部及东北地区农村居民家庭平均每人主要食品消费量（2005年）

Major Foods Consumption Per Capita in Whole Year of Rural Households of Eastern, Central, Western and Northeastern Region (2005)

品 名	Item	东部地区 Eastern Region	中部地区 Central Region	西部地区 Western Region	东北地区 Northeastern Region
粮食(原粮)（公斤）	Grain (Unprocessed) (kg)	196.59	222.09	214.23	184.56
#小麦	Wheat	66.66	69.16	76.42	35.94
稻谷	Rice	108.07	133.64	104.94	98.01
大豆	Soybeans	1.60	1.81	1.45	5.69
蔬菜 （公斤）	Fresh Vegetables (kg)	85.96	116.11	97.71	138.84
食油 （公斤）	Edible Oil (kg)	13.20	5.93	5.01	7.92
#植物油	Vegetable Oil	11.98	4.52	4.10	7.46
肉禽及制品（公斤）	Meats, Poultry and Related Products (kg)	22.20	17.58	27.43	18.30
#猪肉	Pork	13.16	12.90	20.66	12.55
牛肉	Beef	0.53	0.43	0.90	0.66
羊肉	Mutton	0.42	0.14	1.87	0.32
家禽	Poultry	5.01	3.07	3.05	3.21
蛋及制品 （公斤）	Eggs and Related Products (kg)	6.05	5.16	2.57	7.44
奶及制品 （公斤）	Milk and Related Products (kg)	3.56	1.01	3.97	1.86
水产品 （公斤）	Aquatic Products (kg)	9.42	4.53	1.39	4.46
食糖 （公斤）	Sugar (kg)	1.21	1.07	1.18	0.76
酒 （公斤）	Liquor (kg)	13.19	7.88	6.51	15.55
瓜果及制品（公斤）	Fruits and Related Products (kg)	17.19	18.16	14.18	27.38
坚果及制品（公斤）	Nuts and Related Products (kg)	1.08	0.74	0.67	0.67

10-32 东、中、西部及东北地区农村居民家庭平均每百户年底耐用消费品拥有量（2005年）

Number of Durable Consumer Goods Owned per 100 Rural Households of Eastern, Central, Western and Northeastern Region (2005)

品 名	Item	东部地区 Eastern Region	中部地区 Central Region	西部地区 Western Region	东北地区 Northeastern Region
洗衣机 （台）	Washing Machine (unit)	55.54	36.39	31.69	63.00
电风扇 （台）	Electric Fan (unit)	213.22	171.37	89.16	32.74
电冰箱 （台）	Refrigerator (unit)	40.11	14.84	10.55	19.67
空调机 （台）	Air Conditioner (unit)	18.71	3.56	0.81	0.33
抽油烟机（台）	Exhaust Fan (unit)	15.02	1.83	1.00	4.80
自行车 （辆）	Bicycle (unit)	146.08	96.23	57.94	81.62
摩托车 （辆）	Motorcycle (unit)	64.54	37.15	32.59	40.49
电话机 （部）	Telephone Set (set)	86.29	57.14	46.02	76.54
移动电话（部）	Mobile Telephone (set)	78.89	55.35	44.14	58.73
组合音响（台）	Hi-Fi Stereo Component System (unit)	18.39	8.44	12.47	9.81
寻呼机 （台）	Beep-pager (unit)	0.53	0.36	0.24	0.21
黑白电视机（台）	Black and White TV Set (unit)	17.22	29.64	22.43	10.45
彩色电视机（台）	Color TV Set (unit)	107.26	81.01	78.40	99.01
录放像机（台）	Video-recorder (unit)	5.51	1.41	2.05	2.44
收录机 （台）	Radio Cassette Player (unit)	12.39	6.88	13.45	9.63
照相机 （架）	Camera (set)	7.48	2.46	2.13	3.77
家用计算机（台）	Computer (set)	6.20	0.95	0.42	1.19

10-33 各地区农村居民家庭平均每人主要食品消费量（2005年）

Per Capita Consumption of Major Food in Rural Households by Region (2005)

单位：公斤 (kg)

地区	Region	粮食 Grain	蔬菜 Vegetables	食油 Edible Oil	猪牛羊肉 Pork, Beef and Mutton	家禽 Poultry	蛋类及其制品 Eggs and Related Products	水产品 Aquatic Products	食糖 Sugar	酒 Liquor
全国	**National Average**	**208.85**	**102.28**	**6.01**	**17.09**	**3.67**	**4.71**	**4.94**	**1.13**	**9.59**
北京	Beijing	128.61	92.41	9.35	17.41	2.93	9.32	4.89	1.27	21.25
天津	Tianjin	152.65	79.00	9.44	12.05	0.65	8.94	7.45	0.41	10.81
河北	Hebei	200.00	57.70	6.75	8.00	0.75	6.27	2.48	0.77	9.16
山西	Shanxi	214.90	80.72	5.54	5.54	0.41	5.74	0.67	0.96	3.40
内蒙古	Inner Mongolia	207.43	76.93	4.35	26.26	2.25	4.29	1.56	1.08	13.53
辽宁	Liaoning	195.35	173.58	7.21	17.86	2.08	8.58	5.74	0.70	13.73
吉林	Jilin	175.02	138.09	6.81	14.41	4.29	8.60	4.02	0.72	14.83
黑龙江	Heilongjiang	183.03	112.64	9.24	9.58	3.32	5.74	3.77	0.84	17.45
上海	Shanghai	145.49	70.59	8.62	19.47	8.90	7.66	19.12	1.92	18.23
江苏	Jiangsu	207.22	108.87	4.95	14.07	5.65	6.38	9.97	1.19	11.24
浙江	Zhejiang	184.28	82.03	5.57	17.77	6.45	4.59	15.47	1.64	25.16
安徽	Anhui	213.46	78.70	6.31	10.70	4.64	4.69	5.18	1.16	12.72
福建	Fujian	190.36	90.48	4.85	18.88	6.16	3.40	14.27	1.95	18.56
江西	Jiangxi	243.94	136.40	7.00	15.61	3.75	3.50	5.43	1.02	9.72
山东	Shandong	194.20	72.86	9.70	8.48	2.66	10.44	4.55	0.57	17.25
河南	Henan	210.91	100.75	4.36	6.43	1.57	8.48	1.30	1.06	5.97
湖北	Hubei	214.80	152.47	3.70	21.07	3.02	4.14	8.11	0.97	10.17
湖南	Hunan	237.95	140.07	8.97	20.56	4.61	3.38	6.23	1.19	5.18
广东	Guangdong	228.28	122.02	6.40	20.91	10.08	2.76	14.48	1.89	3.72
广西	Guangxi	189.45	101.68	5.05	15.44	9.19	1.05	4.21	1.18	7.33
海南	Hainan	188.79	71.19	4.34	18.49	10.02	1.23	15.07	1.10	4.82
重庆	Chongqing	215.62	152.33	4.49	30.29	3.82	6.53	2.30	1.95	10.40
四川	Sichuan	220.98	155.89	4.89	31.59	4.40	4.84	2.19	1.45	8.29
贵州	Guizhou	186.35	135.51	4.01	30.55	1.69	1.28	0.36	0.85	6.26
云南	Yunnan	192.17	98.30	3.26	28.51	2.93	1.67	1.06	1.21	6.72
西藏	Tibet	262.02	23.03	4.53	54.88	0.09	0.64	0.01	3.18	1.24
陕西	Shaanxi	205.22	54.01	6.47	8.02	0.43	2.21	0.35	0.75	3.57
甘肃	Gansu	261.64	43.57	3.61	16.56	0.81	1.66	0.21	0.75	4.88
青海	Qinghai	232.46	43.63	3.46	20.77	0.56	0.54	0.35	1.51	2.96
宁夏	Ningxia	233.26	82.68	4.75	13.25	2.50	2.17	0.45	1.38	2.97
新疆	Xinjiang	235.37	67.89	10.90	12.22	1.70	1.00	0.41	0.45	1.27

10-34 各地区农村居民家庭平均每百户主要耐用消费品拥有量（2005年底）

Number of Durable Consumer Goods Owned Per 100 Rural Households by Region at the Year-end (2005)

地区	Region	大型家具（件）Large Furniture (unit)	洗衣机（台）Washing Machine (unit)	电风扇（台）Electric Fan (unit)	电冰箱（台）Refrigerator (unit)	空调机（台）Air Conditioner (unit)	抽油烟机（台）Exhaust Fan (unit)	自行车（辆）Bicycle (unit)
全　国	**National Average**	**304.26**	**40.20**	**146.35**	**20.10**	**6.40**	**5.98**	**98.37**
北　京	Beijing	278.80	97.07	153.47	100.00	53.47	42.00	196.00
天　津	Tianjin	144.00	94.17	136.50	78.67	42.17	19.83	182.83
河　北	Hebei	246.57	74.17	161.00	30.64	4.48	3.81	174.38
山　西	Shanxi	305.43	69.29	58.19	14.43	1.00	2.57	102.81
内蒙古	Inner Mongolia	169.08	36.12	17.52	12.86	0.19	1.55	60.97
辽　宁	Liaoning	141.69	63.71	58.73	28.04	0.79	7.35	104.29
吉　林	Jilin	89.44	59.06	20.81	14.44	0.19	1.06	67.50
黑龙江	Heilongjiang	70.40	65.22	19.33	16.34	0.04	5.31	72.59
上　海	Shanghai	278.17	85.67	306.17	89.00	84.00	60.00	173.50
江　苏	Jiangsu	322.38	67.88	241.50	36.03	22.24	12.65	162.15
浙　江	Zhejiang	372.52	51.70	294.07	66.48	40.56	37.41	130.89
安　徽	Anhui	293.61	32.71	202.84	21.71	5.32	2.19	114.32
福　建	Fujian	253.79	46.21	194.34	38.13	10.99	9.62	68.13
江　西	Jiangxi	260.69	7.02	176.41	10.53	2.00	1.80	96.90
山　东	Shandong	336.43	40.90	175.50	28.60	4.02	6.00	169.26
河　南	Henan	301.93	55.67	170.57	13.48	5.19	0.48	133.38
湖　北	Hubei	360.79	26.39	179.36	14.82	3.79	3.12	79.09
湖　南	Hunan	503.27	27.30	199.68	13.73	2.54	1.51	50.03
广　东	Guangdong	445.82	29.49	289.77	24.73	18.13	15.94	109.65
广　西	Guangxi	200.09	6.80	241.52	6.67	0.61	1.08	86.06
海　南	Hainan	195.42	3.89	125.28	7.36	0.42	0.97	48.06
重　庆	Chongqing	353.72	21.50	156.28	13.56	2.17	1.33	14.06
四　川	Sichuan	516.33	40.85	170.45	12.33	1.05	0.88	42.98
贵　州	Guizhou	429.96	29.91	44.73	8.79	0.71	1.07	7.46
云　南	Yunnan	102.08	21.25	8.71	6.92	0.38	0.75	30.96
西　藏	Tibet	534.79	6.46	0.42	4.58			32.29
陕　西	Shaanxi	245.95	53.38	88.74	8.02	1.31	0.63	110.00
甘　肃	Gansu	320.17	39.06	26.33	7.06	1.06	0.78	102.50
青　海	Qinghai	303.50	44.00	4.00	18.00	0.17	1.33	39.33
宁　夏	Ningxia	424.67	44.50	25.50	10.17		1.17	120.33
新　疆	Xinjiang	241.74	28.26	17.03	20.13	0.39	1.23	80.97

10-34 续表 continued

地 区	Region	摩托车 (辆) Motorcycle (unit)	电话机 (部) Telephone Set (unit)	黑白电视机 (台) Black and White TV Set (unit)	彩色电视机 (台) Color TV Set (unit)	录放像机 (台) Video-recorder (unit)	收录机 (台) Radio Cassette Player (unit)	照相机 (架) Camera (unit)	家用计算机 (台) Computer (set)
全 国	**National Average**	**40.70**	**58.30**	**21.77**	**84.00**	**3.00**	**10.98**	**4.05**	**2.10**
北 京	Beijing	45.33	105.07	4.40	130.67	8.80	22.40	33.07	29.87
天 津	Tianjin	53.50	84.50	1.33	116.50	4.33	18.67	10.00	6.00
河 北	Hebei	58.17	76.74	14.60	102.14	2.83	11.10	3.50	1.21
山 西	Shanxi	39.29	50.29	21.86	82.33	1.95	17.10	4.81	0.57
内蒙古	Inner Mongolia	49.56	39.71	14.76	87.09	0.68	16.17	2.82	0.29
辽 宁	Liaoning	45.40	87.25	9.05	102.28	4.44	8.94	6.14	2.59
吉 林	Jilin	43.75	71.19	10.38	97.94	1.88	9.63	2.56	0.19
黑龙江	Heilongjiang	34.02	71.34	11.70	97.01	1.16	10.22	2.63	0.71
上 海	Shanghai	72.00	114.83	21.33	157.33	13.50	27.00	18.00	32.00
江 苏	Jiangsu	52.74	89.38	31.41	104.71	6.76	11.76	6.71	2.88
浙 江	Zhejiang	62.63	96.52	20.89	133.63	10.52	14.89	9.22	11.19
安 徽	Anhui	34.65	72.84	32.23	84.65	2.35	7.68	3.06	0.77
福 建	Fujian	75.22	94.18	13.85	109.67	3.96	6.76	5.49	4.89
江 西	Jiangxi	43.39	61.92	35.39	82.33	2.20	3.92	1.84	2.00
山 东	Shandong	65.21	85.86	19.21	90.98	2.95	12.00	7.00	2.29
河 南	Henan	39.14	51.33	26.52	81.69	0.88	6.33	2.14	0.57
湖 北	Hubei	39.15	51.67	27.42	83.18	0.82	4.59	1.88	1.09
湖 南	Hunan	29.86	56.19	33.59	73.62	0.89	5.05	1.89	0.95
广 东	Guangdong	86.88	82.38	8.28	103.91	5.00	9.77	6.52	9.26
广 西	Guangxi	57.14	56.58	29.22	80.91	0.48	5.54	1.60	0.52
海 南	Hainan	77.22	43.75	3.47	77.36	8.06	11.39	1.53	1.53
重 庆	Chongqing	12.56	59.83	24.94	79.22	1.83	3.72	1.28	0.17
四 川	Sichuan	24.85	52.98	30.93	81.80	2.60	6.73	2.58	0.63
贵 州	Guizhou	14.02	32.59	12.99	66.79	0.58	2.41	0.63	0.45
云 南	Yunnan	16.25	23.29	15.46	70.46	2.38	8.33	1.83	0.71
西 藏	Tibet	12.71	15.83	2.50	48.54	3.13	49.17	2.50	0.42
陕 西	Shaanxi	35.81	60.05	22.48	88.20	0.95	7.12	1.98	0.50
甘 肃	Gansu	37.06	54.56	19.67	86.44	1.50	31.44	2.78	0.28
青 海	Qinghai	52.83	46.67	12.67	81.17	2.17	35.17	2.50	
宁 夏	Ningxia	63.50	51.50	22.50	92.67		17.00	3.17	0.17
新 疆	Xinjiang	45.42	36.26	35.16	61.81	9.29	41.55	3.23	

10-35 城乡新建住宅面积和居民住房情况

Floor Space of Newly Built and Housing Conditions of Urban and Rural Residents

年 份 Year	城镇新建住宅面积 (亿平方米) Floor Space of Newly Built Residential Buildings in Urban Areas (100 million sq.m)	农村新建住宅面积 (亿平方米) Floor Space of Newly Built Residential Buildings in Rural Areas (100 million sq.m)	城市人均住宅建筑面积 (平方米) Per Capita Floor Space of Residential Building in Urban Areas (sq.m)	农村人均住房面积 (平方米) Per Capita Floor Space of Residential Building in Rural Areas (sq.m)
1978	0.38	1.00	6.7	8.1
1980	0.92	5.00	7.2	9.4
1985	1.88	7.22	10.0	14.7
1986	2.22	9.84	12.4	15.3
1987	2.23	8.84	12.7	16.0
1988	2.40	8.45	13.0	16.6
1989	1.97	6.76	13.5	17.2
1990	1.73	6.91	13.7	17.8
1991	1.92	7.54	14.2	18.5
1992	2.40	6.19	14.8	18.9
1993	3.08	4.81	15.2	20.7
1994	3.57	6.18	15.7	20.2
1995	3.75	6.99	16.3	21.0
1996	3.95	8.28	17.0	21.7
1997	4.06	8.06	17.8	22.5
1998	4.76	8.00	18.7	23.3
1999	5.59	8.34	19.4	24.2
2000	5.49	7.97	20.3	24.8
2001	5.75	7.29	20.8	25.7
2002	5.98	7.42	22.8	26.5
2003	5.50	7.52	23.7	27.2
2004	5.69	6.80	25.0	27.9
2005	6.61	6.67	26.1	29.7

注：城市人均住宅建筑面积由建设部提供。
a) Data on the per capita floor space of residential buildings in urban areas are provided by the Ministry of Construction.

10-36 农村居民家庭住房情况

Housing Conditions of Rural Households

本表为农村住户抽样调查资料。
Data in this table are obtained from the sample surveys on rural households.

项 目	Item	1990	1995	2000	2004	2005
本年新建房屋	**Houses Newly Built This Year**					
面积 (平方米/人)	Per Capita Floor Space of Houses (sq.m/person)	0.82	0.78	0.87	0.60	0.83
价值 (元/平方米)	Value of Houses (yuan/sq.m)	92.32	200.30	260.23	339.27	373.31
住房结构 (平方米/人)	Structure of Houses (sq.m/person)					
#钢筋混凝土结构	Reinforced Concrete Structure	0.23	0.33	0.47	0.36	0.50
砖木结构	Brick and Wood Structure	0.47	0.37	0.36	0.21	0.29
年末住房情况	**Houses at the End of Year**					
住房面积 (平方米/人)	Per Capita Floor Space of Houses (sq.m/person)	17.83	21.01	24.82	27.90	29.68
住房价值 (元/平方米)	Value of Houses (yuan/sq.m)	44.60	101.64	187.41	226.13	267.76
住房结构 (平方米/人)	Structure of Houses (sq.m/person)					
#钢筋混凝土结构	Reinforced Concrete Structure	1.22	3.10	6.15	9.17	11.17
砖木结构	Brick and Wood Structure	9.84	11.91	13.61	14.09	14.12

10-37 各地区农村居民家庭住房情况（2005年）

Housing Conditions of Rural Households at the Year-end by Region (2005)

地区	Region	住房面积（平方米/人）Per Capita Floor Space of Houses (sq.m/person)	住房价值（元/平方米）Value of Houses (yuan/sq.m)	住房结构（平方米/人）House Structures (sq.m/person)	
				钢筋混凝土结构 Reinforced Concrete Structure	砖木结构 Brick and Wood Structure
全国	**National Average**	**29.68**	**267.76**	**11.17**	**14.12**
北京	Beijing	36.43	650.32	7.68	28.00
天津	Tianjin	26.03	659.85	3.19	22.84
河北	Hebei	28.35	294.58	6.11	21.10
山西	Shanxi	24.15	276.96	5.52	16.24
内蒙古	Inner Mongolia	19.65	167.29	0.15	11.79
辽宁	Liaoning	25.09	343.42	4.30	20.46
吉林	Jilin	20.10	270.28	0.63	16.06
黑龙江	Heilongjiang	20.37	331.97	1.06	13.90
上海	Shanghai	56.56	988.82	31.63	24.68
江苏	Jiangsu	38.59	400.65	21.58	16.63
浙江	Zhejiang	56.65	416.14	36.86	18.09
安徽	Anhui	27.02	238.86	12.37	14.04
福建	Fujian	40.00	315.69	21.23	11.42
江西	Jiangxi	34.10	188.38	19.94	11.52
山东	Shandong	29.64	283.98	7.45	20.72
河南	Henan	27.21	213.83	10.37	15.72
湖北	Hubei	36.05	171.74	18.32	14.46
湖南	Hunan	38.38	177.85	13.56	22.77
广东	Guangdong	25.71	376.90	19.06	5.28
广西	Guangxi	28.67	205.78	18.15	6.48
海南	Hainan	21.82	269.64	5.48	16.18
重庆	Chongqing	32.91	170.26	9.75	15.86
四川	Sichuan	34.61	173.44	11.44	14.81
贵州	Guizhou	23.50	142.95	7.32	11.43
云南	Yunnan	25.24	179.47	3.99	4.73
西藏	Tibet	19.14	189.70	0.35	1.87
陕西	Shaanxi	26.01	216.13	9.45	10.29
甘肃	Gansu	18.71	182.43	1.07	6.56
青海	Qinghai	17.95	157.84	0.99	4.71
宁夏	Ningxia	21.03	185.76	0.95	11.15
新疆	Xinjiang	21.13	160.97	0.98	6.48

主要统计指标解释

一、城镇住户

城镇家庭人口 指居住在一起，经济上合在一起共同生活的家庭成员。凡计算为家庭人口的成员其全部收支都包括在本家庭中。

城镇就业面 指就业人口占家庭人口的百分比。

城镇就业者负担人数 指家庭人口与就业人口之比。

城镇家庭总收入 指家庭成员得到的工薪收入、经营净收入、财产性收入、转移性收入之和，不包括出售财物收入和借贷收入。

城镇家庭可支配收入 指家庭成员得到可用于最终消费支出和其它非义务性支出以及储蓄的总和，即居民家庭可以用来自由支配的收入。它是家庭总收入扣除交纳的所得税、个人交纳的社会保障支出以及记账补贴后的收入。计算公式为：

$$\text{可支配收入}=\text{家庭总收入}-\text{交纳所得税}-\text{个人交纳的社会保障支出}-\text{记帐补贴}$$

城镇家庭总支出 指除借贷支出以外的全部家庭支出。包括消费性支出、购房建房支出、转移性支出、财产性支出、社会保障支出。

城镇家庭消费性支出 指家庭用于日常生活的支出，包括食品、衣着、家庭设备用品及服务、医疗保健、交通和通信、娱乐教育文化服务、居住、杂项商品和服务等八大类支出。

城镇家庭服务性消费支出 指家庭用于支付社会提供的各种非商品性服务费用。

城镇家庭收入分组方法 是将所有调查户依户人均可支配收入由低到高排队，按10%，10%，20%，20%，20%，10%，10%的比例依次分成：最低收入户、低收入户、中等偏下收入户、中等收入户、中等偏上收入户、高收入户、最高收入户等七组。总体中最低5%的户为困难户。

恩格尔系数 指食物支出金额在消费性总支出金额中所占的比例。计算公式为：

$$\text{恩格尔系数}=\frac{\text{食品支出金额}}{\text{消费性总支出金额}}\times 100\%$$

二、农村住户

农村住户 指农村常住户。农村常住户指长期(一年以上)居住在乡镇(不包括城关镇)行政管理区域内的住户，以及长期居住在城关镇所辖行政村范围内的农村住户。户口不在本地而在本地居住一年及以上的住户也包括在本地农村常住户范围内；有本地户口，但举家外出谋生一年以上的住户，无论是否保留承包耕地都不包括在本地农村住户范围内。

常住人口 指全年经常在家或在家居住6个月以上，而且经济和生活与本户连成一体的人口。外出从业人员在外居住时间虽然在6个月以上，但收入主要带回家中，经济与本户连为一体，仍视为家庭常住人口；在家居住，生活和本户连成一体的国家职工、退休人员也为家庭常住人口。但是现役军人、中专及以上(走读生除外)的在校学生、以及常年在外(不包括探亲、看病等)且已有稳定的职业与居住场所的外出从业人员，不算家庭常住人口。家庭常住人口主要作为计算农村住户平均每人收入、消费和积累水平及分析家庭人口状况的依据。

整、半劳动力 整劳动力指男子18周岁到50周岁，女子18周岁到45周岁；半劳动力指男子16周岁到17周岁，51周岁到60周岁；女子16周岁到17周岁，46周岁到55周岁，同时具有劳动能力的人。虽然在劳动年龄之内，但已丧失劳动能力的人，不应算为劳动力；超过劳动年龄，但能经常参加劳动，计入半劳动力数内。常住人口中的职工，若这些职工为劳动力，就包括在本户的整半劳动力中。

总收入 指调查期内农村住户和住户成员从各种来源渠道得到的收入总和。按收入的性质划分为工资性收入、家庭经营收入、财产性收入和转移性收入。

工资性收入 指农村住户成员受雇于单位或个人，靠出卖劳动而获得的收入。

家庭经营收入 指农村住户以家庭为生产经营单位进行生产筹划和管理而获得的收入。农村住户家庭经营活动按行业划分为农业、林业、牧业、渔业、工业、建筑业、交通运输业邮电业、批发和零售贸易餐饮业、社会服务业、文教卫生业和其他家庭经营。

财产性收入 指金融资产或有形非生产性资产的所有者向其他机构单位提供资金或将有形非生产性资产供其支配，作为回报而从中获得的收入。

转移性收入 指农村住户和住户成员无须付出任何对应物而获得的货物、服务、资金或资产所有权等，不包括无偿提供的用于固定资本形成的资金。一般情况下，是指农村住户在二次分配中的所有收入。

现金收入 指农村住户和住户成员在调查期内得到以现金形态表现的收入。按来源分成工资性收入、家庭经营现金收入、财产性收入、转移性收入。

纯收入 指农村住户当年从各个来源得到的总收入相应地扣除所发生的费用后的收入总和。计算方法：

纯收入=总收入-税费支出-家庭经营费用支出
　　-税费支出-生产性固定资产折旧
　　-赠送农村外部亲友支出-记帐补贴

纯收入主要用于再生产投入和当年生活消费支出，也可用于储蓄和各种非义务性支出。"农民人均纯收入"按人口平均的纯收入水平，反映的是一个地区或一个农户农村居民的平均收入水平。

总支出 指农村住户用于生产、生活和再分配的全部支出。家庭经营费用支出、购置生产性固定资产支出、生产性固定资产折旧、税费支出、生活消费支出、财产性支出和转移性支出。

Explanatory Notes on Main Statistical Indicators

I. Urban Households

Population of Urban Households refer to members of the household living and sharing economically together. All income and expenditure of the population of the household are included in the income and expenditure of the household.

Proportion of Urban Employment refer to the proportion of employed population to the population of urban households.

Number of Dependents per Urban Employee refers to the ratio between number of persons in urban households and the number of dependents.

Total Income of Urban Households refers to the sum of wage and salary, net business income, income from properties, and income from transfers of members of the households, excluding income from selling of properties and income from borrowings.

Disposable Income of Urban Households refers to the actual income at the disposal of members of the households which can be used for final consumption, other non-compulsory expenditure and savings. This equals to total income minus income tax, personal contribution to social security and sample household subsidy for keeping diaries. Following formula is used:

Disposable income = total household income - income tax - personal contribution to social security - sample household subsidy for keeping diaries

Total Expenditure of Urban Households refer to all expenditure of the households except expenditure on leading. It includes expenditure on consumption, on purchasing or building houses, on transfers, on properties and on social security.

Consumption Expenditure of Urban Households refers to total expenditure of the sample households for consumption in daily life, including expenditure on eight categories such as food, clothing, household appliances and services, health care and medical services, transport and communications, recreation, education and cultural services, housing, miscellaneous goods and services.

Expenditure of Urban Households on Consumption of Services refers to expenditure of households on services of various kinds provided by the society.

Urban Households by Income Group All households in the sample are grouped, by per capita disposable income of the household, into groups of lowest income, low income, lower middle income, middle income, upper middle income, high income and highest income, each group consisting of 10%, 10%, 20%, 20%, 20%, 10% and 10% of all households respectively. The lowest 5% of households are also referred to as poor households.

Engel Coefficient refers to the percentage of expenditure on food in the total consumption expenditure, using the following formula:

Engel Coefficient = (expenditure on food / total consumption expenditure) x 100%

II. Rural Households

Rural Households refer to resident households in rural areas. Resident households in rural areas are the households residing for more than one year in the areas under the jurisdiction of administration of township governments (excluding county towns), and in the areas under the jurisdiction of administration of villages in county towns. Migrated households residing in the current addresses for over one year with their household registration in other places are included in the resident households of their current addresses. For households with their household registration in one place but all members of the households moving away for living in another place for over one year, they will not be included in the rural households of the area where they are registered, irrespective of whether they still keep their contracted land.

Resident Population refers to population staying at home permanently or for over 6 months during a year and sharing life economically with the household. Members of the household staying away from the household for over 6 months but keeping a close economic relation with the household by sending the majority of income to the household are regarded as resident population of the household. Government staff and workers or retirees living as close members of the household are also considered as resident population. However, servicemen, students of secondary technical schools or schools of higher education and persons with stable jobs and residence outside the household (excluding those visiting relatives or seeking medical service) are not included as resident population of the household. Resident population is used in calculating income, consumption, accumulation on per capita basis of rural households and in analyzing composition of rural households.

Full/Semi Labour Force Full labour force refers to persons capable of work, aged 18-50 for males and 18-45 for females. Semi labour force refers to persons capable of work, aged 16-17 and 51-60 for males and 16-17 and 46-55 for females. Persons at their working ages but not capable of work are not to be included as labour force. Persons not at working ages but participating regularly in work are included in semi labour force. For staff and workers as resident population of the household, they are included as full or semi labour force of the household if they are in the labour force.

Total Income refers to the sum of income earned from various sources by the rural households and their members during the reference period, and is classified as income from wages and salaries, income from household operations, income from properties and income from transfers.

Income from Wages and Salaries refers to income from labour earned by the members of rural households employed by other units or individuals.

Income from Household Operations refers to income by the rural households as units of production and operations. Operations by rural households are classified by economic activities as agriculture, forestry, animal husbandry, fishery, manufacturing, construction, transportation, post and telecommunications, wholesale, retail and catering, social service, culture, education, health, and other household operations.

Income from Properties refers to the income received as returns by owners of financial assets or tangible non-productive assets by providing capitals or tangible non-productive assets to other institutional units.

Income from Transfers refers to the receipt by rural households and their members of goods, services, capitals or rights of assets without giving or repaying accordingly, excluding capitals provided to them for the formation of fixed assets. In general, it refers to all income received by rural households through redistribution.

Cash Income refers to income received by rural households and their members in the form of cash during the reference period. It is classified, by source of income, into income from wages and salaries, cash income from household operations, income from properties and income from transfers.

Net Income refers to the total income of rural households from all sources minus all corresponding expenses. The formula for calculation is as follows:

Net income = total income – taxes and fees paid - household operation expenses – taxes and fees – depreciation of fixed assets for production – subsidy for participating in household survey – gifts to non-rural relatives

Net income is mainly used as input for reproduction and as consumption expenditure of the year, and also used for savings and non-compulsory expenses of various forms."Per capita net income of farmers" is the level of net income averaged by population which reflects the average income level of rural households in a given area.

Total Expenditure refers to total expenses of rural households on production, consumption and redistribution, including expenditure on household operations, on purchase of productive fixed assets, depreciation of productive fixed assets, taxes and fees, expenses on household consumption, expenses on properties and expenses on transfers.

11

城市概况

General Survey of Cities

简要说明

一、本篇资料的主要内容

本篇资料反映我国城市社会、经济发展和城市建设的规模、速度、效益及综合水平等基本情况，主要内容有三部分：

1.全国城市分布情况；

2.省会城市和计划单列市主要经济指标；

3.城市公用事业基本情况及综合水平指标。

其中城市公用事业部分的主要内容包括：城市建设、供水、供气、供热、市政设施、公共交通、城市绿化、环境卫生等。

二、本篇资料的统计范围与统计口径

涉及城市公用事业情况的部分由建设部提供，其执行范围是全国所有设市城市；统计口径为全社会，即在设市城市范围内所有的城市规划管理、投资、建设或经营管理相关设施的单位。

三、本篇的资料来源

全国城市分布情况及省会城市和计划单列市主要经济指标由各省、自治区、直辖市统计局及城市社会经济调查司依据国家统计局制定的《市、县社会经济基本情况统计报表制度》收集整理提供。

城市公用事业基本情况及综合水平指标部分的资料由建设部根据其《城市建设统计报表制度》和《房地产统计报表制度》汇总整理提供。

Brief Introduction

I. Main Content

Data in this chapter show the social and economic development as well as the scale, growth rate, economic efficiency, overall level and other basic conditions of China's cities. The main content is composed of the following 3 parts:

(1) Distribution of cities in China;

(2) Main economic indicators of provincial capitals and important cities separately listed in the national plan;

(3) Indicators reflecting basic conditions of urban public facilities and overall level.

Data on public facilities include urban construction, supply of water, gas and heating, civil facilities, public transportation, urban greenery, environment and sanitation, etc.

II. Scope and Coverage of Statistics

Data on urban public facilities are provided by the Ministry of Construction, covering all cities. Statistically, they cover all units under the jurisdiction of cities engaged in urban planning and management, in investment, construction and operation of relevant facilities.

III. Source of Data

Data on distribution of cities in China and major economic indicators of provincial capitals and important cities separately listed in the national plan are collected and prepared by the statistical bureaus of the provinces, autonomous regions and municipalities directly under the central government and the Department of Urban Socio-economic Surveys of NBS in accordance with the *Statistical Reporting System on the Basic Social and Economic Situation of the Cities and Counties*, which is stipulated by the NBS.

Data on basic conditions and overall level of urban public facilities are collected, prepared and provided by the Ministry of Construction in line with its *Statistical Reporting System of Construction in Cities and Counties* and *Statistical Reporting System on Real Estate Development*.

11-1 全部地级城市数（2005年）

Number of Cities at Prefecture Level (2005)

单位：个 (unit)

地区	Region	合计 Total	按城市市辖区总人口分组 Grouped by Population in City Districts 400万以上 4 million and over	200-400万 2 million-4 million	100-200万 1 million-2 million	50-100万 0.5 million-1 million	20-50万 0.2 million-0.5 million	20万以下 under 0.2 million
合 计	**Total**	**286**	**13**	**25**	**75**	**108**	**61**	**4**
北 京	Beijing	1	1					
天 津	Tianjin	1	1					
河 北	Hebei	11		2	2	4	3	
山 西	Shanxi	11		1	1	7	2	
内蒙古	Inner Mongolia	9			3	2	4	
辽 宁	Liaoning	14	1	1	2	8	2	
吉 林	Jilin	8		1	1	3	3	
黑龙江	Heilongjiang	12		1	2	7	1	1
上 海	Shanghai	1	1					
江 苏	Jiangsu	13	1	4	5	3		
浙 江	Zhejiang	11	1	1	3	5	1	
安 徽	Anhui	17			6	9	2	
福 建	Fujian	9		1	3	1	4	
江 西	Jiangxi	11		1	2	5	2	1
山 东	Shandong	17		4	9	4		
河 南	Henan	17		1	6	7	3	
湖 北	Hubei	12	1	1	4	5	1	
湖 南	Hunan	16	3	1	3	6	3	
广 东	Guangdong	18		1	6	5	6	
广 西	Guangxi	14		1	3	5	5	
海 南	Hainan	2			1	1		
重 庆	Chongqing	1	1					
四 川	Sichuan	18	1		10	5	2	
贵 州	Guizhou	4		1		2	1	
云 南	Yunnan	8		1		3	3	1
西 藏	Tibet							
陕 西	Shaanxi	10	1			7	2	
甘 肃	Gansu	12		1	1	3	6	1
青 海	Qinghai	1			1			
宁 夏	Ningxia	5				1	4	
新 疆	Xinjiang	2			1		1	

注：地级城市未包括拉萨。

a) Number of cities at prefecture level don't include Lhasa.

11-2 沿海开放城市和经济特区城市社会经济指标（2005年）

Main Social and Economic Indicators of Coastal Opening Cities and Cities in Special Economic Zones (2005)

指 标	Item	沿海开放城市合计 Coastal Opening Cities		经济特区城市合计 Cities in Special Economic Zones	
		包括市辖县 Counties Included	不包括市辖县 Counties Excluded	包括市辖县 Counties Included	不包括市辖县 Counties Excluded
土地面积 （万平方公里）	**Total Land Area (10 000 sq.km)**	**14.05**	**3.39**	**0.73**	**0.72**
人口与就业	**Population and Employment**				
年底人口数 （万人）	Population (year-end) (10 000 persons)	9563.99	4423.04	916.04	908.80
#非农业人口	Non-agricultural Population	4783.00	3477.00	854.00	852.00
在岗职工人数	Staff and Workers	1414.00	1069.00	301.00	301.00
地区生产总值 （亿元）	**Gross Regional Product (100 million yuan)**	**34817.20**	**22234.58**	**7243.80**	**7238.94**
第一产业	Primary Industry	1857.44	409.28	94.55	92.52
第二产业	Secondary Industry	17350.47	10594.22	3857.26	3855.97
第三产业	Tertiary Industry	15609.29	11231.08	3291.99	3290.45
固定资产投资	**Investment in Fixed Assets**				
固定资产投资额 （亿元）	Total Investment in Fixed Assets (100 million yuan)	15303.06	10758.29	1956.93	1955.10
#房地产开发投资额 （亿元）	Total Investment in Real Estate Development (100 million yuan)	3554.22	3162.49	611.43	611.43
#住宅	Residential Buildings	2562.13	2252.07	378.79	378.79
全年用电量（亿千瓦小时）	**Annual Electricity Consumption (100 million kwh)**	**3200.42**	**2464.45**	**679.36**	**678.97**
农业	**Agriculture**				
主要农产品产量 （万吨）	Output of Major Agricultural Products (10 000 tons)				
蔬菜	Vegetables	4149.97		246.94	
水果	Fruits	1215.59		36.66	
肉类	Meat	486.32		28.17	
水产品	Aquatic Products	1546.82		76.21	
限额以上工业企业主要指标	**Main Indicators of Industrial Enterprises above Designated Size**				
工业企业单位数 （个）	Number of Industrial Enterprises (unit)	58138.00	38088.00	9764.00	9753.00
#内资企业	Domestic Funded Enterprises	39748.00	24315.00	4296.00	4285.00
工业总产值 （当年价格，亿元）	Gross Industrial Output Value (at current prices, 100 million yuan)	55033.66	40971.01	13928.73	13927.23
#内资企业	Domestic Funded Enterprises	28712.65	18841.09	3422.10	3420.60
主营业务收入 （亿元）	Revenue from Principal Business(100 million yuan)	54786.92	41350.08	13538.62	13537.18
利税总额 （亿元）	Pre-tax Profits (100 million yuan)	5249.42	4004.19	1057.21	1057.02
资产总额 （亿元）	Total Assets (100 million yuan)	38240.23	31233.55	9115.49	9110.91
每百元资产提供利税 （元）	Pre-tax Profits per 100 Yuan Assets (yuan)	13.73	12.82	11.60	11.60

11-2 续表 continued

指 标	Item	沿海开放城市合计 Coastal Opening Cities 包括市辖县 Counties Included	沿海开放城市合计 Coastal Opening Cities 不包括市辖县 Counties Excluded	经济特区城市合计 Cities in Special Economic Zones 包括市辖县 Counties Included	经济特区城市合计 Cities in Special Economic Zones 不包括市辖县 Counties Excluded
运输邮电	**Transport, Post and Telecommunication Services**				
客运量 (亿人)	Passenger Traffic (100 million persons)	25.2		2.1	
货运量 (亿吨)	Freight Traffic (100 million tons)	31.3		1.5	
年底邮政局所数 (个)	Number of Postal Offices at the year-end (unit)	14017.0	9821.0	922.0	889.0
年末固定电话用户数 (万户)	Number of Fixed Telephone Subscribers (year-end) (10 000 households)	4687.7	3160.0	805.2	802.2
年末移动电话用户 (万户)	Number of Mobile Telephone Phone Subscribers (year-end) (10 000 households)	6295.2	4739.6	588.1	586.4
国内贸易	**Domestic Trade**				
社会消费品零售总额 (亿元)	Total Retail Sales of Consumer Goods (100 million yuan)	11583	8483.6	2274.5	2269.1
限额以上批发零售贸易业商品销售总额 (亿元)	Total Sales of Wholesale and Retail Trades above Designated Size (100 million yuan)	27116.3	25457.4	3936.6	3934.3
实际利用外资金额(亿美元)	**Amount of Foreign Capital Actually Utilized (USD 100 million)**	**288.3**	**212.7**	**44.5**	**44.5**
在校学生数 (万人)	**Student Enrollment (10 000 persons)**				
普通高等学校	Number of Regular Institutions of Higher Education	247.7	238.8	17.4	6.5
中等职业学校	Number of Specialized Secondary Schools	161	118.6	10.7	10.7
普通中学	Number of Regular Secondary Schools	616.8	254.3	81.3	80.6
小学	Number of Primary Schools	713.6	281.2	160.9	160.1
成人高等学校	Number of Schools of Higher Education for Adults	78.6	76.1	4.1	4.1
卫生	**Public Health**				
医院、卫生院数 (个)	Number of Hospitals (unit)	3917.0	2011.0	891.0	873.0
医院、卫生院床位数(万张)	Number of Beds in Hospitals (10 000 beds)	35.7	26.1	3.6	3.6
医生数 (万人)	Number of Doctors (10 000 persons)	**19.9**	**14.0**	**2.3**	**2.3**
在岗职工工资总额 (亿元)	**Total Wages of Staff and Workers (100 million yuan)**	**3605.1**	**3017.9**	**818.4**	**301.3**
城乡居民储蓄年末余额 (亿元)	**Outstanding Amount of Savings Deposits of Urban and Rural Households (year-end) (100 million yuan)**	**26621.8**	**21879.7**	**5028.8**	**5024.7**

注：沿海开放城市系指上海、天津、大连、秦皇岛、青岛、烟台、威海、连云港、南通、宁波、温州、福州、广州、湛江、北海共15个城市；经济特区城市系指深圳、珠海、汕头和厦门4个城市。

a) Coastal opening cities refer to the following 15 cities : Shanghai, Tianjin, Dalian, Qinhuangdao, Qingdao, Yantai, Weihai, Lianyungang, Nantong, Ningbo, Wenzhou, Fuzhou, Guangzhou, Zhanjiang and Beihai. Cities in special economic zones refer to following 4 cities: Shenzhen, Zhuhai, Shantou and Xiamen.

11-3　省会城市和计划单列市主要指标（2005年）

Main Indicators of Provincial Capitals and Separate Planning Cities (2005)

包括市辖县。

Counties under the jurisdiction of city governments are included.

城市名称	City	年底总人口（万人）Total Population (year-end) (10 000 persons)	地区生产总值（当年价格）（万元）Gross Regional Product (Current Prices) (10 000 yuan)	工业总产值（万元）Gross Industrial Output Value (10 000 yuan)	客运量（万人）Passenger Traffic (10 000 persons)	货运量（万吨）Freight Traffic (10 000 tons)
北　京	Beijing	1180.7	68863101	69462116	60840	32103
天　津	Tianjin	939.31	36976200	67741031	4679	39485
石家庄	Shijiazhuang	927.3	17867750	20155826	13908	11942
太　原	Taiyuan	340.39	8931620	9213954	3677	17772
呼和浩特	Hohhot	213.49	7436618	4831642	4545	6540
沈　阳	Shenyang	698.57	20841339	21952498	8629	15852
大　连	Dalian	565.33	21522328	25627970	12370	24667
长　春	Changchun	731.5	16784691	17289653	8197	11813
哈尔滨	Harbin	974.84	18304514	11974562	8044	9830
上　海	Shanghai	1360.26	91541800	157675146	9487	71303
南　京	Nanjing	595.8	24111100	40634843	20188	18073
杭　州	Hangzhou	660.45	29426519	54411271	24124	19909
宁　波	Ningbo	556.7	24493099	48909669	28412	17308
合　肥	Hefei	455.7	8535700	8808230	7080	6134
福　州	Fuzhou	614.83	14763142	18601750	10490	10179
厦　门	Xiamen	153.22	10065831	20291174	5401	3613
南　昌	Nanchang	475.17	10077025	7262572	5187	4553
济　南	Jinan	597.44	18766071	22375103	7428	15728
青　岛	Qingdao	740.91	26958172	43166128	19028	37636
郑　州	Zhengzhou	679.7	16606006	17891575	12543	8770
武　汉	Wuhan	801.36	22380000	22854127	15414	19612
长　沙	Changsha	620.92	15199001	9733713	10895	10991
广　州	Guangzhou	750.53	51542283	60319154	40524	37753
深　圳	Shenzhen	181.93	49509078	95676838	12884	9796
南　宁	Nanning	659.54	7233557	3701812	9131	7236
海　口	Haikou	147.3	3013506	2507203	14914	4909
重　庆	Chongqing	3169.16	30704900	25258683	63424	39198
成　都	Chengdu	1082.03	23707644	16614367	38113	26718
贵　阳	Guiyang	350.66	5256159	5740645	21066	6277
昆　明	Kunming	508.47	10615544	10181367	8229	11225
西　安	Xi'an	741.73	12701400	9810221	11323	11511
兰　州	Lanzhou	311.74	5670437	7887816	2546	5973
西　宁	Xining	209.9	2375652	2277411	3349	2494
银　川	Yinchuan	140.6	2885029	3222799	2681	3807
乌鲁木齐	Urumqi	194.15	5625007	5401041	3640	13644

注：工业总产值的统计范围为全部国有及年销售收入500万元以上的非国有工业企业。

a) The gross industrial output value covers all state-owned industrial enterprises and non-state-owned industrial enterprises with annual sales income over 5 million yuan.

11-3 续表 continued

城市名称	City	地方财政预算内收入(万元) Budgetary Revenue of Local Governments (10 000 yuan)	固定资产投资总额(万元) Total Investment in Fixed Assets (10 000 yuan)	城乡居民储蓄年末余额(万元) Outstanding Amount of Savings Deposits of Urban and Rural Households (year-end) (10 000 yuan)	在岗职工人数(万人) Number of Fully-employed Staff and Workers (10 000 persons)	在岗职工工资总额(万元) Total Wages of Fully-employed Staff and Workers (10 000 yuan)
北京	Beijing	9192098	28272000	74775889	444.58	15200513
天津	Tianjin	3318507	15168405	24624100	166.12	4198024
石家庄	Shijiazhuang	658796	9290289	13551916	87.1	1327349
太原	Taiyuan	569525	4385075	10249200	74.31	1378220
呼和浩特	Hohhot	359319	4600000	3795946	30.31	597507
沈阳	Shenyang	1381415	13632196	18471414	95.59	1901719
大连	Dalian	1514247	11104875	16656295	81.21	1777237
长春	Changchun	610338	6504218	10593043	84.74	1503507
哈尔滨	Harbin	980370	6389729	14614904	147.63	2431270
上海	Shanghai	14173976	35425531	84324900	345.28	11028270
南京	Nanjing	2110746	14027220	15954002	88.08	2584598
杭州	Hangzhou	2504565	13866833	21916600	98.44	3010148
宁波	Ningbo	2123797	13363043	14588012	75.68	2198126
合肥	Hefei	576372	4952700	5161608	38.84	739131
福州	Fuzhou	974502	6032595	11550362	79.8	1451880
厦门	Xiamen	989474	4016175	5850735	66.36	1498285
南昌	Nanchang	582783	5255946	6437518	52.64	949918
济南	Jinan	1061547	8569998	10506503	94.26	1966782
青岛	Qingdao	1764118	14565808	13431016	121.32	2428949
郑州	Zhengzhou	1361261	8200000	14360781	87.95	1468387
武汉	Wuhan	1388169	10551808	16731705	137.3	2540734
长沙	Changsha	1080572	8814355	9544151	67.71	1455835
广州	Guangzhou	3712633	15191582	50246879	191.18	6562762
深圳	Shenzhen	4123800	11810542	32293800	159	5163684
南宁	Nanning	451954	3628975	5982307	56.25	985557
海口	Haikou	179149	1371664	3740519	25.05	498116
重庆	Chongqing	2568072	20063180	25021450	207.95	3458237
成都	Chengdu	1414541	14573505	20740894	128.87	2572464
贵阳	Guiyang	624873	3435426	4977423	60.59	964896
昆明	Kunming	906655	5230093	9938095	66.89	1279075
西安	Xi'an	730543	8351046	17167574	119.1	2111433
兰州	Lanzhou	289256	2595851	5817105	51.39	871482
西宁	Xining	117860	1156289	2346265	20.99	373053
银川	Yinchuan	181645	2016507	2649514	29.22	538329
乌鲁木齐	Urumqi	514014	1976289	5957300	45.42	924522

11-4 地级及以上城市国民经济和社会发展主要指标（2005年）

Main Indicators of Economic and Social Development of Cities at Prefecture Level and above (2005)

指标	Item	全国总计 National Total	地级及以上城市合计（市辖区） Prefecture Cities (Districts under City)	地级及以上城市合计占全国比重(%) Percentage of Prefecture Cities to National Total (%)
自然资源	**Natural Resources**			
土地面积（万平方公里）	Area of Land (10 000 sq.km)	960.0	57.4	6.0
人口	**Population**			
年末总人口（万人）	Population at the Year-end (10 000 persons)	130756.0	36285.0	27.8
国民经济核算	**National Accounting**			
地区生产总值（亿元）	Gross Regional Product (100 million yuan)	183084.8	109743.3	59.9
第一产业	Primary Industry	23070.4	4318.7	18.7
第二产业	Secondary Industry	87046.7	55094.1	63.3
#工业	Industry	76912.9	48381.9	62.9
第三产业	Tertiary Industry	72967.7	50330.4	69.0
固定资产投资	**Investment in Fixed Assets**			
固定资产投资总额（亿元）	Total Investment in Fixed Assets (100 million yuan)	88773.6	51472.0	58.0
#房地产开发	Real Estate Development	15909.2	11610.1	73.0
财政	**Government Finance**			
地方财政收入（亿元）	Local Government Revenue (100 million yuan)	14884.2	9094.4	61.1
地方财政支出（亿元）	Local Government Expenditure (100 million yuan)	25154.3	11772.6	46.8
对外贸易	**Foreign Trade**			
货物进出口总额（亿美元）	Total Value of Imports and Exports (100 million USD)	14219.1	8597.0	60.5
出口额	Exports	7619.5	4312.0	56.6
进口额	Imports	6599.5	4285.0	64.9
工业	**Industry**			
规模以上工业企业数（个）	Number of Industrial Enterprises above Designated Size (unit)	271835	139548	51.3
内资企业	Domestic Funded Enterprises	215448	100811	46.8
港澳台投资企业	Enterprises with Funds from Hong Kong, Macao and Taiwan	27559	18911	68.6
外商投资企业	Foreign Funded Enterprises	28828	19826	68.8
工业总产值（亿元）	Gross Industrial Output Value (100 million yuan)	251619.5	162617.2	64.6
内资企业	Domestic Funded Enterprises	171759.3	100310.6	58.4
港澳台投资企业	Enterprises with Funds from Hong Kong, Macao and Taiwan	28311.8	20457.0	72.3
外商投资企业	Foreign Funded Enterprises	51548.4	41849.6	81.2
固定资产净值年平均余额（亿元）	Annual Average Balance of Net Value of Fixed Assets (100 million yuan)	89460.5	56158.5	62.8
主营业务收入（亿元）	Revenue from Principal Business (100 million yuan)	248544.0	160432.9	64.5
本年应交增值税（亿元）	Value-Added Tax Payable (100 million yuan)	8520.9	5295.4	62.1
利润总额（亿元）	Total Profits (100 million yuan)	14802.5	9444.1	63.8
邮电通信业（亿元）	**Post and Telecommunication Services (100 million yuan)**			
邮政业务收入	Revenue from Postal Services	625.5	337.0	53.9
电信业务收入	Revenue from Telecommunication Services	11403.0	4163.1	36.5
国内商业	**Domestic Trade**			
社会消费品零售额（亿元）	Total Retail Sales of Consumer Goods (100 million yuan)	67176.6	40922.1	60.9
教育	**Education**			
普通高等学校	Institutions of Regular Higher Education			
学校数（个）	Number of Institutions (unit)	1792	1646	91.9
在校学生数（万人）	Student Enrollment (10 000 persons)	1561.8	1432.9	91.7
卫生	**Health Care**			
医院、卫生院数（个）	Number of Hospitals and Health Care Centers (unit)	60397	22599	37.4
医生数（万人）	Number of Doctors (10 000 persons)	193.8	92.0	47.5
医院、卫生机构床位数（万张）	Number of Hospital Beds (10 000 beds)	313.5	173.0	55.2

注：本表数据为市辖区数，不包括所辖行政县。货物进出口总额为35个大中城市数据。

a) Data in this table are total value of imports and exports are the data of 35 large and medium-sized cities.

11-5 城市公用事业基本情况

Basic Statistics on City Public Utilities

本表各项指标按全社会范围计算。
Data have covered the public utilities of all city units.

项目	Item	1990	1995	2000	2004	2005
城市及建筑物面积	**City Areas and Floor Space of Buildings**					
建成区面积 (平方公里)	Developed Areas (sq.km)	12856	19264	22439	30406	32521
城市人口密度（人/平方公里)	Population Density of City Districts (persons/sq.km)	279	322	442	865	870
年末实有房屋建筑面积 (亿平方米)	Total Floor Space of Buildings at the year-end (100 million sq.m)	39.8	57.3	76.6	149.1	164.5
年末实有住宅建筑面积 (亿平方米)	Total Floor Space of Residential Buildings at the year-end (100 million sq.m)	20.0	31.0	44.1	96.2	107.7
供水、供气及供热	**Water Supply, Gas Supply and Heating**					
年供水总量 (亿吨)	Annual Volume of Tap Water Supply (100 million tons)	382.3	481.6	469.0	490.3	502.1
#生活用水量	Water Consumption for Residential use	100.1	158.1	200.0	233.5	243.7
人均生活用水 (吨)	Per Capita Water Consumption for Residential Use (ton)	67.9	71.3	95.5	76.9	74.5
用水普及率 (%)	Percentage of Population with Access to Tap Water (%)	48.0	58.7	63.9	88.9	91.1
人工煤气供气量 (亿立方米)	Gaswork Gas Supply (100 million cu.m)	174.7	126.7	152.4	213.7	255.8
#家庭用量	Consumption of Gaswork Gas for Residential Use	27.4	45.7	63.1	51.2	45.9
天然气供气量 (亿立方米)	Natural Gas Supply (100 million cu.m)	64.2	67.3	82.1	169.3	210.5
#家庭用量	Consumption of Natural Gas for Residential Use	11.6	16.4	24.8	45.4	52.1
液化石油气供气量 (万吨)	Liquefied Petroleum Gas (10 000 tons)	219.0	488.7	1053.7	1126.7	1222.0
#家庭用量 (万吨)	Consumption of Liquefied Gas for Residential Use (10 000 tons)	142.8	370.2	532.3	704.1	706.5
供气管道长度 (万公里)	Length of Gas Pipelines (10 000 km)	2.4	4.4	8.9	14.8	16.2
用气普及率 (%)	Percentage of City Population with Access to Gas(%)	19.1	34.3	45.4	81.5	82.1
集中供热面积 (亿平方米)	Area of Centralized Heating (100 million sq.m)	2.1	6.5	11.1	21.6	25.2
市政设施	**Municipal Infra-structure**					
道路长度 (万公里)	Length of Paved Roads (10 000 km)	9.5	13.0	16.0	22.3	24.7
每万人拥有道路长度 (公里)	Length of Paved Roads Per 10 000 Population (km)	3.1	3.8	4.1	6.5	6.9
道路面积 (亿平方米)	Area of Paved Roads (100 million sq.m)	8.9	13.6	19.0	35.3	39.2
人均拥有道路面积 (平方米)	Per Capita Area of Paved Roads (sq.m)	3.1	4.4	6.1	10.3	10.9
排水管道长度 (万公里)	Length of Sewage Pipes (10 000 km)	5.8	11.0	14.2	21.9	24.1
排水管道密度(公里/平方公里)	Density of Sewage Pipes (km/sq.km)	4.5	5.7	6.3	7.2	7.4
公共交通	**Public Traffic**					
公共交通运营车数 (万辆)	Number of Public Vehicles under Operation (Buses and Trolley Buses, etc.) (10 000 units)	6.2	13.7	22.6	28.2	31.3
每万人拥有公交车辆 (标台)	Number of Public Transportation Vehicles Per 10 000 Population (unit)	2.2	3.6	5.3	8.4	8.6
出租汽车数量 (万辆)	Taxis (10 000 units)	11.1	50.4	82.5	90.4	93.7
城市绿化	**Afforestation in Cities**					
园林绿地面积 (万公顷)	Public Green Areas (10 000 hectares)	47.5	67.8	86.5	132.2	146.8
人均公共绿地面积 (平方米)	Per Capita Public Green Areas (sq.m)	1.8	2.5	3.7	7.4	7.9
公园个数 (个)	Number of Parks and Zoos (unit)	1970	3619	4455	6427	7077
公园面积 (万公顷)	Area of Parks and Zoos (10 000 hectares)	3.9	7.3	8.2	13.4	15.8
环境卫生	**Environmental Sanitation**					
清运垃圾 (万吨)	Volume of Garbage Disposal (10 000 tons)	6767	10671	11819	15509	15577
清运粪便 (万吨)	Volume of Disposal of Excrement and Urine (10 000 tons)	2385	3066	2829	3576	3805
每万人拥有公厕 (座)	Number of Public Lavatories per 10 000 Population (unit)	3.0	3.0	2.7	3.2	3.2

注：人均和普及率指标均按城市人口计算，城市人口指市区（不包括市辖县)有常住户口的人。
a) Per capita data and popularization data are calculated by city population, which refers to population permanently registrated in city districts, exluded counties.

11-6 各地区城市建设情况（2005年）

Statistics on City Construction by Region (2005)

地区	Region	建成区面积（平方公里）Developed Areas (sq.km)	征用土地面积（平方公里）Land Put in Requisition for State Construction Projects (sq.km)	城市人口密度（人/平方公里）Population Density of Urban Area (persons/sq.km)	年末实有房屋建筑面积（万平方米）Total Floor Space of Buildings (year-end) (10 000 sq.m)	年末实有住宅建筑面积（万平方米）Total Floor Space of Residential Buildings (year-end) (10 000 sq.m)
全国	**National Total**	**32520.7**	**1263.5**	**870.2**	**1645064.1**	**1076899.6**
北京	Beijing	1200.0		937.2	50507.0	28922.0
天津	Tianjin	530.0		863.5	22578.1	14043.2
河北	Hebei	1316.4	49.0	2131.9	73900.8	52231.5
山西	Shanxi	709.3	11.8	1587.8	40811.0	28663.6
内蒙古	Inner Mongolia	824.4	13.3	538.4	34812.8	21798.9
辽宁	Liaoning	1779.9	71.9	1242.7	74152.6	44977.5
吉林	Jilin	942.9	23.1	785.4	38612.6	25412.4
黑龙江	Heilongjiang	1496.0	21.0	342.4	64005.3	44504.3
上海	Shanghai	819.9	97.2	2718.2	64197.8	37996.5
江苏	Jiangsu	2378.6	117.4	1321.4	124416.8	75836.7
浙江	Zhejiang	1679.7	155.3	1269.8	103567.4	74662.7
安徽	Anhui	1260.4	98.3	1448.8	46232.3	30980.2
福建	Fujian	672.6	31.8	1000.2	44907.5	32307.3
江西	Jiangxi	663.6	41.7	2739.7	40396.3	28004.4
山东	Shandong	2675.5	157.1	921.4	119180.4	69942.9
河南	Henan	1572.0	37.0	5404.8	84213.6	56629.4
湖北	Hubei	1417.3	20.3	628.1	67018.3	43780.1
湖南	Hunan	1032.9	30.3	1134.6	70927.2	45303.3
广东	Guangdong	3619.1	105.1	1362.5	151808.0	100395.0
广西	Guangxi	772.2	28.7	711.4	53195.7	39106.5
海南	Hainan	194.2		2930.9	8812.4	5430.8
重庆	Chongqing	582.5	34.9	1093.1	34998.4	23112.0
四川	Sichuan	1442.9	30.2	254.5	83484.2	55713.6
贵州	Guizhou	371.9	7.7	906.5	16386.7	12817.5
云南	Yunnan	472.4	16.2	497.2	33553.6	22622.3
西藏	Tibet	74.8	0.7	1256.9	1285.8	1145.2
陕西	Shaanxi	561.7	13.3	2531.1	32805.9	21804.1
甘肃	Gansu	507.4	18.1	6030.9	25833.1	15171.7
青海	Qinghai	105.9	1.3	2001.3	4500.0	3300.0
宁夏	Ningxia	248.9	19.6	188.5	8550.8	4986.3
新疆	Xinjiang	595.5	11.5	230.2	25411.9	15297.7

11-7 各地区城市供水情况（2005年）

Basic Statistics on Tap Water Supply in Cities by Region (2005)

地区	Region	年末供水综合生产能力（万立方米/日）Production Capacity of Tap Water Supply (year-end) (10 000 cu.m/day)	年末供水管道长度（公里）Length of Water Supply Pipelines (year-end) (km)	全年供水总量（万立方米）Total Annual Volume of Water Supply (10 000 cu.m)	#生活用水 For Residential Use	#生产用水 For Productive Use	用水人口（万人）Number of Residents with Access to Tap Water (10 000 persons)	人均日生活用水量（升）Per Capita Daily Consumption of Tap Water for Residential Use (liter)
全 国	**National Total**	**24719.8**	**379332.1**	**5020601**	**2437374**	**2098008**	**32723.4**	**204.1**
北 京	Beijing	1065.7	18175.1	144757	92353	36265	1654.7	152.9
天 津	Tianjin	359.0	7093.3	68236	28885	31430	640.5	123.6
河 北	Hebei	830.9	11336.5	150484	69907	65099	1324.1	144.6
山 西	Shanxi	346.0	5939.4	86516	35703	46285	812.8	120.4
内蒙古	Inner Mongolia	308.8	5864.4	61081	25500	31307	537.7	129.9
辽 宁	Liaoning	1339.1	23211.5	282618	103683	130232	1928.8	147.3
吉 林	Jilin	685.0	6770.8	154409	45566	96931	904.8	138.0
黑龙江	Heilongjiang	654.4	9796.2	120157	62193	45801	1127.1	151.2
上 海	Shanghai	1450.6	25482.2	335517	170084	126766	1778.0	262.1
江 苏	Jiangsu	1977.6	43889.6	390460	185906	161320	2408.5	211.5
浙 江	Zhejiang	1256.7	27033.2	261613	119831	113656	1345.9	243.9
安 徽	Anhui	1032.7	8745.3	204886	72959	121785	1021.4	195.7
福 建	Fujian	700.0	7563.3	119814	61662	52841	630.6	267.9
江 西	Jiangxi	654.2	6078.9	147045	57585	70929	667.0	236.5
山 东	Shandong	1385.3	28798.9	275364	134573	121756	2629.4	140.2
河 南	Henan	1026.5	12632.4	183436	79462	84437	1480.4	147.1
湖 北	Hubei	1424.8	16998.9	285230	161817	113411	1616.0	274.3
湖 南	Hunan	1254.6	9862.3	267800	96300	137001	946.8	278.7
广 东	Guangdong	2995.6	45867.0	738573	419159	252800	3586.9	320.2
广 西	Guangxi	656.2	8594.3	132888	64785	58534	652.4	272.0
海 南	Hainan	149.4	2063.6	24015	17269	4241	140.0	337.8
重 庆	Chongqing	405.6	6766.2	71032	39962	25683	669.7	163.5
四 川	Sichuan	880.5	14061.6	171778	110538	54642	1361.6	222.4
贵 州	Guizhou	297.2	3423.6	50101	27985	13068	452.4	169.5
云 南	Yunnan	282.4	5537.5	61818	35361	13554	442.0	219.2
西 藏	Tibet	17.8	373.7	6735	5158	1143	20.9	676.1
陕 西	Shaanxi	355.4	4434.6	71170	38927	21905	734.8	145.1
甘 肃	Gansu	368.9	5520.9	59810	25262	29785	440.0	157.3
青 海	Qinghai	71.8	1000.0	15116	8559	6016	96.5	242.9
宁 夏	Ningxia	127.6	1830.7	24283	10052	11468	161.7	170.3
新 疆	Xinjiang	359.7	4586.1	53859	30388	17917	510.0	163.2

11-8 各地区城市燃气情况（2005年）

Basic Statistics on Supply of Gas in Cities by Region (2005)

地区	Region	人工煤气生产能力（万立方米/日） Production Capacity of Gaswork Gas (10 000 cu.m/day)	管道长度（公里） Length of Gas Pipelines (km)			全年供气总量 Volume of Gas Supply			用气人口（万人） Population with Access to Gas (10 000 persons)		
			人工煤气 Coal Gas	液化石油气 Liquefied Petroleum Gas	天然气 Natural Gas	人工煤气（万立方米） Coal Gas (10 000 cu.m)	液化石油气（吨） Liquefied Petroleum Gas (ton)	天然气（万立方米） Natural Gas (10 000 cu.m)	人工煤气 Coal Gas	液化石油气 Liquefied Petroleum Gas	天然气 Natural Gas
全国	**National Total**	**9423.5**	**51403.7**	**18661.9**	**92043.1**	**2558343**	**12220141**	**2104951**	**4368.6**	**18012.8**	**7104.4**
北京	Beijing		115.0	176.0	7124.0	20211	374358	317397	21.9	340.8	880.0
天津	Tianjin	185.0	1461.3	173.9	6750.8	28803	61503	68966	96.5	122.9	411.5
河北	Hebei	169.9	3605.9	125.2	2550.1	78435	327294	25374	400.9	705.0	142.0
山西	Shanxi	383.1	3483.2	1.4	441.2	82291	42004	10802	394.7	169.7	50.2
内蒙古	Inner Mongolia	195.4	1008.0	80.2	619.0	6887	138348	9444	92.9	294.5	49.6
辽宁	Liaoning	190.8	4897.2	436.5	4979.0	63614	402659	36817	531.5	713.1	566.6
吉林	Jilin	87.4	2138.0	200.6	2776.0	13755	184269	17333	169.2	493.0	166.9
黑龙江	Heilongjiang	232.0	2433.5	156.8	1193.0	40199	228630	19555	289.4	612.3	103.7
上海	Shanghai	1134.3	8468.6		6370.4	199744	452613	174962	662.3	710.9	521.9
江苏	Jiangsu	3811.4	5320.5	2530.5	8051.1	1290834	1129147	87634	234.1	1764.6	380.4
浙江	Zhejiang	29.3	1140.3	3303.7	2892.8	27686	1060572	10428	83.3	1135.2	118.9
安徽	Anhui	35.5	644.4	1010.1	2973.8	8723	613614	11564	67.0	540.9	207.8
福建	Fujian	8.0	228.0	2262.8		1810	378053		11.2	603.5	
江西	Jiangxi	122.8	1588.6	266.1	477.4	31707	174521	1051	130.6	411.6	38.4
山东	Shandong	126.4	5743.3	1025.5	5937.2	47743	572194	116691	356.5	1835.6	381.3
河南	Henan	202.3	1221.3	205.0	5755.2	117592	225864	53337	142.4	573.8	398.7
湖北	Hubei	121.0	158.0	575.4	3976.8	9184	311171	17422	22.3	1142.0	263.9
湖南	Hunan	167.2	695.3	1260.6	1327.9	44064	294718	5632	74.6	647.6	61.6
广东	Guangdong	141.4	2148.1	3537.8	1172.9	29310	4101990	71597	162.9	3222.5	78.5
广西	Guangxi	14.1	440.0	940.3	105.3	4483	315998	84	24.9	550.9	0.5
海南	Hainan			12.5	533.5		66866	6360		113.4	21.1
重庆	Chongqing				7620.8		95577	164614		71.7	509.0
四川	Sichuan	355.0	442.0	44.2	12274.5	128252	164266	598531	32.5	152.2	966.5
贵州	Guizhou	100.8	1930.5	99.2	17.5	19209	53779	6199	124.8	189.3	1.7
云南	Yunnan	78.0	1492.8	141.2	110.0	20287	70436	14500	177.3	141.0	4.9
西藏	Tibet						1500	808		2.8	15.4
陕西	Shaanxi		18.0	36.0	2151.0	4365	121943	76285	27.4	242.9	358.8
甘肃	Gansu	6.0	188.0		147.0	3802	71904	4100	24.0	141.9	117.6
青海	Qinghai				501.1		14339	63606		36.9	32.6
宁夏	Ningxia		314.0		1026.9	3013	22697	68193	8.8	90.4	34.1
新疆	Xinjiang	1526.4	80.0	60.4	2186.8	232340	147314	45665	5.0	240.2	220.4

11-9 各地区城市集中供热情况（2005年）

Basic Statistics on Heating in Cities by Region (2005)

地 区	Region	供应能力 Heating Capacity 蒸 汽（吨/小时）Steam (ton/hour)	供应能力 Heating Capacity 热 水（兆瓦）Hot Water (Mega Watts)	供热总量 Quantity of Heat Supplied 蒸 汽（万吉焦）Steam (10 000 gigajoules)	供热总量 Quantity of Heat Supplied 热 水（万吉焦）Hot Water (10 000 gigajoules)	管道长度 Length of Heating Pipelines 蒸 汽（公里）Steam (km)	管道长度 Length of Heating Pipelines 热 水（公里）Hot Water (km)	供热面积（万平方米）Area of Centralized Heating (10 000 sq.m)
全 国	**National Total**	**106723**	**197976**	**71493**	**139542**	**14772**	**71338**	**252056.2**
北 京	Beijing	2297	30115	812	15142	173	6272	31736.2
天 津	Tianjin	3294	10563	1966	7572	415	8290	14040.9
河 北	Hebei	9290	13917	7825	8796	1080	5388	18552.2
山 西	Shanxi	3133	8578	1868	5945	674	2364	12708.1
内蒙古	Inner Mongolia	844	10887	528	9330	96	3445	11253.9
辽 宁	Liaoning	12583	36051	6435	22508	2312	14093	47620.7
吉 林	Jilin	4749	18925	1813	13518	444	4904	19585.2
黑龙江	Heilongjiang	5937	23952	2496	24076	603	10064	24397.4
上 海	Shanghai							
江 苏	Jiangsu	19744	200	14499	20	1896		9396.6
浙 江	Zhejiang	4569	233	4923	93	650	59	3942.0
安 徽	Anhui	2006	135	1013	35	223	22	313.4
福 建	Fujian		286		57		19	272.0
江 西	Jiangxi							
山 东	Shandong	22770	16744	14326	10338	4353	7867	26197.8
河 南	Henan	4698	2118	2454	1248	857	1252	5361.4
湖 北	Hubei	1404	78	741	16	100	10	849.0
湖 南	Hunan	105		6		8		250.0
广 东	Guangdong							
广 西	Guangxi							
海 南	Hainan							
重 庆	Chongqing							
四 川	Sichuan	160		134		42		15.0
贵 州	Guizhou							
云 南	Yunnan							
西 藏	Tibet							
陕 西	Shaanxi	2240	1806	1682	1402	377	505	3317.9
甘 肃	Gansu	4813	5791	6636	5586	200	2743	6844.0
青 海	Qinghai		173		236		72	110.6
宁 夏	Ningxia	646	5115	241	5437	132	1151	4327.7
新 疆	Xinjiang	1441	12309	1095	8187	137	2818	10964.4

11-10 各地区城市市政设施(2005年)

Basic Statistics on Municipal Infrastructure in Cities by Region (2005)

地 区	Region	年末实有道路长度(公里) Length of Paved Roads (year-end) (km)	年末实有道路面积(万平方米) Area of Paved Roads (year-end) (10 000 sq.m)	城市桥梁(座) Number of City Bridges (unit)	城市排水管道长度(公里) Length of City Sewage Pipes (km)	城市污水日处理能力(万立方米) Daily Disposal Capacity of City Sewage (10 000 cu.m)	城市路灯(盏) Number of Street Lights (unit)
全 国	**National Total**	**247014.9**	**392166.5**	**52123**	**241055.7**	**7989.7**	**12070195**
北 京	Beijing	15948.0	16227.0		6474.5	334.6	268703
天 津	Tianjin	5460.0	6669.0	563	10889.4	157.8	175696
河 北	Hebei	8369.2	16123.5	1283	10262.7	313.0	373206
山 西	Shanxi	4965.3	7137.2	680	3351.5	143.9	316190
内蒙古	Inner Mongolia	3867.0	6502.1	288	4505.5	105.5	431672
辽 宁	Liaoning	10556.1	16337.2	1232	10518.6	410.8	785639
吉 林	Jilin	5423.4	8451.8	570	5085.5	155.8	245129
黑龙江	Heilongjiang	9318.3	11284.8	673	5918.3	281.3	483313
上 海	Shanghai	12227.0	20942.0	8070	6933.0	481.0	301285
江 苏	Jiangsu	28673.5	40829.4	12451	28567.5	1023.9	1295670
浙 江	Zhejiang	12523.2	21774.2	6442	18607.3	412.6	727278
安 徽	Anhui	7985.5	13454.0	1125	7605.7	269.7	293524
福 建	Fujian	4919.4	7703.4	1276	5911.3	249.0	323697
江 西	Jiangxi	3916.1	6667.4	434	3563.8	120.7	361519
山 东	Shandong	25161.8	42605.2	3620	23288.1	538.3	821555
河 南	Henan	7089.6	15653.4	1075	10200.5	267.4	477873
湖 北	Hubei	14170.6	20524.9	1677	9124.3	449.5	332619
湖 南	Hunan	5978.2	9935.8	482	5593.8	275.7	295972
广 东	Guangdong	24289.3	43695.9	4666	27577.1	633.6	1272744
广 西	Guangxi	5075.3	8122.9	583	4116.3	372.4	391972
海 南	Hainan	1132.0	2352.5	128	1925.9	43.2	95400
重 庆	Chongqing	3629.8	5605.3	668	4106.1	168.9	188977
四 川	Sichuan	9021.2	15266.5	1936	9655.7	226.4	711435
贵 州	Guizhou	2203.6	2959.5	302	3599.6	34.5	136740
云 南	Yunnan	2767.0	3836.6	569	2952.4	173.9	183147
西 藏	Tibet	487.0	529.3	32	278.8		13006
陕 西	Shaanxi	3190.6	6457.3	477	3250.2	68.1	225373
甘 肃	Gansu	2960.2	4972.1	315	2721.9	72.9	126258
青 海	Qinghai	557.3	935.9	63	554.4	8.5	29316
宁 夏	Ningxia	1300.8	2626.3	128	956.2	64.1	134971
新 疆	Xinjiang	3848.7	5984.1	315	2959.9	132.7	250316

11-11 各地区城市公共交通情况（2005年）

Basic Statistics on Public Transportation in Cities by Region (2005)

地区	Region	年末公共交通运营数（辆）Number of Public Vehicles under Operation at the Year-end (unit)	公共汽车 Buses	无轨电车 Trolley Buses	轨道交通 Subways, Light Rail, Streetcar	公共交通客运总量（万人次）Number of Passengers Carried of Bus, Trolley Bus (10 000 person-times)	公共汽车 Buses	无轨电车 Trolley Bues	轨道交通 Subways, Light Rail, Streetcar	出租汽车（辆）Number of Taxi (unit)
全国	**National Total**	**313296**	**308379**	**2553**	**2364**	**4836930**	**4606866**	**65015**	**165049**	**936973**
北京	Beijing	21313	19872	473	968	525606	447105	10525	67976	66000
天津	Tianjin	6884	6768		116	90191	89529		661	31939
河北	Hebei	10429	10429			99412	99412			44527
山西	Shanxi	4565	4439	126		71205	68262	2943		29842
内蒙古	Inner Mongolia	3594	3594			36806	36806			32508
辽宁	Liaoning	17669	17503	45	121	321555	311347	3046	7162	81020
吉林	Jilin	8283	8246		37	105139	103729		1410	49239
黑龙江	Heilongjiang	10648	10598	50		138506	138172	334		56952
上海	Shanghai	18680	17509	476	695	337496	266924	11166	59406	47794
江苏	Jiangsu	22281	22197		84	284117	283760		357	41476
浙江	Zhejiang	15981	15792	189		226740	220912	5828		29993
安徽	Anhui	8880	8880			139661	139661			34287
福建	Fujian	7929	7929			149465	149465			13809
江西	Jiangxi	5818	5729	89		83880	80256	3625		9397
山东	Shandong	23455	23186	269		247906	241642	6264		56226
河南	Henan	13213	13022	191		153775	148701	5074		52744
湖北	Hubei	17782	17578	197	7	224224	219082	5013	130	27414
湖南	Hunan	9611	9611			212507	212507			23087
广东	Guangdong	28979	28410	273	296	482699	447908	7671	27120	43831
广西	Guangxi	5239	5239			107331	107331			11970
海南	Hainan	1362	1322		40	26798	25971		827	3988
重庆	Chongqing	7267	7267			111324	111324			16376
四川	Sichuan	10578	10578			192983	192983			24513
贵州	Guizhou	5006	5006			86310	86310			8677
云南	Yunnan	5547	5547			73733	73733			15794
西藏	Tibet	1040	1040			778	778			1351
陕西	Shaanxi	6908	6833	75		114794	113065	1729		22475
甘肃	Gansu	3515	3415	100		48411	46614	1797		18339
青海	Qinghai	1839	1839			37081	37081			6894
宁夏	Ningxia	1448	1448			12206	12206			11183
新疆	Xinjiang	7553	7553			94292	94292			23328

11-12 各地区城市园林和绿地（2005年）

Basic Statistics on Parks, Gardens and Green Areas in Cities by Region (2005)

地 区	Region	城市园林绿地面积（公顷）Area of Urban Gardens and Green Areas (hectare)	#公共绿地 Public Green Areas	公园（个）Number of Parks (unit)	公园面积（公顷）Area of Parks (hectare)	年游人量（万人次）Number of Visitors to Parks and Zoos in the Year (10 000 person-times)
全 国	**National Total**	**1468228.6**	**283758.1**	**7077**	**157815.9**	**179367.4**
北 京	Beijing	44384.4	11364.7	264	11365.0	12294.0
天 津	Tianjin	15740.7	5368.6	183	2325.3	3462.0
河 北	Hebei	44847.6	10317.0	291	5693.6	6822.5
山 西	Shanxi	19316.9	5418.6	157	3851.3	3934.4
内蒙古	Inner Mongolia	19647.1	4984.9	86	3125.8	772.8
辽 宁	Liaoning	74583.3	15386.8	259	8300.4	6507.6
吉 林	Jilin	26863.6	7392.5	69	2526.2	1774.6
黑龙江	Heilongjiang	51415.2	10432.6	152	5382.7	9663.8
上 海	Shanghai	28704.3	11976.1	142	1516.6	13654.3
江 苏	Jiangsu	189069.8	25687.0	539	9924.0	10044.6
浙 江	Zhejiang	56871.7	13142.6	748	6045.6	12691.3
安 徽	Anhui	41896.1	7429.7	140	3970.1	4901.3
福 建	Fujian	27153.4	5862.0	314	4445.6	5226.3
江 西	Jiangxi	25166.8	5633.5	125	2258.9	1777.9
山 东	Shandong	105305.1	27480.2	456	11380.5	11219.9
河 南	Henan	42964.8	12643.7	292	6190.8	6892.4
湖 北	Hubei	56184.0	13616.2	217	5753.0	9236.1
湖 南	Hunan	40723.3	7143.2	150	6589.3	3814.0
广 东	Guangdong	333015.3	39940.5	1492	31275.8	23588.4
广 西	Guangxi	29688.8	5361.8	110	3675.9	2176.5
海 南	Hainan	6685.1	1700.6	35	1124.9	2249.9
重 庆	Chongqing	15938.7	4253.6	94	2001.3	1250.5
四 川	Sichuan	68079.9	11197.8	312	5700.7	10921.3
贵 州	Guizhou	28020.4	2901.3	44	1863.1	2233.2
云 南	Yunnan	16725.7	4298.9	76	4489.3	2464.1
西 藏	Tibet	62.6	14.2	5	108.0	68.0
陕 西	Shaanxi	15003.1	4026.6	88	1447.8	6843.4
甘 肃	Gansu	11548.0	3514.6	83	2249.2	1226.0
青 海	Qinghai	2430.0	562.0	14	265.9	266.9
宁 夏	Ningxia	7726.5	1384.6	28	758.0	687.1
新 疆	Xinjiang	22466.4	3321.9	112	2211.3	702.4

11-13 各地区城市环境卫生情况（2005年）

Basic Statistics on Urban Sanitation in Cities by Region (2005)

地 区	Region	清扫保洁面积（万平方米）Area under Cleaning Program (10 000 sq.m)	生活垃圾清运量（万吨）Volume of Garbage Disposal (10 000 tons)	粪便清运量（万吨）Volume of Excrement and Urine Disposal (10 000 tons)	市容环卫专用车辆总数（台）Number of Special Vehicles for Environmental Sanitation (unit)	公共厕所（座）Number of Public Lavatories (unit)	#水冲式 Water-Closet
全 国	**National Total**	**310806.1**	**15576.8**	**3804.6**	**64205**	**114917**	**70773**
北 京	Beijing	11248.0	454.6	171.7	5851	5635	4551
天 津	Tianjin	4660.1	144.8	25.7	1346	2075	1788
河 北	Hebei	13053.7	680.1	202.6	2948	5745	2266
山 西	Shanxi	7110.5	619.7	571.1	1396	4211	920
内蒙古	Inner Mongolia	4978.8	329.0	108.5	1199	4212	808
辽 宁	Liaoning	19587.6	768.0	148.4	3313	9661	1373
吉 林	Jilin	7615.1	580.4	120.3	2053	5363	730
黑龙江	Heilongjiang	10279.5	1125.8	272.1	3187	10731	1009
上 海	Shanghai	10414.9	622.3	253.9	4352	3640	3570
江 苏	Jiangsu	27101.4	834.8	388.4	5094	10591	9463
浙 江	Zhejiang	17262.6	762.5	205.4	2848	5087	4974
安 徽	Anhui	9006.5	476.6	41.5	1182	3600	2209
福 建	Fujian	6793.7	303.0	43.8	1590	1759	1749
江 西	Jiangxi	5385.0	264.4	21.4	735	1457	1266
山 东	Shandong	31996.3	1046.5	325.7	4121	4327	3845
河 南	Henan	14616.6	756.7	81.2	2678	5661	3841
湖 北	Hubei	12666.4	885.2	92.0	2597	4840	3823
湖 南	Hunan	7559.7	486.0	41.4	1396	2652	2240
广 东	Guangdong	38542.2	1722.6	459.1	6467	6555	6421
广 西	Guangxi	6527.5	204.7	22.3	982	1502	1437
海 南	Hainan	2563.0	81.2	6.3	315	224	176
重 庆	Chongqing	4455.6	237.6	67.5	937	2239	1748
四 川	Sichuan	13103.1	600.7	51.5	2486	4729	4106
贵 州	Guizhou	2163.9	176.5	6.1	561	1071	1021
云 南	Yunnan	4437.2	205.7	101.7	1331	1180	947
西 藏	Tibet	424.4	44.5	2.5	28	119	68
陕 西	Shaanxi	4870.7	370.7	14.0	1033	1717	1397
甘 肃	Gansu	3554.3	297.8	52.8	566	1094	691
青 海	Qinghai	1030.0	54.4	28.0	187	397	389
宁 夏	Ningxia	2127.4	96.4	5.0	332	938	468
新 疆	Xinjiang	5670.5	343.6	3.9	1094	1905	1479

11-14 各地区城市设施水平（2005年）

Level of Public Facilities in Cities by Region (2005)

地区	Region	人均住宅建筑面积（平方米）Per Capita Floor Space of Residential Buildings (sq.m)	城市用水普及率（%）Percentage of Population with Access to Tap Water (%)	城市用气普及率（%）Percentage of Population with Access to Gas (%)	每万人拥有公共交通车辆（标台）Number of Public Transportation Vehicles Per 10 000 Persons (unit)	人均拥有道路面积（平方米）Per Capita Area of Paved Roads (sq.m)	人均公共绿地面积（平方米）Per Capita Public Green Areas (sq.m)	每万人拥有公共厕所（座）Number of Public Lavatories Per 10 000 Population (unit)
全 国	**National Average**	**26.11**	**91.09**	**82.08**	**8.62**	**10.92**	**7.89**	**3.20**
北 京	Beijing	32.86	100.00		17.64	10.55		3.66
天 津	Tianjin	24.97	100.00	98.50	11.23	10.41	8.38	3.24
河 北	Hebei	26.04	99.95	94.20	7.15	12.17	7.79	4.34
山 西	Shanxi	24.79	90.32	68.29	5.25	7.93	6.02	4.68
内蒙古	Inner Mongolia	22.96	83.88	68.18	5.61	10.14	7.78	6.57
辽 宁	Liaoning	21.96	93.83	88.11	8.94	7.95	7.49	4.70
吉 林	Jilin	22.46	83.20	76.23	7.28	7.77	6.80	4.93
黑龙江	Heilongjiang	22.03	79.55	70.96	6.68	7.96	7.36	7.57
上 海	Shanghai	33.07	99.98	100.00	12.95	11.78	6.73	2.05
江 苏	Jiangsu	27.95	96.28	95.11	9.07	16.32	10.27	4.23
浙 江	Zhejiang	34.80	99.10	98.47	11.71	16.03	9.31	3.75
安 徽	Anhui	22.56	90.52	72.29	7.20	11.92	6.58	3.19
福 建	Fujian	32.28	98.68	96.19	12.08	12.06	9.17	2.75
江 西	Jiangxi	25.58	92.64	80.64	8.03	9.26	7.82	2.02
山 东	Shandong	26.47	77.39	75.74	6.92	12.54	8.09	1.27
河 南	Henan	23.40	91.94	69.25	7.77	9.72	7.85	3.52
湖 北	Hubei	24.99	77.62	68.60	7.80	9.86	6.54	2.32
湖 南	Hunan	26.00	91.11	75.43	8.86	9.56	6.87	2.55
广 东	Guangdong	26.46	98.80	95.42	6.45	12.04	11.00	1.81
广 西	Guangxi	25.23	82.28	72.68	6.93	10.24	6.76	1.89
海 南	Hainan	24.18	85.97	82.56	6.49	14.44	10.44	1.38
重 庆	Chongqing	30.68	79.38	68.84	8.70	6.64	5.04	2.65
四 川	Sichuan	27.48	97.22	82.19	7.63	10.90	8.00	3.38
贵 州	Guizhou	20.40	92.75	64.74	8.63	6.07	5.95	2.20
云 南	Yunnan	28.59	82.07	60.01	9.03	7.12	7.98	2.19
西 藏	Tibet	20.86	61.82	53.74	14.88	15.65	0.42	3.52
陕 西	Shaanxi	23.40	93.24	79.82	8.19	8.19	5.11	2.18
甘 肃	Gansu	23.28	85.94	55.36	6.31	9.71	6.86	2.14
青 海	Qinghai	22.00	100.00	72.00	17.84	9.70	5.82	4.11
宁 夏	Ningxia	23.90	62.89	51.84	4.76	10.21	5.38	3.65
新 疆	Xinjiang	22.22	97.86	89.33	13.00	11.48	6.37	3.66

主要统计指标解释

供水综合生产能力 指按供水设施取水、净化、送水、出厂输水干管等环节设计能力计算的综合生产能力。包括在原设计能力的基础上，经挖、革、改增加的生产能力。计算时，以四个环节中最薄弱的环节为主确定能力。

年末供水管道长度 指从送水泵至用户水表之间所有管道的长度。不包括新安装尚未使用的管道。

全年供水总量 指报告期供水企业(单位)供出的全部水量。包括有效供水量和漏损水量。

生活用水量 包括公共服务用水和居民家庭用水。公共服务用水指为城市社会公共生活服务的用水。包括行政事业单位、部队营区和公共设施服务、社会服务业、批发零售贸易业、旅馆饮食业以及其他公共服务业等单位的用水。居民家庭用水指城市范围内所有居民家庭的日常生活用水。包括城市居民、农民家庭、公共供水站用水。

用水普及率 指城市用水人口数与城市人口总数的比率。计算公式：

$$用水普及率=\frac{城市用水人口数}{城市人口总数}\times 100\%$$

人工煤气生产能力 指报告期末人工煤气生产厂制气、净化、输送等环节的综合生产能力，不包括备用设备能力。一般按设计能力计算，如果实际生产能力大于设计能力时，应按实际测定的生产能力计算。测定时应以制气、净化、输送三个环节中最薄弱的环节为主。

供气管道长度 指报告期末从气源厂压缩机的出口或门站出口至各类用户引入管之间的全部已经通气投入使用的管道长度。不包括煤气生产厂、输配站、液化气储存站、灌瓶站、储配站、气化站、混气站、供应站等厂(站)内的管道。

全年供气总量 指全年燃气企业(单位)向用户供应的燃气数量。包括销售量和损失量。

用气普及率 指报告期末使用燃气的城市人口数与城市人口总数的比率。计算公式为：

$$用气普及率=\frac{城市用气人口数}{城市人口总数}\times 100\%$$

城市供热能力 指供热企业(单位)向城市热用户输送热能的设计能力。

城市供热总量 指在报告期供热企业(单位)向城市热用户输送全部蒸汽和热水的总热量。

城市供热管道长度 指从各类热源到热用户建筑物接入口之间的全部蒸汽和热水的管道长度。不包括各类热源厂内部的管道长度。

年末道路长度 指年末道路长度和与道路相通的广场、桥梁、隧道的长度，按车行道中心线计算。在统计时只统计路面宽度在3.5米(含3.5米)以上的各种铺装道路，包括开放型工业区和住宅区道路在内。

城市桥梁 指为跨越天然或人工障碍物而修建的构筑物。包括跨河桥、立交桥、人行天桥以及人行地下通道等。包括永久性桥和半永久性桥。

城市排水管道长度 指所有排水总管、干管、支管、检查井及连接井进出口等长度之和。

城市污水日处理能力 指污水处理厂(或处理装置)每昼夜处理污水量的设计能力。

年末运营车数 指年末公交企业(单位)用于运营业务的全部车辆数。以企业(单位)固定资产台帐中已投入运营的车辆数为准。

城市园林绿地面积 指报告期末用作园林和绿化的各种绿地面积。包括公共绿地、居住区绿地、单位附属绿地、防护绿地、生产绿地、道路绿地和风景林地面积。

不包括：

1.屋顶绿化、垂直绿化、阳台绿化和室内绿化。

2.以物质生产为主的林地、耕地、牧草地、果园和竹园等。

3.城市总体规划中不列入绿地的水域。

公共绿地 指向公众开放的市级、区级、居住区级各类公园、街旁游园，包括其范围内的水域。其中居住区级公园应不小于1万平方米，街旁游园的宽度不小于8米，面积不小于400平方米。

Explanatory Notes on Main Statistical Indicators

Production Capacity of Water Supply refers to the designed comprehensive production capacity of water facilities, covering the 4 links of water collection, purification, conveyance, and outflow through trunk pipelines. Increase capacity through transformation and innovation projects are included as well. The capacity is determined mainly on the weakest of the above-mentioned 4 links.

Length of Water Supply Pipelines at the Year-end refers to the total length of all the pipelines between the water pumps and the user's water meters, excluding pipelines newly installed but not used yet.

Annual Volume of Water Supply refers to the total volume of water supplied by water-works (units) during the reference period, including both the effective water supply and loss during the water supply.

Consumption of Water for Residential Use refers to the water consumption of households for daily life and the water consumption of public service facilities. The latter refers to water consumption for urban public services, including the consumption of government agencies and public institutions, military barracks, public facilities, wholesale and retail outlets, restaurants, hotels, and other units providing public services. Household water consumption refers to consumption of water for daily life of all households in the boundary of cities, including households of urban residents and farmers, and public water supply stations.

Percentage of Urban Population with Access to Tap Water refers to the ratio of the urban population with access to tap water to the total urban population. The formula is:

Percentage of population with access to tap water= (Urban population with access to tap water) / (Urban population)× 100%

Production Capacity of Gaswork Gas refers to the comprehensive production capacity of the urban gasworks in gas generation, purification and delivery at the end of the reference period, excluding capacity of the reserved facilities. In general, it is determined by the designed capacity, and when actual production capacity is larger than the designed capacity, the capacity is determined by the actual measurement on the weakest link in the production, purification and delivery.

Length of Gas Pipelines refers to the total length of pipelines in use between the outlet of the compressor of gaswork or outlet of gas stations and the leading pipe of users, excluding pipelines within gasworks, delivery stations, LPG storage stations, refilling stations, gas-mixing stations and supply stations.

Volume of Gas Supply refers to the total volume of gas provided to users by gas-producing enterprises (units) in a year, including the volume sold and the volume lost.

Percentage of Urban Population with Access to Gas refers to the ratio of the urban population with access to gas to the total urban population at the end of the reference period. The formula is:

Percentage of population with access to gas = (Urban population with access to gas / Urban population) x 100%

Heating Capacity in Urban Area refers to the designed capacity of heating enterprises (units) in supplying heating energy to urban users during the reference period.

Quantity of Heat Supplied in Urban Area refers to the total quantity of heat from steam and hot water supplied to urban users by heating enterprises (units) during the reference period.

Length of Heating Pipelines refers to the total length of steam or hot water pipelines for sources of heat to the leading pipelines of the buildings of the users, excluding internal pipelines in heat generating enterprises.

Length of Paved Roads at the Year-end refers to the length of roads with paved surface including squares bridges and tunnels connected with roads by the end of the year. Length of the roads is measured by the central lines for vehicles for paved roads with a width of 3.5 meters and over, including roads in open-ended factory compounds and residential quarters.

Urban Bridges refer to bridges built to cross over natural or man-made barriers, including bridges over rivers, overpasses for traffic and for pedestrian, underpasses for pedestrian, etc. Both permanent and semi-permanent bridges are included.

Length of Urban Sewage Pipes refers to the total length of general drainage, trunks. branch and inspection wells, connection wells, inlets and outlets, etc.

Daily Disposal Capacity of Urban Sewage refers to the designed 24 hour capacity of sewage disposal by the sewage treatment works or facilities.

Number of Vehicles under Operation at the Year-end refers to the total number of vehicles under operation by public transport enterprises (units) at the end of the year, based on the records of operational vehicles by the enterprises (units).

Area of Urban Gardens and Green Areas refers to the total area occupied for green projects at the end of the reference period, including public green land, green land in residential quarters, green land attached to institutions, protection green land, production green land, roadside green land and forest in scenic spots. It does not include the following:

(1) Greenery and plants on roofs, balconies, indoors and vertical green areas;

(2) Forest, cultivated land, grassland, orchards and bamboo grooves that are for production purpose; and

(3) Water areas that are not included in urban master plan as green land.

Public Green Area refers to green areas open to the public such as municipal, community and neighborhood parks and roadside parks, including waters within parks. Neighborhood parks should occupy an area larger than 10,000 square meters, and the width of roadside parks should occupy an area larger than 400 square meters, with a width of more that 8 meters.

12

环境保护

Environment Protection

简 要 说 明

一、本篇章的主要内容

本篇主要反映我国环境保护事业发展情况。主要内容包括水环境、大气环境、固体废物、声环境、生态环境、自然灾害和环境污染治理投资等内容。

主要反映我国总的水资源、供水、用水情况以及工业废水和生活污水的排放及治理情况；城市空气质量，废气排放及处理情况；工业固体废物的产生、处理及利用情况以及城市生活垃圾清运及处理情况；我国国控城市道路交通和区域环境噪声监测情况；我国的土地利用、耕地变动、森林资源、造林及其自然保护基本情况；地质、地震、海洋、森林灾害及环境污染与破坏事故情况；环境污染治理投资等情况。

二、本篇章的统计范围和调查方法

1． 统计范围：各地区有污染物排放的工业企业、城镇生活及其他排污单位等。

2． 调查方法：工业企业污染排放及处理利用情况对重点调查单位逐个发表填报汇总，对非重点调查单位的排污情况实行整体估算。

重点调查单位指筛选出的排污量占各地区全部工业污染源排污总量85%以上的工业企业单位。非重点调查单位数据的估算方法为对占各地区排污总量15%的非重点工业企业，按废水、化学需氧量、氨氮、二氧化硫、烟尘、粉尘、固体废物等项目的排放进行测算，经汇总生成重点调查数据。以上两方面的数据汇总成为各地区工业污染排放数据。

3． 生活及其他污染情况，依据相关基础数据和技术参数进行估算。

三、本篇章的资料来源

环境污染与治理、生活污染物排放及处理、声环境、工业污染治理投资情况由国家环境保护总局提供。

水资源、城市生活垃圾清运及处理、土地利用和耕地变动、森林资源、海洋灾害等情况分别由水利部、建设部、国土资源部、国家林业局、国家海洋局提供。

Brief Introduction

I.Main Content

This chapter contain information that reflect the development of environment protection in China, including total water resources, water supply and utilization, discharge and treatment of industrial and other waste water; urban air quality, emission and treatment of waste gas; production, treatment and utilization of industrial solid wastes, collection and disposal of consumption wastes in cities; national monitoring of road traffic noise and urban environmental noise in key cities; land use, change in cultivated land, forest resources, afforestation, and forest protection; cases of geological, seismic, marine and forest disasters, environmental pollution or destruction accidents; investment in environment pollution treatment, etc.

II.Coverage of Statistics and Survey Methodologies

1) Coverage of statistics: industrial enterprises and other urban units which discharge pollutants.

2) Survey methodology for discharge and treatment of industrial pollutants: comprehensive survey is conducted on all key industrial enterprises, while overall estimation is carried out for ordinary enterprises.

Key enterprises refer to those enterprises which discharged more than 85% of all pollutants in the region. For ordinary enterprises whose discharge is less than 15% in the total of the region, estimation is made for the volume of their discharge of waste water, oxygen required substances, ammonia and nitrogen, sulphur dioxide, industrial soot and dust, and solid wastes. Data on discharge of pollutants of key and ordinary enterprises make up the total discharge of the region.

3) Data on pollution from consumption and other sources are estimated using relevant statistics and technical parameters.

III.Source of Data

Data on environment pollution and treatment,pollutants from consumption,noise monitoring and on investment in the treatment of industrial pollution are provided by the State Environment Protection Administration.

Data on water resources, collection and disposal of urban consumption wastes, land use and change in cultivated land, forest resources, marine disasters, etc. are provided respectively by Ministry of Water Conservancy, Ministry of Construction, Ministry of Land and Resources, State Forestry Administration and State Oceanic Administration.

12-1 环境保护基本情况
Basic Statistics on Environmental Protection

指　标	Item	2001	2002	2003	2004	2005
水环境	**Water**					
水资源总量 (亿立方米)	Water Resources (100 million cu.m)	26867.8	28261.3	27460.2	24129.6	28053.1
地表水	Surface Water Resources	25933.4	27243.3	26250.7	23126.4	26982.4
地下水	Groundwater Resources	8390.1	8697.2	8299.3	7436.3	8091.1
地表水与地下水资源重复量	Duplicated Measurement between Surface Water and Groundwater	7455.7	7679.2	7089.9	6433.1	7020.4
人均水资源量 (立方米/人)	Per Capita Water Resources (cu.m/person)	2112.5	2207.2	2131.3	1856.3	2151.8
供水总量 (亿立方米)	Water Supply (100 million cu.m)	5567.4	5497.3	5320.4	5547.8	5633.0
#地表水	Surface Water Supply	4450.7	4404.4	4286.0	4504.2	4572.2
地下水	Groundwater Supply	1094.9	1072.4	1018.1	1026.4	1038.8
用水总量 (亿立方米)	Water Use (100 million cu.m)	5567.4	5497.3	5320.4	5547.8	5633.0
#农业	Agriculture	3825.7	3736.2	3432.8	3585.7	3580.0
工业	Industry	1141.8	1142.4	1177.2	1228.9	1285.2
生活	Living Consumption	599.9	618.7	630.9	651.2	675.1
废水排放总量 (亿吨)	Waste Water Discharge (100 million tons)	433	439	459	482	525
#工业废水排放量	Industry	203	207	212	221	243
生活污水排放量	Non-Industrial	230	232	247	261	281
工业废水排放达标量 (亿吨)	Industrial Waste Water Meeting Discharge Standards (100 million tons)	173	183	189	201	222
工业废水排放达标率 (%)	Percentage of Industrial Waste Water Meeting Discharge Standards (%)	85.2	88.3	89.2	90.7	91.2
化学需氧量排放量 (万吨)	Discharge Amount of COD (10 000 tons)	1405	1367	1333	1339	1414
#工业	Industry	608	584	512	510	555
生活	Non-Industrial	797	783	821	829	859
氨氮排放量 (万吨)	Ammonia Nitrogen Discharge (10 000 tons)	125	129	129	133	150
#工业	Industry	41	42	40	42	53
生活	Non-Industrial	84	87	89	91	97
大气环境	**Atmosphere Environment**					
工业废气排放量 (亿标立方米)	Industrial Waste Air Emission (100 million cu.m)	160863	175257	198906	237696	268988
#燃料燃烧	Fuels Burning	93526	103776	116447	139726	155238
生产工艺	Production Process	67337	71481	82459	97971	113749
二氧化硫排放量 (万吨)	Sulphur Dioxide Emission (10 000 tons)	1947	1927	2159	2255	2549
#工业	Industry	1566	1562	1792	1891	2168
生活	Non-Industrial	381	365	367	364	381
烟尘排放量 (万吨)	Soot Emission (10 000 tons)	1070	1013	1049	1095	1183
#工业	Industry	852	804	846	887	949
生活	Non-Industrial	218	209	202	209	234
工业粉尘排放量 (万吨)	Industrial Dust Emission (10 000 tons)	991	941	1021	905	911
工业二氧化硫去除量 (万吨)	Industrial Sulphur Dioxide Removed (10 000 tons)	565	698	749	890	1090
工业烟尘去除量 (万吨)	Industrial Soot Removed (10 000 tons)	12317	13998	15649	18075	20587
工业粉尘去除量 (万吨)	Industrial Dust Removed (10 000 tons)	5322	5570	5995	8529	6454
建成城市烟尘控制区数 (个)	Number of Soot Control Zones Established (unit)	3203	3369	3599	3693	3452
烟尘控制区面积(万平方公里)	Area of Soot Control Zones (10 000 sq.km)	2.2	2.6	3.3	3.7	3.7

12-1 续表 1 continued

指 标	Item	2001	2002	2003	2004	2005
固体废物	**Solid Wastes**					
工业固体废物产生量(万吨)	Industrial Solid Wastes Produced (10 000 tons)	88840	94509	100428	120030	134449
#危险废物	Hazardous Wastes	952	1001	1170	995	1162
工业固体废物综合利用量(万吨)	Industrial Solid Wastes Utilized (10 000 tons)	47290	50061	56040	67796	76993
工业固体废物综合利用率(%)	Ratio of Industrial Solid Wastes Utilized (%)	52.1	52.0	54.8	55.7	56.1
工业固体废物排放量(万吨)	Industrial Solid Wastes Discharged (10 000 tons)	2894	2635	1941	1762	1655
"三废"综合利用产品产值(亿元)	Output Value of Products Made from Waste Gas, Waste Water & Solid Wastes (100 million yuan)	345	386	441	573	756
噪声	**Noise**					
建成城市环境噪声达标区数(个)	Developed Districts of Environmental Noise Meeting National Standard (unit)	3111	3128	3573	3534	3565
城市环境噪声达标区面积(万平方公里)	Area of Urban Environmental Noise Meeting National Standard (10 000 sq.km)	1.5	1.6	2.0	2.1	2.5
生态环境	**Eco-Environment Protection**					
森林面积 (万公顷)	Area of Forest (10 000 hectares)	15894.1	15894.1	17490.9	17490.9	17490.9
森林覆盖率 (%)	Forest Coverage (%)	16.55	16.55	18.21	18.21	18.21
当年造林面积 (万公顷)	Area of Reforestation of the Year (10 000 hectares)	495	777	912	560	365
自然保护区数 (个)	Number of Nature Reserves (unit)	1551	1757	1999	2194	2349
#国家级	National Level	171	188	226	226	243
自然保护区面积 (万公顷)	Area of Nature Reserves (10 000 hectares)	12989	13295	14398	14823	14995
自然保护区面积占辖区面积比重 (%)	Area of Nature Reserves in Regions (%)	12.9	13.2	14.4	14.8	15.0
生态示范区数 (个)	Number of Demonstration Zones of Ecology (unit)	215	322	484	528	528
#国家级	National Level	82	82	82	166	233
湿地面积 (万公顷)	Area of Wetland (10 000 hectares)			3848.6	3848.6	3848.6
湿地面积占国土面积比重(%)	Area of Wetland out of National Surface Area (%)			4.0	4.0	4.0
自然灾害	**Natural Disaster**					
发生地质灾害起数 (次)	Geological Disaster (time)	5793	40246	15489	13555	17751
#滑坡	Landslide	3034	31247	10240	9130	9367
崩塌	Collapse	583	3097	2604	2593	7654
泥石流	Mudflow	1539	4976	1549	1157	566
发生地震灾害次数 (次)	Seismic Disaster (time)	12	5	21	11	13
#5.0级以上	Magnitude above 5 Richter Scale	11	4	17	9	11
海洋赤潮发生次数 (次)	Red Tide (time)	77	79	119	96	82
森林火灾次数 (次)	Forest Fire (time)	4933	7527	10463	13466	11542
#重大	Serious	17	24	14	38	16
特大	Extraordinarily Serious	3	7	7	3	3
森林火灾受灾面积(万公顷)	Fire-Affected Forest Area (10 000 hectares)	4.6	4.8	45.1	14.2	7.4
森林病虫鼠害发生面积(万公顷)	Forest Area Affected by Diseases, Pests and Rats (10 000 hectares)	839.0	841.2	888.7	944.8	961.0
森林病虫鼠害防治面积(万公顷)	Forest Area Prevented and Cured from Diseases, Pests and Rats (10 000 hectares)	587.3	572.0	582.9	639.5	640.7
森林病虫鼠害防治率 (%)	Rate of Prevention and Cure (%)	70.0	68.0	65.6	68.0	66.7

注：森林面积和森林覆盖率2001、2002年为第五次全国森林资源清查数（1994–1998年），包括台湾省数据；2003–2005年为第六次清查数（1999–2003年），包括香港、澳门特别行政区和台湾省数据。

a) Of area of forest and forest coverage, in 2001 and 2002 were the figures of the Fifth National Forestry Survey(1994-1998), including figures of Taiwan, and in 2003-2005 were figures of the Sixth National Forestry Survey(1999-2003), including figures of Hong Kong, Macao and Taiwan.

12-1 续表 2 continued

指　　标	Item	2001	2002	2003	2004	2005
环境污染	**Pollution**					
环境污染与破坏事故次数（次）	Pollution Accidents (time)	1842	1921	1843	1441	1406
#水污染	Water Pollution	1096	1097	1042	753	693
大气污染	Air Pollution	576	597	654	569	538
固体废物污染	Solid Wastes Pollution	39	109	56	47	48
噪声与震动危害	Noise and Vibration Pollution	80	97	50	36	63
其他	Others	51	21	41	25	64
污染直接经济损失　（万元）	Direct Economic Loss Due to Pollution(10 000 yuan)	12272.4	4640.9	3374.9	36365.7	10515.0
污染事故赔款总额　（万元）	Reparations for Pollution Incidents (10 000 yuan)	2948.7	2629.7	1999.1	3487.2	2373.8
污染事故罚款总额　（万元）	Fines to Pollution Incidents (10 000 yuan)	315.2	511.0	392.4	476.7	708.3
环境污染治理投资	**Investment in the Treatment of Environmental Pollution**					
环境污染治理投资总额（亿元）	Total Investment in the Treatment of Environmental Pollution (100 million yuan)	1106.6	1367.2	1627.7	1909.8	2388.0
环境污染治理投资总额占国内生产总值比重　（%）	Total Investment in the Treatment of Environmental Pollution as Percent of GDP (%)	1.01	1.14	1.20	1.19	1.30
城市环境基础设施建设投资额（亿元）	Investment in Urban Environmental Infrastructure (100 million yuan)	595.7	789.1	1072.4	1141.2	1289.7
#燃气	Gas Supply	75.5	88.4	133.5	148.3	142.4
集中供热	Centralized Heating	82.0	121.4	145.8	173.4	220.2
排水	Drainage Works	224.5	275.0	375.2	352.3	368.0
园林绿化	Gardening and Greening	163.2	239.5	321.9	359.5	411.3
市容环境卫生	Environmental Sanitation	50.6	64.8	96.0	107.8	147.8
工业污染治理项目当年投资来源总额　（亿元）	Source of Current Investment in the Treatment of Industrial Pollution (100 million yuan)	174.5	188.4	221.8	308.1	458.2
#国家预算内资金	State Budget	36.3	42.0	18.8	13.7	7.8
环保专项资金	Special Funds for Environmental Protection	8.3	6.8	12.4	11.1	20.6
其他资金	Other Sources	129.8	139.6	190.7	283.3	429.8
工业污染治理项目本年完成投资（亿元）	Investment Completed this Year (100 million yuan)	174.5	188.4	221.8	308.1	458.2
#治理废水	Waste Water	72.9	71.5	87.4	105.6	133.7
治理废气	Waste Gas	65.8	69.8	92.1	142.8	213.0
治理固体废物	Solid Wastes	18.7	16.1	16.2	22.6	27.4
治理噪声	Noise Pollution	0.6	1.0	1.0	1.3	3.1
治理其他	Others	16.5	29.9	25.1	35.7	81.0
实际执行“三同时”项目环保投资总额　（亿元）	"Three Simultaneities" Environmental Investment for New Project (100 million yuan)	336.4	389.7	333.5	460.5	640.1
#新建	New Projects	238.2	238.0	220.1	326.2	467.1
扩建	Expansion	52.1	67.0	56.7	68.8	111.1
改建	Technical Improvement	46.5	84.7	56.7	65.5	61.9

12-2 水资源情况

Water Resources

年份 Year 地区 Region		水资源总量（亿立方米）Total Amount of Water Resources (100 million cu.m)	地表水资源量 Surface Water Resources	地下水资源量 Ground Water Resources	地表水与地下水资源重复量 Duplicated Measurement Between Surface Water and Groundwater	人均水资源量（立方米/人）Per Capita Water Resources (cu.m/person)
	2000	27700.8	26561.9	8501.9	7363.0	2193.9
	2001	26867.8	25933.4	8390.1	7455.7	2112.5
	2002	28261.3	27243.3	8697.2	7679.2	2207.2
	2003	27460.2	26250.7	8299.3	7089.9	2131.3
	2004	24129.6	23126.4	7436.3	6433.1	1856.3
	2005	28053.1	26982.4	8091.1	7020.4	2151.8
北京	Beijing	23.2	7.6	18.5	2.9	151.2
天津	Tianjin	10.6	7.1	4.5	0.9	102.2
河北	Hebei	134.6	58.0	109.7	33.2	197.0
山西	Shanxi	84.1	50.4	72.5	38.8	251.5
内蒙古	Inner Mongolia	456.2	338.7	214.6	97.1	1917.3
辽宁	Liaoning	377.2	336.3	130.2	89.3	896.3
吉林	Jilin	559.7	489.6	122.5	52.4	2066.8
黑龙江	Heilongjiang	744.3	612.0	288.8	156.5	1954.2
上海	Shanghai	24.5	24.5	9.3	9.3	138.0
江苏	Jiangsu	467.0	366.4	122.2	21.7	626.6
浙江	Zhejiang	1014.4	999.4	216.1	201.1	2077.2
安徽	Anhui	719.3	672.2	195.4	148.3	1178.8
福建	Fujian	1401.1	1400.0	397.7	396.5	3975.5
江西	Jiangxi	1510.1	1490.3	385.1	365.2	3513.2
山东	Shandong	415.9	295.9	213.9	93.9	451.0
河南	Henan	558.5	435.9	219.7	97.1	597.2
湖北	Hubei	934.0	903.6	276.2	245.8	1640.6
湖南	Hunan	1671.0	1664.5	393.2	386.6	2649.5
广东	Guangdong	1747.5	1738.5	400.8	391.8	1906.4
广西	Guangxi	1720.8	1720.8	365.7	365.7	3703.8
海南	Hainan	307.3	304.5	79.0	76.2	3722.4
重庆	Chongqing	509.8	509.8	107.7	107.7	1827.4
四川	Sichuan	2922.6	2921.0	590.1	588.5	3569.6
贵州	Guizhou	834.6	834.6	237.9	237.9	2244.4
云南	Yunnan	1846.4	1846.4	660.4	660.4	4161.7
西藏	Tibet	4451.1	4451.1	1013.3	1013.3	161170.6
陕西	Shaanxi	490.6	468.2	135.3	112.9	1322.7
甘肃	Gansu	269.6	260.3	150.2	140.9	1042.4
青海	Qinghai	876.1	857.6	374.2	355.7	16176.9
宁夏	Ningxia	8.5	6.9	24.2	22.5	143.6
新疆	Xinjiang	962.8	910.7	562.6	510.4	4808.9

12-3 供水用水情况

Water Supply and Water Use

年份 地区	Year Region	供水总量 (亿立方米) Water Supply (100 million cu.m)	地表水 Surface Water	地下水 Ground-water	其他 Others	用水总量 (亿立方米) Water Use (100 million cu.m)	农业 Agricul-ture	生产 Produc-tion	生活 Consump-tion	生态 Biological Protection	人均用水量 (立方米/人) Per Capita Water Use (cu.m/person)
	2000	5530.7	4440.4	1069.2	21.1	5497.6	3783.5	1139.1	574.9		435.4
	2001	5567.4	4450.7	1094.9	21.9	5567.4	3825.7	1141.8	599.9		437.7
	2002	5497.3	4404.4	1072.4	20.5	5497.3	3736.2	1142.4	618.7		429.3
	2003	5320.4	4286.0	1018.1	16.3	5320.4	3432.8	1177.2	630.9	79.5	412.9
	2004	5547.8	4504.2	1026.4	17.2	5547.8	3585.7	1228.9	651.2	82.0	426.8
	2005	5633.0	4572.2	1038.8	22.0	5633.0	3580.0	1285.2	675.1	92.7	432.1
北京	Beijing	34.5	7.0	24.9	2.6	34.5	12.7	6.8	13.9	1.1	225.0
天津	Tianjin	23.1	16.0	7.0	0.1	23.1	13.6	4.5	4.5	0.5	222.0
河北	Hebei	201.8	38.5	162.8	0.5	201.8	150.2	25.7	23.7	2.2	295.4
山西	Shanxi	55.7	20.5	34.8	0.5	55.7	32.7	13.9	8.7	0.4	166.6
内蒙古	Inner Mongolia	174.8	87.7	86.2	0.9	174.8	143.9	13.2	12.2	5.6	734.5
辽宁	Liaoning	133.3	68.2	64.3	0.8	133.3	87.2	21.1	23.9	1.1	316.7
吉林	Jilin	98.4	61.6	36.8		98.4	66.4	18.8	11.5	1.7	363.3
黑龙江	Heilongjiang	271.5	158.4	113.1		271.5	192.1	55.5	20.3	3.7	712.9
上海	Shanghai	121.3	120.5	0.8		121.3	18.5	81.3	19.8	1.7	684.2
江苏	Jiangsu	519.7	508.9	10.8		519.7	263.8	207.9	43.1	5.0	697.4
浙江	Zhejiang	209.9	202.8	6.7	0.5	209.9	106.7	58.1	31.3	13.8	429.8
安徽	Anhui	208.0	189.6	17.9	0.6	208.0	113.6	67.7	25.4	1.4	340.9
福建	Fujian	186.9	179.4	6.4	1.1	186.9	101.5	63.5	20.5	1.3	530.2
江西	Jiangxi	208.1	200.1	8.0		208.1	134.6	51.2	21.0	1.3	484.0
山东	Shandong	211.0	106.7	102.7	1.7	211.0	156.3	21.8	30.6	2.4	228.9
河南	Henan	197.8	72.2	125.5	0.1	197.8	114.5	45.9	33.6	3.8	211.5
湖北	Hubei	253.4	244.3	8.2	0.8	253.4	142.1	82.6	28.6	0.1	445.1
湖南	Hunan	328.4	308.8	19.0	0.7	328.4	201.3	80.5	43.5	3.1	520.7
广东	Guangdong	459.0	437.3	21.1	0.6	459.0	230.7	133.9	89.5	4.9	500.7
广西	Guangxi	312.9	298.4	12.0	2.4	312.9	225.4	45.0	38.9	3.6	673.4
海南	Hainan	44.1	40.1	4.0		44.1	35.1	3.2	5.7	0.1	533.6
重庆	Chongqing	71.2	69.5	1.6		71.2	21.4	33.0	16.4	0.4	255.1
四川	Sichuan	212.3	191.1	17.1	4.1	212.3	121.8	56.8	31.7	2.0	259.3
贵州	Guizhou	97.2	91.2	5.6	0.4	97.2	50.5	28.1	17.9	0.7	261.4
云南	Yunnan	146.8	140.2	6.1	0.6	146.8	108.4	18.4	19.1	0.9	330.9
西藏	Tibet	33.2	31.3	1.9		33.2	30.3	0.5	2.5		1201.8
陕西	Shaanxi	78.8	44.4	33.5	0.9	78.8	52.2	12.8	13.0	0.7	212.4
甘肃	Gansu	123.0	92.3	29.5	1.2	123.0	95.0	15.8	9.1	3.1	475.5
青海	Qinghai	30.7	23.7	7.0		30.7	21.1	6.3	3.2	0.2	565.9
宁夏	Ningxia	78.1	72.7	5.4		78.1	72.3	3.5	1.8	0.6	1314.2
新疆	Xinjiang	508.5	448.9	58.6	0.9	508.5	464.4	8.2	10.5	25.5	2539.7

注：生态用水仅包括部分河湖、湿地人工补水和城市环境用水。

a) Water use by biological protection only includes artficial supplement of river & lake, wetland and city entironment.

12-4 各地区废水排放及处理情况（2005年）

Discharge and Treatment of Industrial Waste Water by Region (2005)

地区	Region	废水治理设施数(套) Number of Facilities for Treatment of Waste Water (set)	工业废水排放总量(万吨) Total Volume of Waste Water Discharge (10 000 tons)	#直接排入海的 Volume of Waste Water Directly Discharged into Sea	工业废水排放达标量(万吨) Industrial Waste Water Meeting Discharge Standards (10 000 tons)
全　国	**National Total**	**69231**	**2431121**	**152370**	**2217093**
北　京	Beijing	553	12813		12740
天　津	Tianjin	904	30081	2009	29962
河　北	Hebei	4271	124533	4274	119920
山　西	Shanxi	3560	32099		28526
内蒙古	Inner Mongolia	745	24967		16634
辽　宁	Liaoning	2137	105072	41791	99917
吉　林	Jilin	681	41189		33458
黑龙江	Heilongjiang	1142	45158		41759
上　海	Shanghai	1707	51097	16447	49590
江　苏	Jiangsu	4663	296318	532	288936
浙　江	Zhejiang	5858	192426	5808	185978
安　徽	Anhui	1529	63487		61816
福　建	Fujian	5385	130939	62683	127874
江　西	Jiangxi	1242	53972		49726
山　东	Shandong	4215	139071	9062	136606
河　南	Henan	3315	123476		113518
湖　北	Hubei	2163	92432		80926
湖　南	Hunan	3086	122440		109879
广　东	Guangdong	5971	231568	5241	194284
广　西	Guangxi	2396	145609	806	121873
海　南	Hainan	267	7428	3718	6954
重　庆	Chongqing	1478	84885		79507
四　川	Sichuan	4493	122590		108195
贵　州	Guizhou	1935	14850		10054
云　南	Yunnan	1927	32928		26659
西　藏	Tibet	15	991		
陕　西	Shaanxi	1747	42819		39704
甘　肃	Gansu	792	16798		12301
青　海	Qinghai	130	7619		3396
宁　夏	Ningxia	456	21411		14508
新　疆	Xinjiang	468	20052		11893

12-4 续表 continued

地区	Region	工业废水中化学需氧量排放量(万吨) COD Discharge from Industrial Waste Water (10 000 tons)	工业废水中氨氮排放量(万吨) Ammonia Nitrogen Discharge from Industrial Waste Water (10 000 tons)	生活污水排放量(万吨) Consumption Waste Water Discharge (10 000 tons)	生活污水中化学需氧量排放量(万吨) COD Discharge from Consumption Waste Water (10 000 tons)	生活污水中氨氮排放量(万吨) Ammonia Nitrogen Discharge from Consumption Waste Water (10 000 tons)
全 国	**National Total**	**554.7**	**52.5**	**2813968**	**859.4**	**97.3**
北 京	Beijing	1.1	0.1	88196	10.5	1.3
天 津	Tianjin	5.9	0.6	30280	8.7	1.3
河 北	Hebei	38.9	3.6	83991	27.1	3.3
山 西	Shanxi	16.8	1.4	62997	21.9	2.8
内蒙古	Inner Mongolia	15.5	1.9	31274	14.2	3.1
辽 宁	Liaoning	26.8	3.3	113633	37.6	5.7
吉 林	Jilin	16.1	0.7	56816	24.6	2.9
黑龙江	Heilongjiang	13.7	1.2	68883	36.7	4.2
上 海	Shanghai	3.7	0.2	148613	26.8	3.1
江 苏	Jiangsu	33.8	2.4	223107	62.8	6.0
浙 江	Zhejiang	29.0	3.1	120770	30.5	3.2
安 徽	Anhui	13.6	1.9	93104	30.7	3.4
福 建	Fujian	9.9	1.0	81453	29.5	4.1
江 西	Jiangxi	11.1	0.8	69348	34.6	2.7
山 东	Shandong	35.7	3.2	141306	41.4	5.2
河 南	Henan	34.3	5.4	139088	37.8	5.0
湖 北	Hubei	17.7	2.6	144936	43.9	5.1
湖 南	Hunan	29.4	4.2	133198	60.1	5.9
广 东	Guangdong	29.2	0.9	406835	76.6	9.1
广 西	Guangxi	66.4	5.7	125248	40.5	3.3
海 南	Hainan	1.2	0.1	27846	8.3	0.7
重 庆	Chongqing	11.9	1.2	60336	15.0	1.6
四 川	Sichuan	29.8	2.0	139061	48.6	4.6
贵 州	Guizhou	2.2	0.2	40818	20.3	1.6
云 南	Yunnan	10.7	0.4	42274	17.8	1.5
西 藏	Tibet	0.1		3564	1.3	0.1
陕 西	Shaanxi	14.9	0.3	40549	20.1	2.4
甘 肃	Gansu	5.9	2.1	26930	12.3	1.3
青 海	Qinghai	3.4	0.1	11741	3.8	0.5
宁 夏	Ningxia	10.8	1.3	14406	3.5	0.4
新 疆	Xinjiang	15.3	0.4	43367	11.8	1.8

12-5 工业按行业分废水排放及处理情况（2005年）

Discharge and Treatment of Waste Water by Sector (2005)

行 业	Sector	汇总工业企业数（个）Number of Industrial Enterprises (unit)	工业废水排放总量（万吨）Total Volume of Industrial Waste Water Discharge (10 000 tons)	工业废水排放达标量（万吨）Volume of Industrial Waste Water Meeting Discharge Standards (10 000 tons)	废水治理设施数（套）Number of Facilities for Treatment of Waste Water (set)
行业总计	**Total**	**70514**	**2159779**	**1989533**	**68940**
煤炭开采和洗选业	Mining and Washing of Coal	2968	46650	39309	2517
石油和天然气开采业	Extraction of Petroleum and Natural Gas	211	11252	10545	662
黑色金属矿采选业	Mining and Processing of Ferrous Metal Ores	744	14239	12829	2305
有色金属矿采选业	Mining and Processing of Non-Ferrous Metal Ores	1123	31136	28027	1565
非金属矿采选业	Mining and Processing of Nonmetal Ores	535	12968	11957	681
其他采矿业	Mining of Other Ores	64	496	388	40
农副食品加工业	Processing of Food from Agricultural Products	3594	118964	94645	3447
食品制造业	Manufacture of Foods	2236	42830	38416	1683
饮料制造业	Manufacture of Beverages	1996	43404	37413	1691
烟草制品业	Manufacture of Tobacco	157	2809	2523	126
纺织业	Manufacture of Textile	6001	172232	165960	5267
纺织服装、鞋、帽制造业	Manufacture of Textile Wearing Apparel, Footware, and Caps	599	9185	8954	486
皮革毛皮羽毛(绒)及其制品业	Manufacture of Leather, Fur, Feather and Related Products	837	18338	17205	811
木材加工及木竹藤棕草制品业	Processing of Timber, Manufacture of Wood, Bamboo, Rattan, Palm, and Straw Products	715	6569	5978	419
家具制造业	Manufacture of Furniture	182	797	770	98
造纸及纸制品业	Manufacture of Paper and Paper Products	3911	367422	335581	5154
印刷业和记录媒介的复制	Printing,Reproduction of Recording Media	382	1618	1545	130
文教体育用品制造业	Manufacture of Articles For Culture, Education and Sport Activity	180	862	772	103
石油加工、炼焦及核燃料加工业	Processing of Petroleum, Coking, Processing of Nuclear Fuel	1011	68122	66520	1340
化学原料及化学制品制造业	Manufacture of Raw Chemical Materials and Chemical Products	6791	339052	311922	9142
医药制造业	Manufacture of Medicines	2225	40050	37963	1996
化学纤维制造业	Manufacture of Chemical Fibers	233	48516	45458	304
橡胶制品业	Manufacture of Rubber	542	6118	6031	322
塑料制品业	Manufacture of Plastics	655	2288	2208	276
非金属矿物制品业	Manufacture of Non-metallic Mineral Products	11891	48248	45544	6633
黑色金属冶炼及压延加工业	Smelting and Pressing of Ferrous Metals	2213	169934	163928	3807
有色金属冶炼及压延加工业	Smelting and Pressing of Non-ferrous Metals	1692	33734	29160	1871
金属制品业	Manufacture of Metal Products	3929	21057	20028	4033
通用设备制造业	Manufacture of General Purpose Machinery	2136	15652	15021	1253
专用设备制造业	Manufacture of Special Purpose Machinery	1154	11324	10915	931
交通运输设备制造业	Manufacture of Transport Equipment	1622	24653	23190	2081
电气机械及器材制造业	Manufacture of Electrical Machinery and Equipment	832	8108	7727	709
通信计算机及其他电子设备制造业	Manufacture of Communication Equipment, Computers and Other Electronic Equipment	1035	18745	18164	1195
仪器仪表及文化办公用机械制造业	Manufacture of Measuring Instruments and Machinery for Cultural Activity and Office Work	496	7241	7056	534
工艺品及其他制造业	Manufacture of Artwork and Other Manufacturing	383	2160	2098	451
废弃资源和废旧材料回收加工业	Recycling and Disposal of Waste	90	235	227	80
电力、热力的生产和供应业	Production and Supply of Electric Power and Heat Power	2356	251145	246832	2793
燃气生产和供应业	Production and Supply of Gas	67	4099	3789	70
水的生产和供应业	Production and Supply of Water	175	18819	18419	120
其他行业	Other Sectors	2551	118708	94516	1814

12-6 主要城市工业废水排放及处理情况（2005年）

Discharge and Treatment of Industrial Waste Water in Major Cities (2005)

单位：万吨 (10 000 tons)

城　市	City	工业废水排放量 Total Volume of Waste Water Discharged	工业废水排放达标量 Industrial Waste Water Metting Discharge Standards	工业废水中化学需氧量排放量(吨) COD Discharge from Industrial Waste Water (ton)	工业废水中氨氮排放量（吨） Ammonia Nitrogen Discharge from Industrial Waste Water (ton)	废水治理设施数(套) Number of Facilities for Treatment of Waste Water (set)	本年运行费用(万元) Annual Expenditure for Operation (10 000 yuan)
北　京	Beijing	12813	12740	10979.4	1202.1	553	47316.2
天　津	Tianjin	30081	29962	59090.5	6358.1	904	48748.9
石家庄	Shijiazhuang	24188	23927	92445.4	6051.6	664	19496.9
太　原	Taiyuan	3953	3565	7287.6	517.3	234	25653.6
呼和浩特	Hohhot	2114	1883	9931.7	578.1	75	2684.4
沈　阳	Shenyang	6307	6043	15622.4	229.6	479	7265.0
长　春	Changchun	3906	3660	19064.5	528.5	108	4963.1
哈尔滨	Harbin	4851	4417	10775.9	5416.4	171	8931.5
上　海	Shanghai	51097	49590	36610.3	2481.3	1707	136195.0
南　京	Nanjing	47200	43115	30335.0	1416.4	606	73574.5
杭　州	Hangzhou	85735	83888	113379.0	2883.7	941	47746.8
合　肥	Hefei	6462	6301	8542.6	1503.3	173	5305.5
福　州	Fuzhou	5113	4950	5676.5	376.4	278	10390.0
南　昌	Nanchang	7486	7144	19085.7	2299.9	132	19694.7
济　南	Jinan	5255	5197	8850.1	272.5	254	16234.0
郑　州	Zhengzhou	11640	11354	13958.5	2620.7	465	15469.8
武　汉	Wuhan	26001	24867	27877.5	1484.9	318	19587.4
长　沙	Changsha	4065	3562	4736.9	186.5	301	3934.3
广　州	Guangzhou	20249	18970	14274.2	747.1	716	66726.8
南　宁	Nanning	17155	16089	90796.0	5449.2	408	10538.7
海　口	Haikou	486	469	228.3	3.1	43	718.8
重　庆	Chongqing	84885	79507	118864.6	12184.9	1478	32075.5
成　都	Chengdu	32517	31280	92013.6	10804.5	1234	14691.5
贵　阳	Guiyang	4980	3969	5421.5	628.0	487	5937.4
昆　明	Kunming	4758	4665	3307.2	199.5	472	15521.3
拉　萨	Lhasa						
西　安	Xi'an	16969	16215	43477.2	651.9	506	8125.0
兰　州	Lanzhou	4352	3947	3583.4	267.1	116	13274.0
西　宁	Xining	4343	3104	11027.6	882.8	112	1392.8
银　川	Yinchuan	5317	4553	16779.6	6157.7	126	2263.5
乌鲁木齐	Urumqi	4661	3924	3917.5	1153.0	46	5351.4

12-7 全海域海水水质评价结果（2005年）
Ambient Sea Water Quality (2005)

单位：万平方公里 (10 000 sq.km)

海区	Sea Area	较清洁海域面积 Clean Area	轻度污染海域面积 Lightly Polluted Area	中度污染海域面积 Moderately Polluted Area	严重污染海域面积 Heavily Polluted Area
全国	**National Total**	**5.780**	**3.406**	**1.815**	**2.927**
渤海	Bohai Sea	0.899	0.624	0.291	0.175
黄海	Yellow Sea	2.188	1.387	0.404	0.315
东海	The East China Sea	2.108	1.049	1.073	2.295
南海	South China Sea	0.585	0.346	0.047	0.142

12-8 主要城市空气质量指标（2005年）
Ambient Air Quality in Major Cities (2005)

单位：毫克/立方米 (milligram/cu.m)

城市	City	可吸入颗粒物 (PM_{10}) Paticulate Matters	二氧化硫 (SO_2) Sulphur Dioxide	二氧化氮 (NO_2) Nitrogen Dioxide	空气质量达到及好于二级的天数（天）Days of Air Quality Equal to or Above Grade II (days)
北京	Beijing	0.141	0.050	0.066	234
天津	Tianjin	0.106	0.076	0.047	298
石家庄	Shijiazhuang	0.132	0.054	0.041	283
太原	Taiyuan	0.139	0.077	0.020	245
呼和浩特	Hohhot	0.097	0.050	0.041	312
沈阳	Shenyang	0.118	0.054	0.036	317
长春	Changchun	0.099	0.026	0.035	340
哈尔滨	Harbin	0.104	0.042	0.056	301
上海	Shanghai	0.088	0.061	0.061	322
南京	Nanjing	0.110	0.052	0.054	304
杭州	Hangzhou	0.112	0.060	0.058	301
合肥	Hefei	0.095	0.018	0.025	329
福州	Fuzhou	0.072	0.016	0.042	349
南昌	Nanchang	0.089	0.050	0.031	339
济南	Jinan	0.128	0.060	0.024	262
郑州	Zhengzhou	0.109	0.059	0.039	300
武汉	Wuhan	0.119	0.054	0.050	271
长沙	Changsha	0.122	0.081	0.036	245
广州	Guangzhou	0.088	0.053	0.068	332
南宁	Nanning	0.067	0.058	0.038	354
海口	Haikou	0.040	0.012	0.015	365
重庆	Chongqing	0.120	0.073	0.048	267
成都	Chengdu	0.125	0.077	0.052	293
贵阳	Guiyang	0.076	0.063	0.013	343
昆明	Kunming	0.082	0.055	0.038	363
拉萨	Lhasa	0.070	0.010	0.025	358
西安	Xi'an	0.129	0.044	0.032	291
兰州	Lanzhou	0.158	0.068	0.037	238
西宁	Xining	0.114	0.029	0.026	306
银川	Yinchuan	0.090	0.054	0.025	323
乌鲁木齐	Urumqi	0.114	0.116	0.056	256

12-9 各地区废气排放及处理情况（2005年）

Emission and Treatment of Industrial Waste Gas by Region (2005)

地 区	Region	工业废气排放总量（亿标立方米）Total Volume of Industrial Waste Gas Emission (100 million cu.m)	燃料燃烧过程中废气排放量 Volume of Waste Gas from Process of Fuel Burning	生产工艺过程中废气排放量 Volume of Waste Gas from Process of Production	废气治理设施数(套) Number of Facilities for Treatment of Waste Gas (set)	工业二氧化硫排放量（万吨）Volume of Sulphur Dioxide Emission by Industry (10 000 tons)	生活二氧化硫排放量（万吨）Volume of Sulphur Dioxide Emission by Consumption (10 000 tons)
全 国	**National Total**	**268988**	**155238**	**113749**	**145043**	**2168.4**	**381.0**
北 京	Beijing	3532	2015	1517	2309	10.5	8.5
天 津	Tianjin	4602	3380	1222	2863	24.1	2.4
河 北	Hebei	26518	13142	13377	11746	128.1	21.4
山 西	Shanxi	15142	8565	6576	7335	120.0	31.6
内蒙古	Inner Mongolia	12071	8802	3269	3521	129.6	16.0
辽 宁	Liaoning	20903	10640	10263	7874	96.1	23.6
吉 林	Jilin	4939	3405	1535	3222	30.8	7.5
黑龙江	Heilongjiang	5261	4276	986	3812	43.1	7.7
上 海	Shanghai	8482	3564	4918	3067	37.5	13.8
江 苏	Jiangsu	20197	12748	7449	8488	131.2	6.1
浙 江	Zhejiang	13025	8148	4877	11560	83.1	2.9
安 徽	Anhui	6960	4478	2481	3307	51.5	5.6
福 建	Fujian	6265	3284	2981	5354	43.9	2.2
江 西	Jiangxi	4379	2138	2240	2253	55.5	5.8
山 东	Shandong	24129	14333	9796	10177	171.5	28.7
河 南	Henan	15498	9180	6319	9336	147.1	15.3
湖 北	Hubei	9404	3958	5446	4306	62.6	9.2
湖 南	Hunan	6014	2826	3188	4990	75.5	16.4
广 东	Guangdong	13447	9213	4234	7872	127.4	2.0
广 西	Guangxi	8339	4370	3969	5092	97.5	4.9
海 南	Hainan	910	552	358	372	2.2	
重 庆	Chongqing	3655	2178	1477	2150	68.3	15.4
四 川	Sichuan	8140	4395	3745	6185	114.1	15.9
贵 州	Guizhou	3852	1933	1919	2291	65.9	69.9
云 南	Yunnan	5444	2939	2505	4182	42.9	9.3
西 藏	Tibet	13	13		22	0.1	0.1
陕 西	Shaanxi	4916	3140	1776	3841	80.0	12.2
甘 肃	Gansu	4250	2648	1603	2730	51.7	4.6
青 海	Qinghai	1370	345	1024	592	11.5	0.9
宁 夏	Ningxia	2844	1625	1220	1211	30.2	4.0
新 疆	Xinjiang	4485	3005	1480	2983	34.8	17.1

12-9 续表 continued

地 区	Region	工业二氧化硫去除量（万吨）Volume of Industry Sulphur Dioxide Removed (10 000 tons)	工业烟尘排放量（万吨）Volume of Industrial Soot Emission (10 000 tons)	生活烟尘排放量（万吨）Volume of Consumption Soot Emission (10 000 tons)	工业烟尘去除量（万吨）Volume of Industrial Soot Removed (10 000 tons)	工业粉尘排放量（万吨）Volume of Industrial Dust Emission (10 000 tons)	工业粉尘去除量（万吨）Volume of Industrial Dust Removed (10 000 tons)	建成烟尘控制区数（个）Number of Soot Control Zones Established (unit)	建成烟尘控制区面积（平方公里）Area of Soot Control Zones (sq.km)
全 国	**National Total**	**1090.4**	**948.9**	**233.6**	**20587.1**	**911.2**	**6453.9**	**3452**	**37240.8**
北 京	Beijing	4.7	1.8	4.0	250.1	3.3	128.5	56	832.5
天 津	Tianjin	10.8	7.7	1.4	272.4	1.9	26.1	48	574.6
河 北	Hebei	70.3	56.0	17.3	1960.9	71.3	634.5	108	1604.0
山 西	Shanxi	39.2	91.0	21.2	1232.9	69.5	235.5	184	688.8
内蒙古	Inner Mongolia	20.0	60.4	17.5	1092.7	45.6	123.1	66	619.8
辽 宁	Liaoning	72.4	51.7	22.8	1125.0	45.3	432.9	104	1523.6
吉 林	Jilin	3.3	32.7	8.6	658.7	13.7	187.1	234	951.7
黑龙江	Heilongjiang	7.6	45.4	9.4	650.6	12.4	59.2	295	1149.6
上 海	Shanghai	7.5	5.0	6.6	574.2	1.1	150.5	134	1801.9
江 苏	Jiangsu	73.3	42.6	2.6	1771.5	35.5	388.7	142	3030.7
浙 江	Zhejiang	63.5	19.9	1.3	617.7	23.1	378.8	144	4915.7
安 徽	Anhui	82.4	25.3	4.5	563.4	46.2	200.2	175	850.6
福 建	Fujian	12.4	11.8	1.3	340.5	19.3	195.6	117	1004.2
江 西	Jiangxi	72.5	23.0	1.6	522.4	35.0	270.3	54	803.0
山 东	Shandong	75.5	48.5	13.4	1789.9	37.3	582.1	250	2965.2
河 南	Henan	34.6	85.7	7.1	1848.9	70.4	538.2	256	2343.7
湖 北	Hubei	54.1	26.6	6.4	695.9	33.8	378.1	176	1285.5
湖 南	Hunan	54.6	45.3	8.6	591.8	76.9	277.5	183	1238.6
广 东	Guangdong	25.5	27.1	0.8	727.0	32.1	242.6	161	3429.2
广 西	Guangxi	40.8	53.8	1.2	444.0	55.6	233.2	86	1227.1
海 南	Hainan	1.3	1.0	0.1	51.0	1.1	11.0	9	175.6
重 庆	Chongqing	40.1	13.1	8.5	207.3	21.3	37.6	146	1132.6
四 川	Sichuan	24.9	63.4	15.7	459.3	38.4	182.3	23	567.0
贵 州	Guizhou	17.8	20.5	15.9	491.5	19.1	118.3	57	354.8
云 南	Yunnan	92.7	17.1	5.6	381.1	15.5	163.3	18	317.2
西 藏	Tibet		0.2			0.2		1	65.9
陕 西	Shaanxi	12.0	29.2	10.2	374.1	34.0	84.1	91	657.2
甘 肃	Gansu	67.2	12.4	3.8	359.9	16.6	75.1	46	472.1
青 海	Qinghai		5.7	2.0	71.3	9.3	29.7	12	74.7
宁 夏	Ningxia	4.6	10.2	2.2	312.3	9.0	31.4	16	206.5
新 疆	Xinjiang	4.9	15.0	12.0	148.7	17.3	58.1	60	377.2

12-10 主要城市工业废气排放及处理情况（2005年）

Emission and Treatment of Industrial Waste Gas in Major Cities (2005)

单位：吨 (ton)

城市	City	工业二氧化硫排放量 Volume of Sulphur Dioxide Emission by Industry	工业烟尘排放量 Volume of Industrial Soot Emission	工业粉尘排放量 Volume of Industrial Dust Emission	工业二氧化硫去除量 Volume of Industry Sulphur Dioxide Removed	工业烟尘去除量 Volume of Industrial Soot Removed	工业粉尘去除量 Volume of Industrial Dust Romoved	废气治理设施数(套) Facilities for Treatment of Waste Gas (set)	#脱硫设施 Desulfuri-zation Facilities	本年运行费用(万元) Annual Expenditure for Operation (10 000 yuan)
北　京	Beijing	105473	17688	32511	47003	2500967	1285158	2309	714	56813.4
天　津	Tianjin	241174	76601	19349	107701	2724475	260766	2863	1378	99211.5
石家庄	Shijiazhuang	181460	89624	149802	193427	2917478	829272	1782	569	17604.6
太　原	Taiyuan	150460	56469	37689	74828	2449455	593891	946	454	84371.7
呼和浩特	Hohhot	107676	71590	16571	3136	2178495	72077	286	9	3827.8
沈　阳	Shenyang	46179	51046	9890	11116	1060926	165885	952	369	3906.1
长　春	Dalian	50007	61711	25059	11797	1540351	851222	750	299	11207.8
哈尔滨	Harbin	60319	67959	35947	5375	749043	129864	728	25	4999.4
上　海	Shanghai	375231	49556	10617	74882	5742450	1505314	3067	290	111236.4
南　京	Nanjing	149171	47560	58871	315614	2837822	710469	1043	50	47930.7
杭　州	Hangzhou	125844	35782	60561	40216	987053	434444	1653	194	44399.4
合　肥	Hefei	24264	13338	3602	1381	786955	12624	469	70	3867.8
福　州	Fuzhou	101502	19459	1721	3715	616022	46536	475	15	9213.1
南　昌	Nanchang	27002	24852	7713	14694	546197	226182	182	37	7279.3
济　南	Jinan	79117	24691	29487	61803	1253016	987323	806	178	29071.9
郑　州	Zhengzhou	160953	139179	92731	38366	2517459	885330	2299	56	23790.7
武　汉	Wuhan	133442	46273	14404	45706	2103511	1019451	675	18	32090.5
长　沙	Changsha	58887	43162	100581	14708	29899	118332	471	130	3002.0
广　州	Guangzhou	145009	16106	5112	100132	1234292	668153	1219	135	36349.2
南　宁	Nanning	66509	52457	36679	37209	253123	184590	829	176	6891.6
海　口	Haikou	133	97		22	228		35		179.0
重　庆	Chongqing	683162	131289	212754	400610	2073281	375696	2150	309	72145.6
成　都	Chengdu	122697	156760	32601	23349	791022	169722	1514	248	15256.7
贵　阳	Guiyang	220297	53765	34234	90759	1355104	303707	672	206	10676.9
昆　明	Kunming	102343	12401	8156	425221	864688	782058	1041	83	35720.1
拉　萨	Lhasa									
西　安	Xi'an	94341	39541	25976	9424	566810	58358	950	327	2539.8
兰　州	Lanzhou	60924	18399	16959	838	905194	125746	533	16	10335.9
西　宁	Xining	70185	28491	35357		678806	190888	352		9677.3
银　川	Yinchuan	16727	4244	3223	12084	74498	72144	217	62	3182.1
乌鲁木齐	Urumqi	94482	45444	11105	41738	679721	175736	525	146	9496.5

12-11 工业按行业分废气排放及处理情况（2005年）

行　　业	Sector	废气治理设施数(套) Number of Facilities for Treatment of Waste Gas (set)	工业废气排放总量(亿标立方米) Total Volume of Waste Gas Emission (100 million cu.m)	燃料燃烧过程中废气排放量 Volume of Waste Gas from Fuel Burning
行业总计	**Total**	**144612**	**268052**	**154527**
煤炭开采和洗选业	Mining and Washing of Coal	4427	1935	1468
石油和天然气开采业	Extraction of Petroleum and Natural Gas	437	963	926
黑色金属矿采选业	Mining and Processing of Ferrous Metal Ores	622	944	281
有色金属矿采选业	Mining and Processing of Non-Ferrous Metal Ores	799	598	225
非金属矿采选业	Mining and Processing of Nonmetal Ores	674	1273	1039
其他采矿业	Mining of Other Ores	19	12	7
农副食品加工业	Processing of Food from Agricultural Products	3534	2453	2105
食品制造业	Manufacture of Foods	2269	930	832
饮料制造业	Manufacture of Beverages	2033	836	802
烟草制品业	Manufacture of Tobacco	706	250	145
纺织业	Manufacture of Textile	7817	3020	2956
纺织服装、鞋、帽制造业	Manufacture of Textile Wearing Apparel, Footware, and Caps	508	350	132
皮革毛皮羽毛(绒)及其制品业	Manufacture of Leather, Fur, Feather and Related Products	1211	291	206
木材加工及木竹藤棕草制品业	Processing of Timber, Manufacture of Wood, Bamboo, Rattan, Palm, and Straw Products	2284	901	514
家具制造业	Manufacture of Furniture	834	314	50
造纸及纸制品业	Manufacture of Paper and Paper Products	5055	4515	3974
印刷业和记录媒介的复制	Printing,Reproduction of Recording Media	190	72	28
文教体育用品制造业	Manufacture of Articles For Culture, Education and Sport Activity	144	40	24
石油加工、炼焦及核燃料加工业	Processing of Petroleum, Coking, Processing of Nuclear Fuel	2127	9129	3717
化学原料及化学制品制造业	Manufacture of Raw Chemical Materials and Chemical Products	12421	15887	9419
医药制造业	Manufacture of Medicines	2581	1132	669
化学纤维制造业	Manufacture of Chemical Fibers	627	2886	1176
橡胶制品业	Manufacture of Rubber	1188	563	384
塑料制品业	Manufacture of Plastics	651	577	204
非金属矿物制品业	Manufacture of Non-metallic Mineral Products	45519	49860	12236
黑色金属冶炼及压延加工业	Smelting and Pressing of Ferrous Metals	10249	56190	15221
有色金属冶炼及压延加工业	Smelting and Pressing of Non-ferrous Metals	4794	13183	2882
金属制品业	Manufacture of Metal Products	2418	846	317
通用设备制造业	Manufacture of General Purpose Machinery	3191	1238	434
专用设备制造业	Manufacture of Special Purpose Machinery	1853	736	455
交通运输设备制造业	Manufacture of Transport Equipment	5578	1947	521
电气机械及器材制造业	Manufacture of Electrical Machinery and Equipment	1639	621	268
通信计算机及其他电子设备制造业	Manufacture of Communication Equipment, Computers and Other Electronic Equipment	2272	1543	482
仪器仪表及文化办公用机械制造业	Manufacture of Measuring Instruments and Machinery for Cultural Activity and Office Work	686	525	154
工艺品及其他制造业	Manufacture of Artwork and Other Manufacturing	370	288	45
废弃资源和废旧材料回收加工业	Recycling and Disposal of Waste	42	8	5
电力、热力的生产和供应业	Production and Supply of Electric Power and Heat Power	10009	88347	88175
燃气生产和供应业	Production and Supply of Gas	293	787	158
水的生产和供应业	Production and Supply of Water	117	55	55
其他行业	Other Sectors	2424	2007	1836

Emission and Treatment of Waste Gas by Sector (2005)

生产工艺过程中废气排放量 Volume of Waste Gas from Production Process	工业二氧化硫排放量(万吨) Volume of Sulphur Dioxide Emission (10 000 tons)	工业二氧化硫去除量(万吨) Volume of Sulphur Dioxide Removed (10 000 tons)	工业烟尘排放量(万吨) Volume of Industrial Soot Emission (10 000 tons)	工业烟尘去除量(万吨) Volume of Industrial Soot Removed (10 000 tons)	工业粉尘排放量(万吨) Volume of Industrial Soot Emission (10 000 tons)	工业粉尘去除量(万吨) Volume of Industrial Dust Removed (10 000 tons)
113528	**1980.5**	**1087.8**	**854.9**	**20443.9**	**828.1**	**6439.2**
467	21.0	5.7	10.9	141.8	24.6	9.7
37	3.2	11.6	1.4	9.9	0.1	0.1
663	4.3	1.9	1.7	19.2	3.9	31.7
373	6.7	6.3	2.7	22.4	2.8	31.0
234	5.7	10.9	6.8	30.7	8.8	22.1
5	0.2		0.1	0.1	0.1	0.2
348	15.6	6.4	20.4	97.2	2.1	4.7
97	9.4	3.5	5.1	41.7	0.6	1.2
33	10.7	3.1	9.0	38.1	0.2	0.6
104	1.3	1.2	0.6	6.4	0.2	1.7
64	29.6	8.7	12.8	120.4	0.3	1.0
218	1.5	0.6	0.7	6.3	1.3	5.1
85	2.1	0.6	1.1	7.6		
387	4.8	0.7	5.5	20.7	1.6	10.5
265	0.4	0.5	0.2	6.8	0.2	5.6
541	43.1	16.4	24.1	221.8	1.6	1.0
44	0.2	0.1	0.1	0.7		
16	0.3	0.1	0.2	2.6	0.4	15.1
5412	70.9	89.2	38.2	209.6	18.8	28.8
6469	116.8	111.1	53.6	631.7	17.5	81.6
464	6.4	2.5	4.2	32.5	0.1	0.2
1710	11.5	5.8	4.6	117.8	0.1	1.8
179	4.4	2.3	2.0	24.7		0.3
372	1.3	0.3	0.6	2.4		0.6
37624	178.4	49.7	133.9	508.3	565.7	3971.5
40970	142.2	43.4	69.3	989.8	125.7	1781.2
10301	70.7	434.5	19.2	284.5	18.7	379.3
530	2.6	0.6	1.7	6.3	1.0	3.1
805	5.5	1.4	3.8	33.1	2.3	10.3
281	3.3	2.3	2.1	10.5	1.7	4.7
1426	4.1	1.5	3.0	39.6	3.2	14.1
353	2.7	0.9	1.5	5.0	0.3	0.1
1061	1.7	0.7	0.8	6.1	0.4	5.8
372	1.3	0.2	0.4	1.3		0.4
243	0.5	0.1	0.5	0.9	0.2	0.5
3				0.1		
173	1167.2	260.7	405.2	16704.8	10.8	3.9
629	1.9	0.8	1.4	25.5	0.1	2.2
	0.5	0.2	0.2	1.6		
170	26.4	1.4	5.3	13.8	12.4	7.5

12-12 各地区工业固体废物产生及处理利用情况（2005年）

Production, Treatment and Utilization of Industrial Solid Wastes by Region (2005)

地区	Region	工业固体废物产生量（万吨）Volume of Industrial Solid Wastes Produced (10 000 tons)	#危险废物 Hazardous Wastes	工业固体废物综合利用量（万吨）Volume of Industrial Solid Wastes Utilized (10 000 tons)	工业固体废物贮存量（万吨）Volume of Industrial Solid Wastes in Stocks (10 000 tons)	工业固体废物处置量（万吨）Volume of Industrial Solid Wastes Treated (10 000 tons)	工业固体废物排放量（吨）Volume of Industrial Solid Wastes Discharged (ton)	#危险废物 Hazardous Wastes	"三废"综合利用产品产值（万元）Output Value of Products Made from Utilization of Waste Gas, Water & Solid Wastes (10 000 yuan)
全　国	**National Total**	**134449**	**1161.6**	**76993**	**27876**	**31259**	**16546848**	**5967.0**	**7555064.3**
北　京	Beijing	1238	10.6	969	170	389	91403		94715.0
天　津	Tianjin	1123	15.0	1153		20	44		77228.9
河　北	Hebei	16279	18.5	8374	3072	5051	424149		428703.0
山　西	Shanxi	11183	4.1	5003	785	4900	6046901		249696.5
内蒙古	Inner Mongolia	7363	37.8	3052	3693	661	624958		86505.0
辽　宁	Liaoning	10242	52.6	4268	2429	3551	93938		256174.2
吉　林	Jilin	2457	7.1	1290	1132	33	18642		128649.3
黑龙江	Heilongjiang	3210	19.6	2401	313	530	300		138067.0
上　海	Shanghai	1964	48.8	1892	8	65	1233		91108.9
江　苏	Jiangsu	5757	83.9	5987	197	129	53		931999.9
浙　江	Zhejiang	2514	21.7	2336	25	158	56380		575110.8
安　徽	Anhui	4196	4.5	3357	360	519	450		187615.8
福　建	Fujian	3773	7.4	2650	99	1097	57682		148978.8
江　西	Jiangxi	7007	3.3	1899	573	4591	102819		178811.2
山　东	Shandong	9175	94.3	8683	599	322	1376		935661.8
河　南	Henan	6178	15.1	4244	857	1287	36354		339139.5
湖　北	Hubei	3692	15.8	2748	874	110	167034		462127.9
湖　南	Hunan	3366	34.6	2385	561	415	567050	904.2	263513.6
广　东	Guangdong	2896	129.9	2518	377	387	138538	112.0	365616.3
广　西	Guangxi	3489	64.2	2165	1119	109	1104791	32.0	238923.4
海　南	Hainan	127	1.1	87	39	1	368		14738.3
重　庆	Chongqing	1777	13.1	1329	209	122	1844955	4899.0	81493.7
四　川	Sichuan	6421	21.0	3850	1325	1159	1157015	4.5	505656.7
贵　州	Guizhou	4854	243.3	1658	1424	1937	1312832		121322.2
云　南	Yunnan	4661	30.4	1646	1348	1638	706602	0.3	392999.2
西　藏	Tibet	8			1		73000		
陕　西	Shaanxi	4588	3.9	1103	2189	1286	348679		49489.4
甘　肃	Gansu	2249	28.6	678	1105	481	406347	15.0	91664.6
青　海	Qinghai	649	76.8	142	515	1	27625		5289.7
宁　夏	Ningxia	719		387	90	238	41047		23498.2
新　疆	Xinjiang	1295	54.6	673	458	73	1094286		90565.5

12-13 按行业分工业固体废物产生及处理利用情况（2005年）

Production, Treatment and Utilization of Industrial Solid Wastes by Sector (2005)

行业	Sector	工业固体废物产生量（万吨）Volume of Industrial Solid Wastes Produced (10 000 tons)	#危险废物 Hazardous Wastes	工业固体废物综合利用量（万吨）Volume of Industrial Solid Wastes Utilized (10 000 tons)	工业固体废物贮存量（万吨）Volume of Industrial Wastes in Stocks (10 000 tons)
行业总计	**Total**	**124324**	**1159.89**	**74083**	**24156**
煤炭开采和洗选业	Mining and Washing of Coal	18248	0.08	11379	2342
石油和天然气开采业	Extraction of Petroleum and Natural Gas	149	19.11	87	5
黑色金属矿采选业	Mining and Processing of Ferrous Metal Ores	12728		1915	5165
有色金属矿采选业	Mining and Processing of Non-Ferrous Metal Ores	16313	222.05	4199	5315
非金属矿采选业	Mining and Processing of Nonmetal Ores	1218	76.33	803	265
其他采矿业	Mining of Other Ores	58		24	8
农副食品加工业	Processing of Food from Agricultural Products	1317	0.02	1212	14
食品制造业	Manufacture of Foods	431	0.35	345	68
饮料制造业	Manufacture of Beverages	675	0.01	650	2
烟草制品业	Manufacture of Tobacco	110		47	2
纺织业	Manufacture of Textile	690	15.22	619	2
纺织服装、鞋、帽制造业	Manufacture of Textile Wearing Apparel, Footware, and Caps	30	0.93	28	
皮革毛皮羽毛(绒)及其制品业	Manufacture of Leather, Fur, Feather and Related Products	85	3.29	70	
木材加工及木竹藤棕草制品业	Processing of Timber, Manufacture of Wood, Bamboo, Rattan, Palm, and Straw Products	155	0.14	149	2
家具制造业	Manufacture of Furniture	42	0.28	31	
造纸及纸制品业	Manufacture of Paper and Paper Products	1243	6.29	1112	38
印刷业和记录媒介的复制	Printing,Reproduction of Recording Media	8	0.45	7	
文教体育用品制造业	Manufacture of Articles For Culture, Education and Sport Activity	9	0.27	9	
石油加工、炼焦及核燃料加工业	Processing of Petroleum, Coking, Processing of Nuclear Fuel	1841	74.79	1564	92
化学原料及化学制品制造业	Manufacture of Raw Chemical Materials and Chemical Products	9233	443.50	6448	1467
医药制造业	Manufacture of Medicines	243	20.97	225	5
化学纤维制造业	Manufacture of Chemical Fibers	342	27.73	315	8
橡胶制品业	Manufacture of Rubber	94	0.30	92	
塑料制品业	Manufacture of Plastics	41	0.36	40	
非金属矿物制品业	Manufacture of Non-metallic Mineral Products	3237	2.83	2680	449
黑色金属冶炼及压延加工业	Smelting and Pressing of Ferrous Metals	23506	31.81	17505	2273
有色金属冶炼及压延加工业	Smelting and Pressing of Non-ferrous Metals	4779	70.33	2047	1442
金属制品业	Manufacture of Metal Products	121	9.87	295	3
通用设备制造业	Manufacture of General Purpose Machinery	478	7.78	427	6
专用设备制造业	Manufacture of Special Purpose Machinery	168	2.40	133	3
交通运输设备制造业	Manufacture of Transport Equipment	337	7.75	275	9
电气机械及器材制造业	Manufacture of Electrical Machinery and Equipment	42	3.53	35	2
通信计算机及其他电子设备制造业	Manufacture of Communication Equipment, Computers and Other Electronic Equipment	98	18.07	88	
仪器仪表及文化办公用机械制造业	Manufacture of Measuring Instruments and Machinery for Cultural Activity and Office Work	56	4.03	47	
工艺品及其他制造业	Manufacture of Artwork and Other Manufacturing	9	0.34	9	
废弃资源和废旧材料回收加工业	Recycling and Disposal of Waste	10	0.09	9	
电力、热力的生产和供应业	Production and Supply of Electric Power and Heat Power	25638	67.62	18721	5136
燃气生产和供应业	Production and Supply of Gas	119	0.15	86	24
水的生产和供应业	Production and Supply of Water	22	0.13	13	
其他行业	Other Sectors	401	20.69	343	9

12-13 续表 continued

行业	Sector	工业固体废物处置量（万吨）Volume of Industrial Solid Wastes Treated (10 000 tons)	工业固体废物排放量（万吨）Volume of Industrial Solid Wastes Discharged (10 000 tons)	#危险废物 Hazardous Wastes	“三废”综合利用产品产值（万元）Output Value of Products Made from Utilization of Waste Gas, Waste Water & Solid Wastes (10 000 yuan)
行业总计	**Total**	**27820**	**1493**	**0.59**	**7538685**
煤炭开采和洗选业	Mining and Washing of Coal	5016	444		157507
石油和天然气开采业	Extraction of Petroleum and Natural Gas	56	1		113897
黑色金属矿采选业	Mining and Processing of Ferrous Metal Ores	5516	227		39980
有色金属矿采选业	Mining and Processing of Non-Ferrous Metal Ores	6677	140		26349
非金属矿采选业	Mining and Processing of Nonmetal Ores	148	22		20804
其他采矿业	Mining of Other Ores	26			680
农副食品加工业	Processing of Food from Agricultural Products	50	45		251195
食品制造业	Manufacture of Foods	14	3		110228
饮料制造业	Manufacture of Beverages	17	6		124604
烟草制品业	Manufacture of Tobacco	50	11		3892
纺织业	Manufacture of Textile	52	17		53767
纺织服装、鞋、帽制造业	Manufacture of Textile Wearing Apparel, Footware, and Caps	2	1		3099
皮革毛皮羽毛(绒)及其制品业	Manufacture of Leather, Fur, Feather and Related Products	14			208655
木材加工及木竹藤棕草制品业	Processing of Timber, Manufacture of Wood, Bamboo, Rattan, Palm, and Straw Products	4	1		61683
家具制造业	Manufacture of Furniture	11			5102
造纸及纸制品业	Manufacture of Paper and Paper Products	115	8		293140
印刷业和记录媒介的复制	Printing,Reproduction of Recording Media	1			2487
文教体育用品制造业	Manufacture of Articles For Culture, Education and Sport Activity				424
石油加工、炼焦及核燃料加工业	Processing of Petroleum, Coking, Processing of Nuclear Fuel	132	53		421674
化学原料及化学制品制造业	Manufacture of Raw Chemical Materials and Chemical Products	1513	70	0.03	834714
医药制造业	Manufacture of Medicines	11	3		40121
化学纤维制造业	Manufacture of Chemical Fibers	24	1		73636
橡胶制品业	Manufacture of Rubber	2			27769
塑料制品业	Manufacture of Plastics	2			32410
非金属矿物制品业	Manufacture of Non-metallic Mineral Products	72	169		1921449
黑色金属冶炼及压延加工业	Smelting and Pressing of Ferrous Metals	3692	149		1333548
有色金属冶炼及压延加工业	Smelting and Pressing of Non-ferrous Metals	1295	40		580200
金属制品业	Manufacture of Metal Products	11	2	0.01	112614
通用设备制造业	Manufacture of General Purpose Machinery	32	12	0.49	45829
专用设备制造业	Manufacture of Special Purpose Machinery	21	11	0.06	29182
交通运输设备制造业	Manufacture of Transport Equipment	116	4		78952
电气机械及器材制造业	Manufacture of Electrical Machinery and Equipment	4	1		18462
通信计算机及其他电子设备制造业	Manufacture of Communication Equipment, Computers and Other Electronic Equipment	10			53517
仪器仪表及文化办公用机械制造业	Manufacture of Measuring Instruments and Machinery for Cultural Activity and Office Work	8			17031
工艺品及其他制造业	Manufacture of Artwork and Other Manufacturing				11477
废弃资源和废旧材料回收加工业	Recycling and Disposal of Waste				65251
电力、热力的生产和供应业	Production and Supply of Electric Power and Heat Power	3041	49		324616
燃气生产和供应业	Production and Supply of Gas	9			7814
水的生产和供应业	Production and Supply of Water	10			814
其他行业	Other Sectors	46	3		30113

12-14 主要城市工业固体废物产生及处理利用情况（2005年）

Emission and Treatment of Industrial Sold Waste in Major Cities (2005)

单位：万吨 (10 000 tons)

城市	City	工业固体废物产生量 Industrial Solid Wastes Generated	#危险废物(吨) Hazardous Wastes (ton)	工业固体废物综合利用量 Industrial Solid Wastes Utilized	工业固体废物排放量(吨) Industrial Solid Wastes Discharged (ton)	工业固体废物综合利用率(%) Ratio of Industrial Solid Wastes Utilized (%)
北京	Beijing	1238	10.58	969	91403	67.9
天津	Tianjin	1123	14.96	1153	44	98.3
石家庄	Shijiazhuang	852	14.45	782	1590	91.8
太原	Taiyuan	2084	2.75	936	509519	44.6
呼和浩特	Hohhot	257	2.94	122	465	36.1
沈阳	Shenyang	475	2.33	330	11136	69.3
长春	Changchun	303	1.88	300		98.9
哈尔滨	Harbin	946	1.22	705		74.5
上海	Shanghai	1964	48.77	1892	1233	96.3
南京	Nanjing	1159	21.33	1052		87.9
杭州	Hangzhou	461	3.53	436	3994	93.9
合肥	Hefei	188	1.55	186	22	98.8
福州	Fuzhou	136	0.93	126	112	92.6
南昌	Nanchang	154	0.37	135	2343	88.1
济南	Jinan	874	9.19	846	240	94.7
郑州	Zhengzhou	691	0.23	467		67.6
武汉	Wuhan	847	0.73	770	8160	85.4
长沙	Changsha	110		98	56726	88.1
广州	Guangzhou	540	22.49	520	2485	91.2
南宁	Nanning	304	25.26	245	52109	80.5
海口	Haikou	4	0.09	3	268	94.5
重庆	Chongqing	1777	13.08	1329	1844955	72.1
成都	Chengdu	424	0.22	401	124830	94.5
贵阳	Guiyang	657	155.71	290	69613	43.7
昆明	Kunming	1132	0.41	451	316990	39.4
拉萨	Lhasa					
西安	Xi'an	125	0.17	117	3407	88.1
兰州	Lanzhou	161	11.10	193	2929	96.9
西宁	Xining	184	0.45	95	900	48.7
银川	Yinchuan	67		63	7087	94.8
乌鲁木齐	Urumqi	343	3.68	247	3286	68.5

12-15 各地区城市生活垃圾清运和处理情况（2005年）
Collection, Transport and Disposal of Consumption Wastes in Cities by Region (2005)

地 区	Region	生活垃圾清运量(万吨) Consumption Wastes Collected and Transported (10 000 tons)	无害化处理厂数(座) Number of Factories for Wastes Treatment (unit)	#卫生填埋 Landfill	#堆 肥 Piling	#焚 烧 Burning	无害化处理能力(吨/日) Treatment Capacity (ton/day)	#卫生填埋 Landfill	#堆 肥 Piling	#焚 烧 Burning
全 国	**National Total**	**15576.8**	**471**	**356**	**46**	**67**	**256312**	**211085**	**11767**	**33010**
北 京	Beijing	454.6	17	13	2	2	10350	9330	600	420
天 津	Tianjin	144.8	5	4		1	6800	5600		1200
河 北	Hebei	680.1	17	9	6	2	9648	6348	2050	1250
山 西	Shanxi	619.7	4	3		1	2300	2300		
内蒙古	Inner Mongolia	329.0	11	10	1		4617	4549	50	18
辽 宁	Liaoning	768.0	10	6	3	1	11661	9561	1700	400
吉 林	Jilin	580.4	13	11		2	6900	6375		525
黑龙江	Heilongjiang	1125.8	24	19	1	4	10047	9522	15	510
上 海	Shanghai	622.3	5	2	1	2	8800	5300	1000	2500
江 苏	Jiangsu	834.8	35	30		5	24000	22120		1880
浙 江	Zhejiang	762.5	42	28		14	21528	13768		7760
安 徽	Anhui	476.6	5	4		1	3071	2471		600
福 建	Fujian	303.0	17	12	3	2	7831	5845	546	1020
江 西	Jiangxi	264.4	8	8			3313	3313		
山 东	Shandong	1046.5	44	35	7	1	17513	16003	980	530
河 南	Henan	756.7	28	19	6	2	12573	9506	1645	1422
湖 北	Hubei	885.2	44	42	2		14721	14151	570	
湖 南	Hunan	486.0	7	7			6122	6122		
广 东	Guangdong	1722.6	28	14		14	27715	17415		10300
广 西	Guangxi	204.7	12	7	3	2	4170	3040	670	430
海 南	Hainan	81.2	7	4	2	1	1625	1439	133	53
重 庆	Chongqing	237.6	9	8		1	5210	4210		1000
四 川	Sichuan	600.7	25	14	5	6	9970	7580	1340	1050
贵 州	Guizhou	176.5	8	6	1	1	4112	3846	250	16
云 南	Yunnan	205.7	18	14	3	1	7859	7570	218	71
西 藏	Tibet	44.5	1	1			400	400		
陕 西	Shaanxi	370.7	4	3		1	4204	4154		50
甘 肃	Gansu	297.8	7	7			1510	1510		
青 海	Qinghai	54.4	4	4			1887	1887		
宁 夏	Ningxia	96.4	5	5			2040	2040		
新 疆	Xinjiang	343.6	7	7			3815	3810		5

12-15 续表 continued

地 区	Region	无害化处理量(万吨) Volume of Wastes Disposed (10 000 tons)	#卫生填埋 Landfill	#堆 肥 Piling	#焚 烧 Burning	简 易处理量(万吨) Volume of Wastes Disposed in a Simple Way (10 000 tons)	粪 便清运量(万吨) Collection and Transport of Excrement and Urine (10 000 tons)	粪 便处理量(万吨) Disposal of Excrement and Urine (10 000 tons)	生活垃圾无害化处理率(%) Treatment Rate of Consumption Wastes (%)
全 国	**National Total**	**8051.1**	**6857.1**	**345.4**	**791.0**	**4444.3**	**3804.6**	**2713.8**	**51.7**
北 京	Beijing	436.2	407.1	21.7	7.4		171.7	127.9	96.0
天 津	Tianjin	116.6	87.3		29.3	28.4	25.7	25.7	80.5
河 北	Hebei	311.3	233.1	49.5	28.8	219.4	202.6	196.6	45.8
山 西	Shanxi	81.3	81.3			213.2	571.1	409.8	13.1
内蒙古	Inner Mongolia	140.4	122.6	17.7	0.1	79.0	108.5	23.9	42.7
辽 宁	Liaoning	384.3	326.9	42.8	14.6	279.7	148.4	34.5	50.0
吉 林	Jilin	233.2	216.9		16.3	160.0	120.3	67.3	40.2
黑龙江	Heilongjiang	363.3	339.9	1.0	4.0	400.9	272.1	123.8	32.3
上 海	Shanghai	222.4	69.7	50.2	102.4	399.8	253.9	253.9	35.7
江 苏	Jiangsu	692.1	649.4		42.7	116.7	388.4	338.4	82.9
浙 江	Zhejiang	628.3	431.7		197.6	88.3	205.4	197.3	82.4
安 徽	Anhui	83.9	73.7		10.2	313.2	41.5	9.7	17.6
福 建	Fujian	260.4	215.0	15.1	28.9	37.0	43.8	39.4	85.9
江 西	Jiangxi	129.2	129.2			123.7	21.4	17.7	48.9
山 东	Shandong	609.6	572.0	20.7	12.8	379.4	325.7	322.2	58.2
河 南	Henan	438.0	344.1	44.9	49.0	231.1	81.2	23.4	57.9
湖 北	Hubei	540.4	520.0	20.4		193.5	92.0	58.5	61.0
湖 南	Hunan	192.9	192.9			269.0	41.4	40.2	39.7
广 东	Guangdong	871.6	662.4		174.9		459.1	360.4	50.6
广 西	Guangxi	125.6	104.0	10.1	11.3	59.4	22.3	14.4	61.4
海 南	Hainan	56.1	51.7	3.7	0.7	25.0	6.3	5.6	69.0
重 庆	Chongqing	130.2	103.9		26.2	106.9	67.5	53.9	54.8
四 川	Sichuan	307.8	245.6	31.7	30.4	98.3	51.5	2.6	51.2
贵 州	Guizhou	102.1	92.5	9.1	0.5	61.2	6.1	3.3	57.8
云 南	Yunnan	169.2	159.4	6.9	2.9	26.6	101.7	87.3	82.2
西 藏	Tibet						2.5		
陕 西	Shaanxi	147.5	147.5			159.6	14.0		39.8
甘 肃	Gansu	51.3	51.3			217.1	52.8	0.2	17.2
青 海	Qinghai	54.4	54.4				28.0		100.0
宁 夏	Ningxia	48.5	48.5			4.5	5.0	1.1	50.4
新 疆	Xinjiang	123.4	123.4			153.4	3.9	3.0	35.9

12-16 主要城市道路交通噪声监测情况（2005年）

Monitoring of Urban Road Traffic Noise in Major Cities (2005)

城　市	City	路段总长度（米） Total Length of Roads (m)	超标路段（米） Roads with Excess Noise (m)	路段超标率（%） Percentage of Roads with Excess Noise (%)	路段平均宽度（米） Average Width of Roads (m)	平均车流量（辆/小时） Average Traffic Volume (car/hour)	等效声级 dB(A) Average Noise Value dB(A)
北　京	Beijing	596092	253339	42.5	36.0	5422	69.5
天　津	Tianjin	276491	30138	10.9	28.8	2221	68.0
石家庄	Shijiazhuang	179402	29780	16.6	29.5	1885	67.2
太　原	Taiyuan	137561	28889	21.0	23.0	2125	67.9
呼和浩特	Hohhot	82649	34547	41.8	30.2	2009	69.7
沈　阳	Shenyang	144000	18144	12.6	33.7	2266	68.4
长　春	Changchun	123604	16563	13.4	30.8	2812	68.0
哈尔滨	Harbin	120200	19352	16.1	16.8	2410	68.2
上　海	Shanghai	215600	162778	75.5	19.9	2164	72.0
南　京	Nanjing	165072	54969	33.3	31.0	2021	69.4
杭　州	Hangzhou	189355	41847	22.1	16.3	1833	67.9
合　肥	Hefei	90571			38.6	2487	68.0
福　州	Fuzhou	111230	14126	12.7	22.9	2614	68.3
南　昌	Nanchang	67500	24907	36.9	31.2	3250	69.9
济　南	Jinan	161424	59565	36.9	52.6	2466	69.4
郑　州	Zhengzhou	84115	11776	14.0	43.5	2934	67.6
武　汉	Wuhan	263325	121129	46.0	21.6	2155	69.8
长　沙	Changsha	95800	46463	48.5	32.5	2716	70.0
广　州	Guangzhou	247364	85093	34.4	24.0	3489	69.3
南　宁	Nanning	102000	39780	39.0	19.8	3310	69.7
海　口	Haikou	107280	18774	17.5	34.2	2443	67.7
重　庆	Chongqing	337005	74141	22.0	16.2	1698	67.9
成　都	Chengdu	322912	94613	29.3	44.3	3185	68.7
贵　阳	Guiyang	56780	26743	47.1	36.0	2722	69.6
昆　明	Kunming	91494	30376	33.2	30.2	2272	69.7
拉　萨	Lhasa	52950	13078	24.7	20.1	815	67.8
西　安	Xi'an	204017	29378	14.4	24.3	2910	68.0
兰　州	Lanzhou	125396	23825	19.0	19.7	1479	68.5
西　宁	Xining	85680	32130	37.5	17.1	2074	69.8
银　川	Yinchuan	94280	33563	35.6	32.2	1699	68.0
乌鲁木齐	Urumqi	212920	107098	50.3	42.9	1991	70.0

12-17 国控主要城市区域环境噪声监测情况（2005年）

Monitoring of Urban Environment Noise in Major Cities under National Control Programme (2005)

城 市	City	网格长度（米）Grid Length (m)	网格宽度（米）Grid Width (m)	网格总数（个）Total Number of Grids (unit)	等效声级dB(A) Sound Level dB(A)
北 京	Beijing	1000	1000	448	53.2
天 津	Tianjin	1000	1000	205	54.9
石家庄	Shijiazhuang	500	500	240	54.0
太 原	Taiyuan	750	750	232	53.8
呼和浩特	Hohhot	400	400	204	54.3
沈 阳	Shenyang	750	750	240	54.1
长 春	Changchun	500	500	204	56.4
哈尔滨	Harbin	700	700	216	56.0
上 海	Shanghai	1414	1414	206	57.3
南 京	Nanjing	1000	1000	210	54.0
杭 州	Hangzhou	500	500	235	55.7
合 肥	Hefei	500	500	250	53.7
福 州	Fuzhou	500	500	220	56.2
南 昌	Nanchang	500	500	201	55.9
济 南	Jinan	1000	1000	352	53.5
郑 州	Zhengzhou	500	500	235	55.7
武 汉	Wuhan	1000	1000	210	55.0
长 沙	Changsha	500	500	288	54.0
广 州	Guangzhou	1000	1000	202	55.1
南 宁	Nanning	550	550	200	56.0
海 口	Haikou	400	400	203	55.7
重 庆	Chongqing	500	500	661	54.7
成 都	Chengdu	900	900	215	54.6
贵 阳	Guiyang	500	500	220	55.6
昆 明	Kunming	800	800	223	53.8
拉 萨	Lhasa				
西 安	Xi'an			200	55.4
兰 州	Lanzhou	500	500	211	57.9
西 宁	Xining	375	375	224	52.1
银 川	Yinchuan	500	500	200	53.3
乌鲁木齐	Urumqi	750	750	209	54.9

12-18 各地区土地利用情况（2005年）
Land Use by Region (2005)

单位：万公顷 (10 000 hectares)

地 区	Region	土地调查面积 Area under Land Survey	农用地 Land for Agriculture Use	#园地 Garden Land	#牧草地 Grazing and Pasture Land	建设用地 Land for Construction	居民点及工矿用地 Land for Living Quarters, Mining and Manufacturing Sites	交通用地 Land for Transport Facilities	水利设施用地 Land for Water Conservancy Facilities
全 国	**National Total**	**95068.8**	**65704.7**	**1154.9**	**26214.4**	**3192.2**	**2601.5**	**230.9**	**359.9**
北 京	Beijing	164.1	110.6	12.4	0.2	32.3	26.8	2.9	2.6
天 津	Tianjin	119.2	70.7	3.7	0.1	34.6	26.3	1.8	6.5
河 北	Hebei	1884.3	1306.6	60.9	81.0	173.3	149.9	10.9	12.5
山 西	Shanxi	1567.1	1014.6	29.5	65.8	84.1	75.0	5.8	3.3
内蒙古	Inner Mongolia	11451.2	9513.6	7.3	6572.0	143.9	120.1	14.8	9.0
辽 宁	Liaoning	1480.6	1122.8	59.8	35.0	137.0	113.4	8.8	14.8
吉 林	Jilin	1911.2	1639.7	11.6	104.6	105.0	83.0	6.4	15.6
黑龙江	Heilongjiang	4526.5	3778.5	6.0	222.6	147.4	115.0	11.6	20.8
上 海	Shanghai	82.4	38.0	1.1		24.0	21.9	1.9	0.2
江 苏	Jiangsu	1067.4	677.5	31.8	0.3	183.2	152.3	11.3	19.5
浙 江	Zhejiang	1054.0	871.2	65.5	0.1	94.1	72.6	8.0	13.5
安 徽	Anhui	1401.3	1121.2	34.2	2.9	162.2	130.2	9.2	22.7
福 建	Fujian	1240.2	1076.5	61.9	0.3	58.9	46.1	6.7	6.0
江 西	Jiangxi	1668.9	1419.0	27.3	0.4	90.6	63.8	6.5	20.4
山 东	Shandong	1571.3	1157.2	102.1	3.4	242.2	201.1	16.1	25.0
河 南	Henan	1655.4	1229.0	31.8	1.4	215.2	185.4	11.7	18.2
湖 北	Hubei	1858.9	1466.4	42.7	4.5	136.8	98.5	8.4	29.9
湖 南	Hunan	2118.6	1793.2	49.8	10.5	133.9	105.4	9.2	19.3
广 东	Guangdong	1797.6	1494.1	92.5	2.8	171.5	139.0	11.3	21.2
广 西	Guangxi	2375.6	1789.1	50.9	72.8	91.0	67.9	8.2	14.9
海 南	Hainan	353.5	282.6	53.3	1.9	29.3	21.9	1.4	6.0
重 庆	Chongqing	822.7	694.5	23.5	23.8	56.9	47.2	4.4	5.4
四 川	Sichuan	4840.6	4242.6	72.1	1371.6	156.2	133.4	12.9	9.9
贵 州	Guizhou	1761.5	1528.8	12.0	160.6	54.1	44.6	5.6	3.9
云 南	Yunnan	3831.9	3176.1	82.8	78.3	77.5	60.2	9.5	7.9
西 藏	Tibet	12020.7	7760.3	0.2	6444.4	6.3	4.0	2.3	0.1
陕 西	Shaanxi	2058.0	1848.2	68.7	311.7	79.9	69.7	6.2	4.0
甘 肃	Gansu	4040.9	2387.7	19.8	1261.9	96.7	87.4	6.4	2.9
青 海	Qinghai	7174.8	4370.6	0.7	4036.0	32.0	24.3	2.9	4.7
宁 夏	Ningxia	519.5	417.8	3.4	227.9	20.3	17.9	1.8	0.7
新 疆	Xinjiang	16649.0	6306.1	35.4	5116.1	122.1	97.6	6.1	18.3

12-19 各地区森林资源情况

Forest Resources by Region

地 区	Region	林业用地面积（万公顷）Area of Afforested Land (10 000 hectares)	森林面积（万公顷）Forest Area (10 000 hectares)	#人工林 Man-made Forest	森林覆盖率（%）Forest Coverage Rate (%)	活立木总蓄积量（万立方米）Total Standing Forest Stock (10 000 cu.m)	森林蓄积量（万立方米）Stock Volume of Forest (10 000 cu.m)
全 国	**National Total**	**28492.56**	**17490.92**	**5364.99**	**18.21**	**1361810.00**	**1245584.58**
北 京	Beijing	97.29	37.88	27.08	21.26	1176.36	840.70
天 津	Tianjin	13.44	9.35	8.99	8.14	234.18	140.35
河 北	Hebei	624.55	328.83	179.48	17.69	8657.98	6509.92
山 西	Shanxi	690.94	208.19	99.19	13.29	7309.34	6199.93
内蒙古	Inner Mongolia	4403.61	2050.67	241.29	17.70	128806.70	110153.15
辽 宁	Liaoning	634.39	480.53	267.60	32.97	18546.33	17476.57
吉 林	Jilin	805.57	720.12	148.22	38.13	85359.17	81645.51
黑龙江	Heilongjiang	2026.50	1797.50	172.63	39.54	150153.09	137502.31
上 海	Shanghai	2.25	1.89	1.89	3.17	233.63	33.24
江 苏	Jiangsu	99.88	77.41	74.17	7.54	4073.18	2285.27
浙 江	Zhejiang	654.79	553.92	255.63	54.41	13846.75	11535.85
安 徽	Anhui	412.32	331.99	185.51	24.03	12667.41	10371.90
福 建	Fujian	908.07	764.94	356.98	62.96	49671.38	44357.36
江 西	Jiangxi	1044.69	931.39	275.25	55.86	37435.19	32505.20
山 东	Shandong	284.64	204.64	194.40	13.44	5819.42	3201.65
河 南	Henan	456.41	270.30	161.11	16.19	13370.51	8404.64
湖 北	Hubei	766.00	497.55	145.90	26.77	17518.13	15406.64
湖 南	Hunan	1171.42	860.79	390.39	40.63	30211.67	26534.46
广 东	Guangdong	1048.14	827.00	440.83	46.49	29703.35	28365.63
广 西	Guangxi	1366.22	983.83	449.62	41.41	40287.06	36477.26
海 南	Hainan	194.47	166.66	109.10	48.87	7863.61	7195.16
重 庆	Chongqing	366.84	183.18	62.87	22.25	10580.49	8441.08
四 川	Sichuan	2266.02	1464.34	343.29	30.27	158216.65	149543.36
贵 州	Guizhou	761.83	420.47	183.50	23.83	21022.16	17795.72
云 南	Yunnan	2424.76	1560.03	251.45	40.77	154759.40	139929.16
西 藏	Tibet	1657.89	1389.61	2.76	11.31	229448.04	226606.41
陕 西	Shaanxi	1071.78	670.39	169.21	32.55	33422.35	30775.77
甘 肃	Gansu	745.55	299.63	67.32	6.66	19542.61	17504.33
青 海	Qinghai	556.28	317.20	4.36	4.40	4101.39	3592.62
宁 夏	Ningxia	115.34	40.36	9.81	6.08	478.39	392.85
新 疆	Xinjiang	608.46	484.07	45.90	2.94	31419.68	28039.68

注：1.本表为第六次全国森林资源清查（1999-2003）资料。

2.全国总计数包括台湾省和香港、澳门特别行政区数据。

a) Data in the table are the figures of the Sixth National Forestry Survey (1999-2003).

b) Data of national total include forest resources in Taiwan province and Hong Kong SAR and Macao SAR.

12-20 造 林 面 积

Area of Afforestation

单位：公顷 (hectare)

年份 Year 地区 Region	造林总面积 Total Area of Afforestation	按造林方式分 By Approach 人工造林 Manual Planting	飞机播种 Airplane Planting	按林种用途分 By Function of Forest 用材林 Timber Forests	经济林 By-product Forests	防护林 Protection Forests	薪炭林 Fuel Forests	特种用途林 Forests for Special Purpose
2000	5105138	4345008	760130	1218461	1350277	2430834	82338	23228
2001	4953038	3977324	975714	905518	1068540	2913538	45611	19831
2002	7770971	6896041	874930	898736	964211	5828810	59144	20070
2003	9118894	8432486	686408	1175812	797318	7087319	37070	21374
2004	5598079	5018885	579194	871132	456691	4210768	49966	9522
2005	3647942	3231556	416386	607547	337816	2678214	16074	8291
北京 Beijing	12186	10186	2000	230	875	9262		1819
天津 Tianjin	3591	3591		650	316	2625		
河北 Hebei	304766	276098	28668	51158	19896	232274	1238	200
山西 Shanxi	140260	112728	27532	672	4045	135410	133	
内蒙古 Inner Mongolia	383833	283219	100614	8914	1716	373203		
辽宁 Liaoning	126489	126489		20711	5252	99644	882	
吉林 Jilin	31049	31049		1309	398	28540	536	266
黑龙江 Heilongjiang	84661	84661		11840	458	71700	12	651
上海 Shanghai	3827	3827			147	3393		287
江苏 Jiangsu	54687	54687		9679	8692	36305		11
浙江 Zhejiang	20341	20341		3635	4300	12231	89	86
安徽 Anhui	36095	36095		15027	4488	15727	739	114
福建 Fujian	24218	24218		15364	3212	5386	189	67
江西 Jiangxi	47589	47589		20736	3911	22142	333	467
山东 Shandong	141141	141141		47470	42674	49559	633	805
河南 Henan	186715	173381	13334	77295	39000	69530	737	153
湖北 Hubei	177946	177946		56848	31712	86839	1873	674
湖南 Hunan	136479	136479		30208	10175	95116	11	969
广东 Guangdong	18337	18337		13084	754	3885	608	6
广西 Guangxi	123970	123970		89405	8247	26308	2	8
海南 Hainan	32380	32380		23119	3243	5755	218	45
重庆 Chongqing	109272	109272		21524	11946	74735	1067	
四川 Sichuan	241883	179142	62741	31936	18788	188814	767	1578
贵州 Guizhou	135597	132183	3414	7976	4177	123413		31
云南 Yunnan	207923	163598	44325	34847	39270	132475	1331	
西藏 Tibet	13488	13488		320	1681	10357	1130	
陕西 Shaanxi	198853	89372	109481	8923	1840	187034	1056	
甘肃 Gansu	247601	234335	13266	1400	6585	239616		
青海 Qinghai	46748	46748				46415	333	
宁夏 Ningxia	112924	108580	4344		8356	103149	1419	
新疆 Xinjiang	163053	156386	6667	3227	51662	107372	738	54
大兴安岭 Daxinganling	40	40		40				

注：2005年全国合计造林面积中包括军事管理区80000公顷人工营造的防护林。

a) The areas of afforestation in 2005 include 80,000 hectares afforested in the military precinct by manual planting.

12-21 林业重点工程造林面积

Area of Key Afforestation Projects

单位：万公顷 (10 000 hectares)

年份 Year 地区 Region		造林总面积 Total Area of Afforestation	天然林保护工程 Project on Preservation of Natural Forests	退耕还林工程 Grain for Green Projects	三北及长江流域等防护林建设工程 Projects on Protection Forests in North China and Yangtze River Basin	京津风沙源治理工程 Projects on Harnessing Source of Sand and Dust in Beijing and Tianjin	速生丰产用材林基地建设工程 Projects on Fast-growing Timber Forest Bases
	2000	334.59	42.64	68.36	28.03	170.88	24.69
	2001	317.33	94.81	89.03	21.73	102.87	8.89
	2002	677.74	85.61	442.36	67.64	77.56	4.57
	2003	826.28	68.83	619.61	82.44	53.35	2.04
	2004	518.81	64.14	356.82	44.83	47.33	5.68
	2005	343.14	42.48	220.32	36.82	41.85	1.67
北京	Beijing	0.76		0.08	0.18	0.49	
天津	Tianjin	0.36			0.35	0.01	
河北	Hebei	38.05		20.74	3.02	13.94	0.35
山西	Shanxi	17.62	0.13	8.67	1.93	6.89	
内蒙古	Inner Mongolia	53.83	6.76	26.56		20.51	
辽宁	Liaoning	12.65		10.05	2.60		
吉林	Jilin	2.79		1.76	1.03		
黑龙江	Heilongjiang	8.46		6.57	1.73		0.16
上海	Shanghai						
江苏	Jiangsu	1.63			1.63		
浙江	Zhejiang	0.57			0.57		
安徽	Anhui	2.58		1.70	0.88		
福建	Fujian	0.34			0.34		
江西	Jiangxi	3.91		3.33	0.58		
山东	Shandong	1.36			0.89		0.47
河南	Henan	12.31		10.02	2.29		
湖北	Hubei	13.92	0.45	12.30	1.17		
湖南	Hunan	13.50		12.52	0.40		0.58
广东	Guangdong	0.32			0.32		
广西	Guangxi	9.16		8.23	0.83		0.10
海南	Hainan	1.82		1.67	0.16		
重庆	Chongqing	10.47	0.40	10.07			
四川	Sichuan	22.75	11.39	11.36			
贵州	Guizhou	13.09	0.34	11.33	1.42		
云南	Yunnan	16.40	7.05	8.54	0.81		
西藏	Tibet	0.69	0.20	0.45	0.04		
陕西	Shaanxi	19.46	12.54	6.25	0.68		
甘肃	Gansu	24.76	2.66	20.76	1.34		
青海	Qinghai	4.64	0.13	3.82	0.70		
宁夏	Ningxia	11.29	0.43	8.24	2.62		
新疆	Xinjiang	15.64		7.31	8.33		

注：2005年退耕还林工程中包括军事管理区80000公顷人工营造的防护林。

a) In the Grain for Green Projects, 80,000 hectares of protection forests in the military precinct by manual planting are inclueded.

12-22 各地区湿地面积

Area of Wetlands by Region

地区	Region	湿地面积（千公顷）Area of Wetlands (1 000 hectares)	天然湿地 Natural Wetlands	近岸及海岸 Coasts and Seashores	河流 Rivers	湖泊 Lakes	沼泽 Marshland	人工湿地 Man-made Wetlands	湿地面积占国土面积比重（%）Proportion of Wetlands in Total Area of Territory (%)
全国	**National Total**	**38485.5**	**36200.6**	**5941.7**	**8207.0**	**8351.6**	**13700.3**	**2285.0**	**4.01**
北京	Beijing	34.4	5.0		5.0			29.4	1.93
天津	Tianjin	171.8	133.7	58.1	55.1	12.3	8.2	38.1	14.95
河北	Hebei	1081.9	1042.3	278.8	319.3	307.2	136.9	39.6	5.82
山西	Shanxi	499.9	462.2		454.1	8.1		37.7	3.19
内蒙古	Inner Mongolia	4245.0	4200.8		607.5	495.2	3098.1	44.3	3.66
辽宁	Liaoning	1219.6	1106.8	738.1	252.2	6.3	110.2	112.9	8.37
吉林	Jilin	1203.4	1016.4	5.8	581.4	74.5	354.7	187.0	6.37
黑龙江	Heilongjiang	4314.8	4182.8		460.7	401.9	3320.3	132.0	9.49
上海	Shanghai	319.7	319.4	305.4	7.2	6.8		0.3	53.68
江苏	Jiangsu	1674.7	1651.1	843.5	203.3	604.2		23.6	16.32
浙江	Zhejiang	802.2	695.9	574.3	118.5	3.0	0.1	106.3	7.88
安徽	Anhui	653.9	590.0		239.5	350.5		63.9	4.73
福建	Fujian	443.0	421.2	370.6	31.1	19.5		21.8	3.65
江西	Jiangxi	998.8	872.9		314.9	443.2	114.8	125.9	5.99
山东	Shandong	1784.1	1681.4	1210.9	301.1	165.5	3.9	102.7	11.72
河南	Henan	624.1	482.2		472.7	2.6	6.9	141.9	3.74
湖北	Hubei	927.3	730.5		377.4	294.7	58.4	196.9	4.99
湖南	Hunan	1226.9	1047.5		683.1	359.3	5.1	179.5	5.79
广东	Guangdong	1398.1	1252.0	1017.8	231.7	1.5	1.0	146.0	7.86
广西	Guangxi	656.1	567.5	348.4	219.1			88.6	2.76
海南	Hainan	311.5	256.6	190.0	38.3	17.3	11.0	54.9	9.13
重庆	Chongqing	43.2	31.9		31.6	0.3		11.3	0.52
四川	Sichuan	961.7	919.5		563.9	13.4	342.3	42.1	1.98
贵州	Guizhou	79.4	65.9		58.0	2.3	5.7	13.5	0.45
云南	Yunnan	235.3	220.3		119.8	96.5	4.0	15.0	0.61
西藏	Tibet	5232.0	5231.5		231.1	2538.6	2461.7	0.5	4.26
陕西	Shaanxi	292.9	277.2		252.1	7.3	17.8	15.7	1.42
甘肃	Gansu	1258.1	1131.4		565.6	44.3	521.5	126.7	2.80
青海	Qinghai	4126.0	4087.7		107.5	1232.0	2748.1	38.3	5.72
宁夏	Ningxia	255.6	252.4		104.1	148.3		3.2	3.85
新疆	Xinjiang	1410.2	1264.6		200.2	694.9	369.5	145.5	0.86

注：本表为中国首次湿地调查（1995-2003)资料，不包括台湾省、香港和澳门特别行政区；湿地面积不包括水稻田湿地。

a) Data in the table are the figures of China First Wetlands Survey (1995-2003), excluding the wetlands of Taiwan province, Hong Kong SAR and Macao SAR. Area of wetlands excludes the wetland of paddyfield.

12-23 红树林各地类面积
Site Classification and Area of Sharpleaf Mangrove (Rhizophora Apiculata)

单位：公顷 (hectare)

地 区	Region	红树林各地类总面积 Total Site Area of Sharpleaf Mangrove	现有面积 Established	未成林面积 Unestablished	宜林地面积 Suitable for Planting
全 国	**National Total**	**82757.2**	**22024.9**	**1884.1**	**58848.2**
浙 江	Zhejiang	5452.3	20.6	236.1	5195.6
福 建	Fujian	13410.1	615.1	286.4	12508.6
广 东	Guangdong	32325.9	9084.0	981.3	22260.6
广 西	Guangxi	18029.2	8374.9	380.3	9274.0
海 南	Hainan	13539.7	3930.3		9609.4

注：本表数据为2002年全国红树林资源调查资料。
a) Data in the table are the figures of National Sharpleaf Mangrove Survey in 2002.

12-24 各地区自然保护基本情况（2005年）
Basic Situation of Natural Protection by Region (2005)

地 区	Region	自然保护区 Nature Reserves 个 数（个） Number of Nature Reserves (unit)	面 积（万公顷） Area of Nature Reserves (10 000 hectares)	占辖区面积比重（%） Percentage of Nature Reserves in the Region (%)	珍稀濒危动物繁殖场（个） Number of Farms to Breed Rare or Endangered Animals (unit)	珍稀植物引种栽培场（个） Cultivating Farms of Rare Plants (unit)	生态示范区建设试点地区和单位（个） Number of Experimental Regions or Units of Ecological Demonstration Zones (unit)	已批准国家级生态示范区（个） Number of Approved National-level Ecological Demonstration Zones (unit)
全 国	**National Total**	**2349**	**14994.9**	**15.0**	**164**	**77**	**528**	**233**
北 京	Beijing	20	13.4	8.0			7	4
天 津	Tianjin	8	16.3	14.4			7	2
河 北	Hebei	30	56.5	3.0			37	5
山 西	Shanxi	45	114.4	7.3		2	26	8
内蒙古	Inner Mongolia	189	1413.4	12.0			15	6
辽 宁	Liaoning	83	285.6	11.2	1	1	21	16
吉 林	Jilin	33	224.6	12.4	2	3	10	7
黑龙江	Heilongjiang	170	471.1	10.4			23	15
上 海	Shanghai	4	9.4	14.8			1	1
江 苏	Jiangsu	40	80.9	7.9			51	48
浙 江	Zhejiang	52	26.4	2.6	2	3	23	21
安 徽	Anhui	31	40.8	3.1	5	1	30	9
福 建	Fujian	103	54.1	3.3			13	4
江 西	Jiangxi	128	90.2	5.4	4	5	33	6
山 东	Shandong	72	108.6	6.6			34	20
河 南	Henan	32	75.7	4.5	1	2	24	18
湖 北	Hubei	62	102.9	5.5	8	7	12	6
湖 南	Hunan	91	106.1	5.0	3	7	30	12
广 东	Guangdong	294	341.9	4.6	37	8	13	5
广 西	Guangxi	72	149.8	6.2	46	5	11	3
海 南	Hainan	68	280.7	5.3	17	1	1	1
重 庆	Chongqing	49	88.8	10.8	2	1	2	2
四 川	Sichuan	161	899.4	18.4			35	4
贵 州	Guizhou	128	88.6	5.0	3	2	12	3
云 南	Yunnan	198	422.5	10.7	23	21	21	2
西 藏	Tibet	38	4097.1	34.1			1	
陕 西	Shaanxi	44	98.7	4.8	2	4	18	2
甘 肃	Gansu	54	925.0	20.3	8	4	4	
青 海	Qinghai	10	2092.5	29.0			2	
宁 夏	Ningxia	13	50.7	9.8			3	1
新 疆	Xinjiang	27	2168.8	13.6			8	2

12-25 地质灾害及防治情况
Geological Disasters and Prevention and Cure

年份 地区	Year Region	发生地质灾害起数（次） Geological Disasters (time)	#滑坡 Land-slide	#崩塌 Collapse	#泥石流 Mud-rock Flow	#地面塌陷 Land Subside	人员伤亡（人） Casualties (person)	#死亡人数 Deaths
	2000	19653	13431	2945	1958	347	27697	1179
	2001	5793	3034	583	1539	554	1675	788
	2002	40246	31247	3097	4976	521	2759	853
	2003	15489	10240	2604	1549	574	1333	767
	2004	13555	9130	2593	1157	445	1407	734
	2005	17751	9367	7654	566	137	1223	578
北京	Beijing							
天津	Tianjin							
河北	Hebei	7	1	1	1	4		
山西	Shanxi	3	1	1	1		26	12
内蒙古	Inner Mongolia	2	1	1			5	
辽宁	Liaoning	75	30	7	24	13		
吉林	Jilin	8	3		4	1	4	4
黑龙江	Heilongjiang	11	4	2	4	1		
上海	Shanghai							
江苏	Jiangsu	2				2		
浙江	Zhejiang	375	198	141	32	4	65	36
安徽	Anhui	8320	1528	6445	333	14	44	40
福建	Fujian	6564	5934	599	18	7	128	84
江西	Jiangxi	11	10	1			42	20
山东	Shandong	26	5			20		
河南	Henan	8	3	3		1	15	4
湖北	Hubei	713	588	72	23	24	66	33
湖南	Hunan	12	9	2	1		19	16
广东	Guangdong	155	101	23	1	30	99	66
广西	Guangxi	37	17	20			81	46
海南	Hainan	107	3	104			10	6
重庆	Chongqing	590	488	90	8	2	264	19
四川	Sichuan	175	98	43	28	4	150	71
贵州	Guizhou	121	74	36	3	3	28	14
云南	Yunnan	34	20	6	8		78	52
西藏	Tibet	10	4	2	4		3	3
陕西	Shaanxi	263	198	37	22	3	79	49
甘肃	Gansu	11	10	1			2	2
青海	Qinghai	14	11	3			10	1
宁夏	Ningxia	2	1			1		
新疆	Xinjiang	95	27	14	51	3	5	

12-25 续表 continued

年 份 地 区	Year Region	直接经济损失 (万元) Direct Economic Losses (10 000 yuan)	地质灾害防治项目数 (个) Number of Projects of Prevention of Geological Disasters (unit)	地质灾害防治投资 (万元) Investment of Projects of Prevention of Geological Disasters (10 000 yuan)	滑坡、泥石流治理面积 (公顷) Area Covered by Landslide and Mud-rock Flow Harnessing Projects (hectare)
	2000	494201	429	33197	52848
	2001	348699	999	44639	25714
	2002	509740	1595	110022	29696
	2003	504325	1815	166514	14450
	2004	408828	2247	175231	11642
	2005	357678	3179	166860	5315
北 京	Beijing		1	20	
天 津	Tianjin		2	150	5
河 北	Hebei	185	16	1495	100
山 西	Shanxi		38	2874	33
内蒙古	Inner Mongolia	100			
辽 宁	Liaoning	27504	15	4090	
吉 林	Jilin	2304	19	334	3
黑龙江	Heilongjiang	409	29	11561	5
上 海	Shanghai		2	500	
江 苏	Jiangsu	140	26	6478	29
浙 江	Zhejiang	8500	473	17726	152
安 徽	Anhui	96800	46	3614	30
福 建	Fujian	34844	664	6600	1095
江 西	Jiangxi	138	187	3919	121
山 东	Shandong	131	40	1477	
河 南	Henan	75	30	11850	26
湖 北	Hubei	26320	181	8520	223
湖 南	Hunan	900	94	7946	817
广 东	Guangdong	58747	27	14030	
广 西	Guangxi	756	86	8736	69
海 南	Hainan	15	15	126	
重 庆	Chongqing	6718	363	11057	
四 川	Sichuan	39075	165	16605	
贵 州	Guizhou	1191	123	10228	339
云 南	Yunnan	44877	324	5810	1821
西 藏	Tibet	20	4	3580	
陕 西	Shaanxi	3484	185	5924	448
甘 肃	Gansu	3435		680	
青 海	Qinghai	615	10	200	
宁 夏	Ningxia	10	4	542	
新 疆	Xinjiang	384	10	188	

12-26 森林火灾情况

Forest Fires

年 份 地 区	Year Region	森林火灾次数（次） Forest Fires (time)	森林火警 Fire Alarms	一般火灾 Ordinary Fires	重大火灾 Major Fires	特大火灾 Severe Fires	火场总面积（公顷） Total Area of Fires (hectare)	受灾森林面积（公顷） Destructed Forest Area (hectare)	#天然林 Natural Forest	#人工林 Man-made Forest	伤亡人数（人） Casualties (person)	#死亡人数 Deaths	直接经济损失（万元） Direct Economic Loss (10 000 yuan)
	2000	5934	2722	3144	60	8	167098	88390	46960	40529	178	81	3069
	2001	4933	2984	1929	17	3	192734	46181	32289	11721	58	20	7409
	2002	7527	4450	3046	24	7	131823	47631	17031	17123	98	48	3610
	2003	10463	5582	4860	14	7	1123751	451020	294271	33531	142	72	37000
	2004	13466	6894	6531	38	3	344211	142238	74471	59106	252	131	20213
	2005	11542	6574	4949	16	3	290633	73701	30435	36306	152	92	15029
北 京	Beijing	11	10	1			37	8		8			
天 津	Tianjin	16	16				27	2		2			
河 北	Hebei	251	226	25			2262	219		139			9
山 西	Shanxi	63	12	50	1		2302	1157	591	567	6	5	314
内蒙古	Inner Mongolia	173	65	106	1	1	47229	4300	193	1205			11
辽 宁	Liaoning	230	186	44			541	130	8	122	1	1	43
吉 林	Jilin	37	32	5			42	26		5			20
黑龙江	Heilongjiang	103	91	10		2	132248	24308	24308				
上 海	Shanghai												
江 苏	Jiangsu	172	151	21			882	388		389	1	1	243
浙 江	Zhejiang	718	130	586	2		11672	6945		3836	24	15	
安 徽	Anhui	325	185	140			2686	1169		1169	6		212
福 建	Fujian	309	41	266	2		5220	3429	61	3368	3	2	44
江 西	Jiangxi	355	60	295			9321	4626	529	4098	7	6	1275
山 东	Shandong	90	50	40			539	243		243	6	5	362
河 南	Henan	982	841	141			1694	507	76	431			208
湖 北	Hubei	1055	721	331	3		6640	1709	141	1600	20	18	72
湖 南	Hunan	3204	1589	1612	3		18868	12931	1789	11294	22	19	3193
广 东	Guangdong	212	61	151			2780	1419	96	1385	18	9	381
广 西	Guangxi	688	351	337			13091	2467	6	2389	11	3	195
海 南	Hainan	221	135	86			1128	542	96	458			6
重 庆	Chongqing	117	93	24			348	136	15	121	2	2	53
四 川	Sichuan	252	202	46	4		6818	2257	2046	211	9	2	7305
贵 州	Guizhou	1148	765	383			8848	2045	197	1822	5	2	662
云 南	Yunnan	665	454	211			14664	2353	124	1224	11	2	332
西 藏	Tibet	17	15	2			117	12	12				66
陕 西	Shaanxi	73	49	24			434	268	136	132			2
甘 肃	Gansu	4	4				9	1		1			
青 海	Qinghai	7	2	5			84	82		77			11
宁 夏	Ningxia	16	10	6			57	10		11			
新 疆	Xinjiang	28	27	1			42	12	10	1			8

12-27 森林病虫鼠害防治情况

Prevention of Forest Diseases, Pests and Rats

年份 地区	Year Region	合计 Total 发生面积(公顷) Area of Occurrence (hectare)	防治面积(公顷) Area of Prevention (hectare)	防治率(%) Prevention Rate (%)	森林病害 Forest Diseases 发生面积(公顷) Area of Occurrence (hectare)	防治面积(公顷) Area of Prevention (hectare)	防治率(%) Prevention Rate (%)
	2000	8518580	5741860	67.4	934520	619450	66.3
	2001	8390270	5872910	70.0	804950	582850	72.4
	2002	8412496	5719588	68.0	744980	571240	76.7
	2003	8887362	5829187	65.6	757456	552461	73.0
	2004	9448372	6395228	68.0	757874	567132	75.0
	2005	9610281	6407494	66.7	1012022	706157	69.8
北京	Beijing	36027	34606	96.1	147	133	90.5
天津	Tianjin	30014	27740	92.4	1294	1273	98.4
河北	Hebei	341526	288513	84.5	16447	11700	71.1
山西	Shanxi	298788	125513	42.0	1987	1173	59.0
内蒙古	Inner Mongolia	634667	606001	95.5	14000	12667	90.5
辽宁	Liaoning	447041	359294	80.4	29994	20747	69.2
吉林	Jilin	241599	137995	57.1	87747	26507	30.2
黑龙江	Heilongjiang	443528	403048	90.9	32727	28360	86.7
上海	Shanghai	13874	13874	100.0	1093	1093	100.0
江苏	Jiangsu	85066	53246	62.6	20666	2780	13.5
浙江	Zhejiang	74492	69325	93.1	29086	28466	97.9
安徽	Anhui	261512	210368	80.4	22506	20520	91.2
福建	Fujian	293080	180946	61.7	25014	22206	88.8
江西	Jiangxi	405587	265994	65.6	82867	47820	57.7
山东	Shandong	551206	463020	84.0	163420	130120	79.6
河南	Henan	449019	348733	77.7	78740	67586	85.8
湖北	Hubei	258467	195687	75.7	21587	17613	81.6
湖南	Hunan	219079	156293	71.3	7366	7327	99.5
广东	Guangdong	737393	86127	11.7	26166	22553	86.2
广西	Guangxi	299714	77334	25.8	38034	2454	6.5
海南	Hainan	16134	13866	85.9			
重庆	Chongqing	145333	115333	79.4	37333	22667	60.7
四川	Sichuan	688774	665447	96.6	79827	71273	89.3
贵州	Guizhou	272001	227333	83.6	13334	12000	90.0
云南	Yunnan	404666	298665	73.8	59333	56666	95.5
西藏	Tibet	91000			6667		
陕西	Shaanxi	658913	228140	34.6	26460	11660	44.1
甘肃	Gansu	251226	203648	81.1	39906	30167	75.6
青海	Qinghai	227687	131214	57.6	23400	11593	49.5
宁夏	Ningxia	317320	78198	24.6	553	67	12.1
新疆	Xinjiang	321047	261054	81.3	7800	3440	44.1
大兴安岭	Daxing'anling	94501	80939	85.6	16521	13526	81.9

12-27 续表 continued

年 份 地 区	Year Region	森林虫害 Forest Pest Plague			森林鼠害 Forest Rat Plague		
		发生面积 (公顷) Area of Occurrence (hectare)	防治面积 (公顷) Area of Prevention (hectare)	防治率 (%) Prevention Rate (%)	发生面积 (公顷) Area of Occurrence (hectare)	防治面积 (公顷) Area of Prevention (hectare)	防治率 (%) Prevention Rate (%)
	2000	6692820	4565910	68.2	891240	556500	62.4
	2001	6683790	4592690	68.7	901530	697370	77.4
	2002	6792324	4512293	66.4	875192	636056	72.7
	2003	7184617	4633348	64.0	945289	643378	68.0
	2004	7440329	4948540	67.0	1250169	879557	70.4
	2005	7260937	4985112	68.7	1337324	716225	53.6
北 京	Beijing	35880	34473	96.1			
天 津	Tianjin	28720	26467	92.2			
河 北	Hebei	318759	271653	85.2	6320	5160	81.6
山 西	Shanxi	279220	121220	43.4	17581	3120	17.7
内蒙古	Inner Mongolia	536666	525334	97.9	84001	68000	81.0
辽 宁	Liaoning	403593	332941	82.5	13454	5606	41.7
吉 林	Jilin	138566	107801	77.8	15286	3687	24.1
黑龙江	Heilongjiang	185914	160754	86.5	224887	213934	95.1
上 海	Shanghai	12781	12781	100.0			
江 苏	Jiangsu	64400	50466	78.4			
浙 江	Zhejiang	45406	40859	90.0			
安 徽	Anhui	239006	189848	79.4			
福 建	Fujian	268066	158740	59.2			
江 西	Jiangxi	321873	218174	67.8	847		
山 东	Shandong	387786	332900	85.8			
河 南	Henan	370279	281147	75.9			
湖 北	Hubei	230453	171647	74.5	6427	6427	100.0
湖 南	Hunan	207380	148966	71.8	4333		
广 东	Guangdong	711227	63574	8.9			
广 西	Guangxi	261640	74847	28.6	40	33	82.5
海 南	Hainan	16134	13866	85.9			
重 庆	Chongqing	94000	83333	88.7	14000	9333	66.7
四 川	Sichuan	580987	571020	98.3	27960	23154	82.8
贵 州	Guizhou	226667	193999	85.6	32000	21334	66.7
云 南	Yunnan	340000	236666	69.6	5333	5333	100.0
西 藏	Tibet	17667			66667		
陕 西	Shaanxi	351960	124647	35.4	280493	91833	32.7
甘 肃	Gansu	137446	109760	79.9	73874	63721	86.3
青 海	Qinghai	71360	45486	63.7	132927	74135	55.8
宁 夏	Ningxia	83853	26450	31.5	232914	51681	22.2
新 疆	Xinjiang	251500	219700	87.4	61747	37914	61.4
大兴安岭	Daxing'anling	41747	35593	85.3	36233	31820	87.8

12-28 环境污染与破坏事故情况

Environment Pollution and Destruction Accidents

年份 Year 地区 Region		环境污染与破坏事故次数(次) Number of Pollution and Destruction Accidents (time)	水污染 Water Pollution	大气污染 Air Pollution	固体废物污染 Solid Wastes Pollution	噪声与振动危害 Noise and Vibration Pollution	其他 Others	污染直接经济损失(万元) Direct Economic Losses (10 000 yuan)	污染事故赔、罚款总额(万元) Reparations and Fines on Pollution Accidents (10 000 yuan)
	2000	2411	1138	864	103	266	40	17807.9	3682.6
	2001	1842	1096	576	39	80	51	12272.4	3263.9
	2002	1921	1097	597	109	97	21	4640.9	3140.7
	2003	1843	1042	654	56	50	41	3374.9	2391.5
	2004	1441	753	569	47	36	36	36365.7	3963.9
	2005	1406	693	538	48	63	64	10515.0	3082.1
北京	Beijing								
天津	Tianjin	3		3				5.0	2.0
河北	Hebei	9	4	5				7.1	20.5
山西	Shanxi	4	1	2	1			11.0	10.0
内蒙古	Inner Mongolia	7	3	4				15.7	20.7
辽宁	Liaoning	26	6	5	3		12	46.3	40.1
吉林	Jilin	2	2					7.5	
黑龙江	Heilongjiang	4	3	1				6.1	11.4
上海	Shanghai	9	3	5		1		37.4	18.9
江苏	Jiangsu	27	18	9				1787.6	27.6
浙江	Zhejiang	65	44	13	4		4	404.9	386.2
安徽	Anhui	28	16	10		2		275.4	199.3
福建	Fujian	15	11	3			1	26.9	23.0
江西	Jiangxi	40	20	15	2	3		88.0	76.4
山东	Shandong	44	11	33				86.9	58.4
河南	Henan	14	7	7				15.1	5.1
湖北	Hubei	38	24	12			2	125.5	187.8
湖南	Hunan	202	123	59	4	7	9	340.4	644.2
广东	Guangdong	31	22	4	1		4	6128.1	71.8
广西	Guangxi	215	70	144			1	370.0	339.5
海南	Hainan	14	9	1			4	16.0	25.6
重庆	Chongqing	8	5	3				7.4	19.8
四川	Sichuan	238	114	80	2	37	5	152.5	194.7
贵州	Guizhou	28	17	10	1			57.9	61.8
云南	Yunnan	159	69	69	8	12	1	222.4	284.1
西藏	Tibet								
陕西	Shaanxi	27	15	5	1	1	5	27.9	111.5
甘肃	Gansu	135	67	31	21		16	191.8	176.6
青海	Qinghai	2	1	1				2.4	1.5
宁夏	Ningxia	7	3	4				10.2	22.0
新疆	Xinjiang	5	5					41.6	41.6

12-29 地震灾害情况
Earthquake Disasters

年份 Year / 地区 Region		地震灾害次数(次) Number of Earthquakes (time)	5.0-5.9级 5.0-5.9 Richter scale	6.0-6.9级 6.0-6.9 Richter scale	7.0级以上 Over 7.0 Richter scale	人员伤亡(人) Casualties (person)	#死亡人数 Deaths	直接经济损失(万元) Direct Economic Loss (10 000 yuan)
	2000	10	7	2		2987	10	146792
	2001	12	8	2	1	750	9	148449
	2002	5	4			362	2	14774
	2003	21	10	6	1	7465	319	466040
	2004	11	8	1		696	8	94959
	2005	13	9	2		882	15	262811
黑龙江	Heilongjiang	1	1			12	1	2745
江 西	Jiangxi	1	1			788	13	203759
广 西	Guangxi	1				4	1	2532
四 川	Sichuan	1						653
云 南	Yunnan	3	3			78		31498
西 藏	Tibet	3	2	1				5222
新 疆	Xinjiang	3	2	1				16402

12-30 主要海洋灾害情况（2005年）
Major Marine Disasters (2005)

灾种	Disaster Categories	发生次数(次) Occurrence (time)	人员伤亡、失踪(人) Casualties and Missing People (person)	直接经济损失(亿元) Direct Economic Loss (100 million yuan)
合 计	**Total**	**176**	**371**	**332.4**
风暴潮	Stormy Tides	20	137	329.8
赤 潮	Red Tides	82		0.7
海 浪	Huge Waves	66	234	1.9
溢 油	Leak of Oil	8		

12-31 环境污染治理投资
Investment in the Treatment of Environmental Pollution

指 标	Item	2001	2002	2003	2004	2005
环境污染治理投资总额(亿元)	**Total Investment in the Treatment of Environmental Pollution (100 million yuan)**	**1106.6**	**1367.2**	**1627.7**	**1909.8**	**2388.0**
#城市环境基础设施建设投资	Investment in Urban Environmental Infrastructure	595.7	789.1	1072.4	1141.2	1289.7
#燃气	Gas Supply	75.5	88.4	133.5	148.3	142.4
集中供热	Centralized Heating	82.0	121.4	145.8	173.4	220.2
排水	Drainage Works	224.5	275.0	375.2	352.3	368.0
园林绿化	Gardening and Greening	163.2	239.5	321.9	359.5	411.3
市容环境卫生	Environmental Sanitation	50.6	64.8	96.0	107.8	147.8
工业污染源治理投资	Investment in the Treatment of Industrial Pollution	174.5	188.4	221.8	308.1	458.2
建设项目“三同时”环保投资	"Three Simultaneities" Environmental Investment for New Project	336.4	389.7	333.5	460.5	640.1
环境污染治理投资总额占国内生产总值比重(%)	**Total Investment in the Treatment of Environmental Pollution as Percent of GDP (%)**	**1.01**	**1.14**	**1.20**	**1.19**	**1.30**

12-32 工业污染治理投资来源

Sources of Investment in the Treatment of Industrial Pollution

年份 地区	Year Region	污染治理项目当年投资来源总额(亿元) Sources of Current Investment in the Treatment of Industrial Pollution (100 million yuan)	国家预算内资金 State Budget	环保专项资金 Special Funds for Environmental Protection	其他资金 Other Funds	#企业自筹 Self-raising Funds	#国内贷款 Domestic Loans	#利用外资 Foreign Investment
	2000	234.73	33.12	6.71	194.91	16.52	12.55	9.17
	2001	174.48	36.35	8.32	129.81	7.49	67.11	7.23
	2002	188.37	41.96	6.79	139.62	8.00	43.55	7.25
	2003	221.79	18.75	12.38	190.66	141.94	25.10	6.78
	2004	308.11	13.71	11.13	283.26	227.43	29.02	4.59
	2005	458.19	7.78	20.60	429.81	361.64	38.99	7.09
北京	Beijing	10.89	0.30	1.10	9.48	8.67	0.81	
天津	Tianjin	18.63	0.04	0.32	18.26	12.75	3.38	0.29
河北	Hebei	25.15	0.11	3.08	21.95	21.24	0.46	0.08
山西	Shanxi	19.79	0.49	2.22	17.08	16.24	0.44	0.28
内蒙古	Inner Mongolia	2.57		0.21	2.36	2.19	0.11	
辽宁	Liaoning	36.95	0.90	0.90	35.15	33.35	0.49	
吉林	Jilin	5.15	0.17	0.32	4.66	3.48	1.00	0.18
黑龙江	Heilongjiang	4.56	1.06	0.49	3.01	2.39	0.09	
上海	Shanghai	8.75	0.09	0.15	8.52	1.30	1.32	2.68
江苏	Jiangsu	38.95		1.50	37.44	33.37	2.92	0.78
浙江	Zhejiang	19.95	1.75	0.45	17.75	14.25	1.64	0.05
安徽	Anhui	4.54	0.28	0.56	3.70	3.41	0.11	0.01
福建	Fujian	34.54	0.01	0.29	34.24	29.23	2.08	1.07
江西	Jiangxi	7.23	0.05	0.05	7.13	7.01	0.06	
山东	Shandong	60.51	0.24	0.94	59.32	50.72	6.68	1.11
河南	Henan	20.68	0.50	0.79	19.39	18.23	0.94	
湖北	Hubei	14.81	0.76	0.74	13.31	12.84	0.47	
湖南	Hunan	14.12	0.26	1.47	12.40	9.03	3.19	0.17
广东	Guangdong	37.04	0.01	0.79	36.24	31.49	3.76	0.14
广西	Guangxi	10.37	0.03	0.95	9.39	6.08	3.27	0.04
海南	Hainan	0.38		0.06	0.32	0.32		
重庆	Chongqing	3.91	0.15	0.79	2.97	2.25	0.69	
四川	Sichuan	20.04	0.10	0.70	19.25	15.16	3.97	
贵州	Guizhou	5.93	0.06	0.20	5.67	5.04	0.14	
云南	Yunnan	6.75	0.02	0.25	6.48	5.34	0.62	0.21
西藏	Tibet							
陕西	Shaanxi	12.69	0.08	0.29	12.32	7.62	0.15	
甘肃	Gansu	6.66	0.28	0.70	5.69	4.34	0.17	
青海	Qinghai	0.47			0.47	0.32		
宁夏	Ningxia	1.77		0.01	1.76	1.75	0.01	
新疆	Xinjiang	4.40	0.03	0.27	4.09	2.22	0.02	

12-33 工业污染治理投资完成情况

Investment Completed in the Treatment of Industrial Pollution

年份 地区	Year Region	污染治理项目本年完成投资（万元） Investment Completed in the Treatment of Industrial Pollution This Year (10 000 yuan)	治理废水 Treatment of Waste Water	治理废气 Treatment of Waste Gas	治理固体废物 Treatment of Solid Waste	治理噪声 Treatment of Noise Pollution	治理其他 Treatment of Other Pollution	本年竣工项目数（个） Number of Projects Completed (unit)
	2000	2347894.7	1095897.4	909241.6	114673.0	13692.4	214390.3	21070
	2001	1745280.0	729214.3	657940.4	186967.2	6424.4	164733.7	10277
	2002	1883662.8	714935.1	697864.3	161287.3	10463.5	299112.6	9733
	2003	2218281.0	873747.7	921222.4	161763.4	10139.2	251408.3	9568
	2004	3081059.5	1055868.1	1427974.9	226464.8	13416.1	357335.6	11290
	2005	4581908.7	1337146.9	2129571.3	274181.3	30613.3	810395.9	11158
北京	Beijing	108880.2	4729.1	91382.8	959.0	136.1	11673.2	142
天津	Tianjin	186315.5	28530.0	101090.8	4327.5	1706.9	50660.3	178
河北	Hebei	251519.0	59176.8	116305.3	36208.0	1702.9	38126.0	468
山西	Shanxi	197885.1	48784.3	123163.0	11866.1	347.6	13724.1	583
内蒙古	Inner Mongolia	25678.1	9876.1	14019.5	1331.5	3.0	448.0	63
辽宁	Liaoning	369498.8	31277.4	88477.3	4165.6	763.0	244815.5	277
吉林	Jilin	51531.2	27129.2	16301.5	5103.8	1221.2	1775.5	206
黑龙江	Heilongjiang	45615.2	19381.2	19000.0	2096.7	3.5	5133.8	79
上海	Shanghai	87516.8	26826.2	55718.7	16.0	363.0	4592.9	282
江苏	Jiangsu	389480.7	81596.6	284590.5	1966.0	2178.3	19149.3	674
浙江	Zhejiang	199470.4	72399.4	66931.8	1784.2	1144.8	57210.2	709
安徽	Anhui	45443.1	24121.9	16767.7	2902.0	249.1	1402.4	210
福建	Fujian	345431.2	56397.3	211579.6	19323.7	6973.0	51157.6	704
江西	Jiangxi	72309.6	21513.3	25804.1	3140.3	195.5	21656.4	145
山东	Shandong	605063.4	242718.1	195957.5	77997.4	5200.1	83190.3	1099
河南	Henan	206815.1	101841.9	70823.8	24177.7	438.2	9533.5	589
湖北	Hubei	148096.5	48067.7	40007.5	11408.1	440.1	48173.1	428
湖南	Hunan	141238.9	35289.9	93399.3	9539.1	688.9	2321.7	479
广东	Guangdong	370383.7	124697.2	150468.9	16817.2	2446.9	75953.5	1071
广西	Guangxi	103730.4	33678.3	56863.4	1849.0	505.3	10834.4	307
海南	Hainan	3788.6	1251.1	2133.5	207.0		197.0	18
重庆	Chongqing	39121.3	21950.2	5751.9	9826.3	321.0	1271.9	110
四川	Sichuan	200385.6	55430.2	120498.9	7098.5	930.2	16427.8	929
贵州	Guizhou	59258.3	22078.7	28693.7	7816.0	382.5	287.4	360
云南	Yunnan	67508.1	12572.7	38957.7	8260.4	973.0	6744.3	350
西藏	Tibet							
陕西	Shaanxi	126946.3	82866.0	21870.4	1317.3	94.2	20798.4	293
甘肃	Gansu	66609.6	13883.8	49289.6	1404.4	84.0	1947.8	165
青海	Qinghai	4670.0	206.0	4073.1	12.0		378.9	18
宁夏	Ningxia	17709.8	5327.0	9993.3	889.5	800.0	700.0	69
新疆	Xinjiang	44008.2	23549.3	9656.2	371.0	321.0	10110.7	153

12-34 林业系统营林固定资产投资资金来源

Sources of Funds of Investment in Fixed Assets for Afforestation in Forest System

单位：万元 (10 000 yuan)

年份 地区	Year Region	合计 Sources of Funds This Year	上年底结余资金 Unspent Capitals from Last Year	国家预算内资金 State Budget	#国债资金 National Debts	#中央财政专项资金 Special Funds of Central Finance	国内贷款 Domestic Loans	利用外资 Foreign Investment	自筹资金 Self-raising Funds	其他资金 Other Funds
	2000	1614486	91197	1099858	377841	431435	49052	34453	271273	68653
	2001	2015639	106744	1502046	533967	723542	55248	19971	221322	110308
	2002	3082417	147963	2472167	788071	1417855	68610	30893	246913	115871
	2003	3963491	146493	3033522	935756	1758212	86305	46065	428001	223105
	2004	4080892	138982	3133121	629113	2096696	60593	46015	430620	271561
	2005	4734696	168714	3526236	582436	2467248	82397	63237	551509	342603
北京	Beijing	109381	3408	104585	5682	8650		412	431	545
天津	Tianjin	6171		4288	2500	1409			1883	
河北	Hebei	226355	490	197305	40329	145916	5300	968	14186	8106
山西	Shanxi	174603		168319	27377	116812	999	4022	65	1198
内蒙古	Inner Mongolia	418848	548	379792	60530	304127		19366	17212	1930
辽宁	Liaoning	121087		110410	13922	66779	523	2758	7396	
吉林	Jilin	233552	8470	146345	14097	122321	3367	56	50824	24490
黑龙江	Heilongjiang	197979		170123	20004	141110	289	552	18537	8478
上海	Shanghai	91190	25576	35698					20323	9593
江苏	Jiangsu	235276		4712	2075	2637	9536	732	123433	96863
浙江	Zhejiang	19471	5796	9270	4346	117	130		3760	515
安徽	Anhui	71043	20	48795	7441	38295	2510	3450	9040	7228
福建	Fujian	61061	5172	8839	2850	1773	11250	985	23116	11699
江西	Jiangxi	40084	262	28250	8134	17412	611	4747	3867	2347
山东	Shandong	162168		12135	2682	1156	4006	857	79488	65682
河南	Henan	99383	1036	85138	16792	62531	7357	2442	1652	1757
湖北	Hubei	143784	705	98498	30757	53718	682	6467	24645	12787
湖南	Hunan	124664		113362	24883	82082	600	1030	4881	4791
广东	Guangdong	43822	3177	34492	2263	332			5240	913
广西	Guangxi	186783	18238	93865	17955	55931	5488	3329	52225	13638
海南	Hainan	37864		21863	3417	16702	4774	451	3879	6897
重庆	Chongqing	209357	17	185403	15641	141897		532	2638	20767
四川	Sichuan	513104	31319	456937	52231	360807	465	7386	7028	9969
贵州	Guizhou	206275	6745	198423	19905	162859			310	797
云南	Yunnan	227648	26140	165056	37082	107660	12	332	16448	19660
西藏	Tibet	425		425		425				
陕西	Shaanxi	142831	8515	127184	38207	84547		1512	1065	4555
甘肃	Gansu	253385		239145	34332	200486	12398	87	1751	4
青海	Qinghai	72868	2718	68517	13004	54442	1100	507		26
宁夏	Ningxia	38196		33263	18152	13468		140	4792	
新疆	Xinjiang	135603	1573	81231	40206	33798	11000		39835	1964

注：全国合计数包含国家林业局直属单位的固定资产投资数据。

a) The national total sources of funds include the investment in fixed assets by departments directly under State Forestry Administration.

12–35 林业系统营林固定资产投资完成情况

Investment in Fixed Assets Completed for Afforestation in Forest System

单位：万元　　(10 000 yuan)

年份 地区	Year Region	本年完成投资 Investment Completed During the Year	#国家投资 State Investment	#国债资金 National Debt	本年新增固定资产 Newly Increased Fixed Assets
	2000	1510541	1103624	365907	425135
	2001	1919835	1516932	509195	409064
	2002	2976388	2479492	778882	797275
	2003	3892793	3098907	945705	1283847
	2004	3989023	3202142	632739	1199775
	2005	4593443	3528122	585865	1590725
北京	Beijing	109188	99857	5859	8020
天津	Tianjin	5139	3628	2130	
河北	Hebei	225131	196985	39488	48612
山西	Shanxi	174345	168140	28140	587
内蒙古	Inner Mongolia	417279	378856	61157	180860
辽宁	Liaoning	121087	115563	13922	35389
吉林	Jilin	188849	115268	10991	82365
黑龙江	Heilongjiang	197979	170123	20004	24296
上海	Shanghai	81293	36080	125	166
江苏	Jiangsu	235276	14248	2075	50939
浙江	Zhejiang	13148	9435	5068	1953
安徽	Anhui	69897	47864	7501	41721
福建	Fujian	79789	13047	2775	17322
江西	Jiangxi	39642	28160	7892	11408
山东	Shandong	162168	12136	2682	32186
河南	Henan	106248	95571	20658	65420
湖北	Hubei	142392	91337	29561	64466
湖南	Hunan	124664	113362	24883	86052
广东	Guangdong	39888	18979	2329	3856
广西	Guangxi	173203	101526	21140	93546
海南	Hainan	37864	25058	3417	37864
重庆	Chongqing	211195	192244	15668	95404
四川	Sichuan	469701	455548	49449	34570
贵州	Guizhou	198246	192124	20507	166193
云南	Yunnan	201479	170543	38707	35093
西藏	Tibet	5832			766
陕西	Shaanxi	144717	137573	40813	105093
甘肃	Gansu	253385	239400	34332	106029
青海	Qinghai	72868	72615	13004	62943
宁夏	Ningxia	38196	33263	18152	
新疆	Xinjiang	138149	81528	35184	64678

注：全国合计数包含国家林业局直属单位的固定资产投资数据。

a) The national total source of funds include the investment in fixed assets by departments directly under State Forestry Administration.

主要统计指标解释

水资源总量　指评价区内降水形成的地表和地下产水总量，即地表产流量与降水入渗补给地下水量之和，不包括过境水量。

地表水资源量　指评价区内河流、湖泊、冰川等地表水体中可以逐年更新的动态水量，即当地天然河川径流量。

地下水资源量　指评价区内降水和地表水对饱水岩土层的补给量，包括降水入渗补给量和河道、湖库、渠系、渠灌田间等地表水体的入渗补给量。

地表水与地下水资源重复量　指地表水和地下水相互转化的部分，即天然河川径流量中的地下水排泄量，和地下水补给量中来源于地表水的入渗补给量。

供水总量　指各种水源工程为用户提供的包括输水损失在内的毛供水量之和，不包括海水直接利用量。

地表水源供水量　指地表水体工程的取水量，按蓄、引、提、调四种形式统计。从水库、塘坝中引水或提水，均属蓄水工程供水量；从河道或湖泊中自流引水的，无论有闸或无闸，均属引水工程供水量；利用扬水站从河道或湖泊中直接取水的，属提水工程供水量；跨流域调水指水资源一级区或独立流域之间的跨流域调配水量，不包括在蓄、引、提水量中。

地下水源供水量　指水井工程的开采量，按浅层淡水、深层承压水和微咸水分别统计。城市地下水源供水量包括自来水厂的开采量和工矿企业自备井的开采量。

其他水源供水量　包括污水处理再利用、集雨工程、海水淡化等水源工程的供水量。

用水总量　指分配给各类用户的包括输水损失在内的毛用水量之和，不包括海水直接利用量。

农业用水　指农田灌溉用水、林果地灌溉用水、草地灌溉用水和鱼塘补水。

工业用水　指工矿企业在生产过程中用于制造、加工、冷却、空调、净化、洗涤等方面的用水，按新水取用量计，不包括企业内部的重复利用水量。

生活用水　包括城镇生活用水和农村生活用水。城镇生活用水由居民用水和公共用水（含第三产业及建筑业等用水）组成；农村生活用水除居民生活用水外，还包括牲畜用水在内。

生态用水　仅包括人为措施供给的城镇环境用水和部分河湖、湿地补水，而不包括降水、径流自然满足的水量。

工业废水排放量　指经过企业厂区所有排放口排到企业外部的工业废水量。包括生产废水、外排的直接冷却水、超标排放的矿井地下水和与工业废水混排的厂区生活污水，不包括外排的间接冷却水(清污不分流的间接冷却水应计算在内)。

直接排入海的　指经企业位于海边的排放口，直接排入海的废水量。直接排放指废水经过工厂的排污口直接排入海，而未经过城市下水道或其他中间体，也不受其他水体的影响。

工业废水排放达标量　指报告期内废水中各项污染物指标都达到国家或地方排放标准的外排工业废水量，包括未经处理外排达标的，经废水处理设施处理后达标排放的，以及经污水处理厂处理后达标排放的。

工业废水排放达标率　指工业废水排放达标量占工业废水排放量的百分率，计算公式为：

$$\text{工业废水排放达标率}=\frac{\text{工业废水排放达标量}}{\text{工业废水排放量}}\times 100\%$$

城镇生活污水排放量　指城镇居民每年排放的生活污水。用人均系数法测算。测算公式为：

$$\begin{matrix}\text{城镇生活}\\\text{污水排放量}\end{matrix}=\begin{matrix}\text{城镇生活}\\\text{污水排放系数}\end{matrix}\times\begin{matrix}\text{市镇非}\\\text{农业人口}\end{matrix}\times 365$$

城镇生活污水中化学需氧量(COD)产生量　指城镇居民每年排放的生活污水中的COD的产生量。用人均系数法测算。测算公式为：

$$\begin{matrix}\text{城镇生活污水中}\\COD\ \text{产生量}\end{matrix}=\begin{matrix}\text{城镇生活污水中}\\COD\ \text{产生系数}\end{matrix}\times\begin{matrix}\text{市镇非}\\\text{农业人口}\end{matrix}\times 365$$

化学需氧量(COD)　测量有机和无机物质化学分解所消耗氧的质量浓度的水污染指数。

工业废气排放量　指报告期内企业厂区内燃料燃烧和生产工艺过程中产生的各种排入大气的含有污染物的气体的总量，以标准状态(273K，101325Pa)计算。测算公式为：

$$\begin{matrix}\text{工业废气}\\\text{排放量}\end{matrix}=\begin{matrix}\text{燃料燃烧过程}\\\text{中废气排放量}\end{matrix}+\begin{matrix}\text{生产工艺过程中}\\\text{废气排放量}\end{matrix}$$

生活及其他SO_2排放量　以生活及其他煤炭消费量和其含硫量为基础，根据以下公式计算：

$$\begin{matrix}\text{生活及其他}\\SO_2\text{排放量}\end{matrix}=\begin{matrix}\text{生活及其他}\\\text{煤炭消费量}\end{matrix}\times\text{含硫量}\times 0.8\times 2$$

工业SO_2排放量　指报告期内企业在燃料燃烧和生产工艺过程中排入大气的SO_2总量，计算公式为：

$$\begin{matrix}\text{工业}SO_2\\\text{排放量}\end{matrix}=\begin{matrix}\text{燃料燃烧过程中}\\SO_2\text{排放量}\end{matrix}+\begin{matrix}\text{生产工艺过程中}\\SO_2\text{排放量}\end{matrix}$$

工业烟尘排放量　指企业厂区内燃料燃烧过程中产生的烟气中夹带的颗粒物排放量。

生活及其他烟尘排放量　指除工业生产活动以外的所有社会、经济活动及公共设施的经营活动中燃烧所排放的烟尘纯重量。以生活及其他煤炭消费量为基础进行测算。

工业粉尘排放量　指企业在生产工艺过程中排放的能在空气中悬浮一定时间的固体颗粒物排放量。如钢铁企业的耐火材料粉尘、焦化企业的筛焦系统粉尘、烧结机的粉尘、石灰窑的粉尘、建材企业的水泥粉尘等。不包括电厂排入大气的烟尘。

工业固体废物产生量　指报告期内企业在生产过程中产生的固体状、半固体状和高浓度液体状废弃物的总量，包括危险废物、冶炼废渣、粉煤灰、炉渣、煤矸石、尾矿、放射性废物和其他废物等；不包括矿山开采的剥离废石和掘进废石(煤矸石和呈酸性或碱性的废石除外)。酸性或碱性废石指采掘的废石其流经水、雨淋水的pH值小于4或pH值大于10.5者。

危险废物　指列入国家危险废物名录或根据国家规定的危险废物鉴别标准和鉴别方法认定的，具有爆炸性、易燃性、易氧化性、毒性、腐蚀性、易传染疾病等危险特性之一的废物。

工业固体废物综合利用量　指报告期内企业通过回收、加工、循环、交换等方式，从固体废物中提取或者使其转化为可以利用的资源、能源和其他原材料的固体废物量(包括当年利用往年的工业固体废物贮存量)，如用作农业肥料、生产建筑材料、筑路等。综合利用量由原产生固体废物的单位统计。

工业固体废物综合利用率　指工业固体废物综合利用量占工业固体废物产生量(包括综合利用往年贮存量)的百分率。计算公式为：

$$\text{工业固体废物综合利用率}=\frac{\text{工业固体废物综合利用量}}{\text{工业固体废物产生量}+\text{综合利用往年贮存量}}\times 100\%$$

工业固体废物贮存量　指报告期内企业以综合利用或处置为目的，将固体废物暂时贮存或堆存在专设的贮存设施或专设的集中堆存场所内的数量。专设的固体废物贮存场所或贮存设施必须有防扩散、防流失、防渗漏、防止污染大气、水体的措施。

工业固体废物处置量　指报告期内企业将固体废物焚烧或者最终置于符合环境保护规定要求的场所，并不再回取的工业固体废物量(包括当年处置往年的工业固体废物贮存量)。处置方式有填埋(其中危险废物应安全填埋)、焚烧、专业贮存场(库)封场处理、深层灌注、回填矿井及海洋处置(经海洋管理部门同意投海处置)等。

工业固体废物排放量　指报告期内企业将所产生的固体废物排到固体废物污染防治设施、场所以外的数量，不包括矿山开采的剥离废石和掘进废石(煤矸石和呈酸性或碱性的废石除外)。

“三废”综合利用产品产值　指报告期内利用“三废”作为主要原料生产的产品价值(现行价)；已经销售或准备销售的应计算产品价值，留作生产自用的不应计算产品价值。

生活垃圾清运量　指报告期内收集和运送到垃圾处理厂(场)的生活垃圾数量。生活垃圾指城市日常生活或为城市日常生活提供服务的活动中产生的固体废物以及法律行政规定的视为城市生活垃圾的固体废物。包括：居民生活垃圾、商业垃圾、集市贸易市场垃圾、街道清扫垃圾、公共场所垃圾和机关、学校、厂矿等单位的生活垃圾。

生活垃圾无害化处理率　指报告期生活垃圾无害化处理量与生活垃圾产生量比率。在统计上，由于生活垃圾产生量不易取得，可用清运量代替。计算公式为：

$$\text{生活垃圾无害化处理率}=\frac{\text{生活垃圾无害化处理量}}{\text{生活垃圾产生量}}\times 100\%$$

土地调查面积　指行政区域内的土地调查总面积，包括农用地、建设用地和未利用地。

农用地　指直接用于农业生产的土地，包括耕地、园地、林地、牧草地及其他农用地。

人工林面积　指由人工播种、植苗或扦插造林形成的生长稳定，(一般造林3-5年后或飞机播种5-7年后)每公顷保存株数大于或等于造林设计植树株数80%或郁闭度0.20以上(含0.20)的林分面积。

造林总面积　指报告期内在荒山、荒地、沙丘、退耕地等一切可以造林的土地上，采用人工播种、飞机播种、植苗造林、分植造林等方法新植成片乔木林和灌木林，经过检查验收符合《造林技术规程》要求的单位面积株数，并按《中华人民共和国森林法实施条例》规定，成活率达85%以上(含85%，年降雨量在400毫米以下且无浇灌条件的地区造林成活率达70%以上)的总面积。四旁植树如一侧在四行以上，连片面积0.066公顷(一亩)以上，应统计在造林面积内。造林面积，通常按所有制(国有、国有集体合作、集体和个人)、造林方式(人工、飞机播种)、主要林种用途(用材林、经济林、防护林、薪炭林、特种用途林)分组进行统计。

用材林　指以生产木材为主要目的的森林和林木，包括以生产竹材为主要目的的竹林。

速生丰产林　指在凡具备一定条件的宜林地，经过科学规划设计，相对集中连片，采取集约经营方式，以达到高速度、高质量、高标准地提供林木产品的基地上，选用生长快、成材早、材质好、经济价值高的速生优良树种，通过各项技术措施培育，以缩短林木生长周期，提高林木生长量和木材质量，并达到部颁标准(每亩年生长量0.6立方米以上)或省颁标准而营造的森林。

经济林　指以生产果品，食用油料、饮料、调料，工业原料和药材为主要目的的林木。经济林是人们为了取得林木的果实、叶片、皮层、胶液等产品作为工业原料或者供食用所营造的林木，如油茶、油桐、核桃、樟树、花椒、茶、桑、果等。

防护林　指以防护为主要目的的森林、林木和灌木丛。包括水源涵养林，水土保持林，防风固沙林，农田、牧场防护林，护岸林，护路林等。

薪炭林　指以生产燃料为主要目的的林木。

特种用途林　指以国防、环境保护、科学实验等为主要目的的森林和林木。包括国防林、实验林、母树林、环境保护林、风景林，名胜古迹和革命纪念地的林木，自然保护区的森林。

天然林保护工程　是我国林业的“天”字号工程、一号工程,也是投资最大的生态工程。具体包括三个层次:全面停止长江上游、黄河上中游地区天然林采伐；大幅度调减东北、内蒙古等重点国有林区的木材产量；同时保护好其他地区的天然林资源。主要解决这些区域天然林资源的休养生息和恢复发展问题。

退耕还林还草工程　是我国林业建设上涉及面最广、

政策性最强、工序最复杂、群众参与度最高的生态建设工程。主要解决重点地区的水土流失问题。

三北和长江流域等重点防护林体系建设工程 三北和长江中下游地区等重点防护林体系建设工程,是我国涵盖面最大、内容最丰富的防护林体系建设工程。具体包括三北防护林四期工程、长江中下游及淮河太湖流域防护林二期工程、沿海防护林二期工程、珠江防护林二期工程、太行山绿化二期工程和平原绿化二期工程。主要解决三北地区的防沙治沙问题和其他区域各不相同的生态问题。

京津风沙源治理工程 环北京地区防沙治沙工程,是首都乃至中国的"形象工程",也是环京津生态圈建设的主体工程。虽然规模不大,但是意义特殊。主要解决首都周围地区的风沙危害问题。

野生动植物保护及自然保护区建设工程 野生动植物保护及自然保护区建设工程,是一个面向未来,着眼长远,具有多项战略意义的生态保护工程,也是呼应国际大气候、树立中国良好国际形象的"外交工程"。主要解决基因保存、生物多样性保护、自然保护、湿地保护等问题。

重点地区速生丰产用材林基地建设工程 重点地区以速生丰产用材林为主的林业产业基地建设工程,是我国林业产业体系建设的骨干工程,也是增强林业实力的"希望工程"。主要解决我国木材和林产品的供应问题。

湿地 指天然或人工、长久或暂时性的沼泽地、泥炭地或水域地带,包括静止或流动、淡水、半咸水、咸水体,低潮时水深不超过6米的水域以及海岸地带地区的珊瑚滩和海草床、滩涂、红树林、河口、河流、淡水沼泽、沼泽森林、湖泊、盐沼及盐湖。

红树林 指生长在热带、亚热带低能海岸潮间带上部,受周期性潮水浸淹,以红树植物为主体的常绿灌木或乔木组成的潮滩湿地木本生物群落。

自然保护区 指对有代表性的自然生态系统、珍稀濒危野生动植物物种的天然分布区、水源涵养区、有特殊意义的自然历史遗迹等保护对象所在的陆地、陆地水体或海域,依法划出一定面积进行特殊保护和管理的区域。以县及县以上各级人民政府正式批准建立的自然保护区为准(包括"六五"以前由部门或"革委会"批准且现仍存在的自然保护区)。风景名胜区、文物保护区不计在内。

生态示范区 指省级以上环境保护行政主管部门批准,以省、地、县政府为主按批准的生态示范区建设规划实施的行政区域。包括已经过国家或省级环境保护行政主管部门验收的和正在开展试点工作的。

滑坡 指斜坡上不稳定的岩土体在重力作用下沿一定软面(或滑动带)整体向下滑动的物理地质现象。地表水和地下水的作用以及人为的不合理工程活动对斜坡岩、土体稳定性的破坏,经常是促使滑坡发生的主要因素。在露天采矿、水利、铁路、公路等工程中,滑坡往往造成严重危害。

崩塌 指陡坡上大块的岩土体在重力作用下突然脱离母体崩落的物理地质现象。它可因多裂隙的岩体经强烈的物理风化、雨水渗入或地震而造成,往往毁坏建筑物,堵塞河道或交通路线。

泥石流 指山地突然爆发的包含大量泥沙、石块的特殊洪流,多见于半干旱山地高原地区。其形成条件是地形陡峻,松散堆积物丰富,有特大暴雨或大量冰融水的流出。

地面塌陷 指地表岩、土体在自然或人为因素作用下向下陷落,并在地面形成塌陷坑(洞)的一种动力地质现象。由于其发育的地质条件和作用因素的不同,地面塌陷可分为:岩溶塌陷、非岩溶塌陷。

环境污染与破坏事故 指由于违反环境保护法规的经济、社会活动与行为,以及意外因素的影响或不可抗拒的自然灾害等原因,致使环境受到污染,国家重点保护的野生动植物、自然保护区受到破坏,人体健康受到危害,社会经济和人民财产受到损失,造成不良社会影响的突发性事件。

环境污染治理投资 指在工业污染源治理和城市环境基础设施建设的资金投入中,用于形成固定资产的资金。包括工业新老污染源治理工程投资、建设项目"三同时"环保投资,以及城市环境基础设施建设所投入的资金。

营林固定资产投资 指在报告期内进行的营林基本建设和营林更新改造活动投资。

上年末结余资金 指在上年资金来源中没有形成固定资产投资额而结余的资金。包括尚未用到工程上去的材料价值、未开始安装的需要安装设备价值及结存的现金和银行存款等。

本年完成投资 指从本年1月1日起至本年最后一天止完成的全部投资额。本年完成投资是反映本年的实际投资规模,计算有关投资效果,进行年度国民经济平衡分析的重要指标。

Explanatory Notes on Main Statistical Indicators

Total Water Resources refers to total volume of water resources measured as run-off for surface water from rainfall and recharge for groundwater in a given area, excluding transit water.

Surface Water Resources refers to total renewable resources which exist in rivers, lakes, glaciers and other collectors from rainfall and are measured as run-off of rivers.

Groundwater Resources refers to replenishment of aquifers with rainfall and surface water.

Duplicated Measurement Between Surface Water and Groundwater refers to mutual exchange between surface water and groundwater, i.e. run-off of rivers includes some depletion with groundwater while groundwater includes some replenishment with surface water.

Water Supply refers to gross water supply by supply systems from sources to consumers, including losses during distribution.

Surface Water Supply refers to withdrawals by surface water supply system, broken down with storage, flow, pumping and transfer. Supply from storage projects includes withdrawals from reservoirs; supply from flow includes withdrawals from rivers and lakes with natural flows no matter if there are locks or not; supply from pumping projects includes withdrawals from rivers or lakes with pumping stations; and supply from transfer refers to water supplies transferred from first-level regions of water resources or independent river drainage areas to others, and should not be covered under supplies of storage, flow and pumping.

Groundwater Supply refers to withdrawals from supplying wells, broken down with shallow layer freshwater, deep layer freshwater and slightly brackish water. Groundwater supply for urban areas includes water mining by both waterworks and own wells of enterprises.

Other Water Supply Sources include supplies by wastewater treatment, rain collection, seawater desalinization and other water projects.

Water Use refers to gross water use distributed to users, including loss during transportation, broken down with use by agriculture, industry, living consumption and biological protection.

Water Use by Agriculture includes uses of water by irrigation of farming fields and by forestry, animal husbandry and fishing. Water use by forestry, animal husbandry and fishing includes irrigation of forestry and orchards, irrigation of grassland and replenishment of fishing pools.

Water Use by Industry refers to new withdrawals of water, excluding reuse of water within enterprises.

Water Use by Living Consumption includes use of water for living consumption in both urban and rural areas. Urban water use by living consumption is composed of household use and public use (including services, commerce, restaurants, cargo transportation, posts, telecommunication and construction). Rural water use by living consumption includes both households and animals.

Water Use by Biological Protection includes replenishment of rivers and lakes and use for urban environment.

Waste Water Discharged by Industry refers to the volume of waste water discharged by industrial enterprises through all their outlets, including waste water from production process, directly cooled water, groundwater from mining wells which does not meet discharge standards and sewage from households mixed with waste water produced by industrial activities, but excluding indirectly cooled water discharged (It should be included if the discharge is not separated with waste water).

Waste Water Directly Discharged into Sea refers to the volume of waste water directly discharged into sea through outlets of enterprises situated by sea without going through municipal sewerage networks or any other intermediates or being affected by any other water bodies.

Industrial Waste Water Meeting Discharge Standards refers to volume of industrial waste water discharge which, with or without treatment, reaches national or local standards with regard to all pollutants.

Ratio of Industrial Waste Water Meeting Discharge Standards refers to percentage of industrial waste water meeting discharge standards over total industrial waste water discharge. It is calculated as:

Ratio of industrial waste water meeting discharge standards = industrial waste water meeting discharge standards / total industrial waste water discharge

Urban Non-industrial Waste Water Discharge refers to annual discharge of non-industrial waste water by urban households. It is estimated by per capita coefficient using the formula:

Urban non-industrial waste water discharge = urban non-industrial waste water discharge coefficient× urban non-agricultural population ×365

Volume of Chemical Oxygen Demand (COD) Generated by Urban Non-industrial Waster Water refers to chemical oxygen demand generated through the annual discharge of non-industrial waste water by urban households. It is estimated as:

Volume of chemical oxygen demand (cod) generated by urban non-industrial waster water = Coefficient of COD generated through urban non-industrial waste water × urban non-agricultural population × 365

Chemical Oxygen Demand (COD) refers to index of

water pollution measuring the mass concentration of oxygen consumed by the chemical breakdown of organic and inorganic matter.

Industrial Waste Air Emission refers to discharge into atmosphere of waste air containing pollutants generated from fuel burning and production process in enterprises within a given period of time. It is calculated at standard status (273K, 101325Pa) as:

Industrial waste air emission = emission through fuel burning + emission through production process

SO_2 Emission through Non-industrial and Other Activities is calculated on the basis of consumption of coal by households and other activities and the sulphur content of coal with the following formula:

SO_2 emission through non-industrial and other activities = consumption of coal by households and other activities× sulphur content ×0.8 ×2

SO_2 Emission through Industrial Activities refers to volume of sulphur dioxide emission from fuel burning and production process by enterprises during a given period of time. It is calculated as:

SO_2 emission through industrial activities = SO_2 emission from fuel burning + SO_2 emission from production process

Industrial Soot Emission refers to volume of soot in smoke emitted in process of fuel burning in premises of enterprises.

Soot Emission by Consumption and Others refers to net volume of soot emitted by fuel burning from all social and economic activities and operation of public facilities other than industrial activities. It is calculated on the basis of coal consumption by households and others.

Industrial Dust Emission refers to volume of dust emitted by production process of enterprises and suspended in the air for a given period of time, including dust from refractory material of iron and steel works, dust from coke-screening systems and sintering machines of coke plants, dust from lime kilns and dust from cement production in building material enterprises, but excluding soot and dust emitted from power plants.

Industrial Solid Wastes Produced refers to total volume of solid, semi-solid and high concentration liquid residues produced by industrial enterprises from production process in a given period of time, including hazardous wastes, slag, coal ash, gangue, tailings, radioactive residues and other wastes, but excluding stones stripped or dug out in mining (gangue and acid or alkaline stones not included). A stone is acid or alkaline depending on the pH value of the water below 4 or above 10.5 when the stone is in, or soaked by, the water.

Hazardous Wastes refers to those included in the national hazardous wastes catalogue or specified as any one of the following properties in the national hazardous wastes identification standards: explosive, ignitable, oxidizable, toxic, corrosive or liable to cause infectious diseases or lead to other dangers.

Industrial Solid Wastes Utilized refers to volume of solid wastes from which useful materials can be extracted or which can be converted into usable resources, energy or other materials by means of reclamation, processing, recycling and exchange (including utilizing in the year the stocks of industrial solid wastes of the previous year). Examples of such utilizations include fertilizers, building materials and road materials. The information shall be collected by the producing units of the wastes.

Ratio of Industrial Solid Wastes Utilized refers to the percentage of industrial solid wastes utilized over industrial solid wastes produced (including stocks of the previous years). It is calculated as:

Ratio of industrial solid wastes utilized = volume of industrial solid wastes utilized / (industrial solid wastes produced + stock of previous years) ×100%

Stocks of Industrial Solid Wastes refers to volume of solid wastes placed in special facilities or special sites for purposes of utilization or disposal. The sites or facilities should take measures against dispersion, loss, seepage, and air and water contamination.

Industrial Solid Wastes Disposed refers to quantity of industrial solid wastes which are burnt or placed ultimately in the sites meeting the requirements for environmental protection and not salvaged or recycled (including disposition in the year of those wastes of previous years). The disposition includes landfill (Safe landfills should be conducted for hazardous wastes), incineration, containment spaces, deep underground disposal, backfill in mining pits and disposal at sea.

Industrial Solid Wastes Discharged refers to volume of industrial solid wastes discharged by producing enterprises to disposal facilities or to other sites. The wastes exclude stones stripped or dug from mining (gangue and acid or alkaline waste stones not included).

Output Value of Products Made from Waste Gas, Waste Water and Solid Wastes refers current value of products with waste gas, waste water and solid wastes as main materials of production. Products sold and ready to sell shall be included while those produced for own use shall not be included.

Consumption Wastes Transported refers to volume of consumption wastes collected and transported to disposal factories or sites. Consumption wastes are solid wastes produced from urban households or from service activities for urban households, and solid wastes regarded by laws and regulations as urban consumption wastes, including those from households, commercial activities, markets, cleaning of streets, public sites, offices, schools, factories, mining units and other sources.

Ratio of Consumption Wastes Treated refers to consumption wastes treated over that produced. In practical statistics, as it is difficult to estimate, the volume of consumption wastes produced is replaced with that transported. It is calculated as:

Ratio of consumption wastes treated = consumption wastes treated / consumption wastes produced × 100%

Area under Land Survey refers to the total area of land, under the land survey, within the jurisdiction of the administrative region, including land for agriculture use, land for construction and unused land.

Land for Agriculture Use refers to land directly used for agriculture production, including land for cultivation, gardening, forests, herbage and other agriculture activities.

Cultivated Land at Beginning (End) of the Year refers to total area of cultivated land within the geographic area of statistical survey at the beginning (end) of the year.

Increase of Cultivated Land during the Year refers to the increase of cultivated land during the year as a result of land preparation, reclamation, new development, adjustment of agriculture structure and other reasons.

Decrease of Cultivated Land during the Year refers to the decrease of cultivated land during the year as a result of adjustment of agriculture structure, construction projects, natural disasters, conversion for ecological purpose, and other reasons.

Area of Man-made Forests refer to the area of stable growing forests, planted manually or by airplanes, with a survival rate of 80% or higher of the designed number of trees per hectare, or with a canopy density of or above 0.20 after 3-5 years of manual planting or 5-7 years of airplane planting.

Total Area of Afforestation refers to the total area of land suitable for afforestation, including barren hills, idle land, sand dunes, "grain for green" land, on which acres of arbores or bushes are planted through manual planting, airplane planting, plant seedlings, etc. in accordance with the required density standards of the *Technical Procedures of Afforestation,* and with a survival rate of over 85% in line with the *Implementing Rules of the Forest Law of the People's Republic of China* (or a survival rate of 75% in areas with less that 400 mm of annual rainfall and without irrigation facilities). Included in the this category are trees planted alone the roadsides, riversides, or next to houses that occupy an area over 0.066 hectares, or where more than 4 lines of trees are planted. Total area of afforestation is further classified by ownership (state-owned, state-collective, collective or private), by approach of planting (manual, airplane), and by type of forests (timber, by-products, protection, fuel, special use, etc.).

Timber Forests refer to forests which is mainly for the production of timber, including bamboo groves planted to harvest bamboos.

Fast-growing Timber Forests refer to forests intensively planted and managed through scientific planning to produce fast-growing, high quality timber product. In these forest bases, Superior species of trees with shorter growing span, good quality and high economic value are planted and grow under various technological measures so as to meet the standards set by the Ministry of Forest (annual growth of over 0.6 cubic metres per 0.066 hectares of trees) of by the provincial authorities.

By-product Forests refer to forests that mainly produce fruits, nuts, edible oil, beverages, indigents, raw materials and medicine materials. By-product forests are planted to harvest the fruits, leaves, bark or liquid of trees, and consume them as food or raw materials for the manufacturing industry, such as tea-oil trees, tung oil trees, walnut trees, camphor trees, tea bushes, mulberry trees, fruit trees, etc.

Protection Forests refer to forests, trees and bushes planted mainly for protection or preservation purpose, including water resource conservation forests, water and soil conservation forests, windbreak and dune-fixing forests, farmland and pasture protection forests, riverside protection forests, roadside protection forests, etc.

Fuel Forests refer to forests planted mainly for fuels.

Forests for Special Purpose refer to forests planted mainly for national defence, environment protection or scientific experiments, including national defence forests, experimental forests, mother-tree forests, environment protection forests, scenery forests, trees in historical or scenic spots, forests in natural reserves.

Project on Preservation of Natural Forests is the Number One ecological project in China's forest industry that involves the largest investment. It consists of 3 components: 1) Complete halt of all cutting and logging activities in the natural forests at the upper stream of Yangtze River and the upper and middle streams of the Yellow River. 2) Significant reduction of timber production of key state forest zones in northeast provinces and in Inner Mongolia. 3) Better protection of natural forests in other regions through rehabilitation programmes.

Projects on Converting Cultivated Land to Forests and Grassland (Grain for Green Projects) aiming at preventing soil erosion in key regions, these projects are ecological construction projects in the development of forest industry that have the widest coverage and most sophisticated procedures, with strong policy implications and most active participation of the people.

Projects on Protection Forests in North China and Yangtze River Basin covering the widest areas in China with a rich variety of contents, these projects aim at solving the problem of sand and dust in northeastern China, northern China and northwestern China and the ecological issues in other areas. More specifically, they include phase IV of project on North China protection forests, phase II of project on protection forests at the middle and lower streams of Yangtze River and at the Huihe River and Taihu Lake valley, phase II of project on coastal protection forests, phase II of project on Pearl River protection forests, phase II project on greenery of Taihang Mountain and phase II projects on greenery of plains.

Projects on Harnessing Source of Sand and Dust in Beijing and Tianjin these Beijing-ring projects aim at harnessing the sand and dust weather around Beijing and its vicinities. As the key to the development of Beijing-Tianjin ecological zone, these projects are of particular importance as it concerns the image of China's capital city and the whole country.

Projects on Preserving Wild Animals and Plants and on Construction of Nature Reserves aiming at gene preservation and protection of bio-diversity, nature and wetlands, these projects look into the future with strategic perspective and are integrated with international trends.

Projects on Fast-growing Timber Forests Bases in Key Regions these are key projects for the forest industry to strengthen its capacity in supplying more timber and forest by-products.

Wetlands refer to marshland and peat bog, whether natural or man-made, permanent or temporary; water covered areas, whether stagnant or flowing, with fresh or semi-fresh or salty water that is less than 6 metres deep at low tide; as well as coral beach, weed beach, mud beach, mangrove, river outlet, rivers, fresh-water marshland, marshland forests, lakes, salty bog and salt lakes along the coastal areas.

Mangrove refer to evergreen woody plants or plant communities in tropical or sub-tropical zones which live between the sea and the land in areas which are inundated by tides.

Nature Reserves refer to certain areas of land, waters or sea that are representative in natural ecological systems, or are natural habitats for rare or endangered wild animals or plants, or water conservation zones, or the location of important natural or historic relics, which are demarked by law and put under special protection and management. Nature reserves are designated by the formal approval of governments at and above county level (including those approved by relevant departments or "revolutionary committees" before 1980). Scenic spots and cultural preservation zones are not included.

Ecological Demonstration Zones refer to administrative areas approved by the environment protection agencies of central and provincial governments and established by provincial, prefecture or county governments in line with the approved programme for ecological demonstration zones. They include those evaluated and accepted by the environment protection agencies of central and provincial governments and those under pilot development stage.

Landslides refer to the geological phenomenon of unstable rocks and earth on slopes sliding down along certain soft surface as a result of gravitational force. Role of surface water and underground water, and destruction of the stability of slopes by irrational construction work are usually main factors triggering the landslides. Several damages are often caused by landslides in open mining, in water conservancy projects, and in the construction of railways and highways.

Collapse refers to the geological phenomenon of large mass of rocks or earth suddenly collapsing from the mountain or cliff as a result of gravitational force. Usually caused by weathering of rocks, permeance of rain or earthquakes, collapse often destructs buildings and blocks river course or transport routes.

Mud-rock Flow refers to the sudden rush of flood torrents containing large amount of mud and rocks in mountainous areas. It is found mostly in semi-arid hills or plateaus. High and precipitous topographic features, loose soil mass, heavy rains or melting water contribute to the mud-rock flow.

Land Subside refers to the geological phenomenon of surface rocks or earth subsiding into holes or pits as a result of natural or human factors. Land subside can be classified as karst subside and non-karst subside.

Environment Pollution and Destruction Accidents refer to sudden accidents, due to economic or social activities that are in contrast to environment protection laws or due to unforeseen factors or natural disasters, that lead to the environment pollution, the destruction of protected wild animals, plants or nature reserves, the damage to human health, the economic and property losses, and the negative impact on the society.

Investment in Environment Pollution Harnessing Projects refers to the proportion of investment in fixed assets in the total investment in harnessing industrial pollution and in the construction of urban environment infrastructure facilities. It includes investment in harnessing sources of industrial pollution, investment in environment protection facilities designed concurrently with construction projects, and investment in urban environment infrastructure facilities.

Investment in Fixed Assets for Afforestation refers to the investment in capital construction and updating projects in afforestation during the reference period.

Unspent Capitals from Last Year refer to capitals from the last year that have not been invested in the fixed assets, including value of materials that have not been used yet, the value of equipment yet to be installed, as well as cash in hand and bank deposits.

Completed Investment during the Year reflecting the actual size of investment completed during January 1 and December 31 of the reference year, this indicator is important in estimating investment efficiency and in making annual analysis of the performance of the national economy.

13

农　业
Agriculture

简 要 说 明

一、本篇资料的主要内容及统计范围

本篇资料反映我国农业生产和农村经济的基本情况，内容主要包括乡村从业人员、耕地、农业机械拥有量、农林牧渔业产值、主要农产品产量、水利设施与除涝治碱、农村居民家庭拥有生产性固定资产、国营农场基本情况等方面的统计资料。

农业统计范围包括全社会除军马生产及农业科研机构进行的农业生产以外的所有农业生产活动。即农村各种经济组织和农户经营的农林牧渔业生产活动；各种专业性农、林、牧、渔场的农业生产活动；国家各级机关、团体、学校、部队进行的农业生产活动；集体所有制的乡、镇、村办农场的农业生产活动；以及工矿企业经营的农、林、牧、渔业生产活动。

1.农业：指对各种农作物的种植活动。包括谷物、豆类、薯类、棉花、油料、糖料、麻类、烟叶、蔬菜、园艺作物、水果、坚果、饮料和香料作物、中草药及其他作物的种植。

2.林业：包括林木的栽培（不包括茶园、桑园和果园的栽培、管理和收获等活动），木材和竹材的采运，林产品的采集。

3.畜牧业：包括牲畜饲养和放牧，家禽饲养以及野生动物的捕猎和饲养。

4.渔业：包括水生动物和海藻类植物的养殖和捕捞。

农村社会经济统计范围包括除县城关镇以外所有乡镇的社会经济活动。

二、本篇资料来源及调查方法

1.农村基层组织、乡村从业人员和农业生产基本情况等（13-1至13-8表、13-15至13-22表），由国家统计局农村社会经济调查司根据《农林牧渔业统计报表制度》、《农业产值和价格综合统计报表制度》、《乡村社会经济调查方案》和《农产量抽样调查制度》的有关资料整理提供。

《农林牧渔业统计报表制度》是各省、自治区、直辖市统计局上报国家统计局的全面报表，由各级统计部门根据当地实际情况，采取抽样调查、重点调查或全面调查的办法搜集资料并逐层上报；或利用同级业务部门统计资料。如农业生产条件中的部分指标及林业生产情况、渔业生产情况等指标取自同级业务部门的统计资料。

《农产量抽样调查制度》是国家统计局为取得高质量的农产品产量等相关指标数据，在全国范围内统一抽选样本调查、推算，并由直属调查队伍实施的抽样调查制度。主要以农业普查资料作为有关标识编制抽样框，采取综合运用多阶段、多相、分层、系统随机抽样等多种方法确定调查网点，选取样本，利用了多目标与规模成比例的概率抽样确定样本容量，开展多主题调查。全国共抽选了约2万个村，13万个样本地块进行实割实测调查，并运用这些样本科学地推算全国粮食产量数据，在95%的概率把握程度下，误差系数不超过±2%。农产量抽样调查实行样本轮换制度，五年为一个周期。粮食产量、棉花产量、播种面积、主要畜产品产量等指标来源于《农产量抽样调查制度》。

《乡村社会经济调查方案》是国家统计局为了解乡镇社会经济基本情况、农村劳动力总量规模和转移情况、以及农村固定资产投资情况等内容而专门设置的统计调查制度。制度规定对镇基本情况每年进行一次全面调查，对乡、村基本情况每三年进行一次全面调查；其他内容采用抽样调查方法，调查网点包括乡镇级调查网点、村级调查网点和住户调查网点，前两套网点分别是以全省乡镇一级单位编制抽样框和以全省村一级单位编制抽样框，抽选样本进行直接调查，住户调查网点与农村住户调查网点相同。

2.农村家庭固定资产、经营耕地及农产品出售情况（13-12至13-14表、13-25表、13-26表），由国家统计局农村社会经济调查司根据《农村住户调查方案》的有关资料整理提供。《农村住户调查方案》的说明见本年鉴“十、人民生活”部分。

3.国营农场基本情况资料主要取材于农业部农垦局汇总的统计报表。其调查范围涉及全国除西藏外的30个省、自治区、直辖市。统计方法为逐级上报、全面汇总。指标设置及统计口径均与国家统计局一致。

4.灌溉、水库和除涝、治水、治碱情况及各地区水利设施和除涝、治碱面积资料，主要来源于水利部汇总的统计报表。其统计范围包括各省、自治区、直辖市。资料收集以县为基本统计单位，采取逐级汇总上报的方式。有些特殊指标如灌区数、大型水库、跨县的中小型水库，由地区直接统计，上报省水利厅。

5.受灾面积和成灾面积是与民政部、水利部、国家气象局等部门共同核定的数据。

Brief Introduction

I. Main Content and Statistical Coverage

The data in this chapter show the basic conditions of agricultural production and rural economy, including mainly rural employed labour force, cultivated land, quantity of agricultural machinery, output of farming, forestry, animal husbandry and fishery, output of major products, facilities of water conservancy and efforts to eliminate water-logging and combat alkalinity, productive fixed assets owned by the rural households, basic conditions of the state-owned farms, and basic conditions of township enterprises.

Statistics on agriculture cover all agricultural production activities except horse raising for military purpose and activities undertaken by agriculture research institutions. Included in agriculture statistics are production activities in crop cultivation, forestry, animal husbandry and fishery undertaken by rural economic units of various types and by rural households, production activities of farms specializing in crop cultivation, forestry, animal husbandry and fishery; production activities undertaken by government agencies, institutions, schools and military units; production activities in agriculture undertaken by collective farms run by townships and villages; and production activities in crop cultivation, forestry, animal husbandry and fishery undertaken by manufacturing and mining enterprises.

(1) Agriculture: refers to cultivation of farms crops, including cereals, beans, tuber crops, cotton, oil-bearing crops, sugar crops, hemp, tobacco leaves, vegetables, gardening plants, fruits, nuts, crops for beverages and for perfumes, medicinal herbs and other farm crops.

(2) Forestry: includes the planting of trees (excluding the operation on tea plantations, mulberry fields and orchards), felling and transport of timber and bamboo and collection of forest products.

(3) Animal husbandry: includes the raising and grazing of domestic animals and poultry, and the hunting and raising of wild animals.

(4) Fishery: includes cultivation and catching of aquatic animals and seaweed.

The rural social and economic statistics cover social and economic activities in all townships except that taking place in county towns.

II. Source of Data and Survey Methodology

(1) Data on rural grassroots units, employed labour force and agricultural production are provided by the Department of Rural Socio-economic Surveys, NBS using data from the *Comprehensive Statistical Reporting on Farming, Forestry, Animal Husbandry and Fishery*, the *Comprehensive Statistical Reporting on Agricultural Output and Prices*, the *Rural Social and Economic Survey*, and the *Sample Survey of Farm Crops.*

Comprehensive Statistical Reporting on Farming, Forestry, Animal Husbandry and Fishery is a comprehensive reporting program reported by provincial statistical bureaus to the National Bureau of Statistics. Data required in this reporting program are collected by statistical offices at all levels by means of sample surveys, surveys of key units or full enumeration depending on the local circumstances, or estimated by using information from other government agencies at the same level or from the sample survey of farm crops and rural household survey conducted by NBS. For instance, some data on condition of agriculture production and on forestry and fishery are obtained from statistics collected by other government agencies at the same level.

Sample Survey of Farm Crops is a nation-wide survey designed by NBS and implemented by sample survey teams throughout China with unified sample selection and estimation procedure, in order to obtain high quality data on grain production and related statistics. Using data from the agriculture census as sampling frame, a total of 130,000 sample plots are selected from some 20,000 villages in the country through a comprehensive multi-stage and multi-phase stratified systematic sampling programme. Actual crop cutting and measuring is conducted on these plots to estimate the national production. The survey is characterized by a multi-purpose probability proportional to size sample design that keeps sampling error to ±2% with the confidence probability as 95%. A rotation scheme is used in the sample survey on farm crops with the cycle of a complete rotation being 5 years. Data on crop production, cotton production, crop planting acreage and production of major animal husbandry products are collected are from the *Sample Survey of Farm Crops*.

Rural Social and Economic Survey is a special survey designed by the NBS to understand the basic condition of social and economic activities at township level, the size and transfer of total rural labour force and investment in fixed assets in rural areas. Under this survey programme, a complete survey is conducted every year to collect information on basic condition of social and economic activities for all towns, a similar survey is conducted every 3 years at township and village levels, while sample surveys are used to collect information on other items with the same sampling units as in the Rural Household Survey.

(2) Data on the fixed assets, cultivated land and sales of farm products of rural households are collected and compiled by the Department of Rural Socio-economic Surveys, NBS through the *Rural Household Survey Programme*. Please refer to Chapter 10 (People's Livelihood) of the Yearbook for description of the *Rural Household Survey Programme*.

(3) Data on the basic conditions of the state-owned farms come from the statistical reports tabulated by the Bureau of Reclamation, Ministry of Agriculture. The statistical coverage includes 30 provinces, autonomous regions and municipalities directly under the central government; except Tibet. Data are collected from the grassroots units in accordance with the statistical reporting scheme and tabulated and reported level by level. The content of indicators and calculation methods are consistent with those stipulated by the National Bureau of Statistics.

(4) Data on irrigation and reservoirs, the data on the efforts to eliminate water-logging, prevent floods by water control and combat alkalinity as well as the data on the facilities of water conservancy and the area of water-logging eliminated and the improved area of saline-alkaline land come mainly from statistical reports of the Ministry of Water Conservancy. The statistical coverage includes provinces, autonomous regions and municipalities directly under the central government. County is the basic statistical unit. The data are collected from the counties in accordance with the statistical reporting scheme and tabulated and reported level by level. Data on some special indicators such as the number of irrigated areas, large reservoirs and the medium-sized and small reservoirs that cut across counties are collected directly by the prefectures and reported to the water conservancy departments of the provinces.

(5) Data on disaster-covered areas and disaster-affected areas are figures jointly confirmed by NBS in consultation with Ministry of Civil affairs, Ministry of Water Conservancy and National Bureau of Meteorology.

13-1 农村基层组织和农业基本情况

Basic Conditions of Rural Grass-root Units and Agriculture

指　标	Item	1999	2000	2004	2005
乡镇数 (个)	Number of Township and Town Governments (unit)	44741	43735	36952	35509
#镇数	Number of Town Governments	19184	19692	19171	18888
村民委员会 (个)	Number of Villagers' Committees (unit)	737429	734715	652718	640139
乡村户数 (万户)	Number of Rural Households (10 000 units)	23810.5	24148.7	24971.4	25222.6
乡村从业人员 (万人)	Number of Rural Laborers (10 000 persons)	46896.5	47962.1	49695.3	50387.3
男	Male	24995.7	25517.8	26525.8	26930.6
女	Female	21900.8	22444.3	23169.5	23456.7
按行业分乡村从业人员(万人)	Number of Rural Laborers by Sector (10 000 persons)	46896.5	47962.1	49695.3	50387.3
农林牧渔业	Farming, Forestry, Animal Husbandry & Fishery	32911.8	32797.5	30596.0	29975.5
工业	Industry	3953.0	4108.6	5438.9	6011.5
建筑业	Construction	2531.9	2691.7	3380.5	3653.2
交通运输业、仓储及邮电通信业	Transport, Storage, Post and Telecommunication Services	1115.8	1170.6	1475.9	1567.3
批发零售贸易业餐饮业	Wholesale, Retail Trade and Catering Services	1584.6	1751.8	2701.6	2937.7
其他非农行业	Other Non-agricultural Trades	4799.4	5441.9	6102.4	6242.0
农业机械总动力 (万千瓦)	Total Agricultural Machinery Power (10 000 kw)	48996.1	52573.6	64027.9	68397.8
农用大中型拖拉机 (台)	Number of Large and Medium Agricultural Tractors (unit)	784216	974547	1118636	1395981
农用大中型拖拉机动力 (万千瓦)	Capacity of Large and Medium Agricultural Tractors (10 000 kw)	2772.8	3161.1	3713.1	4293.5
小型拖拉机 (万台)	Number of Mini-tractors (10 000 unit)	1200.3	1264.4	1454.9	1526.9
小型拖拉机动力 (万千瓦)	Capacity of Mini-tractors (10 000 kw)	11008.9	11663.9	13855.4	14660.9
大中型拖拉机配套农具 (万部)	Number of Large and Medium Tractor Towing Farm Machinery (10 000 unit)	132.0	140.0	188.7	226.2
小型拖拉机配套农具 (万部)	Mini-Tractor Towing Farm Machinery (10 000 unit)	1621.0	1788.8	2309.7	2465.0
农用排灌柴油机 (万台)	Number of Diesel Engines (10 000 unit)	645.0	688.1	777.5	809.9
农用排灌柴油机动力(万千瓦)	Capacity of Diesel Engines (10 000 kw)	4934.6	5232.6	5804.2	6034.0
渔用机动船 (艘)	Number of Motorized Fishing Boats (unit)	417379	459888	486878	439604
渔用机动船动力 (万千瓦)	Capacity of Motorized Fishing Boats (10 000 kw)	1253.1	1338.7	1384.2	1376.1
有效灌溉面积 (千公顷)	Irrigated Area (1 000 hectares)	53158	53820	54478	55029
化肥施用量 (万吨)	Consumption of Chemical Fertilizers (10 000 tons)	4124.3	4146.4	4636.6	4766.2
乡村办水电站个数 (个)	Number of Hydropower Stations in Rural Areas (unit)	31678	29962	27115	26726
乡村办水电站发电能力 (万千瓦)	Generating Capacity of Hydropower Station in Rural Areas (10 000 kw)	664.1	698.5	993.8	1099.2
农村用电量 (亿千瓦小时)	Electricity Consumed in Rural Areas(100 million kwh)	2173.4	2421.3	3933.0	4375.7
农作物总播种面积 (千公顷)	Total Sown Area (1 000 hectares)	156373	156300	153553	155488
粮食	Grain Crops	113161	108463	101606	104278
谷物	Cereal	91617	85264	79350	81874
#稻谷	Rice	31284	29962	28379	28847
小麦	Wheat	28855	26653	21626	22793
玉米	Corn	25904	23056	25446	26358
豆类	Beans	11190	12660	12799	12901
薯类	Tubers	10355	10538	9457	9503
油料	Oil-bearing Crops	13906	15400	14431	14318
棉花	Cotton	3726	4041	5693	5062
麻类	Fiber Crops	205	262	332	335
糖料	Sugar Crops	1644	1514	1568	1564
烟叶	Tobacco	1374	1437	1266	1363
蔬菜	Vegetables	13347	15237	17560	17721
茶园面积 (千公顷)	Area of Tea Plantations (1 000 hectares)	1130	1089	1262	1352
果园面积 (千公顷)	Area of Orchards (1 000 hectares)	8667	8932	9768	10035

注：2002年及以后大中型拖拉机中不包括变形拖拉机。

a) Number of large and medium agricultural tractors excluded the transfiguration tractors since 2002.

13-2 主要农牧渔业生产情况

Output of Farming, Animal Husbandry and Fishery

指标	Item	2000	2001	2002	2003	2004	2005
农产品产量 (万吨)	Output of Farm Products (10 000 tons)						
粮食	Grain	46217.5	45263.7	45705.8	43069.5	46946.9	48402.2
谷物	Cereal	40522.4	39648.2	39798.7	37428.7	41157.2	42776.0
#稻谷	Rice	18790.8	17758.0	17453.9	16065.6	17908.8	18058.8
小麦	Wheat	9963.6	9387.3	9029.0	8648.8	9195.2	9744.5
玉米	Corn	10600.0	11408.8	12130.8	11583.0	13028.7	13936.5
豆类	Beans	2010.0	2052.8	2241.2	2127.5	2232.1	2157.7
薯类	Tubers	3685.2	3563.1	3665.9	3513.3	3557.7	3468.5
油料	Oil-bearing Crops	2954.8	2864.9	2897.2	2811.0	3065.9	3077.1
#花生	Peanuts	1443.7	1441.6	1481.8	1342.0	1434.2	1434.2
油菜籽	Rapeseeds	1138.1	1133.1	1055.2	1142.0	1318.2	1305.2
芝麻	Sesame	81.1	80.4	89.5	59.3	70.4	62.5
棉花	Cotton	441.7	532.4	491.6	486.0	632.4	571.4
麻类	Fiber Crops	52.9	68.1	96.4	85.3	107.4	110.5
#黄红麻	Jute and Ambary Hemp	12.6	10.6	15.9	10.0	8.7	8.3
甘蔗	Sugarcane	6828.0	7566.3	9010.7	9023.5	8984.9	8663.8
甜菜	Beetroots	807.3	1088.9	1282.0	618.2	585.7	788.1
烟叶	Tobacco	255.2	235.0	244.7	225.7	240.6	268.3
#烤烟	Flue-Cured Tobacco	223.8	204.5	213.5	201.5	216.3	243.5
蚕茧	Silkworm Cocoons	54.8	65.5	69.8	66.7	73.1	78.0
#桑蚕茧	Mulberry Silkworm Cocoons	50.1	60.2	64.5	61.1	67.7	71.3
茶叶	Tea	68.3	70.2	74.5	76.8	83.5	93.5
水果	Fruits	6225.1	6658.0	6952.0	14517.4	15340.9	16120.1
农产品单位面积产量 (公斤/公顷)	Output of Farm Products per Hectare (kg/hectare)						
谷物	Cereal	4753	4800	4885	4873	5187	5225
棉花	Cotton	1093	1107	1175	951	1111	1129
花生	Peanuts	2973	2888	3011	2654	3022	3076
油菜籽	Rapeseeds	1519	1597	1477	1582	1813	1793
芝麻	Sesames	1034	1061	1180	863	1128	1054
黄红麻	Jute and Ambary Hemp	2516	2046	2868	2462	2719	2670
甘蔗	Sugarcane	57626	60625	64663	64023	65199	63970
甜菜	Beetroots	24518	26807	30232	24925	30829	37523
烤烟	Flue-Cured Tobacco	1763	1732	1792	1768	1889	1956
大牲畜年底头数(万头)	Number of Large Animals (year-end,10 000 heads)	15151.5	14995.9	15189.3	15500.1	15737.8	15947.5
#牛	Cattle and Buffaloes	12866.3	12824.2	13084.8	13467.2	13781.8	14157.5
马	Horses	876.6	826.0	808.8	790.0	763.9	740.0
驴	Donkeys	922.7	881.5	849.9	820.7	791.9	777.2
骡	Mules	453.0	436.2	419.4	395.7	374.0	360.4
骆驼	Camels	32.6	27.9	26.4	26.5	26.2	26.6
肉猪出栏头数 (万头)	Number of Slaughtered Fattened Hogs(10000 heads)	52673.3	54936.7	56684.0	59200.5	61800.7	66098.6
猪年底头数 (万头)	Number of Hogs (year-end,10 000 heads)	44681.5	45743.0	46291.5	46601.7	48189.1	50334.8
羊年底只数 (万只)	Number of Sheep and Goats(year-end,10 000 heads)	29031.9	29826.4	31655.2	34053.7	36639.1	37265.9
山羊	Goats	15715.9	16129.2	17275.9	18320.7	19550.9	19876.1
绵羊	Sheep	13316.0	13697.2	14379.3	15733.0	17088.2	17389.9
肉类产量 (万吨)	Output of Meat (10 000 tons)	6125.4	6333.9	6586.5	6932.9	7244.8	7743.1
#猪牛羊肉	Pork Beef and Mutton	4838.2	5026.0	5227.9	5506.3	5776.8	6157.6
猪肉	Pork	4031.4	4184.5	4326.6	4518.6	4701.6	5010.6
牛肉	Beef	532.8	548.8	584.6	630.4	675.9	711.5
羊肉	Mutton	274.0	292.7	316.7	357.2	399.3	435.5
奶类 (万吨)	Milk (10 000 tons)	919.1	1122.9	1400.4	1848.6	2368.4	2864.8
#牛奶	Cow Milk	827.4	1025.5	1299.8	1746.3	2260.6	2753.4
绵羊毛 (吨)	Sheep Wool (ton)	292502	298254	307588	338058	373902	393172
山羊毛 (吨)	Goat Wool (ton)	33266	34241	35459	36692	37727	36904
羊绒 (吨)	Cashmere (ton)	11057	10968	11765	13528	14515	15435
禽蛋 (万吨)	Poultry Eggs (10 000 tons)	2243.3	2336.7	2462.7	2606.7	2723.7	2879.5
水产品总产量 (万吨)	Total Aquatic Products (10 000 tons)	4278.5	4381.3	4564.5	4704.6	4901.8	5107.6
海水产品	Seawater Aquatic Products	2538.7	2571.7	2646.3	2685.8	2767.8	2838.3
淡水产品	Freshwater Aquatic Products	1739.7	1809.6	1918.2	2018.8	2134.0	2269.3

注：2003年起水果产量包括瓜果类产量。

a) Output of fruits in 2003 includes yield of melon and fruit.

13-3 农村基层组织情况

Basic Conditions of Rural Grass-root Unit

年 份 地 区 Year Region	乡镇数(个) Number of Township and Town Governments (unit)	#镇 数 Town Governments	村民委员会(个) Number of Villager's Committees (unit)	乡村户数(万户) Number of Households (10 000 households)	乡村人口数(万人) Rural Population (10 000 persons)	乡村从业人员(万人) Number of Rural Laborers (10 000 persons)	男 Male	女 Female
1978	52781		690388	17347.0	80320.0	30637.8	16548.4	14089.6
1980	54183		709820	17673.0	81096.0	31835.9	17379.7	14456.2
1985	72153	7956	940617	19077.0	84419.7	37065.1	20153.2	16911.9
1989	55764	11060	746432	21504.0	87831.0	40938.8	22218.3	18720.5
1990	55838	11392	743278	22237.0	89590.3	42009.5	22551.8	19457.7
1991	55542	11882	804153	22566.0	90525.1	43092.5	23121.9	19970.6
1992	48250	14135	806032	22849.0	91154.4	43801.6	23449.9	20351.7
1993	48179	15223	802352	22984.0	91333.5	44255.7	23653.1	20602.6
1994	48075	16433	802052	23165.0	91526.2	44654.1	23854.1	20800.0
1995	47136	17282	740150	23282.0	91674.6	45041.8	24037.4	21004.4
1996	45484	17998	740128	23437.6	91941.0	45288.0	24154.9	21133.1
1997	44689	18402	739447	23406.2	91524.7	46234.3	24633.4	21600.9
1998	45462	19060	739980	23678.0	91960.1	46432.3	24733.1	21699.2
1999	44741	19184	737429	23810.5	92216.3	46896.5	24995.7	21900.8
2000	43735	19692	734715	24148.7	92819.7	47962.1	25517.8	22444.3
2001	40161	19555	709257	24432.2	93382.9	48228.9	25685.4	22543.5
2002	39054	19811	694515	24569.4	93502.5	48526.9	25850.1	22676.7
2003	38028	19588	678589	24793.1	93750.6	48971.0	26121.0	22850.0
2004	36952	19171	652718	24971.4	94253.7	49695.3	26525.8	23169.5
2005	35509	18888	640139	25222.6	94907.5	50387.3	26930.6	23456.7
北 京 Beijing	184	143	3964	142.2	381.8	184.0	95.8	88.2
天 津 Tianjin	140	120	3821	119.8	397.5	178.5	97.8	80.7
河 北 Hebei	1962	944	49678	1448.6	5422.3	2805.9	1504.1	1301.8
山 西 Shanxi	1192	475	28323	638.4	2354.9	1035.7	573.6	462.1
内蒙古 Inner Mongolia	964	411	12129	351.4	1343.9	690.8	390.4	300.4
辽 宁 Liaoning	993	611	11920	695.6	2331.4	1113.5	618.5	495.0
吉 林 Jilin	624	429	9375	383.7	1443.6	685.2	391.1	294.1
黑龙江 Heilongjiang	878	448	8952	494.0	1917.3	948.9	545.1	403.9
上 海 Shanghai	103	100	1875	111.1	338.2	243.5	126.2	117.3
江 苏 Jiangsu	1092	978	18282	1593.2	5322.5	2662.5	1384.6	1277.9
浙 江 Zhejiang	1251	758	34515	1224.6	3790.5	2298.5	1231.7	1066.9
安 徽 Anhui	1466	915	24076	1346.1	5241.4	2939.2	1574.2	1365.0
福 建 Fujian	934	593	14630	682.2	2667.0	1313.0	708.2	604.9
江 西 Jiangxi	1435	772	17233	795.3	3298.5	1638.8	861.1	777.7
山 东 Shandong	1423	1146	83483	2050.4	7030.1	3782.2	2015.3	1767.0
河 南 Henan	2008	776	48145	2025.7	8000.7	4752.4	2517.5	2234.9
湖 北 Hubei	954	737	26682	1016.4	3993.6	1932.8	1027.3	905.4
湖 南 Hunan	2220	1093	44538	1492.5	5475.8	2975.4	1619.6	1355.8
广 东 Guangdong	1223	1207	21825	1540.8	6451.6	3089.5	1616.0	1473.5
广 西 Guangxi	1130	698	14453	986.1	4146.2	2275.4	1202.1	1073.3
海 南 Hainan	200	180	2615	112.6	525.6	256.0	132.6	123.4
重 庆 Chongqing	958	594	10015	718.8	2430.9	1366.9	736.8	630.1
四 川 Sichuan	4658	1869	51198	1979.2	6904.0	3801.5	2018.4	1783.1
贵 州 Guizhou	1385	624	19696	792.3	3276.3	1934.2	1033.0	901.1
云 南 Yunnan	1296	459	12940	877.4	3568.1	2050.9	1069.3	981.6
西 藏 Tibet	685	142	5886	40.4	225.3	108.8	55.3	53.5
陕 西 Shaanxi	1521	843	27809	705.0	2791.9	1437.0	781.2	655.9
甘 肃 Gansu	1251	451	16585	463.7	2074.8	1084.3	570.8	513.5
青 海 Qinghai	392	109	4161	77.6	357.3	186.0	98.2	87.8
宁 夏 Ningxia	191	94	2382	93.6	415.0	212.0	110.6	101.4
新 疆 Xinjiang	796	169	8953	223.9	989.6	403.9	224.3	179.6

注：本表乡村人口数是指户口在乡村的常住人口，具体范围按1964年建镇标准划分，包括后来的新建制镇人口，口径大于人口篇的乡村总人口。

a) Total rural population refers to persons residing and registered in rural areas. This indicator is calculated on the basis of the town classification standards of 1964 which includes rural population in what are now established towns. Therefore, the statistical coverage in the table are larger than the rural population shown in Chapter 4.

13-4 乡村从业人员（年底数）

Rural Laborers at the Year-end

本表分行业从业人员是按从事的主行业划分的，如以农业为主、兼营商业的，仍作为农林牧渔业从业人员。
The number of laborers by sector in this table is classified by main economic activity. For example, those engaged primarily in agriculture and secondarily in commerce are classified as the laborers under farming, forestry, animal husbandry and fishery.

单位：万人 (10 000 persons)

年份 地区	Year Region	农林牧渔业 Farming, Forestry, Animal Husbandry and Fishery	工业 Industry	建筑业 Construction	交通运输业、仓储及邮电通信业 Transport Storage, Post and Communication Services	批发零售贸易业餐饮业 Wholesale, Retail Trade and Catering Services	其他非农行业 Other Nonagricultural Trades
	1978	28455.6					
	1980	29808.4	916.3				
	1985	30351.5	2741.0	1130.1	434.1	462.6	1945.8
	1989	32440.5	3255.6	1501.8	614.2	652.4	2474.3
	1990	33336.4	3228.7	1522.8	635.3	693.2	2593.1
	1991	34186.3	3267.9	1533.8	655.0	722.8	2726.7
	1992	34037.0	3468.2	1658.8	706.3	813.7	3117.6
	1993	33258.2	3659.0	1886.8	799.9	948.8	3703.0
	1994	32690.3	3849.5	2057.3	908.3	1084.3	4064.4
	1995	32334.5	3970.7	2203.6	983.0	1170.4	4379.6
	1996	32260.4	4018.5	2304.3	1027.6	1261.5	4415.7
	1997	32677.9	4031.3	2373.7	1059.0	1386.8	4705.6
	1998	32626.4	3928.6	2453.5	1087.9	1461.9	4874.0
	1999	32911.8	3953.0	2531.9	1115.8	1584.6	4799.4
	2000	32797.5	4108.6	2691.7	1170.6	1751.8	5441.9
	2001	32451.0	4296.0	2797.4	1205.4	1864.5	5614.6
	2002	31990.6	4505.6	2959.0	1259.1	1996.8	5815.8
	2003	31259.6	4937.1	3201.1	1328.2	2059.2	6185.9
	2004	30596.0	5438.9	3380.5	1475.9	2701.6	6102.4
	2005	29975.5	6011.5	3653.2	1567.3	2937.7	6242.0
北京	Beijing	58.6	33.3	17.8	19.2	22.5	32.8
天津	Tianjin	79.6	49.2	12.9	12.2	15.0	9.5
河北	Hebei	1552.8	518.9	275.2	119.4	202.9	136.8
山西	Shanxi	637.4	141.9	62.7	62.7	61.9	69.1
内蒙古	Inner Mongolia	529.2	25.8	32.2	14.1	39.3	50.2
辽宁	Liaoning	686.4	106.1	77.1	44.5	70.0	129.4
吉林	Jilin	502.1	30.8	40.4	19.2	37.3	55.4
黑龙江	Heilongjiang	696.7	50.7	53.2	26.9	60.6	60.8
上海	Shanghai	59.1	116.4	12.0	9.3	15.4	31.3
江苏	Jiangsu	1058.3	598.5	316.4	107.8	156.1	425.4
浙江	Zhejiang	786.9	754.9	145.4	92.2	216.8	302.4
安徽	Anhui	1766.9	299.3	281.6	92.8	202.1	296.4
福建	Fujian	692.2	209.2	87.4	43.5	88.4	192.4
江西	Jiangxi	951.0	206.6	101.2	38.1	70.9	270.9
山东	Shandong	2045.9	534.4	383.7	166.4	272.8	379.0
河南	Henan	3127.7	543.8	377.1	153.5	285.8	264.4
湖北	Hubei	1101.8	123.1	128.5	51.9	95.2	432.4
湖南	Hunan	1951.9	266.9	165.4	78.9	164.9	347.5
广东	Guangdong	1533.5	632.1	214.4	94.9	245.8	368.8
广西	Guangxi	1503.1	86.2	96.7	43.1	77.2	469.2
海南	Hainan	193.4	9.2	8.7	7.2	18.6	18.9
重庆	Chongqing	775.9	109.8	125.0	26.7	61.1	268.4
四川	Sichuan	2317.7	259.1	301.9	76.0	189.4	657.4
贵州	Guizhou	1268.1	81.8	50.3	27.7	57.4	448.9
云南	Yunnan	1690.1	58.9	63.0	40.2	54.4	144.2
西藏	Tibet	85.5	2.6	5.6	3.0	2.8	9.3
陕西	Shaanxi	949.2	90.9	106.6	44.5	71.4	174.4
甘肃	Gansu	761.4	35.3	63.3	24.6	38.8	160.9
青海	Qinghai	128.7	10.1	15.2	5.7	11.2	15.1
宁夏	Ningxia	140.6	14.2	23.2	10.0	13.8	10.2
新疆	Xinjiang	344.1	11.4	9.3	11.1	18.1	10.1

注：工业从业人员中包括村及村以下办的工业从业人员。
a) Number of employed persons of industry includes those working in enterprises at village and lower levels.

13-5 各 地 区 耕 地 面 积

Area of Cultivated Land by Region

地 区	Region	耕地面积（总资源）(千公顷) Cultivated Land (Total Area) (1 000 hectares)	占全国比重 (%) Percentage to Total Area (%)
全国总计	**National Total**	**130039.2**	**100.00**
北 京	Beijing	343.9	0.26
天 津	Tianjin	485.6	0.37
河 北	Hebei	6883.3	5.29
山 西	Shanxi	4588.6	3.53
内蒙古	Inner Mongolia	8201.0	6.31
辽 宁	Liaoning	4174.8	3.21
吉 林	Jilin	5578.4	4.29
黑龙江	Heilongjiang	11773.0	9.05
上 海	Shanghai	315.1	0.24
江 苏	Jiangsu	5061.7	3.89
浙 江	Zhejiang	2125.3	1.63
安 徽	Anhui	5971.7	4.59
福 建	Fujian	1434.7	1.10
江 西	Jiangxi	2993.4	2.30
山 东	Shandong	7689.3	5.91
河 南	Henan	8110.3	6.24
湖 北	Hubei	4949.5	3.81
湖 南	Hunan	3953.0	3.04
广 东	Guangdong	3272.2	2.52
广 西	Guangxi	4407.9	3.39
海 南	Hainan	762.1	0.59
四 川	Sichuan	9169.1	7.05
贵 州	Guizhou	4903.5	3.77
云 南	Yunnan	6421.6	4.94
西 藏	Tibet	362.6	0.28
陕 西	Shaanxi	5140.5	3.95
甘 肃	Gansu	5024.7	3.86
青 海	Qinghai	688.0	0.53
宁 夏	Ningxia	1268.8	0.98
新 疆	Xinjiang	3985.7	3.07

注：本表数据来源于国土资源部、国家统计局、全国农业普查办公室“关于土地利用现状调查数据成果的公报”，耕地面积（总资源）数据为1996年10月31日时点数。据国家统计局初步测算，2001年耕地总资源为127082千公顷，其中：常用耕地面积为105826千公顷，临时性耕地面积为21256千公顷。

a) Data come from the "*Communique of Main Data on Land Use Survey*" issued by the Ministry of Land and Resources, National Bureau of Statistics, and National Agricultural Census Office of China. The cultivated areas is the data at Oct. 31, 1996. According to the estimation by National Bureau of Statistics, area of cultivated land (total area) in 2001 is 127 082 000 hectares, of which, regularly cultivated land is 105 826 000 hectares, and temporarily cultivated land is 21 256 000 hectares.

13-6 农、林、牧、渔业总产值及指数

Gross Output Value of Farming, Forestry, Animal Husbandry and Fishery and Related Indices

本表绝对数按当年价格计算，指数按可比价格计算。2003年执行新国民经济行业分类标准，总产值包括农林牧渔服务业产值。
Data in value terms in this table are calculated at current prices, while the indices are calculated at constant prices.

年份 地区	Year Region	绝对数（亿元） Gross Output Value (100 million yuan)					指数（上年=100） Indices of Gross Output (preceding year=100)				
		农林牧渔业总产值 Total	#农业 Farming	#林业 Forestry	#牧业 Animal Husbandry	#渔业 Fishery	农林牧渔业总产值 Total	#农业 Farming	#林业 Forestry	#牧业 Animal Husbandry	#渔业 Fishery
	1978	1397.0	1117.5	48.1	209.3	22.1					
	1980	1922.6	1454.1	81.4	354.2	32.9	101.4	99.7	112.2	107.0	107.7
	1985	3619.5	2506.4	188.7	798.3	126.1	103.4	99.8	104.5	117.2	118.9
	1989	6534.7	4100.6	284.9	1800.4	348.8	103.1	102.4	100.4	105.5	107.2
	1990	7662.1	4954.3	330.3	1967.0	410.6	107.6	108.0	103.1	107.0	110.0
	1991	8157.0	5146.4	367.9	2159.2	483.5	103.7	100.9	108.0	108.8	107.6
	1992	9084.7	5588.0	422.6	2460.5	613.5	106.4	104.2	107.7	108.8	115.3
	1993	10995.5	6605.1	494.0	3014.4	882.0	107.8	105.2	108.0	110.8	118.4
	1994	15750.5	9169.2	611.1	4672.0	1298.2	108.6	103.2	108.9	116.7	120.0
	1995	20340.9	11884.6	709.9	6045.0	1701.3	110.9	107.9	105.0	114.8	119.4
	1996	22353.7	13539.8	778.0	6015.5	2020.4	109.4	107.8	105.7	111.4	114.0
	1997	23788.4	13852.5	817.8	6835.4	2282.7	106.7	104.5	103.3	110.1	111.5
	1998	24541.9	14241.9	851.3	7025.8	2422.9	106.0	104.9	102.9	107.4	108.8
	1999	24519.1	14106.2	886.3	6997.6	2529.0	104.7	104.3	103.2	104.6	107.2
	2000	24915.8	13873.6	936.5	7393.1	2712.6	103.6	101.4	105.4	106.3	106.5
	2001	26179.6	14462.8	938.8	7963.1	2815.0	104.2	103.6	99.3	106.3	103.9
	2002	27390.8	14931.5	1033.5	8454.6	2971.1	104.9	103.9	107.1	106.0	106.1
	2003	29691.8	14870.1	1239.9	9538.8	3137.6	103.9	100.5	106.9	107.3	105.3
	2004	36239.0	18138.4	1327.1	12173.8	3605.6	107.5	108.5	102.0	107.2	106.0
	2005	39450.9	19613.4	1425.5	13310.8	4016.1	105.7	104.1	103.2	107.8	106.5
北京	Beijing	268.8	100.6	13.3	135.7	9.7	100.3	102.7	102.7	97.3	102.8
天津	Tianjin	258.4	97.5	1.9	102.7	36.3	104.5	100.2	113.6	107.5	110.6
河北	Hebei	2600.8	1258.0	40.1	1124.4	79.4	106.5	105.9	96.9	107.7	104.1
山西	Shanxi	483.8	281.7	16.5	148.6	2.7	97.2	93.0	84.1	103.2	107.4
内蒙古	Inner Mongolia	980.2	473.9	39.8	444.6	7.2	111.2	110.6	82.6	115.2	116.0
辽宁	Liaoning	1671.6	640.1	44.5	636.4	306.7	107.5	103.8	111.0	111.1	107.9
吉林	Jilin	1050.5	518.1	39.9	467.6	14.9	111.7	106.2	116.9	118.2	110.1
黑龙江	Heilongjiang	1294.4	718.6	67.3	461.2	27.4	110.2	109.0	100.7	115.8	105.5
上海	Shanghai	233.4	111.3	11.1	54.3	51.6	89.5	94.2	84.5	76.5	99.1
江苏	Jiangsu	2577.0	1291.1	45.3	599.1	511.9	103.7	101.1	107.5	103.6	110.7
浙江	Zhejiang	1428.3	654.8	83.5	286.0	380.8	102.4	102.7	101.1	105.2	99.9
安徽	Anhui	1666.2	818.5	78.4	553.6	165.6	101.4	97.9	105.2	103.9	106.7
福建	Fujian	1396.1	571.0	96.9	276.5	434.4	102.2	102.7	107.5	95.5	105.4
江西	Jiangxi	1143.0	510.5	87.4	365.1	162.6	106.8	103.4	104.4	112.3	107.9
山东	Shandong	3741.8	2034.0	57.6	1125.0	465.5	105.2	103.9	96.3	107.3	106.7
河南	Henan	3309.7	1790.4	83.9	1251.6	35.3	107.5	107.7	104.7	107.6	122.5
湖北	Hubei	1775.6	932.1	37.3	545.4	236.5	104.2	103.0	106.4	105.1	105.9
湖南	Hunan	2056.2	947.7	101.0	834.5	138.4	105.8	104.5	109.8	106.3	109.6
广东	Guangdong	2447.6	1109.2	66.2	638.6	523.8	104.8	103.4	102.9	105.5	105.7
广西	Guangxi	1448.4	711.9	61.7	511.6	143.6	107.4	105.8	107.0	110.6	105.0
海南	Hainan	475.9	179.6	58.9	95.2	132.2	106.7	105.8	91.6	115.0	108.6
重庆	Chongqing	662.2	358.3	20.0	249.5	23.8	105.2	103.9	100.8	106.9	106.0
四川	Sichuan	2457.5	1037.2	69.9	1230.2	78.5	106.5	102.6	109.1	109.5	112.7
贵州	Guizhou	571.8	335.5	23.9	194.2	9.4	105.9	104.3	99.9	109.8	106.7
云南	Yunnan	1068.6	559.3	105.5	339.7	23.0	106.9	104.3	108.8	110.3	111.4
西藏	Tibet	67.7	25.5	10.1	30.0		101.9	93.4	176.7	92.5	156.7
陕西	Shaanxi	730.7	472.9	25.0	199.0	5.5	108.1	107.7	93.8	111.6	110.4
甘肃	Gansu	521.5	362.9	15.9	129.1	1.1	106.6	107.0	92.1	108.4	100.0
青海	Qinghai	94.0	36.4	1.8	51.7	0.1	105.3	104.1	97.4	107.1	89.2
宁夏	Ningxia	138.0	78.9	5.6	46.0	4.0	106.2	106.9	89.8	107.5	104.2
新疆	Xinjiang	831.1	595.8	15.3	183.5	4.3	107.4	107.0	105.8	109.0	105.3

13-7 主要农业机械拥有量（年底数）

Major Agricultural Machinery at the Year-end

年 份 地 区	Year Region	农业机械总动力（万千瓦） Total Power of Agricultural Machinery (10 000 kw)	农用大中型拖拉机 Large and Medium Agricultural Tractors 数量（台）Number (unit)	动力（万千瓦） Capacity (10 000 kw)	小型拖拉机 Mini-Tractors 数量（台）Number (unit)	动力（万千瓦） Capacity (10 000 kw)	大中型拖拉机配套农具（部） Number of Large and Medium Tractor Towing Farm Machinery (unit)
	1978	11749.9	557358	1755.0	1373000	1171.2	1192000
	1980	14745.7	744865	2369.3	1874000	1615.5	1369000
	1985	20912.5	852357	2743.6	3824000	3367.0	1128000
	1989	28067.0	848220	2814.0	6543000	5848.0	991000
	1990	28707.7	813521	2745.5	6981000	6231.4	974000
	1991	29388.6	784466	2682.4	7304000	6528.6	991000
	1992	30308.4	758904	2630.2	7507000	6604.0	1044000
	1993	31816.6	721216	2532.5	7883400	7042.8	1001000
	1994	33802.5	693154	2463.4	8236687	7399.7	980000
	1995	36118.1	671846	2404.1	8646356	7848.1	991220
	1996	38546.9	670848	2415.1	9189200	8385.2	1049900
	1997	42015.6	689051	2486.6	10484813	9337.2	1157316
	1998	45207.7	725215	2587.9	11220551	10031.5	1203687
	1999	48996.1	784216	2772.8	12002509	11008.9	1320429
	2000	52573.6	974547	3161.1	12643696	11663.9	1399886
	2001	55172.1	829900	2901.7	13050840	12257.9	1469355
	2002	57929.9	911670	3073.4	13393884	12695.0	1578861
	2003	60386.5	980560	3229.8	13777056	13060.2	1698436
	2004	64027.9	1118636	3713.1	14549279	13855.4	1887110
	2005	68397.8	1395981	4293.5	15268916	14660.9	2262004
北 京	Beijing	337.7	9487	40.9	18961	35.9	18515
天 津	Tianjin	611.9	10260	43.5	35360	36.5	14780
河 北	Hebei	8487.2	100894	366.2	1446840	1485.0	183516
山 西	Shanxi	2288.7	35928	127.7	251260	234.8	74607
内蒙古	Inner Mongolia	1922.0	73658	226.2	544600	639.0	100614
辽 宁	Liaoning	1918.1	42777	158.6	235585	267.8	56958
吉 林	Jilin	1471.3	90750	203.0	538024	540.0	171632
黑龙江	Heilongjiang	2234.0	217275	578.9	744126	790.6	318803
上 海	Shanghai	96.5	4210	15.8	8152	7.4	10724
江 苏	Jiangsu	3135.3	41500	153.0	901135	799.8	80792
浙 江	Zhejiang	2111.3	4482	13.1	197453	168.5	6214
安 徽	Anhui	3983.8	36040	119.9	2079830	1669.1	79730
福 建	Fujian	1000.0	1400	5.1	98806	94.0	406
江 西	Jiangxi	1781.3	12800	23.9	147000	119.9	7000
山 东	Shandong	9199.3	227858	720.5	1827326	1538.4	419555
河 南	Henan	7934.2	110840	366.3	2984520	3119.8	239910
湖 北	Hubei	2057.4	76644	182.0	483915	352.6	93583
湖 南	Hunan	3189.9	8820	27.9	168738	169.5	6722
广 东	Guangdong	1782.1	5900	26.5	352000	279.2	7800
广 西	Guangxi	1909.7	16950	57.6	344382	265.3	15273
海 南	Hainan	268.2	5800	20.4	34419	33.5	2645
重 庆	Chongqing	776.0	104	0.5	3910	5.5	156
四 川	Sichuan	2181.7	12728	35.2	124783	155.9	12622
贵 州	Guizhou	1011.5	13900	47.3	48270	53.0	4740
云 南	Yunnan	1666.1	44978	121.4	274764	307.4	11545
西 藏	Tibet	230.9	6658	19.1	79020	89.9	2531
陕 西	Shaanxi	1406.3	35500	117.2	180049	204.6	57100
甘 肃	Gansu	1406.9	18342	57.2	375612	402.7	28905
青 海	Qinghai	327.3	2745	10.4	221664	204.4	3900
宁 夏	Ningxia	555.1	13245	33.4	169500	176.8	14127
新 疆	Xinjiang	1116.3	113508	375.0	348912	414.2	216599

注：2002年及以后大中型拖拉机中不包括变形拖拉机，2001年数据相应做了调整。

a) Number of large and medium agricultural tractors excluded the transfiguration tractors since 2002. The data in 2001 were adjusted accordingly.

13-7 续表 continued

年份 Year 地区 Region	小型拖拉机配套农具（部）Number of Mini-Tractor Towing Farm Machinery (unit)	农用排灌柴油机 Diesel Engines		渔用机动船 Motorized Fishing Boats	
		数量（台）Number (unit)	动力（万千瓦）Capacity (10 000 kw)	数量（台）Number (unit)	动力（万千瓦）Capacity (10 000 kw)
1978	1454000	2657000	2521.6	47176	213.7
1980	2191000	2899000	2717.7	61022	258.5
1985	3202000	2855000	2566.0	172582	367.2
1989	6043000	3867000	3207.0	289205	609.0
1990	6488000	4111000	3348.5	320927	696.0
1991	7327000	4330000	3447.1	329843	733.4
1992	8308000	4377000	3441.6	335875	786.1
1993	8657000	4554275	3613.1	334656	804.4
1994	8662000	4711516	3731.0	351327	831.1
1995	9579774	4912068	3839.0	376813	965.7
1996	10911500	5092934	3984.9	358869	864.1
1997	12530020	5461235	4292.4	400010	1084.0
1998	14378324	5816118	4499.0	411322	1174.4
1999	16210408	6449528	4934.6	417379	1253.1
2000	17887868	6881174	5232.6	459888	1338.7
2001	18821829	7285693	5580.0	480125	1379.7
2002	20033634	7506066	5667.9	485693	1381.2
2003	21171505	7495652	5592.8	478123	1425.9
2004	23096911	7775427	5804.2	486878	1384.2
2005	24649726	8099100	6034.0	439604	1376.1
北京 Beijing	12453	2019	1.4	3	
天津 Tianjin	38040	38080	31.5		
河北 Hebei	1916292	1258359	1116.6	13226	38.4
山西 Shanxi	305347	18143	22.3	30	0.1
内蒙古 Inner Mongolia	739217	169313	155.5	103	0.3
辽宁 Liaoning	281368	147318	132.2	37590	121.7
吉林 Jilin	1443844	289489	208.7	920	1.3
黑龙江 Heilongjiang	877387	196996	174.3	4690	2.7
上海 Shanghai	7542	7		1248	15.3
江苏 Jiangsu	1436421	165102	168.6	54138	97.6
浙江 Zhejiang	201579	85646	44.6	48253	404.2
安徽 Anhui	4897094	337027	239.0	14254	14.7
福建 Fujian	69970	88400	54.1	57210	202.2
江西 Jiangxi	145900	436800	300.3	16732	9.8
山东 Shandong	2841723	1777828	1427.8	38144	119.2
河南 Henan	5346690	533370	518.3	859	1.2
湖北 Hubei	966928	205993	190.5	15560	8.5
湖南 Hunan	38892	968017	443.9	16414	8.1
广东 Guangdong	312347	228895	125.5	68092	220.1
广西 Guangxi	675032	348010	168.1	13971	48.7
海南 Hainan	9100	93649	44.0	19935	52.8
重庆 Chongqing	1955	72261	43.8	5640	2.7
四川 Sichuan	98575	373961	229.9	10300	4.2
贵州 Guizhou	10260	113010	80.5	904	1.2
云南 Yunnan	180819	87663	49.8	320	0.4
西藏 Tibet	14405	2744	2.6		
陕西 Shaanxi	249872	32990	29.0	553	0.2
甘肃 Gansu	695766	15473	15.7	2	
青海 Qinghai	154714	747	1.2	70	0.1
宁夏 Ningxia	193843	3846	2.9	30	
新疆 Xinjiang	486351	7944	11.6	413	0.3

13-8 有效灌溉面积、农用化肥施用量、农村水电站及用电量

Irrigated Area, Consumption of Chemical Fertilizers, Number of Hydropower Stations and Electricity Consumption in Rural Areas

年份 Year 地区 Region	有效灌溉面积（千公顷）Irrigated Area (1 000 hectares)	化肥施用量（万吨）Consumption of Chemical Fertilizer (10 000 tons)					乡村办水电站 Hydropower Station in Rural Areas		农村用电量（亿千瓦时）Electricity Consumed in Rural Area (100 million kwh)
			氮肥 Nitrogenous Fertilizer	磷肥 Phosphate Fertilizer	钾肥 Potash Fertilizer	复合肥 Compound Fertilizer	个数 Number	发电能力（万千瓦）Generating Capacity (10 000 kw)	
1978	44965.0	884.0					82387	228.4	253.1
1980	44888.1	1269.4	934.2	273.3	34.6	27.2	80319	304.1	320.8
1985	44035.9	1775.8	1204.9	310.9	80.4	179.6	55754	380.2	508.9
1989	44917.2	2357.1	1536.8	418.9	120.5	280.9	50862	416.8	790.5
1990	47403.1	2590.3	1638.4	462.4	147.9	341.6	52387	428.8	844.5
1991	47822.1	2805.1	1726.1	499.6	173.9	405.5	49644	456.9	963.2
1992	48590.1	2930.2	1756.1	515.7	196.0	462.4	48082	478.7	1106.9
1993	48727.9	3151.9	1835.1	575.1	212.3	529.4	45153	481.9	1244.9
1994	48759.1	3317.9	1882.0	600.7	234.8	600.6	48722	503.6	1473.9
1995	49281.2	3593.7	2021.9	632.4	268.5	670.8	40699	519.5	1655.7
1996	50381.4	3827.9	2145.3	658.4	289.6	734.7	37743	533.7	1812.7
1997	51238.5	3980.7	2171.7	689.1	322.0	798.1	36117	562.5	1980.1
1998	52295.6	4083.7	2233.3	682.5	345.7	822.0	33185	634.8	2042.2
1999	53158.4	4124.3	2180.9	697.8	365.6	880.0	31678	664.1	2173.4
2000	53820.3	4146.4	2161.5	690.5	376.5	917.9	29962	698.5	2421.3
2001	54249.4	4253.8	2164.1	705.7	399.6	983.7	29183	896.6	2610.8
2002	54354.8	4339.4	2157.3	712.2	422.4	1040.4	27633	812.2	2993.4
2003	54014.2	4411.6	2149.9	713.9	438.0	1109.8	26696	862.3	3432.9
2004	54478.4	4636.6	2221.9	736.0	467.3	1204.0	27115	993.8	3933.0
2005	55029.3	4766.2	2229.3	743.8	489.5	1303.2	26726	1099.2	4375.7
北京 Beijing	181.5	14.8	7.8	1.2	0.6	5.2	28	1.2	42.2
天津 Tianjin	355.2	23.3	11.6	3.7	1.5	6.6			55.2
河北 Hebei	4547.8	303.4	155.2	48.6	24.3	75.4	116	3.7	337.1
山西 Shanxi	1088.6	95.7	41.1	19.0	6.9	28.8	87	2.3	66.9
内蒙古 Inner Mongolia	2702.2	116.7	60.5	20.5	9.2	26.6	3		29.3
辽宁 Liaoning	1527.1	119.9	64.0	11.4	9.6	34.9	146	38.4	183.0
吉林 Jilin	1613.7	138.1	61.3	6.2	10.0	60.7	80	5.5	28.0
黑龙江 Heilongjiang	2394.1	150.9	57.5	33.8	17.7	42.0	14	1.4	36.3
上海 Shanghai	237.3	14.4	8.9	1.5	0.5	3.6			124.5
江苏 Jiangsu	3817.7	340.8	183.0	48.2	21.7	87.9	2		825.1
浙江 Zhejiang	1417.7	94.3	56.1	12.6	7.5	18.1	2273	192.0	520.6
安徽 Anhui	3330.9	285.7	111.1	38.9	30.7	105.0	509	16.8	64.0
福建 Fujian	949.7	122.0	51.3	16.5	24.4	29.8	4959	222.6	160.6
江西 Jiangxi	1831.4	129.4	47.8	25.4	20.8	35.5	1816	60.9	45.1
山东 Shandong	4790.0	467.6	189.8	57.5	44.9	175.5	12	0.4	346.5
河南 Henan	4864.1	518.1	227.2	106.1	50.8	134.1	405	6.3	172.1
湖北 Hubei	2064.6	285.8	142.0	59.8	23.2	60.8	609	35.7	70.1
湖南 Hunan	2690.4	209.9	106.0	25.6	34.9	43.4	4262	81.2	65.2
广东 Guangdong	1317.8	204.6	93.8	19.0	41.6	50.3	5121	184.6	766.4
广西 Guangxi	1519.8	201.3	63.3	25.2	48.0	64.8	313	17.6	34.3
海南 Hainan	168.3	37.3	12.2	2.4	5.1	17.6	38	8.4	3.8
重庆 Chongqing	618.1	79.1	46.5	17.5	3.8	11.2	529	30.3	42.9
四川 Sichuan	2508.3	220.9	121.8	45.1	12.9	40.6	2582	94.2	112.9
贵州 Guizhou	711.6	77.4	44.6	10.1	5.9	16.9	791	30.2	30.2
云南 Yunnan	1485.4	142.7	79.9	22.7	12.0	28.0	603	23.3	41.7
西藏 Tibet	162.6	4.2	1.8	1.3	0.1	1.0	356	3.9	0.6
陕西 Shaanxi	1298.8	147.3	76.7	16.9	10.8	43.0	650	16.1	88.2
甘肃 Gansu	1030.4	75.9	36.6	15.5	4.4	19.5	234	8.1	33.9
青海 Qinghai	176.5	7.0	3.1	1.6	0.3	2.0	50	4.3	3.0
宁夏 Ningxia	423.5	29.9	13.8	3.6	1.1	11.4			9.3
新疆 Xinjiang	3204.3	107.8	53.4	26.4	4.6	23.4	138	10.1	36.5

13-9 农村水电建设和发电量

Rural Hydropower Construction and Amount of Electric Power Generation

年份 地区	Year Region	本年完成投资额（万元） Amount of Investment Completed This Year (10 000 yuan)	年末发电设备容量（千瓦） Capability of Electricity Generation Equipment at the Year-end (kw)	#本年新增发电设备容量 Newly Increased Capability of Electricity Generation Equipment	在建电站规模（千瓦） Scale of Electric Power Plant under Construction (kw)	#当年新开工电站规模 Scale of Newly Started Electric Power Station This Year	发电量（万千瓦时） Amount of Electric Power Generation (10 000 kwh)
	1990	348848	13978100	791000			4181100
	1991	476529	14942700	1009100			4066800
	1992	594081	15728195	964769	4170000		4818494
	1993	792747	16622781	995124	9600000		5841049
	1994	1020937	17566675	1163873	10500000		5771834
	1995	1321689	18721073	1207854	10760000		6316247
	1996	1442828	20095552	1408342			6496723
	1997	1452004	21771773	1780352			7221270
	1998	1585787	23390300	1741631			7560916
	1999	1833853	25562760	2344285	8717000	386000	7715124
	2000	2220993	27487791	2060127	7459500	2384000	8755014
	2001	2133741	28787476	1714454	3547500	1462800	9490187
	2002	2393195	31044576	1883648	5680800	1419000	10366868
	2003	3006249	34157792	2702834	10850143	6385500	10966512
	2004	3770733	38655048	4363322	16652425	5362090	11045527
	2005	4343826	43090145	4964672	17727677	4284511	13571702
北京	Beijing	30	42920				2675
天津	Tianjin		5000				42
河北	Hebei	11142	339262	7352	17695	9945	35233
山西	Shanxi	14576	151730	1075	62930		27853
内蒙古	Inner Mongolia	980	52730		11130	630	8826
辽宁	Liaoning	5795	350879	7010	8055	8055	118563
吉林	Jilin	25764	374973	10725	160515	101380	124821
黑龙江	Heilongjiang	10082	230585	21450	8600		54496
上海	Shanghai						
江苏	Jiangsu		59786				5605
浙江	Zhejiang	296490	2803274	282483	604400	85000	693396
安徽	Anhui	52285	632092	47525	140830	10205	115149
福建	Fujian	644521	5337924	679061	1307796	327705	1756630
江西	Jiangxi	156338	1776889	149916	260000	60000	450785
山东	Shandong	110	68228				12129
河南	Henan	10240	334583	5565	39945	500	81962
湖北	Hubei	293381	2286676	346261	1202940	607800	613942
湖南	Hunan	388886	3578768	379155	1828545	454525	1138861
广东	Guangdong	325388	5507352	304746	400000	120000	1516225
广西	Guangxi	315282	2817420	378025	2116735	376290	808069
海南	Hainan	5576	252024	12710	28820	22020	52678
重庆	Chongqing	150704	1281367	93858	434681	277356	510816
四川	Sichuan	508066	5933084	725963	2249625	474785	2371494
贵州	Guizhou	173357	1254407	126565	1191185	585165	464236
云南	Yunnan	552364	4255881	957902	3750000	43500	1563216
西藏	Tibet		422440				
陕西	Shaanxi	73686	655588	98920	220000	28000	213501
甘肃	Gansu	230471	922361	118755	1291800	600400	352473
青海	Qinghai	25975	337993	34885	224700	84500	167563
宁夏	Ningxia		3200				800
新疆	Xinjiang	54577	748944	162475	166750	6750	199281
新疆兵团	Xinjiang PC Corps	17760	165185	12290			63819
水利部直属	Directly under The Ministry of Water Resources		106600				46563

注：本表由水利部农村水电及电气化发展局提供。农村水电是指国家、集体和个人兴建，直接为农村经济社会发展提供电力的水电站及电网。

a) The table are provided by the Bureau of Rural Electrification, the Ministry of Water Resources. Rural hydropower refers to the water electric power station and power grid, which built by the state, collectivity and individual and directly serves for rural economic and social development.

13-10 灌溉、水库和除涝、治水、治碱情况

Irrigation, Reservoirs, Flood Prevention, Water and Soil Conservation and Improvement of Saline-Alkaline Land

项 目	Item	1990	1995	2000	2003	2004	2005
年底灌区数 (处)	Number of Irrigation Areas at the year-end(set)	5363	5562	5683	5729	5800	5860
3.3万公顷以上	33 000 Hectares and Over	72	74	101	112	111	117
2.0-3.3万公顷	20 000-33 000 Hectares	76	99	141	169	169	170
灌区有效灌溉面积(万公顷)	Effective Irrigated Areas (10 000 hectares)	2123.1	2249.9	2449.3	2524.4	2550.6	2641.9
3.3万公顷以上	33 000 Hectares and Over	604.7	631.4	788.3	938.1	971.4	1023
2.0-3.3万公顷	20 000-33 000 Hectares	189.6	244.4	344.0	408.4	405.7	408
水库 (座)	Number of Reservoirs	83387	84775	85120	85153	85160	85108
大型水库	Large-scale Reservoir	366	387	420	453	460	470
中型水库	Medium-scale Reservoir	2499	2593	2704	2827	2869	2934
小型水库	Small-scale Reservoir	80522	81795	81996	81873	81831	81704
水库库容量 (亿立方米)	Capacity of Reservoirs (100 million cu.m)	4660	4797	5184	5658	5542	5624
大型水库	Large-scale Reservoir	3397	3493	3842	4278	4147	4197
中型水库	Medium-scale Reservoir	690	719	746	783	796	826
小型水库	Small-scale Reservoir	573	585	594	597	599	602
节水灌溉面积 (万公顷)	Water-saving Irrigated Area (10 000 hectares)			1638.9	1944.3	2034.6	2133.8
除涝面积 (万公顷)	Flooded or Waterlogged Area(10 000 hectares)	1933.7	2006.5	2098.9	2113.9	2119.8	2133.9
水土流失治理面积(万公顷)	Area of Soil Erosion under Control (10 000 hectares)	5300	6690	8096	8971	9200	9465
治碱面积 (万公顷)	Improved Area of Saline-Alkaline Land (10 000 hectares)	499.5	543.4	584.1	586.5	596.2	603.2
堤防长度 (万公里)	Total Length of Dikes (10 000 km)	22.0	24.7	27.0	27.8	27.7	27.7
堤防保护面积 (万公顷)	Area of Land Protected by Dikes (10 000 hectares)	3200.0	3060.9	3960.0	4387.5	4393.4	4412.0

注：大型水库库容：1亿立方米以上；中型水库库容：1千万至1亿立方米；小型水库库容：10万至1千万立方米。

a) The capacity of the large-scale reservoir is over 100 million cubic meters, while that of the medium-scale one is from 10 to 100 million cubic meters and that of the small-scale one is from 100 000 to 10 million cubic meters.

13-11 各地区水利设施和除涝、治碱面积（2005年）

Water Conservancy Facilities and Area with Flood Prevention Measures and Improved Area of Saline-Alkaline Land by Region (2005)

地区	Region	水库数（座）Number of Reservoirs (unit)	水库总库容量（亿立方米）Capacity of Reservoirs (100 million cu.m)	除涝面积（千公顷）Area with Flood Prevention Measures (1 000 hectares)	治碱面积（千公顷）Improved Area of Saline-alkaline Land (1 000 hectares)	水土流失治理面积（千公顷）Area of Soil Erosion under Control (1 000 hectares)
全 国	**National Total**	**85108**	**5623.8**	**21339.7**	**6032.0**	**94654.5**
北 京	Beijing	83	93.2	149.8		371.3
天 津	Tianjin	143	27.5	400.1	210.4	38.9
河 北	Hebei	1099	159.7	1642.7	838.9	5981.2
山 西	Shanxi	731	53.9	89.1	211.3	5184.5
内蒙古	Inner Mongolia	487	81.7	277.0	305.4	9221.4
辽 宁	Liaoning	967	356.2	996.1	305.5	5756.1
吉 林	Jilin	1238	307.0	1017.9	137.2	3334.0
黑龙江	Heilongjiang	628	88.3	3270.1	196.9	4110.7
上 海	Shanghai			52.4	28.6	
江 苏	Jiangsu	917	189.1	2794.8	701.3	863.6
浙 江	Zhejiang	3971	385.5	495.0	2.9	2239.1
安 徽	Anhui	4872	195.5	2210.0	101.9	1955.5
福 建	Fujian	2681	139.7	117.8	40.2	1129.4
江 西	Jiangxi	9394	283.2	350.6		3666.3
山 东	Shandong	5555	195.7	2601.1	945.3	3787.0
河 南	Henan	2344	397.1	1903.7	698.0	4122.5
湖 北	Hubei	5807	553.8	1195.6		4099.4
湖 南	Hunan	13326	387.6	471.2		2671.1
广 东	Guangdong	6610	415.4	501.9		1291.1
广 西	Guangxi	4327	250.8	204.2	101.6	1487.6
海 南	Hainan	990	94.5	11.3		28.4
重 庆	Chongqing	2752	48.8			1886.5
四 川	Sichuan	6683	162.6	91.0	0.3	5272.5
贵 州	Guizhou	1961	77.9	50.0		2627.1
云 南	Yunnan	5370	106.1	234.4	5.1	4229.2
西 藏	Tibet	50	11.9	31.6	0.2	17.5
陕 西	Shaanxi	999	69.3	129.5	59.3	8930.6
甘 肃	Gansu	272	88.7	12.5	66.3	7744.1
青 海	Qinghai	152	299.0		9.9	744.3
宁 夏	Ningxia	198	19.4		92.0	1643.9
新 疆	Xinjiang	501	84.7	38.4	973.6	219.8

13-12 农村居民家庭生产性固定资产原值(年底数)

Original Value of Productive Fixed Assets of Rural Household at the Year-end

本表为农村住户抽样调查资料。

Data in this table are obtained from the sample surveys on rural households.

单位：元/户 (yuan/household)

年份 地区	Year Region	固定资产原值合计 Total Original Value	农业 Agriculture	工业 Industry	建筑业 Construction	交通运输及邮电业 Transport, Post and Telecom-munication Services	批发零售贸易及餐饮业 Wholesale and Retail Trade and Catering Services	社会服务业 Social Services	文教卫生业 Education, Culture, and Health Care	其他 Others
	1985	792.53	603.34	42.28		112.84				34.07
	1989	1126.07	800.51	72.37		198.22				54.97
	1990	1258.06	898.93	82.56		215.82				60.45
	1995	2774.27	2088.23	182.73		444.73				58.57
	1999	4045.48	2915.49	274.45		638.02				217.53
	2000	4676.98	3321.66	334.79	29.02	621.04	149.24	60.16	12.86	144.30
	2001	4883.80	3544.09	349.89	27.78	630.31	134.85	49.67	16.41	129.05
	2002	5221.33	3741.01	418.20	34.38	662.36	153.65	56.83	19.96	135.01
	2003	5586.34	4152.75	345.61	41.13	640.47	201.85	58.85	23.55	122.12
	2004	5956.18	4457.13	386.33	52.50	684.43	194.50	60.42	21.54	99.32
	2005	7155.55	5179.46	537.48	62.03	863.38	310.71	107.41	43.00	52.07
北 京	Beijing	7726.96	3315.10	740.00	578.80	1802.00	899.47	348.93	29.33	13.33
天 津	Tianjin	10149.88	5005.94	1150.83	666.67	2340.17	480.83	455.43	6.67	43.33
河 北	Hebei	9335.54	6104.43	1085.80	38.33	1356.43	528.02	123.43	79.88	19.21
山 西	Shanxi	4329.27	2397.03	103.29	118.53	1078.29	304.60	266.40	6.67	54.46
内蒙古	Inner Mongolia	13603.24	13108.47	41.23	73.79	213.61	69.32	15.44	7.18	74.19
辽 宁	Liaoning	7514.68	5895.58	91.83	15.34	802.80	515.05	48.94	102.43	42.70
吉 林	Jilin	11322.78	9880.03	572.25	100.63	587.63	143.94	14.19	2.50	21.63
黑龙江	Heilongjiang	10358.83	9992.76	5.36	1.34	242.86	72.32	0.00	8.93	35.27
上 海	Shanghai	1887.00	842.25	83.33		688.91	4.17	258.33		10.00
江 苏	Jiangsu	7134.61	3181.56	1301.37	246.33	1701.74	399.80	110.48	110.21	83.14
浙 江	Zhejiang	12428.10	4320.96	5038.99	134.08	1966.55	635.63	96.61	86.52	148.76
安 徽	Anhui	5857.13	4799.33	137.19	19.21	453.19	303.30	50.39	53.55	40.97
福 建	Fujian	6465.01	4408.15	238.84	63.72	899.55	678.96	70.19	49.67	55.93
江 西	Jiangxi	4613.47	3443.15	231.56	19.89	643.41	205.94	46.73	11.39	11.40
山 东	Shandong	9262.74	5783.08	975.64	83.50	1421.34	698.35	137.81	64.33	98.70
河 南	Henan	6547.33	4910.71	439.31	60.12	692.95	254.06	70.64	85.36	34.19
湖 北	Hubei	4121.20	3183.41	232.18	26.94	544.41	82.12	26.39	5.64	20.11
湖 南	Hunan	3718.29	2892.95	236.78	18.20	392.66	123.59	24.71	17.16	12.24
广 东	Guangdong	3842.26	2269.54	196.16	50.31	488.64	670.08	96.88	62.11	8.55
广 西	Guangxi	4483.33	3672.71	166.82	0.00	507.20	77.90	16.45	8.79	33.46
海 南	Hainan	7492.18	5689.24	58.61	17.50	496.22	1121.17	23.75	32.50	53.19
重 庆	Chongqing	3103.72	2542.97	58.17	4.47	289.92	128.92	6.11	53.77	19.39
四 川	Sichuan	5119.03	4177.98	73.23	17.68	456.38	249.61	27.26	42.33	74.57
贵 州	Guizhou	4175.40	3547.05	84.56	17.86	394.42	74.50	23.39	7.03	26.58
云 南	Yunnan	6605.73	5776.37	6.32	0.23	748.92	40.75	13.80	0.21	19.13
西 藏	Tibet	31409.38	27596.25	34.79	142.29	3435.10	103.54	54.58	1.56	41.25
陕 西	Shaanxi	5664.80	3227.33	67.55	49.98	889.43	178.44	1157.23	35.00	59.85
甘 肃	Gansu	7025.89	5952.97	93.19	2.89	718.06	126.11	32.00	45.83	54.83
青 海	Qinghai	9440.80	7764.96	111.17		1288.78	130.50	32.33	8.67	104.40
宁 夏	Ningxia	14811.19	9732.29	604.72	21.05	3527.30	422.33	94.50		409.00
新 疆	Xinjiang	11978.32	11048.91	34.89		544.90	109.03	53.61	45.03	141.94

13-13 农村居民家庭平均每百户拥有主要生产性固定资产数量（年底数）

Number of Major Productive Fixed Assets Per 100 Rural Households at the Year-end

本表为农村住户抽样调查资料。

Data in this table are obtained from the sample surveys on rural households.

年份 地区	Year Region	汽车 (辆) Motor Vehicles (set)	大中型拖拉机 (台) Large and Medium Tractors (set)	小型和手扶拖拉机 (台) Mini and Walking Tractors (set)	机动脱粒机 (台) Motorized Threshing Machines (set)	胶轮大车 (辆) Carts with Rubber Tyres (set)	农用水泵 (台) Pumps (unit)	役畜 (头) Draught Animals (unit)	产品畜 (头) Commodity Animals (unit)
	1985	0.25	0.35	2.71	1.91	5.49	1.69	57.15	32.12
	1989	0.28	0.47	4.84	2.61	7.68	3.81	58.67	34.63
	1990	0.28	0.45	5.30	3.55	7.89	3.86	57.27	30.91
	1991	0.24	0.51	6.61	3.85	8.24	4.73	53.93	28.73
	1992	0.28	0.55	7.25	4.16	8.67	5.48	52.95	30.07
	1993	0.33	0.64	8.40	5.30	9.60	8.54	59.98	53.15
	1994	0.40	0.79	8.77	5.15	9.32	7.90	58.79	56.70
	1995	0.51	0.77	9.93	6.33	9.29	9.07	55.99	50.72
	1996	0.78	0.99	12.46	6.87	8.78	10.97	54.99	56.26
	1997	0.82	1.39	14.26	7.41	8.83	12.12	55.58	52.72
	1998	1.01	1.22	14.34	8.58	8.52	13.73	48.39	52.20
	1999	1.09	1.44	16.28	8.35	7.87	14.02	45.02	54.08
	2000	1.32	1.41	16.72	9.59	13.26	17.73	41.75	41.56
	2001	1.20	1.50	17.41	9.28	14.52	19.92	39.67	54.65
	2002	1.29	1.53	18.48	9.62	14.31	21.53	39.38	56.43
	2003	1.40	1.79	18.93	10.06	13.71	21.12	35.52	58.62
	2004	1.43	2.24	18.78	10.12	12.88	22.06	34.83	51.83
	2005	1.76	2.13	20.24	8.69	9.85	21.03	29.33	60.28
北京	Beijing	7.47	1.73	7.20	0.13	0.40	1.33	1.07	36.53
天津	Tianjin	6.67	1.67	18.00	0.67	4.67	19.00	5.50	26.00
河北	Hebei	3.32	2.48	36.43	2.17	7.15	22.99	11.95	60.95
山西	Shanxi	3.00	2.29	19.02	1.62	6.90	3.57	18.50	49.14
内蒙古	Inner Mongolia	1.67	3.08	48.98	3.69	29.66	31.50	65.53	272.23
辽宁	Liaoning	1.96	3.23	14.44	1.64	18.02	33.12	33.10	68.73
吉林	Jilin	1.25	3.69	42.00	4.25	22.22	19.94	53.50	70.00
黑龙江	Heilongjiang	1.47	9.87	49.15	3.48	4.11	22.37	19.02	67.10
上海	Shanghai	0.67	0.50	0.50	2.67		6.83		2.33
江苏	Jiangsu	2.02	0.97	16.99	12.29	18.00	17.36	3.66	16.59
浙江	Zhejiang	2.41	1.56	2.81	15.79	3.42	21.61	2.44	24.26
安徽	Anhui	1.00	2.15	40.16	14.27	5.74	53.09	9.24	27.90
福建	Fujian	1.70	0.77	3.13	5.00	6.32	11.48	10.23	30.77
江西	Jiangxi	0.97	0.12	2.39	21.16	8.08	16.21	41.26	18.84
山东	Shandong	2.86	3.29	29.70	1.91	17.04	41.90	12.05	31.90
河南	Henan	1.41	5.58	44.18	6.51	10.88	31.98	12.92	31.69
湖北	Hubei	1.02	0.86	13.08	1.59	11.15	21.91	26.67	22.28
湖南	Hunan	0.84	0.24	2.16	21.14	3.56	24.49	18.73	25.61
广东	Guangdong	1.00	0.23	6.11	13.95	4.59	17.19	26.95	18.01
广西	Guangxi	0.74	1.39	14.21	20.55	4.29	15.54	54.11	38.96
海南	Hainan	0.49	0.83	9.03	13.69	1.39	24.35	59.15	49.86
重庆	Chongqing	0.44	0.06	0.11	13.06	0.22	9.83	20.94	33.33
四川	Sichuan	1.20	0.23	2.01	20.99	1.06	25.23	23.84	52.05
贵州	Guizhou	1.38	0.31	0.71	5.27	0.98	3.97	68.88	33.79
云南	Yunnan	1.79	0.63	8.00	4.67	4.58	6.92	65.92	61.50
西藏	Tibet	5.63	7.08	31.77	5.00	11.88		253.54	754.38
陕西	Shaanxi	1.53	2.84	17.27	3.06	18.51	11.59	19.65	49.50
甘肃	Gansu	0.78	2.33	33.11	2.78	18.17	7.28	75.46	51.56
青海	Qinghai	3.83	1.00	53.83	3.53	3.50	0.17	52.67	111.67
宁夏	Ningxia	2.50	2.67	49.88	3.14	3.83	8.33	48.33	43.33
新疆	Xinjiang	1.48	4.32	27.61	1.68	47.29	1.81	69.42	443.10

13-14 各地区农村居民家庭土地经营情况（2005年底）

Area of Land Managed by Rural Households at the Year-end by Region (2005)

本表为农村住户抽样调查资料。

Data in this table are obtained from the sample surveys on rural households.

单位：亩/人 (mu/person)

地 区	Region	经营耕地面积 Area of Cultivated Land under Management	经营山地面积 Hilly Area under Management	园地面积 Area of Garden Plot	牧草地面积 Area of Grassland	养殖水面面积 Water Area for Breeding Aquatics
全 国	**National Total**	**2.08**	**0.32**	**0.08**	**3.74**	**0.03**
北 京	Beijing	0.69	0.10	0.13	0.01	0.04
天 津	Tianjin	1.33	0.02	0.02		0.04
河 北	Hebei	1.89	0.09	0.07		
山 西	Shanxi	2.20	0.03	0.16	0.01	
内蒙古	Inner Mongolia	8.29	0.52	0.08	121.91	
辽 宁	Liaoning	3.33	0.12	0.06		0.02
吉 林	Jilin	6.24	0.01	0.04		
黑龙江	Heilongjiang	10.42	0.02	0.01		0.01
上 海	Shanghai	0.43		0.04		0.09
江 苏	Jiangsu	1.12	0.01	0.02		0.11
浙 江	Zhejiang	0.70	0.92	0.13		0.07
安 徽	Anhui	1.68	0.32	0.04		0.05
福 建	Fujian	0,80	0.76	0.26		0.09
江 西	Jiangxi	1.47	0.75	0.06		0.04
山 东	Shandong	1.38	0.04	0.07		0.01
河 南	Henan	1.53	0.02	0.04		
湖 北	Hubei	1.53	0.50	0.04		0.09
湖 南	Hunan	1.17	0.56	0.06	0.02	0.05
广 东	Guangdong	0.66	0.37	0.10		0.10
广 西	Guangxi	1.31	0.63	0.14	0.03	0.03
海 南	Hainan	0.98	0.88	0.39		0.02
重 庆	Chongqing	0.96	0.31	0.05	0.02	0.02
四 川	Sichuan	0.96	0.23	0.05		0.02
贵 州	Guizhou	1.02	0.29	0.03	0.02	
云 南	Yunnan	1.40	0.62	0.11	0.01	
西 藏	Tibet	1.98	0.01		0.11	
陕 西	Shaanxi	1.84	0.32	0.25	0.11	
甘 肃	Gansu	2.65	0.68	0.09	0.15	
青 海	Qinghai	1.95	0.07	0.02	19.85	
宁 夏	Ningxia	4.13		0.05	0.54	0.03
新 疆	Xinjiang	4.11	0.01	0.20	3.26	

13-15 农作物总播种面积

Total Sown Areas of Farm Crops

单位：千公顷 (1 000 hectares)

年份 Year 地区 Region	农作物总播种面积 Total Sown Area	粮食作物播种面积 Sown Area of Grain Crops	谷物 Cereal	#稻谷 Rice	#小麦 Wheat	#玉米 Corn	豆类 Soybeans
1978	150104	120587		34421	29183	19961	
1980	146380	117234		33878	28844	20087	
1985	143626	108845		32070	29218	17694	
1989	146554	112205		32700	29841	20353	
1990	148362	113466		33064	30753	21401	
1991	149586	112314	94073	32590	30948	21574	9163
1992	149007	110560	92520	32090	30496	21044	8983
1993	147741	110509	88912	30355	30235	20694	12377
1994	148241	109544	87537	30171	28981	21152	12736
1995	149879	110060	89310	30744	28860	22776	11232
1996	152381	112548	92207	31406	29611	24498	10543
1997	153969	112912	91964	31765	30057	23775	11164
1998	155706	113787	92117	31214	29774	25239	11671
1999	156373	113161	91617	31283	28855	25904	11190
2000	156300	108463	85264	29962	26653	23056	12660
2001	155708	106080	82596	28812	24664	24282	13268
2002	154636	103891	81466	28202	23908	24634	12543
2003	152415	99410	76810	26508	21997	24068	12899
2004	153553	101606	79350	28379	21626	25446	12799
2005	155488	104278	81874	28847	22793	26358	12901
北京 Beijing	318.0	192.2	176.6	0.8	53.3	119.7	12.3
天津 Tianjin	499.4	287.7	258.4	16.7	98.9	138.8	28.1
河北 Hebei	8785.5	6240.2	5611.3	87.7	2377.1	2677.4	333.1
山西 Shanxi	3795.4	3033.6	2333.4	2.7	721.0	1183.7	346.3
内蒙古 Inner Mongolia	6215.7	4373.6	2734.4	84.5	460.6	1805.8	1077.5
辽宁 Liaoning	3796.7	3052.0	2629.5	568.4	22.3	1792.5	294.5
吉林 Jilin	4954.1	4294.5	3554.4	654.0	9.5	2775.2	632.9
黑龙江 Heilongjiang	10083.7	8650.8	4317.7	1650.3	248.5	2220.2	4032.0
上海 Shanghai	403.6	166.1	155.7	112.7	29.9	4.3	9.3
江苏 Jiangsu	7641.2	4909.5	4464.1	2209.3	1684.4	370.2	345.3
浙江 Zhejiang	2837.9	1510.8	1191.4	1028.5	67.1	62.9	209.1
安徽 Anhui	9172.5	6410.9	5051.3	2149.1	2108.3	670.2	1008.6
福建 Fujian	2481.3	1441.3	1003.5	951.6	5.9	39.1	113.2
江西 Jiangxi	5251.4	3441.5	3166.0	3129.0	15.9	16.5	154.2
山东 Shandong	10736.1	6711.7	6178.1	119.8	3278.7	2731.4	251.7
河南 Henan	13922.7	9153.4	8093.9	511.1	4962.7	2508.3	616.5
湖北 Hubei	7279.4	3926.8	3238.6	2077.4	716.2	389.6	290.0
湖南 Hunan	7977.6	4838.6	4178.5	3795.2	65.7	277.3	276.8
广东 Guangdong	4815.4	2786.5	2291.8	2137.6	6.5	136.7	108.3
广西 Guangxi	6489.2	3496.2	2959.4	2360.4	10.7	575.7	280.3
海南 Hainan	778.1	423.8	314.0	300.4		12.9	11.6
重庆 Chongqing	3444.7	2501.3	1537.1	748.0	279.7	460.3	234.5
四川 Sichuan	9480.2	6564.8	4778.5	2087.5	1262.3	1196.6	585.6
贵州 Guizhou	4804.1	3073.7	1928.3	721.7	410.6	719.5	324.8
云南 Yunnan	6053.8	4253.9	3087.8	1049.3	532.3	1182.6	478.6
西藏 Tibet	235.0	177.7	168.2	1.0	42.0	3.3	9.0
陕西 Shaanxi	4201.8	3263.9	2567.9	147.1	1211.5	1097.1	382.3
甘肃 Gansu	3726.0	2587.2	1811.1	5.1	1000.8	484.8	245.1
青海 Qinghai	476.7	245.6	129.4		96.8	1.1	40.9
宁夏 Ningxia	1099.3	775.9	587.7	71.3	276.0	178.3	70.9
新疆 Xinjiang	3731.2	1492.8	1376.0	69.3	737.2	526.1	98.3

13-15 续表 1 continued

单位：千公顷 (1 000 hectares)

年份 地区	Year Region	薯类 Tubers	油料 Oil-bearing Crops	#花生 Peanuts	#油菜籽 Rapeseeds	棉花 Cotton	麻类 Fiber Crops	#黄红麻 Jute and Ambary Hemp	糖料 Sugar Crops
	1978	11796	6222	1768	2600	4866	751	412	879
	1980	10153	7928	2339	2844	4920	666	314	922
	1985	8572	11800	3318	4494	5140	1231	992	1525
	1989	9097	10504	2946	4993	5203	563	286	1529
	1990	9121	10900	2907	5503	5588	495	300	1679
	1991	9078	11530	2880	6133	6538	453	270	1947
	1992	9057	11489	2976	5976	6835	434	277	1906
	1993	9220	11142	3379	5300	4985	420	274	1687
	1994	9270	12081	3776	5783	5528	372	176	1755
	1995	9519	13102	3809	6907	5422	376	147	1820
	1996	9797	12555	3616	6734	4722	349	147	1846
	1997	9785	12381	3722	6475	4491	327	162	1923
	1998	10000	12919	4039	6527	4459	224	93	1984
	1999	10355	13906	4268	6899	3726	205	65	1644
	2000	10538	15400	4856	7494	4041	262	50	1514
	2001	10217	14631	4991	7095	4810	323	52	1654
	2002	9881	14766	4921	7143	4184	338	55	1872
	2003	9702	14990	5057	7221	5111	337	41	1657
	2004	9457	14431	4745	7271	5693	332	32	1568
	2005	9503	14318	4662	7278	5062	335	31	1564
北 京	Beijing	3.3	8.6	8.3		1.8			
天 津	Tianjin	1.2	5.1	2.3		61.2			
河 北	Hebei	295.9	559.0	438.8	35.4	573.5	2.2	0.3	10.5
山 西	Shanxi	354.0	273.4	14.6	10.1	97.5	0.1		1.2
内蒙古	Inner Mongolia	561.7	694.7	10.0	255.7	1.6	10.3		38.1
辽 宁	Liaoning	128.0	203.3	172.4	0.9	2.8	0.1		2.1
吉 林	Jilin	107.2	288.5	111.9		1.0	1.6		2.8
黑龙江	Heilongjiang	301.1	410.3	23.9	1.9		84.7		80.5
上 海	Shanghai	1.0	32.1	1.2	30.8	1.1			2.8
江 苏	Jiangsu	100.2	846.9	174.3	660.5	368.3	1.5	0.2	4.1
浙 江	Zhejiang	110.3	249.3	18.1	227.2	17.9	0.5	0.3	15.7
安 徽	Anhui	351.0	1303.1	238.5	953.6	375.7	12.8	6.5	5.7
福 建	Fujian	324.6	122.4	107.2	13.8	0.1	0.1	0.1	14.9
江 西	Jiangxi	121.2	577.0	135.1	409.7	63.9	7.8	0.5	17.7
山 东	Shandong	281.9	899.8	884.8	12.4	846.3	0.7	0.6	
河 南	Henan	443.0	1605.8	979.3	407.8	781.6	13.5	13.3	4.8
湖 北	Hubei	398.2	1460.2	171.7	1178.7	390.3	23.6	1.0	10.0
湖 南	Hunan	383.3	898.3	137.5	752.2	150.9	53.7	0.3	19.6
广 东	Guangdong	386.4	318.0	309.4	7.0		0.5	0.5	147.5
广 西	Guangxi	256.5	314.1	243.7	60.6	1.7	5.3	4.8	747.6
海 南	Hainan	98.2	44.7	41.4			0.2	0.1	60.0
重 庆	Chongqing	729.6	252.4	54.4	187.3	0.2	8.5	0.2	2.8
四 川	Sichuan	1200.7	1093.6	264.0	817.2	27.8	37.0	1.8	26.9
贵 州	Guizhou	820.7	555.8	43.3	504.8	1.4	1.3		19.5
云 南	Yunnan	687.5	225.3	42.9	169.1	0.6	27.3		255.2
西 藏	Tibet	0.6	26.1	0.1	26.1				
陕 西	Shaanxi	313.7	276.9	29.6	178.7	70.2	1.1	0.5	0.1
甘 肃	Gansu	531.0	328.9	1.1	157.3	64.0	4.4		4.5
青 海	Qinghai	75.3	161.9		159.7				
宁 夏	Ningxia	117.3	96.9		0.1				
新 疆	Xinjiang	18.5	185.5	2.7	59.9	1160.5	35.9		69.9

13-15 续表 2 continued

单位：千公顷 (1 000 hectares)

年 份 地 区	Year Region	#甘 蔗 Sugarcane	#甜 菜 Beetroots	烟 叶 Tobacco	#烤 烟 Flue-cured Tobacco	蔬 菜 Vegetables	茶园面积 Area of Tea Plantations at Year-end	果园面积 Area of Orchards at Year-end
	1978	549	331	784	613	3331	1048	1657
	1980	480	443	512	397	3163	1041	1783
	1985	965	560	1313	1077	4753	1077	2736
	1989	959	569	1798	1503	6290	1065	5372
	1990	1009	670	1593	1342	6338	1061	5179
	1991	1164	783	1804	1562	6546	1060	5318
	1992	1246	660	2093	1849	7031	1084	5818
	1993	1088	599	2089	1835	8084	1171	6432
	1994	1057	698	1490	1302	8921	1135	7264
	1995	1125	695	1470	1309	9515	1115	8098
	1996	1207	638	1853	1683	10491	1103	8553
	1997	1311	612	2353	2161	11288	1076	8648
	1998	1401	583	1361	1200	12293	1057	8535
	1999	1303	341	1374	1216	13347	1130	8667
	2000	1185	329	1437	1269	15237	1089	8932
	2001	1248	406	1340	1181	16402	1141	9043
	2002	1393	424	1328	1192	17353	1134	9098
	2003	1409	248	1264	1139	17954	1207	9437
	2004	1378	190	1266	1145	17560	1262	9768
	2005	1354	210	1363	1245	17721	1352	10035
北 京	Beijing					88.6		75.7
天 津	Tianjin					129.7		37.1
河 北	Hebei		10.5	3.7	2.6	1104.8		1115.1
山 西	Shanxi		1.2	2.7	2.5	244.9		279.7
内蒙古	Inner Mongolia		38.1	8.2	6.9	221.5		52.1
辽 宁	Liaoning		2.1	19.8	18.5	413.7		317.0
吉 林	Jilin		2.8	22.6	12.6	209.6		67.8
黑龙江	Heilongjiang		80.5	42.1	39.7	333.4		39.5
上 海	Shanghai	2.8				130.9		22.3
江 苏	Jiangsu	4.1		0.6		1194.4	23.9	191.4
浙 江	Zhejiang	15.7		1.8		666.7	154.7	299.8
安 徽	Anhui	5.7		10.8	10.3	664.9	117.6	104.2
福 建	Fujian	14.9		66.8	65.8	632.1	155.2	550.7
江 西	Jiangxi	17.7		11.7	10.6	543.6	38.2	295.8
山 东	Shandong			34.6	33.9	1847.7	14.5	767.9
河 南	Henan	4.8		132.3	127.1	1595.9	33.1	416.6
湖 北	Hubei	10.0		58.4	43.7	1004.8	138.4	265.1
湖 南	Hunan	19.6		100.1	94.8	997.1	80.1	430.8
广 东	Guangdong	147.5		31.6	26.5	1162.7	36.0	996.9
广 西	Guangxi	747.6		20.9	13.9	1094.4	36.9	865.2
海 南	Hainan	60.0		0.3	0.3	172.4	1.5	163.4
重 庆	Chongqing	2.8		51.5	41.5	400.0	25.8	179.3
四 川	Sichuan	26.7	0.2	79.5	58.8	991.5	152.0	462.0
贵 州	Guizhou	19.4	0.1	222.7	206.6	473.3	59.7	118.9
云 南	Yunnan	255.0	0.2	392.6	381.7	492.0	218.5	224.8
西 藏	Tibet					18.0	0.2	1.1
陕 西	Shaanxi	0.1		32.9	32.6	331.7	59.5	817.5
甘 肃	Gansu		4.5	14.2	13.3	306.8	6.3	347.6
青 海	Qinghai			0.2		25.8		4.3
宁 夏	Ningxia			0.1	0.1	51.3		48.6
新 疆	Xinjiang		69.9	0.5	0.3	176.7		477.0

13-16 主要农作物种植结构

Planting Structure of Major Farm Crops

单位：% (%)

项　目	Item	1995	2000	2002	2003	2004	2005
农作物总播种面积	**Total Sown Areas of Farm Crops**	**100.00**	**100.00**	**100.00**	**100.00**	**100.00**	**100.00**
粮食作物	**Grain Crops**	**73.43**	**69.39**	**67.18**	**65.22**	**66.17**	**67.07**
谷物	Cereal	59.59	54.55	52.68	50.40	51.68	52.66
稻谷	Rice	20.51	19.17	18.24	17.39	18.48	18.55
小麦	Wheat	19.26	17.05	15.46	14.43	14.08	14.66
玉米	Corn	15.20	14.75	15.93	15.79	16.57	16.95
谷子	Millet	1.02	0.80	0.74	0.67	0.60	0.55
高粱	Jowar	0.81	0.57	0.55	0.47	0.37	0.37
其它谷物	Other Cereal	2.80	2.21	1.77	1.63	1.57	1.58
豆类	Soybeans	7.49	8.10	8.11	8.46	8.34	8.30
#大豆	Soja	5.42	5.95	5.64	6.11	6.24	6.17
杂豆	Miscellaneous Beans	2.07	2.15	2.47	2.35	2.09	2.13
薯类	Tubers	6.35	6.74	6.39	6.37	6.16	6.11
#马铃薯	Potato	2.29	3.02	3.02	2.97	2.99	3.14
油料作物	**Oil-bearing Crops**	**8.74**	**9.85**	**9.55**	**9.83**	**9.40**	**9.21**
#花生	Peanuts	2.54	3.11	3.18	3.32	3.09	3.00
油菜籽	Rapeseeds	4.61	4.79	4.62	4.74	4.74	4.68
芝麻	Sesame	0.43	0.50	0.49	0.45	0.41	0.38
胡麻籽	Benne	0.41	0.32	0.29	0.29	0.27	0.26
向日葵	Helianthus	0.54	0.79	0.73	0.77	0.61	0.66
棉花	**Cotton**	**3.62**	**2.59**	**2.71**	**3.35**	**3.71**	**3.26**
麻类	**Fiber Crops**	**0.25**	**0.17**	**0.22**	**0.22**	**0.22**	**0.22**
#黄红麻	Jute and Ambary Hemp	0.10	0.03	0.04	0.03	0.02	0.02
苎　麻	Ramee	0.06	0.06	0.08	0.08	0.08	0.08
大　麻	Hemp		0.01	0.01	0.01	0.01	0.01
亚　麻	Flax	0.08	0.06	0.09	0.10	0.10	0.10
糖料	**Sugar Crops**	**1.21**	**0.97**	**1.18**	**1.09**	**1.02**	**1.01**
甘蔗	Sugarcane	0.75	0.76	0.90	0.92	0.90	0.87
甜菜	Beetroots	0.46	0.21	0.27	0.16	0.12	0.14
烟叶	**Tobacco**	**0.98**	**0.92**	**0.86**	**0.83**	**0.82**	**0.88**
#烤烟	Flue-cured Tobacco	0.87	0.81	0.77	0.75	0.75	0.80
药材	**Medicinal Materials**	**0.19**	**0.43**	**0.62**	**0.82**	**0.84**	**0.78**
蔬菜、瓜类	**Vegetables and Melon**	**7.08**	**11.06**	**12.74**	**13.32**	**12.83**	**12.82**
#蔬菜	Vegetables	6.35	9.75	11.22	11.78	11.44	11.40
其他农作物	**Other Farm Crops**	**4.49**	**4.70**	**4.94**	**5.31**	**4.99**	**4.78**
#青饲料	Succulence	1.22	1.37	1.95	2.33	2.18	2.17

13-17 主要农产品产量

Output of Major Farm Products

单位：万吨 (10 000 tons)

年份 地区	Year Region	粮食 Grain	谷物 Cereal	#稻谷 Rice	#小麦 Wheat	#玉米 Corn	豆类 Beans	薯类 Tubers	棉花 Cotton
1978		30476.5		13693.0	5384.0	5594.5		3174.0	216.7
1980		32055.5		13990.5	5520.5	6260.0		2872.5	270.7
1985		37910.8		16856.9	8580.5	6382.6		2603.6	414.7
1989		40754.9		18013.0	9080.7	7892.8		2730.4	378.8
1990		44624.3		18933.1	9822.9	9681.9		2743.3	450.8
1991		43529.3	39566.3	18381.3	9595.3	9877.3	1247.1	2715.9	567.5
1992		44265.8	40169.6	18622.2	10158.7	9538.3	1252.0	2844.2	450.8
1993		45648.8	40517.4	17751.4	10639.0	10270.4	1950.4	3181.1	373.9
1994		44510.1	39389.1	17593.3	9929.7	9927.5	2095.6	3025.4	434.1
1995		46661.8	41611.6	18522.6	10220.7	11198.6	1787.5	3262.6	476.8
1996		50453.5	45127.1	19510.3	11056.9	12747.1	1790.3	3536.0	420.3
1997		49417.1	44349.3	20073.5	12328.9	10430.9	1875.5	3192.3	460.3
1998		51229.5	45624.7	19871.3	10972.6	13295.4	2000.6	3604.2	450.1
1999		50838.6	45304.1	19848.7	11388.0	12808.6	1894.0	3640.6	382.9
2000		46217.5	40522.4	18790.8	9963.6	10600.0	2010.0	3685.2	441.7
2001		45263.7	39648.2	17758.0	9387.3	11408.8	2052.8	3563.1	532.4
2002		45705.8	39798.7	17453.9	9029.0	12130.8	2241.2	3665.9	491.6
2003		43069.5	37428.7	16065.6	8648.8	11583.0	2127.5	3513.3	486.0
2004		46946.9	41157.2	17908.8	9195.2	13028.7	2232.1	3557.7	632.4
2005		48402.2	42776.0	18058.8	9744.5	13936.5	2157.7	3468.5	571.4
北京	Beijing	94.9	90.4	0.5	26.7	62.6	2.4	2.1	0.2
天津	Tianjin	137.5	133.1	12.2	47.4	73.2	3.9	0.6	8.4
河北	Hebei	2598.6	2452.9	51.6	1150.3	1193.8	51.2	94.5	57.7
山西	Shanxi	978.0	882.1	0.9	202.3	616.1	36.7	59.3	10.3
内蒙古	Inner Mongolia	1662.2	1342.1	62.2	143.6	1066.2	164.1	156.0	0.2
辽宁	Liaoning	1745.8	1660.3	416.5	7.9	1135.5	43.6	41.9	0.3
吉林	Jilin	2581.2	2352.5	473.3	2.7	1800.7	152.8	75.9	0.2
黑龙江	Heilongjiang	3092.0	2324.7	1121.5	94.0	1042.9	680.0	87.3	
上海	Shanghai	105.4	101.3	85.5	9.9	2.8	3.2	0.9	0.2
江苏	Jiangsu	2834.6	2696.9	1706.7	728.5	174.8	82.4	55.3	32.3
浙江	Zhejiang	814.7	705.3	644.8	21.8	25.9	47.4	62.0	2.2
安徽	Anhui	2605.3	2385.8	1250.8	808.1	264.9	95.5	124.0	32.5
福建	Fujian	715.2	544.0	526.6	2.0	13.2	24.7	146.5	
江西	Jiangxi	1757.0	1677.6	1667.2	2.7	6.3	24.9	54.6	8.7
山东	Shandong	3917.4	3650.1	95.8	1800.5	1735.4	68.2	199.1	84.6
河南	Henan	4582.0	4277.5	359.8	2577.7	1298.0	74.4	230.1	67.7
湖北	Hubei	2177.4	1956.2	1535.3	208.9	194.9	65.0	156.2	37.5
湖南	Hunan	2678.6	2452.7	2296.2	13.4	134.0	56.7	169.2	19.8
广东	Guangdong	1395.0	1185.1	1117.0	1.9	61.5	24.4	185.5	
广西	Guangxi	1487.3	1384.9	1169.1	1.8	212.0	40.3	62.1	0.1
海南	Hainan	153.0	116.0	110.6		5.4	2.2	34.8	
重庆	Chongqing	1168.2	845.8	521.5	78.6	233.1	42.2	280.3	
四川	Sichuan	3211.1	2581.4	1505.7	427.4	580.8	131.5	498.2	2.5
贵州	Guizhou	1152.1	901.2	472.8	73.0	344.3	37.8	213.1	0.1
云南	Yunnan	1514.9	1259.2	646.3	106.9	449.3	77.2	178.6	
西藏	Tibet	93.4	89.6	0.6	25.6	1.7	3.2	0.6	
陕西	Shaanxi	1043.0	963.9	89.2	401.2	459.7	37.1	42.0	7.8
甘肃	Gansu	836.9	605.4	4.1	264.8	248.5	41.7	189.9	11.1
青海	Qinghai	93.3	49.1		39.3	0.9	11.8	32.5	
宁夏	Ningxia	299.8	266.3	61.1	79.4	121.4	6.0	27.5	
新疆	Xinjiang	876.6	843.0	53.8	396.2	376.7	25.4	8.2	187.4

13-17 续表 1 continued

单位：万吨 (10 000 tons)

年份 地区	Year Region	油料 Oil-bearing Crops	#花生 Peanuts	#油菜籽 Rapeseeds	#芝麻 Sesame	麻类 Fiber Crops	#黄红麻 Jute and Ambary Hemp	甘蔗 Sugarcane	甜菜 Beetroots
	1978	521.8	237.7	186.8	32.2	135.1	108.8	2111.6	270.2
	1980	769.1	360.0	238.4	25.9	143.6	109.8	2280.7	630.5
	1985	1578.4	666.4	560.7	69.1	444.8	411.9	5154.9	891.9
	1989	1295.2	536.3	543.6	33.8	112.4	66.0	4879.5	924.3
	1990	1613.2	636.8	695.8	46.9	109.7	72.6	5762.0	1452.5
	1991	1638.3	630.3	743.6	43.5	88.4	51.3	6789.8	1628.9
	1992	1641.2	595.3	765.3	51.6	93.8	61.9	7301.1	1506.9
	1993	1803.9	842.1	693.9	56.3	96.0	67.2	6419.4	1204.8
	1994	1989.6	968.2	749.2	54.8	74.7	35.5	6092.7	1252.6
	1995	2250.3	1023.5	977.7	58.3	89.7	37.1	6541.7	1398.4
	1996	2210.6	1013.8	920.1	57.5	79.5	36.5	6818.7	1541.5
	1997	2157.4	964.8	957.8	56.6	74.9	43.0	7889.7	1496.8
	1998	2313.9	1188.6	830.1	65.6	49.5	24.8	8343.8	1446.6
	1999	2601.2	1263.9	1013.2	74.3	47.2	16.4	7470.3	863.9
	2000	2954.8	1443.7	1138.1	81.1	52.9	12.6	6828.0	807.3
	2001	2864.9	1441.6	1133.1	80.4	68.1	10.6	7566.3	1088.9
	2002	2897.2	1481.8	1055.2	89.5	96.4	15.9	9010.7	1282.0
	2003	2811.0	1342.0	1142.0	59.3	85.3	10.0	9023.5	618.2
	2004	3065.9	1434.2	1318.2	70.4	107.4	8.7	8984.9	585.7
	2005	3077.1	1434.2	1305.2	62.5	110.5	8.3	8663.8	788.1
北京	Beijing	2.5	2.5						
天津	Tianjin	1.3	0.8						
河北	Hebei	152.7	140.3	4.7	1.5	0.7	0.1		42.7
山西	Shanxi	21.3	2.9	0.8	0.4				4.0
内蒙古	Inner Mongolia	122.2	1.4	28.3	0.9	2.5			138.3
辽宁	Liaoning	36.8	33.0	0.1	0.6				6.3
吉林	Jilin	54.4	28.7		3.5	0.6			7.4
黑龙江	Heilongjiang	60.6	4.8	0.3	0.8	36.1			155.0
上海	Shanghai	6.9	0.4	6.5				14.5	
江苏	Jiangsu	216.0	55.5	158.7	1.8	0.5	0.1	22.2	
浙江	Zhejiang	50.1	4.9	44.7	0.6	0.1	0.1	90.0	
安徽	Anhui	270.7	79.3	182.3	9.0	3.2	1.9	21.3	
福建	Fujian	27.4	25.5	1.8	0.1			93.3	
江西	Jiangxi	76.1	31.7	41.7	2.5	1.3	0.2	78.3	
山东	Shandong	363.9	359.9	3.0	0.2	0.2	0.2		
河南	Henan	449.6	338.3	87.7	22.1	3.8	3.7	25.2	
湖北	Hubei	293.9	60.2	219.1	13.7	4.9	0.3	42.9	
湖南	Hunan	141.0	31.7	108.2	1.0	14.0	0.1	100.4	
广东	Guangdong	77.0	75.9	1.0	0.2	0.1	0.1	1114.2	
广西	Guangxi	63.2	55.1	6.3	0.5	1.1	1.0	5154.7	
海南	Hainan	8.5	8.3		0.2	0.1	0.1	278.9	
重庆	Chongqing	42.7	9.7	31.8	0.7	1.2		11.5	
四川	Sichuan	232.3	62.0	168.7	0.6	6.9	0.4	132.9	0.3
贵州	Guizhou	84.9	7.3	76.5		0.1		67.8	
云南	Yunnan	36.2	5.7	29.0		14.1		1415.5	0.4
西藏	Tibet	6.1		6.1					
陕西	Shaanxi	45.4	7.6	30.3	1.7	0.1		0.2	0.1
甘肃	Gansu	50.3	0.2	26.6		1.7			14.5
青海	Qinghai	31.9		31.6					
宁夏	Ningxia	12.2							0.1
新疆	Xinjiang	38.9	0.6	9.2		17.1			419.1

13-17 续表 2 continued

单位：万吨 (10 000 tons)

年份 地区	Year Region	烟叶 Tobacco	#烤烟 Flue-cured Tobacco	蚕茧 Silkworm Cocoons	#桑蚕茧 Mulberry Silkworm Cocoons	茶叶 Tea	水果 Fruits	#苹果 Apples	#柑桔 Citrus	#梨 Pears	#葡萄 Grapes	#香蕉 Bananas
	1978	124.2	105.2	22.8	17.3	26.8	657.0	227.5	38.3	151.7	10.4	8.5
	1980	84.5	71.7	32.6	25.0	30.4	679.3	236.3	71.3	146.6	11.0	6.1
	1985	242.5	207.5	37.1	33.6	43.2	1163.9	361.4	180.8	213.7	36.1	63.1
	1989	283.0	240.5	48.8	43.5	53.5	1831.9	449.9	456.1	256.5	87.4	140.4
	1990	262.7	225.9	53.4	48.0	54.0	1874.4	431.9	485.5	235.3	85.9	145.6
	1991	303.1	267.0	58.4	55.1	54.2	2176.1	454.0	633.3	249.8	91.6	198.1
	1992	349.9	311.9	69.2	66.0	56.0	2440.1	655.6	516.0	284.6	112.5	245.1
	1993	345.1	303.6	75.7	71.2	60.0	3011.2	907.0	656.1	321.7	135.5	270.1
	1994	223.8	194.0	81.3	77.7	58.8	3499.8	1112.9	680.5	404.3	152.2	289.8
	1995	231.4	207.2	80.0	76.0	58.9	4214.6	1400.8	822.5	494.2	174.2	312.5
	1996	323.4	294.6	50.8	47.1	59.3	4652.8	1704.7	845.7	580.7	188.3	253.6
	1997	425.1	390.8	46.9	42.3	61.3	5089.3	1721.9	1010.2	641.5	203.3	289.2
	1998	236.4	208.8	52.6	47.5	66.5	5452.9	1948.1	859.0	727.5	235.8	351.8
	1999	246.9	218.5	48.5	44.7	67.6	6237.6	2080.2	1078.7	774.2	270.8	419.4
	2000	255.2	223.8	54.8	50.1	68.3	6225.1	2043.1	878.3	841.2	328.2	494.1
	2001	235.0	204.5	65.5	60.2	70.2	6658.0	2001.5	1160.7	879.6	368.0	527.2
	2002	244.7	213.5	69.8	64.5	74.5	6952.0	1924.1	1199.0	930.9	447.9	555.7
	2003	225.7	201.5	66.7	61.1	76.8	14517.4	2110.2	1345.4	979.8	517.6	590.3
	2004	240.6	216.3	73.1	67.7	83.5	15340.9	2367.5	1495.8	1064.2	567.5	605.6
	2005	268.3	243.5	78.0	71.3	93.5	16120.1	2401.1	1591.9	1132.4	579.4	651.8
北京	Beijing						111.9	13.8		14.6	5.1	
天津	Tianjin						68.2	6.6		2.3	9.3	
河北	Hebei	1.0	0.5	0.1	0.1		1397.9	220.2		324.6	86.4	
山西	Shanxi	0.6	0.6	0.4	0.4		314.4	164.8		24.6	11.9	
内蒙古	Inner Mongolia	2.0	1.5	1.2			178.8	6.2		7.8	2.9	
辽宁	Liaoning	3.4	3.2	4.3			451.3	130.0		69.0	58.2	
吉林	Jilin	6.0	2.5	0.2			235.3	25.2		13.5	11.0	
黑龙江	Heilongjiang	7.4	7.4	0.3			352.6	17.7		4.8	2.1	
上海	Shanghai						101.0		18.0	1.9	2.7	
江苏	Jiangsu	0.1		10.6	10.6	1.2	606.4	55.3	5.2	55.6	15.3	
浙江	Zhejiang	0.4		8.5	8.5	14.4	578.0		148.1	31.0	22.0	
安徽	Anhui	2.6	2.5	3.1	3.1	6.0	711.6	27.8	1.2	63.8	17.3	
福建	Fujian	11.7	11.5			18.5	559.1		215.3	14.8	5.9	85.5
江西	Jiangxi	2.1	2.0	0.9	0.9	1.7	325.4		109.8	7.5	0.4	
山东	Shandong	7.5	7.3	6.5	6.3	0.7	2546.8	671.7		106.1	83.1	
河南	Henan	28.8	28.1	2.0	1.5	1.7	1842.2	300.6	3.6	65.5	41.3	
湖北	Hubei	11.1	7.9	1.1	1.1	8.5	566.8	1.2	146.3	50.2	5.0	
湖南	Hunan	21.3	20.4			7.2	519.5		212.0	10.8	5.2	
广东	Guangdong	6.3	5.1	6.5	6.5	4.4	946.5		182.7	4.3		330.2
广西	Guangxi	3.3	2.0	14.8	14.8	2.6	766.8		187.7	12.1	11.9	117.4
海南	Hainan					0.1	220.4		2.0			91.3
重庆	Chongqing	9.0	7.2	3.1	3.1	1.7	154.6	0.6	90.9	18.0	2.1	0.2
四川	Sichuan	18.2	13.2	9.8	9.8	9.8	527.2	24.3	213.7	68.5	16.1	1.8
贵州	Guizhou	36.9	34.5	0.1	0.1	2.3	96.0	1.0	17.2	12.4	2.1	0.9
云南	Yunnan	79.1	77.2	1.9	1.9	11.6	169.7	15.9	21.1	19.7	7.0	24.5
西藏	Tibet						0.9	0.6		0.1		
陕西	Shaanxi	5.9	5.9	2.3	2.3	1.1	906.1	560.1	16.8	62.1	13.9	
甘肃	Gansu	3.4	3.1			0.1	280.7	101.3	0.3	28.3	7.8	
青海	Qinghai	0.1					2.6	0.7		0.5		
宁夏	Ningxia	0.1	0.1				69.6	22.2		1.2	4.8	
新疆	Xinjiang	0.1					511.9	33.0		36.8	128.8	

注：2003年起水果产量包括瓜果类产量。

a) Data of output of fruits after 2003 include yield of melon and fruit.

13-18 主要农产品单位面积产量

Output of Major Farm Products Per Hectare

单位：公斤/公顷 (kg/hectare)

年份 地区	Year Region	谷物 Cereals	棉花 Cotton	花生 Peanuts	油菜籽 Rapeseeds	芝麻 Sesame	黄红麻 Jute and Ambary Hemp	甘蔗 Sugarcane	甜菜 Beetroots	烤烟 Flue-cured Tobacco
	1978		445	1344	718	506	2639	38496	8166	1717
	1980		550	1539	838	333	3497	47562	14242	1806
	1985		807	2008	1248	657	4154	53430	15913	1927
	1989		728	1820	1089	467	2310	50856	16243	1600
	1990		807	2191	1264	702	2421	57118	21668	1683
	1991	4206	868	2189	1212	640	1902	58345	20791	1709
	1992	4342	660	2000	1281	692	2233	58605	22832	1687
	1993	4557	750	2492	1309	747	2449	59012	20124	1654
	1994	4500	785	2564	1295	794	2020	57669	17935	1491
	1995	4659	879	2687	1415	908	2534	58133	20132	1584
	1996	4894	890	2804	1366	969	2487	56470	24150	1750
	1997	4822	1025	2592	1479	919	2649	60158	24475	1809
	1998	4953	1009	2943	1272	1042	2677	59550	24806	1740
	1999	4945	1028	2961	1469	1066	2540	57338	25334	1797
	2000	4753	1093	2973	1519	1034	2516	57626	24518	1763
	2001	4800	1107	2888	1597	1061	2046	60625	26807	1732
	2002	4885	1175	3011	1477	1180	2868	64663	30232	1792
	2003	4873	951	2654	1582	863	2462	64023	24925	1768
	2004	5187	1111	3022	1813	1128	2719	65199	30829	1889
	2005	5225	1129	3076	1793	1054	2670	63970	37523	1956
北京	Beijing	5121	1149	2964		960				
天津	Tianjin	5150	1364	3432		1064				
河北	Hebei	4371	1006	3198	1318	957	2324		40704	1918
山西	Shanxi	3780	1056	1962	758	716			32473	2399
内蒙古	Inner Mongolia	4908	1117	1452	1109	1111			36331	2185
辽宁	Liaoning	6314	959	1915	1190	943			29962	1716
吉林	Jilin	6619		2562		1101			26351	1976
黑龙江	Heilongjiang	5384		2023	1703	1029			19264	1850
上海	Shanghai	6503	1628	3333	2115			51278		
江苏	Jiangsu	6041	876	3182	2402	1533	3217	54146	12750	
浙江	Zhejiang	5920	1204	2676	1967	1528	2681	57270		
安徽	Anhui	4723	864	3324	1912	822	2979	37213		2407
福建	Fujian	5421	880	2377	1308	990	2948	62535		1748
江西	Jiangxi	5299	1365	2344	1017	827	3094	44271		1857
山东	Shandong	5908	1000	4067	2401	1339	3021			2168
河南	Henan	5285	866	3454	2151	1049	2780	53042		2207
湖北	Hubei	6040	961	3505	1859	1334	3430	43113		1804
湖南	Hunan	5870	1309	2305	1439	1272	1979	51329		2150
广东	Guangdong	5171		2452	1424	1006	2617	75557		1908
广西	Guangxi	4680	536	2262	1045	932	1982	68950		1414
海南	Hainan	3696		2016		555	8820	46483		110
重庆	Chongqing	5503	726	1786	1698	975	727	41078		1726
四川	Sichuan	5402	888	2349	2065	1328	2288	49692	15216	2249
贵州	Guizhou	4673	398	1694	1516	671	3148	34861	5554	1668
云南	Yunnan	4078	393	1339	1716	672		55508	16922	2023
西藏	Tibet	5328		2563	2348					
陕西	Shaanxi	3754	1107	2563	1697	1014	1077	36117	19098	1805
甘肃	Gansu	3343	1728	1722	1693				32683	2353
青海	Qinghai	3792			1976				21850	
宁夏	Ningxia	4530			1313				59200	5777
新疆	Xinjiang	6126	1615	2411	1539	920			59960	1288

13-19 主要林产品产量

Output of Major Forest Products

单位：吨 (ton)

年份 地区	Year Region	橡胶 Rubber	松脂 Pine Resin	生漆 Lacquer	油桐籽 Tung-oil Seeds	油茶籽 Tea-oil Seeds	核桃 Walnuts
	1978	101600	337600	2200	391150	478900	118650
	1980	112945	420750	2450	303350	490350	118900
	1985	187901	343946	2168	378770	619229	121917
	1989	242766	486837	2951	334757	667245	160053
	1990	264243	435244	2683	350770	523313	149560
	1995	424025	548133	2976	404929	623128	230867
	1996	402450	580819	3740	407744	696633	237989
	1997	451970	701183	4416	453535	856868	249834
	1998	462344	543156	4577	438680	722846	265121
	1999	489991	571477	5314	448323	792690	274246
	2000	480248	551057	5279	453461	823224	309875
	2001	477437	563689	4925	406716	824731	252347
	2002	527413	563388	6360	389024	854624	340174
	2003	565045	625757	8664	372645	779492	393529
	2004	574739	673310	9641	381428	874861	436862
	2005	513618	767134	14316	368688	875022	499074
北京	Beijing						13787
天津	Tianjin						442
河北	Hebei						47032
山西	Shanxi						53432
内蒙古	Inner Mongolia						
辽宁	Liaoning						25576
吉林	Jilin						2888
黑龙江	Heilongjiang						
上海	Shanghai						
江苏	Jiangsu					170	151
浙江	Zhejiang		1940		162	43361	
安徽	Anhui		5433	220	3208	9743	6300
福建	Fujian	40	72299	892	20928	72597	112
江西	Jiangxi		93164	355	16160	189020	3255
山东	Shandong						20465
河南	Henan		266	955	45802	8079	25339
湖北	Hubei		8334	4413	10315	9928	9051
湖南	Hunan		32850	3022	42523	374516	3761
广东	Guangdong	24784	154593	29	5193	30470	
广西	Guangxi	678	301943	71	60372	117363	339
海南	Hainan	247775	3836				
重庆	Chongqing		4795	794	20041	1991	3272
四川	Sichuan		2911	725	30314	2464	59272
贵州	Guizhou		4882	1328	81669	10558	6840
云南	Yunnan	240341	79663	404	18883	4618	91200
西藏	Tibet						622
陕西	Shaanxi		225	1047	12577	144	63790
甘肃	Gansu			61	541		29675
青海	Qinghai						86
宁夏	Ningxia						627
新疆	Xinjiang						31761

13-20 牲畜饲养情况

Number of Livestock

单位：万头、万只 (10 000 heads)

年份 地区	Year Region	大牲畜年底头数 Large Animals (year-end)	牛 Cattle and Buffaloes	马 Horses	驴 Donkeys	骡 Mules	骆驼 Camels
	1996	13360.6	11031.8	871.5	944.4	478.0	34.5
	1997	14541.8	12182.2	891.2	952.8	480.6	35.0
	1998	14803.2	12441.9	898.1	955.8	473.9	33.5
	1999	15024.8	12698.3	891.4	934.8	467.3	33.0
	2000	15151.5	12866.3	876.6	922.7	453.0	32.6
	2001	14995.9	12824.2	826.0	881.5	436.2	27.9
	2002	15189.3	13084.8	808.8	849.9	419.4	26.4
	2003	15500.1	13467.2	790.0	820.7	395.7	26.5
	2004	15737.8	13781.8	763.9	791.9	374.0	26.2
	2005	15947.5	14157.5	740.0	777.2	360.4	26.6
北 京	Beijing	26.6	24.4	0.2	1.4	0.6	
天 津	Tianjin	49.4	44.4	0.3	3.6	1.1	
河 北	Hebei	1019.1	826.9	33.1	104.1	40.5	
山 西	Shanxi	312.7	218.6	3.9	32.4	31.1	
内蒙古	Inner Mongolia	783.3	576.4	67.9	86.8	43.6	8.5
辽 宁	Liaoning	495.9	344.7	28.2	98.9	24.1	
吉 林	Jilin	634.9	550.0	53.7	16.8	14.5	
黑龙江	Heilongjiang	580.8	527.1	41.3	7.6	4.8	
上 海	Shanghai	5.4	5.5				
江 苏	Jiangsu	73.9	64.6	1.4	6.4	1.5	
浙 江	Zhejiang	35.6	35.5	0.1			
安 徽	Anhui	433.6	431.8	0.4	1.1	0.3	
福 建	Fujian	105.9	105.7				
江 西	Jiangxi	371.9	371.9				
山 东	Shandong	1046.5	970.7	13.1	54.8	8.1	
河 南	Henan	1508.8	1447.0	17.3	29.6	14.2	
湖 北	Hubei	384.3	415.2	1.6	0.4	0.2	
湖 南	Hunan	595.8	606.5	3.9	0.5	0.2	
广 东	Guangdong	372.4	372.3	0.1			
广 西	Guangxi	777.2	735.6	39.6	0.1	4.1	
海 南	Hainan	143.0	143.0				
重 庆	Chongqing	174.5	167.2	2.4	0.2	1.2	
四 川	Sichuan	1253.8	1150.4	88.5	8.8	9.6	
贵 州	Guizhou	873.8	793.2	78.0	0.2	2.4	
云 南	Yunnan	937.6	802.1	78.3	33.3	65.9	
西 藏	Tibet	686.2	632.5	42.0	10.1	1.6	
陕 西	Shaanxi	340.5	309.0	1.2	21.9	8.5	
甘 肃	Gansu	614.7	476.9	24.5	113.3	61.3	2.2
青 海	Qinghai	453.5	406.2	24.5	8.3	13.8	0.7
宁 夏	Ningxia	116.3	98.2	0.4	12.8	4.9	0.1
新 疆	Xinjiang	739.7	504.2	94.2	123.9	2.4	15.1

13-20 续表 continued

单位：万头、万只 (10 000 heads)

年份 地区	Year Region	肉猪出栏头数 Slaughtered Fattened Hogs	猪年底头数 Hogs (year-end)	羊年底只数 Sheep and Goats (year-end)	山羊 Goats	绵羊 Sheep
	1996	41225.2	36283.6	23728.3	12315.8	11412.5
	1997	46483.7	40034.8	25575.7	13480.1	12095.6
	1998	50215.1	42256.3	26903.5	14168.3	12735.2
	1999	51977.2	43144.2	27925.8	14816.3	13109.5
	2000	52673.3	44681.5	29031.9	15715.9	13316.0
	2001	54936.7	45743.0	29826.4	16129.2	13697.2
	2002	56684.3	46291.5	31655.2	17275.9	14379.3
	2003	59200.5	46601.7	34053.7	18320.7	15733.0
	2004	61800.7	48189.1	36639.1	19550.9	17088.2
	2005	66098.6	50334.8	37265.9	19876.1	17389.9
北京	Beijing	448.7	218.8	126.0	28.0	98.1
天津	Tianjin	481.5	255.5	84.7	21.6	63.1
河北	Hebei	4510.6	3064.4	2482.0	1000.2	1481.8
山西	Shanxi	627.1	463.3	1029.3	421.0	608.3
内蒙古	Inner Mongolia	957.7	738.7	5420.0	1711.0	3709.0
辽宁	Liaoning	2301.9	1453.6	995.6	510.7	484.9
吉林	Jilin	1272.4	615.2	430.0	65.0	365.1
黑龙江	Heilongjiang	1392.2	1316.8	1180.3	408.9	771.4
上海	Shanghai	280.0	156.0	30.1	27.6	2.5
江苏	Jiangsu	2974.9	1927.2	1175.0	1155.0	20.0
浙江	Zhejiang	1867.1	1213.2	222.4	105.4	117.0
安徽	Anhui	2629.5	2034.0	921.3	918.5	2.8
福建	Fujian	1879.0	1330.1	136.0	136.0	
江西	Jiangxi	2237.8	1566.7	105.3	105.3	
山东	Shandong	4585.7	3238.7	3404.8	2683.0	721.8
河南	Henan	5568.0	4439.0	3988.0	3509.4	478.6
湖北	Hubei	3428.4	2340.3	337.7	337.0	0.7
湖南	Hunan	6176.3	4435.0	711.3	711.1	0.1
广东	Guangdong	3616.7	2143.5	39.2	39.2	
广西	Guangxi	2831.9	3015.0	260.0	260.0	
海南	Hainan	427.5	393.5	88.9	88.9	
重庆	Chongqing	1993.3	1756.3	303.6	303.5	0.1
四川	Sichuan	7105.0	5744.8	1587.3	1276.2	311.1
贵州	Guizhou	1453.6	1972.9	448.3	428.6	19.7
云南	Yunnan	2733.6	2601.7	976.9	874.3	102.6
西藏	Tibet	18.9	30.2	1698.3	626.1	1072.2
陕西	Shaanxi	930.4	764.1	930.9	709.6	221.3
甘肃	Gansu	700.1	650.2	1526.3	338.8	1187.5
青海	Qinghai	121.8	105.1	1765.7	330.2	1435.5
宁夏	Ningxia	163.1	122.7	505.4	86.4	419.0
新疆	Xinjiang	384.0	228.5	4355.5	659.8	3695.8

13-21 畜 产 品 产 量

Output of Livestock Products

年份 地区	Year Region	肉类产量 (万吨) Output of Meat (10 000 tons)	#猪牛羊肉 Output of Pork, Beef and Mutton	猪肉 Pork	牛肉 Beef	羊肉 Mutton	奶类 (万吨) Milk (10 000 tons)	#牛奶 Cow Milk
	1996	4584.0	3694.7	3158.0	355.7	181.0	735.8	629.4
	1997	5268.8	4249.9	3596.3	440.9	212.8	681.1	601.1
	1998	5723.8	4598.2	3883.7	479.9	234.6	745.4	662.9
	1999	5949.0	4762.3	4005.6	505.4	251.3	806.9	717.6
	2000	6125.4	4838.2	4031.4	532.8	274.0	919.1	827.4
	2001	6333.9	5026.0	4184.5	548.8	292.7	1122.9	1025.5
	2002	6586.5	5228.9	4326.6	584.6	316.7	1400.4	1299.8
	2003	6932.9	5506.3	4518.6	630.4	357.2	1848.6	1746.3
	2004	7244.8	5776.8	4701.6	675.9	399.3	2368.4	2260.6
	2005	7743.1	6157.6	5010.6	711.5	435.5	2864.8	2753.4
北京	Beijing	66.7	39.7	31.3	4.4	4.0	64.2	64.2
天津	Tianjin	57.8	44.9	35.6	6.2	3.0	63.4	63.4
河北	Hebei	571.9	458.0	337.4	86.9	33.7	348.6	340.3
山西	Shanxi	68.2	62.2	47.9	6.9	7.4	73.8	71.3
内蒙古	Inner Mongolia	229.5	193.6	87.6	33.6	72.4	696.9	691.0
辽宁	Liaoning	347.9	240.6	191.2	42.2	7.1	78.8	74.9
吉林	Jilin	260.2	163.3	108.2	51.0	4.2	30.0	29.4
黑龙江	Heilongjiang	173.5	142.3	100.4	31.1	10.7	444.2	440.2
上海	Shanghai	31.3	18.7	18.0	0.1	0.6	23.8	23.8
江苏	Jiangsu	352.3	242.1	218.5	5.7	17.9	57.9	56.6
浙江	Zhejiang	165.3	130.4	125.1	1.4	3.9	26.7	26.7
安徽	Anhui	340.1	265.0	215.6	33.0	16.4	11.0	11.0
福建	Fujian	165.9	138.5	133.5	2.9	2.1	19.8	19.4
江西	Jiangxi	237.1	187.7	175.9	10.2	1.6	12.5	12.5
山东	Shandong	753.9	484.1	367.1	80.7	36.4	221.0	187.1
河南	Henan	685.9	588.3	440.8	100.8	46.7	108.5	104.0
湖北	Hubei	327.3	278.7	256.3	16.3	6.0	12.2	12.2
湖南	Hunan	523.5	466.8	437.0	18.2	11.6	6.9	6.9
广东	Guangdong	384.3	264.2	256.3	7.2	0.7	11.9	11.6
广西	Guangxi	242.9	206.6	186.0	16.9	3.8	5.4	5.4
海南	Hainan	58.2	41.3	37.0	3.0	1.3	0.1	0.1
重庆	Chongqing	178.0	153.3	143.8	5.8	3.6	8.6	8.6
四川	Sichuan	653.6	562.2	513.7	28.5	20.0	59.0	58.6
贵州	Guizhou	167.5	154.7	136.7	12.5	5.5	3.8	3.8
云南	Yunnan	298.6	276.0	244.2	21.7	10.1	32.7	30.9
西藏	Tibet	21.5	21.5	1.2	12.8	7.5	27.0	21.2
陕西	Shaanxi	102.8	89.6	68.4	11.9	9.3	141.7	113.3
甘肃	Gansu	82.1	75.7	50.5	12.8	12.5	31.7	31.2
青海	Qinghai	25.8	25.1	8.6	7.4	9.2	25.0	23.6
宁夏	Ningxia	26.2	22.3	10.7	5.2	6.4	57.9	57.9
新疆	Xinjiang	143.3	120.3	26.2	34.2	59.9	159.8	152.2

13-21 续表 continued

年份 地区	Year Region	绵羊毛 (吨) Sheep Wool (ton)	#细羊毛 Fine Wool	#半细羊毛 Semi-Fine Wool	山羊毛 (吨) Goat Wool (ton)	羊绒 (吨) Cashmere (ton)	禽蛋 (万吨) Poultry Eggs (10 000 tons)	蜂蜜 (万吨) Honey (10 000 tons)
	1996	298102	121020	74099	35284	9585	1965.2	18.3
	1997	255059	116054	55683	25865	8626	1897.1	21.1
	1998	277545	115752	68775	31417	9799	2021.3	20.7
	1999	283152	114103	73700	31849	10180	2134.7	23.0
	2000	292502	117386	84921	33266	11057	2243.3	24.6
	2001	298254	114651	88075	34241	10968	2336.7	25.2
	2002	307588	112193	102419	35459	11765	2462.7	26.5
	2003	338058	120263	110249	36692	13528	2606.7	28.9
	2004	373902	130413	119514	37727	14515	2723.7	29.3
	2005	393172	127862	123068	36904	15435	2879.5	29.3
北京	Beijing	1132	14	1118	224	93	16.0	0.3
天津	Tianjin	831	58	773	68		23.5	
河北	Hebei	36466	6866	14341	3565	890	459.0	0.8
山西	Shanxi	8805	1733	1122	1740	795	56.9	0.3
内蒙古	Inner Mongolia	94902	44841	14943	7558	6395	46.2	0.5
辽宁	Liaoning	10412	3618	6591	1680	1053	224.0	0.2
吉林	Jilin	19971	15431	4452	425	60	100.0	0.8
黑龙江	Heilongjiang	25734	7965	17769	874	791	102.7	1.1
上海	Shanghai	15		15	112		8.4	
江苏	Jiangsu	640	408	232	32	1	182.0	0.7
浙江	Zhejiang	2045		2045	552		44.5	7.9
安徽	Anhui	129	4	125	193	4	122.1	1.1
福建	Fujian						43.9	0.9
江西	Jiangxi						42.1	1.1
山东	Shandong	21581	4315	11250	6291	913	441.8	0.8
河南	Henan	11462	911	7135	2873	433	375.3	2.7
湖北	Hubei	4	1	1	16		121.3	0.8
湖南	Hunan	3	3		13		92.1	1.0
广东	Guangdong				23		33.2	1.4
广西	Guangxi						17.7	0.8
海南	Hainan						2.7	0.1
重庆	Chongqing	4	4		2		39.1	0.6
四川	Sichuan	5801	804	2895	495	21	157.2	3.5
贵州	Guizhou	346	59	287	10	1	11.1	0.2
云南	Yunnan	1959	313	1141	63	4	19.0	0.6
西藏	Tibet	8718	336	2005	1226	906	0.4	
陕西	Shaanxi	5868	2205	1737	1338	793	48.7	0.3
甘肃	Gansu	21134	7064	4534	1794	416	14.5	0.1
青海	Qinghai	16501	663	4382	1151	355	1.4	0.1
宁夏	Ningxia	8936	1168	2001	519	253	7.8	0.1
新疆	Xinjiang	89772	29079	22174	4067	1258	25.0	0.5

13-22 水产品产量

Output of Aquatic Products

单位：万吨　　　　(10 000 tons)

年份 地区	Year Region	水产品总产量 Total Aquatic Products	海水产品 Seawater Aquatic Products	天然生产 Naturally Grown	人工养殖 Artificially Cultured	鱼类 Fish	虾蟹类 Shrimps, Prawns and Crabs	贝类 Shellfish	藻类 Algae	其他 Others
	1978	465.4	359.5	314.5	45.0	256.1	50.6	26.8	26.0	
	1980	449.7	325.7	281.3	44.4	234.1	42.1	23.4	26.2	
	1985	705.2	419.8	348.5	71.2	274.5	70.6	47.3	27.3	
	1989	1151.7	661.2	503.6	157.6	382.9	105.7	137.5	30.0	5.0
	1990	1237.0	713.3	550.9	162.4	423.1	107.0	147.3	27.5	8.2
	1991	1350.8	800.1	609.6	190.5	466.2	119.4	158.6	40.0	15.9
	1992	1557.1	933.7	691.2	242.4	517.6	127.4	204.4	56.8	27.5
	1993	1823.0	1076.0	767.3	308.7	557.4	138.7	288.6	69.4	22.0
	1994	2143.2	1241.5	895.8	345.7	647.4	170.9	323.6	74.5	25.1
	1995	2517.2	1439.1	1026.8	412.3	758.1	184.8	392.3	74.9	29.0
	1996	3288.1	2012.9	1249.0	763.9	823.5	204.7	852.7	92.9	39.1
	1997	3601.8	2176.4	1385.4	791.0	964.2	225.7	824.2	98.0	64.4
	1998	3906.5	2356.7	1496.7	860.0	1056.0	258.6	870.1	104.1	68.0
	1999	4122.4	2471.9	1497.6	974.3	1057.9	277.1	959.3	119.4	58.2
	2000	4278.5	2538.7	1477.5	1061.3	1033.0	297.1	1038.7	122.2	47.8
	2001	4381.3	2571.7	1440.6	1131.1	1014.7	302.5	1078.1	124.9	51.3
	2002	4564.5	2646.3	1433.5	1212.8	1022.3	310.6	1119.3	133.3	60.8
	2003	4704.6	2685.8	1432.4	1253.3	1028.4	298.2	1109.6	141.3	108.2
	2004	4901.8	2767.8	1451.1	1316.7	1017.3	312.4	1111.5	150.5	176.1
	2005	5107.6	2838.3	1453.5	1384.8	1052.0	323.8	1160.4	154.2	148.0
北京	Beijing	6.4								
天津	Tianjin	33.8	4.9	3.8	1.1	1.8	1.4	1.5		0.2
河北	Hebei	98.9	57.2	31.1	26.1	19.2	9.5	24.7		3.8
山西	Shanxi	3.8								
内蒙古	Inner Mongolia	8.3								
辽宁	Liaoning	425.3	364.2	152.0	212.1	91.3	35.0	173.5	39.5	24.9
吉林	Jilin	11.9								
黑龙江	Heilongjiang	44.6								
上海	Shanghai	35.4	15.0	15.0	0.1	10.1	1.7	2.6		0.7
江苏	Jiangsu	388.7	113.4	58.3	55.1	38.1	15.4	51.1	1.9	7.0
浙江	Zhejiang	483.8	402.4	314.3	88.1	208.6	87.0	72.7	3.5	30.6
安徽	Anhui	177.6								
福建	Fujian	602.2	531.9	222.1	309.7	186.8	35.6	247.8	46.8	14.8
江西	Jiangxi	168.7								
山东	Shandong	736.1	626.1	268.1	358.0	173.0	46.8	314.0	53.8	38.4
河南	Henan	51.7								
湖北	Hubei	318.2								
湖南	Hunan	179.2								
广东	Guangdong	695.2	398.0	172.0	225.9	151.7	46.3	181.2	3.9	14.9
广西	Guangxi	284.2	174.0	84.6	89.4	55.9	26.4	84.9		6.7
海南	Hainan	150.0	127.1	108.0	19.1	91.2	18.8	6.4	4.8	5.9
重庆	Chongqing	25.1								
四川	Sichuan	98.2								
贵州	Guizhou	9.5								
云南	Yunnan	23.8								
西藏	Tibet									
陕西	Shaanxi	7.4								
甘肃	Gansu	1.6								
青海	Qinghai	0.1								
宁夏	Ningxia	5.8								
新疆	Xinjiang	7.9								
中国水产总公司	China Aquatic Company	24.3	24.3	24.3		24.3				

13-22 续表 continued

单位：万吨 (10 000 tons)

年份 地区	Year Region	淡水产品 Freshwater Aquatic Products	天然生产 Naturally Grown	人工养殖 Artificially Cultured	鱼类 Fish	虾蟹类 Shrimps, Prawns and Crabs	贝类 Shell-fish	其他 Others
	1978	105.9	29.6	76.2	99.7	3.8	2.4	
	1980	124.0	33.9	90.2	116.3	5.2	2.5	
	1985	285.4	47.6	237.8	276.5	5.5	3.4	
	1989	490.5	73.5	417.0	472.8	9.5	7.3	
	1990	523.7	78.3	445.4	504.9	9.5	7.6	1.8
	1991	550.7	91.5	459.2	530.4	10.7	8.5	1.0
	1992	623.5	90.1	533.4	598.4	12.4	10.5	2.2
	1993	747.0	102.9	644.1	710.6	13.3	16.3	6.7
	1994	901.7	116.7	785.0	859.3	20.3	15.3	6.8
	1995	1078.1	137.3	940.8	1018.6	27.3	20.5	11.6
	1996	1275.2	176.3	1099.0	1177.8	36.3	48.4	12.7
	1997	1425.4	188.6	1236.7	1324.9	47.8	36.4	16.3
	1998	1549.8	228.4	1321.4	1425.2	60.4	45.8	18.3
	1999	1650.5	227.8	1422.7	1517.1	70.7	43.0	19.7
	2000	1739.7	226.4	1513.4	1573.1	88.3	46.3	32.1
	2001	1809.6	214.6	1595.0	1629.0	100.8	52.6	27.2
	2002	1918.2	225.2	1693.0	1710.2	122.4	56.7	28.9
	2003	2018.8	246.8	1772.0	1795.2	138.8	54.1	30.7
	2004	2134.0	242.0	1892.0	1893.4	153.4	53.5	33.7
	2005	2269.3	258.8	2010.5	2017.6	162.9	53.8	35.1
北京	Beijing	6.4		6.4	6.4	0.1		
天津	Tianjin	28.9	1.2	27.7	26.1	2.6	0.1	
河北	Hebei	41.8	8.5	33.2	38.6	2.4	0.5	0.3
山西	Shanxi	3.8	0.1	3.6	3.7			
内蒙古	Inner Mongolia	8.3	2.9	5.3	7.7	0.4		0.1
辽宁	Liaoning	61.2	4.2	56.9	54.4	5.6	0.1	1.0
吉林	Jilin	11.9	2.5	9.4	11.8	0.1		
黑龙江	Heilongjiang	44.6	5.1	39.5	43.8	0.6		0.1
上海	Shanghai	20.3	0.4	20.0	12.6	7.4	0.1	0.2
江苏	Jiangsu	275.2	32.9	242.3	207.8	54.5	8.9	4.1
浙江	Zhejiang	81.4	9.3	72.1	55.9	11.7	4.8	9.0
安徽	Anhui	177.6	37.9	139.7	143.6	20.4	9.9	3.7
福建	Fujian	70.3	8.5	61.8	60.2	3.7	4.9	1.5
江西	Jiangxi	168.7	24.9	143.8	152.9	6.9	5.4	3.5
山东	Shandong	110.0	12.3	97.7	102.3	5.8	1.4	0.5
河南	Henan	51.7	3.5	48.2	49.7	1.4	0.1	0.3
湖北	Hubei	318.2	45.0	273.2	300.8	11.3	4.2	1.9
湖南	Hunan	179.2	18.5	160.7	172.5	2.7	2.4	1.7
广东	Guangdong	297.3	13.0	284.3	262.9	22.0	7.8	4.6
广西	Guangxi	110.2	11.3	98.9	106.0	1.7	1.9	0.7
海南	Hainan	23.0	2.4	20.5	21.6	0.1	0.3	0.9
重庆	Chongqing	25.1	1.3	23.8	24.7	0.1	0.2	0.1
四川	Sichuan	98.2	6.9	91.3	96.5	0.6	0.6	0.6
贵州	Guizhou	9.5	1.2	8.2	9.2	0.2		
云南	Yunnan	23.8	2.6	21.3	23.1	0.6		
西藏	Tibet							
陕西	Shaanxi	7.4	0.6	6.8	7.3			
甘肃	Gansu	1.6	0.1	1.4	1.6			
青海	Qinghai	0.1		0.1	0.1			
宁夏	Ningxia	5.8		5.8	5.8			
新疆	Xinjiang	7.9	1.4	6.6	7.8			0.1
中国水产总公司	China Aquatic Company							

13-23 主要农产品人均占有量

Per Capita Output of Major Farm Products

单位：公斤 (kg)

年份 地区	Year Region	粮食 Grain	棉花 Cotton	油料 Oil-bearing Crops	猪牛羊肉 Pork, Beef and Mutton	水产品 Total Aquatic Products	牛奶 Milk
	1980	327	2.8	7.8		4.6	1.2
	1985	361	3.9	15.0		6.7	2.4
	1989	364	3.4	11.6		10.3	3.4
	1990	393	4.0	14.2		10.9	3.7
	1995	387	4.0	18.7		20.9	4.6
	1997	402	3.7	17.5	34.6	29.3	5.4
	2000	366	3.5	23.4	38.3	33.9	6.6
	2001	356	4.2	22.5	39.5	34.4	8.1
	2002	357	3.8	22.6	40.8	35.6	10.2
	2003	334	3.8	21.8	42.7	36.5	13.6
	2004	362	4.9	23.7	44.6	37.8	17.4
	2005	371	4.4	23.6	47.2	39.2	21.1
北京	Beijing	62	0.1	1.6	25.9	4.2	41.9
天津	Tianjin	132	8.0	1.2	43.2	32.5	61.0
河北	Hebei	380	8.4	22.4	67.0	14.5	49.8
山西	Shanxi	292	3.1	6.4	18.6	1.1	21.3
内蒙古	Inner Mongolia	699	0.1	51.3	81.4	3.5	290.4
辽宁	Liaoning	415	0.1	8.8	57.2	101.1	17.8
吉林	Jilin	953	0.1	20.1	60.3	4.4	10.9
黑龙江	Heilongjiang	812		15.9	37.4	11.7	115.6
上海	Shanghai	59	0.1	3.9	10.5	19.9	13.4
江苏	Jiangsu	380	4.3	29.0	32.5	52.2	7.6
浙江	Zhejiang	167	0.4	10.3	26.7	99.1	5.5
安徽	Anhui	427	5.3	44.4	43.4	29.1	1.8
福建	Fujian	203		7.8	39.3	170.9	5.5
江西	Jiangxi	409	2.0	17.7	43.7	39.2	2.9
山东	Shandong	425	9.2	39.5	52.5	79.8	20.3
河南	Henan	490	7.2	48.1	62.9	5.5	11.1
湖北	Hubei	382	6.6	51.6	48.9	55.9	2.1
湖南	Hunan	425	3.1	22.4	74.0	28.4	1.1
广东	Guangdong	152		8.4	28.8	75.8	1.3
广西	Guangxi	320		13.6	44.5	61.2	1.2
海南	Hainan	185		10.3	50.0	181.7	0.1
重庆	Chongqing	419		15.3	54.9	9.0	3.1
四川	Sichuan	392	0.3	28.4	68.7	12.0	7.2
贵州	Guizhou	310		22.8	41.6	2.5	1.0
云南	Yunnan	341		8.2	62.2	5.4	7.0
西藏	Tibet	338		22.2	77.7		76.8
陕西	Shaanxi	281	2.1	12.2	24.2	2.0	30.6
甘肃	Gansu	324	4.3	19.5	29.3	0.6	12.1
青海	Qinghai	172		58.8	46.4	0.2	43.6
宁夏	Ningxia	505		20.5	37.5	9.8	97.4
新疆	Xinjiang	438	93.6	19.4	60.1	4.0	76.0

13-24 平均每一农林牧渔业从业人员主要农产品生产量

Output of Major Farm Products Per Agricultural Laborer

单位：公斤 (kg)

年份 Year 地区 Region	粮食 Grain	棉花 Cotton	油料 Oil-bearing Crops	猪牛羊肉 Pork, Beef and Mutton	水产品 Total Aquatic Products	牛奶 Milk
1985	1222	13.4	50.8		22.7	8.1
1989	1276	11.9	40.5		36.0	11.9
1990	1357	13.4	47.9		36.7	12.6
1995	1435	14.7	69.2		77.4	17.7
1997	1528	14.2	66.7	131.4	111.3	18.6
2000	1407	13.4	89.9	147.3	130.2	25.2
2001	1387	16.3	87.8	154.0	134.3	31.4
2002	1419	15.3	89.9	162.3	141.7	40.3
2003	1362	15.4	88.9	174.1	148.8	55.2
2004	1518	20.4	99.1	186.8	158.5	73.1
2005	1598	18.9	101.6	203.3	168.6	90.9
北京 Beijing	1630	3.6	42.8	681.0	110.3	1102.3
天津 Tianjin	1718	104.4	16.2	561.1	422.4	792.2
河北 Hebei	1648	36.6	96.9	290.5	62.8	215.9
山西 Shanxi	1531	16.1	33.3	97.4	5.9	111.6
内蒙古 Inner Mongolia	3157	0.3	232.0	367.8	15.7	1312.6
辽宁 Liaoning	2545	0.4	53.7	350.7	619.9	109.1
吉林 Jilin	5169	0.3	109.0	327.1	23.8	58.9
黑龙江 Heilongjiang	4408		86.4	202.8	63.6	627.7
上海 Shanghai	1696	2.9	111.6	300.8	569.0	382.4
江苏 Jiangsu	2585	29.4	197.0	220.8	354.4	51.6
浙江 Zhejiang	1010	2.7	62.1	161.7	599.6	33.1
安徽 Anhui	1463	18.2	152.0	148.8	99.7	6.2
福建 Fujian	1011		38.8	195.7	851.2	27.4
江西 Jiangxi	1838	9.1	79.6	196.3	176.4	13.1
山东 Shandong	1854	40.1	172.2	229.1	348.4	88.5
河南 Henan	1440	21.3	141.3	184.9	16.2	32.7
湖北 Hubei	1973	34.0	266.3	252.5	288.3	11.1
湖南 Hunan	1364	10.1	71.8	237.7	91.3	3.5
广东 Guangdong	912		50.4	172.8	454.6	7.6
广西 Guangxi	985	0.1	41.9	136.9	188.3	3.5
海南 Hainan	797		44.4	214.8	781.0	0.6
重庆 Chongqing	1482		54.2	194.4	31.8	10.9
四川 Sichuan	1371	1.1	99.2	240.0	41.9	25.0
贵州 Guizhou	901		66.4	121.0	7.4	2.9
云南 Yunnan	895		21.4	163.1	14.1	18.3
西藏 Tibet	1094		71.8	251.4	0.1	248.5
陕西 Shaanxi	1094	8.2	47.6	94.0	7.7	118.9
甘肃 Gansu	1098	14.5	66.0	99.4	2.1	40.9
青海 Qinghai	716		244.5	193.0	0.7	181.3
宁夏 Ningxia	2107		85.8	156.5	41.0	406.5
新疆 Xinjiang	2565	548.4	113.9	352.0	23.2	445.4

13-25 农村居民家庭平均每人出售主要农产品

Per Capita Major Farm Products Sold by Rural Households

本表为农村住户抽样调查资料。
Data in this table are obtained from the sample surveys on rural households.

单位：公斤 (kg)

年份 Year / 地区 Region		粮食 Grain	棉花 Cotton	油料 Oil-bearing Corps	麻类 Fiber Corps	烟叶 Tobacco	蔬菜 Vegetables	水果 Fruits
1985		123.49	4.13	14.37	2.80	2.25	53.76	6.78
1989		154.27	3.48	10.70	1.28	2.78	64.05	11.93
1990		180.24	4.31	12.87	1.56	2.67	65.07	13.17
1991		179.44	5.54	13.22	1.32	3.17	68.70	15.74
1992		165.89	4.16	11.27	1.18	3.58	75.58	16.92
1993		159.35	3.26	10.48	0.86	3.19	77.73	19.60
1994		188.53	4.01	10.68	0.50	2.02	72.68	22.64
1995		179.20	4.31	12.02	0.73	2.21	79.96	24.28
1996		203.47	3.90	11.64	0.83	3.07	97.00	29.78
1997		228.01	5.12	11.13	0.57	4.45	106.22	36.21
1998		227.53	5.10	12.39	0.41	2.33	108.72	38.51
1999		243.34	4.43	15.59	0.28	2.42	111.66	43.17
2000		264.74	5.59	18.43	0.47	2.73	132.07	46.43
2001		268.04	7.05	18.31	0.44	2.42	132.94	48.21
2002		281.15	6.94	18.47	0.64	2.59	143.77	49.06
2003		294.35	16.77	19.22	0.71	2.62	147.58	48.83
2004		287.25	19.19	18.88	0.53	2.47	151.57	57.48
2005		375.79	22.06	20.09	0.69	3.69	167.93	61.62
北京	Beijing	155.26	0.56	1.05		0.06	195.67	103.22
天津	Tianjin	184.21	100.33	0.15	0.05		264.84	33.06
河北	Hebei	371.08	59.91	9.27			275.34	94.21
山西	Shanxi	174.22	23.19	5.74	0.03	0.17	209.62	152.19
内蒙古	Inner Mongolia	861.52		101.13	0.45	0.55	149.90	7.61
辽宁	Liaoning	1176.19	0.01	25.06		3.17	319.45	97.68
吉林	Jilin	2152.48		23.34	0.13	2.05	178.18	6.87
黑龙江	Heilongjiang	2001.39		6.26	0.02	5.75	242.27	1.26
上海	Shanghai	80.87	0.11	7.77			86.98	60.49
江苏	Jiangsu	386.36	11.47	19.18	0.02		101.74	3.57
浙江	Zhejiang	83.78	1.97	6.67			229.61	120.97
安徽	Anhui	444.13	25.24	39.37	0.09	0.21	55.83	3.74
福建	Fujian	105.43		4.10		13.87	153.38	160.88
江西	Jiangxi	436.33	9.77	16.78	0.14	1.26	63.82	27.81
山东	Shandong	424.47	58.05	25.07	0.06	0.93	338.87	79.69
河南	Henan	366.64	17.96	22.70	0.60	3.11	116.79	49.22
湖北	Hubei	382.44	55.95	77.73	0.56	2.34	135.09	69.46
湖南	Hunan	184.91	22.43	9.35	1.13	9.05	74.73	44.80
广东	Guangdong	91.04		5.92	0.02	1.62	278.88	48.59
广西	Guangxi	126.75	0.04	3.84	2.58	0.76	131.43	48.91
海南	Hainan	59.51		7.61	0.14	0.01	405.03	112.77
重庆	Chongqing	69.09		6.05	0.51	7.04	104.83	25.35
四川	Sichuan	80.56	0.23	18.18	0.94	3.54	142.03	32.68
贵州	Guizhou	64.87	0.01	11.68		17.04	95.46	5.74
云南	Yunnan	100.27		10.69	3.83	25.46	146.27	21.46
西藏	Tibet	69.24		2.32			5.12	1.41
陕西	Shaanxi	185.89	11.22	8.00		2.51	118.97	220.22
甘肃	Gansu	192.01	36.63	6.91	0.02	0.09	130.79	55.24
青海	Qinghai	68.52		69.72		0.01	34.07	9.95
宁夏	Ningxia	477.98		19.00			244.37	118.84
新疆	Xinjiang	497.28	197.50	21.54	8.24		243.57	163.01

13-26 农村居民家庭平均每人出售主要畜产品及水产品

Sales of Livestock, Poultry, Small Animals and Fishery Per Capita Rural Household

本表为农村住户抽样调查资料。
Data in this table are obtained from the sample surveys on rural households.

单位：公斤 (kg)

年份 Year / 地区 Region	猪肉 Pork	羊肉 Mutton	牛肉 Beef	家禽 Poultry	蛋类 Poultry Eggs	牛羊奶 Milk	蚕茧 Silkworm Cocoons	水产品 Aquatic Products
1985	16.27	0.57	0.52	1.00	2.21	1.02	0.36	1.74
1989	16.79	0.66	0.51	1.59	2.01	1.44	0.51	2.18
1990	17.84	0.71	0.55	1.45	1.89	1.68	0.58	2.05
1991	20.07	0.90	0.76	2.18	2.65	1.91	0.65	2.92
1992	21.17	0.86	0.72	2.23	2.90	1.85	0.70	3.21
1993	23.80	1.02	0.86	2.41	2.89	1.76	0.74	3.10
1994	23.31	1.11	0.93	2.30	3.35	1.81	0.83	2.97
1995	24.17	1.15	0.96	2.42	3.54	1.90	0.79	2.94
1996	25.73	1.68	2.01	2.45	2.58	2.55	0.50	3.27
1997	26.08	1.76	2.33	2.99	3.76	2.76	0.54	4.50
1998	23.04	1.67	1.04	2.42	3.57	2.60	0.65	4.31
1999	28.41	1.85	1.86	3.41	4.07	3.00	0.62	6.20
2000	30.19	2.06	2.40	4.60	6.32	2.67	0.64	5.82
2001	30.86	2.31	2.76	5.03	5.96	3.65	0.80	6.53
2002	32.30	2.50	2.73	6.01	6.54	4.87	0.77	8.04
2003	29.49	2.87	2.71	6.67	7.06	7.29	0.76	7.47
2004	26.62	2.94	2.49	6.87	6.39	7.67	0.79	7.28
2005	32.19	3.26	2.87	9.62	10.52	11.27	0.91	8.54
北京 Beijing	29.71	2.37	0.07	17.82	26.79	27.57		10.74
天津 Tianjin	46.76	0.18	5.35	31.14	48.59	10.18		22.29
河北 Hebei	17.78	2.74	3.42	8.64	36.98	29.50		
山西 Shanxi	12.28	3.39	1.83	1.97	17.25	16.01	0.10	
内蒙古 Inner Mongolia	20.03	48.44	13.98	2.21	4.21	118.08	0.05	
辽宁 Liaoning	62.63	3.22	7.60	28.15	45.86	11.96	1.54	11.59
吉林 Jilin	41.52	1.71	8.96	12.00	7.81	0.93		0.33
黑龙江 Heilongjiang	56.15	2.18	4.70	11.55	6.85	49.21	0.12	1.21
上海 Shanghai	9.11	0.16		0.09	0.06			10.93
江苏 Jiangsu	22.43	0.85	0.34	11.58	30.68	2.20	1.76	20.74
浙江 Zhejiang	39.75	0.53	0.05	21.99	4.13	0.56	4.37	14.31
安徽 Anhui	17.70	0.84	2.34	6.00	2.29		1.07	4.03
福建 Fujian	32.21	0.28	0.57	2.41	1.45	0.21		11.89
江西 Jiangxi	31.84	0.07	0.33	1.81	4.99	0.32	0.42	7.13
山东 Shandong	32.56	1.79	5.53	28.20	20.70	4.16	1.49	7.77
河南 Henan	39.54	1.36	3.96	4.59	13.67	0.04	0.05	4.24
湖北 Hubei	29.70	0.27	0.36	4.47	11.98		0.16	28.59
湖南 Hunan	45.91	0.19	0.20	5.18	1.28		0.01	8.52
广东 Guangdong	27.89	0.02	0.27	40.08	0.13	0.07	0.85	29.23
广西 Guangxi	49.72	0.15	1.06	6.24	0.09		5.22	5.68
海南 Hainan	33.05	0.63	2.26	4.47	0.03	0.03		72.76
重庆 Chongqing	48.85	0.13	0.68	5.65	1.04		2.63	6.15
四川 Sichuan	69.06	0.79	0.93	10.99	2.39	1.42	1.91	6.01
贵州 Guizhou	29.29	0.53	1.03	2.14	0.61	0.42	0.04	0.04
云南 Yunnan	34.16	0.75	1.30	3.43	6.48	11.85	0.80	0.75
西藏 Tibet	0.84	2.85	7.94	0.05	0.16	0.87		
陕西 Shaanxi	18.83	2.28	0.79	1.11	10.43	23.92	0.76	0.31
甘肃 Gansu	5.28	4.06	4.00	0.61	1.48	3.24		0.09
青海 Qinghai	3.51	16.09	8.88	0.11	0.04	11.72		1.05
宁夏 Ningxia	16.71	8.13	9.28	9.03	0.10	100.44		9.53
新疆 Xinjiang	1.63	19.87	10.59	1.93	9.86	25.02	0.05	

注：1992年及以前，蛋类不包括蛋制品，水产品出售量仅指鱼虾出售量。
a) Sales of poultry eggs before 1992 excluded egg products, and sales of aquatic products only referred to the sales of fish and shrimp.

13-27 主要农产品产量与解放前最高年产量比较

Output of Major Agricultural Products in Comparison with Peak Year Prior to 1949

产品名称	Item	解放前最高年 Peak Year prior to 1949		指数(以解放前最高年为100) Indices (peak year prior to 1949=100)		
		年 份 Year	产 量 Output	1949	1952	2005
种植业 (万吨)	**Planting (10 000 tons)**					
粮 食	Grain	1936	15000	75.5	109.3	322.7
#稻 谷	Rice	1936	5735	84.8	119.3	314.9
小 麦	Wheat	1936	2330	59.3	77.8	418.2
玉 米	Corn	1936	1010		166.8	1379.9
大 豆	Soybeans	1936	1130	45.0	84.3	190.9
薯 类	Tubers	1936	635	155.1	257.2	546.2
棉 花	Cotton	1936	84.9	52.3	153.6	673.0
花 生	Peanuts	1933	317	40.0	73.0	452.3
油菜籽	Rapeseeds	1934	191	38.5	48.9	684.4
芝 麻	Sesame	1933	99.1	32.9	48.5	63.1
黄红麻	Jute and Ambary Hemp	1945	5.5	34.6	278.2	2008.9
桑蚕茧	Mulberry Silkworm Cocoons	1931	22.1	14.0	28.1	353.0
茶 叶	Tea	1932	22.5	18.2	36.4	415.5
甘 蔗	Sugarcane	1940	565	46.7	125.9	1532.9
甜 菜	Beetroots	1939	32.9	58.1	145.6	2395.5
烤 烟	Flue-cured Tobacco	1948	17.9	24.0	124.0	1360.3
苹 果	Apples	1926	12.1		97.5	19843.9
柑 桔	Citrus	1926	40.1		51.6	3969.9
香 蕉	Bananas	1927	10.3		106.8	6328.3
畜牧业(万头、万只)	**Animal Husbandry (10 000 head)**					
大牲畜年底头数	Large Animals (year-end)	1935	7151	83.9	106.9	223.0
牛	Cattle and Buffaloes	1935	4827	91.0	117.3	293.3
马	Horses	1935	649	75.1	94.5	114.0
驴	Donkeys	1935	1215	78.1	97.2	64.0
骡	Mules	1935	460	32.0	35.6	78.3
猪年底头数	Hogs (year-end)	1934	7853	73.5	114.3	641.0
羊年底只数	Sheep and Goats (year-end)	1937	6252	67.7	98.8	596.1
渔 业	**Fishery**					
水产品 (万吨)	Aquatic Products (10 000 tons)	1936	150	30.0	111.3	3405.1

13-28 受灾面积和成灾面积

Areas Covered and Affected by Natural Disaster

单位：千公顷 (1 000 hectares)

年份 地区	Year Region	受灾面积 Areas Covered	成灾面积 Areas Affected	成灾面积占受灾面积比重(%) Percentage of Disaster Areas Affected to Areas Covered (%)	水灾 Flood 受灾面积 Areas Covered	水灾 Flood 成灾面积 Areas Affected	旱灾 Drought 受灾面积 Areas Covered	旱灾 Drought 成灾面积 Areas Affected
	1978	50790	24457	48.2	2850	2012	40170	17970
	1980	44526	29777	66.9	9146	6070	26111	14174
	1985	44365	22705	51.2	14197	8949	22989	10063
	1989	46991	24449	52.0	11328	5917	29358	15262
	1990	38474	17819	46.3	11804	5605	18175	7805
	1991	55472	27814	50.1	24596	14614	29414	10559
	1992	51333	25859	50.4	9423	4464	32980	17049
	1993	48829	23133	47.4	16387	8611	21098	8657
	1994	55043	31383	57.0	17329	10744	30425	17049
	1995	45821	22267	48.6	12731	7630	23455	10401
	1996	46989	21233	45.2	18146	10855	20151	6247
	1997	53429	30309	56.7	11414	5840	33514	20012
	1998	50145	25181	50.2	22292	13785	14236	5060
	1999	49981	26731	53.5	9020	5071	30156	16614
	2000	54688	34374	62.9	7323	4321	40541	26784
	2001	52215	31793	60.9	6042	3614	38472	23698
	2002	47119	27319	58.0	12378	7474	22207	13247
	2003	54506	32516	59.8	19208	12289	24852	14470
	2004	37106	16297	43.9	7314	3747	17253	8482
	2005	38818	19966	51.4	10932	6047	16028	8479
北京	Beijing	69	18	25.5			32	
天津	Tianjin	122	33	26.9			34	
河北	Hebei	1127	417	37.0	65	45	826	257
山西	Shanxi	1765	1052	59.6	11	5	1688	1016
内蒙古	Inner Mongolia	1814	1047	57.7	281	194	1382	735
辽宁	Liaoning	987	571	57.8	345	210	394	268
吉林	Jilin	1023	642	62.8	364	252	406	242
黑龙江	Heilongjiang	2102	873	41.5	1314	434	438	162
上海	Shanghai	85	42	49.9				
江苏	Jiangsu	1683	751	44.6	64	28	348	154
浙江	Zhejiang	1181	525	44.4	58	24	119	60
安徽	Anhui	2882	1616	56.1	1463	1027	598	287
福建	Fujian	946	429	45.3	282	111	15	6
江西	Jiangxi	1426	613	43.0	555	153	57	28
山东	Shandong	1780	713	40.0	524	342	356	72
河南	Henan	2112	1103	52.2	1100	653	424	142
湖北	Hubei	2580	1414	54.8	900	559	771	380
湖南	Hunan	2074	1184	57.1	495	299	840	536
广东	Guangdong	869	387	44.5	273	178	175	64
广西	Guangxi	1524	838	55.0	520	249	894	544
海南	Hainan	728	375	51.5			260	184
重庆	Chongqing	773	462	59.7	394	293	251	98
四川	Sichuan	1594	649	40.7	960	400	213	86
贵州	Guizhou	758	320	42.2	174	93	442	170
云南	Yunnan	2585	1431	55.4	159	113	2053	1192
西藏	Tibet	43	1	2.8	3		34	
陕西	Shaanxi	1748	888	50.8	400	248	1022	515
甘肃	Gansu	1333	854	64.1	135	89	1100	687
青海	Qinghai	107	33	30.6	1		80	21
宁夏	Ningxia	483	335	69.5	5	3	421	301
新疆	Xinjiang	517	352	68.2	88	48	356	272

13-29 国营农场基本情况

Basic Statistics on State Farms

本表为农垦系统数据。
Data in this table cover those of the land reclamation department.

指 标	Item	2001	2002	2003	2004	2005
农场数 （个）	**Number of Farms (unit)**	**1961**	**1945**	**1967**	**1928**	**1923**
职工人数 （万人）	**Number of Staff and Workers (10 000 persons)**	**366.0**	**355.7**	**353.7**	**339.6**	**335.9**
耕地面积 （千公顷）	**Cultivated Area (1 000 hectares)**	**4814.6**	**4740.7**	**4690.1**	**4820.1**	**5038.1**
农业机械总动力 （亿瓦）	**Total Power of Agricultural Machinery (100 million watts)**	**120.1**	**124.4**	**129.9**	**136.4**	**146.3**
农业机械拥有量（台、辆）	**Ownership of Agricultural Machinery (unit)**					
大中型农用拖拉机	Large and Medium Agricultural Tractors	67302	72000	70000	73800	80000
小型及手扶拖拉机	Mini and Walking Agricultural Tractors	216000	232000	245000	263500	270000
农用排灌动力机械	Machinery for Agricultural Drainage and Irrigation	157000	168600	177000	185600	192000
联合收割机	Combine Harvesters	15000	16300	18000	19000	20000
农用载重汽车	Trucks for Agricultural Use	13000	46000	50000	54954	57299
农用化肥施用量 （万吨）	**Consumption of Chemical Fertilizers (10 000 tons)**	**133.7**	**134.2**	**143.9**	**152.2**	**159.6**
农业总产值 （亿元）	**Gross Agricultural Output Value (100 million yuan)**	**652.8**	**726.4**	**846.3**	**977.9**	**1118.6**
农作物总播种面积（千公顷）	**Sown Area of Farm Crops (1 000 hectares)**	**4750.4**	**4792.6**	**4674.7**	**5019.0**	**5145.0**
粮食作物	Grain	3096.0	3073.7	2831.1	3199.0	3375.8
棉 花	Cotton	605.4	571.6	627.6	666.4	649.4
油 料	Oil-bearing Crops	354.6	405.4	446.9	394.6	371.2
糖 料	Sugar Crops	138.4	148.9	115.1	101.7	100.5
麻 类	Fiber Crops	37.6	44.1	67.0	70.0	53.6
年底实有茶园面积	Area of Tea Plantations (year-end)	32.7	31.2	29.6	30.6	30.3
年底实有桑园面积	Area of Mulberry Plantations (year-end)	3.9	2.3	2.6	2.1	1.6
年底实有果园面积	Area of Orchards (year-end)	210.9	230.0	224.4	231.3	241.3
年底实有橡胶园面积	Area of Rubber Plantations (year-end)	383.6	385.3	404.3	412.4	424.2
主要农产品产量	**Output of Major Farm Products**					
粮食作物 （万吨）	Grain (10 000 tons)	1480.2	1498.9	1342.6	1666.2	1859.0
棉 花 （万吨）	Cotton (10 000 tons)	84.9	99.0	103.4	116.3	124.7
油 料 （万吨）	Oil-bearing Crops (10 000 tons)	52.8	67.3	71.9	65.2	66.9
糖 料 （万吨）	Sugar Crops (10 000 tons)	824.9	913.3	721.7	688.7	667.5
麻 类 （万吨）	Fiber Crops (10 000 tons)	12.0	18.0	19.4	26.7	24.5
茶 叶 （万吨）	Tea (10 000 tons)	3.9	4.7	3.8	3.9	4.6
桑蚕茧 （吨）	Mulberry Silkworm Cocoons (ton)					
水 果 （万吨）	Fruits (10 000 tons)	127.6	147.8	146.4	163.1	178.8
干 胶 （万吨）	Rubber (10 000 tons)	34.7	37.8	39.5	39.0	32.0
畜牧业、渔业生产	**Production of Animal Husbandry and Fishery**					
大牲畜年底头数 （万头）	Number of Large Animals (year-end)(10 000 heads)	217.4	232.6	260.2	281.9	305.0
猪年底头数 （万头）	Number of Hogs (10 000 heads)	500.0	569.8	588.3	652.3	722.8
羊年底只数 （万只）	Number of Sheep and Goats (10 000 heads)	1119.9	1240.0	1509.6	1575.8	1591.6
#绵 羊	Sheep	890.2	945.5	431.8	1154.9	1220.6
畜产品产量 （万吨）	**Output of Livestock Products (10 000 tons)**					
猪牛羊肉	Pork, Beef and Mutton	72.4	78.5	87.7	102.2	121.4
#猪 肉	Pork	54.4	58.6	64.2	74.1	88.2
牛 奶	Milk	134.4	159.2	176.8	210.2	245.5
禽 蛋	Poultry Eggs	19.5	19.9	21.3	21.4	22.4
羊 毛	Sheep Wool	2.1	2.1	2.4	2.7	2.9
水产品总产量 （万吨）	**Total output of Aquatic Products (10 000 tons)**	**55.3**	**63.1**	**65.7**	**70.8**	**75.9**

主要统计指标解释

农林牧渔业总产值 指以货币表现的农、林、牧、渔业全部产品和对农林牧渔业生产活动进行的各种支持性服务活动的价值总量，它反映一定时期内农林牧渔业生产总规模和总成果。1957年以前的农林牧渔业总产值中包括了厩肥和农民自给性手工业(如农民自制衣服、鞋、袜，自己从事粮食初步加工等)。1958年及以后，林业中增加了村及村以下竹木采伐产值；牧业中取消了厩肥产值； 副业中取消了农民自给性手工业产值，增加了村及村以下办的工业产值； 渔业中增加了海洋捕捞水产品产值。1980年及以后，在副业中增加了农民家庭兼营工业商品部分的产值。从1984年起村及村以下工业产值划归工业。从1993年起取消副业，将野生动物的捕猎划入牧业，野生植物采集和农民家庭兼营商品性工业划归农业。从2003年起，执行新的国民经济行业分类标准，农林牧渔业总产值中包括了农林牧渔服务业产值。林业中增加了森林采运业产值。农业中取消了家庭兼营商品性工业产值，将野生林产品的采集划归林业。第一次农业普查以后，由于畜牧业产品年报数据与普查数据之间存在一定的差距，国家统计局农调总队对畜牧业年报数据与普查数据进行衔接，对畜牧业产值进行相应调整。

农林牧渔业总产值的计算方法通常是按农、林、牧、渔业产品及其副产品的产量分别乘以各自单位产品价格求得；少数生产周期较长，当年没有产品或产品产量不易统计的，则采用间接方法匡算其产值；然后将四业产品产值相加即为农林牧渔业总产值。

粮食产量 指全社会的产量。包括国有经济经营的、集体统一经营的和农民家庭经营的粮食产量，还包括工矿企业办的农场和其他生产单位的产量。粮食除包括稻谷、小麦、玉米、高粱、谷子及其他杂粮外，还包括薯类和豆类。其产量计算方法，豆类按去豆荚后的干豆计算；薯类(包括甘薯和马铃薯，不包括芋头和木薯)1963年以前按每4公斤鲜薯折1公斤粮食计算，从1964年开始改为按5公斤鲜薯折1公斤粮食计算。城市郊区作为蔬菜的薯类(如马铃薯等)按鲜品计算，并且不作粮食统计。其他粮食一律按脱粒后的原粮计算。1989年以前全国粮食产量数据主要靠全面报表取得，1989年开始使用抽样调查数据。

棉花产量 指全社会的产量。包括春播棉和夏播棉。产量按皮棉计算。不包括木棉。

油料产量 指全部油料作物的生产量。包括花生、油菜籽、芝麻、向日葵籽、胡麻籽（亚麻籽）和其他油料。不包括大豆、木本油料和野生油料。花生以带壳干花生计算。

水产品产量 指人工养殖的水产品和天然生长的水产品的捕捞量。包括海水的鱼类、虾蟹类、贝类和藻类以及内陆水域的鱼类、虾蟹类和贝类，不包括淡水生植物。水产品产量是通过各级水产和统计部门逐级上报取得数据。1995年及以前，贝类中牡蛎按鲜肉计算；蚶、蛤、蛙按 5 斤鲜品折 1 斤计算。1996年以后则统一按鲜品计算。

猪、牛、羊肉产量 指当年出栏并已屠宰、除去头蹄下水后带骨肉(即胴体重)的重量。包括全社会范围内的产量。1996年前为各级逐级上报数据。1996年第一次农业普查以后，由于畜牧业产品年报数据与普查数据之间存在一定的差距，国家统计局农调总队对畜牧业年报数据与普查数据进行衔接。1999年以后，国家统计局开展了猪、牛、羊、禽等主要畜禽品种的抽样调查，并用抽样数据作为国家定案数据使用。未开展抽样调查的品种，仍使用各级统计部门逐级上报数据。

期初(末)畜禽存栏头(只)数 指报告期初(末)农村各种合作经济组织和国营农场、农民个人、机关、团体、学校、工矿企业、部队等单位以及城镇居民饲养的大牲畜、猪、羊、家禽等畜禽的存栏数。数据上报方式及数据调整情况同猪、牛、羊肉产量。

常用耕地 是指耕地总资源中专门种植农作物并经常进行耕种、能够正常收获的土地。包括当年实际耕种的熟地；弃耕、休闲不满三年，随时可以复耕的地；开荒利用三年以上的土地。在统计口径上包括南方小于1米、北方小于2米宽的沟、渠、路和田埂。不包括临时种植农作物的坡度在25度以上的陡坡地；在河套、湖畔、库区临时开发的成片或零星土地；也不包括已列为国家和省（区、市）退耕计划但临时耕种的土地。常用耕地是国家需要重点保护的耕地，是反映我国农业综合生产能力的一个重要指标。

农作物播种面积 指实际播种或移植有农作物的面积。凡是实际种植有农作物的面积，不论种植在耕地上还是种植在非耕地上，均包括在农作物播种面积中。在播种季节基本结束后，因遭灾而重新改种和补种的农作物面积，也包括在内。它是反映我国耕地面积利用情况的一个重要指标。目前，农作物播种面积主要包括粮食、棉花、油料、糖料、麻类、烟叶、蔬菜和瓜类、药材和其他农作物九大类。

有效灌溉面积 指具有一定的水源，地块比较平整，灌溉工程或设备已经配套，在一般年景下，当年能够进行正常灌溉的耕地面积。在一般情况下，有效灌溉面积应等于灌溉工程或设备已经配备，能够进行正常灌溉的水田和水浇地面积之和。它是反映我国耕地抗旱能力的一个重要指标。

农用化肥施用量 指本年内实际用于农业生产的化肥数量，包括氮肥、磷肥、钾肥和复合肥。化肥施用量要求按折纯量计算数量。折纯量是指把氮肥、磷肥、钾肥分别按含氮、含五氧化二磷、含氧化钾的百分之百成份进行折算后的数量。复合肥按其所含主要成分折算。公式为:

折纯量=实物量 × 某种化肥有效成份含量的百分比

农业机械总动力 指主要用于农、林、牧、渔业的各种动力机械的动力总和。包括耕作机械、排灌机械、收获机械、农用运输机械、植物保护机械、牧业机械、林业机械、渔业机械和其他农业机械〔内燃机按引擎马力折成瓦(特)计算、电动机按功率折成瓦(特)计算〕。不包括专门用于乡、镇、村、组办工业、基本建设、非农业运输、科学试验和教学等非农业生产方面用的动力机械与作业机械。这个指标的统计数据主要来源于农机部门。

乡村从业人员 指乡村人口中劳动年龄在16周岁以上实际参加生产经营活动并取得实物或货币收入的人员，包括劳动年龄内经常参加劳动的人员，也包括超过劳动年龄但经常参加劳动的人员，但不包括户口在家的在外学生、现役军人和丧失劳动能力的人，也不包括待业人员和家务劳动者。从业人员按从事主业时间最长（时间相同按收入）分为农林牧渔业从业人员、工业从业人员、建筑业从业人员、交通运输业、仓储及邮电通信业从业人员、批零贸易业、餐饮业从业人员、其他非农行业从业人员。

Explanatory Notes on Main Statistical Indicators

Gross Output Value of Farming, Forestry, Animal Husbandry and Fishery refers to the total value of products of farming, forestry, animal husbandry and fishery, and total value of services rendered to support farming, forestry, animal husbandry and fishery activities. It reflects the total scale and results of agricultural production during a given period. Prior to 1957, Chinas gross agricultural output value included barnyard manure and handicraft products for self-consumption (clothes, shoes, stockings, and initial grain processing undertaken by peasants). Since 1958, cutting and felling of bamboo and trees by villages and other cooperative organizations under villages have been included in forestry; value of barnyard manure has been excluded from animal husbandry; self consumed handicrafts has been excluded from sideline occupations, while the output value of industries run by villages and cooperative organizations under village had been included in sideline occupations and the output value of fish catches by motor fishing boats has been added to fishery. Since 1980, the value of handicraft products made for sale by individuals in households had been added to sideline occupations. Since 1984, industries run by villages and under villages have been included in the sector of industry. Since 1993, the subdivision of sideline occupations has been canceled, and the hunting of wild animals has been classified into animal husbandry, and the gathering of wild plants and commodity industry run by rural household have been included in farming. A new industrial classification of economic activities was introduced in 2003. Under the new classification, value of services to farming, forestry, animal husbandry and fishery is included in the gross output value of agriculture, value of wood felling and transport is included in forestry, value of industrial output by rural households is not included in agriculture, and the collection of wild forest products is taken from agriculture and included in the forestry. The first agriculture census of China revealed some discrepancy between the production of animal products from the annual reports and that from the census. Efforts were made by the Rural Socio-economic Survey Organization of NBS to adjust the output value of animal husbandry to make the figures from the annual reports consistent with the census data.

Gross output value of agriculture is obtained by first multiplying the output of each product or by product by its price, resulting in the output value of each single item. For a small number of products, annual output of which is not available or difficult to get due to the long production (growing) process involved, the output value is estimated through an indirect approach. The sum of output value of all products of farming, forestry, animal husbandry and fishery is then equal to the gross output value of agriculture.

Grain Output refers to the total output in the whole country including grains produced by state farms, collective units, rural households, as well as by farms affiliated to industrial and mining enterprises and other production units. Grain includes rice, wheat, corn, sorghum, millet and other miscellaneous grains as well as tubers and bean. Output of beans refers to dry beans without pods. The output of tubers (sweet potatoes and potatoes, not including taros and cassava) was converted into that of grain at the ratio 4:1, i.e. 4 kilograms of fresh tubers was equivalent to 1 kilogram of grain up to 1963. Since 1964 the ratio for conversion has been 5:1. Tubers supplied as vegetables (such as potatoes) in cities and suburbs are calculated as fresh vegetables and their output is not included in the output of grain. Output of all other grains refers to husked grain. Data on grain production before 1989 were obtained through Comprehensive Statistical Reporting System. Since 1989, data from sample surveys are used.

Cotton Output refers to the cotton production in the whole country including cotton sown in spring and in autumn. Output is measured as the weight of ginned cotton. Ceiba is not included.

Output of Oil-bearing Crops refers to the total production of oil-bearing crops of various kinds, including peanuts, (dry, in shell) rapeseeds, sesame, sunflower seeds, flax seeds, and other oil-bearing crops. Soybeans, oil-bearing woody plants, and wild oil-bearing crops are not included.

Output of Aquatic Products refers to catches of both artificially cultured and naturally grown aquatic products, including fish, shrimps, crabs and shellfish in sea and inland water as well as seaweed. Freshwater plants are not included. Data on output of aquatic products are reported by aquatic product and statistical agencies level by level. Before 1995, among the shellfish, the oyster was counted as fresh meat; 5 kilograms of ark shell, clams and frogs are equivalent to 1 kilogram of fresh aquatic products; they are all counted as fresh aquatic products since 1996.

Output of Pork, Beef, and Mutton refers to the meat of slaughtered hogs, cattle, sheep and goats with head, feet, and offal taken away. Data refers to the production of the whole country. The first agriculture census of China in 1996 revealed some discrepancy between the production of animal products from the annual reports and that from the census. Efforts were made by the Rural Socio-economic Survey Organization of NBS to adjust the output value of animal husbandry to make the figures from the annual reports consistent with the census data. Since 1999, NBS conducted sample survey for the major animal husbandry products, such as hogs, cattle, sheep and goats and fowls, and the data from sample surveys are used as national finalized data. Those products, which are not covered by the sample survey, are still reported by statistical agencies level by level.

Number of Livestock or Poultry in Stock at Beginning (or End) refers to the total number of large animals, pigs, sheep, fowls, etc. raised by rural cooperative organizations, state farms, rural individuals, government agencies, schools, industrial and mining enterprises, army, and urban residents at the beginning (or end) of the reference period. Data reporting system and data adjustment are the same as that in the output of pork, beef and mutton.

Regularly Cultivated Land refers to farmland among the total land resources, which is exclusively used for farming and is under regular cultivation with harvest in normal years. Included are currently cultivated land, land that has been abandoned or put in idle for less than 3 years and could be re-used for cultivation at any time, and new-claimed land that has been put into cultivation for more than 3 years. According to statistical coverage, it includes the gouges, dykes, roads and ridges of field with 1 meter wide in Southern areas and 2 meters wide in Northern areas. Excluded under this category are steep slope land over 25 degrees under temporary cultivation, land (large or small plots) that is claimed along river bends, lake sides or banks of reservoirs, as well as land that has been designated under the "Green for Grain" programme of the state and provincial governments but is still temporarily under cultivation. The regularly cultivated land is the key protection land of the nation, an important indicator reflecting the comprehensive productivity of agriculture of China.

Sown Area of Crops refers to area of land sown or transplanted with crops regardless of being in cultivated area or non-cultivated area. Area of land re-sown due to natural disasters is also included. This is an important indicator that can reflect the utilization condition of the cultivated land in China. At present, the sown area of crops mainly include the following 9 categories of crops: grain, cotton, oil-bearing crops, sugar crops, fiber crops, Tobacco, Vegetables and melons, medicinal materials and other farm crops.

Irrigated Area refers to areas that are effectively irrigated, i.e. level land, which has water source and complete sets of irrigation facilities to lift and move adequate water for irrigation purpose under normal conditions. Under normal conditions, irrigated area is the sum of watered fields and irrigated fields where irrigation systems or equipment have been installed for regular irrigation purpose. This important indicator reflects drought resistance capacity of the cultivated land in China.

Consumption of Chemical Fertilizers in Agriculture refers to the quantity of chemical fertilizers applied in agriculture in the year, including nitrogenous fertilizer, phosphate fertilizer, potash fertilizer, and compound fertilizer. The consumption of chemical fertilizers is required in calculation to convert the gross weight into weight containing 100% effective component (e.g. 100% nitrogen content in nitrogenous fertilizer, 100% phosphorous pent oxide contents in phosphate fertilizer, 100% potassium oxide contents in potash fertilizer). Compound fertilizer is converted with its major component. The formula is :

Volume of effective component= physical quantity x effective component of certain chemical fertilizer (%)

Total Power of Farm Machinery refers to total mechanical power of machinery used in farming, forestry, animal husbandry, and fishery, including ploughing, irrigation and drainage, harvesting, transport, plant protection, stock breeding, forestry and fishery. The power of internal combustion engines is required to convert horsepower into watts and the power of electric motors is required to be converted into watts. Machinery employed for non-agricultural purposes, such as the machines used in township run and village-run industry, construction, non-agricultural transport, scientific experiments and teaching, is excluded. Data are mainly from agricultural machinery agencies.

Rural Employed Persons refer to rural labor forces aged over 16 years old who are engaged in real production and management activities and receive payment in kind or wages, including those covered within the age frame and regularly participating in production activities, and those who are out of the range of age frame and also participating in production activities regularly. Excluding students studying in other places with their permanent residence registered in local areas, servicemen and persons incapable of working; also excluding those who are waiting for jobs and those engaged in household work. Persons employed are classified as persons engaged in agriculture, forestry, animal husbandry or fishery activities; persons engaged in industrial activities; persons engaged in construction activities; persons engaged in transport, storage and telecommunications activities; persons engaged in whole sales and retail sales trade and catering activities; and persons engaged in other non-agriculture activities, depending upon the longest period of employment in major activities (or using income indicator when period of employment is the same).

14

工业

Industry

简要说明

一、本篇资料的主要内容

本篇资料反映我国工业经济方面的基本情况，包括31个省、自治区、直辖市的主要工业经济统计数据：

1.全部国有及规模以上非国有工业企业单位数和总产值，以及按企业登记注册类型、轻重工业、企业规模、工业行业大类和按地区分组的主要经济指标和经济效益指标；

2.国有及国有控股、外商投资、港澳台商投资和私营工业企业按工业行业大类和按地区分组的主要经济指标和经济效益指标；

3.大中型工业企业按工业行业大类和按地区分组的主要经济指标和经济效益指标；

4.主要工业产品产量和生产能力等。

二、本篇的统计范围

工业统计调查范围为我国境内（除港、澳、台）的全部工业企业。1997年以前，我国工业的统计范围按隶属关系划分，分为乡及乡以上独立核算工业企业和非独立核算生产单位、村办工业、城镇合作工业、农村合作工业、城镇个体工业、农村个体工业六大部分。（1984年以前村办工业不在工业统计范围内）。

1998年及以后年份，工业统计调查范围由按隶属关系划分，改变为按企业规模划分，分为全部国有及年主营业务收入在500万元以上非国有工业企业和年主营业务收入在500万元以下非国有工业企业两部分。

本篇资料中工业行业分类按2002年《国民经济行业分类标准》划分；企业大中小型划分按2003年《统计上大中小型企业划分办法（暂行）》标准执行。

三、数据来源和调查方法

本篇工业企业统计数据主要是根据工业统计年度报表中有关资料整理汇总的，并增加了2004年经济普查的部分数据。工业统计年度报表是全国各省、自治区、直辖市统计局上报给国家统计局的全面报表，由各级统计部门根据当地实际情况采取全面调查的方法向工业企业布置和收集。

Brief Introduction

I. Main Content

Data in this chapter reflect the basic condition of industrial sector including main industrial economic indicators of 31 provinces, autonomous regions and municipalities:

(1) The number and the gross industrial output value of all state-owned industrial enterprises and the non-state-owned enterprises that are above designated size; as well as their main economic indicators and efficiency indicators classified by type of registration, by light and heavy industries, by size of the enterprises, by branch of industry and by province.

(2) Main economic indicators and efficiency indicators of the state-owned industrial enterprises and enterprises where the state holds the majority of shares, of foreign-funded industrial enterprises and enterprises funded by entrepreneurs from Hong Kong, Macao and Taiwan, and of private enterprises, classified by branch of industry and by province;

(3) Output and production capacity of key industrial products.

II. Coverage of Statistics

Industrial statistics covers all industrial enterprises within the territory (excluding Hong Kong, Macao and Taiwan). Before 1997, the industrial statistics was based on types of ownership, consisting of following six parts: industrial enterprises at and above county level with independent accounting system and production units with dependant accounting system, village industrial enterprise, urban joint industrial enterprises, rural joint industrial enterprise, urban individual industrial enterprises, and rural industrial enterprises (village industrial enterprises were not included in this part before 1984).

Since 1998, the coverage of industrial statistics was changed from types of ownership to the size of enterprises, they are: all state-owned industrial enterprises and those non-state industrial enterprises with revenue from principle business over 5 million yuan, and non-state industrial enterprises with revenue from principle business below 5 million yuan.

Data by industries in this chapter are based on the 2002 *National Industrial Classification of all Economic Activities*, and data by size of enterprises are based on the *Preliminary Standards of Enterprises by Size*.

III. Source of Data and Survey Methodology

The industrial enterprises statistics in this chapter are collected from the Annual Report of Industrial Statistics, supplemented by some data from the 2004 economic census. The Annual Report of Industrial Statistics is submitted by statistical bureaus of all provinces, autonomous regions and municipalities through Comprehensive Reports to NBS. Statistical agencies at various levels arrange and collect data through comprehensive reporting system basing of real situation in local areas.

14-1 全部工业企业主要经济指标（2004年）

Main Economic Indicators of All Industrial Enterprises (2004)

单位：亿元 (100 million yuan)

行业	Sector	企业单位数（个）Number of Enterprises (unit)	工业总产值（当年价格）Gross Industrial Output Value (current prices)	资产总计 Total Assets	主营业务收入 Revenue from Principal Business	利润总额 Total Profits	全部从业人员年平均人数(万人) Annual Average Number of Employed Persons (10 000 persons)
总计	**Total**	**1375263**	**222315.93**	**240706.77**	**218442.81**	**13065.39**	**9303.94**
按轻重工业分	**Grouped by Light & Heavy Industries**						
轻工业	Light Industry	576319	72115.18	68562.56	69653.74	3103.66	3909.16
重工业	Heavy Industry	798944	150200.75	172144.21	148789.08	9961.72	5394.78
按企业规模分	**Grouped by Size of Enterprises**						
大型企业	Large-sized Enterprises	2135	69483.38	78771.10	71150.97	5538.15	1378.33
中型企业	Medium-sized Enterprises	25557	63891.30	75407.38	62907.56	3645.76	2130.12
小型企业	Small-sized Enterprises	1347571	88941.24	86528.30	84304.11	3881.48	5795.49
按登记注册类型分	**By Status of Registration**						
内资企业	Domestic Funded	1269098	155178.16	180905.15	152295.27	9258.39	7312.53
国有企业	State-owned Enterprises	25339	23519.12	44694.46	24180.57	1088.92	892.41
集体企业	Collective-owned Enterprises	141772	9819.04	8019.28	9379.74	502.50	688.08
股份合作企业	Cooperative Enterprises	50097	3396.73	2858.35	3197.64	156.18	205.61
联营企业	Joint Ownership Enterprises	6547	1033.43	1368.39	992.73	51.18	43.97
国有联营企业	State Joint Ownership Enterprises	756	522.80	837.46	498.75	26.36	9.85
集体联营企业	Collective Joint Ownership Enterprises	2924	175.11	150.47	164.87	11.22	14.00
国有与集体联营企业	Joint State-collective Enterprises	1064	169.23	217.37	168.36	5.70	9.90
其他联营企业	Other Joint Ownership Enterprises	1803	166.30	163.10	160.75	7.91	10.21
有限责任公司	Limited Liability Corporations	102392	44042.82	60663.84	43798.69	2863.70	1693.26
国有独资公司	State Sole funded Corporations	2083	9960.17	19236.56	10423.19	637.70	370.72
其他有限责任公司	Other Limited Liability Corporations	100309	34082.65	41427.29	33375.50	2226.00	1322.54
股份有限公司	Share-holding Corporations Limited	17427	23120.84	26635.07	22813.23	2140.21	506.51
私营企业	Private Enterprises	902647	49705.23	36224.92	47415.22	2415.94	3225.14
私营独资企业	Private-funded Enterprises	459709	13409.74	7667.78	12828.35	916.10	1138.87
私营合伙企业	Private Partnership Enterprises	92023	2876.23	1747.31	2752.90	212.06	271.41
私营有限责任公司	Private Limited Liability Corporations	327629	31131.92	24776.81	29674.45	1165.92	1689.26
私营股份有限公司	Private Share-holding Corporations Ltd.	23286	2287.34	2033.03	2159.53	121.85	125.60
其他企业	Other Enterprises	22877	540.94	440.82	517.46	39.75	57.55
港、澳、台商投资企业	Enterprises with Funds from Hong Kong, Macao and Taiwan	54910	24386.41	22819.32	23640.82	1225.98	1038.14
合资经营企业(港或澳、台资)	Joint-ventures Enterprises	16745	9793.71	9706.19	9365.57	501.18	307.19
合作经营企业(港或澳、台资)	Cooperative Enterprises	3473	1470.21	1410.85	1446.81	77.67	67.72
港、澳、台商独资经营企业	Enterprises with Sole Investment	34104	11859.65	10259.84	11464.46	524.82	642.03
港、澳、台商投资股份有限公司	Share-holding Corporations Ltd. With Investment	588	1262.85	1442.44	1363.98	122.32	21.21
外商投资企业	Foreign Funded Enterprises	51255	42751.35	36982.30	42506.72	2581.03	953.27
中外合资经营企业	Joint-venture Enterprises	21420	19967.71	17289.99	19533.47	1305.38	381.63
中外合作经营企业	Cooperation Enterprises	2818	1666.62	1757.61	1578.65	149.69	52.52
外资企业	Enterprises with Sole Foreign Funds	26335	19420.38	15339.13	19696.82	884.71	492.27
外商投资股份有限公司	Share-holding Corporations Ltd. with Foreign Investment	682	1696.64	2595.57	1697.78	241.25	26.85

注：本表为2004年经济普查数据，范围包括规模以上工业企业和规模以下工业企业（下表同）。

a) Data in this table are from the first National Economic Census in 2004, which include industrial enterprises above and below designated size. The same as in the following table.

14-2 按行业分全部工业企业主要经济指标（2004年）

单位：亿元

项目	Item	企业单位数（个） Number of Enterprises (unit)	工业总产值（当年价格） Gross Industrial Output Value (current prices)
全国总计	**National Total**	**1375263**	**222315.93**
按行业分	**Grouped by Sector**		
煤炭开采和洗选业	Mining and Washing of Coal	26843	4735.20
石油和天然气开采业	Extraction of Petroleum and Natural Gas	482	4630.17
黑色金属矿采选业	Mining and Processing of Ferrous Metal Ores	10262	980.93
有色金属矿采选业	Mining and Processing of Non-Ferrous Metal Ores	6087	913.53
非金属矿采选业	Mining and Processing of Nonmetal Ores	34981	1151.50
其他采矿业	Mining of Other Ores	264	10.38
农副食品加工业	Processing of Food from Agricultural Products	69669	9543.82
食品制造业	Manufacture of Foods	29896	3288.25
饮料制造业	Manufacture of Beverages	25526	2737.09
烟草制品业	Manufacture of Tobacco	287	2597.21
纺织业	Manufacture of Textile	83103	11655.12
纺织服装、鞋、帽制造业	Manufacture of Textile Wearing Apparel, Footware, and Caps	48286	4668.52
皮革、毛皮、羽毛(绒)及其制品业	Manufacture of Leather, Fur, Feather and Related Products	22699	3133.23
木材加工及木、竹、藤、棕、草制品业	Processing of Timber, Manufacture of Wood, Bamboo, Rattan, Palm, and Straw Products	39938	2002.36
家具制造业	Manufacture of Furniture	23913	1495.46
造纸及纸制品业	Manufacture of Paper and Paper Products	39721	3971.24
印刷业和记录媒介的复制	Printing, Reproduction of Recording Media	41241	1744.24
文教体育用品制造业	Manufacture of Articles For Culture, Education and Sport Activity	14622	1428.45
石油加工、炼焦及核燃料加工业	Processing of Petroleum, Coking, Processing of Nuclear Fuel	7163	9088.84
化学原料及化学制品制造业	Manufacture of Raw Chemical Materials and Chemical Products	75179	14027.74
医药制造业	Manufacture of Medicines	11296	3365.85
化学纤维制造业	Manufacture of Chemical Fibers	3383	1994.19
橡胶制品业	Manufacture of Rubber	15190	2047.60
塑料制品业	Manufacture of Plastics	69751	5253.29
非金属矿物制品业	Manufacture of Non-metallic Mineral Products	157861	9951.20
黑色金属冶炼及压延加工业	Smelting and Pressing of Ferrous Metals	20526	17309.81
有色金属冶炼及压延加工业	Smelting and Pressing of Non-ferrous Metals	15186	6244.08
金属制品业	Manufacture of Metal Products	81028	6359.66
通用设备制造业	Manufacture of General Purpose Machinery	113789	10270.75
专用设备制造业	Manufacture of Special Purpose Machinery	55147	5824.81
交通运输设备制造业	Manufacture of Transport Equipment	53852	14538.43
电气机械及器材制造业	Manufacture of Electrical Machinery and Equipment	60144	12036.69
通信设备、计算机及其他电子设备制造业	Manufacture of Communication Equipment, Computers and Other Electronic Equipment	27339	22594.03
仪器仪表及文化、办公用机械制造业	Manufacture of Measuring Instruments and Machinery for Cultural Activity and Office Work	16716	2408.83
工艺品及其他制造业	Manufacture of Artwork and Other Manufacturing	32580	2119.76
废弃资源和废旧材料回收加工业	Recycling and Disposal of Waste	3555	260.52
电力、热力的生产和供应业	Production and Supply of Electric Power and Heat Power	24607	14904.26
燃气生产和供应业	Production and Supply of Gas	1447	437.98
水的生产和供应业	Production and Supply of Water	11704	590.92

Main Economic Indicators of All Industrial Enterprises by Sector (2004)

(100 million yuan)

资产总计 Total Assets	固定资产原价 Original Value of Fixed Assets	负债合计 Total Liabilities	主营业务收入 Revenue from Principal Business	主营业务成本 Cost of Principal Business	主营业务税金及附加 Taxes and Other Charges on Principal Business	利润总额 Total Profits	全部从业人员年平均人数(万人) Annual Average Number of Employed Persons (10 000 persons)
240706.77	**104614.99**	**136785.02**	**218442.81**	**185401.63**	**3058.89**	**13065.39**	**9303.94**
7801.70	4115.61	4535.68	4802.26	3227.80	101.76	447.62	540.19
6110.39	4567.73	2259.97	4541.43	2202.62	120.37	1744.65	98.16
1052.23	412.10	479.31	971.24	688.67	24.22	146.37	62.00
891.31	401.70	469.95	902.30	671.25	10.07	128.29	54.50
1109.34	608.79	524.77	1106.69	859.00	31.35	90.00	112.88
10.88	4.85	6.36	10.32	8.16	0.34	0.54	0.74
6200.79	2507.33	3673.27	9282.83	8299.25	57.55	333.73	296.24
3400.67	1386.53	1886.66	3154.51	2513.26	23.12	154.18	159.80
3765.19	1539.30	2088.48	2673.21	1869.02	156.59	171.61	122.14
3020.81	728.75	1122.54	2574.53	943.38	1018.52	366.22	20.21
10777.70	4509.76	6714.15	11237.13	10140.21	62.00	317.82	763.46
3556.77	1141.83	1972.88	4445.40	3852.89	26.50	173.15	481.71
2014.93	620.49	1146.36	3003.09	2650.73	18.62	118.28	275.97
1711.41	825.58	911.83	1922.14	1674.17	23.76	95.41	157.52
1253.30	446.02	690.52	1446.61	1229.40	12.35	68.95	107.99
4904.06	2349.02	2998.36	3806.39	3285.11	26.34	182.94	200.90
2205.88	1029.76	1108.66	1681.26	1377.26	15.76	111.86	127.01
1139.70	382.44	598.87	1379.27	1209.73	7.44	47.48	148.56
5326.68	2744.68	2846.86	9123.94	8117.07	318.72	293.31	77.99
14126.70	6178.07	7893.61	13702.91	11175.20	109.02	932.35	444.76
5282.54	1883.14	2731.04	3139.19	2045.16	22.61	264.31	132.48
2254.35	1120.57	1339.44	1932.72	1768.59	10.18	47.00	43.26
2088.00	917.23	1272.74	1951.26	1654.61	23.14	84.38	109.14
5082.98	2068.82	2825.51	5118.38	4474.49	35.16	218.99	291.59
11627.90	5622.12	6618.31	9496.00	7809.14	124.66	622.63	839.75
16130.58	7532.83	9676.44	17434.63	15277.04	89.75	1124.66	309.29
5700.73	2490.77	3652.41	6179.93	5492.88	29.10	312.97	147.24
5535.37	1843.42	3235.20	6108.93	7287.24	41.32	284.17	350.25
10672.88	3296.96	6602.33	9750.08	8172.61	69.06	552.72	528.13
6844.52	2043.53	4222.59	5616.24	4657.45	34.44	287.41	309.65
15455.03	4647.74	9095.53	14167.03	11974.45	217.39	813.19	432.77
10628.82	2731.16	6415.74	11633.22	9849.46	44.66	526.48	445.38
16655.34	4553.04	10174.24	22879.24	20486.21	25.96	823.86	435.48
2243.71	595.85	1280.92	2391.24	2013.14	8.26	110.10	113.95
1729.24	665.33	931.76	2034.70	1745.09	16.39	98.38	199.35
161.10	39.55	95.35	254.00	230.69	1.86	9.05	8.66
37983.19	23287.94	20754.16	15461.90	13534.99	88.25	937.42	278.72
1179.91	680.01	554.36	564.96	506.96	3.09	14.30	17.64
3070.17	2094.64	1377.88	561.70	427.25	9.21	8.60	58.50

14-3 各地区全部工业企业主要经济指标（2004年）

Main Indicators of All Industrial Enterprises by Region (2004)

单位：亿元 (100 million yuan)

地 区	Region	企业单位数（个） Number of Enterprises (unit)	工业总产值（当年价格） Gross Industrial Output Value (current prices)	资产总计 Total Assets	固定资产原价 Original Value of Fixed Assets	负债合计 Total Liabilities
全 国	**National Total**	**1375263**	**222315.93**	**240706.77**	**104614.99**	**136785.02**
北 京	Beijing	31670	5974.70	13451.79	3322.08	4697.74
天 津	Tianjin	25650	6119.08	6143.96	2476.96	3479.69
河 北	Hebei	64630	10194.40	9562.64	4735.21	5684.46
山 西	Shanxi	28883	4173.93	6690.45	3351.30	4247.69
内蒙古	Inner Mongolia	11849	2327.48	3648.07	1866.93	2096.42
辽 宁	Liaoning	54607	9140.61	12249.49	5538.81	7141.77
吉 林	Jilin	16363	3551.72	4611.88	2177.68	2652.30
黑龙江	Heilongjiang	20303	3955.70	5637.04	2990.53	3199.72
上 海	Shanghai	55806	14594.15	15574.41	5842.65	8034.29
江 苏	Jiangsu	188841	29476.66	25274.81	10173.96	15458.40
浙 江	Zhejiang	188919	21227.20	20379.32	7746.86	11707.10
安 徽	Anhui	39265	4236.39	4964.71	2368.23	2953.91
福 建	Fujian	49838	7516.05	6937.00	3014.86	3483.60
江 西	Jiangxi	29467	2736.69	3112.75	1511.75	1881.40
山 东	Shandong	120672	24678.50	20552.12	9398.78	11931.55
河 南	Henan	76895	9236.80	9130.85	4589.39	5490.36
湖 北	Hubei	29262	5329.23	7982.03	4129.67	4585.42
湖 南	Hunan	43925	4341.88	4746.82	2341.41	2796.64
广 东	Guangdong	137650	31519.61	26514.48	10118.86	15143.85
广 西	Guangxi	19081	2242.26	2995.91	1503.99	1810.13
海 南	Hainan	2066	429.42	735.69	306.40	424.16
重 庆	Chongqing	20509	2598.84	3109.97	1320.98	1839.22
四 川	Sichuan	43759	5303.64	7550.00	3515.93	4664.61
贵 州	Guizhou	11121	1546.17	2674.85	1444.60	1693.54
云 南	Yunnan	14403	2344.07	4008.96	1839.66	2106.92
西 藏	Tibet	356	24.85	115.59	73.06	25.99
陕 西	Shaanxi	25785	3150.79	4968.23	2614.74	3149.64
甘 肃	Gansu	11663	1695.79	2673.92	1495.52	1680.73
青 海	Qinghai	2199	388.12	1040.49	639.32	687.33
宁 夏	Ningxia	4019	605.19	952.30	489.34	601.96
新 疆	Xinjiang	5807	1656.02	2716.23	1675.52	1434.48

14-3 续表 continued

单位：亿元 (100 million yuan)

地 区	Region	主营业务收入 Revenue from Principal Business	主营业务成本 Cost of Principal Business	主营业务税金及附加 Taxes and Other Charges on Principal Business	利润总额 Total Profits	全部从业人员年平均人数（万人） Annual Average Number of Employed Persons (10 000 persons)
全 国	**National Total**	**218442.81**	**185401.63**	**3058.89**	**13065.39**	**9303.94**
北 京	Beijing	6225.22	5244.46	48.85	389.85	158.03
天 津	Tianjin	6113.21	5197.60	56.88	408.26	168.93
河 北	Hebei	9954.67	8427.93	115.42	646.57	440.99
山 西	Shanxi	4137.27	3197.32	62.40	282.61	278.13
内蒙古	Inner Mongolia	2330.90	1859.00	37.49	161.40	110.14
辽 宁	Liaoning	9052.39	7696.00	110.39	434.31	354.20
吉 林	Jilin	3354.51	2802.44	73.89	197.13	138.29
黑龙江	Heilongjiang	4012.67	2789.85	114.18	753.10	187.48
上 海	Shanghai	15266.68	12777.87	176.99	1058.84	340.93
江 苏	Jiangsu	28639.41	25208.81	211.08	1196.67	1018.91
浙 江	Zhejiang	20719.19	17862.06	227.64	1106.97	861.59
安 徽	Anhui	4186.60	3407.16	86.55	255.32	235.81
福 建	Fujian	7287.11	6185.11	88.85	427.21	364.53
江 西	Jiangxi	2691.95	2279.37	60.57	122.31	179.17
山 东	Shandong	23885.02	20133.49	259.35	1561.54	935.93
河 南	Henan	8896.40	7361.50	138.36	619.06	530.25
湖 北	Hubei	5117.80	4245.60	98.93	279.07	235.48
湖 南	Hunan	4218.30	3339.51	183.13	230.43	262.40
广 东	Guangdong	30843.68	28557.18	240.30	1478.15	1338.13
广 西	Guangxi	2197.12	1809.14	38.25	131.16	126.67
海 南	Hainan	431.60	341.14	9.60	28.73	14.77
重 庆	Chongqing	2551.98	2074.64	51.46	144.19	144.62
四 川	Sichuan	5195.40	4221.95	88.32	222.27	297.31
贵 州	Guizhou	1467.27	1107.99	64.32	76.67	93.89
云 南	Yunnan	2290.58	1616.54	233.66	222.08	103.53
西 藏	Tibet	25.59	17.07	0.46	3.74	2.31
陕 西	Shaanxi	3026.10	2280.36	85.32	290.04	175.43
甘 肃	Gansu	1697.49	1386.72	51.77	63.97	98.09
青 海	Qinghai	385.11	287.76	5.05	33.74	18.10
宁 夏	Ningxia	569.81	479.35	6.30	16.96	33.11
新 疆	Xinjiang	1671.77	1206.73	33.14	223.05	56.81

14-4 按行业分全部国有及规模以上非国有工业企业主要指标（2005年）

单位：亿元

项 目	Item	企业单位数（个）Number of Enterprises (unit)	工业总产值 Gross Industrial Output Value
全国总计	**National Total**	**271835**	**251619.50**
煤炭开采和洗选业	Mining and Washing of Coal	5787	5722.77
石油和天然气开采业	Extraction of Petroleum and Natural Gas	174	6286.27
黑色金属矿采选业	Mining and Processing of Ferrous Metal Ores	2087	989.59
有色金属矿采选业	Mining and Processing of Non-Ferrous Metal Ores	1529	1140.41
非金属矿采选业	Mining and Processing of Nonmetal Ores	2242	756.51
其他采矿业	Mining of Other Ores	14	8.59
农副食品加工业	Processing of Food from Agricultural Products	14575	10614.95
食品制造业	Manufacture of Foods	5553	3779.39
饮料制造业	Manufacture of Beverages	3519	3089.27
烟草制品业	Manufacture of Tobacco	190	2840.74
纺织业	Manufacture of Textile	22569	12671.65
纺织服装、鞋、帽制造业	Manufacture of Textile Wearing Apparel, Footware, and Caps	11865	4974.63
皮革、毛皮、羽毛(绒)及其制品业	Manufacture of Leather, Fur, Feather and Related Products	6227	3462.79
木材加工及木、竹、藤、棕、草制品业	Processing of Timber, Manufacture of Wood, Bamboo, Rattan, Palm, and Straw Products	5397	1827.71
家具制造业	Manufacture of Furniture	3074	1427.26
造纸及纸制品业	Manufacture of Paper and Paper Products	7461	4161.33
印刷业和记录媒介的复制	Printing, Reproduction of Recording Media	4826	1442.96
文教体育用品制造业	Manufacture of Articles For Culture, Education and Sport Activity	3378	1482.50
石油加工、炼焦及核燃料加工业	Processing of Petroleum, Coking, Processing of Nuclear Fuel	1990	12000.49
化学原料及化学制品制造业	Manufacture of Raw Chemical Materials and Chemical Products	18716	16359.66
医药制造业	Manufacture of Medicines	4971	4250.45
化学纤维制造业	Manufacture of Chemical Fibers	1306	2608.39
橡胶制品业	Manufacture of Rubber	3034	2196.74
塑料制品业	Manufacture of Plastics	12041	5067.89
非金属矿物制品业	Manufacture of Non-metallic Mineral Products	20111	9195.24
黑色金属冶炼及压延加工业	Smelting and Pressing of Ferrous Metals	6649	21470.98
有色金属冶炼及压延加工业	Smelting and Pressing of Non-ferrous Metals	5163	7937.95
金属制品业	Manufacture of Metal Products	13802	6556.76
通用设备制造业	Manufacture of General Purpose Machinery	19981	10610.37
专用设备制造业	Manufacture of Special Purpose Machinery	10260	6085.43
交通运输设备制造业	Manufacture of Transport Equipment	11315	15714.86
电气机械及器材制造业	Manufacture of Electrical Machinery and Equipment	15366	13901.29
通信设备、计算机及其他电子设备制造业	Manufacture of Communication Equipment, Computers and Other Electronic Equipment	8868	26994.38
仪器仪表及文化、办公用机械制造业	Manufacture of Measuring Instruments and Machinery for Cultural Activity and Office Work	3723	2781.05
工艺品及其他制造业	Manufacture of Artwork and Other Manufacturing	5131	2035.68
废弃资源和废旧材料回收加工业	Recycling and Disposal of Waste	438	292.95
电力、热力的生产和供应业	Production and Supply of Electric Power and Heat Power	5527	17785.93
燃气生产和供应业	Production and Supply of Gas	484	514.72
水的生产和供应业	Production and Supply of Water	2492	578.98

注：规模以上非国有企业为年主营业务收入在500万元以上的企业（以下表均同）。

Main Indicators of State-owned and Non-state-owned Industrial Enterprises above Designated Size by Industrial Sector (2005)

(100 million yuan)

工 业 增加值 Value-added of Industry	资 产 总 计 Total Assets	流动资产 合 计 Total Working Capitals	流动资产 年平均余额 Annual Average Balance of Working Capitals	固定资产 原 价 Original Value of Fixed Assets	固定资产净值 年平均余额 Annual Average Balance of Net Value of Fixed Assets
72186.99	**244784.25**	**111031.41**	**105901.69**	**143143.63**	**89460.49**
2888.25	8693.48	3402.87	3155.35	5450.03	3299.49
4813.96	6751.78	1498.44	1425.37	9204.82	4235.32
426.50	1167.20	510.06	458.51	466.11	316.41
427.60	968.64	418.43	384.56	484.37	306.32
280.51	682.49	277.65	269.94	377.50	261.45
2.70	5.87	2.38	2.03	5.44	2.93
2745.96	5750.69	2960.41	2849.91	2732.50	1935.52
1168.32	3252.85	1589.32	1523.54	1645.11	1101.21
1164.73	3513.79	1682.42	1609.46	1948.05	1260.37
2059.99	3261.78	2074.87	1990.63	1250.73	632.65
3240.19	10357.97	5196.31	5000.71	5540.64	3705.94
1419.86	3188.77	1961.71	1855.45	1259.36	849.35
944.38	1955.44	1219.28	1170.07	717.70	492.54
510.86	1338.73	619.91	600.78	722.68	521.39
384.87	1032.78	588.42	567.09	421.64	299.89
1146.40	4660.00	1883.67	1829.30	2912.61	2058.98
463.06	1772.83	849.12	824.63	1119.91	689.49
379.71	1014.56	613.23	595.79	447.21	289.44
1981.64	6490.77	2919.56	2549.66	4966.14	2745.08
4391.92	15175.85	6737.89	6399.50	9228.70	5720.89
1529.80	5549.83	2674.84	2565.24	2419.53	1641.66
485.31	2461.41	1011.71	966.80	1658.52	1068.89
595.36	1956.28	976.60	947.31	1049.97	683.79
1272.05	4432.38	2364.53	2249.24	2207.88	1474.10
2807.92	10370.69	4457.28	4311.32	6325.72	4285.00
5776.90	18950.65	8151.92	7710.36	11522.30	6687.44
1929.65	6569.49	3162.81	2961.17	3528.52	2317.09
1693.38	4769.27	2881.58	2759.27	1986.51	1316.02
2966.96	9886.06	6338.71	6003.47	3739.60	2286.91
1681.56	6391.13	3918.45	3688.61	2466.33	1553.33
3830.52	16108.05	9036.41	8882.34	6565.54	3882.57
3574.13	11062.69	7168.85	6718.82	3680.62	2320.18
5722.11	18063.24	11945.36	11081.37	6943.36	4277.13
733.19	2226.09	1422.33	1350.75	794.04	500.90
570.83	1365.98	796.00	757.59	587.84	398.70
59.93	126.37	86.44	81.46	35.18	24.10
5719.79	39375.46	6578.08	6815.53	33588.59	21907.16
134.52	1186.15	361.06	337.26	796.37	540.12
261.64	2896.75	692.50	651.50	2345.98	1570.75

a) Non-state-owned industrial enterprises above designated size are those with annual revenue from principal business over 5 million yuan. The same a in the following tables.

14-4 续表

单位：亿元

项　目	Item	负债合计 Total Liabilities	流动负债合计 Total Working Liabilities
全国总计	**National Total**	**141509.84**	**108411.70**
按行业分	**Grouped by Sector**		
煤炭开采和洗选业	Mining and Washing of Coal	5332.54	3630.44
石油和天然气开采业	Extraction of Petroleum and Natural Gas	2311.75	1562.87
黑色金属矿采选业	Mining and Processing of Ferrous Metal Ores	563.07	488.75
有色金属矿采选业	Mining and Processing of Non-Ferrous Metal Ores	494.45	369.40
非金属矿采选业	Mining and Processing of Nonmetal Ores	370.90	297.91
其他采矿业	Mining of Other Ores	2.54	2.50
农副食品加工业	Processing of Food from Agricultural Products	3423.48	2947.64
食品制造业	Manufacture of Foods	1821.86	1557.49
饮料制造业	Manufacture of Beverages	1873.27	1636.32
烟草制品业	Manufacture of Tobacco	1074.59	1016.39
纺织业	Manufacture of Textile	6346.76	5382.10
纺织服装、鞋、帽制造业	Manufacture of Textile Wearing Apparel, Footware, and Caps	1816.22	1675.59
皮革、毛皮、羽毛(绒)及其制品业	Manufacture of Leather, Fur, Feather and Related Products	1147.48	1065.29
木材加工及木、竹、藤、棕、草制品业	Processing of Timber, Manufacture of Wood, Bamboo, Rattan, Palm, and Straw Products	733.46	567.71
家具制造业	Manufacture of Furniture	592.68	541.33
造纸及纸制品业	Manufacture of Paper and Paper Products	2869.21	2073.66
印刷业和记录媒介的复制	Printing, Reproduction of Recording Media	916.17	796.61
文教体育用品制造业	Manufacture of Articles For Culture, Education and Sport Activity	543.74	507.86
石油加工、炼焦及核燃料加工业	Processing of Petroleum, Coking, Processing of Nuclear Fuel	3664.86	2745.56
化学原料及化学制品制造业	Manufacture of Raw Chemical Materials and Chemical Products	8543.25	6542.30
医药制造业	Manufacture of Medicines	2875.13	2391.64
化学纤维制造业	Manufacture of Chemical Fibers	1454.84	1118.49
橡胶制品业	Manufacture of Rubber	1158.00	937.32
塑料制品业	Manufacture of Plastics	2467.18	2139.56
非金属矿物制品业	Manufacture of Non-metallic Mineral Products	6224.02	4843.95
黑色金属冶炼及压延加工业	Smelting and Pressing of Ferrous Metals	11428.17	9216.69
有色金属冶炼及压延加工业	Smelting and Pressing of Non-ferrous Metals	4151.87	3259.68
金属制品业	Manufacture of Metal Products	2770.75	2518.52
通用设备制造业	Manufacture of General Purpose Machinery	6172.60	5568.62
专用设备制造业	Manufacture of Special Purpose Machinery	4020.38	3581.53
交通运输设备制造业	Manufacture of Transport Equipment	9918.74	8730.55
电气机械及器材制造业	Manufacture of Electrical Machinery and Equipment	6731.24	6181.30
通信设备、计算机及其他电子设备制造业	Manufacture of Communication Equipment, Computers and Other Electronic Equipment	11329.93	10273.00
仪器仪表及文化、办公用机械制造业	Manufacture of Measuring Instruments and Machinery for Cultural Activity and Office Work	1217.39	1108.79
工艺品及其他制造业	Manufacture of Artwork and Other Manufacturing	750.39	662.87
废弃资源和废旧材料回收加工业	Recycling and Disposal of Waste	81.90	76.38
电力、热力的生产和供应业	Production and Supply of Electric Power and Heat Power	22318.16	9245.45
燃气生产和供应业	Production and Supply of Gas	611.17	407.88
水的生产和供应业	Production and Supply of Water	1385.71	741.73

continued

(100 million yuan)

所有者权益 Owners' Equity	主营业务收入 Revenue from Principal Business	主营业务成本 Cost of Principal Business	主营业务税金及附加 Taxes and Other Charges on Principal Business	利润总额 Total Profits	本年应交增值税 Value Added Tax Payable	全部从业人员年平均人数（万人） Annual Average Employed Persons (10 000 persons)
102882.02	**248544.00**	**209862.52**	**2997.34**	**14802.54**	**8520.94**	**6895.96**
3321.99	5912.45	4040.22	100.68	561.00	448.84	435.81
4436.63	6151.22	2512.53	138.83	2957.79	608.98	85.58
603.97	989.58	694.42	17.33	137.31	65.29	40.59
474.18	1120.13	783.22	8.79	209.53	46.33	41.87
311.59	733.89	542.79	16.57	58.93	38.88	42.96
3.33	8.16	6.12	0.08	1.06	0.42	0.21
2327.21	10366.49	9202.03	48.66	398.71	166.78	222.55
1430.75	3665.75	2867.52	19.22	206.21	141.77	121.02
1640.07	3055.28	2134.77	160.11	221.46	166.26	89.00
2187.19	2850.84	1039.58	1129.40	406.54	329.34	19.67
4006.71	12374.53	11104.35	54.63	437.13	316.51	590.96
1372.55	4780.00	4113.10	19.70	206.16	118.92	346.06
807.96	3315.94	2924.94	14.03	138.50	79.18	228.84
605.27	1749.45	1521.63	11.88	82.43	50.85	83.33
440.09	1387.39	1181.98	6.53	61.89	28.91	71.27
1773.01	4034.25	3479.62	21.54	194.04	138.93	130.14
856.66	1386.55	1139.51	6.76	93.19	58.21	66.90
470.82	1437.53	1254.69	4.30	52.47	27.10	109.80
2817.85	12030.52	11424.49	299.88	-119.27	303.26	74.40
6599.45	16165.21	13447.22	108.43	991.06	534.36	339.99
2672.60	4019.83	2684.60	26.96	338.20	219.28	123.44
1006.57	2567.00	2378.59	8.53	46.20	46.01	42.63
797.27	2144.22	1828.17	19.60	105.19	52.48	79.64
1962.85	4944.73	4335.93	18.56	215.79	114.83	183.28
4135.92	8846.49	7472.54	67.87	420.35	370.85	418.18
7358.60	21594.05	19236.62	104.16	1067.44	761.25	287.49
2413.62	7845.56	6927.89	40.31	426.83	251.28	130.74
1998.52	6394.35	5577.73	25.79	314.23	157.19	223.23
3699.84	10197.83	8534.89	46.63	625.26	322.61	355.12
2366.51	5932.97	4939.69	27.91	324.65	169.39	219.89
6162.78	15562.60	13348.71	235.58	664.01	454.56	352.40
4323.53	13363.92	11395.20	40.51	640.17	316.62	367.21
6719.40	26844.02	24176.35	23.42	891.69	315.23	439.64
1008.04	2735.00	2305.00	6.56	154.35	60.59	88.68
615.57	1969.70	1700.51	9.60	90.82	50.71	125.51
44.47	281.67	255.09	1.16	8.13	5.46	4.24
17022.59	18580.36	16335.43	98.98	1157.73	1139.52	252.69
574.98	662.12	596.70	2.59	16.82	17.06	14.84
1511.04	542.41	418.15	5.27	-1.46	26.89	46.15

14-5 按行业分全部国有及规模以上非国有工业企业主要经济效益指标（2005年）

行 业	Sector	工 业 增加值率 (%) Ratio of Value Added to Gross Industrial Output Value (%)	总资产 贡献率 (%) Ratio of Total Assets to Industrial Output Value (%)
全 国 总 计	**National Total**	**28.69**	**11.82**
按行业分	**Grouped by Sector**		
煤炭开采和洗选业	Mining and Washing of Coal	50.47	13.64
石油和天然气开采业	Extraction of Petroleum and Natural Gas	76.58	55.32
黑色金属矿采选业	Mining and Processing of Ferrous Metal Ores	43.10	19.65
有色金属矿采选业	Mining and Processing of Non-Ferrous Metal Ores	37.50	28.45
非金属矿采选业	Mining and Processing of Nonmetal Ores	37.08	17.79
其他采矿业	Mining of Other Ores	31.46	27.64
农副食品加工业	Processing of Food from Agricultural Products	25.87	12.24
食品制造业	Manufacture of Foods	30.91	12.38
饮料制造业	Manufacture of Beverages	37.70	16.40
烟草制品业	Manufacture of Tobacco	72.52	57.68
纺织业	Manufacture of Textile	25.57	9.26
纺织服装、鞋、帽制造业	Manufacture of Textile Wearing Apparel, Footware, and Caps	28.54	11.76
皮革、毛皮、羽毛(绒)及其制品业	Manufacture of Leather, Fur, Feather and Related Products	27.27	12.79
木材加工及木、竹、藤、棕、草制品业	Processing of Timber, Manufacture of Wood, Bamboo, Rattan, Palm, and Straw Products	27.95	12.15
家具制造业	Manufacture of Furniture	26.97	10.40
造纸及纸制品业	Manufacture of Paper and Paper Products	27.55	9.09
印刷业和记录媒介的复制	Printing, Reproduction of Recording Media	32.09	9.66
文教体育用品制造业	Manufacture of Articles For Culture, Education and Sport Activity	25.61	8.93
石油加工、炼焦及核燃料加工业	Processing of Petroleum, Coking, Processing of Nuclear Fuel	16.51	8.53
化学原料及化学制品制造业	Manufacture of Raw Chemical Materials and Chemical Products	26.85	11.93
医药制造业	Manufacture of Medicines	35.99	11.63
化学纤维制造业	Manufacture of Chemical Fibers	18.61	5.65
橡胶制品业	Manufacture of Rubber	27.10	10.39
塑料制品业	Manufacture of Plastics	25.10	8.87
非金属矿物制品业	Manufacture of Non-metallic Mineral Products	30.54	9.55
黑色金属冶炼及压延加工业	Smelting and Pressing of Ferrous Metals	26.91	11.31
有色金属冶炼及压延加工业	Smelting and Pressing of Non-ferrous Metals	24.31	12.33
金属制品业	Manufacture of Metal Products	25.83	11.44
通用设备制造业	Manufacture of General Purpose Machinery	27.96	10.85
专用设备制造业	Manufacture of Special Purpose Machinery	27.63	8.96
交通运输设备制造业	Manufacture of Transport Equipment	24.38	9.10
电气机械及器材制造业	Manufacture of Electrical Machinery and Equipment	25.71	9.90
通信设备、计算机及其他电子设备制造业	Manufacture of Communication Equipment, Computers and Other Electronic Equipment	21.20	7.42
仪器仪表及文化、办公用机械制造业	Manufacture of Measuring Instruments and Machinery for Cultural Activity and Office Work	26.36	10.44
工艺品及其他制造业	Manufacture of Artwork and Other Manufacturing	28.04	12.00
废弃资源和废旧材料回收加工业	Recycling and Disposal of Waste	20.46	12.36
电力、热力的生产和供应业	Production and Supply of Electric Power and Heat Power	32.16	7.57
燃气生产和供应业	Production and Supply of Gas	26.13	3.58
水的生产和供应业	Production and Supply of Water	45.19	1.83

Main Indicators on Economic Benefit of All State-owned and Non-state-owned Industrial Enterprises above Designated Size by Industrial Sector (2005)

资 产 负债率 (%) Assets-Liability Ratio (%)	流动资产周转次数（次/年）Number of Times of Annual of Turnover Working Capitals (times/year)	工业成本费用利润率 (%) Ratio of Profits to Industrial Cost (%)	全员劳动生产率（元/人.年）Overall Labor Productivity (yuan/person-year)	产品销售率 (%) Proportion of Products Sold (%)
57.81	**2.35**	**6.42**	**104680**	**98.14**
61.34	1.87	10.93	66273	98.39
34.24	4.32	102.76	562528	99.83
48.24	2.16	16.88	105067	97.02
51.05	2.91	23.35	102115	98.09
54.35	2.72	9.14	65304	97.78
43.23	4.02	15.18	125975	96.67
59.53	3.64	4.06	123385	98.03
56.01	2.41	6.02	96536	97.83
53.31	1.90	8.31	130862	97.78
32.94	1.43	30.28	1047313	101.43
61.27	2.47	3.68	54830	97.92
56.96	2.58	4.54	41030	97.48
58.68	2.83	4.40	41268	97.90
54.79	2.91	5.00	61303	96.94
57.39	2.45	4.72	54003	97.97
61.57	2.21	5.09	88091	97.64
51.68	1.68	7.21	69219	97.60
53.59	2.41	3.80	34583	98.04
56.46	4.72	-1.00	266352	99.05
56.30	2.53	6.57	129176	98.02
51.81	1.57	9.29	123932	94.18
59.11	2.66	1.84	113835	98.31
59.19	2.26	5.21	74758	97.39
55.66	2.20	4.59	69404	97.72
60.02	2.05	5.02	67147	97.51
60.30	2.80	5.25	200941	97.97
63.20	2.65	5.80	147594	98.10
58.10	2.32	5.19	75857	98.23
62.44	1.70	6.54	83548	97.37
62.91	1.61	5.79	76474	96.86
61.58	1.75	4.48	108699	99.38
60.85	1.99	5.03	97332	97.58
62.72	2.42	3.43	130156	97.81
54.69	2.02	6.00	82682	98.41
54.93	2.60	4.88	45480	98.13
64.81	3.46	3.03	141313	96.48
56.68	2.73	6.62	226353	99.78
51.53	1.96	2.53	90652	100.49
47.84	0.83	-0.26	56691	97.05

14-6 全部国有及规模以上非国有工业企业主要指标

Main Indicators of All State-owned and Non-state-owned Industrial Enterprises above Designated Size

单位：亿元 (100 million yuan)

年份 Year / 地区 Region		企业单位数(个) Number of Enterprises (unit)	工业总产值 Gross Industrial Output Value	工业增加值 Value-added of Industry	资产总计 Total Assets	流动资产合计 Total Working Capitals
	1998	165080	67737.14	19421.93	108821.87	46600.87
	1999	162033	72707.04	21564.74	116968.89	49630.23
	2000	162885	85673.66	25394.80	126211.24	54338.15
	2001	171256	95448.98	28329.37	135402.49	57804.97
	2002	181557	110776.48	32994.75	146217.78	63468.46
	2003	196222	142271.22	41990.23	168807.70	76163.74
	2004	276474	201722.19	54805.10	215358.00	97183.74
	2005	271835	251619.50	72186.99	244784.25	111031.41
北京	Beijing	6300	6946.07	1677.36	12829.79	3929.77
天津	Tianjin	6144	6774.10	1836.30	6347.92	3254.23
河北	Hebei	9936	11008.12	3167.94	9473.70	4032.25
山西	Shanxi	4441	4850.91	1756.70	7045.09	2820.50
内蒙古	Inner Mongolia	2447	2995.59	1240.43	4595.89	1399.95
辽宁	Liaoning	11510	10814.51	3108.44	11902.12	5330.42
吉林	Jilin	2774	3791.96	1169.39	4506.88	1700.75
黑龙江	Heilongjiang	2887	4714.91	2154.57	5174.47	2169.28
上海	Shanghai	14809	15767.51	4121.72	15905.94	8168.00
江苏	Jiangsu	32224	32707.09	8118.99	25488.86	13427.63
浙江	Zhejiang	40275	23106.76	4830.97	20609.30	10896.23
安徽	Anhui	5277	4567.23	1483.75	5067.10	2127.77
福建	Fujian	12396	8135.98	2291.26	6841.37	3393.30
江西	Jiangxi	4403	2978.88	882.30	3058.34	1265.66
山东	Shandong	27540	30522.86	9375.27	22131.24	9773.02
河南	Henan	10867	10487.38	3379.31	9158.03	3801.11
湖北	Hubei	6813	6066.96	2007.21	8683.39	3004.90
湖南	Hunan	8022	4754.86	1629.79	4611.60	1802.43
广东	Guangdong	35157	35942.74	9416.39	27076.08	15132.34
广西	Guangxi	3687	2547.32	794.61	3009.98	1176.12
海南	Hainan	616	473.06	152.50	791.28	285.11
重庆	Chongqing	2943	2525.87	659.40	3091.96	1418.41
四川	Sichuan	7959	6178.03	2160.22	7908.62	3309.89
贵州	Guizhou	2585	1690.40	585.85	2734.05	1006.96
云南	Yunnan	2362	2596.21	998.83	3964.32	1709.36
西藏	Tibet	197	27.29	15.31	112.43	29.97
陕西	Shaanxi	2997	3397.71	1321.67	5085.87	2010.57
甘肃	Gansu	1733	1988.26	559.62	2483.04	980.14
青海	Qinghai	404	486.86	189.10	1145.49	334.73
宁夏	Ningxia	685	671.54	213.71	1113.10	438.15
新疆	Xinjiang	1445	2102.53	888.08	2837.00	902.48

14-6 续表 1 continued

单位：亿元 (100 million yuan)

年份 Year / 地区 Region		流动资产年平均余额 Annual Average Balance of Working Capitals	固定资产原价 Original Value of Fixed Assets	固定资产净值年平均余额 Annual Average Balance of Net Value of Fixed Assets	负债合计 Total Liabilities	流动负债合计 Total Working Liabilities	所有者权益合计 Total Owners' Equities
1998		45420.55	64832.05	44136.87	69363.79	47773.02	39445.40
1999		47643.44	71847.09	47281.43	72322.98	50070.19	44618.80
2000		51910.37	78646.30	51792.33	76743.84	53052.64	49406.88
2001		56486.77	86293.10	55437.43	79843.42	56138.72	55424.40
2002		60798.36	93887.95	59482.66	85857.42	61663.06	60242.01
2003		71487.80	105557.09	66068.38	99527.97	73413.53	69129.56
2004		90788.50	125761.85	79749.41	124847.41	94649.34	90286.70
2005		105901.69	143143.63	89460.49	141509.84	108411.70	102882.02
北京	Beijing	3701.52	4434.04	2590.44	4706.69	3423.07	8123.10
天津	Tianjin	3058.69	3845.17	2155.41	3713.08	3110.92	2635.75
河北	Hebei	3822.08	6306.27	3894.23	5792.05	4381.92	3681.65
山西	Shanxi	2659.71	4436.30	2855.68	4760.87	3232.73	2179.05
内蒙古	Inner Mongolia	1351.71	3207.14	2022.55	2859.86	1654.15	1702.29
辽宁	Liaoning	5045.59	8202.52	4848.73	6929.21	5323.14	4852.41
吉林	Jilin	1707.86	3167.89	1854.24	2681.32	2063.14	1817.22
黑龙江	Heilongjiang	2060.46	4619.41	2379.94	2900.96	2316.71	2273.02
上海	Shanghai	7833.28	9370.76	5226.52	8037.54	6859.22	7868.41
江苏	Jiangsu	12579.76	13405.21	8758.69	15715.86	13324.75	9771.74
浙江	Zhejiang	10305.43	9522.84	6518.30	12286.57	10136.79	8315.61
安徽	Anhui	2008.12	2953.04	1910.87	3122.73	2197.63	1934.99
福建	Fujian	3260.86	3838.40	2521.27	3605.79	2885.26	3235.55
江西	Jiangxi	1231.43	1824.46	1220.96	1932.22	1352.40	1096.16
山东	Shandong	9437.49	13178.37	8309.62	12917.00	9993.35	9185.90
河南	Henan	3750.85	5955.47	3788.63	5639.20	4166.77	3518.83
湖北	Hubei	3059.06	5393.18	3850.14	4873.08	3103.10	3810.31
湖南	Hunan	1761.49	2932.81	1886.62	2853.91	1807.89	1757.68
广东	Guangdong	14411.12	14453.16	8834.68	15661.24	13320.04	11414.84
广西	Guangxi	1125.00	1908.00	1248.34	1853.42	1278.46	1156.56
海南	Hainan	265.54	486.89	358.52	437.44	246.53	353.84
重庆	Chongqing	1357.20	1677.98	1056.30	1846.58	1397.12	1245.38
四川	Sichuan	3150.69	4845.07	3039.99	4934.81	3354.28	2966.06
贵州	Guizhou	947.98	1711.11	1122.67	1784.20	1105.94	949.45
云南	Yunnan	1587.77	2213.36	1361.54	2068.42	1471.11	1895.91
西藏	Tibet	28.58	88.48	70.49	27.40	17.99	85.03
陕西	Shaanxi	1916.50	3439.54	2155.18	3160.74	2088.06	1907.45
甘肃	Gansu	916.73	1608.21	1117.68	1460.08	942.44	1022.96
青海	Qinghai	329.91	844.71	560.46	773.65	384.94	370.22
宁夏	Ningxia	404.58	661.54	426.84	689.95	442.93	406.51
新疆	Xinjiang	824.72	2612.31	1514.97	1483.96	1028.94	1348.13

14-6 续表 2 continued

单位：亿元 (100 million yuan)

年份 Year / 地区 Region	主营业务收入 Revenue from Principal Business	主营业务成本 Cost of Principal Business	主营业务税金及附加 Taxes and Other Charges on Principal Business	利润总额 Total Profits	本年应交增值税 Value Added Tax Payable	全部从业人员年平均人数(万人) Annual Average Employed Persons (10 000 persons)
1998	64148.86	52797.54	1236.79	1458.11	2827.02	6195.81
1999	69851.73	57339.52	1307.65	2288.24	3105.92	5805.05
2000	84151.75	68653.95	1434.17	4393.48	3685.20	5559.36
2001	93733.34	77259.89	1553.82	4733.43	4018.09	5441.43
2002	109485.77	90243.76	1761.61	5784.48	4476.01	5520.66
2003	143171.53	118638.47	2049.21	8337.24	5487.73	5748.57
2004	198908.87	167246.40	2616.25	11929.30	6912.78	6622.09
2005	248544.00	209862.52	2997.34	14802.54	8520.94	6895.96
北京 Beijing	7278.96	6309.44	54.48	413.50	207.19	116.97
天津 Tianjin	7125.93	6039.33	77.74	551.60	186.29	122.17
河北 Hebei	10745.98	9134.05	94.67	690.38	378.18	292.21
山西 Shanxi	4784.59	3728.70	63.82	261.28	320.37	213.20
内蒙古 Inner Mongolia	3050.96	2420.87	37.41	235.13	166.43	83.70
辽宁 Liaoning	10747.31	9409.07	120.57	355.98	336.47	276.55
吉林 Jilin	3634.64	3109.47	70.29	141.00	135.36	101.83
黑龙江 Heilongjiang	4765.42	3192.67	84.03	1067.09	327.93	136.85
上海 Shanghai	16353.73	13982.81	167.61	939.56	437.98	259.63
江苏 Jiangsu	32098.48	28401.23	196.93	1384.64	805.50	704.24
浙江 Zhejiang	23044.63	20119.25	194.10	1103.53	679.47	659.12
安徽 Anhui	4523.27	3762.86	85.21	218.20	183.97	155.21
福建 Fujian	7848.24	6765.06	79.48	407.55	206.26	290.41
江西 Jiangxi	2909.13	2465.13	49.54	112.41	117.65	112.11
山东 Shandong	30023.87	25293.09	280.62	2164.70	1007.60	738.23
河南 Henan	10114.44	8441.39	142.92	643.39	402.71	362.79
湖北 Hubei	5962.54	4800.91	112.78	371.84	242.86	188.30
湖南 Hunan	4585.31	3627.99	180.20	189.25	205.65	169.25
广东 Guangdong	34781.58	30010.54	227.29	1693.99	956.53	1085.65
广西 Guangxi	2466.79	2060.35	38.02	134.99	120.56	91.21
海南 Hainan	449.76	345.51	9.85	35.04	25.34	12.10
重庆 Chongqing	2515.17	2102.80	41.79	115.59	99.10	92.42
四川 Sichuan	6008.12	4900.53	89.36	326.65	241.67	218.99
贵州 Guizhou	1577.16	1224.83	64.30	70.79	97.40	68.08
云南 Yunnan	2569.71	1871.03	245.62	227.91	177.68	68.83
西藏 Tibet	28.39	18.62	0.43	4.47	2.57	1.99
陕西 Shaanxi	3302.51	2404.23	89.58	400.65	186.20	118.97
甘肃 Gansu	1984.67	1512.58	43.72	59.65	84.28	68.62
青海 Qinghai	462.83	330.52	6.82	72.82	29.98	14.04
宁夏 Ningxia	647.47	556.66	6.86	21.09	26.02	25.58
新疆 Xinjiang	2152.45	1520.98	41.30	387.89	125.75	46.70

14-7 全部国有及规模以上非国有工业企业主要经济效益指标(2005年)

Main Indicators on Economic Benefit of All State-owned and Non-state-owned Industrial Enterprises above Designated Size (2005)

地 区	Region	工业增加值率(%) Ratio of Value Added to Gross Industrial Output Value (%)	总资产贡献率(%) Ratio of Total Assets to Industrial Output Value (%)	资产负债率(%) Assets-Liability Ratio (%)	流动资产周转次数(次/年) Number of Times of Turnover of Working Capitals (times/year)	工业成本费用利润率(%) Ratio of Profits to Industrial Cost (%)	全员劳动生产率(元/人.年) Overall Labor Productivity (yuan-person-year)	产品销售率(%) Proportion of Products Sold (%)
全国总计	**National Total**	**28.69**	**11.82**	**57.81**	**2.35**	**6.42**	**104680**	**98.14**
北 京	Beijing	24.15	5.69	36.69	1.97	5.89	143403	97.89
天 津	Tianjin	27.11	13.64	58.49	2.33	8.45	150301	100.63
河 北	Hebei	28.78	13.52	61.14	2.81	6.97	108415	97.95
山 西	Shanxi	36.21	10.57	67.58	1.80	6.00	82396	96.87
内蒙古	Inner Mongolia	41.41	10.85	62.23	2.26	8.68	148199	97.62
辽 宁	Liaoning	28.74	7.84	58.22	2.13	3.46	112402	98.47
吉 林	Jilin	30.84	8.75	59.49	2.13	4.07	114834	98.57
黑龙江	Heilongjiang	45.70	29.45	56.06	2.31	29.63	157436	97.33
上 海	Shanghai	26.14	10.29	50.53	2.09	6.08	158751	98.89
江 苏	Jiangsu	24.82	10.50	61.66	2.55	4.51	115287	98.20
浙 江	Zhejiang	20.91	11.03	59.62	2.24	5.04	73294	97.81
安 徽	Anhui	32.49	10.72	61.63	2.25	5.14	95599	98.24
福 建	Fujian	28.16	11.19	52.71	2.41	5.52	78898	97.33
江 西	Jiangxi	29.62	10.43	63.18	2.36	4.14	78698	98.48
山 东	Shandong	30.72	16.96	58.37	3.18	7.91	126997	98.23
河 南	Henan	32.22	14.47	61.58	2.70	6.91	93148	98.41
湖 北	Hubei	33.08	9.44	56.12	1.95	6.88	106598	97.86
湖 南	Hunan	34.28	13.61	61.89	2.60	4.65	96297	99.30
广 东	Guangdong	26.20	11.29	57.84	2.41	5.16	86735	97.50
广 西	Guangxi	31.19	11.09	61.58	2.19	5.88	87119	98.08
海 南	Hainan	32.24	9.91	55.28	1.69	8.63	126024	98.97
重 庆	Chongqing	26.11	9.40	59.72	1.85	4.85	71348	98.79
四 川	Sichuan	34.97	9.59	62.40	1.91	5.86	98645	98.72
贵 州	Guizhou	34.66	9.74	65.26	1.66	4.92	86057	96.69
云 南	Yunnan	38.47	17.42	52.18	1.62	10.63	145111	99.28
西 藏	Tibet	56.10	6.81	24.37	0.99	19.33	76979	93.83
陕 西	Shaanxi	38.90	14.39	62.15	1.72	14.46	111094	97.74
甘 肃	Gansu	28.15	8.83	58.80	2.16	3.48	81555	98.08
青 海	Qinghai	38.84	11.07	67.54	1.40	19.14	134656	97.38
宁 夏	Ningxia	31.82	6.07	61.98	1.60	3.36	83530	98.33
新 疆	Xinjiang	42.24	20.46	52.31	2.61	22.55	190176	99.23

14-8 按行业分国有及国有控股工业企业主要指标（2005年）

单位：亿元

行　　业	Sector	企业单位数（个）Number of Enterprises (unit)	工业总产值 Gross Industrial Output Value
全国总计	**National Total**	**27477**	**83749.92**
煤炭开采和洗选业	Mining and Washing of Coal	912	3878.50
石油和天然气开采业	Extraction of Petroleum and Natural Gas	102	5689.39
黑色金属矿采选业	Mining and Processing of Ferrous Metal Ores	119	201.34
有色金属矿采选业	Mining and Processing of Non-Ferrous Metal Ores	310	467.71
非金属矿采选业	Mining and Processing of Nonmetal Ores	297	149.66
其他采矿业	Mining of Other Ores	4	2.56
农副食品加工业	Processing of Food from Agricultural Products	1393	1089.84
食品制造业	Manufacture of Foods	595	476.50
饮料制造业	Manufacture of Beverages	557	843.68
烟草制品业	Manufacture of Tobacco	153	2812.86
纺织业	Manufacture of Textile	905	923.87
纺织服装、鞋、帽制造业	Manufacture of Textile Wearing Apparel, Footware, and Caps	282	110.13
皮革、毛皮、羽毛(绒)及其制品业	Manufacture of Leather, Fur, Feather and Related Products	72	24.30
木材加工及木、竹、藤、棕、草制品业	Processing of Timber, Manufacture of Wood, Bamboo, Rattan, Palm, and Straw Products	243	172.51
家具制造业	Manufacture of Furniture	96	53.61
造纸及纸制品业	Manufacture of Paper and Paper Products	374	523.86
印刷业和记录媒介的复制	Printing, Reproduction of Recording Media	1149	288.11
文教体育用品制造业	Manufacture of Articles For Culture, Education and Sport Activity	92	30.71
石油加工、炼焦及核燃料加工业	Processing of Petroleum, Coking, Processing of Nuclear Fuel	241	9557.83
化学原料及化学制品制造业	Manufacture of Raw Chemical Materials and Chemical Products	1696	5022.50
医药制造业	Manufacture of Medicines	676	1017.76
化学纤维制造业	Manufacture of Chemical Fibers	85	581.23
橡胶制品业	Manufacture of Rubber	184	402.69
塑料制品业	Manufacture of Plastics	414	273.90
非金属矿物制品业	Manufacture of Non-metallic Mineral Products	1835	1197.28
黑色金属冶炼及压延加工业	Smelting and Pressing of Ferrous Metals	407	10162.95
有色金属冶炼及压延加工业	Smelting and Pressing of Non-ferrous Metals	429	2734.77
金属制品业	Manufacture of Metal Products	655	486.49
通用设备制造业	Manufacture of General Purpose Machinery	1573	2481.24
专用设备制造业	Manufacture of Special Purpose Machinery	1323	1794.27
交通运输设备制造业	Manufacture of Transport Equipment	1732	8145.24
电气机械及器材制造业	Manufacture of Electrical Machinery and Equipment	927	1546.74
通信设备、计算机及其他电子设备制造业	Manufacture of Communication Equipment, Computers and Other Electronic Equipment	830	3568.84
仪器仪表及文化、办公用机械制造业	Manufacture of Measuring Instruments and Machinery for Cultural Activity and Office Work	490	285.26
工艺品及其他制造业	Manufacture of Artwork and Other Manufacturing	188	127.02
废弃资源和废旧材料回收加工业	Recycling and Disposal of Waste	17	8.87
电力、热力的生产和供应业	Production and Supply of Electric Power and Heat Power	3829	15887.30
燃气生产和供应业	Production and Supply of Gas	221	290.39
水的生产和供应业	Production and Supply of Water	2070	438.23

Main Indicators of State-owned and State-holding Industrial Enterprises by Industrial Sector (2005)

(100 million yuan)

工 业 增加值 Value-added of Industry	资 产 总 计 Total Assets	流动资产 合 计 Total Working Capitals	流动资产 年平均余额 Annual Average Balance of Working Capitals	固定资产 原 价 Original Value of Fixed Assets	固定资产净值 年平均余额 Annual Average Balance of Net Value of Fixed Assets
27176.67	**117629.61**	**42155.31**	**40705.62**	**83515.49**	**49140.16**
2036.29	7244.15	2741.87	2548.50	4802.03	2822.36
4281.55	6434.96	1429.99	1359.38	8987.33	4091.29
105.17	523.79	202.12	179.30	212.18	124.64
186.29	526.41	227.24	209.68	252.42	144.90
72.20	278.56	102.71	104.68	170.22	111.54
0.52	2.06	1.05	0.95	2.50	0.97
248.96	861.66	423.14	401.78	442.18	287.00
161.40	674.92	329.78	322.65	299.62	196.88
357.68	1296.26	637.64	616.65	677.25	429.18
2050.89	3234.14	2061.82	1978.50	1235.25	623.09
243.67	1325.59	598.27	621.19	845.82	498.55
33.80	138.68	81.97	81.37	62.99	39.88
7.20	36.07	21.15	19.73	16.57	10.15
51.00	301.53	110.75	112.70	199.32	135.25
12.95	52.96	26.03	26.46	20.12	12.29
151.65	1030.81	339.28	340.11	741.70	492.75
115.43	537.10	221.84	219.14	395.52	222.07
9.46	63.93	34.71	35.22	28.15	16.81
1282.89	4515.04	1918.25	1625.43	4088.15	2089.86
1251.56	6551.80	2326.22	2244.02	4968.98	2832.83
370.25	1955.15	914.88	898.93	827.87	524.33
114.56	750.28	257.88	248.81	676.28	378.16
91.95	479.50	237.26	225.90	262.60	156.08
62.85	429.74	189.39	189.98	245.40	160.40
369.38	2560.06	994.36	958.71	1705.47	1091.22
3016.62	11651.49	4392.17	4140.36	8419.83	4446.08
736.25	3278.50	1369.65	1302.26	2061.28	1279.75
123.18	582.11	317.95	310.72	275.58	175.50
704.25	3527.08	2413.01	2295.74	1198.31	661.25
453.83	2725.94	1611.27	1507.24	1117.49	659.62
1918.02	9741.07	5364.14	5273.23	4086.87	2268.32
399.81	1945.71	1262.28	1204.81	601.32	346.95
760.61	3971.52	2420.70	2356.85	1418.57	784.10
93.25	504.08	302.55	287.39	189.96	113.05
43.46	178.14	94.72	89.92	98.70	60.14
1.87	11.37	6.88	5.32	5.39	4.20
4976.34	34362.42	5339.73	5581.85	29204.69	19064.24
76.30	867.30	243.25	228.80	636.04	417.11
203.30	2477.76	587.40	551.35	2035.58	1367.36

14-8 续表

单位：亿元

行业	Sector	负债合计 Total Liabilities	流动负债合计 Total Working Liabilities
全国总计	**National Total**	**66653.58**	**44456.78**
煤炭开采和洗选业	Mining and Washing of Coal	4500.54	3017.18
石油和天然气开采业	Extraction of Petroleum and Natural Gas	2220.78	1481.12
黑色金属矿采选业	Mining and Processing of Ferrous Metal Ores	225.38	187.97
有色金属矿采选业	Mining and Processing of Non-Ferrous Metal Ores	273.81	202.54
非金属矿采选业	Mining and Processing of Nonmetal Ores	166.01	127.96
其他采矿业	Mining of Other Ores	0.50	0.50
农副食品加工业	Processing of Food from Agricultural Products	586.21	505.55
食品制造业	Manufacture of Foods	415.44	361.90
饮料制造业	Manufacture of Beverages	633.99	567.20
烟草制品业	Manufacture of Tobacco	1059.84	1002.32
纺织业	Manufacture of Textile	964.12	724.27
纺织服装、鞋、帽制造业	Manufacture of Textile Wearing Apparel, Footware, and Caps	96.34	83.57
皮革、毛皮、羽毛(绒)及其制品业	Manufacture of Leather, Fur, Feather and Related Products	25.81	22.22
木材加工及木、竹、藤、棕、草制品业	Processing of Timber, Manufacture of Wood, Bamboo, Rattan, Palm, and Straw Products	193.03	117.45
家具制造业	Manufacture of Furniture	31.49	27.57
造纸及纸制品业	Manufacture of Paper and Paper Products	672.10	443.37
印刷业和记录媒介的复制	Printing, Reproduction of Recording Media	259.59	213.58
文教体育用品制造业	Manufacture of Articles For Culture, Education and Sport Activity	32.25	27.51
石油加工、炼焦及核燃料加工业	Processing of Petroleum, Coking, Processing of Nuclear Fuel	2341.18	1629.87
化学原料及化学制品制造业	Manufacture of Raw Chemical Materials and Chemical Products	3669.43	2542.80
医药制造业	Manufacture of Medicines	1020.52	873.68
化学纤维制造业	Manufacture of Chemical Fibers	404.59	308.76
橡胶制品业	Manufacture of Rubber	323.67	258.13
塑料制品业	Manufacture of Plastics	265.10	205.82
非金属矿物制品业	Manufacture of Non-metallic Mineral Products	1655.40	1234.14
黑色金属冶炼及压延加工业	Smelting and Pressing of Ferrous Metals	6633.06	5077.01
有色金属冶炼及压延加工业	Smelting and Pressing of Non-ferrous Metals	2162.20	1540.82
金属制品业	Manufacture of Metal Products	376.72	327.08
通用设备制造业	Manufacture of General Purpose Machinery	2524.09	2223.25
专用设备制造业	Manufacture of Special Purpose Machinery	1896.50	1650.08
交通运输设备制造业	Manufacture of Transport Equipment	6153.39	5352.14
电气机械及器材制造业	Manufacture of Electrical Machinery and Equipment	1356.43	1199.79
通信设备、计算机及其他电子设备制造业	Manufacture of Communication Equipment, Computers and Other Electronic Equipment	2367.33	1998.17
仪器仪表及文化、办公用机械制造业	Manufacture of Measuring Instruments and Machinery for Cultural Activity and Office Work	317.39	266.25
工艺品及其他制造业	Manufacture of Artwork and Other Manufacturing	112.75	84.71
废弃资源和废旧材料回收加工业	Recycling and Disposal of Waste	7.15	6.15
电力、热力的生产和供应业	Production and Supply of Electric Power and Heat Power	19134.65	7700.75
燃气生产和供应业	Production and Supply of Gas	402.65	260.71
水的生产和供应业	Production and Supply of Water	1172.10	602.89

continued

(100 million yuan)

所有者权益 Owners' Equities	主营业务收入 Revenue from Principal Business	主营业务成本 Cost of Principal Business	主营业务税金及附加 Taxes and Other Charges on Principal Business	利润总额 Total Profits	本年应交增值税 Value-added Tax Payable	全部从业人员年平均人数(万人) Annual Average Employed Persons (10 000 persons)
50625.00	**85574.18**	**69302.41**	**2121.74**	**6519.75**	**4098.37**	**1874.85**
2704.64	4101.55	2748.63	62.39	335.36	322.46	322.80
4210.77	5780.30	2404.61	120.98	2743.75	575.27	82.13
298.41	227.70	138.56	4.54	38.32	17.53	11.72
252.59	459.31	296.80	2.91	102.69	20.32	18.64
112.55	150.30	92.19	4.49	13.98	12.69	13.93
1.56	2.48	2.02		0.13	0.12	0.08
275.45	1173.73	1049.62	3.70	29.48	22.26	26.77
259.23	488.98	379.40	2.59	25.80	21.11	16.68
662.26	843.62	550.90	68.54	78.90	55.45	27.46
2174.30	2823.10	1017.36	1129.13	404.77	327.92	18.51
356.96	923.72	835.39	4.33	-2.22	30.38	73.79
42.34	104.36	89.66	0.39	1.38	2.72	11.58
10.25	23.00	19.40	0.08	0.59	0.81	1.88
108.49	170.36	144.15	0.71	3.59	6.51	10.77
21.46	54.95	47.12	0.12	3.64	1.74	1.78
340.93	573.56	492.23	2.03	18.00	25.43	15.88
277.51	283.10	220.29	1.90	16.18	17.27	16.59
31.67	32.50	25.16	0.14	1.50	1.01	2.39
2165.81	9654.34	9353.78	274.00	-197.17	184.50	38.08
2848.33	5108.08	4295.58	41.09	264.61	175.44	111.93
934.64	1113.13	747.99	6.89	94.57	65.34	36.34
345.69	580.37	523.67	2.46	-1.96	17.38	14.26
154.83	403.85	347.54	5.90	9.79	8.98	12.75
162.29	292.68	258.68	0.87	6.47	7.71	8.49
898.70	1193.41	992.36	7.80	13.83	64.20	68.43
4854.55	10537.21	9028.12	57.35	677.69	460.70	140.97
1113.00	2791.74	2315.21	18.21	226.27	117.87	56.06
205.40	486.85	416.89	1.64	16.83	13.47	16.34
989.37	2357.01	1944.65	8.61	127.08	75.66	79.05
825.44	1801.57	1520.53	7.45	52.26	44.50	78.08
3561.14	8071.35	6903.93	170.09	302.36	244.59	152.77
581.37	1488.48	1220.78	4.89	70.80	43.68	37.32
1590.50	3569.31	3095.90	7.60	38.02	71.66	55.92
186.03	287.55	209.99	1.31	19.96	10.93	14.97
65.36	121.39	98.06	0.56	4.64	2.85	5.64
4.22	10.00	8.53	0.05	0.77	0.27	0.20
15226.64	16670.86	14771.35	89.75	985.68	993.81	219.97
464.65	402.45	366.01	1.84	6.06	12.02	11.75
1305.66	415.92	329.36	4.39	-14.69	21.80	42.15

14-9 按行业分国有及国有控股工业企业主要经济效益指标（2005年）

行业	Sector	工业增加值率 (%) Ratio of Value Added to Gross Industrial Output Value (%)	总资产贡献率 (%) Ratio of Total Assets to Industrial Output Value (%)
全国总计	**National Total**	**32.45**	**11.87**
煤炭开采和洗选业	Mining and Washing of Coal	52.50	10.74
石油和天然气开采业	Extraction of Petroleum and Natural Gas	75.25	53.88
黑色金属矿采选业	Mining and Processing of Ferrous Metal Ores	52.23	11.98
有色金属矿采选业	Mining and Processing of Non-Ferrous Metal Ores	39.83	24.97
非金属矿采选业	Mining and Processing of Nonmetal Ores	48.24	12.03
其他采矿业	Mining of Other Ores	20.16	12.44
农副食品加工业	Processing of Food from Agricultural Products	22.84	8.00
食品制造业	Manufacture of Foods	33.87	8.44
饮料制造业	Manufacture of Beverages	42.40	16.36
烟草制品业	Manufacture of Tobacco	72.91	58.06
纺织业	Manufacture of Textile	26.38	3.77
纺织服装、鞋、帽制造业	Manufacture of Textile Wearing Apparel, Footware, and Caps	30.69	3.72
皮革、毛皮、羽毛(绒)及其制品业	Manufacture of Leather, Fur, Feather and Related Products	29.64	4.75
木材加工及木、竹、藤、棕、草制品业	Processing of Timber, Manufacture of Wood, Bamboo, Rattan, Palm, and Straw Products	29.57	4.79
家具制造业	Manufacture of Furniture	24.15	11.01
造纸及纸制品业	Manufacture of Paper and Paper Products	28.95	5.78
印刷业和记录媒介的复制	Printing, Reproduction of Recording Media	40.06	7.22
文教体育用品制造业	Manufacture of Articles For Culture, Education and Sport Activity	30.82	5.13
石油加工、炼焦及核燃料加工业	Processing of Petroleum, Coking, Processing of Nuclear Fuel	13.42	6.71
化学原料及化学制品制造业	Manufacture of Raw Chemical Materials and Chemical Products	24.92	8.54
医药制造业	Manufacture of Medicines	36.38	9.63
化学纤维制造业	Manufacture of Chemical Fibers	19.71	3.70
橡胶制品业	Manufacture of Rubber	22.83	6.47
塑料制品业	Manufacture of Plastics	22.95	4.68
非金属矿物制品业	Manufacture of Non-metallic Mineral Products	30.85	4.58
黑色金属冶炼及压延加工业	Smelting and Pressing of Ferrous Metals	29.68	11.31
有色金属冶炼及压延加工业	Smelting and Pressing of Non-ferrous Metals	26.92	12.50
金属制品业	Manufacture of Metal Products	25.32	6.46
通用设备制造业	Manufacture of General Purpose Machinery	28.38	6.60
专用设备制造业	Manufacture of Special Purpose Machinery	25.29	4.64
交通运输设备制造业	Manufacture of Transport Equipment	23.55	7.95
电气机械及器材制造业	Manufacture of Electrical Machinery and Equipment	25.85	6.93
通信设备、计算机及其他电子设备制造业	Manufacture of Communication Equipment, Computers and Other Electronic Equipment	21.31	3.89
仪器仪表及文化、办公用机械制造业	Manufacture of Measuring Instruments and Machinery for Cultural Activity and Office Work	32.69	7.10
工艺品及其他制造业	Manufacture of Artwork and Other Manufacturing	34.21	5.08
废弃资源和废旧材料回收加工业	Recycling and Disposal of Waste	21.14	9.77
电力、热力的生产和供应业	Production and Supply of Electric Power and Heat Power	31.32	7.46
燃气生产和供应业	Production and Supply of Gas	26.28	2.68
水的生产和供应业	Production and Supply of Water	46.39	1.14

Main Indicators on Economic Benefit of State-owned and State-holding Industrial Enterprises by Industrial Sector (2005)

资产负债率 (%) Assets-Liability Ratio (%)	流动资产周转次数（次/年） Number of Times of Annual of Turnover Working Capitals (times/year)	工业成本费用利润率 (%) Ratio of Profits to Industrial Cost (%)	全员劳动生产率（元/人.年） Overall Labor Productivity (yuan/person-year)	产品销售率 (%) Proportion of Products Sold (%)
56.66	**2.10**	**8.44**	**144954**	**99.25**
62.13	1.61	9.23	63082	97.82
34.51	4.25	99.65	521339	99.97
43.03	1.27	20.84	89704	99.82
52.02	2.19	28.73	99916	98.63
59.60	1.44	10.82	51826	97.07
24.28	2.61	5.76	65292	100.01
68.03	2.92	2.61	93017	99.26
61.55	1.52	5.51	96769	98.96
48.91	1.37	11.24	130277	97.74
32.77	1.43	30.74	1108076	101.46
72.73	1.49	-0.24	33021	98.80
69.47	1.28	1.33	29181	98.31
71.57	1.17	2.61	38355	97.53
64.02	1.51	2.13	47371	96.79
59.47	2.08	7.02	72868	99.03
65.20	1.69	3.24	95469	98.79
48.33	1.29	5.95	69574	98.37
50.45	0.92	4.75	39574	96.74
51.85	5.94	-2.05	336914	99.56
56.01	2.28	5.48	111821	98.76
52.20	1.24	9.22	101881	95.73
53.93	2.33	-0.34	80323	98.85
67.50	1.79	2.51	72103	98.17
61.69	1.54	2.24	74015	98.20
64.66	1.24	1.16	53977	98.11
56.93	2.54	6.97	213990	98.96
65.95	2.14	8.89	131340	98.82
64.72	1.57	3.56	75389	100.53
71.56	1.03	5.65	89086	97.31
69.57	1.20	2.95	58121	96.42
63.17	1.53	3.90	125548	101.12
69.71	1.24	4.94	107123	97.87
59.61	1.51	1.07	136026	97.97
62.96	1.00	7.45	62309	97.00
63.30	1.35	4.01	77079	106.64
62.92	1.88	8.20	94350	88.32
55.68	2.99	6.26	226227	99.85
46.43	1.76	1.46	64921	100.15
47.30	0.75	-3.28	48236	96.78

14-10 国有及国有控股工业企业主要指标
Main Indicators of State-owned and State-holding Industrial Enterprises

单位：亿元 (100 million yuan)

年份 Year / 地区 Region		企业单位数（个） Number of Enterprises (unit)	工业总产值 Gross Industrial Output Value	工业增加值 Value Added of Industry	资产总计 Total Assets	流动资产合计 Total Working Capitals
	1998	64737	33621.04	11076.90	74916.27	29559.03
	1999	61301	35571.18	12132.41	80471.69	31042.81
	2000	53489	40554.37	13777.68	84014.94	32628.81
	2001	46767	42408.49	14652.05	87901.54	33239.63
	2002	41125	45178.96	15935.03	89094.60	33468.77
	2003	34280	53407.90	18837.60	94519.79	36125.14
	2004	35597	70228.99	23213.00	109708.25	39376.20
	2005	27477	83749.92	27176.67	117629.61	42155.31
北京	Beijing	1745	3538.19	952.15	10105.97	2148.70
天津	Tianjin	1497	2628.84	864.79	3267.14	1286.21
河北	Hebei	1233	4023.67	1222.56	5054.91	1859.04
山西	Shanxi	1173	2534.62	949.88	4546.47	1596.40
内蒙古	Inner Mongolia	489	1570.24	682.13	2788.87	778.14
辽宁	Liaoning	1397	5771.15	1659.69	7274.18	2950.46
吉林	Jilin	583	2533.47	746.89	3245.39	1127.09
黑龙江	Heilongjiang	693	3607.17	1807.13	3983.60	1601.70
上海	Shanghai	1461	6018.86	1685.05	8088.32	3352.71
江苏	Jiangsu	958	5048.61	1229.08	5519.08	2213.31
浙江	Zhejiang	811	3401.17	845.29	3865.38	1325.52
安徽	Anhui	619	2418.44	835.34	3282.52	1198.13
福建	Fujian	756	1532.88	442.61	1905.37	655.60
江西	Jiangxi	804	1531.55	416.74	1944.95	774.65
山东	Shandong	1394	7401.03	2707.86	8329.05	3168.71
河南	Henan	1280	4042.05	1289.39	5396.17	1997.22
湖北	Hubei	1058	3161.87	1051.82	6035.77	1826.28
湖南	Hunan	1058	2104.56	781.34	2808.64	1023.99
广东	Guangdong	1806	6375.54	1690.01	6676.89	2654.39
广西	Guangxi	1005	1226.87	388.22	1796.38	611.47
海南	Hainan	247	238.24	84.43	429.69	130.69
重庆	Chongqing	471	1299.08	337.09	1991.72	840.72
四川	Sichuan	928	2488.53	902.99	4473.03	1683.30
贵州	Guizhou	927	1154.51	420.87	2264.10	773.37
云南	Yunnan	652	1672.31	748.61	2816.97	1201.11
西藏	Tibet	170	18.19	10.14	92.46	20.92
陕西	Shaanxi	945	2332.47	956.53	3739.76	1421.50
甘肃	Gansu	456	1573.64	405.32	1938.28	753.94
青海	Qinghai	137	395.56	153.34	961.73	276.72
宁夏	Ningxia	140	372.00	125.08	747.69	268.14
新疆	Xinjiang	584	1734.60	784.29	2259.12	635.18

14-10 续表 1 continued

单位: 亿元 (100 million yuan)

年 份 Year 地 区 Region		流动资产年平均余额 Annual Average Balance of Working Capitals	固定资产原 价 Original Value of Fixed Assets	固定资产净值年平均余额 Annual Average Balance of Net Value of Fixed Assets	负债合计 Total Liabilities	流动负债合 计 Total Working Liabilities	所有者权益合 计 Total Owners' Equities
	1998	36122.72	47913.25	31891.43	35648.27	30625.48	26759.22
	1999	29885.62	53146.30	33938.96	49877.69	31828.59	30566.88
	2000	31485.38	57294.96	36886.64	51239.61	32237.41	32714.81
	2001	32575.86	61782.45	38638.22	52025.60	33144.47	35741.27
	2002	32625.56	64521.95	39728.29	52837.08	34009.59	36139.17
	2003	34327.98	69701.11	42118.40	55990.53	36430.98	38381.02
	2004	37557.64	76599.42	46283.30	62005.79	40771.99	47479.25
	2005	40705.62	83515.49	49140.16	66653.58	44456.78	50625.00
北 京	Beijing	2055.71	3448.59	1999.02	3147.11	1983.61	6958.87
天 津	Tianjin	1242.61	2513.20	1350.66	1966.53	1460.86	1300.61
河 北	Hebei	1744.45	4118.36	2298.91	3235.57	2218.21	1819.34
山 西	Shanxi	1517.94	3263.05	1959.56	3083.21	1840.59	1362.88
内蒙古	Inner Mongolia	758.86	2278.09	1381.92	1793.91	916.71	994.96
辽 宁	Liaoning	2780.44	5955.43	3343.02	4315.87	3098.68	2837.81
吉 林	Jilin	1161.88	2477.64	1350.26	1965.86	1468.17	1271.19
黑龙江	Heilongjiang	1527.10	3953.85	1902.75	2171.08	1689.09	1812.03
上 海	Shanghai	3260.16	5735.86	2991.51	3526.75	2852.59	4561.56
江 苏	Jiangsu	2194.84	3854.76	2263.32	3293.05	2515.76	2224.76
浙 江	Zhejiang	1303.67	2974.77	1907.16	2219.00	1249.00	1639.29
安 徽	Anhui	1139.49	2108.77	1351.20	2062.29	1327.87	1211.54
福 建	Fujian	645.60	1444.25	891.29	1069.96	724.05	835.39
江 西	Jiangxi	758.02	1273.65	796.66	1349.41	894.54	565.60
山 东	Shandong	3046.75	6156.31	3449.24	5012.27	3421.99	3290.99
河 南	Henan	1984.96	3943.10	2363.96	3540.89	2456.65	1855.28
湖 北	Hubei	1811.23	4073.82	2996.94	3460.95	1977.03	2574.82
湖 南	Hunan	1005.39	2004.66	1211.28	1888.12	1079.66	920.52
广 东	Guangdong	2621.40	5153.83	3061.53	3552.69	2355.86	3124.21
广 西	Guangxi	595.87	1303.64	824.29	1130.12	719.01	666.26
海 南	Hainan	119.50	304.23	205.10	233.03	124.48	196.66
重 庆	Chongqing	826.52	1195.37	725.27	1173.61	866.55	818.12
四 川	Sichuan	1609.59	3260.59	1904.79	2877.77	1795.29	1587.51
贵 州	Guizhou	732.84	1487.05	957.85	1503.07	880.97	760.64
云 南	Yunnan	1106.86	1556.29	920.86	1336.24	932.00	1480.73
西 藏	Tibet	19.56	78.71	61.85	23.56	15.18	68.90
陕 西	Shaanxi	1348.42	2723.90	1683.20	2314.09	1534.75	1408.00
甘 肃	Gansu	699.49	1315.35	904.63	1149.79	727.01	788.49
青 海	Qinghai	276.36	754.00	475.92	659.39	324.44	300.72
宁 夏	Ningxia	241.13	489.72	302.32	455.64	259.96	275.41
新 疆	Xinjiang	568.98	2314.67	1303.92	1142.74	746.21	1111.92

14-10 续表 2 continued

单位：亿元 (100 million yuan)

年　份 地　区	Year Region	主营业务收入 Revenue from Principal Business	主营业务成本 Cost of Principal Business	主营业务税金及附加 Taxes and Other Charges on Principal Business	利润总额 Total Profits	本年应交增值税 Value-added Tax Payable	全部从业人员年平均人数(万人) Annual Average Employed Persons (10 000 persons)
	1998	33566.11	27092.45	993.53	525.14	1852.36	3747.78
	1999	35950.70	28919.13	1062.21	997.86	2019.03	3394.58
	2000	42203.12	33473.62	1150.28	2408.33	2320.36	2995.25
	2001	44443.52	35522.47	1250.18	2388.56	2408.97	2675.11
	2002	47844.21	38048.00	1401.82	2632.94	2580.51	2423.63
	2003	58027.15	45987.63	1589.87	3836.20	3025.57	2162.87
	2004	71430.99	57187.96	1921.90	5453.10	3514.68	1973.20
	2005	85574.18	69302.41	2121.74	6519.75	4098.37	1874.85
北　京	Beijing	3867.93	3406.42	47.48	240.13	124.65	53.02
天　津	Tianjin	2738.58	2257.75	57.30	262.66	105.89	40.65
河　北	Hebei	4021.96	3388.22	57.04	224.40	183.21	108.40
山　西	Shanxi	2603.14	1974.50	35.21	160.52	171.49	119.84
内蒙古	Inner Mongolia	1579.37	1271.09	22.31	113.20	102.31	41.74
辽　宁	Liaoning	5968.29	5265.79	90.90	159.68	215.84	116.99
吉　林	Jilin	2451.35	2123.45	61.45	81.30	98.93	60.78
黑龙江	Heilongjiang	3696.64	2300.13	70.80	1023.51	281.77	91.22
上　海	Shanghai	6483.49	5439.38	150.68	510.75	244.55	61.12
江　苏	Jiangsu	5021.00	4279.24	114.44	231.34	212.89	76.98
浙　江	Zhejiang	3802.59	3317.26	103.48	187.31	163.93	34.33
安　徽	Anhui	2481.29	2009.52	71.89	140.52	120.28	70.97
福　建	Fujian	1534.14	1273.30	49.50	81.49	68.73	28.77
江　西	Jiangxi	1526.21	1294.42	35.90	57.16	69.19	47.06
山　东	Shandong	7774.29	6196.85	126.60	747.09	346.22	149.02
河　南	Henan	4098.07	3391.21	85.12	203.81	190.42	145.95
湖　北	Hubei	3064.99	2385.37	89.23	245.19	154.02	76.90
湖　南	Hunan	2080.92	1624.16	134.56	77.99	116.37	61.46
广　东	Guangdong	6261.70	5294.21	129.44	387.31	283.51	69.42
广　西	Guangxi	1242.97	1028.19	30.23	67.70	70.57	37.24
海　南	Hainan	235.23	178.74	8.10	22.44	15.26	5.92
重　庆	Chongqing	1307.55	1081.73	32.59	46.45	62.27	40.43
四　川	Sichuan	2506.44	1969.58	59.28	166.71	127.49	80.21
贵　州	Guizhou	1114.30	838.80	58.97	57.47	73.66	44.23
云　南	Yunnan	1665.15	1110.50	240.14	172.16	129.63	33.21
西　藏	Tibet	18.99	12.96	0.31	1.95	1.89	1.61
陕　西	Shaanxi	2297.68	1610.70	69.25	350.68	136.72	77.89
甘　肃	Gansu	1606.53	1200.12	39.71	48.40	71.01	44.96
青　海	Qinghai	380.86	265.24	6.01	68.40	26.55	9.02
宁　夏	Ningxia	353.09	298.47	5.09	11.53	17.36	13.91
新　疆	Xinjiang	1789.47	1215.09	38.72	370.50	111.75	31.58

14-11 国有及国有控股工业企业主要经济效益指标（2005年）

Main Indicators on Economic Benefit of State-owned and State-holding Industrial Enterprises (2005)

地 区	Region	工 业 增加值率 (%) Ratio of Value-added to Gross Industrial Output Value (%)	总资产贡献率 (%) Ratio of Total Assets to Industrial Output Value (%)	资产负债率 (%) Assets-Liability Ratio (%)	流动资产周转次数 (次/年) Number of Times of Turnover of Working Capitals (times/year)	工业成本费用利润率 (%) Ratio of Profits to Industrial Cost (%)	全员劳动生产率 (元/人.年) Overall Labor Productivity (yuan-person-year)	产品销售率 (%) Proportion of Products Sold (%)
全国总计	**National Total**	**32.45**	**11.87**	**56.66**	**2.10**	**8.44**	**144954**	**99.25**
北 京	Beijing	26.91	4.50	31.14	1.88	6.39	179568	98.99
天 津	Tianjin	32.90	13.91	60.19	2.20	10.77	212730	101.98
河 北	Hebei	30.38	10.44	64.01	2.31	5.96	112780	98.67
山 西	Shanxi	37.48	9.38	67.82	1.71	6.82	79263	97.85
内蒙古	Inner Mongolia	43.44	9.82	64.32	2.08	7.94	163442	98.23
辽 宁	Liaoning	28.76	7.45	59.33	2.15	2.78	141864	99.86
吉 林	Jilin	29.48	8.49	60.57	2.11	3.45	122886	99.45
黑龙江	Heilongjiang	50.10	35.35	54.50	2.42	39.49	198106	97.71
上 海	Shanghai	28.00	11.72	43.60	1.99	8.57	275717	99.20
江 苏	Jiangsu	24.34	11.26	59.67	2.29	4.89	159660	99.41
浙 江	Zhejiang	24.85	13.37	57.41	2.92	5.28	246193	99.72
安 徽	Anhui	34.54	11.20	62.83	2.18	6.15	117694	98.89
福 建	Fujian	28.87	11.89	56.16	2.38	5.74	153834	99.49
江 西	Jiangxi	27.21	9.74	69.38	2.01	4.00	88551	99.49
山 东	Shandong	36.59	15.84	60.18	2.55	10.83	181709	99.06
河 南	Henan	31.90	10.22	65.62	2.06	5.34	88343	98.61
湖 北	Hubei	33.27	9.18	57.34	1.69	9.05	136778	99.63
湖 南	Hunan	37.13	12.74	67.23	2.07	4.24	127132	99.52
广 东	Guangdong	26.51	13.03	53.21	2.39	6.70	243444	98.71
广 西	Guangxi	31.64	10.82	62.91	2.09	5.88	104249	99.69
海 南	Hainan	35.44	11.72	54.23	1.97	10.95	142559	101.30
重 庆	Chongqing	25.95	8.15	58.92	1.58	3.71	83372	99.38
四 川	Sichuan	36.29	9.08	64.34	1.56	7.31	112574	101.24
贵 州	Guizhou	36.45	9.70	66.39	1.52	5.77	95160	99.06
云 南	Yunnan	44.76	20.08	47.44	1.50	13.41	225408	100.13
西 藏	Tibet	55.73	4.68	25.48	0.97	11.80	63093	93.68
陕 西	Shaanxi	41.01	15.87	61.88	1.70	18.95	122802	98.76
甘 肃	Gansu	25.76	9.54	59.32	2.30	3.55	90153	98.96
青 海	Qinghai	38.77	12.16	68.56	1.38	22.44	169998	97.90
宁 夏	Ningxia	33.62	5.62	60.94	1.46	3.37	89951	99.38
新 疆	Xinjiang	45.21	23.85	50.58	3.15	27.10	248324	99.93

14-12 按行业分私营工业企业主要指标（2005年）

单位：亿元

行业	Sector	企业单位数（个） Number of Enterprises (unit)	工业总产值 Gross Industrial Output Value
全国总计	**National Total**	**123820**	**47778.20**
煤炭开采和洗选业	Mining and Washing of Coal	2217	700.25
石油和天然气开采业	Extraction of Petroleum and Natural Gas	14	5.22
黑色金属矿采选业	Mining and Processing of Ferrous Metal Ores	1378	479.88
有色金属矿采选业	Mining and Processing of Non-Ferrous Metal Ores	625	229.34
非金属矿采选业	Mining and Processing of Nonmetal Ores	1074	272.69
其他采矿业	Mining of Other Ores	3	1.41
农副食品加工业	Processing of Food from Agricultural Products	7615	3435.28
食品制造业	Manufacture of Foods	2307	837.68
饮料制造业	Manufacture of Beverages	1486	465.73
烟草制品业	Manufacture of Tobacco	2	1.23
纺织业	Manufacture of Textile	12879	5035.94
纺织服装、鞋、帽制造业	Manufacture of Textile Wearing Apparel, Footware, and Caps	5053	1555.77
皮革、毛皮、羽毛(绒)及其制品业	Manufacture of Leather, Fur, Feather and Related Products	2758	957.57
木材加工及木、竹、藤、棕、草制品业	Processing of Timber, Manufacture of Wood, Bamboo, Rattan, Palm, and Straw Products	3426	932.02
家具制造业	Manufacture of Furniture	1532	468.87
造纸及纸制品业	Manufacture of Paper and Paper Products	3836	1140.85
印刷业和记录媒介的复制	Printing,Reproduction of Recording Media	1828	370.13
文教体育用品制造业	Manufacture of Articles For Culture, Education and Sport Activity	1345	393.42
石油加工、炼焦及核燃料加工业	Processing of Petroleum, Coking, Processing of Nuclear Fuel	981	894.62
化学原料及化学制品制造业	Manufacture of Raw Chemical Materials and Chemical Products	8525	3271.71
医药制造业	Manufacture of Medicines	1573	669.52
化学纤维制造业	Manufacture of Chemical Fibers	711	723.51
橡胶制品业	Manufacture of Rubber	1258	385.55
塑料制品业	Manufacture of Plastics	5689	1619.21
非金属矿物制品业	Manufacture of Non-metallic Mineral Products	9669	3224.39
黑色金属冶炼及压延加工业	Smelting and Pressing of Ferrous Metals	3900	4193.63
有色金属冶炼及压延加工业	Smelting and Pressing of Non-ferrous Metals	2577	1780.13
金属制品业	Manufacture of Metal Products	7230	2322.71
通用设备制造业	Manufacture of General Purpose Machinery	10244	3204.74
专用设备制造业	Manufacture of Special Purpose Machinery	4396	1349.78
交通运输设备制造业	Manufacture of Transport Equipment	4713	1931.20
电气机械及器材制造业	Manufacture of Electrical Machinery and Equipment	6609	2744.77
通信设备、计算机及其他电子设备制造业	Manufacture of Communication Equipment, Computers and Other Electronic Equipment	2265	931.27
仪器仪表及文化、办公用机械制造业	Manufacture of Measuring Instruments and Machinery for Cultural Activity and Office Work	1184	313.37
工艺品及其他制造业	Manufacture of Artwork and Other Manufacturing	2274	703.90
废弃资源和废旧材料回收加工业	Recycling and Disposal of Waste	203	114.50
电力、热力的生产和供应业	Production and Supply of Electric Power and Heat Power	328	88.31
燃气生产和供应业	Production and Supply of Gas	46	15.34
水的生产和供应业	Production and Supply of Water	67	12.77

Main Indicators of Private Enterprises by Industrial Sector (2005)

(100 million yuan)

工业增加值 Value-added of Industry	资产总计 Total Assets	流动资产合计 Total Working Capitals	流动资产年平均余额 Annual Average Balance of Working Capitals	固定资产原价 Original Value of Fixed Assets	固定资产净值年平均余额 Annual Average Balance of Net Value of Fixed Assets
12855.55	**30325.12**	**16426.01**	**15484.96**	**12983.32**	**9586.90**
300.92	412.27	187.50	171.23	188.36	148.01
2.15	6.27	1.55	1.39	5.90	4.06
192.66	381.43	168.10	153.10	150.62	117.16
89.13	138.32	70.72	65.01	63.55	44.75
94.26	150.78	69.58	65.58	78.62	60.43
0.49	0.33	0.14	0.09	0.24	0.18
916.53	1516.11	762.44	725.23	680.31	529.75
241.87	562.99	265.28	249.18	261.00	204.79
148.93	402.24	179.19	168.40	192.10	147.79
0.37	0.24	0.09	0.09	0.10	0.06
1220.36	3354.96	1741.36	1637.03	1634.35	1195.91
435.13	812.77	505.96	484.14	295.67	217.71
257.74	442.03	261.40	248.15	153.92	116.13
258.66	455.51	227.12	217.32	218.06	170.64
126.07	281.40	153.51	146.93	111.30	85.43
308.97	788.18	402.75	385.99	394.21	294.15
100.83	330.26	159.42	150.90	185.49	132.05
97.00	210.30	122.94	117.74	80.53	60.73
279.52	740.36	362.98	337.21	329.23	256.95
874.53	1941.63	1058.45	992.70	840.91	603.83
228.18	626.51	286.59	273.35	278.95	208.30
137.10	463.77	213.48	199.59	236.17	170.78
107.16	244.45	134.88	128.22	114.92	86.12
397.34	1031.00	569.00	541.86	450.66	327.79
973.50	2563.95	1138.89	1106.71	1440.21	1047.85
1030.49	2298.47	1263.09	1173.10	924.35	720.50
415.03	917.45	535.29	503.15	356.22	255.41
602.85	1409.29	848.61	799.74	523.38	379.05
878.52	2123.28	1273.05	1201.28	809.22	567.31
397.09	946.93	571.38	535.56	347.48	249.06
472.92	1340.83	804.39	757.01	455.93	328.44
694.33	1781.86	1161.63	1081.83	538.92	381.22
232.35	649.99	436.54	402.92	185.38	125.85
92.24	258.77	167.98	157.52	71.85	51.45
184.01	359.97	210.67	199.52	131.99	101.17
26.79	35.44	20.68	20.52	10.46	7.24
30.59	293.96	75.57	72.50	203.74	160.67
4.08	16.27	5.75	5.70	9.08	7.41
4.85	34.54	8.06	7.48	29.92	20.75

14-12 续表

单位：亿元

行　业	Sector	负债合计 Total Liabilities	流动负债合计 Total Working Liabilities
全 国 总 计	**National Total**	**18038.87**	**15964.40**
煤炭开采和洗选业	Mining and Washing of Coal	205.60	174.51
石油和天然气开采业	Extraction of Petroleum and Natural Gas	2.62	2.40
黑色金属矿采选业	Mining and Processing of Ferrous Metal Ores	188.16	166.29
有色金属矿采选业	Mining and Processing of Non-Ferrous Metal Ores	64.29	50.40
非金属矿采选业	Mining and Processing of Nonmetal Ores	71.96	59.95
其他采矿业	Mining of Other Ores	0.24	0.22
农副食品加工业	Processing of Food from Agricultural Products	820.05	697.30
食品制造业	Manufacture of Foods	310.57	264.79
饮料制造业	Manufacture of Beverages	226.59	184.43
烟草制品业	Manufacture of Tobacco	0.14	0.14
纺织业	Manufacture of Textile	2103.62	1876.39
纺织服装、鞋、帽制造业	Manufacture of Textile Wearing Apparel, Footware, and Caps	489.89	461.47
皮革、毛皮、羽毛(绒)及其制品业	Manufacture of Leather, Fur, Feather and Related Products	261.09	240.88
木材加工及木、竹、藤、棕、草制品业	Processing of Timber, Manufacture of Wood, Bamboo, Rattan, Palm, and Straw Products	223.27	194.20
家具制造业	Manufacture of Furniture	150.91	137.45
造纸及纸制品业	Manufacture of Paper and Paper Products	476.90	408.32
印刷业和记录媒介的复制	Printing,Reproduction of Recording Media	200.44	178.61
文教体育用品制造业	Manufacture of Articles For Culture, Education and Sport Activity	120.38	112.57
石油加工、炼焦及核燃料加工业	Processing of Petroleum, Coking, Processing of Nuclear Fuel	476.83	429.47
化学原料及化学制品制造业	Manufacture of Raw Chemical Materials and Chemical Products	1136.16	1008.75
医药制造业	Manufacture of Medicines	333.49	268.04
化学纤维制造业	Manufacture of Chemical Fibers	292.88	230.40
橡胶制品业	Manufacture of Rubber	136.47	120.15
塑料制品业	Manufacture of Plastics	597.38	539.56
非金属矿物制品业	Manufacture of Non-metallic Mineral Products	1474.16	1220.18
黑色金属冶炼及压延加工业	Smelting and Pressing of Ferrous Metals	1528.41	1382.99
有色金属冶炼及压延加工业	Smelting and Pressing of Non-ferrous Metals	574.26	511.94
金属制品业	Manufacture of Metal Products	849.71	788.21
通用设备制造业	Manufacture of General Purpose Machinery	1265.79	1156.08
专用设备制造业	Manufacture of Special Purpose Machinery	562.42	514.97
交通运输设备制造业	Manufacture of Transport Equipment	857.98	775.24
电气机械及器材制造业	Manufacture of Electrical Machinery and Equipment	1076.63	1002.03
通信设备、计算机及其他电子设备制造业	Manufacture of Communication Equipment, Computers and Other Electronic Equipment	376.85	350.23
仪器仪表及文化、办公用机械制造业	Manufacture of Measuring Instruments and Machinery for Cultural Activity and Office Work	139.86	129.89
工艺品及其他制造业	Manufacture of Artwork and Other Manufacturing	208.24	184.85
废弃资源和废旧材料回收加工业	Recycling and Disposal of Waste	18.41	16.97
电力、热力的生产和供应业	Production and Supply of Electric Power and Heat Power	191.48	109.48
燃气生产和供应业	Production and Supply of Gas	8.53	5.04
水的生产和供应业	Production and Supply of Water	16.25	9.59

continued

(100 million yuan)

所有者权益 Owners' Equities	主营业务收入 Revenue from Principal Business	主营业务成本 Cost of Principal Business	主营业务税金及附加 Taxes and Other Charges on Principal Business	利润总额 Total Profits	本年应交增值税 Value Added Tax Payable	全部从业人员年平均人数(万人) Annual Average Employed Persons (10 000 persons)
12286.22	**45801.43**	**39914.50**	**352.22**	**2120.65**	**1336.63**	**1692.06**
206.69	681.94	512.21	14.23	65.69	42.03	39.48
3.66	4.57	3.84	0.08	0.30	0.15	0.14
193.27	463.85	337.68	8.18	59.20	29.80	16.84
74.03	222.16	164.41	2.55	31.73	12.10	9.12
78.82	255.37	197.06	5.39	19.21	11.35	12.90
0.09	1.03	0.83	0.01	0.04	0.06	0.06
696.05	3302.19	2916.98	22.05	138.14	54.20	77.67
252.42	796.39	667.15	6.78	40.65	22.10	34.81
175.65	433.86	340.94	18.02	23.84	15.11	17.72
0.10	1.13	1.05	0.00	0.07	0.01	0.02
1251.34	4903.15	4419.36	28.30	179.12	118.04	217.03
322.89	1480.30	1289.43	9.20	58.52	40.45	105.68
180.94	923.94	813.58	6.29	43.56	27.29	52.73
232.25	892.85	777.84	7.96	47.27	24.37	40.87
130.49	450.24	377.40	4.36	22.63	12.43	23.04
311.29	1086.02	957.77	9.23	44.15	34.56	44.53
129.82	353.13	304.46	2.39	15.35	11.51	17.01
89.91	372.13	322.03	2.26	16.52	9.96	22.05
263.53	854.28	751.78	9.43	26.26	46.51	15.69
805.46	3143.71	2714.97	25.90	145.95	85.11	87.40
293.02	590.22	449.03	6.43	37.22	22.99	22.42
170.89	708.99	665.24	2.56	21.38	8.88	9.26
107.98	374.40	319.50	3.24	22.66	12.25	17.41
433.62	1567.49	1379.19	9.58	71.57	39.52	58.17
1089.79	3073.15	2618.93	28.32	165.01	122.27	149.13
770.06	4080.66	3781.40	26.34	121.17	104.34	66.24
343.19	1713.93	1580.90	8.53	48.45	43.18	29.56
559.58	2225.62	1951.50	13.16	99.73	59.93	85.85
857.49	3038.85	2599.46	20.67	162.27	99.40	121.25
384.51	1276.01	1068.90	8.72	75.45	43.75	49.42
482.85	1834.18	1591.06	16.40	85.77	48.39	69.51
705.20	2608.40	2256.35	13.76	127.51	71.41	85.40
273.13	904.07	774.48	3.81	45.13	25.14	36.56
118.91	298.08	240.19	2.01	18.96	10.67	13.76
151.73	668.73	586.56	4.43	30.54	19.59	37.47
17.03	105.04	93.59	0.70	2.71	2.45	1.50
102.48	84.15	65.81	0.72	5.57	4.45	3.48
7.74	15.41	13.12	0.12	0.46	0.37	0.33
18.29	11.82	8.55	0.09	0.91	0.54	0.56

14-13 按行业分私营工业企业主要经济效益指标（2005年）

行业	Sector	工业增加值率(%) Ratio of Value Added to Gross Industrial Output Value (%)
全国总计	**National Total**	**26.91**
煤炭开采和洗选业	Mining and Washing of Coal	42.97
石油和天然气开采业	Extraction of Petroleum and Natural Gas	41.29
黑色金属矿采选业	Mining and Processing of Ferrous Metal Ores	40.15
有色金属矿采选业	Mining and Processing of Non-Ferrous Metal Ores	38.87
非金属矿采选业	Mining and Processing of Nonmetal Ores	34.57
其他采矿业	Mining of Other Ores	35.01
农副食品加工业	Processing of Food from Agricultural Products	26.68
食品制造业	Manufacture of Foods	28.87
饮料制造业	Manufacture of Beverages	31.98
烟草制品业	Manufacture of Tobacco	30.40
纺织业	Manufacture of Textile	24.23
纺织服装、鞋、帽制造业	Manufacture of Textile Wearing Apparel, Footware, and Caps	27.97
皮革、毛皮、羽毛(绒)及其制品业	Manufacture of Leather, Fur, Feather and Related Products	26.92
木材加工及木、竹、藤、棕、草制品业	Processing of Timber, Manufacture of Wood, Bamboo, Rattan, Palm, and Straw Products	27.75
家具制造业	Manufacture of Furniture	26.89
造纸及纸制品业	Manufacture of Paper and Paper Products	27.08
印刷业和记录媒介的复制	Printing, Reproduction of Recording Media	27.24
文教体育用品制造业	Manufacture of Articles For Culture, Education and Sport Activity	24.66
石油加工、炼焦及核燃料加工业	Processing of Petroleum, Coking, Processing of Nuclear Fuel	31.24
化学原料及化学制品制造业	Manufacture of Raw Chemical Materials and Chemical Products	26.73
医药制造业	Manufacture of Medicines	34.08
化学纤维制造业	Manufacture of Chemical Fibers	18.95
橡胶制品业	Manufacture of Rubber	27.79
塑料制品业	Manufacture of Plastics	24.54
非金属矿物制品业	Manufacture of Non-metallic Mineral Products	30.19
黑色金属冶炼及压延加工业	Smelting and Pressing of Ferrous Metals	24.57
有色金属冶炼及压延加工业	Smelting and Pressing of Non-ferrous Metals	23.31
金属制品业	Manufacture of Metal Products	25.95
通用设备制造业	Manufacture of General Purpose Machinery	27.41
专用设备制造业	Manufacture of Special Purpose Machinery	29.42
交通运输设备制造业	Manufacture of Transport Equipment	24.49
电气机械及器材制造业	Manufacture of Electrical Machinery and Equipment	25.30
通信设备、计算机及其他电子设备制造业	Manufacture of Communication Equipment, Computers and Other Electronic Equipment	24.95
仪器仪表及文化、办公用机械制造业	Manufacture of Measuring Instruments and Machinery for Cultural Activity and Office Work	29.44
工艺品及其他制造业	Manufacture of Artwork and Other Manufacturing	26.14
废弃资源和废旧材料回收加工业	Recycling and Disposal of Waste	23.40
电力、热力的生产和供应业	Production and Supply of Electric Power and Heat Power	34.63
燃气生产和供应业	Production and Supply of Gas	26.57
水的生产和供应业	Production and Supply of Water	38.02

Main Indicators on Economic Benefit of Private Industrial Enterprises by Industrial Sector (2005)

总资产贡献率 (%) Ratio of Total Assets to Industrial Output Value (%)	资产负债率 (%) Assets-Liability Ratio (%)	流动资产周转次数（次/年） Number of Times of Annual of Turnover Working Capitals (times/year)	工业成本费用利润率 (%) Ratio of Profits to Industrial Cost (%)	全员劳动生产率 (元/人.年) Overall Labor Productivity (yuan/person-year)	产品销售率 (%) Proportion of Products Sold (%)
13.85	**59.48**	**2.96**	**4.93**	**75976**	**97.29**
30.74	49.87	3.98	11.39	76228	98.80
8.66	41.72	3.30	7.20	149669	99.65
26.56	49.33	3.03	15.61	114388	96.99
34.72	46.48	3.42	17.54	97716	96.42
25.07	47.72	3.89	8.59	73091	97.50
40.71	72.08	11.32	4.25	87165	97.14
15.78	54.09	4.55	4.46	118001	97.59
13.59	55.16	3.20	5.51	69487	97.18
15.28	56.33	2.58	6.17	84067	97.16
33.75	56.71	12.69	6.76	181956	99.55
11.28	62.70	3.00	3.83	56230	97.61
14.48	60.27	3.06	4.16	41175	97.23
18.70	59.07	3.72	5.02	48876	97.87
18.83	49.01	4.11	5.71	63292	97.25
15.41	53.63	3.06	5.41	54708	97.31
12.53	60.51	2.81	4.30	69381	97.64
9.86	60.69	2.34	4.60	59270	97.81
14.74	57.24	3.16	4.68	43992	98.00
12.67	64.40	2.53	3.22	178101	96.05
14.61	58.52	3.17	4.95	100061	97.42
11.86	53.23	2.16	6.91	101788	94.01
8.90	63.15	3.55	3.11	147980	98.16
16.97	55.83	2.92	6.53	61548	97.07
12.90	57.94	2.89	4.84	68312	97.57
13.71	57.50	2.78	5.75	65278	97.45
12.03	66.50	3.48	3.10	155572	97.11
12.27	62.59	3.41	2.95	140395	97.47
13.43	60.29	2.78	4.74	70219	97.15
14.49	59.61	2.53	5.69	72458	96.90
14.56	59.39	2.38	6.38	80357	96.47
12.42	63.99	2.42	4.97	68034	97.17
12.99	60.42	2.41	5.18	81306	97.34
12.10	57.98	2.24	5.29	63554	97.25
13.00	54.05	1.89	6.84	67049	97.27
16.49	57.85	3.35	4.85	49115	97.21
17.22	51.94	5.12	2.77	178931	98.08
5.36	65.14	1.16	7.19	87802	98.40
7.07	52.41	2.70	3.10	124366	98.34
5.78	47.05	1.58	8.29	86430	94.03

14-14 私营工业企业主要指标

Main Indicators of Private Industrial Enterprises

单位：亿元 (100 million yuan)

年份 Year / 地区 Region		企业单位数(个) Number of Enterprises (unit)	工业总产值 Gross Industrial Output Value	工业增加值 Value Added of Industry	资产总计 Total Assets	流动资产合计 Total Working Capitals
	1998	10667	2082.87	509.63	1486.98	776.53
	1999	14601	3244.56	806.48	2289.21	1217.04
	2000	22128	5220.36	1318.48	3873.83	1910.75
	2001	36218	8760.89	2174.41	5901.98	3130.00
	2002	49176	12950.86	3255.83	8759.62	4686.53
	2003	67607	20980.23	5378.76	14525.29	7838.48
	2004	119357	35141.25	8290.00	23724.80	13080.46
	2005	123820	47778.20	12855.55	30325.12	16426.01
北京	Beijing	1504	331.14	82.87	372.58	233.52
天津	Tianjin	1765	638.31	132.04	452.54	292.22
河北	Hebei	4724	2829.00	825.99	1458.18	705.70
山西	Shanxi	1166	839.19	281.52	772.26	405.77
内蒙古	Inner Mongolia	984	452.89	182.79	323.67	157.75
辽宁	Liaoning	5118	1694.83	470.12	1359.29	661.27
吉林	Jilin	1034	330.68	109.49	254.91	115.55
黑龙江	Heilongjiang	984	328.19	99.21	319.74	156.24
上海	Shanghai	5481	1424.51	400.13	1124.10	722.25
江苏	Jiangsu	17752	8041.93	1970.98	4735.39	2883.70
浙江	Zhejiang	24244	8250.03	1665.34	6509.00	3754.27
安徽	Anhui	2725	714.73	215.10	523.57	276.73
福建	Fujian	4743	1359.75	395.39	834.40	459.91
江西	Jiangxi	2079	750.06	236.85	461.83	213.61
山东	Shandong	14309	6754.57	1969.64	2922.00	1335.66
河南	Henan	4940	2537.48	841.79	1060.15	511.02
湖北	Hubei	3009	894.10	297.04	617.16	277.55
湖南	Hunan	4379	1259.64	415.65	620.71	265.20
广东	Guangdong	12145	4475.32	1091.79	2528.56	1506.43
广西	Guangxi	1277	406.91	120.01	266.98	142.35
海南	Hainan	121	40.54	9.48	39.48	17.34
重庆	Chongqing	1570	653.64	161.49	468.44	261.60
四川	Sichuan	3893	1475.48	483.49	973.84	458.98
贵州	Guizhou	851	232.63	73.44	170.96	82.71
云南	Yunnan	925	415.15	106.98	434.13	203.75
西藏	Tibet	11	3.04	1.74	6.98	5.41
陕西	Shaanxi	693	212.07	71.23	199.59	91.63
甘肃	Gansu	567	122.04	51.73	120.40	50.54
青海	Qinghai	123	40.35	15.03	51.71	19.95
宁夏	Ningxia	354	155.88	46.74	174.18	83.12
新疆	Xinjiang	350	114.15	30.47	168.39	74.28

14-14 续表 1 continued

单位：亿元 (100 million yuan)

年份 Year / 地区 Region		流动资产年平均余额 Annual Average Balance of Working Capitals	固定资产原价合计 Original Value of Fixed Assets	固定资产净值年平均余额 Annual Average Balance of Net Value of Fixed Assets	负债合计 Total Liabilities	流动负债合计 Total Working Liabilities	所有者权益合计 Total Owners' Equities
	1998	738.94	681.14	541.58	909.42	771.59	577.55
	1999	1171.31	1034.21	795.95	1367.12	1159.58	922.10
	2000	1806.24	1651.37	1243.72	2208.83	1891.82	1664.99
	2001	2992.85	2741.06	2039.37	3527.40	3037.27	2374.59
	2002	4437.08	3959.95	2909.24	5192.26	4493.43	3567.35
	2003	7275.96	6228.85	4565.14	8781.24	7697.03	5743.95
	2004	11978.21	9992.56	7467.75	14529.31	12866.37	9195.48
	2005	15484.96	12983.32	9586.90	18038.87	15964.40	12286.22
北 京	Beijing	217.12	120.17	86.00	216.85	202.68	155.73
天 津	Tianjin	247.22	166.38	114.48	309.85	297.20	142.69
河 北	Hebei	668.09	703.02	552.11	793.07	691.79	665.11
山 西	Shanxi	371.86	326.59	255.94	496.90	441.34	275.36
内蒙古	Inner Mongolia	149.94	146.70	118.90	192.74	170.31	130.94
辽 宁	Liaoning	615.73	603.56	455.57	760.22	658.63	599.07
吉 林	Jilin	107.69	129.51	106.33	142.82	120.53	112.09
黑龙江	Heilongjiang	142.03	149.33	121.83	180.54	150.84	139.21
上 海	Shanghai	678.41	368.02	257.69	677.34	623.72	446.76
江 苏	Jiangsu	2680.94	1893.11	1316.52	3218.51	2923.17	1516.88
浙 江	Zhejiang	3527.19	2440.69	1791.73	4111.12	3733.75	2397.84
安 徽	Anhui	250.74	216.55	162.00	298.32	257.76	225.26
福 建	Fujian	425.71	366.37	281.38	414.25	376.77	420.15
江 西	Jiangxi	201.77	227.25	177.98	237.83	204.83	223.99
山 东	Shandong	1319.10	1491.13	1137.83	1448.17	1267.51	1473.83
河 南	Henan	499.96	526.03	405.06	516.11	429.14	544.04
湖 北	Hubei	262.00	301.68	223.69	325.20	264.25	291.97
湖 南	Hunan	252.80	308.89	246.92	299.22	223.19	321.49
广 东	Guangdong	1491.91	1095.61	739.93	1567.43	1427.45	961.13
广 西	Guangxi	129.81	110.01	82.79	167.35	142.19	99.62
海 南	Hainan	16.00	16.86	11.42	20.92	17.85	18.56
重 庆	Chongqing	238.16	180.72	128.75	286.49	245.24	181.95
四 川	Sichuan	426.11	449.93	332.75	565.04	454.76	408.80
贵 州	Guizhou	73.69	80.63	63.76	101.64	86.88	69.31
云 南	Yunnan	189.78	227.71	157.40	279.37	221.53	154.76
西 藏	Tibet	5.18	1.39	1.32	1.10	0.70	5.87
陕 西	Shaanxi	84.35	97.21	71.33	117.06	87.55	82.53
甘 肃	Gansu	48.66	61.88	50.28	67.68	52.30	52.73
青 海	Qinghai	18.17	25.97	22.01	27.49	19.32	24.22
宁 夏	Ningxia	74.50	82.51	61.96	112.51	95.04	61.67
新 疆	Xinjiang	70.31	67.90	51.22	85.75	76.18	82.64

14-14 续表 2 continued

单位：亿元 (100 million yuan)

年份 地区 Year Region	主营业务收入 Revenue from Principal Business	主营业务成本 Cost of Principal Business	主营业务税金及附加 Taxes and Other Charges on Principal Business	利润总额 Total Profits	本年应交增值税 Value-added Tax Payable	全部从业人员年平均人数(万人) Annual Average Employed Persons (10 000 Persons)
1998	1846.25	1563.23	21.13	67.25	53.04	160.80
1999	2921.58	2485.20	30.46	121.52	85.49	229.06
2000	4791.50	4121.97	44.91	189.68	143.60	346.42
2001	7982.43	6947.43	68.46	312.56	242.55	541.52
2002	11971.63	10433.80	95.67	490.23	368.39	732.90
2003	19733.77	17194.65	146.14	859.64	589.24	1027.61
2004	33487.25	29452.27	257.14	1429.74	964.44	1515.43
2005	45801.43	39914.50	352.22	2120.65	1336.63	1692.06
北京 Beijing	337.52	280.32	1.25	13.51	10.04	14.70
天津 Tianjin	709.59	635.39	11.27	34.96	12.79	21.41
河北 Hebei	2719.79	2323.23	19.54	191.66	73.37	77.34
山西 Shanxi	779.53	661.11	10.24	20.46	50.94	27.40
内蒙古 Inner Mongolia	427.46	342.55	4.69	20.89	17.58	15.27
辽宁 Liaoning	1586.80	1401.27	10.62	64.05	42.18	59.28
吉林 Jilin	307.92	267.02	2.98	11.49	7.17	13.67
黑龙江 Heilongjiang	318.37	277.64	2.38	12.25	12.20	13.52
上海 Shanghai	1394.20	1208.05	5.02	71.89	39.59	51.66
江苏 Jiangsu	7765.24	7050.20	34.49	247.35	193.90	242.75
浙江 Zhejiang	7930.90	7002.73	50.37	324.51	218.83	305.48
安徽 Anhui	684.63	600.20	4.01	22.90	17.67	33.48
福建 Fujian	1289.40	1125.55	11.11	53.66	30.77	61.75
江西 Jiangxi	717.67	610.14	8.29	28.98	27.44	31.52
山东 Shandong	6489.57	5532.20	57.23	441.74	198.88	186.34
河南 Henan	2388.85	1995.43	26.78	197.62	82.09	85.68
湖北 Hubei	820.32	695.99	8.79	27.23	21.28	42.01
湖南 Hunan	1190.29	950.52	25.45	50.15	42.01	56.48
广东 Guangdong	4318.69	3815.23	24.56	150.08	119.16	183.33
广西 Guangxi	370.45	328.62	2.15	10.00	12.34	18.67
海南 Hainan	39.26	33.65	0.20	1.61	1.82	1.44
重庆 Chongqing	640.54	550.38	6.24	31.13	17.17	30.18
四川 Sichuan	1382.01	1205.15	10.84	45.96	36.17	61.77
贵州 Guizhou	199.65	171.12	3.58	3.85	11.27	10.90
云南 Yunnan	404.97	350.55	2.71	24.00	20.74	16.59
西藏 Tibet	3.12	1.26	0.05	1.50	0.29	0.09
陕西 Shaanxi	193.05	157.39	4.91	6.06	7.74	9.80
甘肃 Gansu	99.65	83.13	0.94	2.43	2.84	7.10
青海 Qinghai	31.11	25.68	0.37	0.90	0.95	1.99
宁夏 Ningxia	148.47	134.19	0.64	1.78	3.96	6.16
新疆 Xinjiang	112.40	98.62	0.53	6.05	3.48	4.31

14-15 私营工业企业主要经济效益指标（2005年）

Main Indicators on Economic Benefit of Private Industrial Enterprises (2005)

地 区	Region	工业增加值率 (%) Ratio of Value-added to Gross Industrial Output Value (%)	总资产贡献率 (%) Ratio of Total Assets to Industrial Output Value (%)	资产负债率 (%) Assets-Liability Ratio (%)	流动资产周转次数（次/年） Number of Times of Annual of Turnover Working Capitals (times/year)	成本费用利润率 (%) Ratio of Profits to Industrial Cost (%)	全员劳动生产率 (元/人.年) Overall Labor Productivity (yuan/person-year)	产品销售率 (%) Proportion of Products Sold (%)
全国总计	**National Total**	**26.91**	**13.85**	**59.48**	**2.96**	**4.93**	**75976**	**97.29**
北 京	Beijing	25.03	7.16	58.20	1.55	4.13	56357	96.90
天 津	Tianjin	20.69	13.75	68.47	2.87	5.26	61660	96.38
河 北	Hebei	29.20	20.94	54.39	4.07	7.80	106802	96.93
山 西	Shanxi	33.55	12.25	64.34	2.10	2.80	102752	95.39
内蒙古	Inner Mongolia	40.36	14.55	59.55	2.85	5.55	119711	96.27
辽 宁	Liaoning	27.74	9.60	55.93	2.58	4.22	79307	95.89
吉 林	Jilin	33.11	9.44	56.03	2.86	3.94	80098	96.35
黑龙江	Heilongjiang	30.23	9.29	56.46	2.24	4.06	73370	97.46
上 海	Shanghai	28.09	11.02	60.26	2.06	5.42	77462	98.10
江 苏	Jiangsu	24.51	11.38	67.97	2.90	3.30	81195	97.61
浙 江	Zhejiang	20.19	10.65	63.16	2.25	4.28	54515	97.17
安 徽	Anhui	30.09	9.60	56.98	2.73	3.49	64244	96.73
福 建	Fujian	29.08	12.58	49.65	3.03	4.41	64032	96.24
江 西	Jiangxi	31.58	15.21	51.50	3.56	4.37	75146	97.73
山 东	Shandong	29.16	25.44	49.56	4.92	7.49	105702	97.68
河 南	Henan	33.17	30.74	48.68	4.78	9.18	98249	98.48
湖 北	Hubei	33.22	10.56	52.69	3.13	3.56	70708	96.28
湖 南	Hunan	33.00	20.34	48.21	4.71	4.82	73587	99.45
广 东	Guangdong	24.40	12.34	61.99	2.89	3.64	59554	97.34
广 西	Guangxi	29.49	10.19	62.69	2.85	2.82	64291	95.86
海 南	Hainan	23.37	9.74	52.99	2.45	4.29	65783	93.92
重 庆	Chongqing	24.71	12.91	61.16	2.69	5.18	53503	98.02
四 川	Sichuan	32.77	10.99	58.02	3.24	3.50	78267	97.71
贵 州	Guizhou	31.57	11.67	59.46	2.71	2.02	67407	93.77
云 南	Yunnan	25.77	12.24	64.35	2.13	6.20	64495	97.63
西 藏	Tibet	57.19	26.06	15.79	0.60	94.24	190349	102.33
陕 西	Shaanxi	33.59	10.59	58.65	2.29	3.44	72705	92.62
甘 肃	Gansu	42.39	6.26	56.21	2.05	2.63	72874	92.61
青 海	Qinghai	37.24	5.06	53.16	1.71	3.07	75689	93.61
宁 夏	Ningxia	29.98	5.16	64.60	1.99	1.21	75831	95.87
新 疆	Xinjiang	26.70	7.08	50.92	1.60	5.50	70700	94.92

14-16 按行业分“三资”工业企业主要指标（2005年）

单位：亿元

行业	Sector	企业单位数（个）Number of Enterprises (unit)	工业总产值 Gross Industrial Output Value
全国总计	**National Total**	**56387**	**79860.23**
煤炭开采和洗选业	Mining and Washing of Coal	26	58.73
石油和天然气开采业	Extraction of Petroleum and Natural Gas	7	491.09
黑色金属矿采选业	Mining and Processing of Ferrous Metal Ores	25	20.00
有色金属矿采选业	Mining and Processing of Non-Ferrous Metal Ores	37	45.10
非金属矿采选业	Mining and Processing of Nonmetal Ores	127	57.71
其他采矿业	Mining of Other Ores	4	5.45
农副食品加工业	Processing of Food from Agricultural Products	2130	3071.71
食品制造业	Manufacture of Foods	1294	1376.69
饮料制造业	Manufacture of Beverages	569	1056.07
烟草制品业	Manufacture of Tobacco	6	6.90
纺织业	Manufacture of Textile	5007	3201.80
纺织服装、鞋、帽制造业	Manufacture of Textile Wearing Apparel, Footware, and Caps	5110	2290.07
皮革、毛皮、羽毛(绒)及其制品业	Manufacture of Leather, Fur, Feather and Related Products	2494	1827.08
木材加工及木、竹、藤、棕、草制品业	Processing of Timber, Manufacture of Wood, Bamboo, Rattan, Palm, and Straw Products	918	426.84
家具制造业	Manufacture of Furniture	1051	788.09
造纸及纸制品业	Manufacture of Paper and Paper Products	1234	1454.58
印刷业和记录媒介的复制	Printing,Reproduction of Recording Media	662	467.78
文教体育用品制造业	Manufacture of Articles For Culture, Education and Sport Activity	1616	900.71
石油加工、炼焦及核燃料加工业	Processing of Petroleum, Coking, Processing of Nuclear Fuel	160	1269.96
化学原料及化学制品制造业	Manufacture of Raw Chemical Materials and Chemical Products	3045	4197.18
医药制造业	Manufacture of Medicines	890	1047.90
化学纤维制造业	Manufacture of Chemical Fibers	276	725.61
橡胶制品业	Manufacture of Rubber	744	848.92
塑料制品业	Manufacture of Plastics	3345	2165.85
非金属矿物制品业	Manufacture of Non-metallic Mineral Products	2435	1685.09
黑色金属冶炼及压延加工业	Smelting and Pressing of Ferrous Metals	489	2751.73
有色金属冶炼及压延加工业	Smelting and Pressing of Non-ferrous Metals	638	1207.14
金属制品业	Manufacture of Metal Products	2792	2395.20
通用设备制造业	Manufacture of General Purpose Machinery	2987	2905.45
专用设备制造业	Manufacture of Special Purpose Machinery	2001	1508.36
交通运输设备制造业	Manufacture of Transport Equipment	2072	6732.20
电气机械及器材制造业	Manufacture of Electrical Machinery and Equipment	3830	5264.68
通信设备、计算机及其他电子设备制造业	Manufacture of Communication Equipment, Computers and Other Electronic Equipment	4637	22712.30
仪器仪表及文化、办公用机械制造业	Manufacture of Measuring Instruments and Machinery for Cultural Activity and Office Work	1235	1848.36
工艺品及其他制造业	Manufacture of Artwork and Other Manufacturing	1830	822.28
废弃资源和废旧材料回收加工业	Recycling and Disposal of Waste	100	97.34
电力、热力的生产和供应业	Production and Supply of Electric Power and Heat Power	396	1893.86
燃气生产和供应业	Production and Supply of Gas	108	174.67
水的生产和供应业	Production and Supply of Water	60	59.72

Main Indicators of Industrial Enterprises with Hong Kong, Macao, Taiwan and Foreign Funds by Industrial Sector (2005)

(100 million yuan)

工业增加值 Value-added of Industry	资产总计 Total Assets	流动资产合计 Total Working Capitals	流动资产年平均余额 Annual Average Balance of Working Capitals	固定资产原价 Original Value of Fixed Assets	固定资产净值年平均余额 Annual Average Balance of Net Value of Fixed Assets
20468.28	**64308.47**	**35303.97**	**33416.06**	**34266.82**	**21419.03**
27.68	95.64	54.31	46.47	34.07	24.73
455.72	183.95	26.28	26.01	76.97	66.93
3.87	17.50	12.63	12.10	4.36	3.83
15.12	97.38	39.31	33.91	33.36	21.43
18.27	48.96	19.88	18.88	32.57	21.21
1.52	4.47	1.72	1.41	4.49	2.30
774.36	1705.94	960.39	934.32	845.48	554.27
461.29	1187.72	615.54	592.75	672.83	408.21
403.89	1088.41	489.24	480.27	780.32	470.61
3.70	15.56	8.35	7.47	11.57	5.63
836.28	2916.57	1545.70	1476.24	1610.66	1039.87
673.10	1485.42	928.74	875.00	631.38	403.93
504.90	1144.02	744.62	698.76	436.56	281.06
114.12	394.51	196.37	188.85	223.82	150.32
209.96	593.85	360.23	349.00	241.20	165.95
379.75	2091.72	797.75	774.72	1389.99	989.22
149.46	571.07	307.20	299.74	355.80	214.17
233.35	646.70	404.56	385.31	302.81	186.91
237.88	759.78	348.49	333.96	559.18	315.50
1202.94	3883.56	1857.75	1748.79	2183.86	1517.15
393.91	1188.30	637.30	592.27	583.35	375.42
134.72	737.56	286.55	268.83	540.77	346.71
241.34	887.25	416.53	412.07	516.42	339.62
554.61	2177.01	1182.19	1103.96	1184.37	765.04
515.32	2239.75	985.30	935.23	1455.92	961.95
583.75	2204.17	1065.56	1033.66	976.47	683.51
266.01	992.53	533.71	485.53	475.13	324.03
597.09	1784.40	1102.21	1059.85	817.76	516.49
832.40	2786.77	1838.23	1719.55	1170.57	698.93
425.22	1543.26	1013.59	950.68	594.28	383.10
1727.33	5494.42	3045.11	3078.65	2638.91	1496.83
1356.96	3834.54	2511.59	2339.00	1583.63	957.80
4555.66	12979.59	8750.58	8004.98	5391.01	3323.64
435.81	1107.02	737.23	700.06	419.22	256.57
241.25	567.69	343.77	324.37	254.42	167.54
16.14	47.36	37.00	32.34	9.90	7.00
825.57	4328.90	954.94	953.09	4886.91	2740.29
31.55	250.30	88.03	82.28	139.93	105.19
26.52	224.95	55.45	55.71	196.60	126.11

14-16 续表

单位：亿元

行业	Sector	负债合计 Total Liabilities	流动负债合计 Total Working Liabilities
全国总计	**National Total**	**36459.37**	**30842.48**
煤炭开采和洗选业	Mining and Washing of Coal	58.64	41.13
石油和天然气开采业	Extraction of Petroleum and Natural Gas	29.96	27.92
黑色金属矿采选业	Mining and Processing of Ferrous Metal Ores	11.95	11.71
有色金属矿采选业	Mining and Processing of Non-Ferrous Metal Ores	60.22	43.54
非金属矿采选业	Mining and Processing of Nonmetal Ores	24.49	19.76
其他采矿业	Mining of Other Ores	1.41	1.41
农副食品加工业	Processing of Food from Agricultural Products	1047.49	940.29
食品制造业	Manufacture of Foods	614.06	536.92
饮料制造业	Manufacture of Beverages	584.74	516.51
烟草制品业	Manufacture of Tobacco	6.43	6.43
纺织业	Manufacture of Textile	1559.64	1391.13
纺织服装、鞋、帽制造业	Manufacture of Textile Wearing Apparel, Footware, and Caps	804.07	751.80
皮革、毛皮、羽毛(绒)及其制品业	Manufacture of Leather, Fur, Feather and Related Products	652.75	614.74
木材加工及木、竹、藤、棕、草制品业	Processing of Timber, Manufacture of Wood, Bamboo, Rattan, Palm, and Straw Products	220.41	169.14
家具制造业	Manufacture of Furniture	344.86	321.01
造纸及纸制品业	Manufacture of Paper and Paper Products	1274.80	837.25
印刷业和记录媒介的复制	Printing,Reproduction of Recording Media	262.49	240.20
文教体育用品制造业	Manufacture of Articles For Culture, Education and Sport Activity	338.76	321.19
石油加工、炼焦及核燃料加工业	Processing of Petroleum, Coking, Processing of Nuclear Fuel	403.02	332.24
化学原料及化学制品制造业	Manufacture of Raw Chemical Materials and Chemical Products	2059.01	1502.95
医药制造业	Manufacture of Medicines	595.05	509.07
化学纤维制造业	Manufacture of Chemical Fibers	370.64	272.78
橡胶制品业	Manufacture of Rubber	486.40	377.12
塑料制品业	Manufacture of Plastics	1141.65	994.46
非金属矿物制品业	Manufacture of Non-metallic Mineral Products	1192.43	911.37
黑色金属冶炼及压延加工业	Smelting and Pressing of Ferrous Metals	1407.03	1097.53
有色金属冶炼及压延加工业	Smelting and Pressing of Non-ferrous Metals	586.40	488.90
金属制品业	Manufacture of Metal Products	932.39	857.80
通用设备制造业	Manufacture of General Purpose Machinery	1535.90	1437.30
专用设备制造业	Manufacture of Special Purpose Machinery	826.08	764.91
交通运输设备制造业	Manufacture of Transport Equipment	2914.35	2651.59
电气机械及器材制造业	Manufacture of Electrical Machinery and Equipment	2216.00	2079.12
通信设备、计算机及其他电子设备制造业	Manufacture of Communication Equipment, Computers and Other Electronic Equipment	8416.46	7710.78
仪器仪表及文化、办公用机械制造业	Manufacture of Measuring Instruments and Machinery for Cultural Activity and Office Work	553.94	531.21
工艺品及其他制造业	Manufacture of Artwork and Other Manufacturing	274.33	255.33
废弃资源和废旧材料回收加工业	Recycling and Disposal of Waste	35.94	35.20
电力、热力的生产和供应业	Production and Supply of Electric Power and Heat Power	2369.10	1081.02
燃气生产和供应业	Production and Supply of Gas	166.90	118.61
水的生产和供应业	Production and Supply of Water	79.17	41.11

continued

(100 million yuan)

所有者权益 Owners' Equities	主营业务收入 Revenue from Principal Business	主营业务成本 Cost of Principal Business	主营业务税金及附加 Taxes and Other Charges on Principal Business	利润总额 Total Profits	本年应交增值税 Value Added Tax Payable	全部从业人员年平均人数(万人) Annual Average Employed Persons (10 000 persons)
27770.72	**78564.46**	**67862.98**	**326.90**	**4140.81**	**1811.52**	**1899.64**
37.00	87.49	55.13	0.43	11.89	4.48	1.00
153.99	267.55	54.91	15.56	179.49	23.66	0.21
5.55	20.33	17.23	0.07	1.99	0.65	0.44
37.15	57.86	41.41	0.25	8.38	1.58	1.34
24.46	55.10	40.64	0.75	3.88	2.59	1.82
3.06	5.51	4.02	0.02	0.93	0.29	0.11
658.45	3006.60	2697.02	7.04	114.92	45.16	53.75
573.66	1358.77	982.58	3.20	92.66	67.78	32.92
503.67	1104.18	741.92	36.10	76.84	64.86	19.58
9.13	8.82	5.35	0.07	1.68	1.07	0.41
1356.93	3116.89	2773.87	5.91	116.40	63.26	148.11
681.35	2221.19	1908.65	5.20	87.15	51.10	178.77
491.27	1754.72	1562.24	4.38	61.72	37.20	146.01
174.10	408.40	357.58	0.75	16.99	10.85	17.08
248.99	768.68	665.37	0.67	33.31	11.43	39.08
799.33	1440.43	1227.80	4.45	75.71	43.94	31.19
308.58	455.23	368.56	0.48	43.50	17.97	18.16
307.94	882.68	775.42	1.07	27.53	12.03	75.62
356.76	1252.57	1139.75	14.60	49.37	42.40	5.40
1825.44	4162.17	3231.17	19.27	343.59	155.59	42.38
591.16	967.03	576.67	3.55	103.23	67.77	22.62
366.93	702.96	651.60	1.01	10.56	12.56	7.99
400.84	829.24	698.74	6.77	41.07	16.93	30.14
1035.36	2120.21	1851.12	3.63	91.32	40.17	82.11
1047.32	1640.73	1372.48	4.06	91.68	59.21	57.56
797.14	2675.27	2477.66	2.13	101.44	64.03	19.43
406.13	1176.40	1066.30	0.95	52.52	21.29	14.88
852.01	2359.27	2053.45	2.44	135.33	38.71	69.41
1250.87	2900.76	2373.94	2.93	248.03	73.65	64.86
716.94	1526.71	1243.66	3.56	117.20	38.87	42.34
2554.29	6739.60	5668.12	156.98	386.88	237.99	78.11
1618.57	5077.56	4352.08	4.99	255.39	92.80	153.16
4563.13	22423.20	20604.30	5.58	725.65	182.02	318.49
553.08	1832.07	1605.12	0.93	92.57	25.66	45.56
293.36	800.70	685.74	2.29	38.76	18.31	60.80
11.42	97.66	92.76	0.05	1.36	0.79	0.92
1926.22	1996.83	1606.43	4.39	287.31	157.98	14.31
83.39	210.30	192.83	0.32	6.56	2.45	2.25
145.79	52.77	39.36	0.07	5.98	2.44	1.30

14-17 按行业分“三资”工业企业主要经济效益指标（2005年）

行 业	Sector	工业增加值率 (%) Ratio of Value Added to Gross Industrial Output Value (%)
全国总计	**National Total**	**25.63**
煤炭开采和洗选业	Mining and Washing of Coal	47.12
石油和天然气开采业	Extraction of Petroleum and Natural Gas	92.80
黑色金属矿采选业	Mining and Processing of Ferrous Metal Ores	19.35
有色金属矿采选业	Mining and Processing of Non-Ferrous Metal Ores	33.52
非金属矿采选业	Mining and Processing of Nonmetal Ores	31.66
其他采矿业	Mining of Other Ores	27.89
农副食品加工业	Processing of Food from Agricultural Products	25.21
食品制造业	Manufacture of Foods	33.51
饮料制造业	Manufacture of Beverages	38.24
烟草制品业	Manufacture of Tobacco	53.62
纺织业	Manufacture of Textile	26.12
纺织服装、鞋、帽制造业	Manufacture of Textile Wearing Apparel, Footware, and Caps	29.39
皮革、毛皮、羽毛(绒)及其制品业	Manufacture of Leather, Fur, Feather and Related Products	27.63
木材加工及木、竹、藤、棕、草制品业	Processing of Timber, Manufacture of Wood, Bamboo, Rattan, Palm, and Straw Products	26.74
家具制造业	Manufacture of Furniture	26.64
造纸及纸制品业	Manufacture of Paper and Paper Products	26.11
印刷业和记录媒介的复制	Printing, Reproduction of Recording Media	31.95
文教体育用品制造业	Manufacture of Articles For Culture, Education and Sport Activity	25.91
石油加工、炼焦及核燃料加工业	Processing of Petroleum, Coking, Processing of Nuclear Fuel	18.73
化学原料及化学制品制造业	Manufacture of Raw Chemical Materials and Chemical Products	28.66
医药制造业	Manufacture of Medicines	37.59
化学纤维制造业	Manufacture of Chemical Fibers	18.57
橡胶制品业	Manufacture of Rubber	28.43
塑料制品业	Manufacture of Plastics	25.61
非金属矿物制品业	Manufacture of Non-metallic Mineral Products	30.58
黑色金属冶炼及压延加工业	Smelting and Pressing of Ferrous Metals	21.21
有色金属冶炼及压延加工业	Smelting and Pressing of Non-ferrous Metals	22.04
金属制品业	Manufacture of Metal Products	24.93
通用设备制造业	Manufacture of General Purpose Machinery	28.65
专用设备制造业	Manufacture of Special Purpose Machinery	28.19
交通运输设备制造业	Manufacture of Transport Equipment	25.66
电气机械及器材制造业	Manufacture of Electrical Machinery and Equipment	25.77
通信设备、计算机及其他电子设备制造业	Manufacture of Communication Equipment, Computers and Other Electronic Equipment	20.06
仪器仪表及文化、办公用机械制造业	Manufacture of Measuring Instruments and Machinery for Cultural Activity and Office Work	23.58
工艺品及其他制造业	Manufacture of Artwork and Other Manufacturing	29.34
废弃资源和废旧材料回收加工业	Recycling and Disposal of Waste	16.58
电力、热力的生产和供应业	Production and Supply of Electric Power and Heat Power	43.59
燃气生产和供应业	Production and Supply of Gas	18.06
水的生产和供应业	Production and Supply of Water	44.40

Main Indicators on Economic Benefit of Industrial Enterprises with Hong Kong, Macao, Taiwan and Foreign Funds by Industrial Sector (2005)

总资产贡献率 (%) Ratio of Total Assets to Industrial Output Value (%)	资产负债率 (%) Assets-Liability Ratio (%)	流动资产周转次数（次/年） Number of Times of Annual of Turnover Working Capitals (times/year)	工业成本费用利润率 (%) Ratio of Profits to Industrial Cost (%)	全员劳动生产率 (元/人.年) Overall Labor Productivity (yuan/person-year)	产品销售率 (%) Proportion of Products Sold (%)
10.55	**56.69**	**2.35**	**5.58**	**107748**	**98.12**
18.81	61.32	1.88	15.82	275565	133.88
119.42	16.29	10.28	295.55	21919974	98.35
15.92	68.27	1.68	10.93	87886	96.94
12.13	61.85	1.71	17.05	112625	99.41
15.41	50.03	2.92	7.85	100137	96.66
27.96	31.53	3.91	20.17	134951	95.39
11.11	61.40	3.22	4.00	144066	98.38
14.35	51.70	2.29	7.36	140125	98.40
16.96	53.72	2.30	7.82	206257	98.36
19.04	41.32	1.18	23.71	90329	127.68
7.34	53.47	2.11	3.89	56463	97.58
10.32	54.13	2.54	4.10	37652	97.73
9.80	57.06	2.51	3.67	34580	97.93
8.55	55.87	2.16	4.33	66829	97.11
8.30	58.07	2.20	4.54	53728	98.29
7.36	60.95	1.86	5.55	121763	97.03
11.41	45.96	1.52	10.56	82303	97.24
6.74	52.38	2.29	3.23	30859	98.16
15.23	53.04	3.75	4.13	440412	99.31
14.22	53.02	2.38	9.00	283879	98.56
15.42	50.08	1.63	11.99	174115	92.65
4.42	50.25	2.61	1.54	168692	97.54
8.56	54.82	2.01	5.24	80077	97.92
7.00	52.44	1.92	4.52	67546	97.97
7.91	53.24	1.75	5.90	89527	97.23
8.80	63.84	2.59	3.93	300361	96.76
8.63	59.08	2.42	4.68	178762	97.49
10.63	52.25	2.23	6.07	86022	98.78
12.12	55.11	1.69	9.31	128331	98.94
10.77	53.53	1.61	8.30	100437	97.79
14.68	53.04	2.19	6.19	221133	99.33
9.77	57.79	2.17	5.29	88595	97.99
7.52	64.84	2.80	3.34	143040	97.90
10.96	50.04	2.62	5.33	95646	98.99
11.12	48.32	2.47	5.11	39680	97.75
5.57	75.88	3.02	1.42	174869	96.24
12.11	54.73	2.10	16.55	576746	99.62
4.39	66.68	2.56	3.18	140086	101.10
4.35	35.19	0.95	12.33	204182	96.71

14-18 “三资”工业企业主要指标
Main Indicators of Industrial Enterprises with Hong Kong, Macao, Taiwan and Foreign Funds

单位：亿元　　(100 million yuan)

年份 地区	Year Region	企业单位数(个) Number of Enterprises (unit)	工业总产值 Gross Industrial Output Value	工业增加值 Value Added of Industry	资产总计 Total Assets	流动资产合计 Total Working Capitals
	1998	26442	16757.90	4055.07	21326.95	9971.87
	1999	26837	18954.23	4850.92	23018.92	11127.85
	2000	28445	23464.55	6090.35	25714.06	12849.54
	2001	31423	27220.91	7128.11	28354.46	14029.75
	2002	34466	32459.28	8573.10	31513.76	16237.04
	2003	38581	44357.81	11599.65	39260.26	21489.84
	2004	57165	65995.21	15240.50	55601.79	30615.15
	2005	56387	79860.23	20468.28	64308.47	35303.97
北 京	Beijing	1319	3081.24	630.48	2302.56	1417.97
天 津	Tianjin	1627	3319.23	773.42	2382.30	1518.92
河 北	Hebei	993	1715.29	510.97	1549.76	664.82
山 西	Shanxi	119	232.97	80.65	354.88	137.09
内蒙古	Inner Mongolia	131	330.46	119.88	799.34	210.72
辽 宁	Liaoning	2197	2328.23	647.51	2214.10	1165.29
吉 林	Jilin	265	902.86	261.57	614.85	257.16
黑龙江	Heilongjiang	202	364.35	122.89	434.62	189.41
上 海	Shanghai	5590	9788.71	2325.08	8401.40	4808.77
江 苏	Jiangsu	7576	13263.86	3256.65	10409.61	5617.73
浙 江	Zhejiang	6807	5644.38	1128.33	5098.38	2879.65
安 徽	Anhui	496	743.81	233.62	677.90	339.07
福 建	Fujian	4943	4753.23	1262.75	3719.82	2102.29
江 西	Jiangxi	497	447.45	129.21	434.21	190.94
山 东	Shandong	4684	5401.41	1625.15	3844.75	1769.67
河 南	Henan	435	610.91	166.07	618.64	307.26
湖 北	Hubei	605	1373.30	452.17	1322.80	559.90
湖 南	Hunan	410	385.43	132.15	412.20	164.30
广 东	Guangdong	15708	22875.53	5942.88	16004.54	9726.66
广 西	Guangxi	390	574.22	151.97	521.25	250.46
海 南	Hainan	99	109.13	33.21	217.07	80.43
重 庆	Chongqing	183	470.15	119.27	519.13	234.90
四 川	Sichuan	485	487.99	153.71	582.87	302.29
贵 州	Guizhou	106	51.68	12.84	91.04	47.20
云 南	Yunnan	183	168.62	49.99	218.16	92.71
西 藏	Tibet	1	2.16	1.26	4.67	1.07
陕 西	Shaanxi	169	227.40	88.72	236.76	121.25
甘 肃	Gansu	46	54.15	10.32	70.81	35.62
青 海	Qinghai	21	47.53	15.48	110.91	40.19
宁 夏	Ningxia	35	62.21	15.65	85.68	41.48
新 疆	Xinjiang	65	42.32	14.44	53.47	28.75

14-18 续表 1 continued

单位：亿元 (100 million yuan)

年份 Year / 地区 Region	流动资产年平均余额 Annual Average Balance of Working Capitals	固定资产原价合计 Original Value of Fixed Assets	固定资产净值年平均余额 Annual Average Balance of Net Value of Fixed Assets	负债合计 Total Liabilities	流动负债合计 Total Working Liabilities	所有者权益合计 Total Owners' Equities
1998	9671.91	11439.70	8313.98	12481.58	9507.28	8844.84
1999	10606.05	12747.02	9062.95	13287.86	10407.35	9730.41
2000	11926.66	14318.30	9808.74	14658.92	11616.67	11054.36
2001	13750.96	16700.30	11111.58	15558.91	12466.43	12794.29
2002	15174.60	18726.88	12097.09	17136.03	14146.01	14359.94
2003	19866.14	21818.93	13722.33	21763.06	18466.50	17473.30
2004	28266.85	29387.92	18572.57	31278.34	26700.51	24298.79
2005	33416.06	34266.82	21419.03	36459.37	30842.48	27770.72
北 京 Beijing	1287.13	1044.16	583.81	1300.95	1106.19	1001.60
天 津 Tianjin	1418.87	1106.47	648.23	1270.17	1190.26	1113.04
河 北 Hebei	638.95	1023.39	677.60	882.76	641.87	667.00
山 西 Shanxi	133.27	264.08	178.92	218.87	143.81	136.02
内蒙古 Inner Mongolia	209.39	487.98	282.63	490.52	248.81	275.23
辽 宁 Liaoning	1121.64	1303.53	779.26	1171.71	977.07	1042.39
吉 林 Jilin	283.24	440.61	232.28	317.18	262.76	297.67
黑龙江 Heilongjiang	181.41	321.65	206.50	279.55	250.60	155.07
上 海 Shanghai	4634.21	4582.64	2636.00	4617.35	4008.60	3784.04
江 苏 Jiangsu	5149.99	5641.16	3869.78	6191.14	5239.37	4218.47
浙 江 Zhejiang	2698.96	2202.85	1540.94	2933.30	2521.63	2165.09
安 徽 Anhui	325.02	388.09	243.86	373.67	298.43	304.23
福 建 Fujian	2022.81	1890.88	1234.12	1960.30	1658.42	1759.53
江 西 Jiangxi	180.06	231.21	165.69	225.62	156.56	182.81
山 东 Shandong	1699.63	2249.50	1501.17	2108.39	1688.10	1716.43
河 南 Henan	306.89	427.67	249.15	395.49	326.27	223.15
湖 北 Hubei	667.21	733.44	442.41	715.94	546.67	606.86
湖 南 Hunan	164.37	262.96	174.35	227.37	164.38	184.83
广 东 Guangdong	9086.29	8103.06	4769.34	9195.26	8252.07	6809.28
广 西 Guangxi	247.76	283.75	179.66	303.82	236.60	217.43
海 南 Hainan	75.07	123.58	115.81	134.13	61.19	82.94
重 庆 Chongqing	210.52	333.15	178.43	303.54	228.86	215.59
四 川 Sichuan	279.35	286.67	193.62	348.34	280.14	234.53
贵 州 Guizhou	45.90	44.57	29.30	60.51	46.75	30.53
云 南 Yunnan	88.20	164.90	104.49	116.52	73.39	101.64
西 藏 Tibet	1.07	3.54	3.36	0.06	0.06	4.61
陕 西 Shaanxi	120.08	165.57	89.39	124.33	103.43	112.43
甘 肃 Gansu	33.92	46.77	30.38	41.45	26.92	29.35
青 海 Qinghai	33.68	36.42	25.37	70.18	49.31	40.74
宁 夏 Ningxia	44.23	39.30	31.91	54.64	31.01	31.05
新 疆 Xinjiang	26.93	33.28	21.27	26.31	22.96	27.16

14-18 续表 2 continued

单位：亿元 (100 million yuan)

年份 地区	Year Region	主营业务收入 Revenue from Principal Business	主营业务成本 Cost of Principal Business	主营业务税金及附加 Taxes and Other Charges on Principal Business	利润总额 Total Profits	本年应交增值税 Value-added Tax Payable	全部从业人员年平均人数(万人) Annual Average Employed Persons (10 000 Persons)
	1998	15604.60	13023.55	98.64	418.61	521.06	775.19
	1999	17966.55	14824.32	111.51	753.93	590.79	791.86
	2000	22545.74	18583.27	129.76	1282.48	738.88	852.96
	2001	26022.08	21677.74	134.78	1442.95	876.37	938.98
	2002	31189.27	25907.35	151.87	1877.22	960.87	1054.34
	2003	43607.63	36604.09	223.65	2777.44	1189.01	1258.67
	2004	65105.85	55649.54	296.90	3875.97	1508.66	1755.26
	2005	78564.46	67862.98	326.90	4140.81	1811.52	1899.64
北京	Beijing	3053.44	2600.90	17.45	167.82	73.27	31.02
天津	Tianjin	3485.21	2969.92	19.82	242.41	63.65	42.81
河北	Hebei	1675.24	1413.68	3.98	162.82	66.21	30.82
山西	Shanxi	229.49	184.38	0.81	12.63	14.71	6.56
内蒙古	Inner Mongolia	428.58	340.69	2.00	39.60	22.01	5.59
辽宁	Liaoning	2266.99	1964.30	16.11	92.58	51.62	52.93
吉林	Jilin	753.55	658.56	21.77	27.13	33.24	8.26
黑龙江	Heilongjiang	373.92	278.60	7.34	19.96	21.31	10.45
上海	Shanghai	10114.16	8706.67	46.76	447.95	195.68	137.40
江苏	Jiangsu	13071.24	11639.98	17.71	589.66	217.65	245.21
浙江	Zhejiang	5631.83	4876.71	8.96	281.96	133.35	162.57
安徽	Anhui	698.85	576.36	5.35	39.27	24.51	15.81
福建	Fujian	4573.60	3973.09	12.73	250.35	93.10	170.75
江西	Jiangxi	434.76	364.91	3.42	22.26	13.66	17.58
山东	Shandong	5237.71	4496.59	25.69	349.90	146.50	148.59
河南	Henan	566.98	480.46	3.86	22.14	20.56	14.89
湖北	Hubei	1359.35	1135.11	11.55	66.60	49.98	23.42
湖南	Hunan	362.15	285.03	3.77	22.92	13.28	12.00
广东	Guangdong	22031.66	19138.03	76.21	1140.02	460.35	712.06
广西	Guangxi	544.25	451.80	3.88	33.14	22.34	13.85
海南	Hainan	95.06	70.77	0.88	5.16	3.92	2.39
重庆	Chongqing	470.26	382.84	7.94	32.30	23.75	7.06
四川	Sichuan	466.31	372.31	3.69	28.08	17.13	11.65
贵州	Guizhou	46.69	40.72	0.04	-4.95	1.77	2.40
云南	Yunnan	167.38	133.37	0.68	14.21	8.97	3.65
西藏	Tibet	1.72	0.98		0.60	0.18	0.06
陕西	Shaanxi	201.02	143.97	2.51	18.45	11.44	4.90
甘肃	Gansu	54.10	48.61	0.76	0.16	2.43	1.21
青海	Qinghai	60.67	44.84	0.32	6.87	1.53	1.41
宁夏	Ningxia	67.97	57.31	0.48	4.53	1.43	1.32
新疆	Xinjiang	40.30	31.49	0.44	4.28	2.00	1.02

14-19 "三资"工业企业主要经济效益指标（2005年）

Main Indicators on Economic Benefit of Industrial Enterprises with Hong Kong, Macao, Taiwan and Foreign Funds (2005)

地 区	Region	工业增加值率 (%) Ratio of Value-added to Gross Industrial Output Value (%)	总资产贡献率 (%) Ratio of Total Assets to Industrial Output Value (%)	资产负债率 (%) Assets-Liability Ratio (%)	流动资产周转次数（次/年） Number of Times of Annual of Turnover Working Capitals (times/year)	成本费用利润率 (%) Ratio of Profits to Industrial Cost (%)	全员劳动生产率 (元/人.年) Overall Labor Productivity (yuan/person-year)	产品销售率 (%) Proportion of Products Sold (%)
全国总计	**National Total**	**25.63**	**10.55**	**56.69**	**2.35**	**5.58**	**107748**	**98.12**
北 京	Beijing	20.46	11.81	56.50	2.37	5.80	203279	96.77
天 津	Tianjin	23.30	14.33	53.32	2.46	7.48	180669	101.52
河 北	Hebei	29.79	16.15	56.96	2.62	10.73	165802	98.25
山 西	Shanxi	34.62	9.46	61.67	1.72	5.90	122893	97.54
内蒙古	Inner Mongolia	36.28	9.31	61.37	2.05	10.22	214310	99.60
辽 宁	Liaoning	27.81	8.19	52.92	2.02	4.27	122337	100.06
吉 林	Jilin	28.97	14.64	51.59	2.66	3.80	316617	98.79
黑龙江	Heilongjiang	33.73	12.52	64.32	2.06	5.78	117549	94.40
上 海	Shanghai	23.75	8.82	54.96	2.18	4.63	169217	98.89
江 苏	Jiangsu	24.55	8.79	59.48	2.54	4.71	132809	98.20
浙 江	Zhejiang	19.99	9.41	57.53	2.09	5.25	69407	97.85
安 徽	Anhui	31.41	11.44	55.12	2.15	5.97	147752	98.63
福 建	Fujian	26.57	10.40	52.70	2.26	5.79	73954	97.33
江 西	Jiangxi	28.88	9.90	51.96	2.41	5.48	73513	97.16
山 东	Shandong	30.09	14.74	54.84	3.08	7.22	109369	98.18
河 南	Henan	27.18	8.94	63.93	1.85	4.09	111551	97.69
湖 北	Hubei	32.93	10.63	54.12	2.04	5.23	193105	96.83
湖 南	Hunan	34.29	10.79	55.16	2.20	7.07	110089	98.66
广 东	Guangdong	25.98	10.92	57.45	2.42	5.48	83460	97.52
广 西	Guangxi	26.47	12.57	58.29	2.20	6.62	109730	97.78
海 南	Hainan	30.44	5.85	61.79	1.27	5.81	139127	97.66
重 庆	Chongqing	25.37	13.32	58.47	2.23	7.49	168944	99.83
四 川	Sichuan	31.50	9.51	59.76	1.67	6.50	131939	97.21
贵 州	Guizhou	24.86	-2.03	66.46	1.02	-9.75	53470	96.38
云 南	Yunnan	29.64	12.10	53.41	1.90	9.25	136856	97.96
西 藏	Tibet	58.21	16.68	1.25	1.62	51.00	224775	88.15
陕 西	Shaanxi	39.01	14.46	52.51	1.67	10.32	181017	96.23
甘 肃	Gansu	19.06	5.69	58.55	1.59	0.30	85312	104.58
青 海	Qinghai	32.57	9.52	63.27	1.80	12.90	110004	99.34
宁 夏	Ningxia	25.16	8.72	63.76	1.54	7.14	118625	102.68
新 疆	Xinjiang	34.12	13.41	49.21	1.50	11.68	141166	93.20

14-20 按行业分大中型工业企业主要指标（2005年）

单位：亿元

行业	Sector	企业单位数（个） Number of Enterprises (unit)	工业总产值 Gross Industrial Output Value
全国总计	**National Total**	**29774**	**167700.72**
煤炭开采和洗选业	Mining and Washing of Coal	707	4257.42
石油和天然气开采业	Extraction of Petroleum and Natural Gas	72	5715.98
黑色金属矿采选业	Mining and Processing of Ferrous Metal Ores	171	430.76
有色金属矿采选业	Mining and Processing of Non-Ferrous Metal Ores	216	634.02
非金属矿采选业	Mining and Processing of Nonmetal Ores	116	211.18
其他采矿业	Mining of Other Ores	2	4.57
农副食品加工业	Processing of Food from Agricultural Products	996	4363.72
食品制造业	Manufacture of Foods	633	2244.65
饮料制造业	Manufacture of Beverages	555	2123.96
烟草制品业	Manufacture of Tobacco	108	2722.03
纺织业	Manufacture of Textile	2635	6790.01
纺织服装、鞋、帽制造业	Manufacture of Textile Wearing Apparel, Footware, and Caps	982	2167.22
皮革、毛皮、羽毛(绒)及其制品业	Manufacture of Leather, Fur, Feather and Related Products	650	1739.89
木材加工及木、竹、藤、棕、草制品业	Processing of Timber, Manufacture of Wood, Bamboo, Rattan, Palm, and Straw Products	234	515.57
家具制造业	Manufacture of Furniture	302	674.56
造纸及纸制品业	Manufacture of Paper and Paper Products	641	2204.08
印刷业和记录媒介的复制	Printing, Reproduction of Recording Media	327	584.83
文教体育用品制造业	Manufacture of Articles For Culture, Education and Sport Activity	370	719.45
石油加工、炼焦及核燃料加工业	Processing of Petroleum, Coking, Processing of Nuclear Fuel	408	10794.36
化学原料及化学制品制造业	Manufacture of Raw Chemical Materials and Chemical Products	1729	9444.61
医药制造业	Manufacture of Medicines	795	2704.40
化学纤维制造业	Manufacture of Chemical Fibers	210	2032.04
橡胶制品业	Manufacture of Rubber	374	1499.32
塑料制品业	Manufacture of Plastics	810	1910.17
非金属矿物制品业	Manufacture of Non-metallic Mineral Products	1868	3896.92
黑色金属冶炼及压延加工业	Smelting and Pressing of Ferrous Metals	970	17484.31
有色金属冶炼及压延加工业	Smelting and Pressing of Non-ferrous Metals	585	4853.03
金属制品业	Manufacture of Metal Products	912	2680.58
通用设备制造业	Manufacture of General Purpose Machinery	1759	5692.23
专用设备制造业	Manufacture of Special Purpose Machinery	1022	3516.25
交通运输设备制造业	Manufacture of Transport Equipment	1725	12628.54
电气机械及器材制造业	Manufacture of Electrical Machinery and Equipment	1934	9001.97
通信设备、计算机及其他电子设备制造业	Manufacture of Communication Equipment, Computers and Other Electronic Equipment	2184	24085.71
仪器仪表及文化、办公用机械制造业	Manufacture of Measuring Instruments and Machinery for Cultural Activity and Office Work	443	1830.33
工艺品及其他制造业	Manufacture of Artwork and Other Manufacturing	375	790.37
废弃资源和废旧材料回收加工业	Recycling and Disposal of Waste	15	42.31
电力、热力的生产和供应业	Production and Supply of Electric Power and Heat Power	1663	14163.49
燃气生产和供应业	Production and Supply of Gas	98	251.52
水的生产和供应业	Production and Supply of Water	178	294.34

Main Indicators of Large and Medium-sized Industrial Enterprises by Industrial Sector (2005)

(100 million yuan)

工业增加值 Value-added of Industry	资产总计 Total Assets	流动资产合计 Total Working Capitals	流动资产年平均余额 Annual Average Balance of Working Capitals	固定资产原价 Original Value of Fixed Assets	固定资产净值年平均余额 Annual Average Balance of Net Value of Fixed Assets
48073.53	**178816.88**	**77623.67**	**74090.35**	**109682.42**	**66133.28**
2247.26	7782.18	2979.21	2761.75	5007.37	2961.27
4303.76	6443.40	1421.52	1353.95	9009.71	4109.78
209.74	752.46	321.72	286.67	300.53	187.16
251.59	691.73	293.20	268.03	339.97	203.83
94.49	334.24	127.38	123.53	183.39	119.75
1.19	3.80	1.35	1.19	4.14	2.14
1154.84	2850.39	1457.27	1396.80	1367.59	922.20
717.47	2015.71	982.60	936.08	1020.86	663.17
836.57	2447.76	1195.08	1143.26	1387.87	854.81
1976.48	3179.75	2029.28	1948.70	1205.67	604.94
1748.74	6452.68	3146.23	3025.13	3564.09	2292.83
618.79	1704.53	1043.93	965.80	650.90	433.91
482.75	1113.72	695.33	665.32	399.75	267.82
142.43	529.90	236.07	230.21	301.94	205.14
182.13	547.22	316.70	303.22	222.18	155.20
620.45	3108.89	1080.72	1055.06	2112.20	1490.29
193.69	761.58	359.07	353.96	504.06	295.15
179.79	561.21	335.70	324.08	256.10	161.27
1664.24	5762.20	2529.70	2189.38	4621.17	2487.09
2532.90	10238.97	4066.42	3852.89	6896.44	4124.94
990.74	3572.66	1754.05	1685.70	1567.98	1014.43
361.61	2009.59	789.85	754.00	1411.82	888.64
397.85	1421.81	679.44	662.06	800.40	513.67
462.10	1931.34	996.81	937.64	936.19	621.27
1200.40	5801.69	2301.16	2233.86	3687.61	2438.85
4794.91	16848.45	6918.33	6579.83	10736.71	6095.46
1248.15	5103.51	2275.78	2137.91	2985.50	1937.38
690.63	2102.30	1272.95	1218.01	848.31	548.08
1586.96	6183.88	4067.29	3849.47	2267.09	1303.82
917.11	4033.33	2446.71	2300.46	1587.77	952.25
2969.57	13424.79	7480.76	7401.09	5494.36	3155.46
2291.05	7391.84	4802.64	4472.41	2434.43	1492.51
4946.46	15550.70	10308.30	9525.67	6088.38	3712.16
431.82	1306.26	803.74	775.46	502.24	319.15
207.13	662.19	383.82	361.49	296.53	194.90
9.92	24.92	12.22	13.85	8.35	5.10
4193.63	31625.77	5097.38	5418.07	26601.09	17065.50
72.69	814.95	224.14	205.76	607.21	395.26
141.49	1724.60	389.85	372.60	1464.47	936.73

14-20 续表

单位：亿元

行　　业	Sector	负债合计 Total Liabilities	流动负债合计 Total Working Liabilities
全国总计	**National Total**	**102529.69**	**77049.41**
煤炭开采和洗选业	Mining and Washing of Coal	4844.34	3227.29
石油和天然气开采业	Extraction of Petroleum and Natural Gas	2227.65	1492.62
黑色金属矿采选业	Mining and Processing of Ferrous Metal Ores	352.38	304.10
有色金属矿采选业	Mining and Processing of Non-Ferrous Metal Ores	344.87	259.64
非金属矿采选业	Mining and Processing of Nonmetal Ores	197.38	156.54
其他采矿业	Mining of Other Ores	1.14	1.14
农副食品加工业	Processing of Food from Agricultural Products	1737.79	1495.91
食品制造业	Manufacture of Foods	1133.88	975.45
饮料制造业	Manufacture of Beverages	1254.27	1101.85
烟草制品业	Manufacture of Tobacco	1031.34	974.80
纺织业	Manufacture of Textile	3967.40	3276.00
纺织服装、鞋、帽制造业	Manufacture of Textile Wearing Apparel, Footware, and Caps	963.61	878.57
皮革、毛皮、羽毛(绒)及其制品业	Manufacture of Leather, Fur, Feather and Related Products	671.48	625.64
木材加工及木、竹、藤、棕、草制品业	Processing of Timber, Manufacture of Wood, Bamboo, Rattan, Palm, and Straw Products	296.82	222.28
家具制造业	Manufacture of Furniture	330.62	299.80
造纸及纸制品业	Manufacture of Paper and Paper Products	1914.04	1257.07
印刷业和记录媒介的复制	Printing,Reproduction of Recording Media	370.86	326.46
文教体育用品制造业	Manufacture of Articles For Culture, Education and Sport Activity	295.34	273.75
石油加工、炼焦及核燃料加工业	Processing of Petroleum, Coking, Processing of Nuclear Fuel	3241.48	2366.35
化学原料及化学制品制造业	Manufacture of Raw Chemical Materials and Chemical Products	5764.69	4150.93
医药制造业	Manufacture of Medicines	1835.87	1531.56
化学纤维制造业	Manufacture of Chemical Fibers	1171.98	878.23
橡胶制品业	Manufacture of Rubber	873.04	684.37
塑料制品业	Manufacture of Plastics	1058.97	903.14
非金属矿物制品业	Manufacture of Non-metallic Mineral Products	3488.13	2563.07
黑色金属冶炼及压延加工业	Smelting and Pressing of Ferrous Metals	10099.02	8018.56
有色金属冶炼及压延加工业	Smelting and Pressing of Non-ferrous Metals	3222.02	2443.13
金属制品业	Manufacture of Metal Products	1210.31	1085.62
通用设备制造业	Manufacture of General Purpose Machinery	3976.63	3573.93
专用设备制造业	Manufacture of Special Purpose Machinery	2620.24	2309.04
交通运输设备制造业	Manufacture of Transport Equipment	8351.79	7320.68
电气机械及器材制造业	Manufacture of Electrical Machinery and Equipment	4562.95	4203.32
通信设备、计算机及其他电子设备制造业	Manufacture of Communication Equipment, Computers and Other Electronic Equipment	9891.26	8960.35
仪器仪表及文化、办公用机械制造业	Manufacture of Measuring Instruments and Machinery for Cultural Activity and Office Work	721.80	655.11
工艺品及其他制造业	Manufacture of Artwork and Other Manufacturing	369.43	314.09
废弃资源和废旧材料回收加工业	Recycling and Disposal of Waste	12.30	10.33
电力、热力的生产和供应业	Production and Supply of Electric Power and Heat Power	16998.97	7281.59
燃气生产和供应业	Production and Supply of Gas	376.49	254.16
水的生产和供应业	Production and Supply of Water	747.13	392.94

continued

(100 million yuan)

所有者权益 Owners' Equity	主营业务收入 Revenue from Principal Business	主营业务成本 Cost of Principal Business	主营业务税金及附加 Taxes and Other Charges on Principal Business	利润总额 Total Profits	本年应交增值税 Value-added Tax Payable	全部从业人员年平均人数（万人） Annual Average Employed Persons (10 000 persons)
75928.60	**169237.88**	**141880.22**	**2469.03**	**11011.76**	**6033.51**	**3798.91**
2898.87	4461.38	2971.45	70.12	405.96	356.12	343.04
4212.34	5804.68	2415.47	121.91	2749.05	579.57	84.27
400.08	450.52	287.93	7.93	81.19	32.92	20.90
346.85	631.47	409.82	4.35	147.79	28.61	24.68
136.86	214.23	139.25	5.30	22.08	16.32	14.88
2.65	4.57	3.53	0.01	0.59	0.22	0.10
1112.60	4359.02	3855.34	15.26	196.96	77.10	92.25
881.55	2207.95	1665.85	8.80	145.59	95.65	63.32
1193.03	2159.42	1449.81	131.88	167.66	129.48	55.35
2148.41	2803.87	1006.12	1128.99	401.79	325.04	17.43
2480.78	6670.73	5977.51	24.88	249.64	180.35	302.90
740.91	2076.79	1729.34	7.18	124.71	49.46	112.27
442.24	1669.98	1463.54	4.98	76.96	36.62	109.83
233.08	497.78	428.17	1.98	27.96	15.23	20.83
216.61	662.84	566.56	1.60	32.68	10.02	32.25
1177.07	2162.90	1844.44	9.16	111.95	78.82	56.44
390.72	571.17	459.32	2.17	49.57	25.76	23.67
265.87	704.77	616.70	1.12	28.47	10.43	51.65
2512.67	10851.37	10372.62	291.27	-163.75	253.89	59.30
4441.14	9465.27	7706.92	65.96	658.74	340.76	184.40
1734.69	2674.66	1719.97	16.37	253.24	158.83	73.59
837.61	2008.96	1861.35	6.31	34.53	36.25	31.30
547.77	1470.08	1253.16	15.38	71.24	32.34	43.02
870.03	1897.49	1659.93	4.63	96.33	37.39	64.43
2302.81	3808.22	3177.67	23.85	192.69	166.97	158.46
6585.55	17740.47	15811.59	80.98	971.35	665.42	224.78
1877.50	4847.54	4146.55	27.80	342.78	167.93	88.42
891.99	2641.82	2273.66	7.03	160.26	52.84	78.06
2193.64	5491.75	4553.89	19.54	361.09	162.38	159.41
1408.86	3466.53	2906.95	14.20	176.97	87.90	117.62
5046.47	12621.73	10820.66	217.99	529.95	366.57	236.33
2820.96	8687.24	7353.13	20.34	428.27	190.65	205.72
5645.55	23995.89	21738.10	14.97	787.01	252.23	333.15
583.81	1807.99	1578.44	2.15	85.27	28.91	46.57
292.73	780.67	667.78	2.70	41.19	18.01	42.82
12.62	35.52	31.29	0.16	0.98	0.64	0.78
14625.72	16190.37	14398.74	85.26	963.29	938.62	195.01
438.47	357.68	327.86	1.74	4.55	12.09	10.69
977.47	282.55	229.81	2.80	-4.81	15.18	18.98

14-21 按行业分大中型工业企业主要经济效益指标（2005年）

行业	Sector	工业增加值率 (%) Ratio of Value-added to Gross Industrial Output Value (%)	总资产贡献率 (%) Ratio of Total Assets to Industrial Output Value (%)
全国总计	**National Total**	**28.67**	**11.98**
煤炭开采和洗选业	Mining and Washing of Coal	52.78	11.54
石油和天然气开采业	Extraction of Petroleum and Natural Gas	75.29	53.98
黑色金属矿采选业	Mining and Processing of Ferrous Metal Ores	48.69	16.97
有色金属矿采选业	Mining and Processing of Non-Ferrous Metal Ores	39.68	27.24
非金属矿采选业	Mining and Processing of Nonmetal Ores	44.74	14.11
其他采矿业	Mining of Other Ores	26.15	21.93
农副食品加工业	Processing of Food from Agricultural Products	26.46	11.86
食品制造业	Manufacture of Foods	31.96	13.56
饮料制造业	Manufacture of Beverages	39.39	18.27
烟草制品业	Manufacture of Tobacco	72.61	58.86
纺织业	Manufacture of Textile	25.75	8.69
纺织服装、鞋、帽制造业	Manufacture of Textile Wearing Apparel, Footware, and Caps	28.55	11.72
皮革、毛皮、羽毛(绒)及其制品业	Manufacture of Leather, Fur, Feather and Related Products	27.75	11.59
木材加工及木、竹、藤、棕、草制品业	Processing of Timber, Manufacture of Wood, Bamboo, Rattan, Palm, and Straw Products	27.62	9.96
家具制造业	Manufacture of Furniture	27.00	9.08
造纸及纸制品业	Manufacture of Paper and Paper Products	28.15	8.15
印刷业和记录媒介的复制	Printing,Reproduction of Recording Media	33.12	10.96
文教体育用品制造业	Manufacture of Articles For Culture, Education and Sport Activity	24.99	7.77
石油加工、炼焦及核燃料加工业	Processing of Petroleum, Coking, Processing of Nuclear Fuel	15.42	7.70
化学原料及化学制品制造业	Manufacture of Raw Chemical Materials and Chemical Products	26.82	11.64
医药制造业	Manufacture of Medicines	36.63	13.13
化学纤维制造业	Manufacture of Chemical Fibers	17.80	5.43
橡胶制品业	Manufacture of Rubber	26.54	9.89
塑料制品业	Manufacture of Plastics	24.19	8.26
非金属矿物制品业	Manufacture of Non-metallic Mineral Products	30.80	8.03
黑色金属冶炼及压延加工业	Smelting and Pressing of Ferrous Metals	27.42	11.29
有色金属冶炼及压延加工业	Smelting and Pressing of Non-ferrous Metals	25.72	12.01
金属制品业	Manufacture of Metal Products	25.76	11.62
通用设备制造业	Manufacture of General Purpose Machinery	27.88	9.49
专用设备制造业	Manufacture of Special Purpose Machinery	26.08	7.79
交通运输设备制造业	Manufacture of Transport Equipment	23.51	8.98
电气机械及器材制造业	Manufacture of Electrical Machinery and Equipment	25.45	9.56
通信设备、计算机及其他电子设备制造业	Manufacture of Communication Equipment, Computers and Other Electronic Equipment	20.54	7.41
仪器仪表及文化、办公用机械制造业	Manufacture of Measuring Instruments and Machinery for Cultural Activity and Office Work	23.59	9.45
工艺品及其他制造业	Manufacture of Artwork and Other Manufacturing	26.21	10.28
废弃资源和废旧材料回收加工业	Recycling and Disposal of Waste	23.45	7.80
电力、热力的生产和供应业	Production and Supply of Electric Power and Heat Power	29.61	7.71
燃气生产和供应业	Production and Supply of Gas	28.90	2.56
水的生产和供应业	Production and Supply of Water	48.07	1.32

Main Indicators on Economic Benefit of Large and Medium-sized Industrial Enterprises by Industrial Sector (2005)

资产负债率 (%) Assets-Liability Ratio (%)	流动资产周转次数（次/年） Number of Times of Annual of Turnover Working Capitals (times/year)	工业成本费用利润率 (%) Ratio of Profits to Industrial Cost (%)	全员劳动生产率（元/人.年） Overall Labor Productivity (yuan/person-year)	产品销售率 (%) Proportion of Products Sold (%)
57.34	**2.28**	**7.05**	**126545**	**98.39**
62.25	1.62	10.39	65510	97.83
34.57	4.29	99.24	510684	99.98
46.83	1.57	22.82	100330	97.14
49.86	2.36	30.49	101933	98.39
59.05	1.73	12.01	63517	97.32
30.08	3.85	14.84	118691	92.90
60.97	3.12	4.78	125180	98.52
56.25	2.36	7.10	113301	97.98
51.24	1.89	9.02	151153	98.31
32.43	1.44	30.87	1133799	101.28
61.48	2.21	3.89	57733	98.19
56.53	2.15	6.41	55115	96.54
60.29	2.51	4.86	43953	97.82
56.01	2.16	5.93	68376	96.48
60.42	2.19	5.19	56480	98.29
61.57	2.05	5.47	109933	97.57
48.70	1.61	9.43	81830	96.86
52.63	2.17	4.20	34811	97.94
56.25	4.96	-1.52	280649	99.18
56.30	2.46	7.50	137357	98.34
51.39	1.59	10.52	134627	95.06
58.32	2.66	1.76	115532	98.79
61.40	2.22	5.13	92488	97.34
54.83	2.02	5.35	71717	97.77
60.12	1.70	5.30	75755	97.32
59.94	2.70	5.81	213314	98.21
63.13	2.27	7.66	141169	98.25
57.57	2.17	6.45	88474	99.08
64.31	1.43	7.02	99554	97.45
64.96	1.51	5.36	77972	96.70
62.21	1.71	4.40	125651	99.80
61.73	1.94	5.17	111367	97.63
63.61	2.52	3.39	148476	97.77
55.26	2.33	4.96	92726	98.76
55.79	2.16	5.59	48369	99.09
49.35	2.56	2.85	126398	95.36
53.75	2.99	6.30	215052	99.84
46.20	1.74	1.22	68003	100.27
43.32	0.76	-1.59	74538	97.60

14-22 大中型工业企业主要指标

Main Indicators of Large and Medium-sized Industrial Enterprises

单位：亿元 (100 million yuan)

年 份 Year 地 区 Region		企业单位数 (个) Number of Enterprises (unit)	工业总产值 Gross Industrial Output Value	工业增加值 Value-added of Industry	资产总计 Total Assets	流动资产合计 Total Working Capitals
	1998	23408	37552.34	11766.31	76095.76	30719.90
	1999	22235	41439.42	13279.95	82143.59	32711.77
	2000	21724	48993.02	15747.32	87309.83	35282.86
	2001	22987	57358.40	18133.44	97372.22	39102.67
	2002	23323	65317.51	20841.19	103516.44	41911.77
	2003	23631	95979.46	29073.42	125131.72	54268.38
	2004	27692	133374.68		154178.47	65765.12
	2005	29774	167700.72	48073.53	178816.88	77623.67
北 京	Beijing	536	5201.59	1248.02	10588.36	2553.55
天 津	Tianjin	548	4990.61	1371.78	4360.25	2183.79
河 北	Hebei	1206	7544.53	2160.88	7404.47	3044.23
山 西	Shanxi	844	3852.99	1387.34	5873.66	2305.43
内蒙古	Inner Mongolia	365	2052.40	847.74	3122.98	1018.20
辽 宁	Liaoning	1013	7898.11	2284.95	9209.77	3981.22
吉 林	Jilin	367	3055.49	917.86	3683.37	1355.29
黑龙江	Heilongjiang	432	4050.82	1947.64	4365.82	1788.04
上 海	Shanghai	1412	10943.26	2680.89	11393.04	5400.00
江 苏	Jiangsu	3377	21002.60	5194.06	17777.29	8881.92
浙 江	Zhejiang	3364	12426.48	2642.87	11732.75	6104.33
安 徽	Anhui	625	3352.58	1129.02	3986.27	1609.94
福 建	Fujian	1202	4961.56	1342.45	4356.28	2123.11
江 西	Jiangxi	441	1943.29	535.66	2249.42	927.85
山 东	Shandong	3101	18850.33	5902.45	16693.39	7267.88
河 南	Henan	1324	6204.19	1687.30	7222.03	2884.49
湖 北	Hubei	803	4363.26	1390.59	7194.07	2365.39
湖 南	Hunan	618	2727.72	951.97	3205.34	1279.62
广 东	Guangdong	4477	24411.45	6114.46	17969.79	10184.97
广 西	Guangxi	444	1626.82	506.31	2057.67	796.26
海 南	Hainan	77	290.33	91.60	521.32	176.58
重 庆	Chongqing	457	1855.63	485.38	2430.55	1099.31
四 川	Sichuan	964	3960.28	1380.07	5689.02	2452.25
贵 州	Guizhou	269	1197.54	431.73	2198.74	779.65
云 南	Yunnan	425	1948.80	822.38	2972.25	1302.37
西 藏	Tibet	11	11.16	6.53	33.11	10.23
陕 西	Shaanxi	473	2813.87	1114.01	4274.26	1652.42
甘 肃	Gansu	214	1471.48	375.71	2035.03	797.28
青 海	Qinghai	56	416.18	161.06	1000.61	283.75
宁 夏	Ningxia	121	499.60	162.33	903.78	335.31
新 疆	Xinjiang	208	1775.77	798.50	2312.19	679.04

14-22 续表 1 continued

单位：亿元 (100 million yuan)

年份 Year / 地区 Region		流动资产年平均余额 Annual Average Balance of Working Capitals	固定资产原价 Original Value of Fixed Assets	固定资产净值年平均余额 Annual Average Balance of Net Value of Fixed Assets	负债合计 Total Liabilities	流动负债合计 Total Working Liabilities	所有者权益合计 Total Owners' Equities
	1998	30074.66	47898.94	31712.58	47836.52	31076.11	28246.56
	1999	31428.90	53515.04	34031.40	49431.10	32270.98	32684.52
	2000	33763.10	58348.15	37293.79	52083.87	33935.97	35165.58
	2001	38325.79	66145.71	41393.89	56338.65	37602.83	40898.91
	2002	40411.83	71606.08	44085.34	59873.02	40870.32	43524.43
	2003	50705.48	82397.76	50512.33	72684.52	52292.76	52297.22
	2004	61628.62	95788.91	58703.28	87698.21	64364.76	66263.47
	2005	74090.35	109682.42	66133.28	102529.69	77049.41	75928.60
北　京	Beijing	2406.59	3665.65	2097.44	3404.04	2259.97	7184.32
天　津	Tianjin	2033.10	2953.43	1578.49	2474.49	2039.74	1886.65
河　北	Hebei	2881.96	5184.69	3070.13	4592.09	3391.00	2812.37
山　西	Shanxi	2179.41	3827.14	2368.97	3977.22	2645.89	1791.27
内蒙古	Inner Mongolia	983.61	2133.54	1316.24	1861.94	1133.13	1261.05
辽　宁	Liaoning	3776.64	6910.54	3915.82	5374.15	4002.55	3715.13
吉　林	Jilin	1379.88	2686.14	1489.62	2198.64	1683.33	1476.38
黑龙江	Heilongjiang	1709.48	4176.87	2040.73	2373.06	1919.02	1992.27
上　海	Shanghai	5192.12	7364.55	3970.27	5596.62	4658.60	5796.42
江　苏	Jiangsu	8376.32	9896.41	6303.07	10920.21	9093.94	6855.82
浙　江	Zhejiang	5778.74	5531.56	3653.03	6889.55	5699.83	4836.16
安　徽	Anhui	1532.74	2429.24	1536.36	2452.19	1691.37	1524.71
福　建	Fujian	2068.62	2488.81	1584.84	2347.16	1844.10	2009.10
江　西	Jiangxi	905.11	1391.89	879.86	1486.23	1017.24	733.24
山　东	Shandong	6962.15	10307.41	6188.66	9993.17	7541.69	6671.89
河　南	Henan	2852.16	4884.70	3001.19	4574.44	3350.02	2647.59
湖　北	Hubei	2461.10	4606.32	3290.91	4019.85	2468.23	3174.22
湖　南	Hunan	1258.74	2072.33	1249.16	2057.31	1311.76	1148.03
广　东	Guangdong	9559.77	9368.30	5656.74	10318.03	8930.17	7651.77
广　西	Guangxi	772.82	1345.31	850.70	1237.10	861.10	820.57
海　南	Hainan	159.98	335.14	250.00	292.75	153.39	228.57
重　庆	Chongqing	1060.91	1338.39	815.79	1433.52	1097.36	997.02
四　川	Sichuan	2318.05	3700.42	2215.69	3565.22	2464.06	2116.05
贵　州	Guizhou	735.29	1410.04	902.92	1420.22	848.98	778.14
云　南	Yunnan	1209.66	1657.86	970.98	1456.06	1049.88	1516.19
西　藏	Tibet	9.69	25.85	18.75	13.06	8.42	20.05
陕　西	Shaanxi	1574.04	3015.01	1856.68	2609.27	1680.96	1647.31
甘　肃	Gansu	744.59	1343.27	911.65	1195.05	757.93	839.98
青　海	Qinghai	282.49	772.63	502.26	684.87	335.41	314.11
宁　夏	Ningxia	310.47	555.24	356.00	553.34	332.40	333.79
新　疆	Xinjiang	614.10	2303.75	1290.34	1158.83	777.93	1148.41

14-22 续表 2 continued

单位: 亿元 (100 million yuan)

年份 地区	Year Region	主营业务收入 Revenue from Principal Business	主营业务成本 Cost of Principal Business	主营业务税金及附加 Taxes and Other Charges on Principal Business	利润总额 Total Profits	本年应交增值税 Value-added Tax Payable	全部从业人员年平均人数(万人) Annual Average Employed Persons (10 000 persons)
	1998	37130.61	29949.73	1003.18	881.94	1956.72	3412.76
	1999	41405.57	33254.65	1075.24	1588.58	2175.16	3110.13
	2000	50120.30	39768.89	1173.45	3183.28	2566.15	2880.60
	2001	58480.45	47033.65	1294.65	3440.56	2843.54	2782.72
	2002	66977.14	53839.14	1471.01	4008.97	3109.76	2710.20
	2003	99710.07	81445.72	1770.28	6522.98	4065.11	3224.30
	2004	134039.04	111168.19	2191.08	9183.91	4990.26	3508.45
	2005	169237.88	141880.22	2469.03	11011.76	6033.51	3798.91
北　京	Beijing	5446.08	4796.62	49.28	324.33	146.48	61.91
天　津	Tianjin	5232.51	4383.51	64.60	463.28	139.38	64.55
河　北	Hebei	7455.87	6359.34	72.36	477.12	293.28	176.02
山　西	Shanxi	3839.74	2991.83	46.48	217.18	257.27	156.56
内蒙古	Inner Mongolia	2181.29	1735.93	28.84	176.63	116.65	53.46
辽　宁	Liaoning	8000.32	6990.98	105.92	268.27	262.38	170.75
吉　林	Jilin	2973.75	2551.30	65.43	118.32	114.67	67.06
黑龙江	Heilongjiang	4116.58	2640.98	78.10	1042.35	303.54	103.49
上　海	Shanghai	11492.51	9895.86	156.32	662.99	302.89	126.87
江　苏	Jiangsu	20803.04	18289.84	153.35	984.73	509.17	367.54
浙　江	Zhejiang	13021.87	11291.01	140.08	661.27	371.31	274.68
安　徽	Anhui	3351.99	2725.11	78.78	188.70	150.35	99.06
福　建	Fujian	4826.41	4127.26	59.79	291.72	123.78	130.74
江　西	Jiangxi	1929.46	1631.60	40.40	78.26	83.92	56.32
山　东	Shandong	19395.06	16221.81	194.50	1486.62	662.96	413.74
河　南	Henan	6454.73	5400.40	100.65	359.02	275.34	214.66
湖　北	Hubei	4434.12	3520.28	99.58	321.63	198.90	109.83
湖　南	Hunan	2683.25	2118.13	141.86	114.52	135.98	75.06
广　东	Guangdong	23806.68	20613.50	169.95	1148.21	620.21	571.33
广　西	Guangxi	1615.90	1317.70	32.21	108.09	86.62	43.05
海　南	Hainan	274.64	209.21	8.36	21.75	14.80	6.13
重　庆	Chongqing	1858.94	1536.04	37.57	88.77	78.16	55.70
四　川	Sichuan	3934.89	3138.94	73.74	245.57	175.52	127.55
贵　州	Guizhou	1157.27	868.02	59.04	66.93	75.43	40.82
云　南	Yunnan	1939.85	1329.81	241.72	200.87	143.96	41.90
西　藏	Tibet	11.99	7.77	0.14	2.24	1.18	0.62
陕　西	Shaanxi	2763.56	1979.09	78.77	387.05	162.20	84.16
甘　肃	Gansu	1522.71	1268.42	40.07	41.41	64.95	43.48
青　海	Qinghai	400.48	282.20	6.03	70.04	27.04	9.79
宁　夏	Ningxia	483.62	411.01	5.88	17.71	21.33	19.01
新　疆	Xinjiang	1828.74	1246.74	39.26	376.19	113.87	33.10

14-23 大中型工业企业主要经济效益指标（2005年）

Main Indicators on Economic Benefit of Large and Medium-sized Industrial Enterprises (2005)

地 区	Region	工业增加值率 (%) Ratio of Value-added to Gross Industrial Output Value (%)	总资产贡献率 (%) Ratio of Total Assets to Industrial Output Value (%)	资产负债率 (%) Assets-Liability Ratio (%)	流动资产周转次数（次/年）Number of Times of Annual of Turnover Working Capitals (times/year)	成本费用利润率 (%) Ratio of Profits to Industrial Cost (%)	全员劳动生产率 (元/人.年) Overall Labor Productivity (yuan/person-year)	产品销售率 (%) Proportion of Products Sold (%)
全国总计	**National Total**	**28.67**	**11.98**	**57.34**	**2.28**	**7.05**	**126545**	**98.39**
北 京	Beijing	23.99	5.31	32.15	2.26	6.18	201597	97.81
天 津	Tianjin	27.49	16.17	56.75	2.57	9.81	212519	100.90
河 北	Hebei	28.64	12.62	62.02	2.59	6.90	122764	98.16
山 西	Shanxi	36.01	10.30	67.71	1.76	6.21	88615	97.02
内蒙古	Inner Mongolia	41.30	11.70	59.62	2.22	9.07	158567	98.17
辽 宁	Liaoning	28.93	7.97	58.35	2.12	3.51	133815	99.14
吉 林	Jilin	30.04	9.18	59.69	2.16	4.17	136875	98.99
黑龙江	Heilongjiang	48.08	33.50	54.36	2.41	34.92	188187	97.41
上 海	Shanghai	24.50	10.44	49.12	2.21	6.12	211318	98.86
江 苏	Jiangsu	24.73	10.43	61.43	2.48	4.98	141320	98.57
浙 江	Zhejiang	21.27	11.58	58.72	2.25	5.37	96216	98.21
安 徽	Anhui	33.68	11.59	61.52	2.19	6.08	113978	98.52
福 建	Fujian	27.06	11.97	53.88	2.33	6.48	102679	97.59
江 西	Jiangxi	27.56	10.43	66.07	2.13	4.34	95119	99.07
山 东	Shandong	31.31	15.39	59.86	2.79	8.41	142661	98.45
河 南	Henan	27.20	11.62	63.34	2.26	5.98	78605	98.42
湖 北	Hubei	31.87	9.67	55.88	1.80	8.08	126610	98.33
湖 南	Hunan	34.90	13.31	64.18	2.13	4.78	126832	99.39
广 东	Guangdong	25.05	11.39	57.42	2.49	5.10	107021	97.31
广 西	Guangxi	31.12	12.45	60.12	2.09	7.30	117620	98.99
海 南	Hainan	31.55	9.67	56.16	1.72	8.85	149453	100.92
重 庆	Chongqing	26.16	9.50	58.98	1.75	5.06	87141	99.19
四 川	Sichuan	34.85	9.95	62.67	1.70	6.80	108202	99.43
贵 州	Guizhou	36.05	10.46	64.59	1.57	6.50	105764	97.53
云 南	Yunnan	42.20	20.67	48.99	1.60	13.12	196291	99.60
西 藏	Tibet	58.54	11.26	39.44	1.24	23.41	105334	95.58
陕 西	Shaanxi	39.59	15.78	61.05	1.76	17.06	132370	98.37
甘 肃	Gansu	25.53	8.26	58.72	2.05	2.93	86416	99.64
青 海	Qinghai	38.70	11.93	68.45	1.42	21.69	164502	97.63
宁 夏	Ningxia	32.49	6.12	61.23	1.56	3.80	85378	98.89
新 疆	Xinjiang	44.97	23.75	50.12	2.98	26.80	241261	99.72

14-24 主要工业产品产量

Output of Major Industrial Products

年份 Year 地区 Region	化学纤维 (万吨) Chemical Fiber (10 000 tons)	纱 (万吨) Yarn (10 000 tons)	布 (亿米) Cloth (100 million m)	机制纸及纸板 (万吨) Machine-made Paper and Paperboards (10 000 tons)	原盐 (万吨) Salt (10 000 tons)	成品糖 (万吨) Refined Sugar (10 000 tons)	啤酒 (万千升) Beer (10 000 kiloliter)
1978	28.46	238.20	110.30	439.00	1953.00	227.00	40.00
1980	45.03	292.60	134.70	535.00	1728.00	257.00	69.00
1985	94.78	353.50	146.70	911.00	1479.00	451.00	310.00
1989	148.09	476.70	189.20	1333.00	2829.00	501.00	643.00
1990	165.42	462.60	188.80	1372.00	2023.00	582.00	692.00
1991	191.03	460.80	181.70	1479.00	2410.00	640.00	838.00
1992	213.04	501.70	190.70	1725.00	2838.00	829.00	1021.00
1993	237.37	501.50	203.00	1914.00	2943.00	771.00	1192.00
1994	280.33	489.50	211.30	2138.00	2996.00	592.00	1415.00
1995	341.17	542.20	260.18	2812.30	2977.72	558.64	1568.82
1996	375.45	512.21	209.10	2638.20	2903.57	640.20	1681.91
1997	471.62	559.83	248.79	2733.20	3082.66	702.58	1888.94
1998	510.00	542.00	241.00	2125.63	2242.52	826.00	1987.67
1999	600.00	567.00	250.00	2159.30	2812.36	861.00	2098.77
2000	694.00	657.00	277.00	2486.94	3128.00	700.00	2231.32
2001	841.38	760.68	290.00	3777.07	3410.51	653.10	2288.93
2002	991.20	850.00	322.39	4666.99	3602.43	926.00	2402.70
2003	1181.15	983.58	353.52	4849.33	3437.70	1083.94	2540.48
2004	1699.80	1291.34	482.10	5413.27	4043.44	1033.70	2948.59
2005	1664.79	1450.54	484.39	6205.42	4661.06	912.37	3126.05
北京 Beijing	0.93	2.10	0.43	16.98			152.30
天津 Tianjin	20.54	7.32	2.85	21.68	234.70		18.24
河北 Hebei	22.67	68.59	30.76	407.91	425.07	3.93	159.17
山西 Shanxi	2.71	10.39	3.63	40.49		0.41	21.14
内蒙古 Inner Mongolia	0.23	3.22	0.83	25.74	215.84	14.75	64.55
辽宁 Liaoning	23.70	17.41	5.71	83.37	180.64	1.13	188.30
吉林 Jilin	24.36	6.71	1.01	50.27			90.22
黑龙江 Heilongjiang	17.83	4.88	1.10	77.04		20.01	202.52
上海 Shanghai	49.78	11.65	1.55	90.33			70.45
江苏 Jiangsu	501.95	335.60	90.46	578.58	500.13		157.65
浙江 Zhejiang	660.33	96.41	96.20	966.98	37.31	0.23	242.62
安徽 Anhui	11.36	38.31	6.66	122.24	56.73		124.44
福建 Fujian	70.12	64.53	21.69	200.00	43.87	6.25	158.22
江西 Jiangxi	18.07	20.44	4.12	73.38	69.51	0.23	60.63
山东 Shandong	95.38	371.77	90.17	1255.85	1434.27		327.73
河南 Henan	39.73	141.80	23.65	653.66	109.95		197.51
湖北 Hubei	11.74	89.82	23.40	112.89	406.21		131.80
湖南 Hunan	8.29	26.06	3.70	222.12	119.13	3.03	56.09
广东 Guangdong	39.91	36.64	40.41	712.53	35.22	126.59	269.49
广西 Guangxi	0.32	11.87	0.55	125.37	10.72	504.34	55.96
海南 Hainan	4.61			2.18	17.00	27.51	11.99
重庆 Chongqing	2.97	6.90	14.55	46.81	61.14	0.87	53.87
四川 Sichuan	26.56	25.48	7.93	135.91	404.20	5.04	126.22
贵州 Guizhou	0.69	1.58	0.44	7.81		1.05	16.58
云南 Yunnan	3.04	1.44	0.14	28.88	67.78	153.57	24.61
西藏 Tibet							4.89
陕西 Shaanxi	0.65	19.43	10.67	61.63	26.25		65.38
甘肃 Gansu	0.60	1.78	0.43	13.42	5.02	1.11	34.01
青海 Qinghai		0.36			115.14		
宁夏 Ningxia	0.30	0.15	0.01	45.58			11.81
新疆 Xinjiang	5.42	27.90	1.34	25.79	85.23	42.32	27.66

注：1.成品糖指标名称1997年及以前为糖，1998-2004年为机制糖；产量包括土糖。
2.啤酒2003年及以前计量单位为万吨。

a) Machined-made sugar was called sugar in 1997 and before, in which the homemade sugar was included.1998-2004 was called machine-made sugar.
b) Unit of beer in 2003 and before was 10 000 tons.

14-24 续表 1 continued

年份 地区 Year Region	卷烟（亿支）Cigarettes (100 million pieces)	家用电冰箱（万台）Household Refrigerators (10 000 units)	房间空气调节器（万台）Air Conditioners (10 000 units)	家用洗衣机（万台）Household Washing Machines (10 000 units)	彩色电视机（万台）Color Television Sets (10 000 units)	原煤（亿吨）Coal (100 million tons)	原油（万吨）Crude Oil (10 000 tons)
1978	1182.00	2.80	0.02	0.04	0.38	6.18	10405.00
1980	1520.00	4.90	1.32	24.53	3.21	6.20	10595.00
1985	2370.00	144.81	12.35	887.20	435.28	8.72	12490.00
1989	3195.00	670.79	37.47	825.40	940.02	10.54	13764.00
1990	3298.00	463.06	24.07	662.68	1033.04	10.80	13831.00
1991	3226.00	469.94	63.03	687.17	1205.06	10.87	14099.00
1992	3285.00	485.76	158.03	707.93	1333.08	11.16	14210.00
1993	3376.00	596.66	346.41	895.85	1435.76	11.50	14524.00
1994	3432.00	768.12	393.42	1094.24	1689.15	12.40	14608.00
1995	3485.02	918.54	682.56	948.41	2057.74	13.61	15004.95
1996	3401.92	979.65	786.21	1074.72	2537.60	13.97	15733.39
1997	3377.42	1044.43	974.01	1254.48	2711.33	13.73	16074.14
1998	3374.00	1060.00	1156.87	1207.31	3497.00	12.50	16100.00
1999	3340.00	1210.00	1337.64	1342.17	4262.00	12.80	16000.00
2000	3397.00	1279.00	1826.67	1442.98	3936.00	12.99	16300.00
2001	3402.10	1351.26	2333.64	1341.61	4093.70	13.81	16395.87
2002	3467.08	1598.87	3135.11	1595.76	5155.00	14.55	16700.00
2003	3580.86	2242.56	4820.86	1964.46	6541.40	17.22	16959.98
2004	18736.35	3007.59	6390.33	2533.41	7431.83	19.92	17587.33
2005	19389.08	2987.06	6764.57	3035.52	8283.22	22.05	18135.29
北京 Beijing	136.78	81.71				0.09	
天津 Tianjin	132.50	19.30	434.43	1.96	64.90		1792.99
河北 Hebei	600.00			9.76		0.86	562.45
山西 Shanxi	125.00					5.54	
内蒙古 Inner Mongolia	172.50				239.09	2.56	
辽宁 Liaoning	229.40	120.43	269.65		550.21	0.64	1260.96
吉林 Jilin	278.50	11.25	0.01	0.01	50.80	0.27	550.57
黑龙江 Heilongjiang	400.00	0.06				0.95	4516.01
上海 Shanghai	798.67	42.68	228.50	242.76	145.46		25.27
江苏 Jiangsu	816.36	318.46	544.98	513.66	403.81	0.28	164.70
浙江 Zhejiang	657.65	228.93	430.11	972.91	128.54		
安徽 Anhui	1040.02	530.42	515.00	443.85	313.42	0.85	
福建 Fujian	604.99				373.90	0.18	
江西 Jiangxi	409.07	26.33	166.67		89.11	0.26	
山东 Shandong	1170.25	612.58	588.08	418.78	1018.60	1.40	2694.54
河南 Henan	1303.29	249.01	44.76	12.33	177.00	1.88	507.16
湖北 Hubei	1123.17	20.39	239.94	60.29		0.10	78.11
湖南 Hunan	1395.31	55.54		18.39		0.57	
广东 Guangdong	1053.57	558.64	2914.52	266.48	4089.62	0.04	1470.03
广西 Guangxi	534.50			2.44		0.07	3.43
海南 Hainan	59.00						10.07
重庆 Chongqing	396.08		277.02			0.36	
四川 Sichuan	686.31	23.00	110.89	42.50	564.67	0.81	13.92
贵州 Guizhou	1041.07	80.17			74.10	1.08	
云南 Yunnan	3157.36					0.65	0.09
西藏 Tibet							
陕西 Shaanxi	631.25	8.08		18.37		1.52	1778.16
甘肃 Gansu	354.98	0.08		11.03		0.36	78.91
青海 Qinghai						0.06	221.49
宁夏 Ningxia	11.50					0.26	
新疆 Xinjiang	70.00					0.39	2406.43

注：1.卷烟2003年及以前计量单位为万箱。
2.原煤1999-2004年产量为经济普查后修订数据。

a) Unit of cigarettes in 2003 and before was 10 000 boxes.
b) Data of coal in 1999-2004 were revised data according to the First National Economic Census.

14-24 续表 2 continued

年 份 Year / 地 区 Region		天然气 (亿立方米) Natural Gas (100 million cu.m)	发电量 (亿千瓦小时) Electricity (100 million kwh)	#水 电 Hydropower	生 铁 (万吨) Pig Iron (10 000 tons)	粗 钢 (万吨) Crude Steel (10 000 tons)	钢 材 (万吨) Rolled Steel (10 000 tons)	水 泥 (万吨) Cement (10000 tons)	平板玻璃 (万重量箱) Plate Glass (10 000 weight cases)
	1978	137.30	2566.00	446.00	3479.00	3178.00	2208.00	6524.00	1784.00
	1980	142.70	3006.00	582.00	3802.00	3712.00	2716.00	7986.00	2466.00
	1985	129.30	4107.00	924.00	4384.00	4679.00	3693.00	14595.00	4942.00
	1989	150.50	5848.00	1183.00	5820.00	6159.00	4859.00	21029.00	8442.00
	1990	152.98	6212.00	1267.00	6238.00	6635.00	5153.00	20971.00	8067.00
	1991	160.73	6775.00	1247.00	6765.00	7100.00	5638.00	25261.00	8712.00
	1992	157.88	7539.00	1307.00	7589.00	8094.00	6697.00	30822.00	9359.00
	1993	167.65	8395.00	1518.00	8739.00	8956.00	7716.00	36788.00	11086.00
	1994	175.59	9281.00	1674.00	9741.00	9261.00	8428.00	42118.00	11925.00
	1995	179.47	10070.30	1905.77	10529.27	9535.99	8979.80	47560.59	15731.71
	1996	201.14	10813.10	1879.66	10722.50	10124.06	9338.02	49118.90	16069.37
	1997	227.03	11355.53	1959.83	11511.41	10894.17	9978.93	51173.80	16630.70
	1998	232.79	11670.00	1988.90	11863.67	11559.00	10737.80	53600.00	17194.03
	1999	251.98	12393.00	1965.80	12539.24	12426.00	12109.78	57300.00	17419.79
	2000	272.00	13556.00	2224.14	13101.48	12850.00	13146.00	59700.00	18352.20
	2001	303.29	14808.02	2774.32	15554.25	15163.44	16067.61	66103.99	20964.12
	2002	326.61	16540.00	2879.74	17084.60	18236.61	19251.59	72500.00	23445.56
	2003	350.15	19105.75	2836.81	21366.68	22233.60	24108.01	86208.11	27702.60
	2004	414.60	22033.09	3535.44	26830.99	28291.09	31975.72	96681.99	37026.17
	2005	509.44	25002.60	3970.17	34375.19	35323.98	37771.14	106884.79	40210.24
北 京	Beijing		213.35	4.71	813.88	827.56	966.29	1183.80	293.42
天 津	Tianjin	8.79	369.06		660.24	955.27	1670.15	518.64	458.29
河 北	Hebei	6.92	1338.63	5.61	6841.25	7424.99	6591.12	7686.04	7598.18
山 西	Shanxi	3.24	1311.97	20.32	3229.80	1654.72	1368.60	2310.68	360.24
内蒙古	Inner Mongolia		1056.59	11.55	922.69	805.49	747.77	1632.25	1144.60
辽 宁	Liaoning	11.72	904.21	56.73	3113.95	3059.05	3235.93	2680.67	1853.96
吉 林	Jilin	5.40	433.43	78.30	408.64	462.01	479.36	1718.62	426.49
黑龙江	Heilongjiang	24.43	596.02	14.70	178.10	247.73	236.69	1214.48	520.81
上 海	Shanghai	6.04	733.97		1582.89	1927.96	2108.63	1045.21	830.61
江 苏	Jiangsu	0.64	2120.00	2.66	2697.28	3301.09	4424.63	9681.49	5233.13
浙 江	Zhejiang	0.03	1456.42	135.11	294.88	540.17	803.45	9128.97	2109.14
安 徽	Anhui		648.41	12.52	1105.71	1109.68	1198.96	3352.56	507.72
福 建	Fujian		778.25	291.00	399.03	391.48	729.67	2791.64	1438.57
江 西	Jiangxi		373.49	67.88	821.73	963.39	1023.33	3700.50	626.36
山 东	Shandong	9.25	1911.39	1.30	3217.30	3188.07	3010.86	14425.85	4761.21
河 南	Henan	20.14	1414.68	67.91	1064.85	1229.17	1338.96	6487.18	3434.69
湖 北	Hubei	1.12	1289.80	813.65	1453.29	1568.97	1580.87	4485.69	1626.88
湖 南	Hunan		644.41	241.28	1027.92	976.58	965.96	3742.32	1091.16
广 东	Guangdong	44.75	2278.59	207.74	535.43	940.42	1415.79	8228.92	2372.73
广 西	Guangxi		446.04	195.82	485.39	496.29	519.88	3306.13	515.74
海 南	Hainan	7.32	82.19	10.64	4.55	0.23	14.86	446.42	
重 庆	Chongqing	3.27	253.90	67.32	246.95	277.01	294.70	2226.15	218.27
四 川	Sichuan	145.23	1018.77	653.35	1060.50	1094.45	1172.20	4480.19	1347.41
贵 州	Guizhou	0.53	797.65	213.35	286.36	239.13	214.89	1685.10	
云 南	Yunnan	0.22	624.20	349.19	845.92	513.41	486.93	2832.62	270.15
西 藏	Tibet		13.34	12.10				128.15	
陕 西	Shaanxi	80.59	548.80	50.54	316.37	307.49	337.80	2164.86	541.14
甘 肃	Gansu	0.84	506.17	165.57	468.72	458.44	452.25	1415.99	339.62
青 海	Qinghai	22.26	215.89	160.58	6.06	50.53	48.47	370.62	90.35
宁 夏	Ningxia		312.87	16.41	25.28	0.62	9.21	567.58	66.42
新 疆	Xinjiang	106.71	310.11	42.33	260.23	312.58	322.93	1245.47	132.95

14-24 续表 3 continued

年份 地区	Year Region	乙烯（万吨） Ethylene (10 000 tons)	硫酸（万吨） Sulfuric Acid (10 000 tons)	纯碱（万吨） Soda Ash (10 000 tons)	烧碱（万吨） Caustic Soda (10 000 tons)	农用氮、磷、钾化肥（万吨） Chemical Fertilizer (10 000 tons)	化学农药原药（万吨） Chemical Pesticide (10 000 tons)	初级形态的塑料（万吨） Primary Plastic (10 000 tons)
	1978	38.00	661.0	132.90	164.00	869.30	53.30	67.90
	1980	49.00	764.3	161.30	192.30	1232.10	53.70	89.80
	1985	65.20	676.4	201.10	235.30	1322.20	21.10	123.40
	1989	139.57	1153.3	304.20	321.10	1802.50	20.80	200.80
	1990	157.20	1196.9	379.50	335.40	1879.70	22.80	227.00
	1991	176.10	1332.9	393.60	354.10	1979.50	25.50	283.00
	1992	200.30	1408.7	455.00	379.50	2047.90	28.10	330.80
	1993	202.70	1336.5	534.90	395.40	1956.30	25.70	359.90
	1994	212.90	1536.5	581.40	429.60	2272.80	29.00	401.40
	1995	240.10	1811.0	597.71	531.82	2548.14	41.65	516.87
	1996	304.00	1883.6	669.29	573.78	2809.04	44.75	576.86
	1997	358.60	2036.9	725.76	574.40	2820.96	52.67	685.76
	1998	377.30	2171.0	744.00	539.37	3010.00	55.90	692.58
	1999	435.00	2356.0	766.00	580.14	3251.00	62.50	871.10
	2000	470.00	2427.0	834.00	667.88	3186.00	60.70	1087.51
	2001	480.60	2696.3	914.37	787.96	3383.01	78.72	1288.71
	2002	543.02	3050.4	1033.15	877.97	3791.00	92.90	1455.67
	2003	611.77	3371.2	1133.56	945.27	3881.31	76.72	1652.08
	2004	629.85	3928.9	1334.70	1041.12	4804.82	82.08	2366.50
	2005	755.54	4544.7	1421.08	1239.98	5177.86	114.73	2308.86
北 京	Beijing	99.05	5.23		13.50	4.20	0.09	138.43
天 津	Tianjin	20.71	11.95	86.87	80.45	16.03	1.28	116.64
河 北	Hebei		97.49	177.37	56.56	214.60	3.35	67.35
山 西	Shanxi		75.67	15.59	40.68	349.45	0.20	29.28
内蒙古	Inner Mongolia		48.92	75.97	30.93	60.89	1.06	20.23
辽 宁	Liaoning	47.13	120.72	74.86	53.59	89.60	2.67	121.56
吉 林	Jilin	51.13	18.04		9.32	17.17	1.15	52.19
黑龙江	Heilongjiang	55.56	10.23	0.04	15.55	49.46	0.20	108.60
上 海	Shanghai	160.44	33.32		41.72	3.14	1.49	237.89
江 苏	Jiangsu	111.71	354.33	221.42	155.19	294.70	33.54	374.52
浙 江	Zhejiang		146.12	13.28	76.74	63.13	19.34	120.08
安 徽	Anhui		202.54	24.09	18.85	235.49	3.67	28.53
福 建	Fujian		41.06	19.23	25.51	64.41	0.92	53.37
江 西	Jiangxi		113.19		24.62	53.54	1.47	15.60
山 东	Shandong	83.77	519.31	260.16	245.35	612.70	11.34	202.99
河 南	Henan	19.16	124.76	118.65	67.84	421.12	5.07	74.98
湖 北	Hubei		440.34	71.13	41.02	408.82	8.01	47.01
湖 南	Hunan		183.86	27.53	33.79	261.39	9.55	37.87
广 东	Guangdong	56.17	172.64	31.91	22.77	39.34	1.19	220.22
广 西	Guangxi		170.22	0.27	24.02	83.94	1.91	7.80
海 南	Hainan		1.27			62.65		
重 庆	Chongqing		150.08	9.18	6.91	130.90	0.42	0.54
四 川	Sichuan		319.41	106.51	75.49	518.28	5.97	71.02
贵 州	Guizhou		341.1		8.84	275.35	0.09	
云 南	Yunnan		600.55	16.20	5.23	265.84	0.11	3.06
西 藏	Tibet							
陕 西	Shaanxi		82.29	21.91	10.47	124.92	0.52	11.37
甘 肃	Gansu	24.57	122.69	18.01	7.31	113.51	0.04	45.92
青 海	Qinghai		6.11	17.38	1.06	161.12	0.05	3.05
宁 夏	Ningxia		18.93	0.94	17.08	80.82	0.02	20.15
新 疆	Xinjiang	26.14	12.29	12.58	29.59	101.35	0.01	78.61

注：初级形态的塑料2004年及以前指标名称为塑料树脂及共聚物，简称塑料。此项指标2004年数据为经济普查后的修订数。

a) Before 2004, the primary plastic was called plastic colophony copolymer, or plastic in abbreviation. And of 2004, it was revised figure according to the First National Economic Census.

14-24 续表 4 continued

年份 Year / 地区 Region	金属切削机床 (万台) Metal-cutting Machine Tools (10 000 units)	汽车 (万辆) Motor Vehicles (10 000 units)	#轿车 Cars	大中型拖拉机 (万台) Tractors (10 000 units)	微型电子计算机 (万台) Micro-Computers (10 000 units)	集成电路 (万块) Integrated Circuit (10 000 units)	移动通信手持机 (万台) Mobile Telephones (10 000 units)
1978	18.3	14.91		11.35		3041	
1980	13.4	22.23	0.54	9.77		1684	
1985	16.7	43.72	0.90	4.50		6385	
1989	17.9	58.35	3.58	3.98	7.54	13156	
1990	13.5	51.40	3.50	3.94	8.21	10838	
1991	16.4	71.42	6.87	5.27	16.25	17049	
1992	22.9	106.67	16.17	5.70	12.62	16099	
1993	26.2	129.85	22.29	3.77	14.66	20101	
1994	20.7	136.69	26.87	4.67	24.57	48462	
1995	20.3	145.27	33.70	6.33	83.57	551686	
1996	17.7	147.52	38.29	8.37	138.83	388987	
1997	18.7	158.25	48.60	8.24	206.55	255455	
1998	11.9	163.00	50.71	6.78	291.40	262577	
1999	14.2	183.20	57.10	6.54	405.00	415000	
2000	17.7	207.00	60.70	4.10	672.00	588000	5248
2001	25.6	234.17	70.36	3.82	877.65	636288	8032
2002	30.9	325.10	109.20	4.54	1463.51	963101	12146
2003	30.6	444.39	207.08	4.88	3216.70	1483101	18231
2004	48.7	509.11	227.63	11.38	5974.90	2355100	23752
2005	51.1	570.49	277.01	16.33	8084.89	2699729	30354
北京 Beijing	1.0	58.70	22.09		649.57	125708	8948
天津 Tianjin	0.1	32.78	32.56	1.17	2.15	51958	6310
河北 Hebei	0.2	19.36					
山西 Shanxi	0.2	0.01			0.68		0
内蒙古 Inner Mongolia		0.69			0.80		99
辽宁 Liaoning	11.3	14.98	1.69		26.67	179	102
吉林 Jilin	0.1	58.16	29.94		0.03	134	
黑龙江 Heilongjiang	0.6	23.61	4.99		3.93		
上海 Shanghai	3.0	48.45	48.09	1.37	2176.17	717607	1939
江苏 Jiangsu	8.4	30.05	14.16	4.34	2996.13	820229	2846
浙江 Zhejiang	6.7	13.13	11.42	1.59	139.57	161285	2791
安徽 Anhui	1.2	34.25	18.16		4.27	19	
福建 Fujian	0.4	6.61	3.70		371.67	13996	1166
江西 Jiangxi	0.4	20.61	4.50	0.08	5.07		
山东 Shandong	8.9	22.41	8.70	4.38	39.44	617	1232
河南 Henan	1.1	3.43		3.04	0.42		
湖北 Hubei	0.4	38.90	14.17	0.15			587
湖南 Hunan	0.2	2.99	0.36			14	
广东 Guangdong	2.5	40.22	36.86		1664.12	563709	4184
广西 Guangxi	0.4	37.67	2.68	0.05	1.74		94
海南 Hainan		7.31	5.88				
重庆 Chongqing	0.5	42.16	15.33	0.01			
四川 Sichuan	0.9	4.76		0.15	0.36	90	
贵州 Guizhou	0.1					908	55
云南 Yunnan	1.0	5.05	0.11				
西藏 Tibet							
陕西 Shaanxi	1.3	4.08	1.61		2.10		
甘肃 Gansu	0.2					243278	
青海 Qinghai	0.1						
宁夏 Ningxia	0.3						
新疆 Xinjiang		0.11					

14-25 工 业 产 品 产 量

Output of Industrial Products

产品名称		Item		2004	2005
化学纤维	(万吨)	Chemical Fiber	(10 000 tons)	1699.80	1664.79
纱	(万吨)	Yarn	(10 000 tons)	1291.34	1450.54
布	(亿米)	Cloth	(100 million m)	482.10	484.39
机制纸及纸板	(万吨)	Machine-made Paper and Paperboard	(10 000 tons)	5413.27	6205.42
家用电冰箱	(万台)	Home Refrigerators	(10 000 sets)	3007.59	2987.06
家用洗衣机	(万台)	Home Washing Machines	(10 000 sets)	2533.41	3035.52
家用吸尘器	(万台)	Vacuum Cleaners	(10 000 sets)	5015.42	4679.31
家用电风扇	(万台)	Electric Fans	(10 000 sets)	14169.67	12022.39
房间空气调节器	(万台)	Air Conditioners	(10 000 sets)	6390.33	6764.57
吸排油烟机	(万台)	Smoke Absorbers	(10 000 sets)	677.44	730.10
合成洗涤剂	(万吨)	Synthetic Detergents	(10 000 tons)	465.17	516.95
原盐	(万吨)	Salt	(10 000 tons)	4043.44	4661.06
成品糖	(万吨)	Refined Sugar	(10 000 tons)	1033.70	912.37
卷烟	(亿支)	Cigarettes	(100 million pieces)	18736.35	19389.08
罐头	(万吨)	Canned Food	(10 000 tons)	533.56	500.32
啤酒	(万千升)	Beer	(10 000 kiloliter)	2948.59	3126.05
精制食用植物油	(万吨)	Refined Edible Vegetable Oil	(10 000 tons)	1682.63	2070.96
中成药	(万吨)	Traditional Chinese Medicine	(10 000 tons)	146.24	106.48
化学药品原药	(万吨)	Chemical Medicines	(10 000 tons)	103.05	126.70
彩色电视机	(万台)	Color Television Sets	(10 000 sets)	7431.83	8283.22
录相机	(万台)	Video Recorders	(10 000 sets)	1963.43	1145.96
组合音响	(万台)	Hi-Fi Stereo Component Players	(10 000 sets)	5466.20	7092.82
照相机	(万台)	Cameras	(10 000 sets)	7891.40	8199.00
#数码照相机	(万台)	Digital Cameras	(10 000 sets)	4207.59	5522.97
农用氮、磷、钾化肥	(万吨)	Chemical Fertilizers	(10 000 tons)	4804.82	5177.86
#氮肥	(万吨)	Nitrogen Fertilizers	(10 000 tons)	3357.73	3809.03
磷肥	(万吨)	Phosphate Fertilizers	(10 000 tons)	1246.78	1206.20
化学农药原药	(万吨)	Chemical Pesticides	(10 000 tons)	82.08	114.73
初级形态的塑料	(万吨)	Primary Plastic	(10 000 tons)	2366.50	2308.86
合成橡胶	(万吨)	Synthetic Rubber	(10 000 tons)	184.04	205.13
橡胶轮胎外胎	(万条)	Tires	(10 000 tires)	32709.37	34390.06
采矿设备	(万吨)	Mining Equipment	(10 000 tone)	196.29	163.46
炼油、化工专用设备	(万吨)	Equipments for Oil Refining and Chemical Industry	(10 000 tons)	61.35	61.54
发电设备	(万千瓦)	Power Generating Equipment	(10 000 kw)	7137.88	9200.00
金属切削机床	(万台)	Metal-cutting Machine Tools	(10 000 units)	48.72	51.14
汽车	(万辆)	Motor Vehicles	(10 000 sets)	509.11	570.49
#载货汽车	(万辆)	Trucks	(10 000 sets)	111.56	149.46
公路客车	(万辆)	Buses	(10 000 sets)	48.17	128.20
轿车	(万辆)	Cars	(10 000 sets)	227.63	277.01
摩托车	(万辆)	Motorcycles	(10 000 sets)	1674.92	1690.93
两轮自行车	(万辆)	Bicycles	(10 000 sets)	7906.22	6900.64

注：1.纱包括纯棉纱、棉混纺纱、纯化纤纱，不包括棉线、代用纤维纱和手工纺纱。
2.布包括纯棉布、棉混纺布、纯化纤布，不包括代用纤维布、手工织布。
3.农用化肥按有效成分100%计算。
4.发电设备指500千瓦以上的,包括水轮发电机组、汽轮发电机和燃气轮发电机。
5.金属切削机床不包括台钻、砂轮机、抛光机。
6.家用电风扇、中成药、化学药品原药、照相机、初级形态的塑料、橡胶轮胎外胎、采矿设备、两轮自行车、内燃机、铁路客车2004年产量作了修订。

a) Yarn includes pure and blended cotton yarn, pure chemical-fiber yarn, but excludes cotton thread, substitute fiber yarn and hand-made yarn.
b) Cloth includes pure and blended cotton cloth, pure chemical-fiber cloth and canvas, but excludes substitute fiber cloth, hand-woven cloth and cord fabric.
c) The output of chemical fertilizers is calculated on the basis of 100 % effective content.
d) Power generating equipment refers to units with a generating capacity of 500 kw and over, including hydroturbine generating units, steam turbine generating units and gas turbine generating units.
e) Metal-cutting machine tools exclude bench drills, grinders and polishing machines.
f) Data on output of the following products in year 2004 were revised: electric fans, traditional Chinese medicines, chemical medicines, cameras, primary plastic, tires, mining equipment, bicycles, internal combustion engines and railway passenger coaches.

14-25 续表 continued

产品名称	Item	2004	2005
大中型拖拉机 (万台)	Large and Medium Tractors (10 000 sets)	11.38	16.33
内燃机 (万千瓦)	Internal Combustion Engines (10 000 kw)	31893.56	36563.46
铁路客车 (辆)	Railway Passenger Coaches (unit)	1867.00	2001.00
铁路货车 (万辆)	Railway Freight Wagons (10 000 units)	3.17	3.92
程控交换机 (万线)	Program-controlled Switchboards (10 000 lines)	7625.22	7720.90
移动通信手持机 (万台)	Mobile Telephones (10 000 units)	23751.58	30354.21
电话单机 (万台)	Telephone Sets (10 000 units)	19515.71	18861.52
传真机 (万台)	Fax Machines (10 000 units)	851.16	1068.15
微型电子计算机 (万台)	Micro-computers (10 000 units)	5974.90	8084.89
#笔记本计算机 (万台)	Notebook PCs (10 000 units)	3238.38	4564.99
显示器 (万台)	Display (10 000 units)	14533.58	15182.77
集成电路 (亿块)	Integrated Circuits (100 million units)	235.51	269.97
复印机械 (万台)	Copying Machines (10 000 units)	324.57	403.56
原煤 (亿吨)	Coal (100 million tons)	19.92	22.05
原油 (万吨)	Crude Petroleum Oil (10 000 tons)	17587.33	18135.29
汽油 (万吨)	Gasoline (10 000 tons)	5277.99	5409.22
柴油 (万吨)	Diesel Oil (10 000 tons)	10178.66	11079.42
天然气 (亿立方米)	Natural Gas (100 million cu.m)	414.60	509.44
发电量 (亿千瓦小时)	Electricity (100 million kwh)	22033.09	25002.60
#水电	Hydropower	3535.44	3970.17
火电	Thermal Power	17955.88	20473.36
生铁 (万吨)	Pig Iron (10 000 tons)	26830.99	34375.19
粗钢 (万吨)	Crude Steel (10 000 tons)	28291.09	35323.98
钢材 (万吨)	Rolled Steel (10 000 tons)	31975.72	37771.14
#重轨	Heavy Rail	172.07	192.67
大型型钢	Rolled-steel, Large	809.46	752.04
中小型型钢	Rolled-steel, Medium and Small	1365.55	2830.73
棒材	Steel Bar	2617.65	2899.58
钢筋	Corrugated Steel Bar	6654.61	6912.72
盘条(线材)	Wire Rod	5148.51	6094.74
特厚板	Heavy Steel Plate	182.38	237.40
厚钢板	Thick Steel Plate	832.85	1154.75
热轧薄板	Hot-roll Thin Steel Plate	241.36	637.55
冷轧薄板	Non-hot-roll Thin Steel Plate	549.60	969.21
中厚宽钢带	Medium Wide Steel Belt	3103.66	3713.87
镀层板(带)	Plated Plate (Belt)	765.20	877.88
无缝钢管	Seamless Steel Pipe	1005.65	1033.32
十种有色金属 (万吨)	Ten Kinds of Nonferrous Metals (10 000 tons)	1441.12	1635.00
#精炼铜	Refined Copper	220.21	260.68
电解铝	Electrolyzed Aluminum	669.04	778.68
氧化铝 (万吨)	Aluminum Oxide (10 000 tons)	697.86	859.22
焦炭 (万吨)	Coke (10 000 tons)	20618.63	25411.70
水泥 (万吨)	Cement (10 000 tons)	96681.99	106884.79
平板玻璃 (万重量箱)	Plain Glass (10 000 weight cases)	37026.17	40210.24
乙烯 (万吨)	Ethylene (10 000 tons)	629.85	755.54
硫酸 (万吨)	Sulfuric Acid (10 000 tons)	3928.89	4544.66
碳酸钠 (纯碱) (万吨)	Soda Ash (10 000 tons)	1334.70	1421.08
氢氧化钠 (烧碱) (万吨)	Caustic Soda (10 000 tons)	1041.12	1239.98
合成氨 (万吨)	Synthetic Ammonia (10 000 tons)	4135.06	4596.25

注：1.拖拉机是指14.7千瓦及以上的轮式和履带式拖拉机。用本厂自产的拖拉机装配的推土机，只计推土机产量，不计拖拉机产量。
2.原煤包括无烟煤、烟煤、褐煤,不包括石煤。原煤2004年产量为经济普查后修订数据。
3.原油包括天然原油和人造原油。

a) Tractors refer to both wheel and crawler tractors with a haulage capacity of 14.7 kw and over. The tractors which are refitted into bulldozers by the same tractor factories are deducted.

b) Coal includes anthracite, bituminous coal and lignite, but excludes stone coal. Data of coal in 2004 were revised according to the First National Economic Census.

c) Crude oil includes natural and synthetic crude oil.

14-26 规模以上工业主要产品生产能力（2004年）

Production Capacity of Main Products of Industrial Enterprises above Designated Size (2004)

产品名称		Item		年末生产能力 Production Capacity (Year-end)
原煤（按核定能力填报）	（万吨）	Coal	(10 000 tons)	174448.6
洗煤	（万处理吨）	Coal Washing	(10 000 tons)	56873.4
天然原油	（万吨）	Crude Petroleum Oil	(10 000 tons)	18276.0
天然气	（亿立方米）	Natural Gas	(100 million cu.m)	537.4
铁矿石原矿	（万实物吨）	Ironstone in Original Iron Ores	(10 000 tons)	35082.9
铜选矿产品含铜量	（万吨）	Copper Content of Copper Dressing Products	(10 000 tons)	72.4
铅选矿产品含铅量	（万吨）	Lead Content of Lead Dressing Products	(10 000 tons)	109.2
锌选矿产品含锌量	（万吨）	Zinc Content of Zinc Dressing Products	(10 000 tons)	218.8
锡选矿产品含锡量	（万吨）	Tin Content of Tin Dressing Products	(10 000 tons)	10.8
钨精矿折合量	（吨）	Concentrated Tungsten	(100 % equivalent, ton)	115840.0
钼精矿折合量	（吨）	Concentrated Molybdenum	(100% equivalent, ton)	117685.7
硫铁矿石（折含硫 35%）	（万折合吨）	Pyrite Ore (converted into 35% sulphur)	(10 000/ton)	1436.4
磷矿石（折含五氧化二磷30%）	（万折合吨）	Phosphorite Ore (converted into 30% phosphorous pentoxide)	(10 000/ton)	3129.2
原盐	（万吨）	Salt	(10 000 tons)	4250.2
方便面	（万吨）	Instant Noodles	(10 000 tones)	532.4
味精	（万吨）	Monosodium Glutamate	(10 000 tons)	186.8
卷烟	（亿支）	Cigarettes	(100 million pieces)	27983.6
纤维板	（万立方米）	Fiberboard	(10 000 cu.m)	2930.8
刨花板	（万立方米）	Flakeboard	(10 000 tones)	858.1
机械化焦炉生产的焦炭	（万吨）	Machine-made Coke	(10 000 tons)	27446.7
硫酸（折100%）	（万吨）	Sulfuric Acid	(100% equivalent, 10 000 tons)	4562.8
烧碱（折100%）	（万吨）	Caustic Soda	(100% equivalent, 10 000 tons)	1266.0
纯碱（碳酸钠）	（万吨）	Soda Ash		1436.4
乙烯	（万吨）	Ethylene		603.4
纯苯	（万吨）	Benzene		262.6
精甲醇	（万吨）	Extracted Methanol	(10 000 tons)	740.9
合成氨	（万吨）	Synthetic Ammonia	(10 000 tons)	5044.0
尿素（折含氮100%）	（万吨）	Urea	(100% equivalent, 10 000 tons)	2852.6
氯化钾（折含氧化钾100%）	（万吨）	Potassium Chloride	(100% equivalent, 10 000 tons)	242.6
涂料（油漆）	（万吨）	Paint	(10 000 tones)	700.6
染料	（万吨）	Dye	(10 000 tones)	170.4
聚丙烯树脂	（万吨）	Polypropylene Colophony	(10 000 tons)	570.9
合成橡胶	（万吨）	Synthetic Rubber	(10 000 tones)	239.2
合成纤维单体	（万吨）	Synthetic Fiber Monomer	(10 000 pieces)	738.7
橡胶轮胎外胎	（万条）	Tires	(10 000 tires)	44113.9
水泥熟料	（万吨）	Cement Chamotte	(10 000 tons)	79389.6
水泥	（万吨）	Cement	(10 000 tons)	131226.2
平板玻璃	（万重量箱）	Flat Glass	(10 000 weight cases)	33311.3
耐火材料制品	（万吨）	Fire-resistant Products	(10 000 tons)	2974.7

14-26 续表 continued

产品名称		Item		年末生产能力 Production Capacity (Year-end)
石墨及炭素制品	(万吨)	Graphite and Carbon Products	(10 000 tons)	1002.4
生铁	(万吨)	Pig Iron	(10 000 tons)	35956.3
粗钢	(万吨)	Crude Steel	(10 000 ton)	35694.1
钢材	(万吨)	Rolled Steel	(10 000 ton)	46317.3
锡冶炼能力	(吨)	Tin Smelting Capacity	(ton)	133743.3
氧化铝生产能力	(万吨)	Production Capacity of Alumina	(10 000 tons)	730.9
金属镁冶炼能力	(万吨)	Magnesium Metal	(10 000 tons)	71.8
铜材加工能力	(万吨)	Processing Capacity of Rolled Steel	(10 000 tons)	683.4
铝材加工能力	(万吨)	Processing Capacity of Aluminium	(10 000 ton)	821.8
电站锅炉	(蒸发量吨)	Boilers in Power Stations	(evaporation/ton)	318129.0
工业锅炉	(蒸发量吨)	Industrial Boilers	(evaporation/ton)	342979.4
叉车	(台)	Forklifts	(unit)	144360.0
滚动轴承	(亿套)	Rolling Bearings	(100 million sets)	102.1
缝纫机	(万台)	Sewing Machines	(10 000 sets)	1433.0
汽车	(万辆)	Motor Vehicles	(10 000 sets)	867.0
汽轮发电机组	(万千瓦)	Steam Turbogenerator Sets	(10 000 kw)	4351.1
家用电冰箱(家用冷冻冷藏箱)	(万台)	Household Refrigerators	(10 000 sets)	4377.0
房间空气调节器	(万台)	Air Conditioners	(10 000 sets)	9633.6
家用洗衣机	(万台)	Household Washing Machines	(10 000 sets)	3654.6
移动通信手持机（手机）	(万台)	Mobile Telephones	(10 000 units)	43014.9
电话单机	(万台)	Telephones	(10 000 units)	26147.7
传真机	(万台)	Fax Machines	(10 000 units)	997.9
程控交换机	(万线)	Program-controlled Switchboards	(10 000 lines)	9868.3
台式微型计算机	(万台)	Microcomputers	(10 000 sets)	4493.1
笔记本计算机	(万台)	Nobebook PCs	(10 000 sets)	5615.3
打印机	(万台)	Printers	(10 000 sets)	5721.8
显示器	(万台)	Displays	(10 000 sets)	21889.2
彩色电视机	(万台)	Color Television Sets	(10 000 sets)	12125.0
黑白电视机	(万台)	Black and White TV Sets	(10 000 sets)	1050.8
激光视盘机	(万台)	CD-Videos	(10 000 sets)	20367.2
组合音响	(万台)	Hi-Fi Stereo Component Players	(10 000 sets)	12001.3
彩色显像管	(万只)	Chromoscopes	(10 000 pieces)	11620.9
集成电路	(亿块)	Integrated Circuits	(100 million pieces)	299.3
照相机	(万台)	Cameras	(10 000 units)	10657.5
#数码照相机	(万台)	Digital Cameras	(10 000 units)	5655.2
发电设备容量总计	(万千瓦)	Installation Capacity of Power Generation	(10 000 kw)	42994.8
1.火力发电设备容量	(万千瓦)	1. Thermal Power Generation	(10 000 kw)	31606.0
2.水力发电设备容量	(万千瓦)	2. Hydro Power Generation	(10 000 kw)	9746.8
3.核能发电设备容量	(万千瓦)	3. Nuclear Power Generation	(10 000 kw)	700.0

注：照相机、橡胶轮胎外轮2004年生产能力作了修订。

a) Revisions were made for the production capacity of cameras and tyres in 2004.

主要统计指标解释

工业　指从事自然资源的开采，对采掘品和农产品进行加工和再加工的物质生产部门。具体包括：(1)对自然资源的开采，如采矿、晒盐等(但不包括禽兽捕猎和水产捕捞)；(2)对农副产品的加工、再加工，如粮油加工、食品加工、缫丝、纺织、制革等；(3)对采掘品的加工、再加工，如炼铁、炼钢、化工生产、石油加工、机器制造、木材加工等，以及电力、自来水、煤气的生产和供应等；(4)对工业品的修理、翻新，如机器设备的修理、交通运输工具(如汽车)的修理等。

工业统计调查单位为独立核算法人工业企业。

独立核算法人工业企业指从事工业生产经营活动的单位。独立核算法人工业企业应同时具备以下条件：①依法成立，有自己的名称、组织机构和场所，能够承担民事责任；②独立拥有和使用资产，承担负债，有权与其他单位签订合同；③独立核算盈亏，并能够编制资产负债表。

本年鉴中涉及的企业登记注册类型：

国有及国有控股企业　指国有企业加上国有控股企业。国有企业(即原全民所有制工业或国营工业)指企业全部资产归国家所有，并按《中华人民共和国企业法人登记管理条例》规定登记注册的非公司制的经济组织。包括国有企业、国有独资公司和国有联营企业。1957年以前的公私合营和私营工业，后均改造为国营工业，1992年改为国有工业，这部分工业的资料不单独分列时，均包括在国有企业内。国有控股企业是对混合所有制经济的企业进行的“国有控股”分类。它是指这些企业的全部资产中国有资产(股份)相对其他所有者中的任何一个所有者占资(股)最多的企业。该分组反映了国有经济控股情况。

集体企业　指企业资产归集体所有，并按《中华人民共和国企业法人登记管理条例》规定登记注册的经济组织。是社会主义公有制经济的组成部分。包括城乡所有使用集体投资举办的企业，以及部分个人通过集资自愿放弃所有权并依法经工商行政管理机关认定为集体所有制的企业。

股份合作企业　指以合作制为基础，由企业职工共同出资入股，吸收一定比例的社会资产投资组建，实行自主经营，自负盈亏，共同劳动，民主管理，按劳分配与按股分红相结合的一种集体经济组织。

联营企业　指两个及两个以上相同或不同所有制性质的企业法人或事业单位法人，按自愿、平等、互利的原则，共同投资组成的经济组织。联营企业包括：

国有联营企业指国有企业与国有企业间的联营；

集体联营企业指集体企业与集体企业间的联营；

国有与集体联营企业指国有企业与集体企业间的联营。

有限责任公司　指根据《中华人民共和国公司登记管理条例》规定登记注册，由两个以上，五十个以下的股东共同出资，每个股东以其所认缴的出资额对公司承担有限责任，公司以其全部资产对其债务承担责任的经济组织。有限责任公司包括国有独资公司以及其他有限责任公司。

股份有限公司　指根据《中华人民共和国企业法人登记管理条例》规定登记注册，其全部注册资本由等额股份构成并通过发行股票筹集资本，股东以其认购的股份对公司承担有限责任，公司以其全部资产对其债务承担责任的经济组织。

私营企业　指由自然人投资设立或由自然人控股，以雇佣劳动为基础的营利性经济组织。包括按照《公司法》、《合伙企业法》、《私营企业暂行条例》规定登记注册的私营有限责任公司、私营股份有限公司、私营合伙企业和私营独资企业。

港、澳、台商投资企业　指企业注册登记类型中的港、澳、台资合资、合作、独资经营企业和股份有限公司之和。

外商投资企业　指企业注册登记类型中的中外合资、合作经营企业、外资企业和外商投资股份有限公司之和。

“三资”企业系指港、澳、台商投资企业和外资企业的简称。

轻工业　指主要提供生活消费品和制作手工工具的工业。按其所使用的原料不同，可分为两大类：(1)以农产品为原料的轻工业，是指直接或间接以农产品为基本原料的轻工业。主要包括食品制造、饮料制造、烟草加工、纺织、缝纫、皮革和毛皮制作、造纸以及印刷等工业；(2)以非农产品为原料的轻工业，是指以工业品为原料的轻工业。主要包括文教体育用品、化学药品制造、合成纤维制造、日用化学制品、日用玻璃制品、日用金属制品、手工工具制造、医疗器械制造、文化和办公用机械制造等工业。

重工业　指为国民经济各部门提供物质技术基础的主要生产资料的工业。按其生产性质和产品用途，可以分为下列三类：(1)采掘(伐)工业，是指对自然资源的开采，包括石油开采、煤炭开采、金属矿开采、非金属矿开采等工业；(2)原材料工业，指向国民经济各部门提供基本材料、动力和燃料的工业。包括金属冶炼及加工、炼焦及焦炭、化学、化工原料、水泥、人造板以及电力、石油和煤炭加工等工业；(3)加工工业，是指对工业原材料进行再加工制造的工业。包括装备国民经济各部门的机械设备制造工业、金属结构、水泥制品等工业，以及为农业提供的生产资料如化肥、农药等工业。

根据上述划分原则，修理业中以重工业产品为修理作业对象的划为重工业，反之划为轻工业。

工业总产值

(1)定义：

工业总产值是以货币形式表现的，工业企业在一定时期内生产的工业最终产品或提供工业性劳务活动的总价值量。它反映一定时间内工业生产的总规模和总水平。

(2)计算原则：

工业生产的原则，即凡是企业在报告期生产的经检验合格的产品，不管是否在报告期销售，均包括在内。

最终产品的原则，即凡是计入工业总产值的产品，必须是本企业生产的经检验合格的，不需要再进行任何加工的最终产品。如果企业有中间产品(半成品)对外销售，则对外销售的中间产品应视为企业的最终产品。

工厂法原则，即工业总产值是以工业企业作为基本计算(核算)单位，即按企业的最终产品计算工业总产值。按这种方法计算的工业总产值，不允许同一产品价值在企业内部重复计算，不能把企业内部各个车间(分厂)生产的成果相加，但允许企业间的重复计算。

(3)内容及计算方法：

1995年全国工业普查对工业总产值(原规定)的内容及计算原则和方法做了某些修订，修订后的工业总产值(新规定)包括三项内容：即本期生产成品价值、对外加工费收入、在制品半成品期末期初差额价值三部分。

本期生产成品价值：指企业本期生产，并在报告期内不再进行加工，经检验、包装入库的全部工业成品(半成品)价值合计，包括企业生产的自制设备及提供给本企业在建工程、其他非工业部门和福利部门等单位使用的成品价值。本期生产成品价值为按自备原材料生产的产品的数量乘以本期不含增值税(销项税额)的产品实际销售平均单价计算；会计核算中按成本价格转帐的自制设备和自产自用的成品，按成本价格计算生产成品价值。生产成品价值中不包括用定货者来料加工的成品(半成品)价值。

对外加工费收入：指企业在报告期内完成的对外承接的工业品加工(包括用定货者来料加工产品)的加工费收入和对外工业修理作业所取得的加工费收入。对外加工费收入按不含增值税(销项税额)的价格计算，可根据会计“产品销售收入”科目的有关资料取得。

对于本企业对内非工业部门提供的加工修理、设备安装的劳务收入，如果企业会计核算基础较好，能取得这部分资料，而且这部分价值所占比重较大，应包括在对外加工费收入中。

自制半成品在制品期末期初差额价值：指企业报告期在制品期末减期初的差额价值，本指标一般可以从会计核算资料中取得。如果会计产品成本核算中不计算半成品、在制品的成本，则总产值中也不包括这部分价值，反之则包括。

(4)工业总产值统计范围变化和计算方法修订情况：

1984年以前工业总产值不包括村办工业，村办工业总产值划归农业。1984年以后工业总产值包括村办工业。

1995年工业普查对工业总产值计算方法做了修订，即从1995年始按新修订(新规定)方法计算工业总产值。新规定与原规定的区别如下：

全价与加工费的计算原则不同：新规定为凡自备原材料，不论其生产繁简程度如何，一律按全价计算工业总产值；凡来料加工，允许按加工费计算工业总产值。原规定则视生产加工的繁简程度不同，规定哪些行业按全价，哪些行业按加工费计算工业总产值。

自制半成品、在产品期末期初差额价值的计算原则不同：新规定要求，凡会计产品成本核算时计算了成本的差额价值，总产值中就应包括，否则可不包括；原规定则按生产周期六个月的界限区分，凡生产周期六个月以上的企业，总产值计算中应包括这部分差额价值，否则可不包括。

计算价格不同：新规定按不含增值税(销项税额)的价格计算；原规定则按含增值税(销项税额)的价格计算。

工业增加值　指工业企业在报告期内以货币表现的工业生产活动的最终成果。

工业增加值有两种计算方法：一是生产法，即工业总产出减去工业中间投入加上应交增值税；二是收入法，即从收入的角度出发，根据生产要素在生产过程中应得到的收入份额计算，具体构成项目有固定资产折旧、劳动者报酬、生产税净额、营业盈余，这种方法也称要素分配法。本年鉴中的工业增加值是以生产法计算的。

生产法工业增加值的计算方法为：

工业增加值=工业总产出-工业中间投入+应交增值税

(1)工业总产出：指工业企业在一定时期内工业生产活动的总成果。工业总产出包括：成品生产价值，对外加工费收入，自制半成品、在产品期末期初差额价值。1995年后用新规定计算的工业总产值代替。

(2)工业中间投入：指工业企业在工业生产活动中消耗的外购物质产品和对外支付的服务费用。服务费用包括支付给物质生产部门(工业、农业、批发零售贸易业、建筑业、运输邮电业)的服务费用和支付给非物质生产部门(如保险、金融、文化教育、科学研究、医疗卫生、行政管理等)的服务费用。工业中间投入的确定须遵循以下原则：必须从外部购入的，并已计入工业总产出的产品和服务价值；必须是本期投入生产，并一次性消耗掉(包括本期摊销的低值易耗品等)的产品和服务价值。

工业中间投入包括直接材料费用、制造费用中的工业中间投入、管理费用中的工业中间投入、销售费用中的工业中间投入和利息支出五部分。

资产总计　指企业拥有或控制的能以货币计量的经济资源，包括各种财产、债权和其他权利。资产按流动性分为流动资产、长期投资、固定资产、无形资产、递延资产和其他资产。该指标根据企业会计“资产负债表”中“资产总计”项目的期末数增列。

流动资产　指企业可以在一年内或者超过一年的一个生产周期内变现或者耗用的资产，包括现金及各种存款、短期投资，应收及预付款项、存货等。

流动资产平均余额　指企业在报告期内全部流动资产的平均余额。

固定资产原价　指企业在建造、购置、安装、改建、扩建、技术改造某项固定资产时所支出的全部货币总额。它一般包括买价、包装费、运杂费和安装费等。

固定资产净值年平均余额　指固定资产净值在报告期内余额的平均数。计算公式为：

$$\text{固定资产净值年平均余额}=\frac{\text{1至12月各月月初、月末固定资产净值之和}}{24}$$

该指标根据“资产负债表”中“固定资产原价”、“累计折旧”指标的期初、期末数计算填列。

固定资产净值指固定资产原价减去历年已提折旧额后的净额。计算公式为：

固定资产净值=固定资产原价-累计折旧

负债合计 指企业所承担的能以货币计量，将以资产或劳务偿付的债务，偿还形式包括货币、资产或提供劳务。负债一般按偿还期长短分为流动负债和长期负债。根据会计“资产负债表”中“负债合计”的年末数填列。

所有者权益 指企业投资人对企业净资产的所有权。企业净资产等于企业全部资产减去全部负债后的余额，包括企业投资人对企业的最初投入的实际到位的资产及资本公积金、盈余公积金和未分配利润。所有者权益合计数小于零，表示企业资不抵债。

主营业务收入 指会计“利润表”中对应指标的本年累计数。未执行2001年《企业会计制度》的企业，用“产品销售收入”的本期累计数代替。

主营业务成本 指会计“利润表”中对应指标的本年累计数。未执行2001年《企业会计制度》的企业，用“产品销售成本”的本期累计数代替。

主营业务税金及附加 指会计“利润表”中对应指标的本年累计数。未执行2001年《企业会计制度》的企业，用“产品销售税金及附加” 的本期累计数代替。

利润总额 指企业生产经营活动的最终成果，是企业在一定时期内实现的盈亏相抵后的利润总额(亏损以“-”号表示)，它等于营业利润加上补贴收入加上投资收益加上营业外净收入再加上以前年度损益调整。

本年应交增值税 指企业在报告期内应交纳的增值税额。它等于本年销项税额加上出口退税加上进项税额转出数减去本年进项税额。小规模纳税企业直接按全年计税销售额乘以征收率计算取得。

从业人员平均人数 是指报告期内每天拥有的从业人员人数。其计算公式为:

$$\text{季平均人数}=\frac{\text{季内各月平均人数之和}}{3}$$

$$\text{月平均人数}=\frac{\text{报告月内每天实有人数之和}}{\text{报告月日历日数}}$$

$$\text{年平均人数}=\frac{\text{年内各月平均人数之和}}{12}$$

总资产贡献率 反映企业全部资产的获利能力，是企业经营业绩和管理水平的集中体现，是评价和考核企业盈利能力的核心指标。计算公式为:

$$\text{总资产贡献率}(\%)=\frac{\text{利润总额}+\text{税金总额}+\text{利息支出}}{\text{平均资金总额}}\times 100\%$$

公式中：税金总额为产品销售税金及附加与应交增值税之和；平均资产总额为期初期末资产之和的算术平均值。

资产负债率 该指标既反映企业经营风险的大小，也反映企业利用债权人提供的资金从事经营活动的能力。计算公式为:

$$\text{资产负债率}(\%)=\frac{\text{负债总额}}{\text{资产总额}}\times 100\%$$

资产与负债均为报告期期末数。

流动资产周转次数 指一定时期内流动资产完成的周转次数，反映投入工业企业流动资金的周转速度。计算公式为:

$$\text{流动资产周转资转}=\frac{\text{产品销售收入}}{\text{全部流动资产平均余额}}$$

公式中：全部流动资产平均余额为期初和期末的流动资产之和的算术平均值。

成本费用利润率 反映企业投入的生产成本及费用的经济效益，同时也反映企业降低成本所取得的经济效益。计算公式为:

$$\text{成本费用利润}(\%)=\frac{\text{利润总额}}{\text{成本费用总额}}\times 100\%$$

公式中：成本费用总额为产品销售成本、销售费用、管理费用、财务费用之和。

全员劳动生产率 该指标反映企业的生产效率和劳动投入的经济效益。计算公式为:

$$\text{全员劳动生产率（元/人）}=\frac{\text{工业增加值}}{\text{全部从业人员平均人数}}$$

产品销售率 该指标反映工业产品已实现销售的程度，是分析工业产销衔接情况，研究工业产品满足社会需求的指标。计算公式为:

$$\text{产品销售率}(\%)=\frac{\text{工业销售产值}}{\text{工业总产值（现价）}}\times 100\%$$

Explanatory Notes on Main Statistical Indicators

Industry refers to the material production sector which is engaged in extraction of natural resources and processing and reprocessing of minerals and agricultural products, including (1) extraction of natural resources, such as mining, salt production (but not including hunting and fishing); (2) processing and reprocessing of farm and sideline produces, such as rice husking, flour milling, wine making, oil pressing, silk reeling, spinning and weaving, and leather making; (3) manufacture of industrial products, such as steel making, iron smelting, chemicals manufacturing, petroleum processing, machine building, timber processing; water and gas production and electricity generation and supply; (4)repairing of industrial products such as the repairing of machinery and means of transport (including cars).

Units of industrial statistics survey corporate industrial enterprises with independent accounting system.

Corporate industrial enterprises with independent accounting system refer to enterprises engaging in industrial production activities, which meet the following requirements: (1)They are established legally, having their own names, organizations, location, able to take civil liability; (2)They possess and use their assets independently, assume liabilities, and are entitled to sign contracts with other units; (3)They are financially independent and compile their own balance sheets.

Enterprises covered in the industrial statistics in the Yearbook include following categories by their registration:

State-owned and State-holding Enterprises refer to state-owned enterprises plus state-holding enterprises. State-owned enterprises (originally known as state-run enterprises with ownership by the whole society) are non-corporate economic entities registered in accordance with the *Regulation of the People's Republic of China on the Management of Registration of Legal Enterprises*, where all assets are owned by the state. Included in this category are state-owned enterprises, state-funded corporations and state-owned joint-operation enterprises. Joint state-private industries and private industries, which existed before 1957, were transformed into state-run industries since 1957, and into state-owned industries after 1992. Statistics on those enterprises are included in the state-owned industries instead of grouping them separately. State-holding enterprises is a sub-classification of enterprises with mixed ownership, referring to enterprises where the percentage of state assets (or shares by the state) is larger than any other single share holder of the same enterprise. This sub-classification illustrates the control of the state over a particular industry.

Collective-owned Enterprises refer to economic entities registered in accordance with the *Regulation of the People's Republic of China on the Management of Registration of Legal Enterprises*, where assets are owned by collectively. Collective enterprises constitute an integral part of the socialist economy with public ownership. They include urban and rural enterprises invested by collectives, and some enterprises registered in industrial and commercial administration agency as collective units where funds are pulled together by individuals who voluntarily give up their right of ownership.

Share-holding Cooperative Enterprises refer to economic units set up on cooperative basis, with funding partly from members of the enterprise and partly from outside investment, where the operation and management is decided by the members who also participate in the production, and the distribution of income is based both on work (labour input) and on shares (capital input).

Joint-operation enterprises refer to economic units that are established by joint investment by two or more corporate enterprises or institutions of the same or different types of ownership on voluntary, equal and mutual-beneficial basis. They include:

a) state-owned joint-operation enterprises (joint operation between state-owned enterprises);

b) collective joint-operation enterprises (joint operation between collective enterprises; and

c) state-collective joint-operation enterprises (joint operation between state and collective enterprises).

Limited Liability Corporations refer to economic units registered in accordance with the *Regulation of the People's Republic of China on the Management of Registration of Corporations*, with capitals from 2 to 49 investors, each investor bears limited liability to the corporation depending on his/her holding of shares, and the corporation bears liability to its debt to the maximum of its total assets.

Share-holding Corporations Ltd. refer to economic units registered in accordance with the *Regulation of the People's Republic of China on the Management of Registration of Corporate Enterprises*, with total registered capitals divided into equal shares and raised through issuing stocks. Each investor bears limited liability to the corporation depending on the holding of shares, and the corporation bears liability to its debt to the maximum of its total assets.

Private Enterprises refer to economic units invested or controlled (by holding the majority of the shares) by natural persons who hire labours for profit-making activities. Included in this category are private limited liability corporations, private share-holding corporations Ltd., private partnership enterprises and private sole investment enterprises registered in accordance with the *Corporation Law, Partnership Enterprise Law and Tentative Regulation on Private Enterprises.*

Enterprises with Funds from Hong Kong, Macao and

Taiwan refers to all industrial enterprises registered as the joint-venture, cooperative, sole (exclusive) investment industrial enterprises and limited liability corporations with funds from Hong Kong, Macao and Taiwan.

Foreign Funded Enterprises refers to all industrial enterprises registered as the joint-venture, cooperative, sole (exclusive) investment industrial enterprises and limited liability corporations with foreign funds.

Enterprises with Hong Kong, Macao, Taiwan and foreign fund refer to all the enterpries with funds from Hong Kong Macao and Taiwan and foreign funded enterprises.

Light Industry refers to the industry that produces consumer goods and hand tools. It consists of two categories, depending on the materials used:

(1) Industries using farm products as raw materials. These are branches of light industry which directly or indirectly use farm products as basic raw materials, including the manufacture of food and beverages, tobacco processing, textile, clothing, fur and leather manufacturing, paper making, printing, etc.

(2) Industries using non farm products as raw materials. These are branches of light industry which use manufactured goods as raw materials, including the manufacture of cultural, educational articles and sports goods, chemicals, synthetic fiber, chemical products for daily use, glass products for daily use, metal products for daily use, hand tools, medical apparatus and instruments, and the manufacture of cultural and clerical machinery.

Heavy Industry refers to the industry which produces capital goods, and provides various sectors of the national economy with necessary material and technical basis. It consists of the following three branches according to the purpose of production or the use of products:

(1) Mining, quarrying and logging industry refers to the industry that extracts natural resources, including extraction of petroleum, coal, metal and non-metal ores.

(2) Raw materials industry refers to the industry that provides various sectors of the national economy with raw materials, fuels and power. It includes smelting and processing of metals, coking and coke chemistry, chemical materials and building materials such as cement, plywood, and power, petroleum refining and coal dressing.

(3) Manufacturing industry refers to the industry that processes raw materials. It includes machine-building industry which equips sectors of the national economy, industries of metal structure and cement products, industries producing means of agricultural production, such as chemical fertilizers and pesticides.

According to the above principle of classification, the repairing trades, which are engaged primarily in repairing products of heavy industry are classified into heavy industry while these engaged in repairing products of light industry are classified into light industry.

Gross Industrial Output Value

(1) Definition: Gross industrial output value is the total volume of final industrial products produced and industrial services provided during a given period. It reflects the total achievements and overall scale of industrial production during a given period.

(2) Principles for calculation:

Statistics on industrial production follow the principle that all products produced by the enterprises and accepted during the reference period are to be included no matter whether they are sold or not during the reference period.

Determination of final products follow the principle that all products that are included in the calculation of grow industrial output value are the final products of the enterprise which have been accepted through quality check and require no further processing. If an enterprise has intermediate (semi-finished) products to sell, these intermediate products are considered as the final products of the enterprise.

Gross industrial output value is calculated following the principle of factory approach, i.e. industrial enterprise is used as the basic accounting unit in calculating the gross industrial output value. By this approach, value of the same product is not to be double counted, and the output value of different workshops (branch factories) should not be added. However, this approach does not exclude the possibility of double counting between enterprises.

(3) Content and calculation method: The old definition of gross industrial output value was modified during the national industrial census in 1995. The revised (new) definition of gross industrial output value consists of 3 components: value of the finished products during the reference period, income from external processing, and value of change in semi-finished products at the end and at the beginning of the reference period.

Value of the finished products during the reference period: refers to the value of all finished (semi-finished) industrial products that are produced during the reference period without the need for further processing, checked for acceptance, packed and put into the warehouse of the enterprise, including the value of own-produced equipment and the value of products provided to the projects under construction of the enterprise, and to other non-industrial or welfare units. Value of finished products during the reference period is calculated by the quantity of products produced using own materials multiplied by the average unit prices at which products are sold (excluding value-added tax). Own-produced equipment and products produced for own use are value at cost prices as in the case of enterprise accounting. Value of finished products does not include the value of finished products (semi-finished products) that are produced using the materials from the clients who make the orders.

Income from external processing: refers to income from contracted external processing of industrial products (including processing of industrial products using materials from the clients), and the income from industrial repairing work provided to other units. Income from external processing is calculated using information from the item "products sales income" in the enterprise accounting at the prices excluding value-added tax.

For income from services such as processing, repairing and installation of equipment provided to non-industrial units within the enterprise, if the accounting work of the enterprise is good enough to separate it from other records, and the share of such services is significant, it should also be included in the income from external processing.

Value of change in semi-finished products at the end and at the beginning of the reference period: refers to the value of change in semi-finished products at the end and at the beginning of the reference period, which generally can be obtained from accounting records of enterprises. If the enterprise accounting excludes the cost of semi-finished products, then it should not be included in the gross industrial output value, and vice versa.

(4) Changes in the coverage and method of calculation of gross industrial output value

Prior to 1984, the value of rural industry run by villages was classified into agriculture instead of industry. Since 1984, it has been included in the gross industrial output value. Method of calculation for the gross industrial output value was modified in the industrial census in 1995. The difference in the new method as compared with the old one is outlined below:

Principle in using full value vs. processing fee: The new method stipulates that all products produced using own materials are to be calculated with full value in reporting the gross industrial output value irrespective of sophistication of production, and for external processing, it allows calculation using processing fee. In the old method, however, the use of full value or processing fee was determined by the degree of sophistication of production in different branches of industries.

Principle in determining the value of change in semi-finished products: The new method requires that value of the change in semi-finished products should be included in the gross industrial output value if it is included in the accounting record of the enterprise, otherwise it should not be included. By the old method, it is determined by the type of enterprises in terms of production cycle. If the production cycle is over 6 months, the value of change in semi-finished products is included in the gross industrial output value, otherwise it is excluded.

Difference in prices: The new method uses prices excluding value-added tax in the calculation of gross industrial output value, while the old method used prices including value-added tax.

Value-added of Industry refers to the final results of industrial production of industrial enterprises in money terms during the reference period.

Industrial value-added can be calculated by two approaches: the production approach, i.e. gross industrial output value minus intermediate input plus value-added tax, and the income approach, i.e. income for various factors used in the course of production, including depreciation of fixed assets, remuneration of labourers, net of production tax, and operating surplus. Value-added of industry in the Yearbook is calculated by production approach as following:

Value-added of industry = gross industrial output industrial intermediate input + value-added tax

(1) Gross industrial output: refers to the total achievements of industrial production during a given period. Gross industrial output includes value of finished products, income from external processing, and value of change in semi-finished products at the end and at the beginning of the reference period. Since 1995, it was substituted by the gross industrial output value by new method.

(2) Industrial intermediate input: refers to purchased goods and paid services consumed during the industrial production of enterprises. Fees paid for services include fees paid for the services provided by material production sectors (industry, agriculture, wholesale and retail trade, construction, transport, post and telecommunications) and by non-material production sectors (insurance, banking, culture, education, scientific research, health and medical care, public administration, etc.). The determination of industrial intermediate input follows the principle that the goods and services must be purchased from outside and included in the gross industrial output, and that the goods and services are inputted into production and consumed (include low-value consumables) during the reference period.

Industrial intermediate input includes 5 components, namely direct consumption of materials, industrial intermediate input in manufacturing cost, industrial intermediate input in management cost, industrial intermediate input in marketing cost and expenditure on interest.

Total Assets refer to all economic resources, in monetary terms, that is owned or controlled by enterprises, including properties, creditors equity and other economic rights of all forms. Classified by the degree of equitability, total assets include circulating assets, long-term investment, fixed assets, intangible assets and deferred assets, and other assets. Data on this indicator can be obtained by the year-end figures of total assets in the *Assets and Liability Table* of accounting records of enterprises.

Working Capitals refer to capitals that an enterprise can cash or use during one year or one production cycle that may exceeds one year, including cash and savings deposits of various forms, short-term investment, money receivable and prepaid money, inventories, etc.

Annual Average Value of Working Capitals refers to the average value of all working capitals of the enterprise during the reference period.

Original Value of Fixed Assets refers to the total value, in monetary terms, that an enterprise spent on fixed assets, through construction, purchase, installation, transformation, expansion or technical upgrading. Generally, it covers cost of purchase, packing, transportation and installation, etc.

Annual Average of Net Value of Fixed Assets refer to average of the net value of fixed assets during the reference period, calculated with the following formula:

Annual Average of Net Value of Fixed Assets = sum of net value of fixed assets at the beginning and at the end of each month from January to December / 24.

Information on this indicator can be obtained from the beginning and ending figures of the original value of fixed assets and cumulative depreciation from the Assets and Liability Table of enterprises.

Net value of fixed assets refers to the original value of fixed assets minus depreciation over the years, i.e.:

Net value of fixed assets = original value of fixed assets cumulative depreciation

Total Liabilities refer to payable liabilities of enterprises that have to repay in terms of money, assets or labour services. In terms of payment, it can be divided into liquid liabilities and long-term liabilities. Data on this item is obtained from the ending figures on total liabilities from the Assets and Liability Table from the enterprises.

Owner's Equity refers to the ownership of net assets of enterprise by its investors. The net assets equal the total assets minus total liabilities of the enterprise, including the actual assets invested into the enterprise by investors, accumulation of capitals and operating surplus and non-distributed profits. The enterprise's assets is less than its liabilities if the sum of owner's equity is smaller than zero.

Revenue from Principal Business refers to the annual accumulation of corresponding item in the "profit table" of the accountant. For enterprises that do not follow the *2001 Enterprise Accounting Standards*, the year-end accumulation of revenue from the sales of products is used as a substitute.

Cost of Principal Business refers to the annual accumulation of corresponding item in the "profit table" of the accountant. For enterprises that do not follow the *2001 Enterprise Accounting Standards*, the year-end accumulation of cost for the sales of products is used as a substitute.

Tax and Extra Charges from Principal Business refer to the annual accumulation of corresponding item in the "profit table" of the accountant. For enterprises that do not follow the *2001 Enterprise Accounting Standards*, the year-end accumulation of tax and extra charges from the sales of products is used as a substitute.

Total Profits refer to the final achievements of production and operation of the enterprises, represented by the total profits after deducting losses (loss is expressed by the negative figure). It is the sum of profits from operation, income from subsidies, investment earnings, net income from activities other than operation, and adjustment of profits and losses of previous years.

Value-added Tax Payable refers to the amount of the value-added tax which should be paid by the enterprises during the reference period. It is the sum of tax on sales, export rebate, and transferred tax on purchases of the current year, minus the tax on purchases of the current year. Value-added tax payable of small-size enterprises is determined by the taxable sales of the year multiplied by the tax rate.

Average Annual Number of Employed Persons Employed persons refer to all those who are employed in enterprises and receive remunerations therefrom, including currently working employees, retirees who are re-employed, teachers of local-run schools, as well as foreigners, staff from Hong Kong, Macao and Taiwan, part-time employees and persons with second job who are employed by the enterprise, and employees of other units temporarily working in the enterprises, but excluding former employees who left the enterprise with their employment records still kept by the enterprises.

Average number of employed persons refers to the number of employees everyday during the reference period, calculated with the following formula:

Monthly average number = sum of actual employees everyday in reference month/number of calendar dates in reference month

Quarterly average number = sum of monthly average number in reference quarter/3

Annual average number = sum of monthly average number in reference year/12

Ratio of Profits, Taxes and Interests to Average Assets reflects the profit-making capability of all assets of the enterprise and is a key indicator manifesting the performance and management and evaluating the profit-making potential of the enterprise. It is calculated as follows:

Ratio of Profits, Taxes and Interests to Average Assets (%) = [(total profits + total taxes + interest payment) / average assets] ×100%

In the above formula, total taxes is the sum of tax and extra charges on the sales of products and value-added tax payable; and average assets is the arithmetic mean of the sum of beginning assets and ending assets.

Ratio of Debts to Assets reflect both the operation risk and the capability of the enterprise in making use of the capital from the creditors. It is calculated as follows:

Ratio of Debts to Assets (%) = (total debts / total assets) ×100%

Both assets and debts are figures at the end of the reference period.

Turnover of Working Capitals refers to the number of times of turnover of working capital in a given period of time, which reflects the speed of the turnover of working capital of industrial enterprises, and is calculated as follows:

Turnover of Working Capital=(sales revenue of products) / (average balance of total working capital)

In the above formula, average balance of total working capital refers to the arithmetic mean of the sum of working capital at the beginning and at the end of the reference period.

Ratio of Profits to Total Industrial Costs refers to the ratio of profits realized in a given period to the total costs in the same period, which reflects the economic efficiency of input cost and is calculated as follows:

Ratio of Profits to Total Industrial Cost (%)=(total profits/ total costs)×100%

Total costs in the above formula is the sum of cost of

products sold, marketing cost, management cost and financial cost.

Overall Labour Productivity is an indicator reflecting the production efficiency of an enterprise and the economic efficiency of its labour input, calculated by the formula:

Overall Labour Productivity (yuan/person) = industrial value-added / average of all persons engaged

Sales Ratio of Products is an indicator reflecting the actual sale of industrial products, analyzing the production-selling and supply-demand relations. It is calculated as:

Sales Ratio of Products (%) = value of industrial sales / gross industrial output value (current prices) * 100%

15

建筑业
Construction

简 要 说 明

一、本篇资料的主要内容

本篇资料反映我国建筑业概况和发展情况。包括建筑业企业基本情况和生产经营情况。主要指标有企业个数、从业人员数、建筑业总产值、建筑业增加值、房屋建筑面积、利润税金、劳动生产率等。此外，还包括勘察设计机构和人员情况的主要指标。

二、本篇的统计范围

根据建筑业发展的实际情况，建筑业统计范围从2002年年报起由原具有建筑业资质等级四级及四级以上的独立核算的建筑业企业调整为具有建筑业资质的独立核算建筑业企业。

三、本篇的资料来源及调查方法

本篇建筑业企业统计数据是根据国家统计局制定的《建筑业统计报表制度》整理汇总的。建筑业统计报表是各级统计部门根据当地实际情况采取全面调查的方法布置、收集，由各省、自治区、直辖市统计局上报的全面报表。

勘察设计机构和人员表依据建设部制定的《勘察设计报表制度》中有关年报资料编制，由建设部提供。

Brief Introduction

I. Main Content

Data in this chapter show the general situation and the development of the construction in China. They cover the situation of production and management of the enterprises of construction, including the number of enterprises, number of employed persons, gross output value and value added of construction industry, floor space of the buildings, profits and taxes of enterprises and labour productivity etc. They also cover the situation of prospecting and designing institutions and the personnel.

II. Coverage of Statistics

According to the development of construction industry, starting from 2002, the coverage of construction statistics has been adjusted to include all the construction enterprises of various types of ownership with qualification certificates and with independent accounting system, instead of the original criteria that required construction enterprises of various types of ownership to have qualification certificates at or above Class 4 with independent accounting system.

III. Source of Data and Survey Methodology

Data on construction enterprises are collected in accordance with the *Reporting System of Construction Statistics* stipulated by the National Bureau of Statistics. The annual reports on construction statistics are assigned and collected by statistical bureaus at various levels through comprehensive reporting system, and provided by statistical bureaus of each province, autonomous region and municipality.

Data on prospecting and designing institutions and the personnel are provided by the Ministry of Construction, based on *Prospecting and Designing Statistical Reporting Scheme* stipulated by the Ministry of Construction.

15-1 建筑业企业概况

Main Indicators on Construction Enterprises

年份 Year	总计 Total	国有企业 State-owned	集体企业 Collective-owned	港澳台商投资企业 Funded from Hong Kong, Macao and Taiwan	外商投资企业 Foreign Funded	其他 Others
企业单位数（个） Number of Enterprises						
1980	6604	1996	4608			
1985	11150	3385	7765			
1989	13106	3927	9179			
1990	13327	4275	9052			
1995	24133	7531	15348	329	312	613
1996	41364	9109	29044	417	388	2406
1997	44017	9650	29872	491	454	3550
1998	45634	9458	28410	629	337	6800
1999	47234	9394	27197	664	341	9638
2000	47518	9030	24756	635	319	12778
2001	45893	8264	19096	622	274	17637
2002	47820	7536	13177	632	279	26196
2003	48688	6638	10425	535	287	30803
2004	59018	6513	8959	511	386	42649
2005	58750	6007	8090	516	388	43749
从业人员（万人） Number of Persons Employed (10 000 persons)						
1980	648.0	481.8	166.2			
1985	911.5	576.7	334.8			
1989	1004.8	614.7	390.1			
1990	1010.7	621.0	389.7			
1995	1497.9	824.3	631.9	5.0	5.4	31.3
1996	2121.9	855.9	1171.4	8.7	8.6	77.3
1997	2101.5	828.6	1148.2	8.2	9.6	106.9
1998	2030.0	738.4	1057.3	9.3	5.1	219.9
1999	2020.1	690.6	993.1	11.5	6.1	318.9
2000	1994.3	635.6	887.5	8.2	4.4	458.6
2001	2110.7	590.7	739.9	7.7	4.3	768.1
2002	2245.2	543.8	579.2	7.4	4.5	1110.4
2003	2414.3	524.3	505.6	7.0	6.0	1371.3
2004	2500.3	467.4	386.4	6.8	8.1	1631.6
2005	2699.9	480.0	361.6	8.6	10.8	1838.9
建筑业总产值（亿元） Gross Output Value (100 million yuan)						
1980	286.93	220.90	66.03			
1985	675.10	474.51	200.59			
1989	1282.98	878.57	404.41			
1990	1345.01	935.19	409.82			
1995	5793.75	3670.25	1899.47	33.60	33.19	157.24
1996	8282.25	4160.21	3695.68	46.85	50.51	329.00
1997	9126.48	4526.52	3925.81	63.72	70.49	539.94
1998	10061.99	4571.44	4012.01	91.94	62.52	1324.08
1999	11152.86	4861.38	4081.79	91.97	64.43	2053.29
2000	12497.60	5053.79	4035.84	99.18	67.49	3241.30
2001	15361.56	5362.81	3775.89	102.55	73.06	6047.25
2002	18527.18	5582.86	3338.50	113.87	91.38	9400.57
2003	23083.87	6060.23	3270.73	123.71	129.39	13499.81
2004	29021.45	7325.61	2756.12	137.03	202.46	18600.23
2005	34552.10	8432.03	2815.20	172.54	249.03	22883.30

注：1.本表1980年至1992年数据为全民和集体所有制建筑业企业数据；1993年至1995年数据为各种经济成分的建制镇以上建筑业企业数据；1996年至2001年数据为资质等级(旧资质)四级及四级以上建筑业企业数据；2002年及以后数据为所有具有资质等级的施工总承包、专业承包建筑业企业（不含劳务分包建筑业企业)数据，与以前各年不可比（以下各表同)。
2.从业人员数1993年至1997年为年平均人数。

a) Data from 1980 to 1992 are the figures of state-owned and collective-owned construction enterprises. Data from 1993 to 1995 are the figures of all economic types of construction enterprises above towns. The statistical coverage from 1996 to 2001 included the fourth and higher grades construction enterprises (old classification of grades), and that since 2002 included all grades construction enterprises, both general constructing contractors and professional contractors (excluding the construction enterprises of work subcontractors). Therefore the data were not comparable with the data of the previous years. The same as in the following table.

b) The number of employed persons refers to the annual average number from 1993 to 1997.

15-2 按登记注册类型分建筑业企业主要经济指标（2005年）

指 标		Item		合 计 Total
企业单位数	(个)	Number of Construction Enterprises	(unit)	58750
从业人员	(万人)	Number of Employed Persons	(10 000 persons)	2699.92
自有固定资产原价	(亿元)	Fixed Assets Owned (original value)	(100 million yuan)	7621.45
自有固定资产净价	(亿元)	Fixed Assets Owned (net value)	(100 million yuan)	5056.50
自有施工机械设备年末总台数	(万台)	Number of Machinery and Equipment Owned	(10 000 set)	879.85
自有施工机械设备年末净值	(亿元)	Net Value of Machinery and Equipment Owned	(100 million yuan)	2503.77
自有施工机械设备年末总功率	(万千瓦)	Total Power of Machinery and Equipment Owned	(10 000 kw)	13765.56
建筑业总产值	(亿元)	Gross Output Value of Construction	(100 million yuan)	34552.10
建筑业增加值	(亿元)	Value Added of Construction	(100 million yuan)	6899.71
#本年固定资产折旧		Depreciation of Fixed Assets		445.28
主营业务应付工资		Wages Payable from Principal Business		3772.16
主营业务应付福利费		Welfare Expenses Payable from Principal Business		396.71
工程结算税金及附加		Taxes and Extra Charges on Project Settle Accounts		1101.40
管理费用中的税金		Taxes in Management Expenses		58.40
住房公积金及住房补贴		Housing Provident Funds and Housing Subsidies		53.50
房屋建筑施工面积	(万平方米)	Floor Space of Buildings under Construction	(10 000 sq.m)	352744.67
房屋建筑竣工面积	(万平方米)	Floor Space of Buildings Completed	(10 000 sq.m)	159406.20
利润总额	(亿元)	Total Profits	(100 million yuan)	906.66
税金总额	(亿元)	Total Tax	(100 million yuan)	1159.79
劳动生产率		Overall Labor Productivity		
按总产值计算	(元/人)	In Terms of Gross Output Value	(yuan/person)	117317
按增加值计算	(元/人)	In Terms of Value-added	(yuan/person)	23427
技术装备率	(元/人)	Value of Machines per Laborer	(yuan/person)	9273
动力装备率	(千瓦/人)	Power of Machines per Laborer	(kw/person)	5.1
房屋建筑面积竣工率	(%)	Rate of Floor Space of Buildings Completed	(%)	45.2
产值利润率	(%)	Ratio of Profit to Gross Output Value	(%)	2.6
产值利税率	(%)	Ratio of Pre-tax Profit to Gross Output Value	(%)	6.0

Main Economic Indicators on Construction Enterprises by Registration Status (2005)

内资企业 Domestic Funded	#国有 State-owned	#集体 Collective-owned	港澳台商投资企业 Funded from Hong Kong, Macao and Taiwan	#港澳台商独资企业 Solely Owned	外商投资企业 Foreign Funded	#外商独资企业 Solely Owned
57846	6007	8090	516	70	388	68
2680.45	480.05	361.57	8.65	1.17	10.82	0.86
7531.95	2352.14	737.95	40.06	5.73	49.45	3.59
4999.99	1428.84	517.10	24.35	4.23	32.16	2.45
872.16	152.34	143.63	3.59	0.27	4.11	0.20
2480.74	638.09	253.08	9.90	1.43	13.14	0.62
13683.58	3442.34	1693.35	41.58	5.79	40.40	2.15
34130.52	8432.03	2815.20	172.54	24.34	249.03	45.26
439.27	144.44	33.50	2.92	0.29	3.09	0.31
3733.76	762.59	381.48	13.92	1.60	24.48	3.10
394.14	85.31	38.05	0.85	0.12	1.72	0.20
1089.83	282.71	92.18	4.62	0.55	6.94	1.07
57.71	12.96	7.49	0.34	0.03	0.35	0.14
53.09	28.00	2.54	0.18	0.04	0.23	0.07
350765.50	56308.81	42257.41	668.22	76.70	1310.94	212.60
158574.01	20505.72	21750.39	213.96	21.66	618.23	71.16
891.34	141.43	80.70	3.62	1.00	11.70	2.33
1147.53	295.66	99.66	4.97	0.58	7.29	1.21
116894	154436	75922	161706	204538	169063	233299
9255	13292	7000	11446	12241	12136	7264
5.1	7.2	4.7	4.8	5.0	3.7	2.5
45.2	36.4	51.5	32.0	28.2	47.2	33.5
2.6	1.7	2.9	2.1	4.1	4.7	5.1
6.0	5.2	6.4	5.0	6.5	7.6	7.8

15-3 建筑业企业主要经济指标

Main Economic Indicators on Construction Enterprises

指　标		Item		2004	2005	2005年比上年增长(%) Growth Rate of 2005 to 2004 (%)
企业单位数	(个)	Number of Construction Enterprises	(unit)	59018	58750	-0.5
从业人员	(万人)	Number of Employed Persons	(10 000 persons)	2500.28	2699.92	8.0
自有固定资产原价	(亿元)	Original Value of Fixed Assets Owned	(100 million yuan)	7148.85	7621.45	6.6
自有固定资产净价	(亿元)	Net Value of Fixed Assets Owned	(100 million yuan)	4844.56	5056.50	4.4
自有施工机械设备年末总台数	(万台)	Total Number of Machinery and Equipment Owned	(10 000 set)	846.64	879.85	3.9
自有施工机械设备年末净值	(亿元)	Net Value of Machinery and Equipment Owned	(100 million yuan)	2324.52	2503.77	7.7
自有施工机械设备年末总功率	(万千瓦)	Total Power of Machinery and Equipment Owned	(10 000 kw)	14584.05	13765.56	-5.6
建筑业总产值	(亿元)	Gross Output Value of Construction	(100 million yuan)	29021.45	34552.10	19.1
建筑业增加值	(亿元)	Value Added of Construction	(100 million yuan)	5615.75	6899.71	22.9
#本年固定资产折旧		Depreciation of Fixed Assets		380.38	455.28	19.7
主营业务应付工资		Wages Payable from Principal Business		3026.53	3772.16	24.6
主营业务应付福利费		Welfare Expenses Payable from Principal Business		312.70	396.71	26.9
工程结算税金及附加		Taxes and Extra Charges on Project Settle Accounts		894.10	1101.40	23.2
管理费用中的税金		Taxes in Management Expenses		42.09	58.40	38.8
住房公积金及住房补贴		Housing Provident Funds and Housing Subsidies		55.50	53.50	-3.6
房屋建筑施工面积	(万平方米)	Floor Space of Buildings under Construction	(10 000 sq.m)	310986	352745	13.4
房屋建筑竣工面积	(万平方米)	Floor Space of Buildings Completed	(10 000 sq.m)	147364	159406	8.2
利润总额	(亿元)	Total Profits	(100 million yuan)	719.25	906.66	26.1
税金总额	(亿元)	Total Tax	(100 million yuan)	936.19	1159.79	23.9
劳动生产率		Overall Labor Productivity				
按总产值计算	(元/人)	In Terms of Gross Output Value	(yuan/person)	107942	117317	
按增加值计算	(元/人)	In Terms of Value-added	(yuan/person)	20887	23427	
技术装备率	(元/人)	Value of Machines per Laborer	(yuan/person)	9297	9273	
动力装备率	(千瓦/人)	Power of Machines per Laborer	(kw/person)	5.8	5.1	
房屋建筑面积竣工率	(%)	Rate of Floor Space of Buildings Completed	(%)	47.4	45.2	
产值利润率	(%)	Ratio of Profit to Gross Output Value	(%)	2.5	2.6	
产值利税率	(%)	Ratio of Pre-tax Profit to Gross Output Value	(%)	5.7	6.0	

15-4 各地区总承包建筑业企业主要经济指标（2005年）

Main Economic Indicators on Construction Enterprises of General Contractors by Region (2005)

地 区	Region	企业单位数 (个) Number of Enterprises (unit)	从业人员 (人) Number of Employed Persons (person)	建筑业总产值 (万元) Gross Output Value of Construction (10 000 yuan)	利税总额 (万元) Total Pre-Tax Profits (10 000 yuan)	按总产值计算的劳动生产率 (元/人) Overall Labor Productivity by Gross Output Value (yuan/person)
全 国	**National Total**	**32389**	**23458604**	**298340854**	**17118175**	**116460**
北 京	Beijing	732	500860	15445466	1048437	162626
天 津	Tianjin	240	179719	5606342	241359	197129
河 北	Hebei	1303	949866	11518883	592573	109527
山 西	Shanxi	713	473696	7673150	331767	141476
内蒙古	Inner Mongolia	547	235627	3565811	306236	83113
辽 宁	Liaoning	1285	709353	12191626	898288	119595
吉 林	Jilin	529	307686	4439649	167934	114371
黑龙江	Heilongjiang	1045	377526	5059099	199351	92593
上 海	Shanghai	1116	576076	15020271	1037411	178302
江 苏	Jiangsu	2590	2950115	37529807	1920350	126876
浙 江	Zhejiang	1921	2803048	42196220	2367870	151247
安 徽	Anhui	1071	855692	8359537	425313	99142
福 建	Fujian	807	614310	7352152	402736	119047
江 西	Jiangxi	817	544667	4889529	267533	87972
山 东	Shandong	3347	2161558	21840280	1357800	91639
河 南	Henan	1451	1093627	9332164	537380	83262
湖 北	Hubei	1272	943670	11523252	614774	128013
湖 南	Hunan	1303	1103072	11302999	671004	105309
广 东	Guangdong	2245	1375914	17017268	1234834	123397
广 西	Guangxi	661	400306	3921538	188851	99854
海 南	Hainan	92	63187	557780	43720	87096
重 庆	Chongqing	1316	751646	7018788	401300	93944
四 川	Sichuan	2270	1563199	13039410	681293	83135
贵 州	Guizhou	457	290873	2610612	123813	98629
云 南	Yunnan	1010	517717	4881770	323108	97633
西 藏	Tibet	140	30307	368306	41400	117771
陕 西	Shaanxi	641	397104	6199099	304259	135431
甘 肃	Gansu	529	372790	2766455	161927	68645
青 海	Qinghai	248	76701	833618	34691	89784
宁 夏	Ningxia	267	62192	989205	47350	74831
新 疆	Xinjiang	424	176500	3290768	143516	114022

15-5 各地区专业承包建筑业企业主要经济指标（2005年）

Main Economic Indicators on Construction Enterprises of Professional Contractors by Region (2005)

地区	Region	企业单位数 (个) Number of Enterprises (unit)	从业人员 (人) Number of Employed Persons (person)	建筑业总产值 (万元) Gross Output Value of Construction (10 000 yuan)	利税总额 (万元) Total Pre-Tax Profits (10 000 yuan)	按总产值计算的劳动生产率 (元/人) Overall Labor Productivity by Gross Output Value (yuan/person)
全国	**National Total**	**26361**	**3540645**	**47180115**	**3546396**	**123046**
北京	Beijing	1881	167151	3494970	218246	142999
天津	Tianjin	837	86803	1937360	156761	181922
河北	Hebei	704	131073	1334048	93537	97544
山西	Shanxi	690	80872	819015	42257	99150
内蒙古	Inner Mongolia	111	27438	247233	11363	67262
辽宁	Liaoning	1768	199753	2624902	221702	101514
吉林	Jilin	360	78075	416171	23031	83184
黑龙江	Heilongjiang	680	53445	669856	45837	82907
上海	Shanghai	1270	143510	3872191	301017	199663
江苏	Jiangsu	3319	447232	6159686	459159	132637
浙江	Zhejiang	2020	316879	4991211	406294	152907
安徽	Anhui	852	138356	1275873	88327	96255
福建	Fujian	896	97490	1387619	107030	129436
江西	Jiangxi	413	57466	770879	85138	127149
山东	Shandong	2244	334282	3250712	302744	97081
河南	Henan	1007	155489	1329334	88176	83935
湖北	Hubei	800	199441	1969913	125448	98203
湖南	Hunan	450	82997	890494	60560	111524
广东	Guangdong	1884	286151	4978621	409067	175735
广西	Guangxi	333	28460	330562	32017	112021
海南	Hainan	30	3639	39145	454	102608
重庆	Chongqing	882	77756	816870	53620	104013
四川	Sichuan	1230	163791	1650612	93061	93191
贵州	Guizhou	123	13491	101642	5990	77845
云南	Yunnan	518	48181	511899	39025	100064
西藏	Tibet	28	4221	37813	3482	89752
陕西	Shaanxi	143	25113	386013	17517	146428
甘肃	Gansu	247	51371	367561	24126	66171
青海	Qinghai	124	8953	75719	807	69563
宁夏	Ningxia	206	13177	140445	10346	71295
新疆	Xinjiang	311	18589	301745	20260	116468

15-6 各地区建筑业总产值

Total Output Value of Construction by Region

单位：万元 (10 000 yuan)

地 区	Region	1999	2000	2001	2002	2003	2004	2005
全 国	**National Total**	**111528640**	**124975961**	**153615626**	**185271753**	**230838663**	**290214510**	**345520968**
北 京	Beijing	6814102	7274774	8879099	10550535	12698521	16569591	18940436
天 津	Tianjin	2227406	2380991	2886808	4061628	5208402	6537068	7543702
河 北	Hebei	4321432	4921005	6145010	7111712	7799313	10040393	12852931
山 西	Shanxi	2397739	2393974	3114390	4469457	5401279	7125750	8492165
内蒙古	Inner Mongolia	1168732	1367309	1782561	2200194	2576575	3545091	3813045
辽 宁	Liaoning	4893444	5980933	7611747	8393428	10170794	12451481	14816528
吉 林	Jilin	1713517	2391840	2740726	2926017	3469281	4111106	4855820
黑龙江	Heilongjiang	2996115	3340903	3723204	4079097	4401878	5159832	5728956
上 海	Shanghai	5683036	6223565	7215808	8222730	11958034	16888002	18892463
江 苏	Jiangsu	13299853	15388416	18218039	21995164	27949354	36556163	43689494
浙 江	Zhejiang	11282810	13837658	17684490	22829906	31272779	38956437	47187431
安 徽	Anhui	2773364	3028240	4215500	5282183	6227073	7887558	9635410
福 建	Fujian	2511292	2711420	3690460	4026874	5493441	6716323	8739771
江 西	Jiangxi	1022296	1164115	1691530	2450718	3593356	4617693	5660408
山 东	Shandong	7672600	8170949	9842204	11511730	14813618	19690062	25090992
河 南	Henan	3169845	3573425	4524908	5367328	6345217	8171347	10661498
湖 北	Hubei	3990201	4541767	5290240	6365491	8729958	11121338	13493165
湖 南	Hunan	3338963	3544202	4897879	5955616	8188402	10278915	12193493
广 东	Guangdong	8719500	8919834	11320549	13417808	15163242	19008399	21995888
广 西	Guangxi	1491385	1509158	1802891	2211684	2818466	3286644	4252101
海 南	Hainan	333933	302139	353453	415089	394053	585834	596925
重 庆	Chongqing	3175927	3486579	4368169	5006543	5862095	6902774	7835658
四 川	Sichuan	6495237	7138102	8228676	10725229	12253374	13093829	14690022
贵 州	Guizhou	966508	1090571	1502008	1811244	2122907	2554529	2712254
云 南	Yunnan	3114900	3092645	3439350	3582375	3967957	4482520	5393669
西 藏	Tibet	134958	168178	186832	216949	293427	290802	406118
陕 西	Shaanxi	2183009	2423046	2797388	3465727	4404362	5230766	6585112
甘 肃	Gansu	1187695	1251202	1473057	1923798	2236860	2938853	3134016
青 海	Qinghai	396528	447162	542130	733550	747325	886406	909337
宁 夏	Ningxia	482827	562352	703722	839121	1080546	1111913	1129649
新 疆	Xinjiang	1569486	2349506	2742800	3122828	3196774	3417093	3592513

15-7 各地区建筑业增加值

Value-added of Construction by Region

单位：万元 (10 000 yuan)

地区	Region	1999	2000	2001	2002	2003	2004	2005
全国	**National Total**	**30222586**	**33410864**	**40235718**	**38224156**	**46547067**	**56157481**	**68997130**
北京	Beijing	1809631	1861649	2215886	1710390	1945971	2254726	2842418
天津	Tianjin	599298	596889	665186	638907	795963	962170	1112972
河北	Hebei	1176002	1255840	1595275	1495270	1688931	2090625	2224625
山西	Shanxi	623871	659211	775992	784804	951478	1181453	1300114
内蒙古	Inner Mongolia	387728	415530	530331	508817	666669	951318	1086085
辽宁	Liaoning	1458714	1650483	2013803	1731074	1968475	2350859	3740812
吉林	Jilin	477403	648043	828044	573885	622364	773526	914531
黑龙江	Heilongjiang	838384	901381	1012242	855445	959828	1056119	1111511
上海	Shanghai	1224694	1381463	1432718	1414863	2153664	2555131	3004728
江苏	Jiangsu	3212848	3700633	4346794	4387544	5609752	7182840	9111895
浙江	Zhejiang	2861430	3521692	4368676	4672740	6342032	7570554	9433162
安徽	Anhui	783765	837832	1195204	1185951	1359808	1642821	2059716
福建	Fujian	662526	710129	954305	815704	1063081	1352426	2058206
江西	Jiangxi	303880	324209	448780	553425	739617	896632	1156546
山东	Shandong	2162466	2269464	2740505	2579653	3157332	4431309	5619079
河南	Henan	915452	1006563	1184251	1070946	1273423	1757295	2400746
湖北	Hubei	1208960	1346062	1438777	1423250	1914661	2031426	2391055
湖南	Hunan	909667	965511	1307676	1279692	1724388	2127828	2480593
广东	Guangdong	2492533	2509568	3212604	2932624	3281041	3951611	4757223
广西	Guangxi	463926	495053	536363	524687	611761	702543	898093
海南	Hainan	77185	68036	78689	89284	88847	125703	129188
重庆	Chongqing	870648	912266	1207981	1139108	1287202	1523812	1714340
四川	Sichuan	1855648	2073881	2442159	2528302	2678743	2678796	2901029
贵州	Guizhou	276657	313945	411845	411619	486887	524574	552401
云南	Yunnan	857556	819742	884943	761495	791021	840071	962823
西藏	Tibet	40991	45811	42524	58839	66508	74479	96805
陕西	Shaanxi	557333	591203	683851	622949	697852	812929	1059230
甘肃	Gansu	388427	402912	459363	483668	549941	638115	719034
青海	Qinghai	137154	162241	161192	150146	158293	173105	202605
宁夏	Ningxia	145697	173888	204157	191314	249257	276254	282562
新疆	Xinjiang	442113	789737	855600	647761	662277	666786	671702

注：1.自2003年起，建筑业增加值核算口径有所调整。为便于比较，本表按新口径对2002年的数据进行了调整。
2.从2004年第一次全国经济普查开始,建筑业增加值按新核算方法核算,其结果与2003年及以前年度数据不完全可比。

a) Since 2003, the statistical coverage of value added of construction have been adjusted. In order to compare, the data in 2002 have been adjusted accordingly.

b) New accounting methods were applied in 2004 during the first national economic census in calculating the value-added of the construction industry, hence the results are not completely comparable with figures for 2003 and earlier years.

15-8 各地区建筑业企业利税总额

Total Pre-Tax Profits of Construction Enterprises by Region

单位：万元 (10 000 yuan)

地区	Region	1999	2000	2001	2002	2003	2004	2005
全国	**National Total**	**4944082**	**5792206**	**7934252**	**9697797**	**12785260**	**16554384**	**20664572**
北京	Beijing	341341	385714	465129	584471	699460	931362	1266684
天津	Tianjin	80172	96435	121086	191909	249833	323474	398120
河北	Hebei	207616	224663	416927	381119	451764	606942	686111
山西	Shanxi	72317	93678	119342	178827	226472	315410	374024
内蒙古	Inner Mongolia	51242	58719	81525	113728	148628	261704	317599
辽宁	Liaoning	183582	255827	388175	406326	513813	695685	1119990
吉林	Jilin	54198	88242	136570	128794	155079	177521	190965
黑龙江	Heilongjiang	109410	134863	168938	176265	232212	223541	245188
上海	Shanghai	278825	342818	386166	480415	800563	1226833	1338429
江苏	Jiangsu	443934	585377	740637	936746	1301495	1795798	2379509
浙江	Zhejiang	571252	740235	1009064	1284708	1776998	2175151	2774163
安徽	Anhui	105523	126076	217112	275184	331071	433945	513639
福建	Fujian	120981	141997	236135	231295	306800	388138	509765
江西	Jiangxi	37586	44866	72464	134489	192964	217852	352670
山东	Shandong	416839	419264	561028	666717	876677	1253724	1660544
河南	Henan	132961	148742	202791	245271	297621	468077	625556
湖北	Hubei	190966	216898	278040	390134	547484	667822	740222
湖南	Hunan	121018	153028	255126	319042	451023	610514	731564
广东	Guangdong	522531	543688	800994	888679	1143533	1437161	1643901
广西	Guangxi	63830	64151	85386	125653	151935	165677	220868
海南	Hainan	17655	14801	19191	30539	30446	49380	44174
重庆	Chongqing	133598	152870	236729	262773	329589	401924	454920
四川	Sichuan	268304	318422	415125	569936	662847	678693	774353
贵州	Guizhou	32956	47008	71097	95505	115146	130300	129803
云南	Yunnan	154874	160638	159381	167754	214679	235271	362133
西藏	Tibet	8358	12805	16876	26030	31152	26312	44882
陕西	Shaanxi	67403	84901	111932	144683	177073	236011	321776
甘肃	Gansu	61307	67918	71882	103144	114195	161628	186053
青海	Qinghai	8921	18312	25542	36704	35963	32344	35497
宁夏	Ningxia	19804	29994	35175	37429	49889	51892	57696
新疆	Xinjiang	64778	19257	28688	83528	168856	174299	163776

15-9 各地区建筑业企业利润总额
Total Profits of Construction Enterprises by Region

单位：万元 (10 000 yuan)

地 区	Region	1999	2000	2001	2002	2003	2004	2005
全 国	**National Total**	**1547982**	**1920635**	**2943904**	**3703532**	**5198716**	**7192468**	**9066623**
北 京	Beijing	135595	163561	187424	251894	299739	379578	612127
天 津	Tianjin	21991	27993	37517	73614	97029	125943	170137
河 北	Hebei	62006	67370	126382	146051	180629	246200	293377
山 西	Shanxi	-882	-514	17683	37332	47523	78450	93202
内蒙古	Inner Mongolia	13076	14561	19053	40988	55627	127165	162376
辽 宁	Liaoning	30962	66730	148186	127030	165123	293520	543863
吉 林	Jilin	790	17339	36912	29628	23497	42391	24960
黑龙江	Heilongjiang	23741	31070	53572	45741	54530	44850	52342
上 海	Shanghai	141889	184252	191779	235432	409236	668703	669130
江 苏	Jiangsu	121082	206569	258129	353159	547982	820677	1119457
浙 江	Zhejiang	235308	318850	458497	606604	832163	997326	1324144
安 徽	Anhui	15904	28127	72552	90671	110443	152987	180314
福 建	Fujian	25773	25831	89109	91740	115820	157343	196898
江 西	Jiangxi	3395	6157	15635	40478	58418	73777	155667
山 东	Shandong	176337	182235	262288	312306	410531	647971	867836
河 南	Henan	37901	31281	58802	75985	94049	191762	255655
湖 北	Hubei	51890	58425	88285	129633	190795	284090	266394
湖 南	Hunan	17230	43938	86497	111240	154992	255705	287689
广 东	Guangdong	199092	203926	373276	373902	571518	689142	705824
广 西	Guangxi	13227	9147	22519	43171	47095	48715	67651
海 南	Hainan	6439	3907	6709	14339	14343	30235	25874
重 庆	Chongqing	41582	49310	90786	99587	137489	180833	199481
四 川	Sichuan	76014	100995	150604	213687	259289	276323	276916
贵 州	Guizhou	1775	9855	17334	25997	45525	43502	38331
云 南	Yunnan	53070	58350	46654	46553	80134	90420	187724
西 藏	Tibet	5033	7385	11402	14307	18879	17795	28184
陕 西	Shaanxi	5799	14497	24786	34906	46895	69938	100824
甘 肃	Gansu	16917	19977	19906	22434	33042	68473	86565
青 海	Qinghai	-3873	3812	5249	13780	13601	6063	5797
宁 夏	Ningxia	5559	13722	13863	12354	15575	16779	21055
新 疆	Xinjiang	13359	-48022	-47485	-11011	67205	65813	46830

15-10 各地区建筑业劳动生产率

Labor Productivity of Construction Enterprises by Region

按建筑业增加值计算。

Calculated in terms of value-added of construction.

单位：元/人 (yuan/person)

地区	Region	1999	2000	2001	2002	2003	2004	2005
全国	**National Average**	**14451**	**15929**	**17621**	**15715**	**17476**	**20887**	**23427**
北京	Beijing	21900	22553	26435	19100	19916	20180	23803
天津	Tianjin	20875	21765	25736	18562	22475	25232	28472
河北	Hebei	12360	13070	15023	13352	15169	18347	18719
山西	Shanxi	15071	16824	18118	13638	15705	20040	20803
内蒙古	Inner Mongolia	11753	11913	13509	12029	15802	23827	23317
辽宁	Liaoning	13948	15062	16867	14737	15966	19910	29271
吉林	Jilin	13355	16594	21197	13709	13900	18141	20870
黑龙江	Heilongjiang	13462	13991	15559	13157	14835	16745	17722
上海	Shanghai	21488	24375	23565	23005	27720	25671	28994
江苏	Jiangsu	14540	16793	18823	17455	20185	23517	26624
浙江	Zhejiang	19013	21228	23593	23291	25842	27910	30270
安徽	Anhui	11195	11738	13259	13375	14501	17982	21109
福建	Fujian	16826	17061	22417	19102	20956	23762	28397
江西	Jiangxi	10455	11240	13428	13089	14578	16720	18762
山东	Shandong	12615	12517	13555	12522	12943	18562	20673
河南	Henan	11656	12766	13628	11577	13257	17613	18768
湖北	Hubei	14105	16268	17315	15535	17932	19852	21722
湖南	Hunan	11787	12697	14987	14337	15700	18870	21511
广东	Guangdong	17523	19829	22559	19978	22056	25699	28617
广西	Guangxi	13273	15308	15449	14606	16816	20351	21270
海南	Hainan	12660	11868	11821	12685	12482	17301	19038
重庆	Chongqing	11656	12859	14526	13636	15246	18571	20763
四川	Sichuan	11589	13118	14223	12897	13062	16022	16619
贵州	Guizhou	12296	14311	16162	15169	16548	18819	19889
云南	Yunnan	14653	15531	16089	14717	13803	16920	17469
西藏	Tibet	16375	17105	16676	19987	16593	24731	27280
陕西	Shaanxi	13599	14559	15160	13090	14769	18886	21881
甘肃	Gansu	11203	11701	12594	10998	11520	14364	15680
青海	Qinghai	13505	15348	15508	12325	12930	16489	19532
宁夏	Ningxia	11699	13895	15211	13036	14177	17650	18603
新疆	Xinjiang	15660	25209	26411	17966	19854	21197	21357

注：自2003年起，建筑业增加值核算口径有所调整,相应的按增加值计算的劳动生产率口径也发生了变化。为便于比较，本表按新口径对2002年的数据进行了调整。

a) Since 2003, the statistical standard of value added of construction has been adjusted, the labor productivity of value added have been changed accordingly. In order to compare, the 2002's data in the table have been adjusted by the new statistical standard correspondingly.

15-11 各地区按登记注册类型分建筑业企业单位数（2005年）

Number of Construction Enterprises by Registration Status and Region (2005)

单位：个 (unit)

地区	Region	合计 Total	内资企业 Domestic Funded	#国有 State-owned	#集体 Collective-owned	港澳台商投资企业 Funded from Hong Kong, Macao and Taiwan	#港澳台商独资企业 Solely Owned	外商投资企业 Foreign Funded	#外商独资企业 Solely Owned
全国	**National Total**	**58750**	**57846**	**6007**	**8090**	**516**	**70**	**388**	**68**
北京	Beijing	2613	2507	234	292	59	3	47	4
天津	Tianjin	1077	1040	139	133	19	2	18	3
河北	Hebei	2007	2000	199	211	4		3	
山西	Shanxi	1403	1393	196	170	7		3	
内蒙古	Inner Mongolia	658	657	20	14			1	
辽宁	Liaoning	3053	2974	339	455	32	3	47	4
吉林	Jilin	889	878	203	113	7		4	
黑龙江	Heilongjiang	1725	1718	224	232	2		5	
上海	Shanghai	2386	2242	162	200	83	3	61	14
江苏	Jiangsu	5909	5790	337	561	53	13	66	23
浙江	Zhejiang	3941	3901	137	202	21	2	19	
安徽	Anhui	1923	1911	190	272	8	3	4	1
福建	Fujian	1703	1644	124	200	41	9	18	5
江西	Jiangxi	1230	1216	201	304	12	2	2	
山东	Shandong	5591	5525	516	1010	35	8	31	5
河南	Henan	2458	2445	296	389	7		6	1
湖北	Hubei	2072	2052	345	304	12	3	8	
湖南	Hunan	1753	1739	245	410	11	3	3	1
广东	Guangdong	4129	4034	514	594	70	9	25	4
广西	Guangxi	994	989	151	297	4		1	
海南	Hainan	122	119	38	33	1		2	1
重庆	Chongqing	2198	2185	119	235	8	2	5	
四川	Sichuan	3500	3486	310	524	7	3	7	1
贵州	Guizhou	580	577	131	143	3			
云南	Yunnan	1528	1525	107	280	3			
西藏	Tibet	168	168	29	55				
陕西	Shaanxi	784	784	128	195				
甘肃	Gansu	776	775	133	154			1	
青海	Qinghai	372	369	66	43	2	1	1	1
宁夏	Ningxia	473	472	76	28	1	1		
新疆	Xinjiang	735	731	98	37	4			

15-12 各地区按登记注册类型分建筑业企业从业人员（2005年）

Number of Staff and Workers in Construction Enterprises by Registration Status and Region (2005)

单位：人 (person)

地 区	Region	合 计 Total	内资企业 Domestic Funded	#国 有 State-owned	#集 体 Collective-owned	港澳台商投资企业 Funded from Hong Kong, Macao and Taiwan	#港澳台商独资企业 Solely Owned	外商投资企业 Foreign Funded	#外商独资企业 Solely Owned
全 国	National Total	26999249	26804543	4800466	3615702	86462	11685	108244	8583
北 京	Beijing	668011	644590	182730	61049	12323	3051	11098	947
天 津	Tianjin	266522	262523	87254	26757	1414	239	2585	68
河 北	Hebei	1080939	1080210	186338	114536	295		434	
山 西	Shanxi	554568	552647	170535	48736	1040		881	
内蒙古	Inner Mongolia	263065	263015	15613	3193			50	
辽 宁	Liaoning	909106	891127	206716	149632	3605	75	14374	376
吉 林	Jilin	385761	381745	140737	30729	883		3133	
黑龙江	Heilongjiang	430971	428138	101774	44202	60		2773	
上 海	Shanghai	719586	702685	131879	41022	9440	290	7461	1678
江 苏	Jiangsu	3397347	3369062	246705	339668	11237	3151	17048	3679
浙 江	Zhejiang	3119927	3084789	76088	158074	5716	122	29422	
安 徽	Anhui	994048	989689	166711	134386	3216	1839	1143	66
福 建	Fujian	711800	702541	125103	83980	6181	281	3078	413
江 西	Jiangxi	602133	600687	167616	184120	1278	42	168	
山 东	Shandong	2495840	2485622	334329	522321	5861	291	4357	631
河 南	Henan	1249116	1247562	287605	175804	773		781	70
湖 北	Hubei	1143111	1139614	300811	147036	1624	136	1873	
湖 南	Hunan	1186069	1178623	264722	210841	6016	1005	1430	390
广 东	Guangdong	1662065	1645629	376152	345266	12656	811	3780	158
广 西	Guangxi	428766	427318	176167	93089	327		1121	
海 南	Hainan	66826	66588	35736	14845	195		43	10
重 庆	Chongqing	829402	827773	72704	82652	1154	40	475	
四 川	Sichuan	1726990	1725842	328299	254416	489	79	659	41
贵 州	Guizhou	304364	304239	178006	36258	125			
云 南	Yunnan	565898	565767	96312	97763	131			
西 藏	Tibet	34528	34528	4473	10324				
陕 西	Shaanxi	422217	422217	128972	79046				
甘 肃	Gansu	424161	424140	95491	106604			21	
青 海	Qinghai	85654	85510	26742	10514	88	53	56	56
宁 夏	Ningxia	75369	75189	23740	3572	180	180		
新 疆	Xinjiang	195089	194934	64406	5267	155			

15-13 建筑业企业技术装备情况

Number and Power of Machinery and Equipment Owned by Construction Enterprises

年份 Year / 地区 Region		自有施工机械设备年末总台数（台）Number of Machinery and Equipment Owned (set)	自有施工机械设备年末总功率（万千瓦）Total Power of Machinery and Equipment Owned (10 000 kw)	自有施工机械设备年末净值（万元）Net Value of Machinery and Equipment Owned (10 000yuan)	技术装备率（元/人）Value of Machines per Laborer (yuan/person)	动力装备率（千瓦/人）Power of Machines per Laborer (kw/person)
	1991	2528110	4250.2	2722151	2572	4.0
	1992	2531578	4431.9	3147398	2719	3.8
	1993	2608091	4948.9	4671699	4105	4.3
	1994	2952629	5712.7	4981982	3446	4.0
	1995	3482784	7056.5	6386383	4264	4.7
	1996	5649612	9804.8	8814352	4154	4.6
	1997	5604603	8668.5	9938659	4729	4.1
	1998	5833748	8656.5	10407189	5127	4.3
	1999	6110175	9077.8	11628317	5756	4.5
	2000	6259885	9228.1	12572317	6304	4.6
	2001	7022174	10251.7	15062491	7136	4.9
	2002	7540011	11022.5	21722927	9675	4.9
	2003	8001782	11712.4	24039576	9957	4.9
	2004	8466386	14584.1	23245244	9297	5.8
	2005	8798527	13765.6	25037702	9273	5.1
北京	Beijing	255804	447.0	793434	11878	6.7
天津	Tianjin	100010	246.0	694258	26049	9.2
河北	Hebei	477019	716.4	975515	9025	6.6
山西	Shanxi	243159	395.5	714124	12877	7.1
内蒙古	Inner Mongolia	133168	204.1	310744	11812	7.8
辽宁	Liaoning	320817	644.8	1311446	14426	7.1
吉林	Jilin	103320	260.9	362546	9398	6.8
黑龙江	Heilongjiang	165903	342.0	679666	15771	7.9
上海	Shanghai	165880	312.9	853164	11856	4.3
江苏	Jiangsu	859275	1386.9	2581452	7598	4.1
浙江	Zhejiang	696671	888.2	2040232	6539	2.8
安徽	Anhui	384176	469.8	889587	8949	4.7
福建	Fujian	207165	306.8	630339	8856	4.3
江西	Jiangxi	160075	232.6	412132	6845	3.9
山东	Shandong	663329	1119.1	1827861	7324	4.5
河南	Henan	446710	627.8	1064058	8518	5.0
湖北	Hubei	513404	778.2	1355518	11858	6.8
湖南	Hunan	438731	574.8	954884	8051	4.8
广东	Guangdong	709852	1247.9	1787736	10756	7.5
广西	Guangxi	194780	254.9	374008	8723	5.9
海南	Hainan	26086	62.0	38491	5760	9.3
重庆	Chongqing	172883	257.8	623514	7518	3.1
四川	Sichuan	459474	672.5	1345255	7790	3.9
贵州	Guizhou	72607	122.6	226746	7450	4.0
云南	Yunnan	218066	304.6	631793	11164	5.4
西藏	Tibet	9206	16.2	49816	14428	4.7
陕西	Shaanxi	172246	258.4	506397	11994	6.1
甘肃	Gansu	242190	251.6	382388	9015	5.9
青海	Qinghai	47756	92.1	151828	17726	10.8
宁夏	Ningxia	39509	81.6	142672	18930	10.8
新疆	Xinjiang	99256	189.6	326098	16715	9.7

注：从2004年起，自有机械设备情况统计改为自有施工机械设备情况统计。

a) Starting from 2004, statistics on machinery and equipment owned refer to construction machinery and equipment owned.

15-14 国有建筑业企业技术装备情况

Number and Power of Machinery and Equipment Owned by State-owned Construction Enterprises

年份 地区	Year Region	自有施工机械设备年末总台数(台) Number of Machinery and Equipment Owned (set)	自有施工机械设备年末总功率(万千瓦) Total Power of Machinery and Equipment Owned (10 000 kw)	自有施工机械设备年末净值(万元) Net Value of Machinery and Equipment Owned (10 000yuan)	技术装备率(元/人) Value of Machinery per Laborer (yuan/person)	动力装备率(千瓦/人) Power of Machinery per Laborer (kw/person)
	1991	1519637	3248.9	2213621	3465	5.1
	1992	1410064	3314.6	2464943	3618	4.9
	1993	1309360	3323.8	2848367	4335	5.1
	1994	1476295	3900.2	3567576	4361	4.8
	1995	1637276	3984.6	4161384	5048	4.8
	1996	1870826	4213.3	4692164	5482	4.9
	1997	1865910	4419.9	5211213	6289	5.3
	1998	1818321	4343.2	5180338	7016	5.9
	1999	1876329	4405.0	5548440	8035	6.4
	2000	1822716	4150.8	5485356	8631	6.5
	2001	1831423	4008.7	5561988	9417	6.8
	2002	1710768	3663.2	6811241	12527	6.7
	2003	1649774	3493.8	6920800	13200	6.7
	2004	1485122	3513.5	6037890	12919	7.5
	2005	1523411	3442.3	6380891	13292	7.2
北　京	Beijing	39857	124.7	242500	13271	6.8
天　津	Tianjin	28704	93.9	230140	26376	10.8
河　北	Hebei	73449	180.0	240106	12886	9.7
山　西	Shanxi	57642	148.7	242858	14241	8.7
内蒙古	Inner Mongolia	4313	12.6	30886	19782	8.0
辽　宁	Liaoning	83683	212.0	392337	18980	10.3
吉　林	Jilin	35387	127.1	146627	10419	9.0
黑龙江	Heilongjiang	45202	115.4	193503	19013	11.3
上　海	Shanghai	27379	78.3	227194	17227	5.9
江　苏	Jiangsu	86511	183.0	302953	12280	7.4
浙　江	Zhejiang	28873	50.7	156608	20583	6.7
安　徽	Anhui	52287	134.6	347370	20837	8.1
福　建	Fujian	20375	55.1	114505	9153	4.4
江　西	Jiangxi	46839	94.9	153638	9166	5.7
山　东	Shandong	78772	178.7	397192	11880	5.4
河　南	Henan	83099	190.2	344214	11968	6.6
湖　北	Hubei	132050	325.0	488543	16241	10.8
湖　南	Hunan	86869	142.2	246973	9330	5.4
广　东	Guangdong	143804	272.1	563276	14975	7.2
广　西	Guangxi	38082	87.8	150911	8566	5.0
海　南	Hainan	14452	41.4	19089	5342	11.6
重　庆	Chongqing	17114	36.3	71363	9816	5.0
四　川	Sichuan	86334	153.9	330489	10067	4.7
贵　州	Guizhou	29186	68.6	133214	7484	3.9
云　南	Yunnan	25450	52.5	100962	10483	5.5
西　藏	Tibet	1290	1.6	7462	16683	3.6
陕　西	Shaanxi	32038	83.1	180693	14010	6.4
甘　肃	Gansu	82850	75.4	121670	12741	7.9
青　海	Qinghai	13143	46.3	77417	28950	17.3
宁　夏	Ningxia	8515	18.0	35706	15040	7.6
新　疆	Xinjiang	19862	58.1	90494	14051	9.0

注：从2004年起，自有机械设备情况统计改为自有施工机械设备情况统计。

a) Starting from 2004, statistics on machinery and equipment owned refer to construction machinery and equipment owned.

15-15 各地区建筑业总产值（2005年）
Total Output Value of Construction by Region (2005)

单位：万元 (10 000 yuan)

地区	Region	建筑业总产值 Total Output Value	建筑工程产值 Output Value of Construction	安装工程产值 Output Value of Installation	其他 Others
全国	**National Total**	**345520968**	**294643840**	**38356612**	**12520517**
北京	Beijing	18940436	17214672	1478306	247458
天津	Tianjin	7543702	5760985	1143472	639244
河北	Hebei	12852931	10584910	1718556	549466
山西	Shanxi	8492165	7383324	867411	241430
内蒙古	Inner Mongolia	3813045	3271565	351668	189812
辽宁	Liaoning	14816528	12107649	2241115	467765
吉林	Jilin	4855820	4268121	540133	47567
黑龙江	Heilongjiang	5728956	4533245	989039	206672
上海	Shanghai	18892463	14824181	3116308	951974
江苏	Jiangsu	43689494	39142150	3883821	663523
浙江	Zhejiang	47187431	41460039	4186319	1541073
安徽	Anhui	9635410	8263623	993979	377809
福建	Fujian	8739771	7450380	1039244	250148
江西	Jiangxi	5660408	4809075	522379	328954
山东	Shandong	25090992	20519720	3437903	1133369
河南	Henan	10661498	8932477	1398086	330936
湖北	Hubei	13493165	11330294	1224140	938730
湖南	Hunan	12193493	10117322	1032761	1043409
广东	Guangdong	21995888	18636517	2624915	734456
广西	Guangxi	4252101	3647529	503990	100581
海南	Hainan	596925	530904	53495	12527
重庆	Chongqing	7835658	6970274	636356	229029
四川	Sichuan	14690022	12442178	1553438	694405
贵州	Guizhou	2712254	2194544	467312	50398
云南	Yunnan	5393669	4759740	502038	131892
西藏	Tibet	406118	374757	7554	23808
陕西	Shaanxi	6585112	5888057	555581	141473
甘肃	Gansu	3134016	2522862	531914	79240
青海	Qinghai	909337	742689	132550	34098
宁夏	Ningxia	1129649	978686	135591	15372
新疆	Xinjiang	3592513	2981373	487239	123901

15-16 各地区按登记注册类型分建筑业总产值（2005年）

Total Output Value of Construction by Registration Status and Region (2005)

单位：万元 (10 000 yuan)

地区	Region	合计 Total	内资企业 Domestic Funded	#国有 State-owned	#集体 Collective-owned	港澳台商投资企业 Funded from Hong Kong, Macao and Taiwan	#港澳台商独资企业 Solely Owned	外商投资企业 Foreign Funded	#外商独资企业 Solely Owned
全国	**National Total**	**345520968**	**341305223**	**84320290**	**28151952**	**1725416**	**243444**	**2490330**	**452592**
北京	Beijing	18940436	18387188	6506988	1239741	229615	47021	323632	22949
天津	Tianjin	7543702	7397444	2827730	410307	79607	2470	66651	1044
河北	Hebei	12852931	12846663	4518820	704782	4786		1482	
山西	Shanxi	8492165	8471347	3636616	289417	10125		10694	
内蒙古	Inner Mongolia	3813045	3812917	387742	30967			128	
辽宁	Liaoning	14816528	14469385	4124351	1387290	62411	2504	284732	4925
吉林	Jilin	4855820	4815439	1609587	208423	14254		26127	
黑龙江	Heilongjiang	5728956	5686997	1618596	477282	891		41068	
上海	Shanghai	18892463	17824528	4011008	784438	365570	18120	702364	296318
江苏	Jiangsu	43689494	43094593	3608334	3632134	228411	105201	366490	100556
浙江	Zhejiang	47187431	46697390	1928540	1777788	112799	606	377242	
安徽	Anhui	9635410	9599470	2678924	815820	25256	18366	10683	2200
福建	Fujian	8739771	8586513	1927344	863654	105019	4158	48240	6839
江西	Jiangxi	5660408	5640860	2027986	1286768	17964	149	1584	
山东	Shandong	25090992	24950120	5282318	3792205	83761	10174	57111	8500
河南	Henan	10661498	10638901	3362910	1065652	14188		8409	200
湖北	Hubei	13493165	13464964	5167951	845627	15045	2273	13156	
湖南	Hunan	12193493	12129033	4170789	1399205	50268	18320	14192	4916
广东	Guangdong	21995888	21632416	6839738	2447108	259791	11320	103681	3591
广西	Guangxi	4252101	4228461	2102268	638898	1742		21898	
海南	Hainan	596925	591636	341361	71254	3150		2139	83
重庆	Chongqing	7835658	7809981	1090190	514558	21069	579	4608	
四川	Sichuan	14690022	14679113	4846373	1447634	6973	1679	3936	394
贵州	Guizhou	2712254	2711350	1876550	173182	904			
云南	Yunnan	5393669	5385209	1389621	636852	8461			
西藏	Tibet	406118	406118	62035	109760				
陕西	Shaanxi	6585112	6585112	3137609	466633				
甘肃	Gansu	3134016	3134010	1223940	447062			6	
青海	Qinghai	909337	908026	501419	47415	1233	325	78	78
宁夏	Ningxia	1129649	1129469	375810	37223	180	180		
新疆	Xinjiang	3592513	3590568	1136846	102876	1945			

15-17 各地区按行业分建筑业总产值（2005年）
Total Output Value of Construction by Branch and Region (2005)

单位：万元 (10 000 yuan)

地区	Region	建筑业总产值 Total Output Value of Construction	房屋和土木工程建筑业 Building and Civil Engineering	房屋工程建筑 Building	土木工程建筑 Civil Engineering	建筑安装业 Construction Installation	建筑装饰业 Construction Decoration	其他建筑业 Other Construction
全国	**National Total**	**345520968**	**298827983**	**205403544**	**93424439**	**29272335**	**12369096**	**5051555**
北京	Beijing	18940436	15594965	11242486	4352478	1821646	1284602	239224
天津	Tianjin	7543702	6100586	2614781	3485805	1046200	229702	167215
河北	Hebei	12852931	11351869	8138071	3213798	1221916	164871	114274
山西	Shanxi	8492165	7874545	2302616	5571929	399528	110940	107153
内蒙古	Inner Mongolia	3813045	3612281	2203522	1408759	165643	13572	21548
辽宁	Liaoning	14816528	12508801	7441680	5067121	1529759	661524	116445
吉林	Jilin	4855820	4290509	2018906	2271603	471468	83063	10780
黑龙江	Heilongjiang	5728956	4990200	2883444	2106756	577163	106435	55158
上海	Shanghai	18892463	14658569	10276677	4381892	2283067	1554440	396387
江苏	Jiangsu	43689494	37139969	29871156	7268814	3962727	1727696	859102
浙江	Zhejiang	47187431	43635909	34143788	9492121	1676769	1396310	478443
安徽	Anhui	9635410	8351435	4759967	3591468	869865	275601	138510
福建	Fujian	8739771	7111809	5546567	1565242	1017051	477826	133086
江西	Jiangxi	5660408	5018886	3364566	1654321	407371	129684	104468
山东	Shandong	25090992	21392205	15638073	5754132	2561297	663545	473945
河南	Henan	10661498	8653509	5268510	3384999	1567198	170750	270041
湖北	Hubei	13493165	11996559	7312933	4683626	780356	316621	399628
湖南	Hunan	12193493	11331087	8264510	3066577	658574	129112	74720
广东	Guangdong	21995888	17003320	11766722	5236599	2614516	2028031	350022
广西	Guangxi	4252101	3711698	2755995	955703	451910	57566	30927
海南	Hainan	596925	531368	425197	106172	42917	11245	11395
重庆	Chongqing	7835658	7006158	5840873	1165285	499216	229327	100956
四川	Sichuan	14690022	13248402	9078041	4170361	982355	278876	180390
贵州	Guizhou	2712254	2441441	1302078	1139363	230833	19548	20432
云南	Yunnan	5393669	4932022	2930396	2001626	280279	109689	71679
西藏	Tibet	406118	355671	231842	123828	37385	1247	11816
陕西	Shaanxi	6585112	6221614	2980938	3240676	288406	37792	37299
甘肃	Gansu	3134016	2698916	1908664	790252	361692	31208	42200
青海	Qinghai	909337	819577	222164	597414	73318	9285	7156
宁夏	Ningxia	1129649	1077984	645180	432804	24437	21443	5785
新疆	Xinjiang	3592513	3166120	2023204	1142916	367474	37548	21371

15-18 各地区按资质等级分总承包建筑业总产值（2005年）

Total Output Value of Construction of General Contractors by Qualification Criteria and by Region (2005)

单位：万元 (10 000 yuan)

地区	Region	合计 Total	特级 Special Grade	一级 First Grade	二级 Second Grade	三级及以下 Third Grade and below
全国	**National Total**	**298340854**	**41200398**	**125971633**	**74720381**	**56448442**
北京	Beijing	15445466	4727091	8242749	1762285	713342
天津	Tianjin	5606342	1151948	3355988	776658	321748
河北	Hebei	11518883	1178708	5256800	3195002	1888373
山西	Shanxi	7673150	1992747	4149433	836181	694790
内蒙古	Inner Mongolia	3565811	159751	1263603	1132101	1010357
辽宁	Liaoning	12191626	1561101	5214675	2774954	2640897
吉林	Jilin	4439649	1070544	1825335	799720	744051
黑龙江	Heilongjiang	5059099	825115	1889230	1564506	780249
上海	Shanghai	15020271	2580756	5544744	3997087	2897684
江苏	Jiangsu	37529807	6666509	13391759	9682411	7789129
浙江	Zhejiang	42196220	7792046	18087934	9675228	6641011
安徽	Anhui	8359537	701066	3170418	2448461	2039592
福建	Fujian	7352152	403328	3236741	2661250	1050833
江西	Jiangxi	4889529	613	2303833	1233227	1351856
山东	Shandong	21840280	1488224	8102686	5839661	6409709
河南	Henan	9332164	436617	4460937	2379713	2054897
湖北	Hubei	11523252	2883935	3999504	2689270	1950544
湖南	Hunan	11302999	1402412	4841999	2615203	2443385
广东	Guangdong	17017268	1326606	7811968	4057732	3820962
广西	Guangxi	3921538	134474	1661955	1217032	908077
海南	Hainan	557780		320593	179454	57733
重庆	Chongqing	7018788		2928888	2713251	1376649
四川	Sichuan	13039410	627814	4693564	4618047	3099985
贵州	Guizhou	2610612	146540	1493240	561216	409616
云南	Yunnan	4881770	574662	1699260	1460694	1147154
西藏	Tibet	368306			309614	58691
陕西	Shaanxi	6199099	1072638	3621388	969425	535648
甘肃	Gansu	2766455		1297790	971589	497075
青海	Qinghai	833618	204232	202863	290521	136003
宁夏	Ningxia	989205		385592	310553	293060
新疆	Xinjiang	3290768	90922	1516166	998337	685343

15-19 各地区按资质等级分专业承包建筑业总产值（2005年）

Total Output Value of Construction of Professional Contractors by Qualification Criteria and by Region (2005)

单位：万元 (10 000 yuan)

地区	Region	合计 Total	一级 First Grade	二级 Second Grade	三级及以下 Third Grade and below
全国	**National Total**	**47180115**	**17668326**	**14693426**	**14818362**
北京	Beijing	3494970	1821763	767679	905527
天津	Tianjin	1937360	976958	361103	599299
河北	Hebei	1334048	489944	544565	299539
山西	Shanxi	819015	300909	233418	284689
内蒙古	Inner Mongolia	247233	63892	116527	66814
辽宁	Liaoning	2624902	779425	859735	985742
吉林	Jilin	416171	80892	162062	173218
黑龙江	Heilongjiang	669856	152010	291905	225942
上海	Shanghai	3872191	1681231	955582	1235379
江苏	Jiangsu	6159686	1965989	2135750	2057948
浙江	Zhejiang	4991211	1673451	1328401	1989359
安徽	Anhui	1275873	366090	472052	437731
福建	Fujian	1387619	569978	493043	324599
江西	Jiangxi	770879	476721	134222	159935
山东	Shandong	3250712	451257	1296167	1503288
河南	Henan	1329334	616687	448231	264416
湖北	Hubei	1969913	631840	942453	395620
湖南	Hunan	890494	303739	328960	257796
广东	Guangdong	4978621	2685450	1135669	1157501
广西	Guangxi	330562	65994	136358	128211
海南	Hainan	39145	21435	10822	6889
重庆	Chongqing	816870	214048	330612	272210
四川	Sichuan	1650612	624095	591498	435020
贵州	Guizhou	101642	1871	48584	51187
云南	Yunnan	511899	175985	184294	151621
西藏	Tibet	37813		19074	18739
陕西	Shaanxi	386013	245007	61665	79342
甘肃	Gansu	367561	124630	147948	94983
青海	Qinghai	75719	28113	13002	34604
宁夏	Ningxia	140445	20639	54383	65423
新疆	Xinjiang	301745	58285	87667	155793

15-20 各地区建筑业企业签订合同情况 (2005年)

Contracts Signed by Construction Enterprises by Region (2005)

单位：万元 (10 000 yuan)

地区	Region	合同总额 Total Value of Contracts	上年结转合同额 Value from Contracts Signed in 2004	本年新签合同额 Value from New Contracts Signed in 2005
全国	**National Total**	**559466764**	**195876588**	**363590176**
北京	Beijing	39096753	15874093	23222661
天津	Tianjin	14091016	4931365	9159651
河北	Hebei	18040286	5806190	12234096
山西	Shanxi	16462214	5734832	10727382
内蒙古	Inner Mongolia	5308017	1754064	3553953
辽宁	Liaoning	22074151	6570754	15503397
吉林	Jilin	8048089	3118827	4929262
黑龙江	Heilongjiang	7410680	2005863	5404817
上海	Shanghai	36337341	13334597	23002745
江苏	Jiangsu	55670531	14892909	40777622
浙江	Zhejiang	77204230	29278664	47925567
安徽	Anhui	14659511	4314081	10345430
福建	Fujian	14380369	5167187	9213182
江西	Jiangxi	8698994	2841321	5857673
山东	Shandong	33297399	9622131	23675268
河南	Henan	17173151	6273106	10900045
湖北	Hubei	25233550	8388874	16844676
湖南	Hunan	20780213	7828982	12951231
广东	Guangdong	42842225	17673187	25169038
广西	Guangxi	7136012	2955201	4180811
海南	Hainan	1088285	396322	691963
重庆	Chongqing	10800870	3883418	6917452
四川	Sichuan	22593784	7829730	14764055
贵州	Guizhou	5127456	2400620	2726836
云南	Yunnan	9465801	3702182	5763618
西藏	Tibet	392110	166725	225386
陕西	Shaanxi	13928034	4916929	9011105
甘肃	Gansu	3631700	1316270	2315430
青海	Qinghai	2007374	904836	1102538
宁夏	Ningxia	1629012	436027	1192985
新疆	Xinjiang	4857604	1557300	3300304

15-21 各地区建筑业企业承包工程完成情况（2005年）

Completion of Contracted Projects by Construction Enterprises by Region (2005)

单位：万元 (10 000 yuan)

地区	Region	直接从建设单位承揽工程完成的产值 Completed Output Value of Projects Contracted Directly from Investors	自行完成施工产值 Own-completed Output Value	分包出去工程的产值 Output Value of Out-sourced Projects	从建设单位以外承揽工程完成的产值 Completeted Output Value of Projects Contracted from Non-investors
全国	**National Total**	**341333798**	**331718759**	**9615039**	**13802209**
北京	Beijing	18819080	17996146	822934	944290
天津	Tianjin	7679721	7234704	445018	308998
河北	Hebei	12747102	12622392	124710	230539
山西	Shanxi	8497507	8317074	180433	175092
内蒙古	Inner Mongolia	3765824	3739940	25884	73104
辽宁	Liaoning	14733089	14616140	116949	200388
吉林	Jilin	4822077	4809864	12213	45956
黑龙江	Heilongjiang	5722191	5658198	63994	70758
上海	Shanghai	19568118	16697715	2870403	2194748
江苏	Jiangsu	40634609	40116738	517871	3572755
浙江	Zhejiang	46534859	45991779	543079	1195651
安徽	Anhui	9467459	9304222	163237	331188
福建	Fujian	8666111	8570423	95687	169348
江西	Jiangxi	5605618	5440839	164779	219569
山东	Shandong	24769666	24498927	270739	592065
河南	Henan	10621548	10436700	184847	224798
湖北	Hubei	13209729	13088603	121126	404562
湖南	Hunan	11843580	11798032	45547	395461
广东	Guangdong	23100580	20946916	2153663	1048972
广西	Guangxi	4067199	4059711	7488	192390
海南	Hainan	594073	592124	1949	4802
重庆	Chongqing	7740758	7549602	191156	286056
四川	Sichuan	14331205	14198160	133045	491862
贵州	Guizhou	2683613	2671867	11746	40387
云南	Yunnan	5330500	5309503	20998	84167
西藏	Tibet	385052	385052		21067
陕西	Shaanxi	6615923	6462497	153426	122614
甘肃	Gansu	3102655	3063941	38714	70075
青海	Qinghai	917459	888851	28608	20485
宁夏	Ningxia	1145313	1111313	34000	18337
新疆	Xinjiang	3611585	3540786	70799	51727

15-22 各地区按登记注册类型分建筑业企业实收资本（2005年）

Paid-up Capitals of Construction Enterprises by Registration Status and Region (2005)

单位：万元 (10 000 yuan)

地区	Region	合计 Total	内资企业 Domestic Funded	#国有 State-owned	#集体 Collective-owned	港澳台商投资企业 Funded from Hong Kong, Macao and Taiwan	#港澳台商独资企业 Solely Owned	外商投资企业 Foreign Funded	#外商独资企业 Solely Owned
全 国	**National Total**	**81713763**	**80398947**	**19745821**	**7551387**	**676271**	**90402**	**638546**	**109911**
北 京	Beijing	7820466	7634519	4484419	277589	101727	12001	84220	5627
天 津	Tianjin	1484088	1436014	510687	101726	21195	5428	26879	9351
河 北	Hebei	2799853	2795777	546482	213034	2052		2024	
山 西	Shanxi	2207431	2192340	996442	106697	13223		1868	
内蒙古	Inner Mongolia	1046422	1045550	71977	14822			872	
辽 宁	Liaoning	3759446	3632886	816384	403989	30881	6934	95679	2361
吉 林	Jilin	1157940	1145155	391730	66407	5227		7558	
黑龙江	Heilongjiang	2585760	2566976	487208	178755	2729		16056	
上 海	Shanghai	3821894	3556997	648418	164442	116628	2935	148269	36130
江 苏	Jiangsu	6904933	6731990	707533	604496	88035	33217	84909	34138
浙 江	Zhejiang	5670795	5609124	287653	267826	24711	614	36960	
安 徽	Anhui	2133943	2123030	449038	230628	8268	3736	2645	470
福 建	Fujian	2418191	2356735	321258	259739	42058	5829	19397	5750
江 西	Jiangxi	1464109	1448657	444773	300014	13518	343	1933	
山 东	Shandong	6154949	6075762	910524	889782	46177	4904	33011	5160
河 南	Henan	3174106	3160901	855771	322826	8910		4295	1000
湖 北	Hubei	3202353	3177715	838055	305250	14587	1342	10051	
湖 南	Hunan	2611517	2577267	649372	387898	25454	6548	8796	5691
广 东	Guangdong	5603049	5471549	1448008	641045	92621	5465	38880	3591
广 西	Guangxi	1373203	1366843	580138	276407	1079		5282	
海 南	Hainan	169935	167048	45916	27321	2000		887	387
重 庆	Chongqing	2454361	2446796	300166	188734	5609	572	1955	
四 川	Sichuan	4452698	4443822	939188	472906	3140	440	5736	200
贵 州	Guizhou	741373	737514	348608	85806	3859			
云 南	Yunnan	1913017	1912238	344742	269284	779			
西 藏	Tibet	217226	217226	47080	48432				
陕 西	Shaanxi	1459539	1459539	528846	192283				
甘 肃	Gansu	1063270	1062939	271085	161587			330	
青 海	Qinghai	429558	428966	147324	34534	536	36	56	56
宁 夏	Ningxia	492574	492514	121599	25540	60	60		
新 疆	Xinjiang	925765	924557	205399	31588	1208			

15-23 各地区建筑业企业资产（2005年）

Assets of Construction Enterprises by Region (2005)

单位：万元 (10 000 yuan)

地 区	Region	资产总计 Total Assets	#流动资产 Circulating Funds	#固定资产 Fixed Assets	#无形及递延资产 Intangible and Deferred Assets
全 国	**National Total**	**314857308**	**228268068**	**57876731**	**6508957**
北 京	Beijing	32714956	22101293	2526673	254439
天 津	Tianjin	7384760	5423150	1425897	90999
河 北	Hebei	9764736	6759659	2282900	301470
山 西	Shanxi	8504544	5950281	1831019	122038
内蒙古	Inner Mongolia	3441532	2367209	843853	108475
辽 宁	Liaoning	12539488	9166384	2752977	290855
吉 林	Jilin	4857475	3620957	1014809	94236
黑龙江	Heilongjiang	7038066	4799360	1674139	95407
上 海	Shanghai	20777866	16988395	2150641	164245
江 苏	Jiangsu	32095807	25444589	4903494	580144
浙 江	Zhejiang	25943721	20490153	3814643	350762
安 徽	Anhui	7716162	5312957	1890340	282575
福 建	Fujian	7725253	5995063	1271563	97363
江 西	Jiangxi	4486360	2991078	1107301	168475
山 东	Shandong	23373281	17147844	4576764	685614
河 南	Henan	9230042	6138981	2490358	337926
湖 北	Hubei	11400957	7346810	2953061	470035
湖 南	Hunan	8213667	5417361	2229265	257520
广 东	Guangdong	25926241	19719394	4131685	454463
广 西	Guangxi	4555245	2835274	1116241	112274
海 南	Hainan	598574	398429	169446	17808
重 庆	Chongqing	6668558	4843338	1368539	142528
四 川	Sichuan	14464214	9545324	3264389	374037
贵 州	Guizhou	2858639	2032844	583557	81713
云 南	Yunnan	6360032	4360647	1474328	146724
西 藏	Tibet	441492	217963	172961	17352
陕 西	Shaanxi	5830474	4143833	1253798	160232
甘 肃	Gansu	3409364	2243816	1040081	39807
青 海	Qinghai	1123283	679821	364194	28109
宁 夏	Ningxia	1627824	1133992	378362	30530
新 疆	Xinjiang	3784693	2651871	819453	150802

15-24 各地区按登记注册类型分建筑业企业资产（2005年）

Assets of Construction Enterprises by Registration Status and Region (2005)

单位：万元 (10 000 yuan)

地 区	Region	合 计 Total	内资企业 Domestic Funded	#国 有 State-owned	#集 体 Collective-owned	港澳台商投资企业 Funded from Hong Kong, Macao and Taiwan	#港澳台商独资企业 Solely Owned	外商投资企业 Foreign Funded	#外商独资企业 Solely Owned
全 国	**National Total**	**314857308**	**310192489**	**94024456**	**24561922**	**2008794**	**235727**	**2656026**	**540475**
北 京	Beijing	32714956	32159730	17188833	1548659	262825	37893	292402	21283
天 津	Tianjin	7384760	7199484	2855637	425114	92034	34244	93242	34176
河 北	Hebei	9764736	9757496	3282952	547010	3264		3976	
山 西	Shanxi	8504544	8469106	4357141	323204	28747		6692	
内蒙古	Inner Mongolia	3441532	3440259	226466	30243			1273	
辽 宁	Liaoning	12539488	12125593	3557038	1275858	85015	7786	328881	3167
吉 林	Jilin	4857475	4816726	1793841	202891	24540		16209	
黑龙江	Heilongjiang	7038066	6991981	1889408	495829	3881		42204	
上 海	Shanghai	20777866	19590485	4650553	741898	344349	5049	843032	326810
江 苏	Jiangsu	32095807	31463965	3806893	2441656	263958	95488	367885	96339
浙 江	Zhejiang	25943721	25604031	1723521	1392030	74301	1331	265389	
安 徽	Anhui	7716162	7687667	2318513	757457	16027	7139	12468	2166
福 建	Fujian	7725253	7556348	2019766	862879	108539	8075	60365	22047
江 西	Jiangxi	4486360	4454090	1858393	881574	29754	739	2516	
山 东	Shandong	23373281	23163307	5024441	3350421	110121	8892	99853	19118
河 南	Henan	9230042	9197047	3184295	726524	26051		6945	1301
湖 北	Hubei	11400957	11360238	4458032	623012	21918	2745	18801	
湖 南	Hunan	8213667	8149838	2977562	959008	49722	8916	14107	7936
广 东	Guangdong	25926241	25388251	8439750	2517305	411944	15446	126047	4865
广 西	Guangxi	4555245	4538413	2332490	687947	3915		12917	
海 南	Hainan	598574	593361	178244	64668	2764		2449	825
重 庆	Chongqing	6668558	6651421	1263180	451187	11610	841	5528	
四 川	Sichuan	14464214	14423795	5001410	1184132	8064	630	32355	363
贵 州	Guizhou	2858639	2850055	1881926	222584	8584			
云 南	Yunnan	6360032	6349387	1366012	636879	10645			
西 藏	Tibet	441492	441492	111956	72608				
陕 西	Shaanxi	5830474	5830474	2883619	477316				
甘 肃	Gansu	3409364	3408952	1211641	401897			412	
青 海	Qinghai	1123283	1121927	543350	78209	1278	54	79	79
宁 夏	Ningxia	1627824	1627363	458752	71922	462	462		
新 疆	Xinjiang	3784693	3780208	1178845	110001	4485			

15-25 各地区建筑业企业负债及所有者权益（2005年）

Liabilities and Owners' Equity of Construction Enterprises by Region (2005)

单位：万元 (10 000 yuan)

地区	Region	负债合计 Total Liabilities	流动负债 Liquid Liabilities	长期负债 Long-term Liabilities	所有者权益 Owners' Equity	#实收资本 Paid-in Capitals
全国	**National Total**	**203627396**	**193364293**	**10263103**	**111225356**	**81713763**
北京	Beijing	21004385	19056002	1948383	11710571	7820466
天津	Tianjin	5418780	5117210	301569	1965981	1484088
河北	Hebei	6022624	5802219	220405	3742112	2799853
山西	Shanxi	6070051	5607898	462153	2429937	2207431
内蒙古	Inner Mongolia	2087680	1916002	171678	1353852	1046422
辽宁	Liaoning	7595359	7410394	184965	4944130	3759446
吉林	Jilin	3383705	3264419	119286	1473770	1157940
黑龙江	Heilongjiang	4261943	4122326	139617	2776123	2585760
上海	Shanghai	15127301	14511606	615695	5650565	3821894
江苏	Jiangsu	21814002	21261237	552765	10281806	6904933
浙江	Zhejiang	16978766	16494150	484616	8964956	5670795
安徽	Anhui	4642443	4414894	227549	3073719	2133943
福建	Fujian	4859565	4726017	133549	2865688	2418191
江西	Jiangxi	2651878	2481690	170188	1834482	1464109
山东	Shandong	15475221	14805240	669981	7898060	6154949
河南	Henan	5589234	5362518	226716	3640808	3174106
湖北	Hubei	6580053	6205695	374357	4820904	3202353
湖南	Hunan	4733123	4297663	435460	3480544	2611517
广东	Guangdong	17652169	16668039	984130	8274072	5603049
广西	Guangxi	2740057	2388505	351552	1815188	1373203
海南	Hainan	347913	235841	112072	250661	169935
重庆	Chongqing	3577338	3360004	217334	3091220	2454361
四川	Sichuan	8466658	8014346	452311	5997557	4452698
贵州	Guizhou	1924725	1790267	134458	933914	741373
云南	Yunnan	4005362	3831034	174328	2354670	1913017
西藏	Tibet	149062	136905	12158	292430	217226
陕西	Shaanxi	4075929	3913689	162240	1754545	1459539
甘肃	Gansu	2018895	1947528	71368	1390468	1063270
青海	Qinghai	690155	666703	23452	433128	429558
宁夏	Ningxia	1054913	1017249	37665	572911	492574
新疆	Xinjiang	2628108	2537003	91105	1156585	925765

15-26 各地区按登记注册类型分建筑业企业所有者权益（2005年）

Owners' Equity of Construction Enterprises by Registration Status and Region (2005)

单位：万元 (10 000 yuan)

地区	Region	合计 Total	内资企业 Domestic Funded	#国有 State-owned	#集体 Collective-owned	港澳台商投资企业 Funded from Hong Kong, Macao and Taiwan	#港澳台商独资企业 Solely Owned	外商投资企业 Foreign Funded	#外商独资企业 Solely Owned
全国	**National Total**	**111225356**	**109580489**	**27169895**	**10040974**	**765081**	**110854**	**879787**	**138229**
北京	Beijing	11710571	11494361	7344618	404574	116608	27145	99602	15820
天津	Tianjin	1965981	1924340	610916	137139	13972	712	27669	8897
河北	Hebei	3742112	3737339	672063	300404	2623		2150	
山西	Shanxi	2429937	2416473	989368	125585	12195		1270	
内蒙古	Inner Mongolia	1353852	1352953	86898	15415			899	
辽宁	Liaoning	4944130	4741516	990517	529126	34580	6764	168034	2377
吉林	Jilin	1473770	1455402	392342	82737	10459		7910	
黑龙江	Heilongjiang	2776123	2748011	490203	199592	3400		24712	
上海	Shanghai	5650565	5324272	1015829	227877	120422	2654	205872	42767
江苏	Jiangsu	10281806	10042327	1046170	903148	115890	43062	123589	42112
浙江	Zhejiang	8964956	8875996	495935	401259	30073	655	58887	
安徽	Anhui	3073719	3061133	762416	301213	8915	3652	3671	470
福建	Fujian	2865688	2797577	441155	313566	42936	5115	25175	7897
江西	Jiangxi	1834482	1816364	579094	377011	16184	483	1934	
山东	Shandong	7898060	7804741	1164336	1243210	51750	5822	41569	6742
河南	Henan	3640808	3633715	839908	410053	8684		-1591	834
湖北	Hubei	4820904	4793920	1271851	396393	16942	1502	10042	
湖南	Hunan	3480544	3442292	833168	493598	27688	6571	10564	7160
广东	Guangdong	8274072	8114667	2025185	847016	111456	5896	47950	2409
广西	Guangxi	1815188	1806266	813429	352740	1259		7662	
海南	Hainan	250661	246976	51335	33120	2452		1234	556
重庆	Chongqing	3091220	3082628	378291	231572	5921	518	2670	
四川	Sichuan	5997557	5985667	1430290	626712	3916	277	7974	181
贵州	Guizhou	933914	930328	459608	102382	3587			
云南	Yunnan	2354670	2353893	395046	340312	776			
西藏	Tibet	292430	292430	69126	57506				
陕西	Shaanxi	1754545	1754545	617886	241031				
甘肃	Gansu	1390468	1390138	390229	223987			330	
青海	Qinghai	433128	432582	160071	37382	537	36	9	9
宁夏	Ningxia	572911	572919	126533	39378	-8	-8		
新疆	Xinjiang	1156585	1154720	226080	45938	1865			

15-27 各地区按登记注册类型分建筑业企业负债（2005年）

Liabilities of Construction Enterprises by Registration Status and Region (2005)

单位：万元 (10 000 yuan)

地区	Region	合计 Total	内资企业 Domestic Funded	#国有 State-owned	#集体 Collective-owned	港澳台商投资企业 Funded from Hong Kong, Macao and Taiwan	#港澳台商独资企业 Solely Owned	外商投资企业 Foreign Funded	#外商独资企业 Solely Owned
全　国	**National Total**	**203627396**	**200607444**	**66854561**	**14520948**	**1243713**	**124873**	**1776239**	**402247**
北　京	Beijing	21004385	20665369	9844215	1144085	146217	10748	192800	5463
天　津	Tianjin	5418780	5275144	2244721	287975	78062	33532	65573	25279
河　北	Hebei	6022624	6020157	2610889	246606	641		1827	
山　西	Shanxi	6070051	6048078	3367774	197619	16552		5422	
内蒙古	Inner Mongolia	2087680	2087306	139568	14828			374	
辽　宁	Liaoning	7595359	7384076	2566521	746733	50435	1022	160847	791
吉　林	Jilin	3383705	3361325	1401499	120153	14081		8299	
黑龙江	Heilongjiang	4261943	4243970	1399205	296237	481		17492	
上　海	Shanghai	15127301	14266214	3634725	514021	223928	2395	637159	284043
江　苏	Jiangsu	21814002	21421638	2760723	1538508	148068	52426	244296	54228
浙　江	Zhejiang	16978766	16728035	1227585	990772	44228	675	206503	
安　徽	Anhui	4642443	4626534	1556097	456244	7112	3487	8798	1696
福　建	Fujian	4859565	4758771	1578610	549313	65603	2960	35191	14151
江　西	Jiangxi	2651878	2637726	1279299	504563	13570	256	582	
山　东	Shandong	15475221	15358566	3860105	2107211	58371	3069	58284	12376
河　南	Henan	5589234	5563332	2344387	316472	17366		8536	468
湖　北	Hubei	6580053	6566318	3186180	226619	4976	1243	8759	
湖　南	Hunan	4733123	4707546	2144393	465410	22034	2345	3544	775
广　东	Guangdong	17652169	17273585	6414565	1670289	300487	9550	78097	2457
广　西	Guangxi	2740057	2732147	1519061	335207	2656		5255	
海　南	Hainan	347913	346385	126909	31548	312		1216	269
重　庆	Chongqing	3577338	3568792	884889	219615	5689	323	2857	
四　川	Sichuan	8466658	8438129	3571120	557420	4148	354	24381	182
贵　州	Guizhou	1924725	1919728	1422318	120203	4997			
云　南	Yunnan	4005362	3995494	970965	296567	9868			
西　藏	Tibet	149062	149062	42830	15103				
陕　西	Shaanxi	4075929	4075929	2265733	236286				
甘　肃	Gansu	2018895	2018814	821412	177910			81	
青　海	Qinghai	690155	689345	383279	40827	741	18	70	70
宁　夏	Ningxia	1054913	1054443	332219	32544	470	470		
新　疆	Xinjiang	2628108	2625488	952765	64063	2620			

15-28 各地区建筑业企业总收入（2005年）

Total Income of Construction Enterprises by Region (2005)

单位：万元 (10 000 yuan)

地区	Region	企业总收入 Total Income of Enterprises	工程结算收入 Revenue of Project Settlement Accounts	#工程结算成本 Costs of Project Settlement Accounts	#工程结算利润 Profits of Project Settlement Accounts	其他业务收入 Revenue from Other Businesses	#其他业务利润 Profits from Other Businesses
全国	**National Total**	**331984913**	**325105381**	**288564361**	**23726136**	**6879532**	**1102605**
北京	Beijing	22055063	21621025	19396614	1482238	434037	83450
天津	Tianjin	8077953	7887793	7087997	560008	190160	10764
河北	Hebei	10796504	10565232	9290610	850278	231272	25739
山西	Shanxi	8887393	8735626	7849954	568286	151768	30207
内蒙古	Inner Mongolia	3721320	3660752	3145436	361945	60568	10998
辽宁	Liaoning	14764768	14488860	12567663	1336784	275908	35640
吉林	Jilin	4678157	4636500	4148878	313620	41657	5558
黑龙江	Heilongjiang	5664967	5588548	5026675	351603	76418	13282
上海	Shanghai	22250793	21678701	19474649	1501447	572092	103562
江苏	Jiangsu	34960932	33612188	29606028	2549072	1348744	141643
浙江	Zhejiang	41282038	40842915	36895411	2453607	439123	65355
安徽	Anhui	9308074	9144055	8149089	621234	164019	25046
福建	Fujian	8659037	8553191	7710701	511009	105847	35703
江西	Jiangxi	4889389	4845035	4257931	382919	44353	11054
山东	Shandong	22313478	21734486	18735080	2024603	578992	83020
河南	Henan	10248300	10107640	8907754	799155	140660	27805
湖北	Hubei	13657202	13286132	11689359	1067512	371071	41283
湖南	Hunan	11360997	11255682	10007470	768268	105315	22927
广东	Guangdong	25689316	25197545	22455259	1725119	491771	128931
广西	Guangxi	3969602	3873745	3440444	259468	95856	19735
海南	Hainan	519725	518428	438343	48242	1297	876
重庆	Chongqing	7278552	7158474	6397279	496175	120078	17369
四川	Sichuan	13656895	13400458	11798318	1007951	256437	48925
贵州	Guizhou	2693643	2652641	2396348	155012	41002	20243
云南	Yunnan	5152300	5061525	4470333	375287	90775	18430
西藏	Tibet	295021	292085	227307	47666	2936	1642
陕西	Shaanxi	6483199	6351496	5645911	416940	131703	24906
甘肃	Gansu	2984681	2855796	2425510	306017	128885	11131
青海	Qinghai	877149	857761	757809	67820	19388	5991
宁夏	Ningxia	1164367	1115498	996756	80060	48869	7775
新疆	Xinjiang	3644101	3525569	3167445	236793	118532	23615

15-29 各地区按登记注册类型分建筑业企业总收入（2005年）

Total Income of Construction by Registration Status and Region (2005)

单位：万元 (10 000 yuan)

地区	Region	合计 Total	内资企业 Domestic Funded	#国有 State-owned	#集体 Collective-owned	港澳台商投资企业 Funded from Hong Kong, Macao and Taiwan	#港澳台商独资企业 Solely Owned	外商投资企业 Foreign Funded	#外商独资企业 Solely Owned
全国	**National Total**	**331984913**	**327169888**	**89853307**	**24901718**	**1878336**	**291485**	**2936688**	**568304**
北京	Beijing	22055063	21329679	8270859	1293213	280203	81562	445180	38814
天津	Tianjin	8077953	7915031	2910688	415363	108298	29231	54624	2710
河北	Hebei	10796504	10790423	3528598	602878	4253		1828	
山西	Shanxi	8887393	8865382	3996398	283373	11318		10694	
内蒙古	Inner Mongolia	3721320	3721192	338700	34893			128	
辽宁	Liaoning	14764768	14276999	4169627	1363807	58859	2413	428911	4925
吉林	Jilin	4678157	4628755	1519790	200846	23253		26149	
黑龙江	Heilongjiang	5664967	5624553	1800986	419405	891		39523	
上海	Shanghai	22250793	21039645	5221586	850121	408743	21563	802405	313134
江苏	Jiangsu	34960932	34355269	4028810	2509078	225901	107692	379762	145329
浙江	Zhejiang	41282038	40750191	2214096	1605477	126919	673	404928	
安徽	Anhui	9308074	9276614	2754912	783078	24302	17312	7159	1306
福建	Fujian	8659037	8495648	2153533	873645	84374	4090	79016	36109
江西	Jiangxi	4889389	4869677	1775782	1006702	18128	173	1584	
山东	Shandong	22313478	22195984	5185994	3029668	78175	2279	39318	8532
河南	Henan	10248300	10228062	3356621	978837	14292		5946	320
湖北	Hubei	13657202	13632122	5312589	820936	15744	2571	9336	
湖南	Hunan	11360997	11300732	3854633	1282532	42075	9151	18190	4921
广东	Guangdong	25689316	25223786	9488471	2172186	319061	11322	146469	11391
广西	Guangxi	3969602	3945971	1989201	657231	1821		21810	
海南	Hainan	519725	514436	281104	62408	3150		2139	83
重庆	Chongqing	7278552	7259865	1212763	455696	14095	582	4592	
四川	Sichuan	13656895	13645792	4870004	1306310	4447	375	6655	394
贵州	Guizhou	2693643	2692894	1848584	153321	749			
云南	Yunnan	5152300	5146342	1428490	592712	5958			
西藏	Tibet	295021	295021	51325	64251				
陕西	Shaanxi	6483199	6483199	3032279	476330				
甘肃	Gansu	2984681	2984675	1106352	423254			6	
青海	Qinghai	877149	875641	512233	40516	1171	308	337	337
宁夏	Ningxia	1164367	1164179	414446	38663	188	188		
新疆	Xinjiang	3644101	3642131	1223853	104990	1969			

15-30 各地区建筑业企业利税总额（2005年）

Total Pre-Tax Profits of Construction Enterprises by Region (2005)

地区	Region	利税总额 合计（万元）Total Pre-tax Profits (10 000 yuan)	利润总额 Total Profits	工程结算税金及附加 Taxes and Extra Charges on Project Settlement Accounts	管理费用中的税金 Taxes in Management Expenses	产值利税率（%）Ratio of Pre-tax Profits to Output Value (%)	资产利税率（%）Ratio of Pre-tax Profits to Assets (%)
全国	**National Total**	**20664572**	**9066623**	**11013963**	**583986**	**6.0**	**6.6**
北京	Beijing	1266684	612127	635516	19041	6.7	3.9
天津	Tianjin	398120	170137	219821	8161	5.3	5.4
河北	Hebei	686111	293377	367372	25362	5.3	7.0
山西	Shanxi	374024	93202	266942	13880	4.4	4.4
内蒙古	Inner Mongolia	317599	162376	135740	19483	8.3	9.2
辽宁	Liaoning	1119990	543863	548344	27783	7.6	8.9
吉林	Jilin	190965	24960	158465	7540	3.9	3.9
黑龙江	Heilongjiang	245188	52342	183194	9651	4.3	3.5
上海	Shanghai	1338429	669130	651713	17586	7.1	6.4
江苏	Jiangsu	2379509	1119457	1203950	56101	5.4	7.4
浙江	Zhejiang	2774163	1324144	1408550	41469	5.9	10.7
安徽	Anhui	513639	180314	313051	20274	5.3	6.7
福建	Fujian	509765	196898	302975	9892	5.8	6.6
江西	Jiangxi	352670	155667	184863	12140	6.2	7.9
山东	Shandong	1660544	867836	721998	70709	6.6	7.1
河南	Henan	625556	255655	334195	35706	5.9	6.8
湖北	Hubei	740222	266394	439683	34145	5.5	6.5
湖南	Hunan	731564	287689	418032	25843	6.0	8.9
广东	Guangdong	1643901	705824	898556	39522	7.5	6.3
广西	Guangxi	220868	67651	144734	8483	5.2	4.8
海南	Hainan	44174	25874	17459	840	7.4	7.4
重庆	Chongqing	454920	199481	243227	12212	5.8	6.8
四川	Sichuan	774353	276916	473868	23569	5.3	5.4
贵州	Guizhou	129803	38331	87204	4269	4.8	4.5
云南	Yunnan	362133	187724	164701	9708	6.7	5.7
西藏	Tibet	44882	28184	13748	2950	11.1	10.2
陕西	Shaanxi	321776	100824	211103	9849	4.9	5.5
甘肃	Gansu	186053	86565	91947	7541	5.9	5.5
青海	Qinghai	35497	5797	27203	2497	3.9	3.2
宁夏	Ningxia	57696	21055	34614	2028	5.1	3.5
新疆	Xinjiang	163776	46830	111195	5752	4.6	4.3

15-31 各地区按登记注册类型分建筑业企业税金总额（2005年）

Taxes of Construction Enterprises by Registration Status and by Region (2005)

单位：万元 (10 000 yuan)

地区	Region	合计 Total	内资企业 Domestic Funded	#国有 State-owned	#集体 Collective-owned	港澳台商投资企业 Funded from Hong Kong, Macao and Taiwan	#港澳台商独资企业 Solely Owned	外商投资企业 Foreign Funded	#外商独资企业 Solely Owned
全 国	**National Total**	**11597949**	**11475341**	**2956632**	**996647**	**49679**	**5799**	**72930**	**12075**
北 京	Beijing	654557	633797	240725	41902	8027	2156	12732	1706
天 津	Tianjin	227982	225730	86694	14864	1403	185	850	74
河 北	Hebei	392734	392483	126298	24274	166		85	
山 西	Shanxi	280823	280114	122916	11388	374		336	
内蒙古	Inner Mongolia	155222	155219	10966	1194			4	
辽 宁	Liaoning	576127	559446	162037	52397	1867	78	14814	152
吉 林	Jilin	166005	164226	50702	8249	726		1053	
黑龙江	Heilongjiang	192846	191629	64257	14890	29		1187	
上 海	Shanghai	669298	643934	166980	24982	9722	531	15642	5576
江 苏	Jiangsu	1260052	1243918	125050	103509	4897	951	11237	3392
浙 江	Zhejiang	1450019	1441982	67612	57748	2927	21	5110	
安 徽	Anhui	333325	332202	91182	29404	832	541	291	74
福 建	Fujian	312868	308230	72450	32992	2706	329	1932	552
江 西	Jiangxi	197003	196356	62469	46260	618	11	29	
山 东	Shandong	792707	788950	188876	117961	2360	117	1398	321
河 南	Henan	369901	369289	111006	38964	426		185	10
湖 北	Hubei	473828	473081	171857	37846	430	48	317	
湖 南	Hunan	443875	441720	140293	57549	1501	442	654	130
广 东	Guangdong	938077	924185	297136	96343	9598	339	4294	58
广 西	Guangxi	153217	152730	62920	36929	68		419	
海 南	Hainan	18300	18107	9552	3095	116		77	7
重 庆	Chongqing	255439	254915	36657	18369	435	21	89	
四 川	Sichuan	497437	497097	174225	50636	156	12	184	13
贵 州	Guizhou	91473	91456	59010	6831	16			
云 南	Yunnan	174409	174250	44657	21998	159			
西 藏	Tibet	16698	16698	3892	4220				
陕 西	Shaanxi	220952	220952	108045	19561				
甘 肃	Gansu	99488	99486	32880	16326			2	
青 海	Qinghai	29700	29653	15881	1205	37	10	10	10
宁 夏	Ningxia	36642	36636	13159	1359	6	6		
新 疆	Xinjiang	116946	116870	36251	3406	77			

15-32 各地区按登记注册类型分建筑业企业利润总额（2005年）

Total Profits of Construction Enterprises by Registration Status and Region (2005)

单位：万元 (10 000 yuan)

地区	Region	合计 Total	内资企业 Domestic Funded	#国有 State-owned	#集体 Collective-owned	港澳台商投资企业 Funded from Hong Kong, Macao and Taiwan	#港澳台商独资企业 Solely Owned	外商投资企业 Foreign Funded	#外商独资企业 Solely Owned
全国	**National Total**	**9066623**	**8913374**	**1414286**	**807038**	**36242**	**10014**	**117007**	**23268**
北京	Beijing	612127	604575	341134	49814	778	1437	6775	3070
天津	Tianjin	170137	174349	37299	11382	-4486	590	273	-685
河北	Hebei	293377	293296	45860	22489	128		-48	
山西	Shanxi	93202	93260	22352	5655	-43		-15	
内蒙古	Inner Mongolia	162376	162375	10559	527			1	
辽宁	Liaoning	543863	520437	125848	55760	1266	271	22161	19
吉林	Jilin	24960	20699	-18722	3450	4440		-179	
黑龙江	Heilongjiang	52342	51423	1188	5412	-8		926	
上海	Shanghai	669130	620383	66540	19965	5554	187	43193	9220
江苏	Jiangsu	1119457	1085189	61079	78719	13650	8229	20618	6792
浙江	Zhejiang	1324144	1306560	119757	40697	3972	1	13613	
安徽	Anhui	180314	179785	34788	17602	40	-57	489	57
福建	Fujian	196898	193287	25476	13799	885	-581	2726	2171
江西	Jiangxi	155667	155077	34575	27749	560	-10	30	
山东	Shandong	867836	862077	125877	146055	3120	2	2639	1057
河南	Henan	255655	256893	40962	40923	593		-1831	12
湖北	Hubei	266394	266092	36038	25449	528	-7	-226	
湖南	Hunan	287689	284925	50417	33477	176	21	2588	1456
广东	Guangdong	705824	698674	109308	59043	4134	-8	3016	143
广西	Guangxi	67651	67449	8421	16439	-16		217	
海南	Hainan	25874	25770	14871	852	90		14	-43
重庆	Chongqing	199481	199061	12547	7266	385	-14	35	
四川	Sichuan	276916	276574	41721	37337	319	48	23	-1
贵州	Guizhou	38331	38597	6609	1109	-266			
云南	Yunnan	187724	187378	798	41567	346			
西藏	Tibet	28184	28184	3357	6583				
陕西	Shaanxi	100824	100824	31765	13690				
甘肃	Gansu	86565	86597	11195	22407			-32	
青海	Qinghai	5797	5823	8998	187	-28	-32	1	1
宁夏	Ningxia	21055	21115	3122	254	-60	-60		
新疆	Xinjiang	46830	46647	546	1379	183			

15-33 各地区按资质等级分总承包建筑业企业利润总额（2005年）

Total Profits of Construction of General Contractors by Qualification Criteria and by Region (2005)

单位：万元 (10 000 yuan)

地区	Region	合计 Total	特级 Special Grade	一级 First Grade	二级 Second Grade	三级及以下 Third Grade and below
全国	**National Total**	**7109477**	**1079283**	**2113299**	**2075421**	**1841474**
北京	Beijing	510774	372073	83441	29569	25691
天津	Tianjin	66437	9785	34422	11054	11176
河北	Hebei	239511	3848	88502	75023	72138
山西	Shanxi	78148	27218	23841	13348	13741
内蒙古	Inner Mongolia	162244	14	28759	78907	54564
辽宁	Liaoning	425856	29683	216210	77097	102867
吉林	Jilin	20195	14998	-6467	3298	8366
黑龙江	Heilongjiang	26103	3540	4309	10220	8033
上海	Shanghai	484280	53448	137723	140052	153057
江苏	Jiangsu	865946	153785	299641	251059	161462
浙江	Zhejiang	1064077	231057	362566	276285	194170
安徽	Anhui	135807	9917	32366	43915	49609
福建	Fujian	139704	15701	37259	64475	22270
江西	Jiangxi	95773	-1	32419	26196	37160
山东	Shandong	669502	26876	153675	209325	279626
河南	Henan	215821	8850	41094	73292	92586
湖北	Hubei	209192	35123	35179	70758	68133
湖南	Hunan	257769	13533	109725	63252	71259
广东	Guangdong	498861	38627	158856	150525	150853
广西	Guangxi	46703	1386	6777	16392	22148
海南	Hainan	26765		18086	6285	2393
重庆	Chongqing	173919		60204	78448	35268
四川	Sichuan	237563	5510	36860	111357	83836
贵州	Guizhou	35602	408	11861	15530	7803
云南	Yunnan	166429	3758	31299	70339	61032
西藏	Tibet	26041			19937	6103
陕西	Shaanxi	95113	12412	36482	27102	19118
甘肃	Gansu	75869		29533	33457	12879
青海	Qinghai	6553	5506	-2235	3555	-273
宁夏	Ningxia	15524		1398	6960	7166
新疆	Xinjiang	37398	2230	9514	18411	7243

15-34 各地区按资质等级分专业承包建筑业企业利润总额（2005年）

Total Profits of Construction of General Contractors by Qualification Criteria and by Region (2005)

单位：万元 (10 000 yuan)

地区	Region	合计 Total	一级 First Grade	二级 Second Grade	三级及以下 Third Grade and below
全国	**National Total**	**1957145**	**537449**	**603980**	**815716**
北京	Beijing	101353	27678	22890	50785
天津	Tianjin	103700	75512	6931	21257
河北	Hebei	53866	12157	23942	17767
山西	Shanxi	15054	1736	7361	5956
内蒙古	Inner Mongolia	133	-3096	-360	3588
辽宁	Liaoning	118007	40550	30782	46675
吉林	Jilin	4766	-265	2466	2564
黑龙江	Heilongjiang	26239	3176	5764	17300
上海	Shanghai	184851	46331	51365	87155
江苏	Jiangsu	253511	59687	81216	112608
浙江	Zhejiang	260067	60524	69904	129639
安徽	Anhui	44507	12972	17361	14174
福建	Fujian	57193	15050	21598	20545
江西	Jiangxi	59893	50897	3379	5618
山东	Shandong	198335	12921	78666	106748
河南	Henan	39834	9487	15923	14425
湖北	Hubei	57202	15454	35403	6346
湖南	Hunan	29920	5208	12239	12473
广东	Guangdong	206963	71752	52245	82966
广西	Guangxi	20948	1026	10508	9414
海南	Hainan	-891	-1289	170	228
重庆	Chongqing	25561	7446	8339	9776
四川	Sichuan	39353	11053	13294	15006
贵州	Guizhou	2728	121	648	1960
云南	Yunnan	21295	1901	11579	7815
西藏	Tibet	2143		28	2115
陕西	Shaanxi	5711	1180	3263	1268
甘肃	Gansu	10696	-3285	12729	1252
青海	Qinghai	-756	-905	-169	318
宁夏	Ningxia	5531	491	913	4127
新疆	Xinjiang	9432	1979	3605	3847

15-35 各地区按登记注册类型分建筑业企业工程结算利润（2005年）

Profits of Project Settlement Accounts of Construction Enterprises by Registration Status and Region (2005)

单位：万元 (10 000 yuan)

地 区	Region	合 计 Total	内资企业 Domestic Funded	#国 有 State-owned	#集 体 Collective-owned	港澳台商投资企业 Funded from Hong Kong, Macao and Taiwan	#港澳台商独资企业 Solely Owned	外商投资企业 Foreign Funded	#外商独资企业 Solely Owned
全 国	**National Total**	**23726136**	**23263413**	**5744448**	**1990331**	**154427**	**26206**	**308296**	**56975**
北 京	Beijing	1482238	1431048	467714	112119	15620	2785	35569	7757
天 津	Tianjin	560008	542202	173984	39045	13274	4340	4532	357
河 北	Hebei	850278	849606	262319	55771	439		233	
山 西	Shanxi	568286	567119	239380	23680	935		232	
内蒙古	Inner Mongolia	361945	361925	25650	2596			20	
辽 宁	Liaoning	1336784	1265856	374745	135616	4984	530	65944	233
吉 林	Jilin	313620	306372	104483	19957	6167		1081	
黑龙江	Heilongjiang	351603	347580	94744	32630	83		3940	
上 海	Shanghai	1501447	1389736	300286	45705	27247	965	84465	23648
江 苏	Jiangsu	2549072	2480423	266025	185591	26535	13314	42114	13615
浙 江	Zhejiang	2453607	2411465	247511	93097	8724	100	33418	
安 徽	Anhui	621234	619388	170674	57048	733	246	1113	226
福 建	Fujian	511009	498381	122344	37423	5850	122	6778	4758
江 西	Jiangxi	382919	381388	129149	64422	1355	24	176	
山 东	Shandong	2024603	2008232	390326	319548	7947	385	8424	3429
河 南	Henan	799155	797906	227235	86457	1598		-349	43
湖 北	Hubei	1067512	1065314	365757	94076	1502	189	696	
湖 南	Hunan	768268	761102	236833	86674	3632	1981	3535	1834
广 东	Guangdong	1725119	1686845	426209	161597	23907	1123	14368	994
广 西	Guangxi	259468	259045	99991	47900	120		302	
海 南	Hainan	48242	47225	23431	3302	621		396	21
重 庆	Chongqing	496175	494938	55499	26617	828	57	409	
四 川	Sichuan	1007951	1006039	281741	105384	1036	92	876	38
贵 州	Guizhou	155012	155059	96253	8305	-47			
云 南	Yunnan	375287	374700	82695	41553	587			
西 藏	Tibet	47666	47666	5175	11147				
陕 西	Shaanxi	416940	416940	195302	38431				
甘 肃	Gansu	306017	306014	133447	43861			3	
青 海	Qinghai	67820	67720	47758	2147	77	-31	22	22
宁 夏	Ningxia	80060	80077	23690	2381	-17	-17		
新 疆	Xinjiang	236793	236103	74101	6253	690			

15-36 各地区建筑业劳动生产率（2005年）

Labor Productivity of Construction Enterprises by Region (2005)

单位：元/人 (yuan/person)

地区	Region	按建筑业总产值计算的劳动生产率 Overall Labor Productivity in Terms of Total Output Value	#国有 State-owned	#集体 Collective-owned
全国	**National Average**	**117317**	**154436**	**75922**
北京	Beijing	158604	176198	138056
天津	Tianjin	192983	228411	110298
河北	Hebei	108144	229033	59525
山西	Shanxi	135875	186589	52336
内蒙古	Inner Mongolia	81860	105940	64515
辽宁	Liaoning	115935	148411	71769
吉林	Jilin	110813	116552	60064
黑龙江	Heilongjiang	91342	112716	76733
上海	Shanghai	182307	198762	151436
江苏	Jiangsu	127657	147159	110198
浙江	Zhejiang	151421	234616	116119
安徽	Anhui	98754	154672	62998
福建	Fujian	120582	146901	98929
江西	Jiangxi	91830	109858	72048
山东	Shandong	92311	141276	66847
河南	Henan	83345	107613	62575
湖北	Hubei	122576	178144	59974
湖南	Hunan	105736	150516	74307
广东	Guangdong	132314	177012	73886
广西	Guangxi	100713	124912	60674
海南	Hainan	87912	94298	52010
重庆	Chongqing	94897	123046	71665
四川	Sichuan	84155	135791	59696
贵州	Guizhou	97668	119984	50787
云南	Yunnan	97853	146894	67967
西藏	Tibet	114400	121637	113155
陕西	Shaanxi	136028	214025	58184
甘肃	Gansu	68339	115575	41052
青海	Qinghai	87689	140454	43903
宁夏	Ningxia	74368	86393	62038
新疆	Xinjiang	114229	138471	135363

15-37 建筑业房屋建筑面积

Floor Space of Buildings of Construction Enterprises

单位：万平方米 (10 000 sq.m)

年份 地区	Year Region	房屋建筑面积 Floor Space of Buildings 施工面积 Floor Space under Construction	竣工面积 Floor Space Completed	#国有 State-owned 施工面积 Floor Space under Construction	竣工面积 Floor Space Completed	#集体 Collective-owned 施工面积 Floor Space under Construction	竣工面积 Floor Space Completed
	1985	35491.8	17072.7	19295.8	8563.1	16196.0	8509.6
	1989	40649.9	19723.4	21399.0	9143.3	19250.9	10580.1
	1990	37923.0	19552.5	20303.2	9361.7	17619.7	10190.9
	1991	41054.2	20256.3	21395.4	9566.2	19658.8	10690.1
	1992	51885.4	24045.5	25896.1	10968.0	25989.3	13077.5
	1993	65374.2	28684.8	32118.1	12085.4	32724.1	16379.0
	1994	78032.2	32383.3	39445.8	14143.0	37004.4	17674.0
	1995	89862.8	35666.3	44562.9	15182.4	41829.5	19262.0
	1996	129087.0	60047.9	48372.8	17491.3	74668.4	39827.3
	1997	128680.3	62244.0	48830.1	18507.5	70795.3	39859.3
	1998	137593.6	65682.6	45866.9	17577.4	71597.6	39338.0
	1999	147262.5	73924.9	47055.7	19868.6	70590.4	39949.1
	2000	160141.1	80714.9	46237.5	20145.0	68112.3	38515.5
	2001	188328.7	97699.0	46627.5	20338.2	61239.2	36115.1
	2002	215608.7	110217.1	44567.3	19628.2	52564.4	30071.3
	2003	259377.1	122827.6	46803.7	18774.1	50488.9	26727.6
	2004	310985.7	147364.0	52397.9	20552.5	42858.3	23393.3
	2005	352744.7	159406.2	56308.8	20505.7	42257.4	21750.4
北京	Beijing	15417.6	4862.4	5420.6	1485.8	1067.3	428.4
天津	Tianjin	3940.6	1484.4	1296.4	366.0	324.0	214.7
河北	Hebei	11261.4	5744.2	1943.0	665.8	891.6	542.5
山西	Shanxi	4048.5	1638.5	1686.4	695.6	359.2	174.7
内蒙古	Inner Mongolia	2958.9	1623.4	35.1	15.9	24.9	24.0
辽宁	Liaoning	10224.9	5111.1	1531.8	581.9	1245.8	695.0
吉林	Jilin	3165.9	1744.7	975.7	519.1	152.6	115.1
黑龙江	Heilongjiang	4467.7	2249.7	781.3	397.7	571.1	309.9
上海	Shanghai	14138.1	5643.3	2353.6	693.1	771.7	407.5
江苏	Jiangsu	52242.2	25391.9	1447.2	673.2	5585.2	2925.7
浙江	Zhejiang	59883.7	24637.1	448.2	151.2	2279.1	967.8
安徽	Anhui	9873.7	5081.3	1994.8	747.2	933.3	553.9
福建	Fujian	10268.3	4191.4	1862.8	655.2	1657.6	643.8
江西	Jiangxi	7281.2	4030.5	1468.1	668.3	2666.1	1530.4
山东	Shandong	25449.9	11883.1	3375.8	1191.1	5081.7	2775.4
河南	Henan	10813.2	4787.1	1715.2	709.9	1803.0	943.1
湖北	Hubei	12091.2	6896.9	3499.0	1683.6	1459.1	862.9
湖南	Hunan	13774.9	6846.0	3242.5	1220.5	2644.4	1442.8
广东	Guangdong	26886.0	10027.9	7606.8	2337.9	5128.6	2195.8
广西	Guangxi	5518.2	2209.7	2168.3	697.8	1517.0	676.0
海南	Hainan	692.4	205.1	339.4	104.2	124.7	56.0
重庆	Chongqing	10722.6	5155.2	1013.9	445.8	745.1	427.8
四川	Sichuan	17924.4	8692.2	3845.4	1522.6	2362.5	1283.1
贵州	Guizhou	3152.8	1149.5	1776.4	530.2	421.5	220.3
云南	Yunnan	4591.2	2470.1	990.9	387.4	770.3	506.2
西藏	Tibet	151.3	114.4	18.7	17.7	47.5	41.3
陕西	Shaanxi	4563.9	1892.9	1887.0	652.4	808.9	343.5
甘肃	Gansu	3008.5	1455.2	695.2	277.4	684.9	371.9
青海	Qinghai	407.6	194.0	58.6	26.3	46.8	29.2
宁夏	Ningxia	1056.6	564.0	304.8	143.2	38.8	20.5
新疆	Xinjiang	2767.6	1429.4	526.0	241.8	43.1	21.5

15-38 各地区劳务分包建筑业企业主要指标（2005年）

Main Indicators of Construction Enterprises of Work Subcontractors by Region (2005)

地 区	Region	企业单位数（个）Number of Enterprises (unit)	从业人数（人）Number of Persons Employed (person)	营业收入（万元）Total Revenue (10 000 yuan)	#工程结算收入 Projects Revenue	税 金（万元）Tax (10 000 yuan)	利润总额（万元）Total Profits (10 000 yuan)	从业人员劳动报酬(万元) Earnings of Employed Persons (10 000 yuan)
全 国	**National Total**	**3101**	**868165**	**1885213**	**1827362**	**58730**	**60645**	**1006214**
北 京	Beijing	64	7017	28036	26758	662	977	9807
天 津	Tianjin	170	12410	60715	50938	1854	1499	13108
河 北	Hebei	198	73751	129875	129637	4248	2776	72061
山 西	Shanxi	78	6949	12816	12677	353	-184	5504
内蒙古	Inner Mongolia	11	499	1465	1464	44	136	453
辽 宁	Liaoning	180	6965	44892	43135	1615	-148	9537
吉 林	Jilin	26	2073	5461	5191	172	145	2026
黑龙江	Heilongjiang	72	3660	8437	8272	277	57	2999
上 海	Shanghai	70	8040	78799	78252	4214	1632	13333
江 苏	Jiangsu	697	163588	398317	391012	16362	23241	207545
浙 江	Zhejiang	249	102365	277841	268513	8166	4654	152776
安 徽	Anhui	154	100854	144465	138626	3821	4440	96127
福 建	Fujian	100	103162	136734	131663	2302	3544	128869
江 西	Jiangxi	20	1344	5736	5736	193	71	1080
山 东	Shandong	275	27332	91938	86737	3408	5279	24128
河 南	Henan	138	34365	62141	58573	1401	2357	34092
湖 北	Hubei	94	33392	85998	83839	1122	1080	38458
湖 南	Hunan	114	42093	63481	62982	2238	2761	37082
广 东	Guangdong	26	5016	11588	10047	389	-237	8983
广 西	Guangxi	25	16086	19961	19488	628	231	14864
海 南	Hainan							
重 庆	Chongqing	76	32642	79252	78638	2165	3104	40777
四 川	Sichuan	109	73379	103025	102059	1979	2891	78217
贵 州	Guizhou	1	95	294	247	8	14	127
云 南	Yunnan	7	1810	3031	3031	71	61	2057
西 藏	Tibet							
陕 西	Shaanxi	10	347	1257	1257	65	22	240
甘 肃	Gansu	24	1514	4190	4077	99	116	1155
青 海	Qinghai	7	323	690	690	22	2	142
宁 夏	Ningxia	21	334	2717	2439	107	-28	340
新 疆	Xinjiang	85	6760	22064	21383	745	153	10329

15-39 勘察设计机构和人员数（2005年）

Number of Prospecting and Designing Institutions and Their Staff and Workers (2005)

地 区	Region	单位数（个）Number of Institutions (unit)	年底职工人数（人）Number of Staff & Workers at Year-end (person)	高级职称 Senior Title	中级职称 Middle Title	初级职称 Junior Title	其他人员 Others
全 国	**National Total**	**14245**	**1077785**	**231619**	**317120**	**220094**	**308952**
北 京	Beijing	584	85654	23967	21545	15865	24277
天 津	Tianjin	215	33069	8359	8210	6346	10154
河 北	Hebei	522	43901	8058	9692	5932	20219
山 西	Shanxi	368	26526	6073	8734	5402	6317
内蒙古	Inner Mongolia	223	14619	3911	5112	3445	2151
辽 宁	Liaoning	831	50112	12441	15651	8713	13307
吉 林	Jilin	372	20032	5709	6635	4117	3571
黑龙江	Heilongjiang	319	18951	5387	6103	2914	4547
上 海	Shanghai	495	62816	9843	13255	13265	26453
江 苏	Jiangsu	975	72316	12598	18471	15479	25768
浙 江	Zhejiang	595	39606	7949	13026	9784	8847
安 徽	Anhui	440	23650	6514	8151	5303	3682
福 建	Fujian	686	34316	4887	10805	9216	9408
江 西	Jiangxi	375	21024	4369	7018	4889	4748
山 东	Shandong	1113	58424	14331	18943	12018	13132
河 南	Henan	606	49961	9036	14715	9164	17046
湖 北	Hubei	571	53228	13240	16939	10437	12612
湖 南	Hunan	448	33276	7791	11441	6548	7496
广 东	Guangdong	1041	81442	12486	23836	17822	27298
广 西	Guangxi	283	17288	4172	6437	4229	2450
海 南	Hainan	103	5815	1254	1861	1427	1273
重 庆	Chongqing	267	22501	5460	6666	3637	6738
四 川	Sichuan	823	62465	13616	19309	13278	16262
贵 州	Guizhou	288	16683	2824	5298	4672	3889
云 南	Yunnan	489	24306	4321	8711	6097	5177
西 藏	Tibet	41	1851	227	597	478	549
陕 西	Shaanxi	480	51266	10377	12452	8850	19587
甘 肃	Gansu	227	21922	4552	7100	4104	6166
青 海	Qinghai	92	4207	805	1523	939	940
宁 夏	Ningxia	85	3783	1005	1109	1059	610
新 疆	Xinjiang	247	17681	4462	6057	3926	3236

15-40 勘察设计单位营业收入情况（2005年）

Business Revenue of Prospecting and Designing Institutions (2005)

地 区	Region	营业收入（亿元）Business Revenue (100 million yuan)	工程勘察收入 Revenue from Prospecting	工程设计收入 Revenue from Designing	工程承包收入 Revenue from Contracted Projects	其他收入 Other Revenue
全 国	**National Total**	**2972.64**	**216.02**	**796.64**	**1349.39**	**610.58**
北 京	Beijing	538.63	15.14	126.85	250.50	146.14
天 津	Tianjin	142.11	10.38	28.33	72.35	31.06
河 北	Hebei	76.82	5.65	17.79	19.58	33.81
山 西	Shanxi	28.78	4.39	11.74	7.48	5.17
内蒙古	Inner Mongolia	19.61	2.59	7.73	7.80	1.48
辽 宁	Liaoning	118.14	4.82	28.53	52.42	32.37
吉 林	Jilin	24.60	3.51	11.80	6.51	2.77
黑龙江	Heilongjiang	16.54	1.26	9.30	2.84	3.13
上 海	Shanghai	305.74	8.73	76.74	159.01	61.26
江 苏	Jiangsu	231.38	15.02	49.14	109.24	57.97
浙 江	Zhejiang	149.50	11.39	48.37	59.47	30.28
安 徽	Anhui	70.47	3.10	16.96	28.95	21.45
福 建	Fujian	50.17	5.44	18.31	23.15	3.26
江 西	Jiangxi	26.88	3.32	8.53	8.13	6.91
山 东	Shandong	105.19	6.47	29.66	41.57	27.49
河 南	Henan	70.98	5.82	24.17	27.95	13.05
湖 北	Hubei	155.80	18.86	40.99	81.98	13.97
湖 南	Hunan	55.80	7.79	20.63	22.28	5.11
广 东	Guangdong	323.88	15.41	74.57	199.56	34.34
广 西	Guangxi	17.66	2.41	7.48	1.89	5.89
海 南	Hainan	6.11	1.05	2.51	1.99	0.55
重 庆	Chongqing	77.97	4.31	14.99	50.14	8.54
四 川	Sichuan	133.07	21.45	42.14	33.30	36.18
贵 州	Guizhou	16.08	4.09	8.68	1.52	1.80
云 南	Yunnan	35.39	5.65	12.82	12.66	4.26
西 藏	Tibet	2.15	0.70	1.15	0.04	0.27
陕 西	Shaanxi	108.41	11.55	30.28	54.28	12.30
甘 肃	Gansu	33.28	9.05	12.08	6.79	5.36
青 海	Qinghai	3.51	1.13	1.80	0.26	0.32
宁 夏	Ningxia	4.52	0.73	2.44	0.74	0.61
新 疆	Xinjiang	21.60	4.59	8.99	4.68	3.34

15-41 建设工程监理企业和人员数(2005年)

Construction Project Supervision Enterprises and Employees (2005)

行业 地区	Sector Region	企业单位数(个) Number of Enterprises (unit)	年末从业人数(人) Persons Engaged (year-end) (person)	#高、中级职称人员 Persons with Senior or Mid-level Certificates	年末注册执业人数(人) Registered Professionals (year-end) (person)	注册监理工程师 Registered Supervisory Engineers	其他注册执业人员 Other Registered Professionals
合　计	**Total**	**5927**	**433193**	**263587**	**98683**	**81348**	**17335**
按行业分	**By Sector**						
房屋建筑工程	Housing Construction Projects	4986	322803	195800	75814	63225	12589
冶炼工程	Metallurgical Projects	57	5685	3786	1743	1437	306
矿山工程	Mining Projects	35	3359	2457	734	627	107
化工、石油工程	Chemical and Petroleum Projects	130	14467	9681	4071	3597	474
水利水电工程	Water Conservancy and Hydro-power Projects	94	14373	8593	2597	1637	960
电力工程	Power Projects	149	23145	13690	3689	3002	687
林业及生态工程	Forestry and Ecological Projects	57	2823	1754	444	348	96
铁路工程	Railway Projects	66	11012	7912	2780	2076	704
公路工程	Highway Projects	44	9471	4589	785	507	278
港口与航道工程	Habour and Navigation Projects	16	2177	1300	374	286	88
航天航空工程	Air and Space Projects	6	495	357	145	134	11
通信工程	Communications Projects	19	2097	980	335	179	156
市政公用工程	Civil and Public Utility Projects	263	20803	12356	5029	4150	879
机电安装工程	Machinery and Electric Installation Projects	5	483	332	143	143	
按地区分	**By Region**						
北　京	Beijing	278	38277	25096	7604	7364	240
天　津	Tianjin	71	8185	4062	1709	1474	235
河　北	Hebei	290	17630	13115	3831	3338	493
山　西	Shanxi	182	12644	8002	3276	1802	1474
内蒙古	Inner Mongolia	200	9359	7508	702	669	33
辽　宁	Liaoning	289	14352	11026	4046	3591	455
吉　林	Jilin	157	8351	6017	1756	1690	66
黑龙江	Heilongjiang	115	7347	5732	1590	1377	213
上　海	Shanghai	232	30998	15291	6673	5213	1460
江　苏	Jiangsu	525	37372	20063	9130	7558	1572
浙　江	Zhejiang	266	22568	11118	5270	4643	627
安　徽	Anhui	186	12619	6843	2732	2363	369
福　建	Fujian	167	11752	6858	3002	2416	586
江　西	Jiangxi	156	8411	4782	1549	1416	133
山　东	Shandong	419	28814	16008	6777	5887	890
河　南	Henan	286	20150	12109	4741	3969	772
湖　北	Hubei	224	14781	10739	4287	3785	502
湖　南	Hunan	165	14134	9395	3213	2528	685
广　东	Guangdong	382	28742	16960	9203	7344	1859
广　西	Guangxi	155	8554	4722	2016	1444	572
海　南	Hainan	34	1535	978	471	471	
重　庆	Chongqing	108	9081	5996	2197	1566	631
四　川	Sichuan	288	21564	13580	3764	3150	614
贵　州	Guizhou	60	4999	2593	1015	545	470
云　南	Yunnan	168	9435	5078	1232	779	453
西　藏	Tibet	16	501	275	55	19	36
陕　西	Shaanxi	191	12151	8367	2037	1749	288
甘　肃	Gansu	117	6885	4503	2105	1096	1009
青　海	Qinghai	52	2361	1328	525	269	256
宁　夏	Ningxia	55	3078	1559	466	415	51
新　疆	Xinjiang	93	6563	3884	1709	1418	291

15-42 建设工程监理营业收入(2005年)

Business Revenue of Construction Project Supervision Enterprises (2005)

单位：亿元 (100 million yuan)

行 业 地 区	Sector Region	营业收入 Business Revenue	工程监理收入 Revenue from Project Supervision	工程招标代理收入 Revenue from Project Bidding	工程造价咨询收入 Revenue from Consultation on Project Budgeting	工程项目管理与咨询服务收入 Revenue from Project Management and Consultation Service	其他收入 Other Revenue
合 计	**Total**	**2796704**	**1928416**	**57473**	**58781**	**232420**	**519614**
按行业分	**By Sector**						
房屋建筑工程	Housing Construction Projects	1792560	1244524	48768	50449	110034	338785
冶炼工程	Metallurgical Projects	52685	31766	597	1254	18694	374
矿山工程	Mining Projects	14373	12980	62	69	26	1235
化工、石油工程	Chemical and Petroleum Projects	109756	82036	345	1263	10519	15593
水利水电工程	Water Conservancy and Hydr-power Projects	141171	74068	1363	1142	13091	51508
电力工程	Power Projects	342844	179227	2258	1468	73190	86701
林业及生态工程	Forestry and Ecological Projects	12601	12152	72	8	6	363
铁路工程	Railway Projects	67354	66223	290	170	373	298
公路工程	Highway Projects	58228	53325	328		1014	3561
港口与航道工程	Habour and Navigation Projects	20847	20152	338	151	89	116
航天航空工程	Air and Space Projects	4441	3191	8		122	1121
通信工程	Communications Projects	21018	20720			278	20
市政公用工程	Civil and Public Utility Projects	156152	125648	2980	2807	4778	19939
机电安装工程	Machinery and Electric Installation Projects	2673	2405	64		205	
按地区分	**By Region**						
北 京	Beijing	524473	233295	4498	5228	56828	224624
天 津	Tianjin	44997	42176	92	187	1189	1352
河 北	Hebei	55056	52707	1488	338	456	68
山 西	Shanxi	43121	41967	350	26	595	183
内蒙古	Inner Mongolia	25645	25513	17		100	15
辽 宁	Liaoning	162808	56407	1295	1159	1043	102904
吉 林	Jilin	27245	26818		267	151	9
黑龙江	Heilongjiang	20669	20616	7		4	42
上 海	Shanghai	343228	211577	14384	24004	15027	78236
江 苏	Jiangsu	198955	178197	4691	3186	7235	5646
浙 江	Zhejiang	135846	122333	2302	3731	4768	2711
安 徽	Anhui	61722	40071	745	984	18780	1142
福 建	Fujian	58941	54137	1695	1847	970	291
江 西	Jiangxi	29357	27900	913	137	141	267
山 东	Shandong	135437	114938	2560	3417	7309	7214
河 南	Henan	138895	58281	1017	1112	64537	13947
湖 北	Hubei	71547	65493	544	582	2818	2111
湖 南	Hunan	95783	51856	111	785	8691	34341
广 东	Guangdong	266210	197317	13545	6559	28190	20600
广 西	Guangxi	35571	31888	1985	858	529	312
海 南	Hainan	5984	5938				46
重 庆	Chongqing	42641	39388	968	921	867	498
四 川	Sichuan	86180	77169	1268	984	1682	5078
贵 州	Guizhou	24304	15768	420	102	7887	127
云 南	Yunnan	48044	32026	204	276	1026	14513
西 藏	Tibet	2606	2248	200			158
陕 西	Shaanxi	35809	33059	848	696	767	439
甘 肃	Gansu	25867	22535	363	111	441	2417
青 海	Qinghai	8443	8342		32		70
宁 夏	Ningxia	10753	10198	288	90	114	63
新 疆	Xinjiang	30564	28258	675	1163	274	194

主要统计指标解释

建筑业统计单位 指从事房屋、构筑物建造和设备安装活动的法人企业。建筑业法人企业应具有建筑业资质并能够独立核算，同时其应具备以下条件：①依法成立，有自己的名称、组织机构和场所，能够承担民事责任；②独立拥有和使用资产，承担负债，有权与其他单位签订合同；③独立核算盈亏，能够编制资产负债表。

建筑业总产值 是以货币形式表现的建筑业企业在一定时期内生产的建筑业产品和提供的服务的总和。建筑业总产值包括：

⑴建筑工程产值：指列入建筑工程预算内的各种工程价值。

⑵安装工程产值：指设备安装工程价值，不包括被安装设备本身的价值。

⑶其他产值：建筑业总产值中除建筑工程、安装工程以外的产值。包括房屋构筑物修理产值、非标准设备制造产值、总包企业向分包企业收取的管理费以及不能明确划分的施工活动所完成的产值。

a.房屋构筑物修理产值：指房屋和构筑物修理所完成的产值，但不包括被修理房屋、构筑物本身价值和生产设备的修理产值。

b.非标准设备制造产值：指加工制造没有定型的非标准生产设备的加工费和原材料价值(如化工厂、炼油厂用的各种罐、槽，矿井生产统一使用的各种漏斗、三角槽、阀门等)以及附属加工厂为本企业承建工程制作的非标准设备的价值。

建筑业增加值 指建筑业企业在报告期内以货币形式表现的建筑业生产经营活动的最终成果。

从2004年第一次全国经济普查开始，建筑业现价增加值按生产法和分配法(收入法)两种方法计算，以收入法的计算结果为准，即从收入的角度出发，根据生产要素在生产过程中应得的收入份额计算。具体计算方法：经济普查年度建筑业增加值按照《经济普查年度GDP核算方案》计算，非经济普查年度建筑业增加值按照《非经济普查年度GDP核算方案》计算。

房屋建筑施工面积 指在报告期内施过工的全部房屋建筑面积，包括本期新开工的房屋面积、上期施工跨入本期继续施工的房屋面积、上期停缓建在本期恢复施工的房屋面积、本期竣工的房屋面积及本期施工后又停缓建的房屋面积。

房屋建筑竣工面积 指在报告期内房屋建筑按照设计要求全部完工，达到了使用条件，经验收鉴定合格，正式移交使用单位的房屋建筑面积。

Explanatory Notes on Main Statistical Indicators

Statistical Unit in Construction refers to corporate enterprise engaged in the construction of buildings and structures and in the installation of equipment. A corporate construction enterprise should have qualification certificates with independent accounting system, and should meet the following 3 requirements: a) being set up in line with relevant legal basis, having its full name, organization and location, and capable of taking civil liabilities; b) independently possessing and using its assets and assuming its liabilities, and entitled to sign contracts with other institutions; and c) making independent accounts of its profits and losses, and capable of compiling its own balance sheet.

Gross Output Value of Construction refers to total of construction products and services, expressed in money terms, produced or rendered by construction and installation enterprises during a given period of time. It includes:

(1) Output value of construction projects, that is the value of projects covered by the project budgets;

(2) Output value of installation projects, that is the value of the installation of equipment, (excluding the value of the equipment to be installed);

(3) Output value of others, that is the output value of construction industry excluding that of construction projects and installation projects. It includes: output value of repair of buildings and structures; output value of non-standard equipment manufacturing; overhead expenses received by contracted enterprises to the sub-contracted enterprises and the completed output value of construction activities that have no clear definition.

a. Output value of repair of buildings and structures, that is the value created through the repairs of buildings or structures, but does not include the value of buildings or structures being repaired and the value of the repair of production equipment;

b. Output value of manufactured non-standard equipment, that is the value of non-standard production equipment including raw materials and manufacturing cost made for the construction project (i.e., chemical plant; kettles or tanks used by refineries; various fillers, triangle tanks, valves used by mines), and the output value of equipment manufactured by subsidiary workshops.

Value-added of Construction refers to the final result of the activities of production and management of construction industry in monetary terms in the reference period.

Starting from the 2004 economic census, value-added of construction is calculated by both production approach and income approach, with the income approach as the final approach, where the calculation is based on the share of production factor in the production process. Specifically, value-added of construction for census years is calculated in accordance with the *Programme of Compilation of GDP and National Accounts for the Year of Economic Census*, and value-added of construction for other years is calculated in accordance with the *Programme of Compilation of GDP and National Accounts for the Non Economic Census Years.*

Floor Space of Buildings Under Construction refers to floor space of buildings under construction during the reference period, including newly started buildings, buildings started earlier and continued during the reference period, and buildings suspended earlier but restarted during the reference period, buildings completed during the reference period, and buildings under construction and then suspended during the reference period.

Floor Space of Buildings Completed refers to the floor space of buildings that are completed in the reference period in accordance with the requirements of the design, up to the standard for putting them into use, and have been checked and accepted by concerned departments as qualified ones.

16

运输和邮电

Transport, Post and Telecommunication Services

简 要 说 明

一、本篇资料的主要内容

本篇资料反映我国交通运输业和邮政、通信业发展的基本状况。

交通运输业资料主要包括：五种运输方式的线路里程、运输设备拥有量、技术质量情况，各种运输方式完成的货物运输量和旅客运输量，铁路运输的固定资产构成及财务主要情况，主要港口码头长度及泊位情况，沿海主要港口货物吞吐量。

邮电通信业资料主要包括：全国邮政局(所)及邮路情况，邮电通信主要电路及设备拥有量，主要的邮电业务完成情况，邮电通信发展水平等资料。

二、各部分资料的调查范围及统计单位

1.铁路资料：包括国家铁路、地方铁路和合资铁路运营情况，不含军用铁路及由厂矿企事业单位自建的铁路专用线和专用铁道。国家铁路和合资铁路运营资料来源于各铁路局及所属运输企业(公司)。地方铁路运营概况资料来源于各省地方铁路管理部门。

2.公路、水运、港口资料：(1)公路和水路线路里程为年末通车和通航里程数，不含在建和未正式投入使用的公路和航道里程；(2)民用汽车拥有量及机动车和汽车驾驶员人数，根据公安部交通管理局所属各省车管部门登记注册的车辆资料和驾驶员资料整理，不含军用车辆；(3)公路运输汽车拥有量，根据交通部门所属各省道路运输管理部门登记注册的从事公路运输的营业性和非营业性运输车辆资料整理，属于民用汽车的一部分；(4)民用运输船舶拥有量，根据交通部所属各省水上航运管理部门登记注册的船舶资料整理，不含渔船、水上施工作业船和军用船舶；(5)公路、水路客货运输量资料，按照交通部和国家统计局1992年联合发布的《公路、水路运输全行业统计工作规定》的要求，由交通部和国家统计局分工负责收集整理；(6)公路、水路运输全行业统计以全面调查和非全面调查两种方式进行，统计范围包括在我国注册从事公路、水路客货运输的全部企事业单位和私人(包括个体联户)；(7)沿海、内河主要港口的生产能力及吞吐量，根据各地港务管理部门注册的港口企业和从事港口生产活动单位的资料整理。

3.管道运输资料：包括输原油、输成品油、输天然气、输其他气体的管线长度、输送能力及完成的运输量。具体包括：油气田企业直接通向炼油厂、化工厂、电站等用户及装车站、油码头的管道，炼油厂通向用户(包括商业石油公司油库)的成品油气管道，独立核算的管道运输企业通向用户及装车(站)栈桥、油码头的管道。管道运输统计数据主要来源于中国石油天然气集团公司和中国石油化工集团公司所属的管道运输企业，由两家集团公司分别负责收集审核本部门统计数据。

4.民航运输资料：统计对象为在我国境内注册从事民用航空运输飞行和通用飞行的航空运输企业和民用航空机场，不包括在我国境内运输飞行的外国航空公司。统计范围为各航空公司从事国内运输、港澳台运输、国际运输的定期航班航线条数及里程、运输量及飞机构成和运营情况、通用飞行完成情况、民用航空机场航班起降架次和客货吞吐量等。

5.邮电通信资料：包括全社会电信和邮政运营企业为社会公众提供的各类电信和邮政服务，不含专用网业务资料。邮电业务量按业务种类分为电信业务量和邮政业务量；按业务范围分为国内业务量和国际及港澳业务量(对台业务量统计在港澳中)。

三、本篇的资料来源

本篇资料由国家统计局服务业调查中心负责整理、编辑。有关交通运输资料分别来源于铁道部、交通部、民航总局、公安部、中国石油天然气集团公司、中国石油化工集团公司和各省、自治区、直辖市统计局。邮电通信业资料来源于信息产业部、国家邮政局。

Brief Introduction

I. Main Content

Data in this chapter cover mainly the basic conditions of the development of transportation, post and telecommunications in China.

Data of transport cover mainly the length of the routes of five means of transportation, the possession of the transport equipment, the technological quality, the freight traffic and passenger traffic accomplished by various means of transportation, the composition of the fixed assets and main financial conditions in the railway transport, the length of major ports and the situation of berths, and cargo handled at principal sea ports.

Data of post and telecommunication cover mainly the situation of post and telecommunication offices and postal routes, the telephone lines, telegraph lines and the possession of the telecommunication facilities, the complete business volume of post and telecommunication services, and the development of the post and telecommunication services, etc.

II. Coverage and Statistical Units

1. Data on railway transportation: including the operation and management of the national, local and joint-venture railways, not including the railways for military purpose, industrial lines and special railways. The data on the operation and management of the national railways and joint-venture railways come from the railway bureaus and the transport enterprises subordinate to them. The data on the operation and management of local railways come from the provincial administrative departments of the local railways.

2. Data on highways, waterways and ports: (1) The length of highways and waterways refer to the length open to traffic or navigation at the end of the year, not including the highways and waterways under construction or not officially put into used ones. (2) The data on the possession of civil motor vehicles and number of drivers are provided by the divisions of vehicle management under the provincial departments of public security, subordinate to the Traffic Management Bureau, Ministry of Public Security, not including those for military use. (3) The data on possession of highway vehicles are provided by the divisions of vehicle management under the provincial departments of public security, subordinate to the Traffic Management Bureau, Ministry of Public Security, including vehicles for business use and non-business use. It is part of the civil motor vehicles. (4) The data on the possession of ships are provided by the divisions of navigation or ports management under the provincial departments of communications, subordinate to the Ministry of Communications, not including fishermen, ships for constructions in water and ships for military use. (5) The data on the passenger traffic and freight traffic by highways and waterways are collected and prepared separately by the Ministry of Communications and the National Bureau of Statistics in accordance with the "*Provisions on the Statistical Work of the Whole Trades of Highway and Waterway Transport*", jointly issued by the Ministry of Communications and the National Bureau of Statistics in 1992. (6) The data on highway and waterway transportation are collected through comprehensive reporting system and non-comprehensive reporting system. The statistical coverage is all the enterprises and institutional units and individuals (including joint-households) registered in the People's Republic of China and engaged in highway or waterway freight or passenger transport business. (7) The data on production capacity and handling capacity of the seaports and inland river ports are from the administrative record of local seaport management offices, with those registered enterprises and production units engaged in this field.

3. Data on the pipeline transport: The data on pipeline transport cover the length, transport capacity and the volume transported of the petroleum (crude oil) pipelines, petroleum products pipelines, natural gas pipelines and other gas pipelines. The coverage of statistics of pipeline transport includes the pipelines leading directly from the enterprises of oil fields or gas fields to the users such as refineries, chemical plants, power stations, etc. and to the loading stations and ports or piers, the petroleum products pipelines leading from the refineries to the

users (including the oil depots of the commercial oil companies) and the pipelines leading from the enterprises engaged in pipeline transport with independent accounting system to the users and causeways and ports or piers. The data sources of the pipeline transport statistics are mainly the enterprises engaged in the pipeline transport subordinate to the China National Petroleum and Natural Gas Corporation Group and China Petrochemical Corporation Group. The two corporations collect and examine the statistical data from the units subordinate to them respectively.

4. Data on the civil aviation transport: The civil aviation transport includes the enterprises engaged in the civil aviation transport flights, flights for general purpose and airports for civil aviation, excluding foreign companies' flights within Chinese territory. The statistical data cover the air lines, length, and transport volume of the domestic transport, the transport between China mainland and Hong Kong, Macao and Taiwan, and the international transport engaged by the air companies as well as the composition of aircraft; the statistical data also cover the data on the operation and performance of the civil aviation, and condition of flights for general purpose.

5. Data on post and telecommunications: Data in this category include telecommunications and post services rendered to the public by telecommunications and postal enterprises, but exclude services provided through dedicated networks. The business volume of post and telecommunications is classified by nature into telecommunication service and postal service, and by customers into the domestic service, international service, and service between the mainland and Hong Kong, Macao (business volume of the service to Taiwan is covered in that for Hong Kong and Macao).

III. Sources of Data

Data in this chapter are arranged and compiled by Survey Centre for Service Industry, NBS. Data on transportation are from Ministry of Railway, Ministry of Communication, Civil Aviation Administration of China, Ministry of Public Security, China Petroleum and Natural Gas Corporation Group, China Petrochemical Corporation Group, and statistical bureaus of provinces, autonomous regions and municipalities directly under the central government. Data on post and telecommunication services come from Ministry of Information Industry and National Postal Office.

16-1 各地区交通运输、邮电通信业职工人数（2005年底）

Number of Staff and Employed Workers in Transport, Post and Telecommunication Services at the Year-end by Region (2005)

单位：人 (person)

地区	Region	铁路运输业 Railway Transport	道路运输业 Road Transport	城市公共交通业 Urban Public Transport	水上运输业 Water Transport	航空运输业 Air Transport	管道运输业 Pipeline Transport	装卸搬运和其他运输服务业 Loading, Unloading and Other Transport Services	邮政业 Post	电信和其他信息传输服务业 Telecommunications and Other Information Transmission Services
全国	**National Total**	**1665588**	**1549025**	**896132**	**498182**	**209868**	**17900**	**252303**	**454434**	**896292**
北京	Beijing	59276	28671	160137	85	29824	121	15537	26494	52965
天津	Tianjin	19568	14320	16214	27313	2156	91	10859	4756	13166
河北	Hebei	77699	91657	21400	22620	760	1054	7422	19912	41289
山西	Shanxi	102135	43942	16880	61	3496		3353	17879	33394
内蒙古	Inner Mongolia	87248	32480	10663	154	2729		1559	12227	24260
辽宁	Liaoning	125566	64804	43536	25223	10483	3285	8364	19700	37014
吉林	Jilin	78373	35491	16642	370	3892	1371	9258	13408	26173
黑龙江	Heilongjiang	118890	69662	13610	3605	3725	477	17260	21113	35292
上海	Shanghai	24468	17807	105758	53416	22269		12070	14528	22737
江苏	Jiangsu	61843	81612	37414	70271	6151	7066	15154	23953	45980
浙江	Zhejiang	25349	63864	31507	22319	7244		8929	20232	35992
安徽	Anhui	28536	54204	25892	16728	2146		4856	13214	26347
福建	Fujian	30951	31307	19478	13605	9142		12148	15630	25768
江西	Jiangxi	58042	45783	12521	7038	2358	14	4579	14908	23209
山东	Shandong	60219	83018	41674	46244	7628	1389	14714	21840	44945
河南	Henan	110594	123332	34700	3533	1691		9059	21366	36215
湖北	Hubei	73836	81500	35040	32995	4566	577	17258	16462	38954
湖南	Hunan	73671	61637	21985	8924	4003		9508	18278	31141
广东	Guangdong	54457	124259	91116	78696	28920	136	26653	36594	94445
广西	Guangxi	46222	53587	15427	19323	3509		9154	12458	25022
海南	Hainan	3305	12437	2056	8895	9749		1688	2686	8292
重庆	Chongqing	26302	37175	22371	27115	2806	126	4870	10398	21662
四川	Sichuan	44203	86302	32585	7234	13785	810	9204	18019	42635
贵州	Guizhou	30843	25044	9537	1747	2564	110	1548	7518	14190
云南	Yunnan	38642	47248	10651	344	5964	3	3959	11030	22842
西藏	Tibet		3261	197	25	641			2028	2713
陕西	Shaanxi	91232	54996	9415	202	7409	552	4016	14650	23994
甘肃	Gansu	50693	27871	15712	77	3007	147	5377	6522	17501
青海	Qinghai	14509	9755	4700	20	669		73	1993	6967
宁夏	Ningxia	13255	10095	1914		596		1073	2466	4704
新疆	Xinjiang	35661	31904	15400		5986	571	2801	12172	16484

16-2 交通运输业基本情况
Basic Conditions of Transport

指 标	Item	2001	2002	2003	2004	2005
运输线路长度 （万公里）	**Length of Transport Routes (10 000 km)**					
铁路营业里程	Railways in Operation	7.01	7.19	7.30	7.44	7.54
公路	Highways	169.80	176.52	180.98	187.07	193.05
#高速公路	Expressway	1.94	2.51	2.97	3.43	4.10
内河	Navigable Inland Waterways	12.15	12.16	12.40	12.33	12.33
民航	Total Civil Aviation Routes	155.36	163.77	174.95	204.94	199.85
管道	Petroleum and Gas Pipelines	2.76	2.98	3.26	3.82	4.40
客运量总计 （万人）	**Total Passenger Traffic (10 000 persons)**	**1534122**	**1608150**	**1587497**	**1767453**	**1847018**
铁路	Railways	105155	105606	97260	111764	115583
公路	Highways	1402798	1475257	1464335	1624526	1697381
水运	Waterways	18645	18693	17142	19040	20227
民航	Civil Aviation	7524	8594	8759	12123	13827
旅客周转量总计（亿人公里）	**Total Passenger-Kilometers (100 million passenger-km)**	**13155.1**	**14125.7**	**13810.5**	**16309.1**	**17466.7**
铁路	Railways	4766.8	4969.4	4788.6	5712.2	6062.0
公路	Highways	7207.1	7805.8	7695.6	8748.4	9292.1
水运	Waterways	89.9	81.8	63.1	66.3	67.8
民航	Civil Aviation	1091.4	1268.7	1263.2	1782.3	2044.9
货运量总计 （万吨）	**Total Freight Traffic (10 000 tons)**	**1401786**	**1483446**	**1561422**	**1706412**	**1862066**
铁路	Railways	193189	204955	221178	249017	269296
公路	Highways	1056312	1116324	1159957	1244990	1341778
水运	Waterways	132675	141832	158070	187394	219648
民航	Civil Aviation	171.0	202.1	219.0	276.7	306.7
管道	Petroleum and Gas Pipelines	19439	20133	21997	24734	31037
货物周转量 （亿吨公里）	**Total Freight Ton-kilometers (100 million ton-km)**	**47710**	**50686**	**53859**	**69445**	**80258**
铁路	Railways	14694	15658	17247	19289	20726
公路	Highways	6330	6782	7099	7841	8693
水运	Waterways	25989	27511	28715.8	41429	49672
民航	Civil Aviation	43.7	51.6	57.9	71.8	78.9
管道	Petroleum and Gas Pipelines	653	683	739	815	1088
民用汽车拥有量 （万辆）	**Possession of Civil Motor Vehicles (10 000 units)**	**1802.04**	**2053.17**	**2382.93**	**2693.71**	**3159.66**
#私人汽车	Private Vehicles	770.78	968.98	1219.23	1481.66	1848.07
其他机动车拥有量 （万辆）	**Possession of Other Motor Vehicles (10 000 units)**	**4724.05**	**6174.09**	**7108.90**	**7785.69**	**8595.42**
民用运输船舶拥有量 （艘）	**Possession of Civil Transport Vessels (unit)**	**210786**	**202977**	**204270**	**210700**	**207294**
机动船	Motor Vessels	169329	165936	163813	166854	165900
驳船	Barges	41457	37041	40457	43846	41394
#私人运输船舶拥有量	Possession of Private Transport Vessels	121721	115108	114297	115503	95838
机动船	Motor Vessels	111633	105697	97837	91188	83380
驳船	Barges	10088	9411	16460	24315	12458
沿海主要港口货物吞吐量 （万吨）	**Volume of Freight Handled in Major Coastal Ports (10 000 tons)**	**142634**	**166628**	**201126**	**246074**	**292777**

16-3 各地区运输线路长度（2005年底）

Length of Transport Routes at the Year-end by Region (2005)

单位：公里 (km)

地区	Region	铁路营业里程 Length of Railways in Operation	内河航道里程 Length of Navigable Inland Waterways	公路里程 Total Length of Highways	等级路 Expressway and Class I to IV Highways	#高速 Express-way	#一级 First Class	#二级 Second Class	等外路 Highways Below Class IV
全国	**National Total**	**75437.6**	**123263**	**1930543**	**1591791**	**41005**	**38381**	**246442**	**338752**
北京	Beijing	1125.4		14696	14481	548	554	2368	215
天津	Tianjin	664.6	88	10836	10791	593	497	1729	44
河北	Hebei	4652.0		75894	67229	2135	2645	12547	8665
山西	Shanxi	3153.9	467	69563	67785	1686	1011	11586	1779
内蒙古	Inner Mongolia	6246.2	2403	79029	70880	1001	2139	8359	8149
辽宁	Liaoning	4171.2	413	53521	53325	1773	1556	13440	196
吉林	Jilin	3561.8	1456	50308	48487	542	1529	7335	1821
黑龙江	Heilongjiang	5654.9	5131	67077	61691	958	1118	7140	5386
上海	Shanghai	269.1	2223	8110	8110	560	302	2306	
江苏	Jiangsu	1615.6	24349	82739	74958	2886	4214	13998	7781
浙江	Zhejiang	1292.3	9652	48600	46167	1866	2955	6569	2432
安徽	Anhui	2353.2	5587	72807	67083	1501	338	9633	5724
福建	Fujian	1613.1	3245	58286	47987	1208	358	6262	10298
江西	Jiangxi	2423.9	5638	62300	43523	1559	565	8555	18777
山东	Shandong	3319.3	1012	80131	80131	3163	4855	21949	
河南	Henan	4098.7	1267	79506	75003	2678	106	21684	4503
湖北	Hubei	2525.4	8181	91131	76075	1649	1093	15225	15055
湖南	Hunan	2902.0	11495	88200	45801	1403	530	5563	42399
广东	Guangdong	2225.2	11844	115337	106476	3140	7301	17147	8861
广西	Guangxi	2728.8	5413	62003	51046	1411	546	6299	10957
海南	Hainan	221.7	343	21162	12671	625	180	1255	8491
重庆	Chongqing	1269.2	4103	38215	30835	748	306	4676	7380
四川	Sichuan	2960.4	10720	114694	79337	1758	1599	10123	35356
贵州	Guizhou	1985.7	3323	46893	35447	577	92	2629	11447
云南	Yunnan	2328.1	2539	167638	111920	1421	248	3325	55718
西藏	Tibet			43716	10905			807	32812
陕西	Shaanxi	3131.2	1066	54492	49274	1226	359	5858	5219
甘肃	Gansu	2300.0	860	41330	32792	1006	141	4969	8538
青海	Qinghai	1091.8	329	29720	26982	171	144	4002	2738
宁夏	Ningxia	791.9	117	13078	13001	670	219	2109	77
新疆	Xinjiang	2761.0		89531	71599	541	883	6993	17932

16-4 运输线路长度
Length of Transportation Routes

单位：万公里　　(10 000 km)

年份 Year	铁路营业里程 Length of Railways in Operation	#国家铁路电气化里程 National Electrified Railways	公路 Length of Highways	#高速公路 Expressway	内河 Length of Navigable Inland Waterways	民航 Length of Civil Aviation Routes	#国际航线 International Routes	管道 Length of Petroleum and Gas Pipelines
1978	5.17	0.10	89.02		13.60	14.89	5.53	0.83
1980	5.33	0.17	88.33		10.85	19.53	8.12	0.87
1981	5.39	0.17	89.75		10.87	21.83	8.28	0.97
1982	5.29	0.18	90.70		10.86	23.27	9.99	1.04
1983	5.41	0.23	91.51		10.89	22.91	9.99	1.08
1984	5.45	0.30	92.67		10.93	26.02	10.74	1.10
1985	5.50	0.42	94.24		10.91	27.72	10.60	1.17
1986	5.57	0.44	96.28		10.94	32.43	10.76	1.30
1987	5.58	0.46	98.22		10.98	38.91	14.89	1.38
1988	5.61	0.57	99.96	0.01	10.94	37.38	12.83	1.43
1989	5.69	0.64	101.43	0.03	10.90	47.19	16.64	1.51
1990	5.78	0.69	102.83	0.05	10.92	50.68	16.64	1.59
1991	5.78	0.78	104.11	0.06	10.97	55.91	17.74	1.62
1992	5.81	0.84	105.67	0.07	10.97	83.66	30.30	1.59
1993	5.86	0.89	108.35	0.11	11.02	96.08	27.87	1.64
1994	5.90	0.90	111.78	0.16	10.27	104.56	35.19	1.68
1995	5.97	0.97	115.70	0.21	11.06	112.90	34.82	1.72
1996	6.49	1.01	118.58	0.34	11.08	116.65	38.63	1.93
1997	6.60	1.20	122.64	0.48	10.98	142.50	50.44	2.04
1998	6.64	1.30	127.85	0.87	11.03	150.58	50.44	2.31
1999	6.74	1.40	135.17	1.16	11.65	152.22	52.33	2.49
2000	6.87	1.49	140.27	1.63	11.93	150.29	50.84	2.47
2001	7.01	1.69	169.80	1.94	12.15	155.36	51.69	2.76
2002	7.19	1.74	176.52	2.51	12.16	163.77	57.45	2.98
2003	7.30	1.81	180.98	2.97	12.40	174.95	71.53	3.26
2004	7.44	1.86	187.07	3.43	12.33	204.94	89.42	3.82
2005	7.54	1.94	193.05	4.10	12.33	199.85	85.59	4.40

16-5 运输线路质量
Quality of Transport Routes

指标	Item	1990	1995	2000	2004	2005
国家铁路营业里程 (公里)	**Length of National Railways in Operation (km)**	**53378**	**54616**	**58656**	**61015**	**62200**
#复线里程 (公里)	Double-Tracking Length (km)	13024	16909	21408	23841	24497
复线里程比重 (%)	Proportion (%)	24.4	31.0	36.5	39.1	39.4
#自动闭塞里程 (公里)	Automatic Blocking Length (km)	10370	12910	18318	22724	24149
自动闭塞里程比重 (%)	Proportion (%)	19.4	23.6	31.2	37.2	38.8
公路线路里程 (公里)	**Length of Highways (km)**	**1028348**	**1157009**	**1402698**	**1870661**	**1930543**
#等级公路里程 (公里)	Expressway and Class I to IV Highways (km)	741040	910754	1216013	1515826	1591791
等级公路里程比重 (%)	Proportion (%)	72.1	78.7	86.7	81.0	82.5
内河航道里程 (公里)	**Length of Navigable Inland Waterways (km)**	**109192**	**110562**	**119325**	**123337**	**123263**
#等级航道里程 (公里)	Standard Waterways (km)		56587	61367	60842	61013
等级航道里程比重 (%)	Proportion (%)		51.2	51.4	49.3	49.5

16-6 客 运 量

Passenger Traffic

单位：万人 (10 000 persons)

年 份 Year	客运量 总 计 Total	铁 路 Railways	国 家 National Railways	地 方 Local Railways	合 资 Joint-venture Railways	公 路 Highways	水 运 Waterways	民 航 Civil Aviation
1978	253993	81491	80729	762		149229	23042	231
1980	341785	92204	91246	958		222799	26439	343
1985	620206	112110	110913	1197		476486	30863	747
1989	791376	113807	112798	1009		644508	31778	1283
1990	772682	95712	94888	824		648085	27225	1660
1991	806048	95080	94208	872		682681	26109	2178
1992	860855	99693	98788	905		731774	26502	2886
1993	996634	105458	104580	878		860719	27074	3383
1994	1092883	108738	108009	729		953940	26165	4038
1995	1172596	102745	102081	664		1040810	23924	5117
1996	1245356	94796	93550	612	634	1122110	22895	5555
1997	1326094	93308	91919	659	730	1204583	22573	5630
1998	1378717	95085	92991	629	1465	1257332	20545	5755
1999	1394413	100164	97725	528	1911	1269004	19151	6094
2000	1478573	105073	101847	519	2707	1347392	19386	6722
2001	1534122	105155	101680	558	2917	1402798	18645	7524
2002	1608150	105606	101741	516	3349	1475257	18693	8594
2003	1587497	97260	93634	412	3214	1464335	17142	8759
2004	1767453	111764	107346	378	4040	1624526	19040	12123
2005	1847018	115583	110651	319	4613	1697381	20227	13827

16-7 旅 客 周 转 量

Passenger-Kilometers

单位：亿人公里 (100 million passenger-km)

年 份 Year	旅客周转量 总 计 Total	铁 路 Railways	国 家 National Railways	地 方 Local Railways	合 资 Joint-venture Railways	公 路 Highways	水 运 Waterways	民 航 Civil Aviation
1978	1743.1	1093.2	1090.8	2.4		521.3	100.6	27.9
1980	2281.3	1383.2	1380.4	2.8		729.5	129.1	39.6
1985	4436.4	2416.1	2412.5	3.6		1724.9	178.7	116.7
1989	6074.6	3037.4	3034.4	3.0		2662.1	188.3	186.8
1990	5628.3	2612.6	2610.1	2.5		2620.3	164.9	230.5
1991	6178.4	2828.1	2824.8	3.2		2871.7	177.2	301.3
1992	6949.4	3152.2	3148.3	4.0		3192.6	198.4	406.1
1993	7858.1	3483.3	3479.4	3.9		3700.7	196.5	477.6
1994	8591.4	3636.1	3632.8	3.2		4220.3	183.5	551.6
1995	9001.9	3545.7	3542.6	3.1		4603.1	171.8	681.3
1996	9164.8	3347.6	3322.0	3.4	22.2	4908.8	160.6	747.8
1997	10055.5	3584.9	3543.5	4.7	36.6	5541.4	155.7	773.5
1998	10636.7	3773.4	3691.0	5.0	77.4	5942.8	120.3	800.2
1999	11299.8	4136.0	4046.3	4.4	85.3	6199.2	107.3	857.3
2000	12261.0	4532.6	4414.7	4.6	113.3	6657.4	100.5	970.5
2001	13155.1	4766.8	4636.6	5.2	125.1	7207.1	89.9	1091.4
2002	14125.7	4969.4	4803.1	5.3	161.1	7805.8	81.8	1268.7
2003	13810.5	4788.6	4622.8	4.0	161.8	7695.6	63.1	1263.2
2004	16309.1	5712.2	5512.0	4.0	196.2	8748.4	66.3	1782.3
2005	17466.7	6062.0	5833.2	3.5	225.2	9292.1	67.8	2044.9

16-8 货 运 量
Freight Traffic

单位：万吨 (10 000 tons)

年份 Year	货运量总计 Total	铁路 Railways	国家 National Railways	地方 Local Railways	合资 Joint-venture Railways	公路 Highways	水运 Waterways	#远洋 Ocean	民航 Civil Aviation	管道 Petroleum and Gas Pipelines
1978	248946	110119	107492	2627		85182	43292	3659	6.4	10347
1980	546537	111279	108584	2695		382048	42676	4292	8.9	10525
1985	745763	130709	127516	3193		538062	63322	6627	19.5	13650
1989	988435	151489	146804	4685		733781	87493	9027	31.0	15641
1990	970602	150681	146209	4472		724040	80094	9408	37.0	15750
1991	985793	152893	147898	4995		733907	83370	10567	45.2	15578
1992	1045899	157627	152317	5310		780941	92490	11191	57.5	14783
1993	1115902	162794	156791	6003		840256	97938	12508	69.4	14845
1994	1180396	163216	157278	5938		894914	107091	13421	82.9	15092
1995	1234937	165982	159473	6509		940387	113194	15251	101.1	15274
1996	1298421	171024	161787	7125	2112	983860	127430	14213	115.0	15992
1997	1278218	172149	162010	7854	2285	976536	113406	20287	124.7	16002
1998	1267427	164309	153435	8035	2839	976004	109555	18892	140.1	17419
1999	1293008	167554	157239	7296	3019	990444	114608	22621	170.0	20232
2000	1358682	178581	166056	8369	4156	1038813	122391	22949	196.7	18700
2001	1401786	193189	179201	9542	4446	1056312	132675	27573	171.0	19439
2002	1483446	204955	187578	11241	6136	1116324	141832	29896	202.1	20133
2003	1561422	221178	199814	13064	8300	1159957	158070	34002	219.0	21997
2004	1706412	249017	217816	14924	16277	1244990	187394	39469	276.7	24734
2005	1862066	269296	231839	17802	19655	1341778	219648	48549	306.7	31037

注：1.从1979年起，公路运输包括社会车辆完成数量，从1984年起，还包括私营运输完成的数量(下表同)。
2.1993年及以后年份铁路货物运输指标口径有调整，增加了行包运量(下表同)。

a) Since 1979, the freight traffic by highways has included the quantities transported by trucks of non-highway departments. Since 1984, it has also included the quantities transported by private trucks. The same as the following table.

b) The indicator standard of railways freight has been adjusted since 1993, increased freight of package. The same as the following table.

16-9 货 物 周 转 量
Freight Ton-Kilometers

单位：亿吨公里 (100 million ton-km)

年份 Year	货物周转量总计 Total	铁路 Railways	国家 National Railways	地方 Local Railways	合资 Joint-venture Railways	公路 Highways	水运 Waterways	#远洋 Ocean	民航 Civil Aviation	管道 Petroleum and Gas Pipelines
1978	9829	5345.2	5333.5	11.7		274.1	3779.2	2487	0.97	430
1980	12026	5716.9	5707.3	9.6		764.0	5052.8	3532	1.41	491
1985	18365	8125.7	8111.6	14.1		1903.2	7729.3	5329	4.15	603
1989	25591	10394.2	10373.0	21.2		3374.8	11186.8	7689	6.90	629
1990	26207	10622.4	10601.2	21.2		3358.1	11591.9	8141	8.20	627
1991	27986	10972.0	10948.1	23.9		3428.0	12955.4	8990	10.10	621
1992	29218	11575.6	11548.5	27.0		3755.4	13256.2	9034	13.42	617
1993	30525	11968.9	11937.7	31.2		4070.5	13860.8	9134	16.61	608
1994	33275	12471.4	12440.0	31.4		4486.3	15686.6	10268	18.59	612
1995	35909	13049.5	13015.3	34.2		4694.9	17552.2	11938	22.30	590
1996	36590	13106.2	12935.0	48.6	122.5	5011.2	17862.5	11254	24.93	585
1997	38385	13269.9	13063.0	50.7	156.2	5271.5	19235.0	14875	29.10	579
1998	38089	12560.1	12304.5	50.7	204.8	5483.4	19405.8	14920	33.45	606
1999	40568	12910.3	12649.8	37.6	222.9	5724.3	21263.0	17014	42.30	628
2000	44321	13770.5	13444.0	43.6	282.9	6129.4	23734.2	17073	50.27	636
2001	47710	14694.1	14368.8	55.4	270.0	6330.4	25988.9	20873	43.72	653
2002	50686	15658.4	15219.1	62.8	376.5	6782.5	27510.6	21733	51.55	683
2003	53859	17246.7	16475.6	69.0	702.1	7099.5	28715.8	22305	57.90	739
2004	69445	19288.8	18285.5	89.1	914.2	7840.9	41428.7	32255	71.80	815
2005	80258	20726.0	19533.4	99.2	1093.5	8693.2	49672.3	38552	78.90	1088

16-10 旅客运输平均运距

Average Transport Distance of Passengers

单位：公里 (km)

年份 Year	总计 Total	铁路 Railways	公路 Highways	水运 Waterways	民航 Civil Aviation
1978	69	134	35	44	1208
1980	67	150	33	49	1153
1985	72	216	36	58	1563
1989	77	267	41	59	1456
1990	73	273	40	61	1388
1991	77	297	42	68	1383
1992	81	316	44	75	1407
1993	79	330	43	73	1412
1994	79	334	44	70	1366
1995	77	345	44	72	1331
1996	74	353	44	70	1346
1997	76	384	46	69	1374
1998	77	406	47	59	1391
1999	82	413	49	56	1407
2000	83	431	49	52	1444
2001	86	453	51	48	1450
2002	88	471	53	44	1476
2003	87	492	53	37	1442
2004	92	511	53	35	1470
2005	95	524	55	34	1479

16-11 货物运输平均运距

Average Transport Distance of Freight

单位：公里 (km)

年份 Year	总计 Total	铁路 Railways	公路 Highways	水运 Waterways	民航 Civil Aviation	管道 Petroleum and Gas Pipelines
1978	395	485	32	873	1521	416
1980	220	514	20	1184	1573	467
1985	243	636	31	1216	2128	442
1989	259	686	46	1279	2228	402
1990	270	705	46	1447	2218	398
1991	284	718	46	1554	2234	399
1992	279	734	48	1433	2330	417
1993	274	735	48	1415	2393	409
1994	282	791	50	1465	2241	406
1995	289	807	50	1551	2206	386
1996	282	766	51	1402	2168	366
1997	300	770	54	1696	2334	362
1998	300	763	56	1771	2388	348
1999	313	768	58	1855	2482	310
2000	326	767	59	1939	2556	340
2001	340	757	60	1959	2557	336
2002	341	760	61	1940	2551	339
2003	345	780	61	1817	2644	336
2004	407	775	63	2211	2595	329
2005	431	770	65	2261	2572	350

16-12 各地区客运量(2005年)

Passenger Traffic by Region (2005)

单位: 万人 (10 000 persons)

地区	Region	合计 Total	铁路 Railways	国家铁路 National Railways	地方铁路 Local Railways	合资铁路 Joint-venture Railways	公路 Highways	水运 Waterways
全国	**National Total**	**1847018**	**115583**	**110651**	**319**	**4613**	**1697381**	**20227**
北京	Beijing	8040	5779	5779			2261	
天津	Tianjin	4514	1550	1550			2961	3
河北	Hebei	80894	5492	5492			75402	
山西	Shanxi	39975	3411	3411			36456	108
内蒙古	Inner Mongolia	31776	3172	3117		55	28604	
辽宁	Liaoning	60100	9533	9514	19		49917	650
吉林	Jilin	27601	4618	4618			22870	113
黑龙江	Heilongjiang	55408	8359	8276	83		46809	240
上海	Shanghai	7985	4313	4313			2468	1204
江苏	Jiangsu	145121	6797	6552		245	138287	37
浙江	Zhejiang	161115	6383	4966		1417	152222	2510
安徽	Anhui	72657	3486	3307		179	68927	244
福建	Fujian	55121	1684	1454		229	52452	985
江西	Jiangxi	41586	3906	3906			37253	427
山东	Shandong	98506	3973	3853	120	1	93178	1355
河南	Henan	97896	5879	5832	47		91920	97
湖北	Hubei	70497	3713	3682		31	66183	601
湖南	Hunan	116091	5661	5484	13	164	109728	702
广东	Guangdong	149896	8900	7682	4	1214	139158	1838
广西	Guangxi	51396	1773	1732	9	32	48740	883
海南	Hainan	26785	24			24	25705	1056
重庆	Chongqing	63308	1332	1262		70	60588	1388
四川	Sichuan	168505	5212	4693		520	159450	3843
贵州	Guizhou	64450	2191	2142		49	61414	845
云南	Yunnan	40792	1782	1567	24	190	38509	501
西藏	Tibet	385					385	
陕西	Shaanxi	38725	3601	3410		191	34780	344
甘肃	Gansu	17804	1316	1316			16247	241
青海	Qinghai	4886	349	349			4525	12
宁夏	Ningxia	7066	309	309			6757	
新疆	Xinjiang	24309	1084	1084			23225	
不分地区	Not Classified by Region	13827						

注: 不分地区合计为民航完成数。

a) The total passenger traffic not classified by region is that completed by civil aviation.

16–13 各地区旅客周转量（2005年）

Passenger-kilometers by Region (2005)

单位：亿人公里 (100 million passenger-km)

地 区	Region	合 计 Total	铁 路 Railways	国家铁路 National Railways	地方铁路 Local Railways	合资铁路 Joint-venture Railways	公 路 Highways	水 运 Waterways
全 国	**National Total**	**17466.7**	**6062.0**	**5833.2**	**3.5**	**225.2**	**9292.1**	**67.8**
北 京	Beijing	137.1	77.6	77.6			59.5	
天 津	Tianjin	117.5	90.7	90.7			26.5	0.4
河 北	Hebei	989.8	504.4	504.4			485.3	
山 西	Shanxi	289.4	108.5	108.5			180.9	
内蒙古	Inner Mongolia	287.3	109.7	105.0		4.7	177.7	
辽 宁	Liaoning	599.9	381.4	381.4	0.1		210.1	8.4
吉 林	Jilin	244.7	151.8	151.8			92.8	0.1
黑龙江	Heilongjiang	432.2	177.6	176.2	1.4		254.3	0.3
上 海	Shanghai	128.4	48.9	48.9			75.1	4.5
江 苏	Jiangsu	1193.6	245.4	239.4		6.0	948.1	0.1
浙 江	Zhejiang	848.5	222.9	186.2		36.8	617.9	7.7
安 徽	Anhui	782.4	300.9	290.9		10.0	481.2	0.3
福 建	Fujian	397.1	85.7	76.6		9.1	310.0	1.4
江 西	Jiangxi	592.4	388.0	385.9		2.1	203.7	0.7
山 东	Shandong	827.8	282.7	280.9	1.5	0.4	539.1	6.0
河 南	Henan	998.3	559.9	559.5	0.4		437.8	0.5
湖 北	Hubei	663.0	300.8	298.2		2.6	358.0	4.2
湖 南	Hunan	1011.5	529.0	506.6		22.4	480.6	1.9
广 东	Guangdong	1448.4	327.9	237.7		90.2	1111.6	8.9
广 西	Guangxi	557.7	116.4	115.8		0.6	438.8	2.6
海 南	Hainan	89.5	1.1			1.1	86.9	1.6
重 庆	Chongqing	280.0	41.1	40.4		0.7	227.2	11.7
四 川	Sichuan	682.3	181.8	161.6		20.2	497.8	2.8
贵 州	Guizhou	312.4	145.7	143.8		1.9	164.9	1.8
云 南	Yunnan	291.0	56.8	50.6	0.1	6.2	233.1	1.1
西 藏	Tibet	18.4					18.4	
陕 西	Shaanxi	486.2	279.1	268.7		10.4	206.5	0.6
甘 肃	Gansu	302.9	197.8	197.8			104.9	0.2
青 海	Qinghai	43.3	18.7	18.7			24.7	
宁 夏	Ningxia	62.4	22.2	22.2			40.3	
新 疆	Xinjiang	306.2	107.7	107.7			198.5	
不分地区	Not Classified by Region	2044.9						

注：不分地区合计为民航完成数。

a) The total passenger-kilometers not classified by region is that completed by civil aviation.

16-14 各地区货运量(2005年)

Freight Traffic by Region (2005)

单位: 万吨 (10 000 tons)

地区	Region	合计 Total	铁路 Railways	国家铁路 National Railways	地方铁路 Local Railways	合资铁路 Joint-venture Railways	公路 Highways	水运 Waterways
全国	**National Total**	**1862066**	**269296**	**231839**	**17802**	**19655**	**1341778**	**219648**
北京	Beijing	32113	2063	1976	87		30050	
天津	Tianjin	39219	6810	3344	3466		19850	12559
河北	Hebei	88342	17151	13360	2439	1352	68652	2539
山西	Shanxi	133662	57366	47697	412	9257	76201	95
内蒙古	Inner Mongolia	69187	18167	16796	992	378	51020	
辽宁	Liaoning	95558	15029	14271	758		74799	5730
吉林	Jilin	34162	6634	6474	160		27441	87
黑龙江	Heilongjiang	61800	16123	15616	507		44376	1301
上海	Shanghai	68636	1278	1278			32684	34674
江苏	Jiangsu	111233	5655	5082	538	34	76301	29277
浙江	Zhejiang	126903	3687	2838	59	790	81448	41768
安徽	Anhui	67125	10386	8638	1462	286	49614	7125
福建	Fujian	41200	4411	3491		919	27579	9210
江西	Jiangxi	33996	5532	4804	728		25025	3439
山东	Shandong	144701	15040	13564	1455	21	120455	9206
河南	Henan	78699	14708	12789	1919		62684	1307
湖北	Hubei	46766	5341	4898	339	104	33481	7944
湖南	Hunan	77534	5879	5252	352	275	67040	4615
广东	Guangdong	119287	8004	6010	606	1388	84861	26422
广西	Guangxi	38226	5723	3998	525	1200	27861	4642
海南	Hainan	10182	491			491	6615	3076
重庆	Chongqing	39329	2055	1921	110	24	33378	3896
四川	Sichuan	67351	7771	7391	239	141	56594	2986
贵州	Guizhou	21770	6168	5524		645	15082	520
云南	Yunnan	62015	5077	4709	218	149	56702	236
西藏	Tibet	356					356	
陕西	Shaanxi	41551	8155	5985		2170	33282	114
甘肃	Gansu	26653	4085	4085			22520	48
青海	Qinghai	6816	1325	1325			5491	
宁夏	Ningxia	8529	2881	2449	432		5648	
新疆	Xinjiang	30041	5353	5353			24688	
不分地区	Not Classified by Region	39123	947	919		28		6832

注：不分地区合计中,包括民航、管道、铁路行包运量及中国远洋运输集团总公司海外公司完成数。

a) The freight traffic not classified by region includes that completed by enterprises directly under the departments of civil aviation, pipelines, railway baggage freight and abroad companies under China Ocean Shipping (Group) Company.

16-15 各地区货物周转量（2005年）

Freight Ton-kilometers by Region (2005)

单位：亿吨公里 (100 million ton-km)

地区	Region	合计 Total	铁路 Railways	国家铁路 National Railways	地方铁路 Local Railways	合资铁路 Joint-venture Railways	公路 Highways	水运 Waterways
全国	**National Total**	**80258.1**	**20726.0**	**19533.4**	**99.2**	**1093.5**	**8693.2**	**49672.3**
北京	Beijing	582.1	496.6	496.5	0.1		85.5	
天津	Tianjin	12593.0	410.6	391.2	15.2	4.1	74.0	12108.4
河北	Hebei	5068.1	2468.6	2100.7	15.2	352.6	691.5	1908.1
山西	Shanxi	1690.9	1298.1	1113.1	1.2	183.8	392.8	0.1
内蒙古	Inner Mongolia	1437.1	1114.8	983.5	6.6	124.7	322.3	
辽宁	Liaoning	3350.5	1196.8	1194.8	2.0		415.5	1738.2
吉林	Jilin	605.9	506.7	506.2	0.5		98.8	0.4
黑龙江	Heilongjiang	1167.4	919.7	913.6	6.1		227.6	20.0
上海	Shanghai	12128.1	46.6	46.6			73.4	12008.1
江苏	Jiangsu	2993.2	477.2	450.4	0.6	26.2	459.2	2056.9
浙江	Zhejiang	3417.0	282.9	238.7	0.1	44.2	372.7	2761.4
安徽	Anhui	1566.1	883.8	857.7	8.1	17.9	422.7	259.7
福建	Fujian	1573.1	200.2	163.8		36.3	238.3	1134.6
江西	Jiangxi	885.2	613.7	609.9	1.6	2.1	186.5	85.1
山东	Shandong	5551.0	1187.2	1141.1	7.7	38.4	711.8	3652.0
河南	Henan	2352.5	1832.0	1811.0	20.9		467.0	53.5
湖北	Hubei	1415.7	721.2	715.1	1.4	4.7	251.2	443.2
湖南	Hunan	1628.6	899.7	869.1	0.9	29.7	538.6	190.3
广东	Guangdong	3860.3	325.6	210.2	3.1	112.4	646.5	2888.2
广西	Guangxi	1098.3	667.1	630.6	2.7	33.8	258.4	172.7
海南	Hainan	448.8	3.2			3.2	55.9	389.7
重庆	Chongqing	625.5	76.0	75.0	0.4	0.6	149.1	400.5
四川	Sichuan	916.6	620.9	612.3	0.7	7.9	263.7	31.9
贵州	Guizhou	646.5	544.3	536.8		7.5	94.2	8.1
云南	Yunnan	680.6	295.7	288.0	1.0	6.7	382.0	2.9
西藏	Tibet	40.7					40.7	
陕西	Shaanxi	1028.8	820.6	767.0		53.7	207.8	0.3
甘肃	Gansu	983.2	845.9	845.9			137.3	0.1
青海	Qinghai	147.1	98.8	98.8			48.3	
宁夏	Ningxia	255.2	187.4	184.4	3.0		67.8	
新疆	Xinjiang	806.6	494.2	494.2			312.4	
不分地区	Not Classified by Region	8714.5	190.2	187.2		2.9		7357.8

注：不分地区合计中,包括民航、管道、铁路行包运量及中国远洋运输集团总公司海外公司完成数。

a) The freight ton-kilometers not classified by region includes that completed by enterprises directly under the departments of civil aviation, pipelines, railway baggage freight and abroad companies under China Ocean Shipping (Group) Company.

16-16 国家营业铁路基本情况

Basic Statistics on National Railways in Operation

项　　目	Item	1985	1990	1995	2000	2004	2005
营业里程　（公里）	**Length of Railways in Operation (km)**	**52119**	**53378**	**54616**	**58656**	**61015**	**62200**
正式营业	In Formal Operation	49433	50310	50866	51262	56822	57589
临时营业	In Temporary Operation	2686	3068	3750	7394	4193	4611
正式营业里程比重　(%)	Proportion of the Length in Formal Operation	94.8	94.3	93.1	87.4	93.1	92.6
复线里程　（公里）	**Double-Tracking Length (km)**	**9989**	**13024**	**16909**	**21408**	**23841**	**24497**
占营业里程比重　(%)	As Percentage of the Length of Railways in Operation	19.2	24.4	31.0	36.5	39.1	39.4
电气化线路里程　（公里）	**Length of Electrified Railways (km)**	**4151**	**6941**	**9703**	**14864**	**18562**	**19408**
占营业里程比重　(%)	As Percentage of Railways in Operation	8.0	13.0	17.8	25.3	30.4	31.2
内燃机牵引线路里程（公里）	**Length of Diesel Engine Routes (km)**	**10822**	**16097**	**24749**	**39497**	**42453**	**42792**
占营业里程比重　(%)	As Percentage of Railways in Operation	20.8	30.2	45.3	67.3	69.6	68.8
调度集中里程　（公里）	**Length under Centralized Traffic Control (km)**	**1307**	**1169**	**1226**	**1200**	**1842**	**1828**
占营业里程比重　(%)	As Percentage of Railways in Operation	2.5	2.2	2.2	2.0	3.0	2.9
自动闭塞里程　（公里）	**Automatic Blocking Length (km)**	**6921**	**10370**	**12910**	**18318**	**22724**	**24149**
占营业里程比重　(%)	As Percentage of Railways in Operation	13.3	19.4	23.6	31.2	37.2	38.8
半自动闭塞里程　（公里）	**Semi-automatic Blocking Length (km)**	**42625**	**38832**	**40859**	**41695**	**39335**	**39390**
占营业里程比重　(%)	As Percentage of Railways in Operation	81.8	72.7	74.8	71.1	64.5	63.3
无缝线路里程　（公里）	**Length of Continuous Welded Rail (km)**	**10439**	**14644**	**21854**	**29975**	**43198**	**47965**
占正线里程比重　(%)	As Percentage of the Trunk Lines	16.7	21.7	40.0	51.1	70.8	54.2
有电气集中的车站　（个）	**Number of Stations with Electric Interlocking (unit)**	**2320**	**3535**	**4587**	**5232**	**5340**	**5213**
占营业车站比重　(%)	As Percentage of Railways Stations in Operation	46.9	62.9	73.9	90.4	95.1	93.7

16-17 铁路机车拥有量

Number of Railway Locomotives

单位：台 (unit)

项　　目	Item	1985	1990	1995	2000	2004	2005
国家铁路	**Number of Locomotives Owned by National Railways**	**11772**	**13592**	**15146**	**14472**	**16066**	**16547**
蒸汽机车	Steam Locomotives	7674	6279	4347	601	82	94
#前进型	Qianjin Model	4429	4188	2985	261	24	24
建设型	Jianshe Model	1216	1644	1329	340	58	70
内燃机车	Diesel Locomotives	3511	5680	8282	10355	11135	11331
#东风4型	Dongfeng Model IV	955	2351	4362	5623	6458	6443
电力机车	Electric Locomotives	587	1633	2517	3516	4849	5122
#韶山1型	Shaoshan Model I	505	816	814	800	670	664
地方铁路	**Number of Locomotives Owned by Local Railways**	**368**	**378**	**398**	**327**	**352**	**348**
蒸汽机车	Steam Locomotives	239	253	260	159	89	59
内燃机车	Diesel Locomotives	129	125	129	168	263	289
合资铁路	**Number of Locomotives Owned by Joint-venture Railways**				**454**	**604**	**578**
蒸汽机车	Steam Locomotives				151	92	40
内燃机车	Diesel Locomotives				303	474	494
电力机车	Electric Locomotives					38	44

16-18 国家铁路客、货车拥有量

Number of National Railway Passenger Coaches and Freight Cars Owned

项 目	Item	1985	1990	1995	2000	2004	2005
客 车 (辆)	**Passenger Coaches (coach)**	**20872**	**27261**	**32404**	**35989**	**39766**	**40328**
软卧车	Soft Berth Coaches	679	1061	1537	2055	3049	3109
硬卧车	Hard Berth Coaches	2633	4351	7607	10139	12550	12942
软座车	Soft Seat Coaches	260	330	574	764	772	759
硬座车	Hard Seat Coaches	13700	17503	18076	17571	16965	16900
软硬座车	Soft and Hard Seat Coaches	114	63	35	25		2
餐 车	Dining Cars	1221	1520	1695	1847	2058	2108
行李邮政车	Luggage and Post Cars	1498	1686	1949	2144	2362	2480
公务车	Business Cars	87	77	87	69	77	78
其 他	Others	680	670	844	1375	1933	1950
货 车 (辆)	**Freight Cars (coach)**	**300886**	**364966**	**432731**	**439943**	**520101**	**541824**
按车型分	Grouped by Type of Car						
棚 车	Covered Cars	52667	66668	80437	92569	96107	99206
敞 车	Open Cars	185684	232999	268179	252977	323970	343480
平 车	Flat Cars	18753	18726	27461	24685	29530	30290
毒品车	Hazardous Materials Cars		1229	1580	1578	2056	2056
罐 车	Tank Cars	31837	33646	37119	37778	40222	38331
保温车	Refrigerator Cars	3991	5150	7030	7909	7696	7419
其 他	Others	7944	6548	10925	22447	20250	21042
按载重量分	Grouped by Capacity of Car						
20吨及以下	20 Tons and Under	1476	949	1458			
25-40吨	25-40 Tons	21520	8699	8786			
40吨及以下	40 Tons and Below				7765	8731	8482
41-49吨	41-49 Tons					7589	7589
50吨	50 Tons	104456	92442	48287	15799	3538	3512
51-59吨	51-59 Tons	16544	15500	27951		54456	52565
60吨	60 Tons	153198	238680	342086	307521	267065	265154
61-69吨	61-69 Tons					175111	195911
65吨	65 Tons	1571	6825	3546			
70吨及以上	70 Tons and Over				5427	3611	8611
73吨及以上	73 Tons and Over	306	329	385			
其他	Others	1815	1542	232			
货车总标记载重量（万吨）	**Total Loading Capacity of Freight Cars (10 000 tons)**	**1612.5**	**2055.3**	**2502.9**	**2619.9**	**3147.0**	**3294.5**
平均每辆车标记载重量 (吨)	**Average Marked Loading Capacity per Car (ton)**	**53.9**	**56.6**	**57.9**	**59.6**	**60.5**	**60.8**

16-19 国家铁路运输固定资产

Fixed Assets of National Railway Transport

单位：亿元 (100 million yuan)

项目	Item	1990	1995	2000	2004	2005
固定资产原值	**Original Value of Fixed Assets**	**1253.9**	**3613.6**	**5268.8**	**8656.1**	**9294.2**
#生产用	Fixed Assets for Productive Purpose	1116.1	3526.0	5205.7	8570.6	9212.1
#机车车辆	Locomotives, Coaches and Freight Cars	312.1	776.9	816.8	2009.5	2255.2
线路	Lines	545.2	1850.7	2854.4	4147.2	4428.4
通信线路	Communications Lines	19.5	43.2	0.2		
通信信号设备	Communications & Signaling Equipment	35.4	80.8	153.6		
房屋及建筑物	Buildings	107.4	489.9	683.1	938.0	966.2
机械动力设备	Machinery and Power Equipment	47.7	84.0	143.6	252.4	265.1
传导设备	Conduction Equipment	34.6	72.5	153.4	253.9	270.2
非生产用	Fixed Assets for Non-productive Purposes	106.8				
未使用	Unused Fixed Assets	24.5	73.2	56.3	72.9	71.2
不需用	Non-required Fixed Assets	1.0	2.1	1.4	5.2	4.6
封存及租出的	Sealed-up for Safekeeping and Leased	4.4	12.3	5.3	7.5	6.4
土地	Land	0.3				
固定资产净值	**Net Value of Fixed Assets**	**889.3**	**2409.4**	**3830.1**	**6288.0**	**6667.8**
固定资产折旧	**Depreciation of Fixed Assets**	**364.6**	**1204.1**	**1438.7**	**2368.2**	**2626.5**

注：1995年起生产用固定资产统计口径变更为在用固定资产，原非生产用固定资产和土地包括其中。

a) Since 1995, the fixed assets for productive purposes have changed to be the fixed assets in use, and included land and the fixed assets for non-productive purpose.

16-20 按货类分国家铁路货物运输量

National Railway Freight Traffic by Category of Cargo

项目	Item	2004			2005		
		货运量（万吨）Freight Traffic (10 000 tons)	货物周转量（百万吨公里）Freight Ton-kilometers (million ton-kilometers)	平均运距（公里）Average Transport Distance (km)	货运量（万吨）Freight Traffic (10 000 tons)	货物周转量（百万吨公里）Freight Ton-kilometers (million ton-kilometers)	平均运距（公里）Average Transport Distance (km)
总计	**Total**	**216961**	**1810994**	**835**	**230920**	**1934612**	**838**
煤	Coal	99210	571298	576	107082	637383	595
焦炭	Coke	7189	66151	920	7918	73831	932
石油	Petroleum	11944	109964	921	12667	118495	935
钢铁	Steel and Iron	16083	178964	1113	17536	198931	1134
金属矿石	Metal Ores	19319	119602	619	22187	138578	625
非金属矿石	Nonmetal Ores	8039	53570	666	8240	54442	661
矿建材料	Mineral Building Materials	7785	40976	526	7820	36294	464
水泥	Cement	3700	15283	413	3470	13301	383
木材	Timber	3237	57387	1773	3501	53606	1531
化肥和农药	Chemical Fertilizers and Pesticides	6392	83276	1303	7163	100246	1400
粮食	Grain	10906	163493	1499	11082	165510	1493
棉花	Cotton	264	8987	3410	283	9875	3486
盐	Salt	1278	9843	770	1287	10382	807
其他	Others	21615	332200	1537	20684	323738	1565

16-21 铁路主要干线客货运输量（2005年）

Passenger and Freight Traffic of Principal Trunk Railways (2005)

线路名称	Name	客运量（万人）Passenger Traffic (10 000 persons)	旅客周转量（百万人公里）Passenger-kilometers (million passenger-km)	线路名称	Name	货运量（万吨）Freight Traffic (10 000 tons)	货物周转量（百万吨公里）Freight Ton-kilometers (million ton-km)
京沪线	Beijing-Shanghai	10892	68439	京沈线	Beijing-Shenyang	1728	85731
新石线	Xinjiang-Rizhao	453	1784	哈大线	Harbin-Dalian	3711	79387
沪杭、浙赣线	Shanghai-Hangzhou, Hangzhou-Ganzhou	6118	40934	津沪线	Tianjin-Shanghai	5406	94987
				沪杭线	Shanghai-Hangzhou	217	4175
鹰厦线	Yingtan-Xiamen	696	6583	京广线	Beijing-Guangzhou	6789	140466
京九线	Beijing-Kowloon	4661	40328	南北同蒲线	Datong-Taiyuan-Fenglingdu	16481	38468
京广线	Beijing-Guangzhou	12634	92643				
石太线	Shijiazhuang-Taiyuan	577	1939	太焦柳线	Taiyuan-Jiaozuo-Liuzhou	8637	72132
石德线	Shijiazhuang-Dezhou	571	2512	京九线	Beijing-Kowloon	3747	89399
焦柳线	Jiaozuo-Liuzhou	1492	9023	兰新线	Lanzhou-Urumqi	4231	91687
京包线	Bingjing-Baotou	1635	7550	滨洲线	Harbin-Manzhouli	4685	31451
包兰线	Baotou-Lanzhou	559	3418	滨绥线	Harbin-Suifenhe	1646	20275
北同蒲线	Taiyuan-Datong	563	1452	京包线	Bingjing-Baotou	3119	55923
南同蒲线	Fenglingdu-Taiyuan	1264	4481	石太线	Shijiazhuang-Taiyuan	5120	23790
陇海线	Lianyungang-Lanzhou	6122	46054	石德线	Shijiazhuang-Dezhou	602	16090
宝中线	Baoji-Zhongwei	89	1630	浙赣线	Hangzhou-Ganzhou	3211	51919
兰新线	Lanzhou-Urumqi	1185	19108	陇海线	Lianyungang-Lanzhou	7212	116595
兰青、青藏线	Lanzhou-Qinghai, Qinghai-Tibet	355	2149	胶济线	Qingdao-Jinan	1819	19101
				京秦线	Beijing-Qinhuangdao	416	10204
湘黔线	Zhuzhou-Guiyang	1579	17506	新石线	Xinjiang-Rizhao	3760	42464
宝成、成渝线	Baoji-Chengdu, Chengdu-Chongqing	2449	13356	宝成线	Baoji-Chengdu	1224	26989
				成昆线	Chengdu-Kunming	2369	31789
襄渝线	Xiangfan-Chongqing	1871	12017	大秦线	Datong-Qinhuangdao	881	107370
贵昆线	Guiyang-Kunming	1115	4887	湘黔线	Zhuzhou-Guiyang	2294	47555
南昆线	Nanning-Kunming	301	891	贵昆线	Guiyang-Kunming	2169	21090
成昆线	Chengdu-Kunming	1446	5815	包兰线	Baotou-Lanzhou	5010	34110
京秦线	Beijing-Qinhuangdao	1176	8036	青藏线	Qinghai-Tibet	834	7535
京哈线	Beijing-Harbin	8465	36926				

16-22 铁路主要车站旅客发送量

Number of Passengers Dispatched from Principal Railway Stations

单位：万人 (10 000 persons)

车站名称	Railway Station	1997	1998	1999	2000	2001	2002	2003	2004	2005
哈尔滨	Harbin	1301	1346	1371	1252	1342	1345	1249	1448	1569
沈阳	Shenyang	1280	1217	1168	1168	1303	1235	1077	1176	1182
长春	Changchun	932	925	973	1062	1085	1069	793	1147	1222
鞍山	Anshan	682	293	300	295	309	306	288	327	312
本溪	Benxi	682	599	569	574	685	617	585	684	724
锦州	Jinzhou	401	416	436	421	429	424	371	415	411
吉林	Jilin	400	396	438	397	443	417	373	438	449
北京	Beijing	1656	1691	1868	1997	2115	2163	1795	2278	2478
北京南	Southern Beijing	443	403	366	382	438	436	374	379	337
北京西	Western Beijing					1652	2102	1896	2429	2622
天津	Tianjin	876	925	1006	1004	1019	1005	855	1040	1099
石家庄	Shijiazhuang	722	732	817	864	927	956	877	1098	1178
太原	Taiyuan	684	642	661	679	767	798	719	879	936
郑州	Zhengzhou	1095	1170	1291	1333	1440	1548	1475	1797	1924
武昌	Wuchang	747	748	772	821	864	883	826	973	1062
洛阳	Luoyang	303	318	339	353	397	375	335	418	440
西安	Xi'an	1023	1031	1096	1063	1211	1245	1196	1517	1669
济南	Jinan	597	645	658	702	728	707	673	787	802
徐州	Xuzhou	619	653	674	632	680	647	611	696	714
南京	Nanjing	776	787	918	897	932	995	940	1069	969
蚌埠	Bangbu	351	358	406	412	442	433	406	460	444
镇江	Zhenjiang	310	309	333	327	342	352	323	365	379
常州	Changzhou	460	465	516	4524	560	581	558	659	694
无锡	Wuxi	662	633	702	704	768	802	785	956	1026
苏州	Suzhou	636	625	685	703	776	843	859	1018	1142
上海	Shanghai	2516	2430	2536	2595	2860	3118	3031	3648	3866
杭州	Hangzhou	395	1008	1074	1061	1025	1192	1129	1406	1462
南昌	Nanchang	666	747	807	795	943	1013	968	1148	1218
广州	Guangzhou	1469	1576	1728	1776	1838	2001	2005	2336	2508
深圳	Shenzhen	644	718	817	758	902	966	940	1189	1250
柳州	Liuzhou	386	366	360	335	323	271	246	257	290
成都	Chengdu	803	845	960	1042	1141	1282	1107	1344	1416
重庆	Chongqing	560	581	695	651	776	754	708	779	801
贵阳	Guiyang	557	571	627	598	610	614	553	605	694
兰州	Lanzhou	387	408	439	444	515	523	477	552	560
乌鲁木齐	Urumqi	352	403	411	399	398	410	359	407	450

16-23 铁路主要车站货物发送量

Volume of Freight Dispatched from Principal Railway Stations

单位：万吨 (10 000 tons)

车站名称	Name of Railway Station	1997	1998	1999	2000	2001	2002	2003	2004	2005
七台河	Qitaihe	1289	1273	1317	1338	1333	1314	1304	1477	1474
恒山	Hengshan	481	386	374	371	441	519	614	579	660
竣德	Junde	584	404	526	418	478	538	572	742	733
鹤岗	Hegang	821	656	725	822	787	803	843	952	1019
双鸭山	Shuangyashan	669	621	722	751	831	832	1011	1103	1181
大官屯	Daguantun	653	643	689	657	683	670	662	748	755
灵山	Lingshan	910	909	957	999	956	935	907	1086	1136
甘井子	Ganjingzi	488	502	470	464	389	270	327	338	333
本溪	Benxi	384	377	356	405	391	518	483	508	589
阜新	Fuxin	686	602	503	531	571	573	529	575	578
白云鄂博	Baiyun'ebo	969	860	808	739	794	850	918	1027	1111
石景山南	Southern Shijingshan	517	564	522	602	572	537	517	343	427
古冶	Guye	970	837	847	866	849	873	843	813	798
唐山南	Tangshannan	429	418	394	404	381	357	351	314	338
沙河驿镇	Shaheyizhen	895	920	826	877	887	829	827	738	753
秦皇岛南	Southern Qinhuangdao	331	406	381	398	489	473	515	524	574
白羊墅	Baiyangshu	1029	856	959	986	1082	1090	1052	1192	978
云岗	Yungang	557	436	438	458	517	603	618	581	556
云岗西	Western Yungang	1087	839	752	846	919	1020	1158	1147	1173
新高山	Xingaoshan	1040	905	868	942	1076	1160	1225	1423	1589
介休	Jiexiu	504	522	488	574	634	587	653	709	837
鹤壁北	Northern Hebi	289	261	316	331	407	408	409	418	398
晋城北	Northern Jincheng	1100	1168	1265	1293	1471	1381	1279	1285	1235
长治北	Northern Changzhi	947	939	947	952	1032	1038	1155	1201	1249
新密	Mixian	452	370	342	345	368	394	446	504	455
平顶山东	Eastern Pingdingshan	2119	2013	1953	1984	2146	2309	2453	2453	2595
武昌东	Eastern Wuchang	553	532	454	429	463	428	469	505	631
邹县	Zouxian	525	650	704	691	983	1139	1155	991	738
青龙山	Qinglongshan	386	380	455	502	532	533	516	516	511
茂名	Maoming	461	433	388	544	525	579	684	841	710

16-24 国家铁路运输主要财务指标

Financial Indicators of National Railway Transport

单位：亿元 (100 million yuan)

指标	Item	1990	1995	2000	2004	2005
运输总收入	**Total Transport Revenue**	**411.1**	**632.1**	**1097.4**	**1794.4**	**2019.1**
客运收入	Revenue from Passenger Traffic	110.9	201.5	369.3	592.9	638.1
货运收入	Revenue from Freight Traffic	272.1	357.6	566.6	943.7	1105.7
行李包裹收入	Revenue from Luggage	8.6	15.8	38.1	47.6	48.8
邮运收入	Revenue from Postal Delivery	1.0	1.9	3.5	3.7	3.7
其他收入	Other Revenue	18.4	55.2	119.9	206.5	222.9
营运成本	**Operation Cost**	**253.9**	**640.6**	**951.1**	**1399.4**	**1589.4**
工资	Wages and Salaries	42.8	139.6	197.4	323.4	354.4
材料	Materials	32.6	85.5	76.9	163.0	222.9
燃料	Fuel	38.5	101.1	140.8	193.8	238.8
电力	Electricity	9.0	32.2	61.7	115.1	135.2
折旧	Depreciation	108.8	73.7	351.4	235.8	261.6
其他	Other Costs	22.3	208.5	122.9	368.3	376.5
营业外收支净额	**Non-operating Net Revenue or Expenditure**	**24.1**	**33.4**	**47.1**	**69.5**	**105.9**
应缴税金	**Taxes Payable**	**21.6**	**32.3**	**37.8**	**72.5**	**93.7**
实现利润	**Profits**	**113.1**	**-64.1**	**33.8**	**48.5**	**85.8**

16-25 国家铁路运输主要技术经济指标

Principal Economic and Technical Indicators of National Railway Transport

指标	Item	2001	2002	2003	2004	2005
货运机车日产量 (万吨公里)	Average Daily Ton-kilometers of Freight Locomotives (10 000 ton-km)	99.9	102.2	105.8	108.7	110.6
内燃机车	Diesel Locomotives	100.7	99.3	101.4	103.4	105.6
电力机车	Electric Locomotives	100.7	106.8	112.8	117.1	118.3
货运机车平均牵引总重 (吨)	Average Total Tonnage of Freight Locomotives (ton)	2760	2789	2829	2934	3038
内燃机车	Diesel Locomotives	2668	2648	2679	2768	2848
电力机车	Electric Locomotives	2985	3028	3071	3198	3335
货运机车日车公里 (公里)	Daily Distance per Freight Locomotive (km)	437	445	450	455	458
客运机车日车公里 (公里)	Daily Distance per Passenger Locomotive (km)	533	557	562	612	650
内燃机车每万吨公里耗油 (公斤)	Oil Consumption of Diesel Locomotives (kg/10 000 ton-km)	25.7	25.9	25.4	25.0	24.6
电力机车每万吨公里耗电 (千瓦小时)	Electricity Consumption of Electric Locomotives (kwh/10 000 ton-km)	113.1	110.8	110.0	111.2	111.8
货物列车出发正点率 (%)	Punctuality Rate of Freight Trains at Departure (%)	97.2	97.3	96.9	96.5	97.0
货物列车运行正点率 (%)	Punctuality Rate of Freight Trains in Running (%)	96.8	96.7	96.5	96.2	96.9
旅客列车出发正点率 (%)	Punctuality Rate of Passenger Trains at Departure (%)	99.8	99.8	99.7	99.8	99.5
旅客列车运行正点率 (%)	Punctuality Rate of Passenger Trains in Running (%)	96.9	97.6	96.5	95.9	98.4
旅客列车技术速度(公里/小时)	Technical Speed of Passenger Trains (km/hr)	69.5	71.4	71.7	73.7	74.2
旅客列车旅行速度(公里/小时)	Traveling Speed of Passenger Trains (km/hr)	60.5	62.0	62.2	64.4	65.2
客运密度 (万人公里/公里)	Density of Passenger Transport (10 000 passenger-km/km)	785.0	807.0	765.0	903.0	938.0
货物列车技术速度(公里/小时)	Technical Speed of Freight Trains (km/hr)	46.7	47.1	47.1	46.7	46.3
货物列车旅行速度(公里/小时)	Running Speed of Freight Trains (km/hr)	39.5	32.4	32.8	32.2	32.1
货运密度 (万吨公里/公里)	Density of Freight Transport (10 000 ton-km/km)	2412	2533	2726	2997	3140
货车周转时间 (天)	Turning Around Time of Freight Cars (day)	5.08	5.10	5.10	4.94	4.90
一次货物作业时间 (小时)	Handling Time of Freight (hour)	22.0	21.2	20.9	17.2	15.2
货车中转停留时间 (小时)	Transfer Waiting Time per Car (hour)	4.6	4.6	4.5	4.4	4.3
货车静载重(准轨) (吨)	Static Load of Freight Cars (Standard Gauge) (ton)	58.1	58.2	58.3	59.3	60.1
货车载重力利用率 (%)	Utilization Rate of Loading Capacity of Freight Cars (%)	97.3	96.7	96.5	98.0	98.7

16-26 民用汽车拥有量

Possession of Civil Vehicles

年份 地区	Year Region	民用汽车总计（万辆）Total (10 000 units)	载客汽车（万辆）Passenger Vehicles (10 000 units)	大型 Large	中型 Medium	小型 Small	微型 Minicar	载货汽车（万辆）Trucks (10 000 units)
	1978	135.84	25.90					100.17
	1980	178.29	35.08					129.90
	1985	321.12	79.45					223.20
	1989	511.32	146.43					346.37
	1990	551.36	162.19					368.48
	1991	606.11	185.24					398.62
	1992	691.74	226.16					441.45
	1993	817.58	285.98					501.00
	1994	941.95	349.74					560.33
	1995	1040.00	417.90					585.43
	1996	1100.08	488.02					575.03
	1997	1219.09	580.56					601.23
	1998	1319.30	654.83					627.89
	1999	1452.94	740.23					676.95
	2000	1608.91	853.73					716.32
	2001	1802.04	993.96					765.24
	2002	2053.17	1202.37	75.48	104.80	789.74	232.34	812.22
	2003	2382.93	1478.81	75.76	115.96	1017.21	269.88	853.51
	2004	2693.71	1735.91	78.06	124.54	1248.89	284.42	893.00
	2005	3159.66	2132.46	82.13	131.65	1618.35	300.32	955.55
北京	Beijing	209.73	188.31	3.64	10.89	152.17	21.60	17.73
天津	Tianjin	67.68	54.27	1.41	2.58	39.82	10.46	11.96
河北	Hebei	198.23	119.98	2.92	2.75	84.94	29.36	70.86
山西	Shanxi	107.44	67.77	1.70	2.73	49.74	13.61	37.96
内蒙古	Inner Mongolia	65.82	38.46	1.23	1.78	28.61	6.83	24.88
辽宁	Liaoning	134.87	89.62	4.20	8.54	70.62	6.26	42.39
吉林	Jilin	65.27	46.56	1.93	1.67	36.25	6.71	17.91
黑龙江	Heilongjiang	85.90	57.67	2.97	3.30	43.29	8.11	26.28
上海	Shanghai	95.16	76.00	3.57	8.00	60.72	3.71	19.16
江苏	Jiangsu	192.25	144.63	4.54	9.72	113.79	16.58	43.35
浙江	Zhejiang	202.92	143.51	3.52	7.28	118.34	14.37	55.90
安徽	Anhui	80.50	43.64	2.87	4.10	29.62	7.05	33.21
福建	Fujian	69.79	44.96	1.56	3.12	36.29	3.99	23.14
江西	Jiangxi	48.36	27.18	1.49	1.99	20.03	3.66	19.89
山东	Shandong	246.96	166.40	4.83	8.25	120.52	32.81	72.89
河南	Henan	152.17	98.88	4.62	6.83	67.21	20.21	49.17
湖北	Hubei	86.24	53.40	3.43	4.22	42.89	2.85	30.96
湖南	Hunan	78.34	49.46	2.92	3.17	39.42	3.95	27.97
广东	Guangdong	372.96	247.44	9.99	20.47	209.42	7.56	118.84
广西	Guangxi	59.14	38.00	2.45	1.81	25.83	7.91	19.48
海南	Hainan	16.40	10.54	0.80	0.60	8.83	0.31	5.61
重庆	Chongqing	46.93	26.07	2.03	1.64	19.14	3.27	20.09
四川	Sichuan	138.00	97.13	4.42	3.48	56.39	32.85	39.39
贵州	Guizhou	46.77	26.25	1.30	1.79	15.72	7.43	17.56
云南	Yunnan	103.60	62.49	1.54	2.91	43.36	14.68	40.38
西藏	Tibet	7.07	3.11	0.18	0.42	2.23	0.29	3.96
陕西	Shaanxi	63.21	42.84	1.76	3.16	30.76	7.16	18.82
甘肃	Gansu	33.74	19.31	1.44	1.40	13.69	2.78	13.62
青海	Qinghai	12.18	7.08	0.45	0.60	5.32	0.71	4.85
宁夏	Ningxia	15.63	8.04	0.52	0.56	6.09	0.87	6.90
新疆	Xinjiang	56.42	33.47	1.91	1.89	27.30	2.36	20.46

16-26 续表 continued

年 份 Year 地 区 Region	载货汽车（万辆） Trucks (10 000 units) 重 型 Heavy	中 型 Light-Heavy	轻 型 Light	微 型 Mini	其他汽车（万辆） Others (10 000 units)	机动车驾驶员（万人） Number of Motor Drivers (10 000 persons)	#汽车驾驶员 Automobile Drivers
1978							192.45
1980							245.23
1985							462.44
1989						1577.99	722.32
1990						1635.85	790.96
1991						1791.57	859.44
1992						2017.83	969.55
1993						2359.42	1112.97
1994						2812.12	1269.23
1995						3501.52	1673.39
1996						4275.26	2100.74
1997						5206.79	2619.25
1998						5944.58	2974.06
1999						6727.49	3361.12
2000						7655.56	3746.51
2001						8455.04	4462.68
2002	148.28	218.69	360.58	84.66	38.58	9362.03	4827.08
2003	136.79	243.70	390.79	82.22	50.61	10611.04	5368.07
2004	153.90	233.94	425.74	79.43	64.80	11769.04	7101.64
2005	168.07	236.66	484.51	66.31	71.66	13069.52	8017.76
北 京 Beijing	2.39	3.42	11.71	0.20	3.69	384.00	370.41
天 津 Tianjin	1.89	1.71	7.57	0.79	1.46	164.50	153.14
河 北 Hebei	20.02	11.87	34.33	4.64	7.39	727.90	458.88
山 西 Shanxi	10.28	8.91	14.82	3.94	1.70	255.03	204.53
内蒙古 Inner Mongolia	10.65	5.59	7.76	0.89	2.49	364.28	261.71
辽 宁 Liaoning	10.57	6.25	24.09	1.48	2.86	416.87	335.01
吉 林 Jilin	4.32	3.82	9.26	0.51	0.80	297.69	239.81
黑龙江 Heilongjiang	5.66	7.48	10.85	2.29	1.95	260.64	239.42
上 海 Shanghai	2.65	8.29	7.09	1.13		276.29	208.27
江 苏 Jiangsu	5.11	18.03	18.48	1.73	4.27	978.79	395.38
浙 江 Zhejiang	3.07	10.16	36.75	5.92	3.50	694.55	431.19
安 徽 Anhui	5.09	12.86	13.74	1.52	3.64	439.73	258.40
福 建 Fujian	1.64	4.07	14.76	2.67	1.70	442.79	176.70
江 西 Jiangxi	7.42	3.95	7.78	0.74	1.29	357.98	108.94
山 东 Shandong	8.79	13.98	44.76	5.36	7.67	1096.06	619.43
河 南 Henan	13.69	10.83	19.94	4.70	4.13	762.52	387.15
湖 北 Hubei	2.93	11.78	13.59	2.67	1.88	588.39	373.74
湖 南 Hunan	4.02	10.56	12.61	0.78	0.91	371.52	248.06
广 东 Guangdong	12.11	18.14	84.45	4.14	6.68	1511.21	783.99
广 西 Guangxi	3.89	5.47	7.38	2.74	1.66	524.87	247.83
海 南 Hainan	1.23	0.91	3.11	0.36	0.25	94.88	46.34
重 庆 Chongqing	2.93	6.70	9.30	1.17	0.76	169.25	127.14
四 川 Sichuan	2.52	15.42	18.12	3.33	1.48	558.55	406.63
贵 州 Guizhou	3.72	3.77	7.21	2.86	2.96	156.94	118.70
云 南 Yunnan	5.89	13.07	17.06	4.36	0.74	375.33	253.51
西 藏 Tibet	2.17	0.94	0.57	0.28		12.37	10.22
陕 西 Shaanxi	2.94	6.97	6.42	2.49	1.55	316.81	208.62
甘 肃 Gansu	2.70	4.03	6.18	0.72	0.81	174.19	132.18
青 海 Qinghai	0.92	1.52	1.95	0.46	0.26	56.66	32.50
宁 夏 Ningxia	1.23	2.00	3.37	0.29	0.69	62.88	32.45
新 疆 Xinjiang	5.61	4.19	9.50	1.16	2.49	176.06	147.49

注：1.小轿车包括在载客汽车中（下表同）。

2.从2002年起，载客汽车和载货汽车的其中分项、其他汽车统计口径有调整与以前年份不可比（下表同）。

a) Cars are included in passenger vehicles. The same as in the following table.

b) Since 2002, the statistical standard of detail item of passenger vehicles and trucks, other vehicles have been adjusted, the data are not comparable with the previous years. The same as in the following table.

16-27 私人汽车拥有量

Possession of Private Vehicles

单位：万辆 (10 000 units)

年份 地区	Year Region	汽车总计 Total	载客汽车 Passenger Vehicles	大型 Large	中型 Medium	小型 Small	微型 Minicar
	1985	28.49	1.93				
	1989	73.12	20.28				
	1990	81.62	24.07				
	1991	96.04	30.36				
	1992	118.20	41.78				
	1993	155.77	59.85				
	1994	205.42	78.62				
	1995	249.96	114.15				
	1996	289.67	143.04				
	1997	358.36	191.27				
	1998	423.65	230.65				
	1999	533.88	304.09				
	2000	625.33	365.09				
	2001	770.78	469.85				
	2002	968.98	623.76	9.89	35.87	408.49	169.51
	2003	1219.23	845.87	7.36	42.51	586.90	209.10
	2004	1481.66	1069.69	7.20	46.95	786.63	228.91
	2005	1848.07	1383.93	7.61	50.88	1079.78	245.66
北京	Beijing	149.31	140.52	0.18	6.04	113.86	20.45
天津	Tianjin	45.02	38.62	0.10	1.12	28.07	9.33
河北	Hebei	133.36	97.00	0.52	1.31	68.33	26.83
山西	Shanxi	58.77	43.03	0.19	0.98	31.63	10.24
内蒙古	Inner Mongolia	44.25	27.78	0.27	0.81	20.93	5.78
辽宁	Liaoning	57.91	47.10	0.33	2.50	40.26	4.00
吉林	Jilin	35.88	29.22	0.28	0.59	22.74	5.61
黑龙江	Heilongjiang	43.88	32.84	0.45	1.28	24.99	6.12
上海	Shanghai	41.00	40.97	0.02	2.80	35.25	2.90
江苏	Jiangsu	109.43	94.21	0.09	3.13	77.52	13.48
浙江	Zhejiang	135.08	102.67	0.07	2.21	87.89	12.49
安徽	Anhui	35.41	22.98	0.44	1.83	15.44	5.27
福建	Fujian	42.07	29.29	0.04	0.83	25.07	3.34
江西	Jiangxi	17.55	11.66	0.15	0.35	8.71	2.45
山东	Shandong	136.07	97.69	0.46	2.66	68.22	26.35
河南	Henan	83.85	61.42	0.83	2.73	42.27	15.59
湖北	Hubei	43.47	29.71	0.33	1.50	25.63	2.25
湖南	Hunan	48.19	29.61	0.43	1.33	24.51	3.35
广东	Guangdong	251.60	183.40	0.75	10.79	164.76	7.10
广西	Guangxi	29.62	21.07	0.19	0.45	14.94	5.50
海南	Hainan	7.67	4.63	0.09	0.17	4.13	0.24
重庆	Chongqing	23.15	15.33	0.18	0.27	12.30	2.58
四川	Sichuan	89.32	66.19	0.14	0.98	37.99	27.07
贵州	Guizhou	30.26	16.27	0.28	0.70	9.70	5.58
云南	Yunnan	66.84	39.52	0.12	0.74	27.12	11.54
西藏	Tibet	4.06	1.49	0.05	0.24	0.99	0.21
陕西	Shaanxi	33.77	25.89	0.17	1.02	19.06	5.63
甘肃	Gansu	12.99	7.12	0.26	0.50	4.79	1.57
青海	Qinghai	5.27	3.17	0.04	0.19	2.44	0.50
宁夏	Ningxia	8.02	4.65	0.06	0.20	3.67	0.72
新疆	Xinjiang	24.97	18.89	0.10	0.64	16.57	1.59

16-27 续表 continued

单位：万辆 (10 000 units)

年份 Year / 地区 Region		载货汽车 Trucks	重型 Heavy	中型 Light-heavy	轻型 Light	微型 Mini	其他汽车 Others
	1985	26.48					
	1989	52.50					
	1990	57.48					
	1991	65.61					
	1992	76.15					
	1993	94.00					
	1994	123.29					
	1995	131.83					
	1996	142.78					
	1997	163.19					
	1998	192.03					
	1999	228.68					
	2000	259.09					
	2001	298.95					
	2002	341.29	48.27	84.40	158.67	49.95	3.94
	2003	367.35	44.47	95.20	176.58	51.09	6.00
	2004	402.82	53.40	94.69	203.85	50.87	9.15
	2005	452.11	62.50	100.34	243.29	45.98	12.04
北京	Beijing	8.29	1.05	1.42	5.65	0.16	0.49
天津	Tianjin	6.18	0.59	0.72	4.20	0.66	0.21
河北	Hebei	34.45	7.71	4.91	18.46	3.38	1.91
山西	Shanxi	15.56	2.32	3.70	6.98	2.56	0.18
内蒙古	Inner Mongolia	15.64	8.46	3.81	2.49	0.89	0.83
辽宁	Liaoning	10.68	1.65	1.16	7.05	0.82	0.13
吉林	Jilin	6.54	1.50	1.27	3.44	0.34	0.12
黑龙江	Heilongjiang	10.79	2.03	2.76	4.50	1.50	0.25
上海	Shanghai	0.04		0.01	0.02		
江苏	Jiangsu	14.61	1.75	5.28	6.57	1.02	0.60
浙江	Zhejiang	32.06	1.27	4.22	22.22	4.36	0.35
安徽	Anhui	12.11	0.95	4.14	6.02	0.99	0.32
福建	Fujian	12.69	0.50	1.90	8.33	1.96	0.10
江西	Jiangxi	5.81	1.64	0.84	2.88	0.45	0.08
山东	Shandong	37.19	4.02	6.03	23.17	3.97	1.20
河南	Henan	21.88	3.43	4.19	10.75	3.51	0.55
湖北	Hubei	13.54	0.88	4.90	5.88	1.88	0.23
湖南	Hunan	18.45	2.31	7.34	8.20	0.60	0.13
广东	Guangdong	67.33	5.88	10.40	47.66	3.39	0.88
广西	Guangxi	8.45	1.19	2.36	3.30	1.60	0.10
海南	Hainan	2.99	0.64	0.60	1.53	0.23	0.04
重庆	Chongqing	7.72	1.19	1.51	4.15	0.88	0.10
四川	Sichuan	22.94	0.93	8.15	11.28	2.58	0.19
贵州	Guizhou	11.61	2.78	2.15	4.61	2.08	2.38
云南	Yunnan	27.19	2.93	8.86	12.37	3.03	0.13
西藏	Tibet	2.57	1.32	0.72	0.34	0.19	
陕西	Shaanxi	7.70	0.65	2.62	2.73	1.70	0.19
甘肃	Gansu	5.79	1.24	1.93	2.36	0.26	0.09
青海	Qinghai	2.07	0.32	0.71	0.83	0.22	0.02
宁夏	Ningxia	3.26	0.42	0.91	1.72	0.22	0.11
新疆	Xinjiang	5.96	0.95	0.85	3.62	0.53	0.13

16-28 新注册民用汽车数量

New Registration Statistics on Civil Vehicles

单位：辆 (unit)

年份 Year / 地区 Region		民用汽车总计 Total	载客汽车 Passenger Vehicles	大型 Large	中型 Medium	小型 Small	微型 Minicar
2002		3371951	2294649	97200	145062	1491479	560908
2003		4337485	3160859	100284	157523	2421951	481101
2004		4511823	3332297	96462	138357	2841668	255810
2005		5286287	4157504	99489	105314	3712056	240645
北京	Beijing	342176	325191	6425	3742	307111	7913
天津	Tianjin	121316	109269	1900	1171	105227	971
河北	Hebei	585438	399056	8565	6741	314168	69582
山西	Shanxi	178795	144871	1931	2422	126507	14011
内蒙古	Inner Mongolia	112964	78522	1507	885	70253	5877
辽宁	Liaoning	179705	140576	3662	4418	127558	4938
吉林	Jilin	90881	77769	2037	1232	66353	8147
黑龙江	Heilongjiang	91195	72552	2711	1897	64561	3383
上海	Shanghai	169715	150646	4745	9773	134182	1946
江苏	Jiangsu	381620	334787	6075	8133	311244	9335
浙江	Zhejiang	402832	334331	4822	7355	316434	5720
安徽	Anhui	116023	73960	3105	3308	63737	3810
福建	Fujian	132951	99187	2091	2469	92409	2218
江西	Jiangxi	76609	52540	1311	1465	46463	3301
山东	Shandong	424576	348305	6457	5736	312805	23307
河南	Henan	252509	189176	5193	8195	152878	22910
湖北	Hubei	115940	85269	3361	3355	77736	817
湖南	Hunan	86596	66973	2862	4174	58160	1777
广东	Guangdong	572551	464614	11307	11090	439605	2612
广西	Guangxi	93461	70835	2580	1423	63485	3347
海南	Hainan	21384	16512	518	309	15264	421
重庆	Chongqing	88429	55757	2303	1647	48432	3375
四川	Sichuan	203896	156020	4507	2413	132266	16834
贵州	Guizhou	73421	51103	1524	1719	45852	2008
云南	Yunnan	149412	103796	1625	2969	90993	8209
西藏	Tibet	14420	8864	238	1806	3941	2879
陕西	Shaanxi	68321	54366	1675	2152	43599	6940
甘肃	Gansu	40880	26930	1491	993	23630	816
青海	Qinghai	7341	4913	123	176	4530	84
宁夏	Ningxia	26736	16261	854	740	13919	748
新疆	Xinjiang	64194	44553	1984	1406	38754	2409

16-28 续表 continued

单位：辆 (unit)

年 份 Year 地 区 Region	载货汽车 Trucks	重 型 Heavy	中 型 Light-heavy	轻 型 Light	微 型 Mini	其他汽车 Others
2002	993761	186498	220969	501985	84309	83541
2003	1075692	168363	259173	576073	72083	100934
2004	1029497	228523	194438	564061	42475	150029
2005	1024034	162859	175576	639557	46042	104749
北 京 Beijing	13354	1673	2523	9158		3631
天 津 Tianjin	10334	470	1004	8743	117	1713
河 北 Hebei	170052	42800	24787	92012	10453	16330
山 西 Shanxi	32192	5674	4427	20196	1895	1732
内蒙古 Inner Mongolia	27302	12168	2684	5012	7438	7140
辽 宁 Liaoning	35499	6468	3414	24724	893	3630
吉 林 Jilin	11886	2147	1598	7452	689	1226
黑龙江 Heilongjiang	16772	2867	1812	11297	796	1871
上 海 Shanghai	19069	1706	6690	10456	217	
江 苏 Jiangsu	39968	6093	9988	23255	632	6865
浙 江 Zhejiang	63646	1932	5085	50318	6311	4855
安 徽 Anhui	35542	4916	6776	22900	950	6521
福 建 Fujian	31028	2500	3402	23136	1990	2736
江 西 Jiangxi	22049	4851	6309	10520	369	2020
山 东 Shandong	67331	7869	6370	51137	1955	8940
河 南 Henan	56256	12026	12032	29639	2559	7077
湖 北 Hubei	28203	3749	5542	18585	327	2468
湖 南 Hunan	18780	2285	3565	11986	944	843
广 东 Guangdong	99308	6003	9308	81083	2914	8629
广 西 Guangxi	19895	3062	4131	12236	466	2731
海 南 Hainan	4565	370	459	3611	125	307
重 庆 Chongqing	31479	5286	10872	15128	193	1193
四 川 Sichuan	45859	3741	13918	27406	794	2017
贵 州 Guizhou	20886	2614	4959	12828	485	1432
云 南 Yunnan	44325	5563	14568	23655	539	1291
西 藏 Tibet	5556	1646	2778	863	269	
陕 西 Shaanxi	12416	4088	2125	5780	423	1539
甘 肃 Gansu	12583	2702	1827	7759	295	1367
青 海 Qinghai	2106	476	209	1336	85	322
宁 夏 Ningxia	9396	1361	835	6834	366	1079
新 疆 Xinjiang	16397	3753	1579	10512	553	3244

16-29 公路运输汽车拥有量

Possession of Vehicles for Highway Transportation

年份 Year 地区 Region	汽车总计 Total (万辆) (10 000 units)	载客汽车 Passenger Vehicles 辆数 (万辆) Number (10 000 units)	客位 (万客位) Number of Seats (10 000 seats)	载货汽车 Trucks 辆数 (万辆) Number (10 000 units)	#普通载货汽车 Ordinary Trucks	吨位 (万吨) Capacity (10 000 tons)	#普通载货汽车 Ordinary Trucks
1990	31.30	10.76	468.92	20.22	19.82	131.61	127.06
1991	31.67	11.53	497.35	19.83	19.36	132.02	126.54
1992	30.87	12.70	528.87	18.17	17.59	125.91	118.42
1993	28.96	12.85	509.56	16.15	15.53	116.20	108.37
1994	27.97	13.05	493.94	14.87	14.22	109.80	101.21
1995	27.49	13.73	480.61	13.75	13.12	103.13	94.56
1996	28.81	15.41	499.58	13.40	12.74	102.08	91.83
1997	29.89	17.01	519.10	12.88	12.22	95.31	85.09
1998	31.88	19.40	536.43	12.48	11.81	90.02	79.51
1999	501.77	92.14	1409.86	409.62	401.28	1481.02	1406.00
2000	702.82	216.81	2524.45	486.02	475.24	1667.70	1573.73
2001	764.39	255.12	2701.68	509.27	496.65	1733.58	1621.40
2002	826.34	289.55	2972.32	536.78	520.27	1808.45	1674.79
2003	924.64	352.19	3430.64	572.45	553.23	1941.52	1788.86
2004	1067.18	439.09	3872.21	628.09	604.93	2338.61	2119.64
2005	733.22	128.40	1859.28	604.82	580.28	2537.75	2282.15
北京 Beijing	12.92	0.53	20.18	12.39	11.60	49.57	42.00
天津 Tianjin	7.38	0.61	18.78	6.77	5.83	34.16	24.11
河北 Hebei	39.85	2.17	47.86	37.68	36.42	237.91	224.34
山西 Shanxi	20.84	2.13	29.93	18.71	18.44	121.27	118.90
内蒙古 Inner Mongolia	22.80	4.22	39.27	18.59	18.20	141.03	136.90
辽宁 Liaoning	32.62	1.81	48.66	30.81	29.13	139.91	123.50
吉林 Jilin	16.94	4.63	44.38	12.32	11.89	49.90	46.05
黑龙江 Heilongjiang	20.94	7.90	58.38	13.04	12.67	50.62	47.51
上海 Shanghai	17.90	1.57	38.85	16.33	14.79	73.88	53.78
江苏 Jiangsu	41.03	8.60	123.70	32.43	30.99	147.99	130.18
浙江 Zhejiang	31.56	7.43	102.88	24.13	22.66	87.98	66.37
安徽 Anhui	26.57	4.35	69.14	22.22	21.59	91.71	86.14
福建 Fujian	16.09	3.26	47.02	12.83	11.76	43.84	31.17
江西 Jiangxi	13.35	2.34	35.98	11.01	10.80	42.50	40.63
山东 Shandong	58.28	10.11	118.15	48.18	45.25	213.90	188.44
河南 Henan	38.28	7.49	146.90	30.79	30.25	151.22	146.99
湖北 Hubei	26.54	6.43	83.00	20.10	19.26	72.30	65.58
湖南 Hunan	23.21	5.85	93.15	17.36	16.98	58.24	54.60
广东 Guangdong	86.71	5.95	144.86	80.76	77.82	236.25	192.59
广西 Guangxi	15.66	3.69	60.05	11.97	11.13	53.03	45.85
海南 Hainan	2.98	0.98	18.57	2.00	1.96	6.06	5.59
重庆 Chongqing	18.48	3.25	47.32	15.23	14.92	42.76	40.96
四川 Sichuan	36.48	7.80	112.87	28.69	28.35	71.01	68.43
贵州 Guizhou	12.91	3.83	49.01	9.08	9.01	29.13	28.57
云南 Yunnan	26.02	5.39	68.97	20.63	20.39	68.87	66.65
西藏 Tibet	2.61	0.54	7.12	2.07	2.04	10.99	10.60
陕西 Shaanxi	16.32	5.26	58.52	11.06	10.57	40.74	35.30
甘肃 Gansu	12.95	3.73	41.46	9.22	8.69	38.31	35.01
青海 Qinghai	4.59	1.01	16.80	3.58	3.53	14.32	13.70
宁夏 Ningxia	7.24	1.47	17.17	5.77	5.64	19.45	18.24
新疆 Xinjiang	23.15	4.08	50.35	19.07	17.73	98.91	93.44

注：1.小轿车包括在载客汽车中。

2.1999年以前数据仅为公路部门营运汽车，1999年为全国营运汽车。2000年起为全国运输汽车(含营运和非营运汽车)。2005年起为全国营运汽车（不含非营运汽车）。

a) Passenger vehicles include cars.

b) Number of vehicles for business transportation only included those owned by the department of highway transportation before 1999, and referred to all working vehicles for business transportation in 1999, and all vehicles for business transportation, including working and non-working vehicles from 2000 to 2004, and all working vehicles for business transportation(doesn't include non-working vehicles) in 2005.

16-30 民用运输船舶拥有量

Possession of Civil Transport Vessels

年份 Year / 地区 Region	机动船 Motor Vessels: 艘数(艘) Number (unit)	机动船 Motor Vessels: 净载重量(吨) Dead Weight Tonnage (ton)	机动船 Motor Vessels: 载客量(客位) Passenger Capacity (seat)	机动船 Motor Vessels: 拖船功率(千瓦) Drawing Power (kw)	驳船 Barges: 艘数(艘) Number (unit)	驳船 Barges: 净载重量(吨) Dead Weight Tonnage (ton)	驳船 Barges: 载客量(客位) Passenger Capacity (seat)
1980	64307	12789410	545042	1514998	119464	5951401	100312
1985	260296	20898230	877963	1665030	132682	8670224	99643
1989	351450	27290103	1095018	1759366	88903	8958617	52459
1990	325858	29090082	1138937	1750351	82482	9066738	62926
1991	307127	29959203	1169982	1845705	78410	9588216	61526
1992	302313	31225749	1177035	1844101	71255	9437823	46337
1993	307285	34682035	1124114	1734606	65196	8891435	43801
1994	293472	39591864	1065140	1678066	59913	8898065	26335
1995	299717	40940087	979985	1707115	57998	9449652	17722
1996	269879	39774235	988046	1616585	56128	9315335	15148
1997	215814	38749289	1022970	1468612	49983	9064891	13879
1998	212093	38896576	983630	1584601	48115	9019417	14914
1999	194590	38911462	929138	1494500	47453	8981998	10306
2000	185018	42640605	1014013	1439743	44658	8640504	18258
2001	169329	45526726	1048915	1370221	41457	8968670	27902
2002	165936	48372587	945387	1433547	37041	8683075	33405
2003	163813	60745234	971514	1269607	40457	9871079	30631
2004	166854	75114059	961562	1197191	43846	11058522	34666
2005	165900	90756392	977846	1480381	41394	11030057	33496
北京 Beijing							
天津 Tianjin	341	4997442	3716	331906	40	84198	
河北 Hebei	88	3012379		465	1	2052	
山西 Shanxi	231	8921	5450				
内蒙古 Inner Mongolia							
辽宁 Liaoning	735	2981843	27591	18467	25	12710	
吉林 Jilin	589	10244	11494	3572	41	15640	
黑龙江 Heilongjiang	1123	46235	15795	50220	396	226648	150
上海 Shanghai	2016	16939040	82126	97542	546	286839	
江苏 Jiangsu	34464	8943490	41284	367871	16777	4628016	1914
浙江 Zhejiang	26873	10114637	63940	54597	2569	256539	
安徽 Anhui	30439	13025088	14340	61696	2933	811238	
福建 Fujian	2890	3661363	25715	5236	147	23795	
江西 Jiangxi	5418	1123022	17345	7731	127	33073	
山东 Shandong	4020	4063385	19709	179032	11536	2665833	
河南 Henan	4687	1908984	6115	3068	431	111635	
湖北 Hubei	4158	1777916	38273	114181	1204	1079010	
湖南 Hunan	8772	842444	74802	14801	469	64501	2335
广东 Guangdong	12885	7093274	68045	40175	82	68691	
广西 Guangxi	8307	2036047	89716	966	10	6740	
海南 Hainan	695	377490	18754	2309	4	5448	
重庆 Chongqing	3274	1937189	115175	101524	634	548766	
四川 Sichuan	8669	383508	155334	20554	2689	72453	19935
贵州 Guizhou	2153	61766	26131	3015	151	22088	
云南 Yunnan	1174	50647	24006	177			
西藏 Tibet							
陕西 Shaanxi	980	11312	17043	356	485	1083	4959
甘肃 Gansu	380	2020	8117		53	421	1628
青海 Qinghai	51		768				
宁夏 Ningxia	390		7062	920	44	2640	2575
新疆 Xinjiang							
不分地区 Not Classified by Region	98	5346706					

注：不分地区数据为中国远洋运输集团总公司海外公司数。

a) Number of civil transport vessels not classified by region is the number of abroad companies under China Ocean Shipping (Group) Company.

16-31 私人运输船舶拥有量
Possession of Private Transport Vessels

年份 Year / 地区 Region	机动船 Motor Vessels 艘数(艘) Number	净载重量(吨) Dead Weight Tonnage (ton)	载客量(客位) Passenger Capacity (seat)	拖船功率(千瓦) Drawing Power (kw)	驳船 Barges 艘数(艘) Number	净载重量(吨) Dead Weight Tonnage (ton)	载客量(客位) Passenger Capacity (seat)
1985	133165	2139297	140722	52736	12253	417664	2267
1989	228988	4654767	298174	67638	13021	581523	12308
1990	206589	4257594	283248	70250	10927	586650	3352
1991	200357	4517888	312280	54028	11673	519506	9075
1992	190262	3976814	326587	60481	9192	503787	11622
1993	190820	5961873	302898	85806	9458	636200	3103
1994	198241	7112807	261908	59848	7379	506187	5116
1995	182060	6942745	276555	78867	7964	749329	180
1996	157370	4821091	289402	55129	6533	657652	1240
1997	147415	6714642	347405	115168	9944	879692	1948
1998	127130	6547095	328884	98537	7290	794618	1850
1999	113359	6070634	343208	85615	7262	775881	606
2000	128654	8244485	387405	168099	13463	1523260	13682
2001	111633	8190264	443140	114209	10088	1142822	20293
2002	105697	8913536	428614	112152	9411	1178379	21346
2003	97837	11668873	409915	187186	16460	2779120	20399
2004	91188	10986632	402764	284623	24315	4631108	24030
2005	83380	12599372	432100	165830	12458	2644012	25993
北京 Beijing							
天津 Tianjin							
河北 Hebei	29	28644					
山西 Shanxi	231	8921	5450				
内蒙古 Inner Mongolia							
辽宁 Liaoning	293	6127					
吉林 Jilin	513	8997	9580	3572	41	15640	
黑龙江 Heilongjiang	748	7594	6954	17741	89	34660	150
上海 Shanghai	155	12955					
江苏 Jiangsu	14575	1894407	9499	72453	6258	1139229	1535
浙江 Zhejiang	20543	2599190	468	5822	766	39057	
安徽 Anhui	9989	4440781	4387	400	21	3221	
福建 Fujian	256	10694	3110				
江西 Jiangxi	3750	519454	12422	1637	19	5660	
山东 Shandong	810	561311		25403	2271	1234109	
河南 Henan							
湖北 Hubei	2793	744429	17718	15007	199	87865	
湖南 Hunan	7543	594825	65061	6587	58	17537	
广东 Guangdong	3078	213677	1182				
广西 Guangxi	3450	352816	56299				
海南 Hainan	327	9443	3802				
重庆 Chongqing	1702	180657	29120	2775	64	17025	
四川 Sichuan	8278	316266	142783	13513	2324	44154	16906
贵州 Guizhou	1994	54454	22921		21	2020	
云南 Yunnan	868	21456	13922				
西藏 Tibet							
陕西 Shaanxi	850	10705	15462		230	774	3199
甘肃 Gansu	314	1569	7192		53	421	1628
青海 Qinghai							
宁夏 Ningxia	291		4768	920	44	2640	2575
新疆 Xinjiang							

16-32 沿海主要港口分货类吞吐量

Volume of Freight Handled in Major Coastal Ports by Type of Freight

单位：万吨 (10 000 tons)

货物种类	Type of Freight	2004			2005		
		合计 Total	出港 Out-port	进港 In-port	合计 Total	出港 Out-port	进港 In-port
总计	**Total**	**246074**	**115876**	**130198**	**292777**	**136085**	**156692**
煤炭	Coal	57113	36396	20717	63514	40155	23359
石油	Petroleum	35051	12926	22125	37637	13397	24241
金属矿石	Metal Ores	31769	7670	24099	41963	9667	32296
钢铁	Steel and Iron	10928	5562	5365	12522	6934	5588
矿建材料	Mineral Building Materials	18529	6607	11922	24439	9191	15248
水泥	Cement	2115	649	1466	2230	965	1265
木材	Timber	1365	539	826	1555	650	905
非金属矿石	Nonmetal Ores	3335	2023	1313	3962	2246	1716
化肥和农药	Chemical Fertilizers and Pesticides	2223	980	1243	2074	717	1357
盐	Salt	685	249	436	822	160	662
粮食	Grain	7164	2795	4369	8590	3583	5007
其他	Others	75797	39480	36317	93469	48420	45048

16-33 沿海主要港口货物吞吐量

Volume of Freight Handled in Major Coastal Ports

单位：万吨 (10 000 tons)

港口	Seaport	1985	1990	1995	2000	2001	2002	2003	2004	2005
总计	**Total**	**31154**	**48321**	**80166**	**125603**	**142634**	**166628**	**201126**	**246074**	**292777**
大连	Dalian	4381	4952	6417	9084	10047	10851	12602	14516	17085
营口	Yingkou	98	237	1156	2268	2520	3127	4009	5978	7537
秦皇岛	Qinhuangdao	4419	6945	8382	9743	11302	11167	12562	15037	16900
天津	Tianjin	1856	2063	5787	9566	11369	12906	16182	20619	24069
烟台	Yantai	689	668	1361	1774	2190	2689	2936	3431	4506
青岛	Qingdao	2611	3034	5103	8636	10398	12213	14090	16265	18678
日照	Rizhao		925	1452	2674	2933	3136	4507	5108	8421
连云港	Lianyungang	929	1137	1716	2708	3058	3316	3752	4352	6016
上海	Shanghai	11291	13959	16567	20440	22099	26384	31621	37896	44317
宁波	Ningbo	1040	2554	6853	11547	12852	15398	18543	22586	26881
汕头	Shantou	201	279	716	1284	1309	1380	1470	1576	1736
广州	Guangzhou	1772	4163	7299	11128	12823	15324	17187	21520	25036
湛江	Zhanjiang	1231	1557	1885	2038	2205	2627	2866	3780	4647
海口	Haikou	170	288	468	808	888	1073	1329	1416	2118
八所	Basuo	388	431	275	378	342	343	425	548	486
三亚	Sanya	78	37	42	48	71	49	61	58	49
其他港口	Other Ports		5092	14687	31479	36228	44645	56984	71388	84295

16-34 沿海主要港口码头泊位数（2005年底）

Number of Berths in Major Coastal Ports at the Year-end (2005)

名 称	Name	总 计 Total			生 产 用 For Productive Use			非 生 产 用 For Nonproductive Use	
		码头长度（米）Length of Quay Line (m)	泊位个数（个）Number of Berths (unit)	#万吨级 10 000 Ton Class	码头长度（米）Length of Quay Line (m)	泊位个数（个）Number of Berths (unit)	#万吨级 10 000 Ton Class	码头长度（米）Length of Quay Line (m)	泊位个数（个）Number of Berths (unit)
总 计	**Total**	**378678**	**3641**	**769**	**340727**	**3110**	**769**	**37951**	**531**
#大 连	Dalian	30715	223	57	26119	192	57	4596	31
营 口	Yingkou	5047	31	15	4758	26	15	289	5
秦皇岛	Qinhuangdao	11446	62	38	10128	41	38	1318	21
天 津	Tianjin	20906	116	54	18962	100	54	1944	16
烟 台	Yantai	7357	43	23	6974	40	23	383	3
青 岛	Qingdao	13961	59	40	13018	52	40	943	7
日 照	Rizhao	7314	35	24	6994	28	24	320	7
连云港	Lianyungang	6891	37	27	6421	32	27	470	5
上 海	Shanghai	23580	183	78	20069	121	78	3511	62
宁 波	Ningbo	28157	334	48	26297	297	48	1860	37
汕 头	Shantou	8918	88	16	8662	82	16	256	6
广 州	Guangzhou	46553	617	49	36301	455	49	10252	162
湛 江	Zhanjiang	10439	85	29	9011	71	29	1428	14
海 口	Haikou	2662	31	2	2662	31	2		
八 所	Basuo	1412	8	6	1412	8	6		
三 亚	Sanya	602	5		602	5			

16-35 内河主要港口码头泊位数（2005年底）

Number of Berths in Major Ports of Inland Rivers at the Year-end (2005)

名 称	Name	总 计 Total			生 产 用 For Productive Use			非生产用 For Nonproductive Use	
		码头长度（米）Length of Quay Line (m)	泊位个数（个）Number of Berths (unit)	#万吨级 10 000 Ton Class	码头长度（米）Length of Quay Line (m)	泊位个数（个）Number of Berths (unit)	#万吨级 10 000 Ton Class	码头长度（米）Length of Quay Line (m)	泊位个数（个）Number of Berths (unit)
总 计	**Total**	**366387**	**7011**	**186**	**354147**	**6833**	**186**	**12240**	**178**
#重 庆	Chongqing	4060	82		3571	66		489	16
万 州	Wanzhou	9655	73		7405	56		2250	17
宜 昌	Yichang	1140	21		920	16		220	5
枝 城	Zhicheng	1205	25		989	20		216	5
武 汉	Wuhan	22495	335		21905	327		590	8
黄 石	Huangshi	3725	74		3378	66		347	8
九 江	Jiujiang	1140	14		1010	12		130	2
安 庆	Anqing	2807	43		2342	33		465	10
池 州	Chizhou	2210	38		2055	36		155	2
铜 陵	Tongling	921	14		856	13		65	1
芜 湖	Wuhu	2080	30		1835	26		245	4
马鞍山	Maanshan	2007	28		2007	28			
南 京	Nanjing	20120	301	32	18338	269	32	1782	32
镇 江	Zhenjiang	15831	230	23	15831	230	23		
泰 州	Taizhou	5855	47	8	5831	46	8	24	1
扬 州	Yangzhou	2739	50	4	2739	50	4		
江 阴	Jiangyin	7842	50	23	7842	50	23		
常 州	Changzhou	6186	105	3	6186	105	3		
南 通	Nantong	8971	73	24	8724	69	24	247	4
上海（内河）	Shanghai	75717	2138		75717	2138			

16-36 民用航空航线及飞机架数

Number of Civil Aviation Routes and Civil Aircrafts

指　　标	Item	1990	1995	2000	2004	2005
民用航空航线条数（条）	**Number of Civil Aviation Routes (line)**	**437**	**797**	**1165**	**1279**	**1257**
国际航线	International Routes	44	85	133	244	233
国内航线	Domestic Routes	385	694	1032	1035	1024
地区航线	Regional Routes	8	18	42	45	43
民用航空航线里程（公里）	**Length of Civil Aviation Routes (km)**	**506762**	**1128961**	**1502887**	**2049394**	**1998501**
国际航线	International Routes	166350	348175	508405	894175	855932
国内航线	Domestic Routes	329493	750794	994482	1155219	1142569
地区航线	Regional Routes	10919	29992	55759	62484	61056
民用航班飞行机场（个）	**Number of Civil Airports (unit)**	**94**	**139**	**139**	**133**	**135**
民用飞机期末架数（架）	**Number of Civil Aircraft (unit)**	**499**	**852**	**982**	**1245**	**1386**
#运输飞机	Aero transport			527	754	863
大中型飞机	Air bus			462	675	785
#波音747	Boeing 747	11	16	19	20	22
波音737	Boeing 737	21	115	186	304	358
波音757	Boeing 757	9	44	48	62	64
波音767	Boeing 767	6	17	16	27	27
MD90	MD-90			22	22	22
MD82	MD-82	25	39	27	26	15
A310	Airbus A310	2	3	3	3	3
A320	Airbus A320			60	93	115
Bae-146	BB-146	10	14	7	7	4
小型飞机	Puddle-jumper			65	79	78
通用飞机	General Aircraft			301	365	383

注：1.1997年以前，民航机场和飞机架数为民航总局直属企业数，1997年起为民航全行业数字(下表同)。

2.1997年以前，地区航线含民航至香港、澳门航线,与国内航线、国际航线并列。1997年起，民航至香港航线统计在国内航线中，航线里程及运输量统计口径也做同样调整。1999年起，地区航线为国内航线的其中项，仍含民航至香港、澳门航线及运量(下表同)。

3.民用飞机合计中含教学校验用飞机。

a) Before 1997, the number of civil airports and aircrafts refers to those owned by enterprises directly under CAAC. Since 1997, it refers to those owned by all enterprises of civil aviation. The same as in the following table.

b) Before 1997, regional routes includes the routes to and from Hong Kong, Macao, and are taken as the parataxis item as the item of domestic routes and international routes. Since 1997, regional routes to and from Hong Kong are taken as domestic routes, and adjustment are also made on the length of aviation routes and traffic volume accordingly. Since 1999, regional routes are taken as a part of domestic routes, and include the aviation routes to and from Hong Kong, Macao. The same as in the following table.

c) Number of civil aircrafts include the teaching aircrafts and check aircrafts.

16-37 民用航空运输量及通用飞行时间

Civil Aviation Traffic and Flying Time of General Aviation

指　　标	Item	1990	1995	2000	2004	2005
客运量　（万人）	**Passenger Traffic (10 000 persons)**	**1660**	**5117**	**6722**	**12123**	**13827**
国际航线	International Routes	114	368	690	1077	1225
国内航线	Domestic Routes	1346	4419	6031	11046	12602
地区航线	Regional Routes	200	330	403	469	509
旅客周转量(万人公里)	**Passenger-tons (10 000 person-km)**	**2304797**	**6813036**	**9705437**	**17822791**	**20449288**
国际航线	International Routes	516910	1149710	2328154	3981054	4524063
国内航线	Domestic Routes	1576554	5287232	7377283	13841737	15925225
地区航线	Regional Routes	211333	376094	502405	643597	709205
货(邮)运量　（吨）	**Freight Traffic (ton)**	**369722**	**1011145**	**1967123**	**2767001**	**3067168**
国际航线	International Routes	81102	229632	492356	704835	771551
国内航线	Domestic Routes	239467	702557	1474767	2062165	2295618
地区航线	Regional Routes	49153	78956	135442	167640	169247
货邮周转量(万吨公里)	**Freight Ton-kilometers(10 000 ton-km)**	**81825**	**222981**	**502683**	**718036**	**788954**
国际航线	International Routes	43830	115894	291550	418793	452450
国内航线	Domestic Routes	31647	96604	211133	299243	336504
地区航线	Regional Routes	6348	10483	19495	26018	26263
总周转量（万吨公里）	**Total Air Traffic Ton-kilometers (10 000 ton-km)**	**249950**	**714385**	**1225007**	**2309985**	**2612724**
国际航线	International Routes	82595	201250	465190	774101	855235
国内航线	Domestic Routes	145156	474660	759818	1535884	1757488
地区航线	Regional Routes	22199	38475	56878	83490	89509
通用飞行时间（小时）	**Flying Time of General Aviation (hr)**	**34919**	**39485**	**48707**	**75277**	**84859**
农林业航空作业	Flight for Agriculture and Forestry	22540	16838	22922	27765	25428
#航空护林	Forest Protection Service	3573	2410	3927	5962	6508
播种造林	Afforestation	4605	1713	4060	3074	1929
工业航空作业	Flight for Industry	12379	22647	24116	35806	36514

16-38 输油(气)管道长度和运输量（2005年底）

Length and Volume of Petroleum and Gas Pipelines at the Year-end (2005)

本表是中国石油天然气集团公司和中国石油化工集团公司数据。
Data in this table are provided by China National Petroleum Corporation and China Petro-chemical Corporation.

项目	Item	输油(气)管道里程(公里) Length of Pipelines (km)	输油(气)能力(万吨) Capacity of Pipeline Transport (10 000 tons)	输油(气)量(万吨或千万立方米) Volume Pipeline Transport (10 000 tons or 10 million cu.m)	输油(气)周转量(万吨公里或千万立方米公里) Ton-kilometer or Cubic Meter-kilometers (10 000 ton-km or 10 million cu.m-km)
总计	**Total**	**43981**	**61635.1**	**31037.1**	**10876584.7**
#输油管	Petroleum Pipelines	20984	53825.7	27014.8	7813865.2
输气管	Gas Pipelines	22997	7809.4	4022.3	3062719.5
输原油管道	**Crude Oil Pipelines**	**15541**	**41507.9**	**23434.1**	**7213138.6**
管道分公司	Pipelines Subsidiary Company	3476	7500.0	4913.1	2995416.0
大庆油田有限责任公司	Daqing Oil Fields Limited Corporation	298	1547.0	1179.5	45973.0
新疆油田分公司	Xinjiang Oil Fields Subsidiary Company	1154	1330.0	1132.5	212360.0
胜利油田有限公司	Shengli Oil Fields Limited Co.	347	1725.0	545.6	41988.8
吉林油田分公司	Jilin Oil Fields Subsidiary Company	19	612.0	503.2	1363.0
华北油田分公司	North China Oil Fields Subsidiary Company	417	237.0	252.0	29682.0
大港油田分公司	Dagang Oil Fields Subsidiary Company	46	877.0	345.5	2353.0
玉门油田分公司	Yumen Oil Fields Subsidiary Company	69	879.0	81.9	1452.0
辽河油田分公司	Liaohe Oil Fields Subsidiary Company	494	1425.0	875.9	91535.0
青海油田分公司	Qinghai Oil Fields Subsidiary Company	439	300.0	208.4	91147.0
江汉油田分公司	Jianghan Oil Fields Subsidiary Company	42	113.9	81.1	2187.6
河南油田分公司	Henan Oil Fields Subsidiary Company	93	380.0	159.7	3654.4
中原油田分公司	Zhongyuan Oil Fields Subsidiary Company	1	800.0	176.2	221.6
茂名石油化工公司	Maoming Petrochemical Co.	170	2000.0	1325.7	99620.4
长庆油田分公司	Changqing Oil Fields Subsidiary Company	1146	1405.0	839.9	250775.0
塔里木油田分公司	Tarim Oil Fields Subsidiary Company	723	593.0	357.9	46649.0
锦州石化分公司	Jinzhou Petrochemical Subsidiary Company	79	750.0	519.0	13649.0
锦西石化分公司	Jinxi Petrochemical Subsidiary Company	30	300.0		
长岭炼油化工公司	Changling Refinery & Petrochemical Corporation	22	730.0	430.6	4736.9
吉林石化分公司	Jilin Petrochemical Subsidiary Company	150	400.0	479.9	79660.0
石化集团管道储运分公司	China Petrochemical Corporation Pipeline	4650	7165.0	5541.1	2690966.0
石家庄炼化股份有限公司	Shijiazhuang Refinery & Petrochemical Limited Co.	155	350.0	203.8	31583.8
荆门分公司	Jingmen Subsidiary Company	285	420.0	277.0	52668.3
金陵分公司	Jinling Subsidiary Company	532	2800.0	743.9	264647.8
西北分公司	Northwest Subsidiary Company	192	825.0	555.6	28761.8
济南分公司	Jinan Subsidiary Company	70	330.0	317.0	22190.0
青岛石油化工厂	Qingdao Petrochemical Factory	60	300.0	198.0	12276.0
巴陵石油化工公司	Baling Petrochemical Co.	18	200.0	175.0	3150.0
保定石油化工厂	Baoding Petrochemical Factory	84	50.0		
湛江东兴石油企业有限公司	Zhanjiangdongxing Petrochemical Limited Co.	10	4204.0	315.1	1198.2
冀东油田分公司	Jidong Oil Fields Subsidiary Company	79	240.0	109.1	8567.0
辽河石油勘探局	Liaohe Petroleum Exploration Bureau	26	120.0	110.0	2860.0
中国石油天然气管道局	China Oil and Gas Pipeline Bureau	166	600.0	481.0	79846.0
输成品油管道	**Refined Oil Pipelines**	**5443**	**12317.8**	**3580.7**	**600726.7**
北京燕山分公司	Beijing Yanshan Subsidiary Company	26	469.0	84.7	640.7
抚顺石化分公司	Fushun Petrochemical Subsidiary Company	268	435.0	283.5	70022.0
锦州石化分公司	jimson Petrochemical Subsidiary Company	126	240.0	155.0	6510.0
锦西石化分公司	Jinxi Petrochemical Subsidiary Company	64	338.0	191.9	5757.0
鞍山炼油厂	Anshan Refinery	52	352.0		
大连石化分公司	Dalian Petrochemical Subsidiary Company	11	80.0	0.5	2.0
中国石化长岭分公司	China Petrochemical Corporation Changling Subsidiary Company	61	52.2	2.8	34.0
大庆石化分公司	Daqing Petrochemical Subsidiary Company	52	188.0	37.3	75.0
天津分公司	Tianjin Subsidiary Company	17	335.0	88.0	264.1
沧州分公司	Cangzhou Subsidiary Company	8	32.9	19.5	82.0
镇海炼化股份有限公司	Zhenhai Refinery & Petrochemical Limited Co.	305	408.9	287.4	27275.0
九江分公司	Jiujiang Subsidiary Company	19	259.5	4.0	18.4
荆门分公司	Jingmen Subsidiary Company	12	56.0	4.2	7.6
武汉石油化工厂	Wuhan Petrochemical Factory	15	349.0	3.4	12.5

16-38 续表 continued

项目	Item	输油(气)管道里程(公里) Length of Pipelines (km)	输油(气)能力(万吨) Capacity of Pipeline Transport (10 000 tons)	输油(气)量(万吨或千万立方米) Volume Pipeline Transport (10 000 tons or 10 million cu.m)	输油(气)周转量(万吨公里或千万立方米公里) Ton-kilometer or Cubic Meter-kilometers (10 000 ton-km or 10 million cu.m-km)
中国石化广州分公司	China Petrochemical Corporation Guangzhou Subsidiary Company	67	2418.0	390.9	1720.3
茂名石油化工公司	Maoming Petrochemical Industrial Co.	152	650.0	156.1	5933.3
齐鲁分公司	Qilu Subsidiary Company	3	60.0	0.5	1.4
管道分公司	Pipelines Subsidiary Company	1447	800.0	495.6	458011.0
大庆油田有限责任公司	Daqing Oil Fields Limited Corporation	36	98.0		
新疆油田分公司	Xinjiang Oil Fields Subsidiary Company	291	130.0		
吉林油田分公司	Jilin Oil Fields Subsidiary Company	11	20.0		
哈尔滨石化分公司	Harbin Petrochemical Subsidiary Company	71	50.0	26.8	366.0
高桥分公司	Gaoqiao Subsidiary Company	139	250.0	191.5	191.5
巴陵石油化工公司	Baling Petrochemical Company	88	223.0	47.6	761.9
金陵石油化工公司	Jinling Petrochemical Company	54	278.0	99.3	999.6
青岛石油化工厂	Qingdao Petrochemical Company	15	280.0	65.0	975.0
湛江东兴石油企业有限公司	Zhanjiangdongxing Petrochemical Limited Co.	29	1222.0	181.4	4129.8
金陵分公司	Jinling Subsidiary Company	47	271.0	253.4	3814.8
安庆分公司	Anqing Subsidiary Company	3	135.0	23.4	18.7
茂名分公司	Maoming Subsidiary Company	217	837.3	356.2	8418.2
西南管道项目部	Xinan Pipelines Division	1740	1000.0	130.7	4684.2
输天然气管道	**Natural Gas Pipelines**	**22451**	**7186.9**	**3740.9**	**3058765.5**
管道分公司	Pipelines Subsidiary Company	3455	850.0	285.2	200379.0
西南油气分公司	Southwest Oil & Gas Subsidiary Company	6591		1125.5	428262.1
大庆油田有限责任公司	Daqing Oil Fields Limited Corporation	209	196.0	73.4	1708.4
胜利油田有限公司	Shengli Oil Fields Limited Corporation	143	40.0	20.7	2956.1
华北油田分公司	North China Oil Fields Subsidiary Company	75	27.0	6.7	471.9
辽河油田分公司	Liaohe Oil Fields Subsidiary Company	788	248.0	41.5	717.2
大港油田分公司	Dagang Oil Fields Subsidiary Company	188	91.0	54.1	5312.2
中原油气高新股份有限公司	Sinopec Zhongyuan Petroleum Co., LTD	150	14.6	9.0	1356.0
南方勘探开发分公司	Southern Prospecting & Exploiture Subsidiary Company	1	60.0	3.4	1.7
江汉油田分公司	Jianghan Oil Fields Subsidiary Company	56	10.0	1.8	101.6
新疆油田分公司	Xinjiang Oil Fields Subsidiary Company	626	188.0	216.3	28403.5
青海油田分公司	Qinghai Oil Fields Subsidiary Company	896	147.0	46.0	12099.6
长庆油田分公司	Changqing Oil Fields Subsidiary Company	182	253.0	9.5	471.9
塔里木油田分公司	Tarim Oil Fields Subsidiary Company	663	1457.0	490.0	70167.6
吉林油田分公司	Jilin Oil Fields Subsidiary Company	239	36.0	9.9	853.2
西气东输管道公司	Gas from West to East Pipeline Transport Company	4133		435.7	1481143.8
北京华油天然气有限公司	Beijing Oil and Natural Gas Co.	2011	640.0	403.4	802201.0
中原油田分公司	Zhongyuan Oil Fields Subsidiary Company	906	326.0	82.2	10445.7
华北分公司	North China Subsidiary Company	219	1790.0	78.2	3722.4
西南分公司	Southwest Subsidiary Company	661	650.7	337.5	7168.9
西北分公司	Northwest Subsidiary Company	144	118.6	10.4	786.5
天然气分公司	Natural Gas Subsidiary Company	117	44.0	0.3	35.1
输其他气体管道	**Other Gas pipelines**	**546**	**622.5**	**281.4**	**3954.0**
大庆油田有限责任公司	Daqing Oil Fields Limited Corporation	9	1.0		
锦西石化分公司	Jinxi Petrochemical Subsidiary Company	1	10.0		
北京燕山分公司	Beijing Yanshan Subsidiary Company	3	21.0		
沧州分公司	Cangzhou Subsidiary Company	1	0.1	0.5	0.5
金陵分公司	Jinling Subsidiary Company	45	8.4	13.5	207.1
镇海炼化股份有限公司	Zhenhai Refinery & Petrochemical Limited Co.	39	63.5	72.4	604.5
武汉石油化工厂	Wuhan Petrochemical Factory	23	16.0		
荆门分公司	Jingmen Subsidiary company	3	1.2		
石家庄炼化股份有限公司	Shijiazhuang Refinery & Petrochemical Limited Co.	37	34.0	4.9	81.6
中国石化广州分公司	China Petrochemical Corporation Guangzhou Subsidiary Company	10	9.8	9.3	38.2
茂名分公司	Maoming Subsidiary Company	36	46.4	45.2	419.6
中国石化长岭分公司	China Petrochemical Corporation Changling Subsidiary Company	24	30.7		
天津分公司	Tianjin Subsidiary Company	35	67.0	8.9	117.7
锦州石化分公司	Jinzhou Petrochemical Subsidiary Company	45	32.0	16.0	720.0
南京化学工业公司	Nanjing Petrochemical Co.	1	12.4	7.5	11.0
茂名石油化工公司	Maoming Petrochemical Co.	110	44.0	71.8	1318.7
巴陵石油化工公司	Baling Petrolchemical Co.	53	79.0	21.6	333.6
安庆分公司	Anqing Subsidiary Company	2	1.0	0.9	1.7
金陵石油化工公司	Jinling Petrochemical Co.	70	145.0	8.9	99.6

注：管道输气量按一千立方米折一吨计算。

a) Gas transport through pipelines is converted from volume to tonnage using the conversion ratio of 1000 cubic meters equal to one ton.

16-39 邮电业务基本情况

Basic Conditions of Post and Telecommunication Services

指 标	Item	2001	2002	2003	2004	2005
邮电业务总量 (亿元)	Business Volume of Post and Telecommunication Service (100 million yuan)	4556.26	5695.80	7019.79	9712.29	12028.54
函件 (亿件)	Number of Letters (100 million pcs)	86.93	106.01	103.84	82.81	73.51
特快专递 (万件)	Pieces of Express Mail Services (10 000 pcs)	12652.7	14036.2	17237.8	19771.9	22880.3
报刊期发数 (万份)	Issue of Newspapers and Magazines (10 000 copies)	21811.1	17620.0	16594.4	14789.3	14601.3
集邮业务 (万枚)	Stamps for Collection (10 000 pcs)	344114	244159	183421	149178	121214
长途电话 (亿次)	Number of Long-distance Calls (100 million times)	219.98	192.79	196.03	226.22	259.24
无线寻呼年末用户 (万户)	Number of Subscribers of Wireless Paging Services at Year-end (10 000 subscribers)	3606.4	1872.1	1057.6	395.2	97.1
移动电话年末用户 (万户)	Number of Mobile Telephone Subscribers at Year-end (10 000 subscribers)	14522.2	20600.5	26995.3	33482.4	39340.6
本地电话年末用户 (万户)	Local Telephone Subscribers of at Year-end (10 000 subscribers)	18036.8	21422.2	26274.7	31175.6	35044.5
城市电话用户 (万户)	Local (Urban) Telephone Subscribers at Year-end (10 000 subscribers)	11193.7	13579.1	17109.7	21025.1	23975.3
#住宅电话	Household Telephone Subscribers	8535.3	10196.7	12533.9	15246.5	17201.2
农村电话用户 (万户)	Rural Telephones Subscribers at Year-end (10 000 subscribers)	6843.1	7843.1	9165.0	10150.5	11069.2
#住宅电话	Household Telephone Subscribers	6197.7	7183.8	8389.7	9240.5	10023.9
邮政局所 (处)	Number of Post & Telecommunications Offices(unit)	57136	76358	63555	66393	65917
邮路及农村投递路线总长度 (万公里)	Length of Postal Routes and Rural Delivery Routes (10 000 km)	659.53	659.22	680.20	686.70	697.15
长途光缆线路长度 (万公里)	Length of Long-distance Optical Cable Lines (10 000 km)	39.91	48.77	59.43	69.53	72.30
长途电话交换机容量(万路端)	Capacity of Long Distance Telephone Exchanges (10 000 lines)	703.58	773.01	869.40	1263.00	1371.63
局用电话交换机容量 (万门)	Capacity of Office Telephone Exchange (10000 lines)	25566	28657	35082	42347	47196
用户交换机容量 (万门)	Capacity of PBXs (10000 lines)	1514.5	1370.5	1294.1	1420.0	1413.9
移动电话交换机容量 (万户)	Capacity of Mobile Telephone Exchanges (10 000 subscribers)	21926.3	27400.3	33698.4	39684.3	48241.7

注：1.邮电业务总量2000年及以前按1990年不变价格计算，2001年起按2000年不变价格计算，按可比价格比上年增长27.6%。

2.邮政局所数1998年及以前为邮电局所；从2002年起统计口径为邮政营销网点，含邮政局所和邮政代办点(下表同)。

a) The business volume of post and telecommunication services before 2000 was calculated at 1990's constant prices and that since 2001 was calculated at 2000's constant prices. The increase rate at constant price in 2001 was 27.6 %.

b) Number of postal and telecommunications offices refers to number of postal offices before 1998. That refers to the postal marketing station, including the postal offices and the postal deputy station, since 2002. The same as the following table.

16-40 邮电业务量

Business Volume of Post and Telecommunication Services

年份 Year / 地区 Region		邮电业务总量（亿元）Business Volume of Post and Telecommunication Services (100 million yuan)	邮政业务总量 Business Volume of Post	电信业务总量 Business Volume of Telecommunication Services	函件（亿件）Number of Letters (100 million pcs)	特快专递（万件）Pieces of Express Mail Services (10 000 pcs)	报刊期发数（万份）Issue of Newspapers and Magazines (10 000 copies)
	1978	34.09	14.92	19.17	28.35		11250
	1980	39.03	17.02	22.01	33.13		16431
	1985	62.21	25.70	36.51	46.78		30172
	1989	123.46			57.28	247.3	17704
	1990	155.54	45.95	109.59	54.87	343.3	20078
	1991	204.38	52.75	151.63	52.11	566.7	23277
	1992	290.94	64.36	226.57	57.18	959.2	25104
	1993	462.71	80.26	382.45	68.70	2156.2	25511
	1994	688.19	95.89	592.30	76.50	4019.5	24096
	1995	988.85	113.34	875.51	79.55	5562.7	21689
	1996	1342.04	133.29	1208.75	78.68	7096.6	21157
	1997	1773.29	144.34	1628.95	68.55	6878.9	21875
	1998	2431.21	166.28	2264.94	65.51	7667.7	22989
	1999	3330.82	198.44	3132.37	60.52	9091.3	25035
	2000	4792.70	232.80	4559.90	77.71	11031.4	20090
	2001	4556.26	457.42	4098.84	86.93	12652.7	21811
	2002	5695.80	494.69	5201.12	106.01	14036.2	17620
	2003	7019.79	541.04	6478.75	103.84	17237.8	16594
	2004	9712.29	564.30	9147.99	82.81	19771.9	14789
	2005	12028.54	625.52	11403.02	73.51	22880.3	14601
北京	Beijing	405.90	33.52	372.37	6.23	1795.1	756
天津	Tianjin	174.55	11.30	163.25	0.84	410.2	208
河北	Hebei	523.44	25.07	498.36	2.57	842.9	590
山西	Shanxi	274.45	17.65	256.79	0.93	298.6	338
内蒙古	Inner Mongolia	197.16	8.94	188.23	0.51	246.0	194
辽宁	Liaoning	443.82	23.57	420.25	1.25	804.4	339
吉林	Jilin	259.70	13.31	246.39	0.63	424.7	189
黑龙江	Heilongjiang	338.36	23.73	314.63	1.30	408.6	386
上海	Shanghai	409.67	38.49	371.18	9.14	1685.5	968
江苏	Jiangsu	723.89	52.95	670.94	7.48	1719.2	1294
浙江	Zhejiang	830.39	31.44	798.95	6.98	1256.2	956
安徽	Anhui	278.18	19.91	258.26	2.11	506.4	738
福建	Fujian	519.42	25.61	493.81	3.54	898.4	501
江西	Jiangxi	259.48	17.64	241.84	1.87	516.6	333
山东	Shandong	711.72	44.71	667.01	4.82	1447.1	823
河南	Henan	549.41	31.81	517.60	2.45	1162.6	686
湖北	Hubei	370.74	23.43	347.31	1.52	685.4	635
湖南	Hunan	366.64	22.28	344.36	1.13	562.0	583
广东	Guangdong	2129.25	59.82	2069.43	9.13	3328.3	1002
广西	Guangxi	323.78	11.72	312.06	1.20	620.7	340
海南	Hainan	74.97	4.09	70.88	0.20	108.1	69
重庆	Chongqing	210.11	10.55	199.56	1.25	348.3	255
四川	Sichuan	458.27	21.69	436.59	2.08	1112.8	927
贵州	Guizhou	172.08	6.88	165.20	0.57	394.7	282
云南	Yunnan	262.18	8.60	253.58	0.80	261.7	318
西藏	Tibet	16.34	1.05	15.29	0.03	38.3	27
陕西	Shaanxi	323.54	16.40	307.13	1.51	396.7	286
甘肃	Gansu	136.46	7.02	129.44	0.51	227.1	175
青海	Qinghai	32.06	1.76	30.30	0.19	48.6	51
宁夏	Ningxia	47.09	2.55	44.54	0.30	59.3	61
新疆	Xinjiang	172.38	8.05	164.33	0.44	265.6	293
不分地区	Not Classified by Region	33.15		33.15			

注：邮电业务总量2000年及以前按1990年不变价格计算，以后按2000年不变价格计算。2001年按可比价格比上年增长27.6%。

a) The business volumes of post and telecommunications before 2000 were calculated at 1990's constant prices and these since 2000 were calculated at 2000's constant prices. The increase rate at constant price in 2001 was 27.6%.

16-40 续表 1 continued

年份 Year / 地区 Region	集邮业务（万枚）Stamps for Collection (10 000 pieces)	长途电话（万次）Number of Long Distance Telephone Calls (10 000 times)	无线寻呼年末用户（万户）Number of Subscribers of Wireless Paging Services at Year-end (10 000 subscribers)	移动电话年末用户（万户）Number of Mobile Telephone Subscribers at Year-end (10 000 subscribers)	互联网上网人数（万人）Number of Internet Users (10 000 persons)
1978		18574			
1980		21404			
1985		38254			
1989		78462	23.7	1.0	
1990	71233	116292	43.7	1.8	
1991	123523	172921	87.4	4.8	
1992	167303	287380	222.0	17.7	
1993	210885	506853	561.4	63.9	
1994	236849	757639	1033.0	156.8	
1995	239250	1013966	1739.2	362.9	
1996	303436	1273951	2536.2	685.3	
1997	451729	1554026	3254.6	1323.3	
1998	502850	1825941	3908.2	2386.3	
1999	522475	1782532	4674.5	4329.6	
2000	453500	2107542	4884.3	8453.3	2250
2001	344114	2199823	3606.4	14522.2	3370
2002	244159	1927910	1872.1	20600.5	5910
2003	183421	1960283	1057.6	26995.3	7950
2004	149178	2262240	395.2	33482.4	9400
2005	121214	2592444	97.1	39340.6	11100
北京 Beijing	15681	85905	0.1	1459.4	428
天津 Tianjin	5000	32398		502.6	229
河北 Hebei	3396	93981	0.1	1785.5	486
山西 Shanxi	3686	44176	0.4	906.2	269
内蒙古 Inner Mongolia	1733	29839	0.3	712.3	116
辽宁 Liaoning	4371	118781	3.9	1358.2	372
吉林 Jilin	1958	33118	2.1	915.7	201
黑龙江 Heilongjiang	3684	54032	3.4	1132.3	316
上海 Shanghai	4422	92222	0.1	1444.2	463
江苏 Jiangsu	9668	199472	1.0	2550.0	790
浙江 Zhejiang	6730	234454	0.1	2686.3	707
安徽 Anhui	4010	65496		1046.9	276
福建 Fujian	4376	126808	0.3	1302.3	397
江西 Jiangxi	3328	51933		798.4	187
山东 Shandong	5198	135397	8.0	2347.3	988
河南 Henan	8769	105510	68.7	1815.0	396
湖北 Hubei	5113	75198	0.2	1401.3	463
湖南 Hunan	3072	85301		1266.2	348
广东 Guangdong	7068	411386		6406.6	1486
广西 Guangxi	1708	51131		1021.1	330
海南 Hainan	681	11775		203.9	69
重庆 Chongqing	2059	26374		943.4	189
四川 Sichuan	3838	87282	0.1	1689.7	609
贵州 Guizhou	882	28452		509.4	109
云南 Yunnan	1767	43064	0.7	898.8	241
西藏 Tibet	296	8788		46.9	9
陕西 Shaanxi	3575	67006	0.4	938.1	314
甘肃 Gansu	1741	29933	0.5	408.4	125
青海 Qinghai	490	8048	0.1	131.6	29
宁夏 Ningxia	842	11061		181.1	32
新疆 Xinjiang	2072	41337	0.4	531.3	126
不分地区 Not Classified by Region		102787	6.2		

16-40 续表 2 continued

年份 地区 Year Region	本地电话年末用户（万户） Number of Subscribers of Local Telephone at Year-end (10 000 subscribers)	城市电话用户 Number of Urban Telephone Subscribers	#住宅电话 Household Telephone Subscribers	农村电话用户 Rural Telephone Subscribers	#住宅电话 Household Telephone Subscribers	公用电话（万户） Public Telephone (10 000 subscribers)
1978	192.5	119.2		73.4		1.2
1980	214.1	134.2		79.9		1.4
1985	312.0	219.0	4.1	93.1	2.0	2.7
1989	568.0	439.6	89.6	128.4	21.3	4.0
1990	685.0	538.4	152.7	146.6	30.7	4.6
1991	845.1	670.8	239.0	174.2	49.5	5.4
1992	1146.9	920.6	415.4	226.3	79.0	8.4
1993	1733.2	1407.4	800.4	325.8	139.5	15.8
1994	2729.5	2246.8	1489.4	482.7	274.9	38.7
1995	4070.6	3263.6	2358.4	807.0	551.4	85.0
1996	5494.7	4277.8	3224.6	1216.9	907.3	138.0
1997	7031.0	5244.4	4057.2	1786.6	1406.6	193.9
1998	8742.1	6259.8	4911.1	2482.3	2070.7	259.5
1999	10871.6	7463.3	5894.4	3408.4	2949.2	297.4
2000	14482.9	9311.6	7219.4	5171.3	4597.8	352.0
2001	18036.8	11193.7	8535.3	6843.1	6197.7	346.2
2002	21422.2	13579.1	10196.7	7843.1	7183.8	985.5
2003	26274.7	17109.7	12533.9	9165.0	8389.7	1561.4
2004	31175.6	21025.1	15246.5	10150.5	9240.5	2215.0
2005	35044.5	23975.3	17201.2	11069.2	10023.9	2681.2
北京 Beijing	943.7	847.7	625.6	96.0	93.8	67.0
天津 Tianjin	428.9	425.3	347.4	3.6	2.5	31.6
河北 Hebei	1581.6	901.3	755.5	680.3	651.0	77.3
山西 Shanxi	873.2	602.5	492.9	270.7	249.8	73.0
内蒙古 Inner Mongolia	525.5	417.6	340.3	107.9	99.5	31.9
辽宁 Liaoning	1626.6	1177.0	962.2	449.6	427.9	109.3
吉林 Jilin	756.0	529.8	429.4	226.2	218.9	50.0
黑龙江 Heilongjiang	1056.5	784.5	648.0	272.0	259.5	73.8
上海 Shanghai	996.7	987.0	685.0	9.6	0.0	35.8
江苏 Jiangsu	3059.1	2089.1	1450.6	970.0	868.1	181.6
浙江 Zhejiang	2231.7	1421.5	849.4	810.1	651.6	217.9
安徽 Anhui	1349.5	680.0	501.8	669.5	642.1	65.5
福建 Fujian	1398.5	982.1	657.1	416.5	369.8	104.5
江西 Jiangxi	829.3	488.1	349.4	341.2	315.7	63.6
山东 Shandong	2637.9	1364.3	1103.5	1273.6	1200.7	153.8
河南 Henan	1796.3	1066.1	830.4	730.2	676.9	142.2
湖北 Hubei	1236.4	887.6	614.9	348.8	313.6	133.2
湖南 Hunan	1227.8	718.2	523.4	509.6	479.0	92.0
广东 Guangdong	3442.5	2614.6	1653.2	827.9	651.9	350.0
广西 Guangxi	869.5	557.2	386.9	312.2	290.2	61.8
海南 Hainan	230.3	170.0	106.0	60.3	51.8	23.7
重庆 Chongqing	688.9	456.5	326.8	232.4	218.0	41.4
四川 Sichuan	1577.4	1101.5	772.2	475.8	439.5	131.4
贵州 Guizhou	466.5	328.3	232.8	138.2	127.9	38.4
云南 Yunnan	597.8	444.0	294.1	153.8	126.6	55.0
西藏 Tibet	52.0	49.0	33.1	3.0	1.7	3.9
陕西 Shaanxi	859.3	561.8	385.5	297.5	276.3	65.3
甘肃 Gansu	548.0	395.3	260.3	152.7	135.9	60.9
青海 Qinghai	113.5	92.8	65.7	20.7	18.5	6.8
宁夏 Ningxia	138.9	98.3	67.1	40.6	36.5	12.3
新疆 Xinjiang	592.7	459.2	318.9	133.5	115.4	57.0
不分地区 Not Classified by Region	312.2	277.0	132.0	35.2	13.3	69.1

注：2002年及以后年份，公用电话用户中包括安装在街道等公共场所的智能网专线接入终端用户，与以前年度的统计口径不同。

a) Number of subscribers of public telephone since 2002 included the smart net special end-users which were installed at the public spatial, such as street. The data are not comparable with those of previous years.

16-41 邮政局所数及邮递线路(年底数)

Post and Telecommunication Services Facilities (Year-end)

年份 Year 地区 Region	邮政局所(处) Number of Post and Telecommunication Offices (unit)	信筒信箱(个) Number of Post Boxes (unit)	邮路总长度(公里) Length of Postal Routes (km)	#汽车邮路 Highway Routes	#铁路邮路 Railway Routes	农村投递线路(公里) Rural Delivery Routes (km)
1978	49623	156398	4863282	572204	150249	4266291
1980	49471	159009	4737124	582058	150819	4138879
1985	53107	174678	1416303	658102	181916	3565758
1989	53092	178289	1526073	675352	196178	3389374
1990	53629	181877	1618200	676747	191313	3364861
1991	54006	181939	1603344	685759	185872	3371424
1992	54891	183289	1646931	712367	189359	3374556
1993	57005	187966	1760506	727380	189704	3377769
1994	60447	193902	1781787	757931	187871	3364730
1995	61898	203011	1886082	819412	183036	3345848
1996	72496	217235	2118940	917151	183884	3358051
1997	79273	231337	2363108	873688	186382	3402946
1998	102225	234716	2853942	930622	189652	3361484
1999	66649	232674	2979007	989122	190056	3348054
2000	58437	239356	3073331	1070304	184925	3364498
2001	57136	225846	3102558	1074092	180399	3492761
2002	76358	217541	3080989	1112806	177685	3511190
2003	63555	275962	3270209	1137480	191351	3531832
2004	66393	222946	3336446	1194578	195998	3530508
2005	65917	202259	3406226	1229802	200180	3565226
北　京 Beijing	892	3595	392589	45097	27898	18203
天　津 Tianjin	456	1728	21996	10671	5754	16144
河　北 Hebei	2679	6613	47300	43946	1431	166054
山　西 Shanxi	1603	3517	75942	24008	6869	105761
内蒙古 Inner Mongolia	1773	2805	60713	43895	6196	109398
辽　宁 Liaoning	1686	7366	144996	34187	4158	94088
吉　林 Jilin	1395	4986	67942	23385	7696	88419
黑龙江 Heilongjiang	2138	5775	95569	36606	12339	117588
上　海 Shanghai	647	4022	211266	39672	14720	26844
江　苏 Jiangsu	3164	10579	124619	80530	4790	253889
浙　江 Zhejiang	2374	15474	131193	48012	3081	134966
安　徽 Anhui	2560	6378	70599	51111	1725	134844
福　建 Fujian	1638	15349	136434	30655	2903	81607
江　西 Jiangxi	1858	6051	75355	44063	7078	114673
山　东 Shandong	5841	11924	173098	62516	10098	243763
河　南 Henan	2739	5259	94534	57201	5656	191083
湖　北 Hubei	2119	17502	80613	43732	6703	190449
湖　南 Hunan	6525	13776	86906	52584	3033	209864
广　东 Guangdong	3939	15258	369332	94928	13575	206151
广　西 Guangxi	1672	7556	69698	45603	3942	108908
海　南 Hainan	503	849	36498	13923		23172
重　庆 Chongqing	2290	3934	87436	29424	3067	73249
四　川 Sichuan	6198	9308	174475	57556	7380	175427
贵　州 Guizhou	1908	2293	64926	24541	6385	68798
云　南 Yunnan	1957	4013	145971	66382	4666	165455
西　藏 Tibet	180	292	15357	14037		116710
陕　西 Shaanxi	1794	5484	98489	29196	10213	125077
甘　肃 Gansu	1386	6489	74556	30179	5312	104848
青　海 Qinghai	219	571	23721	9240	4310	14278
宁　夏 Ningxia	340	849	14028	5949	2355	11010
新　疆 Xinjiang	1444	2664	140075	36973	6847	74506

注：邮路总长度1980年及以前是邮路及农村投递线路总长度之和。

a) Length of postal routes before 1981 included the length of postal routes and rural delivery routes.

16-42 电信主要通信能力(年底数)

Main Communication Capacity of Telecommunications (Year-end)

年份 Year 地区 Region		长途自动交换机容量(路端) Capacity of Long-distance Telephone Exchanges (circuit)	局用电话交换机容量(万门) Capacity of Office Telephone Exchanges (10 000 lines)	移动电话交换机容量(万户) Capacity of Mobile Telephone Exchanges (10 000 subscribers)	长途光缆线路长度(公里) Length of Long Distance Optical Cable Lines (km)	长途微波线路长度(公里) Length of Long Distance Microwave Lines (km)
	1978	1863	405.9			13958
	1980	1969	443.2			13958
	1985	11522	613.4			17275
	1989	103269	1034.7	3.7	1851	26338
	1990	161370	1231.8	5.1	3334	33626
	1991	286325	1492.2	10.5	6490	39282
	1992	521885	1915.1	45.3	14388	54418
	1993	1206091	3040.8	156.1	38666	64368
	1994	2416296	4926.2	371.6	73290	
	1995	3518781	7203.6	796.7	106882	79634
	1996	4162009	9291.2	1536.2	130159	71503
	1997	4368305	11269.2	2585.7	150754	65013
	1998	4491595	13823.7	4706.7	194100	66518
	1999	5032026	15346.1	8136.0	239735	65228
	2000	5635498	17825.6	13985.6	286642	121947
	2001	7035769	25566.3	21926.3	399082	164052
	2002	7730133	28656.8	27400.3	487684	193636
	2003	8693998	35082.5	33698.4	594303	119886
	2004	12629982	42346.9	39684.3	695271	56657
	2005	13716307	47196.1	48241.7	723040	41055
北京	Beijing	444680	1383.9	1782.0	3318	231
天津	Tianjin	248432	622.3	619.0	1860	
河北	Hebei	434630	2159.0	2041.5	18370	1169
山西	Shanxi	289510	1122.3	1088.2	21300	
内蒙古	Inner Mongolia	255214	780.9	773.7	33089	638
辽宁	Liaoning	678810	2022.8	1811.7	19724	
吉林	Jilin	292956	1082.4	1027.3	16757	63
黑龙江	Heilongjiang	319807	1495.3	1304.5	35735	
上海	Shanghai	506857	1356.4	1991.0	4617	123
江苏	Jiangsu	930079	4187.5	3397.0	25699	1740
浙江	Zhejiang	569365	2874.9	3582.2	24801	1898
安徽	Anhui	443825	1622.8	1213.9	25488	951
福建	Fujian	448521	1795.1	1573.7	24854	4994
江西	Jiangxi	400094	1096.3	951.2	16260	2298
山东	Shandong	598016	3437.8	2641.1	26869	601
河南	Henan	585480	2266.0	2089.2	28716	1206
湖北	Hubei	468277	1605.5	1861.8	21672	2334
湖南	Hunan	474425	1562.3	1585.9	28097	5924
广东	Guangdong	2111499	4778.0	7924.8	42643	6423
广西	Guangxi	350375	1285.4	1310.0	32126	832
海南	Hainan	90376	280.6	245.0	642	26
重庆	Chongqing	143316	1057.8	968.1	6601	522
四川	Sichuan	616905	2237.6	1911.4	36497	1546
贵州	Guizhou	235876	690.6	610.3	22258	2855
云南	Yunnan	215272	831.7	1207.0	26619	2
西藏	Tibet	54454	88.8	66.0	9576	
陕西	Shaanxi	314010	1230.9	1190.2	31249	1271
甘肃	Gansu	166938	712.5	433.0	22250	340
青海	Qinghai	84262	142.0	147.0	14671	
宁夏	Ningxia	81661	198.1	211.6	7001	113
新疆	Xinjiang	268000	795.8	682.5	31245	2956
不分地区	Not Classified by Region	594385	393.0		62435	

注：电话交换机容量中不包括用户交换机容量。

a) The capacity of exchanges in this table excludes the capacity of exchanges owned by users.

16-43 邮电通信服务水平

Level of Post and Telecommunication Services

指标	Item	2001	2002	2003	2004	2005
邮政通信水平	**Post and Communication Level**					
平均每一邮政局所服务面积（平方公里）	Average Area Served by Every Post Office (sq.km)	168.0	123.8	148.8	142.4	145.6
平均每一邮政局所服务人口 （万人）	Average People Served by Every Post office (10 000 persons)	2.20	1.70	2.02	1.95	1.97
平均每人每年发函件数 （件）	Annual Average Number of Letters Mailed per Capita (piece)	6.90	8.30	8.08	6.41	5.66
平均每百人每年订报刊数 （份）	Annual Average Number of Newspaper and Magazine Subscribed per 100 Persons (piece)	17.2	13.9	12.9	11.4	11.2
设有邮政局、所的乡(镇)比重 （%）	Percentage of Townships with Post and Telecommunication Offices (%)	77.6	81.9	82.8	82.4	83.8
已通邮的行政村比重 （%）	Percentage of Administrative Village with Post Communication (%)	94.45	97.80	97.98	97.73	98.96
电信通信水平	**Communication Level of Telecommunications**					
移动电话漫游国家和地区 （个）	Number of Country (Territory) Roamed through Mobile Telephone (unit)	90	116	155	184	203
电话普及率（包括移动电话）(部/百人)	Popularization Rate of Telephone (include mobile telephone) (sets/100 persons)	25.90	33.60	42.16	50.03	57.22
移动电话普及率 （部/百人）	Popularization Rate of Mobile Telephone (sets/100 persons)	11.20	16.10	21.02	25.91	30.26
每千人拥有公用电话数 （部）	Per 1 000 Person Public Telephone (Sets)	2.71	7.67	12.08	17.14	20.63
已通固定电话的行政村比重 （%）	Percentage of Administrative Village with Telephone (%)	85.30	87.90	89.94	91.18	94.40

主要统计指标解释

铁路营业里程 又称营业长度(包括正式营业和临时营业里程)，指办理客货运输业务的铁路正线总长度。凡是全线或部分建成双线及以上的线路，以第一线的实际长度计算；复线、站线、段管线、岔线和特殊用途线以及不计算运费的联络线都不计算营业里程。该指标可以反映铁路运输业基础设施的发展水平，也是计算客货周转量、运输密度和机车车辆运用效率等指标的基础资料。

铁路电气化里程 指在全部铁路营业里程中已安装了供电线路及设备，可以供电力机车牵引列车运行的区段的总里程。

铁路自动、半自动闭塞里程 指装有列车自动或人工完成闭塞状态的铁路设备里程。为保证列车安全运行，在一个区间、同一时间内，一般只允许一列列车运行，这种保证列车在这个区间安全间隔运行的技术方法称为“闭塞”。自动或半自动闭塞里程占铁路营业里程的比重是反映铁路现代化的重要标志之一。

公路里程 指在一定时期内实际达到《公路工程[WTBZ]技术标准JTJ01-88》规定的等级公路，并经公路主管部门正式验收交付使用的公路里程数。包括大中城市的郊区公路以及通过小城镇街道部分的公路里程和桥梁、渡口的长度，不包括大中城市的街道、厂矿、林区生产用道和农业生产用道的里程。两条或多条公路共同经由同一路段，只计算一次，不得重复计算里程长度。该指标可以反映公路建设的发展规模，也是计算运输网密度等指标的基础资料。

内河航道里程 也称内河通航里程，指在一定时期内，能通航运输船舶及排筏的天然河流、湖泊水库、运河及通航渠道的长度。包括全年季节性通航累计三个月以上的航道，不包括仅供零散流放竹、木排的河道。该指标可以反映内河水运网的规模、水平和发展情况。

民用航空航线里程 指民航运输定期班机飞行的航线长度的总和。航线长度按机场之间的距离计算，通常有两种计算方法：一是将每条航线长度相加称为重复计算航线里程；一是将两线或两条以上航线经过同一区段里程，只计算一次航线长度称为不重复计算航线里程。一般常用的是后者，该指标可以确切反映民航运输网的规模，是表明民航事业为国民经济服务和方便人民生活程度的主要指标。

输油(气)管道长度 也称输油(气)里程，指油品(或天然气)的实际输送距离，一般按输油(气)管道的单线长度计算。若包括复线和备用线长度则称为输油(气)管道延展长度，是指管道铺设的实际长度。我们通常使用的是不包括复线的“输油(气)管道里程”，该指标可以反映管道运输的发展规模和水平。

货(客)运量 指在一定时期内，各种运输工具实际运送的货物(旅客)数量。该指标是反映运输业为国民经济和人民生活服务的数量指标，也是制定和检查运输生产计划、研究运输发展规模和速度的重要指标。货运按吨计算，客运按人计算。货物不论运输距离长短、货物类别，均按实际重量统计。旅客不论行程远近或票价多少，均按一人一次客运量统计；半价票、小孩票也按一人统计。

货(客)运密度 指在一定时期内某种运输方式在营运线路的某一区段平均每公里线路通过的货物(旅客)运输周转量。计算公式为：

$$货（客）运密度=\frac{货物（旅客）周转量}{营业线路长度}$$

该指标可以反映交通运输线路上的货物(旅客)运输量运输繁忙程度，是平衡运输线路运输能力和通过能力，规划线路建设及改造、配备技术设备，研究运输网布局的重要依据。

货物(旅客)周转量 指在一定时期内，由各种运输工具运送的货物(旅客)数量与其相应运输距离的乘积之总和。该指标可以反映运输业生产的总成果，也是编制和检查运输生产计划，计算运输效率、劳动生产率以及核算运输单位成本的主要基础资料。计算货物周转量通常按发出站与到达站之间的最短距离，也就是计费距离计算。计算公式为：

货物（旅客）周转量=Σ（货物（旅客）运输量×运输距离）

铁路货车平均静载重 指铁路货车在始发站静止状态下平均每车装载的货物重量，用以分析货车完成装车时车辆载重力的利用情况。计算公式为：

$$货车平均静载量=\frac{货物发送吨数}{装车数}$$

静载重的多少取决于运送货物的性质、种类、车辆的类型和装载技术的高低。根据货车的平均标记载重与静载重进行对比，可以反映货车载重能力的利用程度。计算公式为：

$$货车载重力利用率（\%）=\frac{货车平均静载重}{货车平均标记载重}\times 100\%$$

铁路货运机车日产量 指在一定时期内，平均每台货运机车在一昼夜内所完成的总重吨公里数，包括载运货物的重量和车辆本身的自重。该指标从时间和牵引能力两方面反映了机车运用效率。计算公式为：

$$货运机车平均日产量=\frac{货运总重吨公里数}{货运机车台日数}$$

沿海主要港口货物吞吐量 指经水运进出沿海主要港区范围，并经过装卸的货物数量，包括邮件及办理托运手续的行李、包裹以及补给运输船舶的燃、物料和淡水。货物吞吐量按货物流向分为进口、出口吞吐量，按货物交流性质分为外贸货物吞吐量和国内贸易货物吞吐量。货物吞吐量的货类构成及其流向，是衡量港口生产能力大小的重要指标。

民用汽车拥有量　指报告期末，在公安交通管理部门按照《机动车注册登记工作规范》，已注册登记领有民用车辆牌照的全部汽车数量。汽车拥有量统计的主要分类：根据汽车结构分为载客汽车、载货汽车及其他汽车；根据汽车所有者不同分为个人(私人)汽车、单位汽车；根据汽车的使用性质分为营运汽车、非营运汽车；根据汽车大小规格不同载客汽车分为大型、中型、小型和微型，载货汽车分为重型、中型、轻型和微型。

邮电业务总量　指以价值量形式表现的邮电通信企业为社会提供各类邮电通信服务的总数量。邮电业务量按专业分类包括函件、包件、汇票、报刊发行、邮政快件、特快专递、邮政储蓄、集邮、公众电报、用户电报、传真、长途电话、出租电路、无线寻呼、移动电话、分组交换数据通信、出租代维等。计算方法为各类产品乘以相应的平均单价(不变价)之和，再加上出租电路和设备、代用户维护电话交换机和线路等的服务收入。该指标综合反映了一定时期邮电业务发展的总成果，是研究邮电业务量构成和发展趋势的重要指标。计算公式为：

邮电业务总量=Σ（各类邮电业务量×不变单价）

+出租代维及其他业务收入

=邮政业务总量+电信业务总量

无线寻呼用户　无线寻呼是指电话用户通过无线寻呼中心，在规定范围内向携带小型寻呼机的用户发出声音、数字或文字显示信息。在寻呼台办理登记手续携带小型寻呼机的用户，称为无线寻呼用户。

移动电话用户　指通过移动电话交换机进入移动电话网、占用移动电话号码的各类电话用户。包括签约用户和智能网预付费用户。一个移动电话号码统计为一户。

互联网上网人数　指平均每周使用互联网至少1小时的中国公民人数。

本地电话用户　指接入本地电信运营商固定电话网上的电话用户。包括：住宅用户、单位用户、公用电话用户等。按电话用户位置又分为市内电话用户和农村电话用户。1997年以前，“市内电话用户”是指接入县城及县以上城市的电话网上的电话用户；“农村电话用户”是指接入县邮电局农话台及县以下农村电话交换点，以县城为中心(除市话用户外)联通县、乡(镇)、行政村、村民小组的用户。从1997年起，电话用户数分组调整为以用户所在区域划分为“城市电话用户”和“乡村电话用户”，与过去的按市内电话和农村电话划分方法不同。而电话用户总数、电话机总部数统计范围不变。

城市电话用户　指直辖市、省辖市、地级市、县级市的市区、市郊区及县城(包括县人民政府所在地的县城关区或行政建制相当于县人民政府所在地的镇)范围内接入局用交换机的电话用户数，包括分布在农村地区的独立工矿区、林区、驻军等电话用户数。

农村电话用户　指按行政区划属于城市范围以外的乡(镇)、村的电话用户数。

住宅电话用户　指安装在居民住宅或农民家里并按照住宅电话用户登记注册和收费的电话用户。包括私人付费、单位付费和按规定免费安装的住宅电话用户。

长途电话交换机容量　指用于接入长途电话网的电话交换机设备的额定容量，包括国际电话交换机容量。

局用交换机容量　指安装在电信运营企业内用于接续本地固定电话的电话交换机容量，包括现用和备用的人工或自动交换机的全部容量。不包括用户交换机容量。

移动电话交换机容量　指移动电话交换机根据一定话务模型和交换机处理能力计算出来的最大同时服务用户的数量。

Explanatory Notes on Main Statistical Indicators

Length of Railways in Operation refers to the total length of the trunk line under passenger and freight transportation (including both full operation and temporary operation). The calculation is based on the actual length of the first line even if this line has a full or partial double track or more tracks, excluding double tracks, station sidings, tracks under the charge of stations, branch lines, special-purpose lines and the non-payable connecting lines. The length of railways in operation is an important indicator to show the development of the infrastructure for the railway transport, and also the essential data to calculate volume of passenger freight transport, traffic density and utilization efficiency of the locomotives and carriages.

Length of Electrified Railways refers to the length of the section of railways in operation in which the power supply lines and other equipment are installed for the running of electrified locomotives. The proportion of the length of electrified railways to the total length of railways in operation is an important indicator to show the modernization of railways.

Automatic-blocking and Semi-automatic-blocking Length of Railways refer to length of railways installed with equipment to perform automatic or manual blocking of trains. Blocking is a spacing technique by which a section of the railway only allows one train to pass at a time in the aim of ensuring the traffic safety. the proportion of automatic/semi-automatic blocking length to the total length of railways in operation is an important indicator to show the modernization of railways.

Length of Highways refers to the length of highways which are built in conformity with the grades specified by the highway engineering standard formulated by the Ministry of Communications, and have been formally checked and accepted by the departments of highways and put into use. The length of highways includes that of the suburb highways at large and medium-sized cities, highways passing through streets at small cities and towns, and also the length of bridges and ferries. It does not include the length of streets in big and medium-sized cities and highways built for the production purpose at factories, mines, forest areas and agricultural areas. If two or more highways go the same section of the way, the length of the section is only calculated for once and no duplication is allowed. The length of highways is an important indicator to show the development of the highway construction and to provide essential information to calculate the transport network density.

Length of Navigable Inland Waterways it is an indicator reflecting the size and development of inland water network, it refers to the length of the natural rivers, lakes, reservoirs, canals, and ditches open to navigation during a given period, which enables the transport by ships and rafts. It includes the channels open to navigation for over an accumulative 3 months in a year, yet this does not include the river courses, which are only used to float odd logs and bamboo rafts. This indicator can reflect the scale, level and development situation of the inland waterway network.

Length of Civil Aviation Routes refers to the length of all routes for regular civil aviation flights. There are usually two ways to calculate the distance between airports connected by the route length: One is to put the length of all air routes together, called duplicated calculation of the length of the routes; the other is not to allow the duplication in calculation when two or more routes passing the same section of aviation routes. The latter is usually used, as it can precisely show the size of the civil aviation network and indicate the extent of civil aviation serving the national economy and the people.

Length of Oil (Gas) Pipelines used as an indicator to show the development, scale and level of the pipeline transportation, it refers to the actual transport distance of oil (or gas) products, and is in general calculated in the length of single pipeline. If the length of the double pipelines and alternate pipeline are included, it is called the extension length of the oil (gas) pipelines, which indicates the actual length of the pipelines built, excluding double pipelines.

Freight (Passenger) Traffic refers to the volume of freight (passenger) transported with various means. Freight transport is calculated in tons and passenger traffic is calculated in the number of persons. Despite the type of freight and traveling distance, the freight transport is calculated in the actual weight of the goods: and despite the traveling distance and ticket price, the passenger traffic is calculated by the principle that one person can be counted only once in one travel. The passengers who travel with a half price ticket or a child ticket is also calculated as one person. The freight (passenger) traffic provides a quantitative measure to show how the transport industry serves the national economy and people, and is also an important indicator for planning the transport industry and for studying the development scale and speed of the transport industry.

Freight (Passenger) Traffic Density refers to the freight (passenger) traffic volume carried by a particular means of transportation during a given period through one kilometer of a specific section of transportation route. The formula is as follows:

Freight (Passenger) traffic density=[freight ton-kilometers (passenger-kilometers)] / (length of route in operation)

Freight (passenger) traffic density reflects the degree of business of freight (passenger) traffic on transportation routes, and therefore provides important information for balancing transport capability, planning construction and upgrading of transport routes and studying the distribution of transport network.

Freight Ton-kilometers (Passenger-kilometers) refer

to the sum of the products of the volume of transported cargo (passengers) multiplying by the transport distance. It is an important indicator to reflect the achievement of transportation industry. Normally, the shortest distance between the departure station and the destination station (i.e., the payable distance) is the basis to calculate the freight ton-kilometers. This is an important indicator to show the total results of the transport industry, to prepare and examine the transport plan and to measure the efficiency, the labour productivity and the unit cost of transport.

The formula is as follows:

Freight ton-kilometers (passenger-kilometers) = Σ {freight (passenger) traffic×distance of transportation}

Static Load of Freight Cars refers to the average cargo weight as loaded by each freight car under the static condition at the departure station. It is used to show the utilization extent of the loading capacity of the freight cars. The formula is:

Static load (ton) of freight car=(tonnage of goods dispatched) / (number of freight cars loaded)

The static load of freight cars is determined by the nature and type of goods loaded, the type of vehicles, and the technique of loading. The difference between the average marked load and the static load of freight cars reflects the utilization of loading capacity of freight cars. For its calculation the following formula is applied:

Utilization rate of capacity of freight cars (%)=[(Average static load) / (Average marked load)]×100%

Average Daily Haul of Freight Locomotives refers to the average total ton-kilometers accomplished by each freight transport locomotive over day and night during a given period of time. It includes both the weight of the goods carried and the dead weight of the train itself. It is a comprehensive indicator reflecting the locomotive efficiency in terms of both time and the pulling force.

Average daily haul of freight transport locomotive (ton-kilometer)=(Total ton/kilometers of freight) / (Daily number of freight transport locomotive)

Volume of Freight Handled in Major Coastal Ports refers to the volume of cargo passing in and out the harbor area of the major coastal ports and having been loaded and unloaded. The volume includes that of the postal matters, registered luggage and fuels, materials and fresh water as supplies of the ships. The volume of freight handled may be classified by direction of flow as freight for import and freight for export, or by nature of cargo as freight for domestic trade and freight for foreign trade. As an important indicator, the volume of freight handled by type of cargo and by main flow direction reflects the production capacity of ports.

Possession of Civil Motor Vehicles refer to the total numbers of vehicles that are registered and received vehicles license tags according to the *Work Standard for Motor Vehicles Registration* formulated by transport management office under department of public security at the end of reference period. They are divided into following categories according to the structure of motor vehicles: passenger vehicles, trucks and others; and private vehicles and vehicles for units use according to ownerships; working vehicles and non-working vehicles according to kind of usage; large passenger vehicles, medium passenger vehicles, small passenger vehicles and mini passenger vehicle, heavy trucks, light-heavy trucks, light trucks and mini trucks according to sizes of vehicles.

Business Volume of Post and Telecommunications refers to the total amount of post and telecommunication services, expressed in value terms, provided by the post and telecommunications departments for the society. Post and telecommunication services can be classified as letters, parcels, remittance, issue of newspapers and magazines, fast mail service, express mail service, savings deposits, stamps for collection, public and individual telegraph service, facsimiles, long-distance telephone service, leasing of telephone lines, urban paging service, mobile telephone service, data transfer and transmission, etc. The accounting approach is to multiply the service products of all types with their average unit price (constant price) to get sum of business value, plus income from other services such as leasing of telephone lines and equipment, maintenance of telephone switchboards and lines on behalf of customers. This indicator reflects the overall results of post and telecommunications service during a given period, and is important to study the composition of business service and the development of post and telecommunications service.

The formula is as follows:

Business volume of post and telecommunications= Σ (Transaction of post and telecommunication service x constant price) + Income from leasing, maintenance and other services = business volume of postal service + business volume of telecommunications service

Subscribers of Wireless Paging Services Wireless paging service refers the service by which telephone users send audio, digital or character signals to persons carrying small-size pagers within the designated areas through wireless paging centers. The page carriers who have registered in paging centers are counted as paging subscribers.

Mobile Telephone Subscribers refer to the persons who own mobile telephone numbers and are connected with the mobile telephone communication network through the mobile telephone switchboards, including contracted subscribers and prepaid subscribers for intelligent network. One mobile telephone is taken as a subscriber.

Internet Users refer to the number of Chinese citizens who use Internet at least for one hour each week.

Local Telephone Subscribers refer to subscribers that are connected to the local telecommunication service provider through fix line network, including household subscribers, institutional subscribers and public telephones. They are also classified as city subscribers and rural subscribers according to locations. Before 1997, city subscribers referred to those connected to city telephone networks in county towns and cities, while village subscribers referred to those connected to village telephone stations at and below counties. Since 1997, the classification of telephone subscribers was modified on the basis of physical location of the subscribers as urban telephone subscribers and rural telephone subscribers, which is different from the previous classification of categorizing local telephones and rural telephones, while the definition of total subscribers and total number of telephones remain unchanged.

Urban Telephone Subscribers refer to number of telephone subscribers, located at municipalities, cities under the jurisdiction of province, cities at prefecture level, downtown and suburb of city at county level town and county towns (including country towns where county government located, and towns of county level according to the administrative organizational system), that are connected to the public line telephone network, including rural mineral area, forest area, military area.

Rural Telephone Subscribers refer to telephone subscribers, located at counties (towns) and villages outside the range of cities according to administrative jurisdiction.

Household Telephone Subscribers refer to telephone sets installed in the dwelling units of urban or rural residents, and registered as residence subscribers for payment, including 3 types of payment for the service: private payment, public payment and free service.

Capacity of Long Distance Telephone Exchanges refers to the rated capacity of telephone exchanges to connect long distance telephone network, including capacity of international telephone exchanges.

Capacity of Office Telephone Exchanges refers to the capacity (measured in gate) of telephone exchanges installed in the offices of telecommunication service providers for communication between fixed telephones. It includes the capacity of both manual and automatic exchanges in use and for stand-by purpose, excluding the capacity of subscribers exchanges.

Capacity of Mobile Telephone Exchanges refers to the capacity of the maximum services provided to subscribers at one time basing on a certain model and transacting capacity of the mobile telephone exchanges.

17

国内贸易

Domestic Trade

简 要 说 明

一、本篇资料的主要内容

本篇资料反映中国国内市场的发展和批发零售业商品流转、住宿餐饮业经营情况以及主要财务状况。主要内容有限额以上批发和零售业、住宿和餐饮业基本情况、商品流转和经营情况、财务状况；社会消费品零售总额；亿元商品交易市场成交情况以及限额以上连锁零售业、住宿和餐饮业经营情况等。

二、本篇的统计范围

全国批发和零售业、住宿和餐饮业，亿元商品交易市场，限额以上连锁零售业、住宿和餐饮业经营情况。

根据2004年第一次经济普查结果，我们对1993年-2004年社会消费品零售总额进行了调整，社会消费品零售总额指标不包括农业生产资料、居民购买住房；不包括各种经济类型的制造业法人企业、产业活动单位和个体工业直接售给城乡居民（包括本企业职工）和社会集团的商品；不包括农民在田间地头出售的农产品。

限额以上批发和零售业、住宿和餐饮业统计限额标准：批发业，年末从业人员20人及以上，年销售额2000万元及以上；零售业，年末从业人员60人及以上，年销售额500万元及以上；住宿业，有星级标志的宾馆、饭店；餐饮业，年末从业人员40人及以上，年营业额200万元及以上。

三、本篇的资料来源

本篇资料是国家统计局贸易外经司根据批发和零售业、住宿和餐饮业统计报表制度进行搜集和加工整理而得。

四、本篇的统计调查方法

本篇资料中限额以上批发和零售业法人企业及住宿和餐饮业法人企业基本情况报表采用全面调查的方法，逐级汇总上报。限额以下的小型企业及个体户资料采用抽样调查方法推算。

本篇资料中各地区社会消费品零售总额相加不等于全国总计，原因是全国总计根据相关核算资料和部门资料进行了修正和调整。

Brief Introduction

I. Main Content

Data in this chapter reflect the development of China's domestic market, circulation of commodities through wholesale and retail trades, and the operation, management and financial situation of hotels and catering services. Main contents include basic condition of wholesale and retail trades, hotels and catering trade above designated size; circulation of commodities (in operation and financial terms); total retail sales of consumer goods; turnover of large commodity transaction markets (with transaction over 100 million yuan); development of chain stores of retail trades, hotels and catering services above designated size, etc.

II. Coverage of Statistics

Included in this chapter are wholesale and retail sale trades, hotels and catering services, large commodity transaction markets, and chain stores of retail sales above designated size.

Based on results from the 2004 economic census, adjustments were made for total retail sales of consumer goods from 1993 to 2004. Total retail sales of consumer goods do not include means of agricultural production, purchase of housing by residents, direct sales of commodities by manufacturing corporations, establishments or self-employed industries to households (including to their employees) or institutions, or sales of farm products by farmers in or beside the fields.

Criteria for wholesale and retail sale trades, hotels and catering services above designated size is defined as follows: wholesale trade, having 20 or more employees at year-end with annual sales over 20 million yuan; retail sale trade, having 60 or more employees at year-end with annual sales over 5 million yuan; hotels, certified hotels with star-ranking; catering services, having 40 or more employees with annual income over 2 million yuan.

III. Sources of Data

Data in this chapter are collected and processed in accordance with the statistical reporting scheme on wholesale and retail sale trades, hotels and catering services by the Department of Trade and External Economic Relations of the National Bureau of Statistics.

IV. Survey Methodology

Data on basic conditions for all corporate enterprises of wholesale, retail, hotels and catering services above the designated size are collected through comprehensive reporting systems and data are reported level by level. Data on small-size enterprises and individual enterprises below the designated size are collected through sample surveys.

In this chapter, the sum of total retail sales of consumer goods of all provinces is not equal to the national total, as the national total has been adjusted and modified in line with national accounts data and data from other departments.

17-1 国内贸易基本情况

Basic Conditions of Domestic Trade

指　标	Item	2001	2002	2003	2004	2005
法人企业　　（个）	**Number of Corporation Unit　(unit)**					
批发和零售业	Wholesale and Retail Trades	25543	26605	27340	52448	47698
住宿和餐饮业	Hotels and Catering Services	4132	5021	5935	19299	19366
产业活动单位　（个）	**Number of Economic Active Unit (unit)**					
批发和零售业	Wholesale and Retail Trades	47099	60019	57237	163110	129931
住宿和餐饮业	Hotels and Catering Services	6386	7424	8908	26914	26323
从业人员　（万人）	**Persons Employed　(10 000 persons)**					
批发和零售业	Wholesale and Retail Trades	404.6	419.1	406.8	507.7	519.5
住宿和餐饮业	Hotels and Catering Services	77.9	97.8	113.3	262.1	287.4
批发和零售业	**Wholesale and Retail Trades**					
商品购进总额　（亿元）	Total Purchases Value　(100 million yuan)	32489.0	36885.9	45383.9		87530.9
商品销售总额　（亿元）	Total Sales Value　(100 million yuan)	72415.2	81266.2	99446.1	164541.9	164032.9
商品库存总额　（亿元）	Total Inventory　(100 million yuan)	3618.0	3577.9	3898.2		7061.0
社会消费品零售总额　（亿元）	**Total Retail Sales of Consumer Goods　(100 million yuan)**	**43055.4**	**48135.9**	**52516.3**	**59501.0**	**67176.6**
按销售单位所在地分	By Location of Establishments					
市	City	27379.1	31376.5	34608.3	39695.7	45094.3
县	County	5251.4	5566.5	6011.8	6636.0	7485.4
县以下	Under County Level	10424.9	11192.9	11896.2	13169.3	14596.9
按行业分	By Sector					
批发和零售业	Wholesale and Retail Trades	36014.8	40926.6	44659.4	50256.8	56589.2
餐饮业	Catering Services	4465.2	5547.1	6191.4	7550.4	8886.8
其他行业	Others	2575.4	1662.2	1665.5	1693.8	1700.6

注：1.法人企业、产业活动单位和从业人员为限额以上企业及单位数据，其中2004年为第一次经济普查数据，以主营业务收入为限额划分标准，其他年份以商品销售总额为限额划分标准。
2.2001-2003年住宿餐饮业的法人企业、产业活动单位和从业人数仅指餐饮业，不包括住宿业。
3.批发和零售业商品购进、库存总额为限额以上批发和零售业数据，商品销售总额为批发零售企业、单位及个体户数据，其中2004年为第一次经济普查数据。
4.社会消费品零售总额已根据第一次经济普查结果进行调整。

a) Number of corporation units, economic active units and persons employed refer to those enterprises above designated size, of which, data in 2004 were the First National Economic Census results and standard of designated size was revenue of principal business, and in other years, the standard was sales of consumer goods.
b) 2001-2003 number of corporation units, economic active units and persons employed of hotels and catering services only refer to hotels, which catering services are not included.
c) Figures on purchase, inventory by wholesale and retail trades refer to units above designated size. Data on total retail sales of consumer goods refer to wholesale and retail trade enterprises and units and self-employed individuals, and data in 2004 were the First Economic Census results.
d) Data of total retail sales of consumer goods have been adjusted according to the First National Economic Census results.

17-2 消费品市场交易情况

Trade of Consumable Markets in Urban and Rural Areas

项　目	Item	1990	2000	2003	2004	2005
消费品市场数　（个）	**Number of Consumable Markets (unit)**	**72579**	**88811**	**81017**	**71552**	**69520**
城市市场	Urban Areas	13106	26395	27006	25404	25905
农村市场	Rural Areas	59473	62416	54011	46148	43615
消费品市场构成　（%）	**Composition of Consumable Markets (%)**					
城市市场	Urban Areas	18.1	29.7	33.3	35.5	37.3
农村市场	Rural Areas	81.9	70.3	66.7	64.5	62.7

注：本表资料由国家工商行政管理总局提供。
a) Data in this table were obtained from the State Administration for Industry & Commerce.

17-3 社会消费品零售总额

Retail Sale of Consumer Goods

单位：亿元 (100 million yuan)

年份 Year / 地区 Region		社会消费品零售总额 Total Retail Sales of Consumer Goods	按销售单位所在地分 By Location			按行业分 By Sector		
			市 City	县 County	县以下 Under County Level	批发和零售业 Wholesale and Retail Trades	餐饮业 Catering Services	其他行业 Others
	1978	1558.6	505.2	380.4	673.0	1363.7	54.8	140.1
	1980	2140.0	733.6	399.4	1007.0	1768.0	80.0	292.0
	1985	4305.0	1874.5	737.2	1693.3	3272.2	196.9	835.9
	1989	8101.4	3666.8	1329.5	3105.1	6009.5	405.1	1686.8
	1990	8300.1	3888.6	1337.4	3074.1	6127.4	419.8	1752.9
	1991	9415.6	4529.8	1491.2	3394.6	6903.9	492.0	2019.7
	1992	10993.7	5470.3	1689.8	3833.6	7922.2	589.7	2481.8
	1993	14270.4	7138.1	2090.1	5042.2	10892.8	817.8	2559.8
	1994	18622.9	9387.8	2558.7	6676.4	14903.4	1201.4	2518.1
	1995	23613.8	12979.4	3366.3	7268.1	19454.3	1614.7	2544.8
	1996	28360.2	16199.2	3759.7	8401.3	23747.5	2070.0	2542.7
	1997	31252.9	18499.5	4011.6	8741.8	26169.9	2488.2	2594.8
	1998	33378.1	20294.1	4220.2	8863.8	27859.2	2878.8	2640.1
	1999	35647.9	22201.8	4460.8	8985.3	29708.8	3270.3	2668.8
	2000	39105.7	24555.2	4831.1	9719.4	32697.3	3836.1	2572.3
	2001	43055.4	27379.1	5251.4	10424.9	36014.8	4465.2	2575.4
	2002	48135.9	31376.5	5566.5	11192.9	40926.6	5547.1	1662.2
	2003	52516.3	34608.3	6011.8	11896.2	44659.4	6191.4	1665.5
	2004	59501.0	39695.7	6636.0	13169.3	50256.8	7550.4	1693.8
	2005	67176.6	45094.3	7485.4	14596.9	56589.2	8886.8	1700.6
北京	Beijing	2902.8	2459.7	59.4	383.7	2529.4	268.0	105.4
天津	Tianjin	1190.1	1113.0	42.2	34.9	958.4	159.5	72.2
河北	Hebei	2952.9	1398.8	588.4	965.7	2535.2	354.3	63.4
山西	Shanxi	1401.2	902.8	262.3	236.1	1187.4	163.3	50.5
内蒙古	Inner Mongolia	1344.1	903.4	275.9	164.8	1071.7	229.6	42.8
辽宁	Liaoning	2999.0	2523.8	145.5	329.7	2479.2	453.1	66.7
吉林	Jilin	1460.8	1140.7	106.7	213.4	1238.6	217.1	5.1
黑龙江	Heilongjiang	1760.1	1323.0	226.4	210.7	1518.0	204.2	37.9
上海	Shanghai	2973.0	2588.9	21.3	362.8	2611.3	350.3	11.4
江苏	Jiangsu	5699.9	4126.2	327.2	1246.5	4964.8	629.1	106.0
浙江	Zhejiang	4631.7	3046.7	460.6	1124.4	4020.8	533.2	77.7
安徽	Anhui	1765.0	941.2	360.6	463.2	1497.1	240.7	27.2
福建	Fujian	2345.8	1479.4	272.9	593.5	2011.9	286.8	47.1
江西	Jiangxi	1236.2	651.7	271.4	313.1	1096.5	123.3	16.4
山东	Shandong	6126.4	4004.5	605.9	1516.0	5116.7	753.0	256.7
河南	Henan	3358.4	1805.2	657.4	895.8	2780.4	497.5	80.5
湖北	Hubei	2964.6	2057.3	279.1	628.2	2402.4	386.6	175.6
湖南	Hunan	2459.1	1371.4	453.6	634.1	2104.5	317.4	37.2
广东	Guangdong	7882.6	5617.9	332.7	1932.0	6575.3	1174.3	133.0
广西	Guangxi	1397.0	819.2	245.3	332.5	1203.7	166.5	26.8
海南	Hainan	268.6	190.7	19.7	58.2	210.9	46.1	11.6
重庆	Chongqing	1215.8	714.8	163.0	338.0	1042.6	162.0	11.2
四川	Sichuan	2981.4	1446.9	525.9	1008.6	2337.6	545.6	98.2
贵州	Guizhou	606.9	362.7	115.8	128.4	531.8	64.7	10.4
云南	Yunnan	1034.4	564.5	239.3	230.6	823.8	155.5	55.1
西藏	Tibet	73.1	33.0	30.8	9.3	57.9	11.2	4.0
陕西	Shaanxi	1322.4	867.0	233.1	222.3	1151.5	144.3	26.6
甘肃	Gansu	632.8	413.3	99.7	119.8	512.1	99.8	20.9
青海	Qinghai	160.5	105.6	36.4	18.5	132.1	24.4	4.0
宁夏	Ningxia	174.3	131.2	19.6	23.5	141.2	30.0	3.1
新疆	Xinjiang	637.8	442.4	95.3	100.1	509.8	90.6	37.4

注：1.1992年及以前为社会商品零售总额。
2.1993年及以后社会消费品零售总额是根据第一次经济普查结果调整的数据。
3.各地区相加不等于全国总计，原因是全国数据进行了修正。

a) Figures before 1992 refer to retail sales of commodities.
b) Data of total retail sales of consumer goods in 1993 and after are adjusted according to the First National Economic Census results.
c) The sum of provincial figures do not add up to the national total, as the national total was adjusted.

17-4 按登记注册类型分限额以上批发和零售业、住宿和餐饮业基本情况（2005年）

Basic Conditions of Enterprises above Designated Size of Wholesale and Retail Trades, Hotels and Catering Services by Status of Registration (2005)

指标	Item	法人企业（个）Number of Corporation Unit	产业活动单位（个）Number of Economic Active Unit	从业人数（人）Persons Employed (person)
总计	**Total**	**67064**	**156254**	**8068191**
批发业合计	**Wholesale Trade**	**26963**	**56157**	**2244131**
内资企业	**Domestic Funded Enterprises**	**25947**	**54825**	**2134494**
国有企业	State-owned Enterprises	4710	13618	725578
集体企业	Collective-owned Enterprises	1099	3448	104940
股份合作企业	Cooperative Enterprises	354	852	25226
联营企业	Joint Ownership Enterprises	173	263	13581
国有联营企业	State Joint Ownership Enterprises	84	145	9100
集体联营企业	Collective Joint Ownership Enterprises	18	18	868
国有与集体联营企业	Joint State-collective Enterprises	38	59	1664
其他联营企业	Other Joint Ownership Enterprises	33	41	1949
有限责任公司	Limited Liability Corporations	7442	12810	554321
国有独资公司	State Sole Funded Corporations	426	1265	69033
其他有限责任公司	Other Limited Liability Corporations	7016	11545	485288
股份有限公司	Share-holding Corporations Ltd.	1164	10132	305608
私营企业	Private Enterprises	10933	13620	399207
私营独资企业	Private-funded Enterprises	259	384	9706
私营合伙企业	Private Partnership Enterprises	130	160	3769
私营有限责任公司	Private Limited Liability Corporations	10109	12559	369508
私营股份有限公司	Private Share-holding Corporations Ltd.	435	517	16224
其他企业	Other Enterprises	72	82	6033
港、澳、台商投资企业	**Enterprises with Funds from Hong Kong, Macao and Taiwan**	**308**	**376**	**27461**
合资经营企业	Joint-venture Enterprises	62	85	5617
合作经营企业	Cooperative Enterprises	13	14	2032
独资经营企业	Enterprises with Sole Investment	227	264	17024
投资股份有限公司	Share-holding Corporations Ltd. with Investment	6	13	2788
外商投资企业	**Foreign Funded Enterprises**	**708**	**956**	**82176**
中外合资经营企业	Joint-venture Enterprises	117	229	14026
中外合作经营企业	Cooperation Enterprises	14	25	2155
外资企业	Enterprises with Sole Foreign Investment	567	678	64085
外商投资股份有限公司	Share-holding Corporations Ltd. with Foreign Investment	10	24	1910
零售业合计	**Retail Trade**	**20735**	**73774**	**2950527**
内资企业	**Domestic Funded Enterprises**	**20346**	**71673**	**2735193**
国有企业	State-owned Enterprises	2798	11296	348412
集体企业	Collective-owned Enterprises	1799	7411	149741
股份合作企业	Cooperative Enterprises	487	1546	51561
联营企业	Joint Ownership Enterprises	145	239	16458
国有联营企业	State Joint Ownership Enterprises	57	96	7360
集体联营企业	Collective Joint Ownership Enterprises	32	36	1649
国有与集体联营企业	Joint State-collective Enterprises	26	51	3277
其他联营企业	Other Joint Ownership Enterprises	30	56	4172
有限责任公司	Limited Liability Corporations	5561	24740	960190
国有独资公司	State Sole Funded Corporations	152	520	26574
其他有限责任公司	Other Limited Liability Corporations	5409	24220	933616
股份有限公司	Share-holding Corporations Ltd.	1068	10176	473967

注：批发业限额以上是指年末从业人员20人及以上，年销售额2000万元及以上；零售业限额以上是指年末从业人员60人及以上，年销售额500万元及以上；住宿业限额以上是指星级宾馆或饭店；餐饮业限额以上是指年末从业人员40人及以上，年营业额200万元及以上。

a) Enterprise above designated size in wholesale trades refers to that the employed persons are more than 20 persons and above with annual sale value is 20 million yuans and above. Enterprise above designated size in retail trade refers to that the employed person is more than 60 persons and above and annual sale value is 5 million yuans and above. Enterprise avove designated size in accommodation refers to star-rated unit. Enterprise above designated size in restaurants refers to that the employed person is more than 40 persons and above and annual turnover is 2 million yuans and above.

17-4 续表 1 continued

指标	Item	法人企业（个）Number of Corporation Units	产业活动单位（个）Number of Economic Active Units	从业人数（人）Persons Employed (person)
私营企业	Private Enterprises	8377	16029	725041
私营独资企业	Private-funded Enterprises	641	875	43775
私营合伙企业	Private Partnership Enterprises	199	297	13824
私营有限责任公司	Private Limited Liability Corporations	7036	13860	618431
私营股份有限公司	Private Share-holding Corporations Ltd.	501	997	49011
其他企业	Other Enterprises	111	236	9823
港、澳、台商投资企业	**Enterprises with Funds from Hong Kong, Macao and Taiwan**	**134**	**549**	**63603**
合资经营企业	Joint-venture Enterprises	72	400	50803
合作经营企业	Cooperative Enterprises	25	29	5169
独资经营企业	Enterprises with Sole Funds	33	108	4633
投资股份有限公司	Share-holding Corporations Ltd. with Funds	4	12	2998
外商投资企业	**Foreign Funded Enterprises**	**255**	**1552**	**151731**
中外合资经营企业	Joint-venture Enterprises	146	1141	90007
中外合作经营企业	Cooperation Enterprises	50	159	30477
外资企业	Enterprises with Sole Foreign Investment	55	244	30280
外商投资股份有限公司	Share-holding Corporations Ltd. with Foreign Investment	4	8	967
住宿业合计	**Hotels**	**9444**	**11228**	**1529270**
内资企业	**Domestic Funded Enterprises**	**8593**	**10265**	**1269901**
国有企业	State-owned Enterprises	3064	3582	471377
集体企业	Collective-owned Enterprises	709	834	80817
股份合作企业	Cooperative Enterprises	209	247	24994
联营企业	Joint Ownership Enterprises	89	100	16143
国有联营企业	State Joint Ownership Enterprises	43	50	8999
集体联营企业	Collective Joint Ownership Enterprises	15	17	1535
国有与集体联营企业	Joint State-collective Enterprises	16	17	2844
其他联营企业	Other Joint Ownership Enterprises	15	16	2765
有限责任公司	Limited Liability Corporations	1683	2122	321759
国有独资公司	State Sole Funded Corporations	107	134	23813
其他有限责任公司	Other Limited Liability Corporations	1576	1988	297946
股份有限公司	Share-holding Corporations Ltd.	364	447	72331
私营企业	Private Enterprises	2397	2840	272006
私营独资企业	Private-funded Enterprises	705	793	54636
私营合伙企业	Private Partnership Enterprises	142	163	10656
私营有限责任公司	Private Limited Liability Corporations	1398	1704	187895
私营股份有限公司	Private Share-holding Corporations Ltd.	152	180	18819
其他企业	Other Enterprises	78	93	10474
港、澳、台商投资企业	**Enterprises with Funds from Hong Kong, Macao and Taiwan**	**462**	**530**	**149541**
合资经营企业	Joint-venture Enterprises	282	340	93548
合作经营企业	Cooperative Enterprises	87	91	35694
独资经营企业	Enterprises with Sole Funds	86	91	18426
投资股份有限公司	Share-holding Corporations Ltd. with Funds	7	8	1873
外商投资企业	**Enterprises With Foreign Investment**	**389**	**433**	**109828**
中外合资经营企业	Joint-venture Enterprises	221	250	61047
中外合作经营企业	Cooperation Enterprises	84	84	26848
外资企业	Enterprises with Sole Foreign Funds	77	92	20731
外商投资股份有限公司	Share-holding Corporations Ltd. with Foreign Investment	7	7	1202

17-4 续表 2 continued

指　标	Item	法人企业（个）Number of Corporation Units	产业活动单位（个）Number of Economic Active Units	从业人数（人）Persons Employed (person)
餐饮业合计	**Catering Services**	**9922**	**15095**	**1344263**
内资企业	**Domestic Funded Enterprises**	**9099**	**11764**	**1015102**
国有企业	State-owned Enterprises	580	816	83386
集体企业	Collective-owned Enterprises	441	524	38863
股份合作企业	Cooperative Enterprises	319	414	27211
联营企业	Joint Ownership Enterprises	35	38	4299
国有联营企业	State Joint Ownership Enterprises	9	9	994
集体联营企业	Collective Joint Ownership Enterprises	8	8	996
国有与集体联营企业	Joint State-collective Enterprises	3	4	438
其他联营企业	Other Joint Ownership Enterprises	15	17	1871
有限责任公司	Limited Liability Corporations	1398	2139	197741
国有独资公司	State Sole Funded Corporations	16	27	3299
其他有限责任公司	Other Limited Liability Corporations	1382	2112	194442
股份有限公司	Share-holding Corporations Ltd.	245	383	39940
私营企业	Private Enterprises	5893	7219	606772
私营独资企业	Private-funded Enterprises	1582	1777	120259
私营合伙企业	Private Partnership Enterprises	365	399	33203
私营有限责任公司	Private Limited Liability Corporations	3605	4651	420065
私营股份有限公司	Private Share-holding Corporations Ltd.	341	392	33245
其他企业	Other Enterprises	188	231	16890
港、澳、台商投资企业	**Enterprises with Funds from Hong Kong, Macao and Taiwan**	**365**	**748**	**87570**
合资经营企业	Joint-venture Enterprises	152	369	37711
合作经营企业	Cooperative Enterprises	59	75	11325
独资经营企业	Enterprises with Sole Funds	151	299	37867
投资股份有限公司	Share-holding Corporations Ltd. with Funds	3	5	667
外商投资企业	**Enterprises With Foreign Investment**	**458**	**2583**	**241591**
中外合资经营企业	Joint-venture Enterprises	177	859	72832
中外合作经营企业	Cooperation Enterprises	89	329	29143
外资企业	Enterprises with Sole Foreign Funds	180	1352	136849
外商投资股份有限公司	Share-holding Corporations Ltd. with Foreign Investment	12	43	2767

17-5 限额以上批发和零售业、住宿和餐饮业法人企业数

Number of Corporation Units above Designated Size of Wholesale and Retail Trades, Hotels and Catering Services

单位：个 (unit)

年份 地区	Year Region	合计 Total	批发业 Wholesale Trade	零售业 Retail Trade	住宿业 Hotels	餐饮业 Catering Services
	2004	71747	30756	21692	9232	10067
	2005	67064	26963	20735	9444	9922
北京	Beijing	7101	2768	2586	492	1255
天津	Tianjin	1908	1231	407	92	178
河北	Hebei	1385	516	484	252	133
山西	Shanxi	1424	472	562	234	156
内蒙古	Inner Mongolia	1001	308	318	166	209
辽宁	Liaoning	2848	1280	863	354	351
吉林	Jilin	906	326	308	168	104
黑龙江	Heilongjiang	1192	473	376	177	166
上海	Shanghai	3313	1803	493	300	717
江苏	Jiangsu	3751	1202	1256	512	781
浙江	Zhejiang	5173	2757	1095	829	492
安徽	Anhui	1275	460	355	295	165
福建	Fujian	3107	1496	1003	360	248
江西	Jiangxi	942	249	308	219	166
山东	Shandong	4802	1440	1904	446	1012
河南	Henan	4441	1383	2195	349	514
湖北	Hubei	1940	689	592	378	281
湖南	Hunan	1716	413	613	397	293
广东	Guangdong	8601	3928	2141	1042	1490
广西	Guangxi	1295	481	421	272	121
海南	Hainan	586	173	122	254	37
重庆	Chongqing	1274	479	408	150	237
四川	Sichuan	1528	475	437	333	283
贵州	Guizhou	452	151	97	145	59
云南	Yunnan	1699	689	432	501	77
西藏	Tibet	90	12	17	61	
陕西	Shaanxi	901	268	243	222	168
甘肃	Gansu	713	302	212	122	77
青海	Qinghai	211	56	83	44	28
宁夏	Ningxia	392	174	113	46	59
新疆	Xinjiang	1097	509	291	232	65

注：本表至17-26表中的2004年数据为第一次经济普查结果，批发和零售业、餐饮业限额以上划分标准为全年主营业务收入，其他年份限额以上划分标准为商品销售额或年营业额。

a) Data in 2004 from this table to table 17-26 were data of the First National Economic Census. In 2004, data of wholesale and retail trades, catering services above designated size were annual revenue of principal business, and for other years, they were total sales of consumer goods or business revenue.

17-6 限额以上批发和零售业、住宿和餐饮业产业活动单位数

Number of Economic Active Units above Designated Size of Wholesale and Retail Trades, Hotels and Catering Services

单位：个　　(unit)

年 份 地 区	Year Region	合 计 Total	批发业 Wholesale Trade	零售业 Retail Trade	住宿业 Hotels	餐饮业 Catering Services
	2004	190024	63255	99855	9872	17042
	2005	156254	56157	73774	11228	15095
北 京	Beijing	12923	3498	6245	610	2570
天 津	Tianjin	1918	1233	407	99	179
河 北	Hebei	1417	522	488	255	152
山 西	Shanxi	4036	1174	2389	248	225
内蒙古	Inner Mongolia	2020	757	815	195	253
辽 宁	Liaoning	6689	3121	2609	400	559
吉 林	Jilin	1856	436	1089	183	148
黑龙江	Heilongjiang	3218	1733	1110	183	192
上 海	Shanghai	13626	2568	9295	340	1423
江 苏	Jiangsu	10358	3200	5428	541	1189
浙 江	Zhejiang	14013	6315	5146	1592	960
安 徽	Anhui	3074	1548	983	310	233
福 建	Fujian	6120	2228	2962	397	533
江 西	Jiangxi	2236	1047	734	241	214
山 东	Shandong	10417	3304	5343	501	1269
河 南	Henan	15919	4369	10418	439	693
湖 北	Hubei	6383	2632	2881	406	464
湖 南	Hunan	3710	926	1954	434	396
广 东	Guangdong	8928	4006	2261	1055	1606
广 西	Guangxi	4058	1891	1639	321	207
海 南	Hainan	722	192	177	303	50
重 庆	Chongqing	4643	2203	1853	210	377
四 川	Sichuan	5018	1856	2364	372	426
贵 州	Guizhou	1166	413	521	158	74
云 南	Yunnan	4165	1921	1499	603	142
西 藏	Tibet	224	69	94	61	
陕 西	Shaanxi	1633	478	690	230	235
甘 肃	Gansu	2203	857	1070	143	133
青 海	Qinghai	563	260	224	45	34
宁 夏	Ningxia	602	287	201	51	63
新 疆	Xinjiang	2396	1113	885	302	96

17-7 限额以上批发和零售业、住宿和餐饮业从业人数

Number of Persons Employed in Enterprises above Designated Size of Wholesale and Retail Trades, Hotels and Catering Services

单位：人 (person)

年份 地区	Year Region	合计 Total	批发业 Wholesale Trade	零售业 Retail Trade	住宿业 Hotels	餐饮业 Catering Services
	2004	7698168	2244978	2831772	1282173	1339245
	2005	8068191	2244131	2950527	1529270	1344263
北京	Beijing	620368	146426	209681	120133	144128
天津	Tianjin	151821	56896	52322	17647	24956
河北	Hebei	252433	72719	112017	48861	18836
山西	Shanxi	230996	82707	84945	35679	27665
内蒙古	Inner Mongolia	109035	29464	39857	21390	18324
辽宁	Liaoning	302840	76426	129416	51193	45805
吉林	Jilin	111198	29028	46850	23287	12033
黑龙江	Heilongjiang	149892	51765	62166	21064	14897
上海	Shanghai	617469	165542	264523	78888	108516
江苏	Jiangsu	557068	125361	243891	81768	106048
浙江	Zhejiang	478265	141928	134348	120702	81287
安徽	Anhui	181083	59038	68825	33018	20202
福建	Fujian	240721	74878	79857	53422	32564
江西	Jiangxi	135973	45140	43135	26740	20958
山东	Shandong	627310	166142	280547	76407	104214
河南	Henan	440576	136741	202820	58434	42581
湖北	Hubei	301809	80392	123088	50427	47902
湖南	Hunan	252064	55550	91891	61082	43541
广东	Guangdong	979896	233783	257898	217658	270557
广西	Guangxi	179010	57488	61870	42052	17600
海南	Hainan	54198	10772	6490	33233	3703
重庆	Chongqing	177304	60848	50402	38089	27965
四川	Sichuan	253777	63269	99363	54606	36539
贵州	Guizhou	69390	27874	17325	16578	7613
云南	Yunnan	161041	63061	41026	46414	10540
西藏	Tibet	7330	1429	1829	4072	
陕西	Shaanxi	169291	43839	60317	35382	29753
甘肃	Gansu	78074	24792	27221	16405	9656
青海	Qinghai	20930	6117	7540	4413	2860
宁夏	Ningxia	35687	9349	12900	7007	6431
新疆	Xinjiang	121342	45367	36167	33219	6589

17-8 按行业分限额以上批发和零售业商品购、销、存总额（2005年）

Total Purchases, Sales and Inventory of Enterprises above Designated Size of Wholesale and Retail Trades by Sector (2005)

单位：亿元 (100 million yuan)

指标	Item	购进总额 Total Purchases Value	销售总额 Total Sale Value	批发 Wholesale Value	零售 Retail Value	年末库存总额 Inventory (year-end)
总计	**Total**	**87530.9**	**93151.3**	**74921.3**	**18230.0**	**7061.0**
批发业合计	**Wholesale Trade**	**71650.6**	**75510.7**	**72029.7**	**3481.0**	**5274.8**
农畜产品批发业	Wholesale of Farm Produce and Livestock Products	1801.9	1798.0	1780.6	17.4	876.9
食品、饮料及烟草制品批发业	Wholesale of Food, Beverages and Tobaccos	8013.5	9509.4	9324.1	185.3	693.6
#米、面制品及食用油批发业	Wholesale of Rice, Flour and Edible Oil	655.6	693.0	675.1	17.9	170.9
烟草制品批发业	Whole of Tobaccos	5466.7	6682.9	6613.5	69.3	375.7
纺织、服装及日用品批发业	Wholesale of Textiles, Garments and Daily Consumer Articles	4638.6	5417.0	5363.5	53.5	230.4
#服装批发业	Wholesale of Garments	1759.0	2028.3	2004.5	23.8	85.6
文化、体育用品及器材批发业	Wholesale of Culture, Sports Appliances and Equipments	1046.0	1113.6	1070.7	42.9	139.2
医药及医疗器材批发业	Wholesale of Medicines and Medical Appliances	2937.9	3147.6	2616.3	531.2	373.2
矿产品、建材及化工产品批发业	Wholesale of Mineral Products, Building Materials and Chemical Products	37762.5	38924.6	36941.4	1983.1	1797.4
#煤炭及制品批发业	Wholesale of Coal and Related Products	2271.2	2838.4	2757.0	81.5	113.6
石油及制品批发业	Wholesale of Petrolem and Related Products	17177.0	17225.2	15535.6	1689.6	453.1
金属及金属矿批发业	Wholesale of Metal Materials	11860.9	12114.0	12017.3	96.7	695.4
建材批发业	Wholesale of Building Materials	1458.7	1492.4	1446.0	46.5	95.5
化肥批发业	Wholesale of Chemical Fertilizer	1066.6	1110.5	1092.0	18.5	162.5
机械设备、五金交电及电子产品批发	Wholesale of Machinery, Hardware and Electronic Equipment	11828.1	11620.6	10984.0	636.6	878.2
#汽车、摩托车及零配件批发业	Wholesale of Motor Vehicles, Motorcycles and Parts	4122.5	3300.9	2991.5	309.4	191.8
家用电器批发业	Wholesale of Household Electrical Appliances	1738.2	1860.8	1743.0	117.8	221.4
计算机、软件及辅助设备批发业	Wholesale of Computer, Software and Assistant Appliances	1056.3	1095.8	1015.2	80.6	59.2
贸易经纪与代理	Trade Broker and Agency	692.0	697.9	695.6	2.3	15.2
其他批发业	Other Wholesale not Classified Elsewhere	2930.2	3282.1	3253.5	28.5	270.6
零售业合计	**Retail Trade**	**15880.3**	**17640.5**	**2891.6**	**14749.0**	**1786.2**
综合零售业	Integrated Retail	5959.7	6969.0	686.2	6282.8	729.2
#百货零售业	Retail of General Merchandise	3008.9	3618.7	226.8	3391.9	318.5
超级市场零售业	Retail of Supermarkets	2614.9	3093.5	408.0	2685.5	388.5
食品、饮料及烟草制品专门零售业	Retail of Food, Beverages and Tobaccos	311.5	342.2	87.3	254.9	37.1
纺织、服装及日用品专门零售业	Special Retail of Textiles, Garments and Daily Consumer Articles	351.0	429.1	73.2	355.9	67.4
#服装零售业	Retail of Garments	200.5	249.2	43.3	206.0	37.4
文化、体育用品及器材专门零售业	Retail of Culture, Sports Appliances and Equipments	518.4	562.3	104.6	457.7	127.5
#体育用品零售业	Retail of Sports Goods	14.9	16.0	2.3	13.7	4.3
图书零售业	Retail of Books	378.2	379.6	55.4	324.2	87.2
医药及医疗器材专门零售业	Retail of Medicines and Medical Appliances	704.3	764.1	197.5	566.5	134.5
#药品零售业	Retail of Medicines	655.1	706.2	175.5	530.7	126.5
汽车、摩托车、燃料及零配件专门零售业	Retail of Motor Vehicles, Motorcycles, Fuel and Parts	5755.7	6253.9	1364.9	4889.0	428.2
#汽车零售业	Retail of Motor Vehicles	3521.4	3765.8	483.1	3282.7	288.3
机动车燃料零售业	Retail of Fuel of Motor Vehicles	2084.4	2332.2	857.4	1474.8	79.4
家用电器及电子产品专门零售业	Special Retail of Household Electric Appliances and Electronic Products	1833.4	1811.5	258.1	1553.3	205.1
#家用电器零售业	Retail of Household Electric Appliances	1252.4	1211.1	124.1	1087.0	152.8
计算机、软件及辅助设备零售业	Retail of Computer, Software and Assistant Appliances	298.2	311.1	73.1	238.0	24.0
通讯设备零售业	Retail of Communication Equipments	229.8	234.4	44.9	189.6	22.3
五金、家具及室内装修材料专门零售业	Special Retail of Hardware, Furniture and Decoration Materials	233.4	268.0	41.2	226.8	40.6
无店铺及其他零售业	Non-shop and Other Retails	212.9	240.6	78.5	162.1	16.7
#邮购及电子销售业	Distribution of Post and E-commerce	7.8	10.4	1.5	8.9	0.5

17-9 限额以上批发和零售业商品购、销、存总额

Total Purchases, Sales and Inventory of Enterprises above Designated Size of Wholesale and Retail Trades

单位：亿元 (100 million yuan)

年份 地区	Year Region	购进总额 Total Goods Purchase	销售总额 Total Sale Value	批发 Wholesale Value	零售 Retail Value	年末库存总额 Inventory (year-end)
	2004		86928.6	71399.7	15528.9	
	2005	87530.9	93151.3	74921.3	18230.0	7061.0
北京	Beijing	10016.1	10854.4	9098.1	1756.3	1264.2
天津	Tianjin	4192.4	4316.0	3897.8	418.2	204.5
河北	Hebei	1429.2	1600.1	1164.1	436.0	156.8
山西	Shanxi	1634.3	1461.2	1057.5	403.8	121.7
内蒙古	Inner Mongolia	627.8	848.7	610.9	237.8	75.4
辽宁	Liaoning	5622.5	5070.4	4287.0	783.4	292.7
吉林	Jilin	1547.7	1566.2	1241.0	325.2	154.2
黑龙江	Heilongjiang	1051.3	1128.4	802.7	325.8	243.3
上海	Shanghai	10957.5	12050.8	10425.1	1625.7	676.4
江苏	Jiangsu	5268.6	5936.7	4329.3	1607.4	336.9
浙江	Zhejiang	8851.9	9164.1	7787.4	1376.7	454.0
安徽	Anhui	1513.1	1615.5	1276.4	339.1	116.2
福建	Fujian	2796.4	3051.0	2459.0	592.0	192.1
江西	Jiangxi	688.0	765.3	533.2	232.1	76.3
山东	Shandong	4376.4	4722.9	3266.5	1456.4	394.0
河南	Henan	2294.3	2520.8	1873.9	647.0	199.6
湖北	Hubei	2532.8	2673.3	2093.6	579.7	208.5
湖南	Hunan	1184.9	1370.8	909.4	461.4	129.5
广东	Guangdong	11326.6	11933.3	9693.0	2240.4	670.9
广西	Guangxi	1114.3	1168.2	870.0	298.2	69.4
海南	Hainan	239.0	271.8	192.1	79.7	20.8
重庆	Chongqing	1156.1	1248.6	883.5	365.1	168.2
四川	Sichuan	1563.9	1762.4	1291.9	470.4	131.3
贵州	Guizhou	380.3	479.4	359.3	120.1	54.5
云南	Yunnan	1894.2	2034.8	1752.0	282.8	265.3
西藏	Tibet	23.3	29.6	16.5	13.1	5.5
陕西	Shaanxi	988.3	1090.0	796.9	293.1	74.1
甘肃	Gansu	842.7	894.8	748.7	146.1	61.7
青海	Qinghai	115.0	127.1	77.0	50.1	10.5
宁夏	Ningxia	195.8	212.5	159.9	52.6	25.5
新疆	Xinjiang	1105.8	1182.0	967.6	214.3	207.0

17-10 限额以上批发和零售业主要商品分类销售额

Sale Values of Enterprises above Designated Size of Wholesale and Retail Trades by Category of Main Commodities

单位：亿元 (100 million yuan)

项目	Item	销售合计 Total Sale Values		批发 Wholesale Value		零售 Retail Vaule	
		2004	2005	2004	2005	2004	2005
食品、饮料、烟酒类	Food, Beverages, Tobacco and Liquor	11638.7	12692.2	9385.9	9895.9	2252.8	2796.3
粮油类	Grain and Oil	1923.1	1710.9	1637.1	1355.1	286.1	355.8
肉禽蛋类	Meat, Poultry and Eggs	579.1	654.2	304.9	309.4	274.2	344.8
其他食品类	Other Food	2102.3	2537.4	1145.8	1266.7	956.4	1270.6
饮料类	Beverages	424.7	512.6	171.4	247.2	253.3	265.4
烟酒类	Tobacco and Liquor	6609.6	7277.0	6126.8	6717.5	482.8	559.5
服装鞋帽、针、纺织品类	Clothing, Shoes, Hats and Textiles	5506.5	5612.1	3838.8	3593.9	1667.7	2018.2
服装类	Clothing	3091.3	3243.4	1979.2	1880.5	1112.0	1362.8
鞋帽类	Shoes and Hats	689.6	731.3	381.2	363.7	308.4	367.6
针、纺织品类	Knitwear and Textiles	1725.6	1637.4	1478.4	1349.7	247.2	287.7
化妆品类	Cosmetics	505.7	480.1	238.7	145.0	267.1	335.1
金银珠宝类	Gold, Silver and Jewelry	289.5	336.4	73.8	81.3	215.7	255.2
日用品类	Articles for Daily Use	1563.9	1636.8	957.9	917.4	606.0	719.3
#洗涤用品类	Washing Articles	338.1	370.5	144.7	153.5	193.5	217.0
儿童玩具类	Children Toys	84.3	83.8	49.3	44.6	35.0	39.2
五金、电料类	Hardware and Electrical Materials	866.5	620.2	757.3	515.1	109.1	105.1
体育、娱乐用品类	Sports and Recreation Articles	331.9	307.1	223.7	185.6	108.1	121.5
书报杂志类	Newspapers and Magazines	859.4	812.5	516.5	428.0	342.9	384.5
电子出版物及音像制品类	E-journals and Video Products	119.3	69.7	76.3	28.2	43.0	41.5
家用电器和音像器材类	Household Appliances and Video Appliances	3421.9	3568.5	2006.2	1955.5	1415.7	1613.0
中西药品类	Traditional Chinese and Western Medicines	3546.8	3517.3	2512.9	2395.3	1034.0	1122.0
#西药	Western Medicines	2474.6	2511.5	1735.9	1685.2	738.7	826.3
中草药及中成药	Traditional Chinese Medicines	734.1	791.4	522.1	544.8	212.0	246.6
文化办公用品类	Cultural and Offices Appliances	1725.1	1409.8	1345.3	1019.2	379.8	390.6
家具类	Furniture	193.1	253.2	98.7	130.0	94.4	123.1
通讯器材类	Communication Appliances	2330.3	1938.6	1930.6	1484.3	399.7	454.3
煤炭及制品类	Coal and Related Products	2703.5	2828.5	2665.2	2798.8	38.2	29.7
木材及制品类	Wood and Wooden Products	264.9	225.4	250.9	214.2	13.9	11.2
石油及制品类	Petroleum and Related Products	16471.3	18419.1	14167.0	15501.2	2304.2	2917.9
化工材料及制品类	Chemical Materials and Related Products	5044.8	4584.2	4992.7	4545.3	52.1	38.9
#化肥类	Fertilizers	959.7	1165.9	955.5	1164.6	4.2	1.3
金属材料类	Metal Materials	12257.7	10467.6	12119.2	10356.0	138.5	111.6
建筑及装潢材料类	Building and Decoration Materials	1019.2	786.2	898.3	635.1	120.9	151.1
机电产品及设备类	Mechanical and Electrical Products	3932.3	3277.0	3772.2	3116.9	160.1	160.1
#农机类	Agricultural Machineries	168.6	135.3	164.0	132.3	4.6	3.0
汽车类	Automobiles	7275.1	5808.2	3855.9	2592.9	3419.1	3215.4
种子饲料类	Seeds and Feedstuff	218.9	169.9	214.7	168.8	4.2	1.0
棉麻类	Cotton, Hemp	625.4	679.9	624.4	678.2	1.0	1.7
其他类	Others	4216.9	3999.4	3876.1	3561.1	340.8	438.3

17-11 各地区星级住宿业经营情况

Business of Star-ranking Hotels by Region

单位：亿元 (100 million yuan)

年 份 Year / 地 区 Region		营业额 Business Revenue	#客房收入 Revenue from Hotel Rooms	#餐费收入 Revenue from Meals	#商品销售收入 Revenue from Commodities
	2004	1170.5	554.7	438.8	47.9
	2005	1353.3	661.1	507.8	40.4
北 京	Beijing	176.1	91.4	52.1	4.8
天 津	Tianjin	16.8	9.0	4.9	0.6
河 北	Hebei	25.6	10.4	12.6	0.6
山 西	Shanxi	21.9	10.0	9.7	0.8
内蒙古	Inner Mongolia	13.2	6.0	6.5	0.2
辽 宁	Liaoning	47.6	23.8	17.3	1.0
吉 林	Jilin	15.1	6.8	6.5	0.4
黑龙江	Heilongjiang	13.0	7.3	4.0	0.8
上 海	Shanghai	152.7	85.5	43.6	3.2
江 苏	Jiangsu	86.1	41.4	33.9	4.3
浙 江	Zhejiang	128.6	57.7	57.5	3.1
安 徽	Anhui	21.7	10.4	8.5	1.1
福 建	Fujian	43.1	18.7	19.8	0.9
江 西	Jiangxi	14.7	8.1	4.9	0.8
山 东	Shandong	66.7	28.4	29.6	3.8
河 南	Henan	37.2	16.7	15.2	2.4
湖 北	Hubei	31.4	16.0	11.8	1.0
湖 南	Hunan	40.5	19.5	16.0	1.3
广 东	Guangdong	201.9	90.2	81.4	3.4
广 西	Guangxi	25.6	12.9	10.3	0.7
海 南	Hainan	22.4	13.9	6.7	0.2
重 庆	Chongqing	20.2	9.3	8.1	0.9
四 川	Sichuan	35.0	18.1	11.9	1.1
贵 州	Guizhou	9.0	5.2	3.0	0.2
云 南	Yunnan	27.1	15.0	8.5	1.0
西 藏	Tibet	3.0	1.6	0.9	
陕 西	Shaanxi	21.7	10.7	8.9	0.7
甘 肃	Gansu	7.8	4.1	2.9	0.2
青 海	Qinghai	1.9	1.0	0.6	
宁 夏	Ningxia	4.0	1.8	1.7	0.2
新 疆	Xinjiang	21.7	10.4	8.6	0.5

17-12 各地区限额以上餐饮业经营情况

Business of Catering Services above Designated Size by Region

单位：亿元 (100 million yuan)

年份 地区	Year Region	营业额 Business Revenue	#客房收入 Revenue from Hotel Rooms	#餐费收入 Revenue from Meals	#商品销售收入 Revenue from Commodities
	2004	1160.5	59.5	1030.8	43.3
	2005	1260.2	64.0	1124.0	45.4
北京	Beijing	149.2	1.5	139.0	4.6
天津	Tianjin	29.6	0.1	26.8	2.6
河北	Hebei	13.7	0.8	12.3	0.3
山西	Shanxi	19.2	2.0	15.9	1.0
内蒙古	Inner Mongolia	11.8	1.3	10.2	0.2
辽宁	Liaoning	48.1	2.4	43.3	1.1
吉林	Jilin	9.6	1.2	8.0	0.3
黑龙江	Heilongjiang	15.5	0.2	12.8	2.4
上海	Shanghai	169.5	1.0	166.4	1.4
江苏	Jiangsu	107.5	10.1	91.5	2.7
浙江	Zhejiang	88.2	6.9	77.6	1.9
安徽	Anhui	25.0	1.2	21.5	2.0
福建	Fujian	36.3	1.1	34.3	0.4
江西	Jiangxi	15.7	1.3	11.7	2.6
山东	Shandong	82.9	9.8	63.8	7.6
河南	Henan	27.9	1.5	23.1	2.3
湖北	Hubei	36.2	1.6	33.0	1.2
湖南	Hunan	30.4	2.1	27.2	0.8
广东	Guangdong	219.7	10.6	198.5	4.2
广西	Guangxi	9.7	0.8	8.4	0.4
海南	Hainan	3.7		3.4	0.2
重庆	Chongqing	21.8	1.9	18.6	0.6
四川	Sichuan	30.8	1.4	26.7	1.5
贵州	Guizhou	5.1	0.1	4.5	0.4
云南	Yunnan	9.5	0.2	8.5	0.2
西藏	Tibet				
陕西	Shaanxi	25.0	2.1	19.6	2.0
甘肃	Gansu	7.0	0.1	6.9	
青海	Qinghai	1.5	0.1	1.4	
宁夏	Ningxia	3.9	0.4	3.1	0.4
新疆	Xinjiang	6.3	0.1	5.8	0.2

17-13 按登记注册类型分限额以上批发、零售企业资产及负债（2005年）

Assets and Liabilities of Enterprises above Designated Size of Wholesale and Retail Trades by Status of Registration (2005)

单位：亿元 (100 million yuan)

指标	Item	资产总计 Total Assets	#流动资产 Working Capitals	#固定资产 Fixed Assets	负债合计 Total Liabilities	所有者权益合计 Total Owners' Equities
总　计	**Total**	**36532.0**	**26098.7**	**4745.6**	**26342.2**	**10189.2**
批发企业合计	**Wholesale Trade**	**28105.8**	**20985.0**	**2658.5**	**20199.5**	**7906.9**
内资企业	**Domestic Funded Enterprises**	**25894.4**	**19226.0**	**2580.4**	**18659.2**	**7235.8**
国有企业	State-owned Enterprises	8639.2	6114.5	969.1	5943.7	2695.9
集体企业	Collective-owned Enterprises	925.3	738.3	86.7	815.4	109.9
股份合作企业	Cooperative Enterprises	182.8	141.2	20.2	137.6	45.2
联营企业	Joint Ownership Enterprises	132.6	103.5	13.5	88.3	44.3
国有联营企业	State Joint Ownership Enterprises	79.6	59.9	10.4	47.5	32.1
集体联营企业	Collective Joint Ownership Enterprises	3.5	2.8	0.4	2.8	0.6
国有与集体联营企业	Joint State-collective Enterprises	18.7	15.8	1.0	13.6	5.1
其他联营企业	Other Joint Ownership Enterprises	30.7	24.9	1.7	24.2	6.5
有限责任公司	Limited Liability Corporations	8135.9	6482.2	554.3	6116.9	2019.0
国有独资公司	State Sole Funded Corporations	1321.0	907.9	117.2	824.9	496.1
其他有限责任公司	Other Limited Liability Corporations	6814.9	5574.3	437.1	5292.0	1522.9
股份有限公司	Share-holding Corporations Ltd.	3384.7	1827.7	680.4	2080.4	1304.5
私营企业	Private Enterprises	4448.7	3781.2	252.8	3444.2	1004.5
私营独资企业	Private-funded Enterprises	77.3	60.4	8.2	61.2	16.1
私营合伙企业	Private Partnership Enterprises	23.0	20.3	1.7	18.5	4.5
私营有限责任公司	Private Limited Liability Corporations	4218.3	3583.9	233.5	3273.4	945.0
私营股份有限公司	Private Share-holding Corporations Ltd.	130.1	116.5	9.5	91.1	38.9
其他企业	Other Enterprises	45.2	37.5	3.5	32.8	12.5
港、澳、台商投资企业	**Enterprises with Funds from Hong Kong, Macao and Taiwan**	**328.3**	**295.5**	**8.5**	**256.9**	**71.5**
合资经营企业	Joint-venture Enterprises	50.9	43.8	2.1	38.6	12.3
合作经营企业	Cooperative Enterprises	15.4	15.0	0.2	10.8	4.6
独资经营企业	Enterprises with Sole Funds	235.8	221.3	5.0	193.4	42.4
投资股份有限公司	Share-holding Corporations Ltd. with Funds	26.2	15.4	1.2	14.1	12.2
外商投资企业	**Foreign Funded Enterprises**	**1883.1**	**1463.5**	**69.5**	**1283.5**	**599.6**
中外合资经营企业	Joint-venture Enterprises	293.0	241.2	24.0	216.4	76.6
中外合作经营企业	Cooperation Enterprises	79.6	75.8	1.2	79.1	0.5
外资企业	Enterprises with Sole Foreign Funds	1498.1	1142.7	42.8	979.1	519.0
外商投资股份有限公司	Share-holding Corporations Ltd. with Foreign Funds	12.3	3.9	1.6	8.9	3.4

17-13 续表 continued

单位：亿元 (100 million yuan)

指标	Item	资产总计 Total Assets	#流动资产 Working Capitals	#固定资产 Fixed Assets	负债合计 Total Liabilities	所有者权益合计 Total Owners' Equities
零售企业合计	**Retail Trade**	**8426.2**	**5113.7**	**2087.1**	**6142.7**	**2282.3**
内资企业	**Domestic Funded Enterprises**	**7636.9**	**4632.7**	**1877.0**	**5554.5**	**2081.2**
国有企业	State-owned Enterprises	841.2	458.3	270.9	632.8	208.5
集体企业	Collective-owned Enterprises	231.2	133.3	63.8	178.5	52.7
股份合作企业	Cooperative Enterprises	106.2	65.0	28.7	85.8	20.4
联营企业	Joint Ownership Enterprises	80.3	46.7	14.5	59.3	21.0
国有联营企业	State Joint Ownership Enterprises	27.0	15.4	4.9	21.2	5.8
集体联营企业	Collective Joint Ownership Enterprises	5.5	2.2	2.2	3.9	1.6
国有与集体联营企业	Joint State-collective Enterprises	27.1	19.3	3.3	18.1	9.1
其他联营企业	Other Joint Ownership Enterprises	20.6	9.8	4.1	16.1	4.5
有限责任公司	Limited Liability Corporations	2497.5	1589.3	574.1	1933.4	564.1
国有独资公司	State Sole Funded Corporations	140.0	65.6	41.8	89.1	50.8
其他有限责任公司	Other Limited Liability Corporations	2357.5	1523.7	532.3	1844.3	513.3
股份有限公司	Share-holding Corporations Ltd.	2002.6	961.3	631.7	1245.9	755.5
私营企业	Private Enterprises	1857.6	1364.2	289.6	1403.9	453.7
私营独资企业	Private-funded Enterprises	68.6	47.3	13.9	46.0	22.6
私营合伙企业	Private Partnership Enterprises	32.0	20.0	9.7	20.1	11.9
私营有限责任公司	Private Limited Liability Corporations	1639.7	1221.7	247.7	1257.4	382.3
私营股份有限公司	Private Share-holding Corporations Ltd.	117.2	75.1	18.2	80.3	36.8
其他企业	Other Enterprises	20.3	14.5	3.6	15.0	5.3
港、澳、台商投资企业	**Enterprises with Funds from Hong Kong, Macao and Taiwan**	**268.3**	**162.0**	**66.1**	**188.5**	**79.7**
合资经营企业	Joint-venture Enterprises	220.7	125.0	59.4	152.8	67.9
合作经营企业	Cooperative Enterprises	23.3	17.7	2.7	14.7	8.5
独资经营企业	Enterprises with Sole Funds	22.8	18.3	3.7	20.2	2.6
投资股份有限公司	Share-holding Corporations Ltd. with Funds	1.6	1.1	0.3	0.8	0.7
外商投资企业	**Foreign Funded Enterprises**	**521.0**	**319.0**	**144.0**	**399.7**	**121.4**
中外合资经营企业	Joint-venture Enterprises	301.0	172.0	85.7	212.9	88.1
中外合作经营企业	Cooperation Enterprises	128.1	90.9	26.9	112.7	15.4
外资企业	Enterprises with Sole Foreign Funds	91.2	55.8	31.2	73.7	17.5
外商投资股份有限公司	Share-holding Corporations Ltd. with Foreign Funds	0.7	0.4	0.3	0.3	0.3

17-14 按行业分限额以上批发、零售企业资产及负债(2005年)
Assets and Liabilities of Enterprises above Designated Size of Wholesale and Retail Trades by Sector (2005)

单位：亿元 (100 million yuan)

指标	Item	资产总计 Total Assets	#流动资产 Working Capitals	#固定资产 Fixed Assets	负债合计 Total Liabilities	所有者权益合计 Total Owners' Equities
总计	**Total**	**36532.0**	**26098.7**	**4745.6**	**26342.2**	**10189.2**
批发业合计	**Wholesale Trade**	**28105.8**	**20985.0**	**2658.5**	**20199.5**	**7906.9**
农畜产品批发业	Wholesale of Farm Produce and Livestock Product	2656.4	2099.2	213.1	2470.4	186.0
食品、饮料及烟草制品批发业	Wholesale of Food, Beverages and Tobaccos	3838.7	2691.8	584.8	1960.6	1878.2
#米、面制品及食用油批发业	Wholesale of Rice, Flour and Edible Oil	675.1	492.2	78.8	557.1	118.0
烟草制品批发业	Whole of Tobaccos	2171.9	1514.9	352.4	708.0	1463.9
纺织、服装及日用品批发业	Wholesale of Textiles, Garments and Daily Consumer Articles	2058.0	1591.3	143.9	1514.5	543.4
#服装批发业	Wholesale of Garments	712.4	563.9	48.1	513.0	199.4
文化、体育用品及器材批发业	Wholesale of Culture, Sports Appliances and Equipments	582.5	409.8	61.1	380.9	201.6
医药及医疗器材批发业	Wholesale of Medicines and Medical Appliances	1366.0	1101.8	115.1	1093.2	272.8
矿产品、建材及化工产品批发业	Wholesale of Mineral Products, Building Material and Chemical Products	11121.6	7816.4	1195.0	7816.7	3305.2
#煤炭及制品批发业	Wholesale of Coal and Related Products	942.2	681.3	75.7	649.6	292.6
石油及制品批发业	Wholesale of Petrolem and Related Products	3253.0	1648.2	751.5	2000.8	1252.6
金属及金属矿批发业	Wholesale of Metal Materials	4275.2	3426.5	185.1	3193.0	1082.2
建材批发业	Wholesale of Building Materials	735.6	561.2	59.8	557.1	178.5
化肥批发业	Wholesale of Chemical Fertilizer	550.0	475.9	45.1	442.1	107.9
机械设备、五金交电及电子产品批发	Wholesale of Machinery, Hardware and Electronic Equipment	4754.3	3884.6	260.2	3636.6	1117.9
#汽车、摩托车及零配件批发业	Wholesale of Motor Vehicles, Motorcycles and Parts	1059.2	929.7	77.5	842.5	216.9
家用电器批发业	Wholesale of Household Electrical Appliances	707.3	536.2	40.8	583.2	124.1
计算机、软件及辅助设备批发业	Wholesale of Computer, Software and Assistant Appliances	400.8	343.3	8.1	312.4	88.4
贸易经纪与代理	Trade Broker and Agency	303.4	246.8	15.4	241.2	62.2
其他批发业	Other Wholesale not Classified Elsewhere	1424.9	1143.4	69.9	1085.4	339.6
零售业合计	**Retail Trade**	**8426.2**	**5113.7**	**2087.1**	**6142.7**	**2282.3**
综合零售业	Integrated Retail	3803.9	1945.6	1212.6	2814.2	988.5
#百货零售业	Retail of General Merchandise	2352.9	1077.7	830.4	1670.2	681.5
超级市场零售业	Retail of Supermarkets	1310.8	792.6	344.8	1043.6	267.1
食品、饮料及烟草制品专门零售业	Retail of Food, Beverages and Tobaccos	201.1	114.5	51.3	134.1	67.0
纺织、服装及日用品专门零售业	Special Retail of Textiles, Garments and Daily Consumer Articles	239.0	151.3	59.9	178.4	60.7
#服装零售业	Retail of Garments	152.6	89.5	44.2	114.3	38.3
文化、体育用品及器材专门零售业	Retail of Culture, Sports Appliances and Equipments	464.4	260.0	127.7	272.6	191.8
#体育用品零售业	Retail of Sports Goods	10.2	7.4	0.6	9.0	1.2
图书零售业	Retail of Books	322.3	169.9	101.3	185.7	136.6
医药及医疗器材专门零售业	Retail of Medicines and Medical Appliances	409.4	312.0	57.3	323.9	85.6
#药品零售业	Retail of Medicines	375.0	281.0	55.4	296.1	79.0
汽车、摩托车、燃料及零配件专门零售业	Retail of Motor Vehicles, Motorcycles, Fuel and Parts	2141.4	1469.4	409.3	1522.9	618.5
#汽车零售业	Retail of Motor Vehicles	1498.1	1160.4	173.2	1128.1	370.0
机动车燃料零售业	Retail of Fuel of Motor Vehicles	571.7	250.6	227.8	341.2	230.5
家用电器及电子产品专门零售业	Special Retail of Household Electric Appliances and Electronic Products	792.6	656.0	66.9	630.9	161.7
#家用电器零售业	Retail of Household Electric Appliances	563.2	466.3	48.1	469.2	94.0
计算机、软件及辅助设备零售业	Retail of Computer, Software and Assistant Appliances	127.5	104.5	9.9	87.6	39.9
通讯设备零售业	Retail of Communication Equipments	76.2	62.2	7.5	55.5	20.7
五金、家具及室内装修材料专门零售业	Special Retail of Hardware, Furniture and Decoration Materials	192.9	112.4	50.2	146.7	46.2
无店铺及其他零售业	Non-shop and Other Retails	181.5	92.4	51.8	119.0	62.4
#邮购及电子销售业	Distribution of Post and E-commerce	4.1	3.8	0.2	6.1	-2.0

17-15 限额以上批发和零售企业资产及负债

Assets and Liabilities of Enterprises above Designated Size of Wholesale and Retail Trades

单位：亿元 (100 million yuan)

年份 Year / 地区 Region		资产总计 Total Assets	#流动资产 Working Capitals	#固定资产 Fixed Assets	负债合计 Total Liabilities	所有者权益合计 Total Owners' Equities
2004		35589.7	25076.4	4514.5	25740.7	9849.0
2005		36532.0	26098.7	4745.6	26342.2	10189.2
北 京	Beijing	6106.1	4303.8	397.6	4350.7	1755.4
天 津	Tianjin	1285.5	1016.4	114.3	963.9	321.6
河 北	Hebei	679.2	419.8	159.6	531.1	148.1
山 西	Shanxi	735.7	483.6	128.2	542.3	193.4
内蒙古	Inner Mongolia	425.6	296.0	86.7	257.3	168.3
辽 宁	Liaoning	1431.3	1046.9	217.6	1168.7	263.0
吉 林	Jilin	515.6	398.5	84.2	461.7	53.0
黑龙江	Heilongjiang	597.9	434.0	122.6	483.3	114.6
上 海	Shanghai	3926.2	2929.3	376.8	2727.3	1199.0
江 苏	Jiangsu	2053.9	1409.5	322.6	1441.9	611.9
浙 江	Zhejiang	3126.6	2368.7	346.2	2170.0	956.6
安 徽	Anhui	622.0	451.8	94.0	454.2	167.8
福 建	Fujian	1137.9	832.5	123.0	713.2	424.6
江 西	Jiangxi	310.7	215.1	65.5	213.9	96.8
山 东	Shandong	2023.8	1446.9	324.1	1526.5	497.3
河 南	Henan	1005.2	666.0	209.1	803.5	201.8
湖 北	Hubei	1012.3	701.0	181.2	830.9	181.5
湖 南	Hunan	586.0	365.7	128.4	395.2	190.8
广 东	Guangdong	4269.1	3057.3	541.7	3046.5	1222.6
广 西	Guangxi	425.7	258.3	78.6	286.9	138.7
海 南	Hainan	122.3	83.1	25.3	79.1	43.2
重 庆	Chongqing	518.4	413.3	93.4	400.1	118.3
四 川	Sichuan	761.5	440.4	96.1	433.9	327.6
贵 州	Guizhou	227.2	162.6	44.0	162.1	65.1
云 南	Yunnan	946.0	705.3	111.8	610.9	335.0
西 藏	Tibet	26.6	14.4	9.9	12.9	13.7
陕 西	Shaanxi	423.3	280.8	83.4	330.3	92.9
甘 肃	Gansu	268.3	186.7	41.9	183.9	84.4
青 海	Qinghai	50.7	30.6	8.2	27.0	23.7
宁 夏	Ningxia	94.5	65.0	15.3	63.8	30.7
新 疆	Xinjiang	816.8	615.5	114.2	668.9	147.9

17-16 限额以上批发企业资产及负债

Assets and Liabilities of Enterprises above Designated Size of Wholesale Trade

单位：亿元 (100 million yuan)

年份 Year / 地区 Region		资产总计 Total Assets	#流动资产 Working Capitals	#固定资产 Fixed Assets	负债合计 Total Liabilities	所有者权益合计 Total Owners' Equities
2004		27886.7	20580.7	2639.0	20205.3	7681.4
2005		28105.8	20985.0	2658.5	20199.5	7906.9
北京	Beijing	5071.7	3633.6	214.2	3616.2	1455.4
天津	Tianjin	1088.6	897.1	64.6	821.0	267.6
河北	Hebei	446.6	288.0	88.2	345.7	100.9
山西	Shanxi	547.5	367.0	79.5	398.6	148.9
内蒙古	Inner Mongolia	312.1	234.2	36.5	182.5	129.5
辽宁	Liaoning	1046.9	826.6	103.1	905.6	141.7
吉林	Jilin	378.1	334.5	34.2	350.4	28.0
黑龙江	Heilongjiang	445.3	353.9	63.7	360.1	85.2
上海	Shanghai	3023.2	2430.1	152.3	2123.2	900.0
江苏	Jiangsu	1421.0	1039.1	155.5	959.2	461.8
浙江	Zhejiang	2597.8	2035.0	225.7	1795.5	802.3
安徽	Anhui	480.3	367.4	60.1	349.5	130.8
福建	Fujian	936.8	695.0	85.7	586.2	350.6
江西	Jiangxi	231.0	165.9	42.9	159.0	72.0
山东	Shandong	1254.1	963.0	135.9	950.5	303.5
河南	Henan	662.1	465.1	125.1	522.4	139.7
湖北	Hubei	737.7	553.8	86.0	621.6	116.0
湖南	Hunan	375.4	251.9	68.7	250.2	125.2
广东	Guangdong	3352.3	2434.4	369.2	2351.5	1000.8
广西	Guangxi	306.3	187.7	50.1	196.6	109.7
海南	Hainan	94.4	64.2	16.9	57.7	36.7
重庆	Chongqing	421.9	349.2	68.1	328.8	93.1
四川	Sichuan	584.2	316.4	60.1	310.4	273.8
贵州	Guizhou	174.2	126.1	32.3	117.8	56.5
云南	Yunnan	815.9	616.0	87.9	519.5	296.3
西藏	Tibet	15.7	10.5	3.6	8.9	6.8
陕西	Shaanxi	275.1	195.6	35.2	223.9	51.3
甘肃	Gansu	208.9	151.8	24.9	141.9	67.0
青海	Qinghai	31.4	20.1	3.5	14.7	16.7
宁夏	Ningxia	64.1	48.8	6.8	45.3	18.8
新疆	Xinjiang	705.2	563.0	77.8	585.0	120.2

17-17 限额以上零售企业资产及负债

Assets and Liabilities of Enterprises above Designated Size of Retail Trade

单位：亿元 (100 million yuan)

年份 地区	Year Region	资产总计 Total Assets	#流动资产 Working Capitals	#固定资产 Fixed Assets	负债合计 Total Liabilities	所有者权益合计 Total Owners' Equities
	2004	7703.0	4495.7	1875.6	5535.3	2167.7
	2005	8426.2	5113.7	2087.1	6142.7	2282.3
北京	Beijing	1034.5	670.2	183.4	734.5	300.0
天津	Tianjin	196.9	119.3	49.7	142.9	54.0
河北	Hebei	232.6	131.8	71.4	185.4	47.2
山西	Shanxi	188.2	116.5	48.7	143.7	44.5
内蒙古	Inner Mongolia	113.6	61.8	50.2	74.8	38.8
辽宁	Liaoning	384.4	220.3	114.5	263.1	121.3
吉林	Jilin	137.5	64.0	50.0	111.3	25.0
黑龙江	Heilongjiang	152.6	80.1	58.9	123.2	29.4
上海	Shanghai	903.0	499.2	224.5	604.1	299.0
江苏	Jiangsu	632.9	370.3	167.2	482.8	150.1
浙江	Zhejiang	528.8	333.7	120.5	374.5	154.3
安徽	Anhui	141.7	84.4	33.9	104.7	37.1
福建	Fujian	201.1	137.6	37.3	127.0	74.1
江西	Jiangxi	79.7	49.2	22.6	54.9	24.8
山东	Shandong	769.7	483.9	188.2	576.0	193.7
河南	Henan	343.2	200.9	84.0	281.1	62.1
湖北	Hubei	274.7	147.2	95.2	209.2	65.4
湖南	Hunan	210.6	113.8	59.7	145.0	65.6
广东	Guangdong	916.8	622.9	172.5	694.9	221.8
广西	Guangxi	119.3	70.6	28.5	90.3	29.0
海南	Hainan	27.9	18.9	8.3	21.4	6.5
重庆	Chongqing	96.5	64.1	25.3	71.3	25.2
四川	Sichuan	177.3	124.0	36.0	123.5	53.8
贵州	Guizhou	53.0	36.6	11.7	44.3	8.6
云南	Yunnan	130.1	89.3	24.0	91.4	38.7
西藏	Tibet	10.9	3.9	6.3	4.0	6.8
陕西	Shaanxi	148.1	85.2	48.1	106.5	41.7
甘肃	Gansu	59.4	34.9	17.0	42.1	17.4
青海	Qinghai	19.4	10.4	4.6	12.3	7.0
宁夏	Ningxia	30.4	16.1	8.5	18.5	11.9
新疆	Xinjiang	111.6	52.5	36.4	83.9	27.7

17-18 按登记注册类型和行业分限额以上餐饮企业资产及负债(2005年)

Assets and Liabilities of Enterprises above Designated Size of Cetering Services by Status of Registration and Sector (2005)

单位: 亿元 (100 million yuan)

指标	Item	资产总计 Total Assets	#流动资产 Working Capitals	#固定资产 Fixed Assets	负债合计 Total Liabilities	所有者权益合计 Total Owners' Equities
总计	**Total**	**1111.0**	**405.3**	**485.2**	**735.6**	**375.4**
按登记注册类型分	**By Status of Registration**					
内资企业	**Domestic Funded Enterprises**	**865.5**	**329.6**	**366.3**	**570.9**	**294.6**
国有企业	State-owned Enterprises	106.1	25.7	59.0	61.9	44.2
集体企业	Collective-owned Enterprises	37.3	10.2	19.9	26.2	11.1
股份合作企业	Cooperative Enterprises	24.7	7.2	13.6	13.2	11.5
联营企业	Joint Ownership Enterprises	4.1	0.6	3.2	2.7	1.4
国有联营企业	State Joint Ownership Enterprises	2.5	0.3	2.1	1.7	0.7
集体联营企业	Collective Joint Ownership Enterprises	0.2	0.1		0.1	0.1
国有与集体联营企业	Joint State-collective Enterprises					
其他联营企业	Other Joint Ownership Enterprises	1.4	0.2	1.1	0.8	0.6
有限责任公司	Limited Liability Corporations	197.6	72.9	85.4	133.4	64.2
国有独资公司	State Sole Funded Corporations	1.7	0.7	0.9	0.9	0.7
其他有限责任公司	Other Limited Liability Corporations	195.9	72.2	84.5	132.5	63.4
股份有限公司	Share-holding Corporations Ltd.	56.5	20.1	24.5	33.2	23.3
私营企业	Private Enterprises	431.2	189.3	157.9	295.5	135.7
私营独资企业	Private-funded Enterprises	72.4	28.0	36.1	37.9	34.5
私营合伙企业	Private Partnership Enterprises	14.2	6.9	5.6	8.9	5.3
私营有限责任公司	Private Limited Liability Corporations	321.5	145.3	106.4	233.4	88.2
私营股份有限公司	Private Share-holding Corporations Ltd.	23.0	9.2	9.7	15.3	7.7
其他企业	Other Enterprises	7.9	3.5	2.7	4.7	3.2
港、澳、台商投资企业	**Enterprises with Funds from Hong Kong, Macao and Taiwan**	**96.7**	**34.2**	**42.3**	**73.3**	**23.4**
合资经营企业	Joint-venture Enterprises	48.8	14.7	23.4	35.8	13.0
合作经营企业	Cooperative Enterprises	17.8	8.4	6.8	16.0	1.8
独资经营企业	Enterprises with Sole Investment	30.0	10.3	12.1	21.3	8.6
投资股份有限公司	Share-holding Corporations Ltd. with Investment	0.2	0.8		0.1	
外商投资企业	**Foreign Funded Enterprises**	**148.8**	**41.6**	**76.7**	**91.5**	**57.4**
中外合资经营企业	Joint-venture Enterprises	56.7	15.0	25.2	36.3	20.3
中外合作经营企业	Cooperation Enterprises	28.4	10.1	12.8	17.0	11.5
外资企业	Enterprises with Sole Foreign Funds	61.1	15.8	37.8	36.4	24.7
外商投资股份有限公司	Share-holding Corporations Ltd. with Foreign Investment	2.6	0.7	0.9	1.8	0.8
按国民经济行业分	**By Sector**					
正餐服务业	Dinner	959.5	359.6	408.6	643.5	316.0
快餐服务业	Snack	114.2	27.7	62.8	70.1	44.1
饮料及冷饮服务业	Beverages and Cold Drinks	12.3	5.5	5.5	3.7	8.6
其他餐饮服务业	Others	25.0	12.5	8.3	18.3	6.7

17-19 限额以上餐饮企业资产及负债

Assets and Liabilities of Enterprises above Designated Size of Catering Services

单位：亿元 (100 million yuan)

年 份 Year / 地 区 Region		资产总计 Total Assets	#流动资产 Working Capitals	#固定资产 Fixed Assets	负债合计 Total Liabilities	所有者权益合计 Total Owners' Equities
2004		1165.0	389.4	491.0	756.7	408.3
2005		1111.0	405.3	485.2	735.6	375.4
北 京	Beijing	106.0	44.3	31.1	81.5	24.5
天 津	Tianjin	30.3	10.7	12.4	19.8	10.5
河 北	Hebei	15.3	4.4	7.8	10.9	4.4
山 西	Shanxi	22.7	12.2	6.7	14.1	8.6
内蒙古	Inner Mongolia	13.6	5.2	7.7	9.1	4.5
辽 宁	Liaoning	51.6	14.6	32.4	34.0	17.6
吉 林	Jilin	12.4	2.6	6.2	6.3	6.1
黑龙江	Heilongjiang	11.9	5.3	6.0	5.6	6.3
上 海	Shanghai	94.5	43.6	29.1	64.1	30.4
江 苏	Jiangsu	122.4	40.4	58.6	77.1	45.3
浙 江	Zhejiang	81.8	27.6	34.3	56.3	25.5
安 徽	Anhui	17.8	6.2	8.2	11.0	6.8
福 建	Fujian	17.6	6.4	8.1	8.9	8.7
江 西	Jiangxi	19.3	7.1	7.9	11.3	8.1
山 东	Shandong	103.8	39.3	43.8	74.2	29.6
河 南	Henan	23.1	7.8	10.6	14.5	8.6
湖 北	Hubei	31.2	10.5	15.4	23.2	8.0
湖 南	Hunan	27.7	7.4	15.7	17.1	10.6
广 东	Guangdong	173.0	60.7	78.9	112.0	61.0
广 西	Guangxi	9.6	2.4	5.5	6.4	3.2
海 南	Hainan	3.0	1.2	1.4	1.3	1.7
重 庆	Chongqing	22.9	7.2	13.1	15.1	7.7
四 川	Sichuan	36.7	14.2	17.1	22.3	14.3
贵 州	Guizhou	4.4	1.7	1.7	2.8	1.7
云 南	Yunnan	9.8	3.8	4.2	7.2	2.6
西 藏	Tibet					
陕 西	Shaanxi	32.1	12.3	14.4	19.6	12.5
甘 肃	Gansu	5.5	2.3	1.8	3.0	2.6
青 海	Qinghai	1.5	0.6	0.8	0.9	0.7
宁 夏	Ningxia	5.0	1.6	2.6	3.4	1.6
新 疆	Xinjiang	4.4	1.9	1.9	2.7	1.7

17-20 按登记注册类型分限额以上批发、零售企业主要财务指标(2005年)

Main Financial Indicators of Enterprises above Designated Size of Wholesale and Retail Trades by Status of Registration (2005)

单位：亿元 (100 million yuan)

指标	Item	主营业务收入 Revenue from Principal Business	主营业务成本 Cost of Principal Business	主营业务税金及附加 Taxes and Other Charges on Principal Business	主营业务利润 Profits from Principal Business
总计	**Total**	**82892.1**	**75545.3**	**127.6**	**5591.2**
批发企业合计	**Wholesale Trade**	**67701.3**	**62047.9**	**80.2**	**4231.3**
内资企业	**Domestic Funded Enterprises**	**62217.0**	**57528.8**	**75.3**	**3599.2**
国有企业	State-owned Enterprises	18221.6	16491.5	27.3	1404.8
集体企业	Collective-owned Enterprises	1484.5	1406.8	1.9	55.3
股份合作企业	Cooperative Enterprises	555.9	527.3	0.5	23.0
联营企业	Joint Ownership Enterprises	404.0	371.0	0.5	28.2
国有联营企业	State Joint Ownership Enterprises	282.6	259.1	0.4	21.5
集体联营企业	Collective Joint Ownership Enterprises	12.9	12.2		0.5
国有与集体联营企业	Joint State-collective Enterprises	49.3	46.1	0.1	2.4
其他联营企业	Other Joint Ownership Enterprises	59.2	53.7		3.8
有限责任公司	Limited Liability Corporations	18644.5	17242.4	20.4	984.8
国有独资公司	State Sole Funded Corporations	2231.3	1992.8	3.1	186.4
其他有限责任公司	Other Limited Liability Corporations	16413.1	15249.6	17.3	798.4
股份有限公司	Share-holding Corporations Ltd.	11128.9	10375.6	10.0	603.2
私营企业	Private Enterprises	11676.1	11021.6	13.5	492.3
私营独资企业	Private-funded Enterprises	191.9	176.4	1.6	8.7
私营合伙企业	Private Partnership Enterprises	77.0	73.3	0.1	3.1
私营有限责任公司	Private Limited Liability Corporations	11037.0	10420.4	11.4	464.2
私营股份有限公司	Private Share-holding Corporations Ltd.	370.3	351.5	0.5	16.3
其他企业	Other Enterprises	101.6	92.6	1.0	7.7
港、澳、台商投资企业	**Enterprises with Funds from Hong Kong, Macao and Taiwan**	**868.6**	**786.4**	**0.3**	**65.8**
合资经营企业	Joint-venture Enterprises	161.3	142.0	0.1	16.8
合作经营企业	Cooperative Enterprises	43.0	37.3		3.7
独资经营企业	Enterprises with Sole Investment	646.2	594.8	0.2	40.6
投资股份有限公司	Share-holding Corporations Ltd. with Funds	18.2	12.2		4.7
外商投资企业	**Foreign Funded Enterprises**	**4615.7**	**3732.8**	**4.6**	**566.3**
中外合资经营企业	Joint-venture Enterprises	1067.1	735.6	1.5	79.5
中外合作经营企业	Cooperation Enterprises	459.6	453.5		6.0
外资企业	Enterprises with Sole Foreign Funds	3081.8	2537.3	3.1	480.2
外商投资股份有限公司	Share-holding Corporations Ltd. with Foreign Funds	7.1	6.4		0.7

17-20 续表 continued

单位：亿元 (100 million yuan)

指　　标	Item	主营业务收入 Revenue from Principal Business	主营业务成本 Cost of Principal Business	主营业务税金及附加 Taxes and Other Charges on Principal Business	主营业务利润 Profits from Principal Business
零售企业合计	**Retail Trade**	**15190.9**	**13497.4**	**47.4**	**1360.0**
内资企业	**Domestic Funded Enterprises**	**13682.6**	**12215.4**	**45.4**	**1171.5**
国有企业	State-owned Enterprises	1199.1	1023.3	5.2	139.2
集体企业	Collective-owned Enterprises	375.4	337.6	2.8	27.6
股份合作企业	Cooperative Enterprises	215.9	197.5	0.6	16.0
联营企业	Joint Ownership Enterprises	208.0	196.7	0.2	10.4
国有联营企业	State Joint Ownership Enterprises	46.7	42.8		3.7
集体联营企业	Collective Joint Ownership Enterprises	12.6	11.6		0.9
国有与集体联营企业	Joint State-collective Enterprises	121.2	117.6		3.3
其他联营企业	Other Joint Ownership Enterprises	27.5	24.7	0.1	2.5
有限责任公司	Limited Liability Corporations	4579.5	4096.3	13.3	392.2
国有独资公司	State Sole Funded Corporations	120.8	100.5	0.4	18.4
其他有限责任公司	Other Limited Liability Corporations	4458.7	3995.9	12.9	373.9
股份有限公司	Share-holding Corporations Ltd.	3156.1	2808.6	11.1	308.0
私营企业	Private Enterprises	3907.5	3518.4	12.1	274.8
私营独资企业	Private-funded Enterprises	136.7	122.7	0.7	11.5
私营合伙企业	Private Partnership Enterprises	55.9	50.0	0.3	5.3
私营有限责任公司	Private Limited Liability Corporations	3491.6	3139.1	10.4	244.6
私营股份有限公司	Private Share-holding Corporations Ltd.	223.3	206.6	0.7	13.5
其他企业	Other Enterprises	41.0	36.9	0.2	3.3
港、澳、台商投资企业	**Enterprises with Funds from Hong Kong, Macao and Taiwan**	**462.5**	**385.1**	**1.0**	**58.6**
合资经营企业	Joint-venture Enterprises	347.5	282.1	0.9	49.6
合作经营企业	Cooperative Enterprises	60.2	52.1	0.1	7.0
独资经营企业	Enterprises with Sole Investment	53.3	49.6		1.9
投资股份有限公司	Share-holding Corporations Ltd. with Funds	1.4	1.2		0.2
外商投资企业	**Foreign Funded Enterprises**	**1045.8**	**896.9**	**1.0**	**129.9**
中外合资经营企业	Joint-venture Enterprises	554.9	475.5	0.6	74.3
中外合作经营企业	Cooperation Enterprises	338.2	291.1	0.3	34.9
外资企业	Enterprises with Sole Foreign Funds	151.9	129.6	0.1	20.5
外商投资股份有限公司	Share-holding Corporations Ltd. with Foreign Funds	0.8	0.7		0.1

17-21 按行业分限额以上批发、零售企业主要财务指标(2005年)
Main Financial Indicators of Enterprises above Designated Size of Wholesale and Retail Trades by Sector (2005)

单位：亿元 (100 million yuan)

指标	Item	主营业务收入 Revenue from Principal Business	主营业务成本 Cost of Principal Business	主营业务税金及附加 Taxes and Other Charges on Principal Business	主营业务利润 Profits from Principal Business
总计	**Total**	**82892.1**	**75545.3**	**127.6**	**5591.2**
批发企业合计	**Wholesale Trade**	**67701.3**	**62047.9**	**80.2**	**4231.3**
农畜产品批发业	Wholesale of Farm Produce and Livestock Product	1719.0	1605.8	1.2	76.8
食品、饮料及烟草制品批发业	Wholesale of Food, Beverages and Tobaccos	8262.6	6929.4	22.7	1173.9
#米、面制品及食用油批发业	Wholesale of Rice, Flour and Edible Oil	643.0	614.9	0.5	20.3
烟草制品批发业	Whole of Tobaccos	5797.2	4707.9	17.1	975.3
纺织、服装及日用品批发业	Wholesale of Textiles, Garments and Daily Consumer Articles	5080.7	4709.5	4.6	305.5
#服装批发业	Wholesale of Garments	1911.9	1778.5	1.3	116.6
文化、体育用品及器材批发业	Wholesale of Culture, Sports Appliances and Equipments	962.9	841.5	1.6	75.9
医药及医疗器材批发业	Wholesale of Medicines and Medical Appliances	2930.7	2684.0	3.5	188.0
矿产品、建材及化工产品批发业	Wholesale of Mineral Products, Building Material and Chemical Products	34529.8	32431.9	33.1	1489.2
#煤炭及制品批发业	Wholesale of Coal and Related Products	2630.3	2344.4	7.1	249.8
石油及制品批发业	Wholesale of Petroleum and Related Products	14806.2	13994.9	11.9	712.6
金属及金属矿批发业	Wholesale of Metal Materials	10829.8	10284.6	6.7	282.0
建材批发业	Wholesale of Building Materials	1363.8	1282.2	2.7	54.5
化肥批发业	Wholesale of Chemical Fertilizer	1056.7	997.7	0.8	45.3
机械设备、五金交电及电子产品批发	Wholesale of Machinery, Hardware and Electronic Equipment	10432.8	9379.3	10.7	668.5
#汽车、摩托车及零配件批发业	Wholesale of Motor Vehicles, Motorcycles and Parts	2966.7	2583.4	1.5	116.3
家用电器批发业	Wholesale of Household Electrical Appliances	1571.4	1437.0	1.7	114.5
计算机、软件及辅助设备批发业	Wholesale of Computer, Software and Assistant Appliances	984.1	936.8	0.7	29.4
贸易经纪与代理	Trade Broker and Agency	683.9	640.4	0.5	33.4
其他批发业	Other Wholesale not Classified Elsewhere	3098.8	2826.2	2.3	220.0
零售企业合计	**Retail Trade**	**15190.9**	**13497.4**	**47.4**	**1360.0**
综合零售业	Integrated Retail	2889.5	2426.9	15.9	389.4
#百货零售业	Retail of General Merchandise	2692.5	2368.0	5.9	258.5
超级市场零售业	Retail of Supermarkets	266.9	225.1	1.3	34.8
食品、饮料及烟草制品专门零售业	Retail of Food, Beverages and Tobaccos	333.0	259.7	2.0	62.4
纺织、服装及日用品专门零售业	Special Retail of Textiles, Garments and Daily Consumer Articles	205.1	159.1	1.2	38.9
#服装零售业	Retail of Garments	485.6	363.9	4.0	100.6
文化、体育用品及器材专门零售业	Retail of Culture, Sports Appliances and Equipments	14.8	12.1		2.2
#体育用品零售业	Retail of Sports Goods	319.3	233.8	1.5	69.6
图书零售业	Retail of Books	665.6	587.4	1.5	65.8
医药及医疗器材专门零售业	Retail of Medicines and Medical Appliances	613.8	543.0	1.4	59.0
#药品零售业	Retail of Medicines	5463.7	5085.6	8.7	282.1
汽车、摩托车、燃料及零配件专门零售业	Retail of Motor Vehicles, Motorcycles, Fuel and Parts	3539.7	3344.5	5.6	151.9
#汽车零售业	Retail of Motor Vehicles	1781.5	1609.8	2.7	120.6
机动车燃料零售业	Retail of Fuel of Motor Vehicles	1742.5	1618.2	5.2	97.7
家用电器及电子产品专门零售业	Special Retail of Household Electric Appliances and Electronic Products	1162.3	1084.7	4.1	63.8
#家用电器零售业	Retail of Household Electric Appliances	312.4	286.6	0.6	18.2
计算机、软件及辅助设备零售业	Retail of Computer, Software and Assistant Appliances	215.5	199.0	0.4	11.7
通讯设备零售业	Retail of Communication Equipments	239.5	203.4	1.2	26.8
五金、家具及室内装修材料专门零售业	Special Retail of Hardware, Furniture and Decoration Materials	205.7	181.5	0.8	19.7
无店铺及其他零售业	Non-shop and Other Retails	9.4	7.0		2.4
#邮购及电子销售业	Distribution of Post and E-commerce				

17-22 限额以上批发和零售企业主要财务指标

Main Financial Indicators of Enterprises above Designated Size of Wholesale and Retail Trades

单位：亿元 (100 million yuan)

年份 Year / 地区 Region		主营业务收入 Revenue from Principal Business	主营业务成本 Cost of Principal Business	主营业务税金及附加 Taxes and Other Charges on Principal Business	主营业务利润 Profits from Principal Business
	2004	78059.7	71773.3	130.4	4838.4
	2005	82892.1	75545.3	127.6	5591.2
北　京	Beijing	9808.5	9021.8	11.8	775.0
天　津	Tianjin	3880.4	3677.7	4.0	145.1
河　北	Hebei	1470.2	1298.2	2.3	100.0
山　西	Shanxi	1330.3	1177.3	5.2	117.1
内蒙古	Inner Mongolia	800.2	639.1	2.7	128.2
辽　宁	Liaoning	4366.5	3969.2	4.7	212.8
吉　林	Jilin	1481.7	1393.9	1.7	62.9
黑龙江	Heilongjiang	1034.2	938.0	1.8	72.8
上　海	Shanghai	11236.2	9874.1	10.1	737.7
江　苏	Jiangsu	5250.9	4757.0	10.7	360.9
浙　江	Zhejiang	7923.8	7466.2	9.5	429.9
安　徽	Anhui	1480.5	1352.6	2.3	110.2
福　建	Fujian	2683.0	2527.3	5.4	155.4
江　西	Jiangxi	668.2	599.3	1.4	60.6
山　东	Shandong	4045.0	3706.6	9.9	266.4
河　南	Henan	2107.2	1949.8	4.2	153.1
湖　北	Hubei	2228.5	2007.9	4.4	141.2
湖　南	Hunan	1169.3	1001.4	3.4	112.0
广　东	Guangdong	10740.2	10008.5	13.7	614.1
广　西	Guangxi	999.4	911.5	1.9	86.0
海　南	Hainan	264.8	238.6	0.4	25.3
重　庆	Chongqing	1078.0	970.4	2.1	88.7
四　川	Sichuan	1594.4	1335.2	3.0	195.7
贵　州	Guizhou	418.5	347.8	1.1	56.5
云　南	Yunnan	1705.3	1483.0	3.8	184.1
西　藏	Tibet	28.4	22.4	0.1	4.4
陕　西	Shaanxi	1009.7	935.2	2.8	63.6
甘　肃	Gansu	859.8	805.7	1.4	49.7
青　海	Qinghai	100.3	88.7	0.1	9.2
宁　夏	Ningxia	139.8	126.8	0.3	12.0
新　疆	Xinjiang	988.7	914.3	1.4	60.6

17-23 限额以上批发企业主要财务指标

Main Financial Indicators of Enterprises above Designated Size of Wholesale Trade

单位：亿元 (100 million yuan)

年份 地区	Year Region	主营业务收入 Revenue from Principal Business	主营业务成本 Cost of Principal Business	主营业务税金及附加 Taxes and Other Charges on Principal Business	主营业务利润 Profits from Principal Business
	2004	64973.7	60149.7	88.1	3795.3
	2005	67701.3	62047.9	80.2	4231.3
北京	Beijing	8089.2	7479.2	8.2	601.8
天津	Tianjin	3541.2	3376.3	3.3	120.3
河北	Hebei	1087.7	982.6	1.4	78.2
山西	Shanxi	1021.1	897.8	4.2	94.9
内蒙古	Inner Mongolia	596.6	464.3	2.1	104.4
辽宁	Liaoning	3738.7	3419.0	2.9	158.3
吉林	Jilin	1212.3	1152.0	0.7	42.9
黑龙江	Heilongjiang	811.2	745.6	1.1	51.9
上海	Shanghai	9351.0	8229.2	5.7	550.3
江苏	Jiangsu	3965.9	3621.1	5.5	247.8
浙江	Zhejiang	6903.7	6535.4	6.4	345.7
安徽	Anhui	1208.9	1107.8	1.6	86.9
福建	Fujian	2292.2	2168.6	2.3	123.4
江西	Jiangxi	542.9	491.2	0.9	48.0
山东	Shandong	2749.0	2531.2	6.0	167.3
河南	Henan	1592.8	1475.5	2.2	115.2
湖北	Hubei	1770.4	1611.4	2.2	97.1
湖南	Hunan	780.9	660.9	1.8	75.0
广东	Guangdong	8895.4	8362.1	9.3	448.8
广西	Guangxi	797.3	732.6	1.3	63.4
海南	Hainan	224.1	202.1	0.3	21.3
重庆	Chongqing	864.6	781.5	1.3	68.3
四川	Sichuan	1243.0	1030.3	2.1	157.2
贵州	Guizhou	340.9	278.9	0.9	49.5
云南	Yunnan	1486.2	1287.9	3.4	163.5
西藏	Tibet	18.6	15.4		2.3
陕西	Shaanxi	805.6	754.4	0.9	45.0
甘肃	Gansu	759.2	715.9	0.9	41.0
青海	Qinghai	72.9	64.6	0.1	7.5
宁夏	Ningxia	102.9	94.3	0.2	8.2
新疆	Xinjiang	835.0	778.9	1.0	45.8

17-24 限额以上零售企业主要财务指标

Main Financial Indicators of Enterprises above Designated Size of Retail Trade

单位：亿元 (100 million yuan)

年份 地区	Year Region	主营业务收入 Revenue from Principal Business	主营业务成本 Cost of Principal Business	主营业务税金及附加 Taxes and Other Charges on Principal Business	主营业务利润 Profits from Principal Business
	2004	13086.0	11623.6	42.3	1043.1
	2005	15190.9	13497.4	47.4	1360.0
北京	Beijing	1719.4	1542.6	3.6	173.2
天津	Tianjin	339.2	301.4	0.7	24.7
河北	Hebei	382.6	315.5	0.9	21.8
山西	Shanxi	309.2	279.4	1.0	22.2
内蒙古	Inner Mongolia	203.6	174.8	0.6	23.8
辽宁	Liaoning	627.9	550.2	1.8	54.5
吉林	Jilin	269.4	241.9	0.9	19.9
黑龙江	Heilongjiang	223.1	192.5	0.7	21.0
上海	Shanghai	1885.2	1644.9	4.4	187.4
江苏	Jiangsu	1285.0	1135.9	5.2	113.0
浙江	Zhejiang	1020.1	930.9	3.1	84.2
安徽	Anhui	271.6	244.8	0.7	23.3
福建	Fujian	390.8	358.7	3.0	32.1
江西	Jiangxi	125.3	108.1	0.5	12.6
山东	Shandong	1296.0	1175.4	3.9	99.0
河南	Henan	514.4	474.4	2.0	38.0
湖北	Hubei	458.1	396.5	2.2	44.1
湖南	Hunan	388.4	340.5	1.5	37.0
广东	Guangdong	1844.7	1646.3	4.4	165.3
广西	Guangxi	202.1	178.9	0.7	22.5
海南	Hainan	40.7	36.5	0.1	4.0
重庆	Chongqing	213.3	188.9	0.7	20.4
四川	Sichuan	351.4	304.9	0.9	38.5
贵州	Guizhou	77.6	68.9	0.2	7.0
云南	Yunnan	219.1	195.0	0.4	20.6
西藏	Tibet	9.8	7.0	0.0	2.2
陕西	Shaanxi	204.1	180.8	2.0	18.6
甘肃	Gansu	100.5	89.8	0.5	8.7
青海	Qinghai	27.5	24.1		1.6
宁夏	Ningxia	36.9	32.5	0.1	3.8
新疆	Xinjiang	153.7	135.4	0.4	14.8

17-25 按登记注册类型和行业分限额以上餐饮企业主要财务指标(2005年)

Main Financial Indicators of Enterprises above Designated Size of Catering Services by Status of Registration and Sector (2005)

单位: 亿元 (100 million yuan)

指 标	Item	主营业务收入 Revenue from Principal Business	主营业务成本 Cost of Principal Business	主营业务税金及附加 Taxes and Other Charges on Principal Business	主营业务利润 Profits from Principal Business
总 计	**Total**	**1199.3**	**599.8**	**64.3**	**486.0**
按登记注册类型分	**By Status of Registration**				
内资企业	**Domestic Funded Enterprises**	**869.0**	**467.6**	**47.9**	**315.1**
国有企业	State-owned Enterprises	49.1	23.9	2.3	20.1
集体企业	Collective-owned Enterprises	27.7	15.2	1.5	9.7
股份合作企业	Cooperative Enterprises	24.5	13.7	1.3	7.9
联营企业	Joint Ownership Enterprises	3.9	1.9	0.3	1.6
国有联营企业	State Joint Ownership Enterprises	0.9	0.3		0.4
集体联营企业	Collective Joint Ownership Enterprises	0.7	0.4		0.3
国有与集体联营企业	Joint State-collective Enterprises	0.1	0.1		0.1
其他联营企业	Other Joint Ownership Enterprises	2.2	1.1	0.2	0.9
有限责任公司	Limited Liability Corporations	164.4	83.8	9.0	64.4
国有独资公司	State Sole Funded Corporations	1.0	0.5	0.1	0.4
其他有限责任公司	Other Limited Liability Corporations	163.4	83.3	9.0	63.9
股份有限公司	Share-holding Corporations Ltd.	39.7	19.4	2.0	17.0
私营企业	Private Enterprises	547.4	302.7	30.9	190.8
私营独资企业	Private-funded Enterprises	99.6	59.7	5.6	29.3
私营合伙企业	Private Partnership Enterprises	25.4	14.5	1.5	8.3
私营有限责任公司	Private Limited Liability Corporations	392.3	211.0	22.2	143.6
私营股份有限公司	Private Share-holding Corporations Ltd.	30.1	17.5	1.6	9.7
其他企业	Other Enterprises	12.2	7.0	0.6	3.6
港、澳、台商投资企业	**Enterprises with Funds from Hong Kong, Macao and Taiwan**	**96.7**	**41.7**	**5.0**	**46.7**
合资经营企业	Joint-venture Enterprises	46.2	19.1	2.4	24.2
合作经营企业	Cooperative Enterprises	14.6	6.0	0.7	7.7
独资经营企业	Enterprises with Sole Funds	35.6	16.4	1.9	14.7
投资股份有限公司	Share-holding Corporations Ltd. with Funds	0.3	0.2		0.1
外商投资企业	**Foreign Funded Enterprises**	**233.6**	**90.5**	**11.4**	**124.2**
中外合资经营企业	Joint-venture Enterprises	80.5	32.5	4.0	43.6
中外合作经营企业	Cooperation Enterprises	38.7	14.8	1.9	21.7
外资企业	Enterprises with Sole Foreign Funds	113.2	42.7	5.4	58.4
外商投资股份有限公司	Share-holding Corporations Ltd. with Foreign Funds	1.2	0.5	0.1	0.6
按国民经济行业分	**By Sector**				
正餐服务业	Dinner	948.5	496.8	52.2	358.3
快餐服务业	Snack	212.9	84.3	10.3	111.0
饮料及冷饮服务业	Beverages and Cold Drinks	7.5	2.6	0.3	4.5
其他餐饮服务业	Other	30.4	16.1	1.4	12.3

17-26 限额以上餐饮企业主要财务指标

Main Financial Indicators of Enterprises above Designated Size of Catering Services

单位：亿元 (100 million yuan)

年份 Year 地区 Region	主营业务收入 Revenue from Principal Business	主营业务成本 Cost of Principal Business	主营业务税金及附加 Taxes and Other Charges on Principal Business	主营业务利润 Profits from Principal Business
2004	1153.3	582.1	62.2	396.9
2005	1199.3	599.8	64.3	486.0
北京 Beijing	153.3	71.5	8.0	73.8
天津 Tianjin	29.5	14.6	1.5	8.2
河北 Hebei	11.9	7.0	0.6	3.3
山西 Shanxi	19.3	10.2	1.1	7.0
内蒙古 Inner Mongolia	10.0	4.9	0.5	4.2
辽宁 Liaoning	46.9	23.4	2.6	19.8
吉林 Jilin	7.8	4.1	0.4	3.2
黑龙江 Heilongjiang	12.7	7.3	0.9	4.3
上海 Shanghai	157.7	72.0	8.1	65.8
江苏 Jiangsu	105.7	53.6	5.6	38.2
浙江 Zhejiang	83.0	43.2	4.5	34.9
安徽 Anhui	14.7	8.0	0.8	5.6
福建 Fujian	31.1	18.9	1.7	10.5
江西 Jiangxi	14.4	7.4	0.7	5.5
山东 Shandong	77.7	42.2	3.9	28.2
河南 Henan	23.8	15.2	1.1	7.6
湖北 Hubei	35.4	18.0	2.0	14.7
湖南 Hunan	27.3	14.6	1.1	9.9
广东 Guangdong	220.6	105.1	13.0	94.2
广西 Guangxi	9.1	4.5	0.4	4.1
海南 Hainan	2.7	1.5	0.2	1.1
重庆 Chongqing	19.9	10.3	1.1	7.8
四川 Sichuan	28.6	13.9	1.5	12.3
贵州 Guizhou	5.0	2.6	0.3	1.6
云南 Yunnan	8.7	4.4	0.4	3.9
西藏 Tibet				
陕西 Shaanxi	24.3	11.5	1.3	10.7
甘肃 Gansu	6.3	3.4	0.4	1.7
青海 Qinghai	1.5	0.9	0.1	0.3
宁夏 Ningxia	4.7	2.7	0.3	1.4
新疆 Xinjiang	5.8	3.1	0.3	2.2

17-27 按业态分限额以上连锁零售企业基本情况
Basic Conditions of Enterprises above Designated Size of Chain Stores by Business Categories

指标	Indicator	合计 Total		直营店 Under Direct Management		加盟店 Through License Arrangement	
		2004	2005	2004	2005	2004	2005
门店总数（个）	**Number of Stores (unit)**	**77631**	**90476**	**54841**	**61087**	**22790**	**29389**
百货商店	Department Store	3016	3438	1057	1231	1959	2207
超级市场	Supermarket	12877	15421	8370	9655	4507	5766
专业店	Professional Shop	47825	54241	36648	40266	11177	13975
#加油站	Gas Station	20181	21411	19671	20863	510	548
专卖店	Regie Shop	4816	5718	1772	1970	3044	3748
便利店	Neighbourhood Market	8824	11218	6762	7658	2062	3560
仓储会员店	Storage Associator Shop	82	157	82	105		52
家居建材商店	Familia Building Materials Shop	79	94	78	93	1	1
其他	Others	112	189	72	109	40	80
营业面积（万平方米）	**Operational Area (10 000 sq.m)**	**7202.6**	**8202.7**	**6623.4**	**7494.5**	**579.2**	**708.2**
百货商店	Department Store	670.2	793.8	619.7	732.2	50.5	61.7
超级市场	Supermarket	1527.4	1862.1	1327.5	1607.8	199.9	254.3
专业店	Professional Shop	4700.4	5186.5	4407.0	4845.7	293.4	340.8
#加油站	Gas Station	3851.5	4029.0	3764.9	3937.9	86.6	91.1
专卖店	Regie Shop	34.2	41.4	19.1	20.9	15.1	20.5
便利店	Neighbourhood Market	129.7	153.6	110.3	123.9	19.4	29.7
仓储会员店	Storage Associator Shop	22.6	29.6	22.6	29.5		0.1
家居建材商店	Familia Building Materials Shop	113.0	130.0	112.3	129.4	0.7	0.7
其他	Others	4.9	5.6	4.9	5.0	0.1	0.6
从业人员（万人）	**Employed Person (10 000 persons)**	**128.2**	**148.8**	**106.2**	**122.7**	**22.0**	**26.2**
百货商店	Department Store	16.6	18.2	14.2	15.7	2.4	2.4
超级市场	Supermarket	48.0	56.2	39.4	45.9	8.5	10.3
专业店	Professional Shop	50.5	59.5	42.2	49.7	8.3	9.8
#加油站	Gas Station	17.6	19.0	17.2	18.5	0.5	0.5
专卖店	Regie Shop	3.8	4.5	2.2	2.4	1.6	2.1
便利店	Neighbourhood Market	7.1	8.0	6.0	6.4	1.1	1.6
仓储会员店	Storage Associator Shop	0.7	1.0	0.7	1.0		
家居建材商店	Familia Building Materials Shop	1.4	1.2	1.4	1.2		
其他	Others	0.2	0.2	0.1	0.2		

17-27 续表 1 continued

指标	Indicator	合计 Total		直营店 Under Direct Management		加盟店 Through License Arrangement	
		2004	2005	2004	2005	2004	2005
商品购进总额（亿元）	**Total Purchases (100 million yuan)**	**7130.1**	**9044.1**	**6314.6**	**8127.0**	**815.4**	**917.1**
百货商店	Department Store	912.9	921.7	876.4	859.3	36.5	62.3
超级市场	Supermarket	1785.7	2170.2	1490.9	1914.2	294.8	256.0
专业店	Professional Shop	4018.6	5441.0	3587.2	4908.7	431.5	532.3
#加油站	Gas Station	2406.8	3330.0	2359.9	3266.0	46.9	64.0
专卖店	Regie Shop	118.6	150.1	84.9	112.2	33.8	37.9
便利店	Neighbourhood Market	145.0	187.8	126.7	159.7	18.3	28.1
仓储会员店	Storage Associator Shop	63.8	78.8	63.8	78.7		0.1
家居建材商店	Familia Building Materials Shop	79.6	89.1	79.3	88.8	0.4	0.3
其他	Others	5.6	5.5	5.6	5.4	0.1	0.1
统一配送商品购进额（亿元）	**Centralized Purchases and Delivery (100 million yuan)**	**5545.6**	**7036.8**	**5068.7**	**6489.9**	**476.9**	**546.9**
百货商店	Department Store	565.5	494.4	541.6	449.0	23.9	45.3
超级市场	Supermarket	1476.4	1721.3	1243.7	1548.0	232.7	173.3
专业店	Professional Shop	3211.9	4448.3	3025.0	4163.8	186.9	284.5
#加油站	Gas Station	2030.4	2813.5	1991.1	2758.2	39.3	55.3
专卖店	Regie Shop	64.5	78.1	47.7	59.9	16.8	18.2
便利店	Neighbourhood Market	125.6	170.9	109.1	145.3	16.5	25.6
仓储会员店	Storage Associator Shop	62.7	77.1	62.7	77.1		
家居建材商店	Familia Building Materials Shop	33.5	41.6	33.5	41.6		
其他	Others	5.5	5.2	5.5	5.1		
自有配送中心配送商品购进额（亿元）	**Self Centralized Purchases and Delivery (100 million yuan)**	**4481.7**	**5773.6**	**4129.4**	**5318.8**	**352.3**	**454.8**
百货商店	Department Store	538.3	453.9	521.3	423.9	17.0	30.1
超级市场	Supermarket	856.3	1045.8	724.2	929.8	132.1	116.0
专业店	Professional Shop	2948.1	4090.3	2766.5	3809.4	181.6	280.9
#加油站	Gas Station	1915.2	2662.2	1875.8	2606.9	39.3	55.3
专卖店	Regie Shop	57.8	73.0	43.4	57.2	14.5	15.8
便利店	Neighbourhood Market	68.2	94.5	61.0	82.5	7.2	12.0
仓储会员店	Storage Associator Shop	2.7	3.3	2.7	3.3		
家居建材商店	Familia Building Materials Shop	10.3	12.7	10.3	12.7		
其他	Others						
非自有配送中心配送商品购进额（亿元）	**Non-self Centralized Purchases and Delivery (100 million yuan)**	**1063.9**	**1263.2**	**939.4**	**1171.1**	**124.6**	**92.1**
百货商店	Department Store	27.2	40.4	20.3	25.2	6.9	15.3
超级市场	Supermarket	620.1	675.5	519.4	618.2	100.6	57.2
专业店	Professional Shop	263.8	358.0	258.5	354.4	5.3	3.6
#加油站	Gas Station	115.2	151.3	115.2	151.3		
专卖店	Regie Shop	6.7	5.1	4.3	2.7	2.4	2.4
便利店	Neighbourhood Market	57.5	76.4	48.1	62.8	9.3	13.6
仓储会员店	Storage Associator Shop	60.0	73.8	60.0	73.8		
家居建材商店	Familia Building Materials Shop	23.2	28.9	23.2	28.9		
其他	Others	5.5	5.2	5.5	5.1		

17-27 续表 2 continued

指 标	Indicator	合 计 Total 2004	2005	直营店 Under Direct Management 2004	2005	加盟店 Through License Arrangement 2004	2005
商品销售额 （亿元）	**Total Revenue of Sales (100 million yuan)**	**8393.6**	**10668.4**	**7399.5**	**9509.6**	**994.1**	**1158.7**
百货商店	Department Store	929.8	1157.2	869.6	1077.2	60.2	79.9
超级市场	Supermarket	2341.6	2848.8	1945.2	2416.7	396.4	432.2
专业店	Professional Shop	4645.8	6085.9	4158.0	5500.2	487.9	585.8
#加油站	Gas Station	2923.5	3802.3	2869.7	3734.8	53.8	67.5
专卖店	Regie Shop	130.5	155.4	104.3	127.0	26.3	28.4
便利店	Neighbourhood Market	176.4	226.4	153.6	194.5	22.9	31.9
仓储会员店	Storage Associator Shop	70.7	86.1	70.7	86.1		0.1
家居建材商店	Familia Building Materials Shop	94.0	102.9	93.6	102.6	0.4	0.3
其他	Others	4.7	5.6	4.6	5.5	0.1	0.1
零售额 （亿元）	**Retail Sales (100 million yuan)**	**6163.1**	**7810.3**	**5285.3**	**6816.7**	**877.8**	**993.6**
百货商店	Department Store	799.5	993.1	744.4	920.8	55.1	72.3
超级市场	Supermarket	1947.8	2376.0	1561.8	1951.4	386.0	424.6
专业店	Professional Shop	2998.7	3964.3	2607.8	3524.0	390.8	440.2
#加油站	Gas Station	1637.2	2189.5	1612.7	2161.5	24.5	27.9
专卖店	Regie Shop	101.7	110.9	78.9	86.3	22.8	24.5
便利店	Neighbourhood Market	152.0	187.2	129.5	155.6	22.5	31.6
仓储会员店	Storage Associator Shop	69.6	84.6	69.6	84.6		
家居建材商店	Familia Building Materials Shop	89.6	89.0	89.2	88.7	0.4	0.3
其他	Others	4.1	5.3	4.0	5.2	0.1	0.1

17-28 按登记注册类型分限额以上连锁零售企业基本情况

Basic Conditions of Enterprises above Designated Size of Chain Stores by Status of Registration

登记注册类型	Status of Registration	门店总数(个) Number of Stores (unit)		营业面积(万平方米) Operational Area (10 000 sq.m)		从业人员(万人) Employed Persons (10 000 person)	
		2004	2005	2004	2005	2004	2005
合　计	**Total**	**77631**	**90476**	**7202.6**	**8202.7**	**128.2**	**148.8**
内资企业	**Domestic Funded Enterprises**	**73790**	**85223**	**6643.5**	**7488.9**	**111.5**	**127.7**
国有企业	State-owned Enterprises	10720	11960	1423.8	1567.6	11.8	12.6
集体企业	Collective-owned Enterprises	573	1070	22.3	28.1	0.8	1.0
股份合作企业	Cooperative Enterprises	824	946	87.2	104.0	1.5	1.9
联营企业	Joint Ownership Enterprises	284	307	23.9	32.0	1.3	1.9
国有联营企业	State Joint Ownership Enterprises	110	130	1.4	1.6	0.1	0.1
集体联营企业	Collective Joint Ownership Enterprises						
国有与集体联营企业	Joint State-collective Enterprises	165	169	19.3	27.4	1.1	1.7
其他联营企业	Other Joint Ownership Enterprises	9	8	3.2	3.0	0.1	0.1
有限责任公司	Limited Liability Corporations	25871	31701	1067.0	1334.9	36.4	43.2
国有独资公司	State Sole Funded Corporations	1285	1504	26.7	29.7	1.3	1.4
其他有限责任公司	Other Limited Liability Corporations	24586	30197	1040.3	1305.3	35.1	41.8
股份有限公司	Share-holding Corporations Ltd.	24940	27108	3483.6	3777.2	40.2	44.1
私营企业	Private Enterprises	9843	11398	528.8	636.9	19.1	22.7
私营独资企业	Private-funded Enterprises	724	745	16.5	17.7	0.8	0.8
私营合伙企业	Private Partnership Enterprises	121	179	9.5	13.2	0.2	0.3
私营有限责任公司	Private Limited Liability Corporations	8849	10314	482.3	584.3	17.6	21.0
私营股份有限公司	Private Share-holding Corporations Ltd.	149	160	20.4	21.7	0.5	0.6
其他企业	Other Enterprises	735	733	6.9	8.2	0.3	0.3
港、澳、台商投资企业	**Enterprises with Funds from Hong Kong, Macao and Taiwan**	**1272**	**1492**	**189.1**	**233.1**	**3.8**	**5.0**
合资经营企业	Joint-venture Enterprises	1205	1406	187.8	230.6	3.7	4.8
合作经营企业	Cooperative Enterprises	17	26	0.6	1.8		0.1
独资经营企业	Enterprises with Sole Investment	45	55	0.7	0.7	0.1	0.1
投资股份有限公司	Share-holding Corporations Ltd. With Investment	5	5				
外商投资企业	**Foreign Funded Enterprises**	**2569**	**3761**	**370.0**	**480.7**	**13.0**	**16.1**
中外合资经营企业	Joint-venture Enterprises	1952	2399	218.5	280.0	7.4	9.1
中外合作经营企业	Cooperative Enterprises	465	1203	138.1	183.2	5.1	6.5
外资企业	Enterprises with Sole Foreign Investment	152	159	13.3	17.5	0.5	0.5
外商投资股份有限公司	Share-holding Corporations Ltd. with Foreign Investment						

17-28 续表 continued

单位：亿元 (100 million yuan)

登记注册类型	Status of Registration	销售额 Total Sale Value 2004	销售额 Total Sale Value 2005	#零售额 Retail Sale 2004	#零售额 Retail Sale 2005
合　计	**Total**	**8393.6**	**10668.4**	**6163.1**	**7810.3**
内资企业	**Domestic Funded Enterprises**	**7341.5**	**9299.4**	**5229.7**	**6616.1**
国有企业	State-owned Enterprises	1197.6	1434.7	819.2	975.1
集体企业	Collective-owned Enterprises	28.5	28.8	26.6	27.4
股份合作企业	Cooperative Enterprises	119.7	169.2	115.3	149.9
联营企业	Joint Ownership Enterprises	133.4	138.0	94.0	116.4
国有联营企业	State Joint Ownership Enterprises	2.9	3.5	2.5	2.9
集体联营企业	Collective Joint Ownership Enterprises				
国有与集体联营企业	Joint State-collective Enterprises	128.7	132.4	89.7	111.3
其他联营企业	Other Joint Ownership Enterprises	1.8	2.2	1.8	2.2
有限责任公司	Limited Liability Corporations	1556.5	2004.2	1292.7	1644.3
国有独资公司	State Sole Funded Corporations	48.9	61.9	35.8	47.2
其他有限责任公司	Other Limited Liability Corporations	1507.6	1942.2	1256.9	1597.0
股份有限公司	Share-holding Corporations Ltd.	3536.7	4623.2	2164.9	2874.3
私营企业	Private Enterprises	761.2	893.8	709.5	821.7
私营独资企业	Private-funded Enterprises	8.6	9.3	4.8	5.1
私营合伙企业	Private Partnership Enterprises	6.0	12.6	5.9	12.6
私营有限责任公司	Private Limited Liability Corporations	733.2	858.0	685.4	790.3
私营股份有限公司	Private Share-holding Corporations Ltd.	13.4	13.9	13.4	13.8
其他企业	Other Enterprises	7.9	7.6	7.4	7.0
港、澳、台商投资企业	**Enterprises with Funds from Hong Kong, Macao and Taiwan**	**256.9**	**310.3**	**251.8**	**293.0**
合资经营企业	Joint-venture Enterprises	245.3	289.6	244.7	288.7
合作经营企业	Cooperative Enterprises	4.8	18.9	0.6	2.8
独资经营企业	Enterprises with Sole Investment	6.4	1.5	6.4	1.5
投资股份有限公司	Share-holding Corporations Ltd. with Investment	0.3	0.3	0.1	0.1
外商投资企业	**Foreign Funded Enterprises**	**795.2**	**1058.6**	**681.6**	**901.3**
中外合资经营企业	Joint-venture Enterprises	374.3	502.2	352.7	467.2
中外合作经营企业	Cooperative Enterprises	398.4	525.2	307.9	404.5
外资企业	Enterprises with Sole Foreign Investment	22.4	31.2	21.0	29.6
外商投资股份有限公司	Share-holding Corporations Ltd. with Foreign Investment				

17-29 分地区限额以上连锁零售企业基本情况

Basic Conditions of Enterprises above Designated Size of Chain Stores by Region

年份 Year 地区 Region		门店总数（个）Number of Stores (unit)	营业面积（万平方米）Operational Area (10 000 sq.m)	从业人员（万人）Employed Persons (10 000 persons)	销售总额（亿元）Total Sales Value (100 million yuan)	#零售额 Retail Sales
	2004	77631	7202.6	128.2	8393.6	6163.1
	2005	90476	8202.7	148.8	10668.4	7810.3
北京	Beijing	4726	434.1	12.1	1035.6	917.6
天津	Tianjin	1183	103.5	2.0	178.7	177.8
河北	Hebei	2100	233.9	2.6	104.9	87.1
山西	Shanxi	955	56.8	2.0	61.1	49.2
内蒙古	Inner Mongolia	1355	320.5	1.6	138.6	118.2
辽宁	Liaoning	2951	280.6	2.7	245.4	148.4
吉林	Jilin	505	18.1	0.5	14.4	12.6
黑龙江	Heilongjiang	810	32.5	1.1	57.7	49.2
上海	Shanghai	10146	728.7	23.2	1645.6	1177.8
江苏	Jiangsu	9778	510.5	20.6	1318.6	850.2
浙江	Zhejiang	8023	636.5	7.0	678.9	451.5
安徽	Anhui	4882	209.6	5.6	420.5	259.6
福建	Fujian	1924	139.5	2.6	240.8	184.8
江西	Jiangxi	2072	107.9	2.8	221.6	160.1
山东	Shandong	6816	676.9	9.1	975.9	488.6
河南	Henan	1961	92.2	3.4	66.1	58.3
湖北	Hubei	3085	245.6	6.1	391.0	314.8
湖南	Hunan	2935	549.5	6.4	324.6	313.3
广东	Guangdong	8059	1597.2	21.4	1582.1	1312.7
广西	Guangxi	2017	185.3	2.1	189.1	62.9
海南	Hainan	323	5.5	0.3	30.0	30.0
重庆	Chongqing	4663	214.7	4.0	208.0	140.7
四川	Sichuan	3083	101.0	2.7	106.4	91.8
贵州	Guizhou	1199	210.4	1.1	113.8	88.2
云南	Yunnan	1731	38.8	1.9	50.1	38.7
西藏	Tibet	8				
陕西	Shaanxi	612	23.3	1.8	116.7	82.4
甘肃	Gansu	1329	259.3	0.5	82.0	81.8
青海	Qinghai	119	11.3	0.2	5.9	5.8
宁夏	Ningxia	361	105.0	0.6	33.9	28.1
新疆	Xinjiang	666	73.7	0.6	30.3	28.2

注：门店总数全国总计中含港澳台地区和国外。
a) Total number of stores includes that from Hong Kong, Macao and Taiwan province and foreign countries.

17-29 续表 continued

年份 Year 地区 Region		购进总额 (亿元) Total Purchases (100 million yuan)	统一配送 商品购进额 (亿元) Centralized Purchase and Delivery (100 million yuan)	自有配送 商品购进额 Self Centralized Purchase and Delivery	非自有配送 商品购进额 Non-self Centralized Purchase and Delivery
	2004	7130.1	5545.6	4481.7	1063.9
	2005	9044.1	7036.8	5773.6	1263.2
北　京	Beijing	925.0	422.7	192.1	230.6
天　津	Tianjin	180.9	159.1	152.7	6.3
河　北	Hebei	99.7	69.0	59.0	10.1
山　西	Shanxi	55.9	51.1	50.8	0.3
内蒙古	Inner Mongolia	123.8	122.8	122.8	
辽　宁	Liaoning	187.8	16.9	15.7	1.1
吉　林	Jilin	13.9	8.9	8.9	0.1
黑龙江	Heilongjiang	51.8	45.7	40.5	5.2
上　海	Shanghai	1054.8	999.3	484.5	514.8
江　苏	Jiangsu	1093.8	899.4	792.0	107.4
浙　江	Zhejiang	626.9	570.6	534.9	35.6
安　徽	Anhui	397.7	289.3	286.6	2.7
福　建	Fujian	212.8	169.9	150.0	20.0
江　西	Jiangxi	204.1	195.0	60.4	134.7
山　东	Shandong	827.6	639.4	611.4	28.0
河　南	Henan	64.4	50.7	46.6	4.1
湖　北	Hubei	299.3	200.4	200.2	0.2
湖　南	Hunan	244.1	111.2	111.1	
广　东	Guangdong	1498.2	1198.4	1072.7	125.7
广　西	Guangxi	169.7	156.8	152.9	3.9
海　南	Hainan	28.5	27.9	27.8	0.1
重　庆	Chongqing	187.9	157.4	155.4	2.0
四　川	Sichuan	93.2	92.3	77.4	14.9
贵　州	Guizhou	104.8	94.2	94.1	0.1
云　南	Yunnan	49.9	49.1	40.6	8.5
西　藏	Tibet				
陕　西	Shaanxi	109.0	105.1	98.3	6.8
甘　肃	Gansu	79.4	79.0	79.0	
青　海	Qinghai	2.8	2.8	2.8	
宁　夏	Ningxia	30.1	28.2	28.2	
新　疆	Xinjiang	26.4	24.2	24.2	

17-30 按业态分限额以上连锁餐饮企业基本情况

Basic Conditions of Enterprises above Designated Size of Chain Catering Services by Business Categories

指　标	Indicator	合计 Total		直营店 Under Direct Management		加盟店 Through License Arrangement	
		2004	2005	2004	2005	2004	2005
门店总数　（个）	**Number of Stores (unit)**	**7578**	**8514**	**4952**	**5518**	**2626**	**2996**
正　餐	Restaurant	2906	3208	1069	1193	1837	2015
快　餐	Snack Counter	3719	4178	3511	3904	208	274
茶　馆	Tea Shop	192	200	192	200		
咖啡店	Cafe	222	293	115	146	107	147
其他餐饮	Others	539	635	65	75	474	560
营业面积（万平方米）	**Operational Area (10 000 sq.m)**	**352.6**	**390.8**	**226.1**	**247.5**	**126.5**	**143.2**
正　餐	Restaurant	238.3	257.2	124.7	131.6	113.5	125.6
快　餐	Snack Counter	103.2	118.8	96.9	110.3	6.4	8.5
茶　馆	Tea Shop	1.1	1.1	1.1	1.1		
咖啡店	Cafe	7.4	9.8	1.9	2.4	5.5	7.4
其他餐饮	Others	2.6	3.9	1.5	2.1	1.1	1.7
餐位数　（万个）	**Number of Dining-seat (unit)**	**180.1**	**200.4**	**79.7**	**88.3**	**100.4**	**112.2**
正　餐	Restaurant	138.8	151.8	42.6	45.6	96.1	106.3
快　餐	Snack Counter	38.5	44.9	35.9	41.4	2.5	3.5
茶　馆	Tea Shop	0.3	0.4	0.3	0.4		
咖啡店	Cafe	2.4	3.2	0.6	0.8	1.7	2.4
其他餐饮	Others	0.1	0.1	0.1	0.1		
从业人员　（万人）	**Employed Persons (10 000 persons)**	**37.9**	**42.6**	**26.5**	**29.1**	**11.4**	**13.5**
正　餐	Restaurant	19.9	22.4	9.6	10.4	10.3	12.0
快　餐	Snack Counter	17.1	19.0	16.6	18.3	0.6	0.7
茶　馆	Tea Shop	0.1	0.1	0.1	0.1		
咖啡店	Cafe	0.5	0.7	0.2	0.2	0.4	0.5
其他餐饮	Others	0.3	0.4	0.1	0.1	0.2	0.2
餐费收入　（亿元）	**Dining Revenue of Sales (100 million yuan)**	**345.3**	**385.3**	**259.3**	**284.1**	**86.1**	**101.2**
正　餐	Restaurant	164.6	187.0	86.0	96.2	78.5	90.8
快　餐	Snack Counter	170.9	186.1	166.5	179.6	4.4	6.5
茶　馆	Tea Shop	0.3	0.3	0.3	0.3		
咖啡店	Cafe	5.1	6.9	3.2	4.3	1.9	2.6
其他餐饮	Others	4.4	4.9	3.2	3.7	1.2	1.3

17-30 续表 continued

指 标	Indicator	合计 Total 2004	合计 Total 2005	直营店 Under Direct Management 2004	直营店 Under Direct Management 2005	加盟店 Through License Arrangement 2004	加盟店 Through License Arrangement 2005
配送中心数 （个）	**Number of Distribution Centers (unit)**	**271**	**299**	**177**	**186**	**94**	**113**
正 餐	Restaurant	103	107	68	69	35	38
快 餐	Snack Counter	118	127	101	109	17	18
茶 馆	Tea Shop	2	2	2	2		
咖啡店	Cafe	43	58	2	2	41	56
其他餐饮	Others	5	5	4	4	1	1
购进总额 （亿元）	**Total Purchases (100 million yuan)**	**124.6**	**143.3**	**84.9**	**87.4**	**39.7**	**55.9**
正 餐	Restaurant	67.9	86.7	30.0	33.3	37.9	53.3
快 餐	Snack Counter	54.6	54.1	53.5	52.4	1.1	1.7
茶 馆	Tea Shop	0.1	0.1	0.1	0.1		
咖啡店	Cafe	0.8	1.1	0.3	0.3	0.5	0.7
其他餐饮	Others	1.2	1.4	1.1	1.2	0.2	0.2
统一配送商品购进额 （亿元）	**Centralized Purchases and Delivery (100 million yuan)**	**89.3**	**98.7**	**63.2**	**63.6**	**26.1**	**35.1**
正 餐	Restaurant	36.4	46.5	11.6	13.1	24.8	33.4
快 餐	Snack Counter	51.3	50.4	50.3	48.9	1.0	1.4
茶 馆	Tea Shop						
咖啡店	Café	0.3	0.4	0.3	0.3	0.1	0.1
其他餐饮	Others	1.2	1.4	1.1	1.2	0.2	0.2
自有配送商品购进额 （亿元）	**Self Centralized Purchases and Delivery (100 million yuan)**	**64.7**	**71.3**	**51.6**	**50.8**	**13.1**	**20.5**
正 餐	Restaurant	21.0	29.6	8.9	10.5	12.1	19.1
快 餐	Snack Counter	42.3	40.0	41.6	38.9	0.8	1.1
茶 馆	Tea Shop						
咖啡店	Cafe	0.2	0.3	0.1	0.2	0.1	0.1
其他餐饮	Others	1.2	1.4	1.0	1.2	0.2	0.2
非自有配送商品购进额（亿元）	**Non-self Centralized Purchases and Delivery (100 million yuan)**	**24.6**	**27.4**	**11.7**	**12.8**	**12.9**	**14.7**
正 餐	Restaurant	15.4	16.9	2.7	2.6	12.7	14.3
快 餐	Snack Counter	9.0	10.3	8.8	10.0	0.2	0.3
茶 馆	Tea Shop						
咖啡店	Cafe	0.2	0.2	0.2	0.2		
其他餐饮	Others						

17-31 按登记注册类型分限额以上连锁餐饮企业基本情况

Basic Conditions of Enterprises above Designated Size of Chain Catering Services by Status of Registration

登记注册类型	Status of Registration	门店总数（个）Number of Stores (unit)		营业面积（万平方米）Operational Area (10 000 sq.m)		从业人员（万人）Employed Persons (10 000 persons)	
		2004	2005	2004	2005	2004	2005
合　　计	**Total**	**7578**	**8514**	**352.6**	**390.8**	**37.9**	**42.6**
内资企业	**Domestic Funded Enterprises**	**5111**	**5488**	**254.8**	**273.6**	**20.5**	**22.6**
国有企业	State-owned Enterprises	541	614	8.7	10.1	0.4	0.5
集体企业	Collective-owned Enterprises						
股份合作企业	Cooperative Enterprises	54	51	3.0	3.4	0.3	0.3
联营企业	Joint Ownership Enterprises						
国有联营企业	State Joint Ownership Enterprises						
集体联营企业	Collective Joint Ownership Enterprises						
国有与集体联营企业	Joint State-collective Enterprises						
其他联营企业	Other Joint Ownership Enterprises						
有限责任公司	Limited Liability Corporations	2057	2104	120.0	124.8	11.5	12.5
国有独资公司	State Sole Funded Corporations						
其他有限责任公司	Other Limited Liability Corporations	2057	2104	120.0	124.8	11.5	12.5
股份有限公司	Share-holding Corporations Ltd.	113	152	14.7	18.3	0.7	0.9
私营企业	Private Enterprises	2326	2548	106.8	115.4	7.5	8.3
私营独资企业	Private-funded Enterprises	342	392	18.5	18.7	1.3	1.3
私营合伙企业	Private Partnership Enterprises	41	52	4.3	5.1	0.3	0.2
私营有限责任公司	Private Limited Liability Corporations	1870	1949	79.8	85.6	5.5	6.1
私营股份有限公司	Private Share-holding Corporations Ltd.	73	155	4.2	6.0	0.3	0.6
其他企业	Other Enterprises	20	19	1.5	1.5	0.1	0.1
港、澳、台商投资企业	**Enterprises with Funds from Hong Kong, Macao and Taiwan**	**491**	**574**	**21.1**	**24.9**	**5.6**	**5.8**
合资经营企业	Joint-venture Enterprises	256	315	13.2	16.0	1.6	1.7
合作经营企业	Cooperative Enterprises	39	47	2.6	3.0	0.2	0.2
独资经营企业	Enterprises with Sole Investment	196	212	5.2	5.9	3.8	3.8
投资股份有限公司	Share-holding Corporations Ltd. with Investmen						
外商投资企业	**Foreign Funded Enterprises**	**1976**	**2452**	**76.8**	**92.3**	**11.8**	**14.2**
中外合资经营企业	Joint-venture Enterprises	687	816	27.7	32.7	4.4	5.0
中外合作经营企业	Cooperative Enterprises	411	520	13.2	16.3	2.5	3.2
外资企业	Enterprises with Sole Foreign Investment	878	1116	35.8	43.3	4.9	5.9
外商投资股份有限公司	Share-holding Corporations Ltd. With Foreign Investment						

17-31 续表 continued

登记注册类型	Status of Registration	餐位数（万个）Number of Dining-seat (10 000 units)		餐费收入（亿元）Dining Revenue of Sales (100 million yuan)	
		2004	2005	2004	2005
合　计	**Total**	**180.1**	**200.4**	**345.3**	**385.3**
内资企业	**Domestic Funded Enterprises**	**143.2**	**156.2**	**164.8**	**184.4**
国有企业	State-owned Enterprises	1.3	1.5	7.1	7.9
集体企业	Collective-owned Enterprises				
股份合作企业	Cooperative Enterprises	0.9	1.0	2.6	2.7
联营企业	Joint Ownership Enterprises				
国有联营企业	State Joint Ownership Enterprises				
集体联营企业	Collective Joint Ownership Enterprises				
国有与集体联营企业	Joint State-collective Enterprises				
其他联营企业	Other Joint Ownership Enterprises				
有限责任公司	Limited Liability Corporations	112.9	123.0	93.8	107.4
国有独资公司	State Sole Funded Corporations				
其他有限责任公司	Other Limited Liability Corporations	112.9	123.0	93.8	107.4
股份有限公司	Share-holding Corporations Ltd.	2.6	3.0	10.2	11.4
私营企业	Private Enterprises	24.8	27.0	50.4	54.2
私营独资企业	Private-funded Enterprises	5.8	6.3	7.7	7.5
私营合伙企业	Private Partnership Enterprises	0.8	1.0	1.9	2.1
私营有限责任公司	Private Limited Liability Corporations	17.3	18.4	38.7	40.5
私营股份有限公司	Private Share-holding Corporations Ltd.	0.8	1.2	2.0	4.1
其他企业	Other Enterprises	0.7	0.7	0.7	0.7
港、澳、台商投资企业	**Enterprises with Funds from Hong Kong, Macao and Taiwan**	**7.6**	**8.9**	**33.1**	**34.9**
合资经营企业	Joint-venture Enterprises	4.7	5.8	18.0	19.2
合作经营企业	Cooperative Enterprises	0.7	0.9	3.6	3.6
独资经营企业	Enterprises with Sole Investment	2.1	2.3	11.5	12.1
投资股份有限公司	Share-holding Corporations Ltd. with Investment				
外商投资企业	**Foreign Funded Enterprises**	**29.3**	**35.4**	**147.5**	**165.9**
中外合资经营企业	Joint-venture Enterprises	11.2	13.1	58.2	64.9
中外合作经营企业	Cooperative Enterprises	4.9	5.9	28.0	34.7
外资企业	Enterprises with Sole Foreign Investment	13.3	16.3	61.4	66.4
外商投资股份有限公司	Share-holding Corporations Ltd. with Foreign Investment				

17-32 分地区限额以上连锁餐饮企业基本情况

Basic Conditions of Enterprises above Designated Size of Chain Catering Services by Region

年 份 地 区	Year Region	门店总数 (个) Number of Stores (unit)	营业面积 (万平方米) Operational Area (10 000 sq.m)	从业人员 (万人) Employed Persons (10 000 persons)	餐位数 (万个) Number of Dining-seat (10 000 units)	餐费收入 (亿元) Dining Revenue of Sales (100 million yuan)
	2004	7578	352.6	37.9	180.1	345.3
	2005	8514	390.8	42.6	200.4	385.3
北 京	Beijing	1066	51.8	4.9	15.3	54.6
天 津	Tianjin	643	11.8	0.9	2.6	15.7
河 北	Hebei	233	0.2			0.1
山 西	Shanxi	161	4.2	0.3	1.5	3.6
内蒙古	Inner Mongolia	125	21.8	5.1	99.1	52.8
辽 宁	Liaoning	201	8.0	1.3	2.5	13.9
吉 林	Jilin	64				
黑龙江	Heilongjiang	86	0.6	0.1	0.4	1.0
上 海	Shanghai	679	24.7	3.1	7.6	36.2
江 苏	Jiangsu	1113	15.8	2.4	5.8	25.1
浙 江	Zhejiang	473	24.6	2.3	7.7	26.1
安 徽	Anhui	128	9.5	0.4	1.4	3.3
福 建	Fujian	262	7.6	0.8	2.4	9.6
江 西	Jiangxi	52	2.4	0.3	1.1	2.1
山 东	Shandong	355	11.3	0.9	3.6	8.5
河 南	Henan	242	5.8	0.5	1.7	3.2
湖 北	Hubei	250	22.1	2.0	5.4	15.4
湖 南	Hunan	115	4.2	0.5	1.0	4.2
广 东	Guangdong	959	43.3	7.7	13.1	53.4
广 西	Guangxi	20				
海 南	Hainan	22	0.3		0.1	0.3
重 庆	Chongqing	285	98.4	7.3	21.1	42.6
四 川	Sichuan	377	7.4	0.8	2.8	6.1
贵 州	Guizhou	55	2.2	0.2	0.6	1.3
云 南	Yunnan	163	5.0	0.3	1.8	2.9
西 藏	Tibet	8				
陕 西	Shaanxi	129	3.6	0.2	1.1	1.0
甘 肃	Gansu	55	1.2	0.1	0.4	0.9
青 海	Qinghai	32	0.7		0.1	0.2
宁 夏	Ningxia	14				
新 疆	Xinjiang	141	2.2	0.1	0.4	1.0

注：门店总数全国总计中含港澳台地区和国外。

a) Number of stores includes that of Hong Kong, Macao and Taiwan province and foreign countries.

17-32 续表 continued

年份 Year 地区 Region	购进总额（亿元）Total Purchases (100 million yuan)	统一配送商品购进额（亿元）Centralized Purchase and Delivery (100 million yuan)	自有配送商品购进额 Self Centralized Purchase and Delivery	非自有配送商品购进额 Non-self Centralized Purchase and Delivery
2004	124.6	89.3	64.7	24.6
2005	143.3	98.7	71.3	27.4
北京 Beijing	21.1	12.1	7.5	4.6
天津 Tianjin	0.1	0.1		
河北 Hebei	0.1			
山西 Shanxi	1.1	0.7	0.7	
内蒙古 Inner Mongolia	30.3	19.7	12.8	6.9
辽宁 Liaoning	1.3	1.3	1.3	
吉林 Jilin				
黑龙江 Heilongjiang				
上海 Shanghai	0.6	0.6	0.6	
江苏 Jiangsu	12.7	11.4	8.8	2.6
浙江 Zhejiang	11.1	8.7	8.4	0.3
安徽 Anhui	1.3	0.8	0.6	0.1
福建 Fujian	2.2	2.2	0.9	1.3
江西 Jiangxi	0.6	0.3	0.3	
山东 Shandong	3.7	3.7	3.7	
河南 Henan	0.4	0.2	0.2	
湖北 Hubei	0.7	0.5	0.5	
湖南 Hunan	1.6	0.1	0.1	
广东 Guangdong	23.5	15.9	13.9	2.0
广西 Guangxi				
海南 Hainan	0.2			
重庆 Chongqing	25.9	16.9	8.3	8.7
四川 Sichuan	2.1	2.1	1.3	0.8
贵州 Guizhou	0.8			
云南 Yunnan	0.9	0.8	0.8	
西藏 Tibet				
陕西 Shaanxi	0.3	0.3	0.3	0.1
甘肃 Gansu	0.4	0.1	0.1	
青海 Qinghai	0.1	0.1	0.1	
宁夏 Ningxia				
新疆 Xinjiang	0.1	0.1	0.1	

17-33 按登记注册类型分限额以上连锁住宿企业基本情况

Basic Conditions of Enterprises above Designated Size in Chain Hotels by Status of Registration

登记注册类型	Status of Registration	门店总数（个）Number of Stores (unit)		营业面积（万平方米）Operational Area (10 000 sq.m)		从业人员（万人）Employed Persons (10 000 persons)	
		2004	2005	2004	2005	2004	2005
合　计	**Total**	**69**	**84**	**46.9**	**68.8**	**0.7**	**0.9**
内资企业	**Domestic Funded Enterprises**	**61**	**68**	**39.1**	**56.6**	**0.6**	**0.7**
国有企业	State-owned Enterprises	6	6	1.1	1.1		
集体企业	Collective-owned Enterprises	2	2				
股份合作企业	Cooperative Enterprises	4	4	0.2	0.3		
联营企业	Joint Ownership Enterprises						
国有联营企业	State Joint Ownership Enterprises						
集体联营企业	Collective Joint Ownership Enterprises						
国有与集体联营企业	Joint State-collective Enterprises						
其他联营企业	Other Joint Ownership Enterprises						
有限责任公司	Limited Liability Corporations	34	41	35.6	53.0	0.5	0.7
国有独资公司	State Sole Funded Corporations						
其他有限责任公司	Other Limited Liability Corporations	34	41	35.6	53.0	0.5	0.7
股份有限公司	Share-holding Corporations Ltd.	6	6	0.5	0.5		
私营企业	Private Enterprises	9	9	1.6	1.6		
私营独资企业	Private-funded Enterprises	2	2	0.2	0.2		
私营合伙企业	Private Partnership Enterprises						
私营有限责任公司	Private Limited Liability Corporations	7	7	1.4	1.4		
私营股份有限公司	Private Share-holding Corporations Ltd.						
其他企业	Other Enterprises						
港、澳、台商投资企业	**Enterprises with Funds from Hong Kong, Macao and Taiwan**	**7**	**15**	**2.9**	**7.4**		**0.1**
合资经营企业	Joint-venture Enterprises	7	15	2.9	7.4		0.1
合作经营企业	Cooperative Enterprises						
独资经营企业	Enterprises with Sole Investment						
投资股份有限公司	Share-holding Corporations Ltd. with Investment						
外商投资企业	**Foreign Funded Enterprises**	**1**	**1**	**4.8**	**4.8**	**0.1**	**0.1**
中外合资经营企业	Joint-venture Enterprises						
中外合作经营企业	Cooperative Enterprises						
外资企业	Enterprises with Sole Foreign Investment	1	1	4.8	4.8	0.1	0.1
外商投资股份有限公司	Share-holding Corporations Ltd. With Foreign Investment						

17-33 续表 continued

登记注册类型	Status of Registration	床位数（个）Number of Beds (unit)		客房收入（亿元）Revenue from Hotel Rooms (100 million yuan)	
		2004	2005	2004	2005
合　计	**Total**	**11115**	**14733**	**4.2**	**5.7**
内资企业	**Domestic Funded Enterprises**	**9362**	**11333**	**2.8**	**3.4**
国有企业	State-owned Enterprises	604	604	0.1	0.1
集体企业	Collective-owned Enterprises	80	80		
股份合作企业	Cooperative Enterprises	215	270		
联营企业	Joint Ownership Enterprises				
国有联营企业	State Joint Ownership Enterprises				
集体联营企业	Collective Joint Ownership Enterprises				
国有与集体联营企业	Joint State-collective Enterprises				
其他联营企业	Other Joint Ownership Enterprises				
有限责任公司	Limited Liability Corporations	6235	8147	2.2	2.9
国有独资公司	State Sole Funded Corporations				
其他有限责任公司	Other Limited Liability Corporations	6235	8147	2.2	2.9
股份有限公司	Share-holding Corporations Ltd.	1275	1279	0.3	0.3
私营企业	Private Enterprises	953	953	0.1	0.1
私营独资企业	Private-funded Enterprises	205	205		
私营合伙企业	Private Partnership Enterprises				
私营有限责任公司	Private Limited Liability Corporations	748	748	0.1	0.1
私营股份有限公司	Private Share-holding Corporations Ltd.				
其他企业	Other Enterprises				
港、澳、台商投资企业	**Enterprises with Funds from Hong Kong, Macao and Taiwan**	**1170**	**2817**	**0.3**	**1.1**
合资经营企业	Joint-venture Enterprises	1170	2817	0.3	1.1
合作经营企业	Cooperative Enterprises				
独资经营企业	Enterprises with Sole Investment				
投资股份有限公司	Share-holding Corporations Ltd. with Investment				
外商投资企业	**Foreign Funded Enterprises**	**583**	**583**	**1.1**	**1.3**
中外合资经营企业	Joint-venture Enterprises				
中外合作经营企业	Cooperative Enterprises				
外资企业	Enterprises with Sole Foreign Investment	583	583	1.1	1.3
外商投资股份有限公司	Share-holding Corporations Ltd. with Foreign Investment				

17-34 分地区限额以上连锁住宿企业基本情况

Basic Conditions of Enterprises above Designated Size of Chain Hotels by Region

年份 地区	Year Region	门店总数（个） Number of Stores (unit)	营业面积（万平方米） Operational Area (10 000 sq.m)	从业人员（万人） Employed Persons (10 000 persons)	床位数（个） Number of Beds (unit)	客房收入（亿元） Revenue from Hotel Rooms (100 million yuan)
	2004	69	46.9	0.7	11115	4.2
	2005	84	68.8	0.9	14733	5.7
北京	Beijing	68	18.2	0.2	7910	1.8
天津	Tianjin					
河北	Hebei					
山西	Shanxi					
内蒙古	Inner Mongolia					
辽宁	Liaoning					
吉林	Jilin					
黑龙江	Heilongjiang					
上海	Shanghai					
江苏	Jiangsu					
浙江	Zhejiang	15	45.8	0.6	6240	2.7
安徽	Anhui					
福建	Fujian					
江西	Jiangxi					
山东	Shandong	1	4.8	0.1	583	1.3
河南	Henan					
湖北	Hubei					
湖南	Hunan					
广东	Guangdong					
广西	Guangxi					
海南	Hainan					
重庆	Chongqing					
四川	Sichuan					
贵州	Guizhou					
云南	Yunnan					
西藏	Tibet					
陕西	Shaanxi					
甘肃	Gansu					
青海	Qinghai					
宁夏	Ningxia					
新疆	Xinjiang					

17-35 亿元以上商品交易市场基本情况（2005年）
Basic Statistics on Commodity Exchange Markets of Turnover above 100 Million Yuan (2005)

市　　场	Market	市场数量（个）Number of Markets (unit)	摊位数（个）Number of Booths (unit)	营业面积（万平方米）Operating Area (10 000 sq.m)	成交额（亿元）Turnover (100 million yuan)	批　发 Wholesale Trade	零　售 Retail Trade
全　　国	**National Total**	**3323**	**2248803**	**13140.8**	**30020.9**	**24544.2**	**5476.7**
综合市场	**Comprehensive Markets**	**767**	**716587**	**2792.5**	**6077.0**	**4338.0**	**1739.1**
工业品综合市场	Industrial Products Comprehensive Markets	228	369070	1782.8	3665.0	3026.4	638.6
农产品综合市场	Farmer Produces Comprehensive Markets	539	347517	1009.7	2412.0	1311.6	1100.4
专业市场	**Special Markets**	**2214**	**1302933**	**8755.4**	**21281.2**	**17993.0**	**3288.1**
纺织品服装鞋帽市场	Textile, Garments, Footgear, and Hats Markets	409	475842	1392.7	4731.7	4185.4	546.2
食品饮料烟酒市场	Food, Beverages, Tobacco, and Liquor Markets	105	66860	299.1	682.3	642.0	40.3
药材药品及医疗器材市场	Medicinal Materials, Medicine and Medical Instruments Markets	19	22447	82.6	174.4	97.7	76.7
家具市场	Furniture Markets	71	36260	485.9	318.6	172.8	145.7
小商品市场	Merchandise Markets	83	63545	175.9	714.1	652.3	61.8
文化音像书报杂志市场	Culture, Video Books, Newspapers and Magazines Markets	24	8862	47.8	190.2	120.7	69.5
旧货市场	Second Hand Markets	14	5133	26.5	47.2	43.7	3.6
机动车市场	Motor Vehicle Markets	169	34141	620.1	1648.2	892.6	755.6
金属材料市场	Metal Materials Markets	172	45655	823.1	5087.4	4836.3	251.1
煤炭市场	Coal and Charcoal Markets	9	1374	930.4	43.9	42.3	1.6
木材市场	Wood Markets	44	12963	353.4	352.5	291.6	60.9
建材装饰材料市场	Building and Decoration Materials Markets	274	108561	1257.9	1843.4	1394.9	448.5
粮油市场	Grain and Oil Markets	146	58503	336.8	687.6	603.5	84.2
干鲜果品市场	Dried and Fresh Melons and Fruits Markets	102	41993	290.5	634.9	575.4	59.5
水产品市场	Aquatic Products Markets	69	39286	164.9	729.7	673.9	55.9
蔬菜市场	Vegetables Markets	265	174748	797.3	1688.7	1440.6	248.0
肉食禽蛋市场	Meat, Poultry and Eggs Markets	116	43784	168.9	522.6	367.4	155.2
土畜产品市场	Local and Livestock Products Markets	19	26081	68.6	407.7	368.4	39.3
农业生产资料市场	Agricultural Productions Markets	25	6269	83.8	220.0	215.0	5.0
计算机市场	Computer Markets	54	19854	70.8	402.2	241.1	161.1
通讯器材市场	Communication Appliances	13	1960	10.7	67.6	49.2	18.4
花卉市场	Flower Markets	12	8812	267.5	86.4	86.4	
其他市场	**Others Markets**	**342**	**229283**	**1592.9**	**2662.7**	**2213.2**	**449.5**

17-36 亿元以上商品交易市场摊位分类情况（2005年）

Classification of Commodity Transaction Markets of Turnover above 100 Million Yuan (2005)

类别	Classification	摊位数（个）Number of Booths (unit)	成交额（亿元）Turnover (100 million yuan)	批发 Wholesale Trade	零售 Retail Trade
全国	**National Total**	**2248803**	**30020.9**	**24544.2**	**5476.7**
食品、饮料、烟酒类	Food, Beverages, Tobacco and Liquor	781857	7506.2	5673.3	1832.9
粮油类	Grain and Oil	119216	1225.6	901.8	323.9
肉禽蛋类	Meat,Poultry and Eggs	117385	1068.5	557.6	510.8
其他食品类	Other Food	474179	4537.7	3675.0	862.7
饮料类	Beverages	35291	291.5	241.6	49.9
烟酒类	Tobacco and Liquor	35786	383.0	297.3	85.7
服装鞋帽、针、纺织品类	Clothing, Shoes, Hats and Textiles	671133	5811.9	5006.9	805.0
服装类	Clothing	394056	2521.8	1959.8	562.1
鞋帽类	Shoes and Hats	103492	646.6	526.3	120.2
针、纺织品类	Knitwear and Textiles	173585	2643.5	2520.8	122.7
化妆品类	Cosmetics	26635	191.6	154.0	37.6
金银珠宝类	Gold,Silver and Jewelry	6597	110.7	104.9	5.8
日用品类	Articles for Daily Use	161884	1462.7	1267.7	195.0
#洗涤用品类	Washing Articles	33814	312.7	284.5	28.2
儿童玩具类	Children Toys	12551	92.4	83.3	9.1
五金、电料类	Hardware & Electrical Materials	53632	593.0	491.0	102.0
体育、娱乐用品类	Sports & Recreational Articles	9760	97.5	88.2	9.3
书报杂志类	Newspapers and Magazines	3681	45.6	31.2	14.4
电子出版物及音像制品类	E-journals and Video Products	5595	65.2	44.5	20.7
家用电器和音像器材类	Household Appliances and Video Appliance	31910	562.6	443.5	119.1
中西药品类	Traditional Chinese and Western Medicines	20575	192.6	108.0	84.6
#西药类	Western Medicines	1407	13.9	4.2	9.7
中草药及中成药类	Traditional Chinese Medicines	18835	171.0	98.2	72.8
文化办公用品类	Cultural and Offices Appliances	36601	475.1	279.2	195.9
家具类	Furniture	45496	457.5	239.6	217.9
通讯器材类	Communication Appliances	6684	117.5	75.9	41.6
煤炭及制品类	Coal and Related Products	1644	56.5	54.8	1.7
木材及制品类	Wood and Wooden Products	21309	520.8	439.5	81.3
石油及制品类	Petroleum and Related Products	1161	36.8	33.7	3.0
化工材料及制品类	Chemical Materials and Related Products	18589	1095.6	1077.6	18.0
#化肥类	Fertilizers	614	42.7	41.1	1.6
金属材料类	Metal Materials	44510	5152.3	4885.7	266.6
建筑及装潢材料类	Building and Decoration Materials	94093	1446.7	1026.1	420.6
机电产品及设备类	Mechanical & Electrical Products	37606	786.4	714.9	71.5
#农机类	Agricultural Machineries	4198	112.0	103.7	8.3
汽车类	Automobiles	26733	1423.0	739.6	683.4
种子饲料类	Seeds and Feedstuff	1927	53.3	44.5	8.9
棉麻类	Cotton and Hemp	1695	78.0	75.9	2.2
其他类	Others	137496	1681.7	1443.9	237.7

17-37 各地区亿元以上商品交易市场基本情况

Basic Statistics on Commodity Exchange Markets of Turnover above 100 Million Yuan by Region

年 份 Year 地 区 Region		市场数量(个) Number of Markets (unit)	摊位数(个) Number of Booths (unit)	营业面积(万平方米) Operating Area (10 000 sq.m)	成交额(亿元) Turnover (100 million yuan)	批发 Wholesale Trade	零售 Retail Trade
	2000	3087	2115115	8261.6	16358.9	11648.0	4710.9
	2001	3273	2200662	9397.3	17719.1	12562.5	5156.5
	2002	3258	2190814	10313.2	19840.0	15450.9	4389.2
	2003	3265	2148866	10984.0	21514.5	16832.6	4681.9
	2004	3365	2229818	12477.5	26102.7	21116.9	4985.8
	2005	3323	2248803	13140.8	30020.9	24544.2	5476.7
北 京	Beijing	80	55637	411.4	791.6	624.2	167.4
天 津	Tianjin	45	33256	166.1	568.6	499.2	69.4
河 北	Hebei	240	286611	2049.1	2322.9	1936.4	386.5
山 西	Shanxi	22	17139	44.9	113.5	94.6	18.8
内蒙古	Inner Mongolia	32	19862	142.2	178.2	132.1	46.1
辽 宁	Liaoning	160	153937	548.3	1434.0	1023.8	410.2
吉 林	Jilin	48	57632	231.6	306.2	221.9	84.3
黑龙江	Heilongjiang	57	42532	114.8	253.4	198.1	55.3
上 海	Shanghai	51	25368	112.5	2197.0	2066.6	130.4
江 苏	Jiangsu	459	242054	1718.0	4814.6	4031.5	783.2
浙 江	Zhejiang	520	331830	1428.1	6257.3	5255.3	1002.0
安 徽	Anhui	105	68945	379.3	779.8	656.0	123.8
福 建	Fujian	105	35298	157.2	600.3	414.7	185.6
江 西	Jiangxi	72	42592	208.9	514.3	429.7	84.6
山 东	Shandong	378	222348	1769.3	2820.0	2345.1	474.9
河 南	Henan	97	68115	357.2	604.3	501.9	102.5
湖 北	Hubei	112	52776	280.6	507.4	359.8	147.6
湖 南	Hunan	124	101079	307.8	859.4	511.6	347.8
广 东	Guangdong	268	128757	831.5	1940.5	1533.6	407.0
广 西	Guangxi	56	42944	134.8	314.7	224.9	89.8
海 南	Hainan	8	3954	5.9	22.0	10.4	11.6
重 庆	Chongqing	76	53941	284.1	683.4	558.8	124.6
四 川	Sichuan	54	48022	186.5	315.2	251.9	63.3
贵 州	Guizhou	19	15613	35.9	126.5	110.6	15.9
云 南	Yunnan	26	17579	120.8	190.3	173.0	17.3
西 藏	Tibet						
陕 西	Shaanxi	15	13547	23.2	74.4	70.1	4.3
甘 肃	Gansu	35	30493	135.2	120.3	83.8	36.5
青 海	Qinghai	8	3905	16.4	20.2	16.4	3.8
宁 夏	Ningxia	16	11048	745.2	76.0	63.7	12.2
新 疆	Xinjiang	35	21989	194.1	214.6	144.6	70.0

主要统计指标解释

社会消费品零售总额 指批发和零售业、餐饮业、新闻出版业、邮政业和其他服务业等，售予城乡居民用于生活消费的商品和社会集团用于公共消费的商品之总量。社会消费品零售总额包括：

一、批发和零售业企业（单位）：

1.售予城乡居民的各种生活消费品；

2.售予入境旅游的外国人、华侨、港澳台同胞的各类商品；

3.售予行政事业单位、社会团体、军队和武警等机构的商品，以及以零售方式售予各类企业的商品。具体包括：用于非生产和社会交往的办公用品，如通讯设备、计算器具和设备、电讯网络设备、文印设备、音像视听器材和设备、纸张、本册、文具及装订文印材料、家具、日用电器、针纺织品、清洁卫生用品、文体用品、奖品、纪念品、礼品等；供内部人员乘坐的交通工具和燃料；用于办公设施修缮的各类配件、材料、工具等；用于取暖和防暑降温的设备、燃料、材料及食品等；专用于教学的用品和设备；非营利医疗机构的中、西药品、中药材和医疗设备器材；非专用的劳动保护用品；不对外营业的内部食堂用的餐具、炊具、设备、清洁卫生工具和食品、燃料等；军队、武警用于其人员生活的衣着品和个人用品；其他各类非生产性设备和用品。

二、餐饮业出售的主食、菜肴、烟酒饮料和其他商品。

三、新闻出版业、邮政业售予城乡居民、企事业单位、军队和武警等机构的书报杂志、音像制品、邮品等。

四、其他服务业出售的食品、烟酒饮料、服装鞋帽、日常生活用品、医药保健用品、艺术品、工艺美术品、玩具、殡葬用品以及其他消费品。

批发零售业商品购、销、存总额 指各种登记注册类型的批发、零售业企业(单位)以本企业(单位)为总体的，从国内、国外市场购进的商品总量，销售和出口的商品总量、库存商品总量等情况。该指标可以反映商品流转过程中商品的购进、销售、库存之间的比例关系和存在的问题。

商品购进总额 指从本企业(单位)以外的单位和个人购进(包括从境外直接进口)作为转卖或加工后转卖的商品总额。它反映批发零售贸易业从国内、国外市场上购进商品的总量。商品购进总额包括：(1)从工农业生产者购进的商品；(2)从出版社、报社的出版发行部门购进的图书、杂志和报纸；(3)从各种登记注册类型的批发零售贸易企业(单位)购进的商品；(4)从其他单位购进的商品，如从机关、团体、企业等单位购进的剩余物资，从餐饮业、服务业购进的商品，从海关、市场管理部门购进的缉私和没收的商品，从居民手中收购的废旧商品等；(5)从国(境)外直接进口的商品。不包括企业(单位)为自身经营用和未通过买卖行为而收入的商品以及销售退回、商品升溢等。

商品销售总额 指对本企业(单位)以外的单位和个人出售(包括对境外直接出口)的商品总额。它反映批发零售贸易业在国内市场上销售商品以及出口商品的总量。商品销售总额包括：(1)售给城乡居民和社会集团消费用的商品；(2)售给工业、农业、建筑业、运输邮电业、批发零售贸易业、餐饮业、服务业等作为生产、经营使用的商品；(3)售给批发零售贸易业作为转卖或加工后转卖的商品；(4)对国(境)外直接出口的商品。不包括出售本企业(单位)自用的废旧包装用品、未通过买卖行为付出的商品、经本单位介绍，由买卖双方直接结算，本单位只收取手续费的业务、购货退出的商品以及商品损耗和损失等。

批发零售业库存 指报告期末各种登记注册类型的批发零售贸易企业(单位)已取得所有权的商品。它反映批发零售贸易企业(单位)的商品库存情况和对市场商品供应的保证程度。期末库存包括：(1)存放在批发零售贸易业经营单位(如门市部、批发站、经营处)仓库、货场、货柜和货架中的商品；(2)挑选、整理、包装中的商品；(3)已记入购进而尚未运到本单位的商品，即发货单或银行承兑凭证已到而货未到的部分；(4)寄放他处的商品，如因购货方拒绝承付而暂时存放在购货方的商品和已办完加工成品收回手续而未提回的商品；(5)委托其他单位代销(未作销售或调出)尚未售出的商品；(6)代其他单位购进尚未交付的商品。不包括所有权不属于本单位的商品、拨付除批发零售贸易业以外的其他行业所属独立核算加工厂等加工生产尚未收回成品的商品、代国家物资储备部门保管的商品等。

库存总额采用的计算价格是：农副产品采购单位按购进价计算；批发单位按进货价计算；零售单位按核算价格计算，即按什么价格核算就按什么价格计算。

住宿餐饮业营业额 指住宿和餐饮业法人企业、产业活动单位在经营活动中因提供服务或销售商品等取得的收入，包括客房收入、餐费收入、商品销售收入和其他收入。客房收入指住宿和餐饮业法人企业、产业活动单位在经营活动中因提供住宿服务取得的客房收入。餐费收入指住宿和餐饮业法人企业、产业活动单位因为顾客提供就餐服务取得的收入，包括经烹饪、调制加工后出售的各种食品，如主食、炒菜、凉拌菜等的收入。商品销售收入指住宿和餐饮业法人企业、产业活动单位伴随服务而出售商品所取得的收入。其他收入指营业收入中除客房收入、餐费收入、商品销售收入以外的其他收入，包括娱乐、健身和商务服务等。

亿元商品交易市场成交额 指年成交额达到亿元以上，经工商部门批准、专门从事商品批发、零售业务活动的市场。其市场所有摊位成交总额称为商品交易市场成交额。

连锁企业（或称连锁店、连锁公司） 指在核心企业或总店的领导下，由分散的、经营同类商品或服务的企业或活动单位，采取共同方针，实行集中采购和分散销售的有机结合，通过规范化经营，实现规模效益的经济联合组织形式。一般连锁店应由若干个分店组成。其经营特征：(1)经营同类商品；(2)使用统一商号；(3)统一采购配送，采购与销售相分离（部分商品可根据物流合理和保质保鲜原则，由供应商直接送货到门店，其余均由总部统一配送）。

连锁门店包括下列三种形式：

直营连锁：也叫正规连锁。连锁门店均由总部独资或控股开设，在总部的直接领导下统一经营。总部采取纵深似的管理方式，直接下令掌管所有的零售门店，零售门店也必须完全接受总部指挥。他是大型垄断商业资本通过吞并、兼并或独资、控股等途径，发展壮大自身实力和规模的一种形式。

特许连锁：各连锁门店（被特许人）通过合同形式，取得使用总部（特许人）商标、商号、经营技术和销售总部开发的商品的特许权，各加盟连锁门店为独立法人，在总部指导下统一经营。

自由连锁：也称自愿连锁。连锁公司的门店均为独立法人，各自的资产所有权关系不变，在公司总部的指导下共同经营。各成员店使用共同的店名，与总部订阅有关购、销、宣传等方面的合同，并按合同开展经营活动。在合同规定的范围之外，各成员店可以自由活动。根据自愿原则，各成员店可自由加入连锁体系，也可自由退出。

特许连锁加上自由连锁等于加盟连锁。

Explanatory Notes on Main Statistical Indicators

Total Retail Sales of Consumer Goods refer to the sum of retail sales of commodities sold by wholesale, retail, catering, publishing, post and telecommunications and other service industries to urban and rural households for private consumption and to social institutions for public consumption. Retail sales of consumer goods include:

1) Sales by wholesale and retail units:

a) of consumer goods sold to urban and rural households

b) of commodities sold to foreigners, overseas Chinese and Chinese compatriots from Hong Kong, Macao and Taiwan visiting in China

c) of commodities sold to government agencies, institutions, social organizations, military and armed police units, and commodities sold to enterprises in the form of retail sales. More specifically, they include: office facilities and articles for non-production purposes such as communications equipment, computing equipment and instruments, TV and network equipment, printing and copying equipment, audio-visual equipment and instruments, paper, notebooks, stationeries, furniture, electric appliances, knitwear, sanitation and cleaning articles, cultural and sport articles, articles for prizes, souvenirs, etc.; transport vehicles and fuels for employees; materials, spare parts and tools for the maintenance of office facilities; equipment, fuels, materials and food for winter heating or summer cooling purposes; articles and equipment for teaching purpose; Chinese and western medicines and medical equipment and facilities purchased by non profit-making medical institutes; non-specialized work safety articles; cooking utensils, tableware, equipment, cleaning articles, food and fuels purchased by internal cafeterias; clothes and personal articles purchased by military or armed police units for their officials and soldiers; and other equipment and articles for non-production purposes.

2) Sales of stable food, cooked dishes, beverages, tobaccos and other articles by catering units.

3) Sales of books, newspapers, magazines, audio-visual products and post products by publishing, post and telecommunications departments to urban and rural households and to enterprises, institutions, military and armed police units.

4) Sales of food, beverages, tobaccos, clothing, hats, footwear, articles for daily use, medicines, medical and health articles, work of art, handicrafts, toys, funeral articles and other articles by other service industries.

Purchase, Sales and Stock of Commodities by Wholesale and Retail Trades refer to the total volume of commodities purchased, total volume of sales and exports, and the stock of commodities by wholesale and retail enterprises (establishments) of different status of registration from domestic and overseas markets. This indictor reflects the relationship among purchase, sales and stock of commodities in the circulation of goods and reveals the existing problems.

Total Purchases of Commodities refer to the total value of purchases of commodities by the enterprises (establishments) from other establishments or individuals (including direct import from abroad) for the purpose of re-selling, either with or without further processing of the commodities purchased. This indicator is used to show the total value of purchases of commodities by wholesale and retail establishments from domestic and overseas markets. The total purchases include: (1) agricultural and industrial products purchased from producers; (2) books, magazines and newspapers purchased from distribution departments of the publishers; (3) commodities purchased from wholesale and retail establishments of different status of registration; (4) commodities purchased from other units, such as surplus materials purchased from government agencies, enterprises or institutions, commodities purchased from catering and service establishments, confiscated goods purchased from customs authorities or market management agencies, second-hand goods and wastes purchased from residents; and (5) commodities directly imported from abroad. Excluded are commodities purchased by enterprises (establishments) for use in their own business operation, commodities obtained without buying or selling procedures, rejected commodities, etc.

Total Sales of Commodities refer to value of commodities sold by the establishments to other establishments and individuals (including direct export). This indicator is used to show the total value of sales of commodities at domestic markets and export. The total sales include: (1) commodities sold to urban and rural residents and social groups for their consumption; (2) commodities sold to establishments in industry, agriculture, construction, transportation, post and telecommunications, wholesale and retail trades, catering trade and public utility for their production and operation; (3) commodities sold to wholesale and retail establishments for re selling, with or without further processing; and (4)commodities for direct export to other countries. Excluded are selling of waste packaging materials used by the establishments (units) themselves, commodities transferred without buying or selling procedures, commission income from brokerage in transactions whose settlement is directly handled by buyers and sellers, rejected commodities in the purchase, loss in commodities, etc.

Commodity Stock of Wholesale and Retail Enterprises refers to total commodities possessed by wholesale and retail enterprises (units) of various types of registration status at the end of the reference period, which reflects the commodity stock level of various wholesale and retail enterprises and the potential for market supply. It includes: (1) commodities located in storage, garages, counters, and shelves of operating units (such as sale stores, wholesale centers, and operating offices) of wholesale and retail enterprises; (2) commodities in the process of selecting, sorting, and packing; (3) commodities not arrived but recorded as purchase in the account, i.e. commodities not arrived but payment receipts for the commodities from the sellers or the banks arrived; (4) commodities deposited in other places rather than places mentioned above, for instance: commodities in the hold of purchasers temporarily due to the refusal of payment and commodities not taken back after going through the formalities; (5) commodities entrusted to other units to sell but not sold yet; (6) commodities purchased for other units but not delivered yet. Commodities not included as stock are those not owned by the enterprises (units), those allocated to financially independent factories rather than wholesale and retail enterprises for processing but not taken back yet, and finally those put in stock by wholesale and retail enterprises on behalf of the state material reserves units.

For the calculation of the value of commodities stock, the value is calculated at purchasing prices in agricultural goods purchasing units and wholesale units, and at the accounting prices in retail units.

Business Revenue of Hotels and Catering Services: refer to revenue received from providing services or selling commodities by corporate enterprises and establishments engaged in hotel and catering services, including income from hotel rooms, from catering services, from selling of commodities and from other services. Income from hotel rooms refers to income of corporate enterprises and establishments by providing lodging services. Income from catering services refers to income of corporate enterprises and establishments by providing catering services, including selling of cooked or prepared foods such as stable food, cooked dishes or cold dishes. Income from selling of commodities refers to income of corporate enterprises and establishments by selling commodities that accompany the services they provide. Income from other activities refers to income received other than income from hotel rooms, catering services or selling of commodities, such as income from providing recreation, fitness or business services.

Volume of Transaction at Large Commodity Markets (with transaction value over 100 million yuan) refers to markets approved by the industrial and commercial administration departments, which specialize in wholesale and retail of commodities with an annual transaction of over 100 million yuan. The sum of sales of all sellers in the markets makes up the transaction value of the markets.

Chain Enterprises (also called chain stores or chain corporations) refer to a form of joint economic entities under which scattered enterprises or establishments engaged in providing homogeneous commodities or services, with the central leadership of core enterprise or headquarters and guided by common policies, conduct centralized purchase and distributed selling of commodities, in order to gain better efficiency through standardized operation. Consisting of a number of branch stores, the chain stores have in general following features: 1) homogeneous commodities, 2) unique name of stores, 3) centralized purchase and delivery which is separated from distributed selling operation (most commodities are delivered from the headquarters except some items which, from logistics, quality or freshness considerations, might be delivered by the suppliers directly).

Chain stores have 3 categories:

a) Chain stores under direct management: These are formal chain stores invested or controlled by the headquarters. They operate under the direct and unified management from the headquarters. Adopting a direct management approach, the headquarters give orders and control all retail stores, which follow completely the directives from the headquarters. Large monopolized commercial companies develop and expand their business through purchasing, merging, direct investment and controlling of shares.

b) Chain stores through special permit: Through contracts, chain stores (or their owners) obtain licenses from the headquarters to use designated trade marks, names, operation know-how, and to sell the commodity developed by the headquarters. Under this arrangement, each store in the chain is an independent legal entity and operates under the guidance from the headquarters.

c) Chain stores through voluntary arrangement: Under this arrangement, all stores operate together under the guidance of the headquarters, while maintaining their status of independent legal entities with full ownership of their assets. They use the same store name, sign contracts with the headquarters concerning purchase, sale, publicity, etc. and operate under the contract. They are free to engage in other activities which are not bounded in the contract. They could join or leave the chain on voluntary basis.

Chain stores through special permit and those through voluntary arrangement make up chain stores through license arrangement.

18

对外经济贸易

Foreign Trade and Economic Cooperation

简要说明

本篇资料综合反映中国的对外贸易、利用外资、对外经济合作的历年概况，重点反映对外经济贸易的近期发展状况。

一、对外贸易部分

对外贸易统计的主要内容包括：进出口货物的品种、数(重)量、金额、国别(地区)、经营单位、境内目的地、境内货源地、贸易方式、关别等项目。

对外贸易统计的范围是按照联合国的国际贸易统计原则制定的，即凡能引起中华人民共和国关境内物质资源存量增加或减少的进出口货物，除制度另有规定者外，均列入该项统计。

对外贸易统计的资料来源于海关总署，调查方法是全面调查。

特殊说明：1979年及以前为外贸业务统计数字，来源于原对外贸易经济合作部（现为商务部）；1980年及以后为海关进出口统计数字，来源于海关总署。

海关历年出口商品分类金额和海关历年进口商品分类金额按照联合国《国际贸易标准分类》(SITC)进行统计。海关进出口商品分类金额按照海关合作理事会制定的《商品名称和编码协调制度》(HS)目录进行统计。

我国对各国(地区)进出口总额表中，出口货物按中华人民共和国关境外最终目的国(地区)，进口货物按中华人民共和国关境外原产国(地区)统计。各地区进出口商品总值分别按境内经营单位所在地和目的地、货源地列示。经营单位所在地是指中华人民共和国关境内进出口企业报关注册的登记地；境内货源地是指出口货物在中华人民共和国关境内的产地或原始发货地；境内目的地则指进口货物在中华人民共和国关境内的消费、使用地或最终运抵地。

二、利用外资统计部分

利用外资统计的主要内容包括：对外借款、外商直接投资和外商其他投资、外商投资企业登记注册情况。

统计范围是凡经工商行政管理机关核准登记，在中华人民共和国境内所有利用外资的单位和部门，经批准设立的中外合资经营企业、合作经营企业、外资企业、外商投资股份制企业、合作开发项目等具有法人资格的独立核算企业(包括港澳台地区投资企业)，在华从事经营活动的外国及港澳台地区企业及外国公司在中国境内设立的分支机构。

利用外资统计的资料来源于商务部，其中，外商投资企业的登记注册情况资料来源于国家工商行政管理总局，调查方法是全面调查。

特殊说明：利用外资统计1985年及以前为政府统计部门的调查汇总数，1986年及以后全部来源于对外贸易经济合作部（现为商务部）。

三、对外经济合作部分

对外经济合作统计的主要内容包括：对外承包工程、对外劳务合作、对外设计咨询的合同数、合同金额、完成营业额和按国别、地区分的对外经济合作完成营业额等。

统计范围是对外承包工程、对外劳务合作、对外设计咨询。

该制度统计单位是经各级商务部门批准的从事对外承包和劳务合作业务并具有法人地位的对外承包劳务企业。

资料来源是商务部，调查方法是全面调查。

四、对外直接投资部分

对外直接投资统计的内容主要包括：境内投资主体的基本情况、境外企业的基本情况、境内投资主体与境外企业间的投资、收益和分配情况、通过境外企业实现的货物进出口情况、境外企业核准情况。

统计范围主要包括境内投资主体通过直接投资在境外设立的各类公司型企业和非公司型企业。

资料来源是商务部，调查方法是全面调查。

五、其他

历年人民币对美元、日元、港币的年平均汇价，资料来源于国家外汇管理局，各年的年平均汇价是根据当年国家外汇管理局公布的每日汇价进行加权平均计算而得出的。

Brief Introduction

Data in this chapter show the summary data of China's foreign trade, utilization of foreign capital, contracted projects and labour cooperation with the foreign countries or territories over the years, focusing on the recent situation of foreign trade and economic cooperation.

I. Foreign Trade

Data on foreign trade include: varieties of imports and exports, amount (weight), value, countries (regions), imports and exports corporations, destination within territory, origin of goods within territory, means of trade, types of taxes and so on.

The coverage of foreign trade statistics are designed according to principle on international trade by United Nations, that is: all imports or exports that will lead to stock changes of material resources with the territory of People's Republic of China; excluding goods by escape clause.

Sources of data on foreign trade are from General Administration of Customs of the People's Republic of China through comprehensive reporting system.

Special notice: Data in the years prior to 1980 were statistical data of foreign trade and come from the former Ministry of Foreign Trade and Economic Cooperation (current Ministry of Commerce). Since 1980, the data have been the statistical data of customs on imports and exports and come from the General Administration of Customs.

Customs statistics on value term imports and exports by categories are using the *UN Standard International Trade Classification (SITC)*. However, the *Harmonized Commodity Description and Coding System (HS)* stipulated by the Customs Cooperation Council is used in the classification of the import and export commodities.

In the table on China's total imports and exports with related countries and regions, the export commodities are calculated at the customs of the countries (regions) of destination and the import commodities are calculated at the customs of the countries (regions) of origin. The total values of the import and export commodities by region are calculated respectively at the provinces where the import or export corporations are situated and at the provinces of destination or provinces of origin within the boundary of the People's Republic of China. The province where the import or export corporations are situated refers to the province where the import or export corporations have applied to and have been registered at the customs. The province of origin within the boundary of the Peoples Republic of China refers to the province where the export commodities are produced or originally delivered. The province of destination within the boundary of the Peoples Republic of China refers to the province where the import commodities are consumed, used or transported to the destination.

II. Statistics on Utilization of Foreign Capitals

Utilization of foreign capitals includes: foreign loans, foreign direct investments and other foreign investments, and the basic condition of registration of foreign funded enterprises.

The statistics cover all the units and departments which have utilized foreign capital and all the Sino-foreign joint ventures, Sino-foreign cooperative enterprises, ventures exclusively with foreign investment, foreign-funded stock companies, Sino-foreign cooperative development projects and other corporate enterprises (including the enterprises funded by the entrepreneurs from Hong Kong, Macao and Taiwan) with independent accounting system which have been approved by the Chinese government to set up in the boundary of the People's Republic of China.

Data on utilization of foreign capitals are from Ministry of Commerce, of which, data on basic condition of registration of foreign funded enterprises are from State Administration for Industry and Commerce through comprehensive reporting system.

Special notice: data on utilization of foreign capitals before 1985 were survey results fro governmental statistical agencies, since 1986 all data are from Ministry of Commerce (former MOFTEC).

III. Foreign Economic Cooperation

Data on foreign economic cooperation include: contracted projects, labour services cooperation, design and consultation services, contracted volume, complete business turnover, business turnover by countries (regions) and so on.

The statistics cover contracted projects, labour services cooperation and design and consultation service with foreign countries.

The statistical unit in the scheme is the corporate enterprise engaged in contracted projects and labour services cooperation with foreign countries and has been approved by the department of commerce at various levels.

Data on foreign economic cooperation are from Ministry of Commerce through comprehensive reporting system.

IV. Overseas Direct Investment

Contents of statistics on overseas direct investment include basic situation of domestic investors and overseas enterprises they invest in, investment, earnings and their distribution between domestic investors and invested overseas enterprises, import and export of commodities through overseas enterprises, approval of overseas enterprises.

The statistics cover overseas corporate and non-corporate enterprises of various forms established by domestic investors through their investment operation.

V. Others

The average exchange rates of RMB yuan to US dollar, Japanese yen and Hong Kong dollar over the years come from the State Administration of Exchange Control. The annual average exchange rate is calculated as the weighted mean of the daily exchange rates provided by the State Administration of Foreign Exchange in the year.

18-1 对外经济贸易基本情况
Foreign Trade and Economic Cooperation

指标	Item	2001	2002	2003	2004	2005
货物进出口总额（人民币亿元）	**Total Value of Imports and Exports (RMB 100 million yuan)**	**42183.6**	**51378.2**	**70483.5**	**95539.1**	**116921.8**
出口总额	Total Exports	22024.4	26947.9	36287.9	49103.3	62648.1
进口总额	Total Imports	20159.2	24430.3	34195.6	46435.8	54273.7
进出口差额	Balance	1865.2	2517.6	2092.3	2667.5	8374.4
货物进出口总额 （亿美元）	**Total Value of Imports and Exports (USD 100 million)**	**5096.5**	**6207.7**	**8509.9**	**11545.5**	**14219.1**
出口总额	Total Exports	2661.0	3256.0	4382.3	5933.2	7619.5
初级产品	Primary Goods	263.4	285.4	348.1	405.5	490.4
工业制成品	Manufactured Goods	2397.6	2970.6	4034.2	5527.7	7129.2
进口总额	Total Imports	2435.5	2951.7	4127.6	5612.3	6599.5
初级产品	Primary Goods	457.4	492.7	727.6	1172.7	1477.1
工业制成品	Manufactured Goods	1978.1	2459.0	3400.0	4439.6	5122.4
进出口差额	Balance	225.5	304.3	254.7	320.9	1020.0
外商直接投资合同项目 （个）	**Number of Projects for Contracted Foreign Capital (unit)**	**26140**	**34171**	**41081**	**43664**	**44001**
外商投资合同金额 （亿美元）	**Total Amount of Contracted Foreign Capital (USD 100 million)**	**719.76**	**847.51**	**1169.01**	**1565.88**	**1925.93**
外商直接投资	Foreign Direct Investments	691.95	827.68	1150.69	1534.79	1890.65
外商其他投资	Other Foreign Investments	27.81	19.82	18.32	31.09	35.28
实际利用外资额 （亿美元）	**Total Amount of Foreign Capital Actually Utilized (USD 100 million)**	**496.72**	**550.11**	**561.40**	**640.72**	**638.05**
外商直接投资	Foreign Direct Investments	468.78	527.43	535.05	606.30	603.25
外商其他投资	Other Foreign Investments	27.94	22.68	26.35	34.42	34.80
外商投资企业基本情况	**Registered Foreign-funded Enterprises**					
年底登记户数 （户）	Number of Registered Enterprises (household)	202306	208056	226373	242284	260000
投资总额 （亿美元）	Total Investment (USD 100 million)	8750	9819	11174	13112	14640
注册资本 （亿美元）	Registered Capital (USD 100 million)	5058	5521	6226	7285	8120
#外方	Capital from Foreign Partners	3597	4020	4658	5580	6319
对外经济合作 （亿美元）	**Economic Cooperation with Foreign Countries & Territories (USD 100 million)**					
合同金额	Contracted Value	164.55	178.91	209.30	276.98	342.16
#对外承包工程	Contracted Projects	130.39	150.55	176.67	238.44	296.14
对外劳务合作	Labor Services	33.28	27.52	30.87	35.03	42.45
完成营业额	Value of Business Fulfilled	121.39	143.52	172.34	213.69	267.76
#对外承包工程	Contracted Projects	88.99	111.94	138.37	174.68	217.63
对外劳务合作	Labor Services	31.77	30.71	33.09	37.53	47.86

注：从2001年起，外商投资合同金额和实际利用外资额均不包括对外借款（18-14表类同）。

a) From 2001, data of contracted foreign capital and total amount of foreign capital actually utilized don't include foreign loans. The same as in Table 18-14.

18-2 人民币对主要外币年平均汇价（中间价）

Average Exchange Rate of RMB Yuan Against Main Convertible Currencies (Middle Rate)

单位：人民币元 (RMB yuan)

年 份 Year	100美元 100 US Dollars	100日元 100 Japanese Yen	100港元 100 Hong Kong Dollars	100欧元 100 Euros
1985	293.66	1.2457	37.57	
1986	345.28	2.0694	44.22	
1987	372.21	2.5799	47.74	
1988	372.21	2.9082	47.70	
1989	376.51	2.7360	48.28	
1990	478.32	3.3233	61.39	
1991	532.33	3.9602	68.45	
1992	551.46	4.3608	71.24	
1993	576.20	5.2020	74.41	
1994	861.87	8.4370	111.53	
1995	835.10	8.9225	107.96	
1996	831.42	7.6352	107.51	
1997	828.98	6.8600	107.09	
1998	827.91	6.3488	106.88	
1999	827.83	7.2932	106.66	
2000	827.84	7.6864	106.18	
2001	827.70	6.8075	106.08	
2002	827.70	6.6237	106.07	800.58
2003	827.70	7.1466	106.24	936.13
2004	827.68	7.6552	106.23	1029.00
2005	819.17	7.4484	105.30	1019.53

注：欧元自2002年开始进入市场流通。

a) ECU enters the circulating market since 2002.

18-3 货物进出口总额

Total Value of Imports and Exports

本表1978年为外贸业务统计数，1980年起为海关进出口统计数。

Data in 1978 were obtained from the Ministry of Foreign Trade, and the data since 1980 have been obtained from the customs statistics.

年 份 Year	人民币（亿元）100 million Yuan				美元（亿美元）USD 100 million			
	进出口总额 Total Imports & Exports	出口总额 Total Exports	进口总额 Total Imports	差额 Balance	进出口总额 Total Imports & Exports	出口总额 Total Exports	进口总额 Total Imports	差额 Balance
1978	355.0	167.6	187.4	-19.8	206.4	97.5	108.9	-11.4
1980	570.0	271.2	298.8	-27.6	381.4	181.2	200.2	-19.0
1985	2066.7	808.9	1257.8	-448.9	696.0	273.5	422.5	-149.0
1989	4156.0	1956.1	2199.9	-243.8	1116.8	525.4	591.4	-66.0
1990	5560.1	2985.8	2574.3	411.5	1154.4	620.9	533.5	87.4
1991	7225.8	3827.1	3398.7	428.4	1357.0	719.1	637.9	81.2
1992	9119.6	4676.3	4443.3	233.0	1655.3	849.4	805.9	43.5
1993	11271.0	5284.8	5986.2	-701.4	1957.0	917.4	1039.6	-122.2
1994	20381.9	10421.8	9960.1	461.7	2366.2	1210.1	1156.1	54.0
1995	23499.9	12451.8	11048.1	1403.7	2808.6	1487.8	1320.8	167.0
1996	24133.8	12576.4	11557.4	1019.0	2898.8	1510.5	1388.3	122.2
1997	26967.2	15160.7	11806.5	3354.2	3251.6	1827.9	1423.7	404.2
1998	26849.7	15223.6	11626.1	3597.5	3239.5	1837.1	1402.4	434.7
1999	29896.2	16159.8	13736.4	2423.4	3606.3	1949.3	1657.0	292.3
2000	39273.2	20634.4	18638.8	1995.6	4742.9	2492.0	2250.9	241.1
2001	42183.6	22024.4	20159.2	1865.2	5096.5	2661.0	2435.5	225.5
2002	51378.2	26947.9	24430.3	2517.6	6207.7	3256.0	2951.7	304.3
2003	70483.5	36287.9	34195.6	2092.3	8509.9	4382.3	4127.6	254.7
2004	95539.1	49103.3	46435.8	2667.5	11545.5	5933.2	5612.3	320.9
2005	116921.8	62648.1	54273.7	8374.4	14219.1	7619.5	6599.5	1020.0

注：货物进出口差额负数为入超。

a) A negative balance indicates an unfavourable balance of foreign trade.

18-4 按贸易方式分货物进出口总额
Total Value of Imports and Exports by Way of Trade

单位：亿美元 (USD 100 million)

年 份 Year	一般贸易 General Trade		加工贸易 Processing Trade		其他贸易 Other Trade	
	出 口 Exports	进 口 Imports	出 口 Exports	进 口 Imports	出 口 Exports	进 口 Imports
1981-1985	**1100.97**	**1191.40**	**93.73**	**114.73**	**5.80**	**17.46**
1981	208.00	203.66	11.31	15.04	0.79	1.40
1982	222.45	188.85	0.53	2.76	0.22	1.38
1983	201.60	187.68	19.44	22.72	1.26	3.50
1984	231.62	238.49	29.29	31.47	0.49	4.14
1985	237.30	372.72	33.16	42.74	3.04	7.04
1986-1990	**1543.72**	**1609.97**	**738.79**	**679.23**	**42.79**	**249.50**
1986	250.95	352.07	56.20	67.03	2.25	9.90
1987	296.43	287.72	89.94	101.91	8.03	42.47
1988	326.22	352.04	140.60	151.05	8.38	49.61
1989	315.52	356.14	197.85	171.64	12.03	63.62
1990	354.60	262.00	254.20	187.60	12.10	83.90
1991-1995	**2579.30**	**1801.00**	**2469.80**	**1988.80**	**134.80**	**1170.50**
1991	381.20	295.40	324.30	250.30	13.60	92.20
1992	436.80	336.20	396.20	315.40	16.40	154.30
1993	432.00	380.50	442.50	363.70	43.00	295.40
1994	615.60	355.20	569.80	475.70	24.70	325.20
1995	713.70	433.70	737.00	583.70	37.10	303.40
1996-2000	**3993.65**	**2891.89**	**5369.20**	**3672.11**	**254.00**	**1558.30**
1996	628.40	393.60	843.30	622.70	38.80	372.00
1997	779.74	390.30	996.02	702.06	52.14	331.34
1998	742.35	436.80	1044.54	685.99	50.22	279.58
1999	791.35	670.40	1108.82	735.78	49.14	250.81
2000	1051.81	1000.79	1376.52	925.58	63.70	324.57
2001-2005	**9887.71**	**9579.95**	**13136.49**	**8747.85**	**827.77**	**3398.03**
2001	1118.81	1134.56	1474.33	939.74	67.83	361.23
2002	1361.87	1291.11	1799.28	1222.01	94.82	438.59
2003	1820.34	1876.51	2418.51	1629.04	143.45	621.22
2004	2436.06	2481.45	3279.70	2216.94	217.44	913.91
2005	3150.63	2796.33	4164.67	2740.12	304.23	1063.08

18-5 历年出口货物分类金额

Exports Value by Category of Commodities (Customs Statistics)

单位：亿美元 (USD 100 million)

年份 Year	总额 Total	初级产品 Primary Goods	食品及主要供食用的活动物 Food and Live Animals Used Chiefly for Food	饮料及烟类 Beverages and Tobacco	非食用原料 Non-edible Raw Materials	矿物燃料、润滑油及有关原料 Mineral Fuels, Lubricants and Related Materials	动、植物油脂及蜡 Animal and Vegetable Oils, Fats and Wax
1980	181.19	91.14	29.85	0.78	17.11	42.80	0.60
1985	273.50	138.28	38.03	1.05	26.53	71.32	1.35
1989	525.38	150.78	61.45	3.14	42.12	43.21	0.86
1990	620.91	158.86	66.09	3.42	35.37	52.37	1.61
1991	719.10	161.45	72.26	5.29	34.86	47.54	1.50
1992	849.40	170.04	83.09	7.20	31.43	46.93	1.39
1993	917.44	166.66	83.99	9.01	30.52	41.09	2.05
1994	1210.06	197.08	100.15	10.02	41.27	40.69	4.95
1995	1487.80	214.85	99.54	13.70	43.75	53.32	4.54
1996	1510.48	219.25	102.31	13.42	40.45	59.31	3.76
1997	1827.92	239.53	110.75	10.49	41.95	69.87	6.47
1998	1837.09	204.89	105.13	9.75	35.19	51.75	3.07
1999	1949.31	199.41	104.58	7.71	39.21	46.59	1.32
2000	2492.03	254.60	122.82	7.45	44.62	78.55	1.16
2001	2660.98	263.38	127.77	8.73	41.72	84.05	1.11
2002	3255.96	285.40	146.21	9.84	44.02	84.35	0.98
2003	4382.28	348.12	175.31	10.19	50.32	111.14	1.15
2004	5933.26	405.49	188.64	12.14	58.43	144.80	1.48
2005	7619.53	490.37	224.80	11.83	74.84	176.22	2.68

18-5 续表 continued

单位：亿美元 (USD 100 million)

年份 Year	工业制成品 Manufactured Goods	化学品及有关产品 Chemicals and Related Products	轻纺产品、橡胶制品矿冶产品及其制品 Light and Textile Industrial Products, Rubber Products, Minerals Metal-lurgical Products	机械及运输设备 Machinery and Transport Equipment	杂项制品 Miscellaneous Products	未分类的其他商品 Products Not Otherwise Classified
1980	90.05	11.20	39.99	8.43	28.36	2.07
1985	135.22	13.58	44.93	7.72	34.86	34.13
1989	374.60	32.01	108.97	38.74	107.55	87.33
1990	462.05	37.30	125.76	55.88	126.86	116.25
1991	556.98	38.18	144.56	71.49	166.20	136.55
1992	679.36	43.48	161.35	132.19	342.34	
1993	750.78	46.23	163.92	152.82	387.81	
1994	1012.98	62.36	232.18	218.95	499.37	0.12
1995	1272.95	90.94	322.40	314.07	545.48	0.06
1996	1291.23	88.77	284.98	353.12	564.24	0.12
1997	1588.39	102.27	344.32	437.09	704.67	0.04
1998	1632.20	103.21	324.77	502.17	702.00	0.05
1999	1749.90	103.73	332.62	588.36	725.10	0.09
2000	2237.43	120.98	425.46	826.00	862.78	2.21
2001	2397.60	133.52	438.13	949.01	871.10	5.84
2002	2970.56	153.25	529.55	1269.76	1011.53	6.48
2003	4034.16	195.81	690.18	1877.73	1260.88	9.56
2004	5527.77	263.60	1006.46	2682.60	1563.98	11.12
2005	7129.16	357.72	1291.21	3522.34	1941.83	16.06

18-6 历年进口货物分类金额

Imports Value by Category of Commodities (Customs Statistics)

单位：亿美元 (USD 100 million)

年份 Year	总额 Total	初级产品 Primary Goods	食品及主要供食用的活动物 Food and Live Animals Chiefly for Food	饮料及烟类 Beverages and Tobacco	非食用原料 Non-edible Raw Materials	矿物燃料、润滑油及有关原料 Mineral Fuels, Lubricants and Related Materials	动、植物油脂及蜡 Animal and Vegetable Oils, Fats and Waxes
1980	200.17	69.59	29.27	0.36	35.54	2.03	2.39
1985	422.52	52.89	15.53	2.06	32.36	1.72	1.22
1989	591.40	117.54	41.92	2.02	48.35	16.50	8.75
1990	533.45	98.53	33.35	1.57	41.07	12.72	9.82
1991	637.91	108.34	27.99	2.00	50.03	21.13	7.19
1992	805.85	132.55	31.46	2.39	57.75	35.70	5.25
1993	1039.59	142.10	22.06	2.45	54.38	58.19	5.02
1994	1156.14	164.86	31.37	0.68	74.37	40.35	18.09
1995	1320.84	244.17	61.32	3.94	101.59	51.27	26.05
1996	1388.33	254.41	56.72	4.97	106.98	68.77	16.97
1997	1423.70	286.20	43.04	3.20	120.06	103.06	16.84
1998	1402.37	229.49	37.88	1.79	107.15	67.76	14.91
1999	1656.99	268.46	36.19	2.08	127.40	89.12	13.67
2000	2250.94	467.39	47.58	3.64	200.03	206.37	9.77
2001	2435.53	457.43	49.76	4.12	221.27	174.66	7.63
2002	2951.70	492.71	52.38	3.87	227.36	192.85	16.25
2003	4127.60	727.63	59.60	4.90	341.24	291.89	30.00
2004	5612.29	1172.67	91.54	5.48	553.58	479.93	42.14
2005	6599.53	1477.14	93.88	7.83	702.26	639.47	33.70

18-6 续表 continued

单位：亿美元 (USD 100 million)

年份 Year	工业制成品 Manufactured Goods	化学品及有关产品 Chemicals and Related Products	轻纺产品、橡胶制品矿冶产品及其制品 Light and Textile Industrial Products, Rubber Products, Minerals and Metallurgical Products	机械及运输设备 Machinery and Transport Equipment	杂项制品 Miscellaneous Products	未分类的其他商品 Products Not Otherwise Classified
1980	130.58	29.09	41.54	51.19	5.42	3.34
1985	369.63	44.69	118.98	162.39	19.02	24.55
1989	473.86	75.56	123.35	182.07	20.73	72.15
1990	434.92	66.48	89.06	168.45	21.03	89.90
1991	529.57	92.77	104.93	196.01	24.39	111.47
1992	673.30	111.57	192.73	313.12	55.88	
1993	897.49	97.04	285.27	450.23	64.95	
1994	991.28	121.30	280.84	514.67	67.68	6.79
1995	1076.67	172.99	287.72	526.42	82.61	6.93
1996	1133.92	181.06	313.91	547.63	84.86	6.46
1997	1137.50	192.97	322.20	527.74	85.50	9.09
1998	1172.88	201.58	310.75	568.45	84.56	7.54
1999	1388.53	240.30	343.17	694.53	97.01	13.52
2000	1783.55	302.13	418.07	919.31	127.51	16.53
2001	1978.10	321.04	419.38	1070.15	150.76	16.76
2002	2458.99	390.36	484.89	1370.10	198.01	15.64
2003	3399.96	489.75	639.02	1928.26	330.11	12.82
2004	4439.62	654.73	739.86	2528.30	501.43	15.29
2005	5122.39	777.34	811.57	2904.78	608.62	20.08

18-7 进出口货物分类金额

Value of Imports and Exports by Category of Commodities (Customs Statistics)

单位：亿美元 (USD 100 million)

商品类别	Categories of Commodities	2004		2005	
		出口 Exports	进口 Imports	出口 Exports	进口 Imports
总额	**Total Value**	**5933.26**	**5612.29**	**7619.53**	**6599.53**
活动物；动物产品	**Live Animals & Animal Products**	**63.02**	**37.35**	**67.00**	**42.58**
活动物	Live Animals	3.30	2.20	3.29	1.09
肉及食用杂碎	Meat and Edible Haslets	7.07	4.76	7.43	5.87
鱼、甲壳动物、软体动物及其他水生无脊椎动物	Fish; Shellfish; Molluscs and Other Aquatic Invertebrates	40.56	23.40	43.50	28.79
乳品；蛋品；天然蜂蜜；其他食用动物产品	Dairy Products; Eggs; Natural Honey;	2.34	4.48	2.67	4.62
植物产品	**Vegetables; Fruits and Cereals**	**66.05**	**110.31**	**82.82**	**111.61**
食用蔬菜、根及块茎	Edible Vegetables; Roots and Stem Tubers	25.37	4.05	30.52	5.24
食用水果及坚果；甜瓜或柑桔属水果的果皮	Edible Fruits and Nuts; Muskmelon and Orange Peels	9.16	6.19	10.67	6.59
咖啡、茶、马黛茶及调味香料	Coffee; Tea and Spices	8.65	0.32	9.27	0.42
谷物	Cereals	7.40	22.17	14.12	13.94
含油子仁及果实；杂项子仁及果实；工业用或药用植物；稻草、秸秆及饲料	Oil Seeds and Kernels and Oleaginous Fruits; Other Seeds and Kernels and Fruits; Plants for Industrial and Medicinal Use; Straws and Forage	11.96	73.71	13.83	81.59
动植物油、脂及分解产品；精制食用油脂；动植物蜡	**Animal and Vegetable Oils; Fats and Wax; Refined Edible Oils and Fats**	**1.58**	**42.09**	**2.84**	**33.11**
食品、饮料、酒及醋；烟草及代用品的制品	**Food; Beverages; Liquor and Vinegar; Tobacco and Tobacco Substitutes**	**94.12**	**28.10**	**111.96**	**34.58**
肉鱼甲壳和软体动物及其他水生无脊椎动物制品	Meat; Fish and Shellfish Products Mollusks and Other Aquatic Products	34.89	0.26	43.64	0.29
糖及糖食	Sugar and Sugar Products	2.52	3.36	4.18	4.51
谷物、粮食粉、淀粉或乳的制品；糕饼点心	Cereals; Grain; Starches or Milk and Pastry Products	6.53	1.95	7.59	2.39
蔬菜水果坚果或植物其他部分的制品	Products of Vegetables; Fruits and Nuts	25.78	1.42	30.94	1.57
饮料、酒及醋	Beverages; Liquor and Vinegar	7.43	2.61	7.18	4.10
烟草、烟草及烟草代用品的制品	Tobacco; Products of Tobacco & Tobacco Substitutes	5.14	2.92	5.37	3.84
矿产品	**Minerals**	**165.73**	**671.01**	**209.20**	**922.93**
盐；硫磺；泥土及石料；石膏料、石灰及水泥	Salt; Sulphur; Clay and Rock; Plaster Stone; Lime and Cement	15.25	18.01	21.74	21.71
矿砂、矿渣及矿灰	Ore; Slag and Mortar	5.68	172.73	11.23	260.33
矿物燃料、矿物油及蒸馏产品；沥青物质；矿物蜡	Mineral Fuels; Lubricants; Asphalt; Mineral Wax	144.80	480.27	176.23	640.89
化学工业及其相关工业的产品	**Chemicals and Related Products**	**245.80**	**426.02**	**318.53**	**505.83**
有机化学品	Organic Chemicals	90.92	238.46	121.33	280.19
药品	Medicinal and Pharmaceutical Products	11.00	15.72	13.64	19.59
肥料	Fertilizers	13.09	22.88	10.11	30.51
鞣料和染料浸膏；鞣酸及衍生物；染颜料及其他着色料；油漆清漆；油灰及类似胶粘剂；墨水、油墨	Tanning and Dyeing Extracts; Tannic Acid; Coloring and Dyeing Materials; Paint and Lacquer; Putty; Ink and Printing Ink	19.27	29.75	24.84	30.81
精油及香膏；芳香料制品及化妆盥洗品	Essential Oils and Perfumed Materials; Cosmetics	9.30	3.93	12.01	5.01
塑料及其制品；橡胶及其制品	**Plastics and Related Products; Rubber and Related Products**	**169.08**	**327.98**	**232.86**	**388.93**
塑料及其制品	Plastics and Related Products	131.06	280.56	177.83	333.08
橡胶及其制品	Rubber and Related Products	38.03	47.42	55.03	55.85
生皮、皮革、毛皮及制品；鞍具挽具；旅行用品、手提包及类似物品；动物肠线（蚕胶丝除外）制品	**Raw Hides; Leather; Furs and Related Products; Saddle; Travel Articles; Handbags and Similar Containers**	**136.67**	**51.20**	**156.01**	**54.24**
生皮（毛皮除外）及皮革	Raw Hides and Leather	14.01	46.01	15.66	48.27
皮革制品；鞍具挽具；旅行用品、手提包及类似容器；动物肠线制品	Leather Products; Saddle; Travel Articles; Handbags and Similar Containers	102.59	1.83	114.20	2.53
毛皮、人造毛皮及其制品	Furs; Artificial Furs and Related Products	20.07	3.37	26.15	3.44
木及木制品；木炭；软木及软木制品；稻草、秸秆、针茅或其他编结材料制品；篮筐及柳条编结品	**Wood and Wooden Products; Charcoal; Cork and Related Products; Straws; Plaited Products; Baskets and Wickerwork**	**60.64**	**52.35**	**75.70**	**57.46**
木浆及其他纤维状纤维素浆；纸及纸板的废碎品；纸、纸板及其制品	**Paper Pulp and Cellulose Pulp; Paper and Waste Paper; Paperboard and Related Products**	**37.97**	**103.06**	**51.14**	**110.03**
木浆及其他纤维状纤维素浆；纸及纸板的废碎品	Paper Pulp and Cellulose Pulp; Paper and Paper Board Waste	0.16	52.95	0.36	61.83
纸及纸板；纸浆、纸或纸板制品	Paper and Paperboard; Articles of Paper Pulp or Paper and Paperboard Products	28.46	46.38	39.29	43.87

18-7 续表 continued

单位：亿美元 (USD 100 million)

商品类别	Categories of Commodities	2004 出口 Exports	2004 进口 Imports	2005 出口 Exports	2005 进口 Imports
纺织原料及纺织制品	**Textile Materials and Products**	**887.67**	**230.07**	**1076.61**	**234.45**
蚕丝	Natural Silk	10.62	1.40	13.36	1.36
羊毛、动物细毛或粗毛；马毛纱线及其机织物	Wool; Wool Yarn and Woolen Woven Fabrics	17.15	20.89	18.45	21.47
棉花	Cotton	65.87	68.98	74.38	70.78
其他植物纺织纤维；纸纱线及其机织物	Other Textile Fiber; Yarn and Related Woven Fabrics	5.53	4.71	6.18	4.77
化学纤维长丝	Chemical Fiber; Continuous Filament	51.56	38.08	58.90	37.76
化学纤维短纤	Chemical Fiber; Staple Fiber	35.54	34.21	43.87	32.57
絮胎毡呢及无纺织物;特种纱线;线绳索缆及制品	Wadding; Felt and Adhesive-Bond Fabrics; Special Yarn; Thread; Rope; Cable and Related Products	5.95	6.19	8.60	7.07
地毯及纺织材料的其他铺地制品	Carpets and Related Products	7.73	0.59	9.32	0.62
特种机织物；簇绒织物；花边；装饰毯；装饰带；刺绣品	Special Woven Fabrics; Lace; Embroidery	19.75	8.18	27.09	8.46
浸渍、涂布、包覆或层压纺织物；工业用纺织制品	Coated Textiles; Textile Products for Industrial Use	12.35	13.50	17.55	14.50
针织物及钩编织物	Knitwear and Crocheted Fabrics	29.94	18.12	36.52	18.78
针织或钩编织的服装及衣着附件	Knitted or Crocheted Garments & Clothing Accessories	258.03	6.42	308.71	6.95
非针织或钩编织的服装及衣着附件	Garments Not Knitted or Crocheted	289.81	7.93	350.31	8.15
其他纺织制成品；成套物品；旧衣着旧纺织品；碎织物	Other Textile Products; Secondhand Garments	77.84	0.88	103.36	1.19
鞋、帽、伞、杖、鞭及其零件;已加工的羽毛及其制品;人造花;人发制品	**Footwear; Headgear; Umbrellas; Canes; Whips; Processed Feather; Artificial Flowers; Wigs**	**184.17**	**6.08**	**227.73**	**6.71**
鞋靴、护腿和类似品及其零件	Parts of Footwear; Gaiters	152.03	4.75	190.52	5.42
帽类及其零件	Headgear And Accessories	11.80	0.11	14.43	0.13
雨伞阳伞、手杖、鞭子、马鞭及其零件	Umbrellas; Canes; Whips and Accessories	8.39	0.11	9.61	0.09
已加工羽毛、羽绒及其制品；人造花；人发制品	Processed Feathers and Related Products; Artificial Flowers; Wigs	11.96	1.11	13.16	1.07
石料石膏水泥石棉云母及类似材料的制品；陶瓷产品；玻璃及其制品	**Gypsum; Cement; Asbestos; Mica; Ceramic Glass**	**93.36**	**32.48**	**122.57**	**33.84**
石料、石膏、水泥、石棉、云母及类似材料制品	Gypsum; Cement; Asbestos; Mica and Related Products	20.29	4.64	27.57	5.36
陶瓷产品	Ceramics	38.90	3.08	50.37	3.01
玻璃及其制品	Glass and Glassware	34.17	24.75	44.63	25.47
天然或养殖珍珠、宝石或半宝石、贵金属、包贵金属及其制品;仿首饰;硬币	**Natural or Cultivated Pearls; Precious or Semi-Precious Stones; Jewelry of Precious Metal or Rolled Precious Metal; Artificial Jewelry; Coins**	**44.63**	**26.55**	**55.33**	**34.70**
贱金属及其制品	**Base Metals and Related Products**	**437.41**	**485.48**	**570.86**	**565.93**
钢铁	Iron and Steel	114.67	236.91	150.90	262.10
钢铁制品	Iron and Steel Products	137.46	46.41	190.32	56.96
铜及其制品	Copper and Related Products	21.42	104.76	30.55	128.96
镍及其制品	Nickel and Related Products	2.62	13.23	3.05	21.77
铝及其制品	Aluminum and Related Products	51.75	49.31	61.09	50.12
铅及其制品	Lead and Related Products	4.28	0.92	4.85	0.80
锌及其制品	Zinc and Related Products	4.11	6.53	3.82	10.06
锡及其制品	Tin and Related Products	3.39	2.56	2.31	4.05
机器、机械器具、电气设备及零件；录音机及放声机、电视图像声音的录制和重放设备及零附件	**Machinery; Electric Equipment and Accessories; Recorders; Video Recorder and Accessories**	**2477.84**	**2339.14**	**3220.08**	**2711.19**
车辆、航空器、船舶及有关运输设备	**Locomotives; Vehicles; Aircraft; Ship and Related Transportation Equipment**	**209.99**	**194.72**	**284.10**	**198.35**
铁道及电车道机车、车辆及零件；铁道及电车轨道固定装置及零附件;各种机械(电动);交通信号设备	Rail Locomotives; Tramcars and Accessories; Fixed Track Equipment; Signal Equipment for Transportation	54.95	3.46	64.06	4.83
车辆及其零件、附件；但铁道及电车道车辆除外	Vehicles and Related Parts and Accessories	118.23	131.02	165.94	123.09
航空器、航天器及零件	Aircraft; Spacecraft and Parts Thereof	5.21	49.90	7.46	65.61
船舶及浮动结构体	Ships and Related Products	31.60	10.33	46.63	4.82
光学、照相、电影、计量、检验、医疗或外科用仪器设备、精密仪器及设备;钟表;乐器;及其零附件	**Optical; Photographic; Film; Measuring and Checking and Medical Instruments and Equipment; Precision Instruments and Equipment; Clocks; Musical Instruments; Related Parts and Accessories**	**190.87**	**413.35**	**283.98**	**511.88**
其他	**Others**	**366.66**	**34.95**	**470.23**	**41.19**

18-8 我国同各国(地区)海关货物进出口总额

Volume of Imports and Exports by Countries and Regions (Customs Statistics)

单位：万美元 (USD 10 000)

国 别（地区）	Country (Region)	2004			2005		
		进出口总额 Total	出口总额 Exports	进口总额 Imports	进出口总额 Total	出口总额 Exports	进口总额 Imports
总 计	**Total**	**115455433**	**59332558**	**56122875**	**142190617**	**76195341**	**65995276**
亚洲	**Asia**	**66490647**	**29548698**	**36941949**	**80788703**	**36640758**	**44147945**
阿富汗	Afghanistan	5792	5697	95	5272	5121	151
巴林	Bahrain	21297	12057	9240	25594	18700	6894
孟加拉国	Bangladesh	196328	190627	5701	248134	240274	7860
不丹	Bhutan	52	35	17	47	47	0
文莱	Brunei	29895	4789	25106	26087	5314	20773
缅甸	Myanmar	114538	93844	20694	120925	93485	27440
柬埔寨	Cambodia	48171	45177	2993	56334	53603	2731
塞浦路斯	Cyprus	18692	18523	169	29012	28728	284
朝鲜	Korea DPR	138516	79950	58566	158024	108110	49914
中国香港	Hong Kong, China	11266529	10086857	1179672	13669803	12447325	1222478
印度	India	1361404	593601	767803	1870050	893428	976622
印度尼西亚	Indonesia	1347209	625642	721567	1678733	835037	843696
伊朗	Iran	704546	255476	449069	1008327	329659	678668
伊拉克	Iraq	46980	14955	32025	82379	40811	41568
以色列	Israel	248485	154199	94286	302788	195434	107354
日本	Japan	16783577	7350904	9432673	18439396	8398628	10040768
约旦	Jordan	71076	62227	8849	91068	83181	7887
科威特	Kuwait	124811	48405	76406	164897	62847	102050
老挝	Laos	11354	10088	1265	12893	10338	2555
黎巴嫩	Lebanon	49356	48385	970	47623	47204	419
中国澳门	Macao, China	183348	161760	21588	186961	160507	26454
马来西亚	Malaysia	2626080	808606	1817474	3069956	1060635	2009321
马尔代夫	Maldives	809	791	18	1696	1693	3
蒙古	Mongolia	69442	23335	46107	85992	31889	54103
尼泊尔	Nepal	17148	16324	823	19644	18794	850
阿曼	Oman	438951	11102	427849	432990	19099	413891
巴基斯坦	Pakistan	306054	246579	59475	426083	342766	83317
巴勒斯坦	Palestine	992	984	7	2383	2360	23
菲律宾	Philippines	1332816	426872	905944	1755732	468763	1286969
卡塔尔	Qatar	43778	10352	33426	67639	20367	47272
沙特阿拉伯	Saudi Arabia	1029810	277546	752265	1607014	382442	1224572
新加坡	Singapore	2668207	1268760	1399447	3314686	1663226	1651460
韩国	Korea Rep.	9004566	2781156	6223410	11192818	3510778	7682040
斯里兰卡	Sri Lanka	71745	69486	2259	97627	93967	3660
叙利亚	Syria	72067	69265	2801	90637	88863	1774
泰国	Thailand	1734208	580158	1154051	2181119	781930	1399189
土耳其	Turkey	341267	282129	59138	487547	425373	62174
阿联酋	United Arab Emirates	814561	684114	130448	1077544	872984	204560
也门共和国	Republic of Yemen	191625	45770	145855	321479	54710	266769
越南	Vietnam	674202	426003	248199	819674	564390	255284
中华人民共和国	P. R. China	3865454		3865454	5516291		5516291
中国台湾	Taiwan, China	7830374	1354443	6475932	9122989	1654956	7468033
东帝汶	Timor Leste	171	171		127	127	
哈萨克	Kazakhstan	449809	221181	228627	680611	389675	290936
吉尔吉斯	Kirghizia	60229	49274	10955	97220	86715	10505
塔吉克	Tadzhikistan	6893	5356	1537	15794	14374	1420
土库曼	Turkmenistan	9844	8455	1389	10996	9088	1908
乌兹别克	Uzbekistan	57551	17244	40307	68056	23006	45050
亚洲其他国家（地区）	Other Countries (Regions) in Asia	43	43		23	12	11
非洲	**Africa**	**2945928**	**1381322**	**1564606**	**3974373**	**1868160**	**2106213**
阿尔及利亚	Algeria	123960	98052	25908	176815	140442	36373
安哥拉	Angola	491086	19352	471734	695462	37279	658183
贝宁	Benin	68854	57726	11127	109234	95295	13939
博茨瓦纳	Botswana	5240	4954	286	6251	5851	400
布隆迪	Burundi	513	481	32	1222	1189	33
喀麦隆	Cameroon	24892	10002	14891	19662	12987	6675
加那利群岛	Canary Is.	5269	5268	1	3905	3905	

18-8 续表 1 continued

单位：万美元 (USD 10 000)

国 别（地区）	Country (Region)	2004 进出口总额 Total	2004 出口总额 Exports	2004 进口总额 Imports	2005 进出口总额 Total	2005 出口总额 Exports	2005 进口总额 Imports
佛得角	Cape Verde	275	275		519	519	
中非	Central Africa	957	332	625	1608	709	899
塞卜泰(休达)	Ceuta	144	144		159	159	
乍得	Chad	22853	594	22259	20601	1493	19108
科摩罗	Comoros	130	130		183	183	
刚果	Congo	166209	9303	156906	242274	14471	227803
吉布提	Djibouti	7273	7222	51	11200	11146	54
埃及	Egypt	157637	138844	18794	214518	193404	21114
赤道几内亚	Eq. Guinea	100677	1013	99665	145663	1880	143783
埃塞俄比亚	Ethiopia	20844	19406	1439	36971	28400	8571
加蓬	Gabon	41444	1416	40029	39296	4128	35168
冈比亚	Gambia	12435	12423	12	12452	12435	17
加纳	Ghana	59078	51040	8038	76843	67242	9601
几内亚	Guinea	10781	9302	1480	14731	14431	300
几内亚(比绍)	Guinea-Bissau	602	599	3	579	579	
科特迪瓦共和国	Cote d'lvoire	23147	12301	10846	22212	13703	8509
肯尼亚	Kenya	36576	34879	1697	47457	45692	1765
利比里亚	Liberia	19833	18181	1652	16380	14963	1417
利比亚	Libya	67174	25499	41676	130222	36050	94172
马达加斯加	Madagascar	16616	15208	1408	19664	18264	1400
马拉维	Malawi	1881	1877	5	1842	1635	207
马里	Mali	16552	5877	10676	14519	6594	7925
毛里塔尼亚	Mauritania	11473	6433	5040	7836	7430	406
毛里求斯	Mauritius	15784	15119	665	18562	17734	828
摩洛哥	Morocco	115756	94348	21408	148388	120643	27745
莫桑比克	Mozambique	11944	7515	4429	16501	9148	7353
纳米比亚	Namibia	9912	5254	4658	13674	6035	7639
尼日尔	Niger	2501	2500	1	3390	3390	
尼日利亚	Nigeria	218178	171856	46322	283004	230316	52688
留尼汪	Reunion	2364	2364		3134	3133	1
卢旺达	Rwanda	2116	513	1603	2354	1201	1153
圣多美和普林西比	Sao Tome & Principle	156	22	134	55	55	
塞内加尔	Senegal	11225	10831	394	14096	13308	788
塞舌尔	Seychelles	181	178	3	341	340	1
塞拉利昂	Sierra Leone	2986	2826	160	3212	3076	136
索马里	Somalia	1733	952	781	1964	1657	307
南非	South Africa	591211	295190	296020	726902	382597	344305
西撒哈拉	Western Sahara	59	59		2	2	
苏丹	Sudan	252176	81589	170588	390805	129359	261446
坦桑尼亚	Tanzania	28424	21597	6827	47430	30358	17072
多哥	Togo	44513	39865	4647	56997	53810	3187
突尼斯	Tunisia	27922	24509	3413	33963	29554	4409
乌干达	Uganda	8807	7643	1164	9937	7937	2000
布基纳法索	Burkina Faso	13645	1234	12411	17941	1614	16327
民主刚果	Congo DR	13657	3699	9959	22548	4971	17577
赞比亚	Zambia	22215	5104	17111	30056	4850	25206
津巴布韦	Zimbabwe	25424	11306	14118	28329	12537	15792
莱索托	Lesotho	4745	4745		5615	5582	33
梅利利亚	Melilla	280	279		324	324	
斯威士兰	Swaziland	2612	1149	1463	3421	1103	2318
厄立特里亚	Eritrea	805	754	51	824	783	41
马约特岛	Mayotte	69	69		92	92	
非洲其他国家（地区）	Other Countries (Regions) in Africa	122	122		236	196	40
欧洲	**Europe**	**21138553**	**12238620**	**8899933**	**26205911**	**16562821**	**9643090**
比利时	Belgium	937946	585968	351978	1174422	773875	400547
丹麦	Denmark	315174	194597	120577	397924	278888	119036
英国	United Kingdom	1972547	1496696	475850	2450025	1897647	552378
德国	Germany	5411175	2375573	3035602	6325006	3252713	3072293
法国	France	1756959	992139	764820	2064615	1163936	900679
爱尔兰	Ireland	332812	214022	118790	460741	318434	142307
意大利	Italy	1567516	922377	645139	1861418	1168889	692529

18-8 续表 2 continued

单位：万美元 (USD 10 000)

国 别（地区）	Country (Region)	2004 进出口总额 Total	2004 出口总额 Exports	2004 进口总额 Imports	2005 进出口总额 Total	2005 出口总额 Exports	2005 进口总额 Imports
卢森堡	Luxembourg	104660	91752	12908	219037	203960	15077
荷兰	Netherlands	2148823	1851882	296941	2880246	2587574	292672
希腊	Greece	146664	138033	8631	202198	193529	8669
葡萄牙	Portugal	86916	58826	28090	123578	91195	32383
西班牙	Spain	722166	547574	174592	1052130	843966	208164
奥地利	Austria	229042	78060	150982	249229	88307	160922
芬兰	Finland	551505	249362	302143	625407	362594	262813
瑞典	Sweden	519816	185859	333957	569870	257650	312220
阿尔巴尼亚	Albania	6921	6325	596	9025	8321	704
安道尔	Andorra	212	211		324	323	1
保加利亚	Bulgaria	40511	33797	6714	53076	44164	8912
直布罗陀	Gibraltar	75	75		66	66	
匈牙利	Hungary	312655	265096	47559	285902	249349	36553
冰岛	Iceland	7331	4597	2734	12143	7470	4673
列支敦士登	Liechtenstein	3033	666	2367	1897	922	975
马耳他	Malta	52536	27318	25218	53905	30111	23794
摩纳哥	Monaco	2077	1433	644	1922	924	998
挪威	Norway	242631	102851	139780	246587	132191	114396
波兰	Poland	233099	184372	48727	315276	259544	55732
罗马尼亚	Romania	138374	105696	32678	166157	136926	29231
圣马力诺	San Marino	62	62		163	162	1
瑞士	Switzerland	511893	150589	361305	582751	194696	388055
爱沙尼亚	Estonia	22266	20202	2064	36910	31143	5767
拉脱维亚	Latvia	19881	17900	1981	29026	28170	856
立陶宛	Lithuania	28588	27236	1352	37219	36071	1148
格鲁吉亚	Georgia	5706	2288	3417	4342	4076	266
亚美尼亚	Armenia	1384	1169	216	2338	2303	35
阿塞拜疆	Azerbaijan	18395	14374	4021	25805	23365	2440
白俄罗斯	Belorussia	21890	6495	15395	57172	8128	49044
摩尔多瓦	Moldavia	2410	2391	19	5163	5149	14
俄罗斯联邦	Russia	2122553	909812	1212741	2910122	1321128	1588994
乌克兰	Ukraine	248790	144329	104461	327732	249252	78480
塞尔维亚和黑山	Serbian	17576	16320	1256	22249	20108	2141
斯洛文尼亚	Slovenia	24886	20690	4196	32281	26557	5724
克罗地亚	Croatia	36642	34452	2190	61749	57366	4383
捷克	Czech	179333	135108	44224	203919	166741	37178
斯洛伐克	Slovakia	28840	15987	12853	49138	30836	18302
前南斯拉夫马其顿	Macedonia of Former Yugoslavia	2787	2641	147	3415	2150	1265
波黑	Bosnia and Herzegovina	1499	1421	78	12298	1957	10341
欧洲其他国家（地区）	Other Countries (Regions) in Europe						
拉丁美洲	**Latin America**	**4000062**	**1823809**	**2176254**	**5046577**	**2368050**	**2678527**
安提瓜和巴布达	Antigua and Barbuda	11853	11853		14690	14690	
阿根廷	Argentina	410718	85230	325487	512364	132443	379921
阿鲁巴岛	Aruba	381	375	6	578	564	14
巴哈马	Bahamas	9938	9869	70	15564	15545	19
巴巴多斯	Barbados	1062	1038	24	1942	1921	21
伯利兹	Belize	2258	2258		3229	3208	21
玻利维亚	Bolivia	5314	2359	2955	8159	5054	3105
巴西	Brazil	1234697	367410	867286	1481973	482721	999252
开曼群岛	Cayman Is.	247	247		404	404	
智利	Chile	535516	168843	366672	714102	214948	499154
哥伦比亚	Colombia	80478	62927	17551	113530	93015	20515
多米尼加	Dominica	4731	4555	175	5000	4905	95
哥斯达黎加	Costa Rica	79571	15442	64129	115085	22877	92208
古巴	Cuba	52323	32828	19494	87283	63587	23696
库腊索岛	Curacao	4344	4289	56	4857	4753	104
多米尼加共和国	Dominica Rep.	24835	23276	1559	29325	26415	2910
厄瓜多尔	Ecuador	43582	34360	9222	51007	46735	4272
法属圭亚那	French Guyana	110	108	2	153	147	6
格林纳达	Granada	79	79		273	273	
瓜德罗普岛	Guadeloupe	403	382	21	615	615	
危地马拉	Guatemala	43555	39264	4291	56833	47364	9469

18-8 续表 3 continued

单位：万美元 (USD 10 000)

国 别（地区）	Country (Region)	2004 进出口总额 Total	2004 出口总额 Exports	2004 进口总额 Imports	2005 进出口总额 Total	2005 出口总额 Exports	2005 进口总额 Imports
圭亚那	Guyana	2236	2118	118	3478	2721	757
海地	Haiti	2248	2222	26	3047	3020	27
洪都拉斯	Honduras	13480	12314	1166	14798	13381	1417
牙买加	Jamaica	39591	12607	26985	32507	10407	22100
马提尼克岛	Martinique	175	175		410	410	
墨西哥	Mexico	711260	497275	213984	776299	553769	222530
蒙特塞拉特	Montserrat	4	4		8	8	
尼加拉瓜	Nicaragua	10454	10159	295	12817	11400	1417
巴拿马	Panama	220187	218695	1492	317332	315112	2220
巴拉圭	Paraguay	29323	23494	5829	31111	25256	5855
秘鲁	Peru	194130	41841	152290	288687	60888	227799
波多黎各	Puerto Rico	29825	20693	9132	40930	28971	11959
萨巴	Saba	6	6				
圣卢西亚	Saint Lucia	232	229	3	3554	283	3271
圣马丁岛	Saint Martin Is.	144	144		244	244	
圣文森特和格林纳丁斯	Saint Vincent & Grenadines	1320	1320		1521	1521	
萨尔瓦多	El Salvador	20067	19688	379	20440	19390	1050
苏里南	Surinam	3123	3027	96	4600	3868	732
特立尼达和多巴哥	Trinidad and Tobago	7959	7591	368	11909	10043	1866
特克斯和凯科斯群岛	Turks & Caicos Is.	2		2	27	25	2
乌拉圭	Uruguay	31985	20955	11030	45590	28257	17333
委内瑞拉	Venezuela	133347	59553	73794	214197	90785	123412
英属维尔京群岛	Virgin Is. (E)	349	82	267	2218	2218	
圣其茨-尼维斯	St. Kitts-Nevis	20	20		58	58	
荷属安地列斯群岛	Andreas Is. (N)	2488	2488		3772	3772	
拉美其他国家（地区）	Other Countries (Regions) in Latin America	119	119		58	58	
北美洲	**North America**	**18526063**	**13323048**	**5203014**	**23083066**	**17466840**	**5616226**
加拿大	Canada	1551417	816118	735299	1916483	1165367	751116
美国	United States	16959858	12494203	4465655	21151252	16289075	4862177
格陵兰	Greenland	2103	45	2058	3101	167	2934
百慕大群岛	Bermuda	12670	12670		12223	12223	
北美洲其他国家（地区）	Other Countries (Regions) in North America	15	13	3	8	8	
大洋洲及太平洋群岛	**Oceanic and Pacific Islands**	**2350431**	**1017062**	**1333369**	**3090073**	**1288713**	**1801360**
澳大利亚	Australia	2039074	883825	1155249	2725513	1106150	1619363
库克群岛	Cook Islands	91	83	8	591	44	547
斐济	Fiji	3871	3253	618	4527	4300	227
盖比群岛	Gambier Is.	25	25		1	1	
马克萨斯群岛	Marquesas Is.				2	2	
瑙鲁	Nauru	10	10		3	3	
新喀里多尼亚	New Caledonia (Fr)	6604	826	5778	9356	1515	7841
瓦努阿图	Vanuatu	749	723	26	828	780	48
新西兰	New Zealand	249058	107737	141322	267944	135344	132600
诺福克岛	Norfolk Islands	36	36		26	26	
巴布亚新几内亚	Papua New Guinea	29638	5252	24386	37605	6659	30946
社会群岛	Society Is.	391	391		572	572	
所罗门群岛	Solomon Is.	6127	332	5795	10168	508	9660
汤加	Tonga	628	628		294	294	
萨摩亚	Samoa	686	589	98	598	594	4
基里巴斯	Kiribati	87	87		143	141	2
图瓦卢	Tuvalu	224	224		635	635	
密克罗尼西亚联邦	Micronesia Commonwealth	745	745		244	242	2
马绍尔群岛共和国	Marshall. Is.	10458	10458		28097	28097	
帕劳共和国	Republic of Palau	43	43		68	68	
法属波利尼西亚	Polynesia (F)	844	758	85	1673	1566	107
大洋洲其他国家（地区）	Other Countries (Regions) in Oceanic	1042	1038	4	1175	1168	7
国别（地区）不详	**Others**	**3750**		**3750**	**1916**		**1916**

18-9 出口主要货物数量和金额

Main Export Commodities in Volume and Value (Customs Statistics)

金额单位：万美元 (USD 10 000)

品名	Item	2004 数量 Volume	2004 金额 Value	2005 数量 Volume	2005 金额 Value
活猪 (万头)	Live Hogs (10 000 heads)	197	23965	176	22686
活家禽 (万只)	Live Poultry (10 000 heads)	1926	3333	2502	3740
鲜、冻牛肉 (万吨)	Frozen, Fresh Beef (10 000 tons)	2	3033	2	4150
鲜、冻猪肉 (万吨)	Frozen, Fresh Pork (10 000 tons)	29	45954	25	40612
冻鸡 (万吨)	Frozen Chicken (10 000 tons)	7	9245	9	11145
鲜、冻兔肉 (吨)	Frozen, Fresh Rabbit Meat (ton)	6396	1007	8925	2106
水海产品 (万吨)	Aquatic and Seawater Products(10 000 tons)	176	405231	176	434677
鲜蛋 (百万个)	Fresh Eggs (million units)	1047	4028	921	4352
谷物及谷物粉 (万吨)	Cereals and Cereals Flour (10 000 tons)	473	82766	1014	151856
#稻谷和大米 (万吨)	Rice (10 000 tons)	91	23944	69	23234
玉米 (万吨)	Maize (10 000 tons)	232	32571	864	110753
蔬菜 (万吨)	Vegetables (10 000 tons)	470	278114	520	330200
#鲜或冷藏蔬菜 (万吨)	Fresh Vegetables (10 000 tons)	314	106263	353	132755
干豆 (万吨)	Dried Beans (10 000 tons)	80	33092	87	38815
橘、橙 (吨)	Mandarins and Oranges (ton)	333264	9745	426153	12834
鲜苹果 (吨)	Apples (ton)	774131	27441	824050	30631
核桃仁 (吨)	Walnut Meat (ton)	9894	2996	12447	4611
栗子 (吨)	Chestnut (ton)	39928	6327	38896	5306
松子仁 (吨)	Pine Nut Kernels (ton)	9542	6890	11655	7632
大豆 (万吨)	Soybean (10 000 tons)	33	14493	40	16958
花生及花生仁 (万吨)	Peanuts (10 000 tons)	40	29867	45	31959
食用植物油(含棕榈油)(吨)	Edible Vegetable Oil (ton)	65215	6327	225214	17207
食糖 (吨)	Sugar (tons)	85191	2579	358290	11077
天然蜂蜜 (吨)	Natural Honey (ton)	81325	8901	88499	8763
茶叶 (吨)	Tea (ton)	280193	43685	286563	48431
辣椒干 (吨)	Dried Capsicum (ton)	73094	11437	70140	10041
猪肉罐头 (吨)	Canned Pork (ton)	54090	7929	52059	8397
蘑菇罐头 (吨)	Canned Mushroom (ton)	298459	29754	322747	29281
啤酒 (万升)	Beer (10 000 liters)	14080	6849	14694	6955
肠衣 (吨)	Casings (ton)	62229	50411	63094	50816
填充用羽毛；羽绒 (吨)	Feathers and Down for Stuffing (ton)	37590	34776	36466	35784
药材 (吨)	Medical Materials (ton)	169864	26639	203007	28745
烤烟 (吨)	Flue-cured Tobacco (ton)	135206	22148	112128	21776
锯材 (立方米)	Wood Sawn (cu.m)	474626	21755	615324	27859
生丝 (吨)	Raw Silk (ton)	11288	21360	10972	24455
山羊绒 (吨)	Cashmere (ton)	4159	23574	3662	24765
兔毛 (吨)	Rabbit Hair (ton)	2970	4387	1988	3714
棉花（原棉） (吨)	Cotton (Cotton Wool) (ton)	9092	1574	4962	791
苎麻 (吨)	Ramie (ton)	1245	470	1144	458
天然石墨 (吨)	Natural Graphite (ton)	451735	6704	493747	8545
天然碳酸镁；氧化镁 (万吨)	Natural Magnesium Carbonate, Magnesia (10 000 tons)	194	26323	184	30776
萤石（氟石） (万吨)	Fluorite (10 000 tons)	83	11916	73	12879
天然硫酸钡(重晶石)(万吨)	Barite (10 000 tons)	239	7782	308	10695
滑石 (万吨)	Talcum (10 000 tons)	64	6596	56	7051
铝矿砂及其精矿 (万吨)	Aluminum Ores (10 000 tons)		11		14
煤 (万吨)	Coal (10 000 tons)	8666	381124	7168	427214
焦炭、半焦炭 (万吨)	Coke and Semi-coke (10 000 tons)	1501	394868	1276	234058

18-9 续表 1 continued

金额单位：万美元 (USD 10 000)

品名	Item	2004 数量 Volume	2004 金额 Value	2005 数量 Volume	2005 金额 Value
原油 (万吨)	Crude Oil (10 000 tons)	549	132469	807	269601
成品油 (万吨)	Petroleum Products Refined (10 000 tons)	1146	396019	1401	641083
石蜡 (万吨)	Paraffin Wax (10 000 tons)	64	32808	73	46904
仲钨酸铵 (吨)	Tungstates (ton)	5909	3853	8012	13557
氧化锌及过氧化锌 (吨)	Zinc Oxide and Zinc Peroxide (ton)	67063	6029	62205	6920
糠醛 (吨)	Furfural (ton)	26770	2257	38547	3293
合成有机染料 (吨)	Synthetic Organic Dyestuffs (ton)	226477	64533	231418	75569
医药品 (吨)	Medical and Pharmaceutical Products (ton)	353349	323471	398169	377863
#中式成药 (吨)	Medicaments of Chinese Type (ton)	12194	11344	12251	12532
医用敷料 (吨)	Pharmaceutical Goods (ton)	97627	43910	121475	52597
洗衣粉 (吨)	Detergent (ton)	116568	6048	121108	6185
烟花、爆竹 (吨)	Fireworks and Firecrackers (ton)	285395	34786	325592	40229
松香及树脂酸 (吨)	Resin and Resin Acids (ton)	342893	16386	347462	25453
新的充气橡胶轮胎 (万条)	Rubber Tyres (10 000 units)	19969	248675	22522	378137
纸及纸板(未切成形) (万吨)	Paper and Paperboard in Rolls (10 000 tons)	101	82115	167	134403
棉纱线 (吨)	Cotton Yarn (ton)	431031	133380	469532	139995
亚麻及苎麻纱线 (吨)	Flax or Ramie Yarn (ton)	25119	11528	23440	13219
丝织物 (万米)	Silk (10 000 m)	25221	58845	29017	72994
棉机织物 (万米)	Cotton Cloth (10 000 m)	530071	604472	610328	699804
亚麻及苎麻机织物 (万米)	Flax or Ramie Woven Fabric (10 000 m)	23774	39859	25093	45234
合成短纤与棉混纺机织物 (万米)	Synthetic Short Fibre and Cotton-fibre Mixture Woven Fabric (10 000 m)	219155	116259	243356	142141
人造纤维短纤机织物 (万米)	Short Rayon Woven Fabric (10 000 m)	51397	25826	68425	37987
地毯 (万平方米)	Carpets (10 000 sq.m)	13632	77331	17505	93216
棉浴巾 (万条)	Cotton Bath Towels (10 000 units)	27390	42113	40126	63482
塑料编织袋 (周转袋除外) (万条)	Bags of PP or PE Strip(Except Turnover Bags) (10 000 units)	235287	34259	276996	45135
水泥 (万吨)	Cement (10 000 tons)	704	23039	2216	68460
平板玻璃 (万平方米)	Plate Glass (10 000 sq.m)	14454	34621	19925	48225
玻璃制品	Glass Products		143579		182934
家用陶瓷器皿 (吨)	Porcelain and Pottery Ware for Household Use (ton)	1870385	133891	2009261	165945
生铁及镜铁 (万吨)	Pig Iron and Spiegeleisen (10 000 tons)	129	36144	223	66651
硅铁 (万吨)	Ferro-silicon (10 000 tons)	93	67558	94	61402
钢坯及粗锻件 (万吨)	Billet and Crude Forgings (10 000 tons)	606	231252	707	267284
钢材 (万吨)	Rolled Steel (10 000 tons)	1423	833376	2052	1307968
未锻造铜及合金 (吨)	Unwrought Copper and its Alloys (ton)	126276	34509	144671	54982
铜材 (吨)	Rolled Copper (ton)	389924	149652	463560	207366
未锻造铝及合金 (吨)	Unwrought Aluminum and its Alloys (ton)	1683369	279916	1318599	237952
铝材 (吨)	Rolled Aluminum (ton)	430949	111999	711484	195089
未锻造的锌及锌合金 (吨)	Unwrought Zinc and Zinc Alloys (ton)	263149	26911	146845	19583
未锻造的锡及锡合金 (吨)	Unwrought Tin and Tin Alloys (ton)	38915	32106	27014	19865
未锻造的锑、粉末及废碎料(吨)	Unwrought Antimony (ton)	21490	4896	29833	8292
未锻造的锰 (吨)	Unwrought Manganese (ton)	269802	38713	285019	42433
钢铁或铜制标准紧固件 (万吨)	Iron or Copper Nails, Bolts, etc. (10 000 tons)	114	131020	152	183357
搪瓷器 (吨)	Enamelware (ton)	116622	16016	104603	15965
手用或机用工具 (吨)	Hand Tools and Tools for Machines (ton)	944717	234446	1102104	301841
锁 (吨)	Locks (ton)	276216	77812	297673	93271
电扇 (万台)	Fans (10 000 sets)	46822	182505	52044	222116
纺织机械及零件	Textile Machinery		66677		86940
缝纫机（包括工业用）(万架)	Sewing Machines (Including Industrial Use) (10 000 sets)	1170	60611	1199	76826

18-9 续表 2 continued

金额单位：万美元 (USD 10 000)

品名	Item	2004 数量 Volume	2004 金额 Value	2005 数量 Volume	2005 金额 Value
金属加工机床 (万台)	Machine Tools (10 000 sets)	616	53853	682	82050
电子计算器 (万台)	Electric Calculator (10 000 sets)	45689	80518	47545	81662
自动数据处理设备及其部件 (万台)	Automatic Data Processing Machines and Components (10 000 sets)	112979	5991127	130516	7630702
自动数据处理设备的零件 (吨)	Parts for Auto Data Processing Equipment(ton)	1327556	2387829	1406665	2835642
轴承 (万套)	Bearings (10 000 units)	224557	88349	248260	110034
电动机及发电机 (万台)	Electric Motors and Generators (10 000 sets)	336168	291222	326025	340677
静止式变流器 (万个)	Static Converters (10 000 units)	168915	416404	211505	528044
原电池 (万个)	Primary Cells and Batteries (10 000 units)	1992596	95545	2028916	107677
蓄电池 (万个)	Electric Accumulators (10 000 units)	219735	315505	258879	414133
手电筒 (万个)	Flashlights (10 000 units)	67498	29170	71864	36719
有线电话机（包括无绳电话机）(万台)	Line Telephone Sets (10 000 sets)	19900	197692	19830	212310
扬声器 (万个)	Loudspeakers (10 000 units)	188170	180147	196719	211795
收录机及组合音响 (万台)	Sound Recording Apparatus (10 000 sets)	20584	292054	19836	389067
收音机 (万台)	Radio (10 000 sets)	30674	36778	27451	51459
电视机 （包括整套散件）(万台)	TV Sets (including a Complete Set of Spare Parts) (10 000 sets)	6309	548553	8590	841087
电容器 (吨)	Electrical Capacitors (ton)	58394	122953	59306	143838
通断保护电路装置及零件	Electrical Apparatus for Switching or Protecting Electrical Circuits		389112		529827
二极管及类似半导体器件(万个)	Diode and Semi Conductors (10 000 units)	14303577	242684	17480840	336075
电线电缆 (吨)	Insulated Wire or Cable (ton)	1077072	370067	1234080	483929
集装箱 (个)	Containers (unit)	1974716	512529	2046530	587142
汽车和汽车底盘 (辆)	Motor Vehicles and Chassis (unit)	401354	78030	1084309	190396
汽车零件	Parts of Motor Vehicles		440919		658043
自行车 (万辆)	Bicycles (10 000 units)	5175	164070	5385	174927
船舶 (艘)	Ships (unit)	87322	313673	136376	457802
照相机 (万架)	Cameras (10 000 sets)	5631	33179	4594	19255
医疗仪器及器械	Medical Instruments and Appliances		137960		193884
手表 (万只)	Wrist Watches (10 000 units)	96582	97743	80521	92439
日用钟 (万只)	Clocks (10 000 sets)	44910	49123	40614	48556
家具及其零件	Furniture		1016766		1350387
服装 （针织、钩织的除外）	Garments (Excluding Knitwear and Crochet)		2668198		3243219
针织或钩编服装	Garments, Knitted or Crocheted		2342531		2787777
皮鞋 (万双)	Leather Shoes (10 000 pairs)	115311	631778	136046	806543
橡胶或塑料底布鞋（包括球鞋） (万双)	Cloth Shoes With Outer of Rubber or Artificial Plastic Materials (including Gym Shoes) (10 000 pairs)	93228	185833	111567	235821
塑料制品 (万吨)	Plastic Articles (10 000 tons)	633	917685	673	1127745
玩具	Toys		637946		656229
足球、篮球、排球 (万个)	Footballs, Basketballs and Volleyballs (10 000 units)	12025	16150	13292	17904
铅笔 (吨)	Pencils (ton)	47706	12113	52113	13638
伞 (万把)	Umbrellas (10 000 units)	76944	78096	82020	87607
竹编结品 (吨)	Bamboo Products (ton)	84425	16687	78409	15571
藤编结品 (吨)	Rattan Products (ton)	36641	9871	32561	9355
草编结品 (吨)	Straw Mats and Straw Products (ton)	45942	11645	53512	13907
柳编结品 (吨)	Wickerwork (ton)	108780	25446	104061	28134
鬃刷 (万把)	Bristle Brushes (10 000 units)	58966	9238	57337	10395
人造花 (吨)	Artificial Flowers (ton)	284214	57668	280101	61157
热水瓶 (万个)	Vacuum Flasks (10 000 units)	16405	29183	18420	38862
机电产品	Mechanical and Electrical Products		32337023		42674726
高新技术产品	High and New-tech Products		16553560		21824802

18-10 进口主要货物数量和金额

Main Import Commodities in Volume and Value (Customs Statistics)

金额单位：万美元 (USD 10 000)

品 名		Item		2004 数 量 Volume	2004 金 额 Value	2005 数 量 Volume	2005 金 额 Value
谷物及谷物粉	(万吨)	Cereals and Cereals Flour	(10 000 tons)	974	222888	627	140887
#小麦	(万吨)	Wheat	(10 000 tons)	726	164961	354	77287
稻谷和大米	(万吨)	Paddy and Rice	(10 000 tons)	76	25345	52	19945
大豆	(万吨)	Soybean	(10 000 tons)	2023	697917	2659	777879
食用植物油	(万吨)	Edible Vegetable Oil	(10 000 tons)	676	366535	621	281508
其他植物油	(万吨)	Other Vegetable Oils	(10 000 tons)	34	22554	42	28040
食糖	(万吨)	Sugar	(10 000 tons)	121	27558	139	38327
配制的动物饲料	(万吨)	Prepared Feeding Stuff	(10 000 tons)	14	12226	11	12107
天然橡胶（包括胶乳）	(万吨)	Natural Rubber (including Latex)	(10 000 tons)	128	152427	141	185466
合成橡胶（包括胶乳）	(万吨)	Synthetic Rubber (including Latex)	(10 000 tons)	109	141423	109	179810
原木	(万立方米)	Logs	(10 000 cu.m)	2631	280432	2937	324356
纸浆	(万吨)	Paper Pulp	(10 000 tons)	732	356772	759	372551
锯材	(万立方米)	Wood Sawn	(10 000 cu.m)	601	138256	597	150779
棉花(原棉)	(万吨)	Cotton, not Carded or Combed	(10 000 tons)	191	317624	257	319709
羊毛及条	(万吨)	Wool and Wool Tops	(10 000 tons)	25	120715	27	131797
纺织用合成纤维	(万吨)	Synthetic Fibers Suitable for Spinning	(10 000 tons)	99	137760	84	138275
#聚酯纤维	(万吨)	Polyester Fibers	(10 000 tons)	51	53221	35	42324
聚丙烯腈纤维	(万吨)	Polyacryolnitr Fibers	(10 000 tons)	46	77681	47	878823
铁矿砂及其精矿	(万吨)	Iron Ore	(10 000 tons)	20808	1269913	27526	1837278
锰矿砂及其精矿	(万吨)	Manganese Ores	(10 000 tons)	465	58558	458	68348
铜矿砂及其精矿	(万吨)	Copper Ores	(10 000 tons)	287	223804	406	370672
铬矿砂及其精矿	(万吨)	Chromium Ores	(10 000 tons)	217	38134	302	59557
氧化铝	(万吨)	Aluminum Oxide	(10 000 tons)	587	204360	702	259717
煤	(万吨)	Coal	(10 000 tons)	1861	89181	2617	138369
原油	(万吨)	Crude Oil	(10 000 tons)	12281	3391168	12682	4772293
成品油	(万吨)	Petroleum Products Refined	(10 000 tons)	3787	923930	3143	1043465
乙二醇	(万吨)	Ethylene Glycol	(10 000 tons)	340	304785	400	352847
对苯二甲酸	(万吨)	Telephthalic Acid	(10 000 tons)	572	417267	650	521496
己内酰胺	(万吨)	Carprolactam	(10 000 tons)	45	72215	49	107285
碳酸钠（纯碱）	(万吨)	Soda Ash	(10 000 tons)	20	2274	7	1276
医药品	(吨)	Pharmaceutical Products	(ton)	30240	190259	36259	231244
肥料(自然吨)	(万吨)	Chemical Fertilizers, Manufactured (Actual Weight)	(10 000 tons)	1240	228769	1397	305143

18-10 续表 continued

金额单位：万美元 (USD 10 000)

品　　名	Item	2004 数量 Volume	2004 金额 Value	2005 数量 Volume	2005 金额 Value
#尿素 (万吨)	Urea (10 000 tons)	4	549	7	1272
氮、磷、钾复合肥 (万吨)	Compound Fertilizers of Nitrogen, Phosphor and Kalium (10 000 tons)	205	41143	229	52896
磷酸氢二胺 (万吨)	Diammonium Phosphape (10 000 tons)	229	57565	175	49738
氯化钾 (万吨)	Potassium Chloride (10 000 tons)	718	115860	883	182414
原形聚乙烯 (万吨)	Polyethylene in primary Forms (10 000 tons)	366	333021	356	371776
原形聚丙烯 (万吨)	Polypropylene in Primary Forms (10 000 tons)	291	256374	302	301551
原形聚苯乙烯 (万吨)	Polystyrene in Primary Forms (10 000 tons)	380	403329	367	438690
#ABS树脂 (万吨)	ABS Copolymers (10 000 tons)	196	227108	199	257867
原形聚氯乙烯 (万吨)	Polyvinyl Chloride in Primary Forms (10 000 tons)	211	170541	166	141604
聚酯切片 (万吨)	Slices or Chips of Polyethylene Terephthalate (10 000 tons)	18	18067	13	14387
农药 (吨)	Pesticides (ton)	27623	14680	36752	18222
纸及纸板（未切成形）(万吨)	Paper and Paperboard (Unchopped in Shape)(10 000 tons)	611	384852	521	354489
钢材 (万吨)	Rolled Steel (10 000 tons)	2930	2078471	2582	2460845
未锻造的铜及铜合金 (万吨)	Copper and Copper Alloys (10 000 tons)	138	381221	142	494967
铜材 (万吨)	Rolled Copper (10 000 tons)	119	390720	112	437824
未锻造的铝及铝合金 (万吨)	Aluminum and Aluminum Alloys (10 000 tons)	103	157110	64	101849
铝材 (万吨)	Rolled Aluminum (10 000 tons)	61	194375	65	225102
锅炉 (台)	Boilers (set)	557	7514	599	7529
制冷设备用压缩机 (万台)	Compressors for Refrigerating Equipment (10 000 sets)	1992	108823	1774	101309
金属加工机床 (台)	Machine Tools (set)	127138	591546	116567	649615
阀门 (万套)	Valves (10 000 sets)	17645	196375	18772	238035
自动数据处理设备及其部件 (万台)	Automatic Data Processing Machines and Components (10 000 sets)	23766	1445609	32133	1802081
有线电话或电报交换机 (台)	Line Telephonic or Telegraphic Switching Apparatus (set)	27458	4945	35922	11752
收录机及组合音响 (万台)	Sound Recording Apparatus (10 000 sets)	125	7822	305	16208
电视机 (万台)	TV Sets (10 000 sets)	78	14808	71	12386
电视显像管 (万只)	Cathode-ray TV Picture Tube (10 000 sets)	2636	99676	2102	65806
汽车和汽车底盘 (辆)	Motor Vehicles and Chassis (unit)	175914	533362	163031	511451
#小轿车（包括整套散件）(辆)	Cars (including a Complete Set of Spare Parts) (unit)	116085	326945	76542	259413
卡车（包括整套散件）(辆)	Trucks (including a Complete Set of Spare Parts) (unit)	7989	39262	2938	15305
自卸车（包括整套散件）(辆)	Dump Trucks (including a Complete Set of Spare Parts) (unit)	90	1167	110	4501
装有引擎的汽车底盘 (台)	Chassis with Engines (unit)	429	1586	515	1398
汽车零件	Parts of Motor Vehicles		732579		672611
飞机 (架)	Aircraft (unit)	146	423126	214	576610
船舶 (艘)	Ships (unit)	2186	67018	1821	41326
复印机 (台)	Photo or Thermos Copying Apparatus (sets)	60549	2382	1025205	19351
医疗仪器及器械	Medical Instruments and Appliances		195164		221666
机电产品	Mechanical and Electrical Products		30204564		35037841
高新技术产品	High and New-tech Products		16141439		19770797

18-11 各地区按经营单位所在地分货物进出口总额

Total Value of Imports and Exports by Location of China's Foreign Trade Managing Units

单位：万美元 (USD 10 000)

地 区	Region	2000			2004			2005		
		进出口 Total	出 口 Exports	进 口 Imports	进出口 Total	出 口 Exports	进 口 Imports	进出口 Total	出 口 Exports	进 口 Imports
全 国	**National Total**	**47429628**	**24920255**	**22509373**	**115455433**	**59332558**	**56122875**	**142190617**	**76195341**	**65995276**
北 京	Beijing	4962189	1196813	3765376	9457573	2056926	7400647	12550643	3086590	9464052
天 津	Tianjin	1715400	862578	852822	4202861	2085175	2117685	5327680	2738088	2589592
河 北	Hebei	523862	371000	152862	1352585	933926	418659	1607035	1092430	514605
山 西	Shanxi	176438	123687	52751	538249	403447	134802	554565	352849	201716
内蒙古	Inner Mongolia	262205	97017	165188	372171	135447	236724	487625	177362	310263
辽 宁	Liaoning	1903148	1085632	817516	3441086	1891351	1549736	4101327	2343832	1757494
吉 林	Jilin	257042	125683	131359	679045	171475	507570	652772	246616	406157
黑龙江	Heilongjiang	298637	145118	153519	678900	368069	310831	956602	606944	349658
上 海	Shanghai	5470802	2535233	2935569	16000992	7350526	8650467	18633674	9071752	9561922
江 苏	Jiangsu	4563636	2576683	1986953	17084901	8749423	8335478	22792276	12296671	10495605
浙 江	Zhejiang	2783262	1944275	838987	8520488	5813854	2706634	10738966	7680245	3058721
安 徽	Anhui	334684	217198	117486	721156	393681	327474	911939	518850	393088
福 建	Fujian	2122046	1290607	831439	4752701	2939476	1813226	5441119	3484187	1956932
江 西	Jiangxi	162405	119741	42664	352795	199475	153319	406461	243934	162527
山 东	Shandong	2498976	1552884	946092	6065822	3584452	2481370	7673587	4612289	3061298
河 南	Henan	228290	149578	78712	661955	417464	244491	772492	508753	263739
湖 北	Hubei	322286	193555	128731	676581	338219	338362	905475	442868	462607
湖 南	Hunan	251222	165271	85951	544352	310643	233708	600019	374714	225305
广 东	Guangdong	17009888	9191770	7818118	35713062	19157104	16555958	42796497	23815883	18980614
广 西	Guangxi	203379	148891	54488	427722	238559	189164	518150	287663	230487
海 南	Hainan	128786	80289	48497	340169	109255	230915	254234	102254	151979
重 庆	Chongqing	178590	99566	79024	385715	209075	176640	429284	252058	177226
四 川	Sichuan	254520	139437	115083	686699	397970	288728	790196	470161	320036
贵 州	Guizhou	65998	42056	23942	151373	86661	64712	140357	85894	54463
云 南	Yunnan	181276	117509	63767	374117	223861	150256	474344	264173	210172
西 藏	Tibet	13031	11334	1697	19989	13022	6967	20547	16538	4009
陕 西	Shaanxi	214008	131005	83003	364238	239658	124581	457687	307689	149998
甘 肃	Gansu	56953	41495	15458	176315	99638	76677	263027	109100	153928
青 海	Qinghai	15973	11200	4773	57552	45476	12075	41331	32320	9011
宁 夏	Ningxia	44292	32737	11555	90821	64626	26195	96657	68742	27915
新 疆	Xinjiang	226404	120413	105991	563452	304627	258825	794049	503892	290157

18-12 各地区按境内目的地和货源地分货物进出口总额

Imports Value of Commodities by the Places of Their Destination and Exports Value of Commodities by the Places of Their Origin in China

单位：万美元 (USD 10 000)

地区	Region	2000			2004			2005		
		进出口 Total	出口 Exports	进口 Imports	进出口 Total	出口 Exports	进口 Imports	进出口 Total	出口 Exports	进口 Imports
全国	**National Total**	**47429628**	**24920255**	**22509373**	**115455433**	**59332558**	**56122875**	**142190617**	**76195341**	**65995276**
北京	Beijing	2424378	766723	1657655	4281985	1311698	2970287	5348598	1839661	3508937
天津	Tianjin	1715625	767427	948198	4323632	2047852	2275780	5463162	2603215	2859947
河北	Hebei	548711	327814	220897	1527966	970952	557013	1932779	1203361	729417
山西	Shanxi	279154	209094	70060	906929	719609	187320	909317	630492	278824
内蒙古	Inner Mongolia	238627	111400	127227	437479	188709	248769	530418	228743	301676
辽宁	Liaoning	2006747	1058947	947800	3993398	1958552	2034846	4703719	2467162	2236557
吉林	Jilin	298532	148693	149839	748670	191674	556995	736165	276416	459748
黑龙江	Heilongjiang	399259	242393	156866	718284	371991	346293	1046912	578939	467973
上海	Shanghai	5470336	2463961	3006375	15679934	6973125	8706808	18150474	8658271	9492204
江苏	Jiangsu	4919437	2637694	2281743	17954167	8803941	9150226	23847521	12459679	11387843
浙江	Zhejiang	3152170	2048214	1103956	9465921	6115262	3350658	12381057	8155104	4225953
安徽	Anhui	368983	211942	157041	699091	355908	343183	926371	508065	418307
福建	Fujian	2295726	1362282	933444	4984746	3055072	1929674	5679908	3594551	2085358
江西	Jiangxi	205206	118837	86369	481782	260783	220999	495921	265400	230521
山东	Shandong	2824997	1609267	1215730	6941591	3717848	3223743	8911528	4772102	4139425
河南	Henan	312389	158683	153706	735547	440023	295524	906580	561320	345260
湖北	Hubei	389264	189977	199287	755872	325159	430713	999286	419384	579902
湖南	Hunan	299226	163190	136036	608226	314416	293809	695965	385607	310358
广东	Guangdong	17548753	9342792	8205961	36335360	19241067	17094293	43918411	24097511	19820900
广西	Guangxi	228496	164048	64448	483210	231441	251768	576280	287199	289082
海南	Hainan	109420	60853	48567	289983	82492	207491	211989	85204	126785
重庆	Chongqing	185107	106048	79059	373012	187608	185404	423082	239764	183318
四川	Sichuan	277752	143360	134392	669406	348804	320602	767457	409237	358220
贵州	Guizhou	85646	48166	37480	237037	126838	110199	203946	113495	90451
云南	Yunnan	188420	109271	79149	373431	202035	171396	499535	238576	260959
西藏	Tibet	14892	10902	3990	16530	11852	4678	13158	10727	2432
陕西	Shaanxi	238754	132693	106061	455687	262428	193260	614931	384088	230843
甘肃	Gansu	69155	42079	27076	196409	103604	92806	298692	110610	188082
青海	Qinghai	22645	13355	9290	64773	46181	18593	49023	31350	17674
宁夏	Ningxia	53211	35426	17785	113120	73491	39629	118113	80776	37337
新疆	Xinjiang	258610	114724	143886	602259	292142	310117	830318	499333	330985

18-13 各地区外商投资企业货物进出口总额
Value of Imports and Exports of Foreign-funded Enterprises by Region

单位：万美元 (USD 10 000)

地区	Region	2000			2004			2005		
		进出口 Total	出口 Exports	进口 Imports	进出口 Total	出口 Exports	进口 Imports	进出口 Total	出口 Exports	进口 Imports
全国	**National Total**	**23671390**	**11944121**	**11727269**	**66304033**	**33859184**	**32444849**	**83163864**	**44418252**	**38745612**
北京	Beijing	776847	287108	489739	1852699	736179	1116520	2704807	1191406	1513401
天津	Tianjin	1369289	637925	731364	3408834	1705174	1703660	4275954	2199307	2076646
河北	Hebei	158147	101240	56907	426021	265709	160312	556490	345288	211202
山西	Shanxi	41876	15209	26667	68521	51768	16753	90359	51959	38401
内蒙古	Inner Mongolia	18157	13799	4358	27169	15539	11629	82847	41522	41325
辽宁	Liaoning	1229698	624464	605234	2066546	1089760	976786	2427281	1332795	1094486
吉林	Jilin	112274	39197	73077	352083	50537	301546	283386	67967	215420
黑龙江	Heilongjiang	47353	26679	20674	76347	38139	38208	87354	47491	39863
上海	Shanghai	3341054	1426102	1914952	10723174	4948834	5774340	12543267	6157921	6385346
江苏	Jiangsu	3018082	1445340	1572742	13553814	6515156	7038658	18474464	9422831	9051633
浙江	Zhejiang	938993	534851	404142	3262642	1965121	1297521	4238315	2726245	1512071
安徽	Anhui	94779	39993	54786	196206	96541	99665	280560	150275	130284
福建	Fujian	1405740	759713	646027	3116631	1841854	1274777	3577290	2175419	1401871
江西	Jiangxi	31814	16298	15516	115607	52937	62670	155379	64278	91100
山东	Shandong	1392569	792766	599803	3222568	1839654	1382914	4133889	2377119	1756770
河南	Henan	57695	30889	26806	122085	70449	51636	149707	84137	65570
湖北	Hubei	104686	42956	61730	234500	98525	135975	319445	129213	190232
湖南	Hunan	47717	18250	29467	106867	50272	56595	128086	64381	63704
广东	Guangdong	9203696	4951011	4252685	22653047	12171077	10481970	27866744	15467100	12399644
广西	Guangxi	55339	34112	21227	146909	49585	97324	178976	63503	115473
海南	Hainan	45993	30464	15529	143037	34999	108038	93324	39861	53464
重庆	Chongqing	32389	9666	22723	126518	21868	104650	156092	35886	120206
四川	Sichuan	61524	24517	37007	130315	55194	75121	149056	68302	80754
贵州	Guizhou	5690	4012	1678	38766	18883	19883	26798	15210	11588
云南	Yunnan	19658	8113	11545	31640	20989	10651	39961	24183	15778
西藏	Tibet	634	389	245	436	172	264	339	181	158
陕西	Shaanxi	35433	11611	23822	65751	22667	43084	82341	32022	50319
甘肃	Gansu	5657	3832	1825	16665	12594	4071	23118	19028	4090
青海	Qinghai	925	202	723	956	442	514	4942	1335	3607
宁夏	Ningxia	6125	4294	1831	13456	9051	4405	23038	11088	11950
新疆	Xinjiang	11557	9119	2438	17758	11046	6712	18618	13677	4942

18-14 利用外资概况
Utilization of Foreign Capital

项目单位：个；　金额单位：亿美元　　　　(unit) (USD 100 million)

年份 Year	总计 Total 项目 Number of Projects	总计 Total 金额 Value	对外借款 Foreign Loans 项目 Number of Projects	对外借款 Foreign Loans 金额 Value	外商直接投资 Direct Foreign Investments 项目 Number of Projects	外商直接投资 Direct Foreign Investments 金额 Value	外商其他投资额 Other Foreign Investments
合同利用外资额 Total Amount of Contracted Foreign Capital							
1979-1984	3365	281.26	117	169.78	3724	97.50	13.98
1985	3145	102.69	72	35.34	3073	63.33	4.02
1989	5909	114.79	130	51.85	5779	56.00	6.94
1990	7371	120.86	98	50.99	7273	65.96	3.91
1995	37184	1032.05	173	112.88	37011	912.82	6.35
1996	24673	816.10	117	79.62	24556	732.76	3.71
1997	21138	610.58	137	58.72	21001	510.03	41.82
1998	19850	632.01	51	83.85	19799	521.02	27.14
1999	17022	520.09	104	83.60	16918	412.23	24.26
2000	22347	711.30			22347	623.80	87.50
2001	26140	719.76			26140	691.95	27.81
2002	34171	847.51			34171	827.68	19.82
2003	41081	1169.01			41081	1150.69	18.32
2004	43664	1565.88			43664	1534.79	31.09
2005	44001	1925.93			44001	1890.65	35.28
1979-2005	554625	14634.06	1683	1385.38	552942	12856.74	391.91
实际利用外资额 Total Amount of Foreign Capital Actually Utilized							
1979-1984		181.87		130.41		41.04	10.42
1985		47.60		25.06		19.56	2.98
1989		100.60		62.86		33.93	3.81
1990		102.89		65.34		34.87	2.68
1995		481.33		103.27		375.21	2.85
1996		548.05		126.69		417.26	4.10
1997		644.08		120.21		452.57	71.30
1998		585.57		110.00		454.63	20.94
1999		526.59		102.12		403.19	21.28
2000		593.56		100.00		407.15	86.41
2001		496.72				468.78	27.94
2002		550.11				527.43	22.68
2003		561.40				535.05	26.35
2004		640.72				606.30	34.42
2005		638.05				603.25	34.80
1979-2005		8091.50		1471.57		6224.29	395.64

注：本表资料由商务部提供。
a) Data in this table come from the Ministry of Commerce.

18-15 按方式分外商投资额
Amount of Foreign Investment by Type

金额单位：亿美元　　　　(USD 100 million)

指标	Item	2004 项目（个） Number of Projects	2004 合同金额 Contracted Value	2004 实际使用金额 Actually Utilized Value	2005 项目（个） Number of Projects	2005 合同金额 Contracted Value	2005 实际使用金额 Actually Utilized Value
总计	**Total**	**43664**	**1565.88**	**640.72**	**44001**	**1925.93**	**638.05**
外商直接投资	**Foreign Direct Investments**	**43664**	**1534.79**	**606.30**	**44001**	**1890.65**	**603.25**
合资经营企业	Joint-ventures Enterprises	11570	276.41	163.86	10480	324.42	146.14
合作经营企业	Cooperative Operation Enterprises	1343	77.88	31.12	1166	86.91	18.31
外资企业	Foreign Investment Enterprises	30708	1172.75	402.22	32308	1459.09	429.61
外商投资股份制企业	Foreign Investment Share Enterprises	43	7.74	7.77	47	20.22	9.18
合作开发	Cooperative Development			1.09			
其他	Others			0.24			
外商其他投资	**Other Foreign Investment**		**31.09**	**34.43**		**35.28**	**34.80**
对外发行股票	Sale Share		4.48	6.95		0.05	1.60
国际租赁	International Lease		0.36	0.38		1.08	1.08
补偿贸易	Compensation Trade			0.05			0.16
加工装配	Processing and Assembly		26.25	27.05		34.15	31.96

18-16 按国别(地区)分实际外商投资额

Actual Foreign Investment by Countries or Regions

单位：万美元 (USD 10 000)

国别(地区)	Country (Region)	2004 外商直接投资 Foreign Direct Investment	2004 外商其他投资 Foreign Other Investment	2005 外商直接投资 Foreign Direct Investment	2005 外商其他投资 Foreign Other Investment
总计	**Total**	**6062998**	**344300**	**6032459**	**348038**
亚洲	**Asia**	**3761986**	**232647**	**3571889**	**240763**
阿富汗	Afghanistan	2190		1264	
巴林	Bahrain	380		6	
孟加拉国	Bangladesh	749		885	
文莱	Brunei	9605		16039	10
缅甸	Myanmar	878		374	
柬埔寨	Cambodia	2069		276	
塞浦路斯	Cyprus	160		774	
朝鲜	Korea DPR	273		129	
中国香港	Hong Kong, China	1899830	180673	1794879	184920
印度	India	1948		2140	
印度尼西亚	Indonesia	10452		8676	
伊朗	Iran	429		420	
伊拉克	Iraq	549		311	
以色列	Israel	2330		633	
日本	Japan	545157	6746	652977	11662
约旦	Jordan	937		894	
科威特	Kuwait	89		45	
老挝	Laos	425			
黎巴嫩	Lebanon	304		421	
中国澳门	Macao, China	54639	191	60046	826
马来西亚	Malaysia	38504		36139	531
蒙古	Mongolia	15		134	
尼泊尔	Nepal	78		1	
巴基斯坦	Pakistan	454		768	
巴勒斯坦	Palestine			10	
菲律宾	Philippines	23324	13	18890	5
沙特阿拉伯	Saudi Arabia	701		937	
新加坡	Singapore	200814	180	220432	551
韩国	Republic of Korea	624786	542	516834	1618
斯里兰卡	Sri Lanka	526		61	
叙利亚	Syria	64		96	
泰国	Thailand	17868	164	9590	178
土耳其	Turkey	745		2216	
阿联酋	United Arab Emirates	8565		9203	
也门	Republic of Yemen	286		70	
越南	Viet Nam	114		127	
中国台湾	Taiwan, China	311749	34061	215171	40462
亚洲其他国家(地区)	Other Countries (Regions) in Asia		10071	21	
非洲	**Africa**	**77568**		**107086**	
阿尔及利亚	Algeria	206		101	
安哥拉	Angola			18	
贝宁	Benin	270			
佛得角	Cape Verde	70		65	
中非	Central Africa			80	
博茨瓦纳	Botswana	47			
刚果	Congo			10	
吉布提	Djibouti			343	
埃及	Egypt	396		532	
赤道几内亚	Eq. Guinea			68	
埃塞俄比亚	Ethiopia			58	
加蓬	Gabon	65			
冈比亚	Gambia			132	
加纳	Ghana	40		40	
几内亚	Guinea	258		49	
肯尼亚	Kenya	106			
利比里亚	Liberia	285		771	
利比亚	Libyan	15		25	
马达加斯加	Madagascar	318		156	
马里	Mali	11		6	
毛里求斯	Mauritius	60232		90777	
摩洛哥	Morocco	97		166	
纳米比亚	Namibia	80		644	
尼日尔	Niger	10			

18-16 续表 1 continued

单位：万美元 (USD 10 000)

国别(地区)	Country (Region)	2004		2005	
		外商直接投资 Foreign Direct Investment	外商其他投资 Foreign Other Investment	外商直接投资 Foreign Direct Investment	外商其他投资 Foreign Other Investment
尼日利亚	Nigeria	1583		856	
塞舌尔	Seychelles	654		440	
塞拉利昂	Sierra Leone	82		147	
索马里	Somali			170	
南非	South Africa	10940		10635	
苏丹	Sudan	41		60	
坦桑尼亚	Tanzania	15			
多哥	Togo	19		21	
乌干达	Uganda			197	
布基纳法索	Burkina Faso			79	
赞比亚	Zambia	385		289	
津巴布韦	Zimbabwe	325		24	
莱索托	Lesotho			12	
几内亚（比绍）	Guinea Bissau	110			
喀麦隆	Cameroon	590			
索马里	Somalia	10			
突尼斯	Tunisia	60			
布基纳法索	Burkina Faso	98			
厄立特里亚	Eritrea	40			
非洲其他国家（地区）	Other Countries (Regions) in Africa	110		115	
欧洲	**Europe**	**479830**	**363**	**564310**	**1408**
比利时	Belgium	8209		5384	
丹麦	Denmark	6571		10043	
英国	United Kingdom	79282	360	96475	73
德国	Germany	105848		153004	723
法国	France	65674		61506	
爱尔兰	Ireland	456	3	973	
意大利	Italy	28082		32201	
卢森堡	Luxembourg	2878		14200	
荷兰	Netherlands	81056		104358	612
希腊	Greece	2819		184	
葡萄牙	Portugal	3322		413	
西班牙	Spain	15075		19690	
阿尔巴尼亚	Albania	13		15	
奥地利	Austria	9761		7630	
保加利亚	Bulgaria	577		23	
芬兰	Finland	2801		2172	
直布罗陀	Gibraltar	100		155	
匈牙利	Hungary	4996		4545	
冰岛	Iceland	50		15	
列支敦士登	Liechtenstein	4780		286	
马耳他	Malta	73		10	
摩纳哥	Monaco	188		4	
挪威	Norway	178		2624	
波兰	Poland	318		749	
罗马尼亚	Romania	3058		5710	
瑞典	Sweden	12070		11145	
瑞士	Switzerland	20312		20588	
爱沙尼亚	Estonia			53	
阿塞拜疆	Azerbaijan	230		74	
哈萨克	Kazakhstan	196		233	
俄罗斯	Russia	12638		8199	
塔吉克斯坦	Tadzhikistan			21	
乌克兰	Ukraine	1386		126	
乌兹别克斯坦	Uzbekistan	15		1	
南斯拉夫	Yugoslavia	327		78	
斯洛文尼亚	Slovenia			83	
克罗地亚	Croatia			2	
捷克	Czech	3363		552	
斯洛伐克	Slovakia	207		97	
马其顿	Macedonia	14			

18-16 续表 2 continued

单位：万美元 (USD 10 000)

国别（地区）	Country (Region)	2003 外商直接投资 Foreign Direct Investment	2003 外商其他投资 Foreign Other Investment	2004 外商直接投资 Foreign Direct Investment	2004 外商其他投资 Foreign Other Investment
吉尔吉斯	Kirghizia	248		53	
亚美尼亚	Armenia	359			
立陶宛	Lithuania	364		32	
欧洲其他国家（地区）	Other Countries (Regions) in Europe	1936		604	
拉丁美洲	**Latin America**	**904353**	**21280**	**1129333**	**11511**
阿根廷	Argentina	3080		1089	
巴哈马	Bahamas	4800		7467	
巴巴多斯	Barbados	3129		9701	
伯利兹	Belize	1033		2284	
玻利维亚	Bolivia	134		164	
巴西	Brazil	3070		2461	
开曼群岛	Cayman Islands	204258		194754	
智利	Chile	339		636	
哥伦比亚	Colombia	10			
哥斯达黎加	Costa Rica	2		60	
古巴	Cuba	100		30	
多米尼加	Dominica	35		102	
多米尼加共和国	Dominica Rep.	114		204	
厄瓜多尔	Ecuador	10		76	
洪都拉斯	Honduras	539		290	
牙买加	Jamaica	360		100	
墨西哥	Mexico	2129		710	
巴拿马	Panama	3592		4291	
巴拉圭	Paraguay	830		142	
秘鲁	Peru	445		338	
萨尔瓦多	El Salvador	7			
苏里南	Suriname	1629			
特克斯和凯科斯岛	Turks and Caicos Islands	127		350	
乌拉圭	Uruguay			104	
委内瑞拉	Venezuela			276	
维尔京群岛	Virgin Islands	673030	10307	902167	11511
圣其茨-尼维斯	St.Kitts-Nevis	1057		623	
圣文森特和格林纳丁斯	Saint Vincent & Grenadines	127		166	
拉美洲其他国家（地区）	Other Countries (Regions) in Latin America	367	10973	748	
北美洲	**North America**	**497759**	**326**	**372996**	**1315**
加拿大	Canada	61387		45413	
美国	United States	394095	326	306123	1315
百慕大	Bermuda	42277		21400	
北美洲其他国家（地区）	Other Countries (Regions) in North America			60	
大洋洲及太平洋岛屿	**Oceanic and Pacific Islands**	**197437**	**129**	**199898**	**18**
澳大利亚	Australia	66263	129	40093	18
库克群岛	Cook Islands	637		457	
斐济	Fiji	76		105	
瑙鲁	Nauru	700		64	
瓦努阿图	Vanuatu			171	
新西兰	New Zealand	11528		12991	
巴布亚新几内亚	Papua New Guinea	400		20	
所罗门群岛	Solomon Is.	30			
汤加	Tonga	41			
萨摩亚	Samoan	112885		135187	
基里巴斯	Kiribati	30		60	
密克罗尼西亚联邦	Micronesia FS			124	
马绍尔群岛	Marshall Islands	1543		4580	
东萨摩亚	East Samoan	1252		896	
贝劳共和国	Palau	34		57	
其它太平洋岛屿	Other Pacific Islands	1808		4459	
大洋洲其他国家（地区）	Other Countries (Regions) in Oceanic	210		634	
其他	**Others**	**144065**	**89555**	**86947**	**93023**

注：外商其他投资的“其他”项中含当年对外发行股票额。

a) The "Others" item of foreign other investment includes the stock issued in foreign countries at the same year.

18-17 按行业分外商直接投资（2005年）

Foreign Direct Investment by Sector (2005)

行业	Sector	合同项目（个）Number of Projects (unit)	合同金额（万美元）Contracted Value (USD 10 000)	实际使用金额（万美元）Actually Utilized Value (USD 10 000)
总计	**Total**	**44001**	**18906454**	**6032469**
农、林、牧、渔业	Agriculture, Forestry, Animal Husbandry and Fishing	1058	383729	71826
采矿业	Mining	252	101632	35495
制造业	Manufacturing	28928	12735725	4245291
电力、燃气及水的生产和供应业	Production and Supply of Electricity, Gas and Water	390	350216	139437
建筑业	Construction	457	256677	49020
交通运输、仓储和邮政业	Transport, Storage and Post	734	522404	181230
信息传输、计算机服务和软件业	Information Transmission, Computer Services and Software	1493	451206	101454
批发和零售业	Wholesale and Retail Trade	2602	434404	103854
住宿和餐饮业	Hotels and Catering Services	1207	273670	56017
金融业	Financial Intermediation	40	55144	21969
房地产业	Real Estate	2120	1940029	541807
租赁和商务服务业	Leasing and Business Services	2981	858005	374507
科学研究、技术服务和地质勘查业	Scientific Research, Technical Service and Geologic Prospecting	926	175503	34041
水利、环境和公共设施管理业	Management of Water Conservancy, Environment and Public Facilities	139	92130	13906
居民服务和其他服务业	Services to Households and Other Services	329	136616	26001
教育	Education	51	15974	1775
卫生、社会保障和社会福利业	Health, Social Security and Social Welfare	22	16459	3926
文化、体育和娱乐业	Culture, Sports and Entertainment	272	106931	30543
公共管理和社会组织	Public Management and Social Organizations			370

18-18 按行业分外商投资企业年底注册登记情况（2005年）

Registration Status of Foreign Funded Enterprises by Sector at the Year-end (2005)

行业	Sector	企业数(户) Number of Enterprises (unit)	投资总额(亿美元) Total Investment (100 million USD)	注册资本(亿美元) Registered Capital (100 million USD)	#外方 Foreign Investor
总计	**National Total**	**260000**	**14640**	**8120**	**6319**
农、林、牧、渔业	Agriculture, Forestry, Animal Husbandry and Fishing	5752	235	115	95
采矿业	Mining	979	64	42	28
制造业	Manufacturing	179949	8955	5117	4031
电力、燃气及水的生产和供应业	Production and Supply of Electricity, Gas and Water	1820	760	299	180
建筑业	Construction	3927	281	158	108
交通运输、仓储和邮政业	Transport, Storage and Post	4339	459	247	149
信息传输、计算机服务和软件业	Information Transmission, Computer Services and Software	6183	298	172	158
批发和零售业	Wholesale and Retail Trade	12084	285	167	131
住宿和餐饮业	Hotels and Catering Services	6013	276	152	109
金融业	Financial Intermediation	175	47	38	25
房地产业	Real Estate	13265	1852	906	722
租赁和商务服务业	Leasing and Business Services	9075	247	167	138
科学研究、技术服务和地质勘查业	Scientific Research, Technical Service and Geologic Prospecting	5622	257	150	126
水利、环境和公共设施管理业	Management of Water Conservancy, Environment and Public Facilities	793	100	60	41
居民服务和其他服务业	Services to Households and Other Services	3318	97	61	47
教育	Education	209	7	5	3
卫生、社会保障和社会福利业	Health, Social Security and Social Welfare	225	20	11	8
文化、体育和娱乐业	Culture, Sports and Entertainment	2316	151	82	67
其他	Others	3956	251	172	154

18-19 各地区外商投资企业年底注册登记情况

Registration Status of Foreign Funded Enterprises by Region at the Year-end

地区	Region	企业数（户） Number of Enterprises (unit)		投资总额（亿美元） Total Investment (100 million USD)		注册资本（亿美元） Registered Capital (100 million USD)		#外方 Foreign Investor	
		2004	2005	2004	2005	2004	2005	2004	2005
全国	**National Total**	**242284**	**260000**	**13112**	**14640**	**7285**	**8120**	**5580**	**6319**
北京	Beijing	9890	10980	532	607	290	324	207	238
天津	Tianjin	9938	10933	470	568	275	333	221	269
河北	Hebei	3497	3637	201	219	106	125	68	82
山西	Shanxi	705	776	69	77	35	40	21	23
内蒙古	Inner Mongolia	847	914	108	126	56	63	36	41
辽宁	Liaoning	14858	16542	679	815	402	495	280	362
吉林	Jilin	2370	2488	194	207	60	69	42	47
黑龙江	Heilongjiang	2202	2288	95	110	57	69	36	45
上海	Shanghai	26657	28978	1722	2007	923	1086	718	854
江苏	Jiangsu	29939	33321	2170	2657	1083	1321	901	1124
浙江	Zhejiang	17792	19009	834	1019	467	565	339	414
安徽	Anhui	2114	2165	129	155	76	89	48	59
福建	Fujian	17236	17854	689	753	387	431	344	378
江西	Jiangxi	3415	3980	163	185	88	114	67	93
山东	Shandong	19251	20153	694	786	416	471	293	339
河南	Henan	2600	2877	149	206	87	112	56	75
湖北	Hubei	4173	4284	227	258	136	151	85	100
湖南	Hunan	2598	2712	119	158	70	95	53	71
广东	Guangdong	55259	58762	2610	2889	1520	1677	1219	1367
广西	Guangxi	2336	2441	127	147	74	83	54	61
海南	Hainan	2329	2456	86	92	55	58	43	45
重庆	Chongqing	1294	1315	72	80	39	42	26	28
四川	Sichuan	3789	4075	140	166	94	109	55	66
贵州	Guizhou	641	649	22	23	14	15	10	10
云南	Yunnan	1761	1817	79	84	44	47	27	29
西藏	Tibet	86	100	3	4	2	2	1	2
陕西	Shaanxi	2754	2890	125	137	71	78	50	56
甘肃	Gansu	650	658	31	32	19	20	13	14
青海	Qinghai	161	138	10	7	6	4	4	3
宁夏	Ningxia	454	463	41	45	20	20	15	15
新疆	Xinjiang	331	345	14	19	10	11	6	8
国家	State Administration	357		509		300		243	

18-20 按主要国别(地区)分对外直接投资(非金融类)

Overseas Direct Investment by Countries or Regions (Non-Finance)

单位：万美元 (USD 10 000)

国家（地区）	Country or Region	2004年对外直接投资净额 Net Overseas Direct Investment in 2004	2005年对外直接投资净额 Net Overseas Direct Investment in 2005	截至2005年底对外直接投资净额 Accumulated Net Overseas Direct Investment at the End of 2005
合计	**Total**	**549799**	**1226117**	**5720562**
亚洲	**Asia**	**300027**	**437464**	**4062904**
香港	Hong Kong	262839	341970	3650708
印度尼西亚	Indonesia	6196	1184	14093
日本	Japan	1530	1717	15070
澳门	Macao	2658	834	59870
新加坡	Singapore	4798	2033	32548
韩国	Republic of Korea	4023	58882	88222
泰国	Thailand	2343	477	21918
越南	Vietnam	1685	2077	22918
非洲	**Africa**	**31742**	**39168**	**159525**
阿尔及利亚	Algeria	1121	8487	17121
苏丹	Sudan	14670	9113	35153
几内亚	Guinea	1444	1634	4422
马达加斯加	Madagascar	1364	14	4994
尼日利亚	Nigeria	4552	5330	9411
南非	South Africa	1781	4747	11228
欧洲	**Europe**	**17092**	**50502**	**159819**
英国	United Kingdom	2939	2478	10797
德国	Germany	2750	12874	26835
法国	France	1031	609	3382
俄罗斯	Russia	7731	20333	46557
拉丁美洲	**Latin America**	**176272**	**646616**	**1146962**
巴哈马	Bahamas	4356	2295	1469
开曼群岛	Cayman Islands	128613	516275	893559
墨西哥	Mexico	2710	355	14186
英属维尔京群岛	Virgin Is. (E)	38552	122608	198358
北美洲	**North America**	**12649**	**32084**	**126324**
加拿大	Canada	512	3244	10329
美国	United States	11993	23182	82268
大洋洲	**Oceania**	**12015**	**20283**	**65028**
澳大利亚	Australia	12495	19307	58746
新西兰	New Zealand	-490	347	3518

18-21 按行业分对外直接投资（非金融类）

Overseas Direct Investment by Sector (non-financial)

单位：万美元 (USD 10 000)

行　业	Sector	对外直接投资净额 Net Overseas Direct Investment 2004	2005	截至2005年对外直接投资净额 Accumulated Net Overseas Direct Investment at the End of 2005
总　计	**Total**	**549799**	**1226117**	**5720562**
农、林、牧、渔业	Agriculture, Forestry, Animal Husbandry and Fishing	28866	10536	51162
采矿业	Mining	180021	167522	865161
制造业	Manufacturing	75555	228040	577028
电力、燃气及水的生产和供应业	Production and Supply of Electricity, Gas and Water	7849	766	28731
建筑业	Construction	4795	8186	120399
交通运输、仓储和邮政业	Transport, Storage and Post	82866	57679	708297
信息传输、计算机服务和软件业	Information Transmission, Computer Services and Software	3050	1479	132350
批发和零售业	Wholesale and Retail Trade	79969	226012	1141791
住宿和餐饮业	Hotels and Catering Services	203	758	4640
房地产业	Real Estate	851	11563	149520
租赁和商务服务业	Leasing and Business Services	74931	494159	1655360
科学研究、技术服务和地质勘查业	Scientific Research, Technical Service and Geologic Prospecting	1806	12942	60431
水利、环境和公共设施管理业	Management of Water Conservancy, Environment and Public Facilities	120	13	91002
居民服务和其他服务业	Services to Households and Other Services	8814	6279	132338
卫生、社会保障和社会福利业	Health, Social Security and Social Welfare	1		11
文化、体育和娱乐业	Culture, Sports and Entertainment	98	12	538
公共管理和社会组织	Public Management and Social Organizations	5	173	1803

18-22 对外经济合作

Economic Cooperation with Foreign Countries or Regions

年份 Year	合同数(份) Number of Contracts (unit)	对外承包工程 Contracted Projects	对外劳务合作 Labor Cooperation	对外设计咨询 Design Consultation	合同金额(亿美元) Contracted Value (100 million USD)	对外承包工程 Contracted Projects
1976-2005	**455513**	**53074**	**398119**	**4320**	**2286.02**	**1859.05**
1976-1988	7534	3449	4085		105.95	89.00
1989	3100	776	2324		22.12	17.81
1990	5175	920	4255		26.04	21.25
1991	8438	1171	7267		36.09	25.24
1992	9405	1164	8241		65.85	52.51
1993	11605	1393	10212		68.00	51.89
1994	17491	1702	15789		79.88	60.28
1995	19321	1558	17397	366	96.72	74.84
1996	24891	1634	22723	534	102.73	77.28
1997	28442	2085	25743	614	113.56	85.16
1998	25955	2322	23191	442	117.73	92.43
1999	21126	2527	18173	426	130.02	101.99
2000	23565	2597	20474	494	149.43	117.19
2001	39400	5836	33358	206	164.55	130.39
2002	34461	4036	30163	262	178.91	150.55
2003	42059	3708	38043	308	209.30	176.67
2004	60312	6694	53271	347	276.98	238.44
2005	73233	9502	63410	321	342.16	296.14

18-22 续表 continued

年份 Year	对外劳务合作 Labor Cooperation	对外设计咨询 Design Consultation	完成营业额(亿美元) Value of Business Fulfilled (100 million USD)	对外承包工程 Contracted Projects	对外劳务合作 Labor Cooperation	对外设计咨询 Design Consultation
1976-2005	**403.60**	**23.36**	**1728.03**	**1358.18**	**355.82**	**14.04**
1976-1988	16.95		60.91	49.70	11.21	
1989	4.31		16.86	14.84	2.02	
1990	4.78		18.67	16.44	2.23	
1991	10.85		23.63	19.70	3.93	
1992	13.35		30.49	24.03	6.46	
1993	16.11		45.38	36.68	8.70	
1994	19.60		59.78	48.83	10.95	
1995	20.07	1.81	65.88	51.08	13.47	1.33
1996	22.80	2.65	76.96	58.21	17.12	1.64
1997	25.50	2.90	83.83	60.36	21.65	1.82
1998	23.90	1.40	101.34	77.69	22.76	0.89
1999	26.32	1.71	112.35	85.22	26.23	0.90
2000	29.91	2.33	113.25	83.79	28.13	1.34
2001	33.28	0.88	121.39	88.99	31.77	0.63
2002	27.52	0.85	143.52	111.94	30.71	0.87
2003	30.87	1.76	172.34	138.37	33.09	0.88
2004	35.03	3.51	213.69	174.68	37.53	1.47
2005	42.45	3.57	267.76	217.63	47.86	2.27

18-23 按国别(地区)分对外经济合作完成营业额

Turnover of Economic Cooperation with Foreign Countries or Regions

单位：万美元 (USD 10 000)

国别(地区)	Country (Region)	2004				2005			
		合计 Total	承包工程 Contracted Projects	劳务合作 Labour Cooperation	设计咨询 Design Consultation	合计 Total	承包工程 Contracted Projects	劳务合作 Labour Cooperation	设计咨询 Design Consultation
合　计	**Total**	**2136898**	**1746829**	**375329**	**14740**	**2677605**	**2176324**	**478560**	**22721**
亚洲	**Asia**	**1050695**	**814158**	**229675**	**6862**	**1207058**	**931788**	**259950**	**15320**
阿富汗	Afghanistan	3521	3452	44	25	5568	5565		3
巴林	Bahrain	17	12	5		7		7	
孟加拉国	Bangladesh	52364	51426	298	640	61397	60815	90	492
不丹	Bhutan	38	38			14	14		
文莱	Brunei	314	296	18		982	934	48	
缅甸	Myanmar	33557	33120	193	244	28976	28672	166	138
柬埔寨	Cambodia	7659	6215	1437	7	13401	12312	1082	7
塞浦路斯	Cyprus	2271	2170	101		317	233	84	
朝鲜	Korea DPR	3939	3487	437	15	3156	2634	512	10
中国香港	Hong Kong, China	276618	254278	22033	307	202173	178277	23706	190
印度	India	24509	23773	103	633	41290	40100	158	1032
印度尼西亚	Indonesia	28781	26303	2368	110	53458	52363	798	297
伊朗	Iran	38585	37195	430	960	65274	64086	1	1187
伊拉克	Iraq	899	888		11	1259	1136		123
以色列	Israel	10060	1543	8517		10404	5457	4947	
日本	Japan	85961	5335	80383	243	118980	9953	108886	141
约旦	Jordan	12033	5459	6328	246	11212	3982	6339	891
科威特	Kuwait	12654	10298	2328	28	21494	15877	5617	
老挝	Laos	14336	13284	201	851	17013	16953	25	35
黎巴嫩	Lebanon	40	38	2		1182	1181	1	
中国澳门	Macao, China	35006	21776	13074	156	51227	37280	13767	180
马来西亚	Malaysia	22806	21394	948	464	25343	22647	2618	78
马尔代夫	Maldives	129	125	4		794	791	3	
蒙古	Mongolia	24433	23872	547	14	19469	18032	1422	15
尼泊尔	Nepal	3889	3875	14		1445	1442	3	
阿曼	Oman	3416	3345	71		8725	8634	91	
巴基斯坦	Pakistan	58601	57423	517	661	75142	66088	65	8989
巴勒斯坦	Palestine					360	360		
菲律宾	Philippines	12826	12660	142	24	18358	17925	96	337
卡塔尔	Qatar	794	664	130		2410	1643	767	
沙特阿拉伯	Saudi Arabia	12977	11634	1343		33127	31729	1398	
新加坡	Singapore	108536	65626	42907	3	116590	76758	39828	4
韩国	Korea Rep.	38043	10482	27559	2	52596	21215	31381	
斯里兰卡	Sri Lanka	9530	9351	179		9023	8926	82	15
叙利亚	Syrian	1221	1215	6		1815	1810		5
泰国	Thailand	20309	16556	3738	15	30879	30099	780	
土耳其	Turkey	4777	4464	171	142	7409	7170	139	100

18-23 续表 1 continued

单位：万美元 (USD 10 000)

国别(地区)	Country (Region)	2004				2005			
		合计 Total	承包工程 Contracted Projects	劳务合作 Labour Cooperation	设计咨询 Design Consultation	合计 Total	承包工程 Contracted Projects	劳务合作 Labour Cooperation	设计咨询 Design Consultation
阿联酋	United Arab Emirates	35884	32170	3714		34010	28039	5971	
也门共和国	Republic of Yemen	7082	6964	103	15	8916	8751	147	18
越南	Vietnam	30365	27784	1830	751	29923	27530	1577	816
中国台湾	Taiwan, China	10246	2548	7452	246	15701	8151	7335	215
东帝汶	East Timor					768	768		
亚洲其他国家（地区）	Other Countries (Regions) in Asia	1669	1620		49	5471	5456	13	2
非洲	**Africa**	**402013**	**381310**	**18231**	**2472**	**627418**	**609222**	**15388**	**2808**
阿尔及利亚	Algeria	82996	80528	2321	147	106535	105043	1071	421
安哥拉	Angola	8210	7935	212	63	30574	30402	172	
贝宁	Benin	613	567	38	8	208	194	14	
博茨瓦纳	Botswana	23096	22933	163		26531	26384	147	
布隆迪	Burundi	108	105	3		262	238	24	
喀麦隆	Cameroon	1495	1223	272		1855	1726	129	
加那利群岛	Canary Is.	130	130	0		55	55		
佛得角	Cape Verde	388	385	3		169	166	3	
中非	Central Africa	1963	1946	17		2385	2362	23	
乍得	Chad					1796	1796		
科摩罗	Comoros	209	181	28		528	483	45	
刚果（布）	Congo (B)	4238	4160	55	23	11550	11371	122	57
吉布提	Djibouti	714	573	141		991	880	101	10
埃及	Egypt	7386	7381		5	27653	27650	3	
赤道几内亚	Eq. Guinea	2869	2702	161	6	7493	7319	172	2
埃塞俄比亚	Ethiopia	20485	20476	6	3	18296	18218	28	50
加蓬	Gabon	3040	2960	80		4286	4221	65	
冈比亚	Gambia	1183	1154	29		1413	1392	21	
加纳	Ghana	6042	5889	74	79	8329	8246	83	
几内亚	Guinea	7522	7008	514		7697	7495	202	
几内亚(比绍)	Guinea Bissau	3381	3187	194		2746	2561	185	
科特迪瓦	Cote d'Lvoire	1403	1378	25		2619	2592	26	1
肯尼亚	Kenya	5286	5271	15		3599	3532	67	
利比里亚	Liberia	1597	890	693	14	906	85	821	
利比亚	Libyan	7234	6667	517	50	13221	12787	374	60
马达加斯加	Madagascar	1651	1410	224	17	3011	2839	153	19
马拉维	Malawi	529	529			360	360		
马里	Mali	9650	9576	66	8	17687	17658	29	
毛里塔尼亚	Mauritania	4701	3508	1163	30	4380	3455	925	
毛里求斯	Mauritius	8525	2385	6140		9152	4092	5060	
摩洛哥	Morocco	4413	3760	653		4944	4555	383	6
莫桑比克	Mozambique	3869	3707	162		9615	9615		
纳米比亚	Namibia	3075	2644	431		3602	3244	340	18
尼日尔	Niger	1225	1132	93		1945	1901	44	

18-23 续表 2 continued

单位：万美元 (USD 10 000)

国别(地区)	Country (Region)	2004 合 计 Total	2004 承包工程 Contracted Projects	2004 劳务合作 Labour Cooperation	2004 设计咨询 Design Consultation	2005 合 计 Total	2005 承包工程 Contracted Projects	2005 劳务合作 Labour Cooperation	2005 设计咨询 Design Consultation
尼日利亚	Nigeria	49902	48884	928	90	79992	77435	1742	815
卢旺达	Rwanda	1031	1024		7	980	949	31	
圣多美和普林西比	Sao Tome & Principe	36	36			19	19		
塞内加尔	Senegal	1922	1833	89		3429	3307	122	
塞舌尔	Seychelles	1009	953	50	6	2165	2089	71	5
塞拉利昂	Sierra Leone	2632	2402	230		1828	1624	203	1
南非	S. Africa	2800	2289	276	235	8279	7960	319	
苏丹	Sudan	74828	72565	778	1485	134278	132998	502	778
坦桑尼亚	Tanzania	8892	8654	129	109	21167	21012	128	27
多哥	Togo	501	450	51		1255	1227	28	
突尼斯	Tunisia	4127	4039	30	58	6549	6089	2	458
乌干达	Uganda	3705	3582	123		5644	5545	99	
布基纳法索	Burkina Faso	18	18			50	50		
赞比亚	Zambia	10581	10574	7		3339	3273	6	60
津巴布韦	Zimbabwe	4810	4792		18	8992	8932	60	
莱索托	Lesotho	1973	1279	693	1	2523	1671	832	20
斯威士兰	Swaziland	109		109		119		119	
厄立特里亚	Eritrea	1643	1617	26		1921	1854	67	
刚果（金）	Congo (J)	2077	2019	48	10	8314	8271	43	
非洲其他国家（地区）	Other Countries (Regions) in Africa	191	20	171		182		182	
欧洲	**Europe**	**164469**	**139367**	**25049**	**53**	**245061**	**213281**	**29809**	**1971**
比利时	Belgium	8832	8832			10440	10437	3	
丹麦	Denmark	1442	1361	81		326	230	96	
英国	United Kingdom	4514	3680	834		7561	6057	1504	
德国	Germany	26904	20304	6595	5	32438	25529	6906	3
法国	France	9285	9256	11	18	17944	17882	43	19
爱尔兰	Ireland	428		428		1103	296	807	
意大利	Italy	2278	2263	15		3235	3213	20	2
荷兰	Netherlands	680	680			6177	6177		
希腊	Greece	7629	7224	405		8250	7836	414	
葡萄牙	Portugal	6	6			797	797		
西班牙	Spain	2827	2610	217		8355	8103	252	
阿尔巴尼亚	Albania	1410	1382	28		2855	2836	19	
奥地利	Austria	18	11	7		411	401	10	
保加利亚	Bulgaria	107	66	41		909	885	24	
芬兰	Finland	3748	3732	16		1836	1836		
匈牙利	Hungary	60	60			735	735		

18-23 续表 3 continued

单位：万美元 (USD 10 000)

国别(地区)	Country (Region)	2004 合 计 Total	2004 承包工程 Contracted Projects	2004 劳务合作 Labour Cooperation	2004 设计咨询 Design Consultation	2005 合 计 Total	2005 承包工程 Contracted Projects	2005 劳务合作 Labour Cooperation	2005 设计咨询 Design Consultation
冰岛	Iceland					50	50		
马耳他	Malta	42		42		67		67	
摩纳哥	Monaco	740	740			1030	1030		
挪威	Norway	6906	5884	1022		6926	5971	955	
波兰	Poland	406	402	4		2		2	
罗马尼亚	Romania	897	886	11		961	952	9	
瑞典	Sweden	135	120	15		103	93	10	
瑞士	Switzerland	218	213	5		97	92	5	
拉脱维亚	Latvia	12		12					
立陶宛	Lithuania	5	5						
格鲁吉亚	Georgia	685	685			282	282		
亚美尼亚	Armenia					3		3	
阿塞拜疆	Azerbaijan	8787	8784	3		13600	13585	15	
白俄罗斯	Belorussia	1112	1088	24		1134	1134		
哈萨克	Kazakhstan	11250	10914	336		39279	36918	592	1769
吉尔吉斯	Kirghizia	12488	12485	3		15863	15863		
俄罗斯	Russia	33977	19173	14774	30	45360	27341	17991	28
塔吉克	Tadzhikistan	1331	1329	2		744	739		5
乌克兰	Ukraine	1085	1085			5754	5727	27	
乌兹别克	Uzbekistan	4582	4529	53		6835	6834	1	
土库曼	Turkmenistan	5980	5980			1665	1664	1	
南斯拉夫	Yugoslavia	42		42					
塞尔维亚和黑山	Serbia and Montenegro					320	144	31	145
斯洛文尼亚	Slovenia	204	185	19		277	277		
克罗地亚	Croatia	405	405			282	282		
捷克	Czech	2191	2189	2		708	706	2	
斯洛伐克	Slovakia	1		1					
马其顿	Macedonia	819	819			347	347		
波黑	Bosnia and Herzegovina	1		1					
拉丁美洲	**Latin America**	**87370**	**80789**	**6548**	**33**	**146738**	**141309**	**5204**	**225**
安提瓜和巴布达	Antigua & Barbuda	1291	1137	154		799	759	40	
阿根廷	Argentina	4042	3242	800		12908	12267	641	
巴哈马	Bahamas	751	740	11		93	82	11	
巴巴多斯	Barbados	1180	984	196		648	603	38	7
伯利兹	Belize	1418	1380	38		1014	990	24	
玻利维亚	Bolivia	225	225			50			50
巴西	Brazil	6488	6460		28	24868	24868		
智利	Chile	2893	2893			2734	2734		
哥伦比亚	Colombia	343	320	23		2270	2260	10	
多米尼克	Dominica	43	43			933	933		
哥斯达黎加	Costa Rica	13		13		8		8	
古巴	Cuba	7579	7569	10		2103	2091	11	1
多米尼加共和国	Dominica Rep.	3739	3739			645	645		
厄瓜多尔	Ecuador	4288	4244	44		3443	3394	13	36

18-23 续表 4 continued

单位：万美元 (USD 10 000)

国别(地区)	Country (Region)	2004				2005			
		合计 Total	承包工程 Contracted Projects	劳务合作 Labour Cooperation	设计咨询 Design Consultation	合计 Total	承包工程 Contracted Projects	劳务合作 Labour Cooperation	设计咨询 Design Consultation
格林纳达	Grenada					148	148		
圭亚那	Guyana	454	399	55		995	910	36	49
洪都拉斯	Honduras	124	87	37		27		27	
牙买加	Jamaica	564	137	423	4	1625	1482	74	69
墨西哥	Mexico	17320	16479	841		38675	38006	669	
尼加拉瓜	Nicaragua	552	12	540		534	8	526	
巴拿马	Panama	2062	1093	969		3891	3127	764	
秘鲁	Peru	11544	9286	2258		8750	6581	2169	
圣卢西亚	Saint Lucia	41	27	14		101	60	41	
圣文森特和格林纳丁斯	Saint Vincent & Grenadines	40		40					
萨尔瓦多	EL Salvador	16		16		4		4	
苏里南	Suriname	1156	1122	33	1	2359	2310	36	13
特立尼达和	Trinidad & Tobago	160	148	12		5		5	
乌拉圭	Uruguay	206	185	21		185	183	2	
委内瑞拉	Venezuela	18838	18838			36923	36868	55	
北美洲	**North America**	**37160**	**24872**	**12265**	**23**	**52125**	**43246**	**8806**	**73**
加拿大	Canada	1283	1195	86	2	2469	2388	72	9
美国	United States	35877	23677	12179	21	49656	40858	8734	64
大洋洲及太平洋岛屿	**Oceanic & Pacific Islands**	**11460**	**9474**	**1976**	**10**	**9101**	**7035**	**1970**	**96**
澳大利亚	Australia	2412	2235	177		2030	1738	277	15
库克群岛	Cook Islands	385	363	22		88	64	24	
斐济	Fiji	3939	3572	367		1662	1279	353	30
马克萨斯	Marquesas Is.	200		200					
瓦努阿图	Vanuatu	384	383	1		292	164	128	
新西兰	New Zealand	568	356	212		624	206	418	
巴布亚新几内亚	Papua New Guinea	1402	1323	74	5	2137	2036	50	51
社会群岛	Society Islands	80		80		66		66	
汤加	Tonga	635	576	59		255	236	19	
萨摩亚	Samoa	218	90	123	5	950	900	50	
基里巴斯	Kiribati	257	257						
密克罗尼西亚	Micronesia FS	895	274	621		933	361	572	
马绍尔群岛	Marshall Is.	15	15			51	51		
贝劳共和国	Palau	70	30	40		13		13	
其他	**Others**	**8595**	**8055**	**362**	**178**	**67281**	**8895**	**58342**	**44**
国境内	**Inner Country**	**375136**	**288804**	**81223**	**5109**	**322823**	**221548**	**99091**	**2184**

主要统计指标解释

进出口总额 指实际进出我国国境的货物总金额。包括对外贸易实际进出口货物，来料加工装配进出口货物，国家间、联合国及国际组织无偿援助物资和赠送品，华侨、港澳台同胞和外籍华人捐赠品，租赁期满归承租人所有的租赁货物，进料加工进出口货物，边境地方贸易及边境地区小额贸易进出口货物(边民互市贸易除外)，中外合资企业、中外合作经营企业、外商独资经营企业进出口货物和公用物品，到、离岸价格在规定限额以上的进出口货样和广告品(无商业价值、无使用价值和免费提供出口的除外)，从保税仓库提取在中国境内销售的进口货物，以及其他进出口货物。该指标可以观察一个国家在对外贸易方面的总规模。我国规定出口货物按离岸价格统计，进口货物按到岸价格统计。

商品经营单位所在地进、出口额 指所在地海关注册登记的有进出口经营权的企业实际进、出口额。

商品目的地进口额和商品货源地出口额 目的地进口额指进口货物的消费、使用或最终抵运地的实际进口额；货源地出口额指出口货物的产地或原始发货地的实际出口额。

利用外资 指我国各级政府、部门、企业和其他经济组织通过对外借款、吸收外商直接投资以及用其他方式筹措的境外现汇、设备、技术等。

对外借款 指通过对外正式签订借款协议，从境外筹措的资金，包括外国政府贷款、国际金融组织贷款、外国银行商业贷款、出口信贷以及对外发行债券等。1996年及以前还包括对外发行股票。该指标是我国利用外资的重要部分。

外商直接投资 指外国企业和经济组织或个人(包括华侨、港澳台胞以及我国在境外注册的企业)按我国有关政策、法规，用现汇、实物、技术等在我国境内开办外商独资企业、与我国境内的企业或经济组织共同举办中外合资经营企业、合作经营企业或合作开发资源的投资(包括外商投资收益的再投资)，以及经政府有关部门批准的项目投资总额内企业从境外借入的资金。

外商其他投资 指除对外借款和外商直接投资以外的各种利用外资的形式。包括企业在境内外股票市场公开发行的以外币计价的股票（目前主要是在香港证券市场发行的H股和在境内证券市场发行的B股）发行价总额，国际租赁进口设备的应付款，补偿贸易中外商提供的进口设备、技术、物料的价款，加工装配贸易中外商提供的进口设备、物料的价款。

对外直接投资 指我国国内投资者以现金、实物、无形资产等方式在国外及港澳台地区设立、购买国（境）外企业，并以控制该企业的经营管理权为核心的经济活动。

对外承包工程 指各对外承包公司以招标议标承包方式承揽的下列业务：(1)承包国外工程建设项目；(2)承包我国对外经援项目；(3)承包我国驻外机构的工程建设项目；(4)承包我国境内利用外资进行建设的工程项目；(5)与外国承包公司合营或联合承包工程项目时我国公司分包部分；(6)对外承包兼营的房屋开发业务。对外承包工程的营业额是以货币表现的本期内完成的对外承包工程的工作量，包括以前年度签订的合同和本年度新签订的合同在报告期内完成的工作量。

对外劳务合作 指以收取工资的形式向业主或承包商提供技术和劳动服务的活动。我国对外承包公司在境外开办的合营企业，中国公司同时又提供劳务的，其劳务部分也纳入劳务合作统计。劳务合作营业额按报告期内向雇主提交的结算数(包括工资、加班费和奖金等)统计。

对外设计咨询 指以服务成果向业主收费的技术服务项目。包括承担地形地貌测绘，地质资源勘探与普查，建设区域规划，提供设计文件、图纸、生产工艺技术资料和工程技术经济咨询，工程项目的可行性考察、研究和评估，进行技术指导和培训人员等；也包括承担国(境)内利用外资建设工程项目中的设计咨询项目内收取外币部分。

Explanatory Notes on Main Statistical Indicators

Total Imports and Exports at Customs refer to the real value of commodities imported into and exported from the boundary of China. They include the actual imports and exports through foreign trade, imported and exported goods under the processing and assembling trades and materials, supplies and gifts as aid given gratis between governments and by the United Nations and other international organizations, and contributions donated by overseas Chinese, compatriots in Hong Kong and Macao and Chinese with foreign citizenship, leasing commodities owned by tenant at the expiration of leasing period, the imported and exported commodities processed with imported materials, commodities trading in border areas (excluding mutual exchange goods), the imported and exported commodities and articles for public use of the Sino-foreign joint ventures, cooperative enterprises and ventures exclusively with foreign own investment. Also included are import or export of samples and advertising goods for whose CIF or FOB value are beyond the permitted ceiling (excluding goods of no trading or use value and free commodities for export), imported goods sold in China from bonded warehouses and other imported or exported goods. The indicator of the total imports and exports at customs can be used to observe the total size of external trade in a country. In accordance with the stipulation of the Chinese government, imports are calculated at CIF, while exports are calculated at FOB.

Import Export Value by Location of China' s Foreign Trade Managing Units refers to actual value of imports and exports carried out by corporations which have been registered by the local customhouse and are vested with right to run import export business.

Import Value of Commodities by the Places of their Destination and Export Value of Commodities by the Places of their Origin in China: The former indicator refers to the value of import commodities of the places of their consumption, utilization or the places of their final destination. The latter indicator refers to the value of export commodities of the places of their origin or the places of the commodities dispatched.

Utilization of Foreign Capitals refers to remittance, equipment and technology financed from abroad, by loans, foreign direct investment and other forms undertaken by the Chinese governments at all levels, by various departments, enterprises and other economic units.

Foreign Borrowings refer to funds borrowed from abroad through formal signing of borrowing agreements with foreign institutions, including loans of foreign governments, loans of international financial institutions, commercial loans of foreign banks, export credit, and funds raised by Chinese bonds (and shares before 1996) issued abroad. It is an important part of China's utilization of foreign capitals.

Foreign Direct Investment refers to the investments inside China by foreign enterprises and economic organizations or individuals (including overseas Chinese, compatriots from Hong Kong, Macao and Taiwan, and Chinese enterprises registered abroad), following the relevant policies and laws of China, for the establishment of ventures exclusively with foreign own investment, Sino-foreign joint ventures and cooperative enterprises or for co-operative exploration of resources with enterprises or economic organizations in China. It includes the re investment of the foreign entrepreneurs with the profits gained from the investment and the funds that enterprises borrow from abroad in the total investment of projects which are approved by the relevant department of the government.

Overseas Direct Investment refers to enterprises set up or bought by domestic investors in foreign countries and in Hong Kong, Macao and Taiwan, and the economic activities centering on operation and management of those enterprises are under the control of domestic investors. The statistical scope covers various corporation type enterprises and non-corporation type enterprises receiving direct investment from domestic investment entities.

Other Investment by Foreign Entrepreneurs refers to all forms of utilization of foreign capitals other than foreign borrowings and foreign direct investment. It includes the total value of stock shares in foreign currencies issued by enterprises at domestic or foreign stock exchanges (now mainly consisting of H shares issued at Hong Kong Security Market and B shares issued at domestic security markets), rent payable for the imported equipment through international leasing arrangement, cost of imported equipment, technology and materials provided by foreign counterparts in compensation trade and processing and assembly trade.

Contracted Projects with Foreign Countries refer to projects undertaken by Chinese contractors (project contracting companies) through bidding process. They include: (1) overseas civil engineering construction projects financed by foreign investors; (2) overseas projects financed by the Chinese government through its foreign aid programs; (3) construction projects of Chinese diplomatic missions, trade offices and other institutions stationed abroad; (4) construction projects in China financed by foreign investment; (5) sub-contracted projects to be taken by Chinese contractors through a joint umbrella project with foreign contractor(s); (6) housing development projects. The business income from international contracted projects is the work volume of contracted projects completed during the reference period, expressed in monetary terms, including completed work on projects signed in previous years.

Service Cooperation with Foreign Countries refers to

the activities of providing technology and labour services to employers or contractors in the forms of receiving salaries and wages. Labour services providing by contractual joint ventures of Chinese international contracting corporations should be included in the statistics of service co-operation with foreign countries. The business income of labour service cooperation is the income in the form of wages and salaries, overtime pay, bonuses and other remuneration received from the employers during the reference period.

Overseas Design and Consultation Service refers to projects with charges for technical services from overseas operators. It includes geographic and topographic mapping, geological resource prospecting and survey, planning of construction areas, provision of design documents, blueprints, materials on production process and techniques, as well as engineering, technical and economic consultation, and feasibility study, research and evaluation of projects. Also included under this category are the above-mentioned services of foreign-financed projects in China that are paid in foreign currencies.

19

旅　游

Tourism

简 要 说 明

一、本篇资料的主要内容

旅游统计的主要内容包括：旅行社个数、旅行社职工人数、星级饭店个数、入境国际旅游者(外国人、华侨、港澳同胞和台湾同胞)人数、出境居民人数、国内居民(城镇和农村)旅游人数，以及国际、国内旅游收入等。

二、本篇资料的统计范围

包括国际旅游和国内旅游。

三、本篇的资料来源

本篇资料是国家统计局贸易外经司根据公安部和国家旅游局的资料编制的。资料来源：入境国际旅游人数和国内居民出境人数来自公安部出、入境管理资料；各地区接待国际旅游者人数、旅行社接待国际旅游者人数、国内旅游人数和国内旅游收入来自国家旅游局；国际旅游外汇收入1994年以前由国家统计局贸易外经司根据国际旅游者在华花费外汇券统计资料整理提供，1994年及以后由国家旅游局整理提供；旅行社、星级饭店基本情况来自国家旅游局。

四、本篇的统计调查方法

国际、国内旅游收入和国内出游人数等指标采取抽样调查方法，其余指标均为全面调查统计取得。

Brief Introduction

I. Main Content

Data on tourism mainly include: number of travel agencies, number of employees in travel agencies, number of star-hotels, total number of international tourists received (foreigners, overseas Chinese, Chinese compatriots from Hong Kong, Macao and Taiwan), Chinese residents going abroad, domestic tourists (from urban and from rural areas), number of domestic tourists (urban and rural areas), and income from international and domestic tourism.

II. Coverage of Statistics

Data in this chapter include both international and domestic tourism.

III. Sources of Data

Data in this chapter are compiled by the Department of Trade and Foreign Economic Relations of the National Bureau of Statistics on the basis of data from the Ministry of Public Security and State Tourism Administration. Sources of data are as follows: number of international tourists entering into China and Chinese residents going abroad is provided by the Frontier Administration of the Ministry of Public Security; number of international tourists received by province, number of international tourists received by travel agency, number of domestic tourists and earnings from domestic tourism are provided by the State Tourism Administration; figures on the earnings from international tourism before 1994 are provided by the Department of Trade and Foreign Economic Relations Statistics of the National Bureau of Statistics using data on the expenditure of Foreign Exchange Certificates by international tourists, and since 1994, by the State Tourism Administration; data on basic situation of travel agencies and tourist hotels are provided the State Tourism Administration.

IV. Survey Methodology

Data on the earnings from international and domestic tourism and domestic tourists are collected from sample surveys, while statistics on other items are from comprehensive reporting system.

19-1 旅游事业发展情况

Development of Tourism

指 标	Item	2000	2001	2002	2003	2004	2005
旅行社数 （个）	**Total Number of Travel Agencies (unit)**	**8993**	**10532**	**11552**	**13361**	**14927**	
国际旅行社	International Travel Agencies	1268	1310	1349	1364	1460	
国内旅行社	Domestic Travel Agencies	7725	9222	10203	11997	13467	
旅行社职工人数 （人）	**Number of Staff and Workers of Travel Agencies (person)**	**164336**	**192408**	**229147**	**249802**	**246219**	
国际旅行社	International Travel Agencies	68093	72801	89128	100742	89342	
国内旅行社	Domestic Travel Agencies	96243	119607	140019	149060	156877	
星级饭店总数 （个）	**Total Number of Tourist Hotel (unit)**	**10481**	**7358**	**8880**	**9751**	**10888**	
入境旅游人数 （万人次）	**Total Number of International Tourists Arrival to China (10 000 person-times)**	**8344.39**	**8901.29**	**9790.83**	**9166.21**	**10903.82**	**12029.23**
外国人	Foreigners	1016.04	1122.64	1343.95	1140.29	1693.25	2025.51
华 侨	Overseas Chinese	7.55					
港澳同胞	Compatriots from Hong Kong and Macao	7009.93	7434.45	8080.82	7752.73	8842.05	9592.79
台湾同胞	Compatriots from Taiwan	310.86	344.20	366.06	273.19	368.53	410.92
#过夜旅游者人数(万人次)	Tourists (Overnight Visitors) (10 000 person-times)	3123.60	3316.67	3680.26	3297.05	4176.14	4680.90
国内居民出境人数(万人次)	**Total Number of Domestic Resident Outbound (10 000 person-times)**	**1047.26**	**1213.44**	**1660.23**	**2022.19**	**2885.00**	**3102.63**
#因私出境人数	For Private Purpose	563.09	694.67	1007.39	1481.09	2298.00	2514.00
国内旅游人数 （万人次）	**Total Number of Domestic Tourists (10 000 person-times)**	**74400**	**78400**	**87800**	**87000**	**110200**	**121200**
旅游收入	**Tourism Earnings**						
国际旅游外汇收入 （亿美元）	International Tourism Foreign Exchange Earnings (100 million USD)	162.24	177.92	203.85	174.06	257.39	292.96
国内旅游收入 （亿元）	Domestic Tourism Earnings (100 million yuan)	3175.54	3522.36	3878.36	3442.27	4710.71	5285.86

注：2000年星级饭店总数为涉外饭店数。

a) In 2000, the total number of tourist hotels is the number of hotels concerning foreign affairs.

19-2 国际旅游外汇收入及构成

Foreign Exchange Earnings and Its Composition

单位：百万美元 (USD million)

指 标	Item	2004 数额 Value	2004 比重 Percentage (%)	2005 数额 Value	2005 比重 Percentage (%)
总计	**Total**	**25739**	**100.0**	**29296**	**100.0**
长途交通	Long Distance Transportation	6688	26.0	8294	28.3
民航	Civil Aviation	4952	19.2	5928	20.2
铁路	Railway	463	1.8	904	3.1
汽车	Highway	810	3.1	718	2.5
轮船	Waterway	463	1.8	744	2.5
游览	Visiting	1307	5.1	1227	4.2
住宿	Accommodation	3124	12.1	3775	12.9
餐饮	Food and Beverage	1942	7.5	2748	9.4
商品销售	Shopping	5798	22.5	6378	21.8
娱乐	Entertainment	1825	7.1	1702	5.8
邮电通讯	Post and Communication Services	881	3.4	844	2.9
市内交通	Local Transportation	1087	4.2	1030	3.5
其他服务	Other Service	3086	12.0	3299	11.3

19-3 按性别、年龄和事由分外国入境旅游人数

Number of Foreigner Tourists by Sex, Age and Purpose

单位：万人次 (10 000 person-times)

指 标	Item	2004 人数 Persons	2004 比重 Percentage (%)	2005 人数 Persons	2005 比重 Percentage (%)
总 计	**Total**	**1693.25**	**100.0**	**2025.51**	**100.0**
按性别分	**By Sex**				
男	Male	1120.40	66.2	1321.15	65.2
女	Female	572.85	33.8	704.36	34.8
按年龄分	**By Age**				
14岁及以下	14 and under	64.15	3.8	79.93	3.9
15至24岁	15-24	131.97	7.8	164.46	8.1
25至44岁	25-44	828.82	48.9	979.74	48.4
45至64岁	45-64	588.27	34.7	703.84	34.7
65岁以上	65 and over	80.05	4.7	97.55	4.8
按目的分类	**By Purpose**				
会议/商务	Meeting /Business	386.14	22.8	459.81	22.7
观光休闲	Sightseeing and Holiday	741.21	43.8	934.46	46.1
探亲访友	Visiting Relatives and Friends	37.62	2.2	40.54	2.0
服务员工	Services & Crew	175.48	10.4	201.16	9.9
其他	Others	352.80	20.8	389.54	19.2

19-4 按国别分外国入境旅游人数

Number of Foreigner Tourists by Country/Region

单位：万人次 (10 000 person-times)

地 区	Region	1995	1997	1998	1999	2000	2001	2002	2003	2004	2005
总计	**Total**	**588.67**	**742.80**	**710.77**	**843.23**	**1016.04**	**1122.64**	**1343.95**	**1140.29**	**1693.25**	**2025.51**
亚洲	**Asia**	**338.26**	**428.17**	**400.06**	**499.27**	**610.15**	**686.42**	**864.38**	**726.50**	**1073.66**	**1250.63**
#朝鲜	Korea, D.P.Rep.	6.64	7.14	6.12	6.98	7.64	7.71	7.93	7.71	11.21	12.58
印度	India	4.50	6.05	6.57	8.42	12.09	15.94	21.36	21.91	30.94	35.65
印度尼西亚	Indonesia	13.28	14.73	10.46	18.29	22.06	22.42	27.47	23.18	34.98	37.76
日本	Japan	130.52	158.17	157.21	185.52	220.15	238.57	292.56	225.48	333.43	339
马来西亚	Malaysia	25.18	36.13	30.01	37.29	44.10	46.86	59.24	43.01	74.19	89.96
蒙古	Mongolia	26.19	34.29	26.48	35.45	39.91	38.71	45.31	41.83	55.38	64.20
菲律宾	Philippines	21.97	27.67	25.65	29.83	36.39	40.80	50.86	45.77	54.94	65.40
新加坡	Singapore	26.15	31.68	31.64	35.25	39.94	41.50	49.71	37.81	63.68	75.59
韩国	Republic of Korea	52.95	78.11	63.28	99.20	134.47	167.88	212.43	194.55	284.49	354.53
泰国	Thailand	17.33	16.85	14.43	20.64	24.11	29.84	38.63	27.54	46.42	58.63
非洲	**Africa**	**4.08**	**4.91**	**5.43**	**5.21**	**6.56**	**7.32**	**9.85**	**10.42**	**17.34**	**23.80**
欧洲	**Europe**	**159.06**	**201.83**	**187.33**	**211.27**	**248.90**	**268.38**	**282.58**	**259.76**	**377.57**	**478.49**
#英国	United Kingdom	18.49	22.79	24.29	25.89	28.39	30.25	34.30	28.83	41.81	49.96
德国	Germany	16.65	18.47	19.19	21.76	23.91	25.34	28.18	22.20	36.53	45.49
法国	France	11.85	13.13	13.80	15.56	18.50	19.95	22.21	15.61	28.11	37.20
意大利	Italy	6.37	6.51	7.25	7.22	7.78	7.77	9.17	6.58	12.24	19.70
荷兰	Netherlands	3.49	5.23	5.89	7.01	7.60	9.30	10.04	6.79	11.74	14.58
葡萄牙	Portugal	2.56	3.58	3.85	4.02	2.28	2.68	3.61	3.01	3.95	4.38
瑞典	Sweden	3.52	3.85	4.06	4.68	5.36	5.28	6.28	5.00	8.72	11.03
瑞士	Switzerland	3.43	3.03	2.84	2.99	3.07	3.08	3.24	2.37	4.07	5.14
哈萨克	Kazakhstan	9.92	9.49	9.60	6.87	6.71	6.93	6.57	8.97	16.25	18.66
俄罗斯	Russia	48.93	81.37	69.20	83.30	108.02	119.62	127.16	138.07	179.22	222.39
拉丁美洲	**Latin America**	**5.37**	**7.66**	**7.46**	**7.59**	**8.29**	**7.45**	**9.71**	**8.01**	**13.25**	**16.04**
北美洲	**North America**	**64.36**	**79.05**	**87.33**	**95.01**	**113.28**	**120.31**	**141.25**	**105.28**	**165.67**	**198.53**
#加拿大	Canada	12.88	17.41	19.60	21.37	23.66	25.39	29.13	23.03	34.80	42.98
美国	United States	51.49	61.64	67.73	73.64	89.62	94.92	112.12	82.25	130.86	155.55
大洋洲及太平洋岛屿	**Oceanic and Pacific Islands**	**15.85**	**19.35**	**22.48**	**24.38**	**28.18**	**30.97**	**35.37**	**30.01**	**45.21**	**57.36**
#澳大利亚	Australia	12.94	15.68	18.64	20.35	23.41	25.51	29.13	24.54	37.63	48.3
新西兰	New Zealand	2.29	2.83	3.00	3.14	3.76	4.44	5.02	4.34	6.46	7.84
其他	**Others**	**1.69**	**1.83**	**0.68**	**0.50**	**0.68**	**1.79**	**0.81**	**0.30**	**0.52**	**0.65**

19-5 各地区国际旅游外汇收入

Foreign Exchange Earnings by Region

单位：百万美元 (USD million)

地区	Region	1995	1997	1998	1999	2000	2001	2002	2003	2004	2005
北京	Beijing	2182	2248	2384	2496	2768	2946	3115	1904	3173	3619
天津	Tianjin	133	180	202	209	232	280	342	329	413	509
河北	Hebei	42	97	100	124	142	157	167	85	190	209
山西	Shanxi	21	37	38	43	50	59	75	36	81	116
内蒙古	Inner Mongolia	91	107	126	120	126	137	149	138	253	352
辽宁	Liaoning	189	260	262	304	383	463	550	454	613	738
吉林	Jilin	41	59	38	45	58	76	86	66	96	120
黑龙江	Heilongjiang	61	105	121	148	189	250	297	244	302	340
上海	Shanghai	939	1317	1218	1364	1613	1808	2275	2053	3041	3556
江苏	Jiangsu	260	408	529	620	724	822	1050	1132	1763	2260
浙江	Zhejiang	236	345	361	410	514	699	928	873	1300	1716
安徽	Anhui	31	64	51	67	86	106	124	83	141	186
福建	Fujian	484	614	651	725	894	942	1100	915	1065	1305
江西	Jiangxi	25	45	43	50	62	70	72	47	80	104
山东	Shandong	154	204	220	265	315	382	472	370	567	780
河南	Henan	60	95	101	114	124	133	145	63	160	216
湖北	Hubei	73	170	88	105	146	201	284	136	192	276
湖南	Hunan	65	140	156	185	221	271	311	46	313	390
广东	Guangdong	2393	2801	2942	3272	4112	4484	5091	4267	5378	6457
广西	Guangxi	121	178	156	202	307	301	321	164	288	359
海南	Hainan	81	102	96	105	109	106	92	80	82	128
重庆	Chongqing		105	88	97	138	163	218	113	203	264
四川	Sichuan	125	79	84	97	122	166	200	150	289	316
贵州	Guizhou	29	44	48	55	61	69	80	29	80	101
云南	Yunnan	165	264	261	350	339	367	419	340	422	528
西藏	Tibet	11	32	33	36	52	46	52	19	37	44
陕西	Shaanxi	139	225	247	272	280	309	351	198	361	446
甘肃	Gansu	21	28	30	37	55	45	54	21	44	59
青海	Qinghai	2	3	3	4	7	9	10	5	9	11
宁夏	Ningxia	1	1	1	2	3	3	2	1	2	2
新疆	Xinjiang	74	71	82	86	95	99	99	49	91	100

19-6 各地区接待入境旅游人数
Number of International Tourists by Region

单位：万人次 (10 000 person-times)

地 区	Region	1995 总计 Total	1995 #外国人 Foreigners	2000 总计 Total	2000 #外国人 Foreigners	2004 总计 Total	2004 #外国人 Foreigners	2005 总计 Total	2005 #外国人 Foreigners
北 京	Beijing	206.87	166.52	282.09	237.96	315.50	268.10	362.92	311.62
天 津	Tianjin	20.06	16.27	35.62	32.14	61.59	55.93	74.01	67.46
河 北	Hebei	16.50	13.59	41.43	35.90	58.07	53.65	62.65	57.39
山 西	Shanxi	7.12	5.15	16.53	11.66	29.58	18.22	42.15	25.40
内蒙古	Inner Mongolia	30.09	29.46	39.19	38.74	79.99	79.11	100.16	99.56
辽 宁	Liaoning	26.38	21.46	61.22	50.05	108.08	93.77	130.20	111.11
吉 林	Jilin	15.61	14.49	22.27	19.19	32.40	27.67	37.32	30.68
黑龙江	Heilongjiang	16.23	13.94	55.17	50.47	73.28	69.28	82.15	76.42
上 海	Shanghai	136.79	107.54	181.40	143.90	385.45	319.67	444.54	379.93
江 苏	Jiangsu	76.77	48.68	160.95	98.15	306.57	214.24	378.30	262.15
浙 江	Zhejiang	67.27	36.65	112.59	64.75	276.67	177.64	348.05	232.92
安 徽	Anhui	14.29	7.28	31.84	16.79	50.10	31.97	63.29	41.06
福 建	Fujian	90.64	22.41	161.33	49.75	172.90	62.92	197.39	72.36
江 西	Jiangxi	7.36	2.34	16.31	5.54	28.77	9.40	37.25	13.63
山 东	Shandong	45.09	30.43	72.31	48.01	119.31	96.17	155.11	124.78
河 南	Henan	21.84	9.12	32.50	18.21	45.02	24.12	60.05	34.73
湖 北	Hubei	27.09	16.83	45.08	35.74	61.19	50.19	82.57	62.68
湖 南	Hunan	17.73	7.18	45.40	15.79	55.34	41.23	71.98	60.88
广 东	Guangdong	620.68	122.07	1198.94	212.85	1563.65	377.68	1896.99	476.53
广 西	Guangxi	41.85	30.74	122.91	50.80	117.58	69.38	147.71	88.66
海 南	Hainan	28.71	5.75	48.68	9.37	30.86	18.38	43.19	26.94
重 庆	Chongqing			26.61	19.29	43.44	33.89	52.39	41.81
四 川	Sichuan	37.67	24.51	46.20	19.97	96.62	54.65	106.28	68.27
贵 州	Guizhou	13.66	7.79	18.39	7.12	23.10	7.63	27.62	9.26
云 南	Yunnan	59.69	47.38	100.11	66.59	110.10	73.22	150.28	99.65
西 藏	Tibet	6.78	6.54	15.00	13.58	9.58	8.88	12.13	11.10
陕 西	Shaanxi	44.23	39.73	71.28	58.48	80.02	60.93	92.84	74.57
甘 肃	Gansu	9.09	7.07	21.31	14.34	23.67	15.14	28.85	17.20
青 海	Qinghai	1.33	0.87	3.26	1.46	2.89	1.24	3.52	1.46
宁 夏	Ningxia	0.37	0.28	0.78	0.58	0.70	0.54	0.82	0.66
新 疆	Xinjiang	20.36	18.55	25.61	20.84	31.69	27.10	33.11	29.01

19-7 国 内 旅 游 情 况
Statistics of Domestic Tourism

年 份 Year	旅游人数 (百万人次) Domestic Tourists (million person-times)	城镇居民 Urban Residents	农村居民 Rural Residents	旅游收入 (亿元) Tourism Earning (100 million yuan)	城镇居民 Urban Residents	农村居民 Rural Residents	人均花费 (元) Per Capita Expenditure (yuan)	城镇居民 Urban Residents	农村居民 Rural Residents
1994	524	205	319	1023.5	848.2	175.3	195.3	414.7	54.9
1995	629	246	383	1375.7	1140.1	235.6	218.7	464.0	61.5
1996	640	256	383	1638.4	1368.4	270.0	256.2	534.1	70.5
1997	644	259	385	2112.7	1551.8	560.9	328.1	599.8	145.7
1998	695	250	445	2391.2	1515.1	876.1	345.0	607.0	197.0
1999	719	284	435	2831.9	1748.2	1083.7	394.0	614.8	249.5
2000	744	329	415	3175.5	2235.3	940.3	426.6	678.6	226.6
2001	784	375	409	3522.4	2651.7	870.7	449.5	708.3	212.7
2002	878	385	493	3878.4	2848.1	1030.3	441.8	739.7	209.1
2003	870	351	519	3442.3	2404.1	1038.2	395.7	684.9	200.0
2004	1102	459	643	4710.7	3359.0	1351.7	427.5	731.8	210.2
2005	1212	496	716	5285.9	3656.1	1629.7	436.1	737.1	227.6

主要统计指标解释

旅游者人数

(1)入境国际旅游者人数：指来中国参观、访问、旅行、探亲、访友、休养、考察、参加会议和从事经济、科技、文化、教育、宗教等活动的外国人、华侨、港澳同胞和台湾同胞的人数。不包括外国在我国的常驻机构，如使领馆、通讯社、企业办事处的工作人员；来我国常住的外国专家、留学生以及在岸逗留不过夜人员。

(2)出境居民人数：指大陆居民因公务活动或私人事务短期出境的人数。公务活动出境居民人数包括在国际交通工具上的中国服务员工，因私出境居民人数不包括在国际交通工具上的中国服务员工。

(3)国内旅游者人数：指我国大陆居民和在我国常住1年以上的外国人、华侨、港澳台同胞离开常住地在境内其他地方的旅游设施内至少停留一夜，最长不超过6个月的人数。

国际旅游(外汇)收入　指入境旅游的外国人、华侨、港澳同胞和台湾同胞在中国大陆旅游过程中发生的一切旅游支出，其对于国家来说就是国际旅游(外汇)收入。

国际旅行社　指经营对外招徕并接待外国人、华侨、港澳同胞和台湾同胞来中国、归国或回内地旅游业务的旅行社。

国内旅行社　指负责经营招徕、组团、接待国内旅客的旅游业务，以及不对外招徕，负责经营接待国际旅行社或其它涉外部门组织的外国人、华侨、港澳同胞和台湾同胞来中国、归国或回内地的旅游业务的旅行社。

星级饭店　指已评定星级的饭店。

Explanatory Notes on Main Statistical Indicators

Number of Tourists

(1) International tourists refer to foreigners, overseas Chinese, Chinese compatriots from Hong Kong, Macao and Taiwan coming to China for sight-seeing, visits, tours, family reunions, vacations, study tours, conferences and other activities of a business, scientific and technological, cultural, educational and religious nature. It does not include representatives and employees of resident institutions of foreign countries in China such as embassies, consulates, news agencies and offices of foreign companies and organizations, nor does it include long-term foreign experts or students residing in China, or persons in transition without spending a night in China.

(2) Chinese residents going abroad refer to Chinese residents going abroad for short terms for either public business or private purposes. Chinese employees working on international transport carriers are included in those going abroad for public business purpose, not in those for private purpose.

(3) Domestic tourists refer to residents of the mainland of China who stay for one night at least but no more than 6 months at tourist facilities in other places than their permanent residence within the territory of the mainland China, including foreigners, overseas Chinese and Chinese compatriots from Hong Kong, Macao and Taiwan who have resided in China for over one year.

Foreign Exchange Earnings from International Tourism refer to the total expenditures of foreigners, overseas Chinese, Chinese compatriots from Hong Kong, Macao and Taiwan during their stay in the mainland of China, which are earnings of foreign exchange from international tourism from the point of view from China.

International Travel Agencies refer to travel agencies engaged in the promotion, solicitation, organization and reception of tours to the mainland of China by foreigners, overseas Chinese, Chinese compatriots from Hong Kong, Macao and Taiwan.

Domestic Travel Agencies refer to travel agencies engaged in the promotion, solicitation, organization and reception of domestic tourists, and in the reception of foreigners, overseas Chinese, Chinese compatriots from Hong Kong, Macao and Taiwan organized by international travel agencies or other departments concerned, without their own promotion and solicitation programmes.

Star-Hotels refer to hotels rated with stars.

20

金融业
Financial Intermediation

简 要 说 明

一、本篇资料的主要内容

本篇反映我国金融、证券和保险业发展情况。有以下五个部分：一是银行系统机构人员，二是金融机构金融活动情况，三是存贷款利率调整情况，四是直接融资情况，五是保险业务情况。

二、本篇各部分资料来源

1.反映银行系统机构人员情况的表是“20-1银行系统机构、人员数”，由中国人民银行总行人事部门根据有关的行政记录汇总和填报。

2.反映金融机构活动情况的资料包括：“20-2金融机构人民币信贷资金平衡表(资金来源)”，“20-3金融机构人民币信贷资金平衡表(资金运用)”，“20-4金融机构现金收入”，“20-5金融机构现金支出”，“20-6金融机构现金投放与回笼”，“20-7国家银行人民币信贷收支（年底余额）”，“20-8货币供应量（年底余额）”，“20-9货币供应量同比增长率”，“20-12黄金和外汇储备”，“20-13国有商业银行资产负债表（年底余额）”，“20-14外资银行资产负债表（年底余额）”。金融机构信贷资金平衡表及现金收支表的统计范围包括中国人民银行、国家政策性银行、国有商业银行、其他商业银行、城市信用合作社、农村信用合作社、外资银行、财务公司、信托投资公司、金融租赁公司、邮政储蓄机构。中国人民银行总行根据金融机构的基层单位全面填报、并按各自系统汇总的资料，进行归并和汇总，最后得到金融机构的信贷收支及现金收支表。黄金和外汇储备表中的资料取自于中国人民银行的资产负债表，由该行有关部门提供。

3.反映存贷款利率调整情况的“20-10金融机构法定存款利率”，“20-11金融机构法定贷款利率表”，数据来自中国人民银行总行规定的、并对外发布的存贷款利率。

4.反映直接融资情况的“20-15国内有价证券分类发行情况”，“20-16证券市场基本情况”，“20-17上市公司数量”，“20-18股票发行量和筹资额”，“20-19股票交易情况”，资料取自中国证券监督管理委员会编制的《中国证券期货统计年鉴》。

5.反映保险业务情况的“20-20保险系统机构、人员数”，“20-21保险公司业务经济技术指标”，数据取自中国保险监督管理委员会编制的保险统计资料。

Brief Introduction

I. Main Content

Data in this chapter show the development of China's banking, securities and insurance, in the following 5 aspects: (1) The number of the institutions and personnel in the banking system; (2) The financial activities of banking institutions; (3) The changes of the interest rates of the deposits and loans; (4) The direct financing; (5) The business of insurance.

II. Sources of Data:

(1) Table 20-1 showing number of institution and employed person in finance system are prepared by the personnel departments of the Headquarter of the People's Bank of China on the basis of the related administrative registers.

(2) Data on the financial activities of banking institutions are 20-2 credit funds balance sheet of financial institutions (sources of funds), 20-3 credit funds balance sheet of financial institutions (uses of funds), 20-4 cash income of financial institutions, 20-5 cash expenditures of financial institutions, 20-6 cash statistics of financial institutions, 20-7 sources and uses of credit funds of national banks at the year-end, 20-8 money supply at the year-end, 20-9 percentage change of money supply over the last corresponding period, 20-10 nominal interest rates on deposits of financial institutions, 20-11 nominal interest rates on loans of financial institutions, 20-12 gold and foreign exchange reserves, 20-13 balance sheet of domestic business banks at the year-end and 20-14 balance sheet of foreign capital banks at the year-end. the statistics of the credit funds balance sheet of financial institutions, cash revenue and expenditure cover the People's Bank of China, the state policy banks, the state-owned commercial banks, other commercial banks, urban and rural credit cooperatives, foreign banks, financing corporations, trust investment corporations, financing and leasing corporations, and savings deposit institutions under the postal offices. The grassroots units of the above banking institutions fill out the questionnaires and report to the higher authorities. The higher authorities tabulate the data level by level. Finally, the Department of Investigation and Statistics of the Head Office of the People's Bank of China tabulate the data and get the national total. The data in the on the gold and foreign exchange reserves are extracted from the balance sheet of the People's Bank of China and provided by its concerned departments.

(3)Table 20-10 nominal interest rates on deposits of financial institutions and 20-11 nominal interest rates on loans of financial institutions show the changes of the interest rates of savings deposits and loans. Data are from the interest rates of deposits and loans stipulated and published by the Head Office of the People's Bank of China.

(4)Table 20-15 issuance of domestic securities, 20-16 general statistics on securities markets, 20-17 summary for number of listed companies, 20-18 issued share and raised capital, and 20-19 trading summary for stocks show the direct fund raising. Data are from the *Statistical Yearbook on China's Securities and Futures* compiled by China Securities Regulatory Commission.

(5) Table 20-20 number of institutions and employed persons in insurance system and 20-21 economic and technical indicators of insurance companies funded with Chinese and foreign capital show the business of insurance, with data coming from the insurance statistics compiled by China Insurance Regulatory Commission.

20-1 银行系统机构、人员数（2005年底）

Number of Institutions and Employed Persons in Finance System at the Year-end (2005)

项 目	Item	机构数(个) Number of Institution (unit)	年末人数(人) Number of Staff and Workers (person)	#女 性 Female
总 计	**Total**	**82453**	**1800381**	**817624**
中国人民银行	The People's Bank of China	2167	138538	44675
中国工商银行	Industrial and Commercial Bank of China	18764	427383	210263
中国农业银行	Agricultural Bank of China	28234	478895	202174
中国银行	Bank of China	11019	229740	115434
中国建设银行	Construction Bank of China	14088	300288	142678
中国农业发展银行	Agricultural Development Bank of China	2176	59598	18956
交通银行	Bank of Communications	2607	57323	29765
中国进出口银行	The Export-Import Bank of China	16	908	393
浦东发展银行	Shanghai Pudong Development Bank	375	10082	4936
国家开发银行	National Development Bank	38	4708	1790
中信实业银行	CITIC Industrial Bank	418	14577	6983
中国光大银行	China Everbright Bank	416	9734	4861
中国民生银行	China Minsheng Banking Corp., Ltd	242	9447	4966
华夏银行	China Huaxia Bank	294	7761	3758
招商银行	China Merchants Bank	454	20653	11069
广东发展银行	Guangdong Development Bank	500	12284	6158
福建兴业银行	Fujian Industrial Bank	329	9918	4619
深圳发展银行	Shenzhen Development Bank Co., Ltd	240	7142	3417
恒丰银行	Everygrowing Bank Co., Ltd	76	1402	729

20-2 金融机构人民币信贷资金平衡表（资金来源）

Credit Funds Balance Sheet of Financial Institutions (Sources of Funds)

(年底余额) 单位：亿元 (year-end) (100 million yuan)

项 目	Item	2004	2005
资金来源合计	**Funds Sources**	**262740.0**	**302042.8**
各项存款	Total Deposits	241424.3	287169.5
企业存款	Deposits by Enterprises	84669.5	96143.7
财政存款	Fiscal Deposits	6236.2	7996.3
机关团体存款	Deposits by Government Departments & Organizations	8152.4	12052.3
城乡储蓄存款	Urban and Rural Household Savings Deposits	119555.4	141051.0
农业存款	Agricultural Deposits	5526.3	6203.8
委托及信托类存款	Trusted Deposits	3008.6	3461.8
其他类存款	Other Deposits	14276.0	20260.7
金融债券	Financial Bonds	3954.7	5672.8
对国际金融机构负债	Liabilities to International Financial Institutions	562.3	641.6
流通中现金	Currency in Circulation	21468.3	24031.7
其他	Others	-4669.7	-15472.7

注：金融机构包括人民银行、政策性银行、国有独资商业银行、邮政储蓄机构、其他商业银行、城市合作银行、农村信用社、城市信用社、外资银行、信托投资公司、租赁公司、财务公司等。

a) Financial Institutions include People's Bank of China, Policy banks,State-owned commercial banks, savings deposit agencies of postal offices, housing saving banks, urban credit cooperative banks, rural credit agencies of postal savings, other commercial banks, urban cooperative banks, rural credits cooperatives, urban credit cooperatives, foreign-funded banks, trust and investment corporations, leasing companies, financial companies etc.

20-3 金融机构人民币信贷资金平衡表（资金运用）

Credit Funds Balance Sheet of Financial Institutions (Uses of Funds)

(年底余额) 单位：亿元 (year-end) (100 million yuan)

项　目	Item	2004	2005
资金运用合计	**Funds Uses**	**262740.0**	**302042.8**
各项贷款	Total Loans	178197.8	194690.4
短期贷款	Short-term Loans	86840.6	87449.2
工业贷款	Loans to Industrial Sector	23896.6	22516.7
商业贷款	Loans to Commercial Sector	17074.1	16447.6
建筑业贷款	Loans to Construction Sector	2780.1	2983.7
农业贷款	Loans to Agricultural Sector	9843.1	11529.9
乡镇企业贷款	Loans to Township Enterprises	8069.2	7901.8
私营企业及个体贷款	Loans to Private Enterprises and Individuals	2081.6	2180.8
三资企业贷款	Loans to Enterprises with Foreign Funds	2198.4	1975.3
其他短期贷款	Other Short-term Loans	20897.5	21913.5
中长期贷款	Medium-term & Long-term Loans	76702.9	87460.4
委托及信托类贷款	Credit Loans	2721.2	3126.2
其他类贷款	Other Loans	11933.1	16654.6
有价证券及投资	Portfolio Investment	30931.0	34942.1
在国际金融机构资产	Assets with International Financial Institutions	682.9	862.0
金银占款	Position for Bullion & Silver Purchase	337.2	337.2
外汇占款	Position for Foreign Exchanges	52591.0	71211.1
财政借款	Fiscal Debts		

20-4 金融机构现金收入

Cash Income of Financial Institutions

单位：亿元 (100 million yuan)

项　目	Item	2004	2005
收入总计	**Total Income**	**567879.2**	**626978.5**
商品销售收入	Income from Commodity Sales	57943.9	61763.4
服务业收入	Income from Service Trade	22865.0	24091.1
税款收入	Income from Taxes	2880.3	3157.1
城乡个体经营收入	Income from Urban and Rural Individual Business	19109.5	20229.6
储蓄存款收入	Income from Savings Deposits	404743.9	454954.3
其他金融机构收入	Income from Other Financial Institutions	2565.2	2347.2
居民归还贷款收入	Income from Repayment of Loans by Residents	10290.1	11874.9
汇兑收入	Income from Remittances	5444.3	5326.1
有价证券收入	Income from Securities	1148.0	927.8
其他收入	Other Income	40889.2	42307.0
#兑换外币收入	Income from Exchange of Foreign Currencies	185.5	206.7

20-5 金融机构现金支出

Cash Expenditures of Financial Institutions

单位：亿元 (100 million yuan)

项　目	Item	2004	2005
支出总计	**Total Expenditure**	**569601.5**	**629541.8**
工资性支出	Wages	34307.0	36963.0
农副产品采购支出	Purchases of Agricultural and Sideline Products	13058.6	14898.0
行政企事业管理费支出	Government and Enterprises Overhead	27241.3	28585.0
城乡个体经营支出	Expenditure for Individual Business	24773.9	26449.8
储蓄存款支出	Expenditure for Savings Deposits	401910.1	451555.7
其他金融机构支出	Expenditure for Other Financial Institutions	2353.5	2122.6
居民提取贷款支出	Expenditure for Loans by Residents	9466.6	10322.0
汇兑支出	Expenditure for Remittances	3280.0	2981.0
工矿及其它产品采购支出	Expenditure for Purchases of Industrial and Mineral Products	11124.9	12697.3
有价证券支出	Expenditure for Securities	923.0	762.0
其他支出	Other Expenditure	41163.0	42205.3

20-6 金融机构现金投放与回笼

Cash Statistics of Financial Institutions

单位：亿元 (100 million yuan)

年 份 Year	现金收入 Cash Income	现金支出 Cash Expenditures	投 放 Currency Issuance
1957	516.7	512.2	-4.5
1962	633.2	614.0	-19.2
1965	675.7	686.5	10.8
1970	812.8	799.3	-13.5
1975	1128.2	1134.2	6.0
1978	1336.0	1352.6	16.6
1979	1626.4	1682.1	55.7
1980	2033.2	2111.7	78.5
1981	2402.2	2452.3	50.1
1982	2819.6	2862.4	42.8
1983	3428.7	3519.4	90.7
1984	4207.6	4469.9	262.3
1985	5499.1	5694.8	195.7
1986	6613.3	6843.9	230.6
1987	8779.6	9015.7	236.1
1988	12810.5	13490.0	679.5
1989	15057.6	15267.6	210.0
1990	17171.1	17471.4	300.4
1991	21465.1	21998.5	533.4
1992	31248.0	32406.2	1158.2
1993	48883.8	50412.5	1528.7
1994	71247.1	72671.0	1423.9
1995	96725.5	97322.3	596.8
1996	120263.3	121179.9	916.6
1997	141612.6	142988.3	1375.7
1998	203966.5	204993.1	1026.6
1999	233399.0	235650.4	2251.3
2000	277067.1	278264.3	1197.2
2001	321380.2	322416.3	1036.1
2002	365593.0	367182.2	1589.2
2003	455527.9	457995.9	2468.0
2004	567879.2	569601.5	1722.3
2005	626978.5	629541.8	2563.4

注：投放栏中的负数表示现金回笼。

a) The negative amount in currency issuance indicates the amount of cash withdrawn.

20-7 国家银行人民币信贷收支（年底余额）

Sources and Uses of Credit Funds of National Banks at the Year-end

单位：亿元　　(100 million yuan)

项　目	Item	2003	2004
资金来源总计	**Funds Sources**	**164523.9**	**193542.8**
各项存款	Total Deposits	134650.3	153556.6
企业存款	Deposits by Enterprises	41594.9	48491.9
活期存款	Demand Deposits	31504.4	35964.8
定期存款	Time Deposits	10090.6	12527.1
财政存款	Fiscal Deposits	5083.5	6105.7
机关团体存款	Deposits by Government Departments & Organizations	5594.0	6589.9
城镇储蓄存款	Urban and Rural Household Savings Deposits	75834.8	86469.6
活期储蓄	Demand Deposits	25944.2	30206.0
定期储蓄	Time Deposits	49890.6	56263.6
农业存款	Agricultural Deposits	463.3	485.0
其他类存款	Other Deposits	6079.8	5414.6
金融债券	Financial Bonds	5429.8	10095.0
同业往来	Inter-bank Credits	4757.3	4318.5
流通中现金	Currency in Circulation	19746.0	21468.3
对国际金融机构负债	Liabilities to International Financial Institutions	482.6	562.3
其他	Others	-542.0	3542.1
资金运用总计	**Funds Uses**	**164523.9**	**193542.8**
各项贷款	Total Loans	106155.9	116050.9
短期贷款	Short-term Loans	47987.5	46164.0
工业贷款	Loans to Industrial Sector	17639.1	17400.7
商业贷款	Loans to Commercial Sector	15168.8	14079.9
建筑业贷款	Loans to Construction Sector	1938.2	1210.8
农业贷款	Loans to Agricultural Sector	1271.8	1296.6
乡镇企业贷款	Loans to Township Enterprises	1680.5	1786.9
三资企业贷款	Loans to Enterprises with Foreign Funds	1679.7	1352.5
私营企业及个体贷款	Loans to Private Enterprises and Individuals	539.7	741.5
其他短期贷款	Other Short-term Loans	8069.7	8295.1
中长期贷款	Medium-term & Long-term Loans	53141.2	62290.3
其它类贷款	Other Loans	5027.3	7596.6
有价证券及投资	Portfolio Investment	21860.6	22494.9
同业往来	Inter-bank Debts	731.5	1505.4
金银占款	Position for Bullion & Silver Purchase	337.2	337.2
外汇占款	Position for Foreign Exchanges	34565.2	52471.5
财政借款	Fiscal Debts		
在国际金融机构资产	Assets with International Financial Institutions	873.4	682.9

注：1. 本表统计口径包括中国人民银行、政策性银行、国有独资商业银行、邮政储蓄机构。
2. 中国人民银行自2002年12月起对黄金储备和金银占款数据进行了调整。

a) The statistics coverage of the table includes the People's Bank of China, policy banks, state-owned commercial banks and agencies of postal saving.
b) Since December in 2002, the data of gold reserve and position for bullion & silver purchase have been adjusted by the People's Bank of China.

20-8 货币供应量（年底余额）

Money Supply at the Year-end

单位：亿元 (100 million yuan)

年份 Year	货币和准货币 (M_2) Money and Quasi-Money (M_2)	货币 (M_1) Money (M_1)	流通中现金 (M_0) Currency in Circulation (M_0)	活期存款 Demand Deposits	准货币 Quasi-Money	定期存款 Time Deposits	储蓄存款 Saving Deposits	其他存款 Other Deposits
1990	15293.4	6950.7	2644.4	4306.3	8342.7			
1991	19349.9	8633.3	3177.8	5455.5	10716.6			
1992	25402.2	11731.5	4336.0	7395.2	13670.7			
1993	34879.8	16280.4	5864.7	10415.7	18599.4	1247.9	15203.5	2148.0
1994	46923.5	20540.7	7288.6	13252.1	26382.8	1943.1	21518.4	2921.3
1995	60750.5	23987.1	7885.3	16101.8	36763.4	3324.2	29662.2	3777.0
1996	76094.9	28514.8	8802.0	19712.8	47580.1	5041.9	38520.8	4017.4
1997	90995.3	34826.3	10177.6	24648.7	56169.0	6738.5	46279.8	3150.7
1998	104498.5	38953.7	11204.2	27749.5	65544.9	8301.9	53407.5	3835.5
1999	119897.9	45837.3	13455.5	32381.8	74060.6	9476.8	59621.8	4962.0
2000	134610.4	53147.2	14652.7	38494.5	81463.2	11261.1	64332.4	5869.7
2001	158301.9	59871.6	15688.8	44182.8	98430.3	14180.1	73762.4	10487.8
2002	185007.0	70881.8	17278.0	53603.8	114125.2	16433.8	86910.7	10780.7
2003	221222.8	84118.6	19746.0	64372.6	137104.3	20940.4	103617.7	12546.2
2004	254107.0	95969.7	21468.3	74501.4	158137.2	25382.2	119555.4	13199.7
2005	298755.7	107278.7	24031.7	83247.1	191476.9	33100.0	141051.0	17325.9

注：2001年6月起，已将证券公司客户保证金计入货币供应量(M_2)，含在其他存款项内。

a) Since June in 2001, the consignment guarantee money of client at securities company had been calculated as the other deposit of M_2.

20-9 货币供应量同比增长率

Percentage Change of Money Supply Over the Last Corresponding Period

单位：% (%)

年份 Year	货币和准货币 (M_2) Money and Quasi-Money (M_2)	货币 (M_1) Money (M_1)	流通中现金 (M_0) Currency in Circulation (M_0)	活期存款 Demand Deposits	准货币 Quasi-Money	定期存款 Time Deposits	储蓄存款 Saving Deposits	其他存款 Other Deposits
1991	26.5	24.2	20.2	26.7	28.5			
1992	31.3	35.9	36.4	35.6	27.6			
1993								
1994	34.5	26.2	24.3	27.2	41.8	55.7	41.5	36.0
1995	29.5	16.8	8.2	21.5	39.3	71.1	37.9	29.3
1996	25.3	18.9	11.6	22.4	29.4	51.7	29.9	6.4
1997	19.6	22.1	15.6	25.0	18.1	33.7	20.1	-21.6
1998	14.8	11.9	10.1	12.6	16.7	23.2	15.4	21.7
1999	14.7	17.7	20.1	16.7	13.0	14.2	11.6	29.4
2000	12.3	16.0	8.9	18.9	10.0	18.8	7.9	18.3
2001	17.6	12.7	7.1	14.8	15.5	25.9	14.7	9.1
2002	16.8	16.8	10.1	19.2	16.8	21.8	17.8	2.8
2003	19.6	18.7	14.3	20.1	20.1	27.4	19.2	16.4
2004	14.7	13.6	8.7	15.1	15.3	21.2	15.4	5.2
2005	17.6	11.8	11.9	11.7	21.1	30.4	18.0	31.3

注：1.同期比增长率按可比口径计算。因1992年以前口径与1993年口径不一致，故1993年未计算增长率。

2.2001年6月起，已将证券公司客户保证金计入货币供应量(M_2)，含在其他存款项内。

3.1997年初，中国人民银行对金融统计制度进行了调整，因此自1997年起的数据与历史数据不完全可比。

a) Percentage change over the last corresponding period is calculated by the comparable standard. Because the statistical standard before 1992 was no comparable with that in 1993, the change in 1993 was not calculated.

b) Since June of 2001, the consignment guarantee money of client at securities company had been calculated as the other deposit of M_2.

c) The People's Bank of China have been adjusted the system of financial statistics at the beginning of 1997, the data since 1997 are imperfectible comparable with the previous years.

20-10 金融机构法定存款利率

Nominal Interest Rates on Deposits of Financial Institutions

单位：年利率%　　　　(annual interest rate %)

项　　目	Item	1998.3.25 Mar. 25, 1998	1998.7.1 Jul. 1, 1998	1998.12.7 Dec. 7, 1998	1999.6.10 Jun. 10,1999	2002.2.21 Feb. 21,2002	2004.10.29 Oct. 29,2004
个人人民币储蓄存款	**Household Deposits**						
活期	Demand	1.71	1.44	1.44	0.99	0.72	0.72
定期	Time						
三个月	3 Months	2.88	2.79	2.79	1.98	1.71	1.71
半年	6 Months	4.14	3.96	3.33	2.16	1.89	2.07
一年	1 Year	5.22	4.77	3.78	2.25	1.98	2.25
二年	2 Year	5.58	4.86	3.96	2.43	2.25	2.70
三年	3 Year	6.21	4.95	4.14	2.70	2.52	3.24
五年	5 Year	6.66	5.22	4.50	2.88	2.79	3.60
企业单位	**Enterprises Deposits**						
活期	Demand	1.71	1.44	1.44	0.99	0.72	0.72
定期	Time						
三个月	3 Months	2.88	2.79	2.79	1.98	1.71	1.71
半年	6 Months	4.14	3.96	3.33	2.16	1.89	2.07
一年	1 Year	5.22	4.77	3.78	2.25	1.98	2.25
二年	2 Year	5.58	4.86	3.96	2.43	2.25	2.70
三年	3 Year	6.21	4.95	4.14	2.70	2.52	3.24
五年	5 Year	6.66	5.22	4.50	2.88	2.79	3.60
大额可转让定期存单	**CDs**						
1个月	1 month						
3个月	3 months	2.88	2.79	2.79			
6个月	6 months	4.14	3.96	3.33			
9个月	9 months						
12个月	12 months	5.22	4.77	3.78			

20-11 金融机构法定贷款利率

Nominal Interest Rates on Loans of Financial Institutions

单位：年利率%　　　　(annual interest rate %)

项　　目	Item	1997.10.23 Oct. 23,1997	1998.3.25 Mar. 25,1998	1998.7.1 Jul. 1, 1998	1998.12.7 Dec. 7, 1998	1999.6.10 Jun. 10,1999	2002.2.21 Feb.21,2002	2004.10.29 Oct. 29,2004
短期贷款	**Short-term**							
六个月	6 Months	7.65①	7.02①	6.57②	6.12②	5.58③	5.04③	5.22
一年	1 Year	8.64①	7.92①	6.93②	6.39②	5.85③	5.31③	5.58
中长期贷款	**Medium-and Long-term**							
一年以上至三年	3 Years or Less	9.36	9.00	7.11②	6.66②	5.94③	5.49③	5.76
三年以上至五年	5 Years or Less	9.90	9.72	7.65②	7.2②	6.03③	5.58③	5.85
五年以上	More than 5 Years	10.53	10.35	8.01②	7.56②	6.21③	5.76③	6.12

注：1.①在法定贷款利率基础上可上浮10%，下浮10%。农村信用社贷款利率最高可上浮40%，下浮10%。
2.②从1998年11月起，金融机构对小企业贷款利率可在法定贷款利率基础上上浮20%。大中企业上浮10%。农村信用社贷款利率最高可上浮50%；金融机构贷款最低下浮10%。
3.③从1999年9月起，金融机构对中小企业贷款利率可在法定贷款利率基础上上浮30%，对大型企业贷款最高上浮10%；金融机构贷款最低下浮10%。

a) ① The lending rate could be 10% higher or 10% lower than nominal interest rates; for rural credit cooperatives, the lending rate could be 40% higher or 10% lower than nominal interest rates.

b) ② As of November 1998, the lending rate for small-sized enterprises could be 20% higher than nominal interest rates, and the lending rate for medium and large-sized enterprises could be 10% higher than nominal interest rates. For all financial institutions, the lending rate could be 10% lower than nominal interest rates, while, for rural credit cooperatives, the lending rate could be 50% higher than nominal interest rates.

c) ③ As of September 1999, the lending rate for medium and small-sized enterprises could be 30% higher than nominal interest rates; for large-sized enterprises, the lending rate could be as much as 10% higher than nominal interest rates. For all financial institutions, the lending rate could be 10% lower than nominal interest rates.

20-12 黄金和外汇储备

Gold and Foreign Exchange Reserves

年份 Year	黄金储备 (万盎司) Gold (10 000 fine troy ounce)	外汇储备 (亿美元) Foreign Exchange Reserve (USD 100 million)	年份 Year	黄金储备 (万盎司) Gold (10 000 fine troy ounce)	外汇储备 (亿美元) Foreign Exchange Reserve (USD 100 million)
1978	1280	1.67	1992	1267	194.43
1979	1280	8.40	1993	1267	211.99
1980	1280	-12.96	1994	1267	516.20
1981	1267	27.08	1995	1267	735.97
1982	1267	69.86	1996	1267	1050.29
1983	1267	89.01	1997	1267	1398.90
1984	1267	82.20	1998	1267	1449.59
1985	1267	26.44	1999	1267	1546.75
1986	1267	20.72	2000	1267	1655.74
1987	1267	29.23	2001	1608	2121.65
1988	1267	33.72	2002	1929	2864.07
1989	1267	55.50	2003	1929	4032.51
1990	1267	110.93	2004	1929	6099.32
1991	1267	217.12	2005	1929	8188.72

20-13 国有商业银行资产负债表（年底余额）

Balance Sheet of State-owned Commercial Banks at the Year-end

单位：亿元 (100 million yuan)

项目	Item	2004	2005
总资产	**Total Assets**	**172919.9**	**200283.7**
国外资产	Overseas Assets	10736.4	13850.0
储备资产	Reserve Assets	15171.0	16400.9
准备金存款	Bank Reserve	14281.6	15436.2
库存现金	Cash on Hand	889.4	964.7
央行债券	Claims on the Central Bank	6759.7	12921.2
对政府债权	Claims on Government	11320.9	11418.3
对非金融机构债权	Claims on Non-financial Institutions	103707.0	103509.2
对特定存款机构债权	Claims on Special Depository Institutions	7333.4	11501.3
对其他金融机构债权	Claims on Other Financial Institutions	6362.0	8324.2
其他资产	Other Assets	11529.4	22358.7
总负债	**Total Liabilities**	**172919.9**	**200283.7**
对非金融机构负债	Liabilities to Non-financial Institutions	142744.1	162835.1
活期存款	Demand Deposits	43288.8	47508.9
定期存款	Time Deposits	12407.1	16647.4
储蓄存款	Savings Deposits	75682.3	87034.2
其他存款	Other Deposits	2571.8	3357.0
外币存款	Foreign Currency Deposits	8794.1	8287.5
对中央银行负债	Liabilities to Central Bank	2402.3	1802.0
对特定存款机构负债	Liabilities to Special Deposit Institutions	170.0	370.8
对其他金融机构负债	Liabilities to Other Financial Institutions	5247.4	5411.8
#计入广义货币的存款	Broad Sense Currency Deposits	913.7	986.2
国外负债	Overseas Liabilities	1718.7	970.9
债券	Bonds	661.1	1353.8
实收资本	Paid-in Capital	6730.9	8043.9
其他负债	Other Liabilities	13245.5	19495.3

20-14 外资银行资产负债表（年底余额）

Balance Sheet of Foreign Capital Banks at the Year-end

单位：亿元 (100 million yuan)

项目	Item	2004	2005
总资产	**Total Assets**	**5160.0**	**6352.9**
国外资产	Overseas Assets	1486.3	1500.8
储备资产	Reserve Assets	244.5	364.9
准备金	Bank Reserve	243.9	363.6
库存现金	Cash on Hand	0.6	1.3
中央银行债券	Claims on the Central Bank		
对政府债权	Claims on Government	98.0	101.8
对非金融机构债权	Claims on Non-financial Institutions	2558.6	3301.4
对特定存款机构债权	Claims on Special Deposit Institutions	72.3	118.4
对其他金融机构债权	Claims on Other Financial Institutions	0.1	3.0
其他资产	Other Assets	700.1	962.7
总负债	**Total Liabilities**	**5160.0**	**6352.9**
国外负债	Overseas Liabilities	2737.1	3048.9
对非金融机构负债	Liabilities to Non-financial Institutions	1264.1	1695.5
活期存款	Demand Deposits	305.4	469.9
定期存款	Time Deposits	251.9	421.0
储蓄存款	Savings Deposits	0.3	0.4
其他存款	Other Deposits		
外币存款	Foreign Currency Deposits	706.7	804.2
对中央银行负债	Liabilities to Central Bank		
对特定存款机构负债	Liabilities to Special Deposit Institutions	3.7	1.6
对其他金融机构负债	Liabilities to Other Financial Institutions	27.2	42.5
#计入广义货币的存款	Broad Sense Currency Deposits		
债券	Bonds	11.6	21.1
实收资本	Paid-in Capital	472.0	579.4
其他负债	Other Liabilities	644.2	963.8

20-15 国内有价证券分类发行情况（2005年）

Issuance of Domestic Securities (2005)

单位：亿元 (100 million yuan)

种类	Kind	发行额 Total Value of Issued Securities	兑付额 Total Value of Redemption	年底余额 Balance (Year-end)
国债	National Debt	7042.0	1045.5	28774.0
#国库券	Treasury Bonds			
财政证券	Fiscal Bonds			
政策性金融债券	Policy Financial Bonds	5851.7	2053.0	17818.0
其他金融债	Other Financial Bonds	1265.3	29.0	1911.6
企业债	Corporate Bonds	2046.5	37.0	
国家投资债	Government Investment Bonds			
国家投资公司债	Bonds Issued by Government Investment Company			
股票	Shares	13.8	56.7	

注：股票是指A种股票(不含A股可转换债券)，股票兑付额是指筹资额。

a) Shares refer to A shares. The figure shown under the column "total value of redemption" for shares refers to the capital raised.

20-16 证券市场基本情况

General Statistics on Securities Markets

项 目	Item	2004	2005
境内上市公司数（A、B股)(家)	Number of Listed Companies (A and B Shares) in Mainland	1377	1381
境内上市外资股（B股）（家）	Number of Listed Companies of Foreign Fund (B Shares) in Mainland	110	109
境外上市公司数（H股）（家）	Number of Listed Companies (H Shares) Overseas	111	122
股票总发行股本 （亿股）	Total Issued Capital (100 million shares)	7149.43	7629.51
#流通股本 （亿股）	Negotiable Capital (100 million shares)	2577.18	2914.77
股票市价总值 （亿元）	Total Market Capitalization (100 million yuan)	37055.57	32430.28
#股票流通市值 （亿元）	Negotiable Market Capitalization (100 million yuan)	11688.64	10630.51
股票成交量 （百万股）	Stock Trading Volume (million shares)	582773.29	662373.20
股票成交金额 （亿元）	Total Stock Turnover (100 million yuan)	42333.95	31664.78
上证综合指数 （收盘）	Composite Index of Shanghai	1266.50	1161.06
深证综合指数 （收盘）	Composite Index of Shenzhen	315.81	278.75
投资者开户数 （万户）	Total Investors (10 000 accounts)	7211.43	7336.07
平均市盈率	Average P/E Ratio		
上海	Shanghai	24.23	16.33
深圳	Shenzhen	24.63	16.36
平均换手率 （%）	Average Turnover Rate (%)		
上海	Shanghai	288.71	274.37
深圳	Shenzhen	288.29	316.43
国债发行额 （亿元）	T-bonds Issued Volume (100 million yuan)	6923.90	7042.00
企业债发行额 （亿元）	Enterprise Bonds Issued Volume (100 million yuan)	327.00	2046.50
债券成交量 （万手）	Bonds Trading Volume (10 000 pieces)	504218.50	283714.36
债券成交额 （亿元）	Total Bonds Turnover (100 million yuan)	50323.50	28367.85
国债现货成交金额 （亿元）	Turnover of T-bonds Spots (100 million yuan)	2966.46	2780.63
国债回购成交金额 （亿元）	Turnover of T-bonds Repurchase (100 million yuan)	44086.61	23621.17
证券投资基金只数 （只）	Number of Securities Investment Funds (unit)	161	218
证券投资基金规模 （亿元）	Capital of Securities Investment Funds (100 million yuan)	3308.79	4714.18
证券投资基金成交金额(亿元)	Turnover of Securities Investment Funds (100 million yuan)	728.58	773.15
期货总成交量 （万手）	Future Trading Volume (10 000 pieces)	30569.76	32287.41
期货总成交额 （亿元）	Total Future Turnover (100 million yuan)	146935.32	134463.38

注：换手率=全年成交金额/[（本年末流通市值+上年末流通市值)/2]*100%

a) Average Turnover Rate = [Total Stock Turnover/(Negotiable Market Capitalization at the year-end + Negotiable Market Capitalization at the previous year-end)/2]*100%

20-17 上 市 公 司 数 量

Summary for Number of Listed Companies

单位：个 (unit)

年 份 Year	全国合计 National	上交所 Shanghai Stock Exchange	深交所 Shenzhen Stock Exchange	仅发A股公司 A Share Only	发A、H股公司 A & H Share	发A、B股公司 A & B Share	仅发B股公司 B Share Only
1990	10	8	2	10			
1991	14	8	6	14			
1992	53	29	24	53		18	
1993	183	106	77	183	3	34	6
1994	291	171	120	227	6	54	4
1995	323	188	135	242	11	58	12
1996	530	293	237	431	14	69	16
1997	745	383	362	627	17	76	25
1998	851	438	413	727	18	80	26
1999	949	484	465	822	19	82	26
2000	1088	572	516	955	19	86	28
2001	1160	646	514	1025	23	88	24
2002	1224	715	509	1085	28	87	24
2003	1287	780	507	1146	30	87	24
2004	1377	837	540	1236	31	86	24
2005	1381	834	547	1240	32	86	23

20-18 股票发行量和筹资额

Issued Share and Raised Capital

年 份 Year	股票发行量 (亿股) Issued Share (100 million shares)	A 股 A Shares	H股，N股 H, N Shares	B 股 B Shares	股票筹资额 (亿元) Raised Capital (100 million yuan)	A 股 A Shares	#配 股 Rights Issued	H股，N股 H, N Shares	B 股 B Shares
1991	5.00	5.00			5.00	5.00			
1992	20.75	10.00		10.75	94.09	50.00			44.09
1993	95.79	42.59	40.41	12.79	375.47	276.41	81.58	60.93	38.13
1994	91.26	10.97	69.89	10.40	326.78	99.78	50.16	188.73	38.27
1995	31.60	5.32	15.38	10.90	150.32	85.51	62.83	31.46	33.35
1996	86.11	38.29	31.77	16.05	425.08	294.34	69.89	83.56	47.18
1997	267.63	105.65	136.88	25.10	1293.82	825.92	170.86	360.00	80.76
1998	105.56	86.30	12.86	9.90	841.52	778.02	334.97	37.95	25.55
1999	122.93	98.11	23.05	1.77	944.56	893.60	320.97	47.17	3.79
2000	512.03	145.68	359.26	7.10	2103.08	1527.03	519.46	562.21	13.99
2001	141.48	93.00	48.48		1252.34	1182.13	430.63	70.21	
2002	291.74	134.20	157.54		961.75	779.75	56.61	181.99	
2003	281.43	83.64	196.79	1.00	1357.75	819.56	74.79	534.65	3.54
2004	227.92	54.88	171.51	1.53	1510.94	835.71	104.54	648.08	27.16
2005	567.05	13.80	553.25		1882.51	338.13	2.62	1544.38	

20-19 股 票 交 易 情 况

Trading Summary for Stocks

项 目	Item	1995	1999	2000	2001	2002	2003	2004	2005
会员总数	**No. of Members**	**1085**	**628**	**631**	**547**	**437**	**382**	**350**	**328**
上市公司数目（家）	No. of listed Companies	323	949	1088	1160	1224	1287	1377	1381
上市股票数目（只）	No. of listed Stocks	381	1029	1174	1240	1310	1372	1463	1467
A股	A Shares	311	921	1010	1130	1199	1261	1353	1358
B股	B Shares	70	108	114	110	111	111	110	109
股票总发行股本（亿股）	**Total Issued Capital (100 million share)**	**765.63**	**2908.85**	**3613.39**	**4838.35**	**5462.99**	**5997.93**	**6714.74**	**7163.54**
A股	A Shares	704.08	2757.88	3439.60	4650.45	5283.64	5808.31	6505.83	6936.08
B股	B Shares	61.55	150.96	173.79	187.90	179.34	189.62	208.91	227.47
流通股本 （亿股）	**Negotiable Shares (100 million share)**	**234.98**	**952.34**	**1233.32**	**1480.88**	**1679.94**	**1897.32**	**2194.15**	**2498.89**
A股	A Shares	178.98	810.45	1078.33	1315.21	1508.43	1717.93	1996.65	2280.84
B股	B Shares	45.99	141.88	154.99	165.67	171.51	179.39	197.50	218.05
股票市价总值（亿元）	**Total Market Capitalization (100 million yuan)**	**3474**	**26471**	**48091**	**43522**	**38329**	**42458**	**37056**	**32430**
A股	A Shares	3311	26167.6	47456	42246	37527	41520	36309	31811
B股	B Shares	164	303.54	635	1277	803	937	746	620
股票流通市值（亿元）	**Negotiable Market Capitalization (100 million yuan)**	**938**	**8213.96**	**16088**	**14463**	**12485**	**13179**	**11689**	**10631**
A股	A Shares	791	7937.46	15524	13345	11719	12306	10998	10028
B股	B Shares	147	276.49	563	1118	766	873	690	602
股票成交金额（亿元）	**Total Turnover (100 million yuan)**	**4036**	**31319.6**	**60827**	**38305**	**27990**	**32115**	**42334**	**31665**
A股	A Shares	4319	31049.6	60279	33242	27142	31270	41576	31099
B股	B Shares	78	270.04	548	5063	848	845	758	565
总成交股数 （亿股）	**Trading Volume (100 million share)**	**705.31**	**2932.39**	**4758.36**	**3152.28**	**3016.19**	**4163.08**	**5827.73**	**6623.73**
A股	A Shares	681.07	2809.75	4558.00	2463.41	2859.49	3992.28	5672.91	6470.87
B股	B Shares	24.24	122.64	200.36	688.88	156.70	170.80	154.83	152.86
深证综合指数	**Shenzhen Composite Index**								
最高	High	169.66	525.14	654.37	664.85	512.38	449.42	470.55	333.28
最低	Low	112.63	310.65	414.69	439.36	371.79	350.74	315.17	237.18
收盘	Close	113.24	402.18	635.73	475.94	388.76	378.63	315.81	278.75
上证综合指数	**Shanghai Composite Index**								
最高	High	926.41	1756.18	2125.72	2245.44	1748.89	1649.60	1783.01	1328.53
最低	Low	524.43	1047.83	1361.21	1514.86	1339.20	1307.40	1259.43	998.23
收盘	Close	555.29	1366.58	2073.48	1645.97	1357.65	1497.04	1266.50	1161.06

20-20 保险系统机构、人员数（2005年底）

Number of Institutions and Employed Persons in Insurance System (Year-end of 2005)

项　目	Item	机构数（个） Number of Institutions (unit)	职工人数（人） Employed Persons (person)	#女职工 Female
总计	**Total**	**93**	**366559**	**170909**
保险集团公司	**Insurance (Group) Corporations**	**6**	**3631**	**1725**
中资保险公司	**Domestic Funded Insurance Corporations**	**42**	**351787**	**162713**
#总公司	Head Offices	42	7439	2964
省级分公司	Provincial Branches	572	73632	35861
中心支分公司	Branches and Sub-branches in Center Cities	2740	123707	60209
支公司	Sub-branches	6899	94380	38945
营业部	Business Departments	2674	11036	4643
营销服务部	Marketing Departments	29041	41593	20091
中外合资公司	**Joint-venture Insurance Corporations**	**40**	**11141**	**6471**
总公司	Head Offices	40	5483	3079
省级分公司	Provincial Branches	47	3507	2181

注：职工人数不包括营销、代理人员。

a) Number of employed persons excludes people engaged in marketing and agency service.

20-21 保险公司业务经济技术指标（2005年）

Economic and Technical Indicators of Insurance Companies Funded with Chinese and Foreign Capital (2005)

项　目	Item	保　费（亿元） Premium (100 million yuan)	赔款及给付（亿元） Claim and Payment (100 million yuan)
合　计	**Total**	**4932**	**1137**
财产保险公司	**Property Insurance Companies**	**1283**	**691**
企业财产保险	Enterprise Property Insurance	149	92
家庭财产保险	Family Property Insurance	12	3
机动车辆保险	Motor Vehicle Insurance	858	483
工程保险	Engineering Insurance	23	13
责任保险	Liability Insurance	45	18
信用保险	Export Credit Insurance	23	10
保证保险	Guarantee Insurance	18	15
船舶保险	Ship Insurance	25	10
货物运输保险	Freight Transport Insurance	51	20
特殊风险保险	Special Risks Insurance	19	1
农业保险	Agriculture Insurance	7	6
健康险	Health Insurance	5	3
意外伤害保险	Accident Injury Insurance	46	16
其他险	Other Insurance	2	1
人寿保险公司	**Life Insurance Companies**	**3649**	**446**
寿险	Life Insurance	3247	311
健康险	Health Insurance	307	107
人身意外伤害险	Personal Accident Insurance	95	28

主要统计指标解释

信贷资金 指金融机构以信用方式积聚和分配的货币资金。金融机构信贷资金的来源有各项存款、金融债券发行、应付及暂收款、对国际金融机构负债、流通中货币、各项准备、所有者权益和其他项目等；信贷资金的运用有各项贷款、有价证券及投资、应收及预付款、委托投资、金银占款、外汇占款、库存现金、财政借款及在国际金融机构中的资产等。

存款 指企业、机关、团体或居民根据资金必须收回的原则，把货币资金存入银行或其他信贷机构保管并取得一定利息的一种信用活动形式。根据存款对象或性质的不同可划分为企业存款、财政存款、机关团体存款、基本建设存款、储蓄存款、农村存款、委托存款、其他存款等科目。它是银行信贷资金的主要来源。

贷款 指银行或其他信贷机构根据资金必须归还的原则，按一定利率，为企业、个人等提供资金的一种信用活动形式。我国银行贷款分为短期贷款、中期流动资金贷款、中长期贷款、信托贷款、融资租赁、委托贷款、票据融资、各项垫款等。

保险公司 在中国境内的、经过保险监督管理部门批准设立，并依法登记注册的各类商业保险公司。

保险金额 指保险人承担赔偿或者给付保险金责任的最高限额。

保费 指投保人为取得保险人在约定范围内所承担赔偿责任而支付给保险人的费用。

赔款 指保险人根据保险合同的规定，向被保险人支付的赔偿保险责任损失的金额。

给付 包括死伤医疗给付和满期给付。死伤医疗给付是指保险人根据人寿保险及长期健康保险合同的规定，因被保险人在保险期内发生保险责任范围内的保险事故支付给被保险人(或受益人)的金额。满期给付是指被保险人生存期满，保险人按人寿保险合同规定支付给被保险人的满期保险金额。

Explanatory Notes on Main Statistical Indicators

Credit Funds refer to the funds issued as loans by banking institutions. The sources of credit funds of the banking institutions included deposits, issue of financial bonds, account-payable and temporary gathering, liabilities to international financial institutions, currency in circulation, various reserves, owners' rights and interests and other items. The credit funds can be used in forms of loans, securities and investment, account receivable and advance payment, entrusted investment, gold, foreign exchange, cash on hand, government debt and assets in the international financial institutions.

Deposit is a form of credit by which enterprises, institutions, organizations or households can put money into banks and other credit institutions for safekeeping and interest earning under the principle of free withdrawal. According to different depositors, deposits are divided into enterprise deposits, treasury deposits, deposits of government agencies and organizations, capital construction deposits, savings deposits, rural saving deposits, entrusted deposits and other deposits. Deposits are major sources of the credit funds of banks.

Loan is a form of credit by which banks and other credit institutions provide funds at certain interest rate to enterprises and individuals in the light of the principle of unconditional repayment. Loans from Chinese banks include circulating capital loans, fixed assets loans, loans to urban and rural individuals engaged in industrial and commercial business and agricultural loans.

Insurance Companies refer to commercial insurance companies of various forms registered by law and established in China with the approval of insurance regulatory agencies.

Amount Insured refers to the maximum that the insurant will get for the claim of the case insured.

Premium is the fee paid by the insurant to the insurer to obtain the obligation of compensation from the insurance within the agreed terms.

Settled Claim is the compensation paid by the insurer to the insurant in accordance with the insurance contract.

Payment includes payment for death, injury or medical treatment and mature payment. Payment for death, injury or medical treatment refers to the money paid to the insurant (or the beneficiary) in accordance with the life or health insurance contract when the insurant encounters accidents within the insured period covered in the contract. Mature payment refers to the mature payment to the insurant in accordance with the life insurance contract at the end of the insured period.

21

教育和科技

Education, Science and Technology

简 要 说 明

本篇主要反映我国教育事业的发展情况和科学技术活动的基本情况。

一、教育部分的主要内容和资料来源

教育统计资料包括研究生教育、高等教育(普通教育本专科、成人教育本专科)、中等教育(高中阶段教育和初中阶段教育)、初等教育(小学)、学前教育、特殊教育(盲聋哑和弱智儿童学校等)以及教育经费等资料。主要指标包括学校数、在校学生数、招生数、毕业生数、教职工数和专任教师数、教育经费总额及国家财政性教育经费等。

教育事业统计资料、教育经费统计资料由教育部提供;技工学校的资料由劳动和社会保障部提供。

详细资料分别见《中国教育事业统计年鉴》(教育部发展规划司编)和《全国教育经费执行情况统计公告》(教育部、国家统计局和财政部联合发文)。

二、科技部分的主要内容,资料来源及调查方法

科技统计资料主要内容包括:国有企事业单位专业技术人员情况;独立核算的科研机构、高校及各类企事业单位的科技活动人员、科技活动经费筹集及支出、研究与试验发展(R&D)活动、科技成果及奖励等情况;国内外职务及非职务专利申请和授权情况;全国技术市场技术合同成交情况;科协系统科技活动情况;高新技术产业开发区企业主要经济指标情况;综合技术服务部门业务机构及业务活动情况等。

统计范围:科技活动统计资料基本包括了全社会有科技活动的企事业单位,具体包括大中型工业企业、独立核算的科研机构、普通高等学校、规模以上小型工业企业、具有一级资质的建筑企业、地市及以上运输和通信企业、地市及以上农业和卫生业企事业单位、从事软件开发活动的企业、以及从事综合技术服务活动的单位等。

资料来源:全国综合资料、各类企业资料、医疗卫生机构和农业事业等单位资料由国家统计局调查提供;独立核算的科研机构资料、技术市场资料、高新技术产业开发区企业资料由科技部调查提供;高校科技活动资料由教育部调查提供;国防科研机构资料由国防科工委调查提供;专业技术人员资料由中组部和国家统计局调查提供;科协系统科技活动资料由中国科协调查提供;测绘、气象、地震、海洋、产品质量监督抽查、专利等资料,分别由国家测绘局、中国气象局、国家地震局、国家海洋局、国家技术监督及检验检疫局、国家知识产权局等部门调查提供。

统计调查方法:工业企业、独立核算的科研机构、高校的科技活动资料采用全数调查取得;科协、测绘、气象、地震、海洋、产品质量监督抽查、专利资料采用抽样等多种调查方法取得;建筑业、运输业、通信业、软件业、农业和卫生业采用五年为一周期的滚动调查制度。

科技活动统计资料口径变动说明:2000年以前科技活动统计资料只包括大中型工业企业、独立核算的科研机构、普通高等学校,2000年及以后年份扩大到了小型工业、建筑业、运输业、通信业、软件业、农业和卫生等行业企事业单位。

Brief Introduction

Data in this chapter show the development of China's education and the basic conditions of the activities of China's science and technology.

I. Main Content and Sources of Data of Education

The data on education cover the situations on postgraduates, higher education (universities and colleges), secondary education (senior and junior high schools), elementary education (primary schools), preschool education, special education (schools for the blind, deaf-mutes, and the retarded) and expenditure on education. The main indicators cover the number of schools, the number of students enrolled, the number of new students enrolled, the number of graduates, the number of staff and workers, the number of full-time teachers, sources and outlay of education fund, education expenditure from the state budget.

The Ministry of Education mainly provides statistical data on education and education funds. Data on the technical training schools are provided by the Ministry of Labour and Social Security.

Detailed information can be found in "*Statistical Yearbook on China Educational Undertakings*" compiled by Department of Planning and Development, Ministry of Education; and the "*Communiqué on the Implementation of National Education Funds*" compiled jointly by Ministry of Education, National Bureau of Statistics and Ministry of Finance.

II. Main Content, Sources of Data and Statistical Methodology of Science and Technology

Data on technology mainly include: condition of professional scientific and technological personnel of state-owned enterprises and institutions; scientific and technological institutions with independent accounting system, scientific and technological personnel in universities and colleges and various enterprises or institutions, funds raising and expenditure on scientific and technological activities, activities of R&D and scientific and technological achievements and prizes; condition on applied and certified patent applications by services and non-services both domestically and overseas; the situation of signed technological contracts on technological market; scientific and technological activities within scientific and technological system; major economic indicators of high and new-tech industrial zones and the condition of comprehensive technological service agencies and their business activities.

Statistical scope: data on scientific and technological activities include all institutions of the society engaged in those activities, they are mainly: large and medium-sized industrial enterprises, scientific and technological institutions with independent accounting system, universities and colleges, small industrial enterprises above designated size, the construction enterprises with first grade, transportation and telecommunication enterprises at and above prefecture level, agricultural and health care institutions at and above prefecture level, enterprises engaged in software development, units engaged in scientific and technological services and so on.

Sources of data: data on national level, various enterprises, medical and health care institutions and agricultural undertakings are from National Bureau of Statistics; data on scientific and technologic research institutions, technological markets and high and new-tech industrial zones are from Ministry of Science and Technology; data on scientific and technological activities in universities and colleges are from Ministry of Education; data on scientific research institutions for defense are from Commission of Science, Technology and Industry for National Defense. Department of Organization of the Central Committee of the Communist Party of China and National Bureau of Statistics provide the data on the number of scientific and technological personnel. The China Association provides data on the scientific and technological activities of the associations for science and technology for Science and Technology. Data on the development of the mapping, meteorology, seismology, ocean, supervision and checking of the products quality and patents are provided separately by the National

Bureau of Surveying and Mapping, China Meteorological Administration, China Seismological Bureau, National Bureau of Marine Administration, General Administration of Quality Supervision, Inspection and Quarantine and State Intellectual Property Office.

Statistical methodology: data on industrial enterprises, scientific and technological institutions with independent accounting system and scientific and technological activities of universities and colleges are collected through complete surveys. Data on scientific and technological association, mapping, meteorology, seismology, ocean, supervision and checking of the products quality and patent applications are through sample surveys and other surveys. Data on construction, transportation, telecommunication, software industry, agriculture and health care are from rolling survey system with 5 years as one cycle.

Changes of the statistical scope of data on scientific and technological activities: before 2000, data only included large and medium-sized industrial enterprises, scientific research institutions with independent accounting system, and universities and colleges. Since 2000 (inclusive), data include: small industrial enterprises, construction sector, transportation sector, telecommunication sector, software sector, agriculture and health care agencies.

21-1 学校、教职工和专任教师情况（2005年）

Basic Statistics on Schools, Teachers and Staff and Full-time Teachers (2005)

项　目	Item	学校数(所) Number of Schools (unit)	教职工数(人) Teachers and Staff (person)	专任教师(人) Full-time Teachers (person)
高等教育	**Higher Education**			
研究生培养机构	Institutions Providing Postgraduate Programs	(766)		
普通高校	Regular Institutions of Higher Education	(450)		
科研机构	Research Institutions	(316)		
普通高等学校	Regular Institutions of Higher Education	1792	1742073	965839
本科院校	Universities with Full Undergraduate Courses	701	1197846	630010
专科院校	Colleges with Specialized Courses	1091	439967	267855
#职业技术学院	Vocational and Technical Colleges	921	362066	220994
其他机构(教学点)	Other Institutions	(428)	104260	67974
#独立学院	Independent Institutions	295	80986	55476
成人高等学校	Adult Institutions of Higher Education	481	148901	84325
民办的其他高等教育机构	Non-state Institutions of Higher Education	1077	48121	22528
中等教育	**Secondary Education**	**96082**	**6857699**	**5553569**
高中阶段教育	Senior Secondary Education	31532	6824770	2056377
高中	Senior Secondary Schools	17066	5731590	1306589
普通高中	Regular Senior Secondary Schools	16092	5720244	1299460
成人高中	Adult Senior Secondary Schools	974	11346	7129
中等职业教育	Vocational Secondary Education	14466	1093180	749788
普通中专	Regular Specialized Secondary Schools	3207	334800	202994
成人中专	Adult Specialized Secondary Schools	2582	121312	74952
职业高中	Vocational Senior Secondary Schools	5822	389250	282499
技工学校	Technical Schools	2855	204009	161094
其他机构(教学点)	Other Institutions	(2386)	43809	28249
初中阶段教育	Junior Secondary Education	64550	32929	3497192
普通初中	Regular Junior Secondary Schools	61885		3471839
职业初中	Vocational Junior Secondary Schools	601	24009	20240
成人初中	Adult Junior Secondary Schools	2064	8920	5113
初等教育	**Primary Education**	**427697**	**6248248**	**5637144**
普通小学	Regular Primary Schools	366213	6132155	5592453
成人小学	Adult Primary Schools	61484	116093	44691
#扫盲班	Literacy Courses	43572	89361	31685
工读学校	**Schools for Juvenile Delinquents**	**77**	**2584**	**1658**
特殊教育	**Special Education**	**1593**	**42256**	**31937**
学前教育	**Pre-school Education**	**124402**	**1152046**	**721609**

注：1.普通高中的教职工数中包含普通初中的教职工数。
　　2.括号内数据均不计校数。

a) Number of Teachers and Staff in regular senior secondary schools includes that of regular junior secondary schools.

b) Data in "()" don't count number of schools.

21–2 各级各类学历教育学生情况（2005年）

Basic Statistics on Students by Level and Type of Education (2005)

单位：人 (person)

项目	Item	招生数 New Enrollment	在校学生数 Total Enrollment	毕业生数 Graduates	女学生占学生总数的比重(%) Females as % of Total
高等教育	**Students Received Higher Education**				
研究生	Postgraduates	364831	978610	189728	43.39
博士	Doctor's Degree	54794	191317	27677	32.57
硕士	Master's Degree	310037	787293	162051	46.02
普通本专科	Regular Undergraduates and College Students	5044581	15617767	3067956	47.08
本科	Enrolled in Full Undergraduate Courses	2363647	8488188	1465786	45.30
专科	Enrolled in Specialized Courses	2680934	7129579	1602170	49.20
成人本专科	Adult Undergraduates and College Students	1930250	4360705	1667889	51.12
本科	Enrolled in Full Undergraduate Courses	747196	1611140	555799	50.89
专科	Enrolled in Specialized Courses	1183054	2749565	1112090	51.26
其他高等学历教育	Other Degree of Higher Education				
在职人员攻读博士、硕士学位	Employees Enrolled in Graduate Programs Leading to Doctor or Master Degrees	101653	254672		27.29
网络本专科生	Students Enrolled in Internet-based Courses	891046	2652679	759627	48.38
本科	Enrolled in Full Undergraduate Courses	408606	1272292	392310	48.38
专科	Enrolled in Specialized Courses	482440	1380387	367317	48.39
学历文凭考试	Students Taking Exam Leading to Diploma		203545	94202	48.46
自学考试	Students Taking Unified Exams after Completing Self-learning Programs		45698	19466	53.32
中等教育	**Students Received Secondary Education**	**35209758**	**102971534**	**32931917**	
高中阶段教育	Senior Secondary Education	15333932	40309409	10921702	
高中	Senior Secondary Schools	8777317	24309014	6739805	
普通高中	Regular Senior Secondary Schools	8777317	24090901	6615713	46.43
成人高中	Adult Senior Secondary Schools		218113	124092	50.11
中等职业教育	Vocational Secondary Education	6556615	16000395	4181897	
普通中专	Regular Specialized Secondary Schools	2411340	6297671	1567135	53.99
成人中专	Adult Specialized Secondary Schools	479465	1125457	393926	48.30
职业高中	Vocational Senior Secondary Schools	2482117	5824293	1530860	48.29
技工学校	Technical Schools	1183693	2752974	689976	
初中阶段教育	Junior Secondary Education	19875826	62662125	22010215	
普通初中	Regular Junior Secondary Schools	19765246	61718079	21065150	47.33
职业初中	Junior Secondary Vocational Schools	110580	431363	169132	45.92
成人初中	Adult Junior Secondary Schools		512683	775933	43.46
初等教育	**Students Received Primary Education**	**16717440**	**111718265**	**23171154**	
普通小学	Regular Primary Schools	16717440	108640655	20194768	46.82
成人小学	Adult Primary Schools		3077610	2976386	54.72
#扫盲班	Literacy Courses		1924380	1690506	56.98
工读学校	**Schools for Juvenile Delinquents**	**3543**	**8372**	**3514**	**12.06**
特殊教育	**Students Received Special Education**	**49288**	**364409**	**43214**	**35.53**
学前教育	**Students Received Pre-school Education**	**13562405**	**21790290**	**10253729**	**45.09**

注：特殊教育学生数中包括普通中小学随班就读的学生。

a) Students receiving special education include those learning in the same classes of formal regular junior and primary schools.

21-3 各级各类学校数

Number of Schools by Level and Type of School

单位：所 (unit)

年份 Year	普通高等学校 Regular Institutions of Higher Education	普通中学 Regular Secondary Schools	高中 Senior Secondary Schools	初中 Junior Secondary Schools	职业中学 Vocational Secondary Schools	普通小学 Primary Schools	特殊教育学校 Special Schools	学前教育 Pre-primary Education
1978	598	162345	49215	113130		949323	292	163952
1980	675	118377	31300	87077	3314	917316	292	170419
1985	1016	93221	17318	75903	8070	832309	375	172262
1986	1054	92967	17111	75856	8187	820846	423	173376
1987	1063	92857	16930	75927	8381	807406	504	176775
1988	1075	91492	16524	74968	8954	793261	577	171845
1989	1075	89575	16050	73525	9173	777244	662	172634
1990	1075	87631	15678	71953	9164	766072	746	172322
1991	1075	85851	15243	70608	9572	729158	886	164465
1992	1053	84021	14850	69171	9860	712973	1077	172506
1993	1065	82795	14380	68415	9985	696681	1123	165197
1994	1080	82358	14242	68116	10217	682588	1241	174657
1995	1054	81020	13991	67029	10147	668685	1379	180438
1996	1032	79967	13875	66092	10049	645983	1428	187324
1997	1020	78642	13880	64762	10047	628840	1440	182485
1998	1022	77888	13948	63940	10074	609626	1535	181368
1999	1071	77213	14127	63086	9636	582291	1520	181136
2000	1041	77268	14564	62704	8849	553622	1539	175836
2001	1225	80432	14907	65525	7802	491273	1531	111706
2002	1396	80067	15406	64661	7402	456903	1540	111752
2003	1552	79490	15779	63711	6843	425846	1551	116390
2004	1731	79058	15998	63060	6478	394183	1560	117899
2005	1792	77977	16092	61885	6423	366213	1593	124402

21-4 各级各类学校专任教师数

Number of Full-time Teachers by Level and Type of School

单位：万人 (10 000 persons)

年份 Year	普通高等学校 Regular Institutions of Higher Education	普通中学 Regular Secondary Schools	高中 Senior Secondary Schools	初中 Junior Secondary Schools	职业中学 Vocational Secondary Schools	普通小学 Primary Schools	特殊教育学校 Special Schools	学前教育 Pre-primary Education
1978	20.6	318.2	74.1	244.1		522.6	0.4	27.7
1980	24.7	302.0	57.1	244.9	2.3	549.9	0.5	41.1
1985	34.4	265.2	49.2	216.0	14.1	537.7	0.7	55.0
1986	37.2	275.8	51.8	223.9	16.4	541.4	0.8	60.5
1987	38.5	287.0	54.4	232.7	18.5	543.4	0.9	65.1
1988	39.3	296.0	55.7	240.3	20.3	550.1	1.1	67.0
1989	39.7	298.0	55.4	242.7	21.4	554.4	1.2	70.9
1990	39.5	303.3	56.2	247.0	22.4	558.2	1.4	75.0
1991	39.1	309.0	57.3	251.7	23.5	553.2	1.6	76.9
1992	38.8	314.1	57.6	256.5	24.8	552.7	1.9	81.5
1993	38.8	316.7	55.9	260.8	26.2	555.2	2.0	83.6
1994	39.6	323.4	54.7	268.7	27.7	561.1	2.3	86.2
1995	40.1	333.4	55.1	278.4	29.2	566.4	2.5	87.5
1996	40.3	346.5	57.2	289.3	30.8	573.6	2.7	88.9
1997	40.5	358.7	60.5	298.2	32.2	579.4	2.9	88.4
1998	40.7	369.7	64.2	305.5	33.6	581.9	3.0	87.5
1999	42.6	384.1	69.2	314.8	33.6	586.1	3.1	87.2
2000	46.3	400.5	75.7	324.9	32.0	586.0	3.2	85.6
2001	53.2	418.8	84.0	334.8	30.6	579.8	2.9	63.0
2002	61.8	437.6	94.6	343.0	31.0	577.9	3.0	57.1
2003	72.5	453.7	107.1	346.7	28.9	570.3	3.0	61.3
2004	85.8	466.8	119.1	347.7	29.4	562.9	3.1	65.6
2005	96.6	477.1	129.9	347.2	30.3	559.2	3.2	72.2

21-5 各级各类学校招生数

Number of New Students Enrollment by Level and Type of School

单位：万人 (10 000 persons)

年份 Year	普通高等学校 Regular Institutions of Higher Education	普通中学 Regular Secondary Schools	高中 Senior Secondary Schools	初中 Junior Secondary Schools	职业中学 Vocational Secondary Schools	普通小学 Primary Schools	特殊教育学校 Special Schools
1978	40.2	2698.9	692.9	2006.0		3315.4	0.6
1980	28.1	1934.3	383.4	1550.9	30.7	2942.3	0.6
1985	61.9	1606.9	257.5	1349.4	116.1	2298.2	0.9
1986	57.2	1643.9	257.3	1386.6	112.8	2258.2	1.1
1987	61.7	1649.5	255.2	1394.3	113.2	2094.6	1.2
1988	67.0	1584.8	244.3	1340.5	119.5	2123.3	1.2
1989	59.7	1551.5	242.1	1309.4	118.3	2151.5	1.4
1990	60.9	1619.6	249.8	1369.9	123.2	2064.0	1.6
1991	62.0	1655.2	243.8	1411.3	137.8	2072.7	2.0
1992	75.4	1699.7	234.7	1465.0	152.1	2183.2	3.0
1993	92.4	1707.3	228.3	1479.0	161.5	2353.5	3.4
1994	90.0	1859.8	243.4	1616.4	175.3	2537.0	4.0
1995	92.6	2025.9	273.6	1752.3	190.1	2531.8	5.6
1996	96.6	2042.9	282.2	1760.7	188.9	2524.7	4.8
1997	100.0	2128.2	322.6	1805.6	211.2	2462.0	4.6
1998	108.4	2321.0	359.6	1961.4	217.6	2201.4	4.9
1999	159.7	2546.0	396.3	2149.7	194.1	2029.5	5.0
2000	220.6	2736.0	472.7	2263.3	182.7	1946.5	5.3
2001	268.3	2815.9	558.0	2257.9	185.0	1944.2	5.6
2002	320.5	2929.0	676.7	2252.3	216.9	1952.8	5.3
2003	382.2	2947.4	752.1	2195.3	222.1	1829.4	4.9
2004	447.3	2899.7	821.5	2078.2	229.1	1747.0	5.1
2005	504.5	2854.3	877.7	1976.5	259.3	1671.7	4.9

21-6 各级各类学校在校学生数

Number of Students Enrollment by Level and Type of School

单位：万人 (10 000 persons)

年份 Year	普通高等学校 Regular Institutions of Higher Education	普通中学 Regular Secondary Schools	高中 Senior Secondary Schools	初中 Junior Secondary Schools	职业中学 Vocational Secondary Schools	普通小学 Primary Schools	特殊教育学校 Special Schools	学前教育 Pre-primary Education
1978	85.6	6548.3	1553.1	4995.2		14624.0	3.1	787.7
1980	114.4	5508.1	969.8	4538.3	45.4	14627.0	3.3	1150.8
1985	170.3	4706.0	741.1	3964.8	229.5	13370.2	4.2	1479.7
1986	188.0	4889.9	773.4	4116.6	256.0	13182.5	4.7	1629.0
1987	195.9	4948.1	773.7	4174.4	267.6	12835.9	5.3	1807.8
1988	206.6	4761.5	746.0	4015.5	279.4	12535.8	5.8	1854.5
1989	208.2	4554.0	716.1	3837.9	282.3	12373.1	6.4	1847.7
1990	206.3	4586.0	717.3	3868.7	295.0	12241.4	7.2	1972.2
1991	204.4	4683.5	722.9	3960.6	315.6	12164.2	8.5	2209.3
1992	218.4	4770.8	704.9	4065.9	342.8	12201.3	13.0	2428.2
1993	253.6	4739.1	656.9	4082.2	362.6	12421.2	16.9	2552.5
1994	279.9	4981.7	664.9	4316.7	405.6	12822.6	21.1	2630.3
1995	290.6	5371.0	713.2	4657.8	448.3	13195.2	29.6	2711.2
1996	302.1	5739.7	769.3	4970.4	473.3	13615.0	32.1	2666.3
1997	317.4	6017.9	850.1	5167.8	511.9	13995.4	34.1	2519.0
1998	340.9	6301.0	938.0	5363.0	541.6	13953.8	35.8	2403.0
1999	413.4	6771.3	1049.7	5721.6	533.9	13548.0	37.2	2326.3
2000	556.1	7368.9	1201.3	6167.6	503.2	13013.3	37.8	2244.2
2001	719.1	7836.0	1405.0	6431.1	466.4	12543.5	38.6	2021.8
2002	903.4	8287.9	1683.8	6604.1	511.5	12156.7	37.5	2036.0
2003	1108.6	8583.2	1964.8	6618.4	528.2	11689.7	36.5	2003.9
2004	1333.5	8695.4	2220.4	6475.0	569.4	11246.2	37.2	2089.4
2005	1561.8	8580.9	2409.1	6171.8	625.6	10864.1	36.4	2179.0

21-7 各级各类学校毕业生数

Number of Graduates by Level and Type of School

单位: 万人 (10 000 persons)

年份 Year	普通高等学校 Regular Institutions of Higher Education	普通中学 Regular Secondary Schools	高中 Senior Secondary Schools	初中 Junior Secondary Schools	职业中学 Vocational Secondary Schools	普通小学 Primary Schools	特殊教育学校 Special Schools
1978	16.5	2375.3	682.7	1692.6		2287.9	0.3
1980	14.7	1581.0	616.2	964.7	7.9	2053.3	0.4
1985	31.6	1194.9	196.6	998.3	41.3	1999.9	0.4
1986	39.3	1281.0	224.0	1057.0	57.9	2016.1	0.5
1987	53.2	1364.1	246.8	1117.3	75.0	2043.0	0.4
1988	55.3	1407.8	250.6	1157.2	81.0	1930.3	0.5
1989	57.6	1377.5	243.2	1134.3	86.3	1857.1	0.5
1990	61.4	1342.1	233.0	1109.1	89.3	1863.1	0.5
1991	61.4	1308.5	222.9	1085.5	94.5	1896.7	0.6
1992	60.4	1328.4	226.1	1102.3	96.7	1872.4	0.9
1993	57.1	1365.9	231.7	1134.2	102.5	1841.5	1.2
1994	63.7	1361.9	209.3	1152.6	107.6	1899.6	1.4
1995	80.5	1429.0	201.6	1227.4	124.0	1961.5	1.9
1996	83.9	1484.0	204.9	1279.0	139.6	1934.1	2.4
1997	82.9	1664.0	221.7	1442.4	150.1	1960.1	2.8
1998	83.0	1832.0	251.8	1580.2	162.8	2117.4	3.5
1999	84.8	1852.7	262.9	1589.8	167.8	2313.7	3.8
2000	95.0	1908.6	301.5	1607.1	176.3	2419.2	4.3
2001	103.6	2047.4	340.5	1707.0	166.5	2396.9	4.6
2002	133.7	2263.6	383.8	1879.9	145.4	2351.9	4.4
2003	187.7	2453.7	458.1	1995.6	135.5	2267.9	4.5
2004	239.1	2617.4	546.9	2070.4	142.5	2135.2	4.7
2005	306.8	2768.1	661.6	2106.5	170.0	2019.5	4.3

21-8 研究生和留学生数

Number of Postgraduates and Students Studying Abroad

单位: 人 (person)

年份 Year	研究生数 Number of Postgraduates: 招生数 New Enrollment	在学人数 Total Enrollment	毕业生数 Graduates	出国留学人员 Number of Students Studying Abroad	学成回国留学人员 Number of Returned Students
1978	10708	10934	9	860	248
1980	3616	21604	476	2124	162
1985	46871	87331	17004	4888	1424
1986	41310	110371	16950	4676	1388
1987	39017	120191	27603	4703	1605
1988	35645	112776	40838	3786	3000
1989	28569	101339	37232	3329	1753
1990	29649	93018	35440	2950	1593
1991	29679	88128	32537	2900	2069
1992	33439	94164	25692	6540	3611
1993	42145	106771	28214	10742	5128
1994	50864	127935	28047	19071	4230
1995	51053	145443	31877	20381	5750
1996	59398	163322	39652	20905	6570
1997	63749	176353	46539	22410	7130
1998	72508	198885	47077	17622	7379
1999	92225	233513	54670	23749	7748
2000	128484	301239	58767	38989	9121
2001	165197	393256	67809	83973	12243
2002	202611	500980	80841	125179	17945
2003	268925	651260	111091	117307	20152
2004	326286	819896	150777	114682	24726
2005	364831	978610	189728	118515	34987

21-9 分学科研究生情况（2005年）
Number of Postgraduate Students by Field of Study (2005)

单位：人 (person)

项 目	Item	招生数 New Enrollment	博 士 Doctor's Degree	硕 士 Master's Degree	在 校 学生数 Total Enrollment	博 士 Doctor's Degree	硕 士 Master's Degree	毕业生数 Graduates	博 士 Doctor's Degree	硕 士 Master's Degree
分学科研究生数（总计）	**Total**	**364831**	**54794**	**310037**	**978610**	**191317**	**787293**	**189728**	**27677**	**162051**
哲 学	Philosophy	4414	731	3683	11632	2395	9237	2249	436	1813
经济学	Economics	18612	2662	15950	49752	9695	40057	10930	1617	9313
法 学	Law	24770	2305	22465	65272	7520	57752	14103	1191	12912
教育学	Education	12357	1005	11352	29855	3029	26826	5101	455	4646
文 学	Literature	28962	2334	26628	73000	7543	65457	13314	1216	12098
历史学	History	5249	946	4303	13790	3180	10610	2657	547	2110
理 学	Science	45193	10214	34979	120510	33059	87451	22028	5458	16570
工 学	Engineering	131345	20983	110362	369738	79714	290024	72941	9427	63514
农 学	Agriculture	13864	2253	11611	36061	7386	28675	6038	1093	4945
医 学	Medicine	38340	6738	31602	100343	20236	80107	19405	4291	15114
军事学	Military	219	34	185	546	122	424	114	22	92
管理学	Management	41506	4589	36917	108111	17438	90673	20848	1924	18924
分学科研究生数（普通高校）	**Regular Colleges**	**348407**	**48824**	**299583**	**932711**	**172052**	**760659**	**181072**	**24035**	**157037**
哲 学	Philosophy	4244	680	3564	11216	2274	8942	2158	397	1761
经济学	Economics	18106	2464	15642	48229	9033	39196	10506	1433	9073
法 学	Law	24314	2185	22129	63882	7169	56713	13778	1078	12700
教育学	Education	12293	975	11318	29694	2940	26754	5065	437	4628
文 学	Literature	28742	2270	26472	72409	7361	65048	13207	1183	12024
历史学	History	5173	929	4244	13559	3109	10450	2609	540	2069
理 学	Science	38531	7159	31372	101855	23158	78697	18748	3532	15216
工 学	Engineering	125052	19102	105950	351921	73377	278544	69473	8377	61096
农 学	Agriculture	13268	2040	11228	34548	6777	27771	5832	994	4838
医 学	Medicine	37507	6533	30974	98096	19671	78425	18922	4169	14753
军事学	Military	216	34	182	540	122	418	111	22	89
管理学	Management	40961	4453	36508	106762	17061	89701	20663	1873	18790
分学科研究生数（科研机构）	**Research Institutions**	**16424**	**5970**	**10454**	**45899**	**19265**	**26634**	**8656**	**3642**	**5014**
哲 学	Philosophy	170	51	119	416	121	295	91	39	52
经济学	Economics	506	198	308	1523	662	861	424	184	240
法 学	Law	456	120	336	1390	351	1039	325	113	212
教育学	Education	64	30	34	161	89	72	36	18	18
文 学	Literature	220	64	156	591	182	409	107	33	74
历史学	History	76	17	59	231	71	160	48	7	41
理 学	Science	6662	3055	3607	18655	9901	8754	3280	1926	1354
工 学	Engineering	6293	1881	4412	17817	6337	11480	3468	1050	2418
农 学	Agriculture	596	213	383	1513	609	904	206	99	107
医 学	Medicine	833	205	628	2247	565	1682	483	122	361
军事学	Military	3		3	6		6	3		3
管理学	Management	545	136	409	1349	377	972	185	51	134

21-10 高等教育学校（机构）数（2005年）

Number of Schools or Institutions of Higher Education (2005)

单位：所 (unit)

项 目	Item	总计 Total	中央部委 Central Ministries and Agencies	教育部 Ministry of Education	其他部委 Other Ministries	地方部门 Local Ministries and Agencies	教育部门 Ministry of Education	非教育部门 Ministry of Non-Education	民办 Non-state
研究生培养机构	**Institutions Providing Postgraduate Programs**	**766**	**370**	**73**	**297**	**396**	**330**	**66**	
普通高校	Regular Institutions of Higher Education	450	97	73	24	353	330	23	
科研机构	Research Institutions	316	273		273	43		43	
普通高校	**Regular Institutions of Higher Education**	**1792**	**111**	**73**	**38**	**1431**	**834**	**597**	**250**
本科院校	Universities with Full Undergraduate Courses	701	104	73	31	570	505	65	27
专科院校	Colleges with Specialized Courses	1091	7		7	861	329	532	223
#高等职业学校	Vocational and Technical Colleges	921	2		2	702	245	457	217
成人高等学校	**Adult Institutions of Higher Education**	**481**	**17**	**1**	**16**	**462**	**191**	**271**	**2**
民办的其他高等教育机构	**Private Institutions of Higher Education**	**1077**							**1077**

21-11 高等学校（机构）学生数（2005年）

Number of Students in Regular Institutions of Higher Education (2005)

单位：人 (person)

项 目	Item	招生数 New Enrollment	在校学生数 Total Enrollment	毕(结)业生数 Graduates with Degrees or Diplomas	授予学位数 Degrees Conferred
研究生	Postgraduates	364831	978610	189728	185250
博士	Doctor's Degree	54794	191317	27677	26506
硕士	Master's Degree	310037	787293	162051	158744
普通本科、专科生	Regular Undergraduates and College Students	5044581	15617767	3067956	1309692
本科	Enrolled in Full Undergraduate Courses	2363647	8488188	1465786	1309692
专科	Enrolled in Specialized Courses	2680934	7129579	1602170	
成人本科、专科生	Adult Undergraduates and College Students	1930250	4360705	1667889	71170
本科	Enrolled in Full Undergraduate Courses	747196	1611140	555799	71170
专科	Enrolled in Specialized Courses	1183054	2749565	1112090	
网络本科、专科生	Students Enrolled in Internet-based Courses	891046	2652679	759627	23032
本科	Enrolled in Full Undergraduate Courses	408606	1272292	392310	23032
专科	Enrolled in Specialized Courses	482440	1380387	367317	
在职人员攻读博士硕士学位	Employees Enrolled in Graduate Programs Leading to Doctor or Master Degrees	101653	254672		43964
学历文凭考试	Students Taking Exam Leading to Diploma		203545	94202	
电大注册视听生	Students Enrolled in Radio and Television Programs		45698	19466	
自考助学班	Classes for Self-learning Programs	317243	737918	199531	
研究生课程进修班	Postgraduate Courses for Advanced Study		88243	69978	
普通预科生	College Preparatory Courses		23663		
进修及培训	In-service Training Courses		1549563	3464440	
留学生	Overseas Students	60904	78323	44337	3791

21-12 成人本、专科分学科学生数（2005年）

Number of Students in Adult Institutions of Higher Education by Field of Study (2005)

单位：人 (person)

项目	Item	招生数 New Enrollment	本科 Undergraduate Courses	专科 Specialized Courses	在校学生数 Total Enrollment	本科 Undergraduate Courses	专科 Specialized Courses	毕业生数 Graduates	本科 Undergraduate Courses	专科 Specialized Courses
总计	**Total**	**1930250**	**747196**	**1183054**	**4360705**	**1611140**	**2749565**	**1667889**	**555799**	**1112090**
成人高等学校办	**Run by Adult Institutions of Higher Education**	**295336**	**52679**	**242657**	**695637**	**113423**	**582214**	**275587**	**45586**	**230001**
#师范	Teacher Training	67555	39712	27843	160710	87047	73663	67672	36089	31583
哲学	Philosophy	8		8	10		10	22		22
经济学	Economics	17934	547	17387	41677	1172	40505	14893	521	14372
法学	Law	17858	3469	14389	44702	7950	36752	18946	4642	14304
教育学	Education	24894	8871	16023	60005	17542	42463	26994	7066	19928
文学	Literature	63288	23131	40157	146045	50265	95780	53577	19173	34404
#外语	Foreign Language	16564	8885	7679	41581	20485	21096	12551	6904	5647
艺术	Art	9759	2284	7475	23007	5683	17324	8049	2141	5908
历史学	History	866	746	120	2428	1710	718	1029	900	129
理学	Science	10939	8564	2375	26206	19373	6833	12514	9665	2849
工学	Engineering	49586	2090	47496	115957	4554	111403	44770	1232	43538
农学	Agriculture	1416	26	1390	3081	68	3013	353		353
医学	Medicine	22957	2159	20798	62715	4369	58346	41872	78	41794
管理学	Management	85590	3076	82514	192811	6420	186391	60617	2309	58308
普通高等学校办	**Run by Regular Institutions of Higher Education**	**1634914**	**694517**	**940397**	**3665068**	**1497717**	**2167351**	**1392302**	**510213**	**882089**
#师范	Teacher Training	325761	162980	162781	288933	186024	102909	668256	401351	266905
哲学	Philosophy	59	26	33	127	38	89	64		64
经济学	Economics	88861	27459	61402	200404	66387	134017	81689	24582	57107
法学	Law	95830	62824	33006	223902	139072	84830	91107	56030	35077
教育学	Education	98579	42356	56223	218247	84191	134056	100034	26835	73199
文学	Literature	273117	158657	114460	613278	338992	274286	256823	120141	136682
#外语	Foreign Language	88683	55130	33553	199918	120689	79229	61819	38754	23065
艺术	Art	54560	30401	24159	127665	69063	58602	49119	22052	27067
历史学	History	4311	3725	586	12355	9240	3115	6118	4823	1295
理学	Science	65269	52267	13002	147240	114442	32798	68348	51221	17127
工学	Engineering	336956	124432	212524	780487	280959	499528	275681	94428	181253
农学	Agriculture	27290	10700	16590	66442	22429	44013	23788	5149	18639
医学	Medicine	219792	77226	142566	518596	160229	358367	190473	41629	148844
管理学	Management	424850	134845	290005	883990	281738	602252	298177	85375	212802

21-13 普通本、专科分学科学生数（2005年）

Number of Students in Undergraduate and Junior Colleges by Field of Study (2005)

单位：人 (person)

项 目	Item	招生数 New Enrollment	本科 Undergraduate Courses	专科 Specialized Courses	在校学生数 Total Enrollment	本科 Undergraduate Courses	专科 Specialized Courses	毕业生数 Graduates	本科 Undergraduate Courses	专科 Specialized Courses
总 计	**Total**	**5044581**	**2363647**	**2680934**	**15617767**	**8488188**	**7129579**	**3067956**	**1465786**	**1602170**
#师范	Teacher Training	494944	258015	236929	1791585	1055506	736079	449734	223715	226019
哲 学	Philosophy	1797	1797		6323	6323		1275	1275	
经济学	Economics	264219	145512	118707	857757	518989	338768	162977	80710	82267
法 学	Law	199521	108779	90742	697174	414309	282865	163529	76140	87389
教育学	Education	315638	86080	229558	1022708	307402	715306	280134	50342	229792
文 学	Literature	760475	435484	324991	2318665	1455454	863211	415206	226903	188303
#外语	Foreign Languages	302174	147644	154530	944397	523211	421186	178090	83874	94216
艺术	Art	295497	171548	123949	814935	521918	293017	122757	68726	54031
历史学	History	13379	13379		49390	49390		10694	10694	
理 学	Science	270147	268061	2086	967908	959757	8151	164867	163076	1791
工 学	Engineering	1809426	739668	1069758	5477207	2699776	2777431	1090986	517225	573761
农 学	Agriculture	97188	45674	51514	308107	174783	133324	69531	35419	34112
医 学	Medicine	338563	147726	190837	1132165	627249	504916	202577	96011	106566
管理学	Management	974228	371487	602741	2780363	1274756	1505607	506180	207991	298189

21-14 网络本、专科分学科学生数（2005年）

Number of Students Enrolled in Internet-based Courses by Field of Study (2005)

单位：人 (person)

项 目	Item	招生数 New Enrollment	本科 Undergraduate Courses	专科 Specialized Courses	在校学生数 Total Enrollment	本科 Undergraduate Courses	专科 Specialized Courses	毕业生数 Graduates	本科 Undergraduate Courses	专科 Specialized Courses
总 计	**Total**	**891046**	**408606**	**482440**	**2652679**	**1272292**	**1380387**	**759627**	**392310**	**367317**
#师范	Teacher Training	36673	33240	3433	99094	90296	8798	34059	31797	2262
哲 学	Philosophy							9	9	
经济学	Economics	36037	23121	12916	154925	94517	60408	79213	43301	35912
法 学	Law	139167	69999	69168	434069	228510	205559	168704	105057	63647
教育学	Education	41797	11214	30583	149586	33414	116172	48723	3268	45455
文 学	Literature	105202	80478	24724	304196	233215	70981	83640	61935	21705
#外语	Foreign Language	28864	17190	11674	98656	61291	37365	24277	17056	7221
历史学	History	238	238		530	530				
理 学	Science	10353	10058	295	27329	26966	363	9213	9106	107
工 学	Engineering	83129	42859	40270	277825	152291	125534	79145	41726	37419
农 学	Agriculture	11110	1527	9583	32626	2682	29944	11107	1207	9900
医 学	Medicine	32992	11620	21372	86390	24664	61726	26800	9985	16815
管理学	Management	431021	157492	273529	1185203	475503	709700	253073	116716	136357

21-15 中等职业学校（机构)数（2005年）
Number of Secondary Vocational Schools (2005)

单位：个 (unit)

项 目	Item	总 计 Total	中央部门 Central Ministries and Agencies	地方部门 Local Ministries and Agencies	教育部门 Run by Education Department	非教育部门 Run by Non-Education Department	民 办 Non-state
中等职业学校	**Secondary Vocational Schools**	**11611**	**92**	**9502**	**6672**	**2830**	**2017**
普通中等专业学校	Regular Specialized Secondary School	3207	39	2700	1303	1397	468
成人中等专业学校	Adult Specialized Secondary School	2582	35	2381	1659	722	166
职业高中学校	Vocational Junior Secondary School	5822	18	4421	3710	711	1383
其他机构(教学点)(不计校数)	**Other Institutions**	**2386**	**19**	**2127**	**1406**	**721**	**240**

注：中等职业学校未含技工学校数据（以下各表同）。

a) Number of secondary vocational schools excludes the number of skilled-worker schools. The same as in the following tables.

21-16 中等职业学校（机构)学生分科类情况（2005年）
Students in Secondary Vocational Schools by Field of Study (2005)

单位：人 (person)

项 目	Item	招生数 New Enrollment	#初中毕业生 Junior Secondary School Graduates	#应届毕业生 Current Year Graduates	在校学生数 Total Enrollment	毕业生数 Graduates	#获得职业资格证书 With Certificate on Professional Competence
总计	**Total**	**5372922**	**5090379**	**4922138**	**13247421**	**3491921**	**1864778**
农林类	Agriculture and Forestry	210063	189905	175762	530306	173862	89301
资源与环境类	Resources and Environment	43299	30844	28417	84139	16693	9432
能源类	Energy	42498	34956	33300	104139	23436	8296
土木水利工程类	Civil and Hydraulic Engineering	128068	118547	114780	322231	78605	39443
加工制造类	Manufacturing	1118390	1075010	1046487	2504163	470164	302292
交通运输类	Communication & Transportation	169303	155506	148692	393742	90465	53302
信息技术类	Information Technologies	1329689	1289911	1255027	3277913	908377	554442
医药卫生类	Medicine and Health	468960	434093	410106	1226777	331183	90810
商贸与旅游类	Trade and Tourism	453781	439131	430048	1192210	342107	195774
财经类	Finance and Economics	325191	307410	298054	850219	249361	138483
文化艺术与体育类	Culture, Arts and Physical Education	282869	268320	261453	778374	214143	103861
社会公共事物类	Public Affairs	162229	145131	137306	396417	138409	66616
师范类	Teacher Training	249313	228484	223667	698535	232081	108198
其他	Other	389269	373131	359039	888256	223035	104528

21-17 职业技术培训机构基本情况（2005年）
Basic Statistics on Vocational/Technical Training Institutions (2005)

单位：人 (person)

项目	Item	学校数(所) Schools (unit)	注册学生数 Registered Students	结业学生数 Graduates	教职工数 Teachers and Staff	#专任教师 Full-time Teachers
总计	**Total**	**198566**	**48827147**	**59341880**	**526240**	**256004**
职工技术培训学校(机构)	Vocational/Technical Training Schools	4230	1723388	1933667	50589	28541
教育部门和集体办	Run by Education Departments and Collectives	1321	950537	1053748	28377	13587
其他部门办	Run by Other Departments	1014	502024	612280	9644	5970
民办	Run by Private	1895	270827	267639	12568	8984
农村成人文化技术培训学校(机构)	Technical Training Schools for Adult Farmers	166601	37293423	47931805	250694	108821
教育部门和集体办	Run by Education Departments and Collectives	160924	35968830	46870460	232963	101516
#县办	Run by Counties	1071	966532	1246986	10699	6204
乡办	Run by Townships	23799	15383126	20053644	76068	37730
村办	Run by Villages	136054	19619172	25569830	146196	57582
其他部门办	Run by Other Departments	3756	747538	726818	6397	2636
民办	Run by Private	1921	577055	334527	11334	4669
其他培训机构(含社会培训机构)	Others	27735	9810336	9476408	224957	118642
教育部门和集体办	Run by Education Departments and Collectives	959	1028734	999029	14910	7200
其他部门办	Run by Other Departments	1544	734478	880572	11518	5976
民办	Run by Private	25232	8047124	7596807	198529	105466

21-18 普通高中学校和学生情况（2005年）
Statistics on Regular Senior Secondary Schools and Students (2005)

项目	Item	学校数(所) Schools (unit)	高级中学 Senior Secondary Schools	完全中学 Six-grades Secondary Schools	招生数(人) New Enrollment (person)	在校学生数(人) Total Enrollment (person)	毕业生数(人) Graduates (person)
总计	**Total**	**16092**	**6453**	**9639**	**8777317**	**24090901**	**6615713**
教育部门和集体办	Run by Education Departments and Collectives	12016	5210	6806	7626522	21154117	5947983
社会力量办	Run by Non-state/private	3175	1064	2111	914794	2267777	475227
其他部门办	Run by Others	901	179	722	236001	669007	192503
城市	Cities	6251	2299	3952	3014263	8434123	2321628
教育部门和集体办	Run by Education Departments and Collectives	4057	1600	2457	2461714	6961415	1964507
社会力量办	Run by Non-state/private	1676	605	1071	398686	1032796	232482
其他部门办	Run by Others	518	94	424	153863	439912	124639
县镇	Counties and Towns	7661	3428	4233	4883443	13320026	3636709
教育部门和集体办	Run by Education Departments and Collectives	6306	2993	3313	4404255	12149038	3397360
社会力量办	Run by Non-state/private	1162	384	778	431078	1038641	200615
其他部门办	Run by Others	193	51	142	48110	132347	38734
农村	Rural	2180	726	1454	879611	2336752	657376
教育部门和集体办	Run by Education Departments and Collectives	1653	617	1036	760553	2043664	586116
社会力量办	Run by Non-state/private	337	75	262	85030	196340	42130
其他部门办	Run by Others	190	34	156	34028	96748	29130

21-19　普通初中学校和学生情况（2005年）
Statistics on Regular Junior Secondary Schools and Students (2005)

项　目	Item	学校数（所）Number of Schools (unit)	初级中学 Junior Secondary Schools	九年一贯制 9-Year Primary-Secondary Schools	招生数（人）New Enrollment (person)	在校学生数（人）Total Enrollment (person)	毕业生数（人）Graduates (person)
总计	**Total**	**61885**	**51991**	**9894**	**19765246**	**61718079**	**21065150**
教育部门和集体办	Run by Education Departments and Collectives	55291	48320	6971	18089582	56802804	19699833
社会力量办	Run by Non-state/private	4608	2701	1907	1292501	3724158	955603
其他部门办	Run by Others	1986	970	1016	383163	1191117	409714
城市	Cities	**8157**	**5946**	**2211**	**3363494**	**10358204**	**3461482**
教育部门和集体办	Run by Education Departments and Collectives	5722	4792	930	2674757	8378387	2883002
社会力量办	Run by Non-state/private	1554	764	790	487269	1370136	364232
其他部门办	Run by Others	881	390	491	201468	609681	214248
县镇	Counties and Towns	**17323**	**15521**	**1802**	**7576314**	**23513281**	**7852565**
教育部门和集体办	Run by Education Departments and Collectives	15453	14359	1094	6956312	21702627	7383458
社会力量办	Run by Non-state/private	1528	976	552	555821	1607081	397863
其他部门办	Run by Others	342	186	156	64181	203573	71244
农村	Rural	**36405**	**30524**	**5881**	**8825438**	**27846594**	**9751103**
教育部门和集体办	Run by Education Departments and Collectives	34116	29169	4947	8458513	26721790	9433373
社会力量办	Run by Non-state/private	1526	961	565	249411	746941	193508
其他部门办	Run by Others	763	394	369	117514	377863	124222

21-20　职业初中学校和学生情况（2005年）
Statistics on Vocational Junior Secondary Schools and Students (2005)

项　目	Item	学校数（所）Schools (unit)	招生数（人）New Enrollment (person)	在校学生数（人）Total Enrollment (person)	毕业生数（人）Graduates (person)
总计	**Total**	**601**	**110580**	**431363**	**169132**
教育部门和集体办	Run by Education Departments and Collectives	575	105384	415945	165177
社会力量办	Run by Non-state/private	25	4985	14888	3793
其他部门办	Run by Others	1	211	530	162
城市	Cities	**26**	**3515**	**12669**	**5294**
教育部门和集体办	Run by Education Departments and Collectives	18	2936	10959	4796
社会力量办	Run by Non-state/private	7	368	1180	336
其他部门办	Run by Others	1	211	530	162
县镇	Counties and Towns	**144**	**30490**	**112795**	**47609**
教育部门和集体办	Run by Education Departments and Collectives	136	28537	106929	46146
社会力量办	Run by Non-state/private	8	1953	5866	1463
其他部门办	Run by Others				
农村	Rural	**431**	**76575**	**305899**	**116229**
教育部门和集体办	Run by Education Departments and Collectives	421	73911	298057	114235
社会力量办	Run by Non-state/private	10	2664	7842	1994
其他部门办	Run by Others				

21-21 普通小学学校和学生情况（2005年）

Statistics on Regular Primary Schools and Students (2005)

项 目	Item	学校数 (所) Schools (unit)	招生数 (人) New Enrollment (person)	在校学生数 (人) Total Enrollment (person)	毕业生数 (人) Graduates (person)
总计	**Total**	**366213**	**16717440**	**108640655**	**20194768**
教育部门和集体办	Run by Education Departments and Collectives	356528	15711304	102519069	19239852
社会力量办	Run by Non-state/private	6242	650598	3889404	553533
其他部门办	Run by Others	3443	355538	2232182	401383
城市	Cities	**20372**	**2773731**	**17303773**	**2919645**
教育部门和集体办	Run by Education Departments and Collectives	17334	2304756	14605376	2509202
社会力量办	Run by Non-state/private	1806	284988	1570562	208710
其他部门办	Run by Others	1232	183987	1127835	201733
县镇	Counties and Towns	**29050**	**3265166**	**21858606**	**3964944**
教育部门和集体办	Run by Education Departments and Collectives	27299	3068823	20563520	3762480
社会力量办	Run by Non-state/private	1211	146944	968713	142733
其他部门办	Run by Others	540	49399	326373	59731
农村	Rural	**316791**	**10678543**	**69478276**	**13310179**
教育部门和集体办	Run by Education Departments and Collectives	311895	10337725	67350173	12968170
社会力量办	Run by Non-state/private	3225	218666	1350129	202090
其他部门办	Run by Others	1671	122152	777974	139919

21-22 技工学校数、学生数和教职工数

Number of Technical Schools, Students, Teachers and Staff

年 份 Year	学校数 (所) Schools (unit)	招生数 (万人) New Enrollment (10 000 persons)	在校学生数 (万人) Total Enrollment (10 000 persons)	毕业生数 (万人) Graduates (10 000 persons)	教职工数 (万人) Teachers and Staff (10 000 persons)
1985	3548	35.5	74.2	22.6	21.5
1986	3765	39.4	89.2	23.3	24.4
1987	3952	42.3	103.1	26.5	26.2
1988	3996	46.1	116.1	31.1	28.0
1989	4102	47.0	125.8	36.8	29.6
1990	4184	50.6	133.2	41.3	30.8
1991	4269	54.4	142.2	45.4	32.5
1992	4392	60.2	155.6	45.7	33.6
1993	4477	66.4	171.7	49.7	33.5
1994	4430	71.4	187.1	55.7	34.0
1995	4521	74.0	188.6	68.1	33.7
1996	4467	72.7	191.8	68.1	33.5
1997	4395	73.4	193.1	69.9	31.0
1998	4362	59.4	181.3	68.2	31.0
1999	4098	51.5	156.0	66.2	26.9
2000	3792	50.4	140.1	64.6	24.0
2001	3470	55.1	134.7	47.7	22.0
2002	3075	73.3	153.0	45.4	20.3
2003	2970	91.6	193.1	45.3	20.2
2004	2884	109.7	234.5	53.5	20.5
2005	2855	118.4	275.3	69.0	20.4

21-23 各类技工学校情况（2005年）

Statistics on Technical Schools (2005)

指标	Item	合计 Total	国务院各部门 Ministries of the State Council	省、自治区、直辖市 Provinces, Autonomous Regions and Municipalities
学校数 (所)	Number of Schools (unit)	2855	163	2692
在校学生数 (万人)	Number of Students (10 000 persons)	275.3	10.1	265.2
教职工数 (万人)	Teachers and Staff (10 000 persons)	20.4	1.1	19.3
专任教师数 (万人)	Full-time Teachers (10 000 persons)	16.1	0.8	15.3
文化技术理论课指导教师(万人)	Classroom Teachers (10 000 persons)	9.7	0.4	9.3
生产实习课指导教师 (万人)	Practical Training Teachers (10 000 persons)	3.8	0.2	3.6
理论实习一体化教师 (万人)	Classroom-training Teachers(10 000 persons)	2.6	0.1	2.5

21-24 学龄儿童入学率和各级普通学校毕业生升学率

Enrollment Rate of School-age Children and Proportion of Students Entering into Schools of Higher Grade

单位：% (%)

年份 Year	学龄儿童净入学率 Net Enrollment Rate of School-Age Children	小学升初中 Primary School Graduates Entering into Junior Secondary Schools	初中升高级中学 Junior Secondary Graduates Entering into Senior Secondary Schools	高中升高等教育 Senior Secondary Graduates Entering into Institution of Higher Learning
1990	97.8	74.6	40.6	27.3
1991	97.8	77.7	42.6	28.7
1992	97.2	79.7	43.6	34.9
1993	97.7	81.8	44.1	43.3
1994	98.4	86.6	47.8	46.7
1995	98.5	90.8	50.3	49.9
1996	98.8	92.6	49.8	51.0
1997	98.9	93.7	51.5	48.6
1998	98.9	94.3	50.7	46.1
1999	99.1	94.4	50.0	63.8
2000	99.1	94.9	51.2	73.2
2001	99.1	95.5	52.9	78.8
2002	98.6	97.0	58.3	83.5
2003	98.7	97.9	59.6	83.4
2004	98.9	98.1	62.9	82.5
2005	99.2	98.4	69.7	76.3

注：1.初中升高级中学包含升入技工学校。

2.高中升学率为普通高校招生数（含电大普通班）与普通高中毕业生数之比。

a) Data on proportion of junior secondary graduates entering into senior secondary schools include those entering into secondary technical schools.

b) Data on proportion of senior secondary graduates entering into institutions of higher learning refer to the ratio between new entrants into regular institutions of higher learning (including regular classes of TV universities) and graduates of senior secondary schools.

21-25 各地区高等学校普通本、专科学生数（2005年）

Number of Students Enrolled in Undergraduate or Specialized Courses in Institutions of Higher Education by Region (2005)

单位：人 (person)

地 区	Region	学校数(所) Schools (unit)	毕(结)业生数 Graduates	本 科 Undergraduate Courses	专 科 Specialized Courses	授予学位数 Degrees Awarded	招生数 Entrants	本 科 Undergraduate Courses	专 科 Specialized Courses
全 国	**National Total**	**1792**	**3067956**	**1465786**	**1602170**	**1309692**	**5044581**	**2363647**	**2680934**
北 京	Beijing	77	120016	87067	32949	79079	158860	111487	47373
天 津	Tianjin	42	69211	33759	35452	28944	103616	53013	50603
河 北	Hebei	86	180377	65451	114926	59278	250273	93494	156779
山 西	Shanxi	59	88344	36769	51575	32039	127514	54418	73096
内蒙古	Inner Mongolia	33	39474	17033	22441	15717	70913	30182	40731
辽 宁	Liaoning	76	144984	79745	65239	74467	201488	122952	78536
吉 林	Jilin	44	83982	52913	31069	47675	129393	89043	40350
黑龙江	Heilongjiang	62	100791	58337	42454	56546	162842	92616	70226
上 海	Shanghai	58	103435	51963	51472	48770	131804	73863	57941
江 苏	Jiangsu	114	229679	119375	110304	99052	361479	182726	178753
浙 江	Zhejiang	68	133051	54584	78467	48336	197896	100359	97537
安 徽	Anhui	81	116958	48178	68780	42400	198690	80486	118204
福 建	Fujian	53	64792	27130	37662	25381	146657	64964	81693
江 西	Jiangxi	67	97781	42361	55420	38117	207882	79475	128407
山 东	Shandong	99	224611	101436	123175	95453	400573	138521	262052
河 南	Henan	83	165159	61827	103332	54979	277578	106193	171385
湖 北	Hubei	85	187920	100268	87652	89956	315560	147434	168126
湖 南	Hunan	93	150981	59752	91229	54300	250844	106251	144593
广 东	Guangdong	102	157082	61059	96023	54606	306956	136527	170429
广 西	Guangxi	51	64871	21906	42965	19775	116719	42130	74589
海 南	Hainan	15	11788	4725	7063	3644	24480	10426	14054
重 庆	Chongqing	35	59381	32991	26390	27631	112045	59485	52560
四 川	Sichuan	68	139328	79221	60107	70805	267198	124476	142722
贵 州	Guizhou	34	38681	20068	18613	16398	68586	32418	36168
云 南	Yunnan	44	47731	24022	23709	21544	84487	43308	41179
西 藏	Tibet	4	3172	1296	1876	942	7589	4597	2992
陕 西	Shaanxi	72	140592	67423	73169	61866	208879	102558	106321
甘 肃	Gansu	33	49886	23861	26025	20477	71572	37783	33789
青 海	Qinghai	11	8227	4221	4006	2836	11682	5683	5999
宁 夏	Ningxia	13	8817	5858	2959	5353	14775	8200	6575
新 疆	Xinjiang	30	36854	21187	15667	13326	55751	28579	27172

21-25 续表 continued

单位：人 (person)

地区	Region	在校学生数 Enrollment	本科 Undergraduate Courses	专科 Specialized Courses	预计毕业生数 Anticipated Graduates for Next Year	本科 Undergraduate Courses	专科 Specialized Courses
全国	**National Total**	**15617767**	**8488188**	**7129579**	**3881031**	**1785706**	**2095325**
北京	Beijing	548270	419521	128749	141316	98419	42897
天津	Tianjin	331553	190629	140924	84605	41481	43124
河北	Hebei	774006	351561	422445	224414	82350	142064
山西	Shanxi	407036	195628	211408	108508	39919	68589
内蒙古	Inner Mongolia	230902	121176	109726	58204	25148	33056
辽宁	Liaoning	659351	439185	220166	158943	93731	65212
吉林	Jilin	407262	306333	100929	104402	64666	39736
黑龙江	Heilongjiang	540867	347267	193600	132217	74784	57433
上海	Shanghai	442620	268030	174590	116352	58549	57803
江苏	Jiangsu	1159795	640335	519460	270178	130740	139438
浙江	Zhejiang	651307	349599	301708	168166	71237	96929
安徽	Anhui	589075	286655	302420	145220	59561	85659
福建	Fujian	406996	206400	200596	96897	34942	61955
江西	Jiangxi	646086	263015	383071	143335	50907	92428
山东	Shandong	1171284	589829	581455	275077	124859	150218
河南	Henan	851864	389447	462417	205425	80347	125078
湖北	Hubei	1012665	535615	477050	279625	127254	152371
湖南	Hunan	754859	370507	384352	195272	79517	115755
广东	Guangdong	874686	428579	446107	205090	73870	131220
广西	Guangxi	338261	144512	193749	88285	31559	56726
海南	Hainan	69984	33709	36275	18122	7031	11091
重庆	Chongqing	333563	209347	124216	78681	40583	38098
四川	Sichuan	775436	451275	324161	174807	96622	78185
贵州	Guizhou	206754	117644	89110	53873	24346	29527
云南	Yunnan	254687	147367	107320	64447	29371	35076
西藏	Tibet	18979	12747	6232	3856	1703	2153
陕西	Shaanxi	666943	374267	292676	163978	76883	87095
甘肃	Gansu	229459	136915	92544	57668	29208	28460
青海	Qinghai	32753	19856	12897	8474	4333	4141
宁夏	Ningxia	48650	29477	19173	11112	6157	4955
新疆	Xinjiang	181814	111761	70053	44482	25629	18853

21-26 各地区普通高等学校（机构）教职工情况（2005年）

Situations on Teachers and Staff in Regular Schools (Institutions) of Higher Education by Region (2005)

单位：人 (person)

地区 Region	教职工数 Teachers & Staff	校本部教职工 Headquarters	专任教师 Full-time Teachers	正高级 Senior	副高级 Sub-senior	中级 Middle	初级 Junior	无职称 No Rank	行政人员 Administrative Personnel	教辅人员 Teaching Assistants	工勤人员 Workers
全 国 National Total	**1742073**	**1572420**	**965839**	**96552**	**278200**	**311958**	**214714**	**64415**	**254885**	**178514**	**173182**
北 京 Beijing	114253	93391	48815	8925	16360	16198	5271	2061	18688	14472	11416
天 津 Tianjin	39434	36270	21670	2827	7148	6481	4187	1027	6276	4225	4099
河 北 Hebei	75881	69837	42697	4228	12453	12778	9534	3704	11290	7521	8329
山 西 Shanxi	47589	44271	27862	2093	7598	9215	6851	2105	6682	4751	4976
内蒙古 Inner Mongolia	27510	26250	16189	1089	4982	5300	3871	947	4357	3121	2583
辽 宁 Liaoning	82816	75201	43960	5025	14357	13929	9135	1514	13629	9077	8535
吉 林 Jilin	54689	50473	28129	3307	8043	8819	6130	1830	8611	6456	7277
黑龙江 Heilongjiang	65662	58861	35127	4220	11414	9551	8448	1494	9400	6118	8216
上 海 Shanghai	70623	57906	31645	4701	9377	11437	4408	1722	9969	8463	7829
江 苏 Jiangsu	120440	108156	67334	6612	18290	21999	16422	4011	17001	12180	11641
浙 江 Zhejiang	64491	58924	38402	3623	10667	12519	9099	2494	9744	6305	4473
安 徽 Anhui	52947	49694	32438	2343	8581	10595	8597	2322	6679	5454	5123
福 建 Fujian	41874	38676	24351	2322	6499	7229	6320	1981	6641	4298	3386
江 西 Jiangxi	62082	56161	38587	2958	10164	11402	10211	3852	7836	4993	4745
山 东 Shandong	109920	101236	64636	6638	18813	18883	16166	4136	15780	10811	10009
河 南 Henan	75782	70162	46309	2805	12148	15196	12606	3554	9224	7415	7214
湖 北 Hubei	107459	96998	59009	6434	17843	19169	10311	5252	15564	11350	11075
湖 南 Hunan	80766	72453	45272	4104	13444	14543	9842	3339	11419	8422	7340
广 东 Guangdong	90771	82884	54257	5214	15328	18227	11468	4020	13473	9090	6064
广 西 Guangxi	35409	30703	19610	1323	5227	7198	4111	1751	4600	3409	3084
海 南 Hainan	7698	7282	4620	447	1134	1387	1353	299	920	737	1005
重 庆 Chongqing	35787	32844	20184	1886	5782	7191	4311	1014	5706	3151	3803
四 川 Sichuan	78764	71669	44854	3890	11850	14801	11317	2996	10672	7870	8273
贵 州 Guizhou	23664	21945	14353	949	4009	5005	3385	1005	3459	2347	1786
云 南 Yunnan	28894	27237	16819	1460	4735	5894	3577	1153	4495	2933	2990
西 藏 Tibet	2033	1997	1187	29	220	425	445	68	425	163	222
陕 西 Shaanxi	82317	72920	42864	4709	11876	13908	9488	2883	12828	7471	9757
甘 肃 Gansu	26019	23686	14816	1240	3973	4859	3994	750	3667	2493	2710
青 海 Qinghai	5830	5076	3051	215	955	1196	562	123	815	575	635
宁 夏 Ningxia	7177	6673	4059	324	1276	1379	826	254	1152	617	845
新 疆 Xinjiang	23492	22584	12733	612	3654	5245	2468	754	3883	2226	3742

21-27 各地区中等职业学校（机构)学生情况（2005年）

Conditions on Students in Secondary Vocational Schools (Institutions) by Region (2005)

单位：人 (person)

地区	Region	毕业生数 Graduates	#获得职业资格证书 With Professional Qualification Certificates	招生数 New Enrollment	初中毕业 Junior Secondary School Graduates	#应届毕业生 Current Year Graduates	在校学生数 Total Enrollment	预计毕业生数 Graduates for Next Year
全国	**National**	**3491921**	**1864778**	**5372922**	**5090379**	**4922138**	**13247421**	**3919519**
北京	Beijing	61837	30295	63637	61545	58044	208554	61953
天津	Tianjin	37749	15288	44153	43393	41998	135426	43547
河北	Hebei	212430	87869	353544	331230	323375	810472	237390
山西	Shanxi	100235	58506	140586	134073	128063	361634	108067
内蒙古	Inner Mongolia	55109	19959	84486	81504	73607	199875	59913
辽宁	Liaoning	121551	51848	160681	151312	144873	431756	132877
吉林	Jilin	52454	22485	71668	67365	64227	182929	61468
黑龙江	Heilongjiang	72172	44790	117793	76860	73976	260073	68866
上海	Shanghai	61196	28048	55216	51941	51368	206326	60637
江苏	Jiangsu	197237	112757	411801	406796	404404	1060824	256284
浙江	Zhejiang	218780	147221	264499	261810	257307	732778	238289
安徽	Anhui	144932	66592	276347	264525	257150	633437	170958
福建	Fujian	110036	63593	175931	170832	160659	447689	131477
江西	Jiangxi	120609	68970	240940	226545	221408	541604	171923
山东	Shandong	330584	180683	392092	373208	359686	1093400	378698
河南	Henan	316127	153414	437102	384495	374757	1076826	344684
湖北	Hubei	129436	66373	273789	268393	264002	606014	155657
湖南	Hunan	187911	111244	317819	311835	308555	705568	192284
广东	Guangdong	189083	118717	279265	276772	269568	710162	202488
广西	Guangxi	97685	53948	146927	142875	137150	365996	109851
海南	Hainan	12598	5486	24235	24010	23967	58424	14856
重庆	Chongqing	100472	68556	114390	109320	104298	308194	100405
四川	Sichuan	192461	119139	345062	330718	322709	783244	227139
贵州	Guizhou	43770	17985	99706	97515	88065	201373	49907
云南	Yunnan	90520	38956	113619	106112	99540	294946	87780
西藏	Tibet	2930	849	2856	2331	1989	7027	2513
陕西	Shaanxi	127128	69184	192052	180192	172756	427967	136288
甘肃	Gansu	54637	22614	79783	74428	68913	195551	54743
青海	Qinghai	5836	2486	13216	10434	8567	24656	7996
宁夏	Ningxia	15856	6173	28422	22767	21609	58773	17478
新疆	Xinjiang	28560	10750	51305	45243	35548	115923	33103

21-28 各地区中等职业学校（机构)教职工数(2005年)

Number of Teachers and Staff in Secondary Vocational Schools (Institutions) by Region (2005)

单位：人 (person)

地区	Region	教职工数 Teachers & Staff	校本部教职工 Teachers and Staff in Headquarters	专任教师 Full-time Teachers	行政人员 Administrative Personnel	教辅人员 Teaching Assistants	工勤人员 Workers	校办企业职工 Employees in School-run Enterprises	其他附设机构人员 Personnel in Other Subsidiary Units	聘请校外教师 Engaged from Other Schools
全国	**National Total**	**889171**	**867655**	**588694**	**112848**	**66297**	**99816**	**10868**	**10648**	**82306**
北京	Beijing	19382	18798	10621	3848	1828	2501	106	478	1596
天津	Tianjin	12632	12347	7699	2365	859	1424	156	129	975
河北	Hebei	61288	59526	39736	8015	4787	6988	1072	690	4561
山西	Shanxi	27498	26927	18528	3331	2073	2995	276	295	2197
内蒙古	Inner Mongolia	18481	18204	12342	2308	1546	2008	142	135	801
辽宁	Liaoning	36456	35712	23138	5569	2710	4295	401	343	3399
吉林	Jilin	25454	25054	15851	4102	2728	2373	239	161	862
黑龙江	Heilongjiang	23597	22869	15007	3281	1715	2866	124	604	1096
上海	Shanghai	17179	16802	8962	2835	1989	3016	278	99	2961
江苏	Jiangsu	53503	52632	38220	4801	3762	5849	437	434	6007
浙江	Zhejiang	41676	41111	32420	3283	2009	3399	339	226	4447
安徽	Anhui	29623	28960	20220	3601	1897	3242	312	351	3679
福建	Fujian	24245	23902	17457	2850	1482	2113	272	71	3739
江西	Jiangxi	24352	22991	16407	2789	1299	2496	963	398	2312
山东	Shandong	80192	77782	52999	10055	6180	8548	1514	896	3730
河南	Henan	64371	62154	43754	7336	4586	6478	1249	968	5701
湖北	Hubei	36658	35466	24036	4656	2862	3912	579	613	4312
湖南	Hunan	39753	38730	25962	5047	2850	4871	549	474	3250
广东	Guangdong	49087	48427	33734	6080	3587	5026	196	464	4984
广西	Guangxi	29667	28237	18113	3736	2498	3890	237	1193	3336
海南	Hainan	4149	3963	2520	558	287	598	14	172	448
重庆	Chongqing	19248	18817	12520	2703	1485	2109	212	219	2282
四川	Sichuan	48120	47319	31629	5970	3729	5991	316	485	3805
贵州	Guizhou	12617	12374	8012	2173	923	1266	67	176	1675
云南	Yunnan	23630	23412	15787	2587	1572	3466	55	163	2605
西藏	Tibet	1214	1214	835	148	63	168			35
陕西	Shaanxi	29090	28416	18688	4581	2299	2848	437	237	4818
甘肃	Gansu	17612	17357	11526	2032	1474	2325	146	109	1210
青海	Qinghai	2227	2153	1588	210	120	235	46	28	105
宁夏	Ningxia	2650	2631	1729	328	186	388	19		339
新疆	Xinjiang	13520	13368	8654	1670	912	2132	115	37	1039

21-29 各地区普通高中基本情况（2005年）

Basic Statistics on Regular Senior Secondary Schools by Region (2005)

单位：人 (person)

地区	Region	学校数（所） Schools (unit)	招生数 New Enrollment	在校学生数 Total Enrollment	毕业生数 Graduates	教职工数 Teachers and Staff	#专任教师 Full-time Teachers
全国	**National Total**	**16092**	**8777317**	**24090901**	**6615713**	**5720244**	**1299460**
北京	Beijing	335	88605	278358	73260	75837	19875
天津	Tianjin	232	74449	217180	57263	55322	14207
河北	Hebei	816	494683	1391138	396263	345193	73403
山西	Shanxi	581	263159	713699	196934	193835	41583
内蒙古	Inner Mongolia	359	198377	523497	136562	121784	26649
辽宁	Liaoning	476	266111	744229	201852	180016	38208
吉林	Jilin	293	173983	489420	133095	124819	24292
黑龙江	Heilongjiang	475	205541	583567	161301	176524	34093
上海	Shanghai	334	100574	311737	101825	75451	18239
江苏	Jiangsu	849	522503	1453420	426520	337789	88801
浙江	Zhejiang	611	303986	899961	259874	194890	56882
安徽	Anhui	760	434612	1169006	300950	228966	51112
福建	Fujian	627	272124	732456	182591	167811	45328
江西	Jiangxi	617	312575	849204	239755	183459	46565
山东	Shandong	813	672165	1965783	575243	470584	108076
河南	Henan	945	699934	1883854	536570	431625	84038
湖北	Hubei	653	458591	1294487	383420	273146	64433
湖南	Hunan	800	512714	1318513	340207	305413	68324
广东	Guangdong	981	569753	1489863	374445	360341	86079
广西	Guangxi	529	256877	699644	193531	191316	35249
海南	Hainan	107	46433	118165	30677	34331	6590
重庆	Chongqing	277	182950	481388	133654	112965	25774
四川	Sichuan	796	511535	1384573	373219	306141	72408
贵州	Guizhou	473	193814	495193	119161	138949	25638
云南	Yunnan	443	189993	483054	116031	153997	29760
西藏	Tibet	25	12864	33342	7684	9006	1922
陕西	Shaanxi	639	326295	906256	259637	191041	44100
甘肃	Gansu	497	205710	566168	138165	111495	29127
青海	Qinghai	144	37577	100511	25355	22370	6571
宁夏	Ningxia	102	43786	125472	36741	25828	6981
新疆	Xinjiang	503	145044	387763	103928	120000	25153

注：教职工数为普通高中和普通初中之和。

a) Number of teachers and staff is the sum of that of regular senior secondary schools and regular junior secondary schools.

21-30 各地区普通初中基本情况（2005年）

Basic Statistics on Regular Junior Secondary Schools by Region (2005)

单位：人 (person)

地 区	Region	学校数（所） Schools (unit)	招生数 New Enrollment	在校学生数 Total Enrollment	毕业生数 Graduates	专任教师 Full-time Teachers
全 国	**National Total**	**61885**	**19765246**	**61718079**	**21065150**	**3471839**
北 京	Beijing	404	93048	321585	156388	31095
天 津	Tianjin	408	99780	359110	136812	27330
河 北	Hebei	3918	1152019	3704263	1384009	216566
山 西	Shanxi	2698	624244	1897840	632597	118220
内蒙古	Inner Mongolia	1224	313496	1031241	345067	67007
辽 宁	Liaoning	1798	495535	1570269	555596	106439
吉 林	Jilin	1341	319725	1057933	375973	69956
黑龙江	Heilongjiang	2112	435524	1695823	565215	109095
上 海	Shanghai	487	110740	466962	154468	33557
江 苏	Jiangsu	2292	1052992	3462294	1203306	191014
浙 江	Zhejiang	1913	560508	1710877	637297	110015
安 徽	Anhui	3188	1119706	3439620	1125179	145867
福 建	Fujian	1403	537933	1769284	576832	98982
江 西	Jiangxi	2184	645042	2012287	742480	116568
山 东	Shandong	3591	1124890	3959117	1497648	269057
河 南	Henan	5262	1895901	5698301	1983617	289035
湖 北	Hubei	2578	1011186	3172392	1055083	169084
湖 南	Hunan	3760	812790	2972610	1251757	193125
广 东	Guangdong	3301	1626601	4627044	1368854	221224
广 西	Guangxi	2358	813749	2339138	745439	117132
海 南	Hainan	456	167719	466186	130345	21062
重 庆	Chongqing	1137	435286	1253778	384891	68223
四 川	Sichuan	4199	1172825	3470817	1137068	186516
贵 州	Guizhou	2193	710857	2054382	627254	97083
云 南	Yunnan	1814	633119	1905763	614981	101925
西 藏	Tibet	93	43964	120706	29396	6239
陕 西	Shaanxi	2088	698088	2139326	712394	115038
甘 肃	Gansu	1553	485890	1377671	423489	70023
青 海	Qinghai	367	78763	226991	68123	13479
宁 夏	Ningxia	316	103102	280950	87233	15335
新 疆	Xinjiang	1449	390224	1153519	356359	76548

21-31 各地区职业初中基本情况（2005年）

Basic Statistics on Vocational Junior Secondary Schools by Region (2005)

单位：人 (person)

地区	Region	学校数（所）Schools (unit)	招生数 New Enrollment	在校学生数 Total Enrollment	毕业生数 Graduates	教职工数 Teachers and Staff	#专任教师 Full-time Teachers
全国	**National Total**	**601**	**110580**	**431363**	**169132**	**24009**	**20240**
北京	Beijing						
天津	Tianjin						
河北	Hebei	25	4120	13137	7451	1130	949
山西	Shanxi	62	7088	27518	9037	1982	1688
内蒙古	Inner Mongolia	122	14220	54991	26971	5839	4290
辽宁	Liaoning						
吉林	Jilin	33	8569	34037	14802	1880	1491
黑龙江	Heilongjiang	7	710	8058	7521	262	221
上海	Shanghai	1	112	392	408	65	34
江苏	Jiangsu						
浙江	Zhejiang	1			67		
安徽	Anhui	172	37626	136855	49843	6738	6070
福建	Fujian	1	121	310	116	27	21
江西	Jiangxi	3	229	1268	685	98	81
山东	Shandong	1	103	332	620	50	38
河南	Henan	7	852	4434	2953	218	210
湖北	Hubei	31	7294	26524	8961	1446	1308
湖南	Hunan	2	99	358	85	32	29
广东	Guangdong						
广西	Guangxi	10	887	4297	2405	282	208
海南	Hainan						
重庆	Chongqing	2	42	138	91	27	15
四川	Sichuan	12	3256	7864	2479	529	443
贵州	Guizhou	69	11921	36538	11445	2106	1947
云南	Yunnan	16	5947	20093	5787	507	460
西藏	Tibet	1	265	265	84	2	2
陕西	Shaanxi	4	868	2924	807	123	116
甘肃	Gansu	6	55	200	1064	18	16
青海	Qinghai	3	93	439	241	26	23
宁夏	Ningxia	1	1449	3823	875	113	113
新疆	Xinjiang	9	4654	46568	14334	509	467

21-32 各地区普通小学基本情况（2005年）

Basic Statistics on Regular Primary Schools by Region (2005)

单位：人 (person)

地区	Region	学校数（所） Schools (unit)	招生数 New Enrollment	在校学生数 Total Enrollment	毕业生数 Graduates	教职工数 Teachers and Staff	#专任教师 Full-time Teachers
全国	**National Total**	**366213**	**16717440**	**108640655**	**20194768**	**6132155**	**5592453**
北京	Beijing	1403	71020	494482	93486	61352	47948
天津	Tianjin	1062	78373	533003	106447	49629	41076
河北	Hebei	20883	720038	5003578	1174631	343697	320110
山西	Shanxi	24339	548755	3502562	635578	208261	192271
内蒙古	Inner Mongolia	5850	258947	1596381	327773	138645	118988
辽宁	Liaoning	9311	379941	2666155	499069	190548	163589
吉林	Jilin	7393	215380	1625238	330055	163366	137675
黑龙江	Heilongjiang	9995	340241	2204055	443962	188256	163204
上海	Shanghai	650	104637	540362	110428	50031	37954
江苏	Jiangsu	6261	619336	4855321	1055231	289751	261646
浙江	Zhejiang	6101	489600	3424042	552525	177886	162183
安徽	Anhui	20142	815248	5841133	1162472	271815	259493
福建	Fujian	10560	358831	2732702	547122	177134	166465
江西	Jiangxi	14727	669411	3841576	648849	200291	193484
山东	Shandong	15871	1042684	6153703	1133143	410394	377729
河南	Henan	33026	1694358	9868409	1918974	502187	475511
湖北	Hubei	12631	567411	4291881	1020710	232888	215693
湖南	Hunan	17108	710905	4198314	815684	261560	246112
广东	Guangdong	21228	1641550	10670304	1674305	463715	403824
广西	Guangxi	15500	734555	4527888	844177	233177	204788
海南	Hainan	3106	182702	1056730	171364	56516	50598
重庆	Chongqing	9558	365028	2609754	447168	127433	114326
四川	Sichuan	19305	1092214	7145093	1187842	337939	307113
贵州	Guizhou	14258	772201	4737645	742112	196785	183679
云南	Yunnan	18747	733383	4412267	693217	232227	219236
西藏	Tibet	890	54665	327497	47960	14967	14267
陕西	Shaanxi	20711	435948	3400893	724600	203262	186644
甘肃	Gansu	14963	461894	3035794	502605	135276	130841
青海	Qinghai	2898	89280	506853	80983	28551	27478
宁夏	Ningxia	2527	130365	693207	104704	34663	33760
新疆	Xinjiang	5209	338539	2143833	397592	149953	134768

21-33 各地区特殊教育基本情况（2005年）

Basic Statistics on Special Education by Region (2005)

单位：人 (person)

地区	Region	学校数（所） Schools (unit)	招生数 New Enrollment	在校学生数 Total Enrollment	毕业生数 Graduates	教职工数 Teachers and Staff	#专任教师 Full-time Teachers
全国	**National Total**	**1593**	**49288**	**364409**	**43214**	**42256**	**31937**
北京	Beijing	25	635	6353	1043	1000	738
天津	Tianjin	24	182	2608	397	700	484
河北	Hebei	117	1896	11411	911	2482	1909
山西	Shanxi	40	743	5021	483	1125	887
内蒙古	Inner Mongolia	28	483	2844	219	842	667
辽宁	Liaoning	74	698	8296	971	2565	1903
吉林	Jilin	47	630	5489	568	1771	1233
黑龙江	Heilongjiang	72	778	6679	669	2290	1782
上海	Shanghai	28	1114	9972	2286	1598	1002
江苏	Jiangsu	109	3998	30688	4277	3390	2548
浙江	Zhejiang	62	1465	12889	1782	1531	1233
安徽	Anhui	67	2394	17957	2035	1230	952
福建	Fujian	67	4596	35198	6317	1527	1290
江西	Jiangxi	59	2876	18805	1551	681	548
山东	Shandong	139	1955	16126	1589	5236	3719
河南	Henan	123	2624	20287	1401	3125	2551
湖北	Hubei	77	1038	9444	1498	1679	1317
湖南	Hunan	53	1200	9372	766	1243	948
广东	Guangdong	67	3363	25752	3086	1782	1360
广西	Guangxi	52	1607	12769	908	915	572
海南	Hainan	4	228	1786	124	112	74
重庆	Chongqing	43	1840	12463	1702	725	556
四川	Sichuan	83	3916	24788	2160	1447	1174
贵州	Guizhou	39	2096	14676	929	749	603
云南	Yunnan	25	3820	19417	2884	687	518
西藏	Tibet	1	23	208	2	23	19
陕西	Shaanxi	29	900	6627	1011	676	519
甘肃	Gansu	14	915	8339	684	438	303
青海	Qinghai	9	335	2307	195	153	126
宁夏	Ningxia	6	93	877	52	167	140
新疆	Xinjiang	10	847	4961	714	367	262

21-34 各地区各级普通学校生师比（2005年）

Student-Teacher Ratio by Level of Regular Schools by Region (2005)

单位：% (%)

地区	Region	小学 Primary School	初中 Junior Secondary School	普通高中 Regular Senior Secondary School	职业高中 Vocational Senior Secondary School	普通中专 Regular Specialized Secondary School	普通高校 Regular Institution of Higher Education	本科院校 Undergraduate Courses	专科院校 Specialized Courses
总计	**National Total**	**19.43**	**17.80**	**18.54**	**20.62**	**31.02**	**16.85**	**17.75**	**14.78**
北京	Beijing	10.31	10.34	14.01	12.90	32.44	17.35	18.08	11.17
天津	Tianjin	12.98	13.14	15.29	15.21	22.85	17.42	18.16	15.82
河北	Hebei	15.63	17.09	18.95	20.35	31.98	16.98	17.99	15.26
山西	Shanxi	18.22	16.06	17.16	15.13	35.43	14.66	16.76	10.80
内蒙古	Inner Mongolia	13.42	15.24	19.64	14.78	26.10	15.16	17.19	11.60
辽宁	Liaoning	16.30	14.75	19.48	14.86	25.23	16.61	17.76	12.19
吉林	Jilin	11.80	15.28	20.15	14.88	21.99	16.40	17.35	11.70
黑龙江	Heilongjiang	13.50	15.59	17.12	13.03	30.05	16.46	17.46	13.38
上海	Shanghai	14.24	13.91	17.09	18.94	25.74	17.43	17.68	16.24
江苏	Jiangsu	18.56	18.13	16.37	20.36	46.42	17.69	18.05	16.94
浙江	Zhejiang	21.11	15.55	15.82	24.34	34.80	17.60	17.73	17.38
安徽	Anhui	22.51	23.54	22.87	36.59	30.28	17.62	18.55	15.96
福建	Fujian	16.42	17.87	16.16		25.10	16.53	16.80	15.88
江西	Jiangxi	19.85	17.26	18.24	25.42	66.74	15.40	16.86	12.99
山东	Shandong	16.29	14.71	18.19	19.39	29.88	16.57	17.29	15.06
河南	Henan	20.75	19.72	22.42	21.50	43.70	17.03	17.44	16.38
湖北	Hubei	19.90	18.77	20.09	24.01	30.02	17.51	18.00	16.42
湖南	Hunan	17.06	15.39	19.30	22.09	53.90	16.84	18.31	14.82
广东	Guangdong	26.42	20.92	17.31	19.19	23.02	17.37	17.89	16.29
广西	Guangxi	22.11	19.97	19.85	21.61	24.40	17.00	17.21	16.73
海南	Hainan	20.88	22.13	17.93	10.66	41.47	15.81	18.65	12.60
重庆	Chongqing	22.83	18.38	18.68	20.93	41.53	17.63	18.71	13.80
四川	Sichuan	23.27	18.61	19.12	21.40	31.22	18.60	19.20	16.76
贵州	Guizhou	25.79	21.11	19.31	19.13	32.03	15.85	17.66	12.74
云南	Yunnan	20.13	18.81	16.23	16.73	24.75	16.07	17.81	12.34
西藏	Tibet	22.95	19.38	17.35		9.29	14.11	14.07	14.67
陕西	Shaanxi	18.22	18.60	20.55	25.46	28.14	15.59	17.32	10.88
甘肃	Gansu	23.20	19.67	19.44	13.52	19.55	17.43	18.93	14.42
青海	Qinghai	18.45	16.84	15.30	19.76	11.86	13.46	13.69	12.63
宁夏	Ningxia	20.53	18.43	17.97	22.40	54.06	13.01	14.01	11.33
新疆	Xinjiang	15.91	15.58	15.42	11.52	17.37	14.69	16.29	11.28

注：普通高校生师比中专任教师数包括聘请校外教师。

a) Of the student-teacher ratio of regular institution of higher education, full-time teachers include those from other schools.

21-35 每十万人口各级学校平均在校生数（2005年）

Number of Students Per 100 000 Inhabitants by Level (2005)

单位：人 (person)

地区	Region	幼儿园 Kindergartens	小学 Primary Education	初中阶段 Junior Secondary	高中阶段 Senior Secondary	高等学校 Higher Education
全国	**National Total**	**1676**	**8358**	**4781**	**3070**	**1613**
北京	Beijing	1355	3312	2154	3727	6580
天津	Tianjin	1999	5205	3507	3910	4340
河北	Hebei	1791	7348	5460	3375	1443
山西	Shanxi	1923	10502	5773	3462	1611
内蒙古	Inner Mongolia	1207	6696	4556	3132	1303
辽宁	Liaoning	1626	6322	3724	2981	2141
吉林	Jilin	1092	5999	4031	2598	2144
黑龙江	Heilongjiang	988	5774	4464	2413	1887
上海	Shanghai	1659	3102	2683	3341	3838
江苏	Jiangsu	1864	6532	4658	3692	2015
浙江	Zhejiang	2801	7254	3625	3745	1886
安徽	Anhui	1120	9041	5535	2890	1110
福建	Fujian	2354	7783	5040	3581	1427
江西	Jiangxi	1673	8967	4700	3457	1768
山东	Shandong	1803	6703	4313	3631	1598
河南	Henan	1580	10156	5869	3199	1119
湖北	Hubei	988	7134	5317	3345	2176
湖南	Hunan	1227	6268	4439	3190	1452
广东	Guangdong	2576	12850	5572	3035	1462
广西	Guangxi	1816	9261	4793	2320	993
海南	Hainan	1469	12918	5699	2285	1133
重庆	Chongqing	1718	8359	4016	2716	1474
四川	Sichuan	1750	8189	3987	2585	1204
贵州	Guizhou	1771	12135	5356	1840	838
云南	Yunnan	1750	9994	4362	1836	904
西藏	Tibet	350	11952	4415	1473	1139
陕西	Shaanxi	1332	9179	5782	3853	2349
甘肃	Gansu	1334	11591	5261	2983	1211
青海	Qinghai	1532	9404	4219	2398	905
宁夏	Ningxia	1735	11789	4843	3248	1278
新疆	Xinjiang	1495	10921	6114	2699	1329

注：1.高等学校包括普通高等学校和成人高等学校。
2.高中阶段合计数据包括普通高中、成人高中、普通中专、职业高中、技工学校和成人中专，分省数据不含技工学校。
3.初中阶段包括普通初中和职业初中。

a) Institutions of higher education include that of regular institutions of higher education and adult institutions of higher education.
b) Total of senior schools include that of regular senior schools, adult senior schools, regular secondary technical schools, vocational secondary schools, technical worker school, adult technical secondary schools, data classified by region exclude that of technical worker schools.
c) Junior secondary schools include regular junior schools and junior vocational schools.

21-36 各地区教育经费情况

Basic Statistics on Educational Funds by Region

单位：万元 (10 000 yuan)

年份 Year / 地区 Region		合计 Total	国家财政性教育经费 Government Appropriation for Education	#预算内教育经费 Budgetary	社会团体和公民个人办学经费 Funds of Social Organizations and Citizens for Running Schools	社会捐资和集资办学经费 Donations and Fund-raising for Running Schools	学费和杂费 Tuition and Miscellaneous Fees	其他教育经费 Other Educational Funds
	1992	8670490.5	7287505.8	5387381.7		696285.2	439319.3	247380.2
	1993	10599374.4	8677618.3	6443914.0	33322.7	701856.1	871476.9	315100.4
	1994	14887812.6	11747395.6	8839794.7	107795.2	974487.1	1469228.1	588906.6
	1995	18779501.1	14115233.3	10283930.0	203671.5	1628414.0	2012422.5	819759.8
	1996	22623393.5	16717045.5	12119133.6	261998.9	1884189.5	2610391.2	1149798.4
	1997	25317325.7	18625416.3	13577262.1	301746.4	1706587.6	3260792.0	1422783.4
	1998	29490592.0	20324526.0	15655917.0	480314.0	1418537.0	3697474.0	3569741.0
	1999	33490416.4	22871756.1	18157597.3	628957.1	1258694.2	4636107.9	4094901.1
	2000	38490805.8	25626055.7	20856792.0	858537.2	1139556.9	5948304.3	4918351.7
	2001	46376626.2	30570099.5	25823761.9	1280895.2	1128851.8	7456013.5	5940766.2
	2002	54800277.6	34914047.5	31142383.3	1725548.7	1272791.0	9227791.7	7660098.7
	2003	62082653.0	38506236.6	34538582.6	2590147.8	1045926.9	11214984.7	8725357.0
	2004	72425989.2	44658574.8	40278158.0	3478528.8	934203.8	13465517.3	9889164.5
北京	Beijing	4492628.4	2983476.1	2769010.7	37745.6	60087.9	556170.6	855148.2
天津	Tianjin	1239681.8	781629.6	700831.1	54813.0	3724.8	200277.4	199237.0
河北	Hebei	2700904.1	1754771.2	1611233.6	85052.1	21228.6	628424.4	211427.8
山西	Shanxi	1548847.8	1012934.1	887726.3	69805.7	26754.8	320948.9	118404.3
内蒙古	Inner Mongolia	1115216.2	855424.3	779271.5	13407.7	2827.8	161201.5	82354.9
辽宁	Liaoning	2700789.4	1774299.7	1587349.9	127952.6	4743.2	497680.9	296113.0
吉林	Jilin	1454419.1	985194.0	885564.0	15824.8	40669.6	225707.0	187023.7
黑龙江	Heilongjiang	2118830.8	1370091.6	1136687.0	56095.6	5651.8	408207.9	278783.9
上海	Shanghai	3832690.6	2285942.5	1992391.3	256061.9	53493.6	632763.4	604429.2
江苏	Jiangsu	5570009.3	3099409.2	2738972.7	251114.6	172793.2	954845.9	1091846.4
浙江	Zhejiang	5001700.0	2853665.1	2304294.2	400106.7	131551.0	740998.3	875378.9
安徽	Anhui	2216290.6	1386903.9	1310319.1	52513.0	22595.8	486145.1	268132.8
福建	Fujian	2224559.2	1391027.1	1296799.6	216790.8	33020.1	379481.7	204239.5
江西	Jiangxi	1566029.1	831076.3	781880.7	149345.1	5281.9	365917.9	214407.9
山东	Shandong	4267089.0	2561587.9	2237315.5	207910.2	53123.1	939728.6	504739.2
河南	Henan	2999488.5	1966366.2	1831162.2	112167.3	16896.5	593433.3	310625.2
湖北	Hubei	2985501.9	1531661.1	1392406.7	151144.5	16270.3	776666.3	509759.7
湖南	Hunan	2724014.0	1409498.3	1294561.9	190728.7	28256.0	687792.5	407738.5
广东	Guangdong	7087101.0	4217378.9	3898843.8	546894.4	88704.4	1547999.3	686124.0
广西	Guangxi	1605769.3	1060559.5	987753.5	31247.0	7319.9	315160.6	191482.3
海南	Hainan	389305.1	248164.2	207015.2	18016.9	10576.3	70829.7	41718.0
重庆	Chongqing	1434395.3	826797.5	751434.6	29486.5	50415.3	233217.5	294478.5
四川	Sichuan	3091286.6	1828023.3	1684852.1	94934.4	31839.7	569378.6	567110.6
贵州	Guizhou	1142161.9	816926.9	753752.1	35404.2	5430.9	168184.1	116215.8
云南	Yunnan	1750840.6	1391479.8	1315972.3	42652.6	14156.7	169705.7	132845.8
西藏	Tibet	234499.5	222773.7	221771.2		581.7	6449.1	4695.0
陕西	Shaanxi	2047443.0	1144359.2	1074132.2	184644.5	15007.7	450737.5	252694.1
甘肃	Gansu	1031445.1	727916.5	659016.7	21273.6	7037.4	179548.8	95668.8
青海	Qinghai	225275.2	190741.6	184898.7	1129.5	325.7	22727.0	10351.4
宁夏	Ningxia	296236.7	223603.9	207277.8	869.4	729.6	41653.4	29380.4
新疆	Xinjiang	1331540.1	924891.6	793659.8	23395.9	3108.5	133534.4	246609.7

21-37 各类学校教育经费情况（2004年）

Educational Funds in Various School (2004)

单位：万元 (10 000 yuan)

学校类别	Type of Schools	合计 Total	国家财政性教育经费 Government Appropriation for Education	#预算内教育经费 Budgetary	社会团体和公民个人办学经费 Funds of Social Organizations and Citizens for Running Schools	社会捐资和集资办学经费 Donations and Fund-Raising for Running Schools	学费和杂费 Tuition and Miscellaneous Fees	其他教育经费 Other Educational Funds
全国总计	**National Total**	**72425989**	**44658575**	**40278158**	**3478529**	**934204**	**13465517**	**9889165**
#中央	Central Government	8078628	4190227	3679482		122791	1431607	2334002
地方	Local Government	64347362	40468347	36598676	3478529	811413	12033910	7555163
按学校类别分组	**Grouped by Type of Schools**							
高等学校	Institutions of Higher Education	22576459	10098392	9658276	1309226	216321	6938658	4013863
普通高等学校	Regular Institutions of Higher Education	21297613	9697909	9309882	1121982	215440	6476921	3785362
成人高等学校	Institutions of Higher Education for Adults	1278846	400483	348395	187244	882	461737	228501
中等专业学校	Specialized Secondary Schools	2650782	1412520	1314426	54496	4812	860022	318931
中等技术学校	Technical Schools	1878819	995488	927834	24323	2904	648180	207924
中等师范学校	Teacher Training Schools	317577	163560	156504		1027	123045	29946
成人中专学校	Specialized Secondary Schools for Adults	454386	253472	230088	30173	881	88798	81062
技工学校	Technical Schools	488899	233525	178256		313	134384	120677
中学	Secondary Schools	22265210	14001339	12120587	1538898	401724	3427590	2895659
普通中学	Regular Secondary Schools	22230171	13988197	12111111	1529022	401681	3422032	2889239
高级中学	Senior Secondary Schools	9083784	4614816	3844724	651696	205345	1994407	1617519
初级中学	Junior Secondary Schools	13146387	9373381	8266388	877326	196336	1427625	1271720
#农村	Rural	5743899	4682906	4401382		57604	625983	377406
成人中学	Secondary Schools for Adults	35040	13142	9475	9876	43	5558	6420
职业中学	Vocational Schools	1987364	1140547	985944	114603	15018	512749	204447
小学	Primary Schools	18051062	14735198	13525942	461305	254102	1450088	1150369
普通小学	Regular Primary Schools	18045650	14731537	13522577	460081	254101	1449915	1150016
#农村	Rural Areas	10703845	9253267	8857401		113535	899874	437169
成人小学	Primary Schools for Adults	5412	3661	3364	1225		173	353
特殊教育学校	Special Education Schools	193181	170528	150003		4779	3792	14083
幼儿园	Kindergartens	875169	545001	519700		13665	138235	178267
其它	Others	3337863	2321526	1825026		23470		992868

21-38 科技活动基本情况

Basic Statistics on Scientific and Technological Activities

指　　标	Item	2001	2002	2003	2004	2005
科技活动人员（万人）	**Personnel Engaged in S&T Activities (10 000 persons)**	**314.1**	**322.2**	**328.4**	**348.1**	**381.5**
#科学家和工程师	Scientists and Engineers	207.2	217.2	225.5	225.2	256.1
研究与试验发展折合全时人员（万人年）	**Full-time Equivalent of R&D Personnel (10 000 man-year)**	**95.7**	**103.5**	**109.5**	**115.3**	**136.5**
#科学家和工程师	Scientists and Engineers	74.3	81.0	86.2	92.6	111.9
科技经费筹集额（亿元）	**Funding for S&T Activities (100 million yuan)**	**2589.4**	**2938.0**	**3459.1**	**4328.3**	**5250.8**
#政府资金	Government Funds	656.4	776.2	839.3	985.5	1213.1
企业资金	Self-raised Funds by Enterprises	1458.4	1676.7	2053.5	2771.2	3440.3
金融机构贷款	Loans From Finance Institutions	190.8	201.9	259.3	265.0	276.8
科技经费内部支出（亿元）	**Internal Expenditures on S&T Activities (100 million yuan)**	**2312.5**	**2671.5**	**3121.6**	**4004.4**	**4836.2**
#劳务费	Service Fees	549.3	654.6	751.5	968.8	1032.5
固定资产购建费	Purchases or Construction of Fixed Assets	692.3	722.6	852.4	1192.0	1427.9
研究与试验发展经费支出（亿元）	**Expenditure on R&D (100 million yuan)**	**1042.5**	**1287.6**	**1539.6**	**1966.3**	**2450.0**
#基础研究	Basic Research	52.2	73.8	87.7	117.2	131.2
应用研究	Applied Research	175.9	246.7	311.4	400.5	433.5
试验发展	Experimental Development	814.3	967.2	1140.5	1448.7	1885.3
研究与试验发展经费支出相当于国内生产总值比例（%）	**Proportion of Expenditure on R&D to GDP (%)**	**0.95**	**1.07**	**1.13**	**1.23**	**1.34**
科技成果及获奖数（项）	**Achievements in S&T and National Prizes Won**					
科技成果登记数	Number of Major Achievements in Science and Technology	28448	26697	30486	31720	32359
国家技术发明奖	Number of National Invention Prizes Awarded	14	21	19	28	40
国家科学技术进步奖	Number of National Scientific and Technological Progress Prizes Awarded	191	218	216	244	236
技术市场成交额（亿元）	**Transaction Value in Technical Market (100 million yuan)**	**783**	**884**	**1085**	**1334**	**1551**
专利申请受理数（件）	**Total Patent Applications Examined**	**203573**	**252631**	**308487**	**353807**	**476264**
发明	Inventions	63204	80232	105318	130133	173327
实用新型	Utility Models	79722	93139	109115	112825	139566
外观设计	Designs	60647	79260	94054	110849	163371
专利申请授权数（件）	**Total Patent Applications Certified**	**114251**	**132399**	**182226**	**190238**	**214003**
发明	Inventions	16296	21473	37154	49360	53305
实用新型	Utility Models	54359	57484	68906	70623	79349
外观设计	Designs	43596	53442	76166	70255	81349

21-39 科学研究与开发机构基本情况

Basic Statistics on Scientific Research and Development Institutions

项 目	Item	2001	2002	2003	2004	2005
科技活动人员 （万人）	**Personnel Engaged in S&T Activities(10 000 persons)**	**42.7**	**41.5**	**40.6**	**39.8**	**45.6**
#科学家和工程师	Scientists and Engineers	27.6	27.1	26.7	26.3	31.9
研究与试验发展折合全时人员 （万人年）	**Full-time Equivalent of R&D Personnel (10 000 man-year)**	**20.5**	**20.6**	**20.4**	**20.3**	**21.5**
#科学家和工程师	Scientists and Engineers	14.8	15.2	15.5	15.8	16.9
#基础研究	Basic Research	2.4	2.3	2.6	2.7	2.8
应用研究	Applied Research	7.6	8.1	7.9	8.1	8.3
试验发展	Experimental Development	10.3	10.2	9.9	9.5	10.4
科技经费筹集额 （亿元）	**Funding for S&T Activities (100 million yuan)**	**626.0**	**702.7**	**750.6**	**789.1**	**950.4**
#政府资金	Government Appropriation Funds	434.9	498.0	535.0	596.1	763.4
企业资金	Self-raised Funds by Enterprises	25.4	36.3	47.0	49.8	56.2
金融机构贷款	Loans From Finance Institutions	8.6	11.9	11.3	9.1	12.7
科技经费内部支出 （亿元）	**Internal Expenditures on S&T Activities (100 million yuan)**	**557.9**	**620.2**	**681.3**	**706.3**	**829.7**
#劳务费	Service Fees	142.5	159.8	169.1	172.2	155.2
业务费	Operating Expenses	231.9	298.6	313.5	393.5	504.2
固定资产购建费	Purchases or Construction of Fixed Assets	123.9	122.0	138.0	140.5	170.3
研究与试验发展经费支出（亿元）	**Expenditure on R&D (100 million yuan)**	**288.5**	**351.3**	**399.0**	**431.7**	**513.1**
#基础研究	Basic Research	34.6	40.7	46.0	51.7	58.0
应用研究	Applied Research	78.9	121.2	140.3	159.1	176.3
试验发展	Experimental Development	175.0	189.4	212.7	221.0	278.7

注：数据口径为县以上独立核算研究机构及科技信息与文献机构，不包括转制的研究机构。

a) The coverage of statistics includes research institutions, institutions of science and technology information and literature, institutions with independent accounting system at and above county level, excluding the research institutions which are not covered by state budget.

21-40 大中型工业企业科技活动基本情况

Basic Statistics on Science and Technology Activities of Large-sized and Medium-sized Industrial Enterprises

指标	Item	2000	2002	2003	2004	2005
有科技机构的企业 （个）	**Number of Enterprises Having Scientific and Technological Institutions (unit)**	**6187**	**5836**	**6424**	**6467**	**6775**
有科技机构的企业占全部企业的比重 (%)	Percentage of Enterprises Having Scientific and Technological Institutions to Total Number of Enterprises (%)	28.5	25.3	28.8	23.4	23.7
科技机构数 （个）	**Number of Scientific and Technological Institutions**	**7601**	**7192**	**6841**	**9083**	**9352**
科技活动人员 （万人）	**Personnel Engaged in S&T Activities (10 000 persons)**	**138.7**	**136.7**	**141.1**	**144.9**	**167.9**
#科学家和工程师	Scientists and Engineers	76.9	81.3	87.3	84.2	103.1
研究与试验发展折合全时人员 （万人年）	**Full-time Equivalent of R&D Personnel (10 000 man-year)**	**32.9**	**42.4**	**47.8**	**43.8**	**60.6**
#科学家和工程师	Scientists and Engineers	23.8	30.5	34.6	32.7	47.7
科技机构科技活动人员数 （万人）	**Personnel Engaged in S&T Activities in S&T Institutions (10 000 persons)**	**44.0**	**49.8**	**53.1**	**52.8**	**64.3**
#科学家和工程师	Scientists and Engineers	27.5	32.6	35.7	33.8	43.1
科技经费筹集额 （亿元）	**Funding for S&T Activities (100 million yuan)**	**922.8**	**1213.0**	**1588.6**	**2091.0**	**2665.8**
#政府资金	Government Funds	43.2	53.7	51.8	65.0	81.9
企业资金	Self-raised Funds by Enterprises	744.4	1020.3	1339.6	1832.0	2358.6
金融机构贷款	Loans From Finance Institutions	97.3	99.9	156.5	155.0	169.4
科技经费内部支出 （亿元）	**Intramural Expenditures on S&T Activities (100 million yuan)**	**823.7**	**1164.1**	**1467.8**	**2002.0**	**2543.3**
#开发新产品经费支出	Expenditures on New Product Development	388.9	509.2	639.0	821.0	1457.2
科技经费支出占产品销售收入的比重 (%)	Percentage of Expenditures on Science and Technology To Sales Revenue (%)	1.65	1.73	1.52	1.49	1.54
研究与试验发展经费支出（亿元）	**Expenditure on R&D (100 million yuan)**	**353.4**	**560.2**	**720.8**	**954.4**	**1250.3**
技术引进经费支出 （亿元）	**Expenditures for Indraught of Technology(100 million yuan)**	**245.4**	**372.5**	**405.4**	**368.0**	**296.8**
消化吸收经费支出 （亿元）	**Expenditures for Absorb and Digest (100 million yuan)**	**18.2**	**25.7**	**27.1**	**56.0**	**69.4**
购买国内技术支出 （亿元）	**Expenditures for Inner Technology (100 million yuan)**	**26.4**	**42.9**	**54.3**	**70.0**	**83.4**

21-41 高技术行业大中型工业企业科技活动投入情况（2005年）

行　业	Industry	科技活动人员（人）Technological Activities Personnel (person)	研究与试验发展折合全时人员(人年) Full-time Equivalent of R&D Personnel (man-year)
合计	**Total**	**347125**	**173161**
医药制造业	**Medical and Pharmaceutical Products**	**51832**	**19584**
#化学药品原药制造业	Original Chemical Medicine	33255	12574
化学药品制剂制造业	Chemical Medicine Preparation	12947	4976
生物、生化制品制造业	Biology, Biochemistry Products	3400	1534
航空航天器制造业	**Aviation and Aircrafts Manufacturing**	**56305**	**29870**
电子及通信设备制造业	**Electron and Communicate Equipments**	**169125**	**95091**
#通信设备制造业	Communicate Equipments	65856	49679
雷达及配套设备制造业	Radar Equipments	4042	1810
广播电视设备制造业	Broadcast and Television Equipments	3293	1740
电子器件制造业	Electronic Parts	32396	15211
电子元件制造业	Electronic Organs	35869	13672
家用视听设备制造业	Household Audiovisual	23723	11573
其他电子设备制造	Other Electron Equipment	3946	1407
电子计算机及办公设备制造业	**Electronic Computers and Office Equipments**	**45288**	**17484**
#电子计算机整机制造业	Electronic Computer	15890	7452
电子计算机外部设备制造业	Electronic Computer Peripheral Equipments	25908	8943
医疗器械及仪器仪表制造业	**Medical Treatment Instrument and Meter**	**24575**	**11132**
#医疗仪器设备及器械制造业	Medical Treatment Equipments and Instruments	3681	1262
仪器仪表制造业	Instruments and Meters	20894	9870

21-42 高技术行业大中型工业企业科技活动产出情况（2005年）

单位：万元

行　业	Industry	工业总产值 Gross Industrial Output Value	#新产品 New Products
合计	**Total**	**343671086**	**70348165**
医药制造业	**Medical and Pharmaceutical Products**	**42504491**	**5119020**
#化学药品原药制造业	Original Chemical Medicine	10940961	3674771
化学药品制剂制造业	Chemical Medicine Preparation	13118125	1125252
生物、生化制品制造业	Biology, Biochemistry Products	3536508	158905
航空航天器制造业	**Aviation and Aircrafts Manufacturing**	**7972261**	**3735597**
电子及通信设备制造业	**Electron and Communicate Equipments**	**168671291**	**38812363**
通信设备制造业	Communicate Equipments	58048422	16873125
雷达及配套设备制造业	Radar Equipments	1026892	243074
广播电视设备制造业	Broadcast and Television Equipments	2003488	165620
电子器件制造业	Electronic Parts	30392844	5207840
电子元件制造业	Electronic Organs	43032478	3027015
家用视听设备制造业	Household Audiovisual	30621071	13061339
其他电子设备制造	Other Electron Equipment	3546096	234351
电子计算机及办公设备制造业	**Electronic Computers and Office Equipments**	**106669548**	**20826746**
电子计算机整机制造业	Electronic Computer	55701590	12331549
电子计算机外部设备制造业	Electronic Computer Peripheral Equipments	45570911	7827349
医疗器械及仪器仪表制造业	**Medical Treatment Instrument and Meter**	**17853495**	**1854438**
#医疗仪器设备及器械制造业	Medical Treatment Equipments and Instruments	3525030	332455
仪器仪表制造业	Instruments and Meters	14328465	1521983

Basic Statistics on Scientific and Technological Activities Funds of Large-sized and Medium-sized Industrial Enterprises in High-tech Industry (2005)

#科学家和工程师 Scientists & Engineers	科技活动经费支出(万元) Expenditures on Technological Activities (10 000 yuan)	#R&D 经费 R&D Expenditures	#新产品经费 Expenditures for New Products	技术改造经费支出(万元) Expenditures for Technical Renovations (10 000 yuan)
141373	**5755848**	**3624985**	**4156916**	**1590214**
16139	**768073**	**399510**	**447725**	**441007**
10187	503355	273832	300482	299639
4269	183002	91512	97048	115426
1313	50131	22955	28373	14754
19251	**490127**	**277969**	**301632**	**368919**
81907	**3379228**	**2347164**	**2611326**	**611919**
46450	1427238	1196585	1267879	80990
1658	40101	24472	27487	17859
1518	35631	18105	27438	12355
11210	652923	328721	355849	160201
11000	457300	257997	315540	233566
8813	733319	500884	589840	102632
1257	32717	20401	27294	4316
14987	**831659**	**434480**	**617788**	**53753**
6838	426375	211999	271034	15313
7434	362506	207560	307709	35001
9088	**286762**	**165862**	**178445**	**114617**
1078	44381	34481	33142	12635
8010	242380	131381	145303	101982

Basic Statistics on Scientific and Technological Activities Outputs of Large-sized and Medium-sized Industrial Enterprises in High-tech Industry (2005)

(10 000 yuan)

产品销售收入 Total Revenue from the Sale of Products	#新产品 New Products	#出口 Export	利润总额 Profits	专利申请(项) Patent Applications (item)	#发明专利数 Inventions	拥有发明专利数(项) Patent Owned (item)
339217854	**69146633**	**26662498**	**14232287**	**16823**	**9635**	**6658**
40198316	**4693608**	**711093**	**3381953**	**2708**	**1659**	**1134**
11037070	3327695	637561	636757	1133	583	495
12218452	1045794	32611	1108648	1288	920	497
3182347	171308	32898	379937	242	135	49
7813693	**3373540**	**68223**	**324038**	**328**	**106**	**192**
166462526	**38520369**	**13808734**	**6508337**	**11022**	**6796**	**4268**
58340416	16431725	4390800	2778506	6602	5298	2959
924638	258585	74055	65247	9		5
1960208	161757	64059	91584	101	14	13
29586159	5127979	2545856	654021	812	524	540
41670325	3023700	1359491	2097922	947	219	369
30490068	13313107	5312171	641856	2434	719	371
3490713	203515	62302	179202	117	22	11
107221520	**20700912**	**11584410**	**2626516**	**1863**	**876**	**473**
56889725	12278252	4952764	1035621	1020	498	146
45087950	7750678	6038492	1372931	796	372	323
17521800	**1858204**	**490038**	**1391443**	**902**	**198**	**591**
3415789	319050	89164	304844	401	99	90
14106011	1539155	400874	1086599	501	99	501

21-43 高等学校科技活动情况
Basic Statistics on Higher Education for Scientific and Technological Activities

指　　标	Item	2001	2002	2003	2004	2005
科技活动人员　（万人）	**Personnel Engaged in S&T Activities (10 000 persons)**	**36.6**	**38.3**	**41.1**	**43.7**	**47.1**
#科学家和工程师	Scientists and Engineers	35.9	37.6	40.4	36.4	39.5
研究与试验发展机构　（个）	**R&D Institutions　(unit)**	**3481**	**3702**	**3332**	**3681**	**3936**
研究与试验发展折合全时人员　(万人年)	**Full-time Equivalent of R&D Personnel　(10 000 man-year)**	**17.1**	**18.1**	**18.9**	**21.2**	**22.7**
#科学家和工程师	Scientists and Engineers	16.8	18.2	18.6	20.6	22.2
#基础研究	Basic Research	5.1	5.6	5.8	7.5	7.8
应用研究	Applied Research	9.2	9.5	10	10.4	11.1
试验发展	Experimental Development	2.8	3.1	3.1	3.3	3.9
科技经费筹集额　（亿元）	**Funding for S&T Activities　(100 million yuan)**	**200.0**	**247.7**	**307.8**	**391.6**	**460.9**
#政府拨款	Government Appropriation Funds	109.8	137.3	164.8	210.6	251.5
企业资金	Self-raised Funds by Enterprises	72.5	89.6	112.6	148.6	172.9
金融机构贷款	Loans From Finance Institutions	1.0	1.3	1.5	1.3	0.3
科技经费内部支出　（亿元）	**Internal Expenditures on S&T Activities　(100 million yuan)**	**165.9**	**204.2**	**253.9**	**318.2**	**387.5**
#劳务费	Service Fees	29.8	38.2	49.1	58.3	71.5
固定资产购建费	Purchases or Construction of Fixed Assets	51.3	38.3	45.1	81.4	93.9
研究与试验发展经费支出（亿元）	**Expenditure for R&D　(100 million yuan)**	**102.4**	**130.5**	**162.3**	**200.9**	**242.3**
#基础研究	Basic Research	17.0	27.8	32.9	47.9	56.7
应用研究	Applied Research	59.0	67.1	89.7	108.8	125.0
试验发展	Experimental Development	26.4	35.6	39.7	44.2	60.6

21-44 国内、外三种专利申请受理数

Three Kinds of Applications for Patents Received from Domestic and Foreign Country (Region)

单位：项 (item)

指　标	Item	1990	1995	2000	2004	2005
申请受理数合计	**Total Applications Examined**	**41469**	**83045**	**170682**	**353807**	**476264**
发　明	**Inventions**	**10137**	**21636**	**51747**	**130133**	**173327**
国　内	Domestic	5832	10018	25346	65786	93485
职　务	Service	2482	2993	12609	41750	62270
大专院校	Universities and Colleges	509	574	1942	9683	14643
科研单位	Research Institutions	805	865	2228	4543	6726
工矿企业	Industrial and Mineral Enterprises	816	1086	8316	27029	40196
机关团体	Government Agencies and Organizations	352	468	123	495	705
非职务	Non-service	3350	7025	12737	24036	31215
国　外	Foreign	4305	11618	26401	64347	79842
职　务	Service	4018	11045	25334	62113	77575
非职务	Non-service	287	573	1067	2234	2267
实用新型	**Utility Models**	**27615**	**43741**	**68815**	**112825**	**139566**
国　内	Domestic	27488	43429	68461	111578	138085
职　务	Service	7424	8727	17792	35218	46879
大专院校	Universities and Colleges	811	771	965	2844	3843
科研单位	Research Institutions	1521	1376	1616	1881	2661
工矿企业	Industrial and Mineral Enterprises	3830	4739	14912	29933	39649
机关团体	Government Agencies and Organizations	1262	1841	299	560	726
非职务	Non-service	20064	34702	50669	76360	91206
国　外	Foreign	127	312	354	1247	1481
职　务	Service	55	190	259	1020	1171
非职务	Non-service	72	122	95	227	310
外观设计	**Designs**	**3717**	**17668**	**50120**	**110849**	**163371**
国　内	Domestic	3265	15433	46532	101579	151587
职　务	Service	1713	8193	22974	34312	49733
大专院校	Universities and Colleges	13	18	17	470	1435
科研单位	Research Institutions	64	104	278	285	359
工矿企业	Industrial and Mineral Enterprises	1310	6031	22634	33186	47552
机关团体	Government Agencies and Organizations	326	2040	45	371	387
非职务	Non-service	1552	7240	23558	67267	101854
国　外	Foreign	452	2235	3588	9270	11784
职　务	Service	418	2013	3432	8904	11230
非职务	Non-service	34	222	156	366	554

21-45 国内、外三种专利申请授权数

Three Kinds of Patents Granted from Domestic and Foreign Country (Region)

单位：项 (item)

指标	Item	1990	1995	2000	2004	2005
授权数合计	**Total Applications Certified**	**22588**	**45064**	**105345**	**190238**	**214003**
发 明	**Inventions**	**3838**	**3393**	**12683**	**49360**	**53305**
国 内	Domestic	1149	1530	6177	18241	20705
职 务	Service	908	932	2824	12176	14761
大专院校	Universities and Colleges	326	258	652	3484	4453
科研单位	Research Institutions	331	304	910	2406	2423
工矿企业	Industrial and Mineral Enterprises	206	205	1016	6128	7712
机关团体	Government Agencies and Organizations	45	165	246	158	173
非职务	Non-service	241	598	3353	6065	5944
国 外	Foreign	2689	1863	6506	31119	32600
职 务	Service	2496	1748	6222	30089	31555
非职务	Non-service	193	115	284	1030	1045
实用新型	**Utility Models**	**16952**	**30471**	**54743**	**70623**	**79349**
国 内	Domestic	16744	30195	54407	70019	78137
职 务	Service	5100	6766	15519	26218	29191
大专院校	Universities and Colleges	698	623	868	1910	2391
科研单位	Research Institutions	1280	1025	1529	1557	1599
工矿企业	Industrial and Mineral Enterprises	2249	2627	12821	22299	24743
机关团体	Government Agencies and Organizations	873	2491	301	452	458
非职务	Non-service	11644	23429	38888	43801	48946
国 外	Foreign	208	276	336	604	1212
职 务	Service	132	154	261	485	1011
非职务	Non-service	76	122	75	119	201
外观设计	**Designs**	**1798**	**11200**	**37919**	**70255**	**81349**
国 内	Domestic	1411	9523	34652	63068	72777
职 务	Service	751	5344	17789	24171	27566
大专院校	Universities and Colleges	7	10	28	111	555
科研单位	Research Institutions	35	156	248	174	170
工矿企业	Industrial and Mineral Enterprises	598	2554	17482	23830	26658
机关团体	Government Agencies and Organizations	111	2624	31	56	183
非职务	Non-service	660	4179	16863	38897	45211
国 外	Foreign	387	1677	3267	7187	8572
职 务	Service	336	1402	3108	6936	8254
非职务	Non-service	51	275	159	251	318

21-46 按地区分国内三种专利申请受理数和授权数（2005年）

Patent Applications Examined and Granted by Region (2005)

单位：项 (item)

地区	Region	申请受理数 合计 Number of Patent Applications Examined	发明 Inventions	实用新型 Utility Models	外观设计 Designs	授权数合计 Number of Patent Applications Granted	发明 Inventions	实用新型 Utility Models	外观设计 Designs
全国	**National Total**	**383157**	**93485**	**138085**	**151587**	**171619**	**20705**	**78137**	**72777**
北京	Beijing	22572	12102	6940	3530	10100	3476	4498	2126
天津	Tianjin	11657	4470	4690	2497	3045	763	1543	739
河北	Hebei	6401	1273	3618	1510	3585	371	2246	968
山西	Shanxi	1985	610	1036	339	1220	280	695	245
内蒙古	Inner Mongolia	1455	307	708	440	845	98	452	295
辽宁	Liaoning	15672	3267	8192	4213	6195	942	4235	1018
吉林	Jilin	4101	1290	1958	853	2023	391	1255	377
黑龙江	Heilongjiang	6050	1598	3293	1159	2906	407	2067	432
上海	Shanghai	32741	10441	8711	13589	12603	1997	4437	6169
江苏	Jiangsu	34811	6582	11071	17158	13580	1241	6483	5856
浙江	Zhejiang	43221	6776	12723	23722	19056	1110	6778	11168
安徽	Anhui	3516	903	1715	898	1939	238	1072	629
福建	Fujian	9460	1202	3182	5076	5147	242	1793	3112
江西	Jiangxi	2815	713	1280	822	1361	142	717	502
山东	Shandong	28835	4801	13100	10934	10743	903	6502	3338
河南	Henan	8981	1703	4594	2684	3748	356	2304	1088
湖北	Hubei	11534	2038	4835	4661	3860	733	2238	889
湖南	Hunan	8763	2594	3730	2439	3659	533	2137	989
广东	Guangdong	72220	12887	18951	40382	36894	1876	11017	24001
广西	Guangxi	2379	641	1183	555	1225	140	700	385
海南	Hainan	498	176	172	150	200	36	76	88
重庆	Chongqing	6260	918	2412	2930	3591	178	1428	1985
四川	Sichuan	10567	2256	3585	4726	4606	613	1948	2045
贵州	Guizhou	2226	782	1065	379	925	162	533	230
云南	Yunnan	2556	776	905	875	1381	306	563	512
西藏	Tibet	102	12	20	70	44		8	36
陕西	Shaanxi	4166	1693	1817	656	1894	445	1131	318
甘肃	Gansu	1759	712	790	257	547	116	338	93
青海	Qinghai	216	103	83	30	79	24	34	21
宁夏	Ningxia	516	106	185	225	214	40	130	44
新疆	Xinjiang	1851	320	1117	414	921	88	537	296
香港	Hong Kong	2645	552	581	1512	1669	139	361	1169
澳门	Macao	27	11	10	6	3		2	1
台湾	Taiwan	20599	8870	9833	1896	11811	2319	7879	1613

21-47 按国别(地区)分国外专利申请受理数及授权数（2005年）

Patent Applications Examined and Granted by Country (Region) (2005)

单位：项 (item)

国别（地区） Country (Region)		申请受理数 合计 Number of Patent Applications Examined	发明 Inventions	实用新型 Utility Models	外观设计 Designs	授权数合计 Number of Patent Applications Grant	发明 Inventions	实用新型 Utility Models	外观设计 Designs
总　计	**Total**	**92418**	**79421**	**1416**	**11581**	**42058**	**32419**	**1163**	**8476**
日　本	Japan	36221	30976	566	4679	18418	13883	577	3958
马来西亚	Malaysia	46	24	7	15	27	10	4	13
新加坡	Singapore	208	129	14	65	99	47	5	47
泰　国	Thailand	25	10	5	10	19	2	2	15
韩　国	Republic of Korea	9300	8131	143	1026	3273	2509	127	637
塞普路斯	Cyprus	17	17			5	3	1	1
印　度	India	217	198		19	67	38		29
摩纳哥	Monaco	4	3		1	8	7		1
南　非	South Africa	84	81	1	2	38	37		1
德　国	Germany	7502	6411	83	1008	3709	2894	32	783
荷　兰	Holland	3988	3735	8	245	1333	1179	5	149
英　国	United Kingdom	1613	1331	20	262	885	638	16	231
瑞　士	Switzerland	2106	1776	9	321	1103	867	10	226
丹　麦	Denmark	478	379	17	82	283	194	23	66
匈牙利	Hungary	33	31		2	22	22		
奥地利	Austria	284	260	3	21	170	145	3	22
比利时	Belgium	380	340		40	134	116	1	17
法　国	France	3190	2644	65	481	1674	1328	6	340
挪　威	Norway	168	142	1	25	69	62		7
俄罗斯联邦	Russia	50	46	3	1	47	37	10	
卢森堡	Luxembourg	53	48		5	38	37		1
列支敦士登	Liechtenstein	84	52		32	68	28		40
西班牙	Spain	373	179	14	180	161	65	5	91
捷　克	Czech	77	12	5	60	12	3		9
波　兰	Poland	22	18		4	4	1	2	1
爱尔兰	Ireland	82	66	3	13	48	24	7	17
芬　兰	Finland	851	752	3	96	496	402	2	92
意大利	Italy	1632	1046	27	559	691	388	15	288
瑞　典	Sweden	1101	1015	7	79	775	690	2	83
以色列	Israel	237	220	4	13	76	68		8
巴　西	Brazil	82	61	6	15	35	21	1	13
美　国	United States	20395	18000	360	2035	7595	6160	290	1145
加拿大	Canada	724	665	22	37	270	225	12	33
新西兰	New Zealand	84	77		7	24	23		1
澳大利亚	Australia	707	546	20	141	382	266	5	111

21-48 按国际标准分类的发明、实用新型专利申请数和授权数

Inventions and Utility Models of Patent Applications Examined and Granted by International Classifications

单位：项 (item)

分　　类	Item	2004 申请数 Applications Examined	2004 授权数 Applications Granted	2005 申请数 Applications Examined	2005 授权数 Applications Granted
合　计	**Total**	**240026**	**119983**	**287162**	**132654**
A 部(人类生活需要)	**Section A: Personal Use Items**	**47173**	**23159**	**57692**	**25744**
农、林、牧、渔	Agriculture, Forestry, Animal Husbandry and Fishery	5856	2758	6802	3157
烘烤、食用面团	Baking and Edible Doughs	455	162	460	210
屠宰、加工	Butchering and Meat Processing	92	40	113	49
食品、食物及处理	Foods or Foodstuffs and their Treatment	3297	905	3610	1334
烟类及用品	Tobacco, Cigars and Cigarettes	698	300	855	357
服　装	Clothing	1513	722	1433	611
帽类制品	Headwear	232	120	291	123
鞋　类	Footwear	1175	580	1295	635
男用服饰用品、珠宝	Haberdashery and Jewelry	367	329	490	310
手携及旅行用品	Hand or Traveling Articles	1794	874	2140	946
刷类用品	Brushware	592	237	606	307
家具、家庭日用品或设备	Furniture, Domestic Articles and Appliances	10020	4788	10865	5313
医学、兽医学、卫生学	Medical or Veterinary Science and Hygiene	17448	9094	24875	10179
救生、消防	Life-saving and Fire-fighting	762	527	621	458
体育、游戏、娱乐活动	Sports, Games, and Recreation	2872	1723	3236	1755
B 部(作业、运输)	**Section B: Industrial and Transportation**	**41558**	**22138**	**47676**	**24880**
物理或化学的方法或装置	Physical or Chemical Processes or Apparatus	3010	2099	4296	2262
破碎、研磨、粉碎	Crushing, Pulverizing, or Disintegrating	659	365	750	422
分选、分离	Separation of Solid Materials, Electrostatic Separation	274	183	321	172
离心装置、离心机	Centrifugal Apparatus or Equipment	135	66	163	77
喷射、雾化	Spraying or Atomizing General	981	665	1102	579
机械振动的产生和传递	Generation or Transmission of Mechanical Vibrations	79	32	68	42
固体分离、分选	Separating Solids from Solid Wastes	314	184	401	249
清　洁	Janitorial	379	202	523	231
固体废料的处理	Disposal of Solid Waste	182	96	218	121
金属加工、冲裁	Mechanical Metal-working and Stamping	1207	759	1547	837
铸造、粉末冶金	Casting and Powder Metallurgy	700	373	1075	585
机床、其他金属加工	Machine Tools	2687	1425	3397	1647
磨削、抛光	Grinding and Polishing	627	342	851	398
简单工具	Hand Tools, Portable Power Tools, and Workshop Equipment	1447	710	1786	826
手工、切割工具、切断	Hand Cutting Tools, Cutting, and Severing	696	334	997	425
木材加工、保存、钉钉机	Wood Preservation and Nailing or Stapling Machines	618	285	635	321
加工水泥、粘土和石料	Cement, Clay or Stone	685	341	561	431
塑料制品的加工	Plastics	1771	830	2145	1009
压力机	Presses	209	143	330	155
纸品制作、纸的加工	Paper Making and Processing Paper	220	68	206	150
叠层产品	Layered Products	613	289	970	365
印刷、打字机、印刷机	Printing, Lining Machines, and Typewriters	1803	853	2008	1127
装订、图册、文件夹	Bookbinding, Albums, and Files	724	289	704	394

21-48 续表 1 continued

单位：项 (item)

分类	Item	2004 申请数 Applications Examined	2004 授权数 Applications Granted	2005 申请数 Applications Examined	2005 授权数 Applications Granted
绘图具、办公附属用品	Writing or Drafting Devices	1905	687	1828	776
装饰艺术	Decorative Arts	857	319	847	422
一般车辆	Vehicles in General	5860	3078	5561	2982
铁　路	Railways	513	311	465	298
无轨陆用车牌	Land Vehicles other than Rail	3502	1796	3770	1948
船舶、船只、有关设备	Ships and Related Equipment	672	331	624	295
飞行器、航空、宇宙航行	Aircraft and Aviation	293	80	247	104
输送、包装、存贮、搬运	Conveying and Packing Inflammatory Materials	6339	3793	7143	4175
卷扬、提升、牵引	Hoisting, Lifting, and Hauling	1230	644	1586	851
液体的贮运	Opening or Closing Bottles, Jars or Similar Containers	251	135	361	161
鞍具、室内装璜	Saddlery ; Upholstery	19	13	21	7
微观结构技术	Micro-structural Technology	63	13	114	30
超微观技术	Nano-Technology	34	5	55	6
C 部(化学、冶金)	**Section C: Chemistry and Metallurgy**	**21163**	**12349**	**29451**	**14378**
无机化学	Inorganic Chemistry	1117	636	1460	776
水、废污水、泥浆的处理	Treatment of Water, Waste Water, Sewage or Sludge	1971	1093	2104	1259
玻璃、石棉和渣棉	Glass; Mineral of Slag Wool	814	258	785	542
水泥、陶瓷等、隔音材料	Cement, Concrete, Artificial Stone; Ceramics, Refractories	984	405	1213	577
肥料及制造	Fertilizers and Related Products	358	158	350	163
炸药、火柴	Explosives and Matches	74	35	45	54
有机化学	Organic Chemistry	4082	3155	6507	3248
有机高分子化合物	Organic Macromolecular Compounds	2979	2151	4310	2066
染料、涂料、抛光剂等	Dyes, Paints, Polishes, Resins, and Adhesives	1904	984	2853	1230
石油、煤气及炼焦工业	Petroleum, Gas or Coke Industries, Inert Gases	934	521	1656	738
动植物油、脂类	Animal or Vegetable Oils, Fats	402	223	590	339
生化、酒、醋、酶、遗传工程	Biochemistry, Beer, Spirits, Wine, Vinegar, Microbiology, Benzymology, Mutation or Genetic Engineering	2553	1235	3546	1377
糖或淀粉工业	Sugar Industry	28	12	35	9
大小原皮、毛皮、皮革	Skins, Hides, Pelts, Leather	69	38	82	33
黑色冶金	Metallurgy of Iron	510	252	716	444
冶金学、合金或有色合金	Metallurgy, Ferrous or Nonferrous Alloys	845	468	1146	508
金属加工涂料、防腐防锈	Coating Metallic Materials	834	383	1163	561
电解电泳方法及设备	Electrolytic or Electrophoretic Processes	536	275	653	364
晶体生长	Crystal Growth	169	67	237	90
D 部(纺织、造纸)	**Section D: Textiles and Papers Making**	**4795**	**2219**	**5352**	**2432**
线、纤维、纺纱	Natural or Artificial Threads or Fibers, Spinning	920	490	1044	510
纺纱、整经或络经	Yarns, Mechanical Finishing of Yarns or Rope	170	76	215	56
织　造	Weaving	364	159	390	163
编带、花边、针织、整理	Braiding, Lace-Making, Knitting	464	226	582	252
缝纫、绣花、簇绒	Sewing, Embroidery, Tufting	402	192	410	233
织物等的处理、洗涤	Treatment of Textiles, Laundering	1736	781	1993	795
绳、除电缆外的缆绳	Ropes and Cables, other than Electric	87	44	106	74
造纸、纤维素的生产	Paper making, Production of Cellulose	652	251	612	349
E 部(固定建筑物)	**Section E: Fixed Construction**	**14671**	**8028**	**16015**	**8955**
道路、铁路和桥梁的建筑	Construction of Roads, Railways, or Bridges	1178	645	1372	743
水利工程、基础、运土	Hydraulic Engineering, Foundations, Soil-shifting	1222	637	1461	789
给水、排水	Water Supply, Sewage	1783	919	1944	1005

21-48 续表 2 continued

单位：项 (item)

分 类	Item	2004 申请数 Applications Examined	2004 授权数 Applications Granted	2005 申请数 Applications Examined	2005 授权数 Applications Granted
建筑物	Building	4219	2150	4725	2475
锁、钥匙、门窗、保险箱	Locks, Keys, Windows or Door Fittings; Safes	2199	1336	2382	1414
一般门、窗、百叶窗、梯子	Doors, Windows, Shutters, or Roller Blinds in General; Ladders	1716	1024	1778	1110
钻井、采矿	Well Drilling, Mining	2354	1317	2353	1419
F 部(机械工程)	**Section F: Mechanical Engineering**	**28567**	**14581**	**32691**	**15503**
一般机器、发动机、蒸汽机	Machines or Engines in General; Engine Plants in General; Steam Engines	1190	443	1332	559
内燃机等	Combustion Engines	2170	781	2464	987
液力机械和其他发动机	Machines or Engines for Liquids	768	154	970	239
液体变容机械、泵	Positive-displacement Machines for Liquids; Pumps for Liquid or Elastic Fluids	2843	1459	3065	1472
液压调节器、液压技术	Fluid-pressure Adjustors; Hydraulic or Pneumatics in General	410	243	423	257
工程元件或部件	Engineering Elements or Units; General Measures for Producing and Maintaining Effective Functioning of Machines or Installations; Thermal Insulation in General	7385	3830	9047	3988
气体或液体的贮藏或分配	Storage or Distribution of Gases or Liquids	213	119	276	145
照 明	Lighting	1746	985	2301	1142
蒸汽的生产	Steam Generation	131	129	209	100
燃烧设备、燃烧技术	Combustion Apparatus; Combustion Processes	1463	999	1702	1000
采暖、炉灶、通风	Stoves, Ranges, Ventilation	6490	3315	6491	3400
制冷气体的液化和固化	Refrigeration or Cooling, Heat Pump Systems	1552	970	1890	899
干 燥	Drying	300	173	391	204
炉、窑、灶、罐	Furnaces, Kilns, Ovens	442	273	497	315
一般热交换	Heat Exchange in General	912	475	1094	508
武 器	Weapons	285	134	298	157
弹药、爆破	Ammunition, Blasting Caps	267	99	241	131
G 部(物理)	**Section G: Physics**	**38768**	**16944**	**45951**	**18415**
测量、测试	Measurements, Testing	9548	4604	11507	5421
光学技术	Optics	4890	1967	5587	2297
照相术、电影术、电刻术	Photography, Cinematography, Electrography	2510	847	2991	1070
测时技术	Horology	453	260	482	255
控制、调节技术	Controlling, Regulating	997	392	1352	415
计算、推算、计数技术	Computing, Calculating, Counting	10607	4277	12441	4316
核算装置	Measurement Devices	644	404	786	342
信号装置	Signaling	982	390	1558	431
教育、密码、显示、广告等	Education, Cryptography, Advertising, Seals	3178	1343	4153	1343
乐器、声学	Musical Instruments, Acoustics	793	508	931	570
信息的存储	Information Storage	3864	1711	3699	1766
仪器的零部件	Instrument Details	213	110	326	113
核物理、核工程	Nuclear physics, Nuclear Engineering	89	131	138	76
H 部(电学)	**Section H: Electricity**	**43331**	**20565**	**52334**	**22347**
基本电器元件	Basic Electric Elements	16054	8406	18911	10251
电力的发电、变电或配电	Generation, Conversion, or Distribution of Electric Power	4673	2293	5769	2465
基本电子电路	Basic Electronic Circuitry	1607	869	1886	773
电信技术	Telecommunications Techniques	17449	7677	21578	7013
其他类不包括的电技术	Electric Techniques Not Otherwise Provided for	3548	1320	4190	1845

注：此表不包括外观设计分类。

a) Designs patents are excluded in this table.

21-49 国有企事业单位专业技术人员数（年底数）

Number of Scientific and Technical Personnel in State-owned Enterprises and Institutions at the Year-end

单位：人 (person)

年份 地区	Year Region	合计 Total	工程技术人员 Engineering	农业技术人员 Agriculture	科学研究人员 Scientific Research	卫生技术人员 Health Care	教学人员 Teaching
	1990	16483542	4797176	450406	335066	2657588	8243306
	1991	17168413	5024000	463050	341934	2757993	8581436
	1992	17596532	5204950	476853	337146	2827599	8749984
	1993	18124140	5363632	496279	333851	2916255	9014123
	1994	18658689	5535329	519827	321036	2995940	9286557
	1995	19133834	5625850	535731	302879	3035335	9634039
	1996	19920785	5745367	579157	303177	3130788	10162296
	1997	20495006	5719337	611458	302684	3213762	10647765
	1998	20913343	5656735	635929	290537	3254958	11075184
	1999	21430140	5654863	654138	283532	3329706	11507901
	2000	21650807	5551098	670105	274506	3371966	11783132
	2001	21698037	5316327	674644	265554	3390233	12051279
	2002	21860024	5289166	666998	262692	3402326	12238842
	2003	21739699	4992867	683437	275496	3441109	12346790
	2004	21783019	4807869	704576	282002	3532282	12456290
	2005	21978684	4791227	705720	311166	3581181	12589390
北京	Beijing	339209	95517	5323	4832	73343	160194
天津	Tianjin	247879	63530	3822	2570	55000	122957
河北	Hebei	994818	124277	26311	3666	141955	698609
山西	Shanxi	664541	127236	20191	4118	100160	412836
内蒙古	Inner Mongolia	465517	62700	27393	2401	81181	291842
辽宁	Liaoning	728761	123366	26381	8453	151354	419207
吉林	Jilin	559747	90679	27676	4681	106529	330182
黑龙江	Heilongjiang	652998	118318	28008	6244	132515	367913
上海	Shanghai	333321	96815	2834	6140	79626	147906
江苏	Jiangsu	994976	122566	29880	7438	168043	667049
浙江	Zhejiang	667340	94541	18838	6239	135809	411913
安徽	Anhui	714146	90669	19381	3498	93224	507374
福建	Fujian	515774	66294	14212	4165	62967	368136
江西	Jiangxi	605243	72724	19694	3840	110022	398963
山东	Shandong	1504722	228141	49307	13484	270674	943116
河南	Henan	1209542	120339	27869	4978	172439	883917
湖北	Hubei	827515	91442	26670	6528	188315	514560
湖南	Hunan	917466	120619	29207	5881	178642	583117
广东	Guangdong	1193149	138132	17126	5400	242881	789610
广西	Guangxi	723900	110906	24159	3507	120265	465063
海南	Hainan	117455	10128	3699	598	21515	81515
重庆	Chongqing	366102	45747	14585	2833	58146	244791
四川	Sichuan	983303	115058	49240	5515	163317	650173
贵州	Guizhou	510248	60531	27484	1604	73583	347046
云南	Yunnan	647176	91716	37693	4834	102707	410226
西藏	Tibet	38219	3674	1559	509	7062	25415
陕西	Shaanxi	602104	88525	25555	3522	95850	388652
甘肃	Gansu	410195	57693	22161	5907	56119	268315
青海	Qinghai	97080	12832	7964	694	18477	57113
宁夏	Ningxia	121251	21316	9583	716	20859	68777
新疆	Xinjiang	403237	52888	32633	2449	67927	247340

注：1.1991年起，本表中专业技术人员包括社会科学领域专业技术人员及小学教师，但不包括行政机关专业技术人员。
2.分地区数据中不含中央属国有企事业单位人数。

a) Since 1991, the data include the personnel in the social field and the primary school teachers, but exclude the personnel in the administrative agencies.

b) The regional data exclude the personnel in the state-owned enterprises and institutions under the central government.

21-50 开发区高新技术企业主要经济指标（2005年）

Main Economic Indicators of High-tech Enterprises in Development Areas (2005)

开发区	Development Area	企业数（个）Number of Enterprises (unit)	从业人员（人）Number of Employees (person)	总产值（万元）Gross Output Value (10 000 yuan)	总收入（万元）Total Income (10 000 yuan)	出口总额（万美元）Exports (10 000 US dollars)
全　国	**National Total**	**41990**	**5211960**	**289575838**	**344156082**	**11164537**
北　京	Beijing	16343	687769	26040836	48652377	948823
天　津	Tianjin	2239	175377	6274422	7512858	245301
石家庄	Shijiazhuang	519	73427	3103402	3906812	21022
保　定	Baoding	148	42930	1666924	1774411	31240
太　原	Taiyuan	700	83089	4485181	5049331	10953
包　头	Baotou	411	96576	3289103	3215341	36318
沈　阳	Shenyang	1193	84106	4690224	6937657	55993
大　连	Dalian	1684	139780	5251957	6891170	150889
鞍　山	Anshan	371	72636	2332642	2710549	7111
长　春	Changchun	803	123490	8896036	9085646	36467
吉　林	Jilin	564	80478	5657999	5856792	13074
哈尔滨	Harbin	391	106928	4390407	5121516	27575
大　庆	Daqing	280	65203	3351623	3422166	6551
上　海	Shanghai	701	196146	22539765	26692228	1549770
南　京	Nanjing	217	97237	15185247	15930317	718803
常　州	Changzhou	478	75838	4023963	3953364	93953
无　锡	Wuxi	575	163399	12097437	12098435	812457
苏　州	Suzhou	691	226690	13338064	14802779	1680965
杭　州	Hangzhou	619	75065	5876721	8273124	286205
合　肥	Hefei	229	68787	3877009	4255717	34957
福　州	Fuzhou	180	53135	2430148	2407469	95777
厦　门	Xiamen	150	49563	5828873	5953521	374132
南　昌	Nanchang	273	77944	2558955	2838227	28060
济　南	Jinan	363	91494	5865669	6452846	36187
青　岛	Qingdao	196	72251	6858336	7213088	185281
淄　博	Zibo	190	93784	4867078	5080916	67307
潍　坊	Weifang	300	91045	4681532	4924299	50879
威　海	Weihai	182	47919	3614480	3717833	178334
郑　州	Zhengzhou	458	69138	3226976	3772288	18030
洛　阳	Luoyang	299	58520	2056514	2512098	22841
武　汉	Wuhan	907	142391	6289592	7249677	34465
襄　樊	Xiangfan	104	49670	2277097	2625929	5964
长　沙	Changsha	707	112009	5527711	6321246	55689
株　洲	Zhuzhou	164	54471	2384398	2520846	24515
广　州	Guangzhou	1120	114287	7285862	9767051	304493
深　圳	Shenzhen	287	103681	13680078	13164076	826365
珠　海	Zhuhai	366	116219	6386259	6397383	590537
惠　州	Huizhou	155	91657	5688634	5657477	465489
中　山	Zhongshan	401	64429	5152539	5489885	359491
佛　山	Foshan	94	56175	3914923	3765461	244687
南　宁	Nanning	307	50070	1870313	2537381	10134
桂　林	Guilin	233	59288	1635030	1650063	18707
海　南	Hainan	115	21368	1358570	1296828	9278
重　庆	Chongqing	704	166536	7163011	8502683	43849
成　都	Chengdu	351	105785	3315341	3885975	45253
绵　阳	Mianyang	96	45001	1883695	2062286	35371
贵　阳	Guiyang	130	59228	1647407	1681945	17852
昆　明	Kunming	120	39232	2245632	2652997	42041
西　安	Xi'an	3003	188973	7474753	11036545	110623
宝　鸡	Baoji	203	61898	1815336	1722521	8036
杨　凌	Yangling	90	9934	252586	321362	6696
兰　州	Lanzhou	414	40079	1537980	1685811	4061
乌鲁木齐	Urumqi	172	19835	431568	1145479	75686

21-51 各地区技术市场成交额

Transaction Value in Technical Market by Region

单位：万元 (10 000 yuan)

地区	Region	1998	1999	2000	2001	2002	2003	2004	2005
全国	**National Total**	**4358228**	**5234123**	**6507519**	**7827489**	**8841713**	**10846728**	**13343630**	**15513694**
北京	Beijing	815591	921889	1402871	1910065	2211738	2653574	4249975	4895922
天津	Tianjin	200298	220296	262581	306009	363262	420008	450276	507093
河北	Hebei	139090	153795	94143	46784	60406	67969	72718	103827
山西	Shanxi	9758	3955	5258	14693	39014	32251	59960	47980
内蒙古	Inner Mongolia	31332	29348	60287	62359	58197	108452	104085	109939
辽宁	Liaoning	280977	301546	347817	408698	508326	620200	752817	865167
吉林	Jilin	93167	103498	71390	88543	82921	87292.3	107900	122261
黑龙江	Heilongjiang	152569	157121	152382	111035	120110	121165	125715	142585
上海	Shanghai	314060	366324	738952	1061603	1202170	1427790	1716963	2317328
江苏	Jiangsu	330684	416683	449568	529165	594873	765163	897855	1008296
浙江	Zhejiang	162275	188496	276275	316652	389438	530353	581465	386954
安徽	Anhui	39545	48544	61012	64145	75423	87960	90675	142553
福建	Fujian	69363	80868	172601	136941	128988	166779	141395	171959
江西	Jiangxi	38332	51444	69299	62724	62891	83323	93661	111227
山东	Shandong	261922	275121	288135	321938	347650	525682	750850	983614
河南	Henan	176492	201661	211621	212589	178506	192690	203207	263737
湖北	Hubei	187596	230161	276000	338597	348603	412538	461700	501823
湖南	Hunan	220189	246605	286833	293887	323422	369306	408280	417394
广东	Guangdong	248122	344528	482104	539722	684532	805730	572651	1124740
广西	Guangxi	37021	25344	17741	37753	44406	41808	90955	94059
海南	Hainan	41533	82407		83990	9134	11978	1885	10007
重庆	Chongqing	92951	325345	296594	289484	409433	555083	596186	357059
四川	Sichuan	152000	125931	104150	126311	77524	128686	165640	190823
贵州	Guizhou	14071	762	620	599	13484	17892	13533	10488
云南	Yunnan	127222	172339	187742	255279	179496	228718	215555	159175
西藏	Tibet								
陕西	Shaanxi	57765	82537	92560	84615	151554	168022	139129	188977
甘肃	Gansu	28137	25816	26413	27393	54644	77581	119608	172736
青海	Qinghai	2917	4283		4657	12373	8291	12793	11812
宁夏	Ningxia	2643	4654	6402	8872	8496	10047	12827	14131
新疆	Xinjiang	30606	42822	66168	82387	100699	120395	133371	80029

21-52 各地区测绘部门生产完成情况（2005年）

Statistics on Projects Completed by Surveying and Mapping Departments by Region (2005)

地区	Region	大地测量 Geodesy GPS测量（点）Global Positioning System Survey (point)	水准测量（公里）Leveling (kilometer)	测图合计（幅）Mapping (unit)	地图数字化（幅）Digital Map (unit)	地图编制 Drawing Map 地形图（幅）Topographic Map (unit)	专题地图（幅/册）Special Map (unit/Volume)	地图集（册）Atlas (Volume)
全　国	**National Total**	**47508**	**144031**	**492554**	**47272**	**4185**	**2530**	**100**
北　京	Beijing	5383	1403	24373	215		16	3
天　津	Tianjin	1120	5983	4206	485	67	1	1
河　北	Hebei	4420	6643	5274	389	5	251	2
山　西	Shanxi	1497	4850	9478	1475		35	6
内蒙古	Inner Mongolia	634	1456	5453	40	21	12	3
辽　宁	Liaoning	6507	2273	21588	1930	1824	743	5
吉　林	Jilin	184	3244	3702	1400		22	
黑龙江	Heilongjiang	481	17678	235384	934		81	12
上　海	Shanghai			18761			6	3
江　苏	Jiangsu	1875	1965	8359	317		19	3
浙　江	Zhejiang	3824	1959	7707				
安　徽	Anhui	3497	3166	6504	1502	513		
福　建	Fujian	108		2300	486		43	11
江　西	Jiangxi	576	800	2995			36	
山　东	Shandong	815	3305	4250	361	70	75	
河　南	Henan	1494	5192	9095	1913	13	146	3
湖　北	Hubei	5674	7955	5469	1560	15	162	2
湖　南	Hunan	692	3250	3555	3986		199	23
广　东	Guangdong	717	3079	16265	693			
广　西	Guangxi	449	2464	7796	5149	10	38	
海　南	Hainan	222	1353	2651	2498	415	9	3
重　庆	Chongqing	245	1728	4700	1620		9	2
四　川	Sichuan	1754	12968	20385	4119	191	99	1
贵　州	Guizhou	666	60	3042	1837	1018	4	1
云　南	Yunnan	62	1324	4941	73		2	
西　藏	Tibet			45				
陕　西	Shaanxi	1023	14903	29187	7681		182	6
甘　肃	Gansu			3132	6164		19	5
青　海	Qinghai	1364	2435	2888	347		62	
宁　夏	Ningxia			3396	20			2
新　疆	Xinjiang	598	5245	7543	78	21	33	2
国家基础地理信息中心	National Geomatics Center of China	1627	27350	5691			13	
中国测绘科学研究院	China Academy of Surveying and Mapping Science			2439		2		
中国地图出版社	China Atlas Publishing House						213	1

21-53 各地区测绘资料提供情况（2005年）

Statistics on Output of Surveying and Mapping Materials by Region (2005)

地区	Region	地形图合计（张）Topographic Map (unit)	1:10000 (scale)	1:50000 (scale)	大地成果（点）Geodetic Results (point)	航摄成果（片）Aerial Photograph (piece)	挂图（张）Wall Map (unit)	地图集（册）Atlas (volume)
全国	**National Total**	**658939**	**159668**	**132853**	**70843**	**351882**	**5189**	**4733**
北京	Beijing	35410	3845					
天津	Tianjin	15096	788	50	132			
河北	Hebei	9256	5919	2760	778			
山西	Shanxi	9919	7925	1731	826	150		
内蒙古	Inner Mongolia	17534	5056	10451	5068			
辽宁	Liaoning	6199	5899	200	610	16	100	132
吉林	Jilin	7485	4534	2318	1225	17936	639	190
黑龙江	Heilongjiang	18536	3175	14402	651	158387	207	302
上海	Shanghai	253318	1200	112	23000	2800		
江苏	Jiangsu	5814	4653	1115	1873	757	96	494
浙江	Zhejiang	4138	4071	35	1455	213		
安徽	Anhui	7895	7074	629	10520	11096		
福建	Fujian	9616	8096	1312	2025	28537		
江西	Jiangxi	6454	4231	1584	1327	48126	5	
山东	Shandong	5208	3808	1134	2013	365	13	40
河南	Henan	2823	1965	646	1821	2407		
湖北	Hubei	5428	2007	2638	426	3853		
湖南	Hunan	12833	8796	3514	812	11057		
广东	Guangdong	11346	8746	2070	3697			
广西	Guangxi	15077	13316	1257	4246	32400	177	126
海南	Hainan	1108	1010	77				
重庆	Chongqing	25953	3587	1573	345		200	1
四川	Sichuan	35401	20412	10027	3045	3574	181	94
贵州	Guizhou	26039	16058	9113	641	3552	83	67
云南	Yunnan	10942	5622	5112	1461	495	287	
西藏	Tibet	16420	108	306	198		2426	1330
陕西	Shaanxi	4722	2249	2004	338	519	28	
甘肃	Gansu	2134	1104	280	371	19		
青海	Qinghai	2950	310	1355	274	117	590	12
宁夏	Ningxia	4540	3324	1160	179		82	
新疆	Xinjiang	12564	780	8545	1486	25506	75	1945
国家基础地理信息中心	National Geomatics Center of China	56781		45343				

21-54 各地区气象业务站点及观测项目情况（2005年）

Status of Operational Meteorological Stations and Their Observation Items (2005)

单位：个

地区和单位	Region, City and Units	地面观测站 Surface Observation Stations	高空观测站 Upper-air Observation Stations	自动气象站 Automatic Weather Stations	天气雷达观测站 Weather Radar Observation Stations	大气成分观测站 Atmospheric Composition Observation Stations	农业气象观测站 Agro-Meteorological Observation Stations	生态与农业气象试验站 Ecological &Agro-Meteorological Observation Stations
全国	**National Total**	**2405**	**120**	**7813**	**253**	**21**	**769**	**67**
北京	Beijing	21	1	85	2	1	7	
天津	Tianjin	14		18	1		7	
河北	Hebei	142	3	794	11	1	121	
山西	Shanxi	109	1	216	12	1	31	
内蒙古	Inner Mongolia	119	12	163	14	4	24	6
辽宁	Liaoning	53	1	206	6		22	3
吉林	Jilin	54	3	1	6		22	3
黑龙江	Heilongjiang	84	4	234	13		33	3
上海	Shanghai	11	1	168	1		1	
江苏	Jiangsu	70	3	362	14		19	3
浙江	Zhejiang	61	3	479	6		11	1
安徽	Anhui	81	2	896	15		22	3
福建	Fujian	67	2	80	4		23	4
江西	Jiangxi	87	2	369	4	1	18	1
山东	Shandong	116	2	111	16	1	55	1
河南	Henan	119	3	1460	17		30	3
湖北	Hubei	77	3	3	8		28	2
湖南	Hunan	97	3	39	5		22	4
广东	Guangdong	86	4	670	12	1	25	2
广西	Guangxi	92	6	108	5	2	24	5
海南	Hainan	21	3	40	3		6	
重庆	Chongqing	35	1	157	3		13	
四川	Sichuan	156	7	124	14		45	2
贵州	Guizhou	85	2	614	6		18	1
云南	Yunnan	125	5	51	15		21	4
西藏	Tibet	39	5	2	5	1	4	1
陕西	Shaanxi	99	4	40	11	2	18	1
甘肃	Gansu	80	9	20	5	2	22	4
青海	Qinghai	52	7	42	3		17	2
宁夏	Ningxia	24	1	12	3		16	3
新疆	Xinjiang	105	14	14	10	3	36	4
大连市	Dalian	8	1	67	1	1	2	
宁波市	Ningbo	7		117			2	
青岛市	Qingdao	7	1	17	1		3	
厦门市	Xiamen	2	1	34	1		1	
国家卫星气象中心	National Satellite Meteorological Center							
气象科学研究院	Chinese Academy of Meteorological Science							1

21-54 续表 continued

单位：个 (unit)

地区和单位	Region, City and Units	大气本底站 Atmospheric Background Stations	闪电定位监测站 Lightning Location Monitoring Stations	太阳辐射观测 Solar Radiation Observation Stations	沙尘暴监测 Sand and Dust Storm Monitoring	紫外线观测 UV Observation	酸雨观测 Acid Rain Observation	臭氧观测 Ozone Observation	干湿沉降观测 Dry & Wet Deposition Observation	卫星云图接收站点 Satellite Cloud Images Receiving Stations
全　国	**National Total**	**6**	**234**	**105**	**85**	**178**	**299**	**14**	**99**	**435**
北　京	Beijing	1	5	1	1	3	3	1	2	4
天　津	Tianjin		3	1	1	1	1			3
河　北	Hebei		12	1	2		5		1	7
山　西	Shanxi		5	3	3	2	5		1	13
内蒙古	Inner Mongolia		4	8	6		8		33	49
辽　宁	Liaoning		4	4	1	3	18		16	17
吉　林	Jilin			2	2	9	2			8
黑龙江	Heilongjiang	1	22	5	5	14	10	1	8	11
上　海	Shanghai		3	1			1	1		3
江　苏	Jiangsu		16	3	1	14	4			49
浙　江	Zhejiang	1	13	2		11	14	1	2	22
安　徽	Anhui		10	3		8	8	1		6
福　建	Fujian		8	2		2	3			8
江　西	Jiangxi		12	2		12	4			11
山　东	Shandong		9	3	4	15	17			22
河　南	Henan		8	3		20	3			22
湖　北	Hubei		16	2		1	4			30
湖　南	Hunan		5	3			6			12
广　东	Guangdong		6	3		7	5	1		9
广　西	Guangxi		10	3		1	10	2		10
海　南	Hainan			3		2	2			2
重　庆	Chongqing		3	1		1	35			4
四　川	Sichuan		18	7	1	2	6			6
贵　州	Guizhou		9	1		2	2	1		8
云　南	Yunnan	1	5	5		1	5			9
西　藏	Tibet	1		4		5	4			8
陕　西	Shaanxi		9	3	2	1	7		1	13
甘　肃	Gansu		5	6	4	12	4		4	18
青　海	Qinghai	1	4	5	24	2	5	1	27	10
宁　夏	Ningxia			2	1	1	2			3
新　疆	Xinjiang			12	4	13	4		3	13
大连市	Dalian			1	1		2		1	2
宁波市	Ningbo		4			1				10
青岛市	Qingdao		5			7	1			6
厦门市	Xiamen		1			1	1			2
国家卫星气象中心	National Satellite Meteorological Center									5
气象科学研究院	Chinese Academy of Meteorological Science				22	4	88	4		

21-55 各地区地震监测情况（2005年）
Situation of Earthquake Monitoring (2005)

单位：个 (unit)

地区	Region	地震台数 总数 Number of Seismic Stations	国家级台 Number of National Stations	省级台 Number of Provincial Stations	市、县级台 Number of Municipality/County-level Stations	企业台 Number of Enterprise Stations	强震观测点 Number of Strong Motion Observation Spots	宏观观测点 Number of Macro-observation Spots
全国	**National Total**	**1465**	**139**	**287**	**899**	**140**	**359**	**9042**
北京	Beijing	78	4	7	65	2	45	119
天津	Tianjin	9	4	5			34	
河北	Hebei	77	6	29	29	13	19	66
山西	Shanxi	64	5	6	28	25	11	694
内蒙古	Inner Mongolia	49	6	16	23	4		334
辽宁	Liaoning	51	6	12	28	5	2	396
吉林	Jilin	33	5	5	23			500
黑龙江	Heilongjiang	14	6	6	2		64	47
上海	Shanghai	22	2	13	7		28	9
江苏	Jiangsu	77	8	11	54	4	8	194
浙江	Zhejiang	35	3	4	28			3
安徽	Anhui	34	3	9	19	3		626
福建	Fujian	60	4	10	46		4	102
江西	Jiangxi	18	2	1	15			94
山东	Shandong	40	7	18	9	6	3	752
河南	Henan	28	2	10	11	5		662
湖北	Hubei	37	4	6	27		4	
湖南	Hunan	77	2	5	26	44		
广东	Guangdong	39	5	11	23		10	132
广西	Guangxi	8	3	5				630
海南	Hainan	19	2	4	13			238
重庆	Chongqing	4	1		3			8
四川	Sichuan	128	7	19	93	9	16	428
贵州	Guizhou							
云南	Yunnan	226	10	20	195	1	46	867
西藏	Tibet	8	3	5				
陕西	Shaanxi	69	5	9	46	9		439
甘肃	Gansu	90	9	18	57	6	25	817
青海	Qinghai	23	3	8	9	3	9	706
宁夏	Ningxia	28	4	3	20	1	3	98
新疆	Xinjiang	20	8	12			28	81

21-56 国家监督抽查产品质量情况

Results of Sampling Check on Product Quality under State Supervision

年 份 Year	抽查企业(个) Number of Enterprises Selected	无不合格品企业数(个) Number of Enterprises without Products Unqualified	抽查产品 Products Selected in Sampling (类) Number of Types (type)	抽查产品 Products Selected in Sampling (种) Number of Kinds (kind)	合格产品(种) Number of Products Qualified (kind)	样品合格率(%) Rate of Sample Products Qualified (%)
1988	2983		181	4031	3072	76.2
1989	3948	2795	180	5437	4092	75.3
1990	2495	1838	131	3457	2657	76.9
1991	2845	2186	138	3902	3122	90.0
1992	6845	4477	231	9007	6312	70.1
1993	8110	5509	281	9915	6980	70.4
1994	4640	3090	164	6036	4216	69.8
1995	5288	3851	185	6713	5061	75.4
1996	6779	5052	217	8318	6420	77.2
1997	5441	4116	187	6590	5162	78.3
1998	5431	4056	176	6770	5269	77.8
1999	7131	5440	207	8345	6562	78.6
2000	8142	6254	235	9705	7655	78.9
2001	8076	5992	207	9906	7513	75.8
2002	7892	6033	222	8850	6942	78.4
2003	10134	7809	249	11152	8738	78.4
2004	10919	8225	240	12343	9497	76.9
2005	11359	8427	249	12544	9478	75.6

21-57 各地区产品质量情况（2005年）

Quality of Products by Region (2005)

单位：% (%)

地区 Region	产品质量等级品率 Rates of Grade Products			新产品产值率 Rate of New Products	质量损失率 Rate of Loss Due to Bad Quality
	优等品率 Rate of Products with Excellent Quality	一等品率 Rate of Products with First Grade Quality	合格品率 Rate of Products with Qualified Quality		
全国 National Total	**39.00**	**36.42**	**24.56**	**18.47**	**0.38**
北京 Beijing	3.21	2.36	94.42	66.03	0.62
天津 Tianjin	37.42	30.06	32.52	28.04	0.03
河北 Hebei	45.97	39.91	14.11	17.20	0.42
山西 Shanxi	23.61	55.18	21.22	13.54	0.48
内蒙古 Inner Mongolia	40.22	30.71	29.08	0.20	0.38
辽宁 Liaoning	35.76	32.04	32.19	7.24	0.08
吉林 Jilin	76.69	21.07	2.25	23.90	1.13
黑龙江 Heilongjiang	12.61	69.07	18.32	21.81	0.43
上海 Shanghai					
江苏 Jiangsu	53.04	34.49	12.11	12.70	0.29
浙江 Zhejiang	40.54	47.86	11.61	28.45	0.66
安徽 Anhui	28.44	52.96	18.60	19.14	0.67
福建 Fujian	63.99	19.65	16.36	5.89	0.03
江西 Jiangxi	87.71	9.18	3.12	3.77	0.07
山东 Shandong	45.82	24.82	29.37	25.79	0.92
河南 Henan	21.89	61.51	16.60	19.72	0.49
湖北 Hubei	39.70	44.50	15.80	18.15	0.29
湖南 Hunan	52.61	43.60	3.80	24.65	0.38
广东 Guangdong	17.72	68.98	13.31	6.00	0.03
广西 Guangxi	19.48	16.74	63.78	5.81	0.26
海南 Hainan	77.89	3.08	19.03	2.23	0.03
重庆 Chongqing	13.90	76.90	9.20	48.56	0.38
四川 Sichuan	51.91	36.41	11.68	18.94	0.37
贵州 Guizhou	48.28	43.46	8.26	9.74	0.75
云南 Yunnan	56.74	24.44	18.61	22.22	
西藏 Tibet		36.72	63.28		0.15
陕西 Shaanxi	37.42	56.57	6.01	5.89	0.07
甘肃 Gansu					
青海 Qinghai	20.52	0.94	78.53	24.58	
宁夏 Ningxia					
新疆 Xinjiang					

注：本资料由73个重点工业城市抽样数据汇总而成。

a) Sampling data in this table are collected from 73 main industrial cities.

21-58 产品质量监督检查情况（2005年）

Results of Sampling Check under Supervision on the Quality of Products (2005)

项 目	Item	监督检验企业数（个）Number of Enterprises Supervised & Checked	有不合格产品企业所占比例（%）Proportion of Enterprises with Products Unqualified	批次合格率（%）Rate of Batch-time Qualified (%)
全国总计	**Total**	**218612**	**16.72**	**84.59**
农用产品	**Agricultural Products**	**15795**	**19.16**	**81.76**
拖拉机	Tractors	567	12.52	84.97
农用化肥	Chemical Fertilizers	8365	19.61	79.09
化学农药	Chemical Pesticides	1836	14.71	87.29
饲料	Forages	4266	22.08	81.58
农用薄膜	Agricultural Films	563	15.63	88.09
种子	Seeds	198	7.58	91.92
加工食品和饮料	**Food and Beverage**	**79801**	**20.56**	**81.82**
食用植物油	Edible Vegetable Oil	14198	16.40	84.25
糕点糖果	Cake	35544	20.43	81.75
乳制品	Dairy Products	2939	17.42	86.73
罐头	Canned Food	1768	23.59	79.25
白酒	White Spirit	22423	23.26	79.88
啤酒	Beer	907	10.92	94.00
冷冻饮料	Frozen Beverage	2022	28.39	74.38
家用电器	**Household Electric Appliances**	**3309**	**17.14**	**83.90**
收录机、音响设备	Radio and Cassette Players, Hi-fi Stereo Component Systems	570	16.67	80.92
电视机、录像机	TV Sets, Videocorders	124	20.16	78.62
洗衣机	Washing Machines	101	11.88	88.79
电风扇	Electric Fans	205	15.12	86.09
电话机	Telephone Sets	167	14.97	90.42
冰箱、冷藏冷冻箱	Refrigerators, Freezers	89	12.36	88.89
电热器具	Electric Heating Appliances	679	15.76	83.00
厨房电器具	Electric Cooking Utensils	1162	17.47	85.51
抽油烟机	Smoke Absorbers	212	27.36	75.86
轻工产品	**Light Industry Products**	**26670**	**17.34**	**83.41**
纸	Paper	1483	25.62	75.55
纸制品	Paper Products	7157	18.63	81.38
玩具	Toys	379	22.96	39.39

21-58 续表 continued

项　目	Item	监督检验企业数（个）Number of Enterprises Supervised & Checked	有不合格产品企业所占比例（%）Proportion of Enterprises with Products Unqualified	批次合格率（%）Rate of Batch-time Qualified (%)
家具	Furniture	8566	17.22	88.60
铝制品压力锅	Aluminum Products	278	12.23	90.44
眼镜(架、片)	Spectacles (Glass & Frame)	7496	15.14	85.70
灯泡灯管	Electric Bulbs & Fluorescence Tubes	950	15.89	84.85
镇流器	Ballast	159	10.06	91.16
电热、燃气热水器	Water Heaters	202	6.44	94.09
纺织、鞋类产品	**Textile and Shoes**	**10827**	**11.91**	**88.81**
布(印染、色织、坯布)	Cloth	1500	10.73	89.59
毛织品	Wool Fabrics	631	13.47	86.61
丝麻织品	Silk & Fabrics	560	8.57	91.52
针织品	Knit Goods	1750	17.26	85.98
鞋	Shoes	6386	10.85	89.52
化工产品	**Chemical Products**	**6296**	**11.80**	**88.33**
涂料、油漆	Paint	5094	12.15	87.66
化学试剂	Chemical Reagent	1202	10.32	91.42
建材产品	**Building Raw Materials**	**50309**	**12.85**	**88.72**
水泥	Cement	10008	7.98	93.64
水泥预制构件	Cement Prefabricated Components	12821	8.35	91.98
砖瓦	Bricks & Tiles	25630	16.23	85.39
油毡油纸	Asphalt Felts & Oilpaper	211	23.22	79.31
平板玻璃	Plate Glass	229	5.68	95.84
水暖管件	Water Pipe	1410	26.38	81.50
机械、电器产品	**Mechanical and Electrical Products**	**14043**	**9.83**	**90.37**
轴承	Bearings	763	11.80	90.74
阀门、泵	Valves	2812	5.05	92.33
电线	Electric Wire	4504	13.77	86.52
低压电器元件	Low-voltage Electric Elements	3451	9.13	94.07
电动工具	Electric Tools	508	10.43	89.45
消防器材	Fire-fighting Equipment & Materials	611	6.55	93.39
电动机柴油机	Motors & Diesel Engines	1394	8.68	91.16
冶金产品及金属制品	**Metallurgical and Metal Products**	**5019**	**14.21**	**87.00**
线材	Wire Rod	2414	14.21	88.26
型材	Section Steel	2605	14.20	85.61
其他产品	**Others**	**6543**	**20.31**	**77.45**

21-59 各地区出入境货物检验检疫情况（2005年）

货值单位：万美元

地区	Region	总计 Total				工业品检验检疫 Commodity			
		批次 Number of Batch	#不合格 Disqualification	货值 Value	#不合格 Disqualification	批次 Number of Batch	#不合格 Disqualification	货值 Value	#不合格 Disqualification
总计	**National Total**	**14686108**	**88480**	**70098963**	**2194108**	**13127828**	**68041**	**64566051**	**1219082**
北京	Beijing	161883	1431	1216051	5775	139490	984	1160609	4658
天津	Tianjin	339587	3242	3573961	256595	297410	1951	3308042	183671
河北	Hebei	127932	665	1305007	50919	101837	503	1143086	10260
山西	Shanxi	22668	96	226661	1427	20024	95	213496	1423
内蒙古	Inner Mongolia	195255	2749	455972	2370	158910	2540	423713	2332
辽宁	Liaoning	373433	1229	2994564	81763	270919	596	2468498	14062
吉林	Jilin	77054	217	355864	975	49806	163	285586	860
黑龙江	Heilongjiang	132030	1029	234659	854	105960	990	191010	842
上海	Shanghai	1266479	25860	7716941	211296	1189079	24179	7371019	162450
江苏	Jiangsu	1259737	5026	7649836	337475	1208622	4458	7189947	117145
浙江	Zhejiang	1060358	3620	3604566	61606	1005253	3259	3359529	26529
宁波	Ningbo	416295	1861	3188277	77015	397805	1473	3080950	29653
安徽	Anhui	79347	307	329767	6823	66069	300	291551	6812
福建	Fujian	569971	2269	1903084	35933	493929	1531	1636778	15239
厦门	Xiamen	242749	1868	1028115	30512	221317	1714	955406	18642
江西	Jiangxi	53593	340	253129	1286	44810	314	228060	1249
山东	Shandong	841644	7328	5996182	537809	554377	6091	4759366	377662
河南	Henan	50963	357	396638	1507	39839	284	350247	1218
湖北	Hubei	51235	481	359926	6102	42405	370	322940	5174
湖南	Hunan	68759	462	321425	4443	55868	453	292212	4410
广东	Guangdong	4941909	14695	15696959	261300	4722658	8585	14930039	106212
深圳	Shenzhen	1343402	3026	6723925	88197	1135607	2241	6460731	57531
珠海	Zhuhai	452825	290	2253586	2250	421879	185	2228000	1816
广西	Guangxi	142675	782	475105	98956	69289	526	344689	45239
海南	Hainan	17653	203	152148	2964	13113	183	128508	2903
重庆	Chongqing	37514	59	204849	614	33069	58	189868	614
四川	Sichuan	59681	282	320088	1381	51012	210	268619	1193
贵州	Guizhou	16538	86	83572	390	15704	78	76853	365
云南	Yunnan	97558	5632	250244	9433	43504	1031	166193	3661
西藏	Tibet	2311	9	10551	13	1670	6	7274	11
陕西	Shaanxi	31718	116	239698	10283	22309	112	200795	10195
甘肃	Gansu	9435	44	115272	211	4615	30	99314	176
青海	Qinghai	2501	78	33956	224	2385	71	33632	214
宁夏	Ningxia	1868	30	29457	265	1604	26	28602	255
新疆	Xinjiang	137548	2711	398928	5138	125681	2451	370886	4408

注：国家出入境货物检验检疫数据是由全国直属的35个检验检疫局直报国家质检总局汇总得到。

General Statistics on Entry-Exit Inspection and Quarantine of Freight by Region (2005)

(10 000 US$)

动物及动物产品检验检疫		Animal and Its Product		植物及植物产品检验检疫		Plant and Its Product		食品检验检疫		Food	
批次 Number of Batch	#不合格 Disqualification	货值 Value	#不合格 Disqualification	批次 Number of Batch	#不合格 Disqualification	货值 Value	#不合格 Disqualification	批次 Number of Batch	#不合格 Disqualification	货值 Value	#不合格 Disqualification
802361	**7397**	**3022995**	**48845**	**2329638**	**29973**	**6363329**	**1154711**	**1405540**	**16987**	**5048563**	**926134**
14468	46	43739	46	12467	387	28413	1086	20411	263	53392	779
17809	156	88840	1585	70381	1611	330156	88971	38852	1076	233434	69991
25350	20	181095	205	21367	481	141603	42731	22801	160	125865	40632
6310	2	53497	12	2340		12750		2482	1	12943	4
3950	3	24661	8	137835	329	137896	73	34859	209	26267	38
49896	125	240407	403	118047	623	447077	67778	96615	613	494026	67631
7729	31	15542	109	31463	49	67970	23	26801	46	65711	112
2297		8393		98484	908	121013	60	25646	39	42173	12
53216	1128	245443	10378	127769	3154	492010	47121	79210	996	265167	25435
38875	352	185314	3435	97489	1420	815764	247922	47998	533	436984	220116
46638	273	226801	3326	123043	440	270889	36377	50711	333	218791	34935
6748	116	44271	1144	50283	621	169004	55912	18017	371	104751	47234
2206		11766		16415	174	49553	6237	12387	6	32779	11
19930	379	120211	4069	111297	432	243407	17651	72766	547	247867	17480
10852	54	35229	132	28182	138	79043	11807	20559	148	65375	11832
5342	7	17796	3	6945	30	22304	42	4573	25	18877	35
119022	408	687808	3402	268741	3495	1146512	260427	281634	1142	1204193	159172
9080	30	40672	192	7781	164	41255	178	8469	70	36485	243
3619	49	14220	518	5948	239	28925	1708	7422	76	31638	594
6475	6	16599	27	8683	49	21987	355	8248	4	22185	6
163826	2238	433366	16647	429034	8977	907223	170615	194324	4718	696228	140888
105333	241	129469	426	347491	1582	386828	33032	147013	721	237619	29507
23409	13	20580	24	32995	102	20055	1841	27207	101	26370	392
17198	21	21000	821	73603	250	144019	52939	69188	219	122859	52896
2587	12	17701	57	4974	34	17983	365	4136	19	22638	60
6714		16506		2530	1	5972	0	3624	1	8080	0
18698	16	57509	152	7081	48	18574	33	7793	62	43339	129
141		210		825	7	8072	25	380	5	2067	17
8746	1640	6485	1659	53932	3895	92715	7389	44850	4229	69635	5195
459		1240		784	3	3426	3	462	3	2933	3
2272		3941		9480	45	40926	1190	8671		37397	
195		1729		4508	14	14441	36	4698	14	14869	36
88	6	505	9	39	1	79	1	97	7	225	10
156	1	2514	2	251	3	1318	8	2816	266	59564	47035
2727	24	7936	54	17151	267	34168	775	12400	226	24617	699

a) National data of entry-exit inspection and quarantine of freight are collected from the 35 inspection and quarantine bureaus directly under the General Administration of Quality Supervision.

21-60 中国科协系统科技活动情况（2005年）

项 目		Item		总 计 Total
机构和人员		**Number of Associations or Academic Societies and Personnel**		
实有机构	(个)	Number of Associations or Academic Societies	(unit)	6936
从业人员	(人)	Number of Employed Persons	(person)	45793
学会个人会员	(万人)	Number of Personal Members of Academic Societies	(10 000 person)	
学术交流活动		**Academic Exchange**		
境内举办学术交流活动	(次)	Number of Academic Meetings Held in China	(time)	22365
参加人数	(万人次)	Number of Participants	(10 000 person-time)	309.96
科学技术普及（综合）		**S&T Popularization Activities (Overview)**		
举办科普讲座	(次)	Number of S&T Popularization Lectures	(time)	122215
听讲人数	(万人次)	Number of Participants	(10 000 person-time)	15970.15
举办科普展览	(次)	Number of S&T Popularization Exhibitions	(time)	53890
参观人数	(万人次)	Number of Participants	(10 000 person-time)	12832.86
举办科普宣传	(次)	Number of S&T Popularization Propagation	(time)	56504
工作人员	(万人次)	Working Staffs and S&T Personnel	(10 000 person-time)	89.89
科普场馆	(个)	Number of S&T halls and stations	(unit)	
展厅面积	(平方米)	Dimension of Exhibition Hall	(square metre)	
科普教育基地	(个)	Number of Education Bases for S&T Popularization	(unit)	
标准科普画廊建筑总长度	(米)	Length of Building of Galleries for S&T Popularization	(metre)	
本年展览总长度	(米)	Length of Exhibition	(metre)	
科学技术普及专题1（青少年科技教育）		**S&T Popularization Activities specifics Activities for Education in Popular S&T among Adolescent**		
举办青少年科普讲座	(次)	Number of S&T Popularization Lectures for Adolescent	(time)	
听讲人数	(万人次)	Number of Participants	(10 000 person-time)	
举办青少年科普展览	(次)	Number of S&T Popularization Exhibitions for Adolescent	(time)	
参观人数	(万人次)	Number of Participants	(10 000 person-time)	
举办青少年科技竞赛	(次)	Number of S&T Competitions for Adolescent	(time)	9999
参加人数	(万人次)	Number of Participants	(10 000 person-time)	3091.09
举办青少年科技夏冬令营	(次)	Number of Summer-Winter Camps for Adolescent	(time)	3522
参加人数	(万人次)	Number of Participants	(10 000 person-time)	67.77
科学技术普及专题2（全国科普日活动）		**S&T Popularization Activities specifics --National S&T Popularization Day Activities**		
举办科普讲座	(次)	Number of S&T Popularization Lectures	(time)	11648
听讲人数	(万人次)	Number of Participants	(10 000 person-time)	528.68
举办科普展览	(次)	Number of S&T Popularization Exhibitions	(time)	9470
参观人数	(万人次)	Number of Participants	(10 000 person-time)	1882.79
举办科普宣传	(次)	Number of S&T Popularization Propagation	(time)	12698
工作人员	(万人次)	Working Staffs and S&T Personnel	(10 000 person-time)	21.68
开展科技咨询	(次)	Number of S&T Popularization Consultation	(time)	21848
工作人员	(万人次)	Working Staffs and S&T Personnel	(10 000 person-time)	15.47
科学技术普及专题3（科技下乡活动）		**S&T Popularization Activities specifics --Popularization Activities Conducted in Rural Section**		
组织科技下乡次数	(次)	Number of S&T Popularization activities in Rural Section	(time)	54689
举办科普讲座	(次)	Number of S&T Popularization Lectures	(time)	30138
听讲人数	(万人次)	Number of Participants	(10 000 person-time)	1122.70
举办科普展览	(次)	Number of S&T Popularization Exhibitions	(time)	15501
参观人数	(万人次)	Number of Participants	(10 000 person-time)	2644.18
开展科技咨询	(次)	Number of S&T Popularization Consultation	(time)	54607
工作人员	(万人次)	Working Staffs and S&T Personnel	(10 000 person-time)	30.85
国际民间科技交流活动		**International S&T Exchange**		
国外及港澳台地区来访团组	(个)	Visits from Foreign Countries, Hong Kong, Macao and Taiwan	(unit)	3113
来访总人数	(人次)	Total Number of Visitors	(person-time)	37576
派往国外及港澳台地区团组	(个)	Visits to Foreign Countries, Hong Kong, Macao and Taiwan	(unit)	2109
派出总人数	(人次)	Total Number of Visitors	(person-time)	18595
社会、科技服务活动		**Public Service on S&T**		
"金桥工程"本年完成数	(项)	Number of Completed "Golden Bridge Program" Projects	(item)	
完成技术咨询合同	(项)	Number of Consultative Contracts Completed	(item)	44804
反映科技建议	(项)	Number of S&T Proposals	(time)	21983
举办培训班	(次)	Number of Training Courses	(unit)	58200
培训人数	(万人次)	Persons Trained	(10 000 person-time)	982.15
科技传媒情况		**S&T Media**		
主办科技期刊	(种)	Number of Scientific & Technological Journals	(kind)	2155
总印数	(万册)	Printed Copies	(10 000 copies)	11930.16
主办科技报纸	(种)	Number of Scientific & Technological Newspapers	(kind)	115
总印数	(万份)	Printed Copies	(10 000 copies)	15786.6
编著科技图书	(种)	Number of Scientific & Technological books	(kind)	1889
总印数	(万册)	Printed Copies	(10 000 copies)	1132.54

Basic Statistics on Scientific and Technological Activities of China Associations for Science and Technology (2005)

科协小计					学会小计		
Total Number of Associations	中国科协 China Associations	省级科协 Provincial Associations	地级科协 Prefectural Associations	县级科协 County Associations	Total Number of Learned Societies	全国性学会 National Learned Societies	省级学会 Provincial Learned Societies
3136	1	31	397	2707	3800	167	3633
33827	1503	6290	9182	16852	11966	2133	9833
						408	439
9164	45	281	5007	3831	13201	3148	10053
148.95	2.31	10.37	89.39	46.88	161.01	44.07	116.94
100944	288	1695	20062	78899	21271	2059	19212
15175.21	11.26	10347.44	817.45	3999.06	794.94	265.18	529.76
50308	40	1239	10460	38569	3582	495	3087
11687.58	223.20	1089.47	2442.77	7932.14	1145.28	101.10	1044.18
49646	33	695	12836	36082	6858	534	6324
82.86	0.03	1.14	15.36	66.33	7.03	0.26	6.77
688	1	26	157	504			
588775	21000	89441	239608	238726			
8955	482	866	2259	5348			
563221		5500	63785	493936			
1173581		54604	252645	866332			
19708	244	463	4268	14733			
1219.13	10.35	25.95	223.76	959.07			
11095	39	260	2489	8307			
2192.48	222.00	128.66	518.70	1323.12			
9421	9	195	2167	7050	578	67	511
2371.73	0.39	677.81	797.24	896.29	719.36	302.89	416.47
3146	5	69	690	2382	376	41	335
62.66	0.03	0.9	12.46	49.27	5.11	0.54	4.57
11648	1	130	2407	9110			
528.68	0.02	9.14	98.59	420.93			
9470	1	205	2255	7009			
1882.79	1.20	68.30	463.12	1350.17			
12698	3	179	2942	9574			
21.68	0.01	0.37	3.86	17.44			
21848	15	593	3677	17563			
15.47	0.01	0.24	2.83	12.39			
47209	3	789	5547	40870	7480	301	7179
25536	32	419	3696	21389	4602	222	4380
1049.65	0.60	14.06	96.16	938.83	73.05	3.9	69.15
14586		268	2501	11817	915	111	804
2521.35		86.28	522.41	1912.66	122.83	10.11	112.72
44717	423	449	5503	38342	9890	259	9631
28.39	0.05	0.51	3.48	24.35	2.46	0.09	2.37
498	35	196	178	89	2615	784	1831
8894	1169	1944	4288	1493	28682	11761	16921
510	154	205	122	29	1599	503	1096
4217	1349	1640	968	260	14378	5396	8982
7547		1597	2764	3186			
40598		12014	24640	3944	4206	121	4085
17185	6	546	4900	11733	4798	249	4549
49703	40	837	6158	42668	8497	1281	7216
824.61	1.05	7.41	84.81	731.34	157.54	18.64	138.9
73	8	58	7		2082	846	1236
3440.39	108.1	3323.89	8.4		8489.77	5186.61	3303.16
42	1	38	3		73	9	64
11979.1	109.2	11728.6	141.3		3807.5	636.0	3171.5
1039	108	180	266	485	850	179	671
701.57	90.23	156.17	189.01	266.16	430.97	136.85	294.12

主要统计指标解释

普通高等学校 指按照国家规定的设置标准和审批程序批准举办的，通过全国普通高等学校统一招生考试，招收高中毕业生为主要培养对象，实施高等教育的全日制大学、独立设置的学院和高等专科学校、高等职业学校和其他机构。

大学、独立设置的学院主要实施本科层次以上教育，高等专科学校、高等职业学校实施专科层次教育，其他机构是承担国家普通招生计划任务不计校数的机构。包括普通高等学校分校和批准筹建的普通高等学校等。

成人高等学校 指按照国家规定的设置标准和审批程序批准举办的，通过全国成人高等学校统一招生考试，招收具有高中毕业或同等学历的在职从业人员为主要培养对象，利用函授、业余、脱产等多种形式对其实施高等学历教育的学校。包括职工高等学校、农民高等学校、管理干部学院、教育学院、独立函授学院、广播电视大学、其他机构等。其他机构是承担国家成人招生计划任务不计校数的机构。

小学学龄儿童净入学率 指调查范围内已入小学学习的学龄儿童占校内外学龄儿童总数(包括弱智儿童，不包括盲聋哑儿童)的比重。计算公式为:

$$\text{小学学龄儿童净入学率}=\frac{\text{已入学的小学学龄儿童数}}{\text{校内外小学学龄儿童总数}}\times 100\%$$

国家财政性教育经费 包括国家财政预算内教育经费，各级政府征收用于教育的税费，企业办学校教育经费，校办产业、勤工俭学和社会服务收入用于教育的经费。

财政预算内教育经费 指中央、地方各级财政或上级主管部门在年度内安排，并计划拨到教育部门和其他部门主办的各级各类学校、教育事业单位，列入国家预算支出科目的教育经费，包括教育事业拨款、科研经费拨款、基建拨款和其他经费拨款。

科技活动 指在自然科学、农业科学、医药科学、工程与技术科学、人文与社会科学领域(简称科学技术领域)中，与科技知识的产生、发展、传播和应用密切相关的有组织的活动。可分为研究与试验发展(R&D)、研究与试验发展成果应用及相关的科技服务三类活动。该定义是联合国教科文组织考虑成员国特别是发展中国家开展科技统计工作的需要，而对科技活动所作的统计界定。

科技活动人员 指直接从事科技活动、以及专门从事科技活动管理和为科技活动提供直接服务，累计的实际工作时间占全年制度工作时间10%及以上的人员。(1)直接从事科技活动的人员包括：在独立核算的科学研究与技术开发机构、高等学校、各类企业及其他事业单位内设的研究室、实验室、技术开发中心及中试车间(基地)等机构中从事科技活动的研究人员、工程技术人员、技术工人及其它人员；虽不在上述机构工作，但编入科技活动项目(课题)组的人员；科技信息与文献机构中的专业技术人员；从事论文设计的研究生等。(2)专门从事科技活动管理和为科技活动提供直接服务的人员，包括：独立核算的科学研究与技术开发机构、科技信息与文献机构、高等学校、各类企业及其他事业单位主管科技工作的负责人，专门从事科技活动的计划、行政、人事、财务、物资供应、设备维护、图书资料管理等工作的各类人员，但不包括保卫、医疗保健人员、司机、食堂人员、茶炉工、水暖工、清洁工等为科技活动提供间接服务的人员。该指标用来反映投入科技活动人力的规模。

科学家与工程师 指科技活动人员中具有高、中级技术职称(职务)的人员和不具有高、中级技术职称(职务)的大学本科及以上学历人员。该指标用来反映投入科技活动人力的素质。

研究与试验发展(R&D) 指在科学技术领域，为增加知识总量，以及运用这些知识去创造新的应用进行的系统的创造性的活动，包括基础研究、应用研究、试验发展三类活动。国际上通常采用R&D活动的规模和强度指标反映一国的科技实力和核心竞争力。

基础研究 指为了获得关于现象和可观察事实的基本原理的新知识(揭示客观事物的本质、运动规律，获得新发现、新学说)而进行的实验性或理论性研究，它不以任何专门或特定的应用或使用为目的。其成果以科学论文和科学著作为主要形式。用来反映知识的原始创新能力。

应用研究 指为获得新知识而进行的创造性研究，主要针对某一特定的目的或目标。应用研究是为了确定基础研究成果可能的用途，或是为达到预定的目标探索应采取的新方法(原理性)或新途径。其成果形式以科学论文、专著、原理性模型或发明专利为主。用来反映对基础研究成果应用途径的探索。

试验发展 指利用从基础研究、应用研究和实际经验所获得的现有知识，为产生新的产品、材料和装置，建立新的工艺、系统和服务，以及对已产生和建立的上述各项作实质性的改进而进行的系统性工作。其成果形式主要是专利、专有技术、具有新产品基本特征的产品原型或具有新装置基本特征的原始样机等。在社会科学领域，试验发展是指把通过基础研究、应用研究获得的知识转变成可以实施的计划(包括为进行检验和评估实施示范项目)的过程。人文科学领域没有对应的试验发展活动。主要反映将科研成果转化为技术和产品的能力，是科技推动经济社会发展的物化成果。

研究与试验发展人员 指参与研究与试验发展项目研究、管理和辅助工作的人员，包括项目(课题)组人员，企业科技行政管理人员和直接为项目(课题)活动提供服务的辅助人员。反映投入从事拥有自主知识产权的研究开发活动的人力规模。

研究与试验发展人员全时当量 指全时人员数加非全时人员按工作量折算为全时人员数的总和。例如：有两个全时人员和三个非全时人员(工作时间分别为20%、30%和70%)，则全时当量为2+0.2+0.3+0.7=3.2人年。为国际上比较科技人力投入而制定的可比指标。

专业技术人员 指从事专业技术工作和专业技术管理工作的人员，即企事业单位中已经聘任专业技术职务从事专业技术工作和专业技术管理工作的人员，以及未聘任专业技术职务，现在专业技术岗位上工作的人员。包括工程技术人员，农业技术人员，科学研究人员，卫生技术人员，教学人员，经济人员，会计人员，统计人员，翻译人员，图书资料、档案、文博人员，新闻出版人员，律师、公证人员，广播电视播音人员，工艺美术人员，体育人员，艺术人员及企业政治思想工作人员，共十七个专业技术职务类别。用来反映科技人力资源情况。

科技活动经费筹集 指从各种渠道筹集到的计划用于科技活动的经费，包括政府资金、企业资金、事业单位资金、金融机构贷款、国外资金和其他资金等。反映各社会经济主体对促进科技进步所做的努力。

政府资金 指从各级政府部门获得的计划用于科技活动的经费，包括科学事业费、科技三项费、科研基建费、科学基金、教育等部门事业费中计划用于科技活动的经费以及政府部门预算外资金中计划用于科技活动的经费等。

企业资金 指从自有资金中提取或接受其他企业委托的，科研院所和高校等事业单位接受企业委托获得的，计划用于科研和技术开发的经费。不包括来自政府、金融机构及国外的计划用于科技活动的资金。

金融机构贷款 指从各类金融机构获得的用于科技活动的贷款。

科技活动经费内部支出 指报告年内用于科技活动的实际支出，包括劳务费、科研业务费、科研管理费，非基建投资购建的固定资产、科研基建支出以及其他用于科技活动的支出。不包括生产性活动支出、归还贷款支出及转拨外单位支出。反映科技投入实际完成情况。

劳务费 指以货币或实物形式直接或间接支付给从事科技活动人员的劳动报酬及各种费用。包括各种形式的工资、津贴、奖金、福利、离退休人员费用、人民助学金等。反映改善科技人员待遇情况。

固定资产购建费 指报告年内使用非基建投资购建的固定资产和用于科研基建投资的实际支出额，即固定资产实际支出和科研基建投资实际完成额之和。固定资产是指长期使用而不改变原有实物形态的主要物资设备、图书资料、实验材料和标本以及其他设备和家具、房屋、建筑物。反映用于改善科研条件和科研手段方面的投入情况。

新产品 指采用新技术原理、新设计构思研制、生产的全新产品，或在结构、材质、工艺等某一方面比原有产品有明显改进，从而显著提高了产品性能或扩大了使用功能的产品。既包括政府有关部门认定并在有效期内的新产品，也包括企业自行研制开发，未经政府有关部门认定，从投产之日起一年之内的新产品。用来反映科技产出及对经济增长的直接贡献。

专利 是专利权的简称，是对发明人的发明创造经审查合格后，由专利局依据专利法授予发明人和设计人对该项发明创造享有的专有权。包括发明、实用新型和外观设计。反映拥有自主知识产权的科技和设计成果情况。

发明 指对产品、方法或者其改进所提出的新的技术方案。是国际通行的反映拥有自主知识产权技术的核心指标。

实用新型 指对产品的形状、构造或者其结合所提出的适于实用的新的技术方案。反映具有一定技术含量的技术成果情况。

外观设计 指对产品的形状、图案、色彩或者其结合所作出的富有美感并适于工业上应用的新设计。反映拥有自主知识产权的外观设计成果情况。

Explanatory Notes on Main Statistical Indicators

Regular Institutions of Higher Learning refer to educational establishments set up according to the government evaluation and approval procedures, enrolling graduates from senior secondary schools and providing higher education courses and training for senior professionals. They include full-time universities, colleges, high professional schools, high professional vocational schools and others.

Universities and colleges are mainly providing undergraduate courses; those high professional schools and high professional vocational schools are mainly providing professional trainings; and others refer to educational establishments, which are responsible for enrolling students but not covered in the total number of schools, including: branch schools of universities and colleges, and universities and colleges that have been proved and prepared to construct.

Institutions of Higher Learning for Adults refer to educational establishments, set up in line with relevant rules approved by the government, enrolling staff and workers with senior secondary school or equivalent education, and providing higher education courses in many forms of correspondence, spare time, or full time for adults. Professionals thus trained receive a qualification equivalent to graduates studying regular courses at regular universities, colleges and professional colleges. Institutions of higher learning for adults include schools of high education for staff and workers, schools of high education for peasants, colleges for management cadres, pedagogical colleges, independent correspondence colleges, Radio and TV universities and other educational establishments. Other educational establishments are responsible for enrolling adult students but not covered in the number of schools.

Enrollment Rate of Primary School Age Children refers to the proportion of school age children enrolled at schools to the total number of school age children both in and outside schools (including retarded children, but excluding blind, deaf and mute children). The formula is:

Enrollment Rate of Primary School-age Children = (Total Primary School-age Children at Schools)/(Total Primary School age Children Both at and Outside Schools) x 100%

Government Appropriation for Education refers to state budgetary fund for education, taxes and fees collected by governments at all levels that are used for education purpose, education fund for enterprise-run schools, income from school-run enterprises, work-study programme and social services that are used for education purpose.

Budgetary Fund for Education refers to education fund that is planned to allocate to various schools and education institutions by central and local financial departments at various levels within the reference year, which is within the state budgetary expenditure, including: appropriate funds for education, science and research, capital construction and others.

Scientific and Technological Activities (S&T Activities) refer to organized activities which are closely related with the creation, development, dissemination and application of the scientific and technical knowledge in the fields of natural sciences, agricultural science, medical science, engineering and technological science, humanities and social sciences (referred to as scientific and technological fields). S&T activities can be classified in to 3 categories: research and development (R&D) activities, application of R&D results, and related S&T services. This statistical definition is made by UNICHIEF for scientific and technological activities to meet the need of carrying out statistical work in this field for its member countries in particular those developing countries.

Personnel Engaged in S&T Activities refer to personnel directly engaged in S&T activities, in the management of S&T activities, and in providing direct service to S&T activities, who spend over 10% of the total working hours in a year in S&T activities. (1) Personnel directly engaged in S&T activities include researchers, engineers, technicians and other related personnel engaged in S&T activities in independent-accounting R&D institutions, institutions of higher learning, and in research institutes, laboratories, technology development centers and central experiment workshops under enterprises and institutions. Also included are people working in S&T research project teams, professional and technical personnel working in S&T information archiving institutes, and graduate students working on the design of their thesis. (2) Personnel engaged in the management of S&T activities and in providing direct service to S&T activities include senior management people responsible for S&T activities in independent-accounting R&D institutions, S&T information archiving institutes, institutions of higher learning, and in enterprises and institutions where S&T activities are undertaken. Also included are people responsible for the planning, administration, personnel management, financial management, logistics supply, equipment maintenance, information and library management that are related with S&T activities. People providing indirect services are excluded, such as security, medical service, drivers, plumbers, cleaners and those providing catering and related service. This indicator reflects the size of personnel engaged in S&T activities.

Scientists and Engineers refer to persons engaged in S&T activities who have obtained titles of senior and middle level professional positions, and those without such position but have completed university or higher education. This indicator reflects the quality of personnel engaged in S&T activities.

Research and Development (R&D) refers to systematic and creative activities in the field of science and technology aiming at increasing the knowledge and using the knowledge for new application. R&D includes 3 categories of activities: basic research, applied research and experiments and development. The scale and intensity of R&D are widely used internationally to reflect the strength of S&T and the core competitiveness of a country in the world.

Basic Research refers to empirical or theoretical research aiming at obtaining new knowledge on the fundamental principles of phenomena of observable facts to reveal the nature and law of movement of objects and to acquire new discoveries or new theories. Basic research takes no specific or designated application as the aim of the research. Results of basic research are mainly released or disseminated in the form of scientific papers or monographs. This indicator reflects the original innovation capacity of knowledge.

Applied Research refers to creative research aiming at obtaining new knowledge on a specific objective or target. Purpose of the applied research is to identify the possible use of results from basic research, or to explore new (fundamental) methods or new approaches. Results of applied research are expressed in the form of scientific papers, monographs, fundamental models or invention patents. This indicator reflects the exploration of ways to apply the results of basic research.

Experiments and Development refer to systematic activities aiming at using the knowledge from basic and applied researches or from practical experience to develop new products, materials and equipment, to establish new production process, systems and services, or to make substantial improvement on the existing products, process or services. Results of experiment and development activities are embodied in patents, exclusive technology, and monotype of new products or equipment. In social sciences, experiment and development activities refer to the process of converting the knowledge from basic or applied researches into feasible programmes (including conduct of demonstration projects for assessment and evaluation). There are no experiment and development activities in the science of humanities. This indicator reflects the capability of transferring the results of S&T into technique and products, which is the materialized measurement of S&T pushing forward the economic and social development.

R&D Personnel refer to persons engaged in research, management and supporting activities of R&D, including persons in the project teams, persons engaged in the management of S&T activities of enterprises and supporting staff providing direct service to the research projects. This indicator reflects the size of personnel engaged in R&D activities with independent intellectual property.

Full-time Equivalent of R&D Personnel refers to the sum of the full-time persons and the full-time equivalent of part-time persons converted by workload. For instance, if there are 2 full-time persons and 3 part-time workers (20%, 30% and 70% of working hours respectively on R&D activities), the full-time equivalent is 2+0.2+0.3+0.7=3.2 person-years. This is an internationally comparable indicator of input of personnel in S&T activities.

Professional and Technical Personnel refer to persons engaged in professional and technical work or in the management of professional and technical activities, i.e., people with professional or technical positions who are engaged in professional and technical work or in the management of professional and technical activities, and people without professional or technical positions but are working on professional or technical posts. They include professionals and technicians working in 17 categories of technical occupations including engineering, agriculture, scientific researches, medical service, teaching, economic research and application, accounting, statistics, translation, libraries, archives, cultural and museum service, journalism and publication, lawyers, notarization service, radio and television broadcasting, handicraft and fine arts, sports, performing art, and political workers in enterprises. This indicator reflects the condition of human resources in S&T.

Funding for S&T Activities refers to funds obtained from various sources for S&T activities, including government funds, self-raised funds by enterprises, self-raised funds by institutions, loans from financial institutions, foreign funds and other funds. This indicator reflects the efforts made by various social economic entities in promoting the development of S&T.

Government Funds refer to funds obtained from government agencies at all levels to be used for S&T activities, including fund for scientific undertakings, 3 kinds of fund for S&T activities, fund for capital construction for scientific researches, science fund, funds from education expenditures by education departments for S&T activities, and extra-budget fund from government agencies for S&T activities.

Self-raised Funds by Enterprises refers to self-raised funds by enterprises from their own expenditure or from other enterprises and funds received by universities or research institutions from enterprises for scientific research or technical development projects. Excluded in this category are funds from government agencies, financial institutions or from foreign institutions.

Loans from Financial Institutions refer to loans from various financial institutions for S&T activities.

Internal Expenditures on S&T activities refer to the actual expenditures on S&T activities during the reference year, including service fees, expenditure on research activities, expenditure on research management, purchase or construction of fixed assets not included in the investment for capital construction, expenditure on capital construction for scientific researches, and other expenditures on S&T activities. Not included are expenditure on production activities, repayment of loans and transfer expenditure. This indicator reflects the real accomplishment of input in S&T.

Service Fees refer to direct or indirect payment, in cash or in kind, made to personnel engaged in S&T activities as remuneration and other fees. They include, in various forms, salaries, subsidies, bonus, benefits, retirement pension, stipend, etc. This indicator reflects the improvement of treatment toward S&T personnel.

Purchase or Construction of Fixed Assets refers to the fixed assets purchased or constructed using funds other than the investment in capital construction, and the actual expenditure on capital construction for scientific researches. In other words, it is the sum of the actual expenditure on fixed assets and the accomplished investment in capital construction for scientific researches. Fixed assets refer to main materials and equipment, literatures and documents in libraries, materials for experiments, specimen, instruments, furniture, buildings and constructions that can be used for a long time without changing the form and shape of those articles or constructions. This indictor reflects the input in improving the condition of S&T and the means of scientific research.

New Products refer to new products produced with new technology and new design, or products that represent noticeable improvement in terms of structure, material, or production process so as to improve significantly the character or function of the older versions. They include new products certified by relevant government agencies within the period of certification, as well as new products designed and produced by enterprises within a year without certification by government agencies. This indictor reflects the direct contribution of S&T output to economic growth.

Patent is an abbreviation for the patent right and refers to the exclusive right of ownership by the inventors or designers for the creation or inventions, given from the patent offices after due process of assessment and approval in accordance with the Patent Law. Patents are granted for inventions, utility models and designs. This indicator reflects the achievements of S&T and design with independent intellectual property.

Inventions refer to the new technical proposals to the products or methods or their modifications. This is universal core indicator reflecting the technologies with independent intellectual property.

Utility Models refer to the practical and new technical proposals on the shape and structure of the product or the combination of both. This indicator reflects the condition of technological results wih certain technical content.

Designs refer to the aesthetics and industrially applicable new designs for the shape, pattern and color of the product, or their combinations. This indicator reflects the appearance design achievements with independent intellectual property.

22

文化、体育和卫生

Culture, Sports and Public Health

简 要 说 明

一、本篇资料的主要内容

本篇主要反映文化、体育、卫生、新闻出版、广播电影电视事业的发展情况。

文化部分主要包括艺术表演团体、艺术表演场所、公共图书馆、博物馆、文化馆、档案馆、文化站、广播、电影、电视、新闻出版以及文物等文化事业的机构、人员、经费和业务活动情况。体育部分主要包括群众体育和竞技体育，主要内容有体育系统职工情况，竞技体育成绩，体育锻炼达标人数以及与国外体育交往次数和人数等情况。卫生部分主要内容有卫生机构、人员、床位数，医院诊疗人次及入院人数，主要疾病死亡原因及构成，传染病的发病及死亡以及卫生事业费用测算等情况。

二、本篇的资料来源

根据各部门制定的统计报表制度汇总加工整理而成。艺术事业、图书馆事业、群众文化事业的资料主要来自文化部；档案馆资料来自国家档案局；文物资料来自国家文物局；广播、电影、电视资料来自国家广播电影电视总局；新闻出版资料来自国家新闻出版总署；体育部分的资料来自国家体育总局；卫生部分的资料来自卫生部。

详细资料分别见《中国文化文物统计年鉴》（文化部计划财务司编）、《中国新闻出版统计资料汇编》（新闻出版署计财司编）、《广播电影电视资料汇编》（广电总局计财司编）和《中国卫生统计年鉴》（卫生部信息中心编）。

Brief Introduction

I. Main Content:

Data in this chapter mainly show the development of culture, sports, public health, news and publication, radio broadcasting, films and televisions.

Data on culture cover mainly the situations on institutions, personnel and business activities of arts (performing groups and venues), libraries, museums, cultural centers, archives, cultural stations, broadcasting, films, televisions, news and publication. Data on sports cover mass sports (sports for all) and athletics sports, including mainly the number of staff and workers in sports departments,number of stadiums and gymnasiums, achievements in athletic sport events, number of persons who have come up to the National Physical Training Program Standards and the international exchanges of sport delegations. Data on public health include mainly the number of institutions, personnel, hospital beds, number of patients treated and in-patients, major diseases as the causes of death and the proportion to the total deaths, the incidence of, and the deaths caused by infectious diseases, estimation of health cost, etc.

II. Sources of Data

Data are collected and tabulated in accordance with the statistical reporting schemes stipulated by the departments concerned. Data on the causes of arts, libraries, mass culture are provided by the Ministry of Culture. Data on archives are from National Bureau of Archives. Data on broadcasting, film and television are mainly from State Administration of Broadcasting, Film and Television. Data on news and publication are mainly provided by the State Agency of News and Publication. Data on sports are mainly from the State Sports Administration. Data on public health are mainly from the Ministry of Public Health.

Detailed information please refer to "*China Cultural Relics Yearbook*" (Department of Financial Management, Ministry of Culture), "*Collection of China News and Publication Statistical Information*" (Department of Financial Management, State Agency of News and Publication), "*Collection of Broadcasting, Film and Television Statistics*" (Department of Financial Management, State Administration of Broadcasting, Film and Television and "*Annual Statistical Yearbook on National Health Care*" (Information Center, Ministry of Public Health).

22-1 文化、文物单位机构、人员数（2005年）

Number of Institutions and Personnel in Culture and Cultural Relics (2005)

机构类别	Category of Institution	机构数（个） Number of Institutions (unit)	从业人数（人） Number of Employed Persons (person)
文化单位合计	**Culture**	**381512**	**1798718**
艺术表演团体	Arts Performance Troupes	2805	141678
话剧、儿童剧、滑稽剧团	Drama, Children Play and Comedy Troupes	118	8383
歌剧、舞剧、歌舞剧团	Opera, Ballet and Dance Troupe	97	9671
歌舞团、轻音乐团	Song and Dance Troupe, Light Music Troupe	345	21585
乐团、合唱团	Philharmonic and Chorus Troupes	37	2425
文工团、文宣队、乌兰牧骑	Cultural and Performance Troupes and Ulanmuchi (equestrian art troupes)	351	10206
戏曲剧团	Local Opera Troupes	1531	72525
其中：京剧	Local Beijing Opera Troupes	109	7981
曲、杂、木、皮团	Recitation and Ballad Troupes, Acrobatics and Circus Troupes, Puppet Show Troupes and Shadow Play Troupes	189	9218
综合性艺术表演团体	Comprehensive Art performance Troupes	137	7665
艺术表演场所	Arts Centers	1866	35678
剧场	Theaters and Music Halls	770	14157
影剧院	Cinemas	996	19176
音乐厅	Concert Halls	20	473
综合性	General Performing Theaters	35	1334
其他艺术表演场馆	Others	45	538
公共图书馆事业	Public Libraries	2762	50423
群众文化事业	Mass Culture	41588	122500
群众艺术馆	Mass Art Centers	447	13407
文化馆	Cultural Centers	2779	37502
文化站	Cultural Stations	38362	71591
#乡文化站	Township Cultural Stations	34593	62949
艺术教育事业	Culture and Education	189	13464
其他文化事业	Other Cultural Units	332302	1434975
艺术创作机构	Art Creation Institutions	352	2576
艺术研究机构	Art Research Institutions	188	3138
艺术展览机构	Art Exhibition Institutions	56	1271
#美术馆	Art Galleries	37	754
其他	Others	331706	1427990
文物单位合计	**Cultural Relics**	**4030**	**82988**
文物保护管理机构	Agencies of Historical Relics Preservation	2186	34052
文物科研机构	Scientific and Research Historical Relics Agencies	88	3444
其他文物机构	Other Historical Relics Agencies	78	4579
博物馆	Museums	1581	38603
综合性博物馆	Comprehensive Museums	797	16738
历史类博物馆	History Museums	532	16217
艺术类博物馆	Arts Museums	126	3043
自然科技类博物馆	Nature Science and Technology Museums	24	628
其他	Other Museums	102	1977
文物商店	Cultural Relics Agencies	97	2310

22-2 文化、文物单位数

Number of Institutions for Culture and Cultural Relics

单位：个 (unit)

年份 Year / 地区 Region		艺术表演团体 Art Performance Troupes	艺术表演场所 Art Performance Places	文化馆和群众艺术馆 Cultural Centers and Mass Art Centers	公共图书馆 Public Libraries	博物馆 Museums
	1978	3150	1095	2840	1218	349
	1980	3533	1444	3130	1732	365
	1985	3317	1673	3295	2344	711
	1990	2805	2011	3321	2527	1013
	1995	2684	1972	3259	2608	1194
	1996	2664	1934	3284	2620	1219
	1997	2663	1947	3286	2628	1282
	1998	2652	1929	3287	2652	1339
	1999	2632	1911	3294	2669	1363
	2000	2630	1912	3297	2677	1392
	2001	2605	1854	3241	2696	1461
	2002	2587	1829	3243	2697	1511
	2003	2618	1912	3228	2709	1515
	2004	2759	1928	3221	2720	1548
	2005	2805	1866	3226	2762	1581
北京	Beijing	20	39	22	25	34
天津	Tianjin	16	28	19	32	18
河北	Hebei	126	95	175	153	46
山西	Shanxi	156	44	131	122	86
内蒙古	Inner Mongolia	109	27	115	110	33
辽宁	Liaoning	66	59	132	126	39
吉林	Jilin	61	73	81	63	18
黑龙江	Heilongjiang	84	45	144	96	46
上海	Shanghai	85	160	33	28	25
江苏	Jiangsu	129	87	117	103	99
浙江	Zhejiang	273	125	99	90	80
安徽	Anhui	92	90	118	88	43
福建	Fujian	91	76	90	84	82
江西	Jiangxi	79	58	113	104	82
山东	Shandong	117	94	158	145	75
河南	Henan	199	156	204	136	78
湖北	Hubei	99	66	124	102	91
湖南	Hunan	91	83	140	120	73
广东	Guangdong	139	68	139	129	146
广西	Guangxi	118	23	115	95	49
海南	Hainan	22	13	21	20	16
重庆	Chongqing	29	17	42	43	18
四川	Sichuan	84	65	201	141	55
贵州	Guizhou	26	12	95	91	11
云南	Yunnan	135	38	149	149	32
西藏	Tibet	27	24	41	4	2
陕西	Shaanxi	113	107	121	111	82
甘肃	Gansu	76	30	100	92	69
青海	Qinghai	12	1	52	43	15
宁夏	Ningxia	23	12	25	20	6
新疆	Xinjiang	91	47	110	96	28

注：除文化馆和群众艺术馆外,其余指标分地区数据不含中央单位数。

a) Of indicators except culture centers and mass art centers, data of regions don't include central government units.

22-3 艺术表演团体演出情况（2005年）

Basic Statistics on Performance of Art Troupes (2005)

种 类	Item	演出场数（万场）Number of Performances (10 000 shows)	#到农村演出 Shows in Rural Areas	观众人数（万人次）Number of Spectators (10 000 person-times)
总 计	**Total**	**45.9**	**26.9**	**38891**
#国有剧团	Troupes Sponsored by State-owned Units	29.9	15.9	28962
集体经营剧团	Troupes Sponsored by Collective Units	10.7	7.1	7141
按剧种分:	**Grouped by Art Troupes**			
话剧、儿童剧、滑稽剧团	Drama, Children's Play and Comedy Troupes	0.9	0.1	1516
歌舞剧团	Song and Dance Drama Troupes	1.4	0.4	1407
歌舞团、轻音乐团	Song and Dance Troupe, Light Music Troupes	4.0	1.2	3839
文工团、宣传队、乌兰牧骑	Cultural and Performance Troupes and Ulanmuchi (equestrian art troupes)	4.0	2.4	3079
乐团、合唱团	Philharmonic and Chorus Troupes	0.2		231
戏曲剧团	Local Opera Troupes	25.9	20.3	24377
#京 剧	Local Beijing Opera Troupes	1.3	0.8	1181
曲艺、杂技、木偶、皮影团	Recitation and Ballad Troupes, Acrobatics and Circus Troupes, Puppet Show Troupes, and Shadow Play Troupes	8.0	1.8	2783
综合性艺术表演团体	General Art Performing Troupes	1.5	0.7	1659

注：歌舞剧团包括歌剧、舞剧、歌舞剧团（下表同）。

a) Song and dance drama troupes include opera, dance and light music troupes. The same as in the following table.

22-4 艺术表演团体收支情况（2005年）

Income and Expenditures of Art Troupes (2005)

种 类	Item	补贴团数（个）Number of Troupes Receiving Government Subsidies (unit)	总收入（万元）Total Income (10 000 yuan)	#财政补助收入 Government Subsidies	#演出收入 Income from Performance	总支出（万元）Total Expenditures (10 000 yuan)	经费自给率(%) Total Income/Total Expenditures Ratio (%)
总 计	**Total**	**2321**	**527146**	**354766**	**98268**	**514000**	**31.3**
#国有剧团	Troupes Sponsored by State-owned Units	1895	486153	330779	86304	473409	30.4
集体经营剧团	Troupes Sponsored by Collective Units	388	35095	20541	10665	35327	43.1
按剧种分:	Grouped by Art Troupes						
话剧、儿童剧、滑稽剧团	Drama, Children's Play and Comedy Troupes	103	50872	32069	8288	52004	34.5
歌舞剧团	Song and Dance Drama Troupes	86	47699	32216	9481	47309	33.4
歌舞团、轻音乐团	Song and Dance, Light Music Troupes	309	92676	61383	19660	91578	31.7
文工团、宣传队、乌兰牧骑	Cultural and Performance Troupes and Ulanmuchi (equestrian art troupes)	332	25055	18822	2465	24241	23.3
乐团、合唱团	Philharmonic and Chorus Troupes	17	24851	13798	5713	24573	35.7
戏曲剧团	Local Opera Troupes	1234	211211	148835	35747	201287	29.4
#京 剧	Local Beijing Opera Troupes	87	47132	36184	4807	40863	23.2
曲艺、杂技、木偶、皮影团	Recitation and Ballad Troupes, Acrobatics and Circus Troupes, Puppet Show Troupes and Shadow Play Troupes	146	42391	26905	11000	41501	35.9
综合性艺术表演团体	Comprehensive Art Performing Troupes	94	32391	20738	5914	31507	30.5

注：本表各项指标均为文化部系统内数据。

a) Data in this table refer to those under the administration of the Ministry of Culture.

22-5 群众艺术馆、文化馆站业务活动及经费情况（2005年）

Basic Statistics on Activities and Expenditures of Mass Art Centers and Cultural Centers (2005)

项　　目	Item	总　计 Total	群众艺术馆 Mass Art Centers	文化馆 Cultural Centers	文化站 Cultural Stations
单位数 （个）	Number of Units (unit)	41588	447	2779	38362
举办展览 （个）	Number of Exhibitions (unit)	111300	2922	14684	93694
组织文艺活动 （次）	Art Performances and Story-Telling Sessions (times)	391439	17686	85563	288190
举办训练班	Training Courses				
班　次 （次）	Number of Classes (times)	190194	18989	40494	130711
结业人次 （万人次）	Number of Persons Completing Courses (10 000 person-times)	666	55	110	500
群众艺术馆、文化馆负责指导单位	Units Responsible for Guiding Mass Art Centers and Cultural Centers				
农村集镇文化中心 （个）	Cultural Centers in County Towns (unit)	19866	2807	17059	
文化户 （户）	Households Specializing in Cultural Activities (household)	394232	6140	110799	277293
群众业余演出团(队) （个）	Part-time Art Groups (unit)	68641	5982	62659	
总支出 （万元）	Total Expenditures (10 000 yuan)	358640	84932	114032	159675
#修缮费	Maintenance Expenses	11113	4169	2418	4525

注：本表各项指标均为文化部系统内数据。

a) Data in this table refer to those under the administration of the Ministry of Culture.

22-6 公共图书馆业务活动及经费情况（2005年）

Facilities, Services and Expenditures of Public Libraries (2005)

项　　目	Item	总　计 Total	#省级公共图书馆 Public Libraries at Provincial Level	#县级公共图书馆 Public Libraries at County Level
总藏量 （万册、件）	Total Collections (10 000 volumes)	48055	14355	16919
书架总长度 （万米）	Total Length of Bookshelves (10 000 m)	1320	304	348
发放借书证数 （万个）	Number of Library Cards Distributed (10 000 units)	1061	194	446
图书流通情况	Circulation of Books			
总流通人次 （万人次）	Total Number of Circulation (10 000 person-times)	23331	3601	10873
书刊外借册次 （万册次）	Number of Books Borrowed by the Readers (10 000 volume-times)	20268	2696	9651
为读者服务举办各种活动	Service Activities Provided for Readers			
次　数 （次）	Number of Activities (times)	246373	6982	221789
参加人数 （万人次）	Number of Readers Involved (10 000 person-times)	2556	526	938
总支出 （万元）	Total Expenditures (10 000 yuan)	312571	82135	86558
#藏量购置费 （万元）	Purchase Expenses (10 000 yuan)	67290	23495	10919
本年新购藏量 （万册）	Number of Books Purchased During the Year (10 000 volumes)	1935	373	709
公用房屋建筑面积 （万平方米）	Floor Space of Public Buildings (10 000 sq.m)	677	103	316
#书　库 （万平方米）	Stack Rooms (10 000 sq.m)	170	35	74
阅览室座席 （万个）	Seating Capacity of Reading Rooms (10 000 seats)	48	4	29

22-7 博物馆、文物机构业务活动及经费情况（2005年）

Facilities, Services and Expenditures of Museums and Cultural Relic Agencies (2005)

项目	Item	文物保护管理机构 Protection and Management Agencies	文物科研机构 Scientific and Research Agencies	其他文物机构 Other Agencies	博物馆 Museums
藏品 (件)	Number of Collections (piece)	2416460	953314	54279	16199377
#一级品 (件)	Grade One (piece)	5099	2636	213	45677
业务活动	Operations				
陈列展览 (个)	Number of Displays and Exhibitions (unit)	2034			5929
参观人数 (万人次)	Number of Visitors (10 000 person-times)	5837			11819
经费支出 (万元)	Total Expenditures (10 000 yuan)	187185	42453	94321	319861
#修缮费	Maintenance Expenses	18112	2600	5382	21874
增加值 (万元)	Value Added (10 000 yuan)	129892	18577	6808	200343

22-8 摄制电影片产量

Film Production

年份 Year	电影故事片厂 (个) Number of Feature Film Studios (unit)	故事片 (部) Feature Films (film)	美术片 (本) Cartoons (reel)	科学教育片 (本) Popular Science Films (reel)	纪录片 (本) Documentary Films (reel)
1952	4	4	2	41	157
1957	11	40	5	84	272
1962	16	34	17	94	133
1965	16	52	21	240	378
1975	15	27	11	214	313
1978	12	46	26	289	202
1979	17	65	25	349	317
1980	17	82	32	337	242
1981	19	105	33	277	276
1982	19	112	33	284	259
1983	19	127	37	343	299
1984	20	144	37	387	337
1985	20	127	45	357	419
1986	20	134	46	383	417
1987	22	146	45	353	347
1988	22	158	38	344	350
1989	22	136	53	334	259
1990	22	134	51	326	296
1991	22	130	46	351	283
1992	22	170	56	354	307
1993	22	154	47	252	300
1994	22	148	32	182	22
1995	30	146	37	40	111
1996	30	110	58	33	39
1997	31	88	28	34	95
1998	31	82	9	30	54
2000	31	91	1	49	10
2001	27	88	1	56	9
2002	31	100	2	60	7
2003	31	140	2	53	6
2004	31	212	4	30	10
2005	32	260	7	33	2

注：本表电影故事片厂只包括国务院批准的厂。

a) The number of feature film studios in this table only includes those approved by the State Council.

22-9 广播、电视事业发展情况

Basic Statistics on Radio and Television Stations

项目	Item	2004	2005	2005年比2004年增长% Increase Percentage in 2005 over 2004
广播电视系统职工人数(人)	Number of Staff and Workers (person)	581838	595377	2.33
广播电台 (座)	Number of Broadcasting Stations (set)	282	273	-3.19
广播发射台及转播台 (座)	Number of Broadcast Transmission Stations and Relaying Stations (set)	774	788	1.81
广播发射机功率 (千瓦)	Broadcast Power of Transmitters (kw)	69884.4	73877.5	5.71
广播电视台 (座)	Number of Wire Broadcast Stations (set)	1913	1932	0.99
广播综合人口覆盖率 (%)	Listener Rating (%)	94.05	94.48	0.43
电视台 (座)	Number of Television Stations (set)	314	302	-3.82
电视发射台及转播台 (座)	Television Transmission Stations and Relaying Stations (set)	48408	47501	-1.87
电视发射机功率 (千瓦)	Power of Transmitters (kw)	8945.15	8732.01	-2.38
电视综合人口覆盖率 (%)	Viewer Rating (%)	95.29	95.81	0.55

注：广播电台、电视台未包括县级数。

a) Number of broadcasting stations and number of television stations don't include the number at county level.

22-10 广播、电视节目制作时间

Production of Radio and Television Programs

单位：小时 (hour)

项目	Item	1995	2001	2002	2003	2004	2005
广播节目制作	**Production of Radio Programs**	**2332164**	**3494303**	**3774001**	**4301505**	**5267457**	**6139227**
新闻	News Programs	353368	483631	531278	628090	858579	1066880
专题	Special Subject Programs	1054140	1578183	1703554	1861943	1579675	1822621
综艺	General Entertainment Programs	924656	1096440	1161402	1376816	1606519	1937290
广播剧	Radio Play Programs					66053	75456
广告	Advertising Programs		336049	377767	434656	564207	671071
其他	Others					592424	565909
电视节目制作	**Production of TV Programs**	**383513**	**989173**	**1072704**	**1185507**	**2117158**	**2553861**
新闻	News Programs	80800	235336	256883	280273	474218	637956
专题	Special Subject Programs	193391	379490	379240	433083	486311	525528
综艺	General Entertainment Programs	109322	191154	218955	228802	321318	382350
影视剧	TV Play Programs					167511	193771
广告	Advertising Programs		183193	217626	243349	426553	524892
其他	Others					241247	289364

22-11 广播、电视宣传基本情况（2005年）

Basic Statistics on Radio and Television Programs (2005)

项目	Item	节目套数(套) Number of Programs (set)	全年播出时间(小时) Broadcasting Hours	#新闻资讯类 News	#专题服务类 Special Subject	#综艺类 General Entertainment	#广播剧 Radio Play	#广告类 Advertising	#其他类 Others
无线广播合计	**All Radio Broadcasting Stations**	**2306**	**10304214**	**2098876**	**2432727**	**3112522**	**411797**	**927086**	**1321203**
中央台和国际台	China Central Broadcasting and China International Broadcasting	63	450489	178597	185209	72241	263	7820	6357
地方台	Local	2243	9853725	1920279	2247518	3040281	411534	919266	1314846
电视播映合计	**All Television Stations**	**2899**	**12591569**	**1472050**	**1351437**	**1167381**	**5599022**	**1480558**	**1521120**
中央电视台	China Central Television	17	132428	37809	39046	19895	27861	6486	1328
地方台	Local Television	2882	12459141	1434241	1312391	1147486	5571161	1474072	1519792

22-12 图书出版分类构成情况（2005年）

Composition of Books Published in China (2005)

类别	Category	种数（种）Number of Publications (kind)	印数（万册）Printed Copies (10 000 copies)	印张（千印张）Printed Sheets (1 000 sheets)
总计	**Total**	**222473**	**646597**	**49329119**
使用“中国标准书号”合计	Publications with "China International Standard Book Number"	221489	644675	49156871
马列主义、毛泽东思想	Marxism-Leninism, Mao Zedong Thought	454	738	93708
哲学	Philosophy	3921	3242	445533
社会科学总论	General Social Sciences	2842	1966	304955
政治、法律	Politics and Law	10104	11934	1484954
军事	Military Affairs	701	574	70111
经济	Economics	18389	14299	2127093
文化、科学、教育、体育	Culture, Science, Education and Sports	85668	489649	31238319
语言、文字	Languages	11659	16986	2590649
文学	Literature	13428	13974	1711974
艺术	Arts	10622	17976	940943
历史、地理	History and Geography	8525	29402	1866800
自然科学总论	General Natural Sciences	982	3389	214868
数理科学、化学	Mathematics and Chemistry	4669	4281	683236
天文学、地球科学	Astronomy and Geology	999	361	48593
生物科学	Biology	1190	745	130411
医学、卫生	Medicine and Health Care	9565	6515	1138234
农业科学	Agricultural Science	3045	2185	182772
工业技术	Industrial Technology	29511	19698	3286998
交通运输	Transportation	2107	1702	218739
航空、航天	Aeronautics and Aerospace	126	44	7046
环境科学	Environmental Science	1014	3248	152938
综合性图书	General Books	1968	1767	217997
不使用“中国标准书号”图书合计	Publications without "China International Standard Book Number"	984	1922	43328
附录(不使用“中国标准书号”）合计	Appendix (Without "China International Standard Book Number")			128920

22-13 各地区少年儿童读物类图书和课本出版情况（2005年）

Number of Books Published for Children and Textbooks by Region (2005)

地 区	Region	种数(种) Number of Publications (kind) 儿童读物 Books for Children	课 本 Textbooks	总印数（万册） Printed Copies (10 000 copies) 儿童读物 Books for Children	课 本 Textbooks	总印张(千印张) Printed Sheets (1 000 sheets) 儿童读物 Books for Children	课 本 Textbooks
全 国	**National Total**	**9583**	**50028**	**22926**	**352949**	**955545**	**25393488**
中 央	Center Publishing	1489	26670	3008	68112	158664	7188463
地 方	Local Publishing	8094	23358	19918	284837	796881	18205025
北 京	Beijing	517	441	678	814	35380	51726
天 津	Tianjin	208	566	252	2133	14366	166393
河 北	Hebei	163	485	301	14339	12013	904383
山 西	Shanxi	110	45	268	6110	10168	414981
内蒙古	Inner Mongolia	151	578	287	6488	12446	455644
辽 宁	Liaoning	411	1841	819	4799	33878	328300
吉 林	Jilin	398	752	1304	7103	68136	469407
黑龙江	Heilongjiang	39	171	24	3855	2424	280463
上 海	Shanghai	689	2567	1261	11483	49974	914601
江 苏	Jiangsu	756	2437	2219	22752	83023	1431906
浙 江	Zhejiang	926	964	2103	10179	117606	717507
安 徽	Anhui	399	310	873	15293	20428	671142
福 建	Fujian	129	248	288	6529	10587	442129
江 西	Jiangxi	577	353	1993	10004	72518	634525
山 东	Shandong	65	1022	111	16467	6403	1139137
河 南	Henan	383	503	605	20483	29899	1180969
湖 北	Hubei	309	1808	932	13047	25683	976993
湖 南	Hunan	133	726	331	24698	9041	1279282
广 东	Guangdong	225	1335	901	15490	27815	1016826
广 西	Guangxi	294	458	1786	9951	65220	587144
海 南	Hainan	90	43	294	1823	13856	120487
重 庆	Chongqing	112	976	249	7899	4826	510563
四 川	Sichuan	504	907	985	12444	30813	904530
贵 州	Guizhou	11	124	38	5148	573	334742
云 南	Yunnan	5	342	2	9429	42	563912
西 藏	Tibet	8	192	3	702	73	41872
陕 西	Shaanxi	208	1085	296	11120	14460	755751
甘 肃	Gansu	74	173	130	5799	2356	364547
青 海	Qinghai	5	127	3	756	133	51393
宁 夏	Ningxia	13	41	7	1009	585	65770
新 疆	Xinjiang	182	1738	575	6691	22156	428000

22-14 课本出版情况(2005年)

Publication of Textbooks (2005)

项 目	Item	种数 (种) Number of Publication (kind)	#新出版 New Publication	总印数 (万册) Printed Copies (10 000)	总印张 (千印张) Printed Sheets (1 000)	定价总金额 (万元) Total Priced Value (10 000 yuan)
总计	**Total**	**50028**	**17727**	**352949**	**25393488**	**2667702**
大专及以上课本	Textbooks for Colleges and Universities	27459	11277	27756	4890240	661913
中专、技校课本	Textbooks for Secondary Technical Schools	3565	875	6808	913211	108314
中学课本	Textbooks for Secondary Schools	5949	1654	156573	12420044	1104240
小学课本	Textbooks for Primary Schools	6668	1535	152227	6327593	672873
业余教育课本	Textbooks for Spare-time Education	1519	706	3481	292831	43871
扫盲课本	Textbooks for Eliminating Illiteracy	10	4	56	2554	489
教学用书	Teaching Materials	4858	1676	6048	547015	76002

22-15 各地区录像制品出版情况（2005年）

Publication of Video Products by Region (2005)

地 区	Region	录像带 Videotapes		数码激光视盘 VCD		高密度激光视盘 DVD-V	
		种 数 (种) Kind	数 量 (万盒) Volume (10 000 cassettes)	种 数 (种) Kind	数 量 (万张) Volume (10 000 disks)	种 数 (种) Kind	数 量 (万张) Volume (10 000 disks)
全 国	**National Total**	**236**	**5.4**	**14067**	**26880.31**	**4226**	**11511.68**
中 央	Center Publishing House	214	1.45	5242	6971.65	1629	3522.88
地 方	Local Publishing House	22	3.95	8825	19908.66	2597	7988.8
北 京	Beijing			145	527.37	23	21.04
天 津	Tianjin			59	158.37	47	145
河 北	Hebei			269	359.24	7	30.5
山 西	Shanxi	3	0.3	106	78.94		
内蒙古	Inner Mongolia			10	6.75	20	4.53
辽 宁	Liaoning			366	502.83	197	190.55
吉 林	Jilin			350	478.24	35	14.56
黑龙江	Heilongjiang			277	654.42	95	122.5
上 海	Shanghai	16	3.32	832	684.87	81	36.9
江 苏	Jiangsu			363	507.83	32	12.05
浙 江	Zhejiang			319	244.06	150	192.77
安 徽	Anhui			412	397.84	11	6.48
福 建	Fujian			445	1303.27	291	353.99
江 西	Jiangxi			274	259.37	18	12.73
山 东	Shandong			804	3581.55	507	1476.35
河 南	Henan			175	109.61	25	163.16
湖 北	Hubei			224	468.12	31	46.29
湖 南	Hunan			730	629.94	36	125.75
广 东	Guangdong			1381	7988.32	672	4824.92
广 西	Guangxi	3	0.33	254	156.14	27	28.45
海 南	Hainan			22	22.99	1	1
重 庆	Chongqing			70	36.96	22	20
四 川	Sichuan			208	150.04	42	23.87
贵 州	Guizhou			170	124.85	126	82.55
云 南	Yunnan			194	106.1	42	24.49
西 藏	Tibet			7	58.8		
陕 西	Shaanxi			193	120.73	55	26.77
甘 肃	Gansu			34	43.4	3	1.5
青 海	Qinghai						
宁 夏	Ningxia			132	147.74	1	0.1
新 疆	Xinjiang						

22-16 各地区录音制品出版情况（2005年）
Publication of Audio Products by Region (2005)

地 区	Region	录音带 Audio-tapes 种数（种）Kind	录音带 Audio-tapes 数量（万盒）Volume (10 000 cassettes)	激光唱盘 CDs 种数（种）(Kind)	激光唱盘 CDs 数量（万张）Volume (10 000 pieces)	高密度激光唱盘及其他 DVD-A and Others 种数（种）(Kind)	高密度激光唱盘及其他 DVD-A and Others 数量（万张）Volume (10 000 pieces)
全 国	**National Total**	**8433**	**15156.87**	**7493**	**7111.93**	**34**	**23.9**
中 央	Center Publishing House	2209	8214.26	2058	2195.7	15	6.67
地 方	Local Publishing House	6224	6942.61	5435	4916.23	19	17.23
北 京	Beijing	248	155.29	123	39.64		
天 津	Tianjin	95	83.91	48	39.3		
河 北	Hebei	95	165.46	44	20.46	1	0.1
山 西	Shanxi	45	47.93	3	0.95		
内蒙古	Inner Mongolia	2	0.4	91	155.16		
辽 宁	Liaoning	108	122.42	66	32.24		
吉 林	Jilin	13	6.6	171	173.82	1	1.8
黑龙江	Heilongjiang	41	5.1	32	12.1		
上 海	Shanghai	3071	3158.29	1883	764.16		
江 苏	Jiangsu	114	83.17	122	87.41		
浙 江	Zhejiang	160	87.59	54	42.74		
安 徽	Anhui	95	58.95	61	12.61		
福 建	Fujian	57	44.85	70	166.7	1	4
江 西	Jiangxi	113	153.88	211	201.27	1	0.51
山 东	Shandong	143	393.56	788	1088.21	1	0.2
河 南	Henan	136	24.47	8	3.5		
湖 北	Hubei	88	220.51	104	24.51		
湖 南	Hunan	343	426.67	80	141.16		
广 东	Guangdong	816	1311.59	1099	1695.75	11	9.91
广 西	Guangxi	61	49.1	79	31.69	1	0.2
海 南	Hainan	37	30.1	2	4		
重 庆	Chongqing	69	28.39	42	17.92		
四 川	Sichuan	59	33.7	86	52.8		
贵 州	Guizhou	14	4.05	26	8.8		
云 南	Yunnan	18	7.1	60	31.2	1	0.5
西 藏	Tibet			8	7.1		
陕 西	Shaanxi	154	227.32	30	10.93	1	0.01
甘 肃	Gansu	16	8.6	3	1.5		
青 海	Qinghai						
宁 夏	Ningxia	13	3.6	41	48.61		
新 疆	Xinjiang						

22-17 档案馆机构和人员情况

Statistics on Institution and Personnel of Archives Institution

单位：个、人 (unit, person)

年 份 Year	国家综合档案馆 National Comprehensive Archives		国家专门档案馆 National Special Archives		部门档案馆 Department Archives		企业档案馆数 Enterprise Archive Institution	文化事业档案馆数 Culture Archive Institution	科技事业单位档案馆数 Science and Technology Archive Institution
	馆数 Number of Institution	专职人员 Full-time Personnel	馆数 Number of Institution	专职人员 Full-time Personnel	馆数 Number of Institution	专职人员 Full-time Personnel			
1991	2957	21657	211	2038	128	2171	229	19	28
1992	2962	22226	206	2082	122	2258	231	19	28
1993	2980	23624	200	2245	122	1448	221	20	31
1994	2983	23568	205	2294	136	2160	209	20	36
1995	3024	24777	216	2484	144	2168	213	27	38
1996	3011	24542	226	2658	134	2072	232	23	44
1997	3021	24904	223	2578	162	2521	228	26	46
1998	3034	24197	232	3200	149	2411	245	27	46
1999	3046	23530	225	3436	142	2123	304	40	59
2000	3070	23701	234	3319	141	1865	307	53	80
2001	3100	23652	243	3448	142	2086	286	47	84
2002	3110	22825	253	3435	148	2109	299	75	93
2003	3121	23086	260	3514	141	1770	300	75	85
2004	3127	23401	258	3591	149	1932	300	79	99
2005	3142	23413	238	3452	145	2020	301	105	63

22-18 国家综合档案馆基本情况

Basic Statistics on National Comprehensive Archives

年 份 Year	馆藏档案 (万卷、万件) Number of Archives (10 000 volume, pieces)	照片档案 (万张) Photos (10 000 sheets)	开放档案 (万卷、万件) Opening Archives (10 000 volume, pieces)	利用档案 (万卷、万件次) Utilized Archives (10 000 volume, pieces)	档案馆建筑面积 (万平方米) Floor Space of Archive Institutions (10 000 sq.m)
1991	9637.4	371.0	2094.3	937.0	348.1
1992	10003.5	402.4	2018.7	773.8	255.7
1993	10726.8	435.5	2140.7	891.9	275.9
1994	10782.9	449.6	2454.6	674.4	268.3
1995	11318.3	485.5	2790.3	529.3	282.5
1996	11341.4	494.6	2939.2	485.4	297.5
1997	12222.9	553.0	3304.6	501.0	347.6
1998	12276.5	579.7	3556.5	446.5	310.7
1999	12866.8	584.5	3808.2	508.5	328.4
2000	13314.0	631.7	4072.0	494.4	336.2
2001	13756.6	642.8	4129.7	575.4	342.0
2002	14790.7	720.5	4301.1	548.8	351.0
2003	15945.9	797.4	4618.4	602.6	361.4
2004	17601.5	827.9	4868.3	813.9	376.8
2005	18688.7	908.8	5132.3	868.0	393.1

22-19 我国与外国体育活动交往情况

Visits between Chinese and Foreign Sports Delegations

项目	Item	1990	1995	2000	2004	2005
来我国的体育团体	Foreign Sports Delegations Visiting China					
次数 (次)	Number of Times (time)	364	1929	1000		
人数 (人次)	Person-Times (person-time)	3171	38700	20320		
我国派出的体育团体	Chinese Sports Delegations Visiting Foreign Countries					
次数 (次)	Number of Times (time)	607	2787	3880	3321	3028
人数 (人次)	Persons-Times (person-time)	5227	18033	22789	20071	18759

注：自1995年起，来华、出访次数、人数包括地方各级体委组办数。自2003年起不再统计来我国的体育代表团体人数和次数。

a) Number of times and persons of foreign delegations visiting China and these of Chinese sports delegations visiting foreign countries included the visits organized by the local sports commissions since 1995. Since 2003, foreign sports delegations visiting China are not calculated any more.

22-20 群众体育活动情况

Activities of Mass Sports

项目	Item	1990	1995	2000	2003	2004	2005
《国家体育锻炼标准》达标人数 (万人)	Number of Persons Who Have Come up to *the State Physical Training Standards* (10 000 persons)	7478	10608	15202	14146	12662	12234
优秀级 (万人)	Excellent (10 000 persons)	1414	1888	2787			
良好级 (万人)	Good (10 000 persons)	2746	3586	5366			
及格级 (万人)	Pass (10 000 persons)	3318	5135	7048			
县以上体委举办运动会次数 (次)	Number of Sports Meetings Held by Sports Commissions at and above County Level (time)	30158	24880	26196	37764	43440	45401
参加运动会的运动员人数 (万人次)	Number of Athletes Attending Sports Meetings (10 000 persons)	1076	1345	1272			

注：自2002年起达标人数指标统计上不再区分优秀、良好和及格三级。

a) Number of persons who have come up to the State Physical Training Standards since 2002 is not classified as excellent, good and pass.

22-21 体委系统职工人数（2005年）

Number of Staff and Workers in Sports Commissions (2005)

单位：人 (person)

人员分类	Category of Personnel	合计 Total	#优秀运动队 Excellent Sports Teams	#体育运动学校 Physical Education and Sports Schools	#业余体校 Spare-time Sports Schools	#公共体育场馆 Public Stadiums and Gymnasiums	#训练基地 Training Bases
总　计	**Total**	**141849**	**38926**	**17580**	**29749**	**13675**	**2765**
运动员	Athletes	21521	20458	697	225	14	107
专职教练员	Full-time Coaches	25232	4704	4960	14795	446	103
专职文化教师	Full-time Teachers	10567	472	5299	4044	1	33
科技人员	Scientific and Technical Personnel	1186	121	117	85	8	3
医务人员	Medical Personnel	1463	832	308	150	14	38
管理人员	Administrative Personnel	34170	7075	3584	5884	6523	856
其他	Others	47710	5264	2615	4566	6669	1625

22-22 运动员分项创世界纪录情况（2005年）
World Records Chalked up by Chinese Athletes by Events (2005)

单位：项、人/队、次 (item, person/team, times)

项目 Item	项数 Number of Events	#女子 Female	人数 Number of Persons/teams	#女子 Female	次数 Number of Times	#女子 Female
总计 Total	**15**	**10**	**14**	**7**	**21**	**15**
射击 Shooting	4	1	3	2	6	2
举重 Weightlifting	9	9	5	5	13	13
跳伞 Parachuting	2		6		2	

22-23 运动员获世界冠军情况
World Championships Won by Chinese Athletes

单位：项、人、个 (item, person, number)

年份 Year	项数 Number of Events	#女子 Female	人数 Number of Persons	#女子 Female	个数 Number of Times	#女子 Female
1959	1		1		1	
1963	4		7		4	
1965	5	2	9	4	5	2
1971	4	2	7	2	4	2
1975	2	1	9	4	2	1
1978	4	2	4	2	4	2
1979	12	6.5	20	11	12	6.5
1980	3		3		3	
1981	25	12.5	53	32	25	12.5
1982	12	2	31	15	13	2
1983	37	15	50	24	39	17
1984	33	10	46	26	37	10
1985	42	20	70	41	46	23
1986	26	14	56	34	26	14
1987	64	39	72	34	69	41.5
1988	54	36.5	59	30	54	36.5
1989	80	49	83	48	82	50
1990	54	33.5	61	30	54	33.5
1991	88	57.5	86	51	93	61.5
1992	86	69.5	68	52	89	72.5
1993	101	66.5	106	70	103	68.5
1994	79	53.5	86	45	79	53.5
1995	98	49.5	187	86	102	51.5
1996	72	55	58	42	75	57
1997	87	46	96	46	92	50.5
1998	75	49	89	59	83	55
1999	91	43	129	72	92	44
2000	92	52	109	60	110	66.5
2001	79	46.5	138	77	90	54.5
2002	99	58	123	81	110	64
2003	17	15.5	94	62.5	84	49
2004	27	21	175	98	101	56
2005	22	19	159	89	106	63

注：男女混合运动项目，女子按半项和半个计算。

a) For mixed doubles champions, the score for female counts as 0.5.

22-24 卫 生 机 构 数

Number of Health Institutions

单位：个 (unit)

年 份 Year	总 计 Total	医院、卫生院 Hospitals and Health Centers	疗养院 Sanatoriums	门诊部、诊所 Clinics	专科防治院(所、站) Specialized Prevention & Treatment Centers or Stations
1978	169732	64311	389	94395	887
1980	180553	65315	470	102474	1138
1985	200866	59342	640	126604	1566
1989	206724	61613	651	128112	1747
1990	208734	62126	650	129332	1781
1991	209036	62768	642	128665	1818
1992	204787	61006	639	125873	1845
1993	193586	60460	600	115161	1872
1994	191742	67524	587	105984	1905
1995	190057	67460	582	104406	1895
1996	322566	67556	528	237153	1887
1997	315033	67479	506	229474	1893
1998	314097	66614	503	229349	1889
1999	310996	66935	485	226588	1877
2000	324771	66095	471	240934	1839
2001	330348	64840	461	248061	1783
2002	306038	63858	365	219907	1839
2003	291323	62968	305	204468	1749
2004	297540	60864	292	208794	1583
2005	298997	60397	274	207404	1502

22-24 续表 continued

单位：个 (unit)

年 份 Year	疾病预防控制中心(防疫站) Center for Disease Control and Prevention (Epidemic Prevention Stations)	妇幼保健院(所、站) Maternity and Child Care Centers	医学科学研究机构 Research Institutions of Medical Science	其 他 卫生机构 Other Institutions
1978	2989	2571	219	3971
1980	3105	2745	282	5024
1985	3410	2996	323	5985
1989	3591	3112	328	7570
1990	3618	3148	337	7742
1991	3652	3187	335	7969
1992	3673	3187	339	8225
1993	3729	3115	436	8213
1994	3711	3190	437	8404
1995	3729	3179	427	8379
1996	3737	3172	427	8106
1997	3747	3180	426	8328
1998	3746	3191	423	8382
1999	3763	3180	421	7747
2000	3741	3163	405	8123
2001	3813	3132	397	7861
2002	3580	3067	298	13124
2003	3584	3033	284	14932
2004	3588	2998	276	19145
2005	3585	3021	263	22551

注：1.1995年及以前的卫生机构数不含私人诊所。
2.2001年及以前的医院数包括专科疾病防治院；疾病预防控制中心(防疫站)包括预防保健中心。
3.2002年及以后卫生机构数为登记注册数，不包括高中等医学院校、药检机构和非卫生部门办的计划生育指导站。

a) Number of health institutions excluded the private clinics before 1995.
b) Number of hospitals before 2002 included specialized prevention and treatment institutions, and center for disease control and prevention (epidemic prevention stations) included health prevention and care centers.
c) Number of health institutions since 2002 are the number of registrated institutions, and excluding medical colleges, drug test institutions and family planning guidance stations of non-health departments.

22-25 卫生机构人员数

Number of Employed Persons in Health Institutions

单位：万人 (10 000 persons)

年 份 Year	总 计 Total	#卫生技术人员 Medical and Technical Personnel	#医 生 Doctors	#护师、护士 Senior and Junior Nurses	每千人口医生数(人) Number of Doctors per 1 000 Population
1978	310.6	246.4	103.3	40.7	1.08
1980	353.5	279.8	115.3	46.6	1.17
1985	431.3	341.1	141.3	63.7	1.36
1989	478.7	380.9	171.8	92.2	1.56
1990	490.6	389.8	176.3	97.5	1.56
1991	502.5	398.5	178.0	101.2	1.56
1992	514.0	407.4	180.8	104.0	1.57
1993	521.5	411.7	183.2	105.6	1.58
1994	530.7	419.9	188.2	109.4	1.60
1995	537.3	425.7	191.8	112.6	1.62
1996	541.9	431.2	194.1	116.3	1.62
1997	551.6	439.8	198.5	119.8	1.65
1998	553.6	442.4	200.0	121.9	1.65
1999	557.0	445.9	204.5	124.5	1.67
2000	559.1	449.1	207.6	126.7	1.68
2001	558.4	450.8	210.0	128.7	1.69
2002	523.8	427.0	184.4	124.7	1.47
2003	527.5	430.6	186.8	126.6	1.48
2004	535.7	439.3	190.6	130.8	1.50
2005	542.7	446.0	193.8	135.0	1.52

注：2002年及以后医生系执业(助理)医师数，护师(士)系注册护士数，故数据有所减少(下同)。

a) Doctors since 2002 refer to the certified (assistant) doctors, nurses refer to the registration nurses, so the numbers decreased somewhat. The same as in the following table.

22-26 卫生机构床位数

Number of Beds in Health Institutions

单位：万张 (10 000 units)

年 份 Year	总 计 Total	医院、卫生院 Hospitals and Health Centers	疗养院 Sanatoriums	妇幼保健院(所、站) Maternity and Child Care Centers	其他卫生机构 Other Health Institutions	每千人口医院、卫生院床位数(张) Number of Hospital Beds per 1 000 Population (unit)
1978	204.2	184.7	5.1	1.2	13.2	1.93
1980	218.4	197.1	6.8	1.6	12.9	2.02
1985	248.7	222.9	10.6	3.5	11.7	2.14
1989	286.7	253.8	12.3	4.5	16.2	2.28
1990	292.5	259.2	12.3	4.7	16.3	2.32
1991	299.2	265.5	12.5	4.8	16.3	2.32
1992	304.9	270.9	12.5	5.0	16.5	2.34
1993	309.9	276.7	11.9	4.5	16.8	2.36
1994	313.4	280.3	11.8	4.8	16.5	2.36
1995	314.1	279.6	11.6	5.1	17.7	2.39
1996	310.0	283.4	10.9	5.6	10.1	2.34
1997	313.5	286.9	10.4	6.0	10.2	2.35
1998	314.3	287.8	10.2	6.3	10.0	2.40
1999	315.9	289.1	9.9	6.6	10.4	2.39
2000	317.7	290.8	9.7	7.1	10.1	2.38
2001	320.1	290.2	9.5	7.4	13.6	2.39
2002	313.6	290.7	6.9	8.0	8.0	2.32
2003	316.4	295.5	4.8	8.1	8.0	2.34
2004	326.8	304.7	5.4	8.7	8.2	2.40
2005	336.8	313.5	5.2	9.4	8.7	2.45

22-27 按市县分卫生机构床位数和卫生技术人员

Beds and Medical Technical Personnel in Health Institutions by City and County Areas

年 份 Year	卫生机构床位数（万张）Beds in Health Institutions (10 000 units)		卫生技术人员（万人）Medical Technical Personnel (10 000 persons)		#医 生 Doctors		#护师、护士 Senior and Junior Nurses	
	市 City	县 County	市 City	县 County	市 City	县 County	市 City	县 County
1952	12.1	3.9	22.5	46.5	8.1	34.3	4.3	1.8
1957	22.1	7.4	38.2	65.7	13.8	40.8	10.0	2.8
1962	43.7	25.3	57.1	84.3	21.4	47.4	15.5	4.5
1965	45.8	30.8	65.2	88.0	26.9	49.4	17.6	5.9
1970	51.0	59.5	59.6	85.7	24.1	46.1	18.0	11.6
1975	63.7	96.1	95.7	110.0	36.7	51.0	24.0	14.0
1978	71.6	114.0	114.2	132.1	44.2	59.1	25.7	14.9
1980	76.8	121.4	131.3	148.5	52.7	62.6	30.0	16.6
1981	80.3	121.4	143.5	157.6	58.6	65.8	33.4	19.1
1982	83.2	122.1	150.9	163.4	62.8	67.9	35.4	21.0
1983	86.9	124.0	157.4	167.9	66.5	68.7	37.3	22.3
1984	91.9	124.7	164.2	170.2	69.4	68.8	39.3	22.3
1985	96.2	126.7	167.7	173.4	70.9	70.4	39.2	24.5
1986	103.3	126.4	177.4	173.3	74.9	69.5	42.9	25.2
1987	112.7	127.7	188.2	172.6	79.3	68.9	46.1	25.7
1988	125.5	124.8	202.8	169.6	88.6	73.2	53.7	29.2
1989	133.5	123.3	212.1	168.8	95.0	76.8	59.9	32.2
1990	138.7	123.7	218.5	171.3	97.8	78.5	63.4	34.1
1991	144.8	124.0	226.4	172.1	100.3	77.7	66.6	34.6
1992	152.4	122.0	236.3	171.1	104.3	76.5	69.5	34.5
1993	159.6	119.9	243.3	168.5	107.7	75.5	71.5	34.1
1994	170.7	112.4	258.9	161.0	115.0	73.2	76.2	33.2
1995	174.0	109.7	265.9	159.8	118.4	73.4	79.0	33.5
1996	179.1	107.5	272.2	159.0	120.3	73.8	82.3	34.0
1997	184.2	106.1	279.5	160.3	123.5	75.0	85.3	34.6
1998	187.2	104.2	281.9	160.5	124.2	75.7	87.0	34.9
1999	188.7	104.2	283.0	162.9	126.1	78.4	88.6	35.9
2000	191.4	103.4	283.5	165.6	126.8	80.8	89.8	36.9
2001	195.9	101.7	287.2	163.6	129.5	80.5	91.8	36.9
2002								
2003	215.0	101.5	282.8	147.8	121.6	65.2	92.8	33.8
2004	225.3	101.6	293.4	145.5	126.1	64.4	96.8	34.0
2005	234.0	102.8	300.6	145.4	129.1	64.7	100.4	34.6

注：2001及以前按市县分的卫生机构床位数为医院、卫生院床位数。
a) Number of beds in health institutions by city and county before 2001 referred to hospital beds.

22-28 医院、卫生院平均每院床位和人员数

Average Number of Beds and Persons Engaged Per Hospitals and Health Centers

项 目	Item	2004 床位（张）Beds (unit)	2004 人员（人）Personnel (person)	2004 #卫生技术人员 Medical Technical Personnel	2005 床位（张）Beds (unit)	2005 人员（人）Personnel (person)	2005 #卫生技术人员 Medical Technical Personnel
医院合计	**Hospitals**	**128.5**	**170.4**	**135.4**	**130.7**	**170.2**	**135.6**
#综合医院	General Hospitals	137.8	185.9	148.5	141.3	187.4	150.2
中医医院	Hospitals Specialized in Traditional Chinese Medicine	105.4	155.5	126.2	109.8	158.5	128.8
专科医院	Specialized Hospitals	113.4	116.7	85.7	108.9	109.6	80.8
卫生院合计	**Health Centers**	**16.1**	**24.8**	**21.3**	**16.5**	**24.9**	**21.4**
城市街道卫生院	Urban	16.0	32.0	27.5	14.8	30.9	26.7
农村乡(镇)卫生院	Rural	16.1	24.7	21.2	16.6	24.7	21.3

22-29 各地区卫生机构数、医疗机构床位数（2005年）

Number of Health Institutions and Beds by Region (2005)

地区	Region	卫生机构数（个）Health Institutions (unit)	#医院 Hospitals	#卫生院 Health Centers	#门诊部、诊所 Clinics	#疾病预防控制中心（防疫站）Center for Disease Control and Prevention (Epidemic Prevention Stations)	#妇幼保健院(所站) Maternity and Child Care Centers	医疗机构床位数（张）Total Beds (bed)	#医院、卫生院 Hospitals and Health Centers
全国	**National Total**	**298997**	**18703**	**41694**	**207404**	**3585**	**3021**	**3350810**	**3134930**
北京	Beijing	4818	516	152	3841	28	18	79067	75715
天津	Tianjin	2472	271	191	1748	24	23	41513	39491
河北	Hebei	18046	817	1966	14096	192	184	162061	153981
山西	Shanxi	9430	884	1640	6094	157	131	107980	103030
内蒙古	Inner Mongolia	7629	474	1358	4863	146	116	69047	63786
辽宁	Liaoning	14925	915	1077	11433	128	114	177524	161244
吉林	Jilin	8755	563	817	5098	74	71	87279	82118
黑龙江	Heilongjiang	8326	886	933	5716	195	148	119692	112536
上海	Shanghai	2526	247	100	1865	22	24	89758	78411
江苏	Jiangsu	15324	1004	1472	9497	154	112	197515	184237
浙江	Zhejiang	12555	553	2339	6581	138	87	140734	131067
安徽	Anhui	9197	683	2001	5415	132	117	126587	119625
福建	Fujian	7934	357	953	5876	93	89	81645	73187
江西	Jiangxi	10669	486	1520	7914	115	112	84836	79272
山东	Shandong	16323	1121	1786	11138	176	150	247574	231277
河南	Henan	14554	1172	2088	10021	183	167	212407	202289
湖北	Hubei	9459	572	1176	6549	113	96	139147	128651
湖南	Hunan	15008	782	2542	10748	150	135	151297	141566
广东	Guangdong	16318	960	1463	12225	134	124	208936	192839
广西	Guangxi	9416	458	1295	7035	106	103	93532	87112
海南	Hainan	2464	190	312	1759	30	26	18651	17480
重庆	Chongqing	6380	358	1102	4668	43	42	64174	61234
四川	Sichuan	23832	1149	5176	16200	208	197	193171	184347
贵州	Guizhou	6571	383	1456	4174	103	84	61594	58325
云南	Yunnan	10110	648	1483	7262	153	148	106334	98836
西藏	Tibet	1378	97	666	458	81	55	6767	6412
陕西	Shaanxi	11701	833	1769	8228	125	115	106391	99549
甘肃	Gansu	11849	382	1358	9547	103	100	63314	59855
青海	Qinghai	1478	130	406	607	57	24	15088	14747
宁夏	Ningxia	1463	134	266	900	25	21	17754	16836
新疆	Xinjiang	8087	678	831	5848	197	88	79441	75875

22-30 各地区卫生机构人员数（2005年）
Number of Employed Persons in Health Institutions by Region (2005)

单位：人 (person)

地 区	Region	人员合计 Total	#卫生技术人员 Medical Technical Personnel	#执业(助理)医师 Doctors	#注册护士 Nurses
全 国	**National Total**	**5426851**	**4460187**	**1938272**	**1349589**
北 京	Beijing	156969	119943	50642	42897
天 津	Tianjin	77580	61085	24996	19606
河 北	Hebei	274424	229696	105582	54456
山 西	Shanxi	173902	146671	66689	42138
内蒙古	Inner Mongolia	121180	102587	50308	27052
辽 宁	Liaoning	265194	209346	91519	72912
吉 林	Jilin	157021	125702	56411	38917
黑龙江	Heilongjiang	191172	150657	65135	45015
上 海	Shanghai	132004	103479	43956	39379
江 苏	Jiangsu	316054	257137	108700	80543
浙 江	Zhejiang	236197	198148	88050	60259
安 徽	Anhui	193973	159788	66102	47329
福 建	Fujian	118652	100945	44314	34197
江 西	Jiangxi	138697	115986	49701	35679
山 东	Shandong	381760	323759	140628	97886
河 南	Henan	362263	289157	111134	77132
湖 北	Hubei	262263	215037	89507	69442
湖 南	Hunan	254423	212483	92073	59640
广 东	Guangdong	364520	297334	118023	98791
广 西	Guangxi	158370	129151	54563	44596
海 南	Hainan	37189	30056	11811	10860
重 庆	Chongqing	94761	78780	37321	20842
四 川	Sichuan	280516	236028	113697	61231
贵 州	Guizhou	94854	81723	40928	23538
云 南	Yunnan	142175	118429	55837	38001
西 藏	Tibet	10781	8913	4593	1896
陕 西	Shaanxi	165170	136550	60316	38499
甘 肃	Gansu	97139	83016	35246	22405
青 海	Qinghai	22923	19518	8478	6418
宁 夏	Ningxia	27560	22817	10586	7376
新 疆	Xinjiang	117165	96266	41426	30657

22-31 卫生机构各类人员数
Employed Persons in Health Institutions by Type of Occupation

单位：万人 (10 000 persons)

人员分类	Type of Personnel	1990	1995	2000	2004	2005
总计	**Total**	**490.6**	**537.3**	**559.1**	**535.7**	**542.7**
卫生技术人员	Medical Technical Personnel	389.8	425.7	449.1	439.3	446.0
其他技术人员	Other Technical Personnel	8.6	12.1	15.8	20.9	22.6
管理人员	Managerial Personnel	39.7	45.0	42.7	31.6	31.3
工勤人员	Logistics Workers	52.6	54.5	51.6	43.9	42.8
卫生技术人员	**Medical Technical Personnel**	**389.8**	**425.7**	**449.1**	**439.3**	**446.0**
医生	Doctors & Assistant Doctors	176.3	191.8	207.6	190.6	193.8
#医师	Doctors	130.3	145.5	160.3	152.2	155.6
护师、士	Senior Nurses & Nurses	97.5	112.6	126.7	130.8	135.0
药技人员	Pharmacists	40.6	41.9	41.4	35.5	35.0
检验人员	Laboratory Technicians	17.0	18.9	20.1	21.2	21.1
其他	Others	58.4	60.5	53.3	61.1	61.1
平均每千人口有卫生技术人员(人)	**Number of Medical Technical Personnel per 1 000 Population**	**3.5**	**3.6**	**3.6**	**3.5**	**3.5**

22-32 各类医疗机构诊疗人次及入院人数（2005年）
Number of Visits and Inpatients in Medical Institutions (2005)

医疗机构	Medical Institutions	诊疗人次（亿次） Visits (100 million person-times) 合计 Total	#非营利 Non-profit	#营利 Profit	入院人数（万人） Inpatients (10 000 persons) 合计 Total	#非营利 Non-profit	#营利 Profit
总计	**Total**	**23.05**	**22.23**	**0.75**	**7184**	**6987**	**176**
医院	Hospitals	13.87	13.29	0.56	5108	4931	170
#综合医院	General Hospitals	10.58	10.17	0.39	4153	4032	114
中医医院	Hospitals Specialized in Traditional Chinese Medicine	2.14	2.11	0.03	567	557	10
专科医院	Specialized Hospitals	0.95	0.83	0.12	339	297	42
疗养院	Sanitariums	0.02	0.02		28	28	
社区卫生服务中心	Health Service Centers for Community	0.59	0.59		27	26	
卫生院	Health Centers	6.99	6.95	0.02	1641	1629	4
#乡镇卫生院	Rural	6.79	6.75	0.02	1622	1611	3
门诊部	Outpatient Departments	0.42	0.25	0.17	7	5	2
妇幼保健院(所、站)	Maternity and Child Care Centers	0.97	0.96		349	346	
专科疾病防治院(所、站)	Specialized Disease Prevention & Treatment Institutions	0.18	0.17		23	21	

22-33 医疗机构病床使用情况（2005年）
Utilization of Beds in Medical Institutions (2005)

医疗机构	Medical Institutions	病床使用率(%) Utilization Rate (%) 合计 Total	#非营利 Non-profit	#营利 Profit	出院者平均住院日 Average Stay Days in Hospital 合计 Total	#非营利 Non-profit	#营利 Profit
总计	**Total**	**62.9**	**63.5**	**47.8**	**9.2**	**9.2**	**9.4**
医院	Hospitals	70.3	71.4	48.3	10.9	10.9	9.5
#综合医院	General Hospitals	70.4	71.3	46.0	10.2	10.2	8.7
中医医院	Hospitals Specialized in Traditional Chinese Medicine	65.0	65.5	47.0	10.8	10.8	10.6
专科医院	Specialized Hospitals	75.7	78.5	53.5	18.9	19.9	11.7
疗养院	Sanitariums	38.8	38.0	38.2	12.7	12.2	9.2
社区卫生服务中心	Health Service Centers for Community	60.7	60.6	44.0	17.2	17.1	7.9
卫生院	Health Centers	37.8	37.7	41.5	4.7	4.7	7.1
#乡镇卫生院	Rural	37.7	37.7	43.5	4.6	4.6	7.4
妇幼保健院(所、站)	MCH Centers	62.6	62.8		5.3	5.4	
专科疾病防治院(所、站)	Specialized Disease Prevention & Treatment Institutions	57.5	57.5	55.4	20.6	21.1	12.1

22-34 城市前十位疾病死亡原因及构成（2005年）
Death Rate of 10 Major Diseases in Urban Areas (2005)

顺位 No.	疾病死亡原因	Cause of Death	占死亡总人数的% As % of Total Deaths
	十种死因合计	**Total**	**92.03**
1	恶性肿瘤	Malignant Tumour	22.94
2	脑血管病	Cerebrovascular Disease	21.23
3	心脏病	Heart Trouble	17.89
4	呼吸系病	Diseases of the Respiratory System	12.57
5	损伤及中毒	Trauma and Toxicosis	8.25
6	消化系病	Diseases of the Digestive System	3.30
7	内分泌营养和代谢疾病	Endocrine, Nutritional & Metabolic Diseases	2.50
8	泌尿、生殖系病	Disease of the Genitourinary System	1.56
9	精神障碍	Mental Disorders	0.95
10	神经系病	Disease of the Nervous System	0.84
	男性十种死因合计	**Male Total**	**91.55**
1	恶性肿瘤	Malignant Tumour	26.05
2	脑血管病	Cerebrovascular Disease	19.01
3	心脏病	Heart Trouble	16.22
4	呼吸系病	Diseases of the Respiratory System	12.37
5	损伤及中毒	Trauma and Toxicosis	9.27
6	消化系病	Diseases of the Digestive System	3.67
7	内分泌营养和代谢疾病	Endocrine, Nutritional & Metabolic Diseases	1.93
8	泌尿生殖系病	Disease of the Genitourinary System	1.45
9	神经系病	Disease of the Nervous System	0.79
10	精神障碍	Mental Disorders	0.79
	女性十种死因合计	**Female Total**	**89.88**
1	脑血管病	Cerebrovascular Disease	21.82
2	心脏病	Heart Trouble	20.09
3	恶性肿瘤	Malignant Tumour	18.36
4	呼吸系病	Diseases of the Respiratory System	12.83
5	损伤及中毒	Trauma and Toxicosis	6.90
6	内分泌营养和代谢疾病	Endocrine, Nutritional & Metabolic Diseases	3.27
7	消化系病	Diseases of the Digestive System	2.79
8	泌尿生殖系病	Disease of the Genitourinary System	1.70
9	精神障碍	Mental Disorders	1.15
10	神经系病	Disease of the Nervous System	0.97

22-35 农村前十位疾病死亡原因及构成（2005年）

Death Rate of 10 Major Diseases in Rural Areas (2005)

顺位 No.	疾病死亡原因	Cause of Death	占死亡总人数的% As % of Total Deaths
	十种死因合计	**Total**	**91.87**
1	呼吸系病	Diseases of the Respiratory System	23.45
2	脑血管病	Cerebrovascular Disease	21.17
3	恶性肿瘤	Malignant Tumour	20.29
4	心脏病	Heart Trouble	11.77
5	损伤及中毒	Trauma and Toxicosis	8.47
6	消化系病	Diseases of the Digestive System	3.24
7	泌尿生殖系病	Disease of the Genitourinary System	1.32
8	内分泌营养和代谢疾病	Endocrine, Nutritional & Metabolic Diseases	1.17
9	肺结核	Pulmonary Tuberculosis	0.55
10	精神障碍	Mental Disorders	0.44
	男性十种死因合计	**Male Total**	**92.16**
1	恶性肿瘤	Malignant Tumour	23.05
2	呼吸系病	Diseases of the Respiratory System	21.20
3	脑血管病	Cerebrovascular Disease	20.60
4	心脏病	Heart Trouble	10.35
5	损伤及中毒	Trauma and Toxicosis	9.89
6	消化系病	Diseases of the Digestive System	3.85
7	泌尿生殖系病	Disease of the Genitourinary System	1.27
8	内分泌营养和代谢疾病	Endocrine, Nutritional & Metabolic Diseases	0.91
9	肺结核	Pulmonary Tuberculosis	0.67
10	精神障碍	Mental Disorders	0.37
	女性十种死因合计	**Female Total**	**90.95**
1	呼吸系病	Diseases of the Respiratory System	26.60
2	脑血管病	Cerebrovascular Disease	21.95
3	恶性肿瘤	Malignant Tumour	15.93
4	心脏病	Heart Trouble	13.75
5	损伤及中毒	Trauma and Toxicosis	6.49
6	消化系病	Diseases of the Digestive System	2.39
7	内分泌营养和代谢疾病	Endocrine, Nutritional & Metabolic Diseases	1.54
8	泌尿生殖系病	Disease of the Genitourinary System	1.39
9	精神障碍	Mental Disorders	0.54
10	肺结核	Pulmonary Tuberculosis	0.37

注：统计范围包括北京等78个县的资料。

a) Statistics in the table cover full or partial areas of 78 counties, including counties in Beijing.

22-36 法定报告传染病发病及死亡情况（2005年）

Incidence and Death from Infectious Diseases (2005)

病名	Item	发病率 (1/10万) Incidence Disease Rate (per 100 000 persons)	死亡率 (1/10万) Death Rate (per 100 000 persons)	病死率 (%) Mortality Rate per 100 Infectious Disease Patients
总计	**Total**	268.3050	0.7552	0.2815
鼠疫	The Plague	0.0008	0.0002	30.0000
霍乱	Cholera	0.0744	0.0003	0.4111
病毒性肝炎	Viral Hepatitis	91.4222	0.0924	0.1011
痢疾	Dysentery	34.9168	0.0105	0.0300
伤寒副伤寒	Typhoid and Paratyphoid Fever	2.6536	0.0011	0.0404
艾滋病	AIDS	0.4299	0.1006	23.4122
淋病	Gonorrhea	13.7908	0.0001	0.0006
梅毒	Syphilis	9.6707	0.0057	0.0585
脊髓灰质炎	Poliomyelitis	0.0000	*	*
麻疹	Measles	9.4176	0.0042	0.0447
百日咳	Pertussis	0.2940	0.0002	0.0520
白喉	Diphtheria	0.0001	0.0000	0.0000
流脑	Epidemic Encephalitis	0.1773	0.0158	8.8870
猩红热	Scarlet Fever	1.9172	0.0002	0.0080
出血热	Hemorrhage Fever	1.5967	0.0207	1.2981
狂犬病	Hydrophobia	0.1940	0.1940	100.0000
钩端螺旋体病	Leptospirosis	0.1082	0.0034	3.1802
布氏杆菌病	Brucellosis	1.4085	0.0003	0.0217
炭疽	Anthrax	0.0407	0.0009	2.2556
乙脑	Encephalitis B	0.3898	0.0164	4.1985
血吸虫	Schistosomiasis	0.2405	0.0002	0.0636
疟疾	Malaria	3.0329	0.0034	0.1135
登革热	Dengue Fever	0.0031	0.0001	2.5000
新生儿破伤风	Newborn Tetanus	0.1902	0.0211	11.0829
肺结核	Pulmonary Tuberculosis	96.3134	0.2602	0.2701
传染性非典型肺炎	SARS	0.0000	*	*
人禽流感	HpAI	0.0005	0.0004	71.4286

注：1．新生儿破伤风发病率和死亡率单位为1‰。
　　2．*无死亡病例。

a) The unit of incidence disease rate and death rate of newborn baby tetanus is 1‰.
b) * refers that there is no death cases.

22-37 卫 生 总 费 用

Expenditure for Public Health

本表按当年价格计算。
The data in this table are calculated at current prices.

项目	Item	1998	1999	2000	2001	2002	2003	2004
卫生总费用（亿元）	**Total Expenditure for Public Health (100 million yuan)**	**3776.5**	**4178.6**	**4586.6**	**5025.9**	**5790.0**	**6584.1**	**7590.3**
政府预算卫生支出	Government Budgetary Expenditure	587.2	640.9	709.5	800.6	908.5	1116.9	1293.6
社会卫生支出	Social Expenditure	1006.0	1064.6	1171.9	1211.4	1539.4	1788.5	2225.4
居民个人卫生支出	Resident Individual Expenditure	2183.3	2473.1	2705.2	3013.9	3342.1	3678.7	4071.4
卫生总费用构成(%)	**Structure of the Expenditure for Public Health (%)**	**100.0**	**100.0**	**100.0**	**100.0**	**100.0**	**100.0**	**100.0**
政府预算卫生支出	Government Budgetary Expenditure	16.0	15.8	15.5	15.9	15.7	17.0	17.0
社会卫生支出	Social Expenditure	29.1	28.3	25.5	24.1	26.6	27.2	29.3
居民个人卫生支出	Resident Individual Expenditure	54.8	55.9	59	60.0	57.7	55.8	53.6

注：本表卫生费用为测算数。
a) Data in the table are estimated.

主要统计指标解释

文化事业机构　指从事专业文化工作和为专业文化工作服务的独立建制的单位。不包括这些单位另外举办独立核算的其他机构和各部门的业余文化组织。该指标主要反映文化事业机构发展规模水平。

艺术表演团体　指从事戏曲、音乐、舞蹈、杂技等专业艺术表演，有独立帐户的单位，不包括半工半艺、半农半艺和民间职业剧团。该指标主要反映全国专业艺术表演团体发展规模水平。

艺术表演观众人数(人次)　指售票、包场演出或民族地区免费演出的艺术表演观众人次数，不包括彩排审查和内部观摩演出的观看人次数。该指标主要反映全国观看专业艺术表演团体演出的效益规模。

卫生机构　包括医疗机构、疾病预防控制中心(防疫站)、采供血机构、卫生监督及监测(检验)机构、医学科研和在职培训机构、健康教育所等。

医疗机构　包括医院、社区卫生服务中心(站)、疗养院、卫生院、门诊部、诊所(卫生所、医务室)、妇幼保健院(所、站)、专科疾病防治院(所、站)、急救中心(站)和临床检验中心。医疗机构分为非赢利性医疗机构和赢利性医疗机构。

医院　包括综合医院、中医医院、中西医结合医院、民族医院、各类专科医院和护理院。

卫生技术人员　指卫生机构中医生、护理人员 、药剂人员、检验人员等卫生技术人员。

医生　指在医疗、预防保健机构工作且取得《执业医师证书》的执业医师和执业助理医师。

卫生服务总费用　反映全国当年用于医疗卫生保健服务所消耗的资金总额，用筹资来源法测算。政府预算卫生支出指各级政府用于卫生事业的财政预算拨款。社会卫生支出指政府预算外的卫生资金投入，主要表现为社会医疗保险。其中包括如企事业单位和乡村集体经济单位举办医疗卫生机构设施建设费，企业职工医疗卫生费，行政事业单位负担的职工公费医疗超支部分等。居民个人卫生支出指城乡居民用自己可支配的经济收入支付的各项医疗卫生费用和医疗保险费用。

Explanatory Notes on Main Statistical Indicators

Cultural Institutions refer to units, which have their own organizational system and independent accounting system and specialize in or serve cultural development. They exclude other establishments run by these cultural institutions and amateur cultural groups established by various departments. This indicator reflects the development of cultural units.

Art Troupe refers to the troupe which is engaged in drama, opera, music, dance, acrobatics or other art performance, opens independent accounts with banks and has self-supporting accounting system; excluding the troupes which are engaged partly in industrial or agricultural activities, partly in art performance and the professional troupes organized by the people. This indicator reflects the development of national professional art troupes.

Number of Audience at Art Performance refers to the number of attendants at commercial shows, completely booked shows or free shows given in minority national areas, and does not include the number of spectators at rehearsals for examination and internal shows for study.

Health Care Institutions include: medical institutions, disease prevention and control centers (epidemic prevention stations), blood gathering and supplying institutions, health supervision and inspection (check up) institutions, medicinal scientific research and on-job training institutions, health education and so on.

Medical Organizations include: hospitals, health service centers (stations) of communities, nursing homes, health centers, clinics, clinics (health stations and infirmaries), maternity and child care agencies (centers and stations), special disease prevention and curing agencies (centers and stations), first aid centers (stations) and clinical inspection centers. Medical organizations are grouped by two types: profit-making and non-profit-making medical organizations.

Hospitals include: polyclinics, traditional Chinese medical hospitals, hospitals integrated with traditional Chinese therapeutics and western therapeutics, ethical hospitals, various specialties hospitals and nursing hospitals.

Medical Technical Personnel refers to doctors, assistant nurses, pharmacists, and laboratory technicians working in medical institutions.

Doctors refer to certified physicians and certified assistant physicians with certifications working in medical and health care and prevention agencies.

Total Cost of Health Services reflects the total expenditures on medical and health care services for the whole country, calculated on basis of sources of funding. Health expenditure from government budget refers to budgetary allocation for health undertakings by governments at all levels. Social health expenditure refers to non-government budgetary capital input, mainly the health insurance. It includes expenditure on health institutions run by enterprises and rural collective entities, expenditure on medical and health care of employees of enterprises, and excessive health expenditure of government employees that could be covered by the government health care system. Health expenditure on individuals refers to expenditure on health service and health insurance paid by residents from their disposable income.

23

其他社会活动

Other Social Activities

简要说明

本篇章的主要内容和资料来源

本篇主要包括社会活动参与、公检法司、民政事业、劳动保障、残疾人事业、妇女干部等内容。

一、社会活动参与的内容主要包括历届全国人大代表和政协委员情况以及全国工会组织情况。全国人大代表、政协委员数由全国人大和全国政协信息中心提供，依全国人大、政协换届情况每五年更换一次；全国工会组织情况由全国总工会依据统计报表制度整理提供。

二、公检法司的资料主要包括公安机关的刑事案件立案情况和治安案件查处情况，交通、火灾事故情况，检察机关的办案情况，人民法院审理案件和收结案情况，以及律师、公证、调解工作等情况。资料分别由公安部、最高人民法院、最高人民检察院和司法部依据统计报表制度整理提供。

三、民政事业和劳动保障统计资料主要包括社会福利企事业机构、人员、经费情况、优抚和社会救济情况、城镇社区服务和农村社会保障网络情况、婚姻登记情况、离退休人员数量及费用和劳动争议仲裁等情况。资料分别由民政部与劳动和社会保障部依据统计报表制度整理提供。

民政事业统计资料详见《中国民政事业统计年鉴》（民政部财务和机关事务司编），工会资料详见《中国工会统计年鉴》（全国总工会编）。

四、残疾人资料主要包括残疾人康复、教育、就业、扶贫和残联组织建设等情况。资料由中国残疾人联合会整理提供。

五、妇女干部情况主要包括妇联系统的专职干部分年龄、学历、政治面貌和妇女干部的流动等情况。资料由全国妇联提供。

Brief Introduction

Main Content and Source of Data

Data in this chapter show statistics on participation in social activities, public security, procuratorial, legal and judicial affairs, civil affairs, labor protection, disabled persons, survey on female cadres and female conditions and so on.

I. Data on participation cover mainly information on representatives to the National People's Congress (NPC), members of the Chinese People's Political Consultative Conference (CPPCC) and trade unions. Data on number of NPC and CPPCC representatives are provided by NPC and CPPCC information centers. Data on expiration of office terms of NPC and CPPCC are updated every five years. Data on trade unions are from All-China Federation of Trade Unions based on statistical reporting scheme.

II. Data on public security, procuratorial, legal and judicial affairs cover information such as criminal cases registered and offense cases handled by the public security agencies, traffic or fire accidents, cases handled by procurator's offices, cases accepted and settled by the people's courts, and statistics on lawyers, notarization and mediation. Data are from the Ministry of Public Security, the Supreme People's Procuratorate, the Supreme People's Court and the Ministry of Justice based on statistical reporting scheme.

III. Data on civil affairs and labor protection include: condition of institutions and personnel, budget, social welfare relief, urban welfare facilities, rural network of social security, marriage registration, retirement pensions, arbitration of labor disputes, etc. Data on civil affairs and labor protection are from the Ministry of Civil Affairs and the Ministry of Labor and Social Security based on statistical reporting scheme.

Data on civil affairs refer to "*Statistical Yearbook on Civil Affairs of China*" (Department of Financial and Departmental Affair, Ministry of Civil Affairs). Data on trade unions refer to "*Statistical Yearbook on Chinese Trade Unions*" (All-China Federation of Trade Unions).

IV. Data on disabled persons covering information on the rehabilitation, education, employment and poverty alleviation of disabled persons and institutions serving the needs of disabled persons. Data are from the All-China Federation of Disabled Persons,

V. Data on female cadres mainly include the basic information of age, education, membership in political parties and shift of work position of full time cadres within Women's Federation system. Data are from All-China Federation of Women.

23-1 历届全国人民代表大会代表人数

Number of Deputies to All the Previous National People's Congresses

单位：人 (person)

届别	Congress	年份 Year	代表总数 Total Number of Deputies	#女代表 Female Deputies	#少数民族代表 Minority Deputies	占代表总数比重(%) As Percentage to Total Deputies (%) #女代表 Female Deputies	#少数民族代表 Minority Deputies
一 届	First Congress	1954	1226	147	178	12.0	14.5
二 届	Second Congress	1959	1226	150	179	12.2	14.6
三 届	Third Congress	1964	3040	542	372	17.8	12.2
四 届	Fourth Congress	1975	2885	653	270	22.6	9.4
五 届	Fifth Congress	1978	3497	742	381	21.2	10.9
六 届	Sixth Congress	1983	2978	632	403	21.2	13.5
七 届	Seventh Congress	1988	2978	634	445	21.3	14.9
八 届	Eighth Congress	1993	2978	626	439	21.0	14.7
九 届	Ninth Congress	1998	2979	650	428	21.8	14.4
十 届	Tenth Congress	2003	2985	604	414	20.2	13.9

23-2 历届全国政治协商会议委员人数

Number of Deputies to All the Previous Chinese People's Political Consultative Conferences

单位：人 (person)

届别	Congress	年份 Year	委员总数 Total Number of Deputies	#中国共产党委员 Deputies from the Communist Party of China	#少数民族委员 Minority Deputies	占委员总数比重(%) As Percentage to Total Deputies (%) #中国共产党委员 Deputies from the Communist Party of China	#少数民族委员 Minority Deputies
一 届	First Congress	1954	198		19		9.6
二 届	Second Congress	1959	729	40	61	5.5	8.4
三 届	Third Congress	1964	1071	60	78	5.6	7.3
四 届	Fourth Congress	1975	1199	61	81	5.1	6.8
五 届	Fifth Congress	1978	1988	76	143	3.8	7.2
六 届	Sixth Congress	1983	2039	76	185	3.7	9.1
七 届	Seventh Congress	1988	2083	90	225	4.3	10.8
八 届	Eighth Congress	1993	2093	91	241	4.3	11.5
九 届	Ninth Congress	1998	2196	92	258	4.2	11.7
十 届	Tenth Congress	2003	2238	99	103	4.4	4.6

23-3 妇联干部情况

Cadres of the Women's Federation

单位：人 (person)

项目	Item	1990	1995	2004	2005
干部总数	**Total Number of Cadres**	**97566**	**82834**	**57336**	**61565**
#少数民族干部	Number of Minority Cadres	14638	10834	6911	9156
按行政级别分	By Administration Level				
司局级	Department/Bureau Level	132	321	335	255
县处级	County Level	1013	2739	3679	3201
科以下	Section Chief and Below	96421	79774	53322	58109
按干部年龄分	By Age Group				
35岁以下	35 and Below	56761	24570	25998	28355
36-45岁	36-45	30332	47197	23028	24897
46-55岁	46-55	9512	10349	8024	7976
56岁以上	56 and Over	961	718	286	337
按干部政治面貌分	By Political Status				
共产党员	Chinese Communist Party	59097	54038	44868	49516
共青团员	Communist Youth League	21549	13271	4754	4556
民主党派	Democratic Parties	1136	1281	371	599
群众	Mass	15784	14244	7343	6894
按干部文化程度分	By Education Attainments				
博士生	Ph. Doctor			19	13
研究生	Master		698	889	1127
大学本科、大专学历	University / College	17615	30146	45046	50380
高中、中专及以下	Senior Middle School and Below	79951	51990	11382	10045
按行政编制分	By Organization Types				
行政编制	Administration	69158	65336	44810	48994
事业编制	Institution	7217	4944	10570	10912
招聘干部	Recruitment	21191	12554	1956	1659
干部参加学历教育情况	**Cadres Attending the Formal Education**				
博士生	Ph. Doctor			8	43
研究生	Master		149	677	820
大学、大专学历	University / College	6676	4025	6032	6447
干部参加非学历教育情况	**Cadres Attending the Non-formal Education**				
党校培训	Training at Party School			14227	18625
参照公务员管理培训	Training for Civil Servant			13762	23088
岗位培训	Vocational Training	37542	9391	20394	22637
干部流动情况	**Cadres Exchange**				
调入	In	1273	2010	3331	3385
调出	Out	8262	1629	2667	2918
省（区、市）妇联领导进同级	**Cadres at Provincial Level Attending the Same Level**				
党委	CCP Committee	22	13	20	18
人大	People's Congress	24	88	24	33
政协	CPPCC	24	33	30	30

注：妇联干部指在妇联系统工作的专职干部。

a) Cadres of the women's federation refer to the full-time cadres who are working in the system of women's federation.

23-4 工会组织情况

Basic Statistics on Trade Unions

年 份 Year	工会基层组织数（万个） Number of Grassroot Trade Unions (10 000 units)	全国已建工会组织的基层单位的职工与会员人数（万人） Membership and Staff and Workers in Grassroot Trade Unions (10 000 persons)				工会专职工作人员人数(万人) Number of Full-time Personnel of Trade Unions (10 000 persons)
		职工人数 Staff and Workers	#女职工 Female	会员人数 Membership	#女会员 Female	
1952	20.7	1393.2		1002.3		5.3
1957	16.5	2158.3		1746.7		
1962	16.5	2667.1		1922.0		8.6
1978						
1979	32.9	6897.2	2171.7	5147.3		17.9
1980	37.6	7448.2	2518.6	6116.5		24.3
1981	41.1	8183.0	2902.0	6843.9	2412.8	29.1
1982	43.3	8586.6	3065.9	7331.6	2629.3	32.2
1983	44.7	8845.7	3191.8	7693.4	2771.4	33.7
1984	46.6	9243.9	3370.3	8029.1	2950.3	41.9
1985	46.5	9643.0	3596.7	8525.8	3149.2	38.1
1986	50.2	9949.6	3664.3	8908.5	3309.2	45.9
1987	53.6	10411.8	3900.4	9336.5	3486.9	47.0
1988	56.4	10747.4	4434.9	9628.9	3647.0	47.4
1989	58.9	10998.6	4178.7	9909.2	3777.7	48.8
1990	60.6	11156.9	4291.0	10135.6	3897.7	55.6
1991	61.4	11351.4	4394.8	10389.1	3991.6	58.0
1992	61.7	11223.9	4377.1	10322.5	3974.0	58.0
1993	62.7	11103.8	4359.9	10176.1	3949.6	55.4
1994	58.3	11269.6	4483.2	10202.5	4018.1	56.0
1995	59.3	11321.4	4515.3	10399.6	4116.5	46.8
1996	58.6	11181.4	4500.0	10211.9	4093.1	60.5
1997	51.0	10111.5	4004.8	9131.0	3579.4	57.7
1998	50.4	9716.5	3882.0	8913.4	3546.7	48.4
1999	50.9	9683.0	3797.9	8689.9	3406.2	49.7
2000	85.9	11472.1	4534.5	10361.5	3917.3	48.2
2001	153.8	12997.0	5087.9	12152.3	4696.6	
2002	171.3	14461.5	5157.6	13397.8	4665.2	47.2
2003	90.6	13301.6	5079.3	12340.5	4601.2	46.5
2004	102.0	14436.7	5502.6	13694.9	5135.3	45.6
2005	117.4	15985.3	6016.3	15029.4	5574.8	47.7

注：2003年起工会基层组织数统计口径有所调整。

a) Since 2003, coverage of number of grassroot trade unions was adjusted.

23-5 劳动争议处理情况
The Disposal of Labor Disputes

项　　目	Item	2004	2005
上期未结案数　（件）	**Number of Cases Left Over from Last Period　(case)**	**17117**	**17829**
案件受理情况	**Cases Accepted**		
当期案件受理数　（件）	Number of Cases　(case)	260471	313773
#集体劳动争议数	Number of Collective Labour Disputes	19241	19387
#劳动者申诉案件数	Number of Cases Appealed by Laborers	249335	293710
劳动者当事人数　（人）	Number of Persons Involved　(person)	764981	744195
#集体争议劳动者当事人数	Number of Persons Involved in Collective Disputes	477992	409819
争议原因　（件）	Cause of the Disputes　(case)		
变更劳动合同	Change the Labour Contract	4465	7567
解除劳动合同	Relieve the Labour Contract	42881	54858
终止劳动合同	End the Labour Contract	14140	14015
其他	Others	17776	28257
案件处理情况	**Cases Settled**		
结案数　（件）	**Number of Cases Settled　(case)**	**258678**	**306027**
按处理方式分	by Manners of Settlement		
仲裁调解	by Mediation	83400	104308
仲裁裁决	by Arbitration Lawsuit	110708	131745
其他方式	Others	64550	69974
按处理结果分	by Result of Settlement		
用人单位胜诉	Won by Units	35679	39401
劳动者胜诉	Lawsuit Won by Laborers	123268	145352
双方部分胜诉	Lawsuit Partly by Both Parties	94041	121274
本期未结案数　（件）	**Number of Cases Dissettled　(case)**	**18817**	**25575**

23-6　律师、公证和调解工作基本情况

Basic Statistics on Lawyers, Notarization and Mediation

项　目	Item	2000	2001	2002	2003	2004	2005
律师工作	**Lawyers**						
律师事务所　(个)	Number of Law Offices (unit)	9541	10225	10873	11593	11823	12988
律师工作人员　(人)	Number of Lawyers (person)	117260	122585	136684	142534	145196	153846
#专职律师　(人)	Full-time Lawyers (person)	69117	76558	90012	99793	100875	114471
兼职律师　(人)	Part-time Lawyers (person)	15639	13699	12186	6850	6966	7418
聘请担任常年法律顾问的单位　(处)	Number of Units with Permanent Legal Advisors (unit)	247160	254758	265362	271669	282361	276097
民事诉讼代理　(件)	Agent of Civil Cases (case)	640610	667232	767628	781452	853897	965956
经济诉讼代理　(件)	Agent of Economic Cases (case)	438672	402669	381146	405133	357326	376793
刑事辩护　(件)	Defender of Criminal Cases (case)	317108	339549	335267	324454	332688	354229
行政诉讼代理　(件)	Agent of Administrative Action (case)	41785	43800	43703	48115	50778	50389
非诉讼法律事务　(件)	Agent of Non-Litigious Legal Affairs (case)	770087	1162715	827057	876696	904516	933346
涉外及涉港澳台法律事务　(件)	Agent of Foreign-related, Hong Kong, Macao & Taiwan Legal Affairs (case)	30531	10609	26788	20622	37728	36361
解答法律询问　(万件)	Agent of Legal Advisory Services (10 000 cases)	457.40	403.40	487.41	430.25	471.05	441.48
代写法律事务文书　(万件)	Agent of Legal Documents Written on Behalf of Clients (10 000 cases)	111.30	113.90	119.70	120.27	123.16	120.07
公证工作	**Notarization**						
公证处　(个)	Number of Notary Offices (unit)	3189	3186	3157	3175	3164	3160
公证人员　(人)	Notarial Personnel (person)	19211	19303	19460	20015	19913	20789
#公证员　(人)	Notaries (person)	12849	12931	12245	12093	11714	11738
公证员助理　(人)	Assistant Notaries (person)	2103	1995	2556	3018	3644	4138
办理公证文书　(万件)	Number of Notarized Documents (10 000 cases)	1249.7	1007.2	1004.5	1010.4	1021.9	945.22
人民调解工作	**Number of People's Mediation**						
专职司法助理员　(人)	Number of Full-time Judicial Assistants (person)	54638	48682	47173	46088	63438	61666
人民调解委员会　(万个)	Number of People's Mediation Committees (10 000 units)	96.4	92.3	89.1	87.8	85.3	84.71
调解人员　(万人)	Number of Mediators (10 000 persons)	844.5	779.3	716.2	669.2	514.4	509.65
调解民间纠纷　(万件)	Number of Civil Disputes Mediated (10 000 cases)	503.1	486.1	314.1	449.2	441.4	448.68

23-7 国内公证文书分类

Domestic Notarial Documents by Type

分 类	Item	2004 办证件数(件) Number of Notarial Documents Issued (pieces)	2004 比 重 (%) Percentage	2005 办证件数(件) Number of Notarial Documents Issued (pieces)	2005 比 重 (%) Percentage
经济公证	**Notarized Documents on Economic Affairs**	**3915752**	**100.00**	**3115642**	**100.00**
购 销	Purchases and Sales of Products	81717	2.09	55428	1.78
联 营	Joint Business	8864	0.23	10565	0.34
拍 卖	Auctions	43326	1.11	21507	0.69
贷 款	Loans	1950465	49.81	1620008	52.00
担 保	Guarantees	82248	2.10	79276	2.54
招标、投标	Bidding	67795	1.73	66010	2.12
技术合作	Scientific and Technological Contracts	3340	0.09	955	0.03
供用电	Supply and Use of Electric Power	224003	5.72	15005	0.48
劳务合同	Labor Contracts	95010	2.43	80289	2.58
建筑工程承包	Construction Project Contracts	15896	0.41	11932	0.38
工商服务业承包	Industrial and Commercial Service Contracts	23968	0.61	15496	0.50
农林牧副渔业承包	Farming, Forestry, Animal Husbandry, Sideline Production and Fishery Contracts	96043	2.45	77025	2.47
乡镇企业承包	Township Enterprise Contracts	3811	0.10	2303	0.07
财产租赁	Property Leases	17419	0.44	15951	0.51
企业租赁	Leases of Enterprise	2917	0.07	2692	0.09
资产经营协议	Asset Business Contracts	1814	0.05	1216	0.04
还款协议	Payment Contracts	118080	3.02	80371	2.58
土地使用权出让、转让	Selling or Transfer of Right of Land Utilization	40042	1.02	31771	1.02
其他经济合同	Other Business Contracts	301955	7.71	234079	7.51
法人(代表人)资格	Legal Person (agent) Identification	13027	0.33	12341	0.40
法人委托书	Legal Person Trust Deeds	112830	2.88	97964	3.14
公司章程	Corporation Constitutions	6266	0.16	3203	0.10
执行许可证明	Operating Permits	18897	0.48	19499	0.63
提 存	Consignation	11004	0.28	5500	0.18
抵押登记	Mortgage Registration	59955	1.53	66830	2.14
公司会议记录	Minutes of Corporation Meetings	19896	0.51	4440	0.14
其 他	Others	495164	12.65	483986	15.53
民事法律关系公证	**Notarized Documents on Civil Legal Relations**	**3462455**	**100.00**	**3431118**	**100.00**
收 养	Child Adoption	7040	0.20	6395	0.19
解除收养	Adoption Renouncements	2991	0.09	2008	0.06
继承权	Rights of Inheritance	232621	6.72	263560	7.68
遗 嘱	Testaments	72685	2.10	73398	2.14
产 权	Property Rights	36383	1.05	30675	0.89
亲属关系	Kinship Confirmation	40898	1.18	40805	1.19
死 亡	Death Certificates	10940	0.32	11209	0.33
房屋买卖	Purchases and Sales of Houses	362682	10.47	342168	9.97
房屋租赁	House Leases	22901	0.66	23222	0.68
留学协议	Foreign Study Contracts	7840	0.23	6406	0.19
遗赠扶养协议	Donations and Family Fostering	14615	0.42	8327	0.24
委托书	Trust Deeds	560125	16.18	594318	17.32
赠与书	Presentation Documents	113653	3.28	114659	3.34
声明书	Declarations	200202	5.78	215877	6.29
现场监督	Field Supervision	88739	2.56	113544	3.31
签名印鉴属实	Confirmation of Signatures and Seals	48833	1.41	53103	1.55
副本等与原本相符	Confirmation of Copies and Photo-offset Copies to Originals	40544	1.17	44120	1.29
宅基地使用权	Rights to Housing Site	13882	0.40	10025	0.29
证据保全	Evidence Preservation	106956	3.09	112962	3.29
拆迁协议	Housing Demolition Agreements	88747	2.56	68963	2.01
计划生育	Family Planning	192544	5.56	136691	3.98
赡养协议	Agreements on Supporting Parents	9301	0.27	10506	0.31
合伙协议	Partnership Agreements	11923	0.34	8366	0.24
夫妻财产协议	Property Agreements Between Spouses	69860	2.02	57485	1.68
其他民事协议	Other Civil Agreements	504835	14.58	361436	10.53
其 他	Others	600715	17.35	720890	21.01

23-8 涉外公证文书分类

Foreign-Related Notarial Documents by Type

分类	Item	2004		2005	
		办证件数(件) Number of Notarial Documents Issued (pieces)	比重(%) Percentage	办证件数(件) Number of Notarial Documents Issued (pieces)	比重(%) Percentage
合计	**Total**	**2592005**	**100.00**	**2717454**	**100.00**
收养	Child Adoption	22285	0.86	17554	0.65
遗嘱	Testaments	3293	0.13	4265	0.16
出生	Births	381714	14.73	368510	13.56
死亡	Deaths	11812	0.46	15392	0.57
生存、居住	Survival and Residence	9176	0.35	12551	0.46
学历	Schooling	211498	8.16	203673	7.49
经历	Personal Histories	43850	1.69	36623	1.35
国籍	Nationality	48358	1.87	58612	2.16
婚姻状况	Marital Status	201330	7.77	194409	7.15
亲属关系	Kinship Confirmation	304515	11.75	313478	11.54
继承权	Rights of Inheritance	2989	0.12	4311	0.16
受、未受刑事处分	Criminal Records	276506	10.67	282106	10.38
声明书	Announcement	61615	2.38	77590	2.86
委托书	Proxy	34037	1.31	33769	1.24
营业证书	Shop Card	15134	0.58	15732	0.58
公司章程	Corporation Constitutions	2977	0.11	3248	0.12
其他法律文书	Other Legal Documents	57046	2.20	25210	0.93
职称	Professional Certificates	12690	0.49	11386	0.42
法人资格	Legal Person Identification	2599	0.10	3354	0.12
商标注册	Trademark Registrations	335	0.01	243	
贷款	Loans	8643	0.33	6526	0.24
担保	Guarantees	1413	0.05	5320	0.2
其他经济合同	Other Business Contracts	22081	0.85	27462	1.01
副本等与原本相符	Confirmation of Copies and Photo-offset Copies to Originals	352779	13.61	459239	16.9
签名印鉴属实	Confirmation of Copies and Photo-offset Copies to Originals	161250	6.22	194776	7.17
其他	Other	342080	13.20	342115	12.59

23-9 调解民间纠纷分类

Number of Civil Disputes Mediated by Type

项　目	Item	调解纠纷(件) Civil Disputes (cases)		各类纠纷所占比重(%) Percentage	
		2004	2005	2004	2005
合　计	**Total**	**4414233**	**4486825**	**100.0**	**100.0**
婚姻家庭	Family Disputes	1140130	1049969	25.8	23.4
婚　姻	Marriages				
继　承	Rights of Inheritance				
赡抚扶养	Family Fostering				
其　他	Others				
房屋、宅基地	Housing and Housing Sites	398759	388032	9.0	8.6
债　务	Debts				
生产经营	Business				
邻　里	Neighbor Disputes	793917	836919	18.0	18.7
损害赔偿	Compensation for Damages	340021	332514	7.7	7.4
其　他	Others	478318	525756	10.8	11.7

23-10 在押服刑人员基本情况

Basic Statistics of Termers in Custody

单位：人 (person)

指　标	Item	2004	2005
年初在押服刑人数	Termers in Custody at the Beginning of the Year	1562742	1558511
#女性	Female	75870	77279
未成年	Minors	21975	23957
释放人数	Persons Dis-imprisoned	332172	319346
年末在押服刑人数	Termers in Custody at the End of the Year	1558511	1565711

注：1.本表未成年是指14-18岁服刑人员。
2.释放人员是指减刑释放、假释和刑满释放人员。
a) Minors in this table refer to termers at the age between 14 and 18.
b) Persons dis-imprisoned refer to persons commuted, paroled or released after serving the full term of a sentence.

23-11 公安机关立案的刑事案件及构成

Criminal Cases Registered in Public Security Organs and Its Composition

单位：起 (case)

案件类别	Category of Cases	立案(起) Number of Cases Registered (case)		构成(%) Composition (%)	
		2004	2005	2004	2005
合计	**Total**	**4718122**	**4648401**	**100.00**	**100.00**
杀人	Homicide	24711	20770	0.52	0.45
伤害	Injury	148623	155056	3.15	3.34
抢劫	Robbery	341908	332196	7.25	7.15
强奸	Rape	36175	33710	0.77	0.73
拐卖妇女儿童	Abducting Women or Children	3343	2884	0.07	0.06
盗窃	Larceny	3212822	3158763	68.10	67.95
诈骗	Fraud	205844	203083	4.36	4.37
走私	Smuggling	955	925	0.02	0.02
伪造、变造货币,出售、购买、运输、持有、使用假币	Forging Coin, and Selling, Buying, Transporting, Using the False Coin	2315	1858	0.05	0.04
其他	Others	741426	739156	15.71	15.90

注：2005年共破获刑事案件2097369起。
a) The solved criminal cases in 2005 are 2097369 cases.

23-12 公安机关受理、查处治安案件数

Offense Cases Against Public Order Handled by Public Security Organs

单位：起 (case)

案件类别	Category of Cases	2004		2005	
		受理 Number of Cases Accepted to be Treated	查处 Number of Cases Investigated and Treated	受理 Number of Cases Accepted to be Treated	查处 Number of Cases Investigated and Treated
合计	**Total**	**6647724**	**5365787**	**7377600**	**6300772**
扰乱工作、公共秩序	Disturbing Work or Public Order	545030	537187	498871	488611
结伙斗殴、寻衅滋事	Gang Fighting or Picking Quarrels and Making Troubles	120030	102225	123641	109123
侮辱妇女及其他流氓活动	Acting Indecently Towards Women	16455	14889	17404	16524
阻碍国家工作人员执行职务	Obstructing the Government Workers to Perform Their Duty	35148	33663	38505	37092
违反枪支管理规定	Violating Regulations on Management of Firearms	7610	7392	6307	6306
违反爆炸物品管理规定	Violating Regulations on Management of Explosives	45144	44076	46139	45417
殴打他人	Beating Other Body	1193348	935634	1392145	1163672
偷窃财物	Robbing Other People of Their Valuables	1259087	559921	1513770	924095
骗取、抢夺、敲诈勒索财物	Defrauding, Snatching or Extorting and Racketeering Valuables	190694	82518	213207	115702
哄抢公私财物	Making Stirs and Then Robbing Public or Private Valuables	5387	3697	5355	4200
故意损坏公私财物	Intentionally Damaging Public or Private Valuables	134172	92168	168879	128559
伪造倒卖票券、证件	Forging and Fraudulently Selling Bills or Certificates	14811	14552	17523	17338
利用迷信扰乱秩序或骗财	Disturbing Public Order or Defrauding People of Their Valuables by Making Use of Their Superstition	8119	7751	8224	8116
卖淫、嫖娼	Prostitution or Going Whoring	142633	141123	143995	142746
赌博	Gambling	380276	373365	418274	412098
违反户口、居民身份证管理	Violating Regulations on Management of Residence or Identity Cards	734880	725012	788485	785276
其他	Others	1814900	1690614	1976876	1895897

23-13 交通事故情况（2005年）

Basic Statistics on Traffic Accidents (2005)

类别	Type	发生数（起） Number of Traffic Accidents (case)	死亡人数（人） Number of Deaths (person)	受伤人数（人） Number of Injuries (person)	损失折款（万元） Losses Converted into Cash (10 000 yuan)
总计	**Total**	**450254**	**98738**	**469911**	**188401.2**
#重大事故	Grave Accidents	86060	98738	47927	57886.1
#特大事故	Serious Accidents	1924	7639	5627	7811.9
机动车	Vehicles	424409	93614	443361	183841.9
#汽车	Motor Vehicles	303696	69808	300837	167997.4
摩托车	Motorcycles	110209	20773	132124	13789.3
拖拉机	Tractors	10221	2933	10197	1997.1
非机动车	Non-motor-driven Vehicles	13823	1876	13674	1431.8
#自行车	Bicycles	8015	1204	7612	923.2
行人乘车人	Pedestrians and Passengers	11302	2902	12406	3014.4
其他	Others	720	346	470	113.0

注：损失折款指直接损失(以下各表同)。

a) Losses converted into cash refer to direct losses. The same as in the following tables.

23-14 火灾事故情况（2005年）
Basic Statistics on Fires (2005)

项　目	Item	合计 Total	特大 Extraordinarily Serious	重大 Serious	一般 Ordinary
发生（起）	Fires (case)	235941	33	250	235658
死亡（人）	Deaths (person)	2496	160	341	1995
受伤（人）	Injuries (person)	2506	167	115	2224
损失折款（万元）	Losses Converted into Cash (10 000 yuan)	136288	7790	10866	117632
平均每起事故损失（元）	Average Loss of Fire (yuan)	5776	2360606	434640	4992

23-15 各地区交通事故情况（2005年）
Basic Statistics on Traffic Accidents by Region (2005)

地区	Region	发生数（起）Number of Traffic Accidents (case)	死亡人数（人）Number of Deaths (person)	受伤人数（人）Number of Injuries (person)	损失折款（万元）Losses Converted into Cash (10000 yuan)
全　国	**National Total**	**450254**	**98738**	**469911**	**188401.2**
北　京	Beijing	6364	1515	6888	2915.6
天　津	Tianjin	4406	970	4939	2455.8
河　北	Hebei	11187	4075	11449	7646.2
山　西	Shanxi	13342	3819	13575	5782.9
内蒙古	Inner Mongolia	8453	2106	8000	2784.7
辽　宁	Liaoning	10341	2919	9159	5907.0
吉　林	Jilin	9659	2428	6837	4468.2
黑龙江	Heilongjiang	7506	2164	7655	3464.9
上　海	Shanghai	9238	1393	8850	7960.9
江　苏	Jiangsu	27690	7603	25530	12668.1
浙　江	Zhejiang	43266	6881	48262	15718.0
安　徽	Anhui	17474	4355	19771	6118.5
福　建	Fujian	26195	4125	27696	9278.9
江　西	Jiangxi	8585	2428	8370	7697.6
山　东	Shandong	35251	7050	32456	11816.4
河　南	Henan	23778	4587	22831	10674.9
湖　北	Hubei	9585	2417	10555	4958.0
湖　南	Hunan	15013	3832	18271	7131.4
广　东	Guangdong	67756	9959	77591	20882.8
广　西	Guangxi	10717	3489	12562	4405.6
海　南	Hainan	1479	497	1964	638.2
重　庆	Chongqing	10605	1484	13580	2598.5
四　川	Sichuan	29628	4415	30906	10745.4
贵　州	Guizhou	3315	1647	3984	2507.1
云　南	Yunnan	6870	2901	7549	3502.2
西　藏	Tibet	845	540	891	877.8
陕　西	Shaanxi	12011	2698	8905	6241.6
甘　肃	Gansu	5414	1799	5406	2252.8
青　海	Qinghai	952	736	1121	410.9
宁　夏	Ningxia	3803	796	3922	1055.8
新　疆	Xinjiang	9526	3110	10436	2834.5

23-16 各地区火灾事故情况（2005年）

Basic Statistics on Fires by Region (2005)

地 区	Region	发生数 (起) Number of Traffic Accidents (case)	死亡人数 (人) Number of Deaths (person)	受伤人数 (人) Number of Injuries (person)	直接经济损失 (万元) Losses Converted into Cash (10 000 yuan)	人口火灾发生率 (1/10万人) Average Number of Fires Per 100 Thousand People
全 国	**National Total**	**235941**	**2496**	**2506**	**136287.5**	**18.6**
北 京	Beijing	9781	50	114	1671.0	83.8
天 津	Tianjin	4728	40	30	2040.5	50.4
河 北	Hebei	7041	92	65	4605.1	10.3
山 西	Shanxi	3319	55	75	2424.8	10.1
内蒙古	Inner Mongolia	5351	37	60	1956.6	22.7
辽 宁	Liaoning	22889	161	128	9394.6	54.9
吉 林	Jilin	18852	135	147	4928.1	70.8
黑龙江	Heilongjiang	13488	71	58	4750.9	35.9
上 海	Shanghai	5869	54	88	2704.2	43.4
江 苏	Jiangsu	15196	166	115	7429.2	21.1
浙 江	Zhejiang	6755	112	82	7778.0	14.8
安 徽	Anhui	7621	93	98	4956.1	11.8
福 建	Fujian	6579	97	87	6003.0	19.5
江 西	Jiangxi	6674	60	60	5388.2	15.3
山 东	Shandong	16932	48	52	6540.1	18.5
河 南	Henan	7390	61	38	3611.6	7.5
湖 北	Hubei	9250	56	47	5510.5	15.4
湖 南	Hunan	5195	117	121	5476.3	7.8
广 东	Guangdong	13266	298	350	12418.4	17.0
广 西	Guangxi	2678	118	116	5320.4	5.5
海 南	Hainan	1335	15	21	1229.2	16.6
重 庆	Chongqing	7904	57	67	3724.9	25.1
四 川	Sichuan	10676	114	111	7688.2	12.4
贵 州	Guizhou	2299	97	62	2427.1	6.0
云 南	Yunnan	4112	107	83	4456.7	9.7
西 藏	Tibet	254	9	19	535.3	9.7
陕 西	Shaanxi	7489	64	64	4682.8	20.4
甘 肃	Gansu	2526	30	41	2468.5	9.7
青 海	Qinghai	936	14	22	442.6	18.8
宁 夏	Ningxia	3347	7	12	913.6	56.7
新 疆	Xinjiang	6209	61	73	2810.7	32.2

注：全国总计数据包括发生在铁道、交通、军队的火灾情况。

a) The national data include the fires which occurred in railways, traffic and armies.

23-17 检察机关直接立案侦查案件情况（2005年）

Cases under Direct Investigation by Procurator's Offices (2005)

案件分类	Case Item	受案(件) Cases Accepted (case)	立案件数(件) Number of Cases Registered (case)	立案人数(人) Person of Cases Registered (person)	#要案 Key Case	结案件数(件) Number of Cases Settled (case)	结案人数(人) Person of Cases Settled (person)
合计	**Total**	**63053**	**35028**	**41447**	**2799**	**32616**	**38457**
贪污贿赂案件小计	**Sub-total of Cases on Corruption and Bribery**	**48722**	**28322**	**33366**	**2503**	**26492**	**31109**
贪污	Corruption	24382	11792	15005	591	11077	14036
贿赂	Bribery	16224	10446	11225	1527	9701	10365
挪用公款	Misappropriation of Public Funds	7013	5636	6480	289	5268	6057
集体私分	Collective Illegal Possession of Public Funds	847	406	604	91	402	590
巨额财产来源不明	Unstated Source of Large Properties	212	24	25	5	19	21
其他	Others	44	18	27		25	40
渎职案件小计	**Sub-total of Cases on Abuse and Dereliction of Duty**	**14331**	**6706**	**8081**	**296**	**6124**	**7348**
滥用职权	Abuse of Power	4125	1883	2161	133	1703	1932
玩忽职守	Dereliction of Duty	4353	2648	3022	94	2432	2747
徇私舞弊	Fraudulent Practice	3274	955	1129	46	844	994
其他	Others	2579	1220	1769	23	1145	1675

注：结案中含上年旧存（以下各表同）。

a) Data of cases settled include cases turned over from previous year. The same as in the following tables.

23-18 检察机关审查批准、决定逮捕犯罪嫌疑人和提起公诉被告人情况（2005年）

Arrests of Criminal Suspects and Defendants Under Public Prosecution Approved by Procurator's Offices (2005)

案件分类	Item	批捕、决定逮捕合计 Total of Arrests		决定起诉合计 Total of Public Prosecutions	
		件 (case)	人 (person)	件 (case)	人 (person)
合计	**Total**	**581448**	**876419**	**654871**	**981009**
公安、安全、监狱机关提请小计	**Sub-total of Requests by Departments of State and Public Security and Prisons**	**566949**	**860372**	**630063**	**950804**
危害国家安全案	Offences Against State Security	185	296	185	349
危害公共安全案	Offences Against Public Security	49190	57923	75107	83800
破坏社会主义市场经济秩序案	Offences Against Socialist Economic Order	13766	21193	14932	24950
侵犯公民人身、民主权利案	Offences Against Citizens' Personal and Democratic Rights	126161	166134	145416	188574
侵犯财产案	Offences Against Properties	293275	469145	305852	492080
妨害社会管理秩序案	Offences Against Social Management of Order	84163	145357	88354	160702
危害国防利益案	Offences Against National Defense	199	308	207	336
军人违反职责案	Offences on Dereliction of Duty by Servicemen	10	16	10	13
检察机关直接立案侦查案件小计	**Sub-total of Cases Handled by Procuratorates**	**14499**	**16047**	**24808**	**30205**
贪污贿赂案	Offences on Corruption and Bribery	13258	14611	21146	25530
渎职案	Offences on Abuse and Dereliction of Duty	1241	1436	3662	4675

23-19 检察机关处理申诉案件情况（2005年）

Appeals Handled by Procurator's Offices (2005)

案件分类	Cases	受案(件) Cases Accepted (case)	立案复查(件) Cases Registered for Reinvestigation (case)	结案(件) Cases Settled (case)	#改变原决定 Original Decision Changed
合计	**Total**	**8127**	**4217**	**4169**	**600**
不服检察机关处理决定	Appeals against Decision of Procurator's Offices	3623	2482	2442	498
不服不批捕	Appeals against Rejection of Arrest	519	320	315	34
不服不起诉	Appeals against Rejection of Prosecuting	1551	1241	1189	159
不服撤案	Appeals against Withdrawal of the Case	132	78	82	19
不服原免予起诉	Appeals against Original Exemption of Lawsuit	139	103	112	30
其他	Others	1282	740	744	256
不服法院刑事判决裁定	Appeals against Judgment of Criminal Case	4504	1735	1727	102
刑罚执行中被害人申诉	Appeals of the Victim at the Punishment	1093	416	403	13
刑罚执行中被告人申诉	Appeals of the Defendant at the Punishment	1903	685	698	66
刑罚执行完毕后被害人申诉	Appeals of the Victim after the Punishment	363	159	160	8
刑罚执行完毕后被告人申诉	Appeals of the Defendant after the Punishment	1145	475	466	15

23-20 人民法院审理一审案件情况

First Trial Cases by Courts

单位：件 (case)

年份 Year	收案 Cases Accepted	刑事 Criminal	民事 Civil	经济纠纷 Economic Disputes	行政 Administrative	海事海商 Maritime Law and Affairs
1978	447755	146968	300787			
1979	513789	123846	389943			
1980	763535	197856	565679			
1981	906051	232125	673926			
1982	1024160	245219	778941			
1983	1343164	542648	756436	43553	527	
1984	1355460	431357	838307	84813	983	
1985	1319741	246655	846391	225541	916	238
1986	1611282	299720	989409	321220	632	301
1987	1875229	289614	1213219	366110	5940	346
1988	2290624	313306	1455130	513046	8573	569
1989	2913515	392564	1815385	694907	9934	725
1990	2916774	459656	1851897	591462	13006	753
1991	2901685	427840	1880635	566592	25667	951
1992	3051157	422991	1948786	650601	27125	1654
1993	3414845	403267	2089257	892580	27911	1830
1994	3955475	482927	2383764	1051742	35083	1959
1995	4545676	495741	2718533	1275959	52596	2847
1996	5312580	618826	3093995	1515848	79966	3945
1997	5288379	436894	3277572	1478822	90557	4534
1998	5410798	482164	3375069	1450049	98350	5166
1999	5692434	540008	3519244	1529877	97569	5736
2000	5356294	560432	3412259	1290867	85760	6976
2001	5344934	628996	3459025	1149101	100921	6891
2002	5132199	631348	4420123		80728	
2003	5130760	632605	4410236		87919	
2004	5072881	647541	4332727		92613	
2005	5161170	684897	4380095		96178	

注：一审案件指人民法院按照诉讼级别管辖按第一审程序审理的案件。

a) First trial cases refer to cases accepted by people's courts according to the first trial proceedings.

23-21 人民法院审理刑事一审案件收结案情况（2005年）

First Trial Criminal Cases Accepted and Settled by Courts (2005)

单位：件 (case)

项目	Item	收案 Cases Accepted	结案 Cases Settled
合计	**Total**	**684897**	**683997**
危害公共安全罪	Offences Against Public Security	75099	74987
破坏社会主义市场经济秩序罪	Offences Against Socialist Economic Order	15229	15082
侵犯公民人身权利民主权利罪	Offences Against Citizens' Personal and Democratic Rights	177701	178046
侵犯财产罪	Offences Against Properties	304641	303869
妨害社会管理秩序罪	Offences Against Social Management of Order	87501	87221
危害国防利益罪	Offences Against National Defense	216	216
贪污贿赂罪	Offences on Corruption and Bribery	21558	21645
渎职罪	Offences on Dereliction of Duty	2664	2632
其他	Others	288	299
合计中含自诉案件	Private Prosecution of Total	29396	29996

23-22 人民法院审理刑事案件罪犯情况

Criminal Cases Heard by Courts

单位：人 (person)

年份 Year	刑事罪犯总数 Number of Offenders	#青少年罪犯 Young Offenders	不满18岁 Less Than 18 Years	18岁至25岁 Between 18 and 25 Years	青少年罪犯占刑事罪犯比重(%) Proportion of Young Offenders to Total (%)
1997	526312	199212	30446	168766	37.9
1998	528301	208076	33612	174464	39.4
1999	602380	221153	40014	181139	36.7
2000	639814	220981	41709	179272	34.5
2001	746328	253465	49883	203582	34.0
2002	701858	217909	50030	167879	31.0
2003	742261	231715	58870	172845	31.2
2004	764441	248834	70086	178748	32.6
2005	842545	285801	82692	203109	33.9

23-23 人民法院审理婚姻家庭、继承一审案件收结案情况（2005年）
First Trial Civil Cases of Marriages, Family Affairs and Inheritance Accepted and Settled by Courts (2005)

单位：件 (case)

项 目	Item	收 案 Cases Accepted	结 案 Cases Settled	调 解 Mediation	判 决 Judgment	驳 回 Reject	撤 诉 With-drawal	其 他 Other
合 计	**Total**	**1133333**	**1132458**	**512923**	**398241**	**4570**	**208513**	**8211**
婚姻家庭	Marriages and Family Affairs	1114879	1114469	507193	390242	4333	204742	7959
离婚	Divorce	956313	955643	440360	332730	3438	172674	6441
赡养纠纷	Support Disputes	35857	35894	13542	11698	109	10135	410
抚养、扶养关系纠纷	Upbringing Disputes	37280	37056	20173	10501	173	5979	230
抚育费纠纷	Upbringing Fee Disputes	24556	24509	10659	9102	120	4397	231
其他	Others	60873	61367	22459	26211	493	11557	647
继承	Inheritance	18454	17989	5730	7999	237	3771	252
法定继承	Legal Inheritance	9961	9694	3237	4179	118	2039	121
遗嘱继承	Testament Inheritance	1182	1193	341	601	12	223	16
其他	Others	7311	7102	2152	3219	107	1509	115

23-24 人民法院审理合同纠纷一审案件收结案情况（2005年）
First Trial Cases of Contracts Disputes Accepted and Settled by Courts (2005)

单位：件 (case)

项 目	Item	收 案 Cases Accepted	结 案 Cases Settled	调 解 Mediation	判 决 Judgment	驳 回 Reject	撤 诉 With-drawal	其 他 Other
合计	**Total**	**2265362**	**2255651**	**646934**	**930483**	**35701**	**592807**	**49726**
借款合同	Loan Contracts	705018	704528	229375	308003	6986	147551	12613
买卖合同	Trade Contracts	514251	510899	157134	209714	6740	125515	11796
电信合同	Telecom Contracts	119498	119484	40743	15299	234	59330	3878
租赁合同	Lease Contracts	104346	103182	23421	45451	1698	30923	1689
劳动争议	Work Disputes	122480	121516	27944	62608	7115	20988	2861
房地产合同	Real Estate Contracts	93750	94635	17694	52896	1883	20252	1910
供用动力合同	Labor Contracts	77171	77316	18769	21173	1228	35697	449
建设工程合同	Construction Contracts	71829	70129	16854	33353	1730	16406	1786
农村承包合同	Rural Contracts	56565	56221	18793	18210	859	17385	974
承揽合同	Contracts for Work	64345	63902	17197	25583	1088	18258	1776
其他	Others	336109	333839	79010	138193	6140	100502	9994

23-25 人民法院审理权属、侵权纠纷及其他民事一审收结案情况（2005年）

First Trial Cases of Disputes of Right, Infringement of Right and Other Civil Affairs Accepted and Settled by Courts (2005)

单位：件 (case)

项目	Item	收案 Cases Accepted	结案 Cases Settled	调解 Mediation	判决 Judgment	驳回 Reject	撤诉 With-drawal	其他 Other
合计	**Total**	**981400**	**972075**	**239915**	**403578**	**14912**	**164122**	**149548**
人身损害赔偿	Compensate for Personal Harm	447602	440936	152194	212934	3390	67139	5279
所有权及其相关权利	Ownership and Related Rights	258915	256851	62178	117025	6123	66942	4583
特别程序	Special Proceedings	180752	180937	5400	31622	3102	5417	135396
人身权纠纷	Personal Rights	9036	9087	1738	4492	179	2446	232
特殊侵权纠纷	Disputes of Special Infringement of Right	19882	18880	5557	8136	414	4454	319
不当得利	Unjustified Enrichment	9346	9302	1760	4514	272	2457	299
票据、证券、股票纠纷	Disputes of Bill, Securities and Stocks	10739	10748	1625	4554	499	2291	1779
知识产权案件	Intellectual Rights	13424	13393	1184	5282	259	6063	605
海事海商案件	Maritime Affairs	6000	5821	1354	2479	194	1637	157
其他	Other	25704	26120	6925	12540	480	5276	899

23-26 人民法院行政一审案件收结案情况（2005年）

First Trial Administrative Cases Accepted and Settled by Courts (2005)

单位：件 (case)

项目	Item	收案 Cases Accepted	结案 Cases Settled	维持 Affirmation of Original Judgement	撤销 Cancel	驳回 Reject	撤诉 With-drawal	单独赔偿 Separate Compen-sation	其他 Other
合计	**Total**	**96178**	**95707**	**15769**	**11764**	**20698**	**28539**	**2418**	**16519**
土地等资源	Land	18974	18835	3197	3866	3404	5163	297	2908
公安	Public Security	9514	9602	2806	969	1775	2780	401	871
城建	City Construction	19197	18864	2723	2701	4598	5729	550	2563
交通运输	Traffic and Transport	2945	3011	387	241	777	995	81	530
工商	Industry and Commerce	2970	2979	699	322	575	1014	74	295
环保	Environment Protection	1190	1220	120	28	75	222	9	766
计划生育	Family Planning	3480	3342	230	50	217	535	27	2283
税务	Tax	815	828	69	26	107	572	8	46
卫生	Health	930	951	175	70	172	327	27	180
乡政府	Townships Government	3966	3953	372	88	906	1618	105	864
劳动和社会保障	Labour and Social Security	7171	7152	1831	945	1587	1900	26	863
其他	Other	25026	24970	3160	2458	6505	7684	813	4350

23-27 收养、救助类单位情况

Basis Statistics on Social Welfare and Salvation Institutions

指标	Item	床位数（万张） Number of Beds (10 000 units) 2004	2005	比上年增减(%) Increase Rate over Preceding Year	收养救助人数（万人） Inmates (10 000 persons) 2004	2005	比上年增减(%) Increase Rate over Preceding Year	年末床位利用率(%) Bed Utilization Rate (%)
全国合计	**National Total**	**153.3**	**170.4**	**11.2**	**116.5**	**128.1**	**10.0**	**75.2**
收养类单位	**Adopting Institutions**	**146.8**	**164**	**11.7**	**110.9**	**123.7**	**11.5**	**75.4**
优抚类收养单位	Agencies for Martyrs	8.3	8.2	-1.2	5.6	5.8	3.6	70.7
荣誉军人康复医院	Convalescent Hospitals for Honorable Servicemen	0.6	0.6		0.3	0.4	33.3	66.7
复员军人慢性病疗养院	Sanatoriums for Ex-servicemen	0.5	0.6	20.0	0.4	0.4		66.7
复退军人精神病院	Mental Hospitals for Ex-servicemen	1.7	1.5	-11.8	1.2	1.2		80.0
光荣院	Homes for Disabled Veterans	5.5	5.5		3.7	3.8	2.7	69.1
福利类收养单位	Social Welfare Institutions	138.5	155.8	12.5	105.3	117.9	12.0	75.7
社会福利院	Social Welfare Homes	15.7	16.3	3.8	12.1	12.5	3.3	76.7
儿童福利院	Baby Welfare Homes	3	3.2	6.7	2.8	2.9	3.6	90.6
社会福利医院	Social Welfare Hospitals	2.8	2.9	3.6	2.4	2.6	8.3	89.7
城镇老年福利机构	Urban Welfare Homes for the Aged Persons	37.9	41.9	10.6	28	31.2	11.4	74.5
农村五保供养福利机构	Welfare Homes for Rural Households with Livelihood Guaranteed in Five Aspects	77.5	89.5	15.5	59.4	67.9	14.3	75.9
其它收养性单位	Others	1.6	2	25.0	0.6	0.8	33.3	40.0
社区类收养单位	**Community Welfare Units**	**1.8**	**1.8**		**0.8**	**0.7**	**-12.5**	**38.9**
救助类单位	**Salvation Institutions**	**4.7**	**4.6**	**-2.1**	**4.8**	**3.7**	**-22.9**	**80.4**

23-28 民政行业单位基本情况

Basic Conditions of Civil Affairs Agencies

指标	Item	单位数（个） Number of Enterprises 2004	2005	比上年增减(%) Increase Rate over Preceding Year	职工人数（人） Number of Staff and Workers 2004	2005	比上年增减(%) Increase Rate over Preceding Year
全国总计	**National Total**	**103411**	**101442**	**-1.9**	**2129262**	**2034085**	**-4.5**
事业单位	**Institutions**	**66884**	**66533**	**-0.5**	**453053**	**452244**	**-0.2**
提供住宿的社会福利单位	Lodging Providing Social Welfare Institutions	42190	45178	7.1	256992	264854	3.1
优抚类收养单位	Adopting Institutions	1446	1447	0.1	26531	26961	1.6
福利类收养单位	Welfare Institutions	37147	39921	7.5	183554	194502	6.0
社区服务单位	Community Service Institutions	522	622	19.2	6168	5541	-10.2
救助类单位	Salvation Institutions	1026	1119	9.1	17182	14711	-14.4
军队离退休干部休养所	Sanatoriums for Retired and Resigned Persons of the Army	1724	1745	1.2	16001	15713	-1.8
军队供应管理单位	Military Supply and Management Institutions	325	324	-0.3	7556	7426	-1.7
不提供住宿的社会福利单位	No Lodging Social Welfare Institutions	17039	17354	1.8	172448	173941	0.9
烈士纪念建筑物管理单位	Martyrys Management Institutions	938	989	5.4	8692	8871	2.1
社区服务单位	Community Service Institutions	7282	7857	7.9	51656	54363	5.2
殡葬事业单位	Funeral and Interment Institutions	3119	3284	5.3	66287	68588	3.5
福利彩票发行单位	Welfare Lottery Issuing Institutions	1128	1113	-1.3	5864	6169	5.2
其他事业单位	Other Institutions	4572	4111	-10.1	39949	35950	-10.0
老龄事业单位	Aging Population Institutions	7655	4001	-47.7	23613	13449	-43.0
社会福利企业单位	**Social Welfare Enterprises**	**32410**	**31211**	**-3.7**	**1524857**	**1442733**	**-5.4**
#国有	State-owned	1119	1013	-9.5	70247	65314	-7.0
集体	Collective-owned	24202	22029	-9.0	1110773	1041990	-6.2
其他	Other	7089	8169	15.2	343837	335429	-2.4
假肢厂	Artificial Limb Enterprises	40	38	-5.0	2640	2735	3.6
行政机关	**Administrative Departments**	**4117**	**3698**	**-10.2**	**112648**	**84081**	**-25.4**
乡镇民政助理员	**Civil Affairs Assistants in Townships**				**38704**	**55027**	**42.2**

23-29 享受补助、救济人员情况

Persons Receiving Subsidies or Relief Funds

单位：万人 (10 000 persons)

项　目	Item	2001	2002	2003	2004	2005
城市居民最低生活保障人数	**Number of Persons Receiving Lowest Cost-of-living in Urban Area**	**1170.7**	**2064.7**	**2246.8**	**2205.0**	**2234.2**
城市临时救济人次数	**Number of Poor Persons Receiving Temporary Almsgiving in Urban Area**	**213.9**	**321.4**	**348.3**	**285.2**	**234.4**
农村低保和传统救济人次数	**Number of Persons Receiving Lowest Cost-of-living or Traditional Relief in Rural Area**	**385.3**	**497.8**	**1160.5**	**1402.1**	**1891.8**
农村居民最低生活保障人数	Number of Persons Receiving Lowest Cost-of-living in Rural Area	304.6	407.8	367.1	488.0	825.0
#五保户数	Number of Households with Livelihood Guaranteed in Five Aspects		51.1	114.5	165.2	49.7
农村传统救济人数	Number of Persons Receiving Traditional Relief in Rural Area	80.7	90.0	793.4	914.1	1066.8
#五保户数	Number of Households with Livelihood Guaranteed in Five Aspects			173.9	228.7	300.0
农村临时救济人次数	**Number of Poor Persons Receiving Temporary Almsgiving in Rural Area**	**1800.5**	**1677.6**	**2009.8**	**1720.0**	**1359.9**

23-30 社会福利企业基本情况

Basic Statistics on Social Welfare Enterprises

年份 Year	国有和集体 State-owned and Collective-owned			其他 Other		
	单位(个) Number of Units (unit)	职工(人) Number of Staff and Workers (person)	#残疾职工 Disabled Persons	单位(个) Number of Units (unit)	职工(人) Number of Staff and Workers (person)	#残疾职工 Disabled Persons
1985	2214	219189	83051	12554	448829	151250
1986	2551	236371	89421	17211	637747	225708
1987	2976	250329	96605	24714	875974	337944
1988	3692	282947	106095	36701	1180589	875974
1989	4595	310345	119626	36864	1192179	494182
1990	5208	325461	124630	36517	1245072	512941
1991	6329	352112	136183	37889	1342064	565139
1992	6798	373412	142473	42985	1528266	635700
1993	7232	390619	147211	49649	1672141	695046
1994	7373	382519	151523	52805	1800262	757307
1995	7734	368636	148551	52503	1845838	790671
1996	7364	355864	141831	52033	1811820	794003
1997	8024	351354	141778	47485	1747143	767980
1998	7527	322522	133389	42987	1630654	722656
1999	7819	207271	132330	36809	1594894	657955
2000	31580	1377506	605592	9090	280853	123899
2001	31445	1379008	603447	6535	218626	95203
2002	29730	1319581	591930	6028	203602	90910
2003	27505	1261877	567916	6471	242983	110917
2004	25321	1181020	533726	7089	343837	125837
2005	23042	1107304	486646	8169	335429	150570

注：国有和集体办的福利企业数据，1999年以前统计范围仅限民政系统，2000年起扩大到全社会范围。

a) The statistical coverage in 2000 have been adjusted. The state-owned and collective-owned social welfare enterprises before 2000 refer to those managed by the system of civil administration, and those in 2000 refer to all state-owned and collective-owned social welfare enterprises.

23-31 各地区城镇社区服务设施基本情况（2005年）

Basic Statistics on Community Services Facilities in Urban Areas by Region (2005)

单位：个 (unit)

地 区	Region	城镇社区服务设施数 Number of Urban Community Services Facilities	#社区服务单位个数 Number of Community Service Units	城镇便民、利民服务网点 Number of Convenience Stores in Urban Areas
全 国	**National Total**	**194796**	**8479**	**664764**
北 京	Beijing	1897	164	6354
天 津	Tianjin	2139	111	8907
河 北	Hebei	6602	231	19758
山 西	Shanxi	1817	168	12137
内蒙古	Inner Mongolia	4826	240	25485
辽 宁	Liaoning	8898	341	91287
吉 林	Jilin	1999	249	11869
黑龙江	Heilongjiang	5805	583	60068
上 海	Shanghai	8016	104	8702
江 苏	Jiangsu	23506	454	71447
浙 江	Zhejiang	36255	300	50046
安 徽	Anhui	6815	327	18327
福 建	Fujian	5778	366	46220
江 西	Jiangxi	3053	299	8990
山 东	Shandong	9563	399	42947
河 南	Henan	3799	346	13634
湖 北	Hubei	6971	278	22573
湖 南	Hunan	14265	955	38045
广 东	Guangdong	9044	665	11108
广 西	Guangxi	1394	93	2681
海 南	Hainan	434	4	1591
重 庆	Chongqing	1644	98	7968
四 川	Sichuan	7216	397	22660
贵 州	Guizhou	4704	149	12004
云 南	Yunnan	424	137	1365
西 藏	Tibet	70	5	
陕 西	Shaanxi	7038	239	18544
甘 肃	Gansu	1975	272	14475
青 海	Qinghai	360	116	1271
宁 夏	Ningxia	2622	42	2973
新 疆	Xinjiang	5867	347	11328

23-32 离休和退休费
Pensions for Retired and Resigned Persons

年份 Year	费用总额(亿元) Total Pensions (100 million yuan)	民政部门支付 Paid by Civil Affairs Departments	总后事业单位支付 Paid by Units under the General Logistics Departments of PLA	国有单位 Funds of State-owned Units	#单位支付 Paid by Employer Units	城镇集体单位 Funds of Urban Collective Owned Units	其他单位 Funds of Other Ownership Units	平均每人费用(元) Per Capita Funds (yuan)
1980	50.4	3.3		43.4	40.1	7.0		714
1981	62.3	3.3		53.3	50.0	9.0		706
1982	73.1	3.2		62.1	58.9	11.0		709
1983	87.3	3.2		74.0	70.8	13.3		726
1984	106.1	3.0		84.6	81.6	21.2	0.3	766
1985	145.6	3.7		116.1	112.4	29.1	0.4	935
1986	172.2	3.3		140.6	137.3	31.0	0.6	1001
1987	208.1	4.0		171.9	167.9	35.3	0.8	1103
1988	275.1	6.6		220.5	213.9	53.2	1.4	1346
1989	319.4	7.5		258.9	251.4	59.1	1.4	1478
1990	396.2	7.2		319.7	312.5	74.7	1.8	1760
1991	467.5	7.6		380.7	373.1	84.5	2.3	1975
1992	578.5	9.2		474.3	465.1	100.8	3.4	2300
1993	759.3	12.0		623.2	611.2	123.9	12.2	2824
1994	1043.6	17.5		875.9	858.4	146.2	21.5	3656
1995	1305.6	19.4		1093.1	1073.7	182.4	30.1	4335
1996	1552.2	20.1		1308.2	1288.1	204.0	40.0	4923
1997	1790.8	22.7	1.9	1517.6	1493.0	225.2	48.0	5458
1998	2073.7	26.1	3.6	1726.0	1696.3	229.0	114.8	5972
1999	2420.9	29.6	3.1					6614
2000	2733.3	36.4	3.4					7190
2001	3071.2	44.3	3.4					7784
2002	3659.4	51.0	3.6					8881
2003	4148.9	56.7	3.6					9485
2004	4510.9	65.2	3.6					9808
2005	5253.2	71.1	4.5					10761

注：1.从2005年起退职费并入退休费(下两表同)。
2.本表1985-1988年的数字不包括根据1985年有关规定发给离休和退休职工的肉类等价格补贴。
a) Since 2005, pensions for retirees include resignation allowances(The same for the following two tables).
b) Figures of 1985-1988 in this table exclude subsidies on meat, etc. delivered to retired and resigned workers and staff in accordance with relevant regulations issued in 1985.

23-33 按企业、事业、机关分的离休和退休费
Pensions for Retired and Resigned Persons by Enterprises, Institutions and State Organizations

单位：亿元 (100 million yuan)

年份 Year	合计 Total	企业 Enterprises	事业 Institutions	机关 State Organs	其他 Other
1990	396.2	307.1	62.6	26.4	
1995	1305.6	915.6	275.6	114.1	
2000	2733.3	1846.6	635.2	251.6	
2001	3071.2	1988.5	768.9	313.8	
2002	3659.4	2417.2	873.0	369.2	
2003	4148.9	2684.6	1032.4	431.9	
2004	4510.9	2867.3	1157.4	486.2	
2005	5253.2	3280.3	1341.9	561.4	69.6

注：1.本表数字不包括离休和退休职工的医疗卫生费。
2.事业单位包括民政部门和总后事业单位支付的离休和退休费。
a) Figures in this table exclude medical expenditures of retired and resigned persons.
b) Institutions include pensions for retirees of civil affair departments and general logistic departments.

23-34 离休和退休人员保险福利费用及构成

Value and Composition of Social Insurance and Welfare for Retired and Resigned Persons

年 份 Year	合 计 Total	离休金 Pensions for Termination	退休金 Retirement Pensions	退职生活费 Resignation Allowances for Living Expenses	医疗卫生费 Medical Care Expenses	其 他 Others
绝对数（亿元） Absolute Figure (100 million yuan)						
1990	465.2	34.6	239.4	5.0	76.2	110.0
1991	554.4	38.6	271.5	5.7	94.5	144.1
1992	685.6	47.1	338.8	6.7	116.3	176.7
1993	901.7	57.1	435.5	8.6	154.3	246.2
1994	1218.9	103.2	766.5	12.4	192.8	144.0
1995	1522.4	121.9	986.3	15.3	236.3	162.6
1996	1797.7	137.7	1199.3	17.1	265.6	178.0
1997	2043.8	162.6	1423.9	23.5	277.6	156.2
1998	2330.9	167.7	1708.5	24.1	286.9	143.7
1999	2708.3	186.1	2035.2	27.2	320.1	139.7
2000	3040.5	201.1	2305.7	30.3	346.9	156.5
2001	3337.2	223.4	2618.7	27.8	312.9	154.4
2002	3870.7	263.7	3143.0	33.4	266.0	164.6
2003	4359.9	269.5	3592.1	37.6	271.3	189.4
2004	4814.9	281.5	3929.4	38.8	372.8	192.4
2005	5492.4	297.0	4654.0		314.7	226.7
构成（以合计为100） Composition (Total=100)						
1990	100.0	7.4	51.5	1.1	16.4	23.6
1991	100.0	7.0	49.0	1.0	17.0	26.0
1992	100.0	6.9	49.4	1.0	17.0	25.8
1993	100.0	6.3	48.3	1.0	17.1	27.3
1994	100.0	8.5	62.9	1.0	15.8	11.8
1995	100.0	8.0	64.8	1.0	15.5	10.7
1996	100.0	7.7	66.7	1.0	14.8	9.9
1997	100.0	8.0	69.7	1.1	13.6	7.6
1998	100.0	7.2	73.3	1.0	12.3	6.2
1999	100.0	6.9	75.1	1.0	11.8	5.2
2000	100.0	6.6	75.8	1.0	11.4	5.1
2001	100.0	6.7	78.5	0.8	9.4	4.6
2002	100.0	6.8	81.2	0.9	6.9	4.3
2003	100.0	6.2	82.4	0.9	6.2	4.3
2004	100.0	5.8	81.6	0.8	7.7	4.0
2005	100.0	5.4	84.7		5.7	4.1

注：本表不包括民政部门支付的离休和退休费。

a) Data in this table excluded pensions or expenses paid by the civil affairs agencies.

23-35 各地区离休和退休人员数（2005年底）

Number of Retired and Resigned Persons at the Year-end by Region (2005)

单位：万人 (10 000 persons)

地区	Region	合计 Total	离休人员 Retired Veterans	退休人员 Retired Persons	企业 Enterprises	离休人员 Retired Veterans	退休人员 Retired Persons
全国	**National Total**	**5088.2**	**126.4**	**4961.8**	**3842.4**	**64.5**	**3777.9**
北京	Beijing	192.2	5.6	186.6	139.3	2.8	136.4
天津	Tianjin	136.2	2.1	134.2	109.1	1.1	108.0
河北	Hebei	213.8	8.0	205.8	157.9	3.5	154.4
山西	Shanxi	128.1	6.2	121.9	98.4	2.9	95.5
内蒙古	Inner Mongolia	91.7	2.5	89.2	61.5	0.9	60.6
辽宁	Liaoning	382.2	10.5	371.7	310.2	6.2	304.0
吉林	Jilin	158.7	4.5	154.2	123.3	2.2	121.1
黑龙江	Heilongjiang	253.1	8.7	244.4	203.0	4.6	198.4
上海	Shanghai	291.3	3.2	288.1	254.2	1.7	252.4
江苏	Jiangsu	327.5	6.3	321.2	260.5	3.1	257.5
浙江	Zhejiang	176.5	2.9	173.6	130.9	1.2	129.7
安徽	Anhui	154.9	4.6	150.2	110.4	2.2	108.2
福建	Fujian	92.4	1.6	90.8	66.8	0.8	66.0
江西	Jiangxi	144.8	2.4	142.4	113.9	1.4	112.5
山东	Shandong	250.4	11.5	238.9	183.6	5.7	177.9
河南	Henan	236.4	8.6	227.8	167.8	3.7	164.1
湖北	Hubei	274.2	5.4	268.8	211.8	3.3	208.5
湖南	Hunan	188.0	2.9	185.1	139.8	1.5	138.3
广东	Guangdong	257.9	4.9	253.0	196.9	2.4	194.5
广西	Guangxi	120.2	1.9	118.3	75.6	0.8	74.7
海南	Hainan	35.1	0.5	34.6	28.0	0.3	27.8
重庆	Chongqing	112.9	1.0	111.9	81.2	0.6	80.7
四川	Sichuan	274.9	3.4	271.5	190.9	1.9	189.0
贵州	Guizhou	79.7	1.5	78.2	53.5	0.6	52.9
云南	Yunnan	126.1	3.0	123.1	83.8	1.3	82.5
西藏	Tibet	5.8	0.1	5.7	2.7		2.7
陕西	Shaanxi	141.2	4.2	137.0	109.7	2.3	107.3
甘肃	Gansu	75.4	2.1	73.3	54.1	1.1	53.0
青海	Qinghai	25.4	0.8	24.7	17.2	0.3	16.9
宁夏	Ningxia	21.9	0.7	21.2	15.5	0.3	15.2
新疆	Xinjiang	115.0	4.6	110.4	90.8	3.6	87.2

注：本表总计中包括总后勤部、民政部门支付离退休费的人数；分地区数据不包括总后勤部支付离退休费的人数。

a) The national total in this table includes number of retirees whose pensions are paid by the General Logistics Department of PLA and by the Ministry of Civil Affairs and its subodinate agencies in local governments, whereas the number of retirees by province do not include retirees whose pensions are paid by the General Logistics Department of PLA.

23-36 参加基本养老保险人数

Number of People Participated in Basic Pension Insurance

单位：万人 (10 000 persons)

年份 Year	合计 Total	在职职工人数 Number of Employees	企业（含其他）Enterprises (including others)	离休和退休人员数 Number of Retirees	企业（含其他）Enterprises (including others)
1989	5710.3	4816.9	4816.9	893.4	893.4
1990	6166.0	5200.7	5200.7	965.3	965.3
1991	6740.2	5653.7	5653.7	1086.6	1086.6
1992	9456.2	7774.7	7774.7	1681.5	1681.5
1993	9847.6	8008.2	8008.2	1839.4	1839.4
1994	10573.5	8494.1	8494.1	2079.4	2079.4
1995	10979.0	8737.8	8737.8	2241.2	2241.2
1996	11116.7	8758.4	8758.4	2358.3	2358.3
1997	11204.4	8671.0	8671.0	2533.4	2533.4
1998	11203.1	8475.8	8475.8	2727.3	2727.3
1999	12485.4	9501.8	8859.1	2983.6	2863.8
2000	13617.4	10447.5	9469.9	3169.9	3016.5
2001	14182.5	10801.9	9733.0	3380.6	3171.3
2002	14736.6	11128.8	9929.4	3607.8	3349.2
2003	15506.7	11646.5	10324.5	3860.2	3556.9
2004	16352.9	12250.3	10903.9	4102.6	3775.0
2005	17487.0	13120.4	11710.5	4367.5	4005.2

注：从2005年起退职人员数并入退休人员数。

a) Since 2005, number of retirees include resigned people.

23-37 社会保险基本情况

Basic Statistics on Social Insurance

年份 Year	失业保险 Unemployment Insurance			基本医疗保险 Medical Insurance		工伤保险 Work Injury Insurance		年末参加生育保险职工人数（万人）Population Covered Maternity Insurance at the Year-end (10 000 persons)
	年末参保职工人数（万人）Staff and Workers at the Year-end (10 000 persons)	全年发放失业保险金人数（万人）Beneficiaries of Unemployment Insurance Fund (10 000 persons)	全年发放失业保险金（万元）Unemployed Relief (10 000 yuan)	年末参保职工人数（万人）Staff and Workers at the Year-end (10 000 persons)	年末参保离休和退休人员（万人）Retirees (10 000 persons)	年末参保职工人数（万人）Staff and Workers at the Year-end (10 000 persons)	年末享受工伤待遇的人数（万人）Beneficiaries at the Year-end (10 000 persons)	
1994	7968.0	196.5	50755	374.6	25.7	1822.1	5.8	915.9
1995	8238.0	261.3	81964	702.6	43.3	2614.8	7.1	1500.2
1996	8333.1	330.8	138704	791.2	64.5	3102.6	10.1	2015.6
1997	7961.4	319.0	186780	1588.9	173.1	3507.8	12.5	2485.9
1998	7927.9	158.1	203907	1508.7	369.0	3781.3	15.3	2776.7
1999	9852.0	271.4	318722	1509.4	555.9	3912.3	15.1	2929.8
2000	10408.4	329.7	561984	2862.8	924.2	4350.3	18.8	3001.6
2001	10354.6	468.5	832563	5470.7	1815.2	4345.3	18.7	3455.1
2002	10181.6	657.0	1167736	6925.8	2475.4	4405.6	26.5	3488.2
2003	10372.4	741.6	1334448	7974.9	2926.8	4574.8	29.5	3655.4
2004	10583.9	753.5	1374983	9044.5	3359.2	6845.2	51.9	4383.8
2005	10647.7	677.8	1367667	10021.7	3761.2	8478.0	63.0	5408.0

23-38 社会保险基金收支及累计结余

Revenue, Expenses and Reserve of Social Insurance Fund

单位：亿元 (100 million yuan)

年份 Year	合计 Total	基本养老保险 Basic Pension Insurance	失业保险 Unemployment Insurance	医疗保险 Medical Insurance	工伤保险 Work Injury Insurance	生育保险 Maternity Insurance
基金收入 Revenue						
1989	153.6	146.7	6.8			
1990	186.8	178.8	8.0			
1991	225.0	215.7	9.3			
1992	377.4	365.8	11.7			
1993	526.1	503.5	17.9	1.4	2.4	0.8
1994	742.0	707.4	25.4	3.2	4.6	1.5
1995	1006.0	950.1	35.3	9.7	8.1	2.9
1996	1252.4	1171.8	45.2	19.0	10.9	5.5
1997	1458.2	1337.9	46.9	52.3	13.6	7.4
1998	1623.1	1459.0	72.6	60.6	21.2	9.8
1999	2211.8	1965.1	125.2	89.9	20.9	10.7
2000	2644.5	2278.1	160.4	170.0	24.8	11.2
2001	3101.9	2489.0	187.3	383.6	28.3	13.7
2002	4048.7	3171.5	215.6	607.8	32.0	21.8
2003	4882.9	3680.0	249.5	890.0	37.6	25.8
2004	5780.3	4258.4	291.0	1140.5	58.3	32.1
2005	6968.6	5093.3	333.0	1405.3	93.0	44.0
基金支出 Expenses						
1989	120.9	118.8	2.0			
1990	151.9	149.3	2.5			
1991	176.1	173.1	3.0			
1992	327.1	321.9	5.1			
1993	482.2	470.6	9.3	1.3	0.4	0.5
1994	680.0	661.1	14.2	2.9	0.9	0.8
1995	877.1	847.6	18.9	7.3	1.8	1.6
1996	1082.4	1031.9	27.3	16.2	3.7	3.3
1997	1339.2	1251.3	36.3	40.5	6.1	4.9
1998	1636.9	1511.6	56.1	53.3	9.0	6.8
1999	2108.1	1924.9	91.6	69.1	15.4	7.1
2000	2385.6	2115.5	123.4	124.5	13.8	8.3
2001	2748.0	2321.3	156.6	244.1	16.5	9.6
2002	3471.5	2842.9	186.6	409.4	19.9	12.8
2003	4016.4	3122.1	199.8	653.9	27.1	13.5
2004	4627.4	3502.1	211.0	862.2	33.3	18.8
2005	5401.0	4040.3	207.0	1078.7	48.0	27.0
累计结余 Balance at the Year-end						
1989	81.6	68.0	13.6			
1990	117.3	97.9	19.5			
1991	169.7	144.1	25.7			
1992	252.8	220.6	32.1			
1993	303.7	258.6	40.8	0.4	3.1	0.8
1994	365.7	304.8	52.0	0.7	6.8	1.4
1995	516.8	429.8	68.4	3.1	12.7	2.7
1996	696.1	578.6	86.4	6.4	19.7	5.0
1997	831.6	682.8	97.0	16.6	27.7	7.5
1998	791.1	587.8	133.4	20.0	39.5	10.3
1999	1009.8	733.5	159.9	57.6	44.9	13.9
2000	1327.5	947.1	195.9	109.8	57.9	16.8
2001	1622.8	1054.1	226.2	253.0	68.9	20.6
2002	2423.4	1608.0	253.8	450.7	81.1	29.7
2003	3313.8	2206.5	303.5	670.6	91.2	42.0
2004	4493.4	2975.0	386.0	957.9	118.6	55.9
2005	6066.1	4041.0	511.0	1278.1	164.0	72.0

23-39 分地区基本养老保险情况（2005年）

Statistics on Basic Pension Insurance by Region (2005)

地 区	Region	年末参加养老保险人数（万人） Population Covered Pension Insurance at the Year-end (10 000 persons)	职 工 Number of Employees	#企 业（含其他） Enterprise (including others)	离休和退休人员 Number of Retirees	基金收支情况（万元） Revenue and Expenses (10 000 yuan) 基金收入 Revenue	基金支出 Expenses	累计结余 Balance at the Year-end
全 国	**National Total**	**17487.0**	**13120.4**	**11710.5**	**4367.5**	**50933144**	**40403182**	**40410251**
北 京	Beijing	520.0	364.7	364.7	155.2	2410284	1955722	1005233
天 津	Tianjin	308.3	200.6	193.4	107.7	1298614	1020689	599685
河 北	Hebei	707.9	523.7	423.3	184.2	2098343	1658652	1699380
山 西	Shanxi	383.4	285.2	285.2	98.2	1328998	896569	1469883
内蒙古	Inner Mongolia	338.9	252.9	224.6	86.1	890990	792843	466731
辽 宁	Liaoning	1193.6	832.8	760.5	360.8	3539353	2871897	2774913
吉 林	Jilin	455.9	325.0	314.1	131.0	1480386	1007817	1039017
黑龙江	Heilongjiang	768.9	545.7	487.1	223.2	2093315	1672529	1395495
上 海	Shanghai	830.0	539.3	476.8	290.7	3598224	3621200	781724
江 苏	Jiangsu	1345.6	1037.6	952.3	307.9	3875751	3099149	2410226
浙 江	Zhejiang	962.3	801.3	735.2	160.9	2895812	1916798	3714726
安 徽	Anhui	471.7	347.0	338.3	124.8	1200284	1005319	590319
福 建	Fujian	409.6	320.8	266.4	88.9	1052179	848001	797036
江 西	Jiangxi	387.4	282.0	265.0	105.5	824765	686325	539539
山 东	Shandong	1302.4	1053.9	833.8	248.6	3601747	2958846	2937075
河 南	Henan	814.0	619.8	538.6	194.2	1924808	1511691	1756380
湖 北	Hubei	804.0	597.6	539.8	206.4	1806995	1539711	930264
湖 南	Hunan	718.6	523.4	369.2	195.2	1734508	1519918	1246938
广 东	Guangdong	1796.1	1564.9	1423.6	231.2	4576734	2799381	7754623
广 西	Guangxi	288.6	215.3	215.3	73.3	693388	584104	571039
海 南	Hainan	120.9	84.4	65.5	36.5	313119	283228	167331
重 庆	Chongqing	290.2	189.6	188.2	100.5	790803	672952	319855
四 川	Sichuan	793.4	562.7	455.2	230.7	2331002	1806205	1959706
贵 州	Guizhou	183.7	132.0	117.2	51.7	532469	433645	494217
云 南	Yunnan	258.7	176.8	167.8	81.9	862728	713312	714496
西 藏	Tibet	7.7	4.6	4.6	3.1	55794	55638	86
陕 西	Shaanxi	376.1	268.4	268.4	107.8	1052042	832228	530677
甘 肃	Gansu	197.3	142.2	137.5	55.1	608803	504034	378727
青 海	Qinghai	60.0	43.0	43.0	16.9	257911	188014	107950
宁 夏	Ningxia	67.5	51.5	51.5	16.1	214295	159268	276589
新 疆	Xinjiang	302.1	213.1	204.3	89.0	975102	778077	935962
不分地区	Not Classified by Region	22.9	18.7		4.2	13598	9420	44429

注：不分地区合计中，包括中国人民银行、中国农业发展银行数。

a) Data in the category of "Not Classified by Region" include data from the People's Bank of China and Agricultural Development Bank of China.

23-40 分地区失业保险情况（2005年底）

Statistics of Unemployment Insurance at the Year-end by Region (2005)

单位：万人 (10 000 persons)

地 区	Region	参保人数 Population Covered	企业 Enterprises	国有企业 State-owned Enterprises	集体企业 Collective-owned Enterprises	其他企业 Other Enterprises	事业单位 Institutions	领取失业保险金人数 Beneficiaries of Unemployment Insurance
全 国	**National Total**	**10647.7**	**8144.5**	**4362.8**	**1018.8**	**2763.0**	**2280.5**	**362.3**
北 京	Beijing	357.5	268.7	92.6	11.8	164.2	77.3	3.5
天 津	Tianjin	197.5	164.0	93.0	17.8	53.2	33.4	3.8
河 北	Hebei	461.2	337.0	219.1	40.6	77.2	122.6	13.3
山 西	Shanxi	288.5	238.8	208.4	25.8	4.6	48.7	4.8
内蒙古	Inner Mongolia	222.2	157.7	87.1	12.6	58.0	61.0	4.9
辽 宁	Liaoning	607.7	454.6	204.4	119.2	131.0	108.9	46.5
吉 林	Jilin	199.4	155.2	120.8	13.7	20.7	42.1	7.5
黑龙江	Heilongjiang	459.6	418.9	316.5	69.6	32.7	37.8	10.3
上 海	Shanghai	466.1	343.1	89.0	32.5	221.6	62.5	17.8
江 苏	Jiangsu	838.3	675.6	222.7	116.2	336.7	146.9	30.2
浙 江	Zhejiang	444.7	333.6	70.6	34.3	228.7	94.6	7.2
安 徽	Anhui	360.3	268.3	157.5	46.6	64.1	89.1	24.3
福 建	Fujian	266.6	218.9	62.1	19.3	137.4	44.5	8.6
江 西	Jiangxi	230.7	153.9	129.3	10.4	14.2	76.5	6.0
山 东	Shandong	771.1	599.9	376.4	98.9	124.6	165.4	32.2
河 南	Henan	681.9	506.8	335.7	91.2	80.0	168.5	29.2
湖 北	Hubei	391.5	284.1	200.9	26.4	56.9	106.7	14.8
湖 南	Hunan	382.7	250.3	192.6	27.3	30.4	130.0	11.3
广 东	Guangdong	1099.1	977.5	217.9	81.8	677.7	100.8	20.4
广 西	Guangxi	219.9	133.8	96.9	12.2	24.7	85.6	9.4
海 南	Hainan	56.7	41.8	31.0	2.4	8.4	12.7	2.0
重 庆	Chongqing	188.2	150.7	111.8	26.4	12.5	34.9	6.4
四 川	Sichuan	380.5	246.1	135.1	20.0	91.1	132.6	15.6
贵 州	Guizhou	129.3	87.3	75.0	5.5	6.8	41.9	1.3
云 南	Yunnan	180.3	111.1	64.6	9.5	37.0	60.9	9.1
西 藏	Tibet	6.7	2.8	2.8			3.9	
陕 西	Shaanxi	326.7	251.9	196.9	28.6	26.4	72.4	8.6
甘 肃	Gansu	160.0	119.3	96.6	12.3	10.4	40.1	5.4
青 海	Qinghai	33.2	21.6	16.1	0.7	4.9	10.7	1.1
宁 夏	Ningxia	37.2	25.9	22.4	1.1	2.4	11.1	1.2
新 疆	Xinjiang	202.4	145.2	116.9	4.0	24.3	56.3	5.6

23-41 分地区基本医疗保险情况（2005年）
Statistics of Basic Medical Insurance by Region (2005)

地区	Region	年末参保人数（万人） Population Covered at the Year-end (10 000 persons) 合计 Total	职工 Employees	离休和退休人员 Retirees	基金收支情况（万元） Revenue and Expenses (10 000 yuan) 基金收入 Revenue	基金支出 Expenses	累计结余 Balance at the Year-end
全国	**National Total**	**13782.9**	**10021.7**	**3761.2**	**14053007**	**10787360**	**12781199**
北京	Beijing	574.8	419.7	155.1	1020106	777404	560083
天津	Tianjin	299.1	180.8	118.3	322544	311564	48169
河北	Hebei	562.1	422.6	139.6	495703	375205	440793
山西	Shanxi	324.9	251.9	73.0	256014	157503	265953
内蒙古	Inner Mongolia	292.0	206.0	86.0	215838	157638	188131
辽宁	Liaoning	864.2	584.2	280.0	685606	551872	601820
吉林	Jilin	283.0	209.1	73.9	179795	134239	170637
黑龙江	Heilongjiang	602.9	432.5	170.4	423163	332442	318535
上海	Shanghai	728.6	452.7	275.9	1510763	1464370	660798
江苏	Jiangsu	1124.1	821.1	303.0	1179901	905982	1044373
浙江	Zhejiang	639.6	476.5	163.1	840808	567871	1110044
安徽	Anhui	387.1	274.4	112.7	303672	238710	256601
福建	Fujian	333.0	255.8	77.2	404369	259821	557482
江西	Jiangxi	276.7	201.7	75.0	145167	112788	117566
山东	Shandong	861.5	684.8	176.7	820726	631723	641006
河南	Henan	641.5	487.4	154.1	414793	305254	455730
湖北	Hubei	502.0	354.9	147.2	415504	296284	462525
湖南	Hunan	503.4	356.8	146.6	453295	338844	392955
广东	Guangdong	1235.3	1055.0	180.3	1417976	933241	2153549
广西	Guangxi	285.9	203.6	82.3	259445	176180	292685
海南	Hainan	87.2	62.8	24.5	59385	52291	38817
重庆	Chongqing	237.7	145.8	91.9	207123	135065	189379
四川	Sichuan	647.0	426.8	220.2	623791	430297	694515
贵州	Guizhou	180.5	129.0	51.5	117655	85554	106568
云南	Yunnan	320.7	225.2	95.5	387659	335928	296534
西藏	Tibet	15.2	10.4	4.8	16517	16018	5700
陕西	Shaanxi	348.8	247.4	101.3	240267	177114	223500
甘肃	Gansu	176.6	130.4	46.2	123129	111720	78989
青海	Qinghai	62.0	41.6	20.4	78302	62816	82512
宁夏	Ningxia	64.5	47.3	17.2	58171	42951	56174
新疆	Xinjiang	321.1	223.6	97.5	375820	308671	269076

23-42 残疾人事业基本情况
Basic Information of People with Disabilities

项目	Item	2001	2002	2003	2004	2005
康复	**Rehabilitation**					
白内障复明手术	Sight-restoring Cataract Surgery					
白内障复明手术（万例）	Sight-restoring Cataract Surgeries (10 000 Cases)	49.1	51.3	57.4	56.9	57.2
人工晶体植入率 (%)	Artificial Intra-ocular Lens Implantation Rate (%)	78.3	83.0	88.0	88.4	90.1
低视力配用助视器（人）	Vision-aids Provided for Individuals with Low-vision (persons)	26476	28231	30932	32791	35575
聋儿康复	Rehabilitation of Children with Hearing Disability					
年收训聋儿（人）	Hearing and Speech Training (persons)	17934	18771	18465	19620	19765
聋儿入普幼普小率 (%)	Enrollment Rate of Trained Children to Ordinary Kindergartens and Primary Schools (%)	22.5	23.6	24.5	26.8	27.1
培训家长（人）	Parents Trained (persons)	18550	21155	20716	22276	23374
精神病防治康复	Prevention and Treatment of Psychiatric Diseases					
开展精神病防治康复工作市县数（个）	Counties Carried on the Works of Prevention and Treatment of Psychiatric Diseases (units)	551	549	582	701	739
综合防治康复精神病人数（万人）	Prevention and Treatment Provided for Patients with Severe Psychiatric Diseases (10 000 persons)	133.2	207.3	242.6	256.8	274.3
监护率 (%)	Guardianship Rate (%)	91.3	86.7	90.2	92.3	92.4
显好率 (%)	Significant Improvement Rate (%)	73.6	69.5	71.1	72.8	73.5
社会参与率 (%)	Social Involvement Rate (%)	62.6	58.7	60.6	62.0	62.3
肇事率 (%)	Violent Events Rate (%)	0.2	0.3	0.3	0.2	0.2
康复训练与服务（人）	Rehabilitation Training and Service (person)					
肢体残疾康复训练数	Function Training Provided to Persons with Physical Disability	50577	47848	44221	49332	53808
智残儿童康复训练数	Rehabilitation Training Provided to Children with Intellectual Disability	26093	22642	22295	22982	24141
脑瘫儿童康复训练数	Rehabilitation Training Provided to Children with Cerebral Palsy	8607	10003	10539	11014	10819
麻风畸残康复	Rehabilitation of People with Leprosy					
矫治手术（例）	Orthopaedic Surgeries (case)	1730	5814	3852	3714	3903
发放辅助用具（件）	Assistant Devices Provided (unit)	5827	30100	35001	75025	58224
康复训练（人）	Rehabilitation Training (person)	5773	13970	9170	8797	8514
教育	**Education**					
未入学适龄残疾儿童少年（万人）	School-age Disabled Children without Schooling (10 000 persons)	35.6	32.3	30.6	27.5	24.3
职业教育与培训	Vocational Education and Training					
机构数（个）	Facilities (unit)	3927	3871	4143	3335	3250
教育与培训人数(万人)	Number of Educated and Trained (10 000 persons)	48.1	45.3	49.9	57.2	58.8
就业	**Employment**					
城镇残疾人就业状况	Employment of Urban Handicapped					
当年安排就业（万人）	Persons Employed in the Year (10 000 persons)	27.5	30.2	32.7	37.8	39.1
#按比例就业	Employed by Quota Scheme	7.5	7.1	8.4	8.8	11
集中就业	Employed at Welfare Enterprises	6.6	8.5	9.8	10.9	11.4
个体就业	Self-employed	13.4	14.6	14.5	18.1	16.7
未安排就业	Unemployed	101.2	103.2	100.4	119.4	115.9
农村残疾人就业状况	Employment of Rural Handicapped					
就业（万人）	Employed (10 000 persons)	1579.5	1717.8	1685.2	1763.2	1803.4
未就业（万人）	Unemployed (10 000 persons)	379.8	337.3	370.2	330.9	337.6
残疾人就业服务机构(个)	Employment Placement Service Facilities for Disabled Jobseekers (unit)	2991	2998	3005	3022	3048
省	Provinces	30	31	33	33	33
地	Prefectures	71	49	54	46	46
市（含县级市）	Cities (inc. Cities at County Level)	646	652	636	639	648
县	County	1497	1505	1517	1515	1528
市辖区	Districts under the Jurisdiction of Cities	747	761	765	789	793
盲人按摩	**Massage by Persons with Visual Disability**					
保健按摩员培训（人）	Massage Therapists Training (person)	7511	7413	6874	8008	7399
医疗按摩员培训（人）	Keep-fit Massager Training (person)	3728	3853	4821	5864	5075
扶贫	**Poverty Alleviation**					
扶贫开发解决温饱残疾人（万人）	Rural Handicapped Overcome Poverty by Government's Poverty Reduction Program (10 000 persons)	167.8	151.4	123.3	127.9	129.3
尚未解决温饱贫困残疾人（万人）	Rural Handicapped Remained in Poverty (10 000 persons)	1058.4	1022.1	1065.2	1051.8	994
#可扶持贫困残疾人	Rural Handicapped Remained in Poverty Can Be Supported	657.7	634.4	673.7	677.5	672.1
残联组织建设	**Organization Building of Disabled Persons' Federation**					
残疾人工作者数（万人）	Workers for Handicapped (10 000 persons)	7.3	7.5	7.8	8.0	8.1

注：根据1987年全国残疾人抽样调查的结果推算，目前全国各类残疾人的总数约6000万人。

a) According to the calculation from the handicapped survey in 1987, number of total handicapped in China is about 60 million persons now.

23-43 婚姻登记和离婚情况
Number of Marriages and Divorces

年份 Year / 地区 Region		结婚登记对数（万对）Total Number of Registered Marriages (10 000 couples)	内地居民登记结婚 Registered Marriages of Mainland	初婚（万人）First Marriages (10 000 persons)	再婚（万人）Remarriages (10 000 persons)	涉外及港澳台居民登记结婚 Registered Marriages with Foreigner and the Citizen of Hong Kong, Macao, Taiwan	离婚（万对）Divorces (10 000 couples)	粗离婚率（‰）Divorce Rate (‰)
	1985	831.3	829.1	1607.6	50.5	2.2	45.8	0.44
	1989	937.2	935.2	1796.0	74.4	2.0	75.3	0.68
	1990	951.1	948.7	1819.1	78.2	2.4	80.0	0.69
	1991	953.6	951.0	1820.3	81.6	2.6	82.9	0.72
	1992	957.5	954.5	1832.1	76.9	3.0	85.0	0.74
	1993	915.4	912.2	1747.0	77.3	3.3	90.9	0.77
	1994	932.4	929.0	1779.3	78.7	3.4	98.1	0.82
	1995	934.1	929.7	1776.1	83.3	4.4	105.5	0.88
	1996	938.7	934.0	1781.7	86.2	4.7	113.2	0.93
	1997	914.1	909.1	1726.0	92.2	5.1	119.8	0.97
	1998	891.7	886.7	1675.4	97.9	5.0	119.0	0.96
	1999	885.3	879.9	1659.4	100.5	5.4	120.2	0.96
	2000	848.5	842.0	1581.4	102.6	6.5	121.3	0.96
	2001	805.0	797.1	1481.7	112.5	7.9	125.0	0.98
	2002	786.2	778.8	1440.3	117.1	7.3	117.7	0.90
	2003	811.4	803.5	1483.9	123.3	7.8	133.1	1.05
	2004	867.1	860.8	1569.6	152.0	6.4	166.5	1.28
	2005	823.1	816.6	1483.0	163.1	6.4	178.5	1.37
北京	Beijing	9.7	9.6	15.9	3.4	0.09	3.4	
天津	Tianjin	6.4	6.3	10.3	2.4	0.04	1.9	
河北	Hebei	53.8	53.8	97.5	10.1	0.03	8.3	
山西	Shanxi	19.0	19.0	35.4	2.6	0.01	2.9	
内蒙古	Inner Mongolia	15.5	15.4	28.0	2.9	0.01	3.9	
辽宁	Liaoning	26.0	25.7	42.7	9.3	0.26	11.1	
吉林	Jilin	16.8	16.7	29.1	4.6	0.13	7.3	
黑龙江	Heilongjiang	22.8	22.6	39.6	6.1	0.24	9.6	
上海	Shanghai	10.3	10.0	16.4	4.1	0.24	3.9	
江苏	Jiangsu	47.2	47.1	84.7	9.7	0.14	9.7	
浙江	Zhejiang	35.3	34.9	64.2	6.4	0.41	7.3	
安徽	Anhui	44.0	43.9	83.4	4.7	0.09	5.8	
福建	Fujian	27.1	25.8	49.8	4.5	1.40	3.9	
江西	Jiangxi	29.5	29.4	55.4	3.7	0.15	3.9	
山东	Shandong	63.2	63.1	114.9	11.4	0.10	9.9	
河南	Henan	51.3	51.2	96.4	6.2	0.13	9.1	
湖北	Hubei	39.4	39.1	71.7	7.1	0.27	7.6	
湖南	Hunan	46.0	45.4	83.8	8.1	0.54	9.6	
广东	Guangdong	58.9	57.9	111.6	6.3	1.09	8.1	
广西	Guangxi	31.8	31.5	59.7	3.9	0.34	4.8	
海南	Hainan	4.1	4.0	7.5	0.7	0.14	0.6	
重庆	Chongqing	18.5	18.3	29.5	7.4	0.14	7.3	
四川	Sichuan	40.8	40.6	69.4	12.3	0.26	14.1	
贵州	Guizhou	21.1	21.1	38.2	4.1	0.07	3.8	
云南	Yunnan	25.1	25.0	45.7	4.5	0.05	4.7	
西藏	Tibet	0.6	0.6	1.1	0.1		0.1	
陕西	Shaanxi	20.8	20.8	38.1	3.5	0.05	4.0	
甘肃	Gansu	11.5	11.4	21.0	1.9	0.01	2.3	
青海	Qinghai	2.9	2.9	5.2	0.5		0.8	
宁夏	Ningxia	4.1	4.1	7.5	0.7		0.9	
新疆	Xinjiang	19.6	19.6	29.4	9.9		7.8	

注：粗离婚率计算方法：离婚对数除以当期人口平均数。此方法为国际惯用方法。

a) Computational method of divorce rate: number of divorce couples divided by average population at current year. This is an internationally accepted method.

主要统计指标解释

社会福利事业单位　指集中收养社会孤老、残、幼的机构，包括由民政部门管理的社会福利院、儿童福利院、精神病人福利院和城镇集体举办的福利院及农村集体举办的敬老院以及优抚医院和具有收养能力的社区服务中心等。该指标主要反映我国在社会福利性单位投入的水平。

社会福利事业单位收养人数　包括民政部门管理和城镇、农村集体举办的社会福利事业单位中收养的老人、少年儿童、缺乏生活自理能力的残疾人员和精神病人。该指标主要反映收养性社会福利单位的收养能力。

社会福利企业单位　指以安置城镇有一定劳动能力的盲、聋、哑和肢体残疾人员就业为目的，享受国家减免税待遇的国有或集体企业。包括福利工厂、福利商业和服务业、假肢厂和安置农场等单位。该指标主要反映我国对残疾人照顾的特殊政策。

农村五保户　指农村中既无劳动能力，又无经济来源的老、弱、孤、残的农民，其生活由集体供养，实行保吃、保穿、保住、保医、保葬(孤儿保教)，简称“五保”，享受五保待遇的家庭叫五保户。该指标主要反映农村弱势群体的人员数量。

粗离婚率　指当年离婚对数占年平均人口的比重，计算公式为:

$$粗离婚率=\frac{当年离婚对数}{年平均人口数}\times 1000‰$$

聋儿入普幼普小率　指本年度内进入普通幼儿园、普通小学的聋儿数与在训聋儿数(不含当年新收训聋儿数)之比。该指标主要反映经过康复训练的聋儿进入普通幼儿园和普通小学的情况。

综合防治康复精神病人数　指在开展精神病防治康复工作地区，采取不同形式，接受综合性防治康复措施、开放式管理的精神病人数。该指标主要反映精神病患者接受治疗康复情况。

监护率　指通过监护小组、家庭病床、工疗站、社会就业以及精神卫生机构，接受社会化、综合性、开放式治疗与康复的精神病人占经调查摸底、登记在册的精神病人数的百分比。该指标主要反映对精神病患者落实治疗康复措施的情况。

精神病人社会参与率　指生活能自理，并参加生产劳动和社会生活的精神病人数占监护精神病人数的百分比。该指标主要反映精神病人康复状况和参与社会的情况。

未入学适龄残疾儿童少年　指根据义务教育法规定应接受义务教育，但因各种原因未能入学的适龄视力残疾、听力与言语残疾、智力残疾、肢体残疾、精神残疾、多重残疾儿童少年。适龄残疾儿童少年的年龄段参照各省级人民政府依照义务教育法规定的入学年龄。该指标主要反映因各种原因未能入学的适龄残疾儿童的年度变化,为制定残疾儿童义务教育发展规划及其应采取的方针、政策和措施提供依据,同时为各地开展资助残疾儿童就学工作提供依据。

律师　指依法取得律师执业证书，担任法律顾问，民事(刑事、行政)案件代理人、刑事案件辩护人、办理非诉讼业务，解答法律询问，代写法律事务文书等，为社会提供法律服务的人员。

公证人员　指在公证处工作的人员总称，包括公证处主任、副主任、公证员、公证员助理(助理公证员)和其他从事辅助性工作的人员。

公证文书　指公证处根据当事人申请，依照事实和法律，按照法定程序制作的，具有法律效力的司法证明文书。根据公证书用途和使用地，公证书分为国内公证书、国内经济公证书、涉外民事公证书、涉外经济公证书四类。

调解员　指在人民调解委员会担负调解民间纠纷工作的人员，包括调解委员会的委员和调解小组的调解员。该指标主要反映从事人民调解工作的人员数量。

调解民间纠纷　指调解委员会按照法律规定，根据自愿原则，用说服教育的方法调解民间发生的有关民事权利和义务争执的件数，包括调解成功数和调解未成功数。该指标主要反映人民调解委员会的工作量。

立案　指人民检察院对受理的报案、控告、举报或自首及自行发现的犯罪线索、犯罪嫌疑人进行初步调查后，认为存在职务犯罪事实和应追究刑事责任，并决定作为刑事案件进行侦查的诉讼活动，是追究犯罪的开始。该指标主要反映人民检察院依法将职务犯罪线索作为刑事案件进行侦查的诉讼活动。

大案　指贪污、贿赂案数额在5万元以上，挪用公款案数额在10万元以上，集体私分、巨额财产来源不明、隐瞒境外存款案数额在50万元以上以及按照《人民检察院直接受理的渎职、侵权重、特大案件标准(试行)》认定的案件。该指标主要反映人民检察院立案查办的职务犯罪案件中经济损失大、社会危害严重的案件。

要案　指县、处级以上干部的犯罪案件。该指标主要反映国家工作人员中县、处级以上干部因职务犯罪被人民检察院依法立案侦查的情况。

决定逮捕　指人民检察院对直接受理、自行侦查的案件，认为需要逮捕犯罪嫌疑人时，依据法律做出的逮捕决定。该指标主要反映人民检察院对直接受理的案件行使决定逮捕权的情况。

批准逮捕　指人民检察院对公安机关、国家安全机关、监狱管理机关提出逮捕的犯罪嫌疑人进行审查，根据事实，依法做出逮捕决定。该指标主要反映人民检察院对提请逮捕机关提请逮捕犯罪嫌疑人进行审查后依法做出批准逮捕决定的情况。

决定起诉　指人民检察院对公安机关、国家安全机关、监狱管理机关和检察机关内设机构反贪污贿赂部门等移送起诉的案件进行审查，根据事实，做出提起公诉的案件。该指标主要反映人民检察院对各种刑事案件向人民法院提起公诉的情况。

申诉　指经检察机关信访部门审查处理后，移送到检察机关申诉部门的申诉案件，包括不服检察机关处理决定和不服法院刑事判决和裁定的申诉的案件。

受理劳动争议案件数 指劳动争议仲裁委员会根据国家有关规定，对劳动争议当事人的申请予以审查，符合受理条件而正式立案、准备处理的劳动争议案件数。

基本养老保险

1.（参保）职工人数：指报告期末按照国家法律、法规和有关政策规定参加基本养老保险并在社保经办机构已建立缴费记录档案的职工人数，包括中断缴费但未终止养老保险关系的职工人数，不包括只登记未建立缴费记录档案的人数。

2. （参保）离退休人员人数：指报告期末参加基本养老保险的离休、退休和退职人员的人数。

3.基本养老保险基金收入：指根据国家有关规定，由纳入基本养老保险范围的缴费单位和个人按国家规定的缴费基数和缴费比例缴纳的养老保险基金，以及通过其他方式取得的形成基金来源的收入。包括单位和职工个人缴纳的基本养老保险费、基本养老保险基金利息收入、上级补助收入、下级上解收入、转移收入、财政补贴和其他收入。

4.基本养老保险基金支出：指按照国家政策规定的开支范围和开支标准从养老保险基金中支付给参加基本养老保险的离休、通休、退职人员个人的养老金、丧葬抚恤补助，以及由于保险关系转移、上下级之间调剂资金等原因而发生的支出。包括离休金、退休金、退职金、各种补贴、医疗费、死亡丧葬补助费、抚恤救济费、社会保险经办机构管理费、补助下级支出、上解上级支出、转移支出、其他支出等。

5.基本养老保险基金累计结余：指截止报告期末基本养老保险基金收支相抵后的累计余额。

离休、退休、退职人员 指正式办理了离休、退休、退职手续，并享受相应的离休、退休、退职待遇的人员。

基本医疗保险

1.参保人数：指报告期末按国家有关规定参加基本医疗保险的人数。包括参加保险的职工人数和退休人员人数。

2.基金收入：指根据国家有关规定，由纳入基本医疗保险范围的缴费单位和个人，按国家规定的缴费基数和缴费比例缴纳的基金，以及通过其他方式取得的形成基金来源的款项，包括：单位缴纳的社会统筹基金收入、个人缴纳的个人账户基金收入、财政补贴收入、利息收入、其他收入。

3.基金支出：指按照国家政策规定的开支范围和开支标准从社会统筹基金中支付给参加基本医疗保险的职工和退休人员的医疗保险待遇支出，和从个人帐户基金中支付给参加基本医疗保险的职工和退休人员的医疗费用支出，以及其他支出。包括：住院医疗费用支出、门急诊医疗费用支出、个人账户基金支出、其他支出。

4.基金累计结余：指截止报告期末基本医疗保险的社会统筹和个人帐户基金累计结余金额。包括银行存款、财政专户、债券投资和其他。

失业保险

1.参保人数：指报告期末按照国家法律、法规和有关政策规定参加了失业保险的城镇企业事业单位的职工及地方政府规定参加失业保险的其他人员的人数。

2.失业保险基金收入：指按照规定从企业、事业及其他单位筹集的失业保险费及其他并入失业保险基金收入的总额。包括单位和个人缴纳的失业保险费、失业保险基金利息收入、上级补助收入、下级上解收入、转移收入、财政补贴和其他收入。

3.失业保险基金支出：指报告期内为保障失业人员和下岗职工基本生活、促进其再就业等支出的基金总额。包括失业救济金、医疗费、死亡丧葬补助费、抚恤救济费、转业训练费支出、失业保险经办机构管理费、补助下级支出、上解上级支出、转移支出和其他支出。

4.基金累计结余：指截止报告期末失业保险基金收支相抵后的累计余额。

工伤保险

1.参加保险人数：指报告期末依据国家有关规定参加工伤保险的职工人数。

2.享受保险待遇人数：指劳动者因工负伤致残、死亡或因患职业病致残，根据有关规定享受工伤保险待遇职工或供养直系亲属人数。包括伤残人数、职业病人数、因工死亡人数、供养直系亲属人数。

3.基金收入：指根据国家有关规定，由参加工伤保险的单位按国家规定的缴费基数和缴费比例缴纳的工伤保险基金，以及通过其他形式取得的形成基金来源的款项。包括：单位缴纳的社会统筹基金收入、财政补贴收入、利息收入、其他收入。

4.基金支出：指按照国家政策规定的开支范围和开支标准从工伤保险基金中支付给参加工伤保险的人员及供养直系亲属工伤保险待遇支出及其他支出。包括工伤医疗费、伤残补助金、工亡补助金、护理费、丧葬补助费、工伤预防费用、职业康复费用和其他支出。

5.基金累计结余：指截止报告期末工伤保险基金累计结余金额。包括银行存款、财政专户、债券投资和其他。

生育保险

1.参保人数：指报告期末依据有关规定参加生育保险的职工人数。

2.基金收入：指根据国家有关规定，由参加生育保险的单位按照国家规定的缴费基数和缴费比例缴纳的生育保险基金，以及通过其他方式取得的形成基金来源的款项，包括：单位缴纳的基金收入、利息收入和其他收入。

3.基金支出：指按照国家政策规定的开支范围和开支标准，从生育保险基金中支付给参加生育保险的职工，因妊娠、分娩和计划生育手术而享受的待遇及其他支出。包括：生育津贴、医疗费用支出及其他支出。

4.基金累计结余：指截止报告期末生育保险基金累计结余金额。包括银行存款、财政专户、债券投资和其他。

离休、退休、退职人员保险福利费用 指离休、退休、退职人员实际得到的生活费用总额，包括从社会保险经办机构和单位得到的费用。

1.离休金：指按规定支付给离休人员的生活费用。

2.退休金：指按规定支付给退休人员的生活费用。

3.退职生活费：指按规定支付给退职人员的生活费用。

4.医疗卫生费：指单位直接支付给离休、退休、退职人员的医疗费、住院费以及住院伙食补助等费用。

5.其他：指离休金、退休金、退职生活费和医疗卫生费以外的其他保险福利费用，如丧葬抚恤救济费、生活补贴、物价补贴、冬季取暖补贴等。

Explanatory Notes on Main Statistical Indicators

Social Welfare Institutions refer to institutions taking care of old people without children, handicapped people and orphans. They include social welfare institutions run by civil affairs departments, children welfare institutions, social welfare institutions for mental patients, collective-owned old people's homes in rural areas, convalescent homes and community service centers with the capacity of receiving those people. This indicator reflects the input in social welfare institutions.

Number of People Taken in by Social Welfare Institutions refers to the number of old people, children, totally dependent handicapped people and mental patients taken in by social welfare institutions run by civil affairs departments and those run by collective units in urban and rural areas. This indicator reflects the capacity of social welfare institutions.

Social Welfare Enterprises are collective owned enterprises which employ the blind, deaf-mute, and other handicapped people who are able to work in cities and towns and enjoy exemption from state taxes, including welfare plants, welfare commercial services, artificial limb plants and farms, etc. This indicator reflects the preferential policies toward disabled persons.

Rural Households with Livelihood Guaranteed in Five Aspects refer to the households in which there are old people without child, orphans and handicapped people who are unable to work and without financial resources in rural areas. They are taken care of by the collective units and their food, clothing, housing, medical care, funeral expenses (or schooling for orphans) are guaranteed to be provided for. This indicator reflects the total number of disadvantageous groups of rural population.

Crude Divorce Rate refers to proportion of divorced people to the annual average population for the reference year, the formula is:

Crude Divorce rate= number of couples divorced for the reference year/annual average population x 1000 per thousand

Proportion of Deaf Children Enrolled in Ordinary Preschool and Primary Education refers to the proportion of deaf children who are enrolled in ordinary kindergartens or primary schools during the year in the total number of deaf children under rehabilitation programme (not including new comers into the rehabilitation programme during the year). This indicator mainly reflects number of rehabilitated deaf children entering ordinary kindergartens or primary schools.

Number of Mental Patients under Integrated Prevention and Rehabilitation Programme refers to mental disease patients receiving integrated prevention and rehabilitation treatment of various forms under open environment in areas with mental disease rehabilitation programme. This indicator reflects the condition of metal patients receiving rehabilitation treatment.

Supervision Rate refers to the percentage of patients among the total number of registered mental disease patients, who participate in social integrated and open treatment and rehabilitation programme through various forms such as supervision groups, family treatment, employment or guidance from psychiatric institutions. This indicator reflects the implementation of various measures aimed at rehabilitating those metal patients.

Social Participation Rate of Metal Patients refers to proportion of mental disease patients who are able to manage their daily life and participate in economic activities to the total number of mental disease patients under supervision. This indicator reflects the condition of recovery of those metal patients and their participation in social activities.

School-age Disabled Children not in Schools refer to children with disability in sight, listening, speaking, mentality, limbs or multi-disability who are obliged to compulsory education by law but have not been enrolled in schools due to various reasons. The definition of school age for disabled children is decided by the definition of school age as specified by provincial governments in line with the local laws on compulsory education. This indicator reflects the annual change of school-age disable children not entering schools by various reasons. It will provide foundation for the formulation of development plans of compulsory education for those disable children, and for related principles, policies and measures as well. It is also the base for the job of funding those disabled children back to schools across the countries.

Lawyers are certified legal workers according to law, and who are employed by legal counseling firms to act as legal advisers, agents in criminal or civil lawsuits, or defenders in criminal lawsuits, or to handle non-litigious legal affairs, to advise on matters of law or to write legal papers for others, and provide service to the public.

Notary Personnel refers to people working for notary offices including: directors, deputy director, notaries, assistant notaries, and other people providing assistance.

Notary Documents refer to the judicatory notary documents drawn up by the request of the party and are in accordance with facts and laws and following certain legal proceedings. According to usage and locality, the notary documents are divided into following 4 types: domestic notary documents, domestic economic notary documents, foreign-related civil notary documents and foreign-related economic notary documents.

Mediators refer to workers on peoples mediation committees responsible for mediating in civil disputes and cases of slight infraction of the law. They include members of the mediation committees and mediators of mediation groups. This indicator reflects the number of people engaged in meditation.

Mediation of Civil Disputes refers to number of cases made by mediation committees in mediating in civil disputes concerning civil rights and duties through persuasion and education in accordance with the provisions of law on a voluntary basis, so as to solve disputes by helping the parties involved come to an agreement and understanding, including those unsuccessful ones. This indicator reflects the workload of the mediation committees.

Acceptance of Case refers to the decision made by the people's procuratorate office on reported cases, prosecution, impeachment, surrender, self-found criminal clues or suspects after initial investigation to confirm the act of crime and to start legal proceedings of the case as criminal case.

Large Cases refer to cases involving a corruption or bribery of over 50,000 yuan, or a misappropriation of over 100,000 yuan. Cases of collectively illegal possession of public funds, unstated sources of large properties, or disguised overseas savings deposits involving 500,000 yuan, or a case that has been defined by the "Standard on Serious and Large Cases of Misconduct and Tortious that Directly Accepted by People's Procurators Office (trial)". This indicator mainly reflects number of accepted cases of job-related criminals that caused serious economic losses or extremely harmful to the society.

Key Cases refer to cases committed by government officials with a ranking of division director or county administrator. This indicator mainly reflects the recorded and spied on cases by the people's procurators offices toward government official with a ranking of division director or county administrator.

Decision on Arrest refers to decision made by people's procurators office, in accordance with laws, to arrest the suspect (s) in the cases that are accepted and to be investigated by procurators office. This indicator mainly reflects the implementation of the decision on arrest by people's procurators office.

Approval for Arrest refers to the decision made by people's procurators office, in accordance with laws and relevant facts, to approve the arrest of the suspect(s) that is proposed by the public security departments, state security departments or authority of prisons. This indicator reflects approved arrests made by people's procurators office that are proposed by related departments.

Decision on Prosecution refers to the decision made by people's procurators office, in accordance with laws and relevant facts, to institute proceedings to the people's court against the suspect(s) of criminal cases handed over by the public security departments, state security departments or authority of prisons, or by the anti-corruption departments within the procurators office. This indicator reflects the condition of the prosecutions made by people's procurators office toward the people's court.

Appeals refer to cases transferred to the appeal departments of procurator's offices after initial review by departments dealing with complaint letters and calls of the public. Included are appeals against decisions made by procurator's offices and appeals against court rules and verdicts.

Number of Labour Dispute Cases Accepted refers to the number of cases of labour dispute submitted that, after being reviewed by the labour dispute arbitration committees in line with the relevant national regulations, are accepted and registered for treatment.

Basic Pension Insurance

1.Number of staff and workers covered refer to staff and workers participating in basic pension insurance programme in line with national laws, regulations and related policies by the end of reference period, who have already had payment records in social security management agencies, including those who interrupt payment without terminating the insurance programme. Those who have registered in the programme with no payment records are not included.

2. Number of retirees participating in basic pension insurance programme refer to number of retirees participating in basic pension insurance programme by the end of reference period.

3. Revenue of basic pension insurance refer to payments made by employers and individuals participating in pension insurance programs in accordance with the basis and proportion stipulated in state regulations, and income from other sources that become source of pension insurance fund, including the premium paid by employers and staff and works, interest income, subsidies from higher level agencies, income as transfer from subordinate agencies, transferred income, government financial subsidies and other income.

4. Expenses of basic pension insurance refer to payment made to those retired and resigned people covered in pension insurance program in terms of pension or compensation within the scope and standards of expenditure according to related national policies, and expenditure occurred due to shift of the insurance relationship or adjustment of funds among agencies, including pension for resigned people, pension for retired people, pension for people quitting jobs, various subsidies, medical fees, funeral subsidies, compensation pension, management fees for social security agencies, expenses on subsidies to lower subordinates, expenses as transfer to agencies at higher level, transferred expenditure and other expenditure.

5. Balance of basic pension insurance refers to the balance of basic pension insurance at the end of the reference period after deducting expenses from revenue.

Retired or Resigned Personnel refers to people who have formally completed formalities for their retirement or quitting work and enjoy the corresponding retirement treatments.

Basic Medical Care Insurance:

1. Number of people participating in the insurance programme refers to people participating in the basic medical care insurance programme according to related regulations by the end of reference period, including number of staff and workers and retirees participating in this insurance programme.

2. Revenue of insurance programme refer to payments made by employers and individuals participating in medical care insurance programs in accordance with the basis and proportion stipulated in state regulations, and income from other sources that become source of medical insurance fund, including income of social comprehensive funds paid by employers, income from individual accounts, government financial subsidies, interest income and other income.

3. Expenses of insurance programme refer to payment made from social comprehensive funds to those retired and resigned

people covered in basic medical care insurance within the scope and standards of expenditure according to related national policies, and medical care payment made from individual accounts to staff and workers and retirees, and other expenses, including medical expenses of hospital inpatients, medical expenses for outpatients and emergency patients, payment from individual accounts and other expenditure.

4. Balance of basic medical care insurance refer to the balance of medical care insurance of social comprehensive funds and individual accounts at the end of the reference period, including bank savings, special fiscal accounts, investment in bonds and others.

Unemployment Insurance

1. Number of people covered refers to staff and workers in urban enterprises or institutions who have participated in unemployment insurance programme in line relevant policies and regulations, and other people who have participated according to local government regulations, by the end of reference period.

2. Revenue of unemployment insurance refer to payments made by employers and individuals participating in unemployment insurance programme in accordance with relevant regulations and other income contributed to this programme, including unemployment insurance premium made by employers and individuals, interest income, subsidies from higher level agencies, income as transfer from subordinate agencies, transferred income, government financial subsidies and other income.

3. Expenses of unemployment insurance refer to total expenses during the reference period to guarantee the basic livelihood of unemployed people and laid-off staff and workers and to encourage their re-employment. Included are unemployment relief, medical fees, funeral subsidies, compensation pension, training expenses, management fees for unemployment insurance agencies, subsidies to lower level agencies, expenses as transfer to higher level agencies, transferred expenditure and other expenditure.

4. Balance of unemployment insurance refer to the balance of unemployment revenue deducting unemployment expenses at the end of the reference period.

Work Injury Insurance

1. Number of people covered refers to staff and workers who have participated in work injury insurance programme in line with relevant national regulations.

2. Number of beneficiaries refers to staff and workers and their direct dependents who can, in line with relevant regulations, benefit from work injury insurance, as a result of work injury leading to disability or death of the staff/worker, or occupational disease leading to disability. Included in this category are number of injured and disabled people, number of people with occupational diseases, number of deaths at work places, and number of direct dependents.

3. Revenue of work injury insurance refer to payments made by employers participating in work injury insurance programs in accordance with the basis and proportion stipulated in state regulations, and income from other sources that become source of work injury insurance fund, including income of social comprehensive funds paid by employers, government financial subsidies, interest income and other income.

4. Expenses of work injury insurance refer to payments made from work injury insurance funds to those who participated in the work injury insurance programme and their direct dependents within the scope and standards of expenditure according to related national policies, and other expenditure, including medical fees for work injury, injury and disability subsidies, death subsidies, nursing fees, funeral subsidies, injury prevention fees, rehabilitation fees for occupational diseases and other expenditure.

5. Balance of work injury insurance refer to the balance of the work injury funds at the end of the reference period, including bank savings, special fiscal account, investment in bonds and others.

Maternity Insurance

1. Number of people covered refers to staff and workers who have participated in maternity insurance programme according to relevant regulation at the end of the reporting period.

2. Revenue of maternity insurance refers to payments made by employers participating in maternity insurance programs in accordance with the basis and proportion stipulated in state regulations, and income from other sources that become source of maternity insurance fund, including income of funds paid by employers, interest income and other income.

3. Expenses of maternity insurance refer to payments made from maternity insurance funds to staff and workers who participated in maternity insurance programme within the scope and standards of expenditure according to related national policies, expenses paid for pregnancy, child delivery or surgeries related to family planning, and other expenditure, including allowance for child bearing, medical fees and other expenditure.

4. Balance of the maternity insurance refers to the balance of the maternity insurance funds at the end of reference period, including bank savings, special fiscal account, investment in funds and others.

Insurance and Welfare Funds for Retirees refer to the total payment for living expenses actually received by retirees, including payment received from social insurance management agencies and units.

1. Pensions for retired veteran cadres refer to living expenses paid to retired veteran cadres according to related regulations.

2. Pensions for retirement refer to living expenses paid to retired staff and workers according to related regulations.

3. Living allowances for resigned staff and workers refer to living expenses paid to resigned staff and workers according to related regulation.

4. Medical care expenses refer to medical fees, hospitalization cost and per diem subsidies during hospitalizations paid by employers directly to retirees.

5. Others refer to insurance and welfare payments other than the above-mentioned payments, including funeral subsidies, living allowances, price subsidies and heating subsidies during winter.

24

香港特别行政区主要社会经济指标

Main Social and Economic Indicators of Hong Kong Special Administrative Region

简要说明

一、本章资料反映香港特别行政区主要社会、经济发展情况。内容包括：土地、人口、就业、国民收入、国际收支平衡表、工业、能源、建筑、交通、对外贸易、财政金融、教育、房屋、卫生、社会保障等方面。

二、本章由香港特别行政区政府统计处提供所有数据，国家统计局国际统计信息中心负责整理、编辑。

三、在统计工作方面，按中华人民共和国“香港特别行政区基本法”的有关原则，香港特别行政区保留其单独运作的统计系统，并负责编制和发布反映香港特别行政区情况的统计数据。由于香港和内地在使用统计名词及概念方面会有所不同，读者在比较两地数据时，请参考以下资料：

（1）本章内的“《中国统计年鉴》与香港特别行政区统计刊物中使用的指标对照表”列出两地概念相近但名称不同的词汇。

（2）本章末的“主要统计指标解释”，载有一些重要概念的解释。

四、香港特别行政区是单独的关税地区，香港与内地之间的贸易，亦需办理进出口报关。在贸易统计方面，香港特别行政区对外贸易统计数据亦包括香港特别行政区与内地的贸易。

五、在外汇统计及与之有关的各方面，港币是香港特别行政区的法定货币，因此，除港币以外的货币（包括人民币）均视作外币。

六、更详细的统计资料及有关的技术细节，可参阅香港特别行政区政府统计处出版的《香港统计月刊》、《香港统计年刊》及各专题统计出版物。

七、本章节表中的符号使用说明：“－”表示不适用；“空格” 表示没有数字。

Brief Introduction

I. Data in this chapter show main social and economic developments of the Hong Kong Special Administrative Region, including data on land, population, employment, national income, Balance of Payments account, industry, energy, construction, transportation, external trade, finance and banking, education, housing, health and social security.

II. All data in this chapter are provided by the Census and Statistics Department, the Government of the Hong Kong Special Administrative Region, and further tabulated or edited by the International Statistical Information Centre of the National Bureau of Statistics.

III. According to the Basic Law of the Hong Kong Special Administrative Region of the People's Republic of China, Hong Kong Special Administrative Region maintains its independent statistical system, and compiles and disseminates statistics on the Region. As Hong Kong and the mainland of China use different statistical concepts, definitions and terminologies, users are advised to make reference of the following materials when using and comparing data of the mainland of China and the Hong Kong Special Administrative Region:

1. A Comparison of Common Statistical Terms Used in China Statistical Yearbook and Publications Compiled by the Census and Statistics Department, the Government of the Hong Kong Special Administrative Region, which listed similar statistical concepts using different terms.

2. The Explanatory Note at the end of this chapter which gives explanation on important statistical indicators.

IV. As Hong Kong is a separate custom territory, trade between Hong Kong and the mainland of China needs customs declaration procedures. In terms of trade statistics, data on Hong Kong's imports and exports include Hong Kong's trade with the mainland of China.

V. As HK dollar is the legal tender in the Hong Kong Special Administrative Region, all other currencies (including Renminbi) are regarded as foreign currencies in compiling foreign exchange statistics and related statistics.

VI. For more detailed statistics and technical details, users are advised to read the "*Hong Kong Monthly Digest of Statistics*", the "*Hong Kong Annual Digest of Statistics*" and other publications compiled by the Census and Statistics Department, the Government of the Hong Kong Special Administrative Region.

VII. Notations used in this chapter:

"-" indicates not applicable. "(blank)" indicates not available.

24-1 主要统计指标概览
Summary of Key Statistics

项目	Item	2001	2002	2003	2004	2005
人口及生命统计	**Population and Vital Events**					
年中人口 (万人)	Mid-year Population (10 000 persons)	672.5	678.7	680.3	688.3	693.6
粗出生率 (‰)	Crude Birth Rate (‰)	7.2	7.1	6.9	7.2	8.2
粗死亡率 (‰)	Crude Death Rate (‰)	5.0	5.0	5.4	5.4	5.5@
登记死亡人数 (人)	Registered Deaths (person)	33305	34316	36423	37321	38683
婴儿死亡率 (按每千名登记活产婴儿计算)	Infant Mortality Rate (per 1 000 Registered Live Births)	2.7	2.4	2.3	2.5	2.4@
劳动、就业	**Labour and Employment**					
劳动人口 (万人)	Labour Force (10 000 persons)	342.7	348.7	349.6	355.1	358.6@
劳动人口参与率 (%)	Labour Force Participation Rate (%)	61.4	61.8	61.4	61.3	60.9@
失业率 (%)	Unemployment Rate (%)	5.1	7.3	7.9	6.8	5.6@
就业不足率① (%)	Underemployment Rate ① (%)	2.5	3.0	3.5	3.3	2.8@
选定行业的就业人数 (千人)	Number of Employed Persons in Selected Industries (1 000 persons)					
(i)制造业	(i) Manufacturing	326.4	290.2	272.0	235.5	227.7@
(ii)建筑业	(ii) Construction	291.4	286.5	265.9	268.2	270.1@
(iii)批发、零售、进口与出口贸易、饮食及酒店业	(iii) Wholesale, Retail and Importand Export Trades, Restaurants and Hotels	981.1	983.4	991.8	1074.3	1110.6@
(iv)运输、仓库及通讯业	(iv) Transport, Storage and Communications	353.4	345.8	346.1	360.1	362.4@
(v)金融、保险、地产及商用服务业	(v) Financing, Insurance, Real Estate and Business Services	478.1	474.4	469.7	482.2	506.1@
(vi)社区、社会及个人服务业	(vi) Community, Social and Personal Services	798.9	825.1	849.5	864.5	883.5@
实际工资指数②(1992年9月=100)	Real Wage Index② (September 1992=100)	114.6	117.8	118.6	115.5	114.9
对外商品贸易	**External Merchandise Trade**					
进口 (亿港元)	Imports (HKD 100 million)	15682	16194	18058	21111	23295
港产品出口 (亿港元)	Domestic Exports (HKD 100 million)	1535	1309	1217	1260	1360
转口 (亿港元)	Re-exports (HKD 100 million)	13275	14296	16208	18931	21141
贸易价格比率指数 (2000年=100)	Terms of Trade Index (2000=100)	100.9	102.1	101.0	99.3	97.9
对外服务贸易	**External Trade in Services**					
服务出口③ (亿港元)	Exports of Services③ (HKD 100 million)	3208.0	3478.4	3624.2	4295.6	4834.6@
服务进口③ (亿港元)	Imports of Services③ (HKD 100 million)	1941.8	2024.9	2034.0	2425.1	2518.3@
工业生产	**Industrial Production**					
工业生产指数 (2000年=100)	Index of Industrial Production (2000=100)	95.6	86.2	78.3	80.6	82.6
工业电力消费量 (万亿焦耳)	Industrial Electricity Consumption (terajoules)	16759	16112	14851	15430	14636
工业煤气消费量 (万亿焦耳)	Industrial Gas Consumption (terajoules)	1011	987	1015	955	898
批发贸易业、零售贸易业、进出口贸易业、运输业及服务业	**Wholesale Trade, Retail Trade, Import and Export Trades, Transport Services and Other Services**					
增加值 (亿港元)	Value Added (HKD 100 million)					
批发贸易业	Wholesale Trade	136	124	114	127	
零售贸易业	Retail Trade	274	279	264	341	
进出口贸易业	Import and Export Trades	2272	2316	2411	2614	
运输及有关服务	Transport and Related Services	849	895	872	992	
仓库、通讯、财务(银行除外)及商用服务业	Storage, Communications, Financing (Except Banking) and Business Services	910	896	954	1050	

24-1 续表 1 continued

项　目	Item	2001	2002	2003	2004	2005
土地、楼宇、建造及地产	**Land, Building, Construction and Real Estate**					
建造工程完成名义总值 (亿港元)	Gross Value of Construction Work in Nominal Terms (HKD 100 million)	1140	1060	990	932	909
获批准可动工兴建私人居住单位 (个)	Private Residential Flats with Consent to Commence Work (number)					
初次呈交图则④	First Submission④	}26461	}17292	16655	8682	7829
重大修改④	Major Revision④			12497	5373	4912
房屋及物业	**Housing and Property**					
公营房屋⑤	Public Housing⑤					
新落成房屋委员会公营租住房屋单位⑥ (个)	Housing Authority Public Rental Housing Flats Newly Completed⑥ (number)	29817	20390	15148	24682	17153
私人物业	Private Housing					
私人住宅单位落成量	Private Domestic Units Newly Completed	26262	31052	26397	26036	17321
楼宇售价指数 (1999年=100)	Property Price Index (1999=100)					
私人住宅单位	Private Domestic Units	78.7	69.9	61.6	78.0	92.0
私人写字楼(甲级、乙级及丙级)	Private Offices (Grades A, B and C)	78.7	68.4	62.5	99.3	133.1@
楼宇租金指数 (1999年=100)	Property Rental Index (1999=100)					
私人住宅单位	Private Domestic Units	95.4	83.4	73.6	77.7	86.5
私人写字楼(甲级、乙级及丙级)	Private Offices (Grades A, B and C)	101.0	85.4	74.6	78.1	96.4
已登记楼宇买卖合约涉及的价值 (亿港元)	Value of Registered Agreements for Sale and Purchase of Building Units (HKD 100 million)					
住宅	Residential	1509.2	1542.5	1535.8	2767.4	3128.3
非住宅	Non-residential	418.9	311.4	358.4	750.5	826.8
总计	Total	1928.1	1853.9	1894.2	3517.9	3955.1
运输、通讯、旅游	**Transport, Communications and Tourism**					
进出香港货运车辆 (万辆)	Inward/Outward Movement of Goods Vehicle (10 000 vehicles)	912.88	975.51	988.26	974.83	973.40
进出香港货物	Inward and Outward Movements of Cargo					
总卸下 (万吨)	Total Discharged (10 000 tons)	13205	14210	15059	15779	16333
总装上 (万吨)	Total Loaded (10 000 tons)	8552	9265	9993	10693	10914
集装箱吞吐量(万标准集装箱单位)	Container Throughput (10 000 TEUs)	1783	1914	2045	2198	2260
领牌车辆⑦ (千辆)	Motor Vehicles Licensed ⑦ (1 000 vehicles)	525.4	525.6	524.2	532.9	540.6
电话服务 (万条操作线路)	Telephone Services (10 000 working lines)	393	384	382	378	379
访港旅客⑧ (万人次)	Visitor Arrivals⑧ (10 000 person-times)	1372.5	1656.6	1553.7	2181.1	2335.9
酒店入住率 (%)	Hotel Room Occupancy Rate (%)	79	84	70	88	86
政府收支、货币、金融 (亿港元)	**Public Accounts, Money and Finance(HKD 100 million)**					
政府储备结余⑨	Government's Reserve Balances⑨	3725	3114	2753	2960	3107
政府收入总额⑨⑩	Total Government Revenue⑨, ⑩	1756	1775	2073	2636	2470
政府支出总额⑨,⑩	Total Government Spending⑨, ⑩	2389	2392	2475	2422	2331
货币供应量M_3	Money Supply M_3					
港元⑪	Hong Kong Dollar⑪	20166	20042	21229	22196	23453
外币⑫	Foreign Currency⑫	15775	15576	17352	19700	20580
总计	Total	35941	35619	38580	41895	44034
在港使用的贷款及垫款	Loans and Advances for Use in Hong Kong	17901	17429	17085	17924	19265
港汇指数(贸易总值(进口及整体出口)加权)⑬ (2000年1月=100)	Effective Exchange Rate Indices for the Hong Kong Dollar (trade (import and export) - weighted)⑬ (January 2000=100)	104.7	104	100.7	98.3	97.4
居民消费价格指数	**Consumer Price Indices**					
(2004年10月至2005年9月=100)	(Oct. 2004-Sep. 2005 = 100)					
综合消费价格指数	Composite Consumer Price Index	105.7	102.4	99.8	99.4	100.3
甲类消费价格指数	Consumer Price Index (A)	104.8	101.4	99.3	99.3	100.3
乙类消费价格指数	Consumer Price Index (B)	105.9	102.6	99.8	99.4	100.4
丙类消费价格指数	Consumer Price Index (C)	106.3	103.3	100.3	99.6	100.3

24-1 续表 2 continued

项 目	Item	2001	2002	2003	2004	2005
教育 （人）	**Education (persons)**					
小学学生人数	Student Enrolment in Primary Schools	493075	483218	468792	447137	425864
中学学生人数⑭	Student Enrolment in Secondary Schools⑭	465403	465926	470487	476954	482273
教资会资助院校学生人数⑮	Student Enrolment in UGC-funded Institutions⑮	81664	85602	90355	91865	91786@
卫生	**Health**					
医生 （人）	Doctors (persons)	10412	10731	11016	11242	11505
中医⑯ （人）	Chinese Medicine Practitioners⑯ (persons)		2385	4738	4986	5133
病床 （张）	Hospital Beds (beds)	34852	35159	35526	34400	34119
社会保障	**Social Security**					
综合社会保障援助⑨	Comprehensive Social Security Assistance⑨					
个案数目⑰ （个）	Number of Cases⑰ (cases)	247192	271893	290705	296688	297434
发放款项⑱ （亿港元）	Amount⑱ (HKD 100 million)	144.05	161.31	173.06	176.31	177.66
公共福利金⑨	Social Security Allowances⑨					
个案数目⑰ （个）	Number of Cases⑰ (cases)	561208	560215	563908	567859	574135
发放款项⑱ （亿港元）	Amount⑱ (HKD 100 million)	52.41	52.81	52.14	52.45	53.39
交通意外伤亡援助⑨	Traffic Accident Victims Assistance⑨					
获批个案数目 （个）	Number of Cases Authorized for Payment (cases)	6733	7102	7190	7360	7893
发放款项 （亿港元）	Amount (HKD 100 million)	1.42	1.51	1.51	1.54	1.64
治安	**Law and Order**					
举报罪案合计 （件）	Overall Reported Crimes (cases)	73008	75877	88377	81315	77437
暴力罪案总计 （件）	Total Violent Crimes (cases)	13551	14140	14542	13890	13890
犯罪被捕人数总计⑲ （人）	Total Persons Arrested for Crime⑲ (persons)	38829	39665	42051	42991	40804
本地生产总值③	**Gross Domestic Product (GDP)③**					
按2000年不变价格计算	At Constant (2000) Market Prices					
年增长率 （%）	Annual Growth Rate (%)	0.6	1.8	3.2	8.6@	7.3@
本地生产总值 （亿港元）	GDP (HKD 100 million)	13232	13475	13906	15102@	16200@
人均本地生产总值 （港元）	Per Capita GDP (HKD)	196756	198541	204408	219420@	233565@
按当年价格计算	At Current Market Prices					
年增长率 （%）	Annual Growth Rate (%)	-1.2	-1.7	-3.4	4.7@	7.0@
本地生产总值 （亿港元）	GDP (HKD 100 million)	12988	12768	12340	12916@	13821@
人均本地生产总值 （港元）	Per Capita GDP (HKD)	193135	188118	181385	187657@	199261@
本地居民生产总值	**Gross National Product (GNP)**					
按当年价格计算	At Current Market Prices					
本地居民生产总值③ （亿港元）	GNP③ (HKD 100 million)	13274	12824	12625	13150@	13845@
人均本地居民生产总值③ （港元）	Per Capita GNP③ (HKD)	197379	188951	185573	191058@	199616@
国外净要素收入③ （亿港元）	Net External Factor Income Flows ③ (HKD 100 million)	285.43	56.52	284.91	234.1@	24.63@
国际收支平衡表 （亿港元）	**Balance of Payments Account (HKD 100 million)**					
经常帐(20)	Current Account(20)	763.2	968.0	1282.4	1224.9@	1576.9@
资本及金融帐(20)	Capital and Financial Account (20)	-973.6	-1512	-1791	-1846@	-1609@
净误差及(21)	Net Errors and Omissions(21)	210.4	543.8	508.5	621.5@	31.9@
整体的国际收支	Overall Balance of Payments	365.3 (盈余) (in surplus)	-185.4 (赤字) (in deficit)	75.9 (盈余) (in surplus)	254.9@ (盈余) (in surplus)	106.8@ (盈余) (in surplus)
国际投资头寸(22)	**International Investment Position(22)**					
国际投资头寸净值(23) （亿港元）	Net International Investment Position(23) (HKD 100 million)	20680	26774	30598	33018	34819@
对外金融资产 （亿港元）	External Financial Assets (HKD 100 million)	83506	80327	92023	106987	116565@
对外金融负债 （亿港元）	External Financial Liabilities(HKD 100 million)	62827	53554	61425	73969	81747@

注：①数字是指就业不足人士在劳动人口中所占的比例。就业不足人士是指包括在统计前7天内在非自愿情况下工作少于35小时，而在统计前30天内有找寻更多工作，或即使不是找寻工作，但在统计前7天内可担任更多工作的就业人士。根据此定义，因工作量不足而在统计前7天内放取无薪假期的就业人士，若在该7天期间内工作少于35小时，甚或全段期间都在休假，亦会界定为就业不足人士。

②实际工资指数是从名义工资指数中，按甲类消费价格指数的变幅，扣除通胀的影响而得出，显示雇员所赚取工资金额购买力的转变。

③政府统计处在2005年8月中完成一项工作，就是在估计香港国民经济核算统计数字时，采用最新国际指引处理由银行所提供的金融中介服务。由于这项统计发

④2002年及以前没有「初次呈交图则」和「重大修改」细分数字。

⑤数字是以相应的财政年度为根据。例如2005年的数字代表2005至2006财政年度数字。从2005年5月起，房屋委员会建屋落成量的房屋类别重新修订如下列注 ⑥所述。上述建屋量数据是已反映修订后的结果。

⑥房屋委员会的公营租住房屋亦包括那些由剩余居者有其屋计划转作公营租住房屋的单位。中转房屋及那些由公营租住房屋转作出售用途的可租可买计划/重建置业计划的单位则不包括在内。

24-1 续表 3 continued

⑦数字是指期末的数字。
⑧访港旅客数字包括经澳门访港的非澳门居民。
⑨数字是以相应的财政年度为根据。例如2005年的数字代表2005至2006财政年度数字。
⑩2005年的数字有待审计署署长核实。
⑪所列数字已包括外币掉期存款。
⑫所列数字已扣除外币掉期存款。《中华人民共和国香港特别行政区基本法》说明，港元是香港特别行政区的法定货币。外币指港元以外的其他货币，因而人民币亦视作外币。
⑬由2002年1月2日起公布的新系列。
⑭数字涵盖日、夜校。
⑮数字包括教资会资助课程的所有学生及就读自资全日制经评审副学位程度的专上课程的学生人数。2003年以前的研究院研究课程只包括在一般的修业期内及教资会指标内的学生。自2003年起，数字亦包括在一般的修业期内及在教资会指标外但受教资会资助的研究院研究课程学生。
⑯数字自2002年开始提供。
⑰于财政年度终结时的数字。
⑱2001年的数字包括2001年4月2日至2002年4月1日期间所发放的款项。2002年的数字则包括2002年4月2日至2003年3月31日期间所发放的款项。
⑲犯罪被捕人数的计算方法是按罪犯被捕的次数而定，不论有否遭起诉。若某人在两宗或以上事件中被捕，会于每次事件中分别记录。若某人在一宗事件中因多项罪名被捕，则只选其中可被判最重刑罚的一项罪名作统计之用。
(20)经常帐差额的正数显示盈余而负数则显示赤字。在资本及金融帐方面,正数显示净流入而负数则显示净流出。由于对外资产的增加是属于借方帐目，而减少则属贷方帐目，因此负数的储备资产变动净值显示储备资产的增加，而正数则显示减少。
(21)原则上，贷方和借方各项帐目的净总和应相等于零。但实际上,贷方和借方帐目的资料是通过不同的来源搜集，基于各种原因会有差异。为了使贷方和借方帐目的总和相等，便须加进一个余额项目，以反映平衡表的“净误差及遗漏”。
(22)期末头寸。
(23)国际投资头寸净值是对外金融资产总值与对外金融负债总值之差。
"空格" 没有数字。 "@" 数字将于日后修订。

Notes :①Figures refers to the proportion of underemployed persons in the labour force. Underemployed persons comprises those employed persons who have involuntarily worked less than 35 hours during the 7 days before enumeration and have sought additional work during the 30 days before enumeration, or have not sought additional work but have been available for additional work during the 7 days before enumeration. Following this definition, employed persons taking no-pay leave due to slack work during the 7 days before enumeration are also classified as underemployed if they worked less than 35 hours or were on leave even for the whole period during the 7-day period.

②The real wage index indicates changes in the purchasing power of the amount of wages earned and is obtained by deflating the nominal wage index by the Consumer Price Index (A).

③The Census and Statistics Department completed an exercise to implement the latest international guidelines on dealing with financial intermediation services produced by banks in the estimation of national accounts statistics of Hong Kong in mid-August 2005. As a result of this statistical development, figures presented in this table were revised.

④Separate figures for "First submission" and "Major revision" were not available for 2002 and the years before.

⑤Figures are for the corresponding financial year.For example,figures for 2005 represent those for financial year 2005/06. Since May 2005, the housing type classifications of Housing Authority public housing production have been revised as stated in notes ⑥ below. The above production figures have taken into account this reclassification.

⑥Figures also include flats transferred from the surplus of the Home Ownership Scheme. Interim Housing flats and those public rental housing flats transferred to Buy or Rent Option Scheme / Mortgage Subsidy Scheme are not included.

⑦Figures refer to end of period position.

⑧Figures include arrival of non-Macao residents via Macao.

⑨Figures are for the corresponding financial year. For example, figures for 2005 represent those for financial year 2005/06.

⑩Figures for 2005 are subject to audit by the Director of Audit.

⑪Figures are adjusted to include foreign currency swap deposits.

⑫Figures are adjusted to exclude foreign currency swap deposits. Hong Kong dollar is the legal tender in the Hong Kong Special Administrative Region, as stated in "The Basic Law of the Hong Kong Special Administrative Region of the People's Republic of China". Foreign currency refers to any currency other than Hong Kong dollar and thus Chinese Renminbi is also treated as a foreign currency.

⑬New series released since 2 January 2002.

⑭Figures cover both day and evening schools.

⑮Figures refer to all students of University Grants Committee (UGC) - funded programmes and students attending full-time accredited self-financing post-secondary programmes at sub-degree level. For research postgraduate (RPg) programmes, figures before 2003 include only students countedwithin the formal time limit and within the UGC student number target. From 2003 onwards, RPg students counted within the formal time limit and outside the UGC student number target but wholly funded by UGC are also included.

⑯Figures have been made available since 2002.

⑰Figures are as at end of the financial year.

⑱Figures for 2001 include the payments for 2 April 2001 to 1 April 2002. Figures for 2002 include the payments for 2 April 2002 to 31 March 2003.

⑲Persons arrested for crime are counted based on the number of occasions on which the offenders are arrested, whether or not they are prosecuted. If a person is arrested on two or more occasions, each occasion is counted as a ‘separate' person. If a person is arrested on one occasion for several offences, the offence with the maximum permissible penalty, being the heaviest, is chosen for statistical purposes.

(20)A positive value for the balance figure in the current account represents a surplus whereas a negative value represents a deficit. For the capital and financial account, a positive value indicates a net inflow and a negative value indicates a net outflow. As increases in external assets are debit entries and decreases are credit entries, a negative value for net change in reserve assets represents a net increase and a positive value represents a net decrease.

(21)In principle, the net sum of credit entries and debit entries is zero. In practice, discrepancies between the credit and debit entries may however occur for various reasons as the data are collected from different sources. Equality between the sum of credit entries and debit entries is brought about by the inclusion of a balancing item which reflects net errors and omissions.

(22)Position as at end of period.

(23)Net international investment position is the difference between total external financial assets and total external financial liabilities.

"(blank)" Not available. "@" Figures are subject to revision later on.

24-2 按区议会地区划分的香港陆地面积

Land Area of Hong Kong by District Council District

单位：平方公里 (sq. km)

区议会分区	District Council District	2001	2002	2003	2004	2005	2006
总计①	**Total①**	**1099**	**1101**	**1102**	**1103**	**1104**	**1104**
香港岛	**Hong Kong Island**						
中西区	Central and Western	12	12	12	12	12	12
湾仔	Wan Chai	10	10	10	10	10	10
东区	Eastern	19	19	19	19	19	19
南区	Southern	39	39	39	39	39	39
小计	Sub-total	80	80	80	80	80	80
九龙	**Kowloon**						
九龙城	Kowloon City	10	10	10	10	10	10
观塘	Kwun Tong	11	11	11	11	11	11
深水埗	Sham Shui Po	9	9	9	9	9	9
黄大仙	Wong Tai Sin	9	9	9	9	9	9
油尖旺	Yau Tsim Mong	7	7	7	7	7	7
小计	Sub-total	47	47	47	47	47	47
新界	**New Territories**						
离岛	Islands	175	176	176	176	176	176
北区	North	137	137	137	137	137	137
西贡	Sai Kung	136	136	136	136	136	136
沙田	Sha Tin	69	69	69	69	69	69
大埔	Tai Po	148	148	148	148	148	148
荃湾	Tsuen Wan	61	62	62	62	62	62
葵青	Kwai Tsing	22	23	23	23	23	23
屯门	Tuen Mun	84	85	85	85	85	85
元朗	Yuen Long	139	139	139	139	139	139
小计	Sub-total	971	974	975	975	975	976

注：2001年的数字是5月份的数据。2002年及以后的数字则是6月底的数据。

2001年至2003年的数字是根据1999年区议会地区界线计算。而2004年及以后的数字则是根据2004年区议会地区界线计算。

2002年及以后的数字是根据地政总署测绘处提供之1：10 000 比例地图数据库计算。

①2005年及2006年的面积包括不在区议会分区内的落马洲河套。

Notes : Figures for 2001 are as at May of the year. Figures for 2002 and onward are as at end-June of the year.

Figures for 2001 to 2003 were computed in accordance with the 1999 District Council boundaries while those for 2004 and onwards were computed in accordance with 2004 District Council boundaries.

Figures for 2002 and onward were computed with reference to the 1:10 000 Mapping Database of the Lands Department.

①Figures for 2005 and 2006 include land area of Lok Ma Chau Loop which is not covered in District Council Districts.

24-3 土地用途分布情况

Land Usage

单位：平方公里 (sq. km)

类别	Class	2002	2003	2004	2005
住宅	**Residential**				
私人住宅①	Private Residential①	25	24	25	25
公屋②	Public Residential②	17	17	17	17
乡郊居所③	Rural Settlements③	26	26	35	36
商业	**Commercial**				
商业／商贸和办公室	Commercial/Business and Offices	3	3	3	3
工业	**Industrial**				
工业	Industrial	5	6	7	7
工业村	Industrial Estates	3	3	3	3
货仓和贮物处④	Warehouse and Storage④	11	12	15	15
机构	**Institution**				
政府、机构和社区设施	Government, Institution and Community Facilities	21	21	23	23
运输	**Transportation**				
道路	Roads	36	37	38	38
铁路	Railways	1	2	2	3
机场	Airport	13	13	13	13
休憩用地⑤	**Open Space⑤**	**20**	**20**	**21**	**22**
空置土地	**Vacant Land**				
空置发展／正在进行建筑工程的土地	Vacant Development Land/Construction in Progress	33	31	29	26
其他都市或已建设土地	**Other Urban or Built-up Land**				
坟场和火葬场	Cemeteries and Crematoriums	5	6	7	7
公用事业设施	Public Utilities	6	6	6	6
其他用途	Other Uses	14	16	18	20
农业用地	**Agricultural Land**				
农地	Agricultural	54	58	56	55
鱼塘／基围	Fish ponds/Gei wais	13	13	17	18
林地／灌丛／草地	**Woodland/ Shrubland/ Grassland**				
林地	Woodland	190	285	268	257
灌丛	Shrubland	241	230	214	220
草地	Grassland	308	226	249	251
湿地	**Wetland**				
红树林和沼泽⑥	Mangrove and Swamp⑥	4	5	1	5
荒地	**Barren Land**				
劣地	Badland	16	11	5	5
石矿场	Quarries	3	2	2	2
石岸	Rocky Shore	5	2	2	2
水体	**Water Area**				
水塘	Reservoirs	24	24	24	24
河道和明渠	Streams and Nullahs	4	4	3	5
总计⑥	**Total⑥**	**1103**	**1108**	**1 107**	**1108**

注：数字是当年12月的数据。
①由私人发展商发展的住宅用地（乡村屋宇、居屋计划／私人参建计划屋苑和临时房屋区除外）。
②包括居屋计划／私人参建计划屋苑和临时房屋区。
③包括临时建筑物。
④包括露天贮物用地。
⑤包括公园、体育馆和运动场。
⑥在2002年至2005年，部份在高水位线下的红树林和沼泽用地，并没有计算在土地总面积内。

Notes : Figures are as at December of the year.
①Residential land developed by private developers except village houses, Home Ownership Scheme (HOS)/Private Sector Participation Scheme (PSPS) and temporary housing areas.
②Include HOS/PSPS and temporary housing areas.
③Include temporary structures.
④Include open storage areas.
⑤Include parks, stadiums and playgrounds.
⑥From 2002 to 2005, some Mangrove and Swamp areas below the High Water Mark are excluded from the calculation of the land area.

24-4　按地区类别及路边情况划分的大气质量(2005年)

Air Quality by Area Type and Roadside Condition (2005)

单位：微克/立方米　　　　(microgram/cu.m.)

地区类别及路边	Area Type and Roadside	全年平均大气污染浓度 Annual average air pollutant concentrations			
		二氧化硫 Sulphur Dioxide	二氧化氮 Nitrogen Dioxide	总悬浮粒子 Total Suspended Particulates	可吸入悬浮粒子 Respirable Suspended Particulates
市区①	Urban①	23	60	81	55
新市镇②	New Town②	22	49	74	56
郊区③	Rural③	14	14	-	50
路边④	Roadside④	22	96	112	75

注：①包括葵涌、中西区、深水涉、观塘、东区及荃湾。
②包括大埔、沙田、元朗及东涌。
③包括塔门。
④包括铜锣湾、中环及旺角。
"-" 不适用。

Notes: ①Includes Kwai Chung, Central/Western, Sham Shui Po, Kwun Tong, Eastern and Tsuen Wan.
②Includes Tai Po, Sha Tin, Yuen Long and Tung Chung.
③Includes Tap Mun.
④Includes Causeway Bay, Central and Mong Kok.
"-" Not applicable.

24-5　按种类划分的每日平均产生的固体废物

Daily Average Solid Waste Generation by Type

单位：吨　　　　(ton)

种　类	Type	2001	2002	2003	2004	2005
都市固体废物①	Municipal Solid Waste①					
住宅废物②	Domestic②	7550	7520	7400	7010	6830
商业废物③	Commercial③	1190	1340	1430	1670	1900
工业废物④	Industrial④	560	560	610	600	650
小计	Sub-total	9300	9420	9440	9280	9380
拆建废料①⑤	Construction and Demolition Waste ①⑤	6410	10200	6730	6600	6560
特殊废物⑥	Special Waste ⑥	1110	1540	1590	1620	1750
已回收都市固体废物⑦	Recovered Municipal Solid Waste ⑦	5320	5370	6510	6310	7110
总计	**Total**	**22140**	**26530**	**24270**	**23180**	**24800**

注：①都市固体废物包括运往弃置设施的住宅废物、商业废物及工业废物，但不包括拆建废料及已回收都市固体废物。
②住宅废物包括使用后的住宅固体废物，及由公共洁净服务收集的废物。
③商业废物包括所有类型的商业活动产生的固体废物。
④工业废物包括由工业活动产生的固体废物，但不包括化学废物及拆建废料。
⑤拆建废料包括由建筑及拆卸活动所产生的废物，但不包括可运往公众填土区作填海用途的物料。
⑥特殊废物包括弃置于堆填区的动物尸体、屠房废物、报废货物、滤水厂及污水处理后的污泥、污水处理厂的隔滤物、禽畜废物、医疗废物及化学废物。
⑦都市固体废物回收后会在本地或海外循环再造。

Notes : ①Municipal solid waste includes domestic waste, commercial waste and industrial waste delivered to disposal facilities but excludes construction and demolition waste and recovered municipal solid waste.
②Domestic waste covers post-consumer residential solid waste and refuse collected in public cleansing activities.
③Commercial waste covers solid waste arising from all forms of commercial activities.
④Industrial waste covers solid waste arising from industrial activities but excludes chemical waste and construction and demolition waste.
⑤Construction and demolition waste covers waste arising from construction and demolition activities but excludes material delivered to public filling areas for land reclamation and formation.
⑥Special waste includes animal carcasses, abattoir waste, condemned goods, waterworks and sewage treatment sludge, sewage works screening, livestock waste, clinical waste and chemical waste delivered to landfills.
⑦Municipal solid waste recovered will be recycled locally or overseas.

24-6 人口主要指标

Main Indicators of Population

项　　目	Item	2001	2002	2003	2004	2005
年中人口　(万人)	Mid-year Population (10 000 persons)	672.5	678.7	680.3	688.3	693.6
粗出生率　(‰)	Crude Birth Rate (‰)	7.2	7.1	6.9	7.2	8.2
粗死亡率　(‰)	Crude Death Rate (‰)	5.0	5.0	5.4	5.4	5.5@
婴儿死亡率　(‰)	Infant Mortality Rate (‰)	2.6	2.3	2.3	2.7	2.4@
自然增长率　(‰)	Rate of Natural Increase (‰)	2.2	2.1	1.5	1.9	2.7@
总和生育率①②	Total Fertility Rate①②	932	939	901	927	966
登记结婚数　(对)	Registered Marriages (couple)	32825	32070	35439	41376	43018
登记离婚数　(对)	Divorce Decrees (couple)	13425	12943	13829	15604	14873
出生时平均预期寿命　(年)	Expectation of Life at Birth (years)					
男	Male	78.4	78.6	78.5	79	78.8@
女	Female	84.6	84.5	84.3	84.7	84.4@

注：①按每千名没有包括外籍家庭佣工的女性人口计算。

②鉴于近年女性在香港生育的情况有所转变，数字已作出修订。详情请参阅《香港统计月刊》2005年四月号题为「1975年至2004年香港生育趋势」的专题文章。

"@" 数字将于日后修订。

Notes : ①Per 1000 female population excluding foreign domestic helpers.

②Figures have been revised in view of the recent change in the situation of women giving births in Hong Kong. For details, please refer to the feature article entitled "The fertility trend in Hong Kong, 1975-2004" in the April 2005 issue of the Hong Kong Monthly Digest of Statistics.

"@" Figures are subject to revision later on.

24-7 劳动人口及失业状况

Labour Force and Unemployment

项　　目	Item	2001	2002	2003	2004	2005
劳动人口数目(万人)	Labour Force (10 000 persons)	342.7	348.7	349.6	355.1	358.6@
男	Male	196.5	196.5	196.1	197.5	197.8@
女	Female	146.2	152.2	153.5	157.6	160.8@
劳动人口参与率 (%)	Labour Force Participation Rate (%)	61.4	61.8	61.4	61.3	60.9@
就业人数　(万人)	Employed Persons (10 000 persons)	325.2	323.2	321.9	330.9	338.6@
失业人数　(万人)	Unemployed Persons (10 000 persons)	17.5	25.6	27.7	24.2	20.1@
失业率　(%)	Unemployment Rate (%)	5.1	7.3	7.9	6.8	5.6@

注：数字是根据该年四季「综合住户统计调查」所得的数据编制。

"@" 数字将于日后修订。

Note: Figures are compiled based on the data obtained from the General Household Survey for the four quarters of the year.

"@" Figures are subject to revision later on.

24-8 按行业划分的就业人数

Employed Persons by Industry

单位：万人 (10 000 persons)

行业	Industry	2001	2002	2003	2004	2005
制造业	Manufacturing	32.64	29.02	27.20	23.55	22.77@
建筑业	Construction	29.14	28.65	26.59	26.82	27.01@
批发、零售、进出口贸易、饮食及酒店业	Wholesale, Retail and Import/Export Trades, Restaurants and Hotels	98.11	98.34	99.18	107.43	111.06@
运输、仓库及通讯业	Transport, Storage and Communications	35.34	34.58	34.61	36.01	36.24@
金融、保险、地产及商用服务业	Financing, Insurance, Real Estate and Business Services	47.81	47.44	46.97	48.22	50.61@
社区、社会及个人服务业	Community, Social and Personal Services	79.89	82.51	84.95	86.45	88.35@
其他	Others	2.31	2.62	2.41	2.37	2.53@
总计	**Total**	**325.23**	**323.16**	**321.91**	**330.86**	**338.55@**

注：数字是根据该年四季「综合住户统计调查」所得的数据编制。
有关就业统计数字,可分别按"综合住户统计调查"及"雇佣及职位空缺按季统计调查"的结果编制。此两套数字用于反映有关就业情况时，各有优点和局限。上表载列了"综合住户统计调查"的估计数字，是由于其包括的就业人口范围较全面。再者，个别人士，包括有多过一份工作的职位持有者，都只计算一次。但"综合住户统计调查"的就业估计数字有一个主要局限，就是被访者有困难准确地提供其本身所属行业的资料，尤以制造业员工为甚。随着香港制造业机构将部分工序移往中国内地，这些机构在香港的传统运作模式已有改变。就一些已将大部分工序移往中国内地的机构而言，他们应归类为进出口贸易业。不过，由于有关机构的员工，尤其是技师及技工级等员工，未必全部都能清楚理解这个统计分类上的改变，有些被访者仍认为他们是属于制造业而非进出口贸易业，因而使"综合住户统计调查"的有关制造业估计就业人数有高估的现象。
"@" 数字将于日后修订。

Notes : Figures are compiled based on the data obtained from the General Household Survey for the four quarters of the year.
Employment statistics are compiled separately based on the General Household Survey (GHS) and the Quarterly Survey of Employment and Vacancies. Each source has its own merits and limitations in reflecting the employment situation. The GHS estimates are presented here because the omission in terms of coverage of the employed population is negligible. Besides, individual persons, including multiple job holders, are counted only once. However, a major limitation of the GHS estimates is that the respondents might not have reported accurately the industry to which they belong, especially for workers in the manufacturing sector. With the relocation of some production processes to the mainland of China, there is a change in the mode of operation of the traditional manufacturing establishments in Hong Kong. As a result, some of these establishments are more appropriately classified as import/export establishments if the majority of the production activities are carried out in the mainland of China. However, this change in statistical classification may not be readily recognized by all the employed persons, particularly the technicians and craftsmen, of the establishments concerned. Hence, the GHS employment estimate in respect of the manufacturing sector will be overstated to the extent that some respondents mistakenly regard themselves as still being engaged in the manufacturing sector instead of the import/export trades.
"@" Figures are subject to revision later on.

24-9 按每月就业收入划分的就业人数

Employed Persons by Monthly Employment Earnings

单位：万人 (10 000 persons)

每月就业收入(港元)	Monthly employment earnings (HKD)	2001	2002	2003	2004	2005
< 3000	< 3000	9.32	12.58	14.95	16.34	15.34@
3000 － 3999	3000 - 3999	22.74	24.46	25.54	25.63	26.40@
4000 － 4999	4000 - 4999	10.18	11.58	14.42	14.44	13.34@
5000 － 5999	5000 - 5999	14.08	16.92	18.72	19.67	19.68@
6000 － 6999	6000 - 6999	20.52	22.01	22.68	23.84	24.71@
7000 － 7999	7000 - 7999	19.44	20.83	21.36	22.97	23.74@
8000 － 8999	8000 - 8999	25.50	24.61	24.32	25.13	25.31@
9000 － 9999	9000 - 9999	17.83	17.10	17.73	19.53	20.81@
10000 － 14999	10000 - 14999	74.54	66.60	60.59	60.64	63.28@
15000 － 19999	15000 - 19999	36.05	34.31	32.27	32.79	34.44@
20000 － 29999	20000 - 29999	38.07	36.01	34.43	34.26	34.73@
≧30000	≧ 30000	36.98	36.16	34.90	35.61	36.76@
总计	**Total**	**325.23**	**323.16**	**321.91**	**330.86**	**338.55@**
每月就业收入中位数(港元)	Median monthly Employment Earnings (HKD)	10000	10000	10000	9600	9900@

注：数字是根据该年四季「综合住户统计调查」所得的数据编制。
"@" 数字将于日后修订。

Note: Figures are compiled based on the data obtained from the General Household Survey for the four quarters of the year.
"@" Figures are subject to revision later on.

24-10 本地生产总值
Gross Domestic Product

年份 Year	本地生产总值(按当年价格计算) Gross Domestic Product(GDP) At Current Market Prices		本地生产总值与上年比较的实际增长(%) GDP Real Growth Rate over the Preceding Year (%)	人均本地生产总值(按当年价格计算) Per Capita GDP At Current Market Prices	
	(亿港元) (HKD 100 million)	(亿美元) (USD 100 million)		(港元) (HKD)	(美元) (USD)
1990	5990	769	4.0	104996	13480
1991	6903	888	5.7	120015	15444
1992	8051	1040	6.5	138795	17930
1993	9280	1200	6.3	157261	20328
1994	10475	1355	5.6	173554	22458
1995	11157	1442	3.9	181241	23428
1996	12295	1590	4.2	191047	24702
1997	13650	1763	5.1	210350	27170
1998	12928	1669	-5.5	197559	25508
1999	12667	1633	4.0	191736	24715
2000	13148	1688	10.0	197268	25320
2001	12988	1665	0.6	193135	24764
2002	12768	1637	1.8	188118	24121
2003	12340	1585	3.2	181385	23293
2004	12916@	1658@	8.6@	187657@	24096@
2005	13821@	1777@	7.3@	199261@	25622@

注：政府统计处在2005年8月中完成一项工作，就是在估计香港国民经济核算统计数字时，采用最新国际指引处理由银行所提供的金融中介服务。由于这项统计发展，载于本表内的数字已作出修订。
"@" 数字将于日后修订。

Note : The Census and Statistics Department completed an exercise to implement the latest international guidelines on dealing with financial intermediation services produced by banks in the estimation of national accounts statistics of Hong Kong in mid-August 2005. As a result of this statistical development, figures presented in this table were revised.
"@" Figures are subject to revision later on.

24-11 按当年价格计算生产法本地生产总值
Gross Domestic Product by Economic Activity at Current Prices

单位：亿港元 (HKD 100 million)

经济活动	Economic Activity	2000	2001	2002	2003@	2004
农业及渔业	**Agriculture and Fishing**	**9.20**	**10.03**	**10.02**	**8.24**	**8.86@**
工业	**Industry**	**1668.57**	**1550.58**	**1426.74**	**1282.69**	**1246.29@**
采矿及采石业	Mining and Quarrying	2.41	1.74	1.36	1.16	0.72@
制造业	Manufacturing	676.46	597.60	513.96	444.03	444.55@
电力、煤气及水的生产和供应业	Electricity, Gas and Water	369.17	379.57	396.09	388.39	397.26@
建筑业	Construction	620.54	571.67	515.34	449.10	403.76@
服务业	**Services**	**10875.70**	**10882.11**	**10912.72**	**10739.41**	**11303.01@**
批发贸易、零售贸易、进口与出口贸易、饮食及酒店业	Wholesale, Retail and Import and Export Trades, Restaurants and Hotels	3086.00	3099.26	3105.00	3088.72	3450.92@
运输、仓库及通讯业	Transport, Storage and Communications	1189.74	1175.26	1217.66	1174.20	1268.2@
金融、保险、地产及商用服务业	Financing, Insurance, Real Estate and Business Services	2683.99	2514.95	2470.45	2510.85	2668.34@
社区、社会及个人服务业	Community, Social and Personal Services	2499.97	2629.60	2657.46	2619.17	2637.56@
楼宇业权	Ownership of Premises	1416.00	1463.04	1462.14	1346.48	1277.99@
本地生产总值(以要素成本计算)	GDP at Factor Cost	12553.48	12442.71	12349.49	12030.34	12558.16@
生产及进口税	**Taxes on Production and Imports**	**579.08**	**539.17**	**433.25**	**480.57**	**587.29@**
统计差额①	**Statistical Discrepancy①**	**0.001**	**0#**	**-0.001**	**-0.014**	**-1.8%@**
本地生产总值(按当年价格计算)	**GDP at Current Market Prices**	**13147.89**	**12988.13**	**12767.57**	**12339.83**	**12915.68@**

注：政府统计处在2005年8月中完成一项工作，就是在估计香港国民经济核算统计数字时，采用最新国际指引处理由银行所提供的金融中介服务。由于这项统计发展，载于本表内的数字已作出修订。
①统计差额是以支出法编制的本地生产总值与以生产法编制的本地生产总值的差额。这差额是由于使用不同数据来源及估算方法而引起的。统计差额是以占本地生产总值(按当年价格计算)的百分比形式作表达。
"@" 数字将于日后修订。
"0#" 数字少于单位的一半。

Notes : The Census and Statistics Department completed an exercise to implement the latest international guidelines on dealing with financial intermediation services produced by banks in the estimation of national accounts statistics of Hong Kong in mid-August 2005. As a result of this statistical development, figures presented in this table were revised.
①Statistical discrepancy refers to the difference in values of GDP compiled using the expenditure and production approaches, as a result of the adoption of different data sources and estimation methods. It is expressed as a percentage to GDP at current market prices.
"@" Figures are subject to revision later on.
"0#" Magnitude less than half of the unit employed.

24-12 按2000年不变价格计算生产法本地生产总值

Gross Domestic Product by Economic Activity at Constant (2000) Prices

单位：亿港元 (HKD 100 million)

经济活动	Economic Activity	2001	2002	2003	2004@	2005
农业及渔业	**Agriculture and Fishing**	**9.58**	**9.51**	**8.98**	**9.23**	**9.42@**
工业	**Industry**	**1599.25**	**1542.41**	**1463.63**	**1424.30**	**1415.37@**
采矿及采石业	Mining and Quarrying	2.07	1.84	1.88	1.56	1.72@
制造业	Manufacturing	615.01	553.32	496.41	504.79	515.53@
电力、煤气及水的生产和供应业	Electricity, Gas and Water	375.58	389.71	396.85	404.94	418.85@
建筑业	Construction	606.58	597.54	568.50	513.02	479.27@
服务业	**Services**	**11066.25**	**11371.10**	**11886.81**	**13065.81**	**14101.02@**
批发贸易、零售贸易、进口与出口贸易、饮食及酒店业	Wholesale, Retail and Import and Export Trades, Restaurants and Hotels	3093.79	3233.91	3526.94	4060.19	4510.43@
运输、仓库及通讯业	Transport, Storage and Communications	1211.89	1290.80	1299.93	1481.11	1681.26@
金融、保险、地产及商用服务业	Financing, Insurance, Real Estate and Business Services	2696.75	2770.04	2928.28	3311.80	3607.71@
社区、社会及个人服务业	Community, Social and Personal Services	2599.76	2582.96	2598.09	2666.09	2690.30@
楼宇业权	Ownership of Premises	1464.07	1493.39	1533.57	1546.62	1611.33@
生产及进口税	**Taxes on Production and Imports**	**572.82**	**572.28**	**591.56**	**668.54**	**675.50@**
统计差额①	**Statistical Discrepancy①**	**-0.001**	**-0.002**	**-0.003**	**-0.004**	**0#@**
本地生产总值(按2000年不变价格计算)	**GDP at Constant (2000) Market Prices**	**13231.67**	**13474.95**	**13906.10**	**15101.82**	**16199.84@**

注：政府统计处在2005年8月中完成一项工作，就是在估计香港国民经济核算统计数字时，采用最新国际指引处理由银行所提供的金融中介服务。由于这项统计发展，载于本表内的数字已作出修订。

①统计差额是以支出法编制的本地生产总值与以生产法编制的本地生产总值的差额。这差额是由于使用不同数据来源及估算方法而引起的。统计差额是以占本地生产总值(按2000年不变价格计算)的百分比形式作表达。

"@" 数字将于日后修订。

"0#" 数字少于单位的一半。

Notes : The Census and Statistics Department completed an exercise to implement the latest international guidelines on dealing with financial intermediation services produced by banks in the estimation of national accounts statistics of Hong Kong in mid-August 2005. As a result of this statistical development, figures presented in this table were revised.

①Statistical discrepancy refers to the difference in values of GDP compiled using the expenditure and production approaches, as a result of the adoption of different data sources and estimation methods. It is expressed as a percentage to GDP at constant (2000) market prices.

"@" Figures are subject to revision later on.

"0#" Magnitude less than half of the unit employed.

24-13　支出法本地生产总值
Gross Domestic Product by Expenditure Component

单位：亿港元，另有注明除外　　(HKD 100 million, unless otherwise specified)

本地生产总值组成部分	GDP Components	2001	2002	2003	2004@	2005
按当年价格计算	**At Current Market Prices**					
居民消费①	Private Consumption Expenditure ①	7825.87	7478.50	7193.04	7677.69	8047.08@
政府消费	Government Consumption Expenditure	1288.66	1312.91	1301.51	1273.09	1213.32@
国内固定资本形成总额	Gross Domestic Fixed Capital Formation	3330.36	2860.20	2613.67	2748.72	2888.21@
存货变动	Changes in Inventories	-40.60	56.60	91.11	70.76	-50.85@
货物出口(离岸价)	Exports of Goods(f.o.b.)	14809.87	15621.21	17490.89	20270.31	22517.44@
减：货物进口(离岸价)	Less: Imports of Goods(f.o.b.)	15492.22	16015.27	17940.59	20995.45	23110.91@
服务出口①	Exports of Services①	3207.99	3478.36	3624.20	4295.63	4834.55@
减：服务进口	Less: Imports of Services	1941.80	2024.94	2034.00	2425.07	2518.32@
本地生产总值	**GDP**	**12988.13**	**12767.57**	**12339.83**	**12915.68**	**13820.52@**
人均本地生产总值	**Per Capita GDP**	**193135**	**188118**	**181385**	**187657**	**199261@**
物量指数(2000年=100)	**Volume Indices (2000=100)**					
居民消费①	Private Consumption Expenditure ①	102.1	101.1	100.1	107.4	111.0@
政府消费	Government Consumption Expenditure	106.0	108.7	110.7	111.5	108.0@
国内固定资本形成总额	Gross Domestic Fixed Capital Formation	102.6	98.0	98.9	101.9	106.1@
存货变动	Changes in Inventories	-34.0	47.8	71.9	50.8	-37.6@
货物出口(离岸价)	Exports of Goods(f.o.b.)	96.7	105.0	120.0	138.3	153.8@
货物进口(离岸价)	Imports of Goods(f.o.b.)	98.1	105.9	119.7	136.7	148.5@
服务出口①	Exports of Services①	106.4	118.0	127.3	150.1	163.2@
服务进口	Imports of Services	102.0	106.0	103.8	118.9	122.3@
本地生产总值	**GDP**	**100.6**	**102.5**	**105.8**	**114.9**	**123.2@**
人均本地生产总值	**Per Capita GDP**	**99.7**	**100.6**	**103.6**	**111.2**	**118.4@**

注：政府统计处在2005年8月中完成一项工作，就是在估计香港国民经济核算统计数字时，采用最新国际指引处理由银行所提供的金融中介服务。由于这项统计发展，载于本表内的数字已作出修订。
"@" 数字将于日后修订。

Note : The Census and Statistics Department completed an exercise to implement the latest international guidelines on dealing with financial intermediation services produced by banks in the estimation of national accounts statistics of Hong Kong in mid-August 2005. As a result of this statistical development, figures presented in this table were revised.
"@" Figures are subject to revision later on.

24-14　本地居民生产总值
Gross National Product

单位：亿港元，另有注明除外　　(HKD 100 million, unless otherwise specified)

项目	Item	2001	2002	2003	2004	2005
按2000年不变价格计算	**At Constant (2000) Market Prices**					
本地生产总值	GDP	13232	13475	13906	15102@	16200@
国外净要素收入	Net External Factor Income Flows	292	61	318	265	27@
本地居民生产总值	GNP	13524	13536	14224	15367@	16227@
人均本地生产总值（港元）	Per Capita GDP (HKD)	196756	198541	204408	219420@	233565@
人均本地居民生产总值(港元)	Per Capita GNP (HKD)	201100	199437	209087	223273@	233954@
按当年价格计算	**At Current Market Prices**					
本地生产总值	GDP	12988	12768	12340	12916@	13821@
国外净要素收入	Net External Factor Income Flows	285	57	285	234	25@
本地居民生产总值	GNP	13274	12824	12625	13150@	13845@
人均本地生产总值（港元）	Per Capita GDP (HKD)	193135	188118	181385	187657@	199261@
人均本地居民生产总值(港元)	Per Capita GNP (HKD)	197379	188951	185573	191058@	199616@

注：政府统计处在2005年8月中完成一项工作，就是在估计香港国民经济核算统计数字时，采用最新国际指引处理由银行所提供的金融中介服务。由于这项统计发展，载于本表内的数字已作出修订。
"@" 数字将于日后修订。

Note : The Census and Statistics Department completed an exercise to implement the latest international guidelines on dealing with financial intermediation services produced by banks in the estimation of national accounts statistics of Hong Kong in mid-August 2005. As a result of this statistical development, figures presented in this table were revised.
"@" Figures are subject to revision later on.

24-15 香港国际收支平衡表

Hong Kong's Balance of Payments Account

单位：亿港元 (HKD 100 million)

标准组成部分①	Standard Components①	2001	2002	2003	2004	2005
经常帐②	**Current Account②**	**763.15**	**968.00**	**1282.40**	**1224.91@**	**1576.92@**
货物	Goods	-649.70	-394.06	-449.70	-725.14@	-593.47@
服务③	Services③	1266.20	1453.41	1590.20	1870.56@	2316.23@
收益③	Income③	285.43	56.52	284.91	234.1@	24.63@
经常转移	Current Transfers	-138.78	-147.87	-143.01	-154.61@	-170.46@
资本及金融帐②	**Capital and Financial Account②**	**-973.59**	**-1511.79**	**-1790.86**	**-1846.40@**	**-1608.82@**
资本转移	Capital Transfers	-91.55	-156.86	-82.92	-25.61@	-52.37@
直接投资	Direct Investment	969.48	-606.85	633.72	-910.38@	258.45@
有价证券投资	Portfolio Investment	-3220.45	-3024.84	-2646.19	-3063.68@	-1681.00@
金融衍生工具	Financial Derivatives	396.40	515.63	782.88	443.19@	137.54@
其他投资	Other Investment	1337.83	1575.73	-402.47	1964.92@	-164.64@
储备资产(变动净值)④	Reserve Assets (Net Change)④	-365.3	185.41	-75.89	-254.86@	-106.79@
净误差及遗漏⑤	**Net Errors and Omissions⑤**	**210.44**	**543.79**	**508.46**	**621.49@**	**31.9@**
整体的国际收支	**Overall Balance of Payments**	**365.30**	**-185.41**	**75.89**	**254.86@**	**106.79@**
		(盈余)	**(赤字)**	**(盈余)**	**(盈余)**	**(盈余)**
		(in surplus)	**(in deficit)**	**(in surplus)**	**(in surplus)**	**(in surplus)**

注：①根据国际收支平衡表的核算常规，某标准组成部分的净贷方数字以正数显示，而净借方则以负数显示。

②经常帐差额的正数显示盈余而负数则显示赤字。在资本及金融帐方面，正数显示净资金流入而负数则显示净资金流出。由于对外资产的增加是属于借方帐目而减少则属贷方帐目，因此负数的储备资产变动净值显示储备资产的增加，而正数则显示减少。

③政府统计处在2005年8月中完成一项工作，就是在估计香港国民经济核算统计数字时，采用最新国际指引处理由银行所提供的金融中介服务。由于这项统计发展，载于本表内的数字已作出修订。

④在国际收支平衡架构下储备资产变动净值的估计是指交易数字。因计价方式改变(包括价格变动及汇率变动)及分类重组所导致的影响并不包括在内。

⑤原则上，贷方和借方各项账目的净总和应相等于零。但实际上，贷方和借方账目的资料是通过不同的来源搜集，基于各种原因会有差异。为了令贷方和借方账目的总和相等，便须加进一个余额项目，以反映平衡表的「净误差及遗漏」。

"@" 数字将于日后修订

Notes: ①In accordance with the Balance of Payments accounting rules, a net credit for a standard component is represented by a positive value, and a net debit a negative value.

②A positive value for the balance figure in the current account represents a surplus whereas a negative value represents a deficit. For the capital and financial account, a positive value indicates a net capital and financial inflow and a negative value indicates a net outflow.As increases in external assets are debit entries and decreases are credit entries, a negative value for net change in reserve assets represents a net increase and a positive value represents a net decrease.

③The Census and Statistics Department completed an exercise to implement the latest international guidelines on dealing with financial intermediation services produced by banks in the estimation of national accounts statistics of Hong Kong in mid-August 2005. As a result of this statistical development, figures presented in this table were revised.

④The estimates on net change in reserve assets under the Balance of Payments framework are transaction figures. Effects from valuation changes (including price changes and exchange rate changes) and reclassifications are excluded.

⑤In principle, the net sum of credit entries and debit entries is zero. In practice, discrepancies between the credit and debit entries may however occur for various reasons as the data are collected from many sources. Equality between the sum of credit entries and debit entries is brought about by the inclusion of a balancing item which reflects net errors and omissions.

"@" Figures are subject to revision later on

24-16 香港国际投资头寸(期末头寸)

Hong Kong's International Investment Position (Position as at end of period)

单位：亿港元 (HKD 100 million)

概括组成部分	Broad Components	2001	2002	2003	2004	2005
香港资产	**Hong Kong Assets**	**83506.23**	**80327.44**	**92023.13**	**106987.13**	**116565.31@**
在外地的直接投资	Direct Investment Abroad	27492.37	24129.32	26366.97	31336.49	36474.58@
有价证券投资	Portfolio Investment	16030.59	19032.41	25999.22	31163.12	34373.53@
金融衍生工具	Financial Derivatives	1366.72	1756.16	1540.65	1744.50	1335.82@
其它投资	Other Investment	29947.34	26681.50	28925.22	33138.41	34745.31@
储备资产	Reserve Assets	8669.22	8728.05	9191.07	9604.61	9636.08@
香港负债	**Hong Kong Liabilities**	**62826.62**	**53553.76**	**61424.8**	**73969.40**	**81746.80@**
在香港的直接投资	Direct Investment in Hong Kong	32696.53	26222.98	29603.58	35218.62	41320.04@
有价证券投资	Portfolio Investment	9124.93	7294.56	9727.7	12069.35	13756.97@
金融衍生工具	Financial Derivatives	940.22	1653.05	1521.41	1643.02	1323.14@
其它投资	Other Investment	20064.94	18383.16	20572.12	25038.41	25346.66@
国际投资头寸净值①	**Net International Investment Position①**	**20679.61**	**26773.68**	**30598.33**	**33017.73**	**34818.51@**

注：①国际投资头寸净值是对外金融资产总值与对外金融负债总值之差。

"@" 数字将于日后修订。

Notes : ①Net International Investment Position is the difference between total external financial assets and total external financial liabilities.

"@" Figures are subject to revision later on.

24-17 电力、煤气、水消费量

Electricity, Gas and Water Consumption

用　途	Use	2001	2002	2003	2004	2005
电力　(万亿焦耳)	**Electricity　(Terajoules)**					
住宅	Domestic	32799	33394	34365	34134	35811
商业	Commercial	84214	87241	88834	91255	93341
工业	Industrial	16759	16112	14851	15430	14636
街灯	Street Lighting	367	365	384	383	383
出口往中国内地	Export to the Mainland of China	5692	7830	10827	11112	16192
总计	Total	139830	144942	149262	152313	160363
煤气　(万亿焦耳)	**Gas　(Terajoules)**					
住宅	Domestic	14493	14794	15446	15237	15444
商业	Commercial	11060	10860	10542	10945	10919
工业	Industrial	1011	987	1015	955	898
总计	Total	26564	26641	27002	27137	27261
水　(万立方米)	**Water　(10 000 Cubic Meters)**	**94000**	**94900**	**97400**	**95500**	**96800**

24-18 工业生产指数

Index of Industrial Production

(2000年=100) (2000=100)

工业组别/组别内选定工业	Industry Group/Selected Component Industry	2001	2002	2003	2004	2005
所有制造行业	**All Manufacturing Industries**	**95.6**	**86.2**	**78.3**	**80.6**	**82.6**
食品、饮品及烟草制品业	Food, Beverages and Tobacco	98.4	106.4	94.1	99.4	100.5
服装制品业(鞋类除外)	Wearing Apparel, Except Footwear	99.9	93.3	95.1	94.7	84.2
纺织制品业(包括针织)	Textiles(Including Knitting)	99.7	92.5	82.6	79.1	82.5
纸品及印刷业	Paper Products and Printing	98.8	98.6	98.2	95.9	95.9
化学产品、橡胶制品、塑胶制品及非金属矿产制品业	Chemical, Rubber, Plastic and Non-metallic Mineral Products	92.2	76.3	77.3	76.0	77.3
塑胶制品业	Plastic Products	84.8	75.7	69.6	68.1	69.3
基本金属及金属制品业	Basic Metals and Fabricated Metal Products	84.6	64.5	60.3	65.4	71.1
金属制品业(机械及设备除外)	Fabricated Metal Products, Except Machinery and Equipment	89.8	63.4	48.3	49.9	53.2
电器及电子制品、机械、专业设备及光学用品制造业	Electrical and Electronic Products, Machinery, Professional Equipment and Optical Goods	92.1	71.7	56.4	63.0	69.7
电器及电子制品制造业	Consumer Electrical and Electronic Products	100.0	76.4	65.9	61.1	64.4
机械、设备、仪器及零件制造业	Machinery, Equipment, Apparatus, Parts and Components	91.5	76.1	58.9	68.4	77.3
其他产品制造行业	Miscellaneous Manufacturing Industries	94.9	98.5	91.8	95.9	102.6

24-19 按楼宇种类划分的新落成私人楼宇

Private Buildings Newly Completed by Type of Building

楼宇类别	Building Type	2001	2002	2003	2004	2005
住宅楼宇	**Residential**					
楼宇数目 (栋)	Number of blocks	189	870	543	364	402
实用楼面面积 (万平方米)	Usable Floor Area(10 000 sq.m.)	56.3	94.7	39.6	60.1	39.4
商住两用楼宇①	**Residential/Commercial①**					
楼宇数目 (栋)	Number of blocks	56	71	79	51	35
实用楼面面积(万平方米)	Usable Floor Area(10 000 sq.m.)					
住宅	Residential	37.9	36.3	58.6	41.2	29.5
非住宅	Non-residential	8.8	7.8	12.1	3.9	2.6
商业楼宇	**Commercial**					
楼宇数目 (栋)	Number of blocks	14	26	18	19	7
实用楼面面积 (万平方米)	Usable Floor Area(10 000 sq.m.)	8.3	21.0	32.9	43.3	3.9
工业楼宇	**Industrial**					
楼宇数目 (栋)	Number of blocks	27	18	6	3	1
实用楼面面积 (万平方米)	Usable Floor Area(10 000 sq.m.)	7.1	2.0	4.4	3.6	0.9
其他用途楼宇	**Others**					
楼宇数目 (栋)	Number of blocks	153	119	131	203	333
实用楼面面积 (万平方米)	Usable Floor Area(10 000 sq.m.)					
住宅	Residential	2.3	5.0	1.7	1.8	2.0
非住宅	Non-residential	14.8	24.0	9.5	18.1	44.3
总计①	**Total①**					
楼宇数目 (栋)	Number of blocks	439	1104	777	640	778
实用楼面面积 (万平方米)	Usable Floor Area(10 000 sq.m.)					
住宅	Residential	96.5	136.0	99.9	103.2	70.9
非住宅	Non-residential	39.1	54.8	58.8	68.8	51.7

注：①在2004年,数字包括由私人机构参建居屋计划转为私人楼宇的红湾半岛单位。

Note: ①Figures for 2004 include units of the Hunghom Peninsula, which were converted from Private Sector Participation Scheme units to private buildings.

24-20 按楼宇种类划分的获批准可动工兴建私人楼宇

Private Buildings with Consent to Commence Work by Type of Building

年份 Year	住宅楼宇 Residential		商住两用楼宇 Residential/Commercial			商业楼宇 Commercial	
	楼宇数目(栋) Number of Blocks	实用楼面面积(万平方米)① Usable Floor Area (10 000 sq.m.)①	楼宇数目(栋) Number of Blocks	实用楼面面积(万平方米) Usable Floor Area (10 000 sq.m.) 住宅 Residential	非住宅 Non-residential	楼宇数目(栋) Number of Blocks	实用楼面面积(万平方米) Usable Floor Area (10 000 sq.m.)
2000	468	69.9	57	40.2	9.9	32	23.9
2001	212	41.0	74	58.4	9.6	12	16.9
2002	604	58.7	36	17.0	5.8	22	30.7
2003							
初次呈交图则 First submission	268	33.3	40	28.2	4.6	13	14.6
重大修改 Major revision	130	25.6	14	6.7	0.8		
2004							
初次呈交图则 First submission	247	18.0	14	13.6	3.2	7	12.3
重大修改 Major revision	56	7.9	6	5.7	0.1	3	0.5
2005							
初次呈交图则 First submission	216	11.7	22	19.4	3.4	15	29.4
重大修改 Major revision	429	11.3	14	10.0	2.5	6	13.0

24-20 续表 continued

年份 Year	工业楼宇 Industrial		其他用途楼宇 Others			总计 Total		
	楼宇数目(栋) Number of Blocks	实用楼面面积(万平方米) Usable Floor Area (10 000 sq.m.)	楼宇数目(栋) Number of Blocks	实用楼面面积(万平方米) Usable Floor Area (10 000 sq.m.) 住宅 Residential	非住宅 Non-residential	楼宇数目(栋) Number of Blocks	实用楼面面积(万平方米) Usable Floor Area (10 000 sq.m.) 住宅① Residential①	非住宅 Non-residential
2000	20	12.9	131	4.3	24.0	708	114.3	70.7
2001	14	4.6	92	0.8	7.5	404	100.3	38.6
2002	17	10.7	125	3.3	10.9	804	79.0	58.2
2003								
初次呈交图则 First submission	1	0#	227	2.0	31.7	549	63.5	50.9
重大修改 Major revision	1	0.1	12	8.0	12.7	157	40.3	13.6
2004								
初次呈交图则 First submission	3	1.0	146	0.6	36.7	417	32.2	53.2
重大修改 Major revision	2	0.7	10	7.3	4.0	77	20.9	5.3
2005								
初次呈交图则 First submission	7	2.3	96	0.1	24.1	356	31.3	59.2
重大修改 Major revision	1	1.2	13	2.5	16.7	463	23.8	33.3

注：2002年及以前没有「初次呈交图则」和「重大修改」的分类数字。
①包括住宅楼宇内用作非住宅用途的实用楼面面积，例如：会所/康乐设施、管理员办事处/宿舍、电机房等。
"0#" 数字少于单位的一半。

Notes: Separate figures for "First submission" and "Major revision" were not available for 2002 and the years before.
①Including usable floor area in residential buildings for non-domestic use, such as club house/recreational facilities, caretakers' office/quarters, transformer room, etc.
"0#" Magnitude less than half of the unit employed.

24-21 按类型划分的永久性屋宇单位数量(3月底的数字)

Number of Permanent Quarters by Type (as at End March of the Year)

单位：万个 (10 000 units)

楼宇类别	Building Type	2001	2002	2003	2004	2005
公营租住房屋①	Public Rental Housing①	68.52	68.58	68.53	69.15	70.92
资助出售单位②	Subsidized Sale Flats②	38.09	37.17	39.66	39.32	38.88
私人房屋③	Private Housing③	117.06	123.75	127.86	130.78	133.31
总计	**Total**	**223.66**	**229.50**	**236.05**	**239.26**	**243.12**

注：永久性屋宇单位的涵盖范围不包括酒店及院舍内的屋宇单位。

①数字不包括在房屋委员会的租者置其屋计划中已出售的单位。

②数字包括在房屋委员会的租者置其屋计划中已出售的单位。由2002年起，数字不包括可在公开市场买卖的资助出售单位。

③由2002年起，数字包括可在公开市场买卖的资助出售单位。

Notes: The coverage of the permanent quarters excludes quarters in hotels and institutions.

① Figures exclude quarters sold under the Housing Authority Tenants Purchase Scheme.

② Figures also cover quarters sold under the Housing Authority Tenants Purchase Scheme. As from 2002, figures exclude subsidized sale flats that can be traded in open market.

③ As from 2002, figures include flats under subsidized sale flats that can be traded in open market.

24-22 按居所租住权划分的家庭住户数目

Domestic Households by Tenure of Accommodation

单位：万户 (10 000 households)

项　目	Item	2001	2002	2003	2004	2005
总计	**Total**	**207.84**	**213.37**	**217.02**	**223.15**	**228.33@**
自置居所住户	Owner-occupier	108.43	112.32	115.31	119.93	121.82@
全租户	Sole Tenant	83.44	84.72	86.26	89.17	92.43@
合租户	Co-tenant	5.45	5.06	4.77	4.18	4.03@
二房东	Main Tenant	0.36	0.23	0.23	0.17	0.13@
三房客	Sub-tenant	1.20	1.10	0.74	0.67	0.55@
免租	Rent Free	3.39	4.54	4.51	4.17	4.17@
居所由雇主提供	Provided by Employer	5.56	5.39	5.21	4.87	5.19@

注：数字是根据该年四季「综合住户统计调查」所得的数据编制。

"@" 数字将于日后修订。

Notes: Figures are compiled based on the data obtained from the General Household Survey for the four quarters of the year.

"@" Figures are subject to revision later on.

24-23 进出香港货物

Inward and Outward Movements of Cargo

单位：万吨 (10 000 tons)

项 目	Item	2001	2002	2003	2004	2005
卸下	**Discharged**					
空运	By Air	89.4	100.4	103.5	116.5	124.6
水运	By Water	11047.2	11972.9	12855.4	13485.4	14095.6
海运	By Ocean	8850.6	9344.4	9936.3	10461.2	10669.5
河运	By River	2196.6	2628.4	2919.1	3024.2	3426.1
道路运输	By Road	2040.9	2108.5	2075.1	2156.1	2096.4
铁路运输①	By Rail①	27.3	28.3	25.3	20.8	16.6
总计	Total	13204.8	14210.0	15059.4	15778.9	16333.2
装上	**Loaded**					
空运	By Air	118.0	147.5	160.7	192.5	215.6
水运	By Water	6773.8	7278.2	7905.8	8602.5	8918.3
海运	By Ocean	4217.0	4485.7	4925.5	5400.6	5477.2
河运	By River	2556.8	2792.5	2980.3	3201.9	3441.1
道路运输	By Road	1650.9	1828.8	1919.2	1891.3	1775.5
铁路运输①	By Rail①	9.7	10.2	7.6	6.4	4.9
总计	Total	8552.4	9264.7	9993.3	10692.6	10914.3

注：①数字不包括家畜。
Note: ①Figures exclude livestock.

24-24 按主要货物装卸地点划分的集装箱吞吐量

Container Throughput by Main Cargo Handling Location

单位：万标准集装箱单位 (10 000 TEUs)

项 目	Item	2001	2002	2003	2004	2005
集装箱吞吐量	Container Throughput	1782.6	1914.4	2044.9	2198.4	2260.2
集装箱码头	Container Terminals					
抵港	Inward					
载货集装箱	Laden Container	380.2	409.6	433.5	493.9	535.1
空集装箱	Empty Container	157.5	161	157.5	161.5	163.4
离港	Outward					
载货集装箱	Laden Container	559.1	583.3	579.9	648.9	689.2
空集装箱	Empty Container	31.7	35.3	36.1	38.3	40.6
集装箱码头以外	Other than Container Terminals					
海运	Ocean					
抵港	Inward					
载货集装箱	Laden Container	153.7	167.2	184.6	217.3	191.4
空集装箱	Empty Container	13.2	10.3	14.2	9.5	5.4
离港	Outward					
载货集装箱	Laden Container	118.5	143.1	180.8	180.1	118.3
空集装箱	Empty Container	15.6	12	10.9	13.5	10.5
河运	River					
抵港	Inward					
载货集装箱	Laden Container	98.6	115.3	142.9	137.1	173.0
空集装箱	Empty Container	80.2	85.8	85.9	89.7	91.5
离港	Outward					
载货集装箱	Laden Container	108.8	113.7	131.4	111.0	138.2
空集装箱	Empty Container	65.5	77.9	87.2	97.7	103.4

注：标准集装箱单位是以20英尺×8英尺×8英尺的标准集装箱为根据。
Note: TEU refers to Twenty-foot Equivalent Unit (based on a standardized container size of 20 ft. × 8 ft. × 8 ft.).

24-25 通讯及互联网服务
Communications and Internet Services

项目	Item	2001	2002	2003	2004	2005
邮递服务	**Postal Services**					
信件邮件 (亿件物品)	Letter Mail (100 million articles)	13.6	12.7	12.6	12.7	12.7
包裹 (万件)	Parcels (10 000 pcs)	92.3	92.8	94.6	93.8	92.7
电话服务①②(万条操作线路)	**Telephone Services①② (10 000 working lines)**					
住宅	Residential	216.1	213.4	211.9	211.8	211.6
商用	Business	176.5	170.8	170.1	166.2	167.7
总计	Total	392.6	384.2	382.0	378.0	379.3
图文传真②(万条操作线路)	**Fax② (10 000 working lines)**	**41.1**	**54.6**	**49.1**	**45.6**	**41.0**
对外电话通讯量 (万分钟)	**External Telephone Traffic Volume (10 000 minutes)**					
拨出③	Outgoing③	348729	395090	423260	493653	563840
拨入④	Incoming④	194235	175599	167620	203725	216752
对外专用电报通讯量(万分钟)	**External Telex Traffic Volume (10 000 minutes)**					
发出	Outward	195.4	150.1	92.9	62.8	30.0
收到	Inward	247.1	229.1	162.9	102.4	84.3
转接	Transit	303.6	212.2	142.4	87.1	56.5
本地电报机电讯 (万分钟)	**Internal Telex Traffic (10 000 minutes)**	**530.7**	**294.9**	**206.9**	**178.8**	**120.9**
电报⑤ (万件)	**Public Telegram Traffic⑤(10 000 messages)**					
发出	Outward	1.2	0.7	0.5	-	-
收到	Inward	0.5	0.4	0.2	-	-
本地电报⑤ (万件)	**Inland Telegram⑤ (10 000 messages)**	**0.3**	**0#**	**0#**	**-**	**-**
公共无线电传呼接收器②(户)	**Public Radio Paging Receivers② (numbers)**	**253215**	**197405**	**177926**	**157695**	**131740**
公共流动无线电话用户系统②⑥⑦ (户)	**Public Mobile Radiotelephone Subscriber Units②⑥⑦ (numbers)**	**4256422 (5701686)**	**4207465 (6218984)**	**4407569 (7194335)**	**4575069 (8157960)**	**4753916 (8544255)**
互联网服务	**Internet Services**					
持牌互联网服务供应商数目②	**No. of Licensed Internet Service Providers (ISPs)②**	**258**	**235**	**201**	**188**	**186**
持牌互联网服务供应商客户数目②⑧	**No. of Customers of Licensed (ISPs)②⑧**					
以拨号接驳的已登记客户户口(不包括互联网储值卡)⑨	Registered Customer Accounts with Dial-up Access (Excluding Internet Pre-paid Calling Cards)⑨	2018238	1371705	1084368	1003604	974873
作拨号接驳用途的互联网储值卡	Internet Pre-paid Calling Cards for Dial-up Access	18569	14978	20411	9800	4800
以私人租用线路接驳的已登记客户户口⑨	Registered Customer Accounts with Leased Line Access⑨	7066	3439	2739	2259	1925
宽带互联网接驳客户户口⑨⑩	Registered Broadband Internet Access Customer Accounts⑨⑩	623302	989115	1230607	1484486	1648409
互联网使用量⑧	**Internet Traffic Volume⑧**					
客户通过公共电话网络接驳⑪ (万分钟)	Customer Access via Public Switched Telephone Networks⑪ (10 000 minutes)	1105581	555023	356394	189698	105954
客户通过宽带网络接驳⑪ (万亿比特)	Customer Access via Broadband Networks⑪ (terabits)	73607	215296	933728	2949652	5392294

注：①数字包括直通内线式电话线、图文传真线及电文线路的直拨服务。 ②数字为该年年底数字。 ③数字也包括图文传真及数据。
④估计数字。 ⑤由2004年1月1日起，有关的服务已经终止。
⑥数字不包括储值智能卡。包括储值智能卡的数字于括号内展示。 ⑦自2004年开始数字包括第3代流动服务。
⑧数字为根据互联网服务供应商申报的估计数字，并不包括不属于持牌互联网服务供应商客户的使用者。
⑨已登记客户户口指互联网服务供应商的客户户口(包括免费的客户户口)。拥有超过一个客户登入识别码的登记客户户口只算作一个已登记的客户户口。数字不包括只获提供电邮地址的客户户口。
⑩宽带是指采用各类数字式用户线路 (xDSL)、本地多点配送系统(LMDS)、光纤到楼 (FTTB)、电缆调制解调器 (cable modem) 等技术以每秒 1.5 百万比特或以上的速度传送数据的容量。
⑪不包括通过私人租用线路接驳及使用宽带服务的客户。
"-" 不适用。 "0#" 数字少于单位的一半。

Notes : ①Figures inlcude direct dialing in lines, facsimile lines and Datel lines. ②Figures are as at end of the year.
③Figures also include facsimile and data. ④Estimated figures. ⑤Related service has been terminated since 1 January 2004.
⑥Excluding pre-paid SIM cards. Figures including prepaid SIM cards are presented in brackets.
⑦Figures include 3G mobile services starting from 2004.
⑧Estimated figures are based on the returns from the ISPs and do not include users who are not customers of the licensed ISPs.
⑨Registered customer accounts refer to the customer accounts of ISPs (including those free-of-charge customer accounts). For a registered customer account which has more than one user login ID, it is counted as one registered customer account only. Figures do not include customer accounts which are provided with e-mail addresses only.
⑩Broadband means the capacity to transmit data at the rate of 1.5Mbps or above using family of Digital Subscriber Line (xDSL), Local Multipoint Distribution Services (LMDS), Fibre-to-the-Building (FTTB), cable modem or other technologies.
⑪Not including customer access via leased circuits and broadband services.
"-" Not applicable. "0#" Magnitude less than half of the unit employed.

24-26 商品进出口贸易总额
Total Imports and Exports of Goods

单位：亿港元 (HKD 100 million)

贸易种类	Type of Trade	2001	2002	2003	2004	2005
进口	Imports	15681.94	16194.19	18057.70	21111.23	23294.69
港产品出口	Domestic Exports	1535.20	1309.26	1216.87	1259.82	1360.30
转口	Re-exports	13274.67	14295.90	16207.49	18931.32	21141.43
整体出口	Total Exports	14809.87	15605.17	17424.36	20191.14	22501.74
贸易总额	Total Trade	30491.81	31799.36	35482.06	41302.37	45796.43
商品贸易差额	Merchandise Trade Balance	-872.08	-589.03	-633.34	-920.09	-792.95

24-27 商品进口及出口的主要供应地和去向
Imports and Exports of Goods by Major Supplier and Destination

单位：亿港元 (HKD 100 million)

贸易种类/主要国家/地区	Type of Trade/Main Country/Territory	2001	2002	2003	2004	2005
进口(供应地)	**Imports (Supplier)**	**15681.94**	**16194.19**	**18057.7**	**21111.23**	**23294.69**
中国内地	The mainland of China	6819.80	7170.74	7856.25	9182.75	10493.35
日本	Japan	1765.99	1825.69	2139.95	2561.41	2565.01
中国台湾	Taiwan, China	1079.29	1159.06	1252.03	1538.12	1682.27
美国	United States of America	1049.41	914.78	987.3	1119.94	1351.9
新加坡	Singapore	728.98	757.4	905.7	1109.86	1192.52
港产品出口(目的地)	**Domestic Exports (Destination)**	**1535.20**	**1309.26**	**1216.87**	**1259.82**	**1360.3**
美国	United States of America	475.89	419.08	391.3	386.36	446.43
中国内地	The mainland of China	495.47	413.74	367.57	378.98	377.67
英国	United Kingdom	85.78	75.88	77.62	81.9	73.04
荷兰	Netherlands	46.19	34.7	24.73	26.16	53.86
中国台湾	Taiwan, China	53.46	43.88	36.53	46.64	51.42

24-28 商品转口的主要来源和去向
Re-exports of Goods by Major Origin and Destination

单位：亿港元 (HKD 100 million)

贸易种类/主要国家/地区	Type of Trade/Main Country/Territory	2001	2002	2003	2004	2005
转口(目的地)	**Re-exports (Destination)**	**13274.67**	**14295.90**	**16207.49**	**18931.32**	**21141.43**
中国内地	The mainland of China	4965.74	5718.70	7057.87	8506.45	9679.23
美国	United States of America	2821.89	2910.43	2850.84	3029.64	3228.72
日本	Japan	835.51	807.43	911.54	1047.33	1142.58
德国	Germany	457.74	445.67	513.69	579.15	683.67
英国	United Kingdom	467.64	466.44	496.25	576.63	619.44
转口(来源地)	**Re-exports (Origin)**	**13274.67**	**14295.90**	**16207.49**	**18931.32**	**21141.43**
中国内地	The mainland of China	8083.70	8639.67	9671.04	11354.69	13132.11
日本	Japan	1256.49	1357.93	1612.31	1942.47	1860.65
中国台湾	Taiwan, China	803.21	942.75	1071.44	1338.74	1524.96
韩国	Republic of Korea	397.75	472.18	570.00	643.58	740.30
美国	United States of America	651.93	629.00	631.58	617.71	643.04

24-29 涉及外发中国内地加工的贸易

Trade Involving Outward Processing in the Mainland of China

项　目	Item	2001	2002	2003	2004	2005
涉及外发加工贸易的估计货值　（亿港元）	**Estimated Value of Outward Processing Trade　(HKD 100 million)**					
输往中国内地的港产出口货物	Domestic Exports to the Mainland of China	351.72	288.48	249.24	248.25	250.80
输往中国内地的转口货物	Re-exports to the Mainland of China	2243.81	2488.01	3012.23	3616.10	3634.02
输往中国内地的整体出口货物	Total Exports to the Mainland of China	2595.53	2776.50	3261.47	3864.35	3884.82
从中国内地进口的货物	Imports from the Mainland of China	5319.60	5310.34	5649.33	6615.43	6919.79
原产地为中国内地经香港输往其他地方的转口货物	Re-exports of the Mainland of China Origin to Other Places	5783.29	5947.08	6035.92	6851.47	7565.79
涉及外发加工贸易的估计比率　(%)	**Estimated Proportion of Outward Processing Trade　(%)**					
输往中国内地的港产出口货物	Domestic Exports to the Mainland of China	71.0	69.8	68.0	65.7	56.3
输往中国内地的转口货物	Re-exports to the Mainland of China	45.2	43.5	42.7	42.5	37.6
输往中国内地的整体出口货物	Total Exports to the Mainland of China	47.5	45.3	43.9	43.5	38.4
从中国内地进口的货物	Imports from the Mainland of China	78.0	74.0	71.7	72.0	65.9
原产地为中国内地经香港输往其他地方的转口货物	Re-exports of the Mainland of China Origin to Other Places	82.2	82.5	79.5	79.3	79.3

24-30 按主要服务组别划分的服务出口及进口

Exports and Imports of Services by Major Service Group

单位：亿港元　　　　(HKD 100 million)

主要服务组别	Major Service Group	2001	2002	2003	2004	2005
服务出口	**Exports of Services**					
运输	Transportation	936.75	1037.51	1076.88	1351.88	1521.47@
旅游	Travel	463.62	581.34	555.75	700.84	799.94@
保险服务	Insurance Services	35.56	34.21	30.65	31.97	35.06@
金融服务①	Financial Services①	349.66	327.08	293.01	354.60	439.46@
商贸服务及其他与贸易相关的服务	Merchanting and Other Trade-related Services	1064.47	1159.96	1301.83	1465.27	1634.98@
其他服务	Other Services	357.94	338.26	366.09	391.07	403.64@
总计①	Total①	3207.99	3478.36	3624.20	4295.63	4834.55@
服务进口	**Imports of Services**					
运输	Transportation	509.16	485.18	523.05	676.57	730.67@
旅游	Travel	960.57	968.46	891.33	1033.47	1034.92@
保险服务	Insurance Services	40.28	46.18	48.40	47.61	52.62@
金融服务①	Financial Services①	69.69	76.94	68.35	90.70	84.50@
商贸服务及其他与贸易相关的服务	Merchanting and Other Trade-related Services	118.02	146.60	160.08	165.17	182.11@
其他服务	Other Services	244.08	301.58	342.79	411.55	433.50@
总计①	Total①	1941.80	2024.94	2034.00	2425.07	2518.32@
服务出口净额①	**Net Exports of Services①**	**1266.19**	**1453.42**	**1590.20**	**1870.56**	**2316.23@**

注：政府统计处在2005年8月中完成一项工作，就是在估计香港国民经济核算统计数字时，采用最新国际指引处理由银行所提供的金融中介服务。由于这项统计发展，载于本表内的数字已作出修订。

"@" 数字将于日后修订。

Note : The Census and Statistics Department completed an exercise to implement the latest international guidelines on dealing with financial intermediation services produced by banks in the estimation of national accounts statistics of Hong Kong in mid-August 2005. As a result of this statistical development, figures presented in this table were revised.

"@" Figures are subject to revision later on.

24-31 按主要目的地和来源地划分的服务出口及进口

Exports and Imports of Services by Major Destination and Source

单位：亿港元 (HKD 100 million)

目的地/来源地	Destination/Source	2001	2002	2003	2004@	2005
服务出口①	**Exports of Services①**					
中国内地	The mainland of China	764.79	945.47	1022.81	1167.87	
美国	United States of America	702.05	706.06	743.51	875.31	
中国台湾	Taiwan, China	209.38	220.36	253.53	312.30	
日本	Japan	269.45	298.08	254.81	306.97	
英国	United Kingdom	179.66	198.37	190.80	262.55	
其他	Others	951.25	985.30	1086.29	1331.19	
所有目的地	All Destinations	3076.57	3353.63	3551.75	4256.19	4727.11@
服务进口①	**Imports of Services①**					
中国内地	The mainland of China	596.37	608.76	580.80	659.60	
美国	United States of America	302.41	317.04	328.18	354.69	
日本	Japan	129.63	147.74	155.32	209.59	
英国	United Kingdom	118.00	129.03	136.13	175.80	
澳大利亚	Australia	112.72	116.39	125.64	149.47	
其他	Others	665.41	677.79	691.98	858.64	
所有来源地	All Sources	1924.53	1996.76	2018.06	2407.79	2512.67@

注：①由于金融中介服务出口/进口没有按区域细分数字，本统计表内的数字并不包括金融中介服务出口/进口数字，因此载于本统计表内所有目的地/来源地的服务出口/进口数字并不等同于表24-30内香港所有服务出口/进口的相关数字。

"空格" 没有数字 。

"@" 数字将于日后修订。

Notes : ①Since data on geographical breakdowns of exports/imports of financial intermediation services are not available, the figures in respect of exports/imports of financial intermediation services are not included in this table. Hence, the figures for exports/imports of services to/from all destinations/sources in this table are not equal to the corresponding figures for exports/imports of all services of Hong Kong in Table 24-30.

"(blank)" Not available.

"@" Figures are subject to revision later on.

24-32 按主要投资者国家/地区划分的外来直接投资头寸及流动

Position and Flow of Inward Direct Investment by Major Investor Country/Territory

单位：亿港元 (HKD 100 million)

主要投资者国家/地区	Major Investor Country/Territory	以市值计算的外来直接投资 Inward Direct Investment at Market Value					
		年底头寸 Position at End of Year			年间流入 Inflow in Year		
		2002	2003	2004	2002	2003	2004
英属维尔京群岛	British Virgin Islands	7794	9352	10293	594	198	627
中国内地	The Mainland of China	5946	7701	10201	317	380	620
荷兰	Netherlands	2049	2561	3072	103	247	88
百慕大	Bermuda	2732	2548	2722	21	-136	89
美国	United States of America	1866	1876	2435	-110	220	484
日本	Japan	1414	1422	1482	153	142	109
新加坡	Singapore	735	580	871	64	-99	32
英国	United Kingdom	558	481	700	86	45	182
开曼群岛	Cayman Islands	449	531	618	-687	29	65
加拿大	Canada	192	199	291	99	2	51
其他	Others	2489	2351	2533	115	36	303
总计	**Total**	**26223**	**29604**	**35219**	**755**	**1063**	**2651**

注：国家/地区是指直接来源经济体系。这分类未必反映最初资金流出的国家/地区。

Note : Country/territory here refers to the immediate source economy. It does not necessarily reflect the country/territory in which the funds are initially mobilised.

24-33 按主要接受投资国家/地区划分的对外直接投资头寸及流动

Position and Flow of Outward Direct Investment by Major Recipient Country/Territory

单位：亿港元 (HKD 100 million)

主要接受投资国家/地区	Major Recipient Country/Territory	以市值计算的对外直接投资 Outward Direct Investment at Market Value					
		年底头寸 Position at End of Year			年间流出 Outflow in Year		
		2002	2003	2004	2002	2003	2004
英属维尔京群岛	British Virgin Islands	11483	12703	14021	101	248	1368
中国内地	The mainland of China	8430	9312	12116	1243	599	1448
百慕大	Bermuda	768	884	1297	-49	-28	267
英国	United Kingdom	205	473	553	36	46	49
日本	Japan	119	152	421	-171	10	284
新加坡	Singapore	260	300	342	43	21	45
巴拿马	Panama	390	242	286	22	-91	-27
泰国	Thailand	208	216	248	26	-7	32
美国	United States of America	322	204	226	72	-94	31
马来西亚	Malaysia	279	242	222	50	-28	15
其他	Others	1666	1638	1604	-11	-247	50
总计	**Total**	**24129**	**26367**	**31336**	**1362**	**429**	**3561**

注：国家/地区是指首个目的地经济体系。这分类未必反映资金最终被使用的所在国家/地区。

Note: Country/territory here refers to the immediate destination economy. It does not necessarily reflect the country/territory in which the funds are ultimately used.

24-34 按母公司的国家/地区划分的驻港地区总部公司数目

Number of Companies in Hong Kong that are Regional Headquarters by Country/Territory of the Parent Company

项目	Item	2001	2002	2003	2004	2005
驻港地区总部公司数目	**Number of companies in Hong Kong that are regional headquarters**	**944**	**948**	**966**	**1 098**	**1 167**
母公司的国家/地区①	Country/territory of the parent company①					
美国	United States of America	221	233	242	256	262
日本	Japan	160	159	168	198	204
英国	United Kingdom	90	80	86	105	115
中国内地	The mainland of China	70	96	84	106	107
德国	Germany	56	52	56	67	75
荷兰	Netherlands	48	39	38	46	54
法国	France	43	35	44	47	49
新加坡	Singapore	25	26	22	35	45
瑞士	Switzerland	34	36	40	39	38
中国台湾	Taiwan,China	22	21	18	29	33
意大利	Italy	7	10	7	15	20
澳大利亚	Australia	15	13	22	18	18
瑞典	Sweden	16	17	16	16	18
韩国	Korea	13	17	15	15	17
加拿大	Canada	16	23	19	15	16

注：指有关年度6月首个工作日的数字。

地区总部是指一个办事处有权控制/管理区内(即香港及另一个或多个地方)的办事处的运作/业务，而毋须经常请示其香港以外的母公司。就一家联营的驻港地区总部而言，其母公司注册/所在的国家/地区可能会多于一个。

① 2005年以前的数字指母公司注册国家/地区。由2005年开始，数字是指母公司所在的国家/地区。

Notes : Figures refer to the first working day of June of the year.

A regional headquarters is an office that has control over the operations of offices in the region (i.e. Hong Kong plus one or more other places), and manages the business without frequent referrals to its parent company outside Hong Kong.

In the case of a joint-ventured regional headquarters in Hong Kong, there may be more than one country/territory of its parent company/companies.

① Prior to 2005, figures refer to the country/territory where parent companies are incorporated. As from 2005, figures refer to the country/territory where parent companies are located.

24-35 按母公司的国家/地区划分的驻港地区办事处公司数目

Number of Companies in Hong Kong that are Regional Offices by Country/Territory of the Parent Company

项 目	Item	2001	2002	2003	2004	2005
驻港地区办事处公司数目	**Number of companies in Hong Kong that are regional offices**	**2293**	**2171**	**2241**	**2511**	**2631**
母公司的国家/地区①	Coutry/territory of the Parent Company①					
美国	United States of America	420	437	498	557	606
日本	Japan	533	471	442	515	537
英国	United Kingdom	163	163	196	211	215
中国内地	The mainland of China	172	170	148	156	160
德国	Germany	108	96	122	135	139
中国台湾	Taiwan,China	142	121	111	128	133
法国	France	88	91	101	106	110
新加坡	Singapore	77	79	81	97	103
瑞士	Switzerland	68	61	61	70	73
澳大利亚	Republic of Korea	43	52	45	57	69
韩国	Australia	76	49	60	67	68
意大利	Italy	52	38	41	54	53
荷兰	Netherlands	62	57	55	52	50
瑞典	Sweden	27	25	28	33	33
加拿大	Canada	34	28	27	29	25

注：指有关年度6月首个工作日的数字。

地区办事处是指一个办事处有权协调/管理区内(即香港及一个或多个地方)的办事处/运作/业务，但须经常请示其地区总部或香港以外的母公司。

就一家联营的驻港地区办事处而言，其母公司的国家/地区可能会多于一个。

①2005年以前的数字指母公司注册国家/地区。由2005年开始，数字是指母公司所在的国家/地区。

Note: Figures refer to the first working day of June of the year.

A regional office is an office that coordinates offices/operations in the region (i.e. Hong Kong plus one or more other places), and manages the business but with frequent referrals to its parent company outside Hong Kong or its regional headquarters .

In the case of a joint-ventured regional office in Hong Kong, there may be more than one country/territory of its parent company/companies.

①Prior to 2005, figures refer to the country/territory where parent companies are incorporated. As from 2005, figures refer to the country/territory where parent companies are located.

24-36 按居住国家/地区划分的访港旅客人数

Visitor Arrivals by Country/Territory of Residence

单位：万人 (10 000 persons)

居住国家/地区	Country/Territory of residence	2001	2002	2003	2004	2005
中国内地	The mainland of China	444.9	682.5	846.7	1224.6	1254.1
南亚及东南亚	South & Southeast Asia	174.7	190.5	136.0	207.8	241.3
中国台湾	Taiwan, China	241.9	242.9	185.2	207.5	213.1
北亚	North Asia	176.2	185.2	123.5	166.5	185.3
欧洲、非洲及中东	Europe, Africa & the Middle East	117.1	126.3	94.6	138.0	172.6
美洲	The Americas	125.9	134.7	92.6	140.0	156.5
澳大利亚、新西兰及南太平洋	Australia, New Zealand & South Pacific	38.7	41.0	30.6	48.3	62.0
中国澳门	Macao, China	53.2	53.5	44.4	48.4	51.0
总计	**Total**	**1372.5**	**1656.6**	**1533.7**	**2181.0**	**2335.9**
		(+5.1)	**(+20.7)**	**(-6.2)**	**(+40.4)**	**(+7.1)**

注：括号内数字表示与去年同期比较的变动百分比，并根据未进位的数字计算。

Note: Figures in brackets refer to percentage changes over the same period in preceding year and are calculated based on unrounded figures.

24-37 政府储备结余(一般收入帐目及各基金)

Government's Reserve Balances (General Revenue Account and Funds)

单位：亿港元 (HKD 100 million)

项　目	Item	2001/2002	2002/2003	2003/2004	2004/2005	2005/2006
期初储备结余①	Opening Reserve Balances①	4302.78	3725.03	3154.71	2753.43	2959.81
收入②	Revenue②	1755.59	1774.89	2073.38	2635.91	2470.35
开支②	Expenditure②	2388.90	2391.77	2474.66	2422.35	2330.71
盈余/(赤字)	Surplus/(Deficit)	-633.31	-616.88	-401.28	213.56	139.64
在外汇基金的投资亏损拨回/(拨备)	Write-back of Provision/(Provision) for Loss in Investments with the Exchange Fund	55.56	5.87		-7.18	7.18
期末储备结余	Closing Reserve Balances	3725.03	3114.02	2753.43	2959.81	3106.63

注：2005/2006年度的数字有待审计署署长核实。

①在2003/2004年度内，2003年4月1日的结余包括奖券基金的40.69亿元结余。奖券基金由2003年4月1日起纳入政府综合帐目内。这与立法会通过决议成立的其它基金的会计方法一致。

②数额不包括"政府一般收入帐目与各基金之间的转拨"。

Notes: Figures for 2005/2006 are subject to audit by the Director of Audit.

①In 2003/2004, the balance at 1 April 2003 includes the balance of $4,069 million in the Lotteries Fund. The Lotteries Fund has been included in the Consolidated Account of the Government with effect from 1 April 2003. This is consistent with the accounting treatment of other Funds established by resolution of the Legislative Council.

②Figures exclude "Transfers between the General Revenue Account and Funds".

24-38 政府收入(一般收入帐目及各基金)

Government Revenue (General Revenue Account and Funds)

单位：亿港元 (HKD 100 million)

项　目	Item	2001/2002	2002/2003	2003/2004	2004/2005	2005/2006
经营收入	**Operating Revenue**					
直接税	Direct Taxes					
入息税及利得税	Earnings and Profits Tax	777.49	730.28	804.74	967.09	1117.52
间接税	Indirect Taxes					
博彩及彩票税	Bets and Sweeps Tax	115.71	109.21	116.36	120.57	119.38
酒店房租税	Hotel Accommodation Tax	2.03	2.01	1.56	2.48	3.10
印花税	Stamp Duties	86.37	74.58	112.46	158.51	178.67
飞机乘客离境税	Air Passenger Departure Tax	6.66	8.84	7.53	13.50	14.40
应课税品税项	Duties	69.81	66.20	64.22	66.03	64.24
一般差饷	General Rates	127.27	89.23	111.67	126.40	141.46
车辆税	Motor Vehicle Taxes	26.76	25.10	27.24	34.17	38.95
专利税及特权税	Royalties and Concessions	18.81	17.26	16.76	7.75	6.16
其他收入	Other Revenue					
罚款、没收及罚金	Fines, Forfeitures and Penalties	9.26	8.43	8.46	9.49	9.88
物业及投资	Properties and Investments	86.21	80.15	78.70	87.10	98.15
贷款、偿款、供款及其他收入	Loans, Reimbursements, Contributions and Other Receipts	41.54	44.05	31.33	30.25	27.91
公用事业	Utilities	33.66	20.68	28.77	34.01	33.74
各项收费	Fees and Charges	109.16	96.87	105.49	107.93	111.09
投资收入	Investment Income					
政府一般收入帐目	General Revenue Account	2.25	27.66	59.23	49.16	38.57
土地基金	Land Fund	1.06	132.81	171.59	65.60	42.26
经营收入总额	Total Operating Revenue	1514.05	1533.36	1746.11	1880.04	2045.48
非经营收入	**Capital Revenue**					
间接税	Indirect Taxes					
遗产税	Estate Duty	19.28	14.03	14.55	14.69	16.76
其他收入	Other Revenue					
其他	Others	8.37	5.48	15.40	21.86	29.54
从房屋委员会收回的款项	Recovery from Housing Authority	24.75	22.12	3.27	0.38	0.29
基金	Funds					
基本工程储备基金(不包括债券收入)	Capital Works Reserve Fund (exclude proceeds of bond issue)	106.83	121.90	65.49	594.28	309.77
资本投资基金	Capital Investment Fund	28.16	24.32	24.27	84.06	29.43
赈灾基金	Disaster Relief Fund	0.01	0.02	0.04	0.02	0.02
贷款基金	Loan Fund	53.82	44.64	176.23	16.88	19.72
公务员退休金储备基金	Civil Service Pension Reserve Fund	0.05	6.31	11.46	7.71	5.20
创新及科技基金	Innovation and Technology Fund	0.27	2.71	4.25	3.17	1.82
奖券基金①	Lotteries Fund①	-	-	12.31	12.82	12.32
非经营收入总额	Total Capital Revenue	241.54	241.53	327.27	755.87	424.87
政府收入总额	**Total Government Revenue**	**1755.59**	**1774.89**	**2073.38**	**2635.91**	**2470.35**

注：2005/2006年度的数字有待审计署署长核实。

①奖券基金由2003年4月1日起纳入政府综合帐目内。这与立法会通过决议成立的其它基金的会计方法一致。

Notes: Figures for 2005/2006 are subject to audit by the Director of Audit.

①The Lotteries Fund was included in the Consolidated Account of the Government with effect from 1 April 2003. This is consistent with the accounting treatment of other Funds established by resolution of the Legislative Council.

24-39 政府支出(一般收入帐目及各基金)

Government Spending (General Revenue Account and Funds)

单位: 亿港元 (HKD 100 million)

项目	Item	2001/2002	2002/2003	2003/2004	2004/2005	2005/2006
经营开支	**Operating Expenditure**					
经常开支	Recurrent Expenditure					
个人薪酬	Personal Emoluments	519.09	509.66	492.63	465.31	446.65
与员工有关联的开支	Personnel Related Expenses	48.70	48.30	48.81	46.99	43.09
退休金	Pensions	128.99	121.07	134.82	149.00	128.34
部门开支	Departmental Expenses	143.66	155.63	150.73	148.03	152.94
其他费用	Other Charges	313.28	336.55	346.28	350.11	351.10
资助金	Subventions					
教育	Education	251.37	258.94	257.98	254.88	256.06
卫生	Health	295.46	295.53	291.12	278.44	270.75
社会福利	Social Welfare	69.60	68.18	69.22	65.32	63.40
大学及理工学院	Universities and Polytechnics	132.58	131.89	129.04	118.72	113.26
职业训练局	Vocational Training Council	20.67	20.05	19.26	17.66	16.89
杂项	Miscellaneous	32.52	34.24	33.02	28.49	29.14
非经常开支	Non-recurrent	31.51	23.06	59.43	46.11	53.00
经营开支总额	**Total Operating Expenditure**	**1987.43**	**2003.10**	**2032.34**	**1969.06**	**1924.62**
非经营支出	**Capital Spending**					
机器、设备及工程	Plant, Equipment and Works	9.84	9.52	7.64	8.23	6.76
资助金	Subventions					
教育	Education	3.98	4.13	3.55	3.52	3.44
卫生	Health	3.85	3.99	3.73	3.09	2.87
职业训练局	Vocational Training Council	1.07	0.71	0.37	0.27	0.29
杂项	Miscellaneous	0.70	0.70	2.57	0.34	0.20
基金	Funds					
基本工程储备基金	Capital Works Reserve Funds	303.30	309.19	344.86	337.25	289.54
资本投资基金 (证券投资)	Capital Investment Fund (Equity Investments)	3.05	29.40	42.53	60.57	65.50
贷款基金	Loan Fund	72.77	27.89	21.81	25.53	25.20
赈灾基金	Disaster Relief Fund	0.08	0.19	0.16	0.38	0.18
创新及科技基金	Innovation and Technology Fund	2.83	2.95	4.71	3.69	3.65
奖券基金①	Lotteries Fund①	-	-	10.39	10.42	8.46
非经营支出总额	**Total Capital Spending**	**401.47**	**388.67**	**442.32**	**453.29**	**406.09**
政府支出总额	**Total Government Spending**	**2388.90**	**2391.77**	**2474.66**	**2422.35**	**2330.71**

注: 2005/2006年度的数字有待审计署署长核实。
①奖券基金由2003年4月1日起纳入政府综合帐目内。这与立法会通过决议成立的其它基金的会计方法一致。
"-" 不适用。

Note :Figures for 2005/2006 are subject to audit by the Director of Audit.
①The Lotteries Fund was included in the Consolidated Account of the Government with effect from 1 April 2003. This is consistent with the accounting treatment of other Funds established by resolution of the Legislative Council.
"-" Not applicable.

24-40 按用途划分的公共开支

Public Expenditure by Function

单位：亿港元 (HKD 100 million)

项目	Item	2001/2002	2002/2003	2003/2004	2004/2005	2005/2006
公共及对外事务	Community and External Affairs	82.25	80.77	80.76	77.63	79.53
经济	Economic	128.04	127.39	137.48	129.84	137.34
教育	Education	526.76	552.47	547.85	541.23	555.76
环境及食物	Environment and Food	112.07	114.43	108.47	101.45	96.92
卫生	Health	342.13	331.99	342.31	322.28	316.39
房屋	Housing	315.71	235.97	248.55	179.69	158.74
基础建设	Infrastructure	262.72	260.34	271.33	287.74	258.87
保安	Security	275.54	270.68	266.16	255.41	251.11
社会福利	Social Welfare	300.59	322.82	337.86	332.85	338.26
辅助服务	Support	352.22	342.97	350.05	343.25	309.63
总计	**Total**	**2693.59**	**2635.20**	**2710.98**	**2571.37**	**2502.55**

注：2005/2006年度的数字为修订预算。

公共开支包括政府开支(即所有记入政府一般收入帐目的开支及由政府的法定基金(不包括资本投资基金)所支付的开支)，以及营运基金及房屋委员会的开支。但政府只享有权益股的机构(包括法定机构)，例如机场管理局、地铁有限公司和九广铁路公司，其开支则不包括在内。同样地，资本投资基金的垫款及股本投资亦不包括在内，因为这些款项并不代表政府所实际用资源。

Notes: Figures for 2005/2006 are revised estimate.

Public expenditure comprises government expenditure (i.e. all expenditure charged to the General Revenue Account and financed by the Government's statutory funds excluding Capital Investment Fund), and expenditure by the Trading Funds and the Housing Authority. Expenditures by those organisations (including statutory organisations) such as the Airport Authority, the MTR Corporation Ltd and the Kowloon-Canton Railway Corporation, in which the Government has only an equity position, are not included. Similarly, advances and equity investments from the Capital Investment Fund are excluded as they do not reflect the actual consumption of resources by the Government.

24-41 外币兑换率及港汇指数

Exchange Rates and the Effective Exchange Rate Indices

(每单位外币兑换港元， 另有注明除外) (HKD per unit of foreign currency, unless otherwise specified)

项目	Item	2001	2002	2003	2004	2005
年内平均数字①	**Average for the year①**					
澳元	Australian Dollar	4.04	4.25	5.08	5.73	5.93
比利时法郎②	Belgian Franc②	0.173	-	-	-	-
加拿大元	Canadian Dollar	5.04	4.97	5.58	6	6.42
人民币（每百港元）	Chinese Renminbi (per HKD100)	106.04	105.84	105.86	106.21	105.26
德国马克②	Deutsche Mark②	3.57	-	-	-	-
荷兰盾②	Dutch Guilder②	3.17	-	-	-	-
欧元②	Euro②	6.99	7.38	8.81	9.69	9.68
法国法郎②	French Franc②	1.07	-	-	-	-
意大利里拉②	Italian Lira②	0.0036	-	-	-	-
日元	Japanese Yen	0.0643	0.0625	0.0673	0.072	0.0707
马来西亚林吉特	Malaysian Ringgit	2.04	2.04	2.04	2.04	2.05
新台币	New Taiwan Dollar	0.232	0.229	0.227	0.233	0.242
菲律宾比索	Philippines Peso	0.157	0.156	0.146	0.14	0.144
英镑	Pound Sterling	11.24	11.73	12.73	14.27	14.15
韩圆	Korean Won	0.006	0.0063	0.0065	0.0068	0.0076
新加坡元	Singapore Dollar	4.36	4.36	4.47	4.61	4.67
瑞士法郎	Swiss Franc	4.63	5.03	5.79	6.28	6.25
泰铢	Thai Baht	0.175	0.182	0.188	0.193	0.193
美元	US Dollar	7.799	7.799	7.787	7.788	7.777
特别提款权	Special Drawing Right	9.92836	10.1047	10.90920	11.53777	11.48780
港汇指数③ (2000年1月=100)	Effective Exchange Rate Indices for the Hong Kong dollar③ (January 2000=100)					
贸易总值(进口及整体出口)加权	Trade (import and export)-weighted	104.7	104	100.7	98.3	97.4
进口货值加权	Import-weighted	105.1	104.7	101.6	99.2	98.1
整体出口货值加权④	Export-weighted④	104.3	103.3	99.8	97.3	96.7
年底数字⑤	**As at end of year⑤**					
澳元	Australian Dollar	3.99	4.41	5.83	6.06	5.68
比利时法郎②	Belgian Franc②	0.171				
加拿大元	Canadian Dollar	4.9	4.95	6	6.46	6.67
人民币（每百港元）	Chinese Renminbi (per HKD100)	106.04	105.82	106.67	106.38	104.16

24-41 续表 continued

(每单位外币兑换港元， 另有注明除外) (HKD per unit of foreign currency, unless otherwise specified)

项目	Item	2001	2002	2003	2004	2005
德国马克②	Deutsche Mark②	3.53	-	-	-	-
荷兰盾②	Dutch Guilder②	3.13	-	-	-	-
欧元②	Euro②	6.91	8.17	9.77	10.6	9.18
法国法郎②	French Franc②	1.05	-	-	-	-
意大利里拉②	Italian Lira②	0.0036	-	-	-	-
日元	Japanese Yen	0.0594	0.0657	0.0726	0.0758	0.0659
马来西亚林吉特	Malaysian Ringgit	2.04	2.04	2.04	2.05	2.05
新台币	New Taiwan Dollar	0.226	0.228	0.227	0.242	0.239
菲律宾比索	Philippines Peso	0.159	0.15	0.143	0.143	0.15
英镑	Pound Sterling	11.31	12.51	13.83	14.99	13.36
韩圆	Korean Won	0.006	0.0066	0.0065	0.0075	0.0077
新加坡元	Singapore Dollar	4.21	4.49	4.57	4.77	4.67
瑞士法郎	Swiss Franc	4.67	5.61	6.27	6.86	5.9
泰铢	Thai Baht	0.177	0.181	0.196	0.199	0.189
美元	US Dollar	7.797	7.798	7.763	7.774	7.753
特别提款权	Special Drawing Right	9.79010	10.60154	11.53559	12.07310	11.08113
港汇指数③	Effective Exchange Rate Indices					
(2000年1月=100)	for the Hong Kong dollar③					
	(January 2000=100)					
贸易总值(进口及整体出口)加权	Trade (import and export)-weighted	105.9	102.0	98.8	96.0	98.4
进口货值加权	Import-weighted	106.7	102.7	99.8	96.8	99.1
整体出口货值加权④	Export-weighted④	105.1	101.2	97.7	95.2	97.7

注：《中华人民共和国香港特别行政区基本法》说明,港元是香港特别行政区的法定货币。外币指港元以外的其他货币，因而人民币亦视作外币。

①数字是指年内每日电汇或现钞收市中间兑换价的平均值。

②欧元是12个欧洲联盟会员国的统一货币，于1999年1月1日推出。由2002年1月1日开始，欧元的纸币及硬币已取代各参与国家的货币成为法定货币。

③由2002年1月2日起公布的新系列。详情请参阅刊载于《香港统计月刊》2001年12月号题为「新系列港币汇率指数」的专题文章。

④包括转口和港产品出口。

⑤数字是该年最后一个交易日的电汇或现钞收市中间兑换价。

Notes: Hong Kong Dollar is the legal tender in the Hong Kong Special Administrative Region, as stated in "The Basic Law of the Hong Kong Special Administrative Region of the People's Republic of China". Foreign currency refers to any currency other than the Hong Kong currency. Accordingly Chinese Renminbi is also treated as foreign currency.

①Figures are the averages of the daily closing middle-market telegraphic transfer rates or notes rates for the year.

②Euro is a unified currencyf 12 European Union's member countries, which was launched on 1 January 1999. As from 1 January 2002, Euro notes and coins have replaced notes and coins in national currencies of participating countries of the Euro.

③New series released since 2 January 2002. For details, please see the feature article entitled "New Series of Effective Exchange Rate Index for the Hong Kong Dollar" in the December 2001 issue of the "Hong Kong Monthly Digest of Statistics".

④Including re-exports and domestic exports.

⑤Figures are the closing middle-market telegraphic transfer rates or notes rates as at the last trading day of the year.

24-42 货币供应量

Money Supply

单位：亿港元(年底数字) (HKD 100 million, as at end of year)

项　目	Item	2001	2002	2003	2004	2005
法定纸币及硬币的流通量	Legal Tender Notes and Coins in Circulation					
由商业银行发行	Commercial Bank Issues	1075.45	1184.75	1342.15	1467.75	1492.95
由政府发行	Government Issues	59.43	61.43	65.50	66.04	69.64
总计	Total	1134.88	1246.18	1407.65	1533.79	1562.59
由认可机构持有的法定纸币及硬币	Authorized Institutions' Holdings of Legal Tender Notes and Coins	118.61	113.84	128.98	125.76	139.52
由公众持有的法定纸币及硬币	Legal Tender Notes and Coins in Hands of Public	1016.27	1132.34	1278.67	1408.03	1423.07
货币供应量：就外币掉期存款作出调整	Money Supply: Adjusted for Foreign Currency Swap Deposits					
货币供应量 M_1	Money Supply M_1					
港元	Hong Kong Dollar	2298.41	2594.11	3547.52	4126.29	3482.48
外币	Foreign Currency	282.15	362.39	586.71	718.65	864.37
总计	Total	2580.56	2956.50	4134.23	4844.94	4346.84
货币供应量 M_2	Money Supply M_2					
港元①	Hong Kong Dollar①	19987.74	19840.49	21072.69	22085.91	23291.73
外币②	Foreign Currency②	15512.86	15342.77	17061.73	19581.16	20460.75
总计	Total	35500.60	35183.26	38134.42	41667.06	43752.47
货币供应量 M_3	Money Supply M_3					
港元①	Hong Kong Dollar①	20166.35	20042.25	21228.61	22195.57	23453.42
外币②	Foreign Currency②	15774.95	15576.27	17351.83	19699.87	20580.37
总计	Total	35941.30	35618.52	38580.44	41895.44	44033.78
货币供应量：未就外币掉期存款作出调整	Money Supply: Unadjusted for Foreign Currency Swap Deposits					
货币供应量 M_2	Money Supply M_2					
港元	Hong Kong Dollar	19961.38	19821.42	21058.60	22075.17	23283.38
外币	Foreign Currency	15539.23	15361.84	17075.82	19591.89	20469.10
总计	Total	35500.60	35183.26	38134.42	41667.06	43752.47
货币供应量 M_3	Money Supply M_3					
港元	Hong Kong Dollar	20139.98	20023.18	21214.52	22184.83	23445.06
外币	Foreign Currency	15801.32	15595.34	17365.92	19710.61	20588.72
总计	Total	35941.30	35618.52	38580.44	41895.44	44033.78

注：《中华人民共和国香港特别行政区基本法》说明，港元是香港特别行政区的法定货币。外币指港元以外的其他货币，因而人民币亦视作外币。

①所列数字已包括外币掉期存款。

②所列数字已扣除外币掉期存款。

Notes : Hong Kong dollar is the legal tender in the Hong Kong Special Administrative Region, as stated in "The Basic Law of the Hong Kong Special Administrative Region of the People's Republic of China". Foreign currency refers to any currency other than the Hong Kong currency. Accordingly Chinese Renminbi is also treated as foreign currency.

①Figures are adjusted to include foreign currency swap deposits.

②Figures are adjusted to exclude foreign currency swap deposits.

24-43 股票价格指数、证券交易成交额及市场总值
Index of Share Prices, Value of Stock Exchange Turnover and Market Capitalisation

项目	Item	2001	2002	2003	2004	2005
主板	**Main Board**					
股票价格指数	Index of Share Prices					
恒生指数(1964年7月31日=100)	Hang Seng Index (31.7.1964=100)					
最高	High	16164.0	11974.6	12594.4	14266.4	15466.1
最低	Low	8934.2	8858.7	8409.0	10967.7	13355.2
收市	Closing	11397.2	9321.3	12575.9	14230.1	14876.4
分类指数(1984年1月13日= 975.47)	Sectoral Sub-indices (13.1.1984 = 975.47)					
金融	Finance					
最高	High	24970.6	20852.0	26263.6	28798.5	28269.6
最低	Low	15030.9	17060.7	17316.4	23329.6	25776.8
收市	Closing	19497.7	18231.2	26263.6	28237.7	26614.3
公用事业	Utilities					
最高	High	22510.2	23666.8	25070.5	30976.7	32468.4
最低	Low	20022.9	20128.6	21611.2	24616.7	29291.3
收市	Closing	20498.9	21970.5	24878.8	30773.4	31866.0
地产	Properties					
最高	High	20096.0	16635.4	15525.5	18353.2	19482.3
最低	Low	10789.8	10264.4	8837.4	12809.4	16244.6
收市	Closing	15554.8	11103.9	14778.7	18177.6	17977.8
工商业	Commerce and Industry					
最高	High	9102.6	5765.5	5342.9	6136.4	7509.5
最低	Low	4282.2	3817.6	3485.8	4383.6	5670.3
收市	Closing	5508.8	4044.0	5271.7	6076.8	7139.3
恒生综合指数系列①	Hang Seng Composite Index Series①					
(2000年1月3日= 2 000)	(3.1.2000 = 2 000)					
恒生综合指数②	Hang Seng Composite Index②					
最高	High	1397	1444.0	1621.6	1836.8	1998.1
最低	Low	1166	1064.5	1031.3	1388.7	1727.4
收市	Closing	1346	1130.2	1621.6	1832.0	1947.7
恒生香港综合指数②	Hang Seng Hong Kong Composite Index②					
最高	High	1474	1530.3	1688.9	1954.1	2042.2
最低	Low	1215	1145.8	1126.9	1497.2	1836.9
收市	Closing	1421	1215.8	1688.9	1954.1	1976.9
恒生香港大型股指数②	Hang Seng HK LargeCap Index ②					
最高	High	1498	1516.4	1636.5	1865.9	1910.4
最低	Low	1229	1145.9	1115.1	1460.7	1728.4
收市	Closing	1443	1211.1	1636.5	1861.8	1815.0
恒生香港中型股指数②	Hang Seng HK MidCap Index②					
最高	High	1514	1739.8	2049.3	2461.9	2878.6
最低	Low	1261	1267.9	1273.8	1756.3	2295.8
收市	Closing	1462	1345.9	2024.9	2461.9	2850.5
恒生香港小型股指数②	Hang Seng HK SmallCap Index②					
最高	High	1082	1198.7	1573.0	1913.8	2043.8
最低	Low	909	842.9	918.2	1347.3	1745.8
收市	Closing	1025	956.9	1543.3	1913.8	1881.4
恒生中国内地综合指数②	Hang Seng Mainland Composite Index②					
最高	High	1271	1269.0	1503.3	1688.2	1948.0
最低	Low	1004	894.0	825.9	1170.6	1493.5
收市	Closing	1198	950.6	1503.3	1592.1	1901.6
恒生中国企业指数③	Hang Seng China Enterprises Index③					
最高	High	2562.6	2259.8	5020.2	5391.3	5539.4
最低	Low	1560.6	1754.2	2007.5	3546.3	4501.6
收市	Closing	1757.8	1990.4	5020.2	4741.3	5330.3
恒生香港中资企业指数③	Hang Seng China- Affiliated Corp. Index③					
最高	High	2095.1	1398.9	1455.3	1660.1	2032.4
最低	Low	1098.5	957.2	848.0	1129.5	1441.3
收市	Closing	1340.5	1011.1	1427.7	1556.9	1934.9

24-43 续表 1 continued

项 目	Item	2001	2002	2003	2004	2005
恒生综合行业指数②	Hang Seng Composite Industry Indices②					
资源矿产业	Oil & Resources					
最高	High	1658	2173.8	3974.8	4792.0	6447.1
最低	Low	1476	1560.9	1978.4	3080.9	4244.6
收市	Closing	1550	1966.1	3974.8	4531.4	5799.2
工业制品业	Industrial Goods					
最高	High	1592	1991.0	2732.8	2983.5	2752.3
最低	Low	1177	1239.3	1409.4	1957.6	2241.5
收市	Closing	1462	1472.2	2732.8	2495.3	2597.1
消费品制造业	Consumer Goods					
最高	High	1274	1735.7	2444.7	2788.9	2787.3
最低	Low	1022	1232.0	1354.6	2058.5	2428.9
收市	Closing	1238	1353.6	2420.0	2499.8	2669.9
服务业	Services					
最高	High	969	957.4	900.4	1049.5	1220.0
最低	Low	743	631.3	559.6	741.2	919.2
收市	Closing	906	671.1	900.4	992.7	1169.4
公用事业	Utilities					
最高	High	2332	2596.5	2932.3	3548.5	3724.5
最低	Low	2193	2203.1	2398.4	2865.4	3359.0
收市	Closing	2242	2418.2	2932.3	3541.2	3667.4
金融业	Financials					
最高	High	1862	1869.1	2359.3	2580.4	2534.7
最低	Low	1559	1518.2	1546.2	2069.9	2319.8
收市	Closing	1748	1628.0	2359.3	2532.3	2430.7
地产建筑业	Properties & Construction					
最高	High	1571	1630.5	1590.6	1988.9	2158.4
最低	Low	1192	1014.8	896.9	1329.2	1784.9
收市	Closing	1529	1100.0	1527.7	1988.9	2072.2
资讯科技业	Information Technology					
最高	High	1132	1214.9	1171.6	1261.2	1406.8
最低	Low	837	673.8	641.4	837.4	910.1
收市	Closing	1113	753.4	1124.3	980.7	1363.1
综合企业	Conglomerates					
最高	High	1441	1479.9	1392.7	1754.7	1924.8
最低	Low	1110	949.1	919.4	1156.1	1629.5
收市	Closing	1417	1027.5	1362.3	1754.7	1821.5
恒生流通指数系列④	Hang Seng Freefloat Index Series④					
恒生流通综合指数④	Hang Seng Freefloat Composite Index④					
最高	High	-	1235	1701.2	1934.4	2107.3
最低	Low	-	1075	1055.4	1443.7	1818.1
收市	Closing	-	1146	1701.2	1927.0	2044.2
恒生香港流通指数④	Hang Seng Hong Kong Freefloat Index④					
最高	High	-	1231	1559.4	1849.0	1977.8
最低	Low	-	1072	1043.6	1381.5	1737.3
收市	Closing	-	1135	1554.3	1849.0	1909.9
恒生中国内地流通指数④	Hang Seng Mainland Freefloat Index④					
最高	High	-	1436	2658.7	2868.8	3176.7
最低	Low	-	1252	1300.1	1999.7	2557.2
收市	Closing	-	1379	2658.7	2704.3	3084.1
恒生50⑤	Hang Seng 50⑤					
最高	High	-	-	1666.2	1867.5	2051.4
最低	Low	-	-	1053.3	1421.6	1746.7
收市	Closing	-	-	1666.2	1854.1	1959.1
恒生香港25⑤	Hang Seng HK 25⑤					
最高	High	-	-	1512.2	1760.8	1876.3
最低	Low	-	-	1036.0	1344.0	1651.5
收市	Closing	-	-	1507.9	1760.8	1784.5
恒生中国内地25⑤	Hang Seng Mainland 25⑤					
最高	High	-	-	3043.3	3246.1	3743.8
最低	Low	-	-	1485.6	2296.2	2847.5
收市	Closing	-	-	3043.3	3020.2	3557.7

24-43 续表 2 continued

项　目	Item	2001	2002	2003	2004	2005
标准普尔/香港交易所大型股⑥	S&P/HKEx LargeCap Index⑥					
(2003年2月28日= 10 000)	(28.2.2003 = 10 000)					
最高	High	17143.4	13235.6	13645.2	15796.8	17775.1
最低	Low	9835.1	9705.8	9155.3	11911.2	14836.2
收市	Closing	12618.5	10165.5	13645.2	15740.4	17025.5
成交金额（亿港元）	Turnover (HKD 100 million)	19500.9	15990.8	25456.8	39483.5	44981.0
市场总值⑦(亿港元)	Market Capitalisation⑦(HKD 100 million)	38853.4	35591.0	54776.7	66291.8	81133.3
创业板	**Growth Enterprise Market**					
标准普尔/香港交易所创业板⑥	S&P/HKEx GEM Index⑥					
(2003年2月28日=1 000)	(28.2.2003 = 1 000)					
最高	High	3287.0	1978.9	1252.8	1370.3	1013.4
最低	Low	1523.4	903.9	901.4	964.8	863.8
收市	Closing	1839.0	950.5	1186.1	988.6	1007.3
成交金额（亿港元）	Turnover (HKD 100 million)	394.2	439.8	381.5	257.6	223.4
市场总值⑦(亿港元)	Market Capitalisation⑦(HKD 100 million)	609.6	522.2	701.8	667.2	666.0

注：所有最高和最低指数是根据期内每日收市指数所编制。

①于2001年10月3日推出。

②2001年的最高及最低指数指由2001年10月至12月期间的数字。

③在「恒生综合指数系列」推出后，指数的成份股已作出修订，而指数亦以2000年1月3日为基日。

④于2002年9月23日推出，2002年的最高及最低指数指由2002年9月23日至12月底期间的数字。

⑤于2003年1月20日推出，2003的最高及最低指数指由2003年1月20日至12月底期间的数字。

⑥标准普尔/香港交易所大型股和标准普尔/香港交易所创业板指数于2003年3月3日推出，分别追溯至1998年和2001年。

⑦年底数字。

"-" 不适用。

Notes: All high and low indices are compiled based on the daily closing indices in the period.

①Launched on 3 October 2001.

②High and low indices for 2001 refer to the period from October to December 2001.

③Following the launch of the Hang Seng Composite Index Series, its constituents have been revised and the index has been re-based to 3 January 2000.

④Launched on 23 September 2002, high and low indices for 2002 refer to the period from 23 September to end December 2002.

⑤Launched on 20 January 2003, high and low indices for 2003 refer to the period from 20 January 2003 to end December 2003.

⑥S&P/HKEx LargeCap Index and S&P/HKEx GEM Index were launched on 3 March 2003. Relevant series were backdated to 1998 and 2001 respectively.

⑦Year-end figures.

"-" Not applicable.

24-44 居民消费价格指数（2004年10月-2005年9月=100）

Consumer Price Indices (Oct. 2004 - Sep. 2005=100)

项目	Item	权数 Weight	2001	2002	2003	2004	2005
综合消费价格指数	**Composite Consumer Price Index**						
总指数	**All Items**	**100.00**	**105.7**	**102.4**	**99.8**	**99.4**	**100.3**
食品	Food	26.94	101.2	99.1	97.6	98.6	100.4
外出用餐	Meals Bought away from Home	[16.86]	102.1	100.6	99.2	99.4	100.3
食品(不包括外出用餐)	Food, Excluding Meals Bought away from Home	[10.08]	99.7	96.6	95.0	97.4	100.5
住房①	Housing①	29.17	118.2	111.5	106.2	100.6	100.7
私人房屋租金	Private Housing Rent	[23.93]	123.3	115.3	108.0	100.9	100.8
公营房屋租金	Public Housing Rent	[2.49]	91.8	89.3	97.5	99.9	100.0
电力、煤气及水	Electricity, Gas and Water	3.59	92.3	85.9	87.1	97.0	101.0
烟酒	Alcoholic Drinks and Tobacco	0.87	97.3	99.6	99.8	99.7	100.1
服装、鞋	Clothing and Footwear	3.91	94.1	94.8	92.2	98.4	100.0
耐用物品	Durable Goods	5.50	118.4	110.9	103.8	102.1	98.3
杂项物品	Miscellaneous Goods	4.78	91.4	92.9	95.1	98.6	100.0
交通	Transport	9.09	99.7	99.0	98.6	99.1	100.4
杂项服务②	Miscellaneous Services②	16.15	105.2	102.8	99.5	99.3	100.3
教育服务	Educational Services	[4.47]	96.4	97.8	98.5	99.0	100.4
电话及其他通讯服务	Telephone and Other Communications Services	[3.27]	149.0	131.7	114.3	103.8	99.1
医疗服务	Medical Services	[2.57]	96.2	96.8	98.1	99.1	100.1
甲类消费价格指数	**Consumer Price Index (A)**						
总指数	**All Items**	**100.00**	**104.8**	**101.4**	**99.3**	**99.3**	**100.3**
食品	Food	32.10	100.8	98.6	97.0	98.4	100.4
外出用餐	Meals Bought away from Home	[18.63]	101.8	100.1	98.7	99.2	100.3
食品(不包括外出用餐)	Food, Excluding Meals Bought away from Home	[13.47]	99.5	96.5	94.7	97.3	100.6
住房①	Housing①	30.54	114.6	108.1	104.9	100.5	100.6
私人房屋租金	Private Housing Rent	[22.07]	122.8	114.5	107.7	100.8	100.8
公营房屋租金	Public Housing Rent	[6.18]	91.8	89.3	97.5	99.9	100.0
电力、煤气及水	Electricity, Gas and Water	4.84	92.1	84.6	85.7	97.1	101.0
烟酒	Alcoholic Drinks and Tobacco	1.35	97.4	99.7	99.8	99.8	100.0
服装、鞋	Clothing and Footwear	2.81	93.0	95.4	92.6	97.6	100.1
耐用物品	Durable Goods	4.01	116.9	109.9	102.9	101.9	98.0
杂项物品	Miscellaneous Goods	4.68	95.0	96.0	97.0	99.1	99.8
交通	Transport	8.07	101.0	100.4	99.4	99.2	100.4
杂项服务②	Miscellaneous Services②	11.60	107.9	104.3	100.4	99.9	100.0
教育服务	Educational Services	[3.15]	96.8	98.0	98.7	99.1	100.5
电话及其他通讯服务	Telephone and Other Communications Services	[4.21]	146.4	130.0	113.8	103.7	99.1
医疗服务	Medical Services	[1.84]	95.9	96.0	98.7	99.6	100.1
乙类消费价格指数	**Consumer Price Index (B)**						
总指数	**All Items**	**100.00**	**105.9**	**102.6**	**99.8**	**99.4**	**100.4**
食品	Food	27.32	101.3	99.1	97.5	98.6	100.4
外出用餐	Meals Bought away from Home	[17.65]	102.2	100.3	98.7	99.2	100.4
食品(不包括外出用餐)	Food, Excluding Meals Bought away from Home	[9.67]	99.4	96.8	95.1	97.5	100.5
住房①	Housing①	27.70	119.3	112.3	106.6	100.7	100.8
私人房屋租金	Private Housing Rent	[23.89]	123.1	115.0	108.0	100.9	100.9
公营房屋租金	Public Housing Rent	[1.25]	91.8	89.3	97.5	99.9	100.0
电力、煤气及水	Electricity, Gas and Water	3.37	92.4	86.3	87.5	97.0	101.0
烟酒	Alcoholic Drinks and Tobacco	0.79	97.4	99.7	99.8	99.8	100.2
服装、鞋	Clothing and Footwear	4.28	92.4	94.3	91.7	97.5	100.1
耐用物品	Durable Goods	5.67	119.0	111.2	103.9	102.3	98.0
杂项物品	Miscellaneous Goods	4.76	92.1	93.4	95.4	98.7	100.0
交通	Transport	9.05	99.3	98.8	98.3	98.9	100.4
杂项服务②	Miscellaneous Services②	17.06	104.8	102.4	99.4	99.4	100.3
教育服务	Educational Services	[4.96]	96.9	98.1	98.7	99.1	100.4
电话及其他通讯服务	Telephone and Other Communications Services	[3.21]	153.4	134.6	115.8	103.9	99.1
医疗服务	Medical Services	[2.92]	95.3	95.9	97.2	98.9	100.1

24-44 续表 continued

项目	Item	权数 Weight	2001	2002	2003	2004	2005
丙类消费价格指数	**Consumer Price Index (C)**						
总指数	**All Items**	**100.00**	**106.3**	**103.3**	**100.3**	**99.6**	**100.3**
食品	Food	20.41	101.8	100.1	98.8	99.2	100.2
外出用餐	Meals Bought away from Home	[13.74]	102.4	102.1	100.9	100.0	100.1
食品(不包括外出用餐)	Food, Excluding Meals Bought away from Home	[6.67]	100.8	96.7	95.4	97.7	100.3
住房①	Housing①	29.66	121.2	114.5	107.1	100.7	100.7
私人房屋租金	Private Housing Rent	[26.11]	124.1	116.7	108.4	100.9	100.8
电力、煤气及水	Electricity, Gas and Water	2.45	92.6	87.9	89.2	96.9	101.0
烟酒	Alcoholic Drinks and Tobacco	0.42	97.0	99.1	99.7	99.7	100.2
服装、鞋	Clothing and Footwear	4.67	97.7	94.9	92.6	100.4	99.9
耐用物品	Durable Goods	6.99	118.9	111.6	104.5	102.1	98.7
杂项物品	Miscellaneous Goods	4.91	87.1	89.6	92.8	98.1	100.2
交通	Transport	10.35	98.9	98.0	98.4	99.1	100.3
杂项服务②	Miscellaneous Services②	20.14	103.5	102.1	99.1	98.9	100.5
教育服务	Educational Services	[5.33]	95.2	97.0	97.9	98.7	100.5
电话及其他通讯服务	Telephone and Other Communications Services	[2.27]	146.3	129.4	112.8	103.9	99.0
医疗服务	Medical Services	[2.90]	97.7	98.5	98.8	98.9	100.2

注：2004年10月起的消费物价指数是根据2004至2005年住户开支统计调查所得的开支权数编制。较早的指数则是根据旧的开支权数而经过按比例换算与新基期的指数拼接。

①除“私人房屋租金”及“公营房屋租金”外，“住房”类别还包括“管理费及其他住房杂费”和“保养住所材料”。而丙类消费价格指数中的“住房”类别并不包括“公营房屋租金”。

②“杂项服务”包括“教育服务”、“电话及其他通讯服务”、“医疗服务”及其他杂项服务。

Notes: The CPIs from October 2004 onwards are compiled based on expenditure weights obtained from the 2004/05 Household Expenditure Survey. The CPIs for earlier periods are compiled based on old weights and have been re-scaled to the new base period for linking with the new index series.

①Apart from "Private Housing Rent" and "Public Housing Rent", the "Housing" section also includes "Management Fees and Other Housing Charges" and "Materials for House Maintenance". For CPI(C), the "Housing" section does not include "Public Housing Rent".

②"Miscellaneous Services" section includes "Educational Services", "Telephone and Other Communications Services", "Medical Services" and other miscellaneous services.

24-45 按四分位开支组别及商品或服务类别划分的住户每月平均开支
Average Monthly Household Expenditure by Commodity/Service Section by Quartile Expenditure Group

商品或服务类别	Commodity/Service Section	总数 Overall 绝对值 Value	总数 Overall 百分比 (percent)	最低四分位 The Lowest 25% 绝对值 Value	最低四分位 The Lowest 25% 百分比 (percent)	第二四分位 The Second 25% 绝对值 Value	第二四分位 The Second 25% 百分比 (percent)	第三四分位 The Third 25% 绝对值 Value	第三四分位 The Third 25% 百分比 (percent)	最高四分位 The Highest 25% 绝对值 Value	最高四分位 The Highest 25% 百分比 (percent)
食品	Food	4863	25.8	2301	33.9	3978	32.4	5305	29.7	7870	20.4
住房	Housing	5775	30.6	2257	33.3	3766	30.7	5150	28.8	11932	30.9
电力、煤气及水	Electricity, Gas and Water	646	3.4	394	5.8	570	4.6	684	3.8	934	2.4
烟酒	Alcoholic Drinks & Tobacco	152	0.8	108	1.6	153	1.2	177	1.0	171	0.4
服装、鞋	Clothing & Footwear	812	4.3	129	1.9	399	3.3	702	3.9	2020	5.2
耐用物品	Durable Goods	868	4.6	157	2.3	395	3.2	739	4.1	2183	5.7
杂项物品	Miscellaneous Goods	937	5.0	304	4.5	592	4.8	875	4.9	1978	5.1
交通	Transport	1793	9.5	488	7.2	966	7.9	1490	8.3	4231	11.0
杂项服务	Miscellaneous Services	3037	16.1	646	9.5	1446	11.8	2753	15.4	7306	18.9
总数（港元）	**All Sections (HKD)**	**18884**	**100.0**	**6783**	**100.0**	**12264**	**100.0**	**17876**	**100.0**	**38624**	**100.0**
住户总数（户）	**Number of Households (household)**	**1684000**	**100.0**	**421000**	**100.0**	**421000**	**100.0**	**421000**	**100.0**	**421000**	**100.0**

注：住户开支是由2004年10月至2005年9月进行的住户开支统计调查的结果计算出来。

Note:Household expenditures are calculated from the results of the Household Expenditure Survey conducted during October 2004 to September 2005.

24-46 按年龄／教育程度／经济活动身份划分的2003年至2005年曾使用个人计算机的10岁及以上人士数目

Persons Aged 10 and Over Having Used Personal Computer by Age/Educational Attainment/Economic Activity Status, 2003 - 2005

项目	Item	2003			2004			2005		
		人数 Number of Persons	百分比 Percent	比率① Rate①	人数 Number of Persons	百分比 Percent	比率① Rate①	人数 Number of Persons	百分比 Percent	比率① Rate①
年龄组别	**Age Group**									
10-14	10–14	422200	12.2	96.3	418200	11.4	98.0	417900	11.5	98.8
15-24	15–24	833300	24.1	94.3	852000	23.2	95.8	859500	23.6	97.2
25-34	25–34	858600	24.8	79.6	892400	24.3	85.0	838800	23.0	84.1
35-44	35–44	856600	24.7	62.9	908900	24.8	68.4	867800	23.8	67.1
45-54	45–54	388500	11.2	36.1	449200	12.2	40.3	506900	13.9	43.7
55-64	55–64	87900	2.5	16.2	117800	3.2	20.6	128500	3.5	20.5
65岁及以上	65 and Over	17200	0.5	2.2	31300	0.9	4.0	26000	0.7	3.2
合计	**Overall**	**3464400**	**100.0**	**56.2**	**3669700**	**100.0**	**59.5**	**3645500**	**100.0**	**58.8**
教育程度	**Educational Attainment**									
未受教育／幼儿园／小学	No Schooling/Kindergarten/Primary	314100	9.1	17.6	311400	8.5	18.2	308000	8.5	17.6
中学／预科	Secondary/Matriculation	2379400	68.7	67.4	2303700	62.8	69.0	2252500	61.8	68.2
专上教育	Tertiary	770900	22.3	91.6	1054600	28.7	94.3	1084900	29.8	94.6
合计	**Overall**	**3464400**	**100.0**	**56.2**	**3669700**	**100.0**	**59.5**	**3645500**	**100.0**	**58.8**
经济活动身份	**Economic Activity Status**									
从事经济活动	Economically Active	2328500	67.2	64.6	2495300	68.0	68.6	2410700	66.1	68.4
非从事经济活动	Economically Inactive	1135900	32.8	44.4	1174400	32.0	46.4	1234700	33.9	46.1
学生	Students	883200	25.5	97.2	862800	23.5	98.5	921000	25.3	99.2
退休人士	Retired Persons	36700	1.1	4.5	48000	1.3	9.0	55500	1.5	6.5
料理家务者	Home-makers	200700	5.8	26.0	250900	6.8	24.8	241500	6.6	29.2
其他	Others	15300	0.4	22.8	12700	0.3	11.6	16600	0.5	23.6
合计	**Overall**	**3464400**	**100.0**	**56.2**	**3669700**	**100.0**	**59.5**	**3645500**	**100.0**	**58.8**

注：数字是来自2003年5月至8月、2004年6月至8月及2005年5月至8月进行的一项有关信息科技的使用情况和普及程度的住户统计调查，并指在统计前12个月内曾使用个人计算机的10岁及以上人士数目。

①在个别年龄／教育程度／经济活动身分组别中占所有10岁及以上人士的百分比。以所有10至14岁的人士为例，根据上述在2003年进行的住户统计调查所得，96.3% 在统计前12个月内曾使用个人计算机。

Notes : Figures are based on a Household Survey on Information Technology Usage and Penetration conducted during May to August in 2003, June to August in 2004 and May to August in 2005. They refer to the number of persons aged 10 and over who had used personal computer in the twelve months before enumeration.

①As a percentage of all persons aged 10 and over in the respective age/educational attainment/economic activity status groups. For example, among all persons aged 10 – 14, 96.3% had used personal computer in the twelve months before enumeration based on the aboved mentioned Household Survey conducted in 2003.

24-47 按年龄/教育程度/经济活动身份划分的2003年至2005年曾使用互联网服务的10岁及以上人士数目

Persons Aged 10 and Over Having Used Internet Service by Age/Educational Attainment/Economic Activity Status, 2003 - 2005

项　目	Item	2003			2004			2005		
		人　数 Number of Persons	百分比 Percent	比率① Rate①	人　数 Number of Persons	百分比 Percent	比率① Rate①	人　数 Number of Persons	百分比 Percent	比率① Rate①
年龄组别	**Age Group**									
10-14	10-14	401700	12.5	91.6	406200	11.7	95.2	408600	11.6	96.6
15-24	15-24	812300	25.3	91.9	835500	24.0	94.0	850800	24.1	96.2
25-34	25-34	810000	25.2	75.1	857400	24.6	81.7	817800	23.2	81.9
35-44	35-44	773400	24.1	56.8	852000	24.5	64.1	835800	23.7	64.6
45-54	45-54	327100	10.2	30.4	404800	11.6	36.3	476400	13.5	41.1
55-64	55-64	74600	2.3	13.8	100300	2.9	17.5	115600	3.3	18.4
65岁及以上	65 and Over	13700	0.4	1.8	23600	0.7	3.0	21300	0.6	2.6
合计	**Overall**	**3212800**	**100.0**	**52.2**	**3479700**	**100.0**	**56.4**	**3526200**	**100.0**	**56.9**
教育程度	**Educational Attainment**									
未受教育/幼儿园/小学	No Schooling/Kindergarten/Primary	272200	8.5	15.2	282300	8.1	16.5	289100	8.2	16.5
中学/预科	Secondary/Matriculation	2192500	68.2	62.1	2160000	62.1	64.7	2162000	61.3	65.5
专上教育	Tertiary	748100	23.3	88.9	1037300	29.8	92.7	1075100	30.5	93.7
合计	**Overall**	**3212800**	**100.0**	**52.2**	**3479700**	**100.0**	**56.4**	**3526200**	**100.0**	**56.9**
经济活动身份	**Economic Activity Status**									
从事经济活动	Economically Active	2143800	66.7	59.5	2358900	67.8	64.8	2329000	66.1	66.1
非从事经济活动	Economically Inactive	1069000	33.3	41.8	1120800	32.2	44.3	1197100	33.9	44.7
学生	Students	856200	26.7	94.2	844600	24.3	96.4	908700	25.8	97.9
退休人士	Retired Persons	31300	1.0	3.9	38300	1.1	7.2	48600	1.4	5.7
料理家务者	Home-makers	167800	5.2	21.7	226800	6.5	22.4	224700	6.4	27.2
其他	Others	13700	0.4	20.5	11200	0.3	10.1	15100	0.4	21.5
合计	**Overall**	**3212800**	**100.0**	**52.2**	**3479700**	**100.0**	**56.4**	**3526200**	**100.0**	**56.9**

注：数字是来自2003年5月至8月、2004年6月至8月及2005年5月至8月进行的一项有关信息科技的使用情况和普及程度的住户统计调查，并指在统计前12个月内曾使用互联网服务的10岁及以上人士数目。

①在个别年龄/教育程度/经济活动身分组别中占所有10岁及以上人士的百分比。以所有10至14岁的人士为例，根据2003年的住户统计调查所得，91.6% 在统计前12个月内曾使用互联网服务。

Notes : Figures are based on a Household Survey on Information Technology Usage and Penetration conducted during May to August in 2003, June to August in 2004 and May to August in 2005. They refer to the number of persons aged 10 and over who had used Internet service in the twelve months before enumeration.

①As a percentage of all persons aged 10 and over in the respective age/educational attainment/economic activity status groups. For example, among all persons aged 10-14，91.6% had used Internet service in the twelve months before enumeration based on the Household Survey in 2003.

24-48 按行业／就业人数类别划分的2003年至2005年使用个人计算机、连接互联网或有设立网页／网站的机构单位数目

Establishments Using Personal Computers, with Internet Connection or Web Pages/Web Sites by Industry Sector/Employment Size, 2003 - 2005

行业／就业人数	Industry Sector/Employment Size	年份 Year	机构单位数目 Number of Establishments	在机构单位中 Among Establishments 使用个人计算机的机构单位的百分比 % using PCs	连接互联网的机构单位的百分比 % with Internet Connection	有设立网页／网站的机构单位的百分比 % with Web Pages/Web Sites
行业类别	**Industry Sector**					
制造业、电力及煤气业	Manufacturing, Electricity and Gas	2003	17275	52.7	42.0	13.4
		2004	17481	63.1	54.1	16.2
		2005	14624	58.4	46.9	10.4
建筑业	Construction	2003	25147	55.6	37.9	9.1
		2004	22869	49.5	39.3	7.3
		2005	21085	55.4	45.0	7.0
批发贸易、零售贸易、进出口贸易、饮食及酒店业	Wholesale, Retail and Import/Export Trades, Restaurants and Hotels	2003	165855	54.6	49.4	14.4
		2004	165582	59.7	52.5	13.5
		2005	165420	63.6	58.1	17.5
运输、仓储及通讯业	Transport, Storage and Communications	2003	37220	31.5	26.5	6.6
		2004	36310	33.7	23.5	6.6
		2005	34729	28.9	25.8	5.4
金融、保险、地产及商用服务业	Financing, Insurance, Real Estate and Business Services	2003	48865	76.6	68.9	14.9
		2004	48630	82.3	76.9	25.8
		2005	46649	87.2	81.8	20.7
社区、社会及个人服务业	Community, Social and Personal Services	2003	34829	50.5	40.7	17.4
		2004	35257	48.8	37.6	18.4
		2005	31424	44.2	38.5	16.4
合计	Overall	2003	329191	54.8	47.5	13.5
		2004	326128	58.4	50.4	14.8
		2005	313931	60.5	54.7	15.5
就业人数类别	**Employment Size**					
大型	Large	2003	5836	94.2	85.1	62.4
		2004	6405	97.4	89.7	67.7
		2005	6053	97.5	91.5	72.3
中型	Medium	2003	35125	87.7	78.2	31.7
		2004	35060	83.7	76.2	39.2
		2005	32583	88.9	83.6	34.6
小型	Small	2003	288231	50.0	43.0	10.2
		2004	284663	54.5	46.4	10.6
		2005	275295	56.4	50.5	12.0
合计	Overall	2003	329191	54.8	47.5	13.5
		2004	326128	58.4	50.4	14.8
		2005	313931	60.5	54.7	15.5

注：数字是来自2003年和2004年5月至8月，以及 2005年4月至8月进行的一项有关信息科技在工商业的使用情况和普及程度的按年统计调查。

Note : Figures are based on the Annual Survey on Information Technology Usage and Penetration in the Business Sector conducted during May to August in 2003 and 2004, and April to August in 2005.

24-49 按行业／就业人数类别划分的2003年至2005年有通过电子途径预订或购买、获取、售卖或递送货物、服务或资料划分的机构单位数目

Establishments Having Ordered or Purchased, Received, Sold or Delivered Goods, Services or Information through Electronic Means by Industry Sector/Employment Size, 2003 - 2005

行业／就业人数	Industry Sector/Employment Size	年份 Year	机构单位数目 Number of Establish-ments (a)	在机构单位中有通过电子途径进行以下不同层面的商业交易的机构单位数目百分比 Among establishments in column (a),% of establishments having performed the following types of business transactions through electronic means 预订或购买 Order or Purchase	获取 Receipt	售卖 Sale	递送 Delivery
行业类别	**Industry Sector**						
制造业、电力及煤气业	Manufacturing, Electricity and Gas	2003	17275	6.0	45.6	1.6	13.5
		2004	17481	8.7	53.6	1.8	16.4
		2005	14624	11.1	43.5	2.1	10.4
建筑业	Construction	2003	25147	9.8	38.4	0#	9.1
		2004	22869	6.7	44.3	0#	7.3
		2005	21085	8.8	45.7	0.1	8.2
批发贸易、零售贸易、进出口贸易、饮食及酒店业	Wholesale, Retail and Import/Export Trades, Restaurants and Hotels	2003	165855	8.7	53.6	1.2	14.4
		2004	165582	11.6	55.3	1.1	14.2
		2005	165420	18.4	55.7	2.5	17.5
运输、仓库及通讯业	Transport, Storage and Communications	2003	37220	4.3	35.1	0.5	6.6
		2004	36310	3.6	31.6	0.4	6.6
		2005	34729	3.5	28.0	0.8	5.4
金融、保险、地产及商用服务业	Financing, Insurance, Real Estate and Business Services	2003	48865	19.1	67.9	1.6	15.6
		2004	48630	22.4	72.9	2.9	26.0
		2005	46649	22.5	75.1	2.0	21.7
社区、社会及个人服务业	Community, Social and Personal Services	2003	34829	7.9	43.4	1.0	17.6
		2004	35257	11.0	42.5	1.1	19.2
		2005	31424	8.1	36.6	0.2	16.4
合计	Overall	2003	329191	9.6	51.0	1.1	13.6
		2004	326128	11.7	53.0	1.3	15.3
		2005	313931	15.4	52.3	1.8	15.7
就业人数类别	**Employment Size**						
大型	Large	2003	5836	27.9	84.7	8.5	62.6
		2004	6405	32.0	88.1	6.2	67.9
		2005	6053	31.5	90.1	6.4	72.4
中型	Medium	2003	35125	15.4	76.2	2.3	32.7
		2004	35060	23.2	76.7	2.6	40.1
		2005	32583	26.0	79.0	2.8	34.9
小型	Small	2003	288231	8.5	47.2	0.8	10.3
		2004	284663	9.9	49.3	1.0	11.0
		2005	275295	13.7	48.4	1.6	12.2
合计	Overall	2003	329191	9.6	51.0	1.1	13.6
		2004	326128	11.7	53.0	1.3	15.3
		2005	313931	15.4	52.3	1.8	15.7

注：数字是来自2003年和 2004年5月至8月，以及 2005年4月至8月进行的一项有关信息科技在工商业的使用情况和普及程度的按年统计调查。
"0#" 数字少于单位的一半。

Note : Figures are based on the Annual Survey on Information Technology Usage and Penetration in the Business Sector conducted during May to August in 2003 and 2004, and April to August in 2005.
"0#" Magnitude less than half of the unit employed.

24-50 15岁及以上人口教育程度

Educational Attainment of Population Aged 15 and Above

项目	Item	2001		2002		2003		2004		2005	
		人数(万人) Number of Persons (10 000 persons)	百分比 (Percent)	人数(万人) Number of Persons (10 000 persons)	百分比 (Percent)	人数(万人) Number of Persons (10 000 persons)	百分比 (Percent)	人数(万人) Number of Persons (10 000 persons)	百分比 (Percent)	人数(万人) Number of Persons (10 000 persons)	百分比 (Percent)
总计	**Total**										
男	**Male**	**269.39**	**48.28**	**271.09**	**48.04**	**272.16**	**47.80**	**275.52**	**47.54**	**278.28@**	**47.29@**
女	**Female**	**288.53**	**51.72**	**293.19**	**51.96**	**297.23**	**52.20**	**304.08**	**52.46**	**310.16@**	**52.71@**
未受教育/幼儿园	No Schooling/Kindergarten										
男	Male	9.68	1.73	9.34	1.65	9.19	1.61	9.02	1.56	8.69@	1.48@
女	Female	31.22	5.60	29.90	5.30	30.34	5.33	30.24	5.22	29.22@	4.97@
小学	Primary										
男	Male	58.05	10.40	56.07	9.94	54.00	9.48	52.83	9.11	52.08@	8.85@
女	Female	62.63	11.23	62.46	11.07	62.09	10.90	61.33	10.58	62.40@	10.6@
初中	Lower Secondary										
男	Male	52.93	9.49	52.24	9.26	53.91	9.47	53.19	9.18	51.70@	8.79@
女	Female	41.08	7.36	42.63	7.56	43.92	7.71	45.06	7.77	44.93@	7.64@
高中	Upper Secondary										
男	Male	79.60	14.27	80.46	14.26	77.94	13.69	81.40	14.04	83.60@	14.21@
女	Female	88.76	15.91	88.92	15.76	87.49	15.36	90.94	15.69	93.99@	15.97@
预科	Matriculation										
男	Male	11.65	2.09	12.57	2.23	13.71	2.41	13.76	2.37	13.67@	2.32@
女	Female	13.73	2.46	14.09	2.50	16.54	2.91	16.70	2.88	16.61@	2.82@
专上教育	Tertiary										
非学位课程	Non-degree Courses										
男	Male	19.25	3.45	20.90	3.70	22.02	3.87	21.70	3.74	22.52@	3.83@
女	Female	19.91	3.57	21.73	3.85	22.15	3.89	21.41	3.69	22.18@	3.77@
学位课程	Degree Courses										
男	Male	38.23	6.85	39.51	7.00	41.39	7.27	43.61	7.52	46.02@	7.82@
女	Female	31.21	5.59	33.41	5.93	34.71	6.10	38.40	6.63	40.82@	6.94@

注：数字是根据该年四季「综合住户统计调查」所得的数据编制。
"@" 数字将于日后修订。

Note : Figures are compiled based on the data obtained from the General Household Survey for the four quarters of the year.
"@" Figures are subject to revision later on.

24-51 按教育及培训机构类别划分的学生人数

Student Enrolment by Type of Educational and Training Institution

单位：人 (person)

类别	Type	2001	2002	2003	2004	2005
幼儿园①	Kindergarten①	156202	143725	136096	130157	149141@
小学	Primary School	493075	483218	468792	447137	425864@
中学	Secondary School	465403	465926	470487	476954	482273@
日校	Day School	456455	461289	467223	474054	478440@
初中	Lower Secondary	246132	251556	251463	253619	254879@
高中	Upper Secondary	150886	150705	157009	160916	161901@
中六及中七	Secondary 6 and Secondary 7	59437	59028	58751	59519	61660@
夜校	Evening School	8948	4637	3264	2900	3833@
特殊教育学校	Special Education School	9538	9889	10177	8556	7734@
特殊学校	Special School	9381	9648	10082	8468	7697@
普通学校内的特殊班	Special Classes in Ordinary School	157	241	95	88	37@
职业训练局②③	Vocational Training Council②③	58238	59714	59694	60074	61270@
全日制	Full-time	28228	31004	33261	36663	39781@
技工级课程④⑤	Craft Level Courses④⑤	3918	4226	4942	4608	4254@
技术员级课程⑥	Technician Level Courses⑥	15205	15049	13716	11857	9983@
高级技术员级课程⑥	Higher Technician Level Courses⑥	8741	11356	14240	19814	25163@
高级技术员／技术员级课程⑦	Higher Technician/Technician Level Course⑦	364	373	363	384	381@
兼读制	Part-time	30010	28710	26433	23411	21489@
技工级课程④	Craft Level Courses④	8073	6030	5079	4084	3466@
技术员级课程⑥	Technician Level Courses⑥	10893	10623	10755	10074	9977@
高级技术员级课程⑥	Higher Technician Level Courses⑥	11044	12057	10599	9253	8046@
认可专上学院 （全日制）	Approved Post-secondary Colleges (full-time)	4180	4011	4043	3960	4069@
其他学院	Other Colleges	3492	3695	3953	5983	7205@
日间课程	Day Course	2513	2646	2977	4427	5010@
夜间课程	Evening Course	979	1049	976	1556	2195@
教资会资助院校⑧	University Grants Committee (UGC) -funded Institution⑧	81664	85602	90355	91865	91786@
全日制	Full-time	64198	68624	73833	77922	81829@
副学位课程⑨	Sub-degree⑨	13830	16668	20034	23948	26429@
学士学位课程	Undergraduate	44796	45669	46602	47489	49159@
研究院修课课程	Taught Postgraduate	1925	2446	2574	1930	1458@
研究院研究课程⑩	Research Postgraduate ⑩	3647	3841	4623	4555	4783@
兼读制	Part-time	17466	16978	16522	13943	9957@
副学位课程	Sub-degree	4537	4372	4293	3697	2629@
学士学位课程	Undergraduate	3258	3501	3527	3409	2466@
研究院修课课程	Taught Postgraduate	9034	8501	8100	6159	4170@
研究院研究课程 ⑩	Research Postgraduate ⑩	637	604	602	678	691@
香港演艺学院	The Hong Kong Academy forPerforming Arts					
全日制	Full-time	738	743	749	756	752@
非学位程度⑪	Non-degree⑪	452	446	450	440	418@
学位程度	Degree	286	297	299	316	334@
香港公开大学	The Open University of Hong Kong					
大学本部⑨	University-based⑨	26875	25115	22473	20400	18552@
全日制	Full-time	68	85	210	459	1256@
兼读制	Part-time	26807	25030	22263	19941	17296@
李嘉诚专业进修学院③⑨⑫	Li Ka Shing Institute of Professional and Continuing Education③⑨⑫	-	-	9655	9441	9729@
全日制	Full-time	-	-	39	62	86@
兼读制	Part-time	-	-	9616	9379	9643@

24-51 续表 continued

单位：人 (person)

类　别	Type	2001	2002	2003	2004	2005
建造业训练局	Construction Industry Training Authority					
全日制	Full-time	1859	1456	1664	1236	966@
技工级课程④⑬	Craft Level Courses④⑬	1558	1115	1417	1063	719@
技术员级课程⑥⑭	Technician Level Courses⑥⑭	301	341	247	173	247@
制衣业训练局	Clothing Industry Training Authority	486	615	853	1191	913@
全日制	Full-time	396	488	607	646	552@
技工级课程④	Craft Level Courses④	37	47	46	49	51@
技术员级课程⑥	Technician Level Courses⑥	359	441	561	597	501@
兼读制	Part-time	90	127	246	545	361@
技工级课程④	Craft Level Courses④	90	127	246	545	361@
医院管理局⑮	Hospital Authority⑮					
全日制	Full-time	-	108	217	317	305@
菲臘牙科医院⑯	The Prince Philip Dental Hospital⑯					
全日制	Full-time	59	95	90	88	88@
兼读制	Part-time	-	6	-	5	-
毅进计划	Project Yi Jin	4293	4170	4529	6585	5936@
全日制	Full-time	2085	2804	2880	4363	4147@
兼读制	Part-time	2208	1366	1649	2222	1789@
提供成人教育／补习／职业课程的院校③	Institutes Offering Adult Education/Tutorial/Vocational Courses③					
日校	Day school	88251	110916	94552	115236	105934@
日暨夜校	Day cum evening school	-	-	-	12531	43964@
夜校	Evening school	94466	99176	106521	92633	82035@

注：数字只包括就读为期一年或以上长期课程的全日制及兼读制的学生人数。「提供成人教育/补习/职业课程的院校」的数字则包括长短期课程。学校教育的学生人数是指学年开始时（通常在9月），学校学生登记册所录得的学生人数。有关职业训练及专上教育，学年开始和完结月份则会因应各教育及培训机构而有所不同。

①2005年数字包括因应2005年9月实施协调学前服务由幼儿中心转型为幼稚园的幼儿班、低班及高班学生，因此不能与以前的数字作比较。 ②数字指香港专业教育学院、训练及培训发展中心、专业进修中心及工商资讯学院的学生人数。

③数字不包括就读毅进计划课程的学生人数。④技工级课程为中三以上程度课程。 ⑤数字亦包括训练及培训发展中心的操作技工级课程。⑥高级技术员及技术员级课程为中五以上程度课程，而高级技术员级课程为较高程度课程。

⑦高级技术员／技术员级课程为中五以上程度课程，首年须修读共同科目。

⑧除非另有说明，数字指修读教资会资助课程的学生人数。数字亦包括香港教育学院。

⑨数字亦包括就读自资全日制经评审专上课程的学生人数。

⑩2003年以前的数字是指在一般的修业期内及教资会指标内的研究院研究课程的学生人数。自2003年起，数字亦包括在一般的修业期内及在教资会指标外但受教资会资助的研究院研究课程学生。

⑪数字包括证书、深造证书、专业证书、文凭、深造文凭及专业文凭课程的学生人数。 ⑫数字从2003年起开始提供。

⑬数字是指基本工艺课程的学生人数。⑭数字是指建造业管工/技术员训练课程的学生人数。

⑮数字指护士训练课程，并从2002年起开始提供。 ⑯数字指牙科训练课程。

"-" 不适用。 "@" 数字将于日后修订。

Notes: Figures cover both full-time and part-time students attending long programmes lasting for at least one academic year, except for "Institutes offering adult education/tutorial/vocational courses" where long and short programmes are included.

Enrolment for school education refers to the number of pupils enrolled in the school register as at the beginning of a school year (usually in September). For vocational and post-secondary education, beginning and ending months of academic year vary among educational and training institutions.

①Figure for 2005 includes pupils attending nursery, lower and upper classes in kindergartens which have been converted from child care centres upon harmonisation of pre-primary services in September 2005. Accordingly, it is not comparable to figures for earlier years.

②Figures refer to students of the Hong Kong Institute of Vocational Education, Training and Development Centres, Continuing Professional Development Centre and School of Business and Information Systems .

③Figures do not include students attending programmes of the Project Yi Jin.

④Craft level courses are post-secondary 3 courses.

⑤Figures also include operative level courses of Training and Development Centres.

⑥Higher technician and technician level courses are post-secondary 5 courses. Higher technician level courses are more advanced courses.

⑦Higher technician/technician level courses are post-secondary 5 courses with common first year curricula.

⑧Figures refer to students attending UGC-funded programmes unless otherwise specified. Figures also include those for the Hong Kong Institute of Education.

⑨Figures also include students attending full-time accredited self-financing post-secondary programmes.

⑩Figures before 2003 refer to RPg students counted within the formal time limit and within the UGC student number target. Figures from 2003 onwards include also RPg students counted within the formal time limit and outside the UGC student number target but wholly funded by UGC.

⑪Figures include students in certificate, advanced certificate, professional certificate, diploma, advanced diploma and professional diploma courses.

⑫Figures are available from 2003 onwards.

⑬Figures refer to students of basic craft courses.

⑭Figures refer to students of construction supervisor/technician trainee training courses.

⑮Figures refer to nurse training programmes and are available from 2002 onwards.

⑯Figures refer to dental training programmes.

"-" Not applicable.

"@" Figures are subject to revision later on.

24-52 医疗卫生条件

Conditions of Public Health

项 目	Item	2001	2002	2003	2004	2005
注册医护专业人员①（人）	Number of Registered Healthcare Professionals①(persons)					
医生	Doctors	10412	10731	11016	11242	11505
中医②	Chinese Medicine Practitioners②	-	2385	4738	4986	5133
牙医③	Dentists③	1855	1907	1848	1896	1941
药剂师	Pharmacists	1362	1414	1457	1517	1583
护士④	Nurses④	42032	43383	43782	44402	35465
按每千名人口计算的医生数	Doctors per Thousand Population	1.5	1.6	1.6	1.6	1.7@
医疗机构和病床	Number of Medical Institutions and Hospital Beds					
医疗机构 （个）	Medical Institutions (number)	99	98	97	98	99
病床 （张）	Hospital Beds (beds)	34852	35159	35526	34400	34119
按每千名人口计算的病床数	Beds per Thousand Population	5.2	5.2	5.2	5.0	4.9@

注：数字是指该年年底的数字。

①注册医护专业人员的统计资料取自不同的资料来源。医务委员会提供医生的资料，中医药管理委员会提供中医的资料，牙医管理委员会提供牙医的资料，药剂业及毒药管理局提供药剂师的资料，及护士管理局提供护士的资料。医生、牙医及药剂师须每年重新申请执业证明书，而中医及护士则须每三年重新申请执业证明书。医生／牙医的数字包括本地及海外名册上的正式注册医生／牙医。护士的数字包括注册护士及登记护士。

②数字自2002年开始提供，当中并不包括表列中医。表列中医可在中医注册过渡性安排下在香港可合法地执业，直至卫生福利及食物局局长日后在宪报上公布的日期为止。表列中医可按过渡性安排的要求，申请成为注册中医。

③在2003年，有关当局根据香港法例《牙医注册条例》第156章第15(3)条把154名注册牙医的姓名从名册中除去。计及2003年内新增的95名注册牙医后，该年注册牙医的净删减人数为59名。

④护士的数目在2005年下降，是由于根据《护士注册条例》(第164章)第7(3)(e)条及第13(3)(e)条，有超过9000名护士的姓名从名册中除去。

"@" 数字将于日后修订。

Notes: Figures are as at end of the year.

①Statistics on the registered healthcare professionals are maintained by the Medical Council for Doctors, Chinese Medical Council of Hong Kong for Chinese Medicine Practitioners, Dental Council for Dentists, Pharmacy and Poisons Board for Pharmacists, and Nursing Council for Nurses. Annual renewal of practising certificate is required only for doctors, dentists and pharmacists. Chinese medicine practitioners and nurses are required to renew the practising certificates every three years. Figures for doctors/dentists refer to the doctors/dentists with full registration on both the local and overseas lists. Figures for nurses refer to registered nurses and enrolled nurses.

②Figures have been made available since 2002. They do not include listed Chinese medicine practitioners who can practise lawfully in Hong Kong under the transitional arrangements for registration of Chinese medicine practitioners until a date to be announced by the Secretary for Health, Welfare and Food in the Gazette. Listed Chinese medicine practitioners may apply for registration under the requirements of transitional arrangements.

③In accordance with Section 15(3) of the Dentists Registration Ordinance, Cap. 156 Laws of Hong Kong, the names of 154 registered dentists were removed from the register in 2003. Offsetting by 95 new dentists registered in 2003, there was a net decrease of 59 dentists in that year.

④The number of nurses had dropped in 2005 due to the removal of names of more than 9000 nurses from the register/roll in accordance with Section7(3)(e) and Section 13(3)(e) of the Nurses Registration Ordinance (Cap. 164).

"@" Figures are subject to revision later on.

24-53 社会保障

Social Security

社会保障计划	Social Security Scheme	2001/2002	2002/2003	2003/2004	2004/2005	2005/2006
综合社会保障援助	Comprehensive Social Security Assistance					
处理中的个案数目①(个)	Number of Active Cases① (cases)					
年老	Old Age	139288	143585	147433	150399	151918
失明	Blind	294	313	325	320	338
听觉受损	Deaf	278	312	352	381	391
肢体残疾	Physically Disabled	3948	4359	4600	4845	4886
精神病患	Mentally Ill	9208	9992	10665	11374	12055
健康欠佳	Ill Health	20082	20852	22251	23341	23922
单亲	Single Parent	29534	34249	37949	39821	39497
低收入	Low Earnings	9140	10982	14215	16902	18237
失业	Unemployment	31602	43237	48450	44224	40658
其他	Others	3818	4012	4465	5081	5532
总计	Total	247192	271893	290705	296688	297434
发放款项②(亿港元)	Amount② (HKD 100 million)	144.05	161.31	173.06	176.31	177.66
公共福利金	Social Security Allowance					
处理中的个案数目①(个)	Number of Active Cases① (cases)					
伤残津贴	Disability Allowance	103167	105282	107110	109959	113111
高龄津贴	Old Age Allowance	458041	454933	456798	457900	461024
总计	Total	561208	560215	563908	567859	574135
发放款项②（亿港元）	Amount② (HKD 100 million)	52.41	52.81	52.14	52.45	53.39
暴力及执法伤亡赔偿	Criminal and Law Enforcement Injuries Compensation					
获批个案数目(个)	Number of Cases Authorised for Payment (cases)	399	455	387	431	413
交通意外伤亡援助	Traffic Accident Victims Assistance					
获批个案数目(个)	Number of Cases Authorised for Payment (cases)	6733	7102	7190	7360	7893
紧急救济	Emergency Relief					
受助灾民人数（人）	Number of Victims Assisted (persons)	1119	278	93	77	604

注：于财政年度终结时的数字。除特别注明外，财政年度是由4月1日至翌年3月31日。

①处理中的个案包括新申请个案，正在复查中的个案，正领取援助款项的个案和已停止领取援助款项等待复查的个案。

②2001/2002年度的数字包括2001年4月2日至2002年4月1日期间所发放的款项。2002/2003年度的数字则包括 2002年4月2日至2003年3月31日期间所发放的款项。

Notes : Figures are as at end of the financial year. Financial year is from 1 April to 31 March of the next year, unless otherwise specified.

① Active cases refer to cases being handled which include new applications, cases being reviewed, cases being paid and cases suspended for payment pending review.

②Figures for 2001/2002 include the payments for 2 April 2001 to 1 April 2002. Figures for 2002/2003 include the payments for 2 April 2002 to 31 March 2003.

《中国统计年鉴》与香港特别行政区统计刊物中使用的指标对照表

A Comparison of Common Statistical Terms Used in China Statistical Yearbook and Publications Compiled by the Census and Statistics Department, the Government of the Hong Kong Special Administrative Region

对应表号 Table Number	《中国统计年鉴》使用的统计名词 Statistical Terms Used in China Statistical Yearbook	香港特别行政区统计名词及对应英文 Statistical Terms Used in Publications of the Hong Kong Special Administrative Region
1	实际工资指数	实质工资指数 Real wage index
1	增加值	增加价值 Value added
1, 8, 11, 12, 48, 49	建筑业	建造业 Construction
1, 10, 11	按当年价格计算	以当时市价计算 At current market prices
1, 11, 12, 48, 49	批发贸易业	批发业 Wholesale trade
1, 11, 12, 48, 49	零售贸易业	零售业 Retail trade
1, 12	不变价格	固定价格 Constant Prices
1, 12, 14	按不变价格计算	以固定市价计算 At constant market prices
1, 13, 30, 31	服务出口	服务输出 Exports of services
1, 13, 30, 31	服务进口	服务输入 Imports of services
1, 14	国外净要素收入	对外要素收益流动净值 Net External Factor Income Flows
1, 24	集装箱	货柜 Container
1, 44	居民消费价格指数	消费物价指数 Consumer Price Indices
11, 12	生产法本地生产总值	按经济活动划分的本地生产总值 GDP by economic activity
11, 12	生产及进口税	生产及入口税 Taxes on production and imports
11, 12	电力、煤气及水的生产和供应业	电力、燃气及水务业 Electricity, gas and water industries
44, 45	电力、煤气及水	电力、燃气及水 Electricity, gas and water
13	支出法本地生产总值	按开支组成部分划分的本地生产总值 GDP by expenditure component
13	居民消费	私人消费开支 Private consumption expenditure
13	政府消费	政府消费开支 Government consumption expenditure
13	存货变动	存货增减 Changes in inventories
13	货物出口(离岸价)	货品出口(离岸价) Exports of Goods (f.o.b.)
13	货物进口(离岸价)	货品进口(离岸价) Imports of Goods (f.o.b.)
17	水	食水 Water
17	电力	用电量 Electricity consumption
17	煤气	煤气用量 Gas consumption
25	宽带	宽频 Broadband
29	出口货物	出口货品 Exports
29	进口货物	进口货品 Imports
29	转口货物	转口货品 Re-exports
32, 33	百慕大	百慕大群岛 Bermuda
4	大气质量	空气质素 Air Quality
41	马来西亚林吉特	马来西亚元 Malaysian Ringgit
41	韩圆	南韩元 Korean Won
41	菲律宾比索	菲律宾披索 Philippines Peso
44	外出用餐	外出用膳 Meals bought away from home
44, 45	服装、鞋	衣履 Clothing and footwear
44, 45	住房	住屋 Housing
46, 47, 50, 51	幼儿园	幼稚园 Kindergarten
46, 48	计算机	电脑 Computer

主要统计指标解释

年中人口 是以“居住人口”方法编制，在1996年之前是以“广义时点”方法编制。自2000年8月起，“居住人口”方法已取代“广义时点”方法用以编制香港的人口数字，而经修订的人口数字已追溯至1996年。利用“居住人口”方法所编制的人口估计称为“居港人口”。“居港人口”包括“常住居民”和“流动居民”。“常住居民”指两类人士:（a）在统计时点之前的6个月内，在港逗留最少3个月，又或在统计时点之后的6个月内，在港逗留最少3个月的香港永久性居民，不论在统计时点他们是否身在香港；及（b）在统计时点身在香港的香港非永久性居民。至于“流动居民”，是指在统计时点之前的6个月内，在港逗留最少一个月但少于3个月，又或在统计时点之后的6个月内，在港逗留最少1个月但少于3个月的香港永久性居民，不论在统计时点他们是否身在香港。根据新的编制方法，旅客并不包括在香港人口内。

粗出生率 是指某一年内的活产婴儿数目相对该年年中每千名人口的比率。

粗死亡率 是指某一年内的死亡人数相对该年年中每千名人口的比率。

婴儿死亡率 是指某一年内一岁以下婴儿死亡人数相对该年每千名活产婴儿人数的比率。

总和生育率 是指某年的每一千名妇女，若她们在生育龄期（即15至49岁）经历了一如该年的年龄别生育率，一生中活产子女的平均数目。

出生时平均预期寿命 是指某年出生人士，若其一生经历一如该年的年龄性别死亡率所反映的死亡情况，他／她预期能活的年数。

劳动人口 是指15岁及以上陆上非住院人口，并符合就业人口或失业人口定义的人士。

劳动人口参与率 是指劳动人口占所有15岁及以上陆上非住院人口的比例。

就业人口 包括在统计前7天内有做工赚取薪酬或利润或有一份正式工作的15岁及以上人士。无酬家庭从业员及在统计前7天内正休假的就业人士亦包括在内。

失业人口 包括所有十五岁及以上人士在（a）统计前7天内并无职位，且并无为赚取薪酬或利润而工作；（b）统计前7天内随时可工作；及（c）在统计前30天内有找寻工作。一名十五岁或以上的人士，如果他／她符合上述（a）和（b）的条件，但由于相信没有工作可做而在统计前三十天内没有找寻工作，仍会被界定为失业，即所谓「因灰心而不求职的人士」。失业人口亦包括那些并无职位，有找寻工作，但由于暂时生病而不能工作的人士；及并无职位，且随时可工作，但由于已为于稍后时间担当的新工作或开展的业务作出安排；或正期待返回原来的工作岗位而没有找寻工作的人士。

失业率 是指失业人士在劳动人口中所占的比例。

每月就业收入 是指上月从所有工作所获得的收入。就雇员来说，收入包括工资和薪金、花红、佣金、小费、房屋津贴、逾时工作津贴、勤工津贴及其它现金津贴，但不包括补薪。就雇主和自营作业人士而言，收入是指从自己拥有的企业提取作个人及家居用途的款额。如果提取作个人及家居用途的款额资料未能提供，则将会搜集有关从业务所得的净收入数据。

本地生产总值 是指一个国家或地区的所有常住生产单位，在一个指定的期间内，未扣除固定资本消耗的生产总值。

人均本地生产总值 是指该国家或地区在某统计年的本地生产总值除以该地区在该年的人口总数而得的数字。

本地居民生产总值 是指一个经济体系的居民从事各项经济活动而赚取的收益，不论该经济活动是否在该地区的经济领域内进行。换言之，编制本地居民生产总值应包括本地居民在经济领域内或领域以外从事各类经济活动的收益，而扣除非本地居民在经济领域内从事经济活动的收益。计算本地居民生产总值，可用以下方程式:

本地居民生产总值

= 本地生产总值

\+ 本地居民从经济领域外所赚取的要素收益

− 非本地居民从经济领域内所赚取的要素收益

而当中的要素收益组成部分主要分为投资收益及雇员报酬，而投资收益包括直接投资收益、有价证券投资收益及其它投资收益。

人均本地居民生产总值 是指该国家或地区在某统计年的本地居民生产总值除以该年的人口总数而得的数字。

国际收支平衡表 是有系统地载录，在指定期间内，某经济体系与世界各地的各类经济交易的统计表。完整的国际收支平衡表包括以下两个主要核算帐:（a）经常帐；及（b）资本及金融帐。

经常帐 是主要量度实际资源的流动，包括货物的进出口、服务的进口及出口、从外地应收及应付予外地的收益，以及从外地及往外地的经常转移。

货物 包括所有可移动的货物，其拥有权由本地居民转至非本地居民（出口）及由非本地居民转至本地居民（进口）。货物包括一般商品、用作加工的物资、各种运输工具在港口购买的货物、货物修理，以及非货币黄金。

服务 包括由本地居民向非本地居民（出口）和由非本地居民向本地居民（进口）所提供的服务。服务交易是按服务类别分类，分别为运输、旅游、保险服务、金融服务及其它服务。

收益 是提供生产要素而赚取的所得，包括本地居民从非本地居民（应收收益）或非本地居民从本地居民（应付收益）所赚取的所得。收益组成部分主要分为雇员报酬及投资收益，而投资收益包括了直接投资收益、有价证券投资收益及其它投资收益。

经常转移 是指一个经济体系的本地居民，在无同等经济价值报偿的情况下，对非本地居民提供／接受实质及金融资源，而且该资源在转移后会被立刻或于短时间内消耗。

资本帐 是用来量度资本转移及非生产／非金融资产的对外交易。

金融帐 记录本地居民与非本地居民之间的金融资产及负债交易。它显示某经济体系如何融资以进行其对外交易。金融帐内的交易可归类为直接投资、有价证券投资、金融衍生工具、其它投资及储备资产。

资本转移 是指在无经济价值报偿下，固定资产的转移或债务的减免。

直接投资 是指一个经济体系内的某投资者购买设立在另一经济体系内的企业，兼且对该企业有持久利益和在管理方面具有效的控制权。

有价证券投资 是指对非居民的股本证券及债务证券（例如中长期债券、货币市场工具）所作的投资，而投资者对投资于该企业并无持久的利益或在管理方面具影响力。

金融衍生工具 是一种与某种特定的金融工具、指标或商品有联系的金融工具，使特定的金融风险本身能通过这种工具而进行交易（包括在交易所内及场外）。

其它投资 是指不属于直接投资、有价证券投资、金融衍生工具或储备资产，而对非居民的其它金融申索及负债。其它金融申索及负债，包括非作销售的贷款、货币和存款、贸易信贷及财务租赁等。

储备资产 是指一个经济体系的金融当局（在香港是指香港金融管理局）可直接用来支付对外收支赤字，且可用于干预外汇市场以影响汇率，从而间接调节该赤字的外币资产。

国际投资头寸 是在一特定时点上一个经济体系的对外金融资产及负债存量的资产负债表。对外金融资产涵盖对非居民的申索和不牵涉债务人的其它金融资产（例如货币黄金）。另一方面，某经济体系的对外金融负债是指非居民向这经济体系的居民的金融申索。国际投资头寸的分类与国际收支平衡表内的金融帐完全一致，资产及负债分为直接投资、有价证券投资、金融衍生工具和其它投资。国际投资头寸的资产项目亦包括储备资产在内。有关投资组成部分的详细解释，请参阅国际收支平衡表内金融帐组成部分的解释。

国际投资头寸净值 是对外金融资产总值与对外金融负债总值之差。

工业生产指数 量度本地制造业生产量的实际变动，即撇除价格调整因素后的本地生产量变动。

实用楼面面积 指各层楼面面积总和，但不包括楼梯、公共信道空间、升降机等候处、盥洗室、厕所、厨房、及为楼宇提供升降机、空调系统、或类似设施而安装的机械所占用的空间。

获批准可动工兴建楼宇 是指获屋宇署签发《同意书》动工兴建的楼宇。这种《同意书》是发给私人发展计划（包括香港房屋协会的计划）及香港房屋委员会的私人机构参建居屋计划。

初次呈交图则 就一项建筑工程初次呈交建筑事务监督批准的图则。

重大修改 指经过大规模修改的建筑图则，而这些图则必须从根本上接受重新评估。

自置居所住户 是指住户拥有其居住的屋宇单位业权。

全租户 是指住户向居于别处的人士租住整个屋宇单位自住，没有分租，单位内也没有其它的住户。

合租户 是指两个或以上的住户，分别向居于别处的人士租用部分单位居住。

二房东 是指住户向居于别处的人士租住整个屋宇单位，并把部分单位分租予其它住户。

三房客 是指住户向居于同一屋宇单位内的人士租用部分单位居住。

免租 是指住户免费在屋宇单位内居住，不论是否获得业主同意，但不包括本身是业主或由雇主提供居所的住户。

居所由雇主提供 是指住户居住在由其成员之一的雇主提供的居所，包括以象征式租金向雇主租住屋宇单位的住户。假如住户使用由雇主提供的房屋津贴租住居所，则租住权不属于"居所由雇主提供"类别。

进口货物 是指在香港以外出产或制成的货物，输入香港供本地使用或转口，以及再进口的香港产品。其货值是以到岸价值计算。

港产品出口货物 是指香港的天然产品或在香港经过制造工序，以致其基本原料的形状、性质、式样或用途受到永久改变的产品。其货值是以离岸价值计算。

转口货物 是指输出曾经自外地输入香港的货物，而这些货物并没有在香港经过任何制造工序，以致永久改变其形状、性质、式样或用途。其货值是以离岸价值计算。

输往中国内地作外发加工用途的出口货物 是指那些从香港或经香港出口往中国内地加工的原料或半制成品，经加工后成为制成品，并以合约安排再进口香港。

有关外发加工从中国内地输入的进口货物 是指那些加工后从中国内地进口香港的货物，其中全部或部分原料或半制成品是以合约安排从香港或经香港出口往中国内地加工。

原产地为中国内地而涉及外发中国内地加工、并输往其它地方的转口货物 是指那些经香港转口的制成品，其中全部或部分原料或半制成品是以合约安排从香港或经香港出口往中国内地加工，而加工后的货物再进口香港。

直接投资 指一个经济体系内的某投资者购买设立在另一经济体系内的企业，兼且对该企业有持久利益和在管理方面具有效的控制权。为达统计目的，在某企业具有效的控制权是指持有该企业10%或以上的股份。直接投资包括股本资本、再投资收益及其它资本。股本资本是指在分行的股本，以及在附属公司和联营公司所持的股票。再投资收益是指投资者在附属公司及联营公司所应占而未获以股息形式派发的利润。其它资本包括总公司与其附属公司、联营公司和分行间之债务交易。

外来直接投资 是指境外居民在香港的企业所作的直接投资。跨国企业在香港经营的分行或附属公司，是外来直接投资的典型例子。

直接投资头寸 是指某一特定日子香港居民在境外投资的价值或接受外来投资的价值。

直接投资流动 是指某一时段内香港居民于境外的投资或接受境外的投资的投入或撤走。

向外直接投资 是指香港居民投资者在境外的企业所作的直接投资。

贷款基金 提供资金予如房屋贷款和教育贷款等贷款计划。基金收入主要来自政府一般收入帐目转拨的款项、偿还的贷款及贷款利息。

港汇指数 是量度港元相对其它主要贸易伙伴货币汇率变动的加权平均值的指数。在2002年1月1日，欧元的纸币及硬币取代各参与国家的货币成为法定货币。因此，港汇指数的货币篮子亦已更新。由2002年1月2日起，新系列港汇指数（包括14种货币及以2000年1月 ＝ 100）已取代旧港汇指数系列。

外币兑换率 指外币兑港元的电汇或现钞收市中间兑换价。

认可机构 包括持牌银行、有限制牌照银行及接受存款公司。持牌银行可接受任何金额及期限的存款。随着撤销利率限制的最后阶段在2001年7月3日生效，各类存款利率再无任何限制。至于有限制牌照银行，它们可接受金额不少于港币50万元的任何期限的定期存款。接受存款公司则可接受金额不少于港币10万元而期限不少于3个月的定期存款。有限制牌照银行及接受存款公司均无任何存款利率限制。

外币掉期存款 是指顾客在现货市场购买外币，然后存入认可机构，但同时订下远期合约，将该笔外币（本金加利息）在存款到期时售予认可机构。从分析角度来看，这类掉期存款应当作港元定期存款。

货币供应量M_1 是指市民持有的法定纸币和硬币加上持牌银行的客户活期存款。

货币供应量M_2 是指货币供应量M_1所包括的项目，加上持牌银行的客户储蓄及定期存款，再加上持牌银行发行而由非认可机构持有的可转让存款证。

货币供应量M_3 是指货币供应量M_2所包括的各项，加上有限制牌照银行及接受存款公司客户的存款，再加上以上两类认可机构发行而由非认可机构持有的可转让存款证。

恒生指数 是以加权资本市值法计算（即发行股数乘以股价），该指数内的三十三只成份股划分为四个行业类别指数，包括工商、金融、地产及公用事业，其总市值占香港联合交易所有限公司所有上市股份总市值大约百分之六十。

居民消费价格指数（即香港特别行政区所称的"消费物价指数"） 量度住户一般所购买的消费商品和服务价格水平变动情况。居民消费价格指数的按年变动率是一个重要指标，用以量度通胀对消费者的影响。每个项目的开支权数，是其在住户总开支中所占的比重。根据住户开支统计调查的结果，每隔五年更新整套开支权数一次，以确保使用不同开支范围住户的最新开支模式来编制相应的居民消费价格指数。

教育程度 是指某人在学校或其它教育机构修读达到的最高教育水平，不论他／她有否完成该课程。计算教育程度时，只包括正式课程，即须最少为期一个学年，入学须具指定学历资格（大部分由香港公开大学提供的副学位及学位课程除外），以及设有考试或指定评核成绩的程序。

幼儿园 为3至6岁的儿童开设。大部分的幼儿园只开办半日制课程，计有高班、低班及幼儿班，亦有部分幼儿园同时开办全日制课程。所有幼儿园须向教育统筹局注册。

非学位课程 包括所有在香港或以外地区专上学院的副学士学位、高级文凭、专业文凭及其它同等程度的专上课程。

学位课程 包括所有在香港或以外地区专上学院的学士学位、研究生修课及专题研究课程。

社会保障计划 旨在帮助社会上需要经济或物质援助的人士，应付基本及特别需要。这个毋须供款的社会保障制度，包括综合社会保障援助计划、公共福利金计划、暴力及执法伤亡赔偿计划、交通意外伤亡援助计划和紧急救济。

综合社会保障援助计划 是以入息补助方法为那些在经济上无法自给的人士提供安全网，使他们的入息达到一定水平，以应付生活上的基本需要。申请人必须符合居港规定及通过入息及资产审查。

公共福利金计划 是为严重残疾或年龄在65岁或以上的香港居民每月提供现金津贴，以应付因严重残疾或年老而引致的特别需要。这项计划包括普通伤残津贴、高额伤残津贴、普通高龄津贴及高额高龄津贴。除普通高龄津贴外，在本计划下发放的津贴均无须申请人接受经济状况审查。

暴力及执法伤亡赔偿计划 旨在提供经济援助给因暴力罪行或因执法人员使用武器执行职务，以致受伤的人士或这些人士的受养人（如受害人因伤死亡）。此计划无须供款，申请人亦无须接受经济状况审查。

交通意外伤亡援助计划 旨在向道路交通意外受害人或这些人士的受养人（如受害人死亡）迅速提供经济援助。此计划无须考虑受惠人的经济状况，或有关交通意外是因谁人的过失而造成。援助金按受害人的伤亡情况支付；至于财物损失，则不在援助范围内。

紧急救济 提供援助予受天灾或其它不幸事故（例如火灾、台风、水灾、暴雨、山泥倾泻、塌屋）影响的灾民，亦会帮助因楼宇成为危楼而遭发出封闭令撤离家园的受影响人士。

Explanatory Notes on Main Statistical Indicators

Mid-year population is compiled using the "resident population" approach. Population figures before 1996 were compiled using the "extended de facto" approach. Since August 2000, the "resident population" approach has been adopted in place of the "extended de facto" approach for compiling Hong Kong population figures, with revised population figures backdated to 1996. The population estimate compiled under the "resident population" approach is referred to as the "Hong Kong Resident Population", which comprises "Usual Residents" and "Mobile Residents". "Usual Residents" refer to two categories of people : (a) Hong Kong Permanent Residents who have stayed in Hong Kong for at least 3 months during the 6 months before or for at least 3 months during the 6 months after the reference time-point, regardless of whether they are in Hong Kong at the reference time-point; and (b) Hong Kong Non-permanent Residents who are in Hong Kong at the reference time-point. As for "Mobile Residents", they are Hong Kong Permanent Residents who have stayed in Hong Kong for at least 1 month but less than 3 months during the 6 months before or for at least 1 month but less than 3 months during the 6 months after the reference time-point, regardless of whether they are in Hong Kong at the reference time-point. Under the new approach, visitors are not part of the Hong Kong population.

Crude birth rate refers to the number of live births in a given year per 1000 mid-year population of that year.

Crude death rate refers to the number of deaths in a given year per 1000 mid-year population of that year.

Infant mortality rate refers to the number of deaths of age under one in a given year per 1000 live births in that year.

Total fertility rate refers to the average number of children that would be born alive to 1000 women during their lifetime if they were to pass through their childbearing ages 15-49 experiencing the age specific fertility rates prevailing in a given year.

Expectation of life at birth refers to the number of years of life that a person born in a given year is expected to live if he/she was subject to the prevalent mortality conditions as reflected by the set of age-sex specific mortality rates for that year.

Labour force refers to the land-based non-institutional population aged 15 and over who satisfy the criteria for inclusion in the employed population or the unemployed population.

Labour force participation rate refers to the proportion of labour force in the land-based non-institutional population aged 15 and over.

Employed persons refer to those persons aged 15 and over who have been at work for pay or profit during the 7 days before enumeration or have had formal job attachment. Unpaid family workers and persons who were on leave/holiday during the 7 days before enumeration are included.

Unemployed persons refer to those persons aged 15 and over who (a) have not had a job and have not performed any work for pay or profit during the 7 days before enumeration; (b) have been available for work during the 7 days before enumeration; and (c) have sought work during the 30 days before enumeration. If a person aged 15 or over fulfils the conditions (a) and (b) above but has not sought work during the 30 days before enumeration because he/she believed that work was not available, he/she is still classified as unemployed, being regarded as a so-called "discouraged worker". Unemployed population also includes persons without a job who have sought work but have not been available for work because of temporary sickness; and persons without a job who have been available for work but have not sought work because they have made arrangements to take up a new job or to start business on a subsequent date; or were expecting to return to their original jobs.

Unemployment rate refers to the proportion of unemployed persons in the labour force.

Monthly employment earnings refer to earnings from all jobs during the last month. For employees, they include wage and salary, bonus, commission, tips, housing allowance, overtime allowance, attendance allowance and other cash allowances. However, back pays are excluded. For employers and self-employed, they refer to amounts drawn from the self-owned enterprise for personal and household use. If information on the amounts drawn for personal and household use is not available, data on net earnings from business would be collected instead.

Gross Domestic Product (GDP) is a measure of the total value of production of all resident producing units of a country or territory in a specified period, before deducting allowance for consumption of fixed capital.

Per capita GDP is obtained by dividing total GDP in a year by the population of that country or territory in the same year.

Gross National Product (GNP) is a measure of the total income earned by residents of an economy from engaging in various economic activities, irrespective of whether the economic activities are carried out within the economic territory or outside. In other words, in compiling GNP, earnings of residents from various economic activities within or outside the economic territory are included, whereas earnings of non-residents from economic activities within the economic territory are excluded. GNP is computed by the following formula:

GNP = GDP

+ Factor income earned by residents from outside the economic territory

- Factor income earned by non-residents from within the economic territory

where factor income is mainly classified into investment income and compensation of employees. Investment income includes direct investment income, portfolio investment income and other investment income.

Per capita GNP is obtained by dividing GNP in a year by the population of that country or territory in the same year.

Balance of Payments (BOP) account is a statistical statement that systematically summarizes, for a specific time period, the economic transactions of an economy with the rest of the world. A complete BOP account comprises two broad accounts: (a) Current Account; and (b) Capital and Financial Account.

Current account largely measures flow of real resources, including exports and imports of good and services, income receivable and payable abroad, and current transfers from and to abroad.

Goods comprise all movable goods that change ownership from residents to non-residents (exports) and from non-residents to residents (imports). Goods cover general merchandise, goods for processing, goods procured in ports by carriers, repairs on goods, and non-monetary gold.

Services include services rendered by residents to non-residents (exports) and by non-residents to residents (imports). Service transactions are classified by type of services, namely transportation, travel, insurance services, financial services and other services.

Income consists of earnings by residents from non-residents (income receivable) and by non-residents from residents (income payable) for the provision of factors of production. Income is mainly classified into compensation of employees and investment income which includes direct investment income, portfolio investment income and other investment income.

Current transfers are those transactions in which residents of an economy provide/receive real and financial resources that are likely to be consumed immediately or shortly, to/from non-residents without the receipt/provision of equivalent economic values in return.

Capital account measures external transactions in capital transfers, and in acquisition or disposal of non-produced, non-financial assets.

Financial account records transactions in financial assets and liabilities between residents and non-residents. It shows how an economy's external transactions are financed. Transactions in the financial account are classified into direct investment, portfolio investment, financial derivatives, other investment and reserve assets.

Capital transfers are transfers of ownership of a fixed asset or the forgiveness of a liability without receiving any economic value in return.

Direct investment refers to external investment in which an investor of an economy acquires a lasting interest and an effective control over the management of an enterprise located in another economy.

Portfolio investment refers to investment in non-resident equity securities and debt securities (e.g. bonds and notes, money market instruments). Compared with direct investors, portfolio investors in equity and debt securities of non-resident enterprises have no lasting interest or influence in the management of the companies they invest.

Financial derivatives are financial instruments that are linked to a specific financial instrument or indicator or commodity, and through which specific financial risks can be traded in financial markets (including on exchanges and over-the-counter) in their own right.

Other investment refers to other financial claims on and liabilities to non-residents that are not classified as direct investment, portfolio investment, financial derivatives or reserve assets. It includes non-marketable loans, currency and deposits, trade credits and financial leases.

Reserve assets consist of foreign currency assets that are readily available to and controlled by the monetary authority of an economy (in the case of Hong Kong, the Hong Kong Monetary Authority) for directly financing payment imbalances and for indirectly regulating the magnitude of such imbalances through intervention in foreign exchange markets to affect the currency exchange rate of that economy.

International Investment Position (IIP) is a balance sheet showing an economy's stock of external financial assets and liabilities at a particular time point. External financial assets consist of claims on non-residents and other financial assets where no debtor is involved (e.g. monetary gold). On the other hand, an economy's external financial liabilities refer to the financial claims of non-residents on residents of the economy. Fully consistent with the Balance of Payments financial account, IIP is categorized by type of investment. Assets and liabilities are divided into direct investment, portfolio investment, financial derivatives and other investment. The asset side of IIP also includes the reserve assets. For detailed explanation on investment components, please refer to the explanatory notes on the components of the financial account of the Balance of Payments account.

Net IIP is the difference between total external financial assets and total external financial liabilities.

Index of industrial production reflects changes in local manufacturing output in real terms, i.e. changes in the volume of local production after discounting the effect of price changes.

Usable floor area means the aggregate of the areas of the floor or floors in a storey or a building excluding any staircases, public circulation space, lift landings, lavatories, water-closets, kitchens and any space occupied by machinery for any lift, air-conditioning system or similar service provided for the building.

Buildings with consents to commence work refer to buildings with consents to commence building works issued by the Buildings Department. Such "consents" are issued to private development projects (including Hong Kong Housing Society's projects) and Hong Kong Housing Authority's development projects under the Private Sector Participation Scheme.

First submission refers to plans for a building project which are first submitted to the Building Authority for approval.

Major revision refers to building plans which have been so extensively revised that they must be fundamentally reassessed.

Owner-occupier refers to a household which owns the quarters it occupies.

Sole tenant refers to a household which rents the whole quarters it occupies from someone who lives outside the quarters without sharing it with other household(s) or subletting.

Co-tenant refers to two or more households each of which rents part of the quarters from someone who lives outside the quarters.

Main tenant refers to a household which rents the whole quarters it occupies from someone who lives outside the quarters and sublets part of it to other household(s).

Sub-tenant refers to a household which rents part of the quarters from someone who lives in the same quarters.

Rent free refers to a household which occupies an accommodation free, with or without the owner's permission. This does not include owner-occupiers or households occupying accommodation provided by employers.

Accommodation provided by employer refers to a household which occupies an accommodation provided by the employer of one of the household members. This also includes households occupying quarters leased from employers at a nominal rent. If a household member uses housing allowance given by his/her employer for renting accommodation, the tenure is not regarded as accommodation provided by employer.

Imports are goods which have been produced or manufactured in places outside the jurisdiction of Hong Kong and brought into Hong Kong for domestic use or for subsequent re-export as well as Hong Kong products re-imported. Their values are recorded on a c.i.f. (cost, insurance and freight) basis.

Domestic exports are the natural produce of Hong Kong or the products of a manufacturing process in Hong Kong which has changed permanently the shape, nature, form or utility of the basic materials used in manufacture. Their values are recorded on a f.o.b. (free-on-board) basis.

Re-exports are products which have previously been imported into Hong Kong and which are re-exported without having undergone in Hong Kong a manufacturing process which has changed permanently the shape, nature, form or utility of the product. Their values are recorded on a f.o.b. (free-on-board) basis.

Domestic exports to the mainland of China for outward processing refer to raw materials or semi-manufactures exported from or through Hong Kong to the mainland of China for processing with a contractual arrangement for subsequent re-importation of the processed goods into Hong Kong.

Imports from the mainland of China related to outward processing refer to processed goods imported to Hong Kong from the mainland of China, of which all or part of the raw materials or semi-manufactures have been under contractual arrangement exported from or through Hong Kong to the mainland of China for processing.

Re-exports of the mainland of China origin to other places involving outward processing in the mainland of China refer to processed goods re-exported through Hong Kong, of which all or part of the raw materials or semi-manufactures have been exported from or through Hong Kong to the mainland of China for processing with a contractual arrangement for subsequent re-importation of the processed goods into Hong Kong.

Direct investment refers to external investment in which an investor of an economy acquires a lasting interest and an effective control over the management of an enterprise located in another economy. For statistical purpose, an effective control is taken as equivalent to a holding of 10% or more of the equity in an enterprise. Direct investment comprises equity capital, reinvested earnings and other capital. Equity capital means equity in branches, stock and shares in subsidiaries and associates. Reinvested earnings consist of the investors' share of earnings of their subsidiaries or associates not distributed as dividends. Other capital includes inter-company debt transactions between parent companies and their subsidiaries, associates and branches.

Inward direct investment refers to direct investment in a Hong Kong enterprise by a non-Hong Kong resident. Typical examples of inward direct investment are multinational corporations' branches and subsidiaries operating in Hong Kong.

Position of direct investment refers to the value of investment abroad or investment received from abroad of Hong Kong residents on a specified date.

Flow of direct investment refers to the additions/withdrawals of investment abroad or investment received from abroad of Hong Kong residents during a period.

Outward direct investment refers to direct investment by a Hong Kong resident in a non-resident enterprise.

Loan Fund finances loans and advances for such schemes as housing loans and education loans. The main sources of income are appropriations from the General Revenue Account, loan repayments and interest on loans.

Effective Exchange Rate Index (EERI) for the Hong Kong dollar is an index which measure movements in the weighted average of the exchange rate of the Hong Kong dollar against currencies of major trading partners of Hong Kong. On 1 January 2002, Euro notes and coins replaced notes and coins in national currencies of participating countries of the Euro. Hence, the currency basket for compiling EERI was updated. A new series of EERI, which includes 14 currencies and is based on January 2000 as 100, has replaced the old series as from 2 January 2002.

Exchange rates between Hong Kong dollar and other currencies refer to the closing middle market telegraphic transfer rates or notes rates.

Authorized institutions include licensed banks, restricted licence banks and deposit-taking companies. Licensed banks can accept deposits of any size and any term of maturity. With the final phase of interest rate deregulation came into effect on 3 July 2001, there is no restriction on interest rate payable. As for restricted licence banks, they can accept time deposits in amounts of not less than HK$500,000 with any term of maturity. Deposit-taking companies can however accept time deposits in amounts of not less than HK$100,000 with a term of maturity of at least three months. Both restricted licence banks and deposit-taking companies have no restriction on interest rate payable.

Foreign currency swap deposits refer to deposits involving customers buying foreign currencies in the spot market and placing them as deposits with authorized institutions, while at the same time entering into a contract to sell such foreign currencies (principal plus interest) forward in line with the maturity of such deposits. For most analytical purpose, they should be regarded as Hong Kong dollar time deposits.

Money Supply M_1 refers to the sum of legal tender notes and coins held by the public plus customers' demand deposits placed with licensed banks.

Money Supply M_2 refers to the sum of M_1 plus customers' savings and time deposits with licensed banks, plus negotiable certificates of deposits issued by licensed banks held by non-authorized institutions.

Money Supply M_3 refers to the sum of M_2 plus customer deposits with restricted licence banks (RLBs) and deposit-taking companies (DTCs) plus negotiable certificates of deposits issued by RLBs and DTCs held by non-authorized institutions.

Hang Seng Index is a market capitalization-weighted index (shares outstanding multiplied by stock price). The 33 constituent stocks of the Hang Seng Index are grouped under four sub-indices, namely Commerce and Industry, Finance, Properties and Utilities. These stocks account for about 60 percent of the total market capitalization of all stocks listed on the Stock Exchange of Hong Kong Limited.

Consumer Price Index (CPI) measures the changes over time in the price level of consumer goods and services purchased by households. The year-on-year rate of change in the CPI is widely used as an indicator of inflation affecting consumers. Four CPI series are compiled to reflect the impact of consumer price changes on households in different expenditure ranges. The CPI (A), CPI(B) and CPI(C) are compiled based on the expenditure patterns of households in the relatively low, medium and relatively high expenditure ranges respectively. A Composite CPI is compiled based on the overall expenditure pattern of all the above households taken together to reflect the impact of consumer price changes on the household sector as a whole. The expenditure weight of each item is the share of the item in the total expenditure of households. Derived from the results of the Household Expenditure Survey, the set of expenditure weights is updated once every five years to ensure that up-to-date expenditure patterns of households in different expenditure ranges are used in the compilation of the respective CPIs.

Educational attainment refers to the highest level of education ever attained by a person in school or other educational institution, regardless of whether he/she had completed the course. Only formal courses are counted as educational attainment. A formal course shall be one that lasts for at least one academic year, requires specific academic qualifications for entrance (except most sub-degree and degree courses offered by the Open University of Hong Kong) and includes examinations or specific academic assessment procedures.

Kindergartens provide services for children from 3 to 6 years old. Most of the kindergartens operate on a half-day basis offering upper, lower kindergarten classes and nursery classes. Some kindergartens operate full-day kindergarten classes. All kindergartens have to register with the Education and Manpower Bureau.

Non-degree courses refer to sub-degree courses including associate degree, higher diploma, professional diploma and other post-secondary programmes of equivalent standards in tertiary educational institutions within or outside Hong Kong.

Degree courses refer to all first degree, taught postgraduate and research postgraduate courses in tertiary educational institutions within or outside Hong Kong.

Social Security Schemes aim to provide for the basic and special needs of the members of the community who are in need of financial or material assistance. The non-contributory social security system comprises the Comprehensive Social Security Assistance Scheme, Social Security Allowance Scheme, Criminal and Law Enforcement Injuries Compensation Scheme, Traffic Accident Victims Assistance Scheme and Emergency Relief.

Comprehensive Social Security Assistance Scheme provides a safety net for those who cannot support themselves financially. It is designed to bring their income up to a prescribed level to meet their basic needs. An applicant must satisfy the residence requirements and pass both the income and assets tests.

Social Security Allowance Scheme provides a monthly allowance to Hong Kong residents who are severely disabled or who are 65 years of age or above to meet special needs arising from disability or old age. The Scheme includes Normal Disability Allowance, Higher Disability Allowance, Normal Old Age Allowance and Higher Old Age Allowance. Except for Normal Old Age Allowance, the allowances paid under the scheme are non-means tested.

Criminal and Law Enforcement Injuries Compensation Scheme aims to provide financial awards to persons (or to their dependants in cases of death) who are injured as a result of a crime of violence, or by a law enforcement officer using a weapon in the execution of his duty. It is non-contributory and non-means tested.

Traffic Accident Victims Assistance Scheme aims to provide speedy financial assistance to road traffic accident victims (or to their dependants in cases of death). It is non-means tested, and does not take into account the element of fault leading to the occurrence of the accident. Payments are made for personal injuries, while loss of or damage to property is not covered.

Emergency relief is provided for victims of natural and other disasters such as fire, typhoon, flood, rainstorm, landslide, house collapse, and also for evacuees of buildings and premises considered to be dangerous under Closure Orders.

25

澳门特别行政区主要社会经济指标

Main Social and Economic Indicators of Macao Special Administrative Region

简 要 说 明

一、本章资料反映澳门特别行政区主要社会、经济发展情况。内容包括：土地、人口、就业、国民经济核算、工业、能源、建筑、交通通讯、对外贸易、财政金融、物价、教育、卫生、房屋、社会保障等方面。

二、本章涉及的1999年及以前数据均指原名为“澳门地区”的数据。

三、本章由澳门特别行政区政府统计暨普查局提供所有数据，国家统计局国际统计信息中心负责整理、编辑。

四、在统计工作方面，按中华人民共和国“澳门特别行政区基本法”的有关原则，澳门特别行政区保留其单独运作的统计系统，并负责编制和发布反映澳门特别行政区情况的统计数据。由于澳门和内地在使用统计名词及概念方面会有所不同，读者在比较两地数据时，请参考本章末的“主要统计指标解释”。

五、澳门特别行政区是单独的关税地区，澳门与内地之间的贸易，亦需办理进出口报关。在贸易统计方面，澳门特别行政区对外贸易统计数据亦包括澳门特别行政区与内地的贸易。

六、在外汇统计及与之有关的各方面，澳门元是澳门特别行政区的法定货币，因此，除澳门元以外的货币（包括人民币）均视作外币。

七、更详细的统计资料及有关的技术细节，可参阅澳门特别行政区政府统计暨普查局出版的《澳门统计月刊》、《澳门统计年鉴》及各专题统计出版物。

八、本章节表中的符号使用说明：“_”表示绝对数值为零；“空格”表示没有数字或未能提供；“r”表示更正资料；“p”表示临时性数字；“o”表示数据小于本表最小单位半数；“*”或“①”等表示本表下有注解。

Brief Introduction

I. Data in this chapter show main social and economic developments of the Macao Special Administrative Region, including data on land, population, employment, national accounts, industry, energy, construction, transportation, communication, external trade, public finance and banking, prices, education, health, housing and social security.

II. Data of 1999 and previous years in this chapter refer to data of the former Macao region.

III. All data in this chapter are provided by the Statistics and Census Services, the Government of the Macao Special Administrative Region, and further tabulated or edited by the International Statistical Information Centre of the National Bureau of Statistics.

IV. According to the *Basic Law of the Macao Special Administrative Region of the People's Republic of China,* Macao Special Administrative Region maintains its independent statistical system, and compiles and disseminates statistics on the Region. As Macao and the mainland of China use different statistical concepts, definitions and terminology, users are advised to make reference of the Explanatory Note at the end of this chapter when using and comparing data of the mainland of China and the Macao Special Administrative Region.

V. As Macao is a separate custom territory, trade between Macao and the mainland of China needs customs declaration procedures. In terms of trade statistics, data on Macao's imports and exports include Macao's trade with the mainland of China.

VI. As Pataca (MOP) is the legal tender in the Macao Special Administrative Region, all other currencies (including Renminbi) are regarded as foreign currencies in compiling foreign exchange statistics and related statistics.

VII. For more detailed statistics and technical details, users are advised to read Macao Monthly Bulletin of Statistics, Macao Yearbook of Statistics and other publications compiled by the Statistics and Census Services, the Government of the Macao Special Administrative Region.

VIII. Notations used in this chapter:

"_" Indicates absolute value equals zero; "(blank)" indicates no figure provided or not available; "p" indicates provisional data; " o" indicates less than half of the unit employed; "r" indicates rectified data; "*" or "①"indicates see footnotes below.

25-1 主要统计指标概况

Principal Statistical Indicators

项目	Items	2001	2002	2003	2004	2005
人口及生命统计	**Population and Vital Events**					
年中人口估计（万人）	Mid-year Estimates of Population (10 000)	43.4	43.9	44.5	45.7	47.7
出生率（‰）	Crude Birth Rate (‰)	7.5	7.2	7.2	7.2	7.7
死亡率（‰）	Crude Death Rate (‰)	3.1	3.2	3.3	3.4	3.4
劳动、就业	**Labour**					
劳动人口（万人）	Labour Force (10 000)	21.7	21.4	21.6	22.9	24.8
劳动力参与率（%）	Labour Force Participation Rate (%)	64.8	62.3	60.9	61.9	63.1
失业率（%）	Unemployment Rate (%)	6.4	6.3	6.0	4.8	4.1
就业不足率（%）	Underemployment Rate (%)	3.6	3.4	2.7	1.9	1.4
就业人口（万人）	Employed Population (10 000)	20.3	20.1	20.3	21.8	23.8
制造业	Manufacturing	4.4	4.1	3.7	3.6	3.6
批发及零售业	Wholesale and Retail	3.0	3.1	3.3	3.5	3.5
酒店及饮食业	Hotels and Restaurants	2.2	2.3	2.2	2.4	2.5
公共行政、社会及个人服务业	Public Administration, Community, Social and Personal Services	5.6	5.9	6.0	6.9	8.1
对外贸易	**External Trade**					
出口（亿澳门元）	Exports (100 million MOP)	185	189	207	226	198
本地产品出口（亿澳门元）	Domestic Exports (100 million MOP)	151	148	163	173	144
再出口（亿澳门元）	Re-exports (100 million MOP)	33	42	44	52	55
进口（亿澳门元）	Imports (100 million MOP)	192	203	221	279	313
贸易条件指数（1996年=100）	Terms of Trade Index (1996=100)	100.0	99.7	100.9	99.0	95.1
工业生产	**Industrial Production**					
工业电力消耗量（亿千瓦小时）	Electricity Consumption (100 million kwh)	1.5	1.9	2.0	2.1	2.5
建筑（私人部门）	**Construction (Private Sector)**					
新建及扩建私人楼宇单位数目（个）	Units Completed and Extended (No.)	2622	381	1566	1108	1277
新建及扩建私人楼宇总面积（万平方米）	Gross Floor Area of Buildings Completed and Extended (10 000 sq.m)	40	10	24	22	39
新动工的私人楼宇单位数目（个）	Units Started (No.)	812	1326	2658	2757	4947
新动工的私人楼宇总面积（万平方米）	Gross Floor Area of Buildings Started (10 000 sq.m)	16	16	53	72	213
楼宇单位买卖数目（个）	Number of Units Sold (No.)	27016	16831	18556	27823	33644
不动产买卖契约数目（宗）	Deed of Real Estate Transacted (No.)	12992	17513	14400	18623	20022
不动产按揭贷款数目（宗）	Real Estate Mortgage Loans (No.)	8206	9902	9198	13786	14769
运输、通讯、旅游	**Transport, Communications, Tourism**					
进出澳门货运车辆数目（万次）	Lorries Entering and Departing Macao (10 000)	45.8	47.8	47.8	56.6	60.8
进出澳门的客船班（万次）	Ferry Trips Entering and Departing Macao (10 000)	7.4	7.7	7.7	8.6	9.2
澳门国际机场的商业航班（万次）	Commercial Flights at Macao International Airport (10 000)	2.9	3.4	2.9	3.8	4.3
登记车辆（万辆）	Licensed Vehicles (10 000)	11.6	12.4	13.2	14.3	15.4
电话线（万条）	Telephone Lines (10 000)	37.1	45.2	53.9	60.6	70.7
访澳旅客（万人次）	Visitors (10 000)	1028	1153	1189	1667	1871
酒店入住率（%）	Hotel Occupancy Rate (%)	61	67	64	76	71
财政收支、货币、金融（亿澳门元）	**Government Accounts, Money and Finance (100 million MOP)**					
财政总收入①	Total Government Revenue①	156	152	184	239r	230
财政总支出①	Total Government Expenditure①	152	135	157	177r	160
货币供应（广义货币供应量M_2）	Money Supply (M_2)					
澳门元②	MOP②	261	275	297	314	367
港元	HKD	469	512	594	662	701
其他货币	Other Currencies	185	202	220	234	288
总计	Total	916	990	1111	1209r	1357
本地机构及私人贷款及垫款	Loans/Advances to Resident Firms & Individuals	355	336	331	355r	425

25-1 续表 continued

项　　目		Items		2001	2002	2003	2004	2005
居民消费价格指数		**Consumer Price Index**						
(1999年10月至2000年9月=100)		(October/1999 - September/2000=100)						
综合消费价格指数		Composite Consumer Price Index		97.5	94.9	93.5	94.4	98.5
甲类消费价格指数		Consumer Price Index (A)		98.2	95.9	94.6	95.7	100.0
乙类消费价格指数		Consumer Price Index (B)		97.4	94.6	93.1	94.0	97.9
房屋（期末值）		**Housing (End of period balance)**						
公共房屋③	(个)	Public Housing ③	(No.)	9405	9656	7037	6829	6936
教育④		**Education④**						
学前教育学生	(人)	Pre-primary Education	(Students)	13638	12737	11936	11128	
小学生	(人)	Primary Education	(Students)	43709	41535	39278	37216	
中学生	(人)	Secondary Education	(Students)	41132	43999	45600	43851	
高等教育学生	(人)	Higher Education	(Students)	8520	11995	13680	13967	
医疗卫生		**Health**						
死亡登记人数	(人)	Registered Deaths	(No.)	1327	1415	1474	1533	1615
死于心脏病人数	(人)	Deaths of Heart Diseases	(No.)	291	296	329	298r	343
死于癌症人数	(人)	Deaths of Cancers	(No.)	401	439	421	477r	455
婴儿死亡率		Infant Mortality Rate		4.3	3.5	0.6	3.0	3.3
(按每千名出生登记活产婴儿计算)		(per 1000 registered live births)						
社会保障		**Social Security**						
受益人数目	(人)	Beneficiaries	(person)	127703	138514	145677	164165	181117
供款单位数目		Contributors		8919	9421	10078	11013	12305
总发放援助次数	(万次)	Number of Payments Granted	(10 000)	17.7	23.6	30.4	28.3	23.9
总发放金额	(万澳门元)	Amount of Payments Granted	(10 000 MOP)	22132	34610	53003	45302	28556
治安		**Crime**						
罪案数目	(宗)	Number of Crimes		8905	9088	9920	9786	10538
囚犯数目	(期末值,人)	Number of Prisoners	(as at the end of year)	886	928	913	867	897
本地生产总值⑤		**Gross Domestic Product (GDP) ⑤**						
按2002年不变价格计算		At Constant (2002) Prices						
支出法本地生产总值实际增长率(%)		Expenditure-based GDP Real Growth Rate	(%)	2.9	10.1	14.2	28.3r	6.7
本地生产总值	(亿澳门元)	GDP	(100 million MOP)	497.8	548.2	625.8	802.8r	856.3
人均本地生产总值	(万澳门元)	GDP per Capita	(10 000 MOP)	11.5	12.5	14.1	17.5	18.0
按当年价格计算		At Current Prices						
支出法本地生产总值名义增长率(%)		Expenditure-based GDP Nominal Growth Rate	(%)	1.5	10.3	16	30.4r	11.7
本地生产总值	(亿澳门元)	GDP	(100 million MOP)	497.0	548.2	635.7r	829.0r	925.9
人均本地生产总值	(万澳门元)	GDP per Capita	(10 000 MOP)	11.5	12.5	14.3	18.1	19.4

注：① 因2005年自治机构的指定账目未完整，故2005年的总收入及总支出不能与2004年直接比较。
2005年数字在日后得到更多资料时会作出修订。
②《中华人民共和国澳门特别行政区基本法》规定，澳门元是澳门特别行政区的法定货币。
③不包括已出售者。
④不包括特殊教育学生。第n年的学生人数是指n/n+1学年年终学生人数。
⑤本地生产总值(GDP)数列于2005年经主要修订，并将基年由1996年更新为2002年。

Notes:①Because of incomplete data on the revenue and expenditure of the Autonomous Agencies in the specific accounts of 2005, the total revenue and the total expenditure of 2005 are not directly comparable with those of 2004. Figures of 2005 are subject to revisions as more data become available.
②Pataca (MOP) is the legal tender in the Macao Special Administrative Region, as stated in "The Basic Law of the Macao Special Administrative Region of the People's Republic of China".
③Excluding the units that had been sold.
④Excluding students in special education. The number of students of year n refer to the students at the end of academic year n/n+1.
⑤Major revision to GDP series was conducted in 2005 and the base year was renewed from 1996 to 2002.

25-2 按堂区划分的澳门面积
Land Area of Macao by Parish

单位：平方公里 (sq.km)

分　区	Sub-division	2001	2002	2003	2004	2005
总面积	**Total Land Area**	**25.8**	**26.8**	**27.3**	**27.5**	**28.2**
澳门	**Macao Peninsula**	**8.5**	**8.5**	**8.7**	**8.8**	**8.9**
圣安多尼堂区	Santo Antonio	1.1	1.1	1.1	1.1	1.1
望德堂区	Sao Lazaro	0.6	0.6	0.6	0.6	0.6
风顺堂区	Sao Lourenco	0.9	0.9	0.9	1.0	1.0
大堂区	Se	2.9	2.9	3.0	3.0	3.0
花地玛堂区	N.S. de Fatima	3.0	3.0	3.1	3.1	3.2
氹仔	**Island of Taipa**	**6.2**	**6.2**	**6.3**	**6.4**	**6.5**
路环	**Island of Coloane**	**7.6**	**7.6**	**7.6**	**7.6**	**7.6**
路氹填海区	Reclaimed Land between the Islands of Taipa and Coloane	3.5	4.5	4.7	4.7	5.2

25-3 人口主要指标
Main Demographic Indicator

项　目	Item	2001	2002	2003	2004	2005
年中人口估计 （万人）	Mid-year Estimates of Population (10 000 persons)	43.4	43.9	44.5	45.7	47.7
出生率 (‰)	Crude Birth Rate (‰)	7.5	7.2	7.2	7.2	7.7
死亡率 (‰)	Crude Death Rate (‰)	3.1	3.2	3.3	3.4	3.4
婴儿死亡率 (‰)	Infant Mortality Rate (‰)	4.3	3.5	0.6	3.0	3.3
自然增长率 (‰)	Natural Growth Rate (‰)	4.4	4.0	3.9	3.9	4.3
总和生育率	Total Fertility Rate	0.8	0.8	0.8	0.8	0.9
登记结婚数 （宗）	No. of Registered Marriages	1222	1209	1309	1737	1734
离婚数目 （宗）	No. of Registered Divorces	348	385	440	475	573
		1997-2000	1998-2001	1999-2002	2000-2003	2001-2004
出生时平均预期寿命(岁)	Life Expectancy at Birth (years)	78.6	78.9	79.0	79.2	79.3
男	Male	76.8	77.2	77.3	77.4	77.5
女	Female	81.3	81.5	81.8	82.0	82.1

25-4 经济活动人口及失业状况
Labour Force and Unemployment

项　目	Item	2001	2002	2003	2004	2005
劳动人口（万人）	Labour Force (10 000 persons)	21.7	21.4	21.6	22.9	24.8
男	Male	11.6	11.3	11.5	12.2	13.0
女	Female	10.1	10.1	10.0	10.7	11.8
就业人口（万人）	Employed Population (10 000 persons)	20.3	20.1	20.3	21.8	23.8
失业人口（万人）	Unemployed Population (10 000 persons)	1.4	1.3	1.3	1.1	1.0
失业率 (%)	Unemployment Rate (%)	6.4	6.3	6.0	4.8	4.1

25-5 按行业划分的就业人口
Employed Population by Industry

单位：万人 (10 000 persons)

行　　业	Industry	2003	2004	2005
总数	**Total**	**20.26**	**21.80**	**23.78**
农业、畜牧业、狩猎及林业	Agriculture, Farming of Animals, Hunting and Forestry	0.01	0.02	0.01
捕渔业	Fishery	0.05	0.05	0.02
采矿业	Mining and Quarrying			
制造业	Manufacturing	3.71	3.59	3.54
电力、煤气及水的生产与供应业	Electricity, Gas and Water Supply	0.13	0.11	0.13
建筑	Construction	1.63	1.81	2.32
批发及零售业	Wholesale and Retail	3.28	3.52	3.55
酒店及饮食业	Hotels and Restaurants	2.21	2.39	2.49
运输、仓储及通信业	Transport, Storage and Communications	1.42	1.49	1.49
金融、保险业	Financial Intermediation	0.62	0.61	0.65
不动产业务、租赁及向企业提供的服务	Real Estate, Renting and Business Activities	1.19	1.26	1.45
公共行政、社会及个人服务业	Public Administration, Community, Social and personal Services	1.78	1.79	1.88
教育	Education	0.96	1.05	1.03
医疗卫生及社会福利	Health and Social Welfare	0.46	0.51	0.53
团体、社会及个人的其他服务	Other Community, Social and Personal Services	2.35	3.09	4.03
雇用佣人的家庭	Households with Domestic Helpers	0.43	0.50	0.63
国际组织及其他领土以外的机构	International Organizations and Other Extra-territorial Institutions	0.01	0.01	0.02
不详	Unknown	0.02	0.01	0.01

25-6 按行业划分的每月工作收入中位数
Median Monthly Employment Earnings

单位：澳门元 (MOP)

行　　业	Occupation	2003	2004	2005
总数	**Total**	**4801**	**5165**	**5765**
制造业	Manufacturing	2840	2992	3118
电力、煤气及水的生产与供应业	Electricity, Gas and Water Supply	11526	11773	12940
建筑	Construction	4589	4965	5920
批发及零售业	Wholesale and Retail	4354	4550	4889
酒店及饮食业	Hotels and Restaurants	4075	4276	4471
运输、仓储及通信业	Transport, Storage and Communications	5798	5955	6444
金融、保险业	Financial Intermediation	8652	8203	8748
不动产业务、租赁及向企业提供的服务	Real Estate, Renting and Business Activities	3682	3692	4156
公共行政、社会及个人服务业	Public Administration, Community, Social and Personal Services	14075	13909	14543
教育	Education	9150	9054	9515
医疗卫生及社会福利	Health and Social Welfare	7905	9661	9704
团体、社会及个人的其他服务	Other Community, Social and Personal Services	6481	7090	7816
雇用佣人的家庭	Households with Domestic Helpers	2755	2675	2615

25-7 本地生产总值（按当年价格计算）

Gross Domestic Product (At Current Prices)

年 份 Year	本地生产总值① GDP① (亿澳门元) (100 million MOP)	(亿美元) (100 million USD)	本地生产总值与上年比较的实际增长率（%）② GDP Real Growth Rate Over the Preceding Year (%)②	人均本地生产总值 GDP per Capita (澳门元) (MOP)	(美元) (USD)
1992	365.2	45.8	13.3	98475	12352
1993	420.7	52.8	5.2	109563	13751
1994	467.2	58.7	4.3	117737	14791
1995	522.7	65.6	3.3	127715	16032
1996	528.1	66.3	-0.4	127211	15968
1997	532.3	66.7	-0.3	127563	15996
1998	493.6	61.9	-4.6	116884	14649
1999	472.9	59.2	-2.4	110637	13844
2000	489.7	61.0	5.7	113739	14171
2001	497.0	61.9	2.9	114501	14253
2002	548.2	68.2	10.1	125058	15567
2003	635.6	79.2	14.2	142825	17805
2004r	829.0	103.3	28.3	181433	22615
2005③	925.9	115.6	6.7	194458	24274

注：①2005年对本地生产总值(GDP)数列进行了主要修订，并将基年由1996年更新为2002年。
②实际增长率是按2002年不变价格估算的本地生产总值计算而得。
③估算数字在日后得到更多资料时会作出修订。

Notes:①Major revision to GDP series was conducted in 2005 and the base year was renewed from 1996 to 2002.
②The real growth rates are calculated based on GDP at constant (2002) prices.
③The estimates are subject to revisions as more data become available.

25-8 支出法本地生产总值①

Gross Domestic Product (Expenditure-based Estimates)①

单位：亿澳门元 (100 million MOP)

本地生产总值组成部分	GDP Components	2001	2002	2003	2004	2005②
按当年价格计算	**At Current Prices**					
居民消费支出	Private Consumption Expenditure	198.0	202.2	206.7	228.1r	252.2
政府最终消费支出	Government Final Consumption Expenditure	61.1	63.2	68.3	70.9r	79.4
固定资本形成总额	Gross Fixed Capital Formation	51.2	58.0	89.8	134.3r	243.6
存货增加	Changes in Inventories	0.2	2.4	3.2	6.0r	6.1
货物出口	Exports of Goods	184.7	189.3	207.0	225.6	198.2
减：货物进口	Less: Imports of Goods	245.5	259.9	291.6	370.9r	417.5
服务出口	Exports of Services	325.7	382.4	449.9	647.1r	692.0
减：服务进口	Less: Imports of Services	78.3	89.5	97.6	112.1r	128.1
本地生产总值	**GDP**	**497.0**	**548.2**	**635.7r**	**829.0r**	**925.9**
人均本地生产总值（澳门元）	**GDP per Capita (MOP)**	**114501**	**125058**	**142825r**	**181433r**	**194458**
按2002年不变价格计算	**At Constant (2002) Prices**					
居民消费支出	Private Consumption Expenditure	193.5	202.2	209.5	228.2r	245.2
政府最终消费支出	Government Final Consumption Expenditure	61.7	63.2	67.6r	69.4	73.7
固定资本形成总额	Gross Fixed Capital Formation	53.0	58.0	84.5	115.9r	181.9
存货增加	Changes in Inventories	0.2	2.4	3.2	5.9r	5.7
货物出口	Exports of Goods	179.4	189.3	207.0	224.2	198.4
减：货物进口	Less: Imports of Goods	237.6	259.9	294.5	365.2r	397.1
服务出口	Exports of Services	325.1	382.4	447.8	637.4r	677.1
减：服务进口	Less: Imports of Services	77.4	89.5	99.3	113.1	128.5
本地生产总值	**GDP**	**497.8**	**548.2**	**625.8**	**802.8r**	**856.3**
人均本地生产总值（澳门元）	**GDP per Capita (MOP)**	**114648**	**125058**	**140616r**	**175705r**	**179836**

注：①2005年对本地生产总值(GDP)数列进行了主要修订，并将基年由1996年更新为2002年。
②估算数字在日后得到更多资料时会作出修订。

Notes:①Major revision to GDP series was conducted in 2005 and the base year was renewed from 1996 to 2002.
②The estimates are subject to revisions as more data become available.

25-9 生产法本地生产总值①

Gross Domestic Product (Production-Based Estimates)①

单位：亿澳门元 (100 million MOP)

经济活动	Economic Activities	2000	2001	2002	2003	2004②
第二产业	**Secondary Sector**	**63.4**	**55.2**	**55.6**	**63.9**	**72.3**
采矿业	Mining and Quarrying	o	0.1	0.1	0.1	0.1
制造业	Manufacturing	40.8	33.4	31.6	31.0	31.9
电力、煤气及水供应业	Electricity, Gas and Water Supply	11.9	12.6	12.1	13.1	13.0
建筑业	Construction	10.7	9.2	11.8	19.7	27.3
第三产业	**Tertiary Sector**	**365.2**	**369.9**	**408.1r**	**461.2r**	**572.4**
批发零售、维修、酒店、餐厅及酒楼业	Wholesale, Retail, Repair, Hotels and Restaurants	45.2	47.5	55.2	59.0	80.2
运输、仓储及通信业	Transport, Storage and Communications	30.9	27.8	29.8	26.8r	31.1
金融保险、不动产、租赁及商业服务	Financial Intermediation, Real Estate, Renting and Business Activities	96.9	90.9	95.5r	102.1r	121.0
公共行政、社会服务及个人服务(包括博彩业)	Public Administration, Other Community, Social and Personal Services (Including gambling)	192.3	203.7	227.7r	273.4r	340.0
减调整项：间接计算的金融中介服务	**Less: Adjustment for Financial Intermediation Services Indirectly Measured (FISIM)**	**-24.3**	**-23.6**	**-23.4**	**-20.8**	**-19.5**
按基本价格按生产法估算的本地生产总值	**Production-based GDP at Basic Prices**	**404.3**	**401.5**	**440.3r**	**504.4r**	**625.2**
加产品税	**Add: Taxes on Products**	**67.3**	**76.7**	**94.5**	**119.0**	**171.3**
按当年市场价格按生产法估算的本地生产总值	**Production-based GDP at Current Market Prices**	**471.6**	**478.2**	**534.8r**	**623.4r**	**796.5**
按当年市场价格按支出法估算的本地生产总值	**Expenditure-based GDP at Current Market Prices**	**489.7**	**497.0**	**548.2**	**635.7r**	**829.0**
统计差额 (%)	Statistical Discrepancy (%)	-3.7	-3.8	-2.4r	-1.9r	-3.9

注：①2005年对本地生产总值(GDP)数列进行了主要修订，并将基年由1996年更新为2002年。
②估算数字在日后得到更多资料时会作出修订。

Notes:①Major revision to GDP series was conducted in 2005 and the base year was renewed from 1996 to 2002.
②The estimates are subject to revisions as more data become available.

25-10 生产法本地生产总值结构①

Structure of Gross Domestic Product (Production-Based Estimates)①

单位：% (%)

经济活动	Economic Activities	2000	2001	2002	2003	2004②
第二产业	**Secondary Sector**	**15.7**	**13.8**	**12.6r**	**12.7r**	**11.6**
采矿业	Mining and Quarrying					
制造业	Manufacturing	10.1	8.3	7.2	6.2r	5.1
电力、煤气及水供应业	Electricity, Gas and Water Supply	3.0	3.1	2.8	2.6r	2.1
建筑业	Construction	2.6	2.3	2.7	3.9r	4.4
第三产业	**Tertiary Sector**	**90.3**	**92.1**	**92.7r**	**91.5r**	**91.6**
批发零售、维修、酒店、餐厅及酒楼业	Wholesale, Retail, Repair, Hotels and Restaurants	11.2	11.8	12.5r	11.7r	12.8
运输、仓库及通信业	Transport, Storage and Communications	7.6	6.9	6.8	5.3r	5.0
金融、保险、不动产、租赁及商业服务	Financial Intermediation, Real Estate, Renting and Business Activities	24.0	22.6	21.7r	20.2r	19.4
公共行政、社会服务及个人服务(包括博彩业)	Public Administration, Other Community, Social and Personal Services (Including gambling)	47.6	50.7	51.7r	54.2r	54.4
减调整项：间接计算的金融中介服务	**Less: Adjustment for Financial Intermediation Services Indirectly Measured (FISIM)**	**-6.0**	**-5.9**	**-5.3r**	**-4.1r**	**-3.1**
按基本价格按生产法估算的本地生产总值	**Production-based GDP at Basic Prices**	**100.0**	**100.0**	**100.0**	**100.0**	**100.0**

注：①2005年对本地生产总值(GDP)数列进行了主要修订，并将基年由1996年更新为2002年。
②估算数字在日后得到更多资料时会作出修订。

Notes:①Major revision to GDP series was conducted in 2005 and the base year was renewed from 1996 to 2002.
②The estimates are subject to revisions as more data become available.

25-11 电力、燃料及水消耗量
Consumption of Electricity, Fuels and Water

项 目	Item	2001	2002	2003	2004	2005
电力 （万千瓦小时）	**Electricity (10 000 kwh)**					
住户	Domestic	42068	44329	45278	48544	54870
工业	Industrial	15426r	18678r	20289	21499	25260
商业①	Commercial①	104124	109682	111582	120271	135766
燃料	**Fuels**					
重油 （万公升）	Fuel Oil (10 000 liters)	31725	32883	30855	31561	35796
轻柴油 （万公升）	Gas Oil and Diesel (10 000 liters)	10464	12542	15551	21603	19441
汽油 （万公升）	Gasoline (10 000 liters)	4119	4254	4471	4807	5321
液化石油气 （吨）	L.P.G. (ton)	24527	26420	28055	29279	30955
水 （万立方米）	**Water (10 000 cu.m)**	**4837**	**4908**	**5163**	**5339**	**5586**

注：①包括公共照明。
Note: ① Including public lighting.

25-12 按用途划分的建成私人房屋单位及建筑面积
Units and Gross Floor Area Completed by End-use

年 份 Year	住宅 Residential		商业及写字楼 Commercial and Offices		工业 Industrial		其他用途 Other Uses		总计 Total	
	单位数目 (个) No. of Units	建筑面积 (万平方米) Gross Floor Area (10 000 m2)	单位数目 (个) No. of Units	建筑面积 (万平方米) Gross Floor Area (10 000 m2)	单位数目 (个) No. of Units	建筑面积 (万平方米) Gross Floor Area (10 000 m2)	单位数目 (个) No. of Units	建筑面积 (万平方米) Gross Floor Area (10 000 m2)	单位数目 (个) No. of Units	建筑面积 (万平方米) Gross Floor Area (10 000 m2)
1997	6191	57.7	2540	36.3	-	-	365	21.0	9096	115.0
1999	4252	30.8	1085	12.9	2	3.4	50	19.9	5389	66.9
2000	2747	23.0	368	5.5	-	-	31	8.5	3146	37.0
2001	1774	17.4	805	10.8	-	-	43	12.3	2622	40.4
2002	336	3.6	30	0.4	2	0.5	13	5.7	381	10.3
2003	1246	15.4	304	2.5	2	1.4	14	5.0	1566	24.3
2004	962	12.2	134	1.9	1	0.5	11	6.9	1108	21.5
2005	1098	16.1	152	2.3	-	-	27	20.7	1277	39.1

25-13 按用途划分的获批准新动工私人房屋单位及建筑面积
Units and Gross Floor Area Started by End-use

年 份 Year	住宅 Residential		商业及写字楼 Commercial and Offices		工业 Industrial		其他用途 Other Uses		总计 Total	
	单位数目 (个) No. of Units	建筑面积 (万平方米) Gross Floor Area (10 000 m2)	单位数目 (个) No. of Units	建筑面积 (万平方米) Gross Floor Area (10 000 m2)	单位数目 (个) No. of Units	建筑面积 (万平方米) Gross Floor Area (10 000 m2)	单位数目 (个) No. of Units	建筑面积 (万平方米) Gross Floor Area (10 000 m2)	单位数目 (个) No. of Units	建筑面积 (万平方米) Gross Floor Area (10 000 m2)
1997	6299	50.9	1347	12.5	4	4.1	34	17.9	7684	85.3
1999	3157	25.0	442	9.7	1	0.4	19	6.7	3619	41.7
2000	1038	9.9	111	2.2	3	0.6	15	7.6	1167	20.3
2001	600	5.3	196	1.2	2	0.3	14	9.0	812	15.8
2002	1196	10.3	116	1.2	-	-	14	4.2	1326	15.7
2003	2430	31.8	211	10.0	-	-	17	11.4	2658	53.3
2004	2611	37.4	120	4.3	2	0.7	24	29.2	2757	71.5
2005	4447	63.3	456	13.1	6	1.0	38	135.8	4947	213.3

25-14 零售业销售额
Retail Sales

单位：亿澳门元 (100 million MOP)

项　目	Item	2002	2003	2004	2005
零售业销售额总额	**Total Retail Sales**	**52.23**	**62.68**	**75.18**	**87.78**
百货①	Department Stores ①	7.2	8.58	10.85	10.99
超级市场	Supermarkets	5.66	7.25	8.29	9.78
汽车	Motor Vehicles	6.48	9.38	11.83	13.77
钟表金饰	Watches, clocks and jewellery	4.94	4.92	7.38	8.93
成人服装	Adults' clothing	4.63	4.16	5.09	7.01
车辆用燃料	Automotive fuels	2.64	3.00	3.70	5.01
家居用燃料	Fuel for household use	2.31	2.83	3.29	4.29
家庭电器	Household electric appliances	2.62	2.71	2.67	3.48
药房	Pharmacy	1.88	1.93	2.45	3.06
其他	Others	13.87	17.92	19.63	21.46

注：①包括出售粮食、饮品及烟草以外的非专门零售店铺。
Note: ① Including non-specialized retail stores selling merchandise other than food, beverages and tobacco.

25-15 外地进出澳门货物
External Trade by Mode of Transport

单位：万吨 (10 000 tons)

项　目	Mode of Transport	2001	2002	2003	2004	2005
入境①	**Imports ①**					
海路	Sea	156.6	153.9	160.7	177.2	274.3
空路	Air	1.7	1.9	1.7	2.5	2.6
陆路	Land	57.3	72.7	110.4	129.5	198.6
其他②	Others ②	5453.2	5459.1	5667.2	5884.9	6151.2
总数	**Total**	**5668.7**	**5687.7**	**5940.0**	**6194.1**	**6626.6**
出境①	**Exports ①**					
海路	Sea	41.8	26.0	32.2	24.2	21.7
空路	Air	4.0	5.9	6.3	7.8	6.9
陆路	Land	12.6	19.3	16.3	18.3	15.8
其他②	Others ②	4.3	9.6	10.2	15.6	16.8
总数	**Total**	**62.7**	**60.8**	**65.1**	**65.9**	**61.2**

注：①包括直接转运货物。
②包括邮递及以管道运输方式进出澳门的货物。
Notes:①Including quantities of direct transit.
②Including quantities of external trade in Macao by postal parcels and pipelines.

25-16 集装箱流量
Container Flow

单位：次数 (number)

项　目	Item	2001	2002	2003	2004	2005
入境	Inward	32843	35105	36111	42548	40688
出境	Outward	33527	35706	38932	46095	42163
转口	Trans-shipment	10027	14296	11635	13528	11084

25-17 海路集装箱总吞吐量
Seaborne Container Throughput

单位：标准集装箱单位 (TEU)

项　目	Item	2001	2002	2003	2004	2005
入境	Inward	41677	45204r	47094r	54208	50209
出境	Outward	43783	47482r	52815r	62241	55603
转口	Trans-shipment	9225	13486r	12221	14259	11670

注：标准集装箱单位为 20英尺×8英尺×8英尺。
Note: TEU - Twenty-foot Equivalent Unit with standard size of 20 feet × 8 feet × 8 feet.

25-18 通信服务
Communications

项　目		Item		2001	2002	2003	2004	2005
邮递服务		**Postal Service**						
信件邮件	(万件)	Mails	(10 000)	2018	2090	2108	2218	2483
包裹	(万件)	Parcels	(10 000)	0.5	0.5	0.6	0.5	0.6
电话服务	**(万条操作线路)**	**Telephone Service**	**(10 000)**					
固定电话线		Fixed Lines		17.6	17.6	17.5	17.4	17.4
移动电话		Mobile Telephone Lines		15.6	17.3	19.9	22.8	25.9
数码式储值卡		Stored Value GSM Cards		3.9	10.3	16.5	20.4	27.3
对外电话通讯量	**(万分钟)**	**International Calls (10 000 minutes)**						
拨出		Outgoing		15753	15408	15274	16966r	18396*
拨入		Incoming		11390	11345r	12981r	13448r	15003*
传呼用户	**(户)**	**Pagers**	**(No.)**	**6689**	**4627**	**3453**	**2728**	**2513**
国际互联网		**Internet Service**						
登记用户		Registered Subscribers		34403	46874	59401	77174	88592
总使用时数	(万小时)	Total Hours Used	(10 000)	1812	2738	3859	5383	7918

注：*只包括2005年1月至10月之数据。
Note: Figure refers to the period of January to October 2005 only.

25-19 主要商品进出口总额
Values of Major Merchandise Trade

单位：亿澳门元 (100 million MOP)

贸易种类	Trade Type	2001	2002	2003	2004	2005
出口	Exports	184.7	189.3	207.0	225.6	198.2
本地产品出口	Domestic Exports	151.3	147.7	162.6	173.2	143.6
再出口	Re-exports	33.5	41.5	44.4	52.4	54.6
进口	Imports	191.7	203.2	221.0	279.0	313.4
进出口总额	Total Trade	376.4	392.5	428.0	504.7	511.6
进出口差额	Trade Balance	-7.0	-14.0	-14.0	-53.4	-115.2
出口/进口比率 (%)	Exports-to-Imports Ratio(%)	96.4	93.1	93.7	80.9	63.3

25-20 主要商品进口原产地和出口目的地

Values of Imports and Exports by Major Country/Region

单位：亿澳门元 (100 million MOP)

主要国家/地区	Major Country/Region	2001	2002	2003	2004	2005
进口（原产地）	**Imports (Country or Region of Origin)**					
中国内地	Mainland China	81.6	84.8	94.9	123.9	135.2
中国香港	Hong Kong SAR，China	26.6	29.6	27.9	29.5	31.3
欧盟	European Union	24.1	23.9	26.4	34.8	41.2
日本	Japan	10.4	13.7	19.9	26.8	34.1
中国台湾	Taiwan, China	12.8	13.6	12.8	13.5	12.6
美国	United States of America	8.0	8.4	8.7	11.3	12.8
出口（目的地）	**Exports (Country or Region of Destination)**					
美国	United States of America	89.1	91.5	103.2	109.9	96.5
欧盟	European Union	49.2	44.0	47.2	48.8	33.9
中国内地	Mainland China	21.5	29.5	28.4	31.4	29.5
中国香港	Hong Kong SAR，China	13.3	11.8	13.6r	17.0	19.4

25-21 财政收入

Government Revenue

单位：万澳门元 (10 000 MOP)

项　目	Items	2001	2002	2003	2004	2005p
经常收入	**Current Revenue**					
直接税	Direct Tax	754742	887623	1134283	1612446	1806911
间接税	Indirect Tax	84079	92604	98761	129728	149475
费用、罚款及其他金钱制裁	Compulsory Fees，Fines and Penalties	29671	33192	33971	43523	54005
财产收益	Property Income	83898	45458	87209	73100	167778
转移	Transfers	16403	12578	40061	49657	75662
耐用品的出售	Sales of Durable Goods	67	245	21	33	29
劳务及非耐用品的出售	Sales of Services and Non-durable Goods	3374	3997	3938	4206	4803
其他经常收入	Other Current Receipts	1912	23009	2940	17304	13197
资本收入	**Capital Revenue**					
投资资产的出售	Sales of Invested Property	99	25	61	-	391
转移	Transfers	-	100	-	-	-
财务资产	Financial Assets	440	-	-	600	-
财务负债	Financial Liabilities	-	-	-	-	-
其他资本收入	Other Capital Revenue	-	-	-	-	-
非从支付中扣减的退回	Reimbursements Not Deducted from Payments	6795	9599	10779	3892	4619
指定帐目	**Autonomous Agencies**	**582685**	**414264**	**425040**	**451866r**	**23277**
总数①	**Total①**	**1564165**	**1522692**	**1837063**	**2386354r**	**2300147**

注：①2005年数字在日后得到更多资料时会作出修订。

Notes: ①Figures of 2005 are subject to revisions as more data become available.

25-22 财政支出
Government Expenditure

单位：万澳门元 (10 000 MOP)

项　目	Items	2001	2002	2003	2004	2005p
经常支出	**Current Expenditure**					
人员	Personnel	271964	278525	286983	295920	325074
物品及劳务	Goods and Services	53932	54361	57259	66366	77837
利息	Interest	-	-	-	-	-
经常转移	Current Transfers	496145	439137	525171	559490	712599
其他经常支出	Other Current Expenditure	5456	6834	4808	4970	5687
资本支出	**Capital Payments**					
投资	Investment	99305	135055	236169	339416	433827
资本转移	Capital Transfers	3832	2206	2651	12133	6304
财务活动	Financial Transactions	8761	18314	33217	40140	13886
其他资本支出	Other Capital Expenditure	-	-	-	-	-
指定帐目	**Autonomous Agencies**	**582685**	**414264**	**425040**	**24734**	**23277**
总数①	**Total①**	**1522079**	**1348695**	**1571297r**	**1343169**	**1598490**

注：①2005年数字在日后得到更多资料时会作出修订。
①Figures of 2005 are subject to revisions as more data become available.

25-23 货币供应
Money Supply

单位：亿澳门元（年底数字） (100 million MOP (as at end of year))

项　目	Items	2001	2002	2003	2004	2005
狭义货币供应量M_1	**Money Supply (M_1)**	**59.2**	**63.5**	**87.9**	**134.4r**	**127.9**
分类一：澳门元	Classification 1: MOP	35.2	39.3	48.7	62.9	68.5
港元	HKD	23.3	23.6	35.3	67.5	54.0
其他货币	Other Currencies	0.6	0.6	3.8	4.1	5.4
分类二：流通货币（澳门元）	Classification 2: Currency in Circulation (MOP)	19.0	20.5	23.6	27.7r	29.7
活期存款	Demand Deposits	40.2	43.0	64.3	106.7	98.1
广义货币供应量$M_2$①	**Money Supply (M_2) ①**	**915.5**	**989.6**	**1110.9**	**1209.5**	**1356.6**
分类一：澳门元	Classification 1: MOP	261.1	275.4	296.7	313.7r	366.9
港元	HKD	469.1	512.2	594.4	662.1	701.5
其他货币	Other Currencies	185.4	201.9	219.8	233.6	288.3
分类二：狭义货币供应量$M_1$②	Classification 2: Money Supply (M_1) ②	59.2	63.5	87.9	134.4r	127.9
准货币负债③	Quasi-Monetary Liabilities (QML)③	856.3	926.1	1023.0	1075.1	1228.7
储蓄存款	Savings Deposits	193.6	230.7	349.2	427.1	364.3
通知存款	Notice Deposits	8.4	9.3	12.3	12.6	11.6
定期存款	Time Deposits	654.3	686.0	661.5	635.4	852.8

注：《中华人民共和国澳门特别行政区基本法》规定，澳门元是澳门特别行政区的法定货币。
① $M_2 = M_1$ + 准货币负债。
② 自2001年1月起，货币供应量M_1只包括流通货币及活期存款。储蓄存款则变为准货币负债的组成部分。
③ 准货币负债：包括储蓄存款、通知存款、定期存款及存款证明书。

Notes: Pataca (MOP) is the legal tender in the Macao Special Administrative Region, as stated in "The Basic Law of the Macao Special Administrative Region of the People's Republic of China".
① $M_2 = M_1$ + Quasi-Monetary Liabilities (QML).
② Starting from January 2001, the definition of M_1 has been revised. Saving Deposits are reclassified as component of the Quasi-Monetary Liabilities (QML); while M1 includes only Currency in Circulation and Demand Deposits.
③ QML: Quasi-Monetary Liabilities, which consist of savings deposits, notice deposits, time deposits and certificate of deposits.

25-24 外币兑换率

Exchange Rates

(一单位外币兑换的澳门元) (MOP to one unit of foreign currency)

项　目	Items	2001	2002	2003	2004	2005
年内平均数字	**Average for the Year**					
澳元	Australian Dollar	4.1598	4.3703	5.2271	5.9021	6.1064
欧元	Euro	7.1962	7.5984	9.0696	9.9645	9.9721
韩元	South Korean Won	0.0062	0.0065	0.0067	0.0070	0.0078
西班牙比塞塔①	Spanish Peseta①	0.0433				
美元	US Dollar	8.0335	8.0334	8.0214	8.0226	8.0109
新台币	Taiwan Dollar	0.2379	0.2328	0.2332	0.2401	0.2494
法国法郎①	French Franc①	1.0971				
英镑	Pound Sterling	11.5698	12.0766	13.1040	14.6911	14.5820
港元	Hong Kong Dollar	1.0300	1.0300	1.0300	1.0300	1.0300
日元	Japanese Yen	0.0662	0.0643	0.0692	0.0742	0.0729
马来西亚林吉特	Malaysian Ringgit	2.1141	2.1141	2.1109	2.1112	2.1155
新西兰元	New Zealand Dollar	3.3813	3.7306	4.6671	5.3214	5.6436
葡萄牙埃斯库多①	Portuguese Escudo①	0.0359				
德国马克①	Deutsche Mark①	3.6794				
人民币	P.R. China Renminbi	0.9706	0.9706	0.9691	0.9693	0.9778
新加坡元	Singapore Dollar	4.4867	4.4893	4.6034	4.7452	4.8137
瑞士法郎	Swiss Franc	4.7638	5.1812	5.9632	6.4572	6.4424
年底数字	**As at End of Year**					
澳元	Australian Dollar	4.1020	4.5470	5.9869	6.2470	5.8462
欧元	Euro	7.0936	8.4164	10.0413	10.9057	9.4555
韩元	South Korean Won	0.0061	0.0068	0.0067	0.0077	0.0079
西班牙比塞塔①	Spanish Peseta①	0.0426				
美元	US Dollar	8.0313	8.0328	7.9969	8.0095	7.9871
新台币	Taiwan Dollar	0.2290	0.2312	0.2351	0.2522	0.2433
法国法郎①	French Franc①	1.0814				
英镑	Pound Sterling	11.6398	12.8810	14.2269	15.4155	13.7598
港元	Hong Kong Dollar	1.0300	1.0300	1.0300	1.0300	1.0300
日元	Japanese Yen	0.0611	0.0678	0.0747	0.0780	0.0679
马来西亚林吉特	Malaysian Ringgit	2.1135	2.1139	2.1044	2.1078	2.1133
新西兰元	New Zealand Dollar	3.3350	4.2333	5.2388	5.7644	5.4468
葡萄牙埃斯库多①	Portuguese Escudo①	0.0354				
德国马克①	Deutsche Mark①	3.6269				
人民币	P.R. China Renminbi	0.9704	0.9705	0.9662	0.9677	0.9897
新加坡元	Singapore Dollar	4.3402	4.6331	4.6963	4.9003	4.8043
瑞士法郎	Swiss Franc	4.7942	5.7900	6.4395	7.0665	6.0743

注：《中华人民共和国澳门特别行政区基本法》规定，澳门元是澳门特别行政区的法定货币。
外币指澳门元以外的其他货币，因而人民币亦视作外币。
①自2002年1月1日开始，欧元区各国均需采用统一的硬币及纸币，而旧有的货币则相继停用。

Notes: Pataca (MOP) is the legal tender in the Macao Special Administrative Region, as stated in "The Basic Law of the Macao Special Administrative Region of the People's Republic of China". Foreign currency refers to any currency other than the Pataca. Accordingly P.R. China Renminbi is also treated as foreign currency.
①On 1/1/2002, the Euro banknotes and coins were introduced to the Euro zone where member states gradually discontinued the circulations of their original currencies

25-25 居民消费价格指数
(1999年10月至2000年9月=100)
Consumer Price Index
(October/1999 - September/2000=100)

项 目	Items	权数 Weight	2001	2002	2003	2004	2005
综合消费价格指数	**Composite Consumer Price Index**						
总指数	**Global Index**	**100.00**	**97.52**	**94.94**	**93.46**	**94.38**	**98.53**
食品及饮料	Foodstuff and Beverages	31.35	98.30	96.21	95.00	97.13	101.00
服装、鞋	Clothing and Footwear	5.26	90.84	81.56	71.37	73.79	73.13
租金及住屋开支	Rent and Housing Expenses	29.93	97.09	94.05	92.86	92.49	100.14
烟酒	Tobacco and Alcoholic Beverages	1.23	102.59	105.16	105.13	105.46	107.36
家居用品	Household Goods	3.22	94.09	90.59	88.18	89.25	90.14
医疗	Health	2.42	101.30	101.32	100.88	100.81	101.36
交通及通讯	Transport and Communications	9.81	97.35	95.44	94.31	94.94	95.35
教育及消闲	Education and Leisure	10.89	99.02	98.21	98.25	99.65	103.71
其他商品及服务	Other Goods and Services	5.89	98.23	95.42	95.19	94.84	97.12
甲类消费价格指数	**Consumer Price Index (A)**						
总指数	**Global Index**	**100.00**	**98.15**	**95.90**	**94.63**	**95.72**	**100.03**
食品及饮料	Foodstuff and Beverages	35.05	98.23	95.77	94.39	96.76	100.86
服装、鞋	Clothing and Footwear	3.34	90.44	81.10	71.46	74.00	72.48
租金及住屋开支	Rent and Housing Expenses	32.88	97.89	94.85	93.82	93.64	100.19
烟酒	Tobacco and Alcoholic Beverages	1.48	102.70	105.36	105.29	105.47	107.34
家居用品	Household Goods	1.47	95.32	91.60	88.99	89.76	90.47
医疗	Health	2.33	101.93	102.31	102.13	102.25	102.95
交通及通讯	Transport and Communications	7.91	96.55	94.98	93.70	94.01	94.18
教育及消闲	Education and Leisure	12.16	100.52	101.71	102.13	103.90	109.09
其他商品及服务	Other Goods and Services	3.38	99.42	96.82	95.77	95.15	97.10
乙类消费价格指数	**Consumer Price Index (B)**						
总指数	**Global Index**	**100.00**	**97.36**	**94.63**	**93.08**	**93.99**	**97.93**
食品及饮料	Foodstuff and Beverages	31.50	98.28	96.25	95.08	97.09	100.81
服装、鞋	Clothing and Footwear	6.22	91.28	82.09	71.29	73.51	73.13
租金及住屋开支	Rent and Housing Expenses	27.13	97.23	94.27	93.24	92.79	100.40
烟酒	Tobacco and Alcoholic Beverages	1.26	102.60	105.22	105.20	105.57	107.47
家居用品	Household Goods	3.51	94.41	90.88	88.36	89.36	90.25
医疗	Health	2.16	101.72	101.84	101.38	101.40	102.05
交通及通讯	Transport and Communications	10.13	96.66	94.57	93.31	94.18	94.97
教育及消闲	Education and Leisure	11.54	98.33	96.43	96.25	97.45	101.04
其他商品及服务	Other Goods and Services	6.55	97.68	94.79	94.98	94.91	97.43

25-26 按双周开支五等分位及商品与服务分类统计之每户双周平均消费开支

Average Biweekly Household Expenditure By Quintile Of Biweekly Expenditure Group And Section Of Goods And Services

商品与服务分类	Goods and services	总数 Total		最低五分位 The lowest 20%		第二五分位 The second 20%	
		澳门元 MOP	百分比 (%)	澳门元 MOP	百分比 (%)	澳门元 MOP	百分比 (%)
消费开支	**Total expenditure**	**5075**	**100.0**	**1454**	**100.0**	**2870**	**100.0**
食物及非酒精饮品	Food and non-alcoholic beverages	1396	27.5	495	34.0	899	31.3
烟酒	Tobacco and alcoholic beverages	50	1.0	24	1.6	38	1.3
衣履	Clothing and footwear	224	4.4	30	2.1	71	2.5
住屋及燃料	Housing and fuels	1042	20.5	504	34.7	750	26.1
家居设备及日用品	Housing equipment and routine maintenance of the house	142	2.8	17	1.2	33	1.2
医疗	Health	149	2.9	39	2.7	75	2.6
运输	Transport	337	6.6	44	3.0	121	4.2
通讯	Communications	226	4.5	71	4.9	139	4.9
康乐及文化	Recreation and culture	324	6.4	45	3.1	160	5.6
教育	Education	483	9.5	70	4.8	311	10.8
杂项商品及服务	Miscellaneous goods and services	407	8.0	39	2.7	135	4.7
外地消费	Consumption expenses outside Macao	295	5.8	76	5.2	137	4.8
住户数目	**Number of households**	**134332**	**100.0**	**26867**	**20.0**	**26867**	**20.0**

注：从2002年10月至2003年9月进行的住户收支调查获取的结果。

Note: Results are obtained from the Household Budget Survey carried out from October 2002 to September 2003.

25-26 续表 continued

商品与服务分类	Goods and services	第三五分位 The third 20%		第四五分位 The fourth 20%		最高五分位 The highest 20%	
		澳门元 MOP	百分比 (%)	澳门元 MOP	百分比 (%)	澳门元 MOP	百分比 (%)
消费开支	**Total expenditure**	**4057**	**100.0**	**5674**	**100.0**	**11322**	**100.0**
食物及非酒精饮品	Food and non-alcoholic beverages	1263	31.1	1688	29.7	2635	23.3
烟酒	Tobacco and alcoholic beverages	48	1.2	61	1.1	78	0.7
衣履	Clothing and footwear	130	3.2	231	4.1	660	5.8
住屋及燃料	Housing and fuels	891	22.0	1156	20.4	1911	16.9
家居设备及日用品	Housing equipment and routine maintenance of the house	55	1.4	128	2.3	475	4.2
医疗	Health	108	2.7	149	2.6	373	3.3
运输	Transport	196	4.8	335	5.9	988	8.7
通讯	Communications	190	4.7	275	4.8	457	4.0
康乐及文化	Recreation and culture	260	6.4	348	6.1	808	7.1
教育	Education	473	11.7	559	9.8	1001	8.8
杂项商品及服务	Miscellaneous goods and services	247	6.1	439	7.7	1174	10.4
外地消费	Consumption expenses outside Macao	195	4.8	305	5.4	761	6.7
住户数目	**Number of households**	**26866**	**20.0**	**26866**	**20.0**	**26866**	**20.0**

25–27　14岁及14岁以上人口教育程度

Education Levels of Population Aged 14 and Over

项　目	Item	1991		1996		2001	
		人数(万人) Persons (10 000)	百分比 Percentage (%)	人数(万人) Persons (10 000)	百分比 Percentage (%)	人数(万人) Persons (10 000)	百分比 Percentage (%)
总计	**Total**	**28.72**	**100.0**	**31.31**	**100.0**	**34.97**	**100.0**
男	Male	13.74	47.8	14.68	46.9	16.45	47.0
女	Female	14.98	52.2	16.62	53.1	18.52	53.0
从未入学/学前教育	No Education/Pre-primary Education	4.30	15.0	2.63	8.4	2.10	6.0
男	Male	1.51	5.3	0.69	2.2	0.48	1.4
女	Female	2.78	9.7	1.94	6.2	1.62	4.6
小学	Primary Education	12.49	43.5	12.70	40.6	13.64	39.0
男	Male	6.12	21.3	6.08	19.4	6.63	19.0
女	Female	6.38	22.2	6.62	21.1	7.01	20.0
初中	Junior Secondary Education	7.56	26.3	8.93	28.5	9.45	27.0
男	Male	3.75	13.1	4.25	13.6	4.43	12.7
女	Female	3.81	13.3	4.68	14.9	5.02	14.4
高中	Senior Secondary Education	2.88	10.1	4.83	15.4	6.63	19.0
男	Male	1.51	5.3	2.47	7.9	3.32	9.5
女	Female	1.36	4.7	2.36	7.5	3.31	9.5
高等教育	Higher Education						
高等专科	Non-university Degree	0.52	1.8	0.25	0.8	0.75	2.1
男	Male	0.23	0.8	0.09	0.3	0.29	0.8
女	Female	0.28	1.1	0.16	0.5	0.46	1.3
大学	University	0.97	3.4	1.93	6.2	2.39	6.8
男	Male	0.61	2.1	1.09	3.5	1.29	3.7
女	Female	0.36	1.3	0.84	2.7	1.10	3.1
不详	Unknown			0.03	0.1	0.02	0.1
男	Male			0.01		0.01	
女	Female			0.02	0.1		

25–28　按各类型教育机构统计的学生人数①

Students by Type of Educational Institutes①

单位：人　　(No. of Students)

类　别	Type	2000/2001	2001/2002	2002/2003	2003/2004	2004/2005
正规教育	**Regular Education**	**106966**	**106999**	**110266**	**110494**	**108407**
学前教育	Pre-Primary Education	14978	13638	12737	11936	11128
小学	Primary Education	45474	43709	41535	39278	37216
中学	Secondary Education	35850	38751	41551	43251	43851
技术及职业中学	Vocational Technical College	2306	2381	2448	2349	2245
高等教育②	Higher Education②	8358	8520	11995	13680	13967
特殊教育	**Special Education**	**560**	**693**	**587**	**568**	**555**
学前	Pre-Primary Education	19	14	26	37	25
小学	Primary Education	63	110	86	107	82
中学	Secondary Education	19	24	30	32	32
特殊班	Special Classes in Ordinary School	459	545	445	392	416
成人教育③	**Adult Education③**	**65695**	**82401**	**86578**	**96131**	**89480**

注：①学生人数为学年终人数。
②只计算政府认可的高等教育机构。
③成人教育为注册学生人数。

Notes: ①No. of students as at the end of the school-year.
②Referring only to the higher education institutions recognized by the government.
③In adult education, data refer to student enrollments.

25-29 医疗卫生条件

Health

项　目	Items	2001	2002	2003	2004	2005
医护人员（人）	**Medical Personnel in Health Care**					
医生	Doctors	891	921	1009	1024	1105
牙科技术员	Odontologists	84	85	83	82	81
护士	Nurses	960	980	1010	1063	1134
诊断及治疗助理员	Diagnostic and Therapeutic Technical Assistants	235	240	239		
卫生服务助理员	Health Service Assistants	378	388	412		
按每千名人口计算的医生数①	Number of Doctors per 1000 Residents ①	2	2.0r	2.1r	2.2	2.1
医疗机构和病床	**Health Care Establishments and Beds**					
医院（所）	Hospitals (No.)	2	2	2	2	2
病床（张）②	Beds (No.) ②	925r	951r	960r	984	984
按每千名人口计算的病床数	Number of Beds per 1000 Residents	2.1r	2.2r	2.1r	2.1	2.0

注：①不包括牙科医生。

②包括普通住院、深切治疗部及新生婴儿的病床。

Notes: ①Excluding dentists.

②Including beds for general hospitalization, intensive care and newborns.

25-30 按住所租住权划分的家庭住户数目

Number of Households by Tenure of Accommodation

单位：户 (No. of households)

项　目	Item	1993/1994	1998/1999	2002/2003
自置	Owner-occupier	68599	87887	104382
租客	Tenant	20335	21248	17727
二房东	Main tenant	348	233	214
三房客	Sub-tenant	440	269	151
合租者	Co-tenant	4528	6355	3315
由雇主提供	Provided by Employer	4051	2721	1023
免租	Rent-free	8745	9140	7520

25-31 社会保障基金发放次数及金额

Number of Payments and Amounts of Subsidy Granted by Social Security Fund

形式	Type	2003 次数 No. of Payments	2003 金额（万澳门元） Amount (10 000MOP)	2004 次数 No. of Payments	2004 金额（万澳门元） Amount (10 000MOP)	2005 次数 No. of Payments	2005 金额（万澳门元） Amount (10 000MOP)
总计	**Total**	**304068**	**53003**	**283311**	**45302**	**239071**	**28556**
养老金	Old Age Pension	98389	11301	110359	12677	123036	14128
残疾津贴	Disability Pension	7516	860	8019	915	8568	977
社会救济金	Social Security Pension	53836	4024	50973	3802	46986	3506
特别给付	Special Payment	13003	1307	13824	1413	14598	1502
失业津贴	Unemployment Subsidy	12554	2749	6964	1529	8582	1861
疾病津贴	Sickness Subsidy	1487	181	1825	232	1965	235
出生津贴	Birth Subsidy	1900	190	1840	184	2218	222
结婚津贴	Marriage Subsidy	917	92	1243	124	1309	131
丧葬津贴	Funeral Subsidy	500	65	514	67	579	75
因肺尘埃沉着病的给付	**Payments for Pneumoconiosis**	**5**	**182**	**4**	**195**	**2**	**53**
因工作关系所引起的债权	**Credit Advances to Worker of Financially** Troubled Enterprise	**450**	**809**	**249**	**852**	**176**	**230**
援助失业人士	Aid given to the Unemployed	69207	20854	42147	5284	-	13
援助建造业失业人士	Aid given to the Unemployed Manufacturing and Construction Workers	-	-	136	36	113	29
援助特困行业从业员	Aid given to workers engaged in industires with severe difficulties	5748	277	503	85	-	-
职业技能培训班和专业知识进修班(4000名额)	Vocational training and professional improvement courses (4000 placements)	38556	10111	12717	3769	-	-
其他	Other	-	-	31994	14139	30939	5593

主要统计指标解释

本地生产总值 反映每年在澳门特区生产的货物和提供各种服务的总量。本年鉴中的本地生产总值用支出法及生产法估算，支出法等于私人消费支出、政府最终消费支出、固定资本形成总额、库存变化和货物及服务出口净值（出口减进口）的总和。而生产法等于各经济行业的增加值总额的总和，这种方法可以评估澳门特区的产业结构。

婴儿死亡率 参考期内年龄在1岁或以下的死亡人数与出生活婴数目的千分比。

自然增长率 参考期内出生人数和死亡人数差额与平均人口之千分比。

出生率 参考期内出生活婴数目与平均人口之千分比。

死亡率 参考期内死亡人数与平均人口之千分比。

正规教育 指有系统的，且主要为儿童及青少年开办的，由学前教育至大学教育之课程。正规教育课程必须符合下列三个条件:

-课程最少为期一学年;

-有规定入学资格;

-有考试或指定程序评核成绩。

学前教育 分为幼儿教育与小学教育预备班。

1)幼儿教育: 对象是年龄3-4岁的儿童。在报名当年的12月31日年满3岁的幼儿皆可报读。而晋升方面，则无须进行知识的考核。

2)小学教育预备班: 在报名当年的12月31日年满5岁的儿童可报读预备班。为晋升之目的，只设有进度测验。在某些教育机构，小学教育预备班仍被称为学前教育第三年。

小学教育 为期6年，完成小学教育预备班或在报名当年的12月31日年满6岁的儿童可报读小学教育第一年。就读小学的最高年龄为15岁。

中学教育 由两个阶段组成: 初中教育及高中教育。大学预科亦被视为中学教育。

1） 初中教育: 为期3年，合格完成小学教育者可以入读。就读初中最大年龄为18岁，但在特别情况下，经教育机构决定，可以逾越此年限。

2) 高中教育: 为期最少2年，最多3年，合格完成初中教育者可以入读。就读高中最大年龄为21岁，但在特别情况下，经教育机构决定，可以逾越此年限。

技术及职业教育 以培训初级及中级程度的技术及专业人员为目的之课程。

高等教育 由大学、理工学院及相等之学院开办之学位或非学位课程。

特殊教育 指专为有精神、感官、身体、沟通等方面有特殊需要人士所开办的课程。

成人教育 指正规教育系统以外为15岁或以上人士所开办的各种有组织、有系统的学习活动。

劳动人口 在参考期间，可参与生产商品或提供服务之14岁或以上人士的总合。包括就业人口及失业人口。

就业人口 在参考期间，为了金钱或物质的报酬、利润或家庭收入而工作至少1小时的14岁或以上人士的总合。亦包括那些被雇用而没有上班，但与雇主保持正式联系，或拥有1间公司，但因特别原因暂时没有上班的人士。

失业人口 在参考期间，同时符合下列条件的14岁或以上人士的总合。包括: 没有工作或与雇主没有正式工作联系; 可接受有酬工作或自己做生意; 在过去30日曾寻找职业。

就业不足人口 在参考期间，不论其职业身份，非自愿地工作少于35小时，但随时可以接受更多的工作或正在寻找更多工作之就业人口。

劳动力参与率 指劳动人口在14 岁或以上的居住人口中所占的比例。

失业率 指失业人口在劳动人口中所占的比例。

就业不足率 指就业不足人口在劳动人口中所占的比例。

访澳旅客 指任何非以澳门特区为常居地的人士，其连续在澳门的逗留时间少于12个月，旅客之旅游目的并非在澳门特区参与任何有偿活动。

酒店入住率 入住客房数量与可供应客房数量之百分比。

进口 指将产自外地的货物输入澳门特区，但再进口和转运制度下输入者除外。

出口 指将货物输出澳门特区，但暂时出口和转运制度下输出者除外。

本地产品出口 指将产地为澳门特区的货物输出澳门特区。

再出口 指原进口的货物未经加工输出澳门特区，或虽加工，但不能取得澳门特区产地资格。

转运 指仅为运输之目的，货物在澳门特区经过或转船，且其下目的地应于附同之文件中列明。（ 按照新修订对外贸易法(第7/2003号法律)的规定，由2003年9月开始，"直接转运" 改称为 "转运"。）

原产地 指农产品种植之国家或地区、矿业开采之国家或地区以及工业产品全部或部份生产之国家或地区。若生产产品之部份，负责将产品变成确定形式进入澳门特区前的最后一个生产工序之国家或地区，都可被视为原产地。而再包装、再分类及混合不被视为生产工序。

目的地 目的地是指货物实际最后到达的国家或地区(不论在运输途中有或没有中断)。如有中间国家或地区，只要不在中间国家或地区内进行商业交易，最后到达的国家或地区都可被视为目的地。

贸易条件指数 即出口单位价格指数与进口单位价格指数之比率。

单位 指永久性楼宇之一个或多个间格及其附属建筑物。每一个单位具有独立入口与楼宇内之公用地方相通，具有合法条件进行分层物业登记和作独立转让。

楼宇建筑面积 相等于所有层数之面积总和。楼面面积的计算方法是从外墙起量度，同时亦包括大堂面积、楼梯、升降机所占面积以及所有公用地方面积(两个或以上单位合用)。

居民消费价格指数 反映澳门特区家庭于购买一篮子之指定商品或服务时，在不同时间该等商品或服务之价格变动。

狭义货币供应量M_1 为流通货币及活期存款之和。

广义货币供应量M_2 指狭义货币供应量M1加上准货币负债。准货币负债指储蓄存款、通知存款、定期存款和存款证明书。

财务活动 由财务资产及财务负债组成。

Explanatory Notes on Main Statistical Indicators

Gross Domestic Product (GDP): Reflects the total of goods produced and services provided annually in Macao, China. GDP in this statistical yearbook is estimated by using the expenditure and production approaches. The expenditure-based GDP is measured as the sum of private consumption expenditure, government final consumption expenditure, gross fixed capital formation, changes in inventories, and net exports (exports less imports) of goods and services. The production-based GDP, which is measured as the sum of gross value added of all economic activities, can be used to evaluate the structure of the industrial sectors in Macao, China.

Infant Mortality Rate: Deaths of infants under one year old per 1,000 live births within the reference period.

Natural Growth Rate: Surplus (or deficit) of births over deaths per 1,000 residents of the average population within the reference period.

Crude Birth Rate: Live births per 1,000 residents of the average population within the reference period.

Crude Mortality Rate: Deaths per 1,000 residents of the average population within the reference period.

Regular Education: Systematic academic programmes designed in principle, for children and juveniles to access / progress from pre-primary education to university. Three pre-requisites are set up:

-Programme duration of at least one academic year.

-Specific academic qualification for entrance.

-Examination or specific academic assessment procedures included.

Pre-primary Education: Composed of 2 stages: infant education and the preparatory level for primary education.

(1)Infant education: Designed for children aged between 3-4 years old. Children aged 3 as at 31st December of the year of enrolment are also eligible. No knowledge assessment tests are required for progression.

(2)Preparatory level for primary education: Designed for children aged 5 as at 31st December of the year of enrolment. Progress examination is a pre-requisite for advancement access. This type of preparatory level is also called the third year of pre-primary education in some educational institutes.

Primary Education: Lasts for 6 years. Children having completed the preparatory level or aged 6 as at 31st December of the year of enrolment are eligible to the first year of primary education. The maximum age for primary education is 15.

Secondary Education: It is divided into 2 stages: Junior secondary and senior secondary. Pre-university courses are also considered secondary education.

(1)Junior Secondary Education: For a duration of 3 years. Students having successfully completed the primary education are eligible. The maximum age for this level is 18 years old. However, under certain circumstances, the educational institutes can exercise their discretion to accept enrolment beyond the age limit.

(2)Senior Secondary Education: For a duration of 2-3 years. Students having successfully completed the junior secondary level are eligible. The maximum age for this level is 21. However, under certain circumstances, the educational institutes can exercise their discretion to accept enrolment beyond the age limit.

Vocational Technical Secondary Education: Programmes aiming at training vocational technical personels in elementary and intermediate levels.

Higher Education: Degree or non-degree programmes offered by universities, polytechnical institutes or equivalent.

Special Education: Programmes designed for students with mental, sensory, corporal or communication problems, etc.

Adult Education: Practical programmes or courses, outside the regular education, organized for general participation, which are designed for individuals aged 15 and above.

Labour Force: Total number of people aged 14 and above who are available to participate in the production of goods and services during the reference period. It comprises employed population and unemployed population.

Employed Population: Total number of people aged 14 and above who have worked at least 1 hour during the reference period, for pay, profits or family gains, in cash or in kind. It also includes individuals who have a job and are absent from work but maintain a formal job attachment with the employer, or company owners who are temporarily not working due to specific reasons.

Unemployed Population: Total number of people aged 14 and above during the reference period with all of the following conditions:

-Not having a job or any formal job attachment to an employer.

-Available for work with remuneration or running own business.

-Seeking work during the last 30 days.

Underemployed Population: Refers to the employed population who, regardless of their status in employment, worked involuntarily for less than 35 hours during the reference period, and have sought or are available to take on additional work.

Labour Force Participation Rate: The proportion of labor force in the resident population aged 14 and above in Macao, China.

Unemployment Rate: The proportion of unemployed in the labor force.

Underemployment Rate: The proportion of underemployed in the labor force.

Visitor: Any person travelling to a place (ie Macao, China) other than that of his/her usual environment for less than 12 consecutive months and whose main purpose of travel is other than the exercise of an activity remunerated from within the place visited.

Hotel Occupancy Rate: The percentage of rooms occupied by guests in the total number of available rooms.

Imports: The entry of any commodities into Macao, China, except Re-imports and Transit.

Exports: The outgoing from Macao, China, of any commodities, excluding Temporary Exports and Transit.

Domestic Exports: The outgoing from Macao, China, of any commodities with the origin of Macao, China.

Re-exports: The outgoing from Macao, China of any commodities previously imported, without any transformation or even with transformation, the commodities did not obtain the origin of Macao, China.

Transit: Commodities passing through or transhiped in Macao, China for the exclusive purpose of transportation and with their next destination mentioned in the attached documents. (In accordance with the newly revised law of external trade (no. 7/2003), starting from September 2003, the trade type named "direct transit" has been changed to "transit").

Country of Origin: The country or territory where the crops were grown, the minerals were mined and the articles were manufactured wholly or partly. If partly, the origin is considered the country or territory responsible for the last phase of manufacture before the merchandise took its final form. Repacking, sorting or mixing are not considered a manufacture operation.

Country of Destination:The final country or territory to which the goods are delivered, whether or not the transport has been interrupted, and without any commercial transaction in the transit country or territory.

Terms of Trade Index¡GThe ratio of the unit value index of exports to that of imports.

Housing Unit: Division(s) or annex of a permanent building. Each housing unit has independent entrance of access to the common area of the building; can be legally registered with the property registry and can be independently transacted.

Gross Floor Area: The sum of area of each floor in a building measured to the outer surface of the outer walls including the area of lobbies, stairs, lift landings and communal space (shared by 2 or more housing units).

Consumer Price Index: Reflects the price change of a representative "basket" of goods and services consumed by families in Macao, China.

Money Supply (M_1): Refers to the sum of currency in circulation and demand deposits.

Money Supply (M_2): Refers to the sum of money supply M_1 and quasi-monetary liabilities that consist of savings deposits, notice deposits, time deposits and certificates of deposits.

Financial Transactions: Comprise financial assets and financial liabilities.

附录一
APPENDIX I

台湾省主要社会经济指标
Main Social and Economic Indicators of Taiwan Province

附录1-1 主要统计指标概况

Summary of Key Statistics

指 标		Item		2001	2002	2003	2004	2005
人口		**Population**						
年末人口	(万人)	Year-end Population	(10 000 persons)	2241	2252	2261	2269	2277
人口自然增加率	(‰)	Natural Grouth Rate	(‰)	5.94	5.29	4.27	3.59	2.92
人口密度	(人/平方公里)	Population Density	(persons/sq.km)	619	622	625	627	629
性别比	(女=100)	Sex Ratio	(Famale=100)	104	104	104	104	103
离婚率	(对/千人)	Divorce Rate	(couple/1000 persons)	2.53	2.73	2.87	2.77	2.75
劳动、就业		**Labour Force and Employment**						
劳动人口		Labour Force	(10 000 persons)	983	997	1008	1024	1037
劳动人口参与率		Labour Force Participation Rate	(%)	57	57	57	58	58
男		Male		68	68	68	68	68
女		Female		46	47	47	48	48
工业占就业人口比重	(%)	Employed Persons at Industry as Percentage of Total(%)		36	35	35	35	36
服务业占就业人口比重	(%)	Employed Persons at Services as Percentage of Total(%)		56	57	58	58	58
失业率		Unemployment Rate	(%)	4.6	5.2	5.0	4.4	4.1
工业及服务业每月人均薪资(新台币元)		Average Monthly Wage Per Capita	(NT$)	41961	41452	42046	43021	43615
工业		Industry		38940	38709	39655	40868	41872
服务业		Services		45020	44222	44452	45064	45234
生活环境		**Habitation**						
平均每人每月用电量	(千瓦小时)	Per Capita Average Monthly Consmption of Electricity	(kwh)	129	130	136	137	146
平均每人每月用水量	(立方米)	Per Capita Average Monthly Consmption of Water	(cu.m)	10.4	10.1	10.0	10.7	10.7
治安		**Law and Order**						
刑案发生率	(件/10万人)	Reported Crimes	(Case/10 0000 persons)	2197	2241	2195	2306	2442
犯罪人口率	(人/10万人)	Number of Offenders	(person/10 0000 persons)	808	827	706	782	913
刑案破获率	(%)	Crimes Uncover	(%)	55	59	59	60	62
少年犯罪人数(12-17岁)	(人)	Young Offenders Between 12 and 17	(person)	16939	15659	12460	10540	9620
火灾事故情况		**Basic Statistics on Fires**						
火灾发生数	(起)	Fires	(case)	13750	13244	8642	6611	5139
死伤人数	(人)	Deaths and Injuries	(person)	1041	857	995	714	664
交通事故情况		**Basic Statistics on Traffic Accidents**						
机动车肇事率	(件/万辆)	Traffic Accidents of Motor Vehicles	(case/10 000 units)	37	49	65	71	80
死亡	(人)	Deaths	(person)	3344	2861	2718	2634	2894
受伤	(人)	Injuries	(person)	80612	109594	156303	179108	203087
参加医疗保险人数	**(万人)**	**Number of People in Medical Insurance**	**(10 000)**	**2165**	**2187**	**2198**	**2213**	**2231**
参加社会保险人数	**(万人)**	**Number of People in Social Insurance**	**(10 000)**					
公务员、教职人员保险		Official and Teacher Insurance		63	63	62	62	59
劳工保险		Labour Insurance		778	786	810	834	854
农民保险		Farmer Insurance		177	175	171	168	165

附录1-1　续表 1　continued

指　　标	Item	2001	2002	2003	2004	2005
工业	**Industry**					
受雇者劳动生产力指数(2001年＝100)	Productivity Index(%) (2001=100)	100.0	109.2	114.7	120.9	126.6
工业生产指数（2001年＝100）	Index of Industrial Production (2001=100)	100.0	107.9	115.6	127.0	132.2
制造业	Manufacturing	100.0	109.4	117.5	129.9	135.1
建筑业	Construction	100.0	79.3	86.4	90.6	101.0
工业生产总值（新台币亿元）	Gross Industry Product (NT$)	80503	86377	94358	110436	113917
商业及对外贸易	**Business and Foreign Trade**					
营利事业家数（万家）	Number of Enterprises (unit)	105.8	107.0	109.7	113.0	116.9
营利事业销售额（新台币亿元）	Sales Revenue (NT$100 million)	235482	246468	273424	319716	342975
贸易值（亿美元）	Total Value of Imports and Exports (USD100 million)					
出口	Exports	1229	1306	1442	1740	1984
进口	Imports	1072	1125	1273	1679	1826
出（入)超	Balance	156	181	170	61	158
	A Favorable(An Unfavorable)Balance of trad					
对日出（入)超（亿美元）	with Japan (USD100 million)	-131	-153	-207	-304	-309
对美出（入)超（亿美元）	with United States (USD100 million)	94	87	91	65	79
对港出（入)超（亿美元）	with Hong Kong (USD100 million)	251	291	266	277	319
外销订单（亿美元）	Order Form (USD100 million)	1357	1510	1700	2151	2564
运输通信	**Transportation and Communication**					
交通运输客运人数（亿人）	Passenger Traffic (100 million persons)					
铁路	Railway	4.8	5.0	4.8	5.2	5.3
公路	Highway	10.9	10.5	9.9	10.1	10.1
航空	Airway					
国内	National	2461	2189	2005	2100	1929
国际	International	1950	2006	1592	2076	2249
高速公路通行车辆数（万辆次）	Vehicles for Motorway Transportation (10000unit-times)	46470	48590	52472	56317	57381
每百人机动车辆数（辆）	Vehicles per 100persons (unit)	77.9	79.5	81.8	84.5	87.2
港埠货物装卸量（万收费吨）	Inward and Outward Movements Cargo (10000 tons)	55287	60671	63558	68850	68793
旅游（万人次）	Tourism (10000person-times)					
出岛旅游人数	International Tourists	719	732	592	778	821
来台湾旅客人数	Visitor Arrivals	262	298	225	295	338
财政、金融	**Public Accounts and Finance**					
赋税实征净额（新台币亿元）	Revenue (NT$100 million)	12578	12256	12528	13873	15674
直接税	Direct Tax	57.0	53.1	54.8	55.8	59.3
间接税	Indirect Tax	43.0	46.9	45.2	44.2	40.7
外汇存底（亿美元）	Foreign Exchange Reserve (USD100 million)	1222.1	1616.6	2066.3	2417.4	2532.9
汇率	Exchange Rate (NT$ to one unit of foreign currency)					
美元	US Dollar	35.04	34.81	34.02	31.78	32.88
日元	Japanese Yen	0.2688	0.2950	0.3199	0.3118	0.2185
货币供应量M_2（新台币亿元）	Money Supply M_2 (NT$100 million)	197245	202470	214336	230012	245075
年增长率（%）	Aerage Annual Growth Rate (%)	4.4	2.6	5.9	7.4	6.6
存款	Deposits	201607	206098	217592	232565	247091
放款与投资	Loans and Investment	160227	155113	159248	179646	193449

附录1-1　续表 2 continued

指　标	Item	2001	2002	2003	2004	2005
财政、金融	**Public Accounts and Finance**					
重贴现率　（年息百分比率）	Rediscount Rate　(% annual)	2.125	1.625	1.375	1.750	2.250
股价指数（1966年＝100）	Stock Price Index (1966=100)	4907	5226	5162	6034	6092
国际收支平衡　（亿美元）	Balance of Payments (USD100 million)	173.5	336.6	370.9	266.0	200.6
经常帐	Current Account	178.9	256.3	285.7	186.6	161.2
资本帐	Capital Account	-1.6	-1.4	-0.9	-0.8	-1.2
金融帐	Financial Account	-3.8	87.5	62.9	68.3	17.2
物价年增率　（%）	**Price Annual Growth Rate　(%)**					
批发	Wholesale Trade Price	-1.3	0.1	2.5	7.0	0.6
消费者	Consumer Price	-0.01	-0.2	-0.3	1.6	2.3
进口	Imports Price	-1.3	0.4	5.2	8.6	2.4
出口	Exports Price	0.3	-1.5	-1.5	1.6	-2.5
国民经济核算　（新台币亿元）	**National Account　(NT$100 million)**					
本地居民生产总值	Gross National Product　(GNP)	96980	100030	101814	105848	114255
本地生产总值	Gross Domestic Product　(GDP)	95066	97488	98476	102059	111316
民间最终消费支出	Household Final Consumption Expenditure	60426	61495	61866	64283	69384
固定资本形成总额	Gross Fixed Capital Formation	17818	17283	17244	20530	22697
商品及服务出口	Exports of Goods and Services	48398	52459	57220	67115	69883
减：商品及服务进口	Less: Imports of Goods and Services	42984	45235	50122	63235	65410
经济增长率　(%)	Economic Growth Rate　(%)	-2.2	3.6	3.2	5.7	4.1
农业	Agriculture	-2.1	4.7	-0.2	-7.1	-4.1
工业	Industry	-6.0	5.0	4.7	8.3	5.2
服务业	Services	-0.1	2.8	2.6	4.8	3.8
产业结构　(%)	Industry Structure　(%)					
农业	Agriculture	2.0	1.9	1.8	1.7	1.8
工业	Industry	31.1	31.0	30.4	29.5	24.6
服务业	Services	67.0	67.1	67.8	68.7	73.6
平均本地居民生产总值（新台币元）	Per Capita GNP at Current Market Prices　(NT$)	435321	466636	452719	468956	504480
平均本地居民生产总值　（美元）	Per Capita GNP at Current Market Prices　(USD)	12876	12916	13157	14032	15676
国民储蓄总额　（新台币亿元）	Gross Deposits　(NT$100 million)	23228	25347	26434	27680	28577
储蓄率　(%)	Deposit Rate　(%)	24.0	25.3	26.0	26.2	25.0

附录1-2　面积和人口主要指标

Main Indicators of Area and Population

资源来源：台湾省《统计月报》（以下各表同）。
Source: Monthly Statistics Bulletin, Taiwan Province. The same as in the following tables.

项　　目	Item	2001	2002	2003	2004	2005
面积　(万平方公里)	Area (10 000 sq.km)	3.6	3.6	3.6	3.6	3.6
年底人口数　(万人)	Year-end Population (10 000 persons)	2240.6	2252.1	2260.5	2268.9	2277.0
男	Male	1144.2	1148.5	1151.5	1154.2	1156.2
女	Female	1096.4	1103.5	1108.9	1114.8	1120.8
出生率　(‰)	Crude Birth Rate (‰)	11.65	11.02	10.06	9.56	9.06
死亡率　(‰)	Crude Death Rate (‰)	5.7	5.7	5.8	6.0	6.1
婴儿死亡率　(‰)	Infant Mortality Rate (‰)	6.33	6.77	6.41	6.20	5.99
妇女生育率　(‰)	Fertility Rate (‰)	41	39	36	34	
人口自然增长率　(‰)	Natural Population Growth Rate (‰)	5.94	5.29	4.27	3.59	2.92
结婚率　(‰)	Marriage Rate (‰)	7.63	7.69	7.60	5.80	6.21
离婚率　(‰)	Divorce Rate (‰)	2.53	2.73	2.87	2.77	2.75
平均期望寿命　(岁)	Life Expectancy at Birth (years)					
男	Male	72.80	72.45	73.34	73.58	73.82
女	Female	78.48	78.39	79.33	79.63	79.92
人口的年龄构成　(%)	Age-specific Distribution (%)					
0-14岁	0-14	20.81	20.42	19.83	19.34	18.70
15-64岁	15-64	70.39	70.56	70.94	71.19	71.56
65岁及以上	65 and Over	8.81	9.02	9.24	9.48	9.74
性别比（女=100）	Sex Ratio (Female=100)	104.36	104.08	103.84	103.53	103.16
人口密度（人/平方公里）	Population Density (persons/sq.km)	619.1	622.3	624.6	627.0	629.20

附录1-3　劳动力和就业状况

Labor Force and Employment

项　　目	Item	2001	2002	2003	2004	2005
劳动力总人数　(万人)	Labor Force (10 000 persons)	983.2	996.9	1007.6	1024.0	1037.1
男	Male	585.5	589.6	590.4	596.8	601.2
女	Female	397.7	407.4	417.2	427.2	435.9
就业人数　(万人)	Employment (10 000 persons)	938.3	945.4	957.3	978.6	994.2
男	Male	555.3	554.7	557.9	568.0	575.3
女	Female	383.0	390.7	399.4	410.6	419.0
就业人数部门构成　(%)	Distribution of Employment by Industry (%)	100.0	100.0	100.0	100.0	100.0
农、林、渔、牧业	Agriculture, Forestry, Fishery and Hunting	7.5	7.5	7.3	6.6	5.9
工业	Industry					
采矿业	Mining and Quarrying	0.1	0.1	0.1	0.1	0.1
制造业	Manufacturing	27.6	27.1	27.1	27.3	27.4
电、煤气、水	Electricity, Gas, Water	0.4	0.4	0.4	0.4	0.3
建筑业	Construction	7.9	7.7	7.3	7.5	8.0
服务业	Services					
批发、零售业	Wholesale and Retail Trade	17.9	17.9	17.7	17.6	17.4
运输、仓储和通信业	Transport, Storage, Communications	5.2	5.0	5.1	5.0	4.8
金融、保险业	Financing, Insurance	4.0	4.0	3.9	3.9	4.1
教育服务业	Education	5.1	5.2	5.3	5.4	5.5
住宿及餐饮业	Hotels and Restaurants	5.6	6.1	6.1	6.2	6.3
公共行政业	Public Administration	3.5	3.5	3.9	3.8	3.5
其他	Others	15.2	15.6	15.9	16.2	16.7
失业人数　(万人)	Unemployment (10 000 persons)	45.0	51.5	50.3	45.4	42.8
失业率　(%)	Unemployment Rate (%)	4.6	5.2	5.0	4.4	4.1

附录1-4　本地居民生产总值

Gross National Product

年　份 Year	本地居民生产总值 Gross National Product			人均本地居民生产总值 Per Capita Gross National Product	
	新台币亿元 NT $100 million	比上年增长 % Annual Growth Rate over the Preceding Year %	亿美元① USD 100 million①	新台币元 NT $	美元 USD
1992	54598	7.3	2170	264338	10506
1993	60322	6.7	2286	264196	10011
1994	65710	6.8	2483	286191	10812
1995	71291	6.3	2691	336042	12686
1996	77876	5.9	2836	364115	13260
1997	84174	6.3	2933	390103	13592
1998	90066	4.3	2692	413582	12360
1999	93758	5.6	2905	427097	13235
2000	98033	6.4	3139	443087	14188
2001	96980	-1.1	2868	435321	12876
2002	100030	3.1	2893	446636	12916
2003	101814	1.8	2959	452719	13157
2004	105848	4.1	3167	468956	14032
2005	114255	2.5	3550	504480	15676

注：①按当年价格计算。
Note: ①At current market prices.

附录1-5　本地生产总值支出构成

Expenditures on Gross Domestic Product

单位：%　　　　(%)

年　份 Year	本地生产总值（新台币亿元） Gross Domestic Product (NT$ 100 million)	居民消费 Household Consumption Expenditure	政府消费 Government Consumption Expenditure	固定资本形成总额 Gross Fixed Capital Formation	存货增加 Change in Stocks	货物及服务出口 Exports of Goods and Services	减：货物及服务进口 Minus: Imports of Goods and Services
1992	53376.9	56.0	17.0	23.2	1.7	43.4	41.3
1993	59183.8	56.6	15.6	25.2	1.0	44.1	42.5
1994	64636.0	58.3	14.6	24.6	0.8	43.7	42.0
1995	70179.3	58.8	14.2	25.0	0.4	48.0	46.3
1996	76781.3	59.1	14.3	22.5	0.7	47.4	44.0
1997	83287.8	59.7	14.4	22.8	1.5	48.3	46.2
1998	89389.7	59.7	14.3	23.5	1.4	47.8	46.7
1999	92899.3	60.7	13.2	22.9	0.5	48.3	45.5
2000	96633.9	61.9	12.9	23.5	-0.6	54.4	52.1
2001	95066.2	63.6	13.1	18.7	-1.1	50.9	45.2
2002	97488.1	63.1	12.6	17.7	-0.9	53.8	46.4
2003	98475.6	62.8	12.8	17.5	-0.4	58.1	50.9
2004	102058.9	63.0	12.5	20.1	0.6	65.8	62.0
2005	111316.0	62.3	13.4	20.4	-0.2	62.8	58.8

附录1-6　本地生产总值部门构成
Gross Domestic Product by Kind of Economic Activity

单位：% (%)

年份 Year	本地生产总值（新台币亿元） Gross Domestic Product (NT$ 100 million)	农业 Agriculture Forestry, Hunting and Fishery	工业 Industry	制造业 Manufacturing	水、电、煤气业 Electricity Gas & Water	建筑业 Construction
1992	53376.9	3.60	39.87	31.70	2.71	4.98
1993	59183.8	3.64	39.35	20.56	2.71	5.28
1994	64636.0	3.51	37.71	28.99	2.64	5.57
1995	70179.3	3.40	36.37	27.92	2.58	5.43
1996	76781.3	3.19	35.71	27.92	2.48	4.91
1997	83287.8	2.55	35.33	27.75	2.37	4.74
1998	89389.7	2.48	34.67	27.42	2.32	4.41
1999	92899.3	2.57	33.24	26.57	2.26	3.91
2000	96633.9	2.09	32.52	26.48	2.17	3.46
2001	95066.2	1.96	31.17	25.60	2.21	2.98
2002	97488.1	1.86	31.36	26.16	2.21	2.58
2003	98475.6	1.80	30.57	25.77	2.22	2.25
2004	102058.9	1.74	29.54	25.53	1.93	1.72
2005	111315.8	1.80	24.64	21.13	1.59	1.61

附录1-6　续表　continued

单位：% (%)

年份 Year	服务业 Services	批发、零售及餐饮业 Wholesale and Retail Trade, and Restaurants	金融保险 Finance, Insurance	不动产及租赁业 Estate & Tenancy	政府部门服务业 Government Services
1992	56.53	14.98			11.02
1993	57.01	15.30			10.49
1994	58.77	15.61			10.27
1995	60.14	16.35			10.35
1996	61.10	15.48	9.15	10.62	10.36
1997	62.13	15.85	10.39	10.32	10.21
1998	62.85	16.35	10.20	10.21	10.04
1999	64.20	16.99	10.41	10.26	10.14
2000	65.38	17.69	10.31	10.05	10.21
2001	66.87	17.58	10.49	10.32	10.65
2002	66.79	17.72	11.11	10.04	10.49
2003	67.63	18.14	11.40	10.05	10.88
2004	68.72	19.10	11.57	9.90	10.61
2005	73.56	18.19	10.87	8.32	11.30

附录1-7 农业生产指数

Index of Agricultural Production

(2001年=100) (2001=100)

年份 Year	总指数 Total	种植业 Crops	林业 Forestry	畜牧业 Livestock	渔业 Fishery
1981	79.1	113.1	704.6	49.3	73.8
1991	100.7	109.6	223.6	92.5	100.2
1993	104.3	112.3	140.9	98.9	102.8
1994	101.1	108.3	106.3	104.5	90.6
1995	104.8	110.5	124.1	109.7	94.4
1996	105.0	110.2	102.2	114.2	90.0
1997	103.6	111.9	115.0	105.7	91.8
1998	97.9	102.7	145.7	97.9	91.9
1999	99.1	109.7	122.4	94.3	90.0
2000	101.2	104.5	120.8	99.7	98.3
2001	100.0	100.0	100.0	100.0	100.0
2002	104.1	105.5	111.6	98.1	108.1
2003	104.3	102.7	117.1	96.2	115.8
2004	99.9	97.6	121.3	96.1	107.5

附录1-8 主要农产品产量

Output of Major Crops

单位：万吨 (10 000 tons)

年份 Year	稻米 Rice	槟榔 Pinang	菠萝 Pineapple	芒果 Mango	甘蔗 Sugarcane	茶叶 Tea	花生 Peanuts	香蕉 Banana
1991	181.9				453.6	2.1	8.4	19.7
1992	162.8				585.8	2.0	7.6	19.6
1993	182.0	13.7	27.7	21.7	480.3	2.1	7.6	21.3
1994	167.9	13.2	25.2	19.1	550.4	2.4	8.1	18.4
1995	168.7	15.6	25.6	20.8	486.2	2.1	9.2	17.3
1996	157.7	16.0	27.4	20.2	419.0	2.3	8.0	14.1
1997	166.3	15.6	30.1	21.0	390.2	2.4	8.4	20.5
1998	148.9	17.3	31.6	18.7	355.9	2.3	6.8	21.6
1999	155.9	17.0	34.8	20.7	325.6	2.1	6.7	21.3
2000	154.0	17.0	35.8	21.1	289.4	2.0	7.9	19.8
2001	139.6	16.5	38.9	21.3	218.0	2.0	5.6	20.5
2002	146.1	16.2	41.6	21.3	197.3	2.0	7.7	22.7
2003	133.8	16.0	44.8	22.1	169.6	2.1	7.3	22.3
2004	116.5	14.3	45.8	18.2	112.9	2.0	6.8	19.0

附录1-9 工业生产指数

Index of Industrial Production

(2001年=100) (2001=100)

年份 Year	总指数 General	矿业 Mining	制造业 Manufacturing	电、煤气、水 Electricity, Gas & Water	建筑业 Construction
1996	86.09	126.55	84.67	77.73	146.79
1997	91.39	126.49	90.79	82.49	123.07
1998	94.49	118.72	93.68	88.79	123.75
1999	101.45	109.20	100.98	91.80	131.93
2000	108.47	99.95	109.12	98.89	112.60
2001	100.00	100.00	100.00	100.00	100.00
2002	107.92	108.28	109.39	103.31	79.34
2003	115.58	100.24	117.46	107.20	86.38
2004	126.96	95.81	129.85	110.36	90.64
2005	132.20	86.38	135.05	114.46	100.95

附录1-10　主要工业产品产量

Output of Major Industrial Products

年　份 Year	食品 (万吨) Food (10 000 tons)	饮料 (万升) Beverage (10 000 litre)	饲料 (万吨) Feed (10 000 tons)	各种成衣 (万打) Wearing Apparel (10 000 dozens)	纸板 (万吨) Cardboard (10 000 tons)	人造纤维 (万吨) Yarn of man-made staple (10 000 tons)	轮胎 (万条) Tyre (10 000 units)
1995				3775.4		258.3	1218.0
1996				3329.9	321.3	276.6	1332.4
1997	48.0	47745.0	630.1	3230.0	325.4	304.3	1446.0
1998	38.8	51157.2	550.1	3348.0	297.5	319.8	1573.0
1999	38.6	46103.2	582.0	3175.6	307.4	325.5	1702.4
2000	39.4	43689.7	539.5	2760.5	323.4	330.8	1775.8
2001	37.1	44224.1	545.6	2188.5	259.1	314.9	1679.0
2002	38.4	43499.8	523.3	1858.1	323.5	335.8	1932.6
2003	37.4	44741.7	510.8	1597.8	340.4	333.3	2261.9
2004	36.8	39974.5	482.9	1473.1	355.5	334.2	2399.3
2005	41.9	40399.9	483.2	1134.9	337.8	289.7	

附录1-10　续表 1 continued

年　份 Year	瓷砖 (万平方米) Tile (10 000 sq.m)	水泥 (万吨) Cement (10 000 tons)	钢坯 (万吨) Billet (10 000 tons)	可携式电脑 (万台) Notebook Computer (10 000 units)	监视器 (万台) Monitor (10 000 units)	主机板 (万片) Mainboard (10 000 units)
1995	13170.4	2247.8			1775.1	1595.3
1996	10969.3	2153.7	1277.3	378.6	1866.9	2343.2
1997	10666.2	2152.2	1552.3	466.9	2046.1	3110.3
1998	10172.4	1965.2	1659.4	702.0	1640.6	4392.4
1999	9234.9	1828.3	1522.2	995.3	932.1	5424.1
2000	7153.2	1757.2	1619.1	1306.0	569.2	6392.9
2001	4726.0	1812.8	1639.9	1413.0	675.3	5528.0
2002	3959.8	1936.3	1742.3	1446.0	510.5	4914.5
2003	4610.8	1847.4	1763.8	1051.2	421.5	4671.5
2004	5229.9	1905.0	1786.9	687.2	339.3	3098.6
2005	5308.5	1989.1	1715.1	456.0	207.6	2565.3

附录1-10　续表 2 continued

年　份 Year	手机 (万部) Mobile Phone (10 000 units)	印刷电路板 (万平方英尺) Printing Circuit Board (10000 sq. foot)	电子电容器 (亿只) Electron Capacitor (100 million units)	汽车 (万辆) Car (10 000 units)	数控机床 (台) NC Machine Tools (units)	发电量 (亿千瓦小时) Electric Power (100 million K.W.H.)
1995			423.5	39.0	3999	1178.6
1996	0.2	48731	450.4	36.7	4337	1350.0
1997	2.5	64202	570.9	37.6	4439	1436.6
1998	7.9	79275	683.3	40.3	5244	1554.5
1999	77.7	94662	824.8	34.5	4325	1605.7
2000	476.1	120547	1144.0	37.1	5665	1751.7
2001	965.4	92541	1216.7	26.9	3714	1783.6
2002	2151.4	118005	1499.6	33.0	4215	1879.1
2003	3067.7	127722	1990.9	39.2	5288	1971.4
2004	3268.2	135969	2339.8	42.7	7267	2060.8
2005	3610.7	121146	2375.7	44.5	7917	2142.2

附录1-11 能源生产和消费

Production and Consumption of Energy

项　目	Item	2000	2001	2002	2003	2004	2005
供给量总计	**Total Supply**						
（亿升标准油）	**(100 000 kl oil equivalent)**	**1050.4**	**1085.2**	**1132.3**	**1212.2**	**1340.6**	**1353.5**
供给量比重　(%)	Distribution of Supply　(%)	100.0	100.0	100.0	100.0	100.0	100.0
煤炭	Coal	31.1	32.3	33.1	32.6	32.5	31.9
石油	Petroleum	50.9	50.4	49.3	50.8	51.0	51.3
天然气	Natural Gas	6.8	7.1	7.6	7.3	8.0	8.0
水力发电	Hydraulic Power	2.1	2.1	1.4	1.4	1.2	1.5
核能发电	Nuclear Energy Source	9.1	8.1	8.7	8.0	7.3	7.3
消费量总计	**Total Consumption**						
（亿升标准油）	**(100 000 kl oil equivalent)**	**906.4**	**948.3**	**1003.1**	**1034.1**	**1077.9**	**1080.5**
分部门消费比重 (%)	Distribution of Consumption (%)	100.0	100.0	100.0	100.0	100.0	100.0
能源	Energy	6.7	6.7	6.2	6.2	6.3	6.7
运输	Transportation	16.3	15.4	15.2	14.8	14.9	15.3
工业	Industry	48.4	50.4	51.6	51.1	51.5	50.0
农业	Agriculture	1.6	1.6	1.5	1.6	1.6	1.5
住宅	Residence	12.4	12.1	11.7	11.8	11.4	12.3
商业	Commerce	5.8	5.8	5.6	5.8	5.8	6.2
其他	Other	6.1	6.2	6.2	6.7	6.6	6.2
非能源消费	Non-energy Use	2.6	1.8	2.0	2.1	1.7	1.7
平均每人能源消费量	**Per Capita Energy Consumption**						
（千升标准油）	**(kl oil equivalent)**	**4.01**	**4.2**	**4.4**	**4.6**	**4.8**	**4.7**

附录1-12 按用途分的批准动工的建筑面积

Floor Space of Authorized Construction Projects by the Purpose

单位：万平方米　　(10 000 sq.m)

年　份 Year	总计 Total	住宅用 Residential	商业用 Stores & Mercantile	工业用 Industrial	办公用 Office	其他用 Other
1992	3692	1566	898	464	251	153
1993	4754	2177	1264	482	237	203
1994	5816	2858	1536	539	216	236
1995	5526	2646	1534	440	290	268
1996	4571	2063	1086	393	249	345
1997	3846	1459	964	378	290	342
1998	3868	1392	922	461	247	406
1999	4124	1356	894	681	409	360
2000	3502	1037	621	688	304	418
2001	3117	819	438	611	243	585
2002	2439	792	320	331	177	407
2003	2650	1001	436	287	266	330
2004	2787	1176	453	256	144	404

附录1-13 铁路和公路客货运量

Railway and Highway Passenger and Freight Traffic

年 份 Year	铁路 Railway 客运量(万人) Passenger Traffic (10 000 persons)	客运周转量(万人公里) Passenger Kilometers (10 000 p-km)	货运量(万吨) Freight Traffic (10 000 tons)	货物周转量(万吨公里) Freight Ton-kilometers (10 000 ton-km)	公路 Highway 客运量(万人) Passenger Traffic (10 000 persons)	客运周转量(万人公里) Passenger Kilometers (10 000 p-km)	货运量(万吨) Freight Traffic (10 000 tons)	货物周转量(万吨公里) Freight Ton-kilometers (10 000 ton-km)
1991	13778	862101	2626	196114	150248	2498117	25430	1181376
1992	14987	935740	2819	213996	142089	2422747	26796	1221989
1993	15803	955227	3058	201778	135556	1941098	30167	1286684
1994	16099	951518	3123	200674	128921	1799516	31340	1309140
1995	16092	949939	3012	189954	120345	1615089	29100	1249150
1996	17100	903200	2741	158486	116716	1542116	28940	1199090
1997	19700	950700	2657	151385	116280	1441704	27700	1216500
1998	23300	1030500	2656	140434	115483	1429848	36000	1742600
1999	31000	1102000	2600	131400	114900	1424673	35000	1847000
2000	46000	1262400	2230	117900	110400	1465716	34400	1818200
2001	47600	1226900	1930	101000	109100	1523654	30000	1773500
2002	50000	1214700	1820	94100	105400	1574680	28900	1773100
2003	47800	1117800	1670	86400	98800	1484700	30400	1816400
2004	52000	1205100	1700	90900	101200	1538300	34500	2042900
2005	53100	1225500	1930	98200	100700	1603900	35400	2053600

附录1-14 邮政及电信营运量

Telecommunication Services

项 目	Item	2001	2002	2003	2004	2005
邮政	**Post**					
函件 (亿件)	Letters (100 million pieces)					
收寄	Received	28.9	28.8	27.3	28.2	28.1
投递	Mailing	33.1	33.2	32.2	32.8	32.6
包裹 (万件)	Parcels (10 000 pieces)					
收寄	Received	1063.1	797.3	895.3	1210.8	1576.7
投递	Mailing	1095.2	820.9	918.1	1266.8	1672.0
电信	**Telecommunications**					
市内电话用户数 (万户)	Number of Local(Urban) Telephone Subscribers (10 000 Subscribers)	1285.8	1309.9	1335.5	1353.0	1361.5
公共电话话机数 (万部)	Number of Public Telephones (10 000 Subscribers)	13.9	13.5	13.2	12.6	11.9
移动电话用户数 (万户)	Number of Mobile Telephones Subscribers (10 000 Subscribers)	2163.3	2390.5	2509.0	2152.8	1987.6
无线寻呼机用户数 (万户)	Number of Subscribers of Pagering Services (10 000 Subscribers)	175.6	159.8	141.5	133.6	109.5
数字式低功率无线电话用户数 (万户)	Digital low-power Wireless Telephones Subscribers (10 000 Subscribers)	21.1	52.1	63.4	78.8	97.8
整体服务数位网络用户数 (万户)	Number of Subscribers of Local Area Network (10 000 Subscribers)	4.2	3.9	4.8	5.0	5.8
国际互联网用户数 (万户)	Number of Subscribers of Internet Services (10 000 Subscribers)	623.2	745.4	782.8	803.6	727.1
国际电话去话分钟数 (万分钟)	International Call (10 000 minutes)	151442	215391	307674	302469	346829

附录1-15　商品进出口贸易总额

Total Imports and Exports

年　份 Year	按新台币计算（亿元）(NT $ 100 million)			按美元计算（亿美元）(USD 100 million)		
	进出口总额 Total	出口额 Exports	进口额 Imports	进出口总额 Total	出口额 Exports	进口额 Imports
1988	31550	17320	14230	1100	610	500
1989	31340	17480	13860	1190	660	520
1990	32750	18030	14720	1220	670	550
1991	37320	20410	16910	1390	760	630
1992	38650	20480	18170	1530	810	720
1993	42740	22390	20350	1620	850	770
1994	47180	24560	22620	1780	930	850
1995	56920	29500	27430	2150	1120	1040
1996	59920	31770	28150	2180	1160	1020
1997	67580	34820	32760	2370	1220	1140
1998	71970	36930	35040	2160	1110	1050
1999	74930	39170	35760	2330	1220	1110
2000	89850	46160	43690	2880	1480	1400
2001	77570	41380	36190	2300	1230	1070
2002	84012	45075	38937	2431	1306	1125
2003	93361	49524	43837	2714	1442	1272
2004	114454	58178	56276	3419	1740	1679
2005	122518	63746	58772	3810	1984	1826

附录1-16 商品进口来源和出口去向

Origin of Imports and Destination of Exports

单位：亿美元 (USD 100 million)

项目	Item	2001	2002	2003	2004	2005
商品进口来源	**Imports (Major Origin)**					
中国香港	Hong Kong, China	18.5	17.4	17.3	20.9	21.1
日本	Japan	258.5	272.8	326.4	436.3	460.6
韩国	Korea, Rep.	67.1	77.1	86.9	116.3	132.4
新加坡	Singapore	33.7	35.4	38.6	42.9	49.6
马来西亚	Malaysia	42.1	41.5	47.5	54.1	51.9
泰国	Thailand	21.8	21.7	23.7	27.7	28.9
法国	France	21.3	15.5	16.3	20.9	25.4
德国	Germany	42.5	44.2	49.6	58.3	61.8
意大利	Italy	10.8	10.9	11.3	13.4	14.5
英国	United Kingdom	14.4	13.6	14.2	17.3	17.1
加拿大	Canada	10.0	9.5	10.8	12.0	13.2
美国	United States	182.3	180.9	168.2	216.3	211.7
澳大利亚	Australia	30.9	28.3	27.3	34.2	47.3
印度尼西亚	Indonesia	25.2	25.9	29.2	41.1	45.4
菲律宾	Philippines	32.5	36.5	30.8	30.6	28.0
越南	Vietnam	4.2	4.5	4.5	6.0	7.0
沙特阿拉伯	Saudi Arabia	27.5	24.1	42.8	55.6	74.7
荷兰	Netherlands	15.2	14.4	13.0	21.8	20.7
商品出口去向	**Exports (Major Destination)**					
中国香港	Hong Kong, China	269.6	308.5	283.5	298.3	340.4
日本	Japan	127.6	119.8	119.1	132.0	151.1
韩国	Korea, Rep.	32.8	38.7	45.7	53.5	58.9
新加坡	Singapore	40.5	43.8	49.8	63.4	80.3
马来西亚	Malaysia	30.6	31.3	30.5	40.7	42.8
泰国	Thailand	21.3	22.9	25.7	32.2	38.2
法国	France	11.7	11.2	12.5	15.7	14.5
德国	Germany	44.8	38.4	42.1	45.1	44.6
意大利	Italy	12.6	12.5	14.6	17.3	18.0
英国	United Kingdom	33.3	29.1	28.8	33.8	32.6
加拿大	Canada	15.6	15.3	14.7	16.4	16.9
美国	United States	276.5	267.6	259.4	281.2	291.1
澳大利亚	Australia	13.6	15.9	18.8	22.4	23.9
印度尼西亚	Indonesia	14.8	14.6	15.1	18.7	23.6
菲律宾	Philippines	21.5	19.7	23.0	38.9	43.3
越南	Vietnam	17.3	22.9	26.6	34.3	41.0
沙特阿拉伯	Saudi Arabia	3.5	3.4	3.6	4.3	5.0
荷兰	Netherlands	42.3	37.7	41.3	47.1	44.0

附录1-17 出口与进口商品分类

Composition of Exports and Imports

单位：亿美元 (USD 100 million)

年份 Year	出口 Exports 出口额 Total	农产品 Agricultural Products	农产加工品 Processed Agricultural Products	工业产品 Industrial Products	进口 Imports 进口额 Total	资本设备 Capital Goods	原材料 Agricultural & Industrial Raw Materials	消费品 Consumer Goods
1992	814.7	5.1	29.8	779.9	720.1	128.7	498.7	92.7
1993	850.9	4.7	30.1	816.1	770.6	130.1	541.4	99.1
1994	930.5	4.6	33.5	892.4	853.5	136.1	603.0	114.4
1995	1116.6	4.8	38.0	1073.8	1035.5	168.7	745.6	121.2
1996	1159.4	4.7	36.2	1118.6	1023.7	183.6	706.4	133.8
1997	1220.8	3.8	21.7	1195.3	1144.3	217.4	771.3	155.6
1998	1105.8	3.2	16.3	1086.3	1046.7	243.0	667.7	135.9
1999	1215.9	3.8	15.7	1196.4	1106.9	292.4	709.8	104.7
2000	1483.2	3.6	17.5	1462.2	1400.1	392.6	897.8	109.8
2001	1228.7	3.0	16.6	1209.1	1072.4	268.6	704.8	98.9
2002	1306.0	3.5	17.0	1285.5	1125.3	259.2	761.7	104.3
2003	1441.8	3.8	17.7	1420.3	1272.5	260.3	896.7	115.5
2004	1740.1	3.8	20.8	1715.5	1678.9	359.9	1181.5	137.5
2005	1984.3	3.8	21.1	1959.5	1826.2	360.5	1307.9	157.7

附录1-18 旅游人数

Visitor Arrivals and International Tourists

单位：万人次 (10 000 person-times)

项目	Item	1999	2000	2001	2002	2003	2004	2005
总计	**Total**	**241.1**	**262.4**	**261.7**	**297.8**	**224.8**	**295.0**	**337.8**
华侨	Overseas Chinese	29.6	31.3	32.5	62.4	43.6	52.2	58.0
外国人	Foreign Tourists	211.5	231.1	229.2	235.4	181.2	242.8	279.8

附录1-19 居民消费价格指数

Consumer Price Indices

(2001年=100) (2001=100)

年份 Year	总指数 General Index	食品类 Food	服装 Clothing	居住 Housing	交通 Transportation	医药保健 Medicines and Medical Care	教育娱乐 Education and Entertainment	杂项 Miscellaneous
1995	93.2	94.0	104.9	95.4	95.3	87.5	81.1	95.5
1996	96.1	97.7	107.5	97.4	96.5	89.0	87.0	96.4
1997	97.0	97.0	108.3	98.5	97.6	91.1	90.2	97.3
1998	98.6	101.3	102.8	99.7	96.6	91.9	93.1	98.3
1999	98.8	100.5	101.4	99.8	95.9	95.1	95.1	99.8
2000	100.0	100.9	101.7	100.3	99.0	98.7	97.9	100.4
2001	100.0	100.0	100.0	100.0	100.0	100.0	100.0	100.0
2002	99.8	99.8	100.6	98.9	97.8	101.3	100.1	105.1
2003	99.5	99.7	102.0	97.8	98.4	104.7	98.8	104.7
2004	101.1	104.1	105.2	97.7	100.4	106.7	98.9	105.2
2005	103.5	111.8	105.1	98.1	101.7	111.0	98.7	105.0

附录1-20 各级政府财政收入净额
Net Revenue of Treasury

单位：新台币亿元 (NT $ 100 million)

项　目	Item	2000	2001	2002	2003
总　计	**Total**	**27849**	**18963**	**17821**	**18482**
课税收入	Tax	18525	12003	11909	12201
独占及专卖收入	Revenue from Monopoly	773	576	3	
营业盈余及事业收入	Revenue from Enterprises and Institutions	4584	3466	2609	3401
其他收入	Other Revenue	3967	2919	3300	2880
财产利息收入	Revenue from Profit of Public Properties	266	203	129	126
规费收入	Fees	1123	769	1252	764
罚款及赔偿收入	Revenue from Fines & Indemnities	597	420	448	437
捐赠及赠与收入	Receipts from Donations and Contributions	27	37	21	51
财产收回及售价收入	Return of Properties and Sales of Public Properties	1053	872	813	910
杂项收入	Miscellaneous Revenues	901	617	694	591

附录1-21 各级政府财政支出净额
Net Expenditures of Treasury

单位：新台币亿元 (NT $ 100 million)

项　目	Item	1999	2000	2001	2002	2003
总　计	**Total**	**20500**	**31409**	**22713**	**21390**	**22062**
一般行政支出	General Administration	2791	4680	3287	3254	3315
国防支出	National Defense	2866	3578	2476	2252	2277
教育科学文化支出	Expenditures on Education, Science and Culture	4291	6551	4301	4380	4612
经济发展支出	Economic Development	3511	4749	3988	4054	4048
社会福利支出	Social Welfare	2805	5318	3970	3237	3451
社区发展及环境保护支出	Community Development and Environment Protect	903	1061	1091	657	911
退休抚恤支出	Retire Pension	1806	2651	1757	1710	1734
债务支出	Obligations	1409	2704	1716	1710	1593
杂项支出	Miscellaneous	118	119	127	136	120

附录1-22 政　府　公　债
Government Bonds

单位：新台币亿元 (NT $ 100 million)

年　份 Year	总计 Total			台湾省级 Taiwan Provincial			省级及“院”辖市级 Sub-provincial and Municipal Gov't		
	发行额 Issues	偿还额 Redemption	余额 Outstanding	发行额 Issues	偿还额 Redemption	余额 Outstanding	发行额 Issues	偿还额 Redemption	余额 Outstanding
1993	2373	665	72223	2100	475	6135	273	189	1087
1994	1480	725	7976	1480	514	7102		211	876
1995	1250	556	8671	1250	300	8051		256	620
1996	2450	1159	9963	2250	940	9361	200	219	601
1997	1740	1354	10348	1600	1208	9754	140	147	594
1998	1460	1369	10439	1200	1260	9694	260	109	745
1999	2828	815	12452	2828	703	11819		112	633
2000	3625	1274	14803	3465	1194	14090	160	80	713
2001	4570	790	18583	4370	734	17736	200	56	857
2002	4362	800	22145	4262	747	21241	100	53	904
2003	4548	808	25885	4548	752	25036		55	849
2004	5070	2428	28527	4650	2394	27292	420	34	1234
2005	4690	1794	31422	4450	1612	30131	240	183	1292

附录1-23 主要金融指标

Principal Financial Indicators

年份 Year	货币供应额(新台币亿元) Money Supply (NT $100 million)	流动性负债(新台币亿元) Liquid Liabilities (NT $100 million)	储备货币(新台币亿元) Reserve Money (NT $100 million)	存款(新台币亿元) Deposits (NT $100 million)	放款与投资(新台币亿元) Loans & Investments (NT $100 million)	再贴现率(年息%) Rediscount Rate (% annual)	汇率(卖出价)(新台币/美元) Exchange Rates of Selling (NT $/USD)
1991	21584	82874	12653	75728	61897	6.25	25.80
1992	24258	97510	14119	90767	79605	5.63	25.47
1993	27971	113536	15014	104638	95110	5.50	26.72
1994	31393	129901	16688	120405	109556	5.50	26.26
1995	31631	142621	16381	131469	121003	5.50	27.32
1996	34261	156464	16525	142606	130518	5.00	27.54
1997	37153	170188	16413	154213	140847	5.25	32.62
1998	38548	185813	16651	166969	151766	4.75	32.26
1999	45072	206382	16433	180642	156750	4.50	31.44
2000	44921	223182	15834	193087	161757	4.63	33.06
2001	50259	241463	14561	201607	160227	2.13	35.04
2002	54916	257923	15688	206098	159257	1.63	34.81
2003	65528	273890	16194	217469	165351	1.38	34.02
2004	73680	299771	17177	232565	179640	1.75	31.78
2005	78711	325206	17585	247091	193449	2.25	32.88

附录1-24 股票交易

Transactions of Listed Stock

单位：新台币亿元 (NT $ 100 million)

年份 Year	上市股票 Listed Stock			股票成交额 Total Trading Value	股票指数(年平均)(1966年=100) Stock Price Index (year average) (1966=100)
	公司数(家) Number (unit)	总面值 Total Par Value	总市值 Total Market Value		
1992	256	7360	25460	59170	4271.63
1993	285	8910	51450	90570	4214.78
1994	313	10710	65020	188120	6252.99
1995	347	13250	51080	101520	5543.75
1996	382	16270	75240	129080	6003.72
1997	404	20660	96960	372410	8410.56
1998	437	26900	83770	296190	7737.68
1999	462	30540	117870	292920	7426.68
2000	531	36300	81910	305270	7847.21
2001	584	40630	102480	183550	4907.43
2002	638	44097	90949	218740	5225.61
2003	669	47051	128691	203332	5161.90
2004	697	50313	139891	238754	6033.78
2005	691	53900	156339	188189	6092.27

附录1-25 入学率和教育经费

Net Enrollment Rate and Public Expenditures for Education at Current Market Prices

单位：% (%)

年份 Year	粗入学率（6-21岁） Gross Enrollment Rate (age 6-21) 初等教育（6-11岁） Primary Education (age 6-11)	中等教育（12-17岁） Secondary Education (age 12-17)	高等教育（18-21岁） Higher Education (age 18-21)	每千人口高等教育学生数 Higher Education Student per 1000 Population	15岁以上人口识字率 Percentage of Literate Aged 15 and Over	公共教育经费 Public Expenditure for Education 占本地居民生产总值% As % of GNP	占政府支出比重% As % of Expenditures of Government
1991	101.0	95.4	32.4	26.8	92.9	6.5	17.8
1992	101.3	95.6	35.6	28.9	93.2	6.8	17.9
1993	101.8	95.3	37.9	30.5	93.4	7.0	18.4
1994	100.9	95.9	38.3	31.7	93.7	6.8	18.6
1995	101.4	95.7	39.4	32.7	94.0	6.6	19.4
1996	101.1	95.8	40.9	34.3	94.3	6.7	19.5
1997	100.6	97.2	43.1	37.6	94.7	6.6	18.9
1998	99.8	98.6	47.0	40.7	94.9	6.3	18.5
1999	99.7	99.6	50.5	44.6	95.3	6.3	18.8
2000	100.5	99.2	56.1	49.4	95.6	5.7	19.2
2001	99.7	99.4	63.0	54.1	95.8	6.2	18.3
2002	100.0	99.3	67.6	56.8	96.0	6.4	19.8
2003	99.5	99.0	72.4	58.3	97.0	6.2	18.5
2004	101.0	98.2	78.6	58.8	97.2	4.0	18.9
2005	100.3	97.9	82.0	58.7	97.3	4.0	

附录1-26 科技人员数和科研开发经费

Number of Scientists, Engineers and Technicians and Expenditures for R&D

年份 Year	科技人员数（人） Number of Scientists, Engineers and Technicians Engaged in Research and Experimental Development (Headcount) 总计 Total	科学家和工程师 Scientists & Engineers	技术人员 Technicians	辅助人员 Assistant	科研开发经费 Expenditures for Research and Experimental Development 总计（新台币亿元） Total (NT $100 million)	占本地生产总值% As % of GDP	占科研开发经费比重（%） As % of Expenditures for Research and Development 政府经费 Government	民间经费 Private
1991	82436	46173	22844	13419	818	1.70	52.1	47.9
1992	77750	48356	22117	7277	948	1.78	52.2	47.8
1993	90918	54905	23720	12293	1036	1.76	49.5	50.5
1994	95088	58156	24067	12865	1147	1.77	48.2	51.8
1995	105822	66478	25635	13709	1250	1.78	45.9	54.1
1996	116853	71611	28987	16255	1380	1.80	42.7	57.3
1997	129165	76588	34021	18556	1563	1.88	40.8	59.2
1998	129305	83209	30535	15561	1765	1.98	38.3	61.7
1999	134845	87454	31465	15926	1905	2.06	37.9	62.1
2000	137622	87394	33713	16515	1976	2.06	37.5	62.5
2001	138409	89118	33007	16283	2050	2.17	37.0	63.0
2002	150200	94821	37998	17381	2244	2.31	38.1	61.9
2003	157225	96436	43730	17058	2408	2.45	38.1	61.9
2004	168525	91490	59583	17451	2609	2.42	33.9	66.1

附录1-27　医院、病床和医务人员情况

Medical Facilities and Health Personnel

年　份 Year	医疗机构 (所) Number of Medical Care Facilities (unit)	病床数 (床) Beds (unit)	每万人病床数 (床) Beds per 10 000 Population (unit)	从业医务人数 (人) Health Personnel (person)	每万人拥有医务人员(人) Health Personnel per 10 000 Population (person)
1987	12199	86328	43.88	77246	39.27
1988	12215	88572	44.50	83045	41.72
1989	12267	86693	43.12	85599	42.57
1990	12902	89151	43.80	91153	44.79
1991	13661	92785	45.14	96921	47.15
1992	14468	96084	46.30	102977	49.62
1993	15062	100570	47.90	109538	52.17
1994	15752	103733	48.98	114076	53.87
1995	16109	112379	52.62	118248	55.37
1996	16645	114923	53.39	123829	57.53
1997	17398	121162	55.73	137829	66.72
1998	17731	124564	56.80	144070	65.71
1999	17770	122937	55.65	152385	68.98
2000	18082	126476	56.78	159212	71.47
2001	18265	127676	56.98	165855	74.02
2002	18228	133398	59.23	175444	77.90
2003	18777	136331	60.31	183103	81.00
2004	19240	143343	63.18	192611	84.89

附录1-28　家 庭 设 备 普 及 率

Percent of Families Owning Household Appliances

单位：%　　　　(%)

年　份 Year	彩色电视机 Color TV Sets	洗衣机 Washing Machines	电话机 Telephone Sets	空　调 Air Conditioners	有线电视频道设备 Cable TV Sets	家用电脑 Family Computers	汽　车 Automobiles
1985	92.31	77.84	82.12	23.95		2.32	11.91
1986	94.42	79.49	85.25	25.45		2.92	13.63
1987	95.78	81.33	87.20	28.66		3.55	15.54
1988	97.34	83.97	89.11	34.29		3.95	19.21
1989	97.80	86.82	91.51	41.74		5.42	24.90
1990	98.26	88.79	93.08	47.26		6.77	29.07
1991	99.16	89.53	94.75	52.37		9.57	33.67
1992	99.30	90.38	95.13	56.14		11.76	38.94
1993	99.25	91.51	96.00	60.69		13.56	41.05
1994	99.36	92.31	96.53	64.01	43.40	15.29	45.54
1995	99.29	92.83	96.70	67.08	54.20	18.54	47.95
1996	99.32	93.00	97.49	71.65	59.60	22.56	51.16
1997	99.47	93.99	97.54	73.83	66.00	28.39	53.79
1998	99.17	93.86	97.63	76.20	68.10	32.31	54.52
1999	99.31	94.74	98.00	78.89	67.90	38.92	54.33
2000	99.45	95.36	98.04	79.46	72.00	46.49	55.58
2001	99.30	95.00	97.80	80.50	72.30	50.90	55.60
2002	99.60	96.00	97.90	83.10	74.80	56.80	58.20
2003	99.50	96.60	97.80	84.50	76.10	58.70	57.40
2004	99.50	96.90	97.60	85.70	78.50	62.40	58.00

附录二
APPENDIX II

我国经济、社会统计指标同世界主要国家和地区比较

A Comparison of Indicators of Economy and Society Among the People's Republic of China and Other Countries/Areas

附录2-1 国 土 面 积 和 人 口

Territory and Population

资料来源：世界银行世界发展指标数据库。
Sources: World Bank World Development Indicators Database.

国家和地区	Country or Area	国土面积（万平方公里） Area (10 000 sq.km)	2004 年中人口数（万人） Mid-year Population (10 000 persons)	2004 人口增长率(%) Annual Growth Rate(%)	2004 人口密度（人/平方公里） Population Density (persons/sq.km)
世界总计	**World**	**13427.9①**	**636498**	**1.2**	**49**
亚　洲④	**Asia④**	**3187.0**	**382339**	**1.3**	**120**
中　国②	China②	960.0	129608	0.6	136
日　本	Japan	36.5	12776	0.1	351
印　度③	India③	297.3	107972	1.4	363
印度尼西亚	Indonesia	181.2	21759	1.3	120
菲律宾	Philippines	29.8	8162	1.8	274
泰　国	Thailand	51.1	6369	0.9	125
马来西亚	Malaysia	32.9	2489	1.9	76
新加坡	Singapore	0.1	424	1.3	6329
巴基斯坦	Pakistan	77.1	15206	2.4	197
缅　甸	Myanmar	65.8	5000	1.1	76
孟加拉国	Bangladesh	13.0	13921	1.9	1069
土耳其	Turkey	77.0	7173	1.4	93
蒙　古	Mongolia	156.7	251	1.4	2
朝　鲜	Korea,Dem.People's Rep.	12.0	2238	0.5	186
韩　国	Korea,Rep.	9.9	4808	0.5	487
越　南	Viet Nam	32.5	8216	1.0	252
非　洲④	**Africa④**	**3030.9**	**85056**	**2.2**	**28**
埃　及	Egypt	99.5	7264	1.9	73
尼日利亚	Nigeria	91.1	12871	2.2	141
欧　洲④	**Europe④**	**2297.6**	**72634**	**-0.1**	**32**
德　国	Germany	34.9	8252	0.0	236
英　国	United Kingdom	24.2	5987	0.5	247
法　国	France	55.0	6038	0.6	110
意大利	Italy	29.4	5757	-0.1	196
捷　克	Czech Republic	7.7	1022	0.1	132
波　兰	Poland	30.6	3818	0.0	125
罗马尼亚	Romania	23.0	2168	-0.3	94
保加利亚	Bulgaria	11.1	776	-0.8	70
俄罗斯联邦	Russian Federation	1638.1	14385	-0.5	9
北美洲④	**North America④**	**2272.5**	**50667**	**1.2**	**22**
美　国	United States	915.9	29366	1.0	32
加拿大	Canada	909.4	3197	1.1	4
墨西哥	Mexico	190.9	10380	1.5	54
南美洲④	**South America④**	**1783.4**	**36228**	**1.4**	**20**
巴　西	Brazil	845.9	18391	1.4	22
阿根廷	Argentina	273.7	3837	1.0	14
大洋洲④	**Oceania④**	**856.4**	**3223**	**1.2**	**4**
澳大利亚	Australia	768.2	2011	1.2	3
新西兰	New Zealand	26.8	406	1.3	15

注：①是指有定居人口的各大洲面积，未包括尚无定居人口的南极洲。如包括南极洲，全世界陆地面积为14950万平方公里。②中国为年底总人口。③不包括查谟、克什米尔和锡金等地区。④ 2003年数据。

Note: ① refers to Continents with resident excluding the Antarctica. If included, it would be 149.50 million sq.km. ② refers to year-end population. ③excludes Jammu, Kashmir and Sikkim.④data refer to 2003.

附录2-2 按三次产业划分的就业

Employment by Type of Industry

资料来源：世界银行数据库。
Source: World Bank Database.

单位：% (%)

国家和地区	Country or Area	第一产业 Primary Industry		第二产业 Secondary Industry		第三产业 Tertiary Industry	
		2000	2003	2000	2003	2000	2003
中　国	China	50.0	49.1	22.5	21.6	27.5	29.3
孟加拉国	Bangladesh	62.1		10.3		23.5	
印度尼西亚	Indonesia	45.3	46.4	13.5	13.2	41.2	40.4
以色列	Israel	2.2	1.8	24.0	22.6	73.0	74.8
日　本	Japan	5.1	4.6	31.2	28.8	63.1	65.6
哈萨克斯坦	Kazakhstan		35.3	16.3①	17.0	48.1①	47.8
韩　国	Korea,Rep.	10.6	8.8	28.1	27.6	61.2	63.5
马来西亚	Malaysia	18.4	14.3	32.2	32.0	49.5	53.7
蒙　古	Mongolia	48.6	41.8	14.1	15.6	37.2	42.6
巴基斯坦	Pakistan	48.4	42.1②	18.0	20.8②	33.5	37.1②
菲律宾	Philippines	37.4	37.4①	16.0	15.6①	46.5	47.0①
斯里兰卡	Sri Lanka		34.3		23.4		38.7
新加坡	Singapore	0.2	0.2	34.2	24.1	65.4	75.6
泰　国	Thailand	48.5	44.9	17.9	19.7	33.5	35.3
土耳其	Turkey	36.0	33.9	24.0	22.8	40.0	43.4
越　南	Vietnam	65.3	59.7	12.4	16.4	22.3	23.9
埃　及	Egypt	29.6	27.5②	21.3	20.6②	49.1	51.9②
南　非	South Africa	14.5	10.3	24.1	24.5	60.9	65.1
加拿大	Canada	3.3	2.8	22.6	22.5	74.1	74.7
墨西哥	Mexico	17.4	16.3	26.9	25.0	55.2	58.4
美　国	United States	2.6	2.5②	23.0	21.6②	74.4	75.9②
阿根廷	Argentina	0.7	1.3	22.7	19.9	76.2	78.3
巴　西	Brazil		19.8②	20.0①	21.6②	59.4①	58.4②
委内瑞拉	Venezuela	10.2	10.7	22.3	19.8	67.4	69.1
保加利亚	Bulgaria	26.2	10.1	28.3	32.8	45.5	57.1
捷　克	Czech Republic	5.1	4.5	40.0	39.7	54.8	55.8
德　国	Germany	2.6	2.5	33.7	31.9	63.6	65.5
意大利	Italy	5.4	4.9	32.4	32.2	62.1	62.8
荷　兰	Netherlands	3.3	3.0②	21.3	20.3②	72.9	74.1②
波　兰	Poland	18.8	18.4	30.9	28.6	50.4	53.0
罗马尼亚	Romania	42.8	35.7	26.2	29.8	31.0	34.5
俄罗斯联邦	Russian Federation	12.7	10.0	29.6	31.3	57.7	58.7
西班牙	Spain	6.6	5.7	31.3	30.8	62.0	63.6
乌克兰	Ukraine	20.5	18.9	31.4	29.9	48.1	51.2
英　国	United Kingdom	1.5	1.2	25.4	23.5	72.7	75.0
澳大利亚	Australia	5.0	4.0	21.8	21.2	73.2	74.8
新西兰	New Zealand	8.7	8.2	23.2	22.3	67.6	69.3

注：①2001年数据。②2002年数据。
Note: ①Data refer to 2001. ②Data refer to 2002.

附录2-3 国内生产总值及其增长率

Gross Domestic Product and Its Growth Rate

资料来源：国际货币基金组织数据库。
Sources: International Monetary Fund Database.

国家和地区	Country or Area	2005 国内生产总值 (亿本币) GDP of 2005 (national currency 100 million)	国内生产总值增长率（比上年增长%） GDP Growth Rate over the Preceding Year (%)				
			2001	2002	2003	2004	2005
世　界	**World**		**2.6**	**3.1**	**4.1**	**5.3**	**4.8**
中　国	China	183085	8.3	9.1	10.0	10.1	10.2
孟加拉国	Bangladesh	39133	4.8	4.8	5.8	5.9	5.8
印　度	India	341953	4.1	4.2	7.2	8.1	8.3
印度尼西亚	Indonesia	26786641	3.8	4.4	4.7	5.1	5.6
伊　朗	Iran	17686654	3.7	7.5	6.7	5.6	5.9
以色列	Israel	5540	-0.3	-1.2	1.7	4.4	5.2
日　本	Japan	5029054	0.4	0.1	1.8	2.3	2.7
哈萨克斯坦	Kazakhstan	74530	13.5	9.8	9.3	9.6	9.4
韩　国	Korea,Rep.	8121966	3.8	7.0	3.1	4.6	4.0
马来西亚	Malaysia	4945	0.3	4.4	5.4	7.1	5.3
蒙　古	Mongolia	22665	1.0	4.0	5.6	10.7	6.2
缅　甸	Myanmar	102300	11.3	12.0	13.8	3.0	5.0
巴基斯坦	Pakistan	70556	2.5	4.1	5.7	7.1	7.0
菲律宾	Philippines	53793	1.8	4.4	4.5	6.0	5.1
新加坡	Singapore	1944	-2.3	4.0	2.9	8.7	6.4
斯里兰卡	Sri Lanka	23637	-1.5	4.0	6.0	5.4	5.9
泰　国	Thailand	69243	2.2	5.3	7.0	6.2	4.4
土耳其	Turkey	4872	-7.5	7.9	5.8	8.9	7.4
越　南	Vietnam	8068549	6.9	7.1	7.3	7.7	7.5
埃　及	Egypt	5580	3.5	3.2	3.1	4.1	5.0
尼日利亚	Nigeria	129896	3.1	1.5	10.7	6.0	6.9
南　非	South Africa	15233	2.7	3.7	3.0	4.5	4.9
加拿大	Canada	13687	1.8	3.1	2.0	2.9	2.9
墨西哥	Mexico	83743		0.8	1.4	4.2	3.0
美　国	United States	124857	0.8	1.6	2.7	4.2	3.5
阿根廷	Argentina	5323	-4.4	-10.9	8.8	9.0	9.2
巴　西	Brazil	19303	1.3	1.9	0.5	4.9	2.3
委内瑞拉	Venezuela	2805307	3.4	-8.9	-7.7	17.9	9.3
白俄罗斯	Belorussia	636789	4.7	5.0	7.0	11.4	9.2
保加利亚	Bulgaria	419	4.1	4.9	4.5	5.7	5.5
捷　克	Czech Republic	29507	2.6	1.5	3.2	4.7	6.0
法　国	France	16904	2.1	1.3	0.9	2.1	1.4
德　国	Germany	22455	1.2	0.1	-0.2	1.6	0.9
意大利	Italy	14177	1.8	0.3	0.1	0.9	0.1
荷　兰	Netherlands	5019	1.4	0.1	-0.1	1.7	1.1
波　兰	Poland	9722	1.1	1.4	3.8	5.3	3.2
罗马尼亚	Romania	2872	5.7	5.1	5.2	8.4	4.1
俄罗斯联邦	Russian Federation	216650	5.1	4.7	7.3	7.2	6.4
西班牙	Spain	9043	3.5	2.7	3.0	3.1	3.4
乌克兰	Ukraine	4185	9.2	5.2	9.6	12.1	2.6
英　国	United Kingdom	12093	2.2	2.0	2.5	3.1	1.8
澳大利亚	Australia	9269	2.2	4.1	3.1	3.6	2.5
新西兰	New Zealand	1541	3.0	4.8	3.4	4.4	2.2

附录2-4 农业生产指数（2005年）

Agricultural Production Indices (2005)

资料来源：联合国粮农组织数据库。
Source: FAO Database.

（1999-2001年=100） (1999-2001=100)

国家和地区	Country or Area	农业 Agriculture	种植业 Crops	畜牧业 Livestock	食品 Food	非食品 Non Food
世　界	**World**	**111.3**	**111.2**	**111.1**	**111.3**	**114.3**
发达国家	**Developed Countries**	**103.4**	**105.1**	**103.4**	**102.7**	**105.2**
发展中国家	**Developing Countries**	**115.6**	**113.9**	**115.5**	**118.9**	**117.5**
亚　洲	**Asia**	**115.6**	**113.6**	**115.4**	**120.5**	**118.5**
中　国①	China①	129.1	122.2	139.7		
孟加拉国	Bangladesh	109.1	109.7	109.3	105.2	104.0
印　度	India	106.2	102.8	105.5	114.1	120.4
印度尼西亚	Indonesia	122.7	120.8	122.7	138.2	124.0
伊　朗	Iran	114.3	119.2	115.0	106.9	93.1
以色列	Israel	109.9	105.3	110.2	118.2	96.0
日　本	Japan	96.8	94.8	96.8	98.8	94.2
哈萨克斯坦	Kazakhstan	111.1	106.3	111.0	122.6	113.5
朝　鲜	Korea, D.P.Rep.	112.3	111.8	112.8	122.4	104.9
韩　国	Korea, Rep.	95.7	94.1	96.3	102.6	58.2
马来西亚	Malaysia	126.7	128.2	126.0	122.7	135.0
蒙　古	Mongolia	75.2	119.4	75.3	73.0	72.1
缅　甸	Myanmar	124.1	122.5	124.9	132.9	94.2
巴基斯坦	Pakistan	115.3	115.5	113.6	115.6	127.8
菲律宾	Philippines	114.1	115.3	114.4	111.2	100.7
新加坡	Singapore	107.1	115.8	107.1	100.7	
斯里兰卡	Sri Lanka	106.4	104.2	107.0	119.9	103.7
泰　国	Thailand	105.3	105.5	103.6	100.3	120.6
土耳其	Turkey	105.0	104.1	106.1	110.4	92.9
越　南	Vietnam	126.6	124.1	125.8	136.2	136.8
非　洲	**Africa**	**110.2**	**109.7**	**110.6**	**110.7**	**102.0**
埃　及	Egypt	116.8	114.6	117.0	118.9	110.8
尼日利亚	Nigeria	106.1	105.9	106.1	107.7	102.9
南　非	South Africa	111.1	111.1	112.0	111.3	79.4
北美洲	**North and Central America**	**106.8**	**107.0**	**106.5**	**105.6**	**113.5**
加拿大	Canada	106.9	108.5	106.9	108.0	109.2
墨西哥	Mexico	108.8	107.2	109.1	110.6	94.7
美　国	United States	106.4	106.9	105.9	104.3	118.4
南美洲	**South America**	**119.7**	**121.2**	**119.2**	**115.6**	**129.9**
阿根廷	Argentina	113.3	122.2	113.5	99.8	102.1
巴　西	Brazil	126.1	124.0	124.8	123.6	145.8
委内瑞拉	Venezuela	94.3	100.0	94.4	91.2	88.9
欧　洲	**Europe**	**101.2**	**103.9**	**101.4**	**100.9**	**94.1**
白俄罗斯	Belorussia	119.0	124.8	118.5	115.8	191.5
保加利亚	Bulgaria	100.8	107.4	99.3	96.7	136.8
捷　克	Czech Republic	97.9	101.6	97.9	90.8	90.8
法　国	France	97.2	97.4	97.2	98.9	99.2
德　国	Germany	97.1	96.6	97.2	100.2	83.2
意大利	Italy	101.2	105.1	101.4	96.7	105.8
荷　兰	Netherlands	93.3	96.8	93.2	92.3	107.8
波　兰	Poland	101.5	86.8	101.5	107.4	86.0
罗马尼亚	Romania	107.2	111.1	107.5	110.9	73.7
俄罗斯联邦	Russian Federation	111.9	123.4	111.9	103.7	122.4
西班牙	Spain	94.9	87.6	95.0	110.3	83.7
乌克兰	Ukraine	113.2	130.7	113.2	100.8	98.0
英　国	United Kingdom	97.1	98.4	97.2	97.5	87.2
大洋洲	**Oceania**	**98.4**	**94.4**	**100.9**	**101.4**	**76.0**
澳大利亚	Australia	92.4	92.4	95.2	93.4	70.5
新西兰	New Zealand	113.9	105.9	115.3	115.0	97.3

注：① 2000年为基期的总产值指数。
Note: ① Indices of gross agricultural output value, the base year is 2000.

附录2-5 工业生产指数

Industry Production Indices

资料来源：联合国数据库。
Sources: United Nations Database.

(1995年=100) (1995=100)

国家和地区	Country or Area	总指数 General Index			其中：制造业 Of Which: Manufacturing		
		2000	2004	2005	2000	2004	2005
中　国①	China①	162.5	244.1	271.9			
孟加拉国	Bangladesh	131.5	164.8	178.9	132.8	162.8	178.1
印　度	India	131.9	165.6	188.6②	134.9	171.8	197.8②
印度尼西亚	Indonesia				91.5	107.3	113.7③
以色列	Israel	123.0	122.2	127.0	123.6	122.7	127.5
日　本	Japan	105.5	106.0	107.4	105.2	105.4	106.6
韩　国	Korea, Rep.	154.1	194.5	206.6	154.6	195.1	207.1
马来西亚	Malaysia	148.1	180.6	188.0	159.8	194.1	204.0
蒙　古	Mongolia						
巴基斯坦	Pakistan	114.2	177.6	204.8②	116.3	183.5	216.2②
新加坡	Singapore	141.4	159.3	174.1	141.3	158.9	173.9
泰　国	Thailand				111.9	149.8	155.5
土耳其	Turkey	121.2	144.5	152.4	121.3	146.8	153.9
南　非	South Africa	104.5	116.3	118.7	106.0	116.6	120.7
加拿大	Canada	125.9	129.4	132.7	135.0	132.9	139.0
墨西哥	Mexico	142.0	142.1	144.3	145.8	142.9	144.7
美　国	United States	129.2	130.5	134.9	133.2	134.6	140.0
阿根廷	Argentina				101.8	109.2	119.0
巴　西	Brazil	109.6	124.0	127.8	105.8	116.7	119.9
委内瑞拉	Venezuela				95.9	93.7	104.4
保加利亚	Bulgaria	78.2	111.7	119.1	74.7	117.1	126.5
捷　克	Czech Republic	105.7	132.8	141.6	108.2	138.4	148.9
法　国	France	114.9	117.2	117.6	116.3	117.9	118.1
德　国	Germany	114.5	117.3	121.5	116.3	119.4	124.0
意大利	Italy	107.7	104.9	103.1	106.7	102.3	99.8
荷　兰	Netherlands	110.0	112.3	110.9	113.8	113.0	112.8
波　兰	Poland	143.5	179.1	186.4	153.7	198.0	207.0
罗马尼亚	Romania	83.2	101.8	124.9	85.1	109.2	131.8
西班牙	Spain	119.3	122.0	122.2	119.7	121.0	120.7
乌克兰	Ukraine	109.0	170.1	173.7			
英　国	United Kingdom	107.1	103.0	100.9	106.6	103.9	102.7
澳大利亚	Australia	112.5	120.2	120.8	110.1	120.3	119.0
新西兰	New Zealand	104.8	115.5	117.1	104.1	117.4	119.3

注：①工业增加值指数。②2005年12月数字。③2005年第三季度数字。
Note: ①Indices of industrial value-added. ②Data refer to Dec.2005. ③Data refer to third quarter of 2005.

附录2-6　中国主要指标居世界位次

Precedence of Main Indicators of China in the World

资料来源：联合国数据库、《工业产品统计年鉴》；联合国粮农组织数据库。

Sources: United Nations Database, "Industrial Commodity Statistics Yearbook", FAO Database.

指　　标	Item	1978	1990	2000	2003	2004	2005
国内生产总值	**Gross Domestic Product**	**10**	**11**	**6**	**7**	**6**	**4**
人均国民总收入①	**Per Capita GNI①**	**175(188)**	**178(200)**	**141(207)**	**133(206)**	**108(180)**	**110(180)**
进出口贸易额	**Total Value of Imports and Exports**	**27**	**16**	**8**	**4**	**3**	**3**
主要工业产品产量	**Major Industrial Products**						
钢	Crude Steel	5	4	1	1	1	
煤	Coal	3	1	1	1	1	
原　油	Crude Petroleum	8	5	5	5	6	
发电量	Electricity	7	4	2	2	2	
水　泥	Cement	4	1	1	1	1	
化　肥	Fertilizer	3	3	1	1	1	
化学纤维	Chemical Fiber	7	2	2			
棉　布	Woven Cotton Fabrics	1	1	2	1	1	
糖	Sugar	8	6	4			
电视机	Television	8	1	1	1		
主要农业产品产量	**Major Agricultural Products**						
谷　物	Cereals	2	1	1	1	1	1
肉　类②	Meat②	3	1	1	1	1	1
籽　棉	Seed Cotton	3	1	1	1	1	1
大　豆	Soybeans	3	3	4	4	4	4
花　生	Groundnuts in Shell	2	2	1	1	1	1
油菜籽	Rapeseeds	2	1	1	1	1	1
甘　蔗	Sugar Cane	9	4	3	3	3	3
茶　叶	Tea	2	2	2	2	1	1
水　果	Fruit		4	1	1	1	1

注：①括号中所列数为排序的国家和地区数。

②1993年以前为猪、牛、羊肉产量的位次。

Note: ① The number in the parentheses indicates the number of countries or territories the order based on.

②Data refer to pork, beef and mutton prior to 1993.

附录2-7 居民消费价格指数

Consumer Price Indices

资料来源：联合国数据库。
Sources: United Nations Database.

(2000年=100) (2000=100)

国家和地区	Country or Area	总指数 General Index			其中：食品 Of Which: Food		
		2003	2004	2005	2003	2004	2005
中　国①	China①	101.2	103.9	101.8	103.4	109.9	102.9
孟加拉国②	Bangladesh ②	111.5	118.4		110.1	118.3	
印　度③	India③	112.5	116.6	121.5	108.4	111.5	115.0
印度尼西亚	Indonesia	133.0	141.3	156.0	121.2	128.3	140.3
伊　朗	Iran	148.1	192.9	192.9	145.9	164.8	186.3
以色列	Israel	107.5	107.1		108.4	108.0	
日　本	Japan	98.1	98.1	97.8	98.4	99.3	98.4
哈萨克斯坦④	Kazakhstan④	122.0	130.5	140.3			
韩　国	Korea, Rep.	110.7	114.7	117.8	112.4	119.5	122.8
马来西亚	Malaysia	104.4	105.9	109.1	102.7	105.0	108.8
蒙　古(乌兰巴托)	Mongolia(Ulan Bator)	112.8	122.1		105.7	118.8	
缅　甸	Myanmar	259.8	271.6		274.3	277.5	
巴基斯坦	Pakistan	110.5	118.7	129.5	108.6	120.2	132.1
菲律宾④	Philippines④	112.5	120.6	129.8	108.2	116.3	123.8
新加坡	Singapore	101.1	102.8	103.2	101.1	103.2	104.6
斯里兰卡(科伦坡)	Sri Lanka (Colombo)	133.0	143.0	159.7	134.9	145.5	163.0
泰　国（曼谷）	Thailand (Bangkok)	104.1	107.0		104.6	109.4	
土耳其	Turkey	280.4	310.1	380.5	290.0	316.1	112.1
越　南	Vietnam	107.0	115.0		108.7	119.8	
埃　及⑤	Egypt⑤	109.5	127.5	133.7	112.3	100.0	105.0
南　非⑥	South Africa⑥	122.1	123.8	128.0	131.9	134.9	137.9
加拿大	Canada	107.8	109.7	112.2	109.1	111.3	114.1
墨西哥④	Mexico④	116.8	122.3		115.1	122.9	
美　国(加拉加斯)	United States (Caracas)	106.9	109.7	113.4	107.3	111.0	113.6
阿根廷(布宜诺斯艾利斯)	Argentina(Buenos Aires)	141.3	147.5	161.7	157.3	165.1	183.3
巴　西	Brazil	132.9	141.7	151.4	140.8	146.5	117.0
委内瑞拉④	Venezuela④	180.6	219.9	255.0			
白俄罗斯	Belorussia	295.0	348.3	384.3	267.6	320.1	358.2
保加利亚	Bulgaria	116.3	123.4	129.6	105.4	112.5	114.1
捷　克	Czech Republic	106.6	109.7	111.7	104.0	109.0	110.3
法　国	France	105.8	108.0	109.9	110.2	110.9	111.0
德　国	Germany	104.5	106.2	108.3	105.2	104.8	105.3
意大利⑦	Italy⑦	108.2	110.5	112.3	111.3	113.7	113.6
荷　兰	Netherlands	109.9	111.2	113.1	111.7	107.8	106.5
波　兰⑧	Poland⑧	108.4	112.2	114.6	103.0	108.6	110.6
罗马尼亚	Romania	189.9	212.5	231.7	184.1	201.5	213.8
俄罗斯联邦	Russian Federation	159.8	177.3	199.7	151.3	166.9	189.7
西班牙	Spain	106.7	109.9	113.6	109.0	113.2	116.7
乌克兰	Ukraine	110.5	114.5	124.1	106.7	111.4	126.1
英　国⑨	United Kingdom⑨	106.5	109.6	112.7	105.4	106.0	107.3
澳大利亚	Australia	110.5	113.1	116.1	114.4	117.1	120.0
新西兰	New Zealand	107.2	109.7	113.0	109.7	110.6	112.2

注：① 上年为100。②政府官员。③指产业工人。④包含酒精饮料和烟草。⑤包括烟草。⑥2001年=100。⑦不包括烟草。⑧包括酒精饮料。⑨指城市消费者。

Note: ①The base year is preceding year.②Government officials. ③Industrial workers.④Including alcoholic beverages and tobacco.⑤Including tobacco. ⑥The base year is 2001. ⑦Excluding tobacco. ⑧Including alcoholic beverages. ⑨All urban consumers.

附录2-8 进出口贸易额

Total Imports and Exports

资料来源：世界贸易组织数据库。
Source: World Trade Organization Database.

单位：亿美元 (USD 100 million)

国家和地区	Country or Area	2004		2005	
		进口 Imports	出口 Exports	进口 Imports	出口 Exports
世界	**World**	**95450**	**91910**	**107530**	**103930**
中国	China	5612	5933	6601	7620
孟加拉国	Bangladesh	120	83	139	92
印度	India	973	756	1316	898
印度尼西亚	Indonesia	550	722	687	863
伊朗	Iran	352	444	416	584
以色列	Israel	429	386	469	426
日本	Japan	4545	5657	5161	5958
哈萨克斯坦	Kazakhstan	128	201	174	278
韩国	Korea, Rep.	2245	2538	2610	2847
马来西亚	Malaysia	1053	1265	1146	1409
蒙古	Mongolia	10	9	11	10
缅甸	Myanmar	22	24	23	28
巴基斯坦	Pakistan	179	134	253	159
菲律宾	Philippines	423	397	463	412
新加坡	Singapore	1736	1986	2000	2296
斯里兰卡	Sri Lanka	80	58	90	63
泰国	Thailand	944	962	1182	1101
埃及	Egypt	128	77	166	103
尼日利亚	Nigeria	142	311	152	435
南非	South Africa	571	460	665	519
加拿大	Canada	2798	3165	3201	3596
墨西哥	Mexico	2061	1880	2317	2137
美国	United States	15255	8188	17327	9043
阿根廷	Argentina	224	346	287	400
巴西	Brazil	664	965	776	1183
委内瑞拉	Venezuela	168	387	249	562
保加利亚	Bulgaria	145	99	182	117
捷克	Czech Republic	700	690	769	785
法国	France	4709	4521	4958	4592
德国	Germany	7157	9099	7741	9707
意大利	Italy	3553	3538	3797	3668
荷兰	Netherlands	3197	3574	3579	4013
波兰	Poland	897	750	1005	889
罗马尼亚	Romania	327	235	405	277
俄罗斯联邦	Russian Federation	974	1832	1251	2453
西班牙	Spain	2583	1826	2776	1861
乌克兰	Ukraine	290	327	361	343
英国	United Kingdom	4706	3475	5012	3779
澳大利亚	Australia	1094	866	1253	1058
新西兰	New Zealand	232	204	262	217

附录2-9 国际收支(2005年)

Balance of Payments (2005)

资料来源：国际货币基金组织数据库。
Source: International Monetary Fund database.

单位：亿美元 (USD 100 million)

国家和地区	Country or Area	经常帐户 Current Account								资本帐户收支盈余 Capital Account Balance	金融帐户收支盈余 Financial Account Balance	国际收支总盈余 Overall Balance
		商品贸易 Merchandise			服务贸易 Services		要素收入 Factor Income		经常帐户收支盈余 Current Account Balance			
		出口 Exports F.O.B	进口 Imports F.O.B	差额 Trade Balance	贷方 Credit	借方 Debit	贷方 Credit	借方 Debit				
中国	China	5934	-5344	590	624	-721	205	-241	686		1107	2064
印度①	India①	507	-571	-64	237	-225	26	-61	58	26	111	188
印度尼西亚②	Indonesia②	633	-395	237	53	-174	11	-73	73		-9	36
以色列	Israel	366	-385	-19	149	-136	23	-65	15	5	-41	-16
日本②	Japan②	5390	-4069	1321	976	-1355	1133	-276	1721	-48	225	1609
韩国	Korea,Rep.	2577	-2196	382	414	-502	87	-80	276	-18	101	387
巴基斯坦	Pakistan	134	-167	-34	27	-53	2	-26	-8	6	-17	-14
菲律宾	Philippines	387	-451	-64	41	-54	35	-34	21		-30	-16
新加坡②	Singapore②	1579	-1285	293	307	-296	134	-145	282	-2	-251	67
泰国	Thailand	961	-850	111	190	-232	31	-51	71		7	57
土耳其	Turkey	670	-909	-239	240	-113	27	-82	-155		170	43
埃及	Egypt	123	-189	-66	142	-80	6	-8	39		-45	-6
南非	South Africa	484	-485	-1	83	-93	32	-75	-70	1	105	85
加拿大	Canada	3301	-2794	507	475	-573	296	-487	220	34	-236	-28
墨西哥	Mexico	1880	-1968	-88	140	-198	50	-149	-74		123	41
美国	United States	8111	-14731	-6620	3361	-2911	3690	-3449	-6659	-15	6127	-28
阿根廷	Argentina	346	-213	132	52	-68	35	-124	34		-104	-70
巴西	Brazil	965	-628	337	124	-172	32	-237	117	7	-37	66
白俄罗斯	Belarus	139	-160	-21	17	-10	1	-1	-10		9	2
保加利亚	Bulgaria	99	-132	-34	41	-33	4	-8	-18		33	17
捷克	Czech Republic	669	-677	-9	97	-92	27	-82	-56	-6	72	3
法国	France	4211	-4291	-79	1103	-975	1130	-1009	-48	22	55	41
德国	Germany	9097	-7179	1918	1412	-1947	1328	-1326	1034	5	-1224	-18
意大利	Italy	3522	-3413	109	837	-820	532	-714	-151	26	82	-28
荷兰	Netherlands	3043	-2733	310	735	-712	656	-668	232	4	-137	-10
波兰	Poland	816	-872	-56	134	-125	21	-67	-36	10	4	8
罗马尼亚	Romania	235	-302	-67	36	-39	4	-22	-56	6	97	60
俄罗斯联邦	Russian Federation	1835	-963	871	203	-337	96	-225	601	-16	-54	466
西班牙	Spain	1843	-2488	-645	852	-540	290	-449	-492	106	390	-64
英国	United Kingdom	3496	-4569	-1073	1814	-1444	2559	-2078	-419	36	222	4
澳大利亚	Australia	871	-1053	-182	254	-262	133	-341	-400	8	412	12
新西兰	New Zealand	205	-219	-14	78	-69	15	-73	-62	3	89	6

注：①2002年。②2003年。
Note:①Data refer to 2002.②Data refer to 2003.

New Published Statistical Yearbook by China Statistics Press

专栏集锦

中国优秀企业

中国石油天然气集团公司
国家开发投资公司
中国国电集团公司
民航快递有限责任公司
武汉钢铁（集团）公司
鞍山钢铁集团公司
天津荣程联合钢铁集团有限公司
宣化钢铁集团有限责任公司
广西柳州钢铁（集团）公司
广东省大宝山矿业有限公司

中国综合实力百强城市

辽宁省沈阳市
黑龙江省哈尔滨市
山东省济南市
江苏省苏州市
河南省郑州市
黑龙江省大庆市
广东省中山市
内蒙古鄂尔多斯市
贵州省贵阳市
山东省潍坊市
辽宁省盘锦市
湖南省湘潭市
陕西省宝鸡市
湖南省株洲市
河北省张家口市
山东省泰安市

中国知名城市

黑龙江省鹤岗市
河南省漯河市
四川省宜宾市
甘肃省金昌市

中国综合实力百强县（市）

江苏省昆山市
广东省顺德区
江苏省江阴市
江苏省张家港市
江苏省常熟市
广东省南海区
浙江省绍兴县
江苏省太仓市
江苏省吴江市
福建省晋江市
山东省荣成市
浙江省义乌市
山东省蓬莱市
广东省新会区
江苏省靖江市
天津市静海县
江苏省仪征市

中国县域经济百强县（市）

山东省滕州市
江苏省泰兴市
河北省遵化市

中国优秀县（市）

云南省思茅市
贵州省仁怀市
湖南省醴陵市

中国最大的国有投资控股公司之一——

国家开发投资公司

国家开发投资公司是由中央出资设立的、中国最大的国有投资控股公司之一。实收资本158亿元，截至2005年底，公司资产总额936亿元。国投公司共有投资企业251家。

电力：国投公司共投资水、火电站及相关项目48个，投产装机容量1800万千瓦。

煤炭：国投公司在煤炭领域共投资煤炭项目16个，年生产能力1700万吨。

港航：国投公司是港口业的中央级港口经营基金的国家出资人代表，在沿海和长江口拥有16个骨干枢纽港。

化肥：国投公司是中国化肥领域最大的国家出资人代表之一，拥有的钾盐资源工业储量占全国总储量的50%以上。

高科技产业：国投公司拥有一批著名高科技企业，生产提供了国内市场50%的基因工程乙肝疫苗、世界10%的浓缩苹果汁、国内60%汽车塑料燃料箱以及中国市场1/3的手机电池。

金融服务领域：控股国投弘泰信托投资公司，参股中银国际、红塔证券等证券公司，参与组建渤海银行，与瑞士银行集团合资，组建国投瑞银基金管理公司。

资产管理领域：受国家有关部门委托管理中国包装总公司，成为第一家承担国家有关部门托管经营任务的公司，经国家有关部门批准进行国有资产经营公司试点。

在咨询服务领域：公司控股的中投咨询可提供投资咨询、工程咨询和管理咨询等服务，是国家有关部门确定的委托投资咨询评估的咨询公司之一。

洋浦港标准化集装箱专用码头

四川二滩水电站是中国20世纪建成的最大水电站

罗布泊钾肥生产现场

国投新集能源有限公司

中国国电集团公司
CHINA GUODIAN CORPORATION

中国国电集团公司党组书记、
总经理　周大兵

中国国电集团公司成立于2002年12月29日，是在电力体制改革中由原国家电力公司部分企事业单位组建而成的全国五大发电企业集团之一，注册资本金120亿元人民币。

公司成立以来，在集团党组和周大兵总经理的正确领导下，认真贯彻邓小平理论和“三个代表”重要思想，树立和落实科学发展观，确立了“做实、做新、做大、做强”的工作方针。集团公司始终把发展作为第一要务，成立之初党组就确定了近期每年平均“三个四百万”千瓦和2010年超过7000万千瓦，2020年达到1亿千瓦的电源发展目标。

三年来，中国国电集团公司坚持以效益为中心，坚持建设节约型企业，不断深化“强化管理、提高效益”活动，实施精细化管理，并取得优异成绩，截至2005年底，装机规模从成立时的2213万千瓦增长到3506万千瓦，运行电厂遍布全国25个省市区；总资产从成立时的667.5亿元增长到1322.9亿元；主营业务收入从2003年的228.8亿元，增长到428亿元；利润总额从2003年的14.24亿元，增长到23.52亿元；供电煤耗从2003年的371.3克/千瓦时，下降到361克/千瓦时，确保了国有资产的保值增值，为集团公司实现快速、健康、可持续发展奠定了良好基础。

“十一五”期间，中国国电集团公司将按照“投资控股型、规模效益型、资源节约型、集团化、市场化、现代化、国际先进”的发展战略，以发电为主，兼顾多元，立足国内市场，开拓国际市场，通过制度创新、管理创新、科技创新、观念创新，打造集团公司“结构优化、科技领先、管理先进”为一体的核心竞争力，在国内外树立“中国国电”品牌形象。

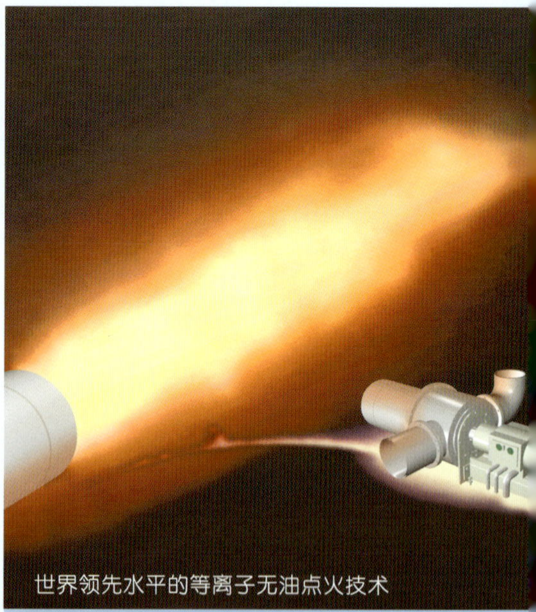

世界领先水平的等离子无油点火技术

60万千瓦机组EDPF-NT系统

创建资源节约环境友好型企业

国电谏电谏壁发电厂（238 万千瓦）

龚嘴水力发电总厂（132 万千瓦）

- 积极开发清洁和可再生能源发电项目
- 风电装机容量居国内首位

国内最大的风电场——新疆达坂城风电场（12.03 万千瓦）

60 万千瓦机组脱硫技术

多项环保、节能技术国内领先

CHINA GUODIAN CORPORATION

“中国十大影响力品牌”——

民航快递

民航快递有限责任公司成立于1996年。由民航多家航空公司和机场共同出资组建，是唯一具有全国配送网络和国内500最具价值品牌的快递、物流专业公司。公司依托全国民航140个机场和国内3075条、国际1184条航线的独特优势，坚持“高标准、严要求、讲效益、上水平”的工作方针，以市场为导向、时效产品为龙头、计算机现代信息管理为手段，为客户提供安全、高效、快捷、诚信的满意服务。

——具有全国地面配送网络，对客户的货件及时配送至全国各地。目前，民航快递覆盖全国大中城市达300多个。

——“民航快递”品牌获中国500最具价值品牌，中国物流协会“安全、快捷、诚信服务满意单位”，中国交通运输协会“全国物流百强企业”，中国品牌年度大奖（NO.1），中国十大影响力品牌等殊荣，已获得国内、国际ISO9000质量认证。

——具有计算机管理信息系统网络，搭建了全国统一的客户服务电话平台。在全国任一城市可拨打95105886电话，民航快递即刻上门为客户提供高效、快捷、诚信的优质服务。

——具备地面各种陆路运输车辆，形成了全国地面陆路运输配送网络。

——拥有各类经营证照，业务运作不断扩展。公司现为中国物流与采购联合会和中国国际货运代理协会常务理事单位。

公司在“十一五”期间，将向着创建国内一流和国际大型快递、物流专业公司迈进。

全国统一客服电话：95105886

民航快递
CHINA AIR EXPRESS

武汉钢铁(集团)公司

武钢是新中国成立后由国家投资建设的第一个特大型钢铁联合企业，于1955年破土动工，1958年9月13日建成投产。武钢厂区坐落在武汉市青山区，占地面积21.17平方公里。所辖的4座铁矿、2座辅助原料矿分布在鄂东、鄂南及河南焦作。2005年，武钢先后与鄂钢、柳钢实现了联合重组。

武钢是中国重要的板材生产基地，拥有从矿山采掘、炼焦、烧结、炼铁、炼钢、轧钢等一整套先进的工艺设备，现已具备年生产钢铁各1000多万吨的能力，主要生产热轧卷板、冷轧卷板、热轧型钢、中厚板、镀锌板、镀锡板、冷轧取向和无取向硅钢片、彩色涂层板、高速线材等几百个品种。此外，武钢还生产焦炭、耐火材料、化工产品、粉末冶金制品、铜硫钴精矿、水渣、氧气、稀有气体等副产品，并对外承担工程建设、机械加工和自动化技术开发。武钢已初步成为以钢铁、工程技术、国际贸易为主，多种产业共同发展的大型企业集团。

近年来，武钢先后获得国家技术创新奖、全国质量管理奖、全国质量效益型先进企业、全国用户满意先进单位、全国企业管理杰出贡献奖和全国先进基层党组织、全国文明单位等荣誉称号。

科技创新居行业领先地位

企业改革不断深化

花园式工厂

年产钢铁1000多万吨

坚持科学发展　立足自主创新　实现跨越升级

鞍山钢铁集团公司

2130冷轧线

鞍山钢铁集团董事会推进委员会主席、鞍钢集团公司党委书记、总经理刘玠

炼钢操作室

鞍钢冷轧板

鞍钢高炉群

转炉炼钢

三号高炉

打造最具国际竞争力的大型钢铁企业集团

“九五”以来，鞍钢从老企业实际出发，加强自主创新和集成创新，走出了“高起点、少投入、快产出、高效益”的技术改造之路，主体技术装备和生产工艺达到国际先进水平，具备1600万吨钢的综合生产能力，实现了跨越式发展。目前鞍钢拥有了一批具有自主知识产权的技术成果，具备了钢铁生产全流程的成套技术集成能力，成为国内首家具有成套技术输出能力的钢铁企业。能够生产700多个品种、25000多个规格钢铁产品，成为以汽车板、家电板、集装箱板、船板、重轨、石油管、管线钢、容器板、冷轧硅钢等为主导产品的精品钢材生产基地。鞍钢大力发展循环经济，加强能源转换、排放物再资源化和环保技术的开发应用，转炉煤气和高炉煤气全部回收利用，水循环利用率达到97%。实施生态恢复再造，植树造林面积达到500万平方米，厂区绿化覆盖率达到35%，被评为花园式工厂。2004年10月，国际专业调查分析机构美国《钢动态》（WSD）对世界主要钢铁企业国际竞争力进行评选，鞍钢列第8位。

“十一五”时期，鞍钢将坚持“高起点、少投入、快产出、高效益”的技术改造方针，加快推进产业优化升级，目标是：成为最具国际竞争力的世界一流大型钢铁企业集团，2010年进入世界500强。

天津荣程联合钢铁集团有限公司

天津荣程联合钢铁集团有限公司（简称荣钢）是以钢铁为主业，兼营国际贸易、矿业投拓、园林绿化、煤化工、综合利用等项目的集合型企业集团，其子公司及生产厂分布在天津市、河北省、广东省、云南省、内蒙古自治区。集团总部设在天津市津南区，东距天津新港20公里，北距天津滨海国际机场22公里，南邻丹拉、津晋高速，具有明显的区位优势。集团公司注册资金42766万元，占地3200亩，总资产已超过50亿元，拥有员工7000余名。现已形成了年产白灰50万吨、焦炭30万吨、烧结矿400万吨、生铁300万吨、钢300万吨、材220万吨的综合生产能力。在2005年公布的中国企业500强中名列302位，首次公布的中国制造业500强排名第151位。2005年集团实现销售收入154.4亿元，利税13.8亿元，上缴税金6亿元，在全国民营企业纳税百强排行榜上名列前茅，已经成为天津市第一大民营企业。

荣钢集团董事长张祥青

荣钢恪守“清洁生产、节能降耗、资源在创新中再生”的建厂方针，全力推行洁净生产，于2004年顺利通过了ISO9001国际质量体系认证，2005年又通过了ISO14001环境管理体系和OHSAS18001职业健康与安全两项认证。荣钢以诚信立企，在区域内拥有众多分销网络终端及渠道，取得了令人瞩目的业绩，在行业内拥有较高的知名度和美誉度。已连续二年被天津市政府命名为“优秀企业”，还荣获了“天津市文明单位”、“中国优秀民营科技企业”、“中国优秀民营企业”等荣誉称号。

荣钢集团在规模不断扩大、效益不断提高、企业不断发展的同时，从来不忘回报社会，积极参与各项社会公益活动。几年来，荣钢先后在赈灾、扶老、助残、救孤、济困、助学、助医以及支持文化、环保、体育等事业方面，捐款捐物累计达2450多万元，为建设社会主义和谐社会做出了突出贡献。荣钢集团秉承“能源与自然和谐、创建可持续发展空间”的经营战略，努力学习和创新，不断提升企业核心竞争力，始终站在钢铁行业的最前沿，努力成为具有国际竞争力的钢铁企业。

宣化钢铁集团有限责任公司

宣钢董事长　刘明哲

宣化钢铁集团有限责任公司创建于1919年，是国家大型企业，也是国家重点钢铁企业之一，2004年宣钢在中国最大500家大企业中名列193位，2005年名列河北“百强企业”第5位。宣钢现有在岗职工21317人，资产总额78亿元。到目前已形成年产铁500万吨、钢420万吨、钢材420万吨的生产能力。宣钢主导产品有，线材、棒材、钢筋、热轧带钢、焊管等，热轧带钢、螺纹钢、焊管荣获河北省名牌产品，螺纹钢荣获国家冶金产品实物质量“金杯奖”。

“十一五”期间，宣钢将按照科学发展、循环经济、做精做强的原则，实施宣钢发展规划，宣钢将成为产品高附加值、装备先进的大型现代化钢铁联合企业。

宣钢总经理　李贵阳

地址：河北省张家口市宣化区牌楼东街30号

电话：0313－8674421

宣钢1800立方米高炉夜景

广西柳州钢铁(集团)公司

广西柳州钢铁（集团）公司于1958年建厂，占地面积5.8平方公里，2005年末资产总额136.42亿元，是集冶金、科研、工程设计、建筑、疗养、商贸、环保于一体的国家大型钢铁联合企业，是广西钢铁生产基地及最大的企业集团，在国家有关部门最新发布的全国500强中位列158名。经过“十五”的建设，柳钢已具备600万吨钢的综合生产能力，可生产中厚板、中小型材、线材、棒材、热轧宽带钢等五大系列数百种规格产品。

柳钢大力推行质量管理体系认证和创名牌工作，并先后于1998年通过GB/T19002：1994质量体系认证，2001年通过2000版GB/T19001质量管理体系认证，2004年11月通过GB/T28001：2001标准建立的职业健康安全管理体系认证。此外，柳钢船用钢板还获得了中国、英国、挪威、法国、美国、日本、德国七国船级社的工厂认证。目前，柳钢执行国际一般水平标准和国际先进水平标准的钢材产品产量占钢材总量的80%以上，获全国冶金行业产品实物质量“金杯奖”的钢材产品产量占钢材产量的60%以上，大部分产品获得广西区名牌产品、区优质产品荣誉称号，其中热轧带肋钢筋为国家免检产品。

柳钢热轧生产线

柳钢办公大楼

广东省大宝山矿业有限公司

广东省大宝山矿业有限公司原名叫广东省大宝山矿。公司位于韶关市曲江区境内。1966年建矿，1995年改制为公司，属国家大型二类企业。公司现有在岗员工2160人，工程技术人员600多人。资产7.47亿元，年工业总产值3.5亿左右。

大宝山资源得天独厚，是南国矿业的一颗明珠。公司属大型金属矿山，有铁矿、铜硫矿和钼矿等资源，在矿床中还伴有钨、铋、金、银等多种金属。现在，年产铁矿石100万吨左右，铜精矿（金属量）8000吨，硫精矿20万吨。钼矿仍未开发，现处于资源勘探调查阶段。

索道运输线

经过四十年的艰苦奋斗，宝山人取得了丰硕的成果。建矿至今，完成工业总产值26.41亿元，实现利税总额6.34亿元，先后获得“全国思想政治工作优秀企业”和“全国模范职工之家”等荣誉称号。近年来，矿山坚持发展为第一要务，选择“以矿为主，一矿多产”的发展战略，大力发展循环经济，加强矿产品的综合利用，将钼矿作为矿山的后续接替资源。在资源日趋紧缺的今天，这颗南国矿业明珠将更加璀璨夺目、熠熠发光。

公司中心区花园

公司铁矿生采场区

插上经济和社会发展腾飞的翅膀

沈阳

2005年，沈阳市以科学发展观为统领，以加快全面振兴与构建和谐社会为主题，以“工业年”活动和筹办“世园会”为主线，经过全市人民的共同努力，推进国民经济和社会事业持续快速健康发展，圆满实现了“十五”计划发展目标。

全市经济快速发展。全年实现地区生产总值2084.1亿元，比上年增长16.0%，为“九五”以来最快增长速度。其中第一产业实现增加值126.3亿元，增长9.4%；第二产业实现增加值906.3亿元，增长22.3%；第三产业实现增加值1051.5亿元，增长11.7%。三次产业比例由2000年的6.7：39.0：54.3调整为6.1：43.5：50.4。地方财政收入完成181.5亿元，增长31.3%，连续五年保持30%以上的增速。政府公共服务能力不断增强，国民经济运行质量进一步提高。

城市建设日新月异。2005年是沈阳城建投入资金较多的一年，共完成城市建设投资123亿元，比上年增长23%。地铁一号线工程破土动工；“南北金廊”、“东西银带”建设全面推进；为迎接“世园会”实施了沈棋路拓宽工程；青年大街、二环路改造全面完成；对461条二级以下街路、240万平方米的小巷全部实施改造。城市公交运营线路比上年增加17条，年内新增公交车500辆，为城乡居民出行创造了便利条件。

工业经济高速发展。中共沈阳市委、市政府将2005年确定为工业年，以工业大发展、快发展为中心，带动国民经济全面快速增长。全年工业经济增长幅度为近十年来最高水平，居全国15个副省级城市首位。全市重点发展的汽车及零部件、装备制造、医药化工、电子信息、农产品加工、黑色金属冶炼、有色金属冶炼、航空航天器制造等八大优势产业的增速，高于全市工业平均增长水平。郊区与县（市）工业也实现快速发展。2005年全市工业经济突破2000亿元大关，达到2195.2亿元，比2004年增长39.6%，在全国15个副省级城市中排名由2001年的12位上升到第8位。

SHENYANG SHENYANG SHENYANG SHENYANG SHENYANG

浑河北岸城市新貌

沈阳中街夜景

沈阳华晨金杯汽车有限公司中华轿车生产线

沈阳世博园标志性建筑——凤之翼

沈阳东西快速干道桥

哈尔滨是一座魅力深厚的城市，是一座创造辉煌的城市。美丽的松花江穿城而过，带来无尽的秀美和丰饶。哈尔滨地处东北亚中心位置，被誉为欧亚大陆桥的明珠。全市现辖八区、十一县(市)，总面积53068平方公里，总人口954.3万。其中市区人口384万，是全国省辖市中面积最大的城市。

哈尔滨是国家重要的老工业基地之一，已形成以机电工业为主体，汽车、医药、食品、机电成套设备制造为重点的门类齐全的工业体系；哈尔滨是国家重要的商品粮基地和大豆、玉米等农作物的主产区。2005年粮食产量达92.5亿公斤，其中商品粮产量约占一半，在省会城市中排第一位；哈尔滨作为我国沿边开放带上的中心城市，对外开放的水平逐步提高，已连续举办了16届“中国·哈尔滨经济贸易洽谈会”，成为我国对外开放的重要窗口城市；哈尔滨是我国最年轻的历史文化名城和中国首批优秀旅游城市。冬季冰雪旅游是哈尔滨旅游精品，也是国家旅游局推向世界35个王牌产品之一。

哈尔滨

Haerbin

“十五”时期，全市人民在市委、市政府的领导下，坚持以经济建设为中心，抢抓机遇，开拓进取，深化改革，努力扩大对外开放，全面推进经济体制改革，国民经济和社会发展取得辉煌成就。改革开放与社会主义现代化建设已进入新的历史发展阶段。国民经济快速发展，综合实力显著增强。2005年全市实现生产总值1830.4亿元，比2000年增长84.0%，年均增长13.0%。人均生产总值由2000年的10563元增加到2005年的18852元，增长80.2%，年均增长12.5%。地方财政一般预算收入98.0亿元，比2000年增长82.8%，年均增长12.8%。对外开放硕果累累，对外贸易增长强劲。2005年进出口总值达27.1亿美元，比2000年增长1.2倍，年均增长17.5%。城市面貌发生巨变，国际大都市步伐加快。截止2005年底，全市拥有铺装道路长度1195.5公里，比2000年增长32.4%，全市拥有桥梁209座，比2000年增长23.7%。人均住宅使用面积由2000年的13.1平方米上升到2005年的16.7平方米。人均公共绿地面积由2000年的4.6平方米上升到2005年的7.1平方米。社会保障体系初步建立，人民生活水平迅速提高。到2005年末，全市城镇养老保险参保职工人数达107万人。城镇职工养老保险覆盖面已达84.3%，城镇职工失业保险覆盖面达88%。城市居民最低生活保障基本实现应保尽保。2005年，哈尔滨市居民家庭人均可支配收入为10065元，比2000年增长78.7%，年均增幅达到12.3%。农村居民人均纯收入为4006元，比2000年增长61.8%，年均增长10.1%。

济南

济南机场候机楼

济南是中国山东省的省会，全省政治、经济、文化、科技、教育中心和全国区域性金融中心城市。辖6区3县1市，总面积8177平方公里，人口600万，其中市区面积3257平方公里，人口344万。

济南是著名的“泉城”，泉水众多，神态各异，历史悠久。域内有名的泉733处，以趵突泉、黑虎泉、珍珠泉、五龙潭、百脉泉、墨泉、梅花泉最为著名。依泉形成融“山泉湖河城”一体的自然风貌，培育了诚信、创新、和谐的地缘文化。济南是中华文明的发祥地之一，国家历史文化名城，齐鲁文化底蕴深厚，历代文人墨客多聚于此。济南区位交通优越，南依泰山，北跨黄河，是黄河中下游和环渤海地区南翼中心城市，连接京津－沪宁两大都市圈和沿海开放与内陆开发的重要枢纽。拥有铁路、航空、高速公路等多元立体交通体系。

“十五”期间，济南经济社会发展站在新的起点：2005年，全市实现生产总值1876.5亿元，比2000年接近翻一番，年均增长14.2%，人均3916美元。地方财政一般预算收入106亿元，是2000年的2.2倍，年均增长16.7%。三次产业比例由2000年的10:43.9:46.1调整为7.1:46:46.9。非公有制经济、高新技术产值比重和经济外向度五年间提高16个、9.9个和3.7个百分点，实际利用外资年均增长26.1%，进出口总额年均增长25.5%，世界500强企业在济已达24家。从2003年开始，高标准实施交通、管网、绿化、供水、康居、设施建设，名城、蓝天保护，河道和容貌整治“十大工程”，完成城建投资850亿元，是“九五”时期的2.2倍。城市基础设施逐步完善、生态环境明显改善、城市形象显著提升、城市承载力明显增强。

未来五年是济南又快又好发展的重要时期，济南市将把握城市化、工业化进程加快和承办十一届全国运动会等新的重大发展机遇，加快建设产业实力雄厚、科技教育发达、服务功能完善、生态环境良好、集聚辐射能力强大、具有深厚历史文化底蕴、独特自然景观、浓郁现代化气息的省会城市和区域中心城市。

趵突泉

济南钢铁集团热轧薄板生产线

中国重汽集团焊装线

齐鲁软件园创业广场

苏州

S U Z H O U

洋苏州——中新合作工业园

新苏州——高新技术开发区

水苏州——美不胜收太湖景

苏州是中国首批公布的24个历史文化名城之一，素有“人间天堂”之美誉。

苏州城是座绵延了2500余年的水乡古城。作为吴文化的发祥地，苏州千百年来贤才辈出，人文荟萃，自唐至清共出状元50名，为全国之最。绘画、书法、诗文流派纷呈，独具魅力；戏曲、医学、建筑自成流派、独树一帜；刺绣、缂丝、宋锦、雕塑、玉石和红木雕刻各有千秋，巧夺天工。拙政园等9个苏州古典园林和“中国戏曲之母”昆曲被联合国教科文组织列入《世界遗产名录》。

改革开放以来，古老的苏州焕发出勃勃生机，社会经济发展取得令人瞩目的成就。美国《新闻周刊》将苏州评为全球九大新兴高科技城市之一；《纽约时报》认为“丝绸之府苏州，而今成为全球经济的高科技前哨阵地”；联合国工业委员会将苏州列为中国最具活力的六大城市与地区之一。苏州还先后获得国家卫生城市、国家环境保护模范城、全国社会治安综合治理工作优秀地区、中国优秀旅游城市、全国文化模范市、全国科技兴市工作先进市、全国创建文明城市工作先进市、全国政务公开先进地区、国际花园城市等荣誉称号。

老苏州——七里山塘传古韵

SUZHOU

崛起的郑州

——中原大地上的璀璨明珠

极目远眺

嵩山少林寺

二七广场

郑州地处中华腹地，九州之中，十省通衢，北临黄河，西依嵩山，东南接黄淮平原。郑州是全国人口第一大省河南的省会，是国家命名的中国历史文化名城、中国优秀旅游城市、国家卫生城市、国家园林城市、全国科技进步先进城市、全国双拥模范城市，名列全国八大古都之一。全市总面积7446.2平方公里，其中市区面积1010.3平方公里，建成区面积262平方公里，全市总人口716万。现辖6区5市1县，建有国家郑州高新技术产业开发区、郑州经济技术开发区和郑州出口加工区，由世界著名建筑设计大师黑川纪章先生设计规划的郑东新区建设已初具规模。

“十五”期间，全市继续发挥商贸优势，努力拉长工业短腿，实现了国民经济又快又好发展和社会事业全面进步。2005年郑州市生产总值达1650亿元，5年平均增长13.6%。在2005年全国地级以上城市综合实力排名中居第23位，并被评为“全国投资环境50优城市”。地方财政一般预算收入达136.1亿元，列全国省会城市第7位。

“十一五”期间，中部六省积极响应中央号召，一场声势浩大的经济大潮正在中部涌动，市委、市政府审时度势，提出了抢抓机遇、全力推进跨越式发展的战略决策，努力将重要的机遇期转化为真正的黄金发展期，不断跨越新的标杆，创造新的业绩，争取早日崛起在中原大地。

初具规模的郑东新区

居住创业两适宜的文明之城

中山

ZHONGSHAN

ZHONGSHAN

中山——中国革命先行者孙中山先生的故乡，是广东省辖地级市，地处珠三角腹地，位于深港、广佛和珠澳三大都市圈的结合部，毗邻港澳，海陆交通发达，年平均温度22度，面积1800平方公里，下辖18个镇、5个街道办事处和1个国家火炬高技术产业开发区。全市常住人口243.46万人，其中户籍人口140.82万人。

中山是中国改革开放先行地区之一。近年来，中山大力推进工业化、城市化和信息化，先后建成了中国包装印刷基地、国家健康科技产业基地、中国电子（中山）基地和中国技术市场科技成果产业化（中山）示范基地等19个国家基地以及一批技术含量较高的工业园区，中山工业形成以高新技术产业为龙头，以电气机械及器材、电子及通信设备、化学原料及化学制品、金属制品、纺织服装等五大产业为支柱产业。小榄五金制品、古镇灯饰、沙溪休闲服装、大涌红木家具、南头空调产品、东凤小家电、黄圃食品加工等区域特色经济蓬勃发展，产品在全国占有较高的市场份额。全球500强中有20余家企业落户中山，国内知名企业如长虹、TCL、中海油、格兰仕等也先后在中山投资设厂。目前，中山正以东部沿海地区开发为契机，加快产业结构调整，推动产业集聚，促进经济结构向高级化发展。2005年全市实现生产总值817.56亿元，工业总产值2495.69亿元，常住人均生产总值33631元（折4167美元）。全市共有名牌名标、免检产品262个。

中山社会主义新农村建设一瞥

工业强市托起经济强市

中山人发扬“敢为天下先”的精神，大力弘扬“博爱、创新、包容、和谐”的新时期中山人精神，积极构建既适宜居住又适宜创业、经济社会协调发展的和谐社会。1994年以来，中山市先后获得全国绿化先进城市、全国科教兴市先进城市、国家卫生城市、全国园林城市、联合国“人居奖”、国家环保模范城市、中国优秀旅游城市、全国畅通工程模范城市、全国双拥模范城、全国社会治安综合治理优秀地市“长安杯”、首批全国文明城市、中国品牌经济城市、全国科技进步先进市等荣誉称号。在城市居民生活水平大幅提高的同时，中山始终坚持利益向下，向农民和外来工倾斜，着力解决农民就业、医保社保及外来工居住和子女就学等问题，初步形成了居住、创业两适宜的良好环境。今日中山，经济繁荣，社会进步，正朝着文明富庶的现代化文明城市迈进。

中山大地激扬绿色乐章

美好人居环境清晰展现

大庆——绿色油化之都，天然百湖之城

大庆市委书记　盖如垠

大庆市长　韩学键

中国最大的石油生产基地和重要的石化工业基地之一，中国优秀旅游城市、国家环境保护模范城市、中国最具魅力城市、中国综合实力百强城市。全市下辖五区四县，面积2.1万平方公里，人口264.4万，其中，市区面积5107平方公里，人口122.3万。在近半个世纪的开发建设中，英雄的大庆人，一次创业，在一片荒原上开发建成了世界级的特大油田，为民族争了光，为国家做出了重要贡献；二次创业，在这片神奇的土地上，又崛起了一座繁荣美丽、文明和谐的现代化城市，续写着一个又一个新的辉煌。今天的大庆正在全力“创建百年油田、构建战略新高、共建和谐社会、加快迈上科学发展新阶段”。2005年，实现地区生产总值1400.7亿元，经济总量占黑龙江省1/4以上。人均GDP5.3万

炼塔林立

黎明湖畔

世纪大道

元，在全国名列前茅。向国家和省财政上缴资金362.2亿元，上缴资金占中央财政收入的1%，占黑龙江省本级财政收入的70%。大庆已累计向国家上缴资金超过万亿元。

40多年来，大庆累计生产原油18.7亿吨，连续27年保持5000万吨以上高产稳产，目前仍保持5000万吨以上油气当量，享有“共和国加油机”的美誉。近年来，大庆接续产业发展不断提速。全市现有大中型石化企业14家，已形成集炼油、化工、化纤、塑料为主体的化工产业群；国家大庆高新技术产业开发区以及轻纺工业园、皮革工业园、橡胶工业园、大豆产业园、省级西城工业园等一大批基础设施配套的产业园区迅速发展，地方工业连续四年以40%以上的速度增长，新兴第三产业和现代农业发展方兴未艾，业已形成以石油为基础，以产值超千亿的石化产业和农产品加工、纺织、新材料、机械制造、电子信息等数个产值超百亿产业为骨干的格局。

大庆十分重视基础设施和生态环境建设，先后投资建设了城乡公路交通、现代文体设施、城市供热供水供电、草原生态恢复、城市绿化美化、水环境治理、绿色能源生产、城市空气质量测控和噪声治理、居住小区改造等一大批现代城市功能项目。城乡道路网络完善，交通顺畅，天蓝地绿水清，居住环境舒适整洁，文化生活丰富多彩，商贸服务发达繁荣，一座“湖在城中、城在绿中”的绿色油化之都、天然百湖之城正在向世人展示其现代都市的风采。

油田冬景

魅力鄂尔多斯

市委书记 云 峰

市长 刘 锦

在中国西部版图上有这样一片土地，它三面被黄河环绕，是中华文明的发祥地之一，它物华天宝、资源富集，有“塞外能源宝库”之美誉，它历史厚重、旷古久远，是一代天骄成吉思汗长眠的圣地，它以亘古、壮美、巍峨的自然景致令无数人魂牵梦绕....，它有一个涂着传奇色彩的名字——鄂尔多斯。

“鄂尔多斯”是蒙古语，汉译为“众多宫殿”，鄂尔多斯市与晋陕宁毗邻，身处于呼包鄂银经济圈腹地，辖七旗一区，东胜区为全市政治、经济、文化中心，已连续三年进入全国百强县之列。全市总面积8.7万平方公里，总人口147万，是一个以蒙古族为主体、汉族居多数的多民族聚居区。

鄂尔多斯得天独厚，物产富集，以“羊、煤、土、气”驰名中外。这里的鄂尔多斯羊绒衫久誉盛名；这里的煤炭总储量达到7656亿吨，占全国总储量的六分之一；天然碱总储量6000万吨；伴生纯碱储量1369万吨；芒硝总储量70亿吨，约占世界总储量的42%以上，高岭土、天然气为世界瞩目。这里有世界级的大型现代化露天煤矿——准格尔露天矿，有世界机械化程度最高的井工开采煤矿——神东矿区，有世界级的整装天然气田——苏里格气田，有世界最大的羊绒制品加工基地，有正在建设的世界级煤液化基地。鄂尔多斯市是正在建设的国家能源重化工基地，也是我国西煤东运、西气东输、西电东送的重要基地。

乘西部大开发的东风，鄂尔多斯经济迅速崛起，逐步形成了煤炭、电力、绒纺、化工、天然气、建材等支柱产业，成为内蒙古自治区发展最快的地区，同时也成为我国中西部地区最具发展活力的城市之一。近年来，在市委、市政府的正确领导下，鄂尔多斯市坚持以科学发展观统领经济社会发展全局，以“战胜自我、推进文明、实现跨越”的鄂尔多斯精神为动力源泉，开拓创新，锐意进取，与时俱进，扎实工作，实施“大煤炭、大煤电、大化工、大循环”四大战略，开创了鄂尔多斯经济社会发展的新局面。2004年，成功挺进中国综合实力百强城市。2005年全市GDP达到550亿元，超“十五”计划250亿元，是2000年的3.7倍；财政收入突破90亿元，超“十五”计划60亿元以上，是2000年的5.9倍；城乡居民收入分别达到11025元和4601元，在2000年的基础上基本实现翻番。全市8个旗区财政收入全部超过亿元，其中东胜区、准格尔旗财政收入突破25亿元。“十一五”鄂尔多斯将会在“优化布局，集中发展”战略指导下，再创奇迹。

这是一片创业的热土，这是一个令人梦想成真的天堂。好客的鄂尔多斯人将以满腔的热情，欢迎海内外有识之士来这里投资兴业、铸就辉煌。

成陵

绒城

市委书记　张传林

市委副书记、市长　张新起

潍坊

Weifang

潍坊市地处山东半岛中部，面积1.58万平方公里，人口852万，是著名的世界风筝都、中国优秀旅游城市、国家环保模范城市，荣获“中国特色城市奖”和“山东省适宜人居环境奖”。

潍坊区位优势明显，是山东半岛的交通枢纽，陆、海、空四通八达。潍坊资源丰富，特别是土地资源、矿产资源、水资源、劳动力资源和电力供应充足。潍坊产业基础较好，农业产业化水平较高，是全国重要的优质农产品生产加工基地；工业基础雄厚，形成了机械装备、纺织服装、海洋化工、食品加工、造纸包装等支柱产业；商贸流通繁荣，现代物流兴旺，是鲁东地区重要的物资集散地；以风筝文化为代表的文化和旅游产业成为重要的城市名片，一年一度的潍坊国际风筝会、鲁台经贸洽谈会和中国（寿光）国际蔬菜科技博览会搭建起对外开放的重要平台。2005年，全市实现GDP1471亿元，财政总收入141.6亿元。

按照建设现代化强市的目标，潍坊确立了“两基地、两中心、一枢纽”的发展定位，即建设以动力机械、海洋化工、纺织和高新技术产业为基础的现代制造业基地，以高级职业技术教育为特色的文化教育产业基地；具有国际影响的世界风筝文化传播交流中心，半岛地区重要的商贸物流中心；联系山东半岛城市群的重要交通枢纽，真正使潍坊成为令本地人为之自豪，令外地人为之向往的地方。

热情好客的潍坊人民，热诚欢迎海内外朋友来潍坊观光旅游，投资兴业，共创美好未来！

潍坊国际风筝会开幕式

宽阔的城市道路

潍坊博物馆

贵阳

Guiyang

贵阳简称“筑”，是贵州省的省会，全省政治、经济和文化中心。全市总面积8034平方公里，人口353万，辖六区一市三县，拥有一个国家经济技术开发区、一个国家高新技术开发区、一个省级经济技术开发区。

贵阳具有四个方面的显著特点：一是区位优势突出。贵阳是大西南重要的交通通信枢纽，川黔、湘黔、黔桂、贵昆铁路交汇于贵阳，322、321、210国道贯穿全境，公路密度居全省之冠。已形成东西三横、南北三纵的现代立体交通网络。二是自然资源突出。丰富的矿产资源，贵阳蕴藏有丰富的铝、磷、煤、铁等52种矿产资源。其中，铝土矿保有储量5亿吨，占全国的五分之一；磷矿保有储量20亿吨，集中了全国70%的优质磷矿，煤炭储量9亿吨。多样的生物资源，贵州是全国四大药材产地之一，各种天然药用资源共有4290种，自古就有“夜郎无闲草、黔地多灵药”的美誉。贵阳市位于天然药用植物资源丰富的黔中经济地带，全市现有中药材资源1250余种，蕴藏量96.3万吨。三是资源优势突出。贵阳是一座以资源开发见长的新兴工业城市，现已建成以食品、机械、化工、冶金、电子、轻工、建材为主，14个工业部门，65个门类的综合性工业体系。主要工业产品和工业行业在全国处于重要的地位。贵阳的铝工业是全国最大的生产基地之一，磷化工是全国的三大生产基地之一，精密光学仪器是全国三大生产基地之一，电子仪器仪表是全国五大生产基地之一。四是旅游资源突出。贵阳是中国优秀旅游城市，是“公园省”贵州的旅游服务中心和游客集散地，境内山环水绕，风光旖旎，民族风情浓郁，民风纯朴，是一个多姿多彩的旅游城市。“美在自然，贵在城边”是贵阳旅游景点的显著特色。城区有大型公园黔灵公园、森林公园，国家风景名胜区红枫湖，位于市郊的花溪公园、天河潭、南江峡谷、百花湖等风景名胜地，景色秀丽，交通便捷。贵阳是中国喀斯特地貌发育最完整和民族民间文化、历史文化保留最丰厚的城市之一。宜人的气候是贵阳得天独厚的自然资源，享有“上有天堂、下有苏杭，气候宜人数贵阳”的美誉，素有“天然空调”之称。今年5月，贵阳又入选“2006中国十佳避暑旅游城市”并排名榜首，荣获“中国避暑之都”的特别称誉。

金阳新区是我市创新城市发展理念，拓展城市空间，开发建设的新城区。目前，金阳新区已提前5年基本完成了第一建设时序17平方公里的基础设施建设，顺利完成了市级行政中心、贵阳一中的搬迁，住宅、医院、商贸广场等公建项目正在全面实施。现正积极引进高新技术企业和一批有实力的房地产商，大力培植产业，聚集人气和商气。按照金阳新区的远景规划，至2020年，用地规模40平方公里，人口规模40万人；至2050年，用地规模106平方公里，人口规模50万人，努力把金阳新区建成生态环保型、园林型、数字化、循环经济和可持续发展的现代化新城区。

近年来，我市以国家实施西部大开发为契机，坚持科学的发展观，抢抓机遇，加快发展，按照建设生态经济市的目标，大力实施“环境立市、工业强市、科教兴市、人才强市和可持续发展”五大战略，经济实力不断增强，基础设施日新月异，投资环境不断改善，城市建设取得历史性突破，各项事业蓬勃发展，经济社会全面进步。2005年全市生产总值525.62亿元，同比增长14.6%；财政总收入133.15亿元，同比增长20.2%。我市相继被评为全国园林绿化先进城市、全国绿化模范城市、中日环境合作示范城市、全国卫生城市、全国科教兴市先进城市、全国双拥模范城市、国家森林城市、全国首家循环经济生态试点城市、联合国人居署授予中国可持续发展试点城市等。

市区全景

在贵阳高新技术产业开发区内的南方汇通世华微硬盘有限公司
是国内第一家生产微硬盘的自主技术企业

金阳的交通

贵阳会展中心

高楼看贵阳

盘锦

P A N J I N

鹤乡

城市一景

小区景色

建造中的船舶修造产业园

红海滩

盘锦是1984年经国家有关部门批准建立的辽宁省省辖市，地处辽河三角洲中心，面积4071平方公里，下辖兴隆台、双台子两区和盘山、大洼两县，全市户籍人口126万，有满族、回族、朝鲜族等34个少数民族。

盘锦作为全国首批小康城市，资源丰富，生态良好。全国第三大油田——辽河油田座落在此，素有“油城”之称。油气储量占全国已探明储量的10%，是我国最大的稠油生产基地之一。在原有石化产业基础上，新型建材、汽车配件、制药和现代服务业近年得到快速发展。地区生产总值多年来始终位居辽宁省前列。2005年，全市地区生产总值实现441.3亿元，比上年增长6.4%，人均生产总值实现4000美元。城市居民人均可支配收入达到11025元，农民人均纯收入5067元。

盘锦作为全国优秀旅游城市和国家生态建设示范区，自然禀赋优越、四季分明、植被繁茂、多水无山。世界第一大苇田和广袤的滨海湿地吸引了丹顶鹤、黑嘴鸥等珍稀鸟类在此栖息，使盘锦享有“鹤乡”和“中国黑嘴鸥之乡”的美誉。作为全国重要的优质米生产基地，“盘锦大米”以其品质上乘而享誉国内，并受到原产地保护。这里河网纵横、海河交汇，渔

环境优美的小洼油田

大型雕塑玉猪龙

浅海采油

业资源丰富，中华绒螯蟹产量居全国首位，是中国北方最大的河蟹人工孵化和养殖基地。

盘锦作为环渤海沿海开放城市，公路、铁路、海运系统四通八达。秦沈高速铁路、沟海铁路、京沈高速公路、盘海营高速公路把盘锦与东北、京津、内蒙和全国紧密相连。

盘锦在以较强的经济实力向全面建设小康社会迈进的同时，教育文化亦进入一个新的发展阶段。教育改革家魏书生民主、科学的教育思想正在实践中一点一滴地形成体系。近年来，人口仅占全省3%的盘锦，每年向清华北大输送优秀学子达全省10%以上。国办唯一不断代的碑林已向社会开放。被文化部和中国美协评为全国首批文化产业示范基地的辽河文化产业园，已吸引了大批的艺术名人来此落户，并创造出优异成绩。东北地区最大的美术馆——辽河美术馆已开始承办国家美术展。

盘锦人杰地灵，热情欢迎有识之士来此发展，共创美好未来。

湘潭

XIANGTAN

中共湘潭市委书记陈润儿（左）、市人民政府市长彭宪法（右）、常务副市长朱明华（中）　在九华工业园调研

君子莲广场夜色迷人

湘钢年产 600 万吨钢工程

湘潭市地处湖南省中部，与长沙市、株洲市构成湖南经济最为雄厚的“金三角”。在世界著名杂志《福布斯》公布的排行榜中，湘潭列中国大陆最适宜投资办厂城市第3位，最佳商业城市第58位。全市总面积5015平方公里，人口284万，其中市区人口80万。2005年，全市人均GDP、人均财政收入、城乡居民人平可支配收入等指标均居全省前列。

湘潭历史悠久，早在十七世纪初期就是全国著名的“米市”和“药都”，素有“金湘潭”的美称，“小南京”的雅号。湘潭人杰地灵，旅游资源丰富，是一代伟人毛泽东、著名军事家彭德怀、世界文化名人齐白石的故乡，是全国绿化先进城市和湖南省文明城市。

湘潭交通便利，铁路湘黔线横穿市境，京广线在市区经过；公路四通八达，107国道和320国道构成境内公路网的主干，上瑞高速、京珠高速穿城而过，为全国地级市高速公路最密集的地区。

湘潭是湖南重要的工业基地，现已形成冶金、机电、化工、纺织、建材五大支柱产业为主体，门类齐全、基础雄厚的工业体系。拥有湘潭电机集团的混合动力大巴和百吨载重汽车、江麓机械集团的塔吊、湘潭钢铁集团的宽厚板以及引进德国技术的汽车尾气三元净化器、无机房电梯等一批处于行业发展前沿、科技含量高的优势产品。

湘潭是享誉中外的湖湘文化发源地，科教事业发达。拥有湘潭大学、湖南科技大学等5所高等院校，在校学生7.53万人。全市拥有科研开发机构280多家及两个博士后流动站，国有企事业单位有各类技术人员近8万人，占职工总人数近30%。

湘潭城市基础设施完善。水、电、气、路基本配套，文化、卫生、体育设施齐全，交通通讯便捷，已成为贯通湖南南北高新技术走廊的核心部分。在市区黄金宝地建立了高新技术产业开发区、昭山旅游经贸开发区、九华工业基地，并提供优惠政策，大力开展招商引资。

湘潭三大桥雄跨湘江

开放的湘潭因实施长株潭经济一体化发展战略而倍受国内外投资者关注，长株潭城市群现为国家中部崛起战略而重点扶持的4个城市群之一。湘潭正抓住历史机遇，实施开放带动、强工富市、科教兴市“三大战略”，大力推进“三化”进程，努力建设成为湖南先进制造业中心、湘中南现代物流中心、长株潭生态休闲中心。

腾飞的宝鸡 投资的热土

市委书记 姚引良

代市长 王宏

宝鸡位于关中平原西部，辖9县3区，总面积1.8万平方公里，总人口376万人，是陕西省第二大城市，设有国家高新技术产业开发区。先后荣获“全国双拥模范城市”、“全国社会治安综合治理优秀城市、“中国优秀旅游城市”、“全国卫生城市”、“国家环保模范城市”、“国家园林城市”、“中国品牌经济城市”、“全国创建文明城市工作先进城市”等称号。连续两年荣获“中国综合实力百强城市”。渭河生态治理建设项目被国家有关部门授予“中国人居环境范例奖”。

宝鸡历史文化悠久，是华夏始祖炎帝的诞生地，也是周秦王朝的发祥地，素有“炎帝故里、周秦故都、佛骨圣地”、“青铜器之乡”和“民间工艺美术之乡”之美誉。宝鸡陆路交通发达，位于中国版图的几何中心，陇海、宝成、宝中铁路在此交汇，是连接西南、西北的交通枢纽，是亚欧大陆桥——陇海线上第三个大“十字”。宝鸡工业基础雄厚，作为西部工业重镇，通过实施“工业强市”战略，现已形成了机械、电子、食品、有色金属四大优势产业为主的35个工业门类。宝鸡生产的钛材居全国前茅，钢桥梁、铁路道岔居全国第二，灯泡居全国第三；通信及导航设备、精密磨齿机床、石油钻采设备、重型汽车、电冰箱、烟酒食品、心脏起搏器等产品成为国内或行业的名优产品。宝鸡城市环境优美，近年来不断加大环境治理和生态建设，已形成“两条林带，一片水面，城在林中，水在城中，依山傍水”的城市景观。通过着力打造“诚信宝鸡”、“平安宝鸡”、“人文宝鸡”、“和谐宝鸡”，使城市品位提高，魅力彰显，人居环境和投资环境更加优越。

水在城中

佛骨圣地法门寺

“十五”期间，市委、市政府领导全市人民以科学发展观为指导，以建设“工业强市、畜牧大市、旅游名市和现代化生态园林大城市”以及创建 “西部最佳投资环境和最佳人居环境”为目标，加快发展、科学发展，经济实现了新跨越，各项社会事业取得全面进步。2005年全市实现生产总值416亿元，财政总收入46亿元，全社会固定资产投资175亿元，比“九五”末年均分别增长11.9%、20.8%和19.9%，综合实力显著增强，大城市雏形已初现，一个和谐奋进新宝鸡正崛起在陕西关中的西部。

西部大开发的热潮持续涌动，奋进腾飞的宝鸡是一方投资热土，我们热忱欢迎海内外朋友到宝鸡观光旅游，投资发展，实现共赢。

宝鸡城市全景

湖南工业重镇——

株洲

市委书记　肖雅瑜

市长　颜石生

株洲市位于湖南省东部，现辖9个县市区，全市总面积11270平方公里，总人口372万，其中城区面积85.6平方公里，常住人口90余万。2005年全市人均生产总值14500元。

株洲交通区位优势突出，是我国南方最大的铁路交通枢纽。京广、浙赣、湘黔三条铁路干线和106、320国道以及京珠（北京至珠海）和上瑞（上海至云南瑞丽）高速公路交汇于市区，也是长（沙）、株（洲）、（湘）潭城市群的重要一隅。

株洲自然和人文历史资源丰富，有国家"神洲第一陵"炎帝陵风景区、神农谷国家森林公园、酒埠江国家地质公园等风景名胜；有李立三、左权、谭震林等老一辈革命家的故居或陵园。

株洲经济实力雄厚，株洲硬质合金集团是亚洲第一、世界第三的合金生产基地，株洲冶炼集团有限公司是亚洲最大的铅锌冶炼基地，株洲电力机车有限公司是全国最大的电力机车生产企业之一。芦淞市场群是中国十大服装批发市场、中南最大的服饰物流中心，年交易额200多亿元。2004和2005年被中国福布斯评为中国最佳商业城市。

根据"十一五"发展规划，株洲被省委、省政府确定为湖南优先发展区域，在中部崛起的战略进程中，株洲迎来了新一轮加速发展机遇。

[上图]
市委市政府奖励在株洲工作的外国专家

[中图]
轨道交通装备制造基地——株洲电力机车有限公司

[下图]
庄严雄伟的炎帝大殿

[右图]
夜幕初临滨江花园

奋进中的张家口

市委书记 刘永瑞

市长 高金浩

城区大清河诱人之夜

历史名城张家口位于河北省西北部，东临首都北京，西连“煤都”大同，南接华北腹地，北靠内蒙古草原，是沟通中原与北疆、连接东部经济带与西部资源产区的纽带。张家口市现辖4区13县。总人口450万人，地域面积3.69万平方公里。其中，中心城区面积845平方公里，2005年末总人口86.5万人。近年来，全市人民在市委、市政府的正确领导下，坚持以经济建设为中心，开拓进取，凝聚实干，全力推进改革开放，经济和社会发展取得了显著成就。

中心城区是张家口经济社会发展的主动力。2005年张家口市中心城区实现生产总值180.04亿元，人均生产总值达2547美元。非农业增加值占GDP的比重98.2%，第三产业增加值占GDP的比重37.5%。实现全部财政收入51.45亿元，年末城市居民储蓄存款余额达179.64亿元，人均储蓄20758元。

城市建设步伐不断加快，城市功能进一步完善，城市面貌发生深刻变化。目前，市区大清河治理已完成一期工程，建成区绿化覆盖率达33.9%，人均公共绿地达到4.4平方米。

消费市场需求旺盛，供给充足、市场繁荣活跃，城市居民生活水平不断提高。2005年市区社会消费品零售总额达77.1亿元。城市居民人均可支配收入7714元。城市居民人均消费性支出5914元，城市居民恩格尔系数为37.5%。

2005年，在中国综合实力百强城市评价中，张家口跻身第91位。

张家口有着独特的风能资源，矿产资源。近年来，张家口正在全力营造对外开放的新格局，这座塞外名城将以新姿欢迎八方来客。

主城区污水处理厂已正式竣工运行

实力雄厚的工业是张家口经济的重要支撑

独特的自然条件造就了华北最大的天然滑雪场

风能正在成为助推张家口经济的丰富资源

泰安

泰山十八盘

市委书记、市人大主任　耿文清

市长　贾学英

泰安因泰山而得名，寓意“国泰民安”。泰安市辖泰山、岱岳两区，新泰、肥城两市，宁阳、东平两县，面积7762平方公里，人口550万。泰城依山而建，山城相依，风光秀丽，荣获“中国优秀旅游城市”、“国家卫生城市”等称号。泰山为五岳之首，它拥有国家重点风景名胜区、世界自然与文化遗产、中国旅游胜地40佳、国家地质公园、“中华十大名山”之首、全国文明风景旅游区等桂冠。

泰安市位于山东省中部，地处中国南北交通要冲，京沪铁路纵贯南北，京沪、京福高速公路在泰安交汇，拟建的京沪高速铁路在泰安设泰山站。泰安市矿产资源丰富，具有储量大、品位高、分布广的特点，是山东省重要的能源、原材料基地。其中，石膏储量居亚洲之冠，岩盐和自然硫折纯储量居全国首位，钾盐、蛇纹岩和玉石居全省首位，铝土矿、铁矿和煤等也位居全省前列。科技教育发达，现有7所高等院校和21个科研单位，并拥有中国科学院、中国工程院两院院士多名，是山东省三大科技文化教育中心之一。

近年来，泰安市认真贯彻落实科学发展观，围绕建设经济强市，突出工业经济、民营经济、招商引资三大重点，经济快速发展，实力明显壮大，2005年实现生产总值855.7亿元，地方财政收入40.6亿元。泰安具有较好的工业基础，形成了以能源、汽车及零部件、无机非金属材料、输变电设备、化工、纺织、食品饮料等行业为骨干的工业体系，拥有国内生产能力最大的玻璃纤维、纸面石膏板、甲酸、三聚氰胺等生产线。旅游服务业活跃兴旺，泰山以其雄伟壮丽的自然风光与悠久灿烂的人文景观，每年吸引一千多万人次的海内外游客前来观光游览，泰安旅游设施完善，旅游商品丰富。商贸流通业繁荣，餐饮业发达。

“投资泰安、稳如泰山”是泰安市的环境品牌，
是投资商对泰安的共同评价。多年来泰安市着力创
诚实守信的投资环境，建造“蓝天、碧水、青山绿
家园”的生活环境，把泰安建成了环境优美、投资
务优良、最宜居住的山水园林旅游城市。泰安像一
璀璨的明珠，在齐鲁大地上绚丽夺目，蓬勃发展。
放的泰安真诚欢迎海内外朋友前来参观游览、投资
业，携手共建美好未来！

天平湖公园

天地广场

泰山广场

鹤岗

在振兴中腾飞的老工业基地——

在我国“金鸡”项下，东北边陲，一座发展中的现代化城市正在崛起，这就是——中国鹤岗。

鹤岗拥有“三金之乡”的美誉。总面积14684平方公里，下辖萝北、绥滨两个边境县和6个行政区，人口110万。

鹤岗市位于黑龙江省东北部，地处小兴安岭向三江平原过渡的缓冲地带，西屏小兴安岭与伊春相邻，东南临松花江与佳木斯接壤，北隔黑龙江与俄罗斯相望，扼守东北要冲，区位优越，交通便利。

鹤岗具有多元的主体资源优势。域内矿产资源和农林资源丰富，煤炭、粮食、木材是三大重要资源。煤炭地质储量19.5亿吨，可采储量9.5亿吨。煤层气总储量347亿立方米。林地面积65万公顷，活立木蓄积量4000万立方米，70%是天然林。耕地面积44万公顷，粮食生产能力40亿斤，是我省水稻、大豆主产区，是发展养殖业用乳、肉、皮、骨等深加工产业具备较好条件的地区。此外，还有石墨、陶砾页岩等30种非金属矿产资源，开发条件优良。

市委书记　刘国中

市长　朱清文

鹤岗具有明显的对俄开放等区位优势。与俄罗斯有235公里的边境线，萝北口岸是全省距哈尔滨最近的国家一类口岸，年吞吐能力48万吨；黑龙江“黄金水道”可运行5000吨级船舶，能以较近的距离到达日本和韩国。

鹤岗具有突出的水、电、土地等生产要素优势。水资源总量38万立方米；电力供应充足，180万千瓦鹤岗电厂为经济发展和人民生活提供了充足的能源。土地资源丰富，后续潜力较大，有能力承载大型资源精深加工和高耗能、高耗水项目。

鹤岗物华天宝，人杰地灵；政通人和，经济兴盛。站在新的起点上，鹤岗百万人民将竭诚与海内外各界朋友携手并肩，坚持“建设两大基地，发展六大产业”成为鹤岗落实科学发展观，构建和谐社会的最强音，把鹤岗建成最具潜质，最富品味的北方边疆名城。

中国食品名城——漯河

漯河市位于河南省中部，1986年升格为省辖市，总面积2617平方公里，总人口253万人。漯河是全国综合改革试点市、全国开拓农村市场试点市、国家农村信息化示范城市、全国卫生先进城市、国家园林城市、全国绿化模范城市、全国首家中国食品名城。

漯河历史悠久，文化灿烂，启于北魏、盛于明清，曾以商贸和水陆交通发达而享誉中原，素有“水旱码头”之称。东汉著名的经学家、文字学家许慎诞生于此，他编纂的《说文解字》是中国乃至世界最早的字典。目前已发现的主要古迹有：曹丕代汉的历史实证“受禅台”和“三绝碑”，早于赵州桥20年、被誉为“天下第一桥”的隋代小商桥。漯河是全省重要的铁路和高速公路“双十字”交通枢纽，淮河两大支流沙河、澧河贯穿全境并在市区交汇，滨河城市特色明显。

近年来，在省委、省政府的正确领导下，全面贯彻科学发展观，漯河经济社会发展取得显著成绩。2005年，全市生产总值达到322亿元，地方财政一般预算收入13.2亿元，规模以上工业完成增加值136.5亿元，城镇居民人均可支配收入7923元、农民人均纯收入3319元，各项主要经济指标的增幅均创近十年来的最好水平。食品加工主导产业优势明显，培育出了全国最大的肉类加工企业之一双汇集团、全国最大的方便面生产企业之一南街村集团、全国第一家葡萄糖饮料生产企业澳的利集团等一批知名食品加工企业；培育出了4家全国食品工业百强企业、8家全省食品工业50强企业。食品工业年加工生猪1400万头、占全省的23%，年加工转化粮食300万吨、占全省的11.1%，鲜冻猪肉出口占全省同类产品出口的90%以上、占全国的四分之一。现有20多个国家和地区的客商投资漯河，5家世界500强企业和一批国内外知名企业在漯河有较大的投资项目。

在第三届中原食品节上，漯河市被中国食品工业协会授予全国首家“中国食品名城”

全国最大的方便面生产企业之一南街村集团

河南省省长李成玉（左三）、副省长史济春（右三）在漯河市委书记刘炳旺（左一）、市长靳克文（右二）等领导的陪同下，到漯河调研指导工作

全国最大的肉类加工企业之一双汇集团

中共金昌市委书记　李建华

金昌市市长　郑玉生

祖国的镍都—金昌

金昌市地处甘肃省河西走廊东段，面积 9600 平方公里，总人口 46.57 万人。因盛产镍而闻名于世，被誉为“祖国的镍都”，是全国最大的镍钴生产基地和铂族贵金属提炼中心之一，也是甘肃省重要的粮油生产和重化工生产基地。

矿产资源得天独厚，全市共发现矿产地 101 处。矿种包括铁、铬、镍、铜、钴、金、银、铂、磷、硅石、萤石、膨润土、建材花岗岩、煤、石油等 41 种。其中镍矿储量丰富，规模巨大，居世界第二、全国第一位。铜、钴等矿产储量居全国第二位。

“十五”以来，全市经济建设取得巨大成就，经济步入持续、健康、协调发展的快车道。2005 年生产总值跨上百亿元台阶，达到 115.87 亿元，是“九五”末的 3.1 倍，经济增长速度年均增长 15.4%；人均生产总值 24950 元，是“九五”末的 3 倍；大口径财政收入 18.7 亿元，是“九五”末的 2.8 倍；人均财政收入 4029 元，是“九五”末的 2.7 倍；规模以上工业增加值 82.8 亿元，是“九五”末的 3.9 倍；城镇居民可支配收入 10175 元，较“九五”末增长 56％；农民人均纯收入 3982 元，较“九五”末增长 44％；我市经济发展速度快于全国平均水平 6 个百分点。

金昌市将以健全的基础设施、优良的投资环境和优质的服务，热忱欢迎海内外朋友来我市投资兴业、携手并进、互利双赢，共创美好未来。

“腾飞的镍都”

西大河风光

永昌县钟鼓楼

金水湖景区

金川集团公司镍、铜、钴生产车间

座落在市中心的人民文化广场

宜宾——中国名酒之都

宜宾，位于四川盆地南缘，川滇黔三省结合部，金沙江、岷江、长江三江交汇处，素有“万里长江第一城”和“酒都”的美誉。辖一区九县，幅员面积13283平方公里，总人口519万人。久负盛名的“五粮液”就产在宜宾。

宜宾历史悠久。有2100多年的建城史，3000多年的酿酒史，酒文化、竹文化、茶文化及僰文化独具魅力，是古丝绸之路的起点，有“西南半壁古戎州”的称号，是国家历史文化名城。

宜宾资源富集。已探明的矿产达53种，是全省最大的煤炭基地。旅游资源独具特色，有“万里长江第一城”、“蜀南竹海天下翠”、“石海洞乡天下奇”、“僰 人故里天下谜”、“神州琼浆五粮液”等国内罕见独特的“五大旅游品牌”，是中国优秀旅游城市。

宜宾经济快速发展。2005年全市地区生产总值366亿元，比上年增长12.5%，“十五”期间年均增长12.4%，经济总量在四川省21个市州中居第4位。地方财政一般预算收入达15亿元。白酒、化工、建材、能源等是经济的支柱产业。拥有全国最大的白酒酿造企业之一——“中国酒业大王”宜宾五粮液集团、全国最大的维卡纤维生产企业之一宜宾丝丽雅集团和全国最大的氯碱化工生产基地之一宜宾天原股份公司。年产原煤1300多万吨。装机600万千瓦的向家坝电站建设已拉开序幕。

宜宾城市建设美好。2005年全市中心城区建城区面积49平方公里，人口58万人。宜宾是国家规划的长江上游一级中心城市。规划到2020年，中心城区人口100万以上，面积100平方公里以上。

宜宾交通设施完善。作为川滇黔结合部的交通枢纽，宜宾交通发达，形成了水陆空的立体交通体系。三江航运直抵上海，内

五粮液鹏程广场

宜宾发展前景美好。宜宾是长江上游成渝地区次区域中心。宜宾是全省规划重点培育的九个大城市之一，将成为四川省及川滇黔结合部区域最具有成长性和发展潜力的区域性中心城市。随着西部大开发向纵深扩进和金沙江水电资源滚动开发的正式启动，宜宾将迎来一个千载难逢的发展机遇。

昆铁路纵贯南北，2级民用机场，可通北京、上海、广州等特大城市。境内外公路网络畅通发达，内昆高速公路贯穿其境已向云南水富、昆明延伸，市区到主要县城半小时经济圈基本形成，基本实现了村村通公路。

宜宾南门大桥

蜀南大道

宜宾市一角

水东门

昆山

KUNSHAN

昆山出口加工区

城市广场

昆山东靠上海，西邻苏州，是江苏省的东大门。昆山历史悠久，人文荟萃，物产丰饶，素有江南“鱼米之乡”美称。

2005年，全市完成GDP730.03亿元，比上年增长24.1%；财政收入116.82亿元，其中地方一般预算收入51.62亿元，分别增长36.1%和36.5%；进出口总额332.19亿美元，增长41.1%；城镇居民人均可支配收入16809元，农民人均纯收入8519元，分别比上年增长12.0%和11.3%。在全国百强县市排名中，昆山居首位。在中国中小城市科学发展三项测评中，昆山名列全国中小城市综合实力100强第一位、最具投资潜力中小城市50强第一位、十佳节约型中小城市第二位。到2005年底，昆山率先实现了江苏全面建设小康社会四大类18项25条指标，被认为走出了一条全面建设小康社会的新时期“昆山之路”。改革开放以来，昆山先后荣获国家卫生城市、国家环保模范城市、全国创建文明城市工作先进市、全国优秀旅游城市、国家园林城市、全国生态市等称号。

一、加快实施产业升级，改善优化经济结构和运行质量。强化外向型经济优势。巩固外资特色，提高外向型经济的比重，推动技术升级和效益升级。加快推进民营经济赶超。推动一大批民营企业进入跨国公司的核心生产体系，较好地解决外源型经济和内源型经济之间的融合问题。积极培育新的支柱产业。近年来，电子信息、精密机械、精细化工、民生用品已成为昆山的支柱产业，光电产业、特种汽车产业正在崛起。

二、创新落实富民安民措施，着力提高城乡居民生活水平。大力实施以“人人有技能、个个有工作、家家有物业”为目标的“三有工程”；不断完善以低保、养老保险、医疗保险、拆迁补偿、征地补偿为主体的农村“五道保障”；建立完善弱势群体帮扶机制，促进共同富裕。

城市交通

体育馆

柏庐路

农民新村

古镇周庄夜景

三、坚持城乡统筹发展理念，不失时机地加快城市化进程。强化城市规划指导；坚持农户动迁、农村新型社区同步建设和基础设施建设先行；完善功能设施配套，加大社会事业投入；加强生态环境建设，目前，昆山市已通过了创建全国生态市省级调研考核。

四、注重强化社会管理，全面推进和谐社会建设。完善“三项机制”。建立招商引资、社会治安、社会稳定、新闻宣传和社情民意五项快速反应机制，治安防范机制和公共安全应急机制。协调好“四个关系”。致力于构建和谐的党群干群关系、政商关系、劳资关系和新老昆山人关系。弘扬六大传统文化。即戏曲文化、水乡旅游文化、政治哲学文化、商业文化、饮食文化和园艺文化，促进传统文化与现代文明的融合，不断丰富城市文化内涵，增添城市魅力。

五、切实加强党的建设，不断增强凝聚力、战斗力和创造力。从昆山实际需要出发，重点建好招商引资、城市规划建设、社会管理三支队伍。加大实施农村“基石工程”，积极推进非公企业党群工作一体化的工作模式，加大社区党建工作力度，切实加强党风廉政建设。

住宅小区

新城区

顺德

佛山市市委常委、常务副市长、顺德区委书记陈云贤

顺德区委副书记、区长周天明

广东顺德位于珠江三角洲中部，北靠广州，毗邻港澳，面积约806平方公里。顺德设县于明景泰三年（1452年），1992年撤县建市，2003年撤市改区。全区现有10个镇（街道），108个行政村，89个居委会。2005年末户籍人口116万人，流动人口86万人。顺德是著名的侨乡，有40多万港澳台同胞和海外侨胞。境内交通发达，公路密度达211公里／百平方公里。

2005年，全区实现地区生产总值856亿元，工农业总产值2062亿元，进出口贸易总额126亿美元，各项税收125亿元，地方一般预算收入47亿元，职工人均工资21091元，农民人均纯收入7360元；城乡居民储蓄余额791亿元。

改革开放以来，顺德始终坚持抢抓机遇和加快发展不动摇，

蓝天白云下的顺德

顺峰山公园俯瞰

德胜广场（德胜夜色）

逐渐由一个传统的农业县发展成为现代新兴的工业城市，区域综合竞争力不断提升，经济社会全面、持续、协调发展。工业制造业拥有家用电器、电子通信、机械装备、纺织服装、精细化工、医药保健、包装印刷、家具制造等八大支柱产业，是我国家电业制造基地，工业企业规模大、门类齐、品牌效应突出，拥有6个中国驰名商标，18个中国名牌产品，50个国家免检产品，48个广东省著名商标，51个广东省名牌产品。农业方面顺德是全国最大的淡水养殖基地和全国最大的花卉种植和销售基地之一。另外拥有“中国厨师之乡”、“中国家具商贸之都”、“中国家具制造重镇”、“中国牛仔服装名镇”和“全国龙舟之乡”之美誉，是世界著名武打影星李小龙的故乡，区内拥有清晖园、碧江金楼、西山庙等名胜古迹。作为珠三角区域性中心城市之一，近年顺德将城市化作为推动经济发展的新动力对地区进行规划和建设，并努力保持地方原来的珠三角水乡风貌特点。今天的顺德正朝着工业化、城市化、国际化和全面建设和谐社会的目标迈进。

中国名牌产品的汇粹

顺德是中国家具制造集散地，龙江镇荣获“中国家具制造重镇”称号

优美的人居环境

市委书记　朱民阳

和谐创新可持续发展的幸福

江阴

市长　王锡南

江阴港夜景

江阴大桥

江阴 位于长江三角洲中部，区域面积 988 平方公里，户籍人口 118 万人。江阴自古钟灵毓秀，人文彬盛，素有“文明礼仪之邦”的美誉。我国明代杰出的地理学家徐霞客、近代民族音乐家刘天华、现代文学家刘半农、文坛老将胡山源、著名电影表演艺术家上官云珠、中国现代机器人之父蒋新松就出生在江阴。

江阴秉承5000年文明历史，坚持科学发展、创新发展、率先发展的理念，实现了经济社会的持续加速和健康协调发展。2005年，全市完成地区生产总值788亿元，财政收入108亿元。江阴占全国的份额可以用“万千百”来概括，在全国万分之一的土地上，占全国近千分之一人口的江阴人，创造了超过全国二百五十分之一的地区生产总值、三百分之一的财政收入，培育了全国百分之一的上市公司，成为首批江苏省全面小康达标县（市）。同时，江阴还获得了全国文化先进市、国家环保模范城市、国家卫生城市、中国优秀旅游城市等50多项全国性的先进荣誉。在全国县域经济基本竞争力评比和百强县评比中，江阴都名列前茅。目前，江阴正在巩固提升全面小康建设水平，向基本实现现代化目标迈进，全力打造和谐创新、可持续发展的幸福江阴。

绿地

江阴城市概貌

振华港机

JIANG
YIN

改革开放以来，江阴的经济和社会事业建设取得了显著成就。2005年，全市完成地区生产总值788亿元、财政收入108亿元、全社会固定资产投资331亿元、工业总产值2420亿元、工业产品销售收入2332亿元，实现工业利税191亿元；全市有各类上市公司18家，占全国的百分之一，被证券界称为“华夏A股第一县”；目前全市有20多个产品市场占有率居全国前列；华西、三房巷、兴澄、阳光、海澜等15家大企业集团跻身“中国大型工业企业1000强”；14家企业名列“中国民营企业500强”。在两个文明建设中已荣获国家卫生城市、国家环保模范城市、全国文化模范市、全国教育先进市、全国创建文明城市工作先进市、全国科技工作先进市、中国优秀旅游城市等50多项全国性荣誉称号。在2005年全国综合经济实力百强县排名中蝉联第三。在首届长三角最具投资价值县市评比中名列十佳首位。成为江苏省首批全面小康达标县级市。

华西村

开发区鸟瞰图

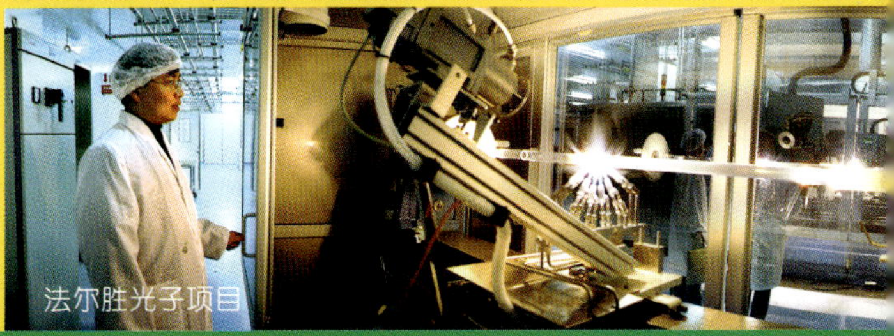
法尔胜光子项目

中国百强县（市）——

江阴

张家港

张家港市位于长江和沿海两大经济带交汇处，是一座新兴的港口工业城市，以境内天然良港—张家港港而命名。全市总面积999平方公里，户籍人口88万人。初步形成“一城四片区”的现代化城市框架，下辖8个建制镇，1个常阴沙管理区。

早在1995年，张家港市两个文明协调发展的典型经验就曾被《人民日报》誉为“伟大理论的成功实践”。近年来，张家港市坚持以邓小平理论和“三个代表”重要思想为指导，始终坚定不移地贯彻落实科学发展观，以争当全省“两个率先”排头兵、构建“和谐张家港”为目标，与时俱进弘扬张家港精神，抢抓机遇率先发展、求真务实科学发展、全面协调统筹发展，百尺竿头更进一步，铸造了三个文明建设的辉煌成就。2005年，全市完成地区生产总值705亿元，人均超过GDP10000美元，实现全口径财政收入108.38亿元；是全国独家摘得“全国文明城市”桂冠的县级市，还被评为国际花园城市、中国优秀旅游城市，创建全国环境优美镇实现了“满堂红”，并率先成为江苏省全国小康达标（县）市。

进入“十一五”开局之年，张家港市将围绕“把张家港市打造成长江三角洲一个富有特色和竞争实力的港口工业城市，一个富有内涵和独特个性的生态园林城市，一个富有精神和文化底蕴的文明法治城市”的奋斗目标，正满怀豪情地向2010年率先基本实现现代化阔步迈进。

江苏省张家港保税物流园区外景

美丽的暨阳湖生态园

张家港市市区人民路一瞥

张家港双山高尔夫球场

繁忙的张家港码头

虞山公园

常熟 ○ 国际花园城市

CHANGSHU

GuoJiHuaYuanChengShi

常熟市是一座具有3000多年历史的国家历史文化名城，也是长江三角洲中心地带新兴的港口工业城市，2004年被联合国环境规划署评为“国际花园城市”。全市总面积1094平方公里，森林覆盖率为20.4%。下辖10个建制镇，1个国营林场。2005年末，全市户籍人口为104万人，暂住人口达到62万多人，城市化率达到62.2%。

进入新世纪以来，常熟市牢固树立富民优先、内外并举、城乡一体、亲近自然、诚信至上五大理念，围绕争当“两个率先”排头兵的目标，坚持加快发展不松劲，科学发展不动摇，牢牢把握工业化、城市化、服务业“三大重点”，积极构建产业、环境、文化“三大特色”，创造了常熟历史上又一发展黄金期，成为江苏省首批进入全面小康社会的县市之一。2005年，全市实现地区生产总值678.78亿元，人均GDP超过8000美元，地方财政一般预算收入37亿元。全市累计注册外资近85亿美元，实际到账外资超过53亿美元；累计建办私营企业11250家，个体工商户56178户，个体、私营经济注册资本超过315亿元。全市拥有5件中国驰名商标，中国名牌产品12只；江苏省著名商标34件，江苏省名牌产品61只；拥有国家授权专利2475项，国际专利4项。

繁华商业街

曾园绿荫

虞城新姿

县城一角

绍兴县位于长江三角洲南翼，地域面积1177平方公里，下辖15个镇，4个街道，302个行政村，70个居委会（社区），户籍人口70.5万，外来人口30万。县人民政府驻地柯桥，陆海空交通便捷，区位优势明显。

绍兴县历史悠久，文化灿烂，名人荟萃，是全国首批24个历史文化名城之一，二千五百年历史绵延不断，素称江南明珠、丝绸之府、文化之邦。

改革开放以来，绍兴县经济持续发展，社会和谐稳定，人民安居乐业，是浙江省首批命名的小康县之一，最近连续四年位居全国十强县行列，形成了经济结构以工业为主、工业结构以轻纺为主、产权结构以民营为主的发展格局，具有独一无二的产业优势、内外兼备的市场优势、率先改革的机制优势、迅速崛起的县城优势和充裕富足的民资民生优势。2005年实现生产总值390亿元，增长15%，人均6850美元；财政总收入42.32亿元，其中地方财政收入20.13亿元，分别增长16.1%和17.7%；城镇居民人均可支配收入18128元，农民人均纯收入9241元，分别增长13.1%和14.4%。基本实现了村村通公交、村村通互联网、村村有放心店、村村响广播、城乡居民洁净水饮用、城镇职工基本养老保险、工伤保险、医疗保险和农村社区卫生服务功能的全覆盖。绍兴县纺织产业集群优势十分明显。作为全球最大的纺织品交易市场——中国轻纺城，拥有近万家贸易公司，经营上万个品种，日客流量10万人次，其中外商2000人次，2005年市场成交额超过450亿元。

新农村

新城

鉴湖

瓜渚湖夜景

古纤道

今日勤劳智慧的绍兴县人民，坚持以科学发展观为指导，牢牢把握“坚持经济中心、推进率先发展”总体要求，全面贯彻“集约发展、创新发展、和谐发展”基本原则，突出市场兴县，加快建设国际纺织之都、现代商贸之城；突出工业强县，加快推进结构优化升级，努力打造先进制造业基地；突出城乡统筹，加快建设社会主义新农村；突出文明创建，加快建设文化强县；突出以人为本，加快构建和谐社会，正谱写着一首世纪腾飞的壮丽诗篇。

中国轻纺城国际贸易区

南海区

中国龙狮运动之乡—
狮舞南海，勇争潮

海纳百川的包容精神
敢为人先的有为精神
团结奋发的龙狮精神

福迪汽车总装车间

南海区位于珠江三角洲腹地，地接广州，毗邻港澳，交通畅达。境内地势平缓，风调雨顺，素称“鱼米之乡”。辖区面积1073.8平方公里，下辖2个街道、6个镇，常住人口111.7万人，流动人口80.8万人，海外侨胞和港澳台同胞40多万人。

南海历史沉积，人文荟萃。康有为、黄飞鸿等名人辈出，西樵山、南国桃园等名胜众多。改革开放以来，南海经济社会全面进步，在全国百强县（市）评比中屡列前茅，先后荣获“国家卫生城市”、“中国优秀旅游城市”、“全国文化先进县”、“全国区域技术创新示范城市”等称号。民营、外源经济相映生辉，拥有“中国铝型材产业基地”、“全国纺织产业升级示范区”、“中国内衣名镇”、“中国日用五金之都”、“中国袜子名镇”等一批著名产业基地和专业镇，汽配、商贸、物流、房地产等成为新的支柱产业。2005年，实现地区生产总值772亿元，增长21.7%；全部财政收入97.8亿元，增长3.8%；金融机构各项存款余额1196.8亿元，增长19%。

现代生态型的南海西部板块——南海科技工业园一隅

太仓

江南丝竹演奏

太仓，一颗镶嵌于中国沿海开放带和长江经济带交汇处的璀璨明珠。已先后荣获国家卫生城市、国家环保模范城市、国家文化和体育先进市、全国生态示范区、中国优秀旅游城市、全国社会治安综合治理先进集体和全国村务公开民主管理示范单位等称号。

新城区一角

郑和下西洋600周年纪念活动

太仓区位独特，是江苏省一个既沿江又沿沪的县(市)。沿江高速、沪嘉浏高速、苏昆太高速、204国道、沪太一级公路、锡太一级公路等使太仓与长三角各大中城市紧密相连。拥有长江深水岸线25公里，太仓港为国家一类口岸、上海国际航运中心的干线港和组合港以及江苏省重点建设的港口。

太仓人文荟萃。是明代著名航海家郑和七下西洋的起锚地。娄东画派影响深远，明清时期的王世贞、张溥、吴梅村等大文学家以及当代的教育家唐文治、著名女物理学家吴健雄、诺贝尔物理学奖获得者朱棣文、中国新舞蹈艺术创始人吴晓邦、丹青大师朱屺瞻等都出自太仓。

太仓经济繁荣。在去年国家有关部门公布的全国百强县(市)中名列第十位。2005年，全市实现地区生产总值300.1亿元，比上年增长20.9%；财政收入45.18亿元，增长42.25%，人均财政收入近万元；城镇居民人均可支配收入、农民人均纯收入分别达到16670元和8401元。建立了较为完善的科技和人才发展体系、教育体系、医疗卫生服务体系、就业促进体系、社会保障体系和救助体系等。

锦绣江南金太仓，正阔步向现代化港口工业城市和滨江卫星城市迈进。

太仓港集装箱码头

吴江市委书记　朱　民

吴江市市长　徐　明

吴江

WUJIANG

“上有天堂，下有苏杭，苏杭中间是吴江”。吴江市位于江苏省的最南端，东临上海，南接杭州，西濒太湖，北依苏州，地处苏浙沪两省一市交会的长三角地区中心腹地。全市总面积为1176平方公里，户籍人口77万，有70万亩耕地和40万亩水面。

吴江古有“鱼米之乡”、“丝绸之府”的美名，今有“电缆之都”、“电子之城”的美誉，近年来更是拥有国家卫生城市、中国优秀旅游城市、全国创建文明城市工作先进市和国家环境保护模范城市等20多项城市荣誉称号。

2005年，全市实现地区生产总值403亿元，同比增长18.5%；完成财政一般预算收入24.69亿元，同比增长17.7%；全社会固定资产投资额210亿元，同比增长10.7%；进出口贸易总额130亿美元。高水平建设小康社会4大类18项25个指标全部完成。在最近《福布斯》公布的中国大陆最佳商业城市排行榜中，吴江前进47位成为上升最快的城市，位列全国县级市第3名。

吴江，经济实现可持续发展，社会事业全面进步，人民生活安康富裕，发展环境不断优化。吴江，是投资者的热土，创业者的福地。

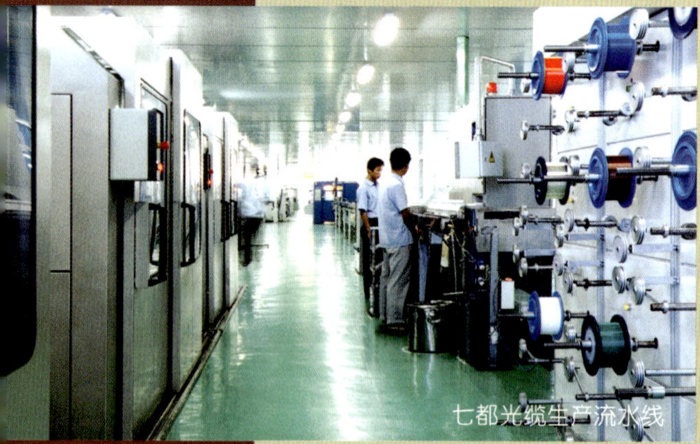

七都光缆生产流水线

企业生产线

塔桥相映

水清鱼肥

盛泽东方市场福建街

荣成

RONGCHENG

荣成市地处山东半岛最东端，三面环海，一线接陆，海岸线长近500公里，东与韩国、日本隔海相望，是我国距离韩国最近的地区。全市现辖3个省级开发区、14个镇区、6个街道办事处、858个行政村、97个居委会，陆地面积1392平方公里，66.6万人口。拥有石岛、龙眼两个国家一类开放港口。不仅是全国第一渔业大县，而且是中国海洋渔业的硅谷，承担着20多个国家“海洋863”计划课题的研发任务。改革开放以来，荣成经济社会得到了快速健康发展，综合实力连续多年居山东县级首位。2005年完成市内生产总值355.34亿元，固定资产投资188.75亿元，实际利用外资3.82亿美元，进出口总值11.77亿美元，财政总收入24.8亿元，其中地方财政收入14亿元。先后荣获国家环保模范城市、中国优秀旅游城市、国家园林城市、全国园林绿化先进城市、中国人居环境范例奖、CCTV首届中国魅力城市、全国城市环境综合整治优秀城市、全国社会治安综合治理模范城市、全国科技先进市等荣誉称号。

电子工业生产流水线

成山橡胶集团全钢子午胎生产车间

中国海岸太阳最早升起的地方

汽车生产线

品牌之都

晋江

江滨公园

晋江地处福建东南沿海，是福建省建设海峡西岸经济区的前沿区域、全国著名侨乡和台湾汉族同胞的主要祖籍地。全市陆域面积649平方公里，海岸线长110公里，现辖13个镇、6个街道、383个行政村，人口103万，旅居海外的侨胞和港、澳、台同胞200多万人，号称“海内外300万晋江人”。1992年撤县设市，2001年被福建省委、省政府列为中等城市，素有“泉南佛国”、“海滨邹鲁”美誉。

改革开放以来，晋江弘扬“诚信、谦恭、团结、拼搏”精神，充分发挥侨乡优势，从“三闲”（闲人、闲房、闲散资金）起步，通过市场途径引进设备、技术和原材料组织商品生产，从遍地开花大办企业到形成专业生产区，并促使产业链上下延伸和相关行业逐步配套，形成了竞争力较强的区域产业集群，构建了富有特色的产业发展环境，并逐步成为我国东南沿海重要的现代制造业基地和品牌之都。地区生产总值从1978年的1.45亿元（包括现石狮市）增长到2004年的438.9亿元，年均增长21.0%；财政总收入从1978年的1476万元（包括现石狮市）增长到2004年的33.11亿元，年均增长23.0%。1992年以来经济综合实力连年居全国前列、福建首位；2004年县域经济社会综合发展指数位居全国百强县（市）第13位。目前，全市拥有13件中国驰名商标、18项中国名牌产品、2项中国出口名牌产品、27项国家免检产品，城市品牌入选“中国50家投资环境诚信安全区”。

同一首歌走进晋江

男篮甲A联赛在晋江

世界男模大赛

第七届中国国际鞋业博览会

第四届全国陶瓷石材博览会

旧城改造新区

晋江世纪公园

义乌

在科学发展观引领下阔步迈向国际性商贸城市

过去的一年，是见证义乌经济新一轮上升足迹的一年，是义乌在科学发展道路上阔步前行的一年。

2005 年，经受了国际市场动荡冲击，克服了土地等资源要素严重制约和各种不利因素的义乌，牢固树立科学发展观，深入实施省委“八八战略”，加快建设文化大市，全面打造“平安义乌”，努力构建和谐社会，切实提高党的执政能力，继续保持了国民经济的旺盛活力和快速增长，经济社会快速协调健康发展。

2005 年，也是检验“十五”计划提出的各项目标任务是否得到圆满完成的一年。“十五”期间，义乌经济社会取得的辉煌成就和发生的历史性变化，让义乌在即将进入一个新的五年经济发展周期时站在了一个新的、更高的历史起点上。

一个改革的义乌，正在不断积聚发展的新动力；一个开放的义乌，已经融入世界经济搏技的大舞台。

——2005 年，全市地区生产总值 300.1 亿元，同比增长 15.1%，完成财政总收入 35 亿元，其中地方财政收入 19.5 亿元，分别同比增长 17.9% 和 17.2%。

——城镇居民人均可支配收入 19010 元，农民人均纯收入 7735 元。

——全市金融机构存款余额 586.2 亿元，贷款余额 355.8 亿元，分别比年初增长 102.8 亿元和 49.7 亿元。

立足 '2005，回首“十五”，义乌的区域经济综合实力大幅度提高。

“十五”时期，全市 GDP 年均增长 15.3%，财政收入年均增长 31.5%，人均 GDP 已经突破 5400 美元，成为区域经济的重要增长点。城市竞争力列浙江省县级市首位，综合实力居全国百强县市第 15 位，并进入了提升经济素质、加快向世界中等发达国家水平迈进的转型发展期。

新的一年，义乌市委、市政府制定出了新的工作要求：以“三个代表”重要思想为指导，贯彻落实党的十六届五中全会和中央经济工作会议精神，以科学发展观总揽全局，把握新形势，立足新起点，确立新任务，落实新举措，树立新作风，加快产业结构升级优化，推进社会主义新农村建设，深化改革，扩大开放，全面创建生态市，建设文化大市，打造“平安义乌”，构建和谐社会，加快国际性商贸城市建设步伐。

新任务，新要求，新目标，新突破。

全面做好 2006 年工作，市委、市政府在牢牢把握发展新形势、立足发展新起点的基础上明确确立了“争取八个方面继续保持领先地位”的新的发展任务：综合实力领先，市场发展领先，国际化发展领先，城乡统筹领先，社会事业发展领先，制度创新领先，生态建设领先和社会和谐领先。

义乌市绣湖广场

义乌市梅湖体育场

义博会开幕式

义乌城市建设宾王商贸区

会展体育中心

新会

XINHUI

新会，地处珠江三角洲西南部，濒临南海，毗邻港澳，区位优势明显。新会人杰地灵、钟灵毓秀、历史悠久，是全国著名侨乡，旅外乡亲和港澳台同胞70多万人。这里，诞生了维新先驱梁启超、理学泰斗陈白沙、史学大师陈垣、武林蔡李佛祖师陈享等诸多名人，有南宋崖海古战场遗址、独树成林的小鸟天堂旅游名胜、千年儒教圣地孔庙、圭峰山国家森林公园、岭南古刹玉台寺、古兜温泉谷等丰富旅游资源。

新会经济综合实力较强，连续5次进入全国最发达100个县行列。先后被命名为中国不锈钢制品生产基地、国家火炬计划江门纺织化纤产业基地、广东银洲湖纸业基地和广东江门市银洲湖石化基地。2005年全区生产总值185.3亿元，增长16.54%；工业总产值572.05亿元，增长27.8%；地方财政一般预算收入9.65亿元，增长22.09%。

由珠江干流西江和潭江汇流而成的银洲湖，通江达海，拥有国家一类货运口岸新会港，成为吸引外来投资的聚宝盆。日本丰田、松下、丸红、住友、新日铁，瑞士ABB等世界500强企业和香港宝源、李锦记、重庆力帆、安徽海螺等大集团都落户银洲湖畔。近三年来，该区域共引进项目500多个，投资总额450多亿元。区域工业产值以每年30%的速度增长。形成了造纸及纸制品、钢铁和钢铁加工、食品、化纤纺织、石化、电力电器、造船、建材等八大临港产业群，涌现了85家年产值超亿元的工业骨干企业，其中10家超10亿元。

小鸟天堂

新会港

与时俱进的靖江统计

靖江市统计局紧紧围绕党和政府中心工作，开拓进取，与时俱进，全面推进统计工作的法制化、规范化、制度化，先后获得"全国统计系统先进集体"、"全国统计执法大检查先进单位"、"全省统计四五普法先进单位"、"全省依法统计先进单位"、"全省乡镇统计网络建设先进集体"等多项荣誉，为全市沿江开发和实现"两个率先"作出了卓越贡献。

靖江市统计局局长卢子飞部署全市统计工作

靖江市政府召开全市统计工作会议

靖江市统计局获得的部分荣誉证书、铜牌等

蓬莱

市委书记　刘树琪

市长　刘炳国

蓬莱市位于胶东半岛最北端，濒临渤、黄二海，总面积1128.6平方公里，人口44.6万，辖7个镇、5个街道、1处省级经济开发区、1 处省级旅游度假区。

蓬莱是区域经济强县。近年来，蓬莱市始终坚持科学发展观，大力实施“抢抓机遇，巧借外力，膨胀总量，跨越发展”战略，明晰了“港口立市、旅游兴市、酒业富民”的产业发展思想，进一步优化经济结构，推进产业升级，加快城市化进程，努力营造发展合力，全市经济和社会各项事业步人跨越发展的快车道。2005年， 全市实现国内生产总值170亿元，地方财政收人7亿元。在新一届全国最发达100县评选中排名第40位。蓬莱是著名的历史文化名城。早在旧石器时代，就有人类繁衍生息，秦皇汉武留下寻仙足迹，汉武帝命名并筑城，苏东坡知五日登州，民族英雄戚继光出生此地并建立了不朽功勋。2100多年以来， 一直是胶东地区政治文化和经济中心，神仙文化、精武文化、港口文化和海洋文化四大文化，为蓬莱积淀了浓厚的历史文化底蕴。

蓬莱是美丽的海滨风景旅游城市。这里有“海市蜃楼”奇观和“八仙过海”美传，有美丽的海滨自然风光，素以“人间仙境”著称于世。这里文物古迹众多， 历史文化积淀深厚，有中国古代四大名楼之一的蓬莱阁，有我国迄今保存最完整的中国古代水军基地——蓬莱水城，有民族英雄戚继光的故居，有亚洲最大的蓬莱海洋极地世界，年接待中外游客200多万人次。2005年，全市景区实现门票收人1.8亿元，综合收人21.6亿元。

蓬莱是重要的港口城市。蓬莱港的前身登州港，是我国古代四大古港之一，是海上丝绸之路的起点和隋唐时期中外文化交流的桥头堡。目前已建成港口3处，拥有蓬莱新港、栾家口港两个国家一类开放口岸，在建和建成的万吨级以上泊位11个，其中5万吨级的6个，10万吨级的1个，年吞吐能力1000万吨以上。依托港口优势和广阔的腹地，蓬莱市坚持以港兴市，规划建设两个临港工

戚继光故里

业区，重点发展石化、造船、能源、建材等工业和汽车及零部件产业。目前全市临港工业引进外资超过200亿元。

蓬莱是资源富集的城市。蓬莱为全国三大优质酿酒葡萄产区之一，围绕打造“中国葡萄酒名城”的品牌，规划了35万亩酿酒葡萄种植基地，建设了18公里葡萄长廊。先后引进中粮长城、天津王朝、新天国际、云南香格里拉、香港华鲁、菲律宾康达、意大利罗迪、德国阿尔玛、英国登龙等国内外知名葡萄酒企业投资。2005年全市葡萄酒生产能力达到10万吨，葡萄种植面积达10万亩，干酒生产能力、产量均居全国县级前茅，成为世界七大葡萄海岸之一。蓬莱是我国黄金重要产区，年产黄金16万两，是全国第三大黄金生产县（市）；蓬莱是我省重要的水产品产区，年水产品产量25万吨。

八仙塑像

蓬莱阁

蓬莱水城

坚持科学发展观　促进静海经济社会健康发展

静海

静海地处天津西南部，交通便利，是北上进京、南下江浙的交通要冲，是国家有关部门批准的沿海开放县。全县总面积1414.9平方公里，耕地105万亩，辖18个乡镇（其中16个建制镇），384个行政村，人口51万。被誉为“华北明珠”的团泊水库，水面9.8万亩，团泊新城已被列入天津市规划发展重点区域。

2005年完成生产总值132.6亿元，同比增长18.2%；财政收入9.55亿元，同比增长26.3%；农民人均纯收入6754元，同比增长11.6%；全社会固定资产投资45亿元，同比增长24.7%。“十五”期间，生产总值年均增长17.1%、财政收入年均增长25.5%、农民人均纯收入年均增长11.7%，累计全社会固定资产投资140亿元，是投资规模最大、水平最高的时期。

“十一五”期间，要用科学发展观统领经济社会发展全局，突出抓好发展第一要务，把“工业立县”、对外开放作为全县发展的主线，加快推进静海新城、团泊新城和钢铁加工业、再生资源综合利用、发酵类生物制药、装备制造业基地建设。坚持可持续发展，着力推进经济结构调整和增长方式转变，构建资源节约型、环境友好型发展模式，统筹社会经济协调发展，努力构建和谐静海，成为率先基本实现现代化的区县之一。到2010年生产总值达到270亿元，年均增长15.3%；人均生产总值达到6290美元，年均增长14.3%；全县财政收入26亿元，年均增长22.3%；全社会固定资产投资累计350亿元；社会消费品零售总额年均增长20%；外贸进出口总额累计35亿美元以上，实际利用外资累计4亿美元，实际利用内资累计150亿元，三次产业比重达到7:60:33。各项社会事业发展取得新突破。

静海县文化广场

企业生产

农村住宅建设

仪征步行街

仪征

——生态型现代滨江工业城市

大连化工

化工园区仓储

仪征是一座生态型现代滨江工业城市，总面积901平方公里，总人口59.3万人，辖11个乡镇和2个办事处。2005年，全市实现地区生产总值106.8亿元，同比增长21.2%；实现财政收入17亿元，增长14.1%；实际利用外资2.35亿美元，招引民资63.5亿元，分别增长95.8%和76.4%。

仪征是长三角地区重要的交通运输枢纽城市之一，长江黄金水道、宁通高速公路、沿江高等级公路、宁启铁路、鲁宁输油管道、甬沪宁输油管道、西气东输天然气管道等多种交通运输设施在仪征交汇。城市依江而建，境内拥有27.6公里长江黄金岸线，现有近20个码头泊位，石油和化学品年吞吐能力达2400万吨，集装箱和散货年吞吐能力达600万吨。仪征产业集聚程度较高，拥有仪征化纤股份公司、台湾大连化工、江苏优士化学、上汽汽车制造仪征分公司、上汽汇众轻型客车仪征厂、长航集团金陵船厂、舜天造船等一批竞争力较强的大企业、大集团，目前已有德国西门子、荷兰飞利浦、美国优尼发、日本东丽等8家世界500强企业和一批国内外知名大企业在仪投资兴业，全市已初步形成了具有比较优势的石油化工、汽车及零部件、高新技术、船舶修造和现代物流五大主导产业。仪征地处南北过渡地带，物种丰富，植被茂盛，有白羊山、铜山2个省级森林公园，森林覆盖率15.4%。全市依山傍水，有登月湖、龙山等3个旅游风景区，生态良好，景色宜人，是安居乐业、休闲度假的好地方。

开放的仪征欢迎您！

上汽汇众伊思坦纳车生产线

仪化股份公司长丝车间

中共枣庄市委副书记、滕州市委书记　牛启忠

滕州市委副书记、市长　杜永光

滕州

TENGZHOU

滕州市位于山东省南部，地处苏鲁豫皖四省交界处的淮海经济区中心位置，总面积1485平方公里，总人口158万，辖21个镇（街道），1226个行政村（居）。滕州历史悠久，文化灿烂，古为“三国五邑之地，文化昌明之邦”，是“科圣”墨子和“工匠祖师”鲁班的故里，还有滕文公、孟尝君、毛遂等许多历史名人，俊彩星驰，各领风骚，留下千古佳话；境内有7300多年前的“北辛文化”遗址，春秋战国时期的滕国、薛国故城遗址和始建于唐代的龙泉古塔等历史文化景观。滕州交通便利，自古就有“九省通衢”之称，京杭大运河、104国道、京福高速公路、京沪铁路及即将建设的京沪高速铁路穿境而过，形成了四通八达的公路、铁路、水路交通网络。滕州资源丰富，产业发达，是全国有名的能源基地、建材之乡，国家重要的商品粮集散地、高效农业生产基地和优质蔬菜基地。滕州青山碧水，风光秀丽，社会和谐，是人居福地，创业热土。

“十五”是新世纪的第一个五年，也是我市经济社会发展取得辉煌成就、实现跨越式发展的五年。“十五”期间，在市委、市政府的正确领导下，坚持以经济建设为中心，强化招商引资龙头，突出重点项目，突出结构调整，突出“亮点”培植，突出城市化，不断解放思想、抢抓机遇、干事创业、加快发展，国民经济保持了持续快速健康发展。2005年全市生产总值实现275.57亿元，是2000

盛隆煤焦化公司

腾达不锈钢公司车间内景

韩资企业明正（滕州）新型建筑材料有限公司

滕州城区鸟瞰

滕州市行政审批服务大厅

年的2.5倍，年均增长17.5%；境内财政收入实现22.65亿元，是2000年的3.13倍，年均增长25.7%；地方财政收入实现9.2亿元，是2000年的3.1倍，同口径年均增长33%；县域经济综合实力大幅上升，由2000年的全国159位上升为2004年的117位，连续五年跻身中国县域经济基本竞争力百强县（市），由2001年的59位上升到2005年的31位，在2005年首届全国中小城市百强评选中名列第67位；2003年进入山东省县域经济30强，2006年6月份被省委、省政府授予"县域经济发展先进单位"。农业基础地位得到加强，被评为全国十大粮食生产先进县（市）。招商引资成效突出，2005年实际利用市外资金80.6亿元、境外资金3716万美元，分别是2000年的6.7倍、4倍，"十五"期间全社会固定资产投资累计完成278亿元，是"九五"时期的3.9倍，年均增长44.3%；重点项目建设加快推进，新源热电、盛隆煤焦化、金州玻璃、腾达不锈钢制品、盈泰食品、锦丘煤矿、东大煤矿等40个规模大、发展前景好的重点项目陆续竣工投产，这些重点骨干工业企业的迅速成长对经济的支撑作用有了明显增强。服务业日益繁荣，微山湖湿地红荷景区建设初具规模，成功举办了三届红荷节，2005年全市实现社会消费品零售总额82.91亿元，年均增长13.1%。城市化进程加速推进，城乡面貌明显改观，城市建成区面积40.5平方公里，城市化水平达到41.8%。城乡居民收入稳定增长，生活水平明显提高。2005年在岗职工平均工资12180元，年均增长11.3%，农民人均纯收入4590元，年均增长9.6%。

红荷湾

山东十大名村张汪镇大宗村

新型滨江工贸城市——泰兴

泰兴位于江苏省的几何中心和长江三角洲经济圈的中心地带，是一座新兴滨江工贸城市，素有“银杏之乡”、“教育之乡”、“建筑之乡”的美誉。全市总人口129万人，总面积1253平方公里，辖24个乡镇和1个省级经济开发区。新长铁路、京沪高速、宁通高速、宁靖盐高速和沿江高等级公路穿境而过，拥有25.2公里的长江黄金岸线和国家一类开放港口。境内名、特、优、稀作物种类繁多，银杏产量约占全国总产量三分之一，且品质超群。泰兴大佛指白果获’99昆明世界园艺博览会无公害白果终生冠名权。普通教育和职业技术教育在江苏省乃至全国一直处于领先地位，“中国名校”洋思中学素质教育经验名闻遐迩。全市工业基础较好，主要工业产品涉及化工、医药、纺织、船舶、电子等10大类近6000个品种，靓蓝、减速机、曲轴、氢氧化钾、小提琴等10多个产品产量居全球或全国前茅。建筑业久负盛名，承建工程5次夺得中国工程质量最高荣誉“鲁班奖”。2005年，全市实现GDP174亿元，完成财政收入20.6亿元，外商直接投资1.06亿美元，全部工业实现产值368.6亿元，销售338.5亿元，连续五届跻身全国县域经济基本竞争力百强县（市）行列。

世界500强企业之一——阿克苏[1]·诺贝尔（泰兴）公司

沿江水利设施景区

古银杏公园

开发区一景

发展强劲活力四溢的经济强市

遵化

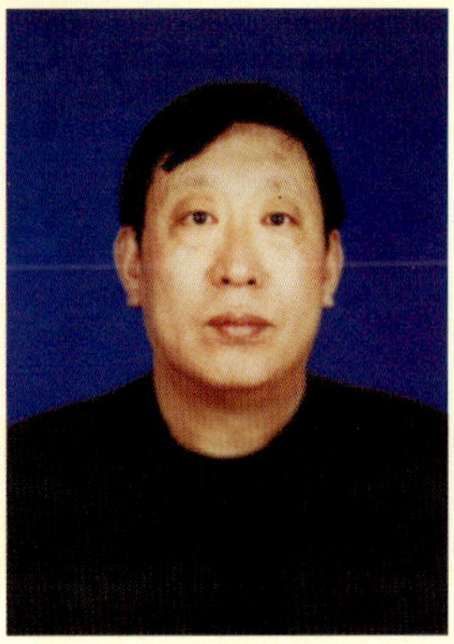

市委书记　侯志宇

市长　赵山

曾以“穷棒子”精神享誉全国，被老一辈无产阶级革命家称为“整个国家的形象”的遵化市，在2005年度全国县域经济基本竞争力评选中名列第55位，连续四年跻身全国百强，并在第二届全国中小城市综合实力百强评比中名列第65位。2005年全市实现生产总值212.6亿元，增长22.0%；财政收入18.3亿元，增长52.5%；城镇居民可支配收入9986元，农民人均纯收入4908元，分别增长19.7%和18.0%。

耕地面积78.5万亩，林地面积116万亩。土地肥沃；盛产板栗、核桃、苹果、柿子、安梨等干鲜果品，年产量达25万吨，享誉海内外的京东板栗年产达1.2万吨。境内已探明的矿藏30多种，有铁矿石储量1.5亿吨、白云石矿储量3.9亿吨。

旅游资源得天独厚。遵化境内有清东陵、明长城世界文化遗产两处，清东陵、万佛园4A级旅游景区两处，鹫峰山、上关湖、卧龙山2A级旅游景区3处。以清东陵为龙头，沿明代古长城分布有始建于后唐时期的汤泉温泉池，是一个景点如珠，底蕴深厚的旅游城市。

城市建设布局合理、功能齐全、设施完备。城镇化率达到47.6%，保持了全省领先水平。人均住房使用面积23.7平方米，万人拥有公交车辆4辆，城市供水普及率100%，城区集中供热普及率61%，城市绿化覆盖率24.6%。全市电话交换机实占容量达到17.7万户，移动用户14.3万户，互联网用户1.1万户。

板栗生产车间

遵化市热电厂

街心公园

清东陵（裕陵）

建龙中宽带生产线

思茅

澜沧景迈1300余年栽培型古茶园

世界茶源　中国茶城　普洱茶都

思茅市地处祖国西南边陲，云南省的西南端，与越南、老挝、缅甸三国接壤，素有“东方多瑙河”之称的澜沧江——湄公河黄金水道纵贯全境，形成得天独厚的“一市连三国，一江通五邻”的独特区位。全市辖九县一区（9个少数民族自治县），总面积4.5万平方公里，是云南省面积最大的州市，总人口256万，生活着汉、哈尼、彝、拉祜、佤、傣等14种世居民族，少数民族人口占60%。思茅资源富集、优势突出，历史悠久，民族众多，风情浓郁，文化厚重，是一块极具开发潜力的绿色宝地。

思茅森林覆盖率64.9%，浩瀚的林海、丰富的物种，使思茅成为云南“动植物王国”的缩影。思茅气候怡人，冬无严寒，夏无酷暑，有“绿海明珠、天然氧吧”的美誉，是最适宜人类居住的地方之一。

思茅是世界茶源、中国茶城、普洱茶都。镇沅千家寨2700余年的野生古茶王树，澜沧邦崴千余年的过渡型古茶树，景迈万亩千年栽培型古茶山，都印证了思茅处于世界茶树原生地中心地带，是“普洱茶”原产地和集散地，是“世界茶文化的摇篮”和“茶马古道”的源头。2003年5月8日，中国茶叶流通协会正式命名思茅为“中国茶城”。2005年末，全市有茶园134万余亩，其中现代茶园74.1万亩。

思茅矿产资源丰富。岩盐储量达43亿吨；已探明黄金储量103.7吨，占云南省的80%以上；铁矿储量仅澜沧县惠民铁矿就有21亿吨。

思茅是云南“西电东送”、“云电外送”的重要水电基地，全市水资源总量828亿m^3，已建成和正在建设大中型水电站15座，其中糯扎渡电站装机585万千瓦。

随着中国——东盟自由贸易区建立，澜沧江——湄公河次区域合作推进，昆曼高速公路的全线竣工，思茅将成为中国面向东南亚大通道上的前沿城市。

2005年，全市生产总值为106.3亿元，财政总收入11亿元，农民人均纯收入1553元。

“十一五”时期，思茅将积极培植壮大茶叶、林产、水电、矿产四个支柱，加快建设“绿色思茅、生态思茅、文化思茅”，着力打造“世界茶源、中国茶城、普洱茶都”，促进经济社会又快又好发展。

镇沅千家寨2700年野生古茶王树

澜沧邦崴过渡型古茶树

昆曼国际大通道一景

绿海明珠——思茅

仁怀

市长房国兴会见泰国公主

国酒大道一瞥

仁怀市政大楼

“十五”期间，仁怀市按照“培植特色产业，发展特色经济，建设特色城市”的发展思路，聚精会神搞建设，一心一意谋发展，强力推进农业产业化、工业化、城镇化进程，把发展作为第一要务，把酒业作为主要经济支柱来培育，带动了经济链条的整体良性互动，市域经济快速发展，取得了辉煌成就。表现在经济总量跃上新台阶，“三化”建设迈出新步伐，基础设施得到新加强，改革开放谱写新篇章，社会事业取得新进步，人民生活又有新改善。

2005年实现地区生产总值59.84亿元，比2000年的20.62亿元，净增39.22亿元，增长190.2%；地方财政收入2005年达到3.39亿元，比2000年的1.3亿元，净增2.09亿元，增长160.77%；社会固定资产投资2005年完成15.39亿元，比2000年的全市投资6.26亿元，净增9.13亿元，增长145.85%；农民人均纯收入2005年达到2496元，比2000年的1181元，增长111.35%；城镇居民可支配收入2005年达到7500元，比2000年的5376元，增长39.50%；高中阶段毛入学率，2005年达到30.7%，比2000年的25.2%增长了5.5个百分点。名列贵州省“经济十强县（市）”第6位，西部百强县（市）第48位。

中国酒都认定证书

经中国食文化研究会组织酒文化专家、学者考察审核，贵州省仁怀市符合《中国酒都认定标准ICO1000-JD》的条款规定，认定为中国酒都。

特发此证

Guizhou Renhuai City passed the checking of the experts and scholars, meets the regulations of 《China Wine City Identified Criterion ICO1000-JD》,and is identified-China Wine City by the Organization of the Leaned Society of Chinese Cooking Culture.

Issue this certificate.

证书编号：中食认jw-2004-0001

认定发证机构：中国食文化研究会

二00四年七月十八日

中国酒都认定证书

茅台酒之源——红高粱

市领导接过中国酒都牌匾